One method of reducing a part of the earth's surface is by aerial photography. The two photographs on this page are semi-controlled mosaics and are made by matching together a series of vertical aerial photographs. Although an accurate map cannot be made directly from such a mosaic, it does illustrate one way that a map can be made. Each of the mosaics is approximately the scale of its corresponding map. On a map, cultural and physical features are represented by means of signs, symbols, and certain conventions. By comparing the mosaic with the map in each case, one can ascertain how various features on the earth have been represented on the map and how they, and other features, appear from the air. For example, the darkest areas on the Pittsburgh mosaic are wooded areas which are shown in green on the map. The heavily built-up area of Pittsburgh is depicted by a red screen on the map. The major buildings, roads, and bridges are easily recognized.

The part of the Strasburg, Virginia, Quadrangle selected lies in the folded Appalachians just east of Woodstock, Virginia, and across the "Great Valley" of the Shenandoah River. The valley, occupied by the meanders of both forks of the Shenandoah River, is divided at this point by Massanutten Mountain. The latter is a complex synclinal mass, made mostly of sandstone. The three northeast trending parallel ridges of the mountain can be readily recognized and compared. Notice that the shading on the map and the shadows on the mosaic do not agree. The photographs were taken in the morning, placing the western slopes of the ridges in shadow. The general practice of the cartographer, however, is to render the relief as if the light source was from the northwest. The comparison, nevertheless, facilitates an understanding of how contours and relief shading are used to represent surface configuration.

PITTSBURGH WEST 1:24 000
U.S. GEOLOGICAL SURVEY

GOODE'S

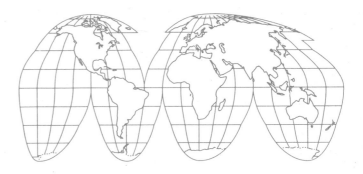

WORLD ATLAS

TWELFTH EDITION

edited by

Edward B. Espenshade, Jr.

Professor of Geography, Northwestern University

RAND McNALLY & COMPANY · CHICAGO

CONTENTS

vi • ACKNOWLEDGMENTS

vii • INTRODUCTION

xii • MAP SYMBOLS

1 PLANETS AND EARTH-SUN RELATIONS

2 – 3 • MAP PROJECTIONS

World Maps

4 – 5 • POLITICAL

6 – 7 • PHYSICAL

8 – 9 • CLIMATIC REGIONS

10 – 11 • TEMPERATURE
Surface Temperature Regions
January Normal Temperature
Normal Annual Range in Temperature
July Normal Temperature

12 – 13 • PRESSURE, WINDS, AND SEASONAL RAINFALL
January: Pressure and Predominant Winds
Rainfall, Nov. 1 to April 30
July: Pressure and Predominant Winds
Rainfall, May 1 to Oct. 31

14 – 15 • ANNUAL RAINFALL AND OCEAN CURRENTS
Inset: Variability of Annual Rainfall

16 – 17 • NATURAL VEGETATION

18 – 19 • GREAT SOIL GROUPS

20 – 21 • DENSITY OF POPULATION

22 – 23 • PREDOMINANT ECONOMIES

24 – 25 • MAJOR AGRICULTURAL REGIONS

Resources and Leading Primary Products

26 • Wheat

26 • Rye, Tea

27 • Corn

27 • Oats, Coffee

28 • Barley, Cacao

28 • Rice, Millet and Grain Sorghum

29 • Cane Sugar, Beet Sugar

29 • Rubber, Grapes

30 • Fruits
Bananas, Citrus Fruit, Dates,
Deciduous Fruit, Pineapples

30 • Tobacco, Fisheries

31 • Vegetable Oils
Castor Bean, Copra, Cottonseed, Flaxseed,
Oil Palm, Olive, Peanut, Rapeseed, Sesame
Seed, Soybeans, Sunflower Seed, Tung Nuts

32 • Vegetable and Other Fibers
Abaca (Manila Hemp), Cotton, Flax,
Hemp, Jute, Kapok, Phormium Tenax,
Ramie, Rayon, Silk, Sisal

33 • Cattle

33 • Swine

34 • Sheep

34 • Wood Products

35 • Water Power

35 • Mineral Fertilizers
Phosphate, Potash, Pyrites, Sulfur

36 – 37 • Mineral Fuels
Coal, Petroleum, Natural Gas

38 – 39 • Iron Ore and Ferroalloys
Chromium, Cobalt, Iron Ore, Manganese,
Molybdenum, Nickel, Tungsten, Vanadium

40 • Copper

40 • Aluminum Ore, Tin

41 • Lead

41 • Zinc

42 – 43 • SURFACE TRANSPORT FACILITIES

44 • OCEAN TRANSPORTATION

45 • TRADE
Exports
Imports

46 • LANGUAGES AND RELIGIONS

Polar Regions

47 • SOUTHERN LANDS AND SEAS. Scale 1:60,000,000

48 • NORTHERN LANDS AND SEAS. Scale 1:60,000,000

North America

49 • NORTH AMERICA. Scale 1:40,000,000

United States and Southern Canada—Special Maps

50 – 51 • Physiography. Scale 1:12,000,000

52 • Precipitation and Glaciation
   Average Annual Precipitation;
   Precipitation, Nov. 1 to April 30;
   Precipitation, May 1 to Oct. 31
   Glacial Lakes: Agassiz, Lahontan
   and Bonneville, and Laurentian

53 • Climate (U.S.)
   Early Frost; Late Frost; Frost-free period;
   Highs and Lows; Sunshine, Dec.-Feb.; Sunshine,
   June-Aug.; Moisture Regions; Thermal Efficiency

54 – 55 • Vegetation. Scale 1:14,000,000

56 – 57 • Land Use (U.S.). Scale 1:12,000,000

58 • Population

58 • Types of Farming

59 • Agriculture (U.S.)
   Corn, Wheat, Cotton, Fruits and Nuts,
   Cattle, Milk Cows, Hogs, Sheep

60 • Minerals
   Coal, Petroleum, Natural Gas, Iron Ore

60 • Manufacturing

61 • Transportation
   Railroads and Standard Time,
   Air Routes and Waterways

62 – 63 • UNITED STATES OF AMERICA. Scale 1:12,000,000
   Insets: Alaska; Scale 1:36,000,000
   Hawaii; Scale 1:12,000,000

64 • ALASKA, STATE OF. Scale 1:12,000,000
   Inset: Aleutian Islands; Scale 1:12,000,000

65 • UNITED STATES AND CANADA—CITIES
   AND ENVIRONS. Scale 1:1,000,000
   Vancouver, Seattle, San Francisco, Portland

66 – 67 • NORTHWESTERN U.S.A. Scale 1:4,000,000

68 – 69 • SOUTHWESTERN U.S.A. Scale 1:4,000,000

70 – 71 • NORTHERN INTERIOR U.S.A. Scale 1:4,000,000

72 – 73 • CENTRAL U.S.A. Scale 1:4,000,000

74 – 75 • UNITED STATES—CITIES AND ENVIRONS.
   Scale 1:1,000,000
   Los Angeles, Salt Lake City, Dallas-Fort Worth,
   San Antonio, St. Louis, Kansas City, Duluth,
   Sault Ste. Marie, Minneapolis-St. Paul,
   Chicago-Milwaukee, Detroit, Buffalo, Cleveland,
   Pittsburgh, Cincinnati, Indianapolis, Louisville

76 – 77 • WESTERN GULF REGION OF U.S.A. AND PART
   OF MEXICO. Scale 1:4,000,000
   Inset: Houston-Galveston; Scale 1:1,000,000

78 – 79 • SOUTHEASTERN U.S.A. Scale 1:4,000,000

80 – 81 • NORTHEASTERN U.S.A., PART OF. Scale 1:4,000,000

82 – 83 • NORTHERN NEW ENGLAND, EASTERN GATEWAY
   OF CANADA, AND NEWFOUNDLAND. Scale 1:4,000,000
   Inset: Boston & Vicinity; Scale 1:1,000,000

84 • UNITED STATES—CITIES AND ENVIRONS.
   Scale 1:1,000,000
   New York, Providence, Baltimore, Philadelphia,
   New Orleans, Atlanta, Norfolk, Birmingham

85 • CANADA—CITIES AND ENVIRONS. Scale 1:1,000,000
   Montreal, Quebec, Toronto, Ottawa,
   Calgary, Winnipeg, Edmonton

86 – 87 • CANADA. Scale 1:12,000,000
   Inset: Newfoundland; Scale 1:12,000,000

88 – 89 • GULF AND CARIBBEAN LANDS. Scale 1:16,000,000
   Insets: Panama; Scale 1:1,000,000
   Puerto Rico and Virgin Islands;
   Scale 1:4,000,000
   St. Thomas Island; Scale 1:500,000

90 – 91 • MEXICO—CENTRAL. Scale 1:4,000,000
   Inset: Mexico City; Scale 1:1,000,000

92 – 93 • CENTRAL AMERICA. Scale 1:4,000,000
   Insets: Yucatan Peninsula; Scale 1:4,000,000
   Leeward and Windward Islands;
   Scale 1:4,000,000

94 – 95 • WEST INDIES—WESTERN. Scale 1:4,000,000
   Cuba, Bahamas, Jamaica, Hispaniola
   Inset: Havana; Scale 1:1,000,000

South America

96 • SOUTH AMERICA. Scale 1:40,000,000

97 • SOUTH AMERICA—SPECIAL MAPS
   Annual Rainfall—Vegetation—
   Population—Economic

98 – 99 • SOUTH AMERICA—NORTHERN. Scale 1:16,000,000
   Insets: Caracas, Bogotá; Scale 1:4,000,000

100 • SOUTH AMERICA—SOUTHERN. Scale 1:16,000,000
   Insets: Buenos Aires, Rio de Janeiro;
   Scale 1:1,000,000

101 • SOUTH AMERICA—CITIES AND ENVIRONS.
   Scale 1:4,000,000
   Rio de Janeiro, Santiago, Buenos Aires

Europe

102 – 103 • EUROPE AND WESTERN ASIA. Scale 1:16,000,000

104 – 105 • EUROPE—PHYSIOGRAPHY. Scale 1:16,000,000
    Insets: Physiographic Provinces, Europe
      during the Ice Age

106 – 107 • EUROPE—LAND USE. Scale 1:20,000,000
    Insets: Vegetation, Minerals; Scale 1:40,000,000

108 – 109 • EUROPE—LANGUAGES. Scale 1:20,000,000
    Insets: Population, Annual Rainfall;
      Scale 1:40,000,000

110 • ENGLAND—CENTRAL MANUFACTURING REGION
AND LONDON. Scale 1:1,000,000

111 • EUROPE—CITIES AND ENVIRONS. Scale 1:1,000,000
    Brussels, Amsterdam, Vienna,
    Munich, Hamburg, Berlin

112 – 113 • WESTERN EUROPE. Scale 1:10,000,000

114 – 115 • MEDITERRANEAN LANDS. Scale 1:10,000,000

116 – 117 • BRITISH ISLES AND NORTH SEA LANDS.
Scale 1:4,000,000
    Inset: Shetland Islands; Scale 1:4,000,000

118 – 119 • SOUTHERN SCANDINAVIA AND THE EAST
BALTIC REPUBLICS. Scale 1:4,000,000

120 – 121 • CENTRAL EUROPE. Scale 1:4,000,000

122 – 123 • FRANCE. Scale 1:4,000,000
    Insets: Paris, Ruhr, Marseille; Scale 1:1,000,000

124 – 125 • SPAIN AND PORTUGAL. Scale 1:4,000,000
    Insets: Madrid, Rome, Lisbon,
      Naples; Scale 1:1,000,000

126 – 127 • ITALY, YUGOSLAVIA, BULGARIA
AND GREECE. Scale 1:5,000,000
    Inset: Crete; Scale 1:4,000,000

128 – 129 • SOUTHWESTERN SOVIET UNION—INDUSTRIAL.
Scale 1:4,000,000

130 – 131 • SOVIET UNION. Scale 1:20,000,000

132 – 133 • SOVIET UNION IN EUROPE—EASTERN EUROPE
AND ASIA MINOR. Scale 1:10,000,000

134 – 135 • SOVIET UNION IN ASIA: SIBERIA. Scale 1:16,000,000

136 • SOVIET UNION—URAL INDUSTRIAL AREA.
Scale 1:4,000,000
    Moscow, Leningrad; Scale 1:1,000,000

137 • SOVIET UNION—SPECIAL MAPS
    Population—Economic. Scale 1:45,000,000

Asia

138 – 139 • EURASIA. Scale 1:40,000,000
    Insets: Palestine, The Region of Singapore;
      Scale 1:4,000,000

140 • ASIA—SPECIAL MAPS
    Annual Rainfall—Population

141 • ASIA—SPECIAL MAPS
    Vegetation—Economic

142 – 143 • INDIA. Scale 1:10,000,000
    Insets: Languages, Economic
      Bombay, Calcutta; Scale 1:1,000,000

144 – 145 • ASIA—SOUTHWESTERN. Scale 1:16,000,000
    Insets: India Political; Scale 1:40,000,000
      Khyber Pass; Scale 1:4,000,000

146 – 147 • CHINA AND JAPAN. Scale 1:16,000,000

148 • PART OF EASTERN CHINA. Scale 1:4,000,000

149 • CHINA—SPECIAL MAPS—CITIES
    Economic, Population
    Canton, Shanghai; Scale 1:1,000,000

150 – 151 • CHINA—EASTERN. Scale 1:10,000,000
    Inset: Peking; Scale 1:1,000,000

152 • KOREA AND JAPAN. Scale 1:10,000,000

153 • SOUTHERN JAPAN. Scale 1:4,000,000
    Insets: Tokyo, Osaka; Scale 1:1,000,000

154 – 155 • INDONESIA AND THE PHILIPPINES. Scale 1:16,000,000
    Inset: Philippines; Scale 1:4,000,000

Pacific Ocean and Australia

156 – 157 • PACIFIC OCEAN. Scale 1:50,000,000
    Inset: Hawaii; Scale 1:4,000,000

158 – 159 • AUSTRALIA AND NEW ZEALAND. Scale 1:16,000,000

160 • AUSTRALIA—SOUTHEASTERN. Scale 1:8,000,000

161 • AUSTRALIA—SPECIAL MAPS—CITIES
    Economic—Annual Rainfall—
    Vegetation—Population
    Melbourne, Sydney; Scale 1:1,000,000

Africa

162 • AFRICA—SPECIAL MAPS
    Annual Rainfall—Vegetation—
    Population—Economic

163 • AFRICA. Scale 1:40,000,000

164 – 165 • AFRICA—NORTHERN. Scale 1:16,000,000
    Insets: Azores, Cape Verde Is.; Scale 1:16,000,000

167 • AFRICA—SOUTHERN. Scale 1:16,000,000
    Insets: Natal; Scale 1:4,000,000
      Johannesburg and Pretoria;
        Scale 1:1,000,000
      Cape Town; Scale 1:1,000,000

168 • AFRICA—REGIONAL
    Eastern Horn; Scale 1:16,000,000
    Lower Nile Valley; Scale 1:4,000,000
    The Suez Canal; Scale 1:1,000,000
    Johannesburg and Pretoria; Scale 1:4,000,000

169 • WORLD COMPARISON

170 • PRINCIPAL COUNTRIES

171 • GLOSSARY

172 • ABBREVIATIONS AND PRONUNCIATIONS

173 • PRONOUNCING INDEX

ACKNOWLEDGMENTS

This is the twelfth edition of *Goode's World Atlas* which was first published more than thirty years ago. The name of Dr. Goode, the original editor who was a distinguished cartographer and designed the early editions, is still retained and suggests the high standards which all those who have participated in the preparation of the book have sought to attain. The practice of including systematic improvements and revisions of the maps and data with each new edition is continued.

Sources. Every effort has been made to assemble the latest and most authentic source materials for use in compiling the atlas. For the general physical-political maps, national and state surveys, recent military maps, and hydrographic charts have been utilized. For the specialized maps, the source materials are even more varied. They include both published and unpublished items in the form of maps, descriptions in articles and books, statistics, and correspondence with geographers and others. To the various agencies and organizations, official and unofficial, who have cooperated, appreciation and thanks are expressed. Noteworthy among these organizations and agencies are: Food and Agriculture Organization of The United Nations for production statistics on livestock, crop and forest products, and statistics on world trade; the Office of the Geographer, The Department of State, for the map of Surface Transport Facilities, and other items; the Office of Foreign Agricultural Relations, Department of Agriculture, for information on crop and livestock production and distribution; the Bureau of Mines, Department of the Interior, for information on mineral production; various branches of the National Military Establishment and the Weather Bureau, Department of Commerce, for information on temperature, wind, pressure, and ocean currents; the Maritime Commission and the Department of Commerce, for statistics on ocean trade; the American Geographical Society, for use of its library and permission to use the Miller cylindrical projection; The University of Chicago Press, owners of the copyright, for permission to use Goode's Homolosine equal-area projection; and McGraw-Hill Book Company, for cooperation in permitting the use of Glenn Trewartha's map of climatic regions and Petterson's diagram of zones of precipitation.

Other acknowledgments. The variety and complexity of the problems involved in the preparation of a world atlas make highly desirable the participation of specialists in some of the problems. In the preparation of the new edition of *Goode's World Atlas* the editor has been ably assisted by several such experts. He expresses his deep appreciation and thanks to all of them. He is particularly indebted to the experts listed below who have assumed primary responsibility for certain maps.

The editor's grateful thanks are due to the staff of Rand McNally & Company. It is not possible to cite individual contributions, but the varied skills of geographers, cartographers, and many others are involved. Their faithful and careful work has contributed much to the final result.

EDWARD B. ESPENSHADE, JR.
Northwestern University
May, 1964

Cooperating Experts

A. W. KÜCHLER
Department of Geography
University of Kansas

THOBURN C. LYON
Consultant
Cartography and Air Navigation

A. C. ORVEDAL
Soil Scientist
Division of Soil Survey
United States Department of Agriculture

ERWIN RAISZ
Cartographer
Cambridge, Massachusetts

GLENN T. TREWARTHA
Department of Geography
University of Wisconsin

J. PARKER VAN ZANDT
President
Aviation Research Institute

WALTER H. VOSKUIL
Mineral Economist
Illinois Geological Survey

DERWENT WHITTLESEY
Late Professor of Geography
Harvard University

BOGDAN ZABORSKI
Professor of Geography
University of Ottawa

INTRODUCTION

Utility of maps. There are many kinds of maps, and they are useful in countless ways. It would be difficult to list all the ways in which even a simple road map, for example, is or may be useful. A knowledge of location, relative size, direction, distance, or of other facts which are set down in an atlas is necessary to an understanding of much about which one reads today. The changing world and the widespread commitments of the United States place new emphasis on map study. An atlas has become a prime necessity for understanding the course of world events. Three outstanding attributes may be noted in connection with the maps of this atlas. They are characteristics common to maps of the most varied kinds and utilities.

(1) The maps show facts of areal distribution, both qualitative and quantitative. For example, the world vegetation map (pp. 16-17) is based on observations made by many hundreds of individuals. The map shows hundreds of varied vegetative units and thirty-two types of vegetation. Thousands of words would be required to state the facts portrayed by the map. These facts can be presented best on a map and can be grasped quickly from a map. The information embodied in the world vegetation map is chiefly qualitative. It was reduced from a general, undefined form to a particular, classified form, and so its utility was greatly enhanced. The world rainfall map (pp. 14-15) provides quantitative facts concerning annual precipitation, by means of isohyets (lines connecting points of equal rainfall). Here again, a single map conveys factual information far better than could be done by volumes of words and tables.

(2) The maps in *Goode's World Atlas* also serve to illustrate innumerable facts of significance that are associated with location and areal distribution. For example, the climatic-regions map (pp. 8-9) shows the areal distribution of types of climate which are determined from a synthesis of thousands of rainfall and temperature statistics.

(3) Finally, many useful comparisons may be made between different maps, between two maps in some instances, between three or more in others, with a view to establishing relationships between the various types of information entered on the maps. Useful comparisons may also be made, of course, between different places on the same map as well as between different aspects of the same place as shown on two or more

maps. For example, compare the areas of dense population (pp. 20-21) with areas which have an intensive subsistence rice or non-rice agriculture (pp. 24-25). There are few agricultural areas in the world, with the exception of those in Europe, which have similar population densities. Note also on the agricultural-regions map the absence of nomadic herding in the Western Hemisphere, whereas extensive areas exist in Asia and Africa.

Reading maps. An ability to read maps is acquired through practice, in the same manner as the ability to read a written text. The effectiveness of any written text depends both on the skill of the writer and on that of the reader. Similarly, the value of a particular map depends both on the effectiveness of the cartography and on the map-reading ability of the user. Of particular importance in reading maps is a knowledge of map scales, projections, and symbolism.

Understanding scales. A function of all maps is to provide a reduced representation of the earth's surface. Since part or all of the earth's surface is depicted on a single page of this atlas, the question arises, "What is the relation of map size to earth size?" This proportional relationship is the scale of a map. The scale is given in three forms on most maps of this atlas to facilitate answering this question.

To aid further in understanding scales, a comparison of scale is given in a series of maps on the next page. A comparison of diagrams A, B, C, and D illustrates how progressively smaller-scale maps (of constant page size) increase the size of the area covered but reduce the detail which can be expressed. On the second map and on each later map, the area covered by the previous map is outlined within the map, to provide a direct comparison of the areas covered. On the first map, individual buildings are shown. On the final map, even many cities are omitted.

To aid the student in acquiring accurate concepts of the relative size of continents and of some countries and regions, uniform scales for comparable areas are used as far as possible. Continental maps are given on a uniform scale of 1:40,000,000 (one inch to 640 miles). In similar fashion, series of regions comparable in area appear in groups of maps on uniform scales of 1:16,000,000 (one inch to 250 miles), 1:12,000,000 (one inch to 190 miles), 1:4,000,000 (one inch to 64 miles), and on larger scales. The maximum size of the scale utilized for any

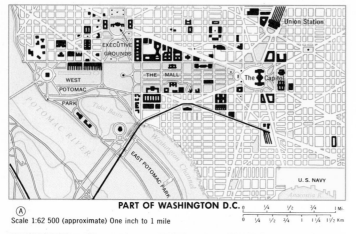

PART OF WASHINGTON D.C.
Ⓐ Scale 1:62 500 (approximate) One inch to 1 mile

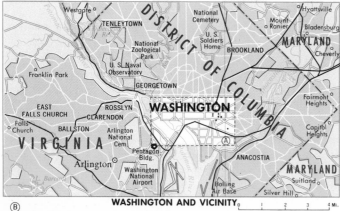

WASHINGTON AND VICINITY
Ⓑ Scale 1:250 000 (approximate) One inch to 4 miles

WASHINGTON TO BALTIMORE
Ⓒ Scale 1:1 000 000 (approximate) One inch to 16 miles

WASHINGTON TO NEW YORK
Ⓓ Scale 1:4 000 000, one inch to 64 miles. Conic Projection

given region is a partial measure of the importance of the region and of interest in it.

Understanding projections. There is no way of representing the curved surface of the globe on a flat surface without some distortion of the useful features desired on flat maps. On large-scale maps covering areas of only a few square miles, this distortion is negligible. In maps representing large areas, as in maps of a large country, a continent, or the whole world, the distortion inevitably is considerable, and, unless understood, it may result in serious misconceptions. The distortion may involve distances, directions, or the shapes and sizes of areas.

A map projection is an orderly system of parallels and meridians on which a map can be drawn. There are hundreds of map projections in use, but none avoids distortion of the spatial relationships that only a globe map can show truthfully. It is not possible to have truth of area, shape, angle, and scale all in the same flat map. It is possible, however, to select from the many types of projections one which is accurate for a particular property or which is a compromise (limiting the distortion of one or more elements at the expense of the others) that is relatively satisfactory for a particular need.

Truth of area is of prime importance in many maps. Most of the maps made for geographical study, particularly those used to show the areal distribution of an item, are drawn on equal-area projections. In an equal-area projection any square inch on the map represents the same number of square miles on the earth's surface as any other square inch on the map. Continents, oceans, islands, states, all are shown in their true relative size. Close to the importance of equality of area is truth of shape. This characteristic is to some extent an esthetic quality, but it is also a practical one. The student becomes familiar with the true shape of a continent or an island or a body of water as it appears on a globe map. Distortion of these shapes almost beyond recognition on a flat map is incongruous and a source of bewilderment to the student. Truth of direction is especially important in the study of the distribution of factors of significance in world relations. To show the latitudinal or zonal distribution of such factors, it is obviously desirable that lines of latitude be parallel, or better, straight lines parallel with the equator.

Most of the maps used in this atlas are drawn on projections that give equality of area, good land and ocean shapes, and parallel latitudinal directions. To provide these and other qualities desired for particular maps, some distortion of other elements is inevitable. The student should make himself aware of the nature of such distortions and make allowances for them in his use of the maps. One of the more practical procedures is to compare the projection grid of the flat map with the grid of the globe map. He should first verify the fundamental characteristics of the globe grid as listed here:

(1) On the globe map all longitude lines are equal in length and meet at the poles.

(2) All latitude lines are parallel.

(3) The length of the latitude lines, that is, the circumference of latitude circles, decreases from the equator to the points representing the poles. At latitude 60°, the circumference of the latitude circle is one-half the circumference of the equatorial circle.

(4) Distances along lines of longitude between any two latitude lines are equal.

(5) All latitude and longitude lines meet at right angles. With item (1) in mind, the student will observe that the projection used on pages 44-45 has latitude lines of equal length. This results in considerable exaggeration of areas in the higher latitudes. With item (5) in mind, he will note that the projection used on pages 6-7 has oblique angles at the junction of latitude and longitude lines in the higher latitudes, and that this partly causes distortion of land shapes in such areas as Alaska and Greenland. In this projection, however, truth of area has been maintained.

Some illustration of the construction of the more commonly used projections and indication of their properties are helpful in making clear the nature of inherent distortions. Pages 2 and 3 are designed to provide this help. They also illustrate the seven projections used in this atlas.

Few of the several hundred projections in use can be constructed graphically by methods of descriptive geometry. Most of them are derived from mathematical formulas designed to afford the properties desired. In some cases it is easier to visualize the general form and characteristics of a projection if the earth's surface is considered to be projected upon a plane, a cone, or a cylinder. The last two surfaces, when they are cut and unrolled, form a plane surface. These surfaces provide one general classification of projections: azimuthal (on a plane), conic, or cylindrical (fig. 1, 2, and 5, pp. 2 and 3). In each class the characteristics of the projections may be changed by varying the systematic arrangement or spacing of the latitude and longitude lines.

Figure 1, A (p. 2) is a true plane projection with the point of projection at the center of the globe. This geometrical projection of the earth grid on a tangent plane is called a gnomonic projection. In the illustration the plane is tangent to the equator, but it could be placed tangent to the poles, or to any other point on the earth's surface. Several other distinctive map projections can be obtained by changing the origin point of the projection. For example, the projection obtained from an origin point on the surface of the globe diametrically opposite the point of contact of the tangent plane is called a stereographic projection, and the projection from an origin point at infinity is called an orthographic projection. None of these perspective projections obtained from projection on a plane is used in this atlas, but the mathematically derived Lambert azimuthal equal-area projection (fig. 1, B, p. 2) may be considered in this general class. The polar aspect of the Lambert azimuthal equal-area projection is used for the map of the Northern Lands and Seas (p. 48); the oblique aspect is used for the series of continental maps. Besides its equal-area quality, the projection gives relatively good shapes to continental areas as a whole.

Conic projections may be thought of as derived from a tangent cone (fig. 2) or from an intersecting cone (fig. 3). In the latter case, the resulting projection is said to have "two standard parallels" along which the scale is exact (since the cone and the sphere coincide throughout the length of the parallels). In maps of areas covering a wide range of longitude, the projection used in this atlas is a modified conic of the latter type (De Lisle's). In this projection, as here used, the shapes are excellent, and the departure from the equal-area quality is almost negligible. (See Canada, pp. 86-87, and Siberia, pp. 134-135). The scale between the two standard parallels is too small along the parallels, and outside the standard parallels is too great along the parallels. The use of two standard parallels, however, provides a much better opportunity of extending the area within which the scale is reasonably accurate than the use of a single standard parallel, as in the simple conic.

Another modification of the conic principle is the Bonne projection (fig. 3, C, p. 2), used on pages 114-115 for the map of the Mediterranean lands. It has a selected standard parallel, and other parallels are arcs of concentric circles truly divided for points of intersection with the meridians. The scale along all the parallels is true everywhere, but the central meridian is the only one along which it is true. By construction, however, it is equal-area, and reasonably correct representation of shape is obtained in narrow zones along the standard parallel and central meridian, where the intersections are at right angles, or nearly so.

The polyconic projection (fig. 4, p. 2) is used for the United States and some other areas of similar position and size. In the case of the polyconic projection, the earth may be considered as made up of a series of tangent cones. As each base is developed, the result is as shown, somewhat exaggerated, in figure 4, B, page 2. The area of the projection used for the map of the United States (fig. 4, C, page 2) is the central portion of figure 4, B, beneath the word "Pole." In this projection the central meridian crosses all parallels at right angles, as on the globe; other intersections become noticeably oblique only at considerable distance from the central meridian. The scale is true on the central meridian and on each parallel. Shapes, as a result, are very good. Meridian-scale errors, however, increase rapidly with increasing distance from the central meridian. The projection is thus not well adapted to areas of wide longitudinal extent. The departure, however, from equality of area is slight where it has been used for maps in this atlas.

The cylindrical class of projections may be visualized as perspective projections on a tangent or intersecting cylinder (fig. 5, page 3). Many of the cylindrical projections in use, however, are mathematical modifications of the true perspective forms. As a general class, the cylindrical projections have the following characteristics: (1) latitude lines which are straight, parallel, and equal in length; (2) longitude lines which are straight, parallel, equal in length, and equally spaced; (3) meridians and parallels which intersect at right angles (fig. 5, page 3). Since the latitude lines are all drawn equal in length, an increasing distortion of scale occurs along the parallels with increasing distance from the standard parallel or parallels of tangency.

Mercator's projection (fig. 5, C, page 3), which belongs to this general class, is one of the better-known projections. For nearly four hundred years it has been used widely for world distributional maps, in spite of the facts (1) that it is impossible with this projection to show the entire surface of the earth, the poles being at infinity; and (2) that distances and areas grow rapidly larger with increase of latitude, until the distortion becomes enormous in higher latitudes. This is made apparent by

a comparison of the relative size of areas in figures 5, C, and 6. The distortion of area is so great that the use of the Mercator projection for world maps showing areal distributions of most kinds is pedagogically unsound and misleading. The projection was designed by Mercator primarily for use of navigators, and for that use it is incomparable. On it, the navigator can draw a straight line (called a rhumb line) between any two points, read the angle between the rhumb line and any meridian that it crosses, set his compass on that angle, and go direct to his destination without change of compass. This advantage is so great that no other projection has yet taken the place of the Mercator in marine navigation.

A variation of the Mercator is the transverse or oblique Mercator. The grid is derived from a cylinder tangent along a selected great circle (fig. 7). The resulting projection is conformal, but its grid bears no resemblance to that of the ordinary Mercator and may be mistaken for that of a conic projection. Although the transverse Mercator projection is not used in this atlas, it illustrates a special-purpose projection which is being used more and more because of its value in air navigation for maps of great-circle strips.

Miller's projection (fig. 5, D) is a recent "compromise projection." It has been used in the atlas (with permission of the American Geographical Society) for climatic maps showing barometric pressures, winds, and temperatures, and for the map of ocean communications. A continuous grid without interruptions, and straight-line parallels were desirable for the best presentation of the features listed above. Miller's projection meets these requirements and provides a compromise between the distortion of areas and shapes. Mercator's projection was not suitable because of its excessive area distortion, although shapes of areas are excellent. Use of continuous grids for the whole world which were strictly equal-area would result in considerable distortion of shapes. The student will note, however, that even on the Miller projection there is still considerable distortion of areas and shapes in the higher latitudes (cf. fig. 5, D, 5, C, and 6). Changes in scale according to latitude are indicated in the legend of the map and should be carefully noted. For example, compare on the graphic scale (page 44) a distance of one thousand miles at the equator with the same distance at latitude 60° or 80°.

Figure 6 illustrates three projections which are purely conventional in design. They cannot be readily related to the three general classes just discussed. They are not projections in the sense of being projected on a plane, a cone, or a cylinder; rather, they all are based on mathematical formulas. The sinusoidal projection (fig. 6, C, page 3) is used for the large-scale sectional maps of South America and Africa and for the map showing world surface transport facilities. It is an equal-area projection. On these continental maps it is most accurate along the equator where the two continents are widest. The placement of the central meridian through the center of the continents results in relatively little distortion of scale or shapes in the narrower southern parts of the continents. The scale is true along all parallels and the central meridian, but it increases on other meridians in conformity with their increasing obliquity. On the world map (pp. 42-43) the extent of the distortion is reduced by the technique of interrupting the projection and of using a separate central meridian for different land masses.

Mollweide's equal-area projection (fig. 6, A, page 3), designed to show the entire globe as an uninterrupted unit, gives an elliptical picture of the earth. The ellipse is drawn to enclose an area equal to that of a globe on the same scale. The central meridian is divided so that the areas of the bands between the parallels are truthfully proportional. Mollweide's projection is thus an equal-area projection, but there is little uniformity in linear scale. So that the areas of greater distortion in the outer parts of the projection will be eliminated, it, like the sinusoidal projection, may be interrupted and a new central meridian established through each continent (cf. the two forms, fig. 6, A and B, page 3).

Most of the world distribution maps in this atlas are drawn on Goode's homolosine equal-area projection (fig. 6, D, page 3). This projection is derived by combining the sinusoidal projection for latitudes up to 40° north and south with the homolographic projection (Mollweide) for areas poleward of these latitudes. In this manner an equal-area projection is obtained which has some of the better qualities of both the sinusoidal and homolographic. Further improvement of shapes is obtained by application of the principle of interruption, so that extremely oblique intersections are eliminated. The result has a number of distinct advantages: (1) It presents the entire surface of the earth, which Mercator's projection cannot do. (2) It is strictly an equal-area projection, with no distortion of the size of areas. (3) On it the parallels of latitude are represented by straight lines trending with the equator, a real advantage in the study of comparative latitudes. (4) On it the grid is interrupted in the oceans so as to give each continent in turn the advantage of being in the center of the projection, thus providing better shapes for the continents than any uninterrupted world map can give. No map projection has been devised which displays to better advantage the distribution of most world phenomena which are studied best from the equatorial aspect.

Symbolism. The signs, symbols, and conventions shown on maps are a form of "shorthand" indicating a variety of phenomena (page xii). Many of them are self-explanatory. Compare also the aerial mosaics with the adjacent topographic maps of Pittsburgh and Strasburg areas (inside cover). A complete legend (page xii) provides a key to the physical-political reference maps.

Two systems of measurement are used in connection with the maps in this atlas. The English system of measures, which is conventional in this country, is utilized, although admittedly it is somewhat irrational and cumbersome. Since much of the world uses the metric system of measurement and the centigrade thermometer, most measures are given also in these scientific terms, or conversion scales are provided. A linear scale in miles is placed alongside a linear scale in kilometers, with the zero points together. Heights and depths may be read in feet or in meters from opposite scales. Comparative scales in the margins permit ready conversion of temperature and precipitation values from one system to another.

Surface configuration on the continental and regional maps is shown in a different manner from the tenth edition of this

atlas. A combination of two techniques is utilized which gives a striking three-dimensional effect. General elevation above sea level is indicated as previously by layer-tints, altitudinal zones, each of which has a different hue and is defined by a generalized contour line. The hues for the zones, however, have been selected so that their values increases with elevation in preference to the more conventional layer-tint colors. Thus, although shades of green are still used for the lowlands below 1,000 feet, hues of light tan, buff, and yellow are used for successively higher elevations and areas of more than 10,000 feet are left white. Each of the hues increases in value with increasing elevation and thus visually appears closer to the observer.

An oblique shading in gray has been utilized to indicate local relief, particularly the direction and steepness of slopes. This has been superimposed over the layer tints and a much more realistic and readily visualized impression of the surface configuration is obtained. The three-dimensional effect is more noticeable where it is important in the higher mountainous areas whose slopes are steepest, because the shadow contrast is greatest in the very areas where the color values are highest.

This new presentation of relief is designed to overcome some of the serious weaknesses of the layer-tints system used previously. Steepness of slope, the ruggedness of the terrain, and significant relief features which have differences in elevation with a value less than the layer-tint interval are distinguished and can be visualized. No longer should the nearly level high plateau area be confused with an adjacent mountain area. The improved symbolism for representation of surface configuration should facilitate the reading of the maps and should reduce some of the misconceptions obtained when layer-tints alone were utilized.

Place Names. Place names are used to distinguish particular places and features—cities, towns, bays, peninsulas—from other similar features. Many place names consist of two parts —a specific and a generic part. For example, Lake Michigan consists of the specific term "Michigan" modifying the generic term "lake."

If the world used one alphabet and one language, no particular difficulty would arise in the use of place names. Unfortunately, people use many languages and various alphabets. Moreover, some of the people of the world, the Chinese and the Japanese, for example, use non-alphabet languages. In order to make some languages intelligible to American readers, their letters and symbols must be converted into the Roman alphabet. It has been the practice of many people to transform place names further by transcribing or translating part or all of them into English. The recent war, which brought far corners of the earth to our attention, and the increasing facilities for communication in recent years make this practice no longer desirable. In this atlas, a "local-name policy" generally has been used for the cities and towns and for all local topographic and water features. However, for a few major cities the Anglicized form is preferred and the local name is given in parentheses. In countries where more than one official language is used such as South Africa, the spelling of the name is in the form of the dominant local language. The generic parts of local names for topographic and water features are self-explanatory in many cases because of the associated map symbol or type style. A complete list of foreign generic terms is given in the glossary on page 171, and a short list of "geographical equivalents" is given on pages 6 and 7.

A distinctive feature of *Goode's World Atlas* is the pronouncing index which has been completely revised. The variable vowel sounds of English and the differences among other languages make the correct pronunciation of place names difficult. The correct pronunciation of many names differs from the pronunciation that may seem natural. Under these circumstances, the pronouncing index of more than thirty thousand names should be very helpful to the student.

Economic maps and statistics. The statistics presented in this atlas are not intended to take the place of statistical reference works. Instead of having been planned to present an absolute index to production and trade, they were planned to give a picture of the relative importance of countries and regions in the particulars involved. The maps have been reserved chiefly to present facts of distribution. However, the general magnitude of production is indicated by graded point symbols in the case of minerals, and the density of the uniform dot pattern indirectly provides a similar assessment for crop production. Marginal graphs show the relative importance of different areas by percentage values of world totals.

No single year affords, for this purpose, a satisfactory base for production and trade statistics. For this reason, the percentages and world totals used have been computed with few exceptions, from averages of a period of three or four years. The base period of years varies, but the latest year for which data are available at time of publication has been used. Few realize that there is a necessary gap of several years between the date of a publication such as this and the date of the statistics used. Organizations issuing statistical data of the sort used in the atlas require two or three years to gather, tabulate, and publish their materials. An additional year is required to incorporate and publish the data within this atlas. Publishers often are reluctant to date their statistical materials, since few users understand the reason for the gap in time. The dates of the base period used are indicated on each graph. In general the averages and percentages will provide the student with a sufficiently accurate picture of the relative importance of areas, despite the fact they are not for the current year. An exception occurs in the case of a product which is subject to major or rapid expansion or contraction of production either nationally, regionally, or on a world wide basis. This occurs more commonly in mineral products than in agricultural products. An important example is petroleum where notable shifts in proven reserves, production, and trade movements have occurred within the last five years.

EDWARD B. ESPENSHADE, JR.
Northwestern University
May, 1964

MAP SYMBOLS

CULTURAL FEATURES

Political Boundaries

— — — — International

— — — — Intercolonial

— — — Secondary: State, Provincial, etc.

Disputed or Indefinite

Parks, Indian Reservations

City Limits

Cities, Towns and Villages
(Except for scales of 1:20,000,000 or smaller)

PARIS   1,000,000 and over

◎ Ufa   500,000 to 1,000,000

⊙ Győr   50,000 to 500,000

○ Agadir   25,000 to 50,000

○ Moreno   0 to 25,000

TŌKYŌ   National Capitals

Boise   Secondary Capitals

Transportation

———— Railroads

- - - - - Railroad Ferries

———— Roads

· · · · · · · Caravan Routes

✈ Airports

Other Cultural Features

Dams

Pipelines

▲ Pyramids

Ruins

WATER FEATURES

Lakes and Reservoirs

Fresh Water

Fresh Water: Intermittent

Salt Water

Salt Water: Intermittent

Other Water Features

Salt Basins, Flats

Swamps

Ice Caps and Glaciers

Rivers

Canals

Aqueducts

Ship Channels

Falls

Rapids

Springs

Water Depths

Fishing Banks

Sand Bars

Reefs

LAND FEATURES

△ Peaks, Spot Heights

= Passes

Sand

Contours

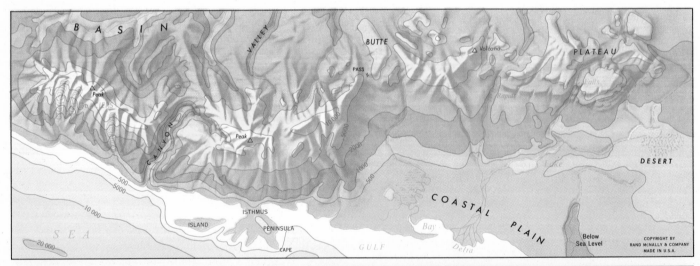

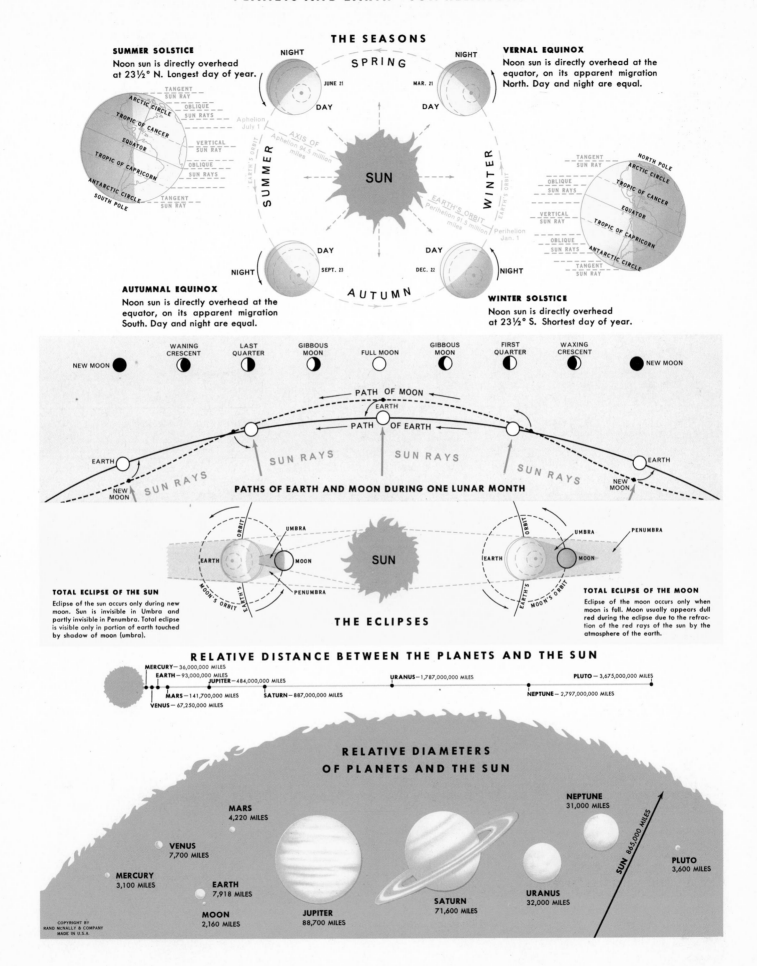

THE SEASONS

SUMMER SOLSTICE
Noon sun is directly overhead at 23½° N. Longest day of year.

VERNAL EQUINOX
Noon sun is directly overhead at the equator, on its apparent migration North. Day and night are equal.

SPRING

NIGHT · JUNE 21 · DAY

NIGHT · MAR. 21 · DAY

Aphelion July 1

AXIS OF
Aphelion 94.5 million miles

SUMMER

WINTER

SUN

EARTH'S ORBIT

EARTH'S ORBIT
Perihelion 91.5 million miles

Perihelion Jan. 1

DAY · SEPT. 23 · NIGHT

DAY · DEC. 22 · NIGHT

AUTUMN

TANGENT SUN RAY
ARCTIC CIRCLE
OBLIQUE SUN RAYS
TROPIC OF CANCER
EQUATOR · VERTICAL SUN RAY
TROPIC OF CAPRICORN
OBLIQUE SUN RAYS
ANTARCTIC CIRCLE
SOUTH POLE · TANGENT SUN RAY

TANGENT SUN RAY
NORTH POLE
ARCTIC CIRCLE
OBLIQUE SUN RAYS
TROPIC OF CANCER
EQUATOR
VERTICAL SUN RAY
TROPIC OF CAPRICORN
OBLIQUE SUN RAYS
ANTARCTIC CIRCLE
TANGENT SUN RAY

AUTUMNAL EQUINOX
Noon sun is directly overhead at the equator, on its apparent migration South. Day and night are equal.

WINTER SOLSTICE
Noon sun is directly overhead at 23½° S. Shortest day of year.

NEW MOON · WANING CRESCENT · LAST QUARTER · GIBBOUS MOON · FULL MOON · GIBBOUS MOON · FIRST QUARTER · WAXING CRESCENT · NEW MOON

PATH OF MOON
EARTH
PATH OF EARTH
EARTH
SUN RAYS · SUN RAYS · SUN RAYS
EARTH
NEW MOON
NEW MOON

PATHS OF EARTH AND MOON DURING ONE LUNAR MONTH

ORBIT · UMBRA
EARTH · MOON
MOON'S ORBIT · PENUMBRA
EARTH'S

SUN

ORBIT · UMBRA · PENUMBRA
EARTH · MOON
EARTH'S · MOON'S ORBIT

TOTAL ECLIPSE OF THE SUN
Eclipse of the sun occurs only during new moon. Sun is invisible in Umbra and partly invisible in Penumbra. Total eclipse is visible only in portion of earth touched by shadow of moon (umbra).

THE ECLIPSES

TOTAL ECLIPSE OF THE MOON
Eclipse of the moon occurs only when moon is full. Moon usually appears dull red during the eclipse due to the refraction of the red rays of the sun by the atmosphere of the earth.

RELATIVE DISTANCE BETWEEN THE PLANETS AND THE SUN

MERCURY—36,000,000 MILES
EARTH—93,000,000 MILES
JUPITER—484,000,000 MILES
URANUS—1,787,000,000 MILES
PLUTO—3,675,000,000 MILES
MARS—141,700,000 MILES
SATURN—887,000,000 MILES
NEPTUNE—2,797,000,000 MILES
VENUS—67,250,000 MILES

RELATIVE DIAMETERS OF PLANETS AND THE SUN

MARS 4,220 MILES
VENUS 7,700 MILES
NEPTUNE 31,000 MILES
MERCURY 3,100 MILES
EARTH 7,918 MILES
PLUTO 3,600 MILES
MOON 2,160 MILES
JUPITER 88,700 MILES
SATURN 71,600 MILES
URANUS 32,000 MILES
SUN 865,000 MILES

PROJECTIONS

A map projection is merely an orderly system of parallels and meridians on which a flat map can be drawn. There are hundreds of projections, but no one represents the earth's spherical surface without some distortion. The distortion is relatively small for most practical purposes when a small part of the sphere is projected. For larger areas, a sacrifice of some property is necessary.

Most projections are designed to preserve on the flat map some particular property of the sphere. By varying the systematic arrangement or spacing of the latitude and longitude lines, a projection may be made either equal-area or conformal. Although most projections are derived from mathematical formulas, some are easier to visualize if thought of as projected upon a plane, or upon a cone or cylinder which is then unrolled into a plane surface. Thus, many projections are classified as plane (azimuthal), conic, or cylindrical.

For a fuller discussion of map projections, see Preface. Figures with asterisks indicate projections used in this atlas.

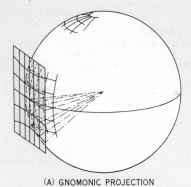

(A) GNOMONIC PROJECTION

A geometric or perspective projection on a tangent plane with the origin point at the center of the globe. Shapes and distances rapidly become increasingly distorted away from the center of the projection. Important in navigation, because all straight lines are great circles.

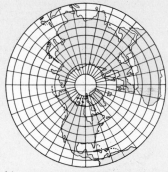

(B) LAMBERT EQUAL AREA PROJECTION*

A mathematically designed azimuthal equal-area projection. Excellent for continental areas. For larger areas away from the center, distortion of distances and shapes is appreciable.

FIGURE 1.–TYPICAL PLANE PROJECTIONS

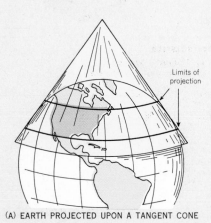

(A) EARTH PROJECTED UPON A TANGENT CONE

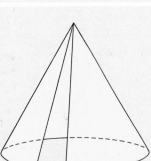

(B) CONE CUT FROM BASE TO APEX

A perspective projection on a tangent cone with the origin point at the center of the globe. At the parallel of tangency, all elements of the map are

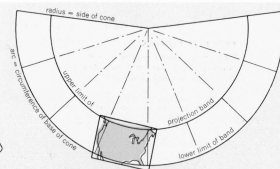

(C) CONE DEVELOPED INTO A PLANE SURFACE

true- angles,distances,shapes,areas. Away from the tangent parallel, distances increase rapidly, giving bad distortion of shapes and areas.

FIGURE 2.–SIMPLE CONIC PROJECTIONS

(A) EARTH PROJECTED UPON AN INTERSECTING CONE

This modification of the conic has two standard parallels, or lines of intersection. It is not an equal-area projection, the space being reduced in size between the standard parallels and

(B) CONIC PROJECTION WITH TWO STANDARD PARALLELS*

progressively enlarged beyond the standard parallels. Careful selection of the standard parallels provides, however, good representation for areas of limited latitudinal extent.

(C) BONNE PROJECTION*

An equal-area modification of the conic principle. Distances are true along all parallels and the central meridian; but away from it, increasing obliqueness of intersections and longitudinal distances, with their attendant distortion of shapes, limits the satisfactory area.

FIGURE 3.–MODIFIED CONIC PROJECTIONS

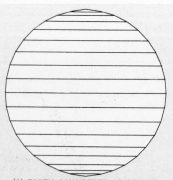

(A) EARTH CONSIDERED AS FORMED BY BASES OF CONES

This variation is not equal-area. Parallels are non-concentric circles truly divided. Distances along the straight central meridian are also true, but

(B) DEVELOPMENT OF THE CONICAL BASES

along the curving meridians are increasingly exaggerated. Representation is good near the central meridian, but away from it there is marked distortion.

(C) POLYCONIC PROJECTION*

FIGURE 4.–POLYCONIC PROJECTION

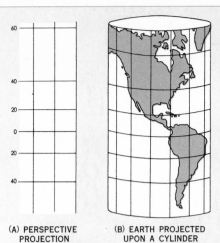
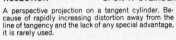

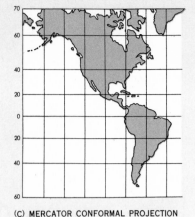

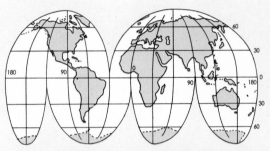

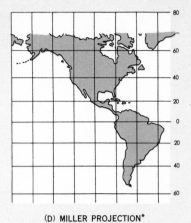

(A) PERSPECTIVE PROJECTION

A perspective projection on a tangent cylinder. Because of rapidly increasing distortion away from the line of tangency and the lack of any special advantage, it is rarely used.

(B) EARTH PROJECTED UPON A CYLINDER

(C) MERCATOR CONFORMAL PROJECTION

Mercator's modification increases the latitudinal distances in the same proportion as longitudinal distances are increased. Thus, at any point shapes are true, but areas become increasingly exaggerated. Of value in navigation, because a line connecting any two points gives the true direction between them.

(D) MILLER PROJECTION*

This recent modification is neither conformal nor equal-area. Whereas shapes are less accurate than on the Mercator, the exaggeration of areas has been reduced somewhat.

FIGURE 5.–CYLINDRICAL PROJECTIONS

(A) MOLLWEIDE'S HOMOLOGRAPHIC PROJECTION

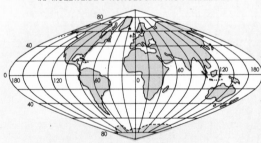

(C) SINUSOIDAL PROJECTION*

(B) GOODE'S INTERRUPTED HOMOLOGRAPHIC PROJECTION

(D) GOODE'S INTERRUPTED HOMOLOSINE PROJECTION*

Although each of these projections is equal-area, differences in the spacing and arrangement of latitude and longitude lines result in differences in the distribution and relative degree of the shape and distance distortion within each grid. On the homolographic, there is no uniformity in scale. It is different on each parallel and each meridian. On the sinusoidal, only distances along all latitudes and the central meridian are true. The homolosine combines the homolographic, for areas poleward of 40°, with the sinusoidal. The principle of interruption permits each continent in turn the advantage of being in the center of the projection, resulting in better shapes.

FIGURE 6.–EQUAL AREA PROJECTIONS OF THE WORLD

A conformal projection in which a selected great circle of the globe is considered as the "equator" of the ordinary Mercator projection, with the cylinder tangent along the great circle. It is used chiefly for charts of great-circle air routes between distant cities.

FIGURE 7.–TRANSVERSE MERCATOR PROJECTION

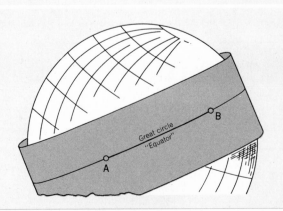

A-510000-26
Copyright by Rand McNally & Co.
Made in U.S.A.

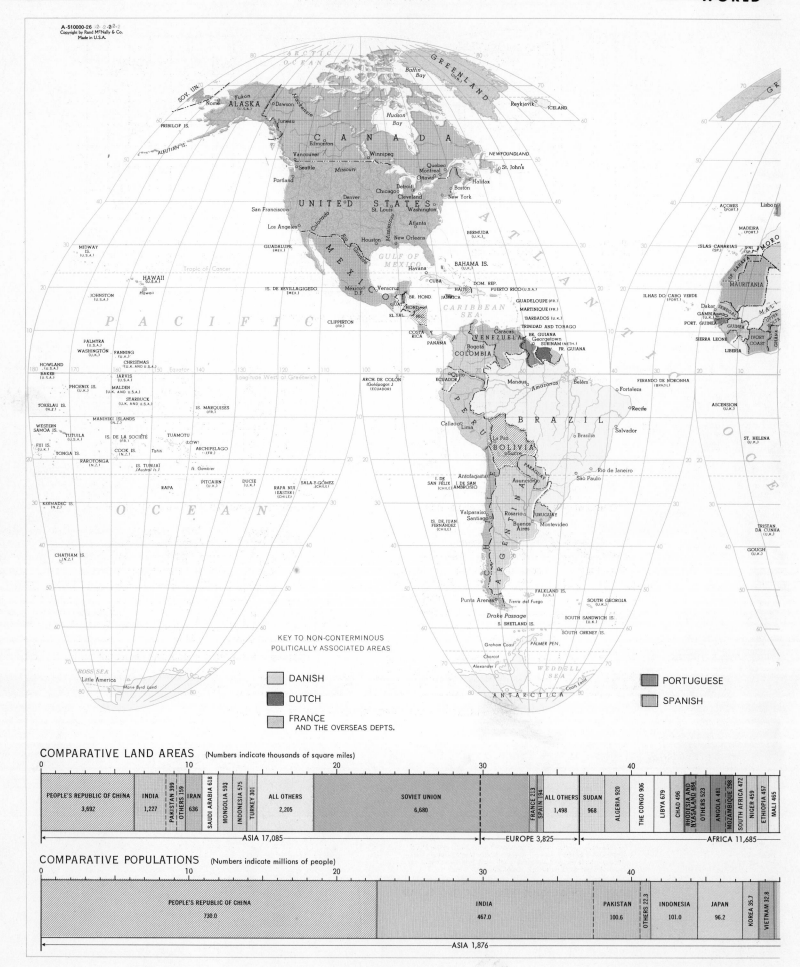

KEY TO NON-CONTERMINOUS
POLITICALLY ASSOCIATED AREAS

DANISH

DUTCH

FRANCE
AND THE OVERSEAS DEPTS.

PORTUGUESE

SPANISH

COMPARATIVE LAND AREAS (Numbers indicate thousands of square miles)

| | PEOPLE'S REPUBLIC OF CHINA 3,692 | INDIA 1,227 | PAKISTAN 399 | OTHERS 159 | IRAN 636 | SAUDI ARABIA 618 | MONGOLIA 593 | INDONESIA 575 | TURKEY 301 | ALL OTHERS 2,205 | SOVIET UNION 6,680 | FRANCE 213 | SPAIN 194 | ALL OTHERS 1,498 | SUDAN 968 | ALGERIA 920 | THE CONGO 906 | LIBYA 679 | CHAD 496 | RHODESIA AND NYASALAND 484 | OTHERS 523 | ANGOLA 481 | MOZAMBIQUE 298 | SOUTH AFRICA 472 | NIGER 459 | ETHIOPIA 457 | MALI 465 |

ASIA 17,085 — EUROPE 3,825 — AFRICA 11,685

COMPARATIVE POPULATIONS (Numbers indicate millions of people)

| PEOPLE'S REPUBLIC OF CHINA 730.0 | INDIA 467.0 | PAKISTAN 100.6 | OTHERS 22.3 | INDONESIA 101.0 | JAPAN 96.2 | KOREA 35.7 | VIETNAM 32.8 |

ASIA 1,876

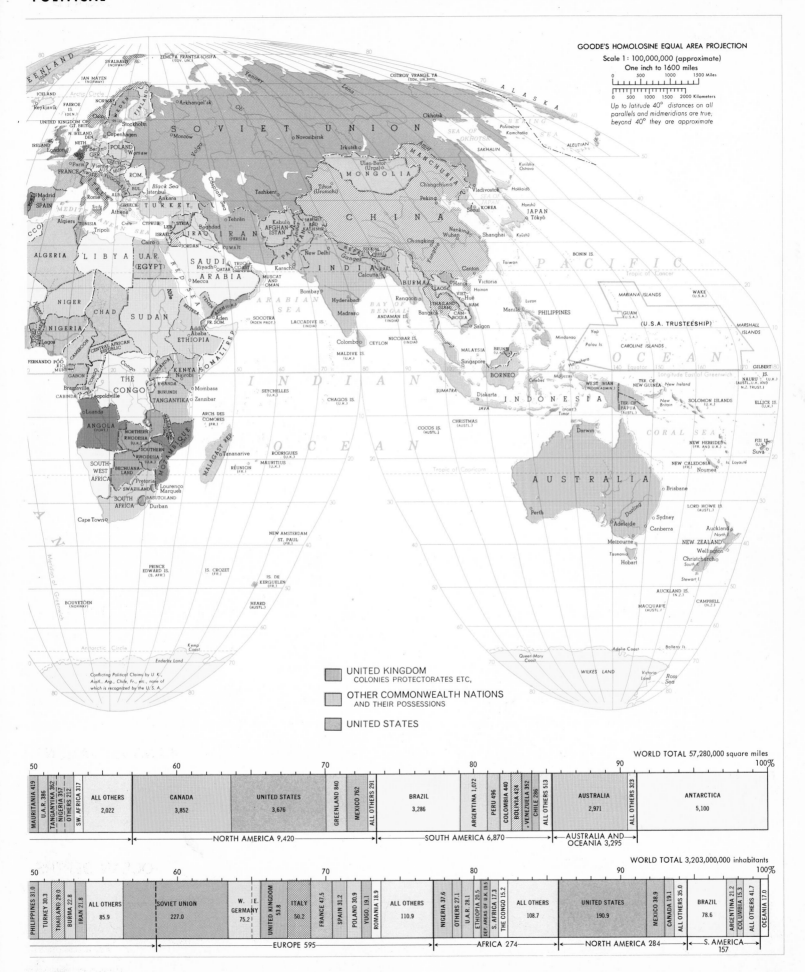

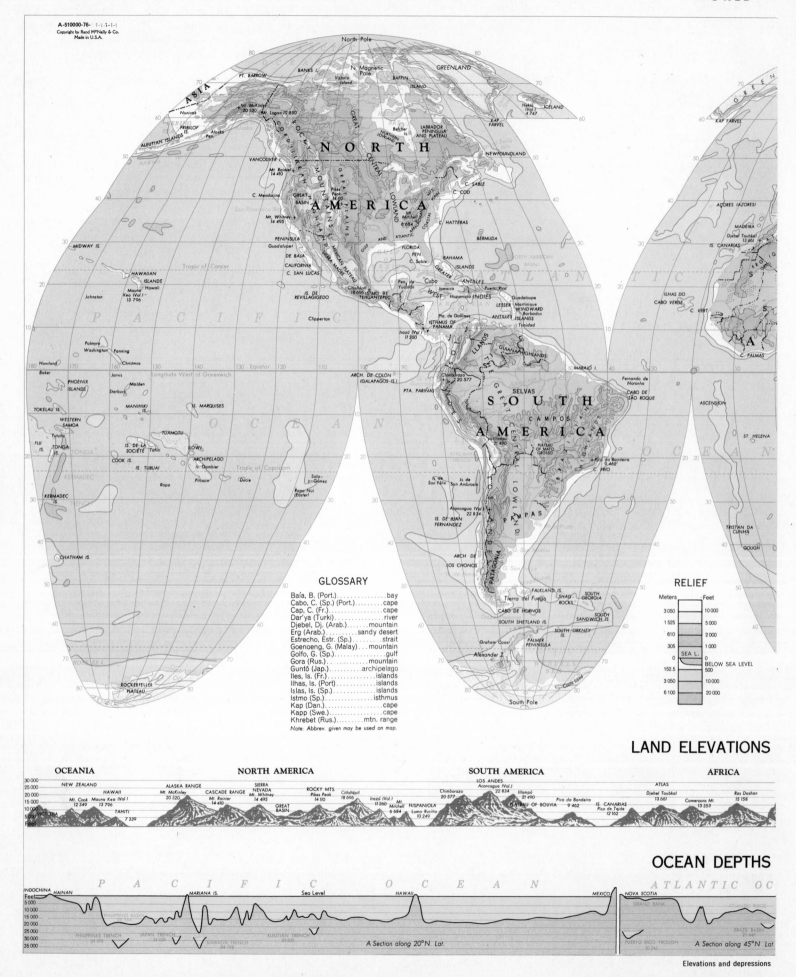

GLOSSARY

Baía, B. (Port.) . . . . bay
Cabo, C. (Sp.) (Port.) . . . . cape
Cap, C. (Fr.) . . . . cape
Dar'ya (Turki) . . . . river
Djebel, Dj. (Arab.) . . . . mountain
Erg (Arab.) . . . . sandy desert
Estrecho, Estr. (Sp.) . . . . strait
Goenoeng, G. (Malay) . . . mountain
Golfo, G. (Sp.) . . . . gulf
Gora (Rus.) . . . . mountain
Guntō (Jap.) . . . . archipelago
Iles, Is. (Fr.) . . . . islands
Ilhas, Is. (Port) . . . . islands
Islas, Is. (Sp.) . . . . islands
Istmo (Sp.) . . . . isthmus
Kap (Dan.) . . . . cape
Kapp (Swe.) . . . . cape
Khrebet (Rus.) . . . . mtn. range

Note: Abbrev. given may be used on map.

RELIEF

Meters	Feet
3 050	10 000
1 525	5 000
610	2 000
305	1 000
0	SEA L. 0
	BELOW SEA LEVEL
152.5	500
3 050	10 000
6 100	20 000

LAND ELEVATIONS

OCEANIA   NORTH AMERICA   SOUTH AMERICA   AFRICA

OCEAN DEPTHS

A Section along 20°N. Lat.   *A Section along 45°N. Lat.*

Elevations and depressions

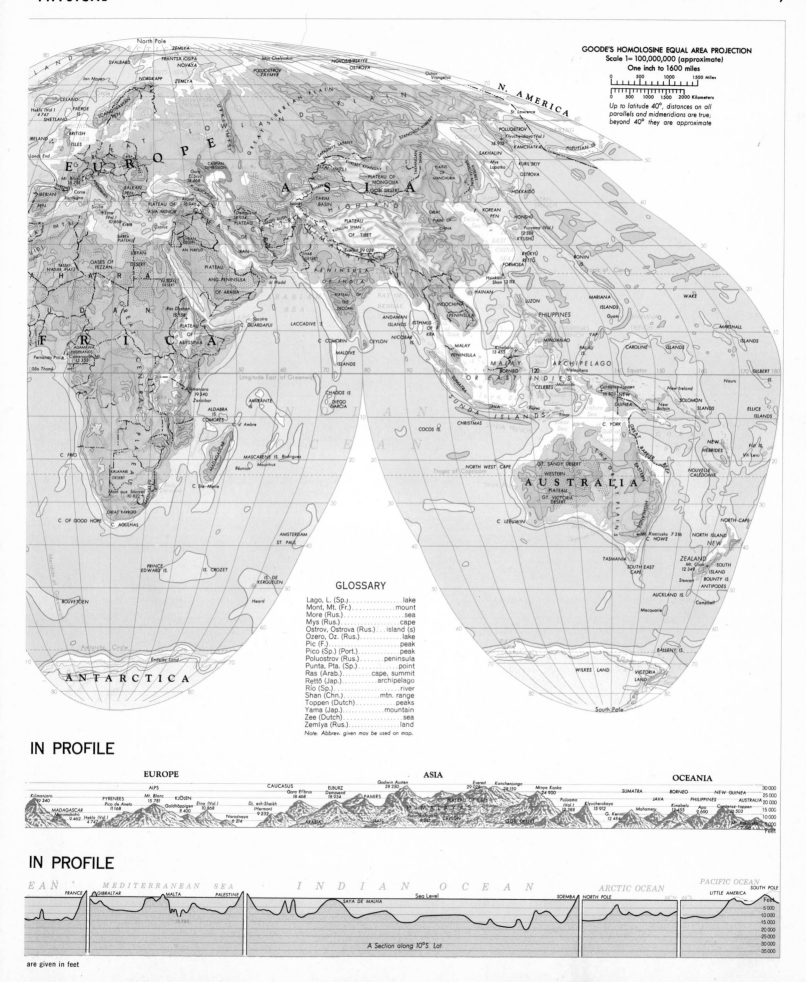

GOODE'S HOMOLOSINE EQUAL AREA PROJECTION
Scale 1= 100,000,000 (approximate)
One inch to 1600 miles

Up to latitude 40°, distances on all
parallels and midmeridians are true;
beyond 40° they are approximate

GLOSSARY

Lago, L. (Sp.) . . . . lake
Mont, Mt. (Fr.) . . . . mount
More (Rus.) . . . . sea
Mys (Rus.) . . . . cape
Ostrov, Ostrova (Rus.) . . . island (s)
Ozero, Oz. (Rus.) . . . . lake
Pic (F.) . . . . peak
Pico (Sp.) (Port.) . . . . peak
Poluostrov (Rus.) . . . . peninsula
Punta, Pta. (Sp.) . . . . point
Ras (Arab.) . . . . cape, summit
Rettō (Jap.) . . . . archipelago
Río (Sp.) . . . . river
Shan (Chn.) . . . . mtn. range
Toppen (Dutch) . . . . peaks
Yama (Jap.) . . . . mountain
Zee (Dutch) . . . . sea
Zemlya (Rus.) . . . . land
Note: Abbrev. given may be used on map.

IN PROFILE

EUROPE   ASIA   OCEANIA

IN PROFILE

A Section along 10°S. Lat.

are given in feet

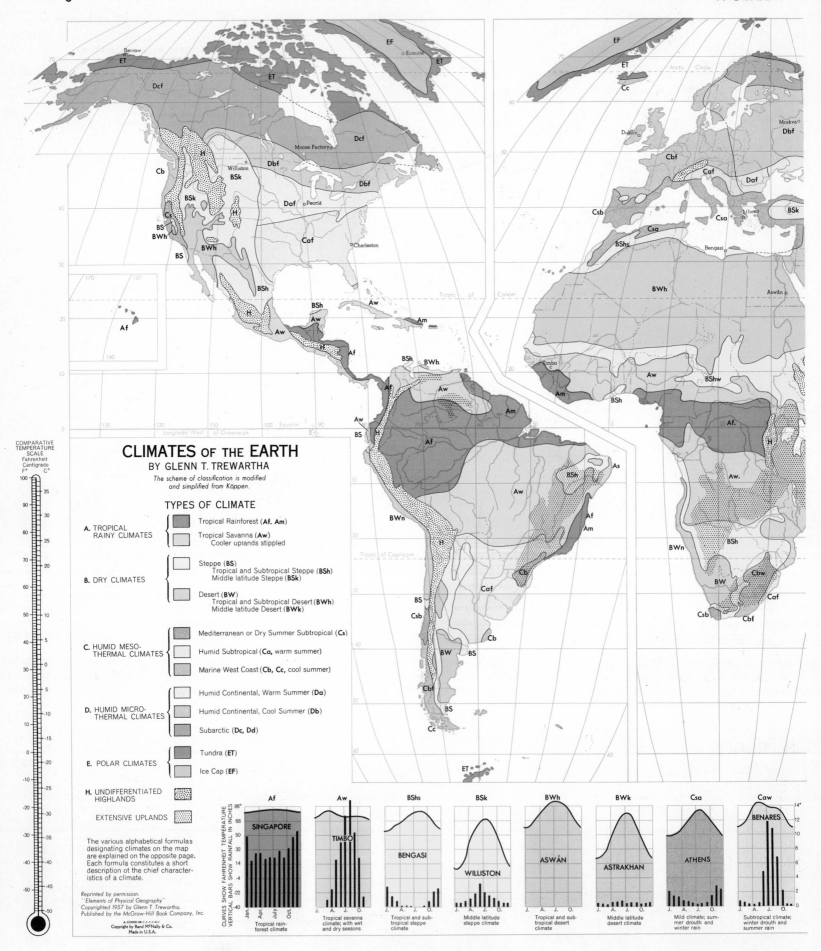

CLIMATES of the EARTH
BY GLENN T. TREWARTHA

*The scheme of classification is modified
and simplified from Köppen.*

TYPES OF CLIMATE

A. TROPICAL RAINY CLIMATES
- Tropical Rainforest (**Af, Am**)
- Tropical Savanna (**Aw**)
  Cooler uplands stippled

B. DRY CLIMATES
- Steppe (**BS**)
  Tropical and Subtropical Steppe (**BSh**)
  Middle latitude Steppe (**BSk**)
- Desert (**BW**)
  Tropical and Subtropical Desert (**BWh**)
  Middle latitude Desert (**BWk**)

C. HUMID MESO-THERMAL CLIMATES
- Mediterranean or Dry Summer Subtropical (**Cs**)
- Humid Subtropical (**Ca**, warm summer)
- Marine West Coast (**Cb, Cc**, cool summer)

D. HUMID MICRO-THERMAL CLIMATES
- Humid Continental, Warm Summer (**Da**)
- Humid Continental, Cool Summer (**Db**)
- Subarctic (**Dc, Dd**)

E. POLAR CLIMATES
- Tundra (**ET**)
- Ice Cap (**EF**)

H. UNDIFFERENTIATED HIGHLANDS

EXTENSIVE UPLANDS

The various alphabetical formulas
designating climates on the map
are explained on the opposite page.
Each formula constitutes a short
description of the chief characteristics of a climate.

Reprinted by permission:
"Elements of Physical Geography"
Copyrighted 1957 by Glenn T. Trewartha.
Published by the McGraw-Hill Book Company, Inc.

A-610000-66-1-1-1-1-0-1
Copyright by Rand McNally & Co.
Made in U.S.A.

COMPARATIVE
TEMPERATURE
SCALE
Fahrenheit
Centigrade
F°   C°

CURVES SHOW FAHRENHEIT TEMPERATURE
VERTICAL BARS SHOW RAINFALL IN INCHES

Af	Aw	BShs	BSk	BWh	BWk	Csa	Caw
SINGAPORE	TIMBO	BENGASI	WILLISTON	ASWÂN	ASTRAKHAN	ATHENS	BENARES
Tropical rain-forest climate	Tropical savanna climate; with wet and dry seasons	Tropical and sub-tropical steppe climate	Middle latitude steppe climate	Tropical and subtropical desert climate	Middle latitude desert climate	Mild climate; summer drouth and winter rain	Subtropical climate; winter drouth and summer rain

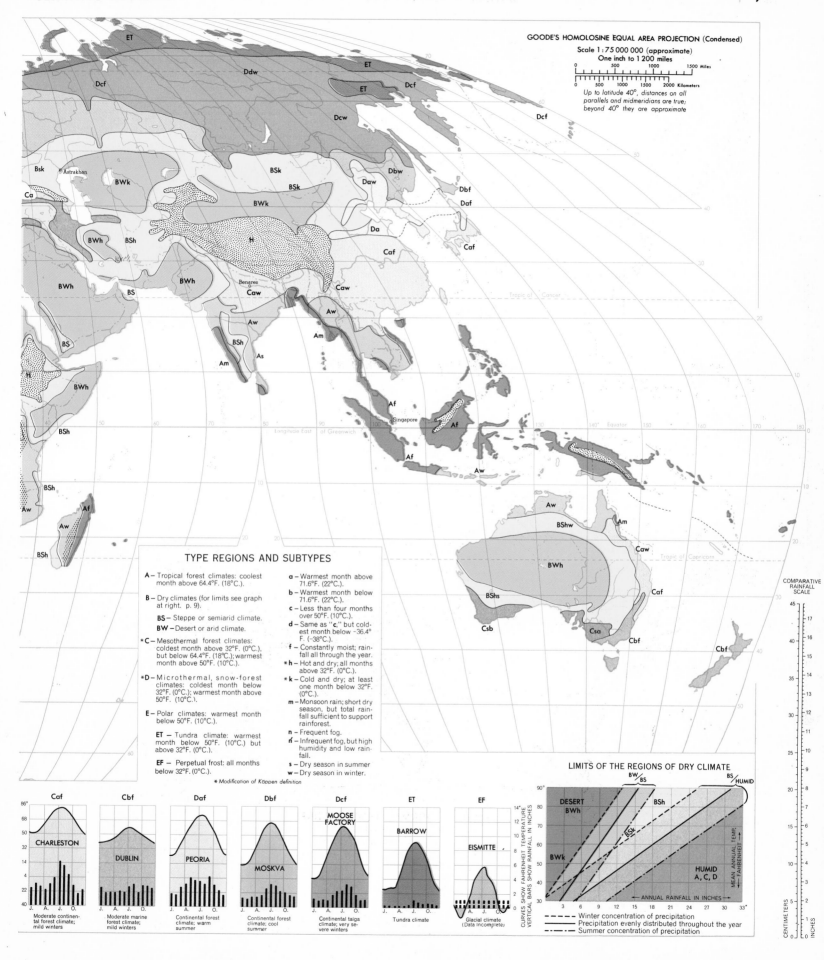

GOODE'S HOMOLOSINE EQUAL AREA PROJECTION (Condensed)

Scale 1 : 75 000 000 (approximate)
One inch to 1 200 miles

Up to latitude 40°, distances on all
parallels and midmeridians are true;
beyond 40° they are approximate

TYPE REGIONS AND SUBTYPES

A – Tropical forest climates: coolest month above 64.4°F. (18°C.).

B – Dry climates (for limits see graph at right. p. 9).

   BS – Steppe or semiarid climate.

   BW – Desert or arid climate.

*C – Mesothermal forest climates: coldest month above 32°F. (0°C.), but below 64.4°F. (18°C.); warmest month above 50°F. (10°C.).

*D – Microthermal, snow-forest climates: coldest month below 32°F. (0°C.); warmest month above 50°F. (10°C.).

E – Polar climates: warmest month below 50°F. (10°C.).

   ET – Tundra climate: warmest month below 50°F. (10°C.) but above 32°F. (0°C.).

   EF – Perpetual frost: all months below 32°F. (0°C.).

a – Warmest month above 71.6°F. (22°C.).

b – Warmest month below 71.6°F. (22°C.).

c – Less than four months over 50°F. (10°C.).

d – Same as "c," but coldest month below −36.4° F. (−38°C.).

f – Constantly moist; rainfall all through the year.

*h – Hot and dry; all months above 32°F. (0°C.).

*k – Cold and dry; at least one month below 32°F. (0°C.).

m – Monsoon rain; short dry season, but total rainfall sufficient to support rainforest.

n – Frequent fog.

n̄ – Infrequent fog, but high humidity and low rainfall.

s – Dry season in summer

w – Dry season in winter.

*Modification of Köppen definition

CURVES SHOW FAHRENHEIT TEMPERATURE
VERTICAL BARS SHOW RAINFALL IN INCHES

Caf
CHARLESTON

Moderate continental forest climate; mild winters

Cbf
DUBLIN

Moderate marine forest climate; mild winters

Daf
PEORIA

Continental forest climate; warm summer

Dbf
MOSKVA

Continental forest climate; cool summer

Dcf
MOOSE FACTORY

Continental taiga climate; very severe winters

ET
BARROW

Tundra climate

EF
EISMITTE

Glacial climate (Data incomplete)

COMPARATIVE
RAINFALL
SCALE

LIMITS OF THE REGIONS OF DRY CLIMATE

BW/BS   BS/HUMID

DESERT
BWh

BWk

BSk

BSh

HUMID
A, C, D

MEAN ANNUAL TEMP. FAHRENHEIT

← ANNUAL RAINFALL IN INCHES →

- - - - Winter concentration of precipitation
——— Precipitation evenly distributed throughout the year
–·–·– Summer concentration of precipitation

CENTIMETERS

INCHES

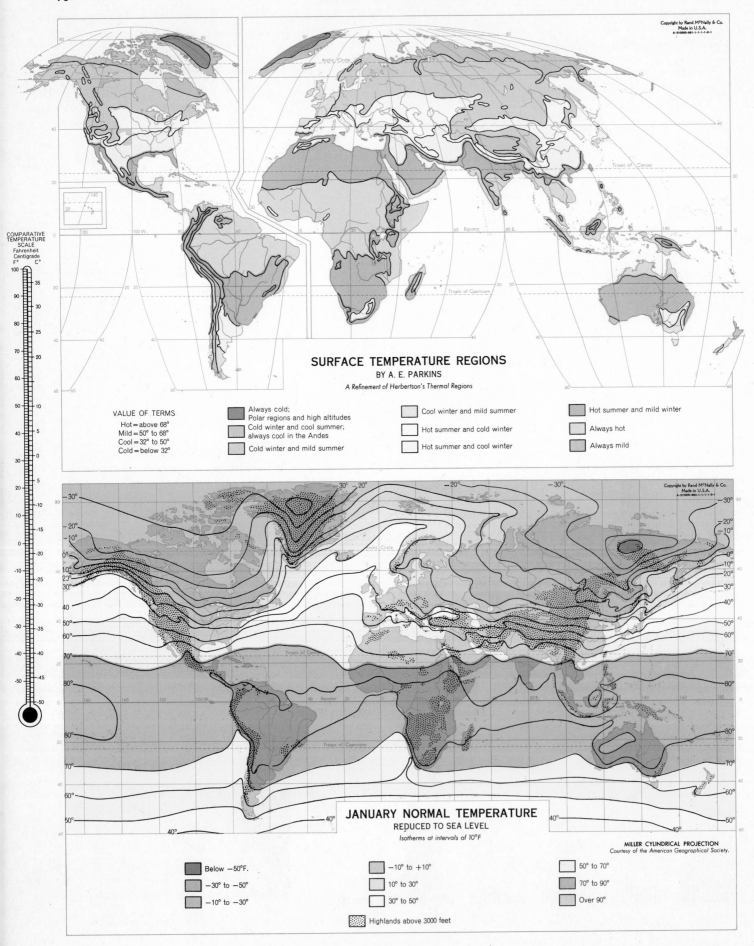

COMPARATIVE
TEMPERATURE
SCALE
Fahrenheit
Centigrade
F°   C°

SURFACE TEMPERATURE REGIONS
BY A. E. PARKINS
A Refinement of Herbertson's Thermal Regions

VALUE OF TERMS

Hot = above 68°
Mild = 50° to 68°
Cool = 32° to 50°
Cold = below 32°

Always cold;
Polar regions and high altitudes

Cold winter and cool summer;
always cool in the Andes

Cold winter and mild summer

Cool winter and mild summer

Hot summer and cold winter

Hot summer and cool winter

Hot summer and mild winter

Always hot

Always mild

JANUARY NORMAL TEMPERATURE
REDUCED TO SEA LEVEL
Isotherms at intervals of 10°F

MILLER CYLINDRICAL PROJECTION
Courtesy of the American Geographical Society.

Below −50°F.

−30° to −50°

−10° to −30°

−10° to +10°

10° to 30°

30° to 50°

50° to 70°

70° to 90°

Over 90°

Highlands above 3000 feet

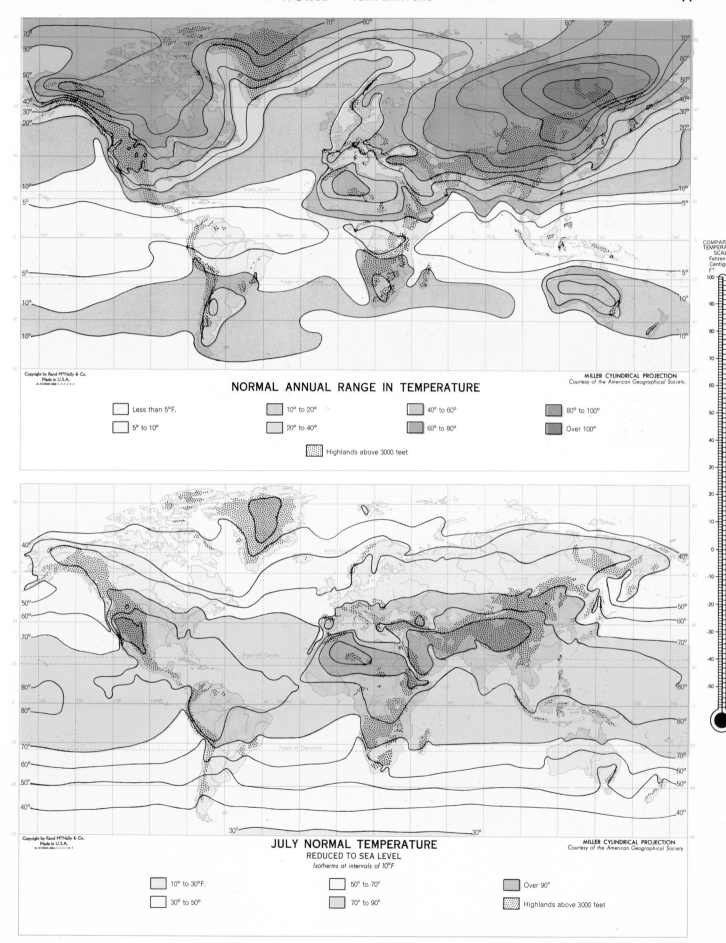

MILLER CYLINDRICAL PROJECTION
Courtesy of the American Geographical Society.

NORMAL ANNUAL RANGE IN TEMPERATURE

Less than 5°F.	10° to 20°	40° to 60°	80° to 100°
5° to 10°	20° to 40°	60° to 80°	Over 100°

Highlands above 3000 feet

COMPARATIVE
TEMPERATURE
SCALE
Fahrenheit
Centigrade
F°   C°

MILLER CYLINDRICAL PROJECTION
Courtesy of the American Geographical Society.

JULY NORMAL TEMPERATURE
REDUCED TO SEA LEVEL
Isotherms at intervals of 10°F

10° to 30°F.	50° to 70°	Over 90°
30° to 50°	70° to 90°	Highlands above 3000 feet

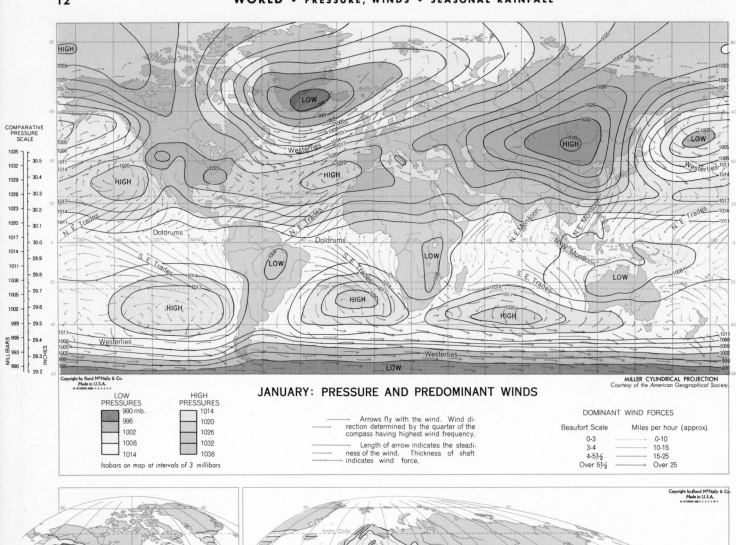

JANUARY: PRESSURE AND PREDOMINANT WINDS

MILLER CYLINDRICAL PROJECTION
Courtesy of the American Geographical Society.

COMPARATIVE
PRESSURE
SCALE

MILLIBARS	INCHES
1035	30.5
1032	30.4
1029	30.4
1026	30.3
1023	30.2
1020	30.1
1017	30.0
1014	29.9
1011	29.8
1008	29.7
1005	29.6
1002	29.5
999	29.4
996	29.4
993	29.3
990	29.2

LOW PRESSURES		HIGH PRESSURES	
990 mb.		1014	
996		1020	
1002		1026	
1008		1032	
1014		1038	

Isobars on map at intervals of 3 millibars

Arrows fly with the wind. Wind direction determined by the quarter of the compass having highest wind frequency.

Length of arrow indicates the steadiness of the wind. Thickness of shaft indicates wind force.

DOMINANT WIND FORCES

Beaufort Scale	Miles per hour (approx)
0-3	0-10
3-4	10-15
4-5½	15-25
Over 5½	Over 25

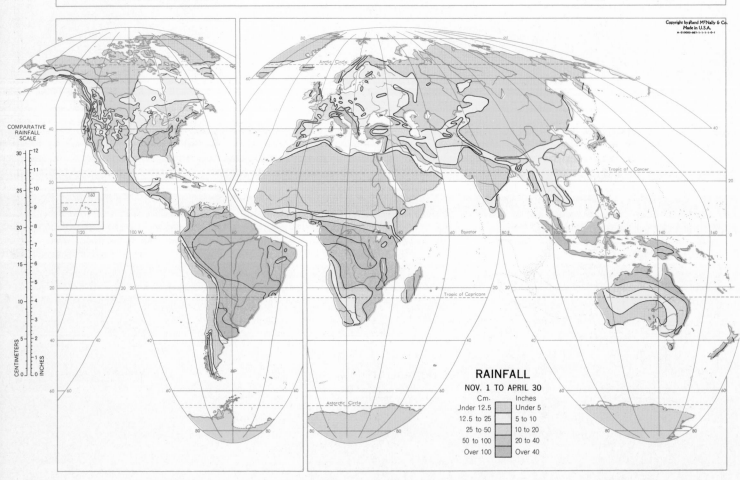

COMPARATIVE
RAINFALL
SCALE

CENTIMETERS	INCHES
30	12
	11
25	10
	9
20	8
	7
15	6
	5
10	4
	3
5	2
	1
0	0

RAINFALL

NOV. 1 TO APRIL 30

Cm.		Inches
Under 12.5		Under 5
12.5 to 25		5 to 10
25 to 50		10 to 20
50 to 100		20 to 40
Over 100		Over 40

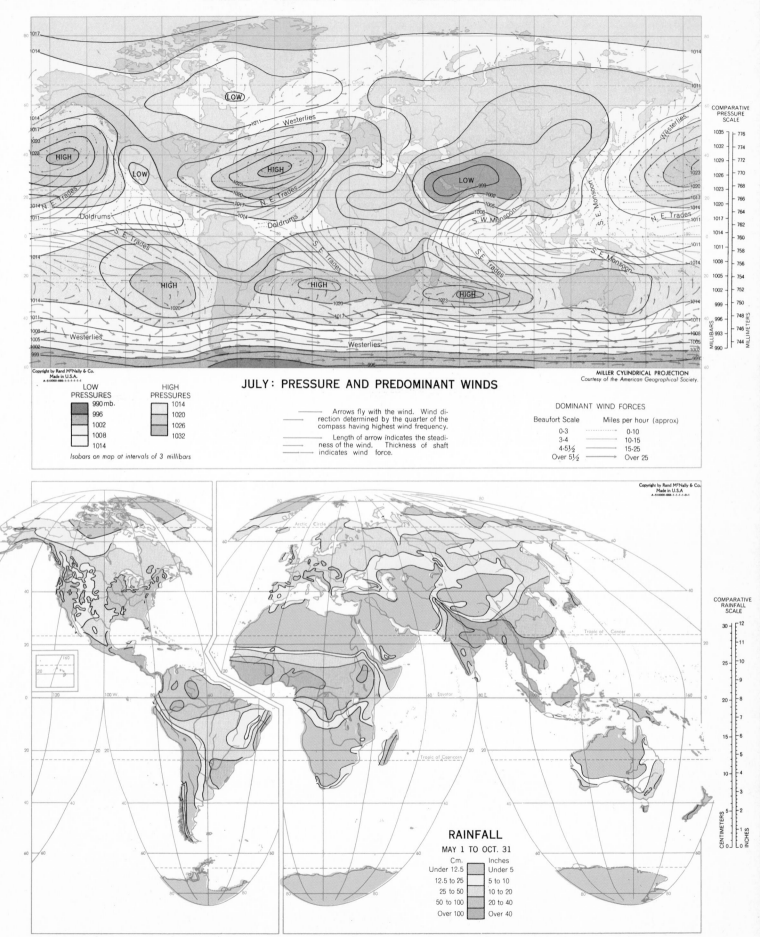

JULY: PRESSURE AND PREDOMINANT WINDS

MILLER CYLINDRICAL PROJECTION
Courtesy of the American Geographical Society.

Copyright by Rand McNally & Co.
Made in U.S.A.
A-510000-888-1-1-1-1-1

COMPARATIVE
PRESSURE
SCALE

LOW PRESSURES	HIGH PRESSURES
990 mb.	1014
996	1020
1002	1026
1008	1032
1014	

Isobars on map at intervals of 3 millibars

Arrows fly with the wind. Wind direction determined by the quarter of the compass having highest wind frequency.

Length of arrow indicates the steadiness of the wind. Thickness of shaft indicates wind force.

DOMINANT WIND FORCES

Beaufort Scale	Miles per hour (approx)
0-3	0-10
3-4	10-15
4-5½	15-25
Over 5½	Over 25

Copyright by Rand McNally & Co.
Made in U.S.A
A-510000-888-1-1-1-1-0-1

COMPARATIVE
RAINFALL
SCALE

RAINFALL

MAY 1 TO OCT. 31

Cm.	Inches
Under 12.5	Under 5
12.5 to 25	5 to 10
25 to 50	10 to 20
50 to 100	20 to 40
Over 100	Over 40

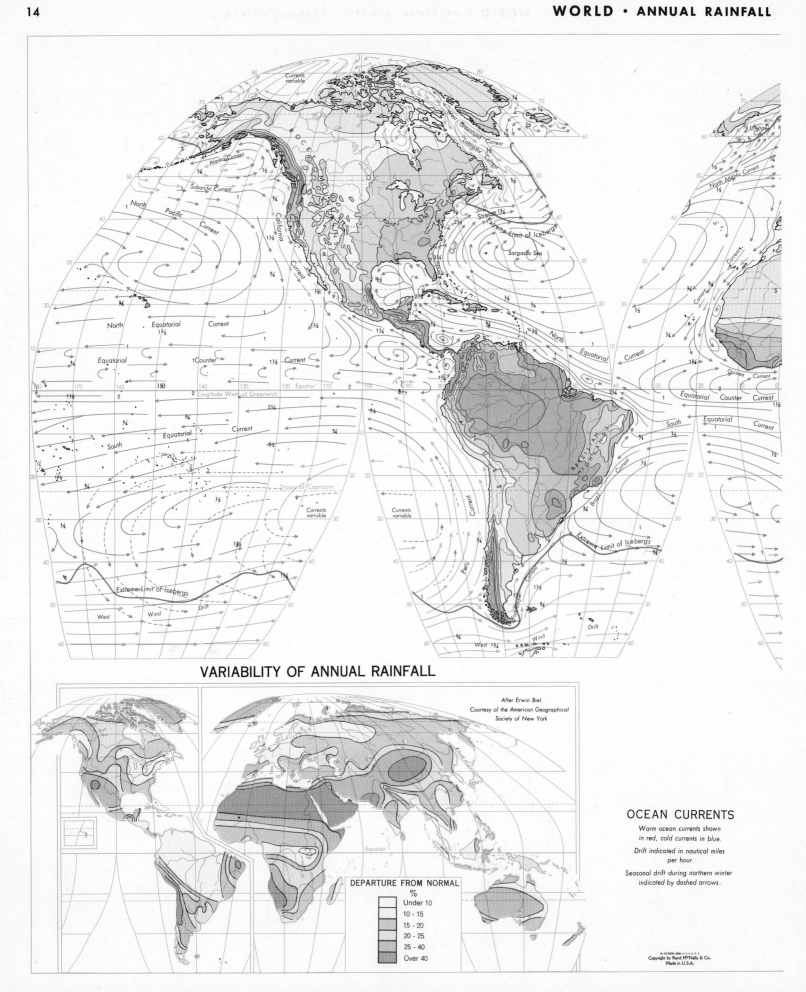

VARIABILITY OF ANNUAL RAINFALL

After Erwin Biel.
Courtesy of the American Geographical
Society of New York

OCEAN CURRENTS

Warm ocean currents shown
in red, cold currents in blue.

Drift indicated in nautical miles
per hour.

Seasonal drift during northern winter
indicated by dashed arrows.

DEPARTURE FROM NORMAL
%
Under 10
10 - 15
15 - 20
20 - 25
25 - 40
Over 40

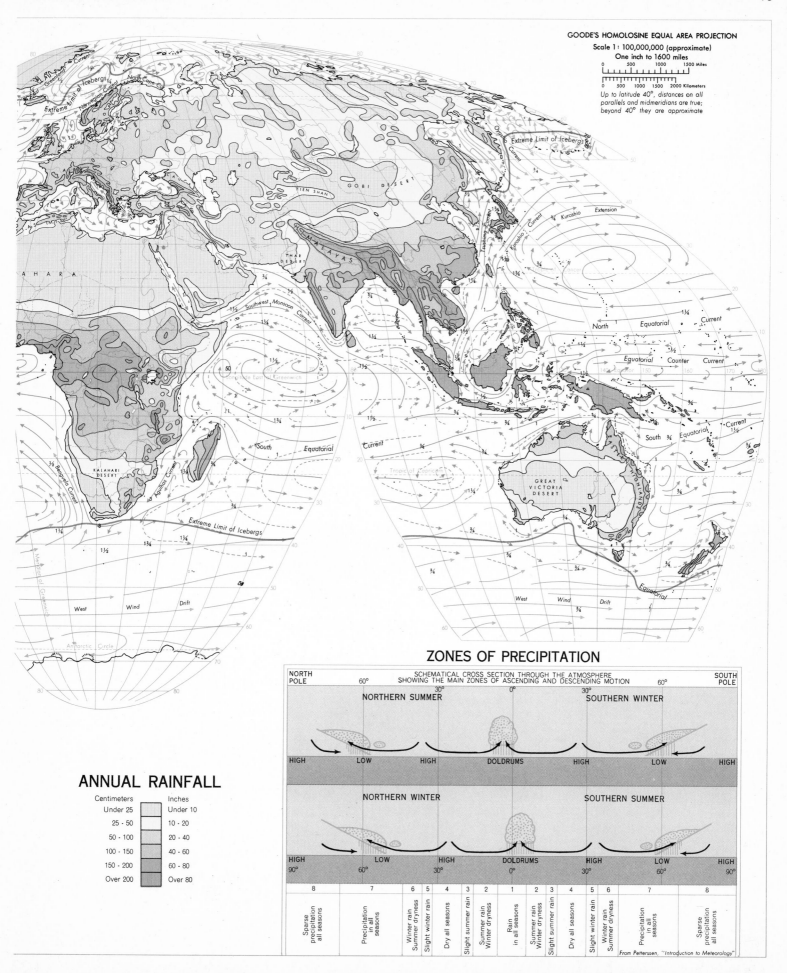

GOODE'S HOMOLOSINE EQUAL AREA PROJECTION
Scale 1 : 100,000,000 (approximate)
One inch to 1600 miles

Up to latitude 40°, distances on all
parallels and midmeridians are true;
beyond 40° they are approximate

ANNUAL RAINFALL

Centimeters		Inches
Under 25		Under 10
25 - 50		10 - 20
50 - 100		20 - 40
100 - 150		40 - 60
150 - 200		60 - 80
Over 200		Over 80

ZONES OF PRECIPITATION

NORTH POLE	60°	SCHEMATICAL CROSS SECTION THROUGH THE ATMOSPHERE SHOWING THE MAIN ZONES OF ASCENDING AND DESCENDING MOTION	60°	SOUTH POLE

NORTHERN SUMMER   0°   SOUTHERN WINTER
30°   30°

| HIGH | LOW | HIGH | DOLDRUMS | HIGH | LOW | HIGH |

NORTHERN WINTER   SOUTHERN SUMMER

| HIGH | LOW | HIGH | DOLDRUMS | HIGH | LOW | HIGH |
| 90° | 60° | 30° | 0° | 30° | 60° | 90° |

8	7	6	5	4	3	2	1	2	3	4	5	6	7	8
Sparse precipitation all seasons	Precipitation in all seasons	Winter rain Summer dryness	Slight winter rain	Dry all seasons	Slight summer rain	Summer rain Winter dryness	Rain in all seasons	Summer rain Winter dryness	Slight summer rain	Dry all seasons	Slight winter rain	Winter rain Summer dryness	Precipitation in all seasons	Sparse precipitation all seasons

From Pettersen, "Introduction to Meteorology"

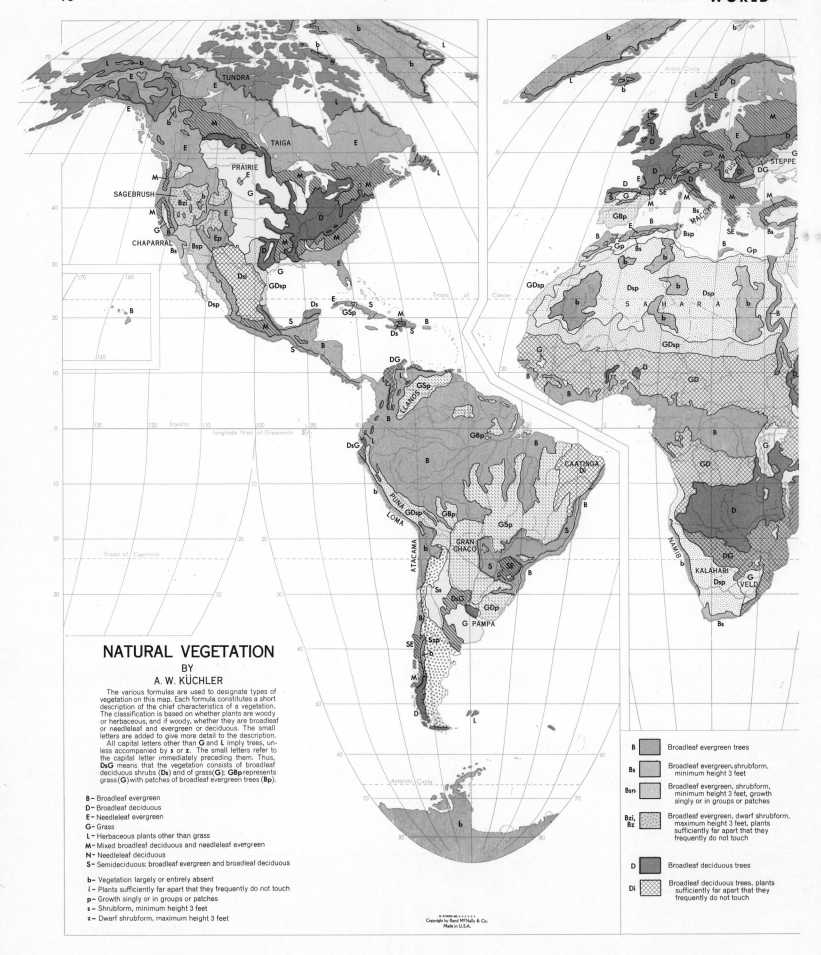

NATURAL VEGETATION

BY
A. W. KÜCHLER

The various formulas are used to designate types of vegetation on this map. Each formula constitutes a short description of the chief characteristics of a vegetation. The classification is based on whether plants are woody or herbaceous, and if woody, whether they are broadleaf or needleleaf and evergreen or deciduous. The small letters are added to give more detail to the description. All capital letters other than **G** and **L** imply trees, unless accompanied by **s** or **z**. The small letters refer to the capital letter immediately preceding them. Thus, **DsG** means that the vegetation consists of broadleaf deciduous shrubs (**Ds**) and of grass (**G**); **GBp** represents grass (**G**) with patches of broadleaf evergreen trees (**Bp**).

B – Broadleaf evergreen
D – Broadleaf deciduous
E – Needleleaf evergreen
G – Grass
L – Herbaceous plants other than grass
M – Mixed broadleaf deciduous and needleleaf evergreen
N – Needleleaf deciduous
S – Semideciduous: broadleaf evergreen and broadleaf deciduous

b – Vegetation largely or entirely absent
i – Plants sufficiently far apart that they frequently do not touch
p – Growth singly or in groups or patches
s – Shrubform, minimum height 3 feet
z – Dwarf shrubform, maximum height 3 feet

A-510000-86-1-1-1-1-1-1
Copyright by Rand McNally & Co.
Made in U.S.A.

B	Broadleaf evergreen trees
Bs	Broadleaf evergreen, shrubform, minimum height 3 feet
Bsn	Broadleaf evergreen, shrubform, minimum height 3 feet, growth singly or in groups or patches
Bzi, Bz	Broadleaf evergreen, dwarf shrubform, maximum height 3 feet, plants sufficiently far apart that they frequently do not touch
D	Broadleaf deciduous trees
Di	Broadleaf deciduous trees, plants sufficiently far apart that they frequently do not touch

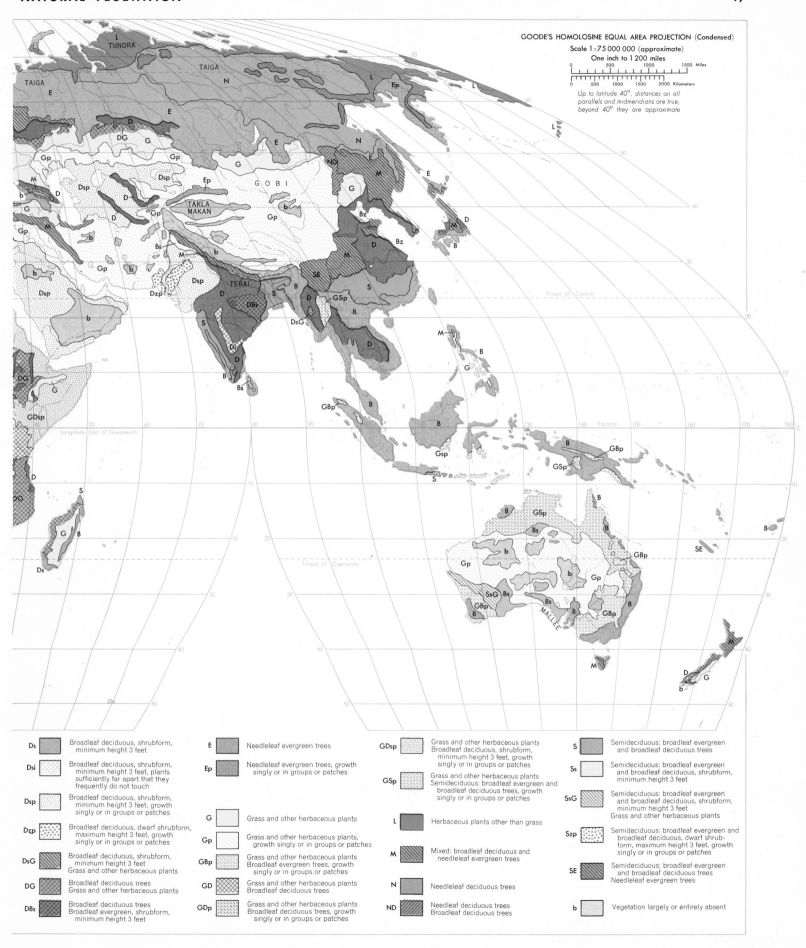

GOODE'S HOMOLOSINE EQUAL AREA PROJECTION (Condensed)
Scale 1:75 000 000 (approximate)
One inch to 1 200 miles

Up to latitude 40°, distances on all parallels and midmeridians are true; beyond 40° they are approximate

Ds		Broadleaf deciduous, shrubform, minimum height 3 feet
Dsi		Broadleaf deciduous, shrubform, minimum height 3 feet, plants sufficiently far apart that they frequently do not touch
Dsp		Broadleaf deciduous, shrubform, minimum height 3 feet, growth singly or in groups or patches
Dzp		Broadleaf deciduous, dwarf shrubform, maximum height 3 feet, growth singly or in groups or patches
DsG		Broadleaf deciduous, shrubform, minimum height 3 feet Grass and other herbaceous plants
DG		Broadleaf deciduous trees Grass and other herbaceous plants
DBs		Broadleaf deciduous trees Broadleaf evergreen, shrubform, minimum height 3 feet

E		Needleleaf evergreen trees
Ep		Needleleaf evergreen trees, growth singly or in groups or patches
G		Grass and other herbaceous plants
Gp		Grass and other herbaceous plants, growth singly or in groups or patches
GBp		Grass and other herbaceous plants Broadleaf evergreen trees, growth singly or in groups or patches
GD		Grass and other herbaceous plants Broadleaf deciduous trees
GDp		Grass and other herbaceous plants Broadleaf deciduous trees, growth singly or in groups or patches

GDsp		Grass and other herbaceous plants Broadleaf deciduous, shrubform, minimum height 3 feet, growth singly or in groups or patches
GSp		Grass and other herbaceous plants Semideciduous: broadleaf evergreen and broadleaf deciduous trees, growth singly or in groups or patches
L		Herbaceous plants other than grass
M		Mixed: broadleaf deciduous and needleleaf evergreen trees
N		Needleleaf deciduous trees
ND		Needleaf deciduous trees Broadleaf deciduous trees

S		Semideciduous: broadleaf evergreen and broadleaf deciduous trees
Ss		Semideciduous: broadleaf evergreen and broadleaf deciduous, shrubform, minimum height 3 feet
SsG		Semideciduous: broadleaf evergreen and broadleaf deciduous, shrubform, minimum height 3 feet Grass and other herbaceous plants
Szp		Semideciduous: broadleaf evergreen and broadleaf deciduous, dwarf shrubform, maximum height 3 feet, growth singly or in groups or patches
SE		Semideciduous: broadleaf evergreen and broadleaf deciduous trees Needleleaf evergreen trees
b		Vegetation largely or entirely absent

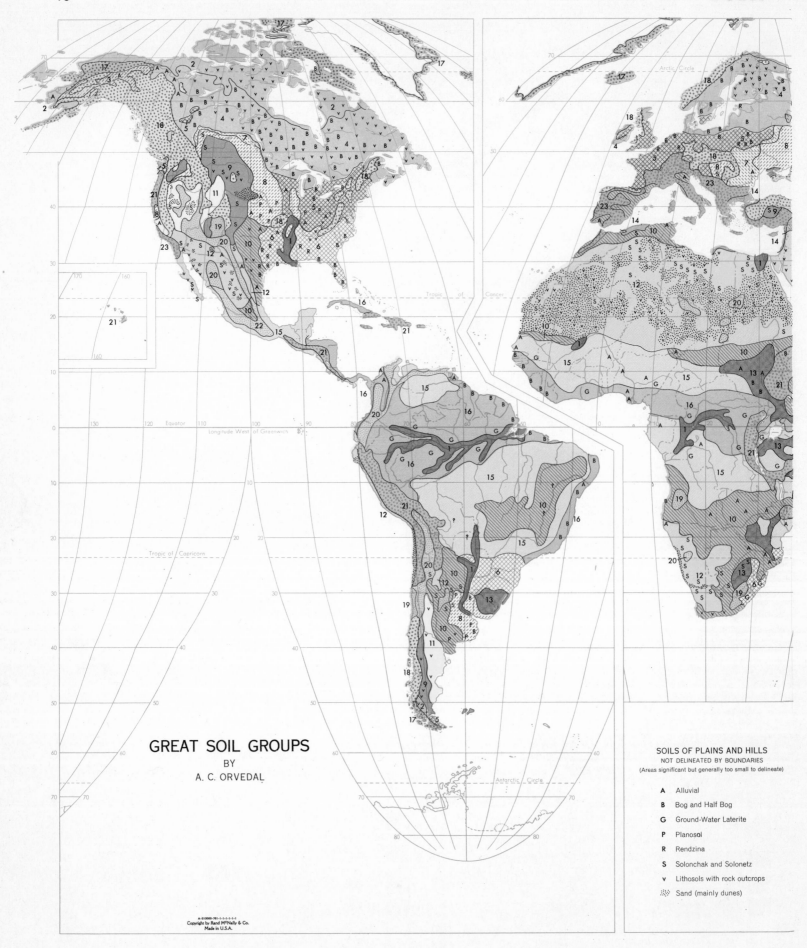

GREAT SOIL GROUPS
BY
A. C. ORVEDAL

SOILS OF PLAINS AND HILLS
NOT DELINEATED BY BOUNDARIES
(Areas significant but generally too small to delineate)

A   Alluvial

B   Bog and Half Bog

G   Ground-Water Laterite

P   Planosol

R   Rendzina

S   Solonchak and Solonetz

v   Lithosols with rock outcrops

Sand (mainly dunes)

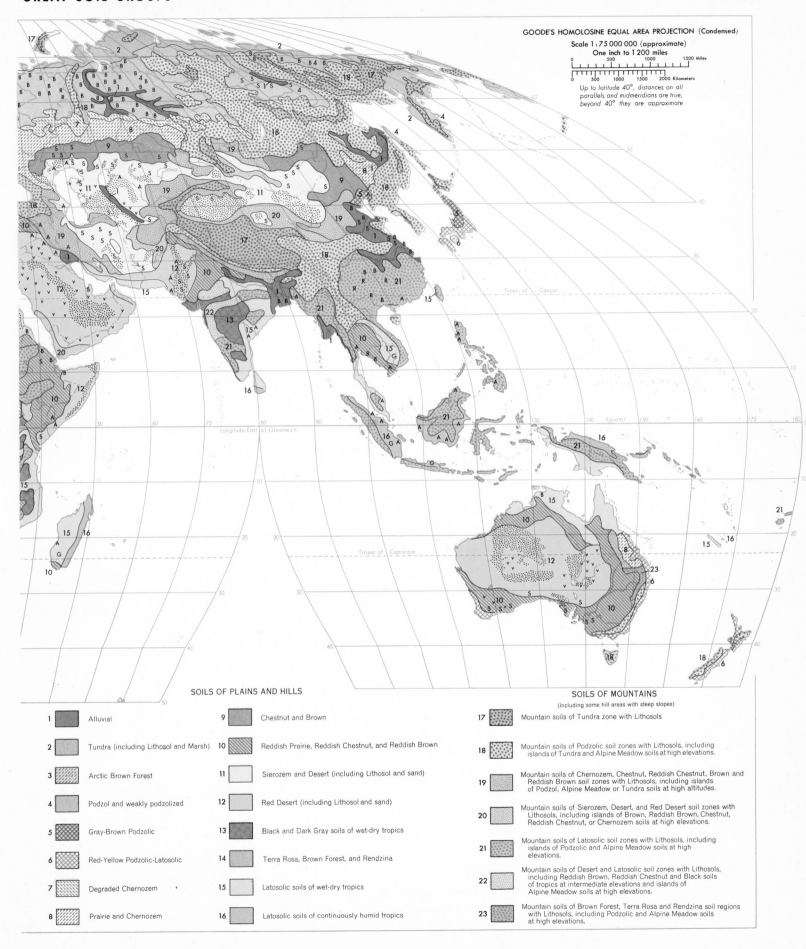

GOODE'S HOMOLOSINE EQUAL AREA PROJECTION (Condensed)

Scale 1 : 75 000 000 (approximate)

One inch to 1 200 miles

Up to latitude 40°, distances on all
parallels and midmeridians are true,
beyond 40° they are approximate

SOILS OF PLAINS AND HILLS

1	Alluvial
2	Tundra (including Lithosol and Marsh)
3	Arctic Brown Forest
4	Podzol and weakly podzolized
5	Gray-Brown Podzolic
6	Red-Yellow Podzolic-Latosolic
7	Degraded Chernozem
8	Prairie and Chernozem
9	Chestnut and Brown
10	Reddish Prairie, Reddish Chestnut, and Reddish Brown
11	Sierozem and Desert (including Lithosol and sand)
12	Red Desert (including Lithosol and sand)
13	Black and Dark Gray soils of wet-dry tropics
14	Terra Rosa, Brown Forest, and Rendzina
15	Latosolic soils of wet-dry tropics
16	Latosolic soils of continuously humid tropics

SOILS OF MOUNTAINS
(Including some hill areas with steep slopes)

17	Mountain soils of Tundra zone with Lithosols
18	Mountain soils of Podzolic soil zones with Lithosols, including islands of Tundra and Alpine Meadow soils at high elevations.
19	Mountain soils of Chernozem, Chestnut, Reddish Chestnut, Brown and Reddish Brown soil zones with Lithosols, including islands of Podzol, Alpine Meadow or Tundra soils at high altitudes.
20	Mountain soils of Sierozem, Desert, and Red Desert soil zones with Lithosols, including islands of Brown, Reddish Brown, Chestnut, Reddish Chestnut, or Chernozem soils at high elevations.
21	Mountain soils of Latosolic soil zones with Lithosols, including islands of Podzolic and Alpine Meadow soils at high elevations.
22	Mountain soils of Desert and Latosolic soil zones with Lithosols, including Reddish Brown, Reddish Chestnut and Black soils of tropics at intermediate elevations and islands of Alpine Meadow soils at high elevations.
23	Mountain soils of Brown Forest, Terra Rosa and Rendzina soil regions with Lithosols, including Podzolic and Alpine Meadow soils at high elevations.

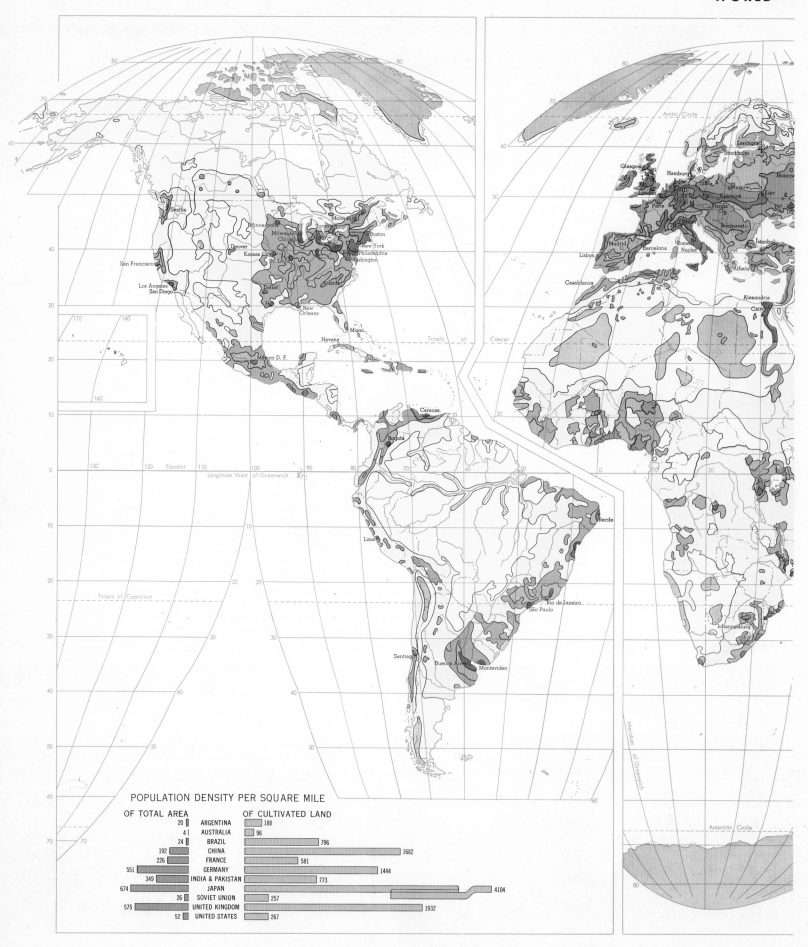

POPULATION DENSITY PER SQUARE MILE

OF TOTAL AREA		OF CULTIVATED LAND	
20	ARGENTINA	188	
4	AUSTRALIA	96	
24	BRAZIL	796	
192	CHINA	1682	
226	FRANCE	581	
551	GERMANY	1444	
349	INDIA & PAKISTAN	773	
674	JAPAN	4104	
26	SOVIET UNION	257	
575	UNITED KINGDOM	1932	
52	UNITED STATES	267	

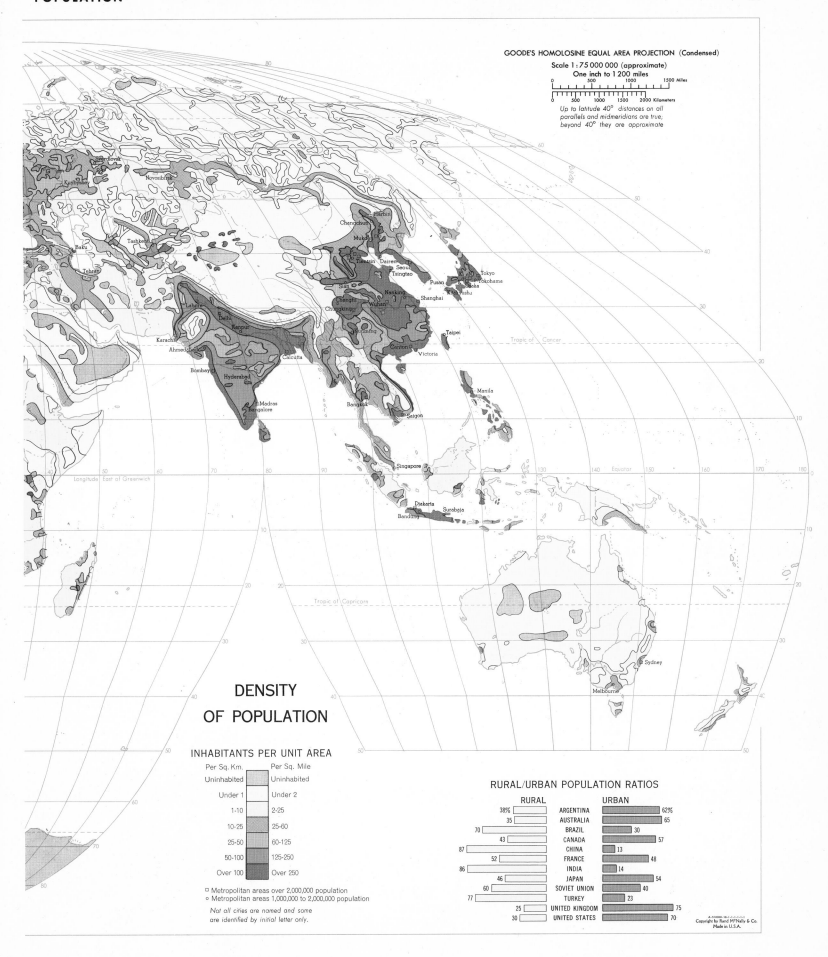

GOODE'S HOMOLOSINE EQUAL AREA PROJECTION (Condensed)

Scale 1 : 75 000 000 (approximate)

One inch to 1 200 miles

Up to latitude 40° distances on all
parallels and midmeridians are true;
beyond 40° they are approximate

DENSITY
OF POPULATION

INHABITANTS PER UNIT AREA

Per Sq. Km.	Per Sq. Mile
Uninhabited	Uninhabited
Under 1	Under 2
1-10	2-25
10-25	25-60
25-50	60-125
50-100	125-250
Over 100	Over 250

□ Metropolitan areas over 2,000,000 population
○ Metropolitan areas 1,000,000 to 2,000,000 population

*Not all cities are named and some
are identified by initial letter only.*

RURAL/URBAN POPULATION RATIOS

RURAL		URBAN
38%	ARGENTINA	62%
35	AUSTRALIA	65
70	BRAZIL	30
43	CANADA	57
87	CHINA	13
52	FRANCE	48
86	INDIA	14
46	JAPAN	54
60	SOVIET UNION	40
77	TURKEY	23
25	UNITED KINGDOM	75
30	UNITED STATES	70

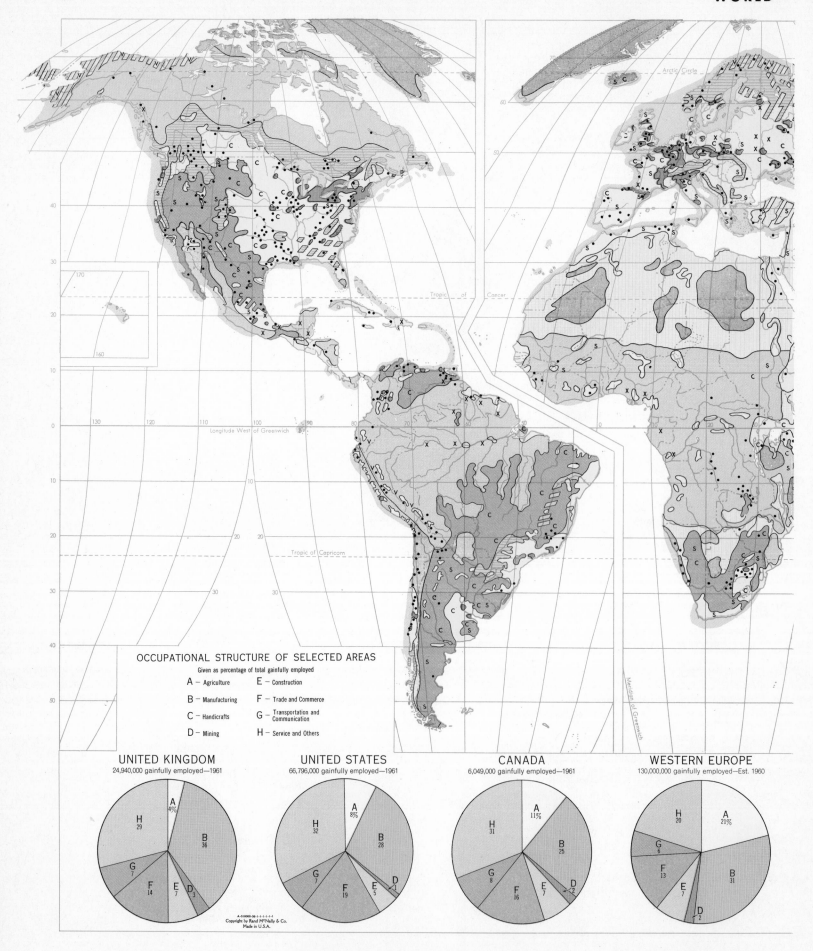

OCCUPATIONAL STRUCTURE OF SELECTED AREAS

Given as percentage of total gainfully employed

A — Agriculture   E — Construction

B — Manufacturing   F — Trade and Commerce

C — Handicrafts   G — Transportation and Communication

D — Mining   H — Service and Others

UNITED KINGDOM
24,940,000 gainfully employed—1961

A 4% · B 36 · D 3 · E 7 · F 14 · G 7 · H 29

UNITED STATES
66,796,000 gainfully employed—1961

A 8% · B 28 · D 1 · E 5 · F 19 · G 7 · H 32

CANADA
6,049,000 gainfully employed—1961

A 11% · B 25 · D 2 · E 7 · F 16 · G 8 · H 31

WESTERN EUROPE
130,000,000 gainfully employed—Est. 1960

A 21% · B 31 · D 2 · E 7 · F 13 · G 6 · H 20

A-510000-36-1-1-1-1-1-1
Copyright by Rand McNally & Co.
Made in U.S.A.

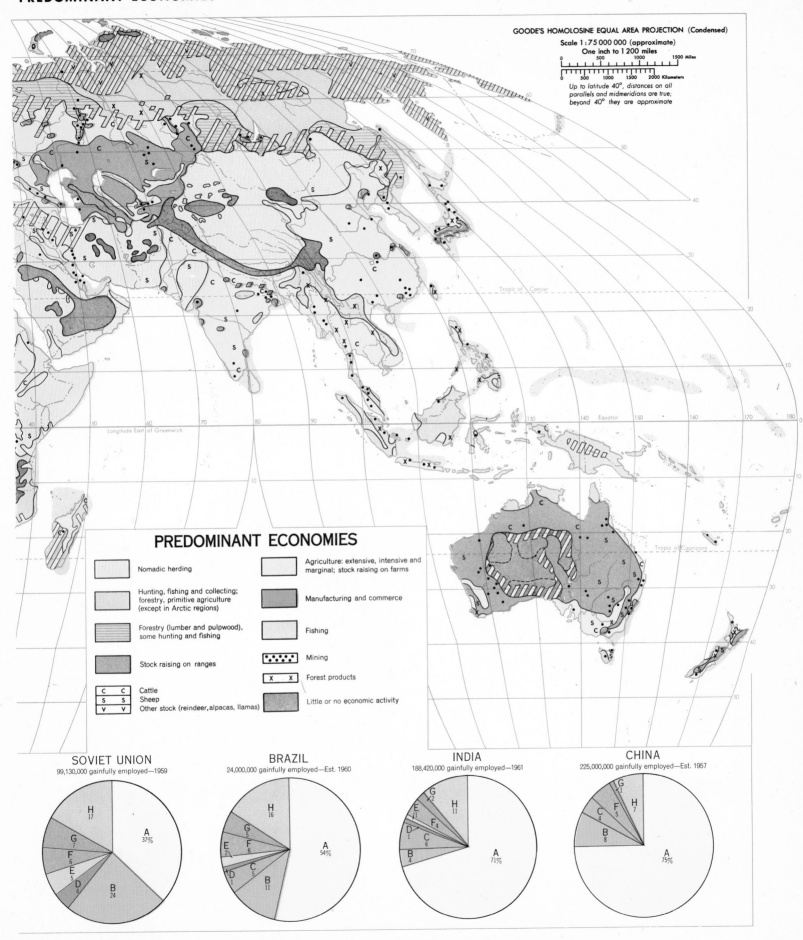

GOODE'S HOMOLOSINE EQUAL AREA PROJECTION (Condensed)

Scale 1 : 75 000 000 (approximate)

One inch to 1 200 miles

Up to latitude 40°, distances on all
parallels and midmeridians are true;
beyond 40° they are approximate

PREDOMINANT ECONOMIES

Nomadic herding

Hunting, fishing and collecting;
forestry, primitive agriculture
(except in Arctic regions)

Forestry (lumber and pulpwood),
some hunting and fishing

Stock raising on ranges

C C Cattle
S S Sheep
V V Other stock (reindeer, alpacas, llamas)

Agriculture: extensive, intensive and
marginal; stock raising on farms

Manufacturing and commerce

Fishing

Mining

Forest products

Little or no economic activity

SOVIET UNION
99,130,000 gainfully employed—1959

A 37%
B 24
D 4
E 5
F 6
G 7
H 17

BRAZIL
24,000,000 gainfully employed—Est. 1960

A 54%
B 11
C 5
D 1
E 2
F 6
G 5
H 16

INDIA
188,420,000 gainfully employed—1961

A 71%
B 4
C 6
D 1
E 1
F 4
G 2
H 11

CHINA
225,000,000 gainfully employed—Est. 1957

A 75%
B 8
C 4
F 5
G 1
H 7

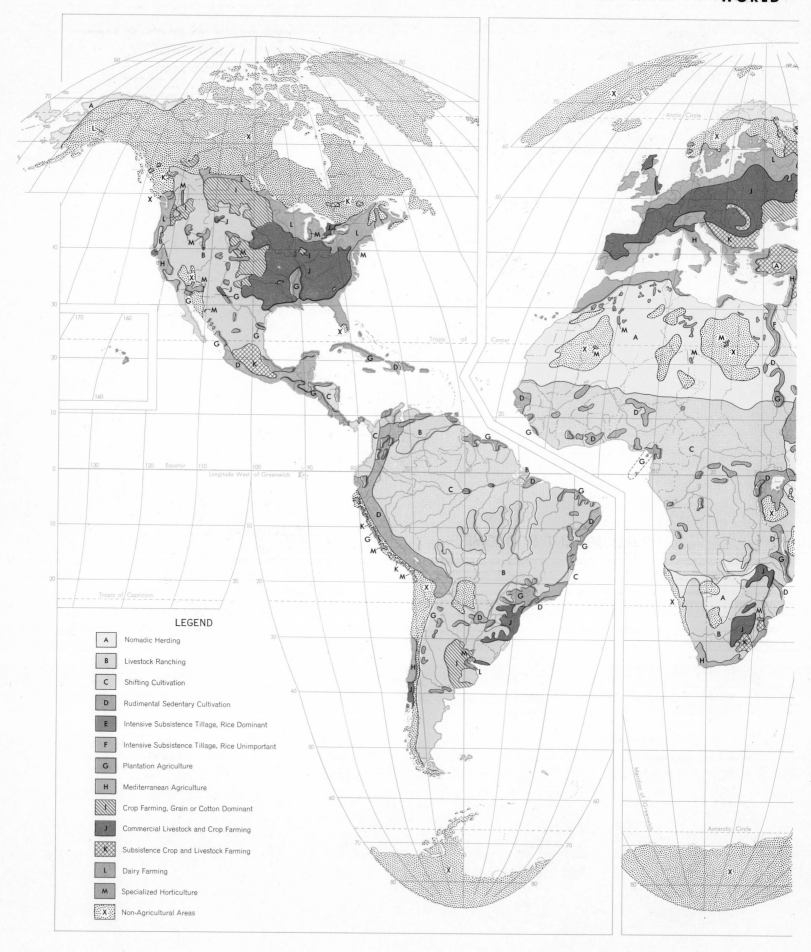

LEGEND

A Nomadic Herding

B Livestock Ranching

C Shifting Cultivation

D Rudimental Sedentary Cultivation

E Intensive Subsistence Tillage, Rice Dominant

F Intensive Subsistence Tillage, Rice Unimportant

G Plantation Agriculture

H Mediterranean Agriculture

I Crop Farming, Grain or Cotton Dominant

J Commercial Livestock and Crop Farming

K Subsistence Crop and Livestock Farming

L Dairy Farming

M Specialized Horticulture

X Non-Agricultural Areas

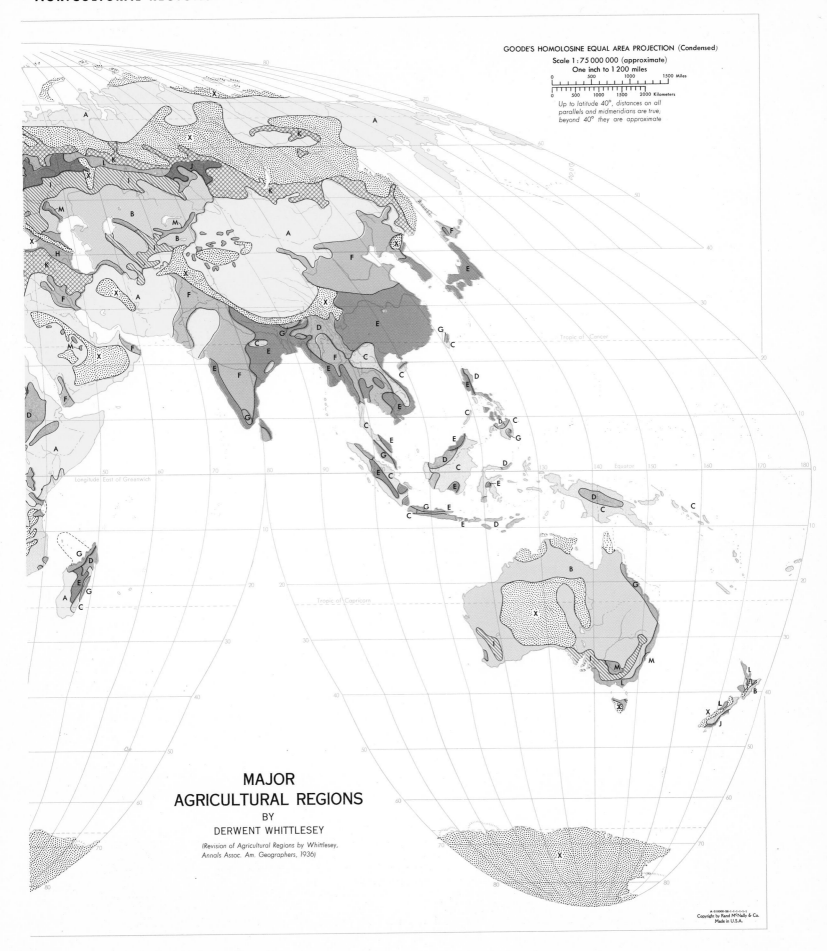

GOODE'S HOMOLOSINE EQUAL AREA PROJECTION (Condensed)

Scale 1 : 75 000 000 (approximate)

One inch to 1 200 miles

*Up to latitude 40°, distances on all
parallels and midmeridians are true;
beyond 40° they are approximate*

MAJOR
AGRICULTURAL REGIONS
BY
DERWENT WHITTLESEY

*(Revision of Agricultural Regions by Whittlesey,
Annals Assoc. Am. Geographers, 1936)*

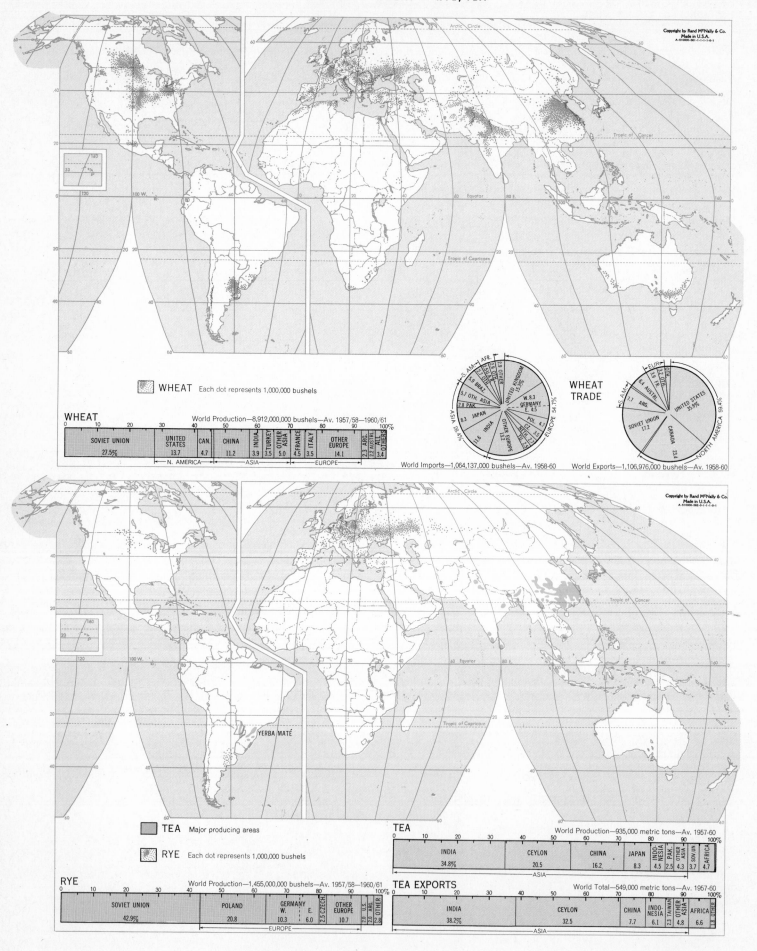

WHEAT   Each dot represents 1,000,000 bushels

WHEAT

World Production—8,912,000,000 bushels—Av. 1957/58—1960/61

SOVIET UNION 27.5%	UNITED STATES 13.7	CAN. 4.7	CHINA 11.2	INDIA 3.9	TURKEY 3.5	OTHER ASIA 5.0	FRANCE 4.5	ITALY 3.5	OTHER EUROPE 14.1	2.3 ARG. / 2.2 AUSTRL. / ALL OTHERS 3.4

← N. AMERICA →   ← ASIA →   ← EUROPE →

WHEAT TRADE

World Imports—1,064,137,000 bushels—Av. 1958-60

World Exports—1,106,976,000 bushels—Av. 1958-60

YERBA MATÉ

TEA   Major producing areas

RYE   Each dot represents 1,000,000 bushels

RYE

World Production—1,455,000,000 bushels—Av. 1957/58—1960/61

SOVIET UNION 42.9%	POLAND 20.8	GERMANY W. 10.3 / E. 6.0	2.5 CZECH	OTHER EUROPE 10.7	2.0 U.S. / 2.3 ARG. / OTHER 2.8	

← EUROPE →

TEA

World Production—935,000 metric tons—Av. 1957-60

INDIA 34.8%	CEYLON 20.5	CHINA 16.2	JAPAN 8.3	INDO-NESIA 4.5	PAK. 2.5	OTHER ASIA 4.3	SOV. UN 3.7	AFRICA 4.7

← ASIA →

TEA EXPORTS

World Total—549,000 metric tons—Av. 1957-60

INDIA 38.2%	CEYLON 32.5	CHINA 7.7	INDO-NESIA 6.1	TAIWAN 2.3	OTHER ASIA 4.8	AFRICA 6.6 / 1.8 OTHER

← ASIA →

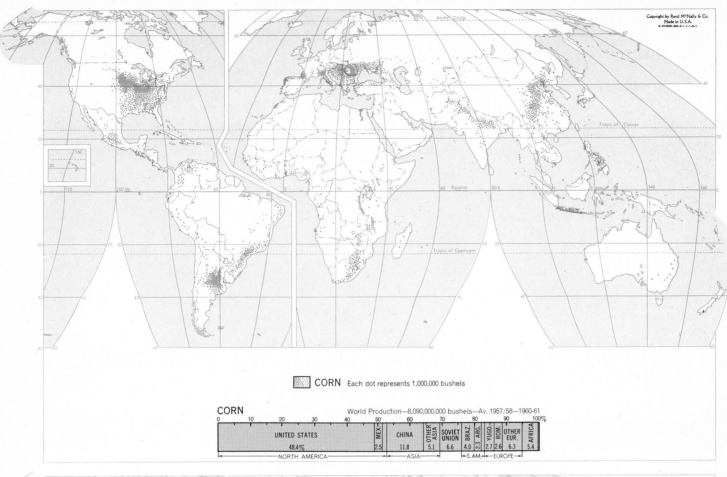

[CORN] **CORN** Each dot represents 1,000,000 bushels

CORN   World Production—8,090,000,000 bushels—Av. 1957/58—1960-61

| 0 | 10 | 20 | 30 | 40 | 50 | 60 | 70 | 80 | 90 | 100% |

| UNITED STATES 48.4% | MEX. 2.5 | CHINA 11.8 | OTHER ASIA 5.1 | SOVIET UNION 6.6 | BRAZ. 4.0 | ARG. 2.3 | YUGO. 2.7 | ROM. 2.6 | OTHER EUR. 6.3 | AFRICA 5.4 |

‹—— NORTH AMERICA ——›   ‹—— ASIA ——›   ‹— S. AM. —›‹— EUROPE —›

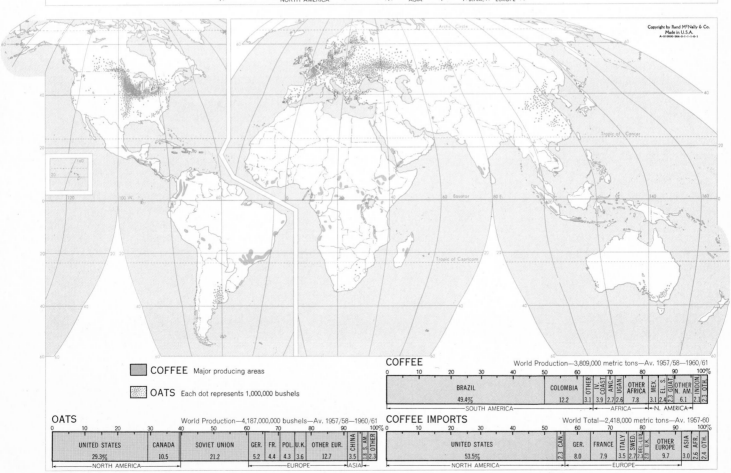

[COFFEE] **COFFEE** Major producing areas

[OATS] **OATS** Each dot represents 1,000,000 bushels

COFFEE   World Production—3,809,000 metric tons—Av. 1957/58—1960/61

| 0 | 10 | 20 | 30 | 40 | 50 | 60 | 70 | 80 | 90 | 100% |

| BRAZIL 49.4% | COLOMBIA 12.2 | OTHER S. AM. 3.1 | IV. COAST 3.9 | ANG. 2.7 | UGAN. 2.6 | OTHER AFRICA 7.8 | MEX. 3.1 | EL. S. 2.4 | GUAT. 2.3 | OTHER N. AM. 6.1 | INDON. 2.1 | OTH. 2.3 |

‹—— SOUTH AMERICA ——›   ‹—— AFRICA ——›   ‹— N. AMERICA —›

OATS   World Production—4,187,000,000 bushels—Av. 1957/58—1960/61

| 0 | 10 | 20 | 30 | 40 | 50 | 60 | 70 | 80 | 90 | 100% |

| UNITED STATES 29.3% | CANADA 10.5 | SOVIET UNION 21.2 | GER. 5.2 | FR. 4.4 | POL. 4.3 | U.K. 3.6 | OTHER EUR. 12.7 | CHINA 3.5 | S. AM. 1.8 | OTHER 2.3 |

‹—— NORTH AMERICA ——›   ‹———— EUROPE ————›   ‹— ASIA —›

COFFEE IMPORTS   World Total—2,418,000 metric tons—Av. 1957-60

| 0 | 10 | 20 | 30 | 40 | 50 | 60 | 70 | 80 | 90 | 100% |

| UNITED STATES 53.5% | CAN. 2.3 | GER. 8.0 | FRANCE 7.9 | ITALY 3.5 | SWED. 2.7 | BEL. LUX. 2.0 | U.K. | OTHER EUROPE 9.7 | ASIA 3.0 | AFR. 2.6 | OTH. 2.4 |

‹—— NORTH AMERICA ——›   ‹———— EUROPE ————›

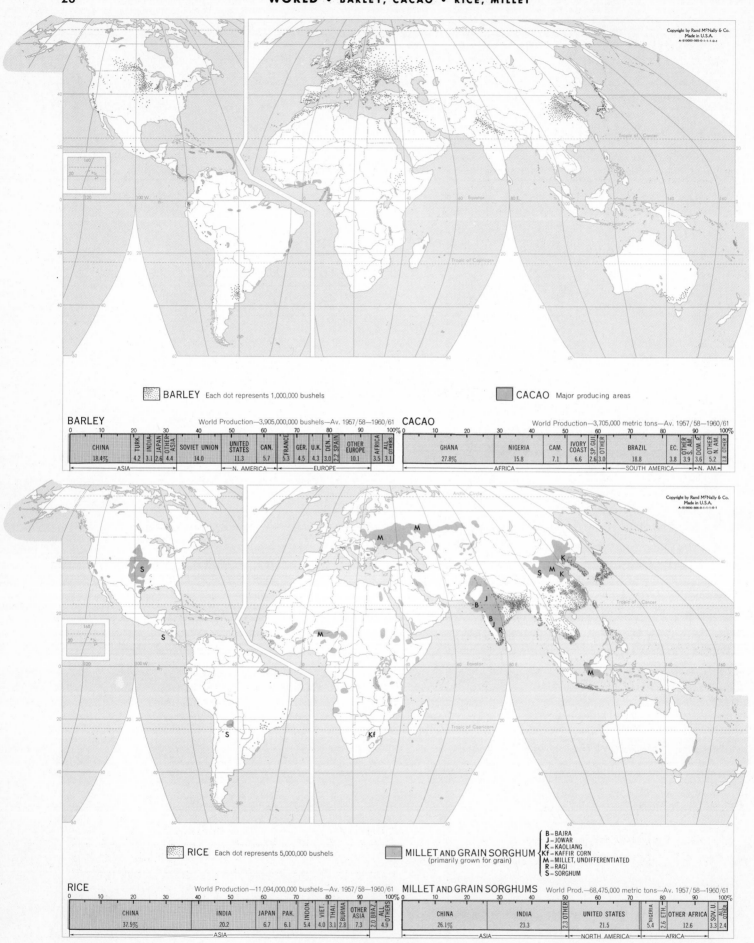

BARLEY Each dot represents 1,000,000 bushels

CACAO Major producing areas

BARLEY
World Production—3,905,000,000 bushels—Av. 1957/58—1960/61

CHINA 18.4%	TURK. 4.2	INDIA 3.1	JAPAN 2.6	OTHER ASIA 4.4	SOVIET UNION 14.0	UNITED STATES 11.3	CAN. 5.7	FRANCE 5.3	GER. 4.5	U.K. 4.3	DEN. 3.0	SPAIN 2.2	OTHER EUROPE 10.1	AFRICA 3.5	ALL OTHERS 3.1

ASIA — N. AMERICA — EUROPE

CACAO
World Production—3,705,000 metric tons—Av. 1957/58—1960/61

GHANA 27.8%	NIGERIA 15.8	CAM. 7.1	IVORY COAST 6.6	SP. GUI. 2.6	OTHER 3.0	BRAZIL 18.8	EC. 3.8	OTHER S. AM. 3.9	DOM. R. 3.6	OTHER N. AM. 5.2	1.8 OTHER

AFRICA — SOUTH AMERICA — N. AM.

RICE Each dot represents 5,000,000 bushels

MILLET AND GRAIN SORGHUM
(primarily grown for grain)

B = BAJRA
J = JOWAR
K = KAOLIANG
Kf = KAFFIR CORN
M = MILLET, UNDIFFERENTIATED
R = RAGI
S = SORGHUM

RICE
World Production—11,094,000,000 bushels—Av. 1957/58—1960/61

CHINA 37.5%	INDIA 20.2	JAPAN 6.7	PAK. 6.1	INDON. 5.4	VIET. 4.0	THAI. 3.1	BURMA 2.8	OTHER ASIA 7.3	BRAZ. 2.0	ALL OTHERS 4.9

ASIA

MILLET AND GRAIN SORGHUMS
World Prod.—68,475,000 metric tons—Av. 1957/58—1960/61

CHINA 26.1%	INDIA 23.3	OTHER 2.3	UNITED STATES 21.5	NIGERIA 5.4	ETH. 2.6	OTHER AFRICA 12.6	SOV. U. 3.3	OTHER 2.4

ASIA — NORTH AMERICA — AFRICA

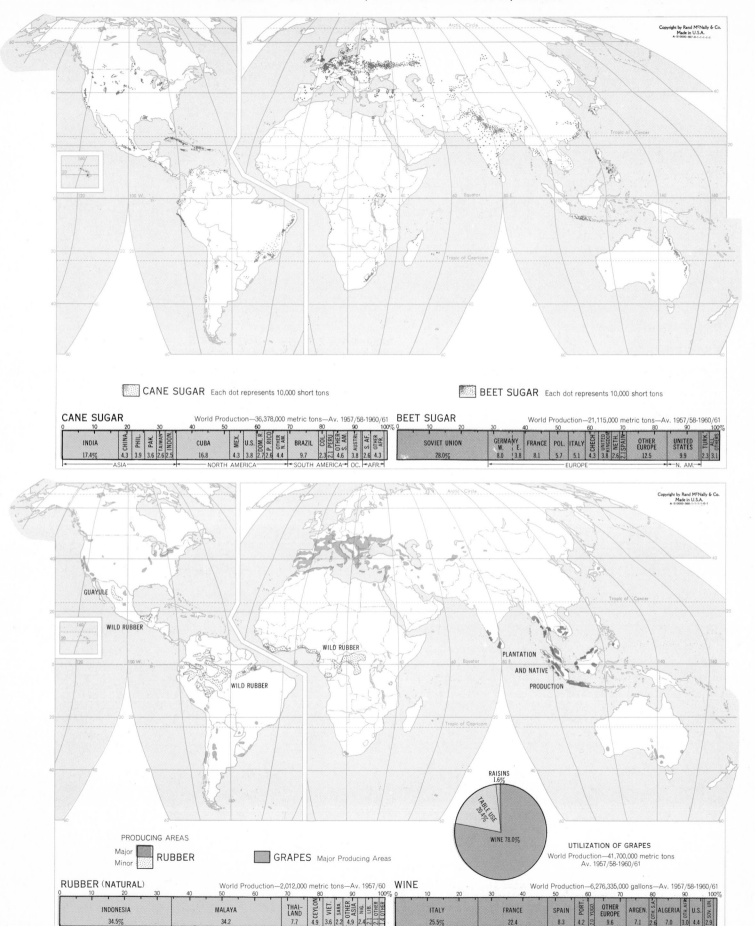

Copyright by Rand McNally & Co.
Made in U.S.A.
A-510000-587-0-1-1-1-1-1

▨ CANE SUGAR Each dot represents 10,000 short tons

▨ BEET SUGAR Each dot represents 10,000 short tons

CANE SUGAR

World Production—36,378,000 metric tons—Av. 1957/58-1960/61

INDIA 17.4%	CHINA 4.3	PHIL. 3.9	PAK. 3.6	TAIWAN 2.6	INDON. 2.5	CUBA 16.8	MEX. 4.3	U.S. 3.8	DOM. R. 2.7	P. RICO 2.6	OTHER N. AM. 4.4	BRAZIL 9.7	COL. 2.3	PERU 2.1	OTHER S. AM. 4.6	AUSTRL. 3.8	S. AF. 2.6	OTHER AFR. 4.3

ASIA — NORTH AMERICA — SOUTH AMERICA — OC. — AFR.

BEET SUGAR

World Production—21,115,000 metric tons—Av. 1957/58-1960/61

SOVIET UNION 28.0%	GERMANY W. 8.0	GERMANY E. 3.8	FRANCE 8.1	POL. 5.7	ITALY 5.1	CZECH. 4.3	UNITED KINGDOM 3.8	NETH. 2.6	SPAIN 2.1	OTHER EUROPE 12.5	UNITED STATES 9.9	TURK. 2.3	ALL OTHERS 3.1

EUROPE — N. AM.

Copyright by Rand McNally & Co.
Made in U.S.A.
A-510000-588-1-1-1-1-0-1

GUAYULE

WILD RUBBER

WILD RUBBER

WILD RUBBER

WILD RUBBER

PLANTATION AND NATIVE PRODUCTION

RAISINS 1.6%

TABLE USE 20.4%

WINE 78.0%

UTILIZATION OF GRAPES
World Production—41,700,000 metric tons
Av. 1957/58-1960/61

PRODUCING AREAS

Major / Minor ▨ RUBBER

▨ GRAPES Major Producing Areas

RUBBER (NATURAL)

World Production—2,012,000 metric tons—Av. 1957/60

INDONESIA 34.5%	MALAYA 34.2	THAI-LAND 7.7	CEYLON 4.9	VIET. 3.6	SARA. 2.2	OTHER ASIA 4.9	NIG. 2.1	LIB. 2.1	OTHER 4

ASIA — AFR.

WINE

World Production—6,276,335,000 gallons—Av. 1957/58-1960/61

ITALY 25.5%	FRANCE 22.4	SPAIN 8.3	PORT. 4.2	YUGO. 2.1	OTHER EUROPE 9.6	ARGEN. 7.1	OTH. S.A. 2.6	ALGERIA 7.0	OTH. AF. 3.0	U.S. 4.4	SOV. UN. 2.9

EUROPE — S. AM. — AFRICA — N.A.

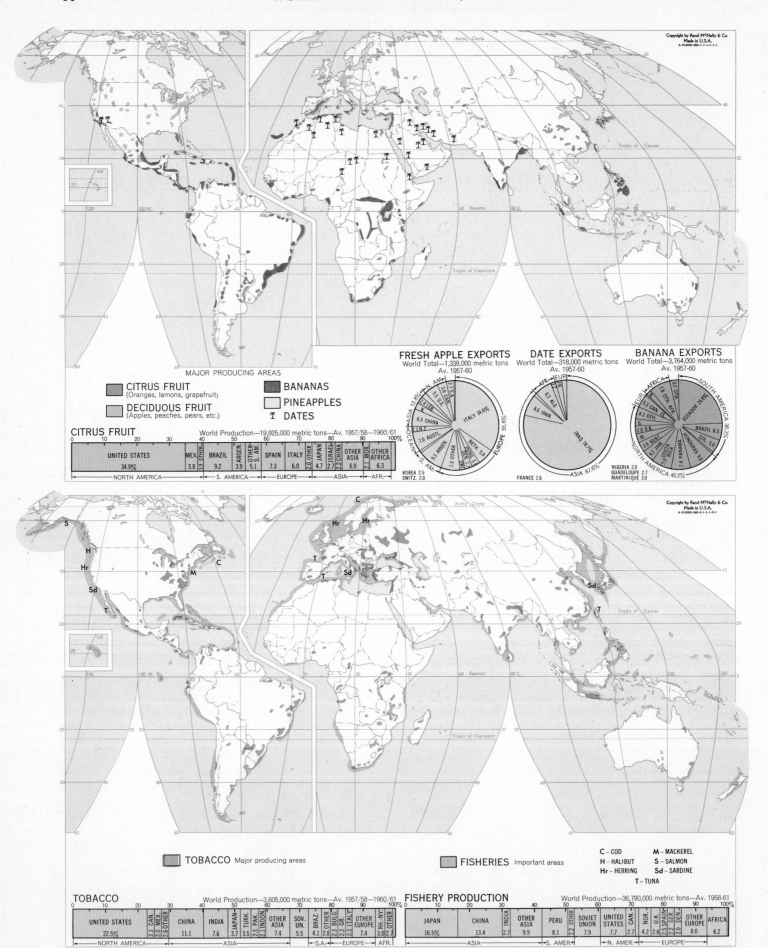

Copyright by Rand McNally & Co.
Made in U.S.A.
A-510000-569-1-1-1-1-1-1

MAJOR PRODUCING AREAS

- ◼ CITRUS FRUIT (Oranges, lemons, grapefruit)
- ◼ DECIDUOUS FRUIT (Apples, peaches, pears, etc.)
- ◼ BANANAS
- ◻ PINEAPPLES
- ⊤ DATES

FRESH APPLE EXPORTS
World Total—1,338,000 metric tons
Av. 1957-60

EUROPE 55.6%
ITALY 34.6%
EUROPE
N. AM. 12.6%
2.7 S.A.
3.6 CAN.
5.5 U.S.
2.1 LEB.
6.3 CHINA
2.3 N.Z.
1.0 AUSTL.
9.3 ARGEN.
7.3 OTHER
NETH. 5.5
DEN. 3.1
ASIA
S. AM.
OCEANIA
KOREA 2.5
SWITZ. 2.0

DATE EXPORTS
World Total—318,000 metric tons
Av. 1957-60

IRAQ 78.7%
ASIA 87.6%
8.0 IRAN
6.2 ALG.
AFR. EUR.
FRANCE 2.6

BANANA EXPORTS
World Total—3,764,000 metric tons
Av. 1957-60

SOUTH AMERICA 36.3%
ECUADOR 24.8%
BRAZIL 6.3
COL. 5.0
HONDURAS 5.6
PANAMA
COSTA RICA
9.9 GUAT.
2.8 D.R.
4.3 OTH.
EUR. AFRICA
2.2 OTH.
2.8 OTH. AFR.
NORTH AMERICA 45.2%
NIGERIA 2.0
GUADELOUPE 2.7
MARTINIQUE 3.0
7.4

CITRUS FRUIT
World Production—19,925,000 metric tons—Av. 1957/58—1960/61

UNITED STATES 34.9%	MEX. 3.8	OTHER 1.9	BRAZIL 9.2	ARGEN. 3.9	OTHER S. AM. 5.1	SPAIN 7.3	ITALY 6.0	OTHER 2.0	JAPAN 4.7	ISRAEL 2.7	CHINA 2.2	OTHER ASIA 6.9	MOR. 2.1	OTHER AFRICA 6.3
NORTH AMERICA			S. AMERICA			EUROPE			ASIA				AFR.	

Copyright by Rand McNally & Co.
Made in U.S.A.
A-510000-560-0-1-1-1-0-1

- ◼ TOBACCO   Major producing areas
- ◼ FISHERIES   Important areas

C – COD   M – MACKEREL
H – HALIBUT   S – SALMON
Hr – HERRING   Sd – SARDINE
T – TUNA

TOBACCO
World Production—3,605,000 metric tons—Av. 1957/58—1960/61

UNITED STATES 22.5%	CAN. 2.3	MEX. 2.0	OTHER 2.6	CHINA 11.1	INDIA 7.6	JAPAN 3.7	TURK. 3.5	PAK. 2.5	INDON. 2.1	OTHER ASIA 7.4	SOV. UN. 5.5	BRAZ. 4.1	BULG. 2.8	GR. 2.3	ITALY 2.3	OTHER EUROPE 7.4	RH.-NY. 3.0	OTHER 2.7
NORTH AMERICA				ASIA							S.A.		EUROPE				AFR.

FISHERY PRODUCTION
World Production—36,790,000 metric tons—Av. 1958-61

JAPAN 16.5%	CHINA 13.4	INDIA 2.7	OTHER ASIA 9.9	PERU 8.1	OTHER 2.7	SOVIET UNION 7.9	UNITED STATES 7.7	CAN. 2.7	NOR. 4.2	U.K. 2.6	SPAIN 2.5	GER. 2.2	DEN. 2.0	OTHER EUROPE 8.0	AFRICA 6.2
ASIA				S. AMER.			N. AMER.		EUROPE					

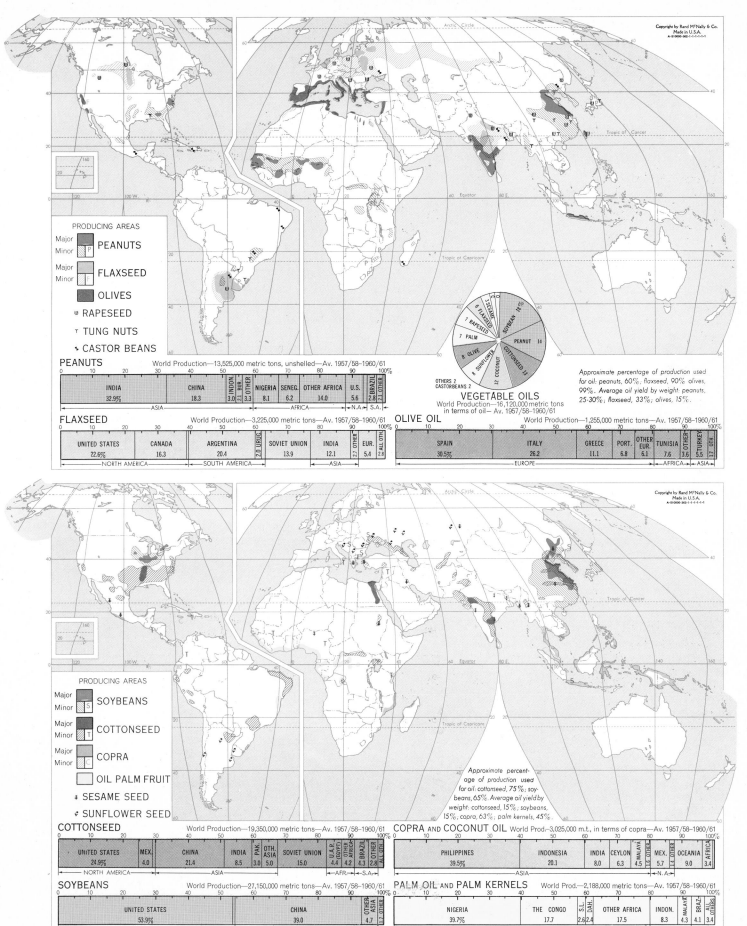

PRODUCING AREAS

Major / Minor		
	PEANUTS P	
	FLAXSEED F	
	OLIVES	
ѡ	RAPESEED	
т	TUNG NUTS	
✦	CASTOR BEANS	

VEGETABLE OILS

World Production—16,120,000 metric tons
in terms of oil— Av. 1957/58–1960/61

(Pie chart: SOYBEAN 18%, PEANUT 14, COTTONSEED 13, COCONUT 12, SUNFLOWER 8, OLIVE 8, PALM 7, RAPESEED 7, FLAXSEED 6, SESAME 3, OTHERS 2, CASTORBEANS 2)

Approximate percentage of production used for oil: peanuts, 60%; flaxseed, 90% olives, 99%. Average oil yield by weight: peanuts, 25-30%; flaxseed, 33%; olives, 15%.

PEANUTS
World Production—13,525,000 metric tons, unshelled—Av. 1957/58–1960/61

		10	20	30	40	50	60	70	80	90	100%
INDIA 32.9%	CHINA 18.3	INDON. 3.0	BUR. 2.1	OTHER 3.3	NIGERIA 8.1	SENEG. 6.2	OTHER AFRICA 14.0	U.S. 5.6	BRAZIL 2.8	OTHER 2.1

ASIA — AFRICA — N.A. — S.A.

FLAXSEED
World Production—3,225,000 metric tons—Av. 1957/58–1960/61

	10	20	30	40	50	60	70	80	90	100%
UNITED STATES 22.6%	CANADA 16.3	ARGENTINA 20.4	URUG. 2.0	SOVIET UNION 13.9	INDIA 12.1	OTHER 2.7	EUR. 5.4	ALL OTH. 2.8

NORTH AMERICA — SOUTH AMERICA — ASIA

OLIVE OIL
World Production—1,255,000 metric tons—Av. 1957/58–1960/61

	10	20	30	40	50	60	70	80	90	100%
SPAIN 30.5%	ITALY 26.2	GREECE 11.1	PORT. 6.8	OTHER EUR. 6.1	TUNISIA 7.6	OTHER 3.6	TURKEY 5.5	OTH. 1.7

EUROPE — AFRICA — ASIA

PRODUCING AREAS

Major / Minor		
	SOYBEANS S	
	COTTONSEED T	
	COPRA C	
	OIL PALM FRUIT	
✦	SESAME SEED	
✦	SUNFLOWER SEED	

Approximate percentage of production used for oil: cottonseed, 75%; soybeans, 65%. Average oil yield by weight: cottonseed, 15%; soybeans, 15%, copra, 63%; palm kernels, 45%.

COTTONSEED
World Production—19,350,000 metric tons—Av. 1957/58–1960/61

	10	20	30	40	50	60	70	80	90	100%
UNITED STATES 24.9%	MEX. 4.0	CHINA 21.4	INDIA 8.5	PAK. 3.0	OTH. ASIA 5.0	SOVIET UNION 15.0	U.A.R. (EGYPT) 4.4	OTHER AFRICA 4.2	BRAZIL 4.3	OTHER 2.8	ALL OTH.

NORTH AMERICA — ASIA — AFR. — S.A.

SOYBEANS
World Production—27,150,000 metric tons—Av. 1957/58–1960/61

	10	20	30	40	50	60	70	80	90	100%
UNITED STATES 53.9%	CHINA 39.0	OTHER ASIA 4.7	OTHER 2.4

NORTH AMERICA — ASIA

COPRA and COCONUT OIL
World Prod.—3,025,000 m.t., in terms of copra—Av. 1957/58–1960/61

	10	20	30	40	50	60	70	80	90	100%
PHILIPPINES 39.5%	INDONESIA 20.1	INDIA 8.0	CEYLON 6.3	MALAYA 4.5	MEX. 5.7	OTHER 1.4	OCEANIA 9.0	AFRICA 3.4

ASIA

PALM OIL and PALM KERNELS
World Prod.—2,188,000 metric tons—Av. 1957/58–1960/61

	10	20	30	40	50	60	70	80	90	100%
NIGERIA 39.7%	THE CONGO 17.7	S.L. 2.6	DAH. 2.4	OTHER AFRICA 17.5	INDON. 8.3	MALAYA 4.3	BRAZ. 4.1	ALL OTHERS 3.4

AFRICA — ASIA

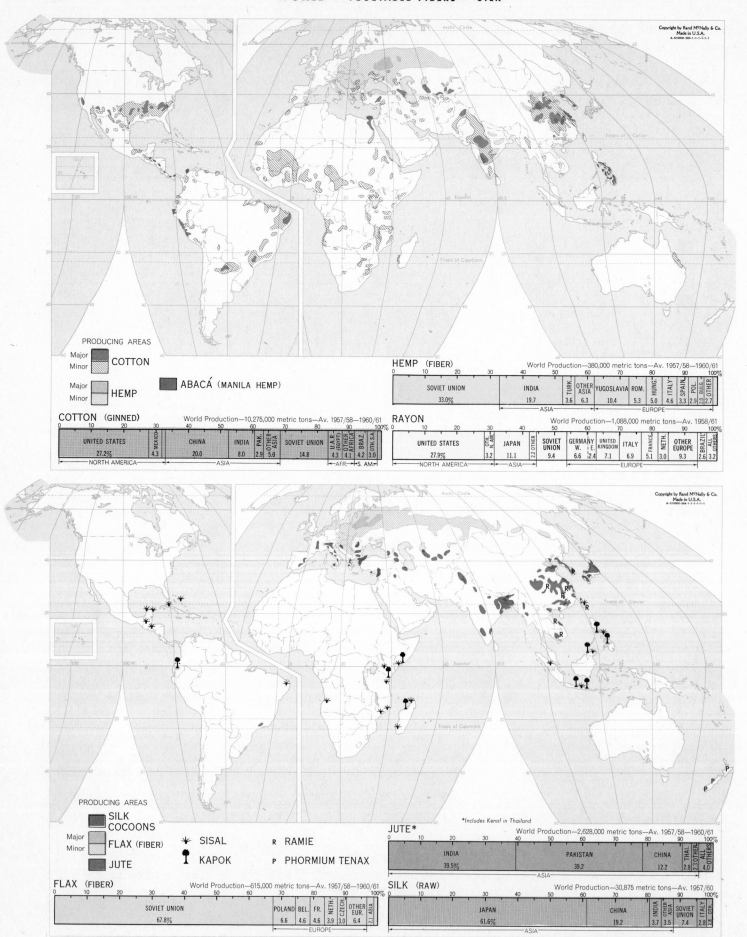

Copyright by Rand McNally & Co.
Made in U.S.A.
A-510000-560-1-1-1-1-1-1

PRODUCING AREAS

Major / Minor — **COTTON**

Major / Minor — **HEMP**

■ **ABACÁ** (MANILA HEMP)

HEMP (FIBER)
World Production—380,000 metric tons—Av. 1957/58—1960/61

SOVIET UNION 33.0%	INDIA 19.7	TURK. 3.6	OTHER ASIA 6.3	YUGOSLAVIA 10.4	ROM. 5.3	HUNG. 5.0	ITALY 4.6	SPAIN 3.3	POL. 2.9	BULG. 2.0	OTHER 2.7

ASIA — EUROPE

COTTON (GINNED)
World Production—10,275,000 metric tons—Av. 1957/58—1960/61

UNITED STATES 27.2%	MEXICO 4.3	CHINA 20.0	INDIA 8.0	PAK. 2.9	OTHER ASIA 5.0	SOVIET UNION 14.8	U.A.R. (EGYPT) 4.3	OTHER AFRICA 4.1	BRAZ. 4.2	OTH. S.A. 3.0

NORTH AMERICA — ASIA — AFR. — S. AM.

RAYON
World Production—1,088,000 metric tons—Av. 1958/61

UNITED STATES 27.9%	OTH. N. AM. 3.2	JAPAN 11.1	OTHER 2.2	SOVIET UNION 9.4	GERMANY W. 6.6	E. 2.4	UNITED KINGDOM 7.1	ITALY 6.9	FRANCE 5.1	NETH. 3.0	OTHER EUROPE 9.3	BRAZIL 2.6	ALL OTHERS 3.2

NORTH AMERICA — ASIA — EUROPE

Copyright by Rand McNally & Co.
Made in U.S.A.
A-510000-364-1-1-1-1-1-1

PRODUCING AREAS

■ **SILK COCOONS**

Major / Minor — **FLAX (FIBER)**

■ **JUTE**

✳ **SISAL**   R **RAMIE**

♟ **KAPOK**   P **PHORMIUM TENAX**

*Includes Kenaf in Thailand

JUTE*
World Production—2,628,000 metric tons—Av. 1957/58—1960/61

INDIA 39.5%	PAKISTAN 39.2	CHINA 12.2	THAI. 2.8	OTHER 2.3	ALL OTHERS 4.0

ASIA

FLAX (FIBER)
World Production—615,000 metric tons—Av. 1957/58—1960/61

SOVIET UNION 67.8%	POLAND 6.6	BEL. 4.6	FR. 4.6	NETH. 3.9	CZECH 3.0	OTHER EUR. 6.4	ASIA 2.1

EUROPE

SILK (RAW)
World Production—30,875 metric tons—Av. 1957/60

JAPAN 61.6%	CHINA 19.2	INDIA 3.7	OTHER ASIA 3.5	SOVIET UNION 7.4	ITALY 2.8	OTH. 1.3

ASIA

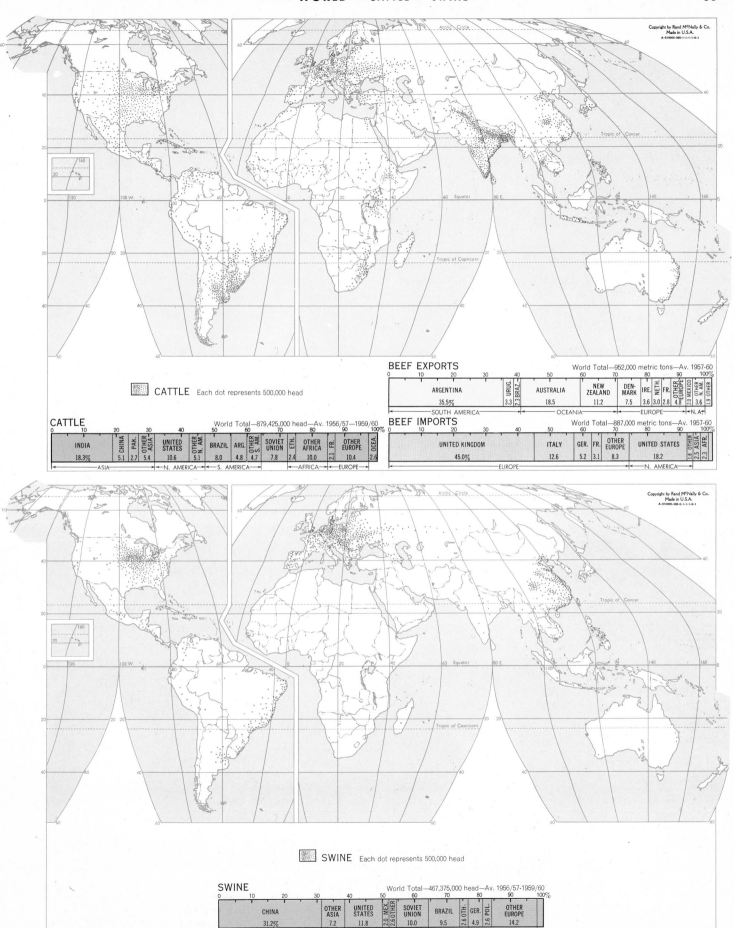

CATTLE Each dot represents 500,000 head

CATTLE   World Total—879,425,000 head—Av. 1956/57—1959/60

INDIA 18.3%	CHINA 5.1	PAK. 2.7	OTHER ASIA* 5.4	UNITED STATES 10.6	OTHER N. AM. 5.1	BRAZIL 8.0	ARG. 4.8	OTHER S. AM. 4.7	SOVIET UNION 7.8	ETH. 2.4	OTHER AFRICA 10.0	FR. 2.1 / OTHER EUROPE 10.4	OCEA. 2.6
ASIA				N. AMERICA		S. AMERICA			AFRICA			EUROPE	

BEEF EXPORTS   World Total—952,000 metric tons—Av. 1957-60

0 10 20 30 40 50 60 70 80 90 100%

ARGENTINA 35.5%	URUG. 3.3	BRAZ. 2.3	AUSTRALIA 18.5	NEW ZEALAND 11.2	DEN-MARK 7.5	IRE. 3.6	NETH. 3.0	FR. 2.8	OTHER EUROPE 4.8	MEXICO 2.0	OTHER N. AM. 3.6	OTHER 1.9
SOUTH AMERICA			OCEANIA		EUROPE					N. A.		

BEEF IMPORTS   World Total—887,000 metric tons—Av. 1957-60

0 10 20 30 40 50 60 70 80 90 100%

UNITED KINGDOM 45.0%	ITALY 12.6	GER. 5.2	FR. 3.1	OTHER EUROPE 8.3	UNITED STATES 18.2	OTHER 1.8 / ASIA* 2.5 / AFR. 2.3
EUROPE					N. AMERICA	

SWINE Each dot represents 500,000 head

SWINE   World Total—467,375,000 head—Av. 1956/57—1959/60

0 10 20 30 40 50 60 70 80 90 100%

CHINA 31.2%	OTHER ASIA 7.2	UNITED STATES 11.8	MEX. 2.0	OTHER 2.6	SOVIET UNION 10.0	BRAZIL 9.5	OTH. 2.6	GER. 4.9 / POL. 2.6	OTHER EUROPE 14.2
ASIA		N. AMERICA				S. AMER.		EUROPE	

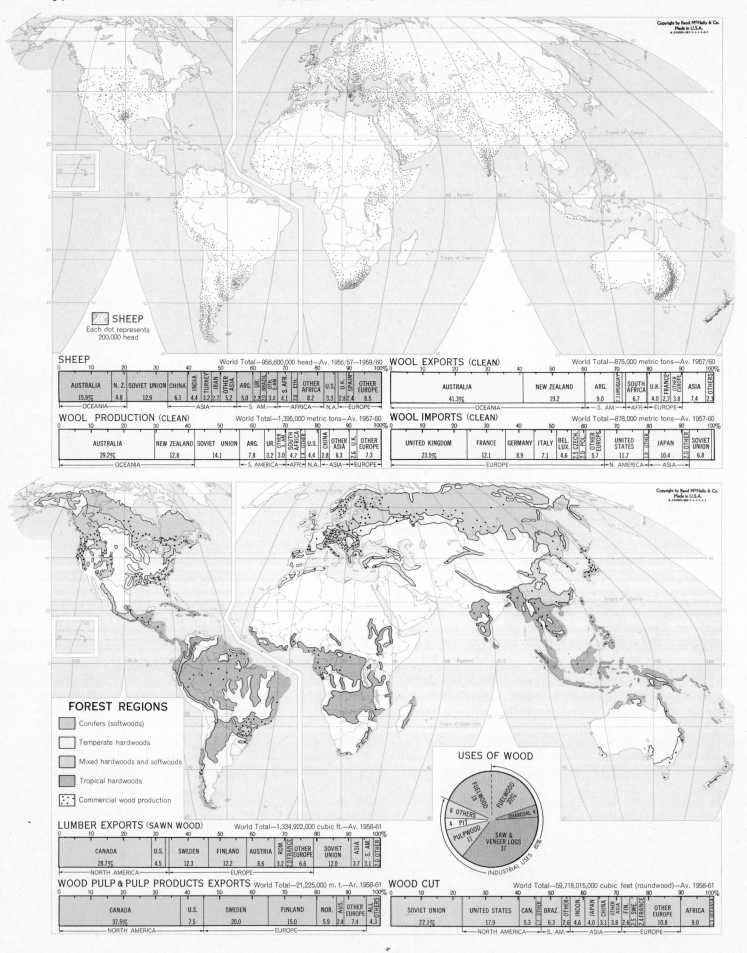

SHEEP
Each dot represents 200,000 head

SHEEP
World Total—956,600,000 head—Av. 1956/57—1959/60

AUSTRALIA 15.9%	N. Z. 4.8	SOVIET UNION 12.9	CHINA 6.1	INDIA 4.4	TURKEY 3.2	IRAN 2.7	OTHER ASIA 5.2	ARG. 5.0	UR. 2.2	BRAZIL 2.0	OTH. S. AM. 3.4	S. AFR. 4.1	ETH. 2.0	OTHER AFRICA 8.2	U.S. 3.3	U.K. 2.8	SPAIN 2.4	OTHER EUROPE 8.5	

OCEANIA — ASIA — S. AM. — AFRICA — N.A. — EUROPE

WOOL EXPORTS (CLEAN)
World Total—875,000 metric tons—Av. 1957/60

AUSTRALIA 41.3%	NEW ZEALAND 19.2	ARG. 9.0	URUGUAY 2.3	SOUTH AFRICA 6.7	U.K. 4.0	FRANCE 2.7	OTHER EUROPE 3.8	ASIA 7.4	OTHERS 2.3

OCEANIA — S. AM. — AFR. — EUROPE

WOOL PRODUCTION (CLEAN)
World Total—1,395,000 metric tons—Av. 1957-60

AUSTRALIA 29.2%	NEW ZEALAND 12.8	SOVIET UNION 14.1	ARG. 7.8	UR. 3.2	OTHER S. AM. 3.0	SOUTH AFRICA 4.7	OTHER 1.8	U.S. 4.4	CHINA 2.8	OTHER ASIA 6.3	U.K. 2.6	OTHER EUROPE 7.3

OCEANIA — S. AMERICA — AFR. — N.A. — ASIA — EUROPE

WOOL IMPORTS (CLEAN)
World Total—878,000 metric tons—Av. 1957-60

UNITED KINGDOM 23.5%	FRANCE 12.1	GERMANY 8.9	ITALY 7.1	BEL. LUX. 4.6	CZECH. 2.5	POL. 2.0	OTHER EUROPE 5.7	UNITED STATES 11.7	OTHER 1.9	JAPAN 10.4	OTHER 2.0	SOVIET UNION 6.8

EUROPE — N. AMERICA — ASIA

FOREST REGIONS
- Conifers (softwoods)
- Temperate hardwoods
- Mixed hardwoods and softwoods
- Tropical hardwoods
- Commercial wood production

USES OF WOOD
FUELWOOD 18
FUELWOOD 20%
CHARCOAL 4
6 OTHERS
4 PIT
PULPWOOD 11
SAW & VENEER LOGS 37
INDUSTRIAL USES 62%

LUMBER EXPORTS (SAWN WOOD)
World Total—1,334,922,000 cubic ft.—Av. 1958-61

CANADA 28.7%	U.S. 4.5	SWEDEN 12.3	FINLAND 12.2	AUSTRIA 8.6	ROM. 3.2	FRANCE 2.0	OTHER EUROPE 6.6	SOVIET UNION 12.0	ASIA 3.7	S. AM. 3.1	OTHER 2.0

NORTH AMERICA — EUROPE

WOOD PULP & PULP PRODUCTS EXPORTS
World Total—21,225,000 m. t.—Ar. 1958-61

CANADA 37.5%	U.S. 7.5	SWEDEN 20.0	FINLAND 15.0	NOR. 5.9	AUS. 2.4	OTHER EUROPE 7.4	ALL OTHERS 4.3

NORTH AMERICA — EUROPE

WOOD CUT
World Total—59,718,015,000 cubic feet (roundwood)—Av. 1958-61

SOVIET UNION 22.1%	UNITED STATES 17.9	CAN. 5.3	OTHER 1.7	BRAZ. 6.3	OTHER 2.6	INDON. 4.6	JAPAN 4.0	CHINA 3.1	OTHER ASIA 3.8	FIN. 2.5	SWE. 2.4	FRANCE 2.1	OTHER EUROPE 10.8	AFRICA 9.0	OCEANIA 1.0

NORTH AMERICA — S. AM. — ASIA — EUROPE

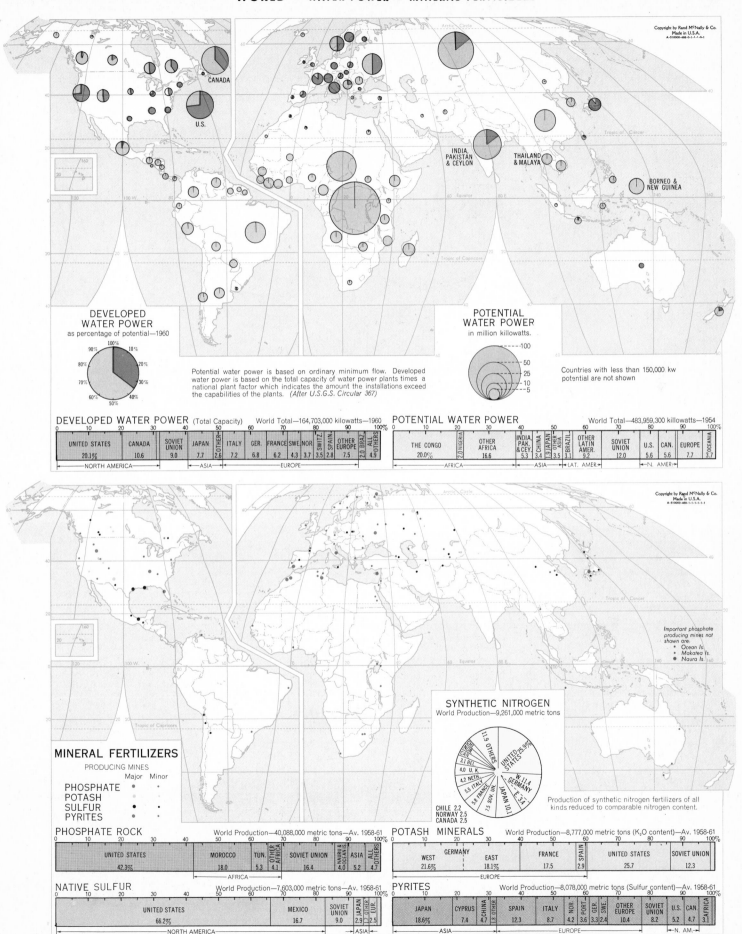

Copyright by Rand McNally & Co.
Made in U.S.A.
A-510000-460-0-1-1-1-0-1

DEVELOPED WATER POWER
as percentage of potential—1960

100% 10%
90% 20%
80% 30%
70% 40%
60% 50%

Potential water power is based on ordinary minimum flow. Developed water power is based on the total capacity of water power plants times a national plant factor which indicates the amount the installations exceed the capabilities of the plants. *(After U.S.G.S. Circular 367)*

POTENTIAL WATER POWER
in million killowatts.

-- 100
-- 50
-- 25
-- 10
-- 5

Countries with less than 150,000 kw potential are not shown

DEVELOPED WATER POWER (Total Capacity) — World Total—164,703,000 kilowatts—1960

UNITED STATES 20.1%	CANADA 10.6	SOVIET UNION 9.0	JAPAN 7.7	OTHER 2.6	ITALY 7.2	GER. 6.8	FRANCE 6.2	SWE. 4.3	NOR. 3.7	SWITZ. 3.5	SPAIN 2.8	OTHER EUROPE 7.5	BRAZ. 2.0	ALL OTHERS 4.9
NORTH AMERICA			ASIA		EUROPE									

POTENTIAL WATER POWER — World Total—483,959,300 killowatts—1954

THE CONGO 20.0%	NIGERIA 2.0	OTHER AFRICA 16.6	INDIA, PAK. & CEY. 5.3	CHINA 3.4	OTHER ASIA 3.5	JAPAN 1.3	BRAZIL 3.1	OTHER LATIN AMER. 9.2	SOVIET UNION 12.0	U.S. 5.6	CAN. 5.6	EUROPE 7.7	OCEANIA 3.7
AFRICA			ASIA				LAT. AMER.		N. AMER.				

Copyright by Rand McNally & Co.
Made in U.S.A.
A-510000-460-1-1-1-1-1-1

Important phosphate producing mines not shown are:
● Ocean Is.
* Makatea Is.
● Naura Is.

SYNTHETIC NITROGEN
World Production—9,261,000 metric tons

11.9 OTHERS
3.0 DEN
NOR
CAN
3.1 BEL
4.0 U.K.
4.2 NETH.
5.5 ITALY
5.8 FRANCE
7.5 SOV. UN.
JAPAN 10.1
E. 3.4
W. 11.4 GERMANY
UNITED STATES 25.9%

CHILE 2.2
NORWAY 2.5
CANADA 2.5

Production of synthetic nitrogen fertilizers of all kinds reduced to comparable nitrogen content.

MINERAL FERTILIZERS
PRODUCING MINES

Major Minor
PHOSPHATE
POTASH
SULFUR
PYRITES

PHOSPHATE ROCK — World Production—40,088,000 metric tons—Av. 1958-61

UNITED STATES 42.3%	MOROCCO 18.0	TUN. 5.3	OTHER AFRICA 4.1	SOVIET UNION 16.4	NAURU & OCEANIS 4.0	ASIA 5.2	ALL OTHERS 4.7
	AFRICA						

POTASH MINERALS — World Production—8,777,000 metric tons (K₂O content)—Av. 1958-61

WEST 21.6%	EAST 18.1%	FRANCE 17.5	SPAIN 2.9	UNITED STATES 25.7	SOVIET UNION 12.3
GERMANY					
EUROPE					

NATIVE SULFUR — World Production—7,603,000 metric tons—Av. 1958-61

UNITED STATES 66.2%	MEXICO 16.7	SOVIET UNION 9.0	JAPAN 1.7	OTHER EUR. 2.5
NORTH AMERICA		ASIA		

PYRITES — World Production—8,078,000 metric tons (Sulfur content)—Av. 1958-61

JAPAN 18.6%	CYPRUS 7.4	CHINA 4.7	OTHER 1.8	SPAIN 12.3	ITALY 8.7	NOR. 4.2	PORT. 3.6	GER. 3.3	SWE. 2.4	OTHER EUROPE 10.4	SOVIET UNION 8.2	U.S. 5.2	CAN. 4.7	AFRICA 3.1
ASIA				EUROPE								N. AM.		

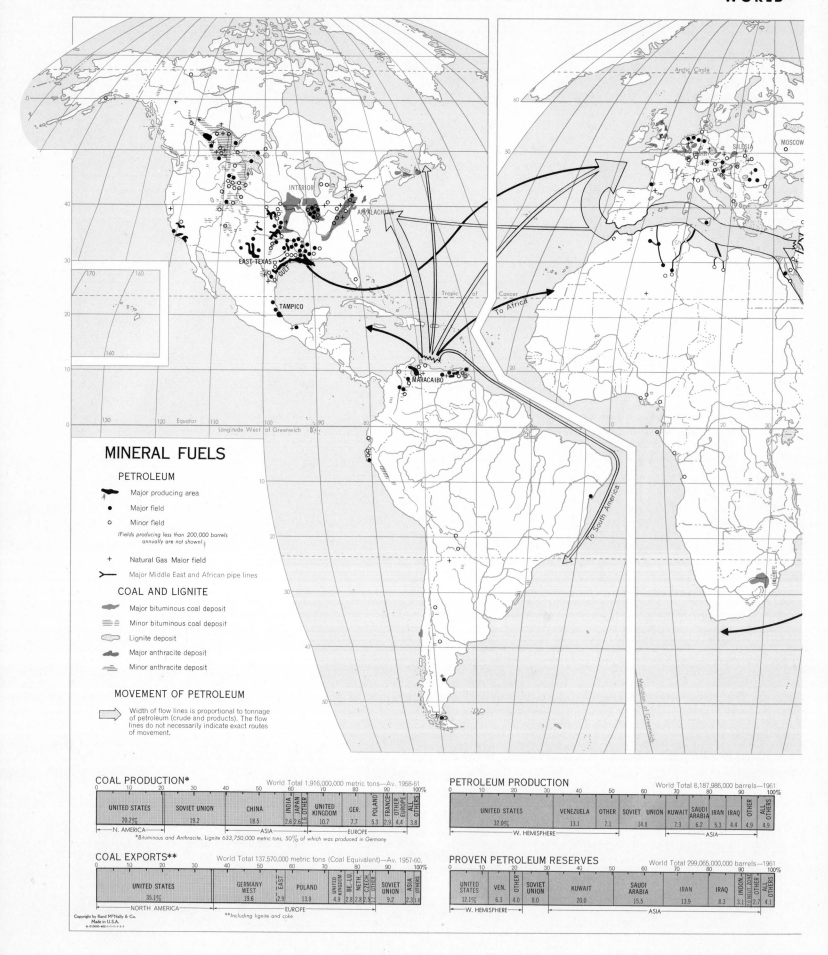

MINERAL FUELS

PETROLEUM

▬ Major producing area

● Major field

○ Minor field

(Fields producing less than 200,000 barrels annually are not shown)

+ Natural Gas Major field

⊢ Major Middle East and African pipe lines

COAL AND LIGNITE

▬ Major bituminous coal deposit

≡ Minor bituminous coal deposit

▭ Lignite deposit

▬ Major anthracite deposit

≡ Minor anthracite deposit

MOVEMENT OF PETROLEUM

⇨ Width of flow lines is proportional to tonnage of petroleum (crude and products). The flow lines do not necessarily indicate exact routes of movement.

COAL PRODUCTION*

World Total 1,916,000,000 metric tons—Av. 1958-61

UNITED STATES	SOVIET UNION	CHINA	INDIA	JAPAN	OTHER	UNITED KINGDOM	GER.	POLAND	FRANCE	OTHER EUROPE	ALL OTHERS
20.2%	19.2	18.5	2.6	2.6	1.6	10.7	7.7	5.3	2.9	4.4	3.8

├── N. AMERICA ──┤ ├──────── ASIA ────────┤ ├────────── EUROPE ──────────┤

*Bituminous and Anthracite. Lignite 633,750,000 metric tons, 50% of which was produced in Germany

COAL EXPORTS**

World Total 137,570,000 metric tons (Coal Equivalent)—Av. 1957-60.

UNITED STATES	GERMANY WEST	EAST	POLAND	UNITED KINGDOM	BE-LU.	NETH.	CZECH.	SOVIET UNION	ASIA	OTHERS
35.1%	19.6	2.9	13.9	4.9	2.8	2.5	1.7	9.2	2.3	1.8

├── NORTH AMERICA ──┤ ├─────────────── EUROPE ───────────────┤

**Including lignite and coke

PETROLEUM PRODUCTION

World Total 8,187,986,000 barrels—1961

UNITED STATES	VENEZUELA	OTHER	SOVIET UNION	KUWAIT	SAUDI ARABIA	IRAN	IRAQ	OTHER	ALL OTHERS
32.0%	13.1	7.1	14.8	7.3	6.2	5.3	4.4	4.9	4.9

├────────── W. HEMISPHERE ──────────┤ ├──────────── ASIA ────────────┤

PROVEN PETROLEUM RESERVES

World Total 299,065,000,000 barrels—1961

UNITED STATES	VEN.	OTHER	SOVIET UNION	KUWAIT	SAUDI ARABIA	IRAN	IRAQ	INDON.	NEUT. ZONE	OTHER	ALL OTHERS
12.1%	6.3	4.0	8.0	20.0	15.5	13.9	8.3	3.1	2.0	2.7	4.1

├── W. HEMISPHERE ──┤ ├──────────────────── ASIA ────────────────────┤

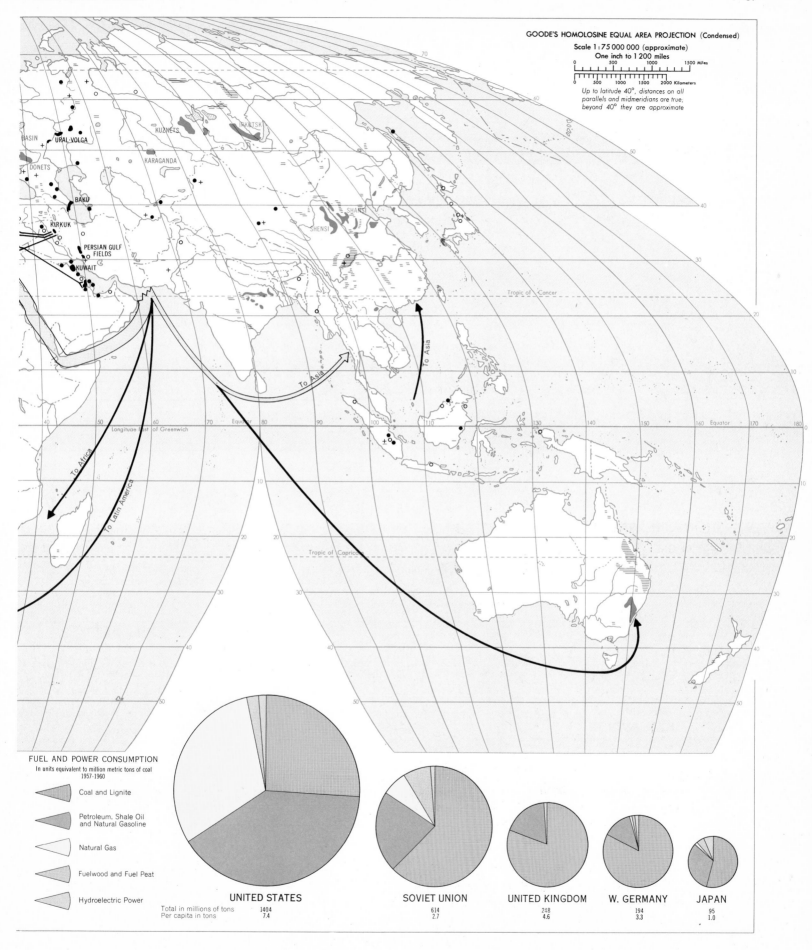

GOODE'S HOMOLOSINE EQUAL AREA PROJECTION (Condensed)

Scale 1 : 75 000 000 (approximate)

One inch to 1 200 miles

Up to latitude 40°, distances on all parallels and midmeridians are true; beyond 40° they are approximate

To Africa

To Latin America

To Asia

To Asia

BASIN

URAL-VOLGA

DONETS

BAKU

KIRKUK

PERSIAN GULF FIELDS

KUWAIT

KUZNETS

KARAGANDA

IRKUTSK

SHANSI

SHENSI

Tropic of Cancer

Longitude East of Greenwich

Equator

Equator

Tropic of Capricorn

FUEL AND POWER CONSUMPTION

In units equivalent to million metric tons of coal
1957-1960

Coal and Lignite

Petroleum, Shale Oil and Natural Gasoline

Natural Gas

Fuelwood and Fuel Peat

Hydroelectric Power

	UNITED STATES	SOVIET UNION	UNITED KINGDOM	W. GERMANY	JAPAN
Total in millions of tons	1404	614	248	194	95
Per capita in tons	7.4	2.7	4.6	3.3	1.0

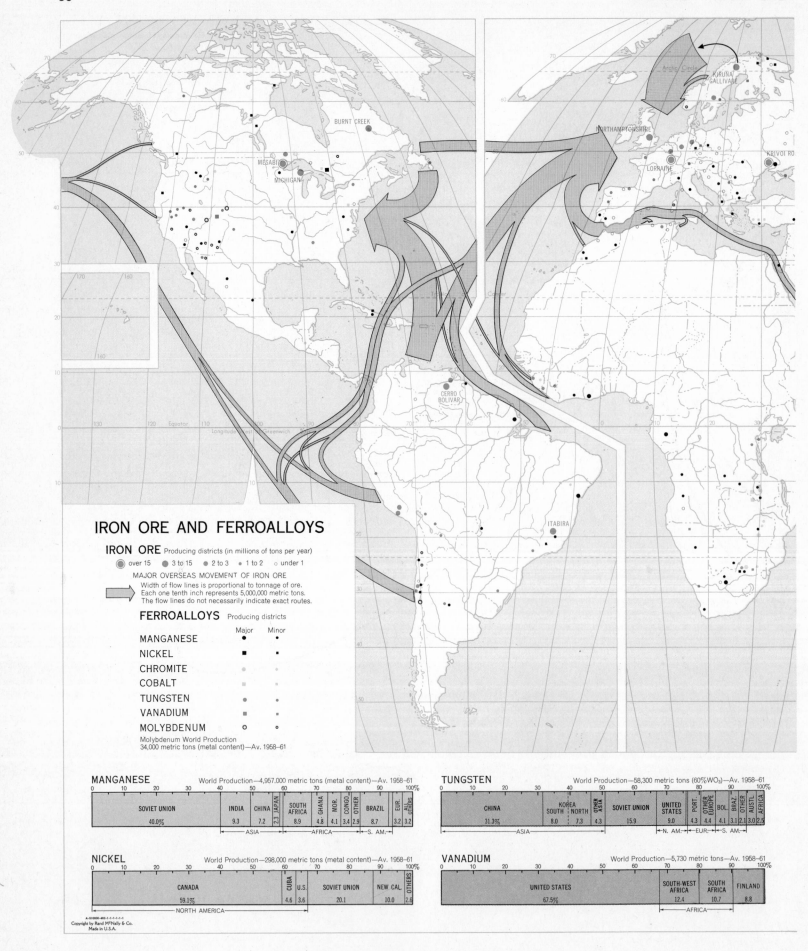

BURNT CREEK

MESABI

MICHIGAN

KIRUNA
GALLIVARE

NORTHAMPTONSHIRE

LORRAINE

KRIVOI RO

CERRO
BOLIVAR

ITABIRA

IRON ORE AND FERROALLOYS

IRON ORE Producing districts (in millions of tons per year)

⦿ over 15   ● 3 to 15   ● 2 to 3   • 1 to 2   ○ under 1

MAJOR OVERSEAS MOVEMENT OF IRON ORE

Width of flow lines is proportional to tonnage of ore.
Each one tenth inch represents 5,000,000 metric tons.
The flow lines do not necessarily indicate exact routes.

FERROALLOYS Producing districts

	Major	Minor
MANGANESE	●	•
NICKEL	■	▪
CHROMITE	●	•
COBALT	■	▪
TUNGSTEN	●	•
VANADIUM	■	▪
MOLYBDENUM	○	◦

Molybdenum World Production
34,000 metric tons (metal content)—Av. 1958–61

MANGANESE   World Production—4,957,000 metric tons (metal content)—Av. 1958–61

0	10	20	30	40	50	60	70	80	90	100%

| SOVIET UNION 40.0% | INDIA 9.3 | CHINA 7.2 | JAPAN 2.3 | SOUTH AFRICA 8.9 | GHANA 4.8 | MOR. 4.1 | CONGO 3.4 | OTHER 2.9 | BRAZIL 8.7 | EUR. 3.2 | ALL OTHERS 3.2 |

←— ASIA —→   ←—— AFRICA ——→   ←S. AM.→

TUNGSTEN   World Production—58,300 metric tons (60%WO₃)—Av. 1958–61

| CHINA 31.3% | KOREA SOUTH 8.0 | NORTH 7.3 | OTHER ASIA 4.3 | SOVIET UNION 15.9 | UNITED STATES 9.0 | PORT. 4.3 | OTHER EUROPE 4.4 | BOL. 4.1 | BRAZ. 3.1 | OTHER 2.1 | AUSTL 3.0 | AFRICA 2.5 |

←——— ASIA ———→   N. AM.   ← EUR. →   S. AM.

NICKEL   World Production—298,000 metric tons (metal content)—Av. 1958–61

| CANADA 59.1% | CUBA 4.5 | U.S. 3.6 | SOVIET UNION 20.1 | NEW CAL. 10.0 | OTHERS 2.6 |

←———— NORTH AMERICA ————→

VANADIUM   World Production—5,730 metric tons—Av. 1958–61

| UNITED STATES 67.5% | SOUTH-WEST AFRICA 12.4 | SOUTH AFRICA 10.7 | FINLAND 8.8 |

←—— AFRICA ——→

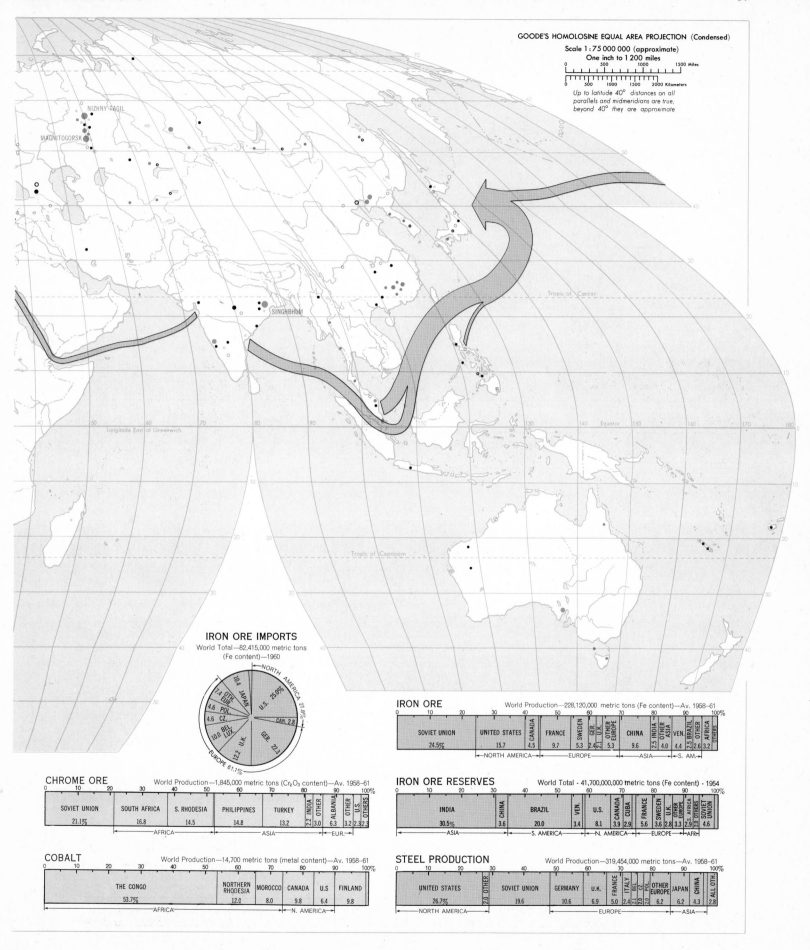

GOODE'S HOMOLOSINE EQUAL AREA PROJECTION (Condensed)

Scale 1:75 000 000 (approximate)
One inch to 1 200 miles

Up to latitude 40° distances on all
parallels and midmeridians are true,
beyond 40° they are approximate

IRON ORE IMPORTS

World Total—82,415,000 metric tons
(Fe content)—1960

NORTH AMERICA 27.8%
U.S. 25.0%
CAN. 2.8
GER. 22.3
U.K. 12.2
BEL. LUX. 10.0
CZ. 4.6
POL. 4.6
OTH. EUR. 7.4
JAPAN 10.4
EUROPE 61.1%

IRON ORE

World Production—228,120,000 metric tons (Fe content)—Av. 1958–61

SOVIET UNION 24.5%	UNITED STATES 15.7	CANADA 4.5	FRANCE 9.7	SWEDEN 5.3	GER. 2.4	U.K. 2.1	OTHER EUROPE 5.3	CHINA 9.6	INDIA 2.5	OTHER ASIA 4.0	VEN. 4.4	BRAZIL 2.5	OTHER 2.6	AFRICA 3.2	OTHERS

NORTH AMERICA — EUROPE — ASIA — S. AM.

CHROME ORE

World Production—1,845,000 metric tons (Cr₂O₃ content)—Av. 1958–61

SOVIET UNION 21.1%	SOUTH AFRICA 16.8	S. RHODESIA 14.5	PHILIPPINES 14.8	TURKEY 13.2	INDIA 2.2	OTHER 3.0	ALBANIA 6.3	OTHER 3.2	U.S. 2.3	OTHERS 2.3

AFRICA — ASIA — EUR.

IRON ORE RESERVES

World Total - 41,700,000,000 metric tons (Fe content) - 1954

INDIA 30.5%	CHINA 3.6	BRAZIL 20.0	VEN. 3.4	U.S. 8.1	CANADA 3.9	CUBA 2.9	FRANCE 5.6	SWEDEN 3.6	U.K. 2.8	OTHER EUROPE 3.3	S. AFRICA 2.9	OTHERS 2.9	SOVIET UNION 4.6

ASIA — S. AMERICA — N. AMERICA — EUROPE — AFR.

COBALT

World Production—14,700 metric tons (metal content)—Av. 1958–61

THE CONGO 53.7%	NORTHERN RHODESIA 12.0	MOROCCO 8.0	CANADA 9.8	U.S 6.4	FINLAND 9.8

AFRICA — N. AMERICA

STEEL PRODUCTION

World Production—319,454,000 metric tons—Av. 1958–61

UNITED STATES 26.7%	OTHER 2.0	SOVIET UNION 19.6	GERMANY 10.6	U.K. 6.9	FRANCE 5.0	ITALY 2.4	BEL. 2.1	CZ. 2.0	POL. 2.0	OTHER EUROPE 6.2	JAPAN 6.2	CHINA 4.3	ALL OTH. 2.8

NORTH AMERICA — EUROPE — ASIA

NIZHNY TAGIL
MAGNITOGORSK
SINGHBHUM

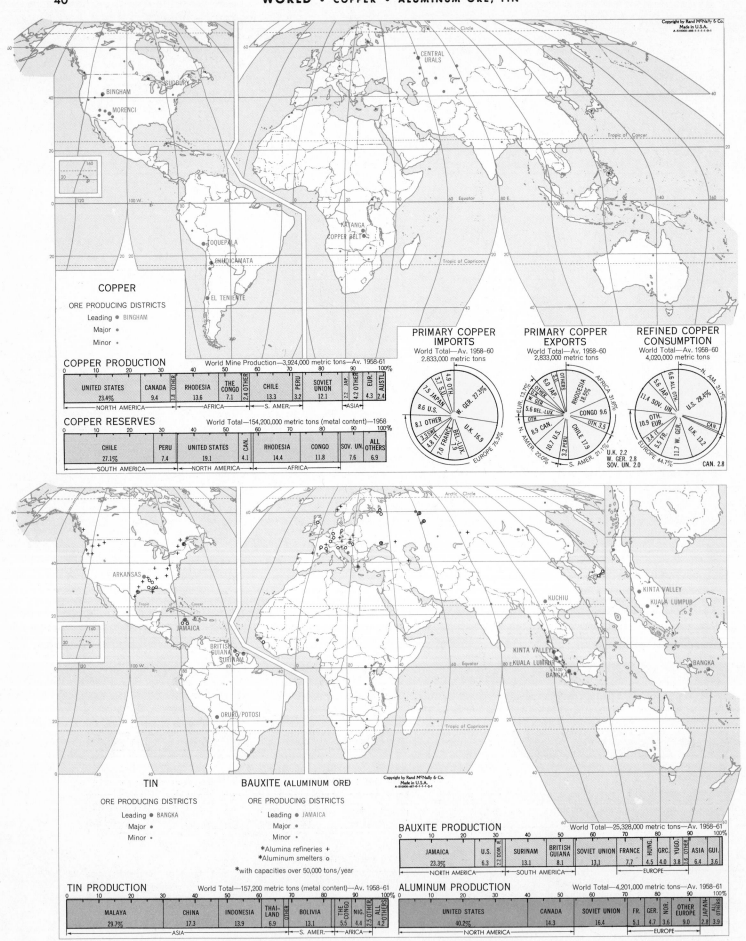

Copyright by Rand McNally & Co.
Made in U.S.A.
A-510000-466-1-1-1-1-0-1

COPPER

ORE PRODUCING DISTRICTS

Leading ● BINGHAM

Major ●

Minor ·

COPPER PRODUCTION

World Mine Production—3,924,000 metric tons—Av. 1958-61

0	10	20	30	40	50	60	70	80	90	100%			
UNITED STATES 23.4%		CANADA 9.4	OTHER 1.8	RHODESIA 13.6	THE CONGO 7.1	OTHER 2.4	CHILE 13.3	PERU 3.2	SOVIET UNION 12.1	JAP. 2.2	OTHER 4.2	EUR. 4.3	AUSTL. 2.4

— NORTH AMERICA —   — AFRICA —   — S. AMER. —   — ASIA —

COPPER RESERVES

World Total—154,200,000 metric tons (metal content)—1958

0	10	20	30	40	50	60	70	80	90	100%	
CHILE 27.1%		PERU 7.4	UNITED STATES 19.1	CAN. 4.1	RHODESIA 14.4	CONGO 11.8		SOV. UN. 7.6	ALL OTHERS 6.9		

— SOUTH AMERICA —   — NORTH AMERICA —   — AFRICA —

PRIMARY COPPER IMPORTS
World Total—Av. 1958-60
2,833,000 metric tons

4.9 OTH.
3.7 S.U.
7.5 JAPAN
8.6 U.S.
8.1 OTHER
3.3 SWE.
4.8 IT.
7.0 FRANCE
BEL.-LUX. 7.9
U.K. 16.9
W. GER. 27.3%
EUROPE 75.3%

PRIMARY COPPER EXPORTS
World Total—Av. 1958-60
2,833,000 metric tons

3.6 JAP.
6.0 JAP.
OTHER
U.K. GER.
W. GER.
5.6 BEL.-LUX.
OTH.
8.9 CAN.
10.7 U.S.
3.2 PERU
CHILE 17.9
RHODESIA 18.5%
AFRICA 31.6%
CONGO 9.6
OTH. 3.5
EUR. 13.7%
N. AMER. 22.0%
S. AMER. 21.2%
U.K. 2.2
W. GER. 2.8
SOV. UN. 2.0

REFINED COPPER CONSUMPTION
World Total—Av. 1958-60
4,020,000 metric tons

6.6 ALL OTH.
5.6 JAP.
11.4 SOV. UN.
OTH.
10.9 EUR.
3.4 IT.
5.5 FR.
11.7 W. GER.
N. AM. 31.7%
U.S. 28.4%
CAN.
U.K. 13.2
EUROPE 44.7%
CAN. 2.8

TIN

ORE PRODUCING DISTRICTS

Leading ● BANGKA

Major ●

Minor ·

BAUXITE (ALUMINUM ORE)

ORE PRODUCING DISTRICTS

Leading ● JAMAICA

Major ●

Minor ·

*Alumina refineries +

*Aluminum smelters ○

*with capacities over 50,000 tons/year

Copyright by Rand McNally & Co.
Made in U.S.A.
A-510000-467-0-1-1-1-2-1

BAUXITE PRODUCTION
World Total—25,328,000 metric tons—Av. 1958-61

0	10	20	30	40	50	60	70	80	90	100%				
JAMAICA 23.3%		U.S. 6.3	DOM. 2.2	SURINAM 13.1	BRITISH GUIANA 8.1	SOVIET UNION 13.1		FRANCE 7.7	HUNG. 4.5	GRC. 4.0	YUGO. 3.8	OTHER 1.6	ASIA 6.4	GUI. 3.6

— NORTH AMERICA —   — SOUTH AMERICA —   — EUROPE —

TIN PRODUCTION
World Total—157,200 metric tons (metal content)—Av. 1958-61

0	10	20	30	40	50	60	70	80	90	100%	
MALAYA 29.7%		CHINA 17.3	INDONESIA 13.9	THAILAND 6.9	OTHER	BOLIVIA 13.1	THE CONGO 5.5	NIG. 4.4	OTHER 2.5	ALL OTHERS 4.7	

— ASIA —   — S. AMER. —   — AFRICA —

ALUMINUM PRODUCTION
World Total—4,201,000 metric tons—Av. 1958-61

0	10	20	30	40	50	60	70	80	90	100%			
UNITED STATES 40.2%		CANADA 14.3	SOVIET UNION 16.4	FR. 5.1	GER. 4.7	NOR. 3.6	OTHER EUROPE 9.0	JAPAN 2.8	ALL OTHERS 3.9				

— NORTH AMERICA —   — EUROPE —

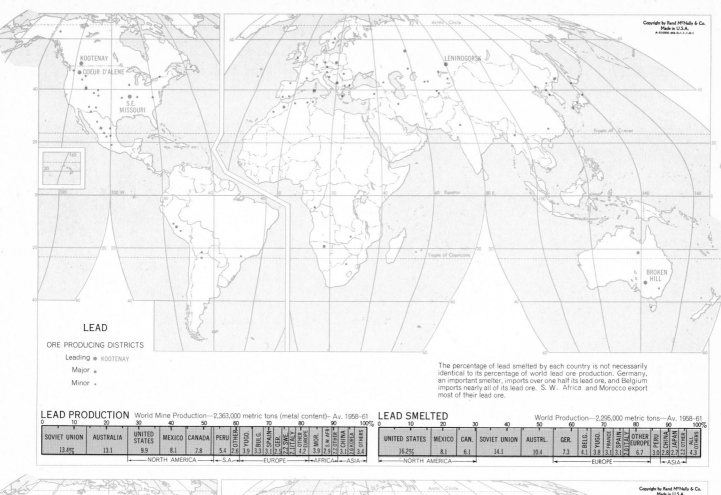

LEAD

ORE PRODUCING DISTRICTS

Leading ● KOOTENAY

Major ●

Minor ·

The percentage of lead smelted by each country is not necessarily identical to its percentage of world lead ore production. Germany, an important smelter, imports over one half its lead ore, and Belgium imports nearly all of its lead ore. S. W. Africa and Morocco export most of their lead ore.

LEAD PRODUCTION — World Mine Production—2,363,000 metric tons (metal content)- Av. 1958–61

SOVIET UNION	AUSTRALIA	UNITED STATES	MEXICO	CANADA	PERU	OTHER	YUGO.	BULG.	SPAIN	GER.	SWE.	ITALY	OTHER EUROPE	MOR.	S.W. AFR.	OTHER	CHINA	KOREA	OTHERS
13.4%	13.1	9.9	8.1	7.8	5.4	2.6	3.9	3.3	3.1	2.5	2.2	2.1	4.2	3.9	2.9	2.0	2.0	2.0	3.4

← NORTH AMERICA → ← S.A. → ← EUROPE → ← AFRICA → ← ASIA →

LEAD SMELTED — World Production—2,295,000 metric tons—Av. 1958–61

UNITED STATES	MEXICO	CAN.	SOVIET UNION	AUSTRL.	GER.	BELG.	YUGO.	FRANCE	SPAIN	ITALY	OTHER EUROPE	PERU	CHINA	JAPAN	OTHER	ALL OTHERS
16.2%	8.1	6.1	14.1	10.4	7.3	4.1	3.8	3.1	3.1	2.0	6.7	3.0	2.8	2.7	2.2	4.3

← NORTH AMERICA → ← EUROPE → ← ASIA →

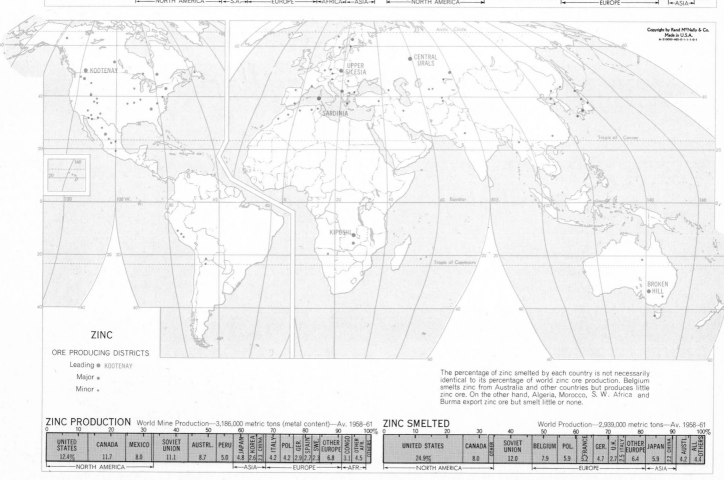

ZINC

ORE PRODUCING DISTRICTS

Leading ● KOOTENAY

Major ●

Minor ·

The percentage of zinc smelted by each country is not necessarily identical to its percentage of world zinc ore production. Belgium smelts zinc from Australia and other countries but produces little zinc ore. On the other hand, Algeria, Morocco, S. W. Africa and Burma export zinc ore but smelt little or none.

ZINC PRODUCTION — World Mine Production—3,186,000 metric tons (metal content)—Av. 1958–61

UNITED STATES	CANADA	MEXICO	SOVIET UNION	AUSTRL.	PERU	JAPAN	KOREA	CHINA	ITALY	POL.	GER.	SPAIN	SWE.	OTHER EUROPE	CONGO	OTHER AFR.	OTHERS
12.4%	11.7	8.0	11.1	8.7	5.0	4.8	2.6	2.3	4.2	4.2	2.9	2.7	2.3	6.8	3.1		4.5

← NORTH AMERICA → ← ASIA → ← EUROPE → ← AFR. →

ZINC SMELTED — World Production—2,939,000 metric tons—Av. 1958–61

UNITED STATES	CANADA	OTHER	SOVIET UNION	BELGIUM	POL.	FRANCE	GER.	U.K.	ITALY	OTHER EUROPE	JAPAN	CHINA	AUSTL.	ALL OTHERS
24.9%	8.0		12.0	7.9	5.9	5.2	4.7	2.7	2.5	6.4	5.9	2.2	4.2	4.4

← NORTH AMERICA → ← EUROPE → ← ASIA →

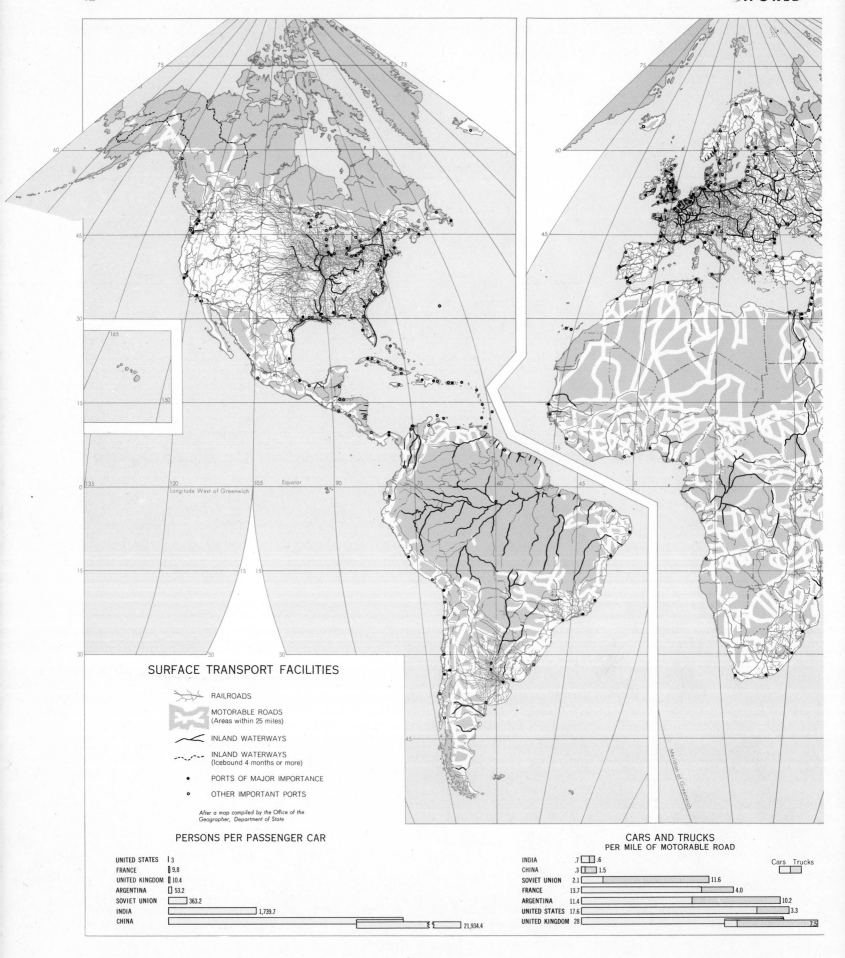

SURFACE TRANSPORT FACILITIES

⟋⟍ RAILROADS

▨ MOTORABLE ROADS
(Areas within 25 miles)

∿ INLAND WATERWAYS

╍╍ INLAND WATERWAYS
(Icebound 4 months or more)

● PORTS OF MAJOR IMPORTANCE

○ OTHER IMPORTANT PORTS

*After a map compiled by the Office of the
Geographer, Department of State*

PERSONS PER PASSENGER CAR

UNITED STATES	3
FRANCE	9.8
UNITED KINGDOM	10.4
ARGENTINA	53.2
SOVIET UNION	363.2
INDIA	1,739.7
CHINA	21,934.4

CARS AND TRUCKS
PER MILE OF MOTORABLE ROAD

Cars　Trucks

INDIA	.7	.6
CHINA	.3	1.5
SOVIET UNION	2.1	11.6
FRANCE	13.7	4.0
ARGENTINA	11.4	10.2
UNITED STATES	17.6	3.3
UNITED KINGDOM	28	7.5

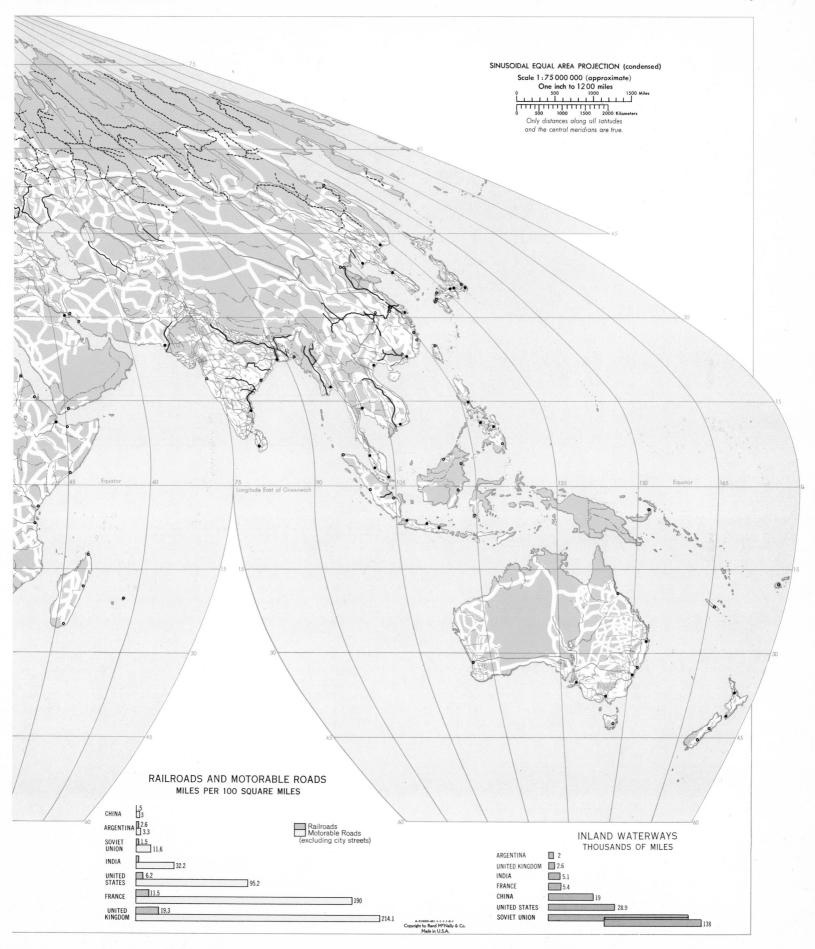

SINUSOIDAL EQUAL AREA PROJECTION (condensed)
Scale 1:75 000 000 (approximate)
One inch to 1200 miles

*Only distances along all latitudes
and the central meridians are true.*

RAILROADS AND MOTORABLE ROADS
MILES PER 100 SQUARE MILES

	Railroads	Motorable Roads
CHINA	.5	.3
ARGENTINA	2.6	3.3
SOVIET UNION	1.5	11.6
INDIA		32.2
UNITED STATES	6.2	95.2
FRANCE	11.5	190
UNITED KINGDOM	19.3	214.1

☐ Railroads
☐ Motorable Roads
(excluding city streets)

INLAND WATERWAYS
THOUSANDS OF MILES

ARGENTINA	2
UNITED KINGDOM	2.6
INDIA	5.1
FRANCE	5.4
CHINA	19
UNITED STATES	28.9
SOVIET UNION	138

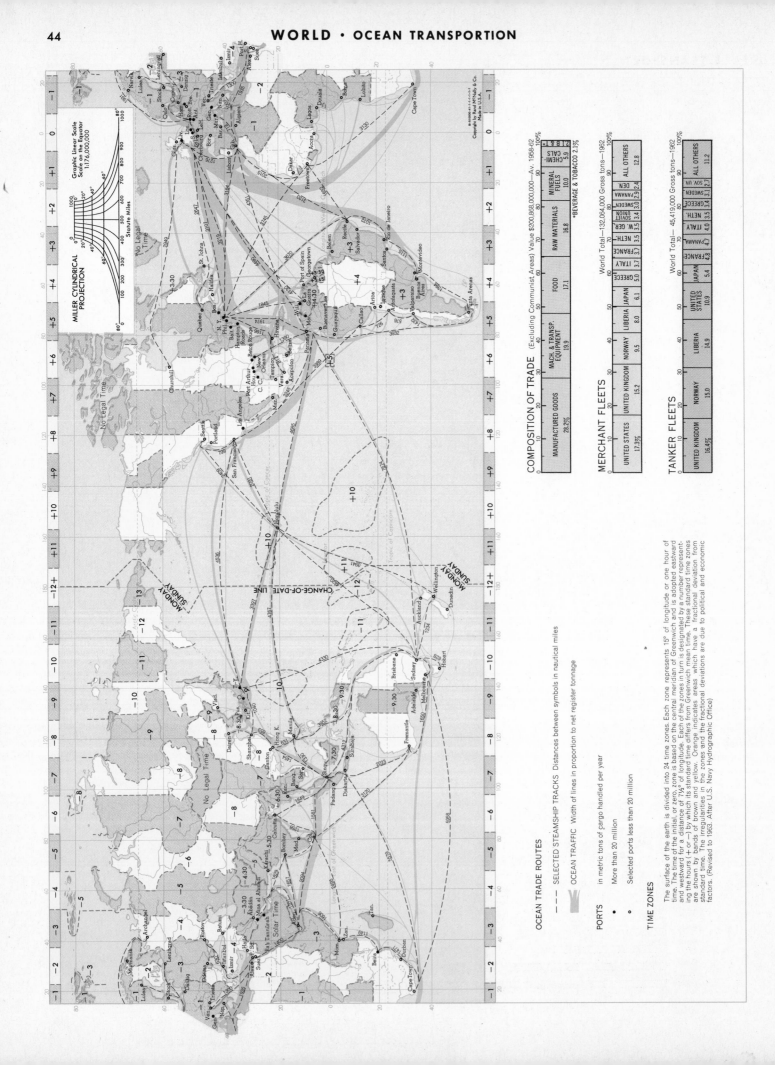

MILLER CYLINDRICAL
PROJECTION

Graphic Linear Scale
Scale on the Equator
1:176,000,000

Statute Miles

COMPOSITION OF TRADE (Excluding Communist Areas) Value $200,868,000,000—Av. 1958-62

MANUFACTURED GOODS	MACH. & TRANSP. EQUIPMENT	FOOD	RAW MATERIALS	MINERAL FUELS	CHEMI-CALS
28.2%	19.9	17.1	16.8	10.0	5.9

*BEVERAGE & TOBACCO 2.1%

MERCHANT FLEETS   World Total—132,064,000 Gross tons—1962

UNITED STATES	UNITED KINGDOM	NORWAY	LIBERIA	JAPAN	ITALY	FRANCE	NETH.	SOVIET UNION	W. GER.	SWEDEN	DEN.	PANAMA	ALL OTHERS
17.3%	15.2	9.5	8.0	6.1	5.0	3.7	3.7	3.5	3.5	3.4	3.0	2.9	2.4	12.8

TANKER FLEETS   World Total—45,419,000 Gross tons—1962

UNITED KINGDOM	NORWAY	LIBERIA	UNITED STATES	JAPAN	PANAMA	FRANCE	ITALY	NETH.	SWEDEN	GREECE	SOV. UN.	ALL OTHERS
16.4%	15.0	14.9	10.9	5.4	4.8	4.7	4.0	3.5	3.4	3.1	2.7	11.2

OCEAN TRADE ROUTES

--- SELECTED STEAMSHIP TRACKS   Distances between symbols in nautical miles

⚓ OCEAN TRAFFIC   Width of lines in proportion to net register tonnage

PORTS   in metric tons of cargo handled per year

● More than 20 million

○ Selected ports less than 20 million

TIME ZONES

The surface of the earth is divided into 24 time zones. Each zone represents 15° of longitude or one hour of time. The time of the initial, or zero, zone is based on the central meridian of Greenwich and is adopted eastward and westward for a distance of 7½° of longitude. Each of the zones in turn is designated by a number representing the hours (+ or −) by which its standard time differs from Greenwich mean time. These standard time zones are shown by bands of brown and yellow. Orange indicates areas which have a fractional deviation from standard time. The irregularities in the zones and the fractional deviations are due to political and economic factors. (Revised to 1963. After U.S. Navy Hydrographic Office)

WORLD • EXPORTS • IMPORTS

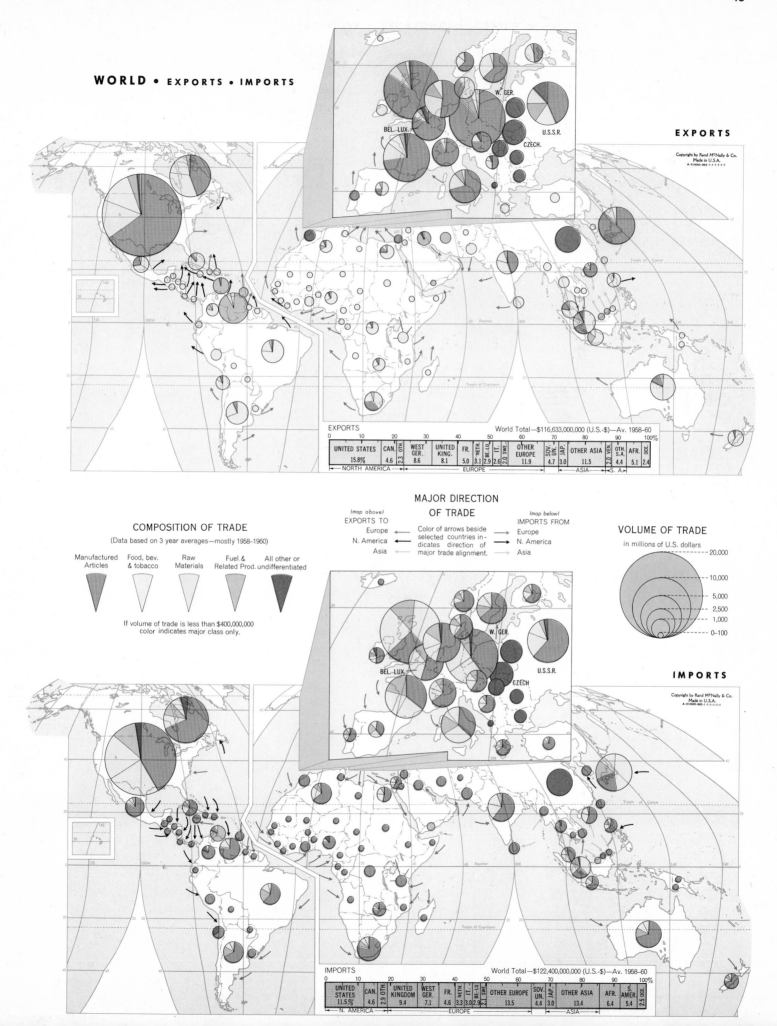

EXPORTS

W. GER.

BEL.-LUX.

U.S.S.R.

CZECH.

EXPORTS											World Total—$116,633,000,000 (U.S.-$)—Av. 1958–60						
0		10		20		30		40	50		60		70	80	90	100%
UNITED STATES 15.8%			CAN. 4.6	OTH. 2.3	WEST GER. 8.6	UNITED KING. 8.1	FR. 5.0	NETH. 3.1	BE.-LU. 2.9	IT. 2.6	SWE. 2.0	OTHER EUROPE 11.9	SOV. UN. 4.7	JAP. 3.0	OTHER ASIA 11.5	VEN. 2.0	OTH. S.A. 4.4	AFR. 5.1	OCE. 2.4
←— NORTH AMERICA —→				←——————————— EUROPE ———————————→									←—————— ASIA ——————→			←— S. A. —→

COMPOSITION OF TRADE

(Data based on 3 year averages—mostly 1958–1960)

Manufactured Articles Food, bev. & tobacco Raw Materials Fuel & Related Prod. All other or undifferentiated

If volume of trade is less than $400,000,000 color indicates major class only.

MAJOR DIRECTION OF TRADE

(map above)
EXPORTS TO
Europe ←—
N. America ←—
Asia ←—

Color of arrows beside selected countries indicates direction of major trade alignment.

(map below)
IMPORTS FROM
Europe —→
N. America —→
Asia —→

VOLUME OF TRADE

in millions of U.S. dollars

— 20,000
— 10,000
— 5,000
— 2,500
— 1,000
— 0–100

IMPORTS

W. GER.

BEL.-LUX.

U.S.S.R.

CZECH.

IMPORTS												World Total—$122,400,000,000 (U.S.-$)—Av. 1958–60					
0		10		20		30		40		50		60	70	80		90	100%
UNITED STATES 11.5%		CAN. 4.6	OTH. 2.9	UNITED KINGDOM 9.4		WEST GER. 7.1	FR. 4.6	NETH. 3.3	BE.-LU. 2.9	IT. 2.9	SWE. 2.1	OTHER EUROPE 13.5	SOV. UN. 4.4	JAP. 3.0	OTHER ASIA 13.4	AFR. 6.4	S. AMER. 5.4	OCE. 2.5
←— N. AMERICA —→				←——————————— EUROPE ———————————→									←—————— ASIA ——————→			

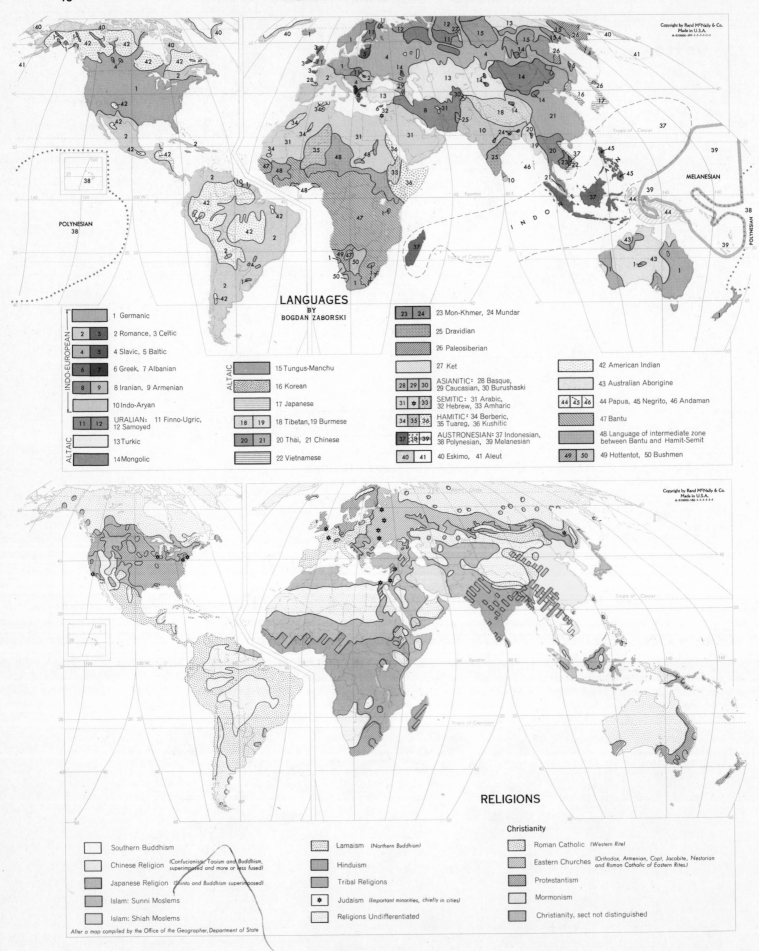

LANGUAGES
BY
BOGDAN ZABORSKI

INDO-EUROPEAN
- 1 Germanic
- 2 Romance, 3 Celtic
- 4 Slavic, 5 Baltic
- 6 Greek, 7 Albanian
- 8 Iranian, 9 Armenian
- 10 Indo-Aryan

URALIAN: 11 Finno-Ugric, 12 Samoyed

ALTAIC
- 13 Turkic
- 14 Mongolic
- 15 Tungus-Manchu
- 16 Korean
- 17 Japanese
- 18 Tibetan, 19 Burmese
- 20 Thai, 21 Chinese
- 22 Vietnamese

- 23 Mon-Khmer, 24 Mundar
- 25 Dravidian
- 26 Paleosiberian
- 27 Ket
- **ASIANITIC:** 28 Basque, 29 Caucasian, 30 Burushaski
- **SEMITIC:** 31 Arabic, 32 Hebrew, 33 Amharic
- **HAMITIC:** 34 Berberic, 35 Tuareg, 36 Kushitic
- **AUSTRONESIAN:** 37 Indonesian, 38 Polynesian, 39 Melanesian
- 40 Eskimo, 41 Aleut
- 42 American Indian
- 43 Australian Aborigine
- 44 Papua, 45 Negrito, 46 Andaman
- 47 Bantu
- 48 Language of intermediate zone between Bantu and Hamit-Semit
- 49 Hottentot, 50 Bushmen

RELIGIONS

- Southern Buddhism
- Chinese Religion *(Confucianism, Taoism and Buddhism, superimposed and more or less fused)*
- Japanese Religion *(Shinto and Buddhism superimposed)*
- Islam: Sunni Moslems
- Islam: Shiah Moslems
- Lamaism *(Northern Buddhism)*
- Hinduism
- Tribal Religions
- ✡ Judaism *(Important minorities, chiefly in cities)*
- Religions Undifferentiated

Christianity
- Roman Catholic *(Western Rite)*
- Eastern Churches *(Orthodox, Armenian, Copt, Jacobite, Nestorian and Roman Catholic of Eastern Rites.)*
- Protestantism
- Mormonism
- Christianity, sect not distinguished

After a map compiled by the Office of the Geographer, Department of State

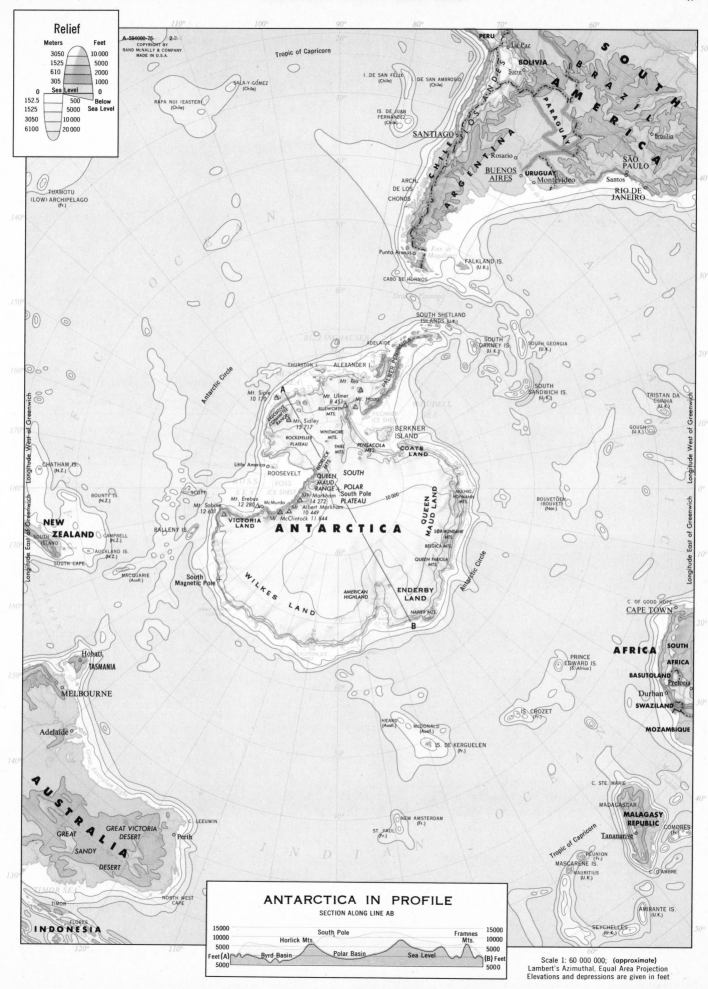

Relief

Meters		Feet
3050		10 000
1525		5000
610		2000
305		1000
0	Sea Level	0
		Below
152.5		500 Sea Level
1525		5000
3050		10 000
6100		20 000

A-594000-76-
COPYRIGHT BY
RAND McNALLY & COMPANY
MADE IN U.S.A.

ANTARCTICA IN PROFILE

SECTION ALONG LINE AB

15000	South Pole		15000
10000	Horlick Mts.	Framnes Mts.	10000
5000			5000
Feet (A)	Byrd Basin	Polar Basin	Sea Level	(B) Feet
5000			5000

Scale 1: 60 000 000; (approximate)
Lambert's Azimuthal, Equal Area Projection
Elevations and depressions are given in feet

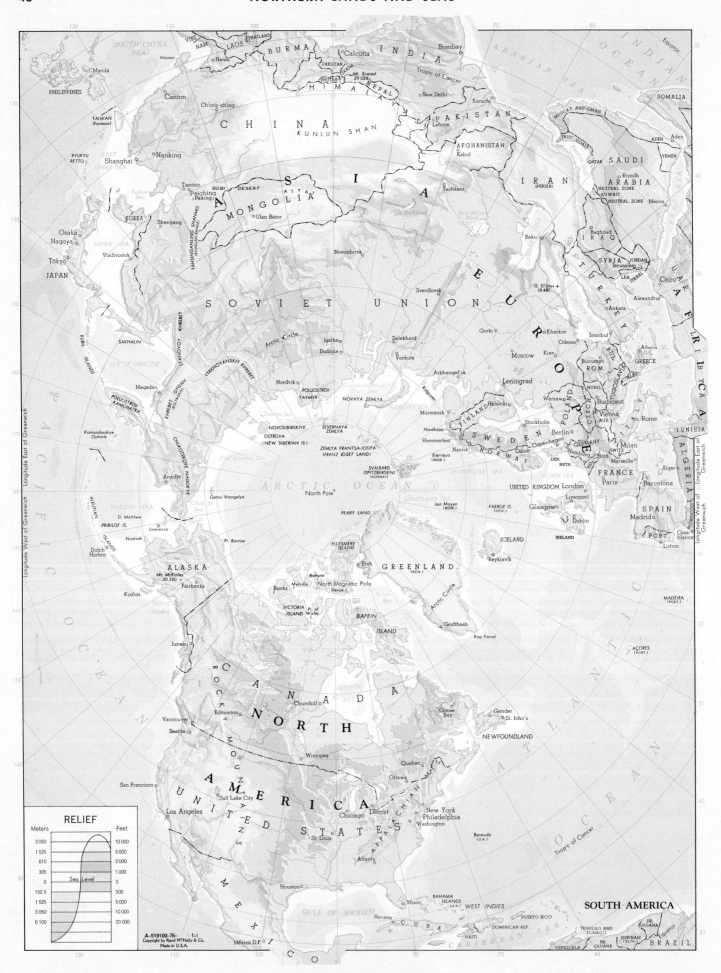

RELIEF

Meters		Feet
3 050		10 000
1 525		5 000
610		2 000
305		1 000
0	Sea Level	0
152.5		500
1 525		5 000
3 050		10 000
6 100		20 000

A-519100-76-   1-1
Copyright by Rand McNally & Co.
Made in U.S.A.

Elevations and depressions are given in feet
LAMBERT AZIMUTHAL EQUAL-AREA PROJECTION
Scale 1:60,000,000 (approximate)

Relief

Meters	Feet
3050	10 000
1525	5000
610	2000
305	1000
0 Sea Level	0 Sea Level
152.5	500 Below Sea Level
1525	5000
3050	10 000
6100	20 000

A-520000-76- 1- 1-1-1
COPYRIGHT BY
RAND McNALLY & COMPANY
MADE IN U.S.A.

0   200   400   600   800   1000 Miles
0   400   800   1200 1600 Kilometers

Scale 1:40 000 000; one inch to 630 miles. Lambert's Azimuthal Equal Area Projection
Elevations and depressions are given in feet

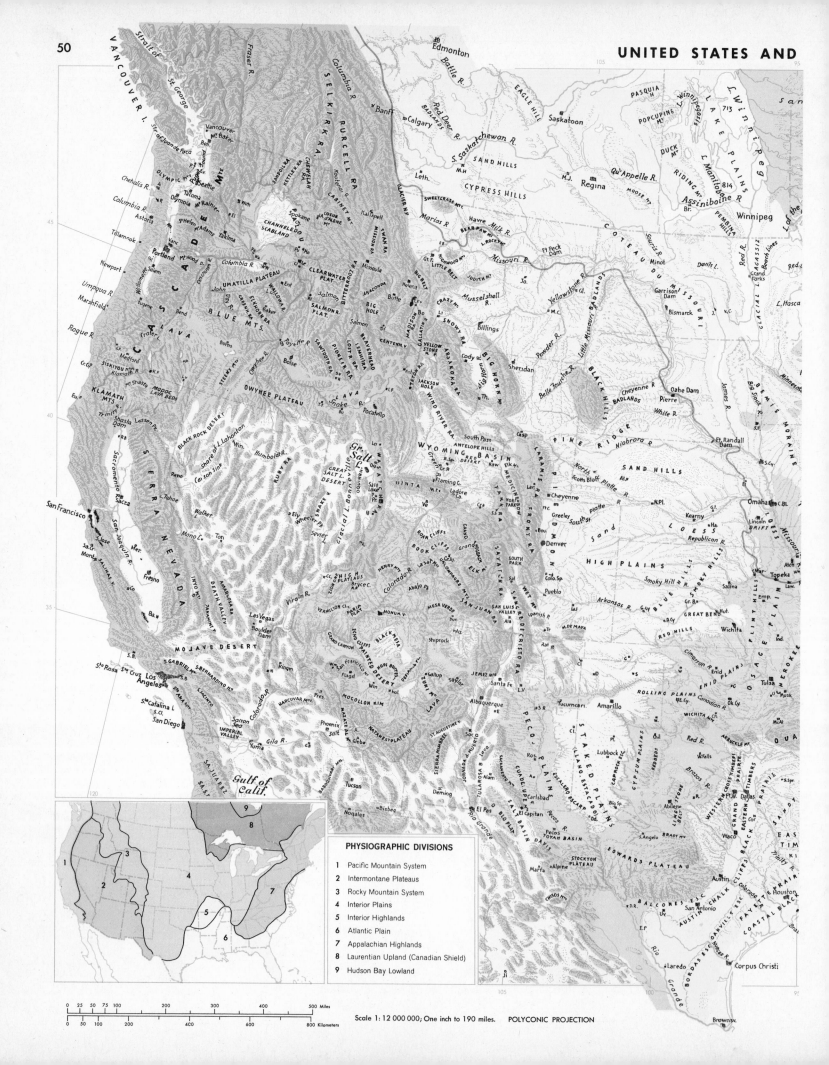

PHYSIOGRAPHIC DIVISIONS

1   Pacific Mountain System
2   Intermontane Plateaus
3   Rocky Mountain System
4   Interior Plains
5   Interior Highlands
6   Atlantic Plain
7   Appalachian Highlands
8   Laurentian Upland (Canadian Shield)
9   Hudson Bay Lowland

0 25 50 75 100   200   300   400   500 Miles

0 50 100   200   400   600   800 Kilometers

Scale 1 : 12 000 000; One inch to 190 miles.   POLYCONIC PROJECTION

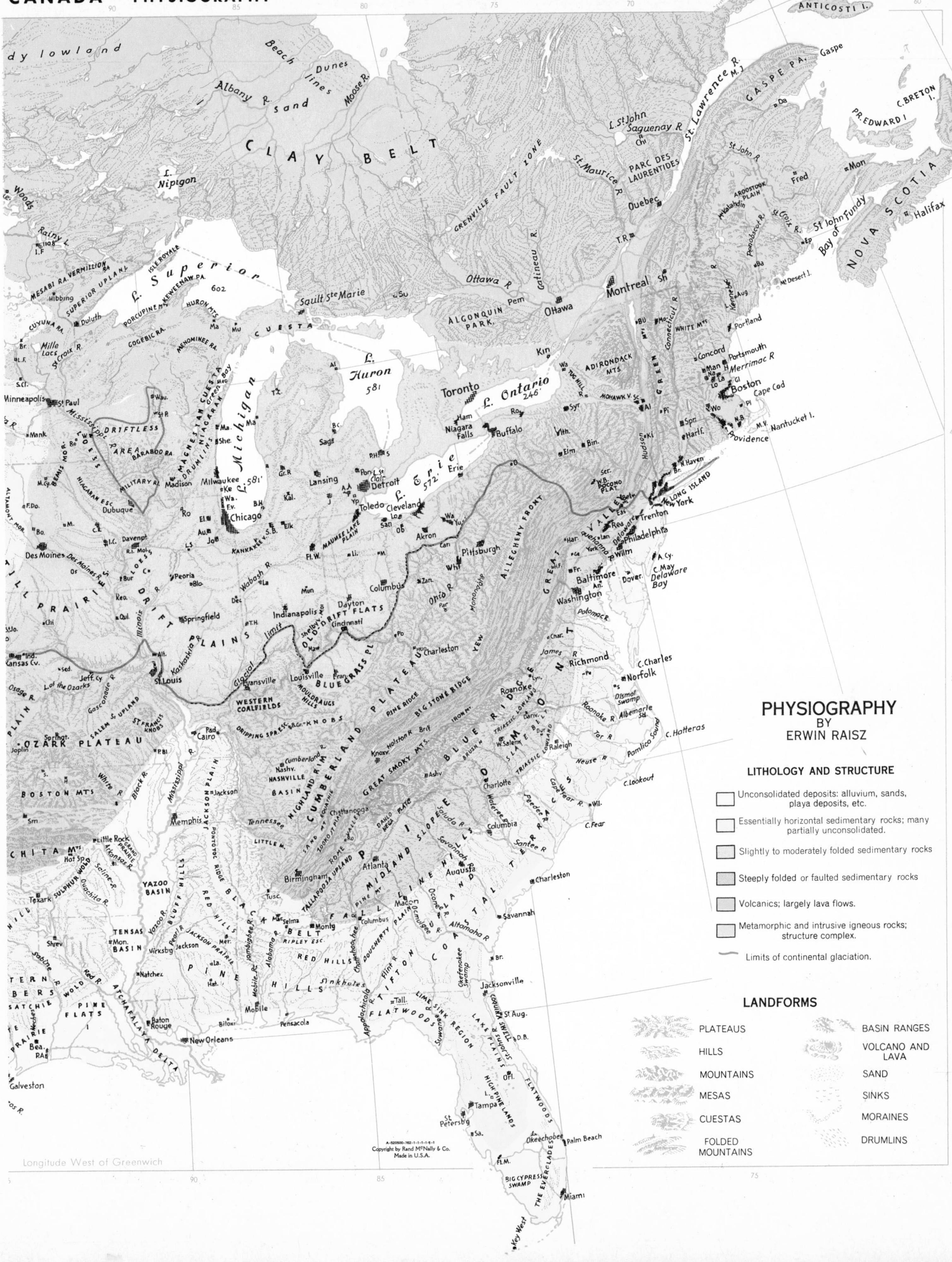

CLAY BELT

dy lowland

Beach Dunes sand lines

Albany R.

Moose R.

L. Nipigon

GRENVILLE FAULT ZONE

St. Lawrence R.

GASPE PA. Gaspe

PARC DES LAURENTIDES

L. St. John Saguenay R.

St. Maurice R.

Quebec

Ottawa R. Gatineau R.

ALGONQUIN PARK

Ottawa

Montreal

NOVA SCOTIA

PR. EDWARD I.

C. BRETON I.

ANTICOSTI I.

Bay of Fundy

Halifax

St. John R.

AROOSTOOK PLAIN

WHITE MTS.

GREEN MTS.

ADIRONDACK MTS.

Portland

Concord Portsmouth

Boston Cape Cod

Providence Nantucket I.

L. Superior

Woods

Rainy L.

MESABI RA. VERMILION

ISLE ROYALE

SUPERIOR UPLAND

KEWEENAW PA. 602

Hibbing Duluth

PORCUPINE RA. HURON MTS.

CUYUNA RA.

GOGEBIC RA.

MENOMINEE RA.

Mille Lacs

CUESTA

Sault Ste Marie

Toronto

L. Ontario 246

Niagara Falls Buffalo

L. Huron 581

Minneapolis St. Paul

DRIFTLESS AREA

MAGNESIAN CUESTA

NIAGARA CUESTA

DRUMLIN

BARABOO RA.

MILITARY RI.

Madison Milwaukee

L. Michigan 581'

Chicago

Detroit L. St. Clair

Toledo Cleveland

L. Erie 572'

Erie

Dubuque

NIAGARA ESC.

LOESS

Lansing

Syr.

MOHAWK V.

Hudson R.

New York

LONG ISLAND

Trenton

Philadelphia

Akron

Pittsburgh

ALLEGHENY FRONT

GREAT VALLEY

Baltimore

Washington

Dover

C. May Delaware Bay

Davenport

Des Moines

Des Moines R.

Peoria

Wabash R.

Columbus

Ohio R.

Monongahela

Springfield

Indianapolis

Dayton

Cincinnati

OLD DRIFT FLATS

Glacial limit

TILL PRAIRIES

DRIFT PLAINS

KANKAKEE

MAUMEE LAKE PLAIN

Ft. W.

St. Louis

Evansville

Louisville

BLUE GRASS PL.

WESTERN COALFIELDS

MOULDRAUGS HILLS

DRIPPING SPRING ESC.

KNOBS

CUMBERLAND PLATEAU

PINE RIDGE

BIG STONE RIDGE

Charleston

Richmond

Norfolk

C. Charles

C. Hatteras

Roanoke R.

Albemarle Sd.

Pamlico Sound

BLUE RIDGE

PIEDMONT

Knoxville

GREAT SMOKY MTS.

Chattanooga

HIGHLAND RIM

NASHVILLE BASIN

Nashville

Memphis

JACKSON PLAIN

BOSTON MTS

OZARK PLATEAU

SALEM UPLAND

ST. FRANCIS KNOBS

Joplin

Springf.

Little Rock

Hot Spgs

OUACHITA MTS

Ouachita R.

YAZOO BASIN

PINE HILLS

TENSAS BASIN

Jackson

BLACK BELT

RED HILLS

FALL BELT

Birmingham

TALLAPOOSA UPLAND

Montg.

Selma

RIPLEY ESC.

PINE HILLS

Mobile R.

Baton Rouge

New Orleans

ATCHAFALAYA DELTA

Galveston

PRAIRIE

PINE FLATS

Natchez

Biloxi

Pensacola

Atlanta

Augusta

Macon

Columbia

Charleston

Savannah

Altamaha R.

COASTAL PLAIN

FALL LINE

MIDLAND SLOPE

DOUGHERTY PLAIN

TIFTON FLATWOODS

OKEFENOKEE SWAMP

Jacksonville

St. Aug.

LIME SINK REGION

HIGH PINE LANDS

Tampa

St. Petersburg

FLATWOODS

BIG CYPRESS SWAMP

THE EVERGLADES

Okeechobee Palm Beach

Miami

Key West

PHYSIOGRAPHY
BY ERWIN RAISZ

LITHOLOGY AND STRUCTURE

- Unconsolidated deposits: alluvium, sands, playa deposits, etc.
- Essentially horizontal sedimentary rocks; many partially unconsolidated.
- Slightly to moderately folded sedimentary rocks
- Steeply folded or faulted sedimentary rocks
- Volcanics; largely lava flows.
- Metamorphic and intrusive igneous rocks; structure complex.
- Limits of continental glaciation.

LANDFORMS

PLATEAUS		BASIN RANGES	
HILLS		VOLCANO AND LAVA	
MOUNTAINS		SAND	
MESAS		SINKS	
CUESTAS		MORAINES	
FOLDED MOUNTAINS		DRUMLINS	

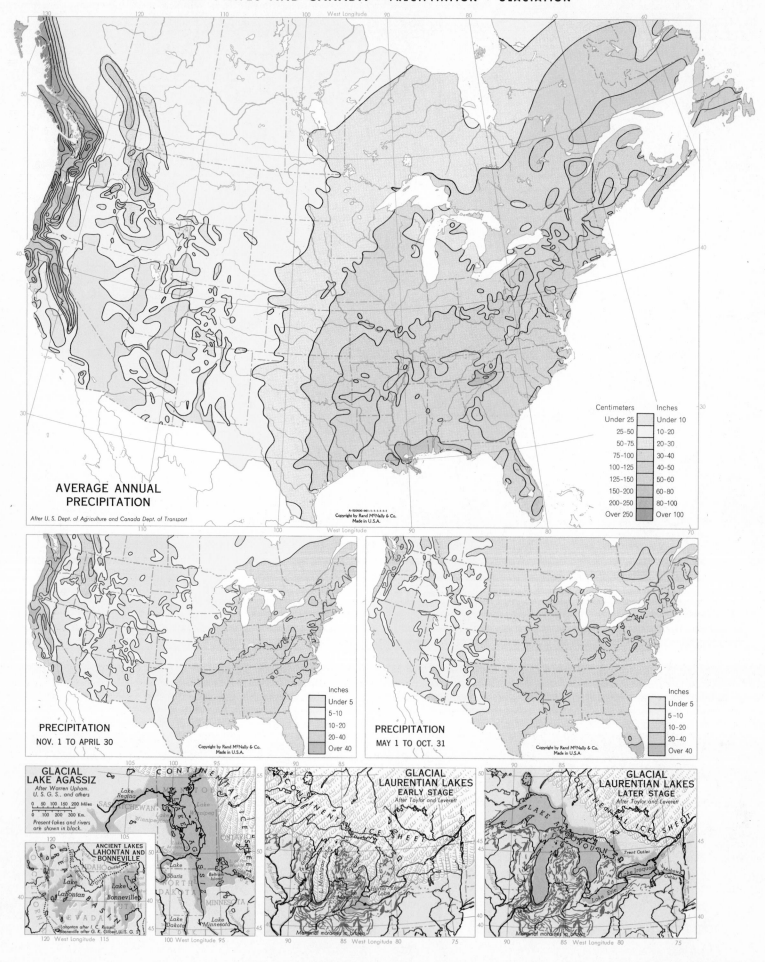

AVERAGE ANNUAL
PRECIPITATION

After U. S. Dept. of Agriculture and Canada Dept. of Transport

A-520500-961-1-1-1-1-1-1
Copyright by Rand McNally & Co.
Made in U.S.A.

Centimeters	Inches
Under 25	Under 10
25–50	10–20
50–75	20–30
75–100	30–40
100–125	40–50
125–150	50–60
150–200	60–80
200–250	80–100
Over 250	Over 100

PRECIPITATION

NOV. 1 TO APRIL 30

Copyright by Rand McNally & Co.
Made in U.S.A.

Inches
Under 5
5–10
10–20
20–40
Over 40

PRECIPITATION

MAY 1 TO OCT. 31

Copyright by Rand McNally & Co.
Made in U.S.A.

Inches
Under 5
5–10
10–20
20–40
Over 40

GLACIAL
LAKE AGASSIZ
After Warren Upham,
U. S. G. S. and others
0 50 100 150 200 Miles
0 100 200 300 Km.
Present lakes and rivers
are shown in black.

ANCIENT LAKES
LAHONTAN AND
BONNEVILLE

Lahontan after I. C. Russell
Bonneville after G. K. Gilbert, U. S. G. S.

GLACIAL
LAURENTIAN LAKES
EARLY STAGE
After Taylor and Leverett

Marginal moraines in black

GLACIAL
LAURENTIAN LAKES
LATER STAGE
After Taylor and Leverett

Marginal moraines in black

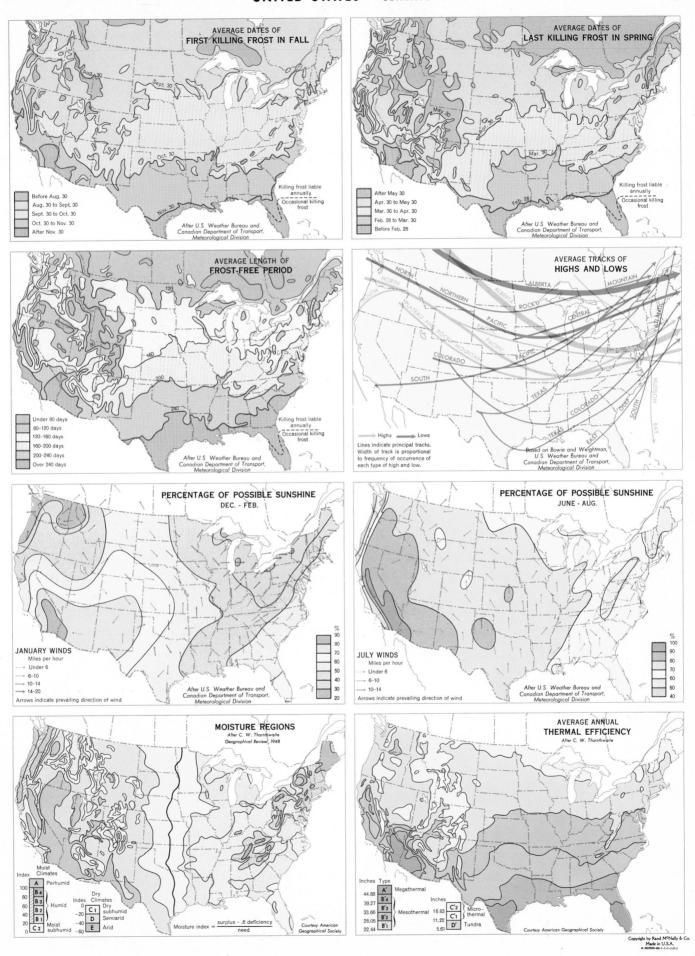

AVERAGE DATES OF FIRST KILLING FROST IN FALL

Before Aug. 30
Aug. 30 to Sept. 30
Sept. 30 to Oct. 30
Oct. 30 to Nov. 30
After Nov. 30

Killing frost liable annually
Occasional killing frost

After U.S. Weather Bureau and Canadian Department of Transport, Meteorological Division

AVERAGE DATES OF LAST KILLING FROST IN SPRING

After May 30
Apr. 30 to May 30
Mar. 30 to Apr. 30
Feb. 28 to Mar. 30
Before Feb. 28

Killing frost liable annually
Occasional killing frost

After U.S. Weather Bureau and Canadian Department of Transport, Meteorological Division

AVERAGE LENGTH OF FROST-FREE PERIOD

Under 80 days
80–120 days
120–160 days
160–200 days
200–240 days
Over 240 days

Killing frost liable annually
Occasional killing frost

After U.S. Weather Bureau and Canadian Department of Transport, Meteorological Division

AVERAGE TRACKS OF HIGHS AND LOWS

Highs   Lows

Lines indicate principal tracks. Width of track is proportional to frequency of occurrence of each type of high and low.

Based on Bowie and Weightman, U.S. Weather Bureau and Canadian Department of Transport, Meteorological Division

PERCENTAGE OF POSSIBLE SUNSHINE DEC. - FEB.

JANUARY WINDS
Miles per hour
Under 6
6–10
10–14
14–20
Arrows indicate prevailing direction of wind

%
90
80
70
60
50
40
30
20

After U.S. Weather Bureau and Canadian Department of Transport, Meteorological Division

PERCENTAGE OF POSSIBLE SUNSHINE JUNE - AUG.

JULY WINDS
Miles per hour
Under 6
6–10
10–14
Arrows indicate prevailing direction of wind

%
100
90
80
70
60
50
40

After U.S. Weather Bureau and Canadian Department of Transport, Meteorological Division

MOISTURE REGIONS
After C. W. Thornthwaite
Geographical Review, 1948

Index   Moist Climates
100   A   Perhumid
80   B4
60   B3   Humid
40   B2
20   B1   Moist
0   C2   subhumid

Index   Dry Climates
0   C1   Dry subhumid
-20   D   Semiarid
-40   E   Arid
-60

Moisture index = surplus − .6 deficiency / need

Courtesy American Geographical Society

AVERAGE ANNUAL THERMAL EFFICIENCY
After C. W. Thornthwaite

Inches   Type
44.88   A'   Megathermal
39.27   B'4
33.66   B'3   Mesothermal
28.05   B'2
22.44   B'1

Inches
16.83   C'2   Microthermal
11.22   C'1
5.61   D'   Tundra

Courtesy American Geographical Society

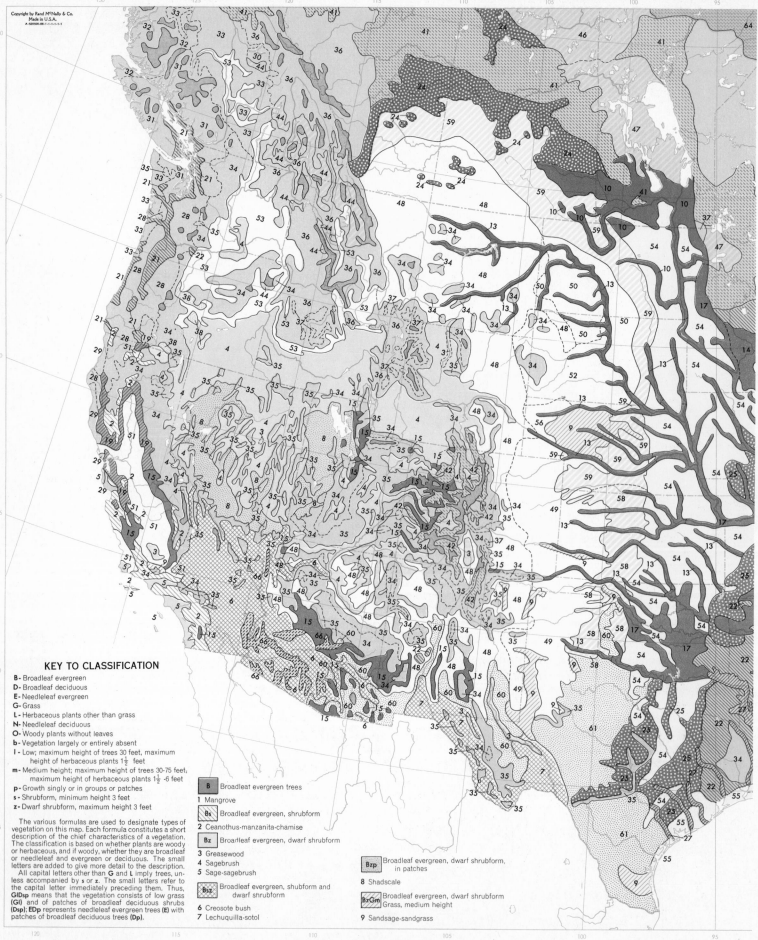

Copyright by Rand McNally & Co.
Made in U.S.A.
A-520500-86-1-1-1-1-1-1

KEY TO CLASSIFICATION

B - Broadleaf evergreen
D - Broadleaf deciduous
E - Needleleaf evergreen
G - Grass
L - Herbaceous plants other than grass
N - Needleleaf deciduous
O - Woody plants without leaves
b - Vegetation largely or entirely absent
l - Low; maximum height of trees 30 feet, maximum height of herbaceous plants 1½ feet
m - Medium height; maximum height of trees 30-75 feet, maximum height of herbaceous plants 1½ -6 feet
p - Growth singly or in groups or patches
s - Shrubform, minimum height 3 feet
z - Dwarf shrubform, maximum height 3 feet

The various formulas are used to designate types of vegetation on this map. Each formula constitutes a short description of the chief characteristics of a vegetation. The classification is based on whether plants are woody or herbaceous, and if woody, whether they are broadleaf or needleleaf and evergreen or deciduous. The small letters are added to give more detail to the description.

All capital letters other than **G** and **L** imply trees, unless accompanied by **s** or **z**. The small letters refer to the capital letter immediately preceding them. Thus, **GlDsp** means that the vegetation consists of low grass (**Gl**) and of patches of broadleaf deciduous shrubs (**Dsp**); **EDp** represents needleleaf evergreen trees (**E**) with patches of broadleaf deciduous trees (**Dp**).

B Broadleaf evergreen trees

1 Mangrove

Bs Broadleaf evergreen, shrubform

2 Ceanothus-manzanita-chamise

Bz Broadleaf evergreen, dwarf shrubform

3 Greasewood
4 Sagebrush
5 Sage-sagebrush

Bsz Broadleaf evergreen, shubform and dwarf shrubform

6 Creosote bush
7 Lechuquilla-sotol

Bzp Broadleaf evergreen, dwarf shrubform, in patches

8 Shadscale

BzGm Broadleaf evergreen, dwarf shrubform Grass, medium height

9 Sandsage-sandgrass

0 25 50 75 100   200   300   400   500 Miles

0 50 100   200   400   600   800 Kilometers

Scale 1:14 000 000; One inch to 220 miles.

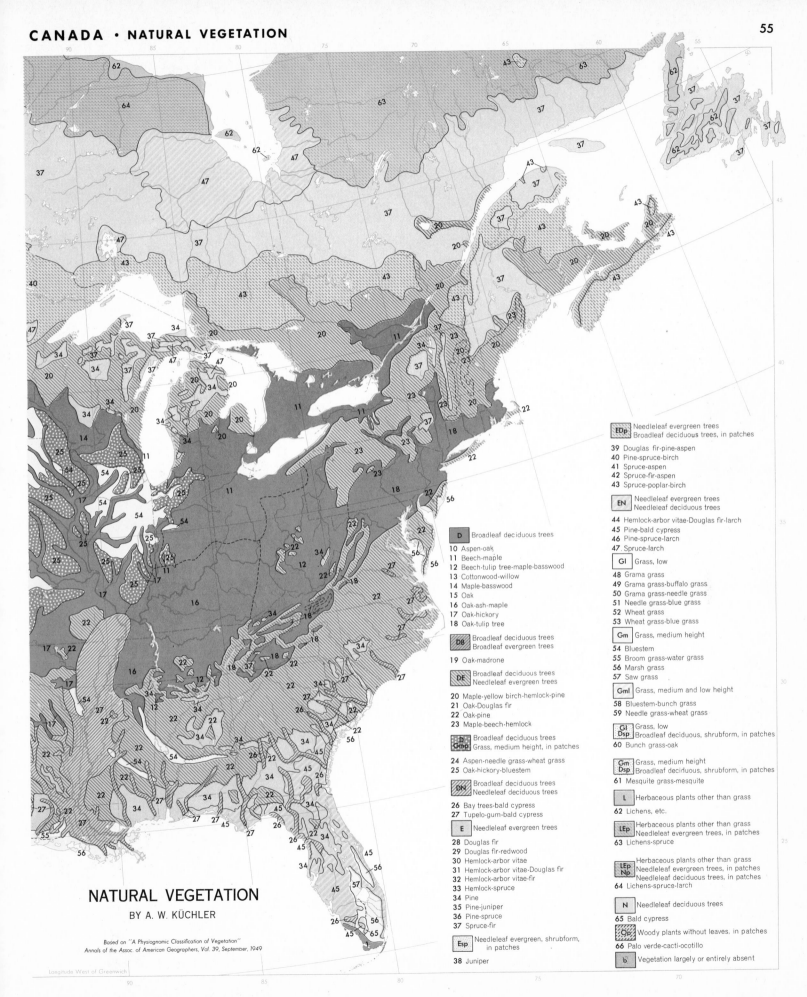

NATURAL VEGETATION

BY A. W. KÜCHLER

Based on "A Physiognomic Classification of Vegetation"
Annals of the Assoc. of American Geographers, Vol. 39, September, 1949

Longitude West of Greenwich

D Broadleaf deciduous trees

10 Aspen-oak
11 Beech-maple
12 Beech-tulip tree-maple-basswood
13 Cottonwood-willow
14 Maple-basswood
15 Oak
16 Oak-ash-maple
17 Oak-hickory
18 Oak-tulip tree

DB Broadleaf deciduous trees
Broadleaf evergreen trees

19 Oak-madrone

DE Broadleaf deciduous trees
Needleleaf evergreen trees

20 Maple-yellow birch-hemlock-pine
21 Oak-Douglas fir
22 Oak-pine
23 Maple-beech-hemlock

D Gmp Broadleaf deciduous trees
Grass, medium height, in patches

24 Aspen-needle grass-wheat grass
25 Oak-hickory-bluestem

DN Broadleaf deciduous trees
Needleleaf deciduous trees

26 Bay trees-bald cypress
27 Tupelo-gum-bald cypress

E Needleleaf evergreen trees

28 Douglas fir
29 Douglas fir-redwood
30 Hemlock-arbor vitae
31 Hemlock-arbor vitae-Douglas fir
32 Hemlock-arbor vitae-fir
33 Hemlock-spruce
34 Pine
35 Pine-juniper
36 Pine-spruce
37 Spruce-fir

Esp Needleleaf evergreen, shrubform,
in patches

38 Juniper

EDp Needleleaf evergreen trees
Broadleaf deciduous trees, in patches

39 Douglas fir-pine-aspen
40 Pine-spruce-birch
41 Spruce-aspen
42 Spruce-fir-aspen
43 Spruce-poplar-birch

EN Needleleaf evergreen trees
Needleleaf deciduous trees

44 Hemlock-arbor vitae-Douglas fir-larch
45 Pine-bald cypress
46 Pine-spruce-larch
47 Spruce-larch

Gl Grass, low

48 Grama grass
49 Grama grass-buffalo grass
50 Grama grass-needle grass
51 Needle grass-blue grass
52 Wheat grass
53 Wheat grass-blue grass

Gm Grass, medium height

54 Bluestem
55 Broom grass-water grass
56 Marsh grass
57 Saw grass

Gml Grass, medium and low height

58 Bluestem-bunch grass
59 Needle grass-wheat grass

Gl Dsp Grass, low
Broadleaf deciduous, shrubform, in patches

60 Bunch grass-oak

Gm Dsp Grass, medium height
Broadleaf deciduous, shrubform, in patches

61 Mesquite grass-mesquite

L Herbaceous plants other than grass

62 Lichens, etc.

LEp Herbaceous plants other than grass
Needleleaf evergreen trees, in patches

63 Lichens-spruce

LEp Np Herbaceous plants other than grass
Needleleaf evergreen trees, in patches
Needleleaf deciduous trees, in patches

64 Lichens-spruce-larch

N Needleleaf deciduous trees

65 Bald cypress

Op Woody plants without leaves, in patches

66 Palo verde-cacti-ocotillo

b Vegetation largely or entirely absent

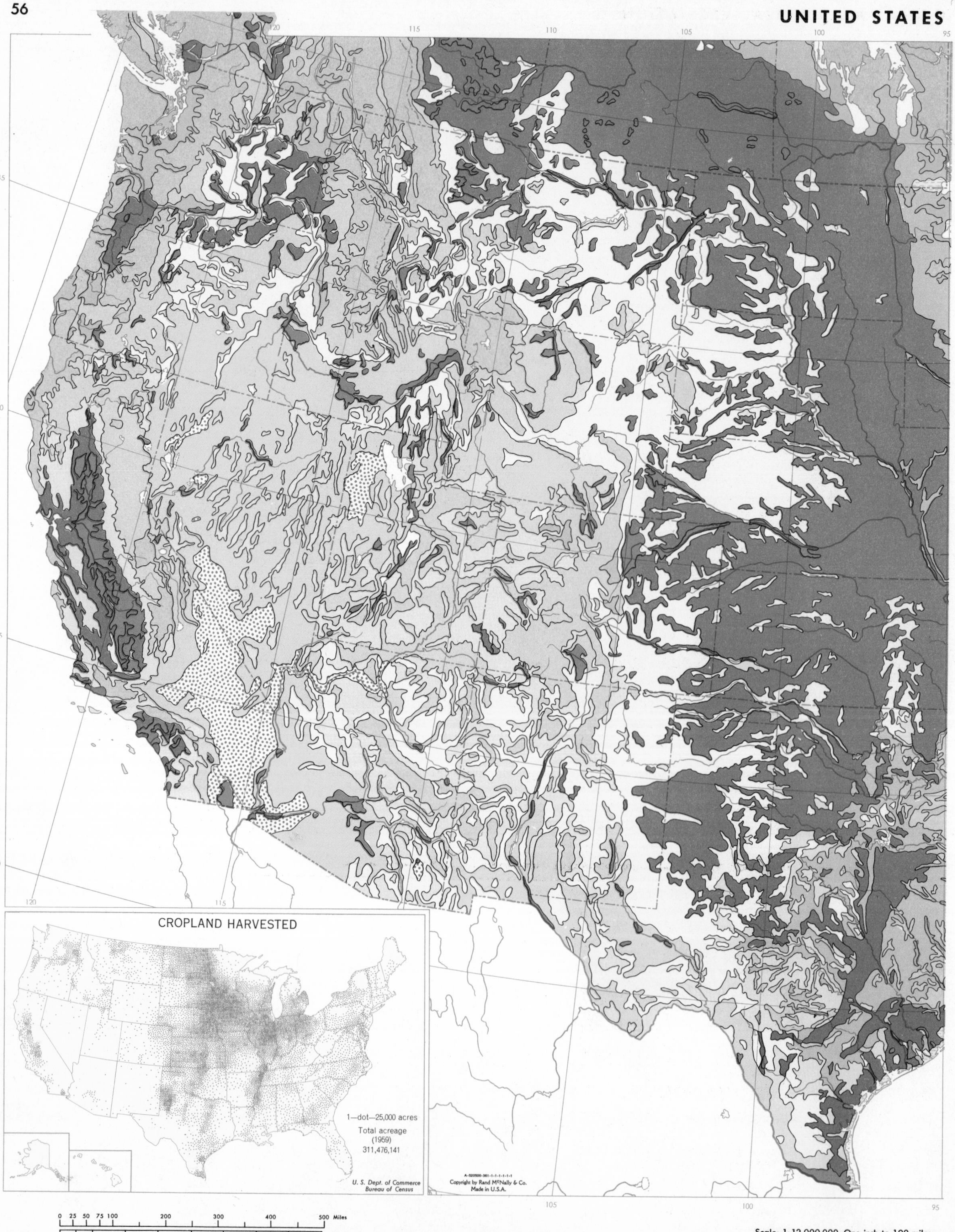

CROPLAND HARVESTED

1—dot—25,000 acres

Total acreage
(1959)
311,476,141

U. S. Dept. of Commerce
Bureau of Census

A-520500-381-1-1-1-1-1-1
Copyright by Rand McNally & Co.
Made in U.S.A.

0   25 50 75 100   200   300   400   500 Miles

0   50   100   200   400   600   800 Kilometers

Scale: 1:12 000 000; One inch to 190 miles.

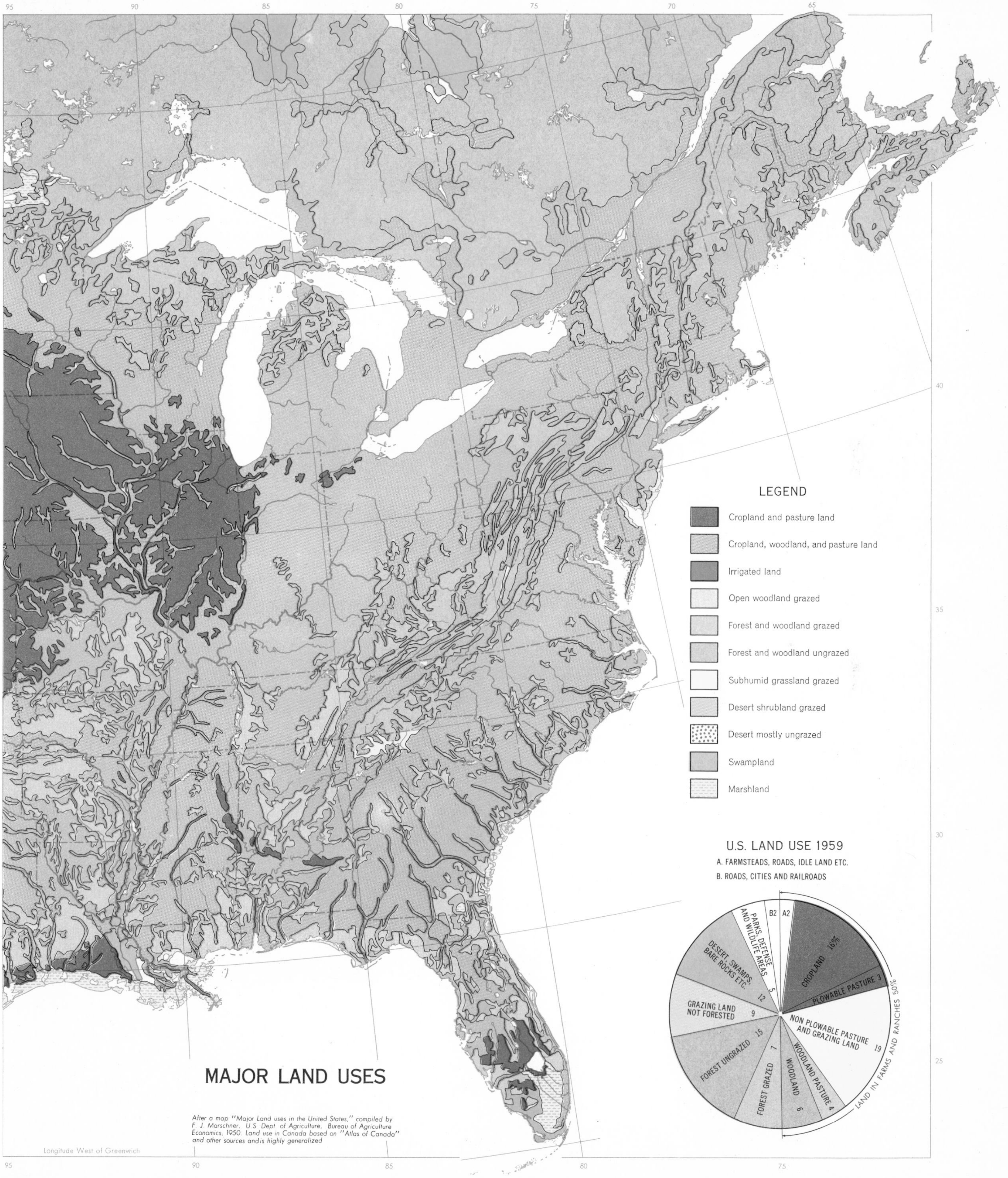
MAJOR LAND USES
LEGEND
Cropland and pasture land
Cropland, woodland, and pasture land
Irrigated land
Open woodland grazed
Forest and woodland grazed
Forest and woodland ungrazed
Subhumid grassland grazed
Desert shrubland grazed
Desert mostly ungrazed
Swampland
Marshland
U.S. LAND USE 1959
A. FARMSTEADS, ROADS, IDLE LAND ETC.
B. ROADS, CITIES AND RAILROADS
CROPLAND 16%
PLOWABLE PASTURE 3
NON PLOWABLE PASTURE AND GRAZING LAND 19
WOODLAND PASTURE 4
WOODLAND 6
FOREST GRAZED 7
FOREST UNGRAZED 15
GRAZING LAND NOT FORESTED 9
DESERT SWAMPS, BARE ROCKS ETC. 12
PARKS, DEFENSE AND WILDLIFE AREAS 5
B2
A2
LAND IN FARMS AND RANCHES 50%
After a map "Major Land uses in the United States," compiled by F. J. Marschner, U.S. Dept. of Agriculture, Bureau of Agriculture Economics, 1950. Land use in Canada based on "Atlas of Canada" and other sources and is highly generalized
Longitude West of Greenwich
95
90
85
80
75
70
65
40
35
30
25

LAMBERT CONFORMAL CONIC PROJECTION

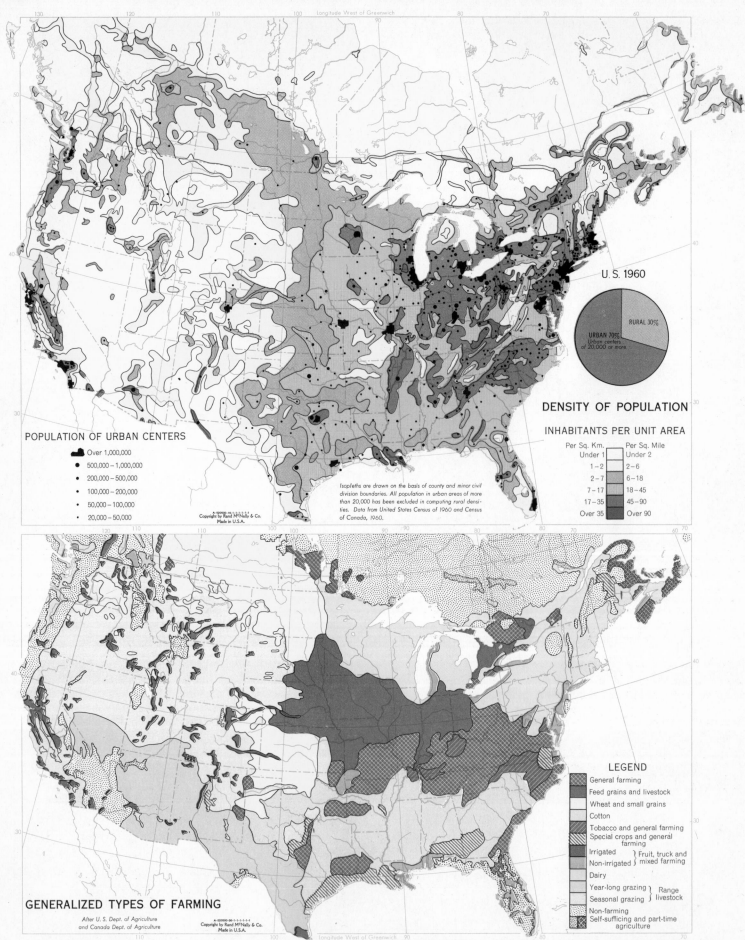

POPULATION OF URBAN CENTERS

Over 1,000,000
500,000 – 1,000,000
200,000 – 500,000
100,000 – 200,000
50,000 – 100,000
20,000 – 50,000

U. S. 1960

RURAL 30%

URBAN 70%
Urban centers
of 20,000 or more

DENSITY OF POPULATION

INHABITANTS PER UNIT AREA

Per Sq. Km.	Per Sq. Mile
Under 1	Under 2
1 – 2	2 – 6
2 – 7	6 – 18
7 – 17	18 – 45
17 – 35	45 – 90
Over 35	Over 90

Isopleths are drawn on the basis of county and minor civil
division boundaries. All population in urban areas of more
than 20,000 has been excluded in computing rural densities. Data from United States Census of 1960 and Census
of Canada, 1960.

Copyright by Rand McNally & Co.
Made in U.S.A.

GENERALIZED TYPES OF FARMING

After U. S. Dept. of Agriculture
and Canada Dept. of Agriculture

Copyright by Rand McNally & Co.
Made in U.S.A.

LEGEND

General farming
Feed grains and livestock
Wheat and small grains
Cotton
Tobacco and general farming
Special crops and general
farming
Irrigated } Fruit, truck and
Non-irrigated } mixed farming
Dairy
Year-long grazing } Range
Seasonal grazing } livestock
Non-farming
Self-sufficing and part-time
agriculture

Scale 1: 28 000 000; One inch to 440 miles.   LAMBERT CONFORMAL CONIC PROJECTION

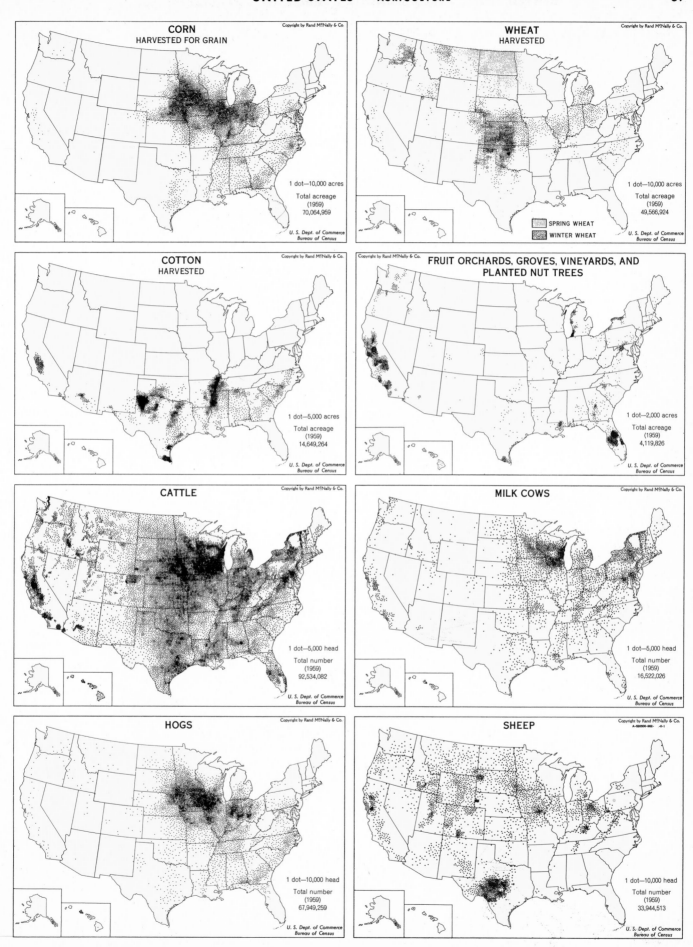

CORN
HARVESTED FOR GRAIN

Copyright by Rand McNally & Co.

1 dot—10,000 acres

Total acreage
(1959)
70,064,959

U. S. Dept. of Commerce
Bureau of Census

WHEAT
HARVESTED

Copyright by Rand McNally & Co.

1 dot—10,000 acres

Total acreage
(1959)
49,566,924

SPRING WHEAT
WINTER WHEAT

U. S. Dept. of Commerce
Bureau of Census

COTTON
HARVESTED

Copyright by Rand McNally & Co.

1 dot—5,000 acres

Total acreage
(1959)
14,649,264

U. S. Dept. of Commerce
Bureau of Census

Copyright by Rand McNally & Co.

**FRUIT ORCHARDS, GROVES, VINEYARDS, AND
PLANTED NUT TREES**

1 dot—2,000 acres

Total acreage
(1959)
4,119,826

U. S. Dept. of Commerce
Bureau of Census

CATTLE

Copyright by Rand McNally & Co.

1 dot—5,000 head

Total number
(1959)
92,534,082

U. S. Dept. of Commerce
Bureau of Census

MILK COWS

Copyright by Rand McNally & Co.

1 dot—5,000 head

Total number
(1959)
16,522,026

U. S. Dept. of Commerce
Bureau of Census

HOGS

Copyright by Rand McNally & Co.

1 dot—10,000 head

Total number
(1959)
67,949,259

U. S. Dept. of Commerce
Bureau of Census

SHEEP

Copyright by Rand McNally & Co.
A-520500-962-   -0-1

1 dot—10,000 head

Total number
(1959)
33,944,513

U. S. Dept. of Commerce
Bureau of Census

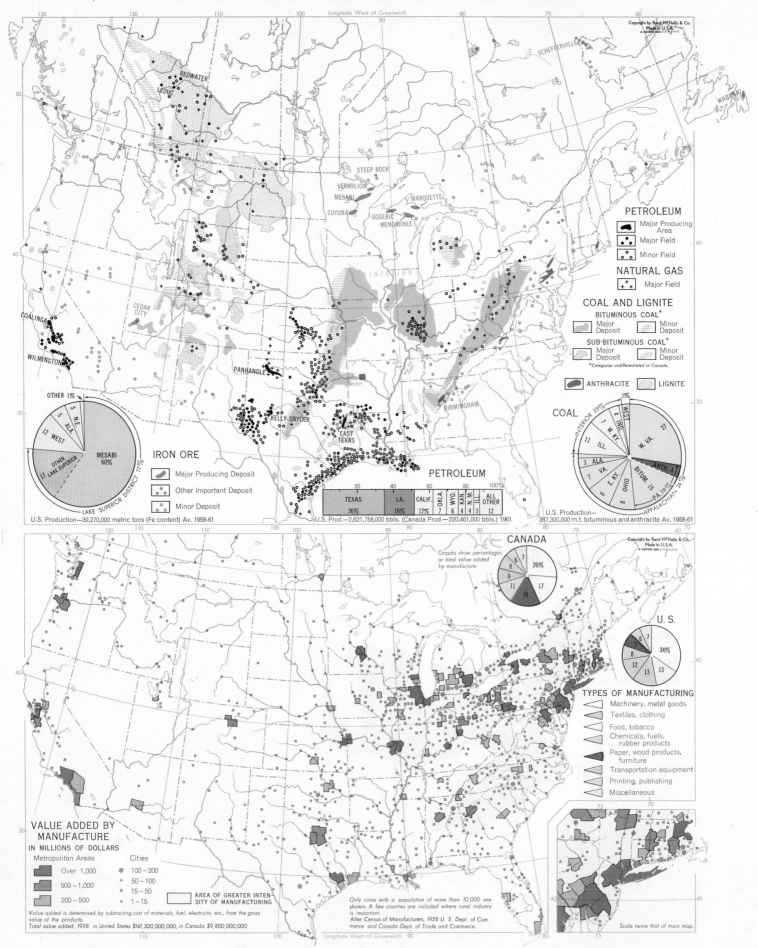

PETROLEUM

- Major Producing Area
- Major Field
- Minor Field

NATURAL GAS

- Major Field

COAL AND LIGNITE

BITUMINOUS COAL*
- Major Deposit
- Minor Deposit

SUB-BITUMINOUS COAL*
- Major Deposit
- Minor Deposit

*Categories undifferentiated in Canada.

- ANTHRACITE
- LIGNITE

COAL

U.S. Production—387,300,000 m.t. bituminous and anthracite Av. 1958-61

IRON ORE

- Major Producing Deposit
- Other Important Deposit
- Minor Deposit

U.S. Production—39,270,000 metric tons (Fe content) Av. 1958-61

PETROLEUM

TEXAS	LA.	CALIF.	OKLA.	WYO.	KAN.	N.M.	ALL OTHER
36%	16%	12%	7	6	4	4 3	12

U.S. Prod.—2,621,758,000 bbls. (Canada Prod.—220,461,000 bbls.) 1961

CANADA

Graphs show percentages or total value added by manufacture.

26% 17 16 11 9 8 6 7

U.S.

34% 13 13 12 8 7 6 7

TYPES OF MANUFACTURING

- Machinery, metal goods
- Textiles, clothing
- Food, tobacco
- Chemicals, fuels, rubber products
- Paper, wood products, furniture
- Transportation equipment
- Printing, publishing
- Miscellaneous

VALUE ADDED BY MANUFACTURE

IN MILLIONS OF DOLLARS

Metropolitan Areas
- Over 1,000
- 500 – 1,000
- 200 – 500

Cities
- 100 – 200
- 50 – 100
- 15 – 50
- 1 – 15

AREA OF GREATER INTENSITY OF MANUFACTURING

Value added is determined by subtracting cost of materials, fuel, electricity, etc., from the gross value of the products.
Total value added, 1958: in United States $141,300,000,000, in Canada $9,800,000,000

Only cities with a population of more than 10,000 are shown. A few counties are included where rural industry is important.
After Census of Manufacturers, 1958 U. S. Dept. of Commerce and Canada Dept. of Trade and Commerce.

Scale twice that of main map.

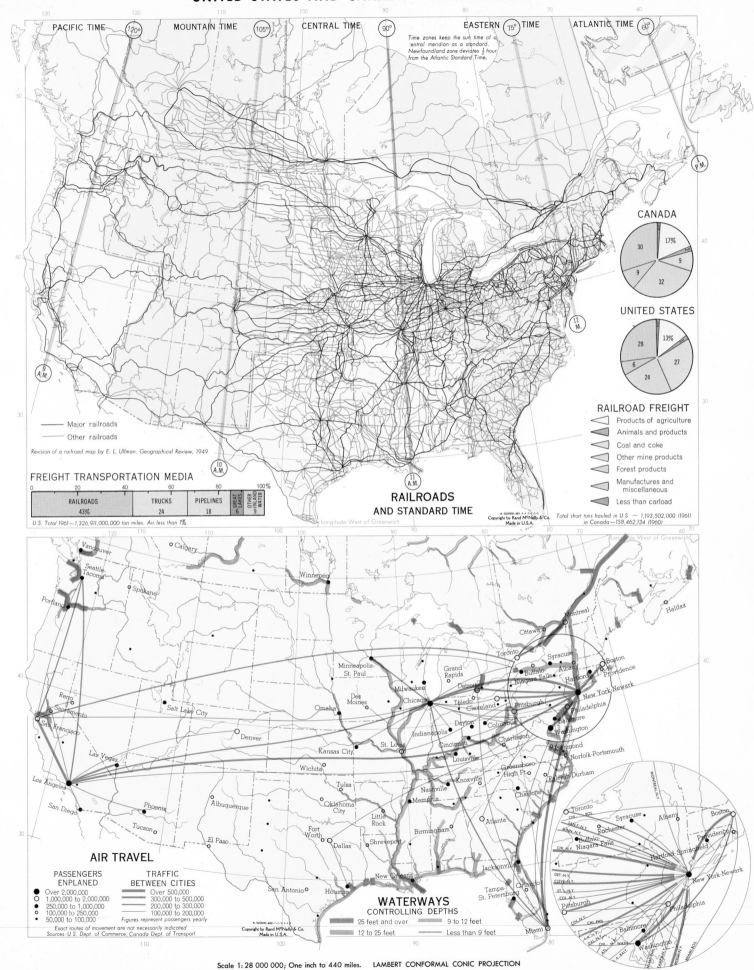

PACIFIC TIME 120° MOUNTAIN TIME 105° CENTRAL TIME 90° EASTERN 75° TIME ATLANTIC TIME 60°

Time zones keep the sun time of a
central meridian as a standard.
Newfoundland zone deviates ½ hour
from the Atlantic Standard Time.

CANADA

17%
30   9
9   32

UNITED STATES

13%
28   27
6
24

RAILROAD FREIGHT

▷ Products of agriculture
▷ Animals and products
▷ Coal and coke
▷ Other mine products
▷ Forest products
▷ Manufactures and miscellaneous
▷ Less than carload

— Major railroads
— Other railroads

Revision of a railroad map by E. L. Ullman, Geographical Review, 1949

FREIGHT TRANSPORTATION MEDIA

0	20	40	60	80	100%

RAILROADS 43% | TRUCKS 24 | PIPELINES 18 | GREAT LAKES 6 | OTHER INLAND WATER 9

U.S. Total 1961—1,326,911,000,000 ton miles. Air, less than 1%

RAILROADS
AND STANDARD TIME

Copyright by Rand McNally & Co.
Made in U.S.A.

Longitude West of Greenwich

Total short tons hauled in U.S — 1,193,502,000 (1961)
in Canada—158,462,134 (1960)

AIR TRAVEL

PASSENGERS ENPLANED
● Over 2,000,000
○ 1,000,000 to 2,000,000
○ 250,000 to 1,000,000
○ 100,000 to 250,000
• 50,000 to 100,000

TRAFFIC BETWEEN CITIES
━━ Over 500,000
━━ 300,000 to 500,000
━━ 200,000 to 300,000
━━ 100,000 to 200,000
Figures represent passengers yearly

Exact routes of movement are not necessarily indicated
Sources: U.S. Dept. of Commerce; Canada Dept. of Transport

Copyright by Rand McNally & Co.
Made in U.S.A.

WATERWAYS
CONTROLLING DEPTHS
25 feet and over   9 to 12 feet
12 to 25 feet   Less than 9 feet

Scale 1: 28 000 000; One inch to 440 miles.   LAMBERT CONFORMAL CONIC PROJECTION

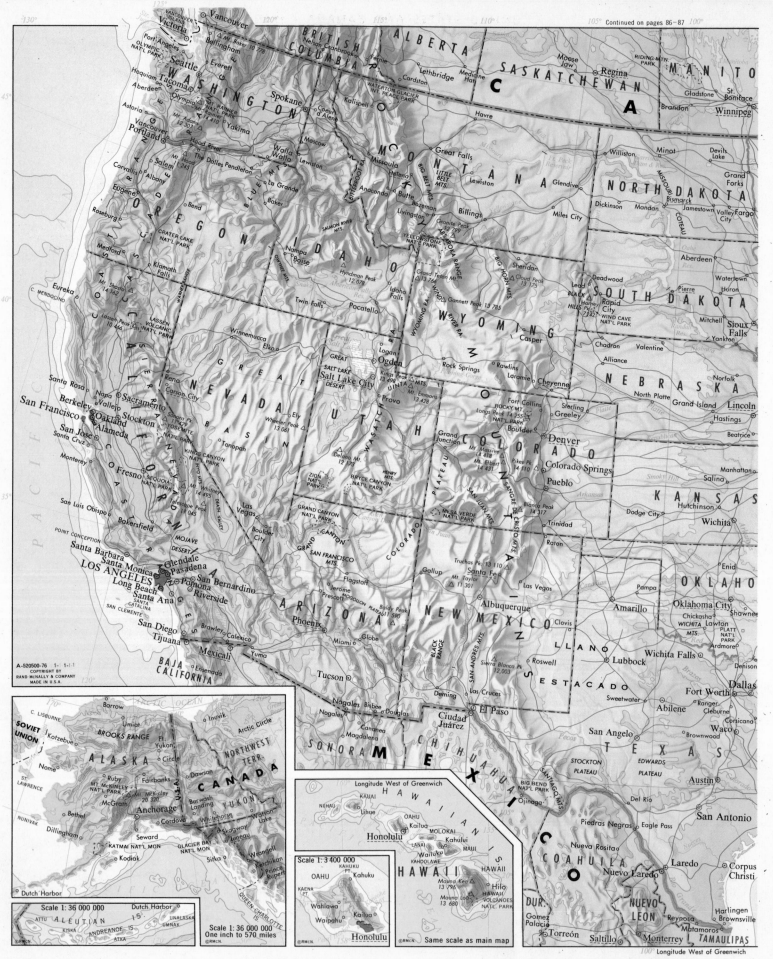

Continued on pages 86-87

Scale 1:12 000 000; one inch to 190 miles. Polyconic Projection
Elevations and depressions are given in feet

Longitude West of Greenwich

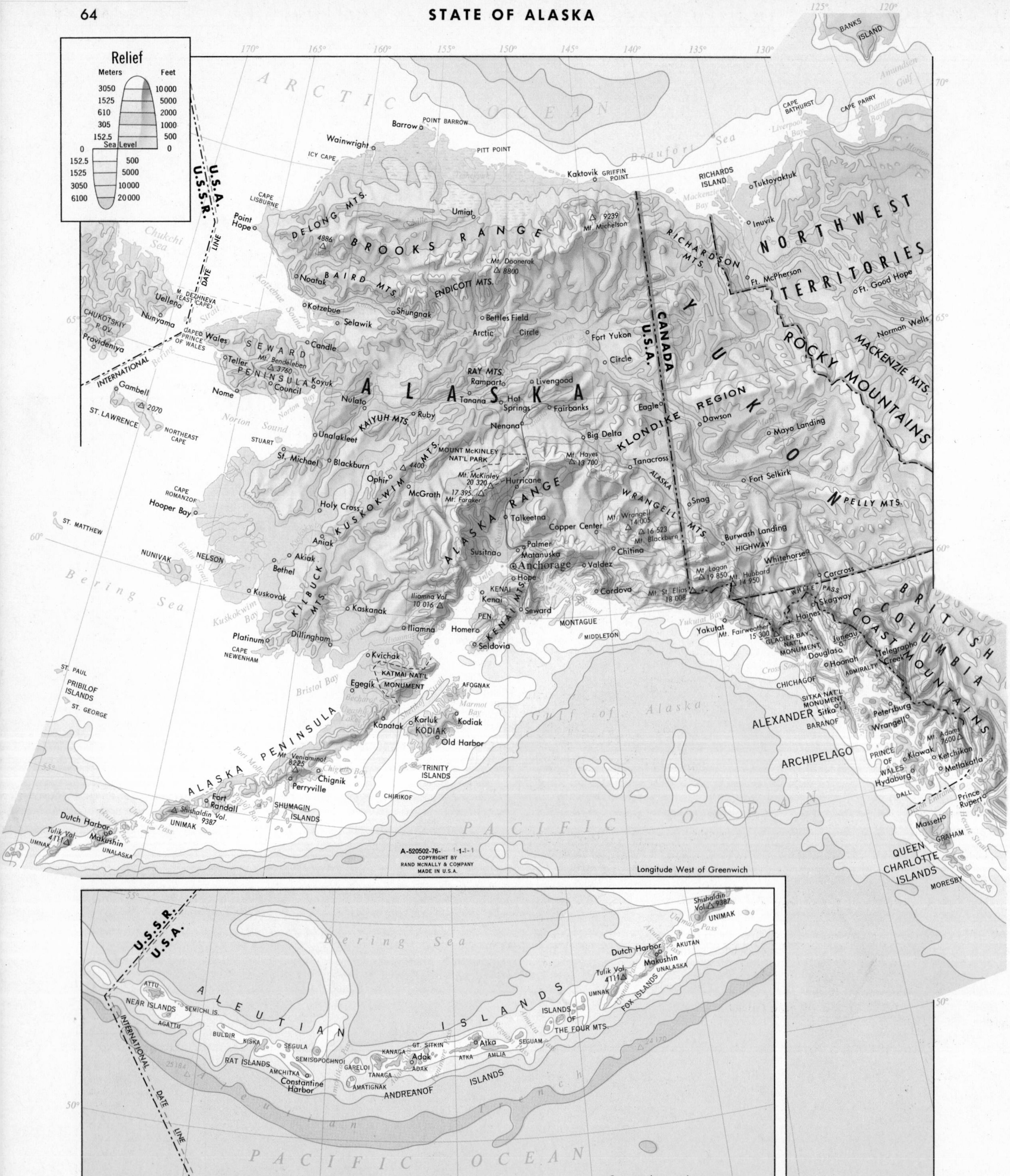

Relief

Meters   Feet
3050   10 000
1525   5000
610   2000
305   1000
152.5   500
0   Sea Level
152.5   500
1525   5000
3050   10 000
6100   20 000

ARCTIC OCEAN

Beaufort Sea

U.S.A.
U.S.S.R.
DATE LINE

CAPE BATHURST   CAPE PARRY

Point Barrow
Barrow
Wainwright
ICY CAPE
PITT POINT
Kaktovik   GRIFFIN POINT
RICHARDS ISLAND
Tuktoyaktuk
Inuvik

CAPE LISBURNE
DELONG MTS.
Umiat
9239   Mt. Michelson
Ft. McPherson
Ft. Good Hope

NORTHWEST TERRITORIES

Point Hope
BROOKS RANGE
4886
Mt. Doonerak 8800
RICHARDSON MTS.
Norman Wells

Chukchi Sea
M. DEZHNEVA (EAST CAPE)
Uelleno
BAIRD MTS.
ENDICOTT MTS.
ROCKY MOUNTAINS
MACKENZIE MTS.

CHUKOTSKIY P.OV.
Providniya
Nunyama
CAPE PRINCE OF WALES
Wales
Noatak
Kotzebue
Shungnak
Selawik
Bettles Field
Arctic Circle
Fort Yukon
YUKON
CANADA
U.S.A.

Gambell
ST. LAWRENCE
NORTHEAST CAPE
2070
Teller
Candle
Circle
KLONDIKE REGION
Eagle
Dawson

SEWARD PENINSULA
Mt. Bendeleben 3760
Koyuk
RAY MTS.
Ramparto
Livengood
Nome
Council
Nulato
Tanana
Hot Springs
Fairbanks
Big Delta
Mayo Landing

STUART
KAIYUH MTS.
Ruby
Nenana
Fort Selkirk
PELLY MTS.

Unalakleet
St. Michael
Blackburn
MOUNT McKINLEY NAT'L PARK
4400
Mt. Hayes 13 700
Tanacross
ALASKA HIGHWAY

Ophir
McGrath
Mt. McKinley 20 320
17 395 Mt. Foraker
Hurricane
WRANGELL MTS.
Snag

Holy Cross
KUSKOKWIM MTS.
Talkeetna
Mt. Wrangell 14 005
16 523 Mt. Blackburn
Burwash Landing
HIGHWAY

Aniak
Susitna
Palmer
Copper Center
Chitina
Whitehorse

Akiak
Bethel
Matanuska
Anchorage
Valdez
Mt. Logan 19 850
Mt. Hubbard 14 950

KILBUCK MTS.
Hope
Cordova
Mt. St. Elias 18 008
Carcross
Skagway

Kuskokvak
ALASKA RANGE
KENAI
Kenai
Seward
Yakutat
Mt. Fairweather 15 300
GLACIER BAY NAT'L MONUMENT
Haines
Juneau

Platinum
Iliamna Vol. 10 016
KENAI PEN.
Homer
Seldovia
MONTAGUE
MIDDLETON
COAST MOUNTAINS
Douglas
Hoonah

Dillingham
Iliamna
Telegraph Creek
BRITISH COLUMBIA

CAPE NEWENHAM
Kvichak
KATMAI NAT'L MONUMENT
AFOGNAK
SITKA NAT'L MONUMENT
Sitka
Petersburg
Wrangell

Egegik
Kanatak
Karluk
Kodiak
Old Harbor
CHICHAGOF
BARANOF
ALEXANDER
ARCHIPELAGO
Klawak
Ketchikan
Metlakatla

Bristol Bay
ALASKA PENINSULA
Mt. Veniaminof 8225
Chignik
Perryville
TRINITY ISLANDS
Gulf of Alaska
PRINCE OF WALES
Hydaburg
DALL
Prince Rupert

ST. PAUL
PRIBILOF ISLANDS
ST. GEORGE
Fort Randall
Shishaldin Vol. 9387
UNIMAK
SHUMAGIN ISLANDS
CHIRIKOF

Dutch Harbor
Makushin
Tulik Vol. 4111
UNALASKA
UMNAK
PACIFIC OCEAN

QUEEN CHARLOTTE ISLANDS
MORESBY

A-520502-76- 1-1-1
COPYRIGHT BY
RAND McNALLY & COMPANY
MADE IN U.S.A.

Longitude West of Greenwich

Aleutian Islands inset

U.S.S.R.
U.S.A.
Bering Sea
Shishaldin Vol. 9387
UNIMAK
AKUTAN
Dutch Harbor
Makushin
Tulik Vol. 4111
UNALASKA
UMNAK
FOX ISLANDS

ATTU
NEAR ISLANDS
SEMICHI IS.
AGATTU
ALEUTIAN ISLANDS
ISLANDS OF THE FOUR MTS.
SEGUAM
AMLIA

BULDIR
KISKA
SEGULA
GT. SITKIN
Atka
ATKA

RAT ISLANDS
AMCHITKA
SEMISOPOCHNOI
KANAGA
Adak
ADAK

INTERNATIONAL DATE LINE
GARELOI
TANAGA
AMATIGNAK
Constantine Harbor
ANDREANOF ISLANDS

PACIFIC OCEAN

Longitude East of Greenwich   Longitude West of Greenwich   Same scale as main map

0 50 100 200 300 400 Miles
0 100 200 300 400 500 600 Kilometers

Scale 1: 12 000 000; one inch to 190 miles.   Conic Projection
Elevations and depressions are given in feet

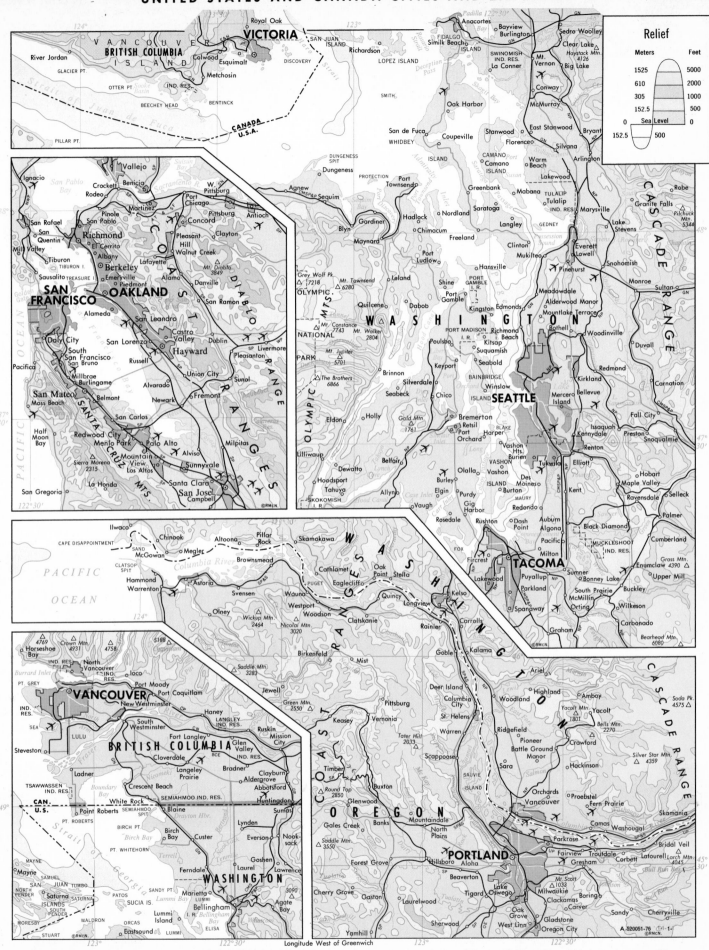

Scale 1:1 000 000; one inch to 16 miles.

Elevations and depressions are given in feet.

Longitude West of Greenwich

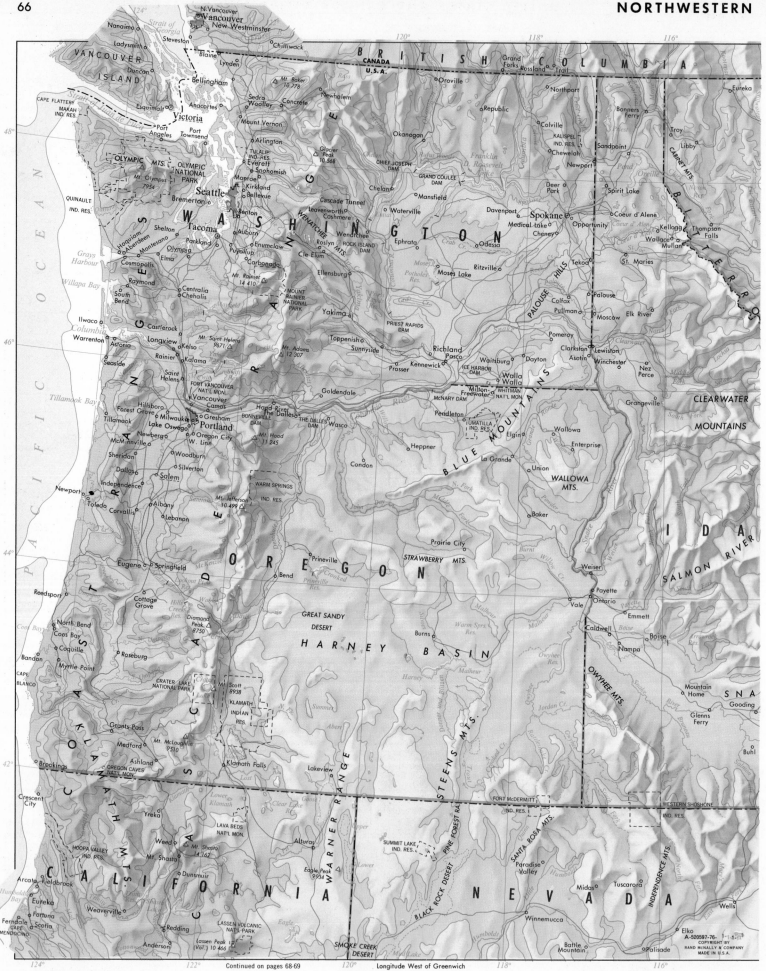

Continued on pages 68-69

Longitude West of Greenwich

Scale 1: 4 000 000; one inch to 64 miles. Conic Projection
Elevations and depressions are given in feet

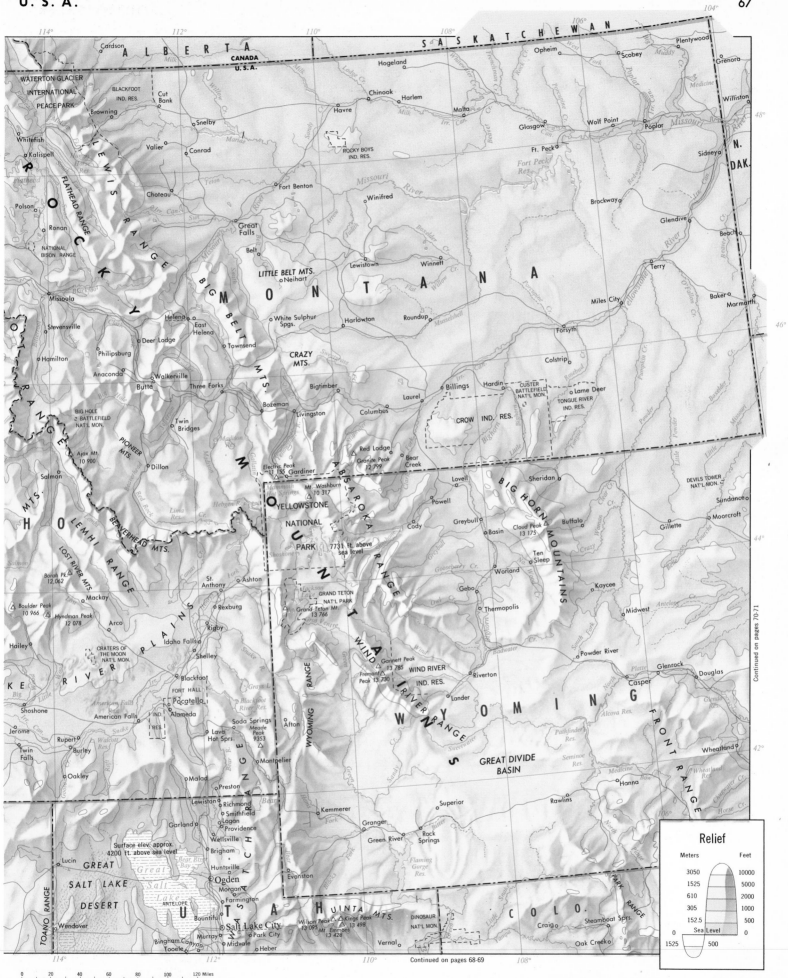

Continued on pages 70-71

Continued on pages 68-69

Relief

Meters		Feet
3050		10000
1525		5000
610		2000
305		1000
152.5		500
0	Sea Level	0
1525		500

0 20 40 60 80 100 120 Miles

0 20 40 60 80 100 120 140 160 180 200 Kilometers

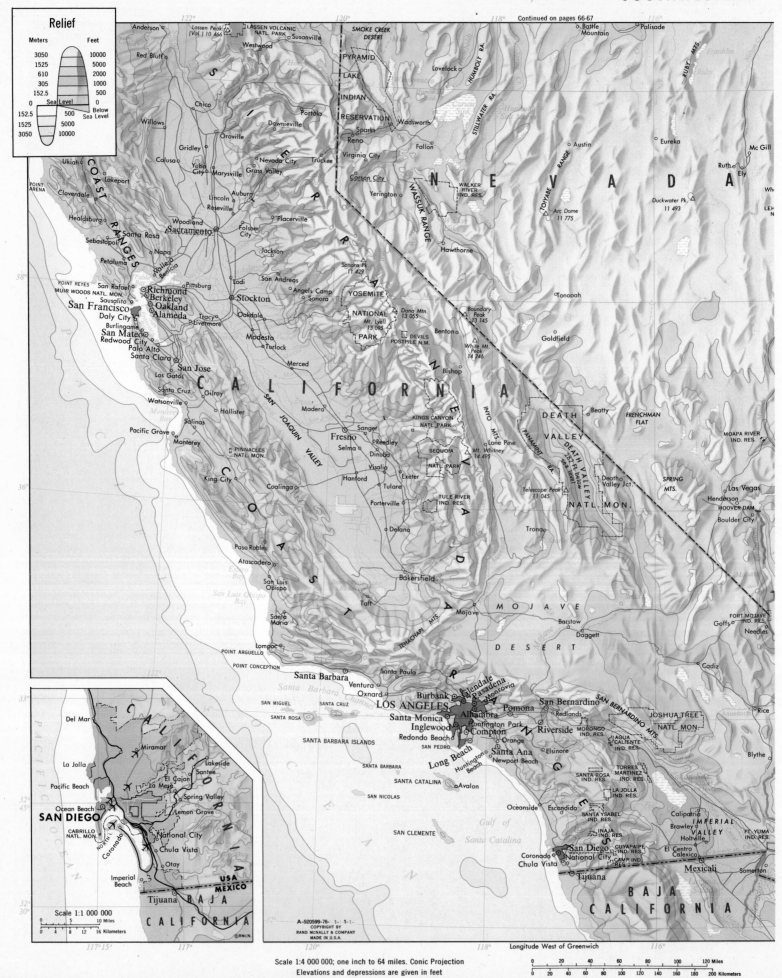

Continued on pages 66-67

Relief

Meters		Feet
3050		10000
1525		5000
610		2000
305		1000
152.5		500
0	Sea Level	0
152.5		Below Sea Level
500		500
1525		5000
3050		10000

Scale 1:4 000 000; one inch to 64 miles. Conic Projection
Elevations and depressions are given in feet

A-520599-76- 1- 1-1
COPYRIGHT BY
RAND McNALLY & COMPANY
MADE IN U.S.A.

Longitude West of Greenwich

Scale 1:1 000 000

San Diego inset

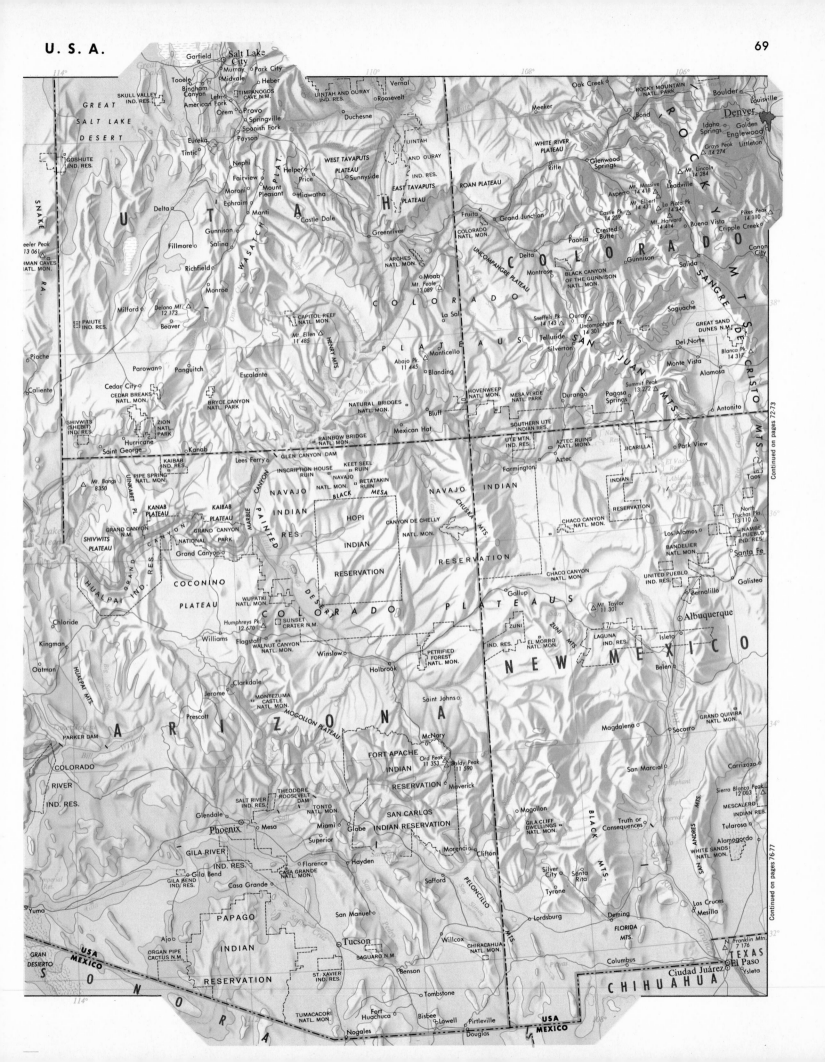

Continued on pages 72-73

Continued on pages 76-77

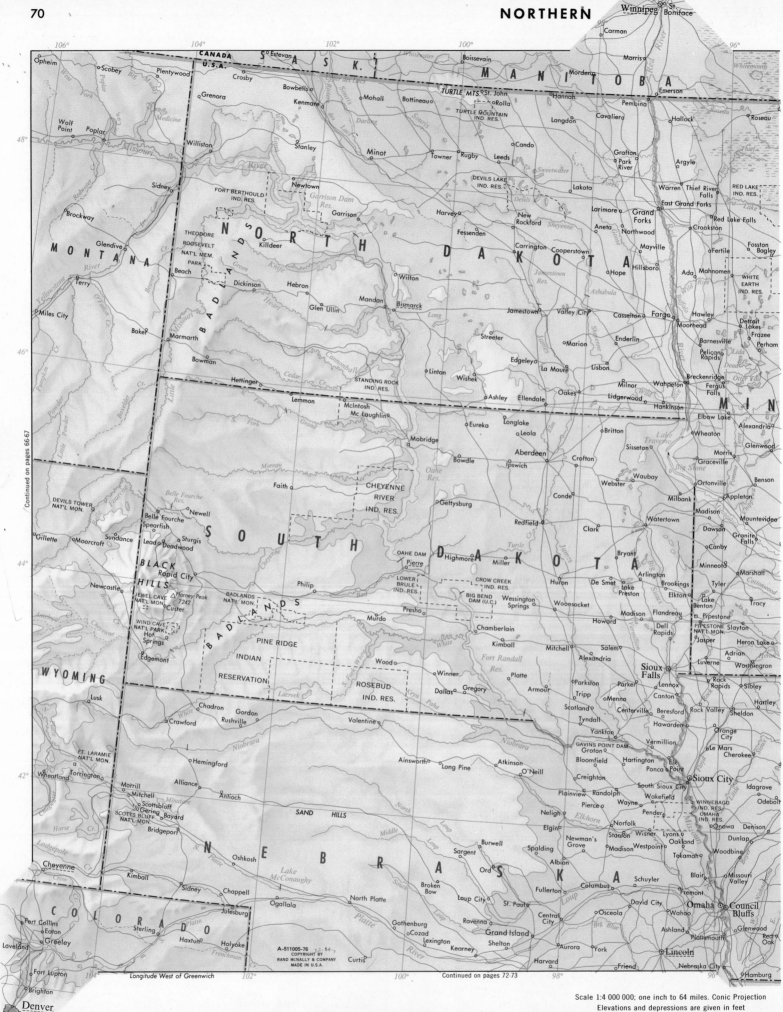

Scale 1:4 000 000; one inch to 64 miles. Conic Projection
Elevations and depressions are given in feet

Continued on pages 66-67

Continued on pages 72-73

A-511005-76   1-4
COPYRIGHT BY
RAND McNALLY & COMPANY
MADE IN U.S.A.

Longitude West of Greenwich

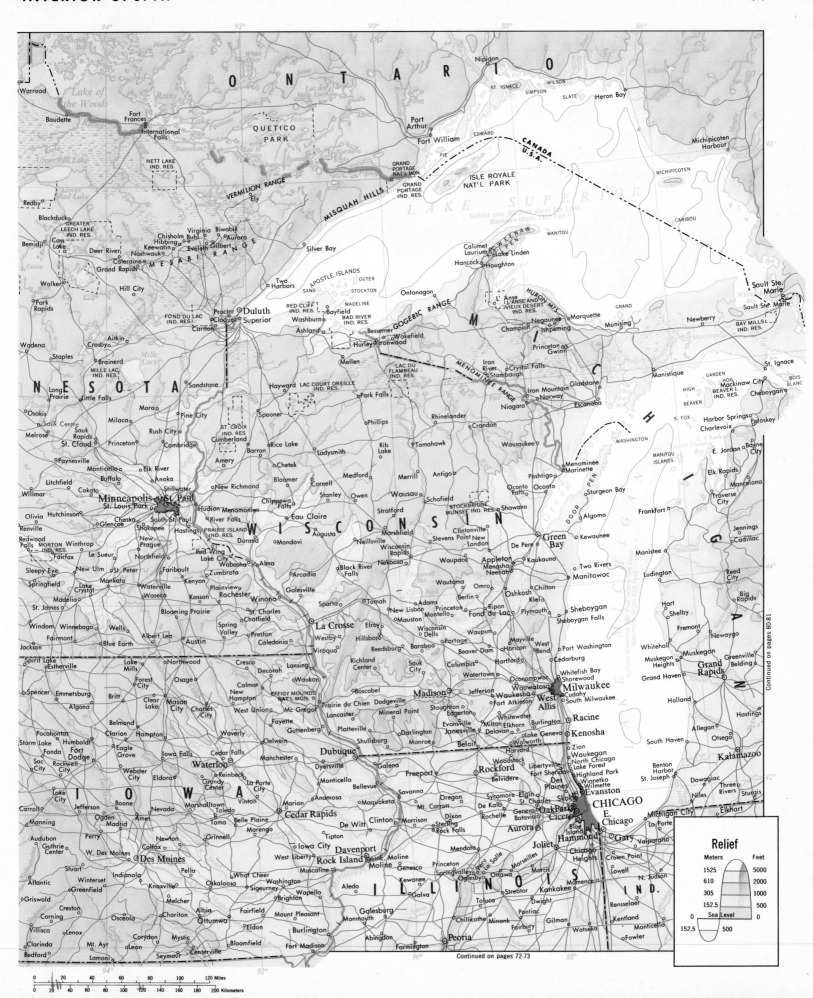

Continued on pages 80-81

Continued on pages 72-73

Relief

Meters	Feet
1525	5000
610	2000
305	1000
152.5	500
0 Sea Level	0
152.5	500

0 20 40 60 80 100 120 Miles

0 20 40 60 80 100 120 140 160 180 200 Kilometers

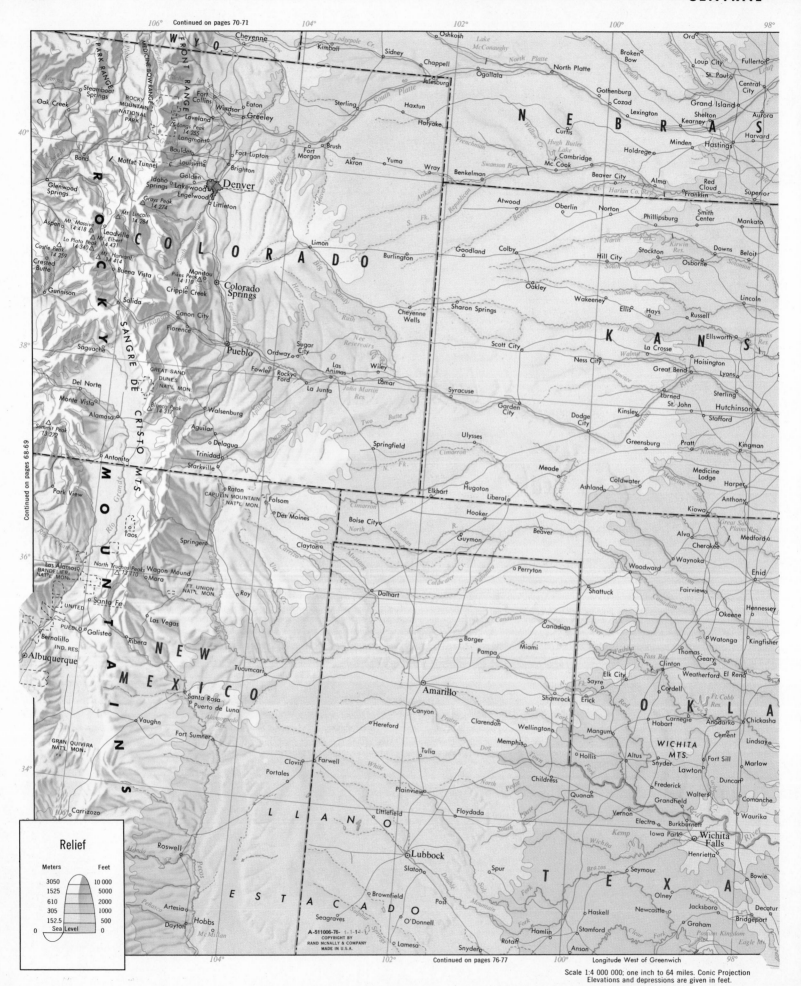

Continued on pages 70-71

Continued on pages 68-69

Continued on pages 76-77

Relief

Meters	Feet
3050	10 000
1525	5000
610	2000
305	1000
152.5	500
0	Sea Level 0

A-511006-76- 1-1-1-1-1
COPYRIGHT BY
RAND McNALLY & COMPANY
MADE IN U.S.A.

Longitude West of Greenwich

Scale 1:4 000 000; one inch to 64 miles. Conic Projection
Elevations and depressions are given in feet.

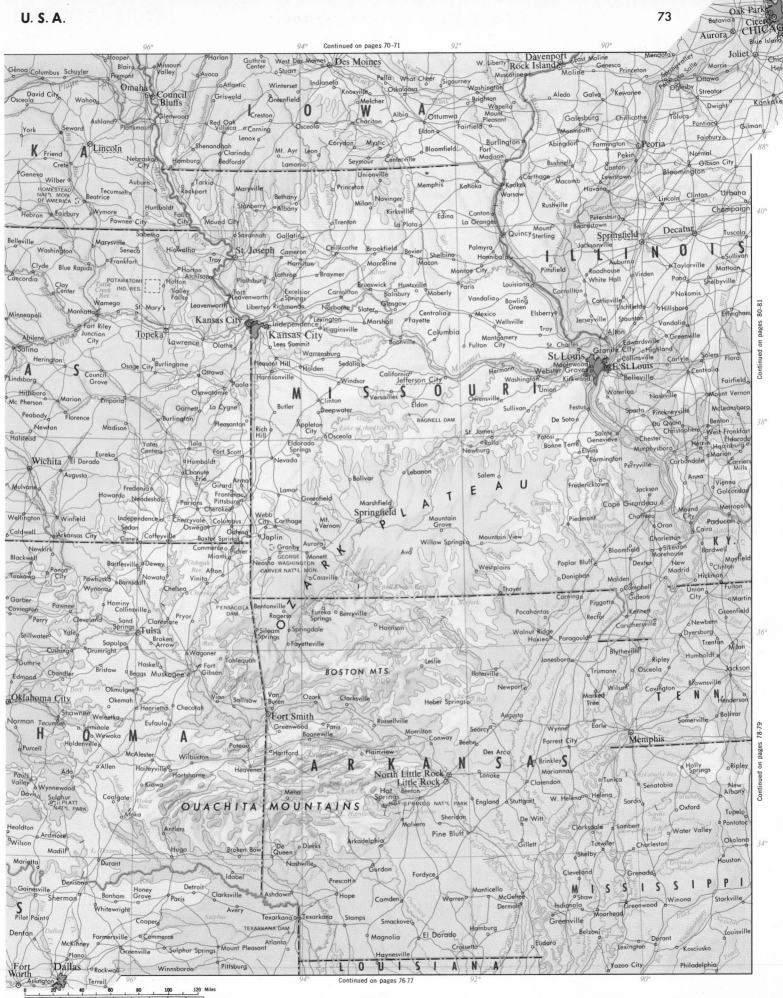

Continued on pages 70-71
Continued on pages 80-81
Continued on pages 78-79
Continued on pages 76-77

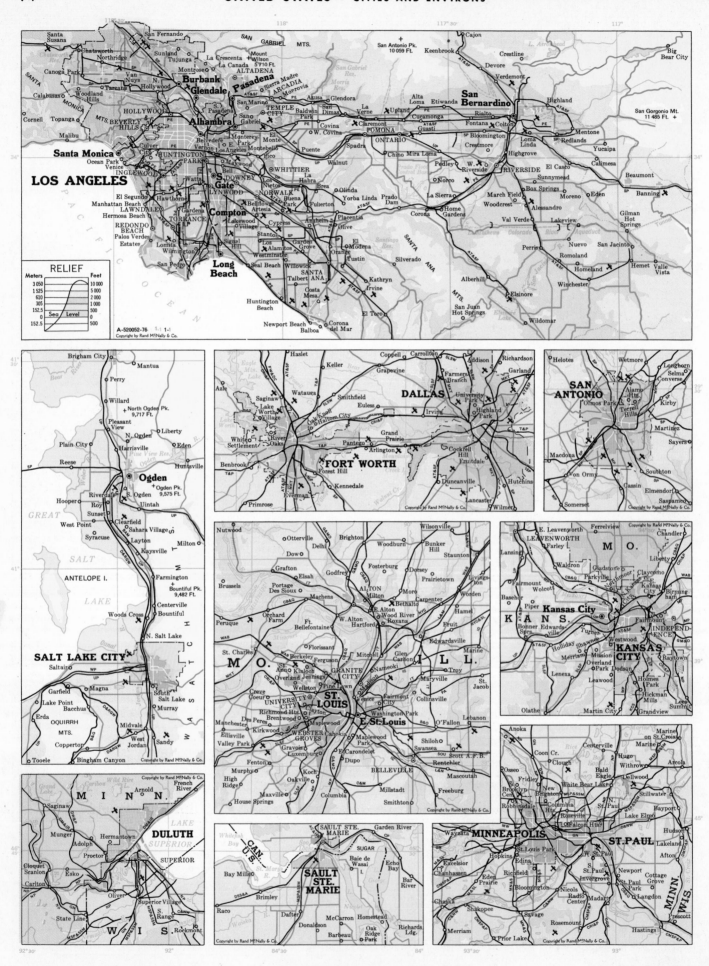

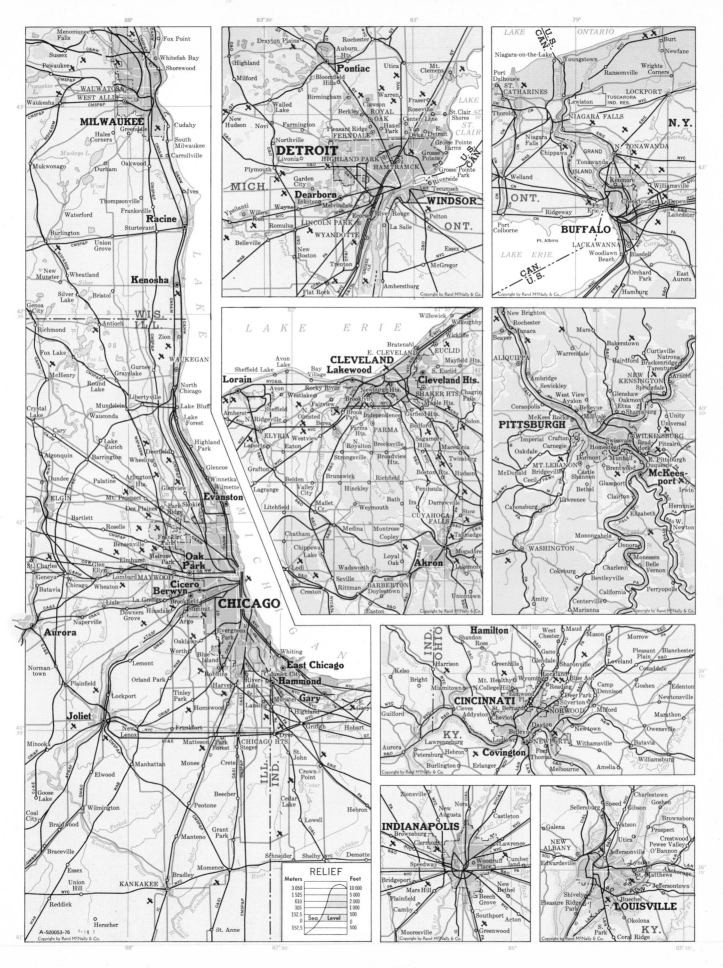

Scale 1:1 000 000; One inch to 16 miles
Elevations and depressions are given in feet

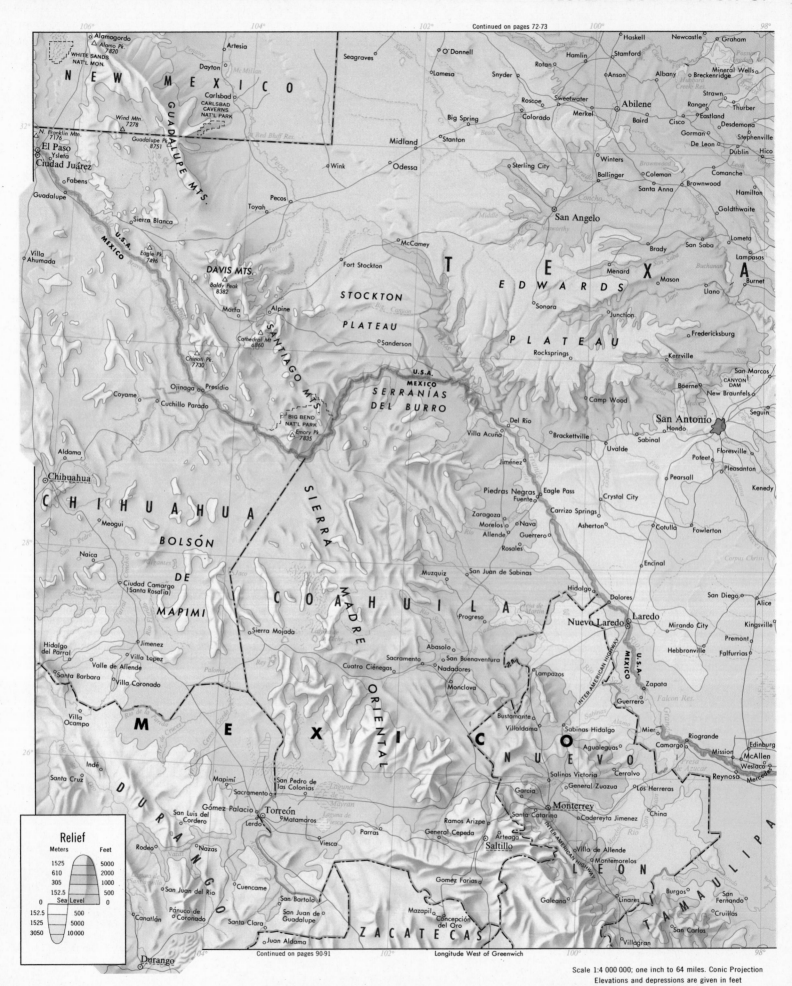

Continued on pages 72-73

Continued on pages 90-91

Longitude West of Greenwich

Scale 1:4 000 000; one inch to 64 miles. Conic Projection
Elevations and depressions are given in feet

Relief

Meters		Feet
1525		5000
610		2000
305		1000
152.5		500
0	Sea Level	0
152.5		500
1525		5000
3050		10 000

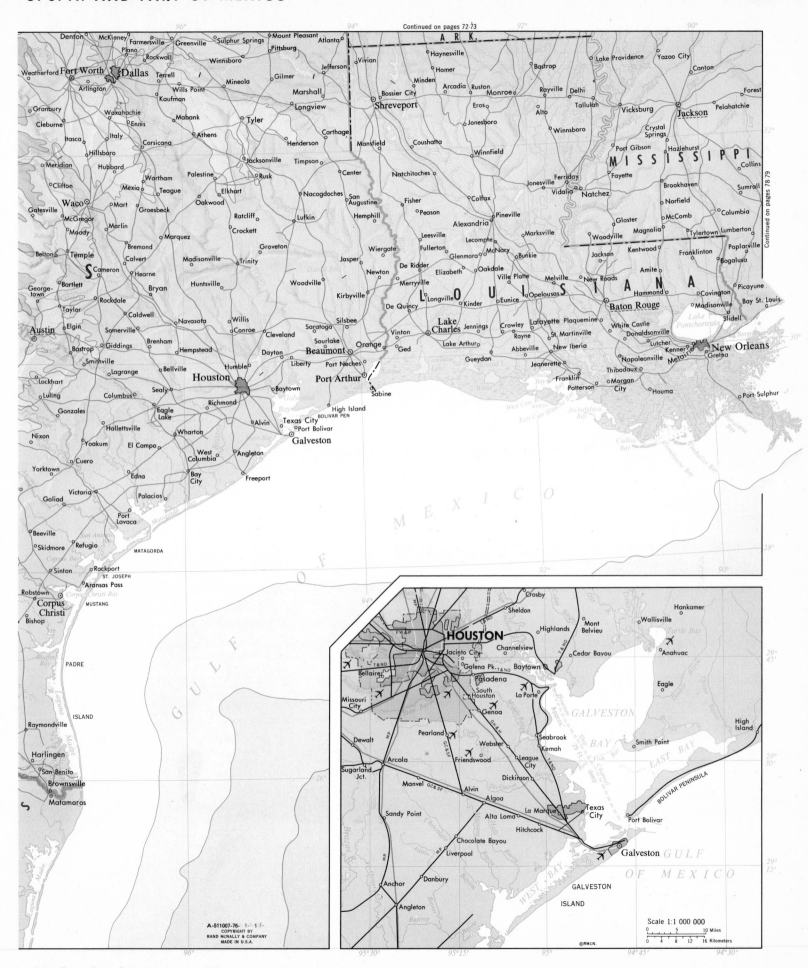

Continued on pages 72-73

Continued on pages 78-79

ARK.

MISSISSIPPI

LOUISIANA

GULF OF MEXICO

Fort Worth Dallas
Shreveport
Jackson
Baton Rouge
New Orleans
Houston
Beaumont
Port Arthur
Galveston
Lake Charles
Alexandria
Natchez
Vicksburg
Corpus Christi
Brownsville
Matamoros

Scale 1:1 000 000

HOUSTON

GALVESTON BAY

GALVESTON ISLAND

GULF OF MEXICO

0 20 40 60 80 100 120 Miles
0 20 40 60 80 100 120 140 160 180 200 Kilometers

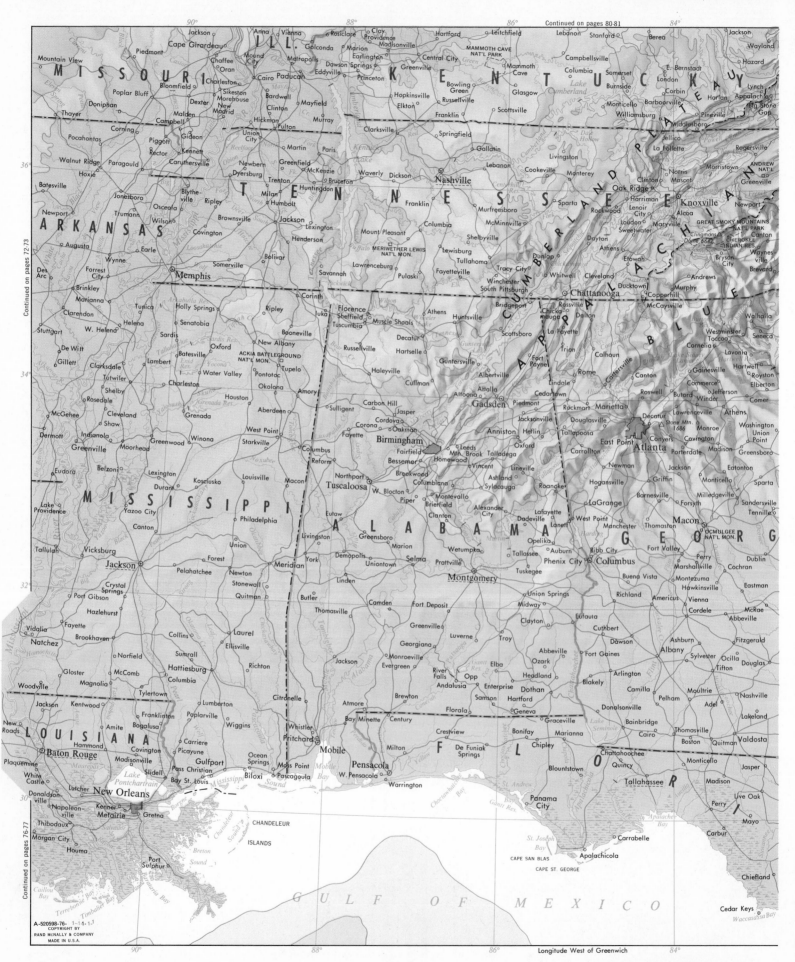

Continued on pages 80-81

Scale 1:4 000 000; one inch to 64 miles. Conic Projection
Elevations and depressions are given in feet

Longitude West of Greenwich

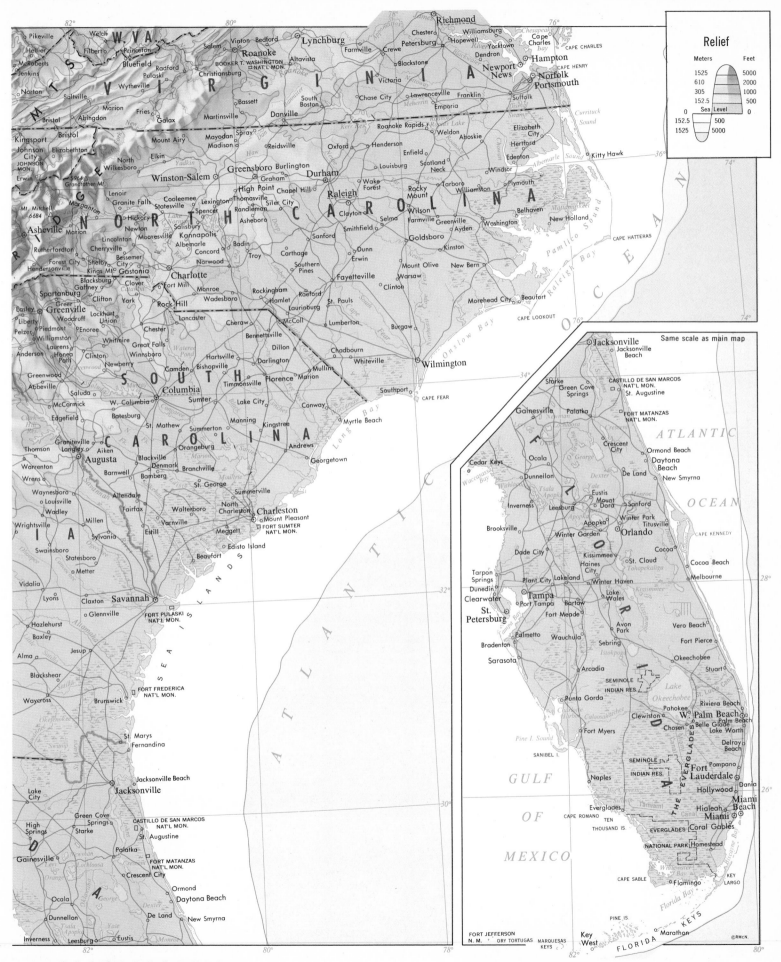

Relief

Meters		Feet
1525		5000
610		2000
305		1000
152.5		500
0	Sea Level	0
152.5	500	
1525	5000	

Same scale as main map

0 10 20 30 40 50 60 70 80 90 100 110 120 Miles
0 20 40 60 80 100 120 140 160 180 200 Kilometers

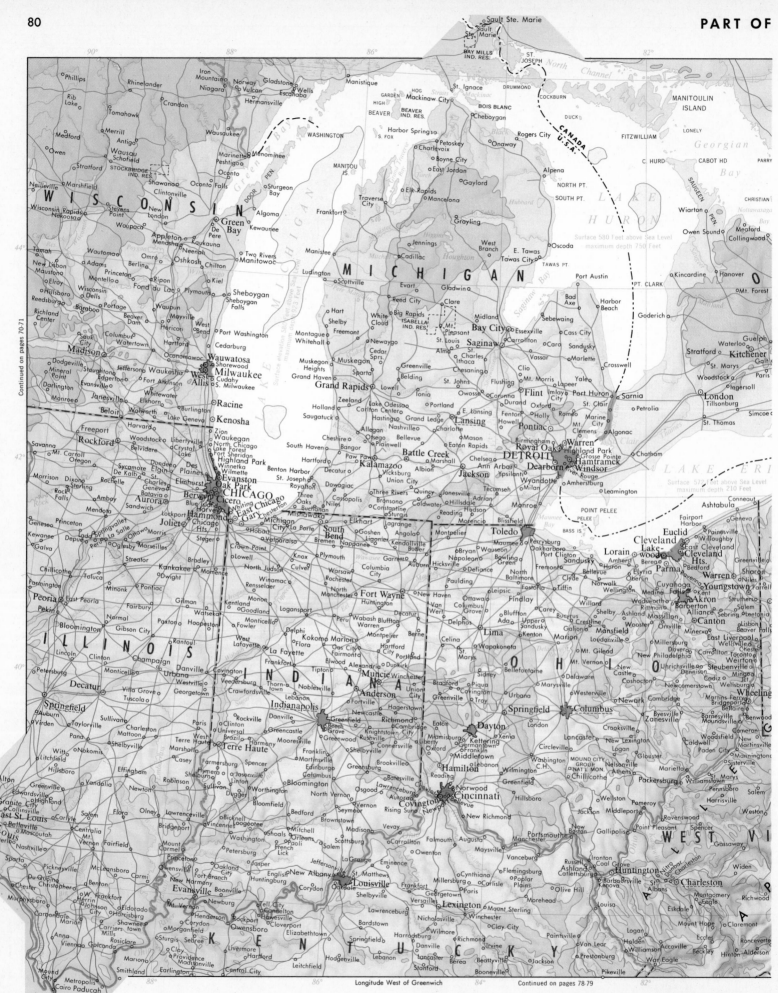

Continued on pages 78-79

Scale 1:4 000 000; one inch to 64 miles. Conic Projection

Elevations and depressions are given in feet

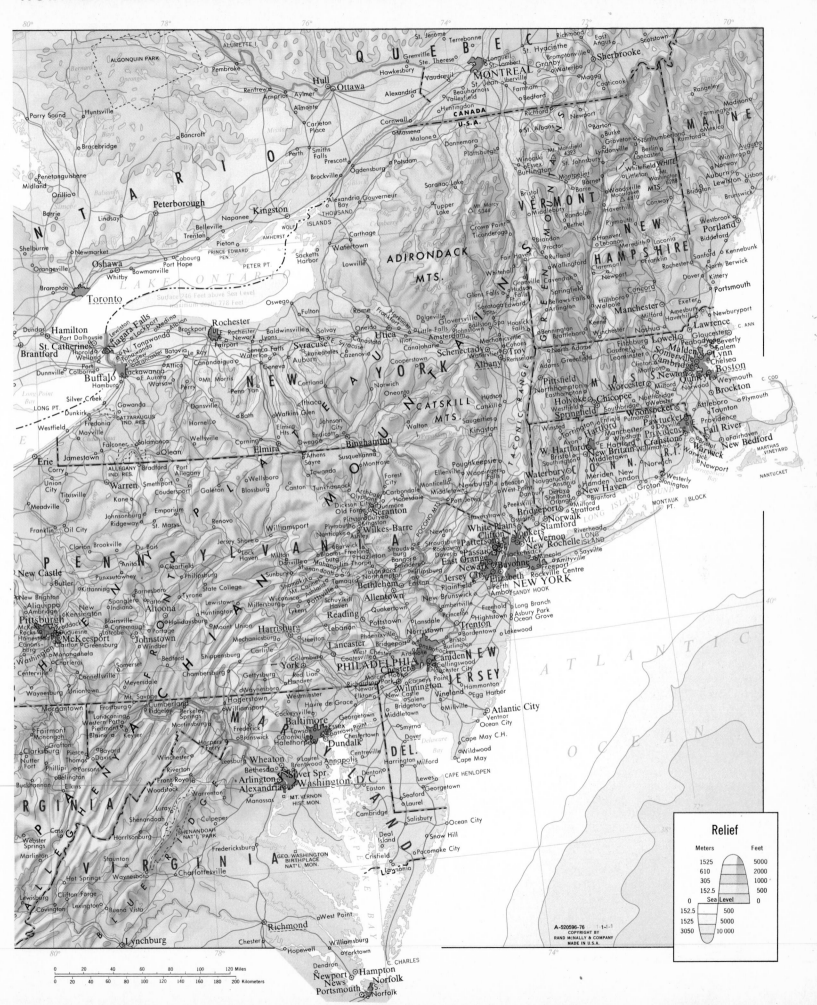

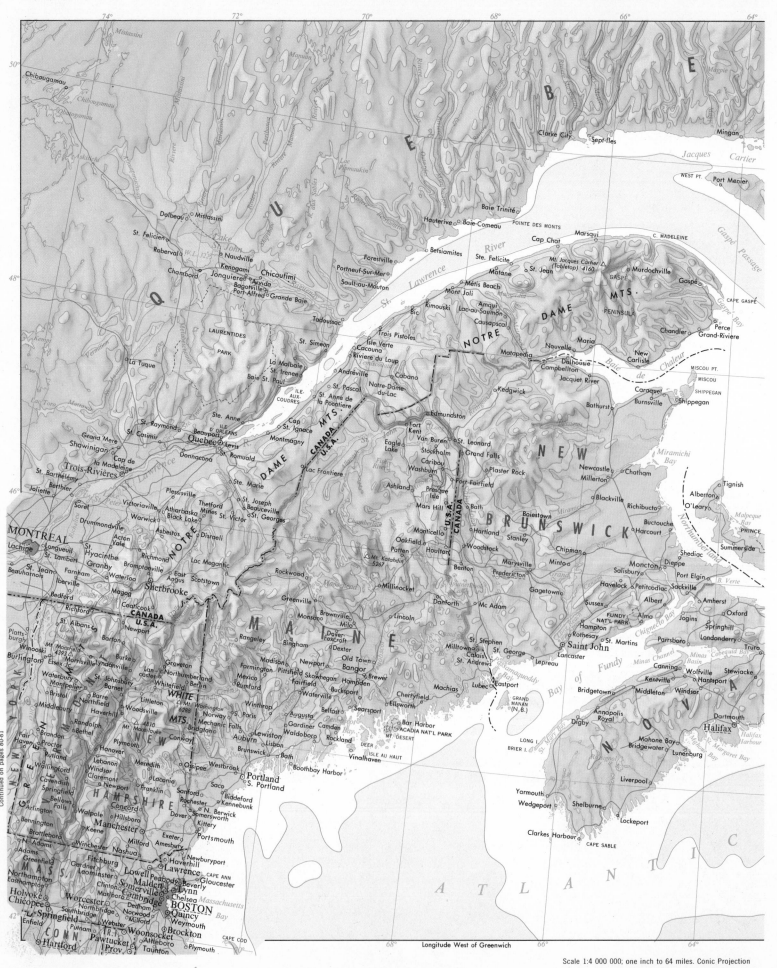

Scale 1:4 000 000; one inch to 64 miles. Conic Projection
Elevations and depressions are given in feet.

Longitude West of Greenwich

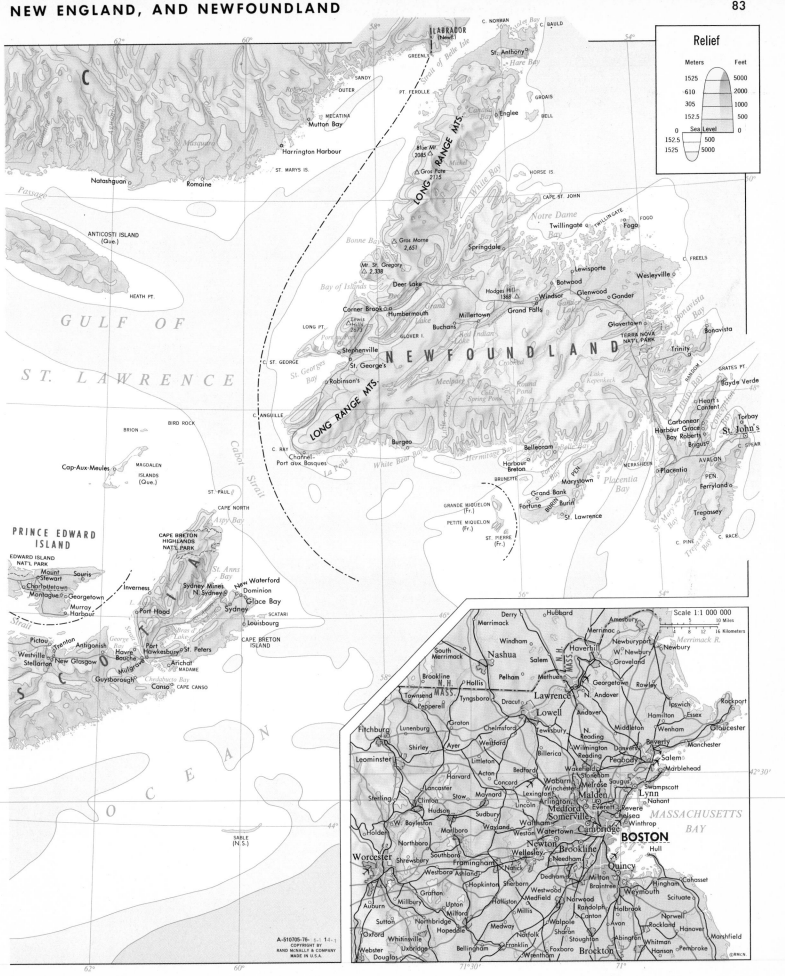

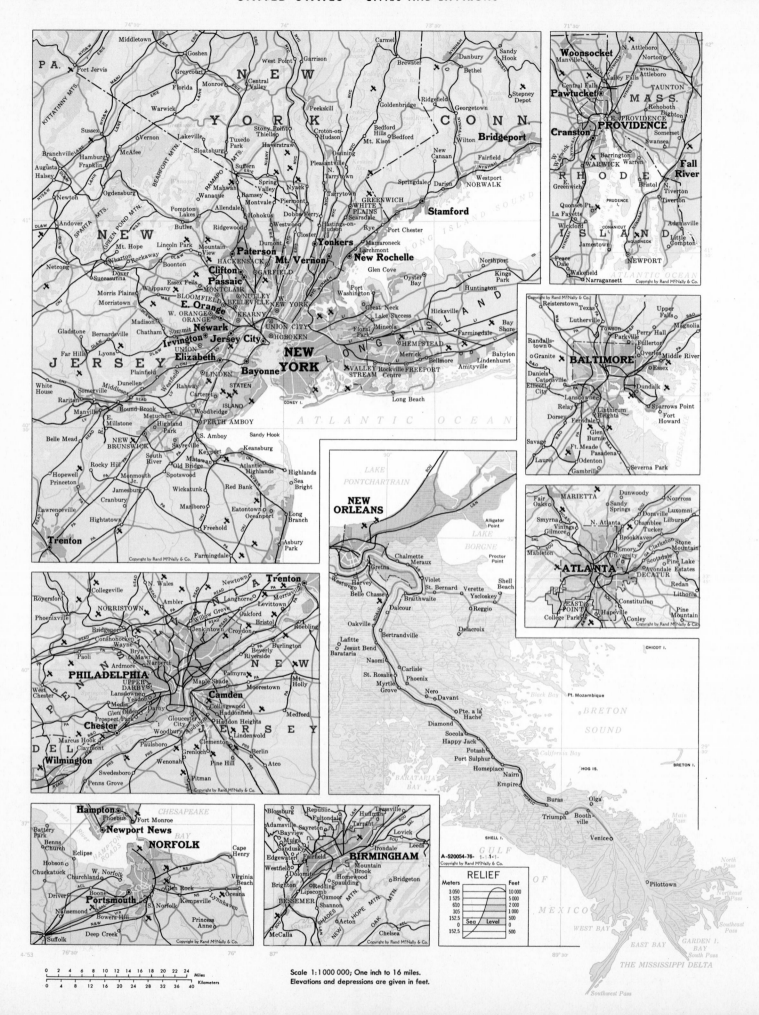

Scale 1:1 000 000; One inch to 16 miles.
Elevations and depressions are given in feet.

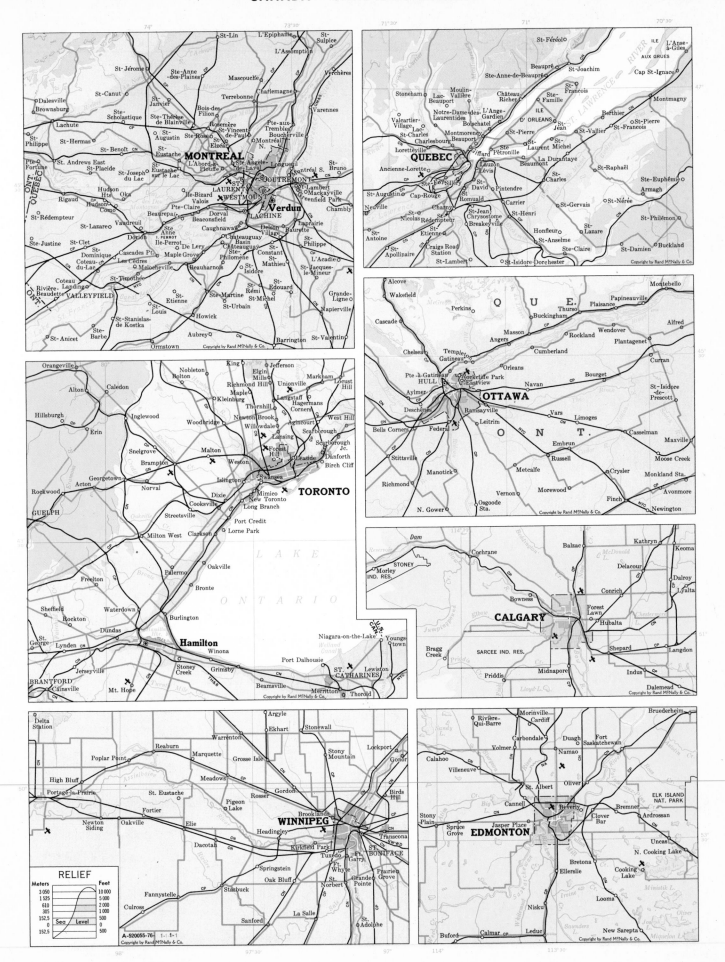

MONTREAL

St-Lin
L'Épiphanie
St-Sulpice
St-Jérôme
L'Assomption
Ste-Anne-des-Plaines
Mascouche
Verchères
Dalesville
St-Canut
Terrebonne
Charlemagne
Brownsburg
Ste-Thérèse de Blainville
Bois-des-Filion
Lachute
Rosemère
Varennes
St-Janvier
St-Augustin
Pte-aux-Trembles
St-Vincent-de-Paul
Boucherville
St-Philippe
St-Hermas
Ste-Rose
Montréal N.
St-Benoît
St-Eustache
St-Bruno
St-Andrews East
L'Abord-à-Plouffe
Ste-Angèle-de-Laval
Longueuil
Montréal S.
Pte-Fortune
St-Placide
St-Eustache sur le Lac
OUTREMONT
Rigaud
Hudson Hts
Oka
ST LAURENT
WESTMOUNT
St-Lambert
Mackayville
Greenfield Park
Hudson Como
Ile-Bizard
Valois
St-Rédempteur
Beaurepair
Pte-Claire
VERDUN
Chambly
St-Lazare
Vaudreuil
Dorval
Beaconsfield
LACHINE
Ste-Anne
Delson Village
Laprairie
St-Justine
I. Perrot
Dorion
Caughnawaga
Baurette
Ste-Dominique
Ile-Perrot
De Léry
Châteauguay Basin
St-Philippe
Coteau-du-Lac
Cascades Pt.
Les Cèdres
Maple Grove
Châteauguay
L'Acadie
Coteau Landing
Mélocheville
Beauharnois
Ste-Philomène
St-Isidore
St-Mathieu
St-Jacques-le-Mineur
Rivière-Beaudette
VALLEYFIELD
St-Timothée
St-Rémi
St-Edouard
St-Stanislas-de Kostka
Ste-Martine
St-Michel
Grande-Ligne
St-Louis
St-Urbain
Napierville
St-Etienne
Howick
St-Barbe
St-Anicet
Aubrey
Barrington
St-Valentin
Ormstown

Copyright by Rand McNally & Co.

QUEBEC

St-Féréol
ILE AUX GRUES
L'Anse-à-Giles
Beaupré
St-Joachim
Cap St-Ignace
Stoneham
Lac-Beauport
Moulin-Vallière
Château-Richer
Ste-Anne-de-Beaupré
Ste-Famille
St-François
Montmagny
Valcartier-Village
Notre-Dame-des-Laurentides
L'Ange-Gardien
Boischatel
ILE D'ORLEANS
Berthier
St-Charles
Montmorency
Beauport
St-Pierre
St-Jean
St-Vallier
St-Pierre
St-François
Loretteville
Charlesbourg
Giffard
Ste-Pétronille
St-Laurent Michel
La Durantaye
Ancienne-Lorette
QUEBEC
Lauzon
Beaumont
St-Raphaël
Ste-Euphémie
St-Augustin
Sillery
Lévis
St-Charles
Ste-Néree
Cap-Rouge
St-David
Pintendre
St-Gervais
Neuville
Charny
St-Romuald
Carrier
St-Henri
St-Nicolas
St-Jean-Chrysostome
Breakeyville
Honfleur
St-Lazare
St-Philémon
St-Antoine
St-Etienne
Ste-Claire
St-Damien
St-Apollinaire
Craigs Road Station
Buckland
St-Lambert
St-Isidore-Dorchester
Armagh

Copyright by Rand McNally & Co.

TORONTO

Orangeville
King
Jefferson
Nobleton
Bolton
Elgin Mills
Unionville
Markham
Locust Hill
Alton
Caledon
Richmond Hill
Maple
Langstaff
Hagermans Corners
Hillsburgh
Inglewood
Kleinburg
Thornhill
Newton Brook
Agincourt
West Hill
Erin
Woodbridge
Willowdale
Scarborough
Snelgrove
Malton
Lansing
Scarborough Jc.
Brampton
Weston
Forest Hill
Leaside
Danforth
Georgetown
Acton
Islington
Swansea
Birch Cliff
Rockwood
Norval
Dixie
Mimico
TORONTO
GUELPH
Cooksville
New Toronto
Streetsville
Long Branch
Palermo
Oakville
Port Credit
Freelton
Lorne Park
Milton West
Clarkson
Sheffield
Waterdown
Rockton
Bronte
Burlington
St. George
Dundas
Lynden
Hamilton
LAKE ONTARIO
Jerseyville
Winona
BRANTFORD
Stoney Creek
Grimsby
Cainsville
Mt. Hope
Beamsville
Merritton
Thorold
Niagara-on-the-Lake
Youngstown
Port Dalhousie
ST. CATHARINES
Lewiston
U.S. CAN.

Copyright by Rand McNally & Co.

OTTAWA

Alcove
Montebello
Wakefield
Perkins
QUE.
Papineauville
Thurso
Plaisance
Cascade
Buckingham
Wendover
Alfred
Chelsea
Templeton
Masson
Rockland
Plantagenet
Gatineau
Angers
Cumberland
Curran
Pte-à-Gatineau
Rockcliffe Park
Orleans
St-Isidore-de-Prescott
HULL
Eastview
Navan
Aylmer
OTTAWA
Bourget
Deschênes
Ramsayville
Bells Corners
Leitrim
Vars
Limoges
Federal
Casselman
Stittsville
Embrun
Maxville
Manotick
Russell
Moose Creek
Richmond
Metcalfe
Crysler
Monkland Sta.
Vernon
Morewood
Avonmore
N. Gower
Osgoode Sta.
Finch
Newington
ONT.

Copyright by Rand McNally & Co.

CALGARY

Dam
Reservoir
Cochrane
Balzac
McDonald L.
Kathryn
Keoma
Morley IND. RES.
STONEY
Delacour
Dalroy
Conrich
Lyalta
Bowness
Forest Lawn
CALGARY
Hubalta
Bragg Creek
Shepard
Langdon
SARCEE IND. RES.
Priddis
Midnapore
Indus
Priddis
Dalemead

Copyright by Rand McNally & Co.

WINNIPEG

Delta Station
Argyle
Ekhart
Stonewall
Warrenton
Reaburn
Marquette
Grosse Isle
Stony Mountain
Lockport
Poplar Point
Gonor
High Bluff
Meadows
Birds Hill
Portage-la-Prairie
St. Eustache
Pigeon Lake
Rosser
Gordon
St. Albert
Fortier
Brooklands
Newton Siding
Oakville
Elie
Headingley
WINNIPEG
Transcona
Dacotah
Kirkfield Park
Tuxedo
ST. BONIFACE
Springstein
Ft. Whyte
Ft. Garry
Prairie Grove
Oak Bluff
St. Norbert
Grande Pointe
Fannystelle
Starbuck
St. Adolphe
Culross
La Salle
Sanford

A-520055-76-   1- 1- 1- 1
Copyright by Rand McNally & Co.

EDMONTON

Rivière-Qui-Barre
Morinville
Cardiff
Bruederheim
Duagh
Fort Saskatchewan
Carbondale
Calahoo
Volmer
Namao
ELK ISLAND NAT. PARK
Villeneuve
St. Albert
Oliver
Cannell
Beverly
Stony Plain
EDMONTON
Clover Bar
Bremner
Spruce Grove
Jasper Place
Ardrossan
Bretona
Uncas
Ellerslie
N. Cooking Lake
Nisku
Looma
Cooking Lake
Buford
Calmar
Leduc
New Sarepta

Copyright by Rand McNally & Co.

RELIEF

Meters		Feet
3 050		10 000
1 525		5 000
610		2 000
305		1 000
152.5		500
0	Sea Level	0
152.5		500

0 2 4 6 8 10 12 14 16 18 20 22 24 Miles
0 4 8 12 16 20 24 28 32 36 40 Kilometers

Scale 1:1 000 000; One inch to 16 miles.
Elevations and depressions are given in feet.

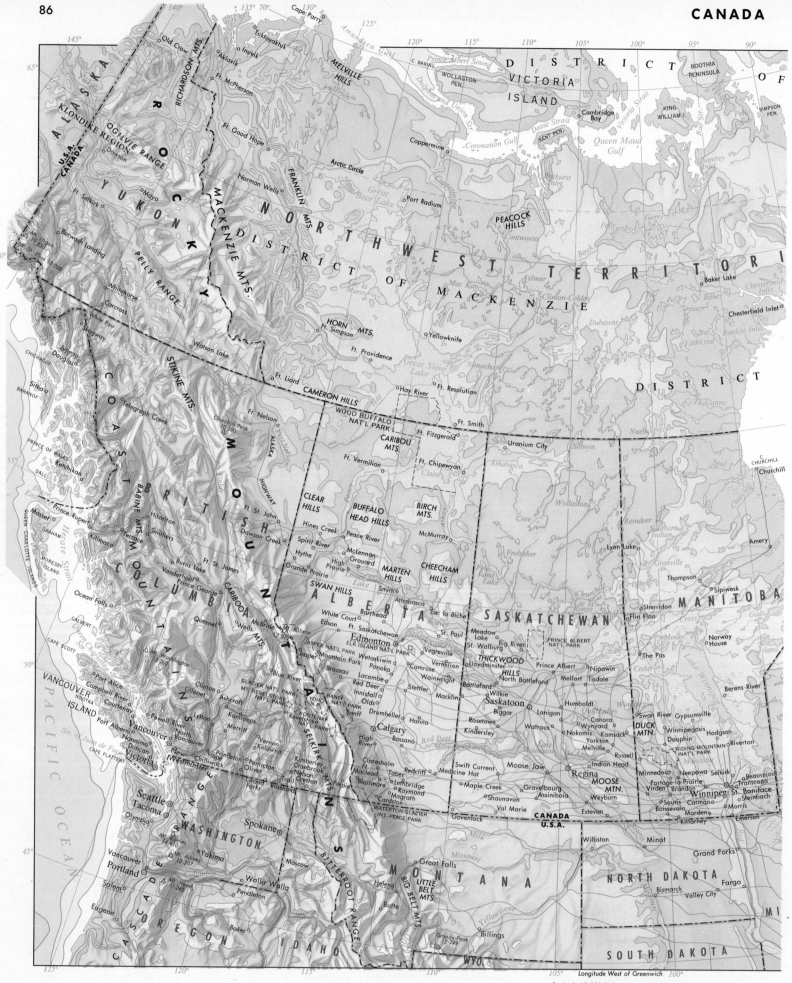

Scale 1: 12 000 000; one inch to 190 miles. Conic Projection

Elevations and depressions are given in feet

Longitude West of Greenwich

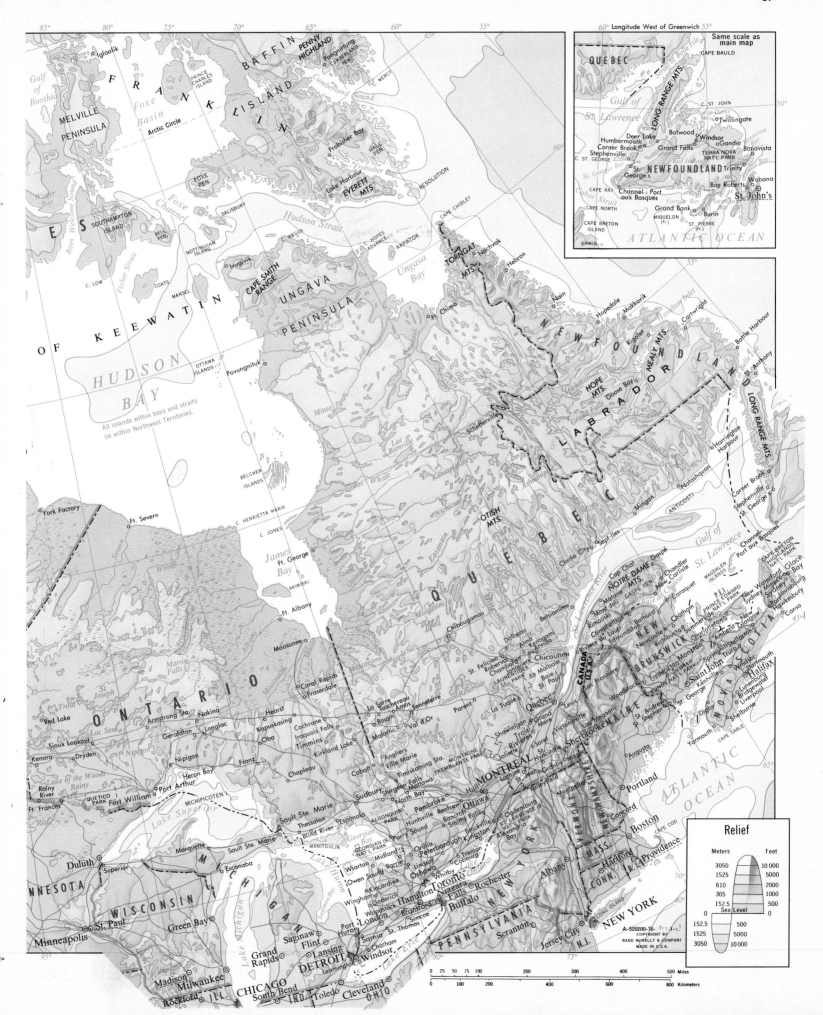

Longitude West of Greenwich

Relief

Meters		Feet
3050		10 000
1525		5000
610		2000
305		1000
152.5		500
Sea Level		0
152.5	500	
1525	5000	
3050	10 000	

A-520200-76-
COPYRIGHT BY
RAND McNALLY & COMPANY
MADE IN U.S.A.

0 25 50 75 100   200   300   400   500 Miles

0   100   200   400   600   800 Kilometers

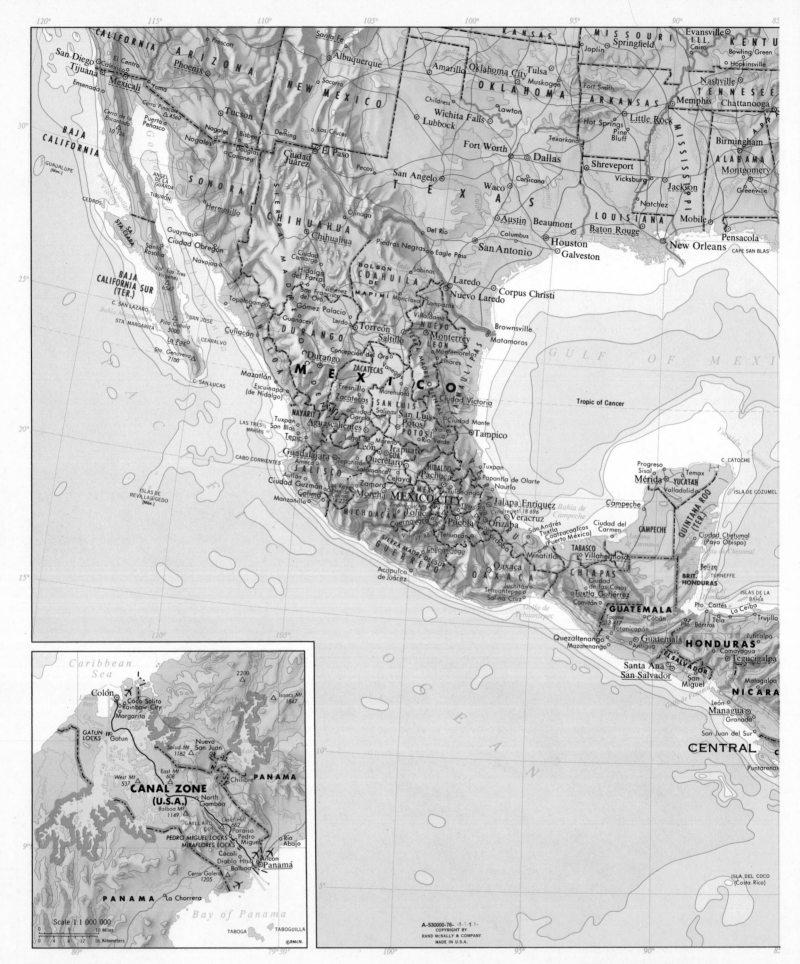

Scale 1:16 000 000; one inch to 250 miles. Polyconic Projection
Elevations and depressions are given in feet

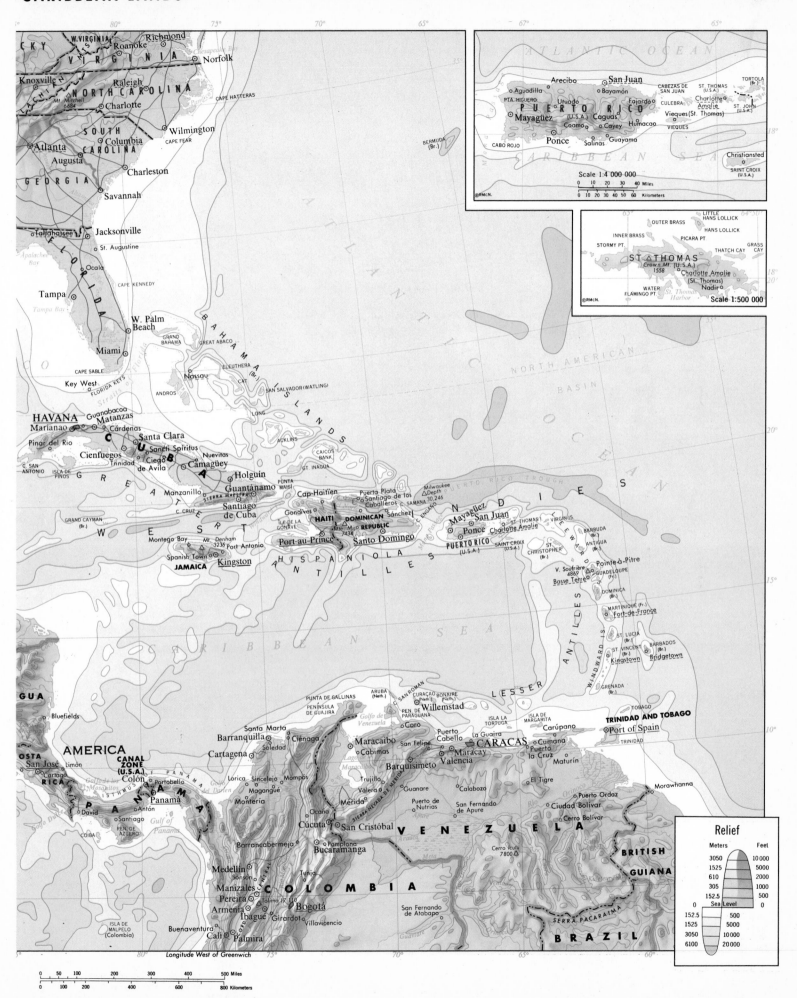

Puerto Rico inset

Scale 1:4 000 000

0 10 20 30 40 Miles
0 10 20 30 40 50 60 Kilometers

ⓇRMcN.

Aguadilla
PTA. HIGUERO
Arecibo · San Juan
Bayamón
Utuado
PUERTO RICO
(U.S.A.)
Mayagüez
Coamo
Caguas
Cayey
Humacao
CABEZAS DE
SAN JUAN
CULEBRA
Fajardo
Vieques (St. Thomas)
VIEQUES
ST. THOMAS
CHARLOTTE
AMALIE
ST. JOHN
(U.S.A.)
TORTOLA
(Br.)
CABO ROJO
Ponce
Salinas
Guayama
CARIBBEAN SEA
ATLANTIC OCEAN
Christiansted
SAINT CROIX
(U.S.A.)

St. Thomas inset

Scale 1:500 000

ⓇRMcN.

LITTLE HANS LOLLICK
OUTER BRASS · HANS LOLLICK
INNER BRASS · PICARA PT · THATCH CAY · GRASS CAY
STORMY PT.
ST. △ THOMAS
Crown Mt. (U.S.A.)
1558
Charlotte Amalie
(St. Thomas)
Nadir
WATER
FLAMINGO PT.
St. Thomas Harbor

Main map

KY
W. VIRGINIA
Roanoke
Richmond
Knoxville
VIRGINIA
Norfolk
RALEIGH
Raleigh
NORTH CAROLINA
Mt. Mitchell 6684
Charlotte
Wilmington
SOUTH
Columbia
CAROLINA
Atlanta
Augusta
GEORGIA
Charleston
Savannah
Chesapeake Bay
CAPE HATTERAS
CAPE FEAR
Tallahassee
Jacksonville
St. Augustine
Ocala
FLORIDA
Tampa
Tampa Bay
Apalachee Bay
CAPE KENNEDY
W. Palm Beach
Miami
CAPE SABLE
Key West
FLORIDA KEYS
Straits of Florida
GRAND BAHAMA
GREAT ABACO
BAHAMA ISLANDS
Nassau
ELEUTHERA (Br.)
CAT
ANDROS
LONG
SAN SALVADOR (WATLING)
ACKLINS
CAICOS BANK
GT. INAGUA
HAVANA
Guanabacoa
Matanzas
Marianao
Cárdenas
Pinar del Rio
Santa Clara
CUBA
Sancti Spíritus
Cienfuegos
Ciego de Avila
Nuevitas
Trinidad
Camagüey
Holguín
C. SAN ANTONIO
ISLA DE PINOS
GREAT
Manzanillo
SIERRA MAESTRA
Guantánamo
PUNTA MAISI
Cap-Haïtien
Puerto Plata
Santiago de los Caballeros
Milwaukee △ Depth 30,246
Sánchez
SAMANA
C. ENGAÑO
GRAND CAYMAN (Br.)
C. CRUZ
Santiago de Cuba
WEST
Montego Bay
Mt. Denham 3236
Port Antonio
Spanish Town
JAMAICA
Kingston
INDIES
Gonaïves
ÎLE DE LA GONÂVE
HAITI
Mte. Mijo 7434
Port-au-Prince
DOMINICAN REPUBLIC
Santo Domingo
HISPANIOLA
ANTILLES
Mayagüez
San Juan
Ponce
Charlotte Amalie
PUERTO RICO (U.S.A.)
PUERTO RICO TROUGH
ST. THOMAS
VIRGIN IS.
SAINT CROIX (U.S.A.)
ST. CHRISTOPHER (Br.)
Barbuda (Br.)
ANTIGUA (Br.)
LEEWARD
V. Soufrière 4869 △
Pointe-à-Pitre
Basse-Terre
GUADELOUPE (Fr.)
DOMINICA (Br.)
MARTINIQUE (Fr.)
Fort-de-France
ISLANDS
ATLANTIC OCEAN
NORTH AMERICAN BASIN
BERMUDA (Br.)
ST. LUCIA (Br.)
ST. VINCENT (Br.)
BARBADOS (Br.)
WINDWARD IS.
Kingstown
Bridgetown
GRENADA (Br.)
CARIBBEAN SEA
LESSER
ANTILLES
TOBAGO
PUNTA DE GALLINAS
ARUBA (Neth.)
C. SAN ROMAN
CURAÇAO (Neth.)
BONAIRE (Neth.)
PEN. DE PARAGUANÁ
Willemstad
ISLA LA TORTUGA
ISLA DE MARGARITA
Carúpano
TRINIDAD AND TOBAGO
Port of Spain
GUA
Bluefields
AMERICA
Santa Marta
Barranquilla
Cartagena
Ciénaga
Soledad
PENÍNSULA DE GUAJIRA
Golfo de Venezuela
Coro
Maracaibo
Cabimas
San Felipe
Puerto Cabello
La Guaira
CARACAS
Cumaná
Puerto la Cruz
TRINIDAD
Maracay
Valencia
Barquisimeto
Maturín
OSTA
San José
Limón
CANAL ZONE (U.S.A.)
Colón
Portobello
Lorica
Sincelejo
Mompós
Magangué
Valera
Guanare
Calabozo
El Tigre
Morawhanna
RICA
PANAMA
Panamá
Antón
Gulf of Panama
Golfo de los Mosquitos
GULF OF DARIEN
Montería
Trujillo
Mérida
SIERRA NEVADA DE MÉRIDA
Puerto de Nutrias
San Fernando de Apure
Puerto Ordaz
Ciudad Bolívar
Cerro Bolívar
David
Santiago
PEN. DE AZUERO
COIBA
Barrancabermeja
Ocaña
Cúcuta
San Cristóbal
Pamplona
Bucaramanga
VENEZUELA
Cerro Icutú 7800 △
BRITISH GUIANA
Medellín
Sonsón
Tunja
Meta
Manizales
COLOMBIA
Pereira
Tolima 17,110
Bogotá
San Fernando de Atabapo
Armenia
Ibagué
Girardot
Villavicencio
ISLA DE MALPELO (Colombia)
Buenaventura
Cali
Palmira
SERRA PACARAIMA
BRAZIL
Guaviare
ISTHMUS

Longitude West of Greenwich

0 50 100   200   300   400   500 Miles
0 100 200   400   600   800 Kilometers

Relief

Meters	Feet
3050	10 000
1525	5000
610	2000
305	1000
152.5	500
Sea Level	0
152.5	500
1525	5000
3050	10 000
6100	20 000

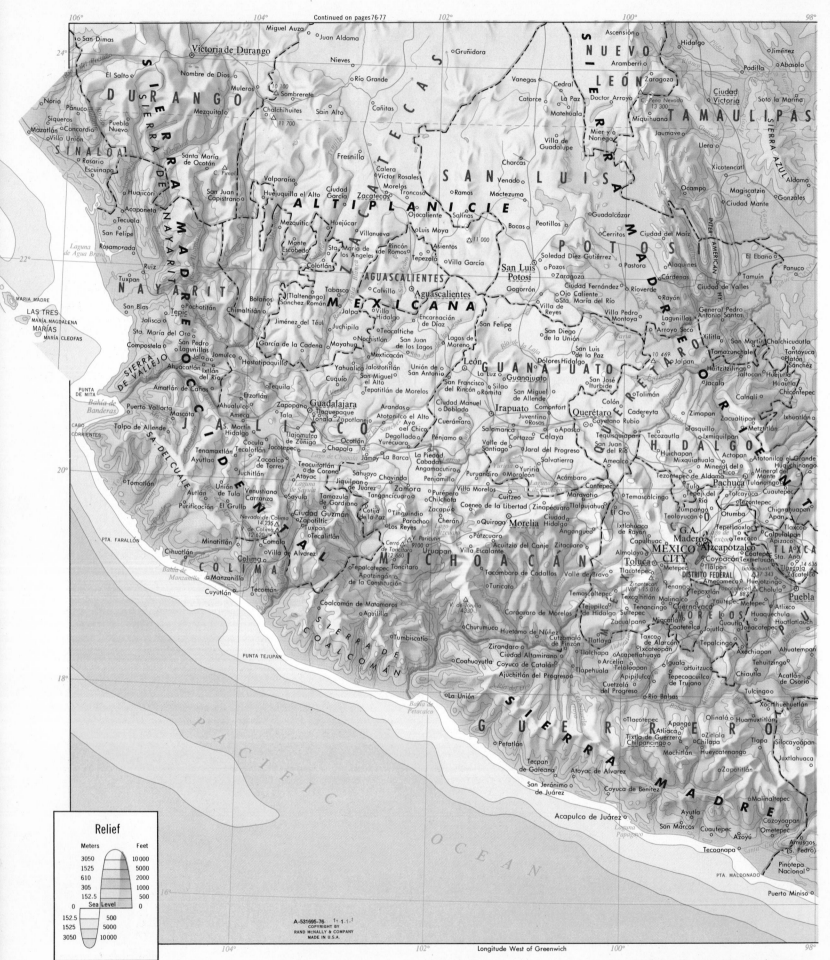

Continued on pages 76-77

Relief

Meters	Feet
3050	10 000
1525	5000
610	2000
305	1000
152.5	500
0 Sea Level	0
152.5	500
1525	5000
3050	10000

A-531695-76
COPYRIGHT BY
RAND McNALLY & COMPANY
MADE IN U.S.A.

Longitude West of Greenwich

Scale 1:4 000 000; one inch to 64 miles. Conic Projection
Elevations and depressions are given in feet

GULF OF MEXICO

BAHÍA DE CAMPECHE

Tropic of Cancer

Laguna Almagre

Laguna de San Andres

PTA. JEREZ

Altamira
Ciudad Madero
Tampico
Villa Cuauhtémoc
Tampico Alto

Laguna Tamiahua

CABO ROJO
ARRECIFE BLANQUILLA
ISLA DE LOBOS

Ozuluama
Tamiahua
Tancoco
Alamo
Túxpan

ARRECIFE TANQUIJO
ARRECIFE TÚXPAN

Tihuatlán
Poza Rica
Mecapalapa
Tecolutla
Furbero
Gutiérrez Zamora
Coyutla
Coxquihui
Nautla
Hueytlalpan
Cuetzalan del Progreso
Tlapacoyan
Vega de Alatorre
Zacatlán
Atempan
Misantla
Zacapoaxtla
Jalacingo
Teziutlán
Altotonga
Naolinco
Perote
Las Vigas
△14 048
Jalapa Enríquez
Libres
Nauhcampatépetl
PUNTA ZEMPOALA
Coatepec
Teocelo
Antigua Veracruz
PUEBLA
Huamantla
Malinalcueyetl
San Juan
Ixtenco
18 696
Huatusco
Coscomatepec
Citlaltépetl (Vol.)
Veracruz Llave
Tepeaca
Ciudad Serdán
Orizaba
Córdoba
Medellín
ARRECIFE CABEZA
Acatzingo de Hidalgo
Nogales
Omealca
Tlalixcoyan
Atoyatempan
Maltrata
Cotaxtla
Alvarado
Tlacotepec
San Martín (Vol.)
△6000
PTA. ZAPOTITLÁN
Tehuacán
Ajalpan
Zoquitlán
Tlacotálpan
Santiago Tuxtla
San Andrés Tuxtla
San Gabriel Chilac
Huatla de Jiménez
Ojitlán (S. Lucas)
Jalapo de Díaz (S. Felipe)
Cosamaloápan
Chacaltianguis
Catemaco
Pajapan
Chazumba
S. Miguel
Teotitlán del Camino
Tuxtepec
Tesechoacan
Soteapan
Coatzacoalcos (Puerto México)
Petlalcingo
Tepelmeme
Cuicatlán
Playa Vicente
San Juan Evangelista
Jáltipan
Minatitlán
Cosoleacaque
Huajuapan de León
Coixtlahuaca
Acayucan
Sayula
Texistepec
Tamazulapan del Progreso
Tejúpan (Santiago)
Jesús Carranza
Tlaxiaco
Nochíxtlan (Asunción)
Talea de Castro (San Miguel)
Puebla Viejo
Sta. María Asunción
Ixtlán de Juárez
Villa Alta (San Ildefonso)
ISTMO
Putla de Guerrero
Chalcatongo (Sta. Catarina)
San Mateo (Etlatongo)
Hidalgo Yalalag
Zempoaltépetl
11 142△
Zacatepec (Santiago)
DE
Itundujia Sta. Cruz
Yosonotú
Oaxaca de Juárez
Tlacolula de Matamoros
Zaachila
Zimatlán de Alvarez
Mazatlán (San Juan)
Guichicovi (San Juan)
TEHUANTEPEC
Yucuñuti (Sta. Catarina)
Ocotlán de Morelos
Sola de Vega (S. Miguel)
Táviche
Ejutla de Crespo
INTER-AMERICAN HY.
Ixtepec
Ixtaltepec (Asunción)
Zanatepec (Sto. Domingo)
Huazolotitlán (Sta. María)
Miahuatlán
Las Vacas
Jalapa del Marqués
Unión Hidalgo
Jamiltepec
Tehuantepec (Sto. Domingo)
Juchitán de Zaragoza
Ixhuatán (San Francisco)
SIERRA DE OAXACA
DEL SUR
Loxicha (Sta. Catarina)
Salina Cruz
Pluma Hidalgo
Golfo de Tehuantepec
Pochutla (San Pedro)
Puerto Ángel

OAXACA

YUCATÁN
Progreso
Sisal
Hunucmá
Mérida
Umán
Maxcanú
Halachó
Becal
Calkini
Dzitbalché
Hecelchakán

CAMPECHE
Lerma
Campeche
Seybaplaya
Champotón
Pustunich
Sabancuy
Chicbul
Mamantel

ISLA DEL CARMEN
San Pedro
Ciudad del Carmen
Frontera
PUNTA FONTERA
Paraíso
Allende
Comalcalco
Palizada
Jonuta
Balancán
MÉXICO
GUATEMALA
TABASCO
Cárdenas
Villahermosa
Cunduacán
San Carlos
Emiliano Zapata
Huimanguillo
Teapa
Tacotalpa
Palenque
Pichucalco
Tenosique
Chapultenango
Tecpatán
Yajalón
Simojovel
Pantepec
Bachajón
Compañía
Jitotol
Ocosingo
MESETA DE AGUA ESCONDIDA
Tuxtla Gutiérrez
9400
Cancuc
Berriozabal
Bohom
Oxchuc
Ciudad de las Casas
Ocozocoautla
Chiapa de Corzo
Suchiapa
Acala
Teopisca
Amatenango
Cintalapa
Las Cruces
Socoltenango
Las Rosas
Comitán
Venustiano Carranza
8202△
Villa Flores
Trinitaria
Arriaga
La Concordia
SA. CUCHUMATANES
Tonalá
GUATEMALA
CORD. DE CHIAPAS
SIERRA MADRE
Pijijiapan
Cuauhtémoc
Jacaltenango
Mapastepec
Escuintla
Huixtla

CHIAPAS

Continued on pages 92-93

Scale 1:1 000 000
0   5   10 Miles
0 4 8 12 16 Kilometers
®RMcN.

DISTRITO FEDERAL

MÉXICO
HIDALGO
TLAXCALA
PUEBLA
MORELOS

Morelos
Nicolás Romero
Cuautitlán
Tutitlán
Teotihuacán
Otumba
Apan
Cahuacán
Coacalco
Chiconautla
Pyramid of Teotihuacán
Calpulalpan
San Bartolo
Ixtlahuaca
Atizapán
Tlalnepantla
Tulpetlac
Tepetlaoxtoc
Jiquipilco
Cerro La Catedral 13 000
Mazatla
Tepotzotlán
San Jerónimo
Nanacamilpa
Temoaya
Atzcapotzalco
Gustavo A. Madero
Texcoco
Mimiapan
Chimalpa
MEXICO CITY
Coatlinchán
Naucalpan
Chicoloapan
Lago de Texcoco
Cuajimalpa
Ixtacalco
Huixquilucan
Villa Obregón
Ixtapalapa
Los Reyes
Río Frío
Texmelucan
Toluca
Lerma
Coyoacán
Ayotla
INTER-AMERICAN HY.
Contreras
Tláhuac
Ixtapaluca
Capultitlán
Metepec
Mexicalcingo
Tlálpan
Xochimilco
Cerro Muneco 12 655
San Andrés
Tecómitl
Chalco
Tlalmanalco
Almoloya
Ajusco
Topilejo
Milpa Alta
Nevado de Toluca (Z-inántecatl)
Cerro Ajusco 12 850
Oxtotepec
Ixtacihuatl 17 343
Coatepec
Tenango
Tenango
Amecameca
Tres Cumbres
Ozumba
Popocatépetl 17 883
Huitzilac
Tepoztlán
Tlalnepantla
Tlayacapan
Cuernavaca

Rio Lerma
Rio Grande

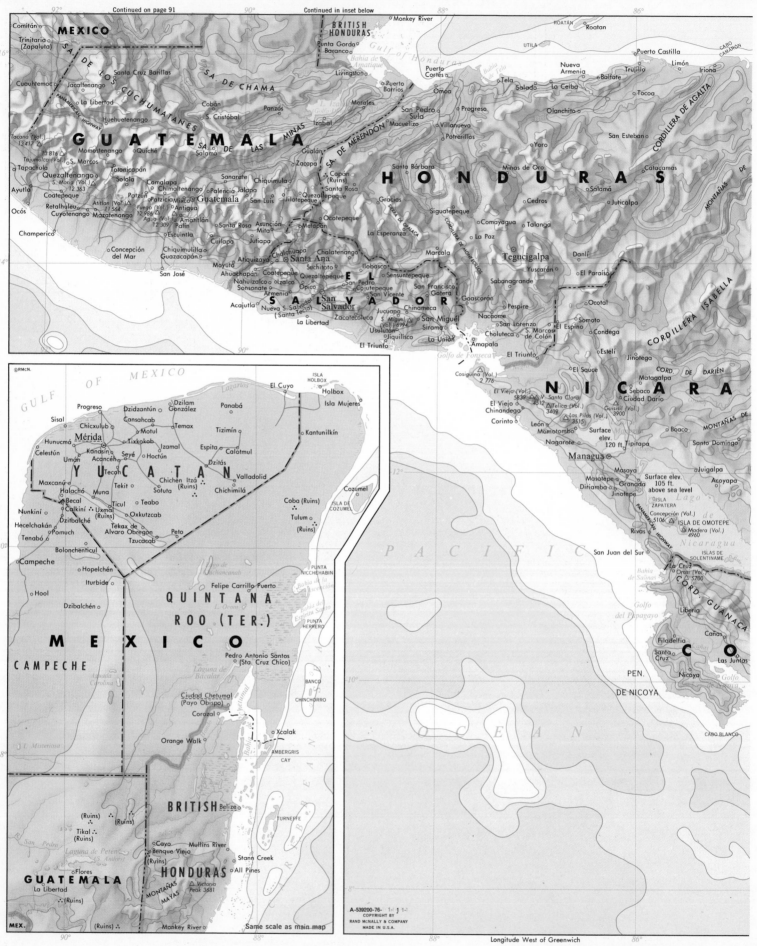

Continued on page 91
Continued in inset below

MEXICO

BRITISH
HONDURAS

GUATEMALA

HONDURAS

EL SALVADOR

NICARA

Tegucigalpa

Managua

GULF OF MEXICO

YUCATAN

MEXICO

CAMPECHE

QUINTANA
ROO (TER.)

GUATEMALA

BRITISH
HONDURAS

MEX.

Same scale as main map

PACIFIC OCEAN

Longitude West of Greenwich

Scale 1:4 000 000; one inch to 64 miles. Sinusoidal Projection

Elevations and depressions are given in feet

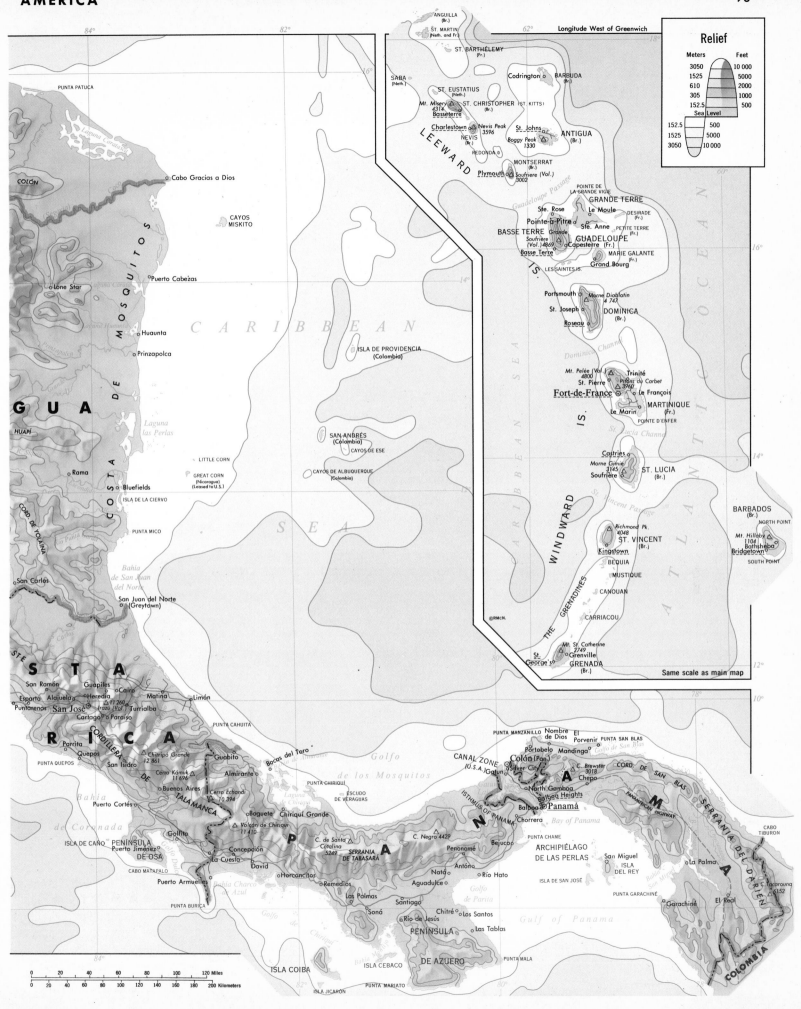

AMERICA

Longitude West of Greenwich

ANGUILLA (Br.)
ST. MARTIN (Neth. and Fr.)
ST. BARTHÉLEMY (Fr.)

SABA (Neth.)
Codrington • BARBUDA (Br.)

ST. EUSTATIUS (Neth.)
Mt. Misery 4314 △ ST. CHRISTOPHER (ST. KITTS)
Basseterre (Br.)

Charlestown ○ △ Nevis Peak 3596
NEVIS (Br.)
△ Boggy Peak 1330
REDONDA

St. Johns ○ ANTIGUA (Br.)

LEEWARD IS.

MONTSERRAT (Br.)
Plymouth ○ △ Soufriere (Vol.) 3002

Guadeloupe Passage

POINTE DE LA GRANDE VIGIE
Ste. Rose • Le Moule • GRANDE TERRE
Pointe-à-Pitre • DÉSIRADE (Fr.)
BASSE TERRE • Grande • Ste. Anne
Soufriere (Vol.) 4869 △ GUADELOUPE • Capesterre (Fr.)
Basse Terre ○ PETITE TERRE (Fr.)
LES SAINTES IS. • MARIE GALANTE (Fr.)
Grand Bourg

Portsmouth • △ Morne Diablotin 4747
St. Joseph • DOMINICA (Br.)
Roseau ○

Dominica Channel

CARIBBEAN SEA

ISLA DE PROVIDENCIA (Colombia)

Mt. Pelée (Vol.) 4800 • Trinité
St. Pierre ⊙ Pitons du Carbet 3960
Fort-de-France ○ MARTINIQUE (Fr.)
Le François
SAN ANDRÉS (Colombia)
CAYOS DE ESE
Le Marin • POINTE D'ENFER

St. Lucia Channel

LITTLE CORN
Castries ○
GREAT CORN (Nicaragua) (Leased to U.S.)
CAYOS DE ALBUQUERQUE (Colombia)
Morne Gimie 3145 △ ST. LUCIA (Br.)
Soufriere

St. Vincent Passage

BARBADOS (Br.)
NORTH POINT

Richmond Pk. 4048 △
ST. VINCENT (Br.)
Mt. Hillaby 1104 △ Bathsheba
Bridgetown ○
SOUTH POINT

Kingstown ○
BEQUIA

WINDWARD IS.

MUSTIQUE

CANOUAN

THE GRENADINES

CARRIACOU

© RMcN.

Mt. St. Catherine 2749 △ Grenville
St. George's ○ GRENADA (Br.)

ATLANTIC OCEAN

Same scale as main map

PUNTA PATUCA

COLÓN

Cabo Gracias a Dios

CAYOS MISKITO

○ Lone Star

Puerto Cabezas

MOSQUITOS

○ Huaunta

CARIBBEAN

○ Prinzapolca

GUA

HUAPÍ

Laguna las Perlas

○ Rama

COSTA DE

○ Bluefields

ISLA DE LA CIERVO

SEA

PUNTA MICO

San Carlos ○

Bahía de San Juan del Norte

San Juan del Norte (Greytown)

STA

RICA

San Ramón ○ Guapiles ○ Cairo ○
Esparta ○ Alajuela ○ Heredia ○ ○ Matina
Puntarenas ○ Irazú (Vol.) △ Turrialba
San José ○ 11 260 ○ Limón
Cartago ○ Paraíso

PUNTA CAHUITA

CORDILLERA

Parrita ○
Quepos ○
PUNTA QUEPOS
San Isidro ○
△ Chirripó Grande 12 861
DE
Cerro Kámuk △ 11 696
Buenos Aires ○ Cerro Echandi △ 10 394
TALAMANCA
Puerto Cortés ○
○ Boquete
○ Volcán de Chiriquí 11 410
Golfito ○
Concepción ○ △ C. de Santa Cotalina 5249
PENÍNSULA DE OSA
Puerto Jiménez ○
La Cuesta ○ David ○
SERRANÍA DE TABASARÁ
CABO MATAPALO
Puerto Armuelles ○
○ Horconcitos
PUNTA BURICA
Remedios ○
Las Palmas ○
Sona ○ Santiago ○
Chitré ○ ○ Los Santos
Río de Jesús ○
ISLA COIBA
PENÍNSULA DE AZUERO
Las Tablas ○
PUNTA MALA
ISLA CEBACO
PUNTA MARIATO
ISLA JICARÓN

Bocas del Toro
Guabito ○
Almirante ○
PUNTA CHIRIQUÍ
Chiriquí Grande ○
Laguna de Chiriquí
ESCUDO DE VERAGUAS

Golfo de los Mosquitos

PUNTA MANZANILLO • Nombre de Dios • El Porvenir • PUNTA SAN BLAS
CANAL ZONE (U.S.A.)
Portobelo ○ Mandinga ○ Golfo de San Blas
Colón (Pan.) ○ Gatún
Silver City ○ △ C. Brewster 3018
CORD. DE SAN BLAS
North Gamboa ○ Chepo ○
Balboa Heights ○
Balboa ○ △ Panamá
Chorrera ○
PANAMÁ
Bejuco ○
C. Negro △ 4429
Penonomé ○ Punta Chame
Natá ○ Antón ○
Río Hato ○
Aguadulce ○
ARCHIPIÉLAGO DE LAS PERLAS
San Miguel ○
ISLA DEL REY
PUNTA GARACHINÉ

Bay of Panama

Gulf of Panama

ISTHMUS OF PANAMÁ

PANAMERICAN HIGHWAY

SERRANÍA DEL DARIÉN

CABO TIBURÓN

○ La Palma
△ C. Tacarouna 6152
El Real ○
Garachiné ○

COLOMBIA

0 20 40 60 80 100 120 Miles
0 20 40 60 80 100 120 140 160 180 200 Kilometers

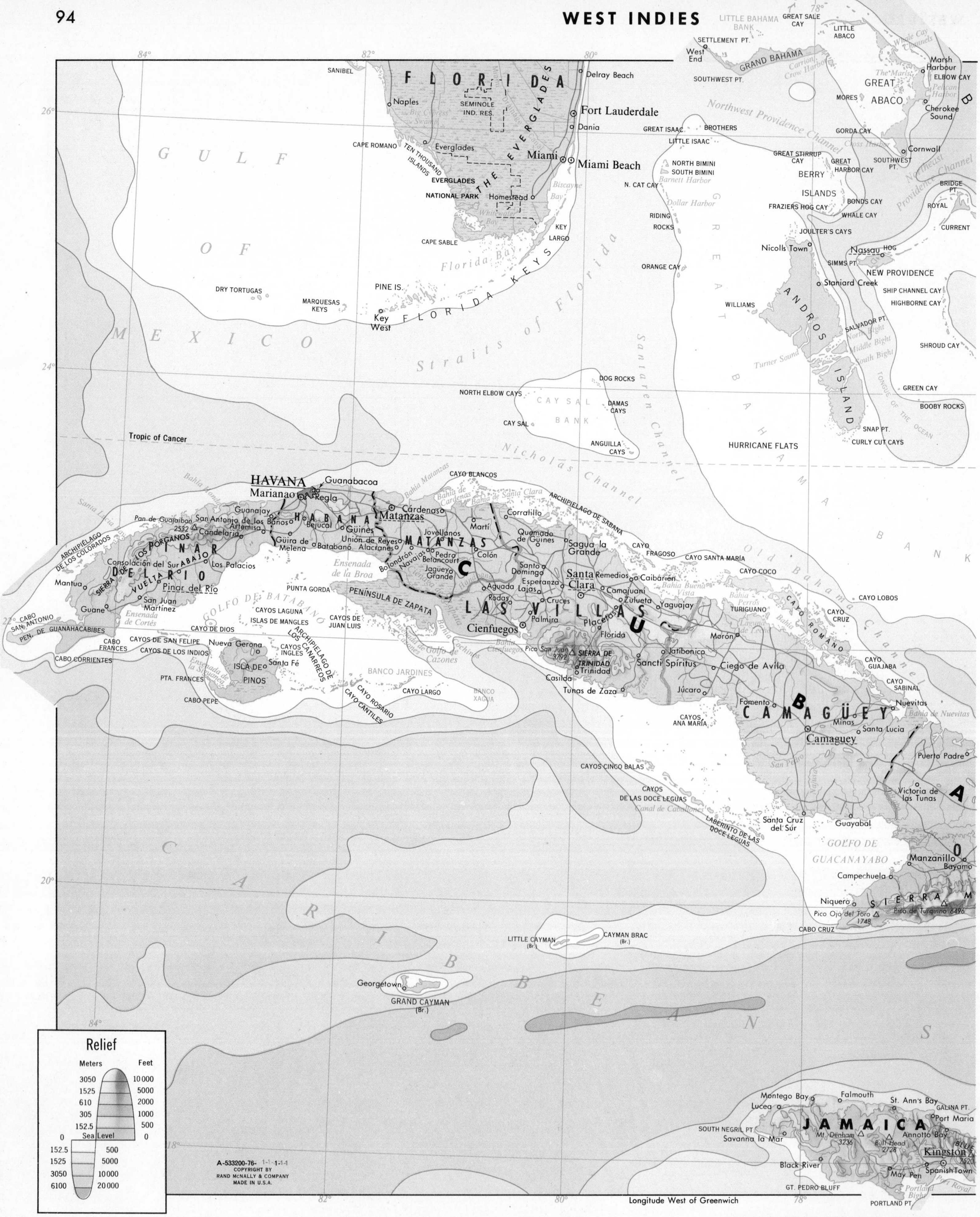

GULF OF MEXICO

FLORIDA

SANIBEL

Naples

Delray Beach

CAPE ROMANO
TEN THOUSAND ISLANDS

Everglades
SEMINOLE IND. RES.
BIG CYPRESS SWAMP
THE EVERGLADES

Fort Lauderdale
Dania

Miami
Miami Beach

EVERGLADES
NATIONAL PARK

Homestead

Biscayne Bay

CAPE SABLE

KEY LARGO

Florida Bay

DRY TORTUGAS

MARQUESAS KEYS

PINE IS.

Key West

FLORIDA KEYS

Straits of Florida

Tropic of Cancer

Santaren Channel

CAY SAL BANK
DOG ROCKS
NORTH ELBOW CAYS
CAY SAL
DAMAS CAYS
ANGUILLA CAYS

HURRICANE FLATS

Nicholás Channel

GREAT BAHAMA BANK
LITTLE BAHAMA BANK
GREAT SALE CAY
SETTLEMENT PT.
West End
GRAND BAHAMA
SOUTHWEST PT.
LITTLE ABACO
GREAT ABACO
MARSH HARBOUR
ELBOW CAY
Cherokee Sound
Cornwall
GORDA CAY
GREAT ISAAC
LITTLE ISAAC
BROTHERS
Northwest Providence Channel
GREAT STIRRUP CAY
GREAT HARBOR CAY
SOUTHWEST
BRIDGE PT.
BERRY ISLANDS
NORTH BIMINI
SOUTH BIMINI
Barnett Harbor
N. CAT CAY
Dollar Harbor
RIDING ROCKS
ORANGE CAY
FRAZIERS HOG CAY
BONDS CAY
WHALE CAY
ROYAL
CURRENT
JOULTER'S CAYS
Nicolls Town
Nassau
HOG
SIMMS PT.
NEW PROVIDENCE
Staniard Creek
SHIP CHANNEL CAY
HIGHBORNE CAY
WILLIAMS
ANDROS ISLAND
SALVADOR PT.
SHROUD CAY
Turner Sound
NORTH BIGHT
MIDDLE BIGHT
SOUTH BIGHT
GREEN CAY
TONGUE OF THE OCEAN
SNAP PT.
CURLY CUT CAYS
BOOBY ROCKS

HAVANA
Guanabacoa
Marianao
Regla
CAYO BLANCOS
Bahía de Matanzas
Bahía de Cárdenas
ARCHIPIÉLAGO DE SABANA
Pan de Guajaibon 2532
San Antonio de los Baños
Guanajay
Artemisa
Candelaria
HABANA
Bejucal
Güines
Güira de Melena
Batabanó
Unión de Reyes
Cárdenas
Matanzas
Jovellanos
Martí
Corralillo
Quemado de Güines
Sagua la Grande
CAYO FRAGOSO
CAYO SANTA MARÍA
Colón
MATANZAS
Pedro Betancourt
Jagüey Grande
Navajas
Bolondrón
Santo Domingo
Esperanza
Lajas
Aguada
Cruces
Rodas
Palmira
Santa Clara
Remedios
Caibarién
Camajuaní
Zulueta
Yaguajay
CAYO COCO
CAYO SANTA MARÍA
Bahía Buena Vista
Bahía Perros
CAYO LOBOS
PINAR DEL RIO
PÓRGANOS
Consolación del Sur
Los Palacios
Mantua
Guane
SIERRA
ABAJO
VUELTA
Pinar del Río
San Juan Martínez
ARCHIPIÉLAGO DE LOS COLORADOS
Santa María
CABO SAN ANTONIO
PEN. DE GUANAHACABIBES
CABO CORRIENTES
CABO FRANCÉS
Ensenada de Cortés
CAYOS DE SAN FELIPE
Nueva Gerona
CAYOS DE LOS INDIOS
ARCHIPIÉLAGO DE LOS CANARREOS
Santa Fé
ISLA DE PINOS
PTA. FRANCES
CABO PEPE
GOLFO DE BATABANÓ
CAYOS LAGUNA
ISLAS DE MANGLES
CAYOS DE JUAN LUIS
PUNTA GORDA
PENÍNSULA DE ZAPATA
CAYO DE DIOS
CAYO ROSARIO
CAYO CANTILES
CAYO LARGO
Banco Jardines
BANCO XAGUA
Ensenada de la Broa
Cienfuegos
LAS VILLAS
Placetas
Florida
Morón
TURIGUANO
CAYO ROMANO
CAYO GUAJABA
CAYO CRUZ
Jatibonica
Ciego de Ávila
Pico San Juan 3792
SIERRA DE TRINIDAD
Sancti Spíritus
Casilda
Trinidad
Tunas de Zaza
Júcaro
CAYO SABINAL
Nuevitas
Bahía de Nuevitas
Fomento
CAMAGÜEY
Minas
Santa Lucía
Camaguey
Puerto Padre
CAYOS ANA MARÍA
CAYOS CINCO BALAS
CAYOS DE LAS DOCE LEGUAS
Canal de Caballones
LABERINTO DE LAS DOCE LEGUAS
Santa Cruz del Sur
Guayabal
GOLFO DE GUACANAYABO
Campechuela
Niquero
SIERRA
Pico Ojo del Toro 1748
Pico de Turquino 6496
CABO CRUZ
Manzanillo
Bayamo
Victoria de las Tunas

CARIBBEAN SEA

LITTLE CAYMAN (Br.)
CAYMAN BRAC (Br.)
Georgetown
GRAND CAYMAN (Br.)

JAMAICA
Montego Bay
Falmouth
St. Ann's Bay
Lucea
GALINA PT.
Port Maria
SOUTH NEGRIL PT.
Mt. Denham 3236
Bull Head 2728
Annotto Bay
Savanna la Mar
Kingston
BLUE
Black River
May Pen
Spanish Town
GT. PEDRO BLUFF
PORTLAND PT.
PORTLAND BIGHT

Longitude West of Greenwich

Scale 1:4 000 000; one inch to 64 miles. Conic Projection
Elevations and depressions are given in feet.

Relief

Meters		Feet
3050		10 000
1525		5000
610		2000
305		1000
152.5		500
0	Sea Level	0
152.5		500
1525		5000
3050		10 000
6100		20 000

A-533200-76-
COPYRIGHT BY
RAND McNALLY & COMPANY
MADE IN U.S.A.

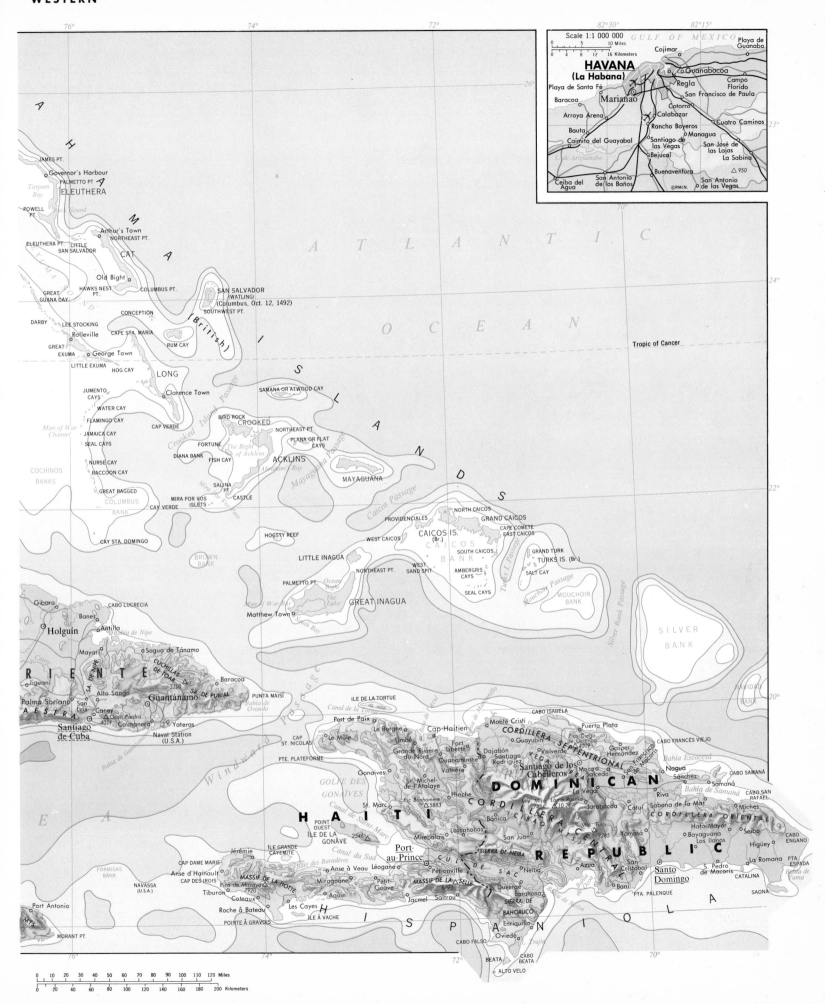

GULF OF MEXICO

Cojimar
Playa de Guanabo
Guanabacoa
Playa de Santa Fé
Regla
Baracoa
Marianao
Campo Florido
San Francisco de Paula
Cotorro
Arroya Arena
Calabazar
Cuatro Caminos
Bauta
Rancho Boyeros
Managua
Caimito del Guayabal
Santiago de las Vegas
San José de las Lajas
Bejucal
La Sabina
△ 950
Buenaventura
Ceiba del Agua
San Antonio de los Baños
San Antonio de las Vegas
©RMCN.

A T L A N T I C

JAMES PT.
Governor's Harbour
PALMETTO PT
ELEUTHERA
Tarpum Bay
POWELL PT.
Rock Sound
A
H
A
M
A

ELEUTHERA PT.
LITTLE SAN SALVADOR
CAT
Old Bight
HAWKS NEST PT.
COLUMBUS PT.
SAN SALVADOR
(WATLING)
(Columbus, Oct. 12, 1492)
SOUTHWEST PT.
O C E A N

GREAT GUANA CAY
CONCEPTIÓN
(British)
DARBY
LEE STOCKING
CAPE STA. MARIA
RUM CAY
Rolleville
GREAT EXUMA
George Town
Tropic of Cancer
LITTLE EXUMA
HOG CAY
LONG
JUMENTO CAYS
Clarence Town
WATER CAY
SAMANA OR ATWOOD CAY
FLAMINGO CAY
CAP VERDE
BIRD ROCK
CROOKED
I S L A N D S
JAMAICA CAY
FORTUNE
NORTHEAST PT.
PLANA OR FLAT CAYS
SEAL CAYS
DIANA BANK
FISH CAY
ACKLINS
NURSE CAY
RACCOON CAY
The Bight of Acklins
Abraham' Bay
GREAT RAGGED
SALINA PT.
MAYAGUANA
COLUMBUS BANK
CAY VERDE
MIRA POR VOS ISLETS
CASTLE
Mira Por Vos Pass
Mayaguana Passage
Man of War Channel
COCHINOS BANKS

CAY STA. DOMINGO
HOGSTY REEF
Caicos Passage
NORTH CAICOS
GRAND CAICOS
CAPE COMETE
BROWN BANK
PROVIDENCIALES
WEST CAICOS
CAICOS IS. (Br.)
EAST CAICOS
SOUTH CAICOS
LITTLE INAGUA
CAICOS BANK
GRAND TURK
TURKS IS. (Br.)
NORTHEAST PT.
WEST SAND SPIT
AMBERGRIS CAYS
SALT CAY
PALMETTO PT.
Ocean Bight
The Lake
SEAL CAYS
MOUCHOIR BANK
Matthew Town
GREAT INAGUA
South Bay
Man of War Bay
Mouchoir Passage
SILVER BANK

Gibara
CABO LUCRECIA
Holguín
Banes
Antilla
Bahía de Nipe
Mayarí
Sagua de Tánamo
CUCHILLAS DE TOAR
△ 3100
Baracoa
R I E N T E
SA. DE NIPE
Alto Songo
Guantánamo
PUNTA MAISÍ
NAVIDAD BANK
Jiguaní
SA. DE PURIAL
Bahía de Ovando
Palma Soriano
San Luis
Caney
△ Gran Piedra
ILE DE LA TORTUE
Caimanera
Yateras
Santiago de Cuba
Naval Station (U.S.A.)
Canal de la Tortue
CABO ISABELA
Port de Paix
AESTRA
Bahía de Guantánamo
Le Môle
Cap-Haitien
Monte Cristi
Puerto Plata
CORDILLERA SEPTENTRIONAL
CABO FRANCÉS VIEJO
CAP ST. NICOLAS
Le Borgne
Limbé
Fort Liberté
Pico Diego de Ocampo △4009
Guayubin
Gasper Hernández
Windward Passage
Grande Riviere du Nord
Valverde
VEGA
San Francisco de Macoris
Ouanaminthe
Dajabón
Bahía Escocesa
PTE. PLATEFORME
Vallière
Santiago Rodriguez
Santiago de los Caballeros
Salcedo
Moca
Gonaives
Riva
Nagua
CABO SAMANÁ
GOLFE DES GONAIVES
St. Michel-de-l'Atalaye
La Vega
CABO SAN RAFAEL
HAITI
Pic Bonhomme
Hinche
Mte. Miée △10,249
Loma Rucilla
DOMINICAN
Samaná
Bahía de Samaná
St. Marc
Jarabacoa
Cotui
Sabana de la Mar
POINT OUEST
ILE DE LA GONÂVE
Mirebalais
Lascahobas
CORDILLERA CENTRAL
Bánica
Bonao
Los Llanos
Miches
CORDILLERA ORIENTAL
Jérémie
ILE GRANDE CAYEMITE
△2548
Mte. Tina △9285
Hato Mayor
Bayaguana
Seibo
Port-au-Prince
Petionville
San Juan
Yamasá
REPUBLIC
Higüey
CABO ENGANO
Anse d'Hainault
MASSIF DE LA HOTTE
Pico de Macaya △7720
Miragoâne
Petit Goave
Léogane
MASSIF DE LA SELLE △8793
SIERRA DE NEIBA
Azua
San Cristóbal
Bani
La Romana
PTA. ESPADA
CAP DAME MARIE
CAP DES IROIS
Neiba
GUL DE SAC
Santo Domingo
S. Pedro de Macoris
CATALINA
Bahía de Yuma
NAVASSA (U.S.A.)
Tiburon
Coteaux
Aquin
Duverge
Barahona
SIERRA DE BAHORUCO
PTA. PALENQUE
SAONA
FORMIGAS BANK
Roche à Bateau
Les Cayes
ILE À VACHE
Jacmel
Saltrou
Enriquillo
L. Trujin
Port Antonio
POINTE À GRAVOIS
H I S P A N I O L A
MORANT PT.
BEATA
CABO FALSO
Oviedo
CABO BEATA
ALTO VELO

SOUTH AMERICA

Longitude West of Greenwich

Scale 1:40 000 000; one inch to 630 miles. Lambert's Azimuthal, Equal Area Projection
Elevations and depressions are given in feet

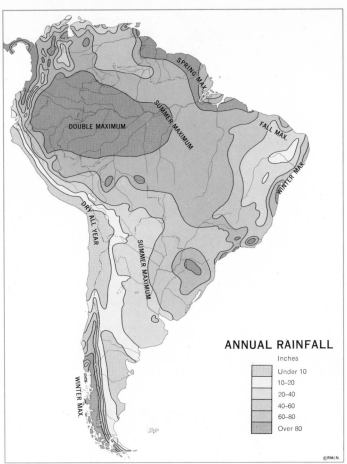

SPRING MAX.

SUMMER MAXIMUM

DOUBLE MAXIMUM

FALL MAX.

WINTER MAX.

DRY ALL YEAR

SUMMER MAXIMUM

WINTER MAX.

ANNUAL RAINFALL

Inches

	Under 10
	10–20
	20–40
	40–60
	60–80
	Over 80

©RMCN.

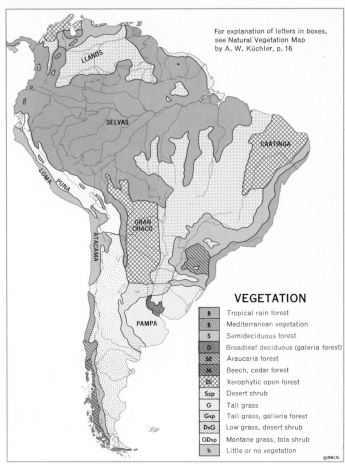

For explanation of letters in boxes,
see Natural Vegetation Map
by A. W. Küchler, p. 16

LLANOS

SELVAS

CAATINGA

LOMA

PUNA

ATACAMA

GRAN CHACO

PAMPA

VEGETATION

B	Tropical rain forest
B	Mediterranean vegetation
S	Semideciduous forest
D	Broadleaf deciduous (galeria forest)
SE	Araucaria forest
M	Beech, cedar forest
Di	Xerophytic open forest
Szp	Desert shrub
G	Tall grass
Gsp	Tall grass, galleria forest
DsG	Low grass, desert shrub
GDsp	Montane grass, tola shrub
b	Little or no vegetation

©RMCN.

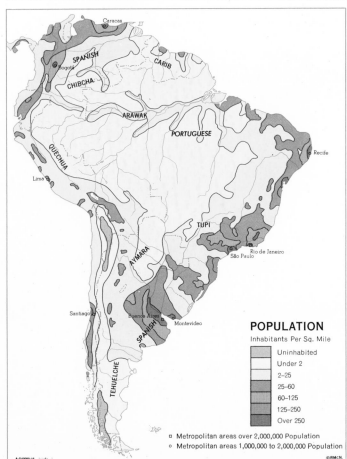

Caracas

SPANISH

Bogotá

CHIBCHA

CARIB

ARAWAK

PORTUGUESE

QUECHUA

Lima

Recife

TUPI

Rio de Janeiro
São Paulo

AYMARA

Santiago

Buenos Aires
Montevideo

SPANISH

TEHUELCHE

POPULATION

Inhabitants Per Sq. Mile

	Uninhabited
	Under 2
	2–25
	25–60
	60–125
	125–250
	Over 250

□ Metropolitan areas over 2,000,000 Population
○ Metropolitan areas 1,000,000 to 2,000,000 Population

A-540000-16 |-|-|-1-|

©RMCN.

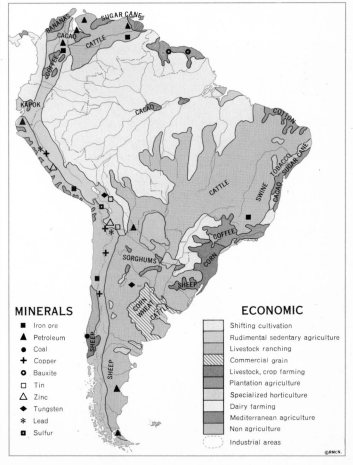

BANANAS
CACAO
COFFEE
KAPOK

SUGAR CANE

CATTLE

CACAO

CATTLE

COTTON

SWINE   TOBACCO   SUGAR CANE   CACAO

COFFEE

CORN

SORGHUMS

SHEEP

CORN
WHEAT
CATTLE

SHEEP

SHEEP

MINERALS

■ Iron ore
▲ Petroleum
● Coal
+ Copper
○ Bauxite
□ Tin
△ Zinc
◆ Tungsten
✳ Lead
⊡ Sulfur

ECONOMIC

	Shifting cultivation
	Rudimental sedentary agriculture
	Livestock ranching
	Commercial grain
	Livestock, crop farming
	Plantation agriculture
	Specialized horticulture
	Dairy farming
	Mediterranean agriculture
	Non agriculture
	Industrial areas

©RMCN.

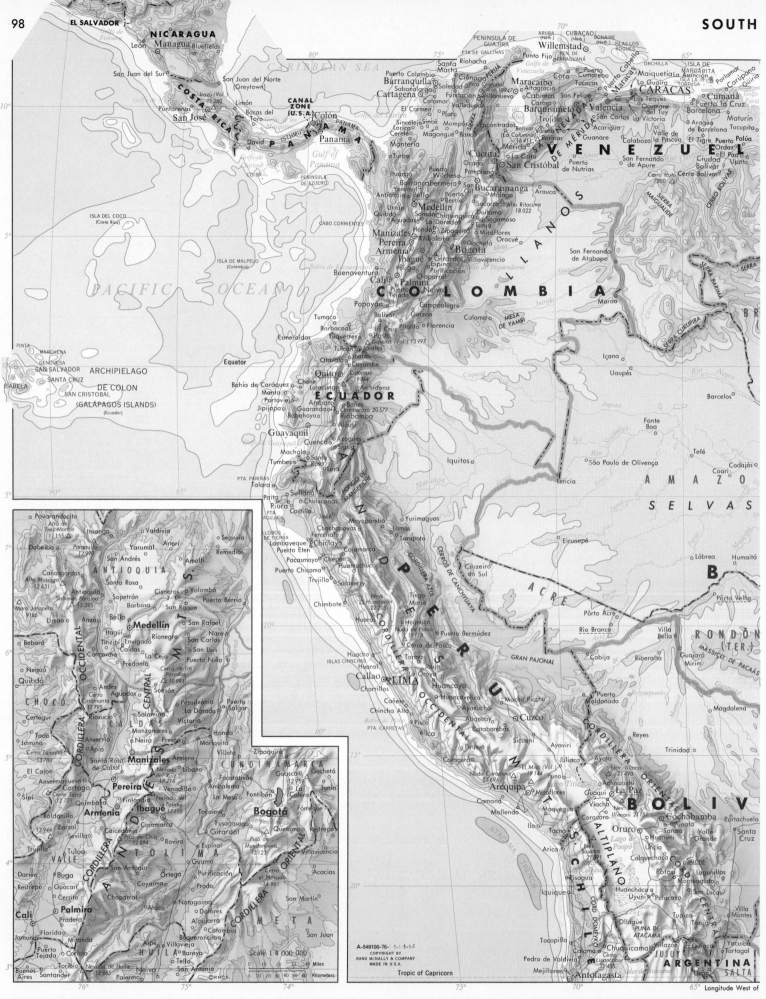

Scale 1:16 000 000; one inch to 250 miles. Sinusoidal Projection
Elevations and depressions are given in feet

Longitude West of

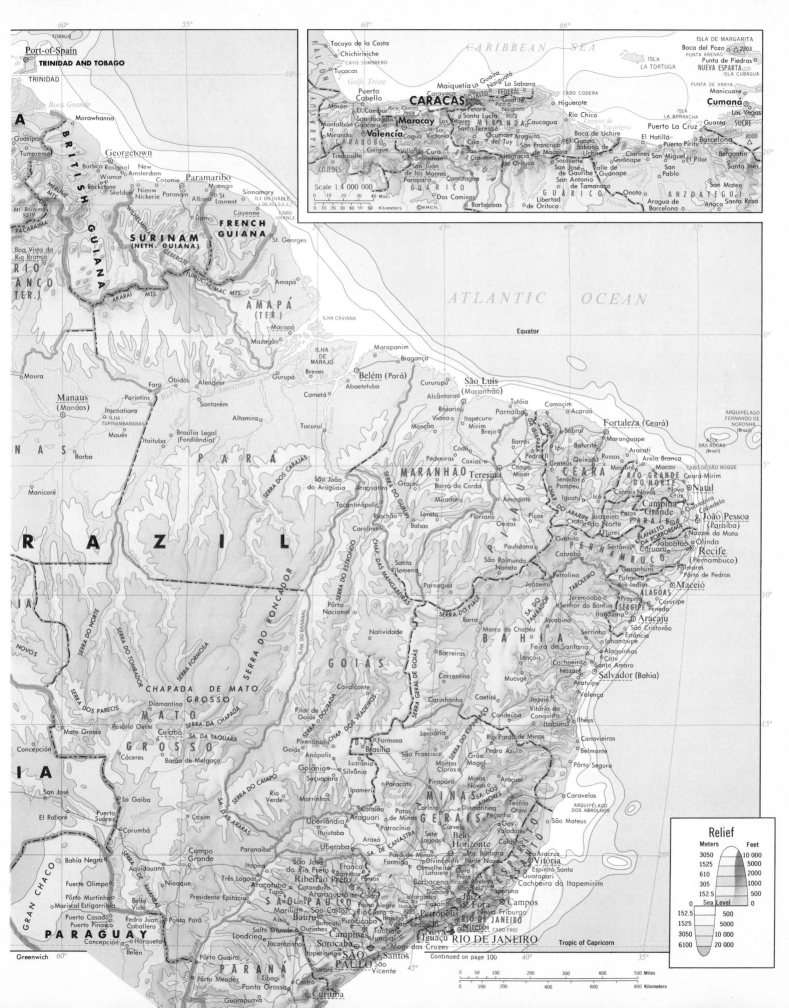

TRINIDAD AND TOBAGO
Port-of-Spain
TRINIDAD

CARACAS

Cumaná

Maracay

Valencia

BRITISH GUIANA
Georgetown
New Amsterdam

SURINAM (NETH. GUIANA)
Paramaribo

FRENCH GUIANA
Cayenne

Manaus (Manáos)

AMAPÁ (TER.)

PARÁ

ATLANTIC OCEAN

Equator

Belém (Pará)

São Luís (Maranhão)

Fortaleza (Ceará)

MARANHÃO
Teresina

CEARÁ

RIO GRANDE DO NORTE
Natal

PARAÍBA
João Pessoa (Paraíba)

PERNAMBUCO
Recife (Pernambuco)

BRAZIL

ALAGOAS
Maceió

SERGIPE
Aracaju

BAHIA
Salvador (Bahia)

GOIÁS

CHAPADA DE MATO GROSSO

MATO GROSSO

Brasília

MINAS GERAIS
Belo Horizonte

ESPÍRITO SANTO
Vitória

RIO DE JANEIRO

SÃO PAULO

PARANÁ
Curitiba

PARAGUAY

GRAN CHACO

Tropic of Capricorn

Continued on page 100

Relief
Meters / Feet
3050 / 10 000
1525 / 5000
610 / 2000
305 / 1000
152.5 / 500
Sea Level / 0
152.5 / 500
1525 / 5000
3050 / 10 000
6100 / 20 000

ISLA DE MARGARITA
NUEVA ESPARTA

CARIBBEAN SEA

Scale 1:4 000 000

0 10 20 30 40 Miles
0 10 20 30 40 50 60 Kilometers

0 50 100 200 300 400 500 Miles
0 100 200 400 600 800 Kilometers

Greenwich

Continued on pages 98-99

Relief

Meters	Feet
3050	10 000
1525	5000
610	2000
305	1000
152.5	500
0 Sea Level	0
152.5	500 Below
1525	Sea Level
3050	5000
6100	10 000
	20 000

0   50   100   200   300   400   500 Miles
0   100   200   400   600   800 Kilometers

BUENOS AIRES

Scale 1:1 000 000
0   5   10 Miles
0   4   8   12   16 Kilometers

©R.M.C.N.

SERRA DAS ARARAS

RIO DE JANEIRO

Scale 1:1 000 000
0   5   10 Miles
0   4   8   12   16 Kilometers

©R.M.C.N.

A-549200-76- 1- 1-1-1
COPYRIGHT BY
RAND McNALLY & COMPANY
MADE IN U.S.A.
Longitude West of Greenwich

Scale 1:16 000 000; one inch to 250 miles. Sinusoidal Projection
Elevations and depressions are given in feet

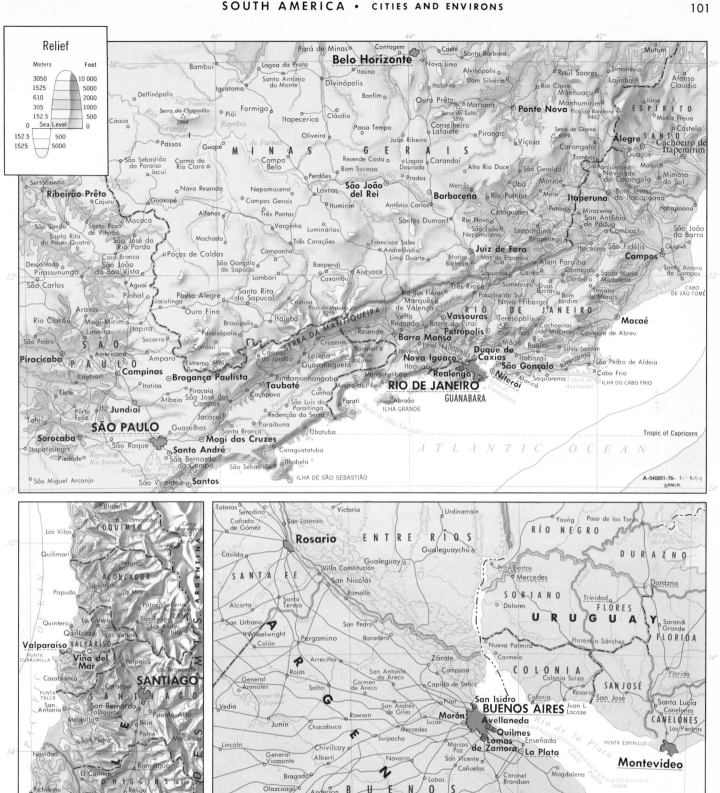

Relief

Meters	Feet
3050	10 000
1525	5000
610	2000
305	1000
152.5	500
0 Sea Level	0
152.5	500
1525	5000

Bambuí
Pará de Minas
Contagem
Caeté
Santa Bárbara
Mutum
Belo Horizonte
Nova Lima
Alvinópolis
Simonésia
Lagoa da Prata
Santo Antônio do Monte
Itaúna
Raúl Soares
Lajinha
Afonso Claudio
Delfinópolis
Iguatama
Divinópolis
Itabirito
Dom Silvério
Rio Casca
Manhuaçu
Manhumirim
ESPIRITO
Piúi
Formiga
Itapecerica
Cláudio
Bonfim
Ouro Prêto
Mariana
Serra do Salto
5896
Pico da Bandeira
9462
Iúna
Muniz Freire
Ponte Nova
Piranga
Serra de Grama
6099
SANTO
Cássia
Passa Tempo
Conselheiro Lafaiete
Alegre
Castelo
Cachoeiro de Itapemirim
Passos
Guapé
MINAS GERAIS
João Ribeiro
Carangola
Porciúncula
Navidade do Carangola
Muqui
Mimoso do Sul
Sertãozinho
Carmo do Rio Claro
Perdões
Bom Sucesso
Lagoa Dourada
Viçosa
Ubá
Tombos
Muriaé
Ribeirão Prêto
Cajuru
Nova Resende
Campo Belo
Alto Rio Doce
São Geraldo
Rio Pomba
Italva
São Fidélis
São Simão
Mocóca
Alfenas
Três Pontas
Lavras
Santos Dumont
Leopoldina
Pirapetinga
Itaocara
Miracema
Campos
São João da Barra
Santa Rosa de Viterbo
São José do Rio Pardo
Campos Gerais
Itumirim
Antônio Carlos
São João Nepomuceno
Cataguases
Santo Amaro de Campos
Descalvado
Casa Branca
Machado
Varginha
Luminárias
Francisco Sales
Andrelândia
Mar de Espanha
Palma
Cantagalo
Santa Maria Madalena
CABO DE SÃO TOMÉ
Pirassununga
São João da Boa Vista
Poços de Caldas
Campanha
Juiz de Fora
Matias Barbosa
Alem Paraíba
Cordeiro
São Carlos
Aguaí
Baependi
Lima Duarte
Carmo
Trajano de Morais
Macaé
Rio Claro
Mogi-Mirim
Limeira
Pinhal
Pouso Alegre
Santa Rita do Sapucaí
Caxambú
Sumidouro
Duas Barras
Araras
Itapira
Jacutinga
São Gonçalo do Sapucaí
Aiuruoca
Rio das Flores
Três Rios
Paraíba do Sul
Bom Jardim
Nova Friburgo
Cordeiro
São Pedro
Piracicaba
SÃO
Socorro
Ouro Fino
Cristina
Pico do Itatiaia
9255
Marquês de Valença
RIO DE JANEIRO
Teresópolis
Cachoeiras de Macacu
Casimiro de Abreu
Campinas
Amparo
Extrema 6890
Brasópolis
Itajubá
Volta Redonda
Vassouras
Barra do Piraí
Petrópolis
Serra dos Órgãos 7359
Rio Bonito
Silva Jardim
São Pedro de Aldeia
PAULO
Paraisópolis
SERRA DA MANTIQUEIRA
Campos do Jordão
Barra Mansa
Piraí
Mangaratiba
Magé
Itaboraí
Cabo Frio
Bragança Paulista
Itatiba
Piracaia
Lorena
Resende
Bananal
Nova Iguaçu
Duque de Caxias
Araruama
Lagoa de Araruama
Americana
Atibaia
São José dos Campos
Taubaté
Guaratinguetá
Itaguaí
São Gonçalo
ILHA DO CABO FRIO
Sorocaba
Tietê
Jundiaí
Mogi das Cruzes
Pindamonhangaba
Cunha
Angra dos Reis
Realengo
Niterói
Pôrto Feliz
Itu
Jacareí
Caçapava
São Luís do Paraitinga
RIO DE JANEIRO
Maricá
Saquarema
Tatuí
Guarulhos
Redenção da Serra
Parati
Abraão
GUANABARA
Bahia de Guanabara
SÃO PAULO
São Roque
São Branca
Paraibuna
Ubatuba
ILHA GRANDE
Tropic of Capricorn
Itapetininga
Piedade
São Bernardo do Campo
Mogi das Cruzes
Caraguatatuba
Represa de Rio Sorocaba
São Miguel Arcanjo
Santo André
ATLANTIC OCEAN
Represa de Guarapiranga
São Sebastião
Ilhabela
A-540051-76- 1-1-1-1
©RMcN
Sorocaba
Santo André
São Vicente
Santos
ILHA DE SÃO SEBASTIÃO

Illapel
Totoras
Serodino
Victoria
Young
Paso de los Toros
Salamanca
Cañada de Gómez
San Lorenzo
Urdinarrain
RÍO NEGRO
Los Vilos
COQUIMBO
Cerro Mercedario 22,211
Rosario
ENTRE RÍOS
Embalse del Río Negro
DURAZNO
Quilimari
Casilda
Gualeguay
Gualeguaychú
Fray Bentos
Mercedes
Petorca
Villa Constitución
Durazno
Quintero
ACONCAGUA
San Nicolás
SORIANO
Trinidad
FLORES
URUGUAY
Papudo
La Ligua
La Mora
Alcorta
Santa Teresa
Ramallo
Dolores
Sarandí Grande
Cerro Aconcagua 22,834
Putaendo
San Felipe
Los Andes Portillo
San Pedro
San Urbano
FLORIDA
Valparaíso
VALPARAISO
Quillota
Las Vegas
Wheelwright
Colón
Zárate
Nueva Palmira
Carmelo
Viña del Mar
Polpaico
Pérgamo
Baradero
COLONIA
Colonia Suiza
Florida
Casablanca
Arrecifes
Campana
Rojas
San Antonio de Areco
Capilla de Señor
Rosario
San José
Santa Lucía
General Arenales
Salto
Carmen de Areco
San Isidro
BUENOS AIRES
Juan L. Lacaze
CANELONES
Vedia
Pilar
San Andrés de Giles
Morón
Colonia
PUNTA ESPINILLO
Las Piedras
SANTIAGO
Curacaví
ARGENTINA
Avellaneda
Junín
Rawson
Luján
Mercedes
Quilmes
Ensenada
San Bernardo
Talagante
Melipilla
Boín
Puente Alto
Chacabuco
Suipacha
Lomas de Zamora
La Plata
Montevideo
San Pedro
Lincoln
Chivilcoy
Alberti
Navarro
Marcos Paz
San Vicente
Cañuelas
Magdalena
PUNTA PIEDRAS
Navidad
Rancagua
Bragado
Lobos
Coronel Brandsen
PUNTA INDIO
O'HIGGINS
Cerro Palomo 4,800
Reñgo
Peléquen
General Viamonte
Olazcoaga
Anderson
Roque Pérez
Monte
Altamirano
San Fernando
Nueve de Julio
Veinticinco de Mayo
General Belgrano
General Paz
Chascomús
Papinas
COLCHAGUA
Cerro Tinguiririca 13,845
Saladillo
BUENOS
Carlos Casares
ATLANTIC
Pichilemu
San Vicente
Bolívar
AIRES
Las Flores
Castelli
OCEAN
Bahia Samborombón
Licantén
Curepto
San Enrique
General Alvear
Chascomús
PUNTA NORTE
CHILE
El Carmen
General Guido
Molina
Tapalqué
Cachari
Dolores
General Lavalle
Santa Cruz
San Fernando
Talca
San Javier
Panimávida
Cerro Campanario 13,130
Maipú
Azul
Rauch
General Conesa
TALCA
Mariposa
Linares
Longitude West of Greenwich

0 10 20 30 40 50 60 70 80 90 100 110 120 Miles
0 20 40 60 80 100 120 140 160 180 200 Kilometers

Relief

Meters	Feet
3050	10 000
1525	5000
610	2000
305	1000
152.5	500
0 Sea Level	0 Sea Level
152.5	500 Below Sea Level
1525	5000
3050	10 000

Longitude West of Greenwich   Longitude East of Greenwich   Continued on pages 164-165

Scale 1: 16 000 000; one inch to 250 miles. Conic Projection
Elevations and depressions are given in feet

0 50 100   200   300   400   500 Miles
0   100   200   400   600   800 Kilometers

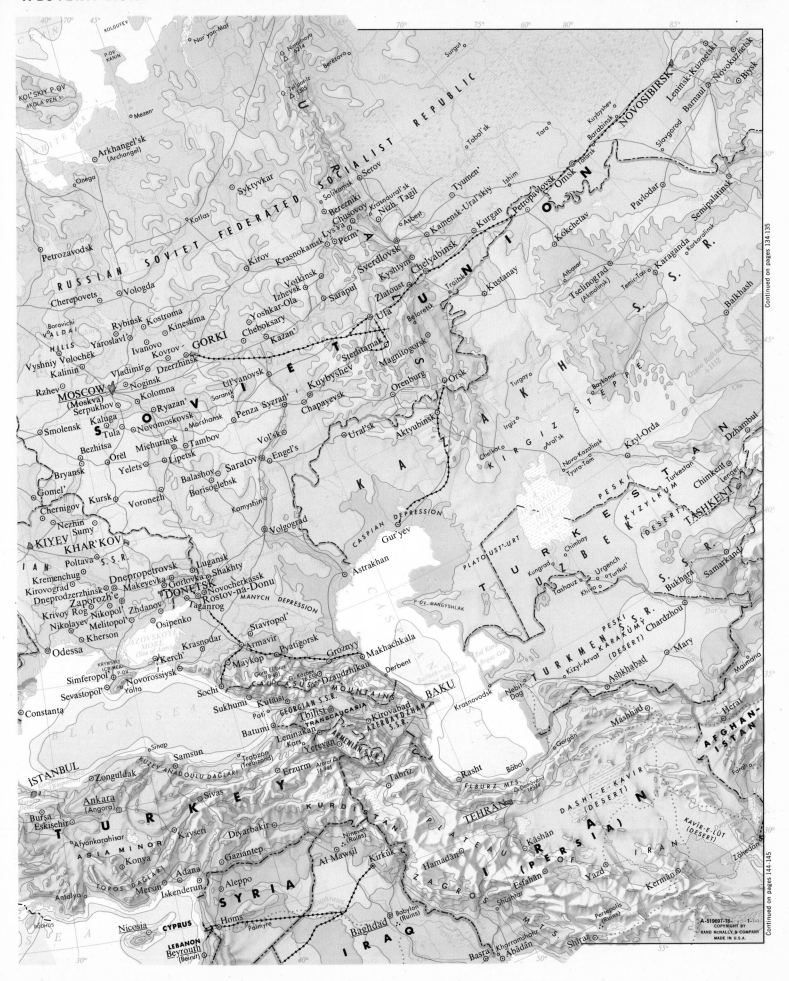

Continued on pages 134-135

Continued on pages 144-145

Scale 1:16 000 000; one inch to 250 miles. Conic Projection
Elevations and depressions are given in feet.

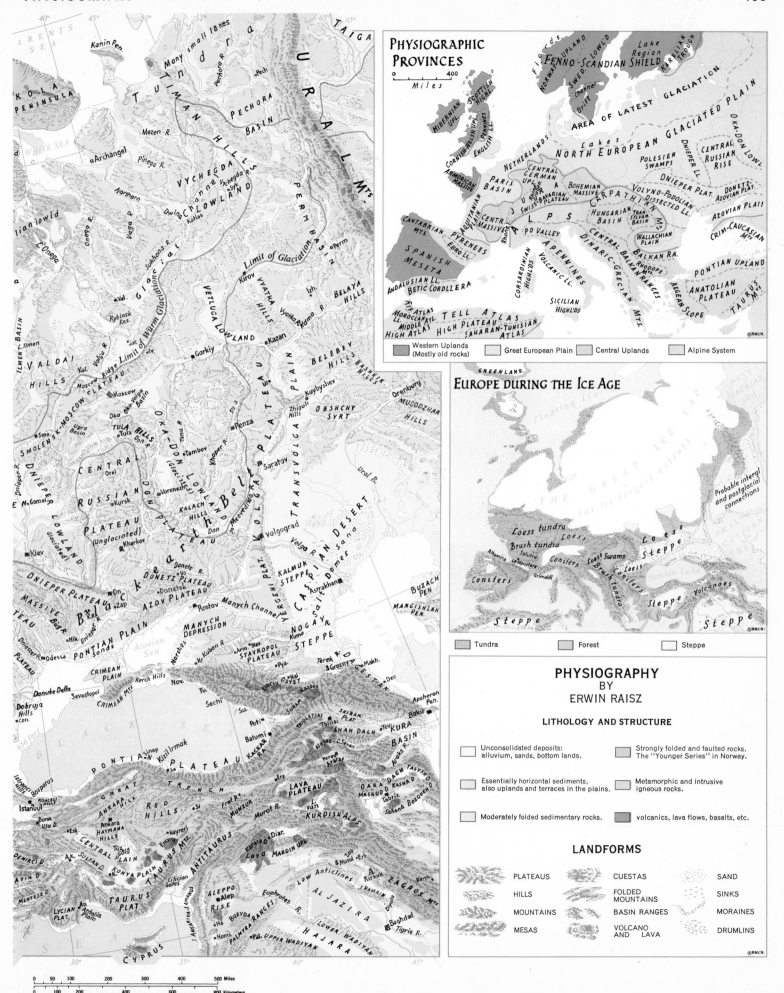

PHYSIOGRAPHIC PROVINCES

0 400
Miles

Western Uplands (Mostly old rocks) | Great European Plain | Central Uplands | Alpine System

EUROPE DURING THE ICE AGE

THE GREAT ICE CAP (at its largest extent)

Probable intergl and postglacial connections

Tundra | Forest | Steppe

PHYSIOGRAPHY
BY
ERWIN RAISZ

LITHOLOGY AND STRUCTURE

Unconsolidated deposits: alluvium, sands, bottom lands.

Essentially horizontal sediments, also uplands and terraces in the plains.

Moderately folded sedimentary rocks.

Strongly folded and faulted rocks. The "Younger Series" in Norway.

Metamorphic and intrusive igneous rocks.

volcanics, lava flows, basalts, etc.

LANDFORMS

PLATEAUS | CUESTAS | SAND

HILLS | FOLDED MOUNTAINS | SINKS

MOUNTAINS | BASIN RANGES | MORAINES

MESAS | VOLCANO AND LAVA | DRUMLINS

0 50 100   200   300   400   500 Miles
0   100   200   400   600   800 Kilometers

MAJOR LAND USES

Cropland-wheat important	Oases and important cotton areas
Cropland-rye important	Chiefly pasture land (meadow, alpine pastures) with some cropland
Cropland-corn important	Sparse pasture land (heath, maquis, steppe)
Cropland-oats and barley important	Sparse grass, desert shrub; seasonally grazed
Cropland and pasture with some woodland	Tundra; seasonally grazed
Intensive grape culture for wine	Forest and woodland
Mediterranean agriculture (including olives, grapes, grains and specialized vegetables)	Waste and unproductive areas

COPYRIGHT BY
RAND McNALLY & COMPANY
MADE IN U.S.A.

0 100 200 300 400 500 600 Miles

0 200 400 600 800 1000 Kilometers

Scale 1:20,000,000; one inch to 315 miles Conic Projection

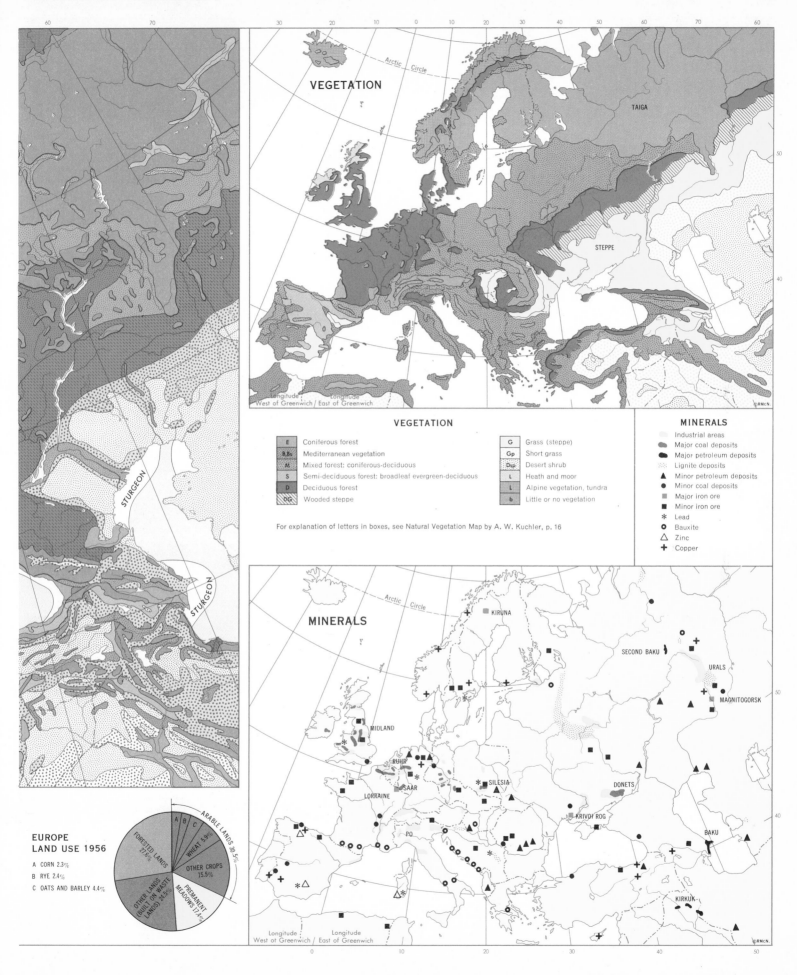

VEGETATION

E	Coniferous forest	G	Grass (steppe)
B,Bs	Mediterranean vegetation	Gp	Short grass
M	Mixed forest: coniferous-deciduous	Dsp	Desert shrub
S	Semi-deciduous forest: broadleaf evergreen-deciduous	L	Heath and moor
D	Deciduous forest	L	Alpine vegetation, tundra
DG	Wooded steppe	b	Little or no vegetation

For explanation of letters in boxes, see Natural Vegetation Map by A. W. Kuchler, p. 16

MINERALS

- Industrial areas
- Major coal deposits
- Major petroleum deposits
- Lignite deposits
- Minor petroleum deposits
- Minor coal deposits
- Major iron ore
- Minor iron ore
- Lead
- Bauxite
- Zinc
- Copper

VEGETATION (map labels: TAIGA, STEPPE, Arctic Circle, Longitude West of Greenwich / Longitude East of Greenwich)

MINERALS (map labels: KIRUNA, SECOND BAKU, URALS, MAGNITOGORSK, MIDLAND, RUHR, SAAR, LORRAINE, SILESIA, DONETS, KRIVOI ROG, PO, BAKU, KIRKUK, Arctic Circle, Longitude West of Greenwich / Longitude East of Greenwich)

EUROPE LAND USE 1956

A CORN 2.3%
B RYE 2.4%
C OATS AND BARLEY 4.4%

ARABLE LANDS 30.5%
WHEAT 5.9%
OTHER CROPS 15.5%
FORESTED LANDS 27.6%
OTHER LANDS (BUILT ON WASTE LANDS) 24.5%
PERMANENT MEADOWS 17.4%

STURGEON

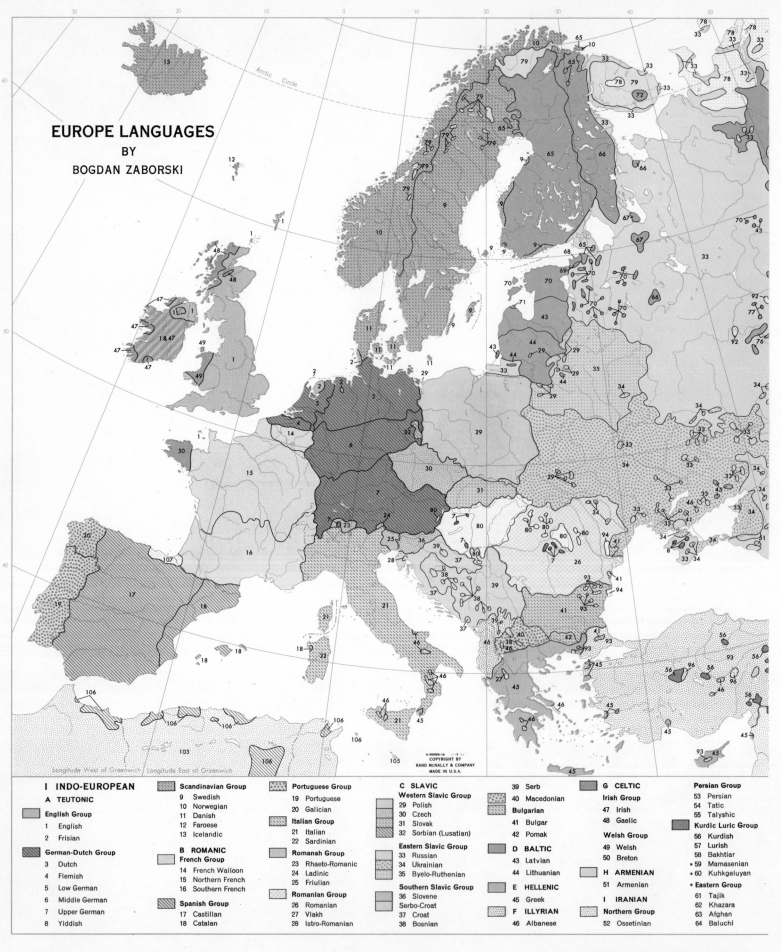

EUROPE LANGUAGES
BY
BOGDAN ZABORSKI

I INDO-EUROPEAN

A TEUTONIC

English Group
1 English
2 Frisian

German-Dutch Group
3 Dutch
4 Flemish
5 Low German
6 Middle German
7 Upper German
8 Yiddish

Scandinavian Group
9 Swedish
10 Norwegian
11 Danish
12 Faroese
13 Icelandic

B ROMANIC

French Group
14 French Walloon
15 Northern French
16 Southern French

Spanish Group
17 Castilian
18 Catalan

Portuguese Group
19 Portuguese
20 Galician

Italian Group
21 Italian
22 Sardinian

Romansh Group
23 Rhaeto-Romanic
24 Ladinic
25 Friulian

Romanian Group
26 Romanian
27 Vlakh
28 Istro-Romanian

C SLAVIC

Western Slavic Group
29 Polish
30 Czech
31 Slovak
32 Sorbian (Lusatian)

Eastern Slavic Group
33 Russian
34 Ukrainian
35 Byelo-Ruthenian

Southern Slavic Group
36 Slovene
Serbo-Croat
37 Croat
38 Bosnian

39 Serb
40 Macedonian

Bulgarian
41 Bulgar
42 Pomak

D BALTIC
43 Latvian
44 Lithuanian

E HELLENIC
45 Greek

F ILLYRIAN
46 Albanese

G CELTIC

Irish Group
47 Irish
48 Gaelic

Welsh Group
49 Welsh
50 Breton

H ARMENIAN
51 Armenian

I IRANIAN

Northern Group
52 Ossetinian

Persian Group
53 Persian
54 Tatic
55 Talyshic

Kurdic Luric Group
56 Kurdish
57 Lurish
58 Bakhtiar
*59 Mamasenian
*60 Kuhkgeluyan

Eastern Group
61 Tajik
62 Khazara
63 Afghan
64 Baluchi

0 100 200 300 400 500 600 Miles
0 200 400 600 800 1000 Kilometers

Scale 1:20,000,000; one inch to 315 miles Conic Projection

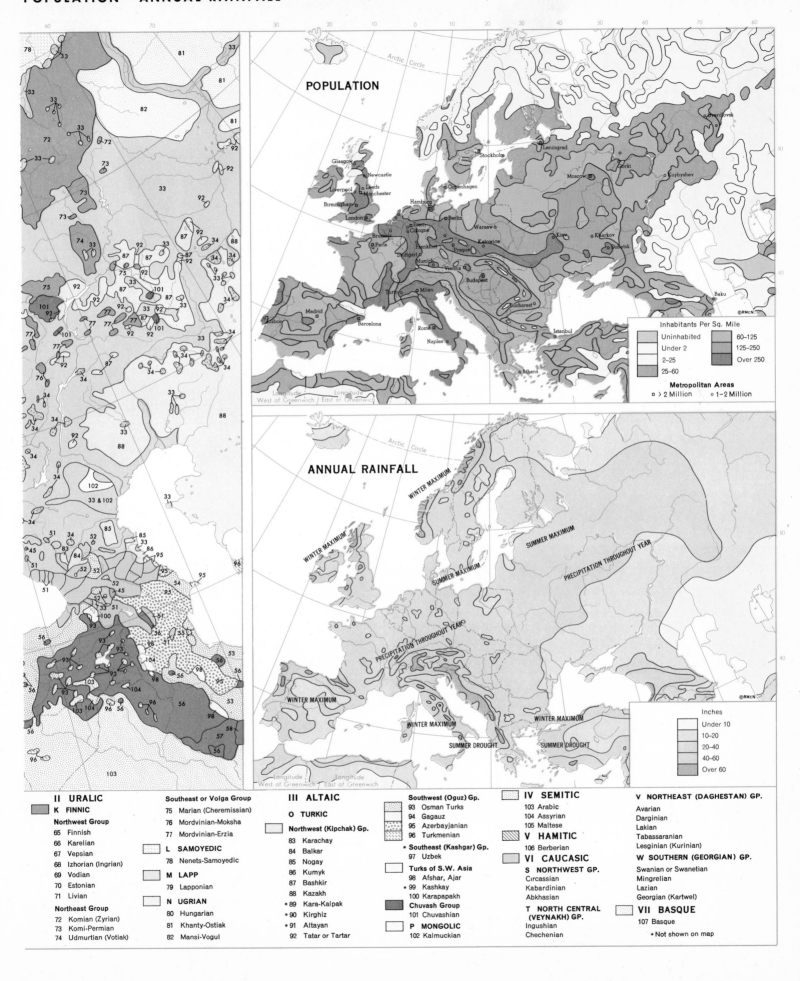

POPULATION

ANNUAL RAINFALL

Inhabitants Per Sq. Mile
- Uninhabited
- Under 2
- 2–25
- 25–60
- 60–125
- 125–250
- Over 250

Metropolitan Areas
- □ > 2 Million
- ○ 1–2 Million

Inches
- Under 10
- 10–20
- 20–40
- 40–60
- Over 60

II URALIC

K FINNIC

Northwest Group
65 Finnish
66 Karelian
67 Vepsian
68 Izhorian (Ingrian)
69 Vodian
70 Estonian
71 Livian

Northeast Group
72 Komian (Zyrian)
73 Komi-Permian
74 Udmurtian (Votiak)

Southeast or Volga Group
75 Marian (Cheremissian)
76 Mordvinian-Moksha
77 Mordvinian-Erzia

L SAMOYEDIC
78 Nenets-Samoyedic

M LAPP
79 Lapponian

N UGRIAN
80 Hungarian
81 Khanty-Ostiak
82 Mansi-Vogul

III ALTAIC

O TURKIC

Northwest (Kipchak) Gp.
83 Karachay
84 Balkar
85 Nogay
86 Kumyk
87 Bashkir
88 Kazakh
* 89 Kara-Kalpak
* 90 Kirghiz
* 91 Altayan
92 Tatar or Tartar

Southwest (Oguz) Gp.
93 Osman Turks
94 Gagauz
95 Azerbayjanian
96 Turkmenian

***Southeast (Kashgar) Gp.**
97 Uzbek

Turks of S.W. Asia
98 Afshar, Ajar
* 99 Kashkay
100 Karapapakh

Chuvash Group
101 Chuvashian

P MONGOLIC
102 Kalmuckian

IV SEMITIC
103 Arabic
104 Assyrian
105 Maltese

V HAMITIC
106 Berberian

VI CAUCASIC

S NORTHWEST GP.
Circassian
Kabardinian
Abkhasian

T NORTH CENTRAL (VEYNAKH) GP.
Ingushian
Chechenian

V NORTHEAST (DAGHESTAN) GP.
Avarian
Darginian
Lakian
Tabassaranian
Lesginian (Kurinian)

W SOUTHERN (GEORGIAN) GP.
Swanian or Swanetian
Mingrelian
Lazian
Georgian (Kartwel)

VII BASQUE
107 Basque

* Not shown on map

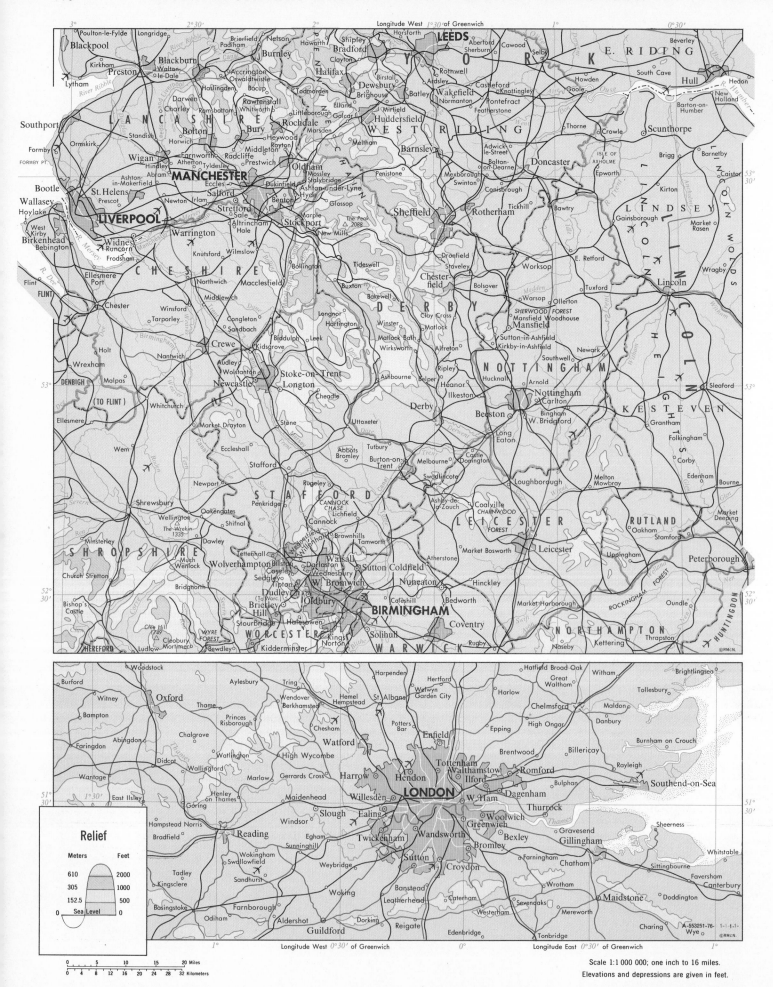

Relief

Meters		Feet
610		2000
305		1000
152.5		500
0	Sea Level	0

0   5   10   15   20 Miles
0 4 8 12 16 20 24 28 32 Kilometers

Scale 1:1 000 000; one inch to 16 miles.
Elevations and depressions are given in feet.

A-553251-76-
Wye
®RMcN

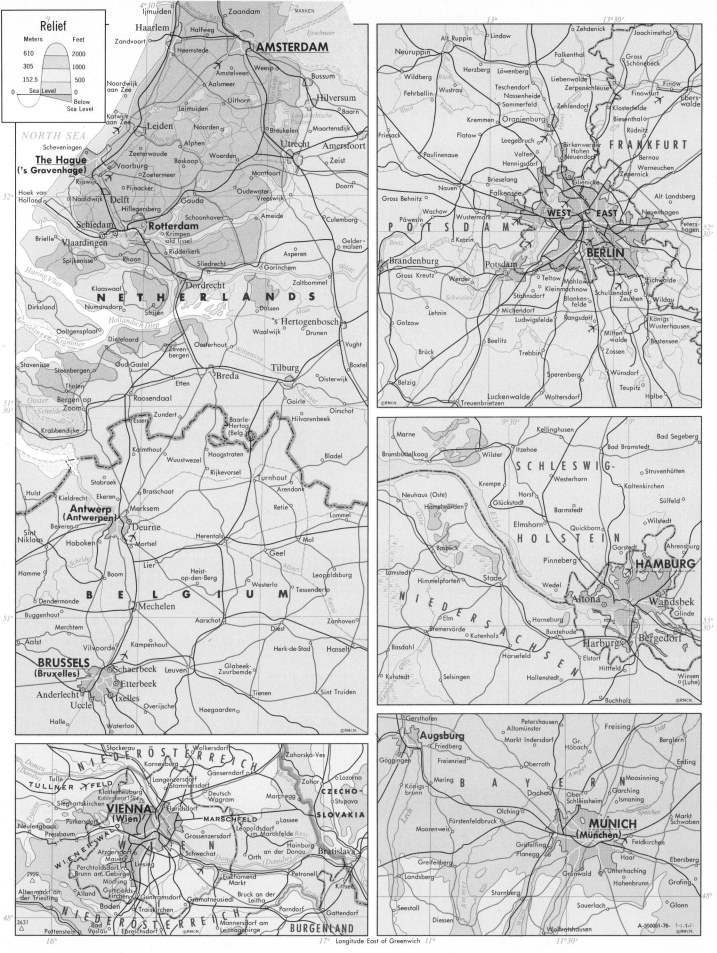

Relief

Meters	Feet
610	2000
305	1000
152.5	500
0 Sea Level	0
	Below Sea Level

Scale 1:1 000 000; one inch to 16 miles.
Elevations and depressions are given in feet.

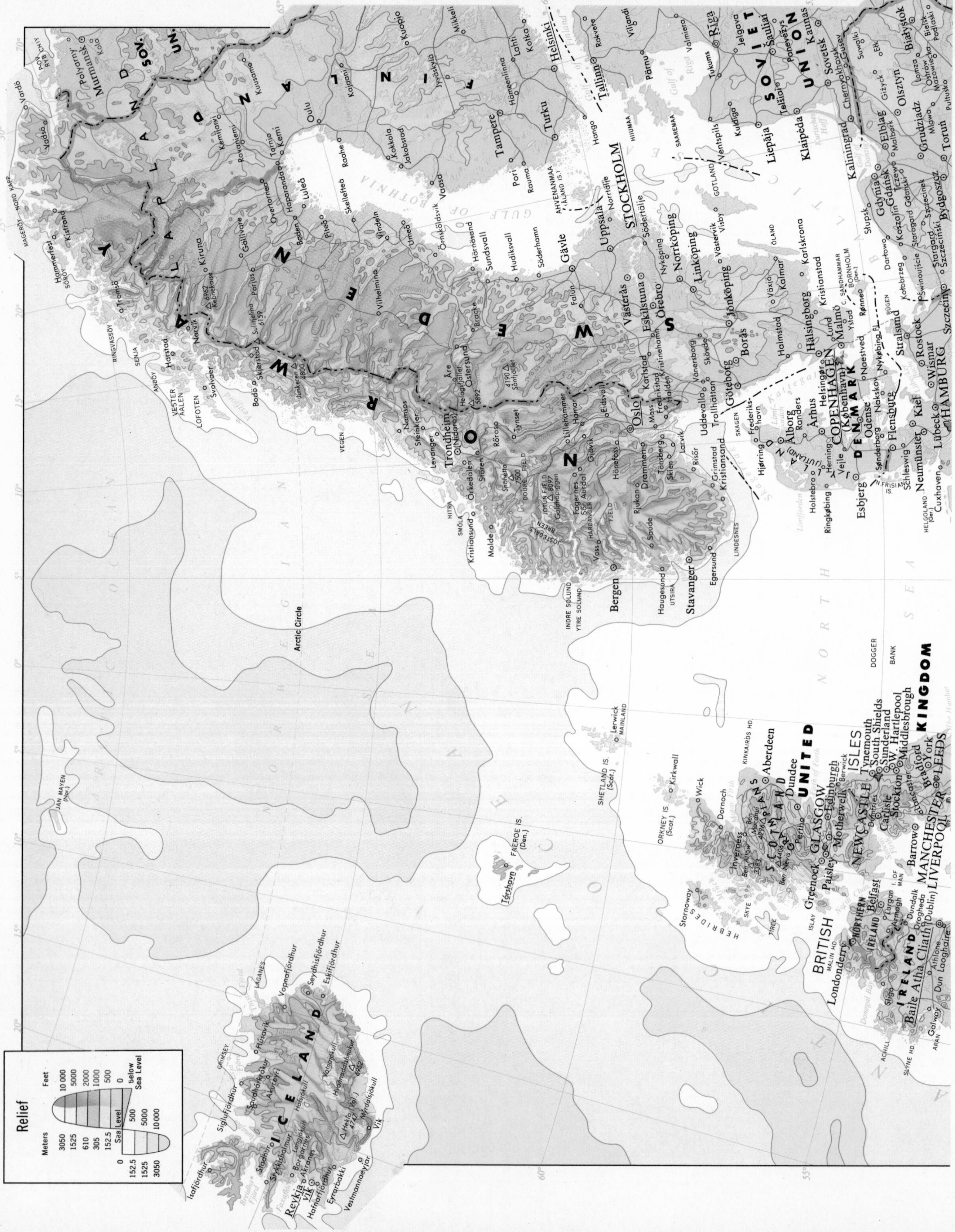
Relief
Meters
Feet
3050
1525
610
305
152.5
Sea Level
0
152.5
1525
3050
10 000
5000
2000
1000
500
0
500
5000
10 000
Below Sea Level
ICELAND
Reykjavík
Akureyri
Húsavík
Siglufjördhur
Ísafjördhur
Seydhisfjördhur
Eskifjördhur
Vopnafjördhur
Vík
Vestmannaeyjar
Hafnarfjördhur
Akranes
Borgarnes
Eyrarbakki
Sauðárkrókur
Vatnajökull
Hofsjökull
Langjökull
Mýrdalsjökull
GRIMSEY
JAN MAYEN (Nor.)
Arctic Circle
FAEROE IS. (Den.)
Tórshavn
SHETLAND IS. (Scot.)
Lerwick
MAINLAND
ORKNEY IS. (Scot.)
Kirkwall
Wick
Dornoch
HEBRIDES
Stornoway
SKYE
TIREE
ISLAY
Inverness
Ben Nevis
Aberdeen
Dundee
Perth
Edinburgh
GLASGOW
Greenock
Paisley
Motherwell
SCOTLAND
UNITED KINGDOM
BRITISH ISLES
NEWCASTLE
Tynemouth
South Shields
Sunderland
W. Hartlepool
Middlesbrough
Stockton
Carlisle
Berwick
Lancaster
Barrow
Bradford
York
LEEDS
MANCHESTER
LIVERPOOL
I. OF MAN
NORTHERN IRELAND
Belfast
Londonderry
Armagh
Dundalk
Drogheda
IRELAND
Baile Atha Cliath (Dublin)
Dun Laoghaire
Athlone
Sligo
Galway
MALIN HD.
ACHILL
SLYNE HD.
ARAN
DOGGER BANK
NORTH SEA
NORWEGIAN SEA
ATLANTIC OCEAN
NORWAY
Bergen
Stavanger
Haugesund
Egersund
Kristiansand
Grimstad
Risør
Skien
Tønsberg
Larvik
Drammen
Oslo
Moss
Fredrikstad
Halden
Hønefoss
Gjøvik
Hamar
Lillehammer
Eidsvoll
Rjukan
Voss
Molde
Kristiansund
Trondheim (Nidaros)
Steinkjer
Levanger
Namsos
Røros
Tynset
Støren
Orkedalen
Bodø
Narvik
Harstad
Tromsø
Hammerfest
Vardø
Vadsø
Kirkenes
NORD KAPP
MAGERØY
SØRØY
SENJA
VESTERÅLEN
LOFOTEN
Svolvær
LINDESNES
JOTUNFJELD
DOVREFJELD
SWEDEN
STOCKHOLM
Uppsala
Västerås
Eskilstuna
Örebro
Norrköping
Linköping
Jönköping
Göteborg
Borås
Trollhättan
Uddevalla
Vänersborg
Karlstad
Kristinehamn
Halmstad
Hälsingborg
Malmö
Lund
Ystad
Kristianstad
Karlskrona
Kalmar
Växjö
Västervik
Visby
GOTLAND
ÖLAND
Nyköping
Södertälje
Gävle
Falun
Söderhamn
Hudiksvall
Sundsvall
Härnösand
Östersund
Åre
Umeå
Örnsköldsvik
Skellefteå
Piteå
Luleå
Boden
Haparanda
Kiruna
Gällivare
Vilhelmina
Kebnekaise
LAPLAND
GULF OF BOTHNIA
FINLAND
Helsinki
Turku
Tampere
Pori
Rauma
Vaasa
Oulu
Kemi
Tornio
Rovaniemi
Kajaani
Kuopio
Jyväskylä
Lahti
Kotka
Hämeenlinna
Mikkeli
Hanko
Kokkola
Jakobstad
Raahe
AHVENANMAA (ÅLAND IS.)
SOVIET UNION
Murmansk
Tallinn
Pärnu
Riga
Liepāja
Ventspils
Klaipėda
Kaunas
Kaliningrad
Sovetsk
Šiauliai
Jelgava
Valmiera
Tukums
Kuldīga
HIIUMAA
SAAREMAA
DENMARK
COPENHAGEN (København)
Odense
Århus
Ålborg
Randers
Esbjerg
Vejle
Herning
Holstebro
Ringkøbing
Frederikshavn
Hjørring
Helsingør
Nakskov
Næstved
Rønne
BORNHOLM (Den.)
JUTLAND
SKAGEN
Flensburg
Kiel
Lübeck
Neumünster
Schleswig
Wismar
Rostock
Stralsund
HAMBURG
Cuxhaven
RÜGEN
HELGOLAND (Ger.)
Szczecin
Kołobrzeg
Koszalin
Słupsk
Gdynia
Gdańsk
Elbląg
Olsztyn
Grudziądz
Bydgoszcz
Toruń
Białystok
Malbork
Tczew
BALTIC SEA
Gulf of Finland
Gulf of Riga
Kattegat
Skagerrak

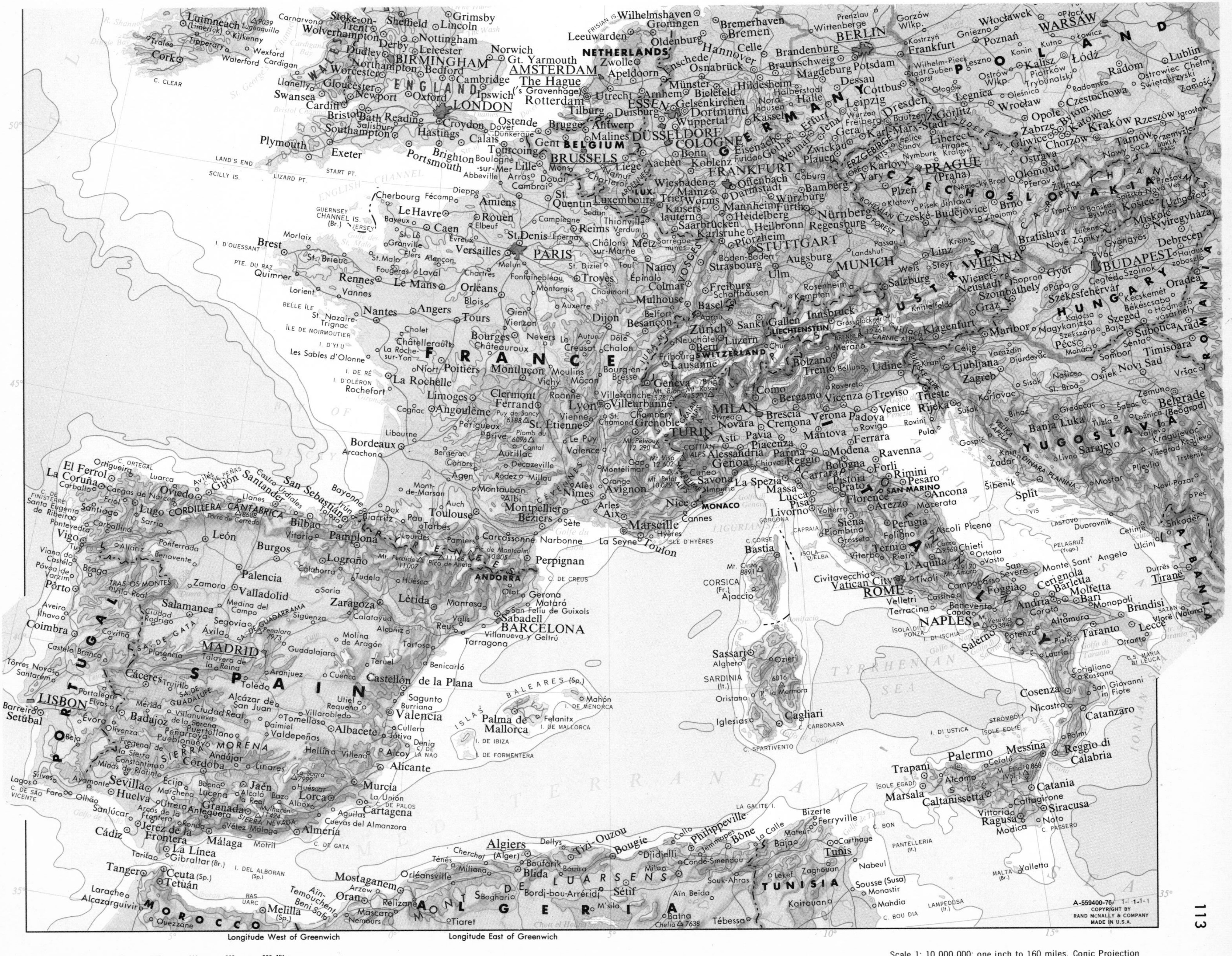

Scale 1: 10 000 000; one inch to 160 miles. Conic Projection
Elevations and depressions are given in feet

A-559400-76
COPYRIGHT BY
RAND MCNALLY & COMPANY
MADE IN U.S.A.

Longitude West of Greenwich · Longitude East of Greenwich

MILES 0 50 100 150 200 250 300
KILOMETERS 0 100 200 300 400 500

Countries / Regions: POLAND, GERMANY, CZECHOSLOVAKIA, AUSTRIA, HUNGARY, YUGOSLAVIA, ALBANIA, ITALY, SWITZERLAND, FRANCE, SPAIN, PORTUGAL, ENGLAND, NETHERLANDS, BELGIUM, MOROCCO, ALGERIA, TUNISIA, SARDINIA, CORSICA

Seas: TYRRHENIAN SEA, ADRIATIC SEA, IONIAN SEA, MEDITERRANEAN SEA, LIGURIAN SEA, ENGLISH CHANNEL

Major cities: WARSAW, BERLIN, PRAGUE, VIENNA, BUDAPEST, BELGRADE, MUNICH, FRANKFURT, COLOGNE, DÜSSELDORF, STUTTGART, BRUSSELS, AMSTERDAM, LONDON, PARIS, MILAN, TURIN, NAPLES, ROME, Vatican City, MONACO, BARCELONA, MADRID, LISBON, BIRMINGHAM, Algiers (Alger), Tunis

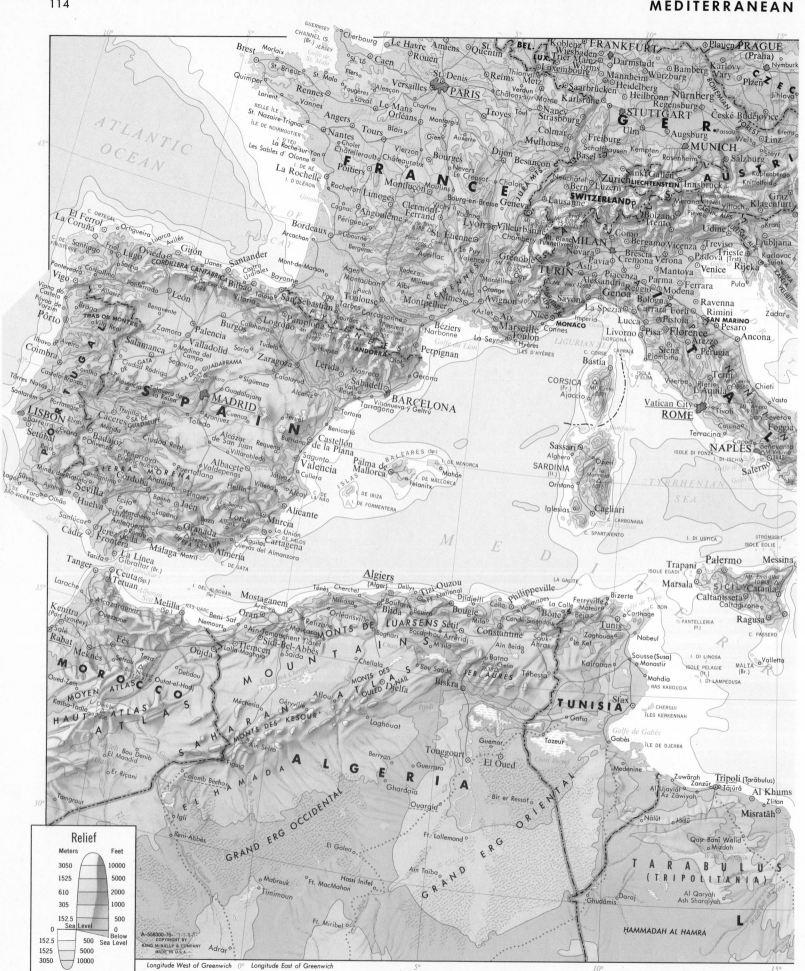

Relief

Meters	Feet
3050	10000
1525	5000
610	2000
305	1000
152.5	500
0 Sea Level	0 Sea Level
152.5	500 Below Sea Level
1525	5000
3050	10000

A-558300-76—
COPYRIGHT BY
RAND MCNALLY & COMPANY
MADE IN U.S.A.

Longitude West of Greenwich 0° Longitude East of Greenwich

Scale 1: 10 000 000; one inch to 160 miles. Bonne's Projection
Elevations and depressions are given in feet

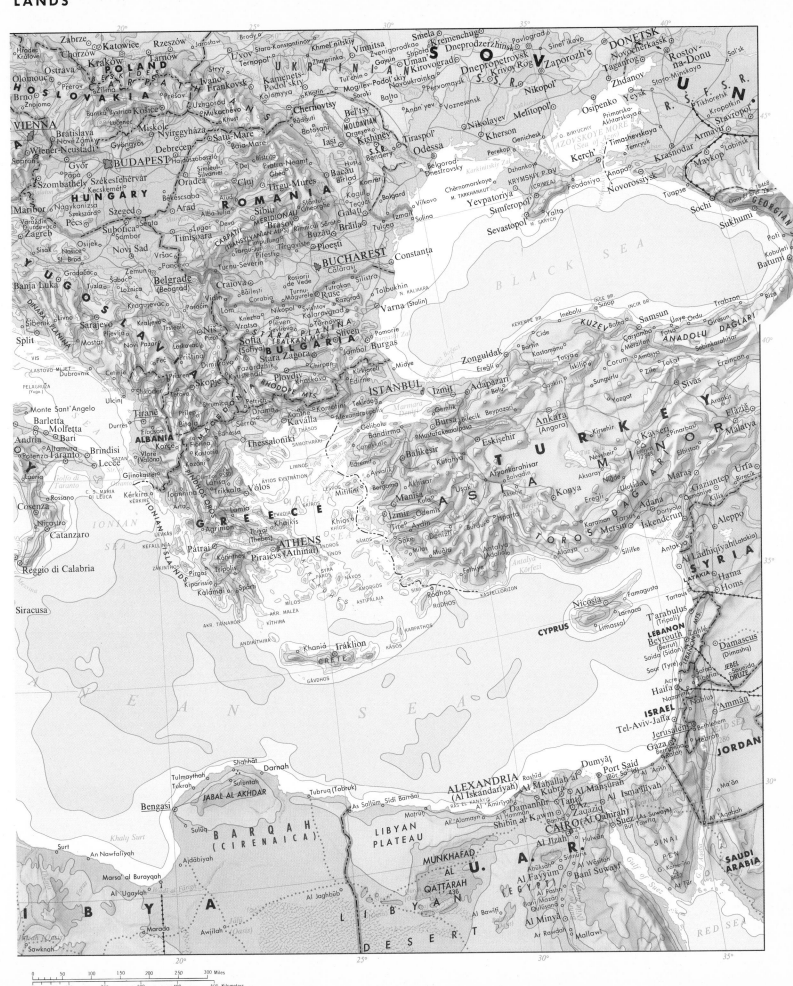

Relief

Meters	Feet
610	2000
305	1000
152.5	500
0 Sea Level	0
152.5	500
1525	5000 Below Sea Level

A-559700-76
COPYRIGHT BY
RAND McNALLY & COMPANY
MADE IN U.S.A.

Longitude West of Greenwich

Scale 1: 4 000 000; one inch to 64 miles. Conic Projection
Elevations and depressions are given in feet

NORWAY

Egersund
Sogndal
Flekkefjord
Kristiansand
Farsund
Mandal
LINDESNES

Arendal
Grimstad
Lillesand

SWEDEN

Alingsås
Ulricehamn
Kungälv
Göteborg Borås
Mölndal
Varberg
Falkenberg
Oskarström

Skagerrak

Skagen SKAGEN
Hjørring Frederikshavn
LAESØ
Brønderslev

Halmstad
Laholm
Ängelholm

Thisted
Løgstør Ålborg Limfjorden
Nykøbing Hobro Mariager
Skive Viborg Randers Grenå
Struer
Holstebro Silkeborg Århus
Rinkøbing Herning Skanderborg

Helsingør
Halsingborg
Landskrona
Hillerød
Nykøbing S.
COPENHAGEN (København)
Lund
Malmö

JYLLAND

DENMARK

Horsens
Holbæk Roskilde
Kalundborg SJAELLAND Ringsted Køge
SAMSØ Slagelse
Ringkøbing Fjord
Varde Vejle Fredericia
Esbjerg Kolding Odense Nyborg Korsør Naestved
FYN
Ribe Assens Fåborg Svendborg Vordingborg
BLÅVANDS HUK Haderslev
FANØ Åbenrå Rudkøbing
RØMØ Tønder Sønderborg ALS Nakskov MØN
SYLT Maribo FALSTER
FØHR Flensburg AERØ LANGELAND Nykøbing Fl.
SCHLESWIG LOLLAND
Schleswig FEHMARN (Ger.)
Husum Kiel Bay

NORTH FRISIAN IS.

Tralleborg
Barth
BALTIC SEA

Tønning Eckernförde Rendsburg
Heide Kiel Neustadt
HOLSTEIN Neumünster
Itzehoe Lübecker Bucht
Bad Oldesloe Lübeck Wismar Güstrow
Elmshorn

Rostock

HELGOLAND (Ger.)

Cuxhaven
Bremerhaven Schwerin
ISLANDS Stade Bergedorf MECKLENBURG
NORDERNEY LANGEOOG HAMBURG Lüneburg Ludwigslust
JUIST Norden Wilhelmshaven Parchim Perleberg
BORKUM Emden Leer Bremen LÜNEBURGER Pritzwalk
FRISIAN Norden HEIDE Wittenberge
TERSCHELLING AMELAND Oldenburg Soltau Ülzen Salzwedel
Delfzijl Papenburg Verden HEIDE Stendal
VLIELAND Leeuwarden Groningen Delmenhorst Gardelegen Tangermünde
Harlingen Meppen NIEDERSACHSEN Celle GERMANY
TEXEL Nienburg Hannover Braunschweig Neuhaldensleben
Den Helder Emmen Lingen Nordhorn Rheine Minden Hameln Hildesheim Wolfenbüttel Magdeburg Schönebeck
Meppel Rheine Osnabrück Herford Goslar Halberstadt
Alkmaar NETHERLANDS Zwolle Almelo Gronau Bielefeld Detmold Einbeck Quedlinburg Blankenburg Staßfurt Bernberg
Zaandam Hengelo WEST Herford Northeim Aschersleben
Haarlem AMSTERDAM Deventer Enschede Münster GERMANY Göttingen Sangerhausen Eisleben Halle
Apeldoorn Coesfeld Gütersloh Paderborn Nordhausen Merseburg
The Hague Leiden Utrecht Rheden Arnhem Lippstadt Heiligenstadt Sondershausen
('s Gravenhage) Delft Nijmegen Kleve Ahlen Soest Mühlhausen Eisenach THÜRINGEN Weimar
Vlaardingen Rotterdam Bochum Hamm Dortmund Arnsberg Kassel Eschwege Erfurt
Dordrecht Wesel Gelsenkirchen Iserlohn Gotha Arnstadt Rudolstadt
Breda 's Hertogenbosch Duisburg ESSEN Hagen NORDRHEIN WESTFALEN Bad Hersfeld Schmalkalden Ilmenau Saalfeld
Bergen Helmond Oberhausen Mülheim Lüdenscheid Meiningen Suhl
op Zoom Tilburg Mönchengladbach Wuppertal Siegen Marburg Zella-Mehlis Sonneberg
Eindhoven Solingen Gummersbach Giessen Hildburghausen Neustadt b.C.
Weert DÜSSELDORF NORDRHEIN Bad Hersfeld Coburg
Turnhout Roermond Cologne WESTERWALD TAUNUS FRANKFURT Bad Kissingen
Antwerp (Köln) Siegburg AM MAIN Schweinfurt
Mechelen Heerlen Düren Bonn Ahrweiler Neuwied Wiesbaden Höchst Hanau Offenbach Aschaffenburg
BELGIUM Maastricht Aachen Andernach Koblenz Mainz Darmstadt Würzburg
Leuven Eupen Verviers Mayen Bad Homburg Kitzingen
Herstal Spa EIFEL HUNSRÜCK Bingen Bad Bayreuth
Liège Malmedy Bad Kreuznach Forchheim
Seraing Wittlich Kirn Bamberg
Namur Kreuznach Erlangen
LUX.

Kings Lynn
Norwich Great Yarmouth
Lowestoft
Ely Bury St. Edmunds
Ipswich
Colchester Harwich
Chelmsford
Ham Southend-on-Sea
Gravesend Margate
Gillingham Ramsgate
Sheerness NORTH FORELAND
Chatham Canterbury
Maidstone Dover
Folkestone
Hastings
Bexhill
Eastbourne

The Wash
DOGGER BANK 60—120 Ft.

NORTH SEA

DOWNS Strait of Dover

FLANDERS Oostende Zeebrügge
Brugge Gent
Calais St. Omer Torhout Roeselare
Ieper Kortrijk Aalst BRUSSELS Anderlecht
Dunkerque Armentières Tourcoing Nivelles
Boulogne-sur-Mer Lille Roubaix BELGIUM Leuven
Étaples Béthune Jumet Charleroi
Hesdin Douai Denain Valenciennes La Louvière Dinant
Crécy Arras Cambrai Maubeuge Namur
FRANCE Hautmont Givet
St. Valéry Abbeville Fourmies ARDENNES Bastogne
Le Tréport

0 10 20 30 40 50 60 70 80 90 100 110 120 Miles
0 20 40 60 80 100 120 140 160 180 200 Kilometers

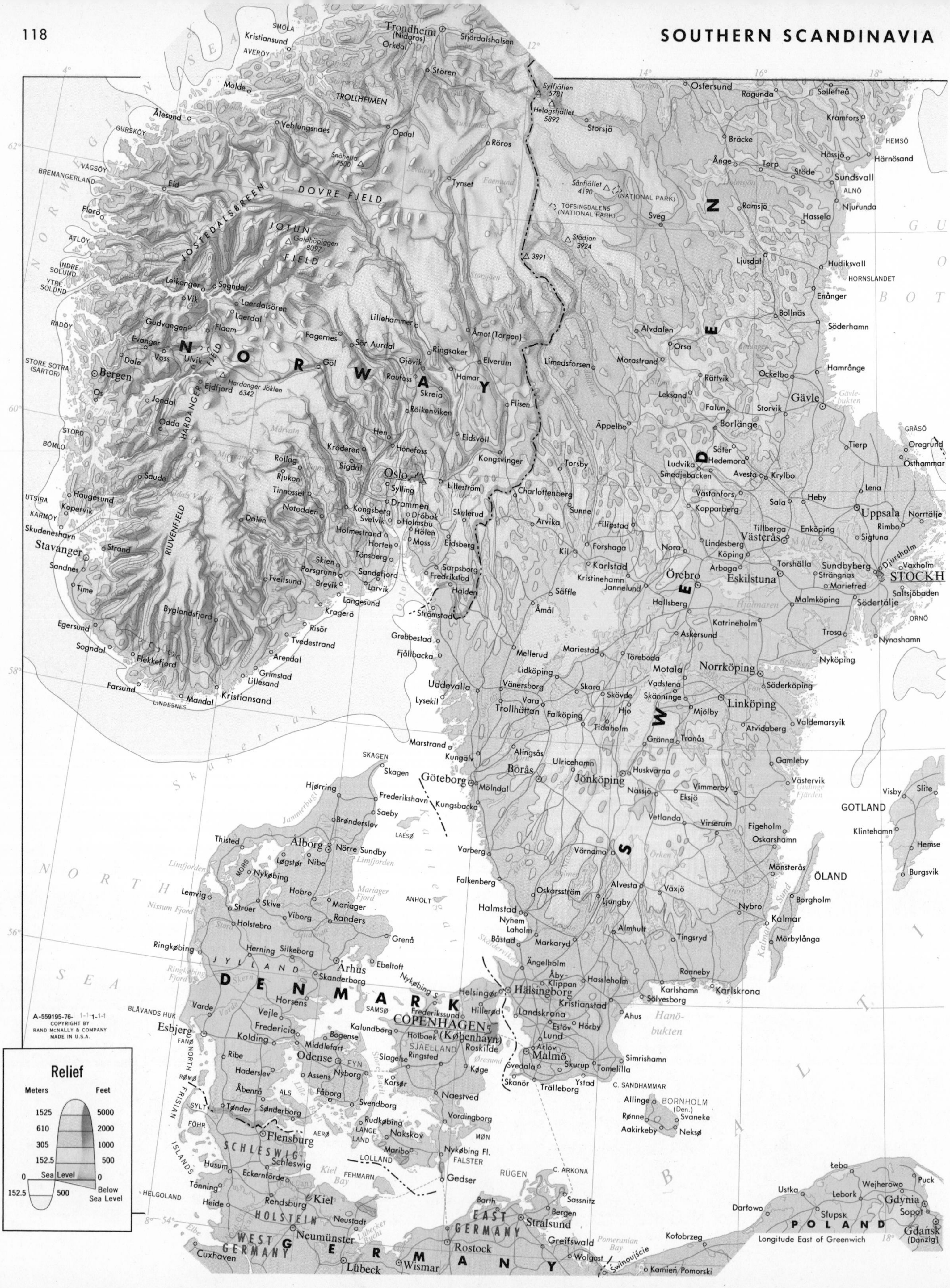

SOUTHERN SCANDINAVIA

NORWEGIAN SEA

SMØLA
Trondheim (Nidaros)
Kristiansund
Averøy
Orkdal
Stjørdalshalsen
Molde
Ålesund
Veblungsnaes
TROLLHEIMEN
Opdal
Støren
Røros
Østersund
Ragunda
Sollefteå
Sylfjällen 5781
Helagsfjället 5892
Storsjö
Bräcke
Kramfors
HEMSÖ
Härnösand
Ånge
Torp
Stöde
Sundsvall
ALNÖ
GURSKØY
VÅGSØY
BREMANGERLAND
Flore
Eid
DOVRE FJELD
Snøhetta 7500
Tynset
Fæmunden
Sänfjället 4190
(NATIONAL PARK)
Sveg
Ramsjö
Hassela
Njurunda

NORWEGIAN SEA
ATLØY
INDRE SOLUND
YTRE SOLUND
RADØY
JOSTEDALSBREEN
JOTUN FJELD
Galdhøpiggen 8097
FJELD
TÖFSINGDALENS (NATIONAL PARK)
Stådjan 3924
3891
Ljusdal
Hudiksvall
HORNSLANDET
Leikanger
Sogndal
Laerdalsøren
Lillehammer
Åmot (Torpen)
Älvdalen
Morastrand
Orsa
Enånger
Bollnäs
Söderhamn
Vik
Laerdal
Flaam
Åsgårdsen
Limedsforsen
Rättvik
Ockelbo
Hamrånge
Gudvangen
Fagernes
Sør Aurdal
Ringsaker
Gjøvik
Elverum
Äppelbo
Leksand
Falun
Gävle
Gävle-bukten
Evanger
Voss
Ulvik
Gøl
Raufoss
Hamar
Borlänge
Storvik
GRÄSÖ
Dale
Bergen
Ejdfjord 6342
Hardanger Jøklen
Skreia
Flisen
Säter
Hedemora
Tierp
Oregrund
Os
Jondal
Skulerud
Röikenviken
Ludvika
Avesta
Krylbo
Östhammar
Odda
Hen
Hønefoss
Eidsvoll
Torsby
Smedjebacken
Kongsvinger
Lena
STORD
Kröderen
Sigdal
Kongsvinger
Sunne
Västanfors
Sala
Heby
BØMLO
Rollag
Oslo
Sylling
Lillestrøm
Charlottenberg
Kopparberg
Enköping
Sigtuna
Uppsala
Haugesund
Kopervik
Rjukan
Tinnoset
Drammen
Arvika
Filipstad
Nora
Tillberga
Västerås
Norrtälje
KARMØY
Notodden
Kongsberg
Svelvik
Drøbak
Holmsbu
Eidsberg
Kil
Forshaga
Köping
Lindesberg
Arboga
Torshälla
Sundbyberg
Djursholm
Skudeneshavn
Dalen
Holmestrand
Hølen
Moss
Karlstad
Kristinehamn
Örebro
Hallsberg
Eskilstuna
Strängnäs
Mariefred
STOCKH
UTSIRA
Stavanger
Saude
Skien
Porsgrunn
Horten
Sandefjord
Tønsberg
Sarpsborg
Fredrikstad
Åmål
Säffle
Jannelund
Katrineholm
Malmköping
Södertälje
Saltsjöbaden
Sandnes
Time
Tveitsund
Brevik
Larvik
Halden
Askersund
Trosa
ORNÖ
Strand
Langesund
Kragerø
Strömstad
Mellerud
Mariestad
Töreboda
Motala
Norrköping
Söderköping
Nynashamn
Egersund
Byglandsfjord
Risør
Grebbestad
Lidköping
Vänersborg
Skara
Skövde
Skänninge
Vadstena
Linköping
Nyköping
Sogndal
Flekkefjord
Tvedestrand
Fjällbacka
Uddevalla
Vara
Falköping
Hjo
Tidaholm
Mjölby
Atvidaberg
Valdemarsvik
Farsund
Grimstad
Lillesand
Lysekil
Trollhättan
Gränna
Tranås
Gamleby
Mandal
Kristiansand
LINDESNES
Marstrand
Kungälv
Alingsås
Ulricehamn
Huskvarna
Vimmerby
Västervik
Gullänge Fjärden

SKAGERRAK
SKAGEN
Skagen
Göteborg
Borås
Mölndal
Jönköping
Nässjö
Eksjö
Visby
Slite
GOTLAND
Hjørring
Frederikshavn
Kungsbacka
Vetlanda
Virserum
Figeholm
Klintehamn
Saeby
LAESØ
Varberg
Värnamo
Oskarshamn
Hemse
Burgsvik
Brønderslev
Falkenberg
Alvesta
Växjö
Mönsterås
ÖLAND
Thisted
Ålborg
Nørre Sundby
Nibe
Limfjorden
Oskarsström
Ljungby
Borgholm
NORTH
Lemvig
Løgstør
Nykøbing
Hobro
Halmstad
Nyhem
Alvesta
Almhult
Tingsryd
Nybro
Kalmar
Mörbylånga
Struer
Skive
Viborg
Mariager
Randers
Laholm
Markaryd
Ringkøbing
Herning
Silkeborg
Grenå
Ängelholm
Åby
Klippan
Hasslehoim
Rønneby
Karlskrona
NORTH SEA
JYLLAND
Århus
Ebeltoft
Nykøbing S.
Helsingør
Hälsingborg
Kristianstad
Karlshamn
Ahus
Hanö-bukten
Varde
Vejle
Horsens
Skanderborg
SAMSØ
Hillerød
Landskrona
Eslöv
Hörby
Sölvesborg
Esbjerg
FANØ
Kolding
Fredericia
Middelfart
Bogense
Kalundborg
Frederikssund
COPENHAGEN (København)
Roskilde
Lund
Arlöv
Malmö
Simrishamn
BLÅVANDS HUK
Ribe
Haderslev
Odense
FYN
Slagelse
Ringsted
Køge
Svedala
Skurup
Tomelilla
RØMØ
FRISIAN
SYLT
Åbenrå
ALS
Assens
Nyborg
Korsør
Naestved
Skanør
Trälleborg
Ystad
C. SANDHAMMAR
Allinge
BORNHOLM (Den.)
FØHR
Tønder
Sønderborg
Fåborg
Svendborg
Vordingborg
MØN
Rønne
Svaneke
Nekse
HELGOLAND
Husum
AERØ
LANGE LAND
Rudkøbing
Nakskov
Maribo
Nykøbing Fl.
FALSTER
Aakirkeby
SCHLESWIG-HOLSTEIN
Flensburg
Schleswig
Kiel Bay
FEHMARN
LOLLAND
Gedser
RÜGEN
C. ARKONA
Łeba
Ustka
Lebork
Wejherowo
Puck
Eckernförde
Husum
Tønning
Heide
Rendsburg
Kiel
Neustadt
Lübecker Bucht
Barth
Sassnitz
Bergen
Stralsund
Kołobrzeg
Darłowo
Słupsk
Sopot
Gdynia
WEST GERMANY
HOLSTEIN
Neumünster
Lübeck
Wismar
EAST GERMANY
Greifswald
Wolgast
Świnoujście
Kamień Pomorski
POLAND
Gdańsk (Danzig)
Cuxhaven
Elbe
GERMANY
Rostock
Pomeranian Bay

Relief

Meters	Feet
1525	5000
610	2000
305	1000
152.5	500
0 Sea Level	0
152.5	500 Below Sea Level

Longitude East of Greenwich

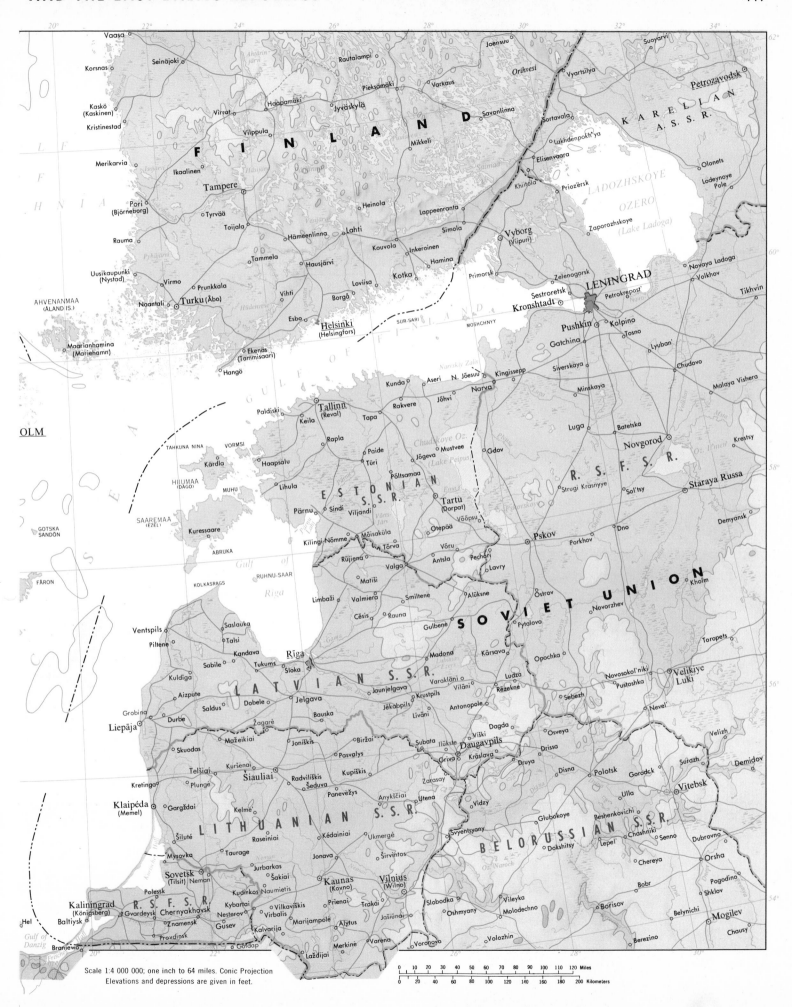

Scale 1:4 000 000; one inch to 64 miles. Conic Projection
Elevations and depressions are given in feet.

Continued on pp. 122 123

Continued on pp. 126 127

Longitude East of Greenwich

Scale 1:4 000 000; one inch to 64 miles. Conic Projection
Elevations and depressions are given in feet.

A-559500-76- -1- -1-
COPYRIGHT BY
RAND M^cNALLY & COMPANY
MADE IN U.S.A.

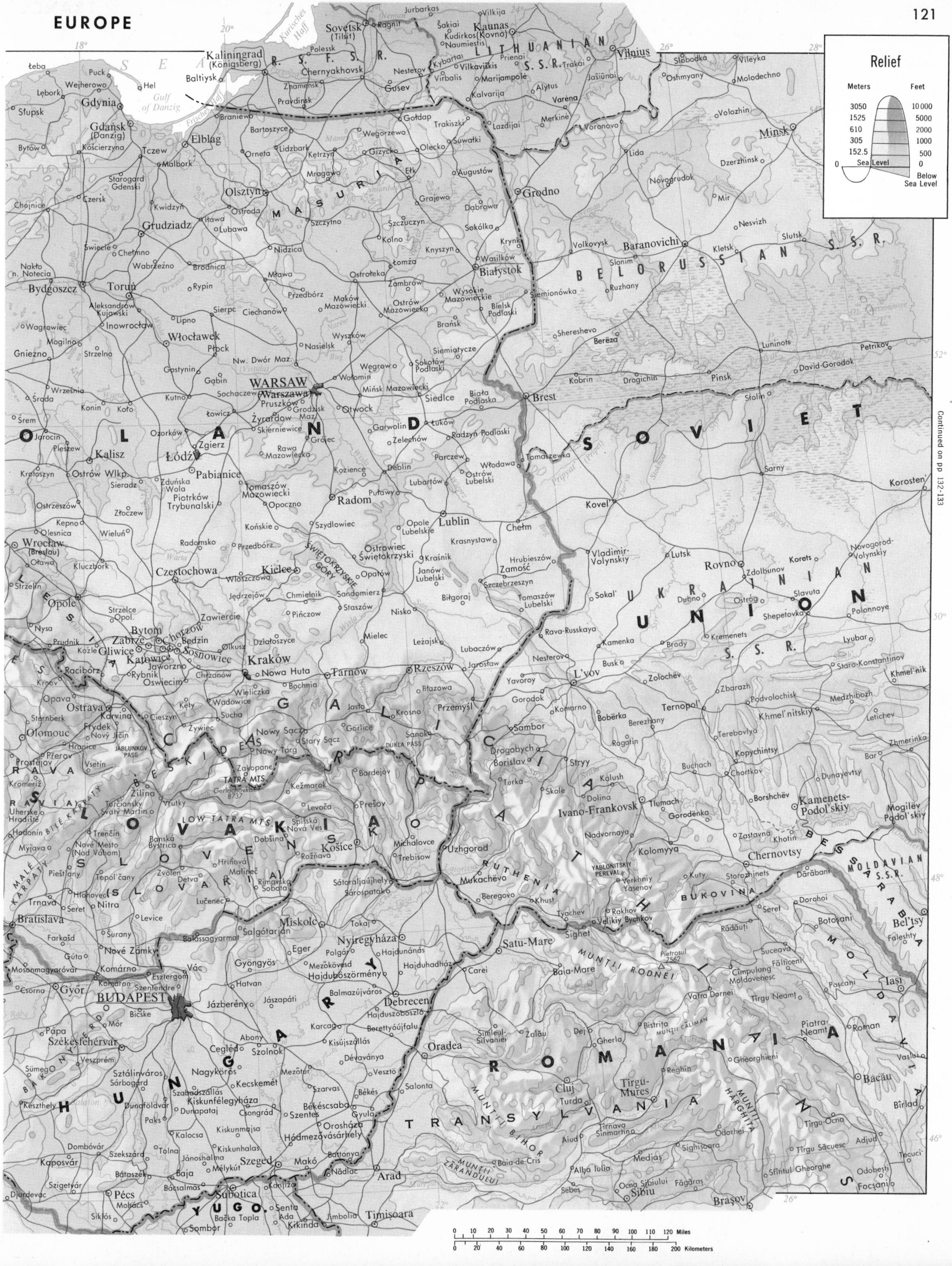

Relief

Meters	Feet
3050	10 000
1525	5000
610	2000
305	1000
152.5	500
Sea Level	0
	Below Sea Level

Continued on pp 132-133

SEA

Kurisches Haff

Gulf of Danzig

Frisches Haff

R. S. F. S. R.

Kaliningrad (Königsberg)

Baltiysk (Pillau)

łeba Puck Hel
Wejherowo Lębork
Gdynia
Gdańsk (Danzig)
Słupsk Kościerzyna
Bytów Kartuzy
Chojnice Tczew
Czersk Starogard Gdenski
Nakło n. Notecią
Grudziadz Malbork Braniewo Bartoszyce
Elblag Orneta Lidzbark
Kwidzyn Iława Ostroda Olsztyn
Chełmno Brodnica Lubawa Mrągowo Szczytno
Toruń Rypin Nidzica Mława
Bydgoszcz Aleksandrów Kujawski Lipno Ciechanów
Inowrocław Sierpc Nasielsk
Mogilno Włocławek Płock Nw. Dwór Maz. (Visula)
Gniezno Strzelno Gostynin Gabin Sochaczew
Września Gabin Łowicz Żyrardów Pruszków
Środa Kutno Łowicz Skierniewice Grodzisk Maz.

Ragnit Jurbarkas Vilkija
Sovétsk (Tilsit) Polessk Šakiai Kudirkos (Kovno) KAUNAS
Chernyakhovsk Nesterov Kybartai Naumiestis
Zhaméngk Gusev Virbalis Marijampolė
Pravdinsk Kalvarija

LITHUANIAN S. S. R.
Vilnius
Prienai Trakai
Alytus Varėna
Merkine Voronovo Volozhin

Gołdap Trakiszki Lazdijai Jašiunai
Wegorzewo Suwałki Oshmyany Molodechno
Gizycko Augustów Lida
Ełk Grajewo Dzerzhinsk
Grodno Novogrudok Mir Nesvizh
Kolno Szczuczyn Dabrowa Slutsk
Łomża Sokółka Volkovysk Baranovichi Kletsk
Zambrów Wysokie Mazowieckie Bielsk Podlaski Slonim Ruzhany
Białystok Siemionówka Bereza Luninots Petrikov
Ostrów Mazowiecka Brańsk Shereshevo David-Gorodok
Wyszków Sokołów Podlaski Siemiatycze Kobrin Drogichin Pinsk Stolin

BELORUSSIAN S. S. R.
Minsk
Volozhin Slobodka Vileyka

WARSAW (Warszawa)
Wołomin Mińsk Mazowiecki Biała Podlaska Brest
Otwock Siedlce Łuków Radzyń Podlaski Drogichin
Garwolin Zelechów Parczew Włodawa Kovel'
Dęblin Lubartów Ostrów Lubelski Tomaszewka
Kozienice Puławy Chełm Sarny
Radom Lublin Korosten

SOVIET

O L A N D
Kalisz Łódź Zgierz Pabianice Tomaszów Mazowiecki
Krotoszyn Sieradz Zduńska Wola Piotrków Trybunalski Opoczno
Ostrów Wlkp. Radomsko Przedbórz Końskie Szydłowiec
Ostrzeszów Kepno Wieluń Włoszczowa Kielce
Wrocław (Breslau) Oleśnica Częstochowa Jędrzejów Chmielnik
Oława Kluczbork Zawiercie Pińczów Staszów
Strzelin Opole Strzelce Opol. Olkusz Działoszyce Nisko
Nysa Prudnik Bytom Chorzów Będzin Miechów
Koźle Gliwice Katowice Sosnowiec Kraków Tarnów
Racibórz Rybnik Jaworzno Chrzanów Bochnia Rzeszów

Świętokrzyskie Góry
Ostrowiec Świetokrzyski Opatów Kraśnik Janów Lubelski
Opole Lubelskie Krasnystaw Hrubieszów Zamość
Sandomierz Biłgoraj Szczebrzeszyn Tomaszów Lubelski
Mielec Leżajsk Lubaczów Rava-Russkaya
Nowa Huta Jarosław Nesterov Yavoroy

UKRAINIAN UNION S. S. R.
Vladimir-Volynskiy Lutsk Rovno Novogorod-Volynskiy
Sokal' Dubno Ostróg Slavuta Polonnoye
L'vov Zdolbunov Shepetovka Korosten
Gorodok Busk Zoloch'év Kremenets Staro-Konstantinov
Komarno Boberka Brody Lyubar Khmel'nik
Przemyśl Bóbrka Berezhany Khmel'nitskiy Letichev
Krosno Sambor Rogatin Ternopol' Medzhibozh
Gorlice Sanok Drogobych Podvolochisk Zbarazh
Dukla Pass Borislav Stryj Buchach Chortkov Dunayetsy
Bardejov Skole Dolina Kałush Borshchév Bar
Zakopane TATRA MTS. Turka Kopychintsy Kamenets-Podol'skiy Mogilév-Podol'skiy
Gerlachovka 8737 Kezmarok Michalovce Ivano-Frankovsk Gorodenka Zastavna Khotin

GALICIA
BESKIDES
CARPATH
RUTHENIA
BUKOVINA
MOLDAVIAN S. S. R.

LOW TATRA MTS.
Spišská Nová Ves Nadvornaya Kolomyya Chernovtsy
Dobšiná Levoča Prešov Uzhgorod Yablonitskiy Pereval Kuty Storozhinets Dărăbani
Rožňava Košice Trebišov Mukachevo Yerkhniy Yasenov Rakhov Bel'tsy
Michalovce Beregovo Khust Tyachev Velikiy Bychkov Rădăuti Faleshty

SLOVAKIA
(SLOVENSKO)
Turčiansky Svätý Martin Hriňová Malinec
Zvolen Detva Rimavská Sobota Sátoraljaújhely Sárospatak
Banská Bystrica Lučenec Tokaj
Žilina Vrutky Zvolen
Trenčín Nové Mesto (Nad Váhom) Piešťany Topol'čany
Nitra Levice Balassagyarmat Salgótarján Miskolc
Nové Zámky Komárno Vác Esztergom
Bratislava Surány Nyíregyháza Satu-Mare Sighet

Hodonín Olomouc Ostrava Karviná Cieszyn Żywiec Nowy Targ
Prostějov Přerov Frýdek Nový Jičín Nowy Sącz Stary Sącz
Kroměříž Hranice Vsetín Jablunkov Pass

MORAVA **SLEZSKO** **BESKIDES**

Sternberk Opava Zábreh
Šumperk

HUNGARY
BUDAPEST
Bicske Jászberény Jászapáti Karcag Püspökladány
Székesfehérvár Mór Cegléd Szolnok Berettyóújfalu Debrecen
Veszprém Nagykórós Kecskemét Mezőtúr Hajdúszoboszló
Pápa Dunaföldvár Szarvas Gyoma Hajdúdorog
Keszthely Sztálinváros Csongrád Békés Gyula Hajdúnánás
Sümeg Sárbogárd Kiskunfélegyháza Szentes Hajdúhadház
Dombóvár Paks Kiskunhalas Hódmezővásárhely Hajdúböszörmény
Szekszárd Kalocsa Szeged Makó Mezőkövesd
Kaposvár Tolna Baja Kiskunmajsa Battonya Oroszháza Nyíregyháza
Szigetvár Bátaszék Mélykút Nádlac Gyöngyös Eger Polgár
Pécs Mohács Bácsalmás Arad Hatvan Hajdúböszörmény

Vác Gyöngyös Mezőkövesd Polgár Balmazújváros
Eger Mezőtúr Nyíregyháza Hajdúböszörmény

ROMANIA
TRANSYLVANIA
Satu-Mare Baia-Mare Baia de Cris Simleul Silvaniei Zalău Dej Gherla Bistrita Reghin
Carei Oradea Salonta Aiud Turda Cluj Tirgu-Mures Gheorghieni Piatra Neamt
Alba Iulia Sebeş Mediaş Sighişoara Odorhei Tirgu Ocna
Ocna Sibiului Fǎgǎras Sibiu Braşov Sfîntul Gheorghe

MUNTII RODNEI Pietrosul 7562
MUNTII CĂLIMAN MUNTII HARGHITA
MUNTII BIHOR MUNTII ZARANDULUI

Vatra Dornei Tirgu Neamt Roman Bîrlad
Cîmpulung Moldovenesc Pascani Fǎlticeni Vaslui
Suceava Iaşi Bacău Tecuci
Botoşani Dorohoi Focşani Odobeşti

MOLDAVIA
Kamenets-Podol'skiy Mogilév-Podol'skiy Zhmerinka
Seret Storozhinets Rădăuti

YUGO.
Djurdjevac Virovitica Subotica Senta Ada Kikinda
Sombor Sombor Jimbolia Timişoara

Malé Karpaty Esztergom Szentendre
Mosonmagyaróvár Győr Tatabánya Komárom
Csorna Kapuvár Farkasd Gúta Nové Zámky

0 10 20 30 40 50 60 70 80 90 100 110 120 Miles
0 20 40 60 80 100 120 140 160 180 200 Kilometers

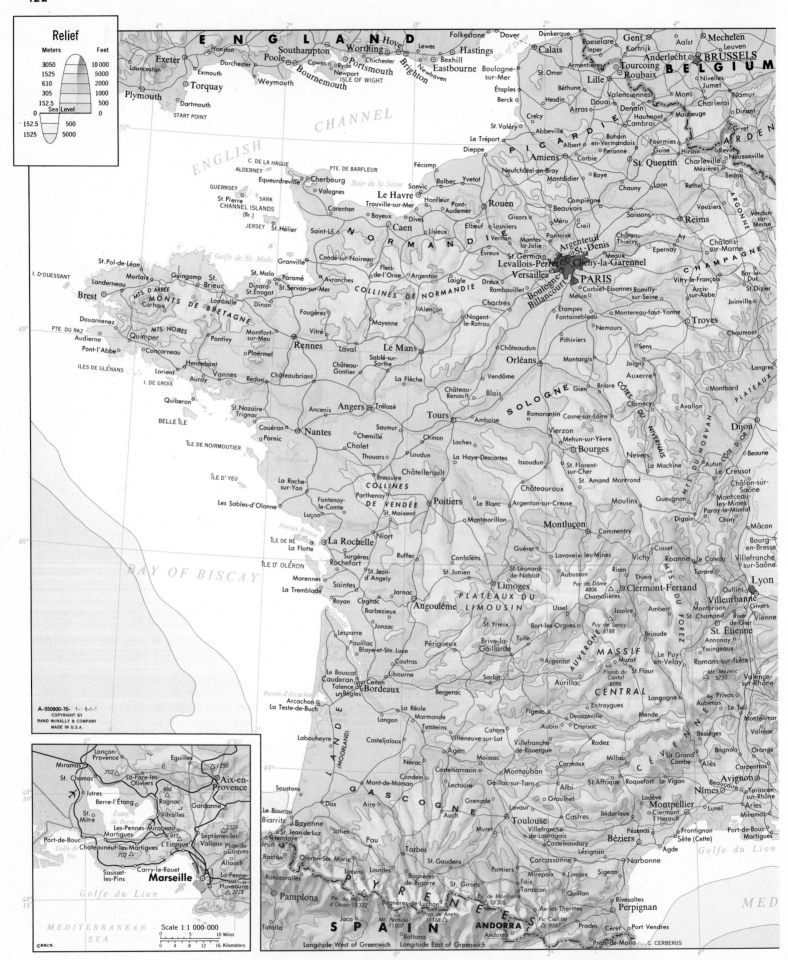

Relief

Meters		Feet
3050		10 000
1525		5000
610		2000
305		1000
152.5		500
0	Sea Level	0
-152.5		500
-1525		5000

START POINT

ENGLAND

ENGLISH CHANNEL

Str. of Dover

BELGIUM

BRUSSELS

ARDEN

PICARDIE

CHAMPAGNE

NORMANDIE

COLLINES DE NORMANDIE

PARIS

Versailles

Boulogne-Billancourt

MONTS DE BRETAGNE

MTS. NOIRES

MTS. D'ARRÉE

Brest

Rennes

Le Mans

Orléans

SOLOGNE

CÔTES DU NIVERNAIS

MTS DU MORVAN

PLATEAU

Dijon

CÔTE D'OR

BAY OF BISCAY

Nantes

Angers

Tours

Bourges

Lyon

COLLINES DE VENDÉE

Poitiers

La Rochelle

PLATEAUX DU LIMOUSIN

Limoges

Clermont-Ferrand

Puy de Dôme 4806

AUVERGNE

Puy de Sancy 6188

MASSIF

CENTRAL

Plomb du Cantal 6096

Mt. Mézenc 5750

St. Étienne

Bordeaux

GASCOGNE

LANDE (MOORLAND)

CÉVENNES

Nîmes

Montpellier

Toulouse

Golfe du Lion

PYRÉNÉES

Pic de Montcalm 10305

Pic Carlitte 9587

ANDORRA

SPAIN

Mt. Perdido 11007

Pico de Aneto 11168

Pic du Midi d'Ossau 10322

Pamplona

C. CERBERUS

Longitude West of Greenwich   Longitude East of Greenwich

A-550900-76- 1- 1-1-1
COPYRIGHT BY
RAND MCNALLY & COMPANY
MADE IN U.S.A.

Aix-en-Provence

Marseille

MEDITERRANEAN SEA

Golfe du Lion

Golfe de Fos

Étang de Berre

Scale 1:1 000 000

0   2   4   6   8   10 Miles

0 4 8 12 16 Kilometers

®rmcn.

Scale 1:4 000 000; one inch to 64 miles. Conic Projection
Elevations and depressions are given in feet

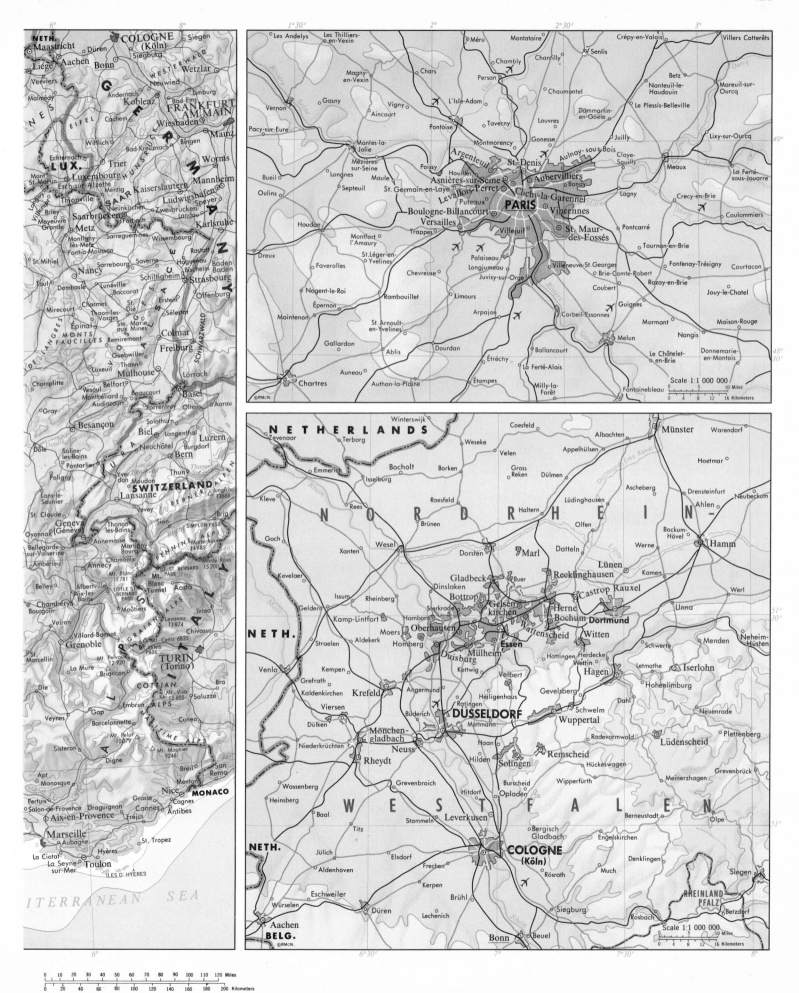

Map 1 (left panel — France/Germany/Switzerland/Italy):

NETH.
Maastricht · Düren · COLOGNE (Köln) · Siegen
Liège · Aachen · Bonn · Siegburg
Verviers · Andernach · Neuwied · Wetzlar
Malmédy · EIFEL · Koblenz · WESTERWALD · Limburg
Mont St. Martin · Cochem · Bad Ems · FRANKFURT AM MAIN
Echternach · Wittlich · Bingen · Wiesbaden · Mainz
LUX. · Trier · Bad Kreuznach · HUNSRÜCK
Luxembourg · Merzig · Kaiserslautern · Worms · Mannheim
Esch-sur-Alzette · SAAR · Neunkirchen · Ludwigshafen
Longwy · Thionville · Saarbrücken · Zweibrücken · Speyer · Landau
Briey · Forbach · Wissembourg · Karlsruhe
Moyeuvre-Grande · Metz · Sarreguemines · Rastatt
Montigny-lès-Metz · Saverne · Hagenau · Baden-Baden
Pont-à-Mousson · Sarrebourg · Bischheim · Offenburg
St. Mihiel · Nancy · Lunéville · Schiltigheim · Strasbourg
Toul · Dombasle · Baccarat · Erstein · SCHWARZWALD
Mirecourt · Charmes · St. Dié · Sélestat · Lörrach
Épinal · Thaon-les-Vosges · Ste. Marie aux Mines · Colmar
MONTS FAUCILLES · Remiremont · Guebwiller · Freiburg
Champlitte · Luxeuil · Thann · Mulhouse
Vesoul · Belfort · Basel
Gray · Montbéliard · Beaucourt · Porrentruy · Olten · Aarau
Besançon · Audincourt · Solothurn · Langenthal
Dôle · Salins-les-Bains · Biel · Neuchâtel · Burgdorf · Luzern
Poligny · Pontarlier · Bern · Thun
Lons-le-Saunier · Yverdon · Moudon · SWITZERLAND
St. Claude · Lausanne · BERNER ALPEN · Jungfrau 13668
Geneva (Genève) · Vevey · Brig · SIMPLON PASS
Oyonnax · Thonon-les-Bains · Sion · PENNINE ALPS · Matterhorn 14685
Bellegarde-sur-Valserine · Annemasse · Martigny · Monte Rosa 15200
Ambérieu · Annecy · Bourg · Chamonix · GT. ST. BERNARD PASS
Belley · Mt. Blanc 15781 · Aosta · Ivrea
Aix-les-Bains · LITTLE ST. BERNARD PASS · Blanc Tunnel · Chivasso
Chambéry · Moûtiers · GRAIAN ALPS · Levanna 11874
Bourgoin · Voiron · Mt. Cenis 6835 · Mt. Cenis Pass
Grenoble · Mt. Pelvoux 12920 · TURIN (Torino)
St. Marcellin · La Mure · Briançon · COTTIAN ALPS · Mt. Viso 12602 · Saluzzo
Die · Embrun · Gap · Bra · Cuneo
Veynes · Barcelonnette · MARITIME ALPS
Mt. Pelat 10079
Sisteron · Digne · Mt. Mounier 9246
Apt · Manosque · Breil · San Remo
Pertuis · Grasse · Menton · MONACO
Aix-en-Provence · Draguignan · Cannes · Nice · Cagnes · Antibes
Marseille · Aubagne · Fréjus
La Ciotat · Hyères · St. Tropez
La Seyne-sur-Mer · Toulon · ILES D'HYÈRES
MEDITERRANEAN SEA

Scale bar:
0 10 20 30 40 50 60 70 80 90 100 110 120 Miles
0 20 40 60 80 100 120 140 160 180 200 Kilometers

Map 2 (top right — Paris region):

Les Andelys · Les Thilliers-en-Vexin · Méru · Montataire · Crépy-en-Valois · Villers Cotterêts
Magny-en-Vexin · Chars · Chambly · Chantilly · Senlis · Betz
Vernon · Gasny · Vigny · L'Isle-Adam · Persan · Chaumontel · Nanteuil-le-Haudouin · Mareuil-sur-Ourcq
Pacy-sur-Eure · Aincourt · Pontoise · Taverny · Louvres · Le Plessis-Belleville
Mantes-la-Jolie · Montmorency · Gonesse · Juilly · Lixy-sur-Ourcq
Bueil · Mézières-sur-Seine · Maule · Argenteuil · St. Denis · Aulnay-sous-Bois · Claye-Souilly · Meaux
Longnes · Poissy · Houilles · Asnières-sur-Seine · Aubervilliers · Bondy · La Ferté-sous-Jouarre
Oulins · Septeuil · St. Germain-en-Laye · Levallois-Perret · Clichy-la-Garenne · Lagny · Crécy-en-Brie
Dreux · Houdan · Puteaux · PARIS · Vincennes · Pontcarré · Coulommiers
Boulogne-Billancourt · Versailles · Villejuif · St. Maur-des-Fossés · Tournan-en-Brie
Faverolles · Trappes · St. Léger-en-Yvelines · Palaiseau · Villeneuve-St. Georges · Fontenay-Trésigny · Courtacon
Nogent-le-Roi · Montfort l'Amaury · Chevreuse · Longjumeau · Brie-Comte-Robert · Rozay-en-Brie · Jouy-le-Chatel
Rambouillet · Limours · Juvisy-sur-Orge · Coubert · Guignes
Épernon · Arpajon · Corbeil-Essonnes · Guignes · Maison-Rouge
Maintenon · St. Arnoult-en-Yvelines · Mormant · Nangis
Gallardon · Ablis · Dourdan · Ballancourt · Melun · Le Châtelet-en-Brie · Donnemarie-en-Montois
Chartres · Auneau · Authon-la-Plaine · Étampes · Étréchy · La Ferté-Alais · Milly-la-Forêt · Fontainebleau

Scale 1:1 000 000
0 5 10 Miles
0 4 8 12 16 Kilometers
©RMCN.

Map 3 (bottom right — Netherlands/Nordrhein-Westfalen):

NETHERLANDS
Winterswijk · Coesfeld · Münster · Warendorf
Zevenaar · Terborg · Weseke · Albachten
Emmerich · Weseke · Velen · Appelhülsen · Hoetmar
Bocholt · Borken · Gross Reken · Dülmen · Ascheberg · Drensteinfurt · Neubeckum
Kleve · Isselburg · Raesfeld · Lüdinghausen · Ahlen
Rees · NORDRHEIN · Haltern · Olfen · Bockum-Hövel
Goch · Brünen · Werne · Hamm
Xanten · Wesel · Dorsten · Marl · Datteln · Recklinghausen · Lünen · Kamen · Werl
Kevelaer · Gladbeck · Buer · Castrop Rauxel · Unna
NETH. · Issum · Dinslaken · Bottrop · Gelsenkirchen · Herne · Bochum · Dortmund
Geldern · Rheinberg · Sterkrade · Hamborn · Wattenscheid · Witten · Schwerte · Menden · Neheim-Hüsten
Straelen · Kamp-Lintfort · Moers · Oberhausen · Herdecke · Wetter
Aldekerk · Homberg · Mülheim · Essen · Hattingen · Hagen · Iserlohn
Venlo · Kempen · Duisburg · Kettwig · Velbert · Gevelsberg · Hohenlimburg · Letmathe
Grefrath · Angermund · Heiligenhaus · Schwelm · Dahl
Kaldenkirchen · Krefeld · Büderich · Ratingen · Schwelm · Hohenlimburg
Viersen · Mettmann · DÜSSELDORF · Wuppertal · Radevormwald · Neuenrade
Dülken · Mönchen-gladbach · Haan · Solingen · Remscheid · Plettenberg
Niederkrüchten · Neuss · Hilden · Hückeswagen · Lüdenscheid
Rheydt · Grevenbroich · Burscheid · Wipperfürth · Meinerzhagen · Grevenbrück
Wassenberg · Hitdorf · Opladen · Berneustadt · Olpe
Heinsberg · Baal · Leverkusen · Bergisch Gladbach · Engelskirchen
NETH. · Titz · Stommeln · Bergisch Gladbach · Denklingen
WESTFALEN · Jülich · Elsdorf · COLOGNE (Köln) · Rösrath · Much · Siegen
Aldenhoven · Frechen · Kerpen · RHEINLAND-PFALZ
Eschweiler · Brühl · Siegburg · Rosbach · Betzdorf
Würselen · Düren · Lechenich
Aachen
BELG. · Bonn · Beuel

Scale 1:1 000 000
0 5 10 Miles
0 4 8 12 16 Kilometers
©RMCN.

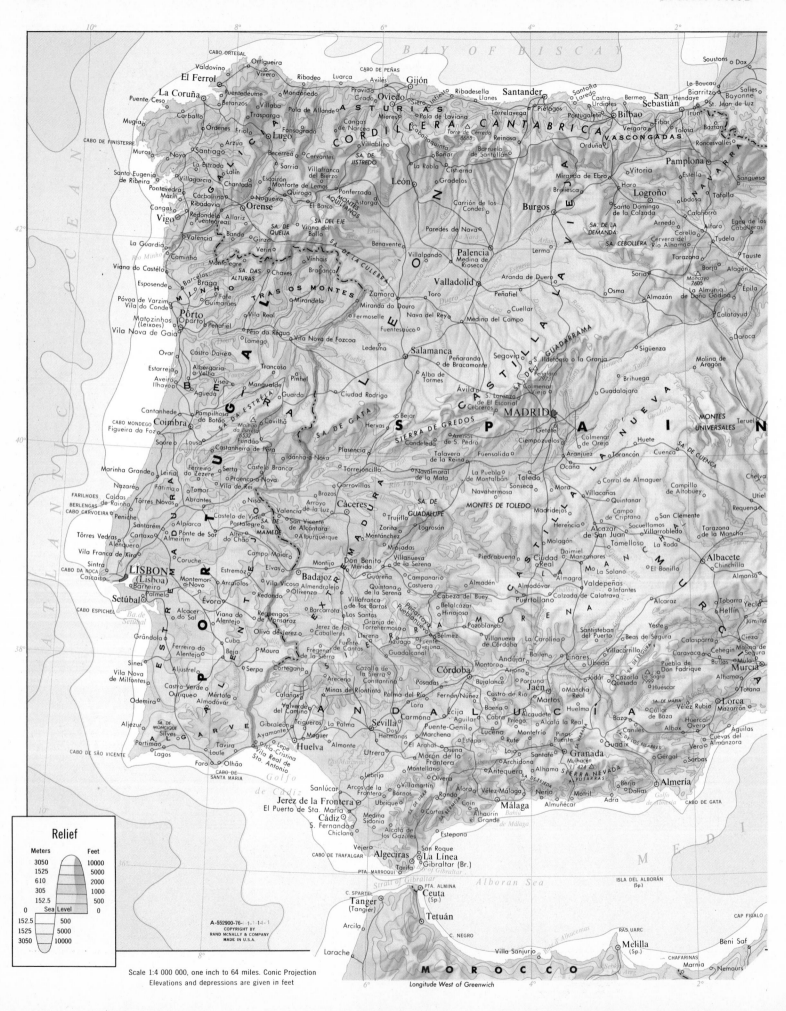

BAY OF BISCAY

ATLANTIC OCEAN

Valdovino
Ortigueira
CABO ORTEGAL
El Ferrol
La Coruña
Puente Ceso
Mugía
CABO DE FINISTERRE
Noya
Muros
Santa Eugenia
de Ribeira
Pontevedra
Marín
Vigo
Redondela
La Guardia
Caminha
Viana do Castélo
Esposende
Póvoa de Varzim
Vila do Conde
Matozinhos
(Leixoes)
Vila Nova de Gaia
Ovar
Estarreja
Aveiro
Ilhavo

Vivero
Ribadeo
Luarca
CABO DE PEÑAS
Avilés
Gijón
Oviedo
Santander
Ortigueira
Puentedeume
Villalba
Mondoñedo
Pravia
Grado
Siero
Infesto
Ribadesella
Llanes
Laredo
Castro Urdiales
Bermeo
San Sebastián
Biarritz
Bayonne
Soustons
Dax

Betanzos
Ordenes
Friol
Trasparga
Fonsagrada
Pola de Allande
Mieres
Pola de Laviana
Torrelavega
Piélagos
Santoña
Portugalete
Bilbao
Vergara
Éibar
Tolosa
Irún
Hendaye
St. Jean de Luz

Santiago
Arzúa
Lugo
Becerreá
Cervantes
Cangas
de Narcea
Villablino
SA. DE
JISTREDO
Torre de Cerredo
8688
Cabañaquinta
Boñar
Reinosa
Barruelo
de Santullán
Orduña
VASCONGADAS
Vitoria

La Estrada
Lalín
Chantada
Sarria
Villafranca
del Bierzo
León
La Robla
Cistierna
Gradelos
Miranda de Ebra
Briviesca
Haro
Santo Domingo
de la Calzada
Pamplona
Estella
Sangüesa

GALICIA
Carballo
Carballino
Ribadavia
Orense
Nogueira
Quiroga
Ponferrada
Astorga
Carrión de los
Condes
Paredes de Nava
Burgos
Lerma
SA. DE LA
DEMANDA
Arnedo
Calahorra
Tafalla

Cangas
Allariz
Puentéareas
SA. DEL EJE
Viana del
Bollo
Benavente
Villalpando
Palencia
Medina de
Rioseco
Aranda de Duero
Osma
Soria
SA. CEBOLLERA
Cervera del
Río Alhama
Corella
Alfaro
Tudela
Tauste
Borja
Alagón
Épila

CORDILLERA CANTABRICA
NAVARRA
Roncesvalles
Logroño
Lodosa
Egea de los
Caballeros

Valencia
Bande
Ginzo
Verín
Vinhais
Bragança
Zamora
Toro
Valladolid
Peñafiel
Cuéllar
Medina del Campo
Tarazona
Almazán
Calatayud
Daroca

La Guardia
Redondela
Viana do Castélo
Monfalegre
Barcelos
Braga
Fafe
Guimarães
Vila Real
Mirandela
Miranda do Douro
Fermoselle
Nava del Rey
Molina de
Aragón

SA. DAS
ALTURAS
Chaves
TRAS OS MONTES
LEÓN

Pôrto
Oporto
Penafiel
Castro Daire
Lamego
Peso da Régua
Vila Nova de Fozcoa
Fuentesaúco
Ledesma
Salamanca
Peñaranda
de Bracamonte
Segovia
S. Ildefonso o la Granja
Sigüenza
Brihuega
Guadalajara

Albergaria-
a-Velha
Agueda
Viseu
Manguaide
Trancoso
Pinhel
Guarda
Alba de
Tormes
Ávila
Peñalara
7973
Colmenar
Viejo

BEIRA
Cantanhede
Coimbra
Figueira da Foz
CABO MONDEGO
Pampilhosa
do Botão
SA. DA ESTRELA
Malhão
da Estrela
6532
Covilhã
Fundão
Ciudad Rodrigo
Béjar
Hervás
Peñaranda
de Bracamonte
S. Lorenzo de
El Escorial
Cebreros
MADRID
Getafe
Guadalajara
Montes
Universales
Teruel

Marinha Grande
Leiria
Nazaré
FARILHOES
Caldas
da Rainha
BERLENGAS
CABO CARVOEIRA
Peniche
Ferreiro
do Zezere
Serta
Vila de Rei
Castelo Branco
Praença-a-Nova
Idanha-a-Nova
Plasencia
Navalmoral
de la Mata
Talavera
de la Reina
Fuénsalida
Candeleda
Arenas
de S. Pedro
SIERRA DE GREDOS
Ciempozuelos
Colmenar
de Oreja
Aranjuez
Tarancón
Huete
Cuenca
SA. DE CUENCA
Chelva
Utiel
Requena

Fátima
Tomar
Abrantes
Garrovillas
Torrejoncillo
Cáceres
Navahermosa
Toledo
Mora
Sonseca
Corral de Almaguer
Villacañas
Quintanar
San Clemente
Tarazona
de la Mancha

Santarém
Alpiarça
Ponte de Sor
Arroyo
Valencia
de la Luz
San Vicente
de Alcántara
Brozas
SA. DE
GUADALUPE
Madridejos
Herencia
Alcázar
de San Juan
Campo
de Criptana
Socuéllamos
Villarrobledo
La Roda

Tôrres Novas
Cartaxo
Alenquer
Alpiarça
Almeirim
Alter
do Chão
Portalegre
SA. DE
MAMEDE
Alburquerque
Zorita
Logrosán
Trujillo
Montánchez
MONTES DE TOLEDO
Piedrabuena
Ciudad
Real
Daimiel
Manzanares
Tomelloso
La Solana
El Bonillo
Albacete
Chinchilla

Tôrres Vedras
Vila Franca de Xira
Sintra
CABO DA ROCA
Cascais
LISBON
(Lisboa)
Barreiro
Palmela
Montemor-
o-Novo
Arraiolos
Campo Maior
Elvas
Montijo
Don Benito
Mérida
Guareña
Villanueva
de la Serena
Campanario
Almadén
Almodóvar
Valdepeñas
Infantes
Alcaraz
Almansa

Setúbal
Ba. de
Setúbal
CABO ESPICHEL
Alcácer
do Sal
Viana do
Alentejo
Évora
Redondo
Vila Viçosa
Olivenza
Badajoz
Almendralejo
Villafranca
de los Barros
Los Santos
Granja de
Torrehermosa
Cabeza del Buey
Belalcázar
Hinojosa
Puertollano
Calzada de Calatrava
Almagro
Tobarra
Hellín
Yecla

Grândola
Ferreira do
Alentejo
Beja
Cuba
Reguengos
de Monsaraz
Barcarrota
Jerez de los
Caballeros
Llerena
Azuaga
Peñarroya
Pueblonuevo
Bélmez
Villanueva
de Córdoba
Pozoblanco
La Carolina
Villacarrillo
Santisteban
del Puerto
Beas de Segura
Calasparra
Cieza
Jumilla

Sines
Vila Nova
de Milfontes
Aljustrel
Serpa
Moura
Oliva de Jerez
Fuente
de Cantos
Fregenal
de la Sierra
Guadalcanal
Andújar
Bailén
Linares
Úbeda
Yeste
Caravaca
Cehegín
Molina de
Segura
Murcia

Odemira
Castro Verde
Mértola
Almodôvar
Cortegana
Aracena
Cazalla
de la Sierra
Constantina
Posadas
Bujalance
Arjona
Porcuna
Jaén
Mancha
Real
Martos
Jódar
Cazorla
La Sagra
7999
Huéscar
Puebla de
Don Fadrique
Mula
Alhama
Totana
Lorca
Mazarrón

SA. DE
MONCHIQUE
Silves
Aljezur
Calañas
Minas de Ríotinto
Valverde
del Camino
Palma del Río
Fernán-Núñez
Castro del Rio
Baena
Cabra
Priego
Alcalá la Real
Santafé
Montefrío
Pinos-
Puente
Baza
Caniles
Albox
Huércal
Overa
Cuevas del
Almanzora
Vera

Portimão
Lagos
Gibraleón
Trigueros
La Palma
Huelva
Almonte
Sevilla
Dos
Hermanas
Carmona
Écija
Aguilar
Marchena
Lucena
Loja
Archidona
Granada
Mulhacén
11 424
Sierra Nevada
ALPUJARRAS
SA. DE MARIA
Gérgal
Sorbas
Almería

Loulé
Faro
Olhão
Tavira
Sta. Cristina
Lepe
Ayamonte
Vila Real de
Sto. Antonio
Moguer
Utrera
El Arahal
Osuna
Morón de la
Frontera
Montellano
Olvera
Antequera
Alhama
SA. DE TEJEDA
Vélez-Málaga
Nerja
Adra
Berja
Dalías
CABO DE GATA

CABO DE
SANTA MARIA
Golfo
de Cádiz
Sanlúcar
Arcos de la
Frontera
Villamartín
Bornos
Ubrique
Ronda
Coín
Alhaurín
el Grande
Málaga
Almuñécar
Motril
Golfo de Almería

Jerez de la Frontera
El Puerto de Sta. María
Cádiz
S. Fernando
Chiclana
Medina
Sidonia
Alcalá de
los Gazules
Estepona
Bahía
de Málaga

Vejero
CABO DE TRAFALGAR
PTA. MARROQUI
San Roque
Algeciras
La Línea
Gibraltar (Br.)
Tarifa
Strait of Gibraltar
ISLA DEL ALBORÁN
(Sp.)
Alboran Sea
MEDI

C. SPARTEL
Tanger
(Tangier)
PTA. ALMINA
Ceuta
(Sp.)
M

Arcila
Tetuán
C. NEGRO
RAS UARC
CAP FIGALO

Larache
Villa Sanjurjo
Melilla
(Sp.)
MOROCCO
Marmia
Beni Saf
Nemours
CHAFARINAS

PORTUGAL
ESTREMADURA
ALGARVE
ALENTEJO
ANDALUCIA
MADRE
SIERRA MORENA
CASTILLA LA NUEVA
CASTILLA LA VIEJA
MURCIA
ARAGON
MONTES UNIVERSALES

Relief

Meters		Feet
3050		10000
1525		5000
610		2000
305		1000
152.5		500
0	Sea Level	0
152.5		500
1525		5000
3050		10000

Scale 1:4 000 000, one inch to 64 miles. Conic Projection
Elevations and depressions are given in feet

Longitude West of Greenwich

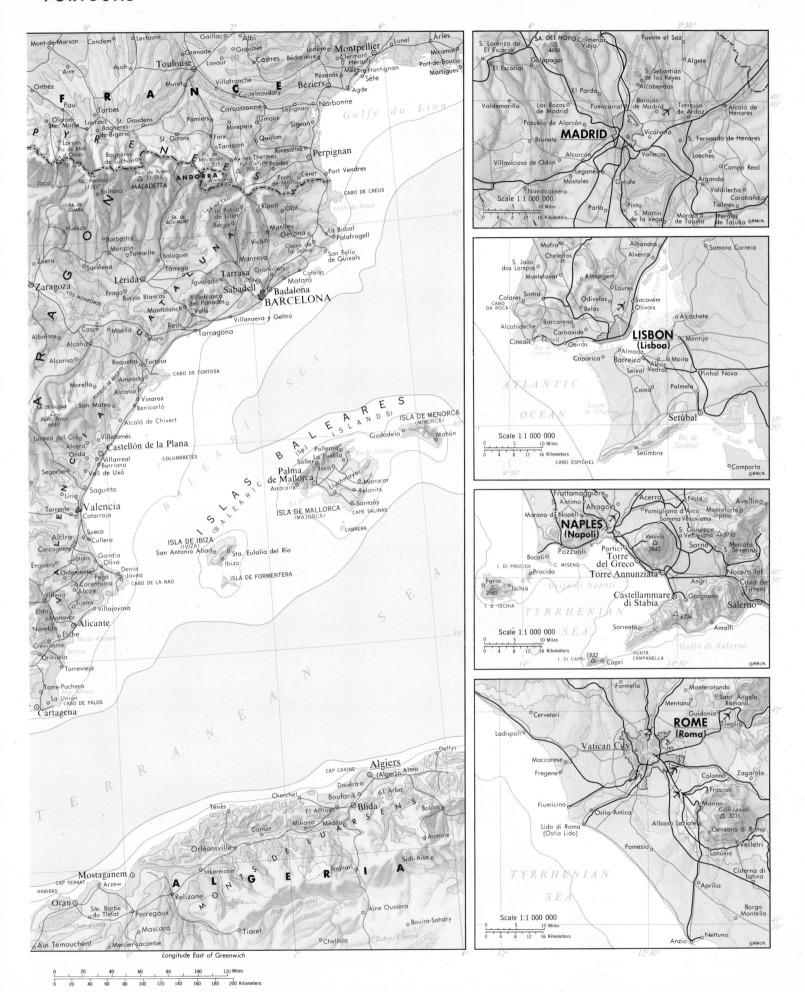

Continued on pp. 120-121

Continued on pp. 122-123

AUSTRIA

SWITZERLAND

FRANCE

FR.

CARNIC ALPS
KARAWANKEN
BRENNER PASS
St. Gotthard Tunnel
Jungfrau 13 668
LEPONTINE ALPI
St. Moritz
Simplon Tunnel
Locarno
Bellinzona
Lugano
Como
Lecco
Bergamo
Varese
ALPI OROBIE
Sondrio
Tirano
Bolzano
Merano
Bressanone
Pieve di Cadore
Tolmezzo
Villach
Klagenfurt
Dravograd
Maribor
Murska Sobota
Ptuj
Čakovec
Varaždin
Koprivnica
Szigetvár

H U N G A R Y

Monte Rosa 15 200
Matterhorn
GR. ST. BERNARD PASS
LITTLE ST. BERNARD PASS
Mont Blanc 15 778
GRAIAN ALPS
MT. CENIS PASS
Aosta
Ivrea
Biella
Novara
Vercelli
Vigevano
Pavia
Lodi
MILAN (Milano)
Monza
Treviglio
Crema
Cremona
Brescia
Chiari
Verona
Villafranca
Mantova (Mantua)
Este
Padova (Padua)
Vicenza
Treviso
Conegliano
Pordenone
Udine
Cividale del Friuli
Gorizia
Monfalcone
Trieste (Trst)
Ljubljana
Kranj
Škofja Loka
Idrija
Novo Mesto
Zagreb
Čazma
Bjelovar
Daruvar
Virovitica

SLOVENIJA
HRVATSKA (CROATIA)
SLAV

TURINO (Torino)
Chieri
Asti
Alessandria
Casale
Tortona
Novi
Acqui
Alba
Bra
Savigliano
Fossano
Cuneo
Mondovi
COTTIAN ALPS
Mt. Viso 12 602
Saluzzo
Pinerolo
Susa
MARITIME ALPS
Nice
MONACO
Ventimiglia
S. Remo
Imperia
Albenga
Savona
Genoa (Genova)
Rapallo
Chiavari
Sestri Levante
La Spezia
Carrara
Massa
Viareggio
Lucca
Pisa
Livorno (Leghorn)
Pistoia
Prato
Florence (Firenze)
Empoli
Pontedera
Poggibonsi
Volterra
Siena
Arezzo
Cortona

LIGURIA
PIEMONTE
LOMBARDIA
EMILIA
ROMAGNA
TOSCANA
VENETO
MARCHE
UMBRIA
LAZIO
ABRUZZI
MOLISE
CAMPANIA
PUGLIA
BASILICATA
CALABRIA

Piacenza
Codogno
Parma
Reggio
Modena
Carpi
Mirandola
Bologna
Imola
Faenza
Forli
Cesena
Rimini
Ravenna
Comacchio
Ferrara
Copparo
Adria
Rovigo
Chioggia
Venice (Venezia)
Golfo di Venezia
G. of Trieste
Pula
Rovinj
Poreč
Pazin
Rijeka (Fiume)
ISTRA
CRES
RAB
PAG
Zadar
Šibenik
Split
Knin
Sinj
Makarska
Korčula
Lastovo
Hvar
Vis
Brač
Šolta

ADRIATIC SEA

BOSNA
Banja Luka
Bihać
Bosanski Novi
Prijedor
Bosanska Gradiška
Jajce
Travnik
Donji Vakuf
Bugojno
Livno
Glamoč

LIGURIAN SEA

Gorgona
CAPRAIA
C. CORSE
Calvi
Mt. Cinto 8891
Corte
Ajaccio
Mt. Incudine
Sartène
Bonifacio
Porto-Vecchio

CORSICA (Fr.)

ISOLA D' ELBA
Piombino
Portoferraio
I. DI MONTECRISTO
I. DEL GIGLIO
I. DI GIANNUTRI
PIANOSA
Grosseto
Orbetello
Massa Marittima
Montepulciano
Orvieto
Viterbo
Civitavecchia
Tarquinia (Corneto)
C. Linaro
Rieti
Terni
Spoleto
Foligno
Perugia
Assisi
Gubbio
Città di Castello
Fabriano
Macerata
Fermo
Ascoli Piceno
San Benedetto del Tronto
Teramo
Penne
M. Corno 9560
L'Aquila
Chieti
Pescara
Ortona
Vasto
Termoli
Vieste
TESTA DEL GARGANO
Monte Sant'Angelo
Manfredonia
Golfo di Manfredonia
Foggia

Vatican City
ROME (Roma)
Frascati
Tivoli
Guidonia
Albano Laziale
Velletri
Aprilia
Anzio
Sabaudia
Terracina
Gaeta
Minturno
Sezze
Fondi
Sora
Frosinone
Ferentino
Cassino
Isernia
Campobasso
Agnone
Larino
San Severo
San Marco
Lucera
Cerignola
Andria
Barletta
Trani
Molfetta
Bari
Bitonto
Ruvo
Corato
Minervino
Canosa
Bovino
Ariano
Benevento
Caserta
Santa Maria
Capua
Aversa
Avellino
Nola
NAPLES (Napoli)
Pozzuoli
I. DI ISCHIA
I. DI CAPRI
Sorrento
Torre del Greco
Vesuvio 3842
Salerno
Eboli
Golfo di Salerno
P. LICOSA
Potenza
Matera
Altamura
Gravina
Gioia del Colle
Spinazzola
Rionero
Lavello
Taranto
Ginosa
Pisticci
Moliterno
Sala Consilina
Lauria
Castrovillari
Corigliano
Rossano
Cosenza
San Giovanni in Fiore
Nicastro
Catanzaro
Vibo Valentia
Polistena
Palmi
Bagnara
Reggio di Calabria
Messina
Milazzo
Taormina
Acireale
Catania
Paterno
Adrano
Mt. Etna (Vol.) 10 868
Caltagirone
Gela
Ragusa
Modica
Siracusa
Noto

TYRRHENIAN SEA

ISOLE EOLIE
STROMBOLI (Vol.)
SALINA
LIPARI
PANAREA
FILICUDI
ALICUDI
VULCANO
DI USTICA

SICILIA
Palermo
Bagheria
Cefalù
Termini
Trapani
Marsala
Mazara del Vallo
Castelvetrano
Sciacca
Agrigento
Marsala
Monreale
Partinico
Corleone
Alcamo
Caltanissetta
Enna
Piazza
Armerina

SARDINIA
Sassari
Alghero
Bosa
Oristano
Golfo di Oristano
Arborea
Cagliari
Golfo di Cagliari
Carbonara
Iglesias
Villacidro
Carloforte
I. DI S. PIETRO
I. DI S. ANTIOCO
Porto Torres
Tempio Pausania
Olbia
ASINARA
CAPRERA
Nuoro
Dorgali
Golfo di Orosei
La Marmora 6015
Lanusei
C. COMINO
C. SPARTIVENTO
C. CARBONARA
Quartu Sant'Elena

Scale 1:4 000 000; one inch to 64 miles. Conic Projection
Elevations and depressions are given in feet

AEGEAN SEA
Same scale as main map
AKR. SPATHA
Kastélli
Khaniá (Canea)
Réthimnon
Iráklion (Candia)
Neápolis
Sitía
AKR. SIDHEROS
CRETE (Greece)
Khóra Sfakíon
Ano Viánnos
Ierápetra
AKR. LITHINON
GÁVDHOS
GAIDHOURONISI
MEDITERRANEAN SEA

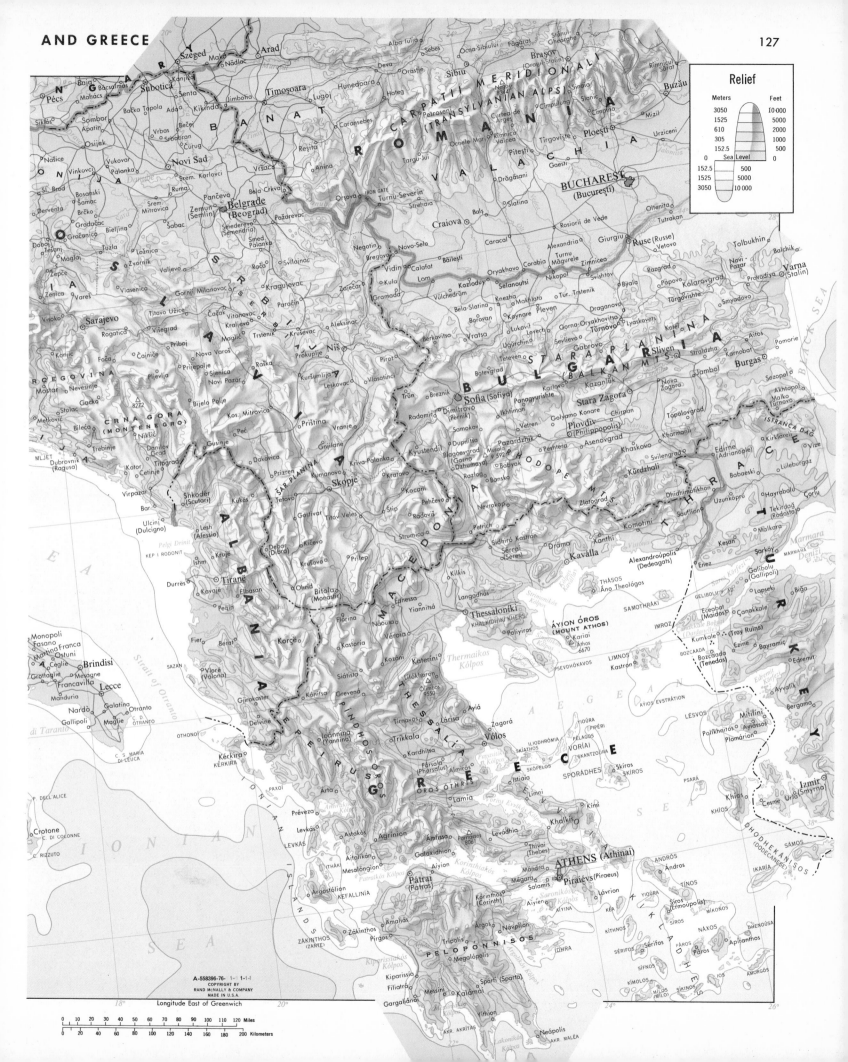

Relief

Feet				
5000	2000	1000	500	0

Meters				
1525	610	305	152.5	Sea Level
				0
				152.5

KOSTROMA

Kostroma

Kineshma

Ples

Vichuga

Furmanov

Rodniki

Kokhma

IVANOVO

Ivanovo

Shuya

Teykovo

Nerekhta

Gavrilov-Yam

Gavrilov Posad

Suzdal'

Velikoye

Pereslavl'-Zalesskiy

Kol'chugino

Karabanovo

Pokrov

Kirzhach

Vladimir

V L A D I M I R

Sudogda

Melenki

Kasimov

Spassk-Ryazanskiy

Spas-Klepiki

Sobinka

Gus'-Khrustal'nyy

Urshel'skiy

Orekhovo-Zuyevo

Pavlovsky Posad

Lyubertsy

Ramenskoye

Bronnitsy

Kolomna

Yegor'yevsk

Zaraysk

Kashira

Ozëry

Venëv

Skopin

Ryazhsk

Sapozhok

Sasovo

Ryazan'

R Y A Z A N'

Mikhaylov

Dankov

Lebedyan'

Michurinsk

TAMBOV

Gryazi

Lipetsk

L I P E T S K

Usman'

Zadonsk

Yelets

Yefremov

Livny

Novosil

Maloarkhangelsk

Kolpny

Dmitrovsk

Kromy

Orël

O R Ë L

Mtsensk

Bolkhov

Kosel'sk

Belëv

Chern'

Chekalin

Aleksin

Tula

T U L A

Novomoskovsk

Venëv

Bogoroditsk

Stalinogorsk

Uzlovaya

Serpukhov

Podol'sk

MOSCOW

Moskva

Kuntsevo

Babushkin

Shchelkovo

Noginsk

Shchëlkovo

Zvenigorod

Istra

Ruza

Vysokovsk

Volokolamsk

Klin

Dmitrov

Taldom

Kalyazin

Kashin

Uglich

Myshkin

Rybinsk

Tutayev

Yaroslavl'

Y A R O S L A V L'

Rostov

Danilov

Lyubim

Poshekhon'ye-Volodarsk

Gryazovets

Vologda

VOLOGDA

Cherepovets

V O L O G D A

Ustyuzhna

Ves'yegonsk

Krasny Kholm

Bezhetsk

Kesova Gora

Kimry

Kalinin

(Tver')

Staritsa

Zubtsov

Rzhev

Sychëvka

Gzhatsk

Vyaz'ma

Mozhaysk

Naro-Fominsk

Borovsk

Maloyaroslavets

Medyn'

Vereya

Tarusa

Kaluga

Yukhnov

Mosal'sk

Mnyov

Meshchovsk

Sukhinichi

Kirov

Lyudinovo

Zhizdra

Bryansk

B R Y A N S K

Karachev

Trubchevsk

Pochep

Starodub

Novozybkov

Zlynka

Klintsy

Surazh

Mglin

Klimovichi

Kostyukovichi

Cherikov

Krichëv

Chausy

Mogilëv

M O G I L Ë V

Shklov

Bykhov

Rogachëv

Bobruysk

Berezino

Borisov

Cherven'

Minsk

M I N S K

Dzerzhinsk

Slutsk

Nesvizh

Kletsk

Lyuban'

BRE

Luninets

B R E S T

Kuznetsovo

Vysokovsk

Narofominsk

VOLGA

MOSCOW RA

O S K V A

S M O L E N S K

F.

Nikitinka

Belyy

Yartsevo

Dukhovshchina

Dorogobuzh

Yel'nya

Pochinok

Smolensk

Demidov

Roslavl'

Spas-Demensk

Monastyrshchina

Krasnyy

Mstislavl'

Dubrovno

Orsha

Orsha

Gorki

Vitebsk

V I T E B S K

Senno

Chashniki

Beshenkovichi

Lepel'

Ulla

Gorodok

Nevel'

Velikiye Luki

Novosokol'niki

Velizh

Toropets

Kholm

Kun'ya

Usvyaty

Gorodok

Surazh

B E L O R U S S I A N   S. S. R.

BELORUSSIAN

Polotsk

Disna

Glubokoye

Dokshitsy

Ushachi

Lepel'

Begoml'

Pleshchenitsy

Vileyka

Molodechno

M O L O D E C H N O

Vileyka

Volozhin

N E S V I Z H

Stolbtsy

Baranovichi

P S K O V

Pskov

Ostrov

Palkino

Novorzhev

Opochka

Pustoshka

Sebezh

Idritsa

Osveya

Drissa

Verkhnedvinsk

Dagda

Ludza

Rēzekne

Kārsava

Viļaka

Balvi

Gulbene

Madona

Līvāni

Varakļāni

Krustpils

Jēkabpils

Daugavpils

Griva

Ilūkste

Zarasai

Vidzy

Braslav

L A T V I A N   S. S. R.

LATVIAN

Alūksne

Valka

Valga

Smiltene

Cēsis

Antsla

Võru

Tartu

(Dorpat)

Elva

Võõpsu

Petseri

Laura

E S T O N I A N   S. S. R.

ESTONIAN

Jõgeva

Tapa

Rakvere

N. Jõesuu

Narva

Kingisepp

Jõhvi

Kunda

Aseri

Põltsamaa

Viljandi

L. Pskov

Tallinn

GULF OF FINLAND

N O V G O R O D

Novgorod

Staraya Russa

Soltsy

Shimsk

Dno

Porkhov

Dedovichi

Bologoye

Okulovka

Valday

Borovichi

Krestsy

Malaya Vishera

Chudovo

Lyuban'

Tosno

Kolpino

Pushkin

Pavlovsk

Gatchina

LENINGRAD

L E N I N G R A D

Krasnoye Selo

Petrokrepost'

Volkhov

Tikhvin

Tosno

Luga

Batetska

Strugi Krasnye

Gdov

Slantsy

Kingisepp

V A L D A I

V A L D A I   H I L L S

Ostashkov

Selizharovo

Kuvshinovo

Vyshniy Volochëk

Torzhok

Likhoslavl'

Spirovo

Udomlya

Maksatikha

Krasnyy Kholm

Demyansk

Lychkovo

Molvotitsy

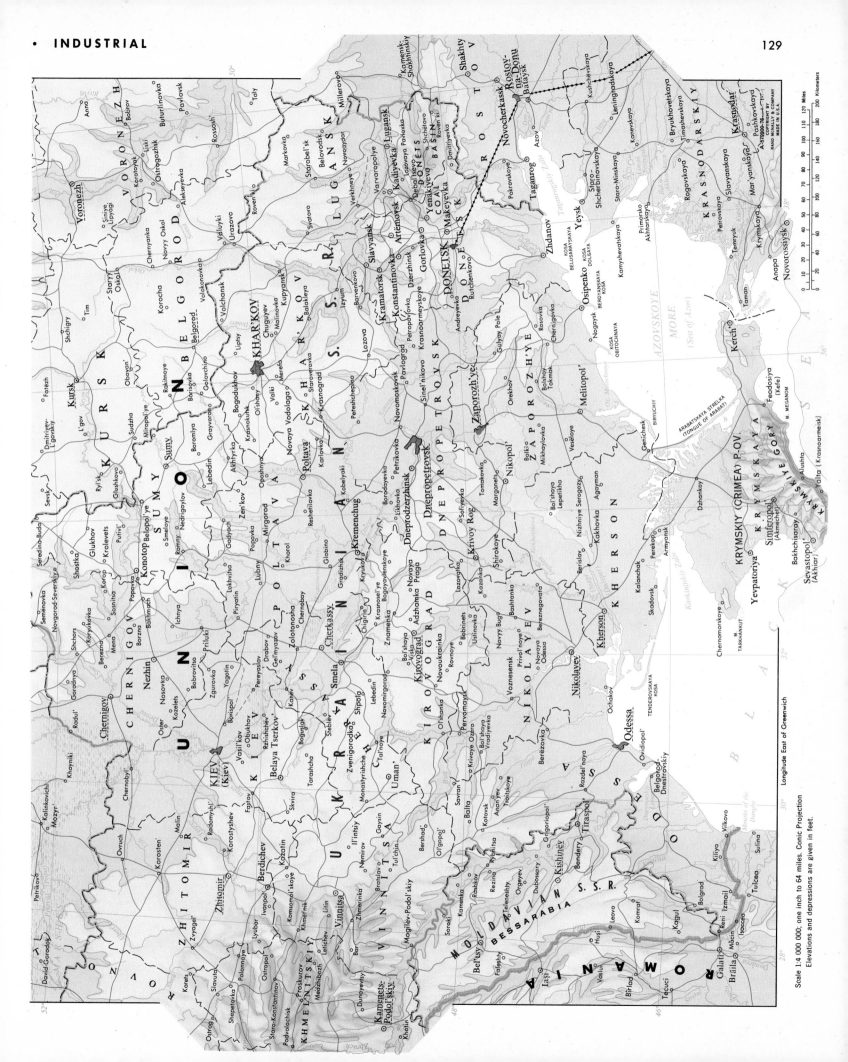

Scale 1:4 000 000; one inch to 64 miles. Conic Projection
Elevations and depressions are given in feet.

Longitude East of Greenwich

ATLANTIC OCEAN

ARCTIC

SVALBARD (SPITSBERGEN) (Nor.)

ZEMLYA FRANTSA-IOSIFA (FRANZ JOSEF LAND)

BARENTS SEA

NOVAYA ZEMLYA

ZEMLYA

KARSKOYE MORE (Kara Sea)

BELYY

UNITED KINGDOM
Glasgow
Aberdeen
Edinburgh
Newcastle

NORTH SEA

NORWAY
Bergen
Oslo

SWEDEN
Göteborg
Stockholm
Norrköping

Trondheim

Gulf of Bothnia
Vaasa
Luleå
Kemi

FINLAND
Turku
Helsinki

LAPLAND

Vardö
Hammerfest
Narvik

Murmansk
KOLA PEN.
KOL'SKIY POL.
Kirovsk

WHITE SEA

P-OV KANIN
Mezen'

PECHORA BASIN

P-OV YAMAL

Dikson

P-OV GYDANSKIY

DENMARK
COPENHAGEN
Ålborg
Kiel
Malmö

Kaliningrad
Gdańsk

POLAND
WARSAW
Poznań
Łódź
Kraków

GERMANY
HAMBURG
Bremen
BERLIN
Leipzig

PRAGUE
CZECHO-
SLOVAKIA
Brno
Ostrava

ESTONIAN S.S.R.
Tallinn
Tartu

LATVIAN S.S.R.
Riga

LITHUANIAN S.S.R.
Kaunas
Vilnyus

LENINGRAD
Vyborg
Pskov'

Velikiye Luki

BELORUSSIAN S.S.R.
Minsk
Mogilev
Gomel'
Baranovichi
Brest
Pinsk

Vitebsk

Velikiy Ustyug

KOMI A.S.R.
Syktyvkar
Ust'-Kulom

Ust'-Tsil'ma
Pechora
Troitsko-Pechorsk

Nar'yan-Mar

Khal'mer-Yu
Vorkuta

Salekhard
Novyy Port
Tazovskoye

MOSCOW
(Moskva)
Serpukhov
Smolensk
Kalinin
Yaroslavl'
Ivanovo
Vladimir

Kaluga
Bryansk
Orël
Tula
Ryazan'
Novomoskovsk

GORKI
Shuya
Murom
Orekhovo-Zuyevo

Kostroma
Kazan'

Kirov
Glazov
Perm'
Chusovoy

Gubakha
Krasnotur'insk

WESTERN SIBERIAN LOWLAND

Khanty Mansiysk
Surgut

Narym
Kolpashevo

KIYEV
UKRAINIAN S.S.R.
Zhitomir
L'vov
Chernovtsy
Vinnitsa
Berdichev

Sumy
Khar'kov
Poltava
Kursk
Yelets
Lipetsk
Voronezh

Saransk
Alatyr'
Penza
Tambov
Ul'yanovsk

Izhevsk
Kungur
Krasno-
ufimsk

Sverdlovsk
Nizhniy Tagil
Nev'yansk
Alapayevsk
Tavda

Irbit
Tyumen'

Tomsk

KUZBAS

Anzhero-Sudzhensk
Kemerovo

ROMANIA
BUCHAREST
Ploesti
Galati
Sibiu
Oradea
Cluj
Iaşi
Kishinev
MOLD. S.S.R.

Dnepropetrovsk
Krivoy Rog
Zaporozh'ye

DONETSK
Lugansk

Saratov
Syzran'
Kuybyshev
Buzuluk
Buguruslan
Abdulino

Ufa
Sterlitamak
Zlatoust

Birsk

Chelyabinsk
Shadrinsk
Kamyshlov
Yalutorovsk

Ishim
Tara

Novosibirsk
Leninsk
Gur'yevsk
Kiselëvsk
Novokuznetsk
Chesnokovka

Odessa
Nikolayev
Kherson

Simferopol'
Sevastopol'
Kerch'

Rostov-na-Donu
Zhdanov
Shakhty
Krasnodar

Volgograd
Kamyshin

Ural'sk

Orenburg
Orsk
Magnitogorsk
Mednogorsk
Karialy

Verkhne-Ural'sk
Sol'-Iletsk

Kurgan
Petropavlovsk
Kustanay

Omsk
Tatarsk
Kuybyshev
Kargat

Cherlak
Stepnyak

Pavlodar

Barnaul
Rubtsovsk
Biysk
Gorno-Altaysk

BLACK SEA

Zonguldak
Sinop
Samsun
Trabzon
Batumi

Novorossiysk
Sochi
Maykop
Armavir
Stavropol'
Groznyy

CAUCASUS MTS.

GEORGIAN S.S.R.
Tbilisi

ARMENIAN S.S.R.
Yerevan

Astrakhan

CASPIAN DEPRESSION

Gur'yev

KAZAKH

KIRGIZ STEPPE

Aktyubinsk
Temir

Chelkar

Turgay
Igiz

Atbasar

Tselinograd
(Akmolinsk)

Temir Tau
Karaganda
Karkaralinsk

Balkhash

Semipalatinsk
Leninogorsk
Zyryanovsk

G. Belukha
15,157

Ayaguz

TURKEY
TOROS DAGLARI
Sivas
Tokat
Erzincan
Erzurum
Kars
Malatya
Diyarbakır

KURDISTAN

AZERBAYDZHAN S.S.R.
BAKU
Kirovabad
Krasnovodsk

CASPIAN SEA

Aral'sk
Novo-Kazalinsk
Tyura-Tam

PLATO UST'-URT

ARAL'SKOYE MORE (ARAL SEA)

Kounradskiy

Urdzhar

Zaysan

DZUNGA

SYRIA
Aleppo
Al Mawsil

Tabriz
Lenkoran'
Rasht

ELBURS MTS.

Krasnovodsk

TURKMEN S.S.R.
Ashkhabad

PESKI KARAKUMY (DESERT)

Tashauz

UZBEK S.S.R.

Chimbay
Turkul'

PESKI KYZYL KUM (DESERT)

Kzyl-Orda

Turkestan

Chimkent
Arys

Dzhambul

PESKI MUYUN-KUM

TASHKENT

Frunze
KIRGIZ S.S.R.

Tokmak
Alma-Ata

Panfilov

Przheval'sk

Tihua (Urumchi)

CHINA

IRAQ
Baghdad
Kirkük
Hit
Tikrit

IRAN
TEHRAN
Hamadan
Kermanshah
Qom

ZAGROS MTS.

Mashhad

Bukhara
Chardzhou
Samarkand
Kokand
Andizhan
Fergana
Namangan

TADZHIK S.S.R.
Dushanbe

Sufu

TIEN SHAN

KOPET MTS.

Mary

Scale 1:20 000 000; one inch to 315 miles.
Lambert's Azimuthal, Equal Area Projection
Elevations and depressions are given in feet

Relief

Feet	Meters
10000	3050
5000	1525
2000	610
1000	305
500	152.5
Sea Level	Sea Level
0	0
500	152.5
5000	1525
10000	3050

Below
Sea Level

Continued on pages 112-113

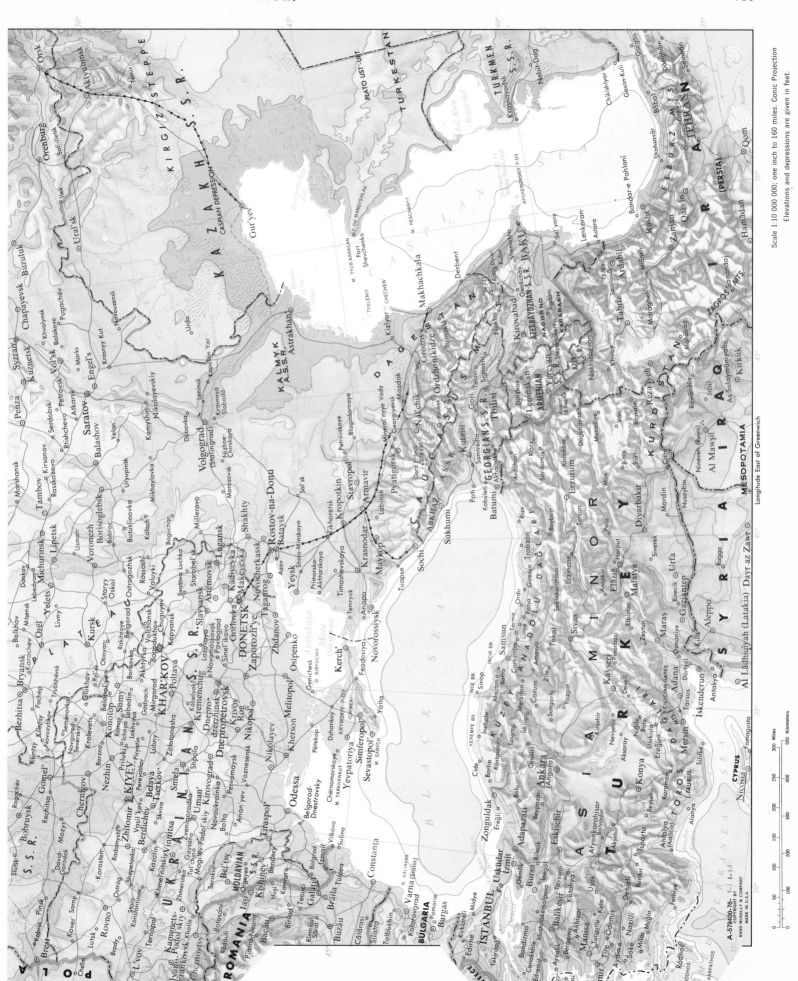

Scale 1:10 000 000; one inch to 160 miles. Conic Projection

Elevations and depressions are given in feet.

Continued on pp. 114-115

Scale 1:16 000 000; one inch to 250 miles Conic Projection
Elevations and depressions are given in feet.

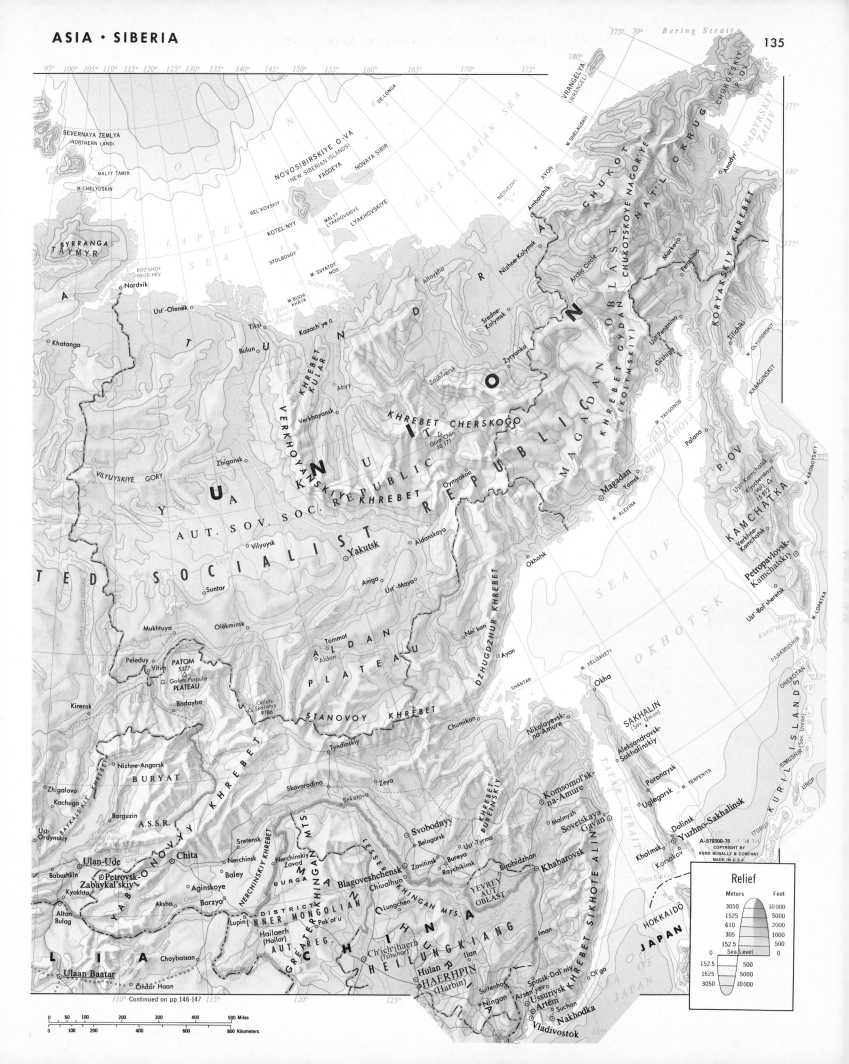

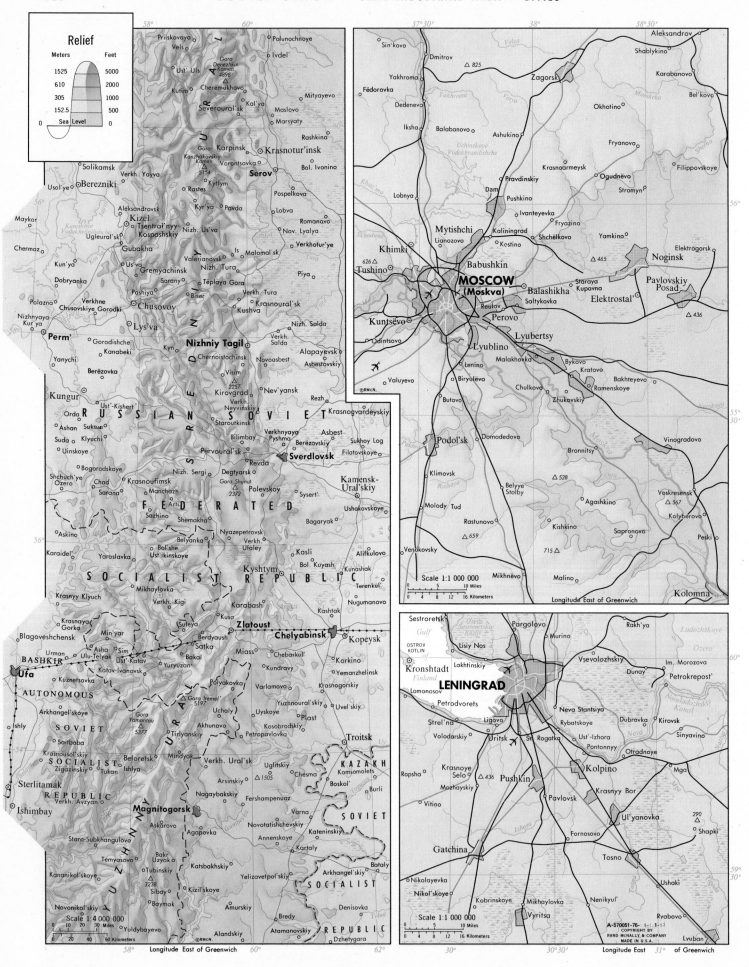

Relief

Meters	Feet
1525	5000
610	2000
305	1000
152.5	500
Sea Level	0

Scale 1:4 000 000

Longitude East of Greenwich

Scale 1:1 000 000

Longitude East of Greenwich

Scale 1:1 000 000

Longitude East of Greenwich

A-570051-76—1-1-14
COPYRIGHT BY
RAND McNALLY & COMPANY
MADE IN U.S.A.

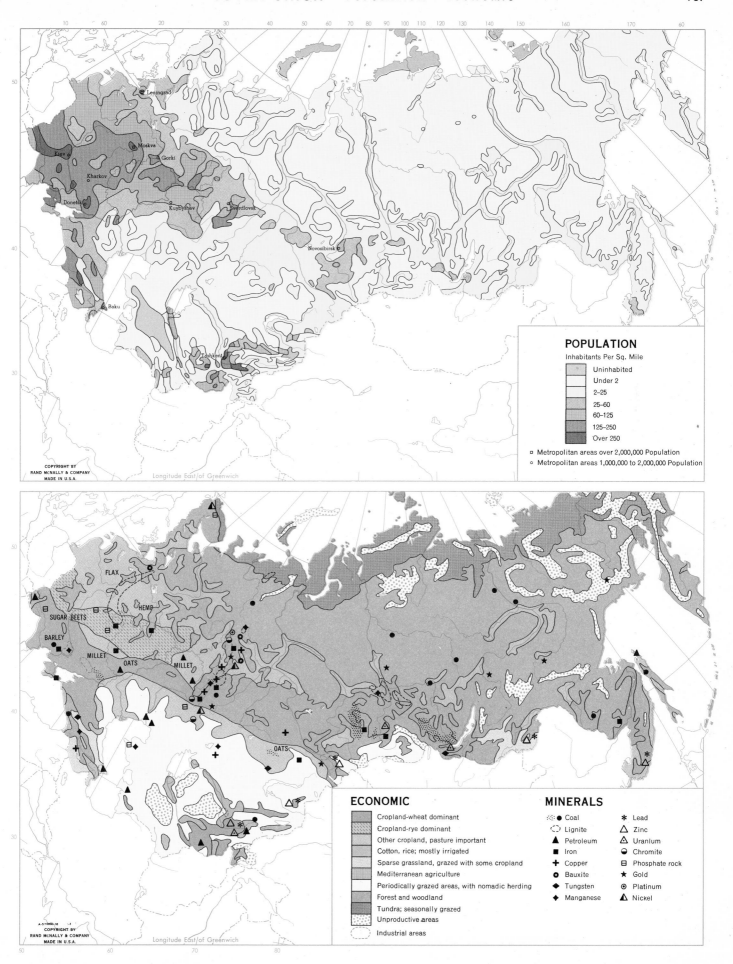

POPULATION

Inhabitants Per Sq. Mile

Uninhabited
Under 2
2–25
25–60
60–125
125–250
Over 250

▫ Metropolitan areas over 2,000,000 Population
○ Metropolitan areas 1,000,000 to 2,000,000 Population

Longitude East/of Greenwich

ECONOMIC

Cropland-wheat dominant
Cropland-rye dominant
Other cropland, pasture important
Cotton, rice; mostly irrigated
Sparse grassland, grazed with some cropland
Mediterranean agriculture
Periodically grazed areas, with nomadic herding
Forest and woodland
Tundra; seasonally grazed
Unproductive areas

Industrial areas

MINERALS

● Coal
○ Lignite
▲ Petroleum
■ Iron
✛ Copper
◉ Bauxite
◆ Tungsten
◆ Manganese

✳ Lead
△ Zinc
△ Uranium
◠ Chromite
⊟ Phosphate rock
★ Gold
◉ Platinum
△ Nickel

Longitude East/of Greenwich

Relief

Meters	Feet
3050	10 000
1525	5000
610	2000
305	1000
0	Sea Level
	0 Below Sea Level
152.5	500
1525	5000
3050	10 000
6100	20 000

A-519695-76- 1-1-1-1
COPYRIGHT BY
RAND MCNALLY & COMPANY
MADE IN U.S.A.

Scale 1:40 000 000; one inch to 630 miles. Lambert's Azimuthal, Equal Area Projection
Elevations and depressions are given in feet

Continued on page 163

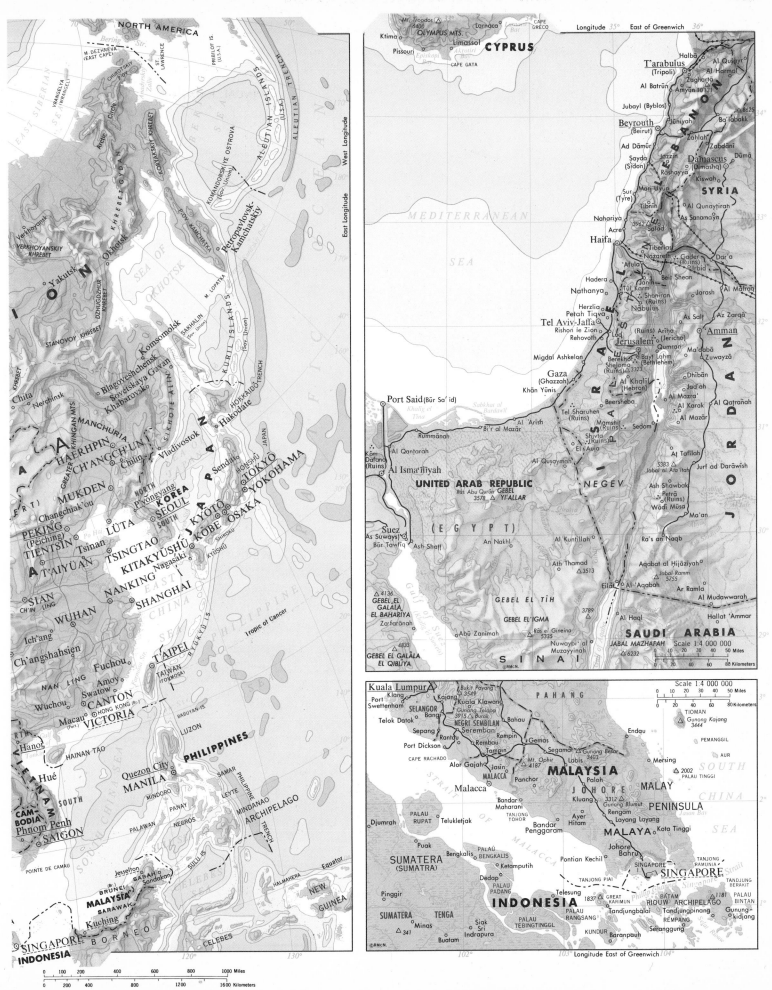

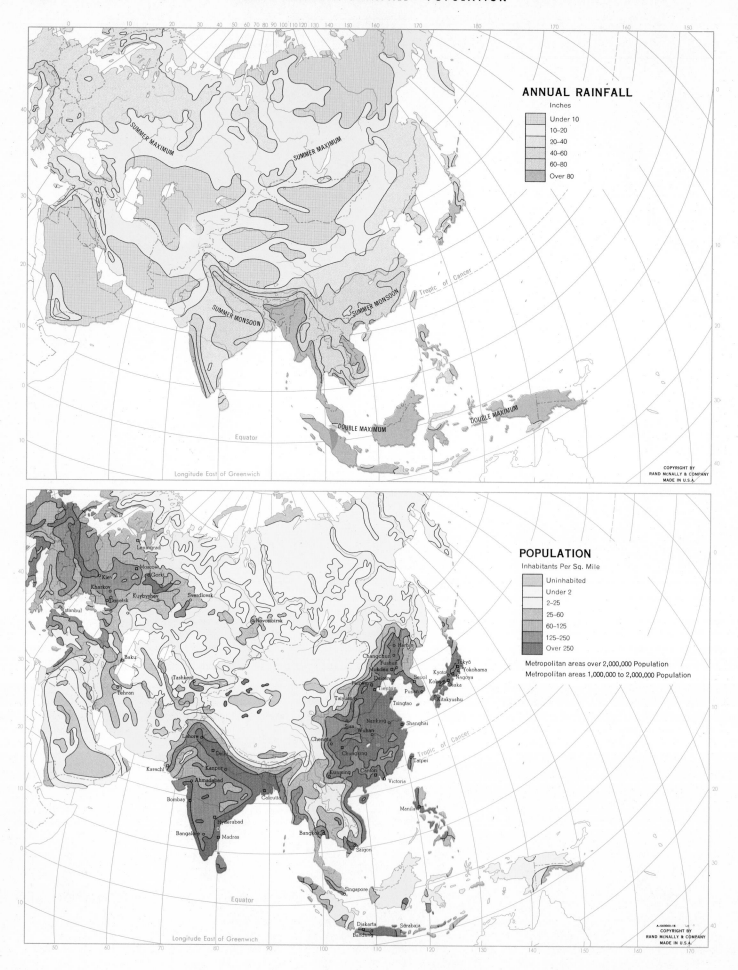

ANNUAL RAINFALL

Inches

Under 10
10–20
20–40
40–60
60–80
Over 80

SUMMER MAXIMUM

SUMMER MAXIMUM

SUMMER MONSOON

SUMMER MONSOON

SUMMER MONSOON

Tropic of Cancer

DOUBLE MAXIMUM

DOUBLE MAXIMUM

Equator

Longitude East of Greenwich

COPYRIGHT BY
RAND MCNALLY & COMPANY
MADE IN U.S.A.

POPULATION

Inhabitants Per Sq. Mile

Uninhabited
Under 2
2–25
25–60
60–125
125–250
Over 250

Metropolitan areas over 2,000,000 Population
Metropolitan areas 1,000,000 to 2,000,000 Population

Leningrad
Kiev
Moscow
Gorki
Kharkov
Donetsk
Kuybyshev
Sverdlovsk
Istanbul
Novosibirsk
Baku
Changchun
Harbin
Fushun
Mukden
Tokyō
Yokohama
Tashkent
Dairen
Peiping
Seoul
Kyoto
Nagoya
Kobe
Osaka
Tehran
Tientsin
Pusan
Taiyuan
Kitakyushu
Tsingtao
Nanking
Sian
Wuhan
Shanghai
Lahore
Chengtu
Delhi
Chungking
Tropic of Cancer
Karachi
Kanpur
Kunming
Canton
Taipei
Ahmadabad
Victoria
Bombay
Calcutta
Manila
Hyderabad
Bangalore
Madras
Bangkok
Saigon
Singapore
Equator
Longitude East of Greenwich
Djakarta
Surabaja
Bandung

A-640000-18
COPYRIGHT BY
RAND MCNALLY & COMPANY
MADE IN U.S.A.

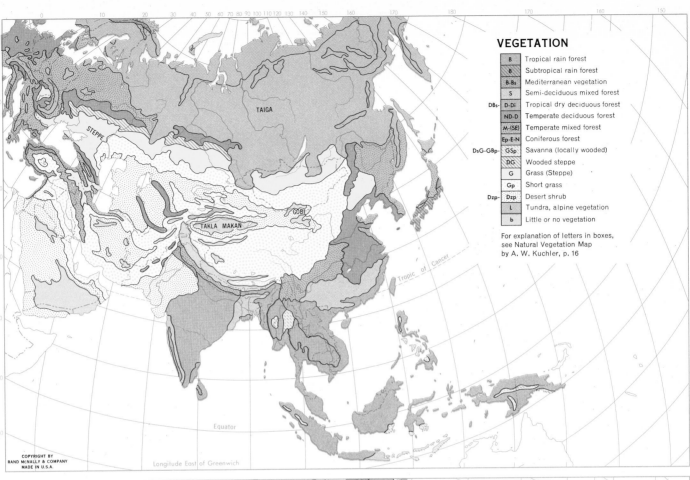

VEGETATION

	B	Tropical rain forest
	B	Subtropical rain forest
	B-Bs	Mediterranean vegetation
	S	Semi-deciduous mixed forest
DBs-	D-Di	Tropical dry deciduous forest
	ND-D	Temperate deciduous forest
	M-(SE)	Temperate mixed forest
	Ep-E-N	Coniferous forest
DsG-GBp-	GSp	Savanna (locally wooded)
	DG	Wooded steppe
	G	Grass (Steppe)
	Gp	Short grass
Dzp-	Dzp	Desert shrub
	L	Tundra, alpine vegetation
	b	Little or no vegetation

For explanation of letters in boxes,
see Natural Vegetation Map
by A. W. Kuchler, p. 16

Longitude East of Greenwich

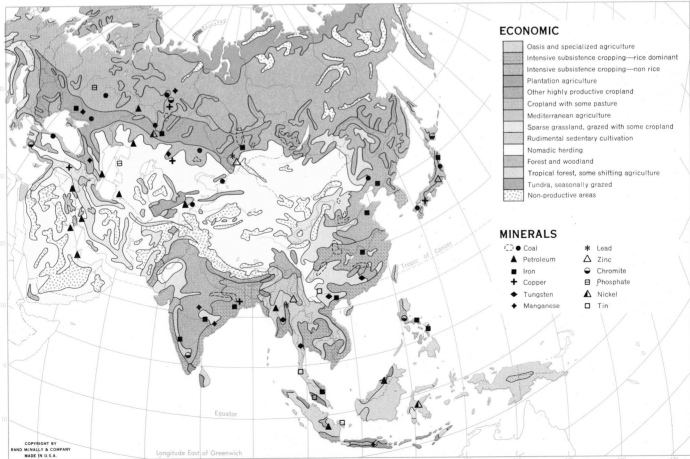

ECONOMIC

	Oasis and specialized agriculture
	Intensive subsistence cropping—rice dominant
	Intensive subsistence cropping—non rice
	Plantation agriculture
	Other highly productive cropland
	Cropland with some pasture
	Mediterranean agriculture
	Sparse grassland, grazed with some cropland
	Rudimental sedentary cultivation
	Nomadic herding
	Forest and woodland
	Tropical forest, some shifting agriculture
	Tundra, seasonally grazed
	Non-productive areas

MINERALS

●	Coal	✳	Lead
▲	Petroleum	△	Zinc
■	Iron	◓	Chromite
✚	Copper	⊟	Phosphate
◆	Tungsten	◮	Nickel
◆	Manganese	□	Tin

Longitude East of Greenwich

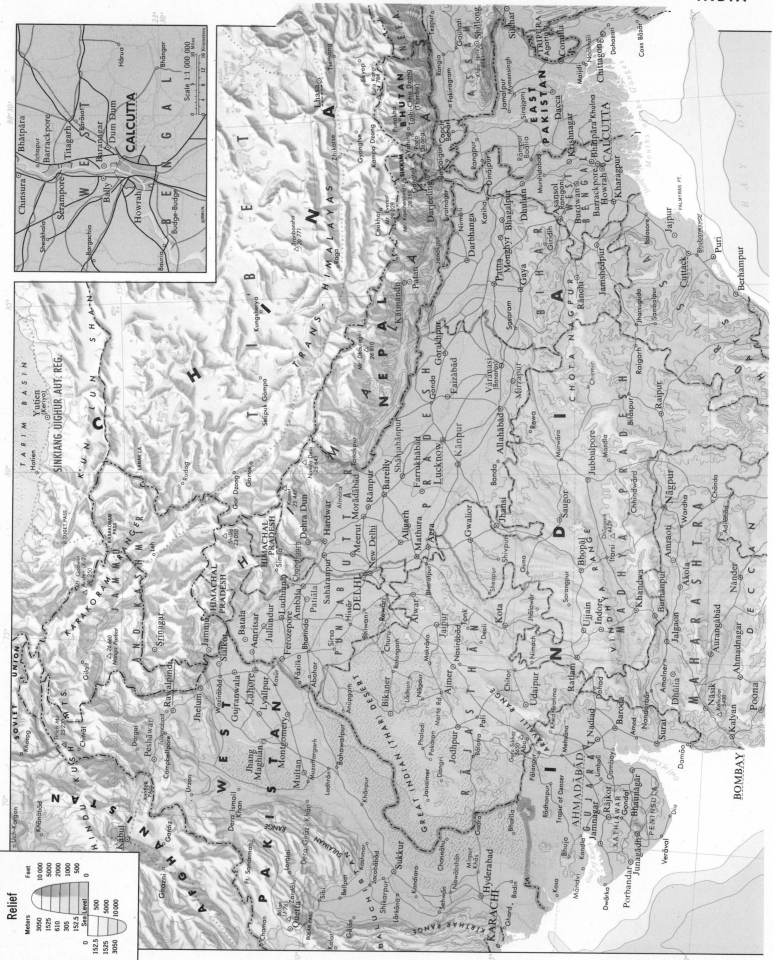

Relief

Meters	Feet	
3050	10 000	
1525	5000	
610	2000	
305	1000	
152.5	500	
0	Sea Level	0
152.5		500
1525		5000
3050		10000

Scale 1:1 000 000

WEST BENGAL

CALCUTTA

Chinsura
Bhātpāra
Barrackpore
Ichāpur
Sheakhāla
Serāmpore
Titāgarh
Bārāsat
Dum Dum
Bhāngar
Hārua
Bally
Barāngar
Bauria
Budge-Budge
Sheakhāla
Bargachia
Howrah

©RMCN

SINKIANG UIGHUR AUT. REG.

TARIM BASIN

KUN LUN SHAN

TIBET

TRANS HIMALAYAS

HIMALAYAS

NEPAL

T'IB ET

SOVIET UNION

AFGHANISTAN

HINDU KUSH MTS.

KARAKORAM RANGE

JAMMU AND KASHMIR

HIMACHAL PRADESH

PUNJAB

WEST PAKISTAN

RAJASTHAN

GREAT INDIAN (THAR) DESERT

ARAVALLI RANGE

GUJARAT

KATHIAWAR PENINSULA

MADHYA PRADESH

VINDHYA RANGE

DECCAN

MAHARASHTRA

UTTAR PRADESH

BIHAR

WEST BENGAL

ORISSA

CHOTA NAGPUR

SIKKIM

BHUTAN

N.E.F.A.

ASSAM

EAST PAKISTAN

TRIPURA

BAY OF BENGAL

BOMBAY

New Delhi
DELHI

Lhasa

Mt. Everest
29 028

Kanchenjunga
28 146

Nanda Devi
25 645

Mt. Godwin
Austen (K2)
28 250

Nanga Parbat
26 660

Trisul Mt.
23 420

KARACHI

CALCUTTA

TROPIC OF CANCER

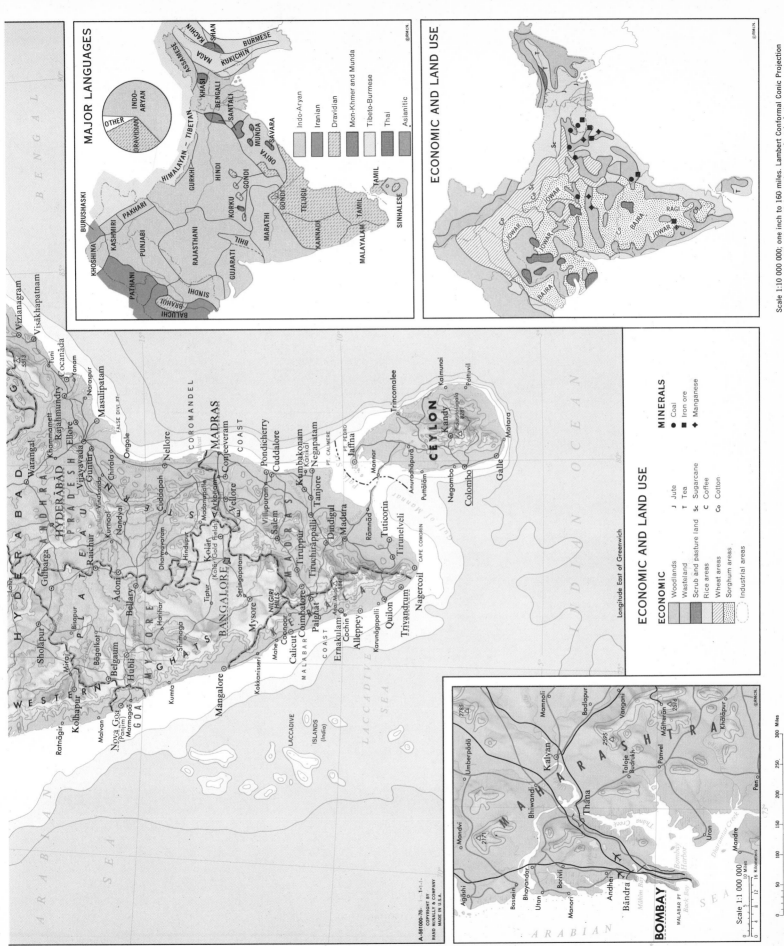

MAJOR LANGUAGES

Indo-Aryan
Iranian
Dravidian
Mon-Khmer and Munda
Tibeto-Burmese
Thai
Asianitic

OTHER
INDO-ARYAN
DRAVIDIAN

BURUSHASKI
KHOSHINA
KASHMIRI
PAKHARI
PATHANI
PUNJABI
SINDHI
BALUCHI
BRAHUI
GUJARATI
RAJASTHANI
BHIL
MARATHI
KORKU
GONDI
HINDI
GURKHI
HIMALAYAN – TIBETAN
KHASI
SANTALI
MUNDA
SAVARA
ORIYA
GONDI
TELUGU
KANNADA
TAMIL
MALAYALAM
TAMIL
SINHALESE
BENGALI
ASSAMESE
NAGA
KUKICHIN
KACHIN
SHAN
BURMESE

ECONOMIC AND LAND USE

JOWAR
BAJRA
RAGI

Scale 1:10 000 000; one inch to 160 miles. Lambert Conformal Conic Projection
Elevations and depressions are given in feet

B E N G A L

Vizianagram
Visākhapatnam

Tuni
Cocanāda
Rajahmundry
Masulipatam
Ellore
Narsapur
Vanam
Khammameti
Warangal
HYDERĀBĀD
ANDHRA
PRADESH
Vijayavada
Guntūr
Chirala
Ongole
Nellore
FALSE DIV.PT.

COROMANDEL
COAST

MADRAS

Conjeeveram
Pondicherry
Cuddalore
Kumbakonam
Karikāl
Negapatam

Gulbarga
Raichur
Kurnool
Nandyāl
Cuddapah
Madanapalle
Arkonam
Vellore
Villupuram
Tanjore

HYDERĀBĀD
Bisapur
Adoni
Bellary
Kolār (Gold Fields)
Kolār
Salem
Tiruppur
Tiruchirāppalli
Dindigul
Madura
Rāmnad
PT. CALIMERE

CEYLON
Trincomalee
Kalmunai
Pottuvil
Kandy
Adam's Peak
8281
Matara
Galle
Colombo
Negombo
Anurādhāpura
Puttalam
PT. PEDRO
Jaffna
Mannar

PLATEAU
DECCAN

Sholapur
Miraj
Bisapur
Bāgalkot
Belgaum
Hubli
MYSORE
Harihar
Shimoga
Tiptur
Seringapatam
BANGALORE
Mysore
NILGIRI HILLS
Coonoor
Coimbatore
Palghat
Alai-Mudi
8841
Ernakulam
Cochin
Alleppey
Quilon
Trivandrum
Nagercoil
CAPE COMORIN
Tuticorin
Tirunelveli
Karunāgapalli

Ratnāgiri
Kolhāpur
Malvan
Nova Goa (Panjim)
Marmagāō
GOA
Kumta
Mangalore
Kokkaniseri
Mahe
Calicut
MALABAR COAST
K E R A L A

WESTERN GHATS

A R A B I A N
S E A

LACCADIVE
ISLANDS (India)

L A C C A D I V E
S E A

I N D I A N   O C E A N

Longitude East of Greenwich

ECONOMIC AND LAND USE

ECONOMIC

Woodlands
Wasteland
Scrub and pasture land
Rice areas
Wheat areas
Sorghum areas
Sugarcane
Industrial areas

J Jute
T Tea
Sc Sugarcane
C Coffee
Co Cotton

MINERALS

● Coal
■ Iron ore
◆ Manganese

BOMBAY

M A H A R A S H T R A

Mamnoli
Bodlapur
Vangani
Khadapur
2785
2516
Umberpāda
Kalyan
Māthera
2595
Mandvi
Bhiwandi
Taloje Budrukh
Panvel
Thāna
2171
Bombay Harbour
Uran
Thāna Creek
Pen
Dharamtar Creek
Mandre
Agāshi
Uttan
Bhayandar
Borivli
Malabar Pt
Malhim Bay
Back Bay
Andheri
Bāndra
Manori
MALABAR PT
A R A B I A N
S E A

Scale 1:1 000 000

Scale 1:10 000 000

A-561000-76-
COPYRIGHT BY
RAND MCNALLY & COMPANY
MADE IN U.S.A.

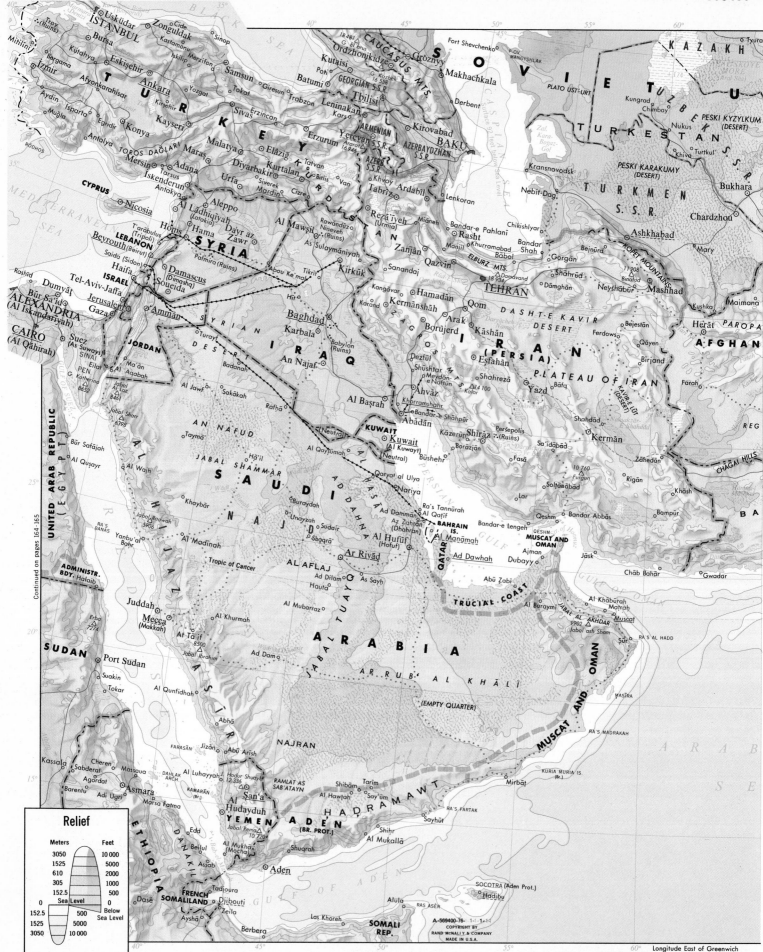

Relief

Meters		Feet
3050		10 000
1525		5000
610		2000
305		1000
152.5		500
0	Sea Level	0
152.5		Below 500
1525	Sea Level	5000
3050		10 000

Continued on pages 164-165

A-569400-76- 1-1- 1-1
COPYRIGHT BY
RAND M C NALLY & COMPANY
MADE IN U.S.A.

Longitude East of Greenwich

Scale 1:16 000 000; one inch to 250 miles. Polyconic Projection
Elevations and depressions are given in feet

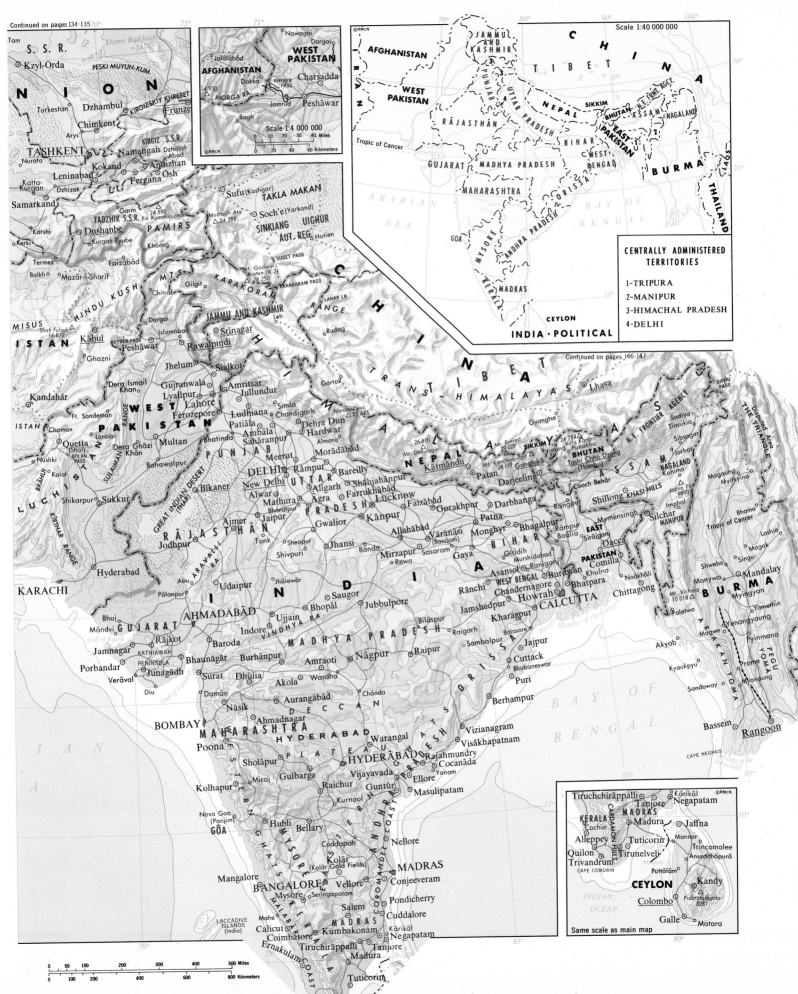

Southwestern

Continued on pages 134·135

WEST PAKISTAN
AFGHANISTAN
Scale 1:4 000 000

Scale 1:40 000 000

CHINA

AFGHANISTAN

WEST PAKISTAN

JAMMU AND KASHMIR

PUNJAB

TIBET

NEPAL

SIKKIM

BHUTAN

N.E. FRNT. AGCY.

RĀJASTHĀN

UTTAR PRADESH

ASSAM

NAGALAND

Tropic of Cancer

BIHAR

EAST PAKISTAN

BURMA

GUJARAT

MADHYA PRADESH

WEST BENGAL

THAILAND

MAHARASHTRA

ORISSA

ARABIAN SEA

BAY OF BENGAL

GOA

MYSORE

ANDHRA PRADESH

KERALA

MADRAS

CEYLON

CENTRALLY ADMINISTERED TERRITORIES

1-TRIPURA
2-MANIPUR
3-HIMACHAL PRADESH
4-DELHI

INDIA · POLITICAL

CEYLON

Same scale as main map

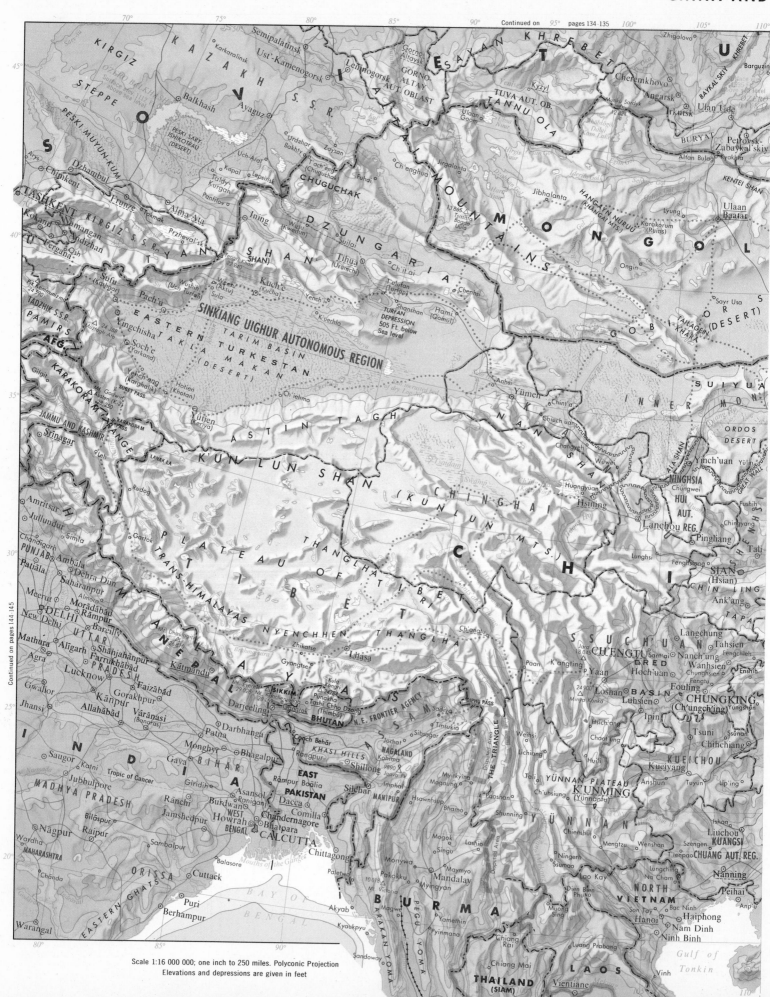

Continued on pages 134-135

Continued on pages 144-145

Scale 1:16 000 000; one inch to 250 miles. Polyconic Projection
Elevations and depressions are given in feet

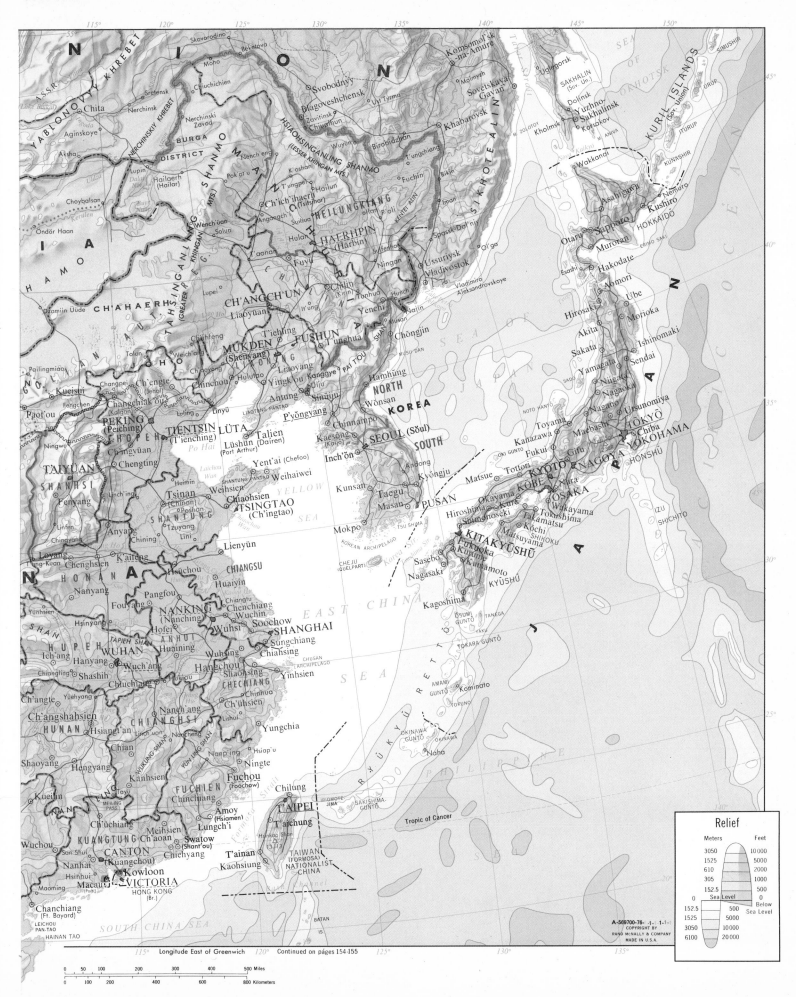

Relief

Meters		Feet
1525		5000
610		2000
305		1000
152.5		500
0 Sea Level		0

LIAONING

Kaip'ing
Hsingch'eng CHÜHUA TAO
Suichung
Chienchangying Ch'ienwei
Linyü
LIAONING
Hsiungyüen 3714
PANTAO
Fuchow
LIAOTUNG
Fuhsien
P'itzuwo
P'ulantien
Lü TA Talien (Dairen)
Lüshun (Port Arthur)
CH'ANGHSING TAO
HSICHUNG TAO
FENGMING TAO
KUANGLU TAO
TACH'ANGSHAN TAO
CH'ANGSHAN LIEHTAO
CH'ANGTZU TAO

Hsihoying SHAN
PEICHING SHIH
PEKING (Peiching)
Haitien
Shuni Changkochuang
Tsunhua
Chihsien
T'unghsien
Sanho
Yut'ien
Fengjun
Hsiangho Paoti
Ts'aiyü
Langfang
Huanghoutien
Wangch'ingt'o
Tinghsing
Paikouchen
Shengfang
Kuch'eng
Wanhsien
T'anghsien
Ch'ingyüan
Jench'iu
Luling
Yahungch'iao Kuyeh
T'ANGSHAN
Luanhsien
Lot'ing
Ningho Lut'ai
TIENTSIN (T'ienching)
T'angku
Koku
Taku

Chienchangying
Funing Ch'inhuangtao
Ch'angli
Ch'inghsien
Ch'ik'ou

POHAI

HOPEH
Tinghsien Lihsien
Ankuo Hochien
Tungeh'angshou
Chengting
Huoly
Wuchi Shentse
Chiaoyang
Shenhsien
Shihmen (Shihkiachwang)
Yangch'uanchan
Chaohsien
Yüanshih
Ningching
Chiaoho
Yenshan
Shangchialin
Pot'ou
Tsanghsien
Yangsanmu
Yangerhchuang
T'ingho
P'englai Ch'aoshui
Huanghsien
Longk'ou
Yent'ai (Chefoo)
Weihaiwei

SHANHSI
Hsiyang
TAIHANG SHAN
Hsingt'ai Weihsien
Hengshui
Chinghsien
Ningchin
Wuch'iao
Tehsien
Huimin Pinhsien
Liching
Hsihsienchen
Moup'ing SHAN
Jungch'eng
Wenteng

Neich'iu
Hsingchiawan
Hsiaching
Kaot'ang
Shangho
Ch'uti
Pohsing
Yangchiaokou
Kuangjao
Chaoyüen 2743 CHIAOW
SHIHTZU SHAN 2861
2707

Nankung
Linch'ing
Ch'ingp'ing
Yuch'eng
Ch'ingch'eng
Changch'iu Chouts'un Itu
AL SHAN
2285 Laiyang
1968
SHAN Hsiatsʻun

Kuangp'ing
Kuant'ao Kuanhsien
Liaoch'eng
Tsinan (Chinan)
Fouts'un
Changtien
Weihsien
Shoukuang
Ch'angi
P'ingtu
Chiangchanchi

Ch'iuhsien
Yungnien
Linchang
Taming
Hsinhsien
Ch'angch'ing
TAHSIEN
Poshan 3284
Lineh'ü
Anch'iu
Kaomi
Chimo 3871

Hantan
Shulyehen Liuyüan Nahlo
T'ai SHAN
5800 T'aian
T'ussuk'ou SHAN
Yüehchuang
Chingchih
Chiaohsien
Chuch'eng
TSINGTAO (Ch'ingtao)

Anyang
Ch'uwang
Sh'ouchang
Yenchuang
T'IENMA SHAN
Ch'ingfeng Tungp'in

SHANTUNG

P'engchengchen
Puhsien
Tungping
Ningyang CHIUNÜ SHAN
Wenshang
T'ai'an 2427
Ishui
5956
Ch'ihsien
T'aok'ou P'uyang
Tzuyang Ch'ufou Ssushui
4100
Chining Tungt'antien Tapingi
Chühsien
Jihchao

Hsinhsiang
Chihsien
Tungming Kotse
Chinhsiang
KUANKU SHAN
Feihsien
Chiaotso
Ch'angyüan
Yenching
Kaoch'eng
T'enghsien
Lini

SHANHSI HONAN
Chenghsien (Chengchow) K'aifeng
Ts'aohsien
Lungku
Ch'ingk'ouchen Wan
Haichow Wan

YELLOW SEA

Yuhsien
Hsincheng Weishih
Ch'ihsien
Shanhsien
Fenghsien
Chinganchi
T'aierhchuang
Tunghai
Lienyün

Hsiangch'eng
Linying Yencheng
Lohochai
Yüch'eng
Shangch'iu
Hsiai
Tangshan
Kuanhu
T'anch'eng
Hsinp'u
Kuanyün

Yehhsien
Hsüch'ang
Yenling
Chech'eng
Hsüchou (Süchow)
Suining
Such'ien
Tashanchen

Wuyang
Hsip'ing
Huaiyang
Lui
Pohsien
Linhuanchi
Foutzuchi
Shuyang

Shangts'ai
Hsiangch'eng
Koyang
Suhsien
Lingpi
Talichi
Ssuhsien
Ch'ingyang
Yangho
Chunghsing
Founing

Suip'ing
Shenchih
Nengch'eng
T'aiho
Kuchen
Haoch'engchi
Huaiyin
Huaian
Yench'eng

Junan
Chiehshouchi
Hukouchi
Santo
Wuyuch'ang

Chengyang
Chiuhsihsien
Fouyang
Pangfou
Kaoyu
Hsinghua
Paichü
Tungt'ai

Wulitien
Changhutien
Kushih
Luchia
Huaiyüan
Fengyang
Mingkuang
CHUNGCHIA SHAN 1135
Shaopo
Taihsien
Chiangyen
Jukao

Hsinyang
Kuangshan
Huangch'uan
Yenchianchi
Shouhsien
Tingyüan
Liuho Chiangtu
Chenchiang
T'ach'iao
Huangch'iao
Chichiashih
Chinshachen

Chut'anghsien
Wenshussu
Shuanglunho
Hochiu
Ch'ienshanchi
Chihhochen Laian
Ch'hsien
CHIANGSU
Chenchiang
T'aihsing
Nantung
Lingtienchen

TAPIEH SHAN
HUPEH
Tienerhwan
Hsuanhuatien
Erhliangtien
Yuwangcheng
Shangch'eng
4200
Yanshiat'an
Livan
Tushan
Shuangho
T'aoch'ichen
Huailinchen
Hofei
Tienfou
Chekao
Hsiensien
Tangt'u
NANKING (Nanching)
Tanyang
Chingchiang
Chiangyin
Wuchin
Ch'angshu
CH'UNGMING TAO

Chiliping
Hsintien
Lihuang
Wuwei
Taifou
Tungpo
Wanchih
Meichu
Wuhu
Kaoshun
Lishui
1358
Ishing
Liyang
Wuhsi Ch'angshu
Huangli
Taichʻiao Paoshan
HENG SHAN
SHANGHAI SHIH
Ch'ienshanchen
Shihhoientun
T'aoch'iehen
Huhu
Huch'iang
Langch'in
Wusieh
Soochow (Wuhsien)
Waikang
Luchih Nanhsiang
New Shanghai
SHANGHAI
Ch'ingp'u
Nanhui
Peich'iao

A-560796-76- 1-1-1-1-1
COPYRIGHT BY
RAND McNALLY & COMPANY
MADE IN U.S.A.

Longitude East of Greenwich

| 0 10 20 30 40 | Miles |
| 0 10 20 30 40 50 60 | Kilometers |

Scale 1:4 000 000 one inch to 64 miles. Conic Projection
Elevations and depressions are given in feet

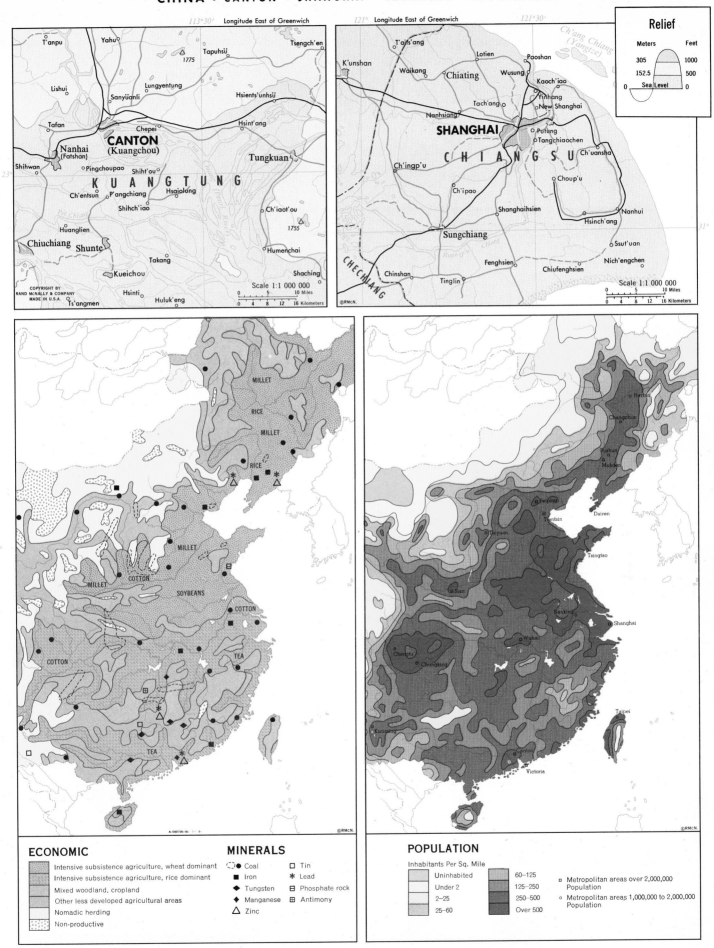

Relief

Meters		Feet
305		1000
152.5		500
0	Sea Level	0

CANTON map

T'anpu, Yahu, Tapuhsü, Tsengch'en
Lishui, Lungyentung, Hsients'unhsü
Sanyüanli, Hsint'ang
Tafan, Chepei
CANTON (Kuangchou), Tungkuan
Nanhai (Fatshan)
Shihwan, Pingchoupao, Shiht'ou
K U A N G T U N G
Ch'entsun, P'angchiang, Hsaiolung
Shihch'iao, Ch'iaot'ou
Huanglien
Chiuchiang, Shunte, Takang
Kueichou, Shaching
Hsinti, Huluk'eng
Ts'angmen

Scale 1:1 000 000
0 5 10 Miles
0 4 8 12 16 Kilometers

COPYRIGHT BY
RAND McNALLY & COMPANY
MADE IN U.S.A.

SHANGHAI map

K'unshan, T'ajts'ang, Lotien, Paoshan, Ch'ang Chiang (Yangtze)
Waikang, Chiating, Wusung, Kaoch'iao
Tach'ang, Yinhang
Nanhsiang, New Shanghai
SHANGHAI, Putung, Tangchiaochen, Ch'uansha
C H I A N G S U
Ch'ingp'u
Ch'ipao, Choup'u
Shanghaihsien, Nanhui
Hsinch'ang
Sungchiang, Ssut'uan
CHECHIANG, Chinshan, Tinglin, Fenghsien, Chiufenghsien, Nich'engchen

Scale 1:1 000 000
0 5 10 Miles
0 4 8 12 16 Kilometers

©RMCN.

ECONOMIC

- Intensive subsistence agriculture, wheat dominant
- Intensive subsistence agriculture, rice dominant
- Mixed woodland, cropland
- Other less developed agricultural areas
- Nomadic herding
- Non-productive

MINERALS

- ◖ Coal
- ■ Iron
- ◆ Tungsten
- ◆ Manganese
- △ Zinc
- □ Tin
- ✳ Lead
- ⊟ Phosphate rock
- ⊞ Antimony

POPULATION

Inhabitants Per Sq. Mile

- Uninhabited
- Under 2
- 2–25
- 25–60
- 60–125
- 125–250
- 250–500
- Over 500

□ Metropolitan areas over 2,000,000 Population
○ Metropolitan areas 1,000,000 to 2,000,000 Population

A-560700-16- 1- 1-
©RMCN.
©RMCN.

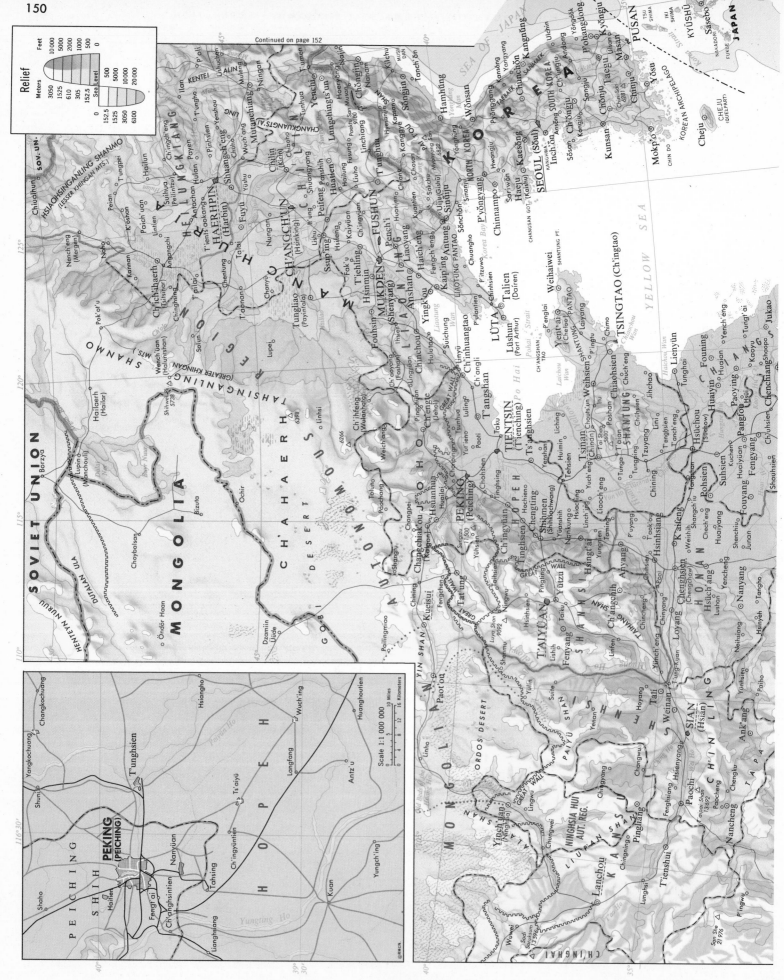

Continued on page 152

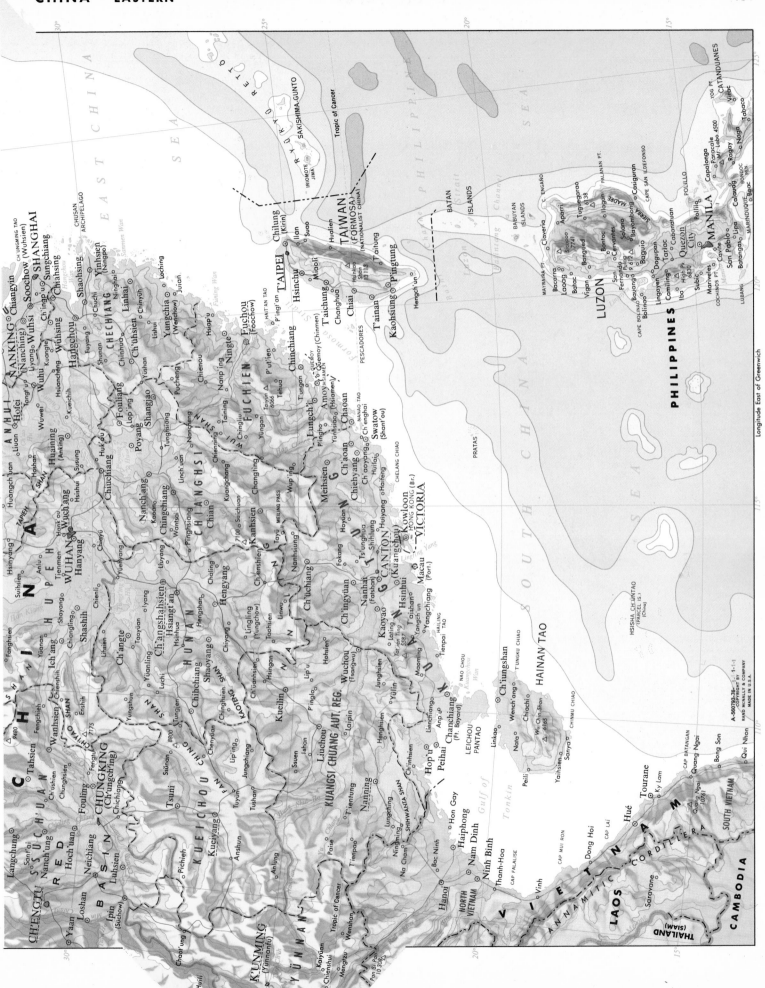

Scale 1:10 000 000; one inch to 160 miles. Lambert Conformal Conic Projection
Elevations and depressions are given in feet

A-560703-76   1-1-[-]
COPYRIGHT BY
RAND M!NALLY & COMPANY
MADE IN U.S.A.

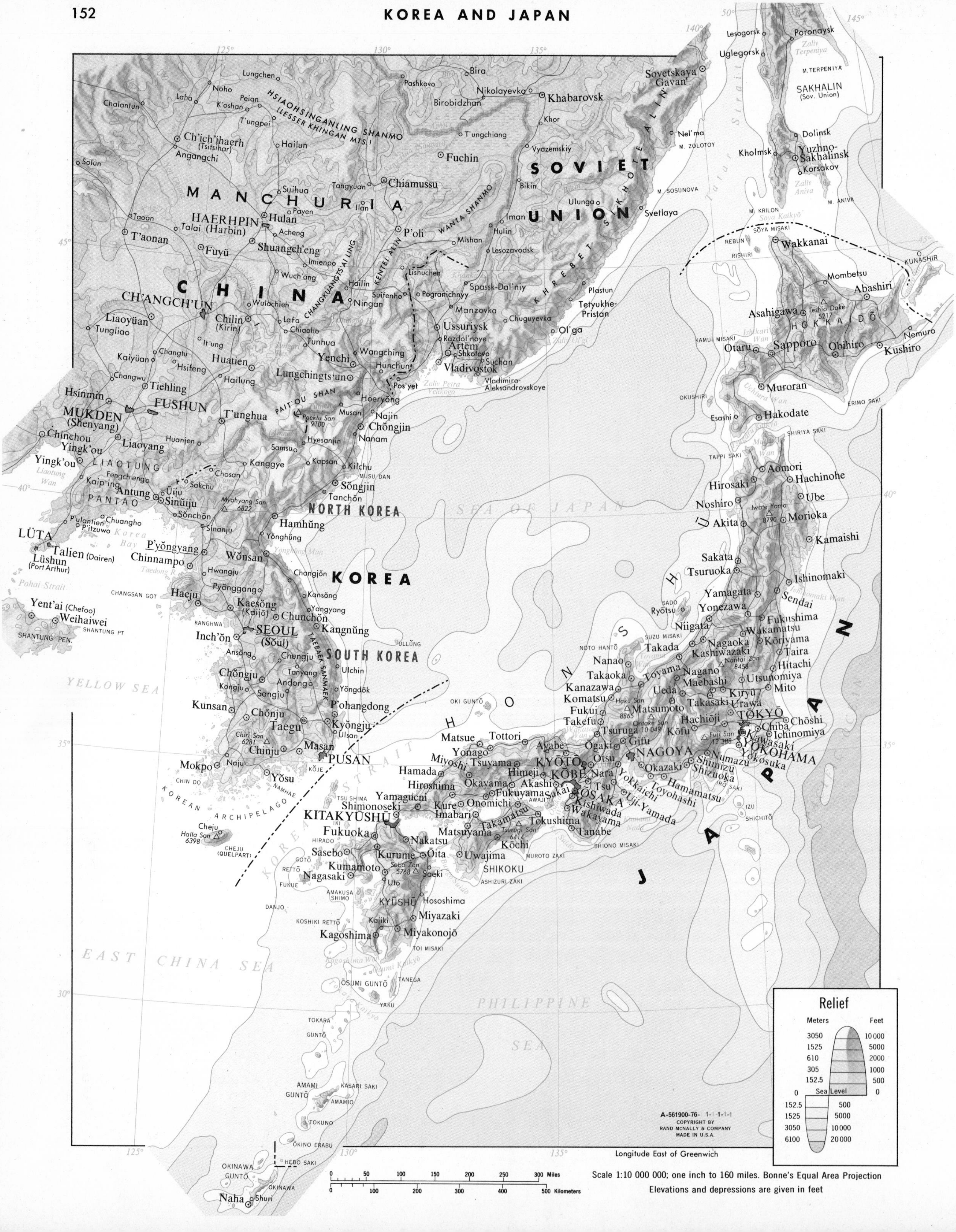

MANCHURIA

CHINA

SOVIET UNION

SAKHALIN (Sov. Union)

HOKKAIDŌ

NORTH KOREA

KOREA

SOUTH KOREA

SEOUL (Sŏul)

PUSAN

YELLOW SEA

SEA OF JAPAN

J A P A N

HONSHU

SHIKOKU

KYŪSHŪ

TŌKYŌ

KYŌTO

ŌSAKA

NAGOYA

YOKOHAMA

KOBE

KITAKYŪSHŪ

EAST CHINA SEA

PHILIPPINE SEA

Lungchen, Noho, Chalantun, Laha, Peian, K'oshan, T'ungpei, Ch'ich'ihaerh (Tsitsihar), Angangchi, Solun, Taoan, HAERHPIN, Hulan, Talai (Harbin), Acheng, Suihua, Tangyüan, Chiamussu, Payen, Ilan, Fuchin, Shuangch'eng, Imienpo, Hailin, P'oli, Mishan, Hulin, Lesozavodsk, Wuch'ang, Lafa, Chiaoho, Lishuchen, Suifenho, Pogranichnyy, Spassk-Dal'niy, Manzovka, Ningan, Hailin, Chuguyevka, Ol'ga, Ussuriysk, Razdol'noye, Artëm, Shkotovo, Suchan, Vladivostok, Vladimiro-Aleksandrovskoye, Pos'yet, Hoeryŏng, Najin, Chŏngjin, Nanam

Pashkovo, Bira, Nikolayevka, Khabarovsk, Birobidzhan, Khor, T'ungchiang, Vyazemskiy, Bikin, Iman, Ulunga, Svetlaya, Sovetskaya Gavan', Plastun, Tetyukhe-Pristan', Nel'ma

Lesogorsk, Poronaysk, Uglegorsk, Zaliv Terpeniya, Kholmsk, Dolinsk, Yuzhno-Sakhalinsk, Korsakov

Wakkanai, Rebun, Rishiri, Abashiri, Mombetsu, Asahigawa, Teshio Dake 5217, Nemuro, Kushiro, Obihiro, Sapporo, Otaru, Muroran, Hakodate, Esashi, Okushiri, Kunashir

MUKDEN (Shenyang), Chinchou, Liaoyang, Yingk'ou, LIAOTUNG, Antung, Sinŭiju, Ŭiju, Sakchu, Chosan, Kanggye, Hyesanjin, Kapsan, Kilchu, Najin, Musan, Paektu San 9100, Samsu, Kanggye, Sŏngjin, Tanchŏn, Myohyang San 6822, Hamhŭng, Yŏnghŭng, Wŏnsan, Changjŏn, Kosŏng

Yaku, ŌSUMI GUNTŌ, Tanega, AMAMI GUNTŌ, Kasari Saki, Amamio, Tokuno, Okino Erabu, OKINAWA GUNTŌ, Naha, Shuri, HEDO SAKI

A-561900-76- 1-1-1-1-1
COPYRIGHT BY
RAND McNALLY & COMPANY
MADE IN U.S.A.

Longitude East of Greenwich

Scale 1:10 000 000; one inch to 160 miles. Bonne's Equal Area Projection
Elevations and depressions are given in feet

Relief

Meters		Feet
3050		10 000
1525		5000
610		2000
305		1000
152.5		500
0	Sea Level	0
152.5		500
1525		5000
3050		10 000
6100		20 000

0 50 100 150 200 250 300 Miles
0 100 200 300 400 500 Kilometers

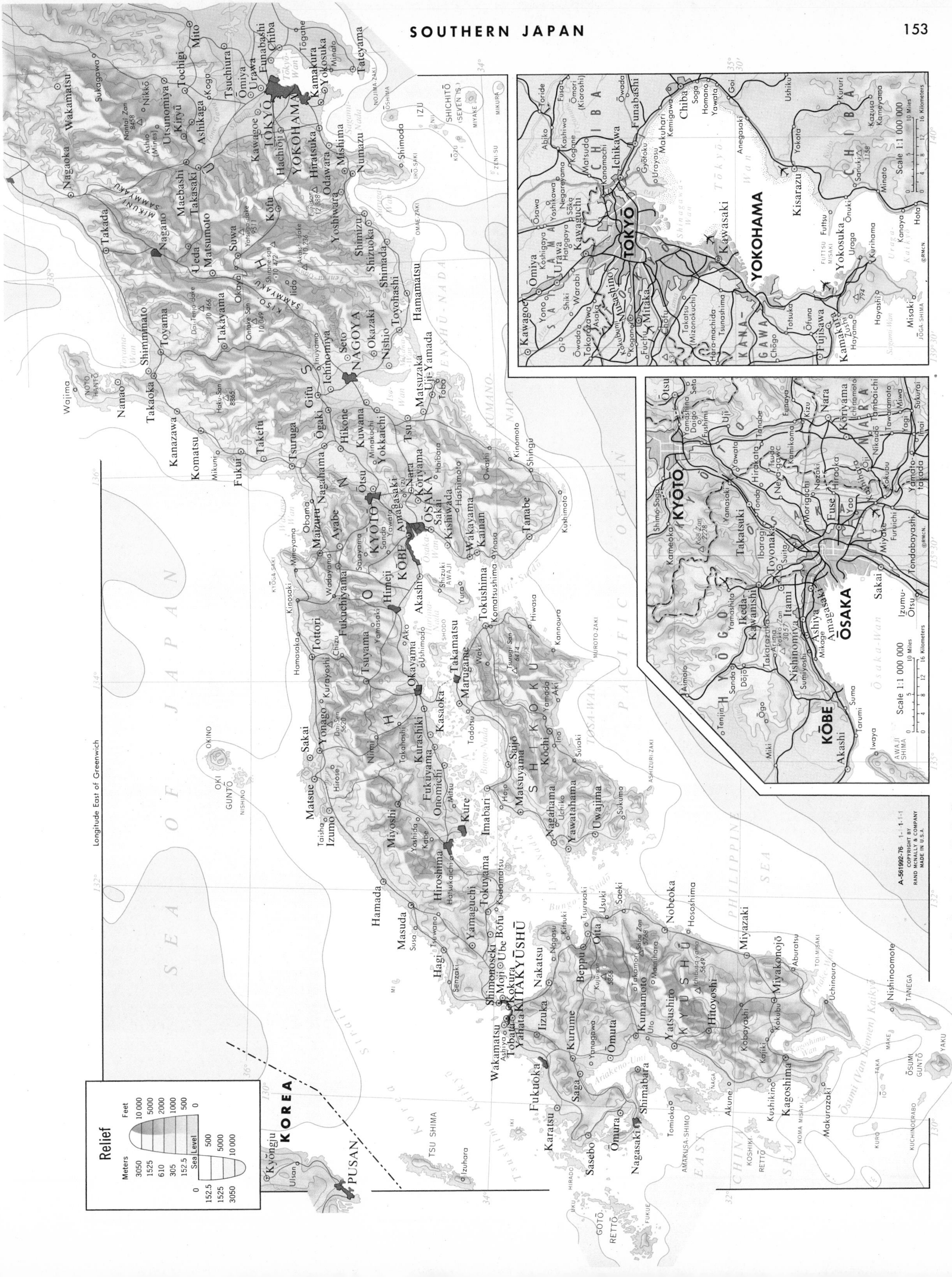

KOREA

SEA OF JAPAN

PACIFIC OCEAN

PHILIPPINE SEA

EAST CHINA SEA

HONSHŪ

SHIKOKU

KYŪSHŪ

TOKYO
YOKOHAMA
NAGOYA
KYOTO
OSAKA
KOBE
KITAKYŪSHŪ

PUSAN

Relief

Meters	Feet
3050	10 000
1525	5000
610	2000
305	1000
152.5	500
0 Sea Level	0
152.5	500
1525	5000
3050	10 000

Longitude East of Greenwich

Scale 1:4 000 000; one inch to 64 miles. Conic Projection
Elevations and depressions are given in feet.

TOKYO-YOKOHAMA
CHIBA
KANAGAWA
Scale 1:1 000 000

KYOTO-OSAKA
KOBE
Scale 1:1 000 000

A-561992-76 1-.1-1-1
COPYRIGHT BY
RAND McNALLY & COMPANY
MADE IN U.S.A.

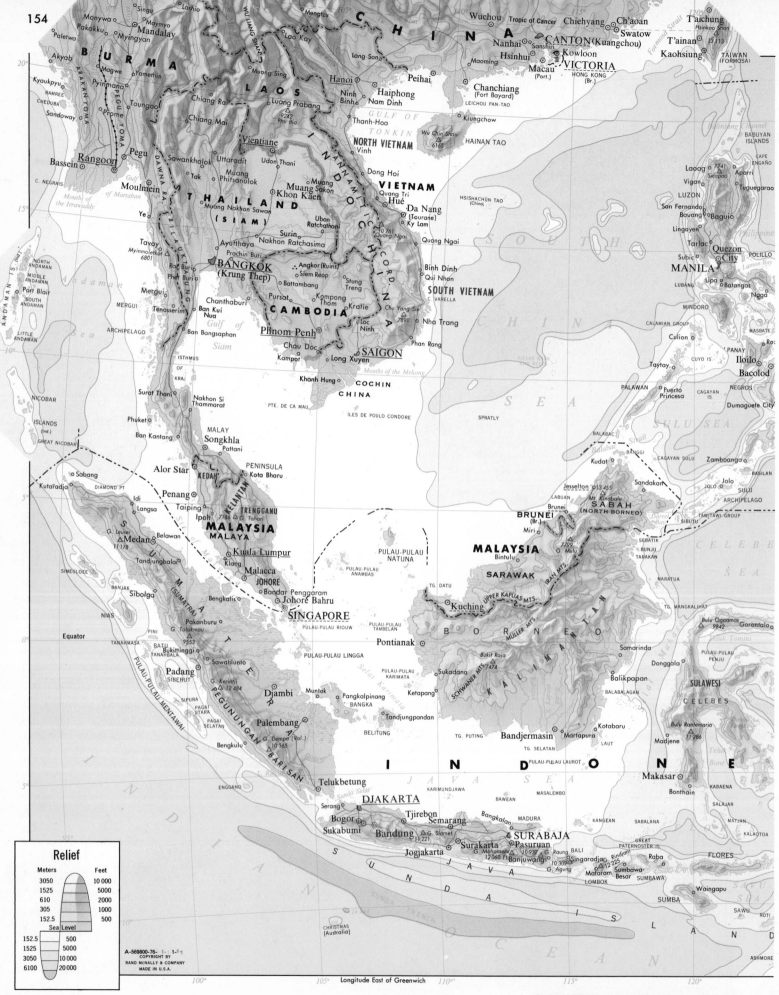

Scale 1:16 000 000; one inch to 250 miles. Polyconic Projection
Elevations and depressions are given in feet

Relief

Meters	Feet
3050	10 000
1525	5000
610	2000
305	1000
152.5	500
Sea Level	
152.5	500
1525	5000
3050	10 000
6100	20 000

A-569800-76- 1- 1-1-1
COPYRIGHT BY
RAND McNALLY & COMPANY
MADE IN U.S.A.

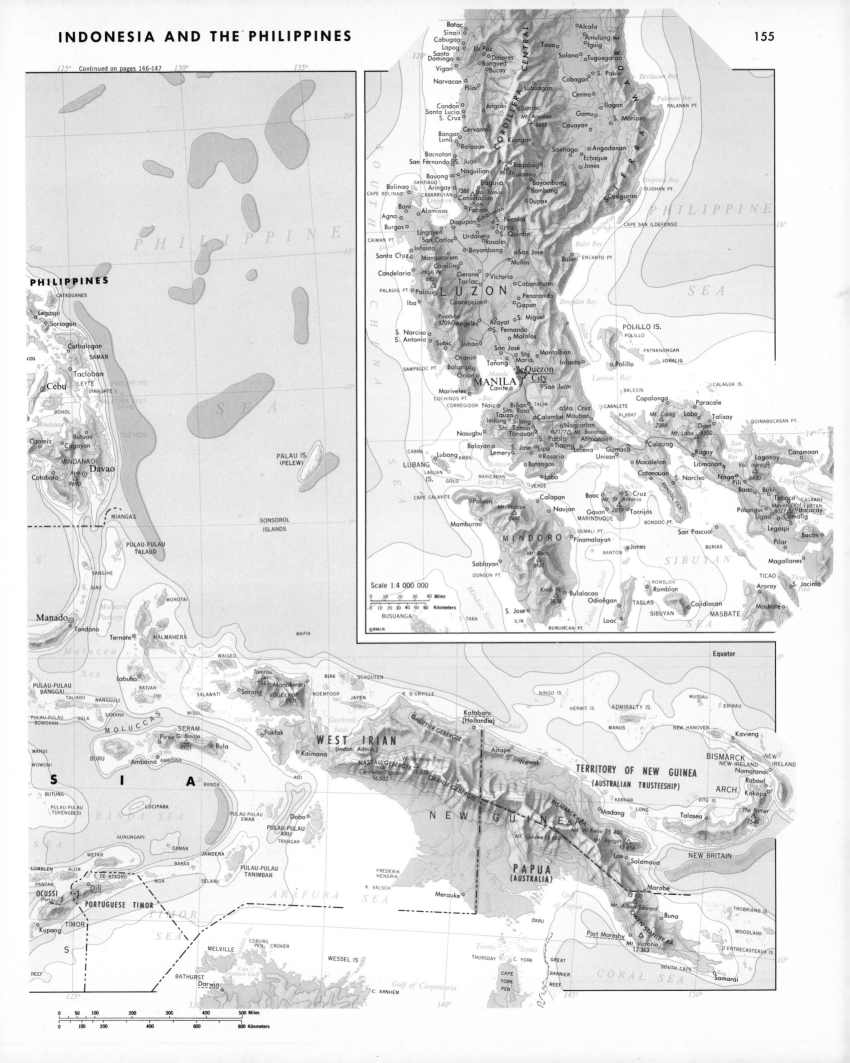

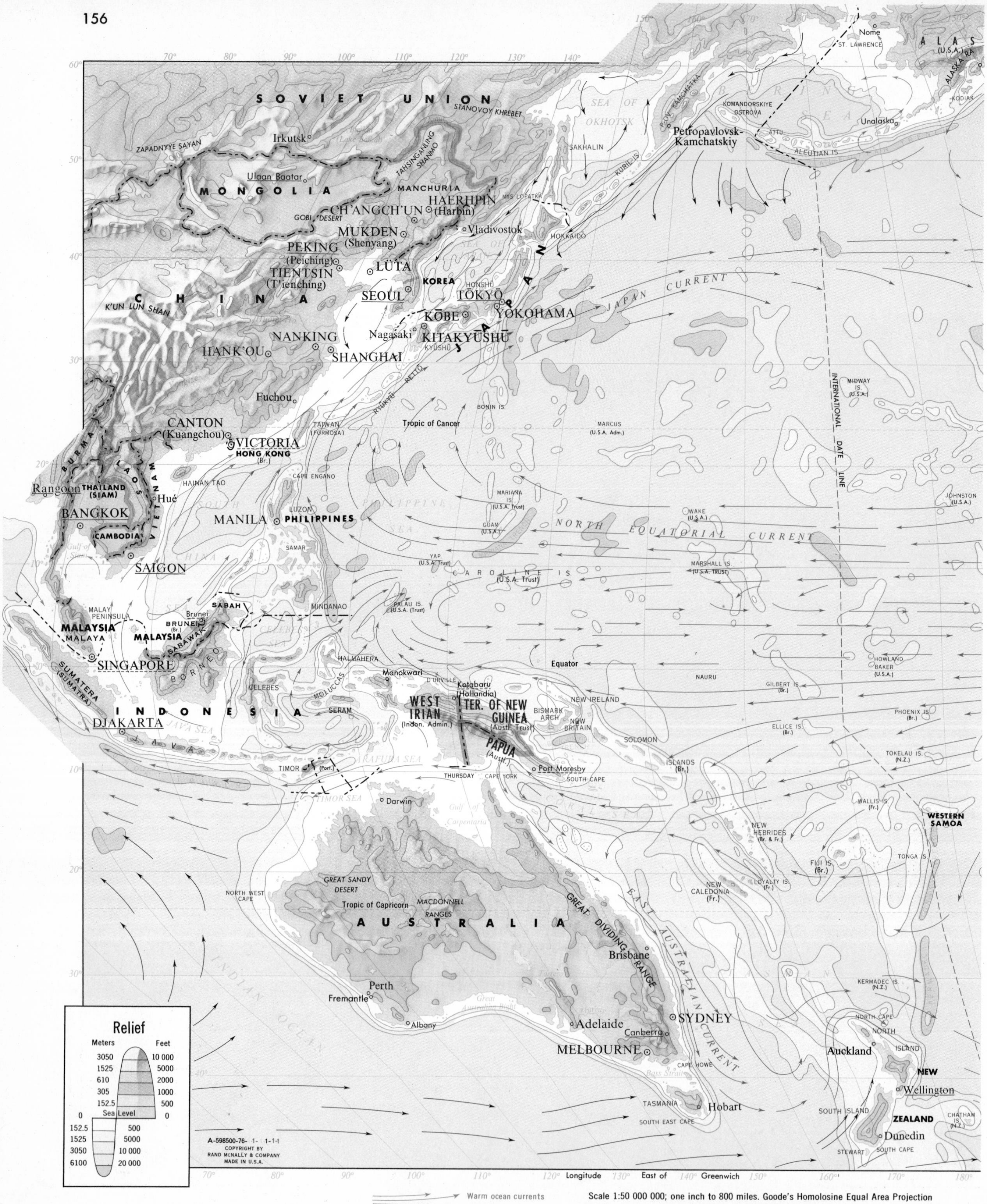

SOVIET UNION

STANOVOY KHREBET

ZAPADNYYE SAYAN

Irkutsk

Sea OF OKHOTSK

Komandorskiye Ostrova

Nome

ST. LAWRENCE

ALAS (U.S.A.)

ALASKA RA

KODIAK

Unalaska

Petropavlovsk-Kamchatskiy

ATTU

ALEUTIAN IS.

BERING SEA

MONGOLIA

Ulaan Baatar

MANCHURIA

GOBI DESERT

TAHSINGANLING SHANMO

HAERHPIN (Harbin)

MYS LOPATKA

CH'ANGCH'UN

Vladivostok

SAKHALIN

HOKKAIDO

KURILE IS.

PEKING (Peiching)

MUKDEN (Shenyang)

LUTA

KOREA

SEA OF JAPAN

HONSHU

TIENTSIN (T'ienching)

SEOUL

TOKYO

JAPAN CURRENT

CHINA

K'UN LUN SHAN

KOBE

YOKOHAMA

Nagasaki

KITAKYUSHU

KYUSHU

NANKING

HANK'OU

SHANGHAI

Fuchou

RYUKYU RETTO

BONIN IS.

Tropic of Cancer

MARCUS (U.S.A. Adm.)

MIDWAY IS. (U.S.A.)

INTERNATIONAL DATE LINE

JOHNSTON (U.S.A.)

CANTON (Kuangchou)

TAIWAN (FORMOSA)

VICTORIA

HONG KONG (Br.)

CAPE ENGANO

HAINAN TAO

BURMA

Rangoon

THAILAND (SIAM)

LAOS

Hué

LUZON

MANILA

PHILIPPINES

PHILIPPINE SEA

MARIANA IS. (U.S.A. Trust)

GUAM (U.S.A.)

WAKE (U.S.A.)

NORTH EQUATORIAL CURRENT

BANGKOK

CAMBODIA

VIETNAM

SAMAR

YAP (U.S.A. Trust)

CAROLINE IS. (U.S.A. Trust)

MARSHALL IS. (U.S.A. TRUST)

SAIGON

Gulf of Siam

MINDANAO

PALAU IS. (U.S.A. Trust)

MALAY PENINSULA

SABAH

BRUNEI (Br.)

SARAWAK

MALAYSIA MALAYA

MALAYSIA

BORNEO

HOWLAND BAKER (U.S.A.)

SINGAPORE

SUMATERA (SUMATRA)

CELEBES

MOLUCCAS

HALMAHERA

Manokwari

D'URVILLE

Kotabaru (Hollandia)

Equator

NAURU

GILBERT IS. (Br.)

PHOENIX IS. (Br.)

INDONESIA

SERAM

WEST IRIAN (Indon. Admin.)

TER. OF NEW GUINEA (Austl. Trust)

BISMARK ARCH.

NEW IRELAND

NEW BRITAIN

ELLICE IS. (Br.)

DJAKARTA

JAVA SEA

JAVA

PAPUA (Aust.)

Port Moresby

SOLOMON

ISLANDS (Br.)

TOKELAU IS. (N.Z.)

TIMOR

(Port.)

ARAFURA SEA

THURSDAY

CAPE YORK

SOUTH CAPE

CORAL SEA

WALLIS IS. (Fr.)

WESTERN SAMOA

TIMOR SEA

Darwin

Gulf of Carpentaria

NEW HEBRIDES (Br. & Fr.)

FIJI IS. (Br.)

TONGA IS.

NORTH WEST CAPE

GREAT SANDY DESERT

Tropic of Capricorn

MACDONNELL RANGES

GREAT DIVIDING RANGE

EAST AUSTRALIAN CURRENT

LOYALTY IS. (Fr.)

NEW CALEDONIA (Fr.)

AUSTRALIA

Brisbane

INDIAN OCEAN

Perth

Fremantle

Albany

Adelaide

Canberra

SYDNEY

MELBOURNE

CAPE HOWE

KERMADEC IS. (N.Z.)

NORTH CAPE

NORTH ISLAND

Auckland

NEW

Wellington

Great Australian Bight

Bass Strait

TASMANIA

Hobart

SOUTH EAST CAPE

SOUTH ISLAND

CHATHAM IS. (N.Z.)

ZEALAND

Dunedin

STEWART

SOUTH CAPE

Relief

Meters		Feet
3050		10 000
1525		5000
610		2000
305		1000
152.5		500
0	Sea Level	0
152.5		500
1525		5000
3050		10 000
6100		20 000

A-598500-76- 1- 1-1
COPYRIGHT BY
RAND MCNALLY & COMPANY
MADE IN U.S.A.

Longitude East of Greenwich

Warm ocean currents

Cold ocean currents

Scale 1:50 000 000; one inch to 800 miles. Goode's Homolosine Equal Area Projection

Elevations and depressions are given in feet

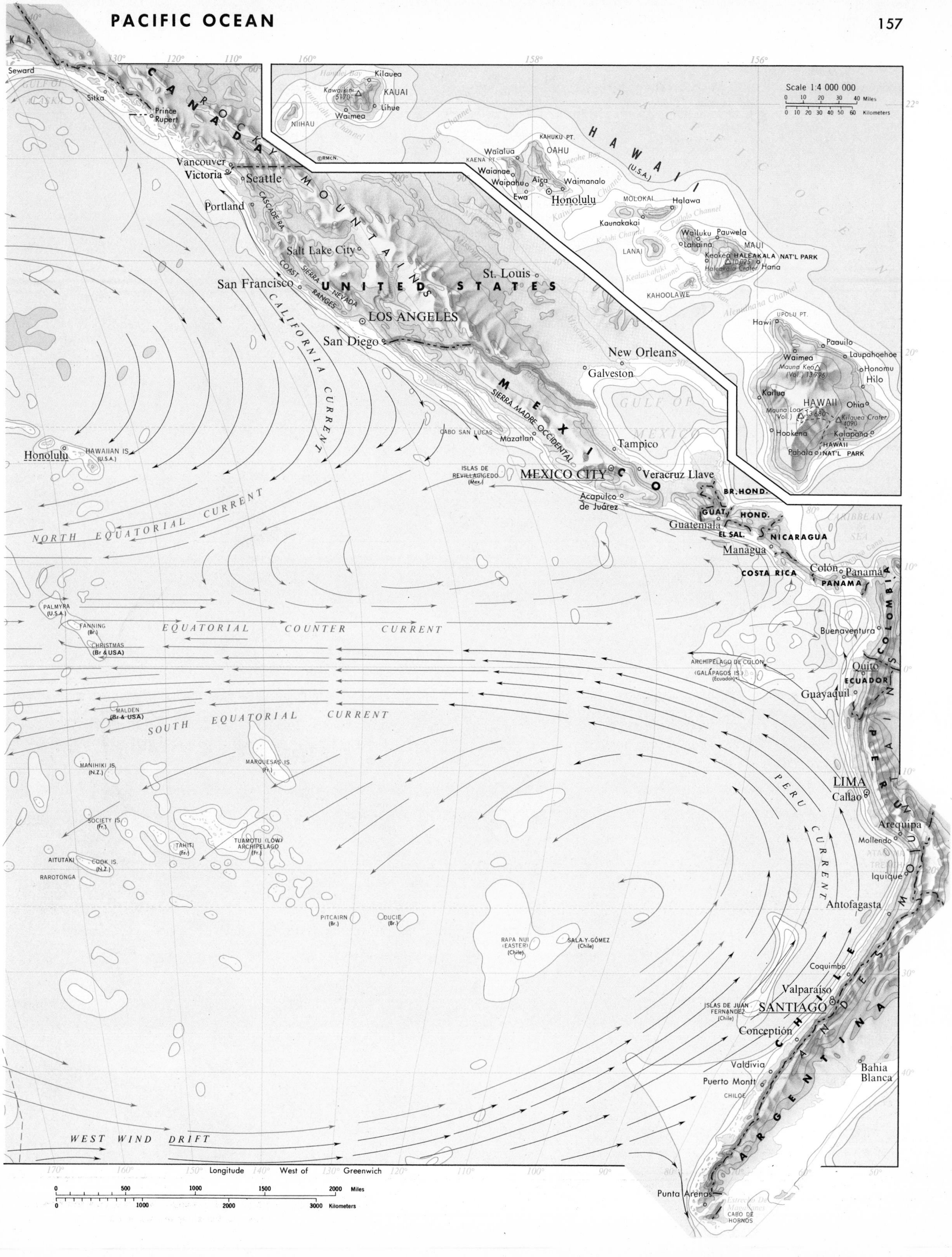

Scale 1:4 000 000

0 10 20 30 40 Miles

0 10 20 30 40 50 60 Kilometers

Seward

Sitka

Prince Rupert

Vancouver

Victoria

Seattle

Portland

CANADA

ROCKY MOUNTAINS

CASCADE RA.

Salt Lake City

San Francisco

SIERRA NEVADA

COAST RANGES

CALIFORNIA CURRENT

UNITED STATES

St. Louis

LOS ANGELES

San Diego

New Orleans

Galveston

MEXICO

SIERRA MADRE OCCIDENTAL

CABO SAN LUCAS

Mazatlan

Tampico

ISLAS DE REVILLAGIGEDO (Mex.)

MEXICO CITY

Veracruz Llave

Acapulco de Juárez

GUAT.

BR. HOND.

HOND.

Guatemala

EL SAL.

NICARAGUA

Managua

COSTA RICA

Colón

Panamá

PANAMA

COLOMBIA

Buenaventura

ARCHIPELAGO DE COLON (GALÁPAGOS IS.) (Ecuador)

Quito

ECUADOR

Guayaquil

LIMA

Callao

PERU

PERU CURRENT

Arequipa

Mollendo

Iquique

Antofagasta

Coquimbo

Valparaíso

SANTIAGO

ISLAS DE JUAN FERNÁNDEZ (Chile)

Conceptión

Valdivia

Puerto Montt

CHILOE

ANDES

CHILE

ARGENTINA

Bahia Blanca

Punta Arenas

CABO DE HORNOS

Honolulu

HAWAIIAN IS. (U.S.A.)

NORTH EQUATORIAL CURRENT

PALMYRA (U.S.A.)

FANNING (Br.)

CHRISTMAS (Br. & USA)

EQUATORIAL COUNTER CURRENT

MALDEN (Br. & USA)

SOUTH EQUATORIAL CURRENT

MANIHIKI IS. (N.Z.)

MARQUESAS IS. (Fr.)

SOCIETY IS. (Fr.)

TAHITI (Fr.)

TUAMOTU (LOW) ARCHIPELAGO (Fr.)

AITUTAKI COOK IS. (N.Z.)

RAROTONGA

PITCAIRN (Br.)

DUCIE (Br.)

RAPA NUI (EASTER) (Chile)

SALA-Y-GÓMEZ (Chile)

WEST WIND DRIFT

0 500 1000 1500 2000 Miles

0 1000 2000 3000 Kilometers

Longitude West of Greenwich

Hawaii inset

Hanalei Bay

Kilauea

KAUAI

Kawaikini 5170

Waimea

Lihue

NIIHAU

Kauai Channel

HAWAII (U.S.A.)

KAHUKU PT.

Waialua

OAHU

KAENA PT.

Waianae

Waipahu

Aiea

Ewa

Waimanalo

Honolulu

Kaneohe Bay

MOLOKAI

Halawa

Kaunakakai

LANAI

Wailuku

Pauwela

Lahaina

Keokea

MAUI

HALEAKALA NAT'L PARK

10,025

Haleakala Crater

Hana

KAHOOLAWE

UPOLU PT.

Hawi

Paauilo

Waimea

Mauna Kea (Vol.) 13,796

Laupahoehoe

Honomu

Hilo

Kailua

HAWAII

Ohia

Mauna Loa (Vol.) 13,680

Kilauea Crater 4090

Hookena

Kalapana

Pahala

HAWAII NAT'L PARK

Alenuihaha Channel

Kalohi Channel

Pailolo Channel

Kealaikahiki Channel

PACIFIC OCEAN

GULF OF MEXICO

CARIBBEAN SEA

ATLANTIC OCEAN

Continued on pages 154-155

Relief

Meters	Feet
3050	10 000
1525	5000
610	2000
305	1000
152.5	500
0 Sea Level	0
152.5	500
1525	5000 Below Sea Level
3050	10 000
6100	20 000

A-590200-76- 1-1-1- -1
COPYRIGHT BY
RAND McNALLY & COMPANY
MADE IN U.S.A.

Longitude 115° East of Greenwich

Scale 1:16 000 000; one inch to 250 miles. Lambert's Azimuthal, Equal Area Projection
Elevations and depressions are given in feet

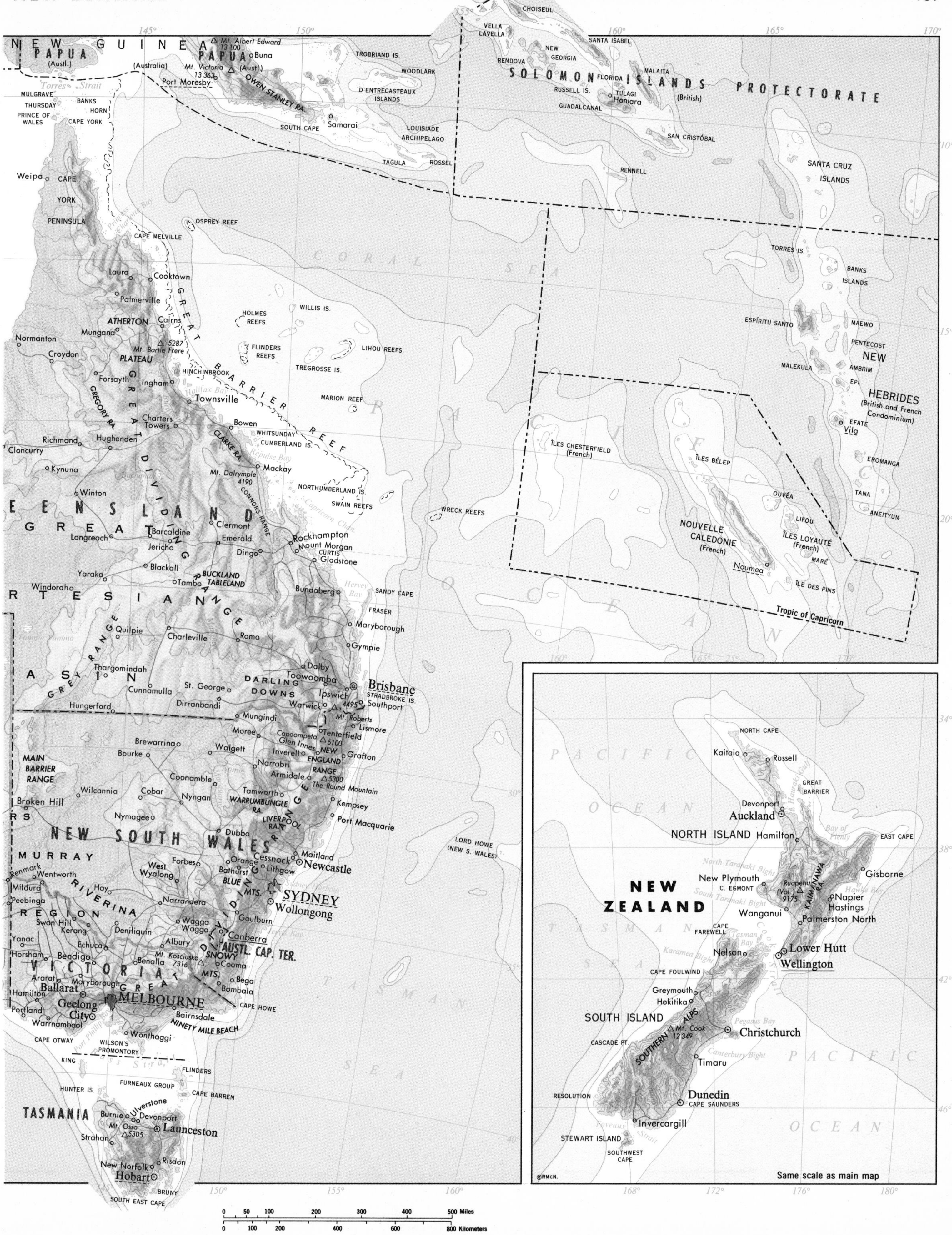

NEW GUINEA

PAPUA (Austl.)

PAPUA (Australia) (Austl.)

△ Mt. Albert Edward 13,100

△ Mt. Victoria 13,363 Buna

Port Moresby

OWEN STANLEY RA.

TROBRIAND IS.

WOODLARK

D'ENTRECASTEAUX ISLANDS

Samarai

SOUTH CAPE

LOUISIADE ARCHIPELAGO

TAGULA ROSSEL

CHOISEUL

VELLA LAVELLA

RENDOVA NEW GEORGIA

RUSSELL IS.

GUADALCANAL

SANTA ISABEL

FLORIDA

TULAGI Honiara

MALAITA

SOLOMON ISLANDS PROTECTORATE (British)

SAN CRISTÓBAL

RENNELL

SANTA CRUZ ISLANDS

TORRES IS.

BANKS ISLANDS

ESPÍRITU SANTO

MAEWO

PENTECOST

MALEKULA

AMBRIM EPI

NEW HEBRIDES (British and French Condominium)

EFATE Vila

EROMANGA

TANA

ANEITYUM

MULGRAVE

THURSDAY

BANKS

HORN

PRINCE OF WALES

CAPE YORK

Torres Strait

Weipa CAPE YORK

PENINSULA

Normanton

Croydon

Laura Cooktown

Palmerville

ATHERTON PLATEAU Cairns

Mungana △5287 Mt. Bartle Frere

Forsayth Ingham

HINCHINBROOK

Townsville

Richmond Hughenden

Charters Towers Bowen

GREGORY RA.

CLARKE RA.

WHITSUNDAY

CUMBERLAND IS.

Cloncurry

Kynuna

Winton

△ Mt. Dalrymple 4190

Mackay

CONNORS RANGE

NORTHUMBERLAND IS.

SWAIN REEFS

OSPREY REEF

HOLMES REEFS

FLINDERS REEFS

WILLIS IS.

LIHOU REEFS

TREGROSSE IS.

MARION REEF

WRECK REEFS

CORAL SEA

ÎLES CHESTERFIELD (French)

ÎLES BÉLEP

NOUVELLE CALÉDONIE (French)

Nouméa

ÎLES LOYAUTÉ (French)

OUVÉA

LIFOU

MARÉ

ÎLE DES PINS

Tropic of Capricorn

PACIFIC OCEAN

QUEENSLAND

GREAT DIVIDING RANGE

Longreach Barcaldine

Jericho Clermont

Blackall Emerald

Dingo

Rockhampton Mount Morgan CURTIS Gladstone

Yaraka

BUCKLAND TABLELAND

Tambo

Windoraho

ARTESIAN

Bundaberg

Hervey Bay

SANDY CAPE

FRASER

Maryborough

GREY RANGE

Quilpie

Charleville Roma

Gympie

BASIN

Thargomindah

Cunnamulla

Hungerford

St. George

Charleville

DARLING DOWNS

Dalby Toowoomba

Ipswich Brisbane

Warwick STRADBROKE IS. Southport

△4495 Mt. Roberts

Lismore

MAIN BARRIER RANGE

Broken Hill

Brewarrina

Bourke

Wilcannia

Cobar

Moree

Mungindi

Narrabri

△5100 Tenterfield

Glen Innes

Inverell NEW ENGLAND RANGE

Grafton

△5300 The Round Mountain

Armidale

Tamworth

MURRAY

RIVERINA REGION

Renmark

Wentworth

Mildura

Peebinga

Swan Hill

Yanac

Horsham

VICTORIA

Ararat

Hamilton

Portland

Ballarat

Geelong City

Warrnambool

CAPE OTWAY

WARRUMBUNGLE RA.

LIVERPOOL RA.

Kempsey

Port Macquarie

NEW SOUTH WALES

Nymagee

Nyngan

Coonamble

Dubbo

Forbes

West Wyalong

Narrandera

Hay

Deniliquin

Echuca

Kerang

Bendigo

Maryborough

Benalla

Albury

Wagga Wagga

Orange Bathurst

Cessnock Lithgow

BLUE MTS.

Goulburn

Cooma

△ Mt. Kosciusko 7316

SNOWY MTS.

Bombala

Bega

Bairnsdale

Wonthaggi

WILSON'S PROMONTORY

Maitland Newcastle

SYDNEY Wollongong

Canberra AUSTL. CAP. TER.

CAPE HOWE

NINETY MILE BEACH

MELBOURNE

GREAT DIVIDING RANGE

LORD HOWE (NEW S. WALES)

TASMAN SEA

KING

FURNEAUX GROUP

FLINDERS

CAPE BARREN

HUNTER IS.

TASMANIA

Burnie Ulverstone

Devonport

△ Mt. Ossa 5305

Strahan

New Norfolk

Launceston

Risdon

Hobart

BRUNY

SOUTH EAST CAPE

NEW ZEALAND

NORTH CAPE

Kaitaia Russell

GREAT BARRIER

Devonport

Auckland

NORTH ISLAND Hamilton

EAST CAPE

Bay of Plenty

New Plymouth C. EGMONT

△ Egmont (Vol.)

KAIMANAWA RA.

△ Ruapehu 9175

Gisborne

Napier Hastings

Wanganui

Palmerston North

CAPE FAREWELL

Nelson

Lower Hutt

Wellington

CAPE FOULWIND

Greymouth

Hokitika

SOUTH ISLAND

SOUTHERN ALPS

CASCADE PT. △ Mt. Cook 12,349

Christchurch

Timaru

Dunedin CAPE SAUNDERS

RESOLUTION

Invercargill

STEWART ISLAND

SOUTHWEST CAPE

PACIFIC OCEAN

Pegasus Bay

Canterbury Bight

South Taranaki Bight

North Taranaki Bight

Hawke Bay

Karamea Bight

Tasman Bay

© RMcN

Same scale as main map

0 50 100 200 300 400 500 Miles

0 100 200 400 600 800 Kilometers

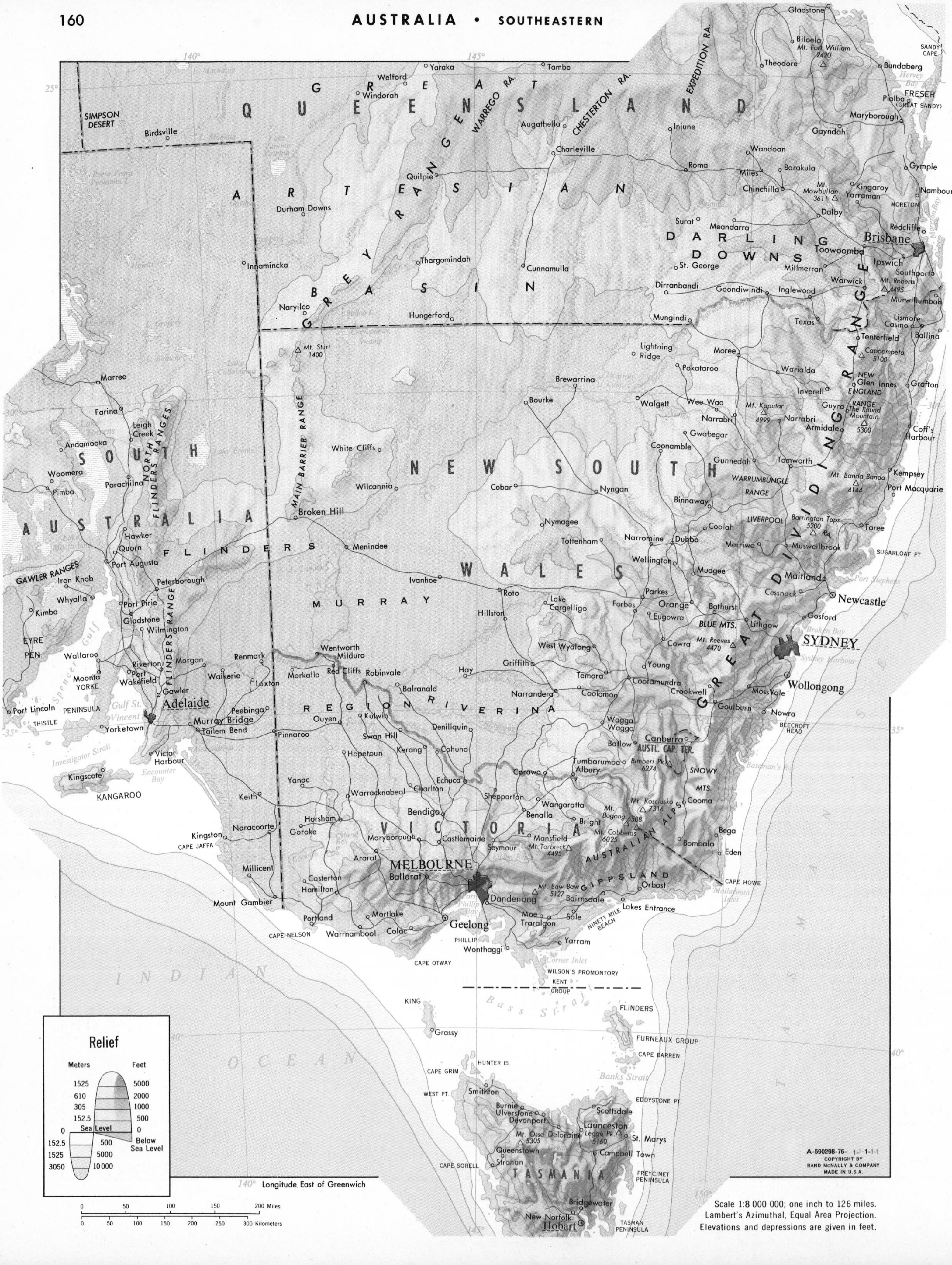

SIMPSON DESERT

QUEENSLAND

GREAT ARTESIAN BASIN

GREY RANGE

GREAT DIVIDING RANGE

WARREGO RA.

CHESTERTON RA.

EXPEDITION RA.

Gladstone
Biloela
Mt. Fort William 2420
Theodore
Bundaberg
Pialba (GREAT SANDY)
FRESER
SANDY CAPE
Hervey Bay

Welford
Yaraka
Tambo
Windorah
Augathella
Injune
Maryborough
Gayndah
Gympie
Nambour
MORETON

Birdsville
Durham Downs
Quilpie
Charleville
Roma
Wandoan
Barakula
Miles
Chinchilla
Kingaroy
Yarraman

Innamincka
Thargomindah
Cunnamulla
Surat
Meandarra
Dalby
Mt. Mowbullan 3611

DARLING DOWNS

Brisbane
Ipswich
Southport
Redcliffe
Toowoomba
Millmerran
St. George
Dirranbandi
Goondiwindi
Inglewood
Warwick
Mt. Roberts 4495
Murwillumbah

Naryilco
Hungerford
Mungindi
Texas
Tenterfield
Casino
Lismore
Ballina

Mt. Sturt 1400
Lightning Ridge
Moree
Warialda
Inverell
Glen Innes
Capoompeta 5100
Grafton

NEW ENGLAND RANGE
The Round Mountain 5300
Coff's Harbour

Marree
Brewarrina
Walgett
Wee Waa
Narrabri
Mt. Kaputar 4999
Guyra
Armidale

SOUTH AUSTRALIA

NORTH FLINDERS RANGES

Farina
Leigh Creek
Bourke
Cobar
Nyngan
Coonamble
Gunnedah
Tamworth
Kempsey
Port Macquarie

Andamooka
Woomera
Pimba

FLINDERS RANGES

White Cliffs
NEW SOUTH WALES
WARRUMBUNGLE RANGE
Mt. Banda Banda 4144

Hawker
Quorn

MAIN BARRIER RANGE

Wilcannia
Nymagee
Coonabarabran
LIVERPOOL RANGE
Barrington Tops 5200
Taree
SUGARLOAF PT.

GAWLER RANGES
Iron Knob
Whyalla
Kimba

Peterborough
Broken Hill
Menindee
Tottenham
Narromine
Dubbo
Coolah
Merriwa
Muswellbrook

FLINDERS
Port Augusta
Wilmington
Gladstone

Ivanhoe
Roto
Wellington
Mudgee
Maitland
Port Stephens

EYRE PEN.
Wallaroo
Moonta
Port Pirie
YORKE
Port Wakefield

L. Torrens

Hillston
Lake Cargelligo
Parkes
Forbes
Orange
Bathurst
Eugowra
BLUE MTS.
Mt. Reeves 4470
Lithgow
Cessnock
Newcastle
Gosford

MURRAY

West Wyalong
Young
Cowra
Broken Bay
SYDNEY
Sydney Harbour

Whyalla
Kimba
Riverton
Morgan
Renmark
Wentworth
Mildura
Hay
Griffith
Temora
Cootamundra
Crookwell
Goulburn
Moss Vale
Wollongong

Port Lincoln
THISTLE
Adelaide
Gawler
Waikerie
Loxton
Morkalla
Red Cliffs
Robinvale
Balranald
Narrandera
Coolamon
Wagga Wagga
Ballow
Canberra
AUSTL. CAP. TER.
Nowra
BEECROFT HEAD

Victor Harbour
Murray Bridge
Tailem Bend
Pinnaroo
Ouyen
Kulwin
Swan Hill
Deniliquin
REGION RIVERINA
Tumbarumba
Albury
Bimberi Pk. 6274
SNOWY MTS.
Cooma
Bateman's Bay

Kingscote
KANGAROO
Yorketown
Keith
Yanac
Kerang
Cohuna
Corowa
Mt. Kosciusko 7316
Bega

Kingston
CAPE JAFFA
Naracoorte
Horsham
Goroke
Maryborough
Castlemaine
Seymour
Benalla
Wangaratta
Bright
Mt. Bogong 6508
Mt. Cobberas 6025
AUSTRALIAN ALPS
Bombala
Eden
CAPE HOWE

Millicent
Ararat
MELBOURNE
Ballarat
Mansfield
Mt. Torbreck 4495
GIPPSLAND
Orbost
Mallacoota Inlet

Mount Gambier
Casterton
Hamilton
Bendigo
Dandenong
Mt. Baw Baw 5127
Bairnsdale
Lakes Entrance

VICTORIA

Portland
Mortlake
Colac
Geelong
Moe
Traralgon
Sale
NINETY MILE BEACH

CAPE NELSON
Warrnambool
PHILLIP
Wonthaggi
Yarram
Corner Inlet

CAPE OTWAY
WILSON'S PROMONTORY
KENT GROUP

KING
Grassy
FLINDERS
FURNEAUX GROUP
CAPE BARREN

BASS STRAIT

CAPE GRIM
HUNTER IS.
Banks Strait
EDDYSTONE PT.

WEST PT.
Smithton
Burnie
Ulverstone
Devonport
Scottsdale
Launceston
Legge Pk. 5160
St. Marys

Mt. Ossa 5305
Deloraine
Campbell Town
FREYCINET PENINSULA

Queenstown
Strahan
TASMANIA

CAPE SORELL
Bridgewater
New Norfolk
Hobart
TASMAN PENINSULA

INDIAN OCEAN

Relief

Meters		Feet
1525		5000
610		2000
305		1000
152.5		500
0	Sea Level	0
152.5		500 Below Sea Level
1525		5000
3050		10 000

140° Longitude East of Greenwich

0 50 100 150 200 Miles

0 50 100 150 200 250 300 Kilometers

A-590298-76- 1- 1-1-1
COPYRIGHT BY
RAND McNALLY & COMPANY
MADE IN U.S.A.

Scale 1:8 000 000; one inch to 126 miles.
Lambert's Azimuthal, Equal Area Projection.
Elevations and depressions are given in feet.

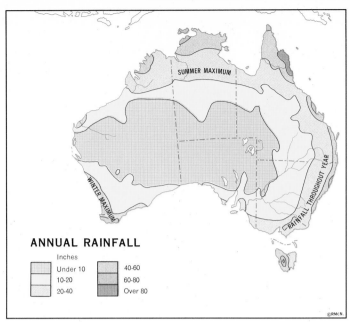

ANNUAL RAINFALL

Inches

Under 10
10-20
20-40

40-60
60-80
Over 80

©RMcN.

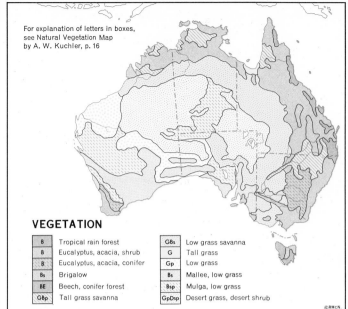

For explanation of letters in boxes,
see Natural Vegetation Map
by A. W. Kuchler, p. 16

VEGETATION

B	Tropical rain forest	GBs	Low grass savanna
B	Eucalyptus, acacia, shrub	G	Tall grass
B	Eucalyptus, acacia, conifer	Gp	Low grass
Bs	Brigalow	Bs	Mallee, low grass
BE	Beech, conifer forest	Bsp	Mulga, low grass
GBp	Tall grass savanna	GpDsp	Desert grass, desert shrub

©RMcN.

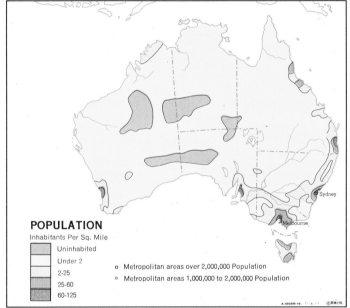

POPULATION

Inhabitants Per Sq. Mile

Uninhabited
Under 2
2-25
25-60
60-125

□ Metropolitan areas over 2,000,000 Population

○ Metropolitan areas 1,000,000 to 2,000,000 Population

A-590200-16- ©RMcN.

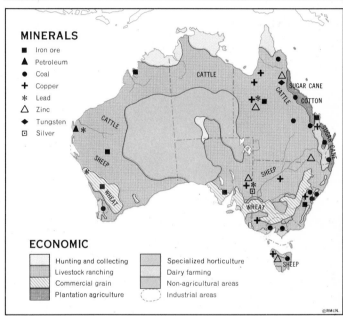

MINERALS

■ Iron ore
▲ Petroleum
● Coal
✛ Copper
✳ Lead
△ Zinc
◆ Tungsten
⊡ Silver

ECONOMIC

Hunting and collecting
Livestock ranching
Commercial grain
Plantation agriculture

Specialized horticulture
Dairy farming
Non-agricultural areas
Industrial areas

©RMcN.

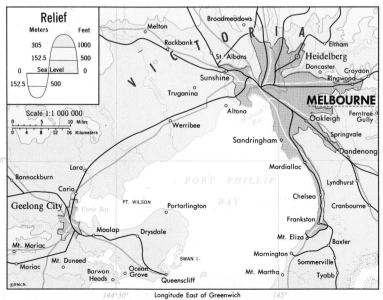

Relief

Meters		Feet
305		1000
152.5		500
0	Sea Level	0
152.5		500

Scale 1:1 000 000

0   5   10 Miles
0 4 8 12 16 Kilometers

©RMcN.

144°30'   Longitude East of Greenwich   145°

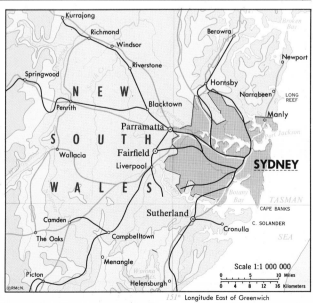

Scale 1:1 000 000

0   5   10 Miles
0 4 8 12 16 Kilometers

©RMcN.

151°   Longitude East of Greenwich

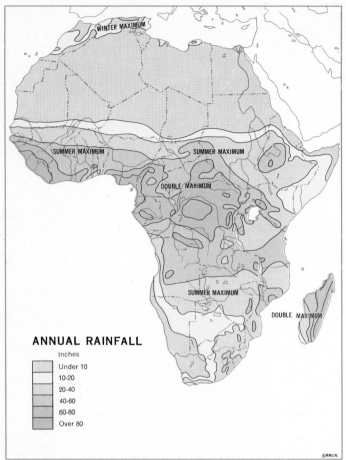

ANNUAL RAINFALL

Inches

	Under 10
	10-20
	20-40
	40-60
	60-80
	Over 80

©RMcN.

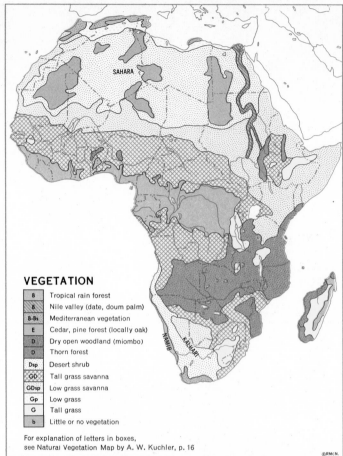

VEGETATION

B	Tropical rain forest
B	Nile valley (date, doum palm)
B-Bs	Mediterranean vegetation
E	Cedar, pine forest (locally oak)
D	Dry open woodland (miombo)
D	Thorn forest
Dsp	Desert shrub
GD	Tall grass savanna
GDsp	Low grass savanna
Gp	Low grass
G	Tall grass
b	Little or no vegetation

For explanation of letters in boxes,
see Natural Vegetation Map by A. W. Kuchler, p. 16

©RMcN.

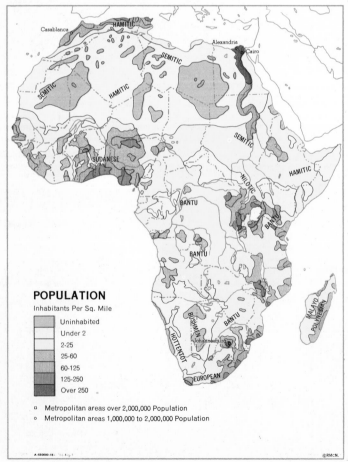

POPULATION

Inhabitants Per Sq. Mile

	Uninhabited
	Under 2
	2-25
	25-60
	60-125
	125-250
	Over 250

▫ Metropolitan areas over 2,000,000 Population

◦ Metropolitan areas 1,000,000 to 2,000,000 Population

A-580000-18 -

©RMcN.

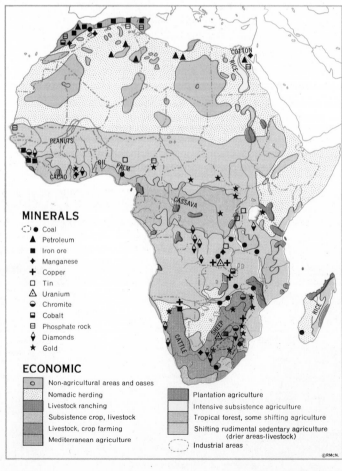

MINERALS

⬭•	Coal
▲	Petroleum
■	Iron ore
◆	Manganese
+	Copper
☐	Tin
△	Uranium
◡	Chromite
⬓	Cobalt
⊟	Phosphate rock
◈	Diamonds
★	Gold

ECONOMIC

	Non-agricultural areas and oases
	Nomadic herding
	Livestock ranching
	Subsistence crop, livestock
	Livestock, crop farming
	Mediterranean agriculture
	Plantation agriculture
	Intensive subsistence agriculture
	Tropical forest, some shifting agriculture
	Shifting rudimental sedentary agriculture (drier areas-livestock)
	Industrial areas

©RMcN.

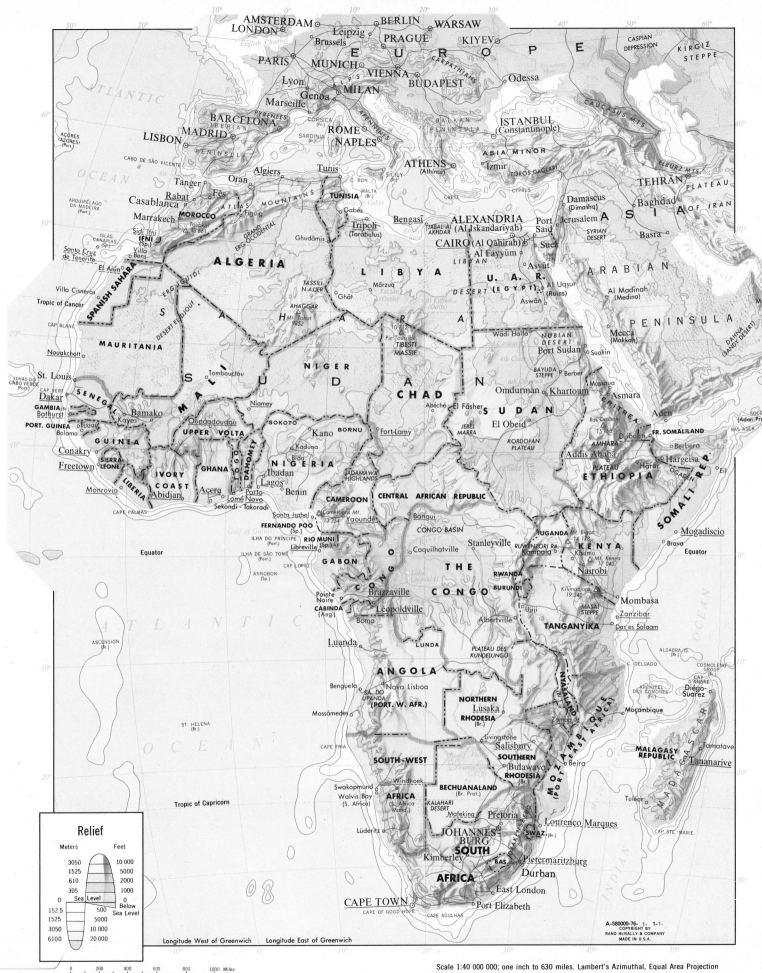

Scale 1:40 000 000; one inch to 630 miles. Lambert's Azimuthal, Equal Area Projection
Elevations and depressions are given in feet.

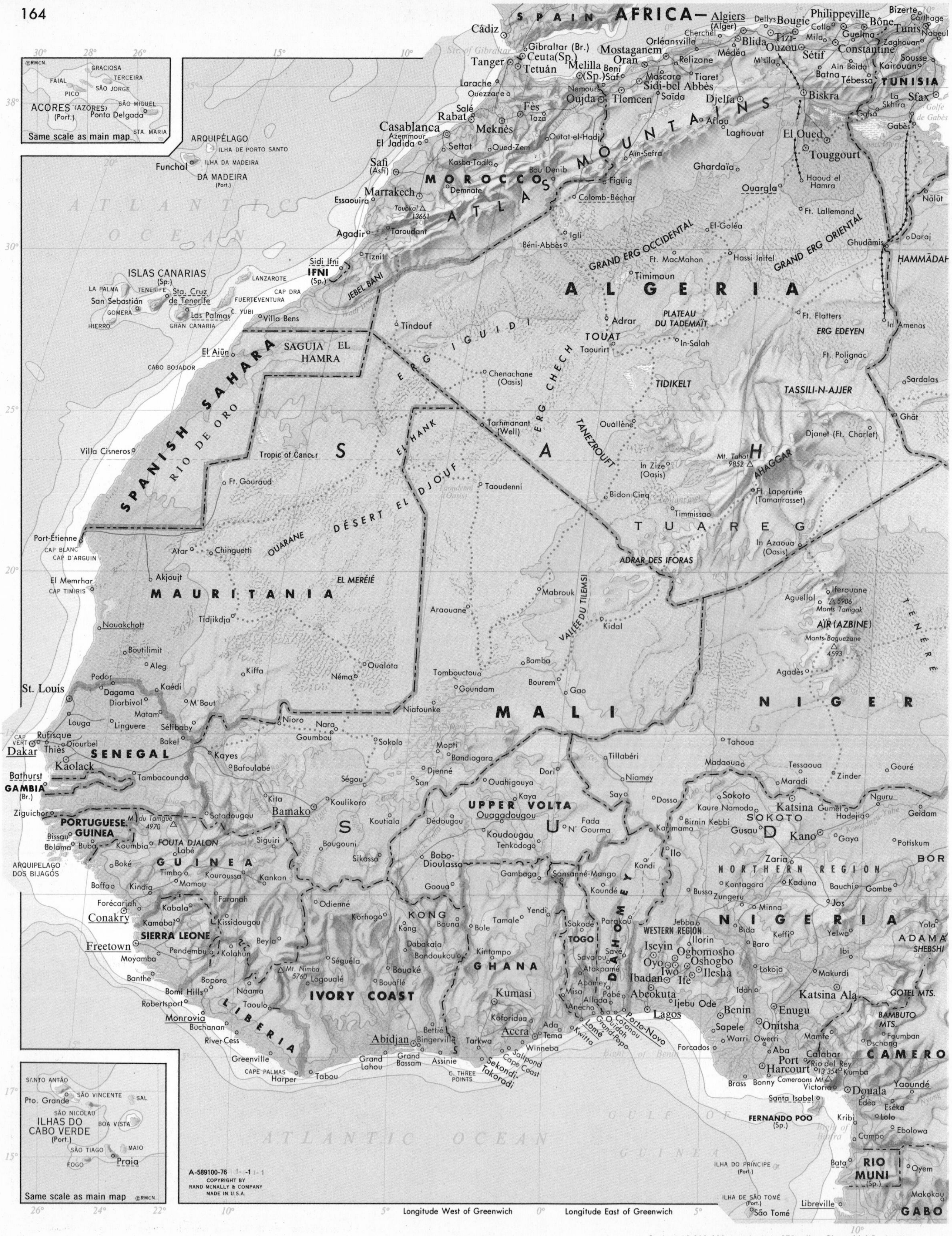

SPAIN AFRICA—

Inset (top left): Azores
©RMCN.
GRACIOSA
FAIAL TERCEIRA
PICO SÃO JORGE
SÃO MIGUEL
STA. MARIA
Ponta Delgada
ACÔRES (AZORES)
(Port.)
Same scale as main map

ARQUIPÉLAGO
ILHA DE PORTO SANTO
ILHA DA MADEIRA
Funchal
DA MADEIRA
(Port.)

ISLAS CANARIAS
(Sp.)
LA PALMA
TENERIFE LANZAROTE
San Sebastián Sta. Cruz de Tenerife
GOMERA CAP DRA FUERTEVENTURA
HIERRO Las Palmas C. YUBI
GRAN CANARIA Villa Bens

ATLANTIC OCEAN

Cádiz
Str. of Gibraltar
Gibraltar (Br.)
Tanger Ceuta (Sp.)
Tetuán
Larache Melilla (Sp.) Beni Saf
Salé Rabat Fès Taza
Casablanca Meknès
El Jadida Azemmour
Settat Oued-Zem
Safi (Asfi) Kasba-Tadla
Marrakech Demnate
Essaouira Toubkal △ 13661
Agadir Taroudant
Tiznit
Sidi Ifni
IFNI (Sp.)
JEBEL BANI

Algiers (Alger) Dellys
Cherchell Orléansville Bougie Philippeville Bône Bizerte
Blida Médéa Tizi Ouzou Mila Guelma Carthage
Mostaganem Sétif Constantine Tunis Nabeul
Oran Relizane Aïn Beïda Souss
Sidi-bel Abbès Mascara Batna Tébessa **TUNISIA**
Saïda Djelfa Biskra La Sfax
Tlemcen Gafsa Golfe de Gabès
Oujda Gabès
Laghouat El Oued
Aflou Touggourt
Ghardaïa Ouargla
El-Goléa Haoud el Hamra
Ft. Lallemand
Colomb-Béchar
GRAND ERG OCCIDENTAL **GRAND ERG ORIENTAL** Ghudâmis **HAMMÂDAH**
Béni-Abbès Ft. MacMahon Hassi Inifel Daraj
Igli Timimoun
A L G E R I A Nâlût
El-Golèa
Adrar **ERG EDEYEN**
PLATEAU DU TADEMAÏT Ft. Flatters In Amenas
TOUAT In-Salah Ft. Polignac
Taourirt **TIDIKELT**
Chenachane (Oasis) **TASSILI-N-AJJER** Sardalas
Ouallène Ghât
Tarhmanant (Well) **TANEZROUFT** In Zize (Oasis) Djanet (Ft. Charlet)
Taoudenni (Oasis) Mt. Tahat 9852 △ **AHAGGAR**
Bidon Cinq Ft. Laperrine (Tamanrasset)
Timmissao
T U A R E G
In Azaoua (Oasis)
ADRAR DES IFORAS

MOROCCO ATLAS MOUNTAINS

SPANISH SAHARA
El Aiún SAGUIA EL HAMRA
CABO BOJADOR
RIO DE ORO
Villa Cisneros Tropic of Cancer
Ft. Gouraud
S A H A R A
ERG IGUIDI
ERG CHECH
EL HANK
DÉSERT EL DJOUF

Port-Étienne
CAP BLANC
CAP D'ARGUIN
El Memrhar
CAP TIMIRIS
Atar Chinguetti
OUARÂNE
Akjoujt
EL MERÉIÉ
M A U R I T A N I A
Tidjikdja
Mabrouk
Araouane Kidal
Kiffa Oualata Néma
Tombouctou **M A L I**
Goundam Bamba
Niafounké Bourem **N I G E R**
Gao

Aguellal Iferouane
△5906 Monts Tamgak
AÏR (AZBINE)
Monts Bagzane △ 4593
Agadès
T E N E R E

Nouakchott
Boutilimit
Aleg
St. Louis
Podor Dagana
Diorbivol Kaédi
Matam M'Bout
Louga Linguere Sélibaby
Rufisque Bakel
CAP VERT Thiès Diourbel
Dakar **S E N E G A L** Kayes
Bathurst Kaolack Bafoulabé
GAMBIA (Br.) Tambacounda Kita
Ziguinchor
PORTUGUESE GUINEA Satadougou
Bissau Mt. du Tangue △ 4970
Bolama Buba Koumbia
ARQUIPÉLAGO DOS BIJAGÓS Boké **FOUTA DJALON** Labé
Boffao Kindia Siguiri
Forécariah Kabala Faranah Kankan
Conakry Kamabai Mamou
Freetown Kissidougou
Moyamba **SIERRA LEONE** Beyla
Banthe Pendembu Kolahun
Bopôro Mt. Nimba 5760 △
Monrovia Naama
Buchanan Taoulé Logoualé
River Cess **L I B E R I A**
Greenville
CAPE PALMAS
Harper Tabou

Nioro Nara
Goumbou Sokolo
Mopti
Bandiagara
Dori Tillabéri
Ouahigouya Niamey
UPPER VOLTA Dosso
Ouagadougou Say
Kaya Fada N' Gourma
Koudougou
Tenkodogo Ilo
Bobo-Dioulasso
Sikasso Gambaga Karimama
Koutiala Sansanné-Mango
Dédougou Kandi
Gaoua Bussa
Odienné Yendi Kontagora
Korhogo **TOGO**
Bouna Tamale Sokodé
KONG Kong Savé Parakou
Dabakala Atakpamé **WESTERN REGION**
Bondoukou Savalou
Séguéla Kintampo **DAHOMEY**
Bouaflé Bouaké Abomey Allada
IVORY COAST Sunyani **GHANA** Pobé
Kumasi Anécho
Koforidua Porto-Novo
Bettié Koumassi **Lagos**
Grand Lahou Winneba **Accra** Lomé
Abidjan Bingerville Saltpond Kwitta
Grand Bassam Assinie Grand-Popo
C. THREE POINTS Sekondi
Takoradi

Tahoua
Madaoua Tessaoua Gouré
Birnin Kebbi Maradi Zinder Nguru
Kaure Namoda Sokoto Katsina Gumel Geidam
Gusau Katsina Hadejia
SOKOTO Kano Gaya
Zaria Potiskum
NORTHERN REGION Kaduna
Zungeru Bauchi Gombe
Minna Jos BOR
N I G E R I A
Bida Keffi
Jebba Ilorin Baro Lokoja Makurdi
Iseyin Ogbomosho Yelwa Ibi Yola
Oyo Oshogbo Ilesha **ADAMA** SHEBSHI
Iwo Ife Idah
Ibadan Abeokuta Benin Enugu Katsina Ala
Ijebu Ode Onitsha **GOTEL MTS.**
Ode Sapele **BAMBUTO MTS.**
Benin City Owerri Mamfe Fournban Dschang
Forcados Aba **CAMERO**
Warri Port Harcourt Calabar
Brass Bonny Cameroons Mt. 13 354 △ Kumba
Santa Isabel Douala Yaoundé
FERNANDO POO (Sp.) Kribi Edéa Eséka
ILHA DO PRÍNCIPE (Port.) Bata **RIO MUNI** (Sp.) Oyem Makokou
ILHA DE SÃO TOMÉ (Port.) **GABO**
São Tomé Libreville Ebolowa

ATLANTIC OCEAN
GULF OF GUINEA
Bight of Benin

Inset (bottom left): Cape Verde
SANTO ANTÃO
SÃO VICENTE SAL
Pto. Grande
SÃO NICOLAU BOA VISTA
ILHAS DO CABO VERDE (Port.)
SÃO TIAGO MAIO
FOGO **Praia**
Same scale as main map ©RMCN.

A-589100-76
COPYRIGHT BY
RAND McNALLY & COMPANY
MADE IN U.S.A.

Longitude West of Greenwich | Longitude East of Greenwich

Scale 1:16 000 000; one inch to 250 miles. Sinusoidal Projection
Elevations and depressions are given in feet

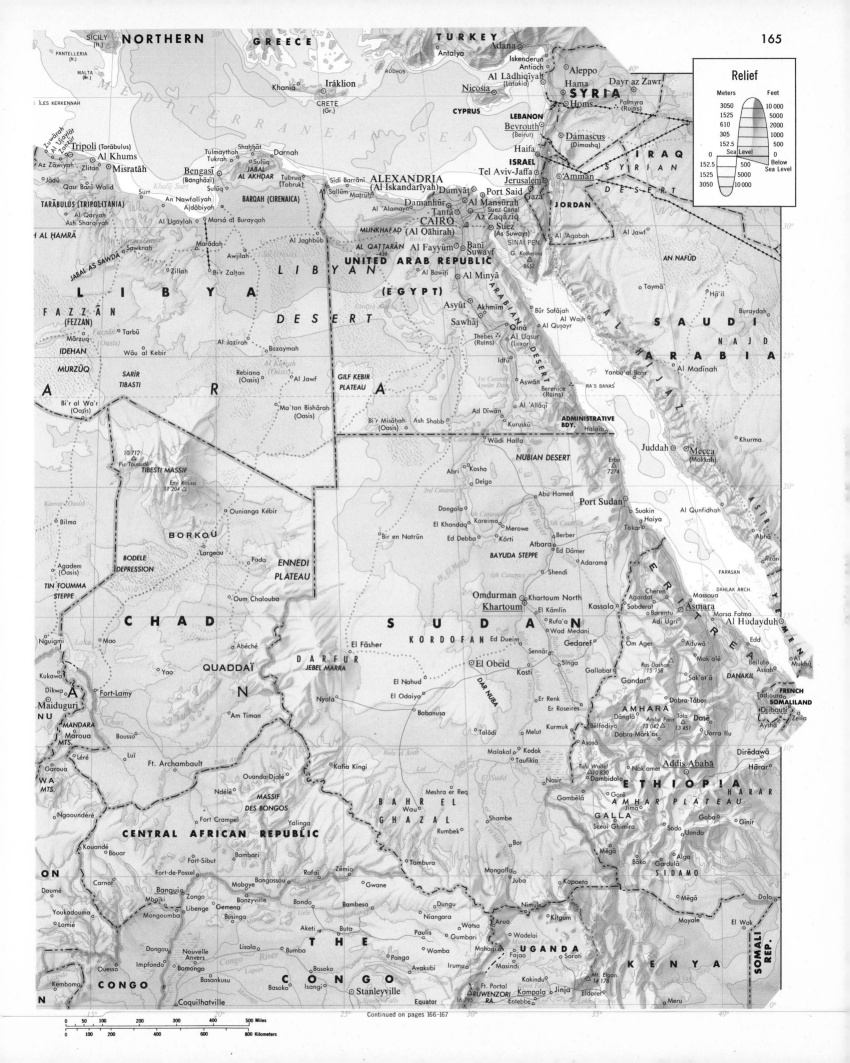

NORTHERN

SICILY (It.)
PANTELLERIA (It.)
MALTA (Br.)
ÎLES KERKENNAH

GREECE
Khaniá
Iráklion
CRETE (Gr.)
RÓDHOS

TURKEY
Antalya
Adana
Iskenderun
Antioch
Aleppo
Al Lādhiqīyah (Latakia)
Hama
Dayr az Zawr
Nicosia
CYPRUS
SYRIA
Homs
Palmyra (Ruins)

Zuwārah
Al Ujaylāt
Zanzur
Tripoli (Tarābulus)
Al Khums
Misrātāh
Az Zāwiyah
Zlitan
Jādū
Qasr Banī Walid

MEDITERRANEAN SEA

LEBANON
Beyrouth (Beirut)
Damascus (Dimashq)
Haifa
Tel Aviv-Jaffa
ISRAEL
Jerusalem
Gaza
'Ammān
JORDAN
IRAQ
Al 'Aqabah
Al Jawf
SYRIAN DESERT

Relief
Meters   Feet
3050   10 000
1525   5000
610   2000
305   1000
152.5   500
0   Sea Level
Sea Level
152.5   500
1525   5000
3050   10 000 Below Sea Level

Tulmaythah
Tukrah
Shahhāt
Darnah
Sulūq
Tubruq (Tobruk)
Bengasi (Banghāzī)
JABAL AL AKHDAR
Sulūq
Sīdī Barrānī
As Sallūm
Matrūh
ALEXANDRIA (Al Iskandarīyah)
Dumyāt
Port Said
Suez Canal

TARĀBULUS (TRIPOLITANIA)
Al Qaryah
Ash Sharqīyah
Surt
An Nawfalīyah
Ajdābiyah
Al Ugaylah
Marsá al Burayqah
BARQAH (CIRENAICA)
Al 'Alamayn
Damanhūr
Tanta
Az Zaqāzīq
Al Mansūrah
CAIRO (Al Qāhirah)
Suez (As Suways)
Al 'Aqabah
SINAI PEN.
G. Katherina 8652

H AL HAMRĀ
Sawknah
Marādah
Awjilah
Al Jaghbūb
MUNKHAFAD AL QATTĀRAH -436
Al Fayyūm
Banī Suwayf
AN NAFŪD

JABAL AS SAWDA
Zillah
Bi'r Zaltān
UNITED ARAB REPUBLIC
(EGYPT)
Al Bawītī
Al Minyā
Taymā
Hā'il
Buraydah

FAZZĀN (FEZZAN)
IDEHAN
MURZŪQ
Mārzuq
Tarbū
Wāu al Kebir
Buzaymah
LIBYAN
DESERT
Asyūt
Akhmīm
Sawhāj
Būr Safājah
Al Wajh
Al Qusayr
SAUDI
NAJD
ARABIA

Bi'r al Wa'r (Oasis)
Rebiana (Oasis)
Al Jawf
GILF KEBIR PLATEAU
S A H A R A
Thebes (Ruins)
Al Uqsur (Luxor)
Idfū
Aswān
Aswān Dam
Yanbu' al Bahr
Al Madīnah

SARĪR TIBASTI
Ma'tan Bishārah (Oasis)
Berenice (Ruins)
RA'S BANĀS

Bi'r al Wa'r
10 712 Pic Toussidé
TIBESTI MASSIF
Emi Koussi 11 204
Bi'r Misāhah (Oasis)
Ash Shabb
Ad Dīwān
Al 'Allāqī
Kuruskū
ADMINISTRATIVE BDY.
Halaib
Erba 7274
Juddah
Mecca (Makkah)
Khurma

Bilma
Ounianga Kébir
Wādi Halfa
NUBIAN DESERT
Abri
Kosha
Delgo
Port Sudan
Suakin
Al Qunfidhah
Haiya
Tokar
Abhā
Jīzan

BORKOU
Agadem (Oasis)
Largeau
Fada
ENNEDI PLATEAU
Bir en Natrûn
Dongola
El Khandaq
Kareima
Merowe
Kōrti
Abu Hamed
Berber
Atbara
Ed Dâmer
FARASAN
DAHLAK ARCH.
Cheren
Massaua

BODELE DEPRESSION
Ed Debba
BAYUDA STEPPE
Shendi
Adarama
Agordat
Sabderat
Barentu

TIN TOUMMA STEPPE
Oum Chalouba
Omdurman
Khartoum North
El Kāmlīn
Kassala
Asmara
Al Hudayduh

Nguigmi
Mao
CHAD
Abéché
El Fāsher
Ed Dueim
Rufa'a
Wad Medani
Gedaref
Om Ager
Aduwā
Edd

Kukawa
Yao
QUADDAÏ
DARFUR
JEBEL MARRA
El Obeid
KORDOFAN
Sennār
Sīnga
Gallabat
Gondar
Mak'alē
Beilul
Assab
Al Mukhā

Dikwa
Fort-Lamy
El Nahud
Kosti
Ras Dashan 15 158
Sak'ot'ā
DANAKIL

Maiduguri
MANDARA MTS.
Maroua
Bousso
Am Timan
Nyala
El Odaiyo
Babanusa
Er Renk
Er Roseires
Dānglā
Tāla 13 451
Dasē
FRENCH SOMALILAND
Tadjoura
Djibouti
Aysha
Zeila

Garoua
Léré
Luï
Ft. Archambault
Talōdi
Kurmuk
Bélfodiyo
Dabra-Mārk'os
Uorra Hu
Amba Farit 13 042
Dīrēdawā
Hārar

WA MTS.
Ndélé
Bahr El Arab
Malakal
Kodok
Taufikia
Asosā
Tulu Wallel 10 830
Dambidolo
Nak'amer
Addis Ababa
Hārar

Garoua
Kouandé
Bouar
Fort-Sibut
Ouanda-Djalé
MASSIF DES BONGOS
Meshra er Req
Nasir
Gambēla
Gorē
ETHIOPIA
GALLA
AMHAR PLATEAU
HARAR
Dirēdawā

CENTRAL AFRICAN REPUBLIC
Bambari
Kafia Kingi
BAHR EL GHAZAL
Wau
Rumbek
Bor
Shambe
Jima
Sodo
Uondo
Ginir

ON
Doumé
Carnot
Fort-Crampel
Yalinga
Tambura
Mongalla
Juba
Kapoeta
SIDAMO
Bāko
Gardulā
Dolo

Ngaoundéré
Bangui
Zongo
Bangassou
Rafaï
Zémio
Gwane
Nimule
Mēga
Moyale
El Wok

Youkadouma
Lomié
Mbaïki
Libenge
Gemena
Bondo
Bambesa
Dungu
Niangara
Watsa
Akubi
Arua
Kitgum
Soroti
SOMALI REP.

THE
Dongou
Nouvelle Anvers
Lisala
Buta
Paulis
Wadelai
Fajao
UGANDA
Masindi
KENYA
Mt. Elgon 14 178
Meru

CONGO
Kemboma
Impfondo
Bomongo
Basankusu
Basoko
Isangi
Stanleyville
CONGO
Coquilhatville
Ft. Portal
RUWENZORI RA. 16 795
Equator
Kampala
Entebbe
Jinja
Eldoret

Continued on pages 166-167

0 50 100 200 300 400 500 Miles
0 100 200 400 600 800 Kilometers

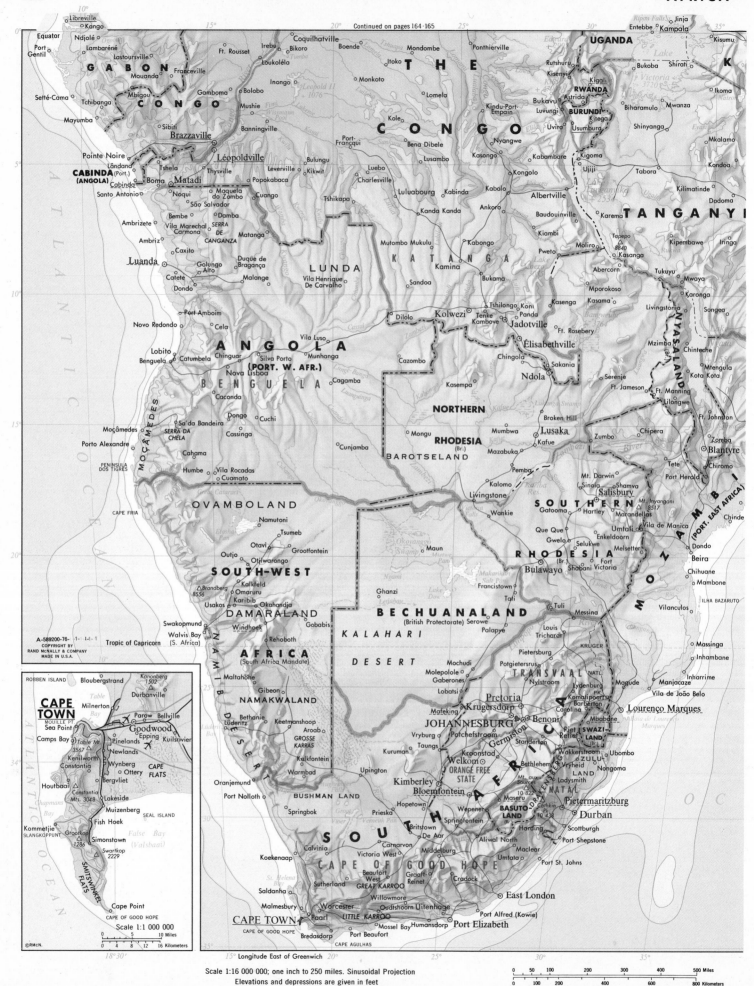

Continued on pages 164·165

CAPE TOWN

Scale 1:1 000 000

0   5   10 Miles

0   4   8   12   16 Kilometers

©RMCN.

Scale 1:16 000 000; one inch to 250 miles. Sinusoidal Projection
Elevations and depressions are given in feet

A-589200-76- 1· 1·1·1
COPYRIGHT BY
RAND McNALLY & COMPANY
MADE IN U.S.A.

0   50 100   200   300   400   500 Miles

0   100   200   400   600   800 Kilometers

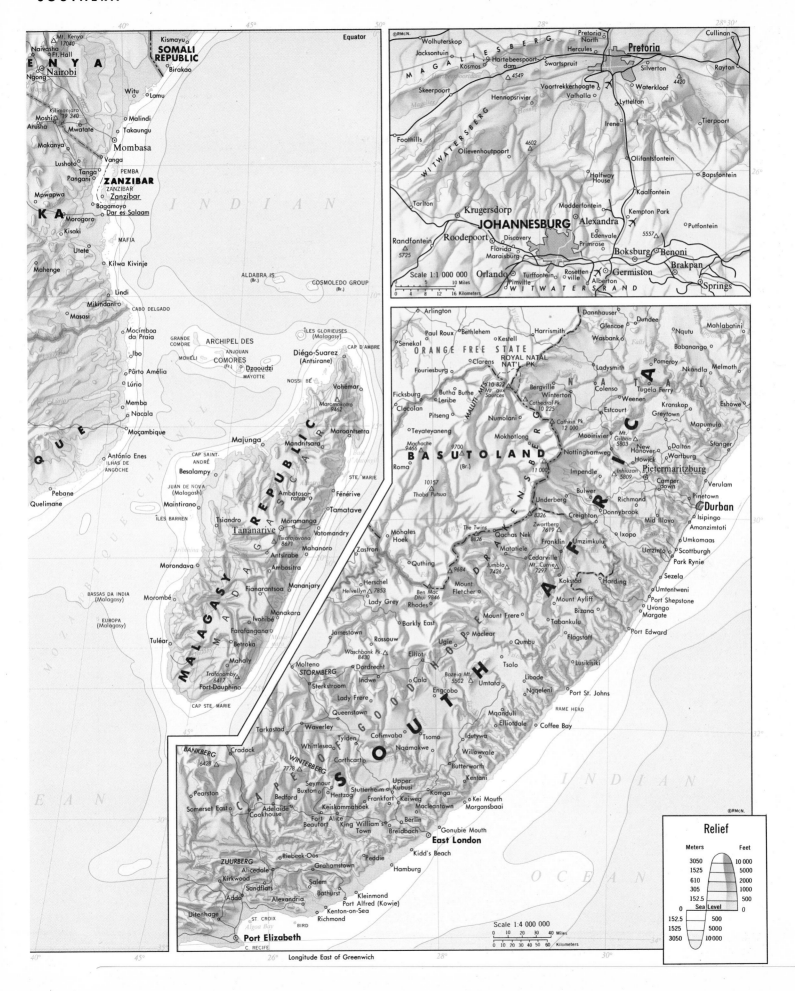

SOMALI
REPUBLIC

Kismayu

Birakao

Mt. Kenya
17,040
Naivasha
Ft. Hall
Ngong
Nairobi

E N Y A

Witu

Lamu

Kilimanjaro
19,340
Moshi
Arusha
Mwatate
Takaungu

Makanya
Malindi

Lushoto
Vanga
Tanga
Pangani
PEMBA

Mpwapwa
ZANZIBAR
ZANZIBAR
Zanzibar

KA
Morogoro
Bagamoyo
Dar es Salaam

Kisaki
MAFIA

Utete

Mahenge
Kilwa Kivinje

Lindi

Mikindani
Masasi
CABO DELGADO

Mocímboa
da Praia

Ibo

ÎLES GLORIEUSES
(Malagasy)

Pôrto Amélia

ALDABRA IS.
(Br.)

COSMOLEDO GROUP
(Br.)

GRANDE
COMORE
ARCHIPEL DES
MOHÉLI
ANJOUAN
COMORES
(Fr.)
Dzaoudzi
MAYOTTE

Diégo-Suarez
(Antsirane)
CAP D'AMBRE

NOSSI BÉ

Vohémar

QUE

Memba

Nacala

Moçambique

Maromokotro
9462

Maroantsetra

Pebane

Quelimane

ILHAS DE
ANGOCHE
ANTÓNIO Enes

JUAN DE NOVA
(Malagash)

CAP SAINT-
ANDRÉ

Besalampy

Majunga

Mandritsara

Ambatoso-
ratra

Fénérive

STE. MARIE

G

Maintirano

ÎLES BARREN

Tsiandro

A
L
A
G
A
S
Y

Moramanga

Vatomandry

Tananarive

Tsiafajavona
8671
Antsirabe
Mahanoro

Morondava

Ambositra

BASSAS DA INDIA
(Malagasy)

Fianarantsoa
Mananjary

Morombé

Manakara

EUROPA
(Malagasy)

Ivohibé

Betroka
Farafangana

Tuléar

A
D
A
G
A
S
C
A
R

R
E
P
U
B
L
I
C

Mahaly
Trafonomby
6417
Fort-Dauphino

CAP STE. MARIE

Equator

INDIAN

MOZAMBIQUE CHANNEL

©RMcN.
Arlington

Paul Roux
Senekal
Bethlehem
Kestell
Harrismith
Dannhauser
Glencoe
Dundee
Nqutu
Mahlabatini

ORANGE FREE STATE
Fouriesburg
Clarens
Wasbank
Babanango
Melmoth

Ficksburg
Butha Buthe
Leribe
**ROYAL NATAL
NAT'L PK.**
10,822
Mt. aux
Sources
Bergville
Winterton
Colenso
Weenen
Ladysmith
Pomeroy
Nkandla
Greytown
Kranskop
Eshowe

Clocolan
Pitseng
Cathedral Pk.
10,225
Cathkin Pk.
12,000
Estcourt
Mapumulo

Teyateyaneng
Numolani
Mokhotlong
Mooirivier
Mt.
Gilboa
5803
New
Hanover
Dalton
Stanger

BASUTOLAND
(Br.)
Roma
Machache
9466
9700
11,000
Nottinghamweg
Inhluzani
5809
Howick
Wartburg
Pietermaritzburg
Verulam

Thaba Putsua
10,157
Impendle
Bulwer
Richmond
Camper
down
Pinetown
Durban

Mohales
Hoek
The Twins
8826
Underberg
8326
Creighton
Donnybrook
Mid Illovo
Isipingo
Amanzimtoti

Zastron
Qachas Nek
Zwartberg
7619
Franklin
Umzimkulu
Ixopo
Umkomaas

Quthing
Matatiele
Cedarville
Mt. Currie
7297
Kokstad
Harding
Umzinto
Scottburgh
Park Rynie

Herschel
9684
Jumbla
7426
Sezela

Helvellyn
7853
Ben Mac
Dhui 9846
Mount
Fletcher
Mount Ayliff
Bizana
Umtentweni
Port Shepstone

Lady Grey
Rhodes
Qumbu
Tabankulu
Flagstaff
Uvongo
Margate

Barkly East
Mount Frere
Port Edward

Jamestown
Rossouw
Ugie
Maclear
Tsolo
Libode
Ngqeleni
Port St. Johns

Molteno
Dordrecht
Elliot
Cala
Bazeia Mt.
5562
Umtata
RAME HEAD

Waschbank Pk.
8430
Indwe
Engcobo
Mqanduli
Coffee Bay

STORMBERG
Sterkstroom
Lady Frere
Mandu
Elliotdale

Tarkastad
Queenstown
Cofimvaba
Tsomo
Idutywa
Willowvale

Waverley
Tylden
Ngamakwe
Butterworth

BANKBERG
6428
Cradock
Whittlesea
Cathcart
Kentani

WINTERBERG
7778
Seymour
Stutterheim
Upper
Kubusi
Komga

Pearston
Bedford
Buxton
Hertzog
Frankfort
Keiweg
Kei Mouth
Morgansbaai

Somerset East
Adelaide
Keiskammahoek
Berlin

Cookhouse
Fort
Beaufort
Alice
King William's
Town
Breidbach
Gonubie Mouth
Maclantown

ZUURBERG
Riebeek-Oos
Peddie
East London

Alicedale
Grahamstown
Kidd's Beach
Kirkwood
Salem
Hamburg

Addo
Sandflats
Bathurst
Kleinmond
Port Alfred (Kowie)

Uitenhage
Alexandria
Kenton-on-Sea
Richmond

ST. CROIX
Algoa Bay
BIRD

Port Elizabeth
C. RECIFE

C
A
P
E
O
F
G
O
O
D
H
O
P
E

S
O
U
T
H

A
F
R
I
C
A

N
A
T
A
L

DRAKENSBERG

INDIAN

OCEAN

Longitude East of Greenwich

Scale 1:4 000 000

0   10 20 30   40 Miles

0 10 20 30 40 50 60 Kilometers

©RMcN.

Relief

Meters   Feet
3050   10 000
1525   5000
610   2000
305   1000
152.5   500
Sea Level   0
152.5   500
1525   5000
3050   10 000

©RMcN.
Wolhuterskop
Pretoria
North
Cullinan

Jacksontuin
MAGALIESBERG
Kosmos
Hercules
Pretoria

Harteespoort-
dam
Swartspruit
Silverton
Rayton

Skeerpoort
4549
Voortrekkerhoogte
Vathalla
Waterkloof
4420

Foothills
Hennopsrivier
Lyttelton
Tierpoort

WITWATERSBERG
Olievenhoutpoort
4602
Irene

Olifantsfontein
Bapsfontein

Tarlton
Halfway
House
Kaalfontein

Krugersdorp
Modderfontein
Kempton Park

Randfontein
JOHANNESBURG
Alexandra
Putfontein

Roodepoort
Discovery
Edenvale

5725
Florida
Maraisburg
Primrose
5557

Scale 1:1 000 000
Orlando
Turffontein
Rosetten-
ville
Boksburg
Benoni

0   5   10 Miles
Pimville
Alberton
Germiston
Brakpan

0 4 8 12 16 Kilometers
WITWATERSRAND
Springs

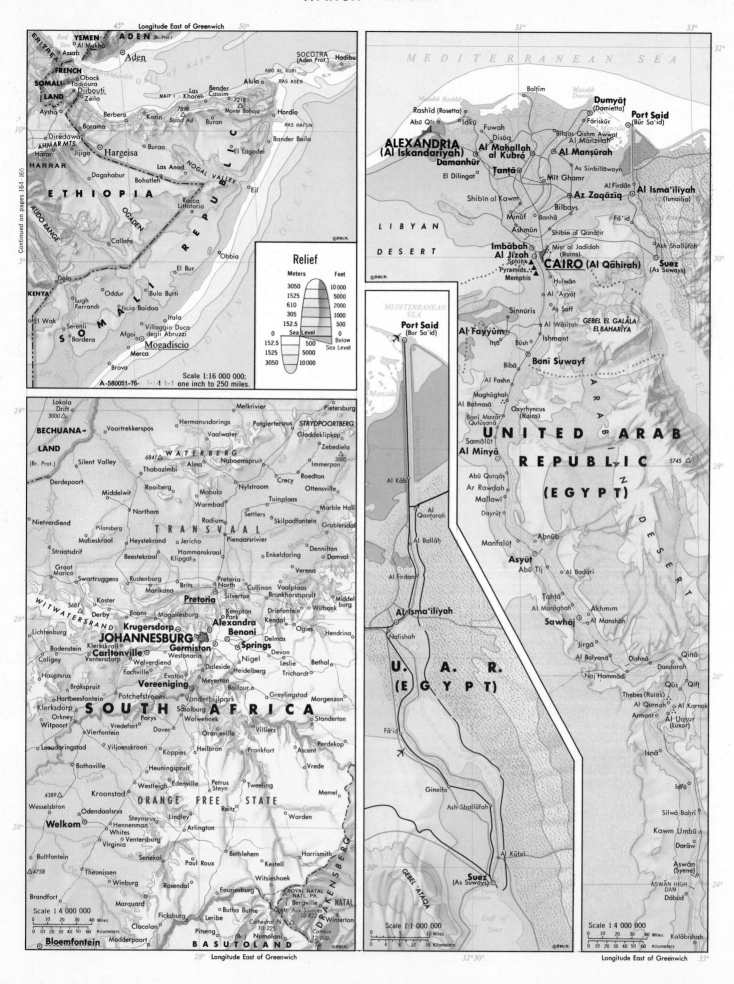

Continued on pages 164-165

Longitude East of Greenwich

Relief

Meters		Feet
3050		10 000
1525		5000
610		2000
305		1000
152.5		500
0	Sea Level	0
	Below	Sea Level
152.5		500
1525		5000
3050		10 000

Scale 1:16 000 000;
A-580051-76- 1-·1 1-1   one inch to 250 miles.

ETHIOPIA

SOMALI REPUBLIC

Mogadiscio

Scale 1:4 000 000
0 10 20 30 40 Miles
0 10 20 30 40 50 60 Kilometers

BECHUANA-LAND
(Br. Prot.)

TRANSVAAL

WATERBERG

WITWATERSRAND

Pretoria

JOHANNESBURG
Alexandra
Benoni
Springs
Germiston
Carltonville
Vereeniging

SOUTH AFRICA

ORANGE FREE STATE

Welkom

Bloemfontein

BASUTOLAND

Longitude East of Greenwich

MEDITERRANEAN SEA

ALEXANDRIA
(Al Iskandariyah)
Damanhūr

Dumyāt
(Damietta)
Port Said
(Būr Sa'īd)

CAIRO (Al Qāhirah)
Suez (As Suways)

LIBYAN DESERT

UNITED ARAB REPUBLIC
(EGYPT)

Al Minyā

Asyūt

MEDITERRANEAN SEA

Port Said
(Būr Sa'īd)

Al Ismā'īlīyah

U. A. R.
(EGYPT)

Suez (As Suways)

Scale 1:1 000 000
0   5   10 Miles
0 4 8 12 16 Kilometers

DESERT

Thebes (Ruins)
Al Uqsur
(Luxor)

Aswān (Syene)

ASWĀN HIGH DAM

Scale 1:4 000 000
0 10 20 30 40 Miles
0 10 20 30 40 50 60

Longitude East of Greenwich

WORLD COMPARISONS

General Information

Equatorial diameter of the earth, 7,926.68 miles
Polar diameter of the earth, 7,899.99 miles
Diameter of the mean sphere of the earth, 7,917.78 miles
Equatorial circumference of the earth, 24,902.45 miles
Polar circumference of the earth, 24,818.60 miles
Mean distance from the earth to the sun, 92,900,000 miles
Mean distance from the earth to the moon, 238,857 miles
Total area of the earth, 196,940,400 square miles

Highest elevation on the earth's surface, Mt. Everest, Asia, 29,028 feet
Lowest elevation on the earth's land surface, shores of the Dead Sea, Asia,—1,286 feet.
Greatest known depth of the ocean, south of the Mariana Islands, Pacific Ocean, 36,198 feet
Total land area of the earth, including inland water and Antarctica, 57,280,000 square miles

Area of Africa, 11,685,000 square miles
Area of Antarctica, 5,100,000 square miles
Area of Asia, 17,085,000 square miles
Area of Europe, 3,825,000 square miles
Area of North America, 9,420,000 square miles
Area of Oceania, incl. Australia, 3,295,000 square miles
Area of South America, 6,870,000 square miles
Population of the earth (est. 1/1/1964), 3,193,000,000

Principal Islands and Their Areas

Island	Area Sq. Miles
Baffin, Arctic Region	183,810
Banks, Arctic Region	23,230
Borneo, Asia	286,967
Bougainville, Oceania	3,880
Celebes, Indonesia	72,986
Ceylon, Indian Ocean	25,332
Corsica, Mediterranean Sea	3,367
Crete, Mediterranean Sea	3,238
Cuba, West Indies	44,217
Cyprus, Mediterranean Sea	3,572
Devon, Arctic Region	20,861
Ellesmere, Arctic Region	82,119
Formosa, China Sea	13,885
Great Britain, Europe	88,756
Greenland, Arctic Region	840,000
Hainan Tao, South China Sea	13,127
Hawaii, Oceania	4,030
Hispaniola, West Indies	29,530
Hokkaidō, Japan	29,950
Honshū, Japan	88,930
Iceland, Arctic Region	39,800
Ireland, Europe	32,596
Jamaica, West Indies	4,411
Java, Indonesia	50,745
Kyūshū, Japan	16,215
Luzon, Philippines	40,814
Madagascar, Indian Ocean	227,800
Melville, Arctic Region	16,141
Mindanao, Philippines	36,906
Mindoro, Philippines	3,794
Negros, Philippines	4,903
New Britain, Oceania	14,592
Newfoundland, Canada	42,734
New Guinea, Oceania	316,856
North East Land, Arctic Region	6,350
North Island (New Zealand), Oceania	44,281
Nouvelle Caledonie, Oceania	5,671
Novaya Zemlya, Arctic Region	31,390
Palawan, Philippines	4,500
Panay, Philippines	4,448
Prince of Wales, Arctic Region	12,830
Puerto Rico, West Indies	3,435
Sakhalin, Soviet Union	29,344
Samar, Philippines	5,124
Sardinia, Mediterranean Sea	9,301
Seram, Indonesia	6,046
Sicily, Mediterranean Sea	9,926
Shikoku, Japan	7,245
Somerset, Arctic Region	9,370
Southampton, Hudson Bay	15,700
South Island (New Zealand) Oceania	58,093
Sumatra, Indonesia	182,859
Tasmania, Australia	26,215
Tierra del Fuego, S.A.	18,600
Timor, Asia	13,094
Vancouver, Canada	12,408
Victoria, Arctic Region	81,930
Vrangelya, Arctic Region	2,819
West Spitsbergen, Arctic Region	15,260

Principal Lakes, Oceans, Seas, and Their Areas

Lake Country	Area Sq. Miles
Aral'skoye More (Aral Sea) Sov. Un.	26,518
Arctic O.	5,427,000
Athabasca, L., Can.	3,120
Atlantic O.	31,744,000
Balkhash, Ozero (L.), Sov. Un.	6,678
Baltic Sea, Eur.	163,000
Baykal, Ozero (L.), Sov. Un.	12,159
Bering Sea, Asia-N.A.	876,000
Black Sea, Eur.-Asia	178,000
Caribbean Sea, N.A.-S.A.	750,000
Caspian Sea, Sov. Un.	152,084
Chad, L., Chad	6,300
Ch'ing Hai (Koko Nor) (L.), China	1,650
East China Sea, Asia	482,000
Erie, L., U. S.-Can.	9,940
Eyre, L., Austl.	3,700
Gairdner, L., Austl.	1,500
Great Bear L., Can.	12,275
Great Salt L., U. S.	1,700
Great Slave L., Can.	10,980
Hudson Bay, Can.	476,000
Huron, L., U. S.-Can.	23,010
Indian O.	28,371,000
Japan, Sea of, Asia	389,000
Ladozhskoye Ozero (Lake Ladoga), Sov. Un.	7,092
Leopold II, L., Con. L.	1,700
Manitoba, L., Can.	1,817
Mediterranean Sea, Eur.-Afr.-Asia	967,000
Mexico, G. of, N. A.	596,000
Michigan, L., U. S.	22,400
Nicaragua, Lago de (L.), Nic.	2,972
North Sea, Eur.	222,000
Nyasa, L., Afr.	10,900
Okhotsk, Sea of, Pac. O.	590,000
Onezhskoye Ozero (Lake Onega), Sov. Un.	3,821
Ontario, L., U. S.-Can.	7,540
Pacific O.	63,855,000
Red Sea, Afr.-Asia	169,000
Rudolf, L., Ken.-Eth.	2,473
Superior, L., U. S.-Can.	31,820
Tanganyika, L., Tan.-Con. L.	10,965
Titicaca, Lago (L.), Bol.-Peru	3,500
Torrens, L., Austl.	2,200
Vänern, L., Swe.	2,156
Van Gölü (L.), Tur.	1,470
Victoria, L., Tan.	26,828
Winnipeg, L., Can.	9,465
Winnipegosis, L., Can.	2,103
Yellow Sea, China	480,000

Principal Mountains and Their Heights

Mountain Country	Height in Feet
Aconcagua, Argentina	22,834
Albert Edward, Papua	13,100
Altar, Ecuador	17,457
Annapurna, Nepal	26,504
Antisana, Ecuador	18,714
Antofalla, Argentina	21,129
Apo, Philippines	9,690
Ararat, Turkey	16,946
Azufre (Copiapó), Chile	19,947
Balbi, Solomon I.	9,000
Bandeira, Brazil	9,462
Barriere Juliana, West Irian	15,420
Bejeda, Ethiopia	15,158
Belukha, Soviet Union	15,157
Blanc, France-Italy	15,781
Blanca, Colorado, U. S.	14,317
Bolívar (La Columna), Venezuela	16,411
Bona, Alaska, U. S.	16,421
Borah, Idaho, U. S.	12,662
Cameroons, Cam.	13,353
Cano, Cape Verde Is.	9,760
Carstensz-Toppen, West Irian	16,503
Cayambe, Ecuador	19,170
Chimborazo, Ecuador	20,577
Citlaltépetl, Mexico	18,696
Colima, Mexico	14,235
Cook, New Zealand	12,349
Cotopaxi, Ecuador	19,344
Cristobal Colón, Colombia	18,947
Damavand, Iran	18,934
Dhaulagiri, Nepal	28,810
Dos Conos, Argentina	22,507
Dykh-Tau, Soviet Union	17,054
Elbert, Colorado, U. S.	14,431
El'brus, Soviet Union	18,468
Elgon, Kenya	14,178
El Misti, Peru	19,144
Emi Koussi, Chad	11,204
Erebus, Antarctica	12,280
Etna, Italy	10,868
Everest, Nepal-China	29,028
Finsteraarhorn, Switzerland	14,026
Foraker, Alaska, U. S.	17,395
Fuji-san, Japan	12,388
Galdhöpiggen, Norway	8,400
Gasherbrum, India	26,470
Godwin Austen (K-2), Pak.	28,250
Gosainthan, China	26,291
Gran Paradiso, Italy	13,323
Gunnbjörn, Greenland	12,139
Gurla Mandhata, China	25,355
Hekla, Iceland	4,747
Hood, Oregon, U. S.	11,245
Hsinkao Shan, Taiwan	13,113
Huascarán, Peru	22,205
Huila, Colombia	18,865
Hvannadalshnukur, Iceland	6,952
Illampu, Bolivia	21,490
Illimani, Bolivia	21,151
Incahuasi, Argentina-Chile	21,719
Ixtacihuatl, Mexico	17,343
Jabal Al Loz, Saudi Arabia	8,461
Jabal Razih, Saudi Arabia	11,999
Jungfrau, Switzerland	13,668
Kailas, China (Tibet)	22,028
Kāmet, India	25,447
Kanchenjunga, Nepal-Sikkim	28,159
Karisimbi, Con. L.	14,787
Kazbek, Soviet Union	16,558
Kenya, Kenya	17,040
Kerintji, Indonesia	12,484
Kilimanjaro, Tanganyika	19,340
Kinabalu, Malaysia	13,455
Klyuchevskaya, Soviet Union	15,912
Kommunizma, Soviet Union	24,590
Korab, Albania	9,068
Kosciusko, Australia	7,316
Krakatoa (Rakata), Indonesia	2,667
Kwanmo, Korea	8,336
Lassen, California, U. S.	10,466
Lenina, Soviet Union	23,382
Leuser, Indonesia	11,178
Llullaillaco, Argentina-Chile	22,146
Logan, Canada	19,850
McKinley, Alaska, U. S.	20,320
Makalu, China-Nepal	27,790
Markham, Antarctica	15,100
Maromokotro, Malagasy	9,462
Matterhorn, Switz.-Italy	14,685
Mauna Kea, Hawaii, U. S.	13,796
Mauna Loa, Hawaii, U. S.	13,680
Mercedario, Argentina-Chile	22,211
Minya Konka, China	24,900
Mitchell, North Carolina, U. S.	6,684
Musala, Bulgaria	9,592
Muztagh Ata, China	24,388
Namcha Barwa, China	25,445
Nanda Devi, India	25,645
Nanga Parbat, Pak.	26,660
Negoi, Romania	8,344
Neiges, Piton des, Reunion	10,069
Ojos del Salado, Argentina-Chile	22,590
Ólimbos, Greece	9,550
Orohena, Tahiti	7,618
Paricutín, Mexico	9,100
Pelée, Martinique	4,800
Pic du Midi d'Ossau, France	10,322
Pidurutalagala, Ceylon	8,281
Pikes Peak, Colorado, U. S.	14,110
Pissis, Argentina	22,546
Pobeda, China-Soviet Union	24,409
Popocatépetl, Mexico	17,883
Pulog, Philippines	9,612
Qurnet es Sa'uda, Lebanon	10,131
Rainier, Washington, U. S	14,410
Rakaposhi, India	25,551
Rindjani, Indonesia	12,225
Rosa, Monte, Italy-Switzerland	15,200
Ruapehu, New Zealand	9,175
Ruwenzori, Con. L.-Uganda	16,821
St. Elias, U.S.-Canada	18,008
Sajama, Bolivia	21,391
Sanford, Alaska, U. S.	16,208
Sangay, Ecuador	17,749
Semeroe, Indonesia	12,060
Shasta, California, U. S.	14,162
Shkhara, Soviet Union	17,059
Sources, Mt. aux, Basutoland-S. Afr.	10,822
Tengri Khan, Soviet Union	22,940
Thabantshonyana, Basutoland	11,425
Tina, Dominican Republic	9,285
Tirich Mir, Pak.	25,426
Tocorpuri, Bolivia-Chile	22,162
Toubkal, Morocco	13,661
Tupungato, Argentina-Chile	22,310
Ulugh Muztagh, China	25,340
Vesuvio (Vesuvius), Italy	3,842
Victoria, Papua	13,363
Vinson Massif, Ant.	16,864
Weisshorn, Switzerland	14,803
Whitney, California, U. S.	14,495
Wilhelmina-Top, West Irian	15,518
Wrangell, Alaska, U. S.	14,005
Yerupaja, Peru	21,758

Principal Rivers and Their Lengths

River Continent	Length in Miles
Albany, North America	610
Aldan, Asia	1,392
Amazonas, South America	3,900
Amu Dar'ya (Oxus), Asia	1,628
Amur, Asia	2,802
Araguaia, South America	1,630
Arkansas, North America	1,450
Athabasca, North America	765
Back, North America	605
Brahmaputra, Asia	1,800
Branco, South America	580
Brazos, North America	870
Canadian, North America	906
Churchill, North America	1,000
Colorado, North America	1,450
Columbia, North America	1,214
Congo, Africa	2,900
Cumberland, North America	687
Danube, Europe	1,770
Darling, Australia	1,750
Dnepr (Dnieper), Europe	1,420
Dnestr (Dniester), Europe	876
Don, Europe	1,224
Donets, Europe	735
Elbe, Europe	720
Euphrates, Asia	1,675
Fraser, North America	850
Gambia, Africa	680
Ganges, Asia	1,550
Gila, North America	630
Godāvari, Asia	930
Hsi Chiang, Asia	1,590
Hwang Ho (Yellow), Asia	2,903
Indus, Asia	1,980
Irrawaddy, Asia	1,425
Japurá, South America	1,400
Juruá, South America	1,200
Kama, Europe	1,261
Kolyma, Asia	1,615
Lena, Asia	2,653
Loire, Europe	625
Mackenzie, North America	2,635
Madeira, South America	2,060
Magdalena, South America	950
Marañón, South America	1,000
Mekong, Asia	2,600
Meuse, Europe	575
Mississippi, North America	2,348
Mississippi-Missouri-Red Rock, N. A.	3,860
Missouri-Red Rock, N. A.	2,683
Murray, Australia	1,600
Negro, South America	1,305
Nelson, North America	1,600
Neman, Eur.	582
Niger, Africa	2,590
Nile, Africa	4,132
Obitsu-Irtysh, Asia	3,461
Oder, Europe	565
Ohio, N. A.	981
Oka, Europe	920
Orange, Africa	1,155
Orinoco, South America	1,800
Ottawa, North America	696
Paraguay, South America	1,290
Paraná, South America	2,450
Parnaíba, South America	850
Peace, North America	1,195
Pechora, Europe	1,118
Pecos, North America	735
Pilcomayo, South America	1,550
Plata-Paraguay, S. America	2,300
Purús, South America	1,900
Red, North America	1,018
Rhein, Europe	820
Rhône, Europe	500
Rio Grande, North America	1,885
Roosevelt, South America	950
St. Lawrence, North America	1,900
Salado, South America	870
Salween, Asia	1,730
São Francisco, South America	1,800
Saskatchewan, North America	1,205
Sava, Europe	585
Senegal, Africa	1,000
Snake, North America	1,038
Sung Hua (Sungari), Asia	1,140
Syr Dar'ya, Asia	1,653
Tajo (Tagus), Europe	625
Tennessee, N. A.	652
Tigris, Asia	1,150
Tisza, Europe	607
Tobol, Asia	1,093
Tocantins, South America	1,640
Ucayali, South America	1,220
Ural, Europe	1,522
Uruguay, South America	1,025
Verkhnyaya Tunguska (Angara), Asia	1,549
Vilyuy, Asia	1,513
Volga, Europe	2,293
White, North America	690
Wisla (Vistula), Europe	630
Xingú, South America	1,230
Yangtze, Asia	3,430
Yellowstone, North America	671
Yenisey, Asia	2,566
Yukon, North America	1,800
Zambezi, Africa	1,659

PRINCIPAL COUNTRIES AND REGIONS OF THE WORLD

Political Division or Region	Area in sq. miles	Population 1/1/64 est.	Pop. per sq. mi.
Aden (U.K.)	111,100	1,250,000	11
Afghanistan	251,000	15,000,000	60
Africa	11,685,000	278,000,000	24
Alabama (U.S.)	51,609	3,414,000	66
Alaska (U.S.)	586,400	256,000	0.4
Albania	11,099	1,800,000	162
Alberta (Can.)	255,285	1,422,000	5.6
Algeria	917,537	11,200,000	12
American Samoa (U.S.)	76	22,000	289
Andorra	175	11,000	63
Angola (Port.)	481,351	5,050,000	10
Antarctica	5,100,000	....	....
Antigua (incl. Barbuda) (U.K.)	171	58,000	339
Argentina	1,072,070	21,800,000	20
Arizona (U.S.)	113,909	1,598,000	14
Arkansas (U.S.)	53,104	1,834,000	35
Asia	17,085,000	1,860,500,000	109
Australia (Br. Comm.)	2,971,081	11,065,000	3.7
Austria	32,374	7,175,000	222
Azores Is. (Port.)	894	331,000	370
Bahama Is. (U.K.)	4,375	116,000	27
Bahrain	231	162,000	701
Barbados (U.K.)	166	235,000	1,416
Basutoland (U.K.)	11,716	725,000	62
Bechuanaland (U.K.)	275,000	365,000	1.3
Belgium	11,778	9,300,000	790
Bermuda (U.K.)	21	58,000	2,762
Bhutan	19,300	710,000	37
Bolivia	424,163	3,650,000	8.6
Bonin Is. (U.S. Admin.)	40	200	5.0
Brazil	3,286,478	78,700,000	24
British Columbia (Can.)	366,255	1,710,000	4.7
Br. Comm. of Nations	11,177,751	777,440,000	70
British Guiana (U.K.)	83,000	620,000	7.5
British Honduras (U.K.)	8,866	100,000	11
Brunei (U.K.)	2,226	95,000	43
Bulgaria	42,729	8,100,000	190
Burma	261,789	23,000,000	88
Burundi (Urundi)	10,747	2,600,000	242
California (U.S.)	158,693	17,947,000	113
Cambodia	66,606	5,900,000	89
Cameroon	183,569	4,650,000	25
Canada (Br. Comm.)	3,851,809	19,100,000	5.0
Canal Zone (U.S.)	553	47,000	85
Canary Is. (Sp.)	2,808	990,000	353
Cape Verde Is. (Port.)	1,552	218,000	140
Cayman Is. (U.K.)	100	8,000	80
Central African Republic	238,200	1,275,000	5.4
Central America	200,412	13,247,000	66
Ceylon (Br. Comm.)	25,332	10,850,000	428
Chad	495,800	2,850,000	5.7
Channel Is. (U.K.)	75	109,000	1,453
Chile	286,397	8,050,000	28
China (excl. Taiwan)	3,691,500	710,000,000	192
Colombia	439,513	15,300,000	35
Colorado (U.S.)	104,247	1,978,000	19
Congo (Republic of Congo; capital Brazzaville)	132,000	850,000	6.4
Congo, The (Republic of the Congo; capital Léopoldville)	905,565	15,200,000	17
Connecticut (U.S.)	5,009	2,683,000	536
Cook Is. (N.Z.)	90	19,000	211
Costa Rica	19,600	1,350,000	69
Cuba	44,217	7,000,000	158
Cyprus	3,572	590,000	165
Czechoslovakia	49,367	14,000,000	284
Dahomey	44,696	2,200,000	49
Delaware (U.S.)	2,057	485,000	236
Denmark	16,619	4,710,000	283
Denmark and Possessions	857,159	4,783,000	5.6
Dist. of Columbia (U.S.)	69	785,000	11,377
Dominica (U.K.)	305	62,000	203
Dominican Republic	18,704	3,400,000	182
Ecuador	104,506	4,800,000	46
El Salvador	8,260	2,725,000	330
England & Wales (U.K.)	58,344	47,500,000	814
Ethiopia	457,267	21,000,000	46
Europe	3,825,000	595,800,000	156
Faeroe Is. (Den.)	540	36,000	67
Falkland Is. (excl. Deps.) (U.K.)	4,618	2,100	0.5
Fernando Poo (Sp.)	785	68,000	87
Fiji (U.K.)	7,040	441,000	63
Finland	130,119	4,565,000	35
Florida (U.S.)	58,560	5,751,000	98
France	212,822	48,000,000	226
France and Possessions	276,238	49,500,000	179
French Guiana (Fr.)	35,100	36,000	1.0
French Polynesia (Fr.)	1,550	80,000	52
French Somaliland (Fr.)	8,500	70,000	8.2
Gabon	103,100	475,000	4.6
Gambia (U.K.)	4,008	320,000	80
Georgia (U.S.)	58,876	4,180,000	71
Germany (Entire)	137,743	74,950,000	544
Germany, East	41,815	17,100,000	409
Germany, West (incl. West Berlin)	95,928	57,850,000	603
Ghana (Br. Comm.)	91,843	7,450,000	81
Gibraltar (U.K.)	2	28,000	14,000
Gilbert & Ellice Is. (U.K.)	369	50,000	136
Greece	50,547	8,450,000	167
Greenland (Den.)	840,000	37,000	0.04
Grenada (U.K.)	133	91,000	684
Guadeloupe (Fr.)	687	298,000	434
Guam (U.S.)	212	66,000	311
Guatemala	42,042	4,150,000	99
Guinea	94,925	3,300,000	35
Haiti	10,714	4,500,000	420
Hawaii (U.S.)	6,424	715,000	111
Honduras	43,277	2,040,000	47
Hong Kong (U.K.)	398	3,675,000	9,234
Hungary	35,919	10,110 000	281
Iceland	39,800	190,000	4.8
Idaho (U.S.)	83,557	700,000	8.4
Ifni (Sp.)	580	52,000	90
Illinois (U.S.)	56,400	10,457,000	185
India (incl. part of Kashmir) (Br. Comm.)	1,227,275	467,700,000	381
Indiana (U.S.)	36,291	4,825,000	133
Indonesia	574,670	101,000,000	176
Iowa (U.S.)	56,290	2,806,000	50
Iran	636,300	22,500,000	35
Iraq	171,599	7,700,000	45
Ireland	27,136	2,825,000	104
Isle of Man (U.K.)	227	48,000	211
Israel	7,815	2,435,000	312
Italy	116,303	50,650,000	436
Ivory Coast	124,503	3,500,000	28
Jamaica (Br. Comm.)	4,411	1,685,000	382
Japan	142,726	96,200,000	674
Jordan	37,301	1,825,000	49
Kansas (U.S.)	82,264	2,244,000	27
Kentucky (U.S.)	40,395	3,073,000	76
Kenya (Br. Comm.)	224,960	8,950,000	40
Korea (Entire)	85,255	37,500,000	440
Korea, North	47,255	10,300,000	218
Korea, South	38,000	27,200,000	716
Kuwait	6,000	350,000	58
Laos	91,400	1,950,000	21
Lebanon	4,000	1,940,000	485
Liberia	43,000	1,360,000	32
Libya	679,360	1,275,000	1.9
Liechtenstein	61	18,000	295
Louisiana (U.S.)	48,523	3,394,000	70
Luxembourg	998	325,000	326
Macao (Port.)	6	175,000	29,167
Madeira Is. (Port.)	308	269,000	873
Maine (U.S.)	33,215	1,003,000	30
Malagasy Republic (Madagascar)	227,800	5,950,000	26
Malaysia (Br. Comm.)	128,522	10,815,000	84
Maldive Is.	115	93,000	809
Mali	464,874	4,450,000	9.6
Malta (U.K.)	122	330,000	2,705
Manitoba (Can.)	251,000	960,000	3.8
Martinique (Fr.)	425	305,000	718
Maryland (U.S.)	10,577	3,300,000	312
Massachusetts (U.S.)	8,257	5,301,000	642
Mauritania	419,230	800,000	1.9
Mauritius (incl. Deps.) (U.K.)	808	735,000	910
Mexico	761,602	39,000,000	51
Michigan (U.S.)	58,216	8,133,000	140
Midway Is. (U.S.)	2	2,500	1,250
Minnesota (U.S.)	84,068	3,557,000	42
Mississippi (U.S.)	47,716	2,261,000	47
Missouri (U.S.)	69,686	4,402,000	63
Monaco	0.8	22,000	27,500
Mongolia	592,700	1,050,000	1.8
Montana (U.S.)	147,138	711,000	4.8
Montserrat (U.K.)	32	13,000	406
Morocco	171,305	12,700,000	74
Mozambique (Port.)	297,846	6,900,000	23
Muscat & Oman	82,000	575,000	7.0
Nauru (Austl.)	8	5,000	625
Nebraska (U.S.)	77,227	1,483,000	19
Nepal	54,362	9,800,000	180
Netherlands	12,978	12,050,000	928
Netherlands and Poss.	68,492	12,620,000	184
Neth. Antilles (Neth.)	371	204,000	550
Nevada (U.S.)	110,540	388,000	3.5
New Brunswick (Can.)	28,354	618,000	22
New Caledonia (incl. Deps.) (Fr.)	6,531	82,000	13
Newfoundland (Can.)	156,185	489,000	3.1
New Guinea Ter. (Austl.)	94,430	1,535,000	16
New Hampshire (U.S.)	9,304	643,000	69
New Hebrides (Fr.-U.K.)	5,700	65,000	11
New Jersey (U.S.)	7,836	6,430,000	821
New Mexico (U.S.)	121,666	1,029,000	8.5
New York (U.S.)	49,576	17,676,000	357
New Zealand (Br. Comm.)	103,736	2,575,000	25
Nicaragua	48,600	1,650,000	34
Niger	458,995	3,250,000	7.1
Nigeria (Br. Comm.)	356,669	37,600,000	105
Niue (N.Z.)	100	5,000	50
Norfolk I. (Austl.)	13	900	69
North America	9,420,000	283,900,000	30
North Carolina (U.S.)	52,712	4,771,000	91
North Dakota (U.S.)	70,665	644,000	9.1
Northern Ireland (U.K.)	5,459	1,450,000	266
Northern Rhodesia (U.K.)	288,130	3,550,000	12
Northwest Ters. (Can.)	1,304,903	24,000	0.02
Norway	125,064	3,685,000	29
Nova Scotia (Can.)	21,425	766,000	36
Nyasaland (U.K.)	45,747	3,200,000	70
Oceania	3,295,000	17,000,000	5.2
Ohio (U.S.)	41,222	10,369,000	252
Oklahoma (U.S.)	69,919	2,477,000	35
Ontario (Can.)	412,582	6,525,000	16
Oregon (U.S.)	96,981	1,887,000	19
Pacific Is. Tr. Ter. (U.S.)	672	85,000	126
Pakistan (incl. part of Kashmir) (Br. Comm.)	399,373	100,600,000	252
Panama	29,209	1,185,000	41
Papua (excl. N. Gui. Ter.) (Austl.)	90,600	560,000	6.2
Paraguay	157,047	1,875,000	12
Pennsylvania (U.S.)	45,333	11,504,000	254
Peru	496,223	11,900,000	24
Philippines	115,707	31,200,000	270
Pitcairn (excl. Deps.) (U.K.)	2	130	65
Poland	120,348	30,850,000	256
Portugal	35,340	9,025,000	255
Portugal and Possessions	837,733	22,523,000	27
Portuguese Guinea (Port.)	13,948	555,000	40
Portuguese Timor (Port.)	7,332	535,000	73
Prince Edward I. (Can.)	2,184	107,000	49
Puerto Rico (U.S.)	3,435	2,564,000	746
Qatar	8,500	65,000	7.6
Quebec (Can.)	594,860	5,525,000	9.3
Reunion (Fr.)	969	360,000	372
Rhode Island (U.S.)	1,214	878,000	723
Rio Muni (Sp.)	10,045	192,000	19
Romania	91,698	18,875,000	206
Rwanda (Ruanda)	10,169	2,875,000	283
St. Helena (incl. Deps.) (U.K.)	160	5,350	33
St. Kitts-Nevis-Anguilla (U.K.)	153	62,000	405
St. Lucia (U.K.)	238	92,000	387
St. Pierre & Miquelon (Fr.)	93	5,000	54
St. Vincent (U.K.)	150	84,000	560
San Marino	23	17,000	739
Sao Tome & Principe (Port.)	372	65,000	175
Saskatchewan (Can.)	251,700	938,000	3.7
Saudia Arabia	617,800	7,000,000	11
Scotland (U.K.)	30,411	5,250,000	173
Senegal	76,124	3,300,000	43
Seychelles (U.K.)	156	45,000	288
Sierra Leone (Br. Comm.)	27,925	2,600,000	93
Sikkim	2,744	170,000	62
Solomon Is. (Austl.)	4,320	60,000	14
Solomon Is., British (U.K.)	11,500	135,000	12
Somali Republic	246,202	2,000,000	8.1
South Africa	472,926	17,300,000	36
South America	6,870,000	157,800,000	23
South Carolina (U.S.)	31,055	2,458,000	79
South Dakota (U.S.)	77,047	709,000	9.2
Southern Rhodesia (U.K.)	150,333	4,080,000	27
S. W. Africa (S. Afr.)	317,887	565,000	1.8
Soviet Union	8,599,300	227,000,000	26
Spain	194,345	31,200,000	161
Spain and Possessions	308,540	31,695,000	103
Spanish Sahara (Sp.)	102,703	27,000	0.3
Sudan	967,500	13,000,000	13
Surinam (Neth.)	55,143	366,000	6.6
Svalbard (Nor.)	24,101	4,000 (winter only)	...
Swaziland (U.K.)	6,705	290,000	43
Sweden	173,666	7,620,000	44
Switzerland	15,941	5,825,000	365
Syria	71,498	5,000,000	70
Taiwan (Formosa) (Nationalist China)	13,884	11,900,000	857
Tanganyika (Br. Comm.)	361,800	9,800,000	27
Tennessee (U.S.)	42,244	3,668,000	87
Texas (U.S.)	267,339	10,313,000	39
Thailand	198,500	29,200,000	147
Tibet (China)	471,660	1,300,000	2.8
Togo	21,850	1,580,000	72
Tokelau (Union) Is. (N.Z.)	4	2,000	500
Tonga (U.K.)	270	70,000	260
Trinidad & Tobago (Br. Comm.)	1,980	925,000	467
Trucial Coast	32,300	115,000	3.6
Tunisia	48,332	4,400,000	91
Turkey	301,381	30,300,000	101
Turks & Caicos Is. (U.K.)	166	6,000	36
Uganda (Br. Comm.)	92,525	7,250,000	78
United Arab Republic (Egypt)	386,000	28,300,000	73
United Kingdom	94,214	54,200,000	575
United Kingdom and Poss.	1,118,573	75,427,000	67
United States	3,675,633	190,700,000	52
United States and Poss.	3,680,757	193,525,000	53
Upper Volta	105,869	4,600,000	43
Uruguay	72,172	2,450,000	34
Utah (U.S.)	84,916	985,000	12
Vatican City	0.2	1,000	5,000
Venezuela	352,143	8,250,000	23
Vermont (U.S.)	9,609	393,000	41
Vietnam (Entire)	125,881	33,000,000	262
Vietnam, North	59,933	17,500,000	292
Vietnam, South	65,948	15,500,000	235
Virgin Is. (U.S.-U.K.)	192	45,000	234
Virginia (U.S.)	40,815	4,237,000	104
Wales (incl. Monmouthshire) (U.K.)	8,017	2,655,000	331
Washington (U.S.)	68,192	3,030,000	44
Western Samoa	1,130	120,000	106
West Irian (Indon. Admin.)	160,600	775,000	4.8
West Virginia (U.S.)	24,181	1,748,000	72
Wisconsin (U.S.)	56,154	4,136,000	74
World	57,280,000	3,193,000,000	56
Wyoming (U.S.)	97,914	351,000	3.6
Yemen	75,300	5,000,000	66
Yugoslavia	98,766	19,200,000	194
Yukon (Can.)	207,076	16,000	0.08
Zanzibar (Br. Comm.)	1,020	327,000	321

GLOSSARY OF FOREIGN GEOGRAPHICAL TERMS

Annam ... Annamese
Arab ... Arabic
Bantu ... Bantu
Bur ... Burmese
Camb ... Cambodian
Celt ... Celtic
Chn ... Chinese
Czech ... Czech
Dan ... Danish
Du ... Dutch
Fin ... Finnish
Fr ... French
Ger ... German
Gr ... Greek
Hung ... Hungarian
Ice ... Icelandic
India ... India
Indian ... American Indian
Indon ... Indonesian
It ... Italian
Jap ... Japanese
Kor ... Korean
Mal ... Malayan
Mong ... Mongolian
Nor ... Norwegian
Per ... Persian
Pol ... Polish
Port ... Portuguese
Rom ... Romanian
Rus ... Russian
Siam ... Siamese
So. Slav ... Southern Slavonic
Sp ... Spanish
Swe ... Swedish
Tib ... Tibetan
Tur ... Turkish
Yugo ... Yugoslav

å, *Nor., Swe* ... brook, river
aa, *Dan., Nor* ... brook
aas, *Dan., Nor* ... ridge
ab, *Per* ... water, river
abad, *India, Per* ... town, city
ada, *Tur* ... island
adrar, *Arab* ... mountain
air, *Indon* ... stream
akrotírion, *Gr* ... cape
älf, *Swe* ... river
alp, *Ger* ... mountain
altipiano, *It* ... plateau
alto, *Sp* ... height
archipel, *Fr* ... archipelago
archipiélago, *Sp* ... archipelago
arquipélago, *Port* ... archipelago
arroyo, *Sp* ... brook, stream
ås, *Nor., Swe* ... ridge
austral, *Sp* ... southern
baai, *Du* ... bay
bab, *Arab* ... gate, port
bach, *Ger* ... brook, stream
backe, *Swe* ... hill
bad, *Ger* ... bath, spa
bahía, *Sp* ... bay, gulf
bahr, *Arab* ... sea, lake
baia, *It* ... bay, gulf
baía, *Port* ... bay
baie, *Fr* ... bay, gulf
bajo, *Sp* ... depression
bak, *Indon* ... stream
bakke, *Dan., Nor* ... hill
balkan, *Tur* ... mountain range
bana, *Jap* ... point, cape
banco, *Sp* ... bank
bandar, *Mal., Per.* ... town, port, harbor
bang, *Siam* ... village
bassin, *Fr* ... basin
batang, *Indon., Mal* ... river
ben, *Celt* ... mountain, summit
bender, *Arab* ... harbor, port
bereg, *Rus* ... coast, shore
berg, *Du., Ger., Nor., Swe.* ... mountain, hill
bir, *Arab* ... well
birket, *Arab* ... pond, pool
bit, *Arab* ... house
bjaerg, *Dan., Nor* ... mountain
bocche, *It* ... mouth
bogaz, *Tur* ... strait
bois, *Fr* ... forest, wood
boloto, *Rus* ... marsh
bolsón, *Sp* flat-floored desert valley
boreal, *Sp* ... northern
borg, *Dan., Nor., Swe* castle, town
borgo, *It* ... town, suburb
bosch, *Du* ... forest, wood
bouche, *Fr* ... river mouth
bourg, *Fr* ... town, borough
bro, *Dan., Nor., Swe* ... bridge
brücke, *Ger* ... bridge
bucht, *Ger* ... bay, bight
bugt, *Dan., Nor., Swe* ... bay, gulf
bulu, *Indon* ... mountain
burg, *Du., Ger* ... castle, town
buri, *Siam* ... town
burun, burnu, *Tur* ... cape
by, *Dan., Nor., Swe* ... village
caatinga, *Port. (Brazil)* ... open brushland
cabezo, *Sp* ... summit
cabo, *Port., Sp* ... cape
campo, *It., Port., Sp* ... field
campos, *Port. (Brazil)* ... plains
cañon, *Sp* ... canyon
cap, *Fr* ... cape
capo, *It* ... cape
casa, *It., Port., Sp* ... house
castello, *It., Port* ... castle, fort
castillo, *Sp* ... castle
càte, *Fr* ... hill
çay, *Tur* ... stream, river
cayo, *Sp* ... rock, shoal, islet
cerro, *Sp* ... hill
champ, *Fr* ... field
chang, *Chn* ... village, middle
château, *Fr* ... castle
chen, *Chn* ... market town
chiang, *Chn* ... river
chott, *Arab* ... salt lake
chou, *Chn* capital of district; island
chu, *Tib* ... water, stream
cidade, *Port* ... town, city
cima, *Sp* ... summit, peak
città, *It* ... town, city
ciudad, *Sp* ... town, city
cochilha, *Port* ... ridge
col, *Fr* ... pass
colina, *Sp* ... hill
cordillera, *Sp* ... mountain chain
costa, *It., Port., Sp* ... coast
côte, *Fr* ... coast
cuchilla, *Sp* ... mountain ridge
dag, *Tur* ... mountain
dake, *Jap* ... peak, summit
dal, *Dan., Du., Nor., Swe* ... valley
dan, *Kor* ... point, cape
danau, *Indon* ... lake
dar, *Arab* ... house, abode, country
darya, *Per* ... river, sea
dasht, *Per* ... plain, desert
deniz, *Tur* ... sea
désert, *Fr* ... desert
deserto, *It* ... desert
desierto, *Sp* ... desert
détroit, *Fr* ... strait
dijk, *Du* ... dam, dike
djebel, *Arab* ... mountain
do, *Kor* ... island
dorf, *Ger* ... village
dorp, *Du* ... village
duin, *Du* ... dune
dzong, *Tib.* ... fort, administrative capital
eau, *Fr* ... water
ecuador, *Sp* ... equator
eiland, *Du* ... island
elv, *Dan., Nor* ... river, stream
embalse, *Sp* ... reservoir
erg, *Arab* ... dune, sandy desert
est, *Fr., It* ... east
estado, *Sp* ... state
este, *Port., Sp* ... east
estrecho, *Sp* ... strait
étang, *Fr* ... pond, lake
état, *Fr* ... state
eyjar, *Ice* ... islands
feld, *Ger* ... field, plain
festung, *Ger* ... fortress
fiume, *It* ... river
fjäll, *Swe* ... mountain
fjärd, *Swe* ... bay, inlet
fjeld, *Nor* ... mountain, hill
fjord, *Dan., Nor* ... fiord, inlet
fjördur, *Ice* ... fiord, inlet
fleuve, *Fr* ... river
flod, *Dan., Swe* ... river
flói, *Ice* ... bay, marshland
fluss, *Ger* ... river
foce, *It* ... river mouth
fontein, *Du* ... a spring
forêt, *Fr* ... forest
fors, *Swe* ... waterfall
forst, *Ger* ... forest
fos, *Dan., Nor* ... waterfall
fu, *Chn* ... town, residence
fuente, *Sp* ... spring, fountain
fuerte, *Sp* ... fort
furt, *Ger* ... ford
gang, *Kor* ... stream, river
gangri, *Tib* ... mountain
gat, *Dan., Nor* ... channel
gâve, *Fr* ... stream
gawa, *Jap* ... river
gebergte, *Du* ... mountain range
gebiet, *Ger* ... district, territory
gebirge, *Ger* ... mountains
ghat, *India* ... pass, mountain range
gobi, *Mong* ... desert
goenoeng, *Mal* ... mountain
gol, *Mong* ... river
göl, gölü, *Tur* ... lake
golf, *Du., Ger* ... gulf, bay
golfe, *Fr* ... gulf, bay
golfo, *It., Port., Sp* ... gulf, bay
gomba, gompa, *Tib* ... monastery
gora, *Rus., So. Slav* ... mountain
góra, *Pol* ... mountain
gorod, *Rus* ... town
grad, *Rus., So. Slav* ... town
guba, *Rus* ... bay, gulf
gundung, *Indon* ... mountain
guntō, *Jap* ... archipelago
haf, *Swe* ... sea, ocean
hafen, *Ger* ... port, harbor
haff, *Ger* ... gulf, inland sea
hai, *Chn* ... sea, lake
hama, *Jap* ... beach, shore
hamada, *Arab* ... rocky plateau
hamn, *Swe* ... harbor
hamun, *Per* ... swampy lake, plain
hantō, *Jap* ... peninsula
hassi, *Arab* ... well, spring
haus, *Ger* ... house
haut, *Fr* ... summit, top
hav, *Dan., Nor* ... sea, ocean
havn, *Dan., Nor* ... harbor, port
havre, *Fr* ... harbor, port
háza, *Hung* ... house, dwelling of
heim, *Ger* ... hamlet, home
hem, *Swe* ... hamlet, home
higashi, *Jap* ... east
hisar, *Tur* ... fortress
hissar, *Arab* ... fort
ho, *Chn* ... river
hoek, *Du* ... cape
hof, *Ger* ... court, farm house
höfn, *Ice* ... harbor
hoku, *Jap* ... north
holm, *Dan., Nor., Swe* ... island
hora, *Czech* ... mountain
horn, *Ger* ... peak
hoved, *Dan., Nor* ... cape
hsien, *Chn* district, district capital
hu, *Chn* ... lake
hügel, *Ger* ... hill
huk, *Dan., Swe* ... point
hus, *Dan., Nor., Swe* ... house
île, *Fr* ... island
ilha, *Port* ... island
indsö, *Dan., Nor* ... lake
insel, *Ger* ... island
insjö, *Swe* ... lake
irmak, irmagi, *Tur* ... river
isla, *Sp* ... island
isola, *It* ... island
istmo, *It., Sp* ... isthmus
istrova, *Rus* ... islands
järvi, jaur, *Fin* ... lake
jebel, *Arab* ... mountain
jima, *Jap* ... island
jökel, *Nor* ... glacier
joki, *Fin* ... river
jökull, *Ice* ... ice-covered mountain
kaap, *Du* ... cape
kai, *Jap* ... bay, gulf, sea
kaikyō, *Jap* ... channel, strait
kalat, *Per* ... castle, fortress
kale, *Tur* ... fort
kali, *Mal* ... river
kand, *Per* ... village
kang, *Chn* mountain ridge; village
kap, *Dan., Ger* ... cape
kapp, *Nor., Swe* ... cape
kasr, *Arab* ... fort, castle
kawa, *Jap* ... river
kefr, *Arab* ... village
kei, *Jap* ... creek, river
ken, *Jap* ... prefecture
khor, *Arab* ... bay, inlet
khrebet, *Rus* ... mountain range
kiang, *Chn* ... large river
king, *Chn* ... capital city, town
kita, *Jap* ... north
ko, *Jap* ... lake
köbstad, *Dan* ... market-town
kol, *Mong* ... lake
kólpos, *Gr* ... gulf
kong, *Chn* ... river
kopf, *Ger* ... head, summit, peak
köpstad, *Swe* ... market-town
korfezi, *Tur* ... gulf
kosa, *Rus* ... cape
kou, *Chn* ... river mouth
köy, *Tur* ... village
kraal, *Du. (Africa)* ... native village
ksar, *Arab* ... fortified village
kuala, *Mal* ... river mouth
kuh, *Per* ... mountain
kum, *Tur* ... sand
kuppe, *Ger* ... summit
küste, *Ger* ... coast
kyo, *Jap* ... town, capital
la, *Tib* ... mountain pass
labuan, *Mal* ... anchorage, port
lac, *Fr* ... lake
lago, *It., Port., Sp* ... lake
lagoa, *Port* ... lake, marsh
laguna, *It., Port., Sp* ... lagoon, lake
lahti, *Fin* ... bay, gulf
län, *Swe* ... county
landsby, *Dan., Nor* ... village
liehtao, *Chn* ... archipelago
liman, *Tur* ... bay, port
ling, *Chn* ... pass, ridge, mountain
llanos, *Sp* ... plains
loch, *Celt. (Scotland)* ... lake, bay
loma, *Sp* ... long, low hill
lough, *Celt. (Ireland)* ... lake, bay
machi, *Jap* ... town
man, *Kor* ... bay
mar, *Port., Sp* ... sea
mare, *It., Rom* ... sea
marisma, *Sp* ... marsh, swamp
mark, *Ger* ... boundary, limit
massif, *Fr* ... block of mountains
mato, *Port* ... forest, thicket
me, *Siam* ... river
meer, *Du., Ger* ... lake, sea
mer, *Fr* ... sea
mesa, *Sp* ... flat-topped mountain
meseta, *Sp* ... plateau
mina, *Port., Sp* ... mine
minami, *Jap* ... south
minato, *Jap* ... harbor, haven
misaki, *Jap* ... cape, headland
mont, *Fr* ... mount, mountain
montagna, *It* ... mountain
montagne, *Fr* ... mountain
montaña, *Sp* ... mountain
monte, *It., Port., Sp.* ... mount, mountain
more, *Rus., So. Slav* ... sea
morro, *Port., Sp* ... hill, bluff
mühle, *Ger* ... mill
mund, *Ger* ... mouth, opening
mündung, *Ger* ... river mouth
mura, *Jap* ... township
myit, *Bur* ... river
mys, *Rus* ... cape
nada, *Jap* ... sea
nadi, *India* ... river, creek
naes, *Dan., Nor* ... cape
nafud, *Arab* ... desert of sand dunes
nagar, *India* ... town, city
nahr, *Arab* ... river
nam, *Siam* ... river, water
nan, *Chn., Jap* ... south
näs, *Nor., Swe* ... cape
nez, *Fr* ... point, cape
nishi, nisi, *Jap* ... west
njarga, *Fin* ... peninsula
nong, *Siam* ... marsh
noord, *Du* ... north
nor, *Mong* ... lake
nord, *Dan., Fr., Ger., It., Nor., Swe* ... north
norte, *Port., Sp* ... north
nos, *Rus* ... cape
nyasa, *Bantu* ... lake
ö, *Dan., Nor., Swe* ... island
occidental, *Sp* ... western
ocna, *Rom* ... salt mine
odde, *Dan., Nor* ... point, cape
oedjoeng, *Mal* ... point, cape
oeste, *Port., Sp* ... west
oka, *Jap* ... hill
oost, *Du* ... east
oriental, *Sp* ... eastern
óros, *Gr* ... mountain
ost, *Ger., Swe* ... east
öster, *Dan., Nor., Swe* ... eastern
ostrov, *Rus* ... island
oued, *Arab* ... river, stream
ouest, *Fr* ... west
ozero, *Rus* ... lake
pää, *Fin* ... mountain
padang, *Mal* ... plain, field
pampas, *Sp. (Argentina)* ... grassy plains
pará, *Indian (Brazil)* ... river
pas, *Fr* ... channel, passage
paso, *Sp* ... passage
passo, *It., Port* ... passage, strait
patam, *India* ... city, town
pei, *Chn* ... north
pélagos, *Gr* ... open sea
pegunungan, *Indon* ... mountains
peña, *Sp* ... rock
peresheyek, *Rus* ... isthmus
pertuis, *Fr* ... strait
peski, *Rus* ... desert
pic, *Fr* ... mountain peak
pico, *Port., Sp* ... mountain peak
piedra, *Sp* ... stone, rock
ping, *Chn* ... plain, flat
planalto, *Port* ... plateau
planina, *Yugo* ... mountains
playa, *Sp* ... shore, beach
pnom, *Camb* ... mountain
poelau, *Mal* ... island
pointe, *Fr* ... point
polder, *Du., Ger* ... reclaimed marsh
polje, *So. Slav* ... field
poluostrov, *Rus* ... peninsula
pont, *Fr* ... bridge
ponta, *Port* ... point, headland
ponte, *It., Port* ... bridge
pore, *India* ... city, town
porthmós, *Gr* ... strait
porto, *It., Port* ... port, harbor
potamós, *Gr* ... river
p'ov, *Rus* ... peninsula
prado, *Sp* ... field, meadow
presqu'île, *Fr* ... peninsula
proliv, *Rus* ... strait
pu, *Chn* ... commercial village
pueblo, *Sp* ... town, village
puerto, *Sp* ... port, harbor
pulau, *Mal* ... island
punkt, *Ger* ... point
punt, *Du* ... point
punta, *It., Sp* ... point
pur, *India* ... city, town
puy, *Fr* ... peak
qal'a, qal'at, *Arab* ... fort, village
qasr, *Arab* ... fort, castle
rann, *India* ... wasteland
ras, *Arab* ... cape, head
reka, *Rus., So. Slav* ... river
represa, *Port* ... reservoir
rettō, *Jap* ... island chain
ría, *Sp* ... estuary
ribeira, *Port* ... stream
riberão, *Port* ... river
rio, *It., Port* ... stream, river
río, *Sp* ... river
rivière, *Fr* ... river
roca, *Sp* ... rock
rt, *Yugo* ... cape
rud, *Per* ... river
saari, *Fin* ... island
sable, *Fr* ... sand
sahara, *Arab* ... desert, plain
saki, *Jap* ... cape
sal, *Sp* ... salt
salar, *Sp* ... salt flat, salt lake
salto, *Sp* ... waterfall
san, *Jap., Kor* ... mountain, hill
sat, satul, *Rom* ... village
schloss, *Ger* ... castle
sebkha, *Arab* ... salt marsh
see, *Ger* ... lake, sea
şehir, *Tur* ... town, city
selat, *Indon* ... stream
selvas, *Port. (Brazil)* ... tropical rain forests
seno, *Sp* ... bay
serra, *Port* ... mountain chain
serranía, *Sp* ... mountain ridge
seto, *Jap* ... strait
severnaya, *Rus* ... northern
shahr, *Per* ... town, city
shan, *Chn* ... mountain, hill, island
shatt, *Arab* ... river
shi, *Jap* ... city
shima, *Jap* ... island
shōtō, *Jap* ... archipelago
si, *Chn* ... west, western
sierra, *Sp* ... mountain range
sjö, *Nor., Swe* ... lake, sea
sö, *Dan., Nor* ... lake, sea
söder, södra, *Swe* ... south
soengai, soengei, *Mal* ... river
song, *Annam* ... river
sopka, *Rus* ... peak, volcano
source, *Fr* ... a spring
spitze, *Ger* ... summit, point
staat, *Ger* ... state
stad, *Dan., Du., Nor., Swe.* ... city, town
stadt, *Ger* ... city, town
stato, *It* ... state
step, *Rus* ... treeless plain, steppe
straat, *Du* ... strait
strand, *Dan., Du., Ger., Nor., Swe* ... shore, beach
stretto, *It* ... strait
strom, *Ger* ... river, stream
ström, *Dan., Nor., Swe* stream, river
stroom, *Du* ... stream, river
su, suyu, *Tur* ... water, river
sud, *Fr., Sp* ... south
süd, *Ger* ... south
suidō, *Jap* ... channel
sul, *Port* ... south
sund, *Dan., Nor., Swe* ... sound
sungai, sungei, *Indon., Mal* ... river
sur, *Sp* ... south
syd, *Dan., Nor., Swe* ... south
tafelland, *Ger* ... plateau
take, *Jap* ... peak, summit
tal, *Ger* ... valley
tandjoeng, tanjong, *Mal* ... cape
tao, *Chn* ... island
târg, târgul, *Rom* ... market, town
tell, *Arab* ... hill
teluk, *Indon* ... bay, gulf
terra, *It* ... land
terre, *Fr* ... earth, land
thal, *Ger* ... valley
tierra, *Sp* ... earth, land
tō, *Jap* ... east; island
tonle, *Camb* ... river, lake
top, *Du* ... peak
torp, *Swe* ... hamlet, cottage
tsangpo, *Tib* ... river
tsi, *Chn* ... village, borough
tso, *Tib* ... lake
tsu, *Jap* ... harbor, port
tundra, *Rus* ... treeless arctic plains
tung, *Chn* ... east
tuz, *Tur* ... salt
udde, *Swe* ... cape
ufer, *Ger* ... shore, river bank
umi, *Jap* ... sea, gulf
ura, *Jap* ... bay, coast, creek
ust'ye, *Rus* ... river mouth
valle, *It., Port., Sp* ... valley
vallée, *Fr* ... valley
valli, *It* ... lake
vár, *Hung* ... fortress
város, *Hung* ... town
varoš, *So. Slav* ... town
veld, *Du* ... open plain, field
verkh, *Rus* ... top, summit
ves, *Czech* ... village
vest, *Dan., Nor., Swe* ... west
vik, *Swe* ... cove, bay
vila, *Port* ... town
villa, *Sp* ... town
villar, *Sp* ... village, hamlet
ville, *Fr* ... town, city
vostok, *Rus* ... east
wad, wadi, *Arab.* ... intermittent stream
wald, *Ger* ... forest, woodland
wan, *Chn., Jap* ... bay, gulf
weiler, *Ger* ... hamlet, village
westersch, *Du* ... western
wüste, *Ger* ... desert
yama, *Jap* ... mountain
yarimada, *Tur* ... peninsula
yug, *Rus* ... south
zaki, *Jap* ... cape
zaliv, *Rus* ... bay, gulf
zapad, *Rus* ... west
zee, *Du* ... sea
zemlya, *Rus* ... land
zuid, *Du* ... south

ABBREVIATIONS OF
GEOGRAPHICAL NAMES AND TERMS

Afg	Afghanistan
Afr	Africa
Ala	Alabama
Alb	Albania
Alg	Algeria
And	Andorra
Ang	Angola
Ant	Antarctica
Arc. O	Arctic Ocean
Arch	Archipelago
Arg	Argentina
Ariz	Arizona
Ark	Arkansas
A. S. S. R.	Autonomous Soviet Socialist Republic
Atl. O	Atlantic Ocean
Aus	Austria
Austl	Australia
Aut	Autonomous
B	Bay, Bahia
Ba. Is	Bahama Is.
Barb	Barbados
Bas	Basutoland
Bdy	Boundary
Bech	Bechuanaland
Bel	Belgium
Bg	Berg
Bhu	Bhutan
Bk	Bank
Bol	Bolivia
Br	British
Braz	Brazil
Br. Comm.	British Commonwealth of Nations
Br. Gu	British Guiana
Br. Hond	British Honduras
Brit. Prot.	British Protectorate
Bru	Brunei
Bul	Bulgaria
Bur	Burma
C	Cerro, Cape
Calif	California
Cam	Cameroun
Camb	Cambodia
Can	Canal, Canada
Can. Is	Canary Is.
Cen. Afr. Rep.	Central African Republic
Cen. Am	Central America
C. H	Court House
Chan	Channel
Co	County
Col	Colombia
Colo	Colorado
Con. B.	Congo; capital Brazzaville
Con. L.	Congo, The; capital; Léopoldville
Conn	Connecticut
Cor	Corsica
C. R	Costa Rica
Cr	Creek
C. V. Is	Cape Verde Is.
C. Z	Canal Zone
Czech	Czechoslovakia
D. C	District of Columbia
Del	Delaware
Den	Denmark
Dept	Department
Des	Desert
D. F	Distrito Federal
Dist	District
Div	Division
Dom. Rep.	Dominican Republic
E	East
Ec	Ecuador
Elec	Electric
Eng	England
E. Pak	East Pakistan
Eth	Ethiopia
Eur	Europe
Faer	Faeroe Is.
Falk. Is	Falkland Is.
Fd	Fjord
Fin	Finland
Fk	Fork
Fla	Florida
For	Forest
Fr	France
Fr. Gu	French Guiana
Fr. Som	French Somaliland
Ft	Fort
G	Gulf
Ga	Georgia
Gam	Gambia
Ger	Germany
Gib	Gibraltar
Grc	Greece
Grnld	Greenland
Gt	Great
Gt. Brit	Great Britain
Guad	Guadeloupe

Guat	Guatemala
Gui	Guinea
Hai	Haiti
Har., Hbr	Harbor
Hd	Head
Hond	Honduras
Hts	Heights
Hung	Hungary
I	Island
Ice	Iceland
Ill	Illinois
In	Inset
Ind	Indiana
Ind. O	Indian Ocean
Indon	Indonesia
Ind. Res	Indian Reservation
Int., Intl	International
Ire	Ireland
Is	Islands
Isr	Israel
Isth	Isthmus
It	Italy
Jam	Jamaica
Jap	Japan
Jc	Junction
Kans	Kansas
Ken	Kenya
Km	Kilometer, Kilometers
Kor	Korea
Kur. Is	Kuril Is.
Kuw	Kuwait
Ky	Kentucky
L	Lake, Loch, Lough
La	Louisiana
Lat	Latitude
Leb	Lebanon
Le. Is	Leeward Is.
Lib	Liberia
Liech	Liechtenstein
Long	Longitude
Lux	Luxembourg
M	Mile, Miles
Mad. Is	Madeira Islands
Mala	Malaysia
Malag. Rep.	Malagasy Republic
Mand	Mandate
Mart	Martinique
Mass	Massachusetts
Max	Maximum
Max. surf. elev.	Maximum surface elevation
Md	Maryland
Medit	Mediterranean
Mex	Mexico
Mi	Mile, Miles
Mich	Michigan
Minn	Minnesota
Miss	Mississippi
Mo	Missouri
Mong	Mongolia
Mont	Montana
Mor	Morocco
Moz	Mozambique
Mt	Mount
Mtn	Mountain
Mts	Mountains
Mus. & Om	Muscat & Oman
N	North
N. A	North America
Natl	National
Natl. Mon.	National Monument
N. C	North Carolina
N. Cal	New Caledonia
N. D	North Dakota
Nebr	Nebraska
Nep	Nepal
Neth	Netherlands
Nev	Nevada
New Hebr	New Hebrides
N. Gui. Ter.	New Guinea Ter.
N. H	New Hampshire
Nic	Nicaragua
Nig	Nigeria
N. Ire	Northern Ireland
N. J	New Jersey
N. Mex	New Mexico
Nor	Norway
N. Rh	Northern Rhodesia
N. Y	New York
Nya	Nyasaland
N. Z	New Zealand
O	Ocean
Obs	Observatory
Okla	Oklahoma
Ore	Oregon
P	Pass
Pa	Pennsylvania
Pac. O	Pacific Ocean
Pan	Panama

Pap	Papua
Par	Paraguay
Pass	Passage
Pen	Peninsula
Phil	Philippines
Pk	Peak, Park
Plat	Plateau
Pln	Plain
Pol	Poland
Port	Portugal
Port. Gui	Portuguese Guinea
Port. Tim	Portuguese Timor
Poss	Possession
P. R	Puerto Rico
Prot	Protectorate
Prov	Province
Pt	Point
Pta	Punta
Pte	Pointe
R	River, Rio, Rivière
Ra	Range, Ranges
Reg	Region
Rep	Republic
Res	Reservation, Reservoir
Rf	Reef
R. I	Rhode Island
Rom	Romania
R. R	Railroad
R. S. F. S. R.	Russian Soviet Federated Socialist Republic
Rw	Rwanda
Ry	Railway
Rys	Railways
S	San, Santo, South
Sa	Serra, Sierra
S. A.	South America
Sal	Salvador
Sard	Sardinia
Sau. Ar	Saudi Arabia
S. C	South Carolina
Scot	Scotland
S. D	South Dakota
Sd	Sound
S. L	Sierra Leone
Sol. Is	Solomon Is.
Som	Somali Republic
Sov. Un	Soviet Union
Sp	Spain
Sp. Gui	Spanish Guinea
Spr., Sprs	Spring, Springs
Sp. Sah	Spanish Sahara
S. Rh	Southern Rhodesia
S. S. R	Soviet Socialist Republic
St	Saint
Sta	Santa
Ste	Sainte
Str	Strait
Strm	Stream
Sud	Sudan
Sur	Surinam
S. Afr	South Africa
S. W. Afr	South-West Africa
Swaz	Swaziland
Swe	Sweden
Switz	Switzerland
Swp	Swamp
Syr	Syria
Tan	Tanganyika
Tas	Tasmania
Tenn	Tennessee
Ter	Territory
Tex	Texas
Thai	Thailand
Trin	Trinidad and Tobago
Tr. Coast	Trucial Coast
Tun	Tunisia
Tur	Turkey
U. A. R.	United Arab Republic
Ug	Uganda
U. K.	United Kingdom of Gt. Brit. and N. Ire.
Ur	Uruguay
U. S., U. S. A.	United States of America
Va	Virginia
Val	Valley
Ven	Venezuela
Viet	Vietnam
Vir. Is	Virgin Is.
Vol	Volcano
Vt	Vermont
W	West
Wash	Washington
W. I.	West Indies
Wind. Is	Windward Islands
W. Irian	West Irian
Wis	Wisconsin
W. Pak	West Pakistan
W. Sam	Western Samoa
W. Va	West Virginia
Wyo	Wyoming
Yugo	Yugoslavia
Zan	Zanzibar

PRONUNCIATION OF
GEOGRAPHICAL NAMES

Key to the Sound Values of Letters and Symbols
Used in the Index to Indicate Pronunciation

ă—ăt, căt, băttle
å—åppeal, finål
ā—rāte, elāte
â—inanimâte, senâte
ä—cälm, ärm
à—àsk, bàth
á—márine, sofá (short neutral or inde-terminate sound)
â—fâre, prepâre
ch—church, choose
dh—as th in other, either
ē—bē, ēve
ĕ—crĕate, ĕvent
ĕ—bĕt, ĕnd
ẽ—recẽnt (short neutral or indeterminate sound)
ẽ—cratẽr, cindẽr
g—gō, gāme
gh—guttural g
ĭ—wĭll, bĭt
ĭ—short neutral or indeterminate sound
ī—rīde, bīte
κ—guttural k as ch in German ich
ng—sing
ŋ—baŋk, liŋger
N—indicates nasalized preceding vowel
ŏ—nŏd, ŏdd
ŏ—cŏmmit, cŏnnect
ō—ōld, bōld
ô—ôbey, hôtel
ô—ôrder, nôrth
oi—boil
ōō—fōōd, rōōt
ŏŏ—fŏŏt, wŏŏd
ou—thou, out
s—as in soft, so, sane
sh—dish, finish
th—thin, thick
ū—pūre, cūre
û—ûnite, ûsurp
û—ûrn, fûr
ŭ—stŭd, ŭp
ū—as in French tu or as "y" in study
ŭ—circŭs, sŭbmit
zh—as z in azure
'—indeterminate vowel sound

In many cases the spelling of foreign geographic names does not even remotely indicate the pronunciation to an American, i. e., Slupca in Poland is pronounced swōōp′tsà; Jujuy in Argentina is pronounced hōō-hwē′; Spezia in Italy is spät′sĕ-ä.

This condition is hardly surprising, however, when we consider that in our own language Worcester, Massachusetts, is pronounced wōōs′tẽr; Sioux City, Iowa, sōō sĭ′tĭ; Schuylkill Haven, Pennsylvania, skōōl′kĭl; Poughkeepsie, New York, pŏ-kĭp′sĕ.

The indication of pronunciation of geographic names presents several peculiar problems:

(1) Many foreign tongues use sounds that are not present in the English language and which an American cannot normally articulate. Thus, though the nearest English equivalent sound has been indicated, only approximate results are possible.

(2) There are several dialects in each foreign tongue which cause variation in the local pronunciation of names. This also occurs in identical names in the various divisions of a great language group, as the Slavic or the Latin.

(3) Within the United States there are marked differences in pronunciation, not only of local geographic names, but also of common words, indicating that the sound and tone values for letters as well as the placing of the emphasis vary considerably from one part of the country to another.

(4) A number of different letter and diacritical combinations could be used to indicate essentially the same or approximate pronunciations.

Some variation in pronunciation other than that indicated in this index may be encountered, but such a difference does not necessarily indicate that either is in error, and in many cases it is a matter of individual choice as to which is preferred. In fact, an exact indication of pronunciation of many foreign names using English letters and diacritical marks is extremely difficult and sometimes impossible.

A PRONOUNCING INDEX

of over 30,000 Geographical Names

This universal index includes in a single alphabetical list all important names that appear on the reference maps. Each place name is preceded by the page number of the map on which it appears. Place names are followed by the pronunciation of the name (see facing page for an explanation of the pronunciation system); the location; and the approximate geographic coordinates.

State locations are listed for all places in the United States. All other place name entries show only country locations. When a name is only shown on an inset map the name of the inset on which it appears is listed.

All minor political divisions are followed by a descriptive term (Dist., Reg., Prov., State, etc.) and by the country in which they are located.

The names of physical features and points of interest that are shown on the maps are listed in the index. Each entry is followed by a descriptive term (Bay, Hill, Mtn., Is., Plat., etc.) to indicate its nature.

The system of alphabetizing used in the index is standard. When more than one name with the same spelling is shown, including both political and physical names, the order of precedence is as follows: *first*, place names, *second*, political divisions, and *third*, physical features.

Local official names are used on the maps for nearly all cities and towns, with the exception of about fifty major world cities for which Anglicized conventional names have been preferred. For these exceptions the index gives a cross reference to the official local name.

Page	Name Pronunciation Region	Lat. °′	Long. °′
123	Aachen (ä'kĕn)...Ger. (Ruhr In.)	50·46 N	6·07 E
118	Aakirkeby (ô-kĭr'kĕ-bü).....Den.	55·04 N	15·00 E
120	Aalen (ä'lĕn)...............Ger.	48·49 N	10·08 E
111	Aalsmeer..Neth. (Amsterdam In.)	52·16 N	4·44 E
111	Aalst..........Bel. (Brussels In.)	50·58 N	4·00 E
120	Aarau (är'ou).............Switz.	47·22 N	8·03 E
111	Aarschot......Bel. (Brussels In.)	50·59 N	4·51 E
164	Aba.......................Nig.	5·13 N	7·14 E
144	Ābādān (ä-bŭ-dän')..........Iran	30·15 N	48·30 E
99	Abaetetuba (ä'bȧĕ-tĕ-tōō'bȧ) Braz.	1·44 S	48·45 W
69	Abajo Pk. (ä-bȧ'-hŏ)........Utah	38·50 N	109·35 W
134	Abakan (ŭ-bȧ-kän').....Sov. Un.	53·43 N	91·28 E
134	Abakan (R.)...........Sov. Un.	53·00 N	91·06 E
98	Abancay (ä-bän-kä'ê).......Peru	13·44 S	72·46 W
152	Abashiri (ä-bä-shē'rê)........Jap.	44·00 N	144·13 E
90	Abasolo (ä-bä-sō'lô)........Mex.	24·05 N	98·24 W
76	Abasolo...................Mex.	27·13 N	101·25 W
165	Abaya L. (ȧ-bä'yȧ)..........Eth.	6·24 N	38·22 E
165	Abbai R. (ȧ-bä'ê)...........Eth.	9·45 N	37·23 E
78	Abbeville (ăb'ê-vĭl)..........Ala.	31·35 N	85·15 W
122	Abbeville (ȧb-vēl')...........Fr.	50·08 N	1·49 E
78	Abbeville (ăb'ê-vĭl)..........Ga.	31·53 N	83·23 W
77	Abbeville...................La.	29·59 N	92·07 W
79	Abbeville..................S. C.	34·09 N	82·25 W
126	Abbiategrasso (äb-byä'tȧ-gräs'sō) It.	45·23 N	8·52 E
110	Abbots Bromley (ăb'ŭts brŭm'lê).Eng.	52·49 N	1·52 W
65	Abbotsford (ăb'ŭts-fērd) Can. (Vancouver In.)	49·03 N	122·17 W
168	Abd Al Kuri I. (ăbd-ĕl-kōō'rê) Som. (Horn of Afr. In.)	12·21 N	51·00 E
132	Abdulino (äb-dōō-lē'nō)..Sov. Un.	53·40 N	53·45 E
165	Abéché (ȧ-bĕ-shā')..........Chad	13·48 N	20·39 E
118	Åbenrå (ô'bĕn-rô)..........Den.	55·03 N	9·20 E
164	Abeokuta (ä-bȧ-ô-kōō'tȧ)....Nig.	7·14 N	3·19 E
166	Abercorn (ăb'ēr-kôrn).....N. Rh.	8·45 S	31·23 E
116	Aberdare (ăb-ēr-dâr').......Wales	51·45 N	3·35 W
116	Aberdeen (ăb-ēr-dēn').......Scot.	57·10 N	2·05 W
78	Aberdeen.................Miss.	33·49 N	88·33 W
70	Aberdeen.................S. D.	45·28 N	98·29 W
66	Aberdeen.................Wash.	47·00 N	123·48 W
110	Aberford (ăb'ēr-fērd)........Eng.	53·49 N	1·21 W
116	Abergavenny (ăb'ēr-gȧ-vĕn'ĭ) Wales	51·45 N	3·05 W
66	Abert L. (ā'bērt)............Ore.	42·39 N	120·24 W
116	Aberystwyth (ă-bēr-ĭst'wĭth) Wales	52·25 N	4·04 W
136	Abestovskiy (ä-bĕs'tôv-skĭ) Sov. Un. (Urals In.)	57·46 N	61·23 E
144	Abhā..................Sau. Ar.	17·47 N	42·29 E
164	Abidjan (ä-bêd-zhäɴ').Ivory Coast	5·26 N	4·06 W
153	Abiko (ä-bē-kō).Jap. (Tōkyō In.)	35·53 N	140·01 E
73	Abilene (ăb'ĭ-lēn)..........Kans.	38·54 N	97·12 W
76	Abilene....................Tex.	32·25 N	99·45 W
110	Abingdon......Eng. (London In.)	51·38 N	1·17 W
71	Abingdon (ăb'ĭng-dŭn)........Ill.	40·48 N	90·21 W
79	Abingdon..................Va.	36·42 N	81·57 W
83	Abington (ăb'ĭng-tŭn) Mass. (Boston In.)	42·07 N	70·57 W
69	Abiquiu Res.............N. Mex.	36·26 N	106·42 W
87	Abitibi (L.) (ăb-ĭ-tĭb'ĭ)......Can.	48·27 N	80·20 W
87	Abitibi (R.)................Can.	49·30 N	81·10 W
133	Abkhaz A.S.S.R.........Sov. Un.	43·10 N	40·45 E
123	Ablis (ȧ-blē')......Fr. (Paris In.)	48·31 N	1·50 E
168	Abnūb (ȧb-nōōb') U. A. R. (Nile In.)	27·18 N	31·11 E
	Åbo, see Turku		
142	Abohar..................India	30·12 N	74·13 E
164	Abomey (ȧb-ô-mā').....Dahomey	7·13 N	2·04 E
121	Abony (ŏ'bô-ny')..........Hung.	47·12 N	20·00 E
144	Abou Kemal (ä'bōō kĕ'mȧl) U. A. R.	34·27 N	40·46 E
155	Abra (R.) (ä'brä) Phil. (Manila In.)	17·16 N	120·38 E
101	Abraão (äbrȧ-ouɴ') Braz. (Rio de Janeiro In.)	23·10 S	44·10 W
95	Abraham's B.............Ba. Is.	22·20 N	73·50 W
110	Abram (ā'brăm)............Eng.	53·31 N	2·36 W
124	Abrantes (ȧ-brän'tĕs).......Port.	39·28 N	8·13 W
165	Abri.......................Sud.	20·36 N	29·57 E
99	Abrolhos, Arquipélago dos (Arch.) (ä-rōōê-pĕ'lä-gô-dôs-ä-brô'l-yōs) Braz.	17·58 S	38·40 W
119	Abruka (I.) (ȧ-brōō'kȧ)..Sov. Un.	58·09 N	22·30 E
126	Abruzzi and Molise (Reg.) (ä-brōōt'sē, mô'lê-zā)........It.	42·10 N	13·55 E
67	Absaroka Ra. (Mts.) (ȧb-sȧ-rō'kȧ).Wyo.	44·50 N	109·47 W
142	Abu (ȧ'bōō)..............India	24·38 N	72·45 E
144	Abū Arīsh (ä'bōō ȧ-rēsh').Sau. Ar.	16·48 N	43·00 E
165	Abu Hamed (ä'bōō hä'mĕd)..Sud.	19·37 N	33·21 E
115	Abūksāh...............U. A. R.	29·29 N	30·40 E
98	Abunã (R.) (ȧ-bōō-nä').Bol-Braz..	10·25 S	67·00 W
168	Abū Qīr (ä'bōō kēr') U. A. R. (Nile In.)	31·18 N	30·06 E
168	Abū Qurqāş (ä'bōō kōōr-käs') U. A. R. (Nile In.)	27·57 N	30·51 E
139	Abu Qurûn, Ras (Mt.) U. A. R. (Palestine In.)	30·22 N	33·32 E
153	Aburatsu (ä'bōō-rät'sōō).....Jap.	31·33 N	131·20 E
168	Abū Tīj.......U. A. R. (Nile In.)	27·03 N	31·19 E
144	Abū Zabī..............Sau. Ar.	24·15 N	54·28 E
139	Abū Zanīmah U. A. R. (Palestine In.)	29·03 N	33·08 E
139	Abyad (R.).Jordan (Palestine In.)	30·07 N	36·01 E
118	Åby-Klippan (ô'bü klĭp'pȧn).Swe.	56·08 N	13·09 E
135	Abyy..................Sov. Un.	68·24 N	145·08 E
98	Acacias (ȧ-kȧ'sēäs).....Col. (In.)	3·59 N	73·44 W
82	Acadia Natl. Park (ȧ-kā'dĭ-ȧ) Maine	44·19 N	68·01 W
92	Acajutla (ä-kä-hōōt'lä).......Sal.	13·37 N	89·50 W
91	Acala (ä-kä'-lä)............Mex.	16·38 N	92·49 W
90	Acàmbaro (ä-käm'bä-rō)....Mex.	20·03 N	100·42 W
92	Acancéh (ä-kän-sĕ') Mex. (Yucatan In.)	20·50 N	89·27 W
90	Acapetlahuaya (ä-kä-pĕt'lä-hwä'yä).Mex.	18·24 N	100·04 W
90	Acaponeta (ä-kä-pô-nā'tȧ)...Mex.	22·31 N	105·25 W
90	Acaponeta (R.)............Mex.	22·47 N	105·23 W
90	Acapulco de Juárez (ä-kä-pōōl'kō-dĕ-ᴋwä'-rāz).Mex.	16·49 N	99·57 W
99	Acaraú (ä-kȧrhȧ-ōō').......Braz.	2·55 S	40·04 W
98	Acarigua (äkȧ-rē'gwä).......Ven.	9·29 N	69·11 W
90	Acatlán de Osorio (ä-kät-län'dā ô-sō'rē-ō).Mex.	18·11 N	98·04 W
91	Acatzingo de Hidalgo (ä-kät-zĭŋ'gō dā ê-dhäl'gō).Mex.	18·58 N	97·47 W
91	Acayucan (ä-kä-yōō'kän)....Mex.	17·56 N	94·55 W
80	Accoville (äk'kô-vĭl)......W. Va.	37·45 N	81·50 W
164	Accra (ă'krȧ).............Ghana	5·40 N	0·15 W
110	Accrington (ăk'rĭng-tŭn).....Eng.	53·45 N	2·22 W
125	Acerra (ä-chĕ'r-rä).It. (Naples In.)	40·42 N	14·22 E
98	Achacachi (ä-chä-kä'chê).....Bol.	16·11 S	68·32 W
152	Acheng (ä'chĕng').........China	45·32 N	126·59 E
116	Achill (ă-chĭl')..............Ire.	53·55 N	10·05 W
134	Achinsk (ȧ-chênsk').....Sov. Un.	56·13 N	90·32 E
126	Acireale (ä-chê-rā-ä'lā)........It.	37·37 N	15·12 E
78	Ackia Battle Ground Natl. Mon. (ă-ᴋyŭ').Miss.	34·22 N	89·05 W
95	Acklins (I.) (ăk'lĭns)......Ba. Is.	22·30 N	73·55 W
95	Acklins, The Bight of (B.).Ba. Is.	22·35 N	74·20 W
91	Acolman (ä-kôl-mȧ'n) Mex. (Mexico City In.)	19·38 N	98·56 W
101	Aconcagua (ä-kôn-kä'gwä) (Prov.) Chile (Santiago In.)	32·20 S	71·00 W
101	Aconcagua, Cerro (Mtn.) Arg. (Santiago In.)	32·38 S	70·00 W
101	Aconcagua (R.) Chile (Santiago In.)	32·43 S	70·53 W
164	Açores (Azores) Is. (ȧ-zōrz') (ä-zô'rês).Atl. O.	37·44 N	29·25 W
92	Acoyapa (ä-kô-yä'pä)........Nic.	11·54 N	85·11 W
126	Acqui (äk'kwē)..............It.	44·41 N	8·22 W
139	Acre (ä'kēr)...Isr. (Palestine In.)	32·56 N	35·05 E
98	Acre (State) (ä'krā)........Braz.	8·40 S	70·45 W
98	Acre (R.).................Braz.	10·33 S	68·34 W
84	Acton (ăk'tŭn) Ala. (Birmingham In.)	33·21 N	86·49 W
85	Acton........Can. (Toronto In.)	43·38 N	80·02 W
75	Acton.....Ind. (Indianapolis In.)	39·39 N	85·58 W
83	Acton........Mass. (Boston In.)	42·29 N	71·26 W
82	Acton Vale.................Can.	45·39 N	72·33 W
90	Actopan (äk-tô-pän').......Mex.	20·16 N	98·57 W
91	Actópan (R.) (äk-tŏ'pän)....Mex.	19·25 N	96·31 W
90	Acuitzio del Canje (ä-kwēt'zê-ō dĕl kän'hȧ).Mex.	19·28 N	101·21 W
95	Acul, Baie de l' (B.) (ä-kōōl').Hai.	19·55 N	72·20 W
164	Ada (ä'dä)...............Ghana	5·57 N	0·31 E
70	Ada (ā'dŭ)................Minn.	47·17 N	96·32 W
80	Ada.......................Ohio	40·45 N	83·45 W
73	Ada......................Okla.	34·45 N	96·43 W
127	Ada (ä'dä)................Yugo.	45·48 N	20·06 E
64	Adak (ă-dăk')............Alaska	56·50 N	176·48 W
64	Adak (I.)................Alaska	51·40 N	176·28 W
64	Adak Str.................Alaska	51·42 N	177·16 W
	Adalia, see Antalya		
164	Adamawa (Reg.) (ä-dä-mä'wä) Nig.-Cam.	8·39 N	11·58 E
81	Adams (ăd'ămz)...........Mass.	42·35 N	73·10 W
71	Adams.....................Wis.	43·55 N	89·48 W
64	Adams, Mt...............Alaska	55·40 N	130·25 W
66	Adams, Mt................Wash.	46·15 N	121·19 W
84	Adamsville (ăd'ămz-vĭl) Ala. (Birmingham In.)	33·36 N	86·57 W
84	Adamsville.....Ga. (Atlanta In.)	33·45 N	84·31 W
84	Adamsville, R. I. (Providence In.)	41·33 N	71·04 W
133	Adana (ä'dä-nä)............Tur.	37·05 N	35·20 E
133	Adapazari (ä-dä-pä-zä'rê)....Tur.	40·45 N	30·20 E
165	Adarama (ä-dä-rä'mä).......Sud.	17·11 N	34·56 E
126	Adda (R.) (äd'dä)............It.	45·43 N	9·31 E
144	Ad Dahna (Des.)........Sau. Ar.	26·05 N	47·15 E
144	Ad Dam (äd däm')......Sau. Ar.	20·45 N	44·12 E
144	Ad Dammān............Sau. Ar.	26·27 N	49·59 E
139	Ad Damur....Leb. (Palestine In.)	33·44 N	35·27 E
144	Ad Dawhah.............Sau. Ar.	20·02 N	51·28 E
144	Ad Dilam..............Sau. Ar.	23·47 N	47·03 E
165	Addis Ababā...............Eth.	9·00 N	38·44 E
74	Addison (ă'dĭ-sŭn) Tex. (Dallas, Fort Worth In.)	32·58 N	96·50 W
165	Ad Dīwān.............U. A. R.	22·44 N	32·15 E
167	Addo (ădō)....S. Afr. (Natal In.)	33·33 S	25·43 E
75	Addyston (ăd'ê-stŭn) Ohio (Cincinnati In.)	39·09 N	84·42 W
78	Adel (ā-dĕl')................Ga.	31·08 N	83·55 W
167	Adelaide (ăd-ĕl'ād) S. Afr. (Natal In.)	32·41 S	26·07 E
160	Adelaide (ăd'ê-lād)........Austl.	34·46 S	139·08 E
47	Adelaide I.................Ant.	67·15 S	68·40 W
144	Aden (ä'dĕn)..............Aden	12·48 N	45·00 E
138	Aden......................Asia	14·35 N	47·45 E
144	Aden, G. of................Aden	11·45 N	45·45 E
155	Adi (I.) (ä'dē).........W. Irian	4·25 S	133·52 E
114	Adige R. (ä'dê-jā).....Aus.-Switz.	46·34 N	10·51 E
126	Adige, Fiume (R.) (fyōō'mĕ-ä'dê-jā).It.	46·38 N	10·43 E
142	Ādilābād (ŭ-dĭl-ä-bäd').....India	19·47 N	78·30 E
143	Adini.....................India	15·42 N	77·18 E
81	Adirondack, Mts. (ăd-ĭ-rŏn'dăk) N. Y.	43·45 N	74·40 W
165	Adi Ugri (ä-dē ōō'grē).......Eth.	14·54 N	38·52 E
121	Adjud (äd'zhōōd)..........Rom.	46·05 N	27·12 E
64	Admiralty (I.)............Alaska	57·50 N	133·50 W
65	Admiralty Inlet (ăd'mĭrȧl-tê) Wash. (Seattle In.)	48·10 N	122·45 W
155	Admiralty Is........N. Gui. Ter.	1·40 S	146·45 E
74	Adolph (ā'dolf) Minn. (Duluth In.)	46·47 N	92·17 W
122	Adour (R.) (ȧ-dōōr').........Fr.	43·43 N	0·38 W
124	Adra (ä'drä)................Sp.	36·45 N	3·02 W
126	Adrano (ä-drä'nō)............It.	37·42 N	14·52 E
164	Adrar des Iforas (Reg.) (ä-drär') Alg.	20·22 N	1·44 E
126	Adria (ä'drê-ä).............. It.	45·03 N	12·01 E
80	Adrian (ā'drĭ-ăn)..........Mich.	41·55 N	84·00 W
70	Adrian....................Minn.	43·39 N	95·56 W
	Adrianople, see Edirne		
126	Adriatic Sea...............Eur.	41·30 N	14·27 E
164	Adrir......................Alg.	27·53 N	0·15 W
100	Adrogué (ȧdrō-gā').....Arg. (In.)	34·33 S	58·24 W
165	Aduwā.....................Eth.	14·02 N	38·58 E
110	Adwick-le-Street (ăd'wĭk-lê-strēt') Eng.	53·35 N	1·11 W
135	Adycha (R.) (ä'dĭ-chȧ)..Sov. Un.	66·11 N	136·45 E
129	Adzhamka (ȧd-zhäm'kȧ).Sov. Un.	48·33 N	32·28 E
132	Adz'va (R.) (ädz'vȧ)....Sov. Un.	67·00 N	59·20 E
115	Aegean Sea (ê-jē'ăn)....Eur.-Asia	39·04 N	24·56 E
118	Aerø (I.) (âr'ö).............Den.	54·52 N	10·22 E
138	Afghanistan (ăf-găn-ĭ-stăn')..Asia	33·00 N	63·00 E
168	Afgoi (äf-gô'ĭ) Som. (Horn of Afr. In.)	2·08 N	45·08 E
164	Aflou (ä-flōō')..............Alg.	33·59 N	2·04 E
64	Afognak (I.) (ä-fŏg-nȧk')..Alaska	58·28 N	151·35 W
125	Afragola (ä-frȧ'gō-lä) It. (Naples In.)	40·40 N	14·19 E
7	Africa (ăf'rĭ-kȧ)		
74	Afton (ăf'tŭn).............Minn. (Minneapolis, St. Paul In.)	44·54 N	92·47 W

Page	Name Pronunciation Region	Lat. °′	Long. °′
73	Afton....................Okla.	36·42 N	94·56 W
67	Afton....................Wyo.	42·42 N	110·52 W
139	'Afula (ä-fōō'lȧ) Isr. (Palestine In.)	32·36 N	35·17 E
133	Afyonkarahisar (ä-fē-ōn-kä-rȧ-hē-sär').Tur.	38·45 N	30·20 E
165	Agadem (Oasis) (ä'gȧ-dĕm).Niger	16·50 N	13·15 E
164	Agadès (ä'gȧ-dĕs)..........Niger	17·01 N	7·55 E
164	Agadir (ä-gȧ-dēr)..........Mor.	30·30 N	9·37 W
92	Agalta, Cord. de (Mts.) (kôr-dēl-yĕ'rä-dĕ-ä-gä'l-tä).......Hond.	15·15 N	85·42 W
136	Agapovka (ä-gä-pôv'kä) Sov. Un. (Urals In.)	53·18 N	59·10 E
142	Agartala.................India	23·53 N	91·22 E
143	Agāshi......India (Bombay In.)	19·28 N	72·46 E
136	Agashkino (ȧ-gäsh'kĭ-nô) Sov. Un. (Moscow In.)	55·18 N	38·13 E
65	Agate Bay (ăg'ĭt) (ăg'ȧt) Wash. (Vancouver In.)	48·45 N	122·20 W
64	Agattu (I.) (ȧ'gä-tōō)....Alaska	52·14 N	173·40 E
129	Agayman (ȧ-gä-ē-män')..Sov. Un.	46·39 N	34·20 E
133	Agdam (āg'dām)........Sov. Un.	40·00 N	47·00 E
122	Agde (ägd)................Fr.	43·19 N	3·30 E
122	Agen (ȧ-zhäN')..............Fr.	44·13 N	0·31 E
85	Agincourt (ä'zhĕN-kōōr') Can. (Toronto In.)	43·47 N	79·16 W
135	Aginskoye (ä-hĭn'skô-yĕ).Sov. Un.	51·15 N	113·15 E
65	Agnew (ăg'nū).Wash. (Seattle In.)	48·06 N	123·15 W
155	Agno (äg'nō)...Phil. (Manila In.)	16·07 N	119·49 E
155	Agno (R.)......Phil. (Manila In.)	15·42 N	120·28 E
126	Agnone (än-yō'nā)...........It.	41·49 N	14·23 E
165	Agordat (ä-gōr'dät).........Eth.	15·34 N	37·54 E
142	Agra (ä'grä)..............India	27·18 N	78·00 E
126	Agri (R.) (ä'grē).............It.	40·15 N	16·21 E
127	Agrínion (ȧ-grē'nyôn)........Grc.	38·38 N	21·06 E
92	Agua (Vol.) (ä'gwä)........Guat.	14·28 N	90·43 W
90	Agua Blanca, Río (R.) (rē'ō-ä-gwä-blä'n-kä).Mex.	21·46 N	102·54 W
90	Agua Brava, Laguna de (L.) (lä-gōō'nä-dĕ-ä'gwä-brä'vä)...Mex.	22·04 N	105·40 W
68	Agua Caliente Ind. Res. (ä'gwä kal-yĕn'tä).Calif.	33·50 N	116·24 W
94	Aguada (ä-gwä'dȧ).........Cuba	22·25 N	80·50 W
92	Aguada L....Mex. (Yucatan In.)	18·46 N	89·40 W
98	Aguadas (ä-gwä'-dȧs)...Col. (In.)	5·37 N	75·27 W
89	Aguadilla (ä-gwä-dēl'yä) P. R. (Puerto Rico In.)	18·27 N	67·10 W
93	Aguadulce (ä-gwä-dōōl'sä)...Pan.	8·15 N	80·33 W
91	Agua Escondida, Meseta de (Plat.) (mĕ-sĕ'tä-dĕ-ä'gwä-ĕs-kôn-dē'dä).Mex.	16·54 N	91·35 W
101	Aguai (ägwä-ē') Braz. (Rio de Janeiro In.)	22·04 S	46·57 W
76	Agualeguas (ä-gwä-lā'gwäs).Mex.	26·19 N	99·33 W
76	Aguanaval, R. (ȧ-guä-nä-väl').Mex.	25·12 N	103·28 W
92	Aguán R. (ä-gwȧ'n).......Hond.	15·22 N	87·00 W
83	Aguanus (R.) (ȧ-gwā'nŭs)...Can.	50·45 N	62·03 W
90	Aguascalientes (ä'gwäs-käl-yĕn'tās).Mex.	21·52 N	102·17 W
124	Agueda (ä-gwā'dȧ).........Port.	40·36 N	8·26 W
124	Agueda (R.) (ä-gĕ-dä)........Sp.	40·50 N	6·44 W
164	Aguellal (ä-gĕl-yäl).........Niger	19·05 N	8·10 E
72	Aguilar (ä-gē-lär')...........Colo.	37·24 N	104·38 W
124	Aguilar.....................Sp.	37·32 N	4·39 W
124	Aguilas (ä'gē-läs)............Sp.	37·26 N	1·35 W
90	Aguililla (ä-gē-lēl-yä).......Mex.	18·44 N	102·44 W
98	Aguja, Pta. (Pt.) (pŭn'tä ȧ-gōō' hä).Peru	6·00 S	81·15 W
166	Agulhas, C. (ä-gōōl'yäs)...S. Afr.	34·47 S	20·00 E
154	Agung, Gunung (Mtn.) (ä-gōōng').Indon.	8·41 S	115·07 E
155	Agusan (R.) (ä-gōō'sän).....Phil.	8·12 N	126·07 E
164	Ahaggar (Mts.) (ȧ-hȧ-gär')...Alg.	23·14 N	6·00 E
123	Ahlen (ä'lĕn).....Ger. (Ruhr In.)	51·45 N	7·52 E
142	Ahmadābād (ŭ-mĕd-ā-bād').India	23·04 N	72·38 E
142	Ahmadnagar (ä'mûd-nû-gûr).India	19·09 N	74·45 E
168	Ahmar Mts.Eth. (Horn of Afr. In.)	9·22 N	42·00 E
165	Ahmara Plat...............Eth.	10·09 N	37·21 E
79	Ahoskie (ā-hŏs'kē)..........N. C.	36·15 N	77·00 W
111	Ahrensburg (ä'rĕns-bōōrg) Ger. (Hamburg In.)	53·40 N	10·14 E
120	Ahrweiler (är'vī-lĕr).........Ger.	50·34 N	7·05 E
119	Ahtärin-järvi (L.)...........Fin.	62·46 N	24·25 E
90	Ahuacatlán (ä-wä-kät-län')..Mex.	21·05 N	104·28 W
92	Ahuachapan (ä-wä-chä-pän')..Sal.	13·57 N	89·53 W
90	Ahualulco (ä-wä-lōōl'kō)....Mex.	20·43 N	103·57 W
90	Ahuatempan (ä-wä-tĕm-pän).Mex.	18·11 N	98·02 W
118	Ahus (ô'hōōs).............Swe.	55·56 N	14·19 E
144	Ahvāz....................Iran	31·15 N	48·54 E
118	Ahvenanma (Åland Is.) (ä'vĕ-nȧn-mô) (ô'länd).Fin.	60·36 N	19·55 E
157	Aica...............Hawaii (In.)	21·18 N	157·52 W
79	Aiken (ā'kĕn)..............S. C.	33·32 N	81·43 W
99	Aimorés, Serra dos (Mts.) (sĕ'r-rä-dôs-ī-mō-rĕ's).Braz.	17·40 S	42·38 W
153	Aimoto (ī-mô-tō).Jap. (Ōsaka In.)	34·59 N	135·09 E
164	Aïn Beida (ä'ēn bā-dä')......Alg.	35·57 N	7·25 E
123	Aincourt (ăN-kōō'r).Fr. (Paris In.)	49·04 N	1·47 E
125	Aïne Ousséra (ĕn ōō-sā-rȧ)....Alg.	35·25 N	2·50 E
164	Aïn Sefra (ä'ēn sĕf'rä).........Alg.	32·49 N	0·39 W
83	Ainsle, L. (ān'slē)...........Can.	46·08 N	61·23 W
70	Ainsworth (ānz'wûrth).....Nebr.	42·32 N	99·51 W
114	Aïn Taïba (ä'ēn tä'ē-bä)......Alg.	30·20 N	5·30 E
113	Aïn-Temouchent (ä'ēntĕ-mōō-shaN').Alg.	35·20 N	1·23 W
98	Aipe (ī'-pĕ)............Col. (In.)	3·13 N	75·15 W
122	Aire (âr)....................Fr.	43·42 N	0·17 W
110	Aire (R.)..................Eng.	53·42 N	1·00 W
139	Airhitam, Selat (Str.) Indon. (Singapore In.)	0·58 N	102·38 E
164	Aïr ou Azbine (Mts.).......Niger	18·28 N	7·51 E
122	Aisne (R.) (ĕn)..............Fr.	49·28 N	3·32 E
155	Aitape (ä-ē-tä'pȧ)....N. Gui. Ter.	3·00 S	142 10 E
71	Aitkin (āt'kĭn)............Minn.	46·32 N	93·43 W
127	Aitolikón (ȧ-tō'lĭ-kôn).......Grc.	38·27 N	21·21 E
127	Aitos (ä-ē'tōs)..............Bul.	42·42 N	27·17 E
157	Aitutaki (I.) (ī-tōō-tä'kē).Cook Is.	19·00 S	162·00 W
121	Aiud (ä'ē-ōōd).............Rom.	46·19 N	23·40 E
101	Aiuruoca (äē'ōō-rōōô'-kȧ) Braz. (Rio de Janeiro In.)	21·57 S	44·36 W
101	Aiuruoca (R.) Braz. (Rio de Janeiro In.)	22·11 S	44·35 W
122	Aix-en-Provence (ĕks-prô-vȧNs) Fr. (Marseille In.)	43·32 N	5·27 E
123	Aix-les-Bains (ĕks'-lā-baN')....Fr.	45·42 N	5·56 E
127	Aiyien.....................Grc.	37·37 N	22·12 E
127	Aíyina (I.).................Grc.	37·43 N	23·35 E
127	Aíyion.....................Grc.	38·13 N	22·04 E
119	Aizpute (ä'ēz-pōō-tĕ)....Sov. Un.	56·44 N	21·37 E
126	Ajaccio (ä-yät'chō)..........Fr.	41·55 N	8·42 E
91	Ajalpan (ä-häl'pän)........Mex.	18·21 N	97·14 W
158	Ajana (āj-än'ēr)...........Austl.	28·00 S	114·45 E
67	Ajax Mt. (ā'jăks).........Mont.	45·19 N	113·43 W
165	Ajdabiyah.................Libya	30·56 N	20·16 E
144	Ajman...............Tr. Coast	25·15 N	54·30 E
142	Ajmer (ŭj-mēr')............India	26·26 N	74·42 E
69	Ajo (ä'hô).................Ariz.	32·20 N	112·55 W
90	Ajuchitlán del Progreso (ä-hōō-chet-lȧn).Mex.	18·11 N	100·32 W
91	Ajusco (ä-hōō's-kō) Mex. (Mexico City In.)	19·13 N	99·12 W
91	Ajusco, Cerro (sĕ'r-rô-ä-hōō's-kō) Mex. (Mexico City In.)	19·12 N	99·16 W
153	Akaishi-dake (Mtn.) (ä-kī-shē dä'kä).Jap.	5·30 N	138·00 E
99	Akarai Mts. (ä'kȧ-rä'ē).Braz.-Sur.	1·30 N	57·40 W
153	Akashi (ä'kä-shē).Jap. (Ōsaka In.)	34·38 N	134·59 E
165	Aketi (ä-kȧ-tē)...........Con. L.	2·58 N	23·57 E
133	Akhaltsikhe (ăkȧ'l-tsĭ-kĕ) Sov. Un.	41·40 N	42·50 E
165	Akhdar, Jabal al (Mts.)....Libya	32·45 N	21·52 E
144	Akhdar, Jabal al (Mts.) Mus. & Om.-Sau. Ar.	23·30 N	56·43 E
127	Akhelóös (R.) (ä-hĕ'lô-ōs)....Grc.	38·45 N	21·26 E
133	Akhisar (äk-hĭs-sär')........Tur.	38·58 N	27·58 E
129	Akhtarskaya, Bukhta (B.) (bōōk'tä ȧK-tär'skȧ-yȧ).Sov. Un.	45·53 N	38·22 E
127	Akhtopol (äK'tô-pōl)........Bul.	42·08 N	27·54 E
129	Akhtyrka (äK-tür'kȧ)....Sov. Un.	50·18 N	34·53 E
136	Akhunovo (ä-kû'nô-vô) Sov. Un. (Urals In.)	54·13 N	59·36 E
153	Aki (ä'kē)..................Jap.	33·31 N	133·51 E
64	Akiak (äk'yȧk)...........Alaska	61·00 N	161·02 W
87	Akimiski (I.) (ä-kĭ-mĭ'skĭ)...Can.	52·54 N	80·22 W
152	Akita (ä'kē-tä)..............Jap.	39·40 N	140·12 E
164	Akjoujt.............Mauritania	19·45 N	14·30 W
86	Aklavik (äk'lä-vĭk).........Can.	68·28 N	135·26 W
153	Ako (ä'kô)..................Jap.	34·44 N	134·22 E
142	Akola (ȧ-kô'lä).............India	20·47 N	77·00 E
87	Akpatok (I.) (ȧk'pȧ-tŏk)....Can.	60·30 N	67·10 W
112	Akranes...................Ice.	64·18 N	21·40 W
127	Akrítas, Akr. (C.)...........Grc.	37·45 N	23·53 E
72	Akron (ăk'rŭn)............Colo.	40·09 N	103·14 W
75	Akron.......Ohio (Cleveland In.)	41·05 N	81·30 W
139	Akrotiri B..Cyprus (Palestine In.)	34·38 N	33·18 E
133	Aksaray (äk-sȧ-rī')..........Tur.	38·30 N	34·05 E
133	Akşehir (äk'shȧ-hēr).........Tur.	38·20 N	31·20 E
133	Aksehir (L.)................Tur.	38·40 N	31·30 E
135	Aksha (äk'shȧ).........Sov. Un.	50·28 N	113·00 E
	Aksu, see Wensu		
146	Ak Su (R.)...............China	40·34 N	77·15 E
133	Aktyubinsk (äk'tyōō-bēnsk) Sov. Un.	50·20 N	57·00 E
153	Akune (ä'kōō-nȧ)...........Jap.	32·03 N	130·16 E
112	Akureyri (ä-kōō-rȧ'rē)........Ice.	65·39 N	18·01 W
64	Akutan (I.) (ä-kōō-tän')...Alaska	53·58 N	169·54 W
63	Alabama (State)(ăl-ȧ-băm'ȧ).U. S.	32·50 N	87·30 W
78	Alabama (R.)...............Ala.	31·20 N	87·39 W
155	Alabat (I.) (ä-lä-bät') Phil. (Manila In.)	14·14 N	122·05 E
155	Alaca (ä-lä-kä).Phil. (Manila In.)	17·56 N	121·39 E
133	Alacam (ä-lä-chäm')........Tur.	41·30 N	35·40 E
94	Alacranes (ä-lä-krä'nȧs)....Cuba	22·45 N	81·35 W
144	Alaflau (Des.)...........Sau. Ar.	24·00 N	44·47 E
99	Alagôas (ä-lä-gō'äzh).......Braz.	9·50 S	36·33 W
99	Alagoinhas (ä-lä-gō-ēn'yäzh).Braz.	12·13 S	38·12 W
124	Alagón (ä-lä-gōn')...........Sp.	41·46 N	1·07 W
124	Alagón (R.).................Sp.	39·53 N	6·42 W
90	Alahuatán (R.) (ä-lä-wä-tȧ'n).Mex.	18·30 N	100·00 W
93	Alajuela (ä-lä-hwa'lä........C.R.	10·01 N	84·14 W
134	Alakol (L.)............Sov. Un.	45·45 N	81·13 E
157	Alalakeiki Chan. (ä-lä-lä-kā'kē) Hawaii (In.)	20·40 N	156·30 W
165	Al 'Alamayn............U. A. R.	30·53 N	28·52 E
165	Al 'Allāqī..............U. A. R.	23·06 N	32·47 E
65	Alameda (ăl-ȧ-mā'dȧ) Calif. (San Francisco In.)	37·46 N	122·15 W
67	Alameda.................Idaho	42·51 N	112·29 W
65	Alameda (R.) Calif. (San Francisco In.)	37·36 N	122·02 W
155	Alaminos (ä-lä-mē'nôs) Phil. (Manila In.)	16·09 N	119·58 E
115	Al 'Āmirīyah..........U. A. R.	31·01 N	29·52 E
65	Alamo (ă'lȧ-mō) Calif. (San Francisco In.)	37·51 N	122·02 W
91	Alamo (ä'lä-mô)............Mex.	21·07 N	99·35 W
76	Alamo, R. (ä'lä-mô)........Mex.	26·33 N	99·35 W
69	Alamogordo (ăl-ȧ-mō-gôr'dō) N. Mex.	32·55 N	106·00 W
74	Alamo Heights (ă'lȧ-mō) Tex. (San Antonio In.)	29·28 N	98·27 W
76	Alamo Pk. (ă'lȧ-mō pēk)..N. Mex.	32·50 N	105·55 W
69	Alamosa (ăl-ȧ-mō'sȧ).......Colo.	37·25 N	105·50 W
136	Alandskiy (ä-länt'skĭ) Sov. Un. (Urals In.)	52·14 N	59·48 E
133	Alanya....................Tur.	36·40 N	32·10 E
167	Alaotra (L.) (ä-lä-ō'trȧ) Malag. Rep.	17·15 S	48·17 E
136	Alapayevsk (ä-lä-pä'yĕfsk) Sov. Un. (Urals In.)	57·50 N	61·35 E
139	Al Aqabah.Jordan (Palestine In.)	29·32 N	35·00 E
90	Alaquines (ā-lȧ-kē'nȧs)......Mex.	22·07 N	99·35 W
139	Al 'Arīsh (a-rēsh') U. A. R. (Palestine In.)	31·08 N	33·48 E
150	Ala Shan (Mtns.) (ä'lä-shän') China	38·02 N	105·20 E
62	Alaska (State) (ȧ-lăs'kȧ).....U. S.	65·00 N	158·00 W
64	Alaska, G. of.............Alaska	57·42 N	147·40 W
64	Alaska Hy................Alaska	63·00 N	142·00 W
64	Alaska Pen...............Alaska	55·50 N	162·10 W
64	Alaska Ra................Alaska	62·00 N	152·18 W
132	Alatyr' (ä'lä-tür)........Sov. Un.	54·55 N	46·30 E
98	Alausí (ȧ-lou-sē')............Ec.	2·15 S	78·45 W
168	Al 'Ayyāţ (ä-ē-yät') U. A. R. (Nile In.)	29·38 N	31·18 E
126	Alba (äl'bä)..................It.	44·41 N	8·02 E
124	Albacete (äl-bä-thā'tā)........Sp.	39·00 N	1·49 W
123	Albachten (äl-bȧ'K-tĕn) Ger. (Ruhr In.)	51·55 N	7·31 E
168	Al Badārī.....U. A. R. (Nile In.)	26·59 N	31·29 E
124	Alba de Tormes (äl-bȧ dā tôr'mās) Sp.	40·48 N	5·28 W
168	Al Bahnasā...U. A. R. (Nile In.)	28·35 N	30·30 E
121	Alba Iulia (äl-bä yōō'lyȧ)...Rom.	46·05 N	23·32 E
125	Albalate (äl-bä-lä'tä).........Sp.	41·07 N	0·34 W
168	Al Ballāḩ (bä'lä) U. A. R. (Suez In.)	30·46 N	32·20 E
168	Al Balyanā....U. A. R. (Nile In.)	26·12 N	32·00 E
102	Albania (ăl-bā'nĭ-ȧ).........Eur.	41·45 N	20·00 E
125	Albano, Lago (L.) (lä'-gō-äl-bä'nō) It. (Rome In.)	41·45 N	12·44 E
125	Albano Laziale (äl-bä'nō lät-zē-ä'lā).It. (Rome In.)	41·44 N	12·43 E
158	Albany (ôl'bȧ-nĭ)..........Austl.	35·00 S	118·00 E
65	Albany.Calif. (San Francisco In.)	37·54 N	122·18 W
78	Albany.....................Ga.	31·35 N	84·10 W
73	Albany.....................Mo.	40·14 N	94·18 W
81	Albany...................N. Y.	42·40 N	73·50 W
66	Albany....................Ore.	44·38 N	123·06 W
76	Albany....................Tex.	32·43 N	99·17 W
87	Albany (R.)...............Can.	51·45 N	83·30 W
144	A'l Basrah................Iraq	30·27 N	47·52 E
139	Al Batrūn (bä-trōōn') Leb. (Palestine In.)	34·16 N	35·39 E
165	Al Bawīţī.............U. A. R.	28·19 N	29·00 E
155	Albay G. (äl-bä'ē) Phil. (Manila In.)	13·09 N	123·52 E
79	Albemarle (ăl'bē-märl)......N. C.	35·24 N	80·36 W
79	Albemarle Sd.............N. C.	36·00 N	76·17 W
126	Albenga (äl-bĕŋ'gä)..........It.	44·04 N	8·13 E
124	Alberche (R.) (äl-bĕr'chȧ).....Sp.	40·08 N	4·19 W
158	Alberga, The (R.) (ăl-bŭr'gȧ) Austl.	27·15 S	135·00 E
124	Albergaria a-Velha (äl-bĕr-gȧ-rē'-ȧ-ä-vāl'yȧ).Port.	40·47 N	8·31 W
74	Alberhill (ăl'bēr-hĭl) Calif. (Los Angeles In.)	33·43 N	117·23 W
82	Albert (ăl'bērt)............Can.	45·44 N	64·46 W
122	Albert (ȧl-bâr')..............Fr.	50·00 N	2·49 E
86	Alberta (Prov.) (ăl-bûr'tȧ)...Can.	54·33 N	117·10 W
155	Albert Edward, Mt. (ăl'bērt ĕd'wērd).Austl.	8·25 S	147·25 E
101	Alberti (ȧl-bĕ'r-tē) Arg. (Buenos Aires In.)	35·01 S	60·16 W
111	Albert Kanal (can.) Bel. (Brussels In.)	51·07 N	5·07 E
165	Albert L. (ăl'bērt) (ȧl-bâr') Con. L.-Ug.	2·00 N	30·16 E
71	Albert Lea (ăl'bērt lē')......Minn.	43·38 N	93·24 W
82	Alberton (ăl'bēr-tŭn)........Can.	46·50 N	64·02 W
167	Alberton.................S. Afr. (Johannesburg & Pretoria In.)	26·16 S	28·08 E
78	Albertville (ăl'bērt-vĭl).......Ala.	34·15 N	86·10 W
166	Albertville (ȧl-bêr-vēl')....Con. L.	5·59 S	29·12 E
123	Albertville.................Fr.	45·42 N	6·25 E
122	Albi (äl-bē')................Fr.	43·54 N	2·07 E
71	Albia (ăl bĭ-ȧ).............Iowa	41·01 N	92·44 W
99	Albina (äl-bē'nä).........Fr. Gu.	5·30 N	54·33 W
75	Albino, Pt. (äl-bē'nō) Can. (Buffalo In.)	42·50 N	79·05 W
80	Albion (ăl'bĭ-ŭn)...........Mich.	42·15 N	84·50 W
70	Albion....................Nebr.	41·42 N	99·00 W
81	Albion....................N. Y.	43·15 N	78·10 W
124	Alboran, Isla del (I.) (ē's-lä-dĕl-äl-bō-rä'n).Sp.	35·58 N	3·02 W
124	Alboran Sea.............Medit.	35·54 N	4·26 W
118	Ålborg (ôl'bŏr)............Den.	57·02 N	9·55 E
124	Albox (äl-bōk')..............Sp.	37·23 N	2·08 W
69	Albuquerque (ăl-bû-kûr'kē) N. Mex.	35·05 N	106·40 W
93	Albuquerque, Cayus de (I.) (ăl-bû-kûr'kē).Col.	12·12 N	81·24 W
144	Al Buraymī............Sau. Ar.	23·45 N	55·39 E
124	Alburquerque (äl-bōōr-kĕr'kā).Sp.	39·13 N	6·58 W
160	Albury (ôl'bēr-ē)..........Austl.	36·00 S	147·00 E
125	Alcabideche (äl-kȧ-bē-dā'chȧ) Port. (Lisbon In.)	38·43 N	9·24 W
124	Alcacer do Sal (äl-kä'sĕr dōō säl') Port.	38·24 N	8·33 W
125	Alcalá de Chivert (äl-kä-lä'dā chē-vĕrt').Sp.	40·18 N	0·12 E
125	Alcalá de Henares (äl-kä-lä' dā ā na'rās). Sp. (Madrid In.)	40·29 N	3·22 W
124	Alcalá de los Gazules (äl-kä-lä' dā lōs gä-thōō'lȧs).Sp.	36·29 N	5·44 W
124	Alcalá la Real (äl-kä-lä'lä rā-äl').Sp.	37·27 N	3·57 W
126	Alcamo (äl'kȧ-mō)...........It.	37·58 N	13·03 E
125	Alcanadre (R.) (äl-kä-nä'drȧ). Sp.	41·41 N	0·18 W
125	Alcanar (äl-kä-när')..........Sp.	40·35 N	0·27 E
125	Alcañiz (äl-kän-yēth')........Sp.	41·03 N	0·08 W
99	Alcântara (äl-kän'tȧ-rȧ).....Braz.	2·17 S	44·29 W
124	Alcaraz (äl-kä-räth')..........Sp.	38·39 N	2·28 W
124	Alcaudete (äl-kou-dhā'tā).....Sp.	37·38 N	4·05 W

ăt; finăl; rate; senâte; ärm; ȧsk; sofȧ; fâre; ch-choose; dh-as th in other; bē; ēvent; bĕt; recĕnt; cratēr; g-go; gh-guttural g; bĭt; ĭ-short neutral; rīde; K-guttural k as ch in German ich;

Page	Name Pronunciation Region	Lat. °′	Long. °′
124	Alcázar de San Juan (äl-kä′thär dā sän hwän′) Sp.	39·22 N	3·12 W
114	Alcazarquivir Mor.	35·01 N	5·48 W
125	Alcira (ä-thē′rä) Sp.	39·09 N	0·26 W
78	Alcoa (ăl-kō′ȧ) Tenn.	35·45 N	84 00 W
125	Alcobendas (äl-kō-bĕn′dȧs) Sp. (Madrid In.)	40·32 N	3·39 W
125	Alcochete (äl-kō-chā′ta) Port. (Lisbon In.)	38·45 N	8·58 W
125	Alcora (äl-kō′rä) Sp.	40·05 N	0·12 W
125	Alcorisa (äl-kō-rē′sä) Sp.	40·53 N	0·20 W
125	Alcorón (äl-kô-rō′n) Sp. (Madrid In.)	40·22 N	3·50 W
101	Alcorta (äl-kôr′tä) Arg. (Buenos Aires In.)	33·32 S	61·08 W
67	Alcova Res. (ăl-kō′vȧ) Wyo.	42·31 N	106·33 W
85	Alcove (ăl-kōv′) Can. (Ottawa In.)	45·41 N	75·55 W
125	Alcoy (äl-koi′) Sp.	38·42 N	0·30 W
125	Alcudia, Ba. de (B.) (bä-ē′ä-dĕ-äl-kōō-dhē′ä) Sp.	39·48 N	3·20 E
167	Aldabra Is. (äl-dä′brä) Afr.	9·16 S	46·17 E
90	Aldama (äl-dä′mä) Mex.	22·54 N	98·04 W
76	Aldama Mex.	28·50 N	105·54 W
135	Aldan Sov. Un.	58·46 N	125·19 E
135	Aldan (R.) Sov. Un.	63·30 N	132·14 E
135	Aldan Plat Sov. Un.	57·42 N	130·28 E
135	Aldanskaya Sov. Un.	61·52 N	135·29 E
123	Aldekerk (ȧl′dĕ-kĕ′rk) Ger. (Ruhr In.)	51·26 N	6·26 E
123	Aldenhoven (ȧl′dĕn-hō′vĕn) Ger. (Ruhr In.)	50·54 N	6·18 E
65	Aldergrove (ôl′dēr-grōv) Can. (Vancouver In.)	49·03 N	122·28 W
122	Alderney (I.) (ôl′dēr-nĭ) Chan. Is.	49·43 N	2·11 W
110	Aldershot (ôl′dēr-shŏt) Eng. (London In.)	51·14 N	0·46 W
80	Alderson (ôl-dēr-sŭn) W. Va.	37·40 N	80·40 W
65	Alderwood Manor (ôl′dēr-wŏŏd măn′ŏr) Wash. (Seattle In.)	47·49 N	122·18 W
73	Aledo (ȧ-le′dō) Ill.	41·12 N	90·47 W
164	Aleg Mauritania	17·10 N	13·57 W
101	Alegre (àlĕ′-grĕ) Braz. (Rio de Janeiro In.)	20·41 S	41·32 W
100	Alegre (R.) Braz. (In.)	22·22 S	43·34 W
100	Alegrete (ä-lå-grā′tä) Braz.	29·46 S	55·44 W
136	Aleksandrov (ä-lyĕk-sän′ drôf) Sov. Un. (Moscow In.)	56·24 N	38·45 E
136	Aleksandrovsk (ä-lyĕk-sän′drôfsk) Sov. Un. (Urals In.)	59·11 N	57·36 E
135	Aleksandrovsk-Sakhalinskiy (ä-lyĕk-sän′drôfsk-sŭ-kŭ-lyēn′skē) Sov. Un.	51·02 N	142·21 E
121	Aleksandrow Kujawski (ä-lĕk-säh′drōōv kōō-yav′skē) Pol.	52·54 N	18·45 E
129	Alekseyevka (ä-lyĕk-sā-yĕf′kȧ) Sov. Un.	50·39 N	38·40 E
128	Aleksin (ä-lyĕ-sēn) Sov. Un.	54·31 N	37·07 E
127	Aleksinac (ä-lyĕk-sē-nȧk′) Yugo.	43·33 N	21·42 E
101	Alem Paraíba (ä-lĕ′m-pȧ-rȧē′bȧ) Braz. (Rio de Janeiro In.)	21·54 S	42·40 W
122	Alençon (ȧ-läN-sôN′) Fr.	48·26 N	0·08 E
99	Alenquer (ä-lĕŋ-kĕr′) Braz.	1·58 S	54·44 W
124	Alenquer Port.	39·04 N	9·01 W
124	Alentjo (Reg.) (ä-lĕŋ-tä′zhōō) Port.	38·05 N	7·45 W
157	Alenuihaha Chan. (ä′lā-nōō-ē-hä′hä) Hawaii (In.)	20·20 N	156·05 W
115	Aleppo (ȧ-lĕp-ō) Syria	36·10 N	37·18 E
122	Alès (ä-lĕs′) Fr.	44·07 N	4·06 E
126	Alessandria (ä-lĕs-sän′drē-ä) It.	44·53 N	8·35 E
74	Alessandro (ä-lĕs-san′drō) Calif. (Los Angeles In.)	33·52 N	117·16 W
	Alessio, see Lesh		
118	Ålesund (ô′lĕ-sōōn′) Nor.	62·28 N	6·14 E
64	Aleutian Is. (ȧ-lu′shăn) Alaska	52·40 N	177·30 E
64	Aleutian Trench Alaska	50·40 N	177·10 E
135	Alevina, Mys (C.) Sov. Un.	58·49 N	151·44 E
64	Alexander Arch. (ăl-ĕg-zăn′dēr) Alaska	57·05 N	138·10 W
78	Alexander City Ala.	32·55 N	85·55 W
47	Alexander I Ant.	71·00 S	71·00 W
167	Alexandra (äl-ex-än′-drȧ) S. Afr. (Johannesburg & Pretoria In.)	26·07 S	28·07 E
158	Alexandria (ăl-ĕg-zăn′drĭ-ȧ) Austl.	19·00 S	136·56 E
81	Alexandria Can.	45·50 N	74·35 W
80	Alexandria Ind.	40·20 N	85·20 W
77	Alexandria La.	31·18 N	92·28 W
70	Alexandria Minn.	45·53 N	95·23 W
127	Alexandria Rom.	43·55 N	25·21 E
70	Alexandria S. D.	43·39 N	97·45 W
167	Alexandria (ăl-ĕx-ăn-drĭ-ȧ) S. Afr. (Natal In.)	33·40 S	26·26 E
81	Alexandria (ăl-ĕg-zăn′drĭ-ȧ) Va.	38·50 N	77·05 W
	Alexandria, see Al Iskandarīyah		
81	Alexandria Bay N. Y.	44·20 N	75·55 W
127	Alexandroúpolis (Dedeagats) (ä-lĕk-sän-drōō′pō-lĭs) (dĕ′dĕ-ä-gäts) Grc.	40·51 N	25·51 E
124	Alfaro (äl-färō) Sp.	42·08 N	1·43 W
168	Al Fashn U. A. R. (Nile In.)	28·47 N	30·53 E
165	Al Fayyūm U. A. R.	29·14 N	30·48 E
101	Alfenas (äl-fĕ′nȧs) Braz. (Rio de Janeiro In.)	21·26 S	45·55 W
127	Alfiós (R.) Grc.	37·33 N	21·50 E
168	Al Firdān (fer-dän′) U. A. R. (Nile In.)	30·43 N	32·20 E
101	Alfonso Claudio (äl-fōn′sô-klou′dēô) Braz. (Rio de Janeiro In.)	20·05 S	41·05 W
85	Alfred (ăl′frĕd) Can. (Ottawa In.)	45·34 N	74·52 W
110	Alfreton (ăl′fēr-tŭn) Eng.	53·06 N	1·23 W
165	Alga Eth.	5·56 N	38·09 E
124	Algarve (Reg.) (äl-gär′vĕ) Port	37·15 N	8·12 W
124	Algeciras (äl-hä-thē′räs) Sp.	36·08 N	5·25 W
164	Alger (Algiers) (àl-zhā′) (ăl-jēr) Alg.	36·51 N	2·56 E
163	Algeria (ăl-gē′rĭ-ȧ) Afr.	34·58 N	2·00 E
125	Algete (äl-hā′tā) Sp. (Madrid In.)	40·36 N	3·30 W
126	Alghero (äl-gâ′rō) It.	40·32 N	8·22 E
	Algiers, see Alger		
77	Algoa (ăl-gō′ȧ) Tex. (In.)	29·24 N	95·11 W
167	Algoa B. (ăl′gôȧ) S. Afr. (Natal In.)	33·51 S	24·50 E
65	Algoma Wash. (Seattle In.)	47·17 N	122·15 W
71	Algoma Wis.	44·38 N	87·29 W
71	Algona Iowa	43·04 N	94·11 W
80	Algonac (ăl′gô-năk) Mich.	42·35 N	82·30 W
75	Algonquin (ăl-gŏŋ′kwĭn) Ill. (Chicago In.)	42·10 N	88·17 W
81	Algonquin Park Can.	45·50 N	78·20 W
124	Alhama (äl-hä′mä) Sp.	37·00 N	3·59 W
124	Alhama Sp.	37·50 N	1·24 W
74	Alhambra (ăl-hăm′brȧ) Calif. (Los Angeles In.)	34·05 N	118·08 W
115	Al Ḩammām U. A. R.	30·46 N	29·42 E
125	Alhandra (äl-yän′drȧ) Port. (Lisbon In.)	38·55 N	9·01 W
139	Al Haql Sau. Ar. (Palestine In.)	29·15 N	34·57 E
139	Al Harmal Leb. (Palestine In.)	34·23 N	36·22 E
144	Al Hasā (Plain) Sau. Ar.	27·00 N	47·48 E
124	Alhaurín el Grande (ä-lou-rēn′ĕl-grä′n-dĕ) Sp.	36·40 N	4·40 W
144	Al Hijaz (Reg.) Sau. Ar.	23·45 N	39·08 E
125	Alhos Vedros (äl′yōs-vā′drōs) Port. (Lisbon In.)	38·39 N	9·02 W
124	Alhucemas, Baie d′ (B.) Mor.	35·18 N	5·50 W
144	Al Hudaydah Yemen	14·43 N	43·03 E
144	Al Hufūf (Hofuf) (hô-fōōf′) Sau. Ar.	25·15 N	49·43 E
127	Aliákmon (R.) (ål-ê-ák′-mōn) Grc.	40·26 N	22·17 E
125	Alicante (ä-lê-kän′tā) Sp.	38·20 N	0·30 W
125	Alicante, Bahia de (B.) (bä-ē′ä-dĕ-ä-lê-kän′tā) Sp.	38·12 N	0·22 W
76	Alice (ăl′ĭs) Tex.	27·45 N	98·04 W
167	Alice (ăl-ĭs) S. Afr. (Natal In.)	32·47 S	26·51 E
167	Alicedale (ăl′ĭs-dāl) S. Afr. (Natal In.)	33·18 S	26·04 E
158	Alice Springs (ăl′ĭs) Austl.	23·38 S	133·56 E
126	Alicudi (I.) (ä-lē-kōō′dē) It.	38·34 N	14·21 E
136	Alifkulovo (ä-lĭf-kŭ′lô-vô) Sov. Un. (Urals In.)	55·57 N	62·06 E
142	Alīgarh (ä-lê-gŭr′) India	27·58 N	78·08 E
118	Alingsås (ä′lĭŋ-sôs) Swe.	57·57 N	12·30 E
75	Aliquippa (ăl-ĭ-kwĭp′ȧ) Pa. (Pittsburgh In.)	40·37 N	80·15 W
168	Al Iskandarīyah (Alexandria) U. A. R. (Nile In.)	31·12 N	29·58 E
168	Al Ismā′īlīyah (Ismailia) (ēs-mä-ēl′ē-à) U. A. R. (Suez In.)	30·35 N	32·17 E
166	Aliwal North (ä-lē-wäl′) S. Afr.	31·09 S	28·26 E
139	Al Jafr (L.) Jordan (Palestine In.)	30·17 N	36·20 E
165	Al Jaghbūb Libya	29·46 N	24·32 E
165	Al Jawf Libya	24·14 N	23·15 E
144	Al Jawf Sau. Ar.	29·45 N	39·30 E
165	Al Jazirah Libya	25·47 N	21·25 E
124	Aljezur (äl-zhā-zōōr′) Port.	37·18 N	8·52 W
168	Al Jīzah U. A. R. (Nile In.)	30·01 N	31·12 E
165	Al Jufrah (Oasis) Libya	29·30 N	15·16 E
124	Aljustrel (äl-zhōō-strĕl′) Port.	37·44 N	8·23 W
168	Al Kāb U. A. R. (Suez In.)	30·56 N	32·19 E
139	Al Karak (kĕ-räk′) Jordan (Palestine In.)	31·11 N	35·42 E
168	Al Karnak (kär′nak) U. A. R. (Nile In.)	25·42 N	32·43 E
144	Al Khābūrah Mus. & Om.	23·45 N	57·30 E
139	Al Khalīl (Hebron) Jordan (Palestine In.)	31·31 N	35·07 E
165	Al Khums Libya	32·35 N	14·10 E
144	Al Khurmah Sau. Ar.	21·37 N	41·44 E
117	Alkmaar (älk-mär′) Neth.	52·39 N	4·42 E
168	Al Kūbrī (kōō′brē) U. A. R. (Suez In.)	30·01 N	32·35 E
165	Al Kufrah (Oasis) Libya	24·45 N	22·45 E
139	Al Kuntillah U. A. R. (Palestine In.)	29·59 N	34·42 E
144	Al Kuwayt (Kuwait) (koo-wit) Kuwait	29·04 N	47·59 E
164	Allada (ä-lä′dä) Dahomey	6·44 N	2·08 E
115	Al Lādhiqīyah (Latakia) Syr.	35·32 N	35·51 E
82	Allagash (R.) (ăl′ȧ-găsh) Maine	46·50 N	69·24 W
142	Allahābād (ŭl-ŭ-hä-bäd′) India	25·32 N	81·53 E
68	All American can. (ăl ȧ-mĕr′ĭ-kăn) Calif.	32·43 N	115·12 W
111	Alland Aus. (Vienna In.)	48·04 N	16·05 E
124	Allariz (äl-yä-rēth′) Sp.	42·10 N	7·48 W
78	Allatoona (R.) (ăl′ȧ-tōōn′ȧ) Ga.	34·05 N	84·57 W
122	Allauch (ä-lĕ′ōō) Fr. (Marseille In.)	43·21 N	5·30 E
135	Allaykha (ä-lī′kȧ) Sov. Un.	70·32 N	148·53 E
80	Allegan (ăl′ê-găn) Mich.	42·30 N	85·55 W
81	Allegany Ind. Res. (ăl-ê-gā′nĭ) N. Y.	42·05 N	78·55 W
81	Allegheny (R.) Pa.	41·10 N	79·20 W
63	Allegheny Mts U. S.	37·35 N	81·55 W
80	Allegheny Plat U. S.	39·00 N	81·15 W
81	Allegheny Front (Mts.) U. S.	38·12 N	80·03 W
73	Allen (ăl′ĕn) Okla.	34·51 N	96·26 W
116	Allen, Lough (B.) (lŏk ăl′ĕn) Ire.	54·07 N	8·09 W
84	Allendale (ăl′ĕn-dāl) N. J. (New York In.)	41·02 N	74·08 W
79	Allendale S. C.	33·00 N	81·19 W
91	Allende (äl-yĕn′dȧ) Mex.	18·23 N	92·49 W
76	Allende Mex.	28·20 N	100·50 W
81	Allentown (ăl′en-toun) Pa.	40·35 N	75·30 W
143	Alleppey (à-lĕp′ē) India	9·33 N	76·22 E
120	Aller R. (äl′ēr) Ger.	52·43 N	9·50 E
70	Alliance (ȧ-lī′ȧns) Nebr.	42·06 N	102·53 W
80	Alliance Ohio	40·55 N	81·10 W
122	Allier (R.) (à-lyā′) Fr.	46·43 N	3·03 E
84	Alligator Pt. (al′ĭ-gā-tēr) La. (New Orleans In.)	30·57 N	89·41 W
118	Allinge (äl′ĭŋ-ĕ) Den.	55·16 N	14·48 E
92	All Pines (ôl pīnz) Br. Hond. (Yucatan In.)	16·55 N	88·15 W
144	Al Luhayyah Yemen	15·58 N	42·48 E
65	Allyn (ăl′ĭn) Wash. (Seattle In.)	47·23 N	122·51 W
125	Alma (ä-mà) Alg.	36·44 N	1·27 E
82	Alma (ăl′mȧ) Can.	45·36 N	65·01 W
79	Alma Ga.	31·33 N	82·31 W
80	Alma Mich.	43·25 N	84·40 W
72	Alma Nebr.	40·08 N	99·21 W
87	Alma Can.	48·29 N	71·42 W
168	Alma S. Afr. (Johannesburg & Pretoria In.)	24·30 S	28·05 E
71	Alma Wis.	44·21 N	91·57 W
134	Alma-Ata (ăl′mà ȧ′tà) Sov. Un.	43·19 N	77·08 E
125	Almada (äl-mä′dä) Port. (Lisbon In.)	38·40 N	9·09 W
124	Almadén (àl-mà-dhän′) Sp.	38·47 N	4·50 W
144	Al Madīnah Sau. Ar.	24·26 N	39·42 E
139	Al Mafraq Jordan (Palestine In.)	32·21 N	36·13 E
91	Almagre, Laguna (L.) (lä-gōō′nä-äl-mä′grĕ) Mex.	22·48 N	97·45 W
124	Almagro (äl-mä′grō) Sp.	38·52 N	3·41 W
168	Al Mahallah al Kubrá U. A. R. (Nile In.)	31·00 N	31·10 E
144	Al Manāmah Bahrain	26·01 N	50·33 E
68	Almanor (R.) (ăl-măn′ôr) Calif.	40·11 N	121·20 W
124	Almansa (äl-män′sä) Sp.	38·52 N	1·09 W
168	Al Manshāh U. A. R. (Nile In.)	26·31 N	31·46 E
124	Almansor (R.) (äl-män-sôr) Port.	38·41 N	8·27 W
168	Al Manşūrah U. A. R. (Nile In.)	31·02 N	31·25 W
168	Al Manzilah (măn′za-la) U. A. R. (Nile In.)	31·09 N	32·05 E
124	Almanzora (R.) (äl-män-thō′rä) Sp.	37·20 N	2·25 W
168	Al Marāghah U. A. R. (Nile In.)	26·41 N	31·35 E
125	Almargem (äl-mär-zhĕN) Port. (Lisbon In.)	38·51 N	9·16 W
144	Al Mawsil Iraq	36·00 N	42·53 E
124	Almazán (äl-mä-thän′) Sp.	41·30 N	2·33 W
139	Al Mazār Jordan (Palestine In.)	31·04 N	35·41 E
139	Al Mazra′ Jordan (Palestine In.)	31·17 N	35·33 E
124	Almeirim (äl-māī-rēN′) Port.	39·13 N	8·31 W
117	Almelo (äl′mē-lō) Neth.	52·20 N	6·42 E
124	Almendralejo (äl-män-drä-lä′hō) Sp.	38·43 N	6·24 W
124	Almería (äl-mā-rē′ä) Sp.	36·52 N	2·28 W
124	Almeria, Golfo de (G.) (gôl-fô-dĕ-ăl-māī-reN′) Sp.	36·45 N	2·26 W
124	Almería (R.) Sp.	37·00 N	2·40 W
118	Almhult (älm′hōōlt) Swe.	56·35 N	14·08 E
124	Almina, Pta. (äl-mē′nä) Mor.	35·58 N	5·17 W
168	Al Minyā U. A. R. (Nile In.)	28·04 N	30·45 E
93	Almirante (äl-mē-rän′tä) Pan.	9·18 N	82·24 W
93	Almirante, Bahia de (B.) (bä-ē′ä-dĕ-äl-mē-rȧn′tā) Pan.	9·22 N	82·07 W
127	Almirós Grc.	39·13 N	22·47 E
124	Almodóvar (äl-mō-dhō′vär) Sp.	38·43 N	4·10 W
142	Almoi India	29·41 N	79·42 E
90	Almoloya (äl-mō-lō′yä) Mex.	19·32 N	99·44 W
91	Almoloya Mex. (Mexico City In.)	19·11 N	99·28 W
81	Almonte (ăl-mŏn′tē) Can.	45·15 N	76·15 W
124	Almonte (äl-mōn′tā) Sp.	37·16 N	6·32 W
124	Almonte (R.) Sp.	39·35 N	5·50 W
142	Almora India	29·20 N	79·40 E
144	Al Mubarraz Sau. Ar.	22·31 N	46·27 E
139	Al Mudawwarah Jordan (Palestine In.)	29·20 N	36·01 E
144	Al Mukallā Aden	14·27 N	49·05 E
144	Al Mukhā Yemen	13·43 N	43·27 E
124	Almuñécar (äl-mōōn-yā′kär) Sp.	36·44 N	3·43 W
118	Alnö (I.) Swe.	62·20 N	17·39 E
65	Aloha (ä′lō-hä) Ore. (Portland In.)	45·29 N	122·52 W
155	Alor (I.) (ä′lôr) Indon.	8·07 S	125·00 E
124	Álora (ä′lō-rä) Sp.	36·49 N	4·42 W
139	Alor Gajah Mala (Singapore In.)	2·23 N	102·13 E
154	Alor Star (ä′lôr stär) Mala.	6·24 N	100·08 E
65	Alouette (R.) (ä-lōō-ĕt′) Can. (Vancouver In.)	49·16 N	122·32 W
80	Alpena (ăl-pē′nȧ) Mich.	45·05 N	83·30 W
111	Alphen Neth. (Amsterdam In.)	52·07 N	4·38 E
124	Alpiarca (äl-pyȧr′sȧ) Port.	39·38 N	8·37 W
76	Alpine (ăl′pīn) Tex.	30·21 N	103·41 W
114	Alps (Mts.) (ălps) Eur.	46·18 N	8·42 E
98	Alpujarra (äl-pōō-Kȧ′r′rä) Col. (In.)	3·23 N	74·56 W
124	Alpujarras (Mts.) (äl-pōō-här′räs) Sp.	36·55 N	3·25 W
168	Al Qāhirah (Cairo) U. A. R. (Nile In.)	30·03 N	31·17 E
168	Al Qanţarah U. A. R. (Suez In.)	30·51 N	32·20 E
165	Al Qaryah ash Shargiyah Libya	30·36 N	13·13 E
144	Al Qatīf Sau. Ar.	26·30 N	50·00 E
139	Al Qaţranah Jordan (Palestine In.)	31·15 N	36·04 E
144	Al Qaysumah Sau. Ar.	28·30 N	46·27 E
139	Al Quarayyah Sau. Ar. (Palestine In.)	28·43 N	36·11 E
139	Al Qunaytirah Syr. (Palestine In.)	33·09 N	35·49 E
144	Al Qunfidhah Sau. Ar.	18·48 N	41·20 E
168	Al Qurnah (kōōr′na) U. A. R. (Nile In.)	25·44 N	32·39 E
139	Al Quşaymah U. A. R. (Palestine In.)	30·40 N	34·23 E
165	Al Quşayr U. A. R.	26·14 N	34·11 E
139	Al Qusayr U. A. R. (Palestine In.)	34·32 N	36·33 E
118	Als (äls) Den.	55·06 N	9·40 E
123	Alsace (Reg.) (äl-sȧ′s) Fr.	48·25 N	7·24 E
148	Al Shan (Mts.) (äī′shän) China	37·27 N	120·35 E
118	Alsterån (R.) Swe.	56·54 N	15·50 E
74	Altadena (ăl-tȧ-dē′nä) Calif. (Los Angeles In.)	34·12 N	118·08 W
100	Alta Gracia (äl′tä grä′sē-a) Arg.	31·41 S	64·19 W

Page	Name Pronunciation Region	Lat. °′	Long. °′
98	Altagracia................Ven.	10·42 N	71·34 W
99	Altagracia de Orituco (ä′l-tȧ-grȧ′ sēȧ-dĕ-ôrē-tōō′kô). Ven. (In.)	9·53 N	66·22 W
134	Altai Ter...............Sov. Un.	53·39 N	78·52 E
146	Altai Mts. (äl′tī′)..........Asia	49·11 N	87·15 E
74	Alta Loma (ăl′tȧ lō′mä) Calif. (Los Angeles In.)	34·07 N	117·35 W
77	Alta Loma (ăl′tȧ lō-mȧ) Tex. (In.)	29·22 N	95·05 W
79	Altamaha (R.) (ôl-tȧ-mȧ-hô′)..Ga.	31·50 N	82·00 W
99	Altamira (äl-tä-mē′rä)......Braz.	3·13 S	52·14 W
91	Altamira.................Mex.	22·25 N	97·55 W
100	Altamirano (äl-tä-mê-rā′nō)..Arg.	35·26 S	58·12 W
126	Altamura (äl-tä-mōō′rä).......It.	40·40 N	16·35 E
135	Altan Bulag.............Mong.	50·18 N	106·31 E
79	Altavista (äl-tä-vēs′tȧ).......Va.	37·08 N	79·14 W
112	Alten (R.) (äl′tĕn)..........Nor.	69·40 N	24·09 E
120	Altenburg (äl-tĕn-bŏŏrgh)....Ger.	50·59 N	12·27 E
111	Altenmarkt an der Triesting Aus. (Vienna In.)	48·02 N	16·00 E
124	Alter do Chão (äl-tĕr′dŏŏ shäɴ′ōɴ).Port.	39·13 N	7·38 W
90	Altiplanicie Mexicana (Plat.) (äl-tē-plä-nē′syĕ-mĕ-ᴋē-kȧ-nä) Mex.	22·38 N	102·33 W
98	Altiplano (Plat.) (äl-tē-plȧ′nō) Bol.	18·38 S	68·20 W
111	Alt Landsberg (ält länts′bĕrgh) Ger. (Berlin In.)	52·34 N	13·44 E
77	Alto (ăl′tō).................La.	32·21 N	91·52 W
98	Alto Marañón, Rio (R.) (rê′ō-ȧl′tô-mä-rän-yŏ′n).Peru	8·18 S	77·13 W
111	Altomünster (äl′tō-mün′stĕr) Ger. (Munich In.)	48·24 N	11·16 E
85	Alton (ôl′tŭn).Can. (Toronto In.)	43·52 N	80·05 W
74	Alton.........Ill. (St. Louis In.)	38·53 N	90·11 W
161	Altona....Austl. (Melbourne In.)	37·52 S	144·50 E
111	Altona (äl′tō-nȧ) Ger. (Hamburg In).	53·33 N	9·54 E
78	Altoona (ăl-tōō′nȧ)..........Ala.	34·01 N	86·15 W
81	Altoona...................Pa.	40·25 N	78·25 W
65	Altoona.....Wash. (Portland In.)	46·16 N	123·39 W
101	Alto Rio Doce (äl′tô-rē′ô-dō′sĕ) Braz. (Rio de Janeiro In.)	21·02 S	43·23 W
95	Alto Songo (äl-fō-sôŋ′gō)....Cuba	20·10 N	75·45 W
91	Altotonga (äl-tō-tôŋ′gä).....Mex.	19·44 N	97·13 W
95	Alto Velo (I.) (äl-tô-vĕ′lō) Dom. Rep.	17·30 N	71·35 W
110	Altrincham (ôl′trĭng-ăm).....Eng.	53·18 N	2·21 W
111	Alt Ruppin (ält rōō′ppēn) Ger. (Berlin In.)	54·56 N	12·48 E
66	Alturas (ăl-tōō′rȧs).........Calif.	41·29 N	120·33 W
72	Altus (ăl′tŭs)..............Okla.	34·38 N	99·20 W
165	Al ‘Ugaylah...............Libya	30·15 N	19·07 E
165	Al Ujaylāt................Libya	32·45 N	12·27 E
128	Alūksne (ä′lŏŏks-nĕ).....Sov. Un.	57·24 N	27·04 E
168	Alula (ä-lōō′lä) Som. (Horn of Afr. In.)	11·53 N	50·40 E
81	Alumette I. (ȧ-lü-mĕt′)......Can.	45·50 N	77·00 W
168	Al Uqşur (Luxor) U. A. R. (Nile In.)	25·38 N	32·59 E
129	Alushta (ä′lŏŏsh-tȧ).....Sov. Un.	44·39 N	34·23 E
72	Alva (ăl′vȧ)...............Okla.	36·46 N	98·41 W
65	Alvarado (ăl-vȧ-rā′dō) Calif (San Francisco In.)	37·35 N	122·05 W
91	Alvarado (äl-vä-rä′dhō).....Mex.	18·48 N	95·45 W
91	Alvarado, Luguna de (L.) (lä-gŏŏ′nä-dĕ-äl-vä-rȧ′dô)..Mex.	18·44 N	96·45 W
118	Älvdalen (ĕlv′dä-lĕn)........Swe.	61·14 N	14·04 E
125	Alverca (al-vĕr′kȧ) Port. (Lisbon In.)	38·53 N	9·02 W
118	Alvesta (äl-vĕs′tä)..........Swe.	56·55 N	14·29 E
77	Alvin (ăl′vĭn)..........Tex. (In.)	29·25 N	95·14 W
101	Alvinópolis (äl-vēnō′pō-lês) Braz. (Rio de Janeiro In.)	20·07 S	43·03 W
65	Alviso (ăl-vī′sō) Calif. (San Francisco In.)	37·26 N	121·59 W
144	Al Wajh................Sau. Ar.	26·15 N	36·32 E
142	Alwar (ŭl′wŭr).............India	27·39 N	76·39 E
168	Al Wāsiţah....U. A. R. (Nile In.)	29·21 N	31·15 E
119	Alytus (ä′lê-tŏŏs).......Sov. Un.	54·25 N	24·05 E
118	Åmå (ô′môl)...............Swe.	59·05 N	12·40 E
90	Amacuzac (R.) (ä-mä-kōō-zȧk) Mex.	18·00 N	99·03 W
158	Amadeus, (L.) (ăm-ȧ-dē′ŭs).Austl.	24·30 S	131·25 E
87	Amadjuak (L.) (ä-mădj′wăk).Can.	64·50 N	69·20 W
153	Amagasaki (ä′mä-gä-sä′kê) Jap. (Osaka In.)	34·43 N	135·25 E
153	Amakusa-Shimo (I.) (ämä-kōō′sä shē-mō).Jap.	32·24 N	129·35 E
98	Amalfi (ä′mȧ′l-fē)......Col. (In.)	6·55 N	75·04 W
125	Amalfi (ä-mä′l-fê).It. (Naples In.)	40·23 N	14·36 E
127	Amaliás (ȧ-mäl′yȧs)........Grc.	37·48 N	21·23 E
142	Amalner..................India	21·07 N	75·06 E
99	Amambay, Cordillera de (Mts.) Braz.	20·06 S	57·08 W
152	Amami Guntō (Is.) (ä′mä′mē gŏŏn′tō′).Jap.	28·25 N	129·00 E
152	Amamio (I.) (ä-mä′mē-ō)....Jap.	28·10 N	129·55 E
167	Amanzimtoti...S. Afr. (Natal In.)	30·02 S	30·54 E
99	Amapá (ä-mä-pȧ′).........Braz.	2·14 N	50·48 W
99	Amapá (Ter.)..............Braz.	1·15 N	52·15 W
92	Amapala (ä-mä-pä′lä)......Hond.	13·16 N	87·39 W
99	Amarante (ä-mä-rän′tā).....Braz.	6·17 S	42·43 W
68	Amargosa (R.) (ȧ′mär-gō′sȧ) Calif.	35·55 N	116·45 W
72	Amarillo (ăm-ȧ-rĭl′ō)........Tex.	35·14 N	101·49 W
126	Amaro, Mt. (ä-mä′rō).........It.	42·07 N	14·07 E
133	Amasya (ä-mä′sê-ȧ).........Tur.	40·40 N	35·50 E
91	Amatenango (ä-mä-tā-naŋ′gō) Mex.	16·30 N	92·29 W
64	Amatignak (I.) (ä-mȧ′tê-näk) Alaska	51·12 N	178·30 W
92	Amatique, Bahía de (B.) (bä-ē′ä-dĕ-ä-mä-tē′kā).Guat.-Br. Hond.	15·58 N	88·50 W
92	Amatitlán (ä-mä-tê-tlän′)..Guat.	14·27 N	90·39 W
90	Amatlán de Cañas (ä-mät-län′dā kän-yäs).Mex.	20·50 N	104·22 W
98	Amazonas Selvas (Reg.) (ä-mä-thō′näs).Braz.	4·15 S	64·30 W
99	Amazonas, Rio (R.) (rē′ō-ä-mä-thō′näs).Braz.	2·03 S	53·18 W
142	Ambala (ŭm-bä′lŭ).........India	30·31 N	76·48 E
98	Ambalema (äm-bä-lā′mä) Col. (In.)	4·47 N	74·45 W
135	Ambarchik (ŭm-bär′chĭk) Sov. Un.	69·39 N	162·18 E
98	Ambato (äm-bä′tō)..........Ec.	1·15 S	78·44 W
167	Ambatosoratra (ämbä′tōō-sōōr-ä′trŭ).Malag. Rep.	17·44 S	48·41 E
120	Amberg (äm′bĕrgh).........Ger.	49·26 N	11·51 E
95	Ambergris Cays (Is.) (ăm′bẽr-grēs kāz) Caicos	21·20 N	71·40 W
92	Ambergris I. Br. Hond. (Yucatan In.)	18·04 N	87·43 W
123	Ambérieu (äɴ-bā-rê-û′).......Fr.	45·57 N	5·21 E
122	Ambert (äɴ-bĕr′).............Fr.	45·32 N	3·41 E
155	Ambil (I.) (äm′bēl) Phil. (Manila In.)	13·51 N	120·25 E
84	Ambler (ăm′blẽr) Pa. (Philadelphia In.)	40·09 N	75·13 W
155	Amboina (ăm-boi′nȧ)......Indon.	3·45 S	128·17 E
155	Amboina (I.).............Indon.	4·50 S	128·45 E
122	Amboise (äɴ-bwăz′)..........Fr.	47·25 N	0·56 E
167	Ambositra (äɴ-bô-sē′trä) Malag. Rep.	20·31 S	47·28 E
80	Amboy (ăm′boi).............Ill.	41·41 N	89·15 W
65	Amboy.....Wash. (Portland In.)	45·55 N	122·27 W
167	Ambre, Cap d′ (C.)..Malag. Rep.	12·06 S	49·15 E
75	Ambridge (ăm′brĭdj) Pa. (Pittsburgh In.)	40·36 N	80·13 W
159	Ambrim (I.)..........New Heb.	16·28 S	158·17 E
166	Ambriz...................Ang.	7·50 S	15·10 E
166	Ambrizete.................Ang.	7·15 S	12·50 E
64	Amchitka P. (ăm-chĭt′kȧ)..Alaska	51·30 N	179·36 W
90	Amealco (ä-mā-äl′kō).......Mex.	20·12 N	100·08 W
90	Ameca (ä-mĕ′kä)...........Mex.	20·34 N	104·02 W
91	Amecameca (ä-mȧ-kä-mā′kä) Mex. (Mexico City In.)	19·06 N	98·46 W
111	Ameide...Neth. (Amsterdam In.)	51·57 N	4·57 E
117	Ameland (I.).............Neth.	53·29 N	5·54 E
75	Amelia (ȧ-mēl′yā) Ohio (Cincinnati In.)	39·01 N	84·12 W
68	American (R.) (ȧ-mĕr′ĭ-kăn) Calif.	38·37 N	121·19 W
101	Americana (ä-mĕ-rê-kȧ′nȧ) Braz. (Rio de Janeiro In.)	22·46 S	47·19 W
67	American Falls (ȧ-mĕr-ĭ-kăn).Idaho	42·45 N	112·53 W
67	American Falls Res........Idaho	42·56 N	113·18 W
69	American Fork.............Utah	40·20 N	111·50 W
47	American Highland.........Ant.	72·00 S	79·00 E
78	Americus (ȧ-mĕr′ĭ-kŭs).......Ga.	32·04 N	84·15 W
111	Amersfoort (ä′mĕrz-fōrt) Neth. (Amsterdam In.)	52·08 N	5·23 E
86	Amery (ā′mẽr-ê)...........Can.	56·32 N	93·58 W
71	Amery....................Wis.	45·19 N	92·24 W
71	Ames (āmz)...............Iowa	42·00 N	93·36 W
83	Amesbury (āmz′bẽr-ê) Mass. (Boston In.)	42·51 N	70·56 W
127	Ámfissa (ȧm-fĭ′sȧ)..........Grc.	38·32 N	22·26 E
135	Amga (ŭm-gä′).........Sov. Un.	61·08 N	132·09 E
135	Amga (R.)............Sov. Un.	61·41 N	133·11 E
135	Amgun (R.)...........Sov. Un.	53·33 N	137·57 E
165	Amhara (Prov.) (äm-hä′rä)..Eth.	11·30 N	36·45 E
82	Amherst (ăm′hẽrst).........Can.	45·49 N	64·14 W
75	Amherst.....Ohio (Cleveland In.)	41·24 N	82·13 W
81	Amherst (I.)...............Can.	44·10 N	76·40 W
122	Amiens (ä-myäɴ′)............Fr.	49·54 N	2·18 E
142	Amio Tsönag Tsho (L.)....China	31·38 N	91·18 E
47	Amirante Is.............Ind. O.	6·02 S	52·30 E
77	Amite (ă-mēt′)..............La.	30·43 N	90·32 W
77	Amite R...................La.	30·45 N	90·48 W
75	Amity (ăm′ĭ-tĭ) Pa. (Pittsburgh In.)	40·02 N	80·11 W
84	Amityville (ăm′ĭ-tĭ-vĭl) N. Y. (New York In.)	40·41 N	73·24 W
64	Amlia (I.) (ȧ′m-lêä).......Alaska	52·00 N	173·28 W
139	‘Ammān (äm′ mȧn) Jordan (Palestine In.)	31·57 N	35·57 E
111	Ammer L. (äm′mĕr) Ger. (Munich In.)	48·00 N	11·08 E
74	Amnicon R. (ăm′nė-kŏn) Wis. (Duluth In.)	46·35 N	91·56 W
	Amnok, see Yalu		
	Amnok, see Yalu (R.)		
142	Amod....................India	21·47 N	72·58 E
127	Amorgós (I.) (ä-môr′gōs).....Grc.	36·47 N	25·47 E
78	Amory (ăm′o-rē)..........Miss.	33·58 N	88·27 W
87	Amos (ā′mŭs)..............Can.	48·31 N	78·04 W
118	Åmot (Torpen) (ô′mōt) (tôr′pĕn) Nor.	61·08 N	11·17 E
	Amoy, see Hsiamen		
101	Amparo (äm-pȧ′-rô) Braz. (Rio de Janeiro In.)	22·43 S	46·44 W
111	Amper R. (äm′pĕr) Ger. (Munich In.)	48·18 N	11·32 E
125	Amposta (äm-pōs′tä).........Sp.	40·42 N	0·34 E
82	Amqui.....................Can.	48·27 N	67·27 W
142	Amraoti (ŭm-rŭ-ô′tê).......India	20·58 N	77·47 E
142	Amritsar (ŭm-rĭt′sŭr).......India	31·43 N	74·52 E
111	Amstelveen Neth. (Amsterdam In.)	52·18 N	4·51 E
111	Amsterdam (äm-stẽr-däm′) Neth. (Amsterdam In.)	52·21 N	4·52 E
81	Amsterdam (ăm′stẽr-dăm)..N. Y.	42·55 N	74·10 W
47	Amsterdam (I.).........Ind. O.	37·52 S	77·32 E
120	Amstetten (äm′stĕt-ĕn)......Aus.	48·09 N	14·53 E
165	Am Timan (äm′tê-män′)....Chad	11·18 N	20·30 E
144	Amu Dar′ya (Oxus) (R.) (ä-mŏŏ-dä′rēä).Asia	40·40 N	62·47 E
142	Amu Dar′ye (R.) (ä-mōō dä′rēä) Afg.-Sov. Un.	36·50 N	66·58 E
64	Amukta P. (ä-mōōk′tȧ)....Alaska	52·30 N	172·00 W
155	Amulung (ä′mōō′lōōng) Phil. (Manila In.)	17·51 N	121·43 E
86	Amundsen G. (ä′mŭn-sĕn)...Can.	70·17 N	23·28 W
47	Amundsen Sea.............Ant.	72·00 S	110·00 W
118	Amungen (L.)..............Swe.	61·07 N	16·00 E
150	Amur R. (ä-mŏŏr′) China and Sov. Un.	49·38 N	127·25 E
136	Amurskiy (ä-mûr′skĭ) Sov. Un. (Urals In.)	52·35 N	59·36 E
152	Amurskiy, Zaliv (B.) (zä′lĭf ä-mŏŏr′skĭ).Sov. Un.	43·20 N	131·40 E
90	Amusgos (San Pedro) (ä-mōō′s-gôs) (sän-pĕ′drō).Mex.	16·39 N	98·09 W
155	Amuyao, Mt. (ä-mōō-yä′ō) Phil. (Manila In.)	17·04 N	121·09 E
127	Amvrakikos Kólpos (G.).....Grc.	39·00 N	21·00 E
139	Amyun.......Leb. (Palestine In.)	34·18 N	35·48 E
135	Anabar (R.) (ăn-ȧ-bär′)..Sov. Un.	71·15 N	113·00 E
99	Anaco (ä-nȧ′kô)........Ven. (In.)	9·29 N	64·27 W
67	Anaconda (ăn-ȧ-kŏn′dȧ)....Mont.	46·07 N	112·55 W
65	Anacortes (ăn-ȧ-kôr′tĕz) Wash. (Seattle In.)	48·30 N	122·37 W
72	Anadarko (ăn-ȧ-där′kō).....Okla.	35·05 N	98·14 W
135	Anadyr (ŭ-nȧ-dĭr′)......Sov. Un.	64·47 N	177·01 E
135	Anadyr (R.)...........Sov. Un.	65·30 N	172·45 E
139	Anadyrskiy Zaliv (B.)...Sov. Un.	64·10 N	178·00 W
74	Anaheim (ăn′ȧ-hīm) Calif. (Los Angeles In.)	33·50 N	117·55 W
77	Anahuac (ä-nä′wäk)....Tex. (In.)	29·46 N	94·41 W
143	Anai Mudi Mt.............India	15·28 N	77·10 E
94	Ana María, Cayos (Is.) (kä′yōs-ä′nȧ mȧ-rē′ȧ).Cuba	21·55 N	78·50 W
154	Anambas, Pulau-Pulau (Is.) (ä-näm-bäs).Indon.	2·41 N	106·38 E
71	Anamosa (ăn-ȧ-mō′sȧ).......Iowa	42·06 N	91·18 W
129	Anan′yev (ȧ-nä′nyĕf)....Sov. Un.	47·43 N	29·59 E
129	Anapa (ȧ-nä′pä)........Sov. Un.	44·54 N	37·19 E
99	Anápolis (ä-nȧ′pō-lês).......Braz.	16·17 S	48·47 W
100	Añatuya (ȧ-nyä-tōō′yȧ)......Arg.	28·22 S	62·45 W
122	Ancenis (äɴ-sē-nē′)...........Fr.	47·24 N	1·12 W
100	Anchieta (ȧn-chyĕ′tä)..Braz. (In.)	22·49 S	43·24 W
64	Anchitka (I.) (än-chĕ′t-kä).Alaska	51·25 N	178·10 E
148	Anch′ iu (än′chê)..........China	36·26 N	119·12 E
110	Ancholme (R.) (ăn′chŭm)...Eng.	53·28 N	0·27 W
77	Anchor (ăŋ′kẽr)........Tex. (In.)	29·13 N	95·28 W
64	Anchorage (ăŋ′kẽr-ȧj).....Alaska	61·12 N	149·48 W
75	Anchorage....Ky. (Louisville In.)	38·16 N	85·32 W
85	Ancienne-Lorette (äɴ-syĕn′ lō-rĕt′).Can. (Quebec In.)	46·48 N	71·21 W
88	Ancon (äŋ-kōn′) C. Z. (Panama Canal In.)	8·55 N	79·32 W
126	Ancona (än-kō′nä)............It.	43·37 N	13·32 E
100	Ancud (äŋ-kōōdh′).........Chile	41·52 S	73·45 W
100	Ancud, G. de (gôl-fô-dĕ-äŋ-kōōdh′).Chile	41·15 S	73·00 W
100	Andalgalá (ȧ′n-däl-gȧ-lȧ′)....Arg.	27·35 S	66·14 W
124	Andalucia (Reg.) (än-dä-lōō-sê′ä).Sp.	37·35 N	5·40 W
78	Andalusia (ăn-dȧ-lōō′zhĭȧ)....Ala.	31·19 N	86·19 W
154	Andaman Is. (ăn-dȧ-măn′)..India	11·38 N	92·17 E
154	Andaman Sea..............Asia	12·44 N	95·45 E
111	Anderlecht (än′dẽr-lĕkt) Bel. (Brussels In.)	50·49 N	4·16 E
120	Andernach (än′dẽr-näᴋ)......Ger.	50·25 N	7·23 E
101	Anderson (ȧ′n-dĕr-sōn) Arg. (Buenos Aires In.)	35·15 S	60·15 W
66	Anderson (ăn′dẽr-sŭn)......Calif.	40·28 N	122·19 W
80	Anderson..................Ind.	40·05 N	85·50 W
79	Anderson.................S. C.	34·30 N	82·40 W
86	Anderson (R.)..............Can.	68·32 N	125·12 W
98	Andes (ăn′dēz) (än′dās).Col. (In.)	5·40 N	75·54 W
96	Andes Mts................S. A.	13·00 S	75·00 W
143	Andhei.......India (Bombay In.)	19·08 N	72·50 E
143	Andhra Pradesh (State).....India	22·00 N	78·50 E
115	Andikíthira (I.).............Grc.	35·50 N	23·20 E
134	Andizhan (än-dê-zhän′)..Sov. Un.	40·51 N	72·39 E
152	Andong (än′dŭng′)..........Kor.	36·31 N	128·42 E
125	Andorra (än-dôr′rä).........And.	42·38 N	1·30 E
125	Andorra...................Eur.	42·32 N	1·18 E
83	Andover (ăn′dô-vẽr) Mass. (Boston In.)	42·39 N	71·08 W
84	Andover....N. J. (New York In.)	40·59 N	74·45 W
112	Andöy (I.) (änd-ûê).........Nor.	69·12 N	14·58 E
125	Andraitx (än-drȧ-ĭtsh′).......Sp.	39·34 N	2·25 E
64	Andreanof Is. (än-drȧ-ä′nôf) Alaska	51·10 N	177·00 W
101	Andrelândia (än-drĕ-lȧ′n-dyȧ) Braz. (Rio de Janeiro In.)	21·45 S	44·18 W
82	Andréville................Can.	47·40 N	69·44 W
78	Andrew Johnson Natl Mon. (ăn′drōō jŏn′sŭn).Tenn.	36·15 N	82·55 W
78	Andrews (ăn′drōōz)........N. C.	35·12 N	83·48 W
79	Andrews..................S. C.	33·25 N	79·32 W
129	Andreyevka (än-drȧ-yĕf′kȧ) Sov. Un.	48·03 N	37·03 E
126	Andria (än′drê-ä)............It.	41·17 N	15·55 E
127	Andros (än′dhrôs)...........Grc.	37·50 N	24·54 E
94	Andros I. (ăn′drŏs)........Ba. Is.	24·30 N	78·00 W
127	Andrós (I.) (ȧn′dhrôs).......Grc.	37·59 N	24·55 E
82	Androscoggin (R.) (ăn-drŭs-kŏg′ĭn).Maine	44·25 N	70·45 W
124	Andújar (än-dŏŏ′här)..........Sp.	38·04 N	4·03 W
164	Anécho (ȧ-nā′chō)..........Togo	6·25 N	1·36 E
153	Anegasaki (ä′mȧ-gä-sä′kê) Jap. (Tōkyō In.)	35·29 N	140·02 E
159	Aneityum (I.) (ä-nȧ-ē′tê-ŭm) New Hebr.	20·15 S	169·49 E
70	Aneta (ă-nē′tȧ)............N. D.	47·41 N	97·57 W
155	Angadanan (äŋ-gȧ-dä′nȧn) Phil. (Manila In.)	16·45 N	121·45 E
155	Angaki (än-gä′kê) Phil. (Manila In.)	17·10 N	120·40 E

ăt; finăl; rāte; senâte; ärm; ȧsk; sofȧ; fâre; ch-choose; dh-as th in other; bē; êvent; bĕt; recĕnt; cratẽr; g-go; gh-guttural g; bĭt; ĭ-short neutral; rīde; ᴋ-guttural k as ch in German ich;

Page	Name Pronunciation Region	Lat. °′	Long. °′
90	Angamacutiro (än'gä-mä-kōō-tē'rō). Mex.	20·08 N	101·44 W
150	Angangchi (än'gäng'kē'). China	47·05 N	123·58 E
90	Angangueo (än-gäŋ'gwå-ō). Mex.	19·36 N	100·18 W
	Angara (R.), see Verkhnyaya Tunguska		
134	Angarsk. Sov. Un.	52·48 N	104·15 E
118	Ånge (ông'ĕ). Swe.	62·31 N	15·39 E
99	Angel, Salto (Falls) (säl'tō-ä'n-hĕl). Ven.	5·44 N	62·27 W
88	Angel De La Guarda (I.) (ä'n-hĕl-dĕ-lä-gwä'r-dä). Mex.	29·30 N	113·00 W
155	Angeles (än'hå-lās) Phil. (Manila In.)	15·09 N	120·35 E
118	Ängelholm (ĕng'ĕl-hôlm). Swe.	56·14 N	12·50 E
77	Angelina R. (ăn-jė lē'nȧ). Tex.	31·30 N	94·53 W
68	Angels Camp (ān'jĕls kămp') Calif.	38·03 N	120·33 W
112	Angermanälven (R.). Swe.	64·02 N	17·15 E
123	Angermund (än'ngĕr-mŭnd) Ger. (Ruhr In.)	51·20 N	6·47 E
120	Angermünde (äng'ĕr-mûn-dĕ). Ger.	53·02 N	14·00 E
85	Angers (äN-zhā') Can. (Ottawa In.)	41·31 N	75·29 W
122	Angers. Fr.	47·29 N	0·36 W
154	Angkor (Ruins) (äng'kôr). Camb.	13·52 N	103·50 E
116	Anglesey (I.) (ăŋ'g'l-sė). Wales	52·28 N	4·35 W
77	Angleton (aŋ'g'l-tŭn). Tex. (In.)	29·10 N	95·25 W
87	Angliers. Can.	47·29 N	79·16 W
49	Angmagssalik (äŋ-mä'sȧ-lĭk) Grnld.	65·40 N	37·40 W
167	Angoche, Ilhas de (Is.) (ē'läs-dĕ-än-gō'chä). Moz.	16·03 S	40·17 E
100	Angol (äŋ-gōl'). Chile	37·47 S	72·43 W
80	Angola (ăŋ-gō'lȧ). Ind.	41·35 N	85·00 W
163	Angola (Portuguese West Africa) Afr.	14·15 S	16·00 E
	Angora, see Ankara		
122	Angoulême (äŋ-gōō-lâm'). Fr.	45·40 N	0·09 E
101	Angra dos Reis (aŋ'-grä dōs rā'ēs) Braz. (Rio de Janeiro In.)	23·01 S	44·17 W
125	Angri (ä'n-grê). It. (Naples In.)	40·30 N	14·35 E
94	Anguilla, Cays (Is.) (ăŋ-gwĭl'ȧ) Ba. Is.	23·30 N	79·35 W
93	Anguilla I. St. Kitts-Nevis-Anguilla (Le. & Wind. Is. In.)	18·15 N	62·54 W
83	Anguille, C. (äŋ-gē'yĕ). Can.	47·58 N	59·35 W
118	Anholt (I.) (än'hŏlt). Den.	56·43 N	11·34 E
146	Anhsi. China	40·36 N	95·49 E
147	Anhui (Anhwei) (Prov.). China	31·23 N	116·53 E
64	Aniak (ä-nyä'k). Alaska	61·32 N	159·35 W
125	Aniene (ä-nyĕ'nĕ). It. (Rome In.)	41·54 N	12·49 E
69	Animas (R.) (ä'nê-mås). Colo.	37·03 N	107·50 W
127	Anina (ä-nē'nä). Rom.	45·03 N	21·50 E
81	Anita (ȧ-nē'ȧ). Pa.	41·05 N	79·00 W
152	Aniva, Mys (Pt.) (mĭs ȧ-nē'vȧ) Sov. Un.	46·08 N	143·13 E
152	Aniva, Zaliv (B.) (zä'lĭf ȧ-nē'vȧ) Sov. Un.	46·28 N	143·30 E
167	Anjouan (I.) (äN-zhwäN) Comores, Arch. des	12·14 S	44·47 E
150	Ank'ang. China	32·38 N	109·10 E
133	Ankara (Angora) (än'kȧ-rȧ) (äŋ-gō'rȧ). Tur.	39·55 N	32·50 E
151	Anking (Huaining) (än'kĭng') China	30·32 N	117·00 E
120	Anklam (än'kläm). Ger.	53·52 N	13·43 E
166	Ankoro (äŋ-kō'rō). Con. L.	6·48 S	26·45 E
148	Ankou (än'gō̤ ŭ). China	38·27 N	115·19 E
151	Anlu (än'lōō'). China	31·18 N	113·40 E
151	Anlung. China	25·01 N	105·32 E
81	Ann, C. (ăn). Mass.	42·40 N	70·40 W
73	Anna (ăn'ȧ). Ill.	37·28 N	89·15 W
129	Anna (än'ä). Sov. Un.	51·31 N	40·27 E
[illegible]	Annaberg-Buchols (än'ȧ-bĕrgh). Ger.	50·35 N	13·02 E
	An Nafud (Des.). Sau. Ar.	28·23 N	39·30 E
	An Najaf (än nä-jäf'). Iraq	31·30 N	44·31 E
	An Nakhl. U. A. R. (Palestine In.)	29·55 N	33·45 E
	Annamitic Cord. Mts. (ă-nȧ-mĭt'ĭk kôr-dĭl-yä'rȧ). Laos-Viet.	17·34 N	105·38 E
8[illegible]	Annapolis (ă-năp'ô-lĭs). Md.	39·00 N	76·25 W
82	Annapolis Royal. Can.	44·44 N	65·32 W
80	Ann Arbor (ăn är'bĕr). Mich.	42·15 N	83·45 W
165	An Nawfalīyah. Libya	30·57 N	17·38 E
123	Annecy (än'sē'). Fr.	45·54 N	6·07 E
123	Annemasse (än'mäs'). Fr.	46·09 N	6·13 E
136	Annenskoye (ä-nĕn'skō-yĕ) Sov. Un. (Urals In.)	53·09 N	60·25 E
78	Anniston (ăn'ĭs-tŭn). Ala.	33·39 N	85·47 W
163	Annobon (I.) (ăn-nō-bōn'). Atl. O.	2·00 S	3·30 E
122	Annonay (ȧ-nô-nĕ'). Fr.	45·16 N	4·36 E
94	Annotto Bay (än-nō'tō). Jam.	18·15 N	76·45 W
74	Anoka (ȧ-nō'kȧ) Minn. (Minneapolis, St. Paul In.)	45·12 N	93·24 W
98	Anori (ȧ-nō'rê). (Col. In.)	7·01 N	75·09 W
127	Áno Theológos. Grc.	40·37 N	24·41 E
126	Áno Viánnos. Grc. (Inset)	35·52 N	25·26 E
151	Anp'u. China	21·28 N	110·00 E
120	Ansbach (äns'bäk). Ger.	49·18 N	10·35 E
95	Anse à Veau (äNs' ä-vō'). Hai.	18·30 N	73·25 W
95	Anse d' Hainault (äNs'dĕnō). Hai	18·45 N	74·25 W
98	Anserma (ä'n-sĕ'r-mȧ). Col. (In.)	5·13 N	75·47 W
98	Ansermanuevo(ä'n-sĕ'r-mä-nwĕ'vō) Col. (In.)	4·47 N	75·59 W
150	Anshan. China	41·00 N	123·00 E
151	Anshun (än-shōōn'). China	26·12 N	105·50 E
76	Anson (ăn'sŭn). Tex.	32·45 N	99·52 W
158	Anson B. Austl.	13·10 S	34·25 E
152	Ansŏng (än'sŭng'). Kor.	37·00 N	127·12 E
81	Ansonia (ăn-sō'nĭ-ȧ). Conn.	41·20 N	73·05 W
150	Antachan. China	41·20 N	125·20 E
133	Antakya (än-täk'yä). U. A. R.	36·20 N	36·10 E
133	Antalya (Adalia) (än-tä'lê-ä) (ä-dä'lê-ä). Tur.	37·00 N	30·50 E
133	Antalya Körfezi (G.). Tur.	36·40 N	31·20 E
47	Antarctica.	80·15 S	127·00 E
67	Antelope Cr. (ăn'tê-lōp). Wyo.	43·29 N	105·42 W
74	Antelope I. Utah (Salt Lake City In.)	40·39 N	112·07 W
124	Antequera (än-tĕ-kĕ'rä). Sp.	37·01 N	4·34 W
72	Anthony (ăn'thô-nê). Kans.	37·08 N	98·01 W
123	Antibes (äN-tēb'). Fr.	43·36 N	7·12 E
83	Anticosti I. (ăn-tĭ-kŏs'tê). Can.	49·40 N	62·00 W
71	Antigo (ăn'tĭ-gō). Wis.	45·09 N	89·11 W
83	Antigonish (ăn-tĭ-gô-nêsh'). Can.	45·39 N	61·59 W
92	Antigua (än-tē'gwä). Guat.	14·32 N	90·43 W
91	Antigua (R.). Mex.	19·16 N	96·36 W
93	Antigua I. N. A. (Le. & Wind. Is. In.)	17·07 N	61·32 W
91	Antigua Veracruz (än-tē'gwä vā-rä-krōōz'). Mex.	19·18 N	96·17 W
95	Antilla (än-tē'lyä). Cuba	20·50 N	75·50 W
89	Antilles, Greater (Is.). N. A.	20·30 N	79·15 W
89	Antilles, Lesser (Is.). N. A.	12·15 N	65·00 W
65	Antioch (ăn'tĭ-ŏk) Calif. (San Francisco In.)	38·00 N	121·48 W
75	Antioch. Ill. (Chicago In.)	42·29 N	88·06 W
70	Antioch. Nebr.	42·05 N	102·36 W
98	Antioquia (än-tê-ō'kêä). Col. (In.)	6·34 N	75·49 W
98	Antioquia (Dept.). Col. (In.)	6·48 N	75·42 W
73	Antlers (ănt'-lērz). Okla.	34·14 N	95·38 W
100	Antofagasta (än-tô-fä-gäs'tä) Chile	23·32 S	70·21 W
100	Antofalla, Salar de (Des.) (sä-lär'de ȧn'tō-fä'lä). Arg.	26·00 S	67·52 W
93	Antón (än-tōn'). Pan.	8·24 N	80·15 W
167	Antongil, Baie d' (B.) (äN-tôN-zhēl'). Malagasy	16·15 S	50·15 E
101	Antonio Carlos (än-tō'nĕōō-kä'r-lôs) Braz. (Rio de Janeiro In.)	21·19 S	43·45 W
167	António Enes (än-to'nyō ĕn'ēs) Moz.	16·13 S	39·58 E
72	Antonito (ăn-tô-nē'tō). Colo.	37·04 N	106·01 W
128	Antonopole (än'tô-nô-pō lyĕ) Sov. Un.	56·19 N	27·11 E
116	Antrim Mts. (ăn'trĭm). N. Ire.	54·60 N	6·15 W
167	Antsirabe (änt-sê-rä'bä) Malag. Rep.	19·49 S	47·16 E
	Antsirane, see Diégo-Suarez		
128	Antsla (änt'slȧ). Sov. Un.	57·49 N	26·29 E
100	Antuco (Vol.) (än-tōō'kō). Chile	37·30 S	72·30 W
150	Antung (än'tōōng'). China	40·10 N	124·30 E
148	Antungwei (ändōōngwä). China	35·08 N	119·19 E
	Antwerp, see Antwerpen		
111	Antwerpen (Antwerp) (änt'wĕrpĕn). Bel. (Brussels In.)	51·13 N	4·24 E
150	Antz'u. China (Peking In.)	39·23 N	116·44 E
142	Anun (R.). Nepal	27·18 N	86·51 E
142	Anūpgarh (ŭ-nōōp'-gŭr). India	29·22 N	73·20 E
143	Anurādhapura (ŭ-nōō'rä-dŭ-pōō'rŭ) Ceylon	8·24 N	80·25 E
148	Anyang (än'yäng). China	36·05 N	114·22 E
119	Anykščiai (aniksh-chä'ê). Sov. Un.	55·34 N	25·04 E
98	Anzá (än-zä'). Col. (In.)	6·19 N	75·51 W
134	Anzhero-Sudzhensk ((än'zhâ-rô-sōōd'zhĕnsk). Sov. Un.	56·08 N	86·08 E
125	Anzio (änt'zê-ō). It. (Rome In.)	41·28 N	12·39 E
99	Anzoategui (State) (än-zôä'tĕ-gê) Ven. (In.)	9·38 N	64·45 W
152	Aomori (äô-mō'rê). Jap.	40·45 N	140·52 E
126	Aosta (ä-ôs'tä). It.	45·45 N	7·20 E
165	Aouk, Bahr (R.) (ä-ōōk'). Chad	9·30 N	20·45 E
78	Apalachicola (ăp-ȧ-lăch-ĭ-kō'lȧ) Fla.	29·43 N	84·59 W
91	Apan (ä-pä'n) Mex. (Mexico City In.)	19·43 N	98·27 W
90	Apango (ä-päŋ'gō). Mex.	17·41 N	99·22 W
98	Apaporis (R.) (ä-pä-pô'rĭs). Col.	0·48 N	72·32 W
154	Aparri (ä-pär'rē). Phil.	18·15 N	121·40 E
90	Apasco (ä-pä's-kō). Mex.	20·33 N	100·43 W
127	Apatin (ŏ'pŏ-tĭn). Yugo.	45·40 N	19·00 E
90	Apatzingán de la Constitución (ä-pät-zĭŋ-gän'dä lä cōn-stĭ-tōō-sê-ōn'). Mex.	19·07 N	102·21 W
117	Apeldoorn (ä'pĕl-dōōrn). Neth.	52·14 N	5·55 E
98	Apía (ä-pē'ä). Col. (In.)	5·07 N	75·58 W
90	Apipilulco (ä-pĭ-pĭ-lōōl'kō). Mex.	18·09 N	99·40 W
127	Apíranthos. Grc.	37·07 N	25·32 E
72	Apishapa (R.) (ăp-ĭ-shä'pȧ). Colo.	37·40 N	104·08 W
90	Apizaco (ä-pê-zä'kō). Mex.	19·18 N	98·11 W
155	Apo (Mtn.) (ä'pō). Phil.	6·56 N	125·05 E
79	Apoka (ä-pŏp'kȧ). Fla. (In.)	28·37 N	81·30 W
79	Apoka (L.). Fla. (In.)	28·38 N	81·50 W
71	Apostle Is. (ă-pŏs'l). Wis.	97·03 N	90·55 W
78	Appalachia (ăpȧ-lăch'ĭ-ȧ). Va.	36·54 N	82·49 W
63	Appalachian Mts. (ăp-ȧ-lăch'ĭ-ȧn). U. S.	37·20 N	82·00 W
78	Appalachicola R. (ăpȧ-lăch'ĭ-cōlȧ) Fla.	30·11 N	85·00 W
118	Äppelbo (ĕp-ĕl-bōō). Swe.	60·30 N	14·02 E
123	Appelhülsen (ä'pĕl-hül'-sĕn) Ger. (Ruhr In.)	51·55 N	7·26 E
126	Appennino (Mts.) (äp-pĕn-nê'nô) It.	43·48 N	11·06 E
120	Appenzell (äp'ĕn-tsĕl). Switz.	47·19 N	9·22 E
70	Appleton (ăp' l-tŭn). Minn.	45·10 N	96·01 W
71	Appleton. Wis.	44·14 N	88·27 W
73	Appleton City. Mo.	38·10 N	94·02 W
79	Appomattox (R.) (ăp-ô-măt'ŭks) Va.	37·22 N	78·09 W
125	Aprília (ä-prē'lyȧ). It. (Rome In.)	41·36 N	12·40 E
133	Apsheronskiy, P-Ov. (pen.) Sov. Un.	40·20 N	50·30 E
123	Apt (äpt). Fr.	43·54 N	5·19 E
	Apulia (Reg.), see Puglia		
98	Apure (R.) (ä-pōō'rä). Ven.	8·08 N	68·46 W
98	Apurimac (R.) (ä-pōō-rê-mäk') Peru	11·39 S	73·48 W
115	Aqaba, G. of (ä'kȧ-bȧ). Asia	28·30 N	34·40 E
139	Aqaba (R.) U. A. R. (Palestine In.)	29·58 N	34·05 E
139	Aqabat al Hijaziyah Jordan (Palestine In.)	29·45 N	35·55 E
69	Aqua (R.) (ä'gwä). Ariz.	33·43 N	112·22 W
99	Aquidauana (ä-kē-däwä'nä). Braz.	20·24 S	55·46 W
84	Aquidneck (ȧ-kwĭd'nĭk) R. I. (Providence In.)	41·31 N	71·14 W
124	Aquilianos, Montes (Mts.) (mô'n-tĕs-ä-kē-lyä'nôs). Sp.	42·27 N	6·35 W
95	Aquin (ä-kăn'). Hai.	18·20 N	73·25 W
153	Ara (R.) (ä-rä). Jap. (Tōkyō In.)	35·40 N	139·52 E
	Araba, see Ha'arava (R.)		
168	Araba, Wadi. U. A. R. (Nile In.)	29·02 N	32·10 E
129	Arabatskaya Strelka (Spit) (Tongue of Arabat) (ä-rä-bat' skȧ-yȧ strĕl'kȧ) (ä-rȧ-băt') Sov. Un.	45·50 N	35·05 E
165	Arabian Des. (ȧ-rā'bĭ-ăn). U. A. R.	27·06 N	32·49 E
163	Arabian Pen. Asia	28·00 N	40·00 E
138	Arabian Sea (ȧ-rā'bĭ-ăn). Asia	16·00 N	65·15 E
99	Aracaju (ä-rä'kä-zhōō'). Braz.	11·00 S	37·01 W
99	Aracati (ä-rä'kä-tē'). Braz.	4·31 S	37·41 W
99	Araçatuba (ä-rä-sȧ-tōō'bä). Braz.	21·14 S	50·19 W
99	Aracruz (ä-rä-krōō's). Braz.	19·58 S	40·11 W
99	Araçuaí (ä-rä-sōō-ä-ē'). Braz.	16·57 S	41·56 W
121	Arad (ŏ'rŏd). Rom.	46·10 N	21·18 E
156	Arafura Sea (ä-rä-fōō'rä). Oceania	8·40 S	130·00 E
125	Aragon (Reg.) (ä-rä-gōn'). Sp.	40·55 N	0·45 W
124	Aragón (R.). Sp.	42·35 N	1·10 W
99	Aragua (State) (ä-rä'gwä) Ven. (In.)	10·00 N	67·05 W
99	Aragua de Barcelona (ä-rä'gwä dä bär-thä-lō'nä). Ven. (In.)	9·29 N	64·48 W
99	Araguaía (R.) (ä-rä-gwä'yä). Braz.	8·37 S	49·43 W
99	Araguari (ä-rä-gwä'rê). Braz.	18·43 S	48·03 W
98	Araguatins (ä-rä-gwä-tēns). Braz.	5·41 S	48·04 W
99	Aragüita (ärä-gwê'tä). Ven. (In.)	10·13 N	66·28 W
115	Araj (Oasis) (ä-räj'). U. A. R.	29·05 N	26·51 E
144	Arak. Iran	34·08 N	49·57 E
146	Arakanyoma (Mts.) (ŭ-rŭ-kŭn'yō'mȧ). Bur.	19·51 N	94·13 E
127	Arakhthos (R.) (är'äK-thôs). Grc.	39·10 N	21·05 E
	Aral Sea, see Aral'skoye More		
134	Aral'sk (ȧ-rälsk'). Sov. Un.	46·47 N	62·00 E
103	Aral'skoye More (Aral Sea) Sov. Un.	45·17 N	60·02 E
133	Aralsor (L.) (ȧ-räl'sôr'). Sov. Un.	49·00 N	48·20 E
90	Aramberri (ä-räm-bĕr-rē'). Mex.	24·05 N	99·47 W
116	Aran (I.) (ăr'ăn). Ire.	53·04 N	9·59 W
116	Aran (I.). Ire.	54·60 N	8·25 W
124	Aranda de Duero (ä-rän'dä dā dwā'rō). Sp.	41·43 N	3·45 W
90	Arandas (ä-rän'däs). Mex.	20·43 N	102·18 W
124	Aranjuez (ä-rän-hwāth'). Sp.	40·02 N	3·24 W
77	Aransas Pass (ȧ-răn'sȧs pȧs). Tex.	27·55 N	97·09 W
142	Aransol. India	23·45 N	86·58 E
164	Araouane. Mali	18·54 N	3·33 W
133	Arapkir (ä-räp-kēr'). Tur.	39·00 N	38·10 E
99	Araraquara (ä-rä-rä-kwä'rä). Braz.	21·47 S	48·08 W
101	Araras (ä-rä'räs) Braz. (Rio de Janeiro In.)	22·21 S	47·22 W
99	Araras, Serra das (Mts.) (sĕ'r-rä-däs-ä-rä'räs). Braz.	18·03 S	53·23 W
100	Araras, Serra das (Mts.). Braz.	23·30 S	53·00 W
100	Araras, Serra das (Mts.). Braz.(In.)	22·24 S	43·15 W
160	Ararat (ăr'ȧrăt). Austl.	37·12 S	38·00 E
133	Ararat (Mtn.). Tur.	39·50 N	44·20 E
99	Arari (L.) (ä-rä'rē). Braz.	0·30 S	48·50 W
99	Araripe, Chapadodo (Plain) (shä-pä'dä-dô-ä-rä-rē'pĕ). Braz.	5·55 S	40·42 W
101	Araruama (ä-rä-rōō-ä'mä) Braz. (Rio de Janeiro In.)	22·53 S	42·19 W
101	Araruama, Lagoa de (L.) (lä-gôä-dĕ-ä-rä-rōō-ä'mä) Braz. (Rio de Janeiro In.)	23·00 S	42·15 W
133	Aras (R.) (ä-räs). Iran-Sov. Un.	39·15 N	47·10 E
99	Aratuípe (ä-rä-tōō-ē'pĕ). Braz.	13·12 S	38·58 W
98	Arauca (ä-rou'kä). Col.	6·56 N	70·45 W
98	Arauca (R.). Ven.	7·13 N	68·43 W
142	Aravalli Ra. (ä-rä'vŭ-lē). India	29·15 N	72·59 E
99	Araxá (ä-rä-shä'). Braz.	19·41 S	46·46 W
99	Araya, Punta de (Pt.) (pŭn'tä-dĕ-ä-rä'yä). Ven. (In.)	10·40 N	64·15 W
155	Arayat (ä-rä'yät) Phil. (Manila In.)	15·10 N	120·44 E
118	Arboga (är-bō'gä). Swe.	59·26 N	15·50 E
126	Arborea (är-bō-rĕ'ä). It.	39·50 N	8·36 E
116	Arbroath (är-brōth'). Scot.	56·36 N	2·25 W
123	Arc (R.) (ärk). Fr. (Marseille In.)	43·32 N	5·17 E
122	Arcachon (är-kä-shôN'). Fr.	44·39 N	1·12 W
122	Arcachon, Bassin d' (Basin) (bä-sĕn' där-kä-shôN'). Fr.	44·42 N	1·50 W
74	Arcadia (är-kā'dĭ-ȧ) Calif. (Los Angeles In.)	34·08 N	118·02 W
79	Arcadia. Fla. (In.)	27·12 N	81·51 W
77	Arcadia. La.	32·33 N	92·56 W
71	Arcadia. Wis.	44·15 N	91·30 W
66	Arcata (är-kȧ'tȧ). Calif.	40·54 N	124·05 W
68	Arc Dome Mtn. (ärk dōm). Nev.	38·51 N	117·21 W
90	Arcelia (är-sä'lê-ä). Mex.	18·19 N	100·14 W
81	Archbald (ärch'bôld). Pa.	41·30 N	75·35 W
69	Arches Natl. Mon. (är'ches). Utah	38·45 N	109·35 W
98	Archidona (är-chē-do'nä). Ec.	1·01 S	77·49 W
124	Archidona (är-chē-dô'nä). Sp.	37·08 N	4·24 W
157	Archipelago (I.). Oceania	16·50 S	142·00 W
124	Arcila (är-sē'lä). Mor.	35·30 N	6·05 W
122	Arcis-sur-Aube (är-sēs'sûr-ōb'). Fr.	48·31 N	4·04 E
67	Arco (är'kō). Idaho	43·39 N	113·15 W
74	Arcola (är'kō'lȧ) Minn. (Minneapolis, St. Paul In.)	45·07 N	92·46 W
77	Arcola. Tex. (In.)	29·30 N	95·28 W
124	Arcos de la Frontera (är'kōs-dĕ-lä-frôn-tĕ'rä). Sp.	36·44 N	5·48 W
48	Arctic Ocean (ärk'tĭk)		

ng-sing; ŋ-baŋk; N-nasalized n; nŏd; cŏmmit; ōld; ôbey; ôrder; fōōd; fŏŏt; ou-out; s-soft; sh-dish; th-thin; pūre; ûnite; ûrn; stŭd; circŭs; ü-as "y" in study; '-indeterminate vowel.

Page	Name Pronunciation Region	Lat. °′	Long. °′
127	Arda (R.) (är'dä) . . . . Bul.	41·36 N	25·18 E
144	Ardabīl . . . . Iran	38 15 N	48·00 E
133	Ardahan (är-dȧ-hän') . . . . Tur.	41·10 N	42·40 E
118	Ardals Fd. (är-däls) . . . . Nor.	58·53 N	7·55 E
132	Ardatov (är-dȧ-tôf') . . . . . Sov. Un.	54·58 N	46·10 E
117	Ardennes (Mts.) (ȧr-dĕn') . . . . Bel.	50·01 N	5·12 E
124	Ardila (R.) (är-dē'là) . . . . Port.	38·12 N	9·20 W
73	Ardmore (ärd'mōr) . . . . Okla.	34·10 N	97·08 W
84	Ardmore . . . Pa. (Philadelphia In.)	40·01 N	75·18 W
85	Ardrossan (är-dros'ăn) Can. (Edmonton In.)	53·33 N	113·08 W
110	Ardsley (ärdz'lē) . . . . Eng.	53·43 N	1·33 W
112	Åre . . . . Swe.	63·12 N	13·12 E
124	Arecena (ä-rĕ-sĕ'nä) . . . . Sp.	37·53 N	6·34 W
89	Arecibo (ä-rȧ-sē'bō) P. R. (Puerto Rico In.)	18·28 N	66·45 W
99	Areia Branca (ä-rĕ'yä-brä'n-kă) Braz.	4·58 S	37·02 W
68	Arena, Pt. (ä-rā'nȧ) . . . . Calif.	38·57 N	123·40 W
99	Arenas, Punta (Pt.) (pōōn'tä-rĕ'näs) . Ven. (In.)	10·57 N	64·24 W
124	Arenas de San Pedro (ä-rā'nȧs dā sän pā'drō) . Sp.	40·12 N	5·04 W
118	Arendal (ä'rĕn-däl) . . . . Nor.	58·29 N	8·44 E
111	Arendonk . . . . . . Bel. (Brussels In.)	51·19 N	5·07 E
98	Arequipa (ä-rā-kē'pä) . . . . Peru	16·27 S	71·30 W
126	Arezzo (ä-rĕt'sō) . . . . It.	43·28 N	11·54 E
124	Arga (R.) (är'gä) . . . . Sp.	42·35 N	1·55 W
125	Arganda (är-gän'dä) Sp. (Madrid In.)	40·18 N	3·27 W
136	Argazi L. (är'gä-zĭ) Sov. Un. (Urals In.)	55·24 N	60·37 E
136	Argazi R. . . . . Sov. Un. (Urals In.)	55·33 N	57·30 E
122	Argentan (ȧr-zhäN-täN') . . . . . . Fr.	48·45 N	0·01 W
122	Argentat (ȧr-zhäN-tä') . . . . Fr.	45·07 N	1·57 E
123	Argenteuil (är-zhäN-tû'y') Fr. (Paris In.)	48·56 N	2·15 E
96	Argentina (är-jĕn-tē'nȧ) . . . . . S. A.	35·30 S	67·00 W
100	Argentino (L.) (är-Kĕn-tē'nō) . Arg.	50·15 S	72·45 W
122	Argenton-sur-Creuse (är-zhäN'tôN-sür-krôs) . Fr.	46·34 N	1·28 E
127	Arges (R.) (ȧr'zhĕsh) . . . . Rom.	44·27 N	25·22 E
75	Argo (är'go) . . . . . Ill. (Chicago In.)	41·47 N	87·49 W
127	Argolikos Kólpos (G.) . . . . Grc.	37·20 N	23·00 E
122	Argonne (Mts.) (ȧ'r-gôn) . . . . . . Fr.	49·21 N	5·54 E
127	Argos (är'gŏs) . . . . Grc.	37·38 N	22·45 E
127	Argostólion (är-gŏs-tô'lē-ōn) . . Grc.	38·10 N	20·30 E
68	Arguello, Pt. (är-gwāl'yō) . . . Calif.	34·35 N	120·40 W
135	Argun R. (ȧr-gōōn') Sov. Un.-China	50·15 N	118·45 E
85	Argyle (ȧr'gīl) Can. (Winnipeg In.)	50·11 N	97·27 W
70	Argyle . . . . Minn.	48·21 N	96·48 W
118	Århus (ôr'hōōs) . . . . Den.	56·09 N	10·10 E
153	Ariakeno-Umi (Sea) (ä-rē'ä-Kä'nō ōō'nē) . Jap.	33·03 N	130·18 E
153	Ariake-Wan (B.) (ä'rē-ä'kȧ wän) Jap.	31·18 N	131·15 E
126	Ariano (ä-rê-ä'nō) . . . . It.	41·09 N	15·11 E
98	Ariari (ä-ryä'rê) (R.) . . . . Col. (In.)	3·34 N	73·42 W
98	Arica (ä-rē'kä) . . . . Chile	18·34 S	70·14 W
83	Arichat (ä-rĭ-shät') . . . . Can.	45·33 N	61·03 W
122	Ariège (R.) (ȧ-rê-ĕzh') . . . . Fr.	43·26 N	1·29 E
65	Ariel (ā'rĭ-ĕl) Wash. (Portland In.)	45·57 N	122·34 W
121	Ariesul R. (ä-rê-ā'shōōl) . . . . Rom.	46·25 N	23·15 E
95	Ariguanabo, L. de (lä'gō-dĕ-ä-rē-gwä-nä'bō) Cuba (Havana In.)	22·17 N	82·33 W
139	Arīhā (Jericho) Jordan (Palestine In.)	31·51 N	35·28 E
72	Arikaree (R.) (ă-rĭ-kȧ-rē') . . . Colo.	39·51 N	102·18 W
153	Arima (ä'rê-mä') . Jap. (Ōsaka In.)	34·17 N	135·16 E
155	Aringay (ä-rĭŋ-gä'ê) Phil. (Manila In.)	16·25 N	120·20 E
99	Arinos (R.) (ä-rē'nôzsh) . . . . . Braz.	12·09 S	56·49 W
99	Aripuanã (R.) (ȧ-rê-pwän'yȧ) Braz.	7·06 S	60·29 W
139	Arish (R.) (ȧ-rēsh') U. A. R. (Palistine In.)	29·53 N	33·39 E
62	Arizona (State) (ăr-ĭ-zō'nȧ) . . U. S.	34·00 N	113·00 W
124	Arjona (är-hō'nä) . . . . Sp.	37·58 N	4·03 W
135	Arka (R.) . . . . Sov. Un.	60·12 N	142·30 E
78	Arkabutla Res. (är-kȧ-bŭt'lȧ) Miss.	34·48 N	88·53 W
73	Arkadelphia (är-kȧ-dĕl'fĭ-ȧ) . . Ark.	34·06 N	93·05 W
63	Arkansas (State) (är'kăn-sô) (är-kăn'sȧs) . U. S.	34·50 N	93·40 W
73	Arkansas City . . . . Kans.	37·04 N	97·02 W
73	Arkansas R. . . . . Okla.	35·20 N	94·56 W
132	Arkhangel'sk (Archangel) (ȧr-Kän'gĕlsk) . Sov. Un.	64·30 N	40·25 E
136	Arkhangel'skiy (är-kän-gĕl'skĭ) Sov. Un. (Urals In.)	52·52 N	61·53 E
136	Arkhangel'skoye (är-kän-gĕl' skô-yĕ) . Sov. Un. (Urals In.)	54·25 N	56·48 E
116	Arklow (ärk'lō) . . . . Ire.	52·47 N	6·10 W
118	Arkona, C. (är'kō-nä) . . . . Ger.	54·43 N	13·43 E
143	Arkonam (är-kō-nām') . . . . . . India	13·05 N	79·43 E
124	Arlanza (R.) (är-län-thä') . . . . Sp.	42·08 N	3·45 W
124	Arlanzón (R.) (är-län-thōn') . . . Sp.	42·12 N	3·58 W
120	Arlberg Tun. (ärl'bĕrgh) . . . . . Aus.	47·05 N	10·15 E
122	Arles (ärl) . . . . Fr.	43·42 N	4·38 E
78	Arlington (är'lĭng-tun') . . . . Ga.	31·25 N	84·42 W
83	Arlington . . . . Mass. (Boston In.)	42·26 N	71·13 W
70	Arlington (är'-lĕng-tŭn) . . . . S. D.	44·23 N	97·09 W
74	Arlington (är'lĭng-tŭn) Tex. (Dallas, Fort Worth In.)	32·44 N	97·07 W
168	Arlington . S. Afr. (Johannesburg & Pretoria In.)	28·02 S	27·52 E
81	Arlington . . . . Vt.	43·05 N	73·05 W
81	Arlington . . . . Va.	38·55 N	77·10 W
65	Arlington . . . . . Wash. (Seattle In.)	48·11 N	122·08 W
75	Arlington Heights (är'lĕng-tŭn-hī'ts) . Ill. (Chicago In.)	42·05 N	87·59 W
118	Arlöv (är'lûf) . . . . Swe.	55·38 N	13·05 E
158	Arltunga (ärl-tōōŋ'gä) . . . . . . Austl.	23·19 S	134·45 E
73	Arma (är'mȧ) . . . . Kans.	37·34 N	94·43 W
85	Armagh (är-mä') (är-mäK') Can. (Quebec In.)	46·45 N	70·36 W
116	Armagh . . . . N. Ire.	54·21 N	6·25 W
168	Armant (är-mänt') U. A. R. (Nile In.)	25·37 N	32·32 E
98	Armaro (är-mȧ'rō) . . . . . . Col. (In.)	4·58 N	74·54 W
133	Armavir (är-mȧ-vĭr') . . . . Sov. Un.	45·00 N	41·00 E
98	Arm'enia (ȧr-mĕ'nê-ȧ) . . . Col. (In.)	4·33 N	75·40 W
92	Armenia (är-mä'nê-ä) . . . . Sal.	13·44 N	89·31 W
130	Armenian, S. S. R. . . . . . . Sov. Un.	41·00 N	44·39 E
122	Armentières (ȧr-mäN-tyâr') . . . . Fr.	50·43 N	2·53 E
90	Armeria, Rio de (R.) (rê'ō-dĕ-är-mȧ-rē'ä) . Mex.	19·36 N	104·10 W
75	Armherstburg (ärm'hĕrst-bōōrgh) Can. (Detroit In.)	42·06 N	83·06 W
160	Armidale (är'mĭ-dāl) . . . . Austl.	30·27 S	151·50 E
70	Armour (är'mĕr) . . . . S. D.	43·18 N	98·21 W
87	Armstrong Station (ärm'strŏng) . Can.	50·21 N	89·00 W
129	Armyansk (ärm'yȧnsk) . . Sov. Un.	46·06 N	33·42 E
124	Arnedo (är-nā'dō) . . . . Sp.	42·12 N	2·03 W
117	Arnhem (ärn'hĕm) . . . . Neth.	51·58 N	5·56 E
158	Arnhem, C. . . . . Austl.	12·15 S	137·00 E
158	Arnhem Land, (Reg.) (ärn'hĕm-lănd) . Austl.	13·15 S	133·00 E
126	Arno (R.) (ä'r-nô) . . . . It.	43·45 N	10·42 E
110	Arnold (är'nŭld) . . . . Eng.	53·00 N	1·08 W
74	Arnold (ȧr'nŭld) Minn. (Duluth In.)	46·53 N	92·06 W
75	Arnold . . . . . . Pa. (Pittsburgh In.)	40·35 N	79·45 W
81	Arnprior (ärn-prī'ĕr) . . . . Can.	45·25 N	76·20 W
117	Arnsberg (ärns'bĕrgh) . . . . Ger.	51·25 N	8·02 E
120	Arnstadt (ärn'shtät) . . . . Ger.	50·51 N	10·57 E
166	Aroab (är'ō-āb) . . . . S. W. Afr.	25·40 S	19·45 E
82	Aroostook (ȧ-rōōs'tŏŏk) . . . . Maine	46·44 N	68·15 W
155	Aroroy (ä-rô-rō'ê) Phil. (Manila In.)	12·30 N	123·24 E
123	Arpajon (ăr-pă-jō'n) Fr. (Paris In.)	48·35 N	2·15 E
100	Arpoador, Ponta do (Pt.) (pô'n-tä-dô-är'pôȧ-dō'r) . Braz. (In.)	22·59 S	43·11 W
124	Arraiolos (är-rī-ō'lōzh) . . . . . . Port.	38·47 N	7·59 W
139	Ar Ramta . Jordan (Palestine In.) .	29·31 N	35·57 E
116	Arran (I.) (ă'rȧn) . . . . Scot.	55·39 N	5·30 W
122	Arras (ä-räs') . . . . Fr.	50·21 N	2·40 E
168	Ar Rawdah . . . U. A. R. (Nile In.)	27·47 N	30·52 E
101	Arrecifes (är-rȧ-sē'fäs) Arg. (Buenos Aires In.)	34·03 S	60·05 W
101	Arrecifes (R.) Arg. (Buenos Aires In.)	34·07 S	59·50 W
122	Arrée, Mts. d' (är-rā') . . . . Fr.	48·27 N	4·00 W
91	Arriaga (är-rêä'gä) . . . . Mex.	16·15 N	95·00 W
144	Ar Riyād . . . . Sau. Ar.	24·31 N	46·47 E
125	Arrone (R.) . . . . It. (Rome In.)	41·57 N	12·17 E
74	Arrowhead, L. (lăk ăr'ōhĕd) Calif. (Los Angeles In.)	34·17 N	117·13 W
67	Arrow R. (ăr'ō) . . . . Mont.	47·29 N	109·53 W
66	Arrowrock Res. (ăr'ō-rŏk) . . Idaho	43·40 N	115·30 W
95	Arroya Arena (är-rō'yä-rĕ'nä) Cuba (Havana In.)	23·01 N	82·30 W
91	Arroy Caribe (R.) (är-ro'i-kȧ-rē'bĕ) . Mex.	18·18 N	90·38 W
124	Arroyo de la Luz (är-rō'yō-dĕ-lä-lōō'z) . Sp.	39·39 N	6·46 W
90	Arroyo Grande (R.) (är-rô'yō-grä'n-dĕ) . Mex.	23·30 N	98·45 W
90	Arroyo Seco (är-rō'yō sä'kō) . Mex.	21·31 N	99·44 W
144	Ar Rub Al Khālī (Empty Quarter) (Des.) . Sau. Ar.	20·30 N	51·45 E
135	Arsen'yev . . . . Sov. Un.	44·13 N	133·32 E
136	Arsinskiy (är-sĭn'skĭ) Sov. Un. (Urals In.)	53·46 N	59·54 E
127	Årta (är'tä) . . . . Grc.	39·08 N	21·02 E
76	Arteaga (är-tä-ä'gä) . . . . Mex.	25·28 N	100·50 W
135	Artëm (ȧr-tyôm') . . . . Sov. Un.	43·28 N	132·29 E
94	Artemisa (är-tȧ-mē'sä) . . . . . . Cuba	22·50 N	82·45 W
129	Artëmovsk (ȧr-tyŏm'ŏfsk) Sov. Un.	48·37 N	38·00 E
72	Artesia (är-tē'sĭ-ȧ) . . . . N. Mex.	32·44 N	104·23 W
160	Artesian Basin, The (är-tē'zhăn) . Austl.	26·45 S	141·40 E
95	Arthur's Town . . . . Ba. Is.	24·40 N	74·30 W
136	Arti (är'tĭ) . . . Sov. Un. (Urals In.)	56·20 N	58·38 E
95	Artibonite (R.) (är-tê-bô-nē'tā) Hai.	19·00 N	72·25 W
100	Artigas (är-tē'gäs) . . . . Ur.	32·33 S	53·29 W
155	Aru, Pulau-Pulau (Is.) . . . . . Indon.	6·20 S	133·00 E
165	Arua (ä'rōō-ä) . . . . Ug.	3·04 N	31·01 E
98	Aruba (ä-rōō'bȧ) (I.) Neth. Antilles	12·29 N	70·00 W
167	Arusha (ȧ-rōō'shä) . . . . Tan.	3·18 S	36·43 E
165	Aruwimi R. (ä-rōō-wē'mê) Con. L.	1·04 N	28·31 E
82	Arvida . . . . Can.	48·25 N	71·11 W
118	Arvika (är-vē'kȧ) . . . . Swe.	59·41 N	12·35 E
132	Arzamas (är-zä-mäs') . . . . Sov. Un.	55·20 N	43·52 E
125	Arzew (är-zȧ-ōō') . . . . Alg.	35·50 N	0·20 W
124	Arzua (är-thōō'ä) . . . . Sp.	42·54 N	8·19 W
120	As (äsh') . . . . Czech.	50·12 N	12·13 E
152	Asahigawa (ä-sä'hê-gä'wä) . . . Jap.	43·50 N	142·09 E
153	Asahi-Gawa (Strm.) (ä-sä'hê-gä'wä) . Jap.	35·01 N	133·40 E
153	Asaka (ä-sä'kä) . . Jap. (Tōkyō In.)	35·47 N	139·36 E
136	Asbest (äs- bĕst') Sov. Un. (Urals In.)	57·02 N	61·28 E
82	Asbestos (ăs bĕs'tōs) . . . . Can.	45·49 N	71·52 W
84	Asbury Park (ăz'bĕr-ĭ) N. J. (New York In.)	40·13 N	74·01 W
92	Ascencion, Bahía de la (B.) (bä-ē'ä-dĕ-lä-äs-sĕn-sê-ōn') Mex. (Yucatan In.)	19·39 N	87·30 W
90	Ascensión (äs-sĕn-sê-ōn') . . . . Mex.	24·21 N	99·54 W
163	Ascension (I.) (ȧ-sĕn'shŭn) . Atl. O.	8·00 S	13·00 W
168	Ascent (ăs-ĕnt') . . . . S. Afr. (Johannesburg & Pretoria In.)	27·14 S	29·06 E
120	Aschaffenburg (ä-shäf'ĕn-bōōrgh) Ger.	49·58 N	9·12 E
123	Ascheberg (ä'shĕ-bĕrg) Ger. (Ruhr In.)	51·47 N	7·38 E
120	Aschersleben (äsh'ĕrs-lā-bĕn) . Ger.	51·46 N	11·28 E
126	Ascoli Piceno (äs'kô-lēpê-chā'nō) It.	42·50 N	13·55 E
127	Asenovgrad . . . . Bul.	42·00 N	24·49 E
168	Aser, Ras (C.) Som. (Horn of Afr. In.)	11·55 N	51·30 E
128	Aseri (á'sĕ-rĭ) . . . . Sov. Un.	59·26 N	26·58 E
	Asfi, see Safi		
136	Asha (ä'shä) . Sov. Un. (Urals In.)	55·01 N	57·17 E
70	Ashabula (L.) (ăsh'ȧ-bū-lȧ) . . N. D.	47·07 N	97·51 W
136	Ashan (ä'shän) Sov. Un. (Urals In.)	57·08 N	56·25 E
110	Ashbourne (ăsh'bŭrn) . . . . Eng.	53·01 N	1·44 W
78	Ashburn (ăsh'bŭrn) . . . . Ga.	31·42 N	83·42 W
158	Ashburton (R.) (ăsh'bûr-tŭn) Austl.	22·30 S	115·30 E
110	Ashby-de-la-Zouch (ăsh'bĭ-dê-lȧ zōōsh') . Eng.	52·44 N	1·23 W
86	Ashcroft . . . . Can.	50·47 N	121·02 W
73	Ashdown (ăsh'doun) . . . . Ark.	33·41 N	94·07 W
79	Asheboro (ăsh'bŭr-ô) . . . . N. C.	35·41 N	79·50 W
76	Asherton (ăsh'ēr-tŭn) . . . . Tex.	28·26 N	99·45 W
79	Asheville (ăsh'vĭl) . . . . N. C.	35·35 N	82·35 W
153	Ashikaga (ä'shê-kä'gȧ) . . . . Jap.	36·22 N	139·26 E
153	Ashiya (ä'shê-yä') . . . . Jap.	33·54 N	130·40 E
153	Ashiya . . . . Jap. (Osaka In.)	34·44 N	135·18 E
153	Ashizuri-Zaki (Pt.) (ä-shē-zōō-rē zä-kē) . Jap.	32·43 N	133·04 E
103	Ashkhabad (ŭsh-kä-bät') . Sov. Un.	39·45 N	58·13 E
78	Ashland (ăsh'lȧnd) . . . . Ala.	33·15 N	85·50 W
72	Ashland . . . . Kans.	37·11 N	99·46 W
80	Ashland . . . . Ky.	38·25 N	82·40 W
82	Ashland . . . . Maine	46·37 N	68·26 W
83	Ashland . . . . Mass. (Boston In.)	42 16 N	71·28 W
70	Ashland . . . . Nebr.	41·02 N	96·23 W
80	Ashland . . . . Ohio	40·50 N	82·15 W
66	Ashland . . . . Ore.	42·12 N	122·42 W
81	Ashland . . . . Pa.	40·45 N	76·20 W
71	Ashland . . . . Wis.	46·34 N	90·55 W
70	Ashley (ăsh'lē) . . . . N. D.	46·03 N	99·23 W
81	Ashley . . . . Pa.	41·15 N	75·55 W
154	Ashmore Rf. (ăsh'mōr) . . . . Indon.	12·08 S	122·45 E
168	Ashmūn (ȧsh-mōōn') U. A. R. (Nile In.)	30·19 N	30·57 E
165	Ash Shabb (Shĕb) . . . . U. A. R.	22·34 N	29·52 E
168	Ash Shallūfah (Shȧl'lōō-fȧ) U. A. R. (Suez In.)	30·09 N	32·33 E
139	Ash Shaṭṭ U. A. R. (Palestine In.)	29·58 N	32·36 E
139	Ash Shawbak Jordan (Palestine In.)	30·31 N	35·35 E
139	Ash Shīdīyah (R.) Jordan (Palestine In.)	29·53 N	36·49 E
80	Ashtabula (ăsh-tȧ-bū'lȧ) . . . . Ohio	41·55 N	80·50 W
67	Ashton (ăsh'tŭn) . . . . Idaho	44·04 N	111·28 W
110	Ashton-in-Makerfield (ăsh'tŭn-ĭn-māk'ĕr-fēld) . Eng.	53·29 N	2·39 W
110	Ashton-under-Lyne (ăsh'tŭn-ŭn-dĕr-līn') . Eng.	53·29 N	2·04 W
87	Ashuanipi (L.) (ăsh-wȧ-nĭp'ĭ) . Can.	52·40 N	67·42 W
82	Ashuapmuchuan (R.) (ăsh-wăp-mōō-chwăn') . Can.	49·10 N	73·10 W
136	Ashukino (ȧ-shōō'kĭ-nô) Sov. Un. (Moscow In.)	56·10 N	37·57 E
7	Asia (ā'zhȧ)		
103	Asia Minor (ā'zhȧ) . . . . Asia	38·18 N	31·18 E
90	Asientos (ä-sê-ĕn'tōs) . . . . Mex.	22·13 N	102·05 W
126	Asinara, Golfo di (G.) (gôl'fô-dē-ä-sē-nä'rä) . . It.	40·58 N	8·28 E
126	Asinara (I.) (ä-sē-nä'rä) . . . . It.	41·02 N	8·22 E
144	Asīr (Reg.) (ä-sēr') . . . . . . Sau. Ar.	19·30 N	21·27 E
136	Askarovo (äs-kä-rô'vô) Sov. Un. (Urals In.)	53·21 N	58·32 E
118	Askersund (äs'kĕr-sōōnd) . . . . Swe.	58·43 N	14·53 E
136	Askino (äs'kĭ-nô) Sov. Un. (Urals In.)	56·06 N	56·29 E
82	Askitichi (L.) (ăs-kĭ-tĭ'chĭ) . . . Can.	49·15 N	73·55 W
165	Asmara (äs-mä'rä) . . . . Eth.	15·17 N	38·56 E
123	Asnières-sur-Seine (ä-nyâr'-sür-sĕ'n) . Fr. (Paris In.)	48·55 N	2·18 E
165	Asosā . . . . Eth.	10·13 N	34·28 E
66	Asotin (ȧ-sō'tĭn) . . . . Wash.	46·19 N	117·01 W
69	Aspen (ăs'pĕn) . . . . Colo.	39·15 N	106·55 W
111	Asperen . . . Neth. (Amsterdam In.)	51·52 N	5·07 E
83	Aspy B. (ăs'pê) . . . . Can.	46·26 N	60·17 W
168	Assab (ȧs-säb') Eth. (Horn of Afr. In.)	12·52 N	42·39 E
168	Aş Şaff . . . . U. A. R. (Nile In.)	29·33 N	31·23 E
165	As Sallūm . . . . U. A. R.	31·34 N	25·09 E
139	As Salt . . . . . Jordan (Palestine In.)	32·02 N	35·44 E
142	Assam (State) (ăs-săm') . . . . . India	30·45 N	90·55 E
144	As Sayh . . . . Sau. Ar.	24·00 N	47·45 E
118	Assens (äs'sĕns) . . . . Den.	55·16 N	9·54 E
168	As Sinbillāwayn U. A. R. (Nile In.)	30·53 N	31·37 E
86	Assiniboia . . . . Can.	49·36 N	106·10 W
85	Assiniboine R. (ă-sĭn'ĭ-boin) Can. (Winnipeg In.)	50·02 N	97·56 W
164	Assinie (ȧ-sê-nē') . . . . . Ivory Coast	4·52 N	3·16 W
99	Assis (ȧ-sē's) . . . . Braz.	22·39 S	50·21 W
144	As Sulaymānīyah . . . . Iraq	35·47 N	45·23 E
168	As Suways (Suez) U.A.R. (Suez In.)	29·58 N	32·34 E
127	Astakós (äs'tä-kôs) . . . . Grc.	38·42 N	21·00 E
133	Astara . . . . Sov. Un.	38·30 N	48·50 E
126	Asti (äs'tē) . . . . It.	44·54 N	8·12 E
146	Astin Tagh (Mts.) . . . . China	36·58 N	85·09 E
115	Astipálaia (I.) . . . . Grc.	36·31 N	26·19 E
124	Astorga (äs-tôr'gä) . . . . Sp.	42·28 N	6·03 W
65	Astoria (ăs-tō'rĭ-ȧ) Ore. (Portland In.)	46·11 N	123·51 W

ăt; finăl; rāte; senâte; ärm; àsk: sofȧ; fâre; ch-choose; dh-as th in other; bē; êvent; bĕt; recĕnt; cratēr; g-go; gh-guttural g; bĭt; ĭ-short neutral; rīde; K-guttural k as ch in German ich;

Page	Name Pronunciation Region	Lat. °′	Long. °′
85	Astotin Cr. (ăs-tō-tĕN') Can. (Edmonton In.)	53·43 N	113·00 W
133	Astrakhan' (ăs-trȧ-kän') . Sov. Un.	46·15 N	48·00 E
166	Astrida (ăs-trē'dȧ) . . . . Rw.	2·37 S	29·48 E
124	Asturias (Reg.) (ăs-tōō'ryȧs) . . Sp.	43·21 N	6·00 W
100	Asunción (ä-sōōn-syōn') . . . . . . Par.	25·25 S	57·30 W
	Asuncion, see Ixtaltepec		
	Asunción, see Nochixtlán		
92	Asuncion Mita (ȧ-sōōn-syō'n-mē'tȧ) . . Guat.	14·19 N	89·43 W
117	Åsunden (L.) (ô'sōōn-dĕn) . . . Swe.	57·46 N	13·16 E
168	Aswān (Syene) (ä-swän') (sē-ā'nē) . U. A. R. (Nile In.)	24·05 N	32·57 E
165	Aswān Dam . . . . U. A. R.	23·50 N	31·30 E
168	Aswān High Dam U. A. R. (Nile In.)	23·58 N	32·53 E
168	Asyūt (ä-syōōt') U. A. R. (Nile In.)	27·10 N	31·10 E
100	Atacama, Puna de (Reg.) (pōō'nä-dĕ-ätä-kȧ'mä) . Chile	23·15 S	68·45 W
98	Atacama, Puna de (Plat.) (pōō'nä-dĕ-ä-tä-kȧ'mä) . Bol.	21·35 S	66·58 W
96	Atacama, Desierto de (Des.) (dĕ-syĕ'r-tô-dĕ-ä-tä-kȧ'mä) Chile-Peru	23·50 S	69·00 W
100	Atacama, Salar de (L.) (sȧ-lȧr'dĕ-ätä-kȧ'mä) . Chile	23·38 S	68·15 W
98	Ataco (ä-tȧ'kŏ) . . . . Col. (In.)	3·36 N	75·22 W
139	'Ata'Itah, Jabal al (Mts.) Jordan (Palestine In.)	30·48 N	35·19 E
164	Atakpamé (ä'tȧk-pȧ-mā') . . . Togo	7·37 N	1·09 E
136	Atamanovskiy (ä-tä-mä'nôv-skĭ) Sov. Un. (Urals In.)	52·15 N	60·47 E
168	Ataqa Gebel (Plat.) U. A. R. (Suez In.)	29·59 N	32·20 E
164	Atar (ä-tär') . . . . Mauritania	20·45 N	13·16 W
68	Atascadero (ăt-ăs-kȧ-dâ'rō) . Calif.	35·29 N	120·40 W
76	Atascosa R. (ăt-ăs-kō'sȧ) . . . . Tex.	28·50 N	98·17 W
165	Atbara (ät'bȧ-rä) . . . . Sud.	17·45 N	30·01 E
165	Atbara R. . . . . Sud.	17·14 N	34·27 E
134	Atbasar (ät'bȧ-sär') . . . . . Sov. Un.	51·42 N	68·28 E
77	Atchafalaya B. (ăch-ȧ-fȧ-lī'ȧ) . La.	29·25 N	91·30 W
77	Atchafalaya R. . . . . La.	30·53 N	91·51 W
73	Atchison (ăch'ĭ-sŭn) . . . . Kans.	39·33 N	95·08 W
84	Atco (ăt'kō) N. J. (Philadelphia In.)	39·46 N	74·53 W
91	Atempan (ä-tĕm-pä'n) . . . . . . Mex.	19·49 N	97·25 W
90	Atenguillo (R.) (ä-tĕn-gē'l-yō) Mex.	20·18 N	104·35 W
86	Athabasca (ăth-ȧ-băs'kȧ) . . . . Can.	54·41 N	113·11 W
86	Athabasca (L.) . . . . Can.	59·04 N	109·10 W
86	Athabasca (R.) . . . . Can.	57·21 N	112·02 W
82	Atharbaska (ăth-ȧr-băs'kȧ) . . Can.	46·03 N	71·54 W
78	Athens (ăth'ĕnz) . . . . Ala.	34·47 N	86·58 W
78	Athens . . . . Ga.	33·55 N	83·24 W
80	Athens . . . . Ohio	39·20 N	82·10 W
81	Athens . . . . Pa.	42·00 N	76·30 W
78	Athens . . . . Tenn.	35·26 N	84·36 W
77	Athens . . . . Tex.	32·13 N	95·51 W
	Athens, see Athínai		
110	Atherstone (ăth'ēr-stŭn) . . . . . Eng.	52·34 N	1·33 W
110	Atherton (ăth'ēr-tŭn) . . . . Eng.	53·32 N	2·29 W
159	Atherton Plat. (ădh-ĕr-tŏn) . Austl.	17·00 S	144·30 E
167	Athi (R.) (ä'tē) . . . . Ken.	2·31 S	35·28 E
127	Athínai (Athens) (ä-thē'nĕ) . . . Grc.	38·00 N	23·38 E
116	Athlone (ăth-lōn') . . . . Ire.	53·24 N	7·30 W
127	Athos (Mtn.) (ăth'ŏs) . . . . Grc.	40·10 N	24·15 E
139	Ath Thamad U. A. R. (Palestine In.)	29·41 N	34·17 E
116	Athy (ȧ-thī) . . . . Ire.	52·59 N	7·08 W
101	Atibaia (ä-tē-bȧ'yȧ) Braz. (Rio de Janeiro In.)	23·08 S	46·32 W
87	Atikonak (L.) . . . . Can.	52·34 N	63·49 W
85	Atim Cr. . . . Can. (Edmonton In.)	53·34 N	113·59 W
155	Atimonan (ä-tē-mō'nän) Phil. (Manila In.)	13·59 N	121·56 E
92	Atiquizaya (ä'tē-kē-zä'yä) . . . . Sal.	14·00 N	89·42 W
92	Atitlan (Vol.) (ä-tē-tlän') . . . Guat.	14·35 N	91·11 W
92	Atitlan L. (ä-tē-tlän') . . . . . . Guat.	14·38 N	91·23 W
91	Atizapán (ä'tē-zä-pän') Mex. (Mexico City In.)	19·33 N	99·16 W
64	Atka (ăt'kȧ) . . . . Alaska	52·18 N	174·18 W
64	Atka (I.) . . . . Alaska	51·58 N	174·30 W
133	Atkarsk (ät-kärsk') . . . . . . Sov. Un.	51·50 N	45·00 E
70	Atkinson (ăt'kĭn-sŭn) . . . . Nebr.	42·32 N	98·58 W
84	Atlanta (ăt-lăn'tȧ) Ga. (Atlanta In.)	33·45 N	84·23 W
73	Atlanta . . . . Tex.	33·09 N	94·09 W
71	Atlantic (ăt-lăn'tĭk) . . . . Iowa	41·23 N	94·58 W
84	Atlantic Highlands N. J. (New York In.)	40·25 N	74·04 W
81	Atlantic City . . . . N. J.	39·20 N	74·30 W
6	Atlantic Ocean		
164	Atlas Mts. (ăt'lăs) . . . . . Alg.-Mor.	31·22 N	4·57 W
90	Atliaca (ät-lê-ä'kä) . . . . Mex.	17·38 N	99·24 W
86	Atlin (L.) (ăt'lĭn) . . . . Can.	59·34 N	133·20 W
90	Atlixco (ät-lēz'kō) . . . . Mex.	18·52 N	98·27 W
118	Atlöy (I.) (ät-lûê) . . . . Nor.	61·24 N	4·46 E
78	Atmore (ăt'mōr) . . . . Ala.	31·01 N	87·31 W
73	Atoka (ȧ-tō'kȧ) . . . . Okla.	34·23 N	96·07 W
73	Atoka Res. . . . . Okla.	34·30 N	96·05 W
90	Atotonilco el Alto (ä'tô-tô-nēl'kō ĕl äl'tō) . Mex.	20·35 N	102·32 W
90	Atotonilco el Grande (ä'tô-tô-nēl-kō ĕl grän'dä) Mex.	20·17 N	98·41 W
164	Atoui R. (ȧ-tōō-ē') Mauritania-Sp. Sah.	21·00 N	15·32 W
90	Atoyac (ä-tô-yäk') . . . . Mex.	20·01 N	103·28 W
91	Atoyac (R.) . . . . Mex.	16·27 N	97·28 W
90	Atoyac (R.) . . . . Mex.	18·35 N	98·16 W
90	Atoyac de Alvarez (ä-tô-yäk'dä äl'vä-rāz) . Mex.	17·13 N	100·29 W
91	Atoyatempan (ä-tō'yä-tĕm-pän') Mex.	18·47 N	97·54 W
144	Atrak, Rud-e (R.) . . . . Iran	37·42 N	55·30 E
118	Atran (R.) . . . . Swe.	57·02 N	12·43 E
99	Atrato, Rio (R.) (rē'ō-ä-trä'tō) . Col.	7·00 N	77·12 W
98	Atrato (R.) (ä-trä'tō) . . . Col. (In.)	5·48 N	76·19 W
139	Aṭ Tafīlah (tä-fē'la) Jordan (Palestine In.)	30·50 N	35·36 E
144	At Tāif . . . . Sau. Ar.	21·03 N	41·00 E
78	Attalla (ȧ-tăl'yȧ) . . . . Ala.	34·01 N	86·05 W
87	Attawapiskat (R.) (ăt'ȧ-wȧ-pĭs'kăt) . Can.	52·31 N	86·22 W
120	Atter See (L.) (Kammer) . . . . Aus.	47·57 N	13·25 E
81	Attica (ăt'ĭ-kȧ) . . . . N. Y.	42·55 N	78·15 W
84	Attleboro (ăt''l-bŭr-ô) Mass. (Providence In.)	41·56 N	71·15 W
116	Attow, Ben (Mtn.) (bĕn ăt'tō) Scot.	57·15 N	5·25 W
77	Attoyac Bay (ă-toi'yăk) . . . . . Tex.	31·45 N	94·23 W
64	Attu (I.) (ăt-tōō') . . . . Alaska	53·08 N	173·18 E
115	Aṭ Ṭūr . . . . U. A. R.	28·09 N	33·47 E
118	Atvidaberg (ôt-vē'dȧ-bĕrgh) . . Swe.	58·12 N	15·55 E
72	Atwood (ăt'wŏŏd) . . . . Kans.	39·48 N	101·06 W
91	Atzcapotzalco (ät'zkä-pô-tzäl'kō) Mex. (Mexico City In.)	19·29 N	99·11 W
111	Atzgersdorf . . . . . Aus. (Vienna In.)	48·10 N	16·17 E
157	Auau Chan (ä'ōō-ä'ōō) Hawaii (In.)	20·55 N	156·50 W
123	Aubagne (ō-bän'y') . . . . Fr.	43·18 N	5·34 E
122	Aube (R.) (ōb) . . . . Fr.	48·42 N	3·49 E
122	Aubenas (ōb'-nä') Fr.	44·37 N	4·22 E
123	Aubervilliers (ō-bĕr-vē-yā') Fr. (Paris In.)	48·54 N	2·23 E
122	Aubin (ō-băN') . . . . Fr.	44·29 N	2·12 E
85	Aubrey (ô-brē') Can. (Montreal In.)	45·08 N	73·47 W
78	Auburn (ô'bŭrn) . . . . Ala.	32·35 N	85·26 W
68	Auburn . . . . Calif.	38·52 N	121·05 W
73	Auburn . . . . Ill.	39·36 N	89·46 W
80	Auburn . . . . Ind.	41·20 N	85·05 W
82	Auburn . . . . Maine	44·04 N	70·24 W
83	Auburn . . . . Mass. (Boston In.)	42·11 N	71·51 W
73	Auburn . . . . Nebr.	40·23 N	95·50 W
81	Auburn . . . . N. Y.	42·55 N	76·35 W
65	Auburn . . . . Wash. (Seattle In.)	47·18 N	122·14 W
75	Auburn Hts. . . Mich. (Detroit In.)	42·37 N	83·13 W
122	Aubusson (ō-bü-sôN') . . . . Fr.	45·57 N	2·10 E
122	Auch (ōsh) . . . . Fr.	43·38 N	0·35 E
78	Aucilla (R.) (ô-sĭl'ȧ) . . . . . Fla.-Ga.	30·15 N	83·55 W
159	Auckland (ôk'lănd) . . . . N. Z. (In.)	37·43 S	174·53 E
47	Auckland Is. . . . . N. Z.	50·30 S	166·30 E
122	Aude (ōd) . . . . Fr.	42·55 N	2·08 E
122	Audierne (ō-dyĕrn') . . . . Fr.	48·02 N	4·31 W
123	Audincourt (ō-dăn-kōōr') . . . . . . Fr.	47·30 N	6·49 E
110	Audley (ôd'lĭ) . . . . Eng.	53·03 N	2·18 W
168	Audo Ra. . Eth. (Horn of Afr. In.)	6·58 N	41·18 E
71	Audubon (ô'dŏŏ-bŏn) . . . . Iowa	41·43 N	94·57 W
84	Audubon . N. J. (Philadelphia In.)	39·54 N	75·04 W
120	Aue (ou'ē) . . . . Ger.	50·35 N	12·44 E
160	Augathella (ôr'gȧ'thĕ-lȧ) . . . Austl.	25·49 S	146·40 E
166	Aughrabies Falls (ô-grä'bēs) S. Afr.	28·30 S	20·00 E
111	Augsburg (ouks'bŏŏrgh) Ger. (Munich In.)	48·23 N	10·55 E
73	Augusta (ô-gŭs'tȧ) . . . . Ark.	35·16 N	91·21 W
79	Augusta . . . . Ga.	33·26 N	82·00 W
73	Augusta . . . . Kans.	37·41 N	96·58 W
80	Augusta . . . . Ky.	38·45 N	84·00 W
82	Augusta . . . . Maine	44·19 N	69·42 W
84	Augusta . . . . N. J. (New York In.)	41·07 N	74·44 W
71	Augusta . . . . Wis.	44·40 N	91·09 W
121	Augustow (ou-gōōs'tōōf) . . . . . Pol.	53·52 N	23·00 E
123	Aulnay-sous-Bois (ō-nĕ'sōō-bwä') Fr. (Paris In.)	48·56 N	2·30 E
122	Aulne (R.) (ōn) . . . . Fr.	48·08 N	3·53 W
125	Aumale (ō-mäl') . . . . Alg.	36·05 N	3·40 E
123	Auneau (ō-nŏ') . . . . Fr. (Paris In.)	48·28 N	1·45 E
166	Auob (R.) (ä'wŏb) . . . . . S. W. Afr.	25·00 S	19·00 E
139	Aur (I.) . . . . Mala. (Singapore In.)	2·27 N	104·51 E
142	Aurangābād (ou-rŭŋ-gä-bäd') India	19·56 N	75·19 E
122	Auray (ō-rĕ') . . . . Fr.	47·42 N	3·00 W
122	Aurillac (ō-rē-yȧk') . . . . Fr.	44·57 N	2·27 E
75	Aurora (ô-rō'rȧ) . Ill. (Chicago In.)	41·45 N	88·18 W
75	Aurora . . . . . . Ind. (Cincinnati In.)	39·04 N	84·55 W
71	Aurora . . . . Minn.	47·31 N	92·17 W
73	Aurora . . . . Mo.	36·58 N	93·42 W
72	Aurora . . . . Nebr.	40·54 N	98·01 W
118	Aursunden (L.) (äûr-sûndĕn) . Nor.	62·42 N	11·10 E
80	Au Sable (R.) (ô-sä'b'l) . . . . . Mich.	44·40 N	84·25 W
81	Ausable (R.) . . . . N. Y.	44·25 N	73·50 W
	Aussig, see Usti nad Labem		
71	Austin (ôs'tĭn) . . . . Minn.	43·40 N	92·58 W
68	Austin . . . . Nev.	39·30 N	117·05 W
77	Austin . . . . Tex.	30·15 N	97·42 W
158	Austin (L.) . . . . Austl.	27·45 S	117·30 E
77	Austin Bay (ôs'tĭn bĭ-ōō') Tex. (In.)	29·17 N	95·21 W
7	Australia (ôs-trā'lĭ-ȧ)		
160	Australian Alps (Mts.) . . . . . Austl.	37·10 S	147·55 E
160	Australian Capital Ter. (ôs-trā'lĭ-ăn) . Austl.	35·30 S	148·40 E
102	Austria (ôs'trĭ-ȧ) . . . . Eur.	47·15 N	11·53 E
123	Authon-la-Plaine (ō-tōN-lă-plĕ'n) Fr. (Paris In.)	48·27 N	1·58 E
90	Autlán (ä-ōōt-län') . . . . Mex.	19·47 N	104·24 W
122	Autun (ō-tŭN') . . . . Fr.	46·58 N	4·14 E
122	Auvergne (Mts.) (ō-vĕrn'y') . . . Fr.	45·12 N	2·31 E
122	Auxerre (ō-sâr') . . . . Fr.	47·48 N	3·32 E
85	Aux Grues, Ile (I.) (ō grü) Can. (Quebec In.)	47·05 N	70·32 W
73	Ava (ā'vȧ) . . . . Mo.	36·56 N	92·40 W
165	Avakubi (ä-vȧ-kōō'bē) . . . . Con. L.	1·19 N	27·32 E
122	Avallon (ȧ-vȧ-lôN') . . . . Fr.	47·30 N	3·58 E
75	Avalon (ăv'ȧ-lŏn) Pa. (Pittsburgh In.)	40·31 N	80·05 W
68	Avalon . . . . Calif.	33·21 N	118·22 W
83	Avalon Pen. . . . . Can.	47·23 N	53·10 W
124	Aveiro (ä-vä'rōō) . . . . Port.	40·38 N	8·38 W
100	Avelar (ȧ'vĕ-lä'r) . . . . . Braz. (In.)	22·20 S	43·25 W
100	Avellaneda (ä-vĕl-yä-nä'dhä) Arg. (In.)	34·25 S	58·23 W
125	Avellino (ä-vĕl-lē'nō) It. (Naples In.)	40·40 N	14·46 E
118	Averöy (I.) (ävĕr-ûê) . . . . Nor.	63·40 N	7·16 E
126	Aversa (ä-vĕr'sä) . . . . It.	40·58 N	14·13 E
73	Avery (ā'vēr-ĭ) . . . . Tex.	33·34 N	94·46 W
118	Avesta (ä-vĕs'tä) . . . . Swe.	60·16 N	16·09 E
122	Aveyron (R.) (ä-vȧ-rôN) . . . . . . Fr.	44·07 N	1·45 E
126	Avezzano (ä-vät-sä'nō) . . . . It.	42·03 N	13·27 E
126	Avigliano (ä-vēl-yä'nō) . . . . It.	40·45 N	15·44 E
122	Avignon (ȧ-vē-nyôN') . . . . Fr.	43·55 N	4·50 E
124	Avila (ä-vē-lä) . . . . Sp.	40·39 N	4·42 W
124	Avilés (ä-vē-läs') . . . . Sp.	43·33 N	5·55 W
73	Avoca (ȧ-vō'kȧ) . . . . Iowa	41·29 N	95·16 W
81	Avon (ā'vŏn) . . . . Conn.	41·40 N	72·50 W
116	Avon (R.) (ā'vŭn) . . . . Eng.	52·05 N	1·55 W
83	Avon (ā'vŏn) . . Mass. (Boston In.)	42·08 N	71·03 W
75	Avon . . . . Ohio (Cleveland In.)	41·27 N	82·02 W
84	Avondale . . . . Ga. (Atlanta In.)	33·47 N	84·16 W
75	Avon Lake . . Ohio (Cleveland In.)	41·31 N	82·01 W
85	Avonmore (ā'vōN-mōr) Can. (Ottawa In.)	45·11 N	74·58 W
79	Avon Park (ā'vŏn pärk') . Fla. (In.)	27·35 N	81·29 W
122	Avranches (ȧ-vränsh') . . . . Fr.	48·43 N	1·34 W
153	Awaji (ä'wä-jē) . . . . Jap.	34·23 N	135·00 E
153	Awaji-Shima (I.) (ä'wä-jē shē-mä) Jap. (Osaka In.)	34·32 N	135·02 E
165	Awash R. (ȧ-wäsh') . . . . Eth.	9·19 N	40·30 E
116	Awe, Loch (L.) (lŏk ôr) . . . . . Scot.	56·22 N	5·04 W
165	Awjilah . . . . Libya	29·07 N	21·21 E
122	Ax-les-Thermes (äks'lā tĕrm') . . Fr.	42·43 N	1·50 E
90	Axochiapan (äks-ō-chyä'pän) . Mex.	18·29 N	98·49 W
122	Ay (ȧ'ē) . . . . Fr.	49·05 N	3·58 E
132	Ay (R.) . . . . Sov. Un.	55·55 N	57·55 E
153	Ayabe (ä'yä-bĕ) . . . . Jap.	35·16 N	135·17 E
100	Ayacucho (ä-yä-kōō'chō) . . . . . Arg.	37·05 S	58·30 W
98	Ayacucho . . . . Peru	12·12 S	74·03 W
134	Ayaguz (ä-yä-gōōz') . . . . . Sov. Un.	48·00 N	80·12 E
124	Ayamonte (ä-yä-mô'n-tĕ) . . . . . Sp.	37·14 N	7·28 W
135	Ayan (ȧ-yän') . . . . Sov. Un.	56·26 N	138·18 E
98	Ayata (ä-yä'tä) . . . . Bol.	15·17 S	68·43 W
98	Ayaviri (ä-yä-vē'rē) . . . . Peru	14·46 S	70·38 W
129	Aydar (R.) (ī-där') . . . . . . Sov. Un.	49·15 N	38·48 E
79	Ayden (ā'dĕn) . . . . N. C.	35·27 N	77·25 W
133	Aydin (ȧ'ĭ-dĭn) . . . . Tur.	37·40 N	27·40 E
83	Ayer (âr) . . . . . . Mass. (Boston In.)	42·33 N	71·36 W
139	Ayer Hitam . Mala. (Singapore In.)	1·55 N	103·11 E
127	Ayiá (ä-yē'ä) . . . . Grc.	39·42 N	22·47 E
127	Ayiassos . . . . Grc.	39·06 N	26·25 E
127	Áyion Óros (Mount Athos) (Reg.) Grc.	40·20 N	24·15 E
127	Áyios Evstrátion (I.) . . . . Grc.	39·30 N	24·58 E
110	Aylesbury (ālz'bēr-ĭ) Eng. (London In.)	51·47 N	0·49 W
85	Aylmer (āl'mēr) Can. (Ottawa In.)	45·24 N	75·50 W
86	Aylmer (L.) . . . . Can.	64·27 N	108·22 W
90	Ayo el Chico (ä'yō el chē'kō) . Mex.	20·31 N	102·21 W
135	Ayon (I.) (ī-ôn') . . . . Sov. Un.	70·04 N	168·33 E
91	Ayotla (ä-yōt'lä) Mex. (Mexico City In.)	19·18 N	98·55 W
116	Ayr (âr) . . . . Scot.	55·27 N	4·40 W
116	Ayr (L.) . . . . Scot.	55·25 N	4·20 W
168	Ayshā . . . . Eth. (Horn of Afr. In.)	10·48 N	42·32 E
92	Ayutla (ä-yōōt'lä) . . . . Guat.	14·44 N	92·11 W
90	Ayutla . . . . Mex.	16·50 N	99·16 W
90	Ayutla . . . . Mex.	20·09 N	104·20 W
154	Ayutthaya (ä-yōōt'hē'ä) . . . . Thai.	14·16 N	100·37 E
127	Ayvalik (äĭ-vä'lĕk) . . . . Tur.	39·19 N	26·40 E
164	Azemmour (ä-zē-mōōr') . . . . . Mor.	33·20 N	8·21 W
130	Azerbaydzhan (Azerbaijan) (S. S. R.) (ä'zēr-bä-ē-jän') . Sov. Un.	40·38 N	47·25 E
82	Aziscoos (L.) (ăz'ĭ kōōs') . . . Maine	45·03 N	70·50 W
74	Azle (ăz'lē) Tex. (Dallas, Fort Worth In.)	35·54 N	97·33 W
98	Azogues (ä-sō'gās) . . . . Ec.	2·47 S	78·45 W
129	Azov (ȧ-zôf') (ā'zŏf) . . . . . Sov. Un.	47·07 N	39·19 E
	Azov, Sea of, see Azovskoye More		
129	Azovskoye More (Sea of Azov) (ȧ-zôf'skô-yĕ mô'rĕ) . Sov. Un.	46·00 N	36·20 E
90	Azoyú (ä-zô-yōō') . . . . Mex.	16·42 N	98·46 W
69	Aztec (ăz'tĕk) . . . . N. Mex.	36·40 N	108·00 W
69	Aztec Ruins Natl. Mon. . N. Mex.	36·50 N	108·00 W
95	Azua (ä'swä) . . . . Dom. Rep.	18·30 N	70·45 W
124	Azuaga (ä-thwä'gä) . . . . Sp.	38·15 N	5·42 W
93	Azuero, Peninsula de (Pen.) (ä-swä'rō) . Pan.	7·30 N	80·34 W
76	Azucar, Presa de (Res.) (prĕ'sä-dĕ-ä-zōō'kär) . Mex.	26·06 N	98·44 W
100	Azufre, Cerro (Copiapó) (Vol.) (sĕr'rō ä-sōō'frä) (kō-pē-äpō') Chile	26·10 S	69·00 W
101	Azul (ä-sōōl') Arg. (Buenos Aires In.)	36·46 S	59·51 W
90	Azul, Sierra (Mts.) (sē-ĕ'r-rä-zōō'l) Mex.	23·20 N	98·28 W
98	Azul, Cordillera (Mts.) (kô'r-dē-lyĕ'rä-zōō'l) . Peru	7·15 S	75·30 W
74	Azusa (ȧ-zōō'sȧ) Calif. (Los Angeles In.)	34·08 N	117·55 W
144	Az Zahrān (Dhahran) (dä-rän') Sau. Ar.	26·13 N	50·00 E
168	Az Zaqāzīq . . . . U. A. R. (Nile In.)	30·36 N	31·36 E
139	Az Zarqā' . . Jordan (Palestine In.)	32·03 N	36·07 E
165	Az Zawiyah . . . . Libya	32·28 N	11·55 E
123	Baal (bäl) . . . . Ger. (Ruhr In.)	51·02 N	6·17 E
155	Baao (bä'ō) . . . . Phil. (Manila In.)	13·27 N	123·22 E
111	Baarle-Hertog . . . Bel. (Brussels In.)	51·26 N	4·57 E
111	Baarn . . . . Neth. (Amsterdam In.)	52·12 N	5·18 E
127	Babaeski (bä'bä-ĕs'kĭ) . . . . Tur.	41·25 N	27·05 E
98	Babahoyo (bä-bä-ō'yō) . . . . Ec.	1·56 S	79·24 W
167	Babanango . . . S. Afr. (Natal In.)	28·24 S	31·11 E
165	Babanusa . . . . Sud.	11·30 N	27·55 E
155	Babar (I.) (bä'bär) . . . . Indon.	7·50 S	129·15 E

Page	Name Pronunciation Region	Lat. °′	Long. °′
144	Bābel . . . . Iran	36·30 N	52·48 E
165	Bab-el-Mandeb Str.		
	(bäb'ĕl män-dĕb') . Afr.-Asia	13·17 N	42·49 E
76	Babia, Arroyo de la		
	(är-rō'yō dā lä bä'bê-ȧ) . Mex.	28·26 N	101·50 W
86	Babine (L.) (băb'ēn) . . . . Can.	54·34 N	126·47 W
86	Babine Mts. . . . . Can.	55·35 N	128·26 W
135	Babushkin (bä'bo͝osh-kĭn)		
	Sov. Un.	51·47 N	106·08 E
136	Babushkin . Sov. Un. (Moscow In.)	55·52 N	37·42 E
154	Babuyan Is. (bä-bo͞o-yän') . . . Phil.	4·30 N	122·38 E
127	Babyak (bäb'zhȧk) . . . . Bul.	41·59 N	23·42 E
84	Babylon (băb'ĭ-lŏn)		
	N. Y. (New York In.)	40·42 N	73·19 W
144	Babylon (Ruins) . . . . Iraq	32·15 N	45·23 E
155	Bacacay (bä-kä-kī')		
	Phil. (Manila In.)	13·17 N	123·48 E
92	Bacalar, Laguna de (L.)		
	(lä-go͞o-nä-dĕ-bä-kä-lär')		
	Mex. (Yucatan In.)	18·50 N	88·31 W
151	Bacarra (bä-kär'rä) . . . . Phil.	18·22 N	120·40 E
121	Bacău . . . . Rom.	46·34 N	27·00 E
123	Baccarat (bȧ-kȧ-rȧ') . . . . Fr.	48·29 N	6·42 E
74	Bacchus (băk'ŭs)		
	Utah (Salt Lake City In.)	40·40 N	112·06 W
91	Bachajón (bä-chä-hōn') . . . . . Mex.	17·08 N	92·18 W
127	Bačka Topola (Bäch'kä Tô'pô-lä')		
	Yugo.	45·48 N	19·38 E
143	Back Bay (băk)		
	India (Bombay In.)	18·55 N	72·45 E
158	Backstairs Pass. (băk-stârs')		
	Austl.	35·50 S	138·15 E
151	Bac Ninh (bäk'nēn') . . . . Viet.	21·10 N	106·02 E
155	Bacnotan (bäk-nô-tän')		
	Phil. (Manila In.)	16·43 N	120·21 E
155	Baco, Mt. (bä'kô)		
	Phil. (Manila In.)	12·50 N	121·11 E
125	Bacoli (bä-kō-lē')		
	It. (Naples In.)	40·33 N	14·05 E
154	Bacolod (bä-kō'lôd) . . . . Phil.	10·42 N	123·03 E
155	Bacon (bä-kōn') . Phil. (Manila In.)	13·02 N	124·04 E
121	Bácsalmás (bäch'ôl-mäs) . . . Hung.	46·07 N	19·18 E
110	Bacup (băk'ŭp) . . . . Eng.	53·42 N	2·12 W
70	Bad (R.) (băd) . . . . S. D.	44·04 N	100·58 W
124	Badajoz (bä-dhä-hōth') . . . . Sp.	38·52 N	6·56 W
125	Badalona (bä-dhä-lō'nä) . . . . . . Sp.	41·27 N	2·15 E
144	Badanah . . . . Sau. Ar.	30·49 N	40·45 E
80	Bad Axe (băd' ăks) . . . . Mich.	43·50 N	82·55 W
111	Bad Bramstedt (bät bräm'shtĕt)		
	Ger. (Hamburg In.)	53·55 N	9·53 E
123	Bad Ems (bät ĕms) . . . . Ger.	50·20 N	7·45 E
111	Baden (bä'dĕn) . . Aus. (Vienna In.)	48·00 N	16·14 E
120	Baden . . . . Switz.	47·28 N	8·17 E
120	Baden-Baden (bä'dĕn-bä'dĕn) . Ger.	48·46 N	8·11 E
120	Baden Württemberg (State)		
	(bä'dĕn vür'tĕm-bĕrgh) . Ger.	48·38 N	9·00 E
120	Bad Freienwalde		
	(bät frī'ĕn-väl'dĕ) . Ger.	52·47 N	14·00 E
120	Bad Hersfeld (bät hĕrsh'fĕlt) . Ger.	50·53 N	9·43 E
117	Bad Homberg (bät hōm'bĕrgh)		
	Ger.	50·14 N	8·35 E
79	Badin (bă'dĭn) . . . . N. C.	35·23 N	80·08 W
120	Bad Ischl (bät ĭsh''l) . . . . Aus.	47·46 N	13·37 E
120	Bad Kissingen (bät kĭs'ĭng-ĕn) . Ger.	50·12 N	10·05 E
120	Bad Kreuznach (bät kroits'näk)		
	Ger.	49·52 N	7·53 E
70	Badlands (Reg.) (băd' lănds)		
	N. D.	46·43 N	103·22 W
70	Badlands (Reg.) . . . . S. D.	43·43 N	102·36 W
70	Badlands Natl. Mon. . . . . S. D.	43·56 N	102·37 W
143	Badlapur . . . . India (Bombay In.)	19·12 N	73·12 E
120	Bad Oldesloe (bät ôl'dĕs-lōĕ) . Ger.	53·48 N	10·21 E
120	Bad Reichenhall (bät rī'kĕn-häl)		
	Ger.	47·43 N	12·53 E
71	Bad River Ind. Res. (băd) . . . Wis.	46·41 N	90·36 W
111	Bad Segeburg (bät sĕ'gĕ-bo͝orgh)		
	Ger. (Hamburg In.)	53·56 N	10·18 E
120	Bad Tölz (bät tûltz) . . . . Ger.	47·46 N	11·35 E
111	Bad Vöslau . . . . . Aus. (Vienna In.)	47·58 N	16·13 E
67	Badwater Cr. (băd'wô-tēr) . . Wyo.	43·13 N	107·55 W
124	Baena (bä-ā'nä) . . . . Sp.	37·38 N	4·20 W
101	Baependi (bä-ȧ-pĕn'dĭ)		
	Braz. (Rio de Janeiro In.)	21·57 S	44·51 W
49	Baffin B. (băf'ĭn) . . . . Can.	72·00 N	65·00 W
77	Baffin B. . . . . Tex.	27·11 N	97·35 W
49	Baffin I. . . . . Can.	67·20 N	71·00 W
164	Bafoulabe (bä-fo͞o-lä-bā') . . . . Mali	13·58 N	10·51 W
144	Bāfq (bäfk) . . . . Iran	31·48 N	55·23 E
133	Bafra (bäf'rä) . . . . Tur.	41·30 N	35·50 E
155	Bagabag (bä-gä-bäg')		
	Phil. (Manila In.)	16·38 N	121·16 E
143	Bāgalkot . . . . India	16·14 N	75·40 E
167	Bagamoyo (bä-gä-mō'yō) . . . . Tan.	6·28 S	38·49 E
136	Bagaryak (bȧ-gȧr-yäk')		
	Sov. Un. (Urals In.)	56·13 N	61·32 E
100	Bagé (bä-zhā') . . . . Braz.	31·17 S	54·07 W
145	Bagh (bäk) . Afg. (Khyber Pass In.)	33·47 N	70·45 E
144	Baghdad (bägh-däd') (băg'dăd)		
	Iraq	33·14 N	44·22 E
126	Bagheria (bä-gå-rē'ä) . . . . It.	38·03 N	13·32 E
70	Bagley (băg'lē) . . . . Minn.	47·31 N	95·24 W
126	Bagnara (bän-yä'rä) . . . . It.	38·17 N	15·52 E
73	Bagnell Dam (băg'nĕl) . . . . . . Mo.	38·13 N	92·40 W
122	Bagnères-de-Bigorre		
	(bän-yâr'dē-bē-gor') . Fr.	43·40 N	0·70 E
122	Bagnères-de-Luchon		
	(bän-yâr' dē-lü chôN') . Fr.	42·46 N	0·36 E
122	Bagnols (bä-nyôl') . . . . Fr.	44·09 N	4·37 E
164	Bagoe R. (bȧ-gō'ȧ) . . . . Mali	12·22 N	6·34 W
82	Bagotville (bȧ-gô-vēl') . . . . Can.	48·20 N	70·58 W
146	Bagrash Köl (L.) . . . . China	42·06 N	88·01 E
164	Baguezane, Monts (Mt.)		
	(bȧ-gē-zän') . Niger	17·45 N	8·40 E
155	Baguio (bä-gē-ō')		
	Phil. (Manila In.)	16·24 N	120·36 E
168	Bahaja, Monte (Mt.)		
	Som. (Horn of Afr. In.)	11·00 N	49·38 E
89	Bahama Is. (bȧ-hā'mȧ) . . . . . N. A.	26·15 N	76·00 W
139	Bahau . . . . . Mala. (Singapore In.)	2·48 N	102·25 E
142	Bahawalpur (bŭ-hä'wŭl-po͞or)		
	W. Pak.	29·29 N	71·41 E
	Bahia, see Salvador		
88	Bahía, Islas de la (I.)		
	(ē's-läs-dĕ-lä-bä-ē'ä) . Hond.	16·15 N	86·30 W
100	Bahia Blanca (bä-ē'ä bläŋ'kä) Arg.	38·45 S	62·07 W
98	Bahía de Caraquez		
	(bä-ē'ä dā kä-rä'kĕz) . Ec.	0·45 S	80·29 W
99	Bahía Negra (bä-ē'ä nā'grä) . . Par.	20·11 S	58·05 W
100	Bahias, Cabo dos (C.)		
	(kȧ'bô-dôs-bä-ē'äs) . Arg.	44·55 S	65·35 W
95	Bahoruco, Sierra de (Mts.)		
	(sē-ĕ'r-rä-dĕ-bä-ō-ro͞o'kô)		
	Dom. Rep.	18·10 N	71·25 W
144	Bahrain Is. (bä-rān') . . . . Asia	26·15 N	51·17 E
165	Bahr el Ghazal (Prov.)		
	(bär ĕl ghä-zäl') . Sud.	7·56 N	27·15 E
115	Baḥrīyah (Oasis) (bȧ-hȧ-rē'yȧ)		
	U. A. R.	28·34 N	29·01 E
121	Baia de Cris (bä'yä dā krēs')		
	Rom.	46·11 N	22·40 E
121	Baia-Mare (bä'yä-mä'rā) . . . Rom.	47·40 N	23·35 E
82	Baie-Comeau . . . . Can.	49·15 N	68·12 W
74	Baie de Wasai (bā dē wä-sä'ē)		
	Mich. (Sault Ste. Marie In.)	46·27 N	84·15 W
82	Baie St. Paul (bā'sănt-pôl') . . Can.	47·26 N	70·33 W
82	Baie Trinite . . . . Can.	49·24 N	67·21 W
	Baikal, see Baykal'skiy Khrebet		
	Baikal, L., see Baykal Ozero		
116	Baile Atha Cliath (Dublin)		
	(bŏ'lĕ ô'hŏ clē'ŏh) (dŭb'lĭn) . Ire.	53·20 N	6·15 W
124	Bailén (bä-ē-län') . . . . Sp.	38·05 N	3·48 W
127	Băilești (bă-ĭ-lĕsh'tē) . . . . Rom.	44·01 N	23·21 E
78	Bainbridge (bān'brĭj) . . . . Ga.	30·52 N	84·35 W
65	Bainbridge I. . . Wash. (Seattle In.)	47·39 N	122·32 W
76	Baird (bârd) . . . . Tex.	32·22 N	99·28 W
75	Bairdford (bârd'fŏrd)		
	Pa. (Pittsburgh In.)	40·37 N	79·53 W
64	Baird Mts. . . . . Alaska	67·35 N	160·10 W
160	Bairnsdale (bârnz'dāl) . . . . . . Austl.	137·50 S	47·39 E
122	Baïse (R.) (bä-ēz') . . . . Fr.	43·52 N	0·23 E
121	Baja (bŏ'yŏ) . . . . Hung.	46·11 N	18·55 E
113	Baja . . . . Tun.	36·52 N	9·20 E
88	Baja California (State)		
	(bä-hä) . Mex.	30·15 N	117·25 W
88	Baja California (Ter.) . . . . Mex.	26·00 N	113·30 W
154	Bajak (I.) . . . . Indon.	2·08 N	97·15 E
136	Bakal (bä'kăl) . Sov. Un. (Urals In.)	54·57 N	58·50 E
164	Bakel (bä-kĕl') . . . . Senegal	14·52 N	12·26 W
67	Baker (bā'kēr) . . . . Mont.	46·21 N	104·12 W
66	Baker . . . . Ore.	44·46 N	117·52 W
156	Baker (I.) . . . . Oceania	1·00 N	176·00 W
86	Baker (L.) . . . . Can.	63·51 N	96·10 W
66	Baker, Mt . . . . Wash.	48·46 N	121·52 W
75	Baker Cr. . . . . Ill. (Chicago In.)	41·13 N	87·47 W
86	Baker Lake . . . . Can.	64·18 N	96·26 W
68	Bakersfield (bā'kērz-fēld) . . Calif.	35·23 N	119·00 W
75	Bakerstown (bā'kerz-toun)		
	Pa. (Pittsburgh In.)	40·39 N	79 56 W
110	Bakewell (bāk'wĕl) . . . . Eng.	53·12 N	1·40 W
129	Bakhchisaray (bȧk'chē-sȧ-rī')		
	Sov. Un.	44·46 N	33·54 E
129	Bakhmach (bȧk-mäch') . . Sov. Un.	51·09 N	32·47 E
144	Bakhtegān, Daryachch-ye (L.)		
	Iran	29·29 N	54·31 E
136	Bakhteyevo (bȧk-tyĕ'yĕ-vô)		
	Sov. Un. (Moscow In.)	55·35 N	38·32 E
165	Bāko (bä'kō) . . . . Eth.	5·47 N	36·39 E
121	Bakony-Erdo (Mts.) (bȧ-kōn'y')		
	Hung.	46·57 N	17·30 E
164	Bakoy R. (bȧ-kô'ē) . . . . Mali	12·49 N	9·51 W
136	Bakr Uzyak (bȧkr o͞oz'yȧk)		
	Sov. Un. (Urals In.)	52·59 N	58·43 E
133	Baku (bȧ-ko͞o') . . . . Sov. Un.	40·28 N	49·45 E
154	Balabac (I.) (bä'lä-bäk) . . . . . Phil.	8·00 N	116·28 E
154	Balabac Str. . . . . Indon.-Phil.	7·23 N	116·30 E
139	Ba'labakk . . . . Leb. (Palestine In.)	34·00 N	36·13 E
154	Balabalagan (I.) (bä-lä-bä'lä-gän)		
	Indon.	2·00 S	117·15 E
136	Balabanovo (bȧ-lȧ-bä'nô-vô)		
	Sov. Un. (Moscow In.)	56·10 N	37·44 E
134	Balagansk (bä-lä-gänsk')		
	Sov. Un.	53·58 N	103·09 E
125	Balaguer (bä-lä-gĕr') . . . . Sp.	41·48 N	0·50 E
134	Balakhta (bȧ'lȧk-tȧ') . . . . Sov. Un.	55·22 N	91·43 E
129	Balakleya (bȧ'lȧ-klā'yȧ) . Sov. Un.	49·28 N	36·51 E
133	Balakovo (bȧ'lȧ-kô'vô) . . Sov. Un.	52·00 N	47·40 E
91	Balancán (bä-läŋ-kän') . . . . . . Mex.	17·47 N	91·32 W
155	Balanga (bä-läŋ'gä)		
	Phil. (Manila In.)	14·41 N	120·31 E
155	Balaoan (bä-lou'än)		
	Phil. (Manila In.)	16·49 N	120·24 E
136	Balashikha (bȧ-lȧ'shĭ-kȧ)		
	Sov. Un. (Moscow In.)	55·48 N	37·58 E
133	Balashov (bȧ'lȧ-shôf) . . . . Sov. Un.	51·30 N	43·00 E
142	Balasore (bä-lä-sōr') . . . . India	21·38 N	86·59 E
121	Balassagyarmat		
	(bô'lôsh-shô-dyôr'môt) . Hung.	48·04 N	19·19 E
121	Balaton L. (bô'lô-tôn) . . . . . . Hung.	46·47 N	17·55 E
155	Balayan (bä-lä-yän')		
	Phil. (Manila In.)	13·56 N	120·44 E
155	Balayan B. . . . . Phil. (Manila In.)	13·46 N	120·46 E
74	Balboa (băl-bō'ȧ)		
	Calif. (Los Angeles In.)	33·36 N	117·54 W
88	Balboa (bäl-bô'ä)		
	C. Z. (Panama Canal In.)	8·55 N	79·34 W
93	Balboa Heights . . . . Pan.	8·59 N	79·33 W
88	Balboa Mt.		
	C. Z. (Panama Canal In.)	9·05 N	79·44 W
100	Balcarce (bäl-kär'sā) . . . . Arg.	37·49 S	58·17 W
127	Balchik . . . . Bul.	43·24 N	28·13 E
74	Bald Eagle (bôld ē'g'l)		
	Minn. (Minneapolis, St. Paul In.)	45·06 N	93·01 W
74	Bald Eagle L.		
	Minn. (Minneapolis, St. Paul In.)	45·08 N	93·03 W
142	Baldin . . . . W. Pak.	24·47 N	69·51 E
74	Baldwin Park (bôld'wĭn)		
	Calif. (Los Angeles In.)	34·05 N	117·58 W
81	Baldwinsville (bôld'wĭns-vĭl) . N. Y.	43·10 N	76·20 W
69	Baldy Pk. (bôl'dê) . . . . Ariz.	33·55 N	109·35 W
76	Baldy Pk. (bôl'dê pēk) . . . . . . Tex.	30·38 N	104·11 W
125	Baleares, Islas (Balearic Is.)		
	(ē's-läs bä-lĕ-ä'rĕs) . Sp.	39·25 N	1·28 E
	Balearic Is., see Baleares, Islas		
125	Balearic Sea (băl-ē-ăr'ĭk) . . . . . Eur.	39·40 N	1·05 E
155	Baler (bä-lâr') . . Phil. (Manila In.)	15·46 N	121·33 E
155	Baler B. . . . . . . Phil. (Manila In.)	15·51 N	121·40 E
155	Balesin (I.) . . . Phil. (Manila In.)	14·28 N	122·10 E
135	Baley (bȧl-yā') . . . . Sov. Un.	51·29 N	116·12 E
92	Balfate (bäl-fä'tē) . . . . Hond.	15·48 N	86·24 W
168	Balfour (băl'fo͝or) . S. Afr.		
	(Johannesburg & Pretoria In.)	26·41 S	28·37 E
154	Bali (I.) (bä'lē) . . . . Indon.	8·00 S	115·22 E
133	Balikesir (bä-lĭ-kĕ-sēr') . . . . . . Tur.	39·40 N	27·50 E
154	Balikpapan (bä'lĕk-pä'pän) . Indon.	1·13 N	116·52 E
154	Balintang Chan. (bä-lĭn-täng')		
	Phil.	19·50 N	121·08 E
	Balkan Mts., see Stara Planina		
142	Balkh (bälk) . . . . Afg.	36·48 N	66·50 E
134	Balkhash (bȧl-kăsh') . . . . Sov. Un.	46·58 N	75·00 E
134	Balkhash, Ozero (L.) . . . . Sov. Un.	45·58 N	72·15 E
129	Balki (bäl'kĭ) . . . . Sov. Un.	47·22 N	34·56 E
123	Ballancourt (bä-läN-ko͞or')		
	Fr. (Paris In.)	48·31 N	2·23 E
160	Ballarat (băl'ȧ-răt) . . . . Austl.	37·37 S	144·00 E
158	Ballard (I.) (băl'ȧrd) . . . . Austl.	29·15 S	120·45 E
116	Ballater (băl'ȧ-tēr) . . . . Scot.	57·05 N	3·06 W
47	Balleny Is. (băl'ĕ nē) . . . . Ant.	67·00 S	164·00 E
160	Ballina (băl-ĭ-nä') . . . . Austl.	28·50 S	153·35 E
116	Ballina . . . . Ire.	54·06 N	9·05 W
116	Ballinasloe (băl'ĭ-nȧ-slō') . . . . . . Ire.	53·20 N	8·09 W
76	Ballinger (băl'ĭn-jēr) . . . . Tex.	31·45 N	99·58 W
81	Ballston Spa (bôls'tŭn spä') . N. Y.	43·05 N	73·50 W
142	Bally . . . . India (Calcutta In.)	22·38 N	88·20 E
121	Balmazújváros		
	(bŏl'mŏz-o͞o'y'vä'rôsh) . Hung.	47·35 N	21·23 E
160	Balonne (R.) (băl-ōn') . . . . . . Austl.	27·00 S	149·10 E
142	Balotra . . . . India	25·56 N	72·12 E
160	Balranald (băl'-rȧn-ăld) . . . . Austl.	34·42 S	143·30 E
127	Balş (bälsh) . . . . Rom.	44·21 N	24·05 E
81	Balsam (L.) (bôl'sȧm) . . . . Can.	44·30 N	78·50 W
99	Balsas (bäl'säs) . . . . Braz.	7·09 S	46·04 W
90	Balsas (R.) . . . . Mex.	18·15 N	102·08 W
129	Balta (bäl'tȧ) . . . . Sov. Un.	47·57 N	29·38 E
112	Baltic Sea (bôl'tĭk) . . . . Eur.	55·20 N	16·50 E
168	Balṭīm (bȧl-tēm')		
	U. A. R. (Nile In.)	31·33 N	31·04 E
84	Baltimore (bôl'tĭ-môr)		
	Md. (Baltimore In.)	39·20 N	76·38 W
119	Baltiysk (bäl-tēysk') . . . . . Sov. Un.	54·40 N	19·55 E
145	Baluchistan (Reg.)		
	(bȧ-lo͞o-chĭ-stän') . W. Pak.	27·45 N	66·58 E
90	Balurte, Río del		
	(rē'ō-dĕl-bä-lo͞o'r-tĕ) . Mex.	23·09 N	105·42 W
85	Balzac (bôl'zăk) . Can. (Calgary In.)	51·13 N	114·00 W
164	Bamako (bä-mä-kō') . . . . Mali	12·45 N	7·50 W
164	Bamba (bäm-bä') . . . . Mali	17·13 N	1·30 W
155	Bambang (bäm-bäng')		
	Phil. (Manila In.)	16·24 N	121·08 E
165	Bambari (bäm-bȧ-rē)		
	Cen. Afr. Rep.	5·44 N	20·40 E
120	Bamberg (bäm'bĕrgh) . . . . Ger.	49·53 N	10·52 E
79	Bamberg (băm'bûrg) . . . . S. C.	33·17 N	81·04 W
165	Bambesa (bäm-bĕ'sä) . . . . . Con. L.	3·46 N	26·09 E
101	Bambuí (bä'm-bo͞o'-ē)		
	Braz. (Rio de Janeiro In.)	20·01 S	45·59 W
164	Bambuto Mts. (bäm-bo͞o'tō)		
	Nig.-Cam.	6·22 N	11·14 E
110	Bampton (băm'tŭn)		
	Eng. (London In.)	51·42 N	1·33 W
144	Bampūr (bŭm-po͞or') . . . . Iran	27·15 N	60·22 E
155	Banahao, Mt. (bä-nä-hä'ô)		
	Phil. (Manila In.)	14·04 N	121·45 E
101	Bananal (bä-nä-näl')		
	Braz. (Rio de Janeiro In.)	22·42 S	44·17 W
99	Bananal, Ilha do (I.)		
	(ē'lä-dô-bä-nä-näl') . Braz.	12·09 S	50·27 W
	Banaras, see Vārānasi		
142	Banās (R.) (bän-äs') . . . . India	25·20 N	74·51 E
165	Banas, Ra's (C.) . . . . U. A. R.	23·48 N	36·39 E
127	Banat (Reg.) (bä-nät')		
	Yugo.-Rom.	45·35 N	21·05 E
154	Ban Bangsaphan . . . . Thai.	11·19 N	99·27 E
98	Banco (bän'-kô) . . . . Col.	8·58 N	74·01 W
81	Bancroft (băn'krŏft) . . . . Can.	45·05 N	77·55 W
142	Banda (băn'dä) . . . . India	25·36 N	80·21 E
155	Banda (I.) . . . . Indon.	4·40 S	129·56 E
160	Banda Banda, Mt.		
	(băn'dȧ băn'dȧ) . Austl.	31·09 S	152·15 E
164	Bandama R. (bän-dä'mä)		
	Ivory Coast	6·19 N	5·40 W
144	Bandar Abbās (Hbr.) (bän-där'		
	ȧb-bäs') . Iran	27·04 N	56·22 E
144	Bandar-e Lengeh (Hbr.) . . . . . Iran	26·44 N	54·47 E
133	Bandar-e Pahlanī (bän-där') . Iran	37·30 N	49·30 E
144	Bandar-e-Shāhpūr (Hbr.) . . . . Iran	30·27 N	48·45 E
139	Bandar Maharani		
	(bän-där' mä-hä-rä'nē)		
	Mala. (Singapore In.)	2·02 N	102·34 E
139	Bandar Penggaram		
	Mala. (Singapore In.)	1·51 N	102·56 E
144	Bandar Shah (Hbr.) . . . . Iran	37·00 N	54·08 E
155	Banda Sea (bän'dä) . . . . Indon.	6·05 S	127·28 E
101	Bandeira, Pico da (Pk.) (pē'ko͞o dä		
	bän-dā'rä) . Braz. (Rio de Janeiro		
	In.)	20·27 S	41·47 W

Page	Name Pronunciation Region	Lat. °'	Long. °'
69	Bandelier Natl. Mon. (băn-dĕ-lēr') N. Mex.	35·50 N	106·45 W
90	Banderas, Bahía de (B.) (bä-ē'ä-dĕ-băn-dĕ'räs). Mex.	20·38 N	103·25 W
168	Bander Beila Som. (Horn of Afr. In.)	9·40 N	50·45 E
164	Bandiagara (băn-dê-ȧ-gä'rä). Mali	14·19 N	3·39 W
133	Bandirma (băn-dĭr'mȧ) Tur.	40·25 N	27·50 E
154	Bandjermasin (băn-jĕr-mä'sĕn) Indon.	3·18 S	114·32 E
124	Bando (bä'n-dô) Sp.	42·02 N	7·58 W
66	Bandon (băn'dŭn) Ore.	43·06 N	124·25 W
143	Bāndra India (Bombay In.)	19·04 N	72·49 E
154	Bandung Indon.	7·00 S	107·22 E
95	Banes (bä'näs) Cuba	21·00 N	75·45 W
86	Banff (bănf) Can.	51·17 N	115·30 W
116	Banff Scot.	57·39 N	2·37 W
86	Banff Natl. Park Can.	51·45 N	116·04 W
100	Bánfield (bá'n-fyĕ'ld) Arg. (In.)	34·30 S	58·24 W
143	Bangalore (băŋ'gȧ'lôr) India	13·03 N	77·39 E
155	Bangar (băŋ-gär') Phil. (Manila In.)	16·54 N	120·24 E
165	Bangassou (bäɴ-gȧ-sōō') Cen. Afr. Rep.	4·47 N	22·49 E
155	Bangeta, Mt. N. Gui. Ter.	6·20 S	147·00 E
155	Banggai, Pulau-Palau (Is.) (bäng-gī') Indon.	1·05 S	123·45 E
154	Banggi (I.) Mala.	7·12 N	117·10 E
165	Banghāzī (Bengasi) (bĕn-gä'zē) Libya	32·08 N	20·06 E
139	Bangi Mala. (Singapore In.)	2·54 N	101·48 E
154	Bangka (I.) (băŋ'kȧ) Indon.	2·24 S	106·55 E
154	Bangkalan (bäng-kȧ-län') Indon.	6·07 S	112·50 E
	Bangkok, see Krung Thep		
82	Bangor (băn'gĕr) Maine	44·47 N	68·47 W
80	Bangor Mich.	42·20 N	86·05 W
81	Bangor Pa.	40·55 N	75·10 W
116	Bangor (băŋ'ĕr) (băŋ'ŏr) Wales	53·13 N	4·05 W
69	Bangs, Mt. (băngs) Ariz.	36·45 N	113·50 W
155	Bangued (bän-gād') Phil. (Manila In.)	17·36 N	120·38 E
165	Bangui (bäɴ-gē') Cen. Afr. Rep.	4·28 N	18·35 E
166	Bangweulu, L. (băng-wē-ōō'lōō) N. Rh.	10·30 S	30·15 E
168	Banhā U. A. R. (Nile In.)	30·24 N	31·11 E
95	Bani (bä'-nē) Dom. Rep.	18·15 N	70·25 W
155	Bani (bä'nē) Phil. (Manila In.)	16·11 N	119·51 E
164	Bani (R.) Mali	13·00 N	5·36 W
164	Bani, Jebel (Mts.) (jĕb'ĕl bä'nē) Mor.	28·39 N	9·33 W
95	Bánica (bä'-nē-kä) Dom. Rep.	19·00 N	71·35 W
168	Banī Mazār U. A. R. (Nile In.)	28·29 N	30·48 E
168	Banī Suwayf U. A. R. (Nile In.)	29·05 N	31·06 E
126	Banja Luka (bän-yä-lōō'kȧ) Yugo.	44·45 N	17·11 E
154	Banjuwangi (bän-jōō-wäŋ'gē) Indon.	8·15 S	114·15 E
154	Ban Kantang (bän-kän'täng') Thai.	7·26 N	99·28 E
167	Bankberg (Mts.) (bȧŋk'bûrg) S. Afr. (Natal In.)	32·10 S	25·11 E
65	Banks (bănks) Ore. (Portland In.)	45·37 N	123·07 W
159	Banks (Is.) Austl.	10·10 S	143·08 E
161	Banks, C. Austl. (Sydney In.)	34·01 S	151·17 E
49	Banks I. Can.	73·00 N	123·00 W
159	Banks Is. New Hebr.	13·38 S	168·23 E
160	Banks Str. Austl.	40·45 S	148·00 E
154	Ban Kui Nua Thai.	12·04 N	99·50 E
116	Bann (R.) (băn) N. Ire.	54·50 N	6·29 W
74	Banning (băn'ĭng) Calif. (Los Angeles In.)	33·56 N	116·53 W
166	Banningville Con. L.	3·19 S	17·28 E
79	Bannister (R.) (băn'ĭs-tẽr) Va.	36·45 N	79·17 W
161	Bannockburn Austl. (Melbourne In.)	38·03 S	144·11 E
98	Baños (bä'-nyôs) Ec.	1·30 S	78·22 W
121	Banská Bystrica (bän'skä bē'strē-tzä) Czech.	48·46 N	19·10 E
127	Bansko (bän'skō) Bul.	41·51 N	23·33 E
110	Banstead (băn'stĕd) Eng. (London In.)	51·18 N	0·09 W
164	Banthe (băn'thĕ) S. L.	7·36 N	12·34 W
155	Banton (bän-tōn') Phil. (Manila In.)	12·54 N	121·55 E
116	Bantry (băn'trĭ) Ire.	51·39 N	9·30 W
116	Bantry B. Ire.	51·25 N	10·09 W
165	Banzyville (bäɴ-zē-vēl') Con. L.	4·14 N	21·11 E
164	Baoule R. (bȧ-ōō-lā') Mali	14·00 N	9·08 W
167	Bapsfontein (băps-fŏn-tān') S. Afr. (Johannesburg & Pretoria In.)	26·01 S	28·26 E
98	Baqueroncito (bä-kĕ-rô'n-sē-tô) Col. (In.)	3·18 N	74·40 W
129	Bar (bär) Sov. Un.	49·02 N	27·44 E
127	Bar Yugo.	42·05 N	19·09 E
134	Barabinsk (bá'rȧ-bĭnsk) Sov. Un.	55·18 N	78·00 E
71	Baraboo (bâr'ȧ-bōō) Wis.	43·29 N	89·44 W
95	Baracoa (bä-rä-kō'ä) Cuba	20·20 N	74·25 W
95	Baracoa Cuba (Havana In.)	23·03 N	82·34 W
101	Baradeo (bä-rä-dĕ'ŏ) Arg. (Buenos Aires In.)	33·50 S	59·30 W
95	Baradères, Baie des (B.) (bä-rä-dâr') Hai.	18·35 N	73·35 W
95	Barahona (bä-rä-ô'nä) Dom. Rep.	18·15 N	71·10 W
125	Barajas de Madrid (bä-rä'häs dā mä-drēdh') Sp. (Madrid In.)	40·28 N	3·35 W
165	Baraka R. (bȧ-rä'kȧ) Eth.	16·44 N	37·34 E
142	Baranagar India (Calcutta In.)	22·38 N	88·25 E
92	Baranco (bä-räŋ'kō) Br. Hond.	16·01 N	88·55 W
64	Baranof (I.) (bä-rä'nôf) Alaska	56·48 N	136·08 W
121	Baranovichi (bä'rä-nô-vē'chē) Sov. Un.	53·08 N	25·59 E
139	Baranpauh Indon. (Singapore In.)	0·40 N	103·28 E
100	Barão de Juperanã (bä-rouɴ-dĕ-zhōō-pe-rä'nȧ) Braz. (In.)	22·21 S	43·41 W
99	Barão de Melgaço (bä-rouɴ-dĕ-mĕl-gä'sō) Braz.	16·12 S	55·48 W
142	Bārāsat India (Calcutta In.)	22·42 N	88·29 E
84	Barataria (bä-rȧ-tä'rē-ȧ) La. (New Orleans In.)	29·44 N	90·08 W
77	Barataria B. La.	29·13 N	89·90 W
98	Baraya (bä-rä'yä) Col. (In.)	3·10 N	75·04 W
101	Barbacena (bär-bä-sā'nȧ) Braz. (Rio de Janeiro In.)	21·15 S	43·46 W
98	Barbacoas (bär-bä-kō'äs) Col.	1·39 N	78·12 W
99	Barbacoas (bär-bä-kô'äs) Ven. (In.)	9·30 N	66·58 W
93	Barbados I. (bär-bā'dōz) N. A. (Le. & Wind. Is. In.)	13·30 N	59·48 W
125	Barbastro (bär-bäs'trō) Sp.	42·05 N	0·05 E
74	Barbeau (bár-bō') Mich. (Sault Ste. Marie In.)	46·17 N	84·16 W
75	Barberton (bär'bẽr-tŭn) Ohio (Cleveland In.)	41·01 N	81·37 W
166	Barberton S. Afr.	25·48 S	31·04 E
122	Barbezieux (bärb'zyû') Fr.	45·30 N	0·11 W
78	Barbourville (bär'bẽr-vĭl) Ky.	36·52 N	83·58 W
98	Barbosa (bär-bô'-sȧ) Col. (In.)	6·26 N	75·19 W
80	Barboursville (bär'bẽrs-vĭl) W. Va.	38·20 N	82·20 W
93	Barbuda I. (bär-bōō'dȧ) Barbados (Le. & Wind. Is. In.)	17·40 N	61·37 W
159	Barcaldine (bär'kôl-dīn) Austl.	28·30 S	145·43 E
125	Barcarena (bär-kä-rĕ'-nä) Port. (Lisbon In.)	38·29 N	9·17 W
124	Barcarrota (bär-kär-rō'tä) Sp.	38·31 N	6·50 W
126	Barcellona (bär-chĕl-lō'nä) It.	38·07 N	15·15 E
125	Barcelona (bär-thȧ-lō'nä) Sp.	41·25 N	2·08 E
99	Barcelona (bär-sȧ-lō'nä) Ven. (In.)	10·09 N	64·41 W
123	Barcelonnette (bär-sĕ-lô-nĕt') Fr.	44·24 N	6·42 E
98	Barcelos (bär-sĕ'lôs) Braz.	1·04 S	63·00 W
124	Barcélos (bär-thȧ'lōs) Port.	41·34 N	8·39 W
144	Bardar-e Pahlant Iran	37·16 N	49·15 E
139	Bardawīl, Sabkhat al (B.) U. A. R. (Palestine In.)	31·20 N	33·24 E
121	Bardejov (bär'dyĕ-yôf) Czech.	49·18 N	21·18 E
168	Bardera (bär-dā'rä) Som. (Horn of Afr. In.)	2·13 N	42·24 E
116	Bardsey (I.) (bärd'sē) Wales	52·45 N	4·50 W
80	Bardstown (bärds'toun) Ky.	37·50 N	85·30 W
78	Bardwell (bärd'wĕl) Ky.	36·51 N	88·57 W
130	Barents Sea (bä'rĕnts) Sov. Un.	72·14 N	37·28 E
165	Barentu (bär-rĕn'tōō) Eth.	15·06 N	37·39 E
122	Barfleur, Pte. de (Pt.) (bȧr-flûr') Fr	49·43 N	1·17 W
142	Bargāchia India (Calcutta In.)	22·39 N	88·07 E
135	Barguzin (bär'gōō-zĭn) Sov. Un.	53·44 N	109·28 E
82	Bar Harbor (bär här'bẽr) Maine	44·22 N	68·13 W
126	Bari (bä'rē) It.	41·08 N	16·53 E
98	Barinas (bä-rē'näs) Ven.	8·36 N	70·14 W
86	Baring, C. (bâr'ĭng) Can.	70·07 N	119·48 W
154	Barisan, Pegunungan (Mts.) (bä-rē-sän') Indon.	2·38 S	101·45 E
154	Barito (Strm.) (bä-rē'tō) Indon.	2·10 S	114·38 E
167	Barkly East (bärk'lē ēst) S. Afr. (Natal In.)	30·58 S	27·37 E
158	Barkly Tableland (Reg.) (bär'klē) Austl.	18·15 S	145·55 E
122	Bar-le-Duc (băr-lē-dük') Fr.	48·47 N	5·05 E
158	Barlee (L.) (bär-lē') Austl.	29·45 S	119·00 E
126	Barletta (bär-lĕt'tä) It.	41·19 N	16·20 E
111	Barmstedt (bärm'shtĕt) Ger. (Hamburg In.)	53·47 N	9·46 E
134	Barnaul (bär-nä-ōōl') Sov. Un.	53·18 N	83·23 E
81	Barnesboro (bärnz'bẽr-ô) Pa.	40·45 N	78·50 W
78	Barnesville (bärnz'vĭl) Ga.	33·03 N	84·10 W
70	Barnesville Minn.	46·38 N	96·25 W
80	Barnesville Ohio	39·55 N	81·10 W
81	Barnet (bär'nĕt) Vt.	44·20 N	72·00 W
110	Barnetby (bär'nĕt-bĭ) Eng.	53·34 N	0·26 W
94	Barnett Hbr. Ba. Is.	25·40 N	79·20 W
73	Barnsdall (bärnz'dôl) Okla.	36·38 N	96·14 W
110	Barnsley (bärnz'lĭ) Eng.	53·33 N	1·29 W
116	Barnstaple (bärn'stā-p'l) Eng.	51·06 N	4·05 W
79	Barnwell (bärn'wĕl) S. C.	33·14 N	81·23 W
164	Baro (bä'rō) Nig.	8·34 N	6·25 E
142	Baroda (bä-rō'dä) India	22·21 N	73·12 E
165	Baro R. Eth.	7·40 N	34·17 E
166	Barotseland (Reg.) (bȧ-rŏt'sē-lănd) N. Rh.	16·00 S	22·52 E
165	Barqah (Cirenaica) (Prov.) Libya	31·09 N	21·45 E
98	Barquisimeto (bär-kē-sē-mä'tō) Ven.	10·04 N	69·16 W
99	Barra (bär'rä) Braz.	11·04 S	43·11 W
142	Barrackpore India (Calcutta In.)	22·46 N	88·22 E
99	Barra do Corda (bär'rä dŏŏ cōr-dä) Braz.	5·33 S	45·13 W
116	Barra Is. (băr'rȧ) Scot.	56·57 N	6·85 W
101	Barra Mansa (bär'rä män'sä) Braz. (Rio de Janeiro In.)	22·35 S	44·09 W
98	Barrancabermeja (bär-räŋ'kä-bĕr-mā'hä) Col.	7·06 N	73·49 W
98	Barranquilla (bär-rän-kēl'yä) Col.	10·57 N	75·00 W
99	Barras (bä'r-räs) Braz.	4·13 S	42·14 W
81	Barre (băr'ē) Vt.	44·15 N	72·30 W
101	Barre do Piraí (bär-rĕ-dô-pē'rä-ē') Braz. (Rio de Janeiro In.)	22·30 S	43·49 W
99	Barreiras (bär-rā'-räs) Braz.	12·13 S	44·59 W
125	Barreiro (bär-rĕ'ē-rōō) Port. (Lisbon In.)	38·39 N	9·05 W
160	Barren, C. (băr'ĕn) Austl.	40·20 S	149·00 E
167	Barren, Îles (Is.) Malag. Rep.	18·18 S	43·57 E
78	Barren (R.) Ky.	37·00 N	86·20 W
99	Barretos (bär-rā'tōs) Braz.	20·40 S	48·36 W
86	Barrhead (băr-hĕd) (băr'ĭd) Can.	54·10 N	114·20 W
81	Barrie (băr'ĭ) Can.	44·25 N	79·45 W
85	Barrington (bă-rēng-tŏn) Can. (Montreal In.)	45·07 N	73·35 W
75	Barrington Ill. (Chicago In.)	42·09 N	88·08 W
84	Barrington R. I. (Providence In.)	41·44 N	71·16 W
160	Barrington Tops (Mtn.) Austl.	32·00 S	151·25 E
74	Bar River (bär) Can. (Sault Ste. Marie In.)	46·27 N	84·02 W
71	Barron (băr'ŭn) Wis.	45·24 N	91·51 W
64	Barrow (băr'ō) Alaska	71·20 N	156·00 W
116	Barrow Eng.	54·10 N	3·15 W
158	Barrow (I.) Austl.	21·05 S	11·30 E
64	Barrow, Pt. Alaska	71·20 N	156·00 W
158	Barrow Creek Austl.	21 23 S	133·55 E
116	Barrow R. (bă-rä) Ire.	52·35 N	7·05 W
124	Barruelo de Santullán (bär-rōō-ā-lō dā sän-tōō-lyän') Sp.	42·55 N	4·19 W
74	Barry (băr'rĭ) Mo. (Kansas City In.)	39·14 N	94·36 W
68	Barstow (bär'stō) Calif.	34·53 N	117·03 W
120	Barth (bärt) Ger.	54·20 N	12·43 E
73	Bartholomew Bay. (bär-thŏl'ō-mū bī-ōō') Ark.	33·53 N	91·45 W
82	Barthurst (băr-thŭrst') Can.	47·38 N	65·40 W
99	Bartica (bär'tĭ-kȧ) Br. Gu.	6·23 N	58·32 W
133	Bartin (bär'tĭn) Tur.	41·35 N	32·12 E
159	Bartle Frere, Mt. (bärt'l frēr') Austl.	17·30 S	145·46 E
73	Bartlesville (bär'tlz-vĭl) Okla.	36·44 N	95·58 W
75	Bartlett (bärt'lĕt) Ill. (Chicago In.)	41·59 N	88·11 W
77	Bartlett Tex.	30·48 N	97·25 W
81	Barton (bär'tŭn) Vt.	44·45 N	72·05 W
110	Barton-on-Humber (bär'tŭn-ŏn-hŭm'bẽr) Eng.	53·41 N	0·26 W
121	Bartoszyce (bär-tô-shĭ'tsȧ) Pol.	54·15 N	20·50 E
79	Bartow (bär'tō) Fla. (In.)	27·51 N	81·50 W
129	Barvenkovo (bär'vĕn-kô'vô) Sov. Un.	48·55 N	36·59 E
160	Barwon (R.) (bär'wŭn) Austl.	29·45 S	148·25 E
161	Barwon Heads Austl. (Melbourne In.)	38·17 S	144·59 E
120	Barycz R. (bä'rĭch) Pol.	51·30 N	16·38 E
165	Basankusu (bȧ-sän-kōō'sōō) Con. L.	1·14 N	19·45 E
111	Basbeck (bäs'bĕk) Ger. (Hamburg In.)	53·40 N	9·11 E
111	Basdahl (bäs'däl) Ger. (Hamburg In.)	53·27 N	9·00 E
74	Basehor (bās'hôr) Kans. (Kansas City In.)	39·08 N	94·55 W
120	Basel (bä'z'l) Switz.	47·32 N	7·35 E
167	Bashee (R.) (bă-shē') S. Afr. (Natal In.)	31·47 S	28·25 E
151	Bashi Chan (bäsh'ē) Phil.	21·20 N	120·22 E
132	Bashkir (A.S.S.R.) (bȧsh-kēr') Sov. Un.	54·12 N	57·15 E
129	Bashtanka (bȧsh-tän'kȧ) Sov. Un.	47·32 N	32·31 E
154	Basilan (I.) Phil.	6·37 N	122·07 E
126	Basilicata (Reg.) (bä-zē-lē-kä'tä) It.	40·30 N	15·55 E
67	Basin (bā'sĭn) Wyo.	44·22 N	108·02 W
110	Basingstoke (bā'zĭng-stōk) Eng. (London In.)	51·14 N	1·06 W
126	Baška (bäsh'ka) Yugo.	44·58 N	14·44 E
133	Baskale (bäsh-kä'lĕ) Tur.	38·10 N	44·00 E
133	Baskunchak (L.) Sov. Un.	48·20 N	46·40 E
165	Basoko (nä-sō'kō) Con. L.	0·52 N	23·50 E
165	Basoko Con. L.	1·22 N	23·40 E
86	Bassano (bäs-sän'ō) Can.	50·44 N	112·35 W
126	Bassano It.	45·46 N	11·44 E
167	Bassas da India (I.) (bäs'säs dä ēn'dē-ȧ) Malag. Rep.	21·23 S	39·42 E
154	Bassein (bŭ-sēn') Bur.	16·46 N	94·47 E
143	Bassein India (Bombay In.)	19·20 N	72·47 E
79	Basset (băs'sĕt) Va.	36·45 N	81·58 W
93	Basse Terre (bäs' târ') Basse Terre (Le. & Wind. Is. In.)	16·00 N	61·43 W
93	Basseterre St. Kitts-Nevis-Anguilla (Le. & Wind. Is. In.)	17·20 N	62·42 W
93	Basse Terre I. Guad. (Le. & Wind. Is. In.)	16·10 N	62·14 W
80	Bass Is. (băs) Ohio	41·40 N	82·50 W
160	Bass Str. Austl.	39·40 S	145·40 E
71	Basswood (L.) (băs'wŏŏd) Can.-Minn.	48·10 N	91·36 W
118	Båstad (bô'stät) Swe.	56·26 N	12·46 E
126	Bastia (bäs'tē-ä) Fr.	42·43 N	9·27 E
117	Bastogne (bäs-tôn'y') Bel.	50·02 N	5·45 E
77	Bastrop (băs'trŭp) La.	32·47 N	91·55 W
77	Bastrop Tex.	30·08 N	97·18 W
77	Bastrop Bay Tex. (In.)	29·07 N	95·22 W
166	Basutoland (bȧ-sōō'tō-lănd) Afr.	29·45 S	28·07 E
164	Bata (bä'tä) Rio Muni	1·53 N	9·48 E
94	Batabanó (bä-tä-bä-nō') Cuba	22·45 N	82·20 W
94	Batabano, Golfo de (G.) (gôl-fô-dĕ-bä-tä-bä'nô) Cuba	22·10 N	83·05 W
155	Batac Phil. (Manila In.)	17·56 N	120·29 E
142	Batala India	31·54 N	75·18 E
136	Bataly (bȧ-tä'lĭ) Sov. Un. (Urals In.)	52·51 N	62·03 E
139	Batam I. (bä-tām') Indon. (Singapore In.)	1·03 N	104·00 E
155	Batan (bä-tän') Phil. (Manila In.)	13·20 N	124·00 E
151	Batan Is. Phil.	20·58 N	122·20 E
151	Batangan, C. Viet.	15·18 N	109·10 E
155	Batangas (bä-tän'gäs) Phil. (Manila In.)	13·45 N	121·04 E
121	Bataszék (bä'tȧ-sĕk) Hung.	46·07 N	18·40 E
75	Batavia (bȧ-tā'vĭ-ȧ) Ill. (Chicago In.)	41·51 N	88·18 W
81	Batavia N. Y.	43·00 N	78·15 W
75	Batavia Ohio (Cincinnati In.)	39·05 N	84·10 W
129	Bataysk (bȧ-tīsk') Sov. Un.	47·08 N	39·44 E
79	Batesburg (bāts'bûrg) S. C.	33·53 N	81·34 W
73	Batesville (bāts'vĭl) Ark.	35·46 N	91·39 W
80	Batesville Ind.	39·15 N	85·15 W
78	Batesville Miss.	34·17 N	89·55 W
128	Batetska (bȧ-tĕ'tskȧ) Sov. Un.	58·36 N	30·21 E
82	Bath (bȧth) Can.	46·31 N	67·36 W
116	Bath Eng.	51·24 N	2·20 W
82	Bath Maine	43·54 N	69·50 W
81	Bath N. Y.	42·25 N	77·20 W
75	Bath Ohio (Cleveland In.)	41·11 N	81·38 W
93	Bathsheba Barbados (Le. & Wind. Is. In.)	13·13 N	60·30 W

Page	Name Pronunciation	Region	Lat. °′	Long. °′
159	Bathurst (băth'ŭrst)	Aust.	33·28 S	149·30 E
164	Bathurst	Gam.	13·23 N	16·45 W
167	Bathurst (băt-hûrst)	S. Afr. (Natal In.)	33·26 S	26·53 E
64	Bathurst, C. (băth'ŭrst)	Can.	70·33 N	127·55 W
158	Bathurst (I.)	Austl.	11·19 S	130·13 E
86	Bathurst Inlet	Can.	67·25 N	106·50 W
155	Batian (I.)	Indon.	1·07 S	127·52 E
144	Batin, Wādī al (R.)	Sau. Ar.	27·17 N	44·13 E
155	Batjan (I.) (bät-jän')	Indon.	1·07 S	127.52 E
144	Bātlaq-E Gāvkhūn (L.)	Iran	31·40 N	52·48 E
110	Batley (băt'lĭ)	Eng.	53·43 N	1·37 W
164	Batna (bät'nä)	Alg.	35·41 N	6·12 E
77	Baton Rouge (băt'ŭn rōōzh')	La.	30·28 N	91·10 W
154	Battambang (bát-tám-bäng')	Camb.	13·14 N	103·15 E
84	Battery Park (băt'ēr-ĭ)	Va. (Norfolk In.)	36·59 N	76·36 W
80	Battle Creek (băt''l krēk')	Mich.	42·20 N	85·15 W
86	Battleford (băt''l-fērd)	Can.	52·44 N	108·30 W
65	Battle Ground (băt''l ground)	Wash. (Portland In.)	45·47 N	122·32 W
87	Battle Harbour (băt''l här'bēr)	Can.	52·17 N	55·33 W
66	Battle Mountain	Nev.	40·40 N	116·56 W
121	Battonya (bät-tô'nyä)	Hung.	46·17 N	21·00 E
154	Batu (I.) (bä'tōō)	Indon.	0·10 S	99·55 E
133	Batumi (bŭ-tōō'mē)	Sov. Un.	41·40 N	41·30 E
99	Baturité (bä-tōō-rê-tā')	Braz.	4·16 S	38·47 W
155	Bauang (bä'wäng)	Phil. (Manila In.)	16·31 N	120·19 E
164	Bauchi (bá-ōō'chē)	Nig.	10·19 N	9·51 E
166	Baudouinville (bō-dwăN-vēl')	Con. L.	7·12 S	29·39 E
83	Bauld, C.	Can.	51·38 N	55·10 W
85	Baurette (bō-rĕt')	Can. (Montreal In.)	45·24 N	73·32 W
142	Bāuria	India (Calcutta In.)	22·29 N	88·08 E
99	Bauru (bou-rōō')	Braz.	22·21 S	48·57 W
119	Bauska (bou'skȧ)	Sov. Un.	56·24 N	24·12 E
95	Bauta (bá'ōō-tä)	Cuba (Havana In.)	22·14 N	82·33 W
120	Bautzen (bout'sĕn)	Ger.	51·11 N	14·27 E
	Bavaria, see Bayern			
160	Baw Baw, Mt. (bá-bá)	Austl.	37·50 S	146·17 E
154	Bawean (I.) (bá'vē-än)	Indon.	5·50 S	112·40 E
110	Bawtry (bô'trĭ)	Eng.	53·26 N	1·01 W
79	Baxley (băks'lĭ)	Ga.	31·47 N	82·22 W
161	Baxter (băks'tēr)	Austl. (Melbourne In.)	38·12 S	145·10 E
73	Baxter Springs (băks'tēr sprĭngs')	Kans.	37·01 N	94·44 W
95	Bayaguana (bä-yä-gwä'nä)	Dom. Rep.	18·45 N	69·40 W
114	Bay al Kabīr Wadi (R.)	Libya	29·52 N	14·28 E
155	Bayambang (bä-yäm-bäng')	Phil. (Manila In.)	15·50 N	120·26 E
94	Bayamo (bä-yä'mō)	Cuba	20·25 N	76·35 W
89	Bayamón	P. R. (Puerto Rico In.)	18·27 N	66·13 W
134	Bayan-Aul (bä'yän-oul')	Sov. Un.	50·43 N	75·37 E
70	Bayard (bā'ērd)	Nebr.	41·45 N	103·20 W
81	Bayard	W. Va.	39·15 N	79·20 W
133	Bayburt (bä'ĭ-bŏŏrt)	Tur.	40·15 N	40·10 E
80	Bay City (bā)	Mich.	43·35 N	83·55 W
77	Bay City	Tex.	28·59 N	95·58 W
146	Baydarag Gol (R.)	Mong.	46·09 N	98·52 E
132	Baydaratskaya Guba (B.)	Sov. Un.	69·20 N	66·10 E
83	Bayde Verde	Can.	48·06 N	52·50 W
120	Bayern (Bavaria) (State) (bī'ērn) (bȧ-vâ-rĭ-ȧ)	Ger.	49·00 N	11·16 E
122	Bayeux (bá-yû')	Fr.	49·19 N	0·41 W
71	Bayfield (bā'fēld)	Wis.	46·48 N	90·51 W
135	Baykal, Ozero (Baikal, L.) (bī'kăl') (bī'kŏl)	Sov. Un.	53·00 N	109·28 E
135	Baykals'kiy Khrebet (Baikal Mts.)	Sov. Un.	53·30 N	102·00 E
134	Baykit (bī-kēt')	Sov. Un.	61·43 N	96·39 E
134	Baykonur (bī-kō-nōōr')	Sov. Un.	47·46 N	66·11 E
136	Baymak (bȧy'mäk)	Sov. Un. (Urals In.)	52·35 N	58·21 E
78	Bay Minette (bā'mĭn-ĕt')	Ala.	30·52 N	87·44 W
74	Bay Mills (bā mĭlls)	Mich. (Sault Ste. Marie In.)	46·27 N	84·36 W
71	Bay Mills Ind. Res.	Mich.	46·19 N	85·03 W
155	Bayombong (bä-yôm-bông')	Phil. (Manila In.)	16·28 N	121·09 E
122	Bayonne (bá-yôn')	Fr.	43·28 N	1·30 W
84	Bayonne (bā-yōn')	N. J. (New York In.)	40·40 N	74·07 W
77	Bayou Bodcau Res. (bī'yōō bŏd'kō)	La.	32·49 N	93·22 W
74	Bayport (bā'pōrt)	Minn. (Minneapolis, St. Paul In.)	45·02 N	92·46 W
127	Bayramiç	Tur.	39·48 N	26·35 E
120	Bayreuth (bī-roit')	Ger.	49·56 N	11·35 E
83	Bay Roberts (bā rŏb'ērts)	Can.	47·36 N	53·12 W
81	Bays, L. of (bās)	Can.	45·15 N	79·00 W
78	Bay St. Louis (bā' sânt lōō'ĭs)	Miss.	30·19 N	89·20 W
84	Bay Shore (bā' shôr)	N. Y. (New York In.)	40·44 N	73·15 W
139	Bayt Lahm (Bethlehem) (bĕth'lē-hĕm)	Jordan (Palestine In.)	31·42 N	35·13 E
77	Baytown (bā'town)	Tex. (In.)	29·44 N	95·01 W
165	Bayuda Steppe (bá-yōō'dá)	Sud.	17·27 N	31·43 E
84	Bayview (bā'vū)	Ala. (Bırmıngham In.)	33·34 N	86·59 W
65	Bayview	Wash. (Seattle In.)	48·29 N	122·28 W
75	Bay Village (bā)	Ohio (Cleveland In.)	41·29 N	81·56 W
124	Baza (bä'thä)	Sp.	37·29 N	2·46 W
133	Bazar-Dyuzi, Gora (Mt.) (bä'zär-dyōōz'ĭ)	Sov. Un.	41·20 N	47·40 E
166	Bazaruto, Ilha (I.) (ē'lä-bä-zä-rōō'tō)	Moz.	21·42 S	36·10 E
167	Bazeia Mt. (bă-zēȧ)	S. Afr. (Natal In.)	31·33 S	28·23 E
124	Baztán (bäth-tän')	Sp.	43·12 N	1·30 W
70	Beach (bēch)	N. D.	46·55 N	104·00 W
81	Beacon (bē'kŭn)	N. Y.	41·30 N	73·55 W
85	Beaconsfield (bē'kŭnz-fēld)	Can. (Montreal In.)	45·26 N	73·51 W
84	Beafort Mtn. (bē'fōrt)	N. J. (New York In.)	41·08 N	74·23 W
76	Beals Cr. (bēls)	Tex.	32·10 N	101·14 W
85	Beamsville	Can. (Toronto In.)	43·10 N	79·29 W
67	Bear Creek (bâr krēk)	Mont.	45·11 N	109·07 W
78	Bear Cr. (bâr)	Ala.	34·27 N	88·00 W
74	Bear Cr.	Tex. (Dallas, Fort Worth In.)	32·56 N	97·09 W
81	Bear Cr. Flood Control Res.	Pa.	41·07 N	75·45 W
73	Beardstown (bērds'toun)	Ill.	40·01 N	90·26 W
65	Bearhead Mtn. (bâr'hĕd)	Wash. (Seattle In.)	47·01 N	121·49 W
67	Bear L.	Idaho-Utah	41·56 N	111·10 W
67	Bear R.	Idaho	42·17 N	111·42 W
74	Bear R.	Utah (Salt Lake City In.)	41·28 N	112·10 W
67	Bear River B.	Utah	41·25 N	112·20 W
124	Beas de Segura (bā'äs dā sā-gōō'rä)	Sp.	38·16 N	2·53 W
95	Beata (I.) (bĕ-ä'tä)	Dom. Rep.	17·40 N	71·40 W
95	Beata, Cabo (C.) (kȧ'bô-bĕ-ä'tä)	Dom. Rep.	17·40 N	71·20 W
73	Beatrice (bē'ȧ-trĭs)	Nebr.	40·16 N	96·45 W
68	Beatty (bēt'ē)	Nev.	36·58 N	116·48 W
80	Beattyville (bēt'ē-vĭl)	Ky.	37·35 N	83·40 W
122	Beaucaire (bō-kâr')	Fr.	43·49 N	4·37 E
82	Beauceville (bōs'vēl)	Can.	46·12 N	70·46 W
123	Beaucourt (bō-kōōr')	Fr.	47·30 N	6·54 E
79	Beaufort (bō'fērt)	N. C.	34·43 N	76·40 W
79	Beaufort	S. C.	32·25 N	80·40 W
64	Beaufort Sea	Alaska	70·30 N	138·40 W
166	Beaufort West	S. Afr.	32·20 S	22·45 E
85	Beauharnois (bō-ăr-nwä')	Can. (Montreal In.)	45·23 N	73·52 W
74	Beaumont (bō'mŏnt)	Calif. (Los Angeles In.)	33·57 N	116·57 W
85	Beaumont	Can. (Quebec In.)	46·50 N	71·01 W
77	Beaumont	Tex.	30·05 N	94·06 W
122	Beaune (bōn)	Fr.	47·02 N	4·49 E
85	Beauport (bō-pôr')	Can. (Quebec In.)	46·52 N	71·11 W
85	Beaupré (bō-prā')	Can. (Quebec In.)	47·03 N	70·53 W
85	Beaurepaire (bōr-pĕr')	Can. (Montreal In.)	45·25 N	73·53 W
86	Beausejour	Can.	50·07 N	96·39 W
122	Beauvais (bō-vĕ')	Fr.	49·25 N	2·05 E
72	Beaver (bē'vēr)	Okla.	36·46 N	100·31 W
75	Beaver	Pa. (Pittsburgh In.)	40·42 N	80·18 W
69	Beaver	Utah	38·15 N	112·40 W
80	Beaver (I.)	Mich.	45·40 N	85·30 W
86	Beaver (R.)	Can.	54·21 N	111·50 W
72	Beaver City	Nebr.	40·08 N	99·52 W
72	Beaver Cr.	Colo.	39·42 N	103·37 W
72	Beaver Cr.	Kans.	39·44 N	101·05 W
67	Beaver Cr.	Mont.	46·45 N	104·18 W
70	Beaver Cr.	Wyo.	43·46 N	104·25 W
71	Beaver Dam	Wis.	43·29 N	88·50 W
67	Beaverhead Mts. (bē'vēr-hĕd)	Mont.	44·33 N	112·59 W
67	Beaverhead R.	Mont.	45·05 N	112·50 W
80	Beaver Ind. Res.	Mich.	45·40 N	85·30 W
65	Beaverton (bē'vēr-tŭn)	Ore. (Portland In.)	45·29 N	122·49 W
98	Bebara' (bĕ-bä-rä')	Col. (In.)	6·07 N	76·39 W
110	Bebington (bē'bĭng-tŭn)	Eng.	53·20 N	2·59 W
91	Becal (bā-käl')	Mex.	20·25 N	90·04 W
127	Bečej (bĕ'chā)	Yugo.	45·36 N	20·03 E
124	Becerreá (bā-thā'rē-ä)	Sp.	42·49 N	7·12 W
64	Becharof (L.) (bĕk ȧ rôf)	Alaska	57·58 N	156·58 W
65	Becher B. (bēch'ēr)	Can. (Seattle In.)	48·18 N	123·37 W
163	Bechuanaland (bĕch-ōō-ȧ'nȧ-lănd)	Afr.	22·10 S	23·13 E
80	Beckley (bĕk'lĭ)	W. Va.	37·40 N	81·15 W
122	Bédarieux (bā-dȧ-ryû')	Fr.	43·36 N	3·11 E
85	Beddington Cr. (bĕd'ĕng tŭn)	Can. (Calgary In.)	51·14 N	114·13 W
81	Bedford (bĕd'fērd)	Can.	45·10 N	73·00 W
116	Bedford	Eng.	52·10 N	0·25 W
80	Bedford	Ind.	38·50 N	86·30 W
71	Bedford	Iowa	40·40 N	94·41 W
83	Bedford	Mass. (Boston In.)	42·30 N	71·17 W
84	Bedford	N. Y. (New York In.)	41·12 N	73·38 W
75	Bedford	Ohio (Cleveland In.)	41·23 N	81·32 W
81	Bedford	Pa.	40·05 N	78·20 W
167	Bedford	S. Afr. (Natal In.)	32·43 S	26·19 E
79	Bedford	Va.	37·19 N	79·27 W
84	Bedford Hill	N. Y. (New York In.)	41·14 N	73·41 W
110	Bedworth (bĕd'wērth)	Eng.	52·29 N	1·28 W
121	Bedzin (bāN-jēn')	Pol.	50·19 N	19·10 E
73	Beebe (bē'bē)	Ark.	35·04 N	91·54 W
75	Beecher (bē'chŭr)	Ill. (Chicago In.)	41·20 N	87·38 W
65	Beechey Hd. (bē'chĭ hĕd)	Can. (Seattle In.)	48·19 N	123·40 W
75	Beech Grove (bēch grōv)	Ind. (Indianapolis In.)	39·43 N	86·05 W
160	Beecroft Hd. (bē'krŭft)	Austl.	35·03 S	151·15 E
111	Beelitz (bĕ'lētz)	Ger. (Berlin In.)	52·14 N	12·59 E
139	Beer (R.)	Isr. (Palestine In.)	31·23 N	34·30 E
139	Beersheba (bēr-shē'bȧ)	Isr. (Palestine In.)	31·15 N	34·48 E
168	Beestekraal	S. Afr. (Johannes-burg & Pretoria In.)	25·22 S	27·34 E
110	Beeston (bēs't'n)	Eng.	52·55 N	1·11 W
111	Beetz R. (bĕtz)	Ger. (Berlin In.)	52·28 N	12·37 E
77	Beeville (bē'vĭl)	Tex.	28·24 N	97·44 W
160	Bega (bā'gȧ)	Austl.	36·50 S	149·49 E
73	Beggs (bĕgz)	Okla.	35·46 N	96·06 W
122	Bégles (bĕ'gl')	Fr.	44·47 N	0·34 W
142	Behampur	India	20·19 N	85·53 E
165	Beilul	Eth.	13·15 N	42·21 E
166	Beira (bā'rȧ)	Moz.	19·46 S	34·58 E
124	Beira (Reg.) (bĕ'y-rä)	Port.	40·38 N	8·00 W
	Beirut, see Beyrouth			
139	Beit Shean	Isr. (Palestine In.)	32·30 N	35·30 E
124	Beja (bä'zhä)	Port.	38·03 N	7·53 W
124	Bejar	Sp.	40·25 N	5·43 W
144	Bejestān	Iran	34·30 N	58·22 E
144	Bejnurd	Iran	37·29 N	57·13 E
95	Bejucal (bā-hōō-käl')	Cuba (Havana In.)	22·08 N	82·23 W
93	Bejuco (bĕ-kōō'kŏ)	Pan.	8·37 N	79·54 W
121	Békés (bā'kāsh)	Hung.	46·45 N	21·08 E
121	Békéscsaba (bā'kāsh-chô'bô)	Hung.	46·39 N	21·06 E
147	Beketova (bĕk'e-to'vȧ)	Sov. Un.	53·23 N	125·21 E
127	Bela Crkva (bĕ'lä tsĕrk'vä)	Yugo.	44·53 N	21·25 E
124	Belalcázar (bāl-äl-kä'thär)	Sp.	38·35 N	5·12 W
125	Belas (bĕ'-läs)	Port. (Lisbon In.)	38·47 N	9·16 W
127	Bela-Slatina (byā'la slä'tēnä)	Bul.	43·26 N	23·56 E
154	Belawan (bā-lä'wȧn)	Indon.	3·43 N	98·43 E
132	Belaya (R.) (byĕ'lĭ-yȧ)	Sov. Un.	52·45 N	61·15 E
129	Belaya Tserkov' (byĕ'lĭ-yȧ tsĕr'kôf)	Sov. Un.	49·48 N	30·09 E
87	Belcher Is. (bĕl'chēr)	Can.	56·20 N	80·40 W
75	Belden (bĕl'dĕn)	Ohio (Cleveland In.)	41·14 N	82·01 W
80	Belding (bĕl'dĭng)	Mich.	43·05 N	85·25 W
132	Belebey (byĕ'lĕ-bā'ĭ)	Sov. Un.	54·00 N	54·10 E
159	Belef, Isles	N. Cal.	19·30 S	160·32 E
99	Belém (Pará) (bā-lĕN') (pä-rä')	Braz.	1·18 S	48·27 W
69	Belen (bĕ-län')	N. Mex.	34·40 N	106·45 W
100	Belén (bā-lān')	Par.	23·30 S	57·09 W
128	Belëv (byĕl'yĕf)	Sov. Un.	53·49 N	36·06 E
65	Belfair (bĕl'fâr)	Wash. (Seattle In.)	47·27 N	122·50 W
116	Belfast (bĕl'fȧst)	N. Ire.	54·36 N	5·45 W
82	Belfast	Maine	44·25 N	69·01 W
116	Belfast, Lough (B.) (lŏK bĕl'fȧst)	Ire.	54·45 N	7·40 W
165	Bēlfodiyo	Eth.	10·45 N	39·27 E
123	Belfort (bā-fôr')	Fr.	47·40 N	7·50 E
143	Belgaum	India	15·57 N	74·32 E
102	Belgium (bĕl'jĭ-ŭm)	Eur.	51·00 N	2·52 E
129	Belgorod (byĕl'gŭ-rŭt)	Sov. Un.	50·36 N	36·32 E
129	Belgorod (Oblast)	Sov. Un.	50·40 N	36·42 E
129	Belgorod Dnestrovskiy (byĕl'gŭ-rŭd nyĕs-trôf'skē)	Sov. Un.	46·09 N	30·19 E
	Belgrade, see Beograd			
79	Belhaven (bĕl'hā-vĕn)	N. C.	35·33 N	76·37 W
81	Belington (bĕl'ĭng-tŭn)	W. Va.	39·00 N	79·55 W
127	Beli Timok (R.) (Bĕ'lĕ Tĕ'môk)	Yugo.	43·35 N	22·13 E
154	Belitung (I.)	Indon.	3·30 S	107·30 E
92	Belize (bĕ-lēz')	Br. Hond. (Yucatan In.)	17·31 N	88·10 W
92	Belize R.	Br. Hond. (Yucatan In.)	17·16 N	88·56 W
136	Bel'kovo (byĕl'kô-vô)	Sov. Un. (Moscow In.)	56·15 N	38·49 E
135	Bel'kovskiy (I.) (byĕl-kôf'skĭ)	Sov. Un.	75·52 N	133·00 E
74	Bell (bĕl)	Calif. (Los Angeles In.)	33·59 N	118·11 W
83	Bell (I.)	Can.	50·45 N	55·35 W
80	Bellaire (bĕl-âr')	Ohio	40·00 N	80·45 W
77	Bellaire	Tex. (In.)	29·43 N	95·28 W
143	Bellary (bĕl-lä'rē)	India	15·15 N	76·56 E
100	Bella Union (bĕ'l-yä-ōō-nyô'n)	Ur.	30·18 S	57·26 W
100	Bella Vista (bä'lyä vēs'tä)	Arg.	27·07 S	65·14 W
100	Bella Vista	Arg.	28·35 S	58·53 W
100	Bella Vista	Arg. (In.)	34·18 S	58·41 W
99	Bella Vista	Braz.	22·16 S	56·14 W
83	Belle B. (bĕl)	Can.	47·35 N	55·15 W
84	Belle Chasse (bĕl shäs')	La. (New Orleans In.)	29·52 N	90·00 W
80	Bellefontaine (bĕl-fŏn'tān)	Ohio	40·25 N	83·50 W
70	Belle Fourche (bĕl' fōōrsh')	S. D.	44·28 N	103·50 W
70	Belle Fourche (R.)	Wyo.	44·29 N	104·40 W
70	Belle Fourche Res.	S. D.	44·51 N	103·44 W
123	Bellegarde-sur-Valserine (bĕl-gärd'sür-väl-sȧ-rēn')	Fr.	46·06 N	6 50 E
79	Belle Glade (bĕl glād)	Fla. (In.)	26·39 N	80·37 W
122	Belle Île (I.) (bĕl-ēl')	Fr.	47·15 N	3·30 W
87	Belle Isle, Str. of	Can.	51·21 N	55·56 W
84	Belle Mead (bĕl mēd)	N. J. (New York In.)	40·28 N	74·40 W
83	Belleoram	Can.	47·29 N	55·50 W
71	Belle Plaine (bĕl plān')	Iowa	41·52 N	92·19 W
75	Belle Vernon (bĕl vŭr'nŭn)	Pa. (Pittsburgh In.)	40·08 N	79·52 W
81	Belleville (bĕl'vĭl)	Can.	44·15 N	77·25 W
74	Belleville	Ill. (St. Louis In.)	38·31 N	89·59 W
73	Belleville	Kans.	39·49 N	97·37 W
75	Belleville	Mich. (Detroit In.)	42·12 N	83·29 W
84	Belleville	N. J. (New York In.)	40·47 N	74·09 W
71	Bellevue (bĕl'vū)	Iowa	42·14 N	90·26 W
75	Bellevue	Ky. (Cincinnati In.)	39·06 N	84·29 W
80	Bellevue	Mich.	42·30 N	85·00 W
80	Bellevue	Ohio	41·15 N	82·45 W
75	Bellevue	Pa. (Pittsburgh In.)	40·30 N	80·04 W
65	Bellevue	Wash. (Seattle In.)	47·37 N	122·12 W
123	Belley (bĕ-lē')	Fr.	45·46 N	5·41 E
74	Bellflower (bĕl-flou'ēr)	Calif. (Los Angeles In.)	33·53 N	118·08 W
83	Bellingham (bĕl'ĭng-hăm)	Mass. (Boston In.)	42·05 N	71·28 W
65	Bellingham	Wash. (Vancouver In.)	48·46 N	122·29 W
65	Bellingham B.	Wash. (Vancouver In.)	48·44 N	122·34 W

ăt; finăl; rāte; senâte; ärm; ȧsk; sofȧ; fâre; ch-choose; dh-as th in other; bē; ēvent; bĕt; recĕnt; cratēr; g-go; gh-guttural g; bĭt; ĭ-short neutral; rīde: K-guttural k as ch in German ich;

Page	Name Pronunciation Region	Lat. °′	Long. °′
47	Bellingshausen Sea (bĕl'ĭngz houz'n) . Ant.	72·00 S	80·30 W
126	Bellinzona (bĕl-ĭn-tsō'nä) . . . Switz.	46·10 N	9·09 E
84	Bellmore (bĕl-mōr) N. Y. (New York In.)	40·40 N	73·31 W
98	Bello (bĕ'l-yô) . . . Col. (In.)	6·20 N	75·33 W
81	Bellows Falls (bĕl'ōz fôls) . . . Vt.	43·10 N	72·30 W
142	Bellpat . . . W. Pak.	29·08 N	68·00 E
87	Bell Pen . . . Can.	63·50 N	81·16 W
85	Bells Corners . . Can. (Ottawa In.)	45·20 N	75·49 W
65	Bells Mtn. (bĕls) Wash. (Portland In.)	45·50 N	122·21 W
126	Belluno (bĕl-lōō'nō) . . . It.	46·08 N	12·14 E
100	Bell Ville (bĕl vēl') . . . Arg.	32·33 S	62·36 W
166	Bellville S. Afr. (Cape Town In.)	33·54 S	18·38 E
77	Bellville (bĕl'vĭl) . . . Tex.	29·57 N	96·15 W
124	Bélmez (bĕl'mĕth) . . . Sp.	38·17 N	5·17 W
71	Belmond (bĕl'mŏnd) . . . Iowa	42·49 N	93·37 W
65	Belmont . Calif. (San Francisco In.)	37·34 N	122·18 W
99	Belmonte (bĕl-mōn'tä) . . . Braz.	15·58 S	38·47 W
135	Belogorsk . . . Sov. Un.	51·09 N	128·32 E
101	Belo Horizonte (bĕ'lô-re-sô'n-tĕ) Braz. (Rio de Janeiro In.)	19·54 S	43·56 W
72	Beloit (bē-loit') . . . Kans.	39·26 N	98·06 W
71	Beloit . . . Wis.	42·31 N	89·04 W
132	Belomorsk (byĕl-ô-môrsk') Sov. Un.	64·30 N	34·42 E
129	Belopol'ye (byĕ'lô-pôl'yĕ) . Sov. Un.	51·10 N	34·19 E
136	Beloretsk (byĕ'lō-rĕtsk) Sov. Un. (Urals In.)	53·58 N	58·25 E
130	Belorussian (S. S. R.) . . . Sov. Un.	53·30 N	25·33 E
129	Belosarayskaya, Kosa (C.) (kô-sä' byĕ'lô-sä-räy'skä'yä) Sov. Un.	46·43 N	37·18 E
134	Belovo (byĕ'lŭ-vû) . . . Sov. Un.	54·17 N	86·23 E
129	Belovodsk (byĕ-lŭ-vôdsk') Sov. Un.	49·12 N	39·36 E
132	Beloye (L.) . . . Sov. Un.	60·10 N	38·05 E
132	Belozersk (byĕ-lŭ-zyôrsk') . Sov. Un.	60·00 N	38·00 E
110	Belper (bĕl'pēr) . . . Eng.	53·01 N	1·28 W
67	Belt (bĕlt) . . . Mont.	47·11 N	110·58 W
67	Belt Cr. . . . Mont.	47·19 N	110·58 W
77	Belton (bĕl'tŭn) . . . Tex.	31·04 N	97·27 W
77	Belton L. . . . Tex.	31·15 N	97·35 W
129	Bel'tsy (bĕl'tsē) . . . Sov. Un.	47·47 N	27·57 E
134	Belukha, Gol'tsy (Mtn.) . Sov. Un.	49·47 N	86·23 E
74	Belvedere (bĕl-vē-dēr') Calif. (Los Angeles In.)	34·02 N	118·11 W
71	Belvidere . . . Ill.	42·14 N	88·52 W
81	Belvidere . . . Pa.	40·50 N	75·05 W
159	Belyando (R.) (bĕl-yăn'dō) . Austl.	22·09 S	146·48 E
136	Belyanka (byĕl'yăn-kȧ) Sov. Un. (Urals In.)	56·04 N	59·16 E
128	Belynichi (byĕl-ĭ-nĭ'chĭ) . Sov. Un.	54·02 N	29·42 E
128	Belyy (byĕ'lē) . . . Sov. Un.	55·52 N	32·58 E
134	Belyy (I.) . . . Sov. Un.	73·19 N	72·00 E
136	Belyye Stolby (byĕ'lĭ-ye stôl'bĭ) Sov. Un. (Moscow In.)	55·20 N	37·52 E
111	Belzig (bĕl'tsēg) . . Ger. (Berlin In.)	52·08 N	12·35 E
78	Belzoni (bĕl-zō'nē) . . . Miss.	33·09 N	90·30 W
166	Bembe (bĕN'bĕ) . . . Ang.	7·00 S	14·20 E
124	Bembezar (R.) (bĕm-bā-thär') . Sp.	38·00 N	5·18 W
71	Bemidji (bē-mĭj'ĭ) . . . Minn.	47·28 N	94·54 W
166	Bena Dibele (bĕn'ȧ dē-bĕ'lĕ) Con. L.	4·00 S	22·49 E
160	Benalla (bĕn-ăl'ȧ) . . . Austl.	36·30 S	14·600 E
124	Benavente (bā-nä-vĕn'tä) . . . Sp.	42·01 N	5·43 W
74	Benbrook (bĕn'brŏŏk) Tex. (Dallas, Fort Worth In.)	32·41 N	97·27 W
66	Bend (bĕnd) . . . Ore.	44·04 N	121·17 W
64	Bendeleben, Mt. (bĕn-dĕl-bĕn) Alaska	65·18 N	163·45 W
168	Bender Cassim Som. (Horn of Afr. In.)	11·19 N	49·10 E
129	Bendery (bĕn-dyĕ're) . . . Sov. Un.	46·49 N	29·29 E
160	Bendigo (bĕn'dĭ-gō) . . . Austl.	36·39 S	144·20 E
120	Benešov (bĕn'ĕ-shôf) . . . Czech.	49·48 N	14·40 E
126	Benevento (bā-nā-vĕn'tō) . . . It.	41·08 N	14·46 E
138	Bengal, B. of (bĕn-gôl') . . . Asia	17·30 N	87·00 E
	Bengasi, see Banghāzī		
139	Bengkalis (bĕng-kä'lĭs) Indon. (Singapore In.)	1·29 N	102·06 E
154	Bengkulu . . . Indon.	3·46 S	102·18 E
166	Benguela (bĕn-gĕl'ȧ) . . . Ang.	12·35 S	13·28 E
166	Benguela (Reg.) . . . Ang.	13·13 S	16·00 E
116	Ben Hope (Mtn.) (bĕn hōp) . Scot.	58·25 N	4·25 W
84	Ben Hill (bĕn hĭl) Ga. (Atlanta In.)	33·42 N	84·31 W
98	Beni (R.) (bā'nē) . . . Bol.	13·41 S	67·30 W
164	Beni-Abbès (bā'nē ä-bĕs') . . . Alg.	30·11 N	2·13 W
125	Benicarló (bā-nē-kär-lō') . . . Sp.	40·26 N	0·25 E
65	Benicia (bē-nĭsh'ĭ-ȧ) Calif. (San Francisco In.)	38·03 N	122·09 W
164	Benin (bĕn-ēn') . . . Nig.	6·21 N	5·34 E
164	Benin, Bight of . . . Afr.	5·09 N	2·19 E
164	Beni Saf (bā'nē säf') . . . Alg.	35·23 N	1·20 W
72	Benkelman (bĕn-kĕl-mȧn) . . . Nebr.	40·05 N	101·35 W
126	Benkovac (bĕn'kō-väts) . . . Yugo.	44·02 N	15·41 E
167	Ben Mac Dhui (Mtn.) (bĕn măk-dōō'ē) . Bas. (Natal In.)	30·38 S	27·54 E
79	Bennettsville (bĕn'ĕts vĭl) . . S. C.	34·35 N	79·41 W
81	Bennington (bĕn'ĭng-tŭn) . . . Vt.	42·55 N	73·15 W
84	Benns Church (bĕnz' chûrch') Va. (Norfolk In.)	36·47 N	76·35 W
167	Benoni (bĕ-nō'nī) . . . S. Afr. (Johannesburg & Pretoria In.)	26·11 S	28·19 E
92	Benque Viejo (bĕn-kĕ bĭē'hō) Br. Hond. (Yucatan In.)	17·07 N	89·07 W
75	Bensenville (bĕn'sĕn-vĭl) Ill. (Chicago In.)	41·57 N	87·56 W
120	Bensheim (bĕns-hīm) . . . Ger.	49·42 N	8·38 E
69	Benson (bĕn-sŭn) . . . Ariz.	32·00 N	110·20 W
70	Benson . . . Minn.	45·18 N	95·36 W
75	Bentleyville (bent'lē vĭl) Pa. (Pittsburgh In.)	40·07 N	80·01 W
82	Benton (bĕn'tŭn) . . . Can.	45·59 N	67·36 W
73	Benton . . . Ark.	34·34 N	92·34 W
68	Benton . . . Calif.	37·44 N	118·22 W
110	Benton . . . Eng.	53·27 N	2·07 W
80	Benton . . . Ill.	38·00 N	88·55 W
80	Benton Harbor (bĕn'tŭn här'bēr) Mich.	42·05 N	86·30 W
73	Bentonville (bĕn'tŭn-vĭl) . . . Ark.	36·22 N	94·11 W
164	Benue R. (bā'nōō-ā) . . . Nig.	7·49 N	7·54 E
139	Benut (R.) . Mala. (Singapore In.)	1·43 N	103·20 E
80	Benwood (bĕn-wŏŏd) . . . W. Va.	39·55 N	80·45 W
127	Beograd (Belgrade) (bĕ-ō'grăd) (bĕl'grăd) . Yugo.	44·48 N	20·32 E
153	Beppu (bĕ'pōō) . . . Jap.	33·16 N	131·30 E
93	Bequia I. (bĕk-ē'ȧ) N. A. (Le. & Wind. Is. In.)	13·00 N	61·08 W
155	Beraoe, Teloek (B.) . . . W. Irian	2·22 S	131·40 E
127	Berat (bĕ-rät') . . . Alb.	40·43 N	19·59 E
100	Berazategui (bĕ-rä-zä'tĕ-gē) Arg. (In.)	34·31 S	58·12 W
165	Berber (bûr'bĕr) . . . Sud.	18·11 N	34·00 E
168	Berbera (bûr'bûr-ȧ) Som. (Horn of Afr. In.)	10·25 N	45·05 E
122	Berck (bĕrk) . . . Fr.	50·26 N	1·36 E
129	Berdichev (bĕ-dē'chĕf) . . . Sov. Un.	49·53 N	28·32 E
129	Berdyanskaya, Kosa (C.) (kô-sä' bĕr-dyän'skä-yä) . Sov. Un.	46·38 N	36·42 E
136	Berdyaush (bĕr'dyȧûsh) Sov. Un. (Urals In.)	55·10 N	59·12 E
78	Berea (bē-rē'ȧ) . . . Ky.	37·30 N	84·19 W
75	Berea . . . Ohio (Cleveland In.)	41·22 N	81·51 W
121	Beregovo (bĕ'rĕ-gô-vô) . Sov. Un.	48·13 N	22·40 E
139	Berekhot Shelmo (Mt) Jordan (Palestine In.)	31·35 N	35·07 E
165	Berenice (Ruins) (bĕr-ē-nī'sē) U. A. R.	23·56 N	35·18 E
86	Berens River (bĕr'ĕnz) . . . Can.	52·28 N	97·11 W
70	Beresford (bĕr'ĕs-fērd) . . . S. D.	43·05 N	96·46 W
121	Berettyóújfalu (bĕ'rĕt-tyō-ōō'y'fô-lōō) . Hung.	47·14 N	21·33 E
121	Berëza (bĕ-rā'zȧ) . . . Sov. Un.	52·29 N	24·59 E
121	Berezhany (bĕr-yĕ'zhä-nĕ) Sov. Un.	49·25 N	24·58 E
128	Berezina (R.) (bĕr-yĕ'zē-nȧ) Sov. Un.	53·20 N	29·05 E
128	Berezino (bĕr-yä'zê-nô) . Sov. Un.	53·51 N	28·54 E
129	Berezna (bĕr-yôz'nȧ) . . . Sov. Un.	51·32 N	31·47 E
129	Bereznegovata . . . Sov. Un.	47·19 N	32·58 E
136	Berezniki (bĕr-yôz'nyē-kē) Sov. Un. (Urals In.)	59·25 N	56·46 E
129	Berezovka (bĕr-yôz'ôf-kȧ) Sov. Un.	47·12 N	30·56 E
136	Berëzovka . . . Sov. Un. (Urals In.)	57·35 N	57·19 E
132	Berëzovo (bĭr-yô'zĕ-vû) . . Sov. Un.	64·10 N	65·10 E
136	Berëzovskiy (bĕr-yô'zôf-skĭ) Sov. Un. (Urals In.)	56·54 N	60·47 E
125	Berga (bĕr'gä) . . . Sp.	42·05 N	1·52 E
127	Bergama (bĕr'gä-mä) . . . Tur.	39·08 N	27·09 E
126	Bergamo (bĕr'gä-mō) . . . It.	45·43 N	9·41 E
99	Bergantín (bĕr-gän-tē'n) Ven. (In.)	10·04 N	64·23 W
111	Bergedorf (bĕr'gē-dôrf) Ger. (Hamburg In.)	53·29 N	10·12 E
120	Bergen (bĕr'gĕn) . . . Ger.	54·26 N	13·26 E
118	Bergen . . . Nor.	60·24 N	5·20 E
111	Bergen op Zoom Neth. (Amsterdam In.)	51·29 N	3·16 E
122	Bergerac (bĕr-zhĕ-răk') . . . Fr.	44·49 N	0·28 E
123	Bergisch Gladbach (bĕrg'ĭsh-glät'bäk) . Ger. (Ruhr In.)	50·59 N	7·08 E
111	Berglern (bĕrgh'lĕrn) Ger. (Munich In.)	48·24 N	11·55 E
74	Bergs (bûrgs) Tex. (San Antonio In.)	29·19 N	98·26 W
167	Bergville (bĕrg'vĭl) S. Afr. (Natal In.)	28·46 S	29·22 E
166	Bergvliet . S. Afr. (Cape Town In.)	34·03 S	18·27 E
49	Bering Sea (bē'rĭng) . . . Asia-N. A.	58·00 N	175·00 W
64	Bering Str. . . . Alaska	64·50 N	169·50 W
129	Berislav (byĕr'ĭ-släf) . . . Sov. Un.	46·49 N	33·24 E
124	Berja (bĕr'hä) . . . Sp.	36·50 N	2·56 W
65	Berkeley (bûrk'lĭ) Calif. (San Francisco In.)	37·52 N	122·17 W
74	Berkeley . . . Mo. (St. Louis In.)	38·45 N	90·20 W
81	Berkeley Springs (bûrk'lĭ sprĭngz) W. Va.	39·40 N	78·10 W
110	Berkhamsted (bĕrk'hȧm'stĕd) Eng. (London In.)	51·44 N	0·34 W
75	Berkley (bûrk'lĭ) Mich. (Detroit In.)	42·30 N	83·10 W
127	Berkovitsa (bĕ-kō'vē-tsȧ) . . . Bul.	43·14 N	23·08 E
124	Berlengas (Is.) (bĕr-lĕn'gäzh) . Port.	39·25 N	9·33 W
111	Berlin (bĕr-lēn') . . Ger. (Berlin In.)	52·27 N	13·26 E
81	Berlin (bûr-lĭn) . . . N. H.	44·25 N	71·10 W
84	Berlin . . . N. J. (Philadelphia In.)	39·47 N	74·56 W
167	Berlin (bĕr-lĭn) . S. Afr. (Natal In.)	32·53 S	27·36 E
71	Berlin (bûr-lĭn') . . . Wis.	43·58 N	88·58 W
124	Bermeja, Sierra (Mts.) (sē-ĕ'r-rä-bĕr-mĕ'hä) . Sp.	36·35 N	5·03 W
100	Bermejo (R.) (bĕr-mā'hō) . . . Arg.	25·05 S	61·00 W
124	Bermeo (bĕr-mā'yō) . . . Sp.	43·23 N	2·43 W
89	Bermuda (I.) . . . N. A.	32·20 N	65·45 W
120	Bern (bĕrn) . . . Switz.	46·55 N	7·25 E
100	Bernal (bĕr-näl') . . . Arg. (In.)	34·27 S	58·17 W
69	Bernalillo (bĕr-nä-lē'yō) . . N. Mex.	35·20 N	106·30 W
81	Bernard (L.) (bĕr-närd') . . . Can.	45·45 N	79·25 W
84	Bernardsville (bûr nărds'vĭl) N. J. (New York In.)	40·43 N	74·34 W
111	Bernau (bĕr'nou) . Ger. (Berlin In.)	52·40 N	13·35 E
120	Bernburg (bĕrn'bŏŏrgh) . . . Ger.	51·48 N	11·43 E
120	Berndorf (bĕrn'dôrf) . . . Aus.	47·57 N	16·05 E
80	Berne (bûrn) . . . Ind.	40·40 N	84·55 W
120	Berner Alpen (Mts.) . . . Switz.	46·29 N	7·30 E
123	Berneustadt (bĕr'noi'shtät) Ger. (Ruhr In.)	51·01 N	7·39 E
158	Bernier (I.) (bĕr-nēr') . . . Austl.	24·58 S	113·15 E
120	Bernina Pizzo (Pk.) . . . Switz.	46·23 N	9·58 E
120	Beroun (bā'rōn) . . . Czech.	49·57 N	14·03 E
120	Berounka R. (bĕ-rōn'kȧ) . . Czech.	49·53 N	13·40 E
161	Berowra . . . Austl. (Sydney In.)	33·36 S	151·10 E
122	Berre, Étang de (L.) (ā-tôN' dĕ bâr') . Fr. (Marseille In.)	43·27 N	5·07 E
122	Berre-l' Étang (bâr'lā-tôN') Fr. (Marseille In.)	43·28 N	5·11 E
91	Berriozabal (bā'rēō-zä-bäl') . . Mex.	16·47 N	93·16 W
114	Berryan (bĕr-ē-äN') . . . Alg.	32·50 N	3·49 E
68	Berryessa (R.) (bĕ'rĭ ĕs'ȧ) . . . Calif.	38·35 N	122·33 W
94	Berry Is. . . . Ba. Is.	25·35 N	3·49 E
73	Berryville (bĕr'ē-vĭl) . . . Ark.	36·21 N	93·34 W
129	Bershad' (byĕr'shät) . . . Sov. Un.	48·22 N	29·31 E
82	Berthier (bĕr-tyā') . . . Can.	46·04 N	73·14 W
85	Berthier . . . Can. (Quebec In.)	46·56 N	70·44 W
65	Bertrand (R.) (bûr'trănd) Wash. (Vancouver In.)	48·58 N	122·31 W
84	Bertrandville (bûr'trănd-vĭl) La. (New Orleans In.)	29·47 N	90·01 W
116	Berwick (bûr'ĭk) . . . Scot.	55·45 N	2·01 W
81	Berwick (bûr'wĭk) . . . Pa.	41·05 N	76·10 W
75	Berwyn (bûr'wĭn) Ill (Chicago In.)	41·49 N	87·47 W
116	Berwyn Ra. . . . Wales	52·45 N	3·41 W
167	Besalampy (bĕz-ȧ-lȧm-pē') Malag. Rep.	16·48 S	40·40 E
123	Besançon (bĕ-säN-sôn) . . . Fr.	47·14 N	6·02 E
139	Besar, Gunong (Mt.) Mala. (Singapore In.)	2·31 N	103·09 E
128	Besed (R.) (byĕ'syĕt) . Sov. Un.	52·58 N	31·36 E
128	Beshenkovichi (byĕ'shĕn-kō vē'chĭ) . Sov. Un.	55·04 N	29·29 E
121	Beskides (Mts.) (bĕs'kēdz') Czech.-Pol.	49·23 N	19·00 E
122	Bessèges (bĕ-sĕzh') . . . Fr.	44·20 N	4·07 E
84	Bessemer (bĕs'ē-mēr) Ala. (Birmingham In.)	33·24 N	86·58 W
71	Bessemer . . . Mich.	46·29 N	90·04 W
79	Bessemer City . . . N. C.	35·16 N	81·17 W
111	Bestensee (bĕs'tĕn-zā) Ger. (Berlin In.)	52·15 N	13·39 E
124	Betanzos (bĕ-tän'thōs) . . . Sp.	43·18 N	8·14 W
69	Betatakin Ruin (bĕt-ȧ-tăk'ĭn) Ariz.	36·40 N	110·29 W
168	Bethal (bĕth'ăl) . S. Afr. (Johannesburg & Pretoria In.)	26·27 S	29·28 E
74	Bethalto (bȧ-thăl'tō) Ill. (St. Louis In.)	38·54 N	90·03 W
166	Bethanie (bĕth'ȧ-nĭ) . . . S. W. Afr.	26·20 S	16·10 E
73	Bethany . . . Mo.	40·15 N	94·04 W
64	Bethel (bĕth'ĕl) . . . Alaska	60·50 N	161·50 W
84	Bethel . . . Conn. (New York In.)	41·22 N	73·24 W
75	Bethel . . . Pa. (Pittsburgh In.)	40·19 N	80·02 W
81	Bethel . . . Vt.	43·50 N	72·40 W
81	Bethesda (bĕ-thĕs'dȧ) . . . Md.	39·00 N	77·10 W
81	Bethlehem (bĕth'lē-hĕm) . . . Pa.	40·40 N	75·25 W
168	Bethlehem . S. Afr. (Johannesburg & Pretoria In.)	28·14 S	28·18 E
	Bethlehem, see Bayt Lahm		
122	Béthune (bā-tün') . . . Fr.	50·32 N	2·37 E
167	Betroka (bĕ-trōk'ȧ) . . Malag. Rep.	23·13 S	46·17 E
82	Betsiamites . . . Can.	48·55 N	68·39 W
82	Betsiamites, R. . . . Can.	49·10 N	69·15 W
167	Betsiboka (R.) (bĕt-sĭ-bō'kȧ) Malag. Rep.	16·47 S	46·45 E
164	Bettié (bĕt-tyā') . . . Ivory Coast	6·04 N	3·32 W
64	Bettles Field (bĕt'tŭls) . . . Alaska	66·58 N	151·48 W
142	Betwa (R.) (bĕt'wȧ) . . . India	23·56 N	77·37 E
123	Betz (bĕ) . . . Fr. (Paris In.)	49·09 N	2·58 E
123	Betzdorf (bĕtz'dôrf) Ger. (Ruhr In.)	50·47 N	7·53 E
123	Beuel (boi'ĕl) . . . Ger. (Ruhr In.)	50·44 N	7·08 E
111	Beveren . . . Bel. (Brussels In.)	51·13 N	4·14 E
85	Beverly (bĕv'ĕr-lĭ) Can. (Edmonton In.)	53·34 N	113·23 W
110	Beverly . . . Eng.	53·50 N	0·25 W
83	Beverly . . . Mass. (Boston In.)	42·34 N	70·53 W
84	Beverly . . . N. J. (Philadelphia In.)	40·03 N	74·56 W
74	Beverly Hills Calif. (Los Angeles In.)	34·05 N	118·24 W
73	Bevier (bē-vēr') . . . Mo.	39·44 N	92·36 W
110	Bewdley (būd'lĭ) . . . Eng.	52·22 N	2·19 W
117	Bexhill (bĕks'hĭl) . . . Eng.	50·49 N	0·25 E
110	Bexley (bĕks'ly) Eng. (London In.)	51·26 N	0·09 E
164	Beyla (bā'lȧ) . . . Gui.	8·38 N	8·39 W
133	Beypazari (bā-pȧ-zä'rĭ) . . . Tur.	40·10 N	31·40 E
139	Beyrouth (Beirut) (bā-rōōt') Leb. (Palestine In.)	33·53 N	35·30 E
133	Beyşehir (bā-shĕ'h'r) . . . Tur.	38·00 N	31·45 E
133	Beyşehir Gölü (L.) . . . Tur.	38·00 N	31·30 E
129	Beysugskiy, Liman (B.) (lĭ-män' bĕy-sōōg'skĭ) . Sov. Un.	46·07 N	38·35 E
128	Bezhetsk (byĕ-zhĕtsk') . . . Sov. Un.	57·46 N	36·40 E
128	Bezhitsa (byĕ-zhĭ'tsȧ) . . . Sov. Un.	53·19 N	34·18 E
122	Béziers (bā-zyā') . . . Fr.	43·21 N	3·12 E
142	Bhagalpur (bä'gŭl-pōōr) . . . India	25·15 N	86·59 E
146	Bhamo (bŭ-mō') . . . Bur.	24·22 N	97·13 E
142	Bhāngar . . . India (Calcutta In.)	22·30 N	88·36 E
142	Bharatpur (bērt'pōōr) . . . India	27·21 N	77·33 E
142	Bhatinda (bŭ-tĭn-dȧ) . . . India	30·19 N	74·56 E
142	Bhātpāra (bŭt-pä'rȧ) India (Calcutta In.)	22·58 N	88·30 E
142	Bhaunāgār (bäv-nŭg'ŭr) . . . India	21·45 N	72·58 E
143	Bhayandar . . . India (Bombay In.)	19·20 N	72·50 E
142	Bhima (R.) (bē'mȧ) . . . India	17·44 N	75·28 E
142	Bhiwani . . . India	28·53 N	76·08 E
143	Bhiwandi . . . India (Bombay In.)	19·18 N	73·03 E
142	Bhopāl (bō-päl) . . . India	23·20 N	77·25 E
142	Bhorila . . . W. Pak.	24·48 N	70·11 E
142	Bhubaneswar (bōō-bŭ-năsh'vûr) India	20·21 N	85·53 E
142	Bhuj (bōōj) . . . India	23·22 N	69·39 E
138	Bhutan (bōō-tän') . . . Asia	28·00 N	90·00 E
164	Biafra, Bight of . . . Cam.	2·52 N	9·01 E

Page	Name Pronunciation Region	Lat. °′	Long. °′
155	Biak (I.) (bē'āk) ... W. Irian	0·45 S	135·00 E
121	Biała Podlaska (byä'wä pōd-läs'kä). Pol.	52·01 N	23·08 E
120	Białogard (byä-wō'gärd) ... Pol.	54·00 N	16·01 E
121	Białystok (byä-wĭs'tōk) ... Pol.	53·08 N	23·12 E
122	Biarritz (byä-rēts') ... Fr.	43·27 N	1·39 W
168	Bibā (bē'bȧ) ... U. A. R. (Nile In.)	28·54 N	30·59 E
78	Bibb City (bĭb' sĭ'tē) ... Ga.	32·31 N	84·56 W
120	Biberach (bē'bĕräk) ... Ger.	48·06 N	9·49 E
82	Bic (bĭk) ... Can.	48·21 N	68·44 W
80	Bicknell (bĭk'nĕl) ... Ind.	38·45 N	87·20 W
121	Bicske (bĭsh'kĕ) ... Hung.	47·29 N	18·38 E
164	Bida (bē'dä) ... Nig.	9·05 N	6·04 E
82	Biddeford (bĭd'ē-fĕrd) ... Maine	43·29 N	70·29 W
110	Biddulph (bĭd'ŭlf) ... Eng.	53·07 N	2·10 W
164	Bidon Cing ... Alg.	22·22 N	0·33 E
121	Biebrza R. (byĕb'zhȧ) ... Pol.	53·18 N	22·25 E
120	Biel (bēl) ... Switz.	47·09 N	7·12 E
120	Bielefeld (bē'lē-fĕlt) ... Ger.	52·01 N	8·35 E
127	Bieljina (bē-yĕ'lyē-nä) ... Yugo.	44·44 N	19·15 E
126	Biella (byĕl'lä) ... It.	45·34 N	8·05 E
121	Bielsk Podlaski (byĕlsk pŭd-lä'skĭ) Pol.	52·47 N	23·14 E
87	Bienville, Lac (L.) ... Can.	55·32 N	72·45 W
111	Biesenthal (bē'sĕn-täl) Ger. (Berlin In.)	52·46 N	13·38 E
126	Biferno (R.) (bē-fĕr'nō) ... It.	41·49 N	14·46 E
82	Big (L.) (bĭg) ... Can.	45·06 N	67·43 W
65	Big (L.) ... Wash. (Seattle In.)	48·23 N	122·14 W
78	Big (R.) ... Ark.	35·55 N	90·10 W
127	Biga (bē'ghȧ) ... Tur.	40·13 N	27·14 E
73	Big Bay (bĭg' bī'yōō) ... Ark.	33·04 N	91·28 W
71	Big Bay de Noc (bĭg bā dē nok') Mich.	45·48 N	86·41 W
74	Big Bear City (bĭg bâr) Calif. (Los Angeles In.)	34·16 N	116·51 W
74	Big Bear Lake (bĭg bâr lāk) Calif. (Los Angeles In.)	34·14 N	116·54 W
67	Big Belt Mts. (bĭg bĕlt) ... Mont.	46·53 N	111·43 W
70	Big Bend Dam (bĭg bĕnd) ... S. D.	44·11 N	99·33 W
76	Big Bend Natl. Park ... Tex.	29·15 N	103·15 W
78	Big Black (R.) (bĭg blăk) ... Miss.	32·05 N	90·49 W
73	Big Blue (R.) (bĭg blōō) ... Nebr.	40·53 N	97·00 W
76	Big Canyon (bĭg kăn'yŭn) ... Tex.	30·27 N	102·19 W
79	Big Cypress Swp. (bĭg sī'prĕs) Fla. (In.)	26·02 N	81·20 W
64	Big Delta (bĭg dĕl'tȧ) ... Alaska	64·08 N	145·48 W
71	Big Fork (R.) (bĭg fôrk) ... Minn.	48·08 N	93·47 W
86	Biggar ... Can.	52·09 N	108·10 W
67	Big Hole R. (bĭg 'hōl) ... Mont.	45·53 N	113·15 W
67	Big Hole Battlefield Natl. Mon. (bĭg hōl băt''l-fēld). Mont.	45·44 N	113·35 W
67	Big Horn Mts. (bĭg hôrn) ... Wyo.	44·47 N	107·40 W
67	Bighorn R. ... Mont.	45·17 N	107·53 W
65	Big Lake (bĭg lāk) Wash. (Seattle In.)	48·24 N	122·14 W
85	Big L. (bĭg lāk) Can. (Edmonton In.)	53·35 N	113·47 W
80	Big Muddy (R.) ... Ill.	37·55 N	89·10 W
67	Big Muddy Cr. (bĭg mŭd'ĭ). Mont.	48·53 N	105·02 W
80	Big Rapids (bĭg răp'ĭdz) ... Mich.	43·40 N	85·30 W
86	Big River ... Can.	53·50 N	107·20 W
	Big Sandy, see Fraser I.		
69	Big Sandy (R.) (bĭg sănd'ē) ... Ariz.	34·59 N	113·36 W
80	Big Sandy (R.) ... Ky.-W. Va.	38·15 N	82·35 W
72	Big Sandy Cr. ... Colo.	39·08 N	103·36 W
70	Big Sioux (R.) (bĭg sōō) ... S. D.	44·34 N	97·00 W
76	Big Spring (bĭg spring) ... Tex.	32·15 N	101·28 W
70	Big Stone (L.) (bĭg stōn) Minn.-S. Dak.	45·29 N	96·40 W
78	Big Stone Gap ... Va.	36·50 N	82·50 W
67	Bigtimber (bĭg'tĭm-bĕr) ... Mont.	45·50 N	109·57 W
67	Big Wood R. (bĭg wŏŏd) ... Idaho	43·02 N	114·30 W
126	Bihać (bē'häch) ... Yugo.	44·48 N	15·52 E
142	Bihar (State) (bē-här') ... India	23·48 N	84·57 E
166	Biharamulo (bē-hä-rä-mōō'lō) Tan.	2·38 S	31·39 E
121	Bihor, Muntii (Mts.) (bē'hôr) Rom.	46·37 N	22·37 E
164	Bijagós, Arquipelago dos (Is.) (är-kē-pä'lä-gō dōs bē-zhä-gôs') Port. Gui.	10·58 N	16·39 W
143	Bijapur ... India	16·53 N	75·42 E
127	Bijelo Polje (bē'yĕ-lō pō'lyĕ) Yugo.	43·02 N	19·48 E
72	Bijou Cr. (bē'zhōō) ... Colo.	39·41 N	104·13 W
142	Bikaner (bĭ-kă'nûr) ... India	28·07 N	73·19 E
152	Bikin (bē-kēn') ... Sov. Un.	46·41 N	134·29 E
152	Bikin (R.) ... Sov. Un.	46·37 N	135·55 E
166	Bikoro (bē-kō'rō) ... Con. L.	0·45 S	18·51 E
142	Bilāspur (bē-läs'pōōr) ... India	22·08 N	82·12 E
154	Bilauktaung Ra. ... Thai.	14·27 N	98·53 E
124	Bilbao (bĭl-bä'ō) ... Sp.	43·12 N	2·48 W
168	Bilbays ... U. A. R. (Nile In.)	30·26 N	31·37 E
127	Bileća (bē'lĕ-chä) ... Yugo.	42·52 N	18·26 E
133	Bilecik (bē-lĕd-zhĕk') ... Tur.	40·10 N	29·58 E
121	Bilé Karpaty (Mts.) ... Czech.	48·53 N	17·35 E
121	Biłgoraj (bēw-gō'rī) ... Pol.	50·31 N	22·43 E
136	Bilimbay (bē'lĭm-bȧy) Sov. Un. (Urals In.)	56·59 N	59·53 E
160	Billabong (R.) (bĭl'ă-bŏng). Austl.	35·15 S	145·20 E
83	Billerica (bĭl'rĭk-ȧ) Mass. (Boston In.)	42·33 N	71·46 W
110	Billericay ... Eng. (London In.)	51·38 N	0·25 E
67	Billings (bĭl'ĭngz) ... Mont.	45·47 N	108·29 W
69	Bill Williams (L.) (bĭl-wĭl'yumz) Ariz.	34·10 N	113·50 W
165	Bilma (bēl'mä) ... Niger.	18·41 N	13·20 E
78	Biloxi (bĭ-lŏk'sĭ) ... Miss.	30·24 N	88·50 W
168	Bilqas Qishm Awwal U. A. R. (Nile In.)	31·14 N	31·25 E
110	Bilston (bĭl'stŭn) ... Eng.	52·34 N	2·04 W
160	Bimberi Pk. (bĭm'bĕrĭ) ... Austl.	35·45 S	148·50 W
155	Binaja, Gunung (Mtn.) ... Indon.	3·07 S	129·25 E
155	Binalonan (bē-nä-lō'nän) Phil. (Manila In.)	16·03 N	120·35 E
144	Binalud (Mtn.) ... Iran	36·32 N	58·34 E
155	Biñan (bē'nän). Phil. (Manila In.)	14·20 N	121·06 E
120	Bingen (bĭn'gĕn) ... Ger.	49·57 N	7·54 E
164	Bingerville (băn-zhä-vēl') Ivory Coast	5·24 N	3·56 W
110	Bingham (bĭng'ăm) ... Eng.	52·57 N	0·57 W
82	Bingham ... Maine	45·03 N	69·51 W
74	Bingham Canyon Utah (Salt Lake City In.)	40·33 N	112·09 W
81	Binghamton (bĭng'ăm-tŭn) ... N. Y.	42·05 N	75·55 W
153	Bingo-Nada (Sea) (bĭn'gō nä-dä) Jap.	34·06 N	133·14 E
154	Binh Dinh (bĭng'dĭng') ... Viet.	13·55 N	109·00 E
160	Binnaway (bĭn'ă-wā) ... Austl.	31·42 S	149·22 E
139	Bintan, Palau (I.) (bĭn'tän) Indon. (Singapore In.)	1·09 N	104·43 E
154	Bintulu (bēn'tōō-lōō) ... Mala.	3·07 N	113·06 E
135	Bira (bē'rȧ) ... Sov. Un.	49·00 N	133·18 E
152	Bira (R.) ... Sov. Un.	48·55 N	132·25 E
167	Birakao ... Som.	1·14 S	41·47 E
139	Bi'r al Mazār U. A. R. (Palestine In.)	31·03 N	33·24 E
165	Bi'r al Wa'r (Oasis) ... Libya	22·51 N	14·22 E
142	Biratnagar (bĭ-rāt'nŭ-gŭr) ... Nep.	26·35 N	87·18 E
65	Birch Bay. Wash. (Vancouver In.)	48·55 N	122·45 W
65	Birch B. (bûrch) Wash. (Vancouver In.)	48·55 N	122·52 W
85	Birch Cliff (bĕrch klĭf) Can. (Toronto In.)	43·41 N	79·16 W
86	Birch Mts. ... Can.	57·36 N	113·10 W
65	Birch Pt. ... Wash. (Vancouver In.)	48·57 N	122·50 W
167	Bird (I.) (bĕrd) S. Afr. (Natal In.)	33·51 S	26·21 E
95	Bird Rock (I.) (bûrd) ... Ba. Is.	22·50 N	74·20 W
83	Bird Rock (I.) ... Can.	47·53 N	61·00 W
85	Birds Hill (bûrds) Can. (Winnipeg In.)	49·58 N	97·00 W
160	Birdsville (bûrdz'vĭl) ... Aust.	22·50 S	139·31 E
158	Birdum (bûrd'ŭm) ... Austl.	15·45 S	133·25 E
133	Birecik (bē-rĕd-zhĕk') ... Tur.	37·10 N	37·50 E
165	Bir en Natrūn ... Sud.	18·13 N	26·44 E
114	Bir er Ressof (bĕr-ĕr-rĕ-sôf') ... Alg.	32·19 N	7·58 E
144	Bīrjand (bēr'jänd) ... Iran	33·07 N	59·16 E
65	Birkenfeld ... Ore. (Portland In.)	49·59 N	123·20 W
110	Birkenhead (bûr'kĕn-hĕd) ... Eng.	53·23 N	3·02 W
111	Birkenwerder (bēr'kĕn-vĕr-dĕr) Ger. (Berlin In.)	52·41 N	13·22 E
121	Bîrlad ... Rom.	46·15 N	27·43 E
84	Birmingham (bûr'mĭng-häm) Ala. (Birmingham In.)	33·31 N	86·49 W
110	Birmingham ... Eng.	52·29 N	1·53 W
75	Birmingham ... Mich. (Detroit In.)	42·32 N	83·13 W
74	Birmingham Mo. (Kansas City In.)	39·10 N	94·22 W
110	Birmingham, Can. ... Eng.	53·07 N	2·40 W
165	Bi'r Misāḥah (Oasis) ... U. A. R.	22·16 N	28·04 E
164	Birnin Kebbi ... Nig.	12·26 N	4·04 E
135	Birobidzhan (bē'rō-bē-jän') Sov. Un.	48·42 N	133·28 E
132	Birsk (bĭrsk) ... Sov. Un.	55·25 N	55·30 E
110	Birstall (bûr'stôl) ... Eng.	53·44 N	1·39 W
129	Biryuchiy (I.) (bĭr-yōō'chĭ) Sov. Un.	46·07 N	35·12 E
136	Biryulëvo (bēr-yōōl'yô-vô) Sov. Un. (Moscow In.)	55·35 N	37·39 E
134	Biryusa (R.) (bēr-yōō'sä) Sov. Un.	56·43 N	97·30 E
118	Biržai (bêr-zhä'ē) ... Sov. Un.	56·11 N	24·45 E
165	Bi'r Zaltan ... Libya	28·20 N	19·40 E
69	Bisbee (bĭz'bē) ... Ariz.	31·30 N	109·55 W
113	Biscay, B. of (bĭs'kā') ... Eur.	45·19 N	3·51 W
79	Biscayne B. (bĭs-kān') ... Fla. (In.)	25·22 N	80·15 W
123	Bischeim (bĭsh'hīm) ... Fr.	48·40 N	7·48 E
136	Biser (bē'sĕr). Sov. Un. (Urals In.)	58·24 N	58·54 E
126	Biševo (Is.) (bē'shĕ-vō) ... Yugo.	43·58 N	15·41 E
68	Bishop (bĭsh'ŭp) ... Calif.	37·22 N	118·25 W
77	Bishop ... Tex.	27·35 N	97·46 W
110	Bishop's Castle (bĭsh'ŏps käs' l) Eng.	52·29 N	2·57 W
79	Bishopville (bĭsh'ŭp-vĭl) ... S. C.	34·11 N	80·13 W
164	Biskra (bēs'krȧ) ... Alg.	34·52 N	5·39 E
70	Bismarck (bĭz'märk) ... N. D.	46·48 N	100·46 W
155	Bismarck Arch. ... N. Gui. Ter.	3·15 S	150·45 E
155	Bismarck Ra. ... N. Gui. Ter.	5·15 S	144·15 E
164	Bissau (bē-sä'ōō) ... Port. Gui.	11·52 N	15·47 W
77	Bistineau L. (bĭs-tĭ-nō') ... La.	32·19 N	93·45 W
121	Bistrita (bĭs'trĭt-sȧ) ... Rom.	47·09 N	24·29 E
121	Bistrita R. ... Rom.	47·08 N	25·47 E
133	Bitlis (bĭt-lēs') ... Tur.	38·30 N	42·00 E
127	Bitola (Monastir) (bē'tō-lä) (mō'nä-stēr). Yugo.	41·02 N	21·22 E
126	Bitonto (bē-tôn'tō) ... It.	41·08 N	16·42 E
67	Bitter Cr. (bĭt'ĕr) ... Wyo.	41·36 N	108·29 W
120	Bitterfeld (bĭt'ĕr-fĕlt) ... Ger.	51·39 N	12·19 E
66	Bitterroot Ra. (bĭt'ĕr-ōōt) ... Mont.	47·15 N	115·13 W
67	Bitterroot R. ... Mont.	46·28 N	114·10 W
129	Bityug (R.) (bĭt'yōōg) ... Sov. Un.	51·23 N	40·33 E
71	Biwabik (bē-wä'bĭk) ... Minn.	47·32 N	92·24 W
153	Biwa-ko (L.) (bē-wä'kō) Jap. (Ōsaka In.)	35·03 N	135·51 E
134	Biya (R.) (bī'yȧ) ... Sov. Un.	52·22 N	87·28 E
134	Biysk (bēsk) ... Sov. Un.	52·32 N	85·28 E
167	Bizana (bĭz-änä) S. Afr. (Natal In.)	30·51 S	29·54 E
164	Bizerte (bē-zĕrt') ... Tun.	37·23 N	9·52 E
150	Bizuta ... Mong.	41·28 N	115·10 E
126	Bjelovar (byĕ-lō'vär) ... Yugo.	45·54 N	16·53 E
	Bjorneborg, see Pori		
118	Bjorne Fd. (byûr'nĕ fyôrd) ... Nor.	60·11 N	5·26 E
80	Black (L.) (blăk) ... Mich.	45·25 N	84·15 W
81	Black (L.) ... N. Y.	44·30 N	75·35 W
73	Black (R.) ... Ark.	35·47 N	91·22 W
81	Black (R.) ... N. Y.	43·45 N	75·20 W
79	Black (R.) ... S. C.	34·55 N	80·08 W
71	Black (R.) ... Wis.	44·07 N	90·56 W
159	Blackall (blăk'ŭl) ... Austl.	24·23 S	145·37 E
71	Black B. (blăk) ... Can.	48·36 N	88·32 W
84	Black B. ... La. (New Orleans In.)	29·38 N	89·33 W
64	Blackburn (blăk'bûrn) ... Alaska	63·20 N	159·45 W
110	Blackburn ... Eng.	53·45 N	2·28 W
64	Blackburn, Mt. ... Alaska	61·50 N	143·12 W
69	Black Canyon of the Gunnison Natl. Mon. (blăk kăn'yŭn). Colo.	38·35 N	107·45 W
65	Black Diamond (dī'mŭnd) Wash. (Seattle In.)	47·19 N	122·00 W
116	Blackdown Hills (blăk'doun). Eng.	50·58 N	3·19 W
71	Blackduck (blăk'dŭk) ... Minn.	47·41 N	94·33 W
67	Blackfoot (blăk'fŏŏt) ... Idaho	43·11 N	112·23 W
67	Blackfoot Ind. Res. ... Mont.	48·49 N	112·53 W
67	Blackfoot R. ... Mont.	46·53 N	113·33 W
67	Blackfoot River Res. ... Idaho	42·53 N	111·23 W
70	Black Hills (Reg.) ... S. D.	44·08 N	103·47 W
82	Black Lake ... Can.	46·02 N	71·24 W
69	Black Mesa (blăk mā'sȧ) ... Ariz.	36·33 N	110·40 W
69	Black Mts. ... N. Mex.	33·15 N	107·55 W
85	Blackmud Cr. (blăk'mŭd) Can. (Edmonton In.)	53·28 N	113·34 W
110	Blackpool (blăk'pōōl) ... Eng.	53·49 N	3·02 W
94	Black River (blăk') ... Jam.	18·00 N	77·50 W
75	Black R. ... Ohio (Cleveland In.)	41·26 N	82·08 W
151	Black R. ... Viet.	20·56 N	104·30 E
71	Black River Falls ... Wis.	44·18 N	90·51 W
66	Black Rock Des. (rŏk) ... Nev.	40·55 N	119·00 W
79	Blacksburg (blăks'bûrg) ... S. C.	35·09 N	81·30 W
103	Black Sea ... Eur.-Asia	43·01 N	32·16 E
79	Blackshear (blăk'shĭr) ... Ga.	31·20 N	82·15 W
79	Blackstone (blăk'stōn) ... Va.	37·04 N	78·00 W
71	Black Sturgeon (R.) (stû'jŭn). Can.	49·12 N	88·41 W
161	Blacktown (blăk'toun) Austl. (Sydney In.)	33·47 S	150·55 E
82	Blackville (blăk'vĭl) ... Can.	46·44 N	65·50 W
79	Blackville ... S. C.	33·21 N	81·19 W
164	Black Volta R. (vōl'tȧ) Upper Volta	11·21 N	4·21 W
78	Black Warrior (R.) (blăk wŏr'ĭ-ĕr) Ala.	32·37 N	87·42 W
78	Black Warrior (R.), Locust Fk. Ala.	34·06 N	86·27 W
78	Black Warrior (R.), Mulberry Fk. Ala.	34·06 N	86·32 W
116	Blackwater (blăk-wô'tĕr) ... Ire.	52·05 N	9·02 W
73	Blackwater (R.) ... Mo.	38·53 N	93·22 W
79	Blackwater (R.) ... Va.	37·07 N	77·10 W
73	Blackwell (blăk'wĕl) ... Okla.	36·47 N	97·19 W
111	Bladel ... Neth. (Amsterdam In.)	51·22 N	5·15 E
133	Blagodarnoye (blä'gō-där-nō'yĕ) Sov. Un.	45·00 N	43·30 E
127	Blagoevgrad (Gorna Dzhumaya) Bul.	42·01 N	23·06 E
135	Blagoveshchensk (blä'gŏ-vyĕsh'-chĕnsk). Sov. Un.	50·16 N	127·47 E
136	Blagoveshchensk Sov. Un. (Urals In.)	55·03 N	56·00 E
65	Blaine (blān) Wash. (Vancouver In.)	48·59 N	122·49 W
81	Blaine ... W. Va.	39·25 N	79·10 W
70	Blair (blâr) ... Nebr.	41·33 N	96·09 W
86	Blairmore (blâr-mōr) ... Can.	49·38 N	114·20 W
81	Blairsville (blârs'vĭl) ... Pa.	40·30 N	79·40 W
65	Blake (I.) (blāk). Wash. (Seattle In.)	47·37 N	122·28 W
78	Blakely (blāk'lē) ... Ga.	31·22 N	84·55 W
164	Blanc, Cap (C.) ... Mauritania	20·39 N	18·08 W
123	Blanc, Mt. (môn blän) ... Fr.-It.	45·50 N	6·53 E
100	Blanca, Bahia (B.) (bä-ē'ä-blän'kä). Arg.	39·30 S	61·00 W
72	Blanca Pk. (blăn'kȧ) ... Colo.	37·36 N	105·22 W
160	Blanch, L. (blănch) ... Austl.	29·20 S	139·12 E
85	Blanche, R. ... Can. (Ottawa In.)	45·34 N	75·38 W
75	Blanchester (blăn'chĕs-tĕr) Ohio (Cincinnati In.)	39·18 N	83·58 W
100	Blanco, C. (blăŋ'kō) ... Arg.	47·08 S	65·47 W
92	Blanco, Cabo (C.) (kä'bô-blăŋ'kō) C. R.	9·29 N	85·15 W
66	Blanco, C. (blăn'kō) ... Ore.	42·53 N	124·38 W
91	Blanco (R.) ... Mex.	18·42 N	96·03 W
90	Blanco (R.) ... Mex.	24·05 N	99·21 W
94	Blancos, Cayo (I.) (kä'yō-blăŋ'kōs). Cuba	23·15 N	80·55 W
69	Blanding ... Utah	37·40 N	109·31 W
117	Blankenburg (blăŋ'kĕn-bōōrgh) Ger.	51·45 N	13·07 E
111	Blankenfelde (blän'kĕn-fĕl-dĕ) Ger. (Berlin In.)	52·20 N	13·24 E
91	Blanquilla, Arrecife (Reef) (är-rĕ-sē'fĕ-blän-kē'l-yä). Mex.	21·32 N	97·14 W
166	Blantyre (blăn-tīr') ... Nya.	15·48 S	35·07 E
75	Blasdell (blāz'dĕl) N. Y. (Buffalo In.)	42·48 N	78·51 W
126	Blato (blä'tō) ... Yugo.	42·55 N	16·47 E
118	Blåvands Huk (cape) (blô'văns-hōk) Den.	55·36 N	7·35 E
122	Blaye-et-Ste. Luce (blā'ā-sănt-lüs'). Fr.	45·08 N	0·40 W
121	Błazowa (bwä-zhō'vȧ) ... Pol.	49·51 N	22·05 E
164	Blida ... Alg.	36·33 N	2·45 E
87	Blind River (blīnd) ... Can.	46·10 N	83·09 W
80	Blissfield (blĭs-fēld) ... Mich.	41·50 N	83·50 W
110	Blithe (R.) (blĭth) ... Eng.	52·22 N	1·49 W
81	Block (I.) (blŏk) ... R. I.	41·05 N	71·35 W
168	Bloemfontein (blōōm'fŏn-tān) S. Afr. (Johannesburg & Pretoria In.)	29·09 S	26·16 E
122	Blois (blwä) ... Fr.	47·36 N	1·21 E
71	Bloomer (blōōm'ĕr) ... Wis.	45·07 N	91·30 W
80	Bloomfield (blōōm'fēld) ... Ind.	39·00 N	86·55 W
71	Bloomfield ... Iowa	40·44 N	92·21 W
73	Bloomfield ... Mo.	36·54 N	89·55 W
70	Bloomfield ... Nebr.	42·36 N	97·40 W
84	Bloomfield. N. J. (New York In.)	40·48 N	74·12 W
75	Bloomfield Hills Mich. (Detroit In.)	42·35 N	83·15 W
71	Blooming Prairie (blōōm'ĭng prā'rĭ). Minn.	43·52 N	93·04 W

ăt; finăl; rāte; senâte; ärm; ȧsk; sofȧ; fâre; ch-choose; dh-as th in other; bē; ēvent; bĕt; recĕnt; cratĕr; g-go; gh-guttural g; bĭt; ĭ-short neutral; rīde; K-guttural k as ch in German ich;

Page	Name Pronunciation Region	Lat. °′	Long. °′
74	Bloomington (blōōm′ĭng-tŭn) Calif. (Los Angeles In.)	34·04 N	117·24 W
80	Bloomington Ill.	40·30 N	89·00 W
80	Bloomington Ind.	39·10 N	86·35 W
74	Bloomington Minn. (Minneapolis, St. Paul In.)	44·50 N	93·18 W
81	Bloomsburg (blōōmz′bûrg) Pa.	41·00 N	76·25 W
84	Blossburg (blŏs′bûrg) Ala. (Birmingham In.)	33·38 N	86·57 W
81	Blossburg Pa.	41·45 N	77·00 W
166	Bloubergstrand S. Afr. (Cape Town In.)	33·48 S	18·28 E
78	Blountstown (blŭnts′tun) Fla.	30·24 N	85·02 W
120	Bludenz (blōō-dĕnts′) Aus.	47·09 N	9·50 E
83	Blue, Mt. Can.	50·28 N	57·11 W
75	Blue Ash (blōō ăsh) Ohio (Cincinnati In.)	39·14 N	84·23 W
71	Blue Earth (blōō ûrth) Minn.	43·38 N	94·05 W
71	Blue Earth (R.) Minn.	43·55 N	94·16 W
79	Bluefield (blōō′fēld) W. Va.	37·15 N	81·11 W
93	Bluefields (blōō′fēldz) Nic.	12·03 N	83·45 W
75	Blue Island Ill. (Chicago In.)	41·39 N	87·41 W
160	Blue Mts. Austl.	33·35 S	149·00 E
94	Blue Mts. Jam.	18·05 N	76·35 W
66	Blue Mts. Ore.	45·15 N	118·50 W
158	Blue Mud B. (blōō mŭd) Austl.	13·20 S	136·45 E
	Blue Nile, see El Azraq, Bahr		
73	Blue Rapids (blōō răp′idz) Kans.	39·40 N	96·41 W
63	Blue Ridge (Mts.) (blōō rĭj) U. S.	35·30 N	82·50 W
86	Blue River Can.	52·09 N	119·21 W
74	Blue R. Mo. (Kansas City In.)	38·55 N	94·33 W
69	Bluff Utah	37·18 N	109·34 W
80	Bluffton (blŭf-tŭn) Ind.	40·40 N	85·15 W
80	Bluffton (blŭf-tŭn) Ohio	40·50 N	83·55 W
100	Blumenau (blōō′mĕn-ou) Braz.	26·53 S	48·58 W
139	Blumut, Gunong (Mt.) Mala. (Singapore In.)	2·03 N	103·34 E
65	Blyn (blĕn) Wash. (Seattle In.)	48·01 N	123·00 W
116	Blyth (blīth) Eng.	55·03 N	1·34 W
68	Blythe Calif.	33·37 N	114·37 W
73	Blytheville (blīth′vĭl) Ark.	35·55 N	89·51 W
155	Boac Phil. (Manila In.)	13·26 N	121·50 E
92	Boaco (bô-ä′kō) Nic.	12·24 N	85·41 W
99	Boa Vista do Rio Branco (bō′ä vēsh′tä dōō rē′ōō brän′kōō) Braz.	2·46 N	60·45 W
164	Boa Vista I. (bō-ä-vēsh′tà) C. V. Is. (In.)	16·01 N	23·52 W
121	Boberka (bō′bĕr-kà) Sov. Un.	49·36 N	24·18 E
164	Bobo-Dioulasso (bō′bō-dyōō-läs-sō′) Upper Volta	11·13 N	4·13 W
128	Bobr (bô′b'r) Sov. Un.	54·19 N	29·11 E
129	Bobrinets (bô′brē-nyĭts) Sov. Un.	48·04 N	32·10 E
120	Bobr R. (bŭ′br) Pol.	51·44 N	15·13 E
129	Bobrov (bŭb-rôf′) Sov. Un.	51·07 N	40·01 E
129	Bobrovitsa (bŭb-rô′vē-tsà) Sov. Un.	50·43 N	31·27 E
128	Bobruysk (bŏ-brōō′ĭsk) Sov. Un.	53·07 N	29·13 E
99	Boca del Pozo (bô-kä-dĕl-pô′zō) Ven. (In.)	11·00 N	64·21 W
99	Boca de Uchire (bô-kä-dĕ-ōō-chē′rĕ) Ven. (In.)	10·09 N	65·27 W
101	Bocaina, Serra da (Mtn.) (sĕ′r-rä-dá-bô-kä′ē-nä) Braz. (Rio de Janeiro In.)	22·47 S	44·39 W
90	Bocas (bō′käs) Mex.	22·29 N	101·03 W
93	Bocas del Toro (bō′käs dĕl tō′rō) Pan.	9·24 N	82·15 W
121	Bochnia (bōk′nyä) Pol.	49·58 N	20·28 E
123	Bocholt (bō′kōlt) Ger. (Ruhr In.)	51·50 N	6·37 E
123	Bochum (bō′kōōm) Ger. (Ruhr In.)	51·29 N	7·13 E
123	Bockum-Hövel (bō′kōōm-hû′fĕl) Ger. (Ruhr In.)	51·41 N	7·45 E
135	Bodaybo (bō-dī′bō) Sov. Un.	57·12 N	114·46 E
165	Bodele Depression (bō-dá-lā′) Chad	17·21 N	16·38 E
112	Boden Swe.	65·51 N	21·29 E
120	Boden See (L.) (bō′dĕn zā) Ger.	47·48 N	9·22 E
168	Bodenstein (bō′dĕn-stān) S. Afr. (Johannesburg & Pretoria In.)	26·20 S	26·27 E
116	Boderg (bō′dûrg) Ire.	53·51 N	8·06 W
116	Bodmin (bŏd′mĭn) Eng.	50·29 N	4·45 W
116	Bodmin Moor (bŏd′mĭn mōōr) Eng.	50·36 N	4·43 W
112	Bodö (bôd′û) Nor.	67·13 N	14·19 E
166	Boende (bō-ĕn′dā) Con. L.	0·21 S	21·06 E
76	Boerne (bō′ĕrn) Tex.	29·49 N	98·44 W
77	Boeuf R. (bĕf) La.	32·23 N	91·57 W
164	Boffa (bôf′á) Gui.	10·13 N	14·06 W
153	Bōfu (bō′fōō) Jap.	34·03 N	131·35 E
77	Bogalusa (bō-gá-lōō′sá) La.	30·48 N	89·52 W
160	Bogan (R.) (bō′gĕn) Austl.	32·10 S	147·40 E
118	Bogense (bô′gĕn-sĕ) Den.	55·34 N	10·09 E
93	Boggy Pk. (bŏg′ĭ-pēk) Antigua (Le. & Wind. Is. In.)	17·03 N	61·50 W
125	Boghari (bō-gà-rē′) (bō-gä′rē) Alg.	35·50 N	2·48 E
129	Bogodukhov (bŏ-gŏ-dōō′kôf) Sov. Un.	50·10 N	35·31 E
160	Bogong, Mt. Austl.	36·50 S	147·15 E
154	Bogor Indon.	6·45 S	106·45 E
128	Bogoroditsk (bŏ-gŏ′rō-dĭtsk) Sov. Un.	53·48 N	38·06 E
132	Bogorodsk Sov. Un.	56·02 N	43·40 E
136	Bogorodskoye (bŏ-gŏ-rôd′skō-yĕ) Sov. Un. (Urals In.)	56·43 N	56·53 E
98	Bogotá (bō-gō-tä′) Col. (In.)	4·38 N	74·06 W
98	Bogotá, Rio (R.) (rē′ō-bō-gō-tä′) Col. (In.)	4·27 N	74·38 W
134	Bogotol (bŏ′gô-tŏl) Sov. Un.	56·13 N	89·13 E
129	Bogoyavlenskoye (bŏ′gô-yäf′lĕn-skō′yĕ) Sov. Un	48·46 N	33·19 E
133	Boguchar (bō′gōō-chär) Sov. Un.	49·40 N	41·00 E
93	Boguete (bô-gĕ′tĕ) Pan.	8·54 N	82·29 W
129	Boguslav (bō′gōō-släf) Sov. Un.	49·34 N	30·51 E
122	Bohain-en-Vermandois (bô-ăN-ŏN-vâr-mäN-dwä′) Fr.	49·58 N	3·22 E
	Bohemia, see Ceske		
120	Bohemian For. (bô-hē′mĭ-ăn) Ger.	49·35 N	12·27 E
155	Bohol (I.) (bô-hôl′) Phil.	9·28 N	124·35 E
91	Bohom (bŏ-ŏ′m) Mex.	16·47 N	92·42 W
168	Bohotleh (bô-hŏt′lĕ) Som. (Horn of Afr. In.)	8·15 N	46·20 E
82	Boiestown (boiz′toun) Can.	46·27 N	66·25 W
127	Boin (R.) (bô′ēn) Yugo.	44·19 N	17·54 E
80	Bois Blanc (I.) (boi′ blăŋk) Mich.	45·45 N	84·30 W
85	Boischatel (bwä-shä-tĕl′) Can. (Quebec In.)	46·54 N	71·08 W
85	Bois-des-Filion (bōō-ä′dĕ-fē-yōN′) Can. (Montreal In.)	45·40 N	73·46 W
66	Boise (boi′zē) Idaho	43·38 N	116·12 W
72	Boise City Okla.	36·42 N	102·30 W
66	Boise R. Idaho	43·43 N	116·30 W
86	Boissevain (bois′vān) Can.	49·11 N	100·01 W
145	Boizabād Afg.	37·13 N	70·38 E
164	Bojador, Cabo (C.) (kä′bô-bō-hä-dōr′) (bŏj-á-dōr′) Sp. Sah.	26·21 N	16·08 W
164	Boké (bō-kā′) Gui.	10·58 N	14·15 W
118	Bokn Fd. (bôk′'n fyôrd) Nor.	59·12 N	5·37 E
167	Boksburg (bŏks′bûrg) S. Afr. (Johannesburg & Pretoria In.)	26·13 S	28·15 E
164	Bolama (bô-lä′mä) Port. Gui.	11·34 N	15·41 W
142	Bolan Mt. (bô-län′) W. Pak.	35·13 N	67·09 E
90	Bolaños (bō-län′yôs) Mex.	21·40 N	103·48 W
90	Bolaños (R.) Mex.	21·26 N	103·54 W
142	Bolan P. W. Pak.	34·50 N	67·10 E
122	Bolbec (bôl-bĕk′) Fr.	49·37 N	0·26 E
164	Bole (bō′lā) Ghana	9·02 N	2·28 W
120	Boleslawiec (bō-lĕ-slä′vyĕts) Pol.	51·15 N	15·35 E
129	Bolgrad (bŏl-grät) Sov. Un.	45·41 N	28·38 E
155	Bolinao (bō-lē-nä′ō) Phil. (Manila In.)	16·24 N	119·53 E
155	Bolinao, C. Phil. (Manila In.)	16·24 N	119·42 E
101	Bolívar (bō-lē′vär) Arg. (Buenos Aires In.)	36·15 S	61·05 W
98	Bolívar Col.	1·46 N	76·58 W
78	Bolivar (bŏl′ĭ-vár) Mo.	37·37 N	93·22 W
78	Bolivar Tenn.	35·14 N	88·56 W
98	Bolívar, Cerro (Mts.) (sĕr-rô-bô-lē′vär) Ven.	6·25 N	64·52 W
98	Bolívar (La Columna) (Mtn.) (bô-lē′vär) (lä-kô-lōō′m-nä) Ven.	8·44 N	70·54 W
77	Bolivar Pen. (bŏl′ĭ-vár) Tex. (In.)	29·25 N	94·40 W
96	Bolivia (bô-lĭv′ĭ-à) S. A.	17·00 S	64·00 W
128	Bolkhov (bŏl-kôf′) Sov. Un.	53·27 N	35·59 E
110	Bollin (R.) (bŏl′ĭn) Eng.	53·18 N	2·11 W
110	Bollington (bôl′ĭng-tŭn) Eng.	53·18 N	2·06 W
118	Bollnäs (bôl′nĕs) Swe.	61·22 N	16·20 E
118	Bolmen (L.) (bôl′mĕn) Swe.	56·58 N	13·25 E
166	Bolobo (bō′lō-bō) Con. L.	2·14 S	16·18 E
126	Bologna (bō-lōn′yä) It.	44·30 N	11·18 E
128	Bologoye (bŏ-lŏ-gô′yĕ) Sov. Un.	57·52 N	34·02 E
92	Bolonchenticul (bô-lôn-chĕn-tē-kōō′l) Mex. (Yucatan In.)	20·03 N	89·47 W
94	Bolondrón (bô-lôn-drōn′) Cuba	22·45 N	81·25 W
126	Bolseno, Lago di (L.) (lä′gō-dē-bôl-sā′nô) It.	42·35 N	11·40 E
132	Bol'shaya Kinel' (R.) Sov. Un.	53·20 N	52·40 E
129	Bol'shaya Lepetikha (bŏl-shà′ yà lyĕ′pyĕ-tē′kà) Sov. Un.	47·11 N	33·58 E
129	Bol'shaya Viska (vĭs-kä′) Sov. Un.	48·34 N	31·54 E
129	Bol'shaya Vradiyevka (vrà-dyĕf′kà) Sov. Un.	47·51 N	30·38 E
136	Bol'she Ust'ikinskoye (bôl′she ōōs-tyĭ-kĕn′skô-yĕ) Sov. Un. (Urals In.)	55·58 N	58·18 E
135	Bolshoy Anyuy (R.) Sov. Un.	67·58 N	161·15 E
135	Bol'shoy Begichëv (I.) Sov. Un.	74·30 N	114·40 E
135	Bolshoy Chuva (R.) Sov. Un.	58·15 N	111·13 E
136	Bol'shoye Ivonino (ĭ-vô′nĭ-nô) Sov. Un. (Urals In.)	59·41 N	61·12 E
136	Bol'shoy Kuyash (bôl′-shôy kōō′yàsh) Sov. Un. (Urals In.)	55·52 N	61·07 E
129	Bolshoy Tokmak (bŏl-shôy′ tôk-mäk′) Sov. Un.	47·17 N	35·48 E
76	Bolson de Mapimi (bôl-sŏ′n-dĕ-mä-pē′mē) Mex.	28·07 N	104·30 W
110	Bolsover (bōl′zō-vēr) Eng.	53·14 N	1·17 W
125	Boltana (bôl-tä′nä) Sp.	42·28 N	0·03 E
85	Bolton (bōl′tŭn) Can. (Toronto In.)	43·53 N	79·44 W
110	Bolton Eng.	53·35 N	2·26 W
110	Bolton-on-Dearne (bōl′tŭn-ŏn-dûrn) Eng.	53·31 N	1·19 W
133	Bolu (bō′lōō) Tur.	40·45 N	31·45 E
128	Bolva (R.) (bôl′vä) Sov. Un.	53·30 N	34·30 E
133	Bolvadin (bôl-vä-dēn′) Tur.	38·50 N	30·50 E
126	Bolzano (bôl-tsä′nō) It.	46·29 N	9·22 E
166	Boma (bō′mä) Con. L.	5·45 S	13·05 E
160	Bombala (bŭm-bä′lă) Austl.	36·55 S	149·07 E
143	Bombay (bŏm-bā′) India (Bombay In.)	18·58 N	72·50 E
142	Bombay (State) India	27·20 N	72·56 E
143	Bombay Hbr. India (Bombay In.)	18·55 N	72·52 E
164	Bomi Hills Lib.	7·00 N	11·00 W
101	Bom Jardim (bôn zhär-dēN′) Braz. (Rio de Janeiro In.)	22·10 S	42·25 W
101	Bom Jesus do Itabapoana (bôN-zhĕ-sōō′s-dô-ē-tà′bä-pô-ä′nä) Braz. (Rio de Janeiro In.)	21·08 S	41·51 W
118	Bömlo (I.) (bûmlô) Nor.	59·47 N	4·57 E
165	Bomongo Con. L.	1·35 N	18·20 E
101	Bom Sucesso (bôN-sōō-sĕ′sō) Braz. (Rio de Janeiro In.)	21·02 S	44·44 W
113	Bon, C. (bôN) Tun.	37·04 N	11·13 E
98	Bonaire (I.) (bō-när′) Neth. Antilles	12·10 N	68·15 W
124	Boñar (bō-nyär′) Sp.	42·53 N	5·18 W
83	Bonavista (bŏ-ná-vĭs′tá) Can.	48·38 N	53·09 W
83	Bonavista B. Can.	48·48 N	53·20 W
72	Bond (bŏnd) Colo.	39·53 N	106·40 W
165	Bondo (bôn′dô) Con. L.	3·49 N	23·43 E
155	Bondoc Pen. (bôn-dŏk′) Phil. (Manila In.)	13·24 N	122·30 E
155	Bondoc Pt. Phil. (Manila In.)	13·11 N	122·20 E
164	Bondoukou (bŏn-dōō′kōō) Ivory Coast	8·06 N	3·47 W
94	Bonds Cay (I.) (bŏnds kē) Ba. Is.	25·30 N	77·45 W
164	Bone (bōn) Alg.	36·57 N	7·39 E
154	Bone, Teluk (L.) Indon.	4·09 S	121·00 E
101	Bonfim (bôN-fē′N) Braz. (Rio de Janeiro In.)	20·20 S	44·15 W
165	Bongos, Massif des (Mts.) Cen. Afr. Rep.	8·04 N	21·59 E
151	Bong Son Viet.	14·20 N	109·10 E
73	Bonham (bŏn′ăm) Tex.	33·35 N	96·09 W
95	Bonhomme, Pic (Pk.) Hai.	19·10 N	72·20 W
126	Bonifacio (bō-nē-fä′chō) Fr.	41·23 N	9·10 E
126	Bonifacio, Str. of Eur.	41·14 N	9·02 E
78	Bonifay (bŏn-ĭ-fā′) Fla.	30·46 N	85·40 W
156	Bonin Is. (bō′nĭn) Asia	26·30 N	141·00 E
123	Bonn (bôn) Ger. (Ruhr In.)	50·44 N	7·06 E
66	Bonners Ferry (bon′erz fĕr′ĭ) Idaho	48·41 N	116·19 W
74	Bonner Springs (bŏn′ĕr sprĭngz) Kans. (Kansas City In.)	39·04 N	94·52 W
73	Bonne Terre (bŏn târ′) Mo.	37·55 N	90·32 W
66	Bonneville Dam (bŏn′ē-vĭl) Wash.-Ore.	45·37 N	121·57 W
83	Bonnie B. (bŏn′ē) Can.	49·38 N	58·15 W
164	Bonny (bŏn′ē) Nig.	4·29 N	7·13 E
65	Bonny Lake (bŏn′ē lăk) Wash. (Seattle In.)	47·11 N	122·11 W
126	Bonorva (bō-nôr′vä) It.	40·26 N	8·46 E
154	Bonthain (bôn-tīn′) Indon.	5·30 S	119·52 E
155	Bontoc (bôn-tŏk′) Phil. (Manila In.)	17·10 N	121·01 E
94	Booby Rocks (I.) (bōō′bĭ rŏks) Ba. Is.	25·55 N	77·00 W
79	Booker T. Washington Natl. Mon. (bōōk′ĕr tē wŏsh′ĭng-tŭn) Va.	37·07 N	79·45 W
111	Boom Bel. (Brussels In.)	51·05 N	4·22 E
71	Boone (bōōn) Iowa	42·04 N	93·51 W
84	Boone Va. (Norfolk In.)	36·50 N	76·26 W
73	Booneville (bōōn′vĭl) Ark.	35·09 N	93·54 W
80	Booneville Ky.	37·25 N	83·40 W
78	Booneville Miss.	34·37 N	88·35 W
168	Boons S. Afr. (Johannesburg & Pretoria In.)	25·59 S	27·15 E
84	Boonton (bōōn′tŭn) N. J. (New York In.)	40·54 N	74·24 W
80	Boonville Ind.	38·00 N	87·15 W
73	Boonville Mo.	38·57 N	92·44 W
82	Boothbay Harbor (bōōth′bā här′bēr) Maine	43·51 N	69·39 W
87	Boothia, G. of (bōō′thĭ-á) Can.	69·04 N	86·04 W
49	Boothia Pen. Can.	73·30 N	95·00 W
84	Boothville (bōōth′vĭl) La. (New Orleans In.)	29·21 N	89·25 W
110	Bootle (bōōt′l) Eng.	53·29 N	3·02 W
164	Boporo (bô-pō′rō) Lib.	7·13 N	10·47 W
120	Boppard (bŏp′ärt) Ger.	50·14 N	7·35 E
165	Bor (bôr) Sud.	6·13 N	31·35 E
133	Bor (bōr) Tur.	37·50 N	34·40 E
67	Borah Pk. (bō′rä) Idaho	44·12 N	113·47 W
168	Borama (bôr-á-mă) Som. (Horn of Afr. In.)	10·05 N	43·08 E
118	Borås (bōō′rōs) Swe.	57·43 N	12·55 E
144	Borāzjān (bō-räz-jān′) Iran	29·13 N	51·13 E
99	Borba (bôr′bä) Braz.	4·23 S	59·31 W
99	Borborema, Planalto da (Plat.) (plä-nál′tô-dä-bôr-bō-rĕ′mä) Braz.	7·35 S	36·40 W
122	Bordeaux (bôr-dō′) Fr.	44·50 N	0·37 W
81	Bordentown (bôr′dĕn-toun) N. J.	40·05 N	74·40 W
113	Bordj-bou-Arréridj (bôrj-bōō-à-rā-rēj′) Alg.	36·03 N	4·48 E
119	Borgå (bôr′gō) Fin.	60·26 N	25·41 E
112	Borgarnes Ice.	64·31 N	21·40 W
72	Borger (bôr′gēr) Tex.	35·40 N	101·23 W
118	Borgholm (bôrg-hŏlm′) Swe.	56·52 N	16·40 E
77	Borgne L. (bôrn′y') La.	30·03 N	89·36 W
126	Borgomanero (bôr′gō-mä-nâ′rō) It.	45·40 N	8·28 E
125	Borgo Montello (bô′r-zhō-môn-tĕ′lō) It. (Rome In.)	41·31 N	12·48 E
126	Borgo Val di Taro (bô′r-zhō-väl-dē-tà′rō) It.	44·29 N	9·44 E
65	Boring (bōr ĭng) Ore. (Portland In.)	45·26 N	122·22 W
121	Borislav (bô′rĭs-lôf) Sov. Un.	49·17 N	23·24 E
133	Borisoglebsk (bŏ-rē sô-glyĕpsk′) Sov. Un.	51·20 N	42·00 E
128	Borisov (bŏ-rē′sôf) Sov. Un.	54·16 N	28·33 E
129	Borisovka (bŏ-rē-sôf′kà) Sov. Un.	50·38 N	36·00 E
129	Borispol' (bo-rĭs′pol) Sov. Un.	50·17 N	30·54 E
143	Borivli India (Bombay In.)	19·15 N	72·48 E
124	Borja (bôr′hä) Sp.	41·50 N	1·33 W
125	Borjas Blancas (bô′r-Käs-blä′n-käs) Sp.	41·29 N	0·53 E
123	Borken (bōr′kĕn) Ger. (Ruhr In.)	51·50 N	6·51 E
165	Borkou (Reg.) (bôr-kōō′) Chad.	18·11 N	18·28 E
120	Borkum I. (bōr′kōōm) Ger.	53·31 N	6·50 E
118	Borlänge (bôr-lĕŋ′gĕ) Swe.	60·30 N	15·24 E
154	Borneo (I.) (bôr′nē-ō) Asia	0·25 N	112·39 E
118	Bornholm (I.) (bôrn-hôlm) Den.	55·16 N	15·15 E
124	Bornos (bôr′nōs) Sp.	36·48 N	5·45 W
164	Bornu (Reg.) Nig.	11·13 N	12·15 E
129	Borodayevka Sov. Un.	48·44 N	34·09 E
129	Boromlya (bŏ-rôm′'l-yä) Sov. Un.	50·36 N	34·58 E
127	Borovan (bŏ-rô-vän′) Bul.	43·24 N	23·47 E
128	Borovichi (bŏ-rô-vē′chē) Sov. Un.	58·22 N	33·56 E
128	Borovsk (bŏ′rôvsk) Sov. Un.	55·13 N	36·26 E
99	Borracha, Isla la (I.) (ē′s-lä-lä-bôr-rá′chä) Ven. (In.)	10·18 N	64·44 W
158	Borroloola (bŏr-rō-lōō′lá) Austl.	16·15 S	136·19 E
121	Borshchëv (bôrsh-chyôf′) Sov. Un.	48·47 N	26·04 E
122	Bort-les-Orgues (bôr-lā-zôrg) Fr.	45·26 N	2·26 E
144	Borūjerd Iran	33·45 N	48·53 E

ng-sing; ŋ-baŋk; N-nasalized n; nŏd; cŏmmit; ōld; ôbey; ôrder; fōōd; fŏŏt; ou-out; s-soft; sh-dish; th-thin; pūre; ûnite; ûrn; stŭd; circŭs; ü-as "y" in study; ′-indeterminate vowel.

Page	Name Pronunciation Region	Lat. °′	Long. °′
129	Borzna (bôrz'nȧ) Sov. Un.	51·15 N	32·26 E
135	Borzya (bôrz'yȧ) Sov. Un.	50·37 N	116·53 E
126	Bosa (bō'sä) It.	40·18 N	8·34 E
126	Bosanska Dubica (bō'sän-skä dōō'bĭt-sä) Yugo.	45·10 N	16·49 E
126	Bosanska Gradiška (bō'sän-skä grä-dĭsh'kä) Yugo.	45·08 N	17·15 E
126	Bosanski Novi (bō's sän-skĭ nō'vē) Yugo.	45·00 N	16·22 E
126	Bosanski Petrovac (bō'sän-skĭ pĕt'rō-väts) Yugo.	44·33 N	16·23 E
127	Bosanski Šamac (bō'sän-skĭ shä'mȧts) Yugo.	45·03 N	18·30 E
71	Boscobel (bŏs'kô-bĕl) Wis.	43·08 N	90·44 W
136	Boskol' (bȧs-kôl') Sov. Un. (Urals In.)	53·45 N	61·17 E
111	Boskoop Neth. (Amsterdam In.)	52·04 N	4·39 E
120	Boskovice (bŏs'kō-vē-tsĕ) Czech.	49·26 N	16·37 E
127	Bosnia (Reg.) (bŏs'nĭ-ȧ) Yugo.	44·17 N	16·58 E
	Bosporous, see Karadeniz Boğazi		
77	Bossier City (bŏsh'ēr) La.	32·31 N	93·42 W
78	Boston (bôs'tŭn) Ga.	30·47 N	83·47 W
83	Boston Mass. (Boston In.)	42·15 N	71·07 W
75	Boston Heights Ohio (Cleveland In.)	41·15 N	81·30 W
73	Boston Mts. Ark.	35·46 N	93·32 W
161	Botany B. (bŏt'ȧ-nĭ) Austl. (Sydney In.)	33·58 S	151·11 E
127	Botevgrad Bul.	42·54 N	23·41 E
168	Bothaville (bō'tȧ-vĭl) S. Afr. (Johannesburg & Pretoria In.)	27·24 S	26·38 E
65	Bothell (bŏth'ĕl) Wash. (Seattle In.)	47·46 N	122·12 W
112	Bothnia, G. of (bŏth'nĭ-ȧ) Eur.	61·45 N	19·45 E
121	Botosani (bō-tō-shan'ĭ) Rom.	47·46 N	26·40 E
70	Bottineau (bŏt-ĭ-nō') N. D.	48·48 N	100·28 W
123	Bottrop (bŏt'trōp) Ger. (Ruhr In.)	51·31 N	6·56 E
99	Botucatú (bô-tōō-kä-tōō') Braz.	22·50 S	48·23 W
83	Botwood (bŏt'wŏŏd) Can.	49·10 N	55·23 W
164	Bouaflé (bōō-ȧ-flā') Ivory Coast	7·23 N	5·32 W
164	Bouaké (bōō-ȧ-kā') Ivory Coast	7·45 N	5·08 W
165	Bouar (bōō-är) Cen. Afr. Rep.	6·04 N	15·34 E
83	Bouche Can.	45·37 N	61·25 W
85	Boucherville (bōō-shȧ-vēl') Can. (Montreal In.)	45·37 N	73·27 W
164	Bou Denib (bōō-dĕ-nĕb') Mor.	32·14 N	3·04 W
71	Boudette (bōō-dĕt) Minn.	48·42 N	94·34 W
113	Bou Dia, C. (bōō dē'ȧ) Tun.	35·18 N	11·17 E
125	Boufarik (bōō-fȧ-rĕk') Alg.	36·35 N	2·55 E
156	Bougainville Trench (bōō-găN-vēl') Oceania	7·00 S	152·00 E
164	Bougie (bōō-zhē') Alg.	36·46 N	5·00 E
164	Bougouni (bōō-gōō-nē') Mali	11·27 N	7·30 W
114	Bouira (boo-ē'rȧ) Alg.	36·25 N	3·55 W
125	Bouïra-Sahary (bwē-rȧ sȧ'ȧ-rē) Alg.	35·16 N	3·23 E
158	Boulder (bōl'dēr) Austl.	31·00 S	121·40 E
72	Boulder Colo.	40·02 N	105·19 W
68	Boulder City Nev.	35 57 N	114·50 W
66	Boulder Cr. Idaho	42·53 N	116·49 W
67	Boulder Pk. Idaho	43·53 N	114·33 W
67	Boulder R. Mont.	46·10 N	112·07 W
164	Boulé R. (bōō-lā') Mali	10·53 N	7·30 W
123	Boulogne-Billancourt (bōō-lôn'y'-bē-yäN-kōōr') Fr. (Paris In.)	48·50 N	2·14 E
122	Boulogne-sur-Mer (bōō-lôn'y-sür-mâr') Fr.	50·44 N	1·37 E
125	Bou-Mort, Sierra de (Mts.) (sē-ĕ'r-rä-dĕ-bō-ōō-mô'rt) Sp.	42·11 N	1·05 E
164	Bouna (bōō-nä') Ivory Coast	9·14 N	3·56 W
65	Boundary B. (boun'dȧ-rĭ) Can. (Vancouver In.)	49·03 N	122·59 W
68	Boundary Pk. Nev.	37·52 N	118·20 W
84	Bound Brook (bound brŏŏk) N. J. (New York In.)	40·34 N	74·32 W
74	Bountiful (boun'tĭ-fōōl) Utah (Salt Lake City In.)	40·55 N	111·53 W
75	Bountiful Pk. (boun'tĭ-fōōl) Utah (Salt Lake City In.)	40·58 N	111·49 W
47	Bounty Is. N. Z.	47·42 S	179·05 E
164	Bourem (bōō-rĕm') Mali	16·43 N	0·15 W
122	Bourg-en-Bresse (bōōr-gĕN-brĕs') Fr.	46·12 N	5·13 E
122	Bourges (bōōrzh) Fr.	47·06 N	2·22 E
85	Bourget (bōōr-zhĕ') Can. (Ottawa In.)	45·26 N	75·09 W
123	Bourgoin (bōōr-gwăN') Fr.	45·46 N	5·17 E
160	Bourke (bûrk) Austl.	30·10 S	146·00 E
135	Bour Khaya, Guba (B.) Sov. Un.	71·45 N	131·00 E
110	Bourne (bôrn) Eng.	52·46 N	0·22 W
116	Bournemouth (bôrn'mŭth) Eng.	50·44 N	1·55 W
114	Bou Saada (bōō-sä'dä) Alg.	35·13 N	4·17 E
165	Bousso (bōō-sô') Chad	10·33 N	16·45 E
164	Boutilimit (bōō-tē-lē-mē') Mauritania	17·30 N	14·54 W
	Bouvet (I.), see Bouvetøya		
47	Bouvetøya (Bouvet) (I.) Atl. O.	54·26 S	3·24 E
126	Bovino (bō-vē'nō) It.	41·14 N	15·21 E
86	Bow (R.) (bō) Can.	50·33 N	112·25 W
70	Bowbells (bō'bĕls) N. D.	48·50 N	102·16 W
70	Bowdle (bōd''l) S. D.	45·28 N	99·42 W
159	Bowen (bō'ĕn) Austl.	20·02 S	148·14 E
84	Bowers Hill (bou'ērs) Va. (Norfolk In.)	36·47 N	76·25 W
72	Bowie (bōō'ĭ) (bō'ē) Tex.	33·34 N	97·50 W
78	Bowling Green (bōlĭng grēn) Ky.	37·00 N	86·26 W
73	Bowling Green Mo.	39·19 N	91·09 W
80	Bowling Green Ohio	41·25 N	83·40 W
70	Bowman (bō'măn) N. D.	46·11 N	103·23 W
81	Bowmanville (bō'măn-vĭl) Can.	43·50 N	78·40 W
85	Bowness Can. (Calgary In.)	51·06 N	114·13 W
155	Bowokan, Pulau-Pulau (Is.) Indon.	2·20 S	123·45 E
70	Boxelder Cr. (bŏks'ĕl-dēr) Mont.	45·35 N	104·28 W
67	Boxelder Cr. Mont.	47·17 N	108·37 W
74	Box Springs (bŏks sprĭngz) Calif (Los Angeles In.)	33·55 N	117·17 W
111	Boxtel Neth. (Amsterdam In.)	51·40 N	5·21 E
85	Boyer, R. (boi'ēr) Can. (Quebec In.)	46·46 N	70·56 W
70	Boyer (R.) Iowa	41·45 N	95·36 W
116	Boyle (boil) Ire.	53·59 N	8·15 W
80	Boyne City Mich.	45·15 N	85·05 W
116	Boyne R. (boin) Ire.	53·40 N	6·40 W
127	Bozcaada (Tenedos) (bōz-cä'dä) (tĕ'nĕ-dŏs) Tur.	39·50 N	26·05 E
127	Bozcaada (I.) (bōz-cä'dä) Tur.	39·50 N	26·00 E
67	Bozemen (bōz'măn) Mont.	45·41 N	111·00 W
126	Bra (brä) It.	44·41 N	7·52 E
126	Brač (I.) (bräch) Yugo.	43·18 N	16·36 E
126	Bracciano, Lago di (L.) (lä'gō-dē-brä-chä'nō) It.	42·05 N	12·00 E
81	Bracebridge (brās'brĭj) Can.	45·05 N	79·20 W
75	Braceville (brās'vĭl) Ill. (Chicago In.)	41·13 N	88·16 W
118	Bräcke (brĕk'kĕ) Swe.	62·44 N	15·28 E
75	Brackenridge (brăk'ĕn-rĭj) Pa. (Pittsburgh In.)	40·37 N	79·44 W
76	Brackettville (brăk'ĕt-vĭl) Tex.	29·19 N	100·24 W
99	Braço Maior (R.) Braz.	11·00 S	51·00 W
99	Braço Menor (R.) (brä'zō-mĕ-nō'r) Braz.	11·38 S	50·00 W
126	Brádano (R.) (brä-dä'nō) It.	40·43 N	16·22 E
75	Braddock (brăd'ŭk) Pa. (Pittsburgh In.)	40·24 N	79·52 W
79	Bradenton (brā'dĕn-tŭn) Fla. (In.)	27·28 N	82·35 W
110	Bradfield (brăd-fēld) Eng. (London In.)	51·25 N	1·08 W
110	Bradford (brăd'fērd) Eng.	53·47 N	1·44 W
80	Bradford Ohio	40·10 N	84·30 W
81	Bradford Pa.	42·00 N	78·40 W
75	Bradley (brăd'lĭ) Ill. (Chicago In.)	41·09 N	87·52 W
65	Bradner (brăd'nēr) Can. (Vancouver In.)	49·05 N	122·26 W
76	Brady (brā'dĭ) Tex.	31·09 N	99·21 W
124	Braga (brä'gä) Port.	41·20 N	8·25 W
101	Bragado (brä-gä'dō) Arg. (Buenos Aires In.)	35·07 S	60·28 W
99	Bragança (brä-gän'sä) Braz.	1·02 S	46·50 W
124	Bragança Port.	41·48 N	6·46 W
101	Bragança Paulista (brä-gän'sä-pä'ōō-lē's-tȧ) Braz. (Rio de Janeiro In.)	22·58 S	46·31 W
85	Bragg Creek (brăg) Can. (Calgary In.)	50·57 N	114·35 W
145	Brahmaputra (R.) (brä'mȧ-pōō'trȧ) India	26·45 N	92·45 E
145	Brahui (Reg.) W. Pak.	28·32 N	66·15 E
75	Braidwood (brăd'wŏŏd) Ill. (Chicago In.)	41·16 N	88·13 W
129	Brăila (brē'ēlȧ) Rom.	45·15 N	27·58 E
71	Brainerd (brān'ērd) Minn.	46·20 N	94·09 W
83	Braintree (brān'trē) Mass. (Boston In.)	42·14 N	71·00 W
84	Braithwaite (brīth'wīt) La. (New Orleans In.)	29·52 N	89·57 W
167	Brakpan (brăk'păn) S. Afr. (Johannesburg & Pretoria In.)	26·15 S	28·22 E
168	Brakspruit S. Afr. (Johannesburg & Pretoria In.)	26·41 S	26·34 E
85	Brampton (brămp'tŭn) Can. (Toronto In.)	43·41 N	79·46 W
100	Branca, Pedra (Mtn.) (pĕ'drä-brä'N-kä) Braz. (In.)	22·55 S	43·28 W
84	Branchville (branch'vĭl) N. J. (New York In.)	41·09 N	74·44 W
79	Branchville S. C.	33·17 N	80·48 W
99	Branco (R.) (brăŋ'kō) Braz.	2·21 N	60·38 W
166	Brandberg (Mtn.) S. W. Afr.	21·15 S	14·15 E
111	Brandenburg (brän'dĕn-bōōrgh) Ger. (Berlin In.)	52·25 N	12·33 E
120	Brandenburg (Reg.) Ger.	52·12 N	13·31 E
168	Brandfort (brăn'd-fôrt) S. Afr. (Johannesburg & Pretoria In.)	28·42 S	26·29 E
86	Brandon (brăn'dŭn) Can.	49·42 N	99·53 W
81	Brandon Vt.	43·45 N	73·05 W
116	Brandon Hill (brăn-dŏn) Ire.	52·15 N	10·12 W
81	Branford (Brăn'fērd) Conn.	41·15 N	72·50 W
121	Braniewo (brä-nyĕ'vō) Pol.	54·23 N	19·50 E
168	Brankhorstspruit S. Afr. (Johannesburg & Pretoria In.)	24·47 S	28·45 E
121	Brańsk (brän' sk) Pol.	52·44 N	22·51 E
85	Brantford (brănt'fērd) Can. (Toronto In.)	43·09 N	80·17 W
83	Bras d'Or L. (brä-dôr') Can.	45·53 N	60·47 W
99	Brasília (brä-sē'lyä) Braz.	15·49 S	47·39 W
99	Brasília Legal (Fordlândia) (brä-sē'lyä-lĕ-gäl) (fô'rd-län-dyä) Braz.	3·45 S	55·46 W
101	Brasópolis (brä-sô'pô-lēs) Braz. (Rio de Janeiro In.)	22·30 S	45·36 W
127	Brașov (Orașul-Stalin) Rom.	45·39 N	25·35 E
164	Brass (brăs) Nig.	4·28 N	6·28 E
111	Brasschaat (bräs'кät) Bel. (Brussels In.)	51·19 N	5·30 E
75	Bratenahl (bră'tĕn-ôl) Ohio (Cleveland In.)	41·34 N	81·36 W
111	Bratislava (brä'tĭs-lȧ-vä) Czech (Vienna In.)	48·09 N	17·07 E
134	Bratsk (brätsk) Sov. Un.	56·10 N	102·04 E
129	Bratslav (brät'slȧf) Sov. Un.	48·48 N	28·59 E
81	Brattleboro (brăt''l-bŭr-ô) Vt.	42·50 N	72·35 W
120	Braunau (brou'nou) Aus.	48·15 N	13·05 E
120	Braunschweig (broun'shvīgh) Ger.	52·16 N	10·32 E
168	Brava (brä'vä) Som. (Horn of Afr. In.)	1·20 N	44·00 E
118	Bråviken (R.) Swe.	58·40 N	16·40 E
	Bravo del Norte, Rio, see Grande, Rio		
68	Brawley (brô'lĭ) Calif.	32·59 N	115·32 W
116	Bray (brā) Ire.	53·10 N	6·05 W
73	Braymer (brā'mēr) Mo.	39·34 N	93·47 W
77	Brays Bay. (brās'bī'yōō) Tex. (In.)	29·41 N	95.33 W
86	Brazeau Can.	52·31 N	116·00 W
80	Brazil (brȧ-zĭl') Ind.	39·30 N	87·00 W
96	Brazil S. A.	9·00 S	53·00 W
96	Brazilian Highlands (Mts.) (brȧ zĭl yȧn hī-lăndz) Braz.	14·00 S	48·00 W
62	Brazos (R.) (brä'zōs) U. S.	33·10 N	98·50 W
76	Brazos (R.), Clear Fk. Tex.	32·56 N	99·14 W
72	Brazos (R.), Double Mountain Fk. Tex.	33·23 N	101·21 W
72	Brazos (R.), Salt Fk. (sôlt fôrk) Tex.	33·20 N	100·57 E
166	Brazzaville (brȧ-zȧ-vēl') Con. B.	4·10 S	15·18 E
127	Brčko (bĕrch'kō) Yugo.	44·54 N	18·46 E
121	Brda R. (bĕr-dä') Pol.	53·18 N	17·55 E
74	Brea (brē'ȧ) Calif. (Los Angeles In.)	33·55 N	117·54 W
85	Breakeyville Can. (Quebec In.)	46·40 N	71·13 W
70	Breckenridge (brĕk'ĕn-rĭj) Minn.	46·17 N	96·35 W
76	Breckenridge Tex.	32·46 N	98·53 W
75	Brecksville (brĕks'vĭl) Ohio (Cleveland In.)	41·19 N	81·38 W
120	Breclav (brzhĕl'läf) Czech.	48·46 N	16·54 E
116	Brecon Beacons (brĕk'ŭn bē kŭns) Wales	52·00 N	3·55 W
111	Breda (brā-dä') Neth. (Amsterdam In.)	51·35 N	4·47 E
166	Bredasdorp (brā'das-dôrp) S. Afr.	34·15 S	20·00 E
136	Bredy (brĕ'dĭ) Sov. Un. (Urals In.)	52·25 N	60·23 E
120	Bregenz (brā'gĕnts) Aus.	47·30 N	9·46 E
127	Bregovo (brĕ'gō-vō) Yugo.	44·07 N	22·45 E
167	Breidbach (brĕd'băk) S. Afr. (Natal In.)	32·54 S	27·26 E
112	Breidha Fd. (brā'dĭ) Ice.	65·15 N	22·50 W
123	Breil (brĕ'y') Fr.	43·57 N	7·36 E
99	Brejo (brȧ'zhŏŏ) Braz.	3·33 S	42·46 W
118	Bremangerland (I.) (brĕ-mängĕr-länd) Nor.	61·51 N	4·25 E
120	Bremen (brā-mĕn) Ger.	53·05 N	8·50 E
80	Bremen (brē'mĕn) Ind.	41·25 N	86·05 W
120	Bremerhaven (brām-ĕr-hä'fĕn) Ger.	53·33 N	8·38 E
65	Bremerton (brĕm'ēr-tŭn) Wash. (Seattle In.)	47·34 N	122·38 W
111	Bremervörde (brĕ'mĕr-fûr-dĕ) Ger. (Hamburg In.)	53·29 N	9·09 E
85	Bremner (brĕm'nēr) Can (Edmonton In.)	53·34 N	113·14 W
77	Bremond (brĕm'ŭnd) Tex.	31·11 N	96·40 W
77	Brenham (brĕn'ăm) Tex.	30·10 N	96·24 W
120	Brenner P. (brĕn'ēr) Aus.-It.	47·00 N	11·30 E
110	Brentwood (brĕnt'wŏŏd) Eng. (London In.)	51·37 N	0·18 E
81	Brentwood Md.	39·00 N	76·55 W
74	Brentwood Mo. (St. Louis In.)	38·37 N	90·21 W
75	Brentwood Pa. (Pittsburgh In.)	40·22 N	79·59 W
126	Brescia (brā'shä) It.	45·33 N	10·15 E
	Breslau, see Wrocław		
126	Bressanone (brĕs-sä-nō'nä) It.	46·42 N	11·40 E
122	Bressuire (brĕ-swēr') Fr.	46·49 N	0·14 W
122	Brest (brĕst) Fr.	48·24 N	4·30 W
121	Brest Sov. Un.	52·06 N	23·43 E
128	Brest (Oblast) Sov. Un.	52·30 N	26·50 E
122	Bretagne, Monts de (Mts.) (mŏN-dĕ-brĕ-tăN'yĕ) Fr.	48·25 N	3·36 W
122	Breton, Pertvis (Str.) (pâr-twē'brĕ-tôN') Fr.	46·18 N	1·43 W
84	Breton I. (brĕt'ŭn) La. (New Orleans In.)	29·27 N	89·10 W
77	Breton Sd. (brĕt'ŭn) La.	29·38 N	89·15 W
85	Bretona (brĕ-tō'nä) Can. (Edmonton In.)	53·27 N	113·20 W
111	Breukelen Neth. (Amsterdam In.)	52·09 N	5·00 E
78	Brevard (brĕ-värd') N. C.	35·14 N	82·45 W
99	Breves (brā'vĕzh) Braz.	1·32 S	50·13 W
118	Brevik (brĕ'vēk) Nor.	59·04 N	9·39 E
160	Brewarrina (brōō-ēr-rē'nȧ) Austl.	29·54 S	146·50 E
82	Brewer (brōō'ēr) Maine	44·46 N	68·46 W
84	Brewster (brōō'stēr) N. Y. (New York In.)	41·23 N	73·38 W
93	Brewster, Cerro (Mt.) (sĕ'r-rô-brōō'stēr) Pan.	9·19 N	79·15 W
78	Brewton (brōō'tŭn) Ala.	31·06 N	87·04 W
126	Brežice (brĕ'zhē-tsĕ) Yugo.	45·55 N	15·37 E
127	Breznik (brĕs'nēk) Bul.	42·44 N	22·55 E
123	Briancon (brē-äN-sôN') Fr.	44·54 N	6·39 E
122	Briare (brē-är') Fr.	47·40 N	2·46 E
65	Bridal Veil (brīd'ăl vāl) Ore. (Portland In.)	45·33 N	122·10 W
94	Bridge Pt. (brĭj) Ba. Is.	25·35 N	76·40 W
78	Bridgeport (brĭj'pôrt) Ala.	34·55 N	85·42 W
84	Bridgeport Conn. (New York In.)	41·12 N	73·12 W
80	Bridgeport Ill.	38·40 N	87·45 W
75	Bridgeport Ind. (Indianapolis In.)	39·44 N	86·18 W
70	Bridgeport Nebr.	41·40 N	103·06 W
80	Bridgeport Ohio	40·00 N	80·45 W
84	Bridgeport Pa. (Philadelphia In.)	40·06 N	75·21 W
72	Bridgeport Tex.	33·13 N	97·46 W
84	Bridgeton (brĭj'tŭn) Ala. (Birmingham In.)	33·27 N	86·39 W
81	Bridgeton N. J.	39·30 N	75·15 W
82	Bridgetown Can.	44·51 N	65·21 W
93	Bridgetown (brĭj' toun) Barbados (Le. & Wind. Is. In.)	13·08 N	59·37 W
75	Bridgeville (brĭj'vĭl) Pa. (Pittsburgh In.)	40·22 N	80·07 W
160	Bridgewater (brĭj'wô-tēr) Austl.	42·50 S	147·28 E
82	Bridgewater Can.	44·24 N	64·34 W
110	Bridgnorth (brĭj'nôrth) Eng.	52·32 N	2·25 W
82	Bridgton (brĭj'tŭn) Maine	44·04 N	70·45 W
116	Bridlington (brĭd'lĭng-tŭn) Eng.	54·06 N	0·10 W

ăt: finăl; rāte; senâte; ärm; ȧsk; sofȧ; fâre; ch-choose; dh-as th in other; bē; ēvent; bĕt; recĕnt; cratēr; g-go; gh-guttural g; bĭt; ĭ-short neutral; rīde; K-guttural k as ch in German ich;

Page	Name Pronunciation Region	Lat. °′	Long. °′
123	Brie-Comte-Robert (brē-kôNt-ĕ-rō-bâr'). Fr. (Paris In.)	48·42 N	2·37 E
111	Brielle ... Neth. (Amsterdam In.)	51·54 N	4·08 E
82	Brier (I.) (brī'ẽr) ... Can.	44·16 N	66·24 W
78	Brierfield (brī'ẽr-fēld) ... Ala.	33·01 N	86·55 W
110	Brierfield (brī'ẽr fēld) ... Eng.	53·49 N	2·14 W
110	Brierley Hill (brī'ẽr-lê hĭl) ... Eng.	52·28 N	2·07 W
111	Brieselang (brē'zĕ-läng) Ger. (Berlin In.)	52·36 N	12·59 E
123	Briey (brē-ĕ') ... Fr.	49·15 N	5·57 E
120	Brig (brēg) ... Switz.	46·17 N	7·59 E
110	Brigg (brĭg) ... Eng.	53·33 N	0·29 W
74	Brigham City (brĭg'ăm) Utah (Salt Lake City In.)	41·31 N	112·01 W
110	Brighouse (brĭg'hous) ... Eng.	53·42 N	1·47 W
160	Bright (brīt) ... Austl.	36·43 S	147·00 E
75	Bright (brīt). Ind. (Cincinnati In.)	39·13 N	84·51 W
110	Brightlingsea (brī't-lĭng-sē) Eng. (London In.)	51·50 N	1·00 E
84	Brighton (brīt'ŭn) Ala. (Birmingham In.)	33·27 N	86·56 W
72	Brighton ... Colo.	39·58 N	104·49 W
116	Brighton ... Eng.	50·47 N	0·07 W
74	Brighton ... Ill. (St. Louis In.)	39·03 N	90·08 W
71	Brighton ... Iowa	41·11 N	91·47 W
83	Brigus (brĭg'ŭs) ... Can.	47·31 N	53·11 W
124	Brihuega (brê-wā'gä) ... Sp.	40·32 N	2·52 W
74	Brimley (brĭm lē) Mich. (Sault Ste. Marie In.)	46·24 N	84·34 W
127	Brindisi (brēn'dē-zē) ... It.	40·38 N	17·57 E
126	Brinje (brēn'yĕ) ... Yugo.	45·00 N	15·08 E
73	Brinkley (brĭŋk'lĭ) ... Ark.	34·52 N	91·12 W
65	Brinnon (brĭn'ŭn) Wash. (Seattle In.)	47·41 N	122·54 W
83	Brion (brē-ôN') ... Can.	47·47 N	61·26 W
122	Brioude (brē-ōōd') ... Fr.	45·18 N	3·22 E
160	Brisbane (brĭz' bân) ... Austl.	27·30 S	153·10 E
81	Bristol (brĭs' tŭl) ... Conn.	41·40 N	72·55 W
116	Bristol ... Eng.	51·29 N	2·39 W
84	Bristol ... Pa. (Philadelphia In.)	40·06 N	74·51 W
84	Bristol ... R.I. (Providence In.)	41·41 N	71·14 W
79	Bristol ... Tenn.	36·35 N	82·10 W
81	Bristol ... Vt.	44·10 N	73·00 W
79	Bristol ... Va.	36·36 N	82·12 W
75	Bristol ... Wis. (Milwaukee In.)	42·32 N	88·04 W
64	Bristol B. ... Alaska	58·08 N	158·54 W
116	Bristol Chan. ... Eng.	51·20 N	3·47 E
73	Bristow (brĭs'tō) ... Okla.	35·50 N	96·25 W
86	British Columbia (Prov.) (brĭt'ĭsh kŏl'ŭm-bĭ-ȧ). Can.	56·00 N	124·53 W
99	British Guiana (gē-ä'nȧ) ... S. A.	7·00 N	59·40 W
88	British Honduras (hēn-dōō'rȧs) N. A.	17·00 N	88·40 W
168	Brits. .S. Afr. (Johannesburg & Pretoria In.)	25·39 S	27·47 E
166	Britstown (brĭts'toun) ... S. Afr.	30·30 S	23·40 E
71	Britt (brĭt) ... Iowa	43·05 N	93·47 W
70	Britton (brĭt'ŭn) ... S. D.	45·47 N	97·44 W
122	Brive-la-Gaillarde (brēv-lä-gī-yärd'ĕ). Fr.	45·10 N	1·31 E
124	Briviesca (brê-vyās'kȧ) ... Sp.	42·34 N	3·21 W
120	Brno (b'r'nô) ... Czech.	49·18 N	16·37 E
94	Broa, Ensenada de la (B.) (ĕn-sĕ-nä'-dä-dĕ-lä-brō'ȧ). Cuba	22·30 N	82·00 W
78	Broad (R.) (brôd) ... Ga.	34·15 N	83·14 W
79	Broad (R.) ... N. C.	35·38 N	82·40 W
161	Broadmeadows (brôd'mĕd-ōz) Austl. (Melbourne In.)	37·40 S	144·53 E
75	Broadview Heights (brôd'vū) Ohio (Cleveland In.)	41·18 N	81·41 W
81	Brockport (brŏk'pōrt) ... N. Y.	43·15 N	77·55 W
83	Brockton (brŏk'tŭn) Mass. (Boston In.)	42·04 N	71·01 W
81	Brockville (brŏk'vĭl) ... Can.	44·35 N	75·40 W
67	Brockway (brŏk'wā) ... Mont.	47·24 N	105·41 W
121	Brodnica (brôd'nĭt-sȧ) ... Pol.	53·16 N	19·26 E
110	Brody (brô'dĭ) ... Sov. Un.	50·05 N	25·10 E
73	Broken Arrow (brō'kĕn ăr'ō). Okla.	36·03 N	95·48 W
161	Broken B. ... Austl. (Sydney In.)	33·34 S	151·20 E
70	Broken Bow (brō'kĕn bō) ... Nebr.	41·24 N	99·37 W
73	Broken Bow ... Okla.	34·02 N	94·43 W
160	Broken Hill (brōk'ĕn) ... Austl.	31·55 S	141·35 E
166	Broken Hill ... N. Rh.	14·18 S	28·28 E
110	Bromley (brŭm'lĭ) Eng. (London In.)	51·23 N	0·01 E
81	Bromptonville (brŭmp'tŭn-vĭl) Can.	45·30 N	72·00 W
118	Brønderslev (brûn'dĕr-slĕv) .. Den.	57·15 N	9·56 E
136	Bronnitsy (brô-nyĭ'tsĭ) Sov. Un. (Moscow In.)	55·26 N	38·16 E
80	Bronson (brŏn'sŭn) ... Mich.	41·55 N	85·15 W
85	Bronte (brONt) Can. (Toronto In.)	43·24 N	79·43 W
85	Bronte Cr. ... Can. (Toronto In.)	43·25 N	79·53 W
79	Brood (R.) (brōōd) ... S. C.	34·46 N	81·25 W
85	Brook, The (R.) Can. (Ottawa In.)	45·25 N	75·09 W
75	Brookfield (brŏŏk'fēld) Ill. (Chicago In.)	41·49 N	87·51 W
73	Brookfield ... Mo.	39·45 N	93·04 W
84	Brookhaven (brŏŏk'hāv'n) Ga. (Atlanta In.)	33·52 N	84·21 W
78	Brookhaven ... Miss.	31·35 N	90·26 W
66	Brookings (brŏŏk'ĭngs) ... Ore.	42·04 N	124·16 W
70	Brookings ... S. D.	44·18 N	96·47 W
85	Brooklands (brŏŏk'lăndz) Can. (Winnipeg In.)	49·56 N	97·12 W
83	Brookline (brŏŏk'līn) Mass. (Boston In.)	42·20 N	71·08 W
83	Brookline ... N. H. (Boston In.)	42·44 N	71·37 W
75	Brooklyn (brŏŏk'lĭn) Ohio (Cleveland In.)	41·26 N	81·44 W
74	Brooklyn Center Minn. (Minneapolis, St. Paul In.)	45·05 N	93·21 W
75	Brook Park (brŏŏk) Ohio (Cleveland In.)	41·24 N	81·50 W
64	Brooks Range (brŏŏks) ... Alaska	68·20 N	159·00 W
79	Brooksville (brŏŏks'vĭl). Fla. (In.)	28·32 N	82·28 W
80	Brookville (brŏŏk'vĭl) ... Ind.	39·20 N	85 00 W
81	Brookville ... Pa.	41·10 N	79·00 W
78	Brookwood (brŏŏk'wŏŏd) ... Ala.	33·15 N	87·17 W
116	Broom (L.) (brōōm) ... Scot.	57·59 N	5·32 W
158	Broome (brōōm) ... Austl.	18·00 S	122·15 E
94	Brothers (Is.) (brŭd'hẽrs) .. Ba. Is.	26·05 N	79·00 W
120	Broumov (brōō'môf) ... Czech.	50·33 N	15·55 E
95	Brown Bk. ... Ba. Is.	21·30 N	74·35 W
72	Brownfield (broun'fēld) ... Tex.	33·11 N	102·16 W
110	Brownhills (broun'hĭlz) ... Eng.	52·38 N	1·55 W
67	Browning (broun'ĭng) ... Mont.	48·37 N	113·05 W
75	Brownsboro (brounz'bô-rô) Ky. (Louisville In.)	38·22 N	85·30 W
85	Brownsburg (brouns'bûrg) Can. (Montreal In.)	45·40 N	74·24 W
75	Brownsburg Ind. (Indianapolis In.)	39·51 N	86·23 W
65	Brownsmead (brounz'-mēd) Ore. (Portland In.)	46·13 N	123·33 W
80	Brownstown (brounz'toun) ... Ind.	38·50 N	86·00 W
78	Brownsville (brounz'vĭl) ... Tenn.	35·35 N	89·15 W
77	Brownsville ... Tex.	25·55 N	97·30 W
82	Brownville (broun'vĭl) ... Maine	45·20 N	69·04 W
76	Brownwood (broun'wŏŏd) ... Tex.	31·44 N	98·58 W
76	Brownwood L. ... Tex.	31·55 N	99·15 W
124	Brozas (brō'thäs) ... Sp.	39·37 N	6·44 W
158	Bruce, Mt. (brōōs) ... Austl.	22·35 S	118·15 E
78	Bruceton (brōōs'tŭn) ... Tenn.	36·02 N	88·14 W
120	Bruchsal (brŏŏk'zäl) ... Ger.	49·08 N	8·34 E
120	Bruck (brŏŏk) ... Aus.	47·25 N	15·14 E
111	Brück (brük) ... Ger. (Berlin In.)	52·12 N	12·45 E
111	Bruck an der Leitha Aus. (Vienna In.)	48·01 N	16·47 E
85	Bruederheim (brōō'dẽr-hīm) Can. (Edmonton In.)	53·47 N	113·56 W
117	Brugge ... Bel.	51·13 N	3·05 E
123	Brühl (brül) ... Ger. (Ruhr In.)	50·49 N	6·54 E
66	Bruneau R. (brōō-nō') ... Idaho	42·47 N	115·43 W
154	Brunei ... Asia	4·52 N	113·38 E
154	Brunei (brōō-nī') ... Bru.	5·00 N	114·59 E
123	Brünen (brü'nĕn). Ger. (Ruhr In.)	51·43 N	6·41 E
125	Brunete (brōō-nä'tȧ) Sp. (Madrid In.)	40·24 N	4·00 W
83	Brunette (I.) (brōō-nĕt') ... Can.	47·17 N	55·55 W
111	Brunn am Gebirge (brōōn'äm gĕ-bĭr'gĕ) Aus. (Vienna In.)	48·07 N	16·18 E
111	Brunsbüttelkoog (brōōns'büt-tĕl-kōg). Ger. (Hamburg In.)	53·58 N	9·10 E
79	Brunswick (brŭnz'wĭk) ... Ga.	31·08 N	81·30 W
82	Brunswick ... Maine	43·54 N	69·57 W
81	Brunswick ... Md.	39·20 N	77·35 W
73	Brunswick ... Mo.	39·25 N	93·07 W
175	Brunswick ... Ohio (Cleveland In.)	41·14 N	81·50 W
100	Brunswick, Pen. de ... Chile	53·25 S	71·15 W
59	Bruny (I.) (brōō'nē) ... Austl.	43·30 S	47·50 E
72	Brush (brŭsh) ... Colo.	40·14 N	103·40 W
100	Brusque (brōō's-kōōĕ) ... Braz.	27·15 S	48·45 W
74	Brussels (brŭs'ĕls) Ill. (St. Louis In.)	38·57 N	90·36 W
	Brussels, see Bruxelles		
111	Bruxelles (Brussels) (brü-sĕl') (brŭs'ĕls). Bel. (Brussels In.)	50·51 N	4·21 E
80	Bryan (brī'ăn) ... Ohio	41·25 N	84·30 W
77	Bryan ... Tex.	30·40 N	96·22 W
128	Bryansk (b'r-yänsk') ... Sov. Un.	53·12 N	34·23 E
128	Bryansk (Oblast) ... Sov. Un.	52·43 N	32·25 E
70	Bryant (brī'ănt) ... S. D.	44·35 N	97·29 E
65	Bryant ... Wash. (Seattle In.)	48·14 N	122·10 W
69	Bryce Canyon Natl. Park (brīs) Utah	37·35 N	112·15 W
84	Bryn Mawr (brĭn mâr') Pa. (Philadelphia In.)	40·02 N	75·20 W
78	Bryson City (brīs'ŭn) ... N. C.	35·25 N	83·25 W
129	Bryukhovetskaya (b'ryŭk'ô-vyĕt-skä'yä). Sov. Un.	45·56 N	38·58 E
139	Buatam ... Indon. (Singapore In.)	0·45 N	101·49 E
164	Buba (bōō'bȧ) ... Port. Gui.	11·39 N	14·58 W
98	Bucaramanga (bōō-kä'rä-mäŋ'gä) Col.	7·12 N	73·14 W
155	Bucay (bōō-kī'). Phil. (Manila In.)	17·32 N	120·42 E
158	Buccaneer Arch. (bŭk-ȧ-nēr') Austl.	16·05 S	122·00 E
121	Buchach (bŏŏ'chách) ... Sov. Un.	49·04 N	25·25 E
164	Buchanan (bû-kăn'ăn) ... Lib.	6·05 N	10·10 W
80	Buchanan ... Mich.	41·50 N	86·25 W
159	Buchanan (L.) (bû-kân'nŏn). Austl.	21·45 S	21·02 E
76	Buchanan L. (bû-kăn'ăn) ... Tex.	30·55 N	98·40 W
83	Buchans ... Can.	48·49 N	56·54 W
	Bucharest, see București		
111	Buchholtz (bŏŏ'hōltz) Ger. (Hamburg In.)	53·19 N	9·53 E
75	Buck Cr. (bŭk) Ind. (Indianapolis In.)	39·43 N	85·58 W
81	Buckhannon (bŭk-hăn'ŭn) W. Va.	39·00 N	80·10 W
116	Buckhaven (bŭk-hā'v'n) ... Scot.	56·10 N	3·10 W
116	Buckie (bŭk'ĭ) ... Scot.	57·40 N	2·50 W
85	Buckingham (bŭk'ĭng-ăm) Can. (Ottawa In.)	45·35 N	75·25 W
142	Buckingham (R.) (bŭk'ĭng-ăm) India	15·18 N	79·50 E
85	Buckland (bŭk'lănd) Can. (Quebec In.)	46·37 N	70·33 W
159	Buckland Tableland, (Reg.) Austl.	24·31 S	148·00 E
65	Buckley (buk'lē) Wash. (Seattle In.)	47·10 N	122·02 W
82	Bucksport (bŭks'pôrt) ... Maine	44·35 N	68·47 W
82	Buctouche (bük-tōōsh') ... Can.	46·30 N	64·42 W
127	București (Bucharest) (bōō-kōō-rĕsh'tĭ) (bōō-kȧ-rĕst'). Rom.	44·23 N	26·10 E
80	Bucyrus (bū-sī'rŭs) ... Ohio	40·50 N	82·55 W
121	Budapest (bōō'dȧ-pĕsht') ... Hung.	47·30 N	19·05 E
123	Büderich (bü'dĕ-rēk) Ger. (Ruhr In.)	51·15 N	6·41 E
142	Budge-Budge. India (Calcutta In.)	22·28 N	88·08 E
75	Buechel (bĕ-chŭl') Ky. (Louisville In.)	38·12 N	85·38 W
123	Bueil (bwā') ... Fr. (Paris In.)	48·55 N	1·27 E
74	Buena Park (bwā'nȧ pärk) Calif. (Los Angeles In.)	33·52 N	118·00 W
98	Buenaventura (bwā'nä-vĕn-tōō'rä) Col.	3·46 N	77·09 W
95	Buenaventura Cuba (Havana In.)	22·08 N	82·22 W
98	Buenaventura, Bahia de (B.) (bä-ē'ä-dĕ-bwā'nä-vĕn-tōō'rȧ) Col.	3·45 N	79·23 W
72	Buena Vista (bū'nȧ vĭs'tȧ) .. Colo.	38·51 N	106·07 W
78	Buena Vista ... Ga.	32·15 N	84·30 W
81	Buena Vista ... Va.	37·45 N	79·20 W
94	Buena Vista, Bahía (B.) (bä-ē'ä-bwĕ-nä-vē's-tä). Cuba	22·30 N	79·10 W
68	Buena Vista Lake Res. (bū'nȧ vĭs'tȧ) Calif.	35·14 N	119·17 W
100	Buenos Aires (bwā'nōs ī'rās) Arg. (In.)	34·20 S	58·30 W
98	Buenos Aires ... Col. (In.)	3·01 N	76·34 W
93	Buenos Aires ... C. R.	9·10 N	83·21 W
100	Buenos Aires (Prov.) ... Arg.	36·15 S	61·45 W
100	Buenos Aires (L.) ... Arg.-Chile	46·30 S	72·15 W
123	Buer (bür) ... Ger. (Ruhr In.)	51·35 N	7·03 E
71	Buffalo (bŭf'ȧ lō) ... Minn.	45·10 N	93·50 W
75	Buffalo ... N. Y. (Buffalo In.)	42·54 N	78·51 W
67	Buffalo ... Wyo.	44·19 N	106·42 W
73	Buffalo (R.) ... Ark.	35·56 N	92·58 W
167	Buffalo (R.) ... S. Afr. (Natal In.)	28·35 S	30·27 E
78	Buffalo (R.) ... Tenn.	35·24 N	87·10 W
77	Buffalo Bay ... Tex. (In.)	29·46 N	95·32 W
71	Buffalo Cr. ... Minn.	44·46 N	94·28 W
86	Buffalo Head Hills ... Can.	57·16 N	116·18 W
85	Buford (bū'fûrd) Can. (Edmonton In.)	53·15 N	113·55 W
78	Buford (bū'fērd) ... Ga.	34·05 N	84·00 W
69	Buford (L.) ... N. Mex.	36·37 N	107·12 W
129	Bug (R.) (bŏŏk) ... Sov. Un.	48·12 N	30·13 E
98	Buga (bōō'gä) ... Col. (In.)	3·54 N	76·17 W
111	Buggenhout ... Bel. (Brussels In.)	51·01 N	4·10 E
126	Bugojno (bōō-gō ĭ nô) ... Yugo.	44·03 N	17·28 E
121	Bug R. (bōōg) ... Pol.	52·29 N	21·20 E
132	Bugul'ma (bōō-gōōl'mȧ). Sov. Un.	54·40 N	52·40 E
132	Buguruslan (bōō-gōō-rōōs-lán') Sov. Un.	53·30 N	52·32 E
155	Buhi (bōō'ē) ... Phil. (Manila In.)	13·26 N	123·31 E
66	Buhl (būl) ... Idaho	42·36 N	114·45 W
71	Buhl ... Minn.	47·28 N	92·49 W
101	Buin (bōō-ēn') Chile (Santiago In.)	33·44 S	70·44 W
133	Buinaksk (bōō'ē-näksk) .. Sov. Un.	42·40 N	47·20 E
124	Bujalance (bōō-hä-län'thā) ... Sp.	37·54 N	4·22 W
166	Bukama (bōō-kä'mä) ... Con. L.	9·08 S	26·00 E
166	Bukavu ... Con. L.	2·39 S	28·50 E
103	Bukhara (bōō-kä'rä) ... Sov. Un.	39·31 N	64·22 E
154	Bukittingg ... Indon.	0·25 S	100·28 E
166	Bukoba ... Tan.	1·19 S	31·49 E
121	Bukovina (Reg.) (bōō-kô'vĭ-nȧ) Sov. Un.	48·06 N	25·20 E
155	Bula (bōō'lä) ... Indon.	3·17 S	130·27 E
155	Bulalacao (bōō-lȧ-lȧ'kä-ô) Phil. (Manila In.)	12·32 N	121·25 E
166	Bulawayo (bōō-lȧ-wä'yō) ... S. Rh.	20·12 S	28·43 E
64	Buldir (I.) (bŭl dĭr) ... Alaska	52·22 N	175·50 E
102	Bulgaria (bŏŏl-gā'rĭ-ă) ... Eur.	42·12 N	24·13 E
124	Bullaque (R.) (bōō-lä'kȧ) ... Sp.	39·15 N	4·13 W
124	Bullas (bōōl'yäs) ... Sp.	38·07 N	1·48 W
69	Bulldog Cr. (bŭl'dŏg') ... Utah	37·45 N	110·55 W
94	Bull Head (Mtn.) ... Jam.	18·10 N	77·15 W
159	Bulloo (R.) (bŭ-lōō') ... Austl.	25·23 S	143·30 E
65	Bull Run (R.) (bŏŏl) Ore. (Portland In.)	45·26 N	122·11 W
65	Bull Run Res. (bŏŏl) Ore. (Portland In.)	45·29 N	122·11 W
73	Bull Shoals Res. (bŏŏl shōlz) Ark.-Mo.	36·35 N	92·57 W
168	Bulo Burti (bōō'lō bŏŏr'tĭ) Som. (Horn of Afr. In.)	3·53 N	45·30 E
110	Bulphan (bŏŏl'făn) Eng. (London In.)	51·33 N	0·21 E
168	Bultfontein (bŏŏlt'fŏn-tān') S. Afr. (Johannesburg & Pretoria In.)	28·18 S	26·10 E
135	Bulun (bōō-lōōn') ... Sov. Un.	70·48 N	127·27 E
166	Bulungu (bōō-lōōŋ'gōō) ... Con. L.	4·58 S	18·57 E
167	Bulwer (bŏŏl-wẽr) S. Afr. (Natal In.)	29·49 S	29·48 E
165	Bumba (bŏŏm'bȧ) ... Con. L.	2·15 N	22·32 E
155	Buna (bōō'nȧ) ... Pap.	8·58 S	148·38 E
158	Bunbury (bŭn'bŭrĭ) ... Austl.	33·25 S	115·45 E
160	Bundaberg (bŭn'dȧ-bûrg) ... Austl.	24·45 S	152·18 E
153	Bungo-Suidō (Chan.) (bōōŋ'gō sōō-ē'dō). Jap.	33·26 N	131·54 E
74	Bunker Hill (bŭnk'ẽr hĭl) Ill. (St. Louis In.)	39·03 N	89·57 W
77	Bunkie (bŭŋ'kĭ) ... La.	30·55 N	92·10 W
135	Buor Khaya, Mys (C.) .. Sov. Un.	71·47 N	133·22 E
168	Buran (bûr'ăn) Som. (Horn of Afr. In.)	10·38 N	48·30 E
168	Burao ... Som. (Horn of Afr. In.)	9·20 N	45·45 E
84	Buras (bûr'ȧs) La. (New Orleans In.)	29·22 N	89·33 W
144	Buraydah ... Sau. Ar.	26·23 N	44·14 E
74	Burbank (bûr'bănk) Calif. (Los Angeles In.)	34·11 N	118·19 W
159	Burdekin (R.) (bûr'dê-kĭn). Austl.	19·22 S	145·07 E
133	Burdur (bōōr-dŏŏr') ... Tur.	37·50 N	30·15 E

ng-sing; ŋ-baŋk; N-nasalized n; nŏd; cŏmmit; ōld; ôbey; ôrder; fōōd; fŏŏt; ou-out; s-soft; sh-dish; th-thin; pūre; ůnite; ûrn; stŭd; circŭs; ü-as "y" in study; '-indeterminate vowel.

Page	Name Pronunciation Region	Lat. °′	Long. °′
142	Burdwan (bŏŏrd-wän′) . . . . . . India	23·29 N	87·53 E
100	Burdwood, Banco (Bk.) . . . Atl. O.	54·00 S	60·45 W
135	Bureinskiy, Khrebet (Mts.) Sov. Un.	51·15 N	133·30 E
135	Bureya (bŏŏrā′ȧ) . . . . Sov. Un.	49·55 N	130·00 E
135	Bureya (R.) (bŏŏ-rā′yä) . . Sov. Un.	51·00 N	130·14 E
110	Burford (bûr-fẽrd) Eng. (London In.)	51·46 N	1·38 W
147	Burga Dist. . . . . China	50·31 N	120·30 E
127	Burgas (bŏŏr-gäs′) . . . . Bul.	42·29 N	27·30 E
127	Burgaski Zaliv (G.) . . . . Bul.	42·30 N	27·40 E
79	Burgaw (bûr′gô) . . . . N. C.	34·31 N	77·56 W
120	Burgdorf (bŏŏrg′dôrf) . . . . . . Switz.	47·04 N	7·37 E
111	Burgenland (State) Aus. (Vienna In.)	47·58 N	16·57 E
83	Burgeo . . . . Can.	47·36 N	57·39 W
76	Burgos (bŏŏr′gōs) . . . . Mex.	24·57 N	98·47 W
155	Burgos . . . . Phil. (Manila In.)	16·03 N	119·52 E
124	Burgos (bōō′r-gôs) . . . . Sp.	42·20 N	3·44 E
118	Burgsvik (bŏŏrgs′vĭk) . . . . Swe.	57·04 N	18·18 E
142	Burhānpur (bŏŏr′hȧn-pōōr) . India	21·26 N	76·08 E
155	Burias I. (bōō′rē-äs) Phil. (Manila In.)	12·56 N	122·56 E
155	Burias Pass (bōō′rē-äs) Phil. (Manila In.)	13·04 N	123·11 E
93	Burica, Punta (Pt.) (pōō′n-tä-bōō′rē-kä) . Pan.	8·02 N	83·12 W
65	Burien (bŭ′rĭ-ĕn) Wash. (Seattle In.)	47·28 N	122·20 W
83	Burin (bûr′ĭn) . . . . Can.	47·03 N	55·33 W
83	Burin Pen. . . . . Can.	47·04 N	55·14 W
72	Burkburnett (bûrk-bûr′nĕt) . . Tex.	34·04 N	98·35 W
81	Burke (bûrk) . . . . Vt.	44·40 N	72·00 W
158	Burketown (bûrk′toun) . . . . . Austl.	17·50 S	139·30 E
67	Burley (bûr′lĭ) . . . . Idaho	42·31 N	113·48 W
65	Burley . . . . Wash. (Seattle In.)	47·25 N	122·38 W
136	Burli . . . . Sov. Un. (Urals In.)	53·36 N	61·55 E
65	Burlingame (bûr′lĭn-gām) Calif. (San Francisco In.)	37·35 N	122·22 W
73	Burlingame . . . . Kans.	38·45 N	95·49 W
85	Burlington (bûr′lĭng-tŭn) Can. (Toronto In.)	43·19 N	79·48 W
72	Burlington . . . . Colo.	39·17 N	102·26 W
71	Burlington . . . . Iowa	40·48 N	91·05 W
73	Burlington . . . . Kans.	38·10 N	95·46 W
75	Burlington . . . Ky. (Cincinnati In.)	39·01 N	84·44 W
84	Burlington . N. J. (Philadelphia In.)	40·04 N	74·52 W
79	Burlington . . . . N. C.	36·05 N	79·26 W
81	Burlington . . . . Vt.	44·30 N	73·15 W
65	Burlington . . . . Wash. (Seattle In.)	48·28 N	122·20 W
75	Burlington . . Wis. (Milwaukee In.)	42·41 N	88·16 W
138	Burma (bûr′mȧ) . . . . Asia	21·00 N	95·15 E
76	Burnet (bûrn′ĕt) . . . . Tex.	30·46 N	98·14 W
110	Burnham on Crouch (bûrn′ăm-ŏn-krouch) Eng. (London In.)	51·38 N	0·48 E
160	Burnie (bûr′nē) . . . . Austl.	41·15 S	146·05 E
110	Burnley (bûrn′lĕ) . . . . Eng.	53·47 N	2·19 W
66	Burns (bûrnz) . . . . Ore.	43·35 N	119·05 W
78	Burnside (bûrn′sīd) . . . . Ky.	36·57 N	84·33 W
86	Burns Lake (bûrnz lăk) . . . . . Can.	54·12 N	125·38 W
82	Burnsville (bûrnz′vĭl) . . . . Can.	47·44 N	65·07 W
66	Burnt R. (bûrnt) . . . . Ore.	44·26 N	117·53 W
65	Burrard Inlet (bûr′ȧrd) Can. (Vancouver In.)	49·19 N	123·15 W
125	Burriana (bōōr-rē-ä′nä) . . . . Sp.	39·53 N	0·05 W
133	Bursa (bōōr′sȧ) . . . . Tur.	40·10 N	28·10 E
165	Būr Safājah . . . . U. A. R.	26·57 N	33·56 E
168	Būr Sa‘id (Port Said) U. A. R. (Suez In.)	31·15 N	32·19 E
123	Burscheid (bōōr′shīd) Ger. (Ruhr In.)	51·05 N	7·07 E
75	Burt (bŭrt) . . . N. Y. (Buffalo In.)	43·19 N	78·45 W
80	Burt (L.) (bŭrt) . . . . Mich.	45·25 N	84·45 W
139	Būr Tawfīg U. A. R. (Palestine In.)	29·58 N	32·33 E
65	Burton (bûr′tŭn) Wash. (Seattle In.)	47·24 N	122·28 W
110	Burton-on-Trent (bŭr′tŭn-ŏn-trĕnt) . Eng.	52·48 N	1·37 W
78	Burton Res. . . . . Ga.	34·46 N	83·40 W
155	Buru (I.) . . . . Indon.	3·30 S	126·30 E
168	Burullus L. . . . . U. A. R. (Nile In.)	31·20 N	30·58 E
155	Buruncan Pt. (bōō-rōōn′kän) Phil. (Manila In.)	12·11 N	121·23 E
166	Burundi . . . . Afr.	3·00 S	29·30 E
86	Burwash Landing (bûr wăsh) . Can.	61·20 N	139·12 W
70	Burwell (bûr′wĕl) . . . . Nebr.	41·46 N	99·08 W
110	Bury (bĕr′ĭ) . . . . Eng.	53·36 N	2·17 W
135	Buryat A.S.S.R. . . . . Sov. Un.	54·15 N	111·22 E
117	Bury St. Edmunds (bĕr′ĭ-sānt ĕd′mŭndz) . Eng.	52·14 N	0·44 E
100	Burzaco (bōōr-zȧ′kô) . . . Arg. (In.)	34·35 S	58·23 W
168	Būsh (bōōsh) . U. A. R. (Nile In.)	29·13 N	31·08 E
144	Būshehr . . . . Iran	28·48 N	50·53 E
166	Bushman Land (Reg.) (bŏŏsh-măn lănd) . S. Afr.	29·15 S	18·45 E
167	Bushmans (R.) (bŏŏsh′mănz) S. Afr. (Natal In.)	33·29 S	26·09 E
73	Bushnell (bŏŏsh′nĕl) . . . . Ill.	40·33 N	90·28 W
165	Businga (bōō-siŋ′gȧ) . . . . . . Con. L.	3·14 N	20·33 E
121	Busk (bōō′sk) . . . . Sov. Un.	49·58 N	24·39 E
164	Bussa (bōō′sȧ) . . . . Nig.	10·11 N	4·20 E
158	Busselton (bûs′′l-tŭn) . . . . . . Austl.	33·40 S	115·30 E
111	Bussum . . . Neth. (Amsterdam In.)	52·16 N	5·10 E
76	Bustamante (bōōs-tȧ-män′tȧ) Mex.	26·34 N	100·30 W
126	Busto Arsizio (bōōs′tō är-sēd′zē-ō) . It.	45·47 N	8·51 E
155	Busuanga (I.) (bōō-swäŋ′gä) . Phil.	12·20 N	119·43 E
165	Buta (bōō′tȧ) . . . . Con. L.	2·47 N	24·46 E
167	Butha Buthe (bōō-thȧ-bōō′thȧ) Bas. (Natal In.)	28·49 S	28·16 E
78	Butler (bŭt′lẽr) . . . . Ala.	32·05 N	88·10 W
80	Butler . . . . Ind.	41·25 N	84·50 W
73	Butler . . . . Mo.	38·16 N	94·19 W
84	Butler . . . . . . N. J. (New York In.)	41·00 N	74·20 W
81	Butler . . . . Pa.	40·50 N	79·55 W
136	Butovo (bŏŏ-tô′vô) Sov. Un. (Moscow In.)	55·33 N	37·36 E
78	Buttahatchie (R.) (bŭt-ȧ-hăch′ē) Ala.-Miss.	34·02 N	88·05 W
67	Butte (būt) . . . . Mont.	46·00 N	112·31 W
167	Butterworth (bŭ tẽr′wûrth) S. Afr. (Natal In.)	32·20 S	28·09 E
116	Butt of Lewis (C.) (bŭt ŏv lū′ĭs) Scot.	58·34 N	6·15 W
155	Butuan (bōō-tōō′än) . . . . Phil.	8·40 N	125·33 E
155	Butung (I.) . . . . Indon.	5·15 S	124·15 E
129	Buturlinovka (bōō-tōō′lē-nôf′ka) Sov. Un.	50·47 N	40·35 E
111	Buxtehude (bŏŏks-tĕ-hōō′dĕ) Ger. (Hamburg In.)	53·29 N	9·42 E
110	Buxton (bŭks′t′n) . . . . Eng.	53·15 N	1·55 W
65	Buxton . . . . Ore. (Portland In.)	45·41 N	123·11 W
167	Buxton . . . . S. Afr. (Natal In.)	32·36 S	26·39 E
132	Buy (bwē) . . . . Sov. Un.	58·30 N	41·48 E
150	Buyr Nuur (bōō′yĕr nôr) . . Mong.	47·50 N	117·00 E
127	Buzău (bōō-zĕ′ŏŏ) . . . . Rom.	45·09 N	26·51 E
129	Buzâu (R.) . . . . Rom.	45·17 N	27·22 E
165	Buzaymah . . . . Libya	25·14 N	22·13 E
133	Buzuluk (bŏŏ-zŏŏ-lŏŏk′) . Sov. Un.	52·50 N	52·10 E
127	Byala . . . . Bul.	43·26 N	25·44 E
	Byblos, see Jubayl		
121	Bydgoszcz (bĭd′gôshch) . . . . . . Pol.	53·07 N	18·00 E
80	Byesville (bīz-vĭl) . . . . Ohio	39·55 N	81·35 W
118	Bygdin (bügh-dēn′) . . . . Nor.	61·24 N	8·31 E
118	Byglandsfjord (bügh′länds-fyôr) Nor.	58·40 N	7·49 E
128	Bykhovo (bĭ-κô′vô) . . . . . Sov. Un.	53·32 N	30·15 E
136	Bykovo (bĭ-kô′vô) Sov. Un. (Moscow In.)	55·38 N	38·05 E
134	Byrranga, Gory (Mts.) . . Sov. Un.	74·15 N	94·28 E
135	Bytantay (R.) (byȧn′tȧy) Sov. Un.	68·15 N	132·15 E
121	Bytom (bĭ′tŭm) . . . . Pol.	50·21 N	18·55 E
128	Bytosh’ (bī-tôsh′) . . . . Sov. Un.	53·48 N	34·06 E
121	Bytow (bĭ′tŭf) . . . . Pol.	54·10 N	17·30 E
127	Buzîu (R.) . . . . Rom.	45·18 N	26·29 E
100	Caazapa′ (kä-zä-pä′) . . . . Par.	26·14 S	56·18 W
155	Cabagan (kä-bä-gän′) Phil. (Manila In.)	17·27 N	12·46 E
155	Cabalete (I.) (kä-bä-lā′tȧ) Phil. (Manila In.)	14·19 N	122·00 E
94	Caballones, Canal de (Chan.) (kä-nä′l-dĕ-kä-bäl-yô′nĕs) . Cuba	20·45 N	79·20 W
69	Caballo Res. (kä-bä-lyō′) . N. Mex.	33·00 N	107·20 W
124	Cabañaquinta (kä-bän-yä-kē′n-tä) Sp.	43·10 N	5·37 W
155	Cabanatuan (kä-bä-nä-twän′) Phil. (Manila In.)	15·30 N	120·56 E
82	Cabano (kä-bä-nō′) . . . . Can.	47·41 N	68·55 W
160	Cabar (kă′bẽr) . . . . Austl.	31·28 S	145·50 E
155	Cabarruyan (I.) (kä-bä-rōō′yän) Phil. (Manila In.)	16·21 N	120·10 E
99	Cabedelo (kä-bē-dā′lŏŏ) . . . . . Braz.	6·58 S	34·49 W
91	Cabeza, Arrecife (Reef) (är-rĕ-sē′fĕ-kä-bĕ-zä) . Mex.	19·07 N	95·52 W
124	Cabeza del Buey (kȧ-bā′thä dĕl bwā′) . Sp.	38·43 N	5·18 W
98	Cabimas (kä-bē′mäs) . . . . Ven.	10·21 N	71·27 W
166	Cabinda (kä-bĭn′dȧ) . . . . Ang.	5·45 S	12·10 E
163	Cabinda (kä-bĭn′dȧ) . . . . Afr.	5·00 S	10·00 E
66	Cabinet Mts. (kăb′ĭ-nĕt) . . Mont. .	48·13 N	115·52 W
101	Cabo Frio (kä′bô-frē′ô) Braz. (Rio de Janeiro In.)	22·53 S	42·02 W
101	Cabo Frio, Ilha do (ē′lä-dô-kä′bô frē′ô) . Braz. (Rio de Janeiro In.)	23·01 S	42·00 W
80	Cabot Hd. (kăb′ŭt) . . . . Can.	45·15 N	81·20 W
83	Cabot Str. (kăb′ŭt) . . . . Can.	47·35 N	60·00 W
164	Cabo Verde, Ilhas do . . . . Afr. (In.)	15·48 N	26·02 W
124	Cabra (käb′rä) . . . . Sp.	37·28 N	4·29 W
155	Cabra (I.) . . . . . . Phil. (Manila In.)	13·55 N	119·55 E
125	Cabrera (I.) (kä-brā′rä) . . . . Sp.	39·08 N	2·57 E
124	Cabriel (R.) (kä-brē-ĕl′) . . . . . . Sp.	39·41 N	1·32 W
68	Cabrillo Natl. Mon. (kä-brēl′yō) Calif. (San Diego In.)	32·41 N	117·03 W
99	Cabrobo′ (kä-brō-bô′) . . . . . . Braz.	8·34 S	39·13 W
100	Cabuçu (R.) (kä-bōō′-sōō) Braz. (In.)	22·57 S	43·36 W
155	Cabugao (kä-bōō′gä-ô) Phil. (Manila In.)	17·48 N	120·28 E
127	Čačak (chä′chȧk) . . . . Yugo.	43·51 N	20·22 E
101	Caçapava (kä′sä-pȧ′vä) Braz. (Rio de Janeiro In.)	23·05 S	45·42 W
99	Cáceres (kȧ′-sĕ-rĕs) . . . . Braz.	16·11 S	57·32 W
124	Cáceres (kȧ′thȧ-rās) . . . . Sp.	39·28 N	6·20 W
101	Cachapoal (R.) (kä-chä-pô-ȧ′l) Chile (Santiago In.)	34·23 S	70·19 W
101	Cacharí (kä-chä-rē′) Arg. (Buenos Aires In.)	36·23 S	59·29 W
73	Cache (R.) (kȧsh) . . . . Ark.	35·24 N	91·12 W
68	Cache Cr. (kăsh) . . . . Calif.	38·53 N	122·24 W
72	Cache la Poudre (R.) (kȧsh lȧ pōōd′r′) . Colo.	40·43 N	105·39 W
100	Cachi, Nevados de (Pk.) (nĕ-vȧ′dôs-dĕ-kȧ′chē) . Arg.	24·35 S	65·59 W
100	Cachinal (kä-chē-näl′) . . . . . . Chile	24·57 S	69·33 W
99	Cachoeira (kä-shô-ā′rä) . . . . . Braz.	12·32 S	38·47 W
100	Cachoeira do Sul (kä-shô-ā′rä-dô-sōō′l) . Braz.	30·02 S	52·49 W
101	Cachoeiras de Macacu (kä-shô-ā′räs-dĕ-mä-kȧ′kōō) Braz. (Rio de Janeiro In.)	22·28 S	42·39 W
101	Cachoeiro de Itapemirim (kä-shô-ā′rô-dĕ-ē′tä-pĕmē-rē′ɴ) Braz. (Rio de Janeiro In.)	20·51 S	41 06 W
166	Caconda (kä-kōn′dä) . . . . Ang.	13·40 S	15·05 E
77	Caddo L. (kăd′ō) . . . . La.-Tex.	32·37 N	94·15 W
90	Cadereyta (kä-dȧ-rā′tä) . . . . . Mex.	20·42 N	99·47 W
76	Cadereyta Jimenez (kä-dä-rā′tä hē-mā′nāz) . Mex.	25·36 N	99·59 W
125	Cadi, Sierra de (Mts.) (sē-ĕ′r-rä-dĕ-kä′dē) . Sp.	42·17 N	1·34 E
155	Cadig, Mt. (kä′dēg) Phil. (Manila In.)	14·11 N	122·26 E
80	Cadillac (kăd′ĭ-lăk) . . . . Mich.	44·15 N	85·25 W
68	Cadiz (kā′dĭz) . . . . Calif.	34·33 N	115·30 W
80	Cadiz . . . . Ohio	40·15 N	81·00 W
124	Cádiz (kȧ′dēz) . . . . Sp.	36·34 N	6·20 W
124	Cádiz, Golfo de (G.) (gôl-fô-dĕ-kȧ′dēz) . Sp.	36·50 N	7·00 W
122	Caen (käɴ) . . . . Fr.	49·13 N	0·22 W
101	Caeté (kä′ĕ-tĕ′) Braz. (Rio de Janeiro In.)	19·53 S	43·41 W
99	Caetité (kä-ȧ-tē-tā′) . . . . Braz.	14·02 S	42·14 W
166	Cagamba (kä-gä′m-bä) . . . . . . Ang.	13·20 S	19·55 E
155	Cagayan (kä-gä-yän′) . . . . Phil.	8·13 N	124·30 E
154	Cagayan (R.) . . . . Phil.	16·45 N	121·55 E
154	Cagayan Is. . . . . Phil.	9·40 N	120·30 E
154	Cagayan Sulu (I.) (kä-gä-yän sōō′lōō) . Phil.	7·00 N	118·30 E
126	Cagli (käl′yē) . . . . It.	42·33 N	12·38 E
126	Cagliari (käl′yä-rē) . . . . It.	39·16 N	9·08 E
126	Cagliari, Golfo di (G.) (gôl-fô-dē-käl′yä-rē) . It.	39·08 N	9·12 E
123	Cagnes (kän′y′) . . . . Fr.	43·40 N	7·14 E
99	Cagua (kä′-gwä) . . . . Ven. (In.)	10·12 N	67·27 W
89	Caguas (kä′gwäs) P. R. (Puerto Rico In.)	18·12 N	66·01 W
78	Cahaba (R.) (kȧ hä-bä) . . . . . . Ala.	32·50 N	87·15 W
166	Cahama (kä-ȧ′mä) . . . . Ang.	16·15 S	14·15 E
74	Cahokia (kȧ-hō′kĭ-ȧ) Ill. (St. Louis In.)	38·34 N	90·11 W
122	Cahors (kȧ-ôr′) . . . . Fr.	44·27 N	1·27 E
91	Cahuacán (kä-wä-kä′n) Mex. (Mexico City In.)	19·38 N	99·25 W
93	Cahuita, Punta (Pt.) (pōō′n-tä-kä-wē′tȧ) . C. R.	9·47 N	82·41 W
99	Caiapó, Serra do (Mts.) (sĕ′r-rä-dô-kä-yä-pô′) . Braz.	17·52 S	52·37 W
94	Caibarién (kī-bä-rē-ĕn′) . . . . . Cuba	22·35 N	79·30 W
98	Caicedonia (kī-sĕ-dô-nēä) Col. (In.)	4·21 N	75·48 W
95	Caicos Bk. (kī′kōs) . . . . Ba. Is.	21·35 N	72·00 W
95	Caicos Is. . . . . . Turks & Caicos Is.	21·45 N	71·50 W
95	Caicos Passage (Str.) . . . . . . Ba. Is.	21·55 N	72·45 W
77	Caillou B. (kȧ-yōō′) . . . . La.	29·07 N	91·00 W
95	Caimanera (kī-mä-nā′rä) . . . . Cuba	20·00 N	75·10 W
90	Caimanere, Laguna del (lä-gŏŏ′nä-dĕl-kä-ē-mä-nĕ-rĕ) Mex.	22·57 N	106·07 W
155	Caiman Pt. (kī′mȧn) Phil. (Manila In.)	15·56 N	119·33 E
88	Caimito, (R.) (kä-ē-mē′tô) Pan. (Panama Canal In.)	8·50 N	79·45 W
95	Caimito del Guayabal (kä-ē-mē′tō-dĕl-gwä-yä-bä′l) Cuba (Havana In.)	22·12 N	82·36 W
85	Cainsville (kānz′vĭl) Can. (Toronto In.)	43·09 N	80·13 W
159	Cairns (kârnz) . . . . Austl.	17·02 S	145·49 E
93	Cairo (kī′-rô) . . . . C. R.	10·06 N	83·47 W
78	Cairo (kā′rō) . . . . Ga.	30·48 N	84·12 W
73	Cairo . . . . Ill.	36·59 N	89·11 W
	Cairo, see Al Qāhirah		
110	Caistor (kâs′tẽr) . . . . Eng.	53·30 N	0·20 W
98	Cajamarca (kä-κä-mȧ′r-kä) Col. (In.)	4·25 N	75·25 W
98	Cajamarca (kä-hä-mär′kä) . . . Peru	7·16 S	78·30 W
155	Cajidiocan (kä-hē-dyô′kän) Phil. (Manila In.)	12·22 N	122·41 E
127	Čajniče (chī′nĭ-chĕ) . . . . Yugo.	43·32 N	19·04 E
74	Cajon (kȧ-hōn′) Calif. (Los Angeles In.)	34·18 N	117·28 W
101	Cajuru (kȧ-zhōō′-rōō) Braz. (Rio de Janeiro In.)	21·17 S	47·17 W
126	Čakovec (chȧ′kō-vĕts) . . . . . . Yugo.	46·23 N	16·27 E
167	Cala (că-lȧ) . . . . S. Afr. (Natal In.)	31·33 S	27·41 E
	(Natal In.)	31·33 S	27·41 E
164	Calabar (kăl-ȧ-bär′) . . . . Nig.	4·58 N	8·21 E
74	Calabasas (kä-lä-bäs′äs) Calif. (Los Angeles In.)	34·09 N	118·39 W
95	Calabazar (kä-lä-bä-zä′r) Cuba (Havana In.)	23·02 N	82·25 W
98	Calabozo (kä-lä-bō′zō) . . . . Ven.	8·48 N	67·27 W
126	Calabria (Reg.) (kä-lä′brē-ä) . . . It.	39·26 N	16·23 E
127	Calafat (kȧ-lȧ-fȧt′) . . . . Rom.	43·59 N	22·56 E
155	Calagua Is. (kä-läg′wä) Phil. (Manila In.)	14·30 N	123·06 E
85	Calahoo (kă-lȧ-hōō′) Can. (Edmonton In.)	53·42 N	113·58 W
124	Calahorra (kä-lä-ôr′rä) . . . . Sp.	42·18 N	1·58 W
82	Calais (kȧ-lĕ′) . . . . Can.	45·11 N	67·15 W
122	Calais . . . . Fr.	50·56 N	1·51 E
100	Calama (kä-lä′mä) . . . . Chile	22·17 S	68·58 W
98	Calama . . . . Col.	1·55 N	72·33 W
98	Calamar (kä-lä-mär′) . . . . Col.	10·24 N	75·00 W
155	Calamba (kä-läm′bä) Phil. (Manila In.)	14·12 N	121·10 E
154	Calamian Group (Is.) (kä-lä-myän′) . Phil.	12·14 N	118·38 E
124	Calañas (kä-län′yäs) . . . . Sp.	37·41 N	6·52 W
155	Calapan (kä-lä-pän′) Phil. (Manila In.)	13·25 N	121·11 E
115	Călărasi (kŭ-lŭ-rȧsh′ĭ) . . . . . . Rom.	44·09 N	27·20 E
114	Calasparra (kä-lä-spär′rä) . . . . . Sp.	38·13 N	1·40 W
124	Calatayud (kä-lä-tä-yōōdh′) . . . Sp.	41·23 N	1·37 W
155	Calauag (kä-lä-wäg′) Phil. (Manila In.)	13·56 N	122·16 E
155	Calauag B . . . . . Phil. (Manila In.)	14·07 N	122·10 E
65	Calaveras Res. (kăl-ȧ-vẽr′ăs) Calif. (San Francisco In.)	37·29 N	121·47 W
155	Calavite, C. (kä-lä-vē′tā) Phil. (Manila In.)	13·29 N	120·00 E
77	Calcasieu L. (kăl′kȧ-shū) . . . . . . La.	29·58 N	93·08 W
77	Calcasieu R. . . . . La.	30·22 N	93·08 W

ăt; finăl; rāte; senȧte; ärm; ȧsk; sofȧ; fâre; ch-choose; dh-as th in other; bē; ēvent; bĕt; recĕnt; cratẽr; g-go; gh-guttural g; bĭt; ĭ-short neutral; rīde; κ-guttural k as ch in German ich;

Page	Name Pronunciation Region	Lat. °′	Long. °′
142	Calcutta (kăl-kŭt'ȧ) ... India (Calcutta In.)	22·32 N	88·22 E
98	Caldas (kȧ'l-däs) ... Col. (In.)	6·06 N	75·38 W
98	Caldas (Dept.) ... Col. (In.)	5·20 N	75·38 W
124	Caldas de Rainha (käl'däs dä rīn'yă) . Port.	39·25 N	9·08 W
110	Calder (R.) (kôl'dẽr) ... Eng.	53·39 N	1·30 W
110	Calder (R.) ... Eng.	53·48 N	2·25 W
100	Caldera (käl-dā'rä) ... Chile	27·02 S	70·53 W
66	Caldwell (kôld'wĕl) ... Idaho	43·40 N	116·43 W
73	Caldwell ... Kans.	37·04 N	97·36 W
80	Caldwell ... Ohio	39·40 N	81·30 W
77	Caldwell ... Tex.	30·30 N	96·40 W
85	Caledon (kăl'ē-dŏn) Can. (Toronto In.)	43·52 N	79·59 W
71	Caledonia (kăl-ē-dō'nĭ-ȧ) ... Minn.	43·38 N	91·31 W
116	Caledonian Can. (kăl-ē-dō'nĭ-ȧn) Scot.	56·58 N	4·05 W
125	Calella (kä-lĕl'yä) ... Sp.	41·37 N	2·39 E
90	Calera Victor Rosales (kä-lā'rä-vē'k-tôr-rô-sȧ'lĕs) . Mex.	22·57 N	102·42 W
68	Calexico (kȧ-lĕk'sĭ-kō) ... Calif.	32·41 N	115·30 W
85	Calgary (kăl'gȧ-rĭ) Can. (Calgary In.)	51·03 N	114·05 W
78	Calhoun (kăl-ho͞on') ... Ga.	34·30 N	84·56 W
98	Cali (kä'lē) ... Col. (In.)	3·26 N	76·30 W
143	Calicut (kăl'ĭ-kŭt) ... India	11·19 N	75·49 E
69	Caliente (käl-yĕn'tā) ... Nev.	37·38 N	114·30 W
73	California (kăl-ĭ-fôr'nĭ-ȧ) ... Mo.	38·38 N	92·38 W
75	California ... Pa. (Pittsburgh In.)	40·03 N	79·53 W
62	California (State) ... U. S.	38·10 N	121·20 W
88	California, Golfo de (G.) (gôl-fô-dĕ-kä-lê-fôr-nyä) . Mex.	30·30 N	113·45 W
84	California B. ... La. (New Orleans In.)	29·29 N	89·32 W
121	Căliman, Muntii (Mts.) ... Rom.	47·05 N	24·47 E
143	Calimere, Pt ... India	15·25 N	80·05 E
74	Calimesa (kă-lĭ-mā'sȧ) Calif. (Los Angeles In.)	34·00 N	117·04 W
68	Calipatria (kăl-ĭ-pȧt'rĭ-ȧ) ... Calif.	33·03 N	115·30 W
91	Calkini (käl-kê-nē') ... Mex.	20·21 N	90·06 W
160	Callabonna, L. (călă'bŏnȧ) . Austl.	29·35 S	140·28 E
168	Callafo ... Eth. (Horn of Afr. In.)	5·40 N	44·00 E
98	Callao (käl-yä'ô) ... Peru	12·80 S	77·07 W
85	Calmar (kăl'mär) Can. (Edmonton In.)	53·16 N	113·49 W
71	Calmar ... Iowa	43·12 N	91·54 W
90	Calnali (käl-nä-lē') ... Mex.	20·53 N	98·34 W
79	Calooshatchee (R.) (kȧ-loo-sȧ-hăch'ê) . Fla. (In.)	26·45 N	81·41 W
92	Calotmul (kä-lôt-mo͞ol) Mex. (Yucatan In.)	20·58 N	88·11 W
90	Calpulalpan (käl-po͞o-lȧl'pän) Mex.	19·35 N	98·33 W
126	Caltagirone (käl-tä-jē-rō'nȧ) ... It.	37·14 N	14·32 E
126	Caltanissetta (käl-tä-nê-sĕt'tä) . It.	37·30 N	14·02 E
71	Calumet (kă-lū-mĕt') ... Mich.	47·15 S	88·29 W
75	Calumet, L. ... Ill. (Chicago In.)	41·43 N	87·36 W
75	Calumet City ... Ill. (Chicago In.)	41·37 N	87·33 W
77	Calvert (kăl'vẽrt) ... Tex.	30·59 N	96·41 W
86	Calvert (I.) ... Can.	51·40 N	129·02 W
126	Calvi (käl'vē) ... Fr.	42·33 N	8·35 E
90	Calvillo (käl-vēl'yō) ... Mex.	21·51 N	102·44 W
166	Calvinia (kăl-vĭn'ĭ-ȧ) ... S. Afr.	31·20 S	19·50 E
124	Calzada de Calatrava (käl-zä'dä-dĕ-kä-lä-trä'vä) . Sp.	38·42 N	3·44 W
116	Cam (R.) (kăm) ... Eng.	52·15 N	0·05 E
94	Camaguey (kä-mä-gwā') ... Cuba	21·25 N	78·00 W
94	Camaguey (State) ... Cuba	21·30 N	78·10 W
94	Camajuani (kä-mä-hwä'nê) . Cuba	22·25 N	79·50 W
155	Camalig (kä-mä'lēg) Phil. (Manila In.)	13·11 N	123·36 E
98	Camaná (kä-mä'nä) ... Peru	16·37 S	72·33 W
65	Camano (kä-mä'no) Wash. (Seattle In.)	48·10 N	122·32 W
65	Camano I. ... Wash. (Seattle In.)	48·11 N	122·29 W
76	Camargo (kä-mär'gō) ... Mex.	26·19 N	98·49 W
92	Camaron, Cabo (C.) (kȧ'bô-kä-mä-rōn') . Hond.	16·06 N	85·05 W
65	Camas (kăm'ȧs) Wash. (Portland In.)	45·35 N	122·54 W
67	Camas Cr ... Idaho	44·10 N	112·09 W
99	Camatagua (kä-mä-tȧ'gwä) Ven. (In.)	9·49 N	66·55 W
154	Ca Mau, Pte de ... Viet.	8·42 N	103·11 E
142	Cambay (kăm-bā') ... India	22·22 N	72·39 E
142	Cambay, G. of ... India	21·05 N	71·58 E
64	Cambell (kămbĕl') ... Alaska	63·48 N	171·58 W
139	Cambodia (kăm-bō'dĭ-ȧ) ... Asia	14·00 N	105·45 E
116	Camborne (kăm'bôrn) ... Eng.	50·15 N	5·28 W
122	Cambrai (käN-brĕ') ... Fr.	50·10 N	3·15 E
116	Cambrian (Mts.) (kăm'brĭ-ăn) Wales	52·05 N	4·05 W
116	Cambridge (kām'brĭj) ... Eng.	52·12 N	0·11 E
81	Cambridge ... Md.	38·35 N	76·10 W
83	Cambridge ... Mass. (Boston In.)	42·23 N	71·07 W
71	Cambridge ... Minn.	45·35 N	93·14 W
72	Cambridge ... Nebr.	40·17 N	100·10 W
80	Cambridge ... Ohio	40·00 N	81·35 W
86	Cambridge Bay ... Can.	69·15 N	105·00 W
80	Cambridge City ... Ind.	39·45 N	85·15 W
101	Cambuci (käm-bo͞o'sē) Braz. (Rio de Janeiro In.)	21·35 S	41·54 W
101	Cambuí (käm-bo͞o-ē') Braz. (Rio de Janeiro In.)	22·38 S	46·02 W
75	Camby (kăm'bē) Ind. (Indianapolis In.)	39·40 N	86·19 W
78	Camden (kăm'dĕn) ... Ala.	31·58 N	87·15 W
73	Camden ... Ark.	33·36 N	92·49 W
161	Camden ... Austl. (Sydney In.)	34·03 S	150·42 E
82	Camden ... Maine	44·11 N	69·05 W
84	Camden ... N. J. (Philadelphia In.)	39·56 N	75·06 W
79	Camden ... S. C.	34·14 N	80·37 W
73	Cameron (kăm'ẽr-ŭn) ... Mo.	39·44 N	94·14 W
77	Cameron ... Tex.	30·52 N	96·57 W
80	Cameron ... W. Va.	39·40 N	80·35 W
86	Camerons Hills ... Can.	60·13 N	120·20 W
163	Cameroon ... Afr.	5·48 N	11·00 E
164	Cameroons Mt ... Cam.	4·15 N	9·01 E
99	Cametá (kä-mȧ-tä') ... Braz.	1·14 S	49·30 W
155	Camiling (kä-mê-lĭng') Phil. (Manila In.)	15·42 N	120·24 E
78	Camilla (kȧ-mĭl'ȧ) ... Ga.	31·13 N	84·12 W
124	Caminha (kä-mĭn'yȧ) ... Port.	41·52 N	8·44 W
99	Camoçim (kä-mô-sēN') ... Braz.	2·56 S	40·55 W
158	Camooweal ... Austl.	20·00 S	138·13 E
101	Campana (käm-pä'nä) Arg. (Buenos Aires In.)	34·10 S	58·58 W
100	Campana (I.) (käm-pän'yä) . Chile	48·20 S	75·15 W
124	Campanario (käm-pä-nä'rê-ō) .. Sp.	38·51 N	5·36 W
125	Campanella, Punta (C.) (po͝o'n-tä-käm-pä-nĕ'lä) It. (Naples In.)	40·20 N	14·21 E
101	Campanha (käm-pän-yäN') Braz. (Rio de Janeiro In.)	21·51 S	45·24 W
126	Campania (Reg.) (käm-pän'yä) . It.	43·00 N	14·40 E
65	Campbell (kăm'bĕl) Calif. (San Francisco In.)	37·17 N	121·57 W
73	Campbell ... Mo.	36·29 N	90·04 W
47	Campbell Is ... N. Z.	52·30 S	169·00 E
142	Campbellpore ... W. Pak.	33·49 N	72·24 E
86	Campbell River ... Can.	50·00 N	125·24 W
78	Campbellsville (kăm'bĕlz-vĭl) . Ky.	37·19 N	85·20 W
82	Campbellton (kăm'bĕl-tŭn) .. Can.	48·00 N	66·43 W
161	Campbelltown (kăm'bĕl-toun) Austl. (Sydney In.)	34·04 S	150·49 E
116	Campbeltown (kăm'b'l-toun) Scot.	55·25 N	5·50 W
75	Camp Dennison (dĕ'nĭ-sŏn) Ohio (Cincinnati In.)	39·12 N	84·17 W
91	Campeche (käm-pā'chȧ) ... Mex.	19·51 N	90·32 W
88	Campeche (State) ... Mex.	18·55 N	90·20 W
88	Campeche, Bahía de (B.) (bä-ē'ä-dĕ-käm-pā'chā) . Mex.	19·30 N	93·40 W
94	Campechuela (käm-pȧ-chwā'lä) Cuba	20·15 N	77·15 W
167	Camperdown (kăm'pẽr-doun) S. Afr. (Natal In.)	29·14 S	30·33 E
124	Campillo de Altobuey (käm-pēl'yō dā äl-tō-bo͞o'ȧ) . Sp.	39·37 N	1·50 W
99	Campina Grande (käm-pē'nä grän'dĕ) . Braz.	7·15 S	35·49 W
101	Campinas (käm-pē'näzh) Braz. (Rio de Janeiro In.)	22·53 S	47·03 W
68	Camp Ind. Res. (kămp) ... Calif.	32·39 N	116·26 W
164	Campo (käm'pō) ... Cam.	2·32 N	9·54 E
98	Campoalegre (kä'm-pô-ȧlĕ'grĕ) Col.	2·34 N	75·20 W
126	Campobasso (käm'pô-bäs'sō) ... It.	41·35 N	14·39 E
100	Campo Belo (kä'm-pô-bĕ'lô) Braz. (In.)	22·54 S	43·33 W
101	Campo Belo Braz. (Rio de Janeiro In.)	20·52 S	45·15 W
124	Campo de Criptana (käm'pō dā krêp-tä'nä) . Sp.	39·24 N	3·09 W
95	Campo Florido (kä'm-pō flô-rê'dō) Cuba (Havana In.)	23.07 N	82.07 W
99	Campo Grande (käm-po͝o grän'dĕ) Braz.	20·28 S	54·32 W
99	Campo Maior (käm-po͝o mä-yôr') Braz.	4·48 S	42·12 W
124	Campo Maior ... Port.	39·03 N	7·06 W
125	Campo Real (käm'pô rȧ-äl') Sp. (Madrid In.)	40·21 N	3·23 W
164	Campo R ... Cam.	2·23 N	11·07 E
101	Campos (kä'm-pôs) Braz. (Rio de Janeiro In.)	21·46 S	41·19 W
101	Campos do Jordão (kä'm-pôs-dô-zhôr-dou'N) Braz. (Rio de Janeiro In.)	22·45 S	45·35 W
101	Campos Gerais (kä'm-pôs-zhĕ-rȧ'es) Braz. (Rio de Janeiro In.)	21·17 S	45·43 W
166	Camps Bay (kămps) S. Afr. (Cape Town In.)	33·57 S	18·22 E
76	Camp Wood (kămp wo͝od) ... Tex.	29·39 N	100·02 W
86	Camrose (kăm-rōz) ... Can.	53·08 N	112·50 W
95	Camu (R.) (kä'mo͞o) ... Dom. Rep.	19·05 N	70·15 W
82	Canaan (R.) (kā'năn) ... Can.	45·55 N	65·45 W
49	Canada (kăn'ȧ-dă) ... N. A.	50·00 N	100·00 W
83	Canada B. ... Can.	50·51 N	56·22 W
101	Cañada de Gomez (kä-nyä'dä-dĕ-gô'mĕz) Arg. (Buenos Aires In.)	32·49 S	61·24 W
72	Canadian (kȧ-nā'dĭ-ăn) ... Tex.	35·54 N	100·24 W
73	Canadian R. ... Okla.	34·53 N	97·06 W
81	Canajoharie (kăn-ȧ-jō-hăr'ê) N. Y.	42·55 N	74·35 W
127	Çanakkale (chä-näk-kä'lĕ) ... Tur.	40·10 N	26·26 E
127	Çanakkale Boğazi (Dardanelles) (Str.) (chä-näk-kä'lĕ) (där-dȧ-nĕlz') . Tur.	40·05 N	25·50 E
88	Canal Zone N. A. (Panama Canal In.)	9·08 N	80·30 W
81	Canandaigua (kăn-ăn-dā'gwȧ) N. Y.	42·55 N	77·20 W
81	Canandaigua (L.) ... N. Y.	42·45 N	77·20 W
88	Cananea (kä-nä-nĕ'ä) ... Mex.	31·00 N	110·20 W
75	Canard R. ... Can. (Detroit In.)	42·10 N	83·04 W
164	Canarias, Islas (Is.) (ê's-läs-kä-nä'ryäs) . Sp.	20·09 N	17·30 W
94	Canarreos, Arch. de los (Is.) (är-chē-pyĕ'lä-gô-dĕ-lôs-kä-när-rĕ'ōs) . Cuba	21·35 N	82·20 W
92	Cañas (kä'-nyäs) ... C. R.	10·26 N	85·06 W
98	Cañasgordas (kä'nyäs-gô'r-däs) Col. (In.)	6·44 N	76·01 W
92	Cañas R. ... C. R.	10·20 N	85·21 W
81	Canastota (kăn-ȧs-tō'tȧ) ... N. Y.	43·05 N	75·45 W
99	Canastra, Serra de (Mts.) (sĕ'r-rȧ-dĕ-kȧ-nȧ's-trȧ) . Braz.	19·53 S	46·57 W
76	Canatlán (kä-nät-län') ... Mex.	24·30 N	104·45 W
	Canaveral, C., see Kennedy, C.		
99	Canavieiras (kä-nȧ-vē-ā'räs) Braz.	15·40 S	38·49 W
160	Canberra (kăn'bĕr-ȧ) ... Austl.	35·21 S	149·10 E
70	Canby (kăn'bĭ) ... Minn.	44·43 N	96·15 W
98	Canchuaya, Cerros de (Mts.) (sĕ'r-rôs-dĕ-kän-cho͞o-ȧ'ïä) Peru	7·30 S	74·30 W
91	Cancuc (kän-ko͞ok) ... Mex.	16·58 N	92·17 W
94	Candelaria (kän-dĕ-lä'ryä) .. Cuba	22·45 N	82·55 W
155	Candelaria (kän-dȧ-lä'rê-ä) Phil. (Manila In.)	15·39 N	119·55 E
91	Candelaria (R.) (kän-dĕ-lä-ryä) Mex.	18·25 N	91·21 W
124	Candeleda (kän-dhȧ-lā'dhä) ... Sp.	40·09 N	5·18 W
	Candia, see Kráklion		
64	Candle (kăn'd'l) ... Alaska	65·00 N	162·04 W
70	Cando (kăn'dō) ... N. D.	48·27 N	99·13 W
155	Candon (kän-dōn') Phil. (Manila In.)	17·13 N	120·26 E
	Canea, see Khaniá		
101	Canelones (kä-nĕ-lô-nĕs) Ur. (Buenos Aires In.)	34·32 S	56·19 W
101	Canelones (Dept.) Ur. (Buenos Aires In.)	34·34 S	56·15 W
98	Cañete (kän-yā'tȧ) ... Peru	13·06 S	76·17 W
95	Caney (kä-nā') (kā'nĭ) ... Cuba	20·05 N	75·45 W
73	Caney (kā'nĭ) ... Kans.	37·00 N	95·57 W
78	Caney (R.) ... Tenn.	36·10 N	85·50 W
166	Canganza, Sierra de (Mts.) (sĕr'rȧ dä kän-gän'zȧ) . Ang.	7·35 S	15·30 E
124	Cangas (kän'gäs) ... Sp.	42·15 N	8·43 W
124	Cangas de Narcea (kä'n-gäs-dĕ-när-sĕ-ä) . Sp.	43·08 N	6·36 W
126	Canicatti (kä-nê-kät'tē) ... It.	37·18 N	13·58 E
124	Caniles (kä-nē'lȧs) ... Sp.	37·26 N	2·43 W
90	Cañitas (kän-yē'täs) ... Mex.	23·38 N	102·44 W
133	Cankiri (chän-kē'rē) ... Tur.	40·40 N	33·40 E
85	Cannell ... Can. (Edmonton In.)	53·35 N	113·38 W
80	Cannelton (kăn'ĕl-tŭn) ... Ind.	37·55 N	86·45 W
123	Cannes (kȧn) ... Fr.	43·34 N	7·05 E
82	Canning (kăn'ĭng) ... Can.	45·11 N	64·26 W
110	Cannock (kăn'ŭk) ... Eng.	52·41 N	2·02 W
110	Cannock Chase (Reg.) (kăn'ŭk chās) . Eng.	52·43 N	1·54 W
71	Cannon (R.) (kăn'ŭn) ... Minn.	44·18 N	93·24 W
70	Cannonball (R.) (kăn'ŭn-bäl) N. D.	46·17 N	101·35 W
93	Caño, Isla de (I.) (ê's-lä-dĕ-kä'nō) . C. R.	8·38 N	84·00 W
74	Canoga Park (kä-nō'gȧ) Calif. (Los Angeles In.)	34·07 N	118·36 W
72	Canon City (kăn'yŭn) ... Colo.	38·27 N	105·16 W
75	Canonsburg (kăn'ŭnz-bûrg) Pa. (Pittsburgh In.)	40·16 N	80·11 W
79	Canoochee (R.) (kȧ-no͞o'chē) .. Ga.	32·25 N	82·11 W
86	Canora (kȧ-nōrȧ) ... Can.	51·43 N	102·32 W
126	Canosa (kä-nō'sä) ... It.	41·14 N	16·03 E
93	Canouan I. N. A. (Le. & Wind. Is. In.)	12·44 N	61·10 W
92	Cansaheab (kän-sä-ĕ-äb) Mex. (Yucatan In.)	21·11 N	89·05 W
83	Canso (kăn'sō) ... Can.	45·23 N	60·59 W
83	Canso, C. ... Can.	45·21 N	60·46 W
83	Canso, Str. of ... Can.	45·50 N	61·35 W
101	Cantagalo (kän-tä-gȧ'lo) Braz. (Rio de Janeiro In.)	21·59 S	42·22 W
124	Cantanhede (kän-täN-yā'dȧ) . Port.	40·22 N	8·35 W
110	Canterbury (kăn'tẽr-bẽr-ê) Eng. (London In.)	51·17 N	1·06 E
159	Canterbury Bght ... N. Z. (In.)	44·17 S	172·38 E
94	Cantiles, Cayo (I.) (kȳ-ō-kän-tē'lȧs) . Cuba	21·40 N	82·00 W
	Canton, see Kuangchou		
78	Canton ... Ga.	34·13 N	84·29 W
73	Canton ... Ill.	40·34 N	90·02 W
83	Canton ... Mass. (Boston In.)	42·09 N	71·09 W
78	Canton ... Miss.	32·36 N	90·01 W
73	Canton ... Mo.	40·08 N	91·33 W
78	Canton ... N. C.	35·32 N	82·50 W
80	Canton ... Ohio	40·50 N	81·25 W
81	Canton ... Pa.	41·50 N	76·45 W
70	Canton ... S. D.	43·17 N	96·37 W
126	Cantu (kän-to͞o') ... It.	45·43 N	9·09 E
101	Cañuelas (kä-nyo͝oĕ'-lȧs) Arg. (Buenos Aires In.)	35·03 S	58·45 W
99	Canumã (R.) (kä-no͝o-mȧ') .. Braz.	6·20 S	58·57 W
72	Canyon (kăn'yŭn) ... Tex.	34·59 N	101·57 W
65	Canyon (R.) Wash. (Seattle In.)	48·09 N	121·48 W
76	Canyon Dam ... Tex.	29·51 N	98·20 W
69	Canyon De Chelly Natl. Mon. Ariz.	36·14 N	110·00 W
155	Capalonga (kä-pä-lôŋ'gä) Phil. (Manila In.)	14·20 N	122·30 E
126	Capannori (kä-pän'nô-rē) ... It.	43·50 N	10·30 E
125	Caparica (kä-pä-rē'kä) Port. (Lisbon In.)	38·40 N	9·12 W
83	Cap-Aux-Meules ... Can.	47·25 N	61·51 W
99	Capaya (R.) (kä-pä-īä) . Ven. (In.)	10·28 N	66·15 W
82	Cap Chat (kȧp shä') ... Can.	49·07 N	66·42 W
82	Cap de la Madeleine (kȧp dē lȧ mȧ-d'lĕn') . Can.	46·23 N	72·30 W
83	Cape Breton (I.) (kāp brĕt'ŭn) Can.	45·48 N	59·53 W
83	Cape Breton Highlands Natl. Park Can.	46·45 N	61·05 W
79	Cape Charles (kāp chärlz) ... Va.	37·13 N	76·02 W
164	Cape Coast ... Ghana	5·14 N	1·19 W
81	Cape Cod B. (kāp kŏd) ... Mass.	41·50 N	70·20 W
79	Cape Fear (R.) (kāp fēr) ... N. C.	34·43 N	78·41 W
166	Cape Flats (kāp flăts) S. Afr. (Cape Town In.)	34·01 S	18·37 E

ng-sing; ŋ-baŋk; N-nasalized n; nŏd; cŏmmit; ōld; ôbey; ôrder; fo͞od; fo͝ot; ou-out; s-soft; sh-dish; th-thin; pūre; ûnite; ûrn; stŭd; circŭs; ü-as "y" in study; '-indeterminate vowel.

Page	Name Pronunciation Region	Lat. °′	Long. °′
73	Cape Girardeau (jē-rär-dō') Mo.	37·17 N	89·32 W
84	Cape Henry (hĕn'rê) Va. (Norfolk In.)	36·55 N	76·00 W
81	Cape May (kāp mā) N. J.	38·55 N	74·50 W
81	Cape May C. H. (kāp mā) N. J.	39·05 N	75·00 W
166	Cape of Good Hope (Prov.) (kāp ŏv go͝od hôp) S. Afr.	31·50 S	21·15 E
86	Cape Parry (kāp păr'rē) Can.	70·29 N	127·41 W
166	Cape Point S. Afr. (Cape Town In.)	34·21 S	18·29 E
87	Cape Smith Ra. (kāp smĭth) Can.	61·23 N	76·32 W
93	Capesterre Basse Terre (Le. & Wind Is. In.)	16·02 N	61·37 W
166	Cape Town (kāp toun) S. Afr. (Cape Town In.)	33·48 S	18·28 E
159	Cape York Pen. (kāp yôrk) Austl.	12·30 S	142·35 E
95	Cap-Haitian (kȧp ȧ-ē-syän') Hai.	19·45 N	72·15 W
101	Capilla de Señor (kä-pēl'yä dā sän-yôr') Arg. (Buenos Aires In.)	34·18 S	59·07 W
69	Capitol Reef Natl. Mon. (kăp'ĭ-tŏl) Utah	38·15 N	111·10 W
101	Capivari (kä-pē-vȧ'rê) Braz. (Rio de Janeiro In.)	22·59 S	47·29 W
100	Capivari Braz. (In.)	22·39 S	43·19 W
160	Capoompeta (Mtn.) (kȧ-po͞om-pē'tȧ) Austl.	29·15 S	152·12 E
126	Caporetto (kä-pô-rĕt'tō) Yugo.	46·15 N	13·34 E
126	Capraia (I.) (kä-prä'yä) It.	43·02 N	9·51 E
126	Caprara Pt. (kä-prä'rä) It.	41·08 N	8·20 E
126	Caprera (I.) (kä-prā'rä) It.	41·12 N	9·28 E
125	Capri It. (Naples In.)	40·18 N	14·16 E
125	Capri, I. di (ē'-sō-lä-dē-kä'prē) It. (Naples In.)	40·19 N	14·10 E
159	Capricorn Chan. (kăp'rĭ-kôrn) Austl.	22·27 S	151·24 E
85	Cap-Rouge (kȧp ro͞ozh') Can. (Quebec In.)	46·45 N	71·21 W
85	Cap St. Ignace (kĭp săN-tê-nyȧs') Can. (Quebec In.)	47·02 N	70·27 W
126	Capua (kä'pwä) It.	41·07 N	14·14 E
90	Capulhuac (kä-po͞ol-hwäk') Mex.	19·33 N	99·43 W
72	Capulin Mountain Natl. Mon. (kȧ-pū'lĭn) N. Mex.	36·15 N	103·58 W
91	Capultitlán (kä-po͞o'l-tē-tlȧ'n) Mex. (Mexico City In.)	19·15 N	99·40 W
98	Caquetá (R.) (kä-kä-tä') Col.	0·23 S	73·22 W
125	Carabaña (kä-rä-bän'yä) Sp. (Madrid In.)	40·16 N	3·15 W
99	Carabobo (State) (kä-rä-bô'-bô) Ven. (In.)	10·07 N	68·06 W
127	Caracal (kȧ-rȧ-kȧl') Rom.	44·06 N	24·22 E
99	Caracas (kä-rä'käs) Ven. (In.)	10·30 N	66·58 W
90	Carácuaro de Morelos (kä-rä'kwä-rō-dĕ-mô-rĕ-lôs) Mex.	18·44 N	101·04 W
101	Caraguatatuba (kä-rä-gwä-tä-to͞o'bä) Braz. (Rio de Janeiro In.)	23·37 S	45·26 W
99	Carajás, Serra dos (Mts.) (sĕ'r-rä-dôs-kä-rä-zhà's) Braz.	5·58 S	51·45 W
98	Caramanta, Cerro (Mtn.) (sĕ'r-rô-kä-rä-mà'n-tä) Col. (In.)	5·29 N	76·01 W
100	Caramarca (kä-rä-mȧ'r-kä) Arg.	28·29 S	65·45 W
155	Caramoan (kä-rä-mō'än) Phil. (Manila In.)	13·46 N	123·52 E
101	Carandaí (kä-rän-dàē') Braz. (Rio de Janeiro In.)	20·57 S	43·47 W
101	Carangola (kä-ràn'gô'lȧ) Braz. (Rio de Janeiro In.)	20·46 S	42·02 W
127	Caransebes (kȧ-rán-sä'bĕsh) Rom.	45·24 N	22·13 E
100	Carapeguá (kä-rä-pȧ-gwä') Arg.	26·01 S	58·13 W
82	Caraquet (kă-rȧ-kĕt') Can.	47·47 N	64·56 W
93	Carata, Laguna (L.) (lä-go͞o'nä-kä-rä'tä) Nic.	13·59 N	83·41 W
93	Caratasca, Laguna (L.) (lä-go͞o'nä-kä-rä-täs'kä) Hond.	15·20 N	83·45 W
124	Caravaca (kä-rä-vä'kä) Sp.	38·05 N	1·51 W
99	Caravelas (kȧ-rä-vĕl'äzh) Braz.	17·46 S	39·06 W
99	Carayaca (kȧ-rä-ïȧ'kä) Ven. (In.)	10·32 N	67·07 W
100	Caràzinho (kä-rȧ'zē-nyŏ) Braz.	28·22 S	52·33 W
124	Carballino (kär-bäl-yē'nō) Sp.	42·26 N	8·04 W
124	Carballo (kär-bäl'yō) Sp.	43·13 N	8·40 W
65	Carbon (R.) (kär'bŏn) Wash. (Seattle In.)	47·06 N	122·08 W
65	Carbonado (kȧr-bō-nä'dō) Wash. (Seattle In.)	47·05 N	122·03 W
126	Carbonara, C. (kär-bō-nä'rä) It.	39·08 N	9·33 E
85	Carbondale (kär'bŏn-dāl) Can. (Edmonton In.)	53·45 N	113·32 W
73	Carbondale Ill.	37·42 N	89·12 W
81	Carbondale Pa.	41·35 N	75·30 W
83	Carbonear (kär-bô-nēr') Can.	47·43 N	53·16 W
78	Carbon Hill (kär'bŏn hĭl) Ala.	33·53 N	87·34 W
78	Carbur (kär'bûr) Fla.	29·55 N	83·25 W
125	Carcagente (kär-kä-hĕn'tä) Sp.	39·09 N	0·29 W
122	Carcans, Étang de (L.) (ā-taN-dĕ-kär-kän) Fr.	45·12 N	1·00 W
122	Carcassonne (kȧr-kȧ-sôn') Fr.	43·12 N	2·23 E
86	Carcross (kär'krôs) Can.	60·18 N	134·54 W
145	Cardamon Hills (kär'dȧ-mŭm) Ceylon (In.)	9·45 N	77·28 E
94	Cárdenas (kär'dȧ-näs) Cuba	23·00 N	81·10 W
91	Cárdenas (kȧ'r-dĕ-näs) Mex.	17·59 N	93·23 W
90	Cárdenas Mex.	22·01 N	99·38 W
95	Cardenas, Bahía de (B.) (bä-ē'ä-dĕ-kär'dȧ-näs) Cuba	23·10 N	81·10 W
85	Cardiff (kär'dĭf) Can. (Edmonton In.)	53·46 N	113·36 W
116	Cardiff Wales	51·30 N	3·18 W
116	Cardigan (kär'dĭ-găn) Wales	52·05 N	4·40 W
116	Cardigan B Wales	52·35 N	4·40 W
86	Cardston (kärds'tŭn) Can.	49·14 N	113·23 W
121	Carei (kä-rĕ') Rom.	47·42 N	22·28 E
122	Carentan (kä-rôN-täN') Fr.	49·19 N	1·14 W
80	Carey (kā'rê) Ohio	40·55 N	83·25 W
158	Carey (I.) (kâr'ē) Austl.	29·20 S	123·35 E
122	Carhaix (kär-ĕ') Fr.	48·17 N	3·37 W
89	Caribbean Sea (kăr-ĭ-bē'ăn) N. A.-S. A.	14·30 N	75·30 W
86	Cariboo Mts. (kă'rĭ-bo͞o) Can.	53·51 N	122·13 W
82	Caribou Maine	46·51 N	68·01 W
71	Caribou (I.) Can.	47·22 N	85·42 W
74	Caribou L. Minn. (Duluth In.)	46·54 N	92·16 W
86	Caribou Mts Can.	59·20 N	115·30 W
99	Carinhanha (kä-rĭ-nyän'yä) Braz.	14·14 S	43·44 W
126	Carini (kä-rē'nē) It.	38·09 N	13·10 E
	Carinthia, See Kärnten		
81	Carleton Place (kärl'tŭn) Can.	45·15 N	76·10 W
73	Carlinville (kär'lĭn-vĭl) Ill.	39·16 N	89·52 W
116	Carlisle (kär-līl') Eng.	54·54 N	3·03 W
80	Carlisle Ky.	38·20 N	84·00 W
84	Carlisle La. (New Orleans In.)	29·41 N	89·57 W
81	Carlisle Pa.	40·10 N	77·15 W
122	Carlitte, Pic (Pk.) (pĕk'-kär-lēt') Fr.	42·33 N	1·56 E
126	Carloforte (kär'lō-fôr-tȧ) It.	39·11 N	8·18 E
101	Carlos Casares (kär-lôs-kä-sȧ'rĕs) Arg. (Buenos Aires In.)	35·38 S	61·17 W
116	Carlow (kär'lō) Ire.	52·50 N	7·00 W
76	Carlsbad (kärlz'băd) N. Mex.	32·24 N	104·12 W
76	Carlsbad Caverns Natl. Park N. Mex.	32·08 N	104·30 W
110	Carlton (kärl'tŭn) Eng.	52·58 N	1·05 W
74	Carlton Minn. (Duluth In.)	46·40 N	92·26 W
80	Carlton Center (kärl'tŭn sĕn'tēr) Mich.	42·45 N	85·20 W
168	Carltonville S. Afr. (Johannesburg & Pretoria In.)	26·20 S	27·23 E
73	Carlyle (kär-līl') Ill.	38·37 N	89·23 W
126	Carmagnolo (kär-mä-nyô'lä) It.	44·52 N	7·48 E
86	Carman (kär'mȧn) Can.	49·30 N	98·02 W
116	Carmarthen (kär-mär'thĕn) Wales	51·50 N	4·20 W
116	Carmarthen B. (kär-mär'thĕn) Wales	51·33 N	4·50 W
122	Carmaux (kȧr-mō') Fr.	44·05 N	2·09 E
84	Carmel (kär'mĕl) N. Y. (New York In.)	41·25 N	73·42 W
101	Carmelo (kär-mĕ'lo) Ur. (Buenos Aires In.)	33·59 S	58·15 W
90	Carmen, Isla del (I.) (ē's-lä-dĕl-kȧ'r-mĕn) Mex.	18·43 N	91·40 W
91	Carmen, Laguna del (L.) (lä-go͞o'nä-dĕl-kȧ'r-mĕn) Mex.	18·15 N	93·26 W
101	Carmen de Areco (kär'mĕn' dā ä-rä'kō) Arg. (Buenos Aires In.)	34·21 S	59·50 W
100	Carmen de Patagones (kȧ'r-mĕn-dĕ-pä-tä-gô'-nĕs) Arg.	40·47 S	62·56 W
80	Carmi (kär'mī) Ill.	38·05 N	88·10 W
101	Carmo (kȧ'r-mô) Braz. (Rio de Janeiro In.)	21·57 S	42·06 W
101	Carmo do Rio Clara (kȧ'r-mô-dô-rē'ô-klȧ'-rä) Braz. (Rio de Janeiro In.)	20·57 S	46·04 W
124	Carmona (kär-mô'nä) Sp.	37·28 N	5·38 W
158	Carnarvon (kär-när'vŭn) Austl.	24·45 S	113·45 E
166	Carnarvon S. Afr.	31·00 S	22·15 E
116	Carnarvon Wales	53·08 N	4·17 W
116	Carnarvon Bay Wales	53·09 N	4·56 W
65	Carnation (kär-nā'shŭn) Wash. (Seattle In.)	47·39 N	121·55 W
125	Carnaxide (kär-nä-shē'dĕ) Port. (Lisbon In.)	38·44 N	9·15 W
116	Carndonagh (kärn-dō-nä') Ire.	54·75 N	6·75 W
72	Carnegie (kär-nĕg'ĭ) Okla.	35·06 N	98·38 W
75	Carnegie Pa. (Pittsburgh In.)	40·24 N	80·06 W
81	Carneys Point (kär'nês) N. J.	39·45 N	75·25 W
120	Carnic Alps (Mts.) Aus.-It.	46·43 N	12·38 E
125	Carnot (kär nō') Alg.	36·15 N	1·40 E
165	Carnot Cen. Afr. Rep.	4·56 N	16·00 E
116	Carnsore Pt. (kärn'sôr) Ire.	52·10 N	6·16 W
80	Caro (kȧ'rō) Mich.	43·30 N	83·25 W
99	Carolina (kä-rô-lē'nä) Braz.	7·26 S	47·16 W
166	Carolina (kăr-ô-lī'nȧ) S. Afr.	26·07 S	30·09 E
92	Carolina L. (kä-rô-lē'-nä) Mex. (Yucatan In.)	18·41 N	89·40 W
156	Caroline Is. (kăr'ô-līn) Pac. Is. Trust Ter.	9·30 N	143·00 E
98	Caroni (R.) (kä-rō'nē) Ven.	5·49 N	62·57 W
98	Carora (kä-rō'rä) Ven.	10·09 N	70·12 W
115	Carpathians Mts. (kär-pā'thĭ-ăn) Eur.	49·23 N	20·14 E
127	Carpatii Meridionali (Transylvanian Alps) (Mts.) Rom.	45·30 N	23·30 E
158	Capentaria, G. of (kär-pĕn-târ'ĭȧ) Austl.	14·45 S	138·50 E
74	Carpenter (kär'pĕn-tēr) Ill. (St. Louis In.)	38·54 N	89·54 W
122	Carpentras (kär-päN-träs') Fr.	44·04 N	5·01 E
126	Carpi It.	44·48 N	10·54 E
78	Carrabelle (kăr-ȧ-bĕl) Fla.	29·50 N	84·40 W
116	Carrantuohill (kă-răn-to͞o'ĭl) Ire.	52·01 N	9·48 W
126	Carrara (kä-rä'rä) It.	44·05 N	10·05 E
98	Carretas, Punta (Pt.) (po͞o'n-tä-kär-rĕ'tĕ'rȧs) Peru	13·50 S	76·24 W
93	Carriacou I. (kăr-ē-ȧ-ko͞o') N. A. (Le. & Wind. Is. In.)	12·28 N	61·20 W
116	Carrick (kăr'ĭk) Ire.	52·20 N	7·35 W
85	Carrier (kăr'ĭ-ēr) Can. (Quebec In.)	46·43 N	71·05 W
78	Carriere (kȧ-rēr') Miss.	30·37 N	89·37 W
80	Carriers Mills (kăr'ĭ-ērs) Ill.	37·40 N	88·40 W
70	Carrington (kăr'ĭng-tŭn) N. D.	47·26 N	99·06 W
65	Carr Inlet (kăr ĭn'lĕt) Wash. (Seattle In.)	47·20 N	122·42 W
124	Carrion (kär-rē-ōn') Sp.	42·36 N	6·42 W
94	Carrion Crow Hbr. (kăr'ĭŭn krō) Ba. Is.	26·35 N	77·55 W
124	Carrión de los Condes (kär-rē-ōn' dā lōs kōn'dȧs) Sp.	42·20 N	4·35 W
72	Carrizo Cr. (kär-rē'zō) N. Mex.	36·22 N	103·39 W
76	Carrizo Springs Tex.	28·32 N	99·51 W
69	Carrizozo (kär-rē-zō'zō) N. Mex.	33·40 N	105·55 W
71	Carroll (kăr'ŭl) Iowa	42·03 N	94·51 W
78	Carrollton (kăr-ŭl-tŭn) Ga.	33·35 N	84·05 W
73	Carrollton Ill.	39·18 N	90·22 W
80	Carrollton Ky.	38·45 N	85·15 W
80	Carrollton Mich.	43·30 N	83·55 W
73	Carrollton Mo.	39·21 N	93·29 W
80	Carrollton Ohio	40·35 N	81·10 W
74	Carrollton Tex. (Dallas, Fort Worth In.)	32·58 N	96·53 W
75	Carrollville (kăr'ŭl vĭl) Wis. (Milwaukee In.)	42·53 N	87·52 W
65	Carrols (kăr'ŭlz) Wash. (Portland In.)	46·05 N	122·51 W
116	Carron (L.) (kȧ'rŭn) Scot.	57·25 N	5·25 W
122	Carry-le-Rouet (kä-rē'lĕ-ro͞o-ā') Fr. (Marseille In.)	43·20 N	5·10 E
133	Çarşamba (chär-shäm'bä) Tur.	41·05 N	36·40 E
68	Carson (R.) (kär'sŭn) Nev.	39·15 N	119·25 W
68	Carson City Nev.	39·10 N	119·45 W
68	Carson Sink Nev.	39·51 N	118·25 W
155	Carstensz-Toppen (Pk.) (kärs'tĕns) W. Irian	4·00 S	137·10 E
98	Cartagena (kär-tä-hā'nä) Col.	10·30 N	75·40 W
125	Cartagena (kär-tä-Kĕ'nä) Sp.	37·46 N	1·00 W
98	Cartago (kär-tä'gō) Col. (In.)	4·44 N	75·54 W
93	Cartago C. R.	9·52 N	83·56 W
124	Cartaxo (kär-tä'shō) Port.	39·10 N	8·48 W
84	Carteret (kär'tē-rĕt) N. J. (New York In.)	40·35 N	74·13 W
78	Cartersville (kär'tērs-vĭl) Ga.	34·09 N	84·47 W
73	Carthage (kär'thȧj) Ill.	40·27 N	91·09 W
73	Carthage Mo.	37·10 N	94·18 W
81	Carthage N. Y.	44·00 N	75·45 W
79	Carthage N. C.	35·22 N	79·25 W
77	Carthage Tex.	32·09 N	94·20 W
164	Carthage Tun.	37·04 N	10·18 E
167	Carthcart (cärth-că't) S. Afr. (Natal In.)	32·18 S	27·11 E
87	Cartwright (kärt'rīt) Can.	53·36 N	57·00 W
99	Caruaru (kä-ro͞o-ȧ-ro͞o') Braz.	8·19 S	35·52 W
98	Carúpano (kä-ro͞o'pä-nō) Ven.	10·45 N	63·21 W
73	Caruthersville (kȧ-rŭdh'ērz-vĭl) Mo	36·09 N	89·41 W
65	Carver (kärv'ēr) Ore. (Portland In.)	45·24 N	122·30 W
124	Carvoeira, Cabo (C.) (kȧ'bô-kär-vô-ĕ'y-rȧ) Port.	39·22 N	9·24 W
75	Cary (kă'rê) Ill. (Chicago In.)	42·13 N	88·14 W
101	Casablanca (kä-sä-bläŋ'kä) Chile (Santiago In.)	33·19 S	71·24 W
164	Casablanca Mor.	33·32 N	7·41 W
101	Casa Branca (kȧ'sȧ-brȧ'N-kȧ) Braz. (Rio de Janeiro In.)	21·47 S	47·04 W
69	Casa Grande (kä'sä grän'dā) Ariz.	32·50 N	111·45 W
69	Casa Grande Natl. Mon. Ariz.	33·00 N	111·33 W
126	Casale (kä-sä'lä) It.	45·08 N	8·26 E
126	Casalmaggiore (kȧ-säl-mȧd-jō'rä) It.	45·00 N	10·24 E
164	Casamance R. (kȧ-sȧ-mäNs') Senegal	12·58 N	15·15 W
85	Cascade (kăs-kād') Can. (Ottawa In.)	45·35 N	75·51 W
159	Cascade Pt. N. Z. (In.)	43·59 S	168·23 E
62	Cascade Ra U. S.	42·50 N	122·20 W
85	Cascades Point (kăs-kādz') Can. (Montreal In.)	45·19 N	73·58 W
66	Cascade Tun. Wash.	47·41 N	120·53 W
125	Cascais (käs-kȧ-ēzh) Port. (Lisbon In.)	38·42 N	9·25 W
125	Cascais, Ba. de (B.) (bä-ē'ä-dĕ-käs-kī's) Port. (Lisbon In.)	38·41 N	9·24 W
65	Case Inlet (kās) Wash. (Seattle In.)	47·22 N	122·47 W
100	Caseros (kä-sā'rôs) Arg. (In.)	34·21 S	58·34 W
126	Caserta (kä-zĕr'tä) It.	41·04 N	14·21 E
80	Casey (kā'sĭ) Ill.	39·20 N	88·00 W
66	Cashmere (kăsh'mĭr) Wash.	47·30 N	120·28 W
155	Casiguran (käs-sē-go͞o'rän) Phil. (Manila In.)	16·15 N	122·10 E
155	Casiguran Sd. Phil. (Manila In.)	16·02 N	121·51 E
101	Casilda (kä-sē'l-dä) Arg. (Buenos Aires In.)	33·02 S	61·11 W
94	Casilda Cuba	21·50 N	80·00 W
101	Casimiro de Abreu (kä'sē-mē'ro-(dĕ-ȧ-brĕ'o͞o) Braz. (Rio de Janeiro In.)	22·30 S	42·11 W
160	Casino (kȧ-sē'nō) Austl.	28·35 S	153·10 E
98	Casiquiare (R.) (kä-sē-kyä'rä) Ven.	2·11 N	66·15 W
125	Caspe (käs'pȧ) Sp.	41·18 N	0·02 W
67	Casper (kăs'pēr) Wyo.	42·51 N	106·18 W
132	Caspian Dep. (kăs'pĭ-ȧn) Sov. Un.	47·40 N	51·40 E
130	Caspian Sea Sov. Un.	39·30 N	52·00 E
81	Cass (kăs) W. Va.	38·25 N	79·55 W
71	Cass (L.) Minn.	47·23 N	94·28 W
125	Cassá de la Selva (käs-sä'dĕ-lä-sĕl-vä) Sp.	41·52 N	2·52 E
166	Cassai (R.) (kä-sä'ē) Ang.	11·15 S	21·00 E
80	Cass City (kăs) Mich.	43·35 N	83·10 W
85	Casselman (kăs''l-màn) Can. (Ottawa In.)	45·18 N	75·05 W
70	Casselton (kăs''l-tŭn) N. D.	46·53 N	97·14 W
101	Cássia (kȧ'syȧ) Braz. (Rio de Janeiro In.)	20·36 S	46·53 W
74	Cassin (kăs'ĭn) Tex. (San Antonio In.)	29·16 N	98·29 W
166	Cassinga (kä-sĭŋ'gä) Ang.	15·05 S	16·15 E
126	Cassino (käs-sē'nō) It.	41·30 N	13·50 E
71	Cass Lake (kăs) Minn.	47·23 N	94·37 W
80	Cassopolis (kăs-ŏ'pō-lĭs) Mich.	41·55 N	86·00 W
73	Cassville (kăs'vĭl) Mo.	36·41 N	93·52 W
124	Castanheira de Pêra (käs-tän-yā'rä-dĕ-pĕ'rä) Port.	40·00 N	8·07 W
122	Casteljaloux (käs-tĕl-zhä-lo͞o') Fr.	44·20 N	0·04 E
125	Castellammare di Stabia (käs-tĕl-läm-mä'rä-dē-stä'byä) It. (Naples In.)	40·26 N	14·29 E

ăt; finăl; rāte; senâte; ärm; åsk; sofȧ; fâre; ch-choose; dh-as th in other; bē; ēvent; bĕt; recĕnt; cratēr; g-go; gh-guttural g; bĭt; ĭ-short neutral; rīde; K-guttural k as ch in German ich;

Page	Name Pronunciation Region	Lat. °′	Long. °′
101	Castelli (kȧs-tĕ'zhē) Arg. (Buenos Aires In.)	36·07 S	57·48 W
125	Castellón de la Plana (käs-tĕl-yō'n-dĕ-lä-plä'nä) . Sp.	39·59 N	0·05 W
122	Castelnaudary (kȧs'tĕl-nō-dȧ-rē') Fr.	43·20 N	1·57 E
101	Castelo (käs-tĕ'lô) Braz. (Rio de Janeiro In.)	21·37 S	41·13 W
124	Castelo Branco (käs-tā'lo͞o brăŋ'ko͞o) . Port.	39·48 N	7·37 W
124	Castelo de Vide (käs-tā'lo͞o dĭ vē'dĭ) . Port.	39·25 N	7·25 W
122	Castelsarrasin (kȧs'tĕl-sȧ-rȧ-zăN') . Fr.	44·03 N	1·05 E
126	Castelvetrano (käs'tĕl-vē-trä'nō) It.	37·43 N	12·50 E
98	Castilla (kȧs-tē'l-yä) Peru	5·18 S	80·40 W
124	Castilla La Nueva (Reg.) (käs-tē'lyä lä nwā'vȧ) . Sp.	39·15 N	3·55 W
124	Castilla La Vieja (Reg.) (käs-tēl'yä lä vyā'hä) . Sp.	40·48 N	4·24 W
79	Castillo De San Marcos Natl. Mon. (käs-tē'lyā de-sän mär-kōs) Fla.	29·55 N	81·25 W
95	Castle (I.) (kȧs''l) Ba. Is.	22·05 N	74·20 W
116	Castlebar (kȧs''l-bär) Ire.	53·55 N	9·15 W
69	Castle Dale (kȧs''l dāl) Utah	39·15 N	111·00 W
110	Castle Donington (dŏn'ĭng-tŭn) Eng.	52·50 N	1·21 W
110	Castleford (kȧs'l-fẽrd) Eng.	53·43 N	1·21 W
160	Castlemaine (käs''l-mān) Austl.	37·05 S	144·14 E
69	Castle Pk. Colo.	39·00 N	106·50 W
66	Castlerock (kȧs''l-rŏk) Wash.	46·17 N	122·53 W
71	Castle Rock Res. Wis.	44·03 N	89·48 W
75	Castle Shannon (shăn'ŭn) Pa. (Pittsburgh In.)	40·22 N	80·02 W
75	Castleton (kȧs''l-tŏn) Ind. (Indianapolis In.)	39·54 N	86·03 W
85	Castor R. (kăs'tôr) Can (Ottawa In.)	45·16 N	75·14 W
73	Castor (R.) Mo.	36·59 N	89·53 W
122	Castres (kȧs'tr') Fr.	43·36 N	2·13 E
93	Castries (kȧs-trē') St. Lucia (Le. & Wind. Is. In.)	14·01 N	61·00 W
100	Castro (käs'tro͞o) Braz.	24·56 S	50·00 W
100	Castro (käs'tro) Chile	42·27 S	73·48 W
124	Castro Daire (käs'tro͞o dīr'ĭ) . Port.	40·56 N	7·57 W
124	Castro de Río (käs-trô-dĕ-rē'ō) Sp.	37·42 N	4·28 W
123	Castrop Rauxel (käs'trōp rou'ksĕl) . Ger. (Ruhr In.)	51·33 N	7·19 E
124	Castro Urdiales (käs'trō o͝or-dyä'läs) . Sp.	43·23 N	3·11 W
65	Castro Valley Calif. (San Francisco In.)	37·42 N	122·05 W
124	Castro Verde (käs-trō vĕr'dĕ) . Port.	37·43 N	8·05 W
126	Castrovillari (käs'trō-vēl-lyä'rē) . It.	39·48 N	16·11 E
124	Castuera (käs-to͞o-ā'rä) Sp.	38·43 N	5·33 W
95	Cat (I.) Ba. Is.	25·30 N	75·30 W
92	Catacamas (kä-tä-kȧ'mäs) . Hond.	14·52 N	85·55 W
155	Catanduanes (I.) (kä-tä-dwä'nĕs) Phil.	13·55 N	125·00 E
101	Cataguases (kä-tä-gwä'sĕs) Braz. (Rio de Janeiro In.)	21·23 S	42·42 W
77	Catahoula L. (kăt-ȧ-ho͞o'lȧ) . . La.	31·35 N	92·20 W
99	Catalão (kä-tä-louN') Braz.	18·09 S	47·42 W
95	Catalina (I.) (kä-tä-lē'nä) Dom. Rep.	18·20 N	69·00 W
125	Cataluma (Reg.) (kä-tä-lo͞o'mä) Sp.	41·23 N	0·50 E
100	Catamarca (Prov.) (kä-tä-mär'kä) Arg.	27·15 S	67·15 W
99	Catanduva (kä-tȧn-do͞o'vä) . . Braz.	21·12 S	48·47 W
126	Catania (kä-tä'nyä) It.	37·30 N	15·09 E
126	Catania, Golfo di (G.) (gôl-fô-dē-kȧ-tä'nyä) . It.	37·24 N	15·28 E
155	Catanuan (kä-tä-nä'wän) Phil.	13·36 N	122·20 E
126	Catanzaro (kä-tän-dzä'rō) It.	38·53 N	16·34 E
125	Catarroja (kä-tär-rō'hä) Sp.	39·24 N	0·25 W
79	Catawba (L.) S. C.	35·02 N	81·21 W
79	Catawba (R.) (kȧ-tô'bȧ) N. C.	35·25 N	80·55 W
91	Catazajá, Laguna de (L.) (lä-go͞o'nä-dĕ-kä-tä-zä-hä') . Mex.	17·45 N	92·03 W
155	Catbalogan (kät-bä-lō'gän) Phil.	11·45 N	124·52 E
91	Catemaco (kä-tä-mä'kō) Mex.	18·26 N	95·06 W
91	Catemaco, Lago (L.) (lä'gô-kä-tä-mä'kō) . Mex.	18·23 N	95·04 W
110	Caterham (kā'tẽr-ŭm) Eng. (London In.)	51·16 N	0·04 W
166	Catete (kä-tĕ'tĕ) Ang.	9·05 S	13·38 E
76	Cathedral Mt. (kȧ-thē'drȧl) . . Tex.	30·09 N	103·46 W
167	Cathedral Pk. (kȧ-thē'drȧl) S. Afr. (Natal In.)	28·53 S	29·04 E
73	Catherine, L. (kă-thẽr-ĭn) Ark.	34·26 N	92·47 W
167	Cathkin Pk. (kăth'kĭn) S. Afr. (Natal In.)	29·08 S	29·22 E
65	Cathlamet (kăth-lăm'ĕt) Wash. (Portland In.)	46·12 N	123·53 W
80	Catlettsburg (kăt'lĕts-bûrg) . . Ky.	38·20 N	82·35 W
88	Catoche, C. (kä-tô'chĕ) Mex.	21·30 N	87·15 W
84	Catonsville (kā'tŭnz-vĭl) Md. (Baltimore In.)	39·16 N	76·45 W
90	Catorce (kä-tôr'sä) Mex.	23·41 N	100·51 W
81	Catskill (kăts'kĭl) N. Y.	42·15 N	73·50 W
81	Catskill Mts. N. Y.	42·20 N	74·35 W
81	Cattaraugus Ind. Res. (kăt'tȧ-rȧ-gŭs) . N. Y.	42·30 N	79·05 W
99	Catu (kȧ-to͞o) Braz.	12·26 S	38·12 W
166	Catumbela (kä'tŏm-bĕl'ȧ) . . . Ang.	12·30 S	13·35 E
155	Cauayan (kou-ä'yän) Phil. (Manila In.)	16·56 N	121·46 E
98	Cauca (R.) (kou'kä) Col.	7·30 N	75·26 W
99	Caucagua (kä'o͞o-kä'gwä) Ven. (In.)	10·17 N	66·22 W
133	Caucasus Mts. (kô'kȧ-sŭs) . Sov. Un.	43·20 N	42·00 E
122	Cauderan (kō-dā-räN') Fr.	44·50 N	0·40 W
85	Caughnawaga . Can. (Montreal In.)	45·24 N	73·41 W
126	Caulonia (kou-lō'nyä) It.	38·24 N	16·22 E
100	Cauquenes (kou-kā'nās) Chile	35·54 S	72·14 W
98	Caura (R.) (kou'rä) Ven.	6·48 N	64·40 W
82	Causapscal Can.	48·19 N	67·18 W
95	Cauto (R.) (kou'tō) Cuba	18·35 N	76·20 W
142	Cauvery (R.) India	11·15 N	78·06 E
100	Cava (kȧ'vä) Braz. (In.)	22·41 S	43·26 W
125	Cava de' Tirreni (kä'vä-dĕ-tēr-rĕ'nē) . It. (Naples In.)	40·27 N	14·43 E
124	Cavado (R.) (kä-vä'dō) Port.	41·43 N	8·08 W
99	Cavalcante (kä-väl-kän'tā) . . Braz.	13·45 S	47·33 W
70	Cavalier (kăv-ȧ-lēr') N. D.	48·45 N	97·39 W
164	Cavally (R.) . . . Lib.-Ivory Coast	6·06 N	8·09 W
116	Cavan (kăv'ȧn) Ire.	54·01 N	7·00 W
126	Cavarzere (kä-vär'dzā-rā) It.	45·08 N	12·06 E
81	Cavendish (kăv'ĕn-dĭsh) Vt.	43·25 N	72·35 W
99	Caviana, Ilha (I.) (kä-vyä'nä) Braz.	0·45 N	49·33 W
155	Cavite (kä-vē'tä) Phil. (Manila In.)	14·30 N	120·54 E
110	Cawood (kā'wo͝od) Eng.	53·49 N	1·07 W
101	Caxambu (kä-shä'm-bo͞o) Braz. (Rio de Janeiro In.)	21·58 S	44·55 W
99	Caxias (kä'shē-äzh) Braz.	4·48 S	43·16 W
100	Caxias do Sul (kä'shē-äzh-dô-so͞o'l) . Braz.	29·13 S	51·03 W
125	Caxine, Cap (C.) (kăp kăk'sēn) Alg.	36·47 N	2·52 E
166	Caxito (kä-shē'to͞o) Ang.	8·20 S	13·35 E
98	Cayambe (kȧ-īä'm-bĕ) Ec.	0·03 N	79·09 W
99	Cayenne (kā-ĕn') Fr. Gu.	4·56 N	52·18 W
90	Cayetano Rubio (kä-yĕ-tä-nô-ro͞o'byô) . Mex.	20·37 N	100·21 W
89	Cayey . . . P. R. (Puerto Rico In.)	18·05 N	66·12 W
94	Cayman Brac (I.) (kī-män' brȧk) Cayman Is.	19·45 N	79·50 W
92	Cayo (kī'yō) Br. Hond. (Yucatan In.)	17·11 N	89·04 W
94	Cay Sal Bk. (kē-săl) Ba. Is.	23·55 N	80·20 W
81	Cayuga (L.) (kā-yo͞o'gȧ) N. Y.	42·35 N	76·35 W
124	Cazalla de la Sierra (kä-thäl'yä-dĕ-lä-sē-ĕ'r-rä) . Sp.	37·55 N	5·48 W
122	Cazaux, Étang de (L.) (ā-tăN' dĕ kä-zō') . Fr.	44·32 N	0·59 W
81	Cazneovia (kăz-ê-nō'vĭ-ȧ) . . N. Y.	42·55 N	75·50 W
75	Cazenovia Cr. . N. Y. (Buffalo In.)	42·49 N	78·45 W
126	Čazma (chäz'mä) Yugo.	45·44 N	16·39 E
166	Cazombo (kä-zô'm-bō) Ang.	12·25 S	22·40 E
91	Cazones (R.) (kä-zô'nĕs) . . . Mex.	20·37 N	97·28 W
94	Cazones, Ensenada de (B.) (ĕn-sĕ-nä-dä-dĕ-kä-zō'nȧs) . Cuba	22·05 N	81·30 W
94	Cazones, Golfo de (G.) (gôl-fô-dĕ-kä-zō'nȧs) . Cuba	23·55 N	81·15 W
124	Cazorla (kä-thôr'lä) Sp.	37·55 N	2·58 W
124	Cea (R.) (thā'ä) Sp.	42·18 N	5·10 W
	Ceará, see Fortaleza		
99	Ceará (State) (sā-ä-rä') Braz.	5·13 S	39·43 W
99	Ceará-Mirim (sā-ä-rä'mē-rē'N) Braz.	6·00 S	35·13 W
93	Cebaco, Isla (I.) (ē's-lä--sä-bä'kō) Pan.	7·27 N	81·08 W
69	Cebolla Cr. (sē-bōl'yä) Colo.	38·15 N	107·10 W
124	Cebollera, Sierra (Mts.) (sē-ĕ'r-rä-sĕ-bôl-yĕ-rä) . Sp.	42·03 N	2·53 W
124	Cebreros (sĕ-brĕ'rôs) Sp.	40·28 N	4·28 W
155	Cebu (sā-bo͞o') Phil.	10·22 N	123·49 E
75	Cecil (sē'sĭl) . . Pa. (Pittsburgh In.)	40·20 N	80·10 W
86	Cedar (L.) Can.	53·18 N	101·08 W
71	Cedar (R.) Iowa	42·23 N	92·07 W
65	Cedar (R.) . . Wash. (Portland In.)	45·56 N	122·32 W
71	Cedar (R.) West Fk. Iowa	42·49 N	93·10 W
77	Cedar Bay Tex. (In.)	29·54 N	94·58 W
77	Cedar Bayou Tex. (In.)	29·46 N	94·56 W
69	Cedar Breaks Natl. Mon. Utah	37·35 N	112·55 W
71	Cedarburg (sē'dẽr bûrg) Wis.	43·23 N	88·00 W
69	Cedar City Utah	37·40 N	113·10 W
70	Cedar Cr. N. D.	46·05 N	102·10 W
71	Cedar Falls Iowa	42·31 N	92·29 W
78	Cedar Keys Fla.	29·06 N	83·03 W
75	Cedar Lake . . . Ind. (Chicago In.)	41·22 N	87·27 W
75	Cedar L. . . . Ind. (Chicago In.)	41·23 N	87·25 W
71	Cedar Rapids Iowa	42·00 N	91·43 W
80	Cedar Springs Mich.	43·15 N	85·40 W
78	Cedartown (sē'dẽr-toun) Ga.	34·00 N	85·15 W
167	Cedarville (cê-dȧr'vĭl) S. Afr. (Natal In.)	30·23 S	29·04 E
90	Cedral (sā-dräl') Mex.	23·47 N	100·42 W
92	Cedros (sā'drōs) Hond.	14·36 N	87·07 W
88	Cedros (I.) Mex.	28·10 N	115·10 W
158	Ceduna (sē-do͞o'nȧ) Austl.	32·15 S	133·55 E
126	Cefalù (chā-fä-lo͞o') It.	38·01 N	14·01 E
124	Cega (R.) (thā'gä) Sp.	41·25 N	4·27 W
121	Cegléd (tsā'glād) Hung.	47·10 N	19·49 E
127	Ceglie (chĕ'lyĕ) It.	40·39 N	17·32 E
124	Cehegín (thā-ä-hēn') Sp.	38·05 N	1·48 W
95	Ceiba del Agua (sā'-bä-dĕl-ȧ'gwä) Cuba (Havana In.)	22·08 N	82·38 W
166	Cela (sĕ-lȧ) Ang.	11·10 S	15·07 E
90	Celaya (sā-lä'yä) Mex.	20·33 N	100·49 W
154	Celebes (Is.) (sĕl'ê-bēz) (sĕl-ā'bĕs) . Indon.	2·15 S	120·30 E
154	Celebes Sea Indon.	3·45 N	121·52 E
92	Celestún (sĕ-lĕs-to͞o'n) Mex. (Yucatan In.)	20·57 N	90·18 W
80	Celina (sê-lī'nȧ) Ohio	40·30 N	84·35 W
126	Celje (tsĕl'yĕ) Yugo.	46·13 N	15·17 E
120	Celle (tsĕl'ē) Ger.	52·37 N	10·05 E
72	Cement (sê-mĕnt') Okla.	34·56 N	98·07 W
99	Ceniza, Pico (Mtn.) (pē'-kô-sĕ-nē'zä) . Ven. (In.)	10·24 N	67·26 W
122	Cenon (sĕ-nôN') Fr.	44·51 N	0·33 W
77	Center (sĕn'tẽr) Tex.	31·50 N	94·10 W
78	Centerhill Res. (sĕn'tẽr-hĭl) . Tenn.	36·02 N	86·00 W
75	Center Line (sĕn'tẽr līn) Mich. (Detroit In.)	42·29 N	83·01 W
71	Centerville (sĕn'tẽr-vĭl) Iowa	40·44 N	92·48 W
74	Centerville . Minn. (Minneapolis, St. Paul In.)	45·10 N	93·03 W
75	Centerville . . . Pa. (Pittsburgh In.)	40·02 N	79·58 W
70	Centerville S. D.	43·70 N	96·56 W
74	Centerville Utah (Salt Lake City In.)	40·55 N	111·53 W
98	Central, Cordillera (Mts.) (kôr-dēl-yĕ'-rä-sĕn-trȧ'l) . Bol.	19·18 S	65·29 W
98	Central, Cordillera (Mts.) Col. (In.)	3·58 N	75·55 W
95	Central, Cordillera (Cibao Mts.) (kôr-dēl-yā'rȧ sĕn'träl) (sê-bä'ō) Dom. Rep.	19·05 N	71·30 W
163	Central African Republic Afr.	7·50 N	21·00 E
88	Central America (ȧ-mĕr'ĭ-kȧ) N. A.	10·45 N	87·15 W
78	Central City (sĕn'trȧl) Ky.	37·15 N	87·09 W
70	Central City (sĕn'trȧl sĭ'tĭ) . . Nebr.	41·07 N	98·00 W
84	Central Falls (sĕn'trȧl fôlz) R. I. (Providence In.)	41·54 N	71·23 W
80	Centralia (sĕn-trā'lĭ-ȧ) Ill.	38·35 N	89·05 W
73	Centralia Mo.	39·11 N	92·07 W
66	Centralia Wash.	46·42 N	122·58 W
133	Central Plat. Sov. Un.	55·00 N	33·30 E
84	Central Valley N. Y. (New York In.)	41·19 N	74·07 W
81	Centreville (sĕn'tẽr-vĭl) Md.	39·05 N	76·05 W
155	Centro (sĕ'n-trô) . Phil. (Manila In.)	17·16 N	121·48 E
78	Century (sĕn'tů-rĭ) Fla.	30·57 N	87·15 W
	Cephalonia, see Kefallinéa		
122	Céret (sā-rĕ') Fr.	42·29 N	2·47 E
98	Cereté (sĕ-rĕ-tĕ') Col.	8·56 N	75·58 W
126	Cerignola (chā-rê-nyô'lä) It.	41·16 N	15·55 E
126	Cerknica (tsĕr'knê-tsȧ) Yugo.	45·48 N	14·21 E
76	Cerralvo (sĕr-räl'vō) Mex.	26·05 N	99·37 W
88	Cerralvo (I.) Mex.	24·00 N	109·59 W
98	Cerrito (sĕr-rĕ'-tô) Col. (In.)	3·41 N	76·17 W
90	Cerritos (sĕr-rē'tôs) Mex.	22·26 N	100·16 W
98	Cerro Bolívar (sĕr'rō bô-lē'vär) Ven.	7.30 N	63.30 W
98	Cerro de Pasco (sĕr'rō dā päs'kō) Peru	10·45 S	76·14 W
76	Cerro Gordo, Arroyo de (är-rô-yŏ-dĕ-sĕ'r-rō-gôr-dō) Mex.	26·12 N	104·06 W
98	Certegui (sĕr-tĕ'gē) Col. (In.)	5·21 N	76·35 W
155	Cervantes (sĕr-vän'tās) Phil. (Manila In.)	16·59 N	120·42 E
124	Cervantes (thĕr-vän'tās) Sp.	42·43 N	7·04 W
124	Cervera del Río Alhama (thĕr-vä'rȧ dĕl rē'ō-äl-ä'mä) . Sp.	42·02 N	1·55 W
125	Cerveteri (chĕr-vĕ'tĕ-rē) It. (Rome In.)	42·00 N	12·06 E
126	Cesena (chĕ'sĕ-nä) It.	44·08 N	12·16 E
119	Cēsis (sā'sĭs) Sov. Un.	57·19 N	25·17 E
120	Česka Lipa (chĕs'kȧ lē'pa) . Czech.	50·41 N	14·31 E
120	Ceske (Bohemia) (Prov.) (chĕs'kä) (bô-hē'mĭ-ȧ) . Czech.	49·51 N	13·55 E
120	České Budějovice (chĕs'kä bo͞o'dyĕ-yô-vēt-sĕ) . Czech.	49·00 N	14·30 E
120	Ceskomoravaska Vysočina (Hts.) Czech.	49·21 N	15·40 E
127	Cesme (chĕsh'mĕ) Tur.	38·20 N	26·20 E
160	Cessnock Austl.	32·58 S	151·15 E
127	Cetinje (tsĕt'in-yĕ) Yugo.	42·23 N	18·55 E
	Cette, see Sète		
164	Ceuta (Sp.) (thā-o͞o'tä) Afr.	36·04 N	5·36 W
122	Cévennes (sā-vĕn') Fr.	44·20 N	3·48 E
115	Ceyhan (R.) Tur.	37·19 N	36·06 E
138	Ceylon (sê-lŏn') Asia	8·45 N	82·30 E
144	Chāb Bahār Iran	25·18 N	60·45 E
65	Chabot (L.) (sha'bŏt) Calif. (San Francisco In.)	37·44 N	122·06 W
101	Chacabuco (chä-kä-bo͞o'kō) Arg. ((Buenos Aires In.)	34·37 S	60·27 W
91	Chacaltianguis (chä-käl-tê-äŋ'-gwēs) . Mex.	18·18 N	95·50 W
98	Chachapoyas (chä-chä-poi'yäs) Peru	6·16 S	77·48 W
69	Chaco Can. Natl. Mon. (chä'kô) N. Mex.	35·38 N	108·06 W
136	Chad (chăd) . Sov. Un. (Urals In.)	56·33 N	57·11 E
163	Chad Afr.	17·48 N	19·00 E
165	Chad, L. Chad.	14·00 N	14·28 E
79	Chadbourn (chăd'bŭrn) N. C.	34·19 N	78·55 W
70	Chadron (chăd'rŭn) Nebr.	42·50 N	103·10 W
124	Chafarinas (C.) Mor.	35·08 N	2·20 W
73	Chaffee (chăf'ê) Mo.	37·10 N	89·39 W
144	Chāgal Hills Afg.-Pak.	29·15 N	63·28 E
128	Chagodoshcha (R.) (chä-gō-dôsh-chä) . Sov. Un.	59·08 N	35·13 E
93	Chagres R. (chä'grĕs) Pan.	9·18 N	79·22 W
75	Chagrin R. (shȧ'grĭn) Ohio (Cleveland In.)	41·34 N	81·24 W
75	Chagrin Falls (shȧ'grĭn fôls) Ohio (Cleveland In.)	41·26 N	81·23 W
150	Ch'ahaerh (Reg.) (chä'här) . China	44·25 N	115·00 E
152	Chalantun (chä'län-to͞on') . . China	47·59 N	122·56 E
92	Chalatenango (chäl-ä-tĕ-näŋ'gō) Sal.	14·04 N	88·54 W
91	Chalcatongo (chäl-kä-tôŋ'gō) Mex.	17·04 N	97·41 W
90	Chalchihuites (chäl-chê-wē'tås) Mex.	23·28 N	103·57 W
92	Chalchuapa (chäl-chwä'pä) . . . Sal.	14·01 N	89·39 W
91	Chalco (chäl-kō) Mex. (Mexico City In.)	19·15 N	98·54 W
82	Chaleur, B. de (shȧ-lûr') Can.	48·07 N	64·50 W
110	Chalgrove (chăl'grôv) Eng. (London In.)	51·38 N	1·05 W
151	Chaling (chä'lĭng) China	27·00 N	118·30 E
84	Chalmette (shăl-mĕt') La. (New Orleans In.)	29·57 N	89·57 W
122	Châlons-sur-Marne (shȧ-lôN'-sür-märn) . Fr.	48·57 N	4·23 E

ng-sing; ŋ-baŋk; N-nasalized n; nŏd; cŏmmit; ōld; ôbey; ôrder; fo͞od; fo͝ot; ou-out; s-soft; sh-dish; th-thin; pūre; ûnite; ûrn; stŭd; circŭs; ü-as "y" in study; '-indeterminate vowel.

Page	Name Pronunciation	Region	Lat. °′	Long. °′
122	Châlon-sur-Saône	Fr.	46·47 N	4·54 E
100	Chaltel, Cerro (Mtn.) (sĕ′r-rô-chäl′tĕl)	Arg.-Chile	48·10 S	73·18 W
69	Chama (R.) (chä′mä)	N. Mex.	36·19 N	106·31 W
92	Chama, Sierra de (Mts.) (sē-ĕ′r-rä-dĕ-chä-mä)	Guat.	15·48 N	90·20 W
122	Chamalières (shä-mä-lyâr′)	Fr.	45·45 N	2·59 E
142	Chaman (chŭm,-än′)	W. Pak.	30·58 N	66·21 E
142	Chambal (R.) (chŭm-bäl′)	India	26·05 N	76·37 E
70	Chamberlain (chām′bēr-lĭn)	S. D.	43·48 N	99·21 W
82	Chamberlain (L.)	Maine	46·15 N	67·05 W
81	Chambersburg (chām′bērz-bûrg)	Pa.	40·00 N	77·40 W
123	Chambéry (shäm-bā-rē′)	Fr.	45·35 N	5·54 E
84	Chamblee (chăm-blē′)	Ga. (Atlanta In.)	33·53 N	84·18 W
85	Chambly (shäN-blē′)	Can. (Montreal In.)	45·27 N	73·17 W
123	Chambly	Fr. (Paris In.)	49·11 N	2·14 E
87	Chambord	Can.	48·22 N	72·01 W
93	Chame, Punta (Pt.) (po͞o′n-tä-chä′må)	Pan.	8·41 N	79·27 W
92	Chamelecón R. (chä-mĕ-lĕ-kô′n)	Hond.	15·09 N	88·42 W
165	Chamo L. (chä′mō)	Eth.	5·58 N	37·00 E
123	Chamonix (shå-mô-nē′)	Fr.	45·55 N	6·50 E
122	Champagne (Reg.) (shäm-pän′-yĕ)	Fr.	48·53 N	4·48 E
80	Champaign (shăm-pān′)	Ill.	40·10 N	88·15 W
92	Champerico (chăm-pā-rē′kō)	Guat.	14·18 N	91·55 W
71	Champion (chăm′pĭ-ŭn)	Mich.	46·30 N	87·59 W
81	Champlain, L. (shăm-plān′)	N. Y.-Vt.	44·45 N	73·20 W
123	Champlitte (shäN-plēt′)	Fr.	47·38 N	5·28 E
91	Champotón (chăm-pō-tōn′)	Mex.	19·21 N	90·43 W
91	Champotón (R.)	Mex.	19·19 N	90·15 W
100	Chañaral (chän-yä-räl′)	Chile	26·20 S	70·46 W
124	Chanca (R.) (chäŋ′kä)	Sp.-Port.	38·15 N	7·22 W
151	Chanchiang (Fort Bayard)	China	21·20 N	110·28 E
142	Chanda (chăn′dŭ)	India	19·58 N	79·21 E
78	Chandeleur Is. (shăn-dē-lo͞or′)	La.	29·53 N	88·35 W
78	Chandeleur Sd	La.	29·47 N	89·08 W
142	Chandīgarh	India	30·51 N	77·13 E
82	Chandler (chăn′dlēr)	Can.	48·24 N	64·40 W
74	Chandler	Mo. (Kansas City In.)	39·18 N	94·24 W
73	Chandler	Okla.	35·42 N	96·52 W
148	Chang (R.) (jäng)	China	36·17 N	114·31 E
166	Changane (R.)	Moz.	22·42 S	32·46 E
148	Ch'angch'ichuang (chäng′chē′zho͞oäng)	China	37·59 N	116·57 E
150	Ch'angchih	China	35·58 N	112·58 E
148	Ch'angch'ing (chäng′chĭng)	China	36·33 N	116·42 E
148	Changch'iu (zhängchĭŏ)	China	36·50 N	117·29 E
150	Ch'angch'un (Hsinking) (chäng′cho͞on′) (hsĭn′kĭng)	China	43·55 N	125·25 E
148	Ch'anghsing Tao (I.) (chängsĭng dou)	China	39·38 N	121·10 E
150	Ch'anghsintien	China (Peking In.)	39·49 N	116·12 E
151	Changhua (chäng′hwä′)	Taiwan	24·02 N	120·32 E
148	Changhutien (jang′ho͞o′dĭan)	China	32·07 N	114·44 E
148	Ch'angi (jäng′yē)	China	36·51 N	119·23 E
152	Changjōn (chäng′jŭn′)	Kor.	38·38 N	128·02 E
150	Changkochuang	China (Peking In.)	40·09 N	116·56 E
150	Changkuangts'ai Ling (Mts.)	China	43·50 N	127·55 E
148	Ch'angli (chäng′lē′)	China	39·46 N	119·10 E
150	Changpei (chäng′pā′)	China	41·12 N	114·50 E
152	Changsan Cot (I.)	Kor.	38·06 N	124·50 E
148	Ch'angshan Liehtao (Is.) (chäng′shän′ lĭĕdou)	China	39·08 N	122·26 E
148	Ch'angshan Tao (I.) (chäng′shän′ dou)	China	37·56 N	120·42 E
148	Ch'angshu (chäng′sho͞o′)	China	31·40 N	120·45 E
151	Ch'angte (chäng′tĕ′)	China	29·00 N	111·38 E
148	Changtien (jäng′dĭan)	China	36·48 N	118·04 E
151	Changting	China	25·50 N	116·18 E
146	Ch'angtu (chäng′to͞o′)	China	31·06 N	96·30 E
152	Changtu	China	43·00 N	124·02 E
148	Ch'angtzu Tao (I.) (chäng′zho͞o dou)	China	39·02 N	122·44 E
150	Changwu (chäng′wo͞o′)	China	35·12 N	107·45 E
152	Changwu	China	42·21 N	123·00 E
146	Changyeh	China	38·46 N	101·00 E
148	Ch'angyüan (chäng′yü-än′)	China	35·10 N	114·41 E
74	Chanhassen (shăn′hăs-sĕn)	Minn. (Minneapolis, St. Paul In.)	44·52 N	93·32 W
148	Chanhua (jän′ho͞oä)	China	37·42 N	117·49 E
122	Channel Is. (chăn′ĕl)	Eur.	49·20 N	2·40 W
83	Channel-Port aux Basques (pôr′tō båsk)	Can.	47·36 N	59·09 W
77	Channelview (chăn′ĕlvū)	Tex. (In.)	29·46 N	95·07 W
150	Chanping	China	40·12 N	116·10 E
124	Chantada (chän-tä′dä)	Sp.	42·38 N	7·36 W
154	Chanthaburi	Thai.	12·37 N	102·04 E
123	Chantilly (shäN-tē-yē′)	Fr. (Paris In.)	49·12 N	2·30 E
86	Chantrey Inlet (chăn-trē)	Can.	67·49 N	94·30 W
73	Chanute (shå-no͞ot′)	Kans.	37·41 N	95·27 W
134	Chany (L.) (chä′nē)	Sov. Un.	54·15 N	77·31 E
150	Chanyü	China	44·30 N	122·30 E
151	Ch'aoan (chä′ō-än′)	China	23·48 N	117·10 E
148	Ch'aohsien (chou′sĭän)	China	31·37 N	117·50 E
148	Chaohsien	China	37·46 N	114·48 E
154	Chao Phraya, Mae Nam (R.)	Thai.	16·13 N	99·33 E
148	Ch'aoshui (jĭousōōĭ)	China	37·43 N	120·56 E
151	Chaot'ung (chä′ō-to͞ong′)	China	27·18 N	103·50 E
151	Ch'aoyang (chä′ō-yäng′)	China	23·18 N	116 32 E
150	Ch'aoyang (Foshan)	China	41·32 N	120·20 E
148	Chaoyüan (chä′ō-yü-än′)	China	37·22 N	120·23 E
99	Chapada, Serra da (Mts.) (sĕ′r-rä-dä-shä-pä′dä)	Braz.	14·57 S	54·34 W
101	Chapadão, Serra do (Mtn.) (sĕ′r-rä-dô-shä-pä-dou′N)	Braz. (Rio de Janeiro In.)	20·31 S	46·20 W
90	Chapala, Lago de (L.) (lä′gô-dĕ-chä-pä′lä)	Mex.	20·14 N	103·02 W
90	Chapalagana (R.) (chä-pä-lä-gå′nä)	Mex.	22·11 N	104·09 W
98	Chaparral (chä-pär-rä′l)	Col. (In.)	3·44 N	75·28 W
90	Chapata (chä-pä′tä)	Mex.	20·18 N	103·10 W
133	Chapayevsk (chå-pī′ĕfsk)	Sov. Un.	53·00 N	49·30 E
79	Chapel Hill (chăp′'l hĭl)	N. C.	35·55 N	79·05 W
65	Chaplain (L.) (chăp′lĭn)	Wash. (Seattle In.)	47·58 N	121·50 W
87	Chapleau (chăp-lō′)	Can.	47·43 N	83·28 W
166	Chapmans B. (chăp′măns bă)	S. Afr. (Cape Town In.)	34·06 S	18·17 E
70	Chappell (chă-pĕl′)	Nebr.	41·06 N	102·29 W
91	Chapultenango (chä-po͞ol-tē-näŋ′gō)	Mex.	17·19 N	93·08 W
90	Charcas (chär′käs)	Mex.	23·09 N	101·09 W
93	Charco de Azul, Bahia (B.) (bä-ē′ä-chä′r-kô-dĕ-ä-zo͞o′l)	Pan.	8·14 N	82·45 W
103	Chardzhou (chēr-jô′o͞o)	Sov. Un.	38·52 N	63·37 E
122	Charente (shå-räNt′)	Fr.	45·48 N	0·28 W
165	Chari (R.) (shä-rē′)	Chad	11·02 N	15·46 E
110	Charing (chă′rĭng)	Eng. (London In.)	51·13 N	0·49 E
71	Chariton (chăr′ĭ-tŭn)	Iowa	41·02 N	93·16 W
73	Chariton (R.)	Mo.	40·24 N	92·38 W
85	Charlemagne (shärl-mäny′)	Can. (Montreal In.)	45·43 N	73·29 W
117	Charleroi (shår-lē-rwä′)	Bel.	50·25 N	4·35 E
75	Charleroi (shär′lē-roi)	Pa. (Pittsburgh In.)	40·08 N	79·54 W
79	Charles, C. (chärlz)	Va.	37·05 N	75·48 W
85	Charlesbourg (shårl-bo͞or′)	Can. (Quebec In.)	46·51 N	71·16 W
71	Charles City (chärlz)	Iowa	43·03 N	92·40 W
80	Charleston (chärlz′tŭn)	Ill.	39·30 N	88·10 W
78	Charleston	Miss.	34·00 N	90·02 W
73	Charleston	Mo.	36·53 N	89·20 W
79	Charleston	S. C.	32·47 N	79·56 W
80	Charleston	W. Va.	38·20 N	81·35 W
75	Charlestown (chärlz′toun)	Ind. (Louisville In.)	38·46 N	85·39 W
93	Charlestown St. Kitts-Nevis-Anguilla	(Le. & Wind. Is. In.)	17·10 N	62·32 W
166	Charlesville	Con. L.	5·19 S	30·59 E
160	Charleville (chär′lē-vĭl)	Austl.	26·16 S	146·28 E
122	Charleville (shärl-vēl′)	Fr.	49·48 N	4·41 E
80	Charlevoix (shär′lē-voi)	Mich.	45·20 N	86·15 W
71	Charlevoix, L	Mich.	45·17 N	85 43 W
80	Charlotte (shär′lŏt)	Mich.	42·35 N	84·50 W
79	Charlotte	N. C.	35·15 N	80·50 W
89	Charlotte Amalie (St. Thomas) (shär-lŏt′ĕ å-mä′lĭ-å)	Virgin Is. (U. S. A.) (St. Thomas In.)	18·21 N	64·54 W
79	Charlotte Hbr	Fla. (In.)	26·47 N	81·58 W
118	Charlottenberg (shär-lŭt′ĕn-bĕrg)	Swe.	59·53 N	12·17 E
81	Charlottesville (shär′lŏtz-vĭl)	Va.	38·00 N	78·25 W
83	Charlottetown (shär′lŏt-toun)	Can.	46·14 N	63·08 W
158	Charlotte Waters (shär′lŏt)	Austl.	26·00 S	134·50 E
123	Charmes (shärm)	Fr.	48·23 N	6·19 E
110	Charnwood Forest (chärn′wo͝od)	Eng.	52·42 N	1·15 W
85	Charny (shär-nē′)	Can. (Quebec In.)	46·43 N	71·16 W
142	Charol Tsho (L.)	China	34·00 N	81·47 E
123	Chars (shär)	Fr. (Paris In.)	49·09 N	1·57 E
145	Charsadda (chŭr-sä′dä)	W. Pak. (Khyber Pass In.)	34·17 N	71·43 E
159	Charters Towers (chär′tērz)	Austl.	20·03 S	146·20 E
123	Chartres (shärt′r′)	Fr. (Paris In.)	48·26 N	1·29 E
101	Chascomús (chäs-kō-mo͞os′)	Arg. (Buenos Aires In.)	35·32 S	58·01 W
79	Chase City (chās)	Va.	36·45 N	78·27 W
128	Chashniki (chäsh′nyē-kē)	Sov. Un.	54·51 N	29·08 E
74	Chaska (chăs′kå)	Minn. (Minneapolis, St. Paul In.)	44·48 N	93·36 W
122	Châteaubriant (shå-tō-brē-äN′)	Fr.	47·43 N	1·23 W
122	Châteaudun (shå-tō-däN′)	Fr.	48·04 N	1·23 E
122	Château-Gontier (chå-tō′ gôN′tyā′)	Fr.	47·48 N	0·43 W
85	Chateauguay (chå-tō-gā′)	Can. (Montreal In.)	45·22 N	73·45 W
85	Châteauguay, R.	Can. (Montreal In.)	45·13 N	73·51 W
85	Chateauguay Basin	Can. (Montreal In.)	45·22 N	73·44 W
122	Chateauneuf-les-Martigues (shå-tō-nûf′lā-mär-tēg′ĕ)	Fr. (Marseille In.)	43·23 N	5·11 E
122	Château-Renault (shå-tō-rē-nō′)	Fr.	47·36 N	0·57 E
85	Château-Richer (shå-tō′rē-shā′)	Can. (Quebec In.)	46·58 N	71·01 W
122	Châteauroux (shå-tō-ro͞o′)	Fr.	46·47 N	1·39 E
122	Château-Thierry (shå-tō′tyĕr-rē′)	Fr.	49·03 N	3·22 E
122	Châtellerault (shä-tĕl-rō′)	Fr.	46·48 N	0·31 E
71	Chatfield (chăt′fēld)	Minn.	43·50 N	92·10 W
80	Chatham (chăt′ăm)	Can.	42·25 N	82·10 W
82	Chatham	Can.	47·01 N	65·28 W
110	Chatham (chăt′ŭm)	Eng. (London In.)	51·21 N	0·27 E
84	Chatham (chăt′ăm)	N. J. (New York In.)	40·44 N	74·23 W
75	Chatham	Ohio (Cleveland In.)	41·06 N	82·01 W
156	Chatham Is	N. Z.	44·00 S	178·00 W
64	Chatham Str	Alaska	57·00 N	134·40 W
74	Chatsworth (chătz′wûrth)	Calif. (Los Angeles In.)	34·16 N	118·36 W
74	Chatsworth Res.	Calif. (Los Angeles In.)	34·15 N	118·41 W
78	Chattahoochee (chăt-tå-ho͞o′ chē)	Fla.	30·42 N	84·47 W
78	Chattahoochee (R.)	Ala.-Ga.	31·17 N	85·10 W
78	Chattanooga (chăt-å-no͞o′gå)	Tenn.	35·01 N	85·15 W
78	Chattooga (R.) (chå-to͞o′gå)	Ga.-S. C.	34·47 N	83·13 W
82	Chaudiere (R.) (shō-dyĕr′)	Can.	46·26 N	71·10 W
154	Chau Doc (shō-dôk′)	Camb.	10·49 N	104·57 E
122	Chaumont (shō-môN′)	Fr.	48·08 N	5·07 E
123	Chaumontel (shō-mŏN-tĕl′)	Fr. (Paris In.)	49·07 N	2·26 E
135	Chaunskaya Guba (B.)	Sov. Un.	69·15 N	170·00 E
122	Chauny (shō-nē′)	Fr.	49·40 N	3·09 E
128	Chausy (chou′sĭ)	Sov. Un.	53·57 N	30·58 E
81	Chautauqua (L.) (shå-tô′kwå)	N. Y.	42·10 N	79·25 W
132	Chavaniga	Sov. Un.	66·02 N	37·50 E
124	Chaves (chä′vĕzh)	Port.	41·44 N	7·30 W
90	Chavinda (chä-vē′n-dä)	Mex.	20·01 N	102·27 W
91	Chazumba (chä-zo͞om′bä)	Mex.	18·11 N	97·41 W
110	Cheadle (chē′d'l)	Eng.	52·59 N	1·59 W
81	Cheat (R.) (chēt)	W. Va.	39·35 N	79·40 W
120	Cheb (kĕb)	Czech.	50·05 N	12·23 E
136	Chebarkul (chĕ-bår-kûl′)	Sov. Un. (Urals In.)	54·59 N	60·22 E
132	Cheboksary (chyĕ-bôk-sä′rê)	Sov. Un.	56·00 N	47·20 E
80	Cheboygan (shē-boi′găn)	Mich.	45·40 N	84·30 W
164	Chech, Erg (Dune)	Alg.	24·45 N	2·07 W
133	Chechen′ (I.) (chyĕch′ĕn)	Sov. Un.	44·00 N	48·10 E
148	Chech'eng (jĭŭcheng)	China	34·05 N	115·19 E
147	Chechiang (Chekiang) (Prov.)	China	29·28 N	119·33 E
73	Checotah (chē-kō′tå)	Okla.	35·27 N	95·32 W
83	Chedabucto B. (chĕd-å-bŭk-tō)	Can.	45·25 N	61·05 W
154	Cheduba (I.)	Bur.	18·45 N	93·01 E
86	Cheecham Hills (chē′hăm)	Can.	55·56 N	112·06 W
75	Cheektowaga (chēk-tŏ-wä′gå)	N. Y. (Buffalo In.)	42·54 N	78·46 W
	Chefoo, see Yent'ai			
66	Chehalis (chê-hā′lĭs)	Wash.	46·39 N	122·58 W
66	Chehalis R	Wash.	46·47 N	123·17 W
152	Cheju (chĕ′jo͞o′)	Kor.	33·29 N	126·40 E
152	Cheju (Quelpart) (I.)	Kor.	33·20 N	126·25 E
128	Chekalin (chĕ-kä′lĭn)	Sov. Un.	54·05 N	36·13 E
148	Chekao (jĭŭgou)	China	31·47 N	117·44 E
	Chekiang, see Chechiang			
166	Chela, Serrada (Mts.) (sĕr′rå dā shā′lå)	Ang.	15·30 S	13·30 E
66	Chelan (chê-lăn′)	Wash.	47·51 N	119·59 W
151	Chelang Chiao (Pt.)	China	22·38 N	116·00 E
66	Chelan R	Wash.	48·09 N	120·20 W
125	Cheleiros (shĕ-lā′rōzh)	Port. (Lisbon In.)	38·54 N	9·19 W
113	Chelic (Mt.) (shĕl-ĭk)	Alg.	35·22 N	6·47 E
125	Chéliff, Oued (R.) (o͞o-ĕd shä-lēf)	Alg.	36·17 N	1·22 E
134	Chelkar (chyĕl′kär)	Sov. Un.	47·52 N	59·41 E
133	Chelkar (L.)	Sov. Un.	50·30 N	51·30 E
134	Chelkar Tengiz (L.) (chyĕl′kär tĕn′yēz)	Sov. Un.	47·42 N	61·45 E
125	Chellala (chĕl-å′lå)	Alg.	35·12 N	2·20 E
121	Chełm (kĕlm)	Pol.	51·08 N	23·30 E
121	Chełmno (kĕlm′nō)	Pol.	53·20 N	18·25 E
110	Chelmsford (chĕlm′s-fērd)	Eng. (London In.)	51·44 N	0·28 E
83	Chelmsford	Mass. (Boston In.)	42·36 N	71·21 W
84	Chelsea (chĕl′sē)	Ala. (Birmingham In.)	33·20 N	86·38 W
161	Chelsea	Austl. (Melbourne In.)	38·05 S	145·08 E
85	Chelsea	Can. (Ottawa In.)	45·30 N	75·46 W
83	Chelsea	Mass. (Boston In.)	42·23 N	71·02 W
80	Chelsea	Mich.	42·20 N	84·00 W
73	Chelsea	Okla.	36·32 N	95·23 W
116	Cheltenham (chĕlt′'nŭm)	Eng.	51·57 N	2·06 W
125	Chelva (chĕl′vä)	Sp.	39·43 N	1·00 W
136	Chelyabinsk (chĕl-yä-bĕnsk′)	Sov. Un. (Urals In.)	55·10 N	61·25 E
135	Chelyuskin, Mys (C.) (chĕl-yo͞os′kĭn)	Sov. Un.	77·45 N	104·45 E
122	Chemillé (shĕ-mē-yā′)	Fr.	47·13 N	0·46 W
	Chemnitz, see Karl-Marx-Stadt			
81	Chemung (R.) (shê-mŭng)	N. Y.	42·20 N	77·25 W
135	Chĕn, Gora (Mtn.)	Sov. Un.	65·13 N	142·12 E
142	Chenāb (R.) (chê-näb)	W. Pak.	31·33 N	72·28 E
164	Chenachane (Oasis) (shē-nå-shän′)	Alg.	26·14 N	4·14 W
148	Chenchiang (jienjäng)	China	32·13 N	119·24 E
66	Cheney (chē′nå)	Wash.	47·29 N	117·34 W
	Chengchow, see Chenghsien			
151	Ch'enghai	China	23·22 N	116·40 E
148	Chenghsien (Chengchow) (jĕngsĭen) (jĕngjō)	China	34·46 N	113·42 E
146	Ch'enghua	China	47·52 N	87·50 E
151	Chengku	China	33·05 N	107·25 E
150	Ch'engte (Jehol) (chĕng′tĕ′) (rē-hōl′)	China	40·50 N	117·50 E
148	Chengting (chengding)	China	38·10 N	114·35 E
151	Ch'engtu (chĕng′to͞o′)	China	30·30 N	104·10 E
148	Chengyang (chĕn′yäng′)	China	32·34 N	114·22 E
146	Chenhsi	China	43·43 N	92·50 E
151	Ch'enshien	China	25·40 N	113·00 E
149	Ch'entsun	China (Canton In.)	22·58 N	113·14 E
150	Chentung	China	45·28 N	123·42 E
151	Chenyüan (chĕn′yü-än′)	China	27·08 N	108·30 E
149	Chepei	China (Canton In.)	23·07 N	113·23 E
98	Chepén (chĕ-pĕ′n)	Peru	7·17 S	79·24 W
93	Chepo (chä′pō)	Pan.	9·12 N	79·06 W

ăt: finăl; rāte; senâte; ärm; åsk; sofå; fâre; ch-choose; dh-as th in other; bē; ēvent; bĕt; recĕnt; cratēr; g-go; gh-guttural g; bĭt; ĭ-short neutral; rīde; K-guttural k as ch in German ich;

Page	Name Pronunciation Region	Lat. °'	Long. °'
93	Chepo R. .... Pan.	9·10 N	78·36 W
122	Cher (R.) (shâr) .... Fr.	47·14 N	1·34 E
90	Cheran (chā-rän') .... Mex.	19·41 N	101·54 W
79	Cheraw (chē'rô) .... S. C.	34·40 N	79·52 W
122	Cherbourg (shär-bōōr') .... Fr.	49·39 N	1·43 W
164	Cherchel (shĕr-shĕl') .... Alg.	36·38 N	2·09 E
146	Cherchen (R.) (chĕr-chĕn') . China	39·00 N	87·19 E
132	Cherdyn' (chĕr-dyēn') ... Sov. Un.	60·25 N	56·32 E
134	Cheremkhovo (chĕr'yĕm-kō-vō) Sov. Un.	52·58 N	103·18 E
136	Cherëmukhovo (chĕr-yĕ-mŭ-kô-vô) . Sov. Un. (Urals In.)	60·20 N	60·00 E
165	Cheren (chĕr'ĕn) .... Eth.	15·46 N	38·28 E
134	Cherepanovo (chĕr'yĕ pä-nô'vô) Sov. Un.	54·13 N	83·18 E
128	Cherepovets (chĕr-yĕ-pô'vyĕtz) Sov. Un.	59·08 N	35·54 E
128	Chereya (chĕr-ā'yä) .... Sov. Un.	54·38 N	29·16 E
114	Chergui, Chott ech (L.) (chĕr gē) Alg.	34·12 N	0·10 W
114	Chergui I. .... Tun.	34·48 N	11·41 E
128	Cherikov (chĕ'rē-kôf) .... Sov. Un.	53·34 N	31·22 E
129	Cherkassy (chĕr-kä'sĭ) ... Sov. Un.	49·26 N	32·03 E
129	Cherkassy (Oblast) .... Sov. Un.	48·58 N	30·55 E
134	Cherlak (chĭr-läk') .... Sov. Un.	54·04 N	74·28 E
136	Chermoz (chĕr-môz') Sov. Un. (Urals In.)	58·47 N	56·08 E
128	Chern' (chĕrn) .... Sov. Un.	53·28 N	36·49 E
129	Chërnaya Kalitva (R.) (chôr'nȧ yȧ kȧ-lēt'vȧ) . Sov. Un.	50·15 N	39·16 E
129	Chernigov (chĕr-nē'gôf) . Sov. Un.	51·28 N	31·18 E
129	Chernigov (Oblast) (chĕr-nē'gôf) Sov. Un.	51·23 N	31·15 E
129	Chernobay (chĕr-nō-bī') . Sov. Un.	49·41 N	32·24 E
129	Chernobyl' (chĕr-nō-bĭl') . Sov. Un.	51·17 N	30·14 E
134	Chernogorsk (chĕr-nŏ-gôrsk') Sov. Un.	54·01 N	91·07 E
129	Chernogovka (chĕr-nô-gôf'kȧ) Sov. Un.	47·08 N	36·20 E
136	Chernoistochinsk (chĕr-nôy-stô'chĭnsk) . Sov. Un. (Urals In.)	57·44 N	59·55 E
129	Chërnomorskoye (chĕr-nô-môr'skô-yĕ) . Sov. Un.	45·29 N	32·43 E
121	Chernovtsy (Cernăuti) (chĭr-nôf'tsē) (chĕr-nou'tsĕ) Sov. Un.	48·18 N	25·56 E
119	Chernyakhovsk (chĕr-nyä'ĸôfsk) . Sov. Un.	55·38 N	21·17 E
129	Chernyanka (chĕrn-yäŋ'kä) Sov. Un.	50·56 N	37·48 E
70	Cherokee (chĕr-ô-kē') .... Iowa	42·43 N	95·33 W
73	Cherokee .... Kans.	37·21 N	94·50 W
72	Cherokee .... Okla.	36·44 N	98·22 W
78	Cherokee (R.) .... Tenn.	36·22 N	83·22 W
78	Cherokee Indian Res. .... N. C.	35·33 N	83·12 W
94	Cherokee Sd. .... Ba. Is.	26·15 N	76·55 W
73	Cherokees, L. of the (chĕr-ô-kēz') . Okla.	36·32 N	95·14 W
82	Cherryfield (chĕr'ĭ-fēld) ... Maine	44·37 N	67·56 W
65	Cherry Grove . Ore. (Portland In.)	45·27 N	123·15 W
73	Cherryvale .... Kans.	37·16 N	95·33 W
79	Cherryville (chĕr'ĭ-vĭl) .... N. C.	35·32 N	81·22 W
65	Cherryville .... Ore. (Portland In.)	45·22 N	122·08 W
135	Cherskogo, Khrebet (Mts.) Sov. Un.	66·15 N	138·30 E
128	Cherven' (chĕr'vyĕn) .... Sov. Un.	53·43 N	28·26 E
128	Chervonoye (L.) (chĕr-vô'nô-yĕ) Sov. Un.	52·24 N	28·12 E
80	Chesaning (chĕs'ȧ-nĭng) .... Mich.	43·10 N	84·10 W
81	Chesapeake B. (chĕs'ȧ-pēk bā) Md.	38·20 N	76·15 W
110	Chesham (chĕsh'ŭm) Eng. (London In.)	51·41 N	0·37 W
80	Cheshire (chĕsh'ĭr) .... Mich.	42·25 N	86·00 W
110	Cheshire (Co.) .... Eng.	53·16 N	2·30 W
132	Chëshskaya Guba (B.) .. Sov. Un.	67·25 N	46·00 E
136	Chesma (chĕs'mȧ) Sov. Un. (Urals In.)	53·50 N	60·42 E
134	Chesnokovka (chĕs-nŏ-kôf'kȧ) Sov. Un.	53·28 N	83·41 E
110	Chester (chĕs'tĕr) .... Eng.	53·12 N	2·53 W
73	Chester .... Ill.	37·54 N	89·48 W
84	Chester .... Pa. (Philadelphia In.)	39·51 N	75·22 W
79	Chester .... S. C.	34·42 N	81·11 W
79	Chester .... Va.	37·20 N	77·24 W
80	Chester .... W. Va.	40·35 N	80·30 W
110	Chesterfield (chĕs'tĕr-fēld) ... Eng.	53·14 N	1·26 W
159	Chesterfield, Isles .... N. Cal.	19·38 S	160·08 E
86	Chesterfield (Inlet) .... Can.	63·59 N	92·09 W
86	Chesterfield Inlet .... Can.	63·19 N	91·11 W
85	Chestermere L. (chĕs'tĕr-mēr) Can. (Calgary In.)	51·03 N	113·45 W
80	Chesterton (chĕs'tĕr-tŭn) .... Ind.	41·35 N	87·05 W
81	Chestertown (chĕs'tĕr-toun) .. Md.	39·15 N	76·05 W
82	Chesuncook (chĕs'ŭn-kŏŏk) . Maine	46·03 N	69·40 W
71	Chetek (chĕ'tĕk) .... Wis.	45·18 N	91·41 W
92	Chetumal, Bahia de (B.) (bä-ē-ä dĕ chĕt-ōō-mäl') Br. Hond. (Yucatan In.)	18·07 N	88·05 W
69	Chevalon Cr. (shĕv'ȧ-lŏn) .... Ariz.	34·35 N	111·00 W
75	Cheviot (shĕv'ĭ-ŭt) Ohio (Cincinnati In.)	39·10 N	84·37 W
116	Cheviot Hills .... Scot., Eng.	55·20 N	2·40 W
123	Chevreuse (shĕ-vrûz') Fr. (Paris In.)	48·42 N	2·02 E
66	Chewelah (chē-wē'lä) .... Wash.	48·17 N	117·42 W
148	Cheyang (R.) (Sĭyang) .... China	33·42 N	119·40 E
70	Cheyenne (shī-ĕn') .... Wyo.	41·10 N	104·49 W
70	Cheyenne (R.) .... S. D.	44·20 N	102 15 W
70	Cheyenne River Ind. Res. ... S. D.	45·07 N	100·46 W
72	Cheyenne Wells .... Colo.	38·46 N	102·21 W
151	Chiachi .... China	19·10 N	110·28 E
151	Chiahsing .... China	30·45 N	120·50 E
151	Chiai (chĭ'ī') .... Taiwan	23·28 N	120·28 E
151	Chialing (R.) .... China	30·30 N	106·20 E
151	Chian .... China	27·12 N	115·10 E
150	Chian .... China	41·00 N	126·04 E
148	Chiangchanchi .... China	36·39 N	120·31 E
83	Chianghsi (Kiangsi) (Prov.) . China	28·16 N	115·34 E
151	Chiangling .... China	30·30 N	112·10 E
146	Chiang Mai .... Thai.	18·38 N	98·44 E
154	Chiang Rai .... Thai.	19·53 N	99·48 E
147	Chiangsu (Kiangsu) (Prov.) . China	33·51 N	120·09 E
148	Chiangtu (jiang'dōō) .... China	32·24 N	119·24 E
148	Chiangyen (jĭäng'yĭn) .... China	32·33 N	120·07 E
148	Chiangyin (jiäng'in) .... China	31·54 N	120·15 E
148	Chiantochen (jĭäng'tō'jĕn) .. China	32·23 N	120·14 E
148	Chiaochou Wan (B.) (jĭou'zhēō wän) . China	36·10 N	119·55 E
148	Chiaoho (jēou'hŭ) .... China	38·03 N	116·18 E
150	Chiaoho .... China	43·40 N	127·20 E
148	Chiaohsien (jēou'sĭän) .... China	36·18 N	120·01 E
149	Ch'iaot'ou .... China (Canton In.)	22·55 N	113·39 E
148	Chiaotso (jēou'zhōōŭ) .... China	35·17 N	113·11 E
148	Chiaow Shan (Mts.) (jēou shän) China	36·59 N	121·15 E
92	Chiapa, Rio de (R.) (rê-ô-dĕ-chê-ä'pä) . Mex.	16·00 N	92·20 W
91	Chiapa de Corzo (chê-ä'pä dā kôr'zō) . Mex.	16·44 N	93·01 W
88	Chiapas (State) (chê-ä'päs) . Mex.	17·10 N	93·00 W
91	Chiapas, Cordilla de (Mts.) (kôr-dēl-yĕ'rä-dĕ-chyä'räs) Mex.	15·55 N	93·15 W
126	Chiari (kyä'rē) .... It.	45·31 N	9·57 E
120	Chiasso .... Switz.	45·50 N	8·57 E
149	Chiating .... China (Shanghai In.)	31·23 N	121·15 E
90	Chiautla (chyä-ōōt'lä) .... Mex.	18·16 N	98·37 W
126	Chiavari (kyä-vä'rē) .... It.	44·18 N	9·21 E
151	Chiayü .... China	33·00 N	114·00 E
153	Chiba (chē'bä) . Jap. (Tōkyō In.)	35·37 N	140·08 E
153	Chiba (Pref.) .... Jap. (Tōkyō In.)	35·47 N	140·02 E
87	Chibougamau (chē-bōō'gä-mou) Can.	49·57 N	74·23 W
75	Chicago (shĭ-kô-gō) (chĭ-kä'gō) Ill. (Chicago In.)	41·49 N	87·37 W
75	Chicago Heights (shĭ-kô'gō) (chĭ-kä'gō) . Ill. (Chicago In.)	41·30 N	87·38 W
166	Chicapa (R.) (chē-kä'pä) .... Ang.	8·15 S	20·15 E
91	Chicbul (chēk-bōō'l) .... Mex.	18·45 N	90·56 W
64	Chichagof (I.) (chê-chä'gôf) Alaska	57·50 N	137·00 W
92	Chichâncanab, Lago de (L.) (lä'-gô-dĕ-chē-chän-kä-nä'b) Mex. (Yucatan In.)	19·50 N	88·28 W
92	Chichen Itzá (Ruins) (chē-chĕ'n-ē-tsà') . Mex. (Yucatan In.)	20·38 N	88·35 W
116	Chichester (chĭch'ĕs-tĕr) .... Eng.	50·50 N	0·55 W
151	Chichiang .... China	29·05 N	106·40 E
148	Chichiashih (jĭ'jĭä'shē) .... China	32·10 N	120·17 E
150	Ch'ich'ihaerh (Tsitsihar) ... China	47·18 N	124·00 E
92	Chichimila (chē-chē-mē'lä) Mex. (Yucatan In.)	20·36 N	88·14 W
99	Chichiriviche (chē-chē-rē-vē-chĕ) Ven. (In.)	10·56 N	68·17 W
78	Chickamauga (chĭk-ȧ-mô'gȧ) .. Ga.	34·50 N	85·15 W
79	Chickamauga, (R.) .... Tenn.	35·18 N	85·22 W
78	Chickasawhay (R.) (chĭk-ȧ-sô'wā) Miss.	31·45 N	88·45 W
72	Chickasha (chĭk'ȧ-shā) .... Okla.	35·04 N	97·56 W
124	Chiclana (chê-klä'nä) .... Sp.	36·25 N	6·09 W
98	Chiclayo (chê-klä'yō) .... Peru	6·46 S	79·50 W
68	Chico (chē'kō) .... Calif.	39·43 N	121·51 W
65	Chico .... Wash. (Seattle In.)	47·37 N	122·43 W
100	Chico (R.) .... Arg.	44·30 S	66·00 W
100	Chico (R.) .... Arg.	49·15 S	69·30 W
155	Chico (R.) .... Phil. (Manila In.)	17·33 N	121·24 E
91	Chicoloapan (chê-kō-lwä'pän) Mex. (Mexico City In.)	19·24 N	98·54 W
91	Chiconautla (chê-kō-nä-ōō'tlä) Mex. (Mexico City In.)	19·39 N	99·01 W
90	Chicontepec (chê-kōn'tĕ-pĕk') Mex.	20·58 N	98·08 W
81	Chicopee (chĭk'ô-pē) .... Mass.	42·10 N	72·35 W
84	Chicot I. (shē-kō') La. (New Orleans In.)	29·44 N	89·15 W
82	Chicoutimi (shē-kōō'tē-mē') .. Can.	48·27 N	71·03 W
92	Chicxulub (chēk-sōō-lōō'b) Mex. (Yucatan In.)	21·10 N	89·30 W
87	Chidley, C. (chĭd'lĭ) .... Can.	60·32 N	63·56 W
66	Chief Joseph Dam .... Wash.	48·00 N	119·39 W
78	Chiefland (chēf'lănd) .... Fla.	29·30 N	82·50 W
146	Ch'iehmo .... China	38·02 N	85·16 E
148	Chiehshou Hu (L.) (jĭeh'shō hōō) China	32·59 N	119·04 E
151	Chiehyang .... China	23·38 N	116·20 E
120	Chiem See (L.) (Kēm zä) .... Ger.	47·58 N	12·20 E
148	Chienchangying (jĭan'chang'yĭng) China	40·09 N	118·47 E
148	Chienkan (R.) (jĭan'gän) ... China	39·35 N	117·34 E
151	Chienli .... China	29·50 N	112·52 E
151	Chienning .... China	26·50 N	116·55 E
151	Chienou .... China	27·10 N	118·18 E
148	Ch'ienshanchen (chĭan'shän'jen) China	31·05 N	120·24 E
148	Ch'ienshanchi (chĭan'shan'jĭ) China	32·38 N	117·02 E
151	Chienshih .... China	30·40 N	109·45 E
151	Chienshui .... China	23·32 N	102·50 E
148	Ch'ienwei (chĭan'wā) .... China	40·11 N	120·05 E
126	Chieri (kyâ'rē) .... It.	45·03 N	7·48 E
126	Chieti (kyĕ'tē) .... It.	42·22 N	14·22 E
129	Chigirin (chê-gē'rĕn) .... Sov. Un.	49·02 N	32·39 E
90	Chignanuapan (chē'g-nä-nwä-pä'n) Mex.	19·49 N	98 02 W
82	Chignecto B. (shĭg-nĕk'tō) ... Can.	45·33 N	64·50 W
64	Chignik (chĭg'nĭk) .... Alaska	56·14 N	158·12 W
64	Chignik B. .... Alaska	56·18 N	157·22 W
151	Chihchiang .... China	27·25 N	109·45 E
150	Ch'ihfeng (chĭ'fŭng) .... China	42·18 N	118·52 E
148	Chihhochen (zhĭ'hŭ'jen) .... China	32·32 N	117·57 E
148	Ch'ihsien (chĭ'hsyĕn') .... China	34·33 N	114·47 E
148	Chihsien .... China	35·25 N	114·03 E
148	Ch'ihsien .... China	35·36 N	114·13 E
148	Chihsien .... China	37·37 N	115·33 E
148	Chihsien .... China	40·03 N	117·25 E
76	Chihuahua (chê-wä'wä) .... Mex.	28·37 N	106·06 W
88	Chihuahua (State) .... Mex.	29·00 N	107·30 W
166	Chihuane (chē-wä'nȧ) .... Moz.	20·43 S	34·57 E
133	Chikishlyar (chê-kêsh-lyär') Sov. Un.	37·40 N	53·50 E
148	Ch'ik'ou (chē'kō) .... China	38·37 N	117·33 E
90	Chilapa (chê-lä'pä) .... Mex.	17·34 N	99·14 W
90	Chilchota (chêl-chō'tä) .... Mex.	19·40 N	102·04 W
72	Childress (chīld'rĕs) .... Tex.	34·26 N	100·11 W
96	Chile (chē'lā) .... S.A.	53·24 N	2·53 W
100	Chilecito (chê-lâ-sē'tō) .... Arg.	29·06 S	67·25 W
98	Chilí, Pico de (Pk.) (pē'kō-dĕ chē-lē') . Col. (In.)	4·14 N	75·38 W
88	Chilibre (chê-lē'brĕ) Pan. (Panama Canal In.)	9·09 N	79·37 W
148	Ch'ili Hu (L.) (chē'lē hōō) .. China	32·57 N	118·26 E
150	Chilin (Kirin) (chĭl'ĭn') (kĭr'ĭn) China	43·58 N	126·40 E
147	Chilin (Prov.) .... China	44·36 N	124·23 E
148	Chilip'ing (chē'lē'pĭng) .... China	31·28 N	114·41 E
142	Chilka (L.) .... India	19·26 N	85·42 E
100	Chillán (chēl-yän') .... Chile	36·44 S	72·06 W
80	Chillicothe (chĭl-ĭ-kŏth'ê) .... Ill.	41·55 N	89·30 W
73	Chillicothe .... Mo.	39·46 N	93·32 W
80	Chillicothe .... Ohio	39·20 N	83·00 W
86	Chilliwack (chĭl'ĭ-wăk) .... Can.	49·09 N	121·59 W
100	Chiloé, Isla de (I.) (ē's-lä-dĕ-chē-lô-ā') . Chile	43·00 S	76·30 W
90	Chilpancingo (chēl-pän-sēŋ'gō) Mex.	17·32 N	97·30 W
71	Chilton (chĭl'tŭn) .... Wis.	44·00 N	88·12 W
151	Chilung (Kirin) (chĭ'lŭng) . Taiwan	25·02 N	121·48 E
65	Chimacum (chĭm'ȧ-kŭm) Wash. (Seattle In.)	48·01 N	122·47 W
91	Chimalpa (chē-mäl'pä) Mex. (Mexico City In.)	19·26 N	99·22 W
92	Chimaltenango (chê-mäl-tå-näŋ'gō) Guat.	14·39 N	90·48 W
90	Chimaltitan (chêmäl-tē-tän') Mex.	21·36 N	103·50 W
103	Chimbay (chĭm-bī') .... Sov. Un.	43·00 N	59·44 E
98	Chimborazo (Mtn.) (chêm-bô-rä'zō) Ec.	1·35 S	78·45 W
98	Chimbote (chêm-bō'tå) .... Peru	9·02 S	78·33 W
134	Chimkent (chĭm-kĕnt) ... Sov. Un.	42·17 N	69·42 E
148	Chimo (gē'mŭ) .... China	36·22 N	120·28 E
138	China (chī'nȧ) .... Asia	36·45 N	93·00 E
76	China (chē'nä) .... Mex.	25·43 N	99·13 W
92	Chinameca (chē-nä-mä'kä) .... Sal.	13·31 N	88·18 W
	Chinan, see Tsinan		
92	Chinandega (chē-nän-dā'gä) . Nic.	12·38 N	87·08 W
76	Chinati Pk. (chĭ-nä'tē) .... Tex.	92·56 N	104·29 W
145	Chinawin (R.) .... Bur.	23·30 N	94·30 E
98	Chincha Alta (chĭn'chä äl'tä) Peru	13·24 S	76·04 W
98	Chinchas, Islas (Is.) (ē's-läs-chē'n-chäs) . Peru	11·27 S	79·05 W
150	Chincheng .... China	35·30 N	112·50 E
151	Chinchiang .... China	24·58 N	118·40 E
148	Chinch'iao (jĭnchĭou) .... China	31·46 N	116·46 E
160	Chinchilla (chĭn-chĭl'ȧ) .... Austl.	26·44 S	150·36 E
124	Chinchilla (chên-chē'lyä) .... Sp.	38·54 N	1·43 W
92	Chinchorro, Banco (Bk.) (bä'n-kô-chēn-chô'r-rō) Mex. (Yucatan In.)	18·43 N	87·25 W
150	Chinchou .... China	41·00 N	121·00 E
148	Chinchou Wan (B.) (jĭn'zhō wän) . China	39·07 N	121·17 E
166	Chinde (shên'dĕ) .... Moz.	17·39 S	36·34 E
152	Chin Do (I.) .... Kor.	34·30 N	125·43 E
142	Chindwara .... India	22·08 N	78·57 E
146	Chindwin R. (chĭn-dwĭn) .... Bur.	23·30 N	94·34 E
148	Chinganchi (jing'än'jĭ) .... China	34·30 N	116·55 E
148	Ch'ingcheng (chĭng'cheng) .... China	37·12 N	117·43 E
150	Ch'ingch'eng .... China	46·50 N	127·30 E
151	Chingchiang (jĭng'jĭang) .... China	28·00 N	115·30 E
148	Chingchiang .... China	32·02 N	120·15 E
148	Chingchih (jĭng'jē) .... China	36·19 N	119·23 E
148	Ch'ingfeng (chingfeng) .... China	35·52 N	115·05 E
146	Chinghai (Tsinghai) (Prov.) China	36·14 N	95·30 E
146	Ch'ing Hai (Koko Nor) (L.) (kō'kō nor) . China	37·26 N	98·30 E
148	Chinghai Wan (B.) (jĭng'hăĭ wän) . China	36·47 N	122·10 E
150	Ching Ho (R.) (chĭng'hō') . China	34·40 N	108·20 E
151	Chinghsien (jĭng'sĭan) .... China	26·32 N	109·45 E
148	Chinghsien .... China	37·43 N	116·17 E
148	Ch'inghsien (chingsĭan) .... China	38·37 N	116·48 E
150	Chinghsing .... China	47·00 N	123·00 E
150	Ching Hu (L.) (chĭng hōō) .... China	39·00 N	115·45 E
148	Chingk'ouchen (chĭng'kō'jĕn) China	34·52 N	119·07 E
151	Chingliu .... China	26·15 N	116·50 E
150	Chingning .... China	35·28 N	105·50 E
166	Chingola (chĭng-gōlä) .... N. Rh.	12·32 S	27·35 E
148	Ch'ingp'ing (chĭng'pĭng) .... China	36·46 N	116·03 E
150	Chingpo Hu (L.) .... China	44·10 N	129·00 E
149	Ch'ingp'u .. China (Shanghai In.)	31·08 N	121·06 E
148	Ch'ingtao (Tsingtao) (tsĭng'dou) China	36·05 N	120·10 E
166	Chinguar (chĭng-gär) .... Ang.	12·35 S	16·15 E
164	Chinguetti (chĕŋ-gĕt'ĕ) Mauritania	20·34 N	12·34 W
148	Ch'ingyang (chĭng'yäng) ... China	33·25 N	118·13 E
150	Chingyang .... China	36·02 N	107·42 E
148	Ch'ingyüan (chĭng'yōōän) .. China	38·52 N	115·31 E
150	Ch'ingyüan .... China	42·04 N	125·00 E
151	Ch'ingyüang .... China	23·43 N	113·10 E
148	Ch'ingyun (chĭng'yōōn) .... China	37·52 N	117·26 E
150	Ch'ingyütien . China (Peking In.)	39·41 N	116·31 E
148	Chinhsiang (jĭn'sĭäng) .... China	35·03 N	116·20 E

ng-sing; ŋ-baŋk; ɴ-nasalized n; nŏd; cŏmmit; ōld; ôbey; ôrder; fōōd; fŏŏt; ou-out; s-soft; sh-dish; th-thin; pūre; ůnite; ûrn; stŭd; circŭs; ü-as "y" in study; '-indeterminate vowel.

Page	Name Pronunciation Region	Lat. °′	Long. °′
148	Chinhsien (jĭn'sĭăn) . . . China	37·08 N	121·43 E
151	Ch'inhsien . . . China	22·00 N	108·35 E
151	Chinhua . . . China	29·10 N	119·42 E
148	Ch'inhuangtao (chĭnhōōăng'dou) China	39·57 N	119·34 E
148	Chining (jē'nĭng) . . . China	35·26 N	116·34 E
150	Chining . . . China	41·00 N	113·10 E
152	Chinju (chĭn'jōō) . . . Kor.	35·13 N	128·10 E
151	Chinkiang (chĭn'kyăng') . . . China	32·05 N	119·25 E
151	Chinmen . . . China	24·42 N	118·05 E
	Chinmen, see Quemoy		
151	Chinmen (I.) . . . China	24·40 N	118·38 E
151	Chinmu Chiao (Pt.) . . . China	18·10 N	109·40 E
152	Chinnampo (chĭn-nàm'pō) . . . Kor.	38·47 N	125·28 E
74	Chino (chē'nō) Calif. (Los Angeles In.)	34·01 N	117·42 W
122	Chinon (shē-nôɴ') . . . Fr.	47·09 N	0·13 E
67	Chinook (shĭn-ŏŏk') . . . Mont.	48·35 N	109·15 W
65	Chinook (shĭn-ŏŏk') Wash. (Portland In.)	46·17 N	123·57 W
148	Chinshachen (jĭn'shä'jĕn) . . . China	32·08 N	121·06 E
149	Chinshan . . . China (Shanghai In.)	30·53 N	121·09 E
142	Chinsura . . . India (Calcutta In.)	22·53 N	88·24 E
146	Chint'a . . . China	40·11 N	98·45 E
148	Chint'an (jĭn'tän) . . . China	31·47 N	119·34 E
166	Chinteche (chĭn-tĕ'chĕ) . . . Nya.	11·48 S	34·14 E
150	Chinyang (chĭn'yäng') . . . China	35·00 N	112·55 E
151	Chinyüh . . . China	28·40 N	120·08 E
126	Chioggia (kyôd'jä) . . . It.	45·12 N	12·17 E
149	Ch'ipao . . . China (Shanghai In.)	31·06 N	121·16 E
166	Chipera (zhê-pĕ'rä) . . . Moz.	15·16 S	32·30 E
78	Chipley (chĭp'lĭ) . . . Fla.	30·45 N	85·33 W
82	Chipman (chĭp'măn) . . . Can.	46·11 N	65·53 W
78	Chipola (R.) (chĭ-pō'lȧ) . . . Fla.	30·40 N	85·14 W
75	Chippawa (chĭp'ê-wä) Can. (Buffalo In.)	43·03 N	79·03 W
70	Chippewa (R.) (chĭp'ê-wä) . . Minn.	45·07 N	95·41 W
71	Chippewa (R.) . . . Wis.	45·07 N	91·19 W
71	Chippewa Falls . . . Wis.	44·55 N	91·26 W
75	Chippewa Lake Ohio (Cleveland In.)	41·04 N	81·54 W
82	Chiputneticook (L.) (chĭ-pōōt-nĕt'ĭ-kŏŏk) . Can.	45·47 N	67·35 W
92	Chiquimula (chē-kê-mōō'lä) . Guat.	14·47 N	89·31 W
92	Chiquimulilla (chē-kē-mōō-lē'l-yä) Guat.	14·08 N	90·23 W
98	Chiquinquira (chê-kēŋ'kê-rä') . Col.	5·33 N	73·49 W
101	Chiquíta, Laguna Mar (L.) (lä-gōō'nä-mär-chê-kē'tä) Arg. (Buenos Aires In.)	34·25 S	61·10 W
69	Chiracahua Natl. Mon. (chĭ-rä-cä'hwä) . Ariz.	32·02 N	109·18 W
143	Chirald . . . India	15·52 N	80·22 E
134	Chirchik (chĭr-chēk') . . . Sov. Un.	41·28 N	69·18 E
64	Chirikof (I.) (chĭ'rĭ-kôf) . . . Alaska	55·50 N	155·35 W
93	Chiriquí, Golfo de (G.) (gôl-fô-dĕ-chē-rê-kē') . Pan.	7·56 N	82·18 W
93	Chiriquí, Laguna de (L.) (lä-gōō'nä-dĕ-chē-rê-kē') . Pan.	9·06 N	82·02 W
93	Chiriqui, Punta (Pt.) (pōō'n-tä-chē-rê-kē') . Pan.	9·13 N	81·39 W
93	Chiriqui, Volcán de (Vol.) (vôl-kä'n-dĕ-chē-rê-kē') . Pan.	8·48 N	82·37 W
93	Chiriquí Grande (chē-rê-kē' grän'dā) . Pan.	8·57 N	82·08 W
152	Chiri San (Mt.) (chĭ'rĭ-sän') . . Kor.	35·20 N	127·39 E
142	Chirmir . . . India	23·10 N	82·20 E
166	Chiromo . . . Nya.	16·34 S	35·13 E
127	Chirpan . . . Bul.	42·12 N	25·19 E
93	Chirripo, R. (chêr-rē'pō) . . . C. R.	9·50 N	83·20 W
93	Chirripo Grande (Mt.) (chêr-rē'pō grän'dā) . C. R.	9·30 N	83·31 W
71	Chisholm (chĭz'ŭm) . . . Minn.	47·28 N	92·53 W
132	Chistopol' (chĭs-tô'pôl-y') Sov. Un.	55·18 N	50·30 E
135	Chita (chê-tà') . . . Sov. Un.	52·09 N	113·39 E
146	Ch'it'ai . . . China	44·07 N	89·04 E
64	Chitina (chĭ-tē'nà) . . . Alaska	61·28 N	144·35 W
142	Chitor . . . India	24·59 N	74·42 E
142	Chitrāl (chē-träl') . . . W. Pak.	35·58 N	71·48 E
93	Chitré (chē'trā) . . . Pan.	7·59 N	80·26 W
142	Chittagong (chĭt-à-gông') . E. Pak.	22·26 N	90·51 E
150	Chiualhun . . . China	49·59 N	127·15 E
148	Chiuch'eng (jĭō'chĕng) . . . China	37·14 N	116·03 E
146	Chiuch'ian . . . China	39·46 N	98·26 E
151	Chiuchiang . . . China	29·43 N	116·00 E
149	Chiuchiang . . . China (Canton In.)	23·50 N	113·02 E
147	Chiuchichien . . . China	52·23 N	121·04 E
149	Chiufenghsien China (Shanghai In.)	30·55 N	121·38 E
148	Ch'iuhsien (chĭō'sĭän) . . . China	36·43 N	115·13 E
148	Chiuhsihsien (jĭō'sē'sĭän) . . . China	32·20 N	114·42 E
148	Chiuhuang (R.) (jĭō'hooăng) China	33·48 N	119·30 E
166	Chiumbe (R.) (chê-ōōm'bâ) . . Ang.	10·00 S	21·00 E
151	Ch'iungshan . . . China	20·00 N	110·20 E
148	Chiunü Shan (Mts.) (jĭō'nü'shān) . China	35·47 N	117·23 E
126	Chivasso (kê-väs'sō) . . . It.	45·13 N	7·52 E
101	Chivilcoy (chē-vêl-koi') Arg. (Buenos Aires In.)	34·51 S	60·03 W
92	Chixoy R. (chē-ĸoi') . . . Guat.	15·40 N	90·35 W
151	Chiyang . . . China	26·40 N	112·00 E
151	Ch'iyao Shan (Mtn.) . . . China	30·00 N	108·50 E
153	Chizu (chê-zōō') . . . Jap.	35·16 N	134·15 E
69	Chloride (klō'rīd) . . . Ariz.	35·25 N	114·15 W
121	Chmielnik (ĸmyĕl'nēĸ) . . . Pol.	50·36 N	20·46 E
101	Choapa (chô-à'pä) (R.) Chile (Santiago In.)	31·56 S	70·48 W
98	Chocó (chô-kô') (Dept.) . Col. (In.)	5·33 N	76·28 W
77	Chocolate Bay (chŏ'ô-lĭt) (chŏk'lĭt) . Tex. (In.)	29·21 N	95·19 W
78	Choctawhatchee, B. (chôk-tô-hăch'ê) . Fla.	30·15 N	86·32 W
78	Choctawhatchee, R. . . . Fla.-Ga.	30·37 N	85·56 W
120	Chodziez (ĸōj'yĕsh) . . . Pol.	52·59 N	16·55 E
100	Choele Choel (chô-ĕ'lĕ-chôĕ'l) Arg.	39·14 S	66·46 W
153	Chōfu (chō'fōō') . Jap. (Tōkyō In.)	35·39 N	139·33 E
153	Chōgo (chō-gō) . . Jap. (Tōkyō In.)	35·25 N	139·28 E
148	Chohsien (jōōŭ'sĭän) . . . China	39·30 N	115·59 E
159	Choiseul, (I.) (shwä-zûl') . . Sol. Is.	7·30 S	157·30 E
121	Chojnice (ĸoi-nē-tsĕ) . . . Pol.	53·41 N	17·34 E
122	Cholet (shô-lĕ') . . . Fr.	47·06 N	0·54 W
150	Ch'olo (R.) . . . China	47·20 N	121·40 E
90	Cholua (chō-lōō'lä) . . . Mex.	19·04 N	98·19 W
92	Choluteca (chō-lōō-tā'kä) . . . Hond.	13·18 N	87·12 W
92	Choluteco R. . . . Hond.	13·34 N	86·59 W
120	Chomutov (kō'mōō-tôf) . . . Czech.	50·27 N	13·23 E
135	Chona (R.) (chō'nä) . . . Sov. Un.	60·45 N	109·15 E
98	Chone (chô'nĕ) . . . Ec.	0·48 S	80·06 W
152	Chŏngjin (chŭng-jĭn') . . . Kor.	41·48 N	129·46 E
152	Chŏngju (chŭng-jōō') . . . Kor.	36·35 N	127·30 E
152	Chŏnju (chŭn-jōō') . . . Kor.	35·48 N	127·08 E
110	Chorley (chôr'lĭ) . . . Eng.	53·40 N	2·38 W
98	Chorrillos (chôr-rē'l-yōs) . . . Peru	12·17 S	76·55 W
121	Chortkov (chôrt'kôf) . . . Sov. Un.	49·01 N	25·48 E
121	Chorzów (kô-zhōōf') . . . Pol.	50·17 N	19·00 E
152	Chosan (chō-sän') . . . Kor.	40·44 N	125·48 E
79	Chosen (chō'z'n) . . . Fla. (In.)	26·41 N	80·41 W
152	Chōshi (chō'shē) . . . Jap.	35·40 N	140·55 E
120	Choszczno (chôsh'chnô) . . . Pol.	53·10 N	15·25 E
142	Chota Nagpur (Reg.) . . . India	28·20 N	81·40 E
67	Choteau (shō'tō) . . . Mont.	47·51 N	112·10 W
113	Chott el Hodna (L.) . . . Alg.	35·20 N	3·27 E
148	Chou (R.) (jēō) . . . China	31·59 N	114·57 E
148	Chouchiak'ou (jēō'jĭä'kō) . . China	33·39 N	114·40 E
149	Choup'u . . . China (Shanghai In.)	31·07 N	121·33 E
148	Chouts'un (jēō'tsōōn) . . . China	36·49 N	117·52 E
79	Chowan (R.) (chô-wän') . . . N. C.	36·13 N	76·46 W
150	Choybalsan . . . Mong.	47·50 N	114·15 E
159	Christchurch (krīst'chûrch) N. Z. (In.)	43·30 S	172·38 E
80	Christian (I.) (krĭs'chăn) . . . Can.	44·50 N	80·00 W
79	Christiansburg (krĭs'chănz-bûrg) Va.	37·08 N	80·25 W
89	Christiansted Vir. Is. (U. S. A.) (Puerto Rico In.)	17·45 N	64·44 W
154	Christmas (I.) . . . Ind. O.	10·35 S	105·40 E
157	Christmas (I.) Gilbert & Ellice Is.	2·20 N	157·40 W
73	Christopher (krĭs'tô-fēr) . . . Ill.	37·58 N	89·04 W
120	Chrudim (ĸrōō'dyĕm) . . . Czech.	49·57 N	15·46 E
121	Chrzanów (ĸzhä'nōōf) . . . Pol.	50·08 N	19·24 E
148	Ch'üanch'iao (chüän'jĭou) . . China	32·06 N	118·17 E
150	Chuangho . . . China	39·40 N	123·00 E
151	Ch'üanhsien . . . China	25·58 N	111·02 E
149	Ch'uansha . . . China (Shanghai In.)	31·12 N	121·41 E
100	Chubut (Prov.) (chōō-bōōt') . . Arg.	44·00 S	69·15 W
100	Chubut (chōō-bōōt') (R.) . . . Arg.	43·05 S	69·00 W
148	Chuch'eng (chōō'chĕng') . . . China	36·01 N	119·24 E
151	Chuchi . . . China	29·58 N	120·10 E
151	Ch'üchiang . . . China	24·58 N	113·42 E
149	Chu Chiang (Pearl R.) China (Canton In.)	23·04 N	113·28 E
148	Ch'üchou (chü'jēō) . . . China	36·47 N	114·58 E
84	Chuckatuck (chŭck ȧ-tŭck) Va. (Norfolk In.)	36·51 N	76·35 W
93	Chucunague, R. (chōō-kōō-nä'kå) Pan.	8·36 N	77·48 W
128	Chudovo (chŏŏ'dô-vô) . . . Sov. Un.	59·03 N	31·56 S
128	Chudskoye Oz. (Peipus, L.) (chŏŏt'skô-yĕ) . Sov. Un.	58·43 N	26·45 E
148	Ch'üfou (chü'fōō) . . . China	35·37 N	116·59 E
	Chuguchak, see T'ach''eng		
146	Chuguchak (Reg.) (chōō'gōō-chäk') . China	46·09 N	83·58 E
129	Chuguyev (chōō'gŏŏ-yĕf) . Sov. Un.	49·52 N	36·40 E
152	Chuguyevka (chŏŏ-gōō'yĕf-kȧ) Sov. Un.	43·58 N	133·49 E
70	Chugwater Cr. (chŭg'wô-tēr) Wyo.	41·43 N	104·54 W
150	Chuho . . . China	45·18 N	127·52 E
151	Ch'ühsien . . . China	28·58 N	118·58 E
148	Ch'ühsien (chōō'sĭän) . . . China	32·19 N	118·19 E
148	Chühsien (jü'sĭän) . . . China	35·35 N	118·50 E
146	Ch'uhsiung . . . China	25·19 N	101·34 E
148	Chühua Tao (I.) (jü'hōōä dou) China	40·30 N	120·47 E
148	Chüjung (jü'rōōng) . . . China	31·58 N	119·12 E
142	Chukhor . . . China	28·22 N	87·28 E
135	Chukot Natl. Okrug (Reg.) Sov. Un.	68·15 N	170·00 E
135	Chukotskiy (Chukot) P-Ov (Pen.) Sov. Un.	66·12 N	174·35 E
135	Chukotskoye Nagor'ye (Mts.) Sov. Un.	66·00 N	166·00 E
68	Chula Vista (chōō'lȧ vĭs'tȧ) Calif. (San Diego In.)	32·38 N	117·05 W
136	Chulkovo (chōōl-kô vô) Sov. Un. (Moscow In.)	55·33 N	38·04 E
98	Chulucanas (chōō-lōō-kä'näs) Peru	5·13 S	80·13 W
134	Chulum (R.) . . . Sov. Un.	57·52 N	84·45 E
148	Chüma (R.) (jü'mä) . . . China	39·37 N	115·45 E
135	Chumikan (chōō-mē-kän') Sov. Un.	54·47 N	135·09 E
152	Chunchŏn (chōōn-chŭn') . . . Kor.	37·51 N	127·46 E
148	Chungchia Shan (Mts.) (jōōng'jĭä shän) . China	32·42 N	118·19 E
151	Ch'ungch'ing (Chungking) (ch'ungch'ing) (chōōng'kĭng') China	29·38 N	107·30 E
151	Chunghsien . . . China	30·20 N	108·00 E
148	Chunghsing (jōōng'sĭng) . . . China	33·43 N	118·42 E
152	Chungju (chŭng'jōō') . . . Kor.	37·00 N	128·19 E
	Chungking, see Ch'ungch'ing		
151	Ch'ungming Tao (I.) . . . China	31·40 N	122·30 E
150	Chungwei (chōōng'wä) . . . China	37·32 N	105·10 E
134	Chunya (R.) (chōōn'yä') . Sov. Un.	61·45 N	101·28 E
100	Chuquicamata (chōō-kê-kä-mä'tä) Chile	22·08 S	68·57 W
120	Chur (kōōr) . . . Switz.	46·51 N	9·32 E
86	Churchill (chûrch'ĭl) . . . Can.	58·48 N	94·10 W
86	Churchill, C. . . . Can.	59·07 N	93·50 W
86	Churchill (R.) . . . Can.	57·00 N	95·21 W
86	Churchill Pk. . . . Can.	58·10 N	125·14 W
84	Churchland (chûrch-lănd) Va. (Norfolk In.)	36·52 N	76·24 W
110	Church Stretton (chûrch strĕt'ŭn) . Eng.	52·32 N	2·49 W
142	Churu . . . India	28·22 N	75·00 E
90	Churumuco (chōō-rōō-mōō'kō) Mex.	18·39 N	101·40 W
151	Chusan Archipelago (Is.) . . . China	30·00 N	123·00 E
151	Ch'ushien . . . China	30·40 N	106·48 E
69	Chuska, Mts. (chŭs-kȧ) Ariz.-N. Mex.	36·21 N	109·11 W
136	Chusovaya R. (chōō-sô-vä'yȧ) Sov. Un. (Urals In.)	58·08 N	58·35 E
136	Chusovoy (chōō-sô-vôy') Sov. Un. (Urals In.)	58·18 N	57·50 E
134	Chust (chŏŏst) . . . Sov. Un.	41·05 N	71·28 E
148	Chut'angtien (jō'däng'dĭän) China	31·59 N	114·13 E
148	Ch'uti (chü'tē) . . . China	37·07 N	117·17 E
132	Chuvash (A. S. S. R.) (chōō'vàsh) Sov. Un.	55·45 N	46·00 E
76	Chuviscar R. (chōō-vês-kär') Mex.	28·34 N	105·36 W
148	Ch'uwang (chōō'wäng) . . . China	36·08 N	114·53 E
154	Chu Yang Sin (Pk.) . . . Viet.	12·22 N	108·20 E
148	Chüyen (jü'yĕ) . . . China	35·24 N	116·05 E
	Cibao Mts., see Central, Cordillera		
76	Cibolo Cr. (sē'bô-lō) . . . Tex.	29·28 N	98·13 W
75	Cicero (sĭs'ēr-ō) . Ill. (Chicago In.)	41·50 N	87·46 W
133	Cide (jē'dĕ) . . . Tur.	41·50 N	33·00 E
121	Ciechanów (tsyĕ-kä'nōōf) . . . Pol.	52·52 N	20·39 E
94	Ciego de Avila (syā'gō dā ä'vê-lä) Cuba	21·50 N	78·45 W
124	Ciempozuelos (thyĕm-pô-thwā'lōs) Sp.	40·09 N	3·36 W
98	Ciénaga (syā'nä-gä) . . . Col.	11·01 N	74·15 W
94	Cienfuegos (syĕn-fwā'gōs) . . . Cuba	22·10 N	80·30 W
94	Cienfuegos, Bahía (B.) (bä-ē'ä-syĕn-fwā'gōs) . Cuba	22·00 N	80·35 W
93	Ciervo, Isla de la (I.) (ê's-lä-dĕ-lä-syĕ'r-vô) . Nic.	11·56 N	83·20 W
121	Cieszyn (tsyĕ'shĕn) . . . Pol.	49·47 N	18·45 E
124	Cieza (thyā'thä) . . . Sp.	38·13 N	1·25 W
90	Cihuatlán (sē-wä-tlä'n) . . . Mex.	19·13 N	104·36 W
90	Cihuatlán (R.) . . . Mex.	19·11 N	104·30 W
133	Cilician Gates (P.) . . . Tur.	37·30 N	35·30 E
116	Cill Mantainn (Wicklow) (kĭl män'tän) (wĭk'lō) . Ire.	52·59 N	6·06 W
72	Cimarron (R.), North Fk. . . . Colo.	37·13 N	102·30 W
72	Cimarron R. (sĭm-ȧ-rōn') . . . Okla.	36·26 N	98·47 W
127	Cîmpina . . . Rom.	45·08 N	25·47 E
127	Cîmpulung . . . Rom.	45·15 N	25·03 E
121	Cîmpulung Moldovenesc . . . Rom.	47·31 N	25·36 E
125	Cinca (R.) (thēŋ'kä) . . . Sp.	42·09 N	0·08 E
75	Cincinnati (sĭn-sĭ-nàt'ĭ) Ohio (Cincinnati In.)	39·08 N	84·30 W
94	Cinco Balas, Cayos (Is.) (kä'yōs-thēŋ'kō bä'läs) . Cuba	21·05 N	79·25 W
91	Cintalapa (sên-tä-lä'pä) . . . Mex.	16·41 N	93·44 W
91	Cintalapa (R.) . . . Mex.	16·46 N	93·36 W
126	Cinto, Mt. (chēn'tō) . . . Fr.	42·24 N	8·54 E
64	Circle (sûr'k'l) . . . Alaska	65·49 N	144·22 W
80	Circleville (sûr'k'lvĭl) . . . Ohio	39·35 N	83·00 W
	Cirenica, see Bargah		
76	Cisco (sĭs'kō) . . . Tex.	32·23 N	98·57 W
98	Cisneros (sês-nĕ'rôs) . . . Col. (In.)	5.33 N	75·05 W
125	Cisterna di Latina (chēs-tĕ'r-nä-dē-lä-tē'nä) . It. (Rome In.)	41·36 N	12·53 E
124	Cistierna (thês-tyĕr'nä) . . . Sp.	42·48 N	5·08 W
91	Citlaltépetl (Vol.) (sē-tlàl-tĕ'pĕtl) Mex.	19·04 N	97·14 W
78	Citronelle (cĭt-rô'nĕl) . . . Ala.	3·04 N	88·12 W
126	Cittadella (chēt-tä-dĕl'lä) . . . It.	45·39 N	11·51 E
126	Città di Castello (chēt-tä'dē käs-tĕl'lō) . It.	43·27 N	12·17 E
90	Ciudad Altamirano (syōō-dä'd-äl-tä-mē-rä'nō) . Mex.	18·24 N	100·38 W
98	Ciudad Bolívar (syōō-dhädh' bô-lē'vär) . Ven.	8·07 N	63·41 W
76	Ciudad Camargo (Santa Rosalia) (syōō-dhädh' kä-mär'gō) (sän'tä rō-sä'lēä) . Mex.	27·42 N	105·10 W
92	Ciudad Chetumal (Payo Obispo) (syōō-dhädh' chĕt-ōō-mäl) (pä'yō ō-bēs'pō) Mex. (Yucatan In.)	18·30 N	88·17 W
92	Ciudad Dario (syōō-dhädh'dä'rê-ō) . Nic.	12·44 N	86·08 W
91	Ciudad de las Casas (syōō-dä'd-dĕ-läs-kä'säs) . Mex.	16·44 N	92·39 W
91	Ciudad del Carmen (syōō-dä'd-dĕl-kä'r-mĕn) . Mex.	18·39 N	91·49 W
90	Ciudad del Maíz (syōō-dhädh'del mä-ēz') . Mex.	22·24 N	99·37 W
90	Ciudad de Valles (syōō-dhädh dā vä'lyās) . Mex.	21·59 N	99·02 W
125	Ciudadela (thyōō-dhä-dhā'lä) . Sp.	40·00 N	3·52 E
90	Ciudad Fernández (syōō-dhädh'fĕr-nän'dĕz) . Mex.	21·56 N	100·03 W
90	Ciudad Garcia (syōō-dhädh'gär-sē'ä) . Mex.	22·39 N	103·02 W
90	Ciudad Guzmán (syōō-dhädh'gōōz-män') . Mex.	19·40 N	103·29 W
90	Ciudad Hidalgo (syōō-dä'd-ê-dä'l-gō) . Mex.	19·41 N	100·35 W

Page	Name Pronunciation Region	Lat. °′	Long. °′
76	Ciudad Juárez (syōō-dhädh hwä'räz) . Mex.	31·44 N	106·28 W
91	Ciudad Madero (syōō-dä'd-mä-dě'-rô) . Mex.	22·16 N	97·52 W
90	Ciudad Mante (syōō-dä'd-män'tě) . Mex.	22·34 N	98·58 W
90	Ciudad Manuel Doblado (syōō-dä'd-män-wāl' dō-blä'dō) Mex.	20·43 N	101·57 W
88	Ciudad Obregon (syōō-dhädh-ô-brě-gô'n) . Mex.	27·40 N	109·58 W
124	Ciudad Real (thyōō-dhädh'rā-äl') . Sp.	38·59 N	3·55 W
124	Ciudad Rodrigo (thyōō-dhädh'rô-drē'gō) . Sp.	40·38 N	6·34 W
91	Ciudad Serdán (syōō-dä'd-sěr-dà'n) . Mex.	18·58 N	97·26 W
90	Ciudad Victoria (syōō-dhädh'vêk-tō'rê-ä) . Mex.	23·43 N	99·09 W
126	Civadale del Friuli (chē-vê-dä'lā-dĕl-frē-ōō'lē) . It.	46·06 N	13·24 E
126	Civitavecchia (chē'vê-tä-věk'kyä) It.	42·06 N	11·49 E
65	Clackamas (klăc-ká'măs) Ore. (Portland In.)	42·25 N	122·34 W
86	Claire (L.) (klâr) Can.	58·33 N	113·16 W
75	Clairton (klârtŭn) Pa. (Pittsburgh In.)	40·17 N	79·53 W
78	Clanton (klăn'tŭn) Ala.	32·50 N	86·38 W
80	Clare (klâr) Mich.	43·50 N	84·45 W
116	Clare (I.) Ire.	53·46 N	9·60 W
74	Claremont (klâr'mŏnt) Calif. (Los Angeles In.)	34·06 N	117·43 W
81	Claremont (klâr'mŏnt) N. H.	43·20 N	72·20 W
80	Claremont W. Va.	37·55 N	81·00 W
73	Claremore (klâr'mōr) Okla.	36·16 N	95·37 W
116	Claremorris (klâr-mŏr'ĭs) Ire.	53·46 N	9·05 W
158	Clarence Str. (klăr'ěns) Austl.	12·15 S	130·05 E
95	Clarence Town Ba. Is.	23·05 N	75·00 W
73	Clarendon (klâr'ěn-dŭn) Ark.	34·42 N	91·17 W
72	Clarendon Tex.	34·55 N	100·52 W
167	Clarens (clâ-rĕns) S. Afr. (Natal In.)	28·34 S	28·26 E
86	Claresholm (klâr'ěs-hōlm) Can.	50·01 N	113·30 W
71	Clarinda (klá-rĭn'dá) Iowa	40·42 N	95·00 W
99	Clarines (klä-rē'něs) Ven. (In.)	9·57 N	65·10 W
71	Clarion (klăr'ĭ-ŭn) Iowa	42·43 N	93·45 W
81	Clarion Pa.	41·10 N	79·25 W
70	Clark (klärk) S. D.	44·52 N	97·45 W
80	Clark, Pt. Can.	44·05 N	81·50 W
82	Clark City Can.	50·12 N	66·38 W
69	Clarkdale (klärk-dāl) Ariz.	34·45 N	112·05 W
159	Clarke Ra. Austl.	20·30 S	148·00 E
82	Clarkes Harbour (klärks) Can.	43·28 N	65·37 W
67	Clark Fork R. Mont.	47·50 N	115·35 W
79	Clark Hill Res. (klärk-hĭl) Ga.-S. C.	33·50 N	82·35 W
81	Clarksburg (klärkz'bûrg) W. Va.	39·15 N	80·20 W
78	Clarksdale (klärks-dāl) Miss.	34·10 N	90·31 W
85	Clarkson Can. (Toronto In.)	43·31 N	79·38 W
84	Clarkston (klärks'-tŭn) Ga. (Atlanta In.)	33·49 N	84·15 W
66	Clarkston Wash.	46·24 N	117·01 W
73	Clarksville (klärks-vĭl) Ark.	35·28 N	93·26 W
78	Clarksville Tenn.	36·30 N	87·23 W
73	Clarksville Tex.	33·37 N	95·02 W
65	Clatskanie Oreg. (Portland In.)	46·06 N	123·11 W
65	Clatskanie (R.) (klăt-skā'nê) Ore. (Portland In.)	46·06 N	123·11 W
65	Clatsop Spit (klăt-sŏp) Ore. (Portland In.)	46·13 N	124·04 W
101	Cláudio (klou'-dēō) Braz. (Rio de Janeiro In.)	20·26 S	44·44 W
151	Claveria (klä-vâ-rē'ä) Phil.	18·38 N	121·08 E
75	Clawson (klô's'n) Mich. (Detroit In.)	42·32 N	83·09 W
79	Claxton (klăks'tŭn) Ga.	32·07 N	81·54 W
78	Clay (klā) Ky.	37·28 N	87·50 W
65	Clayburn (klā'bûrn) Can. (Vancouver In.)	49·05 N	122·17 W
73	Clay Center (klā sĕn'tēr) Kans.	39·23 N	97·08 W
80	Clay City (klā sĭ'tĭ) Ky.	37·50 N	83·55 W
74	Claycomo (kla-kō'mo) Mo. (Kansas City In.)	39·12 N	94·30 W
110	Clay Cross (klā krŏs) Eng.	53·10 N	1·25 W
123	Claye-Souilly (klĕ-sōō-yē') Fr. (Paris In.)	48·56 N	2·43 E
84	Claymont (klā-mŏnt) Del. (Philadelphia In.)	39·48 N	75·28 W
78	Clayton (klā'tŭn) Ala.	31·52 N	85·25 W
65	Clayton Calif. (San Francisco In.)	37·56 N	122·56 W
110	Clayton Eng.	53·47 N	1·49 W
74	Clayton Mo. (St. Louis In.)	38·39 N	90·20 W
72	Clayton N. Mex.	36·26 N	103·12 W
79	Clayton N. C.	35·40 N	78·27 W
68	Clear, (L.) Calif.	39·05 N	122·50 W
116	Clear, C. (klēr) Ire.	51·24 N	9·15 W
73	Clear Boggy Cr. (klēr bŏg'ĭ krēk) Okla.	34·21 N	96·22 W
69	Clear Cr. Ariz.	34·40 N	111·05 W
67	Clear Cr. Wyo.	44·35 N	106·20 W
81	Clearfield (klēr-fēld) Pa.	41·00 N	78·25 W
74	Clearfield Utah (Salt Lake City In.)	41·07 N	112·01 W
86	Clear Hills Can.	57·11 N	119·20 W
71	Clear Lake Iowa	43·09 N	93·23 W
65	Clear Lake Wash. (Seattle In.)	48·27 N	122·14 W
66	Clear Lake Res. Calif.	41·53 N	121·00 W
77	Clear R. Tex. (In.)	29·34 N	95·13 W
77	Clearwater (klēr-wô'tēr) Fla. (In.)	27·43 N	82·45 W
66	Clearwater Mts. Idaho	45·56 N	115·15 W
73	Clearwater Res. Mo.	37·20 N	91·04 W
66	Clearwater R. Idaho	46·27 N	116·33 W
66	Clearwater R., Middle Fork Idaho	46·10 N	115·48 W
66	Clearwater R., North Fork Idaho	46·34 N	116·08 W
66	Clearwater R., South Fork Idaho	45·46 N	115·53 W
77	Cleburne (klē'bŭrn) Tex.	32·21 N	97·23 W
110	Clee Hill (klē) Eng.	52·24 N	2·37 W
66	Cle Elum (klē ĕl'ŭm) Wash.	47·12 N	120·55 W
84	Clementon (klē'měn-tŭn) N. J. (Philadelphia In.)	39·49 N	75·00 W
110	Cleobury Mortimer (klē'ô-bĕr'ĭ môr'tĭ-měr) Eng.	52·22 N	2·29 W
159	Clermont (klĕr'mŏnt) Austl.	23·02 S	147·46 E
75	Clermont Ind. (Indianapolis In.)	39·48 N	86·19 W
122	Clermont-Ferrand (klěr-môN'fĕr-räN') Fr.	45·47 N	3·03 E
122	Clermont l'Herault (klĕr-mŏN' lā-rō') Fr.	43·38 N	3·22 E
78	Cleveland (klēv'lănd) Miss.	33·45 N	90·42 W
75	Cleveland Ohio (Cleveland In.)	41·30 N	81·42 W
73	Cleveland Okla.	36·18 N	96·28 W
78	Cleveland Tenn.	35·09 N	84·52 W
77	Cleveland Tex.	30·18 N	95·05 W
75	Cleveland Heights Ohio (Cleveland In.)	41·30 N	81·35 W
75	Cleves (klē'vĕs) Ohio (Cincinnati In.)	39·10 N	84·45 W
116	Clew (B.) (klōō) Ire.	53·47 N	9·45 W
79	Clewiston (klē'wĭs-tŭn) Fla. (In.)	26·44 N	80·55 W
123	Clichy-la-Garennel (klē-shē'-lä-gä-rě-nĕl') Fr. (Paris In.)	48·54 N	2·18 E
116	Clifden (klĭf'děn) Ire.	53·31 N	10·04 W
69	Clifton (klĭf'tŭn) Ariz.	33·05 N	109·20 W
84	Clifton N. J. (New York In.)	40·35 N	74·09 W
79	Clifton S. C.	35·00 N	81·47 W
77	Clifton Tex.	31·45 N	97·31 W
81	Clifton Forge Va.	37·50 N	79·50 W
78	Clinch Res. (klĭnch) Tenn.-Va.	36·30 N	83·19 W
78	Clingmans Dome, (Mtn.) (klĭng'măns dōm) N. C.	35·37 N	83·26 W
86	Clinton (klĭn-tŭn) Can.	51·09 N	121·40 W
80	Clinton Ill.	40·10 N	88·55 W
80	Clinton Ind.	39·40 N	87·25 W
71	Clinton Iowa	41·50 N	90·13 W
78	Clinton Ky.	36·39 N	88·56 W
83	Clinton Mass. (Boston In.)	42·25 N	71·41 W
73	Clinton Mo.	38·23 N	93·46 W
79	Clinton N. C.	35·58 N	78·20 W
72	Clinton Okla.	35·31 N	98·56 W
79	Clinton S. C.	34·27 N	81·53 W
78	Clinton Tenn.	36·05 N	84·08 W
65	Clinton Wash. (Seattle In.)	47·59 N	122·22 W
86	Clinton-Colden (L.) Can.	63·58 N	106·34 W
75	Clinton R. Mich. (Detroit In.)	42·36 N	83·00 W
71	Clintonville (klĭn'tŭn-vĭl) Wis.	44·37 N	88·46 W
80	Clio (klē'ō) Mich.	43·10 N	83·45 W
158	Cloates, Pt. (klōts) Austl.	22·47 S	113·45 E
168	Clocolan S. Afr. (Johannesburg & Pretoria In.)	28·56 S	27·35 E
116	Clonakilty B. (klŏn-á-kĭltē) Ire.	51·30 N	8·50 W
158	Cloncurry (klŏn-kŭr'ê) Austl.	20·58 S	140·42 E
116	Clonmel (klŏn-měl) Ire.	52·21 N	7·45 W
74	Cloquet (klô-kā') Minn. (Duluth In.)	46·28 N	92·28 W
71	Cloquet (R.) Minn.	47·02 N	92·17 W
84	Closter (clōs'tēr) N. J. (New York In.)	40·58 N	74·57 W
67	Cloud Pk. (kloud) Wyo.	44·23 N	107·11 W
74	Clough (klou'h) Minn. (Minneapolis, St. Paul In.)	45·08 N	93·14 W
79	Clover (klō'vēr) S. C.	35·08 N	81·08 W
85	Clover Bar (klō'vēr bär) Can. (Edmonton In.)	53·34 N	113·20 W
68	Cloverdale (klō'vēr-dāl) Calif.	38·47 N	123·03 W
65	Cloverdale Can. (Vancouver In.)	49·06 N	122·44 W
80	Cloverport (klō'vēr pōrt) Ky.	37·50 N	86·35 W
72	Clovis (klō'vĭs) N. Mex.	34·24 N	103·11 W
121	Cluj (klōōzh) Rom.	46·46 N	23·34 E
110	Clun (R.) (klŭn) Eng.	52·25 N	2·56 W
122	Cluny (klü-nē') Fr.	46·27 N	4·40 E
159	Clutha (R.) (klōō'thá) N. Z. (In.)	45·26 S	169·15 E
73	Clyde (klīd) Kans.	39·34 N	97·23 W
80	Clyde Ohio	41·15 N	83·00 W
116	Clyde (L.) Scot.	55·35 N	3·50 W
116	Clyde, Firth of (fûrth ŏv klīd) Scot.	55·28 N	5·01 W
116	Clydebank Scot.	55·56 N	4·20 W
124	Côa (R.) (kô'ä) Port.	40·28 N	6·55 W
91	Coacalco (kō-ä-käl'kō) Mex. (Mexico City In.)	19·37 N	99·06 W
68	Coachella, Can. (kō'chĕl-lá) Calif.	30·10 N	115·23 W
90	Coahuayana, Rio de (R.) (rê'ō-dě-kō-ä-wä-yä'nä) Mex.	19·00 N	103·33 W
90	Coahuayutla (kō-ä-wē'lä) Mex.	18·19 N	101·44 W
88	Coahuila (State) (kō-ä-wē'lä) Mex.	27·30 N	103·00 W
75	Coal City (kōl sĭ'tĭ) Ill. (Chicago In.)	41·17 N	88·17 W
90	Coalcomán, Sierra de (Mts.) (syěr'rä dā kō-äl-kō-män') Mex.	18·30 N	102·45 W
90	Coalcomán, Rio de (R.) (rê'ō-dě-kō-äl-kō-män') Mex.	18·30 N	102·48 W
90	Coalcomán de Matamoros (kō-äl-kō-män' dä mä-tä-mō'rôs) Mex.	18·46 N	103·10 W
73	Coalgate (kōl'gāt) Okla.	34·33 N	96·13 W
80	Coal Grove (kōl grōv) Ohio	38·20 N	82·40 W
68	Coalinga (kō-á-lĭŋ'gá) Calif.	36·09 N	120·23 W
110	Coalville (kōl'vĭl) Eng.	52·43 N	1·21 W
89	Coamo (kō-ä'mō) P. R. (Puerto Rico In.)	18·05 N	66·21 W
98	Coari (kō-är'ê) Braz.	4·06 S	63·10 W
86	Coast Mts. (kōst) Can.	57·10 N	131·05 W
62	Coast Ranges, (Mts.) U. S.	41·28 N	123·30 W
90	Coatepec (kō-ä-tā-pěk) Mex.	19·23 N	98·44 W
91	Coatepec Mex.	19·26 N	96·56 W
91	Coatepec Mex. (Mexico City In.)	19·08 N	99·25 W
92	Coatepeque (kō-ä-tā-pā'kā) Guat.	14·40 N	91·52 W
92	Coatepeque Sal.	13·56 N	89·30 W
81	Coatesville (kōts'vĭl) Pa.	40·00 N	75·50 W
90	Coatetelco (kō-ä-tâ-těl'kō) Mex.	18·43 N	99·47 W
81	Coaticook (kō'tĭ-kŏŏk) Can.	45·10 N	71·55 W
91	Coatlinchán (kô-ä-tlē'n-chä'n) Mex. (Mexico City In.)	19·26 N	98·52 W
87	Coats (I.) (kōts) Can.	62·23 N	82·11 W
47	Coats Land (Reg.) Ant.	74·00 S	12·00 W
91	Coatzacoalcos (Puerto Mexico) kō-ät'zä-kō-äl'kōs) (pwě'r-tô-mě'-kē-kō) Mex.	18·09 N	94·26 W
91	Coatzacoalcos (R.) Mex.	17·40 N	94·41 W
92	Coba (Ruins) (kô'bä) Mex. (Yucatan In.)	20·23 N	87·23 W
87	Cobalt (kō'bôlt) Can.	47·21 N	79·40 W
92	Cobán (kō-bän') Guat.	15·28 N	90·19 W
160	Cobberas, Mt. (cŏ-bēr-ăs) Austl.	36·45 S	148·15 E
82	Cobequid B. (kŏb'ê-kwĭd) Can.	45·22 N	63·50 W
116	Cobh (kôv) Ire.	51·52 N	8·09 W
98	Cobija (kô-bē'hä) Bol.	11·12 S	68·49 W
81	Cobourg (kō'bŏŏrgh) Can.	43·55 N	78·05 W
94	Cobre (R.) (kô'brā) Jam.	18·05 N	77·00 W
120	Coburg (kō'bŏŏrg) Ger.	50·16 N	10·57 E
143	Cocanāda (kō-kō-nä'dá) India	16·58 N	82·18 E
125	Cocentaina (kō-thân-tä-ē'ná) Sp.	38·44 N	0·27 W
98	Cochabamba (kō-chä-bäm'bà) Bol.	17·28 S	65·43 W
123	Cochem (kō'kěm) Ger.	50·10 N	7·06 E
143	Cochin (kō-chĭn') India	9·58 N	76·19 E
154	Cochin (Reg.) Viet.	9·45 N	107·20 E
94	Cochinos, Bahia (B.) (bä-ē'ä-kô-chē'nōs) Cuba	22·05 N	81·10 W
95	Cochinos Bks. Ba. Is.	22·20 N	76·15 W
155	Cochinos Pt. (kô-chē'-nôs) Phil. (Manila In.)	14·25 N	120·15 E
78	Cochran (kŏk'răn) Ga.	32·23 N	83·23 W
87	Cochrane (kŏk'răn) Can.	49·01 N	81·06 W
85	Cochrane Can. (Calgary In.)	51·11 N	114·28 W
80	Cockburn (I.) (kŏk-bûrn) Can.	45·55 N	83·25 W
81	Cockeysville (kŏk'ĭz-vĭl) Md.	39·30 N	76·40 W
74	Cockrell Hill (kŏk'rēl) Tex. (Dallas, Fort Worth In.)	32·44 N	96·53 W
98	Coco, Isla del (I.) (ê's-lä-dĕl-kô-kô) C. R.	5·33 N	87·02 W
94	Coco, Cayo (I.) (kä'yō-kô'kô) Cuba	22·30 N	78·30 W
79	Cocoa (kō'kō) Fla. (In.)	28·21 N	80·44 W
79	Cocoa Beach Fla. (In.)	28·09 N	80·37 W
88	Cocoli (kô-kô'lē) C. Z. (Panama Canal In.)	8·58 N	79·36 W
69	Coconino, Plat. (kō kō nē'nō) Ariz.	35·45 N	112·28 W
93	Coco R. (Segovia) (kô-kô) (sě-gô'vyä) Hond.	14·55 N	83·45 W
7	Cocos (Keeling) (kō'kōs) (kē'lĭng) Is. Oceania	11·50 S	90·50 E
88	Coco Solito (kô-kô-sŏ-lē'tô) C. Z. (Panama Canal In.)	9·21 N	79·53 W
82	Cocouna Can.	47·54 N	69·31 W
90	Cocula (kō-kōō'lä) Mex.	20·23 N	103·47 W
90	Cocula (R.) Mex.	18·17 N	99·11 W
98	Codajás (kō-dä-häzh') Braz.	3·44 S	62·09 W
99	Codera, Cabo (C.) (ká'bō-kō-dě'rä) Ven. (In.)	10·35 N	66·06 W
99	Codó (kō'dō) Braz.	4·21 S	43·52 W
126	Codogno (kô-dō'nyō) It.	45·08 N	9·43 E
93	Codrington (kŏd'rĭng-tŭn) Barbuda (Le. & Wind. Is. In.)	17·39 N	61·49 W
67	Cody (kō'dĭ) Wyo.	44·31 N	109·02 W
123	Coesfeld (kûs'fĕld) Ger. (Ruhr In.)	51·56 N	7·10 E
66	Coeur d' Alene (kûr dá-lān') Idaho	47·43 N	116·35 W
66	Coeur d' Alene L. Idaho	47·32 N	116·39 W
66	Coeur d' Alene R. Idaho	47·26 N	116·35 W
167	Coffee Bay (cŏfē bā) S. Afr. (Natal In.)	31·58 S	29·10 E
73	Coffeyville (kŏf'ĭ-vĭl) Kans.	37·01 N	95·38 W
160	Coff's Harbour Austl.	30·20 S	153·10 E
167	Cofimvaba (căfĭm'vä-bá) S. Afr. (Natal In.)	32·01 S	27·37 E
126	Coghinas (R.) (kō'gē-nás) It.	40·31 N	9·00 E
122	Cognac (kôn-yak') Fr.	45·41 N	0·22 W
83	Cohasset (kô-hăs'ĕt) Mass. (Boston In.)	42·14 N	70·48 W
81	Cohoes (kô-hōz') N. Y.	42·50 N	73·40 W
100	Coig (kô'ěk) (R.) Arg.	51·15 S	71·00 W
143	Coimbatore (kō-ēm-bá-tōr') India	11·03 N	76·56 E
124	Coimbra (kô-ēm'brä) Port.	40·14 N	8·23 W
124	Coín (kô-ēn') Sp.	36·40 N	4·45 W
125	Coina (kô-ē'ná) Port. (Lisbon In.)	38·35 N	9·03 W
125	Coina (R.) (kō'y-nä) Port. (Lisbon In.)	38·35 N	9·02 W
98	Coipasa, Salar de (Salt Flat) (sä-lä'r-dě-koi-pä'-sä) Chile	19·12 S	69·13 W
91	Coixtlahuaca (kō-ēks'tlä-wä'kä) Mex.	17·42 N	97·17 W
99	Cojedes (State) (kô-kě'děs) Ven. (In.)	9·50 N	68·21 W
95	Cojimar (kō-hê-mär') Cuba (Havana In.)	23·10 N	82·19 W
92	Cojutepeque (kô-hōō-tě-pā'kå) Sal.	13·45 N	88·50 W
71	Cokato (kō-kā'tō) Minn.	45·03 N	94·11 W
75	Cokeburg (kōk bûgh) Pa. (Pittsburgh In.)	40·06 N	80·03 W
160	Colac (kŏ'lăc) Austl.	38·25 S	143·40 E
125	Colares (kô-lä'rěs) Port. (Lisbon In.)	38·47 N	9·27 W
99	Colatina (kō-lä-tē'nä) Braz.	19·33 S	40·42 W
72	Colby (kōl'bĭ) Kans.	39·23 N	101·04 W
101	Colchagua (Prov.) (kôl-chä'gwä) Chile (Santiago In.)	36·42 S	71·24 W
117	Colchester (kōl'chěs-tēr) Eng.	51·52 N	0·50 E
83	Cold Spring Pd. (kōld) Can.	48·08 N	56·25 W
72	Coldwater (kōld'wô-tēr) Kans.	37·14 N	99·21 W
80	Coldwater Mich.	41·55 N	85·00 W
78	Coldwater (R.) Miss.	34·25 N	90·12 W
72	Coldwater Cr. Tex.	36·10 N	101·45 W

n-sing ŋ-baŋk; N-nasalized n; nŏd; cŏmmit; ōld; ôbey; ôrder; fōōd; fŏŏt; ou-out; s-soft; sh-dish; th-thin; pūre; ûnite; ûrn; stŭd; circŭs; ü-as "y" in study; '-indeterminate vowel.

Page	Name Pronunciation Region	Lat. °′	Long. °′
76	Coleman (kōl'măn) Tex.	31·50 N	99·25 W
167	Colenso (kŏ-lĕnz'ô) S. Afr. (Natal In.)	28·48 S	29·49 E
116	Coleraine (kōl-rān') N. Ire.	54·66 N	6·40 W
71	Coleraine Minn.	47·16 N	93·29 W
110	Coleshill (kōlz'hĭl) Eng.	52·30 N	1·42 W
71	Colfax (kōl'făks) Iowa	41·40 N	93·13 W
77	Colfax La.	31·31 N	92·42 W
66	Colfax Wash.	46·53 N	117·21 W
100	Colhué Huapi (L.) (kôl-wā'ōō'ȧ'pê). Arg.	45·30 S	68·45 W
168	Coligny..S. Afr. (Johannesburg & Pretoria In.)	26·20 S	26·18 E
90	Colima (kōlē'mä) Mex.	19·13 N	103·45 W
90	Colima, Vol. de (vôl-kä'n-dĕ-kô-lē'mä). Mex.	19·30 N	103·38 W
116	Coll (I.) (kŏl) Scot.	56·42 N	6·23 W
84	College Park (kŏl'ĕj) Ga. (Atlanta In.)	33·39 N	84·27 W
84	Collegeville (kŏl'ĕj-vĭl) Pa. (Philadelphia In.)	40·11 N	75·27 W
158	Collie (kŏl'ē) Austl.	33·20 S	116·20 E
158	Collier B. (kŏl-yẽr) Austl.	15·30 S	123·30 E
125	Colli Laziali (Mtn.) (kô'lē-lät-zyȧ'lē). It. (Rome In.)	41·46 N	12·45 E
84	Collingswood (kŏl'ĭngz-wŏŏd) N. J. (Philadelphia In.)	39·54 N	75·04 W
80	Collingwood Can.	44·30 N	80·20 W
78	Collins (kŏl'ĭns) Miss.	31·40 N	89·34 W
74	Collinsville (kŏl'ĭnz-vĭl) Ill. (St. Louis In.)	38·41 N	89·59 W
73	Collinsville Okla.	36·21 N	95·50 W
164	Collo (kôl'ō) Alg.	37·02 N	6·29 E
123	Colmar (kôl'mär) Fr.	48·40 N	7·22 E
124	Colmenar de Oreja (kôl-mä-när'dāōrā'hä). Sp.	40·06 N	3·25 W
125	Colmenar Viejo (kôl-mä-när'vyā'hō) Sp. (Madrid In.)	40·40 N	3·46 W
	Cologne, see Köln		
164	Colomb-Béchar Alg.	31·39 N	2·14 W
98	Colombia (kô-lôm'bê-ä). Col. (In.)	3·23 N	74·48 W
96	Colombia S. A.	3·30 N	72·30 W
143	Colombo (kô-lôm'bō) Ceylon	6·58 N	79·52 E
101	Colón (kō-lōn') Arg. (Buenos Aires In.)	33·55 S	61·08 W
88	Colón (kŏ-lô'n) C. Z. (Panama Canal In.)	9·22 N	79·54 W
94	Colón (kô-lô'n) Cuba	22·45 N	80·55 W
90	Colón (kō-lōn') Mex.	20·46 N	100·02 W
98	Colon, Arch. de (Galápagos Is.) (är-chê-pyĕ'l-ägô-dĕ-kō-lōn') (gä-lá'pägôs). Ec.	0·10 S	87·45 W
93	Colōn, Montañas de (Mts.) (môn-tä'n-yäs-dĕ-kŏ-lô'n) Hond.	14·58 N	84·39 W
101	Colonia (kō-lō'nê-ä) Ur. (Buenos Aires In.)	34·27 S	57·50 W
101	Colonia (Dept.) Ur. (Buenos Aires In.)	34·08 S	57·50 W
101	Colonia Suiza (kô-lô'nêä-sōōē'zä) Ur. (Buenos Aires In.)	34·17 S	57·15 W
125	Colonna (kô-lô'n-nä). It. (Rome In.)	41·50 N	12·48 E
127	Colonne, C. di (kô-lô'n-nĕ). It.	39·02 N	17·15 E
116	Colonsay (I.) (kŏl-ôn-sā') Scot.	56·08 N	6·08 W
100	Coloradas, Lomas (Hills) (lô'mäs-kō-lō-rä'däs). Arg.	43·30 S	68·00 W
76	Colorado (kŏl-ô-rä'dō) Tex.	32·24 N	100·50 W
62	Colorado (State) U. S.	39·30 N	106·55 W
62	Colorado, R. U. S.	36·25 N	112·00 W
100	Colorado, Rio (R.) Arg.	38·30 S	66·00 W
69	Colorado Natl. Mon. Colo.	39·00 N	108·40 W
62	Colorado Plat U. S.	36·20 N	109·25 W
77	Colorado R. Tex.	30·08 N	97·33 W
69	Colorado River Ind. Res. Ariz.	34·03 N	114·02 W
68	Colorado River Aqueducts. Calif.	33·38 N	115·43 W
94	Colorados, Arch. de los (Is.) (är-chē-pyĕ-lä-gô-dĕ-lôs-kô-lô-rä'dōs) Cuba	22·25 N	84·25 W
72	Colorado Springs (kŏl-ô-rä'dō) Colo.	38·49 N	104·48 W
91	Colotepec (R.) (kô-lô'tĕ-pĕk) Mex.	15·56 N	96·57 W
90	Colotlán (kô-lô-tlän') Mex.	22·06 N	103·14 W
90	Colotlán (R.) Mex.	22·09 N	103·17 W
98	Colquechaca (kôl-kä-chä'kä). Bol.	18·47 S	66·02 W
67	Colstrip (kōl'strĭp) Mont.	45·54 N	106·38 W
74	Colton (kōl'tŭn) Calif. (Los Angeles In.)	34·04 N	117·20 W
74	Columbia (kô-lŭm'bĭ-ȧ) Ill. (St. Louis In.)	38·26 N	90·12 W
78	Columbia Ky.	37·06 N	85·15 W
78	Columbia Miss.	31·15 N	89·49 W
73	Columbia Mo.	38·55 N	92·19 W
81	Columbia Pa.	40·00 N	76·25 W
79	Columbia S. C.	34·00 N	81·00 W
78	Columbia Tenn.	35·36 N	87·02 W
80	Columbia City Ind.	41·10 N	85·30 W
65	Columbia City Ore. (Portland In.)	45·53 N	122·49 W
74	Columbia Heights Minn. (Minneapolis, St. Paul In.)	45·03 N	93·15 W
78	Columbiana (kô-lŭm-bĭ-ă'nȧ). Ala.	33·10 N	86·35 W
62	Columbia R. U. S.-Can.	46·20 N	123·00 W
125	Columbretes (I.) (kô-lōōm-brĕ'tĕs). Sp.	39·54 N	0·54 E
78	Columbus (kô-lŭm'bŭs) Ga.	32·29 N	84·56 W
80	Columbus Ind.	39·15 N	85·55 W
73	Columbus Kans.	37·10 N	94·50 W
78	Columbus Miss.	33·30 N	88·25 W
67	Columbus Mont.	45·39 N	109·15 W
70	Columbus Nebr.	41·25 N	97·25 W
69	Columbus N. Mex.	31·50 N	107·40 W
80	Columbus Ohio	40·00 N	83·00 W
77	Columbus Tex.	29·44 N	96·34 W
71	Columbus Wis.	43·20 N	89·01 W
95	Columbus Bk. (kô-lŭm'bŭs). Ba. Is.	22·05 N	75·30 W
80	Columbus Grove Ohio	40·55 N	84·00 W
95	Columbus Pt. Ba. Is.	24·10 N	75·15 W
68	Colusa (kô-lū'sȧ) Calif.	39·12 N	122·01 W
66	Colville (kŏl'vĭl) Wash.	48·33 N	117·53 W
64	Colville (R.) Alaska	69·00 N	156·25 W
66	Colville R. Wash.	48·25 N	117·58 W
65	Colvos Pass. (kŏl'vōs) Wash. (Seattle In.)	47·24 N	122·32 W
65	Colwood (kŏl'wŏŏd) Can. (Seattle In.)	48·26 N	123·30 W
126	Comacchio (kô-mäk'kyō) It.	44·42 N	12·12 E
90	Comala (kō-mä-lä') Mex.	19·22 N	103·47 W
92	Comalapa (kō-mä-lä'-pä) Guat.	14·43 N	90·56 W
91	Comalcalco (kō-mäl-käl'kō). Mex.	18·16 N	93·13 W
72	Comanche (kô-măn'chê) Okla.	34·20 N	97·58 W
76	Comanche Tex.	31·54 N	98·37 W
76	Comanche Cr. Tex.	31·02 N	102·47 W
92	Comayagua (kō-mä-yä'gwä) Hond.	14·24 N	87·36 W
79	Combahee (R.) (kŏm-bȧ-hē'). S. C.	32·42 N	80·40 W
78	Comer (kŭm'ẽr) Ga.	34·02 N	83·07 W
95	Comete, C. (kô-mā'tā) Caicos	21·45 N	71·25 W
142	Comilla (kô-mĭl'ä) E. Pak.	23·33 N	91·17 E
126	Comino, C. (kô-mē'nō) It.	40·30 N	9·48 E
91	Comitán (kô-mê-tän') Mex.	16·16 N	92·09 W
65	Commencement Bay (kŏ-mĕns'mĕnt bā) Wash. (Seattle In.)	47·17 N	122·21 W
122	Commentry (kō-mäN-trē') Fr.	46·16 N	2·44 E
78	Commerce (kŏm'ẽrs) Ga.	34·10 N	83·27 W
73	Commerce Okla.	36·57 N	94·54 W
73	Commerce Tex.	33·15 N	95·52 W
85	Como (kō'mō). Can. (Montreal In.)	45·27 N	74·08 W
126	Como It.	45·48 N	9·03 E
126	Como, Lago di (L.) (lä'gō-dē-kō'mō). It.	46·00 N	9·30 E
100	Comodoro Rivadavia (kō'mō-dō'rō rē-vä-dä'vê-ä). Arg.	45·47 S	67·31 W
90	Comonfort (kô-mōn-fô'rt). Mex.	20·43 N	100·47 W
167	Comores, Archipel des (Is.) (är-chē-pĕ'lä-gô-dĕs-kô-mô'rĕs) Afr.	11·46 S	44·12 E
143	Comorin C. (kŏ'mô-rĭn) Ind.	13·18 N	77·16 E
91	Compainalá (kôm-pä-ē-nä-lä') Mex.	17·05 N	93·11 W
101	Companario, Cerro (Mtn.) (sĕ'r-rô-kôm-pä-nä'ryô) Arg.-Chile (Santiago In.)	35·54 S	70·23 W
122	Compiègne (kôN-pyĕn'y') Fr.	49·25 N	2·49 E
125	Comporta (kôm-pôr'tä) Port. (Lisbon In.)	38·24 N	8·48 W
90	Compostela (kōm-pô-stā'lä). Mex.	21·41 N	104·54 W
74	Compton (kŏmp'tŭn) Calif. (Los Angeles In.)	33·54 N	118·14 W
78	Cona (R.) (kō-nȧ) Ga.	34·40 N	84·51 W
164	Conakry (kô-nȧ-krē') Gui.	9·29 N	13·45 W
84	Conanicut (kŏn'ȧ-nĭ-kŭt) R. I. (Providence In.)	41·34 N	71·20 W
122	Concarneau (kôn-kär-nō') Fr.	47·54 N	3·52 W
99	Concepción (kôn-sĕp'syōn'). Bol.	15·47 S	61·08 W
100	Concepción Chile	36·51 S	72·59 W
93	Concepcion Pan.	8·31 N	82·38 W
100	Concepción Par.	23·29 S	57·18 W
155	Concepcion. Phil. (Manila In.)	15·19 N	120·40 E
88	Concepción (R.) Mex.	30·25 N	112·20 W
92	Concepción (Vol.) Nic.	11·36 N	85·43 W
92	Concepcion del Mar (kôn-sĕp-syōn' dĕl mär'). Guat.	14·07 N	91·23 W
76	Concepcion del Oro (kôn-sĕp-syōn' dĕl ō'rō). Mex.	24·39 N	101·24 W
100	Concepción del Uruguay (kôn-sĕp-syō'n-dĕl-ōō-rōō-gwī'). Arg.	32·31 S	53·13 W
95	Conceptión (I.) Ba. Is.	23·50 N	75·05 W
68	Conception, Pt. Calif.	34·27 N	120·28 W
83	Conception B. (kŏn-sĕp'shŭn). Can.	47·50 N	52·50 W
76	Concho R. (kŏn'chō) Tex.	31·34 N	100·02 W
76	Conchos R. Mex.	29·08 N	105·02 W
76	Conchos R. (kŏn'chōs) Mex.	25·03 N	99·00 W
65	Concord (kŏŋ'kŏrd) Calif. (San Francisco In.)	37·58 N	122·02 W
83	Concord Mass. (Boston In.)	42·28 N	71·21 W
81	Concord N. H.	43·10 N	71·30 W
79	Concord N. C.	35·23 N	80·11 W
100	Concordia (kŏn-kôr'dĭ-ȧ) Arg.	31·18 S	57·59 W
98	Concordia Col. (In.)	6·04 N	75·54 W
73	Concordia Kans.	39·32 N	97·39 W
90	Concordia (kôn-kô'r-dyä). Mex.	23·17 N	106·06 W
66	Concrete (kŏn'krēt) Wash.	48·33 N	121·44 W
70	Conde (kŏn-dē') S. D.	45·10 N	98·06 W
92	Condega (kŏn-dĕ'gä) Nic.	13·20 N	86·27 W
122	Condem (kôN-dĕN) Fr.	43·58 N	0·22 E
113	Condé-Smendou (kôN-dā'smăN-dōō'). Alg.	36·34 N	6·51 E
122	Condé-sur-Noireau (kôN-dā'sür-nwä-rō'). Fr.	48·50 N	0·36 W
99	Condeúba (kōn-dā-ōō'bä). Braz.	14·47 S	41·44 W
66	Condon (kŏn'dŭn) Ore.	45·14 N	120·10 W
78	Conecun (R.) (kô-nē'kŭ) Ala.	31·05 N	86·52 W
126	Conegliano (kō-nāl-yä'nō) It.	45·59 N	12·17 E
69	Conejos (R.) (kô-nā'hōs) Colo.	37·07 N	106·19 W
81	Conemaugh (kŏn'ê-mô) Pa.	40·25 N	78·50 W
84	Coney I. (kō'nĭ) N. Y. (New York In.)	40·34 N	73·27 W
122	Confolens (kôN-fä-läN') Fr.	46·01 N	0·41 E
79	Congaree (R.) (kŏŋ-gȧ-rē'). S. C.	33·53 N	80·55 W
110	Congleton (kŏŋ'g'l-tŭn) Eng.	53·10 N	2·13 W
166	Congo (Reg.) (kŏŋ'gō) Ang.	6·40 S	14·00 E
163	Congo (Republic of Congo). Afr.	3·00 S	13·48 E
163	Congo, The (Republic of The Congo). Afr.	1·00 S	22·15 E
163	Congo Basin Con. L.	2·47 N	20·58 E
163	Congo R. Afr.	2·00 S	17·01 E
110	Conisbrough (kŏn'ĭs-bŭr-ô). Eng.	53·29 N	1·13 W
143	Conjeeveram (kŏn'ĭs-bŭr-ō) India	12·55 N	79·43 E
84	Conley (kŏn'lĭ). Ga. (Atlanta In.)	33·38 N	84·19 W
116	Conn, Lough (B.) (lŏk kŏn). Ire.	53·56 N	9·25 W
116	Connacht (cŏn'ât) Ire.	53·50 N	8·45 W
80	Conneaut (kŏn-ê-ôt') Ohio	41·55 N	80·35 W
63	Connecticut (State) (kŏ-nĕt'ĭ-kŭt) U. S.	41·40 N	73·10 W
81	Connecticut R. U. S.	43·55 N	72·15 W
81	Connellsville (kŏn'nĕlz-vĭl) Pa.	40·00 N	79·40 W
116	Connemara, Mts. (kŏn-nê-mȧ'rȧ) Ire.	53·30 N	9·54 W
80	Connersville (kŏn'ẽrz-vĭl) Ind.	39·35 N	85·10 W
159	Connors Ra. (kŏn'nŏrs) Austl.	22·15 S	149·00 E
67	Conrad (kŏn'răd) Mont.	48·11 N	111·56 W
85	Conrich (kŏn'rĭch) Can. (Calgary In.)	51·06 N	113·51 W
77	Conroe (kŏn'rō) Tex.	30·18 N	95·23 W
101	Conselheiro Lafaiete (kŏn-sĕ-lā'rô-lä-fā'ĕ-tĕ) Braz. (Rio de Janeiro In.)	20·40 S	43·46 W
84	Conshohocken (kŏn-shō-hŏk'ĕn) Pa. (Philadelphia In.)	40·04 N	75·18 W
94	Consolación (kōn-sô-lä-syōn') Cuba	22·30 N	83·55 W
155	Consolacion (kŏn-sô-lä-syô'n) Phil. (Manila In.)	16·20 N	120·21 E
65	Constance, Mt. (kŏn'stăns) Wash. (Seattle In.)	47·46 N	123·08 W
115	Constanța (kōn-stän'tsä) Bul.	44·12 N	28·36 E
166	Constantia (kŏn'stăn-tĭ-ȧ) S. Afr. (Cape Town In.)	34·01 S	18·25 E
166	Constantia Mts. S. Afr. (Cape Town In.)	34·03 S	18·23 E
124	Constantina (kōn-stän-tē'nä). Sp.	37·52 N	5·39 W
164	Constantine (kôN-stäN'tēn'). Alg.	36·28 N	6·38 E
80	Constantine (kŏn'stȧn-tēn). Mich.	41·50 N	85·40 W
64	Constantine Harbor Alaska	51·22 N	179·20 E
100	Constitución (kōn'stĭ-tōō-syōn') Chile	35·24 S	72·25 W
84	Constitution (kŏn-stĭ-tū'shŭn) Ga. (Atlanta In.)	33·41 N	84·20 W
101	Contagem (kōn-tá'zhĕm) Braz. (Rio de Janerio In.)	19·54 S	44·05 W
90	Contepec (kōn-tĕ-pĕk') Mex.	20·04 N	100·07 W
91	Contreras (kôn-trĕ'räs) Mex. (Mexico City In.)	19·18 N	99·14 W
74	Converse (kŏn'vẽrs) Tex. (San Antonio In.)	29·31 N	98·17 W
73	Conway (kŏn'wā) Ark.	35·06 N	92·27 W
81	Conway N. H.	44·00 N	71·10 W
79	Conway S. C.	33·49 N	79·01 W
65	Conway Wash. (Seattle In.)	48·20 N	122·20 W
78	Conyers (kŏn'yẽrz) Ga.	33·41 N	84·01 W
142	Cooch Behār (kōōch bê-här'). India	26·25 N	89·34 E
159	Cook, Mt N. Z. (In.)	43·27 S	170·13 E
78	Cookeville (kŏŏk'vĭl) Tenn.	36·07 N	85·30 W
167	Cookhouse (kŏŏk'hous) S. Afr. (Natal In.)	32·44 S	25·49 E
85	Cooking Lake (kŏŏk'ĭng) Can. (Edmonton In.)	53·10 N	113·08 W
85	Cooking L. (kŏŏk'ĭng) Can. (Edmonton In.)	53·26 N	113·03 W
64	Cook Inlet (kŏŏk) Alaska	60·50 N	151·38 W
157	Cook Is. Oceania	19·20 S	158·00 W
159	Cook Str. N. Z. (In.)	40·37 S	174·15 E
85	Cooksville (kŏŏkz'vĭl) Can. (Toronto In.)	43·34 N	79·37 W
159	Cooktown (kŏŏk'toun) Austl.	15·40 S	145·20 E
79	Cooleemee (kōō-lē'mē) N. C.	35·50 N	80·32 W
158	Coolgardie (kōōl-gär'dē) Austl.	31·00 S	121·25 E
160	Cooma (kōō'mȧ) Austl.	36·22 S	149·10 E
160	Coonamble (kōō-năm'b'l) Austl.	30·50 S	144·27 E
74	Coon Creek (kōōn) Minn. (Minneapolis, St. Paul In.)	45·09 N	93·17 W
143	Coonoort India	10·22 N	76·15 E
73	Cooper (kōōp'ẽr) Tex.	33·23 N	95·40 W
64	Cooper Center (kōōp'ẽr sĕn'tẽr) Alaska	61·54 N	145·30 W
160	Coopers Cr. (kōō'pẽrz) Austl.	27·32 S	141·19 E
81	Cooperstown N. Y.	42·45 N	74·55 W
70	Cooperstown (kōōp'ẽrs-toun) N. D.	47·26 N	98·07 W
160	Coorong, The (L.) (kōō'rŏng) Austl.	36·07 S	139·45 E
78	Coosa (kōō'sȧ) Ala.	32·43 N	86·25 W
79	Coosa (R.) Ala.	34·09 N	85·50 W
78	Coosawattee (R.) (kōō-sȧ-wôt'ē) Ga.	34·37 N	84·45 W
66	Coos Bay (kōōs) Ore.	43·21 N	124·12 W
66	Coos B. (kōōs) Ore.	43·19 N	124·40 W
160	Cootamundra (kōōtȧ-mŭnd'rȧ) Austl.	34·25 S	148·00 E
100	Copacabana (kô'pä-kȧ-bä'nä) Braz. (In.)	22·57 S	43·11 W
91	Copalita (R.) (kô-pä-lē'tä). Mex.	15·55 N	96·06 W
92	Copán (Ruins) (kō-pän'). Hond.	14·50 N	89·10 W
77	Copano B. (kō-pän'ō) Tex.	28·08 N	97·25 W
	Copenhagen, see København		
100	Copiapó (kō-pyä-pō') Chile	27·16 S	70·28 W
75	Copley (kŏp'lē) Ohio (Cleveland In.)	41·06 N	81·38 W
126	Copparo (kôp-pä'rō) It.	44·53 N	11·50 E
74	Coppell (kŏp'pĕl) Tex. (Dallas, Fort Worth In.)	32·57 N	97·00 W
64	Copper (R.) (kŏp'ẽr) Alaska	62·38 N	145·00 W
78	Copperhill (kŏp'ẽr hĭl) Tenn.	35·00 N	84·22 W
86	Coppermine (kŏp'ẽr-mīn) Can.	67·46 N	115·19 W
86	Copperinine (R.) Can.	66·48 N	114·59 W
74	Copperton (kŏp'ẽr-tŭn) Utah (Salt Lake City In.)	40·34 N	112·06 W
165	Coquilhatville (kō-kē'yȧ-vēl') Con. L.	0·01 N	18·17 E
66	Coquille (kô-kēl') Ore.	43·11 N	124·11 W
100	Coquimbo (kô-kēm'bō) Chile	29·58 S	71·31 W
101	Coquimbo (kō-kēm'bō) (Prov.) Chile (Santiago In.)	31·50 S	71·05 W
65	Coquitlam (Mtn.) (kō-kwĭt-lăm) Can. (Vancouver In.)	49·23 N	122·44 W
127	Corabia (kô-rä'bĭ-ȧ) Rom.	43·45 N	24·29 E

ăt; finȧl; rāte; senâte; ärm; ȧsk; sofȧ; fâre; ch-choose; dh-as th in other; bē; êvent; bĕt; recĕnt; cratẽr; g-go; gh-guttural g; bĭt; ĭ-short neutral; rīde; K-guttural k as ch in German ich;

Page	Name Pronunciation Region	Lat. °′	Long. °′
98	Coracora (kō'rä-kō'rä) Peru	15·12 s	73·42 w
79	Coral Gables Fla. (In.)	25·43 N	80·14 w
94	Coralillo (kô-rä-lē-yō) Cuba	73·00 N	80·40 w
87	Coral Rapids (kŏr'ăl) Can.	50·18 N	81·49 w
75	Coral Ridge (kŏr'ăl) Ky. (Louisville In.)	38·05 N	85·42 w
156	Coral Sea (kŏr'ăl) Oceania	13·30 s	150·00 E
160	Corangamite, L. (cŏr-ăŋg'ȧ-mīt) Austl.	38·05 s	142·55 E
75	Coraopolis (kō-rä-ŏp'ô-lĭs) Pa. (Pittsburgh In.)	40·31 N	80·10 w
126	Corato (kô'rä-tô) It.	41·08 N	16·28 E
123	Corbeil-Essonnes (kôr-bā'yĕ-sŏn') Fr. (Paris In.)	48·31 N	2·29 E
65	Corbett (kôr'bĕt) Ore. (Portland In.)	45·31 N	122·17 w
122	Corbie (kôr-bē') Fr.	49·55 N	2·27 E
78	Corbin (kôr'bĭn) Ky.	36·55 N	84·06 w
110	Corby (kôr'bĭ) Eng.	52·50 N	0·32 w
100	Corcovado (Mtn.) (kôr-kô-vä'dōō) Braz. (In.)	22·57 s	43·13 w
100	Corcovado, Golfo (G.) (kôr-kô-vä'dhō) Chile	43·40 s	75·00 w
101	Cordeiro (kôr-dā'rō) Braz. (Rio de Janeiro In.)	22·03 s	42·22 w
78	Cordele (kôr-dēl') Ga.	31·55 N	83·50 w
72	Cordell (kôr-dĕl') Okla.	35·19 N	98·58 w
124	Cordillera Cantabrica (Mts.) (kôr-dēl-yĕ'rä-kän-tä'brē-kä) Sp.	43·05 N	6·05 w
155	Cordillera Central (Mts.) (kôr-dēl-yĕ'rä-sĕn'träl) Phil. (Manila In.)	17·05 N	120·55 E
49	Cordilleran Highlands (Reg.) (kōr dĭl'lŭr ȧn) N. A.	55·00 N	125·00 w
100	Córdoba (kôr'dô-vä) Arg.	30·20 s	64·03 w
91	Cordoba (kô'r-dô-bä) Mex.	18·53 N	96·54 w
124	Córdoba (kô'r-dô-bä) Sp.	37·55 N	4·45 w
100	Córdoba (Prov.) (kôr'dô-vä) Arg.	32·00 s	64·00 w
100	Córdoba, Sa. de (Mts.) Arg.	31·15 s	64·30 w
78	Cordova (kôr'dô-ȧ) Ala.	33·45 N	86·11 w
64	Cordova (kôr'dô-vä) Alaska	60·34 N	145·38 w
124	Corella (kô-rĕl-yä) Sp.	42·07 N	1·48 w
126	Corigliano (kō-rē-lyä'nō) It.	39·35 N	16·30 E
78	Corinth (kŏr'ĭnth) Miss.	34·55 N	88·30 w
	Corinth, see Korinthos		
99	Corinto (kô-rē'n-tō) Braz.	18·20 s	44·16 w
98	Corinto Col. (In.)	3·09 N	76·12 w
92	Corinto (kōr-ĭn'to) Nic.	12·30 N	87·12 w
161	Corio Austl. (Melbourne In.)	38·05 s	144·22 E
161	Corio B. Austl. (Melbourne In.)	38·07 s	144·25 E
116	Cork (kôrk) Ire.	51·54 N	8·25 w
116	Cork Hbr. Ire.	51·44 N	8·15 w
126	Corleone (kôr-lâ-ō'nā) It.	37·48 N	13·18 E
127	Corlu (chôr'lōō) Tur.	41·09 N	27·48 E
78	Cornelia (kôr-nē'lyȧ) Ga.	34·31 N	83·30 w
168	Cornelis R. (kôr-nē'lĭs) S. Afr. (Johannesburg & Pretoria In.)	27·48 s	29·15 E
74	Cornell (kôr-nĕl') Calif. (Los Angeles In.)	34·06 N	118·46 w
71	Cornell Wis.	45·10 N	91·10 w
83	Corner Brook (kôr'nẽr) Can.	48·58 N	57·49 w
160	Corner Inlet Austl.	38·55 s	146·45 E
	Corneta, see Targuinia		
73	Corning (kôr'nĭng) Ark.	36·26 N	90·35 w
71	Corning Iowa	40·58 N	94·40 w
81	Corning N. Y.	42·10 N	77·05 w
126	Corno, M. (Mtn.) (kôr'nō) It.	42·28 N	13·37 E
94	Cornwall Ba. Is.	25·55 N	77·15 w
81	Cornwall (kôrn'wôl) Can.	45·05 N	74·35 w
116	Cornwall Pen. (kôrn'wăl) Eng.	50·25 N	5·04 w
98	Coro (kō'rô) Ven.	11·22 N	69·43 w
98	Corocoro (kō-rô-kō'rô) Bol.	17·15 s	68·21 w
143	Coromandel Coast (kŏr-ô-man'dĕl) India	17·50 N	80·14 E
78	Corona (kô-rō'nȧ) Ala.	33·42 N	87·28 w
74	Corona Calif. (Los Angeles In.)	33·52 N	117·34 w
93	Coronada, Bahia de (B.) (bä-ē'ä-dĕ-kô-rō-nä'dō) C.R.	8·47 N	84·04 w
74	Corona del Mar (kô-rō'nȧ dēl măr) Calif. (Los Angeles In.)	33·36 N	117·53 w
68	Coronado (kŏr-ô-nä'dō) Calif. (San Diego In.)	32·42 N	117·12 w
86	Coronation G. (kŏr-ô-nā'shŭn) Can.	68·07 N	112·50 w
100	Coronel (kō-rô-nĕl') Chile	37·00 s	73·10 w
101	Coronel Brandsen (kŏ-rô-nĕl-brȧ'nd-sĕn) Arg. (Buenos Aires In.)	35·09 s	58·15 w
100	Coronel Dorrego (kŏ-rô-nĕl-dôr-rĕ'gô) Arg.	38·43 s	61·16 w
100	Coronel Oviedo (kŏ-rô-nĕl-ô-vēĕ'dô) Par.	25·28 s	56·22 w
100	Coronel Pringles (kŏ-rô-nĕl-prēn'glĕs) Arg.	37·54 s	61·22 w
100	Coronel Suárez (kŏ-rô-nĕl-swä'rās) Arg.	37·24 s	66·49 w
99	Coronie Sur.	5·51 N	56·17 w
160	Corowa (cŏr-ôwă) Austl.	36·02 s	146·23 E
92	Corozal (cŏr-ŏth-ăl') Br. Hond. (Yucatan In.)	18·25 N	88·23 w
77	Corpus Christi (kôr'pŭs krĭs'tē) Tex.	27·48 N	97·24 w
77	Corpus Christi B. Tex.	27·47 N	97·14 w
76	Corpus Christi L. Tex.	28·08 N	98·20 w
100	Corral (kô-räl') Chile	39·57 s	73·15 w
124	Corral de Almaguer (kô-räl'dā äl-mä-gâr') Sp.	39·45 N	3·10 w
155	Corregidor (I.) (kô-rā-hē-dōr') Phil. (Manila In.)	14·21 N	120·25 E
99	Correntina (kô-rĕn-tē-nȧ) Braz.	13·18 s	44·33 w
116	Corrib, Lough (B.) (lŏk kŏr'ĭb) Ire.	53·56 N	9·19 w
100	Corrientes (kō-ryĕn'tās) Arg.	27·25 s	58·39 w
100	Corrientes (Prov.) Arg.	28·45 s	58·00 w
98	Corrientes, Cabo (kȧ'bô-kō-ryĕn'tās) Col.	5·34 N	77·35 w
94	Corrientes, Cabo (C.) (kȧ'bô-kôr-rē-ĕn'tĕs) Cuba	21·50 N	84·25 w
94	Corrientes, Ensenada de (B.) (ĕn-sĕ-nä-dä-dĕ-kō-ryĕn'tās) Cuba	21·45 N	84·45 w
90	Corrientes, Cabo (C.) Mex.	20·25 N	105·41 w
81	Cory (kŏr'ĭ) Pa.	41·55 N	79·40 w
126	Corse, C. (kôrs) Fr.	42·59 N	9·19 E
126	Corsica (I.) (kô'r-sē-kä) Fr.	42·10 N	8·55 E
77	Corsicana (kôr-sĭ-kăn'ȧ) Tex.	32·06 N	96·28 w
90	Cortazar (kôr-tä-zär') Mex.	20·30 N	100·57 w
126	Corte (kôr'tâ) Fr.	42·18 N	9·10 E
124	Cortegana (kôr-tâ-gä'nä) Sp.	37·54 N	6·48 w
124	Cortes (kôr-tās') Sp.	36·38 N	5·20 w
94	Cortés, Ensenada de (B.) (ĕn-sĕ-nä-dä-dĕ-kôr-tās') Cuba	22·05 N	83·45 w
81	Cortland (kôrt'lănd) N. Y.	42·35 N	76·10 w
126	Cortona (kôr-tō'nä) It.	43·16 N	12·00 E
124	Coruche (kô-rōō'she) Port.	38·58 N	8·34 w
133	Coruh (R.) (chō-rōōk') Tur.	40·30 N	41·10 E
133	Corum (chô-rōōm') Tur.	39·30 N	34·50 E
99	Corumbá (kō-rōōm-bä') Braz.	19·01 s	57·28 w
80	Corunna (kô-rŭn'ȧ) Mich.	43·00 N	84·05 w
99	Coruripe (kō-rōō-rē'pĭ) Braz.	10·09 s	36·13 w
66	Corvallis (kŏr-văl'ĭs) Ore.	44·34 N	123·17 w
110	Corve (R.) (kôr'vē) Eng.	52·28 N	2·43 w
80	Corydon (kŏr'ĭ-dŭn) Ind.	38·10 N	86·05 w
71	Corydon Iowa	40·45 N	93·20 w
80	Corydon Ky.	37·45 N	87·40 w
91	Cosamaloápan (kô-sȧ-mä-lwä'pän) Mex.	18·21 N	95·48 w
91	Coscomatepec (kôs'kōmä-tĕ-pĕk') Mex.	19·04 N	97·03 w
110	Coseley (kôs'lē) Eng.	52·33 N	2·10 w
126	Cosenza (kô-zĕnt'sä) It.	39·18 N	16·15 E
80	Coshocton (kô-shŏk'tŭn) Ohio	40·15 N	81·55 w
92	Cosigüina (Vol.) Nic.	12·59 N	83·35 w
167	Cosmoledo Group (Is.) (kŏs-mô-lā'dō) Afr.	9·42 s	47·45 E
66	Cosmopolis (kŏz-mŏp'ô-lĭs) Wash.	46·58 N	123·47 w
122	Cosne-sur-Loire (kōn-sür-lwär') Fr.	47·25 N	2·57 E
91	Cosoleacaque (kō sō lā-ä-kä'kē) Mex.	18·01 N	94·38 w
74	Costa Mesa (kŏs'tȧ mā'sȧ) Calif. (Los Angeles In.)	33·39 N	118·54 w
89	Costa Rica (kŏs'tȧ rē'kȧ) N. A.	10·30 N	84·30 w
68	Cosumnes (R.) (kŏ-sŭm'nĕz) Calif.	38·21 N	121·17 w
98	Cotabambas (kô-tä-bȧm'bäs) Peru	13·49 s	72·17 w
155	Cotabato (kō-tä-bä'tō) Phil.	7·06 N	124·13 E
91	Cotaxtla (kō-täs'tlä) Mex.	18·49 N	96·22 w
91	Cotaxtla (R.) Mex.	18·54 N	96·21 w
85	Coteau-du-Lac (cō-tō'dü-läk) Can. (Montreal In.)	45·17 N	74·11 w
85	Coteau Landing Can. (Montreal In.)	45·15 N	74·13 w
95	Coteaux Hai.	18·15 N	74·05 w
122	Côte d'Or (hill) (kōt-dŏr') Fr.	47·02 N	4·35 E
90	Cotija de la Paz (kô-tē'-kä-dĕ-lä-pȧ'z) Mex.	19·46 N	102·43 w
164	Cotonou (kô-tô-nōō') Dahomey	6·26 N	2·19 E
98	Cotopaxi (Mtn.) (kō-tô-păk'sē) Ec.	0·40 s	78·26 w
95	Cotorro (kô-tôr-rō) Cuba (Havana In.)	23·03 N	82·17 w
116	Cotswold Hills (kŭtz'wōld) Eng.	51·35 N	2·16 w
74	Cottage Grove (kŏt'âj grōv) Minn. (Minneapolis, St. Paul In.)	44·50 N	92·52 w
66	Cottage Grove Ore.	43·48 N	123·04 w
120	Cottbus (kōtt'bōōs) Ger.	51·47 N	14·20 E
123	Cottian Alps (Mts.) (kŏ'tē-ŭn-ălps) Fr.-It.	44·46 N	7·02 E
70	Cottonwood (R.) (kŏt'ŭn-wŏŏd) Minn.	44·25 N	95·35 w
66	Cottonwood Cr. Calif.	40·24 N	122·50 w
95	Cotui (kô-tōō'-ē) Dom. Rep.	19·05 N	70·10 w
76	Cotulla (kŏ-tŭl'lȧ) Tex.	28·26 N	99·14 w
123	Coubert (kōō-bâr') Fr. (Paris In.)	48·40 N	2·43 E
81	Coudersport (koŭ'dẽrz-port) Pa.	41·45 N	78·00 w
82	Coudres, Ile-aux Can.	47·25 N	70·25 w
122	Couéron (kōō-â-rôN') Fr.	47·16 N	1·45 w
123	Coulommiers (kōō-lô-myā') Fr. (Paris In.)	48·49 N	3·05 E
100	Coulto, Serra do (Mts.) (sĕ'r-rä-dô-kô-ōō'tô) Braz. (In.)	22·33 s	43·27 w
64	Council (koun'sĭl) Alaska	64·55 N	163·40 w
70	Council Bluffs (koun'sĭl blŭf) Iowa	41·16 N	95·53 w
73	Council Grove (koun'sĭl grōv) Kans.	38·39 N	96·30 w
65	Coupeville (kōōp'vĭl) Wash. (Seattle In.)	48·13 N	122·41 w
99	Courantyne (R.) (kôr'ăntĭn) Br. Gu.-Sur.	4·28 N	57·42 w
86	Courtenay (cōōrt-nā') Can.	49·51 N	125·07 w
77	Coushatta (kou-shăt'ȧ) La.	32·02 N	93·21 w
122	Coutras (kōō-trȧ') Fr.	45·02 N	0·07 w
110	Coventry (kŭv'ĕn-trĭ) Eng.	52·25 N	1·29 w
124	Covilhã (kô-vēl'yăN) Port.	40·18 N	7·29 w
74	Covina (kô-vē'nȧ) Calif. (Los Angeles In.)	34·06 N	117·54 w
78	Covington (kŭv'ĭng-tŭn) Ga.	33·36 N	83·50 w
80	Covington Ind.	40·10 N	87·15 w
75	Covington Ky. (Cincinnati In.)	39·05 N	84·31 w
77	Covington La.	30·30 N	90·06 w
80	Covington Ohio	40·10 N	84·20 w
73	Covington Okla.	36·18 N	97·32 w
78	Covington Tenn.	35·33 N	89·40 w
81	Covington Va.	37·50 N	80·00 w
160	Cowal, L. (kou'ăl) Austl.	33·30 s	147·10 E
158	Cowan, (L.) (kou'ȧn) Austl.	32·00 s	122·30 E
66	Cow Cr. (kou) Ore.	42·45 N	123·35 w
116	Cowes (kouz) Eng.	50·43 N	1·25 w
66	Cowlitz R. (kou'lĭts) Wash.	46·30 N	122·45 w
160	Cowra (kou'rȧ) Austl.	33·50 s	148·33 E
99	Coxim (kō-shēN') Braz.	18·32 s	54·43 w
91	Coxquihui (kōz-kē-wē') Mex.	20·10 N	97·34 w
142	Coxs Bazar E. Pak.	21·32 N	92·00 E
98	Coyaima (kô-yȧē'-mä) Col. (In.)	3·48 N	75·11 w
76	Coyame (kō-yä'mā) Mex.	29·26 N	105·05 w
76	Coyanosa Draw (kŏ yȧ-nō'sä) Tex.	30·55 N	103·07 w
91	Coyoacàn (kô-yô-ȧ-kän') Mex. (Mexico City In.)	19·21 N	99·10 w
65	Coyote (R.) (kī'ōt) Calif. (San Francisco In.)	37·27 N	121·57 w
90	Coyuca de Benítez (kō-yōō'kä dā bā-nē'tāz) Mex.	17·04 N	100·06 w
90	Coyuca de Catalán (kō-yōō'kä dā kä-tä-län') Mex.	18·19 N	100·41 w
91	Coyutla (kō-yōō'tlä) Mex.	20·13 N	97·40 w
72	Cozad (kō'zăd) Nebr.	40·53 N	99·59 w
75	Cozaddale (kô-zăd-dāl) Ohio (Cincinnati In.)	39·16 N	84·09 w
90	Cozoyoapan (kô-zō-yô-ä-pȧ'n) Mex.	16·45 N	98·17 w
92	Cozumel (kŏ-zōō-mĕ'l) Mex. (Yucatan In.)	20·31 N	86·55 w
92	Cozumel, Isla de (I.) (ē's-lä-dĕ-kŏ-zōō-mĕ'l) Mex. (Yucatan In.)	20·26 N	87·10 w
66	Crab Cr. (krăb) Wash.	46·47 N	119·43 w
66	Crab Cr. Wash.	47·21 N	119·09 w
167	Cradock (kră'dŭk) S. Afr. (Natal In.)	32·12 s	25·38 E
75	Crafton (krăf'tŭn) Pa. (Pittsburgh In.)	40·26 N	80·04 w
67	Craig (krāg) Colo.	40·32 N	107·31 w
85	Craigs Road Station (krāgz) Can. (Quebec In.)	46·37 N	71·22 w
127	Craiova (krȧ-yō'vȧ) Rom.	44·18 N	23·50 E
81	Cranberry (L.) (krăn'bĕr-ĭ) N. Y.	44·10 N	74·50 w
161	Cranbourne Austl. (Melbourne In.)	38·07 s	145·16 E
86	Cranbrook (krăn'brŏŏk) Can.	49·43 N	115·47 w
84	Cranbury (krăn'bē-rĭ) N. J. (New York In.)	40·19 N	74·31 w
71	Crandon (krăn'dŭn) Wis.	45·35 N	88·55 w
122	Cransac (kräN-zȧk') Fr.	44·28 N	2·19 E
84	Cranston (krăns'tŭn) R. I. (Providence In.)	41·46 N	71·25 w
66	Crater L. (krā'tẽr) Ore.	43·00 N	122·08 w
66	Crater Lake Natl. Park Ore.	4258· N	122·40 w
67	Craters of the Moon Natl. Park (krā'tẽr) Idaho	43·28 N	113·15 w
99	Crateús (krä-tâ-ōōzh') Braz.	5·09 s	40·35 w
99	Crato (krä'tŏŏ) Braz.	7·19 s	39·13 w
70	Crawford (krô'fẽrd) Nebr.	42·41 N	103·25 w
65	Crawford Wash. (Portland In.)	45·49 N	122·24 w
80	Crawfordsville (krô'fẽrdz-vĭl) Ind.	40·00 N	86·55 w
67	Crazy Mts. (krā'zĭ) Mont.	46·11 N	110·25 w
67	Crazy Woman Cr. Wyo.	44·08 N	106·40 w
122	Crécy (krā-sē') Fr.	50·13 N	1·48 E
168	Crecy (krĕ-sē) S. Afr. (Johannesburg & Pretoria In.)	24·38 s	28·52 E
123	Crecy-en-Brie (krā-sē'-ĕN-brē') Fr. (Paris In.)	48·52 N	2·55 E
85	Credit R. Can. (Toronto In.)	43·41 N	79·55 w
86	Cree (L.) (krē) Can.	57·35 N	107·52 w
70	Creighton (krā'tŭn) Nebr.	42·27 N	97·54 w
167	Creighton (cre-tŏn) S. Afr. (Natal In.)	30·02 s	29·52 E
122	Creil (krĕ'y') Fr.	49·18 N	2·28 E
126	Crema (krā'mä) It.	45·21 N	9·53 E
126	Cremona (krā-mō'nä) It.	45·09 N	10·02 E
126	Crépy-en-Valois (krā-pē'-ĕN-vä-lwä') Fr. (Paris In.)	49·14 N	2·53 E
126	Cres (Tsrĕs) Yugo.	44·58 N	14·21 E
126	Cres (I.) Yugo.	44·50 N	14·31 E
79	Crescent (R.) (krĕs'ĕnt) Fla.	29·33 N	81·30 w
65	Crescent Beach Can. (Vancouver In.)	49·03 N	122·58 w
79	Crescent City Fla.	29·26 N	81·35 w
66	Crescent L. Ore.	43·25 N	121·58 w
71	Cresco (krĕs'kō) Iowa	43·23 N	92·07 w
66	Cresent City (krĕs'ĕnt) Calif.	41·46 N	124·13 w
69	Crested Butte (krĕst'ĕd būt) Colo.	38·50 N	107·00 w
74	Crestline (krĕst-līn) Calif. (Los Angeles In.)	34·15 N	117·17 w
80	Crestline Ohio	40·50 N	82·40 w
74	Crestmore (krĕst'môr) Calif. (Los Angeles In.)	34·02 N	117·23 w
86	Creston (krĕs'tŭn) Can.	49·09 N	116·32 w
71	Creston Iowa	41·04 N	94·22 w
75	Creston Ohio (Cleveland In.)	40·59 N	81·54 w
78	Crestview (krĕst'vū) Fla.	30·44 N	86·35 w
75	Crestwood (krĕst'wŏŏd) Ky. (Louisville In.)	38·20 N	85·28 w
75	Crete (krēt) Ill. (Chicago In.)	41·26 N	87·38 w
73	Crete Nebr.	40·38 N	96·56 w
126	Crete (I.) Grc. (Inset)	35·15 N	24·30 E
125	Creus, Cabo de (C.) (kā'-bô-dĕ-krĕ-ōōs) Sp.	42·16 N	3·18 E
122	Creuse (krûz) Fr.	46·51 N	0·49 E
74	Creve Coeur (krēv kŏŏr) Mo. (St. Louis In.)	38·40 N	90·27 w
125	Crevillente (krâ-vē-lyĕn'tâ) Sp.	38·12 N	0·48 w
110	Crewe (krōō) Eng.	53·06 N	2·27 w
79	Crewe Va.	37·09 N	78·08 w
	Crimea Poluostrov (Pen.), see Krymskiy		
120	Crimmitschau (krĭm'ĭt-shou) Ger.	50·49 N	12·22 E
72	Cripple Creek (krĭp''l) Colo.	38·44 N	105·12 w
81	Crisfield (krĭs-fēld) Md.	38·00 N	78·50 w
101	Cristina (krēs-tē'-nä) Braz. (Rio de Janeiro In.)	22·13 s	45·15 w
98	Cristobal Colón, Pico (Pk.) (pē'kô-krēs-tô'bäl-kō-lôn') Col.	11·00 N	74·00 w
121	Crisul Alb R. (krē'shōōl älb) Rom.	46·20 N	22·15 E

ng-sing; ŋ-baŋk; N-nasalized n; nŏd; cŏmmit; ōld; ôbey; ôrder; fōōd; fŏŏt; ou-out; s-soft; sh-dish; th-thin; pūre; ûnite; ûrn; stŭd; circŭs; ü-as "y" in study; '-indeterminate vowel.

Page Name Pronunciation Region Lat. °ʹ Long. °ʹ

127 Crna (R.) (tsʹrʹnȧ)........Yugo. 41·03 N 21·46 E
127 Crna Gora (Montenegro) (Reg.) (tsʹr-nȧ-gōʹrȧ) (mȯn-tȧ-nāʹgrō).Yugo. 42·55 N 18·52 E
126 Črnomelj (chʹrʹnō-mālʹ)....Yugo. 45·35 N 15·11 E
Croatia, see Hrvatska
65 Crockett (krȯkʹĕt) Calif. (San Francisco In.) 38·03 N 122·14 W
77 Crockett............Tex. 31·19 N 95·28 W
168 Crocodile R. (krŏʹkŏ-dīl) S. Afr. (Johannesburg & Pretoria In.) 24·25 S 27·08 E
70 Crofton (krŏfʹtŭn)........S. D. 45·25 N 98·04 W
71 Croix, Lac la (.) (krōō-äʹ läk lä).Can.-Minn. 48·19 N 91·53 W
158 Croker (krŏʹkä)........Austl. 10·45 S 132·25 E
161 Cronulla (krō-nŭlʹȧ) Austl. (Sydney In.) 34·03 S 151·09 E
95 Crooked (I.)........Ba. Is. 22·45 N 74·10 W
83 Crooked (L.)........Can. 48·24 N 56·00 W
73 Crooked Cr. (krōōkʹĕd)....Ill. 40·21 N 90·49 W
66 Crooked Cr........Ore. 42·23 N 118·14 W
95 Crooked Island Passage (Str.) Ba. Is. 22·40 N 74·50 W
66 Crooked R........Ore. 44·07 N 120·30 W
70 Crookston (krōōksʹtŭn)....Minn. 47·44 N 96·35 W
80 Crooksville (krōōksʹvĭl)....Ohio 39·45 N 82·05 W
71 Crosby (krŏzʹbĭ)........Minn. 46·29 N 93·58 W
70 Crosby............N. D. 48·55 N 103·18 W
77 Crosby........Tex. (In.) 29·55 N 95·04 W
81 Cross (L.) (krŏs)........Can. 44·55 N 76·55 W
86 Cross (L.)........Can. 54·40 N 98·47 W
73 Crossett (krŏsʹĕt)........Ark. 33·08 N 91·56 W
94 Cross Hbr........Ba. Is. 25·55 N 77·15 W
77 Cross L........Can. 52·33 N 93·58 W
84 Cross River Res. (krŏs) N. Y. (New York In.) 41·14 N 73·34 W
64 Cross Sd. (krŏs)........Alaska 58·12 N 137·20 W
80 Crosswell (krŏzʹwĕl)........Mich. 43·15 N 82·35 W
127 Crotone (krō-tōʹnĕ)........It. 39·05 N 17·08 E
84 Croton Falls Res. (krōtʹȧn) N. Y. (New York In.) 41·22 N 73·44 W
84 Croton-on-Hudson (krōʹtŭn-ȯn hŭdʹsŭn) . N. Y. (New York In.) 41·12 N 73·53 W
71 Crow (L.)........Can. 49·13 N 93·29 W
72 Crow Cr........Colo. 41·08 N 104·25 W
70 Crow Creek Ind. Res........S. D. 44·17 N 99·17 W
67 Crow Ind. Res. (krō)....Mont. 45·26 N 108·12 W
110 Crowle (kroul)........Eng. 53·36 N 0·49 W
77 Crowley (krouʹlē)........La. 30·13 N 92·22 W
89 Crown, Mt. Vir. Is. (U. S. A.) (St. Thomas In.) 18·22 N 64·58 W
65 Crown Mtn. (kroun) Can. (Vancouver In.) 49·24 N 123·05 W
75 Crown Point (kroun pointʹ) Ind. (Chicago In.) 41·25 N 87·22 W
81 Crown Point........N. Y. 44·00 N 73·25 W
71 Crow Wing (R.) (krō)....Minn. 44·50 N 94·01 W
71 Crow Wing (R.)........Minn. 46·42 N 94·48 W
71 Crow Wing (R.), North Fork. Minn. 45·16 N 94·28 W
71 Crow Wing (R.), South Fork Minn. 44·59 N 94·42 W
159 Croydon (kroiʹdŭn)........Austl. 18·15 S 142·15 E
161 Croydon...Austl. (Melbourne In.) 37·48 S 145·17 E
110 Croydon...Eng. (London In.) 51·22 N 0·06 W
84 Croydon...Pa. (Philadelphia In.) 40·05 N 74·55 W
47 Crozet I. (krȯ-zēʹ)........Ind. O. 46·20 S 51·30 E
94 Cruces (krōōʹsȧs)........Cuba 22·20 N 80·20 W
76 Cruces, Arroyo de (är-rŏʹyȯ-dĕ-krōōʹsĕs).Mex. 26·17 N 104·32 W
76 Cruillas (krōō-ēlʹyäs)....Mex. 24·45 N 98·31 W
94 Cruz, Cabo (C.) (käʹ-bȯ-krōōz) Cuba 19·50 N 77·45 W
94 Cruz, Cayo (I.) (käʹyȯ-krōōz) Cuba 22·15 N 77·50 W
100 Cruz Alta (älʹtä)........Braz. 28·41 S 54·02 W
100 Cruz del Eje (krōōʹs-dĕl-ĕ-kĕ).Arg. 30·46 S 64·45 W
101 Cruzeiro (krōō-zāʹrō) Braz. (Rio de Janeiro In.) 22·36 S 44·57 W
98 Cruzeiro do Sul (krōō-zāʹrō dōō sōōl).Braz. 7·34 S 72·40 W
85 Crysler........Can. (Ottawa In.) 45·13 N 75·09 W
76 Crystal City (krĭsʹtȧl sĭʹtĭ)...Tex. 28·40 N 99·90 W
71 Crystal Falls (krĭsʹtȧl fôls)...Mich. 46·06 N 88·21 W
75 Crystal Lake (krĭsʹtȧl läk) Ill. (Chicago In.) 42·15 N 88·18 W
78 Crystal Springs (krĭsʹtȧl sprĭngz) Miss. 31·58 N 90·20 W
65 Crystal Spr. (krĭsʹtȧl) Calif. (San Francisco In.) 37·31 N 122·26 W
121 Csongrád (chȯnʹgräd)....Hung. 46·42 N 20·09 E
121 Csorna (chȯrʹnä)........Hung. 47·39 N 17·11 E
99 Cúa (kōōʹä)........Ven. 10·10 N 66·54 W
91 Cuajimalpa (kwä-hē-mälʹpä) Mex. (Mexico City In.) 19·21 N 99·18 W
90 Cuale, Sierra del (Mts.) (sē-ĕʹr-rä-dĕl-kwäʹlĕ).Mex. 20·20 N 104·58 W
166 Cuamato (kwä-mäʹtō)....Ang. 17·05 S 15·15 E
166 Cuando (R.) (kwänʹdō)....Ang. 14·15 S 20·00 E
166 Cuango (kwänʹgō)........Ang. 6·15 S 16·53 E
166 Cuanza (R.) (kwänʹzä)....Ang. 9·45 S 15·00 E
100 Cuarto Saladillo (R.) (kwärʹtō-sä-lä-dēʹl-yȯ).Arg. 33·00 S 63·25 W
95 Cuatro Caminos (kwä·trō kä-mēʹnōs).Cuba (Havana In.) 23·01 N 82·13 W
76 Cuatro Ciénegas (kwäʹtrō syäʹnä-gäs).Mex. 26·59 N 102·03 W
92 Cuauhtemoc (kwä-ōō-tĕʹmŏk) Mex. 15·43 N 91·57 W
90 Cuautepec (kwä-ōō-tĕʹpĕk)...Mex. 16·41 N 99·04 W
90 Cuautepec........Mex. 20·01 N 98·19 W
91 Cuautitlán (kwä-ōō-tēt-länʹ) Mex. (Mexico City In.) 19·40 N 99·12 W
90 Cuautla (kwä-ōōʹtlä)........Mex. 18·47 N 98·57 W

124 Cuba (kōōʹbä)............Port. 38·10 N 7·55 W
89 Cuba (kūʹbä)............N. A. 22·00 N 79·00 W
99 Cubagua, Isla (ēʹs-lä-kōō-bäʹgwä) Ven. 10·48 N 64·10 W
166 Cubango (R.) (kōō-bänʹgō)..Ang. 15·45 S 18·00 E
74 Cucamonga (kōō-kȧ-mŏnʹgȧ) Calif. (Los Angeles In.) 34·05 N 117·35 W
166 Cuchi........Ang. 14·40 S 16·50 E
76 Cuchillo Parado (kōō-chēʹlyȯ pä-räʹdō).Mex. 29·26 N 104·52 W
92 Cuchumatanes, Sierra de los (Mts.) Guat. 16·02 N 91·50 W
98 Cúcuta (kōōʹkōō-tä)........Col. 7·56 N 72·30 W
75 Cudahy (kŭdʹȧ-hī) Wis. (Milwaukee In.) 42·57 N 87·52 W
143 Cuddalore (kŭd ȧ-lōrʹ)....India 11·49 N 79·46 E
143 Cuddapah (kŭdʹȧ-pä)....India 14·31 N 78·52 E
158 Cue (kū)........Austl. 27·30 S 118·10 E
124 Cuellar (kwäʹlyär)........Sp. 41·24 N 4·15 W
98 Cuenca (kwĕnʹkä)........Ec. 2·52 S 78·54 W
124 Cuenca........Sp. 40·05 N 2·07 W
124 Cuenca, Sierra de (Mts.) (sē-ĕʹr-rä-dĕʹkwĕʹn-kä).Sp. 40·02 N 1·50 W
76 Cuencame (kwĕn-kä-mäʹ)...Mex. 24·52 N 103·42 W
90 Cuerámaro (kwä-räʹmä-rȯ)..Mex. 20·39 N 101·44 W
91 Cuernavaca (kwĕr-nä-väʹkä) Mex. (Mexico City In.) 18·55 N 99·15 W
77 Cuero (kwäʹrō)........Tex. 29·05 N 97·16 W
90 Cuetzalá del Progreso (kwĕt-zä-lä dĕl prō-grāʹsō).Mex. 18·07 N 99·51 W
91 Cuetzalan del Progreso (kwĕt-zä-län dĕl prō-grāʹsō).Mex. 20·02 N 97·33 W
124 Cuevas del Almanzora (kwĕʹväs-dĕl-äl-män-zō-rä).Sp. 37·19 N 1·54 W
126 Cuglieri (kōō-lyäʹrē)........It. 40·11 N 8·37 E
99 Cuiabá (kōō-yä-bäʹ)........Braz. 15·33 S 56·03 W
91 Cuicatlan (kwē-kä-tlänʹ)....Mex. 17·46 N 96·57 W
92 Cuilapa (kōō-ē-läʹpä)......Guat. 14·16 N 90·20 W
116 Cuillin Sd........Scot. 57·09 N 6·20 W
166 Cuito (R.) (kōō-ēʹtō)........Ang. 14·30 S 19·10 E
90 Cuitzeo (kwētʹzā-ō)........Mex. 19·57 N 101·11 W
90 Cuitzeo, Laguna de (L.) (lä-ōōʹnä-dĕ-kwĕtʹzä-ō).Mex. 19·58 N 101·05 W
95 Cul de Sac (Val.) (kōōl-dē-sáʹk) Dom. Rep.-Hai. 18·35 N 72·05 W
89 Culebra (I.) (kōō-lāʹbrä) P. R. (Puerto Rico In.) 18·19 N 65·32 W
111 Culemborg Neth. (Amsterdam In.) 51·57 N 5·14 E
159 Culgoa (R.) (kŭl-gōʹȧ)....Austl. 29·21 S 147·00 E
88 Culiacán (kōō-lyä-käʹn)....Mex. 24·45 N 107·30 W
154 Culion (kōō-lē-ōnʹ)........Phil. 11·43 N 119·58 E
124 Cúllar de Baza (kōōʹl-yär-dĕ-bäʹzä).Sp. 37·36 N 2·35 W
125 Cullera (kōō-lyäʹrä)........Sp. 39·12 N 0·15 W
167 Cullinan (kōōʹlĭ-nän)......S. Afr. (Johannesburg & Pretoria In.) 25·41 S 28·32 E
78 Cullman (kŭlʹmȧn)........Ala. 34·10 N 86·50 W
81 Culpeper (kŭlʹpĕp-ēr)......Va. 38·30 N 77·55 W
85 Culross (kŭlʹrŏs) Can. (Winnipeg In.) 49·43 N 97·54 W
80 Culver (kŭlʹvẽr)............Ind. 41·15 N 86·25 W
74 Culver City Calif. (Los Angeles In.) 34·00 N 118·23 W
99 Cumaná (kōō-mä-näʹ)...Ven. (In.) 10·28 N 64·10 W
85 Cumberland (kŭmʹbẽr-lănd) Can. (Ottawa In.) 45·31 N 75·25 W
75 Cumberland Ind. (Indianapolis In.) 39·46 N 85·57 W
81 Cumberland..........Md. 39·40 N 78·40 W
65 Cumberland...Wash. (Seattle In.) 47·17 N 121·55 W
71 Cumberland..........Wis. 45·31 N 92·01 W
78 Cumberland, L........Ky. 36·55 N 85·20 W
63 Cumberland (R.)........U. S. 36·30 N 87·40 W
159 Cumberland Is........Austl. 20·29 S 149·46 E
87 Cumberland Pen........Can. 65·59 N 64·05 W
78 Cumberland Plat........Tenn. 35·25 N 85·30 W
87 Cumberland Sd........Can. 65·27 N 65·44 W
98 Cundinamarca (Dept.) (kōōn-dē-nä-mäʹr-kȧ).Col. (In) 4·57 N 74·27 W
91 Cunduacán (kōōn-dōō-ä-känʹ) Mex. 18·04 N 93·23 W
166 Cunene (Kunene) (R.) Ang.-S. W. Afr. 17·00 S 13·00 E
126 Cuneo (kōō-nā-ō)........It. 44·24 N 7·31 E
101 Cunha (kōōʹnyä) Braz. (Rio de Janeiro In.) 23·05 S 44·56 W
166 Cunjamba (kōōn-käʹm-bä)..Ang. 15·45 S 20·15 E
160 Cunnamulla (kŭn-ȧ-mŭlʹȧ).Austl. 28·00 S 145·55 E
88 Cupula, Pico (Mtn.) (pēʹkȯ-kōōʹpōō-lä).Mex. 24·45 N 111·10 W
90 Cuquío (kōō-kēʹō)........Mex. 20·55 N 103·03 W
90 Curaçao (kōō-rä-säʹō) (I.) Neth. Antilles 12·12 N 68·58 W
100 Curacautín (kä-rä-käōʹtē-n) Chile 38·25 S 71·53 W
101 Curacaví (kōō-rä-kä-vēʹ) Chile (Santiago In.) 33·23 S 71·09 W
101 Curaumilla, Punta (Pt.) (kōō-rou-mēʹlyä) Chile (Santiago In.) 33·05 S 71·44 W
101 Curepto (kōō-rĕp-tȯ) Chile (Santiago In.) 35·06 S 72·02 W
101 Curicó (kōō-rē-kōʹ) Chile (Santiago In.) 34·57 S 71·14 W
101 Curico (Prov.) Chile 34·55 S 71·15 W
100 Curitiba (kōō-rē-tēʹbä)....Braz. 25·20 S 49·15 W
94 Curly Cut Cays (Is.)......Ba. Is. 23·40 N 77·40 W
99 Currais Novos (kōōr-räʹēs nŏ-vōs).Braz. 6·02 S 36·39 W
85 Curran (kū-ränʹ) Can. (Ottawa In.) 45·30 N 74·00 W
94 Current (I.) (kŭ-rĕnt)......Ba. Is. 25·20 N 76·50 W
73 Current (R.) (kûrʹĕnt)......Mo. 37·18 N 91·21 W
167 Currie, Mt. (cŭ-rē) S. Afr. (Natal In.) 30·28 S 29·23 E

79 Currituck Sd. (kûrʹĭ-tŭk)....N. C. 36·27 N 75·42 W
127 Curtea de Argeş (kŏŏrʹtĕ-à dĕ ärʹzhĕsh).Rom. 45·09 N 24·40 E
72 Curtis (kûrʹtĭs)........Nebr. 40·36 N 100·29 W
159 Curtis (I.)........Austl. 23·38 S 151·43 E
75 Curtisville (kûrʹtĭs-vĭl) Pa. (Pittsburgh In.) 40·38 N 79·50 W
99 Curuá (R.) (kōō-rōō-äʹ)....Braz. 6·26 S 54·39 W
127 Curug (chōōʹrōōg)........Yugo. 45·27 N 20·06 E
98 Curupira, Serra (Mts.) (sĕrʹrá kōō-rōō-pēʹrȯ) Braz.-Ven. 1·00 N 65·30 W
99 Cururupu (kōō-rōō-rōō-pōōʹ) Braz. 1·45 S 44·56 W
100 Curuzú Cuatiá (kōō-rōō-zōōʹ kwä-tĕ-äʹ).Arg. 29·45 S 57·58 W
99 Curvelo (kōōr-vĕlʹdō)......Braz. 18·47 S 44·14 W
73 Cushing (kushʹĭng)........Okla. 35·58 N 96·46 W
122 Cusset (kü-sĕʹ)........Fr. 46·08 N 3·29 E
70 Custer (kŭsʹtēr)........S. D. 43·46 N 103·36 W
65 Custer...Wash. (Vancouver In.) 48·55 N 122·39 W
67 Custer Battlefield Natʹl. Mon. (kŭsʹtēr bătʹʹl-fēld).Mont. 45·44 N 107·15 W
67 Cut Bank (kŭt băŋk)......Mont. 48·38 N 112·19 W
78 Cuthbert (kŭthʹbẽrt)........Ga. 31·47 N 84·48 W
142 Cuttack (kŭ-tăkʹ)........India 20·38 N 85·53 E
90 Cutzamala (R.) (kōō-tzä-mä-läʹ) Mex. 18·57 N 100·41 W
90 Cutzamalá de Pinzón (kōō-tzä-mä-läʹdĕ-pēn-zōʹn).Mex. 18·28 N 100·36 W
166 Cuvo (R.) (kōōʹvȯ)........Ang. 11·15 S 14·15 E
120 Cuxhaven (kŏŏksʹ hä-fĕn)..Ger. 53·51 N 8·43 E
75 Cuyahoga Falls Ohio (Cleveland In.) 41·08 N 81·29 W
75 Cuyahoga R. (kī-ȧ-hōʹgȧ) Ohio (Cleveland In.) 41·22 N 81·38 W
68 Cuyapaire Ind. Res. (kū-yȧ-pâr) Calif. 32·46 N 116·20 W
154 Cuyo Is. (kōōʹyȯ)........Phil. 10·54 N 120·08 E
92 Cuyotenango (kōō-yȯ-tĕ-näńgō) Guat. 14·30 N 91·35 W
99 Cuyuni (R.) (kōō-yōōʹnē) Br. Gu.-Ven. 6·40 N 60·44 W
90 Cuyutlán (kōō-yōō-tlänʹ)...Mex. 18·54 N 104·04 W
98 Cuzco........Peru 13·36 S 71·52 W
80 Cynthiana (sĭn-thĭ-ănʹȧ)....Ky. 38·20 N 84·20 W
74 Cypress (sīʹprĕs) Calif. (Los Angeles In.) 33·50 N 118·03 W
77 Cypress Cr........Tex. 32·49 N 94·35 W
115 Cyprus (sīʹprŭs)........Asia 34·56 N 31·28 E
102 Czechoslovakia (chĕkʹȯ-slȯ-väʹkĭ-ȧ).Eur. 49·28 N 16·00 E
121 Czersk (chĕrsk)........Pol. 53·47 N 17·58 E
121 Czestochowa (chäN-stȯ kōʹvä).Pol. 50·49 N 19·10 E
164 Dabakala (dä-bä-käʹlä) Ivory Coast 8·16 N 4·36 W
98 Dabeiba (dä-bäʹbä)....Col. (In.) 7·01 N 76·16 W
65 Dabob (däʹbŏb) Wash. (Seattle In.) 47·50 N 122·49 W
65 Dabob B........Wash. (Seattle In.) 47·44 N 122·50 W
165 Dabra-Mārkʹos........Eth. 10·15 N 37·45 E
165 Dabra-Tābor........Eth. 11·53 N 38·09 E
121 Dabrowa (dȯN-brŏʹvȧ)......Pol. 53·37 N 23·18 E
168 Dābūd........U. A. R. (Nile In.) 23·55 N 32·50 E
142 Dacca (däʹkä) (däkʹä)....E. Pak. 23·45 N 90·29 E
111 Dachau (däʹkou) Ger. (Munich In.) 48·16 N 11·26 E
85 Dacotah (dȧ-kōʹtä) Can. (Winnipeg In.) 49·52 N 97·38 W
79 Dade City (dād)........Fla. (In.) 28·22 N 82·09 W
78 Dadeville (dādʹvĭl)........Ala. 32·48 N 85·44 W
155 Daet (Mtn.) (däʹät) Phil. (Manila In.) 14·07 N 122·59 E
74 Dafter (dăfʹtēr) Mich. (Sault Ste. Marie In.) 46·21 N 84·26 W
168 Dagahabur Eth. (Horn of Afr. In.) 8·10 N 43·25 E
164 Dagama (dä-gäʹmä)......Senegal 16·27 N 15·28 W
128 Dagda (dägʹdä)........Sov. Un. 56·04 N 27·30 E
110 Dagenham (dăgʹĕn-ăm) Eng. (London In.) 51·32 N 0·09 E
133 Dagestan (Reg.) (dä-gĕs-tänʹ) Sov. Un. 43·40 N 46·10 E
155 Dagupan (dä-gōōʹpän) Phil. (Manila In.) 16·02 N 120·20 E
123 Dahl (däl)......Ger. (Ruhr In.) 51·18 N 7·33 E
163 Dahomey (dȧ-hô-māʹ)......Afr. 8·48 N 2·00 E
153 Daigo (dī-gō)...Jap. (Osaka In.) 34·57 N 135·49 E
124 Daimiel Manzanares (dī-myĕlʹ män-zä-näʹrĕs).Sp. 39·05 N 3·36 W
Daíren, see Talien
65 Dairy (R.) (dârʹĭ) Ore. (Portland In.) 45·33 N 123·04 W
65 Dairy (R.) East Fk. Ore. (Portland In.) 45·40 N 123·03 W
153 Dai-Sen (Mtn.) (dīʹsĕn)....Jap. 35·22 N 133·35 E
153 Dai-Tenjo-dake (Mtn.) (dī-tĕńjō dĕ-ĸä).Jap. 36·21 N 137·38 E
95 Dajabón (dä-kä-bŏnʹ).Dom. Rep. 19·35 N 71·40 W
158 Dajarra (dȧ-järʹȧ)........Austl. 21·45 S 139·30 E
164 Dakar (dȧ-kärʹ)........Senegal 14·39 N 17·28 W
145 Dakka........Afg. (Khyber Pass In.) 34·13 N 71·02 E
127 Dakovica (däʹkȯ-vē-tsa)...Yugo. 42·23 N 20·28 E
150 Dalai Nor (L.) (dä-līʹnōr).China 48·50 N 116·45 E
118 Dalälven (R.)........Swe. 60·26 N 15·50 E
160 Dalby (dôlʹbĕ)........Austl. 27·10 S 151·15 E
84 Dalcour (dăl-koorʹ) La. (New Orleans In.) 29·49 N 89·59 W
118 Dale (däʹlĕ)........Nor. 60·34 N 5·46 E
78 Dale Hollow (L.) (dāl hŏlʹō).Tenn. 36·33 N 85·03 W
85 Dalemead (däʹlĕ-mēd) Can. (Calgary In.) 51·05 N 113·38 W
118 Dalen (däʹlĕn)........Nor. 59·28 N 8·01 E
168 Daleside........S. Afr. (Johannesburg & Pretoria In.) 26·30 S 28·03 E
85 Dalesville (dālzʹvĭl) Can. (Montreal In.) 45·42 N 74·23 W

ăt; fìnăl; rāte; senāte; ärm; ȧsk; sofá; fâre; ch-choose; dh-as th in other; bē; ĕvent; bĕt; recĕnt; crātēr; g-go; gh-guttural g; bĭt; ᵻ-short neutral; rīde; ĸ-guttural k as ch in German ich;

Page	Name Pronunciation Region	Lat. °'	Long. °'
158	Daley (L.) (dā'lĭ) ... Austl.	14·15 S	131·15 E
158	Daley Waters (dā-lē) ... Austl.	16·15 S	133·30 E
72	Dalhart (dăl'härt) ... Tex.	36·04 N	102·32 W
82	Dalhousie (dăl-hōō'zē) ... Can.	48·03 N	66·24 W
124	Dalías (dä-lē'äs) ... Sp.	36·49 N	2·50 W
64	Dall (I.) (dăl) ... Alaska	54·50 N	133·10 W
66	Dallas (dăl'lås) ... Ore.	44·55 N	123·20 W
70	Dallas ... S. D.	43·13 N	99·34 W
74	Dallas		
	Tex. (Dallas Fort Worth In.)	32·45 N	96·48 W
73	Dallas (L.) ... Tex.	33·16 N	96·54 W
66	Dalles Dam ... Ore.	45·36 N	121·08 W
126	Dalmacija (Reg.) (däl-mä'tsē-yä)		
	Yugo.	43·25 N	16·37 E
85	Dalroy (dăl'roi). Can. (Calgary In.)	51·08 N	113·40 W
159	Dalrymple, Mt. (dăl'rĭm-p'l)		
	Austl.	21·14 S	148·46 E
78	Dalton (dôl'tŭn) ... Ga.	34·46 N	84·58 W
167	Dalton (dŏl'tŏn)		
	S. Afr. (Natal In.)	29·21 S	30·41 E
65	Daly City (dā'lē)		
	Calif. (San Francisco In.)	37·42 N	122·27 W
99	Dam (däm) ... Sur.	4·36 N	54·54 W
168	Damanhūr (dä-män-hōōr')		
	U. A. R. (Nile In.)	30·59 N	30·31 E
142	Damão ... Asia	20·32 N	75·52 E
155	Damar (I.) ... Indon.	7·15 S	129·15 E
166	Damaraland (Reg.)		
	(dă'mȧ-rȧ-lănd). S. W. Afr.	22·15 S	16·15 E
94	Damas Cays (Is.) (dä'mäs). Ba. Is.	23·50 N	79·50 W
	Damascus, see Dimashq		
133	Damavand (Mtn.) ... Iran	36·05 N	52·05 E
166	Damba (däm'bä) ... Ang.	6·50 S	15·20 E
165	Dambidolo ... Eth.	8·46 N	34·46 E
77	Dam B Res. (dăm) ... Tex.	30·52 N	94·30 W
95	Dame Marie, Cap (C.)		
	(dăm mȧrē'). Hai.	18·35 N	74·50 W
144	Dāmghān (dām-gān') ... Iran	35·50 N	54·15 E
	Damietta, see Dumyāţ		
123	Dammartin-en-Goële (däN-mär-tăN-äN-gō-ĕl'). Fr. (Paris In.)	49·03 N	2·40 E
155	Dampier, Straat (Str.) (dăm'pēr)		
	W. Irian	0·40 N	131·15 E
158	Dampier Arch. (däN-pyâr'). Austl.	20·15 S	116·25 E
79	Dan (R.) (dăn) ... N. C.	36·26 N	79·40 W
165	Danakil Des ... Eth.	12·45 N	41·01 E
154	Danau (R.) ... Indon.	4·17 S	105·00 E
84	Danbury (dăn'bēr-ĭ)		
	Conn. (New York In.)	41·23 N	73·27 W
110	Danbury ... Eng. (London In.)	51·42 N	0·34 E
77	Danbury ... Tex. (In.)	29·14 N	95·22 W
168	Dandarah (dĕn'dȧ-rȧ)		
	U. A. R. (Nile In.)	26·08 N	32·42 E
161	Dandenong (dăn'dē-nông)		
	Austl. (Melbourne In.)	37·59 S	145·13 E
110	Dane (R.) (dān) ... Eng.	53·11 N	2·14 W
85	Danforth (dăn'fŭrth)		
	Can. (Toronto In.)	43·42 N	79·15 W
82	Danforth ... Maine	45·38 N	67·53 W
165	Dānglā ... Eth.	11·17 N	36·69 E
142	Dangri ... India	26·43 N	71·32 E
79	Dania (dā'nĭ-ȧ) ... Fla. (In.)	26·01 N	80·10 W
84	Daniels (dă-nĭ-ĕls)		
	Md. (Baltimore In.)	39·19 N	76·49 W
128	Danilov (dä'nē-lôf) ... Sov. Un.	58·12 N	40·08 E
127	Danilov Grad (dä'nē-lôf'gräd)		
	Yugo.	42·31 N	19·08 E
128	Dankov (däŋ'kôf) ... Sov. Un.	53·17 N	39·09 E
92	Danlí (dän'lē) ... Hond.	14·02 N	86·35 W
81	Dannemora (dăn-ē-mō'rȧ) ... N. Y.	44·45 N	73·45 W
167	Dannhauser (dän'hou-zēr)		
	S. Afr. (Natal In.)	28·07 S	30·04 E
81	Dansville (dănz'vĭl) ... N. Y.	42·30 N	77·40 W
129	Danube, Mouths of the (dăn'ūb)		
	Rom.	45·13 N	29·37 E
115	Danube R. ... Eur.	43·41 N	23·35 E
83	Danvers (dăn'vērz)		
	Mass. (Boston In.)	42·34 N	70·57 W
65	Danville (dăn'vĭl)		
	Calif. (San Francisco In.)	37·49 N	122·00 W
80	Danville ... Ill.	40·10 N	87·35 W
80	Danville ... Ind.	39·45 N	86·30 W
80	Danville ... Ky.	37·35 N	84·50 W
81	Danville ... Pa.	41·00 N	76·35 W
79	Danville ... Va.	36·35 N	79·24 W
	Danzig, see Gdańsk		
112	Danzig, G. of (dán'tsĭk) ... Pol.	54·41 N	19·01 E
139	Dar'a ... Syria (Palestine In.)	32·37 N	36·07 E
121	Dărăbani (dă-rā-bän'ĭ) ... Rom.	48·13 N	26·38 E
164	Daraj ... Libya	30·12 N	10·14 E
168	Darāw (dȧ-rä'ōō)		
	U. A. R. (Nile In.)	24·24 N	32·56 E
142	Darbhanga (dŭr-bŭŋ'gä) ... India	26·03 N	85·09 E
84	Darby (där'bĭ)		
	Pa. (Philadelphia In.)	39·55 N	75·16 W
95	Darby (I.) ... Ba. Is.	23·50 N	76·20 W
	Dardanelles (Str.), see Çanakkale Boğazi		
167	Dar es Salaam (där ĕs sȧ-läm')		
	Tan.	6·58 S	39·13 E
165	Darfur (Prov.) (där-fōōr') ... Sud.	13·21 N	23·46 E
145	Dargai (dŭr-gä'ē)		
	W. Pak. (Khyber Pass In.)	34·32 N	71·55 E
164	D'Arguin, Cap (C.) ... Mauritania	20·28 N	17·46 W
98	Darien (dā-rĭ-ĕn') ... Col. (In.)	3·56 N	76·30 W
84	Darien (dâ-rē-ĕn')		
	Conn. (New York In.)	41·04 N	73·28 W
	Daíren, see Talien		
92	Darien, Cordillera de (Mts.) .. Nic.	13·00 N	85·42 W
98	Darien, Golfo del (G.)		
	(gôl-fô-dĕl-dā-rĭ-ĕn'). N. A.-S. A.	9·36 N	77·54 W
93	Darien, Serrania del (Ra.)		
	(sĕr-ä-nē'ä dĕl dä-rē-ĕn'). Pan.	8·13 N	77·28 W
142	Darjeeling (dŭr-jē'lĭng) ... India	27·05 N	88·16 E
110	Darlaston (där'lȧs-tŭn) ... Eng.	52·34 N	2·02 W
70	Darling (L.) (där'lĭng) ... N. D.	48·35 N	101·25 W
160	Darling (R.) ... Austl.	31·50 S	143·20 E
160	Darling Downs (Reg.) ... Austl.	27·22 S	150·50 E
158	Darling Ra. ... Austl.	30·30 S	115·45 E
116	Darlington (där'lĭng-tŭn) ... Eng.	54·32 N	1·35 W
79	Darlington ... S. C.	34·15 N	79·52 W
71	Darlington ... Wis.	42·41 N	90·06 W
120	Darlowo (där-lô'vô) ... Pol.	54·25 N	16·21 E
120	Darmstadt (därm'shtät) ... Ger.	49·53 N	8·40 E
165	Darnah ... Libya	32·44 N	22·41 E
64	Darnley B. (därn'lē) ... Alaska	70·00 N	124·00 W
165	Dar Nuba (Reg.) ... Sud.	12·22 N	30·39 E
124	Daroca (dä-rō-kä) ... Sp.	41·08 N	1·24 W
75	Darrowville (dâr'rō-vĭl)		
	Ohio (Cleveland In.)	41·12 N	81·27 W
116	Dartmoor (därt'mōōr) ... Eng.	50·35 N	4·05 W
82	Dartmouth (därt'mŭth) ... Can.	44·41 N	63·36 W
116	Dartmouth ... Eng.	50·33 N	3·28 W
155	Daru (I.) (dä'rōō) ... Pap.	9·17 S	143·13 E
126	Daruvar (där'rōō-vär) ... Yugo.	45·37 N	17·16 E
154	Darvel B. (där'vĕl) ... Mala.	4·50 N	118·40 E
110	Darwen (där'wĕn) ... Eng.	53·42 N	2·28 W
158	Darwin (där'wĭn) ... Austl.	12·25 S	131·00 E
100	Darwin, Cordillera (Mts.)		
	(kôr-dēl-yĕ'rä-där'wēn)		
	Chile-Arg.	54·40 S	69·30 W
144	Daryācheh-ye Rezācheh (L.). Iran	38·07 N	45·17 E
124	Das Alturas, Serra (Mts.)		
	(sĕ'r-rä-däs-äl-tōō'räs). Port.	40·43 N	7·48 W
165	Dasē ... Eth.	11·00 N	39·51 E
65	Dash Point (dăsh)		
	Wash. (Seattle In.)	47·19 N	122·25 W
144	Dasht (R.) (dŭsht) ... W. Pak.	25·47 N	63·01 E
144	Dasht-E Kavir Des.		
	(dŭsht-ē-ka-vēr'). Iran	34·43 N	53·30 E
155	Dasol B. (dä-sōl')		
	Phil. (Manila In.)	15·53 N	119·40 E
123	Datteln (dät'tĕln). Ger. (Ruhr In.)	51·39 N	7·20 E
154	Datu, Tandjung (C.) ... Indon.	2·08 N	110·15 E
165	Daua R. (dä'wä) ... Eth.	4·34 N	41·34 E
128	Daugavpils (dä'ōō-gäv-pĭls)		
	Sov. Un.	55·52 N	25·32 E
86	Dauphin (dô'fĭn) ... Can.	51·09 N	100·01 W
84	Davant (dȧ'vănt)		
	La. (New Orleans In.)	29·36 N	89·51 W
155	Davao (dä'vä-ō) ... Phil.	7·05 N	125·30 E
71	Davenport (dăv'ĕn-pōrt) ... Iowa	41 34 N	90·38 W
159	Davenport ... N. Z. (In.)	37·29 S	174·47 E
66	Davenport ... Wash.	47·39 N	118·07 W
93	David (dȧ-vēdh') ... Pan.	8·27 N	82·27 W
70	David City (dā'vĭd) ... Nebr.	41·15 N	97·10 W
121	David-Gorodok (dȧ-vēt' gō-rō'dôk)		
	Sov. Un.	52·02 N	27·14 E
73	Davis (dā'vĭs) ... Okla.	34·34 N	97·08 W
81	Davis ... W. Va.	39·15 N	79·25 W
66	Davis L. ... Ore.	43·38 N	121·43 W
76	Davis Mts. ... Tex.	30·45 N	104·17 W
47	Davis Sea ... Ant.	66·00 S	92·00 E
49	Davis Str. ... Can.	66·00 N	60·00 W
155	Davo G. (dä'vō) ... Phil.	6·30 N	125·45 E
120	Davos (dä'vōs) ... Switz.	46·47 N	9·50 E
144	Dawāsir, Wādī ad (R.). Sau. Ar.	20·48 N	44·07 E
110	Dawley (dô'lĭ) ... Eng.	52·38 N	2·28 W
154	Dawna Ra. (dô'nȧ) ... Bur.	17·02 N	98·01 E
86	Dawson (dô'sŭn) ... Can.	64·04 N	139·22 W
78	Dawson ... Ga.	31·45 N	84·29 W
70	Dawson ... Minn.	44·54 N	96·03 W
160	Dawson (R.) ... Austl.	24·20 S	149·45 E
86	Dawson Creek ... Can.	55·49 N	120·21 W
78	Dawson Springs ... Ky.	37·10 N	87·40 W
122	Dax (dȧks) ... Fr.	43·42 N	1·06 W
144	Dayr az Zawr (dā-ēr'ez-zôr') .. Syr.	35·15 N	40·01 E
168	Dayrūţ ... U. A. R. (Nile In.)	27·33 N	30·48 E
75	Dayton (dā'tŭn)		
	Ky. (Cincinnati In.)	39·07 N	84·28 W
72	Dayton ... N. Mex.	32·44 N	104·23 W
80	Dayton ... Ohio	39·45 N	84·15 W
78	Dayton ... Tenn.	35·30 N	85·00 W
77	Dayton ... Tex.	30·03 N	94·53 W
66	Dayton ... Wash.	46·18 N	117·59 W
79	Daytona Beach (dā-tō'nȧ) ... Fla.	29·11 N	81·02 W
81	Dayville (dā'vĭl) ... Conn.	41·50 N	71·55 W
166	De Aar (dē-är') ... S. Afr.	30·45 S	24·05 E
70	Dead (L.) (dĕd) ... Minn.	46·28 N	96·00 W
70	Deadwood (dĕd'wŏŏd) ... S. D.	44·23 N	103 43 W
81	Deal Island (dēl-ī'lȧnd) ... Md.	38·10 N	75·55 W
100	Deán Funes (dĕ-ä'n-fōō-nĕs). Arg.	30·26 S	64·12 W
75	Dearborn (dēr'bŭrn)		
	Mich. (Detroit In.)	42·18 N	83·15 W
116	Dearg, Ben (Mtn.) (bĕn dŭrg)		
	Scot.	57·48 N	4·59 W
86	Dease Str. (dēz) ... Can.	68·50 N	108·20 W
155	De Atauro (I.) (dĕ-ä-tä'ōō-rō)		
	Port. Timor	8·20 S	126·15 E
68	Death Valley ... Calif.-Nev.	36·55 N	117·12 W
68	Death Valley Junction ... Calif.	36·18 N	116·26 W
68	Death Valley Natl. Mon. ... Calif.	36·34 N	117·00 W
129	Debal'tsevo (dyĕb'ál-tsyĕ'vô)		
	Sov. Un.	48·23 N	38·29 E
127	Debar (Dibra) (dĕ'bär) (dē'brä)		
	Yugo.	41·31 N	20·32 E
114	Debdou (dĕb-dōō') ... Mor.	34·01 N	2·50 W
121	Deblin (dăN'blĭn) ... Pol.	51·34 N	21·49 E
121	Debno (dĕb-nô') ... Sov. Un.	50·24 N	25·44 E
164	Debo Swp. (dā'bō) ... Mali	15·33 N	3·28 W
121	Debrecen (dĕ'brĕ-tsĕn) ... Hung.	47·32 N	21·40 E
78	Decatur (dē-kā'tŭr) ... Ala.	34·35 N	87·00 W
84	Decatur ... Ga. (Atlanta In.)	33·47 N	84·18 W
73	Decatur ... Ill.	39·50 N	88·59 W
80	Decatur ... Ind.	40·50 N	84·55 W
80	Decatur ... Mich.	42·10 N	86·00 W
72	Decatur ... Tex.	33·14 N	97·33 W
122	Decazeville (dē-käz'vēl') ... Fr.	44·33 N	2·16 E
143	Decean Plat. (dĕk'ăn) ... India	26·36 N	76 35 E
65	Deception P. (dē-sĕp'shŭn)		
	Wash. (Seattle In.)	48·24 N	122·44 W
120	Decin (dyĕ'chĕn) ... Czech.	50·47 N	14·14 E
71	Decorah (dē-kō'rȧ) ... Iowa	43·18 N	91·48 W
139	Dedap ... Indon. (Singapore In.)	1·19 N	102·22 E
	Dedeagats, see Alexandroupolis		
136	Dedenevo (dyĕ-dyĕ'nyĕ-vô)		
	Sov. Un. (Moscow In.)	56·14 N	37·31 E
83	Dedham (dĕd'ăm)		
	Mass. (Boston In.)	42·15 N	71·11 W
100	Dedo do Deus (Mt.)		
	(dĕ-dô-dô-dĕ'ōōs). Braz. (In.)	22·30 S	43·02 W
164	Dédougou (dā-dōō-gōō')		
	Upper Volta	12·28 N	3·21 W
116	Dee (R.) ... Wales	53·00 N	3·10 W
116	Dee (R.) ... Scot.	57·05 N	2·25 W
79	Deep (R.) (dēp) ... N. C.	35·36 N	79·32 W
84	Deep Creek ... Va. (Norfolk In.)	36·44 N	76·22 W
73	Deep Fk. (R.) ... Okla.	35·35 N	96·42 W
73	Deepwater (dep-wô-tēr) ... Mo.	38·15 N	93·46 W
83	Deer (dēr) ... Can.	49·06 N	57·45 W
82	Deer ... Maine	44·07 N	68·38 W
75	Deerfield (dēr'fēld)		
	Ill. (Chicago In.)	42·10 N	87·51 W
65	Deer Island .. Ore. (Portland In.)	45·56 N	122·51 W
83	Deer Lake ... Can.	49·09 N	57·26 W
67	Deer Lodge (dēr lŏj) ... Mont.	46·23 N	112·42 W
75	Deer Park .. Ohio (Cincinnati In.)	39·12 N	84·24 W
66	Deer Park ... Wash.	47·58 N	117·28 W
71	Deer River ... Minn.	47·20 N	93·49 W
80	Defiance (dē-fī'ăns) ... Ohio	41·15 N	84·20 W
78	DeFuniak Springs (dē fū'nĭ-ăk)		
	Fla.	30·42 N	86·06 W
120	Deggendorf (dĕ'ghĕn-dôrf) ... Ger.	48·50 N	12·59 E
90	Degollado (dā-gō-lyä'dō) ... Mex.	20·27 N	102·11 W
158	DeGrey (R.) (dē grā') ... Austl.	20·20 S	119·25 E
136	Degtyarsk (dĕg-ty'arsk)		
	Sov. Un. (Urals In.)	56·42 N	60·05 E
142	Dehra Dun (dā'rŭ) ... India	30·09 N	78·07 E
121	Dej (dāzh) ... Rom.	47·09 N	23·53 E
71	De Kalb (dē kălb') ... Ill.	41·54 N	88·46 W
85	Delacour (dĕ-lä-kōōr')		
	Can. (Calgary In.)	51·09 N	113·45 W
84	Delacroix (dĕl ȧ-krō')		
	La. (New Orleans In.)	29·46 N	89·47 W
72	Delagua (dĕl-ä'gwä) ... Colo.	37·19 N	104·42 W
79	De Land (dē lănd') ... Fla.	29·00 N	81·19 W
68	Delano (dĕl'ȧ-nō) ... Calif.	35·47 N	119·15 W
69	Delano, Mt. ... Utah	38·25 N	112·25 W
71	Delavan (dĕl'ȧ-văn) ... Wis.	42·39 N	88·38 W
80	Delaware (dĕl'ȧ-wâr) ... Ohio	40·15 N	83·05 W
63	Delaware (State) ... U. S.	38·40 N	75·30 W
73	Delaware (R.) ... Kans.	39·45 N	95·47 W
81	Delaware (R.) ... N. J.-Pa.	41·50 N	75·20 W
81	Delaware B. ... Del.-N. J.	39·05 N	75·10 W
80	Delaware Res. ... Ohio	40·30 N	83·05 W
124	Del Eje, Sierra (Mts.)		
	(sē-ĕ'r-rä-dĕl-ĕ'κĕ). Sp.	42·15 N	6·45 W
120	Delemont (dē-lā-môN') ... Switz.	47·21 N	7·18 E
76	De Leon (dē lē-ŏn') ... Tex.	32·06 N	98·33 W
85	De Léry (dā lā-rī')		
	Can. (Montreal In.)	45·21 N	73·49 W
101	Delfínópolis (dĕl-fē'nô'pō-lēs)		
	Braz. (Rio de Janeiro In.)	20·20 S	46·50 W
111	Delft (dĕlft)		
	Neth. (Amsterdam In.)	52·01 N	4·20 E
117	Delfzijl ... Neth.	53·20 N	6·50 E
100	Delgada Pta. (Pt.)		
	(pōō'n-tä-dĕl-gä'dä). Arg.	43·46 S	63·46 W
167	Delgado, Cabo (C.)		
	(kȧ'bô-dĕl-gä'dō). Moz.	10·30 S	41·00 E
165	Delgo (dĕl'gō) ... Sud.	20·07 N	30·41 E
74	Delhi (dĕl'hī) .. Ill. (St. Louis In.)	39·03 N	90·16 W
142	Delhi ... India	28·54 N	77·13 E
77	Delhi ... La.	32·26 N	91·29 W
125	Del Hoyo, Sierra (Mtn.)		
	(sē-ĕ'r-rä-dĕl-ô'yô)		
	Sp. (Madrid In.)	40·39 N	3·56 W
120	Delitzsch (dā'lĭch) ... Ger.	51·32 N	12·18 E
127	Dell Alice, Pt. (dĕl-ä-lē'chĕ) ... It.	39·23 N	17·10 E
70	Dell Rapids (dĕl) ... S. D.	43·50 N	96·43 W
74	Dellwood (dĕl'wŏŏd)		
	Minn. (Minneapolis,		
	St. Paul In.)	45·05 N	92·58 W
164	Dellys (dĕ'lēs') ... Alg.	36·59 N	3·40 E
68	Del Mar (dĕl mär')		
	Calif. (San Diego In.)	32·57 N	117·16 W
168	Delmas (dĕl'mȧs)		
	S. Afr. (Johannesburg &		
	Pretoria In.)	26·08 S	28·43 E
120	Delmenhorst (dĕl'mĕn-hôrst). Ger.	53·03 N	8·38 E
69	Del Norte (dĕl nôrt') ... Colo.	37·40 N	106·25 W
135	De-Longa (I.) ... Sov. Un.	76·58 N	157·39 E
64	Delong Mts. (dĕ-lŏng) ... Alaska	68·30 N	163·25 W
160	Deloraine (dĕ-lŭ-rān') ... Austl.	41·30 S	146·40 E
80	Delphi (dĕl'fī) ... Ind.	40·35 N	86·40 W
80	Delphos (dĕl'fŏs) ... Ohio	40·50 N	84·20 W
79	Delray Beach (dĕl-rā') .. Fla. (In.)	26·27 N	80·05 W
76	Del Rio (dĕl rē'ō) ... Tex.	29·21 N	100·52 W
85	Delson Village (dĕl'sŭn)		
	Can. (Montreal In.)	45·24 N	73·32 W
69	Delta ... Colo.	38·45 N	108·05 W
69	Delta ... Utah	39·20 N	112·35 W
68	Delta Mendota can. ... Calif.	37·10 N	121·02 W
85	Delta Station. Can. (Winnipeg In.)	50·10 N	98·20 W
127	Delvine (dĕl'vē-nä) ... Alb.	39·58 N	20·10 E
132	Dĕma (R.) (dyĕm'ȧ) ... Sov. Un.	53·40 N	54·30 E
128	Demidov (dzyĕ'mē-dô'f). Sov. Un.	55·16 N	31·32 E
69	Deming (dĕm'ĭng) ... N. Mex.	32·15 N	107·45 W
120	Demmin (dĕm'mēn) ... Ger.	53·54 N	13·04 E
164	Demnate (dĕm-nät) ... Mor.	31·58 N	7·03 W
78	Demopolis (dē-mŏp'ō-lĭs) ... Ala	32·30 N	87·50 W
75	Demotte (dē'mŏt)		
	Ind. (Chicago In.)	41·12 N	87·13 W
154	Dempo, Gunung (Vol.) (dĕm'pō)		
	Indon.	4·04 S	103·11 E
134	Dem'yanka (R.) (dyĕm-yän'kä)		
	Sov. Un.	59·07 N	72·58 E

ng-sing; ŋ-baŋk; N-nasalized n; nŏd; cŏmmit; ōld; ôbey; ôrder; fōōd; fŏŏt; ou-out; s-soft; sh-dish; th-thin; pūre; ûnite; ûrn; stŭd; circŭs; ü-as "y" in study; '-indeterminate vowel.

Page	Name Pronunciation Region	Lat. °′	Long. °′
128	Demyansk (dyěm-yänsk') Sov. Un.	57·39 N	32·26 E
122	Denain (dē-năɴ') Fr.	50·23 N	3·21 E
116	Denbigh (děn'bĭ) Wales	53·15 N	3·25 W
110	Denbigh (Co.) Wales	53·01 N	2·59 W
111	Dendermonde. Bel. (Brussels In.)	51·02 N	4·04 E
79	Dendron (děn'drŭn) Va.	37·02 N	76·53 W
136	Denezhkin Kamen, Gora (Mtn.) (dzyě-ŋě'zhkĕn kăm'ĭěŋ) Sov. Un. (Urals In.)	60·26 N	59·35 E
93	D'Enfer, Pointe (Pt.) Mart. (Le. & Wind. Is. In.)	14·21 N	60·48 W
94	Denham, Mt. Jam.	18·20 N	77·30 W
117	Den Helder (děn hěl'dēr) Neth.	52·55 N	5·45 E
125	Denia (dā'nyä) Sp.	38·48 N	0·06 E
160	Deniliquin (dě-nĭl'ĭ-kwĭn) Austl.	35·20 S	144·52 E
70	Denison (děn'ĭ-sŭn) Iowa	42·01 N	95·22 W
73	Denison Tex.	33·45 N	97·02 W
136	Denisovka (dě-nē'sof-kȧ) Sov. Un. (Urals In.)	52·26 N	61·45 E
133	Denizli (děn-ĭz-lē') Tur.	37·40 N	29·10 E
123	Denklingen (děn'klĕn-gĕn) Ger. (Ruhr In.)	50·54 N	7·40 E
79	Denmark (děn'märk) S. C.	33·18 N	81·09 W
102	Denmark Eur.	56·14 N	8·30 E
49	Denmark Str. Grnld.	66·30 N	27·00 W
168	Dennilton (děn-ĭl-tŭn) S. Afr. (Johannesburg & Pretoria In.)	25·18 S	29·13 E
80	Dennison (děn'ĭ-sŭn) Ohio	40·25 N	81·20 W
81	Denton (děn'tŭn) Md.	38·55 N	75·50 W
73	Denton Tex.	33·12 N	97·06 W
158	D'entrecasteaux, Pt. (dăɴ-tr'kȧs-tō'). Austl.	34·50 S	114·45 E
155	D'entrecasteaux Is. (dăɴ-tr'-kȧs-tō'). Pap.	9·45 S	152·00 E
72	Denver (děn'vēr) Colo.	39·44 N	104·59 W
142	Deoli India	25·52 N	75·23 E
71	De Pere (dē pēr') Wis.	44·25 N	88·04 W
75	Depew (dē-pū'). N. Y. (Buffalo In.)	42·55 N	78·43 W
80	Depue (dē pū) Ill.	41·15 N	89·55 W
73	De Queen (dē kwēn') Ark.	34·02 N	94·21 W
77	De Quincy (dē kwĭn'sĭ) La.	30·27 N	93·27 W
142	Dera Ghāzi Khān (dā'rŭ gä-zē' ĸän'). W. Pak.	30·09 N	70·39 E
142	Dera Ismail Khan (dā'rŭ ĭs-mä-ēl' ĸän'). W. Pak.	31·55 N	70·51 E
133	Derbent (dĕr-bĕnt') Sov. Un.	42·00 N	48·10 E
158	Derby (där'bē) (dûr'bē) Austl.	17·20 S	123·40 E
81	Derby (dûr'bē) Conn.	41·20 N	73·05 W
110	Derby (där'bē) Eng.	52·55 N	1·29 W
168	Derby (där'bĭ) S. Afr. (Johannesburg & Pretoria In.)	25·55 S	27·02 E
110	Derby (Co.) (där'bē) Eng.	53·11 N	1·30 W
168	Derdepoort S. Afr. (Johannesburg & Pretoria In.)	24·39 S	26·21 E
116	Derg, Lough (B.) (lŏk dĕrg). Ire.	53·00 N	8·09 W
77	De Ridder (dē rĭd'ēr) La.	30·50 N	93·18 W
73	Dermott (dûr'mŏt) Ark.	33·32 N	91·24 W
83	Derry (dâr'ĭ). N. H. (Boston In.)	45·52 N	71·22 W
127	Derventa (děr'ven-tȧ) Yugo.	45·58 N	17·58 E
160	Derwent (R.) (dûr'wĕnt) Austl.	42·21 S	146·30 E
110	Derwent (R.) (dĕr'wĕnt) Eng.	52·54 N	1·24 W
73	Des Arc (dāz ärk') Ark.	34·59 N	91·31 W
101	Descalvado (dĕs-käl-vá-dō) Braz. (Rio de Janeiro In.)	21·55 S	47·37 W
85	Deschenes. Can. (Ottawa In.)	45·23 N	75·47 W
85	Deschenes, L. Can. (Ottawa In.)	54·25 N	75·53 W
66	Deschutes R. (dā-shōōt') Ore.	44·25 N	121·21 W
76	Desdemona (děz-dē-mō'nȧ). Tex.	32·16 N	98·33 W
100	Deseado, Rio (R.) (rē'-ō-dā-sā-ä'dhō). Arg.	46·50 S	67·45 W
93	Desirade I. (dā-zē-räs') N. A. (Le. & Wind. Is. In.)	16·21 N	60·51 W
70	De Smet (dē smět') S. D.	44·23 N	97·33 W
71	Des Moines (dē moin') Iowa	41·35 N	93·37 W
72	Des Moines N. Mex.	36·42 N	103·48 W
65	Des Moines. Wash. (Seattle In.)	46·24 N	122·20 W
63	Des Moines (R.) U. S.	43·45 N	94·20 W
129	Desna (R.) (dyěs-nȧ'). Sov. Un.	51·05 N	31·03 E
100	Desolación (dě-sô-lä-syô'n) (I.) Chile	53·05 S	74·00 W
73	De Soto (dē sō'tō) Mo.	38·07 N	90·32 W
74	Des Peres (děs pĕr'ĕs) Mo. (St. Louis In.)	38·36 N	90·26 W
75	Des Plaines (děs plānz') Ill. (Chicago In.)	42·02 N	87·54 W
75	Des Plaines R. Ill. (Chicago In.)	41·39 N	88·05 W
120	Dessau (děs'ou) Ger.	51·50 N	12·15 E
120	Detmold (dět'mōld) Ger.	51·57 N	8·55 E
75	Detroit (dē-troit') Mich. (Detroit In.)	42·22 N	83·10 W
73	Detroit Tex.	33·41 N	95·16 W
70	Detroit Lakes (dē-troit' lākz) Minn.	46·48 N	95·51 W
75	Detroit R. U. S.-Can. (Detroit In.)	42·08 N	83·07 W
121	Detva (dyĕt'vȧ) Czech.	48·32 N	19·21 E
111	Deurne. Bel. (Brussels In.)	51·13 N	4·27 E
111	Deutsch Wagram Aus. (Vienna In.)	48·19 N	16·34 E
85	Deux Montagnes, Lac des (dû mōɴ-tăny'') Can. (Montreal In.)	45·28 N	74·00 W
127	Deva (dā'vä) Rom.	45·52 N	22·52 E
121	Dévaványa (dā'vô-vän-yô). Hung.	47·01 N	20·58 E
133	Develi (dě'vȧ-lē) Tur.	38·20 N	35·10 E
117	Deventer (dĕv'ĕn-tēr) Neth.	52·14 N	6·07 E
70	Devils (L.) (děv''lz) N. D.	47·57 N	99·04 W
76	Devils (R.) Tex.	29·55 N	101·10 W
	Devils I., see Diable, Ile du		
62	Devils Lake N. D.	48·10 N	98·55 W
70	Devils Lake Ind. Res. N. D.	48·08 N	99·40 W
68	Devils Postpile Natl. Mon. Calif.	37·42 N	119·12 W
67	Devils Tower Natl. Mon. Wyo.	44·38 N	105·07 W
127	Devoll (R.) Alb.	40·55 N	20·10 E
168	Devon (děv'ŭn) S. Afr. (Johannesburg & Pretoria In.)	26·23 S	28·47 E
160	Devonport (děv'ŭn-pôrt). Austl.	41·20 S	146·30 E
74	Devore (dē-vôr') Calif. (Los Angeles In.)	34·13 N	117·24 W
77	Dewalt (dū'ălt) Tex. (In.)	29·33 N	95·33 W
65	Dewatto (dē-wát'ō) Wash. (Seattle In.)	47·27 N	123·04 W
73	Dewey (dū'ĭ) Okla.	36·48 N	95·55 W
73	De Witt (dē wĭt') Ark.	34·17 N	91·22 W
71	De Witt Iowa	41·46 N	90·34 W
110	Dewsbury (dūz'bĕr-ĭ) Eng.	53·42 N	1·39 W
82	Dexter (děks'tēr) Maine	45·01 N	69·19 W
73	Dexter Mo.	36·46 N	89·56 W
79	Dexter (L.) Fla.	29·07 N	81·24 W
144	Dezfūl Iran	32·14 N	48·37 E
139	Dezhneva, Mys (East Cape) (dyězh'nyĭf). Sov. Un.	68·00 N	172·00 W
	Dhahran, see AzZahrān		
143	Dharamtar Cr. India (Bombay In.)	18·49 N	72·54 E
143	Dharmavaram India	14·32 N	77·43 E
142	Dhaulagiri, Mt. (dou-lȧ-gē'rē) Nep.	33·50 N	83·32 E
127	Dhenoúsa (I.) Grc.	37·09 N	25·53 E
139	Dhibān. Jordan (Palestine In.)	31·30 N	35·46 E
127	Dhidhimótikhon Grc.	41·20 N	26·27 E
127	Dhodhekánisos (Dodecanese) (Is.) Grc.	38·00 N	26·10 E
142	Dhūlia (dōōl'yȧ) India	20·58 N	74·43 E
142	Dhupgarth (Mt.) India	27·30 N	78·27 E
126	Dia (I.) (dē'ā). Grc. (Inset)	35·27 N	25·17 E
99	Diable, Île du (Devils I.). Fr. Gu.	5·15 N	57·10 W
65	Diablo, Mt. (dyä'blō) Calif. (San Francisco In.)	37·52 N	121·55 W
88	Diablo Heights (dyȧ'blō) C. Z. (Panama Canal In.)	8·58 N	79·34 W
65	Diablo Range (Mts.) Calif. (San Francisco In.)	37·47 N	121·50 W
99	Diamantina (dē-ȧ-män-tē'nȧ) Braz.	14·22 S	56·23 W
99	Diamantina Braz.	18·14 S	43·32 W
158	Diamantina (R.) (dī'man-tē'nȧ) Austl.	25·38 S	139·53 E
84	Diamond (dī'ȧ-mŭnd) La. (New Orleans In.)	29·34 N	89·48 W
66	Diamond Pk. Ore.	43·32 N	122·08 W
154	Diamond Pt. (dī'mŭnd). Indon.	5·30 N	96·45 E
95	Diana Bk. (dī'ăn'ȧ). Ba. Is.	22·30 N	74·45 W
155	Diapitan B. (dyä-pē-tä'n) Phil. (Manila In.)	16·28 N	122·25 E
	Dibra, see Debar		
70	Dickinson (dĭk'ĭn-sŭn) N. D.	46·52 N	102·49 W
77	Dickinson (dĭk'ĭn-sŭn). Tex. (In.)	29·28 N	95·02 W
77	Dickinson Bay Tex. (In.)	29·26 N	95·08 W
78	Dickson (dĭk'sŭn) Tenn.	36·03 N	87·24 W
81	Dickson City Pa.	41·25 N	75·40 W
133	Dicle (R.) (dĭj'lȧ) Tur.	37·50 N	40·40 E
110	Didcot (dĭd'cŏt) Eng. (London In.)	51·35 N.	1·15 W
123	Die (dē) Fr.	44·45 N	5·22 E
95	Diego de Ocampo, Pico (Pk.) (pē'-kō-dyĕ'gō-dĕ-ō-kä'm-pō) Dom. Rep.	19·40 N	70·45 W
100	Diego Ramirez, Islas (Is.) (dē ä'gō rä-mē'räz). Chile	56·15 S	70·15 W
167	Diégo-Suarez (Antsirane) (dē-ä'gō-swȧ'räz) (änt-sē-rän') Malag. Rep.	12·18 S	49·16 E
146	Dien Bien Phan Viet.	21·38 N	102·49 E
82	Dieppe (dē-ĕp') Can.	46·08 N	64·45 W
122	Dieppe Fr.	49·54 N	1·05 E
73	Dierks (dērks) Ark.	34·06 N	94·02 W
111	Diessen (dēs'sĕn) Ger. (Munich In.)	47·57 N	11·06 E
111	Diest Bel. (Brussels In.)	50·59 N	5·05 E
82	Digby (dĭg'bĭ) Can.	44·37 N	65·48 W
84	Dighton (dī-tŭn) Mass. (Providence In.)	41·49 N	71·05 W
123	Digne (dēn'y') Fr.	44·07 N	6·16 E
155	Digoel (R.) W. Irian	7.00 S	140·25 E
122	Digoin (dē-gwăɴ') Fr.	46·28 N	4·06 E
155	Dijohan Pt. (dē-kō-än) Phil. (Manila In.)	16·24 N	122·25 E
122	Dijon (dē-zhōɴ') Fr.	47·21 N	5·02 E
134	Dikson (dĭk'sŏn) Sov. Un.	72·47 N	79·20 E
165	Dikwa (dē'kwȧ) Nig.	12·06 N	13·53 E
155	Dili (dĭl'ē) Port. Timor	8·35 S	125·35 E
114	Di Linosa I. (dē-lē-nō'sȧ) Medit. Sea	36·01 N	12·43 E
133	Dilizhan Sov. Un.	40·45 N	45·00 E
64	Dillingham (dĭl'ĕng-hăm). Alaska	59·10 N	158·38 W
67	Dillon (dĭl'ŭn) Mont.	45·12 N	112·40 W
79	Dillon S. C.	34·24 N	79·28 W
166	Dilolo (dē-lō'lō) Con. L.	10·19 S	22·23 E
139	Dimashq (Damascus) (dä-măs'kŭs). Syria (Palestine In.)	33·31 N	36·18 E
127	Dimbovita (R.) Rom.	44·43 N	25·41 E
127	Dimitrovo (Pernik) (pĕr-nēk'). Bul.	42·36 N	23·04 E
155	Dinagate I. (dē-nä'gät) Phil.	10·15 N	126·15 E
142	Dinājpur India	25·38 N	87·39 E
122	Dinan (dē-năɴ') Fr.	48·27 N	2·03 W
117	Dinant (dē-năɴ') Bel.	50·17 N	4·50 E
126	Dinara Planina (Mts.) (dē'nä-rä plä'nē-nä). Yugo.	43·50 N	16·15 E
143	Dindigul India	10·25 N	78·03 E
155	Dingalan B. (dĭŋ-gä'län) Phil. (Manila In.)	15·19 N	121·33 E
116	Dingle (dĭng''l) Ire.	52·10 N	10·13 W
116	Dingle B. Ire.	52·02 N	10·15 W
159	Dingo (dĭŋ'gō) Austl.	23·45 S	149·26 E
116	Dingwall (dĭng'wôl) Scot.	57·37 N	4·23 W
67	Dinosaur Natl. Mon. (dī'nō-sôr) Utah-Colo.	40·45 N	109·17 W
123	Dinslaken (dēns'lä-kĕn) Ger. (Ruhr In.)	51·33 N	6·44 E
111	Dinterloord Neth. (Amsterdam In.)	51·38 N	4·21 E
68	Dinuba (dĭ-nū'bȧ) Calif.	36·33 N	119·29 W
164	Diorbivol (dē-ôr-bē-vôl'). Senegal	16·07 N	13·52 W
94	Dios, Cayo de (I.) (kä'yō-dĕ-dē-ōs'). Cuba	22·05 N	83·05 W
164	Diourbel (dē-ōōr-bĕl'). Senegal	14·37 N	16·28 W
145	Diphu Pass (dĭ-pōō) China	28·15 N	96·45 E
93	Diquis R. (dē-kēs') C. R.	8·59 N	83·24 W
168	Dirēdawā. Eth. (Horn of Afr. In.)	9·40 N	41·47 E
92	Diriamba (dēr-yäm'bä) Nic.	11·52 N	86·15 W
158	Dirk Hartog (I.) Austl.	26·25 S	113·15 E
111	Dirksland. Neth. (Amsterdam In.)	51·45 N	4·04 E
160	Dirranbandi (dĭ-rȧ-băn'dē). Austl.	28·24 S	148·29 E
69	Dirty Devil (R.) (dûr'tĭ děv''l) Utah	38·20 N	110·30 W
158	Disappointment (L.) Austl.	23·20 S	120·20 E
65	Disappointment, C. (dĭs'ȧ-point'ment). Wash. (Portland In.)	46·16 N	124·11 W
125	D'Ischia, I. (dē'sh-kyä) It. (Naples In.)	40·26 N	13·55 E
167	Discovery (dĭs-cŭv'ēr-ĭ). S. Afr. (Johannesburg & Pretoria In.)	26·10 S	27·53 E
65	Discovery Is. (dĭs-kŭv'ēr-ē) Can. (Seattle In.)	48·25 N	123·13 W
168	Dishnā (dēsh'nȧ) U. A. R. (Nile In.)	26·08 N	32·27 E
49	Disko (dĭs'kō) (I.) Grnld.	70·00 N	54·00 W
79	Dismal Swp. (dĭz'măl). N. C.-Va.	36·35 N	76·34 W
128	Disna (dēs'nȧ) Sov. Un.	55·34 N	28·15 E
82	Disraeli (dĭs-rā'lĭ) Can.	45·53 N	71·23 W
81	District of Columbia U. S.	38·50 N	77·00 W
91	Distrito Federal (Dist.) (dēs-trē'tô-fĕ-dĕ-rä'l). Mex.	19·14 N	99·08 W
168	Disūq (dē-sōōk') U. A. R. (Nile In.)	31·07 N	30·41 E
142	Diu (dē'ōō) Asia	20·48 N	70·58 E
122	Dives (dēv) Fr.	49·18 N	0·05 W
155	Divilacan B. (dē-vē-lä'kän). Phil.	17·26 N	122·25 E
101	Divinópolis (dē-vē-nô'pō-lēs) Braz. (Rio de Janeiro In.)	20·10 S	44·53 W
85	Dixie (dĭk'sĭ). Can. (Toronto In.)	43·36 N	79·35 W
71	Dixon (dĭks'ŭn) Ill.	41·50 N	89·30 W
86	Dixon Ent. Alaska-Can.	54·36 N	132·32 W
133	Diyarbakir (dē-yär-běk'ĭr) Tur.	38·00 N	40·10 E
165	Dja R. Cam.	2·40 N	14·11 E
155	Djailolo Pass Indon.	0·05 S	129·08 E
154	Djakarta (yä-kär'tä) Indon.	6·17 S	106·45 E
154	Djambi (jäm'bē) Indon.	1·45 S	103·28 E
164	Djanet (Fort Charlet) Alg.	24·29 N	9·26 E
114	Djedi R. Alg.	34·18 N	4·39 E
164	Djelfa (jĕl'fä) Alg.	34·40 N	3·17 E
164	Djenné (jĕnnā') Mali	13·55 N	4·26 W
114	Djerba, ɪle de (I.) Tun.	33·53 N	11·26 E
164	Djerid, Chott (L.) (jĕr'ĭd) Tun.	33·15 N	8·29 E
168	Djibouti (jē-bōō-tē') Fr. Som. (Horn of Afr. In.)	11·34 N	43·00 E
113	Djidjelli (jē-jĕ-lē') Alg.	36·49 N	5·47 E
139	Djumrah. Indon. (Singapore In.)	1·48 N	101·04 E
126	Djurdevac (dūr'dyĕ-väts'). Yugo.	46·03 N	17·03 E
118	Djursholm (djōōrs'hōlm) Swe.	59·26 N	18·01 E
129	Dmitriyevka (d'mē-trē-yĕf'kȧ) Sov. Un.	47·57 N	38·56 E
129	Dmitriyev L'govskiy (d'mē'trĭ-yĕf l'gôf'skĭ). Sov. Un.	52·07 N	35·05 E
136	Dmitrov (d'mē'trôf) Sov. Un. (Moscow In.)	56·21 N	37·32 E
128	Dmitrovsk (d'mē'trôfsk). Sov. Un.	52·30 N	35·10 E
129	Dnepr (Dnieper) (R.) (nē'pēr) Sov. Un.	46·47 N	32·57 E
129	Dneprodzerzhinsk (d'nyĕp'rô-zēr-shĭnsk). Sov. Un.	48·32 N	34·38 E
129	Dnepropetrovsk (d'nyĕp'rô-pä-trôfsk). Sov. Un.	48·23 N	34·10 E
129	Dnepropetrovsk (Oblast). Sov. Un.	48·15 N	34·08 E
129	Dnepr Zaliv (B.) (dnyĕp'r zȧ'lĭf). Sov. Un.	46·33 N	31·45 E
129	Dnestr (Dniester) (R.) (nēst'rōōl) (nēs'tēr). Sov. Un.	48·21 N	28·10 E
129	Dnestrovskiy Liman (B.) Sov. Un.	46·13 N	29·50 E
	Dnieper (R.), see Dnepr		
	Dniester (R.), see Dnestr		
128	Dno (d'nô') Sov. Un.	57·49 N	29·59 E
84	Dobbs Ferry (dŏbz' fĕ'rē) N. Y. (New York In.)	41·01 N	73·53 W
158	Dobbyn (dôb'ĭn) Austl.	19·45 S	140·02 E
119	Dobele (dô'bĕ-lĕ) Sov. Un.	56·37 N	23·18 E
120	Döbeln (dû'bĕln) Ger.	51·08 N	13·07 E
155	Dobo Indon.	6·00 S	134·18 E
127	Doboj (dō'boi) Yugo.	44·42 N	18·04 E
136	Dobryanka (dôb-ryän'kȧ) Sov. Un. (Urals In.)	58·27 N	56·26 E
121	Dobšina (dôp'shē-nä) Czech.	48·48 N	20·25 E
99	Doce (R.) (dō'sȧ) Braz.	19·01 S	42·14 W
94	Doce Leguas, Cayos de las (Is.) (kä'yōs-dĕ-läs-dô-sĕ-lĕ'gwȧs) Cuba	20·55 N	79·05 W
90	Doctor Arroyo (dōk-tōr' är-rō'yō) Mex.	23·41 N	100·10 W
110	Doddington (dŏd'dĭng-tŏn) Eng. (London In.)	51·17 N	0·47 E
	Dodecanese (Is.), see Dhodhekánisos		
72	Dodge City (dŏj) Kans.	37·44 N	100·01 W
81	Dodgeville (dŏj'vĭl) N. Y.	43·10 N	74·45 W
71	Dodgeville Wis.	42·58 N	90·07 W
166	Dodoma (dō'dô-mȧ) Tan.	6·13 S	35·36 E
74	Dodson (dŏd's'n) Mo. (Kansas City In.)	38·48 N	94·33 W
71	Dog (L.) (dŏg) Can.	48·42 N	89·24 W
117	Dogger Bk. (dŏg'gēr) Eur.	55·07 N	2·25 E
94	Dog Rocks (I.) Ba. Is.	24·05 N	79·50 W
133	Dogubayazit Tur.	39·35 N	44·00 E

ăt; finăl; rāte; senâte; ärm; åsk; sofȧ; fâre; ch-choose: dh-as th in other; bē; ēvent; bĕt; recĕnt; cratēr; g-go; gh-guttural g; bĭt; ĭ-short neutral; rīde; ĸ-guttural k as ch in German ich;

Page	Name Pronunciation Region	Lat. °′	Long. °′
142	Dohad ... India	22·52 N	74·18 E
127	Doiran (L.) ... Grc.	41·10 N	23·00 E
153	Dōjō (dō-jō) ... Jap. (Osaka In.)	34·51 N	135·14 E
128	Dokshitsy (dôk-shētsĕ) .. Sov. Un.	54·53 N	27·49 E
82	Dolbeau ... Can.	48·52 N	72·16 W
123	Dôle (dōl) ... Fr.	47·07 N	5·28 E
129	Dolgaya, Kosa (C.) (kô'sȧ dôl-gä'yȧ) . Sov. Un.	46·42 N	37·42 E
132	Dolgiy (I.) ... Sov. Un.	69·20 N	59·20 E
121	Dolina (dô-lyē'nä) ... Sov. Un.	48·57 N	24·01 E
152	Dolinsk (dȧ-lēnsk') ... Sov. Un.	47·29 N	142·31 E
94	Dollar Hbr. ... Ba. Is.	25·30 N	79·15 W
165	Dolo ... Som.	4·01 N	42·14 E
84	Dolomite (dŏl'ô-mīt) Ala. (Birmingham In.)	33·28 N	86·57 W
126	Dolomitiche, Alpi (Mts.) (äl-pē-dô-lô'mē-tē'chě) . It.	46·16 N	11·43 E
101	Dolores (dô-lō'rěs) Arg. (Buenos Aires In.)	36·20 S	57·42 W
98	Dolores ... Col. (In.)	3·33 N	74·54 W
155	Dolores (dô-lô-rěs) Phil. (Manila In.)	17·40 N	120·43 E
76	Dolores (dô-lō'rěs) ... Tex.	27·42 N	99·47 W
101	Dolores .... Ur. (Buenos Aires In.)	33·32 S	58·15 W
69	Dolores (R.) ... Colo.-Utah	38·35 N	108·50 W
90	Dolores Hidalgo (dô-lô'rěs-ē-däl'gō) . Mex.	21·09 N	100·56 W
86	Dolphin and Union Str. (dŏl'fĭn ūn'yŭn) . Can.	69·22 N	117·10 W
120	Domažlice (dō'mäzh-lē-tsě) Czech.	49·27 N	12·55 E
123	Dombasle (dôN-bäl') ... Fr.	48·38 N	6·18 E
121	Dombóvár (dŏm'bō-vär) ... Hung.	46·22 N	18·08 E
122	Dôme, Puy de (Pk.) (pwē'dě-dôm') . Fr.	45·47 N	2·54 E
98	Domeyko, Cordillera (Mts.) (kôr-dēl-yĕ'rä-dô-mā'kō) . Chile	20·50 S	69·02 W
93	Dominica Chan. (dŏ-mĭ-nē'kȧ) N. A. (Le. & Wind. Is. In.)	15·00 N	61·30 W
93	Dominica I. N. A. (Le. & Wind. Is. In.)	15·24 N	61·05 W
88	Dominican Republic (dô-mĭn'ĭ-kăn) . N. A.	18·59 N	70·40 W
83	Dominion (dô-mĭn'yŭn) ... Can.	46·13 N	60·01 W
136	Domodedovo (dô-mô-dyě'do-vô) Sov. Un. (Moscow In.)	55·27 N	37·45 E
101	Dom Silvério (doN-sěl-vě'ryō) Braz. (Rio de Janeiro In.)	20·09 S	42·57 W
110	Don (R.) (dŏn) ... Eng.	53·27 N	1·34 W
110	Don (R.) ... Eng.	53·39 N	0·58 W
116	Don (R.) ... Scot.	57·19 N	2·39 W
74	Donaldson (dŏn'ăl-sŭn) Mich. (Sault Ste. Marie In.)	46·19 N	84·22 W
77	Donaldsonville (dŏn'ăld-sŭn-vĭl) La.	30·05 N	90·58 W
78	Donalsonville ... Ga.	31·02 N	84·50 W
120	Donawitz (dō'nȧ-vĭts) ... Aus.	47·23 N	15·05 E
142	Donazari ... E. Pak.	22·18 N	91·52 E
124	Don Benito Mérida (dōn' bȧ-nē'tō-mě'rē-dä) . Sp.	38·55 N	6·08 W
161	Doncaster (doŋ'kȧs-tēr) Austl. (Melbourne In.)	37·47 S	145·08 E
110	Doncaster (doŋ'kăs-tēr) ... Eng.	53·32 N	1·07 W
166	Dondo (dōn'dō) ... Ang.	9·35 S	14·25 E
166	Dondo ... Moz.	19·33 S	34·47 E
116	Donegal (dŏn-ê-gôl') ... Ire.	54·44 N	8·05 W
116	Donegal, Mts. of (dŏn-ê-gôl') . Ire.	54·44 N	8·10 W
116	Donegal Bay (dŏn-ê-gôl') .. N. Ire.	54·35 N	8·36 W
129	Donets (R.) (dō-nyěts') .. Sov. Un.	48·48 N	38·42 E
129	Donets Coal Basin (Reg.) (dō-nyěts') . Sov. Un.	48·15 N	38·50 E
133	Donetsk (Stalino) (dō-nyěts'k) (stä'lĭ-nō) . Sov. Un.	48·00 N	37·35 E
158	Dongara (dôŋ-gă'rȧ) ... Austl.	29·15 S	115·00 E
154	Donggala (dôŋ-gä'lä) ... Indon.	0·45 S	119·32 E
151	Dong Hoi (dông-hō-ē') ... Viet.	17·25 N	106·42 E
166	Dongo (dôŋ'gō) ... Ang.	14·45 S	15·30 E
165	Dongola (dŏŋ'gô-lȧ) ... Sud.	19·21 N	30·19 E
155	Dongon Pt. (dông-ōn') Phil. (Manila In.)	12·43 N	120·35 E
165	Dongou (dôŋ-gōō') ... Con. B.	2·12 N	18·08 E
73	Doniphan (dŏn'ĭ-făn) ... Mo.	36·37 N	90·50 W
126	Donji Vakuf (dōn'yĭ väk'ōōf) Yugo.	44·08 N	17·25 E
76	Don Martin, Presa de (Res.) (prě'sä-dě-dôn-mär-tē'n) . Mex.	27·35 N	100·38 W
82	Donnacona ... Can.	46·40 N	71·46 W
123	Donnemarie-en-Montois (dôn-mä-rē'ěN-môN-twä') Fr. (Paris In.)	48·29 N	3·09 E
66	Donner und Blitzen R. (dŏn'ēr ōōnt blĭ'tsěn) . Ore.	42·45 N	118·57 W
167	Donnybrook (dŏ-nĭ-brŏŏk) S. Afr. (Natal In.)	29·56 S	29·54 E
75	Donora (dŏ-nō'rȧ) Pa. (Pittsburgh In.)	40·10 N	79·51 W
64	Doonerak (dōō'nĕ-răk) ... Alaska	68·00 N	150·34 W
111	Doorn .... Neth. (Amsterdam In.)	52·02 N	5·21 E
71	Door Pen. (dōr) ... Wis.	44·40 N	87·36 W
126	Dora Baltea (dō'rä bäl'tä-ä) ... It.	45·40 N	7·34 E
84	Doraville (dō'rȧ-vĭ.) Ga. (Atlanta In.)	33·54 N	84·17 W
116	Dorchester (dôr'chěs-tēr) .... Eng.	50·45 N	2·34 W
122	Dordogne (R.) (dôr-dôn'yě) ... Fr.	44·53 N	0·16 E
111	Dordrecht (dôr'drěKt) Neth. (Amsterdam In.)	51·48 N	4·39 E
167	Dordrecht (dô'drěKt) S. Afr. (Natal In.)	31·24 S	27·06 E
126	Dorgali (dôr'gä-lē) ... Sard.	40·18 N	9·37 E
164	Dori (dô-rē') ... Upper Volta	13·56 N	0·01 W
85	Dorion (dôr-yō) Can. (Montreal In.)	45·23 N	74·01 W
110	Dorking (dôr'kĭng) Eng. (London In.)	51·12 N	0·20 W
85	D'Orleans, Ile (I.) (dôr-lě-äN', yl) Can. (Quebec In.)	46·56 N	70·27 W
75	Dormont (dôr'mŏnt) Pa. (Pittsburgh In.)	40·24 N	80·02 W
120	Dornbirn (dôrn'bĕrn) ... Aus.	47·24 N	9·45 E
116	Dornoch (dôr'nŏK) ... Scot.	57·55 N	4·01 W
116	Dornoch Firth (dôr'nŏK fûrth) Scot.	57·55 N	3·55 W
128	Dorogobuzh (dôrôgô'-bōō'zh) Sov. Un.	54·57 N	33·18 E
121	Dorohoi (dō-rô-hoi') ... Rom.	47·57 N	26·28 E
	Dorpat, see Tartu		
158	Dorre (I.) (dôr) ... Austl.	25·19 S	113·10 E
74	Dorsey (dôrsĭ) .. Ill. (St. Louis In.)	38·59 N	90·00 W
84	Dorsey ...... Md. (Baltimore In.)	39·11 N	76·45 W
123	Dorsten (dōr'stěn) Ger. (Ruhr In.)	51·40 N	6·58 E
123	Dortmund (dôrt'mōōnt) Ger. (Ruhr In.)	51·31 N	7·28 E
123	Dortmund-Ems Kanal (can.) (dōrt'mōōnd-ěms' kä-näl') Ger. (Ruhr In.)	51·50 N	7·25 E
133	Dörtyal (dûrt'yôl) ... Tur.	36·50 N	36·20 E
85	Dorval (dôr-väl') Can. (Montreal In.)	45·26 N	73·44 W
99	Dos Caminos (dôs-kä-mē'nôs) Ven. (In.)	9·38 N	67·17 W
65	Dosewallips (R.) (dō'sē-wăl'lĭps) Wash. (Seattle In.)	47·45 N	123·04 W
124	Dos Hermanas (dōsĕr-mä'näs) . Sp.	37·17 N	5·56 W
164	Dosso (dôs-ō') ... Niger	13·03 N	3·09 E
78	Dothan (dō'thăn) ... Ala.	31·13 N	85·23 W
122	Douai (dōō-ā') ... Fr.	50·23 N	3·04 E
164	Douala (dōō-ä'lä) ... Cam.	4·00 N	9·37 E
122	Douarnenez (dōō-är'nē-něs') ... Fr.	48·06 N	4·18 W
77	Double Bay. (dŭb''l bī'yōō) Tex. (In.)	29·40 N	94·38 W
125	Douéra (dōō-ā'rȧ) ... Alg.	36·40 N	2·55 E
64	Douglas (dŭg'lăs) ... Alaska	58·18 N	134·35 W
69	Douglas ... Ariz.	31·20 N	109·30 W
78	Douglas ... Ga.	31·30 N	82·53 W
116	Douglas (dŭg'lăs) ..... Isle of Man	54·10 N	4·24 W
83	Douglas (dŭg'lăs) Mass. (Boston In.)	42·04 N	71·45 W
67	Douglas (dŭg'lăs) ... Wyo.	42·45 N	105·21 W
110	Douglas (R.) (dŭg'lăs) ... Eng.	53·38 N	2·48 W
78	Douglas (R.) (dŭg'lăs) ... Tenn.	36·00 N	83·35 W
78	Douglasville (dŭg'lăs-vĭl) ... Ga.	33·45 N	84·47 W
165	Doumé (dōō-mā') ... Cam.	4·14 N	13·26 E
99	Dourada, Serra (Mts.) (sě'r-rä-dôōō-rä'dä) . Braz.	15·11 S	49·57 W
123	Dourdan (dōōr-däN') Fr. (Paris In.)	48·32 N	2·01 E
124	Douro, Rio (R.) (rē'ō-dô'ōō-rō) Port.	41·03 N	8·12 W
110	Dove (R.) (dŭv) ... Eng.	52·53 N	1·47 W
81	Dover (dō vēr) ... Del.	39·10 N	75·30 W
117	Dover ... Eng.	51·08 N	1·19 E
81	Dover ... N. H.	43·15 N	71·00 W
84	Dover ...... N. J. (New York In.)	40·53 N	74·33 W
80	Dover ... Ohio	40·35 N	81·30 W
168	Dover ... S. Afr. (Johannesburg & Pretoria In.)	27·05 S	27·44 E
117	Dover, Str. of ... Eur.	50·50 N	1·15 W
82	Dover-Foxcroft (dō'vēr fôks'krôft) Maine	45·10 N	69·15 W
132	Dovlekanovo (dŏv'lyěk-ȧ-nô-vô) Sov. Un.	54·15 N	55·05 E
118	Dovre Fjeld (Plat.) (dŏv'rě fyěl') Nor.	62·03 N	8·36 E
74	Dow (dou) ..... Ill. (St. Louis In.)	39·01 N	90·20 W
166	Dow, L ... Bech.	21·22 S	24·52 E
80	Dowagiac (dô-wô'jăk) ... Mich.	42·00 N	86·05 W
75	Downers Grove (dou'nērz grōv) Ill. (Chicago In.)	41·48 N	88·00 W
74	Downey (dou'nĭ) Calif. (Los Angeles In.)	33·56 N	118·08 W
68	Downieville (dou'nĭ-vĭl) ... Calif.	39·35 N	120·48 W
72	Downs (dounz) ... Kans.	39·29 N	98·32 W
75	Doylestown (doilz'toun) Ohio (Cleveland In.)	40·58 N	81·43 W
164	Draa, C. (drȧ) ... Mor.	28·39 N	12·15 W
164	Draa, Wadi R. (wä-dĭ drä') .. Mor.	28·00 N	9·31 W
129	Drabov (drä'bôf) ... Sov. Un.	49·57 N	32·14 E
123	Drac (R.) (dräK) ... Fr.	44·50 N	5·47 E
83	Dracut (drā'kŭt) Mass. (Boston In.)	42·40 N	71·19 W
127	Draganovo (drä-gä-nō'vô) ... Bul.	43·13 N	25·45 E
127	Drăgăsani (drä-gá-shän'ĭ) ... Rom.	44·39 N	24·18 E
123	Draguignan (drä-gên-yäN') ... Fr.	43·35 N	6·28 E
166	Drakensberg (Mts.) (drä'kěnz-běrgh) . S. Afr.	29·15 S	29·07 E
96	Drake Passage (drāk păs'ĭj) S. A.-Ant.	57·00 S	65·00 W
127	Dráma (drä'mä) ... Grc.	41·09 N	24·10 E
118	Drammen (dräm'ěn) ... Nor.	59·45 N	10·15 E
120	Drau R. (drou) ... Aus.	46·44 N	13·45 E
126	Drava (R.) (Drä'vä) ... Yugo.	46·37 N	15·17 E
126	Dravograd (Drä'vô-gräd') .. Yugo.	46·37 N	15·01 E
120	Drawsko Pomorskie (dräv'skō pō-mōr'skyě) . Pol.	53·31 N	15·50 E
65	Drayton Hbr. (drā'tŭn) Wash. (Vancouver In.)	48·58 N	122·40 W
75	Drayton Plains Mich. (Detroit In.)	42·41 N	83·23 W
146	Dre Chu (R.) ... China	34·11 N	96·08 E
123	Drensteinfurt (drěn'shtīn-fōōrt) Ger. (Ruhr In.)	51·47 N	7·44 E
120	Dresden (drās'děn) ... Ger.	51·05 N	13·45 E
123	Dreux (drû) ...... Fr. (Paris In.)	48·44 N	1·24 E
168	Driefontein S. Afr. (Johannesburg & Pretoria In.)	25·53 S	29·10 E
127	Drin (R.) (drēn) ... Alb.	42·13 N	20·13 E
127	Drina (R.) (drē'nä) ... Yugo.	44·09 N	19·30 E
127	Drinit, Pellg I (Bght.) ... Alb.	41·42 N	19·17 E
128	Drissa (drĭs'sä) ... Sov. Un.	55·48 N	27·59 E
128	Drissa (R.) ... Sov. Un.	55·44 N	28·58 E
84	Driver ... Va. (Norfolk In.)	36·50 N	76·30 W
118	Dröbak (drû'bäk) ... Nor.	59·40 N	10·35 E
116	Drogheda (drŏ'hē-dȧ) ... Ire.	53·43 N	6·15 W
121	Drogichin (drō-gē'chĭn) .. Sov. Un.	52·10 N	25·11 E
121	Drohobych (drô-hô'bĭch) Sov. Un.	49·21 N	23·31 E
122	Drôme (R.) (drōm) ... Fr.	44·42 N	4·53 E
110	Dronfield (drŏn'fēld) ... Eng.	53·18 N	1·28 W
86	Drumheller (drŭm-hĕl-ēr) ... Can.	51·30 N	112·42 W
80	Drummond (I.) (drŭm'ŭnd) Mich.	46·00 N	83·50 W
82	Drummondville (drŭm'ŭnd-vĭl) Can.	45·53 N	72·33 W
73	Drumright (drŭm'rīt) ... Okla.	35·59 N	96·37 W
111	Drunen ... Neth. (Amsterdam In.)	51·41 N	5·10 E
128	Drut' (R.) (drōōt) ... Sov. Un.	53·40 N	29·45 E
128	Druya (drōō'yȧ) ... Sov. Un.	55·45 N	27·26 E
115	Druze, Jebel (Mts.) ... Syria	32·40 N	36·58 E
121	Drweca R. (d'r-văn'tsȧ) ... Pol.	53·06 N	19·13 E
87	Dryden (drī-děn) ... Can.	49·50 N	92·47 W
161	Drysdale .. Austl. (Melbourne In.)	38·11 S	144·34 E
79	Dry Tortugas (I.) (tôr-tōō'gäz) Fla. (In.)	24·37 N	82·45 W
164	Dschang (dshäng) ... Cam.	5·34 N	10·09 E
85	Duagh ...... Can. (Edmonton In.)	53·43 N	113·24 W
101	Duas Barras (dōō'äs-bá'r-räs) Braz. (Rio de Janeiro In.)	22·03 S	42·30 W
86	Dubawnt (L.) (dōō-bônt') ... Can.	63·27 N	103·30 W
86	Dubawnt (R.) ... Can.	61·30 N	103·49 W
144	Dubayy ... Tr. Coast	25·18 N	55·26 E
160	Dubbo (dŭb'ō) ... Austl.	32·20 S	148·42 E
65	Dublin (dŭb'lĭn) Calif. (San Francisco In.)	37·42 N	121·56 W
78	Dublin ... Ga.	32·33 N	82·55 W
76	Dublin ... Tex.	32·05 N	98·20 W
	Dublin, see Baile Atha Cliath		
121	Dubno (dōō'b nô) ..... Sov. Un.	50·24 N	25·44 E
81	Du Bois (dōō-bois') ... Pa.	41·10 N	78·45 W
129	Dubossary (dōō-bŏ-sä'rĭ) . Sov. Un.	47·16 N	29·11 E
133	Dubovka (dōō-bôf'kȧ) ... Sov. Un.	49·00 N	44·50 E
136	Dubrovka (dōō-brôf'kȧ) Sov. Un. (Leningrad In.)	59·51 N	30·56 E
127	Dubrovnik (Ragusa) (dōō'brôv-něk) (rä-gōō'sä) Yugo.	42·40 N	18·10 E
128	Dubrovno (dōō-brôf'nō) .. Sov. Un.	54·39 N	30·54 E
71	Dubuque (dōō-būk') ... Iowa	42·30 N	90·43 W
69	Duchesne (dōō-shān') ... Utah	40·12 N	110·23 W
69	Duchesne (R.) ... Utah	40·20 N	110·50 W
158	Duchess (dŭch'ěs) ... Austl.	21·30 S	139·55 E
157	Ducie I. (dū-sē') ... Oceania	25·30 S	126·20 W
80	Duck (I.) (dŭk) ... Can.	45·35 N	83·00 W
78	Duck (R.) ... Tenn.	35·55 N	87·40 W
65	Duckabush (R.) (dŭk'ȧ-bōōsh) Wash. (Seattle In.)	47·41 N	123·09 W
86	Duck Mtn. ... Can.	51·43 N	101·07 W
78	Ducktown (dŭk'toun) ... Tenn.	35·03 N	84·20 W
68	Duckwater Pk. (dŭk-wô-tēr) . Nev.	39·00 N	115·31 W
98	Duda (dōō'dä) (R.) ..... Col. (In.)	3·25 N	74·23 W
134	Dudinka (dōō-dĭn'kȧ) .... Sov. Un.	69·15 N	85·42 E
110	Dudley (dŭd'lĭ) ... Eng.	52·31 N	2·04 W
124	Duero (R.) (dwě'rô) ... Sp.	41·30 N	5·10 W
80	Dugger (dŭg'ēr) ... Ind.	39·00 N	87·10 W
126	Dugi Otok (I.) (dōō'gē O'tôk) Yugo.	44·03 N	14·40 E
123	Duisburg (dōō'ĭs-bōōrgh) Ger. (Ruhr In.)	51·26 N	6·46 E
98	Duitama (dōōē-tá'mä) ... Col.	5·48 N	73·09 W
128	Dukhovshchina (dōō-Kôfsh'chēnȧ) Sov. Un.	55·13 N	32·26 E
110	Dukinfield (dŭk'ĭn-fēld) ... Eng.	53·28 N	2·05 W
121	Dukla P. (dōō'klä) ... Pol.	49·25 N	21·44 E
93	Dulce, Golfo (G.) (gōl'fô dōōl'sä) C. R.	8·25 N	83·13 W
	Dulcigno, see Ulčinj		
123	Dülken (dül'kěn) .. Ger. (Ruhr In.)	51·15 N	6·21 E
123	Dülmen (dül'měn) Ger. (Ruhr In.)	51·50 N	7·17 E
74	Duluth (dōō-lōōth') Minn. (Duluth In.)	46·50 N	92·07 W
139	Dūmā .... Syria (Palestine In.)	33·34 N	36·17 E
155	Dumaguete City (dōō-mä-gä'tā) Phil.	9·14 N	123·15 E
168	Dumaît, Masabb (R. Mth.) U. A. R. (Nile In.)	31·36 N	31·45 E
155	Dumali Pt. (dōō-mä'lē) Phil. (Manila Pt.)	13·07 N	121·42 E
116	Dumbarton (dŭm'bȧr-tŭn) .. Scot.	56·00 N	4·35 W
142	Dum Dum ... India (Calcutta In.)	22·37 N	88·25 E
116	Dumfries (dŭm-frēs') ... Scot.	54·05 N	3·40 W
84	Dumont (dōō'mŏnt) N. J. (New York In.)	40·56 N	74·00 W
77	Dumont ... Tex. (In.)	29·40 N	95·14 W
168	Dumyāţ (Damietta) (dōōm-yät') (dăm-ĭ-ĕt'ȧ) . U. A. R. (Nile In.)	31·22 N	31·50 E
121	Dunaföldvar (dōō'nô-fûld'vär) Hung.	46·48 N	18·55 E
121	Dunajec R. (dōō-nä'yěts) ..... Pol.	49·52 N	20·53 E
121	Dunapataj (doo'nô-pô-toi) . Hung.	46·42 N	19·03 E
121	Duna R. (dōō'nä) ... Hung.	46·07 N	18·45 E
136	Dunay (dōō'nĭ) Sov. Un. (Leningrad In.)	59·59 N	30·57 E
129	Dunayevtsy (dōō-nä'yěf-tsĭ) Sov. Un.	48·52 N	26·51 E
116	Dunbar (dŭn'bär) ... Scot.	56·00 N	2·25 W
80	Dunbar ... W. Va.	38·20 N	81·45 W
66	Duncan (dŭŋ'kăn) ... Can.	48·46 N	123·42 W
72	Duncan ... Okla.	34·29 N	97·56 W
116	Duncansby Hd. (dŭn'kănz-bĭ) .. Scot.	58·40 N	3·01 W
74	Duncanville (dŭn'kăn-vĭl) Tex. (Dallas, Fort Worth In.)	32·39 N	96·55 W
116	Dundalk (dŭn'dôk) ... Ire.	54·00 N	6·18 W
84	Dundalk ..... Md. (Baltimore In.)	39·16 N	76·31 W
116	Dundalk B. (dŭn'dôk) ... Ire.	53·55 N	6·15 W

Page	Name Pronunciation Region	Lat. °′	Long. °′
85	Dundas (dŭn-dăs′) Can. (Toronto In.)	43·16 N	79·58 W
75	Dundee (dŭn-dē′) Ill. (Chicago In.)	42·06 N	88·17 W
116	Dundee ... Scot.	56·30 N	2·55 W
167	Dundee ... S. Afr. (Natal In.)	28·14 S	30·16 E
158	Dundras (L.) (dŭn-drås) ... Austl.	32·15 S	132·00 E
158	Dundras Str. (dŭn′drås) ... Austl.	10·35 S	131·15 E
116	Dundrum B. (dŭn-drŭm′) ... Ire.	54·13 N	5·47 W
79	Dunedin (dŭn-ē′dĭn) ... Fla. (In.)	28·00 N	82·43 W
159	Dunedin ... N. Z. (In.)	45·48 S	170·32 E
84	Dunellen (dŭn-ĕl′ĕn) N. J. (New York In.)	40·36 N	74·28 W
116	Dunfermline (dŭn-fĕrm′lĭn) .. Scot.	56·05 N	3·30 W
116	Dungarvin (dŭn-gȧr′vǎn) ... Ire.	52·06 N	7·50 W
65	Dungeness (dŭnj-nĕs′) Wash. (Seattle In.)	48·09 N	123·07 W
65	Dungeness (R.) Wash. (Seattle In.)	48·03 N	123·10 W
65	Dungeness Spit Wash. (Seattle In.)	48·11 N	123·03 W
165	Dungu (do͞oŋ-go͞o′) ... Con. L.	3·48 N	28·32 E
122	Dunkerque (dŭn-kĕrk′) ... Fr.	51·02 N	2·37 E
80	Dunkirk (dŭn′kûrk) ... Ind.	40·20 N	85·25 W
81	Dunkirk ... N. Y.	42·30 N	79·20 W
116	Dun Laoghaire (dŭn-lā′rĕ) ... Ire.	53·16 N	6·09 W
70	Dunlap (dŭn′lăp) ... Iowa	41·53 N	95·33 W
78	Dunlap ... Tenn.	35·23 N	85·23 W
81	Dunmore (dŭn′mōr) ... Pa.	41·25 N	75·30 W
79	Dunn (dŭn) ... N. C.	35·18 N	78·37 W
79	Dunnellon (dŭn-ĕl′ŏn) ... Fla.	29·02 N	82·28 W
81	Dunnville (dŭn′vĭl) ... Can.	42·55 N	79·40 W
66	Dunsmuir (dŭnz′mūr) ... Calif.	41·08 N	122·17 W
84	Dunwoody (dŭn-wo͝od′ĭ) Ga. (Atlanta In.)	33·57 N	84·20 W
75	Du Page R. (do͞o pāj) Ill. (Chicago In.)	41·41 N	88·11 W
75	Du Page R., E. Br. Ill. (Chicago In.)	41·49 N	88·05 W
75	Du Page R., W. Br. Ill. (Chicago In.)	41·48 N	88·10 W
155	Dupax (do͞o′päks) Phil. (Manila In.)	16·16 N	121·06 E
127	Dupnitsa (do͞op′nē-tsȧ) ... Bul.	42·15 N	23·07 E
74	Dupo (dū′pō) .. Ill. (St. Louis In.)	38·31 N	90·12 W
166	Duque de Bragança (do͞o′kå dâ brä-gäN′sä) . Ang.	8·55 S	16·10 E
100	Duque de Caxias (do͞o′kĕ-dĕ-kȧ′shyȧs) Braz. (In.)	22·46 S	43·18 W
75	Duquesne (do͞o-kān′) Pa. (Pittsburgh In.)	40·22 N	79·51 W
73	Du Quoin (do͞o-kwoin′) ... Ill.	38·01 N	89·14 W
123	Durance (R.) (dü-räNs′) ... Fr.	43·46 N	5·52 E
80	Durand (dŭ-rănd′) ... Mich.	42·50 N	84·00 W
71	Durand ... Wis.	44·37 N	91·58 W
69	Durango (do͞o-räŋ′gō) ... Colo.	37·15 N	107·55 W
78	Durango (State) ... Mex.	25·00 N	106·00 W
78	Durant (dŭ-rănt′) ... Miss.	33·05 N	89·50 W
73	Durant ... Okla.	33·59 N	96·23 W
124	Duratón (R.) (do͞o-rä-tōn′) ... Sp.	41·55 N	3·55 W
101	Durazno (do͞o-räz′nō) Ur. (Buenos Aires In.)	33·21 S	56·31 W
101	Durazno (Dept.) Ur. (Buenos Aires In.)	33·00 S	56·35 W
167	Durban (dûr′bǎn) S. Afr. (Natal In.)	29·48 S	31·00 E
166	Durbanville (dûr-bǎn′vĭl) S. Afr. (Cape Town In.)	33·50 S	18·39 E
119	Durbe (do͞or′bĕ) ... Sov. Un.	56·36 N	21·24 E
123	Düren (dü′rĕn) ... Ger. (Ruhr In.)	50·48 N	6·30 E
116	Durham (dûr′ăm) ... Eng.	54·47 N	1·46 W
79	Durham ... N. C.	36·00 N	78·55 W
75	Durham ... Wis. (Milwaukee In.)	42·52 N	88·04 W
160	Durham Downs ... Austl.	27·30 S	141·55 E
127	Durrës (do͞or′ĕs) ... Alb.	41·19 N	19·27 E
155	D'urville, Kap (C.) (dûr′vĭl) W. Irian	1·20 S	138·45 E
81	Duryea (do͞or-yā′) ... Pa.	41·20 N	75·50 W
144	Dushanbe ... Sov. Un.	38·41 N	68·43 E
123	Düsseldorf (düs′ĕl-dôrf) Ger. (Ruhr In.)	51·14 N	6·47 E
111	Dussen ... Neth. (Amsterdam In.)	51·43 N	4·58 E
150	Dutalan Ula (Mtn.) ... Mong.	49·25 N	112·40 E
64	Dutch Harbor (dŭch här′bẽr) Alaska	53·58 N	166·30 W
65	Duvall (do͞o′vâl) Wash. (Seattle In.)	47·44 N	121·59 W
95	Duvergé (do͞o-vĕr-hĕ′) . Dom. Rep.	18·20 N	71·20 W
65	Duwamish (do͞o-wăm′ĭsh) Wash. (Seattle In.)	47·24 N	122·18 W
	Dvina, Western, R., see Zapadnaya Dvina		
132	Dvinskaya Guba (G.) ... Sov. Un.	65·10 N	38·40 E
120	Dvur Kralove nad Labem (dvo͞or′ krä′lō-vā) . Czech.	50·28 N	15·43 E
142	Dwārka ... India	22·18 N	68·59 E
80	Dwight (dwīt) ... Ill.	41·00 N	88·20 W
128	Dyat′kovo (dyät′kō-vō) . Sov. Un.	53·36 N	34·19 E
75	Dyer (dī′ẽr) ... Ind. (Chicago In.)	41·30 N	87·31 W
78	Dyersburg (dī′ẽrz-bûrg) ... Tenn.	36·02 N	89·23 W
71	Dyersville (dī′ẽrz-vĭl) ... Iowa	42·28 N	91·09 W
65	Dyes Inlet (dīz) Wash. (Seattle In.)	47·37 N	122·45 W
146	Dzabhan Gol (R.) ... Mong.	48·19 N	94·08 E
150	Dzamiin Üüde ... Mong.	44·38 N	111·32 E
167	Dzaoudzi (dzou′dzĭ) Comores, Arch. des	12·44 S	45·15 E
103	Dzaudzhikau (dzou-jĭ-kou′) Sov. Un.	48·00 N	44·52 E
129	Dzerzhinsk (dzhĕr-zhĭnsk′) Sov. Un.	48·24 N	37·58 E
128	Dzerzhinsk ... Sov. Un.	53·41 N	27·14 E
132	Dzerzhinsk ... Sov. Un.	56·20 N	43·50 E
134	Dzhalal-Abad (jȧ-läl′ȧ-bät′) Sov. Un.	41·13 N	73·35 E

Page	Name Pronunciation Region	Lat. °′	Long. °′
134	Dzhambul (dzhăm-bo͞ol′) Sov. Un.	42·51 N	71·29 E
129	Dzhankoy (dzhän′koi) ... Sov. Un.	45·43 N	34·22 E
136	Dzhetygara (dzhĕt′-gȧ′rȧ) Sov. Un. (Urals In.)	52·12 N	61·18 E
134	Dzhizak (dzhĕ′zăk) ... Sov. Un.	40·13 N	67·58 E
135	Dzhugdzhur Khrebet (Mts.) (jo͝og-jo͞or′) . Sov. Un.	56·15 N	137·00 E
121	Działoszyce (jyä-wō-shē′tsĕ) .. Pol.	50·21 N	20·22 E
92	Dzibalchén (zē-bäl-chĕ′n) Mex. (Yucatan In.)	19·25 N	89·39 W
92	Dzidzantún (zēd-zän-to͞o′n) Mex. (Yucatan In.)	21·18 N	89·00 W
120	Dzierzoniów (dzyĕr-zhōn′yŭf) . Pol.	50·44 N	16·38 E
92	Dzilam Gonzalez (zē-lä′m-gôn-zä′lĕz) . Mex. (Yucatan In.)	21·21 N	88·53 W
92	Dzitás (zē-tà′s) . Mex. (Yucatan In.)	20·47 N	88·32 W
92	Dzitbalché (dzēt-bäl-chā′) Mex. (Yucatan In.)	20·18 N	90·03 W
146	Dzungaria (Reg.) (dzo͝oŋ-gä′rĭ-ȧ) . China	44·39 N	86·13 E
64	Eagle (ē′g′l) ... Alaska	64·42 N	141·20 W
77	Eagle ... Tex. (In.)	29·40 N	94·40 W
80	Eagle ... W. Va.	38·10 N	81·20 W
69	Eagle (R.) ... Colo.	39·32 N	106·28 W
65	Eaglecliff (ē′g′l-klĭf) Wash. (Portland In.)	46·10 N	123·13 W
75	Eagle Cr. . Ind. (Indianapolis In.)	39·54 N	86·17 W
74	Eagle Ford (ē′g′l fērd) Tex. (Dallas, Fort Worth In.)	32·47 N	96·52 W
71	Eagle Grove ... Iowa	42·39 N	93·55 W
82	Eagle Lake ... Maine	47·03 N	68·38 W
77	Eagle Lake ... Tex.	29·37 N	96·20 W
66	Eagle L ... Calif.	40·45 N	120·52 W
74	Eagle Mountain L. Tex. (Dallas, Fort Worth In.)	32·56 N	97·27 W
76	Eagle Pass ... Tex.	28·49 N	100·30 W
66	Eagle Pk ... Calif.	41·18 N	120·11 W
110	Ealing (ē′lĭng) . Eng. (London In.)	51·29 N	0·19 W
73	Earle (ûrl) ... Ark.	35·14 N	90·28 W
78	Earlington (ûr′lĭng-tǔn) ... S. C.	37·15 N	87·31 W
79	Easley (ēz′lĭ) ... S. C.	34·48 N	82·37 W
88	East, Mt. C. Z. (Panama Canal In.)	9·09 N	79·16 W
74	East Alton (ôl′tǔn) Ill. (St. Louis In.)	38·53 N	90·08 W
81	East Angus (ăŋ′gǔs) ... Can.	45·35 N	71·40 W
75	East Aurora (ô-rō′rȧ) N. Y. (Buffalo In.)	42·46 N	78·38 W
84	East B ... La. (New Orleans In.)	29·03 N	89·16 W
77	East B ... Tex. (In.)	29·30 N	94·41 W
111	East Berlin (bĕr-lēn′) Ger. (Berlin In.)	52·31 N	13·28 E
78	East Bernstadt (bûrn′stȧt) ... Ky.	37·09 N	84·08 W
65	Eastbound (ēst-bound) Wash. (Vancouver In.)	48·42 N	122·42 W
117	Eastbourne (ēst′bōrn) ... Eng.	50·48 N	0·16 E
95	East Caicos (I.) (kī′kōs) ... Caicos	21·40 N	71·35 W
159	East C ... N. Z. (In.)	37·37 S	178·33 E
	East Cape, see Dezhneva, Mys		
74	East Carondelet (kȧ-rŏn′dĕ-lĕt) Ill. (St. Louis In.)	38·33 N	90·14 W
75	East Chicago (shĭ-kô′gō) Ind. (Chicago In.)	41·39 N	87·29 W
147	East China Sea ... Asia	30·28 N	125·52 E
75	East Cleveland (klēv′lǎnd) Ohio (Cleveland In.)	41·33 N	81·35 W
77	East Cote Blanche B. (kōt bläNsh′) . La.	29·30 N	92·07 W
71	East Des Moines (R.) (dē moin′) Iowa	42·57 N	94·17 W
75	East Detroit (dē-troit′) Mich. (Detroit In.)	42·28 N	82·57 W
	Easter (I.), see Rapa Nui		
120	Eastern Alps (Mts.) ... Aus.-Switz.	47·03 N	10·55 E
143	Eastern Ghats (Mts.) ... India	19·35 N	78·08 E
146	Eastern Turkestan (Reg.) (to͞or-kĕ-stän′) (tûr-kĕ-stăn′) China	38·23 N	80·41 E
75	East Gary (gā′rĭ) Ind. (Chicago In.)	41·34 N	87·15 W
70	East Grand Forks (grǎnd fôrks) Minn.	47·56 N	97·02 W
84	East Greenwich (grĭn′ĭj) R. I. (Providence In.)	41·40 N	71·27 W
81	Easthampton (ēst-hămp′tǔn) Mass.	42·15 N	72·45 W
81	East Hartford (härt′fērd) ... Conn.	41·45 N	72·35 W
67	East Helena (hĕ-lē′nȧ) ... Mont.	46·31 N	111·50 W
110	East Ilsley (ĭl′slē) Eng. (London In.)	51·30 N	1·18 W
80	East Jordan (jôr′dǎn) ... Mich.	45·05 N	85·05 W
74	East Kansas City (kǎn′zȧs) Mo. (Kansas City In.)	39·09 N	94·30 W
76	Eastland (ēst′lǎnd) ... Tex.	32·24 N	98·47 W
80	East Lansing (lǎn′sĭng) ... Mich.	42·45 N	84·30 W
74	East Leavenworth (lĕv′ĕn-wûrth) Mo. (Kansas City In.)	39·18 N	94·50 W
80	East Liverpool (lĭv′ēr-po͞ol) .. Ohio	40·40 N	80·35 W
167	East London (lŭn′dǔn) S. Afr. (Natal In.)	33·02 S	27·54 E
74	East Los Angeles (lōs ăŋ′hȧ-lās) Calif. (Los Angeles In.)	34·01 N	118·09 W
87	Eastmain (R.) (ēst′mān) ... Can.	52·12 N	73·19 W
78	Eastman (ēst-mǎn) ... Ga.	32·10 N	83·11 W
84	East Millstone (mĭl′stōn) N. J. (New York In.)	40·30 N	74·35 W
71	East Moline (mō-lēn′) ... Ill.	41·31 N	90·28 W
73	East Nishnabotna (R.) (nĭsh-nȧ-bŏt′nȧ) . Iowa	40·53 N	95·23 W
81	Easton (ēs′tǔn) ... Md.	72·45 N	76·05 W
75	Easton (ēst′ǔn) Ohio (Cleveland In.)	40·57 N	81·45 W
81	Easton ... Pa.	40·45 N	75·15 W
84	Easton L. ... Conn. (New York In.)	41·18 N	73·17 W
84	East Orange (ŏr′ĕnj) N. J. (New York In.)	40·46 N	74·12 W

Page	Name Pronunciation Region	Lat. °′	Long. °′
80	East Peoria (pē-ō′rĭ-ȧ) ... Ill.	40·40 N	89·30 W
75	East Pittsburgh (pĭts′bûrg) Pa. (Pittsburgh In.)	40·24 N	79·50 W
84	East Point ... Ga. (Atlanta In.)	33·41 N	84·27 W
82	Eastport (ēst-pōrt) ... Can.	44·53 N	67·01 W
84	East Providence (prŏv′ĭ-dĕns) R. I. (Providence In.)	41·49 N	71·22 W
110	East Retford (rĕt′fērd) ... Eng.	53·19 N	0·56 W
110	East Riding (Co.) (rīd′ĭng) .. Eng.	53·47 N	0·36 W
81	East Rochester (rŏch′ĕs-tēr) . N. Y.	43·10 N	77·30 W
74	East St. Louis (sānt lo͞o′ĭs) (lo͞o-ĭ) Ill. (St. Louis In.)	38·38 N	90·10 W
130	East Siberian Sea (sī-bĭr′y′n) Sov. Un.	73·00 N	153·28 E
65	East Stanwood (stăn′wo͝od) Wash. (Seattle In.)	48·14 N	122·21 W
81	East Stroudsburg (stroudz′bûrg) Pa.	41·00 N	75·10 W
81	East Syracuse (sĭr′ȧ-kūs) ... N. Y.	43·05 N	76·00 W
69	East Tavaputs Plat. (tă-vă′-pŭts) Utah	39·25 N	109·45 W
80	East Tawas (tô′wǎs) ... Mich.	44·15 N	83·30 W
85	Eastview (ēst′vyo͞o) Can. (Ottawa In.)	45·27 N	75·39 W
68	East Walker (R.) (wôk′ēr) ... Nev.	38·36 N	119·02 W
75	Eaton (ē′tǔn) ... Colo.	40·31 N	104·42 W
80	Eaton ... Ohio	39·45 N	84·40 W
75	Eaton ... Ohio (Cleveland In.)	41·19 N	82·01 W
80	Eaton Rapids (răp′ĭdz) ... Mich.	42·30 N	84·40 W
78	Eatonton (ē′tǔn-tǔn) ... Ga.	33·20 N	83·24 W
84	Eatontown (ē′tǔn-toun) N. J. (New York In.)	40·18 N	74·04 W
71	Eau Claire (ō klâr′) ... Wis.	44·47 N	91·32 W
118	Ebeltoft (ĕ′bĕl-tŭft) ... Den.	56·11 N	10·39 E
111	Ebersberg (ĕ′bĕrs-bĕrgh) Ger. (Munich In.)	48·05 N	11·58 E
120	Ebingen (ā′bĭng-ĕn) ... Ger.	48·13 N	9·04 E
146	Ebi Nuur (L.) (ā′bē) ... China	45·09 N	83·15 E
126	Eboli (ĕb′ō-lē) ... It.	40·38 N	15·04 E
164	Ebolowa ... Cam.	2·54 N	11·09 E
111	Ebreichsdorf ... Aus. (Vienna In.)	47·58 N	16·24 E
125	Ebro, Río (R.) (rē′-ō-ā′brō) ... Sp.	41·22 N	0·17 W
110	Eccles (ĕk′′lz) ... Eng.	53·29 N	2·20 W
80	Eccles ... W. Va.	37·45 N	81·10 W
110	Eccleshall (ĕk′′lz-hôl) ... Eng.	52·51 N	2·15 W
127	Eceabat (Maidos) ... Tur.	40·10 N	26·21 E
155	Echague (ā-chä′gwä) Phil. (Manila In.)	16·43 N	121·40 E
93	Echandi, Cerro (Mt.) (sĕ′r-rô-ĕ-chä′nd) . Pan.	9·05 N	82·51 W
74	Echo Bay (ĕk′ō) Can. (Sault Ste. Marie In.)	46·29 N	84·04 W
123	Echternach (ĕk′tēr-näk) ... Lux.	49·48 N	6·25 E
160	Echuca (ē-cho͞o′kȧ) ... Austl.	36·10 S	144·47 E
124	Écija (ā′thē-hä) ... Sp.	37·20 N	5·07 W
120	Eckernförde ... Ger.	54·27 N	9·51 E
84	Eclipse (ē-klĭps′) Va. (Norfolk In.)	36·55 N	76·29 W
75	Ecorse (ē-kôrs′) Mich. (Detroit In.)	42·15 N	83·09 W
96	Ecuador (ĕk′wȧ-dôr) ... S. A.	0·00 N	78·30 W
165	Edd ... Eth.	13·57 N	41·37 E
165	Ed Dāmer (ĕd dä′mĕr) ... Sud.	17·38 N	33·57 E
165	Ed Debba (dĕb′ȧ) ... Sud.	18·04 N	30·58 E
165	Ed Dueim (do͞o-ām′) ... Sud.	13·56 N	32·22 E
78	Eddyville (ĕd′ĭ-vĭl) ... Ky.	37·03 N	88·03 W
164	Edéa (ĕ-dā′ä) ... Cam.	3·45 N	10·08 E
74	Eden (ē′d′n) Calif. (Los Angeles In.)	33·54 N	117·05 W
74	Eden ... Utah (Salt Lake City In.)	41·18 N	111·49 W
116	Eden (R.) (ē′dĕn) ... Eng.	54·40 N	2·35 W
110	Edenbridge (ē′dĕn-brĭj) Eng. (London In.)	51·11 N	0·05 E
110	Edenham (ē′d′n-ǎm) ... Eng.	52·46 N	0·25 W
74	Eden Prairie (prâr′ĭ) Minn. (Minneapolis, St. Paul In.)	44·51 N	93·29 W
79	Edenton (ē′dĕn-tǔn) ... N. C.	36·02 N	76·37 W
75	Edenton ... Ohio (Cincinnati In.)	39·14 N	84·02 W
167	Edenvale (ĕd′ĕn-vāl) ... S. Afr. (Johannesburg & Pretoria In.)	29·06 S	28·10 E
168	Edenville (ē′d′n-vĭl) S. Afr. (Johannesburg & Pretoria In.)	27·33 S	27·42 E
120	Eder R. (ā′dēr) ... Ger.	51·05 N	8·52 E
164	Edeyen, Erg (Dunes) (ĕ-dā′yĕn) Alg.	27·30 N	7·30 E
79	Edgefield (ĕj′fēld) ... S. C.	33·52 N	81·55 W
70	Edgeley (ĕj′lĭ) ... N. D.	46·24 N	98·43 W
70	Edgemont (ĕj′mŏnt) ... S. D.	43·19 N	103·50 W
71	Edgerton (ĕj′ēr-tǔn) ... Wis.	42·49 N	89·06 W
84	Edgewater (ĕj-wô-tēr) Ala. (Birmingham In.)	33·31 N	86·52 W
127	Édhessa ... Grc.	40·48 N	22·04 E
74	Edina (ē-dī′nȧ) Minn. (Minneapolis, St. Paul In.)	44·55 N	93·20 W
73	Edina ... Mo.	40·10 N	92·11 W
80	Edinburg (ĕd′′n-bûrg) ... Ind.	39·20 N	85·55 W
76	Edinburg ... Tex.	26·18 N	98·08 W
116	Edinburgh (ĕd′′n-bŭr-ō) ... Scot.	55·57 N	3·10 W
127	Edirne (Adrianople) (ĕ-dĭr′nĕ) (ā-drĭ-ǎn-ō′p′l) . Tur.	41·41 N	26·35 E
79	Edisto, (R.) (ĕd′ĭs-tō) ... S. C.	33·10 N	80·50 W
79	Edisto (R.), North Fk ... S. C.	33·42 N	81·24 W
79	Edisto (R.), South Fk ... S. C.	33·43 N	81·35 W
79	Edisto Island ... S. C.	32·32 N	80·20 W
73	Edmond (ĕd′mǔnd) ... Okla.	35·39 N	97·29 W
65	Edmonds (ĕd′mǔndz) Wash. (Seattle In.)	47·49 N	122·23 W
85	Edmonton .. Can. (Edmonton In.)	53·30 N	113·45 W
82	Edmundston (ĕd′mǔn-stǔn) .. Can.	47·23 N	68·20 W
77	Edna (ĕd′nȧ) ... Tex.	28·59 N	96·39 W
127	Edremit (ĕd-rĕ-mĕt′) ... Tur.	39·35 N	27·00 E
127	Edremit Körfezi (G.) ... Tur.	39·28 N	26·35 E
86	Edson (ĕd′sŭn) ... Can.	53·40 N	116·40 W

ăt; finăl; rāte; senâte; ärm; åsk; sofȧ; fâre; ch-choose; dh-as th in other; bē; ēvent; bĕt; recĕnt; cratẽr; g-go; gh-guttural g; bĭt; ĭ-short neutral; rīde; K-guttural k as ch in German ich;

Page	Name Pronunciation Region	Lat. °′	Long. °′
71	Edward (I.) (ĕd′wērd).......Can.	48·21 N	88·29 W
166	Edward (L.).............Con. L.	0·15 S	28·32 E
74	Edwardsville (ĕd′wērdz-vĭl)		
	Ill. (St. Louis In.)	38·49 N	89·58 W
75	Edwardsville .Ind. (Louisville In.)	38·17 N	85·53 W
74	Edwardsville		
	Kans. (Kansas City In.)	39·04 N	94·49 W
66	Eel R. (ēl)............Calif.	40·39 N	124·15 W
80	Eel (R.)...................Ind.	40·50 N	85·55 W
159	Efate (I.) (ā-fä′tā)....New Hebr.	18·02 S	168·29 E
71	Effigy Mounds Natl. Mon.		
	(ĕf′ĭ-jŭ mounds).Iowa	43·04 N	91·15 W
80	Effingham (ĕf′ĭng-hăm).......Ill.	39·05 N	88·30 W
124	Ega (R.) (ā′gä)............Sp.	42·40 N	2·20 W
126	Egadi, Isole (Is.)		
	(ĕ′sō-lĕ-ĕ′gä-dē).It.	38·01 N	12·00 E
124	Egea de los Caballeros (â-kā′á dā		
	lōs kä-bäl-yā′rōs).Sp.	42·07 N	1·05 W
64	Egegik (ĕg′ĕ-jĭt)..........Alaska	58·10 N	157·22 W
121	Eger (ĕ gĕr).............Hung.	47·53 N	20·24 E
	Eger, see Ohre R.		
118	Egersund (ĕ′ghĕr-sōōn′)......Nor.	58·29 N	6·01 E
81	Egg Harbor (ĕg här′bēr)....N. J.	39·30 N	74·35 W
110	Egham (ĕg′ŭm)		
	Eng. (London In.)	51·24 N	0·33 W
146	Egiin Gol (R.) (â-gēn′)....Mong.	49·41 N	100·40 E
159	Egmont, C. (ĕg′mŏnt) .N. Z. (In.)	39·18 S	173·49 E
133	Egridir Gölü (L.) (ā-rĭ-dĭr′)..Tur.	38·10 N	30·00 E
122	Eguilles (ĕ-gwē′)		
	Fr. (Marseille In.)	43·34 N	5·21 E
	Egypt, see United Arab Republic		
124	Eibar (ā′ē-bär)..............Sp.	43·12 N	2·20 W
120	Eichstätt (īk′shtät)..........Ger.	48·54 N	11·14 E
111	Eichwalde (īĸ′väl-dĕ)		
	Ger. (Berlin In.)	52·22 N	13·37 E
118	Eid (īdh)..................Nor.	61·54 N	6·01 E
118	Eidsberg (īdhs′bĕrgh).......Nor.	59·32 N	11·16 E
118	Eidsvoll (idhs′vôl)..........Nor.	60·19 N	11·15 E
120	Eifel (Plat.) (ī′fĕl)..........Ger.	50·08 N	6·30 E
168	Eil......Som. (Horn of Afr. In.)	7·53 N	49·45 E
139	Eilat.......Jordan (Palestine In.)	29·34 N	34·57 E
120	Eilenburg (ī′lĕn-bŏŏrgh)......Ger.	51·27 N	12·38 E
167	Elliot.........S. Afr. (Natal In.)	31·19 S	27·52 E
120	Einbeck (īn′bĕk)............Ger.	51·49 N	9·52 E
117	Eindhoven (īnd′hō-vĕn).....Neth.	51·29 N	5·20 E
98	Eirunepé (ā-rōō-nĕ-pĕ′).....Braz.	6·37 S	69·58 W
120	Eisenach (ī′zĕn-äĸ)..........Ger.	50·58 N	10·18 E
120	Eisenhuttenstadt...........Ger.	52·08 N	14·40 E
120	Eisleben (īs′lā′bĕn)..........Ger.	51·31 N	11·33 E
118	Ejdfjord (ĕĭd′fyōr)..........Nor.	60·28 N	7·04 E
91	Ejutla de Crespo (â-hōōt′lä dā		
	krās′pō).Mex.	16·34 N	96·44 W
119	Ekenäs (Tammisaari)		
	(ĕ′kĕ-nâs) (tȧm′ĭ-sä′rĭ).Fin.	59·59 N	23·25 E
111	Ekeren........Bel. (Brussels In.)	51·17 N	4·27 E
85	Ekhart (ĕk′ärt)		
	Can. (Winnipeg In.)	50·08 N	97·26 W
118	Eksjö (ĕk′shû)..............Swe.	57·41 N	14·55 E
165	El Abyad, Bahr (R.) (White Nile)		
	(bär ĕl ä-byäd′).Sud.	14·09 N	32·27 E
125	El Affroun (ĕl ȧf-froun′).......Alg	36·28 N	2·38 E
164	El Aiún (ĕl ä-ē-ōō′n).....Sp. Sah.	26·45 N	13·15 W
167	Elands (R.)....S. Afr. (Natal In.)	31·48 S	26·09 E
168	Elands R. (ĕ′lȧnds)		
	S. Afr. (Johannesburg &		
	Pretoria In.)	25·11 S	28·52 E
165	El Arab, Buhr (R.)...........Sud.	9·46 N	26·52 E
124	El Arahal (ĕl ä-rä-äl′).........Sp.	37·17 N	5·32 W
139	El ʻAuja (ăl oujȧ)		
	Isr.-U. A. R. (Palestine In.)	30·53 N	34·28 E
133	Elâzig (ĕl-ä′zĕz)............Tur.	38·30 N	39·10 E
165	El Azrag, Bahr (R.) (Blue Nile)		
	(bär ĕläz-räk′).Sud.	13·59 N	33·45 E
78	Elba (ĕl′bȧ).................Ala.	31·25 N	86·01 W
126	Elba, Isola di (I.)		
	(ē-sō-lä-dē-ĕl′bȧ).It.	42·42 N	10·25 E
124	El Barco (ĕl bär′kō)...........Sp.	42·26 N	6·58 W
127	Elbasan (ĕl-bä-sän′′).........Alb.	41·08 N	20·05 E
	Elbe, see Labe R.		
120	Elbe R. (ĕl′bĕ)..............Ger.	53·47 N	9·20 E
69	Elbert, Mt. (ĕl′bērt).........Colo.	39·05 N	106·25 W
78	Elberton (ĕl′bēr-tŭn).........Ga.	34·05 N	82·53 W
122	Elbeuf (ĕl-bûf′)..............Fr.	49·16 N	0·59 E
133	Elbistan (ĕl-bē-stän′)........Tur.	38·20 N	37·10 E
121	Elblag (ĕl′blăŋg)............Pol.	54·11 N	19·25 E
124	El Bonillo (ĕl bō-nēl′yō).......Sp.	38·56 N	2·31 W
94	Elbow Cay (I.)...........Ba. Is.	26·25 N	77·55 W
70	Elbow Lake..............Minn.	46·00 N	95·59 W
85	Elbow R. (ĕl′bō)		
	Can. (Calgary In.)	51·03 N	114·24 W
133	El′brus, Gora (Mt.) (ĕl′brōōs′)		
	Sov. Un.	43·20 N	42·25 E
168	El Buheirat el Murrat el Kubra		
	(Great Bitter).U. A. R.		
	(Suez In.)	30·24 N	32·27 E
168	El Buheirat el Murrat el Sughra		
	(Little Bitter).U. A. R.		
	(Suez In.)	30·10 N	32·36 E
168	El Bur....Som. (Horn of Afr. In.)	4·35 N	46·40 E
133	Elburz Mts. (ĕl′bŏŏrz′).......Iran	36·30 N	51·00 E
68	El Cajon...Calif. (San Diego In.)	32·48 N	116·58 W
99	El Cajon (ĕl-kä-kō′n)...Col. (In.)	4·50 N	76·35 W
99	El Cambur (käm-bōōr′).Ven. (In.)	10·24 N	68·06 W
77	El Campo (kăm′pō)..........Tex.	29·13 N	96·17 W
101	El Carmen (kä′r-mĕn)		
	Chile (Santiago In.)	34·14 S	71·23 W
98	El Carmen (kä′r-mĕn).......Col.	9·54 N	75·12 W
74	El Casco (kăs′kō)		
	Calif. (Los Angeles In.)	33·59 N	117·08 W
68	El Centro (sĕn′trō).........Calif.	32·47 N	115·33 W
65	El Cerrito (sĕr-rē′tō)		
	Calif. (San Francisco In.)	37·55 N	122·19 W
100	El Chaco (Prov.) (chä′kō)....Arg.	26·00 S	60·45 W
125	Elche (ĕl′chā)................Sp.	38·15 N	0·42 W
92	El Cuyo......Mex. (Yucatan In.)	21·30 N	87·42 W
125	Elda (ĕl′dä).................Sp.	38·28 N	0·44 W
120	Elde R. (ĕl′dē)..............Ger.	53·11 N	11·30 E
168	El Dilingat....U. A. R. (Nile In.)	30·48 N	30·32 E
164	El Djouf (Des.) (ĕl djōōf)		
	Mauritania	21·38 N	7·44 W
71	Eldon (ĕl-dŭn).............Iowa	40·55 N	92·15 W
73	Eldon......................Mo.	38·21 N	92·36 W
65	Eldon........Wash. (Seattle In.)	47·33 N	123·02 W
71	Eldora (ĕl-dō′rȧ)...........Iowa	42·21 N	93·08 W
73	El Dorado (ĕl dō-rä′dō)......Ark.	33·13 N	92·39 W
80	Eldorado...................Ill.	37·50 N	88·30 W
73	El Dorado.................Kans.	37·49 N	96·51 W
73	Eldorado Springs (sprĭngz)...Mo.	37·51 N	94·02 W
165	Eldoret (ĕl-dō-rĕt′)..........Ken.	00·31 N	35·18 E
90	El Ebano (ā-bä′nō)..........Mex.	22·13 N	98·26 W
72	Electra (ē-lĕk′trȧ)...........Tex.	34·02 N	98·54 W
67	Electric Pk. (ē-lĕk′trĭk)....Mont.	45·03 N	110·52 W
136	Elektrogorsk (ĕl-yĕk′trô-gôrsk)		
	Sov. Un. (Moscow In.)	55·53 N	38·48 E
136	Elektrostal (ĕl-yĕk′trô-stál)		
	Sov. Un. (Moscow In.)	55·47 N	38·27 E
69	Elephant Butte Res.		
	(ĕl′ē-fănt būt). N. Mex.	33·25 N	107·10 W
125	El Escorial (ĕl-ĕs-kō-ryä′l)		
	Sp. (Madrid In.)	40·38 N	4·08 W
92	El Espino (ĕl-ĕs-pē′nō).......Nic.	13·26 N	86·48 W
95	Eleuthera (I.) (ē-lū′thēr-ȧ)		
	Ba. Is.	25·05 N	76·10 W
95	Eleuthera Pt.............Ba. Is.	24·35 N	76·05 W
73	Eleven Point (R.) (ē-lĕv′ĕn)..Mo.	36·53 N	91·39 W
165	El Fāsher (fä′shĕr)..........Sud.	13·38 N	25·21 E
124	El Ferrol (fā-rōl′)............Sp.	43·30 N	8·12 W
75	Elgin (ĕl′jĭn)....Ill. (Chicago In.)	42·03 N	88·16 W
70	Elgin......................Nebr.	41·58 N	98·04 W
66	Elgin.......................Ore.	45·34 N	117·58 W
116	Elgin......................Scot.	57·40 N	3·30 W
77	Elgin.......................Tex.	30·21 N	97·22 W
65	Elgin.........Wash. (Seattle In.)	47·23 N	122·42 W
85	Elgin Mills (mĭls)		
	Can. (Toronto In.)	43·54 N	79·26 W
164	El Goléa (gō-lā-ä′)..........Alg.	30·39 N	2·52 E
165	Elgon, Mt. (ĕl′gŏn)..........Ken.	1·07 N	34·37 E
90	El Grullo (grōōl-yō)........Mex.	19·46 N	104·10 W
99	El Guapo (gwä′pō).....Ven. (In.)	10·07 N	66·00 W
114	El Hamada (Plat.) (häm′ä-dä)		
	Alg.	30·53 N	1·52 W
164	El Hank (Bluffs) Mauritania-Mali	23·44 N	6·45 W
99	El Hatillo (ä-tē′l-yō)...Ven. (In.)	10·08 N	65·13 W
85	Elie (ē′lē)....Can. (Winnipeg In.)	49·55 N	97·45 W
166	Elila (R.) (ĕ-lē′lȧ)........Con. L.	3·38 S	27·48 E
65	Elisa (I.) (ē-lĭ′sȧ)		
	Wash. (Vancouver In.)	48·43 N	122·37 W
166	Élisabethville..............Con. L.	11·41 S	27·32 E
119	Elisenvaara (ā-lē′sĕn-vä′rȧ)		
	Sov. Un.	61·25 N	29·46 E
77	Elizabeth (ē-lĭz′ȧ-bĕth)........La.	30·50 N	92·47 W
84	Elizabeth...N. J. (New York In.)	40·40 N	74·13 W
75	Elizabeth.....Pa. (Pittsburgh In.)	40·16 N	79·53 W
79	Elizabeth City.............N. C.	36·15 N	76·15 W
79	Elizabethton (ē-lĭz-ȧ-bĕth′tŭn)		
	Tenn.	36·19 N	82·12 W
80	Elizabethtown (ē-lĭz′ȧ-bĕth-toun)		
	Ky.	37·40 N	85·55 W
164	El Jadida..................Mor.	33·14 N	8·34 W
121	Ełk (ĕlk)...................Pol.	53·53 N	22·23 E
78	Elk (R.)...................Tenn.	35·05 N	86·36 W
80	Elk (R.)..................W. Va.	38·30 N	81·05 W
165	El Kāmlin (käm-lēn′).......Sud.	15·09 N	33·06 E
72	Elk City (ĕlk).............Okla.	35·23 N	99·23 W
165	El Khandaq (kän-däk′)......Sud.	18·38 N	30·29 E
80	Elkhart (ĕlk′härt)...........Ind.	41·40 N	86·00 W
72	Elkhart...................Kans.	37·00 N	101·54 W
77	Elkhart....................Tex.	31·38 N	95·35 W
71	Elkhorn (ĕlk′hôrn)..........Wis.	42·39 N	88·32 W
70	Elkhorn (R.)...............Nebr.	42·06 N	97·46 W
79	Elkin (ĕl′kĭn)...............N. C.	36·15 N	80·50 W
81	Elkins (ĕl′kĭnz)............W. Va.	38·55 N	79·50 W
86	Elk Island Natl. Park (ĕlk ī′lănd)		
	Can.	53·21 N	115·47 W
66	Elko (ĕl′kō)................Nev.	40·51 N	115·46 W
70	Elk Point..................S. D.	42·41 N	96·41 W
80	Elk Rapids (răp′ĭdz).......Mich.	44·55 N	85·25 W
66	Elk River (rĭv′ĕr)..........Idaho	46·47 N	116·11 W
71	Elk River.................Minn.	45·17 N	93·33 W
78	Elkton (ĕlk′tŭn).............Ky.	36·47 N	87·08 W
81	Elkton......................Md.	39·35 N	75·50 W
70	Elkton.....................S. D.	44·15 N	96·28 W
168	El Lagodei		
	Som. (Horn of Afr. In.)	9·20 N	49·09 E
110	Elland (el′ănd).............Eng.	53·41 N	1·50 W
69	Ellen, Mt. (ĕl′ĕn)...........Utah	38·05 N	110·50 W
70	Ellendale (ĕl′ĕn-dāl).........N. D.	46·01 N	98·33 W
66	Ellensburg (ĕl′ĕnz-bûrg)....Wash.	47·00 N	120·31 W
81	Ellenville (ĕl′ĕn-vĭl).........N. Y.	41·40 N	74·25 W
85	Ellerslie (ĕl′ērz-lē)		
	Can. (Edmonton In.)	53·25 N	113·30 W
110	Ellesmere (ĕlz′mēr).........Eng.	52·55 N	2·54 W
49	Ellesmere I.................Can.	81·00 N	80·00 W
110	Ellesmere Port.............Eng.	53·17 N	2·54 W
156	Ellice Is. (ĕl′ĭs)..........Oceania	5·20 S	174·00 E
84	Ellicott City (ĕl′ĭ-kŏt sĭ′tē)		
	Md. (Baltimore In.)	39·16 N	76·48 W
75	Ellicott Cr....N. Y. (Buffalo In.)	43·00 N	78·46 W
167	Elliotdale (ĕl-ĭ-ŏt′dāl)		
	S. Afr. (Natal In.)	31·58 S	28·42 E
65	Elliott (el′ĭ-ŭt).Wash. (Seattle In.)	47·28 N	122·08 W
72	Ellis (ĕl′ĭs)...............Kans.	38·56 N	99·34 W
78	Ellisville (ĕl′ĭs-vĭl).........Miss.	31·37 N	89·10 W
74	Ellisville......Mo. (St. Louis In.)	38·35 N	90·35 W
143	Ellore (ĕl-lōr′).............India	16·44 N	80·09 E
72	Ellsworth (ĕlz′wûrth)........Kans.	38·43 N	98·14 W
82	Ellsworth..................Maine	44·33 N	68·26 W
47	Ellsworth Highland..........Ant.	77·00 S	90·00 W
120	Ellwangen (ĕl′văŋ-gĕn).......Ger.	48·57 N	10·08 E
111	Elm (ĕlm)....Ger. (Hamburg In.)	53·31 N	9·13 E
70	Elm (R.)...................S. D.	45·47 N	98·28 W
80	Elm (R.)..................W. Va.	38·30 N	81·05 W
66	Elma (ĕl′mȧ)..............Wash.	47·02 N	123·20 W
114	El Maadid..................Mor.	31·32 N	4·30 W
73	Elm Cr......................Tex.	33·34 N	97·03 W
164	El Memrhar..........Mauritania	19·30 N	16·18 W
74	Elmendorf (ĕl′mĕn-dôrf)		
	Tex. (San Antonio In.)	29·16 N	98·20 W
164	El Meréié (Des.).......Mauritania	19·45 N	8·00 W
74	Elm Fork (ĕlm fôrk)		
	Tex. (Dallas, Fort Worth In.)	32·55 N	96·56 W
75	Elmhurst (ĕlm′hûrst)		
	Ill. (Chicago In.)	41·54 N	87·56 W
81	Elmira (ĕl-mī′rȧ)...........N. Y.	42·05 N	76·50 W
81	Elmira Heights.............N. Y.	42·10 N	76·50 W
98	El Misti (Vol.) (mē′s-tē).....Peru	16·04 S	71·20 W
74	El Modena (mô-dē′nô)		
	Calif. (Los Angeles In.)	33·47 N	117·48 W
74	El Monte (mōn′tâ)		
	Calif. (Los Angeles In.)	34·04 N	118·02 W
69	El Morro Natl. Mon.....N. Mex.	35·05 N	108·20 W
111	Elmshorn (ĕlms′hôrn)		
	Ger. (Hamburg In.)	53·45 N	9·39 E
75	Elmwood Pl. (ĕlm′wŏŏd plās)		
	Ohio (Cincinnati In.)	39·11 N	84·30 W
165	El Nahud (nä′hōōd)..........Sud.	12·39 N	28·18 E
165	El Obeid (ō-bād′)............Sud.	13·15 N	30·15 E
165	El Odaiya (ō-dī′yȧ).........Sud.	12·06 N	28·16 E
65	Elokomin (R.) (ē-lō′kō-mĭn)		
	Wash. (Portland In.)	46·16 N	123·16 W
90	El Oro (ō-rô)...............Mex.	19·49 N	100·04 W
164	El Oued (wĕd′)..............Alg.	33·23 N	6·49 E
98	El Pao (ĕl pä′ō).............Ven.	8·08 N	62·37 W
92	El Paraíso (pä-rä-ē′sō).....Hond.	13·55 N	86·35 W
125	El Pardo (pä′r-dō)		
	Sp. (Madrid In.)	40·31 N	3·47 W
76	El Paso (pas′ō).............Tex.	31·47 N	106·27 W
99	El Pilar (pē-lä′r).......Ven. (In.)	9·56 N	64·48 W
93	El Porvenir (pôr-vâ-nēr′).....Pan.	9·34 N	78·55 W
124	El Puerto de Sta. María		
	(pwĕr tō dā sän tä mä-rē′ä).Sp.	36·36 N	6·18 W
93	El Real (rā-äl).............Pan.	8·07 N	77·43 W
72	El Reno (rē′nō)............Okla.	35·31 N	97·57 W
99	El Roboré (rô-bō-rĕ′).........Bol.	18·23 S	59·43 W
71	Elroy (ĕl′roi)...............Wis.	43·44 N	90·17 W
74	Elsah (ĕl′zȧ)...Ill. (St. Louis In.)	38·57 N	90·22 W
90	El Salto (säl′tō)............Mex.	22·48 N	105·22 E
88	El Salvador................N. A.	14·00 N	89·30 W
92	El Sauce (ĕl-sä′ōō-sĕ).......Nic.	13·00 N	86·40 W
73	Elsberry (ĕlz′bĕr-ĭ)...........Mo.	39·09 N	90·44 W
123	Elsdorf (ĕls′dōrf)..Ger. (Ruhr In.)	50·56 N	6·35 E
74	El Segundo (sĕgŭn′dō)		
	Calif. (Los Angeles In.)	33·55 N	118·24 W
74	Elsinore (ĕl′sĭ-nôr)		
	Calif. (Los Angeles In.)	33·40 N	117·19 W
74	Elsinore L.Calif. (Los Angeles In.)	33·38 N	117·21 W
111	Elstorf (ĕls′tōrf)		
	Ger. (Hamburg In.)	53·25 N	9·48 E
165	El Sudd (Swp.).............Sud.	8·45 N	30·45 E
161	Eltham (ĕl′thăm)		
	Austl. (Melbourne In.)	37·43 S	145·08 E
98	El Tigre (tē′grĕ)............Ven.	8·49 N	64·15 W
133	El′ton (L.).............Sov. Un.	49·10 N	47·00 E
74	El Toro (tō′rō)		
	Calif. (Los Angeles In.)	33·37 N	117·42 W
92	El Triunfo (ĕl-trē-ōō′n-fô)..Hond.	13·06 N	87·00 W
92	El Triunfo..................Sal.	13·17 N	88·32 W
69	El Vado Res............N. Mex.	36·37 N	106·30 W
124	Elvas (ĕl′väzh).............Port.	38·53 N	7·11 W
118	Elverum (ĕl′vĕ-rŏŏm).......Nor.	60·53 N	11·33 E
92	El Viego (ĕl-vyĕ′ĸō).........Nic.	12·44 N	87·03 W
92	El Viejo (Vol.).............Nic.	12·44 N	87·03 W
73	Elvins (ĕl′vĭnz)..............Mo.	37·49 N	90·31 W
165	El Wak (wăk′)..............Ken.	3·00 N	41·00 E
75	Elwood (ĕl′wŏŏd)		
	Ill. (Chicago In.)	41·24 N	88·07 W
80	Elwood.....................Ind.	40·15 N	85·50 W
117	Ely (ē′lĭ)...................Eng.	52·25 N	0·17 E
71	Ely.......................Minn.	47·54 N	91·53 W
68	Ely........................Nev.	39·16 N	114·53 W
75	Elyria (ē-lĭr′ĭ-ȧ)		
	Ohio (Cleveland In.)	41·22 N	82·07 W
119	Ema (R.) (â′mȧ)........Sov. Un.	58·25 N	27·00 E
118	Emån (R.)..................Swe.	57·15 N	15·46 E
133	Emba (R.) (yĕm′bȧ)....Sov. Un.	46·50 N	54·10 E
80	Embarrass (R.) (ĕm-băr′ăs)...Ill.	39·15 N	88·05 W
85	Embrun (ĕm′brŭn)		
	Can. (Ottawa In.)	45·16 N	75·17 W
123	Embrun (äɴ-brûɴ′)............Fr.	44·35 N	6·32 E
120	Emden (ĕm′dĕn)..............Ger.	53·21 N	7·15 E
159	Emerald (ĕm′ēr-ăld).......Austl.	28·34 S	148·00 E
86	Emerson (ĕm′ēr-sŭn).........Can.	49·00 N	97·18 W
65	Emeryville (ĕm′ēr-ĭ-vĭl)		
	Calif. (San Francisco In.)	37·50 N	122·17 W
165	Emi Koussi (Mtn.) (ā′mē kōō-sē′)		
	Chad	19·50 N	18·30 E
126	Emilia (Reg.) (ā-mēl′yä).......It.	44·35 N	10·48 E
91	Emiliano Zapata		
	(ĕ-mē-lyȧ′nô-zä-pȧ′tȧ). Mex.	17·45 N	91·46 W
80	Eminence (ĕm′ĭ-nĕns).........Ky.	38·25 N	85·15 W
155	Emirau (I.) (ā-mē-rä′ōō)		
	N. Gui. Ter.	1·40 S	150·28 E
117	Emmen (ĕm′ĕn).............Neth.	52·48 N	6·55 E
123	Emmerich (ĕm′ēr-ĭk)		
	Ger. (Ruhr In.)	51·51 N	6·16 E
71	Emmetsburg (ĕm′ĕts-bûrg)....Ia.	43·07 N	94·41 W
66	Emmett (ĕm′ĕt).............Idaho	43·53 N	116·30 W
67	Emmons Mt. (ĕm′ŭnz).......Utah	40·43 N	110·20 W
76	Emory Pk. (ĕ′mō-rē pēk)....Tex.	29·13 N	103·20 W
84	Empire (ĕm′pĭr)		
	La. (New Orleans In.)	29·24 N	89·37 W
126	Empoli (ām′pô-lē).............It.	43·43 N	10·55 E
73	Emporia (ĕm-pō′rĭ-ȧ)........Kans.	38·24 N	96·11 W
79	Emporia.....................Va.	37·40 N	77·34 W
81	Emporium (ĕm-pō′rĭ-ŭm).....Pa.	41·30 N	78·15 W
	Empty Quarter, see Ar Al Khālī		
120	Ems R. (ĕms)...............Ger.	52·52 N	7·16 E
120	Ems-Weser (can.) (vä′zĕr)...Ger.	52·23 N	8·11 E

ng-sing; ŋ-baŋk; ɴ-nasalized n; nŏd; cŏmmit; ōld; ôbey; ôrder; fōōd; fŏŏt; ou-out; s-soft; sh-dish; th-thin; pūre; ûnite; ûrn; stŭd; circŭs; ü-as "y" in study; ′-indeterminate vowel.

Page	Name Pronunciation	Region	Lat. °′	Long. °′
118	Enånger (ĕn-ôŋ'gĕr)	Swe.	61·36 N	16·55 E
88	Encantada, Cerro de la (Mtn.) (sĕ'r-rô-dĕ-lä-ĕn-kän-tä'dä)	Mex.	31·58 N	115·15 W
155	Encanto Pt. (ĕn-kän'tō)	Phil. (Manila In.)	15·44 N	121·46 E
100	Encarnación (ĕn-kär-nä-syōn')	Par.	27·26 S	55·52 W
90	Encarnación de Diaz (ĕn-kär-nä-syōn dȧ dē'ȧz)	Mex.	21·34 N	102·15 W
76	Encinal (ĕn'sĭ-nôl)	Tex.	28·02 N	99·22 W
98	Encontrados (ĕn-kōn-trä'dōs)	Ven.	9·01 N	72·10 W
160	Encounter B. (ĕn-koun'tẽr)	Austl.	35·50 S	138·45 E
139	Endau	Mala. (Singapore In.)	2·39 N	103·38 E
139	Endau (R.)	Mala. (Singapore In.)	2·29 N	103·40 E
47	Enderby Land (Reg.) (ĕn'dĕr bĭ)	Ant.	72·00 S	52·00 E
70	Enderlin (ĕn'dẽr-lĭn)	N. D.	46·38 N	97·37 W
81	Endicott (ĕn'dĭ-kŏt)	N. Y.	42·05 N	76·00 W
64	Endicott Mts.	Alaska	67·30 N	153·45 W
127	Enez	Tur.	40·42 N	26·05 E
81	Enfield (ĕn'fēld)	Conn.	41·55 N	72·35 W
110	Enfield	Eng. (London In.)	51·38 N	0·06 W
79	Enfield	N. C.	36·10 N	77·41 W
95	Engano, Cabo (C.) (kȧ'-bô-ĕn-gä-nô)	Dom. Rep.	18·40 N	68·30 W
154	Engaño, C. (ĕn-gän'yō)	Phil.	18·40 N	122·45 E
165	Engare Vaso Nyiro R. (ĕn-gä'rā wä'sô nyē'rô)	Ken.	0·59 N	37·47 E
167	Engcobo (ĕŋg-cô-bô)	S. Afr. (Natal In.)	31·41 S	27·59 E
133	Engel's (ĕn'gēls)	Sov. Un.	51·20 N	45·40 E
123	Engelskirchen (ĕn'gĕls-kēr'ĸĕn)	Ger. (Ruhr In.)	50·59 N	7·25 E
72	Engelwood (ĕn'g'l-wŏŏd)	Colo.	39·39 N	105·00 W
154	Enggano (ĕng-gä'nō)	Indon.	5·22 S	102·18 E
73	England (ĭŋ'glănd)	Ark.	34·33 N	91·58 W
116	England (Reg.) (ĭŋ'glănd)	U. K.	51·35 N	1·40 W
83	Englee (ĕn-glee)	Can.	50·46 N	56·07 W
80	English (ĭn'glĭsh)	Ind.	38·15 N	86·25 W
87	English (R.)	Can.	50·31 N	94·12 W
113	English Chan.	Eng.	49·45 N	3·06 W
125	Énguera (ān'gārä)	Sp.	38·58 N	0·42 W
72	Enid (ē'nĭd)	Okla.	36·25 N	97.52 W
78	Enid Res.	Miss.	34·13 N	89·47 W
166	Enkeldoorn (ĕŋ'k'l-dōōrn)	S. Rh.	19·59 S	30·58 E
168	Enkeldoring (ĕŋ'k'l-dôr-ĭng)	S. Afr. (Johannesburg & Pretoria In.)	25·24 S	28·43 E
118	Enköping (ėn'kû-pĭng)	Swe.	59·39 N	17·05 E
165	Ennedi Plat. (ĕn-nĕd'ė)	Chad.	17·15 N	22·45 W
116	Ennis (ĕn'ĭs)	Ire.	52·54 N	9.05 W
77	Ennis	Tex.	32·20 N	96·38 W
116	Enniscorthy (ĕn-ĭs-kôr'thĭ)	Ire.	52·33 N	6·27 W
116	Enniskillen (ĕn-ĭs-kĭl'ĕn)	N. Ire.	54·20 N	7·25 W
120	Enns R. (ĕns)	Aus.	47·37 N	14·35 E
79	Enoree (ė-nō'rē)	S. C.	34·43 N	81·58 W
79	Enoree, (R.)	S. C.	34·35 N	81·55 W
95	Enriquillo (ĕn-rė-kė'l-yô)	Dom. Rep.	17·55 N	71·15 W
95	Enriquillo, Lago (L.) (lä'gô-ĕn-rė-kė'l-yô)	Dom. Rep.	18·35 N	71·35 W
117	Enschede (ĕns'ĸȧ-dĕ)	Neth.	52·10 N	6·50 E
88	Ensenada (ĕn-sĕ-nä'dä)	Mex.	32·00 N	116·30 W
101	Enseñada	Arg. (Buenos Aires In.)	34·50 S	57·55 W
151	Enshih	China	30·18 N	109·25 E
153	Enshū-Nada (Sea) (ĕn'shōō nä-dä)	Jap.	34·25 N	137·14 E
165	Entebbe (ĕn-tĕb'ĕ)	Ug.	0·01 N	32·29 E
78	Enterprise (ĕn'tẽr-prīz)	Ala.	31·20 N	85·50 W
66	Enterprise	Ore.	45·25 N	117·16 W
66	Entiat, L.	Wash.	45·43 N	120·11 W
122	Entraygues (ĕɴ-trĕg')	Fr.	44·39 N	2·33 E
100	Entre Ríos (Prov.) (ĕn-trā rē'ōs)	Arg.	31·30 S	59·00 W
164	Enugu (ĕ-nōō'gōō)	Nig.	6·13 N	7·18 E
65	Enumclaw (ĕn'ŭm-klô)	Wash. (Seattle In.)	47·12 N	121·59 W
98	Envigado (ĕn-vē-gȧ'dŏ)	Col. (In.)	6·10 N	75·34 W
126	Eolie, Isole (Is.) (ė'sō-lĕ-ĕ-ô'lyĕ)	It.	38·43 N	14·43 E
127	Epeirus (Reg.)	Grc.	39·35 N	20·45 E
122	Epernay (ā-pĕr-nĕ')	Fr.	49·02 N	3·54 E
123	Épernon (ā-pĕr-nôɴ')	Fr. (Paris In.)	48·36 N	1·41 E
69	Ephraim (ē'frȧ-ĭm)	Utah	39·20 N	111·40 W
66	Ephrata (ė frā'tȧ)	Wash.	47·18 N	119·35 W
159	Epi (ā'pė)	New Hebr.	16·59 S	168·29 E
124	Épila (ā'pė-lä)	Sp.	41·38 N	1·15 W
123	Épinal (ā-pē-nȧl')	Fr.	48·11 N	6·27 E
139	Episkopi B.	Cyprus (Palestine In.)	34·34 N	32·41 E
110	Epping (ĕp'ĭng)	Eng. (London In.)	51·41 N	0·06 E
166	Epping	S. Afr. (Cape Town In.)	33·56 S	18·35 E
110	Epworth (ĕp'wûrth)	Eng.	53·31 N	0·50 W
122	Equeurdreville (ā-kûr-dr'vēl')	Fr.	49·38 N	1·42 W
85	Eramosa R. (ĕr-ȧ-mō'sȧ)	Can. (Toronto In.)	43·39 N	80·08 W
165	Erba (Mt.) (ĕr'bȧ)	Sud.	20·53 N	36·45 E
115	Erciyas (Mtn.)	Tur.	38·30 N	35·36 E
74	Erda (ẽr'dä)	Utah (Salt Lake City In.)	40·41 N	112·17 W
111	Erding (ĕr'dēng)	Ger. (Munich In.)	48·19 N	11·54 E
100	Erechim (ĕ-rĕ-shė'ɴ)	Braz.	27·43 S	52·11 W
133	Ereğli (ĕ-rȧ'ĭ-le)	Tur.	37·40 N	34·00 E
133	Ereğli	Tur.	41·15 N	31·25 E
120	Erfurt (ĕr'fŏŏrt)	Ger.	50·59 N	11·04 E
127	Ergene (R.) (ĕr'gĕ-nĕ)	Tur.	41·17 N	26·50 E
124	Erges (R.) (ĕr'-zhĕs)	Port. Sp.	39·45 N	7·01 W
148	Erhlangtien (ẽ'läng'diän)	China	31·33 N	114·07 E
124	Eria (R.) (ā-rē'ä)	Sp.	42·10 N	6·08 W
72	Erick (âr'ĭk)	Okla.	35·14 N	99·51 W
73	Erie (ē'rĭ)	Kans.	37·35 N	95·17 W
81	Erie	Pa.	42·05 N	80·05 W
63	Erie, L.	U. S.-Can.	42·15 N	81·25 W
152	Erimo Saki (C.) (ā'rē-mō sä-kē)	Jap.	41·53 N	143·20 E
85	Erin (ĕ'rĭn)	Can. (Toronto In.)	43·46 N	80·04 W
165	Eritrea (Reg.) (ā-rê-trā'ȧ)	Eth.	16·15 N	38·30 E
120	Erlangen (ĕr'läng-ĕn)	Ger.	49·36 N	11·03 E
75	Erlanger (ẽr'lăng-ẽr)	Ky. (Cincinnati In.)	39·01 N	84·36 W
	Ermoúpolis, see Síros			
143	Ernakulam	India	9·58 N	76·23 E
116	Erne, Upper, Lough (B.) (lŏĸ ûrn)	N. Ire.	54·20 N	7·24 W
116	Erne, Lough (B.)	N. Ire.	54·30 N	7·40 W
159	Eromanga (I.)	New Hebr.	18·58 S	169·18 E
77	Eros (ē'rōs)	La.	32·23 N	92·22 W
165	Er Renk (ẽr rĕnk')	Sud.	11·45 N	32·53 E
114	Er Ricani	Mor.	31·09 N	4·20 W
116	Errigal, Mt. (ĕr-ĭ-gôl')	Ire.	54·60 N	8·13 W
165	Er Roseires (rô-sā'rĕs)	Sud.	11·38 N	34·42 E
123	Erstein (ĕr'shtīn)	Fr.	48·27 N	7·40 E
79	Erwin (ûr'wĭn)	N. C.	35·16 N	78·40 W
79	Erwin	Tenn.	36·07 N	82·25 W
120	Erzgebirge (Ore Mts.) (ĕrts'gĕ-bē'gĕ)	Ger.	50·29 N	12·40 E
133	Erzincan (ĕr-zĭn-jän')	Tur.	39·50 N	39·30 E
133	Erzurum (ĕrz'rōōm')	Tur.	39·55 N	41·10 E
152	Esashi (ĕs'ä-shė)	Jap.	41·50 N	140·10 E
118	Esbjerg (ĕs'byĕrgh)	Den.	55·29 N	8·25 E
119	Esbo (ĕs'bô)	Fin.	60·13 N	24·41 E
124	Escairón (ĕs-kī-rô'n)	Sp.	42·34 N	7.40 W
69	Escalante (ĕs-kȧ-lăn'tē)	Utah	37·50 N	111·40 W
69	Escalante (R.)	Utah	37·40 N	111·20 W
78	Escambia (R.) (ĕs-kăm'bĭ-ȧ)	Fla.	30·38 N	87·20 W
71	Escanaba (ĕs-kȧ-nô'bȧ)	Mich.	45·44 N	87·05 W
71	Escanaba (R.)	Mich.	46·10 N	87·22 W
123	Esch-sur-Alzette	Lux.	49·32 N	6·21 E
120	Eschwege (ĕsh'vā-gē)	Ger.	51·11 N	10·02 E
123	Eschweiler (ĕsh'vī-lẽr)	Ger. (Ruhr In.)	50·49 N	6·15 E
95	Escocesá, Bahia (B.) (bä-ē'ä-ĕs-kō-sĕ'sä)	Dom. Rep.	19·25 N	69·40 W
68	Escondido (ĕs-kŏn-dē'dō)	Calif.	33·07 N	117·07 W
76	Escondido, Rio (R.) (rė'ō-ĕs-kōn-dė'dô)	Mex.	28·30 N	100·45 W
93	Escondido R.	Nic.	12·04 N	84·09 W
93	Escudo de Veraguas I. (ĕs-kōō'dä dā vā-rä'gwäs)	Pan.	9·07 N	81·25 W
90	Escuinapa (ĕs-kwē-nä'pä)	Mex.	22·49 N	105·44 W
92	Escuintla (ĕs-kwēn'tlä)	Guat.	14·16 N	90·47 W
91	Escuintla	Mex.	15·20 N	92·45 W
93	Ese, Cayos de (I.)	Col.	12·24 N	81·07 W
164	Eséka (ĕ-sā'kȧ)	Cam.	3·40 N	11·08 E
144	Esfahān	Iran	32·38 N	51·30 E
124	Esgueva (R.) (ĕs-gĕ'vä)	Sp.	41·48 N	4·10 W
167	Eshowe (ĕsh'ô-wė)	S. Afr. (Natal In.)	28·54 S	31·28 E
80	Eskdale (ĕsk'dāl)	W. Va.	38·05 N	81·25 W
112	Eskifjördhur (ĕs'kê-fyŭr'dōōr)	Ice.	65·04 N	14·01 W
118	Eskilstuna (å'shėl-stü-na)	Swe.	59·23 N	16·28 E
86	Eskimo L. (es'kĭ-mō)	Can.	69·29 N	129·57 W
133	Eskişehir (ĕs-kê-shĕ'h'r)	Tur.	39·40 N	30·20 E
74	Esko (ĕs'kô)	Minn. (Duluth In.)	46·27 N	92·22 W
124	Esla (R.) (ĕs-lä)	Sp.	41·50 N	5·48 W
118	Eslöv (ĕs'lûv)	Swe.	55·50 N	13·17 E
98	Esmeraldas (ĕs-mȧ-räl'däs)	Ec.	0·58 N	79·45 W
95	Espada, Punta (Pt.) (pōō'n-tä-ĕs-pä'dä)	Dom. Rep.	18·30 N	68·30 W
87	Espanola (ĕs-pȧ-nō'lȧ)	Can.	46·11 N	81·59 W
93	Esparta (ĕs-pär'tä)	C. R.	9·59 N	84·40 W
158	Esperance (ĕs'pė-răns)	Austl.	33·45 S	122·07 E
94	Esperenza (ĕs-pĕ-rä'n-zä)	Cuba	22·30 N	80·10 W
125	Espichel, Cabo (C.) (kȧ'bō-ĕs-pē-shĕl')	Port. (Lisbon In.)	38·25 N	9·13 W
98	Espinal (ĕs-pė-näl')	Col. (In.)	4·10 N	74·53 W
99	Espinhaço, Serra do (Mts.) (sĕ'r-rä-dô-ĕs-pė-nȧ-sô)	Braz.	16·06 S	44·56 W
101	Espinillo, Punta (Pt.) (pōō'n-tä-ĕs-pė-nē'l-yô)	Ur. (Buenos Aires In.)	34·49 S	56·27 W
99	Espirito Santo (ĕs-pė'rē-tô-sȧn'tô)	Braz.	20·27 S	40·18 W
99	Espírito Santo (State)	Braz.	19·57 S	40·58 W
92	Espíritu Santo, Bahia del (B.) (bä-ē'ä-dĕl-ĕs-pė'rē-tōō-sän'tô)	Mex. (Yucatan In.)	19·25 N	87·28 W
159	Espiritu Santo (I.) (ĕs-pē'rê-tōō sän'tō)	New Hebr.	15·45 S	166·50 E
92	Espita (ĕs-pē'tä)	Mex. (Yucatan In.)	20·57 N	88·22 W
124	Esposende (ĕs-pō-zĕn'dā)	Port.	41·33 N	8·45 W
100	Esquel (ĕs-kĕ'l)	Arg.	42·47 S	71·22 W
65	Esquimalt (ĕs-kwī'mŏlt)	Can. (Seattle In.)	48·26 N	123·25 W
164	Essaouira	Mor.	31·34 N	9·44 W
111	Essen	Bel. (Brussels In.)	51·28 N	4·27 E
123	Essen (ĕs'sĕn)	Ger. (Ruhr In.)	51·26 N	6·59 E
99	Essequibo (R.) (ĕs-ā-kē'bō)	Br. Gu.	4·26 N	58·17 W
75	Essex (ĕs'ĕks)	Can. (Detroit In.)	42·10 N	82·50 W
75	Essex	Ill. (Chicago In.)	41·11 N	88·11 W
84	Essex	Md. (Baltimore In.)	39·19 N	76·29 W
83	Essex	Mass. (Boston In.)	42·38 N	70·47 W
81	Essex	Vt.	44·30 N	73·05 W
84	Essex Fells (ĕs'ĕks fĕlz)	N. J. (New York In.)	40·50 N	74·16 W
80	Essexville (ĕs'ĕks-vĭl)	Mich.	43·35 N	83·50 W
120	Esslingen (ĕs'slēn-gĕn)	Ger.	48·45 N	9·19 E
62	Estacado, Llano (Plain) (yȧ-nō ĕs-tȧ-cȧ-dō')	U. S.	33·50 N	103·20 W
100	Estados, Isla de los	S. A.	55·05 S	63·00 W
99	Estância (ĕs-tän'sĭ-ä)	Braz.	11·17 S	37·18 W
124	Estarreja (ĕs-tär-rā'zhä)	Port.	40·44 N	8·39 W
167	Estcourt (ĕst-coort)	S. Afr. (Natal In.)	29·04 S	29·53 E
126	Este (ĕs'tā)	It.	45·13 N	11·40 E
92	Estelí (ĕs-tā-lē')	Nic.	13·10 N	86·23 W
124	Estella (ĕs-tāl'yä)	Sp.	42·40 N	2·01 W
124	Estepa (ĕs-tā'pä)	Sp.	37·18 N	4·54 W
124	Estepona (ĕs-tȧ-pō'nä)	Sp.	36·26 N	5·08 W
68	Esteros, B. (ĕs-tā'rōs)	Calif.	35·22 N	121·04 W
86	Estevan (ĕ-stē'văn)	Can.	49·11 N	102·57 W
71	Estherville (ĕs'tẽr-vĭl)	Iowa	43·24 N	94·49 W
79	Estill (ĕs'tĭl)	S. C.	32·46 N	81 15 W
130	Estonian S. S. R. (ĕs-tō'nĭ-ä)	Sov. Un.	59·10 N	25·00 E
125	Estoril (ĕs-tô-rēl')	Port. (Lisbon In.)	38·45 N	9·24 W
100	Estrêla (R.) (ĕs-trĕ'lȧ)	Braz. (In.)	22·39 S	43·16 W
124	Estrêla, Serra da (Mts.) (sĕr'rȧ dä ĕs-trā'lȧ)	Port.	40·25 N	7·45 W
124	Estremadura (Reg.) (ĕs-trā-mä-dōō'rȧ)	Port.	41·35 N	8·36 W
124	Estremoz (ĕs-trā-mōzh')	Port.	38·50 N	7·35 W
99	Estrondo, Serra do (Mts.) (sĕr'rȧ dōō ĕs-trôn'dōō)	Braz.	9·52 S	48·56 W
121	Esztergom (ĕs'tẽr-gōm)	Hung.	47·46 N	18·45 E
49	Etah (ē'tȧ)	Grnld.	78·20 N	72·42 W
123	Étampes (ā-täɴp')	Fr. (Paris In.)	48·26 N	2·09 E
122	Étaples (ā-täp'l')	Fr.	50·32 N	1·38 E
85	Etchemin, R. (ĕch'ĕ-mĭn)	Can. (Quebec In.)	46·39 N	71·03 W
163	Ethiopia (ė-thė-ō'pė-ȧ)	Afr.	7·53 N	37·55 E
74	Etiwanda (ĕ-tĭ-wän'dȧ)	Calif. (Los Angeles In.)	34·07 N	117·31 W
	Etlatongo, see San Mateo			
75	Etna (ĕt'nȧ)	Pa. (Pittsburgh In.)	40·30 N	79·55 W
126	Etna, Mt. (Vol.)	It.	37·48 N	15·00 E
85	Etobicoke Cr.	Can. (Toronto In.)	43·44 N	79·48 W
64	Etolin Str. (ĕt ō lĭn)	Alaska	60·35 S	165·40 W
166	Etosha Pan (ėtō'shä)	S. W. Afr.	19·07 S	15·30 E
78	Etowah (ĕt'ô-wä)	Tenn.	35·18 N	84·31 W
78	Etowah (R.)	Ga.	34·23 N	84·19 W
123	Étréchy (ā-trā-shē')	Fr. (Paris In.)	48·29 N	2·12 E
111	Etten	Neth. (Amsterdam In.)	51·34 N	4·38 E
111	Etterbeek (ĕt'ẽr-bāk)	Bel. (Brussels In.)	50·51 N	4·24 E
90	Etzatlán (ĕt-zä-tlän')	Mex.	20·44 N	104·04 W
158	Eucla (ū'klȧ)	Austl.	31·45 S	128·50 E
75	Euclid (ū'klĭd)	Ohio (Cleveland In.)	41·34 N	81·32 W
73	Eudora (u-dō'rȧ)	Ark.	33·07 N	91·16 W
78	Eufaula (û-fô'lȧ	Ala.	31·53 N	85·09 W
73	Eufaula	Okla.	35·16 N	95·35 W
66	Eugene (û-jēn')	Ore.	44·02 N	123·06 W
74	Euless (ū'lĕs)	Tex. (Dallas, Fort Worth In.)	32·50 N	97·05 W
77	Eunice (ū'nĭs)	La.	30·30 N	92·25 W
117	Eupen (oi'pĕn)	Bel.	50·39 N	6·05 E
144	Euphrates, R. (û-frā'tēz)	Asia	35·52 N	39·53 E
122	Eure (R.) (ûr)	Fr.	49·03 N	1·22 E
66	Eureka (û-rē'kȧ)	Calif.	40·45 N	124·10 W
73	Eureka	Kans.	37·48 N	96·17 W
66	Eureka	Mont.	48·53 N	115·07 W
68	Eureka	Nev.	39·33 N	115·58 W
70	Eureka	S. D.	45·46 N	99·38 W
69	Eureka	Utah	39·55 N	112·10 W
73	Eureka Springs	Ark.	36·24 N	93·43 W
144	Eurgun (Mtn.)	Iran	28·47 N	57·00 E
7	Europe (ū'rŭp)			
79	Eustis (ūs'tĭs)	Fla.	28·50 N	81·41 W
78	Eutaw (ū-tȧ)	Ala.	32·48 N	87·50 W
118	Evanger (ĕ-väŋ'gĕr)	Nor.	60·40 N	6·06 E
75	Evanston (ĕv'ănz-tūn)	Ill. (Chicago In.)	42·03 N	87·41 W
67	Evanston	Wyo.	41·17 N	111·02 W
80	Evansville (ĕv'ănz-vĭl)	Ind.	38·00 N	87·30 W
71	Evansville	Wis.	42·46 N	89·19 W
80	Evart (ĕv'ẽrt)	Mich.	43·55 N	85·10 W
168	Evaton (ĕv'ȧ-tŏn)	S. Afr. (Johannesburg & Pretoria In.)	26·32 S	27·53 E
71	Eveleth (ĕv'ė-lĕth)	Minn.	47·27 N	92·35 W
158	Everard (L.) (ĕv'ẽr-ȧrd)	Austl.	36·20 S	134·10 E
158	Everard Ra.	Austl.	27·15 S	132·00 E
142	Everest, Mt. (ĕv'ẽr-ĕst)	Nep.-China	32·58 N	86·57 E
83	Everett (ĕv'ẽr-ĕt)	Mass. (Boston In.)	42·24 N	71·03 W
65	Everett (ĕv'ẽr-ĕt)	Wash. (Seattle In.)	47·59 N	122·11 W
87	Everett Mts.	Can.	62·34 N	68·00 W
79	Everglades (ĕv'ẽr-glādz)	Fla. (In.)	25·50 N	81·25 W
94	Everglades, The (Swp.)	Fla.	25·35 N	80·55 W
79	Everglades Natl. Park	Fla. (In.)	25·39 N	80·57 W
78	Evergreen (ĕv'ẽr-grēn)	Ala.	31·25 N	87·56 W
75	Evergreen Park	Ill. (Chicago In.)	41·44 N	87·42 W
74	Everman (ĕv'ẽr-măn)	Tex. (Dallas, Fort Worth In.)	32·38 N	97·17 W
65	Everson (ĕv'ẽr-sŭn)	Wash. (Vancouver In.)	48·55 N	122·21 W
124	Évora (ĕv'ô-rä)	Port.	38·35 N	7·54 W
122	Évreux (ā-vrû')	Fr.	49·02 N	1·11 E
127	Evrotas (R.) (ĕv-rō'täs)	Grc.	37·15 N	22·17 E
127	Evvoia (Pen.)	Grc.	38·38 N	23·45 E
157	Ewa (ē'wä)	Hawaii (In.)	21·17 N	158·03 E
155	Ewab, Palau-Palan Is.	Indon.	5·55 S	131·30 E
74	Excelsior (ĕk-sel'sĭ-ŏr)	Minn. (Minneapolis, St. Paul In.)	44·54 N	93·35 W
73	Excelsior Springs	Mo.	39·20 N	94·13 W
116	Exe (R.) (ĕks)	Eng.	50·57 N	3·37 W
68	Exeter (ĕk'sė-tẽr)	Calif.	36·18 N	119·09 W
116	Exeter	Eng.	50·45 N	3·33 W
81	Exeter	N. H.	43·00 N	71·00 W
116	Exmoor (ĕks'mŏŏr)	Eng.	51·10 N	3·55 W
116	Exmouth (ĕks'mŭth)	Eng.	50·40 N	3·20 W
158	Exmouth, G.	Austl.	21·45 S	114·30 E
83	Exploits (R.) (ĕks-ploits')	Can.	48·50 N	56·15 W
90	Extórrax (R.) (ĕx-tó'rȧx)	Mex.	21·04 N	99·39 W
101	Extrema (ĕsh-trĕ'mä)	Braz. (Rio de Janeiro In.)	22·52 S	46·19 W

ăt; finăl; rāte; senȧte; ärm; ȧsk; sofȧ; fâre; ch-choose; dh-as th in other; bē; ėvent; bĕt; recĕnt; cratẽr; g-go; gh-guttural g; bĭt; ĭ-short neutral; rīde; ĸ-guttural k as ch in German ich;

Page	Name Pronunciation Region	Lat. °'	Long. °'
124	Extremadura (Reg.) (ĕks-trā-mä-doo'rä) . Sp.	38·43 N	6·30 W
95	Exuma Sd. (ĕk-sōō'mä) Ba. Is.	24·20 N	76·20 W
166	Eyasi (L.) (â-yä'sê) Tan.	3·41 S	34·14 E
112	Eyja Fd. Ice.	66·21 N	18·20 W
112	Eyrarbakki Ice.	63·51 N	20·52 W
158	Eyre (âr) Austl.	32·15 S	126·20 E
160	Eyre (L.) Austl.	28·43 S	137·50 E
158	Eyre Pen. Austl.	33·30 S	136·00 E
100	Ezeiza (ĕ-zā'zä) Arg. (In.)	34·36 S	58·31 W
127	Ezine (â'zĭ-nâ) Tur.	39·47 N	26·18 E
76	Fabens (fā'bĕnz) Tex.	31·30 N	106·07 W
118	Fåborg (fô'bôrg) Den.	55·06 N	10·19 E
126	Fabriano (fä-brē-ä'nô) It.	43·20 N	12·55 E
98	Facatativá (fä-kä-tä-tê-vä') Col (In.)	4·49 N	74·09 W
165	Fada (fä'dä) Chad	17·06 N	21·18 E
164	Fada N'Gourma (fä'dä''n gōōr'mä) . Upper Volta	12·11 N	00·21 E
135	Faddeya (I.) (fád-yä') Sov. Un.	76·12 N	145·00 E
118	Faemund (L.) (fâ'mōōn') Nor.	62·17 N	11·40 E
126	Faenza (fä-ĕnd'zä) It.	44·16 N	11·53 E
112	Faeroe Is. (fā'rō) Eur.	61·53 N	5·58 W
168	Fafan R. . . Eth. (Horn of Afr. In.)	8·15 N	42·40 E
124	Fafe (fä'fā) Port.	41·30 N	8·10 W
127	Făgăras (fä-gä'rāsh) Rom.	45·50 N	24·55 E
118	Fagerness (fä'ghĕr-nĕs) Nor.	61·00 N	9·10 E
100	Fagnano (fäk-nä'nô) (L.) Arg.-Chile	54·35 S	68·20 W
164	Faial I. (fä-yä'l) Azores (In.)	38·40 N	29·19 W
168	Fā'id (fä-yēd') . U. A. R. (Suez In.)	30·19 N	32·18 E
116	Fair (I.) (fâr) Scot.	59·34 N	1·41 W
64	Fairbanks (fâr'bănks) Alaska	64·50 N	147·48 W
80	Fairbury (fâr'bĕr-ĭ) Ill.	40·45 N	88·25 W
73	Fairbury Nebr.	40·09 N	97·11 W
85	Fairchild Cr. (fâr'chīld) Can. (Toronto In.)	43·18 N	80·10 W
71	Fairfax (fâr'făks) Minn.	44·29 N	94·44 W
79	Fairfax S. C.	32·29 N	81·13 W
84	Fairfield (fâr'fēld) Ala. (Birmingham In.)	33·30 N	86·50 W
161	Fairfield Austl. (Sydney In.)	33·52 S	150·57 E
84	Fairfield . . . Conn. (New York In.)	41·08 N	73·22 W
80	Fairfield Ill.	38·25 N	88·20 W
71	Fairfield Iowa	41·00 N	91·59 W
82	Fairfield Maine	44·35 N	69·38 W
81	Fairhaven (fâr-hā'vĕn) Mass.	41·35 N	70·55 W
81	Fair Haven Vt.	43·35 N	73·15 W
80	Fairmont (fâr'mŏnt) Ind.	40·25 N	85·45 W
71	Fairmont Minn.	43·39 N	94·26 W
81	Fairmont W. Va.	39·30 N	80·10 W
74	Fairmont City . . Ill. (St. Louis In.)	38·39 N	90·05 W
74	Fairmount Kans. (Kansas City In.)	39·12 N	95·55 W
74	Fairmount . Mo. (Kansas City In.)	39·06 N	94·28 W
84	Fair Oaks (fâr ōks) Ga. (Atlanta In.)	33·56 N	84·33 W
81	Fairport (fâr'pōrt) N. Y.	43·05 N	77·30 W
80	Fairport Harbor Ohio	41·45 N	81·15 W
75	Fairview (fâr'vū) Ohio (Cleveland In.)	41·27 N	81·52 W
72	Fairview Okla.	36·16 N	98·28 W
65	Fairview . . . Ore. (Portland In.)	45·32 N	122·26 W
69	Fairview Utah	39·35 N	111·30 W
64	Fairweather, Mt. (fâr-wĕdh'ĕr) Can.	59·12 N	137·22 W
70	Faith (fāth) S. D.	45·02 N	120·02 W
142	Faizābād India	26·50 N	82·17 E
165	Fajao (fä-jä'ō) Ug.	2·13 N	31·44 E
89	Fajardo . . . P. R. (Puerto Rico In.)	18·20 N	65·40 W
155	Fakfak W. Irian	2·56 S	132·25 E
142	Fakiragram India	26·28 N	90·16 E
150	Fak'u China	42·28 N	123·20 E
151	Falalise, C. Viet.	19·20 N	106·18 E
99	Falcón (fäl-kô'n) (State) . Ven. (In.)	11·00 N	68·28 W
81	Falconer (fô'k'n-ĕr) N. Y.	42·10 N	79·10 W
74	Falcon Heights (fô'k'n) Minn. (Minneapolis, St. Paul In.)	44·59 N	93·10 W
76	Falcon Res. (fôk'n) Tex.	26·47 N	99·03 W
164	Faleme R. (fä-lā-mā') Mali-Senegal	13·15 N	11·27 W
129	Faleshty (fä-lâsh'tĭ) Sov. Un.	47·33 N	27·46 E
76	Falfurrias (făl'fōō-rē'ás) Tex.	27·15 N	98·08 W
118	Falkenberg (fäl'kĕn-bĕrgh) . . . Swe.	56·54 N	12·25 E
111	Falkensee (fäl'kĕn-zā) Ger. (Berlin In.)	52·34 N	13·05 E
111	Falkenthal (fäl'kĕn-täl) Ger. (Berlin In.)	52·54 N	13·18 E
116	Falkirk (fôl'kûrk) Scot.	55·59 N	3·55 W
100	Falkland Is. (fôk'lănd) S. A.	50·45 S	61·00 W
118	Falköping (fäl'chûp-ĭng) Swe.	58·09 N	13·30 E
65	Fall City . . . . Wash. (Seattle In.)	47·34 N	121·53 W
75	Fall Cr. (fôl) Ind. (Indianapolis In.)	39·52 N	86·04 W
68	Fallon (făl'ŭn) Nev.	39·30 N	118·48 W
84	Fall River Mass. (Providence In.)	41·42 N	71·07 W
73	Falls City Nebr.	40·04 N	95·37 W
116	Falmouth (făl'mŭth) Eng.	50·08 N	3·04 W
94	Falmouth Jam.	18·30 N	77·40 W
80	Falmouth Ky.	38·40 N	84·20 W
166	False B. (Valsbaai) S. Afr. (Cape Town In.)	34·14 S	18·35 E
143	False Divi Pt. India	20·43 N	81·06 E
95	Falso, Cabo (C.) (kå'bô-fäl-sô) Dom. Rep.	17·45 N	71·55 W
118	Falster (I.) (fäls'tĕr) Den.	54·43 N	12·16 E
121	Fălticeni (fŭl-tê-chân'y') Rom.	47·27 N	26·17 E
118	Falun (fä-lōōn') Swe.	60·38 N	15·35 E
115	Famagusta (fä-mä-gōōs'tä) . Cyprus	35·08 N	33·59 E
100	Famatina, Sierra de (Mts.) (sē-ĕ'r-rä-dĕ-fä-mä-tē'-nä) . Arg.	29·00 S	67·50 W
151	Fan Ching Shan (Mtns.) . . . China	26·46 N	107·42 E
151	Fanghsien China	32·05 N	110·45 E
157	Fanning (I.) (făn'ĭng) Gilbert & Ellice Is.	4·20 N	159·00 W
85	Fannystelle (făn'ĭ-stĕl) Can. (Winnipeg In.)	49·45 N	97·46 W
126	Fano (fä'nō) It.	43·49 N	13·01 E
118	Fanø (I.) (fän'û) Den.	55·24 N	8·10 E
167	Farafangana (fä-rä-făŋ-gä'nä) Malag. Rep.	21·18 S	47·59 E
165	Farâfra (Oasis) (fä-rä'frä) . U. A. R.	27·04 N	28·13 E
144	Farah (fä-rä') Afg.	32·15 N	62·13 E
90	Farallón, Punta (Pt.) (pōō'n-tä-fä-rä-lōn) . Mex.	19·21 N	105·03 W
164	Faranah (fä-rä'nä) Gui.	10·02 N	10·52 W
165	Farasan Dahlak Arch. Eth.	16·45 N	41·08 E
115	Faras R. Libya	30·18 N	17·19 E
115	Faregh, Wadi al R. (wädê ĕl fä-rĕg') . Libya	30·10 N	19·34 E
159	Farewell, C. (fâr-wĕl') N. Z. (In.)	40·37 S	171·46 E
70	Fargo (fär'gō) N. D.	46·53 N	96·48 W
84	Far Hills (fär hĭlz) N. J. (New York In.)	40·41 N	74·38 W
71	Faribault (fâ'rĭ-bō) Minn.	44·19 N	93·16 W
124	Farilhoes (Is.) (fä-rê-lyôNzh') Port.	39·28 N	9·32 W
160	Farina (fá-rē'ná) Austl.	30·03 S	138·20 E
110	Faringdon (fă'rĭng-dŏn) Eng. (London In.)	51·38 N	1·35 W
168	Fāriskūr (fä-rês-kōōr') U. A. R. (Nile In.)	31·19 N	31·46 E
165	Farit, Amba (Mt.) Eth.	10·51 N	37·52 E
121	Farkašd (fär'käsht) Czech.	48·00 N	17·43 E
74	Farley (fär'lē) Mo. (Kansas City In.)	39·16 N	94·49 W
74	Farmers Branch (fär'mĕrz brănch) Tex. (Dallas, Fort Worth In.)	32·56 N	96·53 W
80	Farmersburg (fär'mĕrz-bûrg) . Ind.	39·15 N	87·25 W
73	Farmersville (fär'mĕrz-vĭl) . . . Tex.	33·11 N	96·22 W
84	Farmingdale (färm'ĕng-dāl) N. J. (New York In.)	40·11 N	74·10 W
84	Farmingdale N. Y. (New York In.)	40·44 N	73·26 W
83	Farmingham (färm-ĭng-hăm) Mass. (Boston In.)	42·17 N	71·25 W
73	Farmington (färm-ĭng-tŭn) . . . . Ill.	40·42 N	90·01 W
82	Farmington Maine	44·40 N	70·10 W
75	Farmington . . . Mich. (Detroit In.)	42·28 N	83·23 W
73	Farmington Mo.	37·46 N	90 26 W
69	Farmington N. Mex.	36·40 N	108·10 W
74	Farmington Utah (Salt Lake City In.)	40·59 N	111·53 W
79	Farmville (färm-vĭl) N. C.	35·35 N	77·35 W
79	Farmville Va.	37·15 N	78·23 W
110	Farnborough (färn'bŭr-ô) Eng. (London In.)	51·15 N	0·45 W
116	Farne (I.) (färn) Eng.	55·40 N	1·32 W
81	Farnham (fär'năm) Can.	45·15 N	72·55 W
110	Farningham (fär'nĭng-ŭm) . . . Eng.	51·22 N	0·14 E
110	Farnworth (färn'wŭrth) Eng.	53·34 N	2·24 W
99	Faro (fä'rōō) Braz.	2·05 S	56·32 W
124	Faro Port.	37·01 N	7·57 W
119	Fåron (I.) Swe.	57·57 N	19·10 E
158	Farquhar, C. (fär'kwár) . . . . Austl.	23·50 S	112·55 E
80	Farrell (făr'ĕl) Pa.	41·10 N	80·30 W
142	Farrukhābād (fŭ-rōōk-hä-bäd') India	27·29 N	79·35 E
127	Fársala (Pharsalus) Grc.	39·18 N	22·25 E
118	Farsund (fär'sōōn) Nor.	58·05 N	6·47 E
100	Fartura, Serra da (Mts.) (sĕ'r-rä-dá-fär-tōō'rä) . Braz.	26·40 S	53·15 W
49	Farvel, Kap (C.) Grnld.	60·00 N	44·00 W
72	Farwell (fär'wĕl) Tex.	34·24 N	103·03 W
144	Fasā (fŭ-sä') Iran	28·59 N	53·44 E
127	Fasano (fä-zä'nō) It.	40·50 N	17·22 E
129	Fastov (fäs'tôf) Sov. Un.	50·04 N	29·57 E
129	Fatĕzh Sov. Un.	52·06 N	35·51 E
124	Fatima Port.	39·36 N	9·36 E
133	Fatsa (fät'sä) Tur.	40·50 N	37·30 E
	Fatshan, see Nanhai		
123	Faucilles, Monts (Mts.) (môN' fō-sēl') . Fr.	48·07 N	6·13 E
126	Favara (fä-vä'rä) It.	37·19 N	13·50 E
123	Faverolles (fä-vrôl') . Fr. (Paris In.)	48·42 N	1·34 E
110	Faversham (fă'vēr-sh'm) Eng. (London In.)	51·19 N	0·54 E
112	Faxaflói (B.) Ice.	64·33 N	22·40 W
78	Fayette (fâ-yĕt') Ala.	33·40 N	87·54 W
71	Fayette Iowa	42·49 N	91·49 W
78	Fayette Miss.	31·43 N	91·00 W
73	Fayette Mo.	39·09 N	92·41 W
73	Fayetteville (fâ-yĕt'vĭl) . . . . Ark.	36·03 N	94·08 W
79	Fayetteville N. C.	35·02 N	78·54 W
78	Fayetteville Tenn.	35·10 N	86·33 W
142	Fazilka India	30·30 N	74·02 E
165	Fazzān (Fezzan) Prov. . . . . Libya	26·45 N	13·01 E
165	Fazzān (Oasis) Libya	26·06 N	15·00 E
79	Fear, C. (fēr) N. C.	33·52 N	77·48 W
68	Feather (R.) (fĕth'ĕr) Calif.	38·56 N	121·41 W
68	Feather, Middle Fk. of (R.) . Calif.	39·49 N	121·10 W
68	Feather, North Fk. of (R.) . . Calif.	40·00 N	121·20 W
110	Featherstone (fĕdh'ĕr stŭn) . . Eng.	53·39 N	1·21 W
122	Fécamp (fâ-kăN') Fr.	49·45 N	0·20 E
85	Federal (fĕd'ĕr-ăl) Can. (Ottawa In.)	45·20 N	75·42 W
99	Federal, Distrito (Dist.) (dês-trē'tô-fĕ-dĕ-rä'l) Ven. (In.)	10·34 N	66·55 W
142	Federal Capital Dist. . . . . W. Pak.	29·55 N	67·01 E
136	Fëdorovka (fyô'dô-rôf-kà) Sov. Un. (Moscow In.)	56·15 N	37·14 E
120	Fehmarn I. (fā'märn) Ger.	54·28 N	11·15 E
111	Fehrbellin (fĕr'bĕl-lēn) Ger. (Berlin In.)	52·49 N	12·46 E
101	Feia, Logoa (L.) (lô-gôä-fĕ'yä) Braz. (Rio de Janeiro In.)	21·54 S	41·45 W
148	Feich'eng (fā'chĕng) China	36·18 N	116·45 E
148	Feihsien (fā'ê-hsyĕn') China	35·17 N	117·59 E
99	Feira de Santana (fĕ'ê-rä dä sänt-ăn'ä) . Braz.	12·16 S	38·46 W
125	Felanitx (fā-lä-nēch') Sp.	39·29 N	3·09 E
120	Feldkirch (fĕlt'kĭrk) Aus.	47·15 N	9·36 E
111	Feldkirchen (fĕld'kĕr-kĕn) Ger. (Munich In.)	48·09 N	11·44 E
92	Felipe Carrillo Puerto (fĕ-lē'pĕ-kär-rē'l-yô-pwĕ'r-tô) Mex. (Yucatan In.)	19·36 N	88·04 W
126	Feltre (fĕl'trā) It.	46·02 N	11·56 E
167	Fénérive (fê-nâ-rēv') . Malag. Rep.	17·30 S	49·31 E
150	Fengchen (fŭng'chĕn') China	40·28 N	113·20 E
150	Fengch'eng (fŭng'chŭng') . . . China	40·28 N	124·03 E
151	Fengchieh China	31·02 N	109·30 E
150	Fenghsiang China	34·25 N	107·20 E
149	Fenghsien (fŭng'hsyĕn') China (Shanghai In.)	30·55 N	121·26 E
148	Fenghsien China	34·41 N	116·36 E
148	Fengjun (fĕng'yĕn) China	39·51 N	118·06 E
148	Fengming Tao (I.) (fĕng'mĭng dou) . China	39·19 N	121·15 E
150	Fengt'ai (fŭng'tī') China (Peking In.)	39·51 N	116·19 E
151	Fengtu (fŭng'tōō') China	29·58 N	107·50 E
148	Fengyang (fŭng'yäng') China	32·55 N	117·32 E
64	Fenimore P. (fĕn ĭ mōr) . . . Alaska	51·40 N	175·38 W
80	Fenton (fĕn-tŭn) Mich.	42·50 N	83·40 W
74	Fenton . . . . . . Mo. (St. Louis In.)	38·31 N	90·27 W
150	Fenyang China	37·20 N	111·48 E
129	Feodosiya (Kefe) (fĕ-ô-dō'sē'yá) (kyĕ'fĕ) . Sov. Un.	45·02 N	35·21 E
144	Ferdows Iran	34·00 N	58·13 E
126	Ferentino (fā-rĕn-tē'nō) It.	41·42 N	13·18 E
134	Fergana Sov. Un.	40·16 N	72·07 E
70	Fergus Falls (fûr'gŭs) Minn.	46·17 N	96·03 W
74	Ferguson (fûr-gŭ-sŭn) Mo. (St. Louis In.)	38·45 N	90·18 W
126	Fermo (fĕr'mō) It.	43·10 N	13·43 E
124	Fermoselle (fĕr-mō-säl'yā) . . . Sp.	41·20 N	6·23 W
116	Fermoy (fûr-moi') Ire.	52·05 N	8·06 W
79	Fernandina (fûr-năn-dē'ná) . . . Fla.	30·38 N	81·29 W
99	Fernando de Noronha, Arquipélago (Arch.) (är-kê-pĕ'lä-gô-fĕr-nän-dō-dĕ-nô-rō'n-yä) . Braz.	3·50 S	33·15 W
164	Fernando Poo, Isla de (I.) (ê's-lä-dĕ-fĕr-nän'dōpō') (fĕr-nän'dō-pō'ō) . Afr.	3·22 N	7·37 E
124	Fernān-Núñez (fĕr-nän'nōōn'yāth) Sp.	37·42 N	4·43 W
66	Ferndale (fûrn'dāl) Calif.	40·34 N	124·18 W
84	Ferndale . . . . Md. (Baltimore In.)	39·11 N	76·39 W
75	Ferndale . . . . Mich. (Detroit In.)	42·27 N	83·08 W
65	Ferndale . . Wash. (Vancouver In.)	48·51 N	122·36 W
86	Fernie (fûr'nĭ) Can.	49·29 N	114·56 W
65	Fern Prairie (fûrn prâr'ĭ) Wash. (Portland In.)	45·38 N	122·25 W
161	Ferntree Gully Austl. (Melbourne In.)	37·53 S	145·18 E
83	Ferolle, Pt. (fĕ-rōl') Can.	51·01 N	57·04 W
142	Ferozepore (fê-rōz-pōr') India	30·58 N	74·39 E
126	Ferrara (fĕr-rä'rä) It.	44·50 N	11·37 E
125	Ferrat, Cap (C.) (kăp fĕr-rät) . Alg.	35·49 N	0·29 W
124	Ferreira do Alentejo (fĕr-rĕ'ê-rä dōō ä-lĕN-tā'zhōō) Port.	38·03 N	8·06 W
124	Ferreira do Zezere (fĕr-rĕ'ê-rä dōō zå-zā'rĕ) . Port.	39·49 N	8·17 W
74	Ferrelview (fĕr'rĕl-vū) Mo. (Kansas City In.)	39 18 N	94·40 W
98	Ferreñafe (fĕr-rĕn-yä'fĕ) Peru	6·38 S	79·48 W
77	Ferriday (fĕr'ĭ-dā) La.	31·38 N	91·33 W
83	Ferryland (fĕr'ê-lănd) Can.	46·50 N	47·06 W
113	Ferryville (fĕr-ê-vēl') Tun.	37·12 N	9·51 E
136	Fershampenuaz (fĕr-shäm'pĕn-wäz) Sov. Un. (Urals In.)	53·32 N	59·50 E
70	Fertile (fûr'tĭl) Minn.	47·33 N	96·18 W
164	Fès (fĕs) Mor.	34·08 N	5·00 W
70	Fessenden (fĕs'ĕn-dĕn) N. D.	47·39 N	99·40 W
116	Festiniog (fĕs-tĭn-ĭ-ŏg) Wales	52·59 N	3·58 W
73	Festus (fĕst'ŭs) Mo.	38·12 N	90·22 W
133	Fethiye (fĕt-hē'yĕ) Tur.	36·40 N	29·05 E
	Fezzan, see Fazzān		
167	Fianarantsoa (fyá-nä-rän'tsō'á) Malag. Rep.	21·21 S	47·15 E
168	Ficksburg (fĭks'bûrg) S. Afr. (Johannesburg & Pretoria In.)	28·53 S	27·53 E
65	Fidalgo I. (fĭ-dăl'gō) Wash. (Seattle In.)	48·28 N	122·39 W
66	Fieldbrook (fēld'brŏŏk) Calif.	40·59 N	124·02 W
127	Fier (fyĕr) Alb.	40·43 N	19·34 E
116	Fife Ness (C.) (fīf'nes') Scot.	56·15 N	2·19 W
165	Fifth Cataract Sud.	18·27 N	33·38 E
124	Figalo, Cap (C.) (kăp fê-gä-lô) . Alg.	35·35 N	1·12 W
122	Figeac (fē-zhák') Fr.	44·37 N	2·02 E
118	Figeholm (fē-ghĕ-hōlm) Swe.	57·24 N	16·33 E
124	Figueira da Foz (fê-gwĕy-rä-dä-fô'z) . Port.	40·10 N	8·50 W
164	Figuig Alg.	32·06 N	1·17 W
156	Fiji Is. (fē'jē) Oceania	18·50 S	175·00 E
92	Filadelfia (fĭl-á-dĕl'fĭ-á) . . . . C. R.	10·26 N	85·37 W
136	Filatovskoye (fĭ-lá'tôf-skô-yĕ) Sov. Un. (Urals In.)	56·49 N	62·20 E
79	Filbert (fĭl'bĕrt) W. Va.	37·18 N	81·29 W
47	Filchner Shelf Ice (fĭlk'nĕr) . . Ant.	77·30 S	38·00 W
127	Filiatrá Grc.	37·10 N	21·35 E
126	Filicudi (I.) (fē'le-kōō'dē) . . . . It.	38·34 N	14·39 E
115	Filiġas (R.) Tur.	41·10 N	32·53 E
136	Filippovskoye (fĭ-lĭ-pôf'skô-yĕ) Sov. Un. (Moscow In.)	56·06 N	38·38 E
118	Filipstad (fĭl'ĭps-städh) Swe.	59·44 N	14·09 E
69	Fillmore (fĭl'môr) Utah	39·00 N	112·20 W
166	Fimi (R.) Con. L.	2·46 S	17·30 E
85	Finch (fĭnch) . . . Can. (Ottawa In.)	45·09 N	75·06 W

Page	Name Pronunciation Region	Lat. °′	Long. °′
80	Findlay (fĭnd'lā) . . . Ohio	41·05 N	83·40 W
124	Finisterre, Cabo de (C.) (kä'bô-dĕ-fĭn-ĭs-târ'). Sp.	42·52 N	9·48 W
158	Finke (R.) (fĭŋ'kē) . . . Austl.	25·25 S	134·30 E
102	Finland (fĭn'lănd) . . . Eur.	62·45 N	26·13 E
119	Finland, G. of (fĭn'lănd) . . . Eur.	59·35 N	23·35 E
98	Finlandia (fēn-lä'n-dēä). Col. (In.)	4·38 N	75·39 W
86	Finlay (R.) (fĭn'lā) . . . Can.	56·57 N	124·40 W
111	Finofurt (fē'nō-fōōrt) Ger. (Berlin In.)	52·50 N	13·41 E
111	Finow (fē'nōv) . . Ger. (Berlin In.)	52·50 N	13·44 E
120	Finsterwalde (fĭn'stēr-väl-dĕ). Ger.	51·38 N	13·42 E
133	Firat (R.) (fē-rät') . . . Tur.	39·40 N	38·30 E
65	Fircrest (fûr'krĕst) Wash. (Seattle In.)	47·14 N	122·31 W
126	Firenze (Florence) (fē-rĕnt'sā) . . It.	43·47 N	11·15 E
126	Firenzuola (fē-rĕnt-swô'lä) . . . It.	44·08 N	11·21 E
165	First Cataract . . . U. A. R.	24·00 N	32·52 E
111	Fischa (R.) . . . Aus. (Vienna In.)	48·04 N	16·33 E
111	Fischamend Markt Aus. (Vienna In.)	48·07 N	16·37 E
95	Fish Cay (I.) . . . Ba. Is.	22·30 N	74·20 W
85	Fish Cr. (fĭsh) . . Can. (Calgary In.)	50·52 N	114·21 W
77	Fisher (fĭsh'ēr) . . . La.	31·28 N	93·30 W
87	Fisher Str . . . Can.	62·43 N	84·28 W
166	Fish Hoek (fĭsh'hōōk) S. Afr. (Cape Town In.)	34·13 S	18·26 E
83	Fitchburg (fĭch'bûrg) Mass. (Boston In.)	42·35 N	71·48 W
78	Fitzgerald (fĭts-jĕr'ăld) . . . Ga.	31·42 N	83·17 W
158	Fitzroy (R.) (fĭts-roi') . . . Austl.	18·00 S	124·05 E
159	Fitzroy (R.) . . . Austl.	23·45 S	150·02 E
158	Fitzroy Crossing . . . Austl.	18·08 S	126·00 E
80	Fitzwilliam (I.) (fĭts-wĭl'yăm) Can.	45·30 N	81·45 W
	Fiume, see Rijeka		
125	Fiumicino (fyōō-mē-chē'nô) It. (Rome In.)	41·47 N	12·19 E
118	Fjällbacka (fyĕl'bäk-å) . . . Swe.	58·37 N	11·17 E
118	Flaam (flôm) . . . Nor.	60·51 N	7·01 E
69	Flagstaff (flăg-stȧf) . . . Ariz.	35·15 N	111·40 W
167	Flagstaff (flăg'stäf) S. Afr. (Natal In.)	31·06 S	29·31 E
81	Flagstaff (L.) (flăg-stȧf) . . . Maine	45·05 N	70·30 W
111	Flalow (flä'lōv) . . Ger. (Berlin In.)	52·44 N	12·58 E
71	Flambeau (R.) (flăm-bō') . . . Wis.	45·32 N	91·05 W
67	Flaming Gorge Res . . . Wyo.	41·13 N	109·30 W
79	Flamingo (flȧ-mĭŋ'gō) . . . Fla.	25·10 N	80·55 W
95	Flamingo Cay (I.) (flȧ-mĭŋ'gō) Ba. Is.	22·50 N	75·50 W
89	Flamingo Pt. Vir. Is. (U. S. A.) (St. Thomas In.)	18·19 N	65·00 W
117	Flanders (Reg.) . . . Fr.	50·53 N	2·29 E
70	Flandreau (flăn'drō) . . . S. D.	44·02 N	96·35 W
116	Flannan (Is.) (flăn'ăn) . . . Scot.	58·13 N	8·14 W
67	Flathead L. (flăt'hĕd) . . . Mont.	47·57 N	114·20 W
67	Flathead Ra . . . Mont.	47·50 N	113·40 W
67	Flathead R . . . Mont.	48·45 N	114·20 W
67	Flathead R., Middle Fork . . . Mont.	48·30 N	113·47 W
67	Flathead R., South Fork . . . Mont.	48·05 N	113·45 W
75	Flat Rock (flăt rŏk) Mich. (Detroit In.)	42·06 N	83·17 W
66	Flattery C. (flăt'ēr-ĭ) . . . Wash.	48·22 N	125·10 W
67	Flat Willow Cr. (flat wĭl'ō). Mont.	46·45 N	108·47 W
118	Flekkefjord (flĕk'kē-fyōr) . . . Nor.	58·19 N	6·38 E
80	Flemingsburg (flĕm'ĭngz-bûrg) Ky.	38·25 N	83·45 W
120	Flensburg (flĕns'bōōrgh) . . . Ger.	54·48 N	9·27 E
122	Flers-del-l'Orne (flĕr-dĕ-lôrn') . . Fr.	48·43 N	0·37 W
158	Flinders (Reg.) (flĭn'dērz) . . . Austl.	32·15 S	138·45 E
160	Flinders (I.) . . . Austl.	39·35 S	148·10 E
159	Flinders (R.) . . . Austl.	18·48 S	141·07 E
160	Flinders Ra . . . Austl.	34·09 S	138·56 E
159	Flinders Rfs . . . Austl.	17·30 S	149·02 E
86	Flin Flon . . . Can.	54·50 N	101·52 W
110	Flint . . . Wales	53·15 N	3·07 W
80	Flint . . . Mich.	43·00 N	83·45 W
110	Flint (Co.) . . . Wales	53·13 N	3·06 W
78	Flint (R.) (flĭnt) . . . Ga.	31·25 N	84·15 W
118	Flisen (flē'sĕn) . . . Nor.	60·35 N	12·03 E
80	Flora (flō'rȧ) . . . Ill.	38·40 N	88·25 W
80	Flora . . . Ind.	40·25 N	86·30 W
78	Florala (flŏr-ăl'ȧ) . . . Ala.	31·01 N	86·19 W
84	Floral Park (flôr'ăl pärk) N. Y. (New York In.)	40·42 N	73·42 W
78	Florence (flŏr'ĕns) . . . Ala.	34·46 N	87·40 W
69	Florence . . . Ariz.	33·00 N	111·25 W
72	Florence . . . Colo.	38·23 N	105·08 W
73	Florence . . . Kans.	38·14 N	96·56 W
79	Florence . . . S. C.	34·10 N	79·45 W
65	Florence . . . Wash. (Seattle In.)	48·13 N	122·21 W
	Florence, see Firenze		
98	Florencia (flō-rĕn'sē-ȧ) . . . Col.	1·31 N	75·13 W
101	Florencio Sánchez (flō-rĕn-sēō-sä'n-chĕz). Ur. (Buenos Aires In.)	33.52 S	57·24 W
100	Florencio Varela (flō-rĕn'sē-o vä-rā'lä). Arg. (In.)	34·34 S	58·16 W
99	Flores (flō'rĕzh) . . . Braz.	7·57 S	37·48 W
92	Flores . . . Guat. (Yucatan In.)	16·53 N	89·54 W
101	Flores (Dept.) Ur. (Buenos Aires In.)	33·33 S	57·00 W
154	Flores (I.) . . . Indon.	8·14 S	121·08 E
101	Flores (R.) Arg. (Buenos Aires In.)	36·13 S	60·28 W
154	Flores Sea . . . Indon.	7·09 N	120·30 E
76	Floresville (flō'rĕs-vĭl) . . . Tex.	29·10 N	98·08 W
99	Floriano (flō-rē-ä'nōō) . . . Braz.	6·17 S	42·58 W
100	Florianópolis (flō-rē-ä-nō'pô-lēs) Braz.	27·30 S	48·30 W
98	Florida (flō-rē'-dä) . . . Col. (In.)	3·20 N	76·12 W
94	Florida . . . Cuba	22·10 N	79·50 W
84	Florida (flŏr'ĭ-dȧ) N. Y. (New York In.)	41·20 N	74·21 W
167	Florida . . . S. Afr. (Johannesburg & Pretoria In.)	26·11 S	27·56 E
101	Florida (flō-rē-dhä) Ur. (Buenos Aires In.)	34·06 S	56·14 W
63	Florida (State) (flŏr'ĭ-dȧ) . . . U. S.	30·30 N	84·40 W
101	Florida (Dept.) (flō-rē'dhä) Ur. (Buenos Aires In.)	33·48 S	56·15 W
159	Florida (I.) . . . Sol. Is.	8·56 S	159·45 E
94	Florida, Strs. of . . . N. A.	24·10 N	81·00 W
79	Florida B. (flŏr'ĭ-dȧ) . . . Fla. (In.)	24·55 N	80·55 W
79	Florida Keys (Is.) . . . Fla. (In.)	24·33 N	81·20 W
69	Florida Mts . . . N. Mex.	32·10 N	107·35 W
76	Florido, R. (flō-rē'dō) . . . Mex.	27·21 N	104·48 W
111	Floridsdorf (flō'rĭds-dôrf) Aus. (Vienna In.)	48·16 N	16·25 E
127	Florina (flō-rē'nä) . . . Grc.	40·48 N	21·24 E
74	Florissant (flŏr'ĭ-sănt) Mo. (St. Louis In.)	38·47 N	90·20 W
118	Florö (flôr'ü) . . . Nor.	61·36 N	5·01 E
70	Floyd (R.) (floid) . . . Iowa	42·38 N	96·15 W
72	Floydada (floi-dā'dȧ) . . . Tex.	33·59 N	101·19 W
75	Floyds Fk. (R.) (floi-dz) Ky. (Louisville In.)	38·08 N	85·30 W
126	Flumendosa, R. (flōō-mĕn-dô'sä) It.	39·45 N	9·18 E
80	Flushing (flŭsh'ĭng) . . . Mich.	43·05 N	83·50 W
155	Fly (R.) (flī) . . . Austl.	8·00 S	141·45 E
127	Foča (fō'chä) . . . Yugo.	43·29 N	18·48 E
168	Fochville (fŏk'vĭl) . . . S. Afr. (Johannesburg & Pretoria In.)	26·29 S	27·29 E
121	Focsani (fŏk-shä'nē) . . . Rom.	45·41 N	27·17 E
126	Foggia (fôd'jä) . . . It.	41·30 N	15·34 E
83	Fogo (fō'gō) . . . Can.	49·43 N	54·14 W
83	Fogo (I.) . . . Can.	49·44 N	53·53 W
164	Fogo I . . . C. V. Is. (In.)	14·46 N	24·51 W
120	Fohnsdorf (fōns'dôrf) . . . Aus.	47·13 N	14·40 E
120	Föhr I. (fûr) . . . Ger.	54·47 N	8·30 E
122	Foix (fwä) . . . Fr.	42·58 N	1·34 E
151	Fokang . . . China	23·50 N	113·35 E
126	Foligno (fō-lēn'yō) . . . It.	42·58 N	12·41 E
110	Folkingham (fō'kĭng-ăm) . . . Eng.	52·53 N	0·24 W
117	Folkstone (fōk'stŭn) . . . Eng.	51·05 N	3·04 W
72	Folsom (fŏl'sŭm) . . . N. Mex.	36·47 N	103·56 W
68	Folsom City . . . Calif.	38·40 N	121·10 W
94	Fomento (fō-mĕ'n-tō) . . . Cuba	21·35 N	78·20 W
98	Fómeque (fō'mĕ-kĕ) . . . Col. (In.)	4·29 N	73·52 W
71	Fonda (fŏn'dȧ) . . . Iowa	42·33 N	94·51 W
71	Fond du Lac (fŏn dū lăk') . . . Wis.	43·47 N	88·29 W
71	Fond du Lac Ind. Res . . . Minn.	46·44 N	93·04 W
126	Fondi (fōn'dē) . . . It.	41·23 N	13·25 E
124	Fonsagrada (fôn-sä-grä'dhä) . . Sp.	43·08 N	7·07 W
92	Fonseca, Golfo de (G.) (gôl-fô-dĕ-fōn-sā'kä). Hond.	13·09 N	87·55 W
123	Fontainebleau (fôN-tĕn-blō') Fr. (Paris In.)	48·24 N	2·42 E
74	Fontana (fŏn-tă'nȧ) Calif. (Los Angeles In.)	34·06 N	117·27 W
98	Fonte Boa (fōn'tä bō'ȧ) . . . Braz.	2·32 S	66·05 W
122	Fontenay-le-Comte (fôNt-nĕ'lē-kôNt'). Fr.	46·28 N	0·53 W
123	Fontenay-Trésigny (fôN-tē-hā' tra-sēn-yē'). Fr. (Paris In.)	48·43 N	2·53 E
91	Fontera, Punta (Pt.) (pōō'n-tä-fôn-tĕ'rä). Mex.	18·36 N	92·43 W
98	Fontibón (fōn-tē-bôn') . . Col. (In.)	4·42 N	74·09 W
	Foochow, see Fuchou		
167	Foothills (fōōt-hĭls) . . . S. Afr. (Johannesburg & Pretoria In.)	25·55 S	27·36 E
64	Foraker, Mt. (fôr'ȧ-kēr) . . . Alaska	62·40 N	152·40 W
123	Forbach (fōr'bäk) . . . Fr.	49·12 N	6·54 E
160	Forbes (fôrbz) . . . Austl.	33·24 S	148·05 E
164	Forcados (fôr-kä'dōs) . . . Nig.	5·19 N	5·26 E
120	Forchheim (fôrk'hīm) . . . Ger.	49·43 N	11·05 E
	Fordlândia, see Brasília Legal		
73	Fordyce (fôr'dīs) . . . Ark.	33·48 N	92·24 W
164	Forecariah (fōr-kȧ-rē'ȧ') . . . Gui.	9·31 N	13·14 W
49	Forel, Mt . . . Grnld.	65·50 N	37·41 W
78	Forest (fŏr'ĕst) . . . Miss.	32·22 N	89·29 W
70	Forest (R.) . . . N. D.	48·08 N	97·45 W
71	Forest City . . . Iowa	43·14 N	93·40 W
79	Forest City . . . N. C.	35·20 N	81·52 W
81	Forest City . . . Pa.	41·35 N	75·30 W
65	Forest Grove (grōv) Ore. (Portland In.)	45·31 N	123·07 W
85	Forest Hill (hĭl) Can. (Toronto In.)	43·42 N	79·25 W
74	Forest Hill Tex. (Dallas, Fort Worth In.)	32·40 N	97·16 W
85	Forest Lawn (lôn) Can. (Calgary In.)	51·02 N	113·59 W
82	Forestville (fŏr'ĕst-vĭl) . . . Can.	48·46 N	69·05 W
122	Forez, Mts. du (môN dü fō-rā'). Fr.	44·55 N	3·43 E
116	Forfar (fôr'fȧr) . . . Scot.	57·10 N	2·55 W
125	Forio (Mtn.) (fô'ryō) It. (Naples In.)	40·29 N	13·55 E
75	Forked Cr. (fôrk'd) Ill. (Chicago In.)	41·16 N	88·01 W
78	Forked Deer (R.) . . . Tenn.	35·53 N	89·29 W
126	Forli (fôr-lē') . . . It.	44·13 N	12·03 E
110	Formby (fôrm'bē) . . . Eng.	53·34 N	3·04 W
110	Formby Pt . . . Eng.	53·33 N	3·06 W
125	Formello (fôr-mĕ'lō) It. (Rome In.)	42·04 N	12·25 E
125	Formentera, Isla de (I.) (ē's-lä-dĕ-fôr-mĕn-tā'rä). Sp.	38·43 N	1·25 E
101	Formiga (fôr-mē'gȧ) Braz. (Rio de Janeiro In.)	20·27 S	45·25 W
95	Formigas Bk. (fōr-mē'gäs) . . N. A.	18·30 N	75·40 W
100	Formosa (fôr-mō'sä) . . . Arg.	27·25 S	58·12 W
99	Formosa . . . Braz.	15·32 S	47·10 W
100	Formosa (Prov.) . . . Arg.	24·30 S	60·45 W
	Formosa, see Taiwan (I.)		
99	Formosa, Serra (Mts.) (sĕ'r-rä) Braz.	12·59 S	55·11 W
139	Formosa Str. (fôr-mō'sȧ) . . . Asia	24·30 N	120·00 E
136	Fornosovo (fôr-nô'sô vô) Sov. Un. (Leningrad In.)	59·35 N	30·34 E
73	Forrest City (fŏr'ĕst sĭ'tĭ) . . . Ark.	35·00 N	90·46 W
159	Forsayth (fôr-sīth') . . . Austl.	18·33 S	143·42 E
118	Forshaga (fôrs'hä'gä) . . . Swe.	59·34 N	13·25 E
201	Forst (fôrst) . . . Ger.	51·45 N	14·38 E
78	Forsyth (fôr-sīth') . . . Ga.	33·02 N	83·56 W
67	Forsyth . . . Mont.	46·15 N	106·41 W
87	Fort Albany (fôrt ôl'bȧ nĭ) . . . Can.	52·10 N	81·40 W
99	Fortaleza (Ceará) (fôr'tä-lā'zä) (sā-ä-rä'). Braz.	3·35 S	38·31 W
69	Fort Apache Ind. Res. (ȧ-păch'ē) Ariz.	34·02 N	110·27 W
165	Fort-Archambault (är-chaN-bō') Chad	9·04 N	18·17 E
71	Fort Atkinson (ăt'kĭn-sŭn) . . . Wis.	42·55 N	88·46 W
	Fort Bayard, see Chanchiang		
167	Fort Beaufort (bō'fôrt) S. Afr. (Natal In.)	32·47 S	26·39 E
74	Fort Bellefontaine (bĕl-fōn-tān') Mo. (St. Louis In.)	38·50 N	90·15 W
67	Fort Benton (bĕn'tŭn) . . . Mont.	47·51 N	110·40 W
70	Fort Berthould Ind. Res. (bērth'ōld). N. D.	47·47 N	103·28 W
80	Fort Branch (brănch) . . . Ind.	38·15 N	87·35 W
	Fort Charlet, see Djanet		
87	Fort Chimo . . . Can.	58·18 N	68·08 W
86	Fort Chipewyan . . . Can.	58·46 N	111·15 W
72	Fort Cobb Res . . . Okla.	35·12 N	98·28 W
72	Fort Collins (kŏl'ĭns) . . . Colo.	40·36 N	105·04 W
165	Fort Crampel (kräm-pĕl') Cen. Afr. Rep.	7·10 N	19·07 E
167	Fort-Dauphin (dō-făN') Malag. Rep.	24·59 S	46·58 E
93	Fort-de-France (dē fräNs) Mart. (Le. & Wind. Is. In.)	14·37 N	61·06 W
78	Fort Deposit (dē-pŏz'ĭt) . . . Ala.	31·58 N	86·35 W
165	Fort de Possel (dē pō-sĕl') Cen. Afr. Rep.	5·03 N	19·11 E
71	Fort Dodge (dŏj) . . . Iowa	42·31 N	94·10 W
81	Fort Edward (wērd) . . . N. Y.	43·15 N	73·30 W
75	Fort Erie (ē'rĭ) Can. (Buffalo In.)	42·55 N	78·56 W
158	Fortescue (R.) (fôr'tĕs-kū) . . Austl.	21·25 S	116·50 E
82	Fort Fairfield (fâr'fēld) . . . Maine	46·46 N	67·53 W
86	Fort Fitzgerald (fĭts-jĕr'ăld). Can.	59·48 N	111·50 W
164	Fort Flatters (flȧ-târ') . . . Alg.	28·06 N	6·34 E
87	Fort Frances (frăn'sĕs) . . . Can.	48·41 N	94·29 W
79	Fort Frederica Natl. Mon. (frĕd'ē-rĭ-kȧ). Ga.	31·12 N	85·25 W
78	Fort Gaines (gānz) . . . Ga.	31·35 N	85·03 W
85	Fort Garry (găr'ē) Can. (Winnipeg In.)	49·50 N	97·09 W
87	Fort George (jôrj) . . . Can.	53·40 N	78·58 W
87	Fort George (R.) . . . Can.	53·50 N	78·34 W
73	Fort Gibson (gĭb'sŭn) . . . Okla.	35·50 N	95·13 W
86	Fort Good Hope (gōōd hōp). Can.	66·19 N	128·52 W
164	Fort Gouraud . . . Mauritania	22·45 N	12·38 W
116	Forth, Firth of (fûrth ŏv fôrth) Scot.	56·04 N	3·03 W
167	Fort Hall (hôl) . . . Ken.	0·47 S	37·13 E
67	Fort Hall Ind. Res . . . Idaho	43·02 N	112·21 W
84	Fort Howard (hou'ărd) Md. (Baltimore In.)	39·12 N	76·27 W
69	Fort Huachuca (wä-chōō'kä). Ariz.	31·30 N	110·25 W
85	Fortier (fôr-tyā') Can. (Winnipeg In.)	49·56 N	97·55 W
166	Fort Jameson (jăm'sŭn) . . . N. Rh.	13·35 S	32·43 E
79	Fort Jefferson Natl. Mon. (jĕf'ēr-sŭn). Fla. (In.)	24·42 N	83·02 W
166	Fort Johnston . . . Nya.	14·16 S	35·14 E
82	Fort Kent (kĕnt) . . . Maine	47·14 N	68·37 W
164	Fort Lallemand (lȧ-lē-măN') . . Alg.	31·17 N	6·13 E
165	Fort-Lamy (lȧ-mē') . . . Chad	12·15 N	15·04 E
65	Fort Langley (lăng'lĭ) Can. (Vancouver In.)	49·10 N	122·35 W
164	Fort Laperrine (Tamanrasset) (fôr lȧ-pĕ-rēn'). Alg.	22·34 N	5·34 E
70	Fort Laramie Natl. Mon. (fôrt lăr'ȧ-mĭ). Wyo.	42·10 N	104·34 W
79	Fort Lauderdale (lô'dēr-dāl) Fla. (In.)	26·07 N	80·09 W
86	Fort Liard . . . Can.	60·16 N	123·34 W
95	Fort Liberté (lē-bĕr-tā') . . . Hai.	19·40 N	71·50 W
78	Fort Louden (R.) (fôrt lou'dĕn) Tenn.	35·52 N	84·10 W
72	Fort Lupton (lŭp'tŭn) . . . Colo.	40·04 N	104·45 W
66	Fort McDermitt Ind. Res. (măk Dēr'mĭt). Ore.	42·04 N	118·07 W
86	Fort Macleod (mȧ-kloud') . . . Can.	49·40 N	113·22 W
164	Fort MacMahon (mȧk mȧ-ôN') Alg.	29·55 N	1·49 E
86	Fort McPherson (mȧk-fŭr's'n) Can.	67·37 N	134·59 W
71	Fort Madison (măd'ĭ-sŭn) . . . Iowa	40·40 N	91·17 W
166	Fort Manning (măn'ĭng) . . . Nya.	13·42 S	33·00 E
79	Fort Matanzas (mä-tän'zäs) . . Fla.	29·39 N	81·17 W
79	Fort Meade (mēd) . . . Fla. (In.)	27·45 N	81·48 W
84	Fort Meade . . Md. (Baltimore In.)	39·06 N	76·44 W
79	Fort Mill (mĭl) . . . S.C.	35·03 N	80·57 W
114	Fort Miribel (mē-rē-bĕl') . . . Alg.	28·50 N	2·51 E
68	Fort Mojave Ind. Res. (mō-hä'vä) Calif.	34·59 N	115·02 W
84	Fort Monroe (mŏn-rō') Va. (Norfolk In.)	37·00 N	76·19 W
72	Fort Morgan (môr'găn) . . . Colo.	40·14 N	103·49 W
79	Fort Myers (mī'ĕrz) . . . Fla. (In.)	26·36 N	81·45 W
114	Fort National (fô nȧ-syō-nȧl') Alg.	36·45 N	4·15 E
86	Fort Nelson (nĕl'sŭn) . . . Can.	58·57 N	122·30 W
86	Fort Nelson (R.) (nĕl'sŭn) . . . Can.	58·44 N	122·20 W
78	Fort Payne (pān) . . . Ala.	34·26 N	85·41 W
67	Fort Peck (pĕk) . . . Mont.	47·58 N	106·30 W
67	Fort Peck Res . . . Mont.	47·52 N	106·59 W
79	Fort Pierce (pērs) . . . Fla. (In.)	27·25 N	80·20 W
164	Fort Polignac (pō-lē-nyäk') . . . Alg.	26·35 N	8·24 E
165	Fort Portal (pôr'tăl) . . . Ug.	00·40 N	30·16 E

ăt; finăl; rāte; senâte; ärm; ȧsk; sofȧ; fâre; ch-choose; dh-as th in other; bē; ēvent; bĕt; recĕnt; cratēr; g-go; gh-guttural g; bĭt; ĭ-short neutral; rīde; K-guttural k as ch in German ich;

Page	Name Pronunciation Region	Lat. °′	Long. °′
86	Fort Providence (prŏv'ĭ-dĕns) Can.	61·27 N	117·59 W
79	Fort Pulaski Natl. Mon. (pu-lăs'kĭ). Ga.	31·59 N	80·56 W
64	Fort Randall (răn'd'l) Alaska	55·12 N	162·38 W
62	Fort Randall Dam U. S.	43·05 N	100·15 W
70	Fort Randall Res. S. D.	43·35 N	99·12 W
86	Fort Resolution (rĕz'ō-lū'shŭn) Can.	61·08 N	113·42 W
73	Fort Riley (rī'lĭ) Kans.	39·05 N	96·46 W
166	Fort Rosebery (rōz'bĕr-ĭ) N. Rh.	11·14 S	28·58 E
166	Fort Rousset (fôr rōō-sĕ') Con. B.	0·23 S	15·42 E
86	Fort St. James (fôrt sānt jāmz) Can.	54·28 N	124·19 W
86	Fort St. John (sānt jŏn) Can.	56·28 N	120·57 W
142	Fort Sandeman (săn'da-măn) W. Pak.	31·28 N	69·29 E
85	Fort Saskatchewan (săs-kăt'chōō-ân) Can. (Edmonton In.)	53·42 N	113·14 W
73	Fort Scott (skŏt) Kans.	37·50 N	94·43 W
86	Fort Selkirk (sĕl-kûrk') Can.	62·43 N	137·40 W
87	Fort Severn (sĕv'ērn) Can.	56·58 N	87·50 W
133	Fort Shevchenko (shĕv-chĕn'kô) Sov. Un.	44·30 N	50·18 E
165	Fort Sibut (fôr sê-bü') Cen. Afr. Rep.	5·52 N	19·01 E
72	Fort Sill (fôrt sĭl) Okla.	34·41 N	98·25 W
86	Fort Simpson (sĭmp'sŭn) Can.	61·52 N	121·48 W
73	Fort Smith (smĭth) Ark.	35·23 N	94·24 W
86	Fort Smith Can.	60·09 N	112·08 W
76	Fort Stockton (stŏk'tŭn) Tex.	30·54 N	102·51 W
72	Fort Sumner (sŭm'nēr) N. Mex.	34·30 N	104·17 W
79	Fort Sumter Natl. Mon. (sŭm'tēr). S. C.	32·43 N	79·54 W
75	Fort Thomas (tŏm'ăs) Ky. (Cincinnati In.)	39·05 N	84·27 W
66	Fortuna (fŏr-tū'nȧ) Calif.	40·36 N	124·10 W
83	Fortune (fôr'tŭn) Can.	47·04 N	55·51 W
95	Fortune (I.) Ba. Is.	22·35 N	74·20 W
83	Fortune B. Can.	47·25 N	55·30 W
72	Fort Union Natl. Mon. (ūn'yŭn) N. Mex.	35·51 N	104·57 W
78	Fort Valley (văl'ĭ) Ga.	32·33 N	83·53 W
66	Fort Vancouver Natl. Mon. (văn-kōō'vēr). Wash.	45·50 N	122·36 W
86	Fort Vermilion (vēr-mĭl'yŭn). Can.	58·23 N	115·50 W
166	Fort Victoria S. Rh.	20·07 S	30·47 E
80	Fortville (fôrt-vĭl) Ind.	40·00 N	85·50 W
80	Fort Wayne (wān) Ind.	41·00 N	85·10 W
85	Fort Whyte (whīt) Can. (Winnipeg In.)	49·49 N	97·13 W
87	Fort William (wĭl'yăm) Can.	48·20 N	89·20 W
116	Fort William (wĭl'yăm) Scot.	56·50 N	3·00 W
160	Fort William, Mt. (wĭ 'ĭ-ăm) Austl.	24·45 S	151·15 E
74	Fort Worth (wûrth) Tex. (Dallas, Fort Worth In.)	32·45 N	97·20 W
64	Fort Yukon (yōō'kŏn) Alaska	66·30 N	145·00 W
68	Fort Yuma Ind. Res. (yōō'mä) Calif.	32·54 N	114·47 W
122	Fos, Golfe de (G.) (gôlf'dĕ-fôs') Fr. (Marseille In.)	43·22 N	4·55 E
	Foshan, see Ch'aoyang		
126	Fossano (fôs-sä'nō) It.	44·34 N	7·42 E
74	Fossil Cr. (fŏs-ĭl) Tex. (Dallas, Fort Worth In.)	32·53 N	97·19 W
126	Fossombrone (fôs-sôm-brō'nā) It.	43·41 N	12·48 E
72	Foss Res. Okla.	35·38 N	99·11 W
70	Fosston (fôs'tŭn) Minn.	47·34 N	95·44 W
74	Fosterburg (fŏs'tēr-bûrg) Ill. (St. Louis In.)	38·58 N	90·04 W
80	Fostoria (fŏs-tō'rĭ-ȧ) Ohio	41·10 N	83·20 W
148	Fouch'eng (fōō'chĕng) China	37·53 N	116·08 E
122	Fougères (fōō-zhâr') Fr.	48·23 N	1·14 W
150	Fouhsin China	42·05 N	121·40 E
116	Foula (I.) (fou'lȧ) Scot.	60·08 N	2·04 W
151	Fouliang China	29·18 N	117·18 E
151	Fouling China	29·40 N	107·30 E
159	Foulwind, C. (foul'wĭnd) N. Z. (In.)	41·45 S	171·37 E
164	Foumban (fōōm-bän') Cam.	5·49 N	10·52 E
148	Founing (fōō'nĭng) China	33·55 N	119·54 E
72	Fountain Cr. (foun'tĭn) Colo.	38·36 N	104·37 W
73	Fourche la Fave (R.) (fōōrsh lä fäv') Ark.	34·46 N	93·45 W
168	Fouriesburg (fōō'rēz-bûrg) S. Afr. (Johannesburg & Pretoria In.)	28·38 S	28·13 E
122	Fourmies (fōōr-mē') Fr.	50·01 N	4·01 E
64	Four Mts., Is. of the (fōr) Alaska	52·58 N	170·40 W
165	Fourth Cataract Sud.	18·52 N	32·07 E
164	Fouta Djalon (Mts.) (fōō'tä jä-lôN) Gui.	11·37 N	12·29 W
148	Fouts'un (fōō'tsōōn) China	36·38 N	117·26 E
148	Foutzuchi (fōō'tzŭ'jē) China	33·48 N	118·13 E
148	Fouyang (fōō'yäng) China	32·53 N	115·48 E
159	Foveaux Str. (fô-vō') N. Z. (In.)	46·30 S	167·43 E
72	Fowler (foul'ēr) Colo.	38·04 N	104·02 W
80	Fowler Ind.	40·35 N	87·20 W
158	Fowler, Pt. Austl.	32·05 S	132·30 E
76	Fowlerton (foul'ēr-tŭn) Tex.	28·26 N	98·48 W
65	Fox (I.) (fŏks) Wash. (Seattle In.)	47·15 N	122·08 W
71	Fox (R.) Ill.	41·35 N	88·43 W
71	Fox (R.) Wis.	44·18 N	88·23 W
83	Foxboro (fŏks'bŭrō) Mass. (Boston In.)	42·04 N	71·15 W
86	Foxe Basin (fŏks) Can.	67·35 N	79·21 W
87	Foxe Chan. Can.	64·30 N	79·23 W
87	Foxe Pen. Can.	64·57 N	77·26 W
64	Fox Is. (fŏks) Alaska	53·04 N	167·30 W
75	Fox Lake (lăk) Ill. (Chicago In.)	42·24 N	88·11 W
75	Fox L. Ill. (Chicago In.)	42·24 N	88·07 W
75	Fox Point Wis. (Milwaukee In.)	43·10 N	87·54 W
116	Folye, Lough (B.) (lŏk foil') Ire.	54·69 N	6·75 W
125	Fraga (frä'gä) Sp.	41·31 N	0·20 E
94	Fragoso, Cayo (I.) (kä'yō-frȧ-gō'sō). Cuba	22·45 N	79·30 W
127	Francavilla (fräŋ-kä-vēl'lä) It.	40·32 N	17·37 E
99	France (frä'n-kä) Braz.	20·28 S	47·20 W
102	France (frȧns) Eur.	46·39 N	0·47 E
86	Frances (L.) (frăn'sĭs) Can.	61·27 N	128·28 W
94	Frances, Cabo (C.) (kä'bô-frän-sĕ's). Cuba	21·55 N	84·05 W
94	Frances, Punta (Pt.) (pōō'n-tä-frän-sĕ's). Cuba	21·45 N	83·10 W
95	Frances Viejo, Cabo (C.) (kȧ'bô-frän'sȧs vyā'hō) Dom. Rep.	19·40 N	69·35 W
166	Franceville (fräNs-vēl') Gabon.	1·37 S	13·37 E
101	Francisco Sales (frän-sē's-kô-sà'lĕs). Braz. (Rio de Janeiro In.)	21·42 S	44·26 W
166	Francistown (frăn'sis-toun) Bech.	21·17 S	27·28 E
75	Frankfort (frăŋk'fŭrt) Ill. (Chicago In.)	41·30 N	87·51 W
80	Frankfort Ind.	40·15 N	86·30 W
73	Frankfort Kans.	39·42 N	96·27 W
80	Frankfort Ky.	38·10 N	84·55 W
80	Frankfort Mich.	44·40 N	86·15 W
81	Frankfort N. Y.	43·05 N	75·05 W
168	Frankfort S. Afr. (Johannesburg & Pretoria In.)	27·17 S	28·30 E
167	Frankfort (frănk'fōrt) S. Afr. (Natal In.)	32·43 S	27·28 E
120	Frankfurt (fräŋk'fōōrt) Ger.	52·20 N	14·31 E
111	Frankfurt (Dist.) Ger. (Berlin In.)	52·42 N	13·37 E
120	Frankfurt am Main Ger.	50·07 N	8·40 E
80	Franklin (frănk'lĭn) Ind.	39·25 N	86·00 W
78	Franklin Ky.	36·42 N	86·34 W
77	Franklin La.	29·47 N	91·31 W
83	Franklin Mass. (Boston In.)	42·05 N	71·24 W
72	Franklin Nebr.	40·06 N	99·01 W
81	Franklin N. H.	43·25 N	71·40 W
84	Franklin N. J. (New York In.)	41·08 N	74·35 W
80	Franklin Ohio	39·30 N	84·20 W
81	Franklin Pa.	41·25 N	79·50 W
78	Franklin Tenn.	35·54 N	86·54 W
167	Franklin S. Afr. (Natal In.)	30·19 S	29·28 E
79	Franklin Va.	36·41 N	76·57 W
86	Franklin, Dist. of Can.	70·46 N	105·22 W
68	Franklin (L.) Nev.	40·23 N	115·10 W
66	Franklin D. Roosevelt L. Wash.	48·12 N	118·43 W
86	Franklin Mts. Can.	65·36 N	125·55 W
75	Franklin Park Ill. (Chicago In.)	41·56 N	87·53 W
77	Franklinton (frăŋk'lĭn-tŭn) La.	30·49 N	90·09 W
161	Frankston Austl. (Melbourne In.)	38·09 S	145·08 E
75	Franksville (frănkz'vĭl) Wis. (Milwaukee In.)	42·46 N	87·55 W
87	Franz (frănz) Can.	48·27 N	84·28 W
	Franz Josef Land (Is.), see Zemlya Frantsa Iosifa		
125	Frascati (fräs-kä'tē) It. (Rome In.)	41·49 N	12·45 E
75	Fraser (frā'zēr) Mich. (Detroit In.)	42·32 N	82·57 W
160	Fraser (Great Sandy) (I.) (frā'zēr) Austl.	25·12 S	153·00 E
86	Fraser (R.) Can.	51·41 N	122·19 W
116	Fraserburgh (frā'zēr-bûrg) Scot.	57·40 N	2·01 W
87	Fraserdale (frā'zēr-dāl) Can.	49·51 N	81·40 W
125	Frattamaggiore (frät-tä-mäg-zhyô'rĕ). It. (Naples In.)	40·41 N	14·16 E
101	Fray Bentos (frī bĕn'tōs) Ur. (Buenos Aires In.)	33·10 S	58·19 W
70	Frazee (frȧ-zē') Minn.	46·42 N	95·43 W
94	Fraziers Hog Cay (I.) Ba. Is.	25·25 N	77·55 W
123	Frechen (frĕ'kĕn) Ger. (Ruhr In.)	50·54 N	6·49 E
118	Fredericia (frĕdh-ĕ-rē'tsē-ȧ) Den.	55·35 N	9·45 E
81	Frederick (frĕd'ēr-ĭk) Md.	39·25 N	77·25 W
72	Frederick Okla.	34·23 N	99·01 W
76	Fredericksburg (frĕd'ēr-ĭkz-bûrg). Tex.	30·16 N	98·52 W
81	Fredericksburg Va.	38·20 N	77·30 W
73	Fredericktown (frĕd'ēr-ĭk-toun). Mo.	37·32 N	90·16 W
82	Fredericton (frĕd'ēr-ĭk-tŭn) Can.	45·58 N	66·40 W
155	Frederik Hendrik (I.) (frĕd'ēr-ĭk hĕn'drĕk). W. Irian	7·45 S	137·30 E
118	Frederikshavn (frĕdh'ĕ-rĕks-houn). Den.	57·27 N	10·31 E
118	Frederikssund (frĕdh'ĕ-rĕks-sōōn) Den.	55·51 N	12·04 E
98	Fredonia (frĕ-dō'nyȧ) Col. (In.)	5·55 N	75·40 W
73	Fredonia (frê-dō'nĭ-ȧ) Kans.	36·31 N	95·50 W
81	Fredonia N. Y.	42·25 N	79·20 W
118	Fredrikstad (frȧdh'rĕks-städ). Nor.	59·14 N	10·58 E
74	Freeburg (frē'bûrg) Ill. (St. Louis In.)	38·26 N	89·59 W
84	Freehold (frē'hōld) N. J. (New York In.)	40·15 N	74·16 W
81	Freeland (frē'lănd) Pa.	41·00 N	75·50 W
65	Freeland Wash. (Seattle In.)	48·01 N	122·32 W
83	Freels, C. (frēlz) Can.	49·18 N	53·10 W
85	Freelton (frēl'tŭn) Can. (Toronto In.)	43·24 N	80·02 W
71	Freeport (frē'pōrt) Ill.	42·19 N	89·30 W
84	Freeport N. Y. (New York In.)	40·39 N	73·35 W
77	Freeport Tex.	28·56 N	95·21 W
164	Freetown (frē'toun) S. L.	8·29 N	13·16 W
124	Fregenal de la Sierra (frā-hā-näl' dā lä syĕr'rä). Sp.	38·09 N	6·40 W
125	Fregene (frĕ-zhĕ'-nĕ) It. (Rome In.)	41·52 N	12·12 E
120	Freiberg (frī'bĕrgh) Ger.	50·54 N	13·18 E
111	Freienried (frī'ĕn-rēd) Ger. (Munich In.)	48·20 N	11·08 E
100	Freirina (frā-ĭ-rē'nä) Chile	28·35 S	71·26 W
111	Freising (frī'zĭng) Ger. (Munich In.)	48·25 N	11·45 E
123	Fréjus (frā-zhüs') Fr.	43·28 N	6·46 E
158	Fremantle (frē'măn-t'l) Austl.	32·03 S	116·05 E
65	Fremont (frê-mŏnt') Calif. (San Francisco In.)	37·33 N	122·00 W
80	Fremont Mich.	43·25 N	85·55 W
70	Fremont Nebr.	41·26 N	96·30 W
80	Fremont Ohio	41·20 N	83·05 W
69	Fremont (R.) Utah	38·20 N	111·30 W
67	Fremont Pk. Wyo.	43·05 N	109·35 W
	French, see Loyaute, Iles.		
78	French Broad (R.) (frĕnch brôd) Tenn.-N. C.	35·59 N	83·01 W
99	French Guiana (gē-ä'nȧ) S. A.	4·20 N	53·00 W
80	French Lick (frĕnch lĭk) Ind.	38·35 N	86·35 W
67	Frenchman Cr. (frĕnch-măn) Mont.	48·51 N	107·20 W
72	Frenchman Cr. Nebr.	40·24 N	101·50 W
68	Frenchman F. Nev.	36·55 N	116·11 W
74	French River Minn. (Duluth In.)	46·54 N	91·54 W
	French, see Loyaute, Iles		
163	French Somaliland Afr.	11·35 N	45·08 E
90	Fresnillo (frås-nēl'yô) Mex.	23·10 N	102·52 W
68	Fresno (frĕz'nō) Calif.	36·43 N	119·47 W
98	Fresno (frĕs'-nô) Col. (In.)	5·10 N	75·01 W
68	Fresno (R.) (frĕz'nō) Calif.	37·00 N	120·24 W
68	Fresno Slough Calif.	36·39 N	120·12 W
120	Freudenstadt (froi'den-shtät) Ger.	48·28 N	8·26 E
160	Freycinet Pen. (frā-sē-nĕ') Austl.	42·13 S	148·56 E
69	Fria (R.) (frê-ä) Ariz.	34·03 N	112·12 W
166	Fria, C. (frĭȧ) S. W. Afr.	18·15 S	12·10 E
100	Frias (frē-äs) Arg.	28·43 S	65·03 W
120	Fribourg (frē-bōōr') Switz.	46·48 N	7·07 E
74	Fridley (frĭd'lĭ) Minn. (Minneapolis, St. Paul In.)	45·05 N	93·16 W
120	Frieburg (frī'bōōrgh) Ger.	47·59 N	7·50 E
111	Friedberg (frēd'bĕrgh) Ger. (Munich In.)	48·22 N	11·00 E
120	Friedland (frēt'länt) Ger.	53·39 N	13·34 E
120	Friedrichshafen (frē-drēks-häf'ĕn) Ger.	47·39 N	9·28 E
73	Friend (frĕnd) Nebr.	40·40 N	97·16 W
77	Friendswood (frĕnds'-wŏŏd) Tex. (In.)	29·31 N	95·11 W
79	Fries (frēz) Va.	36·42 N	80·59 W
111	Friesack (frē'säk) Ger. (Berlin In.)	52·44 N	12·35 E
99	Frio, Cabo (C.) (kä'bō-frê'ō) Braz.	22·58 S	42·08 W
76	Frio R. Tex.	29·00 N	99·15 W
124	Friol (frê-ōl') Sp.	43·02 N	7·48 W
121	Frisches Haff B. (frĭsh'ĕs häf) Pol.	54·22 N	19·38 E
117	Frisian (Is.) (frē'zhăn) Neth.	53·30 N	5·20 E
86	Frobisher (L.) (frŏb'ĭsh-ēr) Can.	56·33 N	107·57 W
87	Frobisher Bay Can.	63·48 N	68·31 W
87	Frobisher B. Can.	62·49 N	66·41 W
110	Frodsham (frŏdz'ăm) Eng.	53·18 N	2·48 W
160	Frome, L. (frōōm) Austl.	30·40 S	140·13 E
73	Frontenac (frŏn'tē-năk) Kans.	37·27 N	94·41 W
91	Frontera (frôn-tā'rä) Mex.	18·34 N	92·38 W
122	Frontignan (frôN-tē-nyäN') Fr.	43·26 N	3·45 E
67	Front Ra. (frŭnt) Wyo.	42·17 N	105·53 W
81	Front Royal (frŭnt) Va.	38·55 N	78·10 W
112	Fro Sea (frô) Nor.	63·49 N	9·12 E
126	Frosinone (frō-zē-nō'nā) It.	41·38 N	13·22 E
81	Frostburg (frôst'bûrg) Md.	39·40 N	78·55 W
74	Fruit (frōōt) Ill. (St. Louis In.)	38·50 N	89·51 W
69	Fruita (frōōt-ȧ) Colo.	39·10 N	108·45 W
74	Fruitdale (frōōt'dāl) Tex. (Dallas, Fort Worth In.)	32·43 N	96·46 W
134	Frunze (frōōn'zĕ) Sov. Un.	42·49 N	74·42 E
136	Fryanovo (f'ryä'nô-vô) Sov. Un. (Moscow In.)	56·08 N	38·28 E
136	Fryazino (f'ryä'zĭ-nô) Sov. Un. (Moscow In.)	55·58 N	38·05 E
121	Frydek (frē'dĕk) Czech.	49·43 N	18·22 E
120	Frydlant (frēd'länt) Czech.	50·56 N	15·05 E
147	Fuchien (Fukien) (Prov.) China	25·39 N	117·21 E
147	Fuchin (fōō'chĭn') China	47·13 N	132·11 E
151	Fuchou (Foochow) (fōō'chó) China	26·02 N	119·18 E
148	Fuchow (fōō'chō') China	39·46 N	121·44 E
153	Fuchu (fōō'chōō). Jap. (Tōkyō In.)	35·41 N	139·29 E
151	Fuch'un (R.) China	29·50 N	120·00 E
92	Fuego (Vol.) (fwā'gō) Guat.	14·29 N	90·52 W
125	Fuencarral (fuān-kär-räl') Sp. (Madrid In.)	40·29 N	3·42 W
124	Fuensalida (fwān-sä-lē'dä) Sp.	40·04 N	4·15 W
76	Fuente (fwĕ'n-tĕ) Mex.	28·39 N	100·34 W
124	Fuente de Cantos (fwĕn'tā dā kän'tōs). Sp.	38·15 N	6·18 W
125	Fuente el Saz (fwĕn'tā ĕl säth') Sp. (Madrid In.)	40·39 N	3·30 W
124	Fuente-Ovejuna (fwĕn'tā-ōvā-hōō'nä). Sp.	38·15 N	5·30 W
124	Fuentesaúco (fwĕn-tā-sä-ōō'kō) Sp.	41·18 N	5·25 W
88	Fuerte, Rio del (R.) (rē'ō-dĕl-fōō-ĕ'r-tĕ). Mex.	26·15 N	108·50 W
99	Fuerte Olimpo (fwĕr'tā ō-lēm-pō) Par.	21·10 S	57·49 W
164	Fuerteventura I. (fwĕr'tā-vĕn-tōō'rä). Can. Is.	28·24 N	13·21 W
146	Fuhai China	47·01 N	87·07 E
148	Fuhsien (fōō'siān) China	39·36 N	121·59 E
153	Fuji (R.) Jap.	35·20 N	138·23 E
153	Fuji-san (Mtn.) (fōō'jē sän) Jap.	35·23 N	138·44 E
153	Fujisawa (fōō'jē-sä'wa) Jap. (Tōkyō In.)	35·20 N	139·29 E
	Fukien (Prov.), see Fuchien		
153	Fukuchiyama (fōō'kōō-chē-yä'mä). Jap.	35·18 N	135·07 E
153	Fukue (I.) (fōō-kōō'ä) Jap.	32·40 N	129·02 E
153	Fukui (fōō'kōō-ē) Jap.	36·05 N	136·14 E
153	Fukuoka (fōō'kōō-ō'kä) Jap.	33·35 N	130·23 E
152	Fukushima (fōō'kōō-shē'mä) Jap.	37·45 N	140·29 E
153	Fukuyama (fōō'kōō-yä'mä) Jap.	34·31 N	133·21 E
120	Fulda R. (fōōl'dä) Ger.	51·05 N	9·40 E

ng-sing; ŋ-baŋk: N-nasalized n; nŏd; cŏmmit; ōld; ôbey; ôrder; fōōd; fŏŏt; ou-out; s-soft; sh-dish; th-thin; pūre; ûnite; ûrn; stŭd; circŭs; ü-as "y" in study; '-indeterminate vowel.

Page	Name Pronunciation Region	Lat. °′	Long. °′
74	Fullerton (fōōl'ēr-tŭn) Calif. (Los Angeles In.)	33·53 N	117·56 W
77	Fullerton...La.	31·00 N	93·00 W
84	Fullerton...Md. (Baltimore In.)	39·22 N	76·31 W
70	Fullerton...Nebr.	41·21 N	97·59 W
78	Fulton (fŭl'tŭn)...Ky.	36·30 N	88·53 W
73	Fulton...Mo.	38·51 N	91·56 W
81	Fulton...N. Y.	43·20 N	76·25 W
85	Fulton Cr...Can. (Edmonton In.)	53·30 N	113·24 W
84	Fultondale (fŭl'tŭn-dāl) Ala. (Birmingham In.)	33·37 N	86·48 W
153	Funabashi (fōō'nȧ-bä'shē) Jap. (Tōkyō In.)	35·43 N	139·59 E
153	Funaya (fōō-nä'yä) Jap. (Osaka In.)	34·45 N	135·52 E
164	Funchal (fōōn-shäl')...Mad. Is.	32·41 N	16·15 W
98	Fundacion (fōōn-dä-syō'n)...Col.	10·43 N	74·13 W
124	Fundão (fōōn-douN')...Port.	40·08 N	7·32 W
82	Fundy, B. of (fŭn'dĭ)...Can.	44·50 N	66·05 W
82	Fundy Natl. Park...Can.	45·38 N	65·25 W
148	Funing (fōō'nĭng')...China	39·55 N	119·16 E
151	Funing Wan (B.) (fōō'nĭng').China	26·48 N	120·35 E
148	Funiu Shan (Mts.) (fōō'nēo shän) China	34·25 N	113·28 E
91	Furbero (fōōr-bĕ'rô)...Mex.	20·21 N	97·32 W
128	Furmanov (fûr-mä'nôf)..Sov. Un.	57·14 N	41·11 E
101	Furnas, Represa de (Res.) Braz. (Rio de Janeiro In.)	21·00 S	46·00 W
159	Furneaux Group (Is.) (fûr'nō) Austl.	40·15 S	146·27 E
120	Fürstenfeld (für'stĕn-fĕlt)...Aus.	47·02 N	16·03 E
111	Fürstenfeldbruck (fur'stĕn-fĕld' brōōk). Ger. (Munich In.)	48·11 N	11·16 E
120	Fürstenwalde (für'stĕn-väl-dĕ) Ger.	52·21 N	14·04 E
120	Fürth (fürt)...Ger.	49·28 N	11·03 E
153	Furuichi (fōō'rōō-ē'chē) Jap. (Ōsaka In.)	34·33 N	135·37 E
153	Fusa (fōō'sä)...Jap. (Tōkyō In.)	35·52 N	140·08 E
98	Fusagasugá (fōō-sä-gä-sōō-gä') Col. (In.)	4·22 N	74·22 W
153	Fuse (fōō'sâ)...Jap. (Ōsaka In.)	34·39 N	135·35 E
146	Fushih...China	36·46 N	109·15 E
153	Fushimi (fōō'shē-mē) Jap. (Osaka In.)	34·57 N	135·47 E
150	Fushun (fōō'shōōn')...China	41·50 N	124·00 E
150	Fusung...China	42·12 N	127·12 E
153	Futtsu (fōōt'tsōō') Jap. (Tōkyō In.)	35·19 N	139·49 E
153	Futtsu Misaki (C.) (fōōt'tsōō' mē-sä'kē).Jap. (Tōkyō In.)	35·19 N	139·46 E
168	Fuwah (fōō'wȧ). U. A. R. (Nile In.)	31·13 N	30·35 E
151	Fuyang...China	30·10 N	119·58 E
150	Fuyü (fōō'yōō')...China	45·20 N	125·00 E
118	Fyn (fü'n)...Den.	55·24 N	10·33 E
116	Fyne (L.) (fīn)...Scot.	56·14 N	5·10 W
118	Fyresdal Vand (L.) (fü'rĕs-däl vän).Nor.	59·04 N	7·55 E
166	Gaberones (gä-bē-rō'nĕz)...Bech.	24·28 S	25·59 E
164	Gabès (gä'bĕs)...Tun.	33·51 N	10·04 E
164	Gabès, Golfe de (G.)...Tun.	32·22 N	10·59 E
121	Gabin (gŏN'bēn)...Pol.	52·23 N	19·47 E
163	Gabon (gȧ-bôN')...Afr.	0·30 S	10·45 E
77	Gabriel R. (gā'brĭ-ĕl)...Tex.	30·38 N	97·15 W
127	Gabrovo (gäb'rô-vō)...Bul.	42·52 N	25·19 E
98	Gachetá (gä-chā'tä)...Col (In.)	4·50 N	73·36 W
127	Gacko (gäts'kô)...Yugo.	43·10 N	18·34 E
139	Gader...Jordan (Palestine In.)	32·39 N	35·41 E
78	Gadsden (gădz'dĕn)...Ala.	34·00 N	86·00 W
129	Gadyach (gäd-yäch')...Sov. Un.	50·22 N	33·59 E
127	Gaesti (gä-yĕsh'tê)...Rom.	44·43 N	25·21 E
126	Gaeta (gä-ā'tä)...It.	41·18 N	13·34 E
79	Gaffney (găf'nĭ)...S. C.	35·04 N	81·47 W
164	Gafsa (gäf'sä)...Tun.	34·16 N	8·37 E
82	Gagetown (gāj'toun)...Can.	45·47 N	66·09 W
155	Gagrary (I.) (gä-grä-rē) Phil. (Manila In.)	13·23 N	123·58 E
126	Gaidhouronísi (I.)...Grc. (Inset)	34·53 N	25·45 E
122	Gaillac-sur-Tarn (gä-yäk'sür-tärn').Fr.	43·54 N	1·52 E
88	Gaillard Cut (gä-êl-yä'rd) C. Z. (Panama Canal In.)	9·03 N	79·42 W
79	Gainesville (gānz'vĭl)...Fla.	29·38 N	82·19 W
78	Gainesville...Ga.	34·16 N	83·48 W
73	Gainesville...Tex.	33·38 N	97·08 W
110	Gainsborough (gānz'bŭr-ô)...Eng.	53·23 N	0·46 W
160	Gairdner, L. (gârd'nēr)...Austl.	32·20 S	136·30 E
142	Gajan...W. Pak.	28·45 N	67·30 E
139	Galala, Gebel el (Mts.) U. A. R. (Palestine In.)	28·51 N	32·14 E
125	Galapagar (gä-lä-pä-gär') Sp. (Madrid In.)	40·36 N	4·00 W
	Galápagos Is., see Colon, Archip. de		
116	Galashiels (găl-ȧ-shēlz)...Scot.	55·40 N	2·57 W
129	Galati (gä-lätz'ĭ)...Rom.	45·25 N	28·05 E
127	Galatina (gä-lä-tē'nä)...It.	40·10 N	18·12 E
127	Galaxidhion...Grc.	38·26 N	22·22 E
118	Galdhöpiggen (Mtn.) (gäld-hû-pĭggĕn).Nor.	61·39 N	8·12 E
76	Galeana (gä-lå-ä'nä)...Mex.	24·50 N	100·04 W
71	Galena (gȧ-lē'nȧ)...Ill.	42·26 N	90·27 W
75	Galena...Ind. (Louisville In.)	38·21 N	85·55 W
73	Galena...Kans.	37·06 N	94·39 W
77	Galena Pk...Tex. (In.)	29·44 N	95·14 W
88	Galera, Cerro (Mtn.) (sĕ'r-rô-gä-lĕ'rä) C. Z. (Panama Canal In.)	8·55 N	79·38 W
125	Galera (R.) (gä-lĕ'-rä) It. (Rome In.)	41·58 N	12·21 E
98	Galeras (Vol.) (gä-lĕ'räs)...Col.	0·57 N	77·27 W
65	Gales (R.) (gälz) Ore. (Portland In.)	45·33 N	123·11 W
73	Galesburg (gālz'bûrg)...Ill.	40·56 N	90·21 W
71	Galesville (gālz'vĭl)...Wis.	44·04 N	91·22 W
81	Galeton (gāl'tŭn)...Pa.	41·45 N	77·40 W
127	Galibolu (Gallipoli) (gĕ-lĭb'ô-lōō) (gȧ-lĭp'ô-lē).Tur.	40·25 N	26·40 E
132	Galich (gäl'ĭch)...Sov. Un.	58·20 N	42·38 E
121	Galicia (Reg.) (gȧ-lĭsh'ĭ-ȧ) Pol.-Sov. Un.	49·48 N	21·05 E
124	Galicia (Reg.) (gä-lē'thyä)...Sp.	43·35 N	8·03 W
159	Galilee (L.) (găl'ĭ-lē)...Austl.	22·23 S	145·09 E
139	Galilee, Sea of U. A. R. (Palestine In.)	32·53 N	35·45 E
94	Galina Pt. (gä-lē'nä)...Jam.	18·25 N	76·50 W
80	Galion (găl'ĭ-ŭn)...Ohio	40·45 N	82·50 W
69	Galisteo (gä-lĭs-tā'ō)...N. Mex.	35·20 N	106·00 W
113	Galite, I. La (gä-lēt)...Alg.	37·36 N	8·03 E
165	Galla (Prov.) (gäl'lä)...Eth.	7·22 N	35·28 E
165	Gallabat (găl'ȧ-băt)...Sud.	12·55 N	36·12 E
126	Gallarate (gäl-lä-rä'tä)...It.	45·37 N	8·48 E
123	Gallardon (gä-lär-dôN') Fr. (Paris In.)	48·31 N	1·40 E
73	Gallatin (găl'ȧ-tĭn)...Mo.	39·55 N	93·58 W
78	Gallatin...Tenn.	36·23 N	86·28 W
67	Gallatin R...Mont.	45·12 N	111·10 W
143	Galle (gäl)...Ceylon	6·13 N	80·10 E
125	Gállego (R.) (gäl-yā'gō)...Sp.	42·27 N	0·37 W
98	Gallinas, Pta. de (Pt.) (gä-lyē'näs) Col.	12·10 N	72·10 W
127	Gallipoli (gäl-lē'pô-lē)...It.	40·03 N	17·58 E
	Gallipoli, see Galibolu		
80	Gallipolis (găl-ĭ-pô-lēs)...Ohio	38·50 N	82·10 W
112	Gällivare (yĕl-ĭ-vär'ĕ)...Swe.	68·06 N	20·29 E
124	Gallo (R.) (gäl'yō)...Sp.	40·43 N	1·42 W
69	Gallup (găl'ŭp)...N. Mex.	35·30 N	108·45 W
165	Galnale Doria R...Eth.	5·35 N	40·26 E
116	Galty Mts...Ire.	52·19 N	8·20 W
73	Galva (găl'vȧ)...Ill.	41·11 N	90·02 W
77	Galveston (găl'vĕs-tŭn).Tex. (In.)	29·18 N	94·48 W
77	Galveston B...Tex.	29·39 N	94·45 W
77	Galveston I...Tex. (In.)	29·12 N	94·53 W
116	Galway...Ire.	53·16 N	9·05 W
116	Galway B. (gôl'wā)...Ire.	53·10 N	9·47 W
164	Gambaga (gäm-bä'gä)...Ghana	10·37 N	0·20 W
165	Gambēlā (gäm-bā'lȧ)...Eth.	8·15 N	34·33 E
163	Gambia (găm'bē-ȧ)...Afr.	13·38 N	19·38 W
164	Gambia R...Gam.-Senegal	12·58 N	12·58 W
166	Gamboma (gäm-bō'mä)...Con. B.	2·30 S	16·00 E
84	Gambrills (găm-brĭls) Md. (Baltimore In.)	39·04 N	76·38 W
118	Gamleby (gäm'lĕ-bü)...Swe.	57·54 N	16·20 E
155	Gamu (gä-mōō').Phil. (Manila In.)	17·05 N	121·50 E
142	Gandak (R.)...India	26·37 N	84·22 E
83	Gander (găn'dēr)...Can.	48·59 N	54·32 W
83	Gander (R.)...Can.	48·45 N	55·13 W
83	Gander L...Can.	48·57 N	55·10 W
125	Gandia (gän-dē'ä)...Sp.	38·56 N	0·10 W
142	Ganges, Mouths of (găn'jēz).India	21·18 N	88·40 E
142	Ganges (R.) (găn'jēz)...India	24·32 N	87·58 E
126	Gangi (gän'jē)...It.	37·48 N	14·15 E
146	Gangtok...Sikkim	27·15 N	88·30 E
67	Gannett Pk. (găn'ĕt)...Wyo.	43·10 N	109·38 W
75	Gano (g'nô).Ohio (Cincinnati In.)	39·18 N	84·24 W
111	Gänserndorf...Aus. (Vienna In.)	48·21 N	16·43 E
164	Gao (gä'ō)...Mali	16·17 N	0·00
164	Gaoua (gä-ōō-ä')...Upper Volta	10·21 N	3·11 W
123	Gap (gȧp)...Fr.	44·34 N	6·08 E
155	Gapan (gä-pän).Phil. (Manila In.)	15·18 N	120·56 E
93	Garachiné (gä-rä-chē'nä)...Pan.	8·02 N	78·22 W
93	Garachiné, Punta (Pt.) (pōō'n-tä-gä-rä-chē'nȧ).Pan.	8·08 N	78·35 W
99	Garanhuns (gä-rän-yōōNsh').Braz.	8·49 S	36·28 W
73	Garber (gȧr'bēr)...Okla.	36·28 N	97·35 W
111	Garching (gär'kĕng) Ger. (Munich In.)	48·15 N	11·39 E
76	Garcia (gär-sē'ä)...Mex.	25·90 N	100·37 W
90	Garcia de la Cadena (dĕ-lä-kä-dĕ-nä).Mex.	21·14 N	103·26 W
126	Garda, Lago di (L.) (lä'gō-dē-gär'dä).It.	45·43 N	10·26 E
122	Gardanne (gȧr-dän') Fr. (Marseille In.)	43·28 N	5·29 E
120	Gardelegen (gär-dĕ-lā'ghĕn).Ger.	52·32 N	11·22 E
80	Garden (I.) (gär'd'n)...Mich.	45·50 N	85·50 W
74	Gardena (gär-dē'nȧ) Calif. (Los Angeles In.)	33·53 N	118·19 W
75	Garden City..Mich. (Detroit In.)	42·20 N	83·21 W
72	Garden City...Kan.	37·58 N	100·52 W
74	Garden Grove (gär'd'n grōv) Calif. (Los Angeles In.)	33·47 N	117·56 W
84	Garden Island B. La. (New Orleans In.)	29·03 N	89·07 W
74	Garden River Can. (Sault Ste. Marie In.)	46·33 N	84·10 W
82	Gardiner (gärd'nēr)...Maine	44·12 N	69·46 W
67	Gardiner...Mont.	45·03 N	110·43 W
65	Gardiner...Wash. (Seattle In.)	48·03 N	122·55 W
142	Gardiz...Afg.	33·43 N	69·09 E
81	Gardner...Mass.	42·35 N	72·00 W
165	Gardulā...Eth.	5·43 N	37·40 E
142	Gar Dzong...China	32·28 N	79·50 E
64	Gareloi (I.) (gär-lōō-ä')...Alaska	51·40 N	178·48 W
84	Garfield (gär'fēld) N. J. (New York In.)	40·53 N	74·06 W
74	Garfield Utah (Salt Lake City In.)	40·45 N	112·10 W
75	Garfield Heights Ohio (Cleveland In.)	41·25 N	81·36 W
127	Gargaliánoi (gär-gä-lyä'nē)...Grc.	37·07 N	21·50 E
119	Gargždai (gärgzh'dī)...Sov. Un.	55·43 N	20·09 E
100	Garin (gä-rē'n)...Arg. (In.)	34·10 S	58·44 W
74	Garland (gär'lănd) Tex. (Dallas, Fort Worth In.)	32·55 N	96·39 W
67	Garland...Utah	41·45 N	112·10 W
134	Garm...Sov. Un.	39·12 N	70·28 E
120	Garmisch-Partenkirchen (gär' mēsh pär'tĕn-kēr'kĕn).Ger.	47·38 N	11·10 E
73	Garnett (gär'nĕt)...Kans.	38·16 N	95·15 W
122	Garonne Rivière (R.) (gȧ-rôn) Fr.	44·43 N	0·25 W
165	Garoua (gär'wä)...Cam.	9·16 N	13·24 E
80	Garrett (găr'ĕt)...Ind.	41·20 N	85·10 W
84	Garrison (găr'ĭ-sŭn) N. Y. (New York In.)	41·23 N	73·57 W
70	Garrison...N. D.	47·38 N	101·24 W
70	Garrison Dam Res...N. D.	47·49 N	101·58 W
124	Garrovillas (gä-rô-vēl'yäs)...Sp.	39·42 N	6·30 W
86	Garry (L.) (găr'ĭ)...Can.	66·16 N	99·23 W
111	Garstedt (gär'shtĕt) Ger. (Hamburg In.)	53·40 N	9·58 E
142	Gartok (gär-tŏk')...China	31·11 N	80·35 E
121	Garwolin (gär-vō'lēn)...Pol.	51·54 N	21·40 E
75	Gary (gā'rĭ)...Ind. (Chicago In.)	41·35 N	87·21 W
98	Garzón (gär-thōn')...Col.	2·13 N	75·44 W
155	Gasan (gä-sän').Phil. (Manila In.)	13·19 N	121·52 E
133	Gasan-Kuli...Sov. Un.	37·25 N	53·55 E
80	Gas City (găs)...Ind.	40·30 N	85·40 W
122	Gascogne (Reg.) (gäs-kôn'yĕ).Fr.	43·45 N	1·49 W
73	Gasconade (R.) (găs-kô-nād').Mo.	37·46 N	92·15 W
158	Gascoyne (R.) (găs-koin')..Austl.	25·15 S	117·00 E
74	Gashland (găsh'-lănd) Mo. (Kansas City In.)	39·15 N	94·35 W
123	Gasny (gäs-nē')...Fr. (Paris In.)	49·05 N	1·36 E
82	Gaspé, C...Can.	48·44 N	64·00 W
82	Gaspe (I.)...Can.	48·52 N	65·45 W
82	Gaspé B. (gas'pā) (gäs-pā')..Can.	48·40 N	64·07 W
82	Gaspé Passage...Can.	49·21 N	64·16 W
82	Gaspé Pen...Can.	48·51 N	64·32 W
95	Gasper Hernandez (gäs-pär' ĕr-nän'dāth)...Dom. Rep.	19·40 N	70·15 W
80	Gassaway (găs'ȧ-wā)...W. Va.	38·40 N	80·45 W
65	Gaston (găs'tŭn) Ore. (Portland In.)	45·26 N	123·08 W
79	Gastonia (găs-tô-nĭ-ȧ)...N. C.	35·15 N	81·14 W
100	Gastre (gäs-trĕ)...Arg.	42·12 S	68·50 W
139	Gata, C...Cyprus (Palestine In.)	34·31 N	33·08 E
124	Gata, Cabo de (C.) (kȧ'bô-dĕ-gä'tä).Sp.	36·42 N	2·00 W
124	Gata, Sierra de (Mts.) (syĕr'rȧ dā gä'tä).Sp.	40·12 N	6·39 W
136	Gatchina (gä-chē'nȧ) Sov. Un. (Leningrad In.)	59·33 N	30·08 E
116	Gateshead (gāts'hĕd)...Eng.	54·56 N	1·38 W
77	Gatesville (gāts'vĭl)...Mex.	31·26 N	97·43 W
85	Gatineau (gȧ'tē-nō) Can. (Ottawa In.)	45·29 N	75·38 W
81	Gatineau (R.)...Can.	45·45 N	75·50 W
166	Gatooma (gȧ-tōō'mȧ)...S. Rh.	18·14 S	29·46 E
111	Gattendorf...Aus. (Vienna In.)	48·01 N	17·00 E
88	Gatun (gä-tōōn') C. Z. (Panama Canal In.)	9·16 N	79·25 W
88	Gatun, L. Pan.-C. Z. (Panama Canal In.)	9·13 N	79·24 W
88	Gatun (R.) Pan. (Panama Canal In.)	9·21 N	79·10 W
88	Gatun Locks C. Z. (Panama Canal In.)	9·16 N	79·27 W
142	Gauhati...India	26·09 N	91·51 E
119	Gauja (R.) (gä'ōō-yȧ)...Sov. Un.	57·10 N	24·30 E
155	Gauttier-Gebergte (Mts.) (gō-tyā') W. Irian	2·30 S	138·45 E
126	Gávdhos (I.) (gäv'dôs)..Grc. (In.)	34·48 N	24·08 E
70	Gavins Point Dam (gă'-vĭns) Nebr.	42·47 N	97·47 W
118	Gävle (yĕv'lĕ)...Swe.	60·40 N	17·07 E
118	Gavle-bukten (B.)...Swe.	60·45 N	17·30 E
128	Gavrilov Posad (gȧ'vrē-lôf'ka po-sȧt).Sov. Un.	56·34 N	40·09 E
128	Gavrilov-Yam (gȧ'vrē-lôf yäm') Sov. Un.	57·17 N	39·49 E
160	Gawler (gô'lēr)...Austl.	34·35 S	138·47 E
160	Gawler Ra...Austl.	32·35 S	136·30 E
142	Gaya (gŭ'yä) (gī'ȧ)...India	24·53 N	85·04 E
164	Gaya (gä'yä)...Nig.	11·58 N	9·05 E
80	Gaylord (gā'lôrd)...Mich.	45·00 N	84·35 W
160	Gayndah (gān'dȧh)...Austl.	25·43 S	151·33 E
129	Gaysin...Sov. Un.	48·46 N	29·22 E
	Gaza, see Ghazzah		
133	Gaziantep (gä-zē-än'tĕp)...Tur.	37·10 N	37·30 E
121	Gdańsk (Danzig) (g'dänsk) (dän'tsĭg).Pol.	54·20 N	18·40 E
128	Gdov (g'dôf')...Sov. Un.	58·44 N	27·51 E
121	Gdynia (g'dĕn'yȧ)...Pol.	54·29 N	18·30 E
72	Geary (gē'rĭ)...Okla.	35·36 N	98·19 W
168	Gebel el Galala el Bahariya (Plat.) U. A. R. (Nile In.)	29·23 N	31·50 E
67	Gebo (gĕb'ō)...Wyo.	43·49 N	108·13 W
77	Ged (gĕd)...La.	30·07 N	93·36 W
165	Gedaref...Sud.	14·03 N	35·11 E
115	Gediz (R.)...Tur.	38·44 N	28·45 E
65	Gedney (I.) (gĕd-nē) Wash. (Seattle In.)	48·01 N	122·18 W
120	Gedser...Den.	54·35 N	12·08 E
111	Geel...Bel. (Brussels In.)	51·09 N	5·01 E
161	Geelong (jē-lông') Austl. (Melbourne In.)	38·06 S	144·13 E
155	Geelvink-baai (B.) (gäl'vĭnk) W. Irian	2·20 S	135·30 E
164	Geidam...Nig.	12·49 N	11·49 E
158	Geikie Ra. (gē'kē)...Austl.	17·35 S	125·32 E
120	Geislingen (gis'lĭng-ĕn)...Ger.	48·37 N	9·52 E
75	Geist Res. (gēst) Ind. (Indianapolis In.)	39·57 N	85·59 W
111	Geldermalsen Neth. (Amsterdam In.)	51·53 N	5·18 E
123	Geldern (gĕl'dĕrn) Ger. (Ruhr In.)	51·31 N	6·20 E
127	Gelibolu, Yarimada (Pen.) (gĕ-lĭb'ô-lōō).Tur.	40·23 N	25·10 E
129	Gel'myazov...Sov. Un.	49·49 N	31·54 E
123	Gelsenkirchen (gĕl-zĕn-kĭrk-ĕn) Ger. (Ruhr In.)	51·31 N	7·05 E
139	Gemas (jĕm'ás) Mala. (Singapore In.)	2·35 N	102·37 E
165	Gemena...Con. L.	4·00 N	19·53 E
133	Gemlik (gĕm'lĭk)...Tur.	40·30 N	29·10 E

ăt; finȧl; rāte; senȧte; ärm; ȧsk; sofȧ; fâre; ch-choose; dh-as th in other; bē; ēvent; bĕt; recĕnt; cratẽr; g-go; gh-guttural g; bĭt; ĭ-short neutral; rīde; K-guttural k as ch in German ich;

Page	Name Pronunciation Region	Lat. °′	Long. °′
101	General Alvear (gĕ-nĕ-ràl'àl-vĕ-à'r). Arg. (Buenos Aires In.)	36·04 s	60·02 w
101	General Arenales (ä-rĕ-nä'lĕs) Arg. (Buenos Aires In.)	34·19 s	61·16 w
101	General Belgrano (bĕl-grà'nô) Arg. (Buenos Aires In.)	35·45 s	58·32 w
76	General Cepeda (sĕ-pĕ'dä) Mex.	25·24 N	101·29 w
101	General Conesa (kô-nĕ'sä) Arg. (Buenos Aires In.)	36·30 s	57·19 w
101	General Guido (gē'dô) Arg. (Buenos Aires In.)	36·41 s	57·48 w
101	General Lavalle (là-và'l-yĕ) Arg. (Buenos Aires In.)	36·25 s	56·55 w
100	General Madariaga (män-dà-rêà'gä). Arg.	36·59 s	57·14 w
101	General Paz (pà'z) Arg. (Buenos Aires In.)	35·30 s	58·20 w
90	General Pedro Antonio Santios (pĕ'drô-än-tô'nyô-sän-työs). Mex.	21·37 N	98·58 w
100	General Pico (pē'kô) Arg.	36·46 s	63·44 w
100	General Roca (rô-kä) Arg.	39·01 s	67·31 w
100	General San Martín (sän-màr-tē'n) Arg. (In.)	34·19 s	58·32 w
101	General Viamonte (vēä'môn-tĕ) Arg. (Buenos Aires In.)	35·01 s	60·59 w
76	General Zuazua (zwä'zwä). Mex.	25·54 N	100·07 w
71	Genesco (jĕ-nĕs'cō) Ill.	41·28 N	90·11 w
81	Genesee (R.) (jĕn-ê-sē') N. Y.	42·25 N	78·10 w
78	Geneva (jê-nē'và) Ala.	31·03 N	85·50 w
75	Geneva Ill. (Chicago In.)	41·53 N	88·18 w
73	Geneva Nebr.	40·32 N	97·37 w
81	Geneva N. Y.	42·50 N	77·00 w
80	Geneva Ohio	41·45 N	80·55 w
	Geneva, see Génève		
120	Geneva, L. Switz.	46·28 N	6·30 E
120	Génève (Geneva) (zhĕ-nĕv'). Switz.	46·14 N	6·04 E
129	Genichesk (gå'nê-chyĕsk') Sov. Un.	46·11 N	34·47 E
124	Genil (R.) (hå-nēl') Sp.	37·12 N	4·30 w
73	Genoa (jen'ô-à) Nebr.	41·26 N	97·43 w
77	Genoa Tex. (In.)	29·37 N	95·11 w
	Genoa, see Genova		
75	Genoa City. Wis. (Milwaukee In.)	42·31 N	88·19 w
126	Genova (Genoa) (jĕn'ō-vä) It.	44·23 N	9·52 E
126	Genova, Golfo di (G.) (gôl-fô-dē-jĕn'ō-vä). It.	44·10 N	8·45 E
98	Genovesa (I.) (ĕ's-lä-gĕ-nō-vĕ-sä) Ec.	0·08 N	90·15 w
117	Gent Bel.	51·05 N	3·40 E
120	Genthin (gĕn-tēn') Ger.	52·24 N	12·10 E
125	Genzano di Roma (gzhĕnt-zä'-nô-dē-rô'-mä) It. (Rome In.)	41·43 N	12·49 E
158	Geographe B. (jē-ô-grăf') Austl.	33·00 s	114·00 E
158	Geographic Chan. (jēō'grà-fĭk) Austl.	24·15 s	112·50 E
133	Geokchay (gĕ-ôk'chī) Sov. Un.	40·40 N	47·40 E
79	George (L.) (jôr-ĭj) Fla.	29·10 N	81·50 w
81	George (L.) (jôrj) N. Y.	43·40 N	73·30 w
83	George B. (jôr-ĭj) Can.	45·46 N	61·45 w
74	George L. (jôrg) Can.-U. S. (Sault Ste. Marie In.)	46·26 N	84·09 w
75	George, L. Ind. (Chicago In.)	41·31 N	87·17 w
161	Georges (R.). Austl. (Sydney In.)	33·57 s	151·00 E
95	George Town Ba. Is.	23·30 N	75·50 w
99	Georgetown (jôrj'toun) Br. Gu.	7·45 N	58·04 w
83	Georgetown (jôr-ĭj-toun) Can.	46·09 N	62·32 w
85	Georgetown (jôrg-toun) Can. (Toronto In.)	43·39 N	79·56 w
84	Georgetown. Conn. (New York In.)	41·15 N	73·25 w
81	Georgetown Del.	38·40 N	75·20 w
94	Georgetown Cayman Is.	19·20 N	81·20 w
80	Georgetown Ill.	40·00 N	87·40 w
80	Georgetown Ky.	38·10 N	84·35 w
81	Georgetown Md.	39·25 N	75·55 w
83	Georgetown (jôrg-toun) Mass. (Boston In.)	42·43 N	71·00 w
79	Georgetown (jôr-ĭj-toun) S. C.	33·22 N	79·17 w
77	Georgetown (jôrg-toun) Tex.	30·37 N	97·40 w
81	George Washington Birthplace Natl. Mon. (jôrj wŏsh'ĭng-tŭn) Va.	38·10 N	77·00 w
73	George Washington Carver Natl. Mon. (jôrg wăsh-ĭng-tŭn kär'-vēr). Mo.	36·58 N	94·21 w
63	Georgia (State) (jôr'ji-ă) U. S.	32·40 N	83·50 w
65	Georgia, Str. of Wash. (Vancouver In.)	48·56 N	123·06 w
130	Georgian (S. S. R.) Sov. Un.	42·17 N	43·00 E
78	Georgiana (jôr-jē-ăn'à) Ala.	31·39 N	86·44 w
87	Georgian Is. Natl. Park (jôr'ji-ăn). Can.	45·15 N	81·10 w
158	Georgina (R.) (jôr-jē'nà) Austl.	22·00 s	138·15 E
133	Georgiyevsk (gyôr-gyĕfsk') Sov. Un.	44·05 N	43·30 E
120	Gera (gā'rä) Ger.	50·52 N	12·06 E
100	Geral, Serra (Mts.) (sĕr'rà zhā-räl'). Braz.	28·30 s	51·00 w
99	Geral de Goiás, Serra (Mts.) (zhā-räl'-dĕ-gô-yà's). Braz.	14·22 s	45·40 w
158	Geraldton (jĕr'ăld-tŭn) Austl.	28·40 s	114·35 E
87	Geraldton Can.	49·43 N	87·00 w
124	Gérgal (gĕr'gäl) Sp.	37·08 N	2·29 w
70	Gering (gē'rĭng) Nebr.	41·49 N	103·41 w
121	Gerlachovka Pk. Czech.	49·12 N	20·05 E
80	Germantown (jûr'màn-toun). Ohio	39·35 N	84·25 w
102	Germany (jûr'mà-nĭ) Eur.	51·44 N	8·46 E
167	Germiston (jûr'mĭs-tŭn) S. Afr. (Johannesburg & Pretoria In.)	26·19 s	28·11 E
155	Gerona (hā-rō'nä) Phil. (Manila In.)	15·36 N	120·36 E
124	Gerona (hĕ-rô'-nä) Sp.	41·55 N	2·48 E
110	Gerrards Cross (jĕr'ărds krôs) Eng. (London In.)	51·34 N	0·33 w
125	Gers (R.) (zhĕr) Fr.	43·25 N	0·30 E
111	Gersthofen (gĕrst-hō'fĕn) Ger. (Munich In.)	48·26 N	10·54 E
114	Géryville (zhā-rē-vēl') Alg.	33·42 N	1·06 E
168	Gestro R.. Eth. (Horn of Afr. In.)	5·18 N	41·50 E
125	Getafe (hā-tä'fā) Sp. (Madrid In.)	40·19 N	3·44 w
81	Gettysburg (gĕt'ĭs-bûrg) Pa.	39·50 N	77 15 w
70	Gettysburg S. D.	45·01 N	99·59 w
123	Gevelsberg (gĕ-fĕls'bĕrgh) Ger. (Ruhr In.)	51·18 N	7·20 E
142	Ghāghra (R.) India	27·19 N	81·22 E
163	Ghana (gän'ä) Afr.	8·00 N	2·00 w
166	Ghanzi (gän'zē) Bech.	21·30 s	22·00 E
142	Ghard W. Pak.	24·50 N	68·35 E
164	Ghardaïa (gär-dä'ē-ä) Alg.	32·29 N	3·38 E
164	Ghāt Libya	24·52 N	10·16 E
165	Ghazal, Bahr el (R.) (băr ĕl ghä-zäl'). Sud.	9·11 N	29·37 E
142	Ghazni (gŭz'nē) Afg.	33·43 N	68·18 E
139	Ghazzah (Gaza) Gaza Area (Palestine In.)	31·30 N	34·29 E
121	Gheorghieni Rom.	46·48 N	25·30 E
121	Gherla (gĕr'lä) Rom.	47·01 N	23·55 E
164	Ghugāmis Alg.	30·07 N	9·26 E
126	Giannutri, I. di (jän-nōō'trē) It.	42·15 N	11·06 E
95	Gibara (hē-bä'rä) Cuba	21·05 N	76·10 w
166	Gibeon (gĭb'ē-ŭn) S. W. Afr.	24·45 s	16·40 E
124	Gibraleón (hē-brä-lå-ōn') Sp.	37·24 N	7·00 w
124	Gibraltar (hê-bràl-tä'r) Eur.	36·08 N	5·22 w
124	Gibraltar, Bay of Sp.	35·04 N	5·10 w
124	Gibraltar, Strait of Afr.-Eur.	35·55 N	5·45 w
75	Gibson (gĭb'sŭn) Ind. (Louisville In.)	38·24 N	85·40 w
80	Gibson City Ill.	40·25 N	88·20 w
158	Gibson Des. Austl.	24·45 s	123·15 E
73	Gibson Res. Okla.	36·07 N	95·08 w
77	Giddings (gĭd'ĭngz) Tex.	30·11 N	96·55 w
73	Gideon (gĭd'ē-ŭn) Mo.	36·27 N	89·56 w
122	Gien (zhē-äN') Fr.	47·43 N	2·37 E
120	Giessen (gēs'sĕn) Ger.	50·35 N	8·40 E
85	Giffard (zhē-färd') Can. (Quebec In.)	46·51 N	71·12 w
153	Gifu (gē'fōō) Jap.	35·25 N	136·45 E
65	Gig Harbor (gĭg) Wash. (Seattle In.)	47·20 N	122·36 w
126	Giglio, I. di (jēl'yō) It.	42·23 N	10·55 E
124	Gigüela (R.) (hê-gā'lä) Sp.	39·53 N	2·54 w
124	Gijón (hê-hōn') Sp.	43·33 N	5·37 w
69	Gila (R.) (hē'là) Ariz.	32·41 N	113·50 w
69	Gila Bend Ariz.	32·59 N	112·41 w
69	Gila Bend Ind. Res. Ariz.	33·02 N	112·48 w
69	Gila Cliff Dwellings Natl. Mon. N. Mex.	33·15 N	108·20 w
69	Gila River Ind. Res. Ariz.	33·11 N	112·38 w
71	Gilbert (gĭl'bērt) Minn.	47·27 N	92·29 w
159	Gilbert (R.) (gĭl'bērt) Austl.	17·15 s	142·09 E
156	Gilbert Is. Oceania	1·30 s	173·00 E
167	Gilboa, Mt. (gĭl-bôà) S. Afr. (Natal In.)	29·13 s	30·17 E
165	Gilf Kebir Plat. U. A. R.	24·09 N	25·29 E
142	Gilgit (gĭl'gĭt) Pak.	35·58 N	73·48 E
158	Gillen (L.) (jĭl'ĕn) Austl.	26·15 s	125·15 E
73	Gillett (jĭ-lĕt') Ark.	34·07 N	91·22 w
67	Gillette Wyo.	44·17 N	105·30 w
110	Gillingham (gĭl'ĭng ăm) Eng. (London In.)	51·23 N	0·33 E
80	Gilman (gĭl'măn) Ill.	40·45 N	87·55 w
74	Gilman Hot Springs Calif. (Los Angeles In.)	33·49 N	116·57 w
77	Gilmer (gĭl'mēr) Tex.	32·43 N	94·57 w
84	Gilmore (gĭl'môr). Ga. (Atlanta In.)	33·51 N	84·29 w
68	Gilroy (gĭl-roi') Calif.	37·00 N	121·34 w
155	Giluwe, Mt. N. Gui. Ter.	6·04 s	144·00 E
122	Gimone (R.) (zhē-mōn') Fr.	43·26 N	0·36 E
168	Gineifa (jê-nā'fà) U. A. R. (Suez In.)	30·11 N	32·26 E
139	Gineina, Ras el (Mt.) U. A. R. (Palestine In.)	29·02 N	33·58 E
165	Ginir Eth.	7·13 N	40·44 E
126	Ginosa (jê-nō'zä) It.	40·35 N	16·48 E
124	Ginzo (hēn-thō') Sp.	42·03 N	7·43 w
126	Gioja del Colle (jō'yä dĕl kôl'lā) It.	40·48 N	16·55 E
99	Gi-Paraná (R.) (zhē-pä-rä-nà') Braz.	9·33 s	61·35 w
139	Girâfi (R.). U. A. R. (Palestine In.)	29·48 N	34·43 E
73	Girard (jĭ-rärd') Kans.	37·30 N	94·50 w
98	Girardot (hē-rär-dōt') Col. (In.)	4·19 N	75·47 w
133	Giresun (ghĕr'ĕ-sōōn') Tur.	40·55 N	38·20 E
142	Giridih (jē'rē-dê) India	24·12 N	81·18 E
122	Gironde (Est.) (zhē-rôNd') Fr.	45·31 N	1·00 w
116	Girvan (gûr'văn) Scot.	55·15 N	5·01 w
159	Gisborne (gĭz'bŭrn) N. Z. (In.)	38·40 s	178·08 E
122	Gisors (zhē-zôr') Fr.	49·19 N	1·47 E
127	Giurgiu (jŏŏr'jōō) Rom.	43·53 N	25·58 E
122	Givet (zhē-vĕ') Fr.	50·80 N	4·47 E
122	Givors (zhē-vôr') Fr.	45·35 N	4·46 E
135	Gizhiga (gē'zhi-gà) Sov. Un.	61·59 N	160·46 E
121	Gizycko (gĭ'zhĭ-ko) Pol.	54·03 N	21·48 E
127	Gjinokastër Alb.	40·04 N	20·10 E
118	Gjövik (gyû'vĭk) Nor.	60·47 N	10·36 E
111	Glabeek-Zuurbemde Bel. (Brussels In.)	50·52 N	4·59 E
64	Glacier Bay Natl. Mon. (glā'shēr) Alaska	58·40 N	136·50 w
86	Glacier Natl. Park Can.	51·35 N	120·00 w
66	Glacier Pk. Wash.	48·07 N	121·10 w
65	Glacier Pt. Can. (Seattle In.)	48·24 N	123·59 w
123	Gladbeck (gläd'bĕk) Ger. (Ruhr In.)	51·35 N	6·59 E
168	Gladdeklipkop S. Afr. (Johannesburg & Pretoria In.)	24·17 s	29·36 E
160	Gladstone (glăd'stōn) Austl.	23·45 s	150·00 E
160	Gladstone Austl.	33·15 s	138·20 E
62	Gladstone Can.	50·20 N	99·00 w
71	Gladstone Mich.	45·50 N	87·04 w
84	Gladstone. N. J. (New York In.)	40·43 N	74·39 w
65	Gladstone. Ore. (Portland In.)	45·23 N	122·36 w
80	Gladwin (glăd'wĭn) Mich.	44·00 N	84·25 w
126	Glamoč (gläm'ōch) Yugo.	44·03 N	16·51 E
120	Glarus (glä'rōōs) Switz.	47·02 N	9·03 E
116	Glasgow (glàs'gō) Scot.	55·54 N	4·25 w
78	Glasgow Ky.	37·00 N	85·55 w
73	Glasgow Mo.	39·14 N	92·48 w
67	Glasgow Mont.	48·14 N	106·39 w
83	Glass B. (glàs) Can.	46·12 N	59·57 w
75	Glassport (glàs'pōrt) Pa. (Pittsburgh In.)	40·19 N	79·53 w
120	Glauchau (glou'Kou) Ger.	50·51 N	12·28 E
132	Glazov (glä'zôf) Sov. Un.	58·05 N	52·52 E
120	Glda R. (g'l'dà) Pol.	53·27 N	16·52 E
110	Glen (R.) (glĕn) Eng.	52·44 N	0·18 w
122	Glénans, Iles de (Is.) (ēl-dĕ-glā-näN'). Fr.	47·43 N	4·42 w
84	Glen Burnie (bûr'nē) Md. (Baltimore In.)	39·10 N	76·38 w
69	Glen Canyon Dam (glĕn kăn'yŭn) Ariz.	36·57 N	111·25 w
74	Glen Carbon (kär'bŏn) Ill. (St. Louis In.)	38·45 N	89·59 w
75	Glencoe Ill. (Chicago In.)	42·08 N	87·45 w
71	Glencoe (glĕn'kō) Minn.	44·44 N	94·07 w
167	Glencoe (glĕn-cō) S. Afr. (Natal In.)	28·14 s	30·09 E
84	Glen Cove (kōv) N. Y. (New York In.)	40·51 N	73·38 w
69	Glendale (glĕn'dāl) Ariz.	33·30 N	112·15 w
74	Glendale. Calif. (Los Angeles In.)	34·09 N	118·15 w
75	Glendale. Ohio (Cincinnati In.)	31·16 N	84·22 w
67	Glendive (glĕn'dīv) Mont.	47·08 N	104·41 w
67	Glendo Wyo.	42·32 N	104·54 w
74	Glendora (glĕn-dō'rà) Calif. (Los Angeles In.)	34·08 N	117·52 w
160	Glenelg (R.) Austl.	37·20 s	141·30 E
75	Glen Ellyn (glĕn ĕl'-lĕn) Ill. (Chicago In.)	41·53 N	88·04 w
160	Glen Innes (ĭn'ĕs) Austl.	29·45 s	152·02 E
77	Glenmora (glĕn-mō'rà) La.	30·58 N	92·36 w
66	Glenns Ferry (fĕr'ĭ) Idaho	42·58 N	115·21 w
79	Glennville (glĕn'vĭl) Ga.	31·55 N	81·56 w
84	Glen Olden (ōl'd'n) Pa. (Philadelphia In.)	39·54 N	75·17 w
84	Glen Rock (rŏk). Va. (Norfolk In.)	36·50 N	76·13 w
67	Glenrock (glĕn'rŏk) Wyo.	42·50 N	105·53 w
81	Glens Falls (glĕnz fôlz) N. Y.	43·20 N	73·40 w
75	Glenshaw (glĕn'shô) Pa. (Pittsburgh In.)	40·33 N	79·57 w
70	Glen Ullin (glĕn'ŭl'ĭn) N. D.	46·47 N	101·49 w
65	Glen Valley. Can. (Vancouver In.)	49·09 N	122·30 w
75	Glenview (glĕn'vū) Ill. (Chicago In.)	42·04 N	87·48 w
83	Glenwood (glĕn-wŏŏd) Can.	48·59 N	54·51 w
70	Glenwood Iowa	41·03 N	95·44 w
70	Glenwood Minn.	45·39 N	95·23 w
69	Glenwood Springs Colo.	39·35 N	107·20 w
111	Glienicke (glē'nē-kĕ) Ger. (Berlin In.)	52·38 N	13·19 E
111	Glinde (glĕn'dĕ) Ger. (Hamburg In.)	53·32 N	10·13 E
121	Gliwice (gwĭ-wĭt'sĕ) Pol.	50·18 N	18·40 E
69	Globe (glōb) Ariz.	33·20 N	110·50 w
129	Globino (glô'bē-nô) Sov. Un.	49·22 N	33·17 E
120	Głogów Szprotawa (gwō'gōōv shprō-tä'vä). Pol.	51·40 N	16·04 E
118	Glomma (R.) (glômmä) Nor.	61·22 N	11·02 E
118	Glommen (R.) (glôm'ĕn) Nor.	60·03 N	11·15 E
111	Glonn (glônn). Ger. (Munich In.)	47·59 N	11·52 E
167	Glorieuses, Îles (Is.). Malag. Rep.	11·28 s	47·50 E
110	Glossop (glŏs'ŭp) Eng.	53·26 N	1·57 w
78	Gloster (glŏs'tēr) Miss.	31·10 N	91·00 w
116	Gloucester (glŏs'tēr) Eng.	51·54 N	2·11 w
83	Gloucester Mass. (Boston In.)	42·37 N	70·40 w
84	Gloucester City N. J. (Philadelphia In.)	39·53 N	75·08 w
80	Glouster (glŏs'tēr) Ohio	39·35 N	82·05 w
83	Glover I. (glŭv'ēr) Can.	48·41 N	57·30 w
81	Gloversville (glŭv'ērz-vĭl) N. Y.	43·05 N	74·20 w
83	Glovertown (glŭv'ēr-toun) Can.	48·42 N	54·01 w
128	Glubokoye (glōō-bô-kō'yĕ) Sov. Un.	55·08 N	27·44 E
111	Glückstadt (glük-shtät) Ger. (Hamburg In.)	53·47 N	9·25 E
129	Glukhov (glōō'kôf') Sov. Un.	51·42 N	33·52 E
129	Glushkovo (glōōsh'kô-vō). Sov. Un.	51·21 N	34·43 E
120	Gmünden (g'mōōn'dĕn) Aus.	47·57 N	13·47 E
121	Gniezno (g'nyăz'nō) Pol.	52·32 N	17·34 E
127	Gnjilane (gnyē'lä-nĕ) Yugo.	42·28 N	21·27 E
143	Gôa (Ter.) (gō'ă) Asia	20·40 N	74·13 E
92	Goascorán (gō-äs'kō-rän') Hond.	13·37 N	87·43 w
165	Goba (gō'bä) Eth.	7·17 N	39·58 E
166	Gobabis (gō-bä'bĭs) S. W. Afr.	22·25 s	18·50 E
146	Gobi or Shamo (Des.) (gō'be) Mong.	43·29 N	103·15 E
65	Goble (gō'b'l). Ore. (Portland In.)	46·01 N	122·53 w
123	Goch (gôK) Ger. (Ruhr In.)	51·35 N	6·10 E
142	Godāvari (R.) (gō-dä'vŭ-rē). India	17·42 N	81·15 E
158	Goddards Soak (Swp.) (gŏd'ărdz) Austl.	31·20 s	123·30 E
80	Goderich (gōd'rĭch) Can.	43·45 N	81·45 w
74	Godfrey (gŏd'frē) Ill. (St. Louis In.)	38·57 N	90·12 w
49	Godhavn (gōdh'hävn) Grnld.	69·15 N	53·30 w
86	Gods (L.) (gŏdz) Can.	54·38 N	95·23 w
49	Godthaab (gŏt'hōōb) Grnld.	64·10 N	51·32 w
146	Godwin Austen, Mt. (gŏd wĭn ôs'tĕn). Pak.	36·06 N	76·38 E
68	Goffs (gôfs) Calif.	34·57 N	115·06 w
71	Gogebic (L.) (gô-gē'bĭk) Mich.	46·24 N	89·25 w
71	Gogebic Ra. Mich.	46·37 N	89·48 w
111	Goggingen (gûg'gēn-gēn) Ger. (Munich In.)	48·21 N	10·53 E

ng-sing; ŋ-baŋk; N-nasalized n; nŏd; cŏmmit; ōld; ôbey; ôrder; fōōd; fŏŏt; ou-out; s-soft; sh-dish; th-thin; pūre; ûnite; ûrn; stŭd; circŭs; ü-as "y" in study; '-indeterminate vowel.

Page	Name Pronunciation Region	Lat. °′	Long. °′
90	Gogorrón (gō-gô-rōn′) . . . . Mex.	21·51 N	100·54 W
153	Goi (gō′ē) . . . . . . Jap. (Tōkyō In.)	35·31 N	140·05 E
99	Goiânia (gô-vä′nyä) . . . . Braz.	16·41 S	48·57 W
99	Goiás (gô-yà′s) . . . . Braz.	15·57 S	50·10 W
99	Goiás (State) . . . . Braz.	12·35 S	48·38 W
111	Goirle . . . Neth. (Amsterdam In.)	51·31 N	5·06 E
133	Göksu (R.) (gûk′sōō′) . . . . Tur.	36·40 N	33·30 E
118	Göl (gûl) . . . . Nor.	60·58 N	8·54 E
118	Göla älv (R.) . . . . Swe.	58·11 N	12·03 E
79	Golax (gō′lăks) . . . . Va.	36·41 N	80·56 W
110	Golcar (gŏl′kår) . . . . Eng.	53·38 N	1·52 W
73	Golconda (gŏl-kŏn′då) . . . . Ill.	37·21 N	88·32 W
121	Gołdap (gôl′dăp) . . . . Pol.	54·17 N	22·17 E
72	Golden . . . . Colo.	39·44 N	105·15 W
84	Goldenbridge (gōl′dĕn-brĭj) N. Y. (New York In.)	41·17 N	73·41 W
66	Goldendale (gōl′dĕn-dāl) . . . Wash.	45·49 N	120·48 W
65	Golden Gate (Str.) (gōl′dĕn gāt) Calif. (San Francisco In.)	37·48 N	122·32 W
68	Goldfield (gōld-fēld) . . . . Nev.	37·42 N	117·15 W
88	Gold Hill (Mtn.) C. Z. (Panama Canal In.)	9·03 N	79·08 W
65	Gold Mtn. (gōld) Wash. (Seattle In.)	47·33 N	122·48 W
79	Goldsboro (gōldz-bûr′ō) . . . . . N. C.	35·23 N	77·59 W
76	Goldthwaite (gōld′thwāt) . . . . Tex.	31·27 N	98·34 W
120	Goleniów (gô-lĕ-nyŭf′) . . . . Pol.	53·33 N	14·51 E
135	Golets-Purpula, Gol′tsy (Mtn.) Sov. Un.	59·08 N	115·22 E
93	Golfito (gôl-fē′tō) . . . . C. R.	8·40 N	83·12 W
	Golfo Dulce, see Izabal, L.		
77	Goliad (gō-lĭ-ăd′) . . . . Tex.	28·40 N	97·21 W
155	Golo (gō′lō) . . . . Phil. (Manila In.)	13·38 N	120·17 E
126	Golo (R.) . . . . Cor.	42·28 N	9·18 E
129	Golovchino (gō-lôf′chē-nō) Sov. Un.	50·34 N	35·52 E
166	Golungo Alto (gô-lōōŋ′gō äl′tō) Ang.	9·10 S	14·40 E
127	Golyamo Konare (gō′lå-mō-kō′nä-rĕ) . Bul.	42·16 N	24·33 E
111	Golzow (gōl′tsōv) Ger. (Berlin In.)	52·17 N	12·36 E
164	Gombe . . . . Nig.	10·23 N	11·08 E
128	Gomel′ (gô′mĕl′) . . . . Sov. Un.	52·20 N	31·03 E
128	Gomel′ (Oblast) . . . . Sov. Un.	52·18 N	29·00 E
164	Gomera I. (gô-mä′rä) . . . . Can. Is.	28·00 N	18·01 W
76	Gomez Farias (gō′māz fä-rē′äs) Mex.	24·59 N	101·02 W
76	Gómez Palacio (pä-lä′syō) . . . Mex.	25·35 N	103·30 W
95	Gonaïves (gō-nà-ēv′) . . . . Hai.	19·25 N	72·45 W
95	Gonaïves, Golfe des (G.) (gō-nà-ēv′) . Hai.	19·20 N	73·20 W
95	Gonâve, Ile De La (I.) (gô-nàv′) Hai.	18·50 N	73·30 W
142	Gonda . . . . India	27·13 N	82·00 E
142	Gondal . . . . India	22·02 N	70·47 E
165	Gondar (gŏn′dår) . . . . Eth.	12·39 N	37·30 E
123	Gonesse (gô-nĕs′) . . Fr. (Paris In.)	48·59 N	2·28 E
153	Gonō (R.) (gô′nō) . . . . Jap.	35·00 N	132·25 E
85	Gonor (gō′nŏr) Can. (Winnipeg In.)	50·04 N	96·57 W
167	Gonubie Mouth (gŏn′ōō-bē mouth) . S. Afr. (Natal In.)	32·56 S	28·02 E
90	Gonzales (gôn-zà′lĕs) . . . . Mex.	22·47 N	98·26 W
77	Gonzales (gŏn-zä′lĕz) . . . . Tex.	29·31 N	97·25 W
100	González Catán (gōn-zà′lĕz-kä-tà′n) . Arg. (In.)	34·31 S	58·39 W
166	Good Hope, C. of (kăp ov gŏŏd hōp) . S. Afr. (Cape Town In.)	34·21 S	18·29 E
66	Gooding (gŏŏd′ĭng) . . . . Idaho	42·55 N	114·43 W
80	Goodland (gŏŏd′lănd) . . . . Ind.	40·50 N	87·15 W
72	Goodland . . . . Kans.	39·19 N	101·43 W
166	Goodwood (gŏŏd′wŏŏd) S. Afr. (Cape Town In.)	33·54 S	18·33 E
110	Goole (gōōl) . . . . Eng.	53·42 N	0·52 W
70	Goose (R.) . . . . N. D.	47·40 N	97·41 W
87	Goose Bay . . . . Can.	53·19 N	60·33 W
67	Gooseberry Cr. (gōōs-bĕr′ĭ) . . Wyo.	44·04 N	108·35 W
67	Goose Cr. (gōōs) . . . . Idaho	42·07 N	113·53 W
75	Goose Lake (gōōs lāk) Ill. (Chicago In.)	41·21 N	88·18 W
66	Goose L. . . . . Calif.	41·56 N	120·35 W
142	Gorakhpur (gō′rŭk-pōōr) . . . . India	26·45 N	82·39 E
94	Gorda, Punta (Pt.) (pōō′n-tä-gôr-dä) . Cuba	22·25 N	82·10 W
94	Gorda Cay (gôr′dä) . . . . Ba. Is.	26·05 N	77·30 W
85	Gordon (gôr′dŭn) Can. (Winnipeg In.)	50·00 N	97·20 W
70	Gordon . . . . Nebr.	42·47 N	102·14 W
165	Gorē (gō′rĕ) . . . . Eth.	8·12 N	35·34 E
144	Gorgān . . . . Iran	36·44 N	54·30 E
126	Gorgona (I.) (gôr-gō′nä) . . . . It.	43·27 N	9·55 E
133	Gori (gō′rē) . . . . Sov. Un.	42·00 N	44·08 E
111	Gorinchem (gō′rĭn-kĕm) Neth. (Amsterdam In.)	51·50 N	4·59 E
110	Goring (gôr′ĭng) Eng. (London In.)	51·30 N	1·08 W
126	Gorizia (gô-rē′tsē-yä) . . . . Yugo.	44·56 N	13·40 E
132	Gorki (gôr′kē) . . . . Sov. Un.	56·15 N	44·05 E
132	Gor′kovskoye . . . . Sov. Un.	56·38 N	43·40 E
128	Gor′kovskoye (Gorkov) (L.) (gôr′kôf-skō-yĕ) . Sov. Un.	57·38 N	41·18 E
121	Gorlice (gôr-lē′tsĕ) . . . . Pol.	49·38 N	21·11 E
120	Gorlitz (gûr′lĭts) . . . . Ger.	51·10 N	15·01 E
129	Gorlovka (gôr′lôf-kå) . . . . Sov. Un.	48·17 N	38·03 E
76	Gorman (gôr′măn) . . . . Tex.	32·13 N	98·40 W
127	Gorna-Oryakhovitsa (gôr′nä-ôr-yĕk′ô-vē-tså) . Bul.	43·08 N	25·40 E
127	Gornji Milanovac (gôrn′yē-mē′la-nô-vàts) . Yugo.	44·02 N	20·29 E
134	Gorno-Altay Aut. Oblast . Sov. Un.	51·00 N	86·00 E
134	Gorno-Altaysk (gôr′nŭ-ŭl-tīsk′) Sov. Un.	52·28 N	82·45 E
121	Gorodēnka (gō-rô-deŋ′kä) Sov. Un.	48·40 N	25·30 E
132	Gorodets (Res.) . . . . Sov. Un.	57·00 N	43·55 E
136	Gorodishche (gô-rô′dĭsh-chĕ) Sov. Un. (Urals In.)	57·57 N	57·03 E
129	Gorodnya (gô-rôd′′nyä) . . Sov. Un.	51·54 N	31·31 E
121	Gorodok (gō-rô-dôk′) . . . . Sov. Un.	49·37 N	23·40 E
134	Gorodok . . . . Sov. Un.	50·30 N	103·58 E
128	Gorodok . . . . Sov. Un.	55·27 N	29·58 E
154	Gorontalo (gō-rōn-tä′lo) . . . Indon.	0·40 N	123·04 E
121	Goryn′ R. (gō′rĕn′) . . . . . . Sov. Un.	50·55 N	26·07 E
120	Gorzow Wielkopolski (gō-zhōōv′vyĕl-ko-pōl′skē) . Pol.	53·44 N	15·15 E
80	Goshen (gō′shĕn) . . . . Ind.	41·35 N	85·50 W
75	Goshen . . . . Ky. (Louisville In.)	38·24 N	85·34 W
84	Goshen . . . . N. Y. (New York In.)	41·24 N	74·19 W
75	Goshen . . . . . Ohio (Cincinnati In.)	39·14 N	84·09 W
65	Goshen . . . . Wash. (Vancouver In.)	48·52 N	122·20 W
69	Goshute Ind. Res. (gō-shōōt′) Utah	39·50 N	114·00 W
120	Goslar (gôs′lär) . . . . Ger.	51·55 N	10·25 E
99	Gospa (R.) (gôs-pä) . . . . Ven. (In.)	9·43 N	64·23 W
126	Gospić (gôs′pĭch) . . . . Yugo.	44·31 N	15·03 E
127	Gostivar (gos′tē-vär) . . . . Yugo.	41·46 N	20·58 E
121	Gostynin (gôs-tē′nĭn) . . . . Pol.	52·24 N	19·30 E
118	Göta Can. (yû′tå) . . . . Swe.	58·35 N	15·24 E
118	Göteborg (yû′tĕ-bôrgh) . . . . . . Swe.	57·39 N	11·56 E
164	Gotel Mts. . . . . Nig.-Cam.	7·04 N	11·28 E
92	Gotera (gō-tā′rä) . . . . Sal.	13·41 N	88·06 W
120	Gotha (gō′tå) . . . . Ger.	50·57 N	10·43 E
72	Gothenburg (gŏth′ĕn-bûrg) . Nebr.	40·57 N	100·08 W
118	Gotland (I.) . . . . Swe.	57·35 N	17·35 E
153	Gotō-Rettō (Is.) (gō′tō rĕt′tō) Jap.	33·06 N	128·54 E
119	Gotska Sandön (I.) . . . . Swe.	58·24 N	19·15 E
120	Göttingen (gût′ĭng-ĕn) . . . . . . Ger.	51·32 N	9·57 E
111	Gouda (gou′dä) Neth. (Amsterdam In.)	52·00 N	4·42 E
47	Gough (I.) (gŏf) . . . . Atl. O.	40·00 S	10·00 W
87	Gouin Res. . . . . Can.	77·12 N	75·34 W
160	Goulburn (gōl′bŭrn) . . . . Austl.	34·47 S	149·40 E
164	Goumbou (gōōm-bōō′) . . . . Mali	15·02 N	7·35 W
164	Goundam (gōōn-dän′) . . . . Mali	16·29 N	3·37 W
164	Gouré (gōō-rā′) . . . . Niger	13·53 N	10·44 E
81	Gouverneur (gŭv-ẽr-nōōr′) . . N. Y.	44·20 N	75·25 W
86	Govenlock (gŭvĕn-lŏk) . . . . . . Can.	49·09 N	109·42 W
100	Governador Ilhado (I.) (gô-vĕr-nä-dō′r-ē-là′dô) . Braz. (In.)	22·48 S	43·13 W
100	Governador Portela (pōr-tĕ′là) Braz. (In.)	22·28 S	43·30 W
99	Governador Valadares (vä-lä-dä′rĕs) . Braz.	18·47 S	41·45 W
95	Governor′s Harbour . . . . Ba. Is.	25·15 N	76·15 W
81	Gowanda (gô-wŏn′då) . . . . . . N. Y.	42·30 N	78·55 W
100	Goya (gō′yä) . . . . Arg.	29·06 S	59·12 W
110	Goyt (R.) (goit) . . . . Eng.	53·19 N	2·03 W
166	Graaff-Reinet (gräf′rī′nĕt) . . S. Afr.	32·10 S	24·40 E
126	Gračac (grä′chäts) . . . . Yugo.	44·16 N	15·50 E
127	Gračanica (grá-chän′′i-tsä) . Yugo.	44·42 N	18·19 E
78	Graceville (grās′vĭl) . . . . Fla.	30·57 N	85·30 W
70	Graceville . . . . Minn.	45·33 N	96·25 W
92	Gracias (grä′sê-äs) . . . . Hond.	14·35 N	88·37 W
93	Gracias a Dios, Cabo (C.) (kà′bô-grä-syäs-ä-dyō′s) . . Hond.	15·00 N	83·13 W
164	Graciosa I. (grä-syō′sä) Azores (In.)	39·07 N	27·30 W
127	Gradačac (gra-dä′chats) . . . . Yugo.	44·50 N	18·28 E
124	Gradelos (grä-dĕ-lôs) . . . . Sp.	42·38 N	5·15 W
129	Gradizhsk (grä-dēzhsk′) . Sov. Un.	49·12 N	33·06 E
124	Grado (grä′dō) . . . . Sp.	43·24 N	6·04 W
111	Grafelfing (grä′fĕl-fēng) Ger. (Munich In.)	48·07 N	11·27 E
111	Grafing (grä′fēng) Ger. (Munich In.)	48·03 N	11·58 E
160	Grafton (graf′tŭn) . . . . Austl.	29·38 S	153·05 E
74	Grafton . . . . Ill. (St. Louis In.)	38·58 N	90·26 W
83	Grafton . . . . Mass. (Boston In.)	42·13 N	71·41 W
70	Grafton . . . . N. D.	48·24 N	97·25 W
75	Grafton . . . . . Ohio (Cleveland In.)	41·16 N	82·04 W
81	Grafton . . . . W. Va.	39·20 N	80·00 W
125	Gragnano (grän-yä′nô) It. (Naples In.)	40·27 N	14·32 E
79	Graham (grā′ăm) . . . . N. C.	36·03 N	79·23 W
72	Graham . . . . Tex.	33·07 N	98·34 W
65	Graham . . . . . . Wash. (Seattle In.)	47·03 N	122·18 W
86	Graham (I.) . . . . Can.	53·37 N	131·47 W
167	Grahamstown (grā′ăms′toun) S. Afr. (Natal In.)	33·19 S	26·33 E
123	Graian Alps (Mts.) (grā′yăn) Fr.-It.	45·17 N	6·52 E
99	Grajaú (grå-zhà-ōō′) . . . . Braz.	5·59 S	46·03 W
99	Grajaú (R.) . . . . Braz.	4·24 S	46·04 W
121	Grajewo (grä-yä′vo) . . . . Pol.	53·38 N	22·28 E
101	Grama, Serra de (Mtn.) (sĕ′r-rä-dĕ-grà′må) Braz. (Rio de Janeiro In.)	23·42 S	42·28 W
127	Gramada (grä′mà-dä) . . . . Bul.	43·46 N	22·41 E
111	Gramatneusiedl . Aus. (Vienna In.)	48·02 N	16·29 E
126	Grammichele (gräm-mê-kĕ′lā) . . It.	37·15 N	14·40 E
116	Grampian Mts. (grăm′pĭ-ăn) Scot.	56·30 N	4·55 W
92	Granada (grä-nä′dhä) . . . . Nic.	11·55 N	85·58 W
124	Granada (grä-nä′dä) . . . . Sp.	37·13 N	3·37 W
100	Gran Bajo (Pln.) (grän′bà′kō) Arg.	47·35 S	68·45 W
77	Granbury (grăn′bĕr-ĭ) . . . . Tex.	32·26 N	97·45 W
81	Granby (grăn′bĭ) . . . . Can.	45·30 N	72·40 W
73	Granby . . . . Mo.	36·54 N	94·15 W
72	Granby (L.) . . . . Colo.	40·07 N	105·40 W
164	Gran Canaria I. (grän′kä-nä′rē-ä) . Can. Is.	27·39 N	15·39 W
100	Gran Chaco (Reg.) (grän′chä′kō) Arg.-Par.	25·30 S	62·15 W
71	Grand (I.) . . . . Mich.	46·37 N	86·38 W
82	Grand (L.) . . . . Can.	45·17 N	67·42 W
87	Grand (L.) . . . . Can.	66·15 N	45·59 W
80	Grand (R.) . . . . Can.	43·45 N	80·20 W
80	Grand (R.) . . . . Mich.	42·58 N	85·13 W
73	Grand (R.) . . . . Mo.	39·50 N	93·52 W
70	Grand (R.) . . . . S. D.	45·40 N	101·55 W
70	Grand (R.), North Fork . . . . S. D.	45·52 N	102·49 W
70	Grand (R.), South Fork . . . . S. D.	45·38 N	102·56 W
94	Grand Bahama (I.) . . . . Ba. Is.	26·35 N	78·30 W
83	Grand Bank (grănd băngk) . . Can.	47·05 N	55·44 W
164	Grand Bassam (grän bà-sän′) Ivory Coast	5·14 N	3·51 W
93	Grand Bourg (grän bōōr′) Marie Galante (Le. & Wind. Is. In.)	15·54 N	61·20 W
95	Grand Caicos (I.) (grănd kä-ē′kōs) . Caicos	21·45 N	71·50 W
116	Grand Canal . . . . Ire.	53·21 N	7·15 W
	Grand Canal, see Yün Ho		
69	Grand Canyon (grănd kăn′yŭn) Ariz.	36·05 N	112·10 W
69	Grand Canyon . . . . Ariz.	35·50 N	113·16 W
69	Grand Canyon Natl. Mon. . . Ariz.	36·18 N	113·26 W
69	Grand Canyon Natl. Park . . Ariz.	36·15 N	112·20 W
94	Grand Cayman (I.) (kā′măn) Cayman Is.	19·15 N	81·15 W
66	Grand Coulee Dam (kōō′lē) . Wash.	47·58 N	119·28 W
100	Grande, Bahia (B.) (bä-ē′ä-grän′dĕ) . Arg.	50·45 S	68·00 W
100	Grande, Salinas (F.) (sä-lē′näs) Arg.	29·45 S	65·00 W
98	Grande, Rio (R.) . . . . Bol.	16·49 S	63·19 W
99	Grande, Rio (R.) . . . . Braz.	19·48 S	49·54 W
101	Grande, Ilha (I.) (grän′dĕ) Braz. (Rio de Janeiro In.)	23·11 S	44·14 W
99	Grande, Salto (Falls) (säl-tō) Braz.	16·18 S	39·38 W
101	Grande (R.) . . Chile (Santiago In.)	35·25 S	70·14 W
91	Grande (R.) . . . . Mex.	17·37 N	96·41 W
88	Grande, Ciri (R.) (sē′rē-grän′dĕ) Pan. (Panama Canal In.)	8·55 N	80·04 W
62	Grande, Rio (Bravo del Norte, Rio) (R.) (grän′dā) . . U. S.-Mex.	26·50 N	99·10 W
101	Grande (R.) . Ur. (Buenos Aires In.)	33·19 S	57·15 W
100	Grande, Cuchilla (Mts.) (kōō-chē′l-yä) . Ur.	33·00 S	55·15 W
99	Grande, Boca (Est.) (bō′kä-grä′n-dĕ) . Ven.	8·46 N	60·17 W
82	Grande Baie (grănd bā′) . . . . . Can.	48·17 N	70·53 W
95	Grande Cayemite, Ile (I.) . . . . Hai.	18·45 N	73·55 W
167	Grande Comore (grä′n-dĕ-kô-mô-rĕ) . Comores, Arch. des	11·44 S	42·38 E
92	Grande de Otoro (grän′dā dā ô-tō′rō) . Hond.	14·42 N	88·21 W
164	Grande Erg Occidental (Dunes) Alg.	29·37 N	6·04 E
85	Grande-Ligne (lēn′y′) Can. (Montreal In.)	45·13 N	73·17 W
83	Grande Miquelon (I.) (mĭk-ē-lôn′) Can.	47·03 N	56·20 W
85	Grande Pointe (grănd point′) Can. (Winnipeg In.)	49·47 N	97·03 W
86	Grande Prairie (prâr′ĭ) . . . . . . Can.	55·09 N	118·48 W
93	Grande R. (grän′dĕ) . . . . Nic.	13·01 N	84·21 W
95	Grande Rivière du Nord (rē-vyâr′ dü nôr′) . Hai.	19·35 N	72·10 W
66	Grande Ronde R. (rônd′) . . . . Ore.	45·32 N	117·52 W
68	Gran Desierto (Des.) (grän-dĕ-syĕ′r-tô) . Mex.	32·14 N	114·28 W
93	Grande Terre I. (târ′) Guad. (Le. & Wind. Is. In.)	16·28 N	61·13 W
93	Grande Vigie, Pointe de la (Pt.) (grănd vē-gē′) Grande Terre (Le. & Wind. Is. In.)	16·32 N	61·25 W
82	Grand Falls (fôlz) . . . . Can.	47·02 N	67·46 W
87	Grand Falls . . . . Can.	53·34 N	64·23 W
79	Grandfather, Mt. (grănd-fä-thẽr) N. C.	36·07 N	81·48 W
72	Grandfield (grănd′fēld) . . . . . Okla.	34·13 N	98·39 W
86	Grand Forks (fôrks) . . . . Can.	49·00 N	118·27 W
70	Grand Forks . . . . N. D.	47·55 N	97·05 W
80	Grand Haven (hā′v′n) . . . . . Mich.	43·05 N	86·15 W
72	Grand Island (ī′lănd) . . . . . . Nebr.	40·56 N	98·20 W
75	Grand I. . . . . . . N. Y. (Buffalo In.)	43·03 N	78·58 W
69	Grand Junction (jŭngk′shŭn) Colo.	39·05 N	108·35 W
164	Grand Lahou (là-ōō′) . Ivory Coast	5·08 N	5·06 W
83	Grand Lake (lāk) . . . . Can.	49·00 N	57·10 W
77	Grand L. . . . . La.	29·57 N	91·25 W
74	Grand L. . . . . . Minn. (Duluth In.)	46·54 N	92·26 W
80	Grand Ledge (lĕj) . . . . Mich.	42·45 N	84·50 W
122	Grand-Lieu, L. de (grän′-lyû) . Fr.	46·00 N	1·45 W
82	Grand Manan (I.) (mă-năn) . Can.	44·42 N	66·50 W
82	Grand′Mere (grän mâr′) . . . . Can.	46·36 N	72·43 W
123	Grand Morin (R.) (mō-răn′) Fr. (Paris In.)	48·23 N	2·19 E
124	Grândola (grăn′dô-lå) . . . . Port.	38·10 N	8·36 W
164	Grand-Popo (pô-pô′) . . . . Dahomey	6·27 N	1·52 E
71	Grand Portage Ind. Res. (pōr′tĭj) Minn.	47·54 N	89·34 W
71	Grand Portage Nat′l Mon. . . Mich.	47·59 N	89·47 W
74	Grand Prairie (prĕ′rē) Tex. (Dallas, Fort Worth In.)	32·45 N	97·00 W
69	Grand Quivira Natl. Mon. (kē-vē′rå) . N. Mex.	34·10 N	106·05 W
80	Grand Rapids (răp′ĭdz) . . . . Mich.	43·00 N	85·45 W
71	Grand Rapids . . . . Minn.	47·16 N	93·33 W
82	Grand-Riviere . . . . Can.	48·26 N	64·30 W
93	Grand Soufriere Vol. (sōō-frē-âr′) Guad. (Le. & Wind. Is. In.)	16·06 N	61·42 W
67	Grand Teton Mt. . . . . Wyo.	43·46 N	110·50 W
67	Grand Teton Natl. Park (tē′tŏn) Wyo.	43·54 N	110·15 W
80	Grand Traverse B. (trăv′ẽrs) Mich.	45·00 N	85·30 W
95	Grand Turk (I.) (tûrk) . . Turks Is.	21·30 N	71·10 W
74	Grandview (grănd′vyōō) Mo. (Kansas City In.)	38·53 N	94·32 W
69	Grand Wash (R.) (wŏsh) . . . . Ariz.	36·20 N	113·52 W
67	Granger (grān′jẽr) . . . . Wyo.	41·37 N	109·58 W
66	Grangeville (grānj′vĭl) . . . . . . Idaho	45·56 N	116·08 W

ăt; finăl; rāte; senāte; ärm; àsk; sofà; fâre; ch-choose; dh-as th in other; bē; ēvent; bĕt; recĕnt; cratẽr; g-go; gh-guttural g; bĭt; ĭ-short neutral; rīde; K-guttural k as ch in German ich;

Page	Name Pronunciation Region	Lat. °′	Long. °′
84	Granite (grăn′ĭt) Md. (Baltimore In.)	39·21 N	76·51 W
74	Granite City Ill. (St. Louis In.)	38·42 N	90·09 W
70	Granite Falls (fôlz)........Minn.	44·46 N	95·34 W
79	Granite Falls..............N. C.	35·49 N	81·25 W
65	Granite Falls..Wash. (Seattle In.)	48·05 N	121·59 W
67	Granite Pk..............Mont.	45·13 N	109·48 W
79	Graniteville (grăn′ĭt-vĭl).....S. C.	33·35 N	81·50 W
99	Granito (grä-nē′tō).........Braz.	7·39 S	39·34 W
124	Granja de Torrehermosa (grän′hä dā tôr′rā-ĕr-mō′sä).Sp.	38·21 N	5·38 W
118	Grånna (grĕn′å)............Swe.	58·02 N	14·28 E
125	Granollérs (grä-nôl-yĕrs′).....Sp.	41·36 N	2·19 E
98	Gran Pajonal (Marsh) (grä′n-pä-kô-näl′).Peru	11·14 S	71·45 W
95	Gran Piedra (Mtn.) (grän-pyĕ′drä).Cuba	20·00 N	75·40 W
110	Grantham (grăn′tăm).......Eng.	52·54 N	0·38 W
75	Grant Park (grănt pärk) Ill. (Chicago In.)	41·14 N	87·39 W
66	Grants Pass (grȧnts pȧs).....Ore.	42·26 N	123·20 W
122	Granville (gräN-vēl′)..........Fr.	48·52 N	1·35 W
81	Granville (grăn′vĭl)........N. Y.	43·25 N	73·15 W
86	Granville (L.)..............Can.	56·18 N	99·39 W
99	Grão Mogol (grouN′ mŏŏ-gôl′) Braz.	16·34 S	42·35 W
74	Grapevine (grāp′vīn) Tex. (Dallas, Fort Worth In.)	32·56 N	97·05 W
118	Gräsö (I.)..................Swe.	60·30 N	18·35 E
81	Grass (R.)................N. Y.	44·45 N	75·10 W
89	Grass Cay (I.) Vir. Is. (U.S.A.) (St. Thomas In.)	18·22 N	64·50 W
123	Grasse (gräs)................Fr.	43·39 N	6·57 E
65	Grass Mtn. (grȧs) Wash. (Seattle In.)	47·13 N	121·48 W
68	Grass Valley..............Calif.	39·12 N	121·04 W
83	Grates Pt. (grāts)..........Can.	48·14 N	52·45 W
122	Graulhet (grō-lĕ′)...........Fr.	43·46 N	1·58 E
86	Gravelbourg (grăv′ĕl-bôrg)...Can.	49·55 N	106·53 W
110	Gravesend (grāvz′ĕnd′) Eng. (London In.)	51·26 N	0·22 E
126	Gravina (grä-vē′nä)..........It.	40·48 N	16·27 E
74	Gravois (grav′ois) Mo. (St. Louis In.)	38·33 N	90·20 W
95	Gravois, Pte. (grȧ-vwä′).....Hai.	18·00 N	74·20 W
123	Gray (grâ)...................Fr.	47·26 N	5·35 E
80	Grayling (grā′lĭng)........Mich.	44·40 N	84·40 W
75	Grayslake (grāz′lāk) Ill. (Chicago In.)	42·20 N	88·20 W
72	Grays Pk. (grāz)..........Colo.	39·29 N	105·52 W
129	Grayvoron (grȧ-ē′vô-rôn) Sov. Un.	50·28 N	35·41 E
120	Graz (gräts)................Aus.	47·05 N	15·26 E
94	Great Abaco (I.) (ă′bȧ-kō).Ba. Is.	26·30 N	77·05 W
159	Great Artesian Basin (Reg.) (är-tēzh-ăn bā-sĭn).Austl.	23·16 S	143·37 E
158	Great Australian Bight (ôs-trā′-lĭ-ăn bĭt).Austl.	33·30 S	127·00 E
94	Great Bahama Bk. (bȧ-hā′mȧ) Ba. Is.	25·00 N	78·50 W
159	Great Barrier (I.) (băr′ĭ-ĕr) N. Z. (In.)	37·00 S	175·31 E
159	Great Barrier Rf. (bȧ-rĭ-ĕr rēf) Austl.	16·43 S	146·34 E
62	Great Basin (grāt bā′s′n)....U. S.	40·08 N	117·10 W
86	Great Bear L. (bâr).........Can.	66·10 N	119·53 W
72	Great Bend (bĕnd)........Kans.	38·41 N	98·46 W
	Great Bitter, see el Buheirat el Murrat el Kubra		
116	Great Blasket (Is.) (blăs′kĕt) .Ire.	52·05 N	10·55 W
102	Great Britain (brĭt′n)......U. K.	56·53 N	0·02 W
166	Great Cataract (Falls) (căt′ȧ-răkt) Ang.-S. W. Afr.	17·25 S	14·20 E
93	Great Corn I...............Nic.	12·10 N	82·54 W
67	Great Divide Basin (dĭ-vīd′ bā′s′n).Wyo.	42·10 N	108·10 W
159	Great Dividing Ra. (dĭ-vī-dĭng rānj).Austl.	35·16 S	146·38 E
	Greater Khingan Mts., see Tahsinganling Shanmo		
71	Greater Leech Ind. Res. (grāt′ĕr lēch).Minn.	47·39 N	94·27 W
95	Great Exuma (I.) (ĕk-sōō′mȧ) Ba. Is.	23·35 N	76·00 W
83	Great Falls................Can.	48·58 N	55·37 W
67	Great Falls (fôlz).........Mont.	47·30 N	111·15 W
79	Great Falls................S. C.	34·32 N	80·53 W
166	Great Fish (R.) (fĭsh)..S. W. Afr.	28·00 S	17·45 E
167	Great Fish (R.) S. Afr. (Natal In.)	33·04 S	26·08 E
95	Great Guana Cay (I.) (gwä′nä) Ba. Is.	24·00 N	76·20 W
94	Great Harbor Cay (I.) (kē) Ba. Is.	25·45 N	77·50 W
95	Great Inagua (I.) (ê-nä′gwä).Ba. Is.	21·00 N	73·15 W
142	Great Indian (Thar) Des. (tŭr) India	32·04 N	70·25 E
94	Great Isaac (I.) (ī′zȧk)....Ba. Is.	26·05 N	79·05 W
139	Great Karimun (Is.) Indon. (Singapore In.)	1·11 N	103·12 E
166	Great Karroo (Mts.) (grāt kȧ′rōō) S. Afr.	32·45 S	22·00 E
167	Great Kei (R.) (kē) S. Afr. (Natal In.)	32·17 S	27·30 E
84	Great Neck (nĕk) N. Y. (New York In.)	40·48 N	73·44 W
154	Great Nicobar I. (nĭk-ô-bär′) India	7·00 N	94·18 E
154	Great Paternoster Is. (pă′tĕr-nŏs-tĕr).Indon.	7·35 S	118·00 E
94	Great Pedro Bluff (Hd.).....Jam.	17·50 N	78·05 W
49	Great Plains, The (Reg.) (plāns) N. A.	45·00 N	104·00 W
95	Great Ragged (I.).........Ba. Is.	22·10 N	75·45 W
126	Great St. Bernard Pass (sānt bĕr-närd′).Switz.-It.	45·53 N	7·15 E
94	Great Sale Cay (I.) (sāl kē) Ba. Is.	27·00 N	78·15 W
67	Great Salt L. (sôlt lāk)......Utah	41·19 N	112·48 W
62	Great Salt Lake Des.........U. S.	41·00 N	113·30 W
72	Great Salt Plains Res.......Okla.	36·56 N	98·14 W
72	Great Sand Dunes Natl. Mon. Colo.	37·56 N	105·25 W
158	Great Sandy Des. (săn′dē)..Austl.	21·50 S	123·10 E
66	Great Sandy Des. (săn′dĭ)....Ore.	43·43 N	120·44 W
64	Great Sitkin (I.) (sĭt-kĭn)..Alaska	52·18 N	176·22 W
86	Great Slave (L.) (slāv)......Can.	61·37 N	114·58 W
78	Great Smoky Mts. Natl. Park (smōk-ê).N. C.	35·43 N	83·20 W
94	Great Stirrup Cay (I.) (stĭr-ŭp) Ba. Is.	25·50 N	77·55 W
158	Great Victoria Des. (vĭk-tō′rĭ-ȧ) Austl.	29·45 S	124·30 E
110	Great Waltham (wôl′thŭm)..Eng.	51·47 N	0·27 E
87	Great Whale (R.) (hwāl)....Can.	54·57 N	75·51 W
117	Great Yarmouth (yär-mŭth) Eng.	52·35 N	1·45 E
118	Grebbestad (grĕb-bĕ-städh)..Swe.	58·42 N	11·15 E
139	Greco, C....Cyprus (Palestine In.)	34·57 N	34·11 E
124	Gredos, Sierra de (Mts.) (syĕr′rä dā grā′dōs).Sp.	40·13 N	5·30 W
102	Greece (grēs)...............Eur.	39·00 N	21·30 E
72	Greeley (grē′lĭ)............Colo.	40·25 N	104·41 W
78	Green (R.)..................Ky.	37·13 N	86.30 W
70	Green (R.)................N. D.	47·05 N	103·05 W
62	Green (R.) (grēn)..........U. S.	38·30 N	110·10 W
65	Green (R.)....Wash. (Seattle In.)	47·17 N	121·57 W
65	Greenbank (grēn′bănk) Wash. (Seattle In.)	48·06 N	122·35 W
77	Green Bay...........Tex. (In.)	29·53 N	95·13 W
71	Green Bay.................Wis.	44·30 N	88·04 W
63	Green B..................U. S.	44·55 N	87·40 W
80	Greencastle (grēn-kȧs′′l).....Ind.	39·40 N	86·50 W
94	Green Cay (I.)...........Ba. Is.	24·05 N	77·10 W
79	Green Cove Springs (kōv)....Fla.	29·56 N	81·42 W
75	Greendale (grēn′dāl) Wis. (Milwaukee In.)	42·56 N	87·59 W
80	Greenfield (grēn′fēld)........Ind.	39·45 N	85·40 W
71	Greenfield.................Iowa	41·16 N	94·30 W
81	Greenfield.................Mass.	42·35 N	72·35 W
73	Greenfield..................Mo.	37·23 N	93·48 W
80	Greenfield.................Ohio	39·15 N	83·25 W
78	Greenfield.................Tenn.	36·08 N	88·45 W
85	Greenfield Park Can. (Montreal In.)	45·29 N	73·29 W
75	Greenhills (grēn-hĭls) Ohio (Cincinnati In.)	39·16 N	84·31 W
49	Greenland (grēn′lănd)......N. A.	74·00 N	40·00 W
83	Greenly (I.) (grēn′lê)........Can.	51·23 N	57·15 W
65	Green Mtn....Ore. (Portland In.)	45·52 N	123·24 W
69	Green Mountain Res.........Colo.	39·50 N	106·20 W
81	Green Mts...................Vt.	43·10 N	73·05 W
116	Greenock (grēn′ŭk).........Scot.	55·55 N	4·45 W
84	Green Pond Mtn. (pŏnd) N. J. (New York In.)	41·00 N	74·32 W
69	Greenriver (grēn-rĭv′ĕr).....Utah	39·00 N	110·05 W
67	Green River...............Wyo.	41·32 N	109·26 W
67	Green R., Blacks Fk........Wyo.	41·08 N	110·27 W
67	Green R., Hams Fk.........Wyo.	41·55 N	110·40 W
78	Greensboro (grēnz′bŭro).....Ala.	32·42 N	87·36 W
78	Greensboro (grēns-bûr′ô).....Ga.	33·34 N	83·11 W
79	Greensboro................N. C.	36·04 N	79·45 W
80	Greensburg (grēnz′bûrg).....Ind.	39·20 N	85·30 W
72	Greensburg (grēns-bûrg)....Kans.	37·36 N	99·17 W
81	Greensburg..................Pa.	40·20 N	79·30 W
78	Greenville (grēn′vĭl)........Ala.	31·49 N	86·39 W
73	Greenville...................Ill.	38·52 N	89·22 W
78	Greenville..................Ky.	37·11 N	87·11 W
164	Greenville..................Lib.	5·06 N	8·44 W
82	Greenville................Maine	45·26 N	69·35 W
80	Greenville................Mich.	43·10 N	85·25 W
78	Greenville.................Miss.	33·25 N	91·00 W
79	Greenville.................N. C.	35·35 N	77·22 W
80	Greenville.................Ohio	40·05 N	84·35 W
80	Greenville...................Pa.	41·20 N	80·25 W
79	Greenville.................S. C.	34·50 N	82·25 W
78	Greenville.................Tenn.	36·08 N	82·50 W
73	Greenville..................Tex.	33·09 N	96·07 W
84	Greenwich .Conn. (New York In.)	41·01 N	73·37 W
110	Greenwich (grĭn′ĭj) ..Eng. (London In.)	51·28 N	0·00
73	Greenwood (grēn-wŏŏd).....Ark.	35·13 N	94·15 W
75	Greenwood.Ind. (Indianapolis In.)	39·37 N	86·07 W
78	Greenwood.................Miss.	33·30 N	90·09 W
79	Greenwood.................S. C.	34·10 N	82·10 W
79	Greenwood (R.)............S. C.	34·17 N	81·55 W
84	Greenwood L. N. Y. (New York In.)	41·13 N	74·20 W
79	Greer (grēr)...............S. C.	34·55 N	81·56 W
123	Grefrath (grĕf′rät) Ger. (Ruhr In.)	51·20 N	6·21 E
70	Gregory (grĕg′ô-rĭ).........S. D.	43·12 N	99·27 W
160	Gregory, L. (grĕg′ô-rê).......Austl.	29·47 S	139·15 E
159	Gregory Ra..................Austl.	19·23 S	143·45 E
111	Greifenberg (grī′fĕn-bĕrgh) Ger. (Munich In.)	48·04 N	11·06 E
120	Greifswald (grīfs′vält).......Ger.	54·05 N	13·24 E
120	Greiz (grīts)................Ger.	50·39 N	12·14 E
136	Gremyachinsk (grâ′myȧ-chĭnsk) Sov. Un. (Urals In.)	58·35 N	57·53 E
118	Grenå (grĕn′ô)..............Den.	56·25 N	10·51 E
78	Grenada (grē-nä′da)........Miss.	33·45 N	89·47 W
93	Grenada I. N. A. (Le. & Wind. Is. In.)	12·02 N	61·27 W
78	Grenada Res................Miss.	33·52 N	89·30 W
122	Grenade (grē-näd′)...........Fr.	43·46 N	1·15 E
93	Grenadines, The (Is.) (grĕn′ȧ-dēnz) Grenada-St. Vincent (Le. & Wind. Is. In.)	12·37 N	61·35 W
84	Grenloch (grĕn-lŏk) N. J. (Philadelphia In.)	39·48 N	75·04 W
123	Grenoble (grē-nô′bl′).........Fr.	45·14 N	5·45 E
70	Grenora (grē-nō′rȧ)........N. D.	48·38 N	103·55 W
81	Grenville (grĕn′vĭl).........Can.	45·40 N	74·35 W
93	Grenville Grenada (Le. & Wind. Is. In.)	12·07 N	61·38 W
65	Gresham (grĕsh′ăm) Ore. (Portland In.)	45·30 N	122·25 W
84	Gretna (grĕt′nȧ) La. (New Orleans In.)	29·56 N	90·03 W
111	Grevelingen Krammer, R. Neth. (Amsterdam In.)	51·42 N	4·03 E
127	Grevená (grĕ′vâ-nä).........Grc.	40·02 N	21·30 E
123	Grevenbroich (grĕ′fen-broik) Ger. (Ruhr In.)	51·05 N	6·36 E
123	Grevenbrück (grĕ′fĕn-brük) Ger. (Ruhr In.)	51·08 N	8·01 E
65	Grey, Pt. (grā) Can. (Vancouver In.)	49·22 N	123·16 W
67	Greybull (grā′bŏŏl).........Wyo.	44·28 N	108·05 W
67	Greybull R.................Wyo.	44·13 N	108·43 W
84	Greycourt (grā-kōrt) N. Y. (New York In.)	41·22 N	74·16 W
168	Greylingstad (grā-lĭng′shtȧt) S. Afr. (Johannesburg & Pretoria In.)	26·40 S	29·13 E
159	Greymouth (grā′mouth) N. Z. (In.)	42·27 S	171·17 E
160	Grey Ra..................Austl.	28·40 S	142·05 E
66	Greys Hbr. (grās).........Wash.	46·55 N	124·23 W
167	Greytown (grā′toun) S. Afr. (Natal In.)	29·07 S	30·38 E
	Greytown, see San Juan del Norte		
65	Grey Wolf Pk. (grā wŏŏlf) Wash. (Seattle In.)	48·53 N	123·12 W
68	Gridley (grĭd′lĭ)...........Calif.	39·22 N	121·43 W
78	Griffin (grĭf′ĭn)..............Ga.	33·15 N	84·16 W
64	Griffin Pt.................Alaska	70·05 N	143·21 W
160	Griffith (grĭf-ĭth)..........Austl.	34·16 S	146·10 E
75	Griffith........Ind. (Chicago In.)	41·31 N	87·26 W
129	Grigoriopol′ (grĭ′gor-i-ô′pôl) Sov. Un.	47·09 N	29·18 E
91	Grijalva (R.) (grē-häl′vä)...Mex.	18·15 N	92·45 W
160	Grim, C. (grĭm)...........Austl.	40·43 S	144·30 E
120	Grimma (grĭm′ȧ)............Ger.	51·14 N	12·43 E
85	Grimsby (grĭmz′bĭ) Can. (Toronto In.)	43·11 N	79·33 W
112	Grimsey (I.) (grĭms′å)........Ice.	66·30 N	17·50 W
118	Grimstad (grĭm-städh)......Nor.	58·21 N	8·30 E
71	Grinnel (grĭ-nĕl′)...........Iowa	41·44 N	92·44 W
71	Griswold (grĭz′wŭld)........Iowa	41·11 N	95·05 W
128	Griva (grē′vȧ)..........Sov. Un.	55·51 N	26·31 E
83	Groais (I.).................Can.	50·56 N	55·35 W
119	Grobina (grō′bĭ̤nĭa)......Sov. Un.	56·35 N	21·10 E
168	Groblersdal S. Afr. (Johannesburg & Pretoria In.)	25·11 S	29·25 E
121	Grodno (grôd′nŏ).......Sov. Un.	53·40 N	23·49 E
121	Grodzisk Masowieki (grō′jēsk mä-zō-vyĕts′ke).Pol.	52·06 N	20·40 E
120	Grodzisk Wielkopolski (grō′jēsk vyĕl-ko-pōl′skē).Pol.	52·14 N	16·22 E
77	Groesbeck (grōs′bĕk)........Tex.	31·32 N	96·31 W
122	Groix, I. de (ēl dē grwä′)......Fr.	47·39 N	3·28 W
121	Grójec (grŏŏ′yĕts)...........Pol.	51·53 N	20·52 E
120	Gronau (grō′nou)...........Ger.	52·12 N	7·05 E
117	Groningen (grō′nĭng-ĕn)....Neth.	53·13 N	6·30 E
158	Groote Eyelandt (I.) (grō′tē ī′lănt).Austl.	13·50 S	137·30 E
166	Grootfontein (grōt′fŏn-tān′) S. W. Afr.	18·15 S	19·30 E
166	Grootkop (Mtn.) S. Afr. (Cape Town In.)	34·11 S	18·23 E
168	Groot Marico S. Afr. (Johannesburg & Pretoria In.)	25·36 S	26·23 E
168	Groot R. S. Afr. (Johannesburg & Pretoria In.)	25·13 S	26·20 E
166	Groot Vloer (L.) (grōt′ vlōōr′) S. Afr.	30·00 S	20·16 E
83	Gros Morne (Mtn.) (grō môrn′) Can.	49·37 N	57·45 W
83	Gros Pate (Mtn.)...........Can.	50·16 N	57·25 W
111	Gross Behnitz (grōss bĕ′nētz) Ger. (Berlin In.)	52·35 N	12·45 E
75	Grosse I. (grōs) Mich. (Detroit In.)	42·08 N	83·09 W
85	Grosse Isle (ĭl′) Can. (Winnipeg In.)	50·04 N	97·27 W
166	Grosse Karras (Mts.)..S. W. Afr.	27·10 S	18·30 E
120	Grossenhain (grōs′ĕn-hīn)....Ger.	51·17 N	13·33 E
111	Grossenzersdorf.Aus. (Vienna In.)	48·13 N	16·33 E
75	Grosse Pointe (point′) Mich. (Detroit In.)	42·23 N	82·54 W
75	Grosse Pointe Farms (färm) Mich. (Detroit In.)	42·25 N	82·53 W
75	Grosse Pointe Park (pärk) Mich. (Detroit In.)	42·23 N	82·55 W
126	Grosseto (grôs-sā′tō)..........It.	42·46 N	11·09 E
120	Grossglockner Pk. (glôk′nēr).Aus.	47·06 N	12·45 E
111	Gross Höbach (hû′bäk) Ger. (Munich In.)	48·21 N	11·36 E
111	Gross Kreutz (kroitz) Ger. (Berlin In.)	52·24 N	12·47 E
123	Gross Reken (rĕ′kĕn) Ger. (Ruhr In.)	51·50 N	7·20 E
111	Gross Schonebeck (shō′nĕ-bĕk) Ger. (Berlin In.)	52·54 N	13·32 E
67	Gros Ventre R. (grōvĕn′t′r).Wyo.	43·38 N	110·34 W
81	Groton (grôt′ŭn)..........Conn.	41·20 N	72·00 W
83	Groton.......Mass. (Boston In.)	42·37 N	71·34 W
70	Groton....................Nebr.	42·44 N	97·32 W
127	Grottaglie (grôt-täl′yā)........It.	40·32 N	17·26 E

ng-sing; ŋ-baŋk; N-nasalized n; nŏd; cŏmmit; ōld; ôbey; ôrder; fōōd; fŏŏt; ou-out; s-soft; sh-dish; th-thin; pūre; ûnite; ûrn; stŭd; circŭs; ü-as "y" in study; ′-indeterminate vowel.

Page	Name Pronunciation Region	Lat. °′	Long. °′
86	Grouard........Can.	55·35 N	116·11 W
83	Groveland (grōv'lănd) Mass. (Boston In.)	42·45 N	71·02 W
81	Groveton (grōv'tŭn).......N. H.	44·35 N	71·30 W
77	Groveton........Tex.	31·04 N	95·07 W
133	Groznyy (grôz'nĭ).......Sov. Un.	43·20 N	45·40 E
121	Grudziadz (grōō'jyônts)......Pol.	53·30 N	18·48 E
111	Grumpholds-Kirchen Aus. (Wien In.)	48·03 N	16·17 E
71	Grundy Center (grŭn'dĭ sĕn'tẽr) Iowa	42·22 N	92·45 W
90	Gruñidora (grōō-nyē-dō'rō)..Mex.	24·10 N	101·49 W
111	Grunwald (grōōn'väld) Ger. (Munich In.)	48·04 N	11·34 E
128	Gryazi (gryä'zĭ)........Sov. Un.	52·31 N	39·59 E
128	Gryazovets (gryä'zô-vĕts) Sov. Un.	58·52 N	40·14 E
120	Gryfice (grĭ'fĭ-tsĕ)..........Pol.	53·55 N	15·11 E
120	Gryfino (grĭ'fē-nô)...........Pol.	53·16 N	14·30 E
93	Guabito (gwä-bē'tô)........Pan.	9·30 N	82·33 W
94	Guacanayabo, Golfo de (G.) (gôl-fô-dĕ-gwä-kä-nä-yä'bō)...Cuba	20·30 N	77·40 W
99	Guacara (gwä'-kä-rä)...Ven. (In.)	10·16 N	67·48 W
98	Guacarí (gwä-kä-rē')....Col. (In.)	3·45 N	76·20 W
101	Guaçuí (gwä'-sōō-ē') Braz. (Rio de Janeiro In.)	20·47 S	41·40 W
90	Guadalajara (gwä-dhä-lä-hä'rä) Mex.	20·41 N	103·21 W
124	Guadalajara (gwä-dä-lä-kä'-rä) Sp.	40·37 N	3·10 W
124	Guadalcanal (gwä-dhäl-kä-näl') Sp.	38·05 N	5·48 W
159	Guadalcanal (I.).........Sol. Is.	9·48 S	158·43 E
90	Guadalcázar (gwä-dhäl-kä'zär) Mex.	22·38 N	100·24 W
124	Guadalete (R.) (gwä-dhä-lā'tā).Sp.	38·53 N	5·38 W
124	Guadalhorce (R.) (gwä-dhäl-ôr'thā).Sp.	37·05 N	4·50 W
124	Guadalimar (R.) (gwä-dhä-lē-mär').Sp.	38·29 N	2·53 W
125	Guadalope (R.) (gwä-dä-lô-pĕ).Sp.	40·48 N	0·10 W
124	Guadalquivir, Río (R.) (rē'-ō-gwä-dhäl-kē-vēr').Sp.	5·57 N	6·00 W
76	Guadalupe..............Mex.	31·23 N	106·06 W
124	Guadalupe, Sierra de (Mts.) (Syĕr'rä dā gwä-dhä-lōō'pā).Sp.	39·30 N	5·25 W
88	Guadalupe I.............Mex.	29·00 N	118·45 W
76	Guadalupe Mts.....N. Mex.-Tex.	32·00 N	104·55 W
76	Guadalupe Pk..........Tex.	31·55 N	104·55 W
76	Guadalupe R. (gwä-dhä-lōō'pä) Tex.	29·54 N	99·03 W
124	Guadarrama, Sierra de (Mts.) (gwä-dhär-rä'mä).Sp.	41·00 N	3·40 W
125	Guadarrama (R.)(gwä-dhär-rä'mä) Sp. (Madrid In.)	40·34 N	3·58 W
93	Guadeloupe (Is.) (gwä-dē-lōōp') N. A. (Le. & Wind. Is. In.)	16·07 N	61·19 W
93	Guadeloupe Pass N. A. (Le. & Wind. Is. In.)	16·26 N	62·00 W
94	Guadiana, Bahía de (B.) (bä-ē'ä-dĕ-gwä-dhē-ä'nä).Cuba	22·10 N	84·35 W
124	Guadiana, Rio (R.) (rē'ō-gwä-dvä'nä).Port.	37·43 N	7·43 W
124	Guadiana Alto (R.) (äl'tō).....Sp.	39·02 N	2·52 W
124	Guadiana Menor (R.) (mä'nôr) Sp.	37·43 N	2·45 W
124	Guadiaro (R.) (gwä-dhē-ä'rō)..Sp.	37·38 N	5·25 W
125	Guadiato (R.) (gwä-dhē-ä'tō)..Sp.	38·10 N	5·05 W
124	Guadiela (R.) (gwä-dhē-ā'lä)..Sp.	40·23 N	2·23 W
124	Guadix (gwä-dhēsh').........Sp.	37·18 N	3·09 W
99	Guaire (R.) (gwī'-rĕ)...Ven. (In.)	10·25 N	66·43 W
94	Guajaba, Cayo (I.) (kä'yō-gwä-hä'bä).Cuba	21·50 N	77·35 W
98	Guajará Mirim (gwä-zhä-rä'mē-rēN'.Braz.	10·58 S	65·12 W
98	Guajira, Pen. de (Pen.) (pĕ-nē'ng-sōō-lä-dĕ-gwä-kē'rä) Col.-Ven.	12·35 N	73·00 W
92	Gualán (gwä-län')........Guat.	15·08 N	89·21 W
101	Gualeguay (gwä-lĕ-gwä'y) Arg. (Buenos Aires In.)	33·10 S	59·20 W
101	Gualeguay (R.) Arg. (Buenos Aires In.)	32·49 S	59·05 W
101	Gualeguaychú (gwä-lä-gwī-chōō') Arg. (Buenos Aires In.)	33·01 S	58·32 W
101	Gualeguaychú (R.) Arg. (Buenos Aires In.)	32·58 S	58·27 W
100	Gualicho, Salina (F.) (sä-lē'nä-gwä-lē'chō).Arg.	40·20 S	65·15 W
156	Guam (I.) (gwäm).......Oceania	14·00 N	143·20 E
100	Guaminí (gwä-mē-nē').......Arg.	37·02 S	62·21 W
98	Guamo (gwà'mō)........Col. (In.)	4·02 N	74·58 W
95	Guanabacoa (gwä-nä-bä-kō'ä) Cuba (Havana In.)	23·08 N	82·19 W
100	Guanabara (gwä-nä-bä'rä)..Braz.	23·03 N	43·32 W
100	Guanabara, Baia de (B.) Braz. (In.)	22·44 S	43·09 W
92	Guanacaste Cord. (Mts.) (kôr-dĕl-yĕ'rä-gwä-nä-käs'tä) C. R.	10·54 N	85·27 W
88	Guanacevi (gwä-nä-sĕ-vē')..Mex.	25·30 N	105·45 W
94	Guanahacabibes, Pen. de (pĕ-nēn-sōō-lä-dĕ-gwä-nä hä-kä-bē'bäs) Cuba	21·55 N	84·35 W
94	Guanajay (gwä-nä-hī')......Cuba	22·55 N	82·40 W
90	Guanajuato (gwä-nä-hwä'tō) Mex.	21·01 N	101·16 W
88	Guanajuato (State).........Mex.	21·00 N	101·00 W
99	Guanape (gwä-nä'pĕ)...Ven. (In.)	9·55 N	65·32 W
99	Guanape (R.)........Ven. (In.)	9·52 N	65·20 W
98	Guanare (gwä-nä'rä)........Ven.	8·57 N	69·47 W
100	Guanduçu (R.) (gwä'n-dōō'sōō) Braz. (In.)	22·50 S	43·40 W
94	Guane (gwä'nā)...........Cuba	22·10 N	84·05 W
99	Guanta (gwän'tä)......Ven. (In.)	10·15 N	64·35 W
95	Guantánamo (gwän-tä'nä-mō) Cuba	20·10 N	75·10 W
95	Guantanamo, Bahía de (B.) (bä-ē'ä-dĕ).Cuba	19·35 N	75·35 W
101	Guapé (gwà-pĕ') Braz. (Rio de Janeiro In.)	20·45 S	45·55 W
93	Guapiles (gwä-pē-lĕs).......C. R.	10·05 N	83·54 W
100	Guapimirim (gwä-pē-mē-rē'N) Braz. (In.)	22·31 S	42·59 W
98	Guaporé (R.) (gwä-pô-rā') Bol.-Braz.	12·11 S	63·47 W
98	Guaqui (guä'kē)...........Bol.	16·42 S	68·47 W
125	Guara, Sierra de (Mts.) (sē-ĕ'r-rä-dĕ-gwä'rä).Sp.	42·24 N	0·15 W
99	Guarabira (gwä-rä-bē'rä)....Braz.	6·49 S	35·27 W
98	Guaranda (gwä-rän'dä)........Ec.	1·39 S	78·57 W
99	Guarapari (gwä-rä-pä'rē)....Braz.	20·34 S	40·31 W
101	Guarapiranga, Represa do (Res.) (r'ĕ-prĕ-sä-dô-gwä'rä-pē-rä'n-gä) Braz. (Rio de Janeiro In.)	23·45 S	46·44 W
100	Guarapuava (gwä-rä-pwä'vä) Braz.	25·29 S	51·26 W
101	Guaratinguetá (guä-rä-tĭN-gä-tä') Braz. (Rio de Janeiro In.)	22·49 S	45·10 W
124	Guarda (gwär'dä)..........Port.	40·32 N	7·17 W
124	Guareña (gwä-rā'nyä)........Sp.	38·52 N	6·08 W
99	Guaribe (R.) (gwä-rē'bĕ) Ven. (In.)	9·48 N	65·17 W
99	Guarico (State)........Ven. (In.)	9·42 N	67·25 W
99	Guárico (R.)...........Ven. (In.)	9·50 N	67·07 W
101	Guarulhos (gwà-rōō'l-yôs) Braz. (Rio de Janeiro In.)	32·28 S	46·30 W
101	Guarus (gwà'rōōs) Braz. (Rio de Janeiro In.)	21·44 S	41·19 W
98	Guasca (gwäs'kä).......Col. (In.)	4·52 N	73·52 W
99	Guasipati (gwä-sē-pä'tē).....Ven.	7·26 N	61·57 W
126	Guastalla (gwäs-täl'lä)........It.	44·53 N	10·39 E
74	Guasti (gwäs'tĭ) Calif. (Los Angeles In.)	34·04 N	117·35 W
92	Guatemala (guä-tà-mä'lä)..Guat.	14·37 N	90·32 W
88	Guatemala...............N. A.	15·45 N	91·45 W
99	Guatire (gwä-tē'rĕ).....Ven. (In.)	10·28 N	66·34 W
101	Guaxupé (gwä-shōō-pĕ') Braz. (Rio de Janeiro In.)	21·18 S	46·42 W
94	Guayabal (gwä-yä-bä'l).....Cuba	20·40 N	77·40 W
90	Guayalejo (R.) (gwä-yä-lĕ'hō) Mex.	23·24 N	99·09 W
89	Guayama (gwä-yä'mä) P. R. (Puerto Rico In.)	18·00 N	66·08 W
95	Guayamouc (R.)............Hai.	19·05 N	72·00 W
92	Guayape R.................Hond.	14·39 N	86·37 W
98	Guayaquil (gwī-ä-kēl').......Ec.	2·16 S	79·53 W
98	Guayaquil, Golfo de (G.) (gôl-fô-dĕ).Ec.	3·03 S	82·12 W
98	Guayiare (R.) (gwä-yä'rĕ)....Col.	3·35 N	69·28 W
88	Guaymas (gwä'y-mäs)......Mex.	27·49 N	110·58 W
95	Guayubin (gwä-yōō-bē'n) Dom. Rep.	19·40 N	71·25 W
92	Guazacapán (gwä-zä-kä-pän') Guat.	14·04 N	90·26 W
136	Gubakha (gōō-bä'kä) Sov. Un. (Urals In.)	58·53 N	57·35 E
126	Gubbio (gōōb'byō)...........It.	43·23 N	12·36 E
125	Gudar, Sierra de (Mts.) (syĕr'rä dä gōō'dhär).Sp.	40·28 N	0·47 W
118	Gudenaa (R.)..............Den.	56·20 N	9·47 E
118	Gudinge Fjärden (Fd.)......Swe.	57·43 N	16·55 E
118	Gudvangen (gōōdh'väŋ-gĕn).Nor.	60·52 N	6·45 E
123	Guebwiller (gĕb-vē-lâr').......Fr.	47·53 N	7·10 E
164	Guelma (gwĕl'mä)..........Alg.	36·32 N	7·17 E
85	Guelph (gwĕlf).Can. (Toronto In.)	43·33 N	80·15 W
114	Guemar (gē-mär')...........Alg.	33·32 N	6·42 E
99	Güere (gwĕ'rĕ) (R.)...Ven. (In.)	9·39 N	65·00 W
122	Guéret (gā-rĕ')...............Fr.	46·09 N	1·52 E
122	Guernsey (I.) (gûrn'zĭ)......Eur.	49·27 N	2·36 W
114	Guerrara (gĕr-rä'rä).........Alg.	32·50 N	4·26 E
76	Guerrero (gĕr-rā'rō).........Mex.	26·47 N	99·20 W
76	Guerrero...................Mex.	28·20 N	100·24 W
122	Gueugnon (gû-nyôN')........Fr.	46·35 N	4·01 E
77	Gueydan (gā'dăn)...........La.	30·01 N	92·31 W
100	Guia de Pacobaíba (gwē'ä-dĕ-pä'kō-bī'bä).Braz. (In.)	22·42 S	43·10 W
96	Guiana Highlands (Mts.)...Braz.	3·20 N	60·00 W
91	Guichicovi (San Juan) (gwē-chē-kō'vē).Mex.	16·58 N	95·10 W
125	Guidonia (gwē-dō'nyä) It. (Rome In.)	42·00 N	12·45 E
123	Guignes (gēN'yĕ)...Fr. (Paris In.)	48·38 N	2·48 E
99	Güigüe (gwē'gwĕ)......Ven. (In.)	10·05 N	67·48 W
92	Guija, L. (gē'hä)............Sal.	14·16 N	89·21 W
110	Guildford (gĭl'fẽrd) Eng. (London In.)	51·13 N	0·34 W
75	Guilford (gĭl'fẽrd) Ind. (Cincinnati In.)	39·10 N	84·55 W
124	Guimarães (gē-mä-rănsh')...Port.	41·27 N	8·22 W
163	Guinea (gĭn'ē).............Afr.	10·48 N	12·28 W
163	Guinea, G. of...............Afr.	2·00 N	1·00 E
94	Güines (gwē'näs)...........Cuba	22·50 N	82·05 W
122	Guingamp (găN-găN')........Fr.	48·35 N	3·10 W
94	Güira de Melena (gwē'rä dā mä-lā'nä).Cuba	22·45 N	82·30 W
98	Güiria (gwē-rē'ä)...........Ven.	10·43 N	62·16 W
114	Guir R..............Mor.-Alg.	31·55 N	2·48 W
123	Guise (guēz)................Fr.	49·54 N	3·37 E
92	Guisisil (Vol.) (gē-sē-sēl')....Nic.	12·40 N	86·11 W
142	Gujarat (State).............India	22·54 N	79·00 E
142	Gujranwala (gōōj-rän'va-lä) W. Pak.	32·08 N	74·14 E
118	Gula (R.) (gōō'lä)..........Nor.	62·55 N	10·45 E
143	Gulbarga (gōōl-bûr'gä).......India	17·25 N	76·52 E
128	Gulbene (gōōl-bă'nĕ)....Sov. Un.	57·09 N	26·49 E
78	Gulfport (gŭlf'pōrt)..........Miss.	30·24 N	89·05 W
129	Gulyay Pole............Sov. Un.	47·39 N	36·12 E
155	Gumaca (gōō-mä-kä') Phil. (Manila In.)	13·55 N	122·06 E
165	Gumbari (gōōm-bä-rē)....Con. L.	2·45 N	29·00 E
136	Gumbeyka R. (gōōm-bĕy'kà) Sov. Un. (Urals In.)	53·20 N	59·42 E
164	Gumel.....................Nig.	12·43 N	9·19 E
120	Gummersbach (gōōm'ĕrs-bäk).Ger.	51·02 N	7·34 E
111	Gumpoldskirchen...........Aus.	48·04 N	16·15 E
142	Guna......................India	24·44 N	77·17 E
160	Gunnedah (gŭ'nē-dä).......Austl.	31·00 S	150·10 E
69	Gunnison (gŭn'ĭ-sŭn).......Colo.	38·30 N	107·00 W
69	Gunnison...................Utah	39·10 N	111·50 W
69	Gunnison (R.)..............Colo.	38·50 N	107·55 W
78	Guntersville (gŭn'tẽrz-vĭl)....Ala.	34·20 N	86·19 W
78	Guntersville L..............Ala.	34·30 N	86·20 W
111	Guntramsdorf..Aus. (Vienna In.)	48·04 N	16·19 E
143	Guntūr (gōōn'tōōr)........India	16·22 N	80·29 E
155	Gunungapi (I.) (gōō'nōōng-ä'pē) Indon.	6·52 S	127·15 E
139	Gunungkidjang Indon. (Singapore In.)	0·55 N	104·39 E
73	Gurdon (gûr'dŭn)...........Ark.	33·56 N	93·10 W
99	Gurgucia (R.) (gōōr-gōō'syä) Braz.	8·12 S	43·49 W
75	Gurnee (gûr'nē).Ill. (Chicago In.)	42·22 N	87·55 W
118	Gursköy (I.) (gōōrskûē).....Nor.	62·18 N	5·20 E
99	Gurupá (gōō-rōō-pä').......Braz.	1·28 S	51·32 W
99	Gurupi, Serra do (Mts.) (sĕ'r-rä-dô-gōō-rōō-pē').Braz.	5·32 S	47·02 W
99	Gurupí (R.) (gōō-rōō-pē')...Braz.	2·37 S	46·45 W
142	Guru Sikhar Mt.............India	29·42 N	72·50 E
133	Gur'yev (gōōr'yĕf)......Sov. Un.	47·10 N	51·50 E
134	Gur'yevsk (gōōr-yĭfsk')..Sov. Un.	54·14 N	86·07 E
164	Gusau (gōō-zä'ōō)..........Nig.	12·11 N	6·40 E
119	Gusev (gōō'sĕf)........Sov. Un.	54·35 N	22·15 E
127	Gusinje (gōō-sēn'yĕ)........Yugo.	42·34 N	19·54 E
128	Gus'-Khrustal'nyy (gōōs-Krōō-stäl'ny').Sov. Un.	55·39 N	40·41 E
91	Gustavo A. Madero (gōōs-tä'vô-ä-mä-dĕ'rō) Mex. (Mexico City In.)	19·29 N	99·07 W
120	Gustrow (güs'trō)...........Ger.	53·48 N	12·12 E
121	Gúta (gōō'tä)..............Czech.	47·54 N	17·59 E
120	Gütersloh (gü'tĕrs-lo)........Ger.	51·54 N	8·22 E
73	Guthrie (gŭth'rĭ)..........Okla.	35·52 N	97·26 W
71	Guthrie Center.............Iowa	41·41 N	94·33 W
91	Gutiérrez Zamora (gōō-tĭ-âr'räz zä-mō'rä).Mex.	20·27 N	97·17 W
71	Guttenberg (gŭt'ĕn-bûrg)....Iowa	42·48 N	91·09 W
72	Guymon (gī'mŏn)..........Okla.	36·41 N	101·29 W
83	Guysborough (gīz'bŭr-ō).....Can.	45·25 N	61·30 W
119	Gvardeysk (gvär-dĕysk').Sov. Un.	54·39 N	21·11 E
144	Gwadar (gwä'dŭr).......W. Pak.	25·15 N	62·29 E
165	Gwane (gwän)...........Con. L.	4·49 N	26·46 E
166	Gwelo (gwā'lō)...........S. Rh.	19·15 S	29·48 E
71	Gwinn (gwĭn)...............Mich.	46·15 N	87·30 W
146	Gyangtse (gyäng'tsĕ')......China	29·00 N	89·28 E
142	Gyantse.....................China	28·53 N	89·39 E
135	Gydan, Khrebet (Kolymskiy) (Mts.).Sov. Un.	61·45 N	155·00 E
134	Gydanskiy, P-Ov (Pen.).Sov. Un.	70·42 N	76·03 E
160	Gympie (gĭm'pē)...........Austl.	26·20 S	152·50 E
121	Gyöngyös (dyûn'dyûsh)....Hung.	47·47 N	19·55 E
121	Györ (dyûr)...............Hung.	47·40 N	17·37 E
153	Gyōtoku (gyō'tō-kōō') Jap. (Tōkyō In.)	35·42 N	139·56 E
86	Gypsumville (jĭp'sŭm'vĭl)....Can.	51·49 N	98·42 W
121	Gyula (dyōō'lä)...........Hung.	46·38 N	21·18 E
128	Gzhatsk (g'zhätsk)......Sov. Un.	55·32 N	34·58 E
123	Haan (hän)......Ger. (Ruhr In.)	51·12 N	7·00 E
119	Haapamäki (häp'ä-mĕ-kĕ)....Fin.	62·16 N	24·20 E
119	Haapsalu (häp'sä-lōō)...Sov. Un.	58·56 N	23·33 E
111	Haar (här)......Ger. (Munich In.)	48·06 N	11·44 E
139	Ha'arava (R.) (Araba) Isr. (Palestine In.)	30·32 N	35·16 E
111	Haarlem (här'lĕm) Neth. (Amsterdam In.)	52·22 N	4·37 E
94	Habana (State) (hä-vä'nä)..Cuba	22·55 N	82·15 W
125	Habibas (C.) (hä-bē'bäs).....Alg.	35·50 N	0·45 W
152	Hachinohe (hä'chē-nō'hā)....Jap.	40·29 N	141·40 E
153	Hachiōji (hä'chē-ō'jē).......Jap.	35·39 N	139·18 E
84	Hackensack (hăk'ĕn-săk) N. J. (New York In.)	40·54 N	74·03 W
84	Haddonfield (hăd'ŭn-fēld) N. J. (Philadelphia In.)	39·53 N	75·02 W
84	Haddon Heights (hăd'ŭn hīts) N. J. (Philadelphia In.)	39·53 N	75·03 W
164	Hadejia (hä-dā'jä)..........Nig.	12·32 N	10·04 E
139	Hadera (Kä-dĕ'rä) Isr. (Palestine In.)	32·26 N	34·55 E
118	Haderslev (hä'dhĕrs-lĕv).....Den.	55·17 N	9·28 E
168	Hadibu...Som. (Horn of Afr. In.)	12·40 N	53·50 E
65	Hadlock (hăd'lŏk) Wash. (Seattle In.)	48·02 N	122·46 W
144	Hadramawt (Reg.).Sau. Ar.-Aden	15·15 N	48·32 E
152	Haeju (hä'ĕ-jū)............Kor.	38·03 N	125·42 E
150	Haerhpin (Harbin) (här-bēn') China	45·40 N	126·30 E
112	Hafnarfjördhur.............Ice.	64·02 N	21·32 W
168	Hafun, Ras (C.) (hä-fōōn') Som. (Horn of Afr. In.)	10·15 N	51·35 E
67	Hageland (häge'lănd)......Mont.	48·53 N	108·43 W
123	Hagen (hä'gĕn)...Ger. (Ruhr In.)	51·21 N	7·29 E
85	Hagermans Corners (hăg'ẽr-măns kôr'nẽr).Can. (Toronto In.)	43·51 N	79·19 W
80	Hagerstown (hā'gẽrz-toun)...Ind.	39·55 N	85·10 W
81	Hagerstown.................Md.	39·40 N	77·45 W
153	Hagi (hä'gĭ)................Jap.	34·25 N	131·25 E
122	Hague, C. de la (dē lä äg')....Fr.	49·44 N	1·55 W
	Hague, The, see 's Gravenhagen		
123	Haguenau (ág'nō')...........Fr.	48·47 N	7·48 E
148	Haian (hăī'äN)..............China	32·35 N	120·25 E
153	Haibara (hä'ē-bä'rä)........Jap.	34·29 N	135·57 E
150	Haich'eng..................China	40·58 N	122·45 E
148	Haichou Wan (B.) (hăī'jō wän) China	34·58 N	119·27 E
139	Haifa (hä'ē-fä).Isr. (Palestine In.)	32·48 N	35·00 E
151	Haifeng (hä'ē-fĕng').......China	23·00 N	115·20 E

ăt; finăl; rāte; senâte; ärm; àsk; sofà; fâre; ch-choose; dh-as th in other; bē; ēvent; bĕt; recĕnt; cratẽr; g-go; gh-guttural g; bĭt; ĭ-short neutral; rīde; K-guttural k as ch in German ich;

Page	Name Pronunciation Region	Lat. °′	Long. °′
148	Haifuchen (hāī'fōō'jĕn) ..... China	31·57 N	121·48 E
144	Hā'il (hāl) ..... Sau. Ar.	27·30 N	41·57 E
150	Hailaerh (Hailar) (hä-ê-lär') China	49·10 N	118·40 E
	Hailar, see Hailaerh		
67	Hailey (hā'lĭ) ..... Idaho	43·31 N	114·19 W
73	Haileyville (hā'lĭ-vĭl) ..... Okla.	34·51 N	95·34 W
152	Hailin (hä'ê-lēn') ..... China	44·31 N	129·11 E
151	Hailing Tao (I.) ..... China	21·30 N	112·15 E
150	Hailun (hä'ê-lōōn') ..... China	47·18 N	126·50 E
150	Hailung (hä'ê-lōōng') ..... China	42·32 N	125·52 E
151	Hainan Tao (I.) (hä'e-nän'dou) China	19·00 N	111·10 E
111	Hainburg an der Donau Aus. (Vienna In.)	48·09 N	16·57 E
64	Haines (hānz) ..... Alaska	59·10 N	135·38 W
79	Haines City ..... Fla. (In.)	28·05 N	81·38 W
151	Haiphong (hī'fông') (hä'êp-hŏng) Viet.	20·52 N	106·40 E
89	Haiti (hā'tĭ) ..... N. A.	19·00 N	72·15 W
150	Haitien (hī'tyĕn') China (Peking In.)	39·59 N	116·17 E
165	Haiya ..... Sud.	18·40 N	37·45 E
121	Hajduböszörmeny (hôl'dōō-bû'sûr-mān') . Hung.	47·41 N	21·30 E
121	Hajduhadház (hô'ĭ-dōō-hôd'häz) Hung.	47·32 N	21·32 E
121	Hajdunánás (hô'ĭ-dōō-nä'näsh) Hung.	47·52 N	21·27 E
121	Hajduszoboszló (hô'ĭ-dōō-sô'bôs-lō) . Hung.	47·24 N	21·25 E
152	Hakodate (hä-kō-dä'tå) ..... Jap.	41·46 N	140·42 E
153	Haku-San (Mtn.) (hä'kōō-sän') Jap.	36·11 N	136·45 E
91	Halachó (ä-lä-chō') ..... Mex.	20·28 N	90·06 W
165	Halaib (hä-lä'êb) ..... U. A. R.	22·10 N	36·40 E
157	Halawa (hä-lä'wä) ... Hawaii (In.)	21·12 N	156·55 E
139	Halbā ..... Leb. (Palestine In.)	34·33 N	36·03 E
111	Halbe (häl'bĕ) ... Ger. (Berlin In.)	52·07 N	13·43 E
120	Halberstadt (häl'bĕr-shtät) ... Ger.	51·54 N	11·07 E
155	Halcon, Mt. (häl-kōn') Phil. (Manila In.)	13·19 N	120·55 E
118	Halden (häl'dĕn) ..... Nor.	59·10 N	11·21 E
110	Hale (hāl) ..... Eng.	53·22 N	2·20 W
157	Haleakala Crater (hä'lā-ä'kä-lä) Hawaii (In.)	20·44 N	156·15 W
157	Haleakala Natl. Park . Hawaii (In.)	20·46 N	156·00 W
75	Hales Corners (hālz kŏr'nērz) Wis. (Milwaukee In.)	42·56 N	88·03 W
110	Halesowen (hālz'ō-wĕn) ..... Eng.	52·26 N	2·03 W
81	Halethorpe (hāl-thôrp) ..... Md.	39·15 N	76·40 W
78	Haleyville (hā'lĭ-vĭl) ..... Ala.	34·11 N	87·36 W
65	Half Moon Bay (häf'mōōn) . Calif. (San Francisco In.)	37·28 N	122·26 W
167	Halfway House (häf-wā hous) S. Afr. (Johannesburg & Pretoria In.)	26·00 S	28·08 E
111	Halfweg . . Neth. (Amsterdam In.)	52·23 N	4·45 E
82	Halifax (hăl'ĭ-făks) ..... Can.	44·40 N	63·36 W
110	Halifax ..... Eng.	53·44 N	1·52 W
159	Halifax B. (hăl'ĭ-făx) ..... Austl.	18·56 S	147·07 E
82	Halifax Hbr ..... Can.	44·35 N	63·25 W
139	Halīlah (R.) Jordan (Palestine In.)	30·28 N	35·57 E
152	Halla San (Mt.) (häl'lä-sän) . Kor.	33·20 N	126·37 E
139	Hallat 'Ammar Sau. Ar. (Palestine In.)	29·09 N	36·05 E
111	Halle (häl'lĕ) ... Bel. (Brussels In.)	50·45 N	4·13 E
120	Halle ..... Ger.	51·30 N	11·59 E
77	Hallettsville (hăl'ĕts-vĭl) ..... Tex.	29·26 N	96·55 W
70	Hallock (hăl'ŭk) ..... Minn.	48·46 N	96·57 W
87	Hall Pen (hôl) ..... Can.	63·14 N	65·40 W
77	Halls Bay ..... Tex. (In.)	29·55 N	95·23 W
118	Hallsberg (häls'bĕrgh) ..... Swe.	59·04 N	15·04 E
158	Halls Creek (hôlz) ..... Austl.	18·15 S	127·45 E
82	Halls Strm. (hôls) .... Can.-Maine	45·07 N	71·34 W
155	Halmahera (I.) (häl-mä-hä'rä) Indon.	0·45 N	128·45 E
118	Halmstad (hälm'städ) ..... Swe.	56·40 N	12·46 E
118	Halse Fd. (häl'sĕ fyôrd) ..... Nor.	63·03 N	8·23 E
84	Halsey (hôl'zê) N. J. (New York In.)	41·06 N	74·45 W
118	Hälsingborg (hĕl'sĭng-bôrgh) . Swe.	56·04 N	12·40 E
73	Halstead (hôl'stĕd) ..... Kans.	38·02 N	97·36 W
151	Halt'an Tao (I.) ..... China	25·40 N	119·45 E
123	Haltern (häl'tĕrn) Ger. (Ruhr In.)	51·45 N	7·10 E
74	Haltom City (hôl'tŏm) Tex. (Dallas, Fort Worth In.)	32·48 N	97·17 W
	Halunrshan, see Wenchüan		
111	Halvarenbeek Neth. (Amsterdam In.)	51·29 N	5·10 E
115	Hama (hä'mä) ..... Syr.	35·08 N	36·53 E
144	Hamadān (hŭ-mŭ-dän') ..... Iran	34·45 N	48·07 E
153	Hamamatsu (hä'mä-mät'sōō) . Jap.	34·41 N	137·43 E
118	Hamar (hä'mär) ..... Nor.	60·49 N	11·05 E
153	Hamasaka (hä'mä-sä'kä) ..... Jap.	35·37 N	134·27 E
123	Hamborn (häm'bōrn) Ger. (Ruhr In.)	51·30 N	6·43 E
73	Hamburg (hăm'bûrg) ..... Ark.	33·15 N	91·49 W
111	Hamburg (häm'bōōrgh) Ger. (Hamburg In.)	53·34 N	10·02 E
70	Hamburg ..... Iowa	40·39 N	95·40 W
84	Hamburg ... N. J. (New York In.)	41·09 N	74·35 W
75	Hamburg ..... N. Y. (Buffalo In.)	42·44 N	78·51 W
167	Hamburg (hăm'bûrg) S. Afr. (Natal In.)	33·18 S	27·28 E
81	Hamden (hăm'dĕn) ..... Conn.	41·20 N	72·55 W
119	Hämeenlinna (hĕ'mân-lĭn-nå) . Fin.	61·00 N	24·29 E
74	Hamel (hăm'ĕl) . Ill. (St. Louis In.)	38·53 N	89·51 W
120	Hameln (hä'mĕln) ..... Ger.	52·06 N	9·23 E
111	Hamelwörden (hä'mĕl-vûr-dĕn) Ger. (Hamburg In.)	53·47 N	9·19 E
158	Hamersley Ra. (hăm'ērz-lê) . Austl.	22·15 S	117·50 E
152	Hamhung (häm'hōōng') ..... Kor.	39·57 N	127·35 E
146	Hami (Qomul) (hä'mê) (kô-mōōl') China	42·58 N	93·14 E
160	Hamilton (hăm'ĭl-tŭn) ..... Austl.	37·50 S	142·10 E
85	Hamilton ..... Can. (Toronto In.)	43·15 N	79·52 W
83	Hamilton ..... Mass. (Boston In.)	42·37 N	70·52 W
73	Hamilton ..... Mo.	39·43 N	93·59 W
67	Hamilton ..... Mont.	46·15 N	114·09 W
159	Hamilton ..... N. Z. (In.)	37·45 S	175·28 E
75	Hamilton ... Ohio (Cincinnati In.)	39·22 N	84·33 W
76	Hamilton ..... Tex.	31·42 N	98·07 W
73	Hamilton, L. ..... Ark.	34·25 N	93·32 W
85	Hamilton Hbr . Can. (Toronto In.)	43·17 N	79·50 W
87	Hamilton Inlet ..... Can.	54·20 N	56·57 W
119	Hamina (hä'mê-nå) ..... Fin.	60·34 N	27·15 E
79	Hamlet (hăm'lĕt) ..... N. C.	35·52 N	79·46 W
72	Hamlin (hăm'lĭn) ..... Tex.	32·54 N	100·08 W
123	Hamm (häm) .... Ger. (Ruhr In.)	51·40 N	7·48 E
168	Hammanskraal (hä-mȧns-kräl') S. Afr. (Johannesburg & Pretoria In.)	25·24 S	28·17 E
111	Hamme ..... Bel. (Brussels In.)	51·06 N	4·07 E
111	Hamme-Oste Kanal (Can.) (hä'mĕ-ōs'tĕ kä-näl) Ger. (Hamburg In.)	53·20 N	8·59 E
112	Hammerfest (häm'mĕr-fĕst) . . Nor.	70·38 N	23·59 E
75	Hammond (hăm'ŭnd) Ind. (Chicago In.)	41·37 N	87·31 W
77	Hammond ..... La.	30·30 N	90·28 W
65	Hammond .... Ore. (Portland In.)	46·12 N	123·57 W
81	Hammonton (hăm'ŭn-tŭn) . . N. J.	39·40 N	74·45 W
82	Hampden (hăm'dĕn) ..... Maine	44·44 N	68·51 W
116	Hampshire Downs (hămp'shĭr dounz) . Eng.	51·01 N	1·05 W
110	Hampstead Norris (hămp-stĕd nŏ'rĭs) . Eng. (London In.)	51·27 N	1·14 W
82	Hampton (hămp'tŭn) ..... Can.	45·34 N	65·50 W
71	Hampton ..... Iowa	42·43 N	93·15 W
84	Hampton ..... Va. (Norfolk In.)	37·02 N	76·21 W
84	Hampton Roads (Inlet) (Va. (Norfolk In.)	36·56 N	76·23 W
164	Ḥamrā, Ḥammādah al (Plat.) Libya	29·39 N	10·53 E
118	Hamrånge (häm'rông'ĕ) ..... Swe.	60·56 N	17·00 E
75	Hamtramck (hăm-trăm'ĭk) Mich. (Detroit In.)	42·24 N	83·03 W
144	Hāmūn-I Māshkel (L.) (hä-mōōn'ē mäsh-kĕl') . W. Pak.	28·28 N	64·13 E
152	Han (R.) ..... Kor.	37·10 N	127·40 E
157	Hana (hä'nä) ..... Hawaii (In.)	20·43 N	155·59 W
94	Hanábana (R.) (hä-nä-bä'nä) Cuba	22·30 N	80·55 W
157	Hanalei B. (hä-nä-lā'ê) Hawaii (In.)	22·15 N	159·40 W
120	Hanau (hä'nou) ..... Ger.	50·08 N	8·56 E
151	Han Chiang (R.) ..... China	25·00 N	116·35 E
71	Hancock (hăn'kŏk) ..... Mich.	47·08 N	88·37 W
65	Haney (hă-nê) Can. (Vancouver In.)	49·13 N	122·36 W
68	Hanford (hăn'fērd) ..... Calif.	36·20 N	119·38 W
146	Hangayn Nuruu (Khangai Mts.) Mong.	48·03 N	99·45 E
151	Hangchou (hăng'chō') ..... China	30·17 N	120·12 E
151	Hangchou Wan (B.) (hăng'chō') China	30·20 N	121·25 E
119	Hangö (häŋ'gû) ..... Fin.	59·49 N	22·56 E
77	Hankamer (hăŋ'kȧ-mēr) . Tex. (In.)	29·52 N	94·42 W
151	Han Kiang (R.) (hän'kyäng') China	31·40 N	112·04 E
70	Hankinson (hăŋ'kĭn-sŭn) ... N. D.	46·04 N	96·54 W
151	Hank'ou (hän'kō') ..... China	30·42 N	114·22 E
158	Hann, Mt. (hän) ..... Austl.	16·05 S	126·07 E
86	Hanna (hăn' å) ..... Can.	51·36 N	111·58 W
67	Hanna ..... Wyo.	41·51 N	106·34 W
70	Hannah ..... N. D.	48·58 N	98·42 W
73	Hannibal (hăn'ĭ bǎl) ..... Mo.	39·42 N	91·22 W
120	Hannover (hän-ō'vĕr) ..... Ger.	52·22 N	9·45 E
118	Hanö-bukten (B.) ..... Swe.	55·54 N	14·55 E
151	Hanoi (hä-noi') ..... Viet.	21·04 N	105·50 E
80	Hanover (hăn'ô-vēr) ..... Can.	44·10 N	81·05 W
83	Hanover ..... Mass. (Boston In.)	42·07 N	70·49 W
81	Hanover ..... N. H.	43·45 N	72·15 W
81	Hanover ..... Pa.	39·50 N	77·00 W
100	Hanover (I.) ..... Chile	51·00 S	74·45 W
148	Hanshan (hän'shän') ..... China	31·43 N	118·06 E
89	Hans Lollick (I.) (häns'lôl'ĭk) Vir. Is. (U. S. A.) (St. Thomas In.)	18·24 N	64·55 W
83	Hanson (hăn'sŭn) Mass. (Boston In.)	42·04 N	70·53 W
65	Hansville (hăns'-vĭl) Wash. (Seattle In.)	47·55 N	122·33 W
148	Hantan (hän'tän') ..... China	36·37 N	114·30 E
82	Hantsport (hănts'pōrt) ..... Can.	45·05 N	64·12 W
151	Hanyang (han'yäng') ..... China	30·30 N	114·10 E
148	Haoch'engchi (hou'chĕng'jē) . China	33·19 N	117·33 E
112	Haparanda (hä-pä-rän'dä) ... Swe.	65·54 N	23·57 E
84	Hapeville (hăp'vĭl) Ga. (Atlanta In.)	33·39 N	84·25 W
84	Happy Jack (hăp'ĭ jăk) La. (New Orleans In.)	29·31 N	89·44 W
153	Hara-machida (hä-rä mä-chê'dä) Jap. (Tōkyō In.)	35·32 N	139·28 E
124	Harana, Sierra (Mts.) (sē-ĕ'r-rä-rä'nä) . Sp.	37·17 N	3·28 W
146	Hara Nuur (L.) ..... Mong.	47·47 N	94·01 E
168	Hārar (hä-rär') Eth. (Horn of Afr. In.)	9·43 N	42·10 E
165	Harar (Prov.) ..... Eth.	8·15 N	41·00 E
146	Hara Usa (L.) ..... Mong.	48·00 N	92·32 E
	Harbin, see Haerhpin		
80	Harbor Beach (här'bēr bēch) Mich.	43·50 N	82·40 W
80	Harbor Springs ..... Mich.	45·25 N	85·05 W
83	Harbour Breton (brĕt'ŭn) (brē-tôN') . Can.	47·28 N	55·50 W
83	Harbour Grace (grās) ..... Can.	47·39 N	53·15 W
111	Harburg (här-bōōrgh) Ger. (Hamburg In.)	53·28 N	9·58 E
82	Harcourt (här'côrt) (år-kōōr') Can.	46·28 N	65·14 W
118	Hardanger Fd. (här-däng'ĕr fyôrd) . Nor.	59·58 N	6·30 E
118	Hardanger Fjeld (Mts.) (fyĕl') Nor.	60·15 N	6·56 E
118	Hardanger Jöklen (Mtn.) (yû'kōōl-ĕn) . Nor.	60·33 N	7·23 E
67	Hardin (här'dĭn) ..... Mont.	45·44 N	107·36 W
167	Harding (här'dĭng) S. Afr. (Natal In.)	30·34 S	29·54 E
78	Harding (L.) ..... Ala.-Ga.	32·43 N	85·00 W
142	Hardwar (hûr'dvär) ..... India	29·56 N	78·06 E
68	Hardy (R.) (här'dĭ) ..... Mex.	32·04 N	115·10 W
83	Hare B. (hâr) ..... Can.	51·21 N	55·45 W
168	Hargeisa (här-gä'ê-sȧ) Som. (Horn of Afr. In.)	9·20 N	43·57 E
121	Harghita, Muntii (Mts.) .... Rom.	46·25 N	25·40 E
153	Harima-Nada (Sea) (hä'rê-mä nä-dä) . Jap.	34·34 N	134·37 E
111	Haring Vliet (R.) Neth. (Amsterdam In.)	51·49 N	4·03 E
73	Harlan (här'lăn) ..... Iowa	41·40 N	95·10 W
78	Harlan ..... Ky.	36·50 N	83·19 W
72	Harlan Co. Res. ..... Nebr.	40·03 N	99·51 W
67	Harlem (här'lĕm) ..... Mont.	48·33 N	108·50 W
143	Harlhar ..... India	14·32 N	75·41 E
117	Harlingen (här'lĭng-ĕn) ..... Neth.	53·10 N	5·24 E
77	Harlingen ..... Tex.	26·12 N	97·42 W
110	Harlow (här'lō) . Eng. (London In.)	51·46 N	0·08 E
67	Harlowton (här'lô-tun) ..... Mont.	46·26 N	109·50 W
80	Harmony (här'mô-nĭ) ..... Ind.	39·35 N	87·00 W
66	Harney Basin (här'nĭ) ..... Ore.	43·26 N	120·19 W
66	Harney L. ..... Ore.	43·11 N	119·23 W
70	Harney Pk. ..... S. D.	43·52 N	103·32 W
118	Härnösand (hĕr-nû-sänd) .... Swe.	62·37 N	17·54 E
124	Haro (ä'rō) ..... Sp.	42·35 N	2·49 W
65	Haro Str. (hä'rō) ..... Can.-U. S.	48·27 N	123·11 W
110	Harpenden (här'pĕn-d'n) Eng. (London In.)	51·48 N	0·22 W
72	Harper (här'pēr) ..... Kans.	37·17 N	98·02 W
164	Harper ..... Lib.	4·28 N	7·52 W
65	Harper ..... Wash. (Seattle In.)	47·31 N	122·32 W
81	Harpers Ferry (här'pĕrz) . . W. Va.	39·20 N	77·45 W
133	Harput (kär-pōōt') ..... Tur.	38·45 N	39·10 E
78	Harriman (hăr'ĭ-măn) ..... Tenn.	35·55 N	84·34 W
81	Harrington (hăr'ĭng-tŭn) ..... Del.	38·55 N	75·35 W
87	Harrington Harbour (här'bēr) Can.	50·30 N	59·19 W
144	Harri Rud (R.) ..... Afg.	34·29 N	61·16 E
116	Harris (I.) (hăr'ĭs) ..... Scot.	57·55 N	6·40 W
79	Harris (L.) ..... Fla. (In.)	28·43 N	81·40 W
80	Harrisburg (hăr'ĭs-bûrg) ..... Ill.	37·45 N	88·35 W
81	Harrisburg ..... Pa.	40·15 N	76·50 W
168	Harrismith (hă-rĭs'mĭth) S. Afr. (Johannesburg & Pretoria In.)	28·17 S	29·08 E
73	Harrison (hăr'ĭ-sŭn) ..... Ark.	36·13 N	93·06 W
75	Harrison .... Ohio (Cincinnati In.)	39·16 N	84·45 W
81	Harrisonburg (hăr'-ĭ-sŭn-bûrg) Va.	38·30 N	78·50 W
73	Harrisonville (hăr-ĭ-sŭn-vĭl) ... Mo.	38·39 N	94·21 W
74	Harrisville (hăr'ĭs-vĭl) Utah (Salt Lake City In.)	41·17 N	112·00 W
80	Harrisville ..... W. Va.	39·10 N	81·05 W
80	Harrodsburg (hăr'ŭdz-bûrg) . . Ky.	37·45 N	84·50 W
75	Harrods Cr. (hăr'ŭdz) Ky. (Louisville In.)	38·24 N	85·33 W
110	Harrow (hăr'ō) . Eng. (London In.)	51·34 N	0·21 W
111	Harsefeld (här'zĕ-fĕld') Ger. (Hamburg In.)	53·27 N	9·30 E
112	Harstad (här'städh) ..... Nor.	68·49 N	16·10 E
80	Hart (härt) ..... Mich.	43·40 N	86·25 W
168	Hartbeesfontein S. Afr. (Johannesburg & Pretoria In.)	26·46 S	26·25 E
167	Hartbeespoortdam (L.) .... S. Afr. (Johannesburg & Pretoria In.)	25·47 S	27·43 E
167	Hartebeespoortdam S. Afr. (Johannesburg & Pretoria In.)	25·44 S	27·51 E
78	Hartford (härt'fērd) ..... Ala.	31·05 N	85·42 W
73	Hartford ..... Ark.	35·01 N	94·21 W
81	Hartford ..... Conn.	41·45 N	72·40 W
74	Hartford ..... Ill. (St. Louis In.)	38·50 N	90·06 W
78	Hartford ..... Ky.	37·25 N	86·50 W
80	Hartford ..... Mich.	42·15 N	86·15 W
71	Hartford ..... Wis.	43·19 N	88·25 W
80	Hartford City ..... Ind.	40·35 N	85·25 W
110	Hartington (härt'ĭng-tŭn) .... Eng.	53·08 N	1·48 W
70	Hartington ..... Nebr.	42·37 N	97·18 W
82	Hartland (härt'lănd) ..... Can.	46·19 N	67·32 W
116	Hartland Pt. ..... Eng.	51·03 N	4·40 W
166	Hartley ..... S. Rh.	18·11 S	30·08 E
70	Hartley (härt'lĭ) ..... Iowa	43·12 N	95·29 W
78	Hartselle (härt'sĕl) ..... Ala.	34·24 N	86·55 W
73	Hartshorne (härts'hôrn) ..... Okla.	34·49 N	95·34 W
79	Hartsville (härts'vĭl) ..... S. C.	34·20 N	80·04 W
78	Hartwell (härt'wĕl) ..... Ga.	34·21 N	82·56 W
78	Hartwell Res. ..... Ga.	34·30 N	83·00 W
142	Hārua ..... India (Calcutta In.)	22·36 N	88·40 E
71	Harvard (här'vȧrd) ..... Ill.	42·25 N	88·39 W
83	Harvard ..... Mass. (Boston In.)	42·30 N	71·35 W
72	Harvard ..... Nebr.	40·36 N	98·08 W
69	Harvard, Mt ..... Colo.	38·55 N	106·20 W
67	Harve (här'vĭ) ..... Mont.	48·34 N	109·42 W
75	Harvey ..... Ill. (Chicago In.)	41·37 N	87·39 W
84	Harvey .... La. (New Orleans In.)	29·54 N	90·05 W
70	Harvey ..... N. D.	47·46 N	99·55 W
117	Harwich (här'wĭch) ..... Eng.	51·53 N	1·13 E
120	Harz Mts. (härts) ..... Ger.	51·42 N	10·50 E
139	Hasa (R.) . . Jordan (Palestine In.)	30·57 N	35·51 E
153	Hashimoto (hä'shê-mō'tō) .... Jap.	34·19 N	135·37 E
119	Häsijärvi (L.) (hĕ'sê-yĕr'vê) . Fin.	61·42 N	24·05 E

Page	Name Pronunciation Region	Lat. °′	Long. °′
73	Haskell (hăs'kĕl)...........Okla.	35·49 N	95·41 W
72	Haskell...................Tex.	33·09 N	99·43 W
74	Haslet (hăs'lĕt) Tex. (Dallas, Fort Worth In.)	32·58 N	97·21 W
110	Haslingden (hăz'lĭng dĕn)....Eng.	53·43 N	2·19 W
118	Hassela (häs'ĕl-ô)...........Swe.	62·05 N	16·46 E
111	Hasselt (häs'ĕlt) Bel. (Brussels In.)	50·56 N	5·23 E
164	Hassi Inifel...............Alg.	29·54 N	3·47 E
118	Hässjö (hĕs'shû)...........Swe.	62·36 N	17·33 E
118	Hassleholm (häs'lĕ-hōlm)....Swe.	56·10 N	13·44 E
117	Hastings (hās'tĭngz)........Eng.	50·52 N	0·28 E
80	Hastings..................Mich.	42·40 N	85·20 W
74	Hastings Minn. (Minneapolis, St. Paul In.)	44·44 N	92·51 W
72	Hastings..................Nebr.	40·34 N	98·42 W
159	Hastings.............N. Z. (In.)	39·33 S	176·53 E
84	Hastings-on-Hudson (ŏn-hŭd'sŭn) N. Y. (New York In.)	40·59 N	73·53 W
78	Hatchie (R.) (hăch'ē)......Tenn.	35·28 N	89·14 W
127	Hateg (kät-säg')...........Rom.	45·35 N	22·57 E
110	Hatfield Broad Oak (hăt-fēld brôd ōk).Eng.	51·50 N	0·14 E
153	Hatogaya (hä'tō-gä-yä) Jap. (Tōkyō In.)	35·50 N	139·45 E
153	Hatsukaichi (hät'sōō-kä'ê-chê) Jap.	34·22 N	132·19 E
79	Hatteras, C. (hăt'ēr-ȧs).....N. C.	35·15 N	75·24 W
78	Hattiesburg (hăt'ĭz-bûrg)...Miss.	31·20 N	89·18 W
123	Hattingen (hä'tēn-gĕn) Ger. (Ruhr In.)	51·24 N	7·11 E
121	Hatvan (hôt'vôn)..........Hung.	47·39 N	19·44 E
118	Haugesund (hou'gē-soon')....Nor.	59·26 N	5·20 E
119	Haukivesi (L.) (hou'kê-vĕ'sê).Fin.	62·02 N	29·02 E
168	Hauptsrus S. Afr. (Johannesburg & Pretoria In.)	26·35 S	26·16 E
159	Hauraki, G. (hä-ōō-rä'kê) N. Z. (In.)	36·44 S	175·15 E
119	Hausjärvi (hä'ōōs-yĕr'vê)....Fin.	60·44 N	24·44 E
82	Haut, Isle au (hō).........Maine	44·03 N	68·13 W
144	Hauta (hou'tä)..........Sau. Ar.	23·12 N	45·38 E
114	Haut Atlas (Mts.)..........Mor.	32·10 N	5·49 W
82	Hauterive..................Can.	49·12 N	68·15 W
122	Hautmont (ō-môɴ')...........Fr.	50·14 N	3·50 E
73	Havana (hȧ-vă'nȧ)............Ill.	40·17 N	90·02 W
	Havana, see La Habana		
69	Havasu L. (hăv'ȧ-sōō)......Ariz.	34·26 N	114·09 W
82	Havelock (hăv'lŏk)..........Can.	56·58 N	65·20 W
120	Havel R. (hä'fĕl)...........Ger.	53·09 N	13·10 E
81	Haven (hā-vĕn)...............Pa.	40·31 N	76·14 W
83	Haverhill (hā'vēr-hĭl) Mass. (Boston In.)	42·46 N	71·05 W
81	Haverhill.................N. H.	44·00 N	72·05 W
84	Haverstraw (hā'vēr-strô) N. Y. (New York In.)	41·11 N	73·58 W
83	Havre (hăv'rȧ)...............Can.	45·42 N	61·30 W
81	Havre de Grace (hăv'ēr dē gräs') Md.	39·35 N	76·05 W
79	Haw (R.) (hô)............N. C.	36·17 N	79·46 W
62	Hawaii (State).............U. S.	20·00 N	157·40 W
157	Hawaii (I.).........Hawaii (In.)	19·35 N	155·30 W
62	Hawaiian Is. (hä-wī'ăn)...Oceania	22·00 N	158·00 W
157	Hawaii Vol. Natl. Park (hä-wī'ē) Hawaii (In.)	19·15 N	155·20 W
70	Hawarden (hā'wȧr-dĕn).....Iowa	43·00 N	96·28 W
157	Hawi (hä'wē).......Hawaii (In.)	20·16 N	155·48 W
116	Hawick (hô'ĭk)............Scot.	55·25 N	2·55 W
159	Hawke B. (hôk).......N. Z. (In.)	39·17 S	177·58 E
160	Hawker (hô'kēr)...........Austl.	31·58 S	138·12 E
81	Hawkesbury (hôks'bēr-ĭ)....Can.	45·35 N	74·35 W
83	Hawkesbury, Port...........Can.	45·39 N	60·48 W
78	Hawkinsville (hô'kĭnz-vĭl).....Ga.	32·15 N	83·30 W
95	Hawks Nest Pt...........Ba. Is.	24·05 N	75·30 W
70	Hawley (hô'lĭ)............Minn.	46·52 N	96·18 W
110	Haworth (hā'wûrth)........Eng.	53·50 N	1·57 W
144	Hawtah..............Sau. Ar.	15·58 N	48·26 E
74	Hawthorne (hô'thôrn) Calif. (Los Angeles In.)	33·55 N	118·22 W
68	Hawthorne.................Nev.	38·33 N	118·39 W
72	Haxtun (hăks'tŭn).........Colo.	40·39 N	102·38 W
158	Hay (R.) (hā).............Austl.	123·00 S	136·45 E
86	Hay (R.)...................Can.	60·21 N	117·14 W
153	Hayama (hä-yä'mä) Jap. (Tōkyō In.)	35·16 N	139·35 E
153	Hayashi (hä-yä'shē) Jap. (Tōkyō In.)	35·13 N	139·38 E
69	Hayden (hā'dĕn)...........Ariz.	33·00 N	110·50 W
64	Hayes, Mt. (hāz).........Alaska	63·32 N	146·40 W
86	Hayes (R.).................Can.	55·30 N	94·00 W
77	Haynesville (hānz'vĭl)........La.	32·55 N	93·08 W
127	Hayrabolu...................Tur.	41·14 N	27·05 E
86	Hay River..................Can.	60·50 N	115·53 W
72	Hays (hāz)................Kans.	38·51 N	99·20 W
65	Haystack Mtn. (hā-stăk') Wash. (Seattle In.)	48·26 N	122·07 W
65	Hayward (hā'wērd) Calif. (San Francisco In.)	37·40 N	122·06 W
71	Hayward...................Wis.	46·01 N	91·31 W
78	Hazard (hăz'ȧrd)............Ky.	37·13 N	83·10 W
79	Hazelhurst (hā'z'l-hûrst)......Ga.	31·50 N	82·36 W
78	Hazelhurst.................Miss.	31·52 N	90·23 W
75	Hazel Park...Mich. (Detroit In.)	42·28 N	83·06 W
86	Hazelton (hā'z'l-tŭn).........Can.	55·18 N	127·11 W
81	Hazleton....................Pa.	41·00 N	76·00 W
85	Headingley (hĕd'ĭng-lĭ) Can. (Winnipeg In.)	49·53 N	97·25 W
78	Headland (hĕd'lănd).........Ala.	31·22 N	85·20 W
68	Healdsburg (hēldz'bûrg)....Calif.	38·37 N	122·52 W
73	Healdton (hēld'tŭn)........Okla.	34·13 N	97·28 W
110	Heanor (hēn'ŏr)............Eng.	53·01 N	1·22 W
47	Heard I. (hûrd)..........Ind. O.	53·10 S	74·35 E
77	Hearne (hûrn)...............Tex.	30·53 N	96·35 W
87	Hearst (hûrst)...............Can.	49·36 N	83·40 W
70	Heart (R.) (härt)..........N. D.	46·46 N	102·34 W
83	Heart's Content (härts kŏn'tĕnt) Can.	47·55 N	53·20 W
83	Heath Pt. (hēth)...........Can.	49·06 N	61·45 W
73	Heavener (hēv'nēr).........Okla.	34·52 N	94·36 W
76	Hebbronville (hē'brŭn-vĭl)...Tex.	27·18 N	98·40 W
69	Heber (hē'bēr).............Utah	40·30 N	111·25 W
73	Heber Springs..............Ark.	35·28 N	91·59 W
67	Hebgen Res. (hĕb'gĕn).....Mont.	44·47 N	111·38 W
116	Hebrides, Sea of...........Scot.	56·63 N	6·41 W
87	Hebron (hēb'rŭn)...........Can.	58·11 N	62·56 W
75	Hebron........Ind. (Chicago In.)	41·19 N	87·13 W
75	Hebron......Ky. (Cincinnati In.)	39·04 N	84·43 W
73	Hebron....................Nebr.	40·11 N	97·36 W
70	Hebron....................N. D.	46·54 N	102·04 W
	Hebron, see Al Khalīl		
118	Heby (hĭ'bü)...............Swe.	59·56 N	16·48 E
86	Hecate Str. (hĕk'ȧ-tē).......Can.	53·34 N	130·53 W
91	Hecelchakán (ā-sĕl-chä-kän').Mex.	20·10 N	90·09 W
118	Hedemora (hĭ-dĕ-mō'rä).....Swe.	60·16 N	15·55 E
118	Hedesunda Fd. (hi-de-sōōn'dä) Swe.	60·22 N	16·50 E
110	Hedon (hĕdŭn).............Eng.	53·44 N	0·12 W
152	Hedo Saki (C.) (hā'dō sä'kē).Jap.	26·48 N	128·40 E
111	Heemstede Neth. (Amsterdam In.)	52·20 N	4·36 E
117	Heerlen....................Bel.	50·55 N	5·58 E
78	Heflin (hĕf'lĭn)..............Ala.	33·40 N	85·33 W
120	Heide (hī'dē)...............Ger.	54·13 N	9·06 E
161	Heidelberg (hī'dĕl-bûrg) Austl. (Melbourne In.)	37·45 S	145·04 E
120	Heidelberg (hīdĕl-bĕrgh).....Ger.	49·24 N	8·43 E
120	Heidenheim (hī'dĕn-hīm).....Ger.	48·41 N	10·09 E
168	Heilbron (hīl'brōn).........S. Afr. (Johannesburg & Pretoria In.)	27·17 S	27·58 E
120	Heilbronn (hīl'brōn)........Ger.	49·09 N	9·16 E
123	Heiligenhaus (hī'lē-gĕn-houz) Ger. (Ruhr In.)	51·19 N	6·58 E
120	Heiligenstadt (hī'lē-gĕn-shtät) Ger.	51·21 N	10·10 E
147	Heilungkiang (Prov.) (hā-lōōng' kyăng').China	46·36 N	128·07 E
119	Heinola (hā-nō'lä)............Fin.	61·13 N	26·03 E
123	Heinsberg (hīnz'bĕrgh) Ger. (Ruhr In.)	51·04 N	6·07 E
139	Heisi (R.).U. A. R. (Palestine In.)	29·21 N	34·30 E
111	Heist-op-den-Berg Bel. (Brussels In.)	51·05 N	4·14 E
112	Hekla (Vol.) (hĕk'lȧ).........Ice.	63·53 N	19·37 W
121	Hel (hāl)....................Pol.	54·37 N	18·53 E
118	Helagsfjället (M.)..........Swe.	62·54 N	12·24 E
73	Helena (hē-lē'nä)............Ark.	34·33 N	90·35 W
67	Helena (hĕ-lē'nȧ)..........Mont.	46·35 N	112·01 W
161	Helensburgh (hĕl'ĕnz-bŭr-ô) Austl. (Sydney In.)	34·11 S	150·59 E
116	Helensburgh.................Scot.	56·01 N	4·53 W
118	Helge (R.) (hĕl'gĕ)..........Swe.	56·31 N	13·47 E
120	Helgoland I. (hĕl'gō-länd)....Ger.	54·13 N	7·30 E
79	Hellier (hĕl'yēr).............Ky.	37·16 N	82·27 W
124	Hellín (ĕl-yēn')..............Sp.	38·30 N	1·40 W
144	Helmand (R.) (hĕl'mŭnd)....Afg.	31·00 N	63·48 E
117	Helmond (hĕl'mōnt) (ĕl'môɴ') Neth.	51·35 N	5·04 E
120	Helmstedt (hĕlm'shtĕt)......Ger.	52·14 N	11·03 E
74	Helotes (hē'-lōts) Tex. (San Antonio In.)	29·35 N	98·41 W
69	Helper (hĕlp'ēr)............Utah	39·40 N	110·55 W
	Helsingfors, see Helsinki		
118	Helsingør (hĕl-sĭng-ûr')......Den.	56·03 N	12·33 E
119	Helsinki (Helsingfors) (hĕl'sĕn-kē) (hĕl'sĭng-fôrs').Fin.	60·10 N	24·53 E
167	Helvellyn (Mts.) (hĕl-vĕl-lĭn) S. Afr. (Natal In.)	30·32 S	27·18 E
110	Hemel Hempstead (hĕm'ĕl hĕmp'stĕd) Eng. (London In.)	51·43 N	0·29 W
74	Hemet (hĕm'ĕt) Calif. (Los Angeles In.)	33·45 N	116·57 W
70	Hemingford (hĕm'ĭng-fērd)..Nebr.	42·21 N	103·30 W
77	Hemphill (hĕmp'hĭl).........Tex.	31·20 N	93·48 W
84	Hempstead (hĕmp'stĕd) N. Y. (New York In.)	40·42 N	73·37 W
77	Hempstead..................Tex.	30·07 N	96·05 W
118	Hemse (hĕm'sē)..............Swe.	57·15 N	18·25 E
118	Hemsö (I.)...................Swe.	62·43 N	18·22 E
118	Hen (hĭn)....................Nor.	60·14 N	10·10 E
124	Henares (R.) (ā-nä'räs).......Sp.	40·50 N	2·55 W
122	Hendaye (äɴ-dā')..............Fr.	43·20 N	1·46 W
80	Henderson (hĕn'dēr-sŭn).....Ky.	37·50 N	87·30 W
68	Henderson...................Nev.	36·09 N	115·04 W
79	Henderson...................N. C.	36·18 N	78·24 W
78	Henderson...................Tenn.	35·25 N	88·40 W
77	Henderson...................Tex.	32·09 N	94·48 W
79	Hendersonville (hĕn'dēr-sŭn-vĭl) N. C.	35·17 N	82·28 W
110	Hendon (hĕn'dŭn) Eng. (London In.)	51·34 N	0·13 W
168	Hendrina (hĕn-drē'nȧ).....S. Afr. (Johannesburg & Pretoria In.)	26·10 S	29·44 E
151	Hengch'un (hĕng'chŭn')..Taiwan	22·00 N	120·42 E
117	Hengelo (hĕng'ĕ-lō).........Neth.	52·20 N	6·45 E
151	Henghsien...................China	22·40 N	104·20 E
151	Hengshan (hĕng'shän')......China	27·20 N	112·40 E
148	Hengshui (hĕng'shōō-ē').....China	37·43 N	115·42 E
151	Hengyang...................China	26·58 N	112·30 E
110	Henley on Thames (hĕn'lē ŏn tĕmz).Eng. (London In.)	51·31 N	0·54 W
81	Henlopen, C. (hĕn-lō'pĕn)....Del.	38·45 N	75·05 W
122	Hennebont (ĕn-bôɴ')..........Fr.	47·47 N	3·16 W
168	Hennenman.................S. Afr. (Johannesburg & Pretoria In.)	27·59 S	27·03 E
72	Hennessey (hĕn'ĕ-sĭ).........Okla.	36·04 N	97·53 W
111	Hennigsdorf (hĕ'nĕngz-dōrf) Ger. (Berlin In.)	52·39 N	13·12 E
167	Hennops (R.) (hĕn'ŏps)....S. Afr. (Johannesburg & Pretoria In.)	25·51 S	27·57 E
167	Hennopsrivier..............S. Afr. (Johannesburg & Pretoria In.)	25·50 S	27·59 E
73	Henrietta (hĕn-rĭ-ĕt'ȧ).......Okla.	35·25 N	95·58 W
72	Henrietta (hen-rĭ-ĕ'tȧ).......Tex.	33·47 N	98·11 W
87	Henrietta Maria, C. (hĕn-rĭ-ĕt'ȧ) Can.	55·10 N	82·20 W
69	Henry Mts. (hĕn'rĭ).........Utah	38·55 N	110·45 W
150	Henteyn Nuruu (Mts.)..Sov. Un.	49·40 N	111·00 E
66	Heppner (hĕp'nēr)...........Ore.	45·21 N	119·33 W
144	Herāt (hĕ-rät')..............Afg.	34·28 N	62·13 E
127	Hercegovina (Reg.) (hĕr-tsĕ-gô'vē-nȧ).Yugo.	43·23 N	17·52 E
167	Hercules (hĕr'ku-lēs).......S. Afr. (Johannesburg & Pretoria In.)	25·43 S	28·10 E
123	Herdecke (hĕr'dĕ-kĕ) Ger. (Ruhr In.)	51·24 N	7·26 E
93	Heredia (ā-rā'dhê-ä)........C. R.	10·04 N	84·06 W
116	Hereford (hĕrĕ'fērd)........Eng.	52·05 N	2·44 W
110	Hereford (Co.)..............Eng.	52·22 N	2·52 W
72	Hereford (hĕr'ĕ-fērd)........Tex.	34·47 N	102·25 W
139	Hereidin (R.) U. A. R. (Palestine In.)	31·02 N	34·03 E
124	Herencia (ā-rān'thê-ä)........Sp.	39·23 N	3·22 W
111	Herentals......Bel. (Brussels In.)	51·10 N	4·51 E
120	Herford (hĕr'fôrt)...........Ger.	52·06 N	8·42 E
73	Herington (hĕr'ĭng-tŭn)....Kans.	38·41 N	96·57 W
120	Herisau (hā'rē-zou)........Switz.	47·23 N	9·18 E
111	Herk-de-Stad..Bel. (Brussels In.)	50·56 N	5·13 E
81	Herkimer (hûr'kĭ-mēr).......N. Y.	43·05 N	75·00 W
116	Herma Ness (Prom.) (hûr'mȧ nĕs) Scot.	60·50 N	1·10 W
73	Hermann (hûr'măn)..........Mo.	38·41 N	91·27 W
80	Hermansville (hûr'mănz-vĭl).Mich.	45·40 N	87·35 W
74	Hermantown (hĕr'măn-toun) Minn. (Duluth In.)	46·46 N	92·12 W
168	Hermanusdorings..........S. Afr. (Johannesburg & Pretoria In.)	24·08 S	27·46 E
75	Herminie (hûr-mī'nē) Pa. (Pittsburgh In.)	40·16 N	79·45 W
83	Hermitage B. (hûr'mĭ-tĕj)...Can.	47·31 N	56·30 W
155	Hermit Is. (hûr'mĭt)..N. Gui. Ter.	1·48 S	144·55 E
74	Hermosa Beach (hĕr-mō'sȧ) Calif. (Los Angeles In.)	33·51 N	118·24 W
88	Hermosillo (ĕr-mô-sē'l-yō)...Mex.	29·00 N	110·57 W
123	Herne (hĕr'nĕ)....Ger. (Ruhr In.)	51·32 N	7·13 E
118	Herning (hĕr'nĭng)..........Den.	56·08 N	8·55 E
70	Heron (L.) (hĕr'ŭn)........Minn.	43·42 N	95·23 W
87	Heron Bay...................Can.	48·32 N	86·20 W
70	Heron Lake.................Minn.	43·48 N	95·20 W
92	Herrero, Punta (pt.) (pōō'n-tä-ĕr-rĕ'rō).Mex. (Yucatan In.)	19·18 N	87·24 W
80	Herrin (hĕr'ĭn)................Ill.	37·50 N	89·00 W
167	Herschel (hēr'-shĕl) S. Afr. (Natal In.)	30·37 S	27·12 E
75	Herscher (hēr'shēr) Ill. (Chicago In.)	41·03 N	88·06 W
117	Herstal (hĕr'stäl)............Bel.	50·42 N	5·32 E
110	Hertford (hûrt'fērd)........Eng.	51·46 N	0·05 W
79	Hertford....................N. C.	36·10 N	76·30 W
111	Hertzberg (hĕrtz'bĕrgh) Ger. (Berlin In.)	52·54 N	12·58 E
167	Hertzog (hĕrt'zŏg) S. Afr. (Natal In.)	32·36 S	26·46 E
139	Herzlia........Isr. (Palestine In.)	32·10 N	34·49 E
122	Hesdin(ĕ-dăɴ')................Fr.	50·24 N	1·59 E
120	Hessen (State) (hĕs'ĕn).....Ger.	50·16 N	8·48 E
68	Hetch Hetchy Aqueduct (hĕtch hĕt'-chĭ ăk'wē-dŭkt).Calif.	37·27 N	120·54 W
70	Hettinger (hĕt'ĭn-jēr).......N. D.	45·58 N	102·36 W
168	Heuningspruit............S. Afr. (Johannesburg & Pretoria In.)	27·28 S	27·26 E
168	Heystekrand..............S. Afr. (Johannesburg & Pretoria In.)	25·16 S	27·14 E
110	Heywood (hā'wŏŏd)........Eng.	53·36 N	2·12 W
79	Hialeah (hī-ȧ-lē'-ȧh)....Fla. (In.)	25·49 N	80·18 W
73	Hiawatha (hī-ȧ-wô'thȧ).....Kans.	39·50 N	95·33 W
69	Hiawatha...................Utah	39·25 N	111·05 W
71	Hibbing (hĭb'ĭng)...........Minn.	47·26 N	92·58 W
78	Hickman (hĭk'măn)...........Ky.	34·33 N	89·10 W
74	Hickman Mills Mo. (Kansas City In.)	38·56 N	94·32 W
79	Hickory (hĭk'ō-rĭ)..........N. C.	35·43 N	81·21 W
84	Hicksville (hĭks'vĭl) N. Y. (New York In.)	40·47 N	73·25 W
80	Hicksville...................Ohio	41·15 N	84·45 W
76	Hico (hī'kō).................Tex.	32·00 N	98·02 W
90	Hidalgo (ē-dhäl'gō).........Mex.	24·14 N	99·25 W
76	Hidalgo......................Mex.	27·49 N	99·53 W
88	Hidalgo (State).............Mex.	20·45 N	99·30 W
76	Hidalgo del Parral (ē-dä'l-gō-dĕl-pär-rä'l).Mex.	26·55 N	105·40 W
91	Hidalgo Yalalag (ê-dhäl'gō-yä-lä-läg).Mex.	17·12 N	96·11 W
168	Hiedelberg...............S. Afr. (Johannesburg & Pretoria In.)	26·32 S	28·22 E
164	Hierro I. (yĕ'r-rō).......Can. Is.	27·37 N	18·29 W
80	Higgins (L.) (hĭg'ĭnz).......Mich.	44·20 N	84·45 W
73	Higginsville (hĭg'ĭnz-vĭl)......Mo.	39·05 N	93·44 W
80	High (I.)....................Mich.	45·45 N	85·45 W
85	High Bluff...Can. (Winnipeg In.)	50·01 N	98·08 W
94	Highborne Cay (hībôrn kē).Ba. Is.	24·45 N	76·50 W
74	Highgrove (hī'grōv) Calif. (Los Angeles In.)	34·01 N	117·20 W
77	High Island...........Tex. (In.)	29·34 N	94·24 W
74	Highland (hī'lănd) Calif. (Los Angeles In.)	34·08 N	117·13 W
73	Highland.....................Ill.	38·44 N	89·41 W
75	Highland......Ind. (Chicago In.)	41·33 N	87·28 W
75	Highland......Mich. (Detroit In.)	42·38 N	83·37 W
65	Highland....Wash. (Portland In.)	45·55 N	122·37 W
75	Highland Park..Ill. (Chicago In.)	42·11 N	87·47 W
75	Highland Park Mich. (Detroit In.)	42·24 N	83·06 W
84	Highland Park N. J. (New York In.)	40·30 N	74·25 W

ăt; finăl; rāte; senâte; ärm; ȧsk; sofȧ; fâre; ch-choose; dh-as th in other; bē; êvent; bĕt; recĕnt; cratēr; g-go; gh-guttural g; bĭt; ĭ-short neutral; rīde: ĸ-guttural k as ch in German ich;

Page	Name Pronunciation Region	Lat. °′	Long. °′
74	Highland Park Tex. (Dallas, Fort Worth In.)	32·49 N	96·48 W
84	Highlands (hī-lǎndz) N. J. (New York In.)	40·24 N	73·59 W
77	Highlands.............Tex. (In.)	29·49 N	95·01 W
70	Highmore (hī'-mōr)........S. D.	44·30 N	99·26 W
110	High Ongar (on'gẽr) Eng. (London In.)	51·43 N	0·15 E
155	High Pk.......Phil. (Manila In.)	15·38 N	120·05 E
79	High Point................N. C.	35·55 N	80·00 W
86	High Prairie..............Can.	55·30 N	116·47 W
74	High Ridge....Mo. (St. Louis In.)	38·27 N	90·32 W
86	High River................Can.	50·40 N	113·47 W
79	Highrock (R.) (hī'-rŏk).....N. C.	35·40 N	80·15 W
79	High Springs................Fla.	29·48 N	82·38 W
84	Hightstown (hīts-toun) N. J. (New York In.)	40·16 N	74·32 W
110	High Wycombe (wĭ-kŭm) Eng. (London In.)	51·36 N	0·45 W
89	Higuero, Pta. (Pt.) P. R. (Puerto Rico In.)	18·21 N	67·11 W
99	Higuerote (ē-gě-rô'-tě)..Ven. (In.)	10·29 N	66·06 W
95	Higüey (ē-gwě'y).....Dom. Rep.	18·40 N	68·45 W
119	Hiiumaa (D'Ago) (hē'ōōm-ô).Sov. Un.	58·47 N	22·05 E
153	Hikone (hē'kô-ně)............Jap.	35·15 N	136·15 E
120	Hildburghausen (hĭld'bōōrg hou-zěn).Ger.	50·26 N	10·45 E
123	Hilden (hēl'děn)..Ger. (Ruhr In.)	51·10 N	6·56 E
120	Hildesheim (hĭl'děs-hīm).....Ger.	52·08 N	9·56 E
93	Hillaby, Mt. (hĭl'à-bĭ) Barb. (Le. & Wind. Is. In.)	13·15 N	59·35 W
72	Hill City (hĭl).............Kans.	39·22 N	99·54 W
71	Hill City.................Minn.	46·58 N	93·38 W
111	Hillegersberg Neth. (Amsterdam In.)	51·57 N	4·29 E
118	Hillerød (hē'lě-rûdh)........Den.	55·56 N	12·17 E
73	Hillsboro (hĭlz'bŭr-ō).........Ill.	39·09 N	89·28 W
73	Hillsboro.................Kans.	38·22 N	97·11 W
81	Hillsboro.................N. H.	43·05 N	71·55 W
70	Hillsboro.................N. D.	47·23 N	97·05 W
80	Hillsboro.................Ohio	39·10 N	83·40 W
65	Hillsboro......Ore. (Portland In.)	45·31 N	122·59 W
77	Hillsboro..................Tex.	32·01 N	97·06 W
71	Hillsboro..................Wis.	43·39 N	90·20 W
85	Hillsburgh (hĭlz'bûrg) Can. (Toronto In.)	43·48 N	80·09 W
66	Hills Creek Res............Ore.	43·41 N	122·26 W
80	Hillsdale (hĭls-dāl).........Mich.	41·55 N	84·35 W
157	Hilo (hē'lō).........Hawaii (In.)	19·44 N	155·01 W
111	Hilversum (hĭl'vẽr-sŭm) Neth. (Amsterdam In.)	52·13 N	5·10 E
142	Himachal Pradesh (Ter.)....India	36·03 N	77·41 E
145	Himalaya Mts. (hĭ-mä'là-yà).Asia	29·30 N	85·02 E
153	Himeji (hē'mȧ-jě)............Jap.	34·50 N	134·42 E
111	Himmelpforten (hē'měl-pfōr-těn) Ger. (Hamburg In.)	53·37 N	9·19 E
95	Hinche (hēn'chȧ) (ǎNsh).....Hai.	19·10 N	72·05 W
159	Hinchinbrook (I.) (hĭn-chĭn-brōōk) Austl.	18·23 S	146·57 W
110	Hinckley (hĭnk'lĭ)..........Eng.	52·32 N	1·21 W
110	Hindley (hĭnd'lĭ)............Eng.	53·32 N	2·35 W
145	Hindu Kush Mts. (hĭn'dōō kōōsh') Asia	35·15 N	68·44 E
143	Hindupur (hĭn'dōō-pōōr)....India	13·52 N	77·34 E
86	Hines Creek (hīnz)..........Can.	56·15 N	118·33 W
83	Hingham (hĭng'ǎm) Mass. (Boston In.)	42·14 N	70·53 W
75	Hinkley (hĭnk'-lĭ) Ohio (Cleveland In.)	41·14 N	81·45 W
124	Hinojosa (ē-nô-kô'sä).........Sp.	38·30 N	5·09 W
75	Hinsdale (hĭnz'dāl) Ill. (Chicago In.)	41·48 N	87·56 W
80	Hinton (hĭn'tŭn).........W. Va.	37·40 N	80·55 W
153	Hirado (I.) (hē'rä-dō).......Jap.	33·19 N	129·18 E
153	Hirakata (hē'rä-kä'tä) Jap. (Ōsaka In.)	34·49 N	135·40 E
153	Hiraoka (hē'rä-ō'kä) Jap. (Ōsaka In.)	34·40 N	135·39 E
153	Hiratsuka (hē-rät-sōō'kȧ)....Jap.	35·20 N	139·19 E
146	Hirgis Nuur (L.)..........Mong.	49·18 N	94·21 E
152	Hirosaki (hē'rô-sä'kē)........Jap.	40·31 N	140·38 E
153	Hirose (hē'rô-sä)............Jap.	35·20 N	133·11 E
153	Hiroshima (hē-rô-shē'mȧ)....Jap.	34·22 N	132·25 E
122	Hirson (ēr-sôN')...............Fr.	49·54 N	4·00 E
89	Hispaniola (I.) (hĭ'spǎn-ĭ-ō-lȧ) N. A.	17·30 N	73·15 W
142	Hissar....................India	29·15 N	75·47 E
144	Hit (hĭt)....................Iraq	33·32 N	42·35 E
152	Hitachi (hē-tä'chě)...........Jap.	36·42 N	140·47 E
77	Hitchcock (hĭch'kŏk)...Tex. (In.)	29·21 N	95·01 W
123	Hitdorf (hēt'dōrf).Ger. (Ruhr In.)	51·04 N	6·56 E
153	Hitoyoshi (hē'tô-yō'shē)....Jap.	32·13 N	130·45 E
112	Hitra (I.) (hĭträ)...........Nor.	63·34 N	7·37 E
111	Hittefeld (hē'tě-fěld) Ger. (Hamburg In.)	53·23 N	9·59 E
153	Hiwasa (hē'wȧ-sä)...........Jap.	33·44 N	134·31 E
78	Hiwassee (R.) (hī-wôs'sē)...Tenn.	35·10 N	84·35 W
118	Hjälmaren (L.)..............Swe.	59·07 N	16·05 E
118	Hjo (yō)....................Swe.	58·19 N	14·11 E
118	Hjørring (jûr'ĭng)..........Den.	57·27 N	9·59 E
121	Hlohovec (hlō'hô-věts).....Czech.	48·24 N	17·49 E
160	Hobart (hō'bȧrt)..........Austl.	43·00 S	147·30 E
75	Hobart........Ind. (Chicago In.)	41·31 N	87·15 W
72	Hobart....................Okla.	35·02 N	99·06 W
65	Hobart.......Wash. (Seattle In.)	47·25 N	121·58 W
72	Hobbs (hŏbs)............N. Mex.	32·41 N	104·04 W
146	Hobdo Gol (R.)...........Mong.	49·06 N	91·16 E
111	Hoboken (hō'bō-kěn) Bel. (Brussels In.)	51·11 N	4·20 E
84	Hoboken...N. J. (New York In.)	40·43 N	74·03 W
118	Hobro (hô-brô')............Den.	56·38 N	9·47 E
84	Hobson (hŏb'-sŭn) Va. (Norfolk In.)	36·54 N	76·31 W
161	Hobson's B. (hŏb'sŭnz) Austl. (Melbourne In.)	37·54 S	144·45 E
148	Hochien (hŭ'jĭän)..........China	38·28 N	116·05 E
148	Hochiu....................China	32·19 N	116·17 E
120	Höchst (hûKst).............Ger.	50·06 N	8·37 E
151	Hoch'uan.................China	30·00 N	106·20 E
65	Hockinson (hŏk'-ĭn-sŭn) Wash. (Portland In.)	45·44 N	122·29 W
92	Hoctún (ôk-tōō'n) Mex. (Yucatan In.)	20·52 N	89·10 W
80	Hodgenville (hŏj'ěn-vĭl)......Ky.	37·35 N	85·45 W
83	Hodges Hill (hŏj'ěz)........Can.	49·03 N	55·54 W
86	Hodgson (hŏj-sŭn)..........Can.	51·16 N	97·40 W
121	Hódmezövásárhely (hōd'mě-zû-vô' shôr-hěl-y').Hung.	46·24 N	20·21 E
121	Hodonin (hē'dô-nén)......Czech.	48·50 N	17·06 E
111	Hoegaarden....Bel. (Brussels In.)	50·46 N	4·55 E
111	Hoek van Holland Neth. (Amsterdam In.)	51·59 N	4·05 E
152	Hoeryŏng (hwěr'yŭng).......Kor.	42·28 N	129·39 E
123	Hoetmar (hût'mär) Ger. (Ruhr In.)	51·52 N	7·54 E
120	Hof (hōf)..................Ger.	50·19 N	11·55 E
148	Hofei (hŏ'fā)...............China	31·51 N	117·15 E
112	Hofsjökull (Gl.) (hôfs'yü'kōōl) Ice.	64·55 N	18·40 W
	Hofuf, see Al Hufūf		
94	Hog (I.) (hŏg)............Ba. Is.	25·05 N	77·20 W
80	Hog (I.)..................Mich.	45·50 N	85·20 W
78	Hogansville (hō'gǎnz-vĭl)......Ga.	33·10 N	84·54 W
95	Hog Cay (I.).............Ba. Is.	23·35 N	75·30 W
95	Hogsty Rf................Ba. Is.	21·45 N	73·50 W
111	Hohenbrunn (hō'hěn-brōōn) Ger. (Munich In.)	48·03 N	11·42 E
123	Hohenlimburg (hō'hěn lēm'bōōrg) Ger. (Ruhr In.)	51·20 N	7·35 E
111	Hohen Neuendorf (hō'hēn noi'ěn-dōrf).Ger. (Berlin In.)	52·40 N	13·22 E
120	Hohe Tauern (Mts.) (hō'ě tou'ěrn) Aus.	47·11 N	12·12 E
84	Hohokus (hō-hō-kŭs) N. J. (New York In.)	41·01 N	74·08 W
151	Hohsien....................China	24·20 N	24·20 E
148	Hohsien (hō'syěn').........China	31·44 N	118·20 E
148	Ho Hu (L.) (hŭ'hoo).......China	31·37 N	119·57 E
72	Hoisington (hoi'zĭng-tŭn)...Kans.	38·30 N	98·46 W
153	Hojo (hō'jô)................Jap.	33·58 N	132·50 E
159	Hokitika (hō-kĭ-tē'kä)..N. Z. (In.)	42·43 S	171·12 E
152	Hokkaido (I.) (hôk'kī-dō)....Jap.	43·30 N	142·45 E
151	Hokou (hō'kō')............China	29·58 N	116·20 E
118	Holbaek (hôl'běk)..........Den.	55·42 N	11·40 E
92	Holbox (ôl-bō'x) Mex. (Yucatan In.)	21·33 N	87·19 W
92	Holbox, Isla (I.) (ē's-lä-ôl-bō'x) Mex. (Yucatan In.)	21·40 N	87 21 W
69	Holbrook (hōl'brōōk)........Ariz.	34·55 N	110·15 W
83	Holbrook....Mass. (Boston In.)	42·10 N	71·01 W
83	Holden (hōl'děn) Mass. (Boston In.)	42·21 N	71·51 W
73	Holden.....................Mo.	38·42 N	94·00 W
80	Holden..................W. Va.	37·45 N	82·05 W
73	Holdenville (hōl'děn-vĭl)....Okla.	35·05 N	96·25 W
72	Holdrege (hōl'drěj).........Nebr.	40·25 N	99·28 W
118	Hölen (hûl'ěn)..............Nor.	59·34 N	10·40 E
95	Holguín (ôl-gēn')...........Cuba	20·55 N	76·15 W
81	Holidaysburg (hŏl'ĭ-dāz-bûrg).Pa.	40·30 N	78·30 W
120	Hollabrunn.................Aus.	48·33 N	16·04 E
80	Holland (hŏl'ǎnd)..........Mich.	42·45 N	86·10 W
111	Hollandsch Diep (Chan.) Neth. (Amsterdam In.)	51·43 N	4·25 E
111	Hollenstedt (hō'lěn-shtět) Ger. (Hamburg In.)	53·22 N	9·43 E
74	Holliday (hŏl'ĭ-dā) Mo. (Kansas City In.)	39·02 N	94·48 W
83	Hollis (hŏl'ĭs)..N. H. (Boston In.)	42·30 N	71·29 W
72	Hollis.....................Okla.	34·39 N	99·56 W
68	Hollister (hŏl'ĭs-tẽr).........Calif.	36·50 N	121·25 W
83	Holliston (hŏl'ĭs-tŭn) Mass. (Boston In.)	42·12 N	71·25 W
80	Holly (hŏl'ĭ)...............Mich.	42·45 N	83·30 W
65	Holly.........Wash. (Seattle In.)	47·34 N	122·58 W
78	Holly Springs (hŏl'ĭ sprĭngz) Miss.	34·45 N	89·28 W
74	Hollywood (hŏl'ē-wōōd) Calif. (Los Angeles In.)	34·06 N	118·20 W
79	Hollywood............Fla. (In.)	26·00 N	80·11 W
74	Holmes Park Mo. (Kansas City In.)	38·57 N	94·33 W
159	Holmes Rfs. (hōmz)........Austl.	16·33 S	148·43 E
118	Holmestrand (hôl'mě-strän)..Nor.	59·29 N	10·17 E
118	Holmsbu (hôlms'bōō)........Nor.	59·36 N	10·26 E
118	Holmsjön (L.)..............Swe.	62·23 N	15·43 E
118	Holstebro (hôl'stě-brô').......Den.	56·22 N	8·39 E
78	Holston (R.) (hōl'stŭn).....Tenn.	36·02 N	83·42 W
110	Holt (hōlt).................Eng.	53·05 N	2·53 W
73	Holton (hōl'tŭn)............Kans.	39·27 N	95·43 W
116	Holy (I.) (hō'lĭ)............Wales	53·45 N	4·45 W
116	Holy (I.)...................Eng.	55·43 N	1·48 W
64	Holy Cross (hō'lĭ krôs)....Alaska	62·10 N	159·40 W
116	Holyhead (hŏl'ē-hěd)........Wales	53·48 N	4·45 W
72	Holyoke (hōl'yōk)...........Colo.	40·36 N	102·18 W
81	Holyoke...................Mass.	42·10 N	72·40 W
153	Homano (hō-mä'nō) Jap. (Tōkyō In.)	35·33 N	140·08 E
123	Homberg (hōm'běrgh) Ger. (Ruhr In.)	51·27 N	6·42 E
74	Home Gardens (hōm gär'd'nz) Calif. (Los Angeles In.)	33·53 N	117·32 W
74	Homeland (hōm'lǎnd) Calif. (Los Angeles In.)	33·44 N	117·07 W
84	Homeplace (hōm-plās) La. (New Orleans In.)	29·27 N	89·40 W
64	Homer (hō'mẽr)...........Alaska	59·42 N	151·30 W
77	Homer......................La.	32·46 N	93·05 W
79	Homestead (hōm'stěd)..Fla. (In.)	25·27 N	80·28 W
74	Homestead Mich. (Sault Ste. Marie In.)	46·20 N	84·07 W
75	Homestead...Pa. (Pittsburgh In.)	40·29 N	79·55 W
73	Homestead Natl. Mon. of America Nebr.	40·16 N	96·51 W
84	Homewood (hōm'wōōd) Ala. (Birmingham In.)	33·28 N	86·48 W
75	Homewood......Ill. (Chicago In.)	41·34 N	87·40 W
73	Hominy (hŏm'ĭ-nĭ).........Okla.	36·25 N	96·24 W
78	Homochiho (R.) (hō-mō-chĭt'ō).Miss.	31·23 N	91·15 W
115	Homs (hōms)...............Syr.	34·42 N	36·52 E
147	Honan (Prov.) (hō'nän')....China	33·58 N	112·33 E
98	Honda (hōn'dȧ)...........Col. (In.)	5·13 N	74·45 W
94	Honda, Bahía (B.) (bä-ē'ä-ô'n-dä) Cuba	23·10 N	83·20 W
76	Hondo.....................Tex.	29·20 N	99·08 W
92	Hondo, Rio (R.) (hon-dō') Br. Hond. (Yucatan In.)	18·16 N	88·32 W
72	Hondo (R.)..............N. Mex.	33·22 N	105·06 W
88	Honduras (hŏn-dōō'rǎs).....N. A.	14·30 N	88·00 W
88	Honduras, Gulf of..........N. A.	16·30 N	87·30 W
79	Honea Path (hŭn'ĭ pǎth.....S. C.	34·25 N	82·16 W
118	Hønefoss (hē'ně-fôs).........Nor.	60·10 N	10·15 E
81	Honesdale (hōnz'dāl).........Pa.	41·30 N	75·15 W
68	Honey (R.) (hŭn'ĭ).........Calif.	40·11 N	120·34 W
73	Honey Grove (hŭn'ĭ grōv)...Tex.	33·35 N	95·54 W
85	Honfleur (ôN-flûr') Can. (Quebec In.)	46·39 N	70·53 W
122	Honfleur (ôN-flûr')............Fr.	49·26 N	0·13 E
151	Hon Gay..................Viet.	20·58 N	107·10 E
159	Honiara..................Austl.	9·15 S	159·45 E
116	Honiton (hŏn'ĭ-tŏn)..........Eng.	50·49 N	3·10 W
151	Hong Kong (I.) (hŏng' kŏng').Asia	22·15 N	114·40 E
157	Honolulu (hŏn-ô-lōō'lōō) Hawaii (In.)	21·18 N	157·50 W
157	Honomu (hŏn'ô-mōō) Hawaii (In.)	19·50 N	155·04 W
152	Honshū (I.) (hŏn'shōō)......Jap.	36·50 N	135·20 E
66	Hood, Mt...................Ore.	45·20 N	121·43 W
65	Hood Can. (hōōd) Wash. (Seattle In.)	47·45 N	122·45 W
66	Hood River................Ore.	45·42 N	121·30 W
65	Hoodsport (hōōdz'pōrt) Wash. (Seattle In.)	47·25 N	123·09 W
142	Hoogly (R.) (hōōg'lĭ).......India	21·30 N	87·28 E
111	Hoogstraten...Bel. (Brussels In.)	51·24 N	4·46 E
157	Hookena (hōō-kě-nȧ).Hawaii (In.)	19·23 N	155·51 W
72	Hooker (hōōk'ẽr)...........Okla.	36·49 N	101·13 W
92	Hool (ōō'l)...Mex. (Yucatan In.)	19·32 N	90·22 W
64	Hoonah (hōō'nä)..........Alaska	58·05 N	135·25 W
66	Hoopa Valley Ind. Res. (hōō'pȧ) Calif.	41·18 N	123·35 W
73	Hooper (hōōp'ẽr)..........Nebr.	41·37 N	96·31 W
74	Hooper.Utah (Salt Lake City In.)	41·10 N	112·08 W
64	Hooper Bay..............Alaska	61·32 N	166·02 W
80	Hoopeston (hōōps'tŭn)........Ill.	40·35 N	87·40 W
81	Hoosick Falls (hōō'sĭk).....N. Y.	42·55 N	73·15 W
68	Hoover Dam (hōō'vẽr)......Nev.	36·00 N	115·06 W
84	Hopatcong, L. (hō-pǎt'kong) N. J. (New York In.)	40·57 N	74·38 W
64	Hope (hōp)..............Alaska	60·54 N	149·48 W
73	Hope......................Ark.	33·41 N	93·35 W
86	Hope......................Can.	49·25 N	121·10 W
70	Hope.....................N. D.	47·17 N	97·45 W
87	Hopedale (hōp'dāl)..........Can.	55·26 N	60·11 W
83	Hopedale (hōp'dāl) Mass. (Boston In.)	42·08 N	71·33 W
147	Hopeh (Prov.)............China	39·09 N	115·22 E
92	Hopelchén (o-pěl-chě'n) Mex. (Yucatan In.)	19·47 N	89·51 W
87	Hope Mts..................Can.	53·58 N	62·29 W
87	Hopes Advance, C. (hōps ǎd-vǎns') Can.	61·00 N	69·12 W
158	Hopetoun (hōp'toun)......Austl.	33·50 S	120·15 E
84	Hopewell (hōp'wěl) N. J. (New York In.)	40·23 N	74·45 W
79	Hopewell..................Va.	37·14 N	77·15 W
166	Hopetown (hōp'toun)......S. Afr.	29·35 S	24·10 E
69	Hopi Ind. Res. (hō'pē)......Ariz.	36·20 N	110·30 W
74	Hopkins (hŏp'-kĭns) Minn. (Minneapolis, St. Paul In.)	44·55 N	93·24 W
78	Hopkinsville (hŏp'-kĭns-vĭl)...Ky.	36·50 N	87·28 W
83	Hopkinton (hŏp'-kĭn-tŭn) Mass. (Boston In.)	42·14 N	71·31 W
151	Hop'u.....................China	21·28 N	109·10 E
66	Hoquiam (hō'kwĭ-ǎm).....Wash.	47·00 N	123·53 W
118	Horby (hûr'bü)..............Swe.	55·50 N	13·41 E
93	Horconcitos (ŏr-kôn-sē'-tôs)..Pan.	8·18 N	82·11 W
168	Hordio...Som. (Horn of Afr. In.)	10·43 N	51·05 E
120	Horgen (hôr'gěn)..........Switz.	47·16 N	8·35 E
71	Horicon (hŏr'ĭ-kŏn).........Wis.	43·26 N	88·40 W
144	Hormuz, Str. of (hôr'mŭz')...Asia	26·37 N	15·27 E
	Horn, C., see Hornos, Cabo de		
159	Horn (Is.) (hôrn)..........Austl.	10·30 S	143·30 E
112	Hornavan (L.)..............Swe.	65·54 N	16·17 E
111	Horneburg (hôr'ně-bōōrgh) Ger. (Hamburg In.)	53·30 N	9·35 E
81	Hornell (hôr-něl')...........N. Y.	42·10 N	77·40 W
86	Horn Mts..................Can.	62·12 N	120·29 W
100	Hornos, C. de (Horn, C.) (kȧ'-bô-dě-ŏ'r-nôs) (kä'p-hôr'n) Chile	56·00 S	67·00 W
161	Hornsby (hôrnz' bĭ) Austl. (Sydney In.)	33·43 S	151·06 E
118	Hornslandet (I.)............Swe.	61·40 N	17·58 E
100	Horqueta (ŏr-kě'tä)..........Par.	23·20 S	57·00 W
72	Horse Cr. (hôrs)...........Colo.	38·49 N	103·48 W
70	Horse Cr..................Wyo.	41·33 N	104·39 W
83	Horse Is...................Can.	50·11 N	55·45 W
118	Horsens (hôrs'ěns)..........Den.	55·50 N	9·49 E
65	Horseshoe B. (hôrs-shōō) Can. (Vancouver In.)	49·23 N	123·16 W
110	Horsforth (hôrs'fŭrth).......Eng.	53·50 N	1·38 W
160	Horsham (hôr'shǎm) (hôrs'ǎm) Austl.	36·42 S	142·17 E
111	Horst (hōrst).Ger. (Hamburg In.)	53·49 N	9·37 E
118	Horten (hôr'těn)............Nor.	59·26 N	10·27 E

ng-sing; ŋ-baŋk; N-nasalized n; nŏd; cŏmmit; ōld; ôbey ôrder; fōōd; fŏŏt; ou-out; s-soft; sh-dish; th-thin; pūre; ûnite; ûrn; stŭd; circŭs; ü-as "y" in study; '-indeterminate vowel.

Page	Name Pronunciation Region	Lat. °′	Long. °′
73	Horton (hôr'tŭn) Kans.	39·38 N	95·32 W
64	Horton (R.) (hôr'tŭn) Alaska	68·38 N	122·00 W
110	Horwich (hŏr'ĭch) Eng.	53·36 N	2·33 W
151	Hoshan China	31·30 N	116·25 E
153	Hososhima (hō'sô-shē'mä) Jap.	32·25 N	131·40 E
100	Hoste (ôs'tā) (I.) Chile	55·20 S	70·45 W
90	Hostotipaquillo (ôs-tō'tĭ-pä-kēl'yō) Mex.	21·09 N	104·05 W
153	Hota (hō'tä) Jap. (Tōkyō In.)	35·08 N	139·50 E
146	Hotien (Khotan) (hō'tyĕn') (kō-tän') China	37·11 N	79·50 E
95	Hoto Mayor (ô-tô-mä-yô'r) Dom. Rep.	18·45 N	69·10 W
64	Hot Springs (hŏt sprĭngs) Alaska	65·00 N	150·20 W
73	Hot Springs Ark.	34·29 N	93·02 W
70	Hot Springs S. D.	43·28 N	103·32 W
81	Hot Springs Va.	38·00 N	79·55 W
73	Hot Springs Natl. Park Ark.	34·30 N	93·00 W
95	Hotte, Massif de la (Mts.) Hai.	18·25 N	74·00 W
68	Hotville (hŏt'-vĭl) Calif.	32·50 N	115·24 W
148	Houchen (hō'jĕn) China	36·59 N	118·59 E
123	Houdan (ōō-däN') Fr. (Paris In.)	48·47 N	1·36 E
71	Houghton (hō'tŭn) Mich.	47·06 N	88·36 W
80	Houghton (L.) Mich.	44·20 N	84·45 W
123	Houilles (ōō-yēs') Fr. (Paris In.)	48·55 N	2·11 E
82	Houlton (hōl'tŭn) Maine	46·07 N	67·50 W
77	Houma (hōō'mȧ) La.	29·36 N	90·43 W
81	Housatonic (R.) (hōō-sȧ-tŏn'ĭk) Conn.-Mass.	41·50 N	73·25 W
74	House Springs (hous sprĭngs) Mo. (St. Louis In.)	38·24 N	90·34 W
78	Houston (hūs'tŭn) Miss.	33·53 N	89·00 W
77	Houston Tex. (In.)	29·46 N	95·21 W
77	Houston Ship Chan. Tex. (In.)	29·38 N	94·57 W
166	Houtbaai S. Afr. (Cape Town In.)	34·03 S	18·22 E
158	Houtman Rocks (Is.) (hout'män) Austl.	28·15 S	112·45 E
116	Hove (hōv) Eng.	50·50 N	0·09 W
69	Hovenweep Natl. Mon. (hō'v'n-wēp) Colo.-Utah	37·27 N	108·50 W
73	Howard (hou'ȧrd) Kans.	37·27 N	96·10 W
70	Howard S. D.	44·01 N	97·31 W
110	Howden (hou'dĕn) Eng.	53·44 N	0·52 W
160	Howe, C. (hou) Austl.	37·30 S	150·40 E
80	Howell (hou'ĕl) Mich.	42·40 N	84·00 W
85	Howick (hou'ĭk) Can. (Montreal In.)	45·11 N	73·51 W
167	Howick S. Afr. (Natal In.)	29·29 S	30·16 E
156	Howland (I.) (hou'lȧnd) Oceania	1·00 N	176·00 W
142	Howrah (hou'rä) India (Calcutta In.)	22·33 N	88·20 E
73	Hoxie (hŏk'sĭ) Ark.	36·03 N	91·00 W
116	Hoy (I.) (hoi) Scot.	58·53 N	3·10 W
150	Hoyang China	35·18 N	110·18 E
110	Hoylake (hoi-lāk') Eng.	53·23 N	3·11 W
151	Hoyüan China	23·48 N	114·45 E
120	Hradec Králové (hrä'dĕts krä'lô-vā) Czech.	50·14 N	15·50 E
121	Hranice (hrän'yĕ-tsĕ) Czech.	49·33 N	17·45 E
121	Hrinová (hrēn'yô-vä) Czech.	48·36 N	19·32 E
121	Hron R. Czech.	48·22 N	18·42 E
121	Hrubieszów (hrōō-byä'shōōf) Pol.	50·48 N	23·54 E
126	Hrvatska (Croatia) (Reg.) (hr-väts'kä) Yugo.	45·24 N	15·18 E
149	Hsaiolung China (Canton In.)	22·27 N	113·26 E
146	Hsawnhsup Bur.	24·29 N	94·45 E
148	Hsiaching (sĭä'jĭn) China	36·58 N	115·59 E
148	Hsiai (sĭä'yē) China	34·15 N	116·07 E
151	Hsiamen China	24·28 N	118·20 E
151	Hsiamen (Amoy) (ȧ-moi') China	24·30 N	118·10 E
	Hsian, see Sian		
148	Hsiang (hsē'äng') China	39·43 N	116·08 E
148	Hsiangch'eng (sĭäng'chĕng) China	33·11 N	114·52 E
148	Hsiangch'eng China	33·52 N	113·31 E
150	Hsiangho (hsē'äng'-hō') China (Peking In.)	39·46 N	116·59 E
147	Hsiaohsinganling Shanmo (Lesser Khingan Mts.) China	49·50 N	127·26 E
148	Hsiaoku Ho (R.) (sĭou'gōō hŭ) China	36·29 N	120·06 E
151	Hsiap'u China	27·00 N	120·00 E
148	Hsiats'un (sĭä'ts'ün) China	36·54 N	121·31 E
151	Hsich'ang China	26·50 N	102·25 E
151	Hsi Chiang (R.) China	22·00 N	109·18 E
149	Hsi Chiang (R.) China (Canton In.)	22·47 N	113·01 E
148	Hsichung Tao (I.) (sē'joong'dou) China	39·27 N	121·06 E
149	Hsients'unhsü China (Canton In.)	23·10 N	113·41 E
150	Hsienyang China	34·20 N	108·40 E
150	Hsifeng (hsē'fĕng') China	42·40 N	124·40 E
148	Hsihoying (sē'hŭ'yĭng) China	39·58 N	114·50 E
148	Hsihsienchen (sē'sĭän'jĕn) China	37·21 N	119·59 E
148	Hsi Hu (L.) (sē'hōō) China	32·31 N	116·04 E
150	Hsiliao (R.) China	43·23 N	121·40 E
149	Hsinch'ang China (Shanghai In.)	31·02 N	121·38 E
148	Hsincheng (sĭn'jeng) China	34·24 N	113·43 E
148	Hsinchiachai (sĭn'jĭä'jäĭ) China	36·59 N	117·33 E
142	Hsinchiang (Mts.) China	41·52 N	81·20 E
151	Hsinchu (hsĭn'chōō') Taiwan	24·48 N	121·00 E
151	Hsingan China	25·44 N	110·32 E
151	Hsingcheng (sĭng'chĕng) China	40·38 N	120·41 E
148	Hsingchiawan (sĭng'jĭä'wäN) China	37·16 N	114·54 E
148	Hsinghua (sĭng'hōōȧ) China	32·58 N	119·48 E
148	Hsingt'ai (sĭng'täĭ) China	37·04 N	114·33 E
148	Hsinhsiang (sĭn'sĭäng) China	35·17 N	113·49 E
148	Hsinhsien (sĭn'sĭäN) China	36·14 N	115·38 E
150	Hsinhsien China	38·20 N	112·45 E
151	Hsinhua China	27·45 N	111·20 E
151	Hsinhui China	22·40 N	113·08 E
146	Hsining China	36·52 N	101·36 E
151	Hsinkao Shan (Mtn.) Taiwan	23·38 N	121·05 E
	Hsinking, see Ch'angch'un		
150	Hsinmin China	42·00 N	122·42 E
148	Hsinp'u (sĭn'pōō) China	34·35 N	119·09 E
148	Hsint'ai (sĭn'täĭ) China	35·55 N	117·44 E
149	Hsint'ang China (Canton In.)	23·06 N	113·06 E
149	Hsinti China (Canton In.)	22·43 N	113·20 E
148	Hsintien (sĭn'dĭäN) China	31·33 N	115·17 E
148	Hsinyang (sĭn'yäng) China	32·08 N	114·04 E
150	Hsinyeh China	32·40 N	112·20 E
148	Hsip'ing (sĭ'ping) China	33·21 N	114·01 E
151	Hsisha Ch'üntao (Parcel Is.) China	16·40 N	113·00 E
151	Hsishui China	30·30 N	115·10 E
148	Hsiungyüen China	40·10 N	122·08 E
148	Hsiyang (sē'yäng) China	37·37 N	113·42 E
151	Hsüancheng China	30·52 N	118·48 E
150	Hsuanhua China	40·35 N	115·05 E
148	Hsuanhuatien (sōōäN'hōōȧ'dĭäN) China	31·42 N	114·29 E
148	Hsüch'ang (sü'chäng) China	34·02 N	113·49 E
148	Hsüchou (Süchow) China	34·17 N	117·10 E
148	Hsüi (sü'yē) China	31·02 N	113·49 E
151	Hsün Chiang (R.) China	23·28 N	110·30 E
98	Huacho (wä'chō) Peru	11·13 S	77·29 W
148	Huaian (hōōäĭ'äN) China	33·31 N	119·11 E
147	Huai Ho (R.) (hōōäĭ'hŭ) China	32·07 N	114·38 E
148	Huai Ho (R.) China	33·05 N	117·50 E
150	Huailai China	40·20 N	115·45 E
148	Huailinchen (hōōäĭlĭn'jĕn) China	31·27 N	117·36 E
	Huaining, see Anking		
148	Huaiyang (hōōäĭ'yang) China	33·45 N	114·54 E
148	Huaiyin (hōōäĭ'yĭn) China	33·34 N	118·58 E
148	Huaiyüan (hōōäĭ'yōōäN) China	32·53 N	117·13 E
90	Huajicori (wä-jê-kō'rê) Mex.	22·41 N	105·24 W
91	Huajuapan de León (wäj-wä'päm dā lā-ōn') Mex.	17·46 N	97·45 W
151	Hualien (hwä'lyĕn') Taiwan	23·58 N	121·58 E
98	Huallaga (R.) (wäl-yä'gä) Peru	8·12 S	76·34 W
69	Hualpai Ind. Res. (wäl'pī) Ariz.	35·41 N	113·38 W
69	Hualpai Mts. Ariz.	34·53 N	113·54 W
98	Huamachuco (wä-mä-chōō'kō) Peru	7·52 S	78·11 W
91	Huamantla (wä-män'tlȧ) Mex.	19·18 N	97·54 W
90	Huamuxtitlán (wä-mōōs-tē-tlän') Mex.	17·49 N	98·38 W
98	Huancavelica (wän'kä-vä-lē'kä) Peru	12·47 S	75·02 W
98	Huancayo (wän-kä'yō) Peru	12·09 S	75·04 W
98	Huanchaca (wän-chä'kä) Bol.	20·90 S	66·40 W
146	Huan Chiang (R.) China	36·45 N	106·30 E
148	Huangch'iao (hōōäNg'chĭou) China	32·15 N	120·13 E
148	Huangch'uan (hōōäNg'chōōäN) China	32·07 N	115·01 E
148	Huang Ho, Old Course of the (R.) (hōōäng' hu) China	34·28 N	116·59 E
150	Huanghoutien China (Peking In.)	39·22 N	116·53 E
148	Huanghsien (hōōäNg'sĭäN) China	37·39 N	120·32 E
148	Huangli (hōōäNg'lē) China	31·39 N	119·42 E
149	Huanglien China (Canton In.)	22·53 N	113·09 E
149	Huangp'u Chiang (R.) China (Shanghai In.)	30·56 N	121·16 E
146	Huangyüan China	37·00 N	101·01 E
150	Huanjen China	41·10 N	125·30 E
98	Huánuco (wä-nōō'kō) Peru	9·50 S	76·17 W
98	Huanuni (wä-nōō'-nē) Bol.	18·11 S	66·43 W
93	Huapí, Montañas de (Mts.) (môn-tä'n-yäs-dĕ-wä'-pē') Nic.	12·35 N	84·43 W
90	Huaquechula (wä-kĕ-chōō'-lä) Mex.	18·44 N	98·37 W
98	Huaral (wä-rä'l) Peru	11·28 S	77·11 W
98	Huarás (ōōä'rä's) Peru	9·32 S	77·29 W
98	Huascarán, Nevs. (Pk.) (wäs-kä-rän') Peru	9·05 S	77·50 W
100	Huasco (wäs'kō) Chile	28·32 S	71·16 W
150	Huatien China	42·38 N	126·45 E
91	Huatla de Jiménez (wä'-tlä-dĕ-kē-mĕ'-nĕz) Mex.	18·08 N	96·49 W
90	Huatlatlauch (wä'tlä-tlä-ōō'ch) Mex.	18·40 N	98·04 W
91	Huatusco (wä-tōōs'kō) Mex.	19·09 N	96·57 W
90	Huauchinango (wä-ōō-chē-näŋ'gō) Mex.	20·09 N	98·03 W
93	Huaunta (wä-ōō'n-tä) Nic.	13·30 N	83·32 W
93	Huaunta, Laguna (L.) (lä-gōō'-nä-wä-ōō'n-tä) Nic.	13·35 N	83·46 W
90	Huautla (wä-ōō'tlä) Mex.	21·04 N	98·13 W
148	Huayhe Hu (L.) (hōōäĭ'hŭ'hōō) China	32·49 N	117·00 E
90	Huaynamota, Rió de (R.) (rê'ō-dĕ-wäy-nä-mō'tä) Mex.	22·10 N	104·36 W
148	Huayüan Hu (L.) (hōōȧ'yüan'hoo) China	33·03 N	117·33 E
91	Huazolotitlán (Sta. María) (wäzō-lô-tlē-tlän') Mex.	16·18 N	97·55 W
85	Hubalta (hu-bôl'tȧ) Can. (Calgary In.)	51·02 N	113·58 W
83	Hubbard (hŭb'ĕrd) N. H. (Boston In.)	42·53 N	71·12 W
77	Hubbard Tex.	31·53 N	96·46 W
80	Hubbard (L.) Mich.	44·45 N	83·30 W
64	Hubbard, Mt. Can.	60·24 N	139·00 W
76	Hubbard Creek Res. Tex.	32·50 N	98·55 W
143	Hubli (hōō'blê) India	15·25 N	75·09 E
123	Hückeswagen (hü'kĕs-vä'gĕn) Ger. (Ruhr In.)	51·09 N	7·20 E
110	Hucknall (hŭk'nȯl) Eng.	53·02 N	1·12 W
110	Huddersfield (hŭd'ĕrz-fēld) Eng.	53·39 N	1·47 W
118	Hudiksvall (hōō'dĭks-väl) Swe.	61·44 N	17·05 E
85	Hudson (hŭd'sŭn) Can. (Montreal In.)	45·26 N	74·08 W
83	Hudson Mass. (Boston In.)	42·24 N	71·34 W
80	Hudson Mich.	41·50 N	84·15 W
81	Hudson N. Y.	42·15 N	73·45 W
75	Hudson Ohio (Cleveland In.)	41·15 N	81·27 W
74	Hudson Wis. (Minneapolis, St. Paul In.)	44·59 N	92·45 W
87	Hudson B. Can.	60·15 N	85·30 W
81	Hudson Falls N. Y.	43·20 N	73·30 W
85	Hudson Heights Can. (Montreal In.)	45·28 N	74·09 W
81	Hudson R. N. Y.	41·55 N	73·55 W
87	Hudson Str. Can.	62·34 N	72·13 W
151	Hué (ü-ā') Viet.	16·28 N	107·42 E
124	Huebra (R.) (wĕ'brä) Sp.	40·44 N	6·17 W
92	Huehuetenango (wā-wȧ-tȧ-näŋ'gō) Guat.	15·19 N	91·26 W
90	Huejotzingo (wā-hô-tzĭŋ'gō) Mex.	19·09 N	98·24 W
90	Huejúcar (wā-hōō'kär) Mex.	22·26 N	103·12 W
90	Huejuquilla el Alto (wā-hōō-kēl'yä ĕl äl'tō) Mex.	22·42 N	102·54 W
90	Huejutla (wā-hōō'tlä) Mex.	21·08 N	98·26 W
124	Huelma (wĕl'mä) Sp.	37·39 N	3·36 W
124	Huelva (wĕl'vä) Sp.	37·16 N	6·58 W
124	Huercal-Overa (wĕr-käl' ō-vä'rä) Sp.	37·12 N	1·58 W
72	Huerfano (R.) (wâr'fȧ-nō) Colo.	37·41 N	105·13 W
125	Huésca (wĕs'kä) Sp.	42·07 N	0·25 W
124	Huéscar (wās'kär) Sp.	37·50 N	2·34 W
90	Huetamo de Múñez (wȧ-tä'mō dā-mōōn'yĕz) Mex.	18·34 N	100·53 W
124	Huete (wā'tȧ) Sp.	40·09 N	2·42 W
90	Hueycatenango (wĕy-kȧ-tĕ-nȧ'n-gô) Mex.	17·31 N	99·10 W
91	Hueytlalpan (wā'ī-tläl'pän) Mex.	20·03 N	97·41 W
84	Huffman (hŭf'mȧn) Ala. (Birmingham In.)	33·36 N	86·42 W
72	Hugh Butler (L.) Nebr.	40·21 N	100·40 W
159	Hughenden (hū'ĕn-dĕn) Austl.	20·58 S	144·13 E
158	Hughes (hūz) Austl.	30·45 S	129·30 E
74	Hugo (hū'gō) Minn. (Minneapolis, St. Paul In.)	45·10 N	93·00 W
73	Hugo Okla.	34·01 N	95·32 W
72	Hugoton (hū'gō-tŭn) Kans.	37·10 N	101·28 W
90	Huichapan (wē-chä-pän') Mex.	20·22 N	99·39 W
98	Huila (wē'lȧ) (Dept.) Col. (In.)	3·10 N	75·20 W
98	Huila, Nevado de (Pk.) (nĕ-vä-dô-de-wē'lȧ) Col. (In.)	2·59 N	76·01 W
151	Huilai China	23·02 N	116·18 E
151	Huili China	26·48 N	102·20 E
91	Huimanguillo (wē-män-gēl'yō) Mex.	17·50 N	93·16 W
148	Huimin (hōōĭ mĭn) China	37·29 N	117·32 E
91	Huitzilac (ōōē't-zē-lä'k) Mex. (Mexico City In.)	19·01 N	99·16 W
90	Huitzitzilingo (wē-tzē-tzē-lē'n-go) Mex.	21·11 N	98·42 W
90	Huitzuco (wê-tzōō'kō) Mex.	18·16 N	99·20 W
91	Huixquilucan (ōōē'x-kē-lōō-kä'n) Mex. (Mexico City In.)	19·21 N	99·22 W
91	Huixtla (wēs'tlä) Mex.	15·12 N	92·28 W
151	Huiyang China	23·05 N	114·25 E
148	Hukouchi (hōōgō jē) China	33·22 N	117·07 E
150	Hulan (hōō'län') China	45·58 N	126·32 E
150	Hulan (R.) China	42·20 N	126·30 E
152	Hulin (hōō'lĭn') China	45·45 N	133·25 E
85	Hull (hŭl) Can. (Ottawa In.)	45·26 N	75·43 W
110	Hull Eng.	53·45 N	0·25 W
83	Hull Mass. (Boston In.)	42·18 N	70·54 W
110	Hull (R.) Eng.	53·47 N	0·20 W
111	Hulst (hōōlst) Neth. (Amsterdam In.)	51·17 N	4·01 E
149	Huluk'eng China (Canton In.)	22·41 N	113·25 E
150	Hulutao (hōō'lōō-tä'ō) China	40·40 N	122·55 E
168	Ḩulwān (hĕl'wän) U. A. R. (Nile In.)	29·50 N	31·22 E
89	Humacao (ōō-mä-kä'ō) P. R. (Puerto Rico In.)	18·09 N	65·49 W
98	Humaitá (ōō-mä-ē-tä') Braz.	7·37 S	62·58 W
100	Humaitá Par.	27·08 S	58·18 W
166	Humansdorp (hōō'mäns-dôrp) S. Afr.	33·57 S	24·45 E
166	Humbe (hōōm'bȧ) Ang.	16·50 S	14·55 E
116	Humber (L.) (hŭm'bĕr)		
116	Humber (L.) (hŭm'bĕr) Eng.	53·38 N	0·40 W
83	Humbermouth (hŭm'bĕr-mŭth) Can.	48·54 N	57·35 W
85	Humber R. Can. (Toronto In.)	43·53 N	79·40 W
77	Humble (hŭm'b'l) Tex.	29·58 N	95·15 W
86	Humboldt (hŭm'bōlt) Can.	52·15 N	105·01 W
71	Humboldt Iowa	42·43 N	94·11 W
73	Humboldt Kans.	37·48 N	95·26 W
73	Humboldt Nebr.	40·10 N	95·57 W
62	Humboldt (R.) U. S.	40·30 N	116·50 W
155	Humboldt-Baai (B.) (hŭm'bōlt) W. Irian	2·30 S	141·30 E
66	Humboldt B. Calif.	40·48 N	124·25 W
66	Humboldt R., East Fork Nev.	40·59 N	115·21 W
66	Humboldt R., North Fork Nev.	41·25 N	115·45 W
78	Humbolt Tenn.	35·47 N	88·55 W
68	Humbolt Ra. Nev.	40·12 N	118·16 W
68	Humbolt Salt Marsh Nev.	39·49 N	117·41 W
68	Humbolt Sink Nev.	39·58 N	118·54 W
149	Humenchai China (Canton In.)	22·49 N	113·39 E
69	Humphreys Pk. (hŭm'frĭs) Ariz.	35·20 N	111·40 W
120	Humpolec (hōōm'pō-lĕts) Czech.	49·33 N	15·21 E
92	Humuya R. (ōō-mōō'yä) Hond.	14·38 N	87·36 W
112	Hunaflói (B.) (hōō'nä-flō'ĭ) Ice.	65·41 N	20·44 W
147	Hunan (Prov.) (hōō'nän') China	28·08 N	111·25 E
147	Hunch'un (hōōn'chōōn') China	42·53 N	130·34 E
127	Hunedoara (kōō'nĕd-wä'rȧ) Rom.	45·45 N	22·54 E
102	Hungary (hŭn'gȧ-rĭ) Eur.	46·44 N	17·55 E
160	Hungerford (hŭn'gĕr-fĕrd) Austl.	28·50 S	144·32 E
67	Hungry Horse Res. (hŭŋ'gȧ-rĭ hôrs) Mont.	48·11 N	113·30 W
151	Hung Shui Ho (R.) (hōōng) China	25·00 N	107·22 E
148	Hungtse Hu (L.) (hōōngzhŭ hōō) China	33·17 N	118·37 E
120	Hunsrück (Mts.) (hōōns'rûk) Ger.	49·43 N	7·12 E
120	Hunte R. (hōōn'tĕ) Ger.	52·45 N	8·26 E
159	Hunter Is. (hŭn-tĕr) Austl.	40·33 S	143·36 E
80	Huntingburg (hŭnt'ĭng-bûrg) Ind.	38·15 N	86·55 W
81	Huntingdon (hŭnt'ĭng-dŭn) Can.	45·10 N	74·05 W
65	Huntingdon Can. (Vancouver In.)	49·00 N	122·16 W

Page	Name Pronunciation Region	Lat. °′	Long. °′
78	Huntingdon..............Tenn.	36·00 N	88·23 W
110	Huntingdon (Co.)..........Eng.	52·26 N	0·19 W
80	Huntington................Ind.	40·55 N	85·30 W
84	Huntington.N. Y. (New York In.)	40·51 N	73·25 W
81	Huntington................Pa.	40·30 N	78·00 W
80	Huntington..............W. Va.	38·25 N	82·25 W
74	Huntington Beach Calif. (Los Angeles In.)	33·39 N	118·00 W
74	Huntington Park Calif. (Los Angeles In.)	33·59 N	118·14 W
78	Huntsville (hŭnts′-vĭl).......Ala.	35·43 N	86·36 W
81	Huntsville................Can.	45·20 N	79·15 W
73	Huntsville.................Mo.	39·24 N	92·32 W
77	Huntsville.................Tex.	30·44 N	95·34 W
74	Huntsville Utah (Salt Lake City In.)	41·16 N	111·46 W
91	Hunucmá (hōō-nōōk-mä′)...Mex.	21·01 N	89·54 W
148	Huolu (hōōŭ lōō)..........China	38·05 N	114·20 E
155	Huon G.............N. Gui. Ter.	7·15 S	147·45 E
147	Hupeh (Prov.)...........China	31·20 N	111·58 E
80	Hurd, C. (hûrd)...........Can.	45·15 N	81·45 W
71	Hurley (hûr′lĭ).............Wis.	46·26 N	90·11 W
100	Hurlingham (ōō′r-lēn-gäm) Arg. (In.)	34·20 S	58·38 W
80	Huron (hū′rŏn)............Ohio	41·20 N	82·35 W
70	Huron....................S. D.	44·22 N	98·15 W
63	Huron, L. (hū′rŏn)....U. S.-Can.	45·15 N	82·40 W
71	Huron Mts.(hū′rŏn)........Mich.	46·47 N	87·52 W
75	Huron R......Mich. (Detroit In.)	42·12 N	83·26 W
64	Hurricane (hŭr′ĭ-kān).....Alaska	63·00 N	149·30 W
69	Hurricane.................Utah	37·10 N	113·20 W
94	Hurricane Flats (Shoal) (hŭ-rĭ-kǎn flăts).Ba. Is.	23·35 N	78·30 W
112	Húsavik...................Ice.	66·00 N	17·10 W
129	Huşi (kōōsh′)..........Sov. Un.	46·52 N	28·04 E
118	Huskvarna (hōōsk-vär′nȧ)...Swe.	57·48 N	14·16 E
120	Husum (hōō′zōōm).........Ger.	54·29 N	9·04 E
74	Hutchins (hŭch′ĭnz) Tex. (Dallas, Fort Worth In.)	32·38 N	96·43 W
72	Hutchinson (hŭch′ĭn-sŭn)....Kans.	38·02 N	97·56 W
71	Hutchinson...............Minn.	44·53 N	94·23 W
150	Hut′o Ho (R.) (hōō′tō′hō′).China	38·10 N	114·00 E
148	Huwu (hōō wōō)..........China	31·17 N	119·48 E
117	Huy (û-ē′) (hû′ê)...........Bel.	50·33 N	5·14 E
112	Hvannadalshnukur (Mtn.)....Ice.	64·09 N	16·46 W
147	Hwang Ho (Yellow R.) (hwäng′hō′).China	35·06 N	113·39 E
146	Hwang Ho, Old beds of the.China	40 28 N	106·34 E
126	Hvar (I.) (кhvär)..........Yugo.	43·08 N	16·28 E
152	Hwangju (hwäng′jōō′).......Kor.	38·39 N	125·49 E
64	Hydaburg (hī-dȧ′bûrg)....Alaska	55·18 N	132·40 W
110	Hyde (hīd).................Eng.	53·27 N	2·05 W
143	Hyderābād (hī-dĕr-ȧ-băd′)..India	17·29 N	79·28 E
142	Hyderabad (hī-dĕr-ȧ-băd′) W. Pak.	25·29 N	68·28 E
143	Hyderabad (State).........India	23·29 N	76·50 E
123	Hyères (ē-âr′)..............Fr.	43·09 N	6·08 E
123	Hyères, Iles d′ (Is.) (ēl′dyâr′)..Fr.	42·57 N	6·17 E
152	Hyesanjin (hyĕ′sän-jĭn′).....Kor.	41·11 N	128·12 E
80	Hymera (hī-mē′rȧ)..........Ind.	39·10 N	87·20 W
67	Hyndman Pk. (hīnd′măn)..Idaho	43·38 N	114·04 W
153	Hyōgo (Pref.) (hĭyō′gō) Jap. (Ōsaka In.)	34·54 N	135·15 E
86	Hythe.....................Can.	55·18 N	119·34 W
153	Ia (R.) (ē′ä)....Jap. (Ōsaka In.)	34·54 N	135·34 E
121	Iaşi (yä′shē)...............Rom.	47·10 N	27·40 E
155	Iba (ē′bä)......Phil. (Manila In.)	15·20 N	119·59 E
164	Ibadan (ē-bä′dän)...........Nig.	7·26 N	3·48 E
98	Ibagué (ē-bȧ-gā′).......Col. (In.)	4·27 N	75·13 W
127	Ibar (R.) (ē′bär)...........Yugo.	43·22 N	20·35 E
153	Ibaragi (ē-bä′rä-gē) Jap. (Ōsaka In.)	34·49 N	135·35 E
98	Ibarra (ē-bär′rä)............Ec.	0·19 N	78·08 W
163	Iberian Pen.............Port.-Sp.	41·00 N	0·07 W
82	Iberville (ē-bȧr-vēl′) (ĭ′bĕr-vĭl) Can.	45·14 N	73·01 W
164	Ibi (ē′bē)...................Nig.	8·08 N	9·45 E
99	Ibiapaba, Serra da (Mts.) (sĕ′r-rä-dä-ē-byä-pȧ′bä).Braz.	3·30 S	40·55 W
125	Ibiza (ē-bē′thä)..............Sp.	38·55 N	1·24 E
125	Ibiza, Isla de (Iviza I.) (ē′s-lä-dĕ-ē-bē′zȧ).Sp.	39·07 N	1·05 E
167	Ibo (ē′bō)..................Moz.	12·17 S	40·45 E
144	Ibrahim, Jabal (Mtn.)...Sau. Ar.	20·31 N	41·17 E
168	Ibrahim, Port.U. A. R. (Suez In.)	29·57 N	32·33 E
98	Ica (ē′kä)..................Peru	14·09 S	75·42 W
98	Icá (R.) (ē-kä′).............Braz.	2·56 S	69·12 W
98	Içana (ē-sä′nä).............Braz.	0·15 N	67·19 W
66	Ice Harbor Dam..........Wash.	46·15 N	118·54 W
102	Iceland (īs′lănd)...........Eur.	65·12 N	19·45 W
151	Ich′ang (ē′chäng′).........China	30·38 N	111·22 E
142	Ichāpur......India (Calcutta In.)	22·47 N	88·21 E
153	Ichibusayama (Mt.) (ē′chē-bōō′sȧ-yä′mä).Jap.	32·19 N	131·08 E
153	Ichikawa (ē′chē-kä′wä) Jap. (Tōkyō In.)	35·44 N	139·54 E
153	Ichinomiya (ē′chē-nō-mē′yȧ) Jap.	35·19 N	136·49 E
152	Ichinomiya..............Jap.	35·23 N	140·33 E
153	Ichinomoto (ē-chē′nō-mō-tō) Jap. (Ōsaka In.)	34·37 N	135·50 E
129	Ichnya (ĭch′nyä)........Sov. Un.	50·47 N	32·23 E
99	Icó (ē-kô′).................Braz.	6·25 S	38·43 W
98	Icutú, Cerro (Mtn.) (sĕ′r-rô-ē-kōō-tōō′) Ven.	7·07 N	65·30 W
64	Icy C. (ī′sĭ)..............Alaska	70·20 N	161·40 W
73	Idabel (ī′dȧ-bĕl)...........Okla.	33·52 N	94·47 W
70	Idagrove (ī′dȧ-grōv)........Iowa	42·22 N	95·29 W
164	Idah (ē′dä)..................Nig.	7·08 N	6·45 E
62	Idaho (State) (ī′dȧ-hō)......U. S.	44·00 N	115·10 W
67	Idaho Falls...............Idaho	43·30 N	112·01 W
72	Idaho Springs.............Colo.	39·43 N	105·32 W
124	Idanha-a-Nova (ê-dän′yȧ-ä-nō′vȧ).Port.	39·58 N	7·13 W
146	Ideriin Gol (R.)..........Mong.	48·58 N	98·38 E
168	Idfū (ĕd′fōō)..U. A. R. (Nile In.)	24·57 N	32·53 E
127	Idhra (I.)..................Grc.	37·20 N	23·30 E
154	Idi (ē′dē)................Indon.	4·58 N	97·47 E
168	Idkū (ĕd′kōō).U. A. R. (Nile In.)	31·18 N	30·20 E
168	Idkū L.........U. A. R. (Nile In.)	31·13 N	30·22 E
110	Idle (R.) (īd′′l)............Eng.	53·22 N	0·56 W
126	Idrija (ē′drē-ȧ)............Yugo.	46·01 N	14·01 E
167	Idutywa (ē-dōō-tī′wȧ) S. Afr. (Natal In.)	32·06 S	28·18 E
117	Ieper......................Bel.	50·50 N	2·53 E
126	Ierápetra...........Grc. (Inset)	35·01 N	25·48 E
126	Iesi (yā′sē)..................It.	43·37 N	13·20 E
164	Ife........................Nig.	7·36 N	4·38 E
164	Iferouane (ēf′rōō-än′).......Niger	19·23 N	8·24 E
163	Ifni (ēf′nē)..................Afr.	29·45 N	11·00 W
134	Igarka (ē-gär′kȧ)........Sov. Un.	67·22 N	86·16 E
126	Iglesias (ē-lĕ′syôs)...........It.	39·20 N	8·34 E
164	Igli (ē-glē′).................Alg.	30·32 N	2·15 W
87	Igloolik....................Can.	69·33 N	81·18 W
139	′Igma, Gebel el (Mts.) U. A. R. (Palistine In.)	29·12 N	33·42 E
65	Ignacio (ĭg-nä′cĭ-ō) Calif. (San Francisco In.)	38·05 N	122·32 W
100	Iguaçu (R.) (ē-gwä-sōō′).Braz.(In.)	22·42 S	43·19 W
90	Iguala (ê-gwä′lä)..........Mex.	18·18 N	99·34 W
125	Igualada (ē-gwä-lä′dä).......Sp.	41·35 N	1·38 E
100	Iguassu (R.) (ē-gwä-sōō′)....Braz.	25·45 S	52·30 W
100	Iguassu Falls (Falls)........Braz.	25·40 S	54·16 W
101	Iguatama (ē-gwä-tá′mä) Braz (Rio de Janeiro In.)	20·13 S	45·40 W
99	Iguatu (ē-gwä-tōō′).........Braz.	6·22 S	39·17 W
164	Iguidi, Erg (Dune)..........Alg.	26·22 N	6·53 W
155	Iguig (ē-gēg′).Phil. (Manila In.)	17·46 N	121·44 E
150	Ihsien......................China	41·30 N	121·15 E
148	I Ho (R.) (yē′hŭ)..........China	34·38 N	118·07 E
150	Iian.......................China	46·18 N	129·40 E
153	Iida (ē′ē-dä)...............Jap.	35·39 N	137·53 E
132	Iijoki (R.) (ē′yō′kĭ).........Fin.	65·28 N	27·00 E
153	Iizuka (ē′ē-zōō-kä)..........Jap.	33·39 N	130·39 E
164	Ijebu Ode (ê-jĕ′bōō ōdâ).....Nig.	6·46 N	3·59 E
117	IJsselmeer (L.) (ī′sĕl-mär)....Neth.	52·46 N	5·14 E
119	Ikaalinen (ē′kä-lĭ-nĕn).......Fin.	61·47 N	22·55 E
127	Ikaría (I.) (ē-kä′ryȧ)........Grc.	37·43 N	26·07 E
153	Ikeda-Kawanishi (ē′kȧ-dä kä-wä′ nê-shē).Jap. (Osaka In.)	34·49 N	135·26 E
127	Ikhtiman (ēk′tê-män).........Bul.	42·26 N	23·49 E
153	Iki (I.) (ē′kê)...............Jap.	33·46 N	129·44 E
166	Ikoma (ē-kō′mä).............Tan.	2·08 S	34·47 E
136	Iksha (ĭk′shȧ) Sov. Un. (Moscow In.)	56·10 N	37·30 E
155	Ilagen (ê-lä′gän).Phil. (Manila In.)	17·09 N	121·52 E
151	Ilan (ē′län′)..............Taiwan	24·50 N	121·42 E
121	Iława (ê-lä′vȧ)..............Pol.	53·35 N	19·36 E
85	Ile-Bizard Valois (yl-bē-zär vä-lōō-ä′).Can. (Montreal In.)	45·29 N	73·53 W
133	Ilek (ē′lyĕk)...........Sov. Un.	51·30 N	53·10 E
133	Ilek (R.)...............Sov. Un.	51·20 N	53·10 E
85	Ile-Perrot (yl-pĕ-rōt′) Can. (Montreal In.)	45·21 N	73·54 W
164	Ilesha......................Nig.	7·45 N	4·50 E
110	Ilford (ĭl′fērd)..Eng. (London In.)	51·33 N	0·06 E
116	Ilfracombe (ĭl-frȧ-kōōm′)....Eng.	51·13 N	4·08 W
101	Ilhabela (ē′lä-bĕ′lä) Braz. (Rio de Janeiro In.)	23·47 S	45·21 W
101	Ilha Grande, Baia de (B.) (ēl′yȧ grän′dĕ) Braz. (Rio de Janeiro In.)	23·17 S	44·25 W
124	Ilhavo (ēl′yȧ-vô)...........Port.	40·36 N	8·41 W
99	Ilhéus (ē-lĕ′ōōs)...........Braz.	14·52 S	39·00 W
64	Iliamna (ē-lê-ăm′nä)......Alaska	59·45 N	155·05 W
64	Iliamna (L.)..............Alaska	59·25 N	155·30 W
64	Iliamna Vol.)..............Alaska	60·18 N	153·25 W
134	Ilim (R.) (ē-lyêm′)......Sov. Un.	57·28 N	103·00 E
134	Ilimsk (ē-lyêmsk′)......Sov. Un.	56·47 N	103·43 E
155	Ilin (I.) (ê-lyēn′) Phil. (Manila In.)	12·16 N	120·57 E
129	Il′intsiy................Sov. Un.	49·07 N	29·13 E
127	Iliodhrómia (I.)............Grc.	39·18 N	23·35 E
81	Ilion (ĭl′ĭ-ŭn)...............N. Y.	43·00 N	75·05 W
146	Ili R. (ē′lē)............Sov. Un.	43·46 N	77·41 E
110	Ilkeston (ĭl′kĕs-tŭn)........Eng.	52·58 N	1·19 W
98	Illampu, Nevado (Pk.) (nĕ-vä′dô-ēl-yäm-pōō′).Bol.	15·50 S	68·15 W
155	Illano B. (ēl-yä-nô)........Phil.	7·38 N	123·41 E
101	Illapel (ē-zhä-pĕ′l) Chile (Santiago In.)	31·37 S	71·10 W
120	Iller R. (ĭl′er).............Ger.	47·52 N	10·06 E
98	Illimani, Nevado (Pk.) (nĕ-vä′dô-ēl-yē-mä′nē).Bol.	16·50 S	67·38 W
63	Illinois (State) (ĭl-ĭ-noi′) (ĭl-ĭ-noiz′) U. S.	40·25 N	90·40 W
73	Illinois (R.).................Ill.	40·52 N	89·31 W
128	Il′men′, Ozero (L.) (ô′zĕ-rô el″ men″) (ĭl′mĕn).Sov. Un.	58·18 N	32·00 E
117	Ilmenau (ēl′mē-nou).........Ger.	50·37 N	13·02 E
117	Ilmenau (R.)...............Ger.	53·20 N	10·20 E
164	Ilo (ē′lō)...................Nig.	11·30 N	3·41 E
98	Ilo.........................Peru	17·46 S	71·13 W
92	Ilobasco (ê-lô-bäs′kô)........Sal.	13·57 N	88·46 W
154	Iloilo (ē-lô-ē′lō)............Phil.	10·49 N	122·33 E
92	Ilopango, L. (ē-lô-päŋ′gō).....Sal.	13·48 N	88·50 W
164	Ilorin (ê-lô-rēn′)...........Nig.	8·32 N	4·30 E
128	Ilūkste................Sov. Un.	55·59 N	26·20 E
65	Ilwaco (ĭl-wä′kô) Wash. (Portland In.)	46·19 N	124·02 W
132	Ilych (R.) (ê′l′ĭch).......Sov. Un.	62·30 N	57·30 E
153	Imabari (ē′mä-bä′rē)..........Jap.	34·05 N	132·58 E
153	Imai (ē-mī′).....Jap. (Ōsaka In.)	34·30 N	135·47 E
152	Iman (R.) (ê-män′)......Sov. Un.	45·40 N	134·31 E
135	Iman...................Sov. Un.	46·07 N	133·21 E
132	Imandra (L.) (ē-män′drȧ).Sov. Un.	67·40 N	32·30 E
168	Imbābah (ēm-bä′bȧ) U. A. R. (Nile In.)	30·06 N	31·09 E
100	Imbarié (ēm-bä-ryĕ′)..Braz. (In.)	22·38 S	43·13 W
136	Imeni Morozova (ĭm-yĕ′nyĭ mô rô′zô vȧ) Sov. Un. (Leningrad In.)	59·58 N	31·02 E
128	Imeni Moskvy, Kanal (Moscow Can.) (kȧ-näl′ ĭm-yă′nĭ mŏs-kvĭ).Sov. Un.	56·33 N	37·15 E
152	Imienpo (yēmĭänpŭ).......China	44·59 N	127·56 E
80	Imlay City (ĭm′lā).........Mich.	43·00 N	83·15 W
120	Immenstadt (ĭm′ĕn-shtät)....Ger.	47·34 N	10·12 E
168	Immerpan (ĭmēr-pän).....S. Afr. (Johannesburg & Pretoria In.)	24·29 S	29·14 E
126	Imola (ē′mô-lä)..............It.	44·19 N	11·43 E
126	Imotski (ê-môts′kê)........Yugo.	43·25 N	17·15 E
167	Impendle (ĭm-pĕnd′lȧ) S. Afr. (Natal In.)	29·38 S	29·54 E
126	Imperia (êm-pā′rê-ä)..........It.	43·52 N	8·00 E
75	Imperial (ĭm-pē′rĭ-ăl) Pa. (Pittsburgh In.)	40·27 N	80·15 W
68	Imperial Beach Calif. (San Diego In.)	32·34 N	117·08 W
69	Imperial Res..............Ariz.	32·57 N	114·19 W
68	Imperial Valley...........Calif.	33·00 N	115·22 W
165	Impfondo (ĭmp-fōn′dô)...Con. B.	1·46 N	17·53 E
145	Imphal (ĭmp′hŭl)..........India	24·42 N	94·00 E
127	Imroz (I.) (ĭm′rŏz)..........Tur.	40·10 N	25·27 E
153	Ina (R.) (ê-nä′).Jap. (Ōsaka In.)	34·56 N	135·21 E
68	Inaja Ind. Res. (ê-nä′hä)....Calif.	32·56 N	116·37 W
112	Inari (L.)...................Fin.	69·02 N	26·22 E
164	In Azaoua (Oasis) (ēn-ä-zou′ȧ).Alg.	20·57 N	7·24 E
125	Inca (ēŋ′kä).................Sp.	39·43 N	2·53 E
133	Ince Burun (C.) (ĭn′jȧ)......Tur.	42·00 N	35·00 E
152	Inch′ŏn (ĭn′chŭn)...........Kor.	37·26 N	126·46 E
126	Incudine, Mt. (Mtn.) (ēn-kōō-dē′ nȧ) (ăN-kü-dēn′).Cor.	41·53 N	9·17 E
118	Indals-älven (R.)...........Swe.	62·50 N	16·50 E
155	Indang (ēn′däng′) Phil. (Manila In.)	14·11 N	120·53 E
76	Indé (ēn′dā)................Mex.	25·53 N	105·15 W
73	Independence (ĭn-dê-pĕn′dĕns) Kans.	37·14 N	95·42 W
74	Independence Mo. (Kansas City In.)	39·06 N	94·26 W
75	Independence Ohio (Cleveland In.)	41·23 N	81·39 W
66	Independence...............Ore.	44·49 N	123·13 W
66	Independence Mts.........Nev.	41·15 N	116·02 W
133	Inder (L.)..............Sov. Un.	48·20 N	52·10 E
138	India (ĭn′dĭ-ȧ)..............Asia	23·00 N	77·30 E
71	Indian (L.) (ĭn′dĭ-ăn)......Mich.	46·04 N	86·34 W
81	Indian (R.)................N. Y.	44·05 N	75·45 W
81	Indiana (ĭn-dĭ-ăn′ȧ)..........Pa.	40·40 N	79·10 W
63	Indiana (State)............U. S.	39·50 N	86·45 W
75	Indianapolis (ĭn-dĭ-ăn-ăp′ō-lĭs) Ind. (Indianapolis In.)	39·45 N	86·08 W
65	Indian Arm (R.) (ĭn′dĭ-ăn ärm) Can. (Vancouver In.)	49·21 N	122·55 W
86	Indian Head (ĭn′dĭ-ăn hĕd)..Can.	50·36 N	103·42 W
7	Indian Ocean		
71	Indianola (ĭn-dĭ-ăn-ō′lȧ).....Iowa	41·22 N	93·33 W
78	Indianola.................Miss.	33·29 N	90·35 W
135	Indigirka (R.) (ēn-dê-gēr′kȧ) Sov. Un.	67·45 N	145·45 E
88	Indio (R.) (ē′n-dyô) Pan. (Panama Canal In.)	9·13 N	78·28 W
154	Indochina (Reg.) (ĭn-dô-chī′nȧ) Asia	17·22 N	105·18 E
154	Indonesia (ĭn′dô-nê-zhȧ).....Asia	4·38 S	118·45 E
142	Indore (ĭn-dōr′)............India	22·48 N	76·51 E
154	Indragiri (R.) (ĭn-drȧ-jē′rê).Indon.	0·27 S	102·05 E
142	Indrāvati (R.) (ĭn-drŭ-vä′tê) India	19·15 N	80·54 E
122	Indre (R.) (ăN′dr′)...........Fr.	47·13 N	0·29 E
118	Indre Solund (I.) (ĭndrĕ-sô-lŭnd) Nor.	61·09 N	4·37 E
85	Indus (ĭn′dŭs).Can. (Calgary In.)	50·55 N	113·45 W
142	Indus (R.)..............W. Pak.	26·43 N	67·41 E
167	Indwe (ĭnd′wȧ).S. Afr. (Natal In.)	31·30 S	27·21 E
133	Inebolu (ê-nȧ-bô′lōō)........Tur.	41·50 N	33·40 E
133	Inego (ē′nȧ-gŭ)..............Tur.	40·05 N	29·20 E
155	Infanta (ēn-fän′tä) Phil. (Manila In.)	14·44 N	121·39 E
155	Infanta........Phil. (Manila In.)	15·50 N	119·53 E
124	Infantes (ēn-fän′tås)..........Sp.	38·44 N	3·00 W
91	Inferror, Laguna (L.) (lä-gōō′nä-ēn-fĕr-rôr).Mex.	16·18 N	94·40 W
124	Infiesto (ēn-fyĕ′s-tô)..........Sp.	43·21 N	5·24 W
80	Ingersoll (ĭn′gēr-sŏl).........Can.	43·05 N	81·00 W
159	Ingham (ĭng′ăm)..........Austl.	18·45 S	146·14 E
94	Ingles, Cayos (Is.) (kä′yōs-ē′n-glĕ′s).Cuba	21·55 N	82·35 W
74	Inglewood (ĭn′g′l-wŏŏd) Calif. (Los Angeles In.)	33·57 N	118·22 W
85	Inglewood..Can. (Toronto In.)...	43·48 N	79·56 W
135	Ingoda (R.) (ēn-gō′dȧ)...Sov. Un.	51·29 N	112·32 E
120	Ingolstadt (ĭŋ′gōl-shtät).....Ger.	48·46 N	11·27 E
129	Ingul (R.) (ēn-gōōl′).....Sov. Un.	47·22 N	32.52 E
129	Ingulets (R.) (ēn-gōōl′yĕts′) Sov. Un.	47·12 N	33·12 E
133	Ingur (R.) (ēn-gōōr′)....Sov. Un.	42·30 N	42·00 E
166	Inhambane (ēn-äm-bä′-nĕ)...Moz.	23·47 S	35·28 E
99	Inhambupe (ēn-yäm-bōō′pä) Braz.	11·47 S	38·13 W
166	Inharrime (ēn-yär-rē′mä)....Moz.	24·17 S	35·07 E
100	Inhomirim (ē-nô-mê-rē′N) Braz. (In.)	22·34 S	43·11 W
167	Inhiuzan (Mtn.) S. Afr. (Natal In.)	29·34 S	30·03 E
146	Ining (ē′nĭng′)............China	43·58 N	80·49 E
98	Inirida (R.) (ē-nê-rē′dä)......Col.	2·25 N	70·38 W
160	Injune (ĭn′jōōn)...........Austl.	25·52 S	148·30 E
125	Inkermann (ĭŋ-kĕr-măn).....Alg.	35·55 N	0·57 E
119	Inkeroinem (ĭn′kĕr-oi-nĕn)....Fin.	60·42 N	26·50 E
75	Inkster (ĭngk′stēr) Mich. (Detroit In.)	42·18 N	83·19 W
160	Innamincka (ĭnn-ȧ′mĭn-kȧ).Austl.	27·50 S	140·48 E
89	Inner Brass (I.) (bräs) Vir. Is. (U. S. A.) (St. Thomas In.)	18·23 N	64·58 W

Page	Name Pronunciation Region	Lat. °′	Long. °′
116	Inner Hebrides (Is.) .... Scot.	57·20 N	6·20 W
146	Inner Mongolian Aut. Reg. (mŏŋ-gō′lĭ-ăn). China	40·39 N	104·13 E
86	Innisfail .... Can.	52·01 N	113·57 W
114	Inn R. (ĭn) .... Ger.-Aus.	48·19 N	13·16 E
120	Innsbruck (ĭns′brŏŏk) .... Aus.	47·15 N	11·25 E
153	Ino (ē′nō) .... Jap.	33·34 N	133·23 E
166	Inongo (ê-nôŋ′gō) .... Con. L.	1·58 S	18·27 E
121	Inowroctaw (ē-nō-vrŏts′läf) ... Pol.	52·48 N	18·16 E
164	In Salah (ēn-sà-lä′) .... Alg.	27·13 N	2·22 E
69	Inscription House Ruin (ĭn′skrĭp-shŭn hous rōō′ĭn). Ariz.	36·45 N	110·47 W
90	Inter-American Hy. (ĭn′tēr ȧ-mĕr′ĭ-kăn). Mex.	22·30 N	99·08 W
71	International Falls (ĭn′tēr-năsh′ŭn-ăl fôlz). Minn.	48·34 N	93·26 W
86	Inuvik .... Can.	68·40 N	134·10 W
153	Inuyama (ē′nōō-yä′mä) ...... Jap.	35·24 N	137·01 E
159	Invercargil (ĭn-vēr-kär′gĭl) N. Z. (In.)	47·18 S	167·27 E
160	Inverel (ĭn-vēr-el′) .... Austl.	29·50 S	151·32 E
74	Invergrove (ĭn′vēr-grōv) Minn. (Minneapolis, St. Paul In.)	44·51 N	93·01 W
83	Inverness (ĭn-vēr-nĕs′) ...... Can.	46·14 N	61·20 W
79	Inverness .... Fla.	28·48 N	82·22 W
116	Inverness .... Scot.	57·30 N	4·07 W
160	Investigator Str. (ĭn-vĕst′ĭ′gā-tôr) Austl.	35·33 S	137·00 E
166	Inyangani, Mt. (ên-yän-gä′nê) S. Rh.	18·06 S	32·37 E
68	Inyo Mts. (ĭn′yō) .... Calif.	36·55 N	118·04 W
136	Inzer R. (ĭn′zĕr) Sov. Un. (Urals In.)	54·24 N	57·17 E
164	In Zize (Oasis) (ēn-zē′zē) ..... Alg.	23·25 N	2·36 E
153	Iō (I.) (ē′wō) .... Jap.	30·46 N	130·15 E
127	Ioánnina (Yannina) (yô-ä′nē-nà) (yä′nē-nà). Grc.	39·39 N	20·52 E
65	Ioco .... Can. (Vancouver In.)	49·18 N	122·53 W
73	Iola (ī-ō′lȧ) .... Kans.	37·55 N	95·23 W
80	Ionia (ī-ō′nĭ-ȧ) .... Mich.	43·00 N	85·10 W
127	Ionian Is. (ī-ō′nĭ-ăn) .... Grc.	39·10 N	20·05 E
115	Ionian Sea .... Eur.	38·59 N	18·48 E
127	Ios (I.) (ī′ŏs) .... Grc.	36·48 N	25·25 E
63	Iowa (State) (ī′ô-wȧ) .... U. S.	42·05 N	94·20 W
71	Iowa (R.) .... Iowa	41·44 N	91·50 W
71	Iowa City .... Iowa	41·39 N	91·31 W
71	Iowa Falls .... Iowa	42·32 N	93·16 W
72	Iowa Park .... Tex.	33·57 N	98·39 W
99	Ipamerí (ē-pä-mȧ-rē′) .... Braz.	17·44 S	48·03 W
121	Ipel R. (ê′pĕl) ...... Czech.-Hung.	48·08 N	19·00 E
98	Ipiales (ē-pê-ä′lȧs) .... Col.	0·48 N	77·45 W
151	Ipin (Süchow) .... China	28·50 N	104·40 E
154	Ipoh .... Mala.	4·45 N	101·05 E
160	Ipswich (ĭps′wĭch) .... Austl.	27·40 S	152·50 E
117	Ipswich .... Eng.	52·05 N	1·05 W
83	Ipswich .... Mass. (Boston In.)	42·41 N	70·50 W
70	Ipswich .... S. D.	45·26 N	99·01 W
99	Ipu (ē-pōō) .... Braz.	4·11 S	40·45 W
128	Iput′ (R.) (ê-pōōt′) ...... Sov. Un.	52·53 N	31·57 E
98	Iquique (ē-kē′kĕ) .... Chile	20·16 S	70·07 W
98	Iquitos (ē-kē′tōs) .... Peru	3·39 S	73·18 W
75	Ira (ī′rȧ) .... Ohio (Cleveland In.)	41·11 N	81·35 W
126	Iráklion (Candia) .... Gr. (In.)	35·20 N	25·10 E
138	Iran (Persia) (ē-rän′) .... Asia	31·15 N	53·30 E
144	Iran, Plat. of .... Iran	32·28 N	58·00 E
154	Iran Mts .... Mala.	2·30 N	114·30 E
90	Irapuato (ē-rä-pwä′tō) ...... Mex.	20·41 N	101·24 W
138	Iraq (ē-räk′) .... Asia	32·00 N	42·30 E
93	Irazu Vol. (ē-rä-zōō′) .... C. R.	9·58 N	83·54 W
139	Irbid (ēr-bēd′) Jordan (Palestine In.)	32·33 N	35·51 E
133	Irbil .... Iraq	36·10 N	44·00 E
132	Irbit (ēr-bêt′) .... Sov. Un.	57·40 N	63·10 E
166	Irebu (ē-rā′bōō) .... Con. L.	0·40 S	17·48 E
102	Ireland (īr-lănd) .... Eur.	53·33 N	13·00 W
136	Iremel′, Gora (Mt.) (gà-rä′ ĭ-rĕ′mĕl). Sov. Un. (Urals In.)	54·32 N	58·52 E
167	Irene (ĭ-rē-nē) .... S. Afr. (Johannesburg & Pretoria In.)	25·53 S	28·13 E
134	Irgiz (ĭr-gēz′) .... Sov. Un.	48·30 N	61·17 E
134	Irgiz (R.) .... Sov. Un.	49·30 N	60·32 E
166	Iringa (ê-rĭŋ′gä) .... Tan.	7·44 S	35·43 E
151	Iriomote Jima (I.) (ērē′-ō-mō-tä) Ryūkyū Is.	24·20 N	123·30 E
92	Iriona (ê-rê-ō′nä) .... Hond.	15·53 N	85·12 W
116	Irish Sea (ī′rĭsh) .... Eur.	53·55 N	5·25 W
134	Irkutsk (ĭr-kŏŏtsk′) ...... Sov. Un.	52·16 N	104·00 E
110	Irlam (ûr′lăm) .... Eng.	53·26 N	2·26 W
95	Irois, Cap des (C.) .... Hai.	18·25 N	74·50 W
84	Irondale (ī′ērn-dăl) Ala. (Birmingham In.)	33·32 N	86·43 W
127	Iron Gate (Gorge) .... Yugo.-Rom.	44·43 N	22·32 E
160	Iron Knob (ī-ăn nŏb) ...... Austl.	32·47 S	137·10 E
71	Iron Mountain (ī′ērn) ...... Mich.	45·49 N	88·04 W
71	Iron River .... Mich.	46·09 N	88·39 W
80	Ironton (ī′ērn-tŭn) .... Ohio	38·30 N	82·45 W
71	Ironwood (ī′ērn-wŏŏd) ...... Mich.	46·28 N	90·10 W
80	Iroquois (R.) (ĭr′ô-kwoi) .. Ill.-Ind.	40·55 N	87·20 W
87	Iroquois Falls .... Can.	48·41 N	80·39 W
153	Irō-Saki (C.) (ē′rō sä′kē) .... Jap.	34·35 N	138·54 E
129	Irpen′ (R.) (ĭr-pĕn′) ...... Sov. Un.	50·13 N	29·55 E
145	Irrawaddy (R.) .... Bur.	23·27 N	96·25 E
154	Irrawaddy, Mouths of the (ĭr-ȧ-wäd′ê). Bur.	15·40 N	94·32 E
146	Irrawaddy R .... Bur.	20·39 N	94·38 E
134	Irtysh (R.) (ĭr-tĭsh′) ..... Sov. Un.	58·32 N	68·31 E
165	Irumu (ê-rōō′mōō) .... Con. L.	1·30 N	29·52 E
124	Irun (ê-rōōn′) .... Sp.	43·20 N	1·47 W
74	Irvine (ûr′vĭn) Calif. (Los Angeles In.)	33·40 N	117·45 W
116	Irvine .... Scot.	55·39 N	4·40 W
80	Irvine .... Ky.	37·40 N	84·00 W
85	Irvine Cr... Can. (Edmonton In.)	53·23 N	113·27 W
74	Irving (ûr′vēng) Tex. (Dallas, Fort Worth In.)	32·49 N	96·57 W
84	Irvington (ûr′vēng-tăn) N. J. (New York In.)	40·43 N	74·15 W
75	Irwin (ûr′-wĭn) Pa. (Pittsburgh In.)	40·19 N	79·42 W
136	Is (ēs) .... Sov. Un. (Urals In.)	58·48 N	59·44 E
88	Isaacs, Mt. (ē-sä-ä′ks) Pan. (Panama Canal In.)	9·22 N	79·01 W
90	Isabela (I.) (ê-sä-bĕ′-lä) ..... Mex.	21·56 N	105·53 W
98	Isabela (I.) (ē-sä-bä′lä) .... Ec.	0·47 S	91·35 W
95	Isabela, Cabo (C.) (kä′bô-ê-sä-bĕ′lä). Dom. Rep.	20·00 N	71·00 W
92	Isabella, Cord. (Mts.) (kôr-dēl-yĕ′rä-ē-sä-bĕlä). Nic.	13·20 N	85·37 W
80	Isabella Ind. Res. (ĭs-ȧ-bĕl′-lȧ) Mich.	43·35 N	84·55 W
129	Isaccea (ê-säk′chä) .... Rom.	45·16 N	28·26 E
112	Isafjördhur (ēs′á-fyûr-dōōr) ... Ice.	66·09 N	22·39 W
165	Isangi (ê-säŋ′gē) .... Con. L.	0·48 N	24·13 E
120	Isar R. (ē′zär) .... Ger.	48·27 N	12·02 E
126	Isarco (R.) (ê-sär′kō) .... It.	46·37 N	11·25 E
155	Isaroga, Vol. (ê-sä-rô-gä) Phil. (Manila In.)	13·40 N	123·23 E
125	Ischia (ēs′kyä) .... It. (Naples In.)	40·29 N	13·58 E
168	Iscia Baidoa Som. (Horn of Afr. In.)	3·19 N	44·20 E
126	Iseo, Lago di (L.) (lä′-gō-dē-ê-zĕ′ō). It.	45·50 N	9·55 E
123	Isère (R.) (ê-zâr′) .... Fr.	45·24 N	6·04 E
123	Iserlohn (ē′zĕr-lōn) Ger. (Ruhr In.)	51·22 N	7·42 E
126	Isernia (ê-zĕr′nyä) .... It.	41·35 N	14·14 E
153	Ise-Wan (B.) (ē′sĕ wän) ...... Jap.	34·49 N	136·44 E
164	Iseyin .... Nig.	8·13 N	3·21 E
151	Ishan .... China	24·32 N	108·42 E
152	Ishikari Wan (B.) (ē′shē-kä-rē wän). Jap.	43·30 N	141·05 E
134	Ishim (ĭsh-êm′) .... Sov. Un.	56·07 N	69·13 E
134	Ishim (R.) .... Sov. Un.	53·17 N	67·45 E
136	Ishimbay (ē-shēm-bī′) Sov. Un. (Urals In.)	53·28 N	56·02 E
148	Ishing (yēsĭng) .... China	31·26 N	119·57 E
152	Ishinomaki (ĭsh-nō-mä′kē) .... Jap.	38·22 N	141·22 E
152	Ishinomaki Wan (B.) (ē-shē-nō-mä′kē wän). Jap.	38·10 N	141·40 E
136	Ishly (ĭsh′lĭ). Sov. Un. (Urals In.)	54·13 N	55·55 E
136	Ishlya (ĭsh′lyȧ) Sov. Un. (Urals In.)	53·54 N	57·48 E
127	Ishm .... Alb.	41·32 N	19·35 E
168	Ishmant ...... U. A. R. (Nile In.)	29·17 N	31·15 E
71	Ishpeming (ĭsh′pē-mĭng) .... Mich.	46·28 N	87·42 W
148	Ishui (yē suĭ) .... China	35·49 N	118·40 E
167	Isipingo (ĭs-ĭ-pĭŋg-gō) S. Afr. (Natal In.)	29·59 S	30·58 E
133	Iskenderun (ĭs-kĕn′dĕr-ōōn) .. Tur.	36·45 N	36·15 E
115	İskenderun Körfezi (G.) ..... Tur.	36·22 N	35·25 E
133	Iskilip (ēs′kĭ-lēp′) .... Tur.	40·40 N	34·30 E
127	Iskūr (R.) (ĭs′k′r) .... Bul.	43·05 N	23·37 E
124	Isla-Cristina (ēs′lä-krê-stē′nä) . Sp.	37·13 N	7·20 W
145	Islamabad .... W. Pak.	33·55 N	73·05 E
92	Isla Mujeres (ē′s-lä-mōō-kĕ′rĕs) Mex. (Yucatan In.)	21·25 N	86·53 W
86	Island (I.) (ī′lănd) .... Can.	53·35 N	89·58 W
83	Islands, B. of (ī′lăndz) ...... Can.	49·11 N	58·45 W
116	Islay (I.) (ī′lā) .... Scot.	55·55 N	6·35 W
122	Isle (R.) (ēl) .... Fr.	45·02 N	0·29 E
110	Isle of Axholme (Reg.) (ăks′-hôm) Eng.	53·33 N	0·48 W
116	Isle of Man (măn) .... Eur.	54·26 N	4·21 W
71	Isle Royale Nat′l Park (īl′roi-ăl′) U. S.	47·57 N	88·37 W
69	Isleta (ēs-lā′tä) (ī-lē′tȧ) .. N. Mex.	34·55 N	106·45 W
82	Isle Verte (ēl vĕrt′) .... Can.	48·01 N	69·20 W
85	Islington (ĭs′lĭng-tŏn) Can. (Toronto In.)	43·39 N	79·31 W
	Ismailia, see Al Isma′īlīyah		
168	Ismā′īlīyah Can. U. A. R. (Suez In.)	30·25 N	31·45 E
111	Ismaning (ēz′mä-nēng) Ger. (Munich In.)	48·14 N	11·41 E
168	Isnā (ēs′nȧ) ... U. A. R. (Nile In.)	25·17 N	32·33 E
119	Isojärvi (L.) .... Fin.	61·47 N	22·00 E
133	Isparta (ê-spär′tȧ) .... Tur.	37·50 N	30·40 E
138	Israel .... Asia (Palestine In.)	31·00 N	35·00 E
65	Issaquah (ĭz′sȧ-kwăh) Wash. (Seattle In.)	47·32 N	122·02 W
123	Isselburg (ē′sĕl-bōōrg) Ger. (Ruhr In.)	51·50 N	6·28 E
122	Issoire (ē-swȧr′) .... Fr.	45·32 N	3·13 E
122	Issoudun (ē-sōō-dăN′) .... Fr.	46·56 N	2·00 E
123	Issum (ē′sōōm) ... Ger. (Ruhr In.)	51·32 N	6·24 E
134	Issyk-Kul, Ozero (L.) ... Sov. Un.	42·13 N	76·12 E
142	Istāda, Ab-i (L.) .... Afg.	32·29 N	69·25 E
133	Istanbul (ē-stän-bōōl′) .... Tur.	41·02 N	29·00 E
127	Istiaía (ĭs-tyī′yä) .... Grc.	38·58 N	23·11 E
98	Istmina (ēst-mē′nä) ..... Col. (In.)	5·10 N	76·40 W
79	Istokpoga (L.) (ĭs-tŏk-pō′gȧ) Fla. (In.)	27·20 N	81·33 W
126	Istra (pen.) (ê-strä) .... Yugo.	45·18 N	13·48 E
127	Istranca Dağ (Mts.) (ĭ-strän′jȧ) Bul.-Turk.	41·50 N	27·25 E
122	Istres (ēs′tr′) ... Fr. (Marseille In.)	43·30 N	5·00 E
100	Itá (ē-tá′) .... Par.	25·39 S	57·14 W
99	Itabaiana (ē-tä-bä-yä-nä) ... Braz.	10·42 S	37·17 W
101	Itabapoana (ē-tä′-bä-pôä′nä) Braz. (Rio de Janeiro In.)	21·19 S	40·58 W
101	Itabapoana (R.) Braz. (Rio de Janeiro In.)	21·11 S	41·18 W
101	Itabirito (ē-tä-bê-rē′tô) Braz. Rio de Janeiro (In.)	20·15 S	43·46 W
101	Itaboraí (ē-tä-bō-räē′) Braz. (Rio de Janeiro In.)	22·46 S	42·50 W
99	Itabuna (ē-tä-bōō′nȧ) .... Braz.	14·47 S	39·17 W
101	Itacoara (ē-tä-kô′ä-rä) Braz. (Rio de Janeiro In.)	21·41 S	42·04 W
99	Itacoatiara (ē-tä-kwȧ-tyä′rȧ). Braz.	3·03 S	58·18 W
101	Itaguaí (ē-tä-gwä-ē′) Braz. (Rio de Janeiro In.)	22·52 S	43·46 W
98	Itagüí (ē-tä′gwē) .... Col. (In.)	6·11 N	75·36 W
100	Itagui (R.) .... Braz. (In.)	22·53 S	43·43 W
100	Itaipava (ē-tī-pä′-vä) .. Braz. (In.)	22·23 S	43·09 W
100	Itaipu (ē-tī′pōō) .... Braz. (In.)	22·58 S	43·02 W
99	Itaituba (ê-tä′ĭ-tōō′bȧ) ...... Braz.	4·12 S	56·00 W
100	Itajái (ē-tä-zhī′) .... Braz.	26·52 S	48·39 W
101	Itajubá (ē-tä-zhōō-bá′) Braz. (Rio de Janeiro In.)	22·26 S	45·27 W
168	Itala ...... Som. (Horn of Afr. In.)	2·45 N	46·15 E
102	Italy (ĭt′ȧ-lê) .... Eur.	43·58 N	11·14 E
77	Italy .... Tex.	32·11 N	96·51 W
100	Itambi (ē-tä′m-bê) .... Braz. (In.)	22·44 S	42·57 W
153	Itami (ē′tä′mē′) .. Jap. (Osaka In.)	34·47 N	135·25 E
101	Itapecerica (ē-tä-pĕ-sĕ-rē′kȧ) Braz. (Rio de Janeiro In.)	21·29 S	45·08 W
99	Itapecurú (R.) (ē-tä-pĕ-kōō-rōō′) Braz.	4·05 S	43·49 W
99	Itapēcuru-Mirim (ê-tä-pĕ′kōō-rōō-mê-rēN′) .. Braz.	3·17 S	44·15 W
101	Itaperuna (ē-tȧ-pȧ-rōō′nä) Braz. (Rio de Janeiro In.)	21·12 S	41·53 W
101	Itapetininga (ē-tä-pĕ-tê-nē′N-gä) Braz. (Rio de Janeiro In.)	23·37 S	48·03 W
99	Itapira (ē-tȧ-pē′rä) .... Braz.	20·42 S	51·19 W
101	Itapira . Braz. (Rio de Janeiro In.)	21·27 S	46·47 W
142	Itarsi .... India	22·43 N	77·45 E
77	Itasca (ī-tăs′kȧ) .... Tex.	32·09 N	97·08 W
71	Itasca (L.) .... Minn.	47·13 N	95·14 W
101	Itatiaia, Pico da (Pk.) (pē′-kô-dȧ-ē-tä-tyȧ′ēä) Braz. (Rio de Janeiro In.)	22·18 S	44·41 W
101	Itatiba (ē-tä-tē′bä) Braz. (Rio de Janeiro In.)	23·01 S	46·48 W
101	Itaúna (ē-tä-ōō′nä) Braz. (Rio de Janeiro In.)	20·05 S	44·35 W
101	Itaverá (ē-tä-vĕ-rá′) Braz. (Rio de Janeiro In.)	22·44 S	44·07 W
80	Ithaca (ĭth′ȧ-kȧ) .... Mich.	43·20 N	84·35 W
81	Ithaca .... N. Y.	42·25 N	76·30 W
127	Itháki (I.) (ē′thä-kê) .... Grc.	38·27 N	20·48 E
166	Itoko (ê-tō′kō) .... Con. L.	1·13 S	22·07 E
168	Itsā (ēt′sȧ) .... U. A. R. (Nile In.)	29·13 N	30·47 E
101	Itu (ē-tōō′) Braz. (Rio de Janeiro In.)	23·16 S	47·16 W
148	Itu .... China	36·42 N	118·30 E
98	Ituango (ē-twäŋ′gō) .... Col. (In.)	7·07 N	75·44 W
99	Ituiutaba (ē-tōō-ēōō-tä′bä) .. Braz.	18·56 S	49·17 W
101	Itumirim (ē-tōō-mê-rē′N) Braz. (Rio de Janeiro In.)	21·20 S	44·51 W
91	Itundujia Santa Cruz (ê-tōōn-dōō-hē′ä sä′n-tä krōō′z). Mex.	16·50 N	97·43 W
152	It′ung .... China	43·15 N	125·10 E
92	Iturbide (ē′tōōr-bē′dhå) Mex. (Yucatan In.)	19·38 N	89·31 W
135	Iturup (I.) (ē-tōō-rōōp′) . Sov. Un.	45·35 N	147·15 E
100	Ituzaingo (ê-tōō-zä-ē′n-gô) Arg. (In.)	34·24 S	58·40 W
111	Itzehoe (ē′tzĕ-hō) Ger. (Hamburg In.)	53·55 N	9·31 E
78	Iuka (ī-ū′kȧ) .... Miss.	34·47 N	88·10 W
101	Iúna (ē-ōō′-nä) Braz. (Rio de Janeiro In.)	20·22 S	41·32 W
134	Iva (R.) .... Sov. Un.	53·45 N	99·30 E
160	Ivanhoe (ĭv′ăn-hō) .... Austl.	32·53 S	144·10 E
121	Ivano-Frankovsk (ē-vä′nō frän-kôvsk′). Sov. Un.	48·53 N	24·46 E
128	Ivanovo (ê-vä′nō-vō) .... Sov. Un.	57·02 N	41·54 E
128	Ivanovo (Oblast) .... Sov. Un.	56·55 N	40·30 E
129	Ivanpol′ (ê-vän′pôl) ...... Sov. Un.	49·51 N	28·11 E
136	Ivanteyevka (ê-vån-tyĕ′yĕf-kȧ) Sov. Un. (Moscow In.)	55·58 N	37·56 E
136	Ivdel′ (ĭv′dyĕl) Sov. Un. (Urals In.)	60·42 N	60·27 E
75	Ives (ī′vĕs) . Wis. (Milwaukee In.)	43·48 N	87·49 W
	Iviza I., see Ibiza, Isla de		
167	Ivohibé (ê-vô-hê-bā′). Malag. Rep.	22·28 S	46·59 E
163	Ivory Coast .... Afr.	7·43 N	6·30 W
126	Ivrea (ê-vrĕ′ä) .... It.	45·25 N	7·54 E
87	Ivugivik .... Can.	62·17 N	77·52 W
152	Iwate Yama (Mt.) (ē-wä-tĕ-yä′mä). Jap.	39·50 N	140·56 E
153	Iwaya (ē′wȧ-yȧ) .. Jap. (Osaka In.)	34·35 N	135·01 E
164	Iwo .... Nig.	7·52 N	4·04 E
90	Ixcateopán (ēs-kä-tä-ō-pän′). Mex.	18·29 N	99·49 W
111	Ixelles .... Bel. (Brussels In.)	50·49 N	4·23 E
91	Ixhuatán (San Francisco) (ēs-hwä-tän′). Mex.	16·19 N	94·30 W
90	Ixhautlán (ēs-wàt-län′) ...... Mex.	20·41 N	98·01 W
90	Ixmiquilpan (ēs-mê-kēl′pän). Mex.	20·30 N	99·12 W
167	Ixopo .... S. Afr. (Natal In.)	30·10 S	30·04 E
91	Ixtacalco (ēs-tä-käl′kō) Mex. (Mexico City In.)	19·23 N	99·07 W
91	Ixtacihuatl (Mtn.) (ē′ks-tä-sē-wä′tl). Mex. (Mexico City In.)	19·10 N	98·38 W
91	Ixtaltepec (Asunción) (ēs-täl-tĕ-pĕk′). Mex.	16·33 N	95·04 W
91	Ixtapalapa (ēs′tä-pä-lä′pä) Mex. (Mexico City In.)	19·21 N	99·06 W
91	Ixtapaluca (ēs′tä-pä-lōō′kä) Mex. (Mexico City In.)	19·18 N	98·53 W
91	Ixtepec (ēks-tĕ′pĕk) .... Mex.	16·37 N	95·09 W
91	Ixtlahuaca (ēs-tlä-wä′kä) Mex. (Mexico City In.)	19·34 N	99·46 W
91	Ixtlán de Juárez (ēs-tlän′ dā hwä′râz). Mex.	17·20 N	96·29 W
90	Ixtlán del Río (ēs-tlän′děl rē′ō) Mex.	21·05 N	104·22 W
151	Iyang (ē′yäng′) .... China	28·52 N	112·12 E
153	Iyo-Nada (Sea) (ē′yō nä-dä) .. Jap.	33·33 N	132·07 E
92	Izabal (ē′zä-bäl′) .... Guat.	15·23 N	89·10 W
92	Izabal, L. (Golfo Dulce) (gôl′fō dōōl′sȧ). Guat.	15·30 N	89·04 W
92	Izalco (ē-zäl′kō) .... Sal.	13·50 N	89·40 W
92	Izamal (ē-zä-mä′l). Mex. (Yucatan)	20·55 N	89·00 W

ăt; finăl; rāte: senâte: ärm: ȧsk: sofȧ: fâre: ch-choose: dh-as th in other; bē; ēvent; bĕt; recĕnt; cratēr; g-go; gh-guttural g; bĭt; ĭ-short neutral; rīde; K-guttural k as ch in German ich;

Page	Name Pronunciation Region	Lat. °′	Long. °′
132	Izhevsk (ê-zhyěfsk′) . . . Sov. Un.	56·50 N	53·15 E
132	Izhma (ĭzh′mȧ) . . . Sov. Un.	65·00 N	54·05 E
132	Izhma (R.) . . . Sov. Un.	64·00 N	53·00 E
136	Izhora R. (ēz′hô-rȧ) Sov. Un. (Leningrad In.)	59·36 N	30·20 E
129	Izmail (ēz-mȧ-ēl) . . . Sov. Un.	27·21 N	28·49 E
127	Izmir (Smyrna) (ĭz-mēr′) (smûr′nȧ). Tur.	38·25 N	27·05 E
127	Izmir Körfezi (G.) . . . Tur.	38·43 N	26·37 E
133	Izmit (ĭz-mēt′) . . . Tur.	40·45 N	29·45 E
153	Izu (I.) (ē′zōō) . . . Jap.	34·32 N	139·25 E
153	Izuhara (ē′zōō-hä′rä) . . . Jap.	34·11 N	129·18 E
153	Izumo (ē′zōō-mō) . . . Jap.	35·22 N	132·45 E
153	Izumu-Otsu (ē′zōō-mōō ō′tsōō) Jap. (Ōsaka In.)	34·30 N	135·24 E
111	Jaachimsthal (yä′kēm-stäl) Ger. (Berlin In.)	52·58 N	13·45 E
144	Jabal Rema (Mtn.) . . . Yemen	14·13 N	44·38 E
120	Jablonec (Nad Nisou) (yäb′lô-nyěts). Czech.	50·43 N	15·12 E
121	Jablunkov P. (yäb′lōōn-kôf). Czech.	49·31 N	18·35 E
99	Jaboatão (zhä-bô-ä-touN) . . . Braz.	8·14 S	35·08 W
144	Jabul Hadur Shuayb (Mtn.) Yemen	15·45 N	43·45 E
125	Jaca (hä′kä) . . . Sp.	42·35 N	0·30 W
90	Jacala (hä-kä′lä) . . . Mex.	21·01 N	99·11 W
92	Jacaltenango (hä-käl-tě-näŋ′gō) Guat.	15·39 N	91·41 W
101	Jacareí (zhä-kȧ-rě-ē′) Braz. (Rio de Janeiro In.)	23·19 S	45·57 W
100	Jacarepagua (zhä-kä-rȧ′pä-gwä′) Braz. (In.)	22·55 S	43·22 W
99	Jacarézinho (zhä-kä-rě′zē-nyȯ) Braz.	23·13 S	49·58 W
120	Jachymov (yä′chĭ-môf) . . . Czech.	50·22 N	12·51 E
77	Jacinto City (hä-sēn′tō) (jȧ-sĭn′tō) Tex. (In.)	29·45 N	95·14 W
72	Jacksboro (jăks′bŭr-ô) . . . Tex.	33·13 N	98·11 W
78	Jackson (jăk′sŭn) . . . Ala.	31·31 N	87·52 W
68	Jackson . . . Calif.	38·22 N	120·47 W
78	Jackson . . . Ga.	33·19 N	83·55 W
78	Jackson . . . Ky.	37·32 N	83·17 W
77	Jackson . . . La.	30·50 N	91·13 W
80	Jackson . . . Mich.	42·15 N	84·25 W
71	Jackson . . . Minn.	43·37 N	95·00 W
78	Jackson . . . Miss.	32·17 N	90·10 W
73	Jackson . . . Mo.	37·23 N	89·40 W
80	Jackson . . . Ohio	39·00 N	82·40 W
78	Jackson . . . Tenn.	35·37 N	88·49 W
161	Jackson, Port. Austl. (Sydney In.)	33·50 S	151·18 E
67	Jackson L. . . . Wyo.	43·57 N	110·28 W
167	Jacksontuin . . . S. Afr. (Johannesburg & Pretoria In.)	25·44 S	27·45 E
78	Jacksonville (jăk′sŭn-vĭl) . . . Ala.	33·52 N	85·45 W
79	Jacksonville . . . Fla.	30·20 N	81·40 W
73	Jacksonville . . . Ill.	39·43 N	90·12 W
77	Jacksonville . . . Tex.	31·58 N	95·18 W
79	Jacksonville Beach . . . Fla.	31·18 N	81·25 W
95	Jacmel (zhȧk-měl′) . . . Hai.	18·15 N	72·30 W
76	Jaco, L. (hä′kō) . . . Mex.	27·51 N	103·50 W
142	Jacobābad . . . W. Pak.	28·22 N	28·27 E
99	Jacobina (zhä-kô-bē′nȧ) . . . Braz.	11·13 S	40·30 W
82	Jacques Cartier, Mt. (Tabletop) (zhȧk′kär-tyā′). Can.	48·59 N	65·59 W
85	Jacques-Cartier, R. Can. (Quebec In.)	47·04 N	71·28 W
83	Jacques Cartier Pass . . . Can.	50·04 N	63·43 W
82	Jacquet River (zhȧ-kě′) (jăk′ĕt) Can.	47·54 N	66·01 W
101	Jacuí (zhä-kōō-ē′) Braz. (Rio de Janeiro In.)	21·03 S	46·43 W
101	Jacutinga (zhä-kōō-těn′gä) Braz. (Rio de Janeiro In.)	21·17 S	46·36 W
139	Jad′ah . . . Jordan (Palestine In.)	31·23 N	35·45 E
120	Jade B. (yä′dě) . . . Ger.	53·28 N	8·17 E
166	Jadotville . . . Con. L.	11·01 S	26·52 E
165	Jādū . . . Libya	31·57 N	12·04 E
98	Jaén (Kä-ě′n) . . . Peru	5·38 S	78·49 W
124	Jaén . . . Sp.	37·45 N	3·48 W
160	Jaffa, C. (jăf′ȧ) . . . Austl.	36·58 S	139·29 E
143	Jaffna (jăf′nȧ) . . . Ceylon	9·44 N	80·09 E
94	Jagüey Grande (hä′gwā grän′dā) Cuba	22·35 N	81·05 W
139	Jahore Str.. Mala. (Singapore In.)	1·22 N	103·37 E
95	Jaibo (R.) (hä-ē′bō) . . . Cuba	20·10 N	75·20 W
142	Jaipur . . . India	26·45 N	77·00 E
142	Jaisaimer . . . India	27·00 N	70·54 E
126	Jajce (yī′tsě) . . . Yugo.	44·20 N	17·19 E
112	Jakobstad (yȧ′kôb-städh) . . . Fin.	63·33 N	22·31 E
91	Jalacingo (hä-lä-sĭŋ′gō) . . . Mex.	97·16 N	19·47 W
145	Jalalabād (jŭ-lä-lä-bäd′) Afg. (Khyber Pass In.)	34·25 N	70·27 E
92	Jalapa (hä-lä′pȧ) . . . Guat.	14·38 N	89·58 W
91	Jalapa de Diaz (San Felipe) (dȧ dē-äz′) (sän fā-lē′pā). Mex.	18·06 N	96·33 W
91	Jalapa del Marqués (děl mär-kās′). Mex.	16·30 N	95·29 W
91	Jalapa Enriquez (ěn-rē′käz).. Mex.	19·32 N	96·53 W
142	Jalgaon . . . India	21·08 N	75·33 E
90	Jalisco (hä-lēs′kō) . . . Mex.	21·27 N	104·54 W
88	Jalisco (State) . . . Mex.	20·07 N	104·45 W
127	Jalomita (R.) . . . Rom.	44·37 N	26·42 E
124	Jalón (R.) (hä-lōn′) . . . Sp.	41·22 N	1·46 W
90	Jalostotitlán (hä-lōs-tē-tlän′). Mex.	21·09 N	102·30 W
91	Jalpa (häl′pā) . . . Mex.	18·12 N	93·06 W
90	Jalpa (häl′pä) . . . Mex.	21·40 N	103·04 W
90	Jalpan (häl′pän) . . . Mex.	21·13 N	99·31 W
142	Jalpur . . . India	20·49 N	86·37 E
91	Jaltepec (häl-tȧ-pěk′) . . . Mex.	17·20 N	95·15 W
91	Jaltipan (häl-tȧ-pän′) . . . Mex.	17·59 N	94·42 W
90	Jaltocan (häl-tô-kän′) . . . Mex.	21·08 N	98·32 W
165	Jālū (Oasis) . . . Libya	28·58 N	21·45 E
94	Jamaica (I.) . . . N. A.	18·21 N	77·31 W
95	Jamaica Cay (I.) . . . Ba. Is.	22·45 N	75·55 W
142	Jamalpur . . . E. Pak.	24·56 N	89·58 E
90	Jamay (hä-mī′) . . . Mex.	20·16 N	103·43 W
127	Jambol (yȧm′bôl) . . . Bul.	42·28 N	26·31 E
155	Jamdena (I.) . . . Indon.	7·23 S	130·30 E
73	James (R.) . . . Mo.	36·51 N	93·22 W
79	James (R.) . . . N. C.	36·07 N	81·48 W
62	James (R.) . . . U. S.	46·25 N	98·55 W
81	James (R.) . . . Va.	37·35 N	77·50 W
87	James B. (jāmz) . . . Can.	53·53 N	80·40 W
84	Jamesburg (jāmz′bûrg) N. J. (New York In.)	40·21 N	74·26 W
95	James Pt. . . . Ba. Is.	25·20 N	76·30 W
158	James Ra. . . . Austl.	24·15 S	133·30 E
96	James Ross (I.) . . . Ant.	64·20 S	58·20 W
81	Jamestown (jāmz′toun) . . . N. Y.	42·05 N	79·15 W
70	Jamestown . . . N. D.	46·54 N	98·42 W
84	Jamestown. R. I. (Providence In.)	41·30 N	71·21 W
167	Jamestown . . . S. Afr. (Natal In.)	31·07 S	26·49 E
70	Jamestown Res. . . . N. D.	47·16 N	98·40 W
91	Jamiltepec (hä-mēl-tȧ-pěk′).. Mex.	16·16 N	97·54 W
118	Jammerburgt (B.) . . . Den.	57·20 N	9·28 E
142	Jammu . . . India	32·50 N	32·51 E
142	Jammu and Kashmir (disputed reg.) (kȧsh-mēr′). India & Pak.	39·10 N	75·05 E
142	Jamnagar (jäm-nŭ′gŭr) . . . India	22·33 N	70·03 E
145	Jamrud (jäm′rōōd) W. Pak. (Khyber Pass In.)	34·00 N	71·22 E
142	Jamshedpur (jäm′shād-pōōr) India	22·52 N	86·11 E
98	Jamundí (hä-mōō′n-dē′). Col. (In.)	3·15 N	76·32 W
142	Janakpur . . . Nep.	26·50 N	85·55 E
124	Jándula (R.) (hän′dōō-lȧ) . . . Sp.	38·28 N	3·52 W
71	Janesville (jānz′vĭl) . . . Wis.	42·41 N	89·03 W
139	Janin . . . Jordan (Palestine In.)	32·27 N	35·19 E
112	Jan Mayen (I.) (yän mī′ěn).. Nor.	70·59 N	8·05 W
118	Jannelund (yän′ě-lōōnd) . . . Swe.	59·14 N	14·24 E
121	Jánoshalma (yä′nôsh-hôl-mô) Hung.	46·17 N	19·18 E
121	Janów Lubelski (yä′nōōf lŭ-běl′skĭ) Pol.	50·40 N	22·25 E
99	Januária (zhä-nwä′rê-ä) . . . Braz.	15·31 S	44·17 W
145	Janvo Pk. . . . India	25·32 N	94·33 E
148	Jaoyang (jä′ō-yäng′) . . . China	38·16 N	115·45 E
139	Japan (jȧ-păn′) . . . Asia	36·30 N	133·30 E
152	Japan, Sea of (jȧ-păn′) . . . Asia	40·08 N	132·55 W
155	Japen (I.) (yä′pěn) . . . W. Irian	1·30 S	136·15 E
100	Japeri (zhȧ-pě′rê) . . . Braz. (In.)	22·38 S	43·40 W
98	Japurá (R.) (zhä-pōō-rä′) . . . Braz.	1·30 S	67·54 W
95	Jarabacoa (Kä-rä-bä-kô′ä) Dom. Rep.	19·05 N	70·40 W
90	Jaral del Progreso (hä-räl děl prô-grā′sō). Mex.	20·21 N	101·05 W
124	Jarama (R.) (hä-rä′mä) . . . Sp.	40·33 N	3·30 W
139	Jarash . . . Jordan (Palestine In.)	32·17 N	35·53 E
94	Jardines, Banco (Bk.) (bä′n-kō-här-dē′nås). Cuba	21·45 N	81·40 W
99	Jari (R.) (zhä-rē) . . . Braz.	0·28 N	53·00 W
122	Jarnac (zhär-nȧk′) . . . Fr.	45·42 N	0·09 W
121	Jarocin (yä-rō′tsyěn) . . . Pol.	51·58 N	17·31 E
146	Jaro Pk. (hä′rō) . . . China	30·45 N	101·49 E
121	Jarosław (yȧ-rôs-wäf) . . . Pol.	50·01 N	22·41 E
139	Jasin . . . Mala. (Singapore In.)	2·19 N	102·26 E
119	Jašiūnai (dzȧ-shōō-nȧ′yě) Sov. Un.	54·27 N	25·25 E
144	Jāsk (jäsk) . . . Iran	25·46 N	57·48 E
121	Jaslo (yäs′wō) . . . Pol.	49·44 N	21·28 E
139	Jason B. . . . Mala. (Singapore In.)	1·53 N	104·14 E
80	Jasonville (jā′sŭn-vĭl) . . . Ind.	39·10 N	87·15 W
78	Jasper (jăs′pẽr) . . . Ala.	33·50 N	87·17 W
86	Jasper . . . Can.	52·54 N	118·18 W
78	Jasper . . . Fla.	30·30 N	82·56 W
80	Jasper . . . Ind.	38·20 N	86·55 W
70	Jasper . . . Minn.	43·51 N	96·22 W
77	Jasper . . . Tex.	30·55 N	93·59 W
86	Jasper Natl. Park . . . Can.	53·09 N	117·45 W
85	Jasper Place. Can. (Edmonton In.)	53·32 N	113·36 W
121	Jászapáti (yäs′ô-pä-tē) . . . Hung.	47·29 N	20·10 E
91	Jatate (R.) (hä-tä-tā′) . . . Mex.	16·30 N	91·29 W
94	Jatibonico (hä-tē-bô-nē′kô).. Cuba	22·00 N	79·15 W
125	Játiva (hä′tē-vä) . . . Sp.	38·58 N	0·31 W
100	Jau′ (zhä-ōō′) . . . Braz.	22·16 S	48·31 W
98	Jauja (Kä-ōō′K) . . . Peru	11·43 S	75·32 W
90	Jaumave (hou-mä′vå) . . . Mex.	23·23 N	99·24 W
119	Jaunjelgava (youn′yěl′gȧ-vȧ) Sov. Un.	56·37 N	25·06 E
128	Jaunlatgale (youn′lat′gä-lě) Sov. Un.	57·04 N	27·54 E
154	Java (I.) (jä′vȧ) (jȧ′vȧ) . . . Indon.	8·35 S	111·11 E
98	Javari (R.) (Kä-vä-rē) . . . Col.-Peru	4·25 S	72·07 W
154	Java Sea (jä′vȧ) (jȧ′vȧ) . . . Indon.	5·10 S	110·30 E
125	Jávea (hȧ-vā′ä) . . . Sp.	38·45 N	0·07 E
120	Jawor (yä′vôr) . . . Pol.	51·04 N	16·12 E
121	Jaworzno (yä-vôzh′nô) . . . Pol.	50·11 N	19·18 E
136	Jayva R. (yäy′vȧ) Sov. Un. (Urals In.)	59·13 N	57·17 E
121	Jászberény (yäs′bě-rān′) . . . Hung.	47·30 N	19·56 E
139	Jazzin . . . Leb. (Palestine In.)	33·34 N	35·37 E
77	Jeanerette (jěn-ẽr-et′) (zhän-rět′) La.	29·54 N	91·41 W
114	Jebal Aures (Mts.) . . . Alg.	35·16 N	5·53 E
164	Jebba (jěb′ȧ) . . . Nig.	9·07 N	4·46 E
165	Jebel, Bahr el (R.) . . . Sud.	28·22 N	30·31 E
121	Jedrzejów (yăN-dzhā′yŏŏf) . . . Pol.	50·38 N	20·18 E
85	Jefferson (jěf′ẽr-sŭn) Can. (Toronto In.)	43·55 N	79·26 W
78	Jefferson . . . Ga.	34·05 N	83·35 W
71	Jefferson . . . Iowa	42·10 N	94·22 W
77	Jefferson . . . Tex.	32·47 N	94·21 W
71	Jefferson . . . Wis.	42·59 N	88·45 W
66	Jefferson, Mt. . . . Ore.	44·41 N	121·50 W
73	Jefferson City . . . Mo.	38·34 N	92·10 W
67	Jefferson R. . . . Mont.	45·37 N	112·22 W
75	Jeffersontown (jěf′ẽr-sŭn-toun) Ky. (Louisville In.)	38·11 N	85·34 W
75	Jeffersonville (jěf′ẽr-sŭn-vĭl) Ind. (Louisville In.)	38·17 N	85·44 W
	Jehol, see Ch′engte		
115	Jeib, Wadi el (R.) . . . Jordan-Isr.	30·30 N	35·20 E
119	Jēkabpils (yěk′ȧb-pĭls) . . . Sov. Un.	56·29 N	25·50 E
120	Jelenia Góra (yě-lěn′yȧ gōō′rȧ) Pol.	50·53 N	15·43 E
119	Jelgava (yěl′gȧ-vȧ) . . . Sov. Un.	56·39 N	23·40 E
78	Jellico (jěl′ĭ-kō) . . . Tenn.	36·34 N	84·06 W
113	Jemmapes (zhě-mȧp′) . . . Alg.	36·43 N	7·21 E
120	Jena (yā′nä) . . . Ger.	50·55 N	11·37 E
148	Jench′iu (rěnchēō) . . . China	38·44 N	116·05 E
79	Jenkins (jěŋ′kĭnz) . . . Ky.	37·09 N	82·38 W
84	Jenkintown (jěŋ′kĭn-toun) Pa. (Philadelphia In.)	40·06 N	75·08 W
77	Jennings (jěn′ĭngz) . . . La.	30·14 N	92·40 W
80	Jennings . . . Mich.	44·20 N	85·20 W
74	Jennings . . . Mo. (St. Louis In.)	38·43 N	90·16 W
99	Jequié (zhě-kyě′) . . . Braz.	13·53 S	40·06 W
99	Jequitinhonha (R.) (zhě-kē-tēŋ-ō′n-yä). Braz.	16·47 S	41·19 W
95	Jérémie (zhā-rā-mē′) . . . Hai.	18·40 N	74·10 W
99	Jeremoabo (zhě-rā-mō-ȧ′bō). Braz.	10·03 S	38·13 W
91	Jerez, Punta (Pt.) (pōō′n-tä-Kě-räz′). Mex.	23·04 N	97·44 W
124	Jerez de la Frontera (Kě-räth′ dā lä frôn-tā′rä). Sp.	36·42 N	6·09 W
124	Jerez de los Caballeros (Kě-rath′ dā lōs kä-väl-yā′rôs). Sp.	38·20 N	6·45 W
159	Jericho (jěr′ĭ-kō) . . . Austl.	28·38 S	146·24 E
168	Jericho (jěr-ĭkō) S. Afr. (Johannesburg & Pretoria In.)	25·16 S	27·47 E
	Jericho, see Arīhā		
69	Jerome (jê-rōm′) . . . Ariz.	34·45 N	112·10 W
67	Jerome . . . Idaho	42·44 N	114·31 W
122	Jersey (I.) (jûr′zĭ) . . . Eur.	49·13 N	2·07 W
84	Jersey City. N. J. (New York In.)	40·43 N	74·05 W
81	Jersey Shore . . . Pa.	41·10 N	77·15 W
85	Jerseyville (jẽr′zē-vĭl) Can. (Toronto In.)	43·12 N	80·08 W
73	Jerseyville . . . Ill.	39·07 N	90·18 W
139	Jerusalem (jê-rōō′sȧ-lěm) Isr.-Jordan (Palestine In.)	31·46 N	35·14 E
154	Jesselton . . . Mala.	5·55 N	116·05 E
84	Jesuit Bend (jěz′ū-ĭt) La. (New Orleans In.)	29·45 N	90·02 W
79	Jesup (jěs′ŭp) . . . Ga.	31·36 N	81·53 W
91	Jesús Carranza (hē-sōō′s-kär-rä′n-zä). Mex.	17·26 N	95·01 W
70	Jewel Cave Natl. Mon. . . . S. D.	43·44 N	103·52 W
65	Jewell (jū′ěl).. Ore. (Portland In.)	45·56 N	123·30 W
142	Jhālawār . . . India	24·29 N	79·09 E
142	Jhang Maghian . . . W. Pak.	31·21 N	72·19 E
142	Jhansi (jän′sē) . . . India	25·29 N	78·32 E
142	Jharsuguda . . . India	22·51 N	86·13 E
142	Jhelum (R.) (jā′lŭm) . . . W. Pak.	31·40 N	71·51 E
146	Jibhalanta . . . Mong.	47·49 N	97·00 E
69	Jicarilla Ind. Res. (Kē-kȧ-rēl′yȧ) N. Mex.	36·45 N	107·00 W
93	Jicaron, Isla (I.) (Kē-kä-rōn′). Pan.	7·14 N	81·41 W
121	Jiffa R . . . Rom.	47·35 N	27·02 E
158	Jiggalong (jĭg′ȧ-lông) . . . Austl.	23·20 S	120·45 E
95	Jiguani (Kē-gwä-nē′) . . . Cuba	20·20 N	76·30 W
94	Jigüey, Bahía (B.) (bä-ē′ä-Kē′gwā). Cuba	22·15 N	78·10 W
148	Jihchao (rē′jou) . . . China	35·27 N	119·28 E
120	Jihlava (yē′hlȧ-vȧ) . . . Czech.	49·23 N	15·33 E
168	Jijiga . . . Eth. (Horn of Afr. In.)	9·15 N	42·48 E
125	Jijona (Kē-hō′nȧ) . . . Sp.	38·31 N	0·29 W
124	Jikyop . . . China	28·41 N	91·42 E
124	Jiloca (R.) (Kē-lō′kȧ) . . . Sp.	41·13 N	1·30 W
92	Jilotepeque (Kē-lô-tě-pě′kě) Guat.	14·39 N	89·36 W
165	Jima . . . Eth.	7·41 N	36·52 E
127	Jimbolia (zhĭm-bô′lyȧ) . . . Rom.	45·45 N	20·44 E
90	Jiménez (Kê-mā′nāz) . . . Mex.	24·12 N	98·29 W
76	Jimenez . . . Mex.	27·09 N	104·55 W
76	Jiménez . . . Mex.	29·03 N	100·42 W
90	Jiménez del Téul (tě-ōō′l) . . . Mex.	21·28 N	103·51 W
81	Jim Thorpe (jĭm′ thôrp′) . . . Pa.	40·50 N	75·45 W
120	Jindřichov Hradec (yēn′d′r-zhĭ-kōōf hrä′děts). Czech.	49·09 N	15·02 E
165	Jinja (jĭn′jä) . . . Ug.	0·29 N	33·11 E
92	Jinotega (Kē-nô-tā′gä) . . . Nic.	13·07 N	86·00 W
92	Jinotepe (Kē-nô-tā′pȧ) . . . Nic.	11·52 N	86·12 W
153	Jinzū-Gawa (Strm.) (jēn′zōō gä′wä). Jap.	36·26 N	137·18 E
98	Jipijapa (Kē-pē-hä′pä) . . . Ec.	1·36 S	80·52 W
92	Jiquilisco (Kē-kē-lē′s-kô) . . . Sal.	13·18 N	88·32 W
90	Jiquilpan de Juarez (Kē-kēl′pän dā hwä′räz). Mex.	20·00 N	102·43 W
91	Jiquipilco (hē-kē-pē′l-kô) Mex. (Mexico City In.)	19·32 N	99·37 W
168	Jirgā (jēr′gȧ) .. U. A. R. (Nile In.)	26·20 N	31·51 E
146	Jirgalanta . . . Mong.	48·08 N	91·40 E
124	Jistredo, Sierra de (Mts.) (sē-ě′r-rä-dě-kēs-trě′dô). Sp.	42·50 N	6·15 W
91	Jitotol (Kē-tô-tōl′) . . . Mex.	17·03 N	92·54 W
99	João Pessoa (Paraíba) (zhô-ouN′ pě-sōȧ′) (pä-rä-ē′bȧ). Braz.	7·09 S	34·45 W
101	João Ribeiro (zhô-uN-rē-bā′rō) Braz. (Rio de Janeiro In.)	20·42 S	44·03 W
94	Jobabo (R.) (hō-bä′bä) . . . Cuba	20·50 N	77·15 W
85	Jock R. (jŏk) .. Can. (Ottawa In.)	45·08 N	75·51 W
90	Jocotepec (hô-kō-tȧ-pěk′) . . . Mex.	20·17 N	103·26 W
124	Jodar (hō′där) . . . Sp.	37·54 N	3·20 W
142	Jodhpur (jŏd′pōōr) . . . India	26·23 N	83·00 E
119	Joensuu (yô-ěn′sōō) . . . Fin.	62·35 N	29·46 E
153	Jōga-Shima (I.) (jō′gä shē′mä) Jap. (Tōkyō In.)	35·07 N	139·37 E
128	Jōgeva (yû′gě-vȧ) . . . Sov. Un.	58·45 N	26·23 E
82	Jogins . . . Can.	45·41 N	64·27 W
154	Jogjakarta (yŏg-yȧ-kär′tȧ). Indon.	7·50 S	110·20 E
167	Johannesburg (yô-hän′ěs-bōōrgh) S. Afr. (Johannesburg & Pretoria In.)	26·08 S	27·54 E
66	John Day R. (jŏn dā) . . . Ore.	44·46 N	120·15 W
66	John Day R., Middle Fork . . . Ore.	44·53 N	119·04 W
66	John Day R., North Fork . . . Ore.	45·03 N	118·50 W

ng-sing; ŋ-baŋk; N-nasalized n; nŏd; cŏmmit; ōld; ôbey; ôrder; fōōd; fŏŏt; ou-out; s-soft; sh-dish; th-thin; pūre; ûnite; ûrn; stŭd; circŭs; ü-as "y" in study; ′-indeterminate vowel.

Page	Name Pronunciation Region	Lat. °′	Long. °′
72	John Martin Res. (jŏn mär'tĭn) Colo.	37·57 N	103·04 W
65	Johnson (R.) (jŏn'sŭn) Ore. (Portland In.)	45·27 N	122·20 W
81	Johnsonburg (jŏn'sŭn-bûrg) . . . Pa.	41·30 N	78·40 W
80	Johnson City (jŏn'sŭn) . . . . Ill.	37·50 N	88·55 W
81	Johnson City . . . . N. Y.	42·10 N	76·00 W
79	Johnson City . . . . Tenn.	36·17 N	82·23 W
156	Johnston (I.) (jŏn'stŭn) . . . Oceania	17·00 N	168·00 W
81	Johnstown (jonz'toun) . . . . . . N. Y.	43·00 N	74·20 W
81	Johnstown . . . . Pa.	40·20 N	78·50 W
147	Joho (Prov.) . . . . China	42·31 N	118·12 E
154	Johore (State) (jŭ-hōr') . . . . . Mala.	2·15 N	103·00 E
139	Johore (R.) (jŭ-hōr') Mala. (Singapore In.)	1·39 N	103·52 E
139	Johore Bahru (bä-hŭ-rōō') Mala. (Singapore In.)	1·28 N	103·46 E
128	Jōhvi (yû'vĭ) . . . . Sov. Un.	59·21 N	27·21 E
122	Joigny (zhwȧn-yē') . . . . Fr.	47·58 N	3·26 E
100	Joinville (zhwăN-vēl') . . . . Braz.	26·18 S	48·47 W
122	Joinville . . . . Fr.	48·28 N	5·05 E
96	Joinville (I.) . . . . Ant.	63·80 S	53·80 W
90	Jojutla (hō-hōō'tlä) . . . . Mex.	18·39 N	99·11 W
112	Jökullsá (R.) (yû'kōōls-ô) . . . . . Ice.	65·38 N	16·08 W
90	Jola (kô'lä) . . . . Mex.	21·08 N	104·26 W
75	Joliet (jō-lĭ-ĕt') . . Ill. (Chicago In.)	41·37 N	88·05 W
82	Joliette (zhô-lyĕt') . . . . Can.	46·01 N	73·30 W
154	Jolo (hō-lô) . . . . Phil.	5·59 N	121·05 E
154	Jolo (I.) . . . . Phil.	5·55 N	121·15 E
155	Jomalig (I.) (hô-mä'lēg) Phil. (Manila In.)	14·44 N	122·34 E
90	Jomulco (hô-mōōl'kô) . . . . Mex.	21·08 N	104·24 W
90	Jonacatepec (hō-nä-kä-tȧ-pĕk') Mex.	18·39 N	98·46 W
119	Jonava (yō-nä'vȧ) . . . . . . Sov. Un.	55·05 N	24·15 E
118	Jondal (yōn'dȧl) . . . . Nor.	60.16 N	6·16 E
155	Jones (jōnz) . . . . Phil. (Manila In.)	13·56 N	122·05 E
155	Jones . . . . Phil. (Manila In.)	16·35 N	121·39 E
87	Jones, C. . . . . Can.	54·35 N	79·51 W
73	Jonesboro (jōnz'bŭro) . . . . Ark.	35·49 N	90·42 W
77	Jonesboro . . . . La.	32·14 N	92·43 W
77	Jonesville (jōnz'vĭl) . . . . La.	31·35 N	91·50 W
80	Jonesville . . . . Mich.	42·00 N	84·45 W
119	Joniškis (yô'nĭsh-kĭs) . . . . Sov. Un.	56·14 N	23·36 E
118	Jönköping (yûn'chû-pĭng) . . . . Swe.	57·47 N	14·10 E
82	Jonquière (zhôN-kyâr') . . . . . . Can.	48·24 N	71·16 W
91	Jonuta (hô-nōō'tä) . . . . Mex.	18·07 N	92·09 W
122	Jonzac (zhôN-zȧk') . . . . Fr.	45·27 N	0·27 W
73	Joplin (jŏp'lĭn) . . . . Mo.	37·05 N	94·31 W
138	Jordan (jôr'dăn) . . . . Asia	30·15 N	38·00 E
139	Jordan (R.) . Jordan (Palestine In.)	31·58 N	35·36 E
74	Jordan R. Utah (Salt Lake City In.)	40·42 N	111·56 W
145	Jorhat (jôr-hät') . . . . India	26·43 N	94·16 E
90	Jorullo, Vol. de (vôl-kä'n-dĕ-hô-rōōl'yō) . Mex.	18·54 N	101·38 W
164	Jos (jŏs) . . . . Nig.	9·53 N	8·56 E
158	Joseph Bonaparte, G. (jô'sĕf bō'nȧ-pȧrt) . Austl.	13·30 S	128·40 E
85	Joseph L. (jô'sĕf läk) Can. (Edmonton In.)	53·18 N	113·06 W
68	Joshua Tree Natl. Mon. (jô'shū-ȧ trē) . Calif.	34·02 N	115·53 W
118	Jostedalsbreen (Gl.) (yôstĕ-däls-brĕĕn) . Nor.	61·40 N	6·55 E
118	Jotun Fjeld (Mts.) (yō'tōōn fyel') Nor.	61·44 N	8·11 E
94	Joulter's Cays (Is.) (jōl'tērz) . Ba. Is.	25·20 N	78·10 W
123	Jouy-le-Chatel (zhwē-lĕ-shä-tĕl') Fr. (Paris In.)	48·40 N	3·07 E
94	Jovellanos (hō-vĕl-yä'nōs) . . . Cuba	22·50 N	81·10 W
148	Ju (R.) (rōō) . . . . China	33·07 N	114·18 E
90	Juan Aldama (kōōȧ'n-äl-dȧ'mä) Mex.	24·16 N	103·21 W
66	Juan de Fuca, Str. of (hwän' dā fōō'kä) . Wash.-Can.	48·25 N	124·37 W
167	Juan de Nova (I.) . . . . Malag. Rep.	17·18 S	43·07 E
88	Juan Diaz, (R.) (kōōȧ'n-dē'-äz) Pan. (Panama Canal In.)	9·05 N	79·30 W
96	Juan Fernández, Islasde (Is.) (ē's-läs-dĕ-hwän' fĕr-nän'dāth) Chile	33·30 S	79·00 W
101	Juan L. Lacaze (hōōȧ'n-ĕ'lĕ-lä-kȧ'zĕ) . Ur. (Buenos Aires In.)	34·25 S	57·28 W
94	Juan Luis, Cayos de (Is.) (ka-yōs-dĕ-hwän lōō-ēs') . Cuba	22·15 N	82·00 W
99	Juázeiro (zhōōȧ'zä'rō) . . . . . . Braz.	9·27 S	40·28 W
99	Juazeiro do Norte (zhōōȧ'zä'rō-dô-nôr-tĕ) . Braz.	7·16 S	38·57 W
100	Juárez (hōōȧ'rĕz) . . . . Arg.	37·42 S	59·46 W
165	Juba . . . . Sud.	4·58 N	31·37 E
168	Juba R. (jōō'bȧ) Som. (Horn of Afr. In.)	1·30 N	42·25 E
139	Jubayl (Byblos) (jōō-bīl') Leb. (Palestine In.)	34·07 N	35·38 E
142	Jubbulpore (jŭb-ŭl-pōr') . . . . . India	23·18 N	79·59 E
124	Júcar (R.) (hōō'kär) . . . . Sp.	39·10 N	1·22 W
94	Júcaro (hōō'kȧ-rō) . . . . Cuba	21·40 N	78·50 W
90	Juchipila (hōō-chē-pē'lȧ) . . . . Mex.	21·26 N	103.09 W
88	Juchitan (hōō-chē-tän') . . . . . Mex.	16·15 N	95·00 W
91	Juchitán de Zaragoza (hōō-chē-tän' dā thä-rä-gō'thä) . Mex.	16·27 N	95·03 W
90	Juchitlán (hōō-chē-tlän) . . . . . Mex.	20·05 N	104·07 W
92	Jucuapa (kōō-kwä'pä) . . . . Sal.	13·30 N	88·24 W
144	Juddah . . . . Sau. Ar.	21·30 N	39·15 E
120	Judenburg (jōō'dĕn-bûrg) . . . . Aus.	47·10 N	14·40 E
67	Judith R. (jōō'dĭth) . . . . Mont.	47·20 N	109·36 W
127	Jui . . . . Rom.	44·45 N	23·17 E
151	Juian (jwĭ'än') . . . . China	27·48 N	120·40 E
92	Juigalpa (hwē-gäl'pä) . . . . Nic.	12·02 N	85·24 W
123	Juilly (zhwē-yē') . Fr. (Paris In.) . .	49·01 N	2·41 E
117	Juist (I.) (yōō'ēst) . . . . Ger.	53·41 N	6.50 E
101	Juiz de Fora (zhōō-ēzh' dā fō'rä) Braz. (Rio de Janeiro In.)	21·47 S	43·20 W
100	Jujuy (hōō-hwē') . . . . Arg.	24·14 S	65·15 W
100	Jujuy (Prov.) (hōō-hwē') . . . . . Arg.	23·00 S	65·45 W
148	Jukao (rōōgou) . . . . China	32·24 N	120·33 E
167	Jukskei (R.) . . . . S. Afr. (Johannesburg & Pretoria In.)	25·58 S	27·58 E
72	Julesburg (jōōlz'bûrg) . . . . Colo.	40·59 N	102·16 W
98	Juliaca (hōō-lē-ä'kä) . . . . Peru	15·26 S	70·12 W
49	Julianehaab . . . . Grnld.	60·70 N	46·20 W
123	Jülich (yü'lĕk) . . . . Ger. (Ruhr In.)	50·55 N	6 22 E
126	Julijske Alpe (Mts.) (ū'lēy-skĕ' äl'pĕ) . Yugo.	46·05 N	14 05 E
142	Jullundur . . . . India	31·29 N	75·39 E
142	Julpaiguri . . . . India	26·35 N	88·48 E
167	Jumbla (Mtn.) (jum'blȧ) S. Afr. (Natal In.)	30·29 S	28·52 E
95	Jumento Cays (Is.) (hōō-mĕn'tō) Ba. Is.	23·05 N	75·40 W
117	Jumet (zhü-mĕ') . . . . Bel.	50·28 N	4·30 E
124	Jumilla (hōō-mēl'yä) . . . . Sp.	38·28 N	1·20 W
71	Jump (R.) (jŭmp) . . . . Wis.	45·18 N	90·53 W
85	Jumpingpound Cr. (jŭmp-ĭng-pound) . Can. (Calgary In.)	51·01 N	114·34 W
99	Jumundá (R.) (zhōō-mōō'n-dá') Braz.	1·33 S	57·42 W
142	Junagādh (jŏŏ-nä'gŭd) . . . . . . India	21·33 N	70·25 E
148	Junan (rōō Nän) . . . . China	32·59 N	114·22 E
76	Junction (jŭŋk'shŭn) . . . . Tex.	30·29 N	99·48 W
73	Junction City . . . . Kans.	39·01 N	96·49 W
101	Jundiaí (zhōō'n-dyä-ē') Braz. (Rio de Janeiro In.)	23·12 S	46·52 W
64	Juneau (jōō'nō) . . . . Alaska	58·25 N	134·30 W
148	Jungch'eng (jōōng'chĕng') . . China	37·23 N	122·31 E
151	Jungchiang . . . . China	25·52 N	108·45 E
120	Jungfrau Pk. (yōōng'frou) . . Switz.	46·30 N	7·59 E
151	Junghsien . . . . China	22·48 N	110·38 E
101	Junín (hōō-nē'n) Arg. (Buenos Aires In.)	34·35 S	60·56 W
98	Junín . . . . Col. (In.)	4·47 N	73·39 W
139	Juniyah (jōō-nē'ē) Leb. (Palestine In.)	33·59 N	35·38 E
112	Junkeren (Mtn.) (yōōn'kĕ-rĕn) Nor.	66·29 N	14·58 E
83	Jupiter (jōō'pĭ-tēr) . . . . Can.	49·30 N	63·25 W
65	Jupiter, Mt. . . . Wash. (Seattle In.)	47·42 N	123·04 W
116	Jura (I.) (jōō'rȧ) . . . . Scot.	56·09 N	6·45 W
123	Jura (Mts.) (zhü-rȧ') . . . . . . Switz.	46·55 N	6·49 E
116	Jura, Sd. of (jōō'rȧ) . . . . Scot.	55·45 N	5·55 W
119	Jurbarkas (yōōr-bär'käs) Sov. Un.	55·06 N	22·50 E
139	Jurf ad Darāwīsh Jordan (Palestine In.)	30·41 N	35·51 E
165	Jur R. (jōōr) . . . . Sud.	6·38 N	27·52 E
98	Juruá (R.) (zhōō-rōō-ä') . . . . Braz.	5·27 S	67·39 W
99	Juruena (R.) (zhōō-rōōĕ'nä) Braz.	12·22 S	58·34 W
98	Jutai (zhōō-tȧy) . . . . Braz.	4·26 S	68·16 W
92	Jutiapa (hōō-tē-ä'pä) . . . . Guat.	14·16 N	89·55 W
92	Juticalpa (hōō-tē-käl'pä) . . . . Hond.	14·35 N	86·17 W
90	Juventino Rosas (kōō-vĕn-tē'-nô-rō-säs) . Mex.	20·38 N	101·02 W
123	Juvisy-sur-Orge (zhü-vē-sē'sür ôrzh') . Fr. (Paris In.)	48·41 N	2·22 E
90	Juxtahuaca (hōōs-tlä-hwä'kä) Mex.	17·20 N	98·02 W
127	Južna Morava (R.) (ū'zhnȧ mô'rȧ-vȧ) . Yugo.	42·30 N	22·00 E
118	Jylland (Reg.) . . . . Den.	56·04 N	9·00 E
119	Jyväskylä (yü'vĕs-kü-lĕ) . . . . Fin.	62·14 N	25·46 E
167	Kaalfontein (kärl-fŏn-tān) . . S. Afr. (Johannesburg & Pretoria In.)	26·02 S	28·16 E
154	Kabaena (I.) (kä-bȧ-ā'nä) . Indon.	5·35 S	121·07 E
164	Kabala (kȧ-bä'lȧ) . . . . S. L.	9·43 N	11·39 W
166	Kabalo (kä-bä'lō) . . . . Con. L.	6·09 S	26·52 E
166	Kabambare (kä-bäm-bä'rȧ) Con. L.	4·47 S	27·45 E
153	Kabe (kä'bā) . . . . Jap.	34·32 N	132·30 E
166	Kabinda (kȧ-bēN'dȧ) . . . . . Con. L.	6·13 S	24·16 E
139	Kabir (R.) Leb. (Palestine In.)	34·40 N	36·06 E
166	Kabompo (R.) (kȧ-bôm'pō) N. Rh.	13·52 S	23·45 E
166	Kabongo (kȧ-bông'ô) . . . . . Con. L.	7·58 S	25·10 E
114	Kaboudia, Ras (C.) . . . . Tun.	35·17 N	11·28 E
142	Kābul (kä'bōōl) . . . . Afg.	34·39 N	69·14 E
145	Kabul (R.) (kä'bōōl) . . . . Asia	34·44 N	69·43 E
135	Kachuga (kȧ-chōō-gȧ) . . Sov. Un.	54·09 N	105·43 E
129	Kadiyevka (kȧ-dĭ-yĕf'kȧ) . Sov. Un.	48·34 N	38·37 E
132	Kadnikov (käd'nē-kôf) . . Sov. Un.	59·30 N	40·10 E
164	Kaduna (kä-dōō'nä) . . . . Nig.	10·29 N	7·32 E
164	Kaédi (kä-ā-dē') . . . . . . Mauritania	16·20 N	13·32 W
157	Kaena Pt. (kä'ȧ-nä) . . Hawaii (In.)	21·33 N	158·19 W
152	Kaesong (Kaijo) (kä'ĕ-sŭng) (kī'jō) . Kor.	38·00 N	126·35 E
165	Kafia Kingi (kä'fē-ȧ kĭŋ'gē) . Sud.	9·17 N	24·28 E
166	Kafue (kä'fōō-ȧ) . . . . N. Rh.	15·45 S	28·17 E
166	Kafue (R.) . . . . N. Rh.	15·31 S	26·33 E
129	Kagal'nik (R.) (kä-gäl''nĕk) Sov. Un.	46·58 N	39·25 E
166	Kagera (R.) (kä-gā'rȧ) . . . . . . Tan.	1·17 S	31·04 E
153	Kagoshima (kä'gō-shē'mȧ) . . . Jap.	31·35 N	130·31 E
153	Kagoshima-Wan (B.) (kä'gô-shē'mä wän) . Jap.	31·24 N	130·39 E
129	Kagul (ka-gōōl') . . . . Sov. Un.	45·49 N	28·17 E
154	Kahajan (R.) . . . . Indon.	1·45 S	113·40 E
73	Kahoka (kȧ-hō'kȧ) . . . . Mo.	40·26 N	91·42 W
157	Kahoolawe (I.) (kä-hōō-lä'wē) Hawaii (In.)	20·28 N	156·48 W
71	Kahshahpiwi (R.) . . . . Can.	48·24 N	90·56 W
157	Kahuku Pt. (kä-hōō'kōō) Hawaii (In.)	21·50 N	157·50 W
139	Kaiang . . . . Mala. (Singapore In.)	3·00 N	101·47 E
69	Kaibab Ind. Res. (kä'ē-bȧb) . Ariz.	36·55 N	112·45 W
69	Kaibab Plat . . . . Ariz.	36·30 N	112·10 W
99	Kaieteur Fall (kī-ĕ-tōōr') . Br. Gu.	4·48 N	59·24 W
148	K'aifeng (kāī'fĕng) . . . . China	34·48 N	114·22 E
	Kaijo, see Kaesong		
152	Kaikyo, Sōya (Str.) (sô'yȧ kȧ-ē'kī-ô) . Sov. Un.	45·45 N	141·20 E
157	Kailua (kä'ē-lōō'ȧ) . Hawaii (In.)	19·49 N	155·59 W
155	Kaimana . . . . W. Irian	3·32 S	133·47 E
159	Kaimanawa Ra. (kä'ē-mȧ-nä'wȧ) N. Z. (In.)	39·13 S	176·02 E
153	Kainan (kä'ē-nȧn') . . . . Jap.	34·09 N	135·14 E
148	Kaip'ing (kī-pĭng') . . . . China	40·25 N	122·20 E
164	Kairouan (kĕr-ōō-äN') . . . . Tun.	35·46 N	10·04 E
120	Kaiserslautern (kī-zĕrs-lou'tĕrn) Ger.	49·26 N	7·46 E
159	Kaitaia (kä-ê-tä'ê-ȧ) . . . N. Z. (In.)	35·30 S	173·28 E
157	Kaiwi Chan (kä'ē-wē) . Hawaii (In.)	21·10 N	157·38 W
151	Kaiyüan (kī'yōō-än') . . . . China	23·42 N	103·20 E
150	Kaiyuan (kī'yōō-än') . . . . China	42·30 N	124·00 E
64	Kaiyuh Mts. (kī-yōō') . . . . . Alaska	64·25 N	157·38 W
112	Kajaani (kä'yȧ-nĕ) . . . . Fin.	64·15 N	27·16 E
154	Kajan, Sungai (Strm.) . . . . . Indon.	1·45 N	115·38 E
139	Kajang, Gunong (Mt.) Mala. (Singapore In.)	2·47 N	104·05 E
153	Kajiki (kä'jē-kē) . . . . Jap.	31·44 N	130·41 E
129	Kakhovka (kä-Kôf'kȧ) . . . Sov. Un.	46·46 N	33·32 E
129	Kakhovskoye (L.) (kȧ-Kôf'skô-yĕ) Sov. Un.	47·21 N	33·33 E
165	Kakindu (kȧ-kĭn'dōō) . . . . Ug.	1·06 N	32·59 E
64	Kaktovik (kăk-tō'vĭk) . . . . . Alaska	70·08 N	143·51 W
168	Kalābishah . . . . U. A. R. (Nile In.)	23·26 N	32·55 E
133	Kalach (kȧ-lȧch') . . . . Sov. Un.	50·15 N	40·55 E
146	Kaladan (R.) . . . . Bur.	21·07 N	93·04 E
166	Kalahari Des. (kä-lä-hä'rē) . . Bech.	23·00 S	22·03 E
65	Kalama (kȧ-lăm'ȧ) Wash. (Portland In.)	46·01 N	122·50 W
65	Kalama (R.) . Wash. (Portland In.)	46·03 N	122·47 W
127	Kalámai (kä-lä-mī') . . . . Grc.	37·04 N	22·08 E
80	Kalamazoo (kăl-ȧ-mȧ-zōō') . Mich.	42·20 N	85·40 W
80	Kalamazoo (R.) . . . . Mich.	42·35 N	86·00 W
129	Kalanchak (kä-län-chäk') Sov. Un.	46·17 N	33·14 E
157	Kalapana (kä-lä-pȧ'nä) Hawaii (In.)	19·25 N	155·00 W
144	Kalar (Mtn.) . . . . Iran	31·43 N	51·41 E
142	Kalat (kŭ-lät') . . . . W. Pak.	29·05 N	66·36 E
154	Kalatoa (I.) . . . . Indon.	7·22 S	122·30 E
123	Kaldenkirchen (käl'dĕn-kēr-Kĕn) Ger. (Ruhr In.)	51·19 N	6·13 E
150	Kalgan (kăl-gän') . . . . China	40·45 N	114·58 E
158	Kalgoorlie (kăl-gōōr'lē) . . . . . Austl.	30·45 S	121·35 E
115	Kaliakra, Nos (Pt.) . . . . Rom.	43·25 N	28·42 E
154	Kalimantan (Prov.) . . . . Indon.	1·00 S	113·48 E
128	Kalinin (Tver) (kä'lē-nĕn) (tvĕr) . Sov. Un.	56·52 N	35·57 E
128	Kalinin (Oblast) . . . . Sov. Un.	56·50 N	33·08 E
119	Kaliningrad (Königsberg) (kä-lē-nĕn'grät) (kû'nēks-bĕrgh) Sov. Un.	54·42 N	20·32 E
136	Kaliningrad (kä-lē-nĕn'grät) Sov. Un. (Moscow In.)	55·55 N	37·49 E
129	Kalinkovichi (kä-lēn-ko-vē'chē) Sov. Un.	52·07 N	29·19 E
66	Kalispel Ind. Res. (kăl-ĭ-spĕl') Wash.	48·25 N	117·30 W
67	Kalispell (kăl'ĭ-spĕl) . . . . Mont.	48·12 N	114·18 W
121	Kalisz (kä'lēsh) . . . . Pol.	51·45 N	18·05 E
112	Kalix (R.) (kä'lĕks) . . . . Swe.	67·12 N	21·41 E
166	Kalkfeld (kälk'fĕlt) . . . . S. W. Afr.	21·05 S	16·05 E
166	Kalkfontein (kälk'fōn-tān) S. W. Afr.	27·50 S	18·40 E
118	Kalmar (käl'mär) . . . . Swe.	56·40 N	16·19 E
118	Kalmar Sund (Sd.) (käl'mär) Swe.	56·30 N	16·17 E
129	Kal'mius (R.) (käl''myōōs) Sov. Un.	47 15 N	37·38 E
111	Kalmthout . . . . . Bel. (Brussels In.)	51·23 N	4·28 E
143	Kalmunai . . . . Ceylon	7·22 N	81·49 E
133	Kalmyk A. S. S. R. (kȧl'mĭk) Sov. Un.	46·56 N	46·00 E
121	Kalocsa (kä'lô-chä) . . . . Hung.	46·32 N	19·00 E
157	Kalohi Chan. (kä-lō'hĭ) Hawaii (In.)	20·55 N	157·15 W
166	Kalomo (kä-lō'mō) . . . . N. Rh.	17·06 S	26·22 E
142	Kalsubai Mt . . . . India	24·43 N	73·47 E
111	Kaltenkirchen (käl'tĕn-kēr-Kĕn) Ger. (Hamburg In.)	53·50 N	9·57 E
143	Kālu (R.) . . . . India (Bombay In.)	19·18 N	73·14 E
128	Kaluga (kȧ-lōō'gȧ) . . . . . . Sov. Un.	54·29 N	36·12 E
128	Kaluga (Oblast) . . . . Sov. Un.	54·10 N	34·30 E
118	Kalundborg (kȧ-lōōn''bôr') . . Den.	55·42 N	11·07 E
121	Kalush (kä'lōōsh) . . . . Sov. Un.	49·02 N	24·24 E
119	Kalvarija (käl-vä-rē'yȧ) . Sov. Un.	54·24 N	23·17 E
136	Kal'ya (käl'yȧ) Sov. Un. (Urals In.)	60·17 N	59·58 E
143	Kalyān . . . . . . India (Bombay In.)	19·16 N	73·07 E
128	Kalyazin (käl-yä'zēn) . . . . Sov. Un.	57·13 N	37·55 E
135	Kalyma (R.) . . . . Sov. Un.	66·32 N	152·46 E
132	Kama (L.) . . . . Sov. Un.	55·28 N	51·00 E
132	Kama (R.) (kä'mä) . . . . . . Sov. Un.	56·52 N	54·35 E
164	Kamabai (kä-mȧ-bä'ē) . . . . S. L.	9·13 N	11·56 W
152	Kamaishi (kä'mä-ē'shē) . . . . . . Jap.	39·16 N	142·03 E
153	Kamakura (kä'mȧ-kōō'rä) Jap. (Tōkyō In.)	35·19 N	139·33 E
144	Kamarān (I.) (Br.) . . . . Aden	15·19 N	41·47 E
166	Kambove (käm-bō'vĕ) . . . . Con. L.	10·58 S	26·43 E
135	Kamchatka, P-Ov (Pen.) . Sov. Un.	55·19 N	157·45 E
135	Kamchatka (R.) . . . . Sov. Un.	54·15 N	158·38 E
123	Kamen (kä'mĕn) . Ger. (Ruhr In.)	51·35 N	7·40 E
129	Kamenets Podol'skiy (kä-mă'nĕts pō-dôl'skĭ) . Sov. Un.	48·41 N	26·34 E
126	Kamenjak, Rt (C.) (kä'mĕ-nyäk) Yugo.	44·45 N	13·57 E
129	Kamenka (kä-mĕŋ'kȧ) . . . Sov. Un.	48·02 N	28·43 E
121	Kamenka . . . . Sov. Un.	50·06 N	24·20 E
134	Kamen'-na-Obi (kä-mĭny'nŭ ô'bē) Sov. Un.	53·43 N	81·28 E
129	Kamensk-Shakhtinskiy (kä'mĕnsk shäk'tĭn-skĭ) . Sov. Un.	48·17 N	40·16 E
136	Kamensk-Ural'skiy (kä'mĕn-skĭ ōō-räl'skĭ) Sov. Un. (Urals In.)	56·27 N	61·55 E
120	Kamenz (kä'mĕnts) . . . . Ger.	51·16 N	14·05 E

ăt; finăl; rāte; senâte; ärm; ȧsk; sofȧ; fâre; ch-choose; dh-as th in other; bē; ēvent; bĕt; recĕnt; cratẽr; g-go; gh-guttural g; bĭt; ĭ-short neutral; rīde; K-guttural k as ch in German ich;

Page Name Pronunciation Region Lat. °' Long. °'

153 Kameoka (kä'mä-ōkä) Jap. (Ōsaka In.) 35·01 N 135·35 E
142 Kāmet (Mt.)............India 35·50 N 79·42 E
120 Kamień Pomorski..........Pol. 53·57 N 14·48 E
153 Kamikoma (kä'mê-kō'mä) Jap. (Ōsaka In.) 34·45 N 135·50 E
166 Kamina................Con. L. 8·41 S 25·01 E
71 Kaministikwia (R.) (kȧ-mĭ-nĭ-stĭk'wĭ-ȧ).Can. 48·40 N 89·41 W
86 Kamloops (kăm'lōōps).......Can. 50·41 N 120·19 W
Kammer, see Atter See
142 Kampa Dzong............China 28·23 N 89·42 E
165 Kampala (käm-pä'lä)........Ug. 0·14 N 32·34 E
154 Kampar (Strm.) (käm'pär) Indon. 0·30 N 101·30 E
111 Kampenhout Bel. (Brussels In.) 50·56 N 4·33 E
123 Kamp-Lintfort (kämp-lēnt'fōrt) Ger. (Ruhr In.) 51·30 N 6·34 E
154 Kampot (käm'pōt)........Camb. 10·41 N 104·07 E
120 Kamp R. (kămp)..........Aus. 48·30 N 15·45 E
86 Kamsack (kăm'săk).........Can. 51·32 N 102·00 W
103 Kamskoye (Res.).......Sov. Un. 59·08 N 56·30 E
136 Kamskoye Vodokranilishche (L.) Sov. Un. (Urals In.) 59·03 N 56·48 E
93 Kamuk, Cerro (Mt.) (sĕ'r-rô-kä-mōō'k).C. R. 9·18 N 83·02 W
152 Kamu Misaki (C.) (kä'mōō mê-sä'kē).Jap. 43·25 N 139·35 E
129 Kamyshevatskaya (kȧ-mwēsh'ĕ-văt'skä-yȧ).Sov. Un. 46·24 N 37·58 E
133 Kamyshin (kä-mwēsh'ĭn) Sov. Un. 50·08 N 45·20 E
132 Kamyshlov (kä-mēsh'lôf) Sov. Un. 56·50 N 62·32 E
151 Kan (R.) (kän)...........China 26·50 N 115·00 E
134 Kan (R.)..............Sov. Un. 56·30 N 94·17 E
69 Kanab (kăn'ăb)............Utah 37·00 N 112·30 W
69 Kanab Plat...............Ariz. 36·31 N 112·55 W
136 Kanabeki (kȧ-nä'byĕ-kĭ) Sov. Un. (Urals In.) 57·48 N 57·16 E
64 Kanaga (I.) (kă-nă'gă)....Alaska 52·02 N 177·38 W
153 Kanagawa (Pref.) (kä'nä-gä'wä) Jap. (Tōkyō In.) 35·29 N 139·32 E
153 Kanamachi (kä-nä-mä'chē) Jap. (Tōkyō In.) 35·46 N 139·52 E
136 Kananikol'skoye (kȧ-nȧ-nĭ-kôl' skō-yĕ).Sov. Un. (Urals In.) 52·48 N 57·29 E
92 Kanasín (kä-nä-sē'n) Mex. (Yucatan In.) 20·54 N 89·31 W
64 Kanatak (kă-nă'tŏk)......Alaska 57·35 N 155·48 W
63 Kanawha (R.) (kȧ-nô'wȧ)...U. S. 37·55 N 81·50 W
153 Kanaya (kä-nä'yä) Jap. (Tōkyō In.) 35·10 N 139·49 E
115 Kanayis, Rasel (C.)......U. A. R. 31·14 N 28·08 E
153 Kanazawa (kä'nȧ-zä'wȧ).....Jap. 36·34 N 136·38 E
142 Kanchenjunga, Mt. (kĭn-chĭn-jŏŏŋ'gȧ).Nep. 32·40 N 88·18 E
145 Kandahār (kŭn-dŭ-här')......Afg. 31·43 N 65·58 E
166 Kanda Kanda (kän'dȧ kän'dȧ) Con. L. 6·51 S 23·27 E
132 Kandalaksha (kȧn-dȧ-lȧk'shȧ) Sov. Un. 67·10 N 33·05 E
132 Kandalakshskiy Zaliv (B.) Sov. Un. 66·20 N 35·00 E
119 Kandava (kän'dȧ-vȧ)....Sov. Un. 57·03 N 22·45 E
164 Kandi (käN-dē')........Dahomey 11·09 N 3·02 E
142 Kandiaro............W. Pak. 27·09 N 68·12 E
142 Kandla (kŭnd'lŭ)..........India 23·00 N 70·20 E
143 Kandy (kän'dê)..........Ceylon 7·18 N 80·42 E
81 Kane (kān)................Pa. 41·40 N 78·50 W
157 Kaneohe B. (kä-nä-ō'hä) Hawaii (In.) 21·32 N 157·40 W
129 Kanëv (kä-nyôf')........Sov. Un. 49·46 N 31·27 E
129 Kanevskaya (kȧ-nyĕf'skȧ-yȧ) Sov. Un. 46·07 N 38·58 E
160 Kangaroo (I.) (kăŋ-gȧ-rōō') Austl. 36·05 S 137·05 E
144 Kangāvar (kŭŋ'gā-vär)......Iran 34·37 N 46·45 E
154 Kangean (I.) (kăŋ'gê-än)..Indon. 6·50 S 116·22 E
152 Kanggye (käng'gyĕ).........Kor. 40·55 N 126·40 E
152 Kanghwa (I.) (käng'hwä)....Kor. 37·28 N 126·00 E
152 Kangnŭng(käng'nōōng).......Kor. 37·42 N 128·50 E
166 Kango (käN-gō')..........Gabon 0·14 N 10·07 E
146 K'angting...............China 30·15 N 101·58 E
151 Kanhsien...............China 25·50 N 115·00 E
87 Kaniapiskau (L.) (kă-nĭ-ăp'ĭs-kô) Can. 54·04 N 71·20 W
87 Kaniapiskau (R.)...........Can. 56·52 N 68·53 W
132 Kanin, P-Ov. (Pen.) (kȧ-nēn') Sov. Un. 68·00 N 45·00 E
132 Kanin Nos, Mys (C.)....Sov. Un. 68·40 N 44·00 E
127 Kanjiža (kä'nyê-zhä)......Yugo. 46·05 N 20·02 E
75 Kankakee (kăŋ-kȧ-kē') Ill. (Chicago In.) 41·07 N 87·53 W
80 Kankakee (R.)..............Ill. 41·15 N 88·15 W
164 Kankan (käN-käN) (kän-kän').Gui 10·20 N 9·16 W
150 Kannan.................China 47·50 N 123·30 E
79 Kannapolis (kăn-ăp'ô-lĭs)...N. C. 35·30 N 80·38 W
153 Kannoura (kä'nō-ōō'rä)......Jap. 33·34 N 134·18 E
164 Kano (kä'nō)...............Nig. 12·03 N 8·32 E
166 Kanonberg (Mtn.) S. Afr. (Cape Town In.) 33·49 S 18·37 E
72 Kanopolis Res. (kăn-ŏp'ô-lĭs) Kans. 38·44 N 98·01 W
142 Kānpur (kän'pûr)..........India 26·33 N 80·19 E
62 Kansas (State) (kăn'zȧs)....U. S. 38·30 N 99·40 W
73 Kansas (R.)...............Kans. 39·08 N 95·52 W
74 Kansas City Kans. (Kansas City In.) 39·06 N 94·39 W
74 Kansas City.Mo. (Kansas City In.) 39·05 N 94·35 W
134 Kansk................Sov. Un. 56·14 N 95·43 E
152 Kansŏng.................Kor. 38·09 N 128·29 E
146 Kansu (Prov.) (kän'sōō')...China 38·00 N 102·06 E

154 Kan Tang (kän'täng')......Thai. 7·26 N 99·28 E
92 Kantunilkin (kän-tōō-nēl-kē'n) Mex. (Yucatan In.) 21·07 N 87·30 W
136 Kanzhakovskiy Kamen Gora (kȧn-zhă'kôvs-kēê kȧmĭên) Sov. Un. (Urals In.) 59·38 N 59·12 E
151 Kaoan...................China 28·30 N 115·02 E
148 Kaoch'eng (kä'ō-chĕng')....China 34·56 N 114·57 E
149 Kaoch'iao...China (Shanghai In.) 31·21 N 121·35 E
151 Kaohsiung (kä'ō-syōōng').Taiwan 22·35 N 120·25 E
148 Kaoi (gou'yē).............China 37·37 N 114·39 E
164 Kaolack................Senegal 14·02 N 16·16 W
148 Kaomi (gou'mē)..........China 36·23 N 119·46 E
148 Kaoshun (gou'shōōn).......China 31·22 N 118·50 E
148 Kaot'ang (kä'ō-täng')......China 36·52 N 116·12 E
151 Kaoteng Shan (Mtns.).....China 26·30 N 110·00 E
165 Kaovar (Oasis)...........Niger 19·16 N 13·09 E
151 Kaoyao.................China 23·08 N 112·25 E
148 Kaoyu (gou'yü)............China 32·46 N 119·26 E
151 Kaoyu Hu (L.) (kä'ō-yōō'hōō) China 32·42 N 118·40 E
134 Kapal (kȧ-päl')........Sov. Un. 45·13 N 79·08 E
120 Kapfenberg (käp'fĕn-bĕrgh)..Aus. 47·27 N 15·16 E
165 Kapoeta..................Sud. 4·45 N 33·35 E
121 Kaposvár (kô'pôsh-vär)....Hung. 46·21 N 17·45 E
152 Kapsan (käp'sän').........Kor. 40·59 N 128·22 E
154 Kapuas, Sungai (Strm.) (kä'pōō-äs).Indon. 2·05 S 114·15 E
87 Kapuskasing..............Can. 49·28 N 82·22 W
133 Kapustin Yar (kä'pōōs-tēn yär') Sov. Un. 48·30 N 45·40 E
160 Kaputar, Mt. (kă-pû-tȧr)...Austl. 30·11 S 150·11 E
120 Kapuvár (kô'pōō-vär)......Hung. 47·35 N 17·02 E
134 Kara (kärȧ)...........Sov. Un. 68·42 N 65·30 E
132 Kara (R.).............Sov. Un. 68·30 N 65·20 E
136 Karabanovo (kä'rȧ-bȧ-nō-vô) Sov. Un. (Moscow In.) 56·19 N 38·43 E
136 Karabash (kó-rȧ-bäsh') Sov. Un. (Urals In.) 55·27 N 60·14 E
133 Kara-Bogaz-Gol, Zaliv (B.) (kȧrä' bŭ-gäs').Sov. Un. 41·30 N 53·40 E
128 Karachev (kȧ-rȧ-chôf')...Sov. Un. 53·08 N 34·54 E
142 Karachi..................Pak. 24·59 N 68·56 E
103 Karacumy (Des.)........Sov. Un. 39·08 N 59·53 E
133 Karadeniz Boğazi (Bosporous) (Str.).Tur. 41·10 N 29·10 E
134 Karaganda (kȧ-rȧ-gän'dä) Sov. Un. 49·42 N 73·18 E
136 Karaidel (kä'rī-dĕl) Sov. Un. (Urals In.) 55·52 N 56·54 E
133 Kara-Khobda (R.) (kä-rȧ кôb'dȧ).Sov. Un. 50·40 N 55·00 E
145 Karakoram Pass....India & Pak. 35·35 N 77·45 E
146 Karakoram Ra. (kä'rä kō'rōōm) India & Pak. 35·24 N 76·38 E
146 Karakorum (Ruins)........Mong. 47·25 N 102·22 E
133 Karaköse (kä-rä-kŭ'sĕ).......Tur. 39·50 N 43·10 E
130 Karakumy (kara-kum) (Des.) Sov. Un. 40·00 N 57·00 E
133 Karaman (kä-rä-män').........Tur. 37·10 N 33·00 E
159 Karamea Bght. (kȧ-rȧ-mē'ȧ bĭt) N. Z. (In.) 41·10 S 170·42 E
144 Karand...................Iran 34·08 N 46·19 E
Kara Sea, see Karskoye More
153 Karatsu (kä'rȧ-tsōō).........Jap. 33·28 N 129·59 E
134 Karaul (kä-rä-ōōl')......Sov. Un. 70·13 N 83·46 E
120 Karawanken Mts...........Aus. 46·32 N 14·07 E
144 Karbala (kûr'bȧ-lȧ).........Iraq 32·31 N 43·58 E
121 Karcag (kär'tsäg).........Hung. 47·18 N 20·58 E
127 Kardhítsa.................Grc. 39·23 N 21·57 E
119 Kärdla (kĕrd'lȧ)........Sov. Un. 58·59 N 22·44 E
165 Kareima (kȧ-rä'mȧ)..........Sud. 18·34 N 31·49 E
130 Karelian (A. S. S. R.)...Sov. Un. 62·30 N 32·35 E
166 Karema..................Tan. 6·47 S 30·29 E
134 Kargat (kär-gät').......Sov. Un. 55·17 N 80·07 E
Karghalik, see Yehch'eng
132 Kargopol (kär-gō-pōl'')..Sov. Un. 61·30 N 38·50 E
127 Kariaí....................Grc. 40·14 N 24·15 E
166 Kariba Res...............N. Rh. 17·30 S 28·06 E
166 Karibib (kȧr'ȧ-bĭb)....S. W. Afr. 21·55 S 15·50 E
143 Kārikāl (kä-rê-käl').........India 10·58 N 79·49 E
164 Karimama (kä-rê-mä'mä) Dahomey 12·04 N 3·09 E
154 Karimata, Pulau-Pulau (Is.) (kä-rê-mä'tȧ).Indon. 1·08 S 108·10 E
154 Karimata, Selat (Str.).....Indon. 1·15 S 107·10 E
154 Karimundjawa (I.) (kä'rê-mōōn-yä'vä).Indon. 5·36 S 110·15 E
168 Karin (kȧr'ĭn) Som. (Horn of Afr. In.) 10·43 N 45·50 E
155 Karkar (I.) (kär'kär).N. Gui. Ter. 4·50 S 146·45 E
134 Karkaralinsk (kär-kär-ä-lēnsk') Sov. Un. 49·18 N 75·28 E
129 Karkinitskiy Zailv (B.) (kär-kê-nĕt'skĭ-ê zä'lĭf).Sov. Un. 45·50 N 32·45 E
120 Karl-Marx-Stadt (Chemnitz).Ger. 50·48 N 12·53 E
126 Karlobag (kär-lō-bäg')......Yugo. 44·30 N 15·03 E
126 Karlovac (kär'lō-väts)......Yugo. 45·29 N 15·16 E
129 Karlovka (kär'lôv-kȧ)...Sov. Un. 49·26 N 35·08 E
127 Karlovo (kär'lō-vō).........Bul. 42·39 N 24·48 E
120 Karlovy Vary (kär'lô-vê vä'rê) Czech. 50·13 N 12·53 E
118 Karlshamn (kärls'häm)......Swe. 56·11 N 14·50 E
118 Karlskrona (kärls'krō-nä)....Swe. 56·10 N 15·33 E
120 Karlsruhe (kärls'rōō-ĕ)......Ger. 49·00 N 8·23 E
118 Karlstad (kärl'städ)........Swe. 59·25 N 13·28 E
64 Karluk (kär'lŭk)..........Alaska 57·30 N 154·22 W
118 Karmöy (I.) (kärm-ûe).......Nor. 59·14 N 5·00 E
127 Karnobat (kär-nô'bät).......Bul. 42·39 N 26·59 E
120 Kärnten (Carinthia) (State) (kĕrn'tĕn).Aus. 46·55 N 13·42 E
166 Karonga (kȧ-rōŋ'gȧ).........Nya. 9·52 S 33·57 E
115 Kárpathos (I.)..............Grc. 35·34 N 27·26 E
136 Karpinsk (kär'pĭnsk) Sov. Un. (Urals In.) 59·46 N 60·00 E

133 Kars (kärs)................Tur. 40·35 N 43·00 E
134 Karsakpay (kär-säk-pī')..Sov. Un. 47·47 N 67·07 E
128 Kārsava (kär'sä-vä).....Sov. Un. 56·46 N 27·39 E
145 Karshi (kär'shē)........Sov. Un. 38·30 N 66·08 E
134 Karskiye Vorota, Proliv (Str.) Sov. Un. 70·30 N 58·07 E
134 Karskoye More (Kara Sea) Sov. Un. 74·08 N 65·45 E
136 Kartaly (kȧr'tá lê) Sov. Un. (Urals In.) 53·05 N 60·40 E
143 Karunagapalli.............India 9.09 N 76·34 E
121 Karvina.................Czech. 49·50 N 18·30 E
166 Kasaï (R.)..............Con. L. 3·45 S 19·07 E
166 Kasama (kȧ-sä'mȧ).......N. Rh. 10·15 S 31·13 E
166 Kasanga (kȧ-säŋ'gȧ)........Tan. 8·27 S 31·13 E
153 Kasaoka (kä'sä-ō'kȧ).......Jap. 34·33 N 133·29 E
152 Kasari Saki (C.) (kä'sä-rē sä-kē) Jap. 28·25 N 130·10 E
164 Kasba-Tadla (käs'bȧ-täd'lä).Mor. 32·37 N 5·57 W
166 Kasempa (kȧ-sĕm'pȧ).....N. Rh. 13·15 S 25·41 E
166 Kasenga (kȧ-seŋ'gȧ)......Con. L. 10·27 S 28·42 E
144 Kash (R.) (kŭsh)..........Afg. 32·27 N 64·15 E
144 Kāshān (kä-shän')..........Iran 33·52 N 51·15 E
Kashqar, see Sufu
153 Kashihara (kä'shê-hä'rä) Jap. (Ōsaka In.) 34·35 N 135·38 E
128 Kashin (kä-shēn')......Sov. Un. 57·20 N 37·38 E
128 Kashira (kä-shē'rȧ)......Sov. Un. 54·49 N 38·11 E
153 Kashiwa (kä'shê-wä) Jap. (Tōkyō In.) 35·51 N 139·58 E
152 Kashiwazaki (kä'shē-wä-zä'kê) Jap. 37·06 N 138·17 E
Kashmir, see Jammu and Kashmir
142 Kashmor...............W. Pak. 28·33 N 69·34 E
136 Kashtak (kàsh'tàk) Sov. Un. (Urals In.) 55·18 N 61·25 E
128 Kasimov (kȧ-sē'môf)....Sov. Un. 54·56 N 41·23 E
64 Kaskanak (kăs-kă'năk)....Alaska 60·00 N 158·00 W
80 Kaskaskia (R.) (kăs-kăs'kĭ-ȧ)..Ill. 38·45 N 89·15 W
Kaskinem, see Kaskö
119 Kaskö (Kaskinen) (käs'kû) (käs'kē-nĕn).Fin. 62·24 N 21·18 E
136 Kasli (käs'lĭ).Sov. Un. (Urals In.) 55·54 N 60·46 E
166 Kasongo (kä-sôŋ'gō)......Con. L. 4·31 S 26·42 E
115 Kásos (I.)................Grc. 35·20 N 26·55 E
165 Kassala (kä-sä'lä)...........Sud. 15·26 N 36·28 E
120 Kassel (käs'ĕl).............Ger. 51·19 N 9·30 E
71 Kasson (kăs'ŭn)...........Minn. 44·01 N 92·45 W
133 Kastamonu (kä-stȧ-mō'nōō)..Tur. 41·20 N 33·50 E
126 Kastélli...........Grc. (Inset) 35·13 N 24·11 E
115 Kastellórizon (C.)..........Tur. 36·01 N 30·00 E
127 Kastoría (kȧs-tō'rĭ-ȧ).......Grc. 40·28 N 21·17 E
127 Kastron (käs'trôn)...........Grc. 39·52 N 25·01 E
142 Kasur.................W. Pak. 31·10 N 74·29 E
82 Katahdin, Mt. (kȧ-tä'dĭn)..Maine 45·56 N 68·57 W
166 Katanga (Reg.) (kȧ-täŋ'gȧ) Con. L. 8·35 S 23·59 E
158 Katanning (kȧ-tăn'ĭng).....Austl. 33·45 S 117·45 E
136 Katav-Ivanovsk (kä'tȧf ĭ-vä'nôfsk).Sov. Un. (Urals In.) 54·46 N 58·13 E
136 Kateninskiy (kȧtyĕ'nĭs-kĭ) Sov. Un. (Urals In.) 53·12 N 61·05 E
127 Kateríni.................Grc. 40·18 N 22·36 E
165 Katherina, G. (Pk.)......U. A. R. 28·43 N 34·00 E
158 Katherine (kăth'ĕr-ĭn)......Austl. 14·15 S 132·20 E
142 Kathiawar Pen. (kä'tyȧ-wär') India 27·18 N 70·32 E
85 Kathryn (kăth'rĭn) Can. (Calgary In.) 51·13 N 113·42 W
74 Kathryn..Calif. (Los Angeles In.) 33·42 N 117·45 W
142 Katiha...................India 25·39 N 87·39 E
64 Katmai Natl. Mon. (kăt'mī) Alaska 58·38 N 155·00 W
142 Kātmāndu (kät-män-dōō')...Nep. 27·49 N 85·21 E
121 Katowice.................Pol. 50·15 N 19·00 E
118 Katrineholm (kȧ-trē'nĕ-hōlm) Swe. 59·01 N 16·10 E
136 Katsbakhskiy (kȧts-bäk'skĭ) Sov. Un. (Urals In.) 52·57 N 59·37 E
164 Katsina (kät'sê-nȧ)..........Nig. 13·03 N 7·39 E
164 Katsina Ala (ä'lä)...........Nig. 7·15 N 9·12 E
153 Katsura (R.) (kä'tsōō-rä) Jap. (Ōsaka In.) 34·55 N 135·43 E
134 Katta-Kurgan (kȧ-tȧ-kōōr-gän') Sov. Un. 39·45 N 66·42 E
118 Kattegat (Str.) (kăt'ĕ-gät)...Eur. 56·57 N 11·25 E
134 Katun' (R.) (kȧ-tōōn')...Sov. Un. 51·30 N 86·18 E
111 Katwijkaan Zee Neth. (Amsterdam In.) 52·12 N 4·23 E
157 Kauai (I.).........Hawaii (In.) 22·09 N 159·15 W
157 Kauai Chan. (kä-ōō-ä'ê) Hawaii (In.) 21·35 N 158·52 W
120 Kaufbeuren (kouf'boi-rĕn)...Ger. 47·52 N 10·38 E
77 Kaufman (kôf'măn)..........Tex. 32·36 N 96·18 W
71 Kaukauna (kô-kô'nȧ).........Wis. 44·17 N 88·15 W
157 Kaulakahi Chan. (kä'ōō-lȧ-kä'hê) Hawaii (In.) 22·00 N 159·55 W
157 Kaunakakai (kä'ōō-nȧ-kä'kĭ) Hawaii (In.) 21·06 N 156·59 E
119 Kaunas (Kovno) (kou'nȧs) (kôv'nô).Sov. Un. 54·52 N 23·54 E
164 Kaure Namoda.............Nig. 12·41 N 7·32 E
127 Kavajë (kä-vä'yŭ)..........Alb. 41·11 N 19·36 E
127 Kavála (kä-vä'lä)...........Grc. 40·55 N 24·24 E
127 Kavallas, Kólpos (G.).......Grc. 40·45 N 24·20 E
155 Kavieng (kä-vê-ĕng').N. Gui. Ter. 2·44 S 151·02 E
144 Kavir-E Lut (Des.)...........Iran 31·47 N 58·38 E
153 Kawagoe (kä-wä-gō'ȧ) Jap. (Tōkyō In.) 35·55 N 139·29 E
153 Kawaguchi (kä-wä-gōō-chē) Jap. (Tōkyō In.) 35·48 N 139·44 E
157 Kawaikini (Mtn.) (kä-wä'ê-kĭ-nĭ).Hawaii (In.) 22·05 N 159·33 W
153 Kawasaki (kä-wä-sä'kê) Jap. (Tōkyō In.) 35·32 N 139·43 E

ng-sing; ŋ-baŋk; N-nasalized n; nŏd; cŏmmit; ōld; ōbey; ôrder; fōōd; fŏŏt; ou-out; s-soft; sh-dish; th-thin; pūre; ûnite; ûrn; stŭd; circŭs; ü-as "y" in study; '-indeterminate vowel.

Page	Name Pronunciation Region	Lat. °′	Long. °′
168	Kawm Umbū . . U. A. R. (Nile In.)	24·30 N	32·59 E
164	Kaya (kä'yä) Upper Volta	12·59 N	1·21 W
67	Kaycee (kā-sē') Wyo.	43·43 N	106·38 W
164	Kayes (kāz) Mali	14·20 N	11·33 W
133	Kayseri (kī'sĕ-rē) Tur.	38·45 N	35·20 E
74	Kaysville (kāz'vĭl) Utah (Salt Lake City In.)	41·02 N	111·56 W
135	Kazach'ye Sov. Un.	70·46 N	135·47 E
130	Kazakh S. S. R. (kȧ-zäk') Sov. Un.	48·45 N	59·00 E
132	Kazan' (kȧ-zän') Sov. Un.	55·50 N	49·18 E
129	Kazanka (kȧ-zän'kȧ) Sov. Un.	47·49 N	32·50 E
127	Kazanlŭk (kä'zȧn-lĕk) Bul.	42·47 N	25·23 E
129	Kazatin Sov. Un.	49·43 N	28·50 E
133	Kazbek, Gora (Mt.) (kȧz-bĕk') Sov. Un.	42·45 N	44·30 E
144	Kāzerūn Iran	29·37 N	51·44 E
153	Kazusa Kameyama (kä-zōō-sä kä-mȧ'yä-mä). Jap. (Tōkyō In.)	35·14 N	140·06 E
134	Kazym (R.) (kä-zēm') Sov. Un.	63·30 N	67·41 E
127	Kéa (I.) Grc.	37·36 N	24·13 E
157	Kealaikahiki Chan. (kā-ä'lä-ē-kä-hē'kē) Hawaii (In.)	20·38 N	157·00 W
84	Keansburg (kēnz'bûrg) N. J. (New York In.)	40·26 N	74·08 W
72	Kearney (kär'nĭ) Nebr.	40·42 N	99·05 W
84	Kearny . . . N. J. (New York In.)	40·46 N	74·09 W
65	Keasey (kēz'ĭ). Ore. (Portland In.)	45·51 N	123·20 W
112	Kebnekaise (Mtn.) (kĕp'nĕ-kȧ-ēs'ĕ). Swe.	67·53 N	18·10 E
121	Kecskemét (kĕch'kĕ-māt) . . Hung.	46·52 N	19·42 E
154	Kedah State (kā'dä) Mala.	6·08 N	100·31 E
119	Kédainiai (kē-dī'nĭ-ī) Sov. Un.	55·16 N	23·58 E
82	Kedgwick (kĕdj'wĭk) Can.	47·42 N	67·24 W
74	Keenbrook (kēn'brŏŏk) Calif. (Los Angeles In.)	34·16 N	117·29 W
81	Keene (kēn) N. H.	42·55 N	72·15 W
166	Keetmanshoop (kāt'mȧns-hōp) S. W. Afr.	26·30 S	18·05 E
69	Keet Seel Ruin (kēt sēl) Ariz.	36·46 N	110·32 W
71	Keewatin (kē-wä'tĭn) Minn.	47·24 N	93·03 W
86	Keewatin, Dist. of Can.	61·26 N	97·54 W
127	Kefallinía (Cephalonia) (I.) . . Grc.	38·08 N	20·58 E
	Kefe, see Feodosiya		
164	Keffi (kĕf'ē) Nig.	8·52 N	7·49 E
167	Kei (R.) (kā) . . S. Afr. (Natal In.)	32·57 S	26·50 E
119	Keila (kā'lȧ) Sov. Un.	59·19 N	24·25 E
167	Kei Mouth . . . S. Afr. (Natal In.)	32·40 S	28·23 E
167	Keiskammahoek (kās'kämȧ-hōōk') S. Afr. (Natal In.)	32·42 S	27·11 E
119	Keitele (L.) (kā'tĕ-lĕ) Fin.	62·50 N	25·40 E
167	Keiweg . . . S. Afr. (Natal In.)	32·43 S	27·34 E
154	Kelantan State (kĕ-lăn-tăn'). Mala.	5·11 N	101·51 E
115	Kelkit (R.) Tur.	40·38 N	37·03 E
74	Keller (kĕl'ēr) Tex. (Dallas, Fort Worth In.)	32·56 N	97·15 W
111	Kellinghusen (kĕ'lĕng-hōō-zĕn) Ger. (Hamburg In.)	53·57 N	9·43 E
66	Kellogg (kĕl'ŏg) Idaho	47·32 N	116·07 W
119	Kelme' (kĕl-mȧ) Sov. Un.	55·36 N	22·53 E
86	Kelowna Can.	49·49 N	119·17 W
65	Kelso . . . Wash. (Portland In.)	46·09 N	122·54 W
132	Kem' (kĕm) Sov. Un.	65·00 N	34·48 E
77	Kemah (kē'mȧ) Tex. (In.)	29·32 N	95·01 W
165	Kemboma (kĕm-bō-mȧ') . . . Gabon	0·43 S	13·34 E
112	Kemi (kā'mē) Fin.	65·48 N	24·38 E
112	Kemi (R.) Fin.	67·02 N	27·50 E
153	Kemigawa (kĕ'mē-gä'wä) Jap. (Tōkyō In.)	35·38 N	140·07 E
112	Kemijarvi (kā'mē-yĕr-vē) Fin.	66·48 N	27·21 E
112	Kemi-joki (L.) Fin.	66·37 N	28·13 E
67	Kemmerer (kĕm'ēr-ēr) Wyo.	41·48 N	110·36 W
72	Kemp (L.) (kĕmp) Tex.	33·55 N	99·22 W
123	Kempen (kĕm'pĕn) Ger. (Ruhr In.)	51·22 N	6·25 E
160	Kempsey (kĕmp'sē) Austl.	30·59 S	152·50 E
84	Kempsville (kĕmps'vĭl) Va. (Norfolk In.)	36·49 N	76·10 W
82	Kempt (L.) (kĕmpt) Can.	47·28 N	74·00 W
120	Kempten (kĕmp'tĕn) Ger.	47·44 N	10·17 E
167	Kempton Park (kĕmp'tŏn pärk) S. Afr. (Johannesburg & Pretoria In.)	26·07 S	28·29 E
142	Ken (R.) India	25·00 N	79·55 E
64	Kenai (kĕ-nī') Alaska	60·38 N	151·18 W
64	Kenai Mts. Alaska	60·00 N	150·00 W
64	Kenai Pen. Alaska	64·40 N	150·18 W
116	Kendal (kĕn'dăl) Eng.	54·20 N	1·48 W
168	Kendal . . . S. Afr. (Johannesburg & Pretoria In.)	26·03 S	28·58 E
80	Kendallville (kĕn'dăl-vĭl) . . . Ind.	41·25 N	85·20 W
77	Kenedy (kĕn'ĕ-dĭ) Tex.	28·49 N	97·50 W
167	Kenegha (R.) . . S. Afr. (Natal In.)	30·37 S	28·52 E
166	Kenilworth (kĕn'ĭl-wûrth) S. Afr. (Cape Town In.)	33·59 S	18·28 E
114	Kenitra (Port Lyautey) (kĕ-nē'trȧ). Mor.	34·21 N	6·34 W
70	Kenmare (kĕn-mâr') N. D.	48·41 N	102·05 W
75	Kenmore (kĕn'mōr) N. Y. (Buffalo In.)	42·58 N	78·53 W
82	Kennebec (R.) (kĕn-ē-bĕk'). Maine	44·23 N	69·48 W
82	Kennebunk (kĕn-ē-bŭŋk') . . Maine	43·24 N	70·33 W
74	Kennedale (kĕn'-ē-dāl) Tex. (Dallas, Fort Worth In.)	32·38 N	97·13 W
79	Kennedy, C. Fla. (In.)	28·30 N	80·23 W
77	Kenner (kĕn'ēr) La.	29·58 N	90·15 W
73	Kennett (kĕn'ĕt) Mo.	36·14 N	90·01 W
66	Kennewick (kĕn'ē-wĭk) . . . Wash.	46·12 N	119·06 W
65	Kennydale (kĕn-nē'-dāl) Wash. (Seattle In.)	47·31 N	122·12 W
82	Kenogami (kĕn-ŏ'gä-mē) . . . Can.	48·27 N	71·15 W
87	Kenora (kē-nō'rȧ) Can.	49·48 N	94·22 W
75	Kenosha (kĕ-nō'shȧ) Wis. (Milwaukee In.)	42·34 N	87·50 W
80	Kenova (kē-nō'vȧ) W. Va.	38·20 N	82·35 W
84	Kensico Res. (kĕn'sĭ-kō) N. Y. (New York In.)	41·08 N	73·45 W
80	Kent (kĕnt) Ohio	41·05 N	81·20 W
65	Kent Wash. (Seattle In.)	47·23 N	122·14 W
167	Kentani (kĕnt-änĭ') S. Afr. (Natal In.)	32·31 S	28·19 E
147	Kentei Alin (Mts.) (kĕn'tā'ä-lēn') China	45·54 N	131·45 E
146	Kentei Shan (Mts.) (kĕn'tĭ'shän') Mong.	49·25 N	107·51 E
80	Kentland (kĕnt'lănd) Ind.	40·50 N	87·25 W
80	Kenton (kĕn'tŭn) Ohio	40·40 N	83·35 W
167	Kenton-on-Sea (kĕn'tŏn ŏn sē) S. Afr. (Natal In.)	33·41 S	26·42 E
86	Kent Pen. Can.	68·28 N	108·10 W
63	Kentucky (State) (kĕn-tŭk'ĭ) U. S.	37·30 N	87·35 W
63	Kentucky (L.) U. S.	36·20 N	88·50 W
63	Kentucky (R.) U. S.	38·15 N	85·01 W
82	Kentville (kĕnt'vĭl) Can.	45·04 N	64·31 W
77	Kentwood (kĕnt'wŏŏd) La.	30·56 N	90·31 W
163	Kenya (kĕn'yȧ) Afr.	1·00 N	36·53 E
167	Kenya, Mt Ken.	0·15 S	37·16 E
71	Kenyon (kĕn'yŭn) Minn.	44·15 N	92·58 W
157	Keokea Hawaii (In.)	20·44 N	156·26 W
73	Keokuk (kē'ō-kŭk) Iowa	40·24 N	91·34 W
85	Keoma (kē-ō'mȧ) Can. (Calgary In.)	51·13 N	113·39 W
83	Kepenkeck, L. Can.	48·15 N	54·57 W
121	Kepno (kăŋ'pnō) Pol.	51·17 N	17·59 E
143	Kerala (State) India	16·38 N	76·00 E
160	Kerang (kē-răng') Austl.	35·32 S	143·58 E
129	Kerch' (kĕrch) Sov. Un.	45·20 N	36·26 E
129	Kerchenskiy Proliv (Str.) (Kerch Str.) (kĕr-chĕn'skĭ prô'lĭf). Sov. Un.	45·08 N	36·35 E
133	Kerempe Burun (C.) Tur.	42·00 N	33·20 E
47	Kerguelen, Is. de (kĕr'gȧ-lĕn) Ind. O.	49·50 S	69·30 E
154	Kerintji, Gunung (Mtn.) . . Indon.	1·45 S	101·18 E
146	Keriya (R.) (kĕ'rē-yä) China	37·13 N	81·59 E
	Keriya, see Yutien		
165	Kerkennah, Îles (I.) (kĕr'kĕn-nä) Tun.	34·49 N	11·37 E
145	Kerki (kĕr'kē) Sov. Un.	37·52 N	65·15 E
127	Kérkira Grc.	39·36 N	19·56 E
127	Kérkira (I.) Grc.	39·33 N	19·36 E
156	Kermadec Is. (kēr-măd'ĕk) . . N. Z.	30·30 S	177·00 E
156	Kermadec Tonga Trench (kēr-măd'ĕk tŏŋ'gȧ). Oceania	23·00 S	172·30 W
144	Kermān (kĕr-män') Iran	30·23 N	57·08 E
144	Kermānshāh (kĕr-män-shä') . . Iran	34·01 N	47·00 E
134	Kemerovo Sov. Un.	55·31 N	86·05 E
68	Kern (R.) Calif.	35·31 N	118·37 W
68	Kern, South Fork of (R.) . . Calif.	35·40 N	118·15 W
68	Kern Can. (kûrn) Calif.	36·57 N	119·37 W
123	Kerpen (kĕr'pĕn). Ger. (Ruhr In.)	50·52 N	6·42 E
79	Kerr Res. (kēr) N. C.-Va.	36·30 N	78·38 W
76	Kerrville (kûr'vĭl) Tex.	30·02 N	99·07 W
116	Kerry, Mts. (kĕr'ĭ) Ire.	51·48 N	10·02 W
147	Kerulen (R.) (kĕr'ōō-lĕn) . . . Mong.	47·52 N	113·22 E
127	Kesan (kĕ'shän) Tur.	40·50 N	26·37 E
114	Kesour, Monts des (Mts.) . . . Alg.	32·51 N	0·30 W
168	Kestell (kĕs'tĕl) S. Afr. (Johannesburg & Pretoria In.)	28·19 S	28·43 E
110	Kesteven (Co.) (kĕs'tē-vĕn) . Eng.	52·57 N	0·30 W
121	Keszthely (kĕst'hĕl-lĭ) Hung.	46·46 N	17·12 E
134	Ket' (R.) (kyĕt) Sov. Un.	58·30 N	84·15 E
139	Ketamputih Indon. (Singapore In.)	1·25 N	102·19 E
154	Ketapang (kĕ-tȧ-päng') . . . Indon.	2·00 S	109·57 E
64	Ketchikan (kĕch-ĭ-kăn') . . . Alaska	55·26 N	131·40 W
121	Ketrzyn (kăŋ't'r-zĭn) Pol.	54·04 N	21·24 E
110	Kettering (kĕt'ēr-ĭng) Eng.	52·23 N	0·43 W
80	Kettering Ohio	39·40 N	84·15 W
71	Kettle (R.) (kĕt''l) Minn.	46·20 N	92·57 W
123	Kettwig (kĕt'vēg). Ger. (Ruhr In.)	51·22 N	6·56 E
121	Kety (kăŋ'tĭ) Pol.	49·54 N	19·16 E
111	Ketzin (kĕ'tzēn) . . Ger. (Berlin In.)	52·29 N	12·51 E
81	Keuka (L.) (kē-ū'kȧ) N. Y.	42·30 N	77·10 W
123	Kevelaer (kĕ'fĕ-lăr) Ger. (Ruhr In.)	51·35 N	6·15 E
71	Kewanee (kē-wä'nē) Ill.	41·15 N	89·55 W
71	Kewaunee (kē-wô'nē) Wis.	44·27 N	87·33 W
71	Keweenaw B. (kē'wē-nô) . . Mich.	46·59 N	88·15 W
71	Keweenaw Pen. Mich.	47·28 N	88·12 W
70	Keya Paha (R.) (kē-yȧ pä'hä) S. D.	43·11 N	100·10 W
79	Key Largo (I.) Fla. (In.)	25·11 N	80·15 W
84	Keyport (kē'pōrt) N. J. (New York In.)	40·26 N	74·12 W
65	Keyport . . . . . Wash. (Seattle In.)	47·42 N	122·38 W
81	Keyser (kī'zēr) W. Va.	39·25 N	79·00 W
79	Key West (kē wĕst') . . . Fla. (In.)	24·31 N	81·47 W
121	Kežmarok (kĕzh'mȧ-rôk) . . . Czech.	49·10 N	20·27 E
134	Khabarovo (kŭ-bär-ôvô) . Sov. Un.	69·31 N	60·41 E
135	Khabarovsk (κä-bä'rôfsk) Sov. Un.	48·35 N	135·12 E
146	Khaidik Gol (R.) (κī'dĕk gōl) China	42·35 N	84·04 E
134	Khakass Aut. Oblast . . . Sov. Un.	52·32 N	89·33 E
143	Khālāpur . . . . India (Bombay In.)	18·48 N	73·17 E
168	Khalig El Tina (G.) U. A. R. (Nile In.)	31·12 N	32·42 E
135	Khalkha (R.) China-Mong.	48·00 N	118·45 E
127	Khalkidhiki Khers (Pen.) . . . Grc.	40·30 N	23·18 E
127	Khalkis (κäl'kĭs) Grc.	38·28 N	23·38 E
134	Khal'mer-Yu (kŭl-myĕr'-yōō') Sov. Un.	67·52 N	64·25 E
132	Khalturin (κäl'tōō-rēn) . Sov. Un.	58·28 N	49·00 E
143	Khammameth India	17·09 N	80·13 E
142	Khānābād Afg.	36·43 N	69·11 E
142	Khandwa India	21·53 N	76·22 E
	Khangai Mts., see Hangayn Nuruu		
154	Khanh Hung Viet.	9·45 N	105·50 E
126	Khaniá (Canea) (kä-nĕ'ä). Grc. (In.)	35·29 N	24·04 E
126	Khanión, Kólpos (G.) . . . Grc. (In.)	35·35 N	23·55 E
147	Khanka (L.) (κän'kȧ) . . . Sov. Un.	45·09 N	133·28 E
142	Khānpur W. Pak.	28·42 N	70·42 E
134	Khanty-Mansiysk (κŭn-te' mŭn-sēsk'). Sov. Un.	61·02 N	69·01 E
139	Khān Yūnis . . . Isr. (Palestine In.)	31·21 N	34·19 E
142	Kharagpur (kŭ-rŭg'pōōr) . . . . India	22·26 N	87·21 E
129	Khar'kov (kär'kôf) Sov. Un.	50·00 N	36·10 E
129	Kharkov (Oblast) Sov. Un.	49·33 N	35·55 E
132	Kharlovka Sov. Un.	63·40 N	37·40 E
127	Kharmanli (κär-män'lē) Bul.	41·54 N	25·55 E
165	Khartoum (kär-tōōm') Sud.	15·34 N	32·36 E
165	Khartoum North Sud.	15·43 N	32·41 E
144	Khāsh Iran	28·08 N	61·08 E
142	Khasi Hills Bur.	30·56 N	91·19 E
127	Khaskovo (κäs'kô-vô) Bul.	41·56 N	25·32 E
135	Khatanga (κȧ-tän'gȧ) . . . . Sov. Un.	71·48 N	101·47 E
135	Khatangskiy Zaliv (B.) (kä-tän'g-skē). Sov. Un.	73·45 N	108·30 E
142	Khed Brahma (kād brä'mȧ). India	24·00 N	73·05 E
144	Khersan, Rud-E (R.) Iran	31·17 N	50·38 E
129	Kherson (kĕr-sôn') Sov. Un.	46·38 N	32·34 E
129	Kherson (Oblast) Sov. Un.	46·32 N	32·55 E
142	Khetan (R.) India	10·57 N	78·23 E
119	Khiitola (khē'tō-lȧ) . . . . . Sov. Un.	61·14 N	29·40 E
136	Khimki (κēm'kĭ) Sov. Un. (Moscow In.)	55·54 N	37·27 E
127	Khíos (kē'ôs) Grc.	38·23 N	26·09 E
127	Khíos (I.) Grc.	38·20 N	25·45 E
103	Khiva (kē'vȧ) Sov. Un.	41·15 N	60·30 E
129	Khmel'nik Sov. Un.	49·34 N	27·58 E
133	Khmel'nitskiy (kmĕl'nē'ts-kēē) Sov. Un.	49·29 N	26·54 E
129	Khmel'nitskiy (Oblast) (κmĕl-nēt'skĭ ôb'lȧst'). Sov. Un.	49·27 N	26·30 E
146	Khöbsögol Dalai (Koso Lake) Mong.	51·11 N	99·11 E
128	Kholm (κôlm) Sov. Un.	57·09 N	31·07 E
135	Kholmsk (kŭlmsk) Sov. Un.	47·09 N	142·33 E
133	Khopër (R.) (κô'pēr) . . . Sov. Un.	52·00 N	43·00 E
152	Khor (κôr') Sov. Un.	47·50 N	134·52 E
152	Khor (R.) Sov. Un.	47·23 N	135·20 E
126	Khóra Sfakión Grc. (In.)	35·12 N	24·10 E
134	Khorog (κôr'ôg) Sov. Un.	37·30 N	71·47 E
142	Khorog Sov. Un.	37·10 N	71·43 E
129	Khorol (κô'rôl) Sov. Un.	49·48 N	33·17 E
129	Khorol (R.) Sov. Un.	49·50 N	33·21 E
144	Khorramshahr (kô-ram'shär). Iran	30·36 N	48·15 E
146	Khotan (R.) (kō-tän') China	39·09 N	81·08 E
	Khotan, see Hotien		
129	Khotin (κô'tēn) Sov. Un.	48·29 N	26·32 E
144	Khoybār Sau. Ar.	25·45 N	39·28 E
129	Khoyniki Sov. Un.	51·54 N	30·00 E
142	Khulna E. Pak.	22·50 N	89·38 E
144	Khurramabad (κōō-rä-mä-bäd') Iran	36·57 N	50·30 E
121	Khust (κŏŏst) Sov. Un.	48·10 N	23·18 E
133	Khvalynsk (κvȧ-lĭnsk') . . Sov. Un.	52·30 N	48·00 E
144	Khvoy Iran	38·32 N	45·01 E
145	Khyber Pass (kī'bēr) W. Pak. (Khyber Pass In.)	34·28 N	71·18 E
166	Kiambi (kyäm'bē) Con. L.	7·23 S	27·59 E
73	Kiamichi (R.) (kyȧ-mē'chē). Okla.	34·31 N	95·34 W
155	Kiangan (kyäŋ'gän) Phil. (Manila In.)	16·48 N	121·11 E
	Kiangsi, see Chianghsi		
	Kiangsu, see Chiangsu		
132	Kianta (L.) (kyän'tȧ) Fin.	65·00 N	28·15 E
127	Kičevo (kē'chĕ-vô) Yugo.	41·30 N	20·59 E
71	Kickapoo (R.) (kĭk'ȧ-pōō) . . . Wis.	43·20 N	90·55 W
164	Kidal (kē-dăl') Mali	18·33 N	1·00 E
110	Kidderminster (kĭd'ēr-mĭn-stēr) Eng.	52·23 N	2·14 W
167	Kidd's Beach (kĭdz) S. Afr. (Natal In.)	33·09 S	27·43 E
110	Kidsgrove (kĭdz'grōv) Eng.	53·05 N	2·30 W
120	Kiel (kēl) Ger.	54·19 N	10·08 E
71	Kiel Wis.	43·52 N	88·04 W
120	Kiel B. Ger.	54·33 N	10·19 E
	Kiel Can., see Nord-Ostsee Can.		
121	Kielce (kyĕl'tsĕ) Pol.	50·50 N	20·41 E
111	Kieldrecht (kēl'drĕκt) Bel. (Brussels In.)	51·17 N	4·09 E
129	Kiev (Oblast) Sov. Un.	50·03 N	30 07 E
164	Kiffa (kēf'ȧ) Mauritania	16·52 N	10·53 W
166	Kigali (kē-gä'lē) Rw.	1·59 S	30·05 E
166	Kigoma (kē-gō'mȧ) Tan.	4·44 S	29·41 E
153	Kii-Suido (Chan.) (kē sōō-ē'dō) Jap.	33·53 N	134·55 E
127	Kikinda (κē'kēn-dä) Yugo.	45·49 N	20·30 E
127	Kikladhes (Is.) Grc.	37·30 N	24·45 E
166	Kikwit (kē'kwēt) Con. L.	5·18 S	18·48 E
118	Kil (kēl) Swe.	59·30 N	13·15 E
157	Kilauea (kē-lä-ōō-ä'ä). Hawaii (In.)	22·12 N	159·25 W
157	Kilauea Crater Hawaii (In.)	19·28 N	155·18 W
64	Kilbuck Mts. (kĭl-bŭk) . . . . Alaska	60·05 N	160·00 W
152	Kilchu (kĭl'chōō) Kor.	40·59 N	129·23 E
116	Kildare (kĭl-dâr') Ire.	53·09 N	7·05 W
167	Kilimanjaro (Mtn.) (k -ē-măn-jä'rō). Tan.	3·09 S	37·19 E
166	Kilimatinde (kĭl-ē-mä-tĭn'dȧ). Tan.	5·48 S	34·58 E
119	Kilingi-Nõmme (kē'lĭŋ-gē-nôm'mĕ). Sov. Un.	58·08 N	25·03 E
133	Kilis (kē'lēs) U. A. R.	36·50 N	37·20 E
129	Kiliya (kē'lyȧ) Sov. Un.	45·28 N	29·17 E
116	Kilkenny (kĭl-kĕn-ĭ) Ire.	52·40 N	7·30 W
127	Kilkis (kĭl'kĭs) Grc.	40·59 N	22·51 E
116	Killala (kĭ-lä'lȧ) Ire.	54·11 N	9·10 W
86	Killarney (kĭ-lär'nē) Can.	49·02 N	99·34 W
116	Killarney Ire.	52·03 N	9·05 W
70	Killdeer (kĭl'dēr) N. D.	47·22 N	102·45 W

ăt; finăl; rāte; senâte; ärm; ȧsk; sofȧ; fâre; ch-choose; dh-as th in other; bē; ēvent; bĕt; recĕnt; cratēr; g-go; gh-guttural g; bĭt; ĭ-short neutral; rīde; κ-guttural k as ch in German ich;

Page	Name Pronunciation Region	Lat. °′	Long. °′
116	Kilmarnock (kĭl-mär′nŭk) . . . Scot.	55·38 N	4·25 W
116	Kilrush (kĭl′rŭsh) . . . . Ire.	52·40 N	9·16 W
167	Kilwa Kivinje . . . . Tan.	8·43 S	39·18 E
160	Kimba (kĭm′bȧ) . . . . Austl.	33·08 S	136·25 E
70	Kimball (kĭm-bȧl) . . . . Nebr.	41·14 N	103·41 W
70	Kimball . . . . S. D.	43·44 N	98·58 W
86	Kimberley (kĭm′bẽr-lĭ) . . . . . . Can.	49·48 N	115·55 W
166	Kimberley . . . . S. Afr.	28·40 S	24·50 E
127	Kími . . . . Grc.	38·38 N	24·05 E
127	Kímolos (I.) (kē′mȯ-lȯs) . . . . . Grc.	36·52 N	24·20 E
128	Kimry (kĭm′rė) . . . . Sov. Un.	56·53 N	37·24 E
154	Kinabalu, Mt . . . . Mala.	5·45 N	115·26 E
80	Kincardine (kĭn-kär′dĭn) . . . . . Can.	44·10 N	81·15 W
77	Kinder (kĭn′dẽr) . . . . La.	30·30 N	92·50 W
86	Kindersley (kĭn′dẽrz-lė) . . . . . Can.	51·30 N	109·10 W
164	Kindia (kĭn′dė-ȧ) . . . . Gui.	10·02 N	12·49 W
166	Kindu-Port-Empain . . . . . . Con. L.	2·59 S	25·59 E
132	Kinel′-Cherkassy . . . . Sov. Un.	53·32 N	51·32 E
128	Kineshma (kė-nĕsh′mȧ) . . Sov. Un.	57·27 N	41·02 E
85	King (kĭng) . . . Can. (Toronto In.)	43·56 N	79·32 W
160	King (I.) . . . . Austl.	39·35 S	143·40 E
160	Kingaroy (kĭŋ′gă-roi) . . . . Austl.	26·37 S	151·50 E
68	King City (kĭng sĭ′tĭ) . . . . Calif.	36·12 N	121·08 W
72	Kingfisher (kĭng′fĭsh-ẽr) . . . . . Okla.	35·51 N	97·55 W
158	King George Sd. (jôrj) . . . . . Austl.	35·17 S	118·30 E
128	Kingisepp (kĭŋ-gė-sep′) . . Sov. Un.	59·22 N	28·38 E
158	King Leopold Ranges (lē′ȯ-pōld) Austl.	16·35 S	125·00 E
69	Kingman (kĭng′măn) . . . . Ariz.	35·10 N	114·05 W
72	Kingman (kĭng′măn) . . . . Kans.	37·38 N	98·07 W
68	Kings (R.) . . . . Calif.	36·28 N	119·43 W
68	Kings Canyon Natl. Park (kăn′yŭn) Calif.	36·52 N	118·53 W
110	Kingsclere (kĭngs-clēr) Eng. (London In.)	51·18 N	1·15 W
160	Kingscote (kĭngz′kŭt) . . . . . . Austl.	35·45 S	137·32 E
117	Kings Lynn (kĭngz lĭn′) . . . . . Eng.	52·45 N	0·20 E
79	Kings Mt . . . . N. C.	35·13 N	81·30 W
110	Kings Norton (nôr′tŭn) . . . . . Eng.	52·25 N	1·54 W
158	King Sd . . . . Austl.	16·50 S	123·35 E
84	Kings Park (kĭngz pärk) N. Y. (New York In.)	40·53 N	73·16 W
67	Kings Pk . . . . Utah	40·46 N	110·20 W
79	Kingsport (kĭngz′pōrt) . . . . . Tenn.	36·33 N	82·36 W
160	Kingston (kĭngz′tŭn) . . . . Austl.	37·52 S	139·52 E
81	Kingston . . . . Can.	44·15 N	76·30 W
94	Kingston . . . . Jam.	18·00 N	76·45 W
81	Kingston . . . . N. Y.	42·00 N	74·00 W
81	Kingston . . . . Pa.	41·15 N	75·50 W
65	Kingston . . . . . Wash. (Seattle In.)	47·04 N	122·29 W
93	Kingstown (kĭngz′toun) . . . . St. Vincent (Le. & Wind. Is. In.)	13·10 N	61·14 W
79	Kingstree (kĭngz′trē) . . . . S. C.	33·30 N	79·50 W
76	Kingsville (kĭngz′vĭl) . . . . Tex.	27·32 N	97·52 W
86	King William I. (kĭng wĭl′yăm) Can.	69·25 N	97·00 W
167	King William's Town (kĭng-wĭl′-yŭmz-toun) . S. Afr. (Natal In.)	32·53 S	27·24 E
74	Kinloch (kĭn-lŏk) Mo. (St. Louis In.)	38·44 N	90·19 W
116	Kinnairds Hd. (kĭn-ȧrdś hĕd) Scot.	57·42 N	3·55 W
153	Kinomoto (kē′nō-mōtō) . . . . . . Jap.	33·53 N	136·07 E
153	Kinosaki (kē′nō-sä′kė) . . . . Jap.	35·38 N	134·47 E
116	Kinsale Hbr. (kĭn-sāl′) . . . . Ire.	51·35 N	8·17 W
72	Kinsley (kĭnz′lĭ) . . . . Kans.	37·55 N	99·24 W
79	Kinston (kĭnz′tŭn) . . . . N. C.	35·15 N	77·35 W
164	Kintampo (kēn-täm′pō) . . . . Ghana	8·05 N	1·44 W
116	Kintyre Pen. . . . . Scot.	55·50 N	5·40 W
	Kiorashi, see Ōmori		
72	Kiowa (kī′ȯ-wȧ) . . . . Kans.	37·01 N	98·30 W
73	Kiowa . . . . Okla.	34·42 N	95·53 W
127	Kiparissía . . . . Grc.	37·17 N	21·43 E
127	Kiparissiakós Kólpos (G.) . . . . Grc.	37·28 N	21·15 E
166	Kipembawe (kė-pĕm-bä′wȧ) . Tan.	7·43 S	33·22 E
74	Kirby (kŭr′bĭ) Tex. (San Antonio In.)	29·29 N	98·23 W
77	Kirbyville (kŭr′bĭ-vĭl) . . . . Tex.	30·39 N	93·54 W
135	Kirenga (R.) (kė-rĕŋ′gȧ) . Sov. Un.	56·30 N	103·18 E
135	Kirensk (kē-rĕnsk′) . . . . . . Sov. Un.	57·47 N	108·22 E
145	Kirgizskiy Khrebet (Kirgiz) (Mts.) . Sov. Un.	37·58 N	72·23 E
130	Kirgiz S. S. R. (kĭr-gēz′) . Sov. Un.	41·45 N	74·38 E
130	Kirgiz Steppe (Plain) . . . . Sov. Un.	49·28 N	57·07 E
	Kirin, see Chilin		
	Kirin, see Chilung		
110	Kirkby-in-Ashfield (kûrk′bē-ĭn-ăsh′fēld) . . Eng.	53·06 N	1·16 W
116	Kirkcaldy (kẽr-kô′dĭ) . . . . Scot.	56·06 N	3·15 W
85	Kirkfield Park (kûrk-fēld) Can. (Winnipeg In.)	49·53 N	97·16 W
110	Kirkham (kûrk′ăm) . . . . Eng.	53·47 N	2·53 W
65	Kirkland (kûrk′lănd) Wash. (Seattle In.)	47·41 N	122·12 W
87	Kirkland Lake . . . . Can.	48·14 N	80·06 W
127	Kirklareli (kėrk′lȧr-ĕ′lė) . . . . . Tur.	41·44 N	41·43 E
73	Kirksville (kûrks′vĭl) . . . . Mo.	40·12 N	92·35 W
144	Kirkūk (kĭr-ko͞ok′) . . . . Iraq	35·28 N	44·22 E
116	Kirkwall (kûrk′wôl) . . . . Scot.	58·58 N	2·59 W
74	Kirkwood (kûrk′wo͝od) Mo. (St. Louis In.)	38·35 N	90·24 W
167	Kirkwood . . . . . S. Afr. (Natal In.)	33·26 S	25·24 E
120	Kirn (kėrn) . . . . Ger.	49·47 N	7·23 E
128	Kirov . . . . Sov. Un.	54·04 N	34·19 E
132	Kirov . . . . Sov. Un.	58·35 N	49·35 E
133	Kirovabad (kē-rŭ-vŭ-bät′) Sov. Un.	40·40 N	46·20 E
136	Kirovgrad (kē′rŭ-vŭ-grad) Sov. Un. (Urals In.)	57·26 N	60·03 E
129	Kirovograd (kē-rŭ-vŭ-grät′) Sov. Un.	48·33 N	32·17 E
129	Kirovograd (Oblast) . . . . . Sov. Un.	48·23 N	31·10 E
132	Kirovsk . . . . Sov. Un.	67·40 N	33·58 E
136	Kirovsk (kė-rôfsk′) Sov. Un. (Leningrad In.)	59·52 N	30·59 E
133	Kirsanov (kėr-sȧ′nôf) . . . . Sov. Un.	52·40 N	42·40 E
133	Kirşehir (kėr-shĕ′hēr) . . . . Tur.	39·10 N	34·00 E
142	Kirthar Ra. (kĭr-tŭr) . . . . . W. Pak.	30·40 N	67·20 E
110	Kirton (kûr′tŭn) . . . . Eng.	53·29 N	0·35 W
112	Kiruna (kē-ro͞o′nä) . . . . Swe.	67·49 N	20·08 E
72	Kirwin Res. (kûr′wĭn) . . . . . . Kans.	39·34 N	99·04 W
153	Kiryū (kē′rĭ-o͞o) . . . . Jap.	36·26 N	139·18 E
128	Kirzhach (kėr-zhȧk′) . . . . Sov. Un.	56·08 N	38·53 E
167	Kisaki (kē-sȧ′kē) . . . . Tan.	7·37 S	37·43 E
126	Kisámou, Kólpos (G) . . . Grc. (In.)	35·40 N	23·37 E
153	Kisarazu (kē′sȧ-rȧ′zo͞o) Jap. (Tōkyō In.)	35·23 N	139·55 E
134	Kiselëvsk (kē-sĭ-lyôfsk′) . . Sov. Un.	54·05 N	86·19 E
166	Kisenyi (kē′sĕn′yē) . . . . Rw.	1·43 S	29·15 E
129	Kishinëv (ke-shė-nyôf′) . . Sov. Un.	47·02 N	28·52 E
153	Kishiwada (kē′shė-wä′dä) . . . . Jap.	34·25 N	135·18 E
136	Kishkino (kēsh′kĭ-nô) Sov. Un. (Moscow In.)	55·15 N	38·04 E
64	Kiska (I.) (kĭs′kä) . . . . Alaska	52·08 N	177·10 E
121	Kiskunfélegyháza (kĭsh′ko͝on-fā′lĕd-y′hä′zô) . Hung.	46·42 N	19·52 E
121	Kiskunhalas (kĭsh′ko͝on-hô′lôsh) Hung.	46·24 N	19·26 E
121	Kiskunmajsa (kĭsh′ko͝on-mī′shô) Hung.	46·29 N	19·42 E
167	Kismayu . . . . Som.	0·18 S	42·30 E
153	Kiso-Gawa (Strm.) (kē′sō-gä′wä) Jap.	35·29 N	137·12 E
153	Kiso-Sammyaku (Mts.) (kė′sō säm′myȧ-ko͞o) . Jap.	35·47 N	137·39 E
164	Kissidougou (kē′sė-do͞o′go͞o) . . Gui.	9·19 N	10·26 W
79	Kissimmee (kĭ-sĭm′ė) . . . . Fla. (In.)	28·17 N	81·25 W
79	Kissimmee (L.) . . . . Fla. (In.)	27·58 N	81·17 W
79	Kissimmee (R.) . . . . Fla. (In.)	27·45 N	81·07 W
112	Kistrand (kē′stränd) . . . . Nor.	70·29 N	25·01 E
121	Kisujszallás (kĭsh′o͝o′y′sä′läsh) Hung.	47·12 N	20·47 E
166	Kisumu (kē′so͞o-mo͞o) . . . . Ken.	0·05 S	34·49 E
139	Kiswah . . . . Syr. (Palestine In.)	33·31 N	36·13 E
164	Kita (kē′tȧ) . . . . Mali	13·05 N	9·33 W
152	Kitakami Gawa (R.) (kė′tȧ-kä′mē gä-wä) . Jap.	39·20 N	141·10 E
153	Kitakyūshū (kē′tȧ-kyo͞o′sho͞o′) Jap.	34·15 N	130·23 E
80	Kitchener (kĭch′ĕ-nẽr) . . . . Can.	43·25 N	80·35 W
166	Kitega (kė-tā′gȧ) . . . . Burundi	3·39 S	30·05 E
165	Kitgum (kĭt′go͝om) . . . . Ug.	3·29 N	33·04 E
115	Kíthira (I.) . . . . Grc.	36·15 N	22·56 E
127	Kíthnos (I.) . . . . Grc.	37·24 N	24·10 E
86	Kitimat . . . . Can.	54·01 N	128·11 W
65	Kitsap (kĭt-săp) Wash. (Seattle In.)	47·45 N	122·32 W
153	Kitsuki (kėt′so͝o-kė) . . . . Jap.	33·24 N	131·35 E
81	Kittaning (kĭ-tăn′ĭng) . . . . Pa.	40·50 N	79·30 W
84	Kittatinny Mts. (kĭ-tŭ-tĭ′nė) N. J. (New York In.)	41·16 N	74·44 W
82	Kittery (kĭt′ẽr-ĭ) . . . . Maine	43·07 N	70·45 W
111	Kittsee . . . . Aus. (Vienna In.)	48·05 N	17·05 E
79	Kitty Hawk (kĭt′tė hôk) . . . . N. C.	36·04 N	75·42 W
120	Kitzingen (kĭt′zĭng-ĕn) . . . . Ger.	49·44 N	10·08 E
166	Kivu (L.) . . . . Con. L.	2·00 S	28·30 E
133	Kiyev (kē′yĕf) . . . . Sov. Un.	50·27 N	30·30 E
136	Kizel (kē′zĕl) . Sov. Un. (Urals In.)	59·05 N	57·42 E
133	Kizil Irmak (R.) (kĭz′ĭl ĭr-mäk′) Tur.	40·15 N	34·00 E
136	Kizil′skoye (kĭz′ĭl-skô-yĕ) Sov. Un. (Urals In.)	52·43 N	58·53 E
133	Kizlyar (kĭz-lyär′) . . . . Sov. Un.	44·00 N	46·50 E
153	Kizu (kē′zo͞o) . . . . Jap. (Ōsaka In.)	34·43 N	135·49 E
103	Kizyl-Arvat (kē′zĭl-ŭr-vät′) Sov. Un.	38·55 N	56·33 E
111	Klaaswaal . Neth. (Amsterdam In.)	51·46 N	4·25 E
120	Kladno (kläd′nō) . . . . Czech.	50·10 N	14·05 E
120	Klagenfurt (klä′gĕn-fo͝ort) . . . . Aus.	46·38 N	14·19 E
119	Klaipéda (Memel) (klī′pȧ-dȧ) (mā′mĕl) . Sov. Un.	55·43 N	21·10 E
66	Klamath Falls . . . . Ore.	42·13 N	121·49 W
66	Klamath Ind. Res. (klăm′ȧth) . Ore.	42·48 N	121·40 E
66	Klamath Mts. . . . . Calif.	42·00 N	123·25 W
66	Klamath R. . . . . Calif.	41·27 N	123·35 W
139	Klang . . . . . . Mala. (Singapore In.)	3·02 N	101·27 E
139	Klang (R.) . Mala. (Singapore In.)	3·00 N	101·38 E
118	Klar-älven (R.) . . . . Swe.	60·40 N	13·00 E
65	Klaskanine (R.) (klăs′kȧ-nīn) Ore. (Portland In.)	46·02 N	123·43 W
120	Klatovy (klȧ′tô-vė) . . . . Czech.	49·23 N	13·18 E
64	Klawak (klā′wăk) . . . . Alaska	55·32 N	133·10 W
85	Kleinburg (klīn-bûrg) Can. (Toronto In.)	43·51 N	79·38 W
111	Kleinmachnow (klīn-mäĸ′nō) Ger. (Berlin In.)	52·22 N	13·12 E
167	Kleinmond . . . . S. Afr. (Natal In.)	33·33 S	27·04 E
168	Klerksdorp (klẽrks′dôrp) . . . S. Afr. (Johannesburg & Pretoria In.)	26·52 S	26·40 E
168	Klerkskraal (klẽrks′kräl) . . . S. Afr. (Johannesburg & Pretoria In.)	26·15 S	27·10 E
128	Kletnya (klyĕt′nyȧ) . . . . . Sov. Un.	52·19 N	33·14 E
128	Kletsk (klĕtsk) . . . . Sov. Un.	53·04 N	26·43 E
123	Kleve (klĕ′fĕ) . . . . . Ger. (Ruhr In.)	51·47 N	6·09 E
66	Klickitat R. . . . . Wash.	46·01 N	121·07 W
128	Klimovichi (klē-mȯ-vē′chė) Sov. Un.	53·37 N	31·21 E
136	Klimovsk (klĭ′môfsk) Sov. Un. (Moscow In.)	55·21 N	37·32 E
128	Klin (klėn) . . . . Sov. Un.	56·18 N	36·43 E
118	Klintehamn (klēn′tē-häm) . . . Swe.	57·24 N	18·14 E
128	Klintsy (klĭn′tsĭ) . . . . Sov. Un.	52·46 N	32·14 E
168	Klipgat . . . . S. Afr. (Johannesburg & Pretoria In.)	25·26 S	27·57 E
168	Klip R. (klĭp) . . . . S. Afr. (Johannesburg & Pretoria In.)	27·18 S	29·25 E
126	Ključ (klyo͞och) . . . . Yugo.	44·32 N	16·48 E
120	Klodzko (klôd′skȯ) . . . . Pol.	50·26 N	16·38 E
64	Klondike Reg. (klŏn′dīk) Alaska-Can.	64·12 N	142·38 W
111	Klosterfelde (klōs′tĕr-fĕl-dĕ) Ger. (Berlin In.)	52·47 N	13·29 E
111	Klosterneuburg (klōs-tẽr-noi′bo͞orgh) . Aus. (Vienna In.)	48·19 N	16·20 E
139	Kluang . . . . Mala. (Singapore In.)	2·01 N	103·19 E
121	Kluczbork (klo͞och′bōrk) . . . . . Pol.	50·59 N	18·15 E
128	Klyaz′ma (R.) (klyäz′mȧ) . Sov. Un.	55·49 N	39·19 E
135	Klyuchevskaya (Vol.) (klyo͞o-chĕfskä′yä) . Sov. Un.	56·13 N	160·00 E
136	Klyuchi (klyo͞o′chĭ) Sov. Un. (Urals In.)	57·03 N	57·20 E
127	Knezha (knyā′zhȧ) . . . . Bul.	43·27 N	24·03 E
70	Knife (R.) (nīf) . . . . N. D.	47·06 N	102·33 W
80	Knightstown (nīts′toun) . . . . . Ind.	39·45 N	85·30 W
126	Knin (knēn) . . . . Yugo.	44·02 N	16·14 E
120	Knittelfeld . . . . Aus.	47·13 N	14·50 E
155	Knob Pk. (nŏb) . Phil. (Manila In.)	12·30 N	121·20 E
116	Knockmealdown Mts. (nŏk-mēl′doun) . Ire.	52·13 N	8·09 W
110	Knottingley (nŏt′ĭng-lĭ) . . . . . Eng.	53·42 N	1·14 W
80	Knox (nŏks) . . . . Ind.	41·15 N	86·40 W
71	Knoxville (nŏks′vĭl) . . . . Iowa	41·19 N	93·05 W
78	Knoxville . . . . Tenn.	35·58 N	83·55 W
110	Knutsford (nŭts′fẽrd) . . . . Eng.	53·18 N	2·22 W
121	Knyszyn (knĭ′shĭn) . . . . Pol.	53·16 N	22·59 E
148	Ko (R.) (go͞oŭ) . . . . China	33·04 N	117·16 E
153	Kobayashi (kō′bȧ-yä′shė) . . . . Jap.	31·58 N	130·59 E
153	Kōbe (kō′bĕ) . . . . Jap. (Ōsaka In.)	34·30 N	135·10 E
129	Kobelyaki (kō-bĕl-yä′kė) . Sov. Un.	49·11 N	34·12 E
118	København (Copenhagen) (kû-b′n-houn′) . Den.	55·43 N	12·27 E
120	Koblenz (kō′blĕntz) . . . . Ger.	50·18 N	7·36 E
128	Kobozha (R.) (kȯ-bō′zhȧ) . Sov. Un.	58·55 N	35·18 E
121	Kobrin (kō′brėn′) . . . . Sov. Un.	52·13 N	24·23 E
136	Kobrinskoye (kô-brĭn′skô-yĕ) Sov. Un. (Leningrad In.)	59·25 N	30·07 E
64	Kobuk (R.) (kō′bŭk) . . . . . . Alaska	66·58 N	158·48 W
133	Kobuleti (kȯ-bo͝o-lyā′tė) . Sov. Un.	41·50 N	41·40 E
127	Kocani (kô′chä-nĕ) . . . . Yugo.	41·54 N	22·25 E
126	Kočevje (kô′chāv-ye) . . . . . . Yugo.	45·38 N	14·51 E
74	Koch (kōk) . . . Mo. (St. Louis In.)	38·28 N	90·17 W
120	Kocher R. (kȯĸ′ẽr) . . . . Ger.	49·00 N	9·52 E
153	Kōchi (kō′chė) . . . . Jap.	33·35 N	133·32 E
64	Kodiak (kō′dyăk) . . . . Alaska	57·50 N	152·30 W
64	Kodiak (I.) . . . . Alaska	57·24 N	153·32 W
165	Kodok (ko′dŏk) . . . . Sud.	9·57 N	32·08 E
166	Koekenaap . . . . S. Afr.	31·25 S	18·20 E
164	Koforidua (kō fȯ-rĭ-do͞o′ȧ) . . Ghana	6·12 N	0·30 W
153	Kōfu (kō′fo͞o′) . . . . Jap.	35·41 N	138·34 E
153	Koga (kō′gȧ) . . . . Jap.	36·13 N	139·40 E
153	Kogane (kō′gä-nȧ) Jap. (Tōkyō In.)	35·50 N	139·56 E
153	Koganei (kō′gä-nā) Jap. (Tōkyō In.)	35·42 N	139·31 E
118	Køge (kû′gĕ) . . . . Den.	55·27 N	12·09 E
129	Kogil′nik (R.) (kȯ-gėl-nēk′) Sov. Un.	46·08 N	29·10 E
142	Koh-i Baba Mt. . . . . Afg.	39·39 N	67·09 E
145	Kohima (kȯ-ē′mȧ) . . . . India	25·45 N	94·41 E
153	Koito (R.) (kȯ′ė-tō) Jap. (Tōkyō In.)	35·19 N	139·58 E
152	Kŏje (I.) (kû′jĕ) . . . . Kor.	34·53 N	129·00 E
134	Kokand (kȯ-känt′) . . . . . . Sov. Un.	40·27 N	71·07 E
134	Kokchetav (kôk′chĕ-tȧf) . Sov. Un.	53·15 N	69·13 E
119	Kokemäen (R.) (kȯ′kē-mȧ′ĕn) . Fin.	61·23 N	22·03 E
128	Kokhma (kôĸ′mȧ) . . . . . . Sov. Un.	56·57 N	41·08 E
143	Kokkanisseri . . . . India	12·08 N	74·14 E
112	Kokkola (kô′kȯ-lȧ) . . . . Fin.	63·47 N	22·58 E
80	Kokomo (kō′kȯ-mȯ) . . . . Ind.	40·30 N	86·20 W
	Koko Nor, see Ch′ing Hai		
155	Kokopo (kȯ-kȯ′pō) . . . N. Gui. Ter.	4·25 S	152·27 E
87	Koksoak (R.) (kôk′sȯ-ăk) . . . . Can.	57·42 N	69·50 W
167	Kokstad (kôk′shtät) S. Afr. (Natal In.)	30·33 S	29·27 E
148	Koku (gŏ′go͞o) . . . . China	39·00 N	117·30 E
153	Kokubu (kō′ko͞o-bo͞o) . . . . Jap.	31·42 N	130·46 E
153	Kokubunji (kō′ko͞o-bo͝on′jė) Jap. (Tōkyō In.)	35·43 N	139·29 E
153	Kokuou (kȯ′ko͞o-ȯ′o͞o) Jap. (Ōsaka In.)	34·34 N	135·39 E
153	Kokura (kō′ko͝o-rä) . . . . Jap.	33·53 N	130·54 E
164	Kolahun (kȯ-lä′ho͝on) . . . . Lib.	8·24 N	10·11 W
	Kola Pen., see Kol′skiy P-Ov.		
143	Kolār (kȯl-är′) . . . . India	13·39 N	78·33 E
143	Kolār Gold Fields (kȯl-är′) . . India	13·45 N	79·55 E
127	Kolarovgrad . . . . Bul.	43·15 N	26·54 E
128	Kol′chugino (kȯl-cho͝o′gė-nô) Sov. Un.	56·19 N	39·29 E
118	Kolding (kŭl′dĭng) . . . . Den.	55·29 N	9·24 E
166	Kole (kō′lȧ) . . . . Con. L.	3·19 S	22·46 E
132	Kolguyev (I.) (kȯl-go͝o′yĕf) Sov. Un.	69·00 N	49·00 E
120	Kolin (kō′lēn) . . . . Czech.	50·01 N	15·11 E
119	Kolkasrags (Pt.) (kôl-käs′rȧgz) Sov. Un.	57·46 N	22·39 E
123	Köln (Cologne) . . . Ger. (Ruhr In.)	50·56 N	6·57 E
121	Kolno (kôw′nȯ) . . . . Pol.	53·23 N	21·56 E
121	Koło (kô′wȯ) . . . . Pol.	52·11 N	18·37 E
120	Kołobrzeg (kȯ-lôb′zhĕk) . . . . . . Pol.	54·10 N	15·35 E
136	Kolomna (kȧl-ôm′nȧ) Sov. Un. (Moscow In.)	55·06 N	38·47 E
121	Kolomyya (kō′lȯ-mē′yȧ) . Sov. Un.	48·32 N	25 04 E
128	Kolp′ (R.) (kôlp) . . . . Sov. Un.	59·29 N	35·32 E
134	Kolpashevo (kŭl pȧ shô′vȧ) Sov. Un.	58·16 N	82·43 E
136	Kolpino (kôl′pė-nȯ) Sov. Un. (Leningrad In.)	59·45 N	30·37 E
128	Kolpny (kôlp′nyė) . . . . . . Sov. Un.	52·14 N	36·54 E
132	Kol′skiy P-Ov. (Kola Pen.) Sov. Un.	67·15 N	37·40 E
132	Kolva (R.) . . . . Sov. Un.	61·00 N	57·00 E
166	Kolwezi (kōl-wĕ′zē) . . . . . . Con. L.	10·40 S	25·30 E
136	Kolyberovo (kȯ-lĭ-byȧ′rô-vô) Sov. Un. (Moscow In.)	55·16 N	38·45 E
135	Kolyma (R.) . . . . Sov. Un.	66·30 N	151·45 E

ng-sing; ŋ-baŋk; N-nasalized n; nŏd; cŏmmit; ōld; ôbey; ôrder; fo͞od; fo͝ot; ou-out; s-soft; sh-dish; th-thin; pūre; ûnite; ûrn; stŭd; circŭs; ü-as "y" in study; ′-indeterminate vowel.

Page	Name Pronunciation Region	Lat. °′	Long. °′
	Kolymskiy (Mts.), see Gydan, Khrebet		
134	Kolyvan' (kôl-ê-vän') . . . Sov. Un.	55·28 N	82·59 E
130	Komadorskie Ostrova (Is.) Sov. Un.	55·40 N	167·13 E
164	Komadugu-Yobe R. . . . Nig.	12·14 N	10·00 E
121	Komárno (kô'mär-nô) . . . Czech.	47·46 N	18·08 E
121	Komarno . . . Sov. Un.	49·38 N	23·43 E
121	Komaron (kô'mä-rôm) . . . Hung.	47·45 N	18·06 E
166	Komatipoort (kō-mä'tē-pōrt) S. Afr.	25·21 S	32·00 E
153	Komatsu (kō-mät'sōō) . . . Jap.	36·23 N	136·26 E
153	Komatsushima (kō-mät'sōō-shē'mä) . Jap.	34·04 N	134 32 E
167	Komga (kŏm'gȧ) S. Afr. (Natal In.)	32·36 S	27·54 E
130	Komi (A. S. S. R.) (kômê) Sov. Un.	61·31 N	53·15 E
166	Kommetijie S. Afr. (Cape Town In.)	34·09 S	18·19 E
146	Kommunizma, Pik (Pk.) . Sov. Un.	39·46 N	71·23 E
127	Komotiní . . . Grc.	41·07 N	25·22 E
154	Kompong Thom (kŏm'pŏng-tŏm) Camb.	12·41 N	104·39 E
129	Komrat (kôm-rät') . . . Sov. Un.	46·17 N	28·38 E
136	Komsomolets (kôm-sô-mô'lĕts) Sov. Un. (Urals In.)	53·45 N	63·04 E
133	Komsomolets Zaliv (B.) . . Sov. Un.	45·40 N	52·00 E
135	Komsomol'sk-na-Amure (kŭm-sŭ-môlsk'nŭ-ŭ-mōōr'yĭ) . Sov. Un.	50·46 N	137·14 E
129	Komsomol'skoye (kôm-sô-môl'skô-yĕ) . Sov. Un.	48·42 N	28·44 E
132	Konda (R.) (kôn'dȧ) . . . Sov. Un.	60·50 N	64·00 E
136	Kondas R. (kôn'dȧs) Sov. Un. (Urals In.)	59·30 N	56·28 E
166	Kondoa (kôn-dō'ȧ) . . . Tan.	4·52 S	36·00 E
164	Kong (kông) . . . Ivory Coast	9·05 N	4·41 W
164	Kong (Reg.) . . . Ivory Coast	9·19 N	4·03 W
166	Kongolo (kôŋ'gō'lō) . . . Con. L.	5·20 S	26·58 E
118	Kongsberg (kŭngs'bĕrg) . . . Nor.	59·40 N	9·36 E
118	Kongsvinger (kŭngs'vĭŋ-gĕr) . Nor.	60·12 N	12·00 E
166	Koni (kō'nē) . . . Con. L.	10·32 S	27·27 E
	Königsberg, see Kaliningrad		
111	Königsbrunn (kû'nĕgs-brōōn) Ger. (Munich In.)	48·16 N	10·53 E
111	Königs Wusterhausen (kû'nĕgs vōōs'tĕr-hou-zĕn) Ger. (Berlin In.)	52·18 N	13·38 E
121	Konin (kô'nyên) . . . Pol.	52·11 N	18·17 E
127	Kónitsa (kô'nyē'tsȧ) . . . Grc.	40·03 N	20·46 E
127	Konjic (kôn'yēts) . . . Yugo.	43·38 N	17·59 E
152	Konju . . . Kor.	36·21 N	127·05 E
129	Konotop (kô-nô-tôp') . . . Sov. Un.	51·13 N	33·14 E
121	Końskie (koin''skyĕ) . . . Pol.	51·12 N	20·26 E
129	Konstantinovka (kôn-stȧn-tē'nôf-kȧ) . Sov. Un.	48·33 N	37·42 E
120	Konstanz (kôn'-shtänts) . . . Ger.	47·39 N	9·10 E
164	Kontagora (kōn-tȧ-gō'rä) . . . Nig.	10·27 N	5 30 E
164	Kontcha (kōn'chȧ) . . . Cam.	8·03 N	12·21 E
133	Konya (kōn'yȧ) . . . Tur.	36·55 N	32·25 E
86	Kootenay Natl. Park (kōō'tē-nâ) Can.	51·06 N	117·02 W
86	Kootenay (R.) (kōō'tē-nâ) . . . Can.	50·28 N	115·50 W
153	Kōō-zan (Mtn.) (kōō'zän) Jap. (Ōsaka In.)	34·53 N	135·32 E
118	Kopervik (kô'pĕr-vêk) . . . Nor.	59·18 N	5·20 E
144	Kopet, Mts . . . Iran	37·28 N	58·29 E
136	Kopeysk (kô-pāsk') Sov. Un. (Urals In.)	55·07 N	61·36 E
118	Köping (chû'pĭng) . . . Swe.	59·32 N	15·58 E
118	Kopparberg (kŏp'pȧr-bĕrgh) . . Swe.	59·53 N	15·00 E
168	Koppies . . S. Afr. (Johannesburg & Pretoria In.)	27·15 S	27·35 E
126	Koprivnica (kô'prēv-nē'tsȧ) . Yugo.	46·10 N	16·48 E
121	Kopychintsy (kô-pê-chēn'tsĕ) Sov. Un.	49·06 N	25·55 E
127	Korçë (kôr'chĕ) . . . Alb.	40·37 N	20·48 E
126	Korčula (I.) (kôr'chōō-lȧ) . . Yugo.	42·50 N	17·05 E
165	Kordofan (Prov.) (kôr-dô-făn') Sud.	14·08 N	28·39 E
152	Korea B . . . China-Kor.	39·18 N	123·50 E
139	Korea (kô-rē'ȧ) . . . Asia	38·45 N	130·00 E
152	Korean Arch . . . Kor.	39·05 N	125·35 E
152	Korea Str . . . Kor.-Jap.	33·30 N	128·30 E
121	Korets (kô-rĕts') . . . Sov. Un.	50·35 N	27·13 E
164	Korhogo (kôr-hō'gō) . . Ivory Coast	9·22 N	5·21 W
127	Korinthıakós Kólpos (G.) . . . Grc.	38·15 N	22·33 E
127	Korinthos (Corinth) (kô-rēn'thôs) (kŏr'ĭnth) . Grc.	37·56 N	22·54 E
152	Kōriyama (kō'rê-yä'mä) . . . Jap.	37·18 N	140·25 E
153	Kōriyama . . . Jap. (Ōsaka In.)	34·39 N	135·48 E
136	Korkino (kôr'kē-nŭ) Sov. Un. (Urals In.)	54·53 N	61·25 E
120	Körmend (kûr'mĕnt) . . . Hung.	47·02 N	16·36 E
126	Kornat (I.) (kôr-nät') . . . Yugo.	43·46 N	15·10 E
111	Korneuburg (kôr'noi-bōōrgh) Aus. (Vienna In.)	48·22 N	16·21 E
129	Korocha (kô-rō'chȧ) . . . Sov. Un.	50·50 N	37·13 E
129	Korop (kō'rôp) . . . Sov. Un.	51·33 N	33·54 E
129	Korosten' (kô'rôs-tĕn) . . . Sov. Un.	50·51 N	28·39 E
129	Korostyshev (kô-rôs'tē-shôf) Sov. Un.	50·19 N	29·05 E
129	Korotoyak (kô'rô-tô-yȧk') Sov. Un.	51·00 N	39·06 E
135	Korsakov (kôr'sȧ-kôf') . . . Sov. Un.	46·42 N	143·16 E
119	Korsnas (kôrs'nĕs) . . . Fin.	62·51 N	21·17 E
118	Korsør (kôrs'ûr') . . . Den.	55·19 N	11·08 E
165	Korti (kôr'tê) . . . Sud.	18·08 N	31·39 E
117	Kortrijk . . . Bel.	50·49 N	3·10 E
135	Koryakskiy Khrebet (Mts.) Sov. Un.	62·00 N	168·45 E
129	Koryukovka (kôr-yōō-kôf'kȧ) Sov. Un.	51·44 N	32·24 E
142	Kosa . . . India	23·37 N	68·35 E
120	Kóscian (kŭsh'tsyȧn) . . . Pol.	52·05 N	16·38 E
121	Kóścierzyna (kŭsh-tsyĕ-zhē'nȧ) Pol.	54·08 N	17·59 E
78	Kosciusko (kŏs-ĭ-ŭs'kō) . . . Miss.	33·04 N	89·35 W
160	Kosciusko, Mt . . . Austl.	36·26 S	148·20 E
128	Kosel'sk (kô-zĕlsk') . . . Sov. Un.	54·01 N	35·49 E
165	Kosha (kō'shä) . . . Sud.	20·49 N	30·27 E
150	K'oshan (kō'shän') . . . China	48·00 N	126·30 E
153	Koshigaya (kô'shê-gä'yä) Jap. (Tōkyō In.)	35·53 N	139·48 E
153	Koshiki-Rettō (Is.) (kō-shē'kê rät'tō) . Jap.	31·51 N	129·40 E
142	Kosi (R.) (kô'sē) . . . India	26·00 N	86·20 E
121	Košice (kō'shê-tsĕ') . . . Czech.	48·43 N	21·17 E
167	Kosmos (kŏz'mŏs) S. Afr. (Johannesburg & Pretoria In.)	25·45 S	27·51 E
136	Kosobrodskiy (kä-sô'brôd-skĭ) Sov. Un. (Urals In.)	54·14 N	60·53 E
	Koso Lake, see Khōbsögol Dalai		
127	Kosovska Mitrovica (kô'sôv-skä' mē'trô-vê-tsä') . Yugo.	42·51 N	20·50 E
126	Kostajnica (kôs'tä-ê-nē'tsä) . Yugo.	45·14 N	16·32 E
168	Koster . . . S. Afr. (Johannesburg & Pretoria In.)	25·52 S	26·52 E
165	Kosti (kôs'tê) . . . Sud.	13·09 N	32·39 E
136	Kostino (kôs'tĭ-nô) Sov. Un. (Moscow In.)	55·54 N	37·51 E
128	Kostroma (kôs-trô-mȧ') . . Sov. Un.	57·46 N	40·55 E
128	Kostroma (Oblast) . . . Sov. Un.	57·50 N	41·10 E
120	Kostrzyn' (kôst'chēn) . . . Pol.	52·35 N	14·38 E
136	Kos'va R. (kôs'vȧ) Sov. Un. (Urals In.)	58·44 N	57·08 E
120	Koszalin (kô-shä'lĭn) . . . Pol.	54·12 N	16·10 E
120	Köszeg (kû'sĕg) . . . Hung.	47·21 N	16·32 E
142	Kota . . . India	25·17 N	75·49 E
154	Kotabaru . . . Indon.	3·22 S	116·15 E
155	Kotabaru (Hollandia) (kō'tȧ-bä'rōō) (hôl-län'dĭ-ä) W. Irian	2·30 S	140·45 E
154	Kota Bharu (kō'tȧ bä'rōō) . . Mala.	6·15 N	102·23 E
166	Kota Kota (kō-tȧ kō-tȧ) . . . Nya.	12·52 S	34·16 E
139	Kota Tinggi Mala. (Singapore In.)	1·43 N	103·54 E
127	Kotel (kō-tĕl') . . . Bul.	42·54 N	26 28 E
132	Kotel'nich (kô-tyĕl'nĕch) . Sov. Un.	58·15 N	48·20 E
135	Kotel'nyy (I.) (kô-tyĕl'nē) Sov. Un.	74·51 N	134·09 E
143	Kothapur . . . India	16·48 N	74·15 E
119	Kotka (kŏt'kȧ) . . . Fin.	60·28 N	26·56 E
132	Kotlas (kôt'lȧs) . . . Sov. Un.	61·10 N	46·50 E
136	Kotlin, Ostrov (I.) (ôs-trôf' kôt'lĭn) Sov. Un. (Leningrad In.)	60·02 N	29·49 E
127	Kotor (kō'tôr) . . . Yugo.	42·26 N	18·48 E
128	Kotorosl' (R.) (kô-tô'rôsl) Sov. Un.	57·18 N	39·08 E
126	Kotor Varoš (kô'tôr vä'rôsh) . Yugo.	44·37 N	17·23 E
129	Kotovsk (kô-tôfsk') . . . Sov. Un.	47·49 N	29·31 E
148	Kotse (hō'zhē) . . . China	35·13 N	115·28 E
165	Kotto R. . . . Cen. Afr. Rep.	5·17 N	22·04 E
135	Kotuy (R.) (kô-tōō') . . Sov. Un.	71·00 N	103·15 E
64	Kotzebue (kŏt'sē-bōō) . . . Alaska	66·48 N	162·42 W
64	Kotzebue Sd . . . Alaska	67·00 N	164·28 W
165	Kouandé (kwän-dā') Cen. Afr. Rep.	6·08 N	14·32 E
164	Koudougou (kōō-dōō'gōō) Upper Volta	12·02 N	2·15 W
164	Koulikoro (kōō-lê-kō'rō) . . . Mali	13·00 N	7·29 W
166	Kouilou (R.) . . . Con. B.	4·10 S	11·45 E
164	Koumbia (kōōm'bĭ-ȧ) . . . Gui.	11·35 N	13·01 W
164	Koundé (kōōn-dā') . . . Dahomey	10·19 N	1·42 E
134	Kounradskiy (kŭ-ōōn-rät'skē) Sov. Un.	47·25 N	75·10 E
164	Kouroussa (kōō-rōō'sȧ) . . . Gui.	10·43 N	9·59 W
165	Koussi, Emi (Mt.) (ā'mê kōō-sē') Chad	19·56 N	18·34 E
164	Koutiala (kōō-tê-ä'lä) . . . Mali	12·29 N	5·29 W
119	Kouvola (kō'ŏŏ-vô-lä) . . . Fin.	60·51 N	26·40 E
132	Kovda (L.) (kôv'dȧ) . . Sov. Un.	66·45 N	32·00 E
121	Kovel' (kō'vĕl) . . . Sov. Un.	51·13 N	24·45 E
	Kovno, see Kaunas		
128	Kovrov (kôv-rôf') . . . Sov. Un.	56·23 N	41·21 E
	Kowie, see Port Alfred		
151	Kowloon (kō'lōōn') . . . Hong Kong	22·28 N	114·20 E
148	Koyang (gōōŭ'yăng) . . . China	33·32 N	116·10 E
127	Koynare . . . Bul.	43·23 N	24·07 E
64	Koyuk (kô-yōōk') . . . Alaska	65·00 N	161·18 W
64	Koyukuk (R.) (kô-yōō'kŏŏk) Alaska	66·25 N	153·50 W
127	Kozáni . . . Grc.	40·16 N	21·51 E
129	Kozelets (kôzĕ-lyĕts) . . . Sov. Un.	50·53 N	31·07 E
121	Kozience (kō-zyĕ-nē'tsĕ) . . . Pol.	51·34 N	21·35 E
121	Koźle (kôzh'lĕ) . . . Pol.	50·19 N	18·10 E
127	Kozloduy (kŭz'lô-dwē) . . . Bul.	43·45 N	23·42 E
153	Kōzu (I.) (kō'zōō) . . . Jap.	34·16 N	139·03 E
154	Kra, Isth. of . . . Thai.	9·30 S	99·45 E
167	Kraai (R.) (krä'ê) S. Afr. (Natal In.)	30·50 S	27·03 E
111	Krabbendijke Neth. (Amsterdam In.)	51·26 N	4·05 E
118	Kragerö (krä'gĕr-û) . . . Nor.	58·53 N	9·21 E
127	Kragujevac (krä'gōō'yĕ-vȧts) Yugo.	44·01 N	20·55 E
121	Kraków (krä'kōōf) . . . Pol.	50·05 N	20·00 E
127	Kraljevo (kräl'yĕ-vô) . . . Yugo.	43·39 N	20·48 E
129	Kramatorsk (krȧ-mȧ'tôrsk) Sov. Un.	48·43 N	37·32 E
118	Kramfors (kräm'fôrs) . . . Swe.	62·54 N	17·49 E
126	Kranj (krän') . . . Yugo.	46·16 N	14·23 E
167	Kranskop (kränz'kŏp) S. Afr. (Natal In.)	28·57 S	30·54 E
128	Krāslava (kräs'lȧ-vȧ) . . . Sov. Un.	55·53 N	27·12 E
120	Kraslice (kräs'lê-tsĕ) . . . Czech.	50·19 N	12·30 E
136	Krasnaya Gorka (kräs'nȧ-yȧ gôr'kȧ) . Sov. Un. (Urals In.)	55·13 N	56·43 E
133	Krasnaya Sloboda . . . Sov. Un.	43·20 N	44·30 E
121	Kraśnik (kräsh'nĭk) . . . Pol.	50·53 N	22·15 E
136	Krasnoarmeysk (kräs'nô-ȧr-maśk') Sov. Un. (Moscow In.)	56·06 N	38·09 E
129	Krasnoarmeyskoye . . . Sov. Un.	48·19 N	37·04 E
129	Krasnodar (kräs'nô-dȧr) . Sov. Un.	45·03 N	38·55 E
129	Krasnodarskiy (Oblast) Province (krȧs-nô-där'skĭ ôb'lȧst) Sov. Un.	47·28 N	38·13 E
136	Krasnogorskiy (kräs-nô-gôr'skĭ) Sov. Un. (Urals In.)	54·36 N	61·25 E
129	Krasnograd (kräs'nô-grät) Sov. Un.	49·23 N	35·26 E
136	Krasnogvardeyskiy (krȧ'sno-gvăr-dzyē ĕs-kēē) Sov. Un. (Urals In.)	57·17 N	62·05 E
132	Krasnokamsk (kräs-nô-kämsk') Sov. Un.	58·00 N	55·45 E
129	Krasnokutsk (krȧs-nô-kōōtsk') Sov. Un.	50·03 N	35·05 E
129	Krasnosel'ye (kräs'nô-sĕl'yĕ) Sov. Un.	48·44 N	32·24 E
132	Krasnoslobodsk (kräs'nô-slôbôtsk') Sov. Un.	54·20 N	43·50 E
136	Krasnotur'insk (krŭs-nŭ-tōō-rensk') Sov. Un. (Urals In.)	59·47 N	60·15 E
136	Krasnoufimsk (krŭs-nŭ-ōō-fēmsk') Sov. Un. (Urals In.)	56·38 N	57·46 E
136	Krasnoural'sk (kräs'nô-ōō-rälsk') Sov. Un. (Urals In.)	58·21 N	60·05 E
136	Krasnousol'skiy (kräs-nô-ōō-sôl'skĭ) Sov. Un. (Urals In.)	53·53 N	56·30 E
132	Krasnovishersk (kräs-nô-vêshersk') . Sov. Un.	60·22 N	57·20 E
133	Krasnovodsk (krȧs-nô-vôtsk') Sov. Un.	40·00 N	52.50 E
134	Krasnoyarsk (kräs-nô-yȧrsk') Sov. Un.	56·13 N	93·12 E
136	Krasnoye Selo (kräs'nŭ-yŭ sȧ'lō) Sov. Un. (Leningrad In.)	59·44 N	30·06 E
128	Krasny Kholm (kräs'nê kōlm) Sov. Un.	58·03 N	37·11 E
121	Krasnystaw (kräs-nê-stäf') . . . Pol.	50·59 N	23·11 E
136	Krasnyy Bor (kräs'nê bôr) Sov. Un. (Leningrad In.)	59·41 N	30·40 E
136	Krasnyy Klyuch (kräs'nê klyûch') Sov. Un. (Urals In.)	55·24 N	56·43 E
133	Krasnyy Kut (kräs-nê kōōt') Sov. Un.	50·50 N	47·00 E
154	Kratie (krȧ-tyā') . . . Camb.	12·28 N	106·06 E
136	Kratovo (krä'tô-vô) Sov. Un. (Moscow In.)	55·35 N	38·10 E
127	Kratovo (krä'tô-vô) . . . Yugo.	42·04 N	22·12 E
123	Krefeld (krā'fĕlt) . Ger. (Ruhr In.)	51·20 N	6·34 E
129	Kremenchug (krĕm'ĕn-chōōgh') Sov. Un.	49·04 N	33·26 E
129	Kremenchugskoye (Res.) (krĕm-ĕn-chōōgh'skô-ye) Sov. Un.	49·20 N	32·45 E
121	Kremenets (krĕ-mĕn-yĕts') Sov. Un.	50·06 N	25·43 E
111	Kremmen (krĕ'mĕn) Ger. (Berlin In.)	52·45 N	13·02 E
111	Krempe (krĕm'pĕ) Ger. (Hamburg In.)	53·50 N	9·29 E
120	Krems (krĕms) . . . Aus.	48·25 N	15·36 E
119	Krestsy . . . Sov. Un.	58·18 N	32·26 E
128	Kresttsy (krȧst'sĕ) . . . Sov. Un.	58·16 N	32·25 E
119	Kretinga (krĕ-tĭŋ'gȧ) . . . Sov. Un.	55·55 N	21·17 E
164	Kribi (krē'bê) . . . Cam.	3·03 N	9·58 E
128	Krichëv (krĕ'chôf) . . . Sov. Un.	53·44 N	31·39 E
152	Krillon, Mys (Pt.) (mĭs krĭl' ôn) Sov. Un.	45·58 N	142·00 E
111	Krimpenald Ijssel Neth. (Amsterdam In.)	51·55 N	4·34 E
142	Krishnagar . . . India	23·29 N	88·33 E
118	Kristiansand (krĭs-tyȧn-sän'') . Nor.	58·09 N	7·59 E
118	Kristianstad (krĭs-tyȧn-städ') . Swe.	56·02 N	14·09 E
118	Kristiansund (krĭs-tyȧn-sōōn'') Nor.	63·07 N	7·49 E
118	Kristinehamn (krēs-tē'nĕ-häm') Swe.	59·20 N	14·05 E
119	Kristinestad (krĭs-tē'nĕ-städh) . Fin.	62·16 N	21·28 E
127	Kriva-Palanka (krē-vȧ-pȧ-län'kȧ) Yugo.	42·12 N	22·21 E
129	Krivoy Rog (krê-voi' rôgh') Sov. Un.	47·54 N	33·22 E
129	Krivoye Ozero . . . Sov. Un.	47·57 N	30·21 E
126	Križevci (krē'zhĕv-tsĭ) . . . Yugo.	46·02 N	16·30 E
126	Krk (I.) (k'rk) . . . Yugo.	45·06 N	14·33 E
121	Krnov (k'r'nôf) . . . Czech.	50·05 N	17·41 E
118	Kröderen (krû'dĕ-rĕn) . . . Nor.	60·07 N	9·49 E
129	Krolevets (krô-lĕ'vyĕts) . Sov. Un.	51·33 N	33·21 E
121	Kroměříž (krô'myĕr-zhēzh) . Czech.	49·18 N	17·23 E
128	Kromy (krô'mê) . . . Sov. Un.	52·44 N	35·41 E
135	Kronotskiy, Mys (C.) (krô'nôt'skĭ-ê) . Sov. Un.	54·58 N	163·15 E
136	Kronshtadt (krōn'shtät) Sov. Un. (Leningrad In.)	59·59 N	29·47 E
168	Kroonstad (krōn'shtät) . . . S. Afr. (Johannesburg & Pretoria In.)	27·40 S	27·15 E
133	Kropotkin (krȧ-pôt'kĭn) . Sov. Un.	45·25 N	40·30 E
121	Krosno (krôs'nô) . . . Pol.	49·41 N	21·46 E
121	Krotoszyn (krô-tō'shĭn) . . . Pol.	51·41 N	17·25 E
126	Krško (k'rsh'kô) . . . Yugo.	45·58 N	15·30 E
166	Kruger Natl. Park (krōō'gĕr) (krü'gĕr) . S. Afr.	23·22 S	30·18 E
167	Krugersdorp (krōō'gĕrz-dôrp) S. Afr. (Johannesburg & Pretoria In.)	26·06 S	27·46 E
127	Krujë (krōō'yȧ) . . . Alb.	41·32 N	19·49 E
154	Krung Thep (Bangkok) . . . Thai.	13·50 N	100·29 E
127	Kruševac (krōō'shĕ-vȧts) . . . Yugo.	43·34 N	21·21 E
127	Krušovo (krōō'shô-vô) . . . Yugo.	41·20 N	21·15 E
119	Krustpils (krōōst'pêls) . . . Sov. Un.	56·31 N	25·51 E

ăt; finăl; rāte; senȧte; ärm; ȧsk; sofȧ; fâre; ch-choose; dh-as th in other; bē; ēvent; bĕt; recĕnt; cratẽr; g-go; gh-guttural g; bĭt; ĭ-short neutral; rīde; K-guttural k as ch in German ich;

Page	Name	Pronunciation	Region	Lat. °′	Long. °′
118	Krylbo	(krŭl′bò)	Swe.	60·07 N	16·14 E
129	Krymskaya	(krĭm′skà-yà)	Sov. Un.	44·58 N	38·01 E
129	Krymskaya (Oblast)		Sov. Un.	45·08 N	34·05 E
129	Krymskiye Gory (Mts.)	(krēm′skĭ-yĕ gô′rĭ)	Sov. Un.	65·21 N	117·13 E
129	Krymskiy (Crimea) Poluostrov (Pen.)	(krēm′skĭ pô-lŏō-ôs′trôf)	Sov. Un.	45·18 N	33·30 E
121	Krynki	(krĭn′kĕ)	Pol.	53·15 N	23·47 E
129	Kryukov	(k′r′yŏō-kôf′)	Sov. Un.	49·02 N	33·26 E
139	Ktima		Cyprus (Palestine In.)	34·46 N	32·27 E
139	Kuala Klawang		Mala. (Singapore In.)	2·57 N	102·04 E
139	Kuala Lumpur	(kwä′lä lŏŏm-pōōr′)	Mala. (Singapore In.)	3·08 N	101·42 E
150	Kuan	(kŏō′än′)	China (Peking In.)	39·25 N	116·18 E
148	Kuan (R.)	(gŏōäN)	China	31·56 N	115·19 E
151	Kuangchang		China	25·50 N	116·18 E
149	Kuangchou (Canton)	(kän′tôn′)	China (Canton In.)	23·07 N	113·15 E
151	Kuangchou Wan (B.)		China	20·40 N	111·00 E
	Kuanghsi, see Kwangsi Chuang				
148	Kuangjao	(gŏōäNg′rou)	China	37·04 N	118·24 E
148	Kuanglu Tao (I.)	(gŏōäng′lŏō dou)	China	39·13 N	122·21 E
148	Kuangp'ing	(gŏōäNg′pĭng)	China	36·30 N	114·57 E
148	Kuangshan	(gŏōäNg′shan)	China	32·02 N	114·53 E
146	Kuangsi Chuang (Aut. Reg.)	(gŏōäNg′sē jwäng)	China	23·52 N	108·30 E
151	Kuangte		China	30·40 N	119·20 E
147	Kuangtung (Kwangtung) (Prov.)		China	23·49 N	113·02 E
148	Kuanhsien	(gŏōäN′sĭän)	China	36·30 N	115·28 E
148	Kuanhu	(gŏōäN′hoo)	China	34·26 N	117·59 E
148	Kuankü Shan (Mts.)	(gŏōäN′gŏō shän)	China	35·20 N	117·27 E
148	Kuant'ao	(gŏōäN′tou)	China	36·39 N	115·25 E
150	Kuantien		China	40·40 N	24·50 E
148	Kuanyün	(gŏōäN′yün)	China	34·28 N	119·16 E
133	Kuba	(kŏō′bà)	Sov. Un.	41·05 N	48·30 E
129	Kuban′ (R.)	(kŏō-bän′)	Sov. Un.	45·10 N	37·55 E
133	Kuban (R.)		Sov. Un.	45·20 N	40·05 E
115	Kuban R.		Sov. Un.	45·14 N	38·20 E
132	Kubenskoye (L.)		Sov. Un.	59·40 N	39·40 E
	Kucha, see Kuch'e				
146	Kuch'e (Kucha)	(kŏō′chĕ′) (kō′chä′)	China	41·34 N	82·44 E
148	Kuchen	(kŏō′jĕn)	China	33·20 N	117·18 E
148	Kuch'eng	(kŏō′chĕng′)	China	39·09 N	115·43 E
154	Kuching	(kŏō′chĭng)	Mala.	1·30 N	110·26 E
153	Kuchinoerabo (I.)	(kŏō′chĕ nō ĕr′à-bō)	Jap.	30·31 N	129·53 E
153	Kudamatsu	(kŏō′dà-mä′tsōō)	Jap.	34·00 N	131·51 E
154	Kudat (R.)	(kŏō-dät′)	Mala.	6·56 N	116·48 E
119	Kudirkos Naumiestis	(kŏōdĭr-kôs nä′iō-mē′stĭs)	Sov. Un.	54·51 N	23·00 E
134	Kudymakar	(kŏō-dĭm-kär′)	Sov. Un.	58·43 N	54·52 E
148	Kuei (R.)	(kŏōā)	China	33·30 N	116·56 E
151	Kueichih		China	30·35 N	117·28 E
149	Kueichou		China (Canton In.)	22·46 N	113·15 E
146	Kueichou (Kweichow) (Prov.)		China	27·03 N	106·31 E
151	Kueilin		China	25·18 N	110·22 E
150	Kueisui		China	41·05 N	111·50 E
151	Kueiyang		China	26·45 N	107·00 E
146	K'uerhlo		China	41·37 N	86·03 E
120	Kufstein	(kŏōf′shtīn)	Aus.	47·34 N	12·11 E
111	Kuhstedt	(kŏō′shtĕt)	Ger. (Hamburg In.)	53·23 N	8·58 E
	Kuibyshev, see Kuybyshev				
166	Kuilsrivier		S. Afr. (Cape Town In.)	33·56 S	18·41 E
153	Kujū-san (Mt.)	(kŏō′jŏō-sän′)	Jap.	33·07 N	131·14 E
165	Kukawa	(kŏō-kä′wä)	Nig.	12·55 N	13·35 E
127	Kukës	(kŏō′kĕs)	Alb.	42·03 N	20·25 E
127	Kula	(kŏō′là)	Bul.	43·52 N	23·13 E
133	Kula		Tur.	38·32 N	28·30 E
142	Kula Kangri Mt.		China	33·11 N	90·36 E
135	Kular, Khrebet (Mts.)	(kŏō-lär′)	Sov. Un.	69·00 N	131·45 E
119	Kuldīga	(kŏōl′dē-gà)	Sov. Un.	56·59 N	21·59 E
132	Kulebaki	(kŏō-lĕ-bäk′ĭ)	Sov. Un.	55·22 N	42·30 E
120	Kulmbach	(kŏōlm′bäk)	Ger.	50·07 N	11·28 E
126	Kulpa (R.)	(kŏōl′pà)	Yugo.	45·32 N	14·50 E
134	Kulunda	(kŏō-lŭn′dà)	Sov. Un.	52·38 N	74·00 E
134	Kulundinskoye (L.)		Sov. Un.	52·45 N	77·18 E
152	Kum (R.)	(kŏōm)	Kor.	36·50 N	127·30 E
133	Kuma (R.)	(kŏō′mä)	Sov. Un.	44·50 N	45·10 E
153	Kumamoto	(kŏō′mä-mō′tò)	Jap.	32·49 N	130·40 E
153	Kumano-Nada (Sea)	(kŏō-mä′nō nä-dä)	Jap.	34·03 N	136·36 E
127	Kumanovo	(kŏō-mä′nō-vò)	Yugo.	42·10 N	21·41 E
164	Kumasi	(kŏō-mä′sĕ)	Ghana	6·45 N	1·39 W
164	Kumba	(kŏōm′bä)	Cam.	4·41 N	9·26 E
143	Kumbakonam	(kŏōm′bŭ-kô′nŭm)	India	10·59 N	79·25 E
127	Kumkale		Tur.	39·59 N	26·10 E
143	Kumta		India	14·19 N	75·28 E
136	Kunashak	(kŭ-nä′shàk)	Sov. Un. (Urals In.)	55·43 N	61·35 E
152	Kunashir (I.)	(kŏō-nŭ-shēr′)	Sov. Un.	44·40 N	145·45 E
148	Kunch'eng Hu (L.)	(kŏōN′chĕng hoo)	China	31·36 N	120·57 E
128	Kunda	(kŏō′dä)	Sov. Un.	59·30 N	26·28 E
163	Kundelungu, Plateau des (Plat.)		Bel. Congo′	9·00 S	25·30 E
136	Kundravy	(kŏōn′drà-vĭ)	Sov. Un. (Urals In.)	54·50 N	60·14 E
139	Kundur (I.)	Indon. (Singapore In.)		0·49 N	103·20 E
	Kunene (R.), see Cunene				
118	Kungälv	(kŭng′ĕlf)	Swe.	57·53 N	12·01 E
136	Kungur	(kŏōn-gōōr′)	Sov. Un. (Urals In.)	57·27 N	56·53 E
103	Kungrad	(kŏōn-grät′)	Sov. Un.	42·59 N	59·00 E
118	Kungsbacka	(kŭngs′bä-kà)	Swe.	57·31 N	12·04 E
142	Kungsherya		China	31·33 N	84·38 E
146	K'un Lun Shan (Mts.)	(kŏōn′lŏōn′ shän′)	China	35·26 N	83·09 E
151	K'unming (Yünnanfu)	(kŏōn′mĭng′) (yün′nän′fŏō′)	China	25·10 N	102·50 E
152	Kunsan	(kŏōn′sän′)	Kor.	35·54 N	126·46 E
149	K'unshan	(kŏōn′shän′)	China (Shanghai In.)	31·23 N	120·57 E
136	Kuntsëvo	(kŏōn-tsyô′vò)	Sov. Un. (Moscow In.)	55·43 N	37·27 E
136	Kun′ya		Sov. Un. (Urals In.)	58·42 N	56·47 E
128	Kun′ya (R.)	(kŏōn′yà)	Sov. Un.	56·45 N	30·53 E
112	Kuopio	(kŏō-ô′pĕ-ŏ)	Fin.	62·48 N	28·30 E
155	Kupang		Indon.	10·14 S	123·37 E
134	Kupino	(kŏō-pĭ′nò)	Sov. Un.	54·00 N	77·47 E
119	Kupiškis	(kŏō-pĭsh′kĭs)	Sov. Un.	55·50 N	24·55 E
129	Kupyansk	(kŏōp-yänsk′)	Sov. Un.	49·44 N	37·38 E
133	Kura (R.)	(kŏō′rä)	Sov. Un.	41·10 N	45·40 E
146	Kurak Darya (R.)		China	41·09 N	87·46 E
153	Kurashiki	(kŏō′rä-shē′kĕ)	Jap.	34·37 N	133·44 E
153	Kurayoshi	(kŏō′rä-yō′shĕ)	Jap.	35·25 N	133·49 E
133	Kurdistan (Reg.)	(kŭrd′ĭ-stän)	Tur.-Iran	37·40 N	43·30 E
127	Kŭrdzhali		Bul.	41·39 N	25·21 E
153	Kure	(kŏō′rĕ)	Jap.	34·17 N	132·35 E
119	Kuressaare	(kŏō′rĕ-sä′rĕ)	Sov. Un.	58·15 N	22·26 E
134	Kurgan	(kŏōr-gän′)	Sov. Un.	55·28 N	65·14 E
134	Kurgan Tyube	(kŏōr-gän′ tyŏō′bĕ)	Sov. Un.	38·00 N	68·49 E
144	Kuria Muria Is. (Br.)	(kŏō-rē-à′ mŏō′rē-à)	Aden	17·27 N	56·02 E
153	Kurihama	(kŏō-rē-hä′mä)	Jap. (Tōkyō In.)	35·14 N	139·42 E
135	Kuril Is. (kŏō′rĭl)		Sov. Un.	46·20 N	149·30 E
119	Kurisches Haff (Bay)		Sov. Un.	55·10 N	21·08 E
165	Kurmuk	(kŏōr′mŏōk)	Sud.	10·40 N	34·13 E
143	Kurnool	(kŏōr-nŏōl′)	India	16·00 N	78·04 E
153	Kuro (I.)	(kŏō′rò)	Jap.	30·49 N	129·56 E
161	Kurrajong		Austl. (Sydney In.)	33·33 S	150·40 E
119	Kuršenai	(kŏōr′shä-nī)	Sov. Un.	56·01 N	22·56 E
129	Kursk	(kŏōrsk)	Sov. Un.	51·44 N	36·08 E
129	Kursk (Oblast)	(kŏōrsk)	Sov. Un.	51·30 N	35·13 E
127	Kuršumlija	(kŏōr′shŏōm′lĭ-yä)	Yugo.	43·08 N	21·18 E
166	Kuruman	(kŏō-rōō-män′)	S. Afr.	27·25 S	23·30 E
153	Kurume	(kŏō-rōō-mĕ)	Jap.	33·20 N	130·26 E
153	Kururi	(kŏō′rŏō-rĕ)	Jap. (Tōkyō In.)	35·17 N	140·05 E
165	Kuruskü	(kŏō-rōōs-kŏō′)	U. A. R.	22·33 N	32·24 E
136	Kusa	(kŏō′sà)	Sov. Un. (Urals In.)	55·19 N	59·27 E
129	Kushchëvskaya		Sov. Un.	46·34 N	39·40 E
134	Kushevat		Sov. Un.	65·05 N	65·28 E
148	Kushih	(kŏō′sĕ)	China	32·11 N	115·39 E
153	Kushikino	(kŏō′shĭ-kē′nō)	Jap.	31·44 N	130·19 E
153	Kushimoto	(kŏō′shĭ-mō′tō)	Jap.	33·29 N	135·47 E
152	Kushiro	(kŏō′shē-rò)	Jap.	43·00 N	144·22 E
134	Kush-Murun (L.)	(kŏōsh-mŏō-rōōn′)	Sov. Un.	52·30 N	64·15 E
133	Kushum (R.)	(kŏō-shŏōm′)	Sov. Un.	50·30 N	50·40 E
136	Kushva	(kŏōsh′và)	Sov. Un. (Urals In.)	58·18 N	59·51 E
64	Kuskokwim (R.)		Alaska	61·32 N	160·36 W
64	Kuskokwim B.	(kŭs′kô-kwĭm)	Alaska	59·25 N	163·14 W
64	Kuskokwim Mts.		Alaska	62·08 N	158·00 W
64	Kuskovak	(kŭs-kô′väk)	Alaska	60·10 N	162·50 W
134	Kustanay	(kŏōs-tà-nī′)	Sov. Un.	53·10 N	63·39 E
133	Kutahya	(kû-tä′hyà)	Tur.	39·20 N	29·50 E
133	Kutaisi	(kŏō-tŭ-ē′sē)	Sov. Un.	42·15 N	42·40 E
154	Kutaradja		Indon.	5·30 N	95·20 E
142	Kutch, Gulf of		India	22·45 N	68·33 E
142	Kutch, Rann of (Swp.)		India	23·59 N	69·13 E
111	Kutenholz	(kŏō′tĕn-hôlts)	Ger. (Hamburg In.)	53·29 N	9·20 E
136	Kutim	(kŏō′tĭm)	Sov. Un. (Urals In.)	60·22 N	58·51 E
126	Kutina	(kŏō′tĕ-nà)	Yugo.	45·29 N	16·48 E
121	Kutno (kŏōt′nô)		Pol.	52·14 N	19·22 E
132	Kutno (L.)		Sov. Un.	65·15 N	31·30 E
134	Kutulik	(kŏō tŏō′lyĭk)	Sov. Un.	53·12 N	102·51 E
121	Kuty	(kŏō′tĕ)	Sov. Un.	48·16 N	25·12 E
112	Kuusamo	(kŏō′sà-mò)	Fin.	65·59 N	29·10 E
128	Kuvshinovo	(kŏōv-shē′nô-vò)	Sov. Un.	57·01 N	34·09 E
	Kuwait, see Al Kuwayt				
138	Kuwait		Asia	29·00 N	48·45 E
153	Kuwana	(kŏō′wä-nä)	Jap.	35·02 N	136·40 E
132	Kuybyshev (Kuibyshev)	(kŏō′ē-bĭ-shĭf)	Sov. Un.	53·10 N	50·05 E
134	Kuybyshev		Sov. Un.	55·45 N	76·45 E
132	Kuybyshevskoye (Res.)		Sov. Un.	53·40 N	49·00 E
148	Kuyeh	(gŏō′yĕ)	China	39·46 N	118·23 E
133	Kuzey Anadolu Dağ′ari (Mts.)		Tur.	41·20 N	34·30 E
133	Kuznetsk	(kŏōz-nyĕtsk′)	Sov. Un.	53·00 N	46·30 E
134	Kuznetsk Basin		Sov. Un.	57·15 N	86·15 E
136	Kuznetsovka	(kŏōz-nyĕt′sôf-kà)	Sov. Un. (Urals In.)	54·41 N	56·40 E
128	Kuznetsovo	(kŏōz-nyĕt-sô′vò)	Sov. Un.	56·39 N	36·55 E
126	Kvarnerski Zaliv (B.)	(kvär′nĕr-skĕ′ zä′lĕv)	Yugo.	44·41 N	14·05 E
64	Kvichak (R.)	(kvĭ′häk)	Alaska	59·00 N	156·48 W
166	Kwango (R.)	(kwäng′ō′)	Ang.	8·30 S	18·00 E
	Kwangtung, see Kuangtung				
	Kweichow, see Kueichou				
	Kweitun, see Wusu				
166	Kwenge (R.)	(kwĕn′gĕ)	Con. L.	6·45 S	18·34 E
121	Kwidzyń	(kvē′dzĭn′)	Pol.	53·45 N	18·56 E
166	Kwilu (R.)	(kwē′lōō)	Con. L.	5·00 S	19·20 E
164	Kwitta	(kwĭt′à)	Ghana	6·00 N	1·00 E
135	Kyakhta	(kyäK′ta)	Sov. Un.	51·00 N	107·30 E
142	Kyang Tsho (L.)		China	30·37 N	88·33 E
142	Kyayisu (R.)		India	38·05 N	74·36 E
146	Kyaukpyu (chouk′pyoo′)		Bur.	19·19 N	93·33 E
119	Kybartai	(kē′bär-tī′)	Sov. Un.	54·40 N	22·46 E
151	Ky Lam		Viet.	15·48 N	108·30 E
136	Kyn	(kĭn′)	Sov. Un. (Urals In.)	51·52 N	58·42 E
159	Kynuna	(ki-nōō′nà)	Austl.	21·30 S	142·12 E
165	Kyoga L.		Ug.	1·27 N	33·51 E
153	Kyōga-Saki (C.)	(kyō′gä sa′kĕ)	Jap.	35·46 N	135·14 E
152	Kyŏngju	(kyŭng′yŏō)	Kor.	35·48 N	129·12 E
153	Kyōtō	(kyō′tō′)	Jap. (Ōsaka In.)	35·00 N	135·46 E
153	Kyōto (Pref.)		Jap. (Ōsaka In.)	35·34 N	135·42 E
134	Kyren	(kĭ′rĕn′)	Sov. Un.	51·46 N	102·13 E
119	Kyrön (R.)	(kŭ′rò)	Fin.	63·03 N	22·20 E
136	Kyrya	(kēr′yà)	Sov. Un. (Urals In.)	59·18 N	59·03 E
136	Kyshtym	(kĭsh-tĭm′)	Sov. Un. (Urals In.)	55·43 N	60·33 E
136	Kytlym	(kĭt′lĭm)	Sov. Un. (Urals In.)	59·30 N	59·15 E
153	Kyūshū (I.)	(kyōō′shōō′)	Jap.	32·27 N	131·03 E
127	Kyustendil	(kyŏōs-tĕn-dĭl′)	Bul.	42·16 N	22·39 E
134	Kyzyl (kĭ′zĭl)		Sov. Un.	51·37 N	93·38 E
103	Kyzylkum (Des.)	(kĭ′zĭl kŏōm)	Sov. Un.	42·47 N	64·45 E
146	Kyzylsu (R.)		China	39·26 N	74·30 E
134	Kzyl-Orda	(kzĕl-ôr′dà)	Sov. Un.	44·58 N	65·45 E
120	Laa		Aus.	48·42 N	16·23 E
124	La Almunia de Doña Godina	(lä′äl-mōōn′yä dĕ dò nyä gô-dē′nä)	Sp.	41·29 N	1·22 W
98	La Asunción	(lä ä-sōōn-syōn′)	Ven.	11·02 N	63·57 W
100	La Banda	(lä bän′dä)	Arg.	27·48 S	64·12 W
90	La Barca	(lä bär′kä)	Mex.	20·17 N	102·33 W
164	Labé	(lä-bā′)	Gui.	11·15 N	12·16 W
120	Labe (Elbe) R.	(lä′bĕ) (ĕl′bĕ)	Czech.	50·05 N	15·20 E
86	Laberge (R.)	(là-bērzh′)	Can.	61·08 N	136·42 W
94	Laberinto de las Doce Leguas (Is.)	(lä-bâ-rēn tô dä läs dô′sä lä′gwäs)	Cuba	20·40 N	78·35 W
133	Labinsk		Sov. Un.	44·30 N	40·40 E
139	Labis	(läb′ĭs)	Mala. (Singapore In.)	2·23 N	103·01 E
125	La Bisbal	(lä bēs-bäl′)	Sp.	41·55 N	3·00 E
155	Labo	(lä′bò)	Phil. (Manila In.)	13·39 N	121·14 E
155	Labo		Phil. (Manila In.)	14·11 N	122·49 E
155	Labo, Mt.		Phil. (Manila In.)	14·00 N	122·47 E
85	L'Abord-a-Plouffe	(lä-bōr′dä-plŏōf′)	Can. (Montreal In.)	45·32 N	73·45 W
122	Labouheyre	(lä-bōō-âr′)	Fr.	44·14 N	0·58 W
100	Laboulaye	(lä-bô′ōō-lä-yĕ)	Arg.	34·01 S	63·10 W
87	Labrador (Reg.)	(lăb′rá-dôr)	Can.	53·05 N	63·30 W
98	Lábrea	(lä-brä′à)	Braz.	7·28 S	64·39 W
155	Labuan	(lä-bwä′n)	Phil. (Manila In.)	13·43 N	120·07 E
154	Labuan (I.)	(lä-bōō-än′)	Mala.	5·28 N	115·11 E
155	Labuha		Indon.	0·43 S	127·35 E
85	L'Acadie	(lä-kä-dē′)	Can. (Montreal In.)	45·18 N	73·22 W
85	L'Acadie, Riviére	(rē-vyâr′)	Can. (Montreal In.)	45·24 N	73·21 W
101	La Calera	(lä-kä-lĕ-rä)	Chile (Santiago In.)	32·47 S	71·11 W
98	La Calera		Col. (In.)	4·43 N	73·58 W
113	La Calle	(lä käl′)	Alg.	36·52 N	8·23 E
74	La Canada	(lä kän-yä′dä)	Calif. (Los Angeles In.)	34·13 N	118·12 W
91	Lacantum (R.)	(lä-kän-tōō′m)	Mex.	16·13 N	90·52 W
124	La Carolina	(lä kä-rô-lē′nä)	Sp.	38·16 N	3·48 W
91	La Catedral, Cerro (Mtn.)	(sĕ′r-rô-lä-kä-tĕ-drä′l)	Mex. (Mexico City In.)	19·32 N	99·31 W
82	Lac-au-Saumon		Can.	48·24 N	67·23 W
85	Lac-Beauport	(läk-bō-pōr′)	Can. (Quebec In.)	46·58 N	71·17 W
143	Laccadive Is.	(lăk′á-dĭv)	India	11·00 N	73·02 E
142	Laccadive Sea		Asia	9·10 N	75·17 E
71	Lac Court Oreille Ind. Res.	(läk kôrt-ô-rēl) (läk kŏōr tô-rā′y′)	Wis.	46·04 N	91·18 W
71	Lac du Flambeau Ind. Res.		Wis.	46·12 N	89·50 W
92	La Ceiba	(lä sēbä)	Hond.	15·45 N	86·52 W
98	La Ceja	(lä-sĕ-кä)	Col. (In.)	6·02 N	75·25 W
87	Lac Frontiere		Can.	46·41 N	70·04 W
132	Lacha (L.)	(lä′chä)	Sov. Un.	61·15 N	39·05 E
120	La Chaux de Fonds	(lä shō-dĕ-fôn′)	Switz.	47·07 N	6·47 E
85	L'Achigan, R.	(lä-shē-gän′)	Can. (Montreal In.)	45·49 N	73·48 W
85	Lachine	(lá-shēn′)	Can. (Montreal In.)	45·26 N	73·40 W
160	Lachlan (R.)	(läk′lăn)	Austl.	33·54 S	145·15 E
88	La Chorrera	(lächôr-rä′rä)	Pan. (Panama Canal In.)	8·54 N	79·47 W
85	Lachute	(lá-shōōt′)	Can. (Montreal In.)	45·39 N	74·20 W
123	La Ciotat	(lä syô-tä′)	Fr.	43·13 N	5·35 E
75	Lackawanna	(lak-á-wŏn′á)	N. Y. (Buffalo In.)	42·49 N	78·50 W
86	Lac la Biche		Can.	54·46 N	112·04 W
82	Lac Megantic		Can.	45·34 N	70·53 W
	La Columna, see Bolivar				
86	Lacombe		Can.	52·29 N	113·41 W
91	La Concordia	(lä-kôn-kô′r-dyä)	Mex.	16·07 N	92·40 W
81	Laconia	(lá-kō′nĭ-á)	N. H.	43·30 N	71·30 W
65	La Conner	(lä kŏn′ĕr)	Wash. (Seattle In.)	48·23 N	122·30 W
124	La Coruña	(lä kô-rōō′nyä)	Sp.	43·20 N	8·20 W
70	Lacreek (R.)	(lä′krēk)	S. D.	43·04 N	101·46 W
74	La Cresenta	(lá krĕs′ĕnt-à)	Calif. (Los Angeles In.)	34·14 N	118·13 W

Page	Name Pronunciation Region	Lat. °′	Long. °′
72	La Cross (lȧ-krôs') Kans.	38·30 N	99·20 W
71	La Crosse Wis.	43·48 N	91·14 W
92	La Cruz (lä-kroo'z) C. R.	11·05 N	85·37 W
98	La Cruz (lȧ krooz') Col.	1·37 N	77·00 W
70	Lacs, Riviere des (R.) (rē-vyĕr' de läk) N. D.	48·30 N	101·45 W
85	Lac-St-Charles (läk-sĕN-shärl) Can. (Quebec In.)	46·55 N	71·23 W
93	La Cuesta (lä-kwĕ's-tä) C. R.	8·32 N	82·51 W
124	La Culebra, Sierra de (Mts.) (sē-ĕ'r-rä-dĕ-lä-koo-lĕ-brä) Sp.	41·52 N	6·21 W
73	La Cygne (lȧ-sēn'y') (lȧ-sēn') Kans.	38·20 N	94·45 W
80	Ladd (lăd) Ill.	41·25 N	89·25 W
124	La Demanda, Sierra de (Mts.) (sē-ĕ'r-rä-dĕ-lä-dĕ-mä'n-dä) Sp.	42·10 N	2·35 W
125	Ladíspoli (lä-dē's-pô-lē) It. (Rome In.)	41·57 N	12·05 E
65	Ladner (lăd'nēr) Can. (Vancouver In.)	49·05 N	123·06 W
142	Lādnun (läd'nōōn) India	27·45 N	74·20 E
	Ladoga, Lake, see Ladozhskoye Ozero		
98	La Dorado (lä dô-rä'dä) Col. (In.)	5·28 N	74·42 W
119	Ladozhskoye Ozero (Lake Ladoga) (lȧ-dôsh'skô-yĕ ô'zĕ-rô) Sov. Un.	60·59 N	31·30 E
85	La Durantaye (lä dü-räN-tā') Can. (Quebec In.)	46·51 N	70·51 W
167	Lady Frere (lā-dē frâ'r') S. Afr. (Natal In.)	31·48 S	27·16 E
167	Lady Grey S. Afr. (Natal In.)	30·44 S	27·17 E
66	Ladysmith (lā'dĭ-smĭth) Can.	48·59 N	123·50 W
167	Ladysmith S. Afr. (Natal In.)	28·38 S	29·48 E
71	Ladysmith Wis.	45·27 N	91·07 W
155	Lae (lä'å) N. Gui. Ter.	6·15 S	146·57 E
118	Laerdal (lâr'däl) Nor.	61·03 N	7·24 E
118	Laerdalsören (lâr'däls-û'rĕn) Nor.	61·08 N	7·26 E
118	Laesø (I.) (lâs'û) Den.	57·17 N	10·57 E
92	La Esperanza (lä ĕs-pâ-rän'zä) Hond.	14·20 N	88·21 W
124	La Estrada (lä ĕs-trä'dä) Sp.	42·42 N	8·29 W
152	Lafa (lä'fä) China	43·49 N	127·19 E
122	La-Fare-les-Oliviers (lä-fär'lā-ô-lē-vyā) Fr. (Marseille In.)	43·33 N	5·12 E
78	Lafayette Ala.	32·52 N	85·25 W
65	Lafayette Calif. (San Francisco In.)	37·53 N	122·07 W
78	Lafayette (lă-fâ-yĕt') Ga.	34·41 N	85·19 W
80	La Fayette Ind.	40·25 N	86·55 W
77	Lafayette La.	30·15 N	92·02 W
84	La Fayette R. I. (Providence In.)	41·34 N	71·29 W
123	La Ferté-Alais (lä-fĕr-tā'-ä-lā') Fr. (Paris In.)	48·29 N	2·19 E
123	La Ferté-sous-Jouarre (lȧ fĕr-tā'soo-zhoo-är') Fr. (Paris In.)	48·56 N	3·07 E
84	Lafitte (lă-fēt') La. (New Orleans In.)	29·45 N	90·08 W
122	La Flèche (lȧ flāsh') Fr.	47·43 N	0·03 W
122	La Flotte (lȧ flôt') Fr.	46·09 N	1·20 W
78	La Follette (lä-fŏl'ĕt) Tenn.	36·23 N	84·07 W
77	Lafourche, Bay. (bȧ-yoo'lȧ-foorsh') La.	29·25 N	90·15 W
99	La Gaiba (lä-gī'bä) Braz.	17·54 S	57·32 W
116	Lagan (lā'gǎn) N. Ire.	54·30 N	6·00 W
118	Lagan (R.) Swe.	56·34 N	13·25 E
112	Laganes (Pt.) Ice.	66·21 N	14·02 W
88	Lagarto, R. (lä-gä'r-tô) Pan. (Panama Canal In.)	9·08 N	80·05 W
92	Lagartos L. (lä-gä'r-tôs) Mex. (Yucatan In.)	21·32 N	88·15 W
118	Lågen (R.) (lô'ghĕn) Nor.	59·15 N	9·47 E
164	Laghouat (lä-gwät') Alg.	33·45 N	2·49 E
123	Lagny (län-yē') Fr. (Paris In.)	48·53 N	2·41 E
101	Lagoa da Prata (lȧ-gô'ä-dȧ-prä'tȧ) Braz. (Rio de Janeiro In.)	20·04 S	45·33 W
101	Lagoa Dourada (lȧ-gô'ä-doo-rä'dä) Braz. (Rio de Janeiro In.)	20·55 S	44·03 W
155	Lagonoy (lä-gô-noi') Phil. (Manila In.)	13·44 N	123·31 E
155	Lagonoy G. Phil. (Manila In.)	13·34 N	123·46 E
164	Lagos (lä'gōs) Nig.	6·31 N	3·15 E
124	Lagos (lä'gôzh) Port.	37·08 N	8·43 W
90	Lagos de Moreno (lä'gōs dā mô-rā'nō) Mex.	21·21 N	101·55 W
122	La Grand' Combe (lȧ grän kaNb') Fr.	44·12 N	4·03 E
66	La Grande (lȧ grănd') Ore.	45·20 N	118·06 W
158	La Grange (lȧ grānj) Austl.	18·40 S	122·00 E
78	La Grange (lȧ-grānj') Ga.	33·01 N	85·00 W
75	La Grange Ill. (Chicago In.)	41·49 N	87·53 W
80	Lagrange Ind.	41·40 N	85·25 W
80	La Grange Ky.	38·20 N	85·25 W
73	La Grange Mo.	40·04 N	91·30 W
75	Lagrange Ohio (Cleveland In.)	41·14 N	82·07 W
77	Lagrange Tex.	29·55 N	96·50 W
98	La Grita (lä grē'tä) Ven.	8.02 N	71·59 W
99	La Guaira (lä gwä'ē-rä) Ven. (In.)	10·36 N	66·54 W
124	La Guardia (lä gwär'dē-ä) Sp.	41·55 N	8·48 W
100	Laguna (lä-goo'nä) Braz.	28·19 S	48·42 W
94	Laguna, Cayos (Is.) (kä'yōs-lä-goo'nä) Cuba	22·15 N	82·45 W
155	Laguna de Bay (L.) (lä-goo'nä dȧ bä'ē) Phil. (Manila In.)	14·24 N	121·13 E
69	Laguna Ind. Res. N. Mex.	35·00 N	107·30 W
98	Lagunillas (lä-goo-nēl'yäs) Bol.	19·42 S	63·38 W
90	Lagunillas (lä-goo-nē'l-yäs) Mex.	21·34 N	99·41 W
95	La Habana (Havana) (lä-ä-bä'nä) Cuba (Havana In.)	23·08 N	82·23 W
74	La Habra (lȧ hȧb'rȧ) Calif. (Los Angeles In.)	34·56 N	117·57 W
157	Lahaina (lä-hä'ē-nä) Hawaii (In.)	20·52 N	156·39 W
122	La Haye-Descartes (lȧ å-dȧ-kärt') Fr.	46·58 N	0·42 E
120	Lahn R. (län) Ger.	50·21 N	7·54 E
118	Laholm (lä'hôlm) Swe.	56·30 N	13·00 E
65	La Honda (lā hôn'dȧ) Calif. (San Francisco In.)	37·20 N	122·16 W
142	Lahore (lä-hōr') W. Pak.	31·39 N	74·22 E
120	Lahr (lär) Ger.	48·19 N	7·52 E
119	Lahti (lä'tē) Fin.	60·59 N	27·39 E
151	Lai, C. Viet.	17·08 N	107·30 E
148	Laian (läī'äN) China	32·27 N	118·25 E
148	Laichou Wan (B.) (läī'jō wäN) China	37·22 N	119·19 E
122	Laigle (lĕ'gl') Fr.	48·45 N	0·37 E
151	Laipin (lī'pĭn') China	23·42 N	109·20 E
148	Laiyang (läī'yäNg) China	36·59 N	120·42 E
90	Laja, Río de la (R.) (rē'ō-dĕ-lä-lȧ'kä) Mex.	20·17 N	100·57 W
94	Lajas (lä'häs) Cuba	22·25 N	80·20 W
100	Lajeado (lä-zhĕä'dô) Braz.	29·24 S	51·46 W
100	Lajes (lȧ'-zhĕs) Braz.	27·47 S	50·17 W
101	Lajinha (lä-zhē'nyä) Braz. (Rio de Janeiro In.)	20·08 S	41·36 W
68	La Jolla (lȧ hōl'yȧ) Calif. (San Diego In.)	32·51 N	117·16 W
68	La Jolla Ind. Res. Calif.	33·19 N	116·21 W
72	La Junta (lȧ hoon'tȧ) Colo.	37 59 N	103·35 W
168	Lak Dera (R.) (läk dā'rä) Som. (Horn of Afr. In.)	0·45 N	41·26 E
77	Lake Arthur (är'thŭr) La.	30·06 N	92·40 W
70	Lake Benton (bĕn'tŭn) Minn.	44·15 N	96·17 W
75	Lake Bluff (blŭf) Ill. (Chicago In.)	42·17 N	87·50 W
158	Lake Brown (broun) Austl.	31·03 S	118·30 E
77	Lake Charles (chärlz') La.	30·15 N	93·14 W
79	Lake City Fla.	30·09 N	82·40 W
71	Lake City Iowa	42·14 N	94·43 W
71	Lake City Minn.	44·28 N	92·19 W
79	Lake City S. C.	33·57 N	79·45 W
71	Lake Crystal (krĭs'tǎl) Minn.	44·05 N	94·12 W
116	Lake Dist. (lāk) Eng.	54·25 N	3·20 W
74	Lake Elmo (ĕlmō) Minn. (Minneapolis, St. Paul In.)	45·00 N	92·53 W
75	Lake Forest (fŏr'ĕst) Ill. (Chicago In.)	42·16 N	87·50 W
69	Lake Fork (R.) Utah	40·30 N	110·25 W
71	Lake Geneva (jĕ-nē'vȧ) Wis.	42·36 N	88·28 W
87	Lake Harbour (här'bēr) Can.	62·43 N	69·40 W
74	Lake June (joon) Tex. (Dallas, Fort Worth In.)	32·43 N	96·45 W
79	Lakeland (lāk'lǎnd) Fla. (In.)	28·02 N	81·58 W
78	Lakeland Ga.	31·02 N	83·02 W
74	Lakeland Minn. (Minneapolis, St. Paul In.)	44·57 N	92·47 W
71	Lake Linden (lĭn'dĕn) Mich.	47·11 N	88·26 W
71	Lake Mills (mĭlz') Iowa	43·25 N	93·32 W
75	Lakemore (lāk-mōr) Ohio (Cleveland In.)	41·01 N	81·24 W
80	Lake Odessa Mich.	42·50 N	85·15 W
65	Lake Oswego (ŏs-wē'go) Ore. (Portland In.)	45·25 N	122·40 W
74	Lake Point Utah (Salt Lake City In.)	40·41 N	112·16 W
68	Lakeport (lāk'pōrt) Calif.	39·03 N	122·54 W
70	Lake Preston (prĕs'tǔn) S. D.	44·21 N	97·23 W
77	Lake Providence (prŏv'ĭ-dĕns) La.	32·48 N	91·12 W
68	Lakeside (lāk'sīd) Calif. (San Diego In.)	32·52 N	116·55 W
166	Lakeside S. Afr. (Cape Town In.)	34·05 S	18·28 E
65	Lake Stevens Wash. (Seattle In.)	48·01 N	122·04 W
84	Lake Success (sŭk-sĕs') N. Y. (New York In.)	40·46 N	73·43 W
74	Lakeview (lāk-vū') Calif. (Los Angeles In.)	33·50 N	117·07 W
66	Lakeview Ore.	42·11 N	120·21 W
84	Lakeville (lāk'vĭl) N. Y. (New York In.)	41·12 N	74·16 W
67	Lake Walcott Res. Idaho	42·35 N	113·15 W
79	Lake Wales (wälz') Fla. (In.)	27·54 N	81·35 W
72	Lakewood (lāk'wŏŏd) Colo.	39·44 N	105·06 W
75	Lakewood Ohio (Cleveland In.)	41·29 N	81·48 W
81	Lakewood Pa.	40·05 N	74·10 W
65	Lakewood Wash. (Seattle In.)	47·10 N	122·31 W
65	Lakewood Wash. (Seattle In.)	48·09 N	122·13 W
74	Lakewood Village Calif. (Los Angeles In.)	33·50 N	118·09 W
79	Lake Worth (wûrth') Fla. (In.)	26·37 N	80·04 W
74	Lake Worth Village Tex. (Dallas, Fort Worth In.)	32·49 N	97·26 W
75	Lake Zürich (tsü'rĭk) Ill. (Chicago In.)	42·11 N	88·05 W
119	Lakhdenpokh'ya (l'äk-dĭe'npōkyȧ) Sov. Un.	61·33 N	30·10 E
136	Lakhtinskiy (läk-tĭn'skĭ) Sov. Un. (Leningrad In.)	59·59 N	30·10 E
127	Lakonikós Kólpos (G.) Grc.	36·38 N	22·40 E
70	Lakota (lȧ-kō'tȧ) N. D.	48·04 N	98·21 W
92	La Libertad (lä lē-bĕr-tädh') Guat.	15·31 N	91·44 W
92	La Libertad Guat. (Yucatan In.)	16·46 N	90·12 W
92	La Libertad Sal.	13·29 N	89·20 W
101	La Ligua (lä lē'gwä) Chile (Santiago In.)	32·21 S	71·13 W
124	Lalín (lä-lē'n) Sp.	42·40 N	8·05 W
124	La Línea (lä lē'nā-ä) Sp.	36·11 N	5·22 W
114	Lalla-Maghnia (lä'lä-mäg'nēȧ) Alg.	34·52 N	1·40 W
117	La Louviere (lȧ loo-vyâr') Bel.	50·30 N	4·10 E
90	La Luz (lä looz') Mex.	21·04 N	101·19 W
122	La Machine (lȧ mȧ-shēn') Fr.	46·53 N	3·26 E
82	La Malbaie (lȧ mäl-bā') Can.	47·39 N	70·11 W
124	La Mancha (Mts.) (lä män'chä) Sp.	38·55 N	4·20 W
72	Lamar (lȧ-mär') Colo.	38·04 N	102·44 W
73	Lamar Mo.	37·28 N	94·15 W
126	La Marmora, Pta. (Mtn.) (lä-mä'r-mô-rä) It.	40·00 N	9·28 E
77	La Marque (lȧ-märk) Tex. (In.)	29·23 N	94·58 W
98	Lamas (lä'mäs) Peru	6·24 S	76·41 W
122	Lamballe (läN-bäl') Fr.	48·29 N	2·36 W
166	Lambaréné (läN-bȧ-rȧ-nā') Gabon	0·48 S	10·07 E
101	Lambari (läm-bȧ'rē) Braz. (Rio de Janeiro In.)	21·58 S	45·22 W
98	Lambayeque (läm-bä-yā'kā) Peru	6·41 S	79·58 W
78	Lambert (lăm'bērt) Miss.	34·10 N	90·16 W
81	Lambertville (lăm'bērt-vĭl) N. J.	40·20 N	75·00 W
67	Lame Deer (lām dēr') Mont.	45·36 N	106·40 W
124	Lamego (lä-mā'gō) Port.	41·07 N	7·47 W
68	La Mesa (lä mā'sä) Calif. (San Diego In.)	32·46 N	117·01 W
98	La Mesa Col. (In.)	4·38 N	74·27 W
72	Lamesa Tex.	32·44 N	101·54 W
127	Lamía (lȧ-mē'ȧ) Grc.	38·54 N	22·25 E
155	Lamon B. (lä-mōn') Phil. (Manila In.)	14·35 N	121·52 E
101	La Mora (lä-mō'rä) Chile (Santiago In.)	32·28 S	70·56 W
70	La Moure (lȧ moor') N. D.	46·23 N	98·17 W
101	Lampa (R.) (lä'm-pä) Chile (Santiago In.)	33·15 S	70·55 W
76	Lampasas (lăm-păs'ǎs) Tex.	31·06 N	98·10 W
76	Lampasas R. Tex.	31·18 N	98·08 W
76	Lampazos (läm-pä'zōs) Mex.	27·03 N	100·30 W
113	Lampedusa (I.) (läm-pȧ-doo'sä) It.	35·29 N	12·58 E
111	Lamstedt (läm'shtĕt) Ger. (Hamburg In.)	53·38 N	9·06 E
167	Lamu (lä'moo) Ken.	2·17 S	41·07 E
123	La Mure (lȧ mür') Fr.	44·55 N	5·50 E
128	Lan' (R.) (län') Sov. Un.	52·38 N	27·05 E
157	Lanai (I.) (lä-nä'ē) Hawaii (In.)	20·48 N	157·06 W
142	Lanak La (P.) China	34·40 N	79·50 E
125	La Nao, Cabo de (C.) (kȧ'bô-dĕ-lä-nä'ō) Sp.	38·43 N	0·14 E
116	Lanark (lăn'ǎrk) Scot.	55·40 N	3·50 W
110	Lancashire (Co.) (lăŋ'kȧ-shĭr) Scot.	53·38 N	2·30 W
82	Lancaster (lăŋ'kǎs-tēr) Can.	45·16 N	66·06 W
116	Lancaster Eng.	54·04 N	2·55 W
80	Lancaster Ky.	37·35 N	84·30 W
83	Lancaster Mass. (Boston In.)	42·28 N	71·40 W
81	Lancaster N. H.	44·25 N	71·30 W
75	Lancaster N. Y. (Buffalo In.)	42·54 N	78·42 W
80	Lancaster Ohio	39·40 N	82·35 W
81	Lancaster Pa.	40·05 N	76·20 W
79	Lancaster S. C.	34·42 N	80·45 W
74	Lancaster Tex. (Dallas, Fort Worth In.)	32·36 N	96·45 W
71	Lancaster Wis.	42·51 N	90·44 W
150	Lanchou (län'chō) China	35·55 N	103·55 E
122	Lançon-Provence (läN-sôN'prô-vĕNs') Fr. (Marseille In.)	43·35 N	5·08 E
166	Lândana (län-dä'nä) Ang.	5·15 S	12·07 E
120	Landau (län'dou) Ger.	49·13 N	8·07 E
67	Lander (lăn'dēr) Wyo.	42·49 N	108·24 W
122	Landerneau (läN-dĕr-nō') Fr.	48·28 N	4·14 W
122	Landes (Moorland) (Plain) (läNd) Fr.	44·22 N	0·52 W
111	Landsberg (lănds'boorgh) Ger. (Munich In.)	48·03 N	10·53 E
116	Lands End Pt. Eng.	50·03 N	5·45 W
120	Landshut (länts'hoot) Ger.	48·32 N	12·09 E
118	Landskrona (läns-kroo'nȧ) Swe.	55·51 N	12·47 E
78	Lanett (lȧ-nĕt') Ala.	32·52 N	85·13 W
150	Lanfang China (Peking In.)	39·31 N	116·42 E
127	Langadhás Grc.	40·44 N	24·10 E
139	Langat (R.) Mala. (Singapore In.)	2·46 N	101·33 E
148	Langch'i (läNg'che) China	31·10 N	119·09 E
151	Langchung China	31·40 N	106·05 E
85	Langdon (lăng'dǎn) Can. (Calgary In.)	50·58 N	113·40 W
74	Langdon Minn. (Minneapolis, St. Paul In.)	44·49 N	92·56 W
85	L'Ange-Gardien (läNzh gȧr-dyăN') Can. (Quebec In.)	46·55 N	71·06 W
118	Lange Land Den.	54·52 N	10·46 E
65	Langeley Prairie (lăng'lĭ prâr'ĭ) Can. (Vancouver In.)	49·06 N	122·40 W
123	Langenthal Switz.	47·11 N	7·50 E
111	Langenzersdorf Aus. (Vienna In.)	48·30 N	16·22 E
118	Langesund (läng'ĕ-soon') Nor.	58·59 N	9·38 E
118	Lang Fd. (läng'fyôr') Nor.	62·40 N	7·45 E
84	Langhorne (lăng'hôrn) Pa. (Philadelphia In.)	40·10 N	74·55 W
112	Langjökoll (Gl.) (läng-yû'kool) Ice.	64·40 N	20·31 W
79	Langley (lăng'lĭ) S. C.	33·32 N	81·52 W
65	Langley Wash. (Seattle In.)	48·02 N	122·25 W
65	Langley Ind. Res. Can. (Vancouver In.)	49·12 N	122·31 W
120	Langnau (läng'nou) Switz.	46·56 N	7·46 E
122	Langogne (läN-gōn'y') Fr.	44·43 N	3·50 E
122	Langon (läN-gôN') Fr.	44·34 N	0·16 W
122	Langres (läN'gr') Fr.	47·53 N	5·20 E
122	Langres, Plateaux de (Plat.) (plä-tō'dĕ-läN'grĕ) Fr.	47·39 N	5·00 E
154	Langsa (läng'sä) Indon.	4·33 N	97·52 E
154	Lang Son (läng'sŏn') Viet.	21·52 N	106·42 E
85	Langstaff (lăng'stăf) Can. (Toronto In.)	43·51 N	79·25 W
73	L'Anguille (R.) (läN-gē'y') Ark.	35·23 N	90·52 W
86	Lanigan (lăn'ĭ-gǎn) Can.	51·53 N	105·04 W
146	Lanisung Chiang (Mekong) China	24·45 N	100·31 E
81	Lansdale (lănz'dāl) Pa.	40·20 N	75·15 W
84	Lansdowne (lănz'doun) Md. (Baltimore In.)	39·14 N	76·39 W
84	Lansdowne Pa. (Philadelphia In.)	39·57 N	75·17 W
71	L'Anse (läns) Mich.	46·43 N	88·28 W
85	L'Anse-a-Giles (läNz-ä-zhēl) Can. (Quebec In.)	47·05 N	70·26 W
71	L'Anse and Vieux Desert Ind. Res. Mich.	46·41 N	88·12 W
81	Lansford (lănz'fērd) Pa.	40·50 N	75·50 W
85	Lansing (lăn'sĭng) Can. (Toronto In.)	43·46 N	79·24 W
75	Lansing Ill. (Chicago In.)	41·34 N	87·33 W
71	Lansing Iowa	43·22 N	91·16 W

ăt; finǎl; rāte; senâte; ärm; åsk; sofȧ; fâre; ch-choose; dh-as th in other; bē; ēvent; bĕt; recĕnt; cratēr; g-go; gh-guttural g; bĭt; ĭ-short neutral; rīde; K-guttural k as ch in German ich;

Page	Name Pronunciation Region	Lat. °′	Long. °′
74	Lansing..Kans. (Kansas City In.)	39·15 N	94·53 W
80	Lansing....Mich.	42·45 N	84 35 W
100	Lanús (lä-nōōs')....Arg. (In.)	34·27 S	58·24 W
126	Lanusei (lä-nōō-sĕ'y)....It.	39·51 N	9·34 E
125	Lanúvio (lä-nōō'vyô) It. (Rome In.)	41·41 N	12·42 E
164	Lanzarote I. (län-zȧ-rō'tā).Can. Is.	29·04 N	13·03 W
154	Laoag (lä-wäg')....Phil.	18·13 N	120·38 E
147	Lao Ho (R.) (lä'ō hō')....China	43·37 N	120·05 E
154	Lao Kay (lä'ōkä'ē)....Viet.	22·30 N	102·32 E
122	Laon (läN)....Fr.	49·36 N	3·35 E
98	La Orova (lä-ô-rō'yä)....Peru	11·44 S	76·12 W
138	Laos (lä'ōs) (lȧ-ōs')....Asia	19·30 N	102·45 E
93	La Palma (lä-päl'mä)....Pan.	8·25 N	78·07 W
124	La Palma....Sp.	37·24 N	6·36 W
164	La Palma I....Can. Is.	28·42 N	19·03 W
100	La Pampa (Prov.)....Arg.	37·25 S	67·00 W
100	Lapa Rio Negro (lä-pä-rē'ō-nĕ'grô).Braz.	26·12 S	49·56 W
100	La Paz (lä päz')....Arg.	30·48 S	59·47 W
98	La Paz....Bol.	16·31 S	68·03 W
92	La Paz....Hond.	14·15 N	87·40 W
90	La Paz (lä-pä'z)....Mex.	23·39 N	100·44 W
88	La Paz....Mex.	24·00 N	110·15 W
155	La Paz....Phil. (Manila In.)	17·41 N	120·41 E
80	Lapeer (lȧ-pēr')....Mich.	43·05 N	83·15 W
122	La-Penne-sur-Huveaune (la-pĕn'sür-ü-vōn') Fr. (Marseille In.)	43·18 N	5·33 E
90	La Piedad Cabadas (lä pyâ-dhädh' kä-bä'dhäs).Mex.	20·20 N	102·04 W
112	Lapland (Reg.) (lăp'lȧnd)....Eur.	68·20 N	22·00 E
101	La Plata (lä plä'tä) Arg. (Buenos Aires In.)	34·54 S	57·57 W
73	La Plata (lȧ plā'tȧ)....Mo.	40·03 N	92·28 W
69	La Plata Pk....Colo.	39·00 N	106·25 W
125	La Pobla de Lillet (lä-pô'blä-dĕ-lēl-yĕ't).Sp.	42·14 N	1·58 E
155	Lapog (lä-pôg') Phil. (Manila In.)	17·44 N	120·28 E
83	La Poile B. (lȧ pwäl')....Can.	47·28 N	58·35 W
80	La Porte (lȧ pōrt')....Ind.	41·35 N	86·45 W
75	Laporte....Ohio (Cleveland In.)	41·19 N	82·05 W
77	La Porte....Tex. (In.)	29·40 N	95·01 W
71	La Porte City....Iowa	42·20 N	92·10 W
119	Lappeenranta (lä'pēn-rän'tä)..Fin.	61·04 N	28·08 E
85	Laprairie (lȧ-prâ-rē') Can. (Montreal In.)	45·24 N	73·30 W
127	Lapseki (läp'sä-kê)....Tur.	40·20 N	26·41 E
130	Laptev Sea (läp'tyĭf)....Sov. Un.	75·39 N	120·00 E
125	La Puebla (lä pwā'blä)....Sp.	39·46 N	3·02 E
124	La Puebla de Montalbán (lä pwā'blä dā mōnt-äl-bän') Sp.	39·54 N	4·21 W
121	Lapusul R. (lä'pōō-shōōl)...Rom.	47·29 N	23·46 E
100	La Quiaca (lä kē-ä'kä)....Arg.	22·15 S	65·44 W
126	L'Aquila (lä'kē-lä)....It.	42·22 N	13·24 E
144	Lar (lär)....Iran	27·31 N	54·12 E
161	Lara....Austl. (Melbourne In.)	38·02 S	144·24 E
164	Larache (lä-räsh')....Mor.	35·15 N	6·09 W
62	Laramie (lăr'ȧ-mĭ)....Wyo.	41·20 N	105·40 W
72	Laramie (R.)....Colo.	40·56 N	105·55 W
125	L'Arba (l'är'bȧ)....Alg.	36·35 N	3·10 E
84	Larchmont (lärch'mŏnt) N. Y. (New York In.)	40·56 N	73·46 W
65	Larch Mtn. (lärch) Ore. (Portland In.)	45·32 N	122·06 W
124	Laredo (lȧ-rā'dhō)....Sp.	43·24 N	3·24 W
76	Laredo....Tex.	27·31 N	99·29 W
122	La Réole (lä rȧ-ōl')....Fr.	44·37 N	0·03 W
165	Largeau (lär-zhō')....Chad	17·45 N	19·26 E
94	Largo, Cayo (kä'yō-lär'gō)..Cuba	21·40 N	81·30 W
70	Larimore (lăr'ĭ-môr)....N. D.	47·53 N	97·38 W
126	Larino (lä-rē'nô)....It.	41·48 N	14·54 E
100	La Rioja (lä rê-ōhä')....Arg.	29·18 S	67·42 W
100	La Rioja (Prov.) (lä-rē-ô'-kä).Arg.	28·45 S	68·00 W
127	Lárisa (lä'rê-sȧ)....Grc.	39·38 N	22·25 E
142	Lārkāna....W. Pak.	27·40 N	68·12 E
139	Larnaca (lär'nȧ-kä) Cyprus (Palestine In.)	34·55 N	33·37 E
139	Larnaca (B.) Cyprus (Palestine In.)	34·55 N	33·51 E
72	Larned (lär'nĕd)....Kans.	38·09 N	99·07 W
124	La Robla (lä rōb'lä)....Sp.	42·48 N	5·36 W
124	La Rochelle (lȧ rô-shĕl')....Fr.	46·10 N	1·09 W
122	La Roche-sur-Yon (lȧ rôsh'sûr-yôN').Fr.	46·39 N	1·27 W
124	La Roda (lä rō'dä)....Sp.	39·13 N	2·08 W
95	La Romona (lä-rä-mô'nä) Dom. Rep.	18·25 N	69·00 W
158	Larrey Pt. (lăr'ê)....Austl.	19·15 S	118·15 E
122	Laruns (lȧ-rǎNs')....Fr.	42·58 N	0·28 W
118	Larvik (lär'vēk)....Nor.	59·06 N	10·03 E
99	La Sabana (lä-sä-bȧ'nä).Ven. (In.)	10·38 N	66·24 W
95	La Sabina (lä-sä-bē'nä) Cuba (Havana In.)	22·10 N	82·07 W
124	La Sagra (Mtn.) (lä sä'grä)...Sp.	37·56 N	2·35 E
69	La Sal (lȧ săl')....Utah	38·10 N	109·20 W
75	La Salle (lȧ săl') Can. (Detroit In.)	42·14 N	83·06 W
85	La Salle....Can. (Winnipeg In.)	49·41 N	97·16 W
80	La Salle....Ill.	41·20 N	89·05 W
72	Las Animas (lȧs ă'nĭ-mȧs)...Colo.	38·03 N	103·16 W
168	Las Anod (läs ăn'ŏd) Som. (Horn of Afr. In.)	8·24 N	47·20 E
87	La Sarre....Can.	48·43 N	79·12 W
95	Lascahobas (läs-kä-ō'bȧs)....Hai.	19·00 N	71·55 W
91	Las Cruces (läs-krōō'-sĕs)...Mex.	16·37 N	93·54 W
69	Las Cruces....N. Mex.	32·20 N	106·50 W
95	La Selle, Massif De (Mts.) (lä sĕl').Hai.	18·25 N	72·05 W
100	La Serena (lä-sĕ-rĕ'nä)....Chile	29·55 S	71·24 W
123	La Seyne-sur-Mer (lä-sân'sür-mĕr').Fr.	43·07 N	5·52 E
101	Las Flores (läs flo'rês) Arg. (Buenos Aires In.)	36·01 S	59·07 W
146	Lashio (lăsh'ê-ō)....Bur.	22·58 N	98·03 E
74	La Sierra (lȧ sĭ-ĕr'ȧ) Calif. (Los Angeles In.)	33·54 N	117·29 W
92	Las Juntas (läs-Kōō'n-täs)...C. R.	10·15 N	85·00 W
168	Las Khoreh (läs Kō'rȧ) Som. (Horn of Afr. In.)	11·13 N	48·19 E
124	Las Maismas (Reg.) (läs-mī's-mȧs).Sp.	37·05 N	6·25 W
124	La Solano (lä-sô-lä-nō)....Sp.	38·56 N	3·13 W
164	Las Palmas (läs päl'mäs).Can. Is.	28·07 N	15·28 W
93	Las Palmas....Pan.	8·08 N	81·30 W
126	La Spezia (lä-spĕ'zyä)....It.	44·07 N	9·48 E
101	Las Piedras (läs-pyĕ'drȧs) Ur. (Buenos Aires In.)	34·42 S	56·08 W
92	Las Pilas (Vol.) (läs-pē'läs)...Nic.	12·32 N	86·43 W
91	Las Rosas (läs rō thäs)....Mex.	16·24 N	92·23 W
125	Las Rozas de Madrid (läs rō'thas dä mä-dhrēdh').Sp. (Madrid In.)	40·29 N	3·53 W
111	Lassee....Aus. (Vienna In.)	48·14 N	16·50 E
66	Lassen Pk. (lăs'ĕn)....Calif.	40·30 N	121·32 W
66	Lassen Volcanic Natl. Park..Calif.	40·43 N	121·35 W
85	L'Assomption (lȧs-sôm-syôN) Can. (Montreal In.)	45·50 N	73·25 W
93	Las Tablas (läs tä'bläs)....Pan.	7·48 N	80·16 W
86	Last Mountain (L.) (lȧst moun'tĭn).Can.	51·07 N	105·50 W
166	Lastoursville (lȧs-tōōr-vēl') Gabon	1·00 S	12·49 E
88	Las Tres Marías (I.) (läs-trĕ's mä-rē'äs).Mex.	21·30 N	106·40 W
88	Las Tres Virgenes, Vol. (vē'r-hĕ-nĕs).Mex.	26·00 N	111·45 W
91	Las Vacas (läs-vȧ'käs)....Mex.	16·24 N	95·48 W
101	Las Vegas (läs-vĕ'gäs) Chile (Santiago In.)	30·50 S	70·59 W
68	Las Vegas (läs vā'gäs)....Nev.	36·12 N	115·10 W
72	Las Vegas....N. Mex.	35·36 N	105·13 W
99	Las Vegas (läs-vĕ'gäs)..Ven. (In.)	10·26 N	64·08 W
90	Las Vigas....Mex.	19·38 N	97·03 W
94	Las Villas (State) (läs-vē'l-läs) Cuba	22·15 N	80·50 W
100	Las Vizcachas, Meseta de (Plat.) (mĕ-sĕ'tä-dĕ-läs-vêz-kä'-chȧs) Arg.	49·35 S	71·00 W
98	Latacunga (lä-tä-kōōŋ'gä)....Ec.	1·02 S	78·33 W
	Latakia, see El Ladhiqiya		
115	Latakia (Reg.) (lä-tä-kē'ä) U. A. R.	35·10 N	35·49 E
122	La Teste-de-Buch (lä-tĕst-dĕ-büsh).Fr.	44·38 N	1·11 W
73	Lathrop (lā'thrŭp)....Mo.	39·32 N	94·21 W
	Latium (Reg.), see Lazio		
121	Latoritsa R. (lä-tô'rĭ-tsȧ) Sov. Un.	48·27 N	22·30 E
85	La Tortue, R. (lä tôr-tü') Can. (Montreal In.)	45·12 N	73·32 W
65	Latourell (lȧ-tou'rĕl) Ore. (Portland In.)	45·32 N	122·13 W
122	La Tremblade (lä-trĕN-bläd')..Fr.	45·45 N	1·12 W
81	Latrobe (lȧ-trōb')....Pa.	40·25 N	79·15 W
82	La Tuque (lȧ tük')....Can.	47·27 N	72·49 W
143	Latūr (lä-tōōr')....India	18·20 N	76·35 E
130	Latvian (S. S. R.)....Sov. Un.	57·28 N	24·29 E
160	Launceston (lôn'sĕs-tŭn)....Austl.	41·35 S	147·22 E
116	Launceston (lôrn'stŏn)....Eng.	50·38 N	4·26 W
100	La Unión (lä-ōō-nyô'n)....Chile	40·15 S	73·04 W
90	La Unión (lä ōōn-nyōn')....Mex.	17·59 N	101·48 W
92	La Unión....Sal.	13·18 N	87·51 W
125	La Unión....Sp.	37·38 N	0·50 W
157	Laupahoehoe (lä'ōō-pä-hō'ē-hō-ē) Hawaii (In.)	19·58 N	155·13 W
159	Laura (lôrȧ)....Austl.	15·40 S	144·45 E
128	Laura (lou'rȧ)....Sov. Un.	57·36 N	27·29 E
81	Laurel (lô'rĕl)....Del.	38·30 N	75·40 W
84	Laurel....Md. (Baltimore In.)	39·06 N	76·51 W
78	Laurel....Miss.	31·42 N	89·07 W
67	Laurel....Mont.	45·41 N	108·45 W
65	Laurel....Wash. (Vancouver In.)	48·52 N	122·29 W
65	Laurelwood (lô'rĕl-wōōd) Ore. (Portland In.)	45·25 N	123·05 W
79	Laurens (lô'rĕnz)....S. C.	34·29 N	82·03 W
49	Laurentian Highlands (Reg.) (lô'rĕn-tĭ-ȧn).Can.	49·00 N	74·50 W
82	Laurentides Park (lô'rĕn-tīdz) Can.	47·53 N	71·26 W
126	Lauria (lou'rē-ä)....It.	40·03 N	15·02 E
79	Laurinburg (lô'rĭn-bûrg)....N. C.	34·45 N	79·27 W
71	Laurium (lô'rĭ-ŭm)....Mich.	47·13 N	88·28 W
154	Laurot Pulau-Pulau Is....Indon.	4·44 S	115·43 E
120	Lausanne (lō-zȧn')....Switz.	46·32 N	6·35 E
154	Laut (I.)....Indon.	3·39 S	116·07 E
100	Lautaro (lou-tä'rô)....Chile	38·40 S	72·24 W
85	Lauzon (lō-zōN') Can. (Quebec In.)	46·50 N	71·10 W
66	Lava Beds Natl. Mon. (lä'vȧ bĕds).Calif.	41·38 N	121·44 W
77	Lavaca R. (lȧ-văk'ȧ)....Tex.	29·05 N	96·50 W
67	Lava Hot Springs....Idaho	42·37 N	111·58 W
122	Laval (lȧ-väl')....Fr.	48·05 N	0·47 W
122	Lavaur (lȧ-vōr')....Fr.	43·41 N	1·48 E
122	Lavaveix-les-Mines (lȧ-vȧ-vĕ'lā-mēn').Fr.	46·05 N	2·05 E
95	La Vega (lä-vĕ'-gä)....Dom. Rep.	19·15 N	70·35 W
159	Lavella (I.)....Sol. Is.	7·50 S	155·45 E
126	Lavello (lä-vĕl'lô)....It.	41·05 N	15·50 E
74	La Verne (lȧ vûrn') Calif. (Los Angeles In.)	34·06 N	117·46 W
158	Laverton (lā'vēr-tŭn)....Austl.	28·45 S	122·30 E
99	La Victoria (lä vēk-tō'rē-ä) Ven. (In.)	10·14 N	67·20 W
78	Lavonia (lȧ-vō'nĭ-ȧ)....Ga.	34·26 N	83·05 W
77	Lavon Res....Tex.	33·06 N	96·20 W
101	Lavras (lä'vräzh) Braz. (Rio de Janeiro In.)	21·15 S	44·59 W
127	Lávrion (läv'rĭ-ŏn)....Grc.	37·44 N	24·05 E
74	Lawndale (lôn'dāl) Calif. (Los Angeles In.)	33·54 N	118·22 W
75	Lawrence (lô'rĕns) Ind. (Indianapolis In.)	39·59 N	86·01 W
73	Lawrence....Kans.	38·57 N	95·13 W
83	Lawrence....Mass. (Boston In.)	42·42 N	71·09 W
75	Lawrence....Pa. (Pittsburgh In.)	40·18 N	80·07 W
65	Lawrence..Wash. (Vancouver In.)	48·52 N	122·18 W
75	Lawrenceburg (lô'rĕns-bûrg) Ind. (Cincinnati In.)	39·06 N	84·47 W
80	Lawrenceburg....Ky.	38·00 N	85·00 W
78	Lawrenceburg....Tenn.	35·13 N	87·20 W
78	Lawrenceville (lô-rĕns-vĭl)....Ga.	33·56 N	83·57 W
80	Lawrenceville....Ill.	38·45 N	87·45 W
84	Lawrenceville N. J. (New York In.)	40·17 N	74·44 W
79	Lawrenceville....Va.	36·43 N	77·52 W
81	Lawsonia (lô-sō'nĭ-ȧ)....Md.	38·00 N	75·50 W
72	Lawton (lô'tŭn)....Okla.	34·36 N	98·25 W
139	Layang Layang (lä-yäng' lä-yäng').Mala. (Singapore In.)	1·49 N	103·28 E
74	Layton (lā'tŭn) Utah (Salt Lake City In.)	41·04 N	111·58 W
119	Lazdijai (läzh'dē-yī')....Sov. Un.	54·12 N	23·35 E
126	Lazio (Latium) (Reg.) (lä'zyô) (lā't-zēōōm).It.	42·05 N	12·25 E
70	Lead (lēd)....S. D.	44·22 N	103·47 W
72	Leadville (lĕd'vĭl)....Colo.	39·14 N	106·18 W
87	Leaf (R.) (lēf)....Can.	59·12 N	72·50 W
78	Leaf (R.)....Miss.	31·43 N	89·20 W
77	League City (lēg)....Tex. (In.)	29·31 N	95·05 W
80	Leamington (lĕm'ĭng-tŭn)....Can.	42·05 N	82·35 W
116	Leamington (lĕ'mĭng-tŭn)....Eng.	52·17 N	1·25 W
85	Leaside (lē'sīd) Can. (Toronto In.)	43·42 N	79·22 W
110	Leatherhead (lĕdh'ĕr-hĕd') Eng. (London In.)	51·17 N	0·20 W
74	Leavenworth (lĕv'ĕn-wûrth) Kans. (Kansas City In.)	39·19 N	94·54 W
66	Leavenworth....Wash.	47·35 N	120·39 W
74	Leawood (lē'wōōd) Mo. (Kansas City In.)	38·58 N	94·37 W
121	Leba (lā'bä)....Pol.	54·45 N	17·34 E
139	Lebam R....Mala. (Singapore In.)	1·35 N	104·09 E
74	Lebanon (lĕb'ȧ-nŭn) Ill. (St. Louis In.)	38·36 N	89·49 W
80	Lebanon....Ind.	40·00 N	86·30 W
78	Lebanon....Ky.	37·32 N	85·15 W
73	Lebanon....Mo.	37·40 N	92·43 W
81	Lebanon....N. H.	43·40 N	72·15 W
80	Lebanon....Ohio	39·25 N	84·10 W
66	Lebanon....Ore.	44·31 N	122·53 W
81	Lebanon....Pa.	40·20 N	76·20 W
78	Lebanon....Tenn.	36·10 N	86·16 W
138	Lebanon....Asia	34·00 N	35·00 E
115	Lebanon Mts....Leb.	33·30 N	35·32 E
129	Lebedin (lyĕ'bĕ-dēn)....Sov. Un.	48·56 N	31·35 E
129	Lebedin....Sov. Un.	50·34 N	34·27 E
128	Lebedyan' (lyĕ'bĕ-dyän') Sov. Un.	53·03 N	39·08 E
122	Le Blanc (lĕ-bläN')....Fr.	46·38 N	0·59 E
95	Le Borgne (lē bōrn'y')....Hai.	19·50 N	72·30 W
121	Lebork (lăN-bōōrk')....Pol.	54·33 N	17·46 E
122	Le Boucau (lĕ-bōō-Kō')....Fr.	43·33 N	1·28 W
122	Le Bouscat (lē bōōs-kȧ)....Fr.	44·53 N	0·38 W
124	Lebrija (lā-brē'hä)....Sp.	36·55 N	6·06 W
100	Lebú (lĕ-bōō')....Chile	37·35 S	73·37 W
127	Lecce (lĕt'chā)....It.	40·22 N	18·11 E
126	Lecco (lĕk'kō)....It.	45·52 N	9·28 E
123	Le Châtelet-en-Brie (lĕ-shä-tĕ-lā' ĕN-brē').Fr. (Paris In.)	48·29 N	2·50 E
94	Leche, Laguna de (L.) (lä-gōō'nä-dĕ-lĕ'chĕ).Cuba	22·10 N	78·30 W
76	Leche, Laguna de la (L.)....Mex.	27·16 N	102·45 W
123	Lechenich (lĕ'Kĕ-nĕK) Ger. (Ruhr In.)	50·47 N	6·46 E
120	Lech R. (lĕk)....Ger.	47·41 N	10·52 E
77	Lecompte....La.	31·06 N	92·25 W
122	Le Coteau (lē kō-tō')....Fr.	46·01 N	4·06 E
122	Le Creusot (lĕkrû-zō')....Fr.	46·48 N	4·23 E
122	Lectoure (lĕK-tōōr)....Fr.	43·56 N	0·38 E
124	Ledesma (lā-dĕs'mä)....Sp.	41·05 N	5·59 W
85	Leduc (lĕ-dōōk') Can. (Edmonton In.)	53·16 N	113·34 W
71	Leech (L.) (lēch)....Minn.	47·06 N	94·16 W
84	Leeds (lēdz) Ala. (Birmingham In.)	33·33 N	86·33 W
110	Leeds....Eng.	53·48 N	1·33 W
70	Leeds....N. D.	48·18 N	99·24 W
110	Leeds and Liverpool Can. (lĭv'ēr-pōōl).Eng.	53·36 N	2·38 W
111	Leegebruch (lĕh'gĕn-brōōK) Ger. (Berlin In.)	52·43 N	13·12 E
110	Leek (lēk)....Eng.	53·06 N	2·01 W
120	Leer (lār)....Ger.	53·14 N	7·27 E
116	Lee R. (lē)....Ire.	51·52 N	8·30 W
79	Leesburg (lēz'bûrg)....Fla.	28·49 N	81·53 W
81	Leesburg....Va.	39·10 N	77·30 W
69	Lees Ferry....Ariz.	36·55 N	111·45 W
74	Lees Summit Mo. (Kansas City In.)	38·55 N	94·23 W
95	Lee Stocking (I.)....Ba. Is.	23·45 N	76·05 W
77	Leesville (lēz'vĭl)....La.	31·09 N	93·17 W
80	Leetonia (lē-tō'nĭ-ȧ)....Ohio	40·50 N	80·45 W
117	Leeuwarden (lā'wär-dĕn)...Neth.	52·12 N	5·50 E
158	Leeuwin, C. (lōō'wĭn)....Austl.	34·15 S	114·30 E
89	Leeward Is. (lē'wērd)....N. A.	12·25 N	62·15 W
93	Le Francois Mart. (Le. & Wind. Is. In.)	14·37 N	60·55 W
158	Lefroy (L.) (lē-froi')....Austl.	31·30 S	122·00 E
125	Leganés (lā-gä'nās) Sp. (Madrid In.)	40·20 N	3·46 W
155	Legaspi (lā-gäs'pē) Phil. (Manila In.)	13·09 N	123·44 E
160	Legge Pk. (lĕg)....Austl.	41·33 S	148·10 E
	Leghorn, see Livorno		
126	Legnano (lā-nyä'nō)....It.	45·35 N	8·53 E

ng-sing; ŋ-baŋk; N-nasalized n; nŏd; cŏmmit; ōld; ôbey; ôrder; fōōd; fŏŏt; ou-out; s-soft; sh-dish; th-thin; pūre; ûnite; ûrn; stŭd; circŭs; ü-as "y" in study; '-indeterminate vowel.

Page Name Pronunciation Region Lat. °′ Long. °′

120 Legnica (lĕk-nĭt′sȧ) . . . . . Pol. 51·13 N 16·10 E
142 Leh (lā) . . . . . India 34·10 N 77·40 E
122 Le Havre (lē àv′r′) . . . . . Fr. 49·31 N 0·07 E
69 Lehi (lē′hī) . . . . . Utah 40·25 N 111·55 W
69 Lehman Caves Natl. Mon. (lē′măn) . Nev. 38·54 N 114·08 W
111 Lehnin (lĕh′nēn) . Ger. (Berlin In.) 52·19 N 12·45 E
110 Leicester (lĕs′tēr) . . . . . Eng. 52·37 N 1·08 W
110 Leicester (Co.) . . . . . Eng. 52·40 N 1·12 W
158 Leichhardt, (R.) (līk′härt) . . Austl. 18·30 S 139·45 E
111 Leiden (lī′dĕn) Neth. (Amsterdam In.) 52·09 N 4·29 E
160 Leigh Creek (lē krēk) . . . . . Austl. 30·33 S 138·30 E
118 Leikanger (lī′kăn̤′gĕr) . . . . . Nor. 61·11 N 6·51 E
111 Leimuiden. Neth. (Amsterdam In.) 52·13 N 4·40 E
120 Leine R. (lī′nĕ) . . . . . Ger. 51·58 N 9·56 E
116 Leinster (lĕn-stēr) . . . . . Ire. 52·45 N 7·19 W
80 Leipsic (līp′sĭk) . . . . . Ohio 41·05 N 84·00 W
120 Leipzig (līp′tsĭk) . . . . . Ger. 51·20 N 12·24 E
124 Leiria (lā-rē′ä) . . . . . Port. 39·45 N 8·50 W
78 Leitchfield (lēch′fēld) . . . . . Ky. 37·28 N 86·20 W
111 Leitha (R.) . . . . . Aus. (Vienna In.) 48·04 N 16·57 E
85 Leitrim . . . . . Can. (Ottawa In.) 45·20 N 75·36 W
Leixoes, see Matozinhos
117 Lek (R.) (lĕk) . . . . . Neth. 51·59 N 5·30 E
113 Lekef (lĕkĕf′) . . . . . Tun. 36·14 N 8·42 E
118 Leksand (lĕk′sänd) . . . . . Swe. 60·45 N 14·56 E
65 Leland (lē′lănd) Wash. (Seattle In.) 47·54 N 122·53 W
120 Le Locle (lē lô′kl′) . . . . . Switz. 47·03 N 6·43 E
100 Le Maire, Estrecho de (Str.) (ĕs-trĕ′chô-dĕ-lĕ-mī′rĕ) . Arg. 55·15 S 65·30 W
122 Le Mans (lē mäN′) . . . . . Fr. 48·01 N 0·12 E
93 Le Marin Mart. (Le. & Wind. Is. In.) 14·28 N 60·55 W
70 Le Mars (lē märz′) . . . . . Iowa 42·46 N 96·09 W
155 Lemery (lā-mā-rē′) Phil. (Manila In.) 13·51 N 120·55 E
67 Lemhi Ra. (Mts.) (lĕm′hī) . . Idaho 44·35 N 113·33 W
67 Lemhi R. . . . . . Idaho 44·40 N 113·27 W
70 Lemmon (lĕm′ŭn) . . . . . S. D. 45·55 N 102·10 W
95 Le Môle (lē mōl′) . . . . . Hai. 19·50 N 73·20 W
68 Lemon Grove (lĕm′ŭn-grōv) Calif. (San Diego In.) 32·44 N 117·02 W
75 Lemont (lē′-mŏnt) Ill. (Chicago In.) 41·40 N 87·59 W
93 Le Moule (lē mōōl′) Grande Terre (Le. & Wind. Is. In.) 16·19 N 61·22 W
92 Lempa R. (lĕm′pä) . . . . . Sal. 13·20 N 88·46 W
118 Lemvig (lĕm′vĕgh) . . . . . Den. 56·33 N 8·16 E
118 Lena (lī′nä) . . . . . Swe. 60·01 N 17·40 E
135 Lena (R.) . . . . . Sov. Un. 68·39 N 124·15 E
100 Lençóes Paulista (lĕN-sôNs′ pou-lēs′tȧ) . Braz. 22·30 S 48·45 W
99 Lençóis (lĕn-sóis) . . . . . Braz. 12·38 S 41·28 W
74 Lenexa (lē-nĕx′ă) Mo. (Kansas City In.) 38·58 N 94·44 W
103 Lenger (lyĭn′gyĕr) . . . . . Sov. Un. 41·38 N 70·00 E
139 Lenik (R.) . . Mala. (Singapore In.) 1·59 N 102·51 E
134 Leninabad (lĕ-nyē-nȧ bät′) Sov. Un. 40·15 N 69·49 E
133 Leninakan (lĕ-nyē-nȧ-kän′) Sov. Un. 40·40 N 43·50 E
136 Leningrad (lyĕ-nēn-grät′) Sov. Un. (Leningrad In.) 59·57 N 30 20 E
128 Leningrad (Oblast) . . . . . Sov. Un. 59·15 N 30·30 E
129 Leningradskaya (lyĕ-nĭn-gräd′skȧ-yȧ) . Sov. Un. 46·19 N 39·23 E
136 Lenino (lyĕ′nĭ-nô) Sov. Un. (Moscow In.) 55·37 N 47·41 E
134 Leninogorsk (lyĕ-nĭn ŭ gôrsk′) Sov. Un. 50·29 N 83·25 E
133 Leninsk (lyĕ-nēnsk′) . . . . Sov. Un. 48·40 N 45·10 E
134 Leninsk-Kuznetskiy (lyĕ-nēnsk′ kōōz-nyĕt′skĭ-ē) . Sov. Un. 54·28 N 86·48 E
133 Lenkoran′ (lĕn-kô-rän′) . . Sov. Un. 38·52 N 48·58 E
70 Lennox (lĕn′ŭks) . . . . . S. D. 43·22 N 96·53 W
79 Lenoir (lē-nōr′) . . . . . N. C. 35·54 N 81·35 W
78 Lenoir City . . . . . Tenn. 35·47 N 84·16 W
71 Lenox . . . . . Iowa 40·51 N 94·29 W
120 Leoben (lȧ-ō′bĕn) . . . . . Aus. 47·22 N 15·09 E
95 Léogane (lā-ô-gan′) . . . . . Hai. 18·30 N 72·35 W
70 Leola (lē-ō′lȧ) . . . . . S. D. 45·43 N 99·55 W
83 Leominster (lĕm′ĭn-stĕr) Mass. (Boston In.) 42·32 N 71·45 W
71 Leon (lē′ŏn) . . . . . Iowa 40·43 N 93·44 W
90 León (lȧ-ōn′) . . . . . Mex. 21·08 N 101·41 W
92 León (lĕ-ô′n) . . . . . Nic. 12·28 N 86·53 W
124 León (lĕ-ô′n) . . . . . Sp. 42·38 N 5·33 W
124 Leon (Reg.) (lĕ-ô′n) . . . . . Sp. 41·18 N 5·50 W
126 Leonforte (lā-ôn-fôr′tä) . . . . . It. 37·40 N 14·27 E
76 Leon R. (lē′ŏn) . . . . . Tex. 31·54 N 98·20 W
101 Leopoldina (lā-ô-pôl-dē′nä) Braz. (Rio de Janeiro In.) 21·32 S 42·38 W
111 Leopoldsburg . . Bel. (Brussels In.) 51·07 N 5·18 E
111 Leopoldsdorf im Marchfelde (lā′ô-pôlts-dôrf′) Aus. (Vienna In.) 48·14 N 16·42 E
166 Leopold II (L.) (lā′ô-pōld) . Con. L. 2·16 S 19·00 E
166 Léopoldville (lā-ô-pôld-vēl′) Con. L. 4·28 S 15·16 E
129 Leovo (lȧ-ō′vô) . . . . . Sov. Un. 46·30 N 28·16 E
124 Lepe (lā′pā) . . . . . Sp. 37·15 N 7·12 W
128 Lepel′ (lyĕ-pĕl′) . . . . . Sov. Un. 54·52 N 28·41 E
85 L'Epiphanie (lā-pē-fȧ-nē′) Can. (Montreal In.) 45·51 N 73·29 W
123 Le Plessis-Belleville (lĕ-plĕ-sē′ bĕl-vēl′) . Fr. (Paris In.) 49·05 N 2·46 E
120 Lepontine Alpi (Mts.) (lē-pŏn′tĭn) Switz. 46·28 N 8·38 E
82 Lepreau (lĕ-prō′) . . . . . Can. 45·10 N 66·28 W
134 Lepsinsk . . . . . Sov. Un. 45·32 N 80·47 E
122 Le Puy-en-Velay (lē pwē′) . . . . . Fr. 45·02 N 3·54 E
126 Lercara (lĕr-kä′rä) . . . . . It. 36·47 N 13·36 E
76 Lerdo (lĕr′dō) . . . . . Mex. 25·31 N 103·30 W

165 Léré (lā-rā′) . . . . . Chad 9·42 N 14·14 E
167 Leribe . . . . . Bas. (Natal In.) 28·53 S 28·02 E
125 Lérida (lā′rē-dhä) . . . . . Sp. 41·38 N 0·37 E
91 Lerma (lĕr′mä) . . . . . Mex. 19·49 N 90·34 W
91 Lerma . . . . Mex. (Mexico City In.) 19·17 N 99·30 W
124 Lerma (lĕ′r-mä) . . . . . Sp. 42·03 N 3·45 W
90 Lerma (R.) . . . . . Mex. 20·14 N 101·50 W
81 Le Roy (lē roi′) . . . . . N. Y. 43·00 N 78·00 W
116 Lerwick (lĕr′ĭk) (lûr′wĭk) . . . . Scot. 60·08 N 1·27 W
84 Lery, L. (lĕ′rē) La. (New Orleans In.) 29·48 N 89·45 W
123 Les Andelys (lā-zäN-dē-lē′) Fr. (Paris In.) 49·15 N 1·25 E
95 Les Cayes . . . . . Hai. 18·15 N 73·45 W
85 Les Cèdres (lā-sĕdr′) Can. (Montreal In.) 45·18 N 74·03 W
127 Lesh (Alessio) (lĕshĕ) (ä-lā′sē-ō) Alb. 41·47 N 19·40 E
126 Lésina, Lago di (L.) (lä′gō dē lā′zē-nä) . It. 41·48 N 15·12 E
127 Leskovac (lĕs′kô-vȧts) . . . . . Yugo. 43·00 N 21·58 E
73 Leslie (lĕz′lĭ) . . . . . Ark. 35·49 N 92·32 W
168 Leslie S. Afr. (Johannesburg & Pretoria In.) 26·23 S 28·57 E
132 Lesnoy (lĕs′noi) . . . . . Sov. Un. 66·45 N 34·45 E
152 Lesogorsk (lyĕs′ô-gôrsk) . Sov. Un. 49·28 N 141·59 E
152 Lesozavodsk (lyĕ-sô-zȧ-vôdsk′) Sov. Un. 45·21 N 133·19 E
122 Lesparre (lĕ-spär) . . . . . Fr. 45·18 N 0·57 W
122 Les-Pennes-Mirabeau (lā-pĕn′ mĭ-rä-bō′) . Fr. (Marseille In.) 43·25 N 5·19 E
122 Les Sables-d'Olonne (lā sȧ′bl′dô-lŭn′) . Fr. 46·30 N 1·47 W
93 Les Saintes Is. (lā-săNt′) Guad. (Le. & Wind. Is. In.) 15·50 N 61·40 W
Lesser Khingan Mts. see Hsiaohsinganling Shanmo
86 Lesser Slave L. (lĕs′ēr slāv) . . Can. 55·10 N 116·18 W
122 L'Estaque (lĕs-tȧl) Fr. (Marseille In.) 43·22 N 5·20 E
123 Les Thilliers-en-Vexin (lā-tē-yā′ ĕN-vĕ-săN′) . Fr. (Paris In.) 49·19 N 1·36 E
71 Le Sueur (lē sōōr′) . . . . . Minn. 44·27 N 93·53 W
127 Lésvos (I.) . . . . . Grc. 39·15 N 25·40 E
120 Leszno (lĕsh′nô) . . . . . Pol. 51·51 N 16·35 E
122 Le Teil (lē tā′y′) . . . . . Fr. 44·34 N 4·39 E
86 Lethbridge (lĕth′brĭj) . . . . . Can. 49·40 N 112·39 W
166 Letiahau (R.) . . . . . Bech. 21·16 S 22·17 E
129 Letichev (lyĕ-tē-chĕf′) . . . Sov. Un. 49·22 N 27·29 E
98 Leticia (lĕ-tē′syȧ) . . . . . Col. 4·04 S 69·57 W
123 Letmathe (lĕt′mät-hĕ) Ger. (Ruhr In.) 51·22 N 7·37 E
122 Le Tréport (lē-trā-pôr′) . . . . . Fr. 50·03 N 1·21 E
154 Leuser, Gulung (Mtn.) . . . . . Indon. 3·36 N 97·17 E
111 Leuven . . . . . Bel. (Brussels In.) 50·53 N 4·42 E
127 Levádhia . . . . . Grc. 38·25 N 22·51 E
123 Levallois-Perret (lē-vȧl-wä′pĕ-rĕ′) Fr. (Paris In.) 48·53 N 2·17 E
112 Levanger (lĕ-väng′ĕr) . . . . . Nor. 63·42 N 11·01 E
126 Levanna (Mtn.) (lā-vä′nä) . Fr.-It. 45·25 N 7·14 E
158 Leveque, C. (lē-vĕk′) . . . . . Austl. 16·25 S 123·08 E
123 Leverkusen (lĕ′fĕr-kōō-zĕn) Ger. (Ruhr In.) 51·01 N 6·59 E
166 Leverville (lē-vā-vēl′) . . . . . Con. L. 5·13 S 18·43 E
121 Levice (lā′vĕt-sĕ) . . . . . Czech. 48·13 N 18·37 E
126 Levico (lā′vē-kō) . . . . . It. 46·02 N 11·20 E
122 Le Vigan (lē vē-găN′) . . . . . Fr. 43·59 N 3·36 E
85 Levis (lā-vē′) (lē′vĭs) Can. (Quebec In.) 46·48 N 71·11 W
84 Levittown (lĕ′vĭt-toun) Pa. (Philadelphia In.) 40·08 N 74·50 W
127 Levkás (lyĕfkäs′) . . . . . Grc. 38·49 N 20·43 E
127 Levkás (I.) . . . . . Grc. 38·42 N 20·22 E
121 Levoča (lā′vô-chä) . . . . . Czech. 49·03 N 20·38 E
79 Levy (L.) (lē′vĭ) . . . . . Fla. 29·31 N 82·23 W
81 Lewes (lōō′ĭs) . . . . . Del. 38·45 N 75·10 W
116 Lewes . . . . . Eng. 50·51 N 0·01 E
116 Lewis (I.) (lōō′ĭs) . . . . . Scot. 58·05 N 6·07 W
65 Lewis (R.) East Fk. Wash. (Portland In.) 45·52 N 122·40 E
78 Lewisburg (lū′ĭs-bûrg) . . . . . Tenn. 35·27 N 86·47 W
80 Lewisburg (lū′ĭs-bûrg) . . . . . W. Va. 37·50 N 80·20 W
83 Lewis Hills . . . . . Can. 48·49 N 58·28 W
83 Lewisporte (lū′ĭs-pôrt) . . . . . Can. 49·15 N 55·06 W
67 Lewis Ra. (lū′ĭs) . . . . . Mont. 48·05 N 113·06 W
66 Lewis R. . . . . . Wash. 46·05 N 122·09 W
66 Lewiston (lū′ĭs-tŭn) . . . . . Idaho 46·24 N 116·59 W
82 Lewiston . . . . . Maine 44·05 N 70·14 W
75 Lewiston . . . . . N. Y. (Buffalo In.) 43·11 N 79·02 W
67 Lewiston . . . . . Utah 41·58 N 111·51 W
73 Lewistown (lū′ĭs-toun) . . . . . Ill. 40·23 N 90·06 W
67 Lewistown . . . . . Mont. 47·05 N 109·25 W
81 Lewistown . . . . . Pa. 40·35 N 77·30 W
80 Lexington (lĕk′sĭng-tŭn) . . . . . Ky. 38·05 N 84·30 W
83 Lexington . . . . . Mass. (Boston In.) 42·27 N 71·14 W
78 Lexington . . . . . Miss. 33·08 N 90·02 W
73 Lexington . . . . . Mo. 39·11 N 93·52 W
72 Lexington . . . . . Nebr. 40·46 N 99·44 W
79 Lexington . . . . . N. C. 35·47 N 80·15 W
78 Lexington . . . . . Tenn. 35·37 N 88·24 W
81 Lexington . . . . . Va. 37·45 N 79·20 W
155 Leyte (I.) (lā′tā) . . . . . Phil. 10·35 N 125·35 E
121 Lezajsk (lĕ′zhä-ĭsk) . . . . . Pol. 50·14 N 22·25 E
128 Lezha (R.) (lĕ-zhä′) . . . . Sov. Un. 58·59 N 40·27 E
122 Lézignan (lā-zē-nyăN′) . . . . . Fr. 43·13 N 2·48 E
129 L'gov (lgôf) . . . . . Sov. Un. 51·42 N 35·15 E
142 Lhasa (läs′ä) . . . . . China 29·41 N 91·12 E
148 Lhsien (yĕ′sĭăN) . . . . . China 37·09 N 119·57 E
150 Lianghsiang (lyäng′syän′) China (Peking In.) 39·43 N 116·08 E
136 Lianozovo (lĭ-á-nô′zô-vô) Sov. Un. (Moscow In.) 55·54 N 37·36 E
148 Liaoch'eng (lĭou′chĕng) . . . . China 36·27 N 115·56 E
150 Liao Ho (R.) (lyä′ō hō′) . . . . China 41·40 N 122·40 E
147 Liaoning (Prov.) . . . . . China 41·31 N 122·11 E

148 Liaotung Pantao (Pen.) (lĭou′dōōng băN′dou) . China 39·45 N 122·22 E
150 Liaotung Wan (B.) . . . . . China 40·25 N 121·15 E
150 Liaoyang (lyä′ō-yäng′) . . . . . China 41·18 N 123·10 E
147 Liaoyüan (lyä′ō-yü-än′) . . . . China 43·37 N 123·30 E
86 Liard (R.) (lē-är′) . . . . . Can. 59·43 N 126·42 W
98 Libano (lē′-bä-nô) . . . . . Col. (In.) 4·55 N 75·05 W
124 Libar, Sierra de (Mts.) (sē-ĕ′r-rä-dĕ-lē-bär) . Sp. 39·42 N 5·28 W
66 Libby (lĭb′ē) . . . . . Mont. 48·27 N 115·35 W
165 Libenge (lē-bĕn̤′gä) . . . . . Con. L. 3·39 N 18·40 E
72 Liberal (lĭb′ēr-ăl) . . . . . Kans. 37·01 N 100·56 W
120 Liberec (lē′bĕr-ĕts) . . . . . Czech. 15·47 N 15·06 E
163 Liberia (lī-bē′rĭ-ȧ) . . . . . Afr. 6·30 N 9·55 W
92 Liberia . . . . . C. R. 10·38 N 85·28 W
99 Libertad de Orituco (lē-bĕr-tä′d-dĕ-ŏ-rē-tōō′kô) . Ven. (In.) 9·32 N 66·24 W
80 Liberty (lĭb′ēr-tĭ) . . . . . Ind. 39·35 N 84·55 W
74 Liberty . . . . Mo. (Kansas City In.) 39·15 N 94·25 W
79 Liberty . . . . . S. C. 34·47 N 82·41 W
77 Liberty . . . . . Tex. 30·03 N 94·46 W
74 Liberty. Utah (Salt Lake City In.) 41·20 N 111·52 W
65 Liberty B. . . . . Wash. (Seattle In.) 47·43 N 122·41 W
75 Libertyville (lĭb′ēr-tĭ-vĭl) Ill. (Chicago In.) 42·17 N 87·57 W
155 Libmanan (lĭb-mä′nän) Phil. (Manila In.) 13·42 N 123·04 E
167 Libode (lĭ-bō′dĕ) S. Afr. (Natal In.) 31·33 S 29·03 E
95 Libón, R. . . . . . Hai. 19·30 N 71·45 W
122 Libourne (lē-bōōrn′) . . . . . Fr. 44·55 N 0·12 W
91 Libres (lē′brās) . . . . . Mex. 19·26 N 97·41 W
164 Libreville (lē-br′vēl′) . . . . . Gabon 0·29 N 9·26 E
84 Liburn (lĭb′ûrn) Ga. (Atlanta In.) 33·53 N 84·09 W
163 Libya (lĭb′ē-ä) . . . . . Afr. 27·38 N 15·00 E
165 Libyan Des. (lĭb′ē-ăn) . . . . . Libya 28·23 N 23·34 E
115 Libyan Plat. . . . . . U. A. R. 30·58 N 26·20 E
100 Licancábur, Cerro (Mtn.) (sĕ′r-rô-lē-kän-kä′bōōr) . Chile 22·45 S 67·45 W
101 Licanten (lē-kän-tĕ′n) Chile (Santiago In.) 34·58 S 72·00 W
110 Lichfield (lĭch′fēld) . . . . . Eng. 52·41 N 1·49 W
146 Lichiang . . . . . China 27·06 N 100·08 E
148 Liching (lē′jĭn) . . . . . China 37·24 N 118·12 E
168 Lichtenburg (lĭk′tĕn-bĕrgh) S. Afr. (Johannesburg & Pretoria In.) 26·09 S 26·10 E
75 Lick Cr. (lĭk) Ind. (Indianapolis In.) 39·43 N 86·06 W
80 Licking (R.) (lĭk′ĭng) . . . . . Ky. 38·30 N 84·10 W
126 Licosa, Pt. (lē-kô′sä) . . . . . It. 40·17 N 14·40 E
121 Lida (lē′dä) . . . . . Sov. Un. 53·53 N 25·19 E
70 Lidgerwood (lĭj′ĕr-wood) . . . . N. D. 46·04 N 97·10 W
118 Lidköping (lĕt′chû-pĭng) . . . . . Swe. 58·31 N 13·06 E
125 Lido di Roma (Ostia Lido) (lē′dô-dē-rô′mä) (ô′s-tyä-lē-dô) It. (Rome In.) 41·19 N 12·17 E
121 Lidzbark (lĭts′bärk) . . . . . Pol. 54·07 N 20·36 E
168 Liebenbergs R. . . . . . S. Afr. (Johannesburg & Pretoria In.) 27·35 S 28·25 E
111 Liebenwalde (lē′bĕn-väl-dĕ) Ger. (Berlin In.) 52·52 N 13·24 E
151 Liechou Pan-Tao (Pen.) . . . . China 20·40 N 109·25 E
120 Liechtenstein (lĕk′tĕn-shtīn) . Eur. 47·14 N 9·15 E
117 Liége (lē-āzh′) . . . . . Bel. 50·40 N 5·30 E
151 Lienchiang . . . . . China 21·38 N 110·15 E
148 Lienshui (lĭăN′sōōā) . . . . . China 33·46 N 119·15 E
147 Lienyün . . . . . China 33·10 N 120·01 E
148 Lienyun (lĭăN′yüN) . . . . . China 34·43 N 119·27 E
120 Lienz (lē-ĕnts′) . . . . . Aus. 46·49 N 12·45 E
119 Liepāja (le′pä-yä′) . . . . . Sov. Un. 56·31 N 20·59 E
111 Lier . . . . . Bel. (Brussels In.) 5·08 N 4·34 E
111 Liesing (lē′sĭng) . Aus. (Vienna In.) 48·09 N 16·17 E
120 Liestal (lēs′täl) . . . . . Switz. 47·28 N 7·44 E
81 Lievre, Rivière du (R.) . . . . . Can. 45·00 N 75·25 W
116 Liffey R. (lĭf′ĭ) . . . . . Ire. 53·21 N 6·35 W
159 Lifou, (I.) . . . . . N. Cal. Is. 21·15 S 167·32 E
155 Ligao (lē-gä′ô) . . Phil. (Manila In.) 13·14 N 123·33 E
160 Lightning Ridge . . . . . Austl. 29·23 S 147·50 E
167 Ligonha (R.) (lē-gō′nyȧ) . . . . . Moz. 16·14 S 39·00 E
80 Ligonier (lĭg-ô-nēr′) . . . . . Ind. 41·30 N 85·35 W
136 Ligovo (lē′gô-vô) Sov. Un. (Leningrad In.) 59·51 N 30·13 E
126 Liguria (Reg.) (lē-gōō-rē-ä) . . . . It. 44·24 N 8·27 E
126 Ligurian Sea (lĭ-gū′rĭ-ăn) . . . . Eur. 43·42 N 8·32 E
159 Lihou Rfs. (lē-hōō′) . . . . . Austl. 17·23 S 152·43 E
151 Lihsien (lē′hsyĕn′) . . . . . China 29·42 N 111·40 E
148 Lihsien . . . . . China 38·30 N 115·38 E
148 Lihuang (lē′hōōäNg) . . . . . China 31·32 N 115·46 E
157 Lihue (lē-hōō′ā) . . . . . Hawaii (In.) 21·59 N 159·23 W
119 Lihula (lē′hōō-lä) . . . . . Sov. Un. 58·41 N 23·50 E
128 Likhoslavl′ (lyē-kôslav′′l) Sov. Un. 57·07 N 35·27 E
129 Likhovka (lyē-Kôf′kȧ) . . . Sov. Un. 48·52 N 33 57 E
122 Lille (lēl) . . . . . Fr. 50·38 N 3·01 E
118 Lille Baelt (str.) . . . . . Den. 55·09 N 9·53 E
118 Lillehammer (lēl′ĕ-häm′mĕr) . Nor. 61·07 N 10·25 E
118 Lillesand (lēl′ĕ-sän′) . . . . . Nor. 58·16 N 8·19 E
118 Lilleström (lēl′ĕ-strûm) . . . . . Nor. 59·56 N 11·04 E
65 Lilliwaup (lĭl′ĭ-wŏp) Wash. (Seattle In.) 47·28 N 123·07 W
86 Lillooet . . . . . Can. 50·49 N 122·02 W
166 Lilongwe (lē-lô-än) . . . . . Nya. 13·51 S 33·47 E
80 Lima (lī′mȧ) . . . . . Ohio 40·40 N 84·05 W
98 Lima (lē′mä) . . . . . Peru 12·06 S 76·55 W
124 Lima (R.) . . . . . Port. 41·45 N 8·22 W
101 Lima Duarte (dwä′r-tĕ) Braz. (Rio de Janeiro In.) 21·52 S 43·47 W
67 Lima Res. . . . . . Mont. 44·45 N 112·15 W
139 Limassol (lē-mȧ-sōl′) Cyprus (Palestine In.) 34·39 N 33·02 E
100 Limay (lē-mä′ē) (R.) . . . . . Arg. 39·50 S 69·15 W
119 Limbaži (lēm′bä-zĭ) . . . . Sov. Un. 57·32 N 24·44 E
95 Limbé . . . . . Hai. 19·45 N 72·30 W

Page	Name Pronunciation Region	Lat. °′	Long. °′
142	Limboli ... India	22·39 N	71·49 E
120	Limburg (lem-bōōrg') ... Ger.	50·22 N	8·03 E
118	Limedsforsen (lĕ'mĕs-fôrs'ĕn) . Swe.	60·54 N	13·24 E
101	Limeira (lē-mä'rä) Braz. (Rio de Janeiro In.)	22·34 S	47·24 W
118	Limfjorden (Fd.) ... Den.	56·14 N	7·55 E
118	Limfjorden (Fd.) ... Den.	56·56 N	10·35 E
158	Limmen Bght. (lĭm'ĕn) ... Austl.	14·45 S	136·00 E
127	Limni (lêm'nê) ... Grc.	38·47 N	23·22 E
127	Limnos (I.) ... Grc.	39·58 N	24·48 E
85	Limoges (lē-môzh') Can. (Ottawa In.)	45·20 N	75·15 W
122	Limoges ... Fr.	45·50 N	1·15 E
72	Limon (lī'mŏn) ... Colo.	39 15 N	103·41 W
93	Limón (lē-mōn') ... C. R.	10·01 N	83·02 W
92	Limón (lē-mô'n) ... Hond.	15·53 N	85·34 W
95	Limon (R.) ... Dom. Rep.	18·20 N	71·40 W
88	Limón B. C. Z. (Panama Canal In.)	9·21 N	79·58 W
123	Limours (lē-mōōr') . Fr. (Paris In.)	48·39 N	2·05 E
122	Limousin, Plateaux du (Plat.) (plä-tō' dü lē-mōō-zăN') . Fr.	45·44 N	1·09 E
122	Limoux (lē-mōō') ... Fr.	43·03 N	2·14 E
166	Limpopo R. (lĭm-pō'pō) ... Afr.	23·15 S	27·46 E
101	Linares (lē-nä'räs) Chile (Santiago In.)	35·51 S	71·35 W
76	Linares ... Mex.	24·53 N	99·34 W
124	Linares (lē-nä'rĕs) ... Sp.	38·07 N	3·38 W
101	Linares (Prov.) Chile (Santiago In.)	35·53 S	71·30 W
126	Linaro, C. (lē-nä'rä) ... It.	42·02 N	11·53 E
148	Linchang (lĭn'chäng') ... China	36·19 N	114·40 E
150	Linchiang (lĭn'chäng') ... China	41·45 N	127·00 E
148	Linch'ing (lĭn'chĭng) ... China	36·49 N	115·42 E
151	Linch'uan ... China	27·58 N	116·18 E
101	Lincoln (lĭŋ'kŭn) Arg. (Buenos Aires In.)	34·51 S	61·29 W
68	Lincoln ... Calif.	38·51 N	121·19 W
110	Lincoln ... Eng.	53·14 N	0·33 W
73	Lincoln ... Ill.	40·09 N	89·21 W
72	Lincoln ... Kans.	39·02 N	98·08 W
82	Lincoln ... Maine	45·23 N	68·31 W
83	Lincoln ... Mass. (Boston In.)	42·25 N	71·19 W
73	Lincoln ... Nebr.	40·49 N	96·43 W
110	Lincoln (Co.) ... Eng.	53·12 N	0·29 W
72	Lincoln, Mt. ... Colo.	39·20 N	106·19 W
110	Lincoln Heights (Reg.) ... Eng.	53·23 N	0·39 W
75	Lincoln Park Mich. (Detroit In.)	42·14 N	83·11 W
84	Lincoln Park N. J. (New York In.)	40·56 N	74·18 W
79	Lincolnton –lĭŋ'kŭn-tŭn) ... N. C.	35·27 N	81·15 W
116	Lincoln Wolds (woldz') ... Eng.	53·25 N	0·23 W
78	Lindale (lĭn'dāl) ... Ga.	34·10 N	85·10 W
120	Lindau (lĭn'dou) ... Ger.	47·33 N	9·40 E
78	Linden (lĭn'dĕn) ... Ala.	32·16 N	87·47 W
74	Linden ... Mo. (Kansas City In.)	39·13 N	94·35 W
84	Linden ... N. J. (New York In.)	40·38 N	74·16 W
84	Lindenhurst (lĭn'dĕn-hûrst) N. Y. (New York In.)	40·41 N	73·23 W
84	Lindenwold (lĭn'dĕn-wôld) N. J. (Philadelphia In.)	39·50 N	75·00 W
118	Lindesberg (lĭn'dĕs-bĕrgh) ... Swe.	59·37 N	15·14 E
117	Lindesnes (C.) (lĭn'ĕs-nĕs) ... Nor.	58·00 N	7·05 E
150	Lindho ... China	40·45 N	107·30 E
167	Lindi (lĭn'dê) ... Tan.	9·59 S	39·43 E
165	Lindi R. ... Con. L.	1·00 N	27·13 E
168	Lindley (lĭnd'lê) .S. Afr. (Johannesburg & Pretoria In.)	27·52 S	27·55 E
111	Lindow (lĕn'dōv) . Ger. (Berlin In.)	52·58 N	12·59 E
81	Lindsay (lĭn'zê) ... Can.	44·20 N	78·45 W
72	Lindsay ... Okla.	34·50 N	97·38 W
72	Lindsborg (lĭnz'bôrg) ... Kans.	38·34 N	97·42 W
110	Lindsey (Co.) (lĭn'zĭ) ... Eng.	53·25 N	0·32 W
148	Lineh'ü (lĭn'chü) ... China	36·31 N	118·33 E
78	Lineville (lĭn'vĭl) ... Ala.	33·18 N	85·45 W
150	Linfen ... China	36·00 N	111·38 E
155	Lingayen (lĭŋ'gä-yän') Phil. (Manila In.)	16·01 N	120·13 E
155	Lingayen G. ... Phil. (Manila In.)	16·18 N	120·11 E
120	Lingen (lĭŋ'gĕn) ... Ger.	52·32 N	7·20 E
154	Lingga, Pulau-Pulau (Is.) (lĭng-gä') . Indon.	0·35 S	105·05 E
151	Lingling ... China	26·10 N	111·40 E
148	Lingpi (lĭng'pĭ') ... China	33·33 N	117·33 E
148	Lingtienchen (lĭng'diăN'jĕn) China	31·52 N	121·28 E
151	Lingting Yang (Can.) ... China	22·00 N	114·00 E
164	Linguere (lĭŋ-gĕr') ... Senegal	15·22 N	14·55 W
150	Lingwu ... China	38·05 N	106·18 E
150	Lingyüan ... China	41·12 N	119·20 E
151	Linhai ... China	28·52 N	121·08 E
150	Linhsi ... China	43·30 N	118·02 E
148	Linhuaikuan (lĭnhōōäi'gōōăN) China	32·55 N	117·38 E
148	Linhuanchi (lĭn'hōōaN'jē) ... China	33·42 N	116·33 E
148	Lini (lĭn'yē) ... China	35·04 N	118·21 E
151	Linkao ... China	19·58 N	109·40 E
118	Linköping (lĭn'chû-pĭng) ... Swe.	58·25 N	15·35 E
148	Linmingkuan (lĭN'mĭng'gōōän) China	36·47 N	114·32 E
116	Linnhe (L.) (lĭn'ê) ... Scot.	56·35 N	4·30 W
99	Lins (lê'Ns) ... Braz.	21·42 S	49·41 W
84	Linthicum Heights (lĭn'thĭ-kŭm) Md. (Baltimore In.)	39·12 N	76·39 W
150	Lintien ... China	42·08 N	124·59 E
80	Linton (lĭn'tŭn) ... Ind.	39·05 N	87·15 W
70	Linton ... N. D.	46·16 N	100·15 W
151	Linwu (lĭn'wōō') ... China	25·20 N	112·30 E
148	Linying (lĭn'yĭng') ... China	33·48 N	113·56 E
148	Linyü (lĭn'yü) ... China	40·01 N	119·45 E
120	Linz (lĭnts) ... Aus.	48·18 N	14·18 E
155	Lipa (lê-pä') ... Phil. (Manila In.)	13·55 N	121·10 E
126	Lipari (lē'pä-rê) ... It.	38·29 N	15·00 E
126	Lipari (I.) ... It.	38·32 N	15·04 E
128	Lipetsk (lyĕ'pĕtsk) ... Sov. Un.	52·26 N	39·34 E
128	Lipetsk (Oblast) ... Sov. Un.	52·18 N	38·30 E
151	Lip'ing (lê'pĭng') ... China	26·18 N	109·00 E
121	Lipno (lēp'nô) ... Pol.	52·50 N	19·12 E
117	Lippe (R.) (lĭp'ĕ) ... Ger.	51·36 N	6·45 E
120	Lippstadt (lĭp'shtät) ... Ger.	51·39 N	8·20 E
84	Lipscomb (lĭp'skŭm) Ala. (Birmingham In.)	33·26 N	86·56 W
129	Liptsy (lyēp'tsê) ... Sov. Un.	50·11 N	36·25 E
151	Lip'u ... China	24·38 N	110·35 E
126	Liri (R.) (lē'rē) ... It.	41·49 N	13·30 E
125	Liria (lê'ryä) ... Sp.	39·35 N	0·34 W
165	Lisala (lê-sä'lä) ... Con. L.	2·14 N	21·38 E
125	Lisboa (Lisbon) (lĕzh-bō'ä) (lĭz'bŭn) . Port. (Lisbon In.)	38·42 N	9·05 W
82	Lisbon ... Maine	43·59 N	70·03 W
70	Lisbon ... N. D.	46·21 N	97·43 W
80	Lisbon ... Ohio	40·45 N	80·50 W
	Lisbon, see Lisboa		
116	Lisburn (lĭs'bŭrn) ... N. Ire.	54·35 N	6·05 W
64	Lisburne, C. ... Alaska	68·20 N	165·40 W
150	Lishih ... China	37·32 N	111·12 E
150	Lishu ... China	43·12 N	124·18 E
150	Lishuchen ... China	45·01 N	130·50 E
151	Lishui ... China	28·28 N	120·00 E
148	Lishui (lĭ'shwĭ') ... China	31·41 N	119·01 E
149	Lishui ... China (Canton In.)	23·12 N	113·09 E
122	Lisieux (lē-zyû') ... Fr.	49·10 N	0·13 E
136	Lisiy Nos (lĭ'sĭy nôs) Sov. Un. (Leningrad In.)	60·01 N	30·00 E
129	Liski (lyēs'kê) ... Sov. Un.	50·56 N	39·28 E
75	Lisle (lĭl) ... Ill. (Chicago In.)	41·48 N	88·04 W
123	L'Isle-Adam (lēl-ädăN') Fr. (Paris In.)	49·05 N	2·13 E
160	Lismore (lĭz'môr) ... Austl.	28·48 S	153·18 E
47	Lister, Mt. (lĭs'tĕr) ... Ant.	78·05 S	163·00 E
139	Litani (R.) ... Leb. (Palestine In.)	33·28 N	35·42 E
73	Litchfield (lĭch'fēld) ... Ill.	39·10 N	89·38 W
71	Litchfield ... Minn.	45·08 N	94·34 W
75	Litchfield ... Ohio (Cleveland In.)	41·10 N	82·01 W
160	Lithgow (lĭth'gō) ... Austl.	33·23 S	149·31 E
126	Lithinon, Ark. (C.) ... Grc. (In.)	34·59 N	24·35 E
84	Lithonia (lĭ-thō'nĭ-à) Ga. (Atlanta In.)	33·43 N	84·07 W
130	Lithuanian S. S. R. (lĭth-ū-ā'-nĭ-à) Sov. Un.	55·42 N	23·30 E
129	Litin (lê-tēn) ... Sov. Un.	49·16 N	28·11 E
127	Litókhoron (lē'tô-kô'rôn) ... Grc.	40·05 N	22·29 E
120	Litomerice (lē'tô-myĕr'zhĭ-tsĕ) Czech.	50·33 N	14·10 E
120	Litomyšl (lē'tô-mēsh'l) ... Czech.	49·52 N	16·14 E
161	Little (R.) . Austl. (Melbourne In.)	37·54 S	144·27 E
78	Little (R.) ... Tenn.-Mo.	36·28 N	89·39 W
77	Little R. ... Tex.	30·48 N	96·50 W
94	Little Abaco (I.) (ä'bä-kō) . Ba. Is.	26·55 N	77·45 W
47	Little America ... Ant.	78·30 S	161·30 W
154	Little Andaman I. (ăn-dà-măn') Andaman Is.	10·39 N	93·08 E
94	Little Bahama Bk. (bà-hā'mà) Ba. Is.	26·55 N	78·40 W
67	Little Belt Mts. (bĕlt) ... Mont.	47·00 N	110·50 W
67	Little Bighorn R. (bĭg-hôrn) . Mont.	45·08 N	107·30 W
	Little Bitter, see el Buheirat el Murrat el Sughra		
66	Little Bitterroot R. (bĭt'ēr-ōōt) Mont.	47·45 N	114·45 W
72	Little Blue (R.) ... Nebr.	40·15 N	98·01 W
74	Little Blue R. (blōō) Mo. (Kansas City In.)	38·52 N	94·25 W
110	Littleborough (lĭt''l-bŭr-ô) . . . Eng.	53·39 N	2·06 W
75	Little Calumet R. (kăl-ū-mĕt') Ill. (Chicago In.)	41·38 N	87·38 W
94	Little Cayman (I.) (kā'măn) Cayman Is.	19·40 N	80·05 W
69	Little Colorado (R.) (kŏl-ô-rä'dō) Ariz.	36·05 N	111·35 W
84	Little Compton (kŏmp'tŏn) R. I. (Providence In.)	41·31 N	71·07 W
93	Little Corn I. ... Nic.	12·19 N	82·50 W
95	Little Exuma (I.) (ĕk-sōō'mä) Ba. Is.	23·25 N	75·40 W
71	Little Falls (fôlz) ... Minn.	45·58 N	94·23 W
81	Little Falls ... N. Y.	43·05 N	74·55 W
72	Littlefield (lĭt''l-fēld) ... Tex.	33·55 N	102·17 W
71	Little Fork (R.) (fôrk) ... Minn.	48·24 N	93·30 W
89	Little Hans Lollick (I.) (hans lôl'lĭk) . Vir. Is. (U. S. A.) (St. Thomas In.)	18·25 N	64·54 W
66	Little Humboldt R. (hŭm'bōlt) Nev.	41·10 N	117·40 W
95	Little Inagua (I.) (ê-nä'gwä) Ba. Is.	21·30 N	73·00 W
94	Little Isaac (I.) (ī'zăk) ... Ba. Is.	25·55 N	79·00 W
80	Little Kanawha (R.) (kà-nô'wà) W. Va.	39·05 N	81·30 W
166	Little Karroo (Mts.) (kä-rōō) S. Afr.	33·50 S	21·02 E
87	Little Mecatina (R.) (mĕ cà tĭ nâ) Can.	52·40 N	62·21 W
75	Little Miami R. (mī-ăm'ĭ) Ohio (Cincinnati In.)	39·19 N	84·15 W
75	Little Miami R., E. Fk. Ohio (Cincinnati In.)	39·01 N	84·03 W
73	Little Missouri (R.) (mĭ-sōō'rĭ) Ark.	34·15 N	93·54 W
70	Little Missouri (R.) ... S. D.	45·46 N	103·48 W
83	Little or Gray (R.) (lĭt''l) (grā) . Can.	47·50 N	57·05 W
79	Little Pee Dee (R.) (pē-dē') . S. C.	34·35 N	79·21 W
67	Little Powder R. (pou'dēr) . . Wyo.	44·51 N	105·20 W
73	Little Red (R.) (rĕd) ... Ark.	35·42 N	92·14 W
73	Little Red R. ... Okla.	33·53 N	94·38 W
73	Little Rock (rôk) ... Ark.	34·42 N	92·16 W
123	Little St. Bernard P. (sănt-bēr-närd') (săN bĕr-när') . Fr.-It.	45·49 N	6·50 E
95	Little San Salvador (I.) (săn săl'và-dôr) . Ba. Is.	24·35 N	75·55 W
79	Little Satilla (R.) (sà-tĭl'à) ... Ga.	31·43 N	82·47 W
70	Little Sioux (R.) (sōō) ... Iowa	42·22 N	95·47 W
67	Little Snake R. (snāk) ... Colo.	40·40 N	108·21 W
78	Little Tallapoosa (R.) (tăl-à-pōō'sà) . Ala.	32·25 N	85·28 W
78	Little Tennessee (R.) (tĕn-ĕ-sē') Tenn.	35·36 N	84·05 W
72	Littleton (lĭt''l-tŭn) ... Colo.	39·34 N	105·01 W
83	Littleton ... Mass. (Boston In.)	42·32 N	71·29 W
81	Littleton ... N. H.	44·15 N	71·45 W
80	Little Wabash (R.) (wô'băsh) . Ill.	38·50 N	88·30 W
67	Little Wood R. (wŏŏd) ... Idaho	43·00 N	114·08 W
148	Liuan (lyōō'ăn') ... China	31·45 N	116·29 E
151	Liuchou (lōō'chōō) ... China	24·25 N	109·30 E
148	Liuho (lyōō'hō') ... China	32·22 N	118·50 E
150	Liuho ... China	42·10 N	125·38 E
150	Liup'an Shan (Mts.) ... China	36·20 N	105·30 E
151	Liuyang (lyōō'yäng') ... China	28·10 N	113·35 E
148	Liuyüan (lü'yüăn) ... China	36·09 N	114·37 E
128	Līvāni (lē'vä-nê) ... Sov. Un.	56·24 N	26·12 E
64	Livengood (lĭv'ĕn-gŏŏd) ... Alaska	65·30 N	148·35 W
78	Live Oak (lĭv'ōk) ... Fla.	30·15 N	83·00 W
65	Livermore (lĭv'ēr-mōr) Calif. (San Francisco In.)	37·41 N	121·46 W
80	Livermore ... Ky.	37·30 N	87·05 W
161	Liverpool (lĭv'ēr-pōōl) Austl. (Sydney In.)	33·55 S	150·56 E
82	Liverpool ... Can.	44·02 N	64·44 W
110	Liverpool ... Eng.	53·25 N	2·52 W
77	Liverpool ... Tex. (In.)	29·18 N	95·17 W
64	Liverpool B. ... Alaska	70·25 N	129·35 W
159	Liverpool Ra. ... Austl.	31·47 S	31·00 E
165	Livindo R. ... Gabon	1·09 N	13·30 E
78	Livingston (lĭv'ĭng-stŭn) ... Ala.	32·35 N	88·09 W
92	Livingston ... Guat.	15·50 N	88·45 W
74	Livingston ... Ill. (St. Louis In.)	38·58 N	89·51 W
67	Livingston ... Mont.	45·40 N	110·35 W
78	Livingston ... Tenn.	36·23 N	85·20 W
166	Livingstone (lĭv-ĭng-stôn) . . N. Rh.	17·51 S	25·48 E
166	Livingstonia (lĭv-ĭng-stō'nĭ-à) Nya.	10·35 S	34·07 E
126	Livno (lēv'nô) ... Yugo.	43·50 N	17·03 E
128	Livny (lēv'nê) ... Sov. Un.	52·28 N	37·36 E
75	Livonia (lĭ-vō-nĭ-à) Mich. (Detroit In.)	42·25 N	83·23 W
126	Livorno (Leghorn) (lê-vôr'nō) (lĕg'hôrn) . It.	43·32 N	11·18 E
100	Livramento (lē-vrä-mĕ'n-tō) . Braz.	30·46 S	55·21 W
148	Liyang (lē'yäng') ... China	31·30 N	119·29 E
116	Lizard Pt. (lĭz'àrd) ... Eng.	49·55 N	5·09 W
123	Lizy-sur-Ourcq (lēk-sē'sür-ōōrk') Fr. (Paris In.)	49·01 N	3·02 E
111	Ljmuiden . Neth. (Amsterdam In.)	52·27 N	4·35 E
126	Ljubljana (lyōō'blyà'na) ... Yugo.	46·04 N	14·29 E
126	Ljubuški (lyōō'bŏŏsh-kê) . Yugo.	43·11 N	17·29 E
118	Ljungan (R.) ... Swe.	62·50 N	13·45 E
118	Ljungby (lyŏŏng'bü) ... Swe.	56·49 N	13·56 E
118	Ljusdal (lyōōs'dâl) ... Swe.	61·50 N	16·11 E
118	Ljusnan (R.) ... Swe.	61·55 N	15·33 E
116	Llandudno (lăn-düd'nō) ... Wales	53·20 N	3·46 W
116	Llanelly (lă-nĕl'ĭ) ... Wales	51·44 N	4·09 W
124	Llanes (lyä'nâs) ... Sp.	43·25 N	4·41 W
76	Llano (lă'nō) (lyä'nō) ... Tex.	30·45 N	98·41 W
76	Llano R. ... Tex.	30·38 N	99·04 W
98	Llanos (lyä'nōs) (Reg.) . . Col.-Ven.	4·00 N	71·15 W
90	Llera (lyā'rä) ... Mex.	23·16 N	99·03 W
124	Llerena (lyā-rā'nä) ... Sp.	38·14 N	6·02 W
116	Lleyn Prom. (lĭn) ... Wales	52·55 N	3·10 W
125	Llobregat (R.) (lyô-brĕ-gät') . Sp.	41·55 N	1·55 E
85	Lloyd L. (loid) . Can. (Calgary In.)	50·52 N	114·13 W
86	Lloydminster ... Can.	53·18 N	109·50 W
125	Lluchmayor (lyōōch-mä-yôr') . Sp.	39·28 N	2·53 E
100	Llullaillaco (Vol.) (lyōō-lyī-lyä'kō) . Arg.	24·50 S	68·30 W
166	Loange (R.) (lô-äŋ'gä) ... Con. L.	4·46 S	20·18 E
166	Lobatsi (lō-bä'tsē) ... Bech.	25·13 S	25·35 E
100	Lobería (lō-bĕ-rē'ä) ... Arg.	38·13 S	58·48 W
166	Lobito (lō-bē'tō) ... Ang.	12·15 S	13·35 E
136	Lobnya (lôb'nyá) Sov. Un. (Moscow In.)	56·01 N	37·29 E
101	Lobos (lō'bôs) Arg. (Buenos Aires In.)	35·10 S	59·08 W
94	Lobos, Cayo (I.) (lō'bôs) . . Ba. Is.	22·25 N	77·40 W
91	Lobos, Isla de (I.) (ē's-lä-dĕ-lô'bôs) . Mex.	21·24 N	97·11 W
98	Lobos de Tierra (I.) (lô'bô-dĕ-tyĕ'r-rä) . . Peru	6·29 S	80·55 W
136	Lobva (lôb'vá) Sov. Un. (Urals In.)	59·12 N	60·28 E
136	Lobva R. ... Sov. Un. (Urals In.)	59·14 N	60·17 E
120	Locarno (lô-kär'nō) ... Switz.	46·10 N	8·43 E
122	Loches (lôsh) ... Fr.	47·08 N	0·56 E
151	Loching ... China	28·02 N	120·40 E
79	Lochloosa (L.) (lŏk-lō'sà) ... Fla.	29·33 N	82·07 W
116	Lochy (L.) (lŏk'ĭ) ... Scot.	56·57 N	4·45 W
79	Lockhart (lŏk'härt) ... S. C.	34·47 N	81·30 W
77	Lockhart ... Tex.	29·54 N	97·40 W
81	Lock Haven (lŏk'hā-vĕn) ... Pa.	41·05 N	77·30 W
75	Lockland (lŏk'lănd) Ohio (Cincinnati In.)	39·14 N	84·27 W
85	Lockport (lŏk'pōrt) Can. (Winnipeg In.)	50·05 N	96·58 W
75	Lockport ... Ill. (Chicago In.)	41·35 N	88·04 W
75	Lockport ... N. Y. (Buffalo In.)	43·11 N	78·43 W
84	Lock Raven Res. (lŏk ra'vĕn) Md. (Baltimore In.)	39·28 N	76·38 W
154	Loc Ninh (lōk'nĭng') ... Viet.	12·00 N	106·30 E
85	Locust Hill (lō'kŭst hĭl) Can. (Toronto In.)	43·54 N	79·11 W
139	Lod (lôd) ... Isr. (Palestine In.)	31·57 N	34·55 E
122	Lodève (lô-dĕv') ... Fr.	43·43 N	3·18 E
119	Lodeynoye Pole (lô-dĕy-nô'yĕ) Sov. Un.	60·43 N	33·24 E
67	Lodge Cr. ... Mont.	48·51 N	109·30 W
70	Lodgepole Cr. (lŏj'pōl) ... Wyo.	41·22 N	104·48 W

ng-sing; ŋ-baŋk; N-nasalized n; nŏd; cŏmmit; ōld; ôbey; ôrder; fōōd; fŏŏt; ou-out; s-soft; sh-dish; th-thin; pūre; ûnite; ûrn; stŭd; circŭs; ü-as "y" in study; '-indeterminate vowel.

Page	Name Pronunciation Region	Lat. °′	Long. °′
142	Lodhran ... W. Pak.	29·40 N	71·39 E
68	Lodi (lō'dī) ... Calif.	38·07 N	121·17 W
126	Lodi (lô'dē) ... It.	45·18 N	9·30 E
75	Lodi (lō'dī) .. Ohio (Cleveland In.)	41·02 N	82·01 W
124	Lodosa (lô-dô'-sä) ... Sp.	42·27 N	2·04 W
121	Łódź (wōōdzh) ... Pol.	51·46 N	19·13 E
125	Loeches (lô-āch'ĕs) Sp. (Madrid In.)	40·22 N	3·25 W
112	Lofoten (Is.) (lô'fō-tĕn) ... Nor.	68·26 N	13·42 E
80	Logan (lō'găn) ... Ohio	39·35 N	82·25 W
67	Logan ... Utah	41·46 N	111·51 W
80	Logan ... W. Va.	37·50 N	82·00 W
86	Logan, Mt. ... Can.	60·54 N	140·33 W
80	Logansport (lō'gănz-pōrt) ... Ind.	40·45 N	86·25 W
165	Logone R. (lō-gō'nä) (lô-gôn') Chad-Cam.	10·28 N	15·22 E
164	Logoualé (lô-gwä-lā') . Ivory Coast	7·19 N	7·38 W
124	Logroño (lô-grō'nyō) ... Sp.	42·28 N	2·25 W
124	Logrosán (lô-grô-sän') ... Sp.	39·22 N	5·29 W
118	Løgstør (lûgh-stûr') ... Den.	56·56 N	9·15 E
148	Lohochai (lou'wŭ'jäi) ... China	33·35 N	114·02 E
122	Loir (R.) (lwȧr) ... Fr.	47·40 N	0·07 E
122	Loire (R.) ... Fr.	47·19 N	1·11 W
98	Loja (lō'hä) ... Ec.	3·49 S	79·13 W
124	Loja (lô'-kä) ... Sp.	37·10 N	4·11 W
168	Lokala Drift (lô'kä-lȧ drĭft) . S. Afr. (Johannesburg & Pretoria In.)	24·00 S	26·38 E
129	Lokhvitsa (lôk-vêt'sȧ) ... Sov. Un.	50·21 N	33·16 E
164	Lokoja (lô-kō'yä) ... Nig.	7·50 N	6·39 E
165	Lol R. (lōl) ... Sud.	9·06 N	28·09 E
118	Lolland (lôl'än') ... Den.	54·41 N	11·00 E
164	Lolo (lō'lō) ... Cam.	3·14 N	10·38 E
127	Lom (lōm) ... Bul.	43·48 N	23·15 E
74	Loma Linda (lō'mȧ lĭn'dȧ) Calif. (Los Angeles In.)	34·04 N	117·16 W
110	Lomas de Zamora (lō'mäs dā zä-mō'rä) . Arg. (In.)	34·31 S	58·24 W
75	Lombard (lŏm-bärd) Ill. (Chicago In.)	41·53 N	88·01 W
126	Lombardia (Reg.) (lôm-bär-dē'ä) . It.	45·20 N	9·30 E
155	Lomblen (I.) (lŏm-blĕn') ... Indon.	8·08 S	123·45 E
154	Lombok (I.) (lŏm-bŏk') ... Indon.	9·15 S	116·15 E
154	Lombok Selat (Str.) ... Indon.	9·00 S	115·28 E
164	Lomé (lō-mā') (lō'mā) ... Togo.	6·13 N	1·14 E
166	Lomela (lô-mā'lȧ) ... Con. L.	2·19 S	23·33 E
166	Lomela (R.) ... Con. L.	0·21 S	21·11 E
76	Lometa (lô-mē'tȧ) ... Tex.	31·10 N	98·25 W
165	Lomié (lô-mê-ā') ... Cam.	3·14 N	13·34 E
74	Lomita (lō-mē'tȧ) Calif. (Los Angeles In.)	33·48 N	118·20 W
111	Lommel ... Bel. (Brussels In.)	51·14 N	5·21 E
116	Lomond, Loch (L.) (lŏk lō'mŭnd) Scot.	56·15 N	4·40 W
136	Lomonosov (lô-mô'nô-sof) Sov. Un. (Leningrad In.)	59·54 N	29·47 E
68	Lompoc (lŏm-pōk') ... Calif.	34·39 N	120·30 W
121	Lomza (lôm'zhȧ) ... Pol.	53·11 N	22·04 E
81	Lonaconing (lō-nȧ-kō'nĭng) ... Md.	39·35 N	78·55 W
80	London (lŭn'dŭn) ... Can.	43·00 N	81·20 W
110	London ... Eng. (London In.)	51·30 N	0·07 W
78	London ... Ky.	37·07 N	84·06 W
80	London ... Ohio	39·50 N	83·30 W
82	Londonderry (lŭn'dŭn-dĕr-ĭ) . Can.	45·29 N	63·40 W
116	Londonderry ... N. Ire.	54·60 N	6·80 W
158	Londonderry, C. ... Austl.	13·30 S	127·00 E
99	Londrina (lôn-drē'nä) ... Braz.	21·53 S	51·17 W
80	Lonely (I.) (lōn'lĭ) ... Can.	45·35 N	81·30 W
68	Lone Pine ... Calif.	36·36 N	118·03 W
93	Lone Star ... Nic.	13·58 N	84·25 W
95	Long (I.) ... Ba. Is.	23·25 N	75·10 W
82	Long (I.) ... Can.	44·21 N	66·25 W
155	Long (I.) ... N. Gui. Ter.	5·10 S	147·30 E
70	Long (L.) ... N. D.	46·47 N	100·14 W
65	Long (L.) ... Wash. (Seattle In.)	47·29 N	122·36 W
166	Longa (R.) (lôŋ'gȧ) ... Ang.	10·20 S	15·10 E
79	Long B. ... S. C.	33·30 N	78·54 W
74	Long Beach (lông bēch) Calif. (Los Angeles In.)	33·46 N	118·12 W
84	Long Beach . N. Y. (New York In.)	40·35 N	73·38 W
85	Long Branch (lông brȧnch) Can. (Toronto In.)	43·36 N	79·32 W
84	Long Branch . N. J. (New York In.)	40·18 N	73·59 W
70	Longdon (lông'-dŭn) ... N. D.	48·45 N	98·23 W
110	Long Eaton (ē'tŭn) ... Eng.	52·54 N	1·16 W
116	Longford (lông'fērd) ... Ire.	53·43 N	7·40 W
74	Longhorn (lông-hôrn) Tex. (San Antonio In.)	29·33 N	98·23 W
81	Long I. (lông) ... N. Y.	40·50 N	72·50 W
81	Long Island Sd. (lông ī'lănd) Conn.-N. Y.	41·05 N	72·45 W
123	Longjumeau (lôN-zhü-mō') Fr. (Paris In.)	48·42 N	2·17 E
148	Longk'ou (lōōng'kō) ... China	37·39 N	120·21 E
87	Longlac (lông'lăk) ... Can.	49·41 N	86·28 W
70	Longlake (lông-lāk) ... S. D.	45·52 N	99·06 W
72	Longmont (lông'mŏnt) ... Colo.	40·11 N	105·07 W
123	Longnes (lôN'y') ... Fr. (Paris In.)	48·56 N	1·37 W
110	Longnor (lông'nŏr) ... Eng.	53·11 N	1·52 W
70	Long Pine (lông pīn) ... Nebr.	42·31 N	99·42 W
81	Lont Pt. ... Can.	42·35 N	80·05 W
83	Long Pt. ... Can.	48·46 N	58·47 W
81	Long Point B. ... Can.	42·40 N	80·10 W
71	Long Prairie (lông prâr'ĭ) ... Minn.	45·58 N	94·49 W
83	Long Range Mts. ... Can.	47·45 N	58·52 W
159	Longreach (lông'rēch) ... Austl.	23·32 S	144·17 E
82	Long Reach (R.) ... Can.	45·26 N	66·05 W
161	Long Rf. ... Austl. (Sydney In.)	33·45 S	151·22 E
110	Longridge (lông'rĭj) ... Eng.	53·51 N	2·37 W
72	Longs Pk. (lôngz) ... Colo.	40·17 N	105·37 W
110	Longton (lông'tŭn) ... Eng.	52·59 N	2·08 W
85	Longueuil (lôN-gû'y') Can. (Montreal In.)	45·32 N	73·30 W
65	Longview (lông-vū) Ore. (Portland In.)	46·06 N	123·02 W
77	Longview ... Tex.	32·29 N	94·44 W
77	Longville (lông'vĭl) ... La.	30·36 N	93·14 W
123	Longwy (lôN-wē') ... Fr.	49·32 N	6·14 E
154	Long Xuyen (loung' sōō'yĕn) . Viet.	10·31 N	105·28 E
73	Lonoke (lō'nōk) ... Ark.	34·48 N	91·52 W
123	Lons-le-Saunier (lôN-lē-sō-nyā') . Fr.	46·40 N	5·33 E
101	Lontué (lōn-tōō-ĕ') (R.) Chile (Santiago In.)	35.20 S	70·45 W
155	Looc (lō-ōk') ... Phil. (Manila In.)	12·16 N	121·59 E
80	Loogootee ... Ind.	38·40 N	86·55 W
79	Lookout, C. (lŏŏk'out) ... N. C.	34·34 N	76·38 W
66	Lookout Pt. Res. ... Ore.	43·51 N	122·38 W
85	Looma (lōō'mă) Can. (Edmonton In.)	53·22 N	113·15 W
116	Loop Head (lōōp) ... Ire.	52·32 N	9·59 W
78	Loosahatchie (R.) (lōz-ȧ-hă'chē) Tenn.	35·20 N	89·45 W
111	Loosdrechtsche Plassen (L.) Neth. (Amsterdam In.)	52·11 N	5·09 E
135	Lopatka, Mys (C.) (lô-păt'kȧ) Sov. Un.	51·00 N	156·52 E
163	Lopez, Cap (C.) ... Gabon	0·41 S	9·00 E
155	Lopez B. (lō'päz) Phil. (Manila In.)	14·04 N	122·00 E
65	Lopez I. ... Wash. (Seattle In.)	48·25 N	122·53 W
151	Lop'ing (lō'pĭng') ... China	29·02 N	117·12 E
165	Lopori R. (lō-pō'rē) ... Con. L.	1·23 N	21·18 E
124	Lora (lō'rä) ... Sp.	37·40 N	5·31 W
142	Lora (R.) ... Afg.	31·43 N	67·08 E
75	Lorain (lô-rān') Ohio (Cleveland In.)	41·28 N	82·10 W
142	Loralai (lō-rŭ-lī') ... W. Pak.	30·31 N	68·35 E
124	Lorca (lôr'kä) ... Sp.	37·39 N	1·40 W
159	Lord Howe (I.) (lôrd hou) . Austl.	31·44 S	157·56 E
69	Lordsburg (lôrdz'bûrg) ... N. Mex.	32·20 N	108·45 W
101	Lorena (lô-rā'nȧ) Braz. (Rio de Janeiro In.)	22·45 S	45·07 W
99	Loreto (lō-rā'tō) ... Braz.	7·09 S	45·10 W
85	Loretteville (lô-rĕt-vēl') Can. (Quebec In.)	46·51 N	71·21 W
163	Loriami (R.) ... Con. L.	4·30 S	24·28 E
98	Lorica (lô-rē'kä) ... Col.	9·14 N	75·54 W
122	Lorient (lô-rē'äN') ... Fr.	47·45 N	3·22 W
116	Lorne, Firth of (fûrth ôv lôrn') Scot.	56·10 N	6·09 W
85	Lorne Park (lôrn) Can. (Toronto In.)	43·31 N	79·36 W
120	Lörrach (lûr'äk) ... Ger.	47·36 N	7·38 E
74	Los Alamitos (lōs ăl-ȧ-mē'tôs) Calif. (Los Angeles In.)	33·48 N	118·04 W
69	Los Alamos (ăl-ȧ-môs') ... N. Mex.	35·53 N	106·20 W
65	Los Altos (ăl-tôs') Calif. (San Francisco In.)	37·23 N	122·06 W
101	Los Andes (ăn'dĕs) Chile (Santiago In.)	32·44 S	70·36 W
74	Los Angeles (ăŋ'gĕl-ĕs) (ăn'jĕl-ĕs) (äŋ'hä-lās) Calif. (Los Angeles In.)	34·00 N	118·15 W
100	Los Angeles (äŋ'hä-lās) ... Chile	37·27 S	72·15 W
68	Los Angeles Aqueduct ... Calif.	35·12 N	118·02 W
74	Los Angeles R. Calif. (Los Angeles In.)	33·50 N	118·13 W
101	Los Bronces (lōs brō'n-sĕs) Chile (Santiago In.)	33·09 S	70·18 W
66	Loscha R. (lōs'chă) ... Idaho	46·20 N	115·11 W
100	Los Chonos, Archipelago de (är-chê-pyĕ'lä-gō dĕ lōs chŏ'nôs) Chile	44·35 S	76·15 W
100	Los Estados, Isla de (I.) (ē's-lä dĕ lōs ĕs-tä'dôs) . Arg.	54·45 S	64·25 W
124	Los Filabres, Sierra de (Mts.) (sē-ĕ'r-rä dĕ lōs fē-lä'brĕs) . Sp.	37·19 N	2·48 W
68	Los Gatos (gä'tōs) ... Calif.	37·13 N	121·59 W
151	Loshan (lō'shän') ... China	29·40 N	103·40 E
76	Los Herreras (ĕr-rä-räs) ... Mex.	25·55 N	99·23 W
95	Los Ilanos (lōs ē-lä'nōs) . Dom. Rep.	18·35 N	69·30 W
94	Los Indios, Cayos de (Is.) (kä'yōs dĕ lōs ē'n-dyō's) . Cuba	21·50 N	83·10 W
126	Lošinj (lô'shēn') ... Yugo.	44·30 N	14·29 E
126	Lošinj (I.) ... Yugo.	44·35 N	14·34 E
168	Loskopdam (L.) ... S. Afr. (Johannesburg & Pretoria In.)	25·30 S	29·26 E
125	Los Monegros (Mts.) (mô-nĕ'grōs) . Sp.	41·31 N	0·18 W
74	Los Nietos (nyā'tôs) Calif. (Los Angeles In.)	33·57 N	118·05 W
94	Los Patacios (pä-tä'sē-ōs) ... Cuba	22·35 N	83·15 W
69	Los Pinos (R.) (pē'nôs) Colo.-N. Mex.	36·58 N	107·35 W
90	Los Reyes (rā'yĕs) ... Mex.	19·35 N	102·29 W
91	Los Reyes . Mex. (Mexico City In.)	19·21 N	98·58 W
93	Los Santos (sän'tôs) ... Pan.	7·57 N	80·24 W
124	Los Santos (sän'tôs) ... Sp.	38·38 N	6·30 W
99	Los Teques (tĕ'kĕs) ... Ven. (In.)	10·22 N	67·04 W
67	Lost R. (lôst) ... Idaho	43·56 N	113·38 W
66	Lost R. ... Ore.	42·07 N	121·30 W
67	Lost River Mts. (rĭ'vēr) ... Idaho	44·23 N	113·48 W
101	Los Vilos (vē'lōs) Chile (Santiago In.)	31·56 S	71·29 W
122	Lot (R.) (lôt) ... Fr.	44·32 N	1·08 E
100	Lota (lō'tä) ... Chile	37·11 S	73·14 W
149	Lotien (lō'tyĕn') China (Shanghai In.)	31·25 N	121·20 E
151	Loting (lō'tĭng') ... China	23·42 N	111·35 E
148	Lot'ing (lō'tĭng) ... China	39·26 N	118·53 E
120	Lötschen Tun. (lût'shĕn) ... Switz.	46·26 N	7·54 E
78	Loudon (lou'dŭn) ... Tenn.	35·43 N	84·20 W
80	Loudonville (lou'dŭn-vĭl) ... Ohio	40·40 N	82·15 W
122	Loudun (lōō-dŭN') ... Fr.	47·03 N	0·00
164	Louga (lōō'gä) ... Senegal	15·36 N	16·24 W
110	Loughborough (lŭf'bŭr-ō) ... Eng.	52·46 N	1·12 W
80	Louisa (lōō'ēz-ȧ) ... Ky.	38·05 N	82·40 W
159	Louisade Arch. (lōō-ĭs-äd' är-kĭ-pĕl-ĭ-gō) . Austl.	10·44 S	153·58 E
79	Louisberg (lōō'ĭs-bûrg) ... N. C.	36·05 N	79·19 W
83	Louisbourg (lōō'ĭs-bourg) ... Can.	45·56 N	59·59 W
73	Louisiana (lōō-ē-zē-ăn'ȧ) ... Mo.	39·24 N	91·03 W
63	Louisiana (State) ... U. S.	30·50 N	92·50 W
166	Louis Trichardt (lōō'ĭs trĭch'ärt) S. Afr.	22·52 S	29·53 E
72	Louisville (lōō'ĭs-vĭl) (lōō'ê-vĭl) Colo.	39·58 N	105·08 W
79	Louisville ... Ga.	33·00 N	82·25 W
75	Louisville ... Ky. (Louisville In.)	38·15 N	85·45 W
78	Louisville ... Miss.	33·07 N	89·02 W
166	Loukoléla ... Con B.	1·00 S	17·13 E
124	Loule (lō-lā') ... Port.	37·08 N	8·03 W
120	Louny (lō'nê) ... Czech.	50·20 N	13·47 E
70	Loup (R.) (lōōp) ... Nebr.	41·17 N	97·58 W
70	Loup City ... Nebr.	41·15 N	98·59 W
122	Lourdes (lōōrd) ... Fr.	43·06 N	0·03 W
166	Lourenço Marques, Baia de (B.) (bä-ē'ä dā lôw-rĕn'sô mär'kĕs) . Moz.	26·14 S	33·30 E
125	Loures (lō'rĕzh) . Port. (Lisbon In.)	38·49 N	9·10 W
124	Lousa (lō'zȧ) ... Port.	40·05 N	8·12 W
116	Louth (louth) ... Eng.	53·27 N	0·02 W
122	Louviers (lōō-vyā') ... Fr.	49·13 N	1·11 E
123	Louvres (lōōv'r') ... Fr. (Paris In.)	49·02 N	2·28 E
128	Lovat' (lô-vȧt'y') ... Sov. Un.	57·23 N	31·18 E
127	Lovech (lō'vĕts) ... Bul.	43·10 N	24·40 E
72	Loveland (lŭv'lănd) ... Colo.	40·24 N	105·04 W
75	Loveland ... Ohio (Cincinnati In.)	39·16 N	84·15 W
67	Lovell (lŭv'ĕl) ... Wyo.	44·50 N	108·23 W
68	Lovelock (lŭv'lŏk) ... Nev.	40·10 N	118·37 W
84	Lovick (lŭ'vĭk) Ala. (Birmingham In.)	33·34 N	86·38 W
119	Loviisa (lô'vē-sȧ) ... Fin.	60·28 N	26·10 E
87	Low, C. (lō) ... Can.	62·58 N	86·50 W
166	Lowa (lō'wȧ) ... Con. L.	1·30 S	27·18 E
69	Lowell (lō'ĕl) ... Ariz.	31·25 N	109·55 W
75	Lowell ... Ind. (Chicago In.)	41·17 N	87·26 W
83	Lowell ... Mass. (Boston In.)	42·38 N	71·18 W
80	Lowell ... Mich.	42·55 N	85·20 W
65	Lowell ... Wash. (Seattle In.)	47·57 N	122·12 W
111	Löwenberg (lû' vĕn-bĕrgh) Ger. (Berlin In.)	52·53 N	13·09 E
86	Lower Arrow (L.) (ăr'ō) ... Can.	49·41 N	118·40 W
	Lower Austria (State), see Niederösterreich		
70	Lower Brule Ind. Res. (brü'lā) S. D.	44·15 N	100·21 W
159	Lower Hutt (hŭt) ... N. Z. (In.)	41·08 S	175·00 E
66	Lower Klamath L. (klăm'ȧth) Calif.	41·55 N	121·50 W
66	Lower L. ... Calif.-Nev.	41·21 N	119·53 W
71	Lower Red (L.) (rĕd) ... Minn.	47·58 N	94·31 W
68	Lower Otay Res. (ō'tā) Calif. (San Diego In.)	32·37 N	116·46 W
	Lower Saxony (State), see Niedersachsen		
117	Lowestoft (lō'stŏft) ... Eng.	52·31 N	1·45 E
121	Łowicz (lô'vĭch) ... Pol.	52·06 N	19·57 E
121	Low Tatra Mts. ... Czech.	48·57 N	19·18 E
81	Lowville (lou'vĭl) ... N. Y.	43·45 N	75·30 W
91	Loxicha (Santa Caterina) (lô-zē'chä) (sän-tä kä-tä-rē'nä) . Mex.	16·03 N	96·46 W
160	Loxton (lôks'tŭn) ... Austl.	34·25 S	140·38 E
75	Loyal Oak (loi'ăl ōk) Ohio (Cleveland In.)	41·03 N	81·38 W
150	Loyang ... China	34·45 N	112·32 E
159	Loyauté, Iles ... N. Cal.	21·17 S	168·16 E
144	Loz, Jabal Al (Mtn.) ... Sau. Ar.	28·46 N	35·37 E
127	Ložnica (lôz'nē-tsä) ... Yugo.	44·31 N	19·16 E
111	Lozorno ... Czech. (Vienna In.)	48·21 N	17·03 E
129	Lozova (lô-zô'vȧ) ... Sov. Un.	48·54 N	36·17 E
129	Lozovatka (lô-zô-vät'kȧ) . Sov. Un.	48·03 N	33·19 E
129	Lozovaya Pavlovka (lô-zo-vä'yȧ päv-lôf'kȧ) . Sov. Un.	48·27 N	38·37 E
125	Lozoya, Canal de (kä-nä'l dĕ lô-thō'yä) . Sp. (Madrid In.)	40·36 N	3·41 W
166	Lualaba (lōō-ȧ-lä'bȧ) ... Con. L.	10·02 S	25·16 E
166	Luama (lōō-ä'mȧ) ... Con. L.	4·47 S	27·32 E
150	Luan (R.) ... China	41·25 N	117·15 E
166	Luanda (lōō-än'dä) ... Ang.	8·50 S	13·15 E
154	Luang Prabang (lōō-ang'-prä-băng') . Laos	19·47 N	102·15 E
166	Luanguinga (R.) (lōō-än-gĭŋ'gȧ) Ang.	14·00 S	20·45 E
166	Luangwa (R.) (lōō-äŋ'gwä) N. Rh.	12·38 S	32·41 E
148	Luanhsien (lōōän'sĭän) ... China	39·47 N	118·40 E
124	Luarca (lwä'rkä) ... Sp.	43·33 N	6·30 W
113	Luarsens, Monts de (Mts.) (lwä-sŏŋ) . Alg.	35·44 N	0·50 E
121	Lubaczów (lōō-bä'chōōf) ... Pol.	50·08 N	23·10 E
120	Lubán (lōō'bän') ... Pol.	51·08 N	15·17 E
119	Lubānas Ezers (L.) (lōō-bä'näs ā'zĕrs) . Sov. Un.	56·48 N	26·30 E
155	Lubang (lōō-bäng') Phil. (Manila In.)	13·49 N	120·07 E
155	Lubang (Is.) ... Phil. (Manila In.)	13·47 N	119·56 E
155	Lubao (lōō-bä'ō) . Phil. (Manila In.)	14·55 N	120·36 E
121	Lubartow (lōō-bär'tōōf) ... Pol.	51·27 N	22·37 E
121	Lubawa (lōō-bä'vä) ... Pol.	53·31 N	19·47 E
120	Lübben (lüb'ĕn) ... Ger.	51·56 N	13·53 E
72	Lubbock (lŭb'ŭk) ... Tex.	33·35 N	101·50 W
82	Lubec (lū'bĕk) ... Maine	44·49 N	67·01 W
120	Lübeck (lü'bĕk) ... Ger.	53·53 N	10·42 E
120	Lübecker Bucht (B.) (lü'bĕ-kĕr bōōkt) . Ger.	54·10 N	11·20 E
166	Lubilash (R.) (lōō-bê-lăsh') Con. L.	7·45 S	24·09 E
120	Lubin (lyōō'bĭn) ... Pol.	51·24 N	16·14 E
121	Lublin (lyōō'blĕn') ... Pol.	51·14 N	22·33 E
129	Lubny (lōōb'nê) ... Sov. Un.	50·01 N	33·02 E
155	Lubuagan (lōō-bwä-gä'n) Phil. (Manila In.)	17·24 N	121·11 E
166	Lubudi (R.) (lōō-bōō'dê) . Con. L.	10·03 S	24·28 E
126	Lucca (lōōk'kä) ... It.	43·51 N	10·29 E
116	Luce B. (lūs) ... Scot.	54·45 N	4·45 W
94	Lucea ... Jam.	18·25 N	78·10 W

ăt; finăl; rāte; senâte; ärm; àsk; sofȧ; fâre; ch-choose; dh-as th in other; bē; ēvent; bĕt; recĕnt; cratēr; g-go; gh-guttural g; bĭt; ĭ-short neutral; rīde; K-guttural k as ch in German ich;

Page	Name Pronunciation Region	Lat. °′	Long. °′
155	Lucena (lōō-sä'nä) Phil. (Manila In.)	13·55 N	121·36 E
124	Lucena (loō-thä'nä) Sp.	37·25 N	4·28 W
125	Lucena del Cid (lōō-thä'nä dā thēdh'). Sp.	40·08 N	0·18 W
121	Lučenec (lōō'chå-nyĕts) Czech.	48·19 N	19·41 E
126	Lucera (lōō-châ'rä) It.	41·31 N	15·22 E
151	Luchi China	28·18 N	110·10 E
148	Luchia (lōō'jĭä) China	32·12 N	115·53 E
148	Luchih (lōō'jēĭ) China	31·17 N	120·54 E
67	Lucin (lů-sēn') Utah	41·23 N	113·59 W
155	Lucipara (I.) (lōō-sē-pä'rä). Indon.	5·45 S	128·15 E
111	Luckenwalde (lōōk-ĕn-väl'dĕ) Ger. (Berlin In.)	52·05 N	13·10 E
142	Lucknow (lŭk'nou) India	26·54 N	80·58 E
122	Luçon (lü-sôn') Fr.	46·27 N	1·12 W
95	Lucrecia, Cabo (C.) (kä'bô-lōō-krā'sē-å). Cuba	21·05 N	75·30 W
127	Luda Kamchiya (R.) Bul.	42·46 N	27·13 E
123	Lüdenscheid (lü'dĕn-shīt) Ger. (Ruhr In.)	51·13 N	7·38 E
166	Lüderitz (lü'dēr-ĭts) (lü'dĕ-rĭts) S. W. Afr.	26·35 S	15·15 E
166	Lüderitz B. S. W. Afr.	26·35 S	14·30 E
142	Ludhiana India	31·00 N	75·52 E
123	Lüdinghausen (lü'dēng-hou-zĕn) Ger. (Ruhr In.)	51·46 N	7·27 E
80	Ludington (lŭd'ĭng-tŭn) Mich.	44·00 N	86·25 W
110	Ludlow (lŭd'lō) Eng.	52·22 N	2·43 W
75	Ludlow Ky. (Cincinnati In.)	39·05 N	84·33 W
118	Ludvika (loodh-vē'kå) Swe.	60·10 N	15·09 E
120	Ludwigsburg (lōōt'vēks-bōōrgh) Ger.	48·53 N	9·14 E
111	Ludwigsfelde (lōōd'vēgs-fĕl-dĕ) Ger. (Berlin In.)	52·18 N	13·16 E
120	Ludwigshafen (lōōt'vēks-hä'fĕn) Ger.	49·29 N	8·26 E
120	Ludwigslust (lōōt'vēks-lōōst). Ger.	53·18 N	11·31 E
128	Ludza (lōōd'zå) Sov. Un.	56·33 N	27·45 E
166	Luebo (lōō-ā'bō) Con. L.	5·15 S	21·22 E
166	Lufira (R.) (lōō-fē'rå) Con. L.	9·32 S	27·15 E
77	Lufkin (lŭf'kĭn) Tex.	31·21 N	94·43 W
128	Luga (lōō'gå) Sov. Un.	58·43 N	29·52 E
128	Luga (R.) Sov. Un.	59·00 N	29·25 E
120	Lugano (lōō-gä'nō) Switz.	46·01 N	8·52 E
129	Lugansk (lōō-gänsk') Sov. Un.	48·34 N	39·18 E
129	Lugansk (Oblast) (ôb'lȧst). Sov. Un.	49·08 N	38·37 E
167	Lugenda (R.) (lōō-zhĕn'dä) Moz.	12·16 S	37·29 E
168	Lugh Ferrandi Som. (Horn of Afr. In.)	3·38 N	42·35 E
116	Lugnaquilla, Mt. (lōōk-nȧ-kwĭ-lȧ). Ire.	52·56 N	6·30 W
126	Lugo (lōō'gô) It.	44·28 N	11·57 E
124	Lugo (lōō'gō) Sp.	43·01 N	7·32 W
115	Lugoi Rom.	45·42 N	22·00 E
127	Lugoj Rom.	45·51 N	21·56 E
	Luhe, see Winsen		
151	Luhsien China	28·58 N	105·25 E
165	Luī Chad	9·29 N	16·18 E
148	Lui (lōō'yĭ) China	33·52 N	115·32 E
166	Luilaka (R.) (lōō-ē-lä'kå) Con. L.	2·18 S	21·15 E
116	Luimneach (lĭm'nåk) Ire.	52·39 N	8·35 W
90	Luis Moya (lōōē's-mô-yä) Mex.	22·26 N	102·14 W
101	Luján (lōō-hän') Arg. (Buenos Aires In.)	34·36 S	59·07 W
101	Luján (R.) Arg. (Buenos Aires In.)	34·33 S	58·59 W
147	Lujchow Pen. China	20·40 N	110·30 E
166	Lukanga Swp. (lōō-kăŋ'gȧ). N. Rh.	14·08 S	28·32 E
166	Lukenie (R.) (lōō-kä'nyå). Con. L.	2·48 S	18·45 E
127	Lukovit (lōō'kō-vēt') Bul.	43·13 N	24·07 E
121	Łuków (wōō'kōōf) Pol.	51·57 N	22·25 E
166	Lukuga (R.) (lōō-kōō'gå) Con. L.	5·47 S	27·48 E
132	Lule (R.) Swe.	66·20 N	20·25 E
112	Luleå (lōō'lĕ-ô) Swe.	65·39 N	21·52 E
127	Lüleburgaz (lü'lĕ-bōōr-gäs') Tur.	41·25 N	27·23 E
148	Luling (lū'lĭng) China	39·54 N	118·53 E
77	Luling Tex.	29·41 N	97·38 W
65	Lulu (I.) (lū'lōō) Can. (Vancouver In.)	49·10 N	123·04 W
166	Lulua (R.) (lōō'lōō-å) Con. L.	6·30 S	22·15 E
166	Luluabourg (lōō'lōō-å-bōōrg') Con. L.	6·14 S	22·17 E
79	Lumber (R.) (lŭm'bēr) N. C.	35·12 N	79·35 W
78	Lumberton (lŭm'bēr-tŭn) Miss.	31·00 N	89·25 W
79	Lumberton N. C.	34·37 N	79·00 W
101	Luminárias (lōō-mē-nȧ'ryäs) Braz. (Rio de Janeiro In.)	21·32 S	44·53 W
65	Lummi (I.) Wash. (Vancouver In.)	48·42 N	122·43 W
65	Lummi B. (lŭm'ĭ) Wash. (Vancouver In.)	48·47 N	122·44 W
65	Lummi Island Wash. (Vancouver In.)	48·44 N	122·42 W
155	Luna (lōō'nä). Phil. (Manila In.)	16·51 N	120·22 E
118	Lund (lŭnd) Swe.	55·42 N	13·10 E
163	Lunda (Reg.) (lōōn'dȧ) Ang.	8·53 S	20·00 E
166	Lundi (R.) (lōōn'dē) S. Rh.	21·09 S	30·10 E
116	Lundy (I.) (lŭn'dē) Eng.	51·12 N	4·50 W
120	Lüneberger Heide (Reg.) (lü'nĕ-bōōr-gĕr hī'dĕ). Ger.	53·08 N	10·00 E
120	Lüneburg (lü'nē-bōōrgh) Ger.	53·16 N	10·25 E
122	Lunel (lü-nĕl') Fr.	43·41 N	4·07 E
123	Lünen (lü'nĕn) Ger. (Ruhr In.)	51·36 N	7·30 E
82	Lunenburg (lōō'nĕn-bûrg) Can.	44·24 N	64·16 W
83	Lunenburg Mass. (Boston In.)	42·36 N	71·44 W
123	Lunéville (lü-nȧ-vel') Fr.	48·37 N	6·29 E
166	Lunga (R.) (lōōŋ'gȧ) N. Rh.	12·58 S	26·18 E
152	Lungchen (lōōng'chĕn) China	48·38 N	122·12 E
135	Lungchen (lōōng'chĕn) China	48·47 N	126·43 E
151	Lungch'i China	24·35 N	117·45 E
151	Lungching China	22·20 N	107·02 E
150	Lungchingts'un (lōōng'chĭng'tsōōn'). China	42·45 N	129·30 E
166	Lungé-Bungo (R.) (lŭn'gā bŭn'gō) Ang.	13·00 S	20·15 E
150	Lunghsi China	35·00 N	104·40 E
148	Lungku (lōōng'kō) China	34·52 N	116·48 E
149	Lungyentung. China (Canton In.)	23·12 N	113·21 E
142	Lūni (R.) India	24·64 N	71·10 E
128	Luninets (R.) (lōō-nēn'yets) Sov. Un.	52·14 N	26·54 E
150	Lupei (lōō'pī) China	44·35 N	120·40 E
150	Lupin (Manchouli) (lōō'pĭn') (mȧn-chōō'lē). China	49·25 N	117·15 E
100	Luque (loo'kā) Par.	25·18 S	57·17 W
81	Luray (lū-rā') Va.	38·40 N	78·25 W
116	Lurgan (lûr'gȧn) N. Ire.	54·27 N	6·28 W
167	Lúrio (lōō'rē-ô) Moz.	13·17 S	40·29 E
167	Lúrio (R.) Moz.	13·58 S	37·52 E
166	Lusaka (lōō-sä'kȧ) N. Rh.	15·19 S	28·15 E
166	Lusambo (lōō-säm'bō) Con. L.	4·57 S	23·28 E
142	Lushai Hills Bur.	28·28 N	92·50 E
150	Lushan China	33·45 N	113·00 E
167	Lushoto (lōō-shō'tō) Tan.	4·47 S	38·17 E
148	Lüshun (Port Arthur) (lü'shŭn) China	38·49 N	121·15 E
167	Lusikisiki (lōō-sē-kē-sē'kē) S. Afr. (Natal In.)	31·22 S	29·37 E
70	Lusk (lŭsk) Wyo.	42·46 N	104·27 W
148	Lüta (lüdȧ) China	38·55 N	121·19 E
148	Lut'ai (lōō'tăī) China	39·20 N	117·50 E
77	Lutcher (lŭch'ēr) La.	30·03 N	90·43 W
84	Lutherville (lōō'thŭr-vĭl) Md. (Baltimore In.)	39·26 N	76·38 W
116	Luton (lū'tŭn) Eng.	51·55 N	0·28 W
121	Lutsk (lōōtsk) Sov. Un.	50·45 N	25·20 E
78	Luverne (lū-vûrn') Ala.	31·42 N	86·15 W
70	Luverne (lū-vûrn') Minn.	43·40 N	96·13 W
166	Luvua (R.) (lōō'vōō-ȧ) Con. L.	6·49 S	27·17 E
166	Luvungi (lōō-vōōn'gē) Con. L.	2·54 S	29·00 E
78	Luxapalila Cr. (lŭk-sȧ-pôl'ĭ-lȧ) Ala.	33·36 N	88·08 W
123	Luxembourg (lŭk-sĕm-bûrg) (lük sän-bōōr') (look-sĕm-bōōrgh). Lux.	49·38 N	6·30 E
102	Luxembourg Eur.	49·30 N	6·22 E
74	Luxemburg Mo. (St. Louis In.)	38·32 N	90·17 W
123	Luxeuil (lük-sû'y') Fr.	47·49 N	6·19 E
84	Luxomni (lŭx'ôm-nī) Ga. (Atlanta In.)	33·54 N	84·07 W
	Luxor, see Al Uqsur		
150	Luya Shan (Mtn.) China	38·50 N	111·40 E
132	Luza (R.) (lōō'zȧ) Sov. Un.	60·30 N	47·10 E
120	Luzern (lōō-tsĕrn) Switz.	47·03 N	8·18 E
99	Luziânia (lōō-zyȧ'nēȧ) Braz.	16·17 S	47·44 W
154	Luzon (I.) (lōō-zŏn') Phil.	17·10 N	119·45 E
151	Luzon Str. (lōō-zŏn') Phil.	20·40 N	121·00 E
121	L'vov (l'vōōf) Sov. Un.	49·51 N	24·01 E
135	Lyakhovskiye (Is.) (lya'kō'v-skyē). Sov. Un.	73·45 N	145·15 E
142	Lyallpur (lī'ȧl-pûr) W. Pak.	31·29 N	73·06 E
85	Lyalta Can. (Calgary In.)	51·07 N	113·36 W
136	Lyalya R. (lyȧ'lyȧ) Sov. Un. (Urals In.)	58·58 N	60·17 E
127	Lyaskovets Bul.	43·07 N	25·41 E
166	Lydenburg (lī'dĕn-bûrg) S. Afr.	25·06 S	30·21 E
68	Lyell, Mt. (lī'ĕl) Calif.	37·44 N	119·22 W
81	Lykens (lī'kĕnz) Pa.	40·35 N	76·45 W
121	Lyna R. (lĭn'ȧ) Pol.	53·56 N	20·30 E
78	Lynch (lĭnch) Ky.	36·56 N	82·55 W
79	Lynchburg (lĭnch'bûrg) Va.	37·23 N	79·08 W
65	Lynch Cove (lĭnch) Wash. (Seattle In.)	47·26 N	122·54 W
85	Lynden (lĭn'dĕn) Can. (Toronto In.)	43·14 N	80·08 W
65	Lynden Wash. (Vancouver In.)	48·56 N	122·27 W
161	Lyndhurst. Austl. (Melbourne In.)	38·03 S	145·14 E
75	Lyndon (lĭn'dŭn) Ky. (Louisville In.)	38·15 N	85·36 W
81	Lyndonville (lĭn'dŭn-vĭl) Vt.	44·35 N	72·00 W
83	Lynn (lĭn) Mass. (Boston In.)	42·28 N	70·57 W
84	Lynnhaven (lĭn'hā-vĕn) Va. (Norfolk In.)	36·50 N	76·04 W
86	Lynn Lake (lăk) Can.	56·48 N	101·10 W
74	Lynwood (lĭn'wŏŏd) Calif. (Los Angeles In.)	33·56 N	118·13 W
122	Lyon (lē-ôn') Fr.	45·44 N	4·52 E
79	Lyons (lī'ŭnz) Ga.	32·08 N	82·19 W
72	Lyons Kans.	38·20 N	98·11 W
70	Lyons Nebr.	41·57 N	96·28 W
84	Lyons N. J. (New York In.)	40·41 N	74·33 W
81	Lyons N. Y.	43·05 N	77·00 W
118	Lyse Fd. (lü'sĕ fyôr') Nor.	58·59 N	6·35 E
118	Lysekil (lü'sĕ-kēl) Swe.	58·17 N	11·22 E
136	Lys'va (lĭs'vȧ) Sov. Un. (Urals In.)	58·07 N	57·47 E
110	Lytham (lĭth'ȧm) Eng.	53·44 N	2·58 W
167	Lyttelton (lĭt'l'ton) S. Afr. (Johannesburg & Pretoria In.)	25·51 S	28·13 E
86	Lytton (lĭt'ŭn) Can.	50·16 N	121·29 W
136	Lyuban' (lyōō' bän) Sov. Un. (Leningrad In.)	59·21 N	31·15 E
129	Lyubar (lyōō'bär) Sov. Un.	49·56 N	27·44 E
136	Lyubertsy (lyōō'bĕr-tsē) Sov. Un. (Moscow In.)	55·40 N	37·55 E
128	Lyubim (lyōō-bēm') Sov. Un.	58·24 N	40·39 E
136	Lyublino (lyōōb'lĭ-nô) Sov. Un. (Moscow In.)	55·41 N	37·45 E
128	Lyudinovo (lū-dē'novō). Sov. Un.	53·52 N	34·28 E
146	Lyung Mong.	47·58 N	104·52 E
139	Ma'an (mä-än') Jordan (Palestine In.)	30·12 N	35·45 E
118	Maarianhamina (Mariehamn) (mä'rē-ȧn-hä'mē-na) (mȧ-rē'ĕ-häm''n). Fin.	60·07 N	19·57 E
111	Maartensdijk Neth. (Amsterdam In.)	52·09 N	5·10 E
123	Maas (R.) Neth. (Ruhr In.)	51·32 N	6·07 E
117	Maastricht (mäs'trĭkt) Bel.	50·51 N	5·35 E
165	Maaten Bishidra (Oasis) Libya	23·11 N	22·34 E
65	Mabana (mä-bä-nä) Wash. (Seattle In.)	48·06 N	122·25 W
77	Mabank (mā'bănk) Tex.	32·21 N	96·05 W
168	Mabeskraal S. Afr. (Johannesburg & Pretoria In.)	25·12 S	26·47 E
84	Mableton (mā'b'l-tŭn) Ga. (Atlanta In.)	33·49 N	84·34 W
114	Mabrouk (mȧ-brōōk') Alg.	29·30 N	0·20 E
164	Mabrouk Mali	19·27 N	1·16 W
139	Mabruk (R.) Sau. Ar. (Palestine In.)	29·16 N	35·22 E
168	Mabula (mȧ'bōō-la) S. Afr. (Johannesburg & Pretoria In.)	24·49 S	27·59 E
82	McAdam (măk-ăd'ăm) Can.	45·37 N	67·21 W
101	Macaé (mä-kä-ā') Braz. (Rio de Janeiro In.)	22·22 S	41·47 W
84	McAfee (măk-ȧ'fē) N. J. (New York In.)	41·10 N	74·32 W
99	Macaira (R.) (mä-kī'rä) Ven. (In.)	9·37 N	66·16 W
155	Macalelon (mä-kä-lä-lōn') Phil. (Manila In.)	13·46 N	122·09 E
73	McAlester (măk ăl'ĕs-tēr) Okla.	34·55 N	95·45 W
76	McAllen (măk-ăl'ĕn) Tex.	26·12 N	98·14 W
99	Macapá (mä-kä-pä') Braz.	0·08 N	50·02 W
151	Macau (mä-kȧ'ōō) Asia	22·10 N	113·35 E
99	Macau (mä-kȧ'ōō) Braz.	5·12 S	36·34 W
95	Macaya, Pico de (Pk.) Hai.	18·25 N	74·00 W
86	McBride (măk-brīd') Can.	53·25 N	120·15 W
84	McCalla (măk-kăl'lȧ) Ala. (Birmingham In.)	33·20 N	87·00 W
76	McCamey (mȧ-kā'mĭ) Tex.	31·08 N	102·13 W
125	Maccarese (mäk-kä-rĕ'zĕ) It. (Rome In.)	41·53 N	12·13 E
74	McCarron (măk kăr'ŭn) Mich. (Sault Ste. Marie In.)	46·20 N	84·17 W
78	McCaysville (mȧ-kāz'vĭl) Ga.	34·57 N	84·21 W
110	Macclesfield (măk''lz-fēld) Eng.	53·15 N	2·07 W
110	Macclesfield Can. (măk''lz-fēld) Eng.	53·14 N	2·07 W
79	McColl (mȧ-kōl') S. C.	34·40 N	79·34 W
78	McComb (mȧ-kōm') Miss.	31·14 N	90·27 W
70	McConaughy, L. (măk kō'nō ĭ') Nebr.	41·24 N	101·40 W
72	McCook (mȧ-kōōk') Nebr.	40·13 N	100·37 W
79	McCormick (mȧ-kôr'mĭk) S. C.	33·56 N	82·20 W
116	Macdhui, Ben (Mtn.) (bĕn măk-dōō'ē). Scot.	57·06 N	3·45 W
74	Macdona (măk-dō'nȧ) Tex. (San Antonio In.)	29·20 N	98·42 W
75	McDonald (măk-dŏn'ăld) Pa. (Pittsburgh In.)	40·22 N	80·13 W
158	Macdonald (I.) (măk-dŏn'ăld) Austl.	23·40 S	127·40 E
47	McDonald I. Austl.	53·00 S	72·45 E
85	McDonald L. (măk-dŏn-ăld) Can. (Calgary In.)	51·12 N	113·53 W
158	Macdonnell Ra. (măk-dŏn'ĕl) Austl.	23·40 S	131·30 E
75	Macedonia (măs-ē-dō'nĭ-ȧ) Ohio (Cleveland In.)	41·19 N	81·30 W
127	Macedonia (Reg.) (măs-ē-dō'nĭ-ȧ) Eur.	41·05 N	22·15 E
99	Maceió (mä-sȧ-yō') Braz.	9·33 S	35·35 W
126	Macerata (mä-chä-rä'tä) It.	43·18 N	13·28 E
160	Macfarlane, L. (măc'fär-lān) Austl.	32·10 S	137·00 E
73	McGehee (mȧ-gē') Ark.	33·39 N	91·22 W
68	McGill (mȧ-gĭl') Nev.	39·25 N	114·47 W
65	McGowan (măk-gou'ăn) Wash. (Portland In.)	46·15 N	123·55 W
64	McGrath (măk grăth) Alaska	62·58 N	155·20 W
75	McGregor (măk-grĕg'ēr) Can. (Detroit In.)	42·08 N	82·58 W
71	McGregor Iowa	42·58 N	91·12 W
77	McGregor Tex.	31·26 N	97·23 W
85	McGregor L. (măk-grĕg'ēr) Can. (Ottawa In.)	45·38 N	75·44 W
167	Machache (Mtn.). Bas. (Natal In.)	29·22 S	27·53 E
101	Machado (mä-shä-dô) Braz. (Rio de Janeiro In.)	21·42 S	45·55 W
98	Machala (mä-chä'lä) Ec.	3·18 S	78·54 W
75	McHenry (măk-hĕn'rĭ) Ill. (Chicago In.)	42·21 N	88·16 W
74	Machens (măk'ĕns) Mo. (St. Louis In.)	38·54 N	90·20 W
82	Machias (mȧ-chī'ȧs) Maine	44·22 N	67·29 W
98	Machu Picchu (mä'chōō-pē'k-chōō). Peru	8·01 S	72·24 W
129	Măcin (mȧ-chēn') Rom.	45·15 N	28·09 E
70	McIntosh (măk'ĭn-tŏsh) S. D.	45·54 N	101·22 W
159	Mackay (mȧ-kī') Austl.	21·15 S	149·08 E
67	Mackay (măk-kā') Idaho	43·55 N	113·38 W
158	Mackay (I.) (mȧ-kī') Austl.	22·30 S	127·45 E
86	MacKay (L.) (măk-kā') Can.	64·00 N	113·13 W
65	McKay (R.) Ore.	45·43 N	123·00 W
85	MacKayville (măk-kā-vĭl) Can. (Montreal In.)	45·28 N	73·28 W
75	McKeesport (mȧ-kēz'pōrt) Pa. (Pittsburgh In.)	40·21 N	79·51 W
75	McKees Rocks (mȧ-kēz' rŏks) Pa. (Pittsburgh In.)	40·29 N	80·05 W
78	McKenzie (mȧ-kĕn'zĭ) Tenn.	36·07 N	88·30 W
86	Mackenzie, Dist. of Can.	63·48 N	125·25 W
86	Mackenzie (R.) Can.	63·28 N	124·23 W
64	Mackenzie B. Alaska	69·20 N	137·10 W
86	Mackenzie Mts. (mȧ-kĕn'zĭ). Can.	63·41 N	129·27 W
66	McKenzie R. Ore.	44·07 N	122·20 W
80	Mackinac, Str. of (măk'ĭ-nô) (măk'ĭ-năk). Mich.	45·50 N	84·40 W
80	Mackinaw (R.) Ill.	40·35 N	89·25 W
80	Mackinaw City (măk'ĭ-nô). Mich.	45·45 N	84·45 W
64	McKinley, Mt. (mȧ-kĭn'lĭ). Alaska	63·00 N	151·02 W
73	McKinney (mȧ-kĭn'ĭ) Tex.	33·12 N	96·35 W
86	Macklin (măk'lĭn) Can.	52·22 N	109·51 W

ng-sing; ŋ-baŋk; ɴ-nasalized n; nŏd; cŏmmit; ōld; ōbey; ôrder; fōōd; fŏŏt; ou-out; s-soft; sh-dish; th-thin; pūre; ûnite; ûrn; stŭd; circŭs; ü-as "y" in study; '-indeterminate vowel.

Page	Name Pronunciation Region	Lat. °′	Long. °′
70	McLaughlin (mȧk-lŏf'lĭn) . . . S. D.	45·48 N	100·45 W
80	McLeansboro (mȧ-klānz'bŭr-ō) Ill.	38·10 N	88·35 W
167	Macleantown (măk-lān'toun) S. Afr. (Natal In.)	32·48 S	27·48 E
167	Maclear (mȧ-klēr') S. Afr. (Natal In.)	31·06 S	28·23 E
86	McLennan (măk-lĭn'nȧn) . . . . Can.	55·51 N	117·10 W
66	McLoughlin, Mt. (mȧk-lŏk'lĭn) Ore.	42·27 N	122·20 W
76	McMillan L. (mȧk-mĭl'ȧn) . . . Tex.	32·40 N	104·09 W
65	McMillin (mȧk-mĭl'ĭn) Wash. (Seattle In.)	47·08 N	122·14 W
66	McMinnville (mȧk-mĭn'vĭl) . . Ore.	45·13 N	123·13 W
78	McMinnville . . . Tenn.	35·41 N	85·47 W
86	McMurray (mȧk-mŭr'ĭ) . . . . . Can.	56·45 N	111·15 W
65	McMurray . . . . Wash. (Seattle In.)	48·19 N	122·15 W
69	McNary (mȧk-nâr'ē) . . . Ariz.	34·10 N	109·55 W
77	McNary . . . La.	30·58 N	92·32 W
66	McNary Dam . . . Ore.-Wash.	45·57 N	119·15 W
73	Macomb (mȧ-kōōm') . . . Ill.	40·27 N	90·40 W
122	Mâcon (mä-kôN) . . . Fr.	46·19 N	4·51 E
78	Macon (mā'kŏn) . . . Ga.	32·49 N	83·39 W
78	Macon . . . Miss.	32·07 N	88·31 W
73	Macon . . . Mo.	39·42 N	92·29 W
73	McPherson (mȧk-fŭr's'n) . . . Kans.	38·21 N	97·41 W
160	Macquarie (R.) . . . Austl.	31·43 S	148·04 E
47	Macquarie Is. (mȧ-kwŏr'ē) . Austl.	54·36 S	158·45 E
78	McRae (mȧk-rā') . . . Ga.	32·02 N	82·55 W
78	McRoberts (mȧk-rŏb'ērts) . . . . Ky.	37·12 N	82·40 W
92	Macuelizo (mä-kwĕ-lē'zō) . . Hond.	15·22 N	88·32 W
139	Ma'dabā) . . Jordan (Palestine In.)	31·43 N	35·47 E
163	Madagascar (I.) (măd-ȧ-găs'kȧr) Malag. Rep.	23·30 S	46·00 E
83	Madame (I.) (mȧ-dȧm') . . . . Can.	45·31 N	60·45 W
143	Madanapalle . . . India	13·06 N	78·09 E
155	Madang (mä-däng') . N. Gui. Ter.	5·15 S	145·45 E
164	Madaoua (mȧ-dou'ȧ) . . . Niger	14·04 N	6·03 E
74	Madart (mȧ'dȧrt) Minn. (Minneapolis, St. Paul In.)	44·48 N	93·02 W
81	Madawaska (R.) (măd-ȧ-wôs'kȧ) Can.	45·20 N	77·25 W
88	Madden, L. C. Z. (Panama Canal In.)	9·15 N	79·34 W
164	Madeira, Ilha da (I.) (mä-dā'rä) Mad. Is.	32·41 N	16·15 W
164	Madeira, Arquipelago da (Is.) (är-kē-pĕ'lä-gō-dä-mä-dĕ'y-rä) Port.	33·26 N	16·44 W
98	Madeira (R.) . . . Braz.	6·48 S	62·43 W
82	Madeleine, C. (măd'lĕn') . . . . Can.	49·15 N	65·20 W
71	Madelia (mȧ-dē'lĭ-ȧ) . . . Minn.	44·03 N	94·23 W
71	Madeline (I.) (măd'ĕ-lĭn) . . . Wis.	46·47 N	91·30 W
68	Madera (mȧ-dā'rȧ) . . . Calif.	36·57 N	120·04 W
92	Madera (Vol.) . . . Nic.	11·27 N	85·30 W
142	Madhya Pradesh (State) ((mŭd'vŭ prŭ-dāsh') . India	27·04 N	77·48 E
73	Madill (mȧ-dĭl') . . . Okla.	34·04 N	96·45 W
78	Madison (măd'ĭ-sŭn) . . . Fla.	30·25 N	85·25 W
78	Madison . . . Ga.	33·34 N	83·29 W
74	Madison . . . Ill. (St. Louis In.)	38·40 N	90·09 W
80	Madison . . . Ind.	38·45 N	85·25 W
73	Madison . . . Kans.	38·08 N	96·07 W
82	Madison . . . Maine	44·47 N	69·52 W
70	Madison . . . Minn.	44·59 N	96·13 W
70	Madison . . . Nebr.	41·49 N	97·27 W
84	Madison . . . . N. J. (New York In.)	40·46 N	74·25 W
79	Madison . . . N. C.	36·22 N	79·59 W
70	Madison . . . S. D.	44·01 N	97·08 W
71	Madison . . . Wis.	43·05 N	89·23 W
67	Madison Res . . . Mont.	45·25 N	111·28 W
67	Madison R . . . Mont.	45·15 N	111·30 W
80	Madisonville (măd'ĭ-sŭn-vĭl) . . Ky.	37·20 N	87·30 W
77	Madisonville . . . La.	30·22 N	90·10 W
77	Madisonville . . . Tex.	30·57 N	95·55 W
154	Madjene . . . Indon.	3·34 S	119·00 E
128	Madona (mȧ'dō'nȧ) . . . . . Sov. Un.	56·50 N	26·14 E
143	Madras (mȧ-drȧs') (mŭ-drŭs') India	13·08 N	80·15 E
143	Madras (State) (mŭ-drŭs') (mȧ-drȧs') . India	15·20 N	78·20 E
77	Madre, Laguna L. (lä-gōō'nä mä'drâ) . Mex.	25·08 N	97·41 W
90	Madre, Sierra (Mts.) (sē-ĕ'r-rä-mȧ'drĕ) . Mex.	15·55 N	92·40 W
155	Madre, Sierra (Mts.) Phil. (Manila In.)	16·40 N	122·10 E
100	Madre de Dios, Arch. (mȧ'drä dä dē-ōs') . Chile	50·40 S	76·30 W
98	Madre de Dios, Rio (R.) (rē'ō-mȧ'drä dä dē-ōs') . Bol.	12·07 S	68·20 W
90	Madre del Sur, Sierra (Mts.) (sē-ĕ'r-rä-mȧ'drä dĕlsōōr') . Mex.	17·35 N	100·35 W
71	Madrid (măd'rĭd) . . . Iowa	41·51 N	93·48 W
125	Madrid (mä-drē'd) Sp. (Madrid In.)	40·26 N	3·42 W
124	Madridejos (mä-dhrē-dhä'hōs) . Sp.	39·29 N	3·32 W
66	Mad R. (măd) . . . Calif.	40·38 N	123·37 W
143	Madura (mä-dōō'rȧ) . . . India	9·57 N	78·04 E
154	Madura (I.) (mȧ-dōō'rä) . . Indon.	6·45 S	113·30 E
100	Madureira, Serra do (Mtn.) (sĕ'r-rä-dō-mä-dōō-rā'rȧ) . Braz. (In.)	22·49 S	43·30 W
153	Maebashi (mä-ĕ-bä'shē) . . . Jap.	36·26 N	139·04 E
125	Maella (mä-āl'yä) . . . Sp.	41·10 N	0·07 E
94	Maestra, Sierra (Mts.) (sē-ĕ'r-rȧ-mä-ās'trä) . Cuba	20·05 N	77·05 W
159	Maewo (I.) . . . New Hebr.	15·17 S	168·16 E
166	Mafeking (mȧf'ē-kĭng) . . . . S. Afr.	25·46 S	24·45 E
167	Mafia (I.) (mä-fē'ä) . . . Tan.	7·45 S	39·45 E
100	Mafra (mȧ'frä) . . . Braz.	26·21 S	49·59 W
125	Mafra (mäf'rȧ) . Port. (Lisbon In.)	38·56 N	9·20 W
135	Magadan (mȧ-gȧ-dän') . Sov. Un.	59·39 N	150·43 E
135	Magadan Oblast . . . Sov. Un.	63·00 N	170·30 E
167	Magadi (L.) (mä-gä'dē) . . . . Ken.	2·12 S	37·32 E
167	Magalies (R.) (mä-gä'lyĕs) S. Afr. (Johannesburg & Pretoria In.)	25·51 S	27·42 E

Page	Name Pronunciation Region	Lat. °′	Long. °′
167	Magaliesberg (Mts.) S. Afr. (Johannesburg & Pretoria In.)	25·45 S	27·43 E
168	Magaliesburg . . . S. Afr. (Johannesburg & Pretoria In.)	26·01 S	27·32 E
155	Magallanes (mä-gäl-yä'näs) Phil. (Manila In.)	12·48 N	123·52 E
100	Magallene, Estrecho de (Str.) (ĕs-trĕ'chō-dĕ-mä-gäl-yä'nĕs) Arg.-Chile	52·30 S	68·45 W
98	Magangué (mä-gän'gā) . . . Col.	9·08 N	74·56 W
155	Magat (R.) (mä-gät') Phil. (Manila In.)	16·45 N	121·16 E
101	Magdalena (mäg-dä-lā'nä) Arg. (Buenos Aires In.)	35·05 S	57·32 W
98	Magdalena . . . Bol.	13·17 S	63·57 W
62	Magdalena . . . Mex.	30·34 N	110·50 W
69	Magdalena . . . N. Mex.	34·10 N	107·45 W
100	Magdalena (I.) . . . Chile	44·45 S	73·15 W
88	Magdalena, Bahia (B.) (bä-ē'ä-mäg-dä-lā'nä) . Mex.	24·30 N	114·00 W
98	Magdalena, Rio (R.) . . . Col.	7·45 N	74·04 W
83	Magdalen Is. (măg'dȧ-lĕn) . . . Can.	47·27 N	61·25 W
120	Magdeburg (mäg'dĕ-bōōrgh) . Ger.	52·07 N	11·39 E
100	Magé (mä-zhā') . . . Braz. (In.)	22·39 S	43·02 W
126	Magenta (mȧ-jĕn'tȧ) . . . It.	45·26 N	8·53 E
112	Mageröy (I.) (mä'ghĕr-ûē) . . . Nor.	71·10 N	24·11 E
126	Maggiore, Lago di (L.) . . . It.	46·03 N	8·25 E
168	Maghāghah . . . U. A. R. (Nile In.)	28·38 N	30·50 E
90	Magiscatzin (mä-kēs-kät-zēn') Mex.	22·48 N	98·42 W
127	Maglaj (mȧ'glä-ē) . . . Yugo.	44·34 N	18·12 E
127	Maglić (mäg'lēch) . . . Yugo.	43·36 N	20·36 E
127	Maglie (mäl'yā) . . . It.	40·06 N	18·20 E
74	Magna (măg'nȧ) Utah (Salt Lake City In.)	40·43 N	112·06 W
136	Magnitogorsk (mäg-nyē'tô-gôrsk) . Sov. Un. (Urals In.)	53·26 N	59·05 E
73	Magnolia (măg-nō'lĭ-ȧ) . . . Ark.	33·16 N	93·13 W
84	Magnolia . . . . Md. (Baltimore In.)	39·24 N	76·19 W
78	Magnolia . . . Miss.	31·08 N	90·27 W
123	Magny-en-Vexin (mä-nyē'ĕN-vĕ-sǎN') . Fr. (Paris In.)	49·09 N	1·45 E
81	Magog (mȧ-gŏg') . . . Can.	45·15 N	72·10 W
82	Magpie (L.) (măg'pī) . . . Can.	50·56 N	64·30 W
71	Magpie (R.) . . . Can.	48·13 N	84·50 W
86	Magrath . . . Can.	49·22 N	112·52 W
166	Magude (mä-gōō'dȧ) . . . Moz.	24·58 S	32·39 E
146	Magwe (mŭg-wā') . . . Bur.	20·19 N	94·57 E
133	Mahabād . . . Iran	36·55 N	45·50 E
165	Mahagi (mä-hä'gē) . . . Con. L.	2·14 N	31·12 E
154	Mahakam, Sungai (Strm.) . . Indon.	0·30 S	116·15 E
167	Mahaly (mȧ-hȧl-ē') . . Malag. Rep.	24·09 S	46·20 E
154	Mahameru, Gunung (Mtn.) . . Java	8·00 S	112·50 E
142	Mahānadi (R.) (mŭ-hä-nŭd'ē) India	20·50 N	84·27 E
167	Mahanoro (mȧ-hȧ-nô'rō) Malag. Rep.	19·57 S	48·47 E
81	Mahanoy City (mä-hȧ-noi') . . . Pa.	40·50 N	76·10 W
142	Maharashtra (State) . . . India	20·25 N	75·00 E
139	Mahasham (R.) U. A. R. (Palestine In.)	30·08 N	34·09 E
167	Mahavavy (R.) (mä-hä-vä'vē) Malag. Rep.	17·42 S	46·06 E
142	Mahaweli (R.) . . . India	7·47 N	80·43 E
113	Mahdia (mä-dē'ä) (mä'dē-ȧ) . Tun.	35·30 N	11·09 E
143	Mahe (mä-ā') . . . India	11·42 N	75·39 E
167	Mahenge (mä-hĕŋ'gȧ) . . . Tan.	8·41 S	36·43 E
142	Mahi (R.) . . . India	23·16 N	73·20 E
143	Māhīm Bay . . India (Bombay In.)	19·03 N	72·45 E
167	Mahlabatini (mä'lȧ-bȧ-tē'nē) S. Afr. (Natal In.)	28·15 S	31·29 E
111	Mahlow (mä'lōv) . Ger. (Berlin In.)	52·23 N	13·24 E
70	Mahnomen (mô-nō'mĕn) . . . Minn.	47·18 N	95·58 W
125	Mahón (mä-ōn') . . . Sp.	39·52 N	4·15 E
82	Mahone Bay (mȧ-hōn') . . . Can.	44·27 N	64·24 W
82	Mahone B . . . Can.	44·27 N	64·05 W
84	Mahopac, L. (mā-hō'păk) N. Y. (New York In.)	41·24 N	73·45 W
84	Mahwah (mȧ-wä') N. J. (New York In.)	41·05 N	74·09 W
110	Maidenhead (mād'ĕn-hĕd) Eng. (London In.)	51·30 N	0·44 W
	Maidos, see Eceabat		
110	Maidstone (mād'stŭn) Eng. (London In.)	51·17 N	0·32 E
165	Maiduguri (mä'ē-dä-gōō'rē) . . Nig.	11·53 N	13·12 E
98	Maigualide Sierra (Mts.) (sē-ĕ'r-rä-mī-gwä'lē-dĕ) . Ven.	6·30 N	65·50 W
142	Maijdi . . . E. Pak.	22·59 N	91·08 E
	Maikop, see Maykop		
144	Maimana (mī-mȧ-nä') . . . Afg.	35·53 N	64·38 E
160	Main Barrier Ra. (băr"ēr) . Austl.	31·25 S	141·40 E
63	Maine (State) (mān) . . . U. S.	45·25 N	69·50 W
116	Mainland (I.) (măn-lănd) Scot. (In.)	60·19 N	2·40 W
120	Main R. (mīn) . . . Ger.	49·49 N	9·20 E
123	Maintenon (măN-tē-nôN') Fr. (Paris In.)	48·35 N	1·35 E
167	Maintirano (mä'ēn-tē-rä'nō) Malag. Rep.	18·05 S	44·08 E
120	Mainz (mīnts) . . . Ger.	49·59 N	8·16 E
164	Maio I. (mä'yō) . . . . C. V. Is. (In.)	15·15 N	22·50 W
101	Maipo (mī'pō) (R.) Chile (Santiago In.)	33·45 S	71·08 W
100	Maipo (Vol.) . . . Arg.	34·08 S	69·51 W
101	Maipú (mī'pōō') Arg. (Buenos Aires In.)	36·51 S	57·54 W
99	Maiquetía (mī-kĕ-tē'ä) . Ven. (In.)	10·37 N	66·56 W
95	Maisí, Punta (Pt.) (pōōn'n-tä-mī-sē') . Cuba	20·10 N	74·00 W
123	Maison-Rouge (mā-zôN-rōōzh') Fr. (Paris In.)	48·34 N	3·09 E
168	Mait I. (mät) Som. (Horn. of Afr. In.)	11·24 N	46·38 E

Page	Name Pronunciation Region	Lat. °′	Long. °′
160	Maitland (māt'lȧnd) . . . Austl.	32·45 S	151·40 E
80	Maitland (R.) . . . Can.	45·50 N	81·10 W
153	Maizuru (mä-ĭ'zōō-rōō) . . . Jap.	35·26 N	135·15 E
	Majorca I., see Mallorca, Isle de		
167	Majunga (mȧ-jŭŋ'gä) Malag. Rep.	15·12 S	46·26 E
66	Makah Ind. Res. (mä kī') . . Wash.	48·17 N	124·52 W
165	Mak'alē . . . Eth.	13·31 N	39·19 E
167	Makanya (mä-kän'yä) . . . Tan.	4·15 S	37·49 E
166	Makarikari Salt Pan (L.) . . Bech.	20·38 S	21·31 E
126	Makarska (mȧ'kär-skȧ) . . . . Yugo.	43·17 N	17·05 E
132	Makar'yev . . . Sov. Un.	57·50 N	43·48 E
154	Makasar . . . Indon.	5·08 S	119·28 E
154	Makasar, Selat (Str.) (mȧ-kăs'ẽr) Indon.	2·00 S	118·07 E
153	Make (I.) (mä'kȧ) . . . Jap.	30·43 N	130·49 E
129	Makeyevka (mŭk-yä'ŭf-kŭ) Sov. Un.	48·03 N	38·00 E
133	Makhachkala (mäκ'ȧch-kä'lä) Sov. Un.	43·00 N	47·40 E
167	Makhaleng (R.) . . Bas. (Natal In.)	29·53 S	27·33 E
127	Makhlata (mäκ'lä-tä) . . . Bul.	43·27 N	24·16 E
144	Makkah (Mecca) (mĕk'ä) . Sau. Ar.	21·27 N	39·45 E
87	Makkovik . . . Can.	55·01 N	59·10 W
121	Makó (mô'kō) . . . Hung.	46·13 N	20·30 E
164	Makokou (mȧ-kō-kōō') . . . . Gabon	0·39 N	12·46 E
121	Maków Mazowiecki (mä'kōov mä-zō-vyĕts'kē) . Pol.	52·51 N	21·07 E
153	Makuhari (mä-kōō-hä'rē) Jap. (Tōkyō In.)	35·39 N	140·04 E
153	Makurazaki (mä'kōō-rä-zä'kē) Jap.	31·16 N	130·18 E
164	Makurdi . . . Nig.	7·44 N	8·34 E
64	Makushin (mȧ-kōō'shĭn) . . . Alaska	53·57 N	166·28 W
134	Makushino (mȧ-kōō-shēn'ō) Sov. Un.	55·03 N	67·43 E
143	Malabar Coast (măl'ȧ-bär) . . India	16·30 N	75·33 E
139	Malacca (mȧ-lăk'ȧ) Mala. (Singapore In.)	2·11 N	102·15 E
139	Malacca (State) Mala. (Singapore In.)	2·19 N	102·09 E
154	Malacca, Str. of (mȧ-lăk'ȧ) . . Asia	4·15 N	99·44 E
67	Malad (mȧ-lăd') . . . Idaho	42·11 N	112·15 W
125	Maladetta (Mts.) (mä-lä-dĕt'tä) Sp.	42·30 N	0·38 E
125	Malafede (R.) (mä-lä-fē'dĕ) It. (Rome In.)	41·43 N	12·28 E
98	Málaga (mȧ'lä-gȧ) . . . Col.	6·41 N	72·46 W
124	Málaga . . . Sp.	36·45 N	4·25 W
124	Málaga, Bahía de (B.) (bä-ē'ä-dĕ-mȧ'lä-gä) . Sp.	36·35 N	4·10 W
163	Malagasy Republic . . . Afr.	18·05 S	43·12 E
124	Malagón (mä-lä-gōn') . . . Sp.	39·12 N	3·52 W
159	Malaita (I.) (mȧ-lä'ē-tȧ) . . Sol. Is.	8·38 S	161·15 E
165	Malakal (mȧ-lȧ-käl') . . . Sud.	9·46 N	31·54 E
136	Malakhovka (mȧ-lăk'ôf-kȧ) Sov. Un. (Moscow In.)	55·38 N	38·01 E
166	Malange (mȧ-läŋ'gȧ) . . . Ang.	9·30 S	16·25 E
82	Malapedia (R.) . . . Can.	48·11 N	67·08 W
93	Mala Punta (Pt.) (pōō'n-tä-mä'lä) Pan.	7·32 N	79·44 W
118	Mälaren (L.) . . . Swe.	59·38 N	16·55 E
87	Malartic . . . Can.	48·07 N	78·11 W
133	Malatya (mȧ-lä'tyȧ) . . . Tur.	38·30 N	38·15 E
154	Malaya (Reg.) (mȧ-lā'yȧ) . . . Mala.	3·35 N	101·30 E
128	Malaya Vishera (vē-shā'rȧ) Sov. Un.	58·51 N	32·13 E
154	Malay Pen. (mȧ-lā') (mā'lā) . . Asia	7·46 N	101·06 E
154	Malaysia (mȧ-lā'zhȧ) . . . Asia	4·10 N	101·22 E
116	Mal B. (măl) . . . Ire.	52·51 N	9·45 E
158	Malbon (măl'bŭn) . . . Austl.	21·15 S	140·30 E
121	Malbork (mäl'bôrk) . . . Pol.	54·02 N	19·04 E
125	Malcabran (R.) (mäl-kä-brän') Port. (Lisbon In.)	38·47 N	8·46 W
83	Malden (môl'dĕn) Mass. (Boston In.)	42·26 N	71·04 W
73	Malden . . . Mo.	36·32 N	89·56 W
157	Malden (I.) . . . Oceania	4·20 S	154·30 W
138	Maldive Is. (măl'dīv) . . . Asia	4·30 N	71 30 E
110	Maldon (môrl'dŏn) Eng. (London In.)	51·44 N	0·39 E
100	Maldonado (mäl-dŏ-nä'dô) . . . . Ur.	34·54 S	54·57 W
90	Maldonado, Punta (Pt.) (pōō'n-tä) . Mex.	16·18 N	98·34 W
127	Maléa, Akr. (C.) . . . Grc.	37·31 N	23·13 E
121	Male Karpaty (Mts.) . . . Czech.	48·31 N	17·15 E
159	Malekula (I.) (mä-lä-kōō'lä) New Hebr.	16·44 S	167·45 E
124	Malhão da Estrêla (Mtn.) (mäl-you'N-dä-ĕs-trĕ'lä) . Sp.	40·20 N	7·38 W
66	Malheur L. (mȧ-lōōr') . . . Ore.	43·16 N	118·37 W
66	Malheur R. (mȧ-lōōr') . . . Ore.	43·45 N	117·41 W
164	Mali . . . Afr.	15·45 N	0·15 W
74	Malibu (măl'ĭ-bōō) Calif. (Los Angeles In.)	34·03 N	118·38 W
129	Malin (mȧ-lēn') . . . Sov. Un.	50·44 N	29·15 E
90	Malinalco (mä-lē-näl'kō) . . . . Mex.	18·54 N	99·31 W
90	Malinaltepec (mä-lē-näl-tȧ-pĕk') Mex.	17·01 N	98·41 W
167	Malindi (mä-lēn'dē) . . . Ken.	3·14 S	40·04 E
121	Malineč (mä'lē-nyets') . . . . Czech.	48·31 N	19·40 E
116	Malin Hd . . . N. Ire.	54·84 N	6·70 W
116	Malinmore Hd. (mȧ'lĭn-mōr) . . Ire.	54·45 N	8·30 W
136	Malino (mä'lĭ-nô) Sov. Un. (Moscow In.)	55·07 N	38·12 E
129	Malinovka (mȧ-lē-nôf'kȧ) . Sov. Un.	49·50 N	36·43 E
127	Malkara (mäl'κȧ-rȧ) . . . Tur.	40·51 N	26·52 E
127	Malko Tŭrnovo (mäl'kō-t'r'nô-vȧ) . Bul.	41·59 N	27·28 E
116	Mallaig (măl'āg) . . . Scot.	56·59 N	5·55 W
168	Mallawī (mȧ-lȧ'wē) U. A. R. (Nile In.)	27·43 N	30·49 E
75	Mallet Creek (măl'ĕt) Ohio (Cleveland In.)	41·10 N	81·55 W

ăt; finăl; rāte; senâte; ärm; åsk; sofȧ; fâre; ch-choose; dh-as th in other; bē; ēvent; bĕt; recĕnt; cratẽr; g-go; gh-guttural g; bĭt; ĭ-short neutral; rīde; κ-guttural k as ch in German ich;

Page	Name Pronunciation Region	Lat. °′	Long. °′
125	Mallorca, Isla de (Majorca I.) (ē's-lä-dě-mäl-yô'r-kä) . Sp.	39·18 N	2·22 E
116	Mallow (măl'ō) . Ire.	52·07 N	9·04 W
117	Malmédy (mȧl-mā-dē') . Bel.	50·25 N	6·01 E
166	Malmesbury (mämz'bẽr-ĭ) . S. Afr.	33·30 S	18·35 E
118	Malmköping (mälm'chû'pĭng) Swe.	59·09 N	16·39 E
118	Malmö (mälm'û) . Swe.	55·36 N	12·58 E
135	Malmyzh (mȧl-mēzh') . Sov. Un.	49·58 N	137·07 E
132	Malmyzh . Sov. Un.	56·30 N	50·48 E
128	Maloarkhangelsk (mä'lô-är-кäŋ'gĕlsk) . Sov. Un.	52·26 N	36·29 E
155	Malolos (mä-lō'lōs) Phil. (Manila In.)	14·58 N	120·53 E
136	Malomal'sk (mȧ-lô-mälsk'') Sov. Un. (Urals In.)	58·47 N	59·55 E
81	Malone (mȧ-lōn') . N. Y.	44·50 N	74·20 W
128	Maloyaroslavets (mä'lô-yä-rô-slä-vyěts) . Sov. Un.	55·01 N	36·25 E
132	Malozemel'skaya Tundra (Plains) Sov. Un.	67·30 N	50·00 E
110	Malpas (măl'pȧz) . Eng.	53·01 N	2·46 W
98	Malpelo, Isla de (I.) (mäl-pä'lō) Col.	3·55 N	81·30 W
82	Malpeque B. (môl-pěk') . Can.	46·41 N	63·40 W
67	Malta (môl'tȧ) . Mont.	48·20 N	107·50 W
113	Malta (I.) . Eur.	35·52 N	14·26 E
166	Maltahöhe (mäl'tä-hō'ĕ) S. W. Afr.	24·45 S	16·45 E
85	Malton (môl'tŭn) Can. (Toronto In.)	43·42 N	79·39 W
91	Maltrata (mäl-trä'tä) . Mex.	18·48 N	97·16 W
167	Maluti Mts. (mȧ-lōō-tĭ) Bas. (Natal In.)	29·00 S	28·29 E
143	Malvan . India	16·08 N	73·32 E
73	Malvern (măl'vẽrn) . Ark.	34·21 N	92·47 W
135	Malyy Anyuy (R.) . Sov. Un.	67·52 N	164·30 E
135	Malyy Lyakhovskiye (I.) . Sov. Un.	74·15 N	142·30 E
135	Malyy Tamir (I.) . Sov. Un.	78·10 N	107·30 E
91	Mamantel (mä-män-těl') . Mex.	18·36 N	91·06 W
84	Mamaroneck (măm'á-rō-něk) N. Y (New York In.)	40·57 N	73·44 W
164	Mamau . Gui.	10·26 N	12·07 W
155	Mamberamo (R.) (mäm-bȧ-rä'mō) W. Irian	2·30 S	138·00 E
166	Mambone (mȧm-bŏ'nĕ) . Moz.	21·04 S	35·13 E
155	Mamburao (mäm-bōō'rä-ō) Phil. (Manila In.)	13·14 N	120·35 E
124	Mamede, Serra de (Mts.) (sĕ'r-rä-dĕ-mä-mĕ'dĕ) . Port.	39·29 N	7·11 W
164	Mamfe (mäm'fĕ) . Cam.	9·06 E	5·52 N
153	Mamihara (mä'mē-hä-rä) . Jap.	32·41 E	131·12 N
78	Mammoth Cave (măm'ŏth) . Ky.	37·10 N	86·04 W
78	Mammoth Cave Natl. Park . Ky.	37·20 N	86·21 W
67	Mammoth Hot Springs (măm'ŭth hot sprĭngz) . Wyo.	44·55 N	110·50 W
143	Mamnoli . India (Bombay In.)	19·17 N	73·15 E
98	Mamoré (R.) (mä-mô-rā') . Bol.	13·19 S	65·27 W
121	Mamry L. (mäm'rĭ) . Pol.	54·10 N	21·28 E
139	Mamshit . Isr. (Palestine In.)	31·02 N	35·04 E
125	Manacor (mä-nä-kôr') . Sp.	39·35 N	3·15 E
155	Manado . Indon.	1.29 N	124·50 E
95	Managua (mä-nä'gwä) Cuba (Havana In.)	22·14 N	82·17 W
92	Managua . Nic.	12·10 N	86·16 W
92	Managua, Lago de (L.) (lä'gô-dĕ) Nic.	12·28 N	86·10 W
167	Manakara (mä-nä-kä'rŭ) Malag. Rep.	22·17 S	48·06 E
167	Mananara (R.) (mä-nä-nä'rŭ) Malag. Rep.	23·15 S	48·15 E
167	Mananjary (mä-nän-zhä'rê) Malag. Rep.	20·16 S	48·13 E
	Manáos, see Manaus		
142	Manasaroar (L.) . China	30·40 N	81·58 E
81	Manassas (mȧ-năs'ȧs) . Va.	38·45 N	77·30 W
99	Manaus (Manáos) (mä-nä'ōōzh) Braz.	3·01 S	60·00 W
80	Mancelona (măn-sê-lō'nȧ) . Mich.	44·50 N	85·05 W
124	Mancha Real (män'chä rā-äl') . Sp.	37·48 N	3·37 W
136	Manchazh (män'chȧsh) Sov. Un. (Urals In.)	56·30 N	58·10 E
81	Manchester (măn'chĕs-tẽr) . Conn.	41·45 N	72·30 W
110	Manchester . Eng.	53·28 N	2·14 W
78	Manchester . Ga.	32·50 N	84·37 W
71	Manchester . Iowa	42·30 N	91·30 W
83	Manchester . Mass. (Boston In.)	42·35 N	70·47 W
74	Manchester . Mo. (St. Louis In.)	38·36 N	90·31 W
81	Manchester . N. H.	43·00 N	71·30 W
80	Manchester . Ohio	38·40 N	83·35 W
110	Manchester Ship Canal . Eng.	53·20 N	2·40 W
	Manchouli, see Lupin		
147	Manchuria (Reg.) (măn-chōō'rē-ȧ) China	48·00 N	124·58 E
144	Mand, Rud-e (R.) . Iran	28·30 N	51·43 E
118	Mandal (män'däl) . Nor.	58·03 N	7·28 E
146	Mandalay (măn'dȧ-lā) . Bur.	22·00 N	96·08 E
118	Mandalselv (R.) (män'dälsĕlv) Nor.	58·25 N	7·30 E
70	Mandan (măn'dăn) . N. D.	46·49 N	100·54 W
165	Mandara Mts. (män-dä'rä) . Cam.	10·55 N	14·10 E
139	Mandau Siak (R.) Indon. (Singapore In.)	1·03 N	101·25 E
93	Mandinga (män-dĭŋ'gä) . Pan.	9·32 N	79·04 W
142	Mandla . India	22·43 N	80·23 E
127	Mándra (män'drȧ) . Grc.	38·06 N	23·32 E
167	Mandritsara (mȧn-drēt-sä'rȧ) Malag. Rep.	15·49 S	48·47 E
127	Manduria (män-dōō'rē-ä) . It.	40·23 N	17·41 E
143	Mandve . India (Bombay In.)	18·47 N	72·52 E
143	Māndvi (mŭnd'vē) India (Bombay In.)	19·29 N	72·53 E
142	Māndvi (mŭnd'vē) . India	22·54 N	69·23 E
168	Manfalūț (män-fȧ-loot') U. A. R. (Nile In.)	27·18 N	30·59 E
126	Manfredonia (män-frȧ-dô'nyä) . It.	41·39 N	15·55 E
126	Manfredónia, Golfo di (G.) (gôl-fô-dē) . It.	41·34 N	16·05 E
99	Mangabeiras, Chap. das (Plains) (shä-pä'däs-däs-mäŋ-gä-bä'ê-räzh) . Braz.	8·05 S	47·32 W
143	Mangalore (mŭŋ-gŭ-lōr') . India	12·53 N	74·52 E
101	Mangaratiba (män-gä-rä-tē'bȧ) Braz. (Rio de Janeiro In.)	22·56 S	44·03 W
155	Mangatarem (män'gȧ-tä'rĕm) Phil. (Manila In.)	15·48 N	120·18 E
155	Mangguli (I.) (män-gōō-lē') . Indon.	1·35 S	126·22 E
154	Mangkalihat, Tandjoeng (C.) (mäng'kȧ-lē-hät') . Indon.	1·25 N	119·55 E
94	Mangles, Islas de (ē's-läs-dĕ-mäŋ'gläs) (măn'g'lz) Cuba	22·05 N	83·50 W
167	Mangoky (R.) (män-gō'kē) Malag. Rep.	22·02 S	44·11 E
124	Mangualde (män-gwäl'dĕ) . Port.	40·38 N	7·44 W
100	Mangueira, L. da (L.) (män-gā'ê-rȧ) . Braz.	33·15 S	52·45 W
72	Mangum (măŋ'gŭm) . Okla.	34·52 N	99·31 W
133	Mangyshlak, P.-ov. (Pen.) Sov. Un.	44·30 N	50·40 E
75	Manhattan . Ill. (Chicago In.)	41·25 N	87·29 W
73	Manhattan (măn-hăt'ăn) . Kans.	39·11 N	96·34 W
74	Manhattan Beach Calif. (Los Angeles In.)	33·53 N	118·24 W
101	Manhuaçu (män-ōōá'sōō) Braz. (Rio de Janeiro In.)	20·17 S	42·01 W
101	Manhumirim (män-ōō-mê-rē'ɴ) Braz. (Rio de Janeiro In.)	20·22 S	41·57 W
167	Mania (R.) (män'yä) . Malag. Rep.	19·52 S	46·02 E
99	Manicoré (mä-nê-kō-rā') . Braz.	5·53 S	61·13 W
87	Manicouagan (R.) . Can.	50·24 N	68·29 W
99	Manicuare (mä-nē-kwä'rē) Ven. (In.)	10·35 N	64·10 W
157	Manihiki Is. (mä'nē-hē'kē) Oceania	9·40 S	158·00 W
155	Manila (mȧ-nĭl'ȧ) Phil. (Manila In.)	14·37 N	121·00 E
155	Manila B . Phil. (Manila In.)	14·38 N	120·46 E
133	Manisa (mä'nê-sȧ) . Tur.	38·40 N	27·30 E
80	Manistee (măn-ĭs-tē') . Mich.	44·15 N	86·20 W
80	Manistee (R.) . Mich.	44·25 N	85·45 W
71	Manistique (măn-ĭs-tēk') . Mich.	45·58 N	86·16 W
71	Manistique (L.) . Mich.	46·14 N	85·30 W
71	Manistique (R.) . Mich.	46·05 N	86·09 W
86	Manitoba (Prov.) (măn-ĭ-tō'bȧ) Can.	55·12 N	97·29 W
86	Manitoba (L.) . Can.	50·38 N	98·40 W
72	Manitou (măn'ĭ-tōō) . Colo.	38·51 N	104·58 W
71	Manitou (I.) . Mich.	47·21 N	87·33 W
71	Manitou (L.) . Can.	49·21 N	93·01 W
80	Manitou Is . Mich.	45·05 N	86·00 W
80	Manitoulin I. (măn-ĭ-tōō'lĭn) . Can.	45·45 N	81·30 W
71	Manitowoc (măn-ĭ-tō-wŏk') . Wis.	44·05 N	87·42 W
98	Manizales (mä-nē-zä'lȧs) . Col. (In.)	5·05 N	75·31 W
166	Manjacaze (man'yä-kä'zĕ) . Moz.	24·37 S	33·49 E
144	Manjil (mŭn-jēl') . Iran	36·45 N	49·15 E
142	Mānjra (R.) . India	18·18 N	77·00 E
72	Mankato (măn-kā'tō) . Kans.	39·45 N	98·12 W
71	Mankato . Minn.	44·10 N	93·59 W
125	Manlleu (män-lyā'ōō) . Sp.	42·00 N	2·16 E
161	Manly (măn'lĭ) Austl. (Sydney In.)	33·48 S	151·16 E
143	Mannar (mȧ-när') . Ceylon	9.48 N	80·03 E
142	Mannar, G. of . India	8·47 N	78·33 E
111	Mannersdorf am Leithagebirge Aus. (Vienna In.)	47·58 N	16·36 E
120	Mannheim (män'hīm) . Ger.	49·30 N	8·31 E
71	Manning (măn'ĭng) . Iowa	41·53 N	95·04 W
79	Manning . S. C.	33·41 N	80·12 W
80	Mannington (măn'ĭng-tŭn) . W. Va.	39·30 N	80·55 W
126	Mannu (R.) (mä'n-nōō) . It.	39·32 N	9·03 E
95	Man of War B . Ba. Is.	21·05 N	74·05 W
95	Man of War Chan . Ba. Is.	22·45 N	76·10 W
155	Manokwari (mȧ-nŏk-wä'rē) W. Irian	0·56 S	134·10 E
65	Manor (măn'ẽr) Wash. (Portland In.)	45·45 N	122·36 W
143	Manori . India (Bombay In.)	19·13 N	72·43 E
123	Manosque (mȧ-nôsh') . Fr.	43·51 N	5·48 E
85	Manotick . Can. (Ottawa In.)	45·13 N	75·41 W
125	Manresa (män-rā'sä) . Sp.	41·44 N	1·52 E
87	Mansel (I.) (măn'sĕl) . Can.	61·56 N	81·10 W
98	Manseriche, Pongo de (Water Gap) (pŏ'n-gō-dĕ-män-sĕ-rē'chĕ) . Peru	4·15 S	77·45 W
110	Mansfield (mănz'fēld) . Eng.	53·08 N	1·12 W
77	Mansfield . La.	32·02 N	93·43 W
80	Mansfield . Ohio	40·45 N	82·30 W
66	Mansfield . Wash.	47·48 N	119·39 W
81	Mansfield, Mt . Vt.	44·30 N	72·45 W
110	Mansfield Woodhouse (wŏŏd-hous) . Eng.	53·08 N	1·12 W
99	Manso (R.) . Braz.	13·30 S	51·45 W
98	Manta (män'tä) . Ec.	1·03 S	80·16 W
75	Manteno (măn-tē-nō) Ill. (Chicago In.)	41·15 N	87·50 W
123	Mantes-la-Jolie (mäɴt-ĕ-lä-zhō-lē') Fr. (Paris In.)	48·59 N	1·42 E
69	Manti (măn'tī) . Utah	39·15 N	111·40 W
101	Mantiqueira, Serra da (Mts.) (sĕr'rä dä män-tê-kā'ē-rȧ) Braz. (Rio de Janeiro In.)	22·40 S	45·12 W
126	Mantova (Mantua) (män'tô-vä) (măn'tū-ȧ) . It.	45·09 N	10·47 E
94	Mantua (män-tōō'ä) . Cuba	22·20 N	84·15 W
74	Mantua (măn'tū-ȧ) Utah (Salt Lake City In.)	41·30 N	111·57 W
	Mantua, see Mantova		
82	Manuan (L.) (mä-nōō'ăn) . Can.	50·36 N	70·50 W
82	Manuan, Riviere (R.) . Can.	49·50 N	70·55 W
155	Manui (Is.) (mä-nōō'ē) . Indon.	3·35 S	123·38 E
155	Manus (I.) (mä'nōōs) . N. Gui. Ter.	2·22 S	146·22 E
77	Manvel (măn'vĕl) . Tex. (In.)	29·28 N	95·22 W
84	Manville (măn'vĭl) N. J. (New York In.)	40·33 N	74·36 W
84	Manville . R. I. (Providence In.)	41·57 N	71·27 W
133	Manych (R.) (mä-nĭch') . Sov. Un.	47·00 N	41·10 E
103	Manych Dep . Sov. Un.	46·32 N	42·44 E
133	Manych-Gudilo (Lake) . Sov. Un.	46·40 N	42·50 E
168	Manzala L . U. A. R. (Nile In.)	31·14 N	32·04 E
98	Manzanares (män-sä-nä'rĕs) Col. (In.)	5·15 N	75·09 W
125	Manzanares (R.) (mänz-nä'rĕs) Sp. (Madrid In.)	40·36 N	3·48 W
125	Manzanares, Canal de (kä-nä'l-dĕ-män-thä-nä'rĕs) Sp. (Madrid In.)	40·20 N	3·38 W
94	Manzanillo (män'zä-nēl'yō) . Cuba	20·20 N	77·05 W
90	Manzanillo . Mex.	19·02 N	104·21 W
95	Manzanillo, Bahía de (B.) . Hai.	19·55 N	71·50 W
90	Manzanillo, Bahía de (B.) (bä-ē'ä-dĕ-män-zä-nē'l-yō) . Mex.	19·00 N	104·38 W
93	Manzanillo, Punta (Pt.) . Pan.	9·40 N	79·33 W
152	Manzovka (mȧn-zhô'f-kȧ) Sov. Un.	44·16 N	132·13 E
165	Mao (mä'ŏ) . Chad	14·07 N	15·15 E
151	Maoming . China	21·55 N	110·40 E
91	Mapastepec (ma-päs-tȧ-pĕk') . Mex.	15·24 N	92·52 W
155	Mapia (I.) (mä'pē-ä) . W. Irian	0·57 N	134·22 E
76	Mapimi (mä-pē-mē') . Mex.	25·50 N	103·50 W
85	Maple (mā'p'l) . Can. (Toronto In.)	43·51 N	79·30 W
86	Maple Creek (crēk) . Can.	49·52 N	109·32 W
85	Maple Grove (grōv) Can. (Montreal In.)	45·19 N	73·51 W
75	Maple Heights Ohio (Cleveland In.)	41·25 N	81·34 W
84	Maple Shade (shād) N. J. (Philadelphia In.)	39·57 N	75·01 W
65	Maple Valley (văl'ê) Wash. (Seattle In.)	47·24 N	122·02 W
74	Maplewood (wŏŏd) Mo. (St. Louis In.)	38·37 N	90·20 W
74	Maplewood Park (wŏŏd pärk) Ill. (St. Louis In.)	38·34 N	90·11 W
167	Mapumulo (mä-pä-mōō'lō) S. Afr. (Natal In.)	29·12 S	31·05 E
155	Maqueda Chan. (mä-kā'dä) Phil. (Manila In.)	13·40 N	123·52 E
166	Maquela do Zombo (mȧ-kä'lȧ dōō zôm'bōō) . Ang.	6·08 S	15·15 E
71	Maquoketa (mȧ-kō-kê-tȧ) . Iowa	42·04 N	90·42 W
71	Maquoketa (R.) . Iowa	42·08 N	90·40 W
100	Mar, Serra do (Mts.) (sĕr'rȧ dōō mär') . Braz.	26·30 S	49·15 W
98	Maracaibo (mä-rä-kī'bō) . Ven.	10·38 N	71·45 W
98	Maracaibo, Lago de (L.) (lä'gô-dĕ-mä-rä-kī'bō) . Ven.	9·55 N	72·13 W
99	Maracay (mä-rä-käy') . Ven. (In.)	10·15 N	67·35 W
165	Marādah . Libya	29·10 N	19·07 E
164	Maradi (mȧ-rȧ-dē') . Niger	13·30 N	7·11 E
133	Marāgheh . Iran	37·20 N	46·10 E
167	Maraisburg S. Afr. (Johannesburg & Pretoria In.)	26·12 S	27·57 E
99	Marajó, Ilha de (I.) (mä-rä-zhō') Braz.	0·30 S	50·00 W
166	Marandelles (mȧ-rȧn-dāl'ȧs) S. Rh.	18·08 S	31·36 E
99	Maranguape (mä-räŋ-gwä'pĕ) Braz.	3·48 S	38·38 W
	Maranhão, see São Luis		
99	Maranhão (State) (mä-rän-youɴ) Braz.	5·15 S	45·52 W
160	Maranoa (R.) (mä-rä-nō'ä) . Austl.	27·01 S	148·03 E
125	Marano di Napoli (mä-rä'nô-dē-nä'pô-lē) It. (Naples In.)	40·39 N	14·12 E
98	Marañón, Rio (R.) (rê'ō-mä-rä-nyōn') . Peru	4·26 S	75·08 W
99	Marapanim (mä-rä-pä-nē'ɴ) . Braz.	0·45 S	47·42 W
133	Maras (mä-räsh') . Tur.	37·40 N	36·50 E
79	Marathon (măr'ȧ-thŏn) . Fla. (In.)	24·41 N	81·06 W
75	Marathon . Ohio (Cincinnati In.)	39·09 N	83·59 W
154	Maratua (I.) . Indon.	2·14 N	118·30 E
90	Maravatio (mä-rä-vä'tê-ō) . Mex.	19·54 N	100·25 W
158	Marble Bar (märb''l bär) . Austl.	21·15 S	119·15 E
69	Marble Can. (mär'b'l) . Ariz.	36·21 N	111·48 W
168	Marble Hall (hâll) S. Afr. (Johannesburg & Pretoria In.)	24·59 S	29·19 E
83	Marblehead (mär'b'l-hĕd) Mass. (Boston In.)	42·30 N	70·51 W
120	Marburg (mär'bōōrgh) . Ger.	50·49 N	8·46 E
92	Marcala (mär-kä-lä) . Hond.	14·08 N	88·01 W
126	Marche (Reg.) (mär'kā) . It.	43·35 N	12·33 E
111	Marchegg . Aus. (Vienna In.)	48·18 N	16·55 E
124	Marchena (mär-chā'nä) . Sp.	37·20 N	5·25 W
98	Marchena (I.) (ĕ's-lä-mär-chĕ'nä) Ec.	0·29 N	90·31 W
74	March Field (märch) Calif. (Los Angeles In.)	33·54 N	117·17 W
73	Marceline (mär-sê-lēn') . Mo.	39·42 N	92·56 W
101	Marcos Paz (mär-kōs' päz) Arg. (Buenos Aires In.)	34·49 S	58·51 W
156	Marcus (I.) (mär'kŭs) . Asia	24·00 N	155·00 E
84	Marcus Hook (mär'kŭs hŏŏk) Pa. (Philadelphia In.)	39·49 N	75·25 W
81	Marcy, Mt. (mär'sê) . N. Y.	44·10 N	73·55 W
101	Mar de Espanha (mär-dĕ-ĕs-pä'nyȧ) Braz. (Rio de Janeiro In.)	21·53 S	43·00 W
100	Mar del Plata (mär dĕl plä'ta) Arg.	37·59 S	57·35 W
133	Mardin (mär-dēn') . Tur.	37·25 N	40·40 E
159	Mare (I.) (mȧ-rā') . N. Cal.	21·53 S	168·30 E
116	Maree (L.) (mȧ-rē') . Scot.	57·40 N	5·44 W
71	Marengo (mȧ-rĕŋ'gō) . Iowa	41·47 N	92·04 W
122	Marennes (mȧ-rĕn') . Fr.	45·49 N	1·08 W

Page	Name Pronunciation Region	Lat. °′	Long. °′
123	Mareuil-sur-Ourcq (mä-rû'yĕ-sür-ōōrk'). Fr. (Paris In.)	49·08 N	2·04 E
76	Marfa (mär'fȧ). Tex.	30·19 N	104·01 W
129	Marganets. Sov. Un.	47·41 N	34·33 E
88	Margarita (mär-gōō-rē'tä) C.Z. (Panama Canal In.)	9·20 N	79·55 W
99	Margarita, Isla de (I.) (mär-gȧ-rē'tȧ). Ven. (In.)	11·00 N	64·15 W
116	Margate (mär'gāt). Eng.	51·21 N	1·17 E
167	Margate (mär-gāt') S. Afr. (Natal In.)	30·52 S	30·21 E
82	Marguerite, Riviere (R.). Can.	50·36 N	66·40 W
132	Mari (A. S. S. R.) (mä'rê). Sov. Un.	56·20 N	48·00 E
82	Maria (mȧ-rē'ȧ). Can.	48·10 N	66·04 W
124	Maria, Sierra de (Mts.) (sē-ĕ'r-rä-dĕ-mä-ryä). Sp.	37·42 N	2·25 W
90	María Cleofas (I.) (mä-rē'ä klā'ô-fäs). Mex.	21·17 N	106·14 W
118	Mariager (mä-rê-ägh'ĕr). Den.	56·38 N	10·00 E
118	Mariager Fd. Den.	56·44 N	10·32 E
90	María Madre. Mex.	21·43 N	106·17 W
90	María Magdalena (I.) (mä rē'ä mäg-dä-lā'nä). Mex.	21·25 N	106·23 W
101	Mariana (mä-ryä'nä) Braz. (Rio de Janeiro In.)	20·23 S	43·24 W
156	Mariana Is. (mä-rê-ä'nä) Pac. Is. Trust. Ter.	17·20 N	145·00 E
156	Mariana Trench. Oceania	12·00 N	144·00 E
95	Marianao (mä-rê-ä-nä'ō) Cuba (Havana In.)	23·05 N	82·26 W
73	Marianna (mā-rĭ-ăn'ȧ). Ark.	34·45 N	90·45 W
78	Marianna. Fla.	30·46 N	85·14 W
75	Marianna. Pa. (Pittsburgh In.)	40·01 N	80·05 W
100	Mariano Acosta (mä-rêä'nô-ä-kôs'tä). Arg. (In.)	34·28 S	58·48 W
120	Mariánské Lázně (mär'yán-skĕ'läz'nyĕ). Czech.	49·58 N	12·42 E
67	Marias R. (mȧ-rī'ȧz). Mont.	48·17 N	111·47 W
93	Mariato, Punta (Pt.). Pan.	7·17 N	81·09 W
118	Maribo (mä'rê-bô). Den.	54·46 N	11·29 E
126	Maribor (mä're-bôr). Yugo.	46·33 N	15·37 E
101	Maricá (mä-rē-kä') Braz. (Rio de Janeiro In.)	22·55 S	42·49 W
155	Maricaban (I.) (mä-rê-kä-bän') Phil. (Manila In.)	13·40 N	120·44 E
168	Marico R. (mä'rĭ-cô). S. Afr. (Johannesburg & Pretoria In.)	24·53 S	26·22 E
47	Marie Byrd Land (mȧ rē' bûrd') Ant.	78·00 S	130·00 W
118	Mariefred (mä-rē'ĕ-frĭd). Swe.	59·17 N	17·09 E
93	Marie Galante I. (mȧ-rē' gȧ-lăɴt') Guad. (Le. & Wind. Is. In.)	15·58 N	61·05 W
	Mariehamn, see Maarianhamina		
118	Mariestad (mä-rē'ĕ-städ'). Swe.	58·43 N	13·45 E
84	Marietta (mā-rĭ-ĕt'ȧ) Ga. (Atlanta In.)	33·57 N	84·33 W
80	Marietta. Ohio	39·25 N	81·30 W
73	Marietta. Okla.	33·53 N	97·07 W
65	Marietta. Wash. (Vancouver In.)	48·48 N	122·35 W
134	Mariinsk (mȧ-re'ïnsk). Sov. Un.	56·15 N	87·28 E
119	Marijampole (mä-rē-yäm-pô'lĕ) Sov. Un.	54·33 N	23·26 E
168	Marikana (mă'-rĭ-kä-nȧ). S. Afr. (Johannesburg & Pretoria In.)	25·40 S	27·28 E
99	Marília (mä-rē'lyä). Braz.	22·02 S	49·48 W
155	Marinduque (I.) (mä-rên-dōō'kā) Phil. (Manila In.)	13·14 N	121·45 E
74	Marine (mȧ-rēn') Ill. (St. Louis In.)	38·48 N	89·47 W
74	Marine. Minn. (Minneapolis, St. Paul In.)	45·11 N	92·51 W
80	Marine City. Mich.	42·45 N	82·30 W
74	Marine L. Minn. (Minneapolis, St. Paul In.)	45·13 N	92·55 W
74	Marine on St. Croix (ăɴ sĕɴ krōō-ȧ). Minn. (Minneapolis, St. Paul In.)	45·11 N	92·47 W
71	Marinette (măr-ĭ-nĕt'). Wis.	45·05 N	87·40 W
165	Maringa R. (mȧ-riŋ'gȧ). Con. L.	0·30 N	21·08 E
124	Marinha Grande (mä-rēn'yȧ grän'dĕ). Port.	39·49 N	8·53 W
78	Marion (măr'ĭ-ŭn). Ala.	32·36 N	87·19 W
80	Marion. Ill.	37·40 N	88·55 W
80	Marion. Ind.	40·35 N	85·45 W
71	Marion. Iowa	42·01 N	91·39 W
73	Marion. Kans.	38·21 N	97·02 W
78	Marion. Ky.	37·19 N	88·05 W
79	Marion. N. C.	35·40 N	82·00 W
70	Marion. N. D.	46·37 N	98·20 W
80	Marion. Ohio	40·35 N	83·10 W
79	Marion. S. C.	34·08 N	79·23 W
79	Marion. Va.	36·48 N	81·33 W
79	Marion (R.). S. C.	33·25 N	80·35 W
159	Marion Rf. Austl.	18·57 S	151·31 E
101	Mariposa (mä-rē-pô'sä) Chile (Santiago In.)	35·33 S	71·21 W
68	Mariposa Cr. Calif.	37·14 N	120·30 W
98	Mariquita (mä-rē-kē'tä). Col. (In.)	5·13 N	74·52 W
99	Mariscal Estigarribia (mä-rēs-käl'ĕs-tē-gär-rē'byä) Par.	22·03 S	60·28 W
100	Marisco, Ponta do (Pt.) (pô'n-tä-dô-mä-rē's-kō) Braz. (In.)	23·01 S	43·17 W
123	Maritime Alps (Mts.) (mȧ'rĭ-tĭm ălps). Fr.-It.	44·20 N	7·02 E
127	Maritsa (R.) (mä'rê-tsȧ). Gr.-Tur.	40·43 N	26·19 E
155	Mariveles. Phil. (Manila In.)	14·27 N	120·29 E
139	Marj Uyan. Leb. (Palestine In.)	33·21 N	35·36 E
146	Marka Kul' (L.). Sov. Un.	49·15 N	85·48 E
118	Markaryd (mär'kä-rüd). Swe.	56·30 N	13·34 E
73	Marked Tree (märkt trē). Ark.	35·31 N	90·26 W
111	Marken, I. Neth. (Amsterdam In.)	52·26 N	5·08 E
110	Market Bosworth (bŏz'wûrth) Eng.	52·37 N	1·23 W
110	Market Deeping (dēp'ĭng). Eng.	52·40 N	0·19 W
110	Market Drayton (drā'tŭn). Eng.	52·54 N	2·29 W
110	Market Harborough (här'bŭr-ô) Eng.	52·28 N	0·55 W
110	Market Rasen (rā'zĕn). Eng.	53·23 N	0·21 W
85	Markham (märk'ȧm) Can. (Toronto In.)	43·53 N	79·15 W
47	Markham, Mt. Ant.	82·59 S	159·30 E
129	Markovka (mȧr-kôf'kȧ). Sov. Un.	49·32 N	39·34 E
135	Markovo (mär'kô-vô). Sov. Un.	64·46 N	170·48 E
142	Markrāna. India	27·08 N	74·43 E
133	Marks. Sov. Un.	51·40 N	46·40 E
77	Marksville (märks'vĭl). La.	31·09 N	92·05 W
111	Markt Indersdorf (märkt ēn'dĕrs-dōrf) Ger. (Munich In.)	48·22 N	11·23 E
120	Marktredwitz (märk-rĕd'vĕts). Ger.	50·02 N	12·05 E
111	Markt Schwaben (märkt shvä'bĕn) Ger. (Munich In.)	48·12 N	11·52 E
123	Marl (märl). Ger. (Ruhr In.)	51·40 N	7·05 E
83	Marlboro (märl'bŭr-ô) Mass. (Boston In.)	42·21 N	71·33 W
84	Marlboro. N. J. (New York In.)	40·18 N	74·15 W
80	Marlette (mär-lĕt'). Mich.	43·25 N	83·05 W
77	Marlin (mär'lĭn). Tex.	31·18 N	96·52 W
81	Marlinton (mär'lĭn-tŭn). W. Va.	38·15 N	80·10 W
110	Marlow (mär'lō). Eng. (London In.)	51·33 N	0·46 W
72	Marlow. Okla.	34·38 N	97·56 W
94	Marls, The (Shoals) (märls). Ba. Is.	26·30 N	77·15 W
143	Marmagoā. India	15·09 N	73·58 E
122	Marmande (mȧr-mäɴd'). Fr.	44·30 N	0·10 E
127	Marmara (I.) (mär'mȧ-rȧ). Tur.	40·38 N	27·35 E
133	Marmara Denizi (Sea). Tur.	40·40 N	28·00 E
70	Marmarth (mär'mȧrth). N. D.	46·19 N	103·57 W
91	Mar Muerto (L.) (mär-mōōĕ'r-tô) Mex.	16·13 N	94·22 W
111	Marne (mär'nĕ) Ger. (Hamburg In.)	53·57 N	9·01 E
122	Marne (R.) (märn). Fr.	49·08 N	3·39 E
124	Marnia (mär-nyä). Alg.	35·07 N	2·10 W
98	Maroa (mä-rō'ä). Ven.	2·43 N	67·37 W
167	Maroantsetra (mȧ-rō-äŋ-tsä'trȧ) Malag. Rep.	15·18 S	49·48 E
98	Maro Jarapeto (Mtn.) (mä-rô-hä-rä-pĕ'tô). Col. (In.)	6·29 N	76·39 W
167	Maromokotro (Mtn.). Malag. Rep.	14·00 S	49·11 E
99	Maroni (R.) (mȧ-rō'nē) Fr. Gu.-Sur.	3·02 N	53·54 W
165	Maroua (mär'wä). Cam.	10·41 N	14·14 E
110	Marple (mär'p'l). Eng.	53·24 N	2·04 W
168	Marquard. S. Afr. (Johannesburg & Pretoria In.)	28·41 S	27·26 E
157	Marquesas Is. (mȧr-kĕ'säs) Fr. Polynesia	8·50 S	141·00 W
79	Marquesas Keys (Is.) (mȧr-kē'zȧs) Fla. (In.)	24·37 N	82·15 W
101	Marquês de Valença (mȧr-kĕ's-dĕ-vä-lĕ'n-sȧ) Braz. (Rio de Janeiro In.)	22·16 S	43·42 W
85	Marquette (mär-kĕt') Can. (Winnipeg In.)	50·04 N	97·43 W
71	Marquette. Mich.	46·32 N	87·25 W
77	Marquez (mär-käz'). Tex.	31·14 N	96·15 W
165	Marra, Jebel (Mt.) (jĕb'ĕl mär'ä) Sud.	13·00 N	23·47 E
164	Marrakech (mȧr-rä'kĕsh). Mor.	31·38 N	8·00 W
160	Marree (măr'rē). Austl.	29·38 S	137·55 E
124	Marroqui, Pta. (mä-rō-kē'). Sp.	36·03 N	5·36 W
75	Mars (märz). Pa. (Pittsburgh In.)	40·42 N	80·01 W
165	Marsá al Burayqah. Libya	30·25 N	19·20 E
165	Marsa Fatma. Eth.	14·54 N	40·14 E
126	Marsala (mär-sä'lä). It.	37·48 N	12·28 E
111	Marschfeld (Reg.) Aus. (Vienna In.)	48·14 N	16·37 E
110	Marsden (märz'dĕn). Eng.	53·36 N	1·55 W
122	Marseille (mȧr-sâ'y') Fr. (Marseille In.)	43·18 N	5·25 E
122	Marseille, Canal de (mȧr-sâ-yaɴ') Fr. (Marseille In.)	43·34 N	5·16 E
80	Marseilles (mär-sĕlz'). Ill.	41·20 N	88·40 W
80	Marshall (mär'shȧl). Ill.	39·20 N	87·40 W
80	Marshall. Mich.	42·20 N	84·55 W
70	Marshall. Minn.	44·28 N	95·49 W
73	Marshall. Mo.	39·07 N	93·12 W
77	Marshall. Tex.	32·33 N	94·22 W
156	Marshall Is. Pac. Is. Trust Ter.	10·00 N	165·00 E
71	Marshalltown (mär'shȧl-toun) Iowa	42·02 N	92·55 W
78	Marshallville (mär'shȧl-vĭl). Ga.	32·29 N	83·55 W
83	Marshfield (märsh'fēld) Mass. (Boston In.)	42·06 N	70·43 W
73	Marshfield. Mo.	37·20 N	92·53 W
71	Marshfield. Wis.	44·40 N	90·10 W
94	Marsh Harbour. Ba. Is.	26·30 N	77·00 W
75	Mars Hill (märz' hĭl') Ind. (Indianapolis In.)	39·43 N	86·15 W
82	Mars Hill. Maine	46·34 N	67·54 W
82	Marsqui. Can.	49·13 N	66·08 W
118	Marstrand (mär'stränd). Swe.	57·54 N	11·33 E
136	Marsyaty (mȧrs'yȧ-tĭ) Sov. Un. (Urals In.)	60·03 N	60·28 E
77	Mart (märt). Tex.	31·32 N	96·49 W
154	Martaban, G. of (mär-tŭ-bän') Bur.	16·34 N	96·58 E
154	Martapura. Indon.	3·19 S	114·45 E
86	Marten Hills. Can.	55·40 N	114·09 W
81	Marthas Vineyard (I.) (mär'thȧz vĭn'yȧrd). Mass.	41·25 N	70·35 W
94	Martí (mär-tē'). Cuba	23·00 N	80·55 W
120	Martigny-Bourg (mȧr-tê-nyē') Switz.	46·06 N	7·00 E
122	Martigues (mȧr-tēg') Fr. (Marseille In.)	43·24 N	5·05 E
78	Martin (mär'tĭn). Tenn.	36·20 N	88·45 W
78	Martin (R.). Ala.	32·40 N	86·05 W
127	Martina Franca (mär-tē'nä fräŋ'kä). It.	40·43 N	17·21 E
74	Martin City (mär-tĭn sĭ'tĭ) Mo. (Kansas City In.)	38·53 N	94·35 W
65	Martinez (mär-tē'nĕz) Calif. (San Francisco In.)	38·01 N	122·08 W
74	Martinez. Tex. (San Antonio In.)	29·25 N	98·20 W
87	Martin Falls (mär'tĭn). Can.	51·35 N	86·40 W
93	Martinique I. (mȧr-tê-nēk') N. A. (Le. & Wind. Is. In.)	14·30 N	60·37 W
81	Martinsburg (mär'tĭnz-bûrg) W. Va.	39·30 N	78·00 W
80	Martins Ferry (mär'tĭnz). Ohio	40·05 N	80·45 W
80	Martinsville (mär'tĭnz-vĭl). Ind.	39·25 N	86·25 W
79	Martinsville. Va.	36·40 N	79·53 W
124	Martos (mär'tōs). Sp.	37·43 N	3·58 W
86	Martre, Lac la (L.) (lȧk la märtr). Can.	63·24 N	119·58 W
153	Marugame (mä'rōō-gä'mä). Jap.	34·19 N	133·48 E
118	Mårvatn (L.) (môr-vät'n). Nor.	60·10 N	8·28 E
124	Marvín (mär-vē'n). Sp.	42·24 N	8·40 W
103	Mary (mä'rê). Sov. Un.	37·45 N	61·47 E
129	Mar'yanskaya (mȧr-yȧn'skȧ-yȧ) Sov. Un.	45·04 N	38·39 E
160	Maryborough (mā'rĭ-bŭr-ô). Austl.	25·35 S	152·40 E
160	Maryborough. Austl.	37·00 S	143·50 E
63	Maryland (State) (mĕr'ĭ-lȧnd) U. S.	39·10 N	76·25 W
66	Mary's R. (mā'rĭz). Nev.	41·25 N	115·10 W
83	Marystown (mā'rĭz-toun). Can.	47·11 N	55·11 W
82	Marysville. Can.	45·59 N	66·40 W
68	Marysville (mā'rĭz-vĭl). Calif.	39·09 N	121·37 W
73	Marysville. Kans.	39·49 N	96·38 W
80	Marysville. Ohio	40·15 N	83·25 W
65	Marysville Wash. (Seattle In.)	48·03 N	122·11 W
168	Maryūt (L.). U. A. R. (Nile In.)	31·09 N	30·10 E
74	Maryville (mā'rĭ-vĭl) Ill. (St. Louis In.)	38·44 N	89·57 W
73	Maryville. Mo.	40·21 N	94·51 W
78	Maryville. Tenn.	35·44 N	83·59 W
165	Mārzuq. Libya	26·00 N	14·09 E
163	Masai Steppe. Tan.	5·05 S	36·16 E
154	Masalembo (I.). Indon.	5·40 S	114·28 E
152	Masan (mä-sän'). Kor.	35·10 N	128·31 E
167	Masasi (mä-sä'sê). Tan.	10·41 S	38·05 E
92	Masatepe (mä-sä-tē'pĕ). Nic.	11·57 N	86·10 W
92	Masaya (mä-sä'yä). Nic.	11·58 N	86·05 W
155	Masbate (mäs-bä'tä) Phil. (Manila In.)	12·21 N	123·38 E
155	Masbate (I.). Phil. (Manila In.)	12·19 N	123·03 E
164	Mascara (mäs'kä-rä) (mȧs-kȧ-rȧ') Alg.	35·25 N	0·08 E
47	Mascarene Is. Afr.	20·20 S	56·40 E
78	Mascot (măs'kŏt). Tenn.	36·04 N	83·45 W
90	Mascota (mäs-kō'tä). Mex.	20·33 N	104·45 W
90	Mascota (R.). Mex.	20·33 N	104·52 W
85	Mascouche (mȧs-kōōsh') Can. (Montreal In.)	45·45 N	73·36 W
85	Mascouche (R.) Can. (Montreal In.)	45·44 N	73·45 W
74	Mascoutah (măs-kū'tā) Ill. (St. Louis In.)	38·29 N	89·48 W
166	Maseru (măz'ēr-ōō). Bas.	29·09 S	27·11 E
144	Mashhad. Iran	36·17 N	59·30 E
165	Masindi (mä-sēn'dê). Ug.	1·44 N	31·43 E
144	Masīra (I.). Mus. & Om.	20·43 N	58·58 E
116	Mask, Lough (B.) (lŏk mȧsk). Ire.	53·35 N	9·23 W
136	Maslovo (mȧs'lô-vô) Sov. Un. (Urals In.)	60·08 N	60·28 E
80	Mason (mā'sŭn). Mich.	42·35 N	84·25 W
75	Mason. Ohio (Cincinnati In.)	39·22 N	84·18 W
76	Mason. Tex.	30·46 N	99·14 W
71	Mason City. Iowa	43·08 N	93·14 W
83	Masquaro (L.). Can.	50·34 N	60·40 W
126	Massa (mäs'sä). It.	44·02 N	10·08 E
63	Massachusetts (State) (măs-ȧ-chōō'sĕts). U. S.	42·20 N	72·30 W
82	Massachusetts B. Mass.	42·26 N	70·20 W
126	Massafra (mäs-sä'frä). It.	40·35 N	17·05 E
126	Massa Maritima (mäs'sä mä-rē'tê-mä). It.	43·03 N	10·55 E
165	Massaua (mäs-sä'wä). Eth.	15·40 N	39·19 E
81	Massena (mă-sē'nȧ). N. Y.	44·55 N	74·55 W
86	Massett (măs'ĕt). Can.	54·03 N	132·11 W
122	Massif Central (Plat.) (mȧ-sēf' säɴ-trȧl'). Fr.	45·12 N	3·02 E
80	Massillon (măs'ĭ-lŏn). Ohio	40·50 N	81·35 W
166	Massinga (mä-sĭn'gä). Moz.	23·18 S	35·18 E
69	Massive, Mt. (măs'ĭv). Colo.	39·05 N	106·30 W
85	Masson (măs-sŭn) Can. (Ottawa In.)	45·33 N	75·25 W
153	Masuda (mä-sōō'dȧ). Jap.	34·42 N	131·53 E
121	Masuria (Reg.). Pol.	53·40 N	21·10 E
166	Matadi (mȧ-tä'dê). Con. L.	5·48 S	13·35 E
92	Matagalpa (mä-tä-gäl'pä). Nic.	12·52 N	85·57 W
77	Matagorda B. (măt-ȧ-gôr'dȧ). Tex.	28·32 N	96·13 W
77	Matagorda I. Tex.	28·13 N	96·27 W
164	Matam (mä-tăm'). Senegal	15·41 N	13·20 W
76	Matamoros (mä-tä-mō'rōs). Mex.	25·32 N	103·13 W
77	Matamoros. Mex.	25·52 N	97·30 W
82	Matane (mȧ-tăn'). Can.	48·49 N	67·35 W
166	Matanga (mä-täŋ'gä). Ang.	7·35 S	17·25 E
64	Matanuska (mä-tä-nōōs'kȧ) Alaska	61·32 N	149·38 W
94	Matanzas (mä-tän'zäs). Cuba	23·00 N	81·40 W
94	Matanzas (State). Cuba	22·45 N	81·20 W
94	Matanzas, Bahía (B.) (bä-ē'-ä) Cuba	23·10 N	81·30 W
93	Matapalo, Cabo (C.) (kä'bô-mä-tä-pä'lō). C. R.	8·22 N	83·25 W
82	Matapedia (mă-tȧ-pē'dĭ-ȧ). Can.	48·00 N	66·55 W
82	Matapedia (L.). Can.	48·36 N	67·20 W
101	Mataquito (R.) (mä-tä-kē'tô) Chile (Santiago In.)	35·08 S	71·35 W
143	Matara (mä-tä'rä). Ceylon	5·59 N	80·35 E
154	Mataram. Indon.	8·45 S	116·15 E
125	Mataró (mä-tä-rō'). Sp.	41·33 N	2·27 E

ăt; finăl; rāte; senāte; ärm; ȧsk; sofȧ; fâre; ch-choose; dh-as th in other; bē; ēvent; bĕt; recĕnt; cratēr; g-go; gh-guttural g; bĭt; ĭ-short neutral; rīde; ĸ-guttural k as ch in German ich;

Page	Name Pronunciation Region	Lat. °′	Long. °′
167	Matatiele (mä-tä-tyä'lä) S. Afr. (Natal In.)	30·21 S	28·49 E
84	Matawana (mȧ-tȧ-wŏn'ȧ) N. J. (New York In.)	40·24 N	74·13 W
90	Matehuala (mä-tå-wä'lä) Mex.	23·38 N	100·39 W
126	Matera (mä-tâ'rä) It.	40·42 N	16·37 E
113	Mateur (mȧ-tûr') Tun.	37·09 N	9·43 E
143	Mātherān India (Bombay In.)	18·58 N	73·16 E
74	Mathews, L. (măth'ūz) Calif. (Los Agneles In.)	33·50 N	117·24 W
142	Mathura (mu-tōō'rŭ) India	27·39 N	77·39 E
101	Matias Barbosa (mä-tē'äs-bär-bô-sä) Braz. (Rio de Janeiro In.)	21·53 S	43·19 W
91	Matillas, Laguna (L.) (lä-gōō'nä-mä-tē'l-yäs) Mex.	18·02 N	92·36 W
93	Matina (mä-tē'nä) C. R.	10·06 N	83·20 W
119	Matiši (mä'tē-sē) Sov. Un.	57·43 N	25·09 E
154	Matjan (I.) Indon.	6·52 S	121·45 E
90	Matlalcueyetl, Cerra (sĕ'r-rä-mä-tläl-kwĕ'yĕtl) Mex.	19·13 N	98·02 W
110	Matlock (măt'lŏk) Eng.	53·08 N	1·33 W
110	Matlock Bath (măt'lŏk bàth) Eng.	53·06 N	1·34 W
134	Matochkin Shar (mä'tŏch-kĭn) Sov. Un.	73·57 N	56·16 E
99	Mato Grosso (mät'ōō grōs'ōō) Braz.	15·04 S	59·58 W
99	Mato Grosso (State) Braz.	14·38 S	55·36 W
99	Mato Grosso, Chapada de (Plain) (shä-pä'dä-dĕ) Braz.	13·39 S	55·42 W
124	Matozinhos (Leixoes) (mä-tô-zēn'yōzh) (lĕ'y-shô'-ĕs) Port.	41·10 N	8·48 W
144	Matrah (mȧ-trä') Mus. & Om.	23·36 N	58·27 E
165	Maṭrūḥ U .A. R.	31·19 N	27·14 E
153	Matsudo (mät'sōō-dô) Jap. (Tōkyō In.)	35·48 N	139·55 E
153	Matsue (mät'sōō-ĕ) Jap.	35·29 N	133·04 E
153	Matsumoto (mät'sōō-mō'tô) Jap.	36·15 N	137·59 E
153	Matsuyama (mät'sōō-yä'mä) Jap.	33·48 N	132·45 E
153	Matsuzaka (mät'sōō-zä'kä) Jap.	34·35 N	136·34 E
87	Mattagami (L.) (mȧ-tä-gä'mē) Can.	50·10 N	78·49 W
79	Mattamuskeet (R.) (măt-tȧ-mŭs'kēt) N. C.	35·34 N	76·03 W
81	Mattaponi (R.) (măt'ȧ-ponī') Va.	37·45 N	77·00 W
87	Mattawa (măt'ȧ-wȧ) Can.	46·15 N	78·49 W
82	Mattawin (R.) (măt'ȧ-wĭn) Can.	46·55 N	73·20 W
120	Matterhorn Mt. (măt'ēr-hôrn) Switz.	45·57 N	7·36 E
75	Matteson (mătt'ē-sŭn) Ill. (Chicago In.)	41·30 N	87·42 W
95	Matthew Town (măth'ū toun) Ba. Is.	21·00 N	73·40 W
80	Mattoon (mă-tōōn') Ill.	39·30 N	88·20 W
98	Maturín (mä-tōō-rēn') Ven.	9·48 N	63·16 W
155	Mauban (mä'ōō-bän') Phil. (Manila In.)	14·11 N	121·44 E
122	Maubeuge (mô-bûzh') Fr.	50·18 N	3·57 E
75	Maud (môd) Ohio (Cincinnati In.)	39·21 N	84·23 W
111	Mauer (mou'ĕr) Aus. (Vienna In.)	48·09 N	16·16 E
99	Maués (mȧ-wĕ's) Braz.	3·34 S	57·30 W
157	Maui (I.) (mä'ōō-ē) Hawaii (In.)	20·52 N	156·02 W
101	Maule (R.) (mà'ōō-lĕ) Chile (Santiago In.)	35·45 S	70·50 W
80	Maumee (mô-mē') Ohio	41·30 N	83·40 W
80	Maumee (R.) Ind.-Ohio	41·10 N	84·50 W
80	Maumee B. Ohio	41·50 N	83·20 W
166	Maun (mä-ōōn') Bech.	19·52 S	23·40 E
157	Mauna Kea (Vol.) (mä'ōō-näkä'ä) Hawaii (In.)	19·52 N	155·30 W
157	Mauna Loa (Vol.) (mä'ōō-nälō'ä) Hawaii (In.)	19·28 N	155·38 W
154	Maung Nakhon Sawan Thai.	16·00 N	99·52 E
77	Maurepas L. (mō-rē-pä') La.	30·18 N	90·40 W
163	Mauritania (mô-rē-tā'nĭ-ȧ) Afr.	19·38 N	13·30 W
47	Mauritius I. (mô-rĭsh'ĭ-ŭs) Afr.	20·18 S	57·36 E
65	Maury (mô'rĭ) Wash. (Seattle In.)	47·22 N	122·23 W
71	Mauston (môs'tŭn) Wis.	43·46 N	90·05 W
69	Maverick, (R.) (mă-vûr'ĭk) Ariz.	33·40 N	109·30 W
91	Maxcanú (mäs-kä-nōō') Mex.	20·35 N	89·59 W
85	Maxville (măks'vĭl) Can. (Ottawa In.)	45·17 N	74·52 W
74	Maxville Mo. (St. Louis In.)	38·26 N	90·24 W
135	Maya (R.) (mä'yä) Sov. Un.	58·00 N	135·45 E
95	Mayaguana (I.) Ba. Is.	22·25 N	73·00 W
95	Mayaguana Passage (Str.) Ba. Is.	22·20 N	73·25 W
89	Mayagüez (mä-yä-gwāz') P. R. (Puerto Rico In.)	18·12 N	67·10 W
95	Mayarí (mä-yä-rē') Cuba	20·45 N	75·40 W
95	Mayari (R.) Cuba	20·25 N	75·35 W
92	Mayas, Montañas (Mts.) (mōntăn'äs mä'äs) Br. Hond. (Yucatan In.)	16·43 N	89·00 W
120	Mayen (mī'ĕn) Ger.	50·19 N	7·14 E
122	Mayenne (mȧ-yĕn') Fr.	48·19 N	0·35 W
122	Mayenne (R.) Fr.	48·14 N	0·45 W
78	Mayfield (mā'fēld) Ky.	36·44 N	88·19 W
79	Mayfield Cr. Ky.	36·54 N	88·47 W
75	Mayfield Heights Ohio (Cleveland In.)	41·31 N	81·26 W
66	Mayfield Res. Wash.	46·31 N	122·34 W
133	Maykop (Maikop) (mī-kôp') Sov. Un.	44·35 N	40·10 E
136	Maykor (mī-kôr') Sov. Un. (Urals In.)	59·01 N	55·52 E
146	Maymyo (mī'myō') Bur.	22·14 N	96·32 E
83	Maynard (mā'nȧrd) Mass. (Boston In.)	42·25 N	71·27 W
65	Maynard Wash. (Seattle In.)	47·59 N	122·54 W
65	Mayne (mān) Can. (Vancouver In.)	48·51 N	123·18 W
65	Mayne (I.) Can. (Vancouver In.)	48·52 N	123·14 W
78	Mayo (mā-yō') Fla.	30·02 N	83·08 W
64	Mayo (L.) Alaska	63·50 N	135·30 W
86	Mayo Can.	63·40 N	135·51 W
116	Mayo, Mts. of Ire.	54·01 N	9·01 W
79	Mayodan (mā-yō'dăn) N. C.	36·25 N	79·59 W
155	Mayon (Vol.) (mä-yōn') Phil. (Manila In.)	13·21 N	123·43 E
167	Mayotte (I.) (mȧ-yôt') Comores, Arch. des	13·07 S	45·32 E
94	May Pen Jam.	18·00 N	77·25 W
151	Mayraira Pt. Phil.	18·40 N	120·45 E
76	Mayran, Laguna de (L.) (lä-ōō'nä-dĕ-mī-rän') Mex.	25·40 N	102·35 W
80	Maysville (māz'vĭl) Ky.	38·35 N	83·45 W
166	Mayumba Gabon	3·15 S	10·10 E
81	Mayville (mā'vĭl) N. Y.	42·15 N	79·30 W
70	Mayville N. D.	47·30 N	97·20 W
71	Mayville Wis.	43·30 N	88·45 W
74	Maywood (mā'wŏŏd) Calif. (Los Angeles In.)	33·59 N	118·11 W
75	Maywood Ill. (Chicago In.)	41·53 N	87·51 W
166	Mazabuka (mä-zä-bōō'kä) N. Rh.	16·00 S	27·43 E
99	Mazagão (mä-zȧ-gou'N) Braz.	0·05 S	51·27 W
76	Mazapil (mä-zä-pēl') Mex.	24·40 N	101·30 W
142	Mazar-i-Sharif (mȧ-zär'-ē-shȧ-rēf') Afg.	36·48 N	67·12 E
124	Mazarrón (mä-zär-rô'n) Sp.	36·37 N	1·29 W
99	Mazaruni (R.) (mä-zä-rōō'nē) Br. Gu.	5·58 N	59·37 W
92	Mazatenango (mä-zä-tå-näŋ'gō) Guat.	14·30 N	91·30 W
91	Mazatla Mex. (Mexico City In.)	19·30 N	99·24 W
91	Mazatlán (San Juan) (mä-zä-tlän') (sän hwän') Mex.	17·05 N	95·26 W
90	Mazatlán Mex.	23·14 N	106·27 W
119	Mažeikiai (mȧ-zhā'kē-ī) Sov. Un.	56·19 N	22·24 E
139	Mazhafah, Jabal (Mts.) Sau. Ar. (Palestine In.)	28·56 N	35·05 E
126	Mazzara del Vallo (mät-sä'rä dĕl väl'lō) It.	37·40 N	12·37 E
126	Mazzarino (mät-sä-rē'nō) It.	37·16 N	14·15 E
166	Mbabane (m'bä-bä'nĕ) Swaz.	26·18 S	31·14 E
165	Mbaiki (m'bȧ-ē'kē) Cen. Afr. Rep.	3·54 N	17·57 E
166	Mbigou (m-bē-gōō') Con. B.	2·07 S	12·07 E
165	M'Bomu R. (m'bō'mōō) Con. L.	4·38 N	23·48 E
164	M'Bout (m'bōō') Mauritania	16·03 N	12·31 W
72	Meade (mēd) Kans.	37·17 N	100·21 W
69	Meade, L. Nev.-Ariz.	36·20 N	114·14 W
67	Meade Pk. Idaho	42·19 N	111·16 W
65	Meadowdale (mĕd'ō-dāl) Wash. (Seattle In.)	47·51 N	122·20 W
86	Meadow Lake (mĕd'ō lăk) Can.	54·10 N	108·30 W
85	Meadows (mĕd'ōz) Can. (Winnipeg In.)	50·02 N	97·35 W
81	Meadville (mēd'vĭl) Pa.	41·40 N	80·10 W
80	Meaford (mē'fērd) Can.	44·35 N	80·40 W
87	Mealy Mts. (mē'lē) Can.	53·32 N	57·58 W
160	Meandarra (mē-ăn-dă'rȧ) Austl.	27·47 S	149·40 E
123	Meaux (mō) Fr. (Paris In.)	48·58 N	2·53 E
91	Mecapalapa (mā-kä-pä-lä'pä) Mex.	20·32 N	97·52 W
83	Mecatina (I.) (mā-kȧ-tē'nȧ) Can.	50·50 N	58·33 W
83	Mecatina (R.) (mā-kȧ-tē'nȧ) Can.	50·50 N	59·45 W
	Mecca, see Makkah		
82	Mechanic Falls (mē-kăn'ĭk) Maine	44·05 N	70·23 W
81	Mechanicsburg (mē-kăn'ĭks-bûrg) Pa.	40·15 N	77·00 W
81	Mechanicsville (mē-kăn'ĭks-vĭl) N. Y.	42·55 N	73·45 W
111	Mechelen Bel. (Brussels In.)	51·01 N	4·28 E
114	Mecheria Mor.	33·30 N	0·13 W
120	Mecklenburg (Reg.) (mĕk'lĕn-bōōrgh) Ger.	53·34 N	12·18 E
154	Medan (mā-dän') Indon.	3·35 N	98·35 E
100	Medanosa, Punta (Pt.) (pōō'n-tä-mĕ-dä-nō'sä) Arg.	47·50 S	65·53 W
110	Medden (R.) (mĕd'ĕn) Eng.	53·14 N	1·05 W
125	Médéa (mā-dā'ä) Alg.	36·18 N	2·40 E
98	Medellín (mā-dhĕl-yēn') Col. (In.)	6·15 N	75·34 W
91	Medellín (mĕ-dĕl-yĕ'n) Mex.	19·03 N	96·08 W
114	Medenine (mā-dĕ-nēn') Tun.	33·22 N	10·33 E
83	Medfield (mĕd'fēld) Mass. (Boston In.)	42·11 N	71·19 W
83	Medford (mĕd'fērd) Mass. (Boston In.)	42·25 N	71·07 W
84	Medford N. J. (Philadelphia In.)	39·54 N	74·50 W
72	Medford Okla.	36·47 N	97·44 W
66	Medford Ore.	42·19 N	122·52 W
71	Medford Wis.	45·09 N	90·22 W
84	Media (mē'dĭ-ȧ) Pa. (Philadelphia In.)	39·55 N	75·24 W
121	Medias (mĕd-yäsh') Rom.	46·09 N	24·21 E
66	Medical Lake (mĕd'ĭ-kăl) Wash.	47·34 N	117·40 W
72	Medicine Bow Ra. (mĕd'ĭ-sĭn bō) Colo.-Wyo.	40·55 N	106·02 W
67	Medicine Bow R. Wyo.	41·58 N	106·30 W
86	Medicine Hat (mĕd'ĭ-sĭn hăt) Can.	50·09 N	110·50 W
67	Medicine L. (mĕd'ĭ-sĭn) Mont.	48·24 N	104·15 W
72	Medicine Lodge Kans.	37·17 N	98·37 W
72	Medicine Lodge (R.) Kans.	37·20 N	98·57 W
81	Medina (mē-dī'nȧ) N. Y.	43·15 N	78·20 W
75	Medina Ohio (Cleveland In.)	41·08 N	81·52 W
124	Medina del Campo (mȧ-dē'nä dĕl käm'pō) Sp.	41·18 N	4·54 W
124	Medina de Rioseco (mȧ-dē'nä dä rē-ô-sā'kō) Sp.	41·53 N	5·05 W
76	Medina L. Tex.	29·36 N	98·47 W
76	Medina R. Tex.	29·45 N	99·13 W
124	Medina Sidonia (sē-dō'nyä) Sp.	36·28 N	5·58 W
101	Medio (mĕ'dyō) (R.) Arg. (Buenos Aires In.)	33·40 S	60·30 W
114	Mediterranean Sea (mĕd-ĭ-tēr-ā'nē-ăn) Afr.-Asia-Eur.	36·22 N	13·25 E
113	Medjerda, Oued (R.) (wĕd mĕ-jĕr'dȧ) Tun.	36·43 N	9·54 E
134	Mednogorsk Sov. Un.	51·27 N	57·22 E
133	Medveditsa (R.) (mĕd-vyĕ'dē tsȧ) Sov. Un.	50·10 N	43·40 E
132	Medvezhegorsk (mĕd-vyĕzh'yĕ-gôrsk') Sov. Un.	63·00 N	34·20 E
135	Medvezh'y (Is.) Sov. Un.	71·00 N	161·25 E
83	Medway (mĕd'wā) Mass. (Boston In.)	42·08 N	71·23 W
128	Medyn' (mĕ-dēn') Sov. Un.	54·58 N	35·53 E
129	Medzhibozh (mĕd-zhē-bōzh') Sov. Un.	49·23 N	27·29 E
158	Meekatharra (mē-kȧ-thăr'ȧ) Austl.	26·30 S	118·38 E
69	Meeker (mēk'ēr) Colo.	40·00 N	107·55 W
120	Meerane (mā-rä'nĕ) Ger.	50·51 N	12·27 E
142	Meerut (mē'rōōt) India	28·59 N	77·43 E
165	Mēgā Eth.	6·14 N	35·34 E
127	Megalópolis (mĕg-ȧ lŏ'pô-lĭs) Grc.	37·22 N	22·08 E
129	Meganom, M. (C.) (mĭs mĕ-gȧ-nôm') Sov. Un.	44·48 N	35·17 E
127	Mégara (mĕg'ȧ-rȧ) Grc.	37·59 N	23·21 E
79	Megget (mĕg'ĕt) S. C.	32·44 N	80·15 W
65	Megler (mĕg'lēr) Wash. (Portland In.)	46·15 N	123·52 W
128	Meglino (L.) (mȧ-glē'nō) Sov. Un.	58·32 N	35·27 E
79	Meherrin (R.) (mē-hĕr'ĭn) Va.	36·40 N	77·49 W
142	Mehsāna India	23·42 N	72·23 E
122	Mehun-sur-Yèvre (mē-ŭN-sür-yĕvr') Fr.	47·11 N	2·14 E
148	Meichu (mā'jēōō) China	31·17 N	119·12 E
151	Meihsien China	24·20 N	116·10 E
151	Meiling Pass (mā'lĭng') China	25·22 N	115·00 E
123	Meinerzhagen (mī'nĕrts-hä-gĕn) Ger. (Ruhr In.)	51·06 N	7·39 E
120	Meiningen (mī'nĭng-ĕn) Ger.	50·35 N	10·25 E
120	Meiringen Switz.	46·45 N	8·11 E
100	Mejillones (mĕ-Kē-lyō'nĕs) Chile	23·07 S	70·31 W
164	Meknès (mĕk'nĕs) (mĕk-nĕs') Mor.	33·56 N	5·44 W
	Mekong, see Lanisung Chiang		
154	Mekong, Mouths of the (mē'kông') Viet.	10·09 N	107·15 E
154	Mekong R. Thai.-Laos	17·53 N	103·57 E
161	Melbourne (mĕl'bŭrn) Austl. (Melbourne In.)	37·52 S	145·08 E
79	Melbourne Fla. (In.)	28·02 N	28·37 W
110	Melbourne Eng.	52·49 N	1·26 W
75	Melbourne Ky. (Cincinnati In.)	39·02 N	84·22 W
71	Melcher (mĕl'chēr) Iowa	41·13 N	93·11 W
132	Melekess (mĕl-yĕk ĕs) Sov. Un.	54·20 N	49·30 E
128	Melenki (mĕ-lyĕŋ'kē) Sov. Un.	55·25 N	41·34 E
86	Melfort (mĕl'fôrt) Can.	52·55 N	104·31 W
165	Melik, Wadi el (R.) Sud.	16·48 N	29·30 E
164	Melilla (Sp.) (mā-lēl'yä) Afr.	35·24 N	3·03 W
101	Melipilla (mȧ-lē-pē'lyä) Chile (Santiago In.)	33·40 S	71·12 W
129	Melitopol' (mā-lē-tô'pôl-y') Sov. Un.	46·49 N	35·19 E
168	Melkrivier S. Afr. (Johannesburg & Pretoria In.)	24·01 S	28·23 E
71	Mellen (mĕl'ĕn) Wis.	46·20 N	90·40 W
118	Mellerud (mål'ĕ-rōōdh) Swe.	58·43 N	12·25 E
167	Melmoth S. Afr. (Natal In.)	28·38 S	31·26 E
100	Melo (mā'lō) Ur.	32·18 S	54·07 W
85	Melocheville (mĕ-lôsh-vēl') Can. (Montreal In.)	45·24 N	73·56 W
136	Melozha R. (myĕ'lô-zhȧ) Sov. Un. (Moscow In.)	56·06 N	38·34 E
164	Melrhir Chott (L.) (mĕl'rēr) Alg.	33·52 N	5·22 E
83	Melrose (mĕl'rōz) Mass. (Boston In.)	42·29 N	71·06 W
71	Melrose Minn.	45·39 N	94·49 W
75	Melrose Park Ill. (Chicago In.)	41·54 N	87·52 W
166	Melsetter (mĕl-sĕt'ēr) S. Rh.	19·44 S	32·51 E
110	Meltham (mĕl'thăm) Eng.	53·35 N	1·51 W
161	Melton (mĕl'tăn) Austl. (Melbourne In.)	37·41 S	144·35 E
110	Melton Mowbray (mō'brȧ) Eng.	52·45 N	0·52 W
123	Melun (mĕ-lŭN') Fr. (Paris In.)	48·32 N	2·40 E
165	Melut (mȧ-lōōt') Sud.	10·30 N	32·17 E
86	Melville (mĕl'vĭl) Can.	51·00 N	102·52 W
77	Melville La.	30·39 N	91·45 W
159	Melville, C. Austl.	14·15 S	145·50 E
158	Melville (I.) Austl.	11·30 S	131·12 E
87	Melville (R.) Can.	53·46 N	59·31 W
86	Melville Hills Can.	69·18 N	124·57 W
87	Melville Pen. Can.	67·44 N	84·09 W
75	Melvindale (mĕl'vĭn-dăl) Mich. (Detroit In.)	42·17 N	83·11 W
121	Mélykút (mā'l'kōōt) Hung.	46·14 N	19·21 E
168	Memal (mĕ'mĕl) S. Afr. (Johannesburg & Pretoria In.)	27·42 S	29·35 E
167	Memba (mĕm'bȧ) Moz.	14·12 S	40·35 E
	Memel, see Klaipėda		
120	Memmingen (mĕm'ĭng-ĕn) Ger.	47·59 N	10·10 E
99	Memo (R.) (mĕ'mō) Ven. (In.)	9·32 N	66·30 W
73	Memphis (mĕm'fĭs) Mo.	40·27 N	92·11 W
78	Memphis (mĕm'fĭs) Tenn.	35·07 N	90·03 W
72	Memphis Tex.	34·42 N	100·33 W
168	Memphis (Ruins) U. A. R. (Nile In.)	29·50 N	31·12 E
81	Memphremagog (L.) (mĕm'frē-mā'gŏg) Can.	45·05 N	72·10 W
73	Mena (mē'nȧ) Ark.	34·35 N	94·09 W
129	Mena (mā-nȧ') Sov. Un.	51·31 N	32·14 E
161	Menangle Austl. (Sydney In.)	34·08 S	150·48 E
76	Menard (mē-närd') Tex.	30·56 N	99·48 W
71	Menasha (mē-năsh'ȧ) Wis.	44·12 N	88·29 W
122	Mende (mäNd) Fr.	44·31 N	3·30 E
123	Menden (mĕn'dĕn) Ger. (Ruhr In.)	51·26 N	7·47 E
133	Menderes (R.) (mĕn'dĕr-ĕs) Tur.	37·50 N	28·20 E
100	Mendes (mĕ'n-dĕs) Braz. (In.)	22·32 S	43·44 W

ng-sing; ŋ-baŋk; N-nasalized n; nŏd; cŏmmit; ōld; ôbey; ôrder; fōōd; fŏŏt; ou-out; s-soft; sh-dish; th-thin; pūre; ûnite; ûrn; stŭd; circŭs; ü-as "y" in study; '-indeterminate vowel.

Page	Name Pronunciation	Region	Lat. °′	Long. °′
66	Mendocino, C. (měn'dô-sē'nō)	Calif.	40·25 N	124·22 W
71	Mendota (měn-dō'tȧ)	Ill.	41·34 N	89·06 W
71	Mendota (L.)	Wis.	43·09 N	89·41 W
100	Mendoza (měn-dō'sä)	Arg.	32·48 S	68·45 W
100	Mendoza (Prov.)	Arg.	35·10 S	69·00 W
151	Mengtzu	China	23·22 N	103·20 E
160	Menindee (mě-nĭn-dē)	Austl.	32·23 S	142·30 E
65	Menlo Park (měn'lō pärk)	Calif. (San Francisco In.)	37·27 N	122·11 W
70	Menno (měn'ô)	S. D.	43·14 N	97·34 W
71	Menominee (mê-nŏm'ĭ-nē)	Mich.	45·08 N	87·40 W
71	Menominee (R.)	Mich.-Wis.	45·37 N	87·54 W
75	Menomonee Falls (fôls)	Wis. (Milwaukee In.)	43·11 N	88·06 W
71	Menominee Ra.	Mich.	46·07 N	88·53 W
75	Menomonee R.	Wis. (Milwaukee In.)	43·09 N	88·06 W
71	Menomonie	Wis.	44·53 N	91·55 W
125	Menorca, Isla de (Minorca) (I.) (ê's-lä-dě-mě-nô'r-kä)	Sp.	40·05 N	3·58 E
125	Mentana (měn-tȧ'nä)	It. (Rome In.)	42·02 N	12·40 E
154	Mentawai, Pulau-Pulau (Is.) (měn-tä-vī')	Indon.	1·08 S	98·10 E
123	Menton (mäN-tôN')	Fr.	43·46 N	7·37 E
74	Mentone (měn'tōne)	Calif. (Los Angeles In.)	34·05 N	117·08 W
167	Mentz (R.) (měnts)	S. Afr. (Natal In.)	33·13 S	25·15 E
132	Menzelinsk (měn'zyě-lênsk')	Sov. Un.	55·40 N	53·15 E
158	Menzies (měn'zēz)	Austl.	29·45 S	122·15 E
76	Meogui (mâ-ō'gē)	Mex.	28·17 N	105·28 W
117	Meppel (měp'ěl)	Neth.	52·41 N	6·08 E
120	Meppen (měp'ěn)	Ger.	52·40 N	7·18 E
126	Merabéllou, Kólpos (G.)	Grc. (In.)	35·16 N	25·55 E
73	Meramec (R.) (měr'ȧ-měk)	Mo.	38·06 N	91·06 W
126	Merano (mâ-rä'nō)	It.	46·39 N	11·10 E
83	Merasheen (I.) (mē'rȧ-shēn)	Can.	47·33 N	54·15 W
155	Merauke (mâ-rou'kä)	W. Irian	8·32 S	140·17 E
84	Meraux (mē-rō')	La. (New Orleans In.)	29·56 N	89·56 W
168	Merca (měr'kä)	Som. (Horn of Afr. In.)	1·45 N	44·47 E
125	Mercato San Severino (měr-kȧ'tō sän sě-vě-rē'nō)	It. (Naples In.)	40·34 N	14·38 E
68	Merced (mēr-sěd')	Calif.	37·17 N	120·30 W
68	Merced (R.)	Calif.	37·25 N	120·31 W
101	Mercedario, Cerro (Mtn.) (měr-sā-dhä'rê-ō)	Chile (Santiago In.)	31·58 S	70·07 W
100	Mercedes (měr-sā'dhās)	Arg.	29·04 S	58·01 W
101	Mercedes	Arg. (Buenos Aires In.)	34·41 S	59·26 W
76	Mercedes	Tex.	26·09 N	97·55 W
101	Mercedes	Ur. (Buenos Aires In.)	33·17 S	58·04 W
101	Mercedita (měr-sě-dē'tä)	Chile (Santiago In.)	33·51 S	71·10 W
65	Mercer Island (mûr'sēr)	Wash. (Seattle In.)	47·35 N	122·15 W
101	Mercês (měr-sě's)	Braz. (Rio de Janeiro In.)	21·13 S	43·20 W
139	Merchong (R.)	Mala. (Singapore In.)	3·08 N	103·13 E
111	Merchtem	Bel. (Brussels In.)	50·57 N	4·13 E
125	Mercier-Lacombe (měr-syā' lȧ-kôNb)	Alg.	35·18 N	0·11 W
87	Mercy, C.	Can.	64·48 N	63·22 W
81	Meredith (měr'ê-dĭth)	N. H.	43·35 N	71·35 W
129	Merefa (mâ-rěf'ȧ)	Sov. Un.	49·49 N	36·04 E
92	Merendón, Serrania de (Mts.) (sěr-rä-nē'ȧ-dä mâ-rěn-dōn')	Hond.	15·01 N	89·05 W
110	Mereworth (mě-rě'wûrth)	Eng. (London In.)	51·15 N	0·23 E
	Mergen, see Nench'eng			
154	Mergui (měr-gē')	Bur.	12·29 N	98·39 E
154	Mergui Archip.	Asia	12·04 N	97·02 E
91	Mérida (mā'rê-dhä)	Mex. (Yucatan In.)	20·57 N	89·38 W
98	Mérida	Ven.	8·30 N	71·15 W
98	Mérida, Sierra Nevada de (Mts.) (sē-ě'r-rä-nē-vä'dä-dě-mě'rê-dhä)	Ven.	8·30 N	70·45 W
81	Meriden (měr'ĭ-děn)	Conn.	41·30 N	72·50 W
78	Meridian (mê-rĭd-ĭ-ăn)	Miss.	32·21 N	88·41 W
77	Meridian	Tex.	31·56 N	97·37 W
119	Merikarvia (mā'rē-kär'vē-à)	Fin.	61·51 N	21·30 E
111	Mering (mě'rěng)	Ger. (Munich In.)	48·16 N	11·00 E
78	Meriwether Lewis Natl. Mon. (měr'ĭ-wěth-ēr lōō'ĭs)	Tenn.	35·25 N	87·25 W
76	Merkel (mûr'kěl)	Tex.	32·26 N	100·02 W
119	Merkine (měr'kĭ-nê)	Sov. Un.	54·09 N	24·10 E
111	Merksem	Bel. (Brussels In.)	51·15 N	4·27 E
121	Merkys R. (màr'kĭs)	Sov. Un.	54·23 N	25·00 E
100	Merlo (měr-lô)	Arg. (In.)	34·25 S	58·44 W
165	Merowe	Sud.	18·07 N	31·57 E
74	Merriam (měr-rĭ-yam)	Minn. (Minneapolis, St. Paul In.)	44·44 N	93·36 W
74	Merriam	Mo. (Kansas City In.)	39·01 N	94·42 W
84	Merrick (měr'ĭk)	N. Y. (New York In.)	40·40 N	73·33 W
71	Merrill (měr'ĭl)	Wis.	45·11 N	89·42 W
83	Merrimac (měr'ĭ-măk)	Mass. (Boston In.)	42·50 N	71·00 W
83	Merrimack	N. H. (Boston In.)	42·51 N	71·25 W
81	Merrimack (R.) (měr'ĭ-măk)	Mass.-N. H.	43·10 N	71·30 W
83	Merrimack R.	Mass. (Boston In.)	42·49 N	70·44 W
86	Merritt (měr'ĭt)	Can.	50·10 N	120·48 W
85	Merritton (měr'ĭt-tŭn)	Can. (Toronto In.)	43·14 N	79·13 W
77	Merryville (měr'ĭ-vĭl)	La.	30·46 N	93·34 W
120	Merseburg (měr'zě-bŏŏrgh)	Ger.	51·21 N	11·59 E
110	Mersey (R.) (mûr'zê)	Eng.	52·52 N	2·04 W
116	Mersey (R.)	Eng.	53·15 N	2·51 W
133	Mersin (měr-sēn')	Tur.	37·00 N	34·40 E
139	Mersing	Mala. (Singapore In.)	2·25 N	103·51 E
142	Merta Road (mār'tŭ rōd)	India	26·50 N	73·54 E
116	Merthyr Tydfil (mûr'thēr tĭd'vĭl)	Wales	51·46 N	3·30 W
124	Mértola Almodóvar (měr-tô-lȧ-äl-mô-dô'vär)	Port.	37·39 N	8·04 W
123	Méru (mā-rü')	Fr. (Paris In.)	49·14 N	2·08 E
165	Meru (mā'rōō)	Ken.	00·01 N	37·45 E
99	Merume Mts. (měr-ü'mě)	Br. Gu.	5·45 N	60·15 W
111	Merwerde, Kanal (Can.)	Neth. (Amsterdam In.)	52·15 N	5·01 E
65	Merwin (L.) (měr'wĭn)	Wash. (Portland In.)	45·58 N	122·27 W
133	Merzifon (měr'ze-fōn)	Tur.	40·50 N	35·30 E
123	Merzig (měr'tsēg)	Ger.	49·27 N	6·54 E
69	Mesa (mā'sȧ)	Ariz.	33·25 N	111·50 W
71	Mesabi Ra. (mā-sŏb'bē)	Minn.	47·17 N	93·04 W
127	Mesagne (mā-sän'yā)	It.	40·34 N	17·51 E
69	Mesa Verde Natl. Park. (vēr'dē)	Colo.	37·22 N	108·27 W
69	Mescalero Ind. Res. (měs-kä-lā'rō)	N. Mex.	33·10 N	105·45 W
128	Meshchovsk (myěsh'chěfsk)	Sov. Un.	54·17 N	35·19 E
165	Meshra er Req	Sud.	8·28 N	29·15 E
69	Mesilla (mâ-sē'yä)	N. Mex.	32·15 N	106·45 W
127	Mesolóngion (mě-sô-lôŋ'gê-ôn)	Grc.	38·23 N	21·28 E
126	Messina (mě-sē'nȧ)	It.	38·11 N	15·34 E
166	Messina	S. Afr.	22·17 S	30·13 E
126	Messina, Stretto di (Str.) (strě't-tô dē)	It.	38·10 N	15·34 E
127	Messíni	Grc.	37·05 N	22·00 E
127	Méssiniakós Kólpos (G.)	Grc.	36·59 N	22·00 E
127	Mesta (R.) (mě-stȧ')	Bul.	41·42 N	23·40 E
126	Mestre (měs'trā)	It.	45·29 N	12·15 E
98	Meta (Dept.) (mě'tȧ)	Col. (In.)	3·28 N	74·07 W
98	Meta (R.)	Col.	4·33 N	72·09 W
83	Metabetchouan (R.) (mě-tȧ-bět-chōō-ăn')	Can.	47·45 N	72·00 W
77	Metairie (mě-trâr'ĭ)	La.	30·00 N	90·11 W
100	Metán (mě-tȧ'n)	Arg.	25·32 S	64·51 W
92	Metapán (mâ-tä-pän')	Sal.	14·21 N	89·26 W
85	Metcalfe (mět-käf)	Can. (Ottawa In.)	45·14 N	75·27 W
65	Metchosin	Can. (Seattle In.)	48·22 N	123·33 W
90	Metepec (mâ-tě-pěk')	Mex.	18·56 N	98·31 W
91	Metepec	Mex. (Mexico City In.)	19·15 N	99·36 W
66	Methow R. (mět'hou) (mět hou')	Wash.	48·26 N	120·15 W
83	Methuen (mê-thū'ěn)	Mass. (Boston In.)	42·44 N	71·11 W
82	Metis Beach (mâ-tē') (mā-tĭs')	Can.	48·40 N	68·04 W
127	Metkovic' (mět'kô-vĭch)	Yugo.	43·02 N	17·40 E
64	Metlakatla (mět-lȧ-kăt'lȧ)	Alaska	55·10 N	131·30 W
73	Metropolis (mê-trŏp'ô-lĭs)	Ill.	37·09 N	88·46 W
79	Metter (mět'ēr)	Ga.	32·21 N	82·05 W
123	Mettmann (mět'män)	Ger. (Ruhr In.)	51·15 N	6·58 E
84	Metuchen (mě-tŭ'chěn)	N. J. (New York In.)	40·32 N	74·21 W
123	Metz (mětz)	Fr.	49·08 N	6·10 E
90	Metztitlán (mětz-tět-län')	Mex.	20·36 N	98·45 W
122	Meuse (R.) (mûz) (müz)	Eur.	50·32 N	5·22 E
110	Mexborough (měks'bŭr-ô)	Eng.	53·30 N	1·17 W
77	Mexia (mâ-hē'ä)	Tex.	31·32 N	96·29 W
91	Mexicalcingo (mě-kē-käl-sēn'go)	Mex. (Mexico City In.)	19·13 N	99·34 W
68	Mexicali (mâk-sê-kä'lê)	Mex.	32·28 N	115·29 W
69	Mexican Hat (měk'sĭ-kăn hăt)	Utah	37·10 N	109·55 W
82	Mexico (měk'sĭ-kō)	Maine	44·34 N	70·33 W
73	Mexico	Mo.	39·09 N	91·51 W
88	Mexico (State) (mâk'sē-kō)	Mex.	19·50 N	99·50 W
49	Mexico	N. A.	23·45 N	104·00 W
88	Mexico, G. of	N. A.	25·15 N	93·45 W
91	Mexico City (měk'sĭ-kō)	Mex. (Mexico City In.)	19·28 N	99·09 W
90	Mexticacán (měs'tê-kä-kän')	Mex.	21·12 N	102·43 W
144	Meydān-e Naftūn	Iran	31·45 N	49·17 E
81	Meyersdale (mī'ērz-dāl)	Pa.	39·55 N	79·00 W
168	Meyerton (mī'ēr-tŭn)	S. Afr. (Johannesburg & Pretoria In.)	26·35 S	28·01 E
132	Mezen'	Sov. Un.	65·50 N	44·05 E
132	Mezen' (R.)	Sov. Un.	65·20 N	44·45 E
122	Mézenc, Mt. (mōN-mä-zěN')	Fr.	44·55 N	4·12 E
128	Mezha (R.) (myā'zhȧ)	Sov. Un.	55·53 N	31·44 E
122	Mézières (mā-zyâr')	Fr.	49·45 N	4·40 E
123	Mézières-sur-Seine (mā-zyâr'sür-sân')	Fr. (Paris In.)	48·58 N	1·49 E
121	Mezőkövesd (mě'zû-kû'věsht)	Hung.	47·49 N	20·36 E
121	Mezőtur (mě'zû-tōōr)	Hung.	47·00 N	20·36 E
90	Mezquital (mâz-kê-täl')	Mex.	23·30 N	104·20 W
90	Mezquital (R.)	Mex.	23·07 N	104·52 W
90	Mezquitic (mâz-kê-těk')	Mex.	22·25 N	103·43 W
90	Mezquitic (R.)	Mex.	22·25 N	103·45 W
136	Mga (m'gȧ)	Sov. Un. (Leningrad In.)	59·45 N	31·04 E
128	Mglin (m'glēn')	Sov. Un.	53·03 N	32·52 E
90	Miacatlán (mê'ä-kä-tlän')	Mex.	18·42 N	99·17 W
91	Miahuatlán (mê'ä-wä-tlän')	Mex.	16·20 N	96·38 W
124	Miajadas (mê-ä-hä'däs)	Sp.	39·10 N	5·53 W
69	Miami (mī-ăm'ĭ)	Ariz.	33·20 N	110·55 W
79	Miami	Fla. (In.)	25·45 N	80·11 W
73	Miami	Okla.	36·51 N	94·51 W
72	Miami	Tex.	35·41 N	100·39 W
80	Miami (R.)	Ohio	39·20 N	84·45 W
79	Miami Beach	Fla. (In.)	25·47 N	80·07 W
94	Miami Drainage Can.	Fla.	26·25 N	80·50 W
80	Miamisburg (mī-ăm'iz-bûrg)	Ohio	39·40 N	84·20 W
75	Miamitown (mī-ăm'ĭ-toun)	Ohio (Cincinnati In.)	39·13 N	84·43 W
144	Miāneh	Iran	37·15 N	47·13 E
155	Miangas (I.) (myä'n-gäs)	Phil.	5·30 N	127·00 E
148	Miaochen (mĭou'zhen)	China	31·44 N	121·28 E
151	Miaoli (mê-ou'lĭ)	Taiwan	24·30 N	120·48 E
148	Miao Liehtao (Is.) (miou' lĭĕdou)	China	38·06 N	120·35 E
136	Miass (mī-äs')	Sov. Un. (Urals In.)	55·00 N	60·03 E
120	Miastko (myäst'kô)	Pol.	54·01 N	17·00 E
121	Michalovce (mē'Kä-lôf'tsě)	Czech.	48·44 N	21·56 E
83	Michel (L.) (mê-shěl') (mĭch'ěl)	Can.	50·21 N	56·45 W
64	Michelson, Mt. (mĭch'ěl-sŭn)	Alaska	69·11 N	144·12 W
111	Michendorf (mē'Kěn-dōrf)	Ger. (Berlin In.)	52·19 N	13·02 E
95	Miches (mē'-chěs)	Dom. Rep.	19·00 N	69·05 W
63	Michigan (State) (mĭsh'ĭ-găn)	U. S.	45·55 N	87·00 W
63	Michigan, L.	U. S.	43·20 N	87·10 W
80	Michigan City	Ind.	41·40 N	86·55 W
87	Michikamau (L.)	Can.	54·11 N	63·21 W
71	Michipicoten (I.) (mĕ-shĭ-pĭ-kō'těn)	Can.	47·49 N	85·50 W
71	Michipicoten	Can.	47·56 N	84·42 W
71	Michipicoten Harbour	Can.	47·58 N	84·58 W
128	Michurinsk (mĭ-chōō-rĭnsk')	Sov. Un.	52·53 N	40·32 E
93	Mico, Punta (Pt.) (pōō'n-tä-mē'kô)	Nic.	11·38 N	83·24 W
66	Midas (mī'dăs)	Nev.	41·15 N	116·50 W
166	Middelburg (mĭd'ěl-bûrg)	S. Afr.	31·30 S	25·00 E
168	Middelburg	S. Afr. (Johannesburg & Pretoria In.)	25·47 S	29·30 E
168	Middelwit (mĭd'l'wĭt)	S. Afr. (Johannesburg & Pretoria In.)	24·50 S	27·00 E
154	Middle Andaman I. (ăn-dȧ-măn')	Andaman Is.	12·44 N	93·21 E
77	Middle Bay (mĭd''l bā)	Tex. (In.)	29·38 N	95·06 W
94	Middle Bight (B.) (bĭt)	Ba. Is.	24·20 N	77·35 W
81	Middlebury (mĭd''l-běr-ĭ)	Vt.	44·00 N	73·10 W
76	Middle Concho (kŏn'chō)	Tex.	31·21 N	100·50 W
118	Middelfart (mêd''l-fârt)	Den.	55·30 N	9·45 E
70	Middle Loup (R.) (lōōp)	Nebr.	41·49 N	100·20 W
80	Middleport (mĭd''l-pōrt)	Ohio	39·00 N	82·05 W
84	Middle River	Md. (Baltimore In.)	39·20 N	76·27 W
78	Middlesboro (mĭd''lz-bŭr-ô)	Ky.	36·36 N	83·42 W
116	Middlesbrough (mĭd''lz-brŭ)	Eng.	54·35 N	1·18 W
84	Middlesex (mĭd''l-sěks)	N. J. (New York In.)	40·34 N	74·30 W
110	Middleton (mĭd''l-tŭn)	Eng.	53·04 N	2·12 W
64	Middleton (I.)	Alaska	59·35 N	146·35 W
82	Middletown (mĭd''l-toun)	Can.	44·56 N	65·03 W
81	Middletown	Conn.	41·35 N	72·40 W
81	Middletown	Del.	39·30 N	75·40 W
83	Middletown	Mass. (Boston In.)	42·35 N	71·01 W
84	Middletown	N. Y. (New York In.)	41·26 N	74·25 W
80	Middletown	Ohio	39·30 N	84·25 W
110	Middlewich (mĭd''l-wĭch)	Eng.	53·11 N	2·27 W
125	Midi, Canal du (kä-näl-dü-mē-dē')	Fr.	43·22 N	1·35 E
167	Mid Illovo (mĭd ĭl'ô-vō)	S. Afr. (Natal In.)	29·59 S	30·32 E
81	Midland (mĭd'lănd)	Can.	44·45 N	79·50 W
80	Midland	Mich.	43·40 N	84·20 W
76	Midland	Tex.	32·00 N	102·04 W
85	Midnapore (mĭd'-nȧ-pōr)	Can. (Calgary In.)	50·56 N	114·04 W
74	Midvale (mĭd'vāl)	Utah (Salt Lake City In.)	40·37 N	111·54 W
78	Midway (mĭd'wā)	Ala.	32·03 N	85·30 W
156	Midway Is.	Pac. O.	28·00 N	179·00 W
67	Midwest (mĭd-wěst')	Wyo.	43·25 N	106·15 W
133	Midye (mēd'yě)	Tur.	41·35 N	28·10 E
120	Miedzyrzecz (myăn-dzŭ'zhěch)	Pol.	52·26 N	15·35 E
121	Mielec (myě'lěts)	Pol.	50·17 N	21·27 E
76	Mier (myâr)	Mex.	26·26 N	99·08 W
124	Mieres (myâ'räs)	Sp.	43·14 N	5·45 W
90	Mier y Noriega (myâr'ê nô-rē-ā'gä)	Mex.	22·28 N	100·08 W
120	Miessen (mē'sěn)	Ger.	51·11 N	13·28 E
139	Migdal Ashkelon (mĭg'däl äsh'kě-lōn)	Isr. (Palestine In.)	31·40 N	34·36 E
129	Migorod	Sov. Un.	49·56 N	33·36 E
90	Miguel Auza (mē-gě'l-ä-ōō'zä)	Mex.	24·17 N	103·27 W
100	Miguel Pereira (pě-rä'-rä)	Braz. (In.)	22·27 S	43·28 W
95	Mija, Monte (Mtn.) (mô'n-tě-mē'kä)	Dom. Rep.	19·10 N	71·15 W
125	Mijares (R.) (mē-hä'räs)	Sp.	40·05 N	0·42 W
153	Mikage (mē'kä-gå)	Jap. (Ōsaka In.)	34·42 N	135·15 E
153	Mikawa-Wan (B.) (mē'kä-wä wän)	Jap.	34·43 N	137·09 E
128	Mikhaylov (mē-Kāy'lôf)	Sov. Un.	54·14 N	39·03 E
129	Mikhaylovka	Sov. Un.	47·16 N	35·12 E
133	Mikhaylovka	Sov. Un.	50·05 N	43·10 E
136	Mikhaylovka (mê-kä'ē-lôf-kȧ)	Sov. Un. (Urals In.)	55·35 N	57·57 E
136	Mikhaylovka	Sov. Un. (Leningrad In.)	59·20 N	30·21 E
136	Mikhněvo (mĭk-nyô'vô)	Sov. Un. (Moscow In.)	55·08 N	37·57 E
153	Miki (mē'kê)	Jap. (Ōsaka In.)	34·47 N	134·59 E
167	Mikindani (mē-kên-dä'nê)	Tan.	10·17 S	40·06 E
119	Mikkeli (mĭk'ě-lĭ)	Fin.	61·42 N	27·14 E
127	Míkonos (I.)	Grc.	37·26 N	25·30 E
120	Mikulov (mĭ'kōō-lôf)	Czech.	48·47 N	16·39 E
153	Mikuni (mē'kōō-nê)	Jap.	36·09 N	136·14 E

ăt; finăl; rāte; senâte; ärm; ȧsk; sofȧ; fâre; ch-choose; dh-as th in other; bē; ēvent; bět; recěnt; cratēr; g-go; gh-guttural g; bĭt; ĭ-short neutral; rīde; K-guttural k as ch in German ich;

Page	Name Pronunciation Region	Lat. °′	Long. °′
153	Mikuni-Sammyaku (Mts.) (säm′myä-kōō) . Jap.	36·51 N	138·38 E
153	Mikura (I.) (mē′kōō-rȧ) ...... Jap.	33·53 N	139·26 E
164	Mila (mē′lä) ... Alg.	36·30 N	6.16 E
71	Milaca (mė-lăk′ȧ) ... Minn.	45·45 N	93·41 W
80	Milan (mī′lăn) ... Mich.	42·05 N	83·40 W
73	Milan ... Mo.	40·13 N	93·07 W
78	Milan ... Tenn.	35·54 N	88·47 W
	Milan, see Milano		
126	Milano (Milan) (mė-lä′nō) ..... It.	45·29 N	9·12 E
133	Milas (mė′läs) ... Tur.	37·10 N	27·25 E
126	Milazzo (mė-lät′sō) ... It.	38·13 N	15·17 E
70	Milbank (mĭl′băŋk) ... S. D.	45·13 N	96·38 W
160	Mildura (mĭl-dū′rȧ) ... Austl.	34·10 S	142·18 E
67	Miles City (mīlz) ... Mont.	46·24 N	105·50 W
81	Milford (mĭl′fẽrd) ... Conn.	41·15 N	73·05 W
81	Milford ... Del.	38·55 N	75·25 W
83	Milford .... Mass. (Boston In.)	42·09 N	71·31 W
75	Milford .... Mich. (Detroit In.)	42·35 N	83·36 W
81	Milford ... N. H.	42·50 N	71·40 W
75	Milford ..... Ohio (Cincinnati In.)	39·11 N	84·18 W
69	Milford ... Utah	38·20 N	113·05 W
116	Milford Haven (hāv′n) ..... Wales	51·40 N	5·10 W
113	Miliana (mėl-yä′nä) ... Alg.	36·19 N	1·56 E
158	Miling (mīl′ʻng) ... Austl.	30·30 S	116·25 E
65	Milipitas (mĭl-ĭ-pĭ′tăs) Calif. (San Francisco In.)	37·26 N	121·54 W
67	Milk R. (mĭlk) ... Mont.	48·25 N	108·45 W
68	Mill Cr. ... Calif.	40·07 N	121·55 W
85	Mill Cr. (mĭl). Can. (Edmonton In.)	53·13 N	113·25 W
122	Millau (mē-yō′) ... Fr.	44·06 N	3·04 E
65	Millbrae (mĭl′brā) Calif. (San Francisco In.)	37·36 N	122·23 W
83	Millbury (mĭl′bẽr-ĭ) Mass. (Boston In.)	42·12 N	71·46 W
78	Milledgeville (mĭl′ĕj-vĭl) ...... Ga.	33·05 N	83·15 W
85	Mille Iles, R. des (rė-vyâr′ dā mēl′ēl′) Can. (Montreal In.)	45·41 N	73·40 W
71	Mille Lac Ind. Res. (mĭl lăk′) Minn.	46·14 N	94·13 W
71	Mille Lacs (L.) ... Minn.	46·25 N	93·22 W
71	Mille Lacs, Lac des (L.) (läk dĕ mēl läks) . Can.	48·52 N	90·53 W
79	Millen (mĭl′ĕn) ... Ga.	32·47 N	81·55 W
70	Miller (mĭl′ẽr) ... S. D.	44·31 N	99·00 W
129	Millerovo (mĭl′ĕ-rō-vō) ... Sov. Un.	48·58 N	40·27 E
80	Millersburg (mĭl′ẽrz-bûrg) .... Ky.	38·15 N	84·10 W
80	Millersburg ... Ohio	40·35 N	81·55 W
81	Millersburg ... Pa.	40·35 N	76·55 W
82	Millerton (mĭl′ẽr-tŭn) ... Can.	46·56 N	65·40 W
83	Millertown (mĭl′ẽr-toun) ..... Can.	48·48 N	56·33 W
160	Millicent (mĭl-ĭ′sĕnt) ... Austl.	37·30 S	140·20 E
82	Millinocket (mĭl-ĭ-nŏk′ĕt) . . Maine	45·40 N	68·44 W
83	Millis (mĭl′ĭs) Mass. (Boston In.)	42·10 N	71·22 W
74	Millstadt (mĭl′stăt) Ill. (St. Louis In.)	38·27 N	90·06 W
84	Millstone R. (mĭl′stōn) N. J. (New York In.)	40·27 N	74·38 W
158	Millstream (mĭl′strēm) ..... Austl.	21·45 S	117·10 E
82	Milltown (mĭl′toun) ... Can.	45·13 N	67·19 W
75	Millvale (mĭl′vāl) Pa. (Pittsburgh In.)	40·29 N	79·58 W
65	Mill Valley (mĭl) Calif. (San Francisco In.)	37·54 N	122·32 W
81	Millville (mĭl′vĭl) ... N. J.	39·25 N	75·00 W
123	Milly-la-Forêt (mē-yē′-la-fŏ-rĕ′) Fr. (Paris In.)	48·24 N	2·28 E
166	Milnerton (mĭl′nẽr-tŭn) S. Afr. (Cape Town In.)	33·52 S	18·30 E
70	Milnor (mĭl′nẽr) ... N. D.	46·17 N	97·29 W
82	Milo (mī′lō) ... Maine	44·16 N	69·01 W
	Milo (I.), see Mílos		
127	Mílos (Milo) (I.) (mē′lŏs) .... Grc.	36·45 N	24·35 E
91	Milpa Alta (mē′l-pä-ȧ′l-tä) Mex. (Mexico City In.)	19·11 N	99·01 W
78	Milton (mĭl′tŭn) ... Fla.	30·37 N	87·02 W
74	Milton .... Ill. (St. Louis In.)	38·54 N	90·08 W
83	Milton .... Mass. (Boston In.)	42·16 N	71·03 W
81	Milton ... Pa.	41·00 N	76·50 W
74	Milton . Utah (Salt Lake City In.)	41·04 N	111·44 W
65	Milton .... Wash. (Seattle In.)	47·15 N	122·20 W
71	Milton ... Wis.	42·45 N	89·00 W
66	Milton-Freewater ... Ore.	45·57 N	118·25 W
85	Milton West . . Can. (Toronto In.)	43·31 N	79·53 W
75	Milwaukee . . Wis. (Milwaukee In.)	43·03 N	87·55 W
89	Milwaukee Depth .... Atl. O.	19·45 N	68·00 W
75	Milwaukee R. Wis. (Milwaukee In.)	43·10 N	87·56 W
65	Milwaukie (mĭl-wô′kė) Ore. (Portland In.)	45·27 N	122·38 W
91	Mimiapan (mē-myä-pȧn′) Mex. (Mexico City In.)	19·26 N	99·28 W
85	Mimico (mĭ′mĭ-kō) Can. (Toronto In.)	43·37 N	79·30 W
101	Mimoso do Sul (mē-mô′sō-dô-sōō′l) Braz. (Rio de Janeiro In.)	21·03 S	41·21 W
125	Mina (R.) (mē′nȧ) ... Alg.	35·24 N	0·51 E
153	Minakuchi (mē′nȧ-kōō′chė) . . Jap.	34·59 N	136·06 E
94	Minas (mė′näs) ... Cuba	21·30 N	77·35 W
139	Minas ..... Indon. (Singapore In.)	0·52 N	101·29 E
100	Minas (mē′näs) ... Ur.	34·18 S	55·12·W
92	Minas, Sierra de las (Mts.) (syĕr′rȧ dā läs mē′näs) . Guat.	15·08 N	90·25 W
82	Minas Basin (mī′nȧs) .... Can.	45·19 N	64·10 W
82	Minas Chan. ... Can.	45·13 N	64·55 W
92	Minas de Oro (mė′-näs-dĕ-ŏ-rô) Hond.	14·52 N	87·19 W
124	Minas de Ríontinto (mē′näs dā rē-ô-tēn′tō) . Sp.	37·43 N	6·35 W
99	Minas Gerais (State) (mē′näzh-zhĕ-rȧ′ēs) . Braz.	17·45 S	43·50 W
99	Minas Novas (mē′näzh nō′väzh) Braz.	17·20 S	42·19 W
70	Minatare (L.) (mĭn′ȧ-târ) ... Nebr.	41·56 N	103·07 W
91	Minatitlán (mė-nä-tė-tlän′) . . Mex.	17·59 N	94·33 W
90	Minatitlán ... Mex.	19·21 N	104·02 W
153	Minato (mē′nȧ-tô) Jap. (Tōkyō In.)	35·13 N	139·52 E
116	Minch, The (Chan.) .... Scot.	58·04 N	6·04 W
116	Minch, The Little (Chan.) (mĭnch) . Scot.	56·85 N	6·42 W
151	Min Chiang (R.) ... China	26·30 N	118·30 E
151	Min Chiang (R.) ... China	29·30 N	104·00 E
155	Mindanao (I.) (mĭn-dä-nou′) . Phil.	7·30 N	125·10 E
155	Mindanao Sea ... Phil.	8·55 N	124·00 E
120	Minden (mĭn′dĕn) ... Ger.	52·17 N	8·58 E
77	Minden ... La.	32·36 N	93·19 W
72	Minden ... Nebr.	40·30 N	98·54 W
155	Mindoro (I.) (mĭn-dô′rō) Phil. (Manila In.)	13·04 N	121·06 E
155	Mindoro Str. . . . Phil. (Manila In.)	12·28 N	120·33 E
136	Mindyak (mēn′dyȧk) Sov. Un. (Urals In.)	54·01 N	58·48 E
84	Mineola (mĭn-ė-ō′lȧ) N. Y. (New York In.)	40·43 N	73·38 W
77	Mineola ... Tex.	32·39 N	95·31 W
90	Mineral del Chico (mė-nȧ-räl′dĕl chē′kô) . Mex.	20·13 N	98·46 W
90	Mineral del Monte (mė-nȧ-räl dĕl mōn′tȧ) . Mex.	20·18 N	98·39 W
133	Mineral′nyye Vody ...... Sov. Un.	44·10 N	43·15 E
71	Mineral Point (mĭn′ẽr-ăl) .... Wis.	42·50 N	90·10 W
76	Minerál Wells (mĭn′ẽr-ăl wĕlz) Tex.	32·48 N	98·06 W
80	Minerva (mĭ-nûr′vȧ) .... Ohio	40·45 N	81·10 W
126	Minervino (mē-nĕr-vē′nô) ..... It.	41·07 N	16·05 E
153	Mineyama (mē-nĕ-yä′mä) .... Jap.	35·38 N	135·05 E
82	Mingan (mĭŋ′găn) ... Can.	50·19 N	64·02 W
133	Mingechaur (R.) .... Sov. Un.	41·00 N	47·20 E
158	Mingenew (mĭn′gĕ-nû) ..... Austl.	29·15 S	115·45 E
148	Mingkuang (mĭng′gōōäɴg) . . China	32·41 N	118·00 E
80	Mingo Junction (mĭŋ′gō) .... Ohio	40·15 N	80·40 W
124	Minho (Reg.) (mēn yōō) .... Port.	41·32 N	8·13 W
94	Minho (R.) ... Jam.	17·55 N	77·20 W
124	Minho, Rio (R.) (rė′ō-mė′n-yô) Port.	41·48 N	9·05 W
85	Ministik L. (mĭ-nĭs′tĭk) Can. (Edmonton In.)	53·23 N	113·05 W
164	Minna (mĭn′ä) ... Nig.	9·40 N	6·34 E
73	Minneapoli (mĭn-ė-ăp′ô-lĭ) . . Kans.	39·07 N	97·41 W
74	Minneapolis (mĭn-ė-ăp′ô-lĭs) Minn. (Minneapolis, St. Paul In.)	44·58 N	93·15 W
86	Minnedosa (mĭn-ė-dō′sȧ) .... Can.	50·16 N	99·50 W
70	Minneota (mĭn-ė-ō′tȧ) ...... Minn.	44·34 N	95·59 W
63	Minnesota (State) (mĭn-ė-sō′tȧ) U. S.	46·10 N	90·20 W
70	Minnesota (R.) ... Minn.	45·04 N	96·03 W
71	Minnetonka (L.) (mĭn-ė-tôŋ′kȧ) Minn.	44·52 N	93·34 W
69	Minnie Maud Cr. (mĭn′ĭmôd′) Utah	39·50 N	110·30 W
153	Mino (R.) (mė′nō) Jap. (Ōsaka In.)	34·56 N	135·06 E
124	Miño (R.) (mē′nyō) ... Sp.	42·28 N	7·48 W
80	Minonk (mī′nŏnk) ... Ill.	40·55 N	89·00 W
75	Minooka (mĭ-nōō′kȧ) Ill. (Chicago In.)	41·27 N	88·15 W
	Minorca (I.), see Menorca, Isla de		
70	Minot (mī′nŏt) ... N. D.	48·13 N	101·16 W
128	Minsk (mėnsk) ... Sov. Un.	53·54 N	27·35 E
128	Minsk (Oblast) ... Sov. Un.	53·50 N	27·43 E
121	Mińsk Mazowiecki (mėn′sk mä-zô-vyĕt′skĭ) .... Pol.	52·10 N	21·35 E
110	Minsterley (mĭnstẽr-lē) ...... Eng.	52·38 N	2·55 W
82	Minto (mĭn′tô) ... Can.	46·05 N	66·05 W
87	Minto (L.) ... Can.	57·18 N	75·50 W
126	Minturno (mėn-tōōr′nō) ... It.	41·17 N	13·44 E
168	Minūf (mė-nōōf′) U. A. R. (Nile In.)	30·26 N	30·55 E
134	Minusinsk (mē-nōō-sėnsk′) Sov. Un.	53·47 N	86·43 E
146	Minya Konka (Mt.) (mēn′yȧ kôŋ′kȧ) . China	29·16 N	101·46 E
136	Min′yar (mēn′yȧr) Sov. Un. (Urals In.)	55·06 N	57·33 E
85	Miquelon L. (mĭ′kė-lôn) Can. (Edmonton In.)	53·16 N	112·55 W
90	Miquihuana (mė-kė-wä′nä) . . Mex.	23·36 N	99·45 W
121	Mir (mēr) ... Sov. Un.	53·27 N	26·25 E
124	Mira (R.) (mė′rä) ... Port.	37·29 N	8·15 W
101	Miracema (mē-rä-sĕ′mä) Braz. (Rio de Janeiro In.)	21·24 S	42·10 W
99	Mirador (mė-rȧ-dōr′) .... Braz.	6·19 S	44·12 W
98	Miraflores (mē-rä-flō′rās) ..... Col.	5·10 N	73·13 W
98	Miraflores ... Peru	16·19 S	71·20 W
88	Miraflores Locks C. Z. (Panama Canal In.)	9·00 N	79·35 W
95	Miragoâne (mė-rȧ-gwän′) .... Hai.	18·25 N	73·05 W
101	Miraí (mē-rȧ-ē′) Braz. (Rio de Janeiro In.)	21·13 S	42·36 W
143	Miraj (mė-rŭj′) ... India	16·55 N	74·40 E
74	Mira Loma (mĭ′rȧ lō′mȧ) Calif. (Los Angeles In.)	34·01 N	117·32 W
68	Miramar (mĭr′ă-mär) Calif. (San Diego In.)	32·53 N	117·08 W
122	Miramas ...... Fr. (Marseille In.)	43·35 N	5·00 E
82	Miramichi (R.) ... Can.	46·36 N	66·08 W
82	Miramichi B. (mĭr′ȧ-mė′shē) . Can.	47·14 N	64·45 W
98	Miranda (mē-rä′n-dä) . . . Col. (In.)	3·14 N	76·11 W
99	Miranda ... Ven. (In.)	10·09 N	68·24 W
99	Miranda (State) .... Ven. (In.)	10·17 N	66·41 W
124	Miranda de Ebro (mē-rä′n-dä-dĕ-ĕ′l-brô) . Sp.	42·42 N	2·59 W
124	Miranda de Ebro (mė-rän′dä dōō-dwĕ′rô) . Port.	41·30 N	6·17 W
124	Mirandela (mė-rän-dā′lȧ) .... Port.	41·28 N	7·10 W
76	Mirando City (mĭr-ȧn′dō) .... Tex.	27·25 N	99·03 W
95	Mira Por Vos Islets (Is.) (mē′rä pôr vōs′) . Ba. Is.	22·05 N	74·30 W
95	Mira Por Vos Pass (Str.) . . Ba. Is.	22·10 N	74·35 W
144	Mirbāt ... Mus. & Om.	16·58 N	54·42 E
95	Mirebalais (mēr-bȧ-lĕ′) ...... Hai.	18·50 N	72·05 W
123	Mirecourt (mēr-kōōr′) ... Fr.	48·20 N	6·08 E
122	Mirepoix (mēr-pwä′) ... Fr.	43·06 N	1·52 E
110	Mirfield (mûr′fēld) ... Eng.	53·41 N	1·42 W
154	Miri (mē′rē) ... Mala.	4·13 N	113·56 E
100	Mirim, L. (mė-rėɴ′) . . . . Braz.-Ur.	33·00 S	53·15 W
129	Miropol′ye (mē-rô-pôl′yĕ) Sov. Un.	51·02 N	35·13 E
142	Mīrpur Khās (mēr′pōōr ᴋäs) W. Pak.	25·36 N	69·10 E
142	Mirzapur (mēr′zä-pōōr) ..... India	25·12 N	82·38 E
164	Misa ... Togo	7·00 N	00·34 E
153	Misaki (mē′sȧ-kė) Jap. (Tōkyō In.)	35·08 N	139·37 E
91	Misantla (mė-sän′tlä) .... Mex.	19·55 N	96·49 W
82	Miscou (I.) (mĭs′kō) ... Can.	47·58 N	64·35 W
82	Miscou Pt. ... Can.	48·04 N	64·25 W
125	Miseno, C. (mė-zĕ′nō) It. (Naples In.)	40·33 N	14·12 E
93	Misery, Mt. (mĭz′rē-ĭ) St. Christopher (Le. & Wind. Is. In.)	17·28 N	62·47 W
152	Mishan (mĭ′shäɴ) ... China	45·32 N	132·19 E
80	Mishawaka (mĭsh-ȧ-wôk′ȧ) . . . Ind.	41·45 N	86·15 W
153	Mishima (mė′shė-mä) ... Jap.	35·09 N	138·56 E
100	Misiones (Prov.) (mė-syō′nās) Arg.	27·00 S	54·30 W
93	Miskito, Cayos (Is.) ... Nic.	14·34 N	82·30 W
121	Miskolc (mĭsh′kôlts) .... Hung.	48·07 N	20·50 E
155	Misol (I.) (mė-sōl′) ...... W. Irian	2·00 S	130·05 E
71	Misquah Hills (mĭs-kwä′ hĭlz) Minn.	47·50 N	90·30 W
168	Mişr al Jadīdah (Ruins) U. A. R. (Nile In.)	30·06 N	31·35 E
165	Misratāh ... Libya	32·23 N	14·58 E
87	Missinaibi (R.) (mĭs′ĭn-ä′ė-bė) Can.	50·27 N	83·01 W
74	Mission (mĭsh′ŭn) Mo. (Kansas City In.)	39·02 N	94·39 W
76	Mission ... Tex.	26·14 N	98·19 W
65	Mission City (sĭ′tĭ) Can. (Vancouver In.)	49·08 N	122·19 W
80	Mississinewa (R.) (mĭs-ĭ-sĭn′ė-wä) Ind.	40·30 N	85·45 W
63	Mississippi (State) (mĭs-ĭ-sĭp′ė) U. S.	32·30 N	89·45 W
81	Mississippi (L.) ... Can.	45·05 N	76·15 W
63	Mississippi (R.) ... U. S.	31·50 N	91·30 W
84	Mississippi Delta, The La. (New Orleans In.)	28·59 N	89·14 W
78	Mississippi Sd. ... Miss.	34·16 N	89·10 W
67	Missoula (mĭ-zōō′lȧ) .... Mont.	46·52 N	114·00 W
63	Missouri (State) (mĭ-sōō′rė) . U. S.	38·00 N	93·40 W
63	Missouri (R.) ... U. S.	40·40 N	96·00 W
77	Missouri City .... Tex. (In.)	29·37 N	95·32 W
62	Missouri Coteau, (Plat.) ..... U. S.	47·30 N	101·00 W
70	Missouri Valley ... Iowa	41·35 N	95·53 W
65	Mist (mĭst) . . . Ore. (Portland In.)	46·00 N	123·15 W
82	Mistassibi (R.) (mĭs-tȧ-sĭ′bė) . Can.	49·45 N	71·58 W
82	Mistassini (mĭs-tȧ-sĭ′nė) ..... Can.	48·56 N	71·55 W
87	Mistassini (L.) (mĭs-tȧ-sĭ′nė) . Can.	50·48 N	75·00 W
120	Mistelbach (mĭs′tĕl-bäk) ..... Aus.	48·34 N	16·33 E
92	Misteriosa, L. (mēs-tĕ-ryô′sä) Mex. (Yucatan In.)	18·05 N	90·15 W
126	Mistretta (mė-strĕt′tä) ... It.	37·54 N	14·22 E
90	Mita, Punta de (Pt.) (pōō′n-tä-dĕ-mē′tä) . Mex.	20·44 N	105·34 W
153	Mitaka (mė′tä-kä) Jap. (Tōkyō In.)	35·42 N	139·34 E
74	Mitchell (mĭch′ĕl) Ill. (St. Louis In.)	38·46 N	90·05 W
80	Mitchell ... Ind.	38·45 N	86·25 W
70	Mitchell ... Nebr.	41·56 N	103·49 W
70	Mitchell ... S. D.	43·42 N	98·01 W
159	Mitchell (R.) ... Austl.	15·30 S	142·15 E
79	Mitchell, Mt ... N. C.	35·47 N	82·15 W
168	Mīt Ghamr . . . U. A. R. (Nile In.)	30·43 N	31·20 E
127	Mitilíni ... Grc.	39·09 N	26·35 E
153	Mito (mē′tō′) ... Jap.	36·20 N	140·23 E
153	Mitsu (mēt′sōō) ... Jap.	34·21 N	132·49 E
120	Mittelland (can.) (mĭt′ĕl-länd) Ger.	52·18 N	10·42 E
111	Mittenwalde (mē′tĕn-väl-dĕ) Ger. (Berlin In.)	52·16 N	13·33 E
120	Mittweida (mĭt-vī′dä) .... Ger.	50·59 N	12·58 E
136	Mityayevo (mĭt-yä′yĕ-vô) Sov. Un. (Urals In.)	60·17 N	61·02 E
129	Mius (R.) (mė-ōōs′) ..... Sov. Un.	47·30 N	38·48 E
153	Miwa (mė′wä) . . . Jap. (Ōsaka In.)	34·32 N	135·51 E
92	Mixico (mēs′kô) ... Guat.	14·37 N	90·37 W
90	Mixquiahuala (mēs-kė-wä′lä). Mex.	20·12 N	99·13 W
90	Mixteco (R.) (mės-tā′kō) .... Mex.	17·45 N	98·10 W
153	Miyake (mė′yä-kȧ) Jap. (Ōsaka In.)	34·35 N	135·34 E
153	Miyake (I.) (mė′yä-kȧ) ...... Jap.	34·06 N	139·21 E
153	Miyakonojō (mė′yȧ-kô′nô-jô) . Jap.	31·42 N	131·03 E
153	Miyazaki (mē′yä-zä′kė) ...... Jap.	31·55 N	131·27 E
153	Miyoshi (mė-yō′shė′) ... Jap.	34·48 N	132·49 E
114	Mizdah (mēz′dä) ... Libya	31·29 N	13·09 E
127	Mizil (mē′zėl) ... Rom.	45·01 N	26·30 E
	Mizonokuchi, see Takatsu		
118	Mjölby (myûl′bü) ... Swe.	58·20 N	15·09 E
118	Mjörn (L.) ... Swe.	57·55 N	12·22 E
118	Mjösa (myûsä) ... Nor.	60·41 N	11·25 E
118	Mjösvatn (myûs-vät′n) ...... Nor.	59·55 N	7·50 E
166	Mkalamo (m′kä-lä′mō) ...... Tan.	4·07 S	34·38 E
120	Mladá Boleslav (mlä′dä bô′lĕ-slȧf) Czech.	50·26 N	14·52 E
121	Mława (mwä′vȧ) ... Pol.	53·07 N	20·25 E
127	Mljet (I.) (mlyĕt) ... Yugo.	42·40 N	17·45 E
155	Moa (I.) ... Indon.	8·30 S	128·30 E
69	Moab (mō′ăb) ... Utah	38·35 N	109·35 W
68	Moapa River Ind. Res. (mō-ȧp′ȧ) Nev.	36·44 N	115·01 W

ng-sing; ŋ-baŋk; ɴ-nasalized n; nŏd; cŏmmit; ōld; ôbey; ôrder; fōōd; fŏŏt; ou-out; s-soft; sh-dish; th-thin; pūre; ûnite; ûrn; stŭd; circŭs; ü-as "y" in study; ′-indeterminate vowel.

Page	Name Pronunciation Region	Lat. °′	Long. °′
165	Mobaye (mô-bä'y'). Cen. Afr. Rep.	4·30 N	21·10 E
73	Moberly (mō'bēr-lĭ) Mo.	39·24 N	92·25 W
78	Mobile (mô-bēl') Ala.	30·42 N	88·03 W
78	Mobile (R.) Ala.	31·15 N	88·00 W
78	Mobile B. Ala.	30·26 N	87·56 W
70	Mobridge (mō'brĭj) S. D.	45·32 N	100·26 W
95	Moca (mô'kä) Dom. Rep.	19·25 N	70·35 W
167	Moçambique (mō-sän-bē'kĕ) Moz.	15·07 S	40·48 E
166	Moçâmedes Ang.	15·10 S	12·15 E
166	Moçâmedes (Reg.) (mô-zà-mĕ-dĕs) Ang.	16·00 S	12·15 E
144	Mocha (mō'kä) Yemen	13·11 N	43·20 E
90	Mochitlán (mō-chē-tlän') Mex.	17·10 N	99·19 W
166	Mochudi (mō-chōō'dē) Bech.	24·13 S	26·07 E
167	Mocímboa da Praia (mō-sē'ĕm-bō-à dà prä'ēà) Moz.	11·25 S	40·18 E
101	Mococa (mô-kô'kà) Braz. (Rio de Janeiro In.)	21·29 S	46·58 W
90	Moctezuma (môk'tà-zōō'mä) Mex.	22·44 N	101·06 W
167	Modderfontein S. Afr. (Johannesburg & Pretoria In.)	26·06 S	28·10 E
168	Modderpoort S. Afr. (Johannesburg & Pretoria In.)	29·08 S	27·27 E
126	Modena (mô'dĕ-nä) It.	44·38 N	10·54 E
68	Modesto (mô-dĕs'tō) Calif.	37·39 N	121·00 W
113	Modica (mô'dē-kä) It.	36·50 N	14·43 E
111	Mödling (mûd'lĭng) Aus. (Vienna In.)	48·06 N	16·17 E
99	Moengo Fr. Gu.	5·43 N	54·19 W
166	Moero, L. Con. L.	8·45 S	27·45 E
123	Moers (mûrs) Ger. (Ruhr In.)	51·27 N	6·38 E
72	Moffat Tun. (môf'ăt) Colo.	39·52 N	106·20 W
168	Mogadiscio (mô-gä-dē'shō) Som. (Horn of Afr. In.)	2·08 N	45·22 E
75	Mogadore (môg-à-dōr') Ohio (Cleveland In.)	41·04 N	81·23 W
146	Mogaung (mô-gä'ōōng) Bur.	25·30 N	96.52 E
101	Mogi das Cruzes (mô-gê-däs-krōō'sĕs) Braz. (Rio de Janeiro In.)	23·33 S	46·10 W
101	Mogi-Guaçu (R.) (mô-gê-gwà'sōō) Braz. (Rio de Janeiro In.)	22·06 S	47·12 W
128	Mogilëv (mô-gê-lyôf') Sov. Un.	53·53 N	30·22 E
128	Mogilëv (Oblast) (mô-gê-lyôf') Sov. Un.	53·28 N	30·15 E
129	Mogilëv-Podol'skiy (mô-gê-lyôf) (pô-dôl'skĭ) Sov. Un.	48·27 N	27·51 E
121	Mogilno (mô-gēl'nô) Pol.	52·38 N	17·58 E
101	Mogi-Mirim (mô-gê-mē-rē'N) Braz. (Rio de Janeiro In.)	22·26 S	46·57 W
146	Mogok (mô-gōk') Bur.	23·14 N	96·38 E
69	Mogollon (mō-gô-yōn') N. Mex.	33·25 N	108·45 W
69	Mogollon, Plat. (mō-gô-yōn') Ariz.	34·26 N	111·17 W
168	Mogol R. (mô-gŏl) S. Afr. (Johannesburg & Pretoria In.)	24·12 S	27·55 E
124	Moguer (mô-gĕr') Sp.	37·15 N	6.50 W
121	Mohács (mô'häch) Hung.	45·59 N	18·38 E
167	Mohales Hoek Bas. (Natal In.)	30·09 S	27·28 E
70	Mohall (mō'hôl) N. D.	48·46 N	101·29 W
68	Mohave (L.) (mô-hä'vä) Nev.	35·23 N	114·40 W
81	Mohawk (R.) (mō'hôk) N. Y.	43·15 N	75·20 W
167	Mohéli (I.) (mô-ā-lē') (mô-hā'lē) Comores, Arch. des	12·23 S	43·38 E
147	Moho (mō'hō') China	53·33 N	122·30 E
119	Mõisaküla (mẽē'sà-kü'lä) Sov. Un.	58·07 N	25·12 E
87	Moisie (R.) (mwä-zē') Can.	51·24 N	66·11 W
122	Moissac (mwä-säk') Fr.	44·07 N	1·05 E
125	Moita (mō-ē'tà) Port. (Lisbon In.)	38·39 N	9·00 W
68	Mojave Calif.	35·06 N	118·09 W
68	Mojave (R.) (mô-hä'vä) Calif.	34·46 N	117·24 W
68	Mojave Desert Calif.	35·05 N	117·30 W
153	Moji (mō'jê) Jap.	33·56 N	130·59 E
68	Mokelumne (R.) (mō-kē-lŭm'nē) Calif.	38·12 N	121·09 W
167	Mokhotlong Bas. (Natal In.)	29·18 S	29·06 E
152	Mokpo (môk'pō') Kor.	34·50 N	126·30 E
132	Moksha (R.) (môk-shä') Sov. Un.	54·50 N	43·20 E
111	Mol Bel. (Brussels In.)	51·21 N	5·09 E
126	Molat (I.) (mô'lät) Yugo.	44·15 N	14·40 E
121	Moldavia (Reg.) Rom.	47·20 N	27·12 E
118	Molde (môl'dĕ) Nor.	62·44 N	7·15 E
118	Molde Fd. (môl'dĕ fyōrd) Nor.	62·40 N	7·05 E
121	Moldova R. Rom.	47·17 N	26·27 E
166	Molepolole (mō-lā-pō-lō'lā) Bech.	24·15 S	25·33 E
126	Molfetta (môl-fĕt'tä) It.	41·11 N	16·38 E
101	Molina (mō-lē'nä) Chile (Santiago In.)	35·07 S	71·17 W
124	Molina de Aragón (mô-lē'nä dĕ ä-rä-gô'n) Sp.	41·40 N	1·54 W
124	Molína de Segura (mô-lē'nä dĕ sĕ-gōō'rä) Sp.	38·03 N	1·07 W
71	Moline (mô-lēn') Ill.	41·31 N	90·34 W
166	Moliro Con. L.	8·08 S	30·30 E
126	Moliterno (môl-ē-tĕr'nō) It.	40·13 N	15·54 E
98	Mollendo (mô-lyĕn'dō) Peru	17·02 S	71·59 W
64	Moller, Port (pōrt mōl'ĕr) Alaska	56·18 N	161·30 W
118	Mölndal (mûln'däl) Swe.	57·39 N	12·01 E
129	Molochnaya (R.) (mô-lôch'nà-yà) (rĕ-kä') Sov. Un.	47·05 N	35·22 E
129	Molochnoye, Ozero (L.) (ô'zĕ-rô mô-lôch'nô-yĕ) Sov. Un.	46·35 N	35·32 E
128	Molodechno (mô-lô-dĕch'nô) Sov. Un.	54·18 N	26·57 E
128	Molodechno (Oblast) Sov. Un.	54·27 N	27·38 E
136	Molody Tud (mō-lō-dô'ê tōō'd) Sov. Un. (Moscow In.)	55·17 N	37·31 E
128	Mologa (R.) (mô-lô'gà) Sov. Un.	58·05 N	35·43 E
157	Molokai (I.) (mō-lô-kä'ê) Hawaii (In.)	21·15 N	157·05 E
136	Molokcha R. (mô'lôk-chä) Sov. Un. (Moscow In.)	56·15 N	38·29 E
166	Molopo (R.) (mō-lō-pô) S. Afr.	27·45 S	20·45 E

Page	Name Pronunciation Region	Lat. °′	Long. °′
167	Molteno (môl-tā'nô) S. Afr. (Natal In.)	31·24 S	26·23 E
155	Molucca Pass. (mô-lŭk'à) Indon.	1·55 N	126·30 E
155	Moluccas (Is.) (mô-lŭk'àz) Indon.	2·40 S	127·15 E
155	Molucca Sea Indon.	0·15 N	125·41 E
167	Mombasa (mōm-bä'sä) Ken.	4·01 S	39·43 E
152	Mombetsu (môm'bĕt-sōō') Jap.	44·21 N	142·48 E
75	Momence (mô-mĕns') Ill. (Chicago In.)	41·09 N	87·40 W
92	Momostenango (mô-môs-tā-näŋ'gô) Guat.	15·02 N	91·25 W
92	Momotombo Nig.	12·25 N	86·43 W
155	Mompog Pass (mōm-pōg') Phil. (Manila In.)	13·35 N	122·09 E
98	Mompos (mōm-pōs') Col.	8·05 N	74·30 W
118	Møn (I.) (mûn) Den.	54·54 N	12·30 E
75	Monaca (mŏ-nă'kō) Pa. (Pittsburgh In.)	40·41 N	80·17 W
123	Monaco (mŏn'á-kō) Eur.	43·43 N	7·47 E
116	Monaghan (mŏn'á-găn) Ire.	54·16 N	7·20 W
89	Mona Pass. (mō'nä) N. A.	18·00 N	68·10 W
113	Monastir (mōn-às-tēr') Tun.	35·49 N	10·56 E
	Monastir, see Bitola		
129	Monastyrishche (mô-nàs-tē-rēsh'châ). Sov. Un.	48·57 N	29·53 E
128	Monastyrshchina (mô-nàs-tērsh'chĭ-nà). Sov. Un.	54·19 N	31·49 E
99	Monção (moŋ-souN') Braz.	3·39 S	45·23 W
124	Moncayo (Mtn.) (môn-kä'yō) Sp.	41·44 N	1·48 W
132	Monchegorsk (mōn'chĕ-gôrsk) Sov. Un.	69·00 N	33·35 E
123	Mönchengladbach (mûn'kĕn gläd'bäK) Ger. (Ruhr In.)	51·12 N	6·28 E
124	Moncique, Serra de (Mts.) (sĕr'rä dä môn-chē'kĕ). Port.	37·22 N	8.37 W
76	Monclova (mōn-klō'vä) Mex.	26·53 N	101·25 W
82	Moncton (mŭŋk'tŭn) Can.	46·06 N	64·49 W
124	Mondego, Cabo (C.) (kà'bō môn-dā'gō). Port.	40·12 N	8·55 W
124	Mondêgo (R.) (môn-dĕ'gō) Port.	40·10 N	8·36 W
166	Mondombe (môn-dôm'bâ) Con. L.	0·45 S	23·06 E
124	Mondoñedo (môn-dô-nyā'dō) Sp.	43·35 N	7·18 W
126	Mondoví (mōn-dô'vē') It.	44·23 N	7·53 E
71	Mondovi (mŏn-dō'vĭ) Wis.	44·35 N	91·42 W
75	Monee (mŏ-nĭ) Ill. (Chicago In.)	41·25 N	87·45 W
75	Monessen (mŏ-nĕs'sen) Pa. (Pittsburgh In.)	40·09 N	79·53 W
73	Monett (mô-nĕt') Mo.	36·55 N	93·55 W
124	Monforte de Lemos (môn-fôr'tä dĕ lĕ'môs). Sp.	42·30 N	7·30 W
165	Mongala R. (mōn-gäl'à) Con. L.	3·20 N	21·30 E
165	Mongalla Sud.	5·11 N	31·46 E
142	Monghyr (mōn-gēr') India	25·23 N	86·34 E
138	Mongolia (mŏŋ-gō'lĭ-à) Asia	46·00 N	100·00 E
165	Mongoumba (mŏŋ-gōōm'bà) Con. B.	3·41 N	18·21 E
166	Mongu (mŏŋ-gōō') N. Rh.	15·14 S	23·07 E
92	Monkey River (mŭŋ'kĭ) Br. Hond. (Yucatan In.)	16·22 N	88·33 W
85	Monkland Sta. (mŭngk-lănd) Can. (Ottawa In.)	45·12 N	74·52 W
166	Monkoto (mōn-kō'tô) Con. L.	1·45 S	20·51 E
73	Monmouth (mŏn'mŭth) (mŏn'mouth). Ill.	40·54 N	90·38 W
84	Monmouth Junction (mŏn'mouth jŭngk'shŭn) N. J. (New York In.)	40·23 N	74·33 W
68	Mono (L.) (mō'nō) Calif.	38·04 N	119·00 W
80	Monon (mō'nŏn) Ind.	40·55 N	86·55 W
81	Monongah (mô-nŏŋ'gà) W. Va.	39·25 N	80·10 W
75	Monongahela (mô-nŏn-gà-hē'là) Pa. (Pittsburgh In.)	40·11 N	79·55 W
81	Monongahela (R.) W. Va.	39·30 N	80·10 W
127	Monopoli (mô-nô'pô-lê) It.	40·55 N	17·17 E
125	Monovar (mô-nō'vär) Sp.	38·26 N	0·50 W
126	Monreale (mōn-rā-ä'lā) It.	38·04 N	13·15 E
78	Monroe (mŭn-rō') Ga.	33·47 N	83·43 W
77	Monroe La.	32·30 N	92·06 W
80	Monroe Mich.	41·55 N	83·25 W
84	Monroe N. Y. (New York In.)	41·19 N	74·11 W
79	Monroe N. C.	34·58 N	80·34 W
69	Monroe Utah	38·35 N	112·10 W
65	Monroe Wash. (Seattle In.)	47·52 N	121·58 W
71	Monroe Wis.	42·35 N	89·40 W
79	Monroe (L.) Fla.	28·50 N	81·15 W
73	Monroe City Mo.	39·38 N	91·41 W
78	Monroeville (mŭn-rō'vĭl) Ala.	31·33 N	87·19 W
74	Monrovia (mŏn-rō'vĭ-à) Calif. (Los Angeles In.)	34·09 N	118·00 W
164	Monrovia Lib.	6·21 N	10·59 W
117	Mons (môN') Bel.	50·29 N	3·55 E
82	Monson (mŏn'sŭn) Maine	45·17 N	69·28 W
118	Mönsterås (mŭn'stĕr-ôs) Swe.	57·04 N	16·24 E
146	Montagh Ata (Mt.) China	38·26 N	75·23 E
87	Montagne Tremblante Park. Can.	46·30 N	75·51 W
83	Montague (mŏn'tà-gū) Can.	46·11 N	62·35 W
80	Montague Mich.	43·30 N	86·25 W
64	Montague (I.) Alaska	60·10 N	147·00 W
155	Montalban (mŏnt-äl-bän) Phil. (Manila In.)	14·47 N	121·11 E
99	Montalbán Ven. (In.)	10·14 N	68·19 W
126	Montalcone (môn-täl-kô'nĕ) It.	45·49 N	13·30 E
124	Montalegre (mōn-tä-lā'grĕ). Port.	41·49 N	7·48 W
62	Montana (State) (mŏn-tăn'à) U. S.	47·10 N	111·50 W
124	Montánchez (môn-tän'chāth). Sp.	39·18 N	6·09 W
122	Montargis (môN-tàr-zhē') Fr.	47·59 N	2·42 E
123	Montataire (môN-tà-târ) Fr. (Paris In.)	49·15 N	2·26 E
122	Montauban (môN-tô-bäN') Fr.	44·01 N	1·22 E
81	Montauk Pt. (mŏn-tôk') N. Y.	41·05 N	71·55 W
125	Montbanch (mōnt-bän'ch) Sp.	41·20 N	1·08 E
122	Montbard (môN-bàr') Fr.	47·40 N	4·19 E
123	Montbéliard (môN-bā-lyàr') Fr.	47·32 N	6·45 E

Page	Name Pronunciation Region	Lat. °′	Long. °′
77	Mont Belvieu (mŏnt bĕl'vū) Tex. (In.)	29·51 N	94·53 W
123	Mont Blanc Tunnel (môN bläN) Fr.-It.	45·53 N	6·53 E
122	Montbrison (môN-brê-zôN') Fr.	45·38 N	4·06 E
122	Montcalm, Pic de (Pk.) (pĕk dē môN-kàm'). Fr.	42·43 N	1·13 E
122	Montceau-les-Mines (môN-sō'lā-mēn'). Fr.	46·39 N	4·22 E
84	Montclair (mŏnt-klâr') N. J. (New York In.)	40·49 N	74·13 W
122	Mont-de-Marsan (môN-dē-màr-säN'). Fr.	43·54 N	0·32 W
122	Montdidier (môN-dē-dyā') Fr.	49·42 N	2·33 E
101	Monte (mŏ'n-tĕ) Arg. (Buenos Aires In.)	35·25 S	58·49 W
98	Monteagudo (mōn'tâ-ä-gōō'dhō) Bol.	19·49 S	63·48 W
74	Montebello (mŏn-tê-bĕl'ō) Calif. (Los Angeles In.)	34·01 N	118·06 W
85	Montebello Can. (Ottawa In.)	45·40 N	74·56 W
158	Monte Bello (Is.) Austl.	20·30 S	114·10 E
100	Monte Caseros (mŏ'n-tĕ-kä-sĕ'rôs). Arg.	30·16 S	57·39 W
92	Mont Ecillos, Cord. de (Mts.) (kôr-dēl-yĕ'rä dĕ mô'nt ĕ-sē'l-yōs). Hond.	14·19 N	87·52 W
95	Monte Cristi (mô'n-tĕ-krē's-tē) Dom. Rep.	19·50 N	71·40 W
126	Montecristo, I. di (mōn'tâ-krēs'tō). It.	42·20 N	10·19 E
90	Monte Escobedo (mōn'tâ ĕs-kô-bā'dhō). Mex.	22·18 N	103·34 W
125	Monteforte Irpino (môn-tĕ-fô'r-tĕ ē'r-pē'nō) It. (Naples In.)	40·39 N	14·42 E
124	Montefrío (mōn-tâ-frē'ō) Sp.	37·20 N	4·02 W
94	Montego Bay (mŏn-tē'gō) Jam.	18·30 N	77·55 W
100	Monte Grande (mŏ'n-tĕ grän'dĕ) Arg. (In.)	34·34 S	58·28 W
125	Montelavar (mōn-tĕ-là-vär') Port. (Lisbon In.)	38·51 N	9·20 W
122	Montélimar (môN-tā-lē-mär') Fr.	44·33 N	4·47 E
124	Montellano (mōn-tâ-lyä'nō) Sp.	37·00 N	5·34 W
71	Montello (mŏn-tĕl'ō) Wis.	43·47 N	89·20 W
76	Montemorelos (mōn'tâ-mō-rā'lōs) Mex.	25·14 N	99·50 W
124	Montemor-o-Novo (mōN-tĕ-môr'ōō-nô'vōō). Port.	38·39 N	8·11 W
	Montenegro (Reg.), see Črna Gora		
126	Montepulciano (môn'tâ-pōōl-chä'nō). It.	43·05 N	11·48 E
122	Montereau-faut-Yonne (môN-t'rō'fō-yôn'). Fr.	48·24 N	2·57 E
68	Monterey (mŏn-tĕ-rā') Calif.	36·36 N	121·53 W
78	Monterey Tenn.	36·06 N	85·15 W
68	Monterey B. Calif.	36·48 N	122·01 W
74	Monterey Park Calif. (Los Angeles In.)	34·04 N	118·08 W
98	Montería (mōn-tā-rā'ä) Col.	8·47 N	75·57 W
100	Monteros (mōn-tĕ'rôs) Arg.	27·14 S	65·29 W
125	Monterotondo (môn-tĕ-rô-tô'n-dō) It. (Rome In.)	42·03 N	12·39 E
76	Monterrey (mōn-tĕr-rā') Mex.	25·43 N	100·19 W
126	Monte Sant' Angelo (mô'n-tĕ sän ä'n-gzhĕ-lô). It.	41·43 N	15·59 E
66	Montesano (mŏn-tē-sä'nō) Wash.	46·59 N	123·35 W
99	Montes Claros (mōn-tĕs-klä'rôs) Braz.	16·44 S	43·41 W
78	Montevallo (môn-tê-văl'ō) Ala.	33·05 N	86·49 W
126	Montevarchi (mōn-tâ-vär'kē) It.	43·30 N	11·45 E
101	Montevideo (mōn'tâ-vê-dhā'ō) Ur. (Buenos Aires In.)	34·50 S	56·10 W
69	Monte Vista (mŏn'tê vĭs'tà). Colo.	37·35 N	106·10 W
78	Montezuma (mŏn-tê-zōō'mà) Ga.	32·17 N	84·00 W
69	Montezuma Castle Natl. Mon. Ariz.	34·38 N	111·50 W
111	Montfoort. Neth. (Amsterdam In.)	52·02 N	4·56 E
123	Montfort l'Amaury (mŏN-fôr'lä-mō-rē') Fr. (Paris In.)	48·47 N	1·49 E
122	Montfort-sur-Meu (mŏn-fôr-sür-mû'). Fr.	48·09 N	1·58 W
78	Montgomery (mŏnt-gŭm'ēr-ĭ). Ala.	32·23 N	86·17 W
142	Montgomery W. Pak.	30·43 N	73·04 E
80	Montgomery W. Va.	38·10 N	81·25 W
73	Montgomery City Mo.	38·58 N	91·29 W
73	Monticello (mŏn-tĭ-sĕl'ō) Ark.	33·38 N	91·47 W
78	Monticello Fla.	30·32 N	83·53 W
78	Monticello Ga.	33·00 N	83·11 W
80	Monticello Ill.	40·05 N	88·35 W
80	Monticello Ind.	40·40 N	86·50 W
71	Monticello Iowa	42·14 N	91·13 W
78	Monticello Ky.	36·47 N	84·50 W
82	Monticello Maine	46·19 N	67·53 W
71	Monticello Minn.	45·18 N	93·48 W
81	Monticello N. Y.	41·35 N	74·40 W
69	Monticello Utah	37·55 N	109·25 W
123	Montigny-lès-Metz (môN-tēn-yē'lâ-mĕts'). Fr.	49·06 N	6·07 E
125	Montijo (môn-tē'zhō) Port. (Lisbon In.)	38·42 N	8·58 W
124	Montijo (môn-tē'hō) Sp.	38·55 N	6·35 W
93	Montijo, Bahia (B.) (bä-ē'ä môn-tē'hō). Pan.	7·36 N	81·11 W
82	Mont Joli (môN zhô-lē') Can.	48·37 N	68·09 W
122	Montluçon (môN-lü-sôN') Fr.	46·20 N	2·35 E
85	Montmagny (môN-màn-yē') Can. (Quebec In.)	46·59 N	70·33 W
85	Montmorency (mŏnt-mō-rĕn'sĭ) Can. (Quebec In.)	46·53 N	71·09 W
123	Montmorency (môN-mō-räN-sē') Fr. (Paris In.)	48·59 N	2·19 E
85	Montmorency, Rivière (R.) (rê-vyâr' mŏnt-mō-rĕn'sĭ) Can (Quebec In.)	47·04 N	71·12 W

ăt; finăl; rāte; senâte; ärm; àsk; sofà; fâre; ch-choose; dh-as th in other; bē; ēvent; bĕt; recĕnt; cratēr; g-go; gh-guttural g; bĭt; ĭ-short neutral; rīde; K-guttural k as ch in German ich;

Page	Name Pronunciation Region	Lat. °′	Long. °′
122	Montmorillon (môɴ′mô-rê-yôɴ′) Fr.	46·26 N	0·50 E
126	Montone (R.) (môn-tô′nĕ) It.	44·03 N	11·45 E
124	Montoro (môn-tō′rō) Sp.	38·01 N	4·22 W
80	Montpelier (mŏnt-pēl′yēr) Ind.	40·35 N	85·20 W
67	Montpelier Idaho	42·19 N	111·19 W
80	Montpelier Ohio	41·35 N	84·35 W
81	Montpelier Vt.	44·20 N	72·35 W
122	Montpellier (môɴ-pĕ-lyā′) Fr.	43·38 N	3·53 E
85	Montreal (mŏn-trê-ôl′) Can. (Montreal In.)	45·30 N	73·35 W
85	Montreal North Can. (Montreal In.)	45·36 N	73·38 W
85	Montreal South Can. (Montreal In.)	45·31 N	73·30 W
120	Montreux (môn-trû′) Switz.	46·26 N	6·52 E
74	Montrose (mŏnt-rōz) Calif. (Los Angeles In.)	34·13 N	118·13 W
69	Montrose (mŏn-trōz′) Colo.	38·30 N	107·55 W
116	Montrose Scot.	56·45 N	2·25 W
75	Montrose Ohio (Cleveland In.)	41·08 N	81·38 W
81	Montrose (mŏnt-rōz′) Pa.	41·50 N	75·50 W
82	Monts, Pointe des (Pt.) (pwăɴt′ dā môɴ′) Can.	49·19 N	67·22 W
123	Mont St. Martin (mŏɴ sᴀɴ mär-tᴀɴ′) Fr.	49·34 N	6·13 E
93	Montserrat I. (mŏnt-sĕ-răt′) N. A. (Le. & Wind. Is. In.)	16·48 N	62·00 W
84	Montvale (mŏnt-vāl′) N. J. (New York In.)	41·02 N	74·01 W
154	Monywa (mŏn′yōō-wä) Bur.	22·02 N	95·16 E
126	Monza (mōn′tsä) It.	45·34 N	9·17 E
125	Monzón (mōn-thōn′) Sp.	41·54 N	1·09 E
77	Moody (mōō′dĭ) Tex.	31·18 N	97·20 W
168	Mooi (R.) (mōō′ĭ) S. Afr. (Johannesburg & Pretoria In.)	26·34 S	27·03 E
167	Mooi (R.) S. Afr. (Natal In.)	29·00 S	30·15 E
167	Mooirivier S. Afr. (Natal In.)	29·14 S	29·59 E
161	Moolap Austl. (Melbourne In.)	38·11 S	144·26 E
160	Moonta (mōōn′tȧ) Austl.	34·05 S	137·42 E
158	Moora (mŏŏr′ȧ) Austl.	30·35 S	116·12 E
67	Moorcroft (mōr′krôft) Wyo.	44·17 N	104·59 W
158	Moore (L.) (mōr) Austl.	29·50 S	128·12 E
111	Moorenweis (mō′rĕn-vīz) Ger. (Munich In.)	48·10 N	11·05 E
81	Moore Res. Vt.-N. H.	44·20 N	72·10 W
84	Moorestown (mōrz′toun) N. J. (Philadelphia In.)	39·58 N	74·56 W
75	Mooresville (mōrz′vĭl) Ind. (Indianapolis In.)	39·37 N	86·22 W
79	Mooresville (mōrz′vĭl) N. C.	35·34 N	80·48 W
70	Moorhead (mōr′hĕd) Minn.	46·52 N	96·44 W
78	Moorhead Miss.	33·25 N	90·30 W
	Moorland, see Landes		
86	Moose (L.) (mōōs) Can.	54·14 N	99·28 W
87	Moose (R.) Can.	51·01 N	80·42 W
85	Moose Creek Can. (Ottawa In.)	45·16 N	74·58 W
82	Moosehead (mōōs′hĕd) Maine	45·37 N	69·15 W
86	Moose Jaw (mōōs jô) Can.	50·26 N	105·40 W
82	Mooselookmeguntic (L.) (mōō-sĕ-lŏŏk-mē-gŭn′tĭk) Maine	44·54 N	70·20 W
86	Moose Mtn. Can.	50·10 N	102·54 W
81	Moosilauke (Mtn.) (mōō-sĭ-lȯ′kē) N. H.	44·00 N	71·50 W
111	Moosinning (mō′zē-nēng) Ger. (Munich In.)	48·17 N	11·51 E
87	Moosonee (mōō′sô-nê) Can.	51·20 N	80·44 W
164	Mopti (mŏp′tê) Mali	14·27 N	3·56 W
98	Moquegua (mô-kā′gwä) Peru	17·15 S	70·54 W
121	Mór (mōr) Hung.	47·51 N	18·14 E
71	Mora (mō′rȧ) Minn.	45·52 N	93·18 W
72	Mora N. Mex.	35·58 N	105·17 W
124	Mora (mô-rä) Sp.	39·42 N	3·45 W
125	Mora Sp.	41·06 N	0·25 E
142	Morādābād (mô-rä-dä-bäd′) India	28·57 N	78·48 E
92	Morales (mô-rä′lĕs) Guat.	15·29 N	88·46 W
167	Moramanga (mō-rä-mäŋ′gä) Malag. Rep.	18·48 S	48·09 E
95	Morant Pt. (mô-rănt′) Jam.	17·55 N	76·10 W
118	Morastrand (mō′rä-strănd) Swe.	61·00 N	14·29 E
125	Morata de Tajuña (mô-rä′tä dā tä-hōō′nyä) Sp. (Madrid In.)	40·14 N	3·27 W
121	Morava (Moravia) (Prov.) (mô′rä-vä) (mô-rā′vĭ-ȧ) Czech.	49·21 N	16·57 E
120	Morava R. Czech.	49·53 N	16·53 E
	Moravia, see Morava		
99	Morawhanna (mô-rȧ-hwä′nȧ) Br. Gu.	8·12 N	59·33 W
116	Moray Firth (mŭr′ā) Scot.	57·41 N	3·55 W
118	Mörbylånga (mûr′bü-lōŋ′gä) Swe.	56·32 N	16·23 E
86	Morden (môr′dĕn) Can.	49·08 N	98·19 W
161	Mordialloc (môr-dĭ-ăl′ŏk) Austl. (Melbourne In.)	38·00 S	145·05 E
116	More, Ben (Mtn.) (bĕn môr) Scot.	58·09 N	5·01 W
70	Moreau (R.) (mô-rō′) S. D.	45·13 N	102·22 W
116	Morecambe B. (mōr′kăm) Eng.	53·55 N	3·25 W
160	Moree (mō′rē) Austl.	29·20 S	149·50 E
80	Morehead Ky.	38·10 N	83·25 W
79	Morehead City (mōr′hĕd) N. C.	34·43 N	76·43 W
73	Morehouse (mōr′hous) Mo.	36·49 N	89·41 W
90	Morelia (mô-rā′lyä) Mex.	19·43 N	101·12 W
125	Morella (mô-rāl′yä) Sp.	40·38 N	0·07 W
90	Morelos (mô-rā′lōs) Mex.	22·46 N	102·36 W
76	Morelos Mex.	28·24 N	100·51 W
91	Morelos Mex. (Mexico City In.)	19·41 N	99·29 W
76	Morelos, R. Mex.	25·27 N	99·35 W
65	Morena, Sierra (Mt.) (syĕr′rä mô-rā′nä) Calif. (San Francisco In.)	37·24 N	122·19 W
124	Morena, Sierra (Mts.) (syĕr′rä mô-rā′nä) Sp.	38·15 N	5·45 W
69	Morenci (mô-rĕn′sĭ) Ariz.	33·05 N	109·25 W
80	Morenci Mich.	41·50 N	84·05 W
100	Moreno (mô-rĕ′nō) Arg. (In.)	34·25 S	58·47 W
74	Moreno Calif. (Los Angeles In.)	33·55 N	117·09 W
94	Mores (I.) (mōrz) Ba. Is.	26·20 N	77·35 W
65	Moresby (I.) (mōrz′bĭ) Can. (Vancouver In.)	48·43 N	123·15 W
86	Moresby I. Can	52·54 N	131·00 W
160	Moreton (I.) (môr′tŭn) Austl.	26·53 S	152·42 E
160	Moreton B. (môr′tŭn) Austl.	27·12 S	153·10 E
85	Morewood (mōr′wŏŏd) Can. (Ottawa In.)	45·11 N	75·17 W
67	Morgan (môr′gǎn) Utah	41·04 N	111·42 W
77	Morgan City La.	29·41 N	91·11 W
80	Morganfield (môr′gǎn-fēld) Ky.	37·40 N	87·55 W
167	Morgansbaai S. Afr. (Natal In.)	32·42 S	28·19 E
79	Morganton (môr′gǎn-tǔn) N. C.	35·44 N	81·42 W
81	Morgantown (môr′gǎn-toun) W. Va.	39·40 N	79·55 W
168	Morganzon (môr′gǎnt-sŏn) S. Afr. (Johannesburg & Pretoria In.)	26·44 S	29·39 E
145	Morga Ra. Afg. (Khyber Pass In.)	34·02 N	70·38 E
161	Moriac Austl. (Melbourne In.)	38·15 S	144·12 E
153	Moriguchi (mō′rê-gōō′chê) Jap. (Ōsaka In.)	34·44 N	135·34 E
85	Morinville (mō′-rĭn-vĭl) Can. (Edmonton In.)	53·47 N	113·40 W
152	Morioka (mō′rê-ō′kȧ) Jap.	39·40 N	141·21 E
135	Morkoka (R.) (môr-kô′kȧ) Sov. Un.	65·35 N	111·00 E
122	Morlaix (mŏr-lĕ′) Fr.	48·36 N	3·48 W
85	Morley (mŏr′lē) Can. (Calgary In.)	51·10 N	114·51 W
123	Mormant Fr. (Paris In.)	48·35 N	2·54 E
93	Morne Diablotin, Mt. (mōrn dē-ȧ-blô-tăɴ′) Dominica (Le. & Wind. Is. In.)	15·31 N	61·24 W
93	Morne Gimie, Mt. (mōrn′ zhê-mē′) St. Lucia (Le. & Wind. Is. In.)	13·53 N	61·03 W
161	Mornington Austl. (Melbourne In.)	38·13 S	145·02 E
74	Moro (mō′rō) Ill. (St. Louis In.)	38·56 N	90·01 W
155	Morobe N. Gui. Ter.	8·03 S	147·45 E
165	Morocco (mō-rŏk′ō) Afr.	32·00 N	7·00 W
167	Morogoro (mō-rō-gō′rō) Tan.	6·49 S	37·46 E
90	Moroleón (mô-rō-lā-ōn′) Mex.	20·07 N	101·15 W
167	Morombé (mōō-rōōm′bā) Malag. Rep.	21·39 S	43·34 E
100	Morón (mō-rō′n) Arg. (In.)	34·24 S	58·37 W
94	Morón (mô-rōn′) Cuba	22·05 N	78·35 W
99	Morón (mô-rŏ′n) Ven. (In.)	10·29 N	68·11 W
167	Morondava (mō-rōn-dä′vȧ) Malag. Rep.	20·17 S	44·18 E
124	Morón de la Frontera (mô-rōn′dā lȧf rôn-tā′rä) Sp.	37·08 N	5·20 W
68	Morongo Ind. Res. (mō-rôŋ′gō) Calif.	33·54 N	116·47 W
69	Moroni (mô-rō′nĭ) Utah	39·30 N	111·40 W
155	Morotai (I.) (mō-rô-tä′ē) Indon.	2·12 N	128·30 E
133	Morozovsk Sov. Un.	48·20 N	41·50 E
70	Morrill (mŏr′ĭl) Nebr.	41·59 N	103·54 W
73	Morrilton (mŏr′ĭl-tǔn) Ark.	35·09 N	92·42 W
99	Morrinhos (mô-rēn′yōzh) Braz.	17·45 S	48·56 W
86	Morris (mŏr′ĭs) Can.	49·19 N	97·32 W
80	Morris Ill.	41·20 N	88·25 W
70	Morris Minn.	45·35 N	95·53 W
71	Morrison (mŏr′ĭ-sŭn) Ill.	41·48 N	89·58 W
84	Morris Plains (mŏr′ĭs pláns) N. J. (New York In.)	40·49 N	74·29 W
74	Morris Res. Calif. (Los Angeles In.)	34·11 N	117·49 W
84	Morristown (mŏr′rĭs-toun) N. J. (New York In.)	40·48 N	74·29 W
78	Morristown Tenn.	36·10 N	83·18 W
84	Morrisville (mŏr′ĭs vĭl) Pa. (Philadelphia In.)	40·12 N	74·46 W
82	Morrisville Vt.	44·33 N	72·39 W
99	Morro do Chapéu (môr-ōō dōō-shä-pě′ōō) Braz.	11·34 S	41·03 W
75	Morrow (mŏr′ō) Ohio (Cincinnati In.)	39·21 N	84·07 W
133	Morshansk (môr-shȧnsk′) Sov. Un.	53·25 N	41·35 E
118	Mofs (I.) Den.	56·46 N	8·38 E
126	Mortara (môr-tä′rä) It.	45·13 N	8·47 E
100	Morteros (môr-tĕ′rōs) Arg.	30·47 S	62·00 W
101	Mortes, Rio das (R.) (rē′-o-däs-mô′r-tĕs) Braz. (Rio de Janeiro In.)	21·04 S	44·29 W
71	Morton Ind. Res. (mŏr′tǔn) Minn.	44·35 N	94·48 W
111	Mortsel (môr-sĕl′) Bel. (Brussels In.)	51·10 N	4·28 E
122	Morvan, Mts. du (môr-väɴ′) Fr.	46·45 N	4·00 E
132	Morzhovets (I.) (môr′zhô-vyĕts′) Sov. Un.	66·40 N	42·30 E
128	Mosal′sk (mō-zȧlsk′) Sov. Un.	54·27 N	34·57 E
66	Moscow (mŏs′kō) Idaho	46·44 N	116·57 W
	Moscow, see Moskva		
	Moscow Canal, see Imeni Moskvy, Kanal		
120	Mosel R. (mō′sĕl) (mô-zĕl) Ger.	49·49 N	7·00 E
66	Moses Lake Wash.	47·08 N	119·15 W
66	Moses L. (mō′zĕz) Wash.	47·09 N	119·30 W
168	Moses R. S. Afr. (Johannesburg & Pretoria In.)	25·17 S	29·04 E
119	Moshchnyy (Is.) (môsh′chnĭ) Sov. Un.	59·56 N	28·07 E
167	Moshi (mō′shê) Tan.	3·17 S	37·18 E
136	Moskva (Moscow) (mŏs-kvä′) Sov. Un. (Moscow In.)	55·45 N	37·37 E
128	Moskva (Oblast) Sov. Un.	55·38 N	36·48 E
128	Moskva (R.) Sov. Un.	55·50 N	37·05 E
121	Mosonmagyaróvár Hung.	47·51 N	17·16 E
93	Mosquitos, Costa de (kôs-tä-dĕ-mŏs-kē′tō) Nic.	12·05 N	83·49 W
93	Mosquitos, Gulfo de los (G.) (gōō′l-fô-dĕ-lôs-mŏs-kē′tōs) Pan.	9·17 N	80·59 W
118	Moss (môs) Nor.	59·29 N	10·39 E
65	Moss Beach (môs bēch) Calif. (San Francisco In.)	37·32 N	122·31 W
166	Mossel Bay (mô′sŭl bā) S. Afr.	34·06 S	22·23 E
110	Mossley (môs′lĭ) Eng.	53·31 N	2·02 W
99	Mossoró (mō-sô-rōō′) Braz.	5·13 S	37·14 W
78	Moss Point (môs) Miss.	30·25 N	88·32 W
120	Most (môst) Czech.	50·32 N	13·37 E
164	Mostaganem (mŏs′tä-gȧ-nĕm′) Alg.	36·04 N	0·11 E
127	Mostar (môs′tär) Yugo.	43·20 N	17·51 E
125	Móstoles (môs-tō′lās) Sp. (Madrid In.)	40·19 N	3·52 W
92	Motagua R. (mô-tä′gwä) Guat.	15·29 N	88·39 W
118	Motala (mō-tô′lä) Swe.	58·34 N	15·00 E
116	Motherwell (mŭdh′ēr-wĕl) Scot.	55·45 N	4·05 W
124	Motril (mô-trēl′) Sp.	36·44 N	3·32 W
92	Motul (mō-tōō′l) Mex. (Yucatan In.)	21·07 N	89·14 W
166	Mouanda Gabon	1·37 S	13·09 E
95	Mouchoir Bk. (mōō-shwȧr′) Ba. Is.	21·35 N	70·40 W
95	Mouchoir Passage (Str.) Ba. Is.	21·05 N	71·05 W
123	Moudon Switz.	46·40 N	6·47 E
166	Mouille Pt. S. Afr. (Cape Town In.)	33·54 S	18·19 E
122	Moulins (mōō-lăɴ′) Fr.	46·34 N	3·19 E
85	Moulin Vallie're (mōō-lĕɴ′ vä-lē-ĕr′) Can. (Quebec In.)	46·58 N	71·12 W
154	Moulmein (mōl-mān′) Bur.	16·30 N	97·39 E
114	Moulouya Oued (R.) (mōō-lōō′yȧ) Mor.	34·07 N	3·27 W
78	Moultrie (mōl′trĭ) Ga.	31·10 N	83·48 W
79	Moultrie (Dam) S. C.	33·12 N	80·00 W
73	Mound City (mound) Ill.	37·06 N	89·13 W
73	Mound City Mo.	40·08 N	95·13 W
80	Mound City Group Natl. Mon. Ohio	39·25 N	83·00 W
80	Moundsville (moundz′vĭl) W. Va.	39·50 N	80·50 W
123	Mounier, Mt. (mōō-nyā′) Fr.	44·10 N	6·59 E
84	Mountain Brook (moun′tĭn brŏŏk) Ala. (Birmingham In.)	33·30 N	86·45 W
74	Mountain Creek L. Tex. (Dallas, Fort Worth In.)	32·43 N	97·03 W
65	Mountaindale (dāl) Ore. (Portland In.)	45·37 N	123·02 W
73	Mountain Grove (grōv) Mo.	37·07 N	92·16 W
66	Mountain Home (hōm) Idaho	43·08 N	115·43 W
86	Mountain Park (pärk) Can.	52·57 N	117·22 W
65	Mountain View (moun′tĭn vū) Calif. (San Francisco In.)	37·25 N	122·07 W
73	Mountain View Mo.	36·59 N	91·46 W
84	Mountain View N. J. (New York In.)	40·55 N	74·17 W
79	Mount Airy (âr′ĭ) N. C.	36·28 N	80·37 W
	Mount Athos (Reg.), see Áyion Óros		
167	Mount Ayliff (ā′lĭf) S. Afr. (Natal In.)	30·48 S	29·24 E
71	Mount Ayr (âr) Iowa	40·43 N	94·06 W
80	Mount Carmel (kär′mĕl) Ill.	38·25 N	87·45 W
81	Mount Carmel Pa.	40·50 N	76·25 W
71	Mount Carroll Ill.	42·05 N	89·55 W
75	Mount Clemens (klĕm′ĕnz) Mich. (Detroit In.)	42·36 N	82·52 W
166	Mount Darwin S. Rh.	15·44 S	31·40 E
82	Mount Desert (I.) (dê-zûrt′) Can.	44·15 N	68·08 W
79	Mount Dora (dō′rȧ) Fla. (In.)	28·45 N	81·38 W
161	Mount Duneed Austl. (Melbourne In.)	38·15 S	144·20 E
161	Mount Eliza Austl. (Melbourne In.)	38·11 S	145·05 E
70	Mountevideo (mōn′tȧ-vê-dhä′ō) Minn.	44·56 N	95·42 W
167	Mount Fletcher (flĕ′chēr) S. Afr. (Natal In.)	30·42 S	28·32 E
80	Mount Forest (fŏr′ĕst) Can.	44·00 N	80·45 W
167	Mount Frere (frâr′) S. Afr. (Natal In.)	30·54 S	29·02 E
160	Mount Gambier (găm′bēr) Austl.	37·30 S	140·53 E
80	Mount Gilead (gĭl′ēăd) Ohio	40·30 N	82·50 W
75	Mount Healthy (hĕlth′ê) Ohio (Cincinnati In.)	39·14 N	84·32 W
84	Mount Holly (hŏl′ĭ) N. J. (Philadelphia In.)	39·59 N	74·47 W
85	Mount Hope Can. (Toronto In.)	43·09 N	79·55 W
84	Mount Hope (hōp) N. J. (New York In.)	40·55 N	74·32 W
80	Mount Hope W. Va.	37·55 N	81·10 W
158	Mount Isa (ī′zȧ) Austl.	21·00 S	139·45 E
84	Mount Kisco (kĭs′ko) N. Y. (New York In.)	41·12 N	73·44 W
65	Mountlake Terrace (mount lāk tĕr′ĭs) Wash. (Seattle In.)	47·48 N	122·19 W
75	Mount Lebanon (lĕb′ȧ-nŭn) Pa. (Pittsburgh In.)	40·22 N	80·03 W
64	Mount McKinley Natl. Park (mȧ-kĭn′lĭ) Alaska	63·48 N	153·02 W
158	Mount Magnet (măg-nĕt) Austl.	28·00 S	118·00 E
161	Mount Martha Austl. (Melbourne In.)	38·17 S	145·01 E
159	Mount Morgan (môr-gǎn) Austl.	23·42 S	150·45 E
161	Mount Moriac Austl. (Melbourne In.)	38·13 S	144·12 E
80	Mount Morris (mŏr′ĭs) Mich.	43·10 N	83·45 W
81	Mount Morris N. Y.	42·45 N	77·50 W
79	Mount Olive (ŏl′ĭv) N. C.	35·11 N	78·05 W
69	Mount Peale Utah	38·26 N	109·16 W
71	Mount Pleasant (plĕz′ǎnt) Iowa	40·59 N	91·34 W
80	Mount Pleasant Mich.	43·35 N	84·45 W
79	Mount Pleasant S. C.	32·46 N	79·51 W
78	Mount Pleasant Tenn.	35·31 N	87·12 W
73	Mount Pleasant Tex.	33·10 N	94·56 W
69	Mount Pleasant Utah	39·35 N	111·20 W
75	Mount Prospect (prŏs′pĕkt) Ill. (Chicago In.)	42·03 N	87·56 W
66	Mount Rainier Natl. Park (rȧ-nēr′) Wash.	46·47 N	121·17 W

ng-sing; ŋ-baŋk: ɴ-nasalized n; nŏd; cǒmmit; ōld; ôbey; ôrder; fōōd; fŏŏt; ou-out; s-soft; sh-dish; th-thin; pūre; ûnite; ûrn; stŭd; circǔs; ü-as "y" in study; ′-indeterminate vowel.

Page	Name Pronunciation Region	Lat. °′	Long. °′
86	Mount Revelstoke Natl. Park (rĕv'ĕl-stōk). Can.	51·22 N	120·15 W
81	Mount Savage (săv'āj) Md.	39·45 N	78·55 W
66	Mount Shasta (shăs'tȧ) Calif.	41·18 N	122·17 W
73	Mount Sterling (stûr'lĭng) Ill.	39·59 N	90·44 W
80	Mount Sterling Ky.	38·05 N	84·00 W
83	Mount Stewart (stū'ărt) Can.	46·21 N	62·54 W
81	Mount Union (ūn'yŭn) Pa.	40·25 N	77·50 W
80	Mount Vernon (vûr'nŭn) Ill.	38·20 N	88·50 W
80	Mount Vernon Ind.	37·55 N	87·50 W
73	Mount Vernon Mo.	37·09 N	93·48 W
84	Mount Vernon N. Y. (New York In.)	40·55 N	73·51 W
80	Mount Vernon Ohio	40·25 N	82·30 W
65	Mount Vernon. Wash. (Seattle In.)	48·25 N	122·20 W
155	Mount Wilhelm New Guinea	5·45 S	144·30 E
148	Moup'ing (mō'pĭng) China	37·23 N	121·36 E
99	Moura (mō'rȧ) Braz.	1·33 S	61·38 W
124	Moura Port.	38·08 N	7·28 W
116	Mourne, Mts. (môrn) N. Ire.	54·10 N	6·09 W
123	Moûtiers (mōō-tyâr') Fr.	45·31 N	6·34 E
160	Mowbullan, Mt. (mō'bōō-lȧn) Austl.	26·50 S	151·34 E
90	Moyahua (mô-yä'wä) Mex.	21·16 N	103·10 W
165	Moyale (mô-yä'lä) Ken.	3·28 N	39·04 E
164	Moyamba (mô-yäm'bä) S. L.	8·11 N	12·27 W
114	Moyen Atlas (Mts.) Mor.	32·49 N	5·28 W
123	Moyeuvre Grande Fr.	49·15 N	6·26 E
66	Moyie R. (moi'yē) Idaho	48·50 N	116·10 W
98	Moyobamba (mō-yō-bäm'bä). Peru	6·12 S	76·56 W
92	Moyuta (mô-ē-ōō'tä) Guat.	14·01 N	90·05 W
135	Moyyero (R.) Sov. Un.	67·15 N	104·10 E
163	Mozambique (Portuguese East Africa) (mō-zăm-bēk'). Afr.	20·15 S	33·53 E
84	Mozambique, Pt. La. (New Orleans In.)	29·38 N	89·26 W
167	Mozambique Chan. (mō-zăm-bek') Ind. O.	52·18 S	4·28 E
133	Mozdok (môz-dôk') Sov. Un.	43·45 N	44·35 E
128	Mozhaysh (mô-zhäysh'). Sov. Un.	55·31 N	36·02 E
136	Mozhayskiy (mô-zhäy'skĭ) Sov. Un. (Leningrad In.)	59·42 N	30·08 E
129	Mozyr' (mô-zür') Sov. Un.	52·03 N	29·14 E
166	Mporokoso ('m-pō-rô-kō'sō) N. Rh.	9·28 S	30·06 E
167	Mpwapwa ('m-pwä'pwä) Tan.	6·20 S	36·39 E
167	Mqanduli ('m-kän'dōō-lē) S. Afr. (Natal In.)	31·50 S	28·42 E
121	Mragowo (mrăn'gô-vô) Pol.	53·52 N	21·18 E
164	M'sila (m'sē'lä) Alg.	35·47 N	4·34 E
128	Msta (R.) (m'stá') Sov. Un.	58·33 N	32·08 E
128	Mstislavl' (m'stē-slävl') Sov. Un.	54·01 S	31·42 E
166	Mtengula ('m-tĕn-gōō'lä) Moz.	12·42 S	34·48 E
166	Mtetwe Pan (Basin) ('m-tĕt'wĕ) Bech.	20·00 S	24·18 E
128	Mtsensk (m'tsĕnsk) Sov. Un.	53·17 N	36·33 E
154	Muang Khon Kaen Thai.	16·37 N	102·41 E
154	Muang Lamphum Thai.	18·40 N	98·59 E
154	Muang Phitsanulok Thai.	16·51 N	100·15 E
154	Muang Sakon Thai.	17·00 N	104·06 E
139	Muar (R.) Mala. (Singapore In.)	2·18 N	102·43 E
123	Much (mōōk). Ger. (Ruhr In.)	50·54 N	7·24 E
110	Much Wenlock (mŭch wĕn'lŏk) Eng.	52·35 N	2·33 W
78	Muckalee Cr. (mŭk'ă lē) Ga.	31·55 N	84·10 W
65	Muckleshoot Ind. Res. (mŭck''l-shōōt) Wash. (Seattle In.)	47·21 N	122·04 W
99	Mucugê (mōō-kōō-zhĕ') Braz.	13·02 S	41·19 W
71	Mud (L.) (mŭd) Mich.	46·12 N	84·32 W
68	Mud (L.) Nev.	40·28 N	119·11 W
68	Muddy (R.) (mŭd'ĭ) Nev.	36·56 N	114·42 W
73	Muddy Boggy Cr. (mud'ĭ bôg'ĭ) Okla.	34·42 N	96·11 W
69	Muddy Cr. (mŭd'ĭ) Utah	38·45 N	111·10 W
160	Mudgee (mŭ-jē) Austl.	32·47 S	149·10 E
124	Mugía (mōō-kē'ä) Sp.	43·05 N	9·14 W
133	Muğla (mōōg'lä) Tur.	37·10 N	28·20 E
120	Mühldorf (mül-dôrf) Ger.	48·15 N	12·33 E
120	Mühlhausen (mül'hou-zĕn) Ger.	51·13 N	10·25 E
119	Muhu (I.) (mōō'hōō) Sov. Un.	58·41 N	22·55 E
151	Mui Ron, C Viet.	18·05 N	106·45 E
68	Muir Woods Natl. Mon. (mūr) Calif.	37·54 N	123·22 W
166	Muizenberg (mwĭz-ĕn-bûrg') S. Afr. (Cape Town In.)	34·07 S	18·28 E
121	Mukachëvo (mōō-kȧ-chyô'vô) Sov. Un.	48·25 N	22·43 E
	Mukden, see Shenyang		
135	Mukhtuya (mōōk-tōō'yȧ). Sov. Un.	61·00 N	113·00 E
65	Mukilteo (mū-kĭl-tā'ō) Wash. (Seattle In.)	47·57 N	122·18 W
153	Muko (R.) (mōō'kô) Jap. (Ōsaka In.)	34·52 N	135·17 E
75	Mukwonago (mū-kwō-nȧ'gō) Wis. (Milwaukee In.)	42·52 N	88·19 W
124	Mula (mōō'lä) Sp.	38·05 N	1·12 W
120	Mulde R. (mōōl'dĕ) Ger.	50·30 N	12·30 E
150	Muleng China	44·32 N	130·18 E
150	Muleng (R.) China	44·40 N	130·30 E
90	Muleros (mōō-lā'rōs) Mex.	23·44 N	104·00 W
84	Mulga (mŭl'gȧ) Ala. (Birmingham In.)	33·33 N	86·59 W
83	Mulgrave (mŭl'grāv) Can.	45·37 N	61·22 W
159	Mulgrave (I.) Austl.	10·08 S	142·14 E
124	Mulhacén (Mtn.) Sp.	37·04 N	3·18 W
123	Mülheim (mül'hīm) Ger. (Ruhr In.)	51·25 N	6·53 E
123	Mulhouse (mü-lōōz') Fr.	47·46 N	7·20 E
116	Mull (I.) (mŭl) Scot.	56·40 N	6·19 W
66	Mullan (mŭl'ăn) Idaho	47·26 N	115·50 W
154	Müller Mts. (mül'ēr) Indon.	0·22 N	113·05 E
116	Mullet Pen. Ire.	54·15 N	10·12 W
116	Mullinger (mŭl-ĭn-gär) Ire.	53·31 N	7·26 W
79	Mullins (mŭl'ĭnz) S. C.	34·11 N	79·13 W
92	Mullins River Br. Hond. (Yucatan In.)	17·08 N	88·18 W
142	Multan (mōōl-tän') W. Pak.	30·17 N	71·13 E
65	Multnomah Chan. (mŭl nō mȧ) Ore. (Portland In.)	45·41 N	122·53 W
154	Mulu, Gunung (Mtn.) Mala.	3·56 N	115·11 E
73	Mulvane (mŭl-vān') Kans.	37·30 N	97·13 W
166	Mumbwa (mōōm'bwä) N. Rh.	14·58 S	27·06 E
92	Muna (mōō'nä) Mex. (Yucatan In.)	20·28 N	89·42 W
111	München (Munich) (mün'kĕn) Ger. (Munich In.)	48·08 N	11·35 E
80	Muncie (mŭn'sĭ) Ind.	40·10 N	85·30 W
75	Mundelein (mŭn-dē-lĭn') Ill. (Chicago In.)	42·16 N	88·00 W
98	Mundonueva, Pico de (Pk.) (pē'kô-dĕ-mōō'n-dô-nwĕ'vä) Col. (In.)	4·18 N	74·12 W
91	Muneco, Cerro (Mtn.) (sĕ'r-rô-mōō-nĕ'kō) Mex. (Mexico City In.)	19·13 N	99·20 W
159	Mungana (mŭn-găn'ȧ) Austl.	17·15 S	144·18 E
74	Munger (mŭn'gẽr) Minn. (Duluth In.)	46·48 N	92·20 W
160	Mungindi (mŭn-gĭn'dē) Austl.	32·00 S	148·45 E
75	Munhall (mŭn'hôl) Pa. (Pittsburgh In.)	40·24 N	79·53 W
166	Munhanga (mōōn-hăn'gȧ) Ang.	12·15 S	18·55 E
	Munich, see München		
71	Munising (mū'nĭ-sĭng) Mich.	46·24 N	86·41 W
134	Munku Sardyk (Mtn.) (mōōn'kōō sär-dĭk') Sov. Un.-Mong.	51·45 N	100·30 E
155	Muños (mōōn-nyōth') Phil. (Manila In.)	15·44 N	120·53 E
123	Münster (mün'stẽr). Ger. (Ruhr In.)	51·57 N	7·38 E
75	Munster (mŭn'stẽr) Ind. (Chicago In.)	41·34 N	87·31 W
116	Munster (mŭn-stẽr) Ire.	52·30 N	9·24 W
154	Muntok (mōōn-tŏk') Indon.	2·05 S	105·11 E
101	Munzi Freire (mōō-nĕ'z-frā'rĕ) Braz. (Rio de Janeiro In.)	20·29 S	41·25 W
154	Muong Sing (mōō'ông-sĭng'). Laos	21·06 N	101·17 E
112	Muonio (R.) Fin.-Swe.	68·15 N	23·00 E
101	Muqui (mōō-kōōē) Braz. (Rio de Janeiro In.)	20·56 S	41·20 W
133	Muradiye (mōō-rä'dē-yĕ) Tur.	39·00 N	43·40 E
122	Murat (mü-rä') Fr.	45·05 N	2·56 E
133	Murat (R.) (mōō-rät') Tur.	38·50 N	40·40 E
158	Murchison (R.) (mûr'chĭ-sŭn) Austl.	26·45 S	116·15 E
165	Murchison Falls (mûr'chĭ-sŭn). Ug.	2·19 N	31·50 E
124	Murcia (mōōr'thyä) Sp.	38·00 N	1·10 W
124	Murcia (Reg.) Sp.	38·35 N	1·51 W
70	Murdo (mûr'dô) S. D.	43·53 N	100·42 W
82	Murdochville (mŭr-dŏk'vĭl) Can.	48·56 N	65·37 W
121	Muresul R. (mōō'rĕsh-ōōl) Rom.	46·02 N	21·50 E
122	Muret (mü-rĕ') Fr.	43·28 N	1·17 E
78	Murfreesboro (mûr'frēz-bŭr-ô) Tenn.	35·50 N	86·19 W
103	Murgab (R.) (mōō-rgäb'). Sov. Un.	37·07 N	62·32 E
101	Muriaé (mōō-ryä-ĕ') Braz. (Rio de Janeiro In.)	21·10 S	42·21 W
101	Muriaé (R.) Braz. (Rio de Janeiro In.)	21·20 S	41·40 W
136	Murino (mōō'rĭ-nô) Sov. Un. (Leningrad In.)	60·03 N	30·28 E
120	Müritz See (L.) (mür'ĭts) Ger.	53·20 N	12·33 E
146	Murku Sardyk (Pk.) Sov. Un.-Mong.	51·56 N	100·21 E
132	Murmansk (mōōr-mänsk'). Sov. Un.	69·00 N	33·20 E
132	Murom (mōō'rôm) Sov. Un.	55·30 N	42·00 E
152	Muroran (mōō'rō-rän) Jap.	42·21 N	141·05 E
124	Muros (mōō'rōs) Sp.	42·48 N	9·00 W
153	Muroto-Zaki (Pt.) (mōō'rô-tō zä'kĕ). Jap.	33·14 N	134·12 E
74	Murphy (mŭr'fĭ) Mo. (St. Louis In.)	38·29 N	90·29 W
78	Murphy N. C.	35·05 N	84·00 W
73	Murphysboro (mŭr'fĭz-bŭr-ô) Ill.	37·46 N	89·21 W
78	Murray (mŭr'ĭ) Ky.	36·39 N	88·17 W
74	Murray. Utah (Salt Lake City In.)	40·40 N	111·53 W
79	Murray (R.) (mŭr'ĭ) S. C.	34·07 N	81·18 W
160	Murray Bridge Austl.	35·10 S	139·35 E
159	Murray Reg. (mŭ'rē) Austl.	33·20 S	142·30 E
160	Murray R. Austl.	34·12 S	141·20 E
120	Mur R. (mōōr) Aus.	47·10 N	14·08 E
160	Murrumbidgee (R.) (mŭr-ŭm-bĭd'jē). Austl.	34·30 S	145·20 E
142	Murshidabad (mōōr'shē-dä-bäd') India	24·08 N	87·11 E
126	Murska Sobota (mōōr'skȧ sô'bô-tȧ). Yugo.	46·40 N	16·14 E
142	Murwāra India	23·54 N	80·23 E
160	Murwillumbah (mŭr-wĭl'lŭm-bŭ) Austl.	28·15 S	153·30 E
120	Mürz R. (mürts) Aus.	47·30 N	15·21 E
165	Murzūg Libya	26·00 N	14·09 E
120	Murzzuschlag (mürts'tsōō-shlägh) Aus.	47·37 N	15·41 E
133	Mus (mōōsh) Tur.	38·55 N	41·30 E
127	Musala (Mtn.) Bul.	42·05 N	23·24 E
152	Musan (mōō'sän) Kor.	41·11 N	129·10 E
153	Musashino (mōō-sä'shē-nō) Jap. (Tōkyō In.)	35·43 N	139·35 E
144	Muscat (mŭs-kăt') Mus. & Om.	23·23 N	58·30 E
144	Muscat & Oman Asia	18·50 N	56·45 E
71	Muscatine (mŭs-kȧ-tēn') Iowa	41·26 N	91·00 W
78	Muscle Shoals (mŭs''l shōlz) Ala.	34·44 N	87·38 W
158	Musgrave Ra. (mŭs'grāv) Austl.	26·15 S	131·15 E
166	Mushie (mŭsh'ē) Con. L.	3·04 S	16·50 E
154	Musi, Air (Strm.) (mōō'sē). Indon.	2·40 S	103·42 E
98	Musinga, Alto (Ht.) (ä'l-tô-mōō-sē'n-gä). Col. (In.)	6·40 N	76·13 W
75	Muskego L. (mŭs-kē'gō) Wis. (Milwaukee In.)	42·53 N	88·10 W
80	Muskegon (mŭs-kē'gŭn) Mich.	43·15 N	86·20 W
80	Muskegon (R.) Mich.	43·20 N	85·55 W
80	Muskegon Heights Mich.	43·10 N	86·20 W
80	Muskingum (R.) (mŭs-kĭn'gŭm) Ohio	39·45 N	81·55 W
73	Muskogee (mŭs-kō'gē) Okla.	35·44 N	95·21 W
81	Muskoka (L.) (mŭs-kō'kȧ) Can.	45·00 N	79·30 W
155	Mussau (I.) (mōō-sä'ōō) N. Gui. Ter.	1·30 S	149·32 E
116	Musselburgh (mŭs''l-bŭr-ô) Scot.	55·55 N	3·08 W
67	Musselshell R. (mŭs''l-shĕl). Mont.	46·25 N	108·20 W
133	Mustafakemalpasa Tur.	40·05 N	28·30 E
77	Mustang Bay Tex. (In.)	29·22 N	95·12 W
72	Mustang Cr. (mŭs'tăng) Tex.	36·22 N	102·46 W
77	Mustang I. Tex.	27·43 N	97·00 W
93	Mustique I. (mūs-tēk') N. A. (Le. & Wind. Is. In.)	12·53 N	61·03 W
128	Mustvee (mōōst'vĕ-ĕ) Sov. Un.	58·50 N	26·54 E
147	Musu Dan (C.) (mōō'sōō dän). Kor.	40·51 N	130·00 E
152	Musu Dan (Pt.) (mōō'sōō dän) Sov. Un.	40·48 N	129·50 E
160	Muswellbrook (mŭs'wŭl-brŏŏk) Austl.	32·15 S	150·50 E
150	Mutan (R.) China	45·30 N	129·40 E
150	Mutanchiang China	44·28 N	129·38 E
166	Mutombo Mukulu (mōō-tôm'bō mōō-kōō'lōō) Con. L.	8·12 S	23·56 E
152	Mutsu Wan (B.) (mōōt'sōō wän) Jap.	41·20 N	140·55 E
83	Mutton B. (mŭt''n) Can.	50·47 N	58·58 W
101	Mutum (mōō-tōō'm) Braz. (Rio de Janeiro In.)	19·48 S	41·24 W
134	Muyun-Kum, Peski (Des.) (mōō-yōōn' kōōm'). Sov. Un.	44·30 N	70·00 E
142	Muzaffargarh W. Pak.	30·09 N	71·15 E
76	Muzquiz (mōōz'kēz) Mex.	27·53 N	101·31 W
166	Mwanza (mwän'zä) Tan.	2·31 S	32·52 E
167	Mwatate (mwä-tä'tä) Ken.	3·28 S	38·19 E
166	Mwaya (mwä'yä) Tan.	9·19 S	33·51 E
114	Mya R. (myä') Alg.	29·26 N	3·15 E
146	Myingyan (myĭng-yŭn') Bur.	21·37 N	95·26 E
154	Myinmoletkat (Pk.) Bur.	13·58 N	98·34 E
146	Myitkyina (myĭ'chē-nȧ) Bur.	25·33 N	97·25 E
121	Myjava (mûĕ'yȧ-vä) Czech.	48·45 N	17·33 E
142	Mymensingh (mī-mŭn-sĭng') E. Pak.	24·48 N	90·28 E
152	Myohyang San (Mtn.) (myō'hyang). Kor.	40·00 N	126·12 E
112	Mýrdalsjökull (Gl.) (mür'däls-yû'kōōl). Ice.	63·34 N	18·04 W
79	Myrtle Beach (mûr't'l) S. C.	33·42 N	78·53 W
84	Myrtle Grove (grōv) La. (New Orleans In.)	29·38 N	89·57 W
66	Myrtle Point Ore.	43·04 N	124·08 W
128	Myshkino (mēsh'kē-nô) Sov. Un.	57·48 N	38·21 E
143	Mysore (mī-sōr') India	12·31 N	76·42 E
143	Mysore (State) India	20·15 N	75·32 E
119	Mysovka (mē' sôf-kȧ) Sov. Un.	55·11 N	21·17 E
71	Mystic (mĭs'tĭk) Iowa	40·47 N	92·54 W
136	Mytishchi (mê-tēsh'chi) Sov. Un. (Moscow In.)	55·55 N	37·46 E
166	Mzimba ('m-zĭm'bä) Nya.	11·41 S	33·39 E
120	Naab R. (näp) Ger.	49·38 N	12·15 E
111	Naaldwijk. Neth. (Amsterdam In.)	52·00 N	4·11 E
164	Naama (nä'ä-mä) Lib.	7·18 N	9·31 W
119	Naantali (nän'tȧ-lē) Fin.	60·29 N	22·03 E
158	Nabberu (L.) (năb'ēr-ōō) Austl.	26·05 S	120·35 E
164	Nabeul (nā-bûl') Tun.	36·34 N	10·45 E
168	Naboomspruit S. Afr. (Johannesburg & Pretoria In.)	24·32 S	28·43 E
139	Nābulus. Jordan (Palestine In.)	32·13 N	35·16 E
167	Nacala (nȧ-kä'lȧ) Moz.	14·33 S	40·52 E
92	Nacaome (nä-kä-ō'mȧ) Hond.	13·32 N	87·28 W
114	Naceur, Bou Mt. Mor.	33·50 N	3·55 W
151	Na Cham (nä chäm') Viet.	22·02 N	106·30 E
66	Naches R. (năch'ĕz) Wash.	46·51 N	121·03 W
120	Nachod (näk'ôt) Czech.	50·25 N	16·08 E
87	Nachvak Can.	59·08 N	63·57 W
68	Nacimiento (R.) (nȧ-sĭ-myĕn'tō) Calif.	35·50 N	121·00 W
77	Nacogdoches (năk'ô-dō'chĕz). Tex.	31·36 N	94·40 W
76	Nadadores (nä-dä-dō'räs) Mex.	27·04 N	101·36 W
142	Nadaid India	22·45 N	72·51 E
89	Nadir Vir. Is. (U. S. A.) (St. Thomas In.)	18·19 N	64·53 W
127	Nădlac Rom.	46·09 N	20·52 E
	Nad Nisou, see Jablonec		
	Nad Vahom, see Nové Mesto		
121	Nadvornaya (nȧd-vōōr'nȧ-yȧ) Sov. Un.	48·37 N	24·35 E
134	Nadym (R.) (nȧ'dĭm) Sov. Un.	64·30 N	72·48 E
118	Naestved (nĕst'vĭdh) Den.	55·14 N	11·46 E
168	Nafishah U. A. R.	30·34 N	32·15 E
155	Naga (nä'gä) Phil. (Manila In.)	13·37 N	123·12 E
153	Naga (I.) Jap.	32·09 N	130·16 E
153	Nagahama (nä'gä-hä'mä) Jap.	33·32 N	132·29 E
153	Nagahama Jap.	35·23 N	136·16 E
146	Nagaland (State) India	25·47 N	94·15 E
153	Nagano (nä'gä-nô) Jap.	36·42 N	138·12 E
153	Nagaoka (nä'gȧ-ō'kȧ) Jap.	37·22 N	138·49 E
143	Nagapatam India	10·48 N	79·51 E
92	Nagarote (nä-gä-rô'tĕ) Nic.	12·17 N	86·35 W
153	Nagasaki (nä'gȧ-sä'kē) Jap.	32·48 N	129·53 E
153	Nagasu (nä'gäs-ōō) Jap.	33·31 N	131·22 E
142	Nāgaur India	27·19 N	73·41 E
136	Nagaybakskiy (nȧ-gáy-bák'skĭ) Sov. Un. (Urals In.)	53·33 N	59·33 E
155	Nagcarlan (näg-kär-län') Phil. (Manila In.)	14·07 N	121·24 E
143	Nagercoil India	8·15 N	77·29 E
133	Nagornokarabakh (Reg.) (nu-gôr'nŭ-kŭ-rŭ-bäk') Sov. Un.	40·10 N	46·50 E
153	Nagoya (nä'gō'yȧ) Jap.	35·09 N	136·53 E
142	Nagpur (näg'pōōr) India	21·12 N	79·09 E
95	Nagua (nä'gwä) Dom. Rep.	19·20 N	69·40 W

ăt; finȧl; rāte; senâte; ärm; ȧsk; sofȧ; fâre; ch-choose; dh-as th in other; bē; ēvent; bĕt; recĕnt; cratẽr; g-go; gh-guttural g; bĭt; ĭ-short neutral; rīde; K-guttural k as ch in German ich;

Page	Name Pronunciation Region	Lat. °′	Long. °′
155	Naguilian (nä-gwê-lē'än) Phil. (Manila In.)	16·33 N	120·23 E
120	Nagykanizsa (nôd'y'kô'nê-shô) Hung.	46·27 N	17·00 E
121	Nagykörös (nôd'y'kû'rûsh) Hung.	47·02 N	19·46 E
152	Naha (nä'hä) Ryūkyū Is.	26·02 N	127·43 E
83	Nahant (nȧ-hănt) Mass. (Boston In.)	42·26 N	70·55 W
139	Nahariya Isr. (Palestine In.)	33·01 N	35·06 E
133	Nahr al Khābūr (R.) U. A. R.	35·50 N	41·00 E
125	Nahr-Ouassel (R.) (när-wä-sĕl') Alg.	35·30 N	1·55 E
100	Nahuel Huapi (L.) (nä'wâl wä'pê) Arg.	41·00 S	71·30 W
92	Nahuizalco (nä-wê-zäl'kō) Sal.	13·50 N	89·43 W
155	Naic (nä'ēk) Phil. (Manila In.)	14·20 N	120·46 E
76	Naica (nä-ē'kä) Mex.	27·53 N	105·30 W
99	Naiguatá (nī-gwä-tá') Ven. (In.)	10·37 N	66·44 W
99	Naiguata, Pico (Mtn.) (pē'kô) Ven. (In.)	10·32 N	66·44 W
142	Naihāti India (Calcutta In.)	22·54 N	88·25 E
87	Nain (nīn) Can.	56·29 N	61·52 W
84	Nairn (nărn) La. (New Orleans In.)	29·27 N	89·37 W
116	Nairn (nârn) Scot.	57·35 N	3·54 W
167	Nairobi (nī-rō'bê) Ken.	1·18 S	36·47 E
167	Naivasha (nī-vä'shȧ) Ken.	0·47 S	36·29 E
144	Najd (Des.) Sau. Ar.	25·18 N	42·38 E
168	Naj 'Ḥammādī (näg'hä-mä'dê) U. A. R. (Nile In.)	26·02 N	32·12 E
152	Najin (nä'jĭn) Kor.	42·04 N	136·06 E
144	Najran (Des.) (nŭj-rän') Sau. Ar.	17·29 N	45·30 E
152	Naju (nä'jōō') Kor.	35·02 N	126·42 E
94	Najusa (R.) (nä-hōō'sä) Cuba	21·55 N	77·55 W
150	Nakadorishima (I.) (nä'kä'dô'rê-shê'mä) Jap.	33·00 N	128·20 E
165	Nak'amet Eth.	9·09 N	36·29 E
153	Nakatsu (nä'käts-ōō) Jap.	33·34 N	131·10 E
133	Nakhichevan' (nä-kē-chĕ-vän') Sov. Un.	49·10 N	45·30 E
135	Nakhodka (nŭ-kôt'kŭ) Sov. Un.	43·03 N	133·08 E
154	Nakhon Ratchasima Thai.	14·56 N	102·14 E
154	Nakhon Si Thammarat Thai.	8·27 N	99·58 E
87	Nakina Can.	50·10 N	86·40 W
118	Nakskov (näk'skou) Den.	54·51 N	11·06 E
121	Nakto nad Notecia (näk'wō näd nō-tĕ'chōn) Pol.	53·10 N	17·35 E
152	Naktong (R.) (näk'tŭng) Kor.	36·10 N	128·30 E
133	Nal'chik (nȧl-chēk') Sov. Un.	43·30 N	43·35 E
124	Nalón (R.) (nä-lōn') Sp.	43·15 N	5·38 W
164	Nālūt (nä-lōōt') Libya	31·51 N	10·49 E
144	Namak, Daryacheh-ye (L.) Iran	34·58 N	51·33 E
71	Namakan (L.) (nă'mȧ-kȧn) Minn.	48·20 N	92·43 W
166	Namakwaland (Reg.) (nă-mä'kwȧ'lănd) S. W. Afr.	25·30 S	16·30 E
144	Namakzār E Shahdād (L.) (nŭ-mŭk-zär') Iran	31·20 N	57·59 E
134	Namangan (nȧ-mȧn-gän') Sov. Un.	41·08 N	71·59 E
85	Namao Can. (Edmonton In.)	53·43 N	113·30 W
155	Namatanai (nä'mä-tȧ-nä'ê) N. Gui. Ter.	3·43 S	152·26 E
69	Nambe Pueblo Ind. Res. (näm'bā pwĕb'lō) N. Mex.	35·52 N	105·39 W
160	Nambour (năm'bŏŏr) Austl.	26·48 S	153·00 E
154	Nam Dinh (näm dēnk') Viet.	20·30 N	106·10 E
74	Nameoki (nă'mē-ō-kē) Ill. (St. Louis In.)	38·44 N	90·07 W
152	Namhae (I.) (näm'hī') Kor.	34·23 N	128·05 E
166	Namib Des. (nä-mēb') S. W. Afr.	24·00 S	15·00 E
160	Namoi (R.) (năm'oi) Austl.	30·10 S	148·43 E
114	Namous, Oued en (R.) (nȧ-mōōs') Alg.	31·48 N	00·19 W
66	Nampa (năm'pȧ) Idaho	43·35 N	116·35 W
112	Namsos (näm'sôs) Nor.	64·28 N	11·14 E
142	Nam Tsho (L.) China	30·30 N	91·10 E
117	Namur (nȧ-mür') Bel.	50·29 N	4·55 E
166	Namutoni (nȧ-mōō-tō'nê) S. W. Afr.	18·45 S	17·00 E
154	Nan, Mae Nam (R.) Thai.	18·11 N	100·29 E
91	Nanacamilpa (nä-nä-kä-mē'l-pä) Mex. (Mexico City In.)	19·30 N	98·33 W
66	Nanaimo (nȧ-nī'mō) Can.	49·09 N	123·57 W
152	Nanam (nä'nän') Kor.	41·38 N	129·37 E
153	Nanao (nä'nä-ō) Jap.	37·03 N	136·59 E
151	Nanao Tao (I.) (nä'nä-ō dou) China	23·30 N	117·30 E
151	Nanch'ang (nän'chäng') China	28·38 N	115·48 E
151	Nancheng China	26·50 N	116·40 E
150	Nancheng China	33·02 N	107·00 E
148	Nanch'enghuang Tai (I.) (nan'chĕng'hōōang'dou) China	38·22 N	120·54 E
148	Nanching (Nanking) (nän'jĭng) (nän'kĭng) China	32·04 N	118·46 E
151	Nanch'ung China	30·45 N	106·05 E
123	Nancy (näN-sē') Fr.	48·42 N	6·11 E
84	Nancy Cr. (năn'cē) Ga. (Atlanta In.)	33·51 N	84·25 W
142	Nanda Devi (Mt.) (nän'dä dā'vē) India	30·30 N	80·25 E
142	Nander India	19·13 N	77·21 E
142	Nandurbār India	21·29 N	74·13 E
143	Nandyal India	15·54 N	78·09 E
142	Nanga Parbat (Pk.) India	40·05 N	74·35 E
123	Nangis (näN-zhē') Fr. (Paris In.)	48·33 N	3·01 E
149	Nanhai (Fatshan) China (Canton In.)	23·02 N	113·07 E
149	Nanhsiang China (Shanghai In.)	31·17 N	121·17 E
151	Nanhsiung China	25·10 N	114·20 E
149	Nanhui China (Shanghai In.)	31·03 N	121·45 E
148	Naniana China	35·14 N	116·24 E
151	Nani Dinh Viet.	20·25 N	106·08 E
148	Nani Hu (L.) (näN'yi' hōō) China	31·12 N	119·05 E
	Nanking, see Nanching		
148	Nankung (nän'kōōng') China	37·22 N	115·22 E
151	Nan Ling (Mtns.) China	25·15 N	111·40 E
148	Nanlo (nän'lō') China	36·03 N	115·13 E
158	Nannine (nă-nēn') Austl.	26·50 S	118·30 E
151	Nanning (nän'nĭng') China	22·56 N	108·10 E
151	Nanp'an (R.) China	24·50 N	105·30 E
151	Nanpling China	26·40 N	118·05 E
84	Nansemond (năn'sê-mŭnd) Va. (Norfolk In.)	36·46 N	76·32 W
84	Nansemond R. Va. (Norfolk In.)	36·50 N	76·34 W
146	Nan Shan (Mts.) (nän'shän') China	38·43 N	98·00 E
153	Nantai Zan (Mtn.) (nän-täê zän) Jap.	36·47 N	139·28 E
122	Nantes (näNt') Fr.	47·13 N	1·37 W
123	Nanteuil-le-Haudouin (näN-tû-lē-ō-dwăN') Fr. Paris In.)	49·08 N	2·49 E
81	Nanticoke (năn'tĭ-kōk) Pa.	41·10 N	76·00 W
81	Nantucket (I.) (năn-tŭk'ĕt) Mass.	41·15 N	70·05 W
148	Nantung (nän'tōōng') China	32·02 N	120·51 E
110	Nantwich (nănt'wĭch) Eng.	53·04 N	2·31 W
150	Nanyang China	33·00 N	112·42 E
150	Nanyüan China (Peking In.)	39·48 N	116·24 E
148	Nanyün (näN'yün') China	38·11 N	116·37 E
151	Nao Chou (I.) China	20·58 N	110·58 E
91	Naolinco (nä-ō-lēŋ'kō) Mex.	19·39 N	96·50 W
84	Naomi (nā-ō'mī) La. (New Orleans In.)	29·42 N	89·59 W
127	Náousa (nä'ōō-sȧ) Grc.	40·38 N	22·05 E
68	Napa (năp'ȧ) Calif.	38·20 N	122·17 W
81	Napanee (năp'ȧ-nē) Can.	44·15 N	77·00 W
75	Naperville (nā'pēr-vĭl) Ill. (Chicago In.)	41·46 N	88·09 W
159	Napier (nā'pĭ-ēr) N. Z. (In.)	39·30 S	177·00 E
85	Napierville (nā'pĭ-ēr-vĭl) Can. (Montreal In.)	45·11 N	73·24 W
79	Naples (nă'p'lz) Fla. (In.)	26·07 N	81·46 W
	Naples, see Napoli		
98	Napo (R.) (nä'pō) Peru	1·49 S	74·20 W
80	Napoleon (nȧ-pō'lē-ŭn) Ohio	41·20 N	84·10 W
77	Napoleonville (nȧ-pō'lê-ŭn-vĭl) La.	29·56 N	91·03 W
125	Napoli (Naples) (nä'pô-lē) It. (Naples In.)	40·37 N	14·12 E
125	Napoli, Golfo di (G.) (gôl-fô-dē) It. (Napoli In.)	40·29 N	14·08 E
80	Nappanee (năp'ȧ-nē) Ind.	41·30 N	86·00 W
153	Nara (nä'rä) Jap. (Osaka In.)	34·41 N	135·50 E
164	Nara Mali	15·09 N	7·27 W
153	Nara (Pref.) Jap. (Osaka In.)	34·36 N	135·49 E
128	Nara (R.) Sov. Un.	55·05 N	37·16 E
160	Naracoorte (nȧ-rȧ-kōōn'tē) Austl.	36·50 S	140·50 E
143	Naraspur India	16·32 N	81·43 E
84	Narberth (när'bûrth) Pa. (Philadelphia In.)	40·01 N	75·17 W
122	Narbonne (nȧr-bôn') Fr.	43·12 N	3·00 E
127	Nardò (när-dô') It.	40·11 N	18·02 E
98	Nare (nä'rĕ) Col. (In.)	6·12 N	74·37 W
121	Narew R. (nä'rĕf) Pol.	52·43 N	21·19 E
142	Narmada (R.) India	22·17 N	74·45 E
128	Naroch' (L.) (nä'rôch) Sov. Un.	54·51 N	27·00 E
132	Narodnaya, Gora (Mtn.) (nȧ-rôd'nȧ-yȧ) Sov. Un.	65·10 N	60·10 E
128	Naro Fominsk (nä'rô-fô-mēnsk') Sov. Un.	55·23 N	36·43 E
119	Närpesȧ (R.) Fin.	62·35 N	21·24 E
161	Narrabeen (năr-ȧ-bĭn) Austl. (Sydney In.)	33·44 S	151·18 E
160	Narrabri (nä-rä'brê) Austl.	30·17 S	149·46 E
84	Narragansett (năr-ȧ-găn'sĕt) R. I. (Providence In.)	41·26 N	71·27 W
81	Narragansett B. R. I.	41·20 N	71·15 W
160	Narrandera (nȧ-rȧn-dē'rȧ) Austl.	34·40 S	146·40 E
158	Narrogin (năr'ō-gĭn) Austl.	33·00 S	117·15 E
128	Narva (nȧr'vȧ) Sov. Un.	59·24 N	28·12 E
155	Narvacan (när-vä-kän') Phil. (Manila In.)	17·27 N	120·29 E
128	Narva Jõesuu (nȧr'vȧ ōō-ô-ă'sōō-ōō) Sov. Un.	59·26 N	28·02 E
112	Narvik (när'vēk) Nor.	68·21 N	17·18 E
119	Narvskiy Zaliv (B.) (nȧr'vskĭ zä'lĭf) Sov. Un.	59·35 N	27·25 E
132	Nar'yan-Mar (när'yȧn mär') Sov. Un.	67·42 N	53·30 E
160	Naryilco (năr-ĭl'kô) Austl.	28·40 S	141·50 E
134	Narym (nä-rēm') Sov. Un.	58·47 N	82·05 E
145	Naryn (R.) (nŭ-rĭn') Sov. Un.	41·46 N	73·00 E
110	Naseby (nāz'bĭ) Eng.	52·23 N	0·59 W
74	Nashua (năsh'ŭ-ȧ) Mo. (Kansas City In.)	39·18 N	94·34 W
83	Nashua N. H. (Boston In.)	42·47 N	71·23 W
73	Nashville (năsh'vĭl) Ark.	33·56 N	93·50 W
78	Nashville Ga.	31·12 N	83·15 W
73	Nashville Ill.	38·21 N	89·42 W
80	Nashville Mich.	42·35 N	85·05 W
78	Nashville Tenn.	36·10 N	86·48 W
71	Nashwauk (năsh'wôk) Minn.	47·21 N	93·12 W
127	Našice (nä'shê-tsĕ) Yugo.	45·29 N	18·06 E
121	Nasielsk (nä'syĕlsk) Pol.	52·35 N	20·50 E
142	Nāsik (nä'sĭk) India	20·02 N	73·49 E
165	Nasir (nä-zēr') Sud.	8·30 N	33·06 E
142	Nasirabād India	26·13 N	74·48 E
87	Naskaupi (R.) (năs'kô-pĭ) Can.	53·59 N	61·10 W
94	Nassau (năs'ô) Ba. Is.	25·05 N	77·20 W
155	Nassau-Gebergte (Mts.) W. Irian	3·48 S	136·45 E
111	Nassenheide (nä'sĕn-hī-dĕ) Ger. (Berlin In.)	52·49 N	13·13 E
118	Nässjö (nĕs'shû) Swe.	57·39 N	14·39 E
155	Nasugbu (nȧ-sōōg-bōō') Phil. (Manila In.)	14·05 N	120·37 E
76	Nasworthy L. (năz'wûr-thē) Tex.	31·17 N	100·30 W
151	Nata China	19·30 N	109·38 E
93	Natá (nä-tà') Pan.	8·20 N	8·30 W
98	Natagaima (nä-tä-gī'mä) Col. (In.)	3·38 N	75·07 W
99	Natal (nä-täl') Braz.	6·00 S	35·13 W
166	Natal (Prov.) (nȧ-täl') S. Afr.	28·50 S	30·07 E
83	Natashguan (nä-täsh'kwän) Can.	50·09 N	61·46 W
87	Natashguan (R.) Can.	51·34 N	61·46 W
78	Natchez (năch'ĕz) Miss.	31·35 N	91·20 W
77	Natchitoches (năk'ĭ-tŏsh) (nȧch-ĭ-tŏsh') La.	31·46 N	93·06 W
139	Nathanya Isr. (Palestine In.)	32·19 N	34·52 E
83	Natick (nā'tĭk) Mass. (Boston In.)	42·17 N	71·21 W
135	National Area (Reg.) Sov. Un.	66·30 N	170·30 E
67	National Bison Ra. (Mts.) (năsh'ŭn-ăl bī's'n) Mont.	47·18 N	113·58 W
68	National City Calif. (San Diego In.)	32·38 N	117·01 W
85	Nation R. (nā'shŭn) Can. (Ottawa In.)	45·21 N	75·07 W
99	Natividade (nä-tê-vê-dä'dĕ) Braz.	11·43 S	47·34 W
75	Natrona (nā'trō nȧ) Pa. (Pittsburgh In.)	40·38 N	79·43 W
166	Natron L. (nā'trŏn) Tan.	2·29 S	35·17 E
168	Natrum, Wadi el (Val.) U. A. R. (Nile In.)	30·33 N	30·12 E
154	Natuna, Pulau-Pulau (Is.) Indon.	3·22 N	108·00 E
69	Natural Bridges Natl. Mon. (năt'ŭ-rȧl brĭj'ĕs) Utah	37·20 N	110·20 W
158	Naturaliste, C. (năt-ŭ-rȧ-lĭst') Austl.	33·30 S	115·10 E
91	Naucalpan (nä'ōō-käl-pȧ'n) Mex. (Mexico City In.)	19·28 N	99·14 W
91	Nauchampatepetl (Mtn.) (nä'ōō-chäm-pä-tĕ'pĕtl) Mex.	19·32 N	97·09 W
82	Naudville Can.	48·36 N	71·40 W
111	Nauen (nou'ĕn) Ger. (Berlin In.)	52·36 N	12·53 E
81	Naugatuck (nô'gȧ-tŭk) Conn.	41·25 N	73·05 W
155	Naujan (nä-ōō-hän') Phil. (Manila In.)	13·19 N	121·17 E
120	Naumburg (noum'bŏŏrgh) Ger.	51·10 N	11·50 E
156	Nauru I. Oceania	0·30 S	167·00 E
91	Nautla (nä-ōōt'lä) Mex.	20·14 N	96·44 W
76	Nava (nä'vä) Mex.	28·25 N	100·44 W
124	Nava, L. de la Sp.	42·05 N	4·42 W
124	Nava del Rey (nä-vä dĕl rā'ē) Sp.	41·22 N	5·04 W
124	Navahermosa (nä-vä-ĕr-mō'sä) Sp.	39·39 N	4·28 W
94	Navajas (nä-vä-häs') Cuba	22·40 N	81·20 W
69	Navajo Ind. Res. (năv'ȧ-hō) Ariz.-N. Mex.	36·31 N	109·24 W
69	Navajo Natl. Mon. Ariz.	36·43 N	110·39 W
69	Navajo Res. N. Mex.	36·57 N	107·26 W
125	Navalcarnero (nä-väl-kär-nā'rō) Sp. (Madrid In.)	40·17 N	4·05 W
124	Navalmoral de la Mata (nä-väl'mōräl' dā lä mä'tä) Sp.	39·53 N	5·32 W
85	Navan (nă'vȧn) Can. (Ottawa In.)	45·25 N	75·26 W
100	Navarino (nä-vä-rē'nô) (I.) Chile	55·30 S	68·15 W
124	Navarra (Reg.) (nä-vär'rä) Sp.	42·40 N	1·35 W
101	Navarro (nä-vä'r-rō) Arg. (Buenos Aires In.)	35·00 S	59·16 W
77	Navasota (năv-ȧ-sō'tȧ) Tex.	30·24 N	96·05 W
77	Navasota R. Tex.	31·03 N	96·11 W
95	Navassa (I.) (nȧ-văs'ȧ) N. A.	18·25 N	75·15 W
124	Navia (R.) (nä-vē'ä) Sp.	43·10 N	6·45 W
101	Navidad (nä-vê-dä'd) Chile (Santiago In.)	34·57 S	71·51 W
95	Navidad Bk. (nä-vê-dädh') Ba. Is.	20·05 N	69·00 W
101	Navidade do Carangola (nä-vē-dä'dĕ-dô-kä-rän-gô'la) Braz. (Rio de Janeiro In.)	21·04 S	41·58 W
88	Navojoa (nä-vô-kô'ä) Mex.	27·00 N	109·40 W
127	Návplion Grc.	37·33 N	22·46 E
142	Nawābshāh (nȧ-wäb'shä) W. Pak.	26·20 N	68·30 E
145	Nawagai (nŭ-wŭ-gī') W. Pak. (Khyber Pass In.)	34·40 N	71·18 E
127	Náxos (I.) (nȧk'sôs) Grc.	37·15 N	25·20 E
88	Nayarit (State) (nä-yä-rēt') Mex.	22·00 N	105·15 W
90	Nayarit, Sierra de (Mts.) (sē-ĕ'r-rä-dĕ) Mex.	23·20 N	105·07 W
99	Nazaré (nä-zä-rĕ') Braz.	13·04 S	38·49 W
124	Nazaré (nä-zä-rā') Port.	39·38 N	9·04 W
99	Nazaré da Mata (dä-mä-tä) Braz.	7·46 S	35·13 W
139	Nazareth (năz'ȧ-rĕth) Isr. (Palestine In.)	32·43 N	35·19 E
76	Nazas (nä'zäs) Mex.	25·14 N	104·08 W
76	Nazas, R. Mex.	25·08 N	104·20 W
133	Nazilli (nȧ-zĭ-lē') Tur.	37·40 N	28·10 E
136	Naziya R. (nȧ-zē'yȧ) Sov. Un. (Leningrad In.)	59·48 N	31·18 E
165	Ndélé (n'dā-lā') Cen. Afr. Rep.	8·21 N	20·43 E
166	Ndjolé (n'dzhō-lā') Gabon	0·15 S	10·45 E
166	Ndola (n'dō'lä) N. Rh.	12·52 S	28·44 E
116	Neagh Lough (B.) (lŏk nā) N. Ire.	54·40 N	6·47 W
161	Neapean (R.) Austl. (Sydney In.)	33·40 S	150·39 E
127	Neápolis (nā-ŏp' ô-lĭs) Grc.	36·35 N	23·08 E
126	Neápolis Grc. (In.)	35·17 N	25·37 E
64	Near Is. (nēr) Alaska	52·20 N	172·40 E
116	Neath (nēth) Wales	51·41 N	3·50 W
160	Nebine Cr. (nĕ-bēne') Austl.	27·50 S	147·00 E
133	Nebit-Dag (nyĕ-bēt'däg') Sov. Un.	39·30 N	54·20 E
62	Nebraska (State) (nê-brăs'kȧ) U. S.	41·45 N	101·30 W
73	Nebraska City Nebr.	40·40 N	95·50 W
77	Neches R. (nĕch'ĕz) Tex.	31·03 N	94·40 W
120	Neckar R. (nĕk'är) Ger.	49·16 N	9·06 E
100	Necochea (nā-kô-chā'ä) Arg.	38·30 S	58·45 W
129	Nedrigaylov (nĕ-drĭ-gī'lôf) Sov. Un.	50·49 N	33·52 E
83	Needham (nēd'ăm) Mass. (Boston In.)	42·17 N	71·14 W
68	Needles (nē'd'lz) Calif.	34·51 N	114·39 W
71	Neenah (nē'nȧ) Wis.	44·10 N	88·30 W
86	Neepawa Can.	50·17 N	99·31 W
72	Nee Res. (nē) Colo.	38·26 N	102·56 W
117	Neetze (R.) (nā'tzĕ) Ger.	53·04 N	11·00 E
153	Negareyama (nā'gä-rā-yä'mä) Jap. (Tōkyō In.)	35·52 N	139·54 E
71	Negaunee (nê-gô'nē) Mich.	46·30 N	87·37 W
139	Negev (Des.) (nĕ'gĕv) Isr. (Palestine In.)	30·34 N	34·43 E
127	Negoi (Mtn.) (nā-goi') Rom.	45·33 N	24·38 E
143	Negombo Ceylon	7·39 N	79·49 E
127	Negotin (nĕ'gô-tēn) Yugo.	44·13 N	22·33 E
154	Negrais, C. (nĕ'grĭs) Bur.	16·08 N	93·34 E

ng-sing; ŋ-baŋk; N-nasalized n; nŏd; cŏmmit; ōld; ōbey; ôrder; fōōd; fŏŏt; ou-out; s-soft; sh-dish; th-thin; pūre; ûnite; ûrn; stŭd; circŭs; ü-as "y" in study; '-indeterminate vowel.

Page	Name Pronunciation Region	Lat. °′	Long. °′
139	Negri Sembilan (State)		
	(nā'grē sĕm-bē-län')		
	Mala. (Singapore In.)	2·46 N	101·54 E
100	Negro (R.)..............Arg.	39·50 S	65·00 W
98	Negro, Rio (R.) (rē'ō nā'grōō)		
	Braz.	0·18 S	63·21 W
124	Negro, C. (na'grō)..........Mor.	35·25 N	4·51 W
93	Negro, Cerro (Mt.)		
	(sĕ'r-rô-nā'grô) . Pan.	8·44 N	80·37 W
101	Negro (R.) . Ur. (Buenos Aires In.)	33·17 S	58·18 W
92	Negro R..................Nic.	13·01 N	87·10 W
154	Negros (I.) (nā'grōs)........Phil.	9·50 N	121·45 E
98	Neguá (nā-gwá').......Col. (In.)	5·51 N	76·36 W
66	Nehalem R. (nē-hăl'ĕm)......Ore.	45·52 N	123·37 W
123	Neheim-Hüsten (nĕ'hīm)		
	Ger. (Ruhr In.)	51·28 N	7·58 E
95	Neiba (nâ-ē'bä).......Dom. Rep.	18·30 N	71·20 W
95	Neiba, Bahai de (B.) (bä-ä'ē-dĕ)		
	Dom. Rep.	18·10 N	71·00 W
95	Neiba, Sierra de (Mts.)		
	(sē-ĕr'rä-dĕ) . . Dom. Rep.	18·40 N	71·40 W
151	Neichiang................China	29·38 N	105·01 E
148	Neich'iu (nā'chĭō).........China	37·17 N	114·32 E
67	Neihart (nī'hărt)..........Mont.	46·54 N	110·39 W
150	Neihsiang.................China	33·00 N	111·54 E
71	Neillsville (nēlz'vĭl).........Wis.	44·35 N	90·37 W
98	Neira (nā'rä)..........Col. (In.)	5·10 N	75·32 W
98	Neiva (nâ-ē'vä) (nā'vä) . Col. (In.)	2·55 N	75·16 W
71	Nekoosa (nē-kōō'sȧ)........Wis.	44·19 N	89·54 W
118	Neksø (nĕk'sû)............Den.	55·05 N	15·05 E
70	Neligh (nē'lĭg).............Nebr.	42·06 N	98·02 W
135	Nel'kan (nĕl-kän')......Sov. Un.	57·45 N	136·36 E
143	Nellore (nĕl-lōr')..........India	14·28 N	79·59 E
152	Nel'ma (nĕl-mä')........Sov. Un.	47·34 N	139·05 E
86	Nelson (nĕl'sŭn)...........Can.	49·27 N	117·24 W
110	Nelson...................Eng.	53·50 N	2·13 W
159	Nelson.............N. Z. (In.)	41·15 S	173·22 E
64	Nelson (I.)..............Alaska	60·38 N	164·42 W
160	Nelson, C..................Austl.	38·29 S	141·20 E
86	Nelson (R.)................Can.	56·20 N	93·59 W
68	Nelson Cr..................Nev.	40·22 N	114·43 W
80	Nelsonville (nĕl'sŭn-vĭl)......Ohio	39·30 N	82·15 W
164	Néma (nā'mä)........Mauritania	16·46 N	7·03 W
74	Nemadji R. (nĕ-măd'jē)		
	Wis. (Duluth In.)	46·33 N	92·16 W
119	Neman (ŋĕ'-mȧn).......Sov. Un.	55·02 N	22·01 E
121	Neman R...............Sov. Un.	53·28 N	24·45 E
120	Německý Brod		
	(nyĕ'myĕt-skyĭ brōd') . Czech.	49·38 N	15·34 E
129	Nemirov (nyā-mē'rôf) . . . Sov. Un.	48·56 N	28·51 E
113	Nemours (nē-mōōr')..........Alg.	35·19 N	1·09 W
122	Nemours....................Fr.	48·16 N	2·41 E
152	Nemuro (nā'mōō-rō).........Jap.	43·13 N	145·10 E
152	Nemuro Str..................Jap.	43·07 N	145·10 E
110	Nen (R.) (nĕn).............Eng.	52·32 N	0·19 W
116	Nenagh (nē'nȧ)..............Ire.	52·50 N	8·05 W
64	Nenana (nȧ-nä'nȧ)........Alaska	64·28 N	149·18 W
150	Nench'eng (Mergen).......China	49·02 N	125·15 E
147	Nen Chiang (R.)...........China	47·07 N	123·28 E
148	Nengcheng................China	33·15 N	116·34 E
136	Nenikyul' (nĕ-nyē'kyûl)		
	Sov. Un. (Leningrad In.)	59·26 N	30·40 E
73	Neodesha (nē-ô-dĕ-shô')....Kans.	37·24 N	95·41 W
73	Neosho.....................Mo.	36·51 N	94·22 W
73	Neosho (R.) (nē-ō'shō).....Kans.	38·21 N	95·53 W
138	Nepal (nĕ-pôl')............Asia	28·45 N	83·00 E
69	Nephi (nē'fī)..............Utah	39·40 N	111·50 W
101	Nepomuceno (nĕ-pô-mōō-sĕ'no)		
	Braz. (Rio de Janeiro In.)	21·15 S	45·13 W
126	Nera (R.) (nā'rä).............It.	42·45 N	12·54 E
122	Nérac (nā-räk')...............Fr.	44·08 N	0·19 E
135	Nerchinsk (nyĕr' chĕnsk) . Sov. Un.	51·47 N	116·17 E
135	Nerchinskiy Khrebet (Mts.)		
	Sov. Un.	50·30 N	118·30 E
135	Nerchinskiy Zavod		
	(nyĕr'chĕn-skĭzȧ-vôt') . Sov. Un.	51·35 N	119·46 E
128	Nerekhta (nyĕ-rĕĸ'tȧ) . . . Sov. Un.	57·29 N	40·34 E
127	Neretva (R.) (nĕ'rĕt-vȧ) . . . Yugo.	43·08 N	17·50 E
124	Nerja (nĕr'hä)................Sp.	36·45 N	3·53 W
128	Nerl' (R.) (nyĕrl)......Sov. Un.	56·59 N	37·57 E
84	Nero (nĕr'ō)		
	La. (New Orleans In.)	29·37 N	89·52 W
136	Nerskaya R. (nyĕr'skȧ-yȧ)		
	Sov. Un. (Moscow In.)	55·31 N	38·46 E
128	Nerussa (R.) (nyȧ-rōō'sȧ) . Sov. Un.	52·24 N	34·20 E
116	Ness, Loch (L.) (lŏĸ nĕs) . . . . Scot.	57·23 N	4·20 W
72	Ness City (nĕs)............Kans.	38·27 N	99·55 W
121	Nesterov (ŋĕs'-tzhyé-rôf) . Sov. Un.	50·03 N	23·58 E
119	Nesterov (nyĕs-tä'rôf) . . . Sov. Un.	54·39 N	22·38 E
127	Néstos (R.) (nās'tōs)........Grc.	41·25 N	24·12 E
128	Nesvizh (nyĕs'vēsh).....Sov. Un.	53·13 N	26·44 E
84	Netcong (nĕt'cŏnj)		
	N. J. (New York In.)	40·54 N	74·42 W
102	Netherlands (nĕdh'ēr-lăndz) . . Eur.	53·01 N	3·57 E
	Netherlands Guiana, see Surinam		
71	Nett Lake Ind. Res. (nĕt lăk) . Minn.	48·23 N	93·19 W
125	Nettuno (nĕt-tōō'nô)		
	It. (Rome In.)	41·28 N	12·40 E
123	Neubeckum (noi'bĕ-kōōm)		
	Ger. (Ruhr In.)	51·48 N	8·01 E
120	Neubrandenburg		
	(noi-brän'dĕn-bōōrgh) . Ger.	53·33 N	13·16 E
120	Neuburg (noi'bōōrgh)........Ger.	48·43 N	11·12 E
120	Neuchâtel (nû-shȧ-tĕl')......Switz.	47·00 N	6·52 E
120	Neuchatel, Lac de (L.)......Switz.	46·48 N	6·53 E
111	Neuenhagen (noi'ĕn-hä-gĕn)		
	Ger. (Berlin In.)	52·31 N	13·41 E
123	Neuenrade (noi'ĕn-rä-dĕ)		
	Ger. (Ruhr In.)	51·17 N	7·47 E
122	Neufchâtel-en-Bray		
	(nû-shä-tĕl'ĕɴ-brā') . Fr.	49·43 N	1·25 E
120	Neuhaldensleben		
	(noi-häl'dĕns-lā'bĕn) . Ger.	52·18 N	11·23 E
111	Neuhaus (Oste) (noi' houz) (ôz'tĕ)		
	Ger. (Hamburg In.)	53·48 N	9·02 E
111	Neulengbach . . . Aus. (Vienna In.)	48·13 N	15·55 E
120	Neumarkt (noi'märkt).......Ger.	49·17 N	11·30 E
120	Neumünster (noi'münstĕr) . . . Ger.	54·04 N	10·00 E
120	Neunkirchen (noin'kĭrĸ-ĕn) . . . Aus.	47·43 N	16·05 E
123	Neunkirchen................Ger.	49·21 N	7·20 E
100	Neuquén (nĕ-ōō-kān')........Arg.	38·52 S	68·12 W
100	Neuquen (Prov.)............Arg.	39·40 S	70·45 W
100	Neuquén (R.)...............Arg.	38·45 S	69·00 W
111	Neuruppin (noi'rōō-pēn)		
	Ger. (Berlin In.)	52·55 N	12·48 E
79	Neuse (R.) (nūz)..........N. C.	36·12 N	78·50 W
120	Neusiedler See (L.) (noi-zēd'lēr)		
	Aus.	47·54 N	16·31 E
123	Neuss (nois)......Ger. (Ruhr In.)	51·12 N	6·41 E
120	Neustadt (noi'shtät).........Ger.	49·21 N	8·08 E
120	Neustadt...................Ger.	54·06 N	10·50 E
120	Neustadt bei Coburg		
	(bī kō'bōōrgh) . Ger.	50·20 N	11·09 E
120	Neustrelitz (noi-strā'lĭts).....Ger.	53·21 N	13·05 E
120	Neu Ulm (noi ŏŏ lm')........Ger.	48·23 N	10·01 E
85	Neuville (nü'vĭl) . Can. (Quebec In.)	46·39 N	71·35 W
120	Neuwied (noi'vēdt)..........Ger.	50·26 N	7·28 E
71	Nevada (nē-vä'dȧ)..........Iowa	42·01 N	93·27 W
73	Nevada.....................Mo.	37·49 N	94·21 W
62	Nevada (State)............U. S.	39·30 N	123·20 W
124	Nevada, Sierra (Mts.)		
	(syĕr'rä nā-vä'dhä) . Sp.	37·01 N	3·28 W
62	Nevada, Sierra (Mts.)		
	(sē-ĕ'r-rä nē-vä'dȧ) . U. S.	39·20 N	120·25 W
68	Nevada City..............Calif.	39·16 N	120·01 W
98	Nevado, Cerro el (Mtn.)		
	(sĕ'r-rô-ĕl-nĕ-vä'dô) . Col. (In.)	4·02 N	74·08 W
90	Nevado de Colima (Mtn.)		
	(nā-vä'dhô dā kô-lē'mä) . Mex.	19·34 N	103·39 W
136	Neva R. (nyĕ-vä')		
	Sov. Un. (Leningrad In.)	59·49 N	30·54 E
136	Neva Stantsiya		
	(nyĕ-vä' stän'tsĭ-yȧ)		
	Sov. Un. (Leningrad In.)	59·53 N	30·30 E
128	Nevel' (nyĕ'vĕl)........Sov. Un.	56·03 N	29·57 E
99	Neveri (nĕ-vĕ-rē) (R.) . . Ven. (In.)	10·13 N	64·18 W
122	Nevers (nĕ-vâr')............Fr.	46·59 N	3·10 E
127	Nevesinje (nĕ-vĕ'sēn-yĕ) . . . . Yugo.	43·15 N	18·08 E
116	Nevis, Ben (Mtn.) (bĕn) . . . . Scot.	56·47 N	5·00 W
93	Nevis I. (nē'vĭs)		
	St. Kitts-Nevis-Anguilla		
	(Le. & Wind. Is. In.)	17·05 N	62·38 W
93	Nevis Pk.		
	Nevis (Le. & Wind. Is. In.)	17·11 N	62·33 W
127	Nevrokop (nĕv'rō-kôp')......Bul.	41·35 N	23·46 E
133	Nevşehir (nĕv-shĕ'hĕr).......Tur.	38·40 N	34·35 E
136	Nev'yansk (nĕv-yänsk')		
	Sov. Un. (Urals In.)	57·29 N	60·14 E
79	New (R.) (nū)..............Va.	37·20 N	80·35 W
79	New (R.), South Fork . . Va.-N. C.	36·37 N	81·15 W
75	New Albany (nû ôl'bȧ-nĭ)		
	Ind. (Louisville In.)	38·17 N	85·49 W
78	New Albany...............Miss.	34·28 N	89·00 W
99	New Amsterdam (ăm'stēr-dăm)		
	Br. Gu.	6·14 N	57·30 W
65	Newark (nū'ērk)		
	Calif. (San Francisco In.)	37·32 N	122·02 W
81	Newark....................Del.	39·40 N	75·45 W
110	Newark....................Eng.	53·04 N	0·49 W
84	Newark . . . . N. J. (New York In.)	40·44 N	74·10 W
81	Newark....................N. Y.	43·05 N	77·10 W
80	Newark....................Ohio	40·05 N	82·25 W
75	New Augusta (ô-gŭs'tȧ)		
	Ind. (Indianapolis In.)	39·53 N	86·14 W
80	Newaygo (nū'wā-go).......Mich.	43·25 N	85·50 W
81	New Bedford (bĕd'fērd) . . . . Mass.	41·35 N	70·55 W
80	Newberg (nū'bûrg)..........Ore.	45·17 N	122·58 W
79	New Bern (bûrn)...........N. C.	35·05 N	77·05 W
78	Newbern..................Tenn.	36·05 N	89·12 W
71	Newberry (nū'bĕr-ĭ)........Mich.	46·22 N	85·31 W
79	Newberry..................S. C.	34·15 N	81·40 W
75	New Bethel (bĕth'ĕl)		
	Ind. (Indianapolis In.)	39·30 N	86·00 W
75	New Boston (bôs'tŭn)		
	Mich. (Detroit In.)	42·10 N	83·24 W
80	New Boston................Ohio	38·45 N	82·55 W
76	New Braunfels (nū broun'fĕls)		
	Tex.	29·43 N	98·07 W
74	New Brighton (brī'tŭn) . . . . Minn.		
	(Minneapolis, St. Paul In.)	45·04 N	93·12 W
75	New Brighton . Pa. (Pittsburgh In.)	40·34 N	80·18 W
81	New Britain (brĭt''n)........Conn.	41·40 N	72·45 W
155	New Britain (I.)......N. Gui. Ter.	6·45 S	149·38 E
84	New Brunswick (brŭnz'wĭk)		
	N. J. (New York In.)	40·29 N	74·27 W
87	New Brunswick (Prov.).......Can.	47·14 N	66·30 W
80	Newburg..................Ind.	38·00 N	87·25 W
73	Newburg..................Mo.	37·54 N	91·53 W
81	Newburgh..................N. Y.	41·30 N	74·00 W
75	Newburgh Heights		
	Ohio (Cleveland In.)	41·27 N	81·40 W
116	Newbury (nū'bĕr-ĭ).........Eng.	51·24 N	1·26 W
83	Newbury......Mass. (Boston In.)	42·48 N	70·52 W
83	Newburyport (nū'bĕr-ĭ-pōrt)		
	Mass. (Boston In.)	42·48 N	70·53 W
84	New Canaan (kā-nȧn)		
	Conn. (New York In.)	41·06 N	73·30 W
82	New Carlisle (kär-līl')........Can.	48·01 N	65·22 W
160	Newcastle (nū-kás''l).......Austl.	33·00 S	151·55 E
82	Newcastle..................Can.	47·00 N	65·36 W
81	New Castle.................Del.	39·40 N	75·35 W
110	Newcastle (nū-kás''l) (nû-kás''l)		
	Eng.	53·01 N	2·14 W
80	Newcastle..................Ind.	39·55 N	85·25 W
80	New Castle.................Ohio	40·20 N	82·10 W
80	New Castle.................Pa.	41·00 N	80·25 W
72	Newcastle..................Tex.	33·13 N	98·44 W
70	Newcastle..................Wyo.	43·51 N	104·11 W
116	Newcastle-on-Tyne..........Eng.	55·00 N	1·45 W
158	Newcastle Waters (wô'tērz) . Austl.	17·10 S	133·25 E
80	Newcomerstown		
	(nū'kŭm-ērz-toun) . Ohio	40·15 N	81·40 W
84	New Croton Res. (krō'tŏn)		
	N. Y. (New York In.)	41·15 N	73·47 W
142	New Delhi (dĕl'hī).........India	28·43 N	77·18 E
70	Newell (nū'ĕl)..............S. D.	44·43 N	103·26 W
159	New England Ra. (nû ĭŋ'glănd)		
	Austl.	29·32 S	152·30 E
64	Newenham, C. (nū-ĕn-hăm) . Alaska	58·40 N	162·32 W
75	Newfane (nū-fān)		
	N. Y. (Buffalo In.)	43·17 N	78·44 W
87	Newfoundland (Prov.)		
	(nû-fŭn'lănd') (nū'fŭnd-lănd)		
	(nû'found-lănd')		
	Can. (Newfoundland In.)	48·15 N	56·53 W
159	New Georgia (I.) (jôr'jĭ-ȧ) . Sol. Is.	8·08 S	158·00 E
83	New Glasgow (glȧs'gō)......Can.	45·36 N	62·40 W
155	New Guinea, Territory of . Oceania	3·45 S	145·45 E
155	New Guinea (I.) (gĭne)		
	N. Gui. Ter.	5·45 S	140·00 E
66	Newhalem (nū hā'lŭm).....Wash.	48·44 N	121·11 W
63	New Hampshire (State)		
	(hămp'shĭr) . U. S.	43·55 N	71·40 W
71	New Hampton (hămp'tŭn) . . Iowa	43·03 N	92·20 W
167	New Hanover (hăn'ōvēr)		
	S. Afr. (Natal In.)	29·23 S	30·32 E
155	New Hanover (I.) . . . N. Gui. Ter.	2·37 S	150·15 E
80	New Harmony (nū här'mô-nĭ)		
	Ind.	38·10 N	87·55 W
81	New Haven (hā'vĕn).......Conn.	41·20 N	72·55 W
117	Newhaven..................Eng.	50·45 N	0·10 E
80	New Haven (nū hăv''n)......Ind.	41·05 N	85·00 W
159	New Hebrides (Is.) (hĕb'rĭ-dēz)		
	Oceania	16·02 S	169·15 E
110	New Holland (hŏl'ănd)......Eng.	53·42 N	0·21 W
79	New Holland...............N. C.	35·27 N	76·14 W
84	New Hope Mtn. (hōp)		
	Ala. (Birmingham In.)	33·23 N	86·45 W
75	New Hudson (hŭd'sŭn)		
	Mich. (Detroit In.)	42·30 N	83·36 W
77	New Iberia (ī-bē'rĭ-ȧ).........La.	30·00 N	91·50 W
85	Newington (nū'ĕng-tŏn)		
	Can. (Ottawa In.)	45·07 N	75·00 W
155	New Ireland (I.) (ĭr'lănd)		
	N. Gui. Ter.	3·15 S	152·30 E
63	New Jersey (State) (jûr'zĭ) . . U. S.	40·30 N	74·50 W
75	New Kensington (kĕn'zĭng-tŭn)		
	Pa. (Pittsburgh In.)	40·34 N	79·35 W
73	Newkirk (nū'kûrk).........Okla.	36·52 N	97·03 W
166	Newlands (nû'lănds)		
	S. Afr. (Cape Town In.)	33·58 S	18·28 E
75	New Lenox (lĕn'ŭk)		
	Ill. (Chicago In.)	41·31 N	87·58 W
80	New Lexington (lĕk'sĭng-tŭn) . Ohio	39·40 N	82·10 W
71	New Lisbon (lĭz'bŭn)........Wis.	43·52 N	90·11 W
81	New London (lŭn'dŭn).....Conn.	41·20 N	72·05 W
71	New London...............Wis.	44·24 N	88·45 W
73	New Madrid (măd'rĭd).......Mo.	36·34 N	89·31 W
78	Newman (nū'mȧn)............Ga.	33·22 N	84·47 W
79	Newman (L.)...............Fla.	29·41 N	82·13 W
70	Newman's Grove (nū'mȧn grōv)		
	Nebr.	41·46 N	97·44 W
81	Newmarket (nū'mär-kĕt) . . . . Can.	44·00 N	79·30 W
80	New Martinsville		
	(mär'tĭnz-vĭl) . W. Va.	39·35 N	80·50 W
62	New Mexico (State) (mĕk'sĭ-kō)		
	U. S.	34·30 N	107·10 W
110	New Mills (mĭlz)...........Eng.	53·22 N	2·00 W
75	New Munster (mŭn'stēr)		
	Wis. (Milwaukee In.)	42·35 N	88·13 W
160	New Norfolk (nôr'fŏk).....Austl.	42·50 S	147·17 E
84	New Orleans (ôr'lē-ănz)		
	La. (New Orleans In.)	30·00 N	90·05 W
80	New Philadelphia		
	(fĭl-ȧ-dĕl'fĭ-ȧ) . Ohio	40·30 N	81·30 W
159	New Plymouth (plĭm'ūth)		
	N. Z. (In.)	39·04 S	174·13 E
73	Newport (nū'pōrt)..........Ark.	35·35 N	91·16 W
161	Newport.....Austl. (Sydney In.)	33·39 S	151·19 E
116	Newport (nū-pôrt)..........Eng.	50·41 N	1·25 W
116	Newport...................Wales	51·36 N	3·05 W
110	Newport...................Eng.	52·46 N	2·22 W
75	Newport.....Ky. (Cincinnati In.)	39·05 N	84·30 W
82	Newport...................Maine	44·49 N	69·20 W
74	Newport...................Minn.		
	(Minneapolis, St. Paul In.)	44·52 N	92·59 W
81	Newport...................N. H.	43·20 N	72·10 W
66	Newport...................Ore.	44·39 N	124·02 W
84	Newport . . . R. I. (Providence In.)	41·29 N	71·16 W
78	Newport...................Tenn.	35·55 N	83·12 W
81	Newport...................Vt.	44·55 N	72·15 W
66	Newport...................Wash.	48·12 N	117·01 W
74	Newport Beach (bēch)		
	Calif. (Los Angeles In.)	33·36 N	117·55 W
84	Newport News . . Va. (Norfolk In.)	36·59 N	76·24 W
71	New Prague (nū prāg)......Minn.	44·33 N	93·35 W
94	New Providence (I.)		
	(prŏv'ĭ-dĕns) . Ba. Is.	25·00 N	77·25 W
80	New Richmond (rĭch'mŭnd) . Ohio	38·55 N	84·15 W
71	New Richmond..............Wis.	45·07 N	92·34 W
77	New Roads (rōds)...........La.	30·42 N	91·26 W
84	New Rochelle (rû-shĕl')		
	N. Y. (New York In.)	40·55 N	73·47 W
70	New Rockford (rŏk'fōrd) . . . N. D.	47·40 N	99·08 W
116	New Ross (rôs)..............Ire.	52·25 N	6·55 W
85	New Sarepta . Can. (Edmonton In.)	53·17 N	113·09 W
149	New Shanghai		
	China (Shanghai In.)	31·18 N	121·31 E
	New Siberian Is., see		
	Novosibirskiye O-va		
79	New Smyra (smûr'nȧ)........Fla.	29·00 N	80·57 W
159	New South Wales (State) (wālz)		
	Austl.	32·45 S	146·14 E
110	Newton (nû'tŭn)...........Eng.	53·27 N	2·37 W
80	Newton.....................Ill.	39·00 N	88·10 W
71	Newton.....................Iowa	41·42 N	93·04 W
73	Newton.....................Kans.	38·03 N	97·22 W
83	Newton.......Mass. (Boston In.)	42·21 N	71·13 W

Page	Name Pronunciation Region	Lat. °'	Long. °'
78	Newton . . . . Miss.	32·18 N	89·10 W
84	Newton . . . . N. J. (New York In.)	41·03 N	74·45 W
79	Newton . . . . N. C.	35·40 N	81·19 W
77	Newton . . . . Tex.	30·47 N	93·45 W
85	Newton Brook (brŏŏk) Can. (Toronto In.)	43·48 N	79·25 W
85	Newton Siding (sīd'ĭng) Can. (Winnipeg In.)	49·56 N	98·04 W
75	Newtonsville (nū'tŭnz-vĭl) Ohio (Cincinnati In.)	39·11 N	84·04 W
85	New Toronto (tō-rŏn'tō) Can. (Toronto In.)	43·37 N	79·30 W
70	Newtown (nū'toun) . . . . N. D.	47·57 N	102·25 W
75	Newtown . . . Ohio (Cincinnati In.)	39·08 N	84·22 W
84	Newtown . . . Pa. (Philadelphia In.)	40·13 N	74·56 W
116	Newtownards (nu-t'n-ardz') . . . Ire.	54·35 N	5·39 W
71	New Ulm (ŭlm) . . . . Minn.	44·18 N	94·27 W
83	New Waterford (wô'tēr-fērd) . Can.	46·14 N	60·04 W
65	New Westminster (wĕst'mĭn-stēr) Can. (Vancouver In.)	49·12 N	122·55 W
84	New York (yôrk) N. Y. (New York In.)	40·40 N	73·58 W
63	New York (State) . . . . U. S.	42·45 N	78·05 W
159	New Zealand (zē'lănd) . . . . Oceania	39·14 S	169·30 E
90	Nexapa (R.) (nĕks-ä'pä) . . . . Mex.	18·32 N	98·29 W
153	Neya-gawa (nâ'yä gä'wä) Jap. (Ōsaka In.)	34·47 N	135·38 E
144	Neyshābūr . . . . Iran	36·06 N	58·45 E
136	Neyva R. (nēy'vȧ) Sov. Un. (Urals In.)	57·39 N	60·37 E
129	Nezhin (nyĕzh'ēn) . . . . Sov. Un.	50·03 N	31·52 E
66	Nez Perce (nĕz' pûrs') . . . . Idaho	46·16 N	116·15 W
166	Ngami (R.) (n'gä'mē) . . . . Bech.	20·56 S	22·31 E
142	Nganglaring Tsho (L.) . . . . China	31·42 N	82·53 E
165	Ngaoundéré (n'gōn-dā-rā') . . Cam.	7·19 N	13·30 E
167	Ngong ('n-gông) . . . . Ken.	1·27 S	36·39 E
167	Ngqeleni ('ng-kĕ-lā'nē) S. Afr. (Natal In.)	31·41 S	29·04 E
165	Nguigmi ('n-gēg'mē) . . . . Niger	14·14 N	13·04 E
164	Nguru ('n-gōō'rōō) . . . . Nig.	12·53 N	10·26 E
154	Nha Trang (nyä-träng') . . . . Viet.	12·08 N	108·56 E
164	Naifounke . . . . Mali	16·03 N	4·17 W
71	Niagara (nī-ăg'ȧ-rȧ) . . . . Wis.	45·45 N	88·05 W
75	Niagara Falls . . Can. (Buffalo In.)	43·05 N	79·05 W
75	Niagara Falls . . N. Y. (Buffalo In.)	43·06 N	79·02 W
85	Niagara-on-the-Lake Can. (Toronto In.)	43·16 N	79·05 W
75	Niagara R. U. S.-Can. (Buffalo In.)	43·12 N	79·03 W
164	Niamey (nē-ä-mā') . . . . Niger	13·33 N	2·08 E
165	Niangara (nē-äŋ-gà'rà) . . . . Con. L.	3·36 N	28·00 E
73	Niangua (R.) (nī-ăŋ'gwȧ) . . . . Mo.	37·45 N	92·56 W
154	Nias (I.) (nē'äs') . . . . Indon.	0·58 N	97·43 E
118	Nibe (nē'bĕ) . . . . Den.	56·57 N	9·36 E
88	Nicaragua (nĭk-ȧ-rä'gwȧ) . . . N. A.	12·45 N	86·15 W
92	Nicaragua, Lago de (L.) (lä'gō dĕ) Nic.	11·45 N	85·28 W
126	Nicastro (nê-käs'trō) . . . . It.	38·39 N	16·15 E
92	Nicchehabin, Punta (Pt.) (pōō'n-tä-nĕk-chĕ-ä-bē'n) Mex. (Yucatan In.)	19·50 N	87·20 W
123	Nice (nēs) . . . . Fr.	43·42 N	7·21 E
149	Nich'engchen China (Shanghai In.)	30·54 N	121·48 E
87	Nichicun (L.) (nĭch'ĭ-kŭn) . . . Can.	53·07 N	72·10 W
94	Nicholas Chan. (nĭk'ô-lȧs) . Ba. Is.	23·30 N	80·20 W
80	Nicholasville (nĭk'ô-lȧs-vĭl) . . . Ky.	37·55 N	84·35 W
154	Nicobar Is. (nĭk-ô-bär') . . . . India	8·28 N	94·04 E
65	Nicolai Mtn. (nē-cō lī') Ore. (Portland In.)	46·05 N	123·27 W
91	Nicolás Romero (nē-kô-lá's-rô-mĕ'rô) Mex. (Mexico City In.)	19·38 N	99·20 W
74	Nicolet, L. (nĭ'kŏ-lĕt) Mich. (Sault Ste. Marie In.)	46·22 N	84·14 W
94	Nicolls Town . . . . Ba. Is.	25·10 N	78·00 W
74	Nicols (nĭk'ĕls) Minn. (Minneapolis, St. Paul In.)	44·50 N	93·12 W
65	Nicomeki (R.) Can. (Vancouver In.)	49·04 N	122·47 W
115	Nicosia (nē-kô-sē'ȧ) . . . . Cyprus	35·10 N	33·22 E
92	Nicoya (nē-kō'yä) . . . . C. R.	10·08 N	85·27 W
92	Nicoya, Golfo de (G.) (gôl-fô-dĕ) . C. R.	10·03 N	85·04 W
92	Nicoya, Pen. de . . . . C. R.	10·05 N	86·00 W
	Nidaros, see Trondheim		
121	Nidzica (nê-jĕt'sȧ) . . . . Pol.	53·21 N	20·30 E
120	Niedere Tauern (Mts.) . . . . Aus.	47·15 N	13·41 E
123	Niederkrüchten (nē'dĕr-krük-tĕn) Ger. (Ruhr In.)	51·12 N	6·14 E
111	Niederösterreich (Lower Austria) (State) . Aus. (Vienna In.)	48·24 N	16·20 E
120	Niedersachsen (Lower Saxony) (State) (nē'dĕr-zäĸ-sĕn) . Ger.	52·52 N	8·27 E
120	Nienburg (nē'ĕn-bōōrgh) . . . . Ger.	52·40 N	9·15 E
120	Niesse (R.) (nēs) . . . . Pol.	51·30 N	15·00 E
168	Nietverdiend . . . . S. Afr. (Johannesburg & Pretoria In.)	25·02 S	26·10 E
99	Nieuw Nickerie (nē-nē'kĕ-rē') Sur.	5·51 N	57·00 W
90	Nieves (nyā'vås) . . . . Mex.	24·00 N	102·57 W
133	Niğde (nĭg'dĕ) . . . . Tur.	37·55 N	34·40 E
168	Nigel (nī'jĕl) . . . . S. Afr. (Johannesburg & Pretoria In.)	26·26 S	28·27 E
163	Niger (nī'jēr) . . . . Afr.	18·02 N	8·30 E
164	Niger R. . . . . Afr.	8·22 N	6·11 E
163	Nigeria (nī-jē'rĭ-ȧ) . . . . Afr.	8·57 N	6·30 E
153	Nii (I.) (nē) . . . . Jap.	34·26 N	139·23 E
152	Niigata (nē'ê-gä'tȧ) . . . . Jap.	37·47 N	139·04 E
157	Niihau (nē'ê-hä'ōō) . . Hawaii (In.)	21·50 N	160·05 W
157	Niihau (I.) . . . . Hawaii (In.)	21·50 N	160·05 W
153	Niimi (nē'mē) . . . . Jap.	34·59 N	133·28 E
117	Nijmegen (nī'mā-gĕn) . . . . Neth.	51·50 N	5·52 E
153	Nikaidō (nē'ki-dô) Jap. (Osaka In.)	34·36 N	135·48 E
128	Nikitinka (nê-kĭ'tĭn-kȧ) . Sov. Un.	55·33 N	33·19 E
153	Nikkō (nēk'kō) . . . . Jap.	36·44 N	139·35 E
129	Nikolayev (nē-kô-lä'yĕf) . Sov. Un.	46·58 N	32·02 E
129	Nikolayev (Oblast) (ôb'lȧst) Sov. Un.	47·27 N	31·25 E
152	Nikolayevka . . . . Sov. Un.	48·37 N	134·49 E
136	Nikolayevka (nē-kô-lä'yĕf-kȧ) Sov. Un. (Leningrad In.)	59·29 N	29·48 E
133	Nikolayevskiy . . . . Sov. Un.	50·00 N	45·30 E
135	Nikolayevsk-na-Amure . . Sov. Un.	53·18 N	140·49 E
132	Nikol'sk (nê-kôlsk') . . . . Sov. Un.	59 30 N	45·40 E
136	Nikol'skoye (nê-kôl'skô-yĕ) Sov. Un. (Leningrad In.)	59·27 N	30·00 E
127	Nikopol (nē'kô-pŏl') . . . . Bul.	43·41 N	24·52 E
129	Nikopol' . . . . Sov. Un.	47·36 N	34·24 E
127	Nikšić (nēk'shêch) . . . . Yugo.	42·45 N	18·57 E
101	Nilahue (R.) (nē-lä'wĕ) Chile (Santiago In.)	36·36 S	71·50 W
163	Nile (R.) (nīl) . . . . Afr.	23·00 N	33·00 E
80	Niles (nīlz) . . . . Mich.	41·50 N	86·15 W
80	Niles . . . . Ohio	41·15 N	80·45 W
143	Nilgiri Hills . . . . India	17·05 N	76·22 E
100	Nilópolis (nē-lô'pō-lēs) . Braz. (In.)	22·48 S	43·25 W
142	Nimach . . . . India	24·32 N	74·51 E
164	Nimba, Mt. (nĭm'bȧ) . Ivory Coast	7·40 N	8·33 W
122	Nîmes (nēm) . . . . Fr.	43·49 N	4·22 E
73	Nimrod Res. (nĭm'rŏd) . . . . Ark.	34·58 N	93·46 W
165	Nimule (nê-mōō'lā) . . . . Sud.	3·38 N	32·12 E
160	Ninety Mile Bch . . . . Austl.	38·20 S	147·30 E
133	Nineveh (Ruins) (nĭn'ê-vȧ) . . . Iraq	36·30 N	43·10 E
150	Ningan (nĭŋ'gän') . . . . China	44·20 N	129·20 E
148	Ningchin (nĭng'jĭn) . . . . China	37·39 N	116·47 E
148	Ningching (nĭng'jĭn) . . . . China	37·37 N	114·55 E
146	Ningerh . . . . China	23·14 N	101·14 E
151	Ninghai (nĭng'hī') . . . . China	29·20 N	121·20 E
148	Ningho (nĭng'hō') . . . . China	39·27 N	117·44 E
	Ninghsia, see Yinch'uan		
146	Ninghsia Hui Aut. Reg. . . . . China	37·45 N	106·30 E
151	Ningming . . . . China	22·22 N	107·06 E
155	Ningo Is. . . . . N. Gui. Ter.	1·15 S	143·30 E
151	Ningpo (nĭng-pō') . . . . China	29·56 N	121·30 E
151	Ningte . . . . China	26·38 N	119·33 E
150	Ningwu (nĭng'wōō') . . . . China	39·00 N	112·12 E
148	Ningyang (nĭng'yäng') . . . . China	35·46 N	116·48 E
151	Ninh Binh (nēn bēnk') . . . . Viet.	20·22 N	106·00 E
72	Ninnescah (R.) (nĭn'ĕs-kä) . Kans.	37·37 N	98·31 W
99	Nioaque (nēô-ä'-kĕ) . . . . Braz.	21·14 S	55·41 W
70	Niobrara (R.) (nī-ô-brâr'ȧ) . . Nebr.	42·46 N	98·46 W
164	Nioro (nê-ō'rō) . . . . Mali	15·16 N	9·22 W
122	Niort (nê-ôr') . . . . Fr.	46·17 N	0·28 W
86	Nipawin . . . . Can.	53·24 N	103·52 W
95	Nipe, Bahía de (B.) (bä-ē'ä-dĕ-nē'pā) . Cuba	20·50 N	75·30 W
95	Nipe, Sierra de (Mts.) (sē-ĕ'r-rä-dĕ) . Cuba	20·20 N	75·50 W
87	Nipigon (nĭp'ĭ-gŏn) . . . . Can.	48·58 N	88·17 W
87	Nipigon (L.) . . . . Can.	49·37 N	89·55 W
71	Nipigon B . . . . Can.	48·56 N	88·00 W
82	Nipisiguit (R.) (nĭ-pĭ'sĭ-kwĭt) . Can.	47·26 N	66·15 W
87	Nipissing (L.) (nĭp'ĭ-sĭng) . . . . Can.	45·59 N	80·19 W
94	Niquero (nē-kā'rō) . . . . Cuba	20·00 N	77·35 W
142	Nirmāli . . . . India	26·30 N	86·43 E
127	Niš (nēsh) . . . . Yugo.	43·18 N	21·55 E
124	Nisa (nē'sȧ) . . . . Port.	39·32 N	7·41 W
127	Nišava (R.) (nē'shȧ-vȧ) . . . . Yugo.	43·17 N	22·17 E
153	Nishino (I.) (nēsh'ê-nô) . . . . Jap.	36·06 N	132·49 E
153	Nishinomiya (nēsh'ê-nô-mē'yȧ) Jap. (Ōsaka In.)	34·44 N	135·21 E
153	Nishinoomote (nēsh'ê-nô-ô-mō'tô) Jap.	30·44 N	130·59 E
153	Nishio (nēsh'ê-ô) . . . . Jap.	34·50 N	137·01 E
121	Nisko (nēs'kô) . . . . Pol.	50·30 N	22·07 E
85	Nisku (nĭs-kū') Can. (Edmonton In.)	53·21 N	113·33 W
66	Nisqually R. (nĭs-kwôl'ĭ) . . . Wash.	46·51 N	122·33 W
118	Nissan (R.) . . . . Swe.	57·06 N	13·22 E
118	Nisser Vand (L.) (nĭs'ĕr vän) . Nor.	59·14 N	8·35 E
118	Nissum Fd . . . . Den.	56·24 N	7·35 E
100	Niterói (nē-tĕ-rō'ĭ) . . . . Braz. (In.)	22·53 S	43·07 W
116	Nith (R.) (nĭth) . . . . Scot.	55·13 N	3·55 W
121	Nitra (nē'trȧ) . . . . Czech.	48·18 N	18·04 E
121	Nitra R . . . . Czech.	48·13 N	18·14 E
80	Nitro (nī'trō) . . . . W. Va.	38·25 N	81·50 W
117	Nivelles (nē'vĕl') . . . . Bel.	50·33 N	4·17 E
122	Nivernais, Côtes de (hills) (nē-vĕr-nĕ') . Fr.	47·40 N	3·09 E
77	Nixon (nĭk'sŭn) . . . . Tex.	29·16 N	97·48 W
135	Nizhne-Angarsk (nyēzh'nyĭ-ŭngärsk') . Sov. Un.	55·49 N	108·46 E
133	Nizhne-Chirskaya (nyĭ-ŭn-gärsk') Sov. Un.	48·20 N	42·50 E
135	Nizhne-Kolymsk (kô-lêmsk') Sov. Un.	68·32 N	160·56 E
134	Nizhneudinsk (nêzh'nyĭ-ōōdēnsk') Sov. Un.	54·58 N	99·15 E
136	Nizhniye Sergi (nyēzh'[nyē] sĕr'gē) Sov. Un. (Urals In.)	56·41 N	59·19 E
129	Nizhniye Serogozy (nyēzh'nyĭ sĕ-rô-gô'zĭ) . Sov. Un.	46·51 N	34·25 E
136	Nizhniy Tagil (tŭgēl') Sov. Un. (Urals In.)	57·54 N	59·59 E
136	Nizhnyaya Kur'ya (nyĕ'zhnyȧ-yȧ koor'yȧ) Sov. Un. (Urals In.)	58·01 N	56·00 E
136	Nizhnyaya Salda (nyĕ'zh[nya'ya] säl'da') Sov. Un. (Urals In.)	58·05 N	60·43 E
134	Nizhnyaya Taymyra (R.) . Sov. Un.	72·30 N	95·18 E
134	Nizhnyaya (Lower) Tunguska (R.) (tōōn-gōōs'kä) . Sov. Un.	64·13 N	91·30 E
136	Nishnyaya Tura (tōō'rȧ) Sov. Un. (Urals In.)	58·38 N	59·50 E
136	Nizhnyaya Us'va (ōōs'vȧ) Sov. Un. (Urals In.)	59·05 N	58·53 E
118	Njurunda (nyōō-rōōn'dȧ) . . . . Swe.	62·15 N	17·24 E
167	Nkandla ('n-känd'lä) S. Afr. (Natal In.)	28·40 S	31·06 E
142	Noākhāli . . . . E. Pak.	22·52 N	91·08 E
64	Noatak (nô-ȧ'tȧk) . . . . Alaska	67·22 N	163·28 W
64	Noatak (R.) . . . . Alaska	67·58 N	162·15 W
153	Nobeoka (nō-bā-ō'kȧ) . . . . Jap.	32·36 N	131·41 E
80	Noblesville (nō'bl'z-vĭl) . . . . Ind.	40·00 N	86·00 W
85	Nobleton (nō'bl'tŭn) Can. (Toronto In.)	43·54 N	79·39 W
125	Nocero Inferiore (nô-chĕ'rô-ēn-fĕ-ryô'rĕ) It. (Naples In.)	40·30 N	14·38 E
90	Nochistlán (nô-chēs-tlän') . . . Mex.	21·23 N	102·52 W
91	Nochixtlan (Asunción) (ä-sōōn-syōn') . Mex.	17·28 N	97·12 W
155	Noemfoor (I.) (nōōm'fōr) . W. Irian	1·20 S	134·48 E
69	Nogales (nô-gä'lĕs) . . . . Ariz.	31·20 N	110·55 W
91	Nogales (nô-gä'lĕs) . . . . Mex.	18·49 N	97·09 W
88	Nogales . . . . Mex.	31·15 N	111·00 W
168	Nogal Val. (nô'gȧl) Som. (Horn of Afr. In.)	8·30 N	47·50 E
129	Nogaysk (nô-gīsk') . . . . Sov. Un.	46·43 N	36·21 E
123	Nogent-le-Roi (nŏ-zhôɴ-lĕ-rwä') Fr. (Paris In.)	48·39 N	1·32 E
122	Nogent-le-Rotrou (rō-trōō') . . . Fr.	48·22 N	0·47 E
136	Noginsk (nô-gēnsk') Sov. Un. (Moscow In.)	55·52 N	38·28 E
124	Nogueira (nô-gā'rä) . . . . Sp.	42·25 N	7.43 W
125	Nogueira Pallaresa (R.) (nô-gĕ'y-rä-päl-yä-rĕ-sä) . Sp.	42·18 N	1·03 E
150	Noho (nô'hô') . . . . China	48·23 N	124·58 E
122	Noires, Mts. (nwär) . . . . Fr.	48·07 N	3·42 W
122	Noirmoutier, Île de (I.) (nwȧr-mōō-tyā') . Fr.	47·03 N	3·08 W
153	Nojimā-Zaki (Pt.) (nō'jê-mä zä-kê) . Jap.	34·54 N	139·48 E
86	Nokomis (nô-kō'mĭs) . . . . Can.	51·30 N	104·58 W
80	Nokomis . . . . Ill.	39·15 N	89·10 W
125	Nola (nô'lä) . . . . It. (Naples In.)	40·41 N	14·32 E
79	Nolichucky (nŏl-ĭ-chŭck'ĭ) . . N. C.	39·59 N	82·20 W
132	Nolinsk (nô-lênsk') . . . . Sov. Un.	57·32 N	49·50 E
153	Noma Misaki (C.) (nô'mä mê'sä-kē) . Jap.	31·25 N	130·09 E
90	Nombre de Dios (nôm-brĕ-dĕ-dyô's) . Mex.	23·50 N	104·14 W
93	Nombre de Dios (nô'm-brĕ) . . Pan.	9·34 N	79·28 W
64	Nome (nōm) . . . . Alaska	64·30 N	165·20 W
86	Nonacho (L.) . . . . Can.	61·48 N	111·20 W
166	Nongoma (nŏn-gō'mȧ) . . . . S. Afr.	27·48 S	31·45 E
65	Nooksack (nŏŏk'săk) Wash. (Vancouver In.)	48·55 N	122·19 W
65	Nooksack (R.) Wash. (Vancouver In.)	48·54 N	122·31 W
111	Noorden . . Neth. (Amsterdam In.)	52·09 N	4·49 E
111	Noordwijkaan Zee Neth. (Amsterdam In.)	52·14 N	4·25 E
111	Noordzee, Kanal, (Can.) Neth. (Amsterdam In.)	52·27 N	4·42 E
86	Nootka (I.) (nōōt'kȧ) . . . . Can.	49·38 N	127·38 W
166	Noqui (nô-kē') . . . . Ang.	5·50 S	13·35 E
152	Nor (R.) (nou') . . . . China	46·55 N	132·45 E
75	Nora (nō'rä) Ind. (Indianapolis In.)	39·54 N	86.08 W
118	Nora . . . . Swe.	59·32 N	14·56 E
73	Norborne (nôr'bôrn) . . . . Mo.	39·17 N	93·39 W
74	Norco (nôr'kô) Calif. (Los Angeles In.)	33·57 N	117·33 W
84	Norcross (nôr'krôs) Ga. (Atlanta In.)	33·56 N	84·13 W
85	Nord, Riviere du (rēv-yĕr' dü nôr) Can. (Montreal In.)	45·45 N	74·02 W
120	Norden (nôr'dĕn) . . . . Ger.	53·35 N	7·14 E
120	Norderney I. (nōr'dĕr-nēy) . . . Ger.	53·45 N	6·58 E
118	Nord Fd. (nôr'fyôr) . . . . Nor.	61·50 N	5·35 E
120	Nordhausen (nôrt'hau-zĕn) . . . Ger.	51·30 N	10·48 E
120	Nordhorn (nôrt'hôrn) . . . . Ger.	52·26 N	7·05 E
112	Nord Kapp (C.) (nôr-kapp) . . Nor.	71·07 N	25·57 E
65	Nordland (nôrd'lȧnd) Wash. (Seattle In.)	48·03 N	122·41 W
120	Nördlingen (nûrt'lĭng-ĕn) . . . . Ger.	48·51 N	10·30 E
120	Nord-Ostsee (Kiel) Can. (nōrd-ōzt-zā) (kēl) . Ger.	54·03 N	9·23 E
120	Nordrhein-Westfalen (North Rhine-Westphalia) (State) (nōrd'hīn-vĕst-fä-lĕn) . Ger.	50·50 N	6.53 E
135	Nordvik (nôrd'vĕk) . . . . Sov. Un.	73·57 N	111·15 E
116	Nore R. (nōr) . . . . Ire.	52·34 N	7·15 W
78	Norfield (nôr'fēld) . . . . Miss.	31·24 N	90·25 W
83	Norfolk (nôr'fŏk) Mass. (Boston In.)	42·07 N	71·19 W
70	Norfolk . . . . Nebr.	42·10 N	97·25 W
84	Norfolk . . . . Va. (Norfolk In.)	36·55 N	76·15 W
73	Norfork, L. . . . . Ark.	36·25 N	92·09 W
90	Noria (nō'rē-ȧ) . . . . Mex.	23·04 N	106·20 W
134	Noril'sk (nô rēlsk') . . . . Sov. Un.	69·00 N	87·11 E
80	Normal (nôr'mȧl) . . . . Ill.	40·35 N	89·00 W
73	Norman (nôr'mȧn) . . . . Okla.	35·13 N	97·25 W
79	Norman, L. . . . . N. C.	35·30 N	80·53 W
159	Norman (R.) . . . . Austl.	18·27 S	141·29 E
122	Normandie (Reg.) (nŏr-mäɴ-dē') Fr.	49·02 N	0·17 E
122	Normandie, Collines de (Hills) (kô-lēn'dĕ-nŏr-män-dē') . Fr.	48·35 N	0·30 W
159	Normanton (nôr'mȧn-tŭn) . . Austl.	17·45 S	141·10 E
110	Normanton . . . . Eng.	53·40 N	1·21 W
75	Normantown (nôr'mȧn toun) Ill. (Chicago In.)	41·39 N	88·14 W
86	Norman Wells . . . . Can.	65·26 N	127·00 W
158	Nornalup (nôr-năl'ŭp) . . . . Austl.	35·00 S	117·00 E
118	Norra Dellen (L.) . . . . Swe.	61·57 N	16·25 E
118	Norre Sundby (nû-rĕ-sōōn'bü) Den.	57·04 N	9·55 E
78	Norris (nŏr'ĭs) . . . . Tenn.	36·09 N	84·05 W
78	Norris (R.) . . . . Tenn.	36·17 N	84·10 W
84	Norristown (nŏr'ĭs-town) Pa. (Philadelphia In.)	40·07 N	75·21 W
118	Norrköping (nôr'chûp'ĭng) . . . Swe.	58·37 N	16·10 E
118	Norrtälje (nôr-tĕl'yĕ) . . . . Swe.	59·47 N	18·39 E

ng-sing; ŋ-baŋk; ɴ-nasalized n; nŏd; cŏmmit; ōld; ôbey; ôrder; fōōd; fŏŏt; ou-out; s-soft; sh-dish; th-thin; pūre; ûnite; ûrn; stŭd; circŭs; ü-as "y" in study; '-indeterminate vowel.

Page	Name Pronunciation Region	Lat. °′	Long. °′
158	Norseman (nôrs'măn) ...... Austl.	32·15 S	122·00 E
101	Norte, Punta (Pt.) (pōō'n-tä-nŏr'tĕ) Arg. (Buenos Aires In.)	36·17 S	56·46 W
99	Norte, Serra do (Mts.) (sĕ'r-rä-dô-nôr'te) . Braz.	12·04 S	59·08 W
83	North, C. .... Can.	47·05 N	60·15 W
159	North, C. .... N. Z. (In.)	34·31 S	173·02 E
68	North, I. ... Calif. (San Diego In.)	32·39 N	117·14 W
159	North, I. .... N. Z. (In.)	37·34 S	171·12 E
81	North Adams (ăd'ămz) ..... Mass.	42·40 N	73·05 W
158	Northam (nôr-dhăm) ...... Austl.	31·50 S	116·45 E
168	Northam (nôr'thăm) ...... S. Afr. (Johannesburg & Pretoria In.)	24·52 S	27·16 E
6	North America (à-mĕr'ĭ-kà)		
89	North American Basin (à-mĕr'ĭ-kǎn) . Atl. O.	23·45 N	62·45 W
158	Northampton (nôr-thămp'tŭn) Austl.	28·22 S	114·45 E
116	Northampton (nôrth-ămp'tŭn) Eng.	52·14 N	0·56 W
81	Northampton .... Pa.	40·45 N	75·30 W
110	Northampton (Co.) .... Eng.	52·25 N	0·47 W
154	North Andaman I. (ăn-dǎ-măn') Andaman Is.	13·15 N	93·30 E
83	North Andover (ăn'dô-vēr) Mass. (Boston In.)	42·42 N	71·07 W
65	North Arm (ärm) Can. (Vancouver In.)	49·13 N	123·01 W
84	North Atlanta (ăt-lăn'tǎ) Ga. (Atlanta In.)	33·52 N	84·20 W
84	North Attleboro (ăt''l-bŭr-ô) Mass. (Providence In.)	41·59 N	71·18 W
80	North Baltimore (bôl'tĭ-môr) . Ohio	41·10 N	83·40 W
76	North Basque (băsk) .... Tex.	31·56 N	98·01 W
86	North Battleford (băt''l-fērd) . Can.	52·52 N	108·22 W
87	North Bay .... Can.	46·13 N	79·26 W
66	North Bend (bĕnd) .... Ore.	43·23 N	124·13 W
82	North Berwick (bûr'wĭk) ... Maine	43·18 N	70·46 W
94	North Bght. (bĭt) .... Ba. Is.	24·30 N	77·40 W
94	North Bimini (I.) (bĭ'mĭ-nê) Ba. Is.	25·45 N	79·20 W
	North Borneo, see Sabah		
83	Northboro (nôrth'bŭr-ô) Mass. (Boston In.)	42·19 N	71·39 W
83	Northbridge (nôrth'brĭj) Mass. (Boston In.)	42·09 N	71·39 W
95	North Caicos (I.) (kī'kōs) . Turks & Caicos	21·55 N	72·00 W
72	North Canadian R. (cá nā'dĭ-ǎn) Okla.	36·22 N	99·17 W
63	North Carolina (State) (kăr-ô-lī'nǎ) . U. S.	35·40 N	81·30 W
94	North Cat Cay (I.) .... Ba. Is.	25·35 N	79·20 W
80	North Channel (B.) (chăn'ĕl) . Can.	46·10 N	83·20 W
116	North Chan .... N. Ire.-Scot.	55·15 N	7·56 W
79	North Charleston (chärlz'tŭn) S. C.	32·49 N	79·57 W
75	North Chicago (shĭ-kô'gō) Ill. (Chicago In.)	42·19 N	87·51 W
75	North College Hill (kŏl'ĕj hĭl) Ohio (Cincinnati In.)	39·13 N	84·33 W
76	North Concho (kŏn'chō) ..... Tex.	31·40 N	100·48 W
85	North Cooking Lake (kŏŏk'ĭng lāk) Can. (Edmonton In.)	53·28 N	112·57 W
62	North Dakota (State) (dǎ-kō'tǎ) U. S.	47·20 N	101·55 W
116	North Downs (dounz) .... Eng.	51·11 N	0·01 W
64	Northeast C. (nôrth-ēst) ... Alaska	63·15 N	169·04 W
146	Northeast Frontier Agency (State) India	27·35 N	92·56 E
95	Northeast Pt. .... Ba. Is.	21·25 N	73·00 W
95	Northeast Pt. .... Ba. Is.	22·45 N	73·50 W
94	Northeast Providence Chan. (prŏv'ĭ-dĕns) . Ba. Is.	25·45 N	77·00 W
120	Northeim (nôrt'hīm) .... Ger.	51·42 N	9·59 E
94	North Elbow Cays (Is.) ... Ba. Is.	23·55 N	80·30 W
	Northern Dvina, see Severnaya Dvina		
102	Northern Ireland (ĭr'lǎnd) .. U. K.	54·56 N	8·58 W
	Northern Land (Is.), see Severnaya Zemlya		
71	Northern Light (L.) (nôr'thērn līt) . Can.	46·16 N	90·25 W
164	Northern Region (Div.) ...... Nig.	10·54 N	6·37 E
166	Northern Rhodesia (rô-dē'zhĭ-ǎ) Afr.	14·23 S	24·15 E
158	Northern Territory (State) . Austl.	18·15 S	133·00 E
71	Northfield (nôrth'fēld) ..... Minn.	44·28 N	93·11 W
82	Northfield .... Vt.	44·10 N	72·39 W
160	North Flinders, Ra. (flĭn'dērz) Austl.	31·55 S	138·45 E
117	North Foreland (fōr'lǎnd) ... Eng.	51·20 N	1·30 E
76	North Franklin Mt. (frăŋ'klĭn) Tex.	31·55 N	106·30 W
118	North Frisian Is. .... Den.	55·16 N	8·15 E
88	North Gamboa (gäm-bô'ä) C. Z. (Panama Canal In.)	9·07 N	79·40 W
85	North Gower (gŏw'ēr) Can. (Ottawa In.)	45·08 N	75·43 W
81	Northampton .... Mass.	42·20 N	72·45 W
74	North Hollywood (hŏl'ê-wŏŏd) Calif. (Los Angeles In.)	34·10 N	118·23 W
80	North Judson (jŭd'sŭn) ...... Ind.	41·15 N	86·50 W
74	North Kansas City (kăn'zǎs) Mo. (Kansas City In.)	39·08 N	94·34 W
73	North Little Rock (lĭt''l rŏk) . Ark.	34·46 N	92·13 W
70	North Loup (R.) (lōōp) ..... Nebr.	42·05 N	100·10 W
80	North Manchester (măn'chĕs-tēr) Ind.	41·00 N	85·45 W
74	Northmoor (nôrth'mōōr) Mo. (Kansas City In.)	39·10 N	94·37 W
74	North Ogden (ŏg'dĕn) Utah (Salt Lake City In.)	41·18 N	111·58 W
74	North Ogden Pk. Utah (Salt Lake City In.)	41·23 N	111·59 W
75	North Olmsted (ōlm-stĕd) Ohio (Cleveland In.)	41·25 N	81·55 W
72	North Pease (R.) (pēz) .... Tex.	34·19 N	100·58 W
65	North Pender (I.) (pĕn'dēr) Can. (Vancouver In.)	48·48 N	123·16 W
65	North Plains (plānz) Ore. (Portland In.)	45·36 N	123·00 W
70	North Platte (plăt) .... Nebr.	41·08 N	100·45 W
62	North Platte, (R.) .... U. S.	41·20 N	102·40 W
80	North Pt. .... Mich.	45·00 N	83·20 W
93	North Pt. Barb. (Le. & Wind. Is. In.)	13·22 N	59·36 W
78	Northport (nôrth'pōrt) ...... Ala.	33·12 N	87·35 W
84	Northport .. N. Y. (New York In.)	40·53 N	73·20 W
66	Northport .... Wash.	48·53 N	117·47 W
83	North Reading (rĕd'ĭng) Mass. (Boston In.)	42·34 N	71·04 W
	North Rhine-Westphalia, see Nordrhein-Westfalen		
74	Northridge (nôrth'ridj) Calif. (Los Angeles In.)	34·14 N	118·32 W
75	North Ridgeville (rĭj-vĭl) Ohio (Cleveland In.)	41·23 N	82·01 W
75	North Royalton (roi'ǎl-tŭn) Ohio (Cleveland In.)	41·19 N	81·44 W
74	North St. Paul (sânt pôl') .. Minn. (Minneapolis, St. Paul In.)	45·01 N	92·59 W
74	North Salt Lake (sôlt lāk) Utah (Salt Lake City In.)	40·50 N	111·55 W
86	North Saskatchewan (R.) (săs-kăch'ê-wän) . Can.	53·54 N	112·37 W
112	North Sea .... Eur.	56·09 N	3·16 E
71	North Skunk (R.) (skŭnk) ... Iowa	41·39 N	92·46 W
83	North Sydney (sĭd'nê) .... Can.	46·14 N	60·28 W
159	North Taranaki Bght. (tä-rä-nä'kĭ bĭt) . N. Z. (In.)	38·23 S	172·03 E
84	North Tarrytown (tăr'ĭ-toun) N. Y. (New York In.)	41·05 N	73·52 W
84	North Tiverton (tĭv'ēr-tŭn) R. I. (Providence In.)	41·40 N	71·08 W
75	North Tonawanda (tŏn-ǎ-wŏn'dä) N. Y. (Buffalo In.)	43·02 N	78·53 W
69	North Truchas Pks. (Mts.) (trōō'chäs) . N. Mex.	35·58 N	105·37 W
116	North Uist (I.) (ū'ĭst) .... Scot.	56·99 N	6·56 W
82	Northumberland Str. (nôr thŭm'bēr-lǎnd) . Can.	46·25 N	64·20 W
81	Northumberland .... N. H.	44·30 N	71·30 W
159	Northumberland, Is. .... Austl.	21·42 S	151·30 E
66	North Umpqua R. (ŭmp'kwà) Ore.	43·20 N	122·50 W
65	North Vancouver (văn-kōō'vēr) Can. (Vancouver In.)	49·19 N	123·05 W
80	North Vernon (vûr'nŭn) ..... Ind.	39·05 N	85·45 W
75	Northville (nôrth-vĭl) Mich. (Detroit In.)	42·26 N	83·28 W
84	North Wales (wālz) Pa. (Philadelphia In.)	40·12 N	75·16 W
158	North West, C. (nôrth'wĕst) Austl.	21·50 S	112·25 E
79	Northwest Cape Fear, (R.) (căp fēr) . N. C.	34·34 N	79·46 W
116	Northwest Highlands .... Scot.	56·50 N	5·20 W
94	Northwest Providence Chan. (prŏv'ĭ-dĕns) . Ba. Is.	26·15 N	78·45 W
86	Northwest Territories (tĕr'ĭ-tō'rĭs) . Can.	64·42 N	119·09 W
117	Northwich (nôrth'wĭch) ..... Eng.	53·15 N	2·31 W
79	North Wilkesboro (wĭlks'bûrô) N. C.	36·08 N	81·10 W
71	Northwood (nôrth'wŏŏd) .... Iowa	43·26 N	93·13 W
70	Northwood .... N. D.	47·44 N	97·36 W
67	North Wood Cr. .... Wyo.	44·02 N	107·37 W
65	North Yamhill (R.) (yăm' hĭl) Ore. (Portland In.)	45·22 N	123·21 W
116	North York Moors (yôrk mŏŏrz') Eng.	54·20 N	0·40 W
72	Norton (nôr'tŭn) .... Kans.	39·40 N	99·54 W
84	Norton .... Mass. (Providence In.)	41·58 N	71·08 W
79	Norton .... Va.	36·54 N	82·36 W
64	Norton B. .... Alaska	64·22 N	162·18 W
84	Norton Res. Mass. (Providence In.)	42·01 N	71·07 W
64	Norton Sd. .... Alaska	63·48 N	164·50 W
85	Norval (nôr'vǎl) Can. (Toronto In.)	43·39 N	79·52 W
74	Norwalk (nôr'wôk) Calif. (Los Angeles In.)	33·54 N	118·05 W
84	Norwalk ... Conn. (New York In.)	41·06 N	73·25 W
80	Norwalk .... Ohio	41·15 N	82·35 W
102	Norway (nôr'wā) .... Eur.	63·48 N	11·17 E
82	Norway .... Maine	44·11 N	70·35 W
71	Norway .... Mich.	45·47 N	87·55 W
86	Norway House .... Can.	54·00 N	97·54 W
112	Norwegian Sea (nôr-wē'jǎn) . Eur.	66·54 N	1·43 E
83	Norwell (nôr'wĕl) Mass. (Boston In.)	42·10 N	70·47 W
81	Norwich (nôr'wĭch) .... Conn.	41·20 N	72·00 W
117	Norwich .... Eng.	52·40 N	1·15 E
81	Norwich .... N. Y.	42·35 N	75·30 W
83	Norwood (nôr'wŏŏd) Mass. (Boston In.)	42·11 N	71·13 W
79	Norwood .... N. C.	35·15 N	80·08 W
75	Norwood .... Ohio (Cincinnati In.)	39·10 N	84·27 W
85	Nose Cr. (nōz) . Can. (Calgary In.)	51·09 N	114·02 W
152	Noshiro (nō'shê-rô) .... Jap.	40·09 N	140·02 E
129	Nosovka (nô'sôf-kǎ) .... Sov. Un.	50·54 N	31·35 E
167	Nossi Bé (I.) (nōō'sē bā) Malag. Rep.	13·14 S	47·28 E
166	Nossob (R.) (nô'sŏb) ... S. W. Afr.	24·15 S	19·10 E
120	Noteć R. (nô'tĕch) .... Pol.	52·50 N	16·19 E
113	Noto (nô'tô) .... It.	36·49 N	15·08 E
118	Notodden (nōt'ôd'n) .... Nor.	59·35 N	9·15 E
153	Noto-Hantō (Pen.) (nô'tō hän'tō) Jap.	37·18 N	137·03 E
83	Notre Dame B. (nō't'r dȧm') . Can.	49·48 N	55·27 W
85	Notre-Dame-des-Laurentides (dĕ-lō-räN-tēd') . Can. (Quebec In.)	46·55 N	71·20 W
82	Notre-Dame-du-Lac .... Can.	47·37 N	68·51 W
82	Notre Dame Mts. .... Can.	48·10 N	67·40 W
80	Nottawasaga B. (nŏt'ǎ-wǎ-sā'gǎ) Can.	44·45 N	80·35 W
87	Nottaway (R.) (nôt'ǎ-wā) ... Can.	50·58 N	78·02 W
110	Nottingham (nŏt'ĭng-ǎm) .... Eng.	52·58 N	1·09 W
110	Nottingham (Co.) .... Eng.	53·03 N	1·05 W
87	Nottingham I. .... Can.	62·58 N	78·53 W
167	Nottinghamweg (nŏt-ĭng-hǎm-vĕg) S. Afr. (Natal In.)	29·21 S	30·00 E
79	Nottoway, (R.) (nôt'ǎ-wā) .... Va.	36·53 N	77·47 W
164	Nouakchott .... Mauritania	18·15 N	15·56 W
159	Noumea (nōō-mā'ä) ...... N. Cal.	22·18 S	166·48 E
82	Nouvelle (nōō-vĕl') .... Can.	48·08 N	66·19 W
165	Nouvelle Anvers (äN-vår') . Con. L.	1·42 N	19·08 E
159	Nouvelle Caledonie, (Is.) . Oceania	21·28 S	164·15 E
122	Nouzonville (nōō-zôN-vēl') .... Fr.	49·51 N	4·43 E
99	Nova Cruz (nō'vǎ-krōō'z) ... Braz.	6·22 S	35·20 W
101	Nova Friburgo (frê-bōōr'gōō) Braz. (Rio de Janeiro In.)	22·18 S	42·31 W
143	Nova Goa (Panjim) .... India	15·33 N	73·52 E
100	Nova Iguaçu (nō'vä-ē-gwä-sōō') Braz. (In.)	22·45 S	43·27 W
101	Nova Lima (lē'mä) Braz. (Rio de Janeiro In.)	19·59 S	43·51 W
166	Nova Lisboa (lĕzh-bô'ǎ) ..... Ang.	12·45 S	15·45 E
126	Novara (nô-vä'rä) .... It.	45·24 N	8·38 E
101	Nova Resende Braz. (Rio de Janeiro In.)	21·12 S	46·25 W
87	Nova Scotia (Prov.) (skō'shà) Can.	44·28 N	65·00 W
127	Nova Varoš (nô'vä vä'rôsh) . Yugo.	43·24 N	19·53 E
119	Novaya Ladogo (nô'vä-yà lä-dô-gô) . Sov. Un.	60·06 N	32·16 E
136	Novaya Lyalya (lyä'lyà) Sov. Un. (Urals In.)	59·03 N	60·36 E
129	Novaya Odessa (ô-dĕs'ä) . Sov. Un.	47·18 N	31·48 E
129	Novaya Praga (prä'gà) .. Sov. Un.	48·34 N	32·54 E
135	Novaya Sibir (I.) (sê-bēr') Sov. Un.	75·42 N	150·00 E
129	Novaya Vodolaga (vô-dôl'á-gà) Sov. Un.	49·43 N	35·51 E
134	Novaya Zemlya (I.) (zĕm-lyä') Sov. Un.	72·00 N	54·46 E
127	Nova Zagora (zä'gô-rà) ...... Bul.	42·30 N	26·01 E
125	Novelda (nō-vĕl'dä) .... Sp.	38·22 N	0·46 W
121	Nové Mesto (Nad Váhom) (nô'vĕ myĕs'tô) . Czech.	48·44 N	17·47 E
121	Nové Zámky (zäm'kê) ..... Czech.	47·58 N	18·10 E
128	Novgorod (nôv'gô-rŏt) ... Sov. Un.	58·32 N	31·16 E
128	Novgorod (Oblast) ...... Sov. Un.	58·27 N	31·55 E
126	Novi (nô'vê) .... It.	44·43 N	8·48 W
75	Novi (nō'vĭ) .. Mich. (Detroit In.)	42·29 N	83·28 W
126	Novi Grad (gräd) .... Yugo.	44·09 N	15·34 E
73	Novinger (nŏv'ĭn-jēr) .... Mo.	40·14 N	92·43 W
127	Novi-Pazar (pä-zär') .... Bul.	43·22 N	27·26 E
127	Novi Pazar (pä-zär') .... Yugo.	43·08 N	20·30 E
127	Novi Sad (säd') .... Yugo.	45·15 N	19·53 E
136	Novoasbest (nô-vô-ä-bĕst') Sov. Un. (Urals In.)	57·43 N	60.14 E
129	Novoaydar (nô'vô-ī-där') Sov. Un.	48·57 N	39·01 E
129	Novocherkassk (nô'vô-chĕr-kåsk') Sov. Un.	47·25 N	40·04 E
129	Novogorod-Severskiy .... Sov. Un.	52·01 N	33·14 E
121	Novogrudok (nô-vô-grōō'dôk) Sov. Un.	53·35 N	25·51 E
103	Novo-Kazalinsk (nô-vŭ-kŭ-zǎ-lyēnsk') . Sov. Un.	45·47 N	62·00 E
134	Novokuznetsk (Stalinsk) (nō'vô-kōō'z-nyĕ'tsk) (stä'lênsk) . Sov. Un.	53·43 N	86·59 E
136	Novoladozhskiy Kanal (Can.) (nô-vô-lä'dôzh-skĭ kà-näl') Sov. Un. (Leningrad In.)	59·54 N	31·19 E
126	Novo Mesto (nôvô mās'tô) . Yugo.	45·48 N	15·13 E
129	Novomirgorod (nô'vô-mēr'gô-rôt) Sov. Un.	48·46 N	31·44 E
129	Novomoskovsk (nô'vô-môs-kôfsk') Sov. Un.	48·37 N	35·12 E
136	Novonikol'skiy (nô'vô-nyĭ-kôl'skĭ) Sov. Un. (Urals In.)	52·28 N	57·12 E
166	Novo Redondo (nô'vōō rā-dôn'dōō) . Ang.	11·15 S	13·50 E
129	Novorossiysk (nô'vô-rô-sēsk') Sov. Un.	44·43 N	37·48 E
128	Novorzhev (nô'vô-rzhêv') Sov. Un.	57·01 N	29·17 E
127	Novo-Selo (nô'vô-sĕ'lô) .... Bul.	44·09 N	22·46 E
134	Novosibirsk (nô'vô-sê-bērsk') Sov. Un.	55·09 N	82·58 E
135	Novosibirskiye O-va (New Siberian Is.) (no'vŭ-sĭ-bĭr'skĕ-ĕ) . Sov. Un.	76·45 N	140·30 E
128	Novosil' (nô'vô-sĭl) ...... Sov. Un.	52·58 N	37·03 E
128	Novosokol'niki (nô'vô-sô-kôl'nê-kê) . Sov. Un.	56·18 N	30·07 E
136	Novotatishchevskiy (nô'vô-tà-tyĭsh'chĕv-skĭ) Sov. Un. (Urals In.)	53·22 N	60·24 E
129	Novoukrainka (nô-vô-ōō'krä) Sov. Un.	48·18 N	31·33 E
133	Novouzensk (nô-vô-ōō-zĕnsk') Sov. Un.	50·40 N	48·08 E
128	Novozybkov (nô'vô-zēp'kôf) Sov. Un.	52·31 N	31·54 E
121	Novy Jičin (nô'vē yē'chēn) . Czech.	49·36 N	18·02 E
129	Novyy Bug (bōōk) ...... Sov. Un.	47·43 N	32·33 E
129	Novyy Oskol (ôs-kôl') ... Sov. Un.	50·46 N	37·53 E
134	Novyy Port (nô'vē) ...... Sov. Un.	67·19 N	72·28 E
121	Nowa Huta (nō'vä hōō'tà) ... Pol.	50·04 N	20·20 E
120	Nowa Sól (nō'vä sŭl') .... Pol.	51·49 N	15·41 E
73	Nowata (nô-wä'tǎ) .... Okla.	36·42 N	95·38 W
160	Nowra (nou'rǎ) .... Austl.	34·55 S	150·45 E

ăt; finǎl; rāte; senâte; ärm; àsk; sofǎ; fâre; ch-choose; dh-as th in other; bē; ēvent; bĕt; recĕnt; cratēr; g-go; gh-guttural g; bĭt; ĭ-short neutral; rīde; K-guttural k as ch in German ich;

Page	Name Pronunciation Region	Lat. °′	Long. °′
121	Nowy Dwór Mazowiecki (nō'vĭ dvōōr mä-zō-vyĕts'ke) Pol.	52·26 N	20·46 E
121	Nowy Sacz (nô'vê sônch') . . . . Pol.	49·36 N	20·42 E
121	Nowy Targ (tärk') . . . . Pol.	49·29 N	20·02 E
66	Noxon Res. . . . . Mont.	47·50 N	115·40 W
78	Noxubee (R.) (nŏks'ū-bē) . . . Miss.	33·20 N	88·55 W
124	Noya (nō'yä) . . . . Sp.	42·46 N	8·50 W
153	Nozaki (nō'zä-kê) Jap. (Ōsaka In.)	34·43 N	135·39 E
167	Nqamakwe ('n-gä-mä'kwȧ) S. Afr. (Natal In.)	32·13 S	27·57 E
167	Nqutu ('n-kōō'tōō) S. Afr. (Natal In.)	28·17 S	30·41 E
165	Nubian Des. (nōō'bĭ-ǎn) . . . . . Sud.	21·13 N	33·09 E
98	Nudo Coropuna (Mt.) (nōō'dô kō-rō-pōō'nä) . Peru	15·53 S	72·04 W
98	Nudo de Pasco (Mt.) (dĕ päs'kô) Peru	10·34 S	76·12 W
76	Nueces R. (nû-ā'sås) . . . . Tex.	28·20 N	98·08 W
86	Nueltin (L.) (nwĕl'tin) . . . . . . Can.	60·14 N	101·00 W
92	Nueva Armenia (nwä'vä är-mā'nê-ȧ) . Hond.	15·47 N	86·32 W
99	Nueva Esparta (State) (nwĕ'vä ĕs-pä'r-tä) . Ven. In.	10·50 N	64·35 W
94	Nueva Gerona (ĸĕ-rô'nä) . . . . Cuba	21·55 N	82·45 W
101	Nueva Palmira (päl-mē'rä) Ur. (Buenos Aires In.)	33·53 S	58·23 W
62	Nueva Rosita (nōōĕ'vä rô-sē'tä) Mex.	27·55 N	101·10 W
92	Nueva San Salvador (Santa Tecla) (sän' säl-vȧ-dōr) (sän'tä tĕ'klä) Sal.	13·41 N	89·16 W
101	Nueve de Julio (nwā'vā dā hōō'lyô) Arg. (Buenos Aires In.)	35·26 S	60·51 W
94	Nuevitas (nwā-vē'täs) . . . . . . Cuba	21·35 N	77·15 W
94	Nuevitas, Bahía de (bä-ē'ä dĕ nwā-vē'täs) . Cuba	21·30 N	77·05 W
74	Nuevo (nwā'vō) Calif. (Los Angeles In.)	33·48 N	117·09 W
76	Nuevo Laredo (lä-rā'dhō) . . . Mex.	27·29 N	99·30 W
88	Nuevo Leon (State) (lå-ōn') . Mex.	26·00 N	100·00 W
88	Nuevo San Juan (nwĕ'vô sän ĸōō-ä'n) C. Z. (Panama Canal In.)	9·14 N	79·43 W
136	Nugumanovo (nû-gû-mä'nô-vô) Sov. Un. (Urals In.)	55·28 N	61·50 E
133	Nukha (nōō'kä) . . . . Sov. Un.	41·10 N	47·10 E
64	Nulato (nōō-lä'tō) . . . . Alaska	64·40 N	158·18 W
158	Nullagine (nŭ-lă'jēn) . . . . Austl.	22·00 S	120·07 E
158	Nullarbor Plain, (Reg.) (nŭ-lär'bôr) . Austl.	31·45 S	126·30 E
111	Numansdorp Neth. (Amsterdam In.)	51·43 N	4·25 E
153	Numazu (nōō'mä-zōō) . . . . Jap.	35·06 N	138·55 E
101	No. 1, Canal Arg. (Buenos Aires In.)	36·43 S	58·14 W
101	No. 9, Canal Arg. (Buenos Aires In.)	36·22 S	58·19 W
101	No. 12, Canal Arg. (Buenos Aires In.)	36·47 S	57·20 W
167	Numolani . . . . Bas. (Natal In.)	29·06 S	28·59 E
110	Nuneaton (nün'ē-tǎn) . . . . Eng.	52·31 N	1·28 W
150	Nungan . . . . China	44·25 N	125·10 E
64	Nunivak (I.) (nōō'nĭ-văk) . Alaska	60·25 N	167·42 W
92	Nunkiní (nōōn-kē-nē') Mex. (Yucatan In.)	20·19 N	90·14 W
64	Nunyama (nûn-yä'mȧ) . . Sov. Un.	65·49 N	170·32 W
126	Nuoro (nwô'rō) . . . . It.	40·29 N	9·20 E
134	Nura (R.) (nōō'rä) . . . . . . Sov. Un.	49·48 N	73·54 E
134	Nurata (nōōr'ät'ä) . . . . . . Sov. Un.	40·33 N	65·28 E
120	Nürnberg (nürn'bĕrgh) . . . . . . Ger.	49·28 N	11·07 E
95	Nurse Cay (I.) . . . . Ba. Is.	22·30 N	75·50 W
133	Nusabyin (nōō'sĭ-bên) . . . . Tur.	37·05 N	41·10 E
64	Nushagak (R.) (nū-shă-găk') Alaska	59·28 N	157·40 W
148	Nushan Hu (L.) (nü'shän hōō) China	32·50 N	117·59 E
145	Nushki (nŭsh'kê) . . . . W. Pak.	29·30 N	66·02 E
111	Nuthe R. (nōō'tê) Ger. (Berlin In.)	52·15 N	13·11 E
84	Nutley (nŭt'lê) N. J. (New York In.)	40·49 N	74·09 W
81	Nutter Fort (nŭt'ēr fôrt) . . W. Va.	39·15 N	80·15 W
74	Nutwood (nŭt'wŏŏd) Ill. (St. Louis In.)	39·05 N	90·34 W
139	Nuwaybi 'al Muzayyinah U. A. R. (Palestine In.)	28·59 N	34·40 E
84	Nyack (nī'ăk) N. Y. (New York In.)	41·05 N	73·55 W
165	Nyala . . . . Sud.	12·00 N	24·52 E
166	Nyangwe (nyäng'wā) . . . . . Con. L.	4·09 S	26·16 E
166	Nyasa, L. (nyä'sä) . . . . . Tan.-Moz.	11·32 S	35·15 E
166	Nyasaland (nyä'sä-lănd) . . . . . Afr.	11·15 S	33·45 E
136	Nyazepetrovsk (nyä'zĕ-pĕ-trôvsk') Sov. Un. (Urals In.)	56·04 N	59·38 E
118	Nyborg (nü'bôr'') . . . . Den.	55·20 N	10·45 E
118	Nybro (nü'brō) . . . . Swe.	56·44 N	15·56 E
146	Nyenchhen Thanglha (Mts.) China	29·55 N	88·08 E
118	Nyhem (nü'hĕm) . . . . Swe.	56·39 N	12·50 E
121	Nyiregyháza (nyē'rĕd-y'hä'zä) Hung.	47·58 N	21·45 E
118	Nykøbing (nü'kû-bĭng) . . . . . . Den.	56·46 N	8·47 E
118	Nykøbing Falster . . . . Den.	54·45 N	11·54 E
118	Nykøbing Sjaelland . . . . Den.	55·55 N	11·37 E
118	Nyköping (nü'chû-pĭng) . . . . . Swe.	58·46 N	16·58 E
168	Nyl R. (nĭl) . . . . S. Afr. (Johannesburg & Pretoria In.)	24·30 S	28·55 E
168	Nylstroom (nĭl'strōm) S. Afr. (Johannesburg & Pretoria In.)	24·42 S	28·25 E
160	Nymagee (nī-mȧ-gē') . . . . . . Austl.	32·17 S	146·18 E
120	Nymburk (nêm'bōōrk) . . . . Czech.	50·12 N	15·03 E
116	Nymphe Bk. (nĭmpf) . . . . Ire.	51·36 N	7·35 W
118	Nynashamn (nü-nĕs-häm'n) . . Swe.	58·53 N	17·55 E
160	Nyngan (nĭŋ'gǎn) . . . . Austl.	31·31 S	147·25 E
164	Nyong R. (nyông) . . . . Cam.	3·41 N	12·21 E
120	Nýrány (nêr-zhä'nê) . . . . Czech.	49·43 N	13·13 E
121	Nysa (nē'sȧ) . . . . Pol.	50·29 N	17·20 E
	Nystad, see Uusikaupunki		
132	Nytva . . . . Sov. Un.	58·00 N	55·10 E
135	Nyuya (R.) (nyōō'yȧ) . . . Sov. Un.	60·30 N	111·45 E
70	Oahe Dam (ō-ȧ-hē) . . . . S. D.	44·28 N	100·34 W
70	Oahe Res. . . . . S. Dak.	45·20 N	100·00 W
157	Oahu (I.) (ō-ä'hōō) (ō-ä'hû) Hawaii (In.)	21·38 N	157·48 W
85	Oak Bluff (ōk blŭf) Can. (Winnipeg In.)	49·47 N	97·21 W
67	Oak Creek (ōk krēk') . . . . Colo.	40·20 N	106·50 W
68	Oakdale (ōk'dāl) . . . . Calif.	37·45 N	120·52 W
80	Oakdale . . . . Ky.	38·15 N	85·50 W
77	Oakdale . . . . La.	30·49 N	92·40 W
75	Oakdale . . . . . . Pa. (Pittsburgh In.)	40·24 N	80·11 W
110	Oakengates (ōk'ĕn-gāts) . . . . . Eng.	52·41 N	2·27 W
70	Oakes (ōks) . . . . N. D.	46·10 N	98·50 W
82	Oakfield (ōk'fēld) . . . . Maine	46·08 N	68·10 W
84	Oakford (ōk'fōrd) Pa. (Philadelphia In.)	40·08 N	74·58 W
65	Oak Grove (grōv) Ore. (Portland In.)	45·25 N	122·38 W
110	Oakham (ōk'ǎm) . . . . Eng.	52·40 N	0·38 W
80	Oakharbor (ōk'här'bēr) . . . . . . Ohio	41·30 N	83·05 W
65	Oak Harbor . . Wash. (Seattle In.)	48·18 N	122·39 W
74	Oak Knoll (nōl) Tex. (Dallas, Fort Worth In.)	32·47 N	97·17 W
65	Oakland (ōk'lǎnd) Calif. (San Francisco In.)	37·48 N	122·16 W
70	Oakland . . . . Nebr.	41·50 N	96·28 W
80	Oakland City . . . . Ind.	38·20 N	87·20 W
75	Oaklawn (ōk'lôn) Ill. (Chicago In.)	41·43 N	87·45 W
161	Oakleigh (ōk'lȧ) Austl. (Melbourne In.)	37·54 S	145·05 E
67	Oakley (ōk'lĭ) . . . . Idaho	42·15 N	113·53 W
72	Oakley . . . . Kans.	39·08 N	100·49 W
78	Oakman (ōk'măn) . . . . Ala.	33·42 N	87·20 W
75	Oakmont (ōk'mōnt) Pa. (Pittsburgh In.)	40·31 N	79·50 W
84	Oak Mtn. . Ala. (Birmingham In.)	33·22 N	86·42 W
75	Oak Park (pärk) Ill. (Chicago In.)	41·53 N	87·48 W
65	Oak Point . . . Wash. (Portland In.)	46·11 N	123·11 W
78	Oak Ridge (rĭj) . . . . Tenn.	36·01 N	84·15 W
74	Oak Ridge Park Mich. (Sault Ste. Marie In.)	46·18 N	84·12 W
85	Oakville (ōk'vĭl) Can. (Toronto In.)	43·27 N	79·40 W
85	Oakville . . . . . Can. (Winnipeg In.)	49·56 N	98·00 W
84	Oakville . . . . La. (New Orleans In.)	29·47 N	90·02 W
74	Oakville . . . . . . Mo. (St. Louis In.)	38·27 N	90·18 W
85	Oakville Cr. . . . Can. (Toronto In.)	43·34 N	79·54 W
77	Oakwood (ōk'wŏŏd) . . . . Tex.	31·36 N	95·48 W
75	Oakwood . . . Wis. (Milwaukee In.)	42·51 N	88.30 W
69	Oatman (ōt'mǎn) . . . . Ariz.	34·00 N	114·25 W
88	Oaxaca (State) (wä-hä'kä) . . . Mex.	16·45 N	97·00 W
91	Oaxaca, Sierra de (Mts.) (sē-ĕ'r-rä dĕ) . Mex.	16·15 N	97·25 W
91	Oaxaca de Juárez (ĸōōä'rĕz) . Mex.	17·03 N	96·42 W
134	Ob' (R.) . . . . Sov. Un.	62·15 N	67·00 E
87	Oba (ō'bȧ) . . . . Can.	48·58 N	84·09 W
153	Obama (ō'bȧ-mä) . . . . Jap.	35·29 N	135·44 E
116	Oban (ō'băn) . . . . Scot.	56·25 N	5·35 W
75	O'Bannon (ō-băn'nŏn) Ky. (Louisville In.)	38·17 N	85·30 W
82	Obatogamau (L.) (ō-bȧ-tō'gäm-ô) . Can.	49·38 N	74·10 W
168	Obbia (ŏb'byä) Som. (Horn of Afr. In.)	5·24 N	48·28 E
123	Oberhausen (ō'bĕr-hou'zĕn) Ger. (Ruhr In.)	51·27 N	6·51 E
72	Oberlin (o'bĕr-lĭn) . . . . Kans.	39·49 N	100·30 W
80	Oberlin . . . . Ohio	41.15 N	82·15 W
120	Oberösterreich (Prov.) . . . . Aus.	48·05 N	13·15 E
111	Oberroth (ō'bĕr-rōt) Ger. (Munich In.)	48·19 N	11·20 E
111	Ober-Schleissheim (ō'bĕr-shlīs-hĕm) Ger. (Munich In.)	48·15 N	11·34 E
155	Obi (I.) (ō'bê) . . . . Indon.	1·25 S	128·15 E
99	Óbidos (ō'bê-dŏŏzh) . . . . Braz.	1·57 S	55·32 W
152	Obihiro (ō'bē-hē'rō) . . . . Jap.	42·55 N	142·50 E
78	Obion (R.) . . . . Tenn.	36·10 N	89·25 W
78	Obion (R.), North Fk. (ō-bī'ŏn) Tenn.	35·49 N	89·06 W
129	Obitochnaya, Kosa (C.) (kô-sä' ô-bē-tôch'nȧ-yȧ) Sov. Un.	46·32 N	36·07 E
153	Obitsu (R.) (ō'bēt'sōō) Jap. (Tōkyō In.)	35·19 N	140·03 E
168	Obock (ō-bŏk') Fr. Som. (Horn of Afr. In.)	11·55 N	43·15 E
127	Obol' (R.) (ō-bōl') . . . . . Sov. Un.	55·24 N	29·24 E
129	Oboyan' (ō-bô-yän') . . . . Sov. Un.	51·14 N	36·16 E
134	Obskaya Guba (R.) . . . . . Sov. Un.	67·13 N	73·45 E
129	Obukhov (ō'bōō-ĸôf) . . . . Sov. Un.	50·07 N	30·36 E
79	Ocala (ô-kä'lȧ) . . . . Fla.	29·11 N	82·09 W
90	Ocampo (ô-käm'pō) . . . . Mex.	22·49 N	99·23 W
98	Ocaña (ô-kän'yä) . . . . Col.	8·15 N	73·37 W
124	Ocaña (ô-kä'n-yä) . . . . Sp.	39·58 N	3·31 W
164	Occidental, Grand Erg (Dunes) Alg.	29·30 N	00·45 W
98	Occidental, Cordillera (Mts.) (kôr-dēl-yĕ'rä ôk-sê-dĕn-täl') Col. (In.)	5·05 N	76·04 W
98	Occidental, Cordillera (Mts.) Peru	10·12 S	76·58 W
88	Occidental, Sierra Madre, (Mts.) (sē-ĕ'r-rä-mä'drĕ-ôk-sē-dĕn-tä'l) Mex.	29·30 N	107·30 W
84	Oceana (ō'shē'ǎn-ȧ) Va. (Norfolk In.)	36·51 N	76·01 W
68	Ocean Beach (ō'shǎn bēch) Calif. (San Diego In.)	32·44 N	117·14 W
95	Ocean Bight (B.) . . . . Ba. Is.	21·15 N	73·15 W
81	Ocean City . . . . Md.	38·20 N	75·10 W
81	Ocean City . . . . N. J.	39·15 N	74·35 W
86	Ocean Falls (Fôls) . . . . Can.	52·27 N	127·50 W
161	Ocean Grove Austl. (Melbourne In.)	38·16 S	144·32 E
81	Ocean Grove (grōv) . . . . N. J.	40·10 N	74·00 W
74	Ocean Park (pärk) Calif. (Los Angeles In.)	34·00 N	118·28 W
84	Oceanport (ō'-shǎn-pōrt) N. J. (New York In.)	40·18 N	74·02 W
68	Oceanside (ō'shǎn-sīd) . . . . . . Calif.	33·11 N	117·22 W
78	Ocean Springs (sprĭngs) . . . . . Miss.	30·25 N	88·49 W
127	Ocenele Mari . . . . Rom.	45·05 N	24·17 E
129	Ochakov (ô-chä'kôf) . . . . . Sov. Un.	46·38 N	31·33 E
146	Ochina Ho (R.) . . . . China	41·15 N	100·46 E
150	Ochir . . . . China	45·38 N	115·35 E
78	Ochlockonee R. (ŏk-lô-kō'nē) Fla.-Ga.	30·10 N	84·38 W
78	Ocilla (ô-sĭl'ȧ) . . . . Ga.	31·36 N	83·15 W
118	Ockelbo (ôk'ĕl-bô) . . . . Swe.	60·54 N	16·35 E
79	Ocmulgee, (R.) . . . . Ga.	32·35 N	83·30 W
78	Ocmulgee Natl. Mon. (ôk-mŭl'gē) Ga.	32·45 N	83·28 W
127	Ocna-Sibiului (ōk'nȧ-sê-byōō-lōō-ê) Rom.	45·52 N	24·04 E
95	Ocoa, Bahai de (B.) (bȧ-ä'ē-ô-kô'ȧ) Dom. Rep.	18·20 N	70·40 W
91	Ococingo (ô-kô-sē'n-gô) . . . . . Mex.	17·03 N	92·18 W
92	Ocom, L. (ô-kô'm) Mex. (Yucatan In.)	19·26 N	88·18 W
78	Oconee, (R.) (ô-kō'nē) . . . . Ga.	32·45 N	83·00 W
71	Oconomowoc (ô-kŏn'ô-mô-wŏk') Wis.	43·06 N	88·24 W
71	Oconto (ô-kŏn'tō) . . . . Wis.	44·54 N	87·55 W
71	Oconto (R.) . . . . Wis.	45·08 N	88·24 W
71	Oconto Falls . . . . Wis.	44·53 N	88·11 W
92	Ocós (ô-kōs') . . . . Guat.	14·31 N	92·12 W
92	Ocotal (ō-kô-tāl') . . . . Nic.	13·36 N	86·31 W
92	Ocotepeque (ô-kō-tȧ-pā'kȧ) . Hond.	14·25 N	89·13 W
90	Ocotlán (ō-kô-tlän') . . . . Mex.	20·19 N	102·44 W
91	Ocotlán de Morelos (dā mô-rā'lōs) Mex.	16·46 N	96·41 W
91	Ocozocoautla (ô-kō'zō-kwä-ōō'tlä) Mex.	16·44 N	93·22 W
99	Ocumare del Tuy (ō-kōō-mä'rā del twē') Ven. (In.)	10·07 N	66·47 W
155	Ocussi . . . . Port. Tim.	9·00 S	128·53 E
153	Odawara (ō'dȧ-wä'rä) . . . . Jap.	35·15 N	139·10 E
118	Odda (ôdh-ȧ) . . . . Nor.	60·04 N	6·30 E
168	Oddur . . . . Som. (Horn of Afr. In.)	3·55 N	43·45 E
70	Odebolt (ō'dê-bōlt) . . . . Iowa	42·20 N	95·14 W
124	Odemira (ō-dȧ-mē'rȧ) . . . . Port.	37·35 N	8·40 W
133	Ödemis (û'dĕ-mēsh) . . . . Tur.	38·12 N	28·00 E
168	Odendaalsrus (ō'dĕn-däls-rûs') S. Afr. (Johannesburg & Pretoria In.)	27·52 S	26·41 E
118	Odense (ō'dhĕn-sĕ) . . . . Den.	55·24 N	10·20 E
84	Odenton (ō'dĕn-tǎn) Md. (Baltimore In.)	39·05 N	76·43 W
120	Odenwald (For.) (ō'dĕn-väld) . Ger.	49·39 N	8·55 E
120	Oder R. (ō'dēr) . . . . Ger.	52·40 N	14·19 E
129	Odessa (ô-dĕs'sä) . . . . Sov. Un.	46·28 N	30·44 E
76	Odessa (ô-dĕs'ȧ) . . . . Tex.	31·52 N	102·21 W
66	Odessa . . . . Wash.	47·20 N	118·42 W
129	Odessa (Oblast) . . . . Sov. Un.	46·05 N	29·48 E
124	Odiel (R.) (ō-dê-ĕl') . . . . Sp.	37·47 N	6·42 W
164	Odienné (ō-dê-ĕn-nā') Ivory Coast	9·47 N	7·32 W
110	Odiham (ŏd'ē-ǎm) Eng. (London In.)	51·14 N	0·56 W
138	Odintsovo (ô-dēn'tsô-vô) Sov. Un. (Moscow In.)	55·40 N	37·16 E
155	Odioñgan (ō-dê-ōŋ'gän) Phil. (Manila In.)	12·24 N	121·59 E
125	Odivelas (ō-dê-vā'lyäs) Port. (Lisbon In.)	38·47 N	9·11 W
121	Odobesti (ō-dô-bĕsh't') . . . . . Rom.	45·46 N	27·08 E
72	O'Donnell (ō-dŏn'ĕl) . . . . Tex.	32·59 N	101·51 W
121	Odorhei (ō-dôr-hā') . . . . Rom.	46·18 N	25·17 E
121	Odra R. (ô'drȧ) . . . . Pol.	50·28 N	17·55 E
99	Oeiras (wä-ê-räzh') . . . . Braz.	7·05 S	42·01 W
125	Oeirás (ô-ĕ'y-rä's) Port. (Lisbon In.)	38·42 N	9·18 W
71	Oelwein (ōl'wīn) . . . . Iowa	42·40 N	91·56 W
74	O'Fallon (ō-făl'ŭn) Ill. (St. Louis In.)	38·36 N	89·55 W
67	O'Fallon Cr. . . . . Mont.	46·25 N	104·47 W
126	Ofanto (R.) (ō-fän'tō) . . . . It.	41·08 N	15·33 E
120	Offenbach (ôf'ĕn-bäk) . . . . Ger.	50·06 N	8·50 E
120	Offenburg (ôf'ĕn-bŏŏrgh) . . . . . Ger.	48·28 N	7·57 E
153	Ofuna (ō'fōō-nä) . Jap. (Tōkyō In.)	35·21 N	139·32 E
168	Ogaden Plat. Eth. (Horn of Afr. In.)	6·45 N	44·53 E
153	Ōgaki . . . . Jap.	35·21 N	136·36 E
70	Ogallala (ō-gä-lä'lȧ) . . . . Nebr.	41·80 N	101·44 W
164	Ogbomosho (ŏg-bô-mō'shō) . . . Nig.	8·06 N	4·04 E
71	Ogden (ŏg'dĕn) . . . . Iowa	42·10 N	94·20 W
74	Ogden . . Utah (Salt Lake City In.)	41·14 N	111·58 W
74	Ogden Pk. Utah (Salt Lake City In.)	41·11 N	111·51 W
74	Ogden R. Utah (Salt Lake City In.)	41·16 N	111·54 W
84	Ogdensburg (ŏg'dĕnz-bûrg) N. J. (New York In.)	41·05 N	74·36 W
81	Ogdensburg . . . . N. Y.	44·40 N	75·30 W
79	Ogeechee, (R.) (ô-gē'chê) . . . . . Ga.	32·35 N	81·50 W
168	Ogies . . . . S. Afr. (Johannesburg & Pretoria In.)	26·03 S	29·04 E
86	Ogilvie Ra. (ō'g'l-vĭ) . . . . Can.	64·43 N	138·36 W
80	Oglesby (ō'g'lz-bĭ) . . . . Ill.	41·20 N	89·00 W
126	Oglio (R.) (ōl'yō) . . . . It.	45·15 N	10·19 E

ng-sing; ŋ-baŋk; ɴ-nasalized n; nŏd; cǒmmit; ōld; ōbey; ôrder; fōōd; fŏŏt; ou-out; s-soft; sh-dish; th-thin; pūre; ûnite; ûrn; stŭd; circǎs; ü-as "y" in study; '-indeterminate vowel.

Page	Name Pronunciation Region	Lat. °′	Long. °′
153	Ōgo (ō′gô) Jap. (Ōsaka In.)	34·49 N	135·06 E
154	Ogoamas, Bulu (Mtn.) Indon.	0·45 N	120·15 E
166	Ogooué (R.) Gabon	0·20 S	11·07 E
136	Ogudnëvo (ôg-o͝og-nyô′vô) Sov. Un. (Moscow In.)	56·04 N	38·17 E
126	Ogulin (ō-go͞o-lēn′) Yugo.	45·17 N	15·11 E
157	Ohia (ō-hī′ȧ) Hawaii (In.)	19·35 N	155·01 W
101	O'Higgins (Prov.) (ô-kē′gēns) Chile (Santiago In.)	34·17 S	70·52 W
63	Ohio, (State) (ô′hī′ō) U. S.	40·30 N	83·15 W
80	Ohio R. U. S.	37·25 N	88·05 W
79	Ohoopee (R.) (ô-ho͞o′pē) Ga.	32·32 N	82·38 W
120	Ohre (Eger) R. (ōr′zhĕ) (ā′gĕr) Czech.	50·08 N	12·45 E
127	Ohrid (ō′ĸrēd) Yugo.	41·08 N	20·46 E
127	Ohrid (L.) Alb.-Yugo.	40·58 N	20·35 E
153	Ōi (oi′) Jap. (Tōkyō In.)	35·51 N	139·31 E
118	Oieren (L.) (ûĭĕrĕn) Nor.	59·50 N	11·25 E
153	Oi-Gawa (Strm.) (ō′ē-gä′wȧ) Jap.	35·09 N	138·05 E
81	Oil City (oil sĭ′tĭ) Pa.	41·25 N	79·40 W
111	Oirschot Neth. (Amsterdam In.)	51·30 N	5·20 E
122	Oise (R.) (wäz) Fr.	49·30 N	2·56 E
111	Oisterwijk Neth. (Amsterdam In.)	51·34 N	5·13 E
153	Oita (ō′ē-tä) Jap.	33·14 N	131·38 E
153	Oji (ō′jē) Jap. (Ōsaka In.)	34·36 N	135·43 E
76	Ojinaga (ō-Kē-nä′gä) Mex.	29·34 N	104·26 W
91	Ojitlán (San Lucas) (ōkē-tlän′) (sän-lo͞o′käs) Mex.	18·04 N	96·23 W
90	Ojo Caliente (ōĸō käl-yĕn′tā) Mex.	21·50 N	100·43 W
90	Ojocaliente (ô-ĸô-kä-lyĕ′n-tĕ) Mex.	22·39 N	102·15 W
94	Ojo del Toro, Pico (Pk.) (pē′kô-ô-ĸō-dĕl-tô′rô) Cuba	19·55 N	77·25 W
85	Oka (ō-kä) Can. (Montreal In.)	45·28 N	74·05 W
133	Oka (R.) (ô-kä′) Sov. Un.	52·10 N	35·20 E
134	Oka (R.) (ō-kä′) Sov. Un.	53·28 N	101·09 E
132	Oka (R.) (ô-kȧ′) Sov. Un.	55·10 N	42·10 E
166	Okahandja S. W. Afr.	21·50 S	16·45 E
86	Okanagan (ō′kȧ-näg′ȧn) Can.	49·56 N	120·23 W
66	Okanogan Wash.	48·20 N	119·34 W
66	Okanogan R. Wash.	48·36 N	119·33 W
164	Okano R. (ô′kä′nō) Gabon	0·15 N	11·08 E
78	Okatibbee (R.) (ō′kä-tĭb′ē) Miss.	32·37 N	88·54 W
78	Okatoma Cr. (ô-kȧ-tō′mă) Miss.	31·43 N	89·34 W
153	Okaya (ō′kȧ-yȧ) Jap.	36·04 N	138·01 E
153	Okayama (ō′kȧ-yä′mȧ) Jap.	34·39 N	133·54 E
153	Okazaki (ō′kȧ-zä′kē) Jap.	34·58 N	137·09 E
79	Okeechobee (ō-kē-chō′bē) Fla. (In.)	27·15 N	26·48 W
79	Okeechobee, L. Fla. (In.)	27·00 N	80·49 W
72	Okeene (ô-kēn′) Okla.	36·06 N	98·19 W
79	Okefenokee Swp. (ō′kē-fē-nō′kē) Ga.	30·54 N	82·20 W
73	Okemah (ô-kē′mä) Okla.	35·26 N	96·18 W
117	Oker (R.) (ō′kĕr) Ger.	52·23 N	10·00 E
135	Okha (ŭ-ĸä′) Sov. Un.	53·44 N	143·12 E
136	Okhotino (ô-ĸô′tĭ-nô) Sov. Un. (Moscow In.)	56·14 N	38·24 E
135	Okhotsk (ô-ĸôtsk′) Sov. Un.	59·28 N	143·32 E
139	Okhotsk, Sea of (ô-kôtsk′) Asia	56·45 N	146·00 E
153	Oki-Guntō (Arch.) (ō′kē go͝on′tō) Jap.	36·17 N	133·05 E
152	Okinawa (I.) (ō′kē-nä′wȧ) Ryūkyū Is.	26·30 N	128·30 E
152	Okinawa Guntō (Is.) (go͝on′tō′) Ryūkyū Is.	26·50 N	127·25 E
153	Okino (I.) (ō′kē-nô) Jap.	36·22 N	133·27 E
152	Ōkino Erabu (I.) (ō-kē′nô-ȧ-rä′bo͞o) Jap.	27·18 N	129·00 E
62	Oklahoma (State) (ô-klȧ-hō′mȧ) U. S.	36·00 N	98·20 W
73	Oklahoma City Okla.	35·27 N	97·32 W
79	Oklawaha (R.) (ŏk-lȧ-wô′hô) Fla.	29·13 N	82·00 W
73	Okmulgee (ôk-mŭl′gē) Okla.	35·37 N	95·58 W
75	Okolona (ō-kô-lō′nȧ) Ky. (Louisville In.)	38·08 N	85·41 W
78	Okolona Miss.	33·59 N	88·43 W
166	Okovanggo (R.) Ang.-S. W. Afr.	17·50 S	19·30 E
166	Okovanggo Swp. Bech.	19·30 S	23·02 E
152	Okushiri (I.) (ō′koo-shē′rē) Jap.	42·12 N	139·30 E
65	Olalla (ō-lä′lȧ) Wash. (Seattle In.)	47·26 N	122·33 W
92	Olanchito (ō′län-chē′tô) Hond.	15·28 N	86·35 W
118	Öland (I.) (û-länd′) Swe.	57·03 N	17·15 E
74	Olathe (ô-lā′thē) Mo. (Kansas City In.)	38·53 N	94·49 W
100	Olavarría (ō-lä-vär-rē′ä) Arg.	36·49 S	60·15 W
121	Oława (ô-lä′vȧ) Pol.	50·57 N	17·18 E
101	Olazcoago (ô-läz-kôä′gô) Arg. (Buenos Aires In.)	35·14 S	60·37 W
126	Olbia (ô′l-byä) It.	40·55 N	9·28 E
111	Olching (ōl′ĸēng) Ger. (Munich In.)	48·13 N	11·21 E
94	Old Bahama Chan. (bȧ-hā′mȧ) N. A.	22·45 N	78·30 W
95	Old Bight Ba. Is.	24·15 N	75·20 W
84	Old Bridge (brĭj) N. J. (New York In.)	40·24 N	74·22 W
110	Oldbury (ōld′bẽr-ĭ) Eng.	52·30 N	2·01 W
86	Old Crow (crō) Can.	67·51 N	139·58 W
120	Oldenburg (ôl′dĕn-bo͝orgh) Ger.	53·09 N	8·13 E
81	Old Forge (fôrj) Pa.	41·20 N	75·50 W
110	Oldham (ōld′ȧm) Eng.	53·32 N	2·07 W
64	Old Harbor (här′bẽr) Alaska	57·18 N	153·20 W
116	Old Head of Kinsale (ōld hĕd ŏv kĭn-sāl) Ire.	51·35 N	8·35 W
77	Old R. Tex. (In.)	29·54 N	94·52 W
86	Olds (ōldz) Can.	51·50 N	114·00 W
82	Old Town (toun) Maine	44·55 N	68·42 W
81	Olean (ō-lē-ăn′) N. Y.	42·05 N	78·25 W
82	O'Leary (ō-lĕr′ē) Can.	46·43 N	64·10 W
121	Olecko (ô-lĕt′skô) Pol.	54·02 N	22·29 E
135	Olekma (R.) (ô-lyĕk-mȧ′) Sov. Un.	55·41 N	120·33 E
135	Olëkminsk (ô-lyĕk-mēnsk′) Sov. Un.	60·39 N	120·40 E
135	Olenëk (R.) (ô-lyĕ-nyôk′) Sov. Un.	70·18 N	121·15 E
122	Oléron Île, d' (I.) (ēl′ dō lā-rôɴ′) Fr.	45·52 N	1·58 W
121	Olesnica (ô-lĕsh-nĭ′tsȧ) Pol.	51·13 N	17·24 E
123	Olfen (ōl′fĕn) Ger. (Ruhr In.)	51·43 N	7·22 E
135	Ol'ga (ôl′gȧ) Sov. Un.	43·48 N	135·44 E
84	Olga (ōl′gȧ) La. (New Orleans In.)	29·22 N	89·25 W
152	Ol'gi, Zaliv (B.) (zä′lĭf ôl′gĭ) Sov. Un.	43·43 N	135·25 E
129	Ol'gopol (ôl-gô-pôl′y′) Sov. Un.	48·11 N	29·28 E
124	Olhão (ôl-youɴ′) Port.	37·02 N	7·54 W
167	Olievenhoutpoort S. Afr. (Johannesburg & Pretoria In.)	25·58 S	27·55 E
166	Olifants (R.) (ŏl′ĭ-fănts) S. Afr.	23·58 S	31·00 E
167	Olifantsfontein S. Afr. (Johannesburg & Pretoria In.)	25·58 S	28·19 E
127	Ólimbos Grc.	40·03 N	22·22 E
90	Olinalá (ô-lē-nä-lä′) Mex.	17·47 N	98·51 W
99	Olinda (ô-lē′n-dä) Braz.	8·00 S	34·58 W
74	Olinda (ô-lĭn′dȧ) Calif. (Los Angeles In.)	33·55 N	117·51 W
125	Oliva (ô-lē′vä) Sp.	38·54 N	0·07 W
124	Oliva de Jerez (ô-lē′vä dā hā′rĕth) Sp.	38·33 N	6·55 W
125	Olivais (ô-lē-vȧ′ys) Port. (Lisbon In.)	38·46 N	9·06 W
74	Olive (ŏl′ĭv) Calif. (Los Angeles In.)	33·50 N	117·51 W
80	Olive Hill Ky.	38·15 N	83·10 W
101	Oliveira (ô-lē-vā′rä) Braz. (Rio de Janeiro In.)	20·42 S	44·49 W
124	Olivenza (ō-lē-vĕn′thä) Sp.	38·42 N	7·06 W
86	Oliver (ŏ′lĭ-vẽr) Can.	49·09 N	119·36 W
85	Oliver Can. (Edmonton In.)	53·38 N	113·21 W
74	Oliver (ŏ′lĭvẽr) Wis. (Duluth In.)	46·39 N	92·12 W
85	Oliver L. Can. (Edmonton In.)	53·19 N	113·00 W
71	Olivia (ō-lĭv′ē-ȧ) Minn.	44·46 N	95·00 W
100	Olivos (ōlē′vōs) Arg. (In.)	34·15 S	58·29 W
121	Olkusz (ôl′ko͞osh) Pol.	50·16 N	19·41 E
98	Ollagüe (ô-lyä′gā) Chile	21·17 S	68·17 W
110	Ollerton (ôl′ẽr-tŭn) Eng.	53·12 N	1·02 W
74	Olmos Park (ōl′mŭs pärk′) Tex. (San Antonio In.)	29·27 N	98·32 W
80	Olney (ŏl′nĭ) Ill.	38·45 N	88·05 W
65	Olney (ŏl′nē) Ore. (Portland In.)	46·06 N	123·45 W
72	Olney Tex.	33·24 N	98·43 W
83	Olomane (R.) (ō′lô mȧ′nĕ) Can.	50·50 N	60·30 W
121	Olomouc (ô′lô-mōts) Czech.	49·37 N	17·15 E
119	Olonets (ô-lô′nĕts) Sov. Un.	60·58 N	32·54 E
122	Oloron, Gave d' (Strm.) (gäv-dŏ-lŏ-rŏɴ′) Fr.	43·21 N	0·44 W
122	Oloron-Ste. Marie (ō-lô-rôɴt′săɴt mȧ-rē′) Fr.	43·11 N	1·37 W
125	Olot (ô-lōt′) Sp.	42·09 N	2·30 E
123	Olpe (ōl′pĕ) Ger. (Ruhr In.)	51·02 N	7·51 E
129	Ol'shanka (ôl′shȧŋ-kȧ) Sov. Un.	48·14 N	30·52 E
129	Ol'shany (ôl′shȧn-ē) Sov. Un.	50·02 N	35·54 E
120	Olsnitz (ōlz′nētz) Ger.	50·25 N	12·11 E
121	Olsztyn (ôl′shtēn) Pol.	53·47 N	20·28 E
120	Olten (ôl′tĕn) Switz.	47·20 N	7·53 E
127	Oltenita (ôl-tā′nĭ-tsȧ) Rom.	44·05 N	26·39 E
115	Olt R. Rom.	44·09 N	24·40 E
124	Olvera (ôl-vĕ′rä) Sp.	36·55 N	7·16 W
66	Olympia (ô-lĭm′pĭ-ȧ) Wash.	47·02 N	122·52 W
66	Olympic Mts. Wash.	47·54 N	123·58 W
66	Olympic Natl. Park (ô-lĭm′pĭk) Wash.	47·54 N	123·00 W
66	Olympus Mt. (ô-lĭm′pŭs) Wash.	47·43 N	123·30 W
139	Olympus Mts. Cyprus (Palestine In.)	34·50 N	32·44 E
81	Olyphant (ŏl′ĭ-fănt) Pa.	41·30 N	75·40 W
135	Olyutorskiy, Mys (C.) (ŭl-yo͞o′tŏr-skē) Sov. Un.	59·49 N	167·16 E
153	Omae-Zaki (Pt.) (ō′mä-ȧ zä′kē) Jap.	34·37 N	138·15 E
165	Om Ager Eth.	14·06 N	36·46 E
116	Omagh (ō′mä) N. Ire.	54·35 N	7·25 W
70	Omaha (ō′mȧ-hä) Nebr.	41·18 N	95·57 W
70	Omaha Ind. Res. Nebr.	42·09 N	96·08 W
144	Oman, G. of Asia	24·24 N	58·58 E
166	Omaruru (ō-mä-ro͞o′ro͞o) S. W. Afr.	21·25 S	16·50 E
126	Ombrone (R.) (ôm-brō′nā) It.	42·48 N	11·18 E
165	Omdurman (ŏm-do͞or-män′) Sud.	15·45 N	32·30 E
91	Omealca (ōmȧ-äl′kō) Mex.	18·44 N	96·45 W
90	Ometepec (ô-mā-tȧ-pĕk′) Mex.	16·41 N	98·27 W
153	Ōmiya (ō′mē-yȧ) Jap. (Tōkyō In.)	35·54 N	139·38 E
92	Omoa (ô-mō′rä) Hond.	15·43 N	88·03 W
135	Omolon (R.) (ō′mō) Sov. Un.	67·43 N	159·15 E
153	Ōmori (Kioroshi) (ō′mô-rē) (kē′ô-rō′shē) Jap. (Tōkyō In.)	35·50 N	140·09 E
165	Omo R. (ō′mō) Eth.	5·54 N	36·09 E
92	Omotepe, Isla de (I.) (ē′s-lä-dĕ-ō-mô-tā′pȧ) Nic.	11·32 N	85·30 W
71	Omro (ŏm′rō) Wis.	44·01 N	89·46 W
134	Omsk (ômsk) Sov. Un.	55·12 N	73·19 E
153	Ōmura (ō′mo͞o-rȧ) Jap.	32·56 N	129·57 E
153	Ōmuta (ō-mo͝o-tȧ) Jap.	33·02 N	130·28 E
132	Omutninsk (ô′mo͞o-tēnsk) Sov. Un.	58·38 N	52·10 E
70	Onawa (ŏn-ȧ-wȧ) Iowa	42·02 N	96·05 W
80	Onaway Mich.	45·25 N	84·10 W
125	Onda (ōn′dä) Sp.	39·58 N	0·13 W
121	Ondava R. (ōn′dȧ-vȧ) Czech.	48·51 N	21·40 E
150	Öndör Haan Mong.	47·20 N	110·40 E
132	Onega (ô-nyĕ′gȧ) Sov. Un.	63·50 N	38·08 E
132	Onega (R.) Sov. Un.	63·20 N	39·20 E
	Onega, L., see Onezhskoye Ozero		
81	Oneida (ô-nī′dȧ) N. Y.	43·05 N	75·40 W
81	Oneida (L.) N. Y.	43·10 N	76·00 W
70	O'Neill (ō-nēl′) Nebr.	42·28 N	98·38 W
135	Onekotan (ŭ-nyĕ-kŭ-tän′) Sov. Un.	49·45 N	153·45 E
81	Oneonta (ō-nē-ŏn′tȧ) N. Y.	42·25 N	75·05 W
132	Onezhskaja Guba (B.) Sov. Un.	64·30 N	36·00 E
132	Onezhskiy, P-Ov. (Pen.) Sov. Un.	64·30 N	37·40 E
132	Onezhskoye Ozero (L. Onega) (ô-năsh′skô-yĕ ô′zĕ-rô) Sov. Un.	62·02 N	34·35 E
146	Ongin (ŏn′gĭn′) Mong.	46·00 N	102·46 E
143	Ongole India	15·36 N	80·03 E
167	Onilahy (R.) Malag. Rep.	23·41 S	45·00 E
164	Onitsha (ô-nĭt′shȧ) Nig.	6·13 N	5·47 E
153	Onomichi (ō′nô-mē′chē) Jap.	34·27 N	133·12 E
135	Onon (R.) (ô′nôn) Sov. Un.	50·33 N	114·18 E
135	Onon Gol (R.) (ô′nôn) Sov. Un.	48·30 N	110·38 E
99	Onoto (ô-nŏ′tô) Ven. (In.)	9·38 N	65·03 W
158	Onslow (ŏnz′lō) Austl.	21·53 S	115·00 E
79	Onslow B. (ônz′lō) N. C.	34·22 N	77·35 W
153	Ontake San (Mtn.) (ôn′tä-kā sän) Jap.	35·55 N	137·29 E
74	Ontario (ŏn-tā′rĭ-ō) Calif. (Los Angeles In.)	34·04 N	117·39 W
66	Ontario Ore.	44·02 N	116·57 W
87	Ontario (Prov.) Can.	50·47 N	88·50 W
63	Ontario, L. U. S.-Can.	43·35 N	79·05 W
125	Onteniente (ōn-tā-nyĕn′tā) Sp.	38·48 N	0·35 W
71	Ontonagon (ŏn-tô-năg′ŏn) Mich.	46·50 N	89·20 W
153	Ōnuki (ō′no͞o-kē) Jap. (Tōkyō In.)	35·17 N	139·51 E
158	Oodnadatta (o͞od′nȧ-dȧ′tȧ) Austl.	27·38 S	135·40 E
158	Ooldea Station (o͞ol-dā′ä) Austl.	30·35 S	132·08 E
73	Oologah Res. Okla.	36·43 N	95·32 W
111	Ooltgensplaat Neth. (Amsterdam In.)	51·41 N	4·19 E
78	Oostanaula (R.) (o͞o-stȧ-nô′lȧ) Ga.	34·25 N	85·10 W
117	Oostende (ōst-ĕn′dē) Bel.	51·14 N	2·55 E
111	Oosterhout Neth. (Amsterdam In.)	51·38 N	4·52 E
117	Ooster Schelde (R.) Neth.	51·40 N	3·40 E
92	Opalaca, Sierra de (Mts.) (sē-ĕ′r-rä-dĕ-ô-pä-lä′kä) Hond.	14·30 N	88·29 W
121	Opatow (ô-pä′to͝of) Pol.	50·47 N	21·25 E
121	Opava (ō′pä-vä) Czech.	49·56 N	17·52 E
118	Opdal (ôp′däl) Nor.	62·37 N	9·41 E
78	Opelika (ŏp-ē-lī′kȧ) Ala.	32·39 N	85·23 W
77	Opelousas (ŏp-ē-lo͞o′sȧs) La.	30·33 N	92·04 W
81	Opeongo (L.) (ŏp-ē-ôŋ′gō) Can.	45·40 N	78·20 W
67	Opheim (ô-fīm′) Mont.	48·51 N	106·19 W
64	Ophir (ō′fẽr) Alaska	63·10 N	156·28 W
139	Ophir, Mt. Mala. (Singapore In.)	2·22 N	102·37 E
92	Opico (ô-pē′kō) Sal.	13·50 N	89·23 W
87	Opinaca (R.) (ŏp-ĭ-nä′kȧ) Can.	52·28 N	77·40 W
123	Opladen (ōp′lä-dĕn) Ger. (Ruhr In.)	51·04 N	7·00 E
128	Opochka (ō-pôch′kȧ) Sov. Un.	56·43 N	28·39 E
121	Opoczno (ô-pôch′nô) Pol.	51·22 N	20·18 E
121	Opole (ô-pôl′ā) Pol.	50·42 N	17·55 E
121	Opole Lubelskie (ō-pō′lă lo͞o-bĕl′skyĕ) Pol.	51·09 N	21·58 E
	Oporto, see Pôrto		
66	Oportunity (ŏp-ŏr tū′nĭ tĭ) Wash.	47·37 N	117·20 W
129	Oposhnya (ô-pôsh′nyȧ) Sov. Un.	49·57 N	34·34 E
78	Opp (ŏp) Ala.	31·18 N	86·15 W
74	Oquirrh Mts. (ō′kwẽr) Utah (Salt Lake City In.)	40·38 N	112·11 W
121	Oradea (ô-räd′yä) Rom.	47·02 N	21·55 E
164	Oran (ō-rän′) (ô-räɴ′) Alg.	35·46 N	0·45 W
100	Orán (ô-rȧ′n) Arg.	23·13 S	64·17 W
73	Oran (ôr′ȧn) Mo.	37·05 N	89·39 W
160	Orange (ŏr′ĕnj) Austl.	33·15 S	149·08 E
74	Orange Calif. (Los Angeles In.)	33·48 N	117·51 W
81	Orange Conn.	41·15 N	73·00 W
122	Orange (ô-raɴzh′) Fr.	44·08 N	4·48 E
84	Orange N. J. (New York In.)	40·46 N	74·14 W
77	Orange Tex.	30·07 N	93·44 W
99	Orange, Cabo (C.) (kȧ-bô-rȧ′n-zhĕ) Braz.	4·25 N	51·30 W
79	Orange (L.) Fla.	29·30 N	82·12 W
166	Orange (R.) S. W. Afr.-S. Afr.	29·15 S	17·30 E
79	Orangeburg (ŏr′ĕnj-bûrg) S. C.	33·30 N	80·50 W
94	Orange Cay (I.) (ŏr-ĕnj kē) Ba. Is.	24·55 N	79·05 W
70	Orange City Iowa	43·01 N	96·06 W
166	Orange Free State (Prov.) S. Afr.	28·15 S	26·00 E
85	Orangeville (ŏr′ĕnj-vĭl) Can. (Toronto In.)	43·55 N	80·06 W
168	Orangeville S. Afr. (Johannesburg & Pretoria In.)	27·05 S	28·13 E
92	Orange Walk (wôl′′k) Br. Hond. (Yucatan In.)	18·09 N	88·32 W
155	Orani (ō-rä′nē) Phil. (Manila In.)	14·47 N	120·32 E
111	Oranienburg (ō-rä′nē-ĕn-bo͝orgh) Ger. (Berlin In.)	52·45 N	13·14 E
155	Oranje-Gebergte (Mts.) W. Irian	4·22 S	139·25 E
166	Oranjemund S. W. Afr.	28·33 S	16.20 E
127	Orastie (ô-rûsh′tyā) Rom.	45·50 N	23·14 E
	Orașul-Stalin, see Brașov		
126	Orbetello (ôr-bȧ-tĕl′lō) It.	42·27 N	11·15 E
124	Orbigo (R.) (ôr-bē′gō) Sp.	42·30 N	5·55 W
160	Orbost (ôr′bŭst) Austl.	37·43 S	148·20 E
65	Orcas (I.) (ôr′kȧs) Wash. (Vancouver In.)	48·43 N	122·52 W
74	Orchard Farm (ôr′chẽrd färm) Mo. (St. Louis In.)	38·53 N	90·27 W
75	Orchard Park N. Y. Buffalo In.)	42·46 N	78·46 W
65	Orchards (ôr′chẽdz) Wash. (Portland In.)	45·40 N	122·33 W
98	Orchilla (ôr-kĭl-ȧ) Ven.	11·47 N	66·34 W
70	Ord (ôrd) Nebr.	41·35 N	98·57 W
158	Ord (R.) Austl.	17·30 S	128·40 E
136	Orda (ôr′dȧ) Sov. Un. (Urals In.)	56·50 N	57·12 E
124	Órdenes (ōr′dā-nās) Sp.	43·46 N	8·24 W
150	Ordos Des. China	39·12 N	108·10 E
69	Ord Pk. Ariz.	33·55 N	109·40 W
133	Ordu (ôr′do͝o) Tur.	41·00 N	37·50 E
124	Orduña (ôr-do͞o′nyä) Sp.	42·59 N	3·01 W
72	Ordway (ôrd′wā) Colo.	38·11 N	103·46 W
133	Ordzhonikidze (Ora ghō ɴĭ kĭd ze) Sov. Un.	43·05 N	44·35 E
118	Örebro (û′rē-brō) Swe.	59·16 N	15·11 E
136	Oredezh R. (ô′rĕ-dĕzh) Sov. Un. (Leningrad In.)	59·23 N	30·21 E
71	Oregon Ill.	42·01 N	89·21 W
62	Oregon (State) U. S.	43·40 N	121·50 W
66	Oregon Caves Natl. Mon. (cāvz) Ore.	42·05 N	123·13 W

ăt; finăl; rāte; senāte; ärm; ȧsk; sofȧ; fâre; ch-choose; dh-as th in other; bē; ēvent; bĕt; recĕnt; cratẽr; g-go; gh-guttural g; bĭt; ĭ-short neutral; rīde: ĸ-guttural k as ch in German ich;

Page	Name Pronunciation Region	Lat. °′	Long. °′
65	Oregon City...Ore. (Portland In.)	45·21 N	122·36 W
118	Oregrund (û'rĕ-grŏŏnd)...Swe.	60·20 N	18·26 E
129	Orekhov (ôr-yĕ'kôf)...Sov. Un.	47·34 N	35·51 E
128	Orekhovo-Zuyevo (ôr-yĕ'kô-vô zōō'yĕ-vô).Sov Un.	55·46 N	39·00 E
128	Orël (ôr-yôl')...Sov. Un.	52·54 N	36·03 E
128	Orël (Oblast)...Sov. Un.	52·35 N	36·08 E
129	Orel' (R.)...Sov. Un.	49·08 N	34·55 E
69	Orem (ŏ'rĕm)...Utah	40·15 N	111·50 W
	Ore Mts., see Erzgebirge		
133	Orenburg (ô'rĕn-bŏŏrg)..Sov. Un.	51·50 N	55·05 E
124	Orense (ô-rĕn'sā)...Sp.	42·20 N	7·52 W
118	Øresund (Sd) (ûr'ŭ-sŏŏn)...Den.	55·30 N	12·25 E
94	Organos, Sierra de los (Mts.) (sē-ĕ'r-rä-dĕ-lôs-ŏ'r-gä-nôs).Cuba	22·20 N	84·10 W
69	Organ Pipe Cactus Natl. Mon. (ôr'găn pīp kăk'tŭs).Ariz.	32·14 N	113·05 W
101	Orgãos, Serra das (Mtn.) (sĕ'r-rä-däs-ôr-gouN's) Braz. (Rio de Janeiro In.)	22·30 S	43·01 W
129	Orgeyev (ôr-gyâ'yĕf)...Sov. Un.	47·27 N	28·49 E
146	Orhon Gol (R.)...Mong.	48·33 N	103·07 E
98	Oriental, Cordillera (Mts.) (kôr-dēl-yĕ'rä ō-rê-ĕn-täl').Bol.	14·00 S	68·33 W
98	Oriental, Cordillera (Mts.) (kôr-dēl-yĕ'rä).Col. (In.)	3·30 N	74·27 W
95	Oriental, Cordillera (Mts.) (kôr-dēl-yĕ'rä-ô-ryĕ'n-täl) Dom. Rep.	18·55 N	69·40 W
88	Oriental, Sierra Madre, (Mts.) (sē-ĕ'r-rä-mä'drĕ-ô-ryĕ'n-täl') Mex.	25·30 N	100·45 W
95	Oriente (State) (ō-rê-ĕn'tâ)..Cuba	20·25 N	76·15 W
125	Orihuela (ō'rê-wā'lä)...Sp.	38·04 N	0·55 W
119	Orihvesi (L.) (ô'rĭ-vĕ-sĭ)...Fin.	62·15 N	29·55 E
81	Orillia (ô-rĭl'ĭ-ȧ)...Can.	44·35 N	79·25 W
98	Orinoco, Rio (R.) (rē'ō-ô-rĭ-nō'kō).Ven.	8·32 N	63·13 W
155	Orion (ō-rê-ōn').Phil. (Manila In.)	14·37 N	120·34 E
142	Orissa (State) (ŏ-rĭs'ȧ)...India	25·09 N	83·50 E
126	Oristano (ô-rês-tä'nō)...It.	39·53 N	8·38 E
126	Oristano, Golfo di (G.) (gôl-fô-dē-ō-rês-tä'nō).It.	39·53 N	8·12 E
99	Orituco (R.) (ô-rē-tōō'kō) Ven. (In.)	9·37 N	66·25 W
99	Oriuco (ô-rêōō'kō) (R.).Ven. (In.)	9·36 N	66·25 W
91	Orizaba (ô-rê-zä'bä)...Mex.	18·52 N	97·05 W
118	Orkdal (ôr'k-däl)...Nor.	63·19 N	9·54 E
112	Örkedalen (ûr'kĕ-dä-lĕn)...Nor.	63·13 N	9·53 E
118	Örken (L.) (ûr'kĕn)...Swe.	57·11 N	14·45 E
118	Orkla (R.) (ôr'klå)...Nor.	62·55 N	9·50 E
168	Orkney (ôrk'nĭ)...S. Afr. (Johannesburg & Pretoria In.)	26·58 S	26·39 E
116	Orkney (Is.)...Scot.	59·01 N	2·08 W
79	Orlando (ôr-lăn'dō)...Fla. (In.)	28·32 N	81·22 W
167	Orlando (ôr-lăn-dō)...S. Afr. (Johannesburg & Pretoria In.)	26·15 S	27·56 E
75	Orland Park (ôr-lăn') Ill. (Chicago In.)	41·38 N	87·52 W
85	Orleans (ôr-lå-äN') Can. (Ottawa In.)	45·28 N	75·31 W
122	Orléans (ôr-lå-äN')...Fr.	47·55 N	1·56 E
80	Orleans (ôr-lēnz')...Ind.	38·40 N	86·25 W
164	Orléansville (ôr-lå-äN-vēl')...Alg.	36·14 N	1·32 E
79	Ormond (ôr'mŏnd)...Fla.	29·15 N	81·05 W
110	Ormskirk (ôrms'kĕrk)...Eng.	53·34 N	2·53 W
85	Ormstown (ôrms'toun) Can. (Montreal In.)	45·07 N	74·00 W
122	Orne (R.) (ôrn')...Fr.	49·05 N	0·32 W
121	Orneta (ôr-nyĕ'tä)...Pol.	54·07 N	20·10 E
118	Ornö (I.)...Swe.	59·02 N	18·35 E
112	Örnsköldsvik (ûrn'skôlts-vēk).Swe.	63·10 N	18·32 E
90	Oro, Rio del (R.) (rē'ō dĕl ō'rō) Mex.	18·04 N	100·59 W
76	Oro, Rio del (R.)...Mex.	26·04 N	105·40 W
126	Orobie, Alpi (Mts.) (äl'pē-ô-rō'byĕ).It.	46·05 N	9·47 E
98	Orocué (ô-rô-kwā')...Col.	4·48 N	71·26 W
116	Oronsay, Pass. of (ŏ'rŏn-så)..Scot.	55·55 N	6·25 W
126	Orosei, Golfo di (G.) (gôl-fô-dē-ō-rô-sā'ē).It.	40·12 N	9·45 E
121	Orosháza (ô-rôsh-hä'sô)...Hung.	46·33 N	20·31 E
92	Orosi Vol. (ō-rō'sē)...C. R.	11·00 N	85·30 W
68	Oroville (ōr'ô-vĭl)...Calif.	39·29 N	121·34 W
66	Oroville...Wash.	48·55 N	119·25 W
80	Orrville (ôr'vĭl)...Ohio	40·45 N	81·50 W
118	Orsa (ōr'sä)...Swe.	61·08 N	14·35 E
118	Örsdals Vand (L.) (ûrs-däls vän) Nor.	58·39 N	6·06 E
128	Orsha (ôr'shå)...Sov. Un.	54·29 N	30·28 E
133	Orsk (ôrsk)...Sov. Un.	51·15 N	58·50 E
127	Orşova (ôr'shô-vä)...Rom.	44·43 N	22·26 E
98	Ortega (ôr-tĕ'gä)...Col. (In.)	3·56 N	75·12 W
124	Ortegal, Cabo (C.) (kå'bô-ôr-tå-gäl').Sp.	43·46 N	8·15 W
111	Orth...Aus. (Vienna In.)	48·09 N	16·42 E
125	Orthez (ôr-tĕz')...Fr.	43·29 N	0·43 W
124	Ortigueira (ôr-tê-gā'ē-rä)...Sp.	43·40 N	7·50 W
65	Orting (ôrt'ĭng) Wash. (Seattle In.)	47·06 N	122·12 W
126	Ortona (ôr-tō'nä)...It.	42·22 N	14·22 E
70	Ortonville (ôr-tŭn-vĭl)...Minn.	45·18 N	96·26 W
98	Oruro (ô-rōō'rō)...Bol.	17·57 S	66·59 W
126	Orvieto (ôr-vyâ'tō)...It.	42·43 N	12·08 E
127	Oryakhovo...Bul.	43·43 N	23·59 E
118	Os (ôs)...Nor.	60·24 N	5·22 E
132	Osa (ô'så)...Sov. Un.	57·18 N	55·25 E
93	Osa, Pen. de (ō'sä)...C. R.	8·30 N	83·25 W
71	Osage (ō'sāj)...Iowa	43·16 N	92·49 W
73	Osage (R.)...Mo.	38·10 N	93·12 W
73	Osage City (ō'sāj sĭ'tĭ)...Kans.	38·28 N	95·53 W
153	Ōsaka (ō'sä-kä)..Jap. (Ōsaka In.)	34·40 N	135·27 E
153	Ōsaka (Pref.)...Jap. (Ōsaka In.)	34·45 N	135·36 E
153	Ōsaka-Wan (B.) (wän)...Jap.	34·34 N	135·16 E
71	Osakis (ô-sā'kĭs)...Minn.	45·51 N	95·09 W
71	Osakis (L.)...Minn.	45·55 N	94·55 W
153	Ōsawa (ō'sä-wä).Jap. (Tōkyō In.)	35·54 N	129·48 E
73	Osawatomie (ŏs-ȧ-wăt'ô-mē).Kans.	38·29 N	94·57 W
72	Osborne (ŏz'bŭrn)...Kans.	39·25 N	98·42 W
71	Osceola (ŏs-ê-ō'lå)...Iowa	41·04 N	93·45 W
73	Osceola...Mo.	38·02 N	93·41 W
70	Osceola...Nebr.	41·11 N	97·34 W
73	Osceola...Tenn.	35·42 N	89·58 W
80	Oscoda (ŏs-kō'dȧ)...Mich.	44·25 N	83·20 W
128	Osëtr (R.) (ô'sĕt'r)...Sov. Un.	54·27 N	38·15 E
80	Osgood (ŏz'gŏŏd)...Ind.	39·10 N	85·20 W
85	Osgoode Sta...Can. (Ottawa In.)	45·09 N	75·37 W
134	Osh (ôsh)...Sov. Un.	40·28 N	72·47 E
81	Oshawa (ŏsh'ȧ-wȧ)...Can.	43·50 N	78·50 W
153	Ōshima (I.) (ō'shê'mä)...Jap.	34·47 N	139·35 E
70	Oshkosh (ŏsh'kŏsh)...Nebr.	41·24 N	102·22 W
71	Oshkosh...Wis.	44·01 N	88·35 W
119	Oshmyany (ôsh-myä'nĭ)..Sov. Un.	54·27 N	25·55 E
164	Oshogbo...Nig.	7·53 N	4·23 E
127	Osijek (ôs'ĭ-yĕk)...Yugo.	45·33 N	18·48 E
134	Osinniki (ŭ-sē'nyĭ-kē)...Sov. Un.	53·29 N	85·19 E
129	Osipenko (ŭ-sē'pyĭn-kō)..Sov. Un.	46·45 N	36·47 E
71	Oskaloosa (ŏs-kȧ-lōō'sȧ)...Iowa	41·16 N	92·40 W
118	Oskarshamn (ôs'kärs-häm'n).Swe.	57·16 N	16·24 E
118	Oskarsström (ôs'kärs-strûm).Swe.	56·48 N	12·55 E
129	Oskol (R.) (ôs-kôl')...Sov. Un.	49·25 N	37·41 E
118	Oslo (ôs'lō)...Nor.	59·56 N	10·41 E
118	Oslo Fd (fyôrd)...Nor.	59·03 N	10·35 E
124	Osma (ōs'mä)...Sp.	41·35 N	3·02 W
133	Osmaniye...Tur.	37·10 N	36 30 E
120	Osnabrück (ôs-nä-brük')...Ger.	52·16 N	8·05 E
100	Osorno (ō-sō'r-nō)...Chile	40·42 S	73·13 W
159	Osprey Reef (I.) (ŏs'prå)...Austl.	14·00 S	146·45 E
160	Ossa, Mt. (ŏsȧ)...Austl.	41·45 S	146·05 E
74	Osseo (ŏs'sê-ō)...Minn. (Minneapolis, St. Paul In.)	45·07 N	93·24 W
84	Ossining (ŏs'ĭ-nĭng) N. Y. (New York In.)	41·09 N	73·51 W
82	Ossipee (ŏs'ĭ-pē)...N. H.	43·42 N	71·08 W
118	Ossjöen (L.) (ôs-syûĕn)...Nor.	61·20 N	12·00 E
128	Ostashkov (ôs-täsh'kôf)..Sov. Un.	57·07 N	33·04 E
117	Oste (R.) (ōz'tĕ)...Ger.	53·20 N	9·19 E
129	Oster (ōs'tĕr)...Sov. Un.	50·55 N	30·52 E
118	Oster-daläven (R.)...Swe.	61·40 N	13·00 E
118	Oster Fd. (ûs'tĕr fyôr')...Nor.	60·40 N	5·25 E
118	Ostersund (ûs'tĕr-sŏŏnd)...Swe.	63·09 N	14·49 E
118	Östhammar (ûst'häm'är)...Swe.	60·16 N	18·21 E
125	Ostia Antica (ô's-tyä-än-tē'kä) It. (Rome In.)	41·46 N	12·24 E
	Ostia Lido, see Lido di Roma		
121	Ostrava...Czech.	49·51 N	18·18 E
121	Ostróda (ôs'trŏŏt-å)...Pol.	53·41 N	19·58 E
129	Ostróg (ŏs-trôk')...Sov. Un.	50·21 N	26·40 E
129	Ostrogozhsk (ôs-trô-gôzhk') Sov. Un.	50·53 N	39·03 E
121	Ostrołeka (ôs-trô-woN'kå)...Pol.	53·04 N	21·35 E
129	Ostropol' (ôs-trô-pôl')...Sov. Un.	49·48 N	27·32 E
128	Ostrov (ôs-trôf')...Sov. Un.	57·21 N	28·22 E
121	Ostrowiec Świetokrzyski (ôs-trō'vyĕts shvyĕN-tō-kzhĭ'ske) Pol.	50·55 N	21·24 E
121	Ostrów Lubelski (ôs'trŏŏf lōō'bĕl-skĭ).Pol.	51·32 N	22·49 E
121	Ostrów Mazowiecka (mä-zô-vyĕt'skå).Pol.	52·47 N	21·54 E
121	Ostrow Wielkopolski (ôs'trŏŏv vyĕl-kō-pôl'skē).Pol.	51·38 N	17·49 E
121	Ostrzeszów (ôs-tzhä'shŏŏf)...Pol.	51·26 N	17·56 E
127	Ostuni (ôs-tōō'nē)...It.	40·44 N	17·35 E
127	Osum (R.) (ō'sŏŏm)...Alb.	40·37 N	20·00 E
153	Ōsumi-Guntō (Arch.) (ō'sōō-mê gŏŏn'tō).Jap.	30·34 N	130·30 E
153	Ōsumi (Van Diemen) Kaikyō (Str.) (văn dē'mĕn) (käē'kyō) Jap.	31·02 N	130·10 E
124	Osuna (ô-sōō'nä)...Sp.	37·18 N	5·05 W
128	Osveya (ôs'vĕ-yå)...Sov. Un.	56·00 N	28·08 E
110	Oswaldtwistle (ŏz-wȧld-twĭs''l) Eng.	53·44 N	2·23 W
81	Oswegatchie (R.) (ŏs-wê-găch'ĭ) N. Y.	44·15 N	75·20 W
73	Oswego (ŏs-wē'gō)...Kans.	37·10 N	95·08 W
81	Oswego...N. Y.	43·25 N	76·30 W
121	Oswiecim (ôsh-vyăN'tsyĭm)...Pol.	50·02 N	19·17 E
152	Otaru (ō'tä-rŏŏ)...Jap.	43·07 N	141·00 E
98	Otavalo (ōtä-vä'lō)...Ec.	0·14 N	78·16 W
166	Otavi (ô-tä'vē)...S. W. Afr.	19·35 S	17·20 E
68	Otay (ō'tā)..Calif. (San Diego In.)	32·36 N	117·04 W
128	Otepää (ō'tĕ-på)...Sov. Un.	58·03 N	26·31 E
127	Othonoí (I.)...Grc.	40·51 N	19·26 E
127	Óthris, Óros (Mts.)...Grc.	39·00 N	22·15 E
87	Otish Mts. (ô-tĭsh')...Can.	52·24 N	70·01 W
166	Otjiwarongo (ŏt-jê-wȧ-rôŋ'gō) Ang.	20·20 S	16·25 E
126	Otočac (ō'tō-chåts)...Yugo.	44·53 N	15·15 E
136	Otradnoye (ô-trå'd-nôyĕ) Sov. Un. (Leningrad In.)	59·46 N	30·50 E
127	Otranto (ô'trän-tô) (ô-trän'tō)..It.	40·07 N	18·30 E
127	Otranto, C. di...It.	40·06 N	18·32 E
127	Otranto, Strait of...It.-Alb.	40·30 N	18·45 E
136	Otra R. (ôt'rå) Sov. Un. (Moscow In.)	55·22 N	38·20 E
80	Otsego (ŏt-sē'gō)...Mich.	42·25 N	85·45 W
153	Otsu (ō'tsŏŏ)...Jap. (Ōsaka In.)	35·00 N	135·54 E
118	Ottavand (L.) (ôt'tä-vän)...Nor.	61·53 N	8·40 E
85	Ottawa (ŏt'ȧ-wȧ) Can. (Ottawa In.)	45·25 N	75·43 W
80	Ottawa...Ill.	41·20 N	88·50 W
73	Ottawa...Kans.	38·37 N	95·16 W
80	Ottawa...Ohio	41·00 N	84·00 W
87	Ottawa (R.)...Can.	46·05 N	77·20 W
87	Ottawa Is...Can.	59·50 N	81·00 W
168	Ottensville (ŏt'ĕns-vĭl)...S. Afr. (Johannesburg & Pretoria In.)	24·46 S	29·34 E
118	Otteråen (ôt'ĕr-ôĕn)...Nor.	59·13 N	7·20 E
69	Otter Cr. (ŏt'ĕr)...Utah	38·20 N	111·55 W
81	Otter Cr...Vt.	44·05 N	73·15 W
65	Otter Pt...Can. (Seattle In.)	48·21 N	123·50 W
70	Otter Tail (L.)...Minn.	46·21 N	95·52 W
74	Otterville (ŏt'ĕr-vĭl) Ill. (St. Louis In.)	39·03 N	90·24 W
166	Ottery (ŏt'ĕr-ĭ) S. Afr. (Cape Town In.)	34·02 S	18·31 E
71	Ottumwa (ô-tŭm'wȧ)...Iowa	41·00 N	92·26 W
91	Otumba (ô-tŭm'bä) Mex. (Mexico City In.)	19·41 N	98·46 W
160	Otway, C. (ŏt'wā)...Austl.	38·55 S	153·40 E
100	Otway, Seno (B.) (sĕ'nō-ô't-wä'y) Chile	53·00 S	73·00 W
121	Otwock (ôt'vôtsk)...Pol.	52·05 N	21·18 E
63	Ouachita, (R.)...U. S.	33·25 N	92·30 W
73	Ouachita Mts. (wŏsh'ĭ-tô)...Okla.	34·29 N	95·01 W
165	Ouaddai (Reg.) (wä-dī')...Chad	13·04 N	20·00 E
164	Ouagadougou (wä'gȧ-dōō'gōō) Upper Volta	12·20 N	1·43 W
164	Ouahigouya (wä-ê-gōō'yȧ) Upper Volta	13·34 N	2·22 W
164	Oualata (wä-lä'tä)...Mauritania	17·11 N	6·50 W
164	Ouallene (wäl-lân')...Alg.	24·43 N	1·15 E
95	Ouanaminthe...Hai.	19·35 N	71·45 W
165	Ouanda-Djalé (wän'dȧ jä-lā') Cen. Afr. Rep.	8·56 N	22·46 E
164	Ouarane (Dunes)...Mauritania	20·44 N	10·27 W
164	Ouargla (wär'glä)...Alg.	32·00 N	5·18 E
111	Oude Rijn (R.) Neth. (Amsterdam In.)	52·09 N	4·33 E
111	Oudewater.Neth. (Amsterdam In.)	52·01 N	4·52 E
111	Oud Gastel Neth. (Amsterdam In.)	51·35 N	4·27 E
114	Oudrhes, L. (Mt.)...Mor.	32·33 N	4·49 W
166	Oudtshoorn (outs'hōrn)...S. Afr.	33·33 S	23·36 E
114	Oued-Zem (wĕd-zĕm')...Mor.	33·05 N	5·49 W
122	Ouessant, I. d' (ēl-dwĕ-säN')...Fr.	48·28 N	5·00 W
165	Ouesso...Con. B.	1·38 N	16·04 E
95	Ouest, Pt...Hai.	19·00 N	73·25 W
164	Ouezzane (wĕ-zan')...Mor.	34·48 N	5·40 W
116	Oughter (L.) (lôK oK'tĕr)...Ire.	54·02 N	7·40 W
164	Ouidah (wē-dä')...Dahomey	6·25 N	2·05 E
114	Ouled Nail, Montes des (Mts.).Alg.	34·43 N	2·44 E
123	Oulins (ōō-lăN')...Fr. (Paris In.)	48·52 N	1·27 E
122	Oullins (ōō-lăN')...Fr.	45·44 N	4·46 E
112	Oulu (ō'lōō)...Fin.	64·58 N	25·43 E
112	Oulu-jarvi (L.)...Fin.	64·20 N	25·48 E
165	Oum Chalouba (ōōm shä-lōō'bä) Chad	15·48 N	20·30 E
112	Ounas (R.) (ō'nås)...Fin.	67·46 N	24·40 E
110	Oundle (ôn'd'l)...Eng.	52·28 N	0·28 W
165	Ounianga Kébir (ōō-nê-äŋ'gȧ kē-bēr').Chad	19·04 N	20·22 E
69	Ouray (ōō-rā')...Colo.	38·00 N	107·40 W
99	Ourinhos (ôôô-rê'nyôs)...Braz.	23·04 S	49·45 W
124	Ourique (ō-rē'kĕ)...Port.	37·39 N	8·10 W
101	Ouro Fino (ŏŭ-rô-fē'nō) Braz. (Rio de Janeiro In.)	22·18 S	46·21 W
101	Ouro Prêto (ô'rōō prā'tōō) Braz. (Rio de Janeiro In.)	20·24 S	43·30 W
116	Ouse (R.)...Eng.	53·45 N	1·09 W
87	Outardes, R. aux (ōō-tärdz').Can.	50·33 N	69·10 W
164	Outat el Hadj...Mor.	33·25 N	3·44 W
83	Outer (I.) (out'ĕr)...Can.	51·06 N	58·23 W
71	Outer (I.) (out'ĕr)...Wis.	47·03 N	90·20 W
89	Outer Brass (I.) (bräs)...Vir. Is. (U. S. A.) (St. Thomas In.)	18·24 N	64·58 W
116	Outer Hebrides (Is.)...Scot.	57·20 N	7·50 W
166	Outjo (ōt'yō)...S. W. Afr.	20·05 S	17·10 E
85	Outremont (ōō-trē-môN') Can. (Montreal In.)	45·31 N	73·36 W
160	Ouyen (ōō-ĕn)...Austl.	35·05 S	142·10 E
100	Ovalle (ō-väl'yä)...Chile	30·43 S	71·16 W
166	Ovamboland (Reg.)...S. W. Afr.	18·10 S	15·00 E
95	Ovando, Bahía de (B.) (bä-ē'ä-dĕ-ô-vä'n-dō).Cuba	20·10 N	74·05 W
124	Ovar (ô-vär')...Port.	40·52 N	8·38 W
111	Overijsche...Bel. (Brussels In.)	50·46 N	4·32 E
74	Overland (ō'vĕr-lănd) Mo. (St. Louis In.)	38·42 N	90·22 W
74	Overland Park Mo. (Kansas City In.)	38·59 N	94·40 W
84	Overlea (ō'vĕr-lā) (ō'vĕr-lē) Md. (Baltimore In.)	39·21 N	76·31 W
112	Overtornea...Swe.	66·19 N	23·31 E
129	Ovidiopol' (ô-vê-dê-ô'pôl') Sov. Un.	46·15 N	30·28 E
95	Oviedo (ô-vyĕ'dō)...Dom. Rep.	17·50 N	71·25 W
124	Oviedo (ô-vê-ā'dhō)...Sp.	43·22 N	5·50 W
129	Ovruch (ôv'rŏŏch)...Sov. Un.	51·19 N	28·51 E
153	Owada (ō'wä-dȧ).Jap. (Tōkyō In.)	35·43 N	140·06 E
153	Owada...Jap. (Tōkyō In.)	35·49 N	139·33 E
81	Owasco (L.) (ō-wăs'kō)...N. Y.	42·50 N	76·30 W
153	Owashi (ō'wä-shē)...Jap.	34·03 N	136·12 E
81	Owego (ō-wē'gō)...N. Y.	42·05 N	76·15 W
71	Owen (ō'ĕn)...Wis.	44·56 N	90·35 W
68	Owens (L.) (ō'ĕnz)...Calif.	36·27 N	117·45 W
68	Owens (R.)...Calif.	37·13 N	118·20 W
80	Owensboro (ō'ĕnz-bŭr-ō)...Ky.	37·45 N	87·05 W
80	Owen Sound (ō'ĕn)...Can.	44·30 N	80·55 W
155	Owen Stanley Ra. (stăn'lē)..Pap.	9·00 S	147·30 E
80	Owensville (ō'ĕnz-vĭl)...Ind.	38·15 N	87·40 W
73	Owensville...Mo.	38·20 N	91·29 W
75	Owensville..Ohio (Cincinnati In.)	39·08 N	84·07 W
80	Owenton (ō'ĕn-tŭn)...Ky.	38·35 N	84·55 W
164	Owerri (ô-wĕr'ê)...Nig.	5·26 N	7·04 E
67	Owl Cr. (oul)...Wyo.	43·45 N	108·46 W
80	Owosso (ô-wŏs'ō)...Mich.	43·00 N	84·15 W
66	Owyhee Mts. (ô-wī'hê)...Idaho	43·15 N	116·48 W
66	Owyhee Res...Ore.	43·27 N	117·30 W
66	Owyhee R...Ore.	43·04 N	117·45 W
66	Owyhee R., South Fork...Idaho	42·07 N	116·43 W
91	Oxchuc (ôs-chōōk')...Mex.	16·47 N	92·24 W
78	Oxford (ŏks'fērd)...Ala.	33·38 N	8·46 W

ng-sing; ŋ-baŋk; N-nasalized n; nŏd; cŏmmit; ōld; ōbey; ôrder; fōōd; fŏŏt; ou-out: s-soft; sh-dish; th-thin; pūre; ûnite; ûrn; stŭd; circŭs; ü-as "y" in study; '-indeterminate vowel.

Page	Name Pronunciation Region	Lat. °′	Long. °′
82	Oxford (ŏks'fērd) Can.	45·44 N	63·51 W
110	Oxford Eng. (London In.)	51·43 N	1·16 W
83	Oxford Mass. (Boston In.)	42·07 N	71·52 W
80	Oxford Mich.	42·50 N	83·15 W
78	Oxford Miss.	34·22 N	89·30 W
79	Oxford N. C.	36·17 N	78·35 W
80	Oxford Ohio	39·30 N	84·45 W
92	Oxkutzcab (ôx-kōō'tz-käb) Mex. (Yucatan In.)	20·18 N	89·22 W
84	Oxmoor (ŏks'mŏŏr) Ala. (Birmingham In.)	33·25 N	86·52 W
116	Ox Mts. (ŏks) Ire.	54·05 N	9·05 W
68	Oxnard (ŏks'närd) Calif.	34·08 N	119·12 W
91	Oxtotepec (ôx-tô-tĕ'pĕk) Mex. (Mexico City In.)	19·10 N	99·04 W
168	Oxyrhyncus (Ruins) U. A. R. (Nile In.)	28·37 N	30·48 E
99	Oyapock (ō-yȧ-pŏk'). Braz.-Fr. Gu.	2·45 N	52·15 W
164	Oyem (ô-yĕm) (ô-yăN') Gabon	1·42 N	11·38 E
135	Oymyakon (oi-myŭ-kôn'). Sov. Un.	63·14 N	142·58 E
164	Oyo (ō'yō) Nig.	7·52 N	3·51 E
123	Oyonnax (ô-yô-näks') Fr.	46·16 N	5·40 E
84	Oyster Bay. N. Y. (New York In.)	40·52 N	73·32 W
77	Oyster Bay Tex. (In.)	29·41 N	94·33 W
77	Oyster Cr. (ois'tēr) Tex. (In.)	29·13 N	95·29 W
95	Ozama (R.) (ô-zä'mä). Dom. Rep.	18·45 N	69·55 W
155	Ozamiz (ô-zä'mêz) Phil.	8·06 N	123·43 E
78	Ozark (ō'zärk) Ala.	31·28 N	85·28 W
73	Ozark Ark.	35·29 N	93·49 W
73	Ozarks, L. of the (ō'zärkz) Mo.	38·06 N	93·26 W
73	Ozark Plat. Mo.	36·37 N	93·56 W
128	Ozëry (ô-zyô'rĕ) Sov. Un.	54·53 N	38·31 E
126	Ozieri Sard.	40·38 N	8·53 E
121	Ozorków (ô-zôr'kŏŏf) Pol.	51·58 N	19·20 E
91	Ozuluama (ō'zōō-lōō-ä'mä). Mex.	21·34 N	97·52 W
91	Ozumba (ô-zōō'm-bä) Mex. (Mexico City In.)	19·02 N	98·48 W
146	Paan China	30·08 N	99·00 E
166	Paarl (pärl) S. Afr.	33·45 S	18·55 E
157	Paauilo (pä-ä-ōō'ê-lō). Hawaii (In.)	20·03 N	155·25 W
121	Pabianice (pä-byȧ-nē'tsĕ) Pol.	51·40 N	19·29 E
98	Pacaás Novos, Massiço de (Mts.) (mä-sē'sô-dĕ-pä-kà's-nô'vôs) Braz.	11·03 S	64·02 W
98	Pacaraima, Serra (Mts.) (sĕr'rȧ pä-kä-rä-ē'mȧ) Braz.-Ven.	3·45 N	62·30 W
98	Pacasmayo (pä-käs-mä'yō) Peru	7·24 S	79·30 W
146	Pach'u (pä'chōō') China	39·50 N	78·23 E
90	Pachuca (pä-chōō'kä) Mex.	20·07 N	98·43 W
65	Pacific (pȧ-sĭf'ĭk) Wash. (Seattle In.)	47·16 N	122·15 W
65	Pacifica (pȧ-sĭf'ĭ-kȧ) Calif. (San Francisco In.)	37·38 N	122·29 W
68	Pacific Beach Calif. (San Diego In.)	32·47 N	117·22 W
68	Pacific Grove Calif.	36·37 N	121·54 W
157	Pacific O.		
79	Pacolet (R.) (pă'cō-lĕt) S. C.	34·55 N	81·49 W
123	Pacy-sur-Eure (pä-sē-sür-ûr') Fr. (Paris In.)	49·01 N	1·24 E
154	Padang (pä-däng') Indon.	1·01 S	100·28 E
139	Padang, Palau (I.) Indon. (Singapore In.)	1·12 N	102·21 E
80	Paden City (pā'dĕn) W. Va.	39·30 N	80·55 W
120	Paderborn (pä-dĕr-bôrn') Ger.	51·43 N	8·46 E
110	Padiham (păd'ĭ-hȧm) Eng.	53·48 N	2·19 W
90	Padilla (pä-dēl'yä) Mex.	24·00 N	98·45 W
65	Padilla B. (pä-dĕl'lȧ) Wash. (Seattle In.)	48·31 N	122·34 W
126	Padova (Padua) (pä'dô-vä) (păd'ū-ȧ). It.	45·24 N	11·53 E
77	Padre I. (pä'drā) Tex.	27·09 N	97·15 W
	Padua, see Padova		
78	Paducah (pȧ-dū'kȧ) Ky.	37·05 N	88·36 W
152	Paektu San (Mt.) (pâk'tōō-sän') China-Kor.	42·00 N	128·03 E
126	Pag (I.) (päg) Yugo.	44·30 N	14·48 E
154	Pagai Selatan (I.) Indon.	2·48 S	100·22 E
154	Pagai Utara (I.) Indon.	2·45 S	100·02 E
127	Pagasitikós Kólpos (G.) Grc.	39·15 N	23·00 E
69	Pagosa Springs (pȧ-gō'sȧ) Colo.	37·15 N	107·05 W
157	Pahala (pä-hä'lä) Hawaii (In.)	19·11 N	155·28 W
139	Pahang (State) Mala. (Singapore In.)	3·02 N	102·57 E
154	Pahang R. Mala.	3·39 N	102·41 E
79	Pahokee (pȧ-hō'kē) Fla. (In.)	26·45 N	80·40 W
148	Paichü (bäi'gü) China	33·04 N	120·17 E
150	Paich'uan China	47·22 N	126·00 E
119	Paide (pī'dĕ) Sov. Un.	58·54 N	25·30 E
150	Paiho China	32·30 N	110·15 E
148	Pai Hu (L.) (bäi' hōō) China	32·22 N	117·38 E
119	Päijänna (L.) (pĕ'ē-yĕn-nĕ) Fin.	61·38 N	25·05 E
148	Paikouchen (bäi'gō'jen) China	39·08 N	116·02 E
150	Pailingmiao China	41·42 N	110·55 E
157	Pailolo Chan. (pä-ê-lō'lō) Hawaii (In.)	21·05 N	156·41 W
101	Paine (pī'nĕ). Chile (Santiago In.)	33·49 S	70·44 W
80	Painesville (pānz'vĭl) Ohio	41·40 N	81·15 W
69	Painted Des. (pānt'ĕd) Ariz.	36·15 N	111·35 W
80	Paintsville (pānts'vĭl) Ky.	37·50 N	82·50 W
148	Paip'u (bäi'pōō) China	32·15 N	120·47 E
150	Paise China	24·00 N	106·38 E
116	Paisley (pāz'lĭ) Scot.	55·50 N	4·30 W
98	Paita (pä-ē'tä) Peru	5·11 S	81·12 W
150	Pai T'ou Shan (Mts.) Korea	40·30 N	127·20 E
69	Paiute Ind. Res. Utah	38·17 N	113·50 W
150	Paiyü Shan (Mtns.) China	37·02 N	108·30 E
91	Pajápan (pä-hä'pän) Mex.	18·16 N	94·41 W
154	Pakanburu Indon.	0·43 N	101·15 E
150	Pakhoi (päk'hoi') China	21·58 N	108·51 E
136	Pakhra R. (päk'rá) Sov. Un. (Moscow In.)	55·29 N	37·51 E
138	Pakistan Asia	28·00 N	67·30 E
142	Pakistan, East Asia	24·15 N	89·50 E
142	Pakistan, West Asia	32·20 N	71·30 E
154	Pakokku (pȧ-kŏk'kōō) Bur.	21·29 N	95·00 E
126	Pakrac (pä'kräts) Yugo.	45·25 N	17·13 E
121	Paks (pôksh) Hung.	46·38 N	18·53 E
77	Palacios (pȧ-lä'syōs) Tex.	28·42 N	96·12 W
125	Palafrogell (pä-lä-frô-gĕl) Sp.	41·55 N	3·09 E
126	Palagruža (Is.) (pä'lä-grōō'zhä) Yugo.	42·20 N	16·23 E
123	Palaiseau (pȧ-lĕ-zō'). Fr. (Paris In.)	48·44 N	2·16 E
135	Palana Sov. Un.	59·07 N	159·58 E
155	Palanan B. (pä-lä'nän) Phil. (Manila In.)	17·14 N	122·35 E
155	Palanan Pt. Phil. (Manila In.)	17·12 N	122·40 E
127	Palanka (pä'län-kä) Yugo.	45·14 N	19·24 E
142	Pālanpur (pä'lŭn-pōōr) India	24·08 N	73·29 E
166	Palapye (pȧ-läp'yĕ) Bech.	22·34 S	27·28 E
75	Palatine (păl'ȧ-tīn) Ill. (Chicago In.)	42·07 N	88·03 W
79	Palatka (pȧ-lăt'kȧ) Fla.	29·39 N	81·40 W
155	Palau (Pelew) Is. (pä-lä'ōō) Pac. Is. Trust. Ter.	7·15 N	134·30 E
155	Palauig (pȧ-lou'ĕg) Phil. (Manila In.)	15·27 N	119·54 E
155	Palauig Pt. Phil. (Manila In.)	15·28 N	119·41 E
154	Palawan (I.) (pä-lä'wän) Phil.	9·50 N	117·38 E
119	Paldiski (päl'dĭ-skĭ) Sov. Un.	59·22 N	24·04 E
154	Palembang (pä-lĕm-bäng'). Indon.	2·57 S	104·40 E
92	Palencia (pä-lĕn'sê-ȧ) Guat.	14·40 N	90·22 W
124	Palencia (pä-lĕ'n-syä) Sp.	42·02 N	4·32 W
91	Palenque (pä-lĕŋ'kä) Mex.	17·34 N	91·58 W
95	Palenque, Punta (Pt.) (pōō'n-tä) Dom. Rep.	18·10 N	70·10 W
85	Palermo (pä-lĕr'mô) Can. (Toronto In.)	43·26 N	79·47 W
98	Palermo Col. (In.)	2·53 N	75·26 W
126	Palermo It.	38·08 N	13·24 E
77	Palestine Tex.	31·46 N	95·38 W
139	Palestine (Reg.) (păl'ĕs-tīn) Asia (Palestine In.)	31·33 N	35·00 E
146	Paletwa (pŭ-lĕt'wä) Bur.	21·19 N	92·52 E
143	Palghāt India	10·49 N	76·40 E
142	Pali India	25·53 N	73·18 E
92	Palín (pä-lēn') Guat.	14·42 N	90·42 W
66	Palisade (păl-ĭ-säd') Nev.	40·39 N	116·11 W
91	Palizada (pä-lê-zä'dä) Mex.	18·17 N	92·04 W
142	Palk Str. (pôk) India	10·00 N	79·23 E
101	Palma (päl'mä) Braz. (Rio de Janeiro In.)	21·23 S	42·18 W
125	Palma, Ba. de (B.) (bä-ē'ä-dĕ). Sp.	39·24 N	2·37 E
124	Palma del Río (dĕl rē'ō) Sp.	37·43 N	5·19 W
125	Palma de Mallorca (dĕ-mäl-yô'r-kä). Sp.	39·35 N	2·38 E
99	Palmares (päl-mä'rĕs) Braz.	8·46 S	35·28 W
100	Palmas (päl'mäs) Braz.	26·20 S	51·56 W
164	Palmas, C. Lib.	4·30 N	9·20 W
95	Palma Soriano (sô-rê-ä'nō). Cuba	20·15 N	76·00 W
79	Palm Beach (päm bēch'). Fla. (In.)	26·43 N	80·03 W
99	Palmeira dos Índios (päl-mā'rä-dôs-ē'n-dyôs). Braz.	9·26 S	36·33 W
125	Palmela (päl-mĕ'lä) Port. (Lisbon In.)	38·34 N	8·54 W
64	Palmer (päm'ēr) Alaska	61·38 N	149·15 W
65	Palmer Wash. (Seattle In.)	47·19 N	121·53 W
47	Palmer Pen. Ant.	70·00 S	65·00 W
159	Palmerston North (päm'ēr-stŭn) N. Z. (In.)	40·21 S	175·43 E
159	Palmerville (päm'ēr-vĭl) Austl.	16·08 S	144·15 E
79	Palmetto (pȧl-mĕt'ô) Fla. (In.)	27·32 N	82·34 W
95	Palmetto Pt. Ba. Is.	21·15 N	73·25 W
126	Palmi (päl'mē) It.	38·21 N	15·54 E
98	Palmira (päl-mē'rä) Col. (In.)	3·33 N	76·17 W
94	Palmira Cuba	22·15 N	80·25 W
73	Palmyra (păl-mī'rȧ) Mo.	39·45 N	91·32 W
84	Palmyra N. J. (Philadelphia In.)	40·01 N	75·00 W
157	Palmyra (I.) Oceania	6·00 N	162·20 W
142	Palmyras Pt. India	25·42 N	87·45 E
103	Palmyre Syr.	30·35 N	37·58 E
65	Palo Alto (pă'lō äl'tō) Calif. (San Francisco In.)	37·27 N	122·09 W
72	Paloduro Cr. (pā-lô-dōō'rô). Tex.	36·16 N	101·12 W
139	Paloh Mala. (Singapore In.)	2·11 N	103·12 E
76	Paloma, L. (pä-lō'mä) Mex.	26·53 N	104·02 W
101	Palomo, Cerro el (Mtn.) (sĕ'r-rô-ĕl-pä-lô'mô) Chile (Santiago In.)	34·36 S	70·20 W
125	Palos, Cabo de (C.) (kä'bô-dĕ-pä'lôs). Sp.	39·38 N	0·43 W
74	Palos Verdes Estates (pă'lŭs vûr'dĭs) Calif. (Los Angeles In.)	33·48 N	118·24 W
66	Palouse (pȧ-lōōz') Wash.	46·54 N	117·04 W
66	Palouse Hills Wash.	46·48 N	117·47 W
66	Palouse R. Wash.	47·02 N	117·35 W
133	Palu (pä-loo') Tur.	38·55 N	40·10 E
98	Palúa (pä-lōō'ȧ) Ven.	8·30 N	62·30 W
155	Paluan (pä-lōō'än) Phila. (Manila In.)	13·25 N	120·29 E
135	Pamamushir (I.) Sov. Un.	50·42 N	153·45 E
122	Pamiers (pȧ-myā') Fr.	43·07 N	1·34 E
145	Pamirs (Plat.) Sov. Un.	38·14 N	72·27 E
79	Pamlico R. (păm'lĭ-kō) N. C.	35·25 N	76·59 W
79	Pamlico Sd. N. C.	35·10 N	76·10 W
72	Pampa (păm'pȧ) Tex.	35·32 N	100·56 W
100	Pampa de Castillo (Plat.) (pä'm-pä-dĕ-käs-tē'l-yô). Arg.	45·30 S	67·30 W
155	Pampanga (R.) (päm-päŋ'gä) Phil. (Manila In.)	15·20 N	120·48 E
100	Pampas (Reg.) (päm'päs) Arg.	37·00 S	64·30 W
124	Pampilhosa do Botão (päm-pê-lyō'sȧ-dô-bô-to'uN) Port.	40·21 N	8·23 W
98	Pamplona (päm-plō'nä) Col.	7·19 N	72·41 W
124	Pamplona (päm-plô'nä) Sp.	42·49 N	1·39 W
81	Pamunkey (R.) (pȧ-mŭŋ'kĭ) Va.	37·40 N	77·20 W
80	Pana (pā'nȧ) Ill.	39·25 N	89·05 W
92	Panabá (pä-nä-bä') Mex. (Yucatan In.)	21·18 N	88·15 W
127	Panagyurishte (pȧ-nȧ-gyōō'rêsh-tĕ). Bul.	42·30 N	24·11 E
88	Panamá (păn-ȧ-mä') N. A. (Panama Canal In.)	8·35 N	81·08 W
89	Panama, G. of Pan.	7·45 N	79·20 W
89	Panama, Isth. of Pan.	9·00 N	81·00 W
93	Panama, B. of Pan.	8·50 N	79·08 W
78	Panama City (păn-ȧ mä' sĭ'tĭ). Fla.	30·08 N	85·39 W
68	Panamint Ra. (păn-ȧ-mĭnt') Calif.	36·40 N	117·30 W
126	Panaria (Is.) (pä-nä'rê-ä) It.	38·37 N	15·05 E
126	Panaro (R.) (pä-nä'rô) It.	44·47 N	11·06 E
154	Panay (I.) (pä-nī') Phil.	11·15 N	121·38 E
127	Pančevo (pän'chĕ-vô) Yugo.	44·52 N	20·42 E
139	Panchor Mala. (Singapore In.)	2·10 N	102·43 E
166	Panda (pän'dä') Con. L.	10·59 S	27·24 E
94	Pan de Guajaibon (Mtn.) (pän dä gwä-jä-bōn'). Cuba	22·50 N	83·20 W
154	Pandjang, Selat (Str.) Indon.	1·00 N	102·00 E
119	Panevėžys (pä'nyĕ-vāzh'ēs) Sov. Un.	55·44 N	24·21 E
134	Panfilov (pŭn-fē'lôf) Sov. Un.	44·12 N	79·58 E
165	Panga (päŋ'gä) Con. L.	1·58 N	26·45 E
167	Pangani (pän-gä'nē) Tan.	5·28 S	38·58 E
149	P'angchiang. China (Canton In.)	22·57 N	113·15 E
148	Pangfou (bäng'fōō) China	32·54 N	117·22 E
154	Pangkalpinang (päng-käl'pê-näng') Indon.	2·11 S	106·04 E
142	Pangkong Tsho (L.) China	33·40 N	79·30 E
87	Pangnirtung Can.	66·08 N	65·26 W
69	Panguitch (päŋ'gwĭch) Utah	37·50 N	112·30 W
101	Panimávida (pä-nē-mà'vē-dä) Chile (Santiago In.)	36·44 S	71·26 W
	Panjim, see Nova Goa		
150	Panshih China	42·50 N	126·48 E
151	Pan Si Pan (Mtn.) Viet.	22·25 N	103 50 E
155	Pantar (I.) (pän'tär) Indon.	8·40 S	123·45 E
74	Pantego (păn'tĭ-gō) Tex. (Dallas, Fort Worth In.)	32·45 N	97·06 W
113	Pantelleria (I.) (pän-tĕl-lȧ-rē'ä) It.	36·43 N	11·59 E
91	Pantepec (pän-tȧ-pĕk') Mex.	17·11 N	93·04 W
90	Panuco (pä'nōō-kô) Mex.	22·04 N	98·11 W
90	Pánuco (pä'nōō-kô) Mex.	29·47 N	105·55 W
90	Panuco (R.) Mex.	21·59 N	98·20 W
76	Pánuco de Coronado (pä'nōō-kô dä kō-rô-nä'dhō) Mex.	24·33 N	104·20 W
143	Panvel India (Bombay In.)	18·59 N	73·06 E
92	Panzós (pän-zós') Guat.	15·26 N	89·40 W
99	Pao (pà'ō) (R.) Ven. (In.)	9·52 N	67·57 W
150	Paochang China	41·52 N	115·25 E
150	Paocheng China	33·15 N	106·58 E
150	Paochi China	34·10 N	106·58 E
73	Paola (pā-ō'lȧ) Kans.	38·34 N	94·51 W
80	Paoli (pā-ō'lī) Ind.	38·35 N	86·30 W
84	Paoli Pa. (Philadelphia In.)	40·03 N	75·29 W
69	Paonia (pā-ō'nyȧ) Colo.	38·50 N	107·40 W
146	Paoshan (pä'ô-shän') China	25·14 N	99·03 E
149	Paoshan China (Shanghai In.)	31·25 N	121·29 E
148	Paoti (pä'ô-tē') China	39·44 N	117·19 E
150	Paot'ou China	40·28 N	110·10 E
148	Paoying (pä'ô-yĭng) China	33·14 N	119·20 E
121	Pápa (pä'pô) Hung.	47·18 N	17·27 E
92	Papagayo, Golfo del (G.) (gôl-fô-dĕl-pä-pä-gä'yō). C. R.	10·44 N	85·56 W
90	Papagayo, Laguna (L.) (lä-ōō-nä) Mex.	16·44 N	99·44 W
90	Papagayo (R.) (pä-pä-gä'yō) Mex.	16·52 N	99·41 W
69	Papago Ind. Res. (pä'pä-gō). Ariz.	32·33 N	112·12 W
88	Papantla de Olarte (pä-pän'tlä dä-ô-lä'r-tĕ). Mex.	20·30 N	97·15 W
91	Papatoapan (R.) (pä-pä-tô-ä-pä'n). Mex.	18·00 N	96·22 W
120	Papenburg (päp'ĕn-bōōrgh). Ger.	53·05 N	7·23 E
101	Papinas (pä-pē'näs) Arg. (Buenos Aires In.)	35·30 S	57·19 W
85	Papineauville (pä-pē-nō'vēl) Can. (Ottawa In.)	45·38 N	75·01 W
155	Papua (păp'ōōȧ) Oceania	7·30 S	142·30 E
155	Papua, Gulf of (păp-ōō-ȧ) Pap.	8·20 S	144·45 E
101	Papudo (pä-pōō'dô) Chile (Santiago In.)	32·30 S	71·25 W
100	Paquequer Pequeno (pä-kĕ-kĕ'r-pĕ-kĕ'nô). Braz. (In.)	22·19 S	43·02 W
	Pará, see Belém		
99	Pará (State) (pä-rä') Braz.	4·45 S	53·30 W
101	Pará (pä-rä') (R.) Braz. (Rio de Janeiro In.)	20·21 S	44·38 W
99	Pará, Rio do (R.) (rē'ō-dô-pä-rä') Braz.	1·09 S	48·48 W
128	Para (R.) Sov. Un.	53·45 N	40·58 E
155	Paracale (pä-rä-kä'lä) Phil. (Manila In.)	14·17 N	122·47 E
100	Paracambi (pä-rä-kà'm-bē) Braz. (In.)	22·36 S	43·43 W
99	Paracatu (pä-rä-kä-tōō') Braz.	17·17 S	46·43 W
160	Parachilna (pä-rä-chĭl'nä) Austl.	31·09 S	138·20 E
127	Paraćin (pä'rä-chēn) Yugo.	43·51 N	21·26 E
101	Para de Minas (pä-rä-dĕ-mē'näs) Braz. (Rio de Janeiro In.)	19·52 S	44·37 W
66	Paradise Valley (păr'ȧ-dīs) Nev.	41·28 N	117·32 W
98	Parados, Cerro de los (Mtn.) (sĕ'r-rô-dĕ-lôs-pä-rä'dôs) Col. (In.)	5·44 N	75·13 W
73	Paragould (păr'ȧ-gōōld) Ark.	36·03 N	90·29 W
99	Paraguaçu (R.) (pä-rä-gwä-zōō') Braz.	12·25 S	39·46 W
98	Paraguaná, Pen. de (Pen.) (pĕ-nĕ'ng-sōō-lä-dĕ-pä-rä-gwä-nä'). Ven.	12·00 N	69·55 W
96	Paraguay (păr'ȧ-gwā) S. A.	24·00 S	57·00 W
99	Paraguay, Rio (R.) (rē'ō-pä-rä-gwä'y). S. A.	21·12 S	57·31 W
	Paraíba, see João Pessoa		
99	Paraíba (State) (pä-rä-ē'bä). Braz.	7·11 S	37·05 W

ăt; finăl; rāte; senâte; ärm; àsk; sofȧ; fâre; ch-choose; dh-as th in other; bē; êvent; bĕt; recĕnt; cratēr; g-go; gh-guttural g; bĭt; ĭ-short neutral; rīde; K-guttural k as ch in German ich;

Page	Name Pronunciation Region	Lat. °'	Long. °'
101	Paraiba (R.) Braz. (Rio de Janeiro In.)	23·02 S	45·43 W
101	Paraíba do Sul (dô-sōō'l) Braz. (Rio de Janeiro In.)	22·10 S	43·18 W
101	Paraibuna (pä-räē-bōō'nä) Braz. (Rio de Janeiro In.)	23·23 S	45·38 W
88	Paraiso (pä-rä-ē'sō) C. Z. (Panama Canal In.)	9·02 N	79·38 W
93	Paraíso C. R.	9·50 N	83·53 W
91	Paraíso Mex.	18·24 N	93·11 W
101	Paraisópolis (pä-räē-sô'pō-lēs) Braz. (Rio de Janeiro In.)	22·35 S	45·45 W
101	Paraitinga (pä-rä-ē-tē'n-gä) (R.) Braz. (Rio de Janeiro In.)	23·15 S	45·24 W
164	Parakou (pȧ-rȧ-kōō') Dahomey	9·16 N	2·37 E
99	Paramaribo (pȧ-rȧ-mä'rē-bō) Sur.	5·50 N	55·15 W
161	Paramatta (păr-ȧ-măt'ȧ) Austl. (Sydney In.)	33·49 S	150·59 E
122	Paramé (pȧ-rȧ-mā') Fr.	48·40 N	1·58 W
98	Paramillo (Mtn.) (pä-rä-mē'l-yō) Col. (In.)	7·06 N	75·55 W
135	Paramushir (I.) Sov. Un.	50·45 N	154·00 E
139	Paran (R.) Isr. (Palestine In.)	30·05 N	34·50 E
100	Paraná (pä-rä-nä') Arg.	31·44 S	60·29 W
100	Paraná (State) Braz.	24·25 S	52·00 W
100	Paraná, Rio (R.) Arg.	32·15 S	60·55 W
99	Paraná (R.) Braz.	13·05 S	47·11 W
100	Paranaguá (pä-rä'nä-gwä') Braz.	25·39 S	48·42 W
99	Paranaíba (pä-rä-nȧ-ē'bȧ) Braz.	19·43 S	51·13 W
99	Paranaíba (R.) Braz.	18·58 S	50·44 W
101	Parana Ibicuy (R.) (ē-bē-kōō'ē) Arg. (Buenos Aires In.)	33·27 S	59·26 W
99	Paranam Sur.	5·39 N	55·13 W
100	Paránápanema (R.) (pä-rä'nȧ'pä-nĕ-mä) Braz.	22·28 S	52·15 W
101	Paraopeda (R.) (pä-rä-o-pĕ'dä) Braz. (Rio de Janeiro In.)	20·09 S	44·14 W
99	Parapara (pä-rä-pä-rä) Ven. (In.)	9·44 N	67·17 W
101	Parati (pä-rätē) Braz. (Rio de Janeiro In.)	23·14 S	44·43 W
122	Paray-le-Monial (pȧ-rĕ'lē-mô-nyäl') Fr.	46·27 N	4·14 E
142	Pārbati (R.) India	24·50 N	76·44 E
	Parcel Is., see Hsisha Ch'üntao		
120	Parchin (pär'kēn) Ger.	53·25 N	11·52 E
121	Parczew (pär'chĕf) Pol.	51·38 N	22·53 E
99	Pardo (R.) (pär'dō) Braz.	15·25 S	39·40 W
101	Pardo (R.) Braz. (Rio de Janeiro In.)	21·32 S	46·40 W
120	Pardubice (pär'dōō-bĭt-sĕ) Czech.	50·02 N	15·47 E
99	Parecis, Serra dos (Mts.) (sĕr'rȧ dōs pä-rȧ-sēzh') Braz.	13·45 S	59·28 W
124	Paredes de Nava (pä-rā'dâs dā nä'vä) Sp.	42·10 N	4·41 W
87	Parent Can.	47·56 N	74·30 W
136	Pargolovo (pȧr-gô'lô vô) Sov. Un. (Leningrad In.)	60·04 N	30·18 E
98	Paria, Golfo de (G.) (gôl-fô-dĕ-pä'rē-ä) Ven.	10·33 N	62·14 W
69	Paria (R.) Utah-Ariz.	37·07 N	111·51 W
90	Paricutín, Vol. (pä-rē-kōō-tē'n) Mex.	19·27 N	102·14 W
76	Parida, Rio de la (R.) (rē'ō-dĕ-lä-pä-rē'dä) Mex.	26·23 N	104·40 W
98	Parima, Serra (Mts.) (sĕr'rȧ pä-rē'mȧ) Braz.-Ven.	3·45 N	64·00 W
98	Pariñas, Punta (Pt.) (pōō'n-tä-pä-rē'n-yäs) Peru	4·30 S	81·23 W
99	Parintins (pä-rĭn-tĭnzh') Braz.	2·34 S	56·30 W
74	Paris (păr'ĭs) Ark.	35·17 N	93·43 W
80	Paris Can.	43·15 N	82·20 W
123	Paris (pȧ-rē') Fr. (Paris In.)	48·51 N	2·20 E
80	Paris Ill.	39·35 N	87·40 W
80	Paris Ky.	38·15 N	84·15 W
73	Paris Mo.	39·27 N	91·59 W
78	Paris Tenn.	36·16 N	88·20 W
73	Paris Tex.	33·39 N	95·33 W
93	Parita, Golfo de (G.) (gôl-fô-dĕ-pä-rē'tä) Pan.	8·06 N	80·10 W
67	Park City Utah	40·39 N	111·33 W
70	Parker (pär'kēr) S. D.	43·24 N	97·10 W
69	Parker Dam Calif.-Ariz.	34·20 N	114·00 W
80	Parkersburg (pär'kērz-bûrg) W. Va.	39·15 N	81·35 W
160	Parkes (pärks) Austl.	33·10 S	148·10 E
71	Park Falls (pärk) Wis.	45·55 N	90·29 W
75	Park Forest Ill. (Chicago In.)	41·29 N	87·41 W
65	Parkland (pärk'lănd) Wash. (Seattle In.)	47·09 N	122·26 W
67	Park Ra. Colo.	40·54 N	106·40 W
71	Park Rapids Minn.	46·53 N	95·05 W
75	Park Ridge Ill. (Chicago In.)	42·00 N	87·50 W
70	Park River N. D.	48·22 N	97·43 W
65	Parkrose (pärk'rōz) Ore. (Portland In.)	45·33 N	122·33 W
167	Park Rynie S. Afr. (Natal In.)	30·22 S	30·43 E
70	Parkston (pärks'tŭn) S. D.	43·22 N	97·59 W
69	Park View (vū) N. Mex.	36·45 N	106·30 W
84	Parkville (pärk'vĭl) Md. (Baltimore In.)	39·23 N	76·33 W
74	Parkville Mo. (Kansas City In.)	39·12 N	94·41 W
125	Parla (pär'lä) Sp. (Madrid In.)	40·14 N	3·46 W
126	Parma (pär'mä) It.	44·48 N	10·20 E
75	Parma Ohio (Cleveland In.)	41·23 N	81·44 W
75	Parma Heights Ohio (Cleveland In.)	41·23 N	81·36 W
99	Parnaguá (pär-nä-gwä') Braz.	9·52 S	44·27 W
99	Parnaíba (pär-nä-ē'bä) Braz.	3·00 S	41·42 W
99	Parnaiba (R.) Braz.	3·57 S	42·30 W
127	Parnassós (Mtn.) Grc.	38·33 N	22·35 E
111	Parndorf Aus. (Vienna In.)	48·00 N	16·52 E
119	Pärnu (pĕr'nōō) Sov. Un.	58·24 N	24·29 E
119	Pärnu (R.) Sov. Un.	58·40 N	25·05 E
119	Pärnu Laht (B.) (läkt) Sov. Un.	58·15 N	24·17 E
142	Paro Dzong (pä'rô dzông') Bhu.	27·30 N	89·30 E
160	Paroo (R.) (pä'rōō) Austl.	29·40 S	144·24 E
144	Paropamisus (Mts.) Afg.	34·45 N	63·58 E
127	Páros (pä'rôs) (pā'rŏs) Grc.	37·05 N	25·14 E
127	Páros (I.) Grc.	37·11 N	25·00 E
166	Parow (pă'rô) S. Afr. (Cape Town In.)	33·54 S	18·36 E
69	Parowan (păr'ô-wăn) Utah	37·50 N	112·50 W
100	Parral (pär-rä'l) Chile	36·07 S	71·47 W
76	Parral, R. Mex.	27·25 N	105·08 W
161	Parramatta (R.) (păr-ȧ-măt'ȧ) Austl. (Sydney In.)	33·42 S	150·58 E
76	Parras (pär-räs') Mex.	25·28 N	102·08 W
93	Parrita (pär-rē'tä) C. R.	9·32 N	84·17 W
82	Parrsboro (pärz'bŭr-ô) Can.	45·25 N	64·20 W
80	Parry (I.) Can.	45·15 N	80·00 W
64	Parry, C. (păr'ĭ) Can.	70·20 N	124·31 W
49	Parry Is. Can.	75·30 N	110·00 W
81	Parry Sound Can.	45·20 N	80·00 W
73	Parsons (pär's'nz) Kans.	37·20 N	95·16 W
81	Parsons W. Va.	39·05 N	79·40 W
122	Parthenay (pär-t'nĕ') Fr.	46·39 N	0·16 W
126	Partinico (pär-tē'nē-kô) It.	38·02 N	13·11 E
168	Parys (pȧ-rĭs') S. Afr. (Johannesburg & Pretoria In.)	26·53 S	27·28 E
74	Pasadena (păs-ȧ-dē'nȧ) Calif. (Los Angeles In.)	34·09 N	118·09 W
84	Pasadena Md. (Baltimore In.)	39·06 N	76·35 W
77	Pasadena Tex. (In.)	29·43 N	95·13 W
78	Pascagoula (păs-kȧ-gōō'lȧ) Miss.	30·22 N	88·33 W
78	Pascagoula (R.) Miss.	30·52 N	88·48 W
121	Pascani (päsh-kän'') Rom.	47·46 N	26·42 E
66	Pasco (păs'kō) Wash.	46·13 N	119·04 W
120	Pasewalk (pä'zē-välk) Ger.	53·31 N	14·01 E
136	Pashiya (pä'shĭ-yȧ) Sov. Un. (Urals In.)	58·27 N	58·17 E
152	Pashkovo (pȧsh-kô'vô) Sov. Un.	48·52 N	131·09 E
129	Pashkovskaya (pȧsh-kôf'skȧ-yȧ) Sov. Un.	45·29 N	39·04 E
92	Pasión, Rio de la (R.) (rē'ō-dĕ-lä-pä-syōn') Guat. (Yucatan In.)	16·31 N	90·11 W
100	Paso de los Libres (pä-sô-dĕ-lôs-lē'brĕs) Arg.	29·33 S	57·05 W
101	Paso de los Toros (tô'rôs) Ur. (Buenos Aires In.)	32·43 S	56·33 W
68	Paso Robles (pă'sō rō'blĕs) Calif.	35·38 N	120·44 W
84	Passaic (pă-sā'ĭk) N. J. (New York In.)	40·52 N	74·08 W
84	Passaic R. N. J. (New York In.)	40·42 N	74·26 W
82	Passamaquoddy B. (păs'ȧ-mȧ-kwŏd'ĭ) Can.	45·00 N	66·45 W
101	Passa Tempo (pä's-sä-tĕ'm-pô) Braz. (Rio de Janeiro In.)	21·40 S	44·29 W
120	Passau (päs'ou) Ger.	48·34 N	13·27 E
78	Pass Christian (pȧs krĭs'tyĕn) Miss.	30·20 N	89·15 W
113	Passero, C. (päs-sĕ'rô) It.	36·34 N	15·13 E
100	Passo Fundo (pä'sŏ fōōn'dōō) Braz.	28·16 S	52·13 W
101	Passos (pä's-sōs) Braz. (Rio de Janeiro In.)	20·45 S	46·37 W
98	Pastaza (R.) (päs-tä'zä) Peru	3·05 S	76·18 W
98	Pasto (päs'tô) Col.	1·15 N	77·19 W
90	Pastora (päs-tô-rä) Mex.	22·08 N	100·04 W
154	Pasuruan Indon.	7·45 S	112·50 E
119	Pasvalys (päs-vä-lēs') Sov. Un.	56·04 N	24·23 E
100	Patagonia (Reg.) (păt-ȧ-gō'nĭ-ȧ) Arg.	46·45 S	69·30 W
143	Pātālganga (R.) India (Bombay In.)	18·52 N	73·08 E
142	Patan (pä'tŭn) Nep.	27·23 N	85·24 E
84	Patapsco R. (pȧ-tăps'kō) Md. (Baltimore In.)	39·12 N	76·30 W
126	Paternò (pä-tĕr-nô') It.	37·35 N	14·58 E
84	Paterson (păt'ēr-sŭn) N. J. (New York In.)	40·55 N	74·10 W
67	Pathfinder Res. (păth'fīn-dēr) Wyo.	42·22 N	107·10 W
142	Patiāla (pŭt-ē-ä'lŭ) India	30·25 N	76·28 E
100	Pati do Alferes (pä-tē-dô-äl-fĕ'rĕs) Braz. (In.)	22·25 S	43·25 W
142	Patna (pŭt'nŭ) India	25·33 N	85·18 E
155	Patnanongan (pät-nä-nôŋ'gän) Phil. (Manila In.)	14·50 N	122·25 E
80	Patoka (R.) (pȧ-tō'kȧ) Ind.	38·25 N	87·25 W
135	Patom Plat. Sov. Un.	59·30 N	115·00 E
99	Patos (pä'tōzh) Braz.	7·03 S	37·14 W
65	Patos (pă'tōs) Wash. (Vancouver In.)	48·47 N	122·57 W
100	Patos, Lago dos (L.) (lä'gō-ȧ dozh pä'tōzh) Braz.	31·15 S	51·30 W
99	Patos de Minas (dĕ-mē'näzh) Braz.	18·39 S	46·31 W
127	Pátrai (Patras) (pä-trī') (pȧ-träs') Grc.	38·15 N	21·48 E
127	Patraïkós Kólpos (G.) Grc.	38·16 N	21·19 E
	Patras, see Pátrai		
99	Patrocínio (pä-trō-sē'nē-ōō) Braz.	18·48 S	46·47 W
154	Pattani (pät'ȧ-nē) Thai.	6·56 N	101·13 E
82	Patten (păt''n) Maine	45·59 N	68·27 W
77	Patterson (păt'ēr-sŭn) La.	29·41 N	91·20 W
81	Patton Pa.	40·40 N	78·45 W
93	Patuca, Punta (Pt.) (pōō'n-tä-pä-tōō'kä) Hond.	15·23 N	84·05 W
93	Patuca R. Hond.	15·22 N	84·31 W
81	Patuxent (R.) (pȧ-tŭk'sĕnt) Md.	39·10 N	77·10 W
90	Pátzcuaro (päts'kwä-rô) Mex.	19·30 N	101·36 W
90	Pátzcuaro, Lago de (L.) (lä'gô-dĕ) Mex.	19·36 N	101·38 W
92	Patzicia (pät-zē'syä) Guat.	14·36 N	90·57 W
92	Patzún (pät-zōōn') Guat.	14·40 N	91·00 W
122	Pau (pō) Fr.	43·18 N	0·23 W
122	Pau, Gave de (strm.) (gȧv-dē) Fr.	43·33 N	0·51 W
122	Pauillac (pō-yȧk') Fr.	45·12 N	0·46 W
80	Paulding (pôl'dĭng) Ohio	41·05 N	84·35 W
111	Paulinenaue (pou'lē-nē-nou-ĕ) Ger. (Berlin In.)	52·40 N	12·43 E
165	Paulis Con. L.	2·40 N	28·08 E
99	Paulistana (pȧ'ōō-lēs-tä-nä) Braz.	8·13 S	41·06 W
99	Paulo Afonso, Salto (falls) (säl-tô-pou'lōō äf-fôn'sōō) Braz.	9·33 S	38·32 W
168	Paul Roux (pôrl rōō) S. Afr. (Johannesburg & Pretoria In.)	28·18 S	27·57 E
84	Paulsboro (pôlz'bē-rô) N. J. (Philadelphia In.)	39·50 N	75·16 W
73	Pauls Valley (pôlz văl'ē) Okla.	34·43 N	97·13 W
157	Pauwela (pä-ōō-wä'lä) Hawaii (In.)	20·58 N	156·19 W
98	Pavarandocito (pä-vä-rän-dô-sē'tô) Col. (In.)	7·18 N	76·32 W
136	Pavda (päv'dá) Sov. Un. (Urals In.)	59·16 N	59·32 E
126	Pavia (pä-vē'ä) It.	45·12 N	9·11 E
134	Pavlodar (pȧv-lô-dȧr') Sov. Un.	52·17 N	77·23 E
64	Pavlo'f B. (păv-lôf) Alaska	55·20 N	161·20 W
129	Pavlograd (pȧv-lô-grȧt') Sov. Un.	48·32 N	35·52 E
129	Pavlovsk (pȧv-lôfsk') Sov. Un.	50·28 N	40·05 E
136	Pavlovsk Sov. Un. (Leningrad In.)	59·41 N	30·27 E
136	Pavlovskiy Posad (pȧv-lôf'skĭ pô-sȧt') Sov. Un. (Moscow In.)	55·47 N	38·39 E
100	Pavuna (pȧ-vōō'nȧ) Braz. (In.)	22·48 S	43·21 W
111	Päwesin (pă'vĕ-zēn) Ger. (Berlin In.)	52·31 N	12·44 E
73	Pawhuska (pô-hŭs'kȧ) Okla.	36·41 N	96·20 W
73	Pawnee (pô-nē') Okla.	36·20 N	96·47 W
72	Pawnee (R.) Kans.	38·18 N	99·42 W
73	Pawnee City Nebr.	40·08 N	96·09 W
80	Paw Paw (pô'pô) Mich.	42·15 N	85·55 W
71	Paw Paw (R.) Mich.	42·14 N	86·21 W
84	Pawtucket (pô-tŭk'ĕt) R. I. (Providence In.)	41·53 N	71·23 W
127	Paxoi (I.) Grc.	39·14 N	20·15 E
80	Paxton (păks'tŭn) Ill.	40·35 N	88·00 W
150	Payen (pä'yĕn') China	46·00 N	127·20 E
66	Payette (pȧ-ĕt') Idaho	44·05 N	116·55 W
66	Payette R. Idaho	43·57 N	116·26 W
66	Payette R., North Fork Idaho	44·35 N	116 10 W
66	Payette R., South Fork Idaho	44·07 N	115·43 W
	Payintala, see Tungliao		
132	Pay-Khoy, Khrebet (Mts.) Sov. Un.	68·08 N	63·04 E
87	Payne (L.) (pān) Can.	59·22 N	73·16 W
71	Paynesville (pānz'vĭl) Minn.	45·23 N	94·43 W
139	Payong, Bukit (Mt.) Mala. (Singapore In.)	3·04 N	101·58 E
	Payo Obispo, see Ciudad Chetumal		
100	Paysandú (pī-sän-dōō') Ur.	32·16 S	57·55 W
69	Payson (pā's'n) Utah	40·05 N	111·45 W
127	Pazardzhik (pä-zȧr-dzhek') Bul.	42·10 N	24·22 E
126	Pazin (pä'zēn) Yugo.	45·14 N	13·57 E
73	Peabody (pē'bŏd-ĭ) Kans.	38·09 N	97·09 W
83	Peabody Mass. (Boston In.)	42·32 N	70·56 W
86	Peace (R.) Can.	57·29 N	117·32 W
79	Peace Cr. (pēs) Fla. (In.)	27·16 N	81·53 W
84	Peace Dale (dāl) R. I. (Providence In.)	41·27 N	71·30 W
86	Peace River (rĭv'ēr) Can.	56·19 N	117·22 W
86	Peacock Hills (pē-kŏk' hĭlz) Can.	66·08 N	109·55 W
110	Peak, The (Mt.) (pēk) Eng.	53·23 N	1·52 W
158	Peak Hill Austl.	25·38 S	118·50 E
78	Pearl (R.) (pûrl) Miss.-La.	31·06 N	89·44 W
77	Pearland (pûrl'ănd) Tex. (In.)	29·34 N	95·17 W
	Pearl R., see Chu Chiang		
76	Pearsall (pēr'sôl) Tex.	28·53 N	99·06 W
167	Pearston (pēr'ērstŏn) S. Afr. (Natal In.)	32·36 S	25·09 E
48	Peary Land (Reg.) (pēr'ĭ) Grnld.	82·00 N	40·00 W
72	Pease (R.) (pēz) Tex.	34·07 N	99·53 W
77	Peason (pēz''n) La.	31·25 N	93·19 W
167	Pebane (pĕ-bä'nē) Moz.	17·23 S	37·45 E
127	Peć (pĕch) Yugo.	42·39 N	20·18 E
76	Pecan Bay (pē-kăn') Tex.	32·04 N	99·15 W
99	Peçanha (pā-kän'yȧ) Braz.	18·37 S	42·26 W
71	Pecatonica (R.) (pĕk-ȧ-tŏn-ĭ-kȧ) Ill.	42·21 N	89·28 W
132	Pechenga (pyĕ'chĕŋ-gȧ) Sov. Un.	69·30 N	31·10 E
132	Pechora (R.) Sov. Un.	66·00 N	52·30 E
134	Pechora Basin (pyĕ-chô'rȧ) Sov. Un.	67·55 N	58·37 E
132	Pechorskaya Guba (B.) Sov. Un.	68·40 N	55·00 E
76	Pecos (pā'kôs) Tex.	31·26 N	103·30 W
62	Pecos (R.) U. S.	31·10 N	103·10 W
121	Pécs (pāch) Hung.	46·04 N	18·15 E
167	Peddie S. Afr. (Natal In.)	33·13 S	27·09 E
128	Pededze (R.) (pȧ'dĕd-zĕ) Sov. Un.	57·18 N	27·13 E
74	Pedley (pĕd'lē) Calif. (Los Angeles In.)	33·59 N	117·29 W
99	Pedra Azul (pā'drä-zōō'l) Braz.	16·03 S	41·13 W
99	Pedreiras (pĕ-drā'räs) Braz.	4·30 S	44·31 W
143	Pedro, Pt. (pē'drō) Cey.	15·05 N	80·28 E
92	Pedro Antonio Santos (Sta. Cruz Chico) (pā'drō än-tō'nē-ō sän'tōs) (sän'tä krōōz' chē'kô) Mex. (Yucatan In.)	18·55 N	88·13 W
94	Pedro Betancourt (bā-täŋ-kōrt') Cuba	22·40 N	81·15 W
100	Pedro de Valdivia (pĕ'drô-dĕ-väl-dē'vē-ä) Chile	22·32 S	69·55 W
100	Pedro do Rio (dô-rē'ô) Braz. (In.)	22·20 S	43·09 W
99	Pedro Juan Caballero (hōōá'n-kä-bäl-yĕ'rō) Par.	22·40 S	55·42 W
88	Pedro Miguel (mē-găl') C. Z. (Panama Canal In.)	9·01 N	79·36 W
88	Pedro Miguel Locks (mē-găl') C. Z. (Panama Canal In.)	9·01 N	79·36 W
99	Pedro II (pā'drōō sâ-gōōn'dōō) Braz.	4·20 S	41·27 W
160	Peebinga (pē-bĭng'ȧ) Austl.	34·43 S	140·55 E
116	Peebles (pē'b'lz) Scot.	55·40 N	3·15 W
79	Pee Dee (R.) (pē-dē') S. C.-N. C.	34·01 N	79·26 W
84	Peekskill (pēks'kĭl) N. Y. (New York In.)	41·17 N	73·55 W

Page Name Pronunciation Region Lat. °′ Long. °′
159 Pegasus B. (pĕg′*á*-sŭs) N. Z. 43·18 S 173·37 E
120 Pegnitz R. (pĕgh-nēts) Ger. 49·38 N 11·40 E
125 Pego (pā′gō) Sp. 38·50 N 0·09 W
154 Pegu (pĕ-gōō′) Bur. 17·17 N 96·29 E
146 Pegu Yoma (Mts.) (pĕ-gōō′yō′mä) Bur. 19·16 N 95·59 E
127 Pehčevo (pĕκ′chĕ-vô) Yugo. 41·42 N 22·57 E
150 Peian (pĕ′ê-än′) China 48·05 N 126·26 E
149 Pei-Chiang (R.) China (Canton In.) 22·54 N 113·08 E
148 Peich′iao (bā′chiou) China 31·03 N 121·27 E
148 Peich′enghuang Tao (I.) (bā′chĕng′hōōäng′ dou) China 38·23 N 120·55 E
150 Peiching (Peking) China (Peking In.) 39·55 N 116·23 E
148 Peiching Shih (Dist.) (bā′jĭng′ shē) China 40·07 N 115·56 E
150 Peifeng China 43·00 N 124·59 E
151 Peihai China 21·30 N 109·10 E
151 Peili China 19·08 N 108·42 E
Peilintzu, see Suihua
Peipus, L., see Chudskoye Oz.
148 Pei Wan (B.) (bā′wäɴ) China 36·21 N 120·48 E
150 Peiyün Ho (R.) China (Peking In.) 39·42 N 116·48 E
80 Pekin (pē′kĭn) Ill. 40·35 N 89·30 W
Peking, see Peiching
114 Pelagie, Isole I. Medit. Sea 35·46 N 12·32 E
127 Pélagos (I.) Grc. 39·17 N 24·05 E
78 Pelahatchee (pĕl-á-hăch′ê) Miss. 32·17 N 89·48 W
123 Pelat, Mt. (pē-lá′) Fr. 44·16 N 6·43 E
135 Peleduy (pyĕl-yĭ-dōō′ē) Sov. Un. 59·50 N 112·47 E
93 Pelee, Mt. (Vol.) (pē-lā′) Mart. (Le. & Wind. Is. In.) 14·49 N 61·10 W
80 Pelee, Pt. Can. 41·55 N 82·30 W
80 Pelee I. (pē′lê) Can. 41·45 N 82·30 W
101 Pelequén (pĕ-lĕ-kĕ′n) Chile (Santiago In.) 34·26 S 71·52 W
Pelew, see Palau
78 Pelham (pĕl′hăm) Ga. 31·07 N 84·10 W
83 Pelham N. H. (Boston In.) 42·43 N 71·22 W
71 Pelican (L.) Minn. 46·36 N 94·00 W
94 Pelican Hbr. (pĕl′ĭ-kǎn) Ba. Is. 26·20 N 76·45 W
70 Pelican Rapids (pĕl′ĭ-kǎn) Minn. 46·34 N 96·05 W
71 Pella (pĕl′*á*) Iowa 41·25 N 92·50 W
120 Pell-Worm I. (pĕl′vôrm) Ger. 54·33 N 8·25 E
86 Pelly (L.) Can. 66·08 N 102·57 W
86 Pelly (R.) Can. 62·20 N 133·26 W
86 Pelly B. (pĕl-ĭ) Can. 68·57 N 91·05 W
86 Pelly Ra. Can. 61·47 N 133·32 W
69 Peloncillo Mts. (pĕl-ôn-sĭl′lō) Ariz. 32·40 N 109·20 W
127 Peloponnisos (Reg.) Grc. 37·28 N 22·14 E
100 Pelotas (pā-lō′tăzh) Braz. 31·45 S 52·18 W
75 Pelton (pĕl-tǔn) Can. (Detroit In.) 42·15 N 82·57 W
123 Pelvoux, Mt. (pĕl-vōō′) Fr. 44·56 N 6·24 E
132 Pelym (R.) Sov. Un. 60·20 N 63·05 E
79 Pelzer (pĕl′zēr) S. C. 34·38 N 82·30 W
139 Pemanggil (I.) Mala. (Singapore In.) 2·37 N 104·41 E
166 Pemba (pĕm′b*á*) N. Rh. 15·29 S 27·22 E
167 Pemba (I.) Tan. 5·13 S 40·05 E
70 Pembina (pĕm′bĭ-ná) N. D. 48·58 N 97·15 W
70 Pembina (R.) Can. 49·16 N 98·38 W
81 Pembroke (pĕm′ brōk) Can. 45·50 N 77·00 W
83 Pembroke (pĕm′brōk) Mass. (Boston In.) 42·05 N 70·49 W
116 Pembroke Wales 51·40 N 5·00 W
143 Pen India (Bombay In.) 18·44 N 73·06 E
124 Penafiél (pā-nà-fyĕl′) Port. 41·12 N 8·19 W
124 Penafiel (pā-nyà-fyĕl′) Sp. 41·38 N 4·08 W
124 Peñalara (Mtn.) (pā-nyä-lä′rä) Sp. 40·52 N 3·57 W
90 Pena Nevada, Cerro Mex. 23·47 N 99·52 W
154 Penang (pê-năng′) Mala. 5·21 N 100·09 E
155 Penaranda (pä-nyä-rän′dä) Phil. (Manila In.) 15·20 N 120·59 E
124 Peñaranda de Bracamonte (pā-nyä-rän′dä dā brä-kä-mōn′tå) Sp. 40·54 N 5·11 W
125 Peña Roya (Mtn.) (pā′nyä rō′yä) Sp. 40·18 N 0·42 W
124 Peñarroya-Pueblonuevo (pĕn-yär-rô′yä-pwĕ′blô-nwĕ′vô) Sp. 38·18 N 5·18 W
124 Peñas, Cabo de (C.) (kå′bô-dĕ-pā′nyäs) Sp. 43·42 N 6·12 W
100 Penas, Golfo de (gôl-fô-dĕ-pĕ′n-äs) Chile 47·15 S 77·30 W
76 Penasco R. (pā-näs′kō) Tex. 32·50 N 104·45 W
150 Pench′i China 41·25 N 123·50 E
164 Pendembu (pĕn-dĕm′bōō) S. L. 8·14 N 10·52 W
70 Pender (pĕn′dēr) Nebr. 42·08 N 96·43 W
98 Penderisco (R.) (pĕn-dĕ-rē′s-kô) Col. (In.) 6·30 N 76·21 W
66 Pendleton (pĕn′d′l-tǔn) Ore. 45·41 N 118·47 W
66 Pend Oreille L. (pŏn-dô-rā′) (pĕn-dô-rĕl′) Idaho 48·09 N 116·38 W
66 Pend Oreille R. Wash. 48·44 N 117·20 W
99 Penedo (pâ-nā′dōō) Braz. 10·17 S 36·28 W
81 Penetanguishene (pĕn′ê-tăŋ-gĭ-shēn′) Can. 44·45 N 79·55 W
148 P′engchengchen (pĕng′chĕng′jĕn) China 36·24 N 114·11 E
148 P′englai (pĕng′lăi) China 37·49 N 120·45 E
124 Peniche (pĕ-nē′chå) Port. 39·22 N 9·24 W
75 Peninsula (pĕn-ĭn′sū-l*á*) Ohio (Cleveland In.) 41·14 N 81·32 W
110 Penistone (pĕn′ĭ-stŭn) Eng. 53·31 N 1·38 W
90 Penjamillo (pĕn-hä-mēl′yō) Mex. 20·06 N 101·56 W
90 Penjamo (pān′hä-mō) Mex. 20·27 N 101·43 W
154 Penju, Pulau-Pulau (Is.) Indon. 0·18 S 120·43 E
110 Penk (R.) (pĕnk) Eng. 52·41 N 2·10 W
110 Penkridge (pĕnk′rĭj) Eng. 52·43 N 2·07 W
126 Penne (pĕn′nä) It. 42·28 N 13·57 E
142 Penner (R.) (pĕn′ēr) India 14·43 N 79·09 E
120 Pennine Alpi (Mts.) Switz. 46·02 N 7·07 E
116 Pennine Chain (Mts.) (pĕn-ĭn′) Eng. 53·44 N 1·59 W
80 Pennsboro (pĕnz′bǔr-ô) W. Va. 39·10 N 81 00 W
84 Penns Grove (pĕnz grōv) N. J. (Philadelphia In.) 39·44 N 75·28 W
63 Pennsylvania (State) (pĕn-sĭl-vā′nĭ-*á*) U. S. 41·00 N 78·10 W
81 Penn Yan (pĕn yăn′) N. Y. 42·40 N 77·00 W
87 Penny Highland (pĕnz hī′lănd) Can. 66·55 N 65·30 W
128 Peno (L.) (pā′nô) Sov. Un. 56·55 N 32·28 E
82 Penobscot (R.) Maine 45·00 N 68·36 W
82 Penobscot B. (pê-nŏb′skŏt) Maine 44·20 N 69·00 W
158 Penong (pê-nông′) Austl. 32·00 S 133·00 E
93 Penonomé (pā-nō-nô-mā′) Pan. 8·32 N 80·21 W
161 Penrith Austl. (Sydney In.) 33·45 S 150·42 E
78 Pensacola (pĕn-s*á*-kō′l*á*) Fla. 30·25 N 87·13 W
73 Pensacola Dam Okla. 36·27 N 95·02 W
98 Pensilvania (pĕn-sêl-vá′nyä) Col. (In.) 5·31 N 75·05 W
159 Pentecost (I.) (pĕn′tê-kŏst) New Hebr. 16·05 S 168·28 E
86 Penticton Can. 49·29 N 119·28 W
116 Pentland Firth (pĕnt′l*ă*nd) Scot. 58·44 N 3·25 W
133 Penza (pĕn′zà) Sov. Un. 53·10 N 45·00 E
116 Penzance (pĕn-zăns′) Eng. 50·07 N 5·40 W
120 Penzberg (pĕnts′bĕrgh) Ger. 47·43 N 11·21 E
135 Penzhina (R.) (pyĭn-zē-nŭ) Sov. Un. 62·15 N 166·30 E
135 Penzhino Sov. Un. 63·42 N 168·00 E
135 Penzhinskay′a Guba (B.) Sov. Un. 60·30 N 161·30 E
80 Peoria (pē-ō′rĭ-*á*) Ill. 40·45 N 89·35 W
90 Peotillos (pâ-ō-tel′yōs) Mex. 22·30 N 100·39 W
75 Peotone (pē′ŏ-tôn) Ill. (Chicago In.) 41·20 N 87·47 W
81 Pepacton Res. (pĕp-ăc′tǔn) N. Y. 42·05 N 74·40 W
94 Pepe, Cabo (kä′bô-pĕ′pĕ) (C.) Cuba 21·30 N 83·10 W
83 Pepperell (pĕp′ēr-ĕl) Mass. (Boston In.) 42·40 N 71·36 W
127 Peqin (pĕ-kēn′) Alb. 41·03 N 19·48 E
125 Perales (R.) (pā-rä′lās) Sp. 40·24 N 4·07 W
125 Perales de Tajuña (dä tä-hōō′nyä) Sp. (Madrid In.) 40·14 N 3·22 W
82 Percé (pĕr-sā′) Can. 48·32 N 64·15 W
111 Perchtoldsdorf (pĕrk′tôlts-dôrf) Aus. (Vienna In.) 48·07 N 16·17 E
168 Perdekop S. Afr. (Johannesburg & Pretoria In.) 27·11 S 29·38 E
125 Perdido, Mt. (pĕr-dē′dō) Sp. 42·40 N 0·00
78 Perdido (R.) (pĕr-dī′dō) Ala.-Fla. 30·45 N 87·38 W
101 Perdões (pĕr-dô′ĕs) Braz. (Rio de Janeiro In.) 21·05 S 45·05 W
98 Pereira (pā-rā′rä) Col. (In.) 4·49 N 75·42 W
129 Perekop (pĕr-â-kôp′) Sov. Un. 46·08 N 33·39 E
80 Pere Marquette Mich. 43·55 N 86·10 W
129 Pereshchepino (pĕr′ăsh-chē′pê-nô) Sov. Un. 49·02 N 35·19 E
128 Pereslavl′-Zalesskiy (pâ-râ-sláv′′l zá-lyĕs′kĭ) Sov. Un. 56·43 N 38·52 E
129 Pereyaslav (pĕr-â-yäs′ läv) Sov. Un. 50·05 N 31·25 E
101 Pergamino (pĕr-gä-mē′nō) Arg. (Buenos Aires In.) 33·53 S 60·36 W
70 Perham (pēr′h*ă*m) Minn. 46·37 N 95·35 W
87 Peribonca (R.) (pĕr-ĭ-bŏŋ′kà) Can. 50·57 N 71·19 W
122 Périgueux (pā-rê-gû′) Fr. 45·12 N 0·43 E
98 Perija, Sierra de (Mts.) (sĕ-ĕ′r-rä-dĕ-pĕ-rē′κä) Col. 9·25 N 73·30 W
85 Perkins (pĕr′kĕns) Can. (Ottawa In.) 45·37 N 75·37 W
93 Perlas, Arch. de Las (är-chē-pyĕ′lä-gō-dĕ-läs-pĕr′läs) Pan. 8·29 N 79·15 W
93 Perlas, Laguna las (L.) (lä-gōō′nä-dĕ-läs) Nic. 12·34 N 83·19 W
120 Perleberg (pĕr′lĕ-bĕrg) Ger. 53·06 N 11·51 E
136 Perm′ (pĕrm) Sov. Un. (Urals In.) 58·00 N 56·15 E
Pernambuco, see Recife
99 Pernambuco (State) (pĕr-näm-bōō′kō) Braz. 8·08 S 38·54 W
Pernik, see Dimitrovo
122 Peronne (pā-rôn′) Fr. 49·57 N 2·49 E
91 Perote (pĕ-rô′tĕ) Mex. 19·33 N 97·13 W
136 Perovo (pâ′rô-vô) Sov. Un. (Moscow In.) 55·43 N 37·47 E
122 Perpignan (pĕr-pē-nyäɴ′) Fr. 42·42 N 2·48 E
125 Perregaux (pĕr-rē-gō′) Alg. 35·35 N 0·05 E
74 Perris (pĕr′ĭs) Calif. (Los Angeles In.) 33·46 N 117·14 W
94 Perros, Bahía (B.) (bä-ē′ä-pā′rōs) Cuba 22·25 N 78·35 W
85 Perrot I. (pĕr′ŭt) Can. (Montreal In.) 45·23 N 73·57 W
78 Perry (pĕr′ĭ) Ga. 32·27 N 83·44 W
78 Perry Fla. 30·06 N 83·35 W
71 Perry Iowa 41·49 N 94·40 W
81 Perry N. Y. 42·45 N 78·00 W
73 Perry Okla. 36·17 N 97·18 W
74 Perry Utah (Salt Lake City In.) 41·27 N 112·02 W
84 Perry Hall Md. (Baltimore In.) 39·25 N 76·27 W
75 Perryopolis (pĕ-rê-ŏ′pō-lĭs) Pa. (Pittsburgh In.) 40·05 N 79·45 W
80 Perrysburg (pĕr ĭz-bûrg) Ohio 41·35 N 83·35 W
72 Perryton (pĕr′ĭ-tǔn) Tex. 36·23 N 100·48 W
64 Perryville (pĕr ĭ-vĭl) Alaska 55·58 N 159·28 W
73 Perryville Mo. 37·41 N 89·52 W
123 Persan (pĕr-säɴ′) Fr. (Paris In.) 49·09 N 2·15 E
103 Persepolis (Ruins) (pēr-sĕp′o-lĭs) Iran 30·15 N 53·08 E
Persia, see Iran
144 Persian G. (pûr′zh*á*n) Asia 27·38 N 50·30 E
158 Perth (pûrth) Austl. 31·50 S 116·10 E
81 Perth Can. 44·40 N 76 15 W
116 Perth Scot. 56·24 N 3·25 W
84 Perth Amboy (âm′boi) N. J. (New York In.) 40·31 N 74·16 W
123 Pertuis (pĕr-tüē′) Fr. 43·43 N 5·29 E
80 Peru (pē-rōō′) Ill. 41·20 N 89·10 W
80 Peru Ind. 40·45 N 86·00 W
96 Peru S. A. 10·00 S 75·00 W
126 Perugia (pā-rōō′jä) It. 43·08 N 12·24 E
74 Peruque (pē rō′kĕ) Mo. (St. Louis In.) 38·52 N 90·36 W
129 Pervomaysk (pĕr-vô-mīsk′) Sov. Un. 48·04 N 30·52 E
136 Pervoural′sk (pĕr-vô-ōō-rálsk′) Sov. Un. (Urals In.) 56·54 N 59·58 E
135 Pervyy Kuril′skiy Proliv (Str.) Sov. Un. 51·43 N 154·32 E
126 Pesaro (pā′zä-rō) It. 43·54 N 12·55 E
99 Pescado (pĕs-kä′dō) (R.) Ven. (In.) 9·33 N 65·32 W
Pescadores (Is.) (pĕs-ka-dō′rĕs) Taiwan 23·30 N 119·00 E
126 Pescara (päs-kä′rä) It. 42·26 N 14·15 E
126 Pescara (R.) It. 42·18 N 13·22 E
133 Peschanyy, Mys (C.) Sov. Un. 43·10 N 51·20 E
126 Pescia (pā′shä) It. 43·53 N 11·42 E
145 Peshāwar (pĕ-shä′w*ŭ*r) W. Pak. (Khyber Pass In.) 34·01 N 71·34 E
127 Peshtera Bul. 42·03 N 24·19 E
71 Peshtigo (pĕsh′tê-gō) Wis. 45·03 N 87·46 W
71 Peshtigo (R.) Wis. 45·15 N 88·14 W
103 Peski Sov. Un. 39·46 N 59·47 E
103 Peski Sov. Un. 44·07 N 63·17 E
136 Peski (pyås′kĭ) Sov. Un. (Moscow In.) 55·13 N 38·48 E
124 Pêso da Régua (pā-sōō-dä-rā′gwä) Port. 41·09 N 7·47 W
92 Pespire (pås-pē′râ) Hond. 13·35 N 87·20 W
76 Pesqueria, R. (pås-kå-rē′*á*) Mex. 25·55 N 100·25 W
90 Petacalco, Bahía de (B.) (bä-ē′ä-dĕ-pĕ-tä-käl′kô) Mex. 17·55 N 102·00 W
139 Petah Tiqva (pĕ′tak tĭk′vâ) Isr. (Palestine In.) 32·05 N 34·53 E
68 Petaluma (pét-*á*- lōō′m*á*) Calif. 38·15 N 122·38 W
99 Petare (pĕ-tä′rĕ) Ven. (In.) 10·28 N 66·48 W
90 Petatlán (pā-tä-tlän′) Mex. 17·31 N 101·17 W
92 Petén, Laguna de (L.) (lä-gōō′nä-dĕ-pā-tān′) Guat. (Yucatan In.) 17·05 N 89·54 W
71 Petenwell Res. Wis. 44·10 N 89·55 W
81 Peterborough (pē′tēr-bŭr-ô) Can. 44·20 N 78·20 W
160 Peterborough Austl. 32·53 S 138·58 E
110 Peterborough Eng. 52·35 N 0·14 W
116 Peterhead (pē-tēr-hĕd′) Scot. 57·36 N 3·47 W
81 Peter Pt. Can. 43·50 N 77·00 W
86 Peter Pond L.(pŏnd) Can. 56·03 N 109·23 W
64 Petersburg (pē′tērz-bûrg) Alaska 56·52 N 133·10 W
73 Petersburg Ill. 40·01 N 89·51 W
80 Petersburg Ind. 38·30 N 87·15 W
75 Petersburg Ky. (Cincinnati In.) 39·04 N 84·52 W
79 Petersburg Va. 37·12 N 77·30 W
111 Petershagen (pĕ′tĕrs-hä-gĕn) Ger. (Berlin In.) 52·32 N 13·46 E
111 Petershausen (pĕ′tĕrs-hou-zĕn) Ger. (Munich In.) 48·25 N 11·29 E
95 Pétionville Hai. 18·30 N 72·20 W
82 Petitcodiac (pē-tē-kô-dyåk′) Can. 45·55 N 65·11 W
83 Petite Miquelon (I.) (mē-k′lon′) (mĭk-ē-lŏn′) Can. 46·50 N 56·20 W
93 Petite Terre I. (pē-tēt′târ′) N. A. (Le. & Wind. Is. In.) 16·12 N 61·00 W
95 Petit Goâve (pē-tē′ gō-äv′) Hai. 18·25 N 72·50 W
73 Petit Jean Cr. (pē-tē′ zhäɴ′) Ark. 35·05 N 93·55 W
91 Petlalcingo (pĕ-tläl-sĕŋ′gō) Mex. 18·05 N 97·53 W
92 Peto (pē′tô) Mex (Yucatan In.) 20·07 N 88·49 W
101 Petorca (pā-tōr′kä) Chile (Santiago In.) 32·14 S 70·55 W
80 Petoskey (pê-tŏs′kĭ) Mich. 45·25 N 84·55 W
139 Petra Jordan (Palestine In.) 30·21 N 35·25 E
152 Petra Velikogo, Zaliv (B.) (zä′lĭf pĕt-rä′ vĕ-lĭ′kô-vô) Sov. Un. 42·40 N 131·50 E
127 Petrich (pā′trĭch) Bul. 41·24 N 23·13 E
69 Petrified Forest Natl. Mon. (pĕt′rĭ-fīd fôr′ĕst) Ariz. 34·58 N 109·35 W
129 Petrikovka (pyĕ′trê-kôf-kä) Sov. Un. 48·43 N 34·29 E
129 Petrikov (pyĕ′trê-kô-v) Sov. Un. 52·09 N 28·30 E
126 Petrinja (pā′trēn-yä) Yugo. 45·25 N 16·17 E
136 Petrodvorets (pyĕ-trô-dvô-ryĕts′) Sov. Un. (Leningrad In.) 59·53 N 29·55 E
136 Petrokrepost′ (pyĕ-trô-krĕ-pôst) Sov. Un. (Leningrad In.) 59·56 N 31·03 E
80 Petrolia (pê-trō′lĭ-*á*) Can. 42·50 N 82·10 W
99 Petrolina (pĕ-trō-lē′n*á*) Braz. 9·18 S 40·28 W
111 Petronell Aus. (Vienna In.) 48·07 N 16·52 E
129 Petropavlovka (pyĕ′trô-päv′lôf-κä) Sov. Un. 48·24 N 36·23 E
136 Petropavlovka Sov. Un. (Urals In.) 54·10 N 59·50 E
134 Petropavlovsk (pyĕ-trô-päv′lôfsk) Sov. Un. 54·44 N 69·07 E
135 Petropavlovsk-Kamchatskiy (kăm-chät′skĭ) Sov. Un. 53·13 N 158·56 E
100 Petrópolis (pâ-trô-pô-lēzh′) Braz. (In.) 22·31 S 43·10 W
127 Petroseni Rom. 45·24 N 23·24 E
133 Petrovsk (pyĕ-trôfsk′) Sov. Un. 52·20 N 45·15 E
129 Petrovskaya (pyĕ-trôf′skå-yä) Sov. Un. 45·25 N 37·50 E
133 Petrovskoye Sov. Un. 45·20 N 43·00 E
135 Petrovsk-Zabaykal′skiy (pyĕ-trôfskzä-bī-käl′skĭ) Sov. Un. 51·13 N 109·08 E
119 Petrozavodsk (pyä′trō-zå-vôtsk′) Sov. Un. 61·46 N 34·25 E
168 Petrus Steyn (pä′trōōs stän′) S. Afr. Johannesburg & Pretoria In.) 27·40 S 28·09 E

ăt; finăl; rāte; senâte; ärm; åsk; sof*á*; fâre; ch-choose; dh-as th in other; bē; êvent; bĕt; recĕnt; cratēr; g-go; gh-guttural g; bĭt; ĭ-short neutral; rīde; κ-guttural k as ch in German ich;

Page	Name Pronunciation Region	Lat. °′	Long. °′
128	Petseri (pĕt'sĕ-rē) Sov. Un.	57·48 N	27·33 E
75	Pewaukee (pĭ-wô'kē) Wis. (Milwaukee In.)	43·05 N	88·15 W
75	Pewaukee L. Wis. (Milwaukee In.)	43·03 N	88·18 W
75	Pewee Valley (pe wē) Ky. (Louisville In.)	38·19 N	85·29 W
132	Peza (R.) (pyâ'zà) Sov. Un.	65·35 N	46·50 E
122	Pézenas (pā-zē-nä') Fr.	43·26 N	3·24 E
120	Pforzheim (pfôrts'hīm) Ger.	48·52 N	8·43 E
142	Phalodi India	27·13 N	72·22 E
154	Phan Rang (p'hän'răng') Viet.	11·30 N	108·43 E
	Pharsalus, see Fársala		
78	Phenix City (fē'nĭks) Ala.	32·29 N	85·00 W
154	Phet Buri Thai.	13·07 N	99·53 E
78	Philadelphia (fĭl-à-dĕl'phĭ-à) Miss.	32·45 N	89·07 W
84	Philadelphia Pa. (Philadelphia In.)	40·00 N	75·13 W
70	Philip (fĭl'ĭp) S. D.	44·03 N	101·35 W
164	Philippeville (fē-lēp'vēl') Alg.	36·58 N	6·51 E
155	Philippines (fĭl'ĭ-pēnz) Asia	14·25 N	125·00 E
156	Philippine Sea (fĭl'ĭ-pēn) Asia	16·00 N	133·00 E
155	Philippine Trench Phil.	10·30 N	127·15 E
	Philippopolis, see Plovdiv		
81	Philipsburg (fĭl'lĭps-bĕrg) Pa.	40·55 N	78·10 W
67	Philipsburg Wyo.	46·19 N	113·19 W
160	Phillip (I.) (fĭl'ĭp) Austl.	38·32 S	145·10 E
139	Phillip Chan. Indon. (Singapore In.)	1·04 N	103·40 E
81	Phillipi (fĭ-lĭp'ĭ) W. Va.	39·10 N	80·00 W
71	Phillips (fĭl'ĭps) Wis.	45·41 N	90·24 W
72	Phillipsburg (fĭl'lĭps-bĕrg) Kans.	39·44 N	99·19 W
81	Phillipsburg Pa.	40·45 N	75·10 W
154	Phnom Penh (nŏm'pĕn') Camb.	11·39 N	104·53 E
84	Phoebus (fē'bŭs) Va. (Norfolk In.)	37·02 N	76·19 W
69	Phoenix (fē'nĭks) Ariz.	33·30 N	112·00 W
84	Phoenix La. (New Orleans In.)	29·39 N	89·56 W
156	Phoenix Is. Oceania	4·00 S	174·00 W
84	Phoenixville (fē'nĭks-vĭl) Pa. (Philadelphia In.)	40·08 N	75·31 W
154	Phu Bia (Pk.) Laos	19·36 N	103·00 E
154	Phuket Thai.	7·57 N	98·19 E
148	P'i (R.) (pē') China	32·06 N	116·31 E
126	Piacenza (pyä-chĕnt'sä) It.	45·02 N	9·42 E
126	Pianosa (I.) (pyä-nō'sä) It.	42·13 N	15·45 E
121	Piatra-Neamt (pyä'trà-nä-ämts') Rom.	46·54 N	26·24 E
99	Piauí (State) (pyou'ē) Braz.	7·40 S	42·25 W
99	Piauí, Serra do (Mts.) (sĕr'rà dŏŏ pyou'ē) Braz.	10·45 S	44·36 W
126	Piave (R.) (pyä'vā) It.	45·45 N	12·15 E
126	Piazza Armerina (pyät'sà är-mä-rē'nä) It.	37·23 N	14·26 E
165	Pibor R. (pē'bôr) Sud.	7·21 N	32·54 E
71	Pic (R.) (pĕk) Can.	48·48 N	86·28 W
89	Picara Pt. (pē-kä'rä) Vir. Is. (U. S. A.) (St. Thomas In.)	18·23 N	64·57 W
78	Picayune (pĭk'à yōōn) Miss.	30·32 N	89·41 W
126	Piccole Alpi Dolomitche (Mts.) (pē'k-kô-le-äl'pē-dô-lô'mē-tē'chĕ) It.	46·05 N	12·17 E
125	Pic du Midi d'Ossau (Mtn.) (pēk dü mē-dē' dôs-sō') Fr.	42·51 N	0·25 W
73	Picher (pĭch'ēr) Okla.	36·58 N	94·49 W
151	Pichieh China	27·20 N	105·18 E
101	Pichilemu (pē-chē-lĕ'mōō) Chile (Santiago In.)	34·22 S	72·01 W
91	Pichucalco (pē-chōō-käl'kô) Mex.	17·34 N	93.06 W
91	Pichucalco (R.) Mex.	17·40 N	93·02 W
71	Pickerel (L.) (pĭk'ēr-ĕl) Can.	48·35 N	91·10 W
78	Pickwick (R.) (pĭk'wĭck) Tenn.	35·04 N	88·05 W
74	Pico (pē'kô) Calif. (Los Angeles In.)	34·01 N	118·05 W
125	Pico de Aneto (Mtn.) (pē'kō-dĕ-ä-nĕ'tô) Sp.	42·35 N	0·38 E
164	Pico I. (pē'kōō) Azores (In.)	38·16 N	28·49 W
99	Picos (pē'kōzh) Braz.	7·13 S	41·23 W
161	Picton (pĭk'tŭn) Austl. (Sydney In.)	34·11 S	150·37 E
83	Pictou (pĭk-tōō') Can.	45·43 N	62·44 W
143	Pidurutalagala Mt. (pē'dōō-rōō-tà'là-gä'là) Ceylon	12·27 N	80·45 E
71	Pie (I.) (pī) Can.	48·10 N	89·07 W
101	Piedade (pyā-dä'dĕ) Braz. (Rio de Janeiro In.)	23·42 S	47·25 W
78	Piedmont (pēd'mŏnt) Ala.	33·54 N	85·36 W
65	Piedmont Calif. (San Francisco In.)	37·50 N	122·14 W
73	Piedmont Mo.	37·09 N	90·42 W
79	Piedmont S. C.	34·40 N	82·27 W
81	Piedmont W. Va.	39·30 N	79·05 W
124	Piedrabuena (pyā-drä-bwā'nä) Sp.	39·01 N	4·10 W
101	Piedras, Punta (Pt.) (pōō'n-tä-pyĕ'dräs) Arg. (Buenos Aires In.)	35·25 S	57·10 W
76	Piedras Negras (pyā'dräs nā'gräs) Mex.	28·41 N	100·33 W
119	Pieksämäki (pyĕk'sĕ-mĕ-kē) Fin.	62·18 N	27·14 E
124	Piélagos (pyā'lä-gōs) Sp.	43·23 N	3·55 W
126	Piemonte (Reg.) (pyĕ-mô'n-tĕ) It.	44·30 N	7·42 E
168	Pienaars R. S. Afr. (Johannesburg & Pretoria In.)	25·13 S	28·05 E
168	Pienaarsrivier S. Afr. (Johannesburg & Pretoria In.)	25·12 S	28·18 E
70	Pierce (pērs) Nebr.	42·11 N	97·33 W
81	Pierce W. Va.	39·15 N	79·30 W
84	Piermont (pēr'mŏnt) N. Y. (New York In.)	41·03 N	73·55 W
70	Pierre (pēr) S. D.	44·22 N	100·20 W
121	Piešťany (pyĕsh'tyà-nûĭ) Czech.	48·36 N	17·48 E
167	Pietermaritzburg (pē-tēr-mà-rĭts-bûrg) S. Afr. (Natal In.)	29·36 S	30·23 E
168	Pietersburg (pē'tērz-bûrg) S. Afr. (Johannesburg & Pretoria In.)	23·56 S	29·30 E
81	Pieton Can.	44·00 N	77·15 W
166	Piet Retief (pēt rĕ-tēf') S. Afr.	27·00 S	30·58 E
121	Pietrosul Pk. Rom.	47·35 N	24·49 E
126	Pieve di Cadore (pyā'vā dē kä-dō'rā) It.	46·26 N	12·22 E
71	Pigeon (R.) (pĭj'ŭn) Can.-Minn.	48·05 N	90·13 W
85	Pigeon Lake Can. (Winnipeg In.)	49·57 N	97·36 W
73	Piggott (pĭg'ŭt) Ark.	36·22 N	90·10 W
91	Pijijiapan (pēкē-kē-ä'pän) Mex.	15·40 N	93·12 W
111	Pijnacker Neth. (Amsterdam In.)	52·01 N	4·25 E
72	Pikes Pk. (pīks) Colo.	38·49 N	105·03 W
79	Pikeville (pīk'vĭl) Ky.	37·28 N	82·31 W
120	Piła (pē'là) Pol.	53·09 N	16·44 E
168	Pilansberg (pē'ǎns'bûrg) S. Afr. (Johannesburg & Pretoria In.)	25·08 S	26·55 E
101	Pilar (pē'lär) Arg. (Buenos Aires In.)	34·27 S	58·55 W
100	Pilar Par.	27·00 S	58·15 W
155	Pilar (pē'lär) Phil. (Manila In.)	12·55 N	123·41 E
155	Pilar Phil. (Manila In.)	17·24 N	120·36 E
99	Pilar de Goiás (dĕ-gô'yà's) Braz.	14·47 S	49·33 W
65	Pilchuck (R.) Wash. (Seattle In.)	48·03 N	121·58 W
65	Pilchuck Cr. (pĭl'chŭk) Wash. (Seattle In.)	48·19 N	122·11 W
65	Pilchuck Mtn. Wash. (Seattle In.)	48·03 N	121·48 W
100	Pilcomayo (R.) (pēl-cō-mī'ō) Par.	24·45 S	69·15 W
155	Pili (pē'lē) Phil. (Manila In.)	13·34 N	123·17 E
121	Pilica R. (pē-lēt'sä) Pol.	51·00 N	19·48 E
65	Pillar Pt. (pĭl'ǎr) Can. (Seattle In.)	48·14 N	124·06 W
65	Pillar Rock Wash. (Portland In.)	46·16 N	123·35 W
90	Pilón (R.) (pē-lōn') Mex.	24·13 N	99·03 W
73	Pilot Point (pī'lŭt) Tex.	33·24 N	97·00 W
84	Pilottown (pī'lŭt-toun) La. (New Orleans In.)	29·11 N	89·15 W
	Pilsen, see Plzeň		
119	Piltene (pĭl'tĕ-nĕ) Sov. Un.	57·17 N	21·40 E
90	Pimal, Cerra (Mtn.) (sĕ'r-rä-pē-mäl') Mex.	22·58 N	104·19 W
158	Pimba (pĭm'bà) Austl.	31·15 S	146·50 E
167	Pimville (pĭm'vĭl) S. Afr. (Johannesburg & Pretoria In.)	26·17 S	27·54 E
88	Pinacate, Cerro (Mtn.) (sĕ'r-rō-pē-nä-kä'tĕ) Mex.	31·45 N	113·30 W
155	Pinamalayan (pē-nä-mä-lä'yän) Phil. (Manila In.)	13·04 N	121·31 E
133	Pinarbasi (pē'när-bä'shĭ) Tur.	38·50 N	36·10 E
94	Pinar del Rio (pē-när' dĕl rē'ō) Cuba	22·25 N	83·35 W
94	Pinar del Rio (State) Cuba	22·45 N	83·25 W
155	Pinatubo (Mtn.) (pē-nä-tōō'bô) Phil. (Manila In.)	15·09 N	120·19 E
73	Pinckneyville (pĭnk'nĭ-vĭl) Ill.	38·06 N	89·22 W
121	Pińczow (pēn''chōōf) Pol.	50·32 N	20·33 E
101	Pindamonhangaba (pē'n-dä-mōnyä'n-gä-bä) Braz. (Rio de Janeiro In.)	22·56 S	45·26 W
127	Píndhos Oros (Mts.) Grc.	39·48 N	21·19 E
83	Pine, C (pīn) Can.	46·36 N	53·35 W
71	Pine (R.) Wis.	45·50 N	88·37 W
73	Pine Bluff (pīn blŭf) Ark.	34·13 N	92·01 W
71	Pine City (pīn) Minn.	45·50 N	93·01 W
158	Pine Creek Austl.	13·45 S	132·00 E
68	Pine Cr. Nev.	40·15 N	116·17 W
66	Pine Forest Ra. Nev.	41·35 N	118·45 W
132	Pinega (pē-nyĕ'gà) Sov. Un.	64·40 N	43·30 E
132	Pinega (R.) Sov. Un.	64·10 N	42·30 E
84	Pine Hill (pīn hĭl) N. J. (Philadelphia In.)	39·47 N	74·59 W
65	Pinehurst (pīn'hûrst) Wash. (Seattle In.)	47·56 N	122·13 W
79	Pine Is. Fla. (In.)	24·48 N	81·32 W
79	Pine Island Sd. Fla. (In.)	26·32 N	82·30 W
84	Pine Lake Estates (lāk ĕs-tāts') Ga. (Atlanta In.)	33·47 N	84·13 W
166	Pinelands (pīn'lănds) S. Afr. (Cape Town In.)	33·57 S	18·30 E
74	Pine Lawn (lôn) Mo. (St. Louis In.)	38·42 N	90·17 W
84	Pine Mountain (moun'tĭn) Ga. (Atlanta In.)	33·39 N	84·09 W
70	Pine Ridge Ind. Res. (rĭj) S. D.	43·33 N	102·13 W
126	Pinerola (pē-nä-rô'lō) It.	44·47 N	7·18 E
77	Pines, Lake o' the Tex.	32·50 N	94·40 W
167	Pinetown (pīn'toun) S. Afr. (Natal In.)	29·47 S	30·52 E
74	Pine View Res. (vū) Utah (Salt Lake City In.)	41·17 N	111·54 W
78	Pineville (pīn'vĭl) Ky.	36·48 N	83·43 W
77	Pineville La.	31·20 N	92·25 W
154	Ping, Mae Nam (R.) Thai.	17·54 N	98·29 E
149	Pingchoupao China (Canton In.)	23·01 N	113·11 E
150	Pingchüan China	40·58 N	118·40 E
139	Pinggir Indon. (Singapore In.)	1·05 N	101·12 E
151	P'ingho (pĭng'hō') China	24·30 N	117·02 E
151	Pinghsiang China	27·40 N	113·50 E
150	Pingliang (pĭng'lyäng') China	35·12 N	106·50 E
151	P'inglo (pĭng'lō') China	24·30 N	110·22 E
151	P'ingt'an China	25·30 N	119·45 E
150	Pingting (pĭng'tĭng') China	37·50 N	113·30 E
148	P'ingtu (pĭng'tōō') China	36·46 N	119·57 E
151	P'ingtung Taiwan	22·40 N	120·35 E
150	P'ingwu China	32·20 N	104·40 E
148	P'ingyuan (pĭng'yü-än') China	37·11 N	116·26 E
101	Pinhal (pē-nyà'l) Braz. (Rio de Janeiro In.)	22·11 S	46·43 W
125	Pinhal Novo (nô vōō) Port. (Lisbon In.)	38·38 N	8·54 W
124	Pinhel (pēn-yĕl') Port.	40·45 N	7·03 W
148	Pinhsien (pĭn'siän) China	38·29 N	117·58 E
150	Pinhsien China	45·40 N	127·20 E
154	Pini (I.) (pē'nē) Indon.	0·07 N	98·38 E
127	Piniós (R.) Grc.	40·33 N	21·40 E
68	Pinnacles Natl. Mon. (pĭn'à-k'lz) Calif.	36·30 N	121·00 W
111	Pinneberg (pĭn'ĕ-bĕrg) Ger. (Hamburg In.)	53·40 N	9·48 E
65	Pinole (pĭ-nō'lē) Calif. (San Francisco In.)	38·01 N	122·17 W
94	Pinos, Isla de (I.) (ē's-lä-dĕ-pē'nôs) Cuba	21·40 N	82·45 W
124	Pinos-Puente (pwān'tā) Sp.	37·15 N	3·43 W
90	Pinotepa Nacional (pē-nô-tā'pä nä-syô-näl') Mex.	16·21 N	98·04 W
159	Pins, Ile des N. Cal.	22·44 S	167·44 E
121	Pinsk (pēn'sk) Sov. Un.	52·07 N	26·05 E
98	Pinta (I.) Ec.	0·41 N	90·47 W
85	Pintendre (pĕn-tändr') Can. (Quebec In.)	46·45 N	71·07 W
125	Pinto (pēn'tō) Sp. (Madrid In.)	40·14 N	3·42 W
69	Pioche (pī-ō'chē) Nev.	37·56 N	114·28 W
126	Piombino (pyôm-bē'nō) It.	42·56 N	10·33 E
65	Pioneer (pī'ō-nēr') Wash. (Portland In.)	45·49 N	122·40 W
67	Pioneer Mts. Mont.	45·23 N	112·51 W
121	Piotrków Trybunalski (pyōtr'kōōv trĭ-bōō-nal'skē) Pol.	51·23 N	19·44 E
78	Piper (pī'pēr) Ala.	33·04 N	87·00 W
74	Piper Kans. (Kansas City In.)	39·09 N	94·51 W
127	Pipéri (I.) (pē'per-ē) Grc.	39·19 N	24·20 E
69	Pipe Spring Natl. Mon. (pīp sprĭng) Ariz.	36·50 N	112·45 W
70	Pipestone (pīp'stōn) Minn.	44·00 N	96·19 W
71	Pipestone (R.) Can.	48·34 N	92·22 W
70	Pipestone Natl. Mon. Minn.	44·03 N	96·24 W
82	Pipmaukin, L. (pĭp-mä-kän') Can.	49·36 N	69·55 W
80	Piqua (pĭk'wà) Ohio	40·10 N	84·15 W
101	Piracaia (pē-rä-kà'yä) Braz. (Rio de Janeiro In.)	23·04 S	46·20 W
101	Piracicaba (pē-rä-sē-kä'bä) Braz. (Rio de Janeiro In.)	22·43 S	47·39 W
101	Piraí (pē-rä-ē') Braz. (Rio de Janeiro In.)	22·38 S	43·54 W
101	Piraíba (R.) (pä-rä-ē'bà) Braz. (Rio de Janeiro In.)	21·38 S	41·29 W
134	Piramida, Gol'tsy (Mtn.) Sov. Un.	54·00 N	96·00 E
126	Piran (pē-rà'n) Yugo.	45·31 N	13·34 W
101	Piranga (pē-rà'n-gä) Braz. (Rio de Janeiro In.)	20·41 S	43·17 W
101	Pirapetinga (pē-rä-pĕ-tē'n-gä) Braz. (Rio de Janeiro In.)	21·40 S	42·20 W
99	Pirapóra (pē-rà-pō'rà) Braz.	17·39 S	44·54 W
101	Pirassununga (pē-rä-sōō-nōō'n-gä) Braz. (Rio de Janeiro In.)	22·00 S	47·24 W
99	Pirenópolis (pē-rĕ-nô'pō-lēs) Braz.	15·56 S	48·49 W
127	Pírgos Grc.	37·51 N	21·28 E
99	Piritu, Laguna de (L.) (lä-gōō'nä-dĕ-pē-rē'tōō) Ven. (In.)	10·00 N	64·57 W
120	Pirmasens (pĭr-mä-zĕns') Ger.	49·12 N	7·34 E
120	Pirna (pĭr'nä) Ger.	50·57 N	13·56 E
155	Piroe (pē-rōō') Indon.	3·15 S	128·25 E
127	Pirot (pē'rōt) Yugo.	43·09 N	22·35 E
69	Pirtleville (pûr't'l-vĭl) Ariz.	31·25 N	109·35 W
129	Piryatin (pēr-yä-tēn') Sov. Un.	50·13 N	32·31 E
126	Pisa (pē'sä) It.	43·52 N	10·24 E
98	Pisagua (pē-sä'gwä) Chile	18·43 S	70·12 W
98	Pisco (pēs'kō) Peru	13·43 S	76·07 W
98	Pisco, Bahia de (B.) (bä-ē'ä-dĕ) Peru	13·43 S	77·48 W
81	Piseco (L.) (pĭ-sā'kô) N. Y.	43·25 N	74·35 W
120	Pisek (pē'sĕk) Czech.	49·18 N	14·08 E
100	Pissis, Monte (Vol.) (mô'n-tĕ-pē-sēs') Arg.	27·50 S	68·35 W
139	Pissouri Cyprus (Palestine In.)	34·39 N	32·42 E
126	Pisticci (pēs-tē'chē) It.	40·24 N	16·34 E
126	Pistoia (pēs-tô'yä) It.	43·57 N	11·54 E
83	Pistolet B. (pĭs-tô-lā') Can.	51·40 N	55·43 W
124	Pisuerga (R.) (pē-swĕr'gä) Sp.	41·48 N	4·28 W
98	Pitalito (pē-tä-lē'tō) Col.	1·45 N	75·09 W
75	Pitcairn (pĭt'kârn) Pa. (Pittsburgh In.)	40·29 N	79·47 W
157	Pitcairn (I.) Oceania	24·30 S	133·00 W
112	Pite (R.) (pē'tĕ) Swe.	66·08 N	18·51 E
112	Piteå (pē'tĕ-ô') Swe.	65·21 N	21·10 E
127	Pitesti (pē-tĕsht'') Rom.	44·51 N	24·51 E
158	Pithara (pĭt'ărǎ) Austl.	30·27 S	116·45 E
122	Pithiviers (pē-tē-vyā') Fr.	48·12 N	2·14 E
84	Pitman (pĭt'măn) N. J. (Philadelphia In.)	39·44 N	75·08 W
93	Pitons du Carbet, Mt. Mart. (Le. & Wind. Is. In.)	14·40 N	61·05 W
66	Pit R. (pĭt) Calif.	40·58 N	121·42 W
167	Pitseng Bas. (Natal In.)	29·03 S	28·13 E
65	Pitt (R.) Can. (Vancouver In.)	49·19 N	122·39 W
64	Pitt Pt. (pĭt) Alaska	70·48 N	152·00 W
65	Pittsburg (pĭts'bûrg) Calif. (San Francisco In.)	38·01 N	121·52 W
73	Pittsburg Kans.	37·25 N	94·43 W
65	Pittsburg Ore. (Portland In.)	45·54 N	123·09 W
73	Pittsburg Tex.	32·00 N	94·57 W
75	Pittsburgh Pa. (Pittsburgh In.)	40·26 N	80·01 W
73	Pittsfield (pĭts'fēld) Ill.	39·37 N	90·47 W
82	Pittsfield Maine	44·45 N	69·44 W
81	Pittsfield Mass.	42·25 N	73·15 W
81	Pittston (pĭts'tŭn) Pa.	41·20 N	75·50 W
148	P'itzuwo (Hsinchin) (pē'zhē'wŏ) (sĭn'jĭn) China	39·25 N	122·19 E
101	Piũi (pē-ōō'ē) Braz. (Rio de Janeiro In.)	20·27 S	45·57 W
98	Piura (pē-ōō'rä) Peru	5·13 S	80·46 W
136	Piya (pē'yà) Sov. Un. (Urals In.)	58·34 N	61·12 E
74	Placentia (plă-sĕn'shĭ-à) Calif. (Los Angeles In.)	33·52 N	117·50 W
83	Placentia Can.	47·16 N	53·59 W
83	Placentia B. Can.	47·14 N	54·30 W
68	Placerville (plăs'ēr-vĭl) Calif.	38·43 N	120·47 W
94	Placetas (plä-thā'tās) Cuba	22·10 N	79·40 W
81	Placid (L.) (plăs'ĭd) N. Y.	44·20 N	74·00 W
74	Plain City (plān) Utah (Salt Lake City In.)	41·18 N	112·06 W

Page	Name Pronunciation Region	Lat. °′	Long. °′
75	Plainfield (plān′fēld) Ill. (Chicago In.)	41·37 N	88·12 W
75	Plainfield..Ind. (Indianapolis In.)	39·42 N	86·23 W
84	Plainfield...N. J. (New York In.)	40·38 N	74·25 W
73	Plainview (plān′vū)...Ark.	34·59 N	93·15 W
71	Plainview...Minn.	44·09 N	93·12 W
70	Plainview...Nebr.	42·20 N	97·47 W
72	Plainview...Tex.	34·11 N	101·42 W
80	Plainwell (plan′wĕl)...Mich.	42·25 N	85·40 W
85	Plaisance (plĕ-zäNs′) Can. (Ottawa In.)	45·37 N	75·07 W
95	Plana or Flat Cays (Is.) (plä′nä) Ba. Is.	22·35 N	73·35 W
122	Plan-de-Cuques (plä-dĕ-kük′) Fr. (Marseille In.)	43·22 N	5·29 E
111	Planegg (plä′nĕg) Ger. (Munich In.)	48·06 N	11·27 E
73	Plano (plā′nō)...Tex.	33·01 N	96·42 W
85	Plantagenet (pläN-täzh-nĕ′) Can. (Ottawa In.)	45·33 N	75·00 W
79	Plant City (plånt sĭ′tĭ)..Fla. (In.)	28·00 N	82·07 W
77	Plaquemine (pläk′mēn′)...La.	30·17 N	91·14 W
124	Plasencia (plä-sĕn′thê-ä)...Sp.	40·02 N	6·07 W
136	Plast (plåst)..Sov. Un. (Urals In.)	54·22 N	60·48 E
82	Plaster Rock (plås′tẽr rŏk)...Can.	46·54 N	67·22 W
152	Plastun (plås-tōōn′)...Sov. Un.	44·41 N	136·08 E
100	Plata, R. de la (R.) (dālä plä′tä) Arg.-Ur.	34·35 S	58·15 W
126	Platani (R.) (plä-tä′nē)...It.	37·26 N	13·28 E
95	Plateforme, Pte...Hai.	19·35 N	73·50 W
64	Platinum (plăt′ĭ-nŭm)...Alaska	59·00 N	161·27 W
98	Plato (plä′tō)...Col.	9·49 N	74·48 W
90	Platón Sánchéz (plä-tōn′ sän′chĕz).Mex.	21·14 N	98·20 W
73	Platt Natl. Park (plăt)...Okla.	34·31 N	96·44 W
70	Platte (plăt)...S. D.	43·22 N	98·51 W
73	Platte (R.)...Mo.	40·09 N	94·40 W
62	Platte (R.)...U. S.	40·50 N	100·40 W
71	Platteville (plăt′vĭl)...Wis.	42·44 N	90·31 W
73	Plattsburg (plăts′bûrg)...Mo.	39·33 N	94·26 W
81	Plattsburgh...N. Y.	44·40 N	73·30 W
70	Plattsmouth (plăts′mŭth)...Nebr.	41·00 N	95·53 W
120	Plauen (plou′ĕn)...Ger.	50·30 N	12·08 E
95	Playa de Guanabo (plä-yä-dĕ-gwä-nä′bô) Cuba (Havana In.)	23·10 N	82·07 W
95	Playa de Santa Fe (sä′n-tä-fĕ′) Cuba (Havana In.)	23·05 N	82·31 W
69	Playas (L.) (plä′yås)...N. Mex.	31·50 N	108·30 W
91	Playa Vicente (vē-sĕn′tå)...Mex.	17·49 N	95·49 W
91	Playa Vicente (R.)...Mex.	17·36 N	96·13 W
81	Pleasant (L.) (plĕz′ănt)...N. Y.	43·25 N	74·25 W
65	Pleasant Hill Calif. (San Francisco In.)	37·57 N	122·04 W
73	Pleasant Hill...Mo.	38·46 N	94·18 W
65	Pleasanton (plĕz′ăn-tŭn) Calif. (San Francisco In.)	37·40 N	121·53 W
73	Pleasanton...Kans.	38·10 N	94·41 W
76	Pleasanton...Tex.	28·58 N	98·30 W
75	Pleasant Plain (plĕz′ănt) Ohio (Cincinnati In.)	39·17 N	84·06 W
75	Pleasant Ridge. Mich. (Detroit In.)	42·28 N	83·09 W
75	Pleasure Ridge Park (plĕzh′ẽr rĭj) Ky. (Louisville In.)	38·09 N	85·49 W
74	Pleasant View (plĕz′ănt vū) Utah (Salt Lake City In.)	41·20 N	112·02 W
84	Pleasantville (plĕz′ănt-vĭl) N. Y. (New York In.)	41·08 N	73·47 W
159	Plenty, B. of (plĕn′tê).N. Z. (In.)	37·23 S	177·10 E
67	Plentywood (plĕn′tê-wo͝od).Mont.	48·47 N	104·38 W
128	Ples (plyĕs)...Sov. Un.	57·26 N	41·29 E
128	Pleshcheyevo (L.) (plĕsh-chă′yĕ-vô).Sov. Un.	56·50 N	38·22 E
82	Plessisville (plĕ-sē′vēl′)...Can.	46·12 N	71·47 W
121	Pleszew (plĕ′zhĕf)...Pol.	51·54 N	17·48 E
123	Plettenberg (plĕ′tĕn-bĕrgh) Ger. (Ruhr In.)	51·13 N	7·53 E
127	Pleven (plĕ′vĕn)...Bul.	43·24 N	24·26 E
127	Pljevlja (plĕv′lyä)...Yugo.	43·20 N	19·21 E
121	Płock (pwôtsk)...Pol.	52·32 N	19·44 E
122	Ploërmel (plô-ĕr-mĕl′)...Fr.	47·56 N	2·25 W
127	Ploești (plô-yĕsht′′)...Rom.	44·56 N	26·01 E
127	Plomárion (plô-mä′rĭ-ŏn)...Grc.	38·51 N	26·24 E
122	Plomb du Cantal (Mt.) (plôN′dükäN-täl′). Fr.	45·30 N	2·49 E
127	Plovdiv (Philippopolis) (plôv′dĭf) (fĭl-ĭp-ŏp′ô-lĭs).Bul.	42·09 N	24·43 E
91	Pluma Hidalgo (plōō′mä ē-däl′gō) Mex.	15·54 N	96·23 W
119	Plunge (plo͝on′gā)...Sov. Un.	55·56 N	21·45 E
116	Plymouth (plĭm′ŭth)...Eng.	50·25 N	4·14 W
80	Plymouth...Ind.	41·20 N	86·20 W
81	Plymouth...Mass.	42·00 N	70·45 W
75	Plymouth.....Mich. (Detroit In.)	42·23 N	83·27 W
81	Plymouth...N. H.	43·50 N	71·40 W
79	Plymouth...N. C.	35·50 N	76·44 W
81	Plymouth...Pa.	41·15 N	75·55 W
93	Plymouth Montserrat (Le. & Wind. Is. In.)	16·43 N	62·12 W
71	Plymouth...Wis.	43·45 N	87·59 W
128	Plyussa (R.) (plyōō′så)..Sov. Un.	58·33 N	28·30 E
120	Plzeň (Pilsen)...Czech.	49·46 N	13·25 E
126	Po, Bocche del (Mouth) (bô′chĕ-dĕl-pô′).It.	44·57 N	12·38 E
126	Po, Fiume (R.) (fyōō′mĕ-pō)...It.	45·00 N	11·23 E
150	Poar...China	35·10 N	113·08 E
164	Pobé (pô-bā′)...Dahomey	6·56 N	2·32 E
73	Pocahontas (pō-kȧ-hŏn′tȧs)..Ark.	36·15 N	91·01 W
71	Pocahontas...Iowa	42·43 N	94·41 W
67	Pocatello (pō-kȧ-tĕl′ō)...Idaho	42·54 N	112·30 W
128	Pochëp (pô-chĕp′)...Sov. Un.	52·56 N	32·27 E
128	Pochinok (pô-chē′nôk)...Sov. Un.	54·14 N	32·27 E
132	Pochinski...Sov. Un.	54·40 N	44·50 E
90	Pochotitán (pô-chô-tē-tå′n)..Mex.	21·37 N	104·33 W
91	Pochutla (San Pedro) (pō-chōō′tlä) (sän pā′drō).Mex.	15·46 N	96·28 W
81	Pocomoke City (pō-kō-mōk′).Md.	38·05 N	75·35 W
81	Pocono Mts. (pō-cō′nō)...Pa.	41·10 N	75·05 W
101	Poços de Caldas (pō-sôs-dĕ-käl′dȧs) Braz. (Rio de Janeiro In.)	21·48 S	46·34 W
164	Poder (pô-dôr′)...Senegal	16·35 N	15·04 W
134	Podkamennaya (Stony) Tunguska (R.).Sov. Un.	61·43 N	93·45 E
136	Podol′sk (pô-dôl′′sk) Sov. Un. (Moscow In.)	55·26 N	37·33 E
129	Podvolochisk...Sov. Un.	49·32 N	26·16 E
126	Poggibonsi (pôd-jê-bôn′sê)...It.	43·27 N	11·12 E
128	Pogodino (pô-gô′dê-nô)..Sov. Un.	54·17 N	31·00 E
152	Pohai Str. (pō′hī′)...China	38·05 N	121·40 E
152	P′ohangdong...Kor.	35·57 N	129·23 E
148	Pohsien...China	33·52 N	115·47 E
148	Pohsing (pō′hsĭng′)...China	37·09 N	118·08 E
85	Pointe-a′-Gatineau (pōō-äNt′ä-gä-tē-nō′) Can. (Ottawa In.)	45·28 N	75·42 W
84	Pointe a la Hache (point′ å lå åsh′) La. (New Orleans In.)	29·35 N	89·47 W
93	Pointe-à-Pitre (pwăNt′ å pē-tr′) Guad. (Le. & Wind. Is. In.)	16·15 N	61·32 W
85	Pointe-aux-Pins (pōō-äNt′ ō-pĕN) Can. (Edmonton In.)	53·38 N	113·15 W
85	Pointe-aux-Trembles (pōō-äNt′ ō-träNbl) Can. (Montreal In.)	45·39 N	73·30 W
85	Pointe Claire (pōō-äNt′ klĕr) Can. (Montreal In.)	45 26 N	73 50 W
85	Pointe Fortune (fôr′tün) Can. (Montreal In.)	45·34 N	74·23 W
166	Pointe Noire...Con. B.	4·48 S	11·50 E
64	Point Hope (hōp)...Alaska	68·18 N	166·38 W
80	Point Pleasant (plĕz′ănt)..W. Va.	38·50 N	82·10 W
65	Point Roberts (rŏb′ẽrts) Wash. (Vancouver In.)	48·59 N	123·04 W
123	Poissy (pwȧ-sē′)....Fr. (Paris In.)	48·55 N	2·02 E
122	Poitiers (pwȧ-tyā′)...Fr.	46·35 N	0·18 E
142	Pokaran (pō′kŭr-ŭn)...India	27·00 N	72·05 E
150	Pok′ot′u (pō′kô-tōō′)...China	48·45 N	121·42 E
128	Pokrov (pô′krôf)...Sov. Un.	55·56 N	39·09 E
129	Pokrovskoye (pô-krôf′skô-yĕ) Sov. Un.	47·27 N	38·54 E
128	Pola (R.) (pō′lä)...Sov. Un.	54·44 N	31·53 E
124	Pola de Allade (dĕ-äl-yä′dĕ)...Sp.	43·18 N	6·35 W
124	Pola de Laviana (dĕ-lä-vyä′nä).Sp.	43·15 N	5·29 W
102	Poland (pō′lănd)...Eur.	52·37 N	17·01 E
155	Polangui (pô-läŋ′gē) Phil. (Manila In.)	13·18 N	123·29 E
136	Polazna (pô′låz-nȧ) Sov. Un. (Urals In.)	58·18 N	56·25 E
119	Polessk (pô′lĕsk)...Sov. Un.	54·50 N	21·14 E
133	Poles′ye (Pripyat′ Marshes) Sov. Un.	52·10 N	27·30 E
136	Polevskoy (pô-lĕ′vs-kô′ê) Sov. Un. (Urals In.)	56·28 N	60·14 E
121	Polgár (pôl′gär)...Hung.	47·54 N	21·10 E
150	P′oli (pô′lĭ)...China	45·40 N	130·38 E
126	Policastro, Golfo di (G.)...It.	41·00 N	13·23 E
123	Poligny (pō-lē-nyē′)...Fr.	46·48 N	5·42 E
127	Políkhnitos...Grc.	39·05 N	26·11 E
155	Polillo (pô-lēl′yō) Phil. (Manila In.)	14·42 N	121·56 E
155	Polillo Is......Phil. (Manila In.)	15·05 N	122·15 E
155	Polillo Str.....Phil. (Manila In.)	15·02 N	121·40 E
128	Polist′ (R.) (pô′lĭst)...Sov. Un.	57·42 N	31·02 E
126	Polistena (pō-lês-tā′nä)...It.	40·25 N	16·05 E
127	Poliyiros...Grc.	40·23 N	23·27 E
134	Polkan, Gol′tsy (Mtn.)..Sov. Un.	60·18 N	92·08 E
125	Pollensa (pōl-yĕn′sä)...Sp.	39·50 N	3·00 E
92	Polochic R. (pō-lô-chēk′)...Guat.	15·19 N	89·45 W
129	Polonnoye (pô′lô-nô-yĕ)..Sov. Un.	50·07 N	27·31 E
128	Polotsk (pô′lôtsk)...Sov. Un.	55·30 N	28·48 E
101	Polpaico (pôl-pȧ′y-kô) Chile (Santiago In.)	33·10 S	70·53 W
67	Polson (pōl′sŭn)...Mont.	47·40 N	114·10 W
129	Poltava (pôl-tä′vä)...Sov. Un.	49·35 N	34·33 E
129	Poltava (Oblast)...Sov. Un.	49·53 N	32·58 E
128	Põltsamaa (pŏlt′så-mä)..Sov. Un.	58·39 N	26·00 E
128	Põltsamaa (R.)...Sov. Un.	58·35 N	25·55 E
136	Polunochnoye (pô-lōō-nô′ch-nô′yĕ) Sov. Un. (Urals In.)	60·52 N	60·27 E
134	Poluy (R.) (pôl′wê)...Sov. Un.	65·45 N	68·15 E
136	Polyakovka (pŭl-yä′kôv-kȧ) Sov. Un. (Urals In.)	54·38 N	59·42 E
132	Polyarnyy (pŭl-yär′nē)..Sov. Un.	69·10 N	33·30 E
101	Pomba (pô′m-bȧ) (R.) Braz. (Rio de Janeiro In.)	21·28 S	42·28 W
120	Pomerania (Reg.) (pŏm-ê-rā′nĭ-ȧ) Pol.	53·50 N	15·20 E
118	Pomeranian B. (pō′mĕ-rä-ny-än) Ger.	54·10 N	14·20 E
80	Pomeroy...Ohio	39·00 N	82·00 W
167	Pomeroy (pŏm′ẽr-roi) S. Afr. (Natal In.)	28·36 S	30·26 E
66	Pomeroy (pŏm′ẽr-oi)...Wash.	46·28 N	117·35 W
125	Pomezia (pô-mĕ′t-zyä) It. (Rome In.)	41·41 N	12·31 E
125	Pomigliano d′Arco (pô-mē-lyȧ′nô-d-ä′r-kô) It. (Naples In.)	40·39 N	14·23 E
70	Pomme de Terre (pôm dē tĕr′) Minn.	45·22 N	95·52 W
74	Pomona (pô-mō′nȧ) Calif. (Los Angeles In.)	34·04 N	117·45 W
127	Pomorie...Bul.	42·24 N	27·41 E
142	Pomo Tsho (L.)...China	23·38 N	89·58 E
79	Pompano (pŏm′pă-nô)..Fla. (In.)	26·12 N	80·07 W
84	Pompton Lakes (pŏmp′tŏn) N. J. (New York In.)	41·01 N	74·16 W
92	Pomuch (pô-mōō′ch) Mex. (Yucatan In.)	20·12 N	90·10 W
70	Ponca (pŏn′kȧ)...Nebr.	42·34 N	96·43 W
73	Ponca City...Okla.	36·42 N	97·07 W
85	Ponce (pōn′sā) P. R. (Puerto Rico In.)	18·01 N	66·43 W
143	Pondicherry (pôn-dī-shĕr′ē′) (pŏn-dĭ-shĕr′ê).India	11·58 N	79·48 E
124	Ponferrada (pôn-fĕr-rä′dhä)...Sp.	42·33 N	6·38 W
86	Ponoca (pō-nō′cȧ)...Can.	52·43 N	113·32 W
132	Ponoy...Sov. Un.	66·58 N	41·00 E
132	Ponoy (R.)...Sov. Un.	65·50 N	38·40 E
164	Ponta Delgada (pôn′tȧ dĕl-gä′dȧ) Azores (In.)	37·40 N	25·45 W
100	Ponta Grossa (grō′sȧ)...Braz.	25·09 S	50·05 W
123	Pont-à-Mousson (pôN′tȧ-mōōsôN′) Fr.	48·55 N	6·02 E
99	Ponta Porã...Braz.	22·30 S	55·31 W
123	Pontarlier (pôN′tȧr-lyā′)...Fr.	46·53 N	6·22 E
122	Pont-Audemer (pôN′tōd′mâr′).Fr.	49·23 N	0·28 E
123	Pontcarré (pôN-kȧ-rā′) Fr. (Paris In.)	48·48 N	2·42 E
77	Pontchartrain L. (pôN-shȧr-trăn′) La.	30·10 N	90·10 W
126	Pontedera (pōn-tå-dā′rä)...It.	43·37 N	10·37 E
124	Ponte de Sor (pōŋ′tĕ då sōr′) Port.	39·14 N	8·03 W
110	Pontefract (pŏn′tê-frăkt)...Eng.	53·41 N	1·18 W
101	Ponte Nova (pô′n-tĕ-nô′vȧ) Braz. (Rio de Janeiro In.)	20·26 S	42·52 W
124	Pontevedra (pôn-tĕ-vĕ-drä)...Sp.	42·28 N	8·38 W
166	Ponthierville (pôN-tyā-vēl′) Con. L.	0·28 S	25·19 E
80	Pontiac (pŏn′tĭ-ăk)...Ill.	40·55 N	88·35 W
75	Pontiac.......Mich. (Detroit In.)	42·37 N	83·17 W
154	Pontianak (pôn-tê-ä′nȧk)..Indon.	0·04 S	109·20 E
139	Pontian Kechil Mala (Singapore In.)	1·29 N	103·24 E
122	Pontivy (pôN-tê-vē′)...Fr.	48·05 N	2·57 W
122	Pont-l′Abbe (pôN-lȧ-bā′)...Fr.	47·53 N	4·12 W
123	Pontoise (pôN-twȧz′) Fr. (Paris In.)	49·03 N	2·05 E
136	Pontonnyy (pôn′tôn-nyĭ) Sov. Un. (Leningrad In.)	59·47 N	30·39 E
78	Pontotoc (pŏn-tô-tŏk′)...Miss.	34·11 N	88·59 W
126	Pontremoli (pôn-trĕm′ô-lē)...It.	44·21 N	9·50 E
126	Ponza, Isole di (I.) (ê′sō-lĕ-dē-pōn′tsä)...It.	40·55 N	12·58 E
116	Poole (pōōl)...Eng.	50·43 N	2·00 W
142	Poona (pōō′nŭ)...India	18·38 N	73·53 E
98	Poopó, Lago de (L.) (lä′gô-dĕ-pō-ô-pô′).Bol.	18·16 S	67·57 W
98	Popayán (pō-pä-yän′)...Col.	2·21 N	76·43 W
67	Poplar (pŏp′lẽr)...Mont.	48·08 N	105·10 W
73	Poplar Bluff (blŭf)...Mo.	36·43 N	90·22 W
80	Poplar Plains (plāns)...Ky.	38·20 N	83·40 W
85	Poplar Point. Can. (Winnipeg In.)	50·04 N	97·58 W
67	Poplar R....Mont.	48·34 N	105·20 W
67	Poplar R., West Fork...Mont.	48·59 N	106·06 W
78	Poplarville (pŏp′lẽr-vĭl)...Miss.	30·50 N	89·33 W
91	Popocatépetl (Mtn.) (pô-pô-kä-tā′pĕt′l) Mex. (Mexico City In.)	19·01 N	98·38 W
166	Popokabaca (pō′pô-kȧ-bä′kȧ) Con. L.	5·38 S	16·47 E
129	Popovka (pô′pôf-kȧ)...Sov. Un.	50·03 N	33·41 E
129	Popovka...Sov. Un.	51·13 N	33·08 E
127	Popovo (pô′pô-vō)...Bul.	43·23 N	26·17 E
142	Porbandar (pōr-bŭn′dŭr)...India	21·44 N	69·40 E
98	Porce (pôr-sĕ) (R.)...Col. (In.)	7·11 N	74·55 W
124	Porcuna (pôr-kōō′nä)...Sp.	37·54 N	4·10 W
64	Porcupine (R.)...Alaska	67·00 N	143·25 W
86	Porcupine (R.)...Can.	67·38 N	140·07 W
67	Porcupine Cr. (pôr′kû-pīn).Mont.	46·38 N	107·04 W
67	Porcupine Cr....Mont.	48·27 N	106·24 W
126	Pordenone (pōr-då-nō′nå)...It.	45·58 N	12·38 E
126	Poreč (pô′rĕch)...Yugo.	45·13 N	13·37 E
119	Pori (Björneborg) (pô′rê) (byûr′nĕ-bôrgh)...Fin.	61·29 N	21·45 E
101	Poriúncula (po-rēōō′n-kōō-lä) Braz. (Rio de Janeiro In.)	20·58 S	42·02 W
112	Porjus (pôr′yōōs)...Swe.	66·54 N	19·40 E
128	Porkhov (pôr′Kôf)...Sov. Un.	57·46 N	29·33 E
98	Porlamar (pôr-lä-mär′)...Ven.	11·00 N	63·55 W
122	Pornic (pôr-nēk′)...Fr.	47·08 N	2·07 W
135	Poronaysk (pô′rô-nīsk)..Sov. Un.	49·21 N	143·23 E
120	Porrentruy (pô-räN-trüē′)..Switz.	47·25 N	7·02 E
118	Porsgrunn (pôrs′gro͝on′)...Nor.	59·09 N	9·36 E
98	Portachuelo (pôrt-ä-chwā′lô).Bol.	17·20 S	63·12 W
81	Portage (pôr′tåj)...Pa.	40·25 N	78·35 W
71	Portage...Wis.	43·33 N	89·29 W
74	Portage Des Sioux (dē sōō) Mo. (St. Louis In.)	38·56 N	90·21 W
85	Portage-la-Prairie (lä-prā′rĭ) Can. (Winnipeg In.)	49·58 N	98·18 W
86	Port Alberni (pōr äl-bĕr-nē′).Can.	49·20 N	124·51 W
124	Portalegre (pôr-tä-lā′grĕ)...Port.	39·18 N	7·26 W
72	Portales (pôr-tä′lĕs)...N. Mex.	34·10 N	103·11 W
82	Port-Alfred (ăl′frĕd)...Can.	48·19 N	70·55 W
167	Port Alfred (Kowie) (kou′ĭ) S. Afr. (Natal In.)	33·36 S	26·55 E
86	Port Alice...Can.	50·29 N	127·29 W
81	Port Allegany (ăl-ê-gā′nĭ)...Pa.	41·50 N	78·10 W
166	Port Ambim...Ang.	11·01 S	13·45 E
66	Port Angeles (ăn′jē-lĕs)...Wash.	48·07 N	123·26 W
95	Port Antonio...Jam.	18·10 N	76·25 W
161	Portarlington Austl. (Melbourne In.)	38·07 S	144·39 E
87	Port Arthur (är′thŭr)...Can.	48·28 N	89·12 W
77	Port Arthur...Tex.	29·52 N	93·59 W
	Port Arthur, see Lüshun		
160	Port Augusta (ô-gŭs′tă)...Austl.	32·28 S	137·50 E
83	Port au Port B. (pôr′tō pōr′) Can.	48·41 N	58·45 W
95	Port-au-Prince (prăNs′)...Hai.	18·35 N	72·20 W
80	Port Austin (ôs′tĭn)...Mich.	44·00 N	83·00 W
166	Port Beaufort (bō′fẽrt)...S. Afr.	34·14 S	20·59 E
154	Port Blair (blâr)...Andaman Is.	12·07 N	92·45 E
77	Port Bolivar (bŏl′ĭ-vȧr).Tex. (In.)	29·22 N	94·46 W

ăt; finăl; rāte; senåte; ärm; åsk; sofȧ; fâre; ch-choose; dh-as th in other; bē; ēvent; bĕt; recĕnt; cratẽr; g-go; gh-guttural g; bĭt; ĭ-short neutral; rīde; K-guttural k as ch in German ich;

Page	Name, Pronunciation, Region	Lat. °′	Long. °′
84	Port Chester (chĕs'tẽr) N. Y. (New York In.)	40·59 N	73·40 W
65	Port Chicago (shĭ-kô'gō) Calif. (San Francisco In.)	38·03 N	122·01 W
80	Port Clinton (klĭn'tŭn) Ohio	41·30 N	83·00 W
75	Port Colborne (kōl'bŏrn) Can. (Buffalo In.)	43·53 N	79·13 W
65	Port Coquitlam (kô-kwĭt'lăm) Can. (Vancouver In.)	49·16 N	122·47 W
85	Port Credit (krĕd'ĭt) Can. (Toronto In.)	43·33 N	79·35 W
85	Port Dalhousie (dăl-hōō'zĭ) Can. (Toronto In.)	43·12 N	79·17 W
122	Port-de-Bouc (pôr-dē-bōōk') Fr. (Marseille In.)	43·24 N	5·00 E
95	Port de Paix (pĕ') Hai.	19·55 N	72·50 W
139	Port Dickson (dĭk'sŭn) Mala. (Singapore In.)	2·33 N	101·49 E
65	Port Discovery (B.) (dĭs-kŭv'ẽr-ĭ) Wash. (Seattle In.)	48·05 N	122·55 W
167	Port Edward (ĕd'wẽrd) S. Afr. (Natal In.)	31·04 S	30·14 E
82	Port Elgin (ĕl'jĭn) Can.	46·03 N	64·06 W
167	Port Elizabeth (ē-lĭz'ȧ-bĕth) S. Afr. (Natal In.)	33·57 S	25·37 E
78	Porterdale (pōr'tẽr-dāl) Ga.	33·34 N	83·53 W
68	Porterville (pōr'tẽr-vĭl) Calif.	36·03 N	119·05 W
164	Port Étienne (pôr tā-tyĕn') Mauritania	21·02 N	17·09 W
100	Portezuelo de Tupungato (Vol.) (pôr-tĕ-zwĕ-lō-dĕ-tōō-pōō'n-gä-tô) Arg-Chile	33·30 S	69·52 W
166	Port Francqui (fräN-kē') Con. L.	4·15 S	20·43 E
65	Port Gamble (găm'bŭl) Wash. (Seattle In.)	47·52 N	122·36 W
65	Port Gamble Ind. Res. Wash. (Seattle In.)	47·54 N	122·33 W
166	Port Gentil (zhäN-tē') Gabon	1·30 S	8·45 E
78	Port Gibson (gĭb'sŭn) Miss.	31·56 N	90·57 W
164	Port Harcourt (här'kŭrt) Nig.	4·47 N	7·00 E
158	Port Headland (hĕd'lănd) Austl.	20·30 S	118·30 E
166	Port Herald (hĕr'ăld) Nya.	16·52 S	35·16 E
83	Port Hood (hŏŏd) Can.	46·03 N	61·30 W
81	Port Hope (hōp) Can.	43·55 N	78·10 W
80	Port Huron (hū rŏn) Mich.	43·00 N	82·30 W
125	Portici (pôr'tē-chē). It. (Naples In.)	40·34 N	14·20 E
101	Portillo (pôr-tē'l-yô) Chile (Santiago In.)	32·51 N	70·09 W
124	Portimão (pôr-tē-mo'uN) Port.	37·09 N	8·34 W
84	Port Jarvis (jûr'vĭs) N. Y. (New York In.)	41·22 N	74·41 W
160	Portland (pōrt'lănd) Austl.	38·20 S	142·40 E
80	Portland Ind.	40·25 N	85·00 W
82	Portland Maine	43·40 N	70·16 W
80	Portland Mich.	42·50 N	85·00 W
65	Portland Ore. (Portland In.)	45·31 N	123·41 W
94	Portland Bight (B.) Jam.	17·45 N	77·05 W
94	Portland Pt. Jam.	17·40 N	77·20 W
77	Port Lavaca (lȧ-vä'kȧ) Tex.	28·36 N	96·38 W
160	Port Lincoln (lĭŋ'kŭn) Austl.	34·39 S	135·50 E
65	Port Ludlow (lŭd'lō) Wash. (Seattle In.)	47·26 N	122·41 W
	Port Lyautey, see Kenitra		
160	Port Macquarie (mȧ-kwŏ'rĭ). Austl.	31·25 S	152·45 E
65	Port Madison Ind. Res. (măd'ĭ-sŭn). Wash. (Seattle In.)	47·46 N	122·38 W
94	Port Maria (mȧ-rī'ȧ) Jam.	18·20 N	76·55 W
82	Port Menier (mē-nyā') Can.	49·51 N	64·19 W
65	Port Moody (mōōd'ĭ) Can. (Vancouver In.)	49·17 N	122·51 W
155	Port Moresby (mōrz'bē) Pap.	9·34 S	147·20 E
77	Port Neches (nĕch'ĕz) Tex.	29·59 N	93·57 W
49	Port Nelson (nĕl'sŭn) Can.	56·59 N	92·57 W
82	Portneuf-Sur-Mer (pôr-nûf'sür mēr). Can.	48·40 N	69·10 W
166	Port Nolloth (nŏl'ŏth) S. Afr.	29·10 S	17·00 E
124	Pôrto (Oporto) (pōr'tōō) Port.	41·10 N	8·38 W
98	Pôrto Acre (ä'krĕ) Braz.	9·38 S	67·34 W
100	Pôrto Alegre (ä-lā'grĕ) Braz.	29·58 S	51·11 W
166	Porto Alexandre (ȧ-lĕ-zhän'drĕ) Ang.	16·00 S	11·50 E
167	Pôrto Amélia (ȧ-mĕ'lyä) Moz.	12·59 S	40·32 E
93	Portobelo (pôr'tô-bā'lô) Pan.	9·32 N	79·40 W
99	Pôrto de Pedras (pā'dräzh) Braz.	9·09 S	35·20 W
101	Pôrto Feliz (fĕ-lē's) Braz. (Rio de Janeiro In.)	23·12 S	47·30 W
126	Portoferraio (pōr'tō-fĕr-rä'yō) It.	42·47 N	10·20 E
99	Port-of-Spain (spān) Trin.	10·44 N	61·24 W
126	Portogruaro (pōr'tō-grōō-ä'rō) It.	45·48 N	12·49 E
99	Pôrto Guaira (gwä-ē-rä) Braz.	24·03 S	44·02 W
68	Portola (pôr'tō-lȧ) Calif.	39·47 N	120·29 W
99	Pôrto Mendes (mĕ'n-dĕs) Braz.	24·41 S	54·13 W
99	Pôrto Murtinho (mōōr-tēn'yōō) Braz.	21·43 S	57·43 W
99	Pôrto Nacional (nä-syō-näl') Braz.	10·43 S	48·14 W
164	Porto Novo (pōr'tō-nō'vō) Dahomey	6·31 N	2·32 E
65	Port Orchard (ôr'chẽrd) Wash. (Seattle In.)	47·32 N	122·38 W
65	Port Orchard (B.) Wash. (Seattle In.)	47·40 N	122·39 W
164	Porto Santo, Ilha de (I.) (säN'tōō) Mad. Is.	32·41 N	16·15 W
99	Pôrto Seguro (sā-gōō'rōō) Braz.	16·26 S	38·59 W
126	Porto Torres (tôr'rĕs) It.	40·49 N	8·25 E
126	Porto-Vecchio (vĕk'ē-ô) Fr.	41·36 N	9·17 E
98	Pôrto Velho (väl'yōō) Braz.	8·45 S	63·43 W
98	Portoviejo (pôr-tō-vyā'hō) Ec.	1·11 S	80·28 W
160	Port Phillip B. (fĭl'ĭp) Austl.	37·57 S	144·50 E
160	Port Pirie (pĭ'rē) Austl.	33·10 S	138·00 E
86	Port Radium (rā'dē-ŭm) Can.	66·06 N	118·03 W
94	Port Royal (B.) (roi'ăl) Jam.	17·50 N	76·45 W
	Port Said, see Būr Sa'īd		
167	Port St. Johns (sânt jŏnz) S. Afr. (Natal In.)	31·37 S	29·32 E
167	Port Shepstone (shĕps'tŭn) S. Afr. (Natal In.)	30·45 S	30·23 E
116	Portsmouth (pôrts'mŭth) Eng.	50·45 N	1·03 W
81	Portsmouth N. H.	43·05 N	70·50 W
80	Portsmouth Ohio	38·45 N	83·00 W
84	Portsmouth Va. (Norfolk In.)	36·50 N	76·19 W
93	Portsmouth Dominica (Le. & Wind. Is. In.)	15·33 N	61·28 W
100	Port Stanley Falk. Is.	51·46 S	57·59 W
165	Port Sudan (sōō-dan') Sud.	19·30 N	37·10 E
84	Port Sulphur (sŭl'fẽr) La. (New Orleans In.)	29·28 N	89·41 W
65	Port Susan (B.) (sū-zan') Wash. (Seattle In.)	48·11 N	122·25 W
139	Port Swettenham (swĕt'ĕn-hăm) Mala. (Singapore In.)	3·00 N	101·25 E
79	Port Tampa (tăm'pȧ) Fla. (In.)	27·50 N	82·30 W
65	Port Townsend (tounz'ĕnd) Wash. (Seattle In.)	48·07 N	122·46 W
65	Port Townsend (B.) Wash. (Seattle In.)	48·05 N	122·47 W
102	Portugal (pōr'tû-găl) Eur.	38·15 N	8·08 W
124	Portugalete (pōr-tōō-gä-lā'tā) Sp.	43·18 N	3·05 W
	Portuguese East Africa, see Mozambique		
163	Portuguese Guinea (gĭn'ē) Afr.	12·00 N	20·00 W
	Portuguese India, see Damão, Diu & Gôa		
155	Portuguese Timor (tē-mōr') Asia	4·22 S	126·15 E
	Portuguese West Africa, see Angola		
122	Port Vendres (pôr väN'dr') Fr.	42·32 N	3·07 E
160	Port Wakefield (wāk'fēld) Austl.	34·12 S	138·10 E
84	Port Washington (wôsh'ĭng-tŭn) N. Y. (New York In.)	40·49 N	73·42 W
71	Port Washington Wis.	43·24 N	87·52 W
100	Posadas (pō-sä'dhäs) Arg.	27·32 S	55·56 W
124	Posadas (pō-sä-däs) Sp.	37·48 N	5·09 W
148	Poshan (pō'shän') China	36·32 N	117·51 E
128	Poshekhon'ye Volodarsk (pô-shyĕ'kôn-yĕ vôl'ô-dȧrsk) Sov. Un.	58·31 N	39·07 E
154	Poso, Danau (L.) (pō'sō) Indon.	2·00 S	119·40 E
136	Pospelkova (pôs-pyĕl'kô-vȧ) Sov. Un. (Urals In.)	59·25 N	60·50 E
65	Possession Sd. (pŏ-zĕsh'ŭn) Wash. (Seattle In.)	47·59 N	122·17 W
76	Possum Kingdom Res. (pŏs'ŭm kĭng'dŭm) Tex.	32·58 N	98·12 W
72	Post (pōst) Tex.	33·12 N	101·21 W
126	Postojna (pōs-tōynȧ) Yugo.	45·45 N	14·13 E
152	Pos'yet (pos-yĕt') Sov. Un.	42·27 N	130·47 E
84	Potash (pŏ'tăsh) La. (New Orleans In.)	29·29 N	89·43 W
73	Potawatomi Ind. Res. (pŏt-ȧ-wä'tō mē) Kans.	39·30 N	96·11 W
168	Potchefstroom (pŏch'ĕf-strōm) S. Afr. (Johannesburg & Pretoria In.)	26·42 S	27·06 E
73	Poteau (pô-tō') Okla.	35·03 N	94·37 W
76	Poteet (pô-tēt) Tex.	29·05 N	98·35 W
126	Potenza (pô-tĕnt'sä) It.	40·39 N	15·49 E
126	Potenza (R.) It.	43·09 N	13·00 E
168	Potgiertersrus (pôt-kē'tẽrs-rûs) S. Afr. (Johannesburg & Pretoria In.)	24·09 S	29·04 E
66	Potholes Res. Wash.	47.00 N	119·20 W
133	Poti (pô'tē) Sov. Un.	42·10 N	41·40 E
164	Potiskum Nig.	11·45 N	11·05 E
81	Potomac (R.) (pô-tō'măk) Va.	38·15 N	76·55 W
98	Potosí (pō-tô-sē') Bol.	19·42 S	65·42 W
73	Potosi (pō-tō'sĭ) Mo.	37·56 N	90·46 W
76	Potosi, R. (pō-tô-sē') Mex.	25·04 N	99·36 W
148	Pot'ou (bŭ'tō) China	38·05 N	116·35 E
92	Potrerillos (pō-trȧ-rēl'yôs) Hond.	15·13 N	87·58 W
111	Potsdam (pôts'däm) Ger. (Berlin In.)	52·24 N	13·04 E
81	Potsdam (pŏts'dăm) N. Y.	44·40 N	75·00 W
111	Potsdam (Dist.) (pôts'däm) Ger. (Berlin In.)	52·31 N	12·45 E
111	Pottenstein Aus. (Vienna In.)	47·58 N	16·06 E
110	Potters Bar (pŏt'ẽrz bär) Eng. (London In.)	51·41 N	0·12 W
81	Pottstown (pŏts'toun) Pa.	40·15 N	75·40 W
81	Pottsville (pŏts'vĭl) Pa.	40·40 N	76·15 W
143	Pottuvil Ceylon	6·33 N	81·48 E
81	Poughkeepsie (pō-kĭp'sĭ) N. Y.	41·45 N	73·55 W
154	Poulo Condore, Iles de (Is.) Viet.	8·30 N	106·28 E
65	Poulsbo (pōlz'bōō) Wash. (Seattle In.)	47·44 N	122·38 W
110	Poulton-le-Fylde (pōl'tŭn-lē-fīld') Eng.	53·52 N	2·59 W
101	Pouso Alegre (pō'zōō ä-lā'grĕ) Braz. (Rio de Janeiro In.)	22·13 S	45·56 W
124	Póvoa de Varzim (pō-vō'ȧ dā vär'zēN) Port.	41·23 N	8·44 W
87	Povungnituk Can.	59·12 N	77·51 W
67	Powder River Wyo.	43·06 N	106·55 W
67	Powder R. (pou'dẽr) Mont.-Wyo.	45·18 N	105·37 W
66	Powder R. Ore.	44·55 N	117·35 W
67	Powder R., South Fk. Wyo.	43·13 N	106·54 W
67	Powell (pou'ĕl) Wyo.	44·44 N	108·44 W
69	Powell, L. Utah	37·26 N	110·25 W
95	Powell Pt. Ba. Is.	24·50 N	76·20 W
78	Powell Res. Ky.-Tenn.	36·30 N	83·35 W
86	Powell River Can.	49·54 N	124·25 W
151	Poyang (pō'yäng) China	29·00 N	116·42 E
151	P'oyang Hu (L.) China	29·20 N	116·28 E
71	Poygan (R.) (poi'gȧn) Wis.	44·10 N	89·05 W
127	Požarevac (pô'zhä'rĕ-vȧts) Yugo.	44·38 N	21·12 E
120	Poznań (pôz'nän'') Pol.	52·24 N	16·55 E
124	Pozoblanco (pô-thō-blän'kō) Sp.	38·23 N	4·50 W
91	Pozo Rica (pô-zō-rē'kä) Mex.	20·32 N	97·25 W
90	Pozos (pô'zōs) Mex.	22·05 N	100·50 W
125	Pozuelo de Alarcón (pô-thwā'lō dā ä-lär-kōn') Sp. (Madrid In.)	40·27 N	3·49 W
125	Pozzuoli (pôt-swô'lē) It. (Naples In.)	40·34 N	14·08 E
128	Pra (R.) (prȧ) Sov. Un.	55·00 N	40·13 E
154	Prachin Buri (prä'chēn) Thai.	13·59 N	101·15 E
98	Pradera (prä-dĕ'rä) Col. (In.)	3·24 N	76·13 W
122	Prades (prȧd) Fr.	42·37 N	2·23 E
98	Prado (prä'dô) Col. (In.)	3·44 N	74·55 W
74	Prado Dam (prä'dō) Calif. (Los Angeles In.)	33·53 N	117·39 W
101	Prados (prȧ'dôs) Braz. (Rio de Janeiro In.)	21·05 S	44·04 W
	Prague, see Praha		
120	Praha (Prague) (prä'hȧ) (präg) Czech.	50·05 N	14·30 E
164	Praia (prä'yȧ) C. V. Is. (In.)	15·00 N	23·30 W
100	Praia Funda, Ponta da (Pt.) (pôn'tä-dȧ-prä'yȧ-fōō'n-dä) Braz. (In.)	23·04 S	43·34 W
66	Prairie City (prā'rĭ) Ore.	44·25 N	118·42 W
71	Prairie du Chien (prā'rĭ dōō shēn') Wis.	43·02 N	91·10 W
85	Prairie Grove (prā'rĭ grōv) Can. (Winnipeg In.)	49·48 N	96·57 W
71	Prairie Island Ind. Res. Minn.	44·42 N	92·32 W
85	Prairies, R. des (rē-vyâr' dā prȧ-rē') Can. (Montreal In.)	45·40 N	73·35 W
74	Prairietown (prā'rĭ-toun) Ill. (St. Louis In.)	38·58 N	89·55 W
151	Pratas (Is.) China	20·40 N	116·30 E
126	Prato (prä'tō) It.	43·53 N	11·03 E
122	Prats-de-Mollo (prȧ-dē-mô-lō') Fr.	42·26 N	2·36 E
72	Pratt (prăt) Kans.	37·37 N	98·43 W
78	Prattville (prăt'vĭl) Ala.	32·28 N	86·27 W
119	Pravdinsk Sov. Un.	54·26 N	20·11 E
136	Pravdinskiy (prȧv-dēn'skĭ) Sov. Un. (Moscow In.)	56·03 N	37·52 E
124	Pravia (prä'vē-ä) Sp.	43·30 N	6·08 W
119	Pregolya (R.) (prĕ-gô'lȧ) Sov. Un.	54·37 N	20·50 E
76	Premont (prē-mŏnt') Tex.	27·20 N	98·07 W
120	Prenzlau (prĕnts'lou) Ger.	53·19 N	13·52 E
121	Přerov (przhĕ'rôf) Czech.	49·28 N	17·28 E
91	Presa Aleman (L.) (prä'sä-lĕ-mä'n) Mex.	18·20 N	96·35 W
110	Prescot (prĕs'kŭt) Eng.	53·25 N	2·48 W
69	Prescott (prĕs'kŏt) Ariz.	34·30 N	112·30 W
73	Prescott Ark.	33·47 N	93·23 W
81	Prescott (prĕs'kŭt) Can.	44·45 N	75·35 W
74	Prescott (prĕs'kŏt) Wis. (Minneapolis, St. Paul In.)	44·45 N	92·48 W
70	Presho (prĕsh'ō) S. D.	43·56 N	100·04 W
100	Presidencia Rogue Sáenz Peña (prĕ-sē-dĕ'n-sēȧ-rô'kĕ-sȧ'ĕnz-pĕ'n-yȧ) Arg.	26·52 S	60·15 W
99	Presidente Epitácio (prā-sē-dĕn'tĕ ȧ-pē-tȧ'syōō) Braz.	21·56 S	52·01 W
76	Presidio (prĕ-sĭ'dĭ-ō) Tex.	29·33 N	104·23 W
90	Presidio, Rio del (R.) (rē'ō-dĕl-prĕ-sē'dyô) Mex.	23·54 N	105·44 W
121	Prešov (prĕ'shôf) Czech.	49·00 N	21·18 E
127	Prespa (L.) (prĕs'pä) Alb.-Yugo.	40·49 N	20·50 E
99	Presputnal (R.) (prĕs-pōō-täl') Ven. (In.)	9·55 N	64·32 W
82	Presque Isle (prĕsk'ēl') Maine	46·41 N	68·03 W
111	Pressbaum Aus. (Vienna In.)	48·12 N	16·06 E
110	Preston (prĕs'tŭn) Eng.	53·46 N	2·42 W
67	Preston (pres'tŭn) Idaho	42·05 N	111·54 W
71	Preston (prĕs'tŭn) Minn.	43·42 N	92·06 W
65	Preston Wash. (Seattle In.)	47·31 N	121·56 W
80	Prestonburg (prĕs'tŭn-bûrg) Ky.	37·35 N	82·50 W
110	Prestwich (prĕst'wĭch) Eng.	53·32 N	2·17 W
167	Pretoria (prē-tō'rĭ-ȧ) S. Afr. (Johannesburg & Pretoria In.)	25·43 S	28·16 E
167	Pretoria North (prē-tō'rĭ-ȧ nōōrd) S. Afr. (Johannesburg & Pretoria In.)	25·41 S	28·11 E
127	Préveza (prĕ'vȧ-zä) Grc.	38·58 N	20·44 E
64	Pribilof (Is.) (prĭ'bĭ-lof) Alaska	57·00 N	169·20 W
127	Priboj (prē'boi) Yugo.	43·33 N	19·33 E
69	Price (prīs) Utah	39·35 N	110·50 W
69	Price (R.) Utah	39·21 N	110·35 W
85	Priddis (prĭd'dĭs) Can. (Calgary In.)	50·53 N	114·20 W
85	Priddis Cr. Can. (Calgary In.)	50·56 N	114·32 W
124	Priego (prē-ā'gō) Sp.	37·27 N	4·13 W
119	Prienai (prē-ĕn'ī) Sov. Un.	54·38 N	23·56 E
166	Prieska (prē-ĕs'kȧ) S. Afr.	29·40 S	22·50 E
66	Priest L. (prēst) Idaho	48·30 N	116·43 W
66	Priest Rapids Dam Wash.	46·39 N	119·55 W
66	Priest Rapids Res. Wash.	46·42 N	119·58 W
136	Priiskovaya (prĭ-ēs'kô-vȧ-yȧ) Sov. Un. (Urals In.)	60·50 N	58·55 E
126	Prijedor (prē'yĕ-dôr) Yugo.	44·58 N	16·43 E
127	Prijepolje (prē'yĕ-pô'lyĕ) Yugo.	43·22 N	19·41 E
127	Prilep (prē'lĕp) Yugo.	41·20 N	21·35 E
129	Priluki (prē-lōō'kē) Sov. Un.	50·36 N	32·21 E
119	Primorsk (prē-môrsk') Sov. Un.	60·24 N	28·35 E
129	Primorsko-Akhtarskaya (prē-môr'skô äk-tär'skĭ-ĕ) Sov. Un.	46·03 N	38·09 E
74	Primrose (prĭm'rōz) Tex. (Dallas, Fort Worth In.)	32·36 N	97·28 W
167	Primrose S. Afr. (Johannesburg & Pretoria In.)	26·11 S	28·11 E
86	Prince Albert (prĭns ăl'bẽrt) Can.	53·17 N	105·33 W
86	Prince Albert Natl. Park Can.	54·10 N	105·25 W
86	Prince Albert Sd. Can.	70·23 N	116·57 W
87	Prince Charles I. (chärlz) Can.	67·41 N	74·10 W
82	Prince Edward Natl. Park (ĕd'wẽrd) Can.	46·33 N	63·35 W
83	Prince Edward I. (Prov.) Can.	46·45 N	63·10 W
47	Prince Edward Is. S. Afr.	46·36 S	37·57 E

Page	Name Pronunciation	Region	Lat. °′	Long. °′
81	Prince Edward Pen.	Can.	44·00 N	77·15 W
86	Prince George (jôrj)	Can.	53·51 N	122·57 W
64	Prince of Wales (I.)	Alaska	55·48 N	133·46 W
159	Prince of Wales (I.)	Austl.	10·47 S	142·15 E
64	Prince of Wales, C. (wālz)	Alaska	65·48 N	169·08 W
86	Prince Rupert (roo'pẽrt)	Can.	54·20 N	130·11 W
110	Princes Risborough (prĭns'ĕz rĭz'brŭ)	Eng. (London In.)	51·41 N	0·51 W
84	Princess Anne (prĭn'sĕs ăn)	Va. (Norfolk In.)	36·44 N	76·03 W
159	Princess Charlotte B. (shär'lŏt)	Austl.	13·45 S	144·15 E
47	Princess Martha Coast (mär'thȧ)	Ant.	72·00 S	5·00 W
86	Princeton (prĭns'tŭn)	Can.	49·21 N	120·20 W
80	Princeton	Ill.	41·20 N	89·25 W
80	Princeton	Ind.	38·20 N	87·35 W
78	Princeton	Ky.	37·07 N	87·52 W
71	Princeton	Mich.	46·16 N	87·33 W
71	Princeton	Minn.	45·34 N	93·36 W
73	Princeton	Mo.	40·23 N	93·34 W
84	Princeton	N. J. (New York In.)	40·21 N	74·40 W
79	Princeton	W. Va.	37·21 N	81·05 W
71	Princeton	Wis.	43·50 N	89·09 W
64	Prince William Sd. (wĭl'yăm)	Alaska	60·40 N	147·10 W
164	Príncipe, Ilha do (I.) (ēl'yȧ dô prēn'sē-pĕ)	Afr.	1·42 N	5·38 E
66	Prineville (prīn'vĭl)	Ore.	44.17 N	120.48 W
66	Prineville Res.	Ore.	44·07 N	120·45 W
93	Prinzapolca (prēn-ză-pōl'kă)	Nic.	13·18 N	83·35 W
93	Prinzapolca R.	Nic.	13·23 N	84·23 W
74	Prior Lake (prī'ẽr)	Minn. (Minneapolis, St. Paul In.)	44·43 N	93·26 W
119	Priozërsk (prĭ-ô'zĕrsk)	Sov. Un.	61·03 N	30·08 E
133	Pripyat (Pripet) (R.) (prē'pyăt)	Sov. Un.	51·50 N	29·45 E
	Pripyat' Marshes, see Poles'ye			
127	Priština (prēsh'tĭ-nä)	Yugo.	42·39 N	21·12 E
78	Pritchard (prĭt'chârd)	Ala.	30·44 N	87·04 W
120	Pritzwalk (prēts'välk)	Ger.	53·09 N	12·12 E
122	Privas (prē-väs')	Fr.	44·44 N	4·37 E
129	Privol'noye (prē'vôl-nô-yĕ)	Sov. Un.	47·30 N	32·21 E
127	Prizren (prē'zrĕn)	Yugo.	42·11 N	20·45 E
125	Procida (prô'chē-dă)	It. (Naples In.)	40.31 N	14.02 E
125	Procida, I. di	It. (Naples In.)	40·32 N	13·57 E
74	Proctor (prŏk'tẽr)	Minn. (Duluth In.)	46·45 N	92·14 W
81	Proctor	Vt.	43·40 N	73·00 W
65	Proebstel (prōb'stĕl)	Wash. (Portland In.)	45·40 N	122·29 W
124	Proenca-a-Nova (prô-ān'sȧ-ă-nō'vȧ)	Port.	39·44 N	7·55 W
92	Progreso (prô-grĕ'sô)	Hond.	15·28 N	87·49 W
91	Progreso (prô-grā'sō)	Mex.	21·14 N	89·39 W
76	Progreso	Mex.	27·29 N	101·05 W
134	Prokop'yevsk	Sov. Un.	53·52 N	86·38 E
127	Prokuplje (prô'ko͝op'l-yĕ)	Yugo.	43·16 N	21·40 E
154	Prome (prōm)	Bur.	18·46 N	95·15 E
128	Pronya (R.) (prô'nyă)	Sov. Un.	54·08 N	30·58 E
128	Pronya (R.)	Sov. Un.	54·08 N	39·30 E
99	Propriá (prō-prē-ă')	Braz.	10·17 S	36·47 W
75	Prospect (prŏs'pĕkt)	Ky. (Louisville In.)	38·21 N	85·36 W
84	Prospect Park (prŏs'pĕkt pärk)	Pa. (Philadelphia In.)	39·53 N	75·18 W
66	Prosser (prŏs'ẽr)	Wash.	46·10 N	119·46 W
121	Prostějov (prôs'tyĕ-yôf)	Czech.	49·28 N	17·08 E
65	Protection (I.) (prô-tĕk'shŭn)	Wash. (Seattle In.)	48·07 N	122·56 W
128	Protoka (R.) (prôt'ô-kȧ)	Sov. Un.	55·00 N	36·42 E
127	Provadiya (prō-văd'ē-yȧ)	Bul.	43·13 N	27·28 E
80	Providence (prŏv'ĭ-dĕns)	Ky.	37·25 N	87·45 W
84	Providence	R. I. (Providence In.)	41·50 N	71·23 W
67	Providence	Utah	41·42 N	111·50 W
93	Providencia, Isla de (I.)	Col.	13·21 N	80·55 W
95	Providenciales (I.) (prō-vē-dĕn-sē-ä'lȧs) (prŏ-vĭ-dĕn'shȧlz)	Caicos	21·50 N	72·15 W
64	Provideniya (prô-vĭ-dă'nĭ-yȧ)	Sov. Un.	64·30 N	172·54 W
69	Provo (prō'vō)	Utah	40·15 N	111·40 W
126	Prozor (prô'zôr)	Yugo.	43·48 N	17·59 E
84	Prudence I. (pro͞o'dĕns)	R. I. (Providence In.)	41·38 N	71·20 W
121	Prudnik (pro͞od'nĭk)	Pol.	50·19 N	17·34 E
119	Prunkkala (pro͞oŋk'ȧ-lȧ)	Fin.	60·38 N	22·32 E
120	Prussia (Reg.) (prŭsh'ȧ)	Ger.	50·43 N	8·35 E
121	Pruszków (pro͞osh'ko͞of)	Pol.	52·09 N	20·50 E
129	Prut (R.) (pro͞ot)	Sov. Un.	48·05 N	27·07 E
73	Pryor (prī'ẽr)	Okla.	36·16 N	95·19 W
133	Prypeć (R.)	Sov. Un.	51·50 N	25·35 E
121	Przedbórz (pzhĕd'bo͞ozh)	Pol.	51·05 N	19·53 E
121	Przedbórz	Pol.	53·01 N	20·54 E
121	Przemyśl (pzhĕ'mĭsh'l)	Pol.	49·47 N	22·45 E
134	Przheval'sk (p'r-zhĭ-vălsk')	Sov. Un.	42·25 N	78·18 E
127	Psará (I.) (psă'rȧ)	Grc.	38·39 N	25·26 E
129	Psël (R.) (psĕl)	Sov. Un.	49·45 N	33·42 E
127	Psevdhókavos (Pen.)	Grc.	39·58 N	24·05 E
128	Pskov (pskôf)	Sov. Un.	57·48 N	28·19 E
128	Pskov (Oblast)	Sov. Un.	57·33 N	29·05 E
128	Pskovskoye Ozero (L.) (p'skôv'skô'yĕ ôzē-rô)	Sov. Un.	58·05 N	28·15 E
128	Ptich' (R.) (p'tēch)	Sov. Un.	53·17 N	28·16 E
126	Ptuj (pto͞o'ē)	Yugo.	46·24 N	15·54 E
139	Puak (po͞o'ä)	Indon. (Singapore In.)	1·39 N	101·31 E
151	Pucheng (po͞o'chĕng')	China	28·02 N	118·25 E
121	Puck (po͞otsk)	Pol.	54·43 N	18·23 E
146	Pudog	China	33·29 N	79·26 E
132	Pudozh (po͞o'dôzh)	Sov. Un.	61·50 N	36·50 E
90	Puebla (pwā'blă)	Mex.	19·02 N	98·11 W
124	Puebla de Don Fadrique (pwĕ'blă dā dōn fă-drē'kā)	Sp.	37·55 N	2·55 W
72	Pueblo (pwā'blō)	Colo.	38·15 N	104·36 W
90	Pueblo Nuevo (nwā'vô)	Mex.	23·23 N	105·21 W
91	Pueblo Viejo (vyā'hô)	Mex.	17·23 N	93·46 W
74	Puente (pwĕn'tē)	Calif. (Los Angeles In.)	34·01 N	117·57 W
101	Puente Alto (pwĕ'n-tĕ ȧl'tô)	Chile (Santiago In.)	33·36 S	70·34 W
124	Puenteareas (pwĕn-tā-ă-rā'ăs)	Sp.	42·09 N	8·23 W
124	Puente Ceso (pwĕn'tā thā'sô)	Sp.	43·15 N	8·53 W
124	Puentedeume (pwĕn-tā-dhā-o͞o'mā)	Sp.	43·28 N	8·09 W
124	Puente-Genil (pwĕn'tā-hā-nēl')	Sp.	37·25 N	4·18 W
69	Puerco (R.) (pwĕr'kō)	N. Mex.	35·15 N	107·05 W
100	Puerto Aisén (pwĕ'r-tō ă'y-sĕ'n)	Chile	45·28 S	72·44 W
91	Puerto Ángel (pwĕ'r-tō ăŋ'hāl)	Mex.	15·42 N	96·32 W
93	Puerto Armuelles (pwe'r-tô ăr-mo͞o-ā'lyās)	Pan.	8·18 N	82·52 W
92	Puerto Barrios (pwĕ'r-tô băr'rē-ôs)	Guat.	15·43 N	88·36 W
98	Puerto Bermúdez (pwĕ'r-tō bĕr-mo͞o'dāz)	Peru	10·17 S	74·57 W
98	Puerto Berrío (pwĕ'r-tō bĕr-rē'ō)	Col. (In.)	6·29 N	74·27 W
99	Puerto Cabello (pwĕ'r-tō kă-bĕl'yō)	Ven. (In.)	10·28 N	68·01 W
93	Puerto Cabezas (pwĕ'r-tô kă-bā'zăs)	Nic.	14·01 N	83·26 W
100	Puerto Casado (pwĕ'r-tō kă-să'dō)	Par.	22·16 S	57·57 W
92	Puerto Castilla (pwĕ'r-tô käs-tēl'yō)	Hond.	16·01 N	86·01 W
98	Puerto Chicama (pwĕ'r-tō chē-kă'mă)	Peru	7·46 S	79·18 W
98	Puerto Columbia (pwĕr'tô kô-lôm'bē-ȧ)	Col.	11·08 N	75·09 W
93	Puerto Cortés (pwĕ'r-tô kôr-tās')	C. R.	9·00 N	83·37 W
92	Puerto Cortés (pwĕ'r-tô kôr-tās')	Hond.	15·48 N	87·57 W
98	Puerto Cumarebo (pwĕ'r-tō ko͞o-mă-rĕ'bô)	Ven.	11·25 N	69·17 W
125	Puerto de Beceite (Mts.) (pwĕ'r-tō dĕ bĕ-sĕ'y-tĕ)	Sp.	40·43 N	0·05 W
72	Puerto de Luna (pwĕr'tô dā lo͞o'nă)	N. Mex.	34·49 N	104·36 W
98	Puerto de Nutrias (pwĕ'r-tō dĕ no͞o-trē-ăs')	Ven.	8·02 N	69·19 W
100	Puerto Deseado (pwĕ'r-tō dā-sā-ă'dhō)	Arg.	47·38 S	66·00 W
98	Puerto Eten (pwĕ'r-tō ĕ-tĕ'n)	Peru	6·59 S	79·51 W
93	Puerto Jimenez (pwĕ'r-tô ĸē-mĕ'nĕz)	C. R.	8·35 N	83·23 W
99	Puerto La Cruz (pwĕ'r-tō lă kro͞o'z)	Ven. (In.)	10·14 N	64·38 W
124	Puertollano (pwĕr-tôl-yă'nō)	Sp.	38·41 N	4·05 W
100	Puerto Madryn (pwĕ'r-tō mă-drēn')	Arg.	42·45 S	65·01 W
98	Puerto Maldonado (pwĕ'r-tō măl-dō-nă'dô)	Peru	12·43 S	69·01 W
	Puerto Mexico, see Coatzacoalcos			
90	Puerto Miniso (pwĕ'r-tō mē-nē'sô)	Mex.	16·06 N	98·02 W
100	Puerto Montt (pwĕ'r-tō mô'nt)	Chile	41·29 S	73·00 W
100	Puerto Natales (pwĕ'r-tō nă-tȧ'lĕs)	Chile	51·48 S	72·01 W
98	Puerto Niño (pwĕ'r-tō nē'n-yô)	Col. (In.)	5·57 N	74·36 W
98	Puerto Ordaz (pwĕ'r-tōôr-dȧ's)	Ven.	8·30 N	62·45 W
94	Puerto Padre (pwĕ'r-tō pă'drā)	Cuba	21·10 N	76·40 W
88	Puerto Peñasco (pwĕ'r-tô pĕn-yă's-kô)	Mex.	31·39 N	113·15 W
100	Puerto Pinasco (pwĕ'r-tō pē-nȧ's-kô)	Par.	22·31 S	57·50 W
99	Puerto Píritu (pwĕ'r-tō pē'rē-to͞o)	Ven. (In.)	10·05 N	65·04 W
95	Puerto Plata (pwĕ'r-tô plä'tä)	Dom. Rep.	19·50 N	70·40 W
154	Puerto Princesa (pwẽr-tô prēn-sā'sä)	Phil.	9·45 N	118·41 E
89	Puerto Rico (pwĕr'tô rē'kō)	N. A. (In.)	18·16 N	66·50 W
89	Puerto Rico Trough	N. A.	19·45 N	66·30 W
98	Puerto Salgar (pwĕ'r-tō säl-gär')	Col (In.)	5·30 N	74·39 W
100	Puerto Santa Cruz (pwĕ'r-tō sän'tä kro͞oz')	Arg.	50·04 S	68·32 W
99	Puerto Suárez (pwĕ'r-tō swä'răz)	Bol.	18·55 S	57·39 W
98	Puerto Tejada (pwĕ'r-tō tĕ-ĸä'dä)	Col. (In.)	3·13 N	76·23 W
90	Puerto Vallarta (pwĕ'r-tō väl-yär'tä)	Mex.	20·36 N	105·13 W
100	Puerto Varas (pwĕ'r-tō vä'räs)	Chile	41·16 S	73·03 W
98	Puerto Wilches (pwĕ'r-tō vēl'c-hĕs)	Col.	7·19 N	73·54 W
133	Pugachëv (po͞o'gȧ-chyôf)	Sov. Un.	52·00 N	48·40 E
65	Puget (pū'jĕt)	Wash. (Portland In.)	46·10 N	123·23 W
66	Puget Sd.	Wash.	47·49 N	122·26 W
126	Puglia (Apulia) (Reg.) (po͞o'lyä) (ä-po͞o'lyä)	It.	41·13 N	16·10 E
148	Puhsien (po͞o'sĭän)	China	35·43 N	115·22 E
139	Pukin (R.)	Mala. (Singapore In.)	2·53 N	102·54 E
126	Pula (po͞o'lä)	Yugo.	44·52 N	13·55 E
98	Pulacayo (po͞o-lä-kä'yō)	Bol.	20·12 S	66·33 W
148	P'ulantien (po͞o'lăn'chĕn')	China	39·23 N	121·57 E
78	Pulaski (pŭ-lăs'kĭ)	Tenn.	35·11 N	87·03 W
79	Pulaski	Va.	37·00 N	81·45 W
121	Puławy (po͝o-wä'vē)	Pol.	51·24 N	21·59 E
142	Pulizat (R.)	India	13·58 N	79·52 E
66	Pullman (po͝ol'măn)	Wash.	46·44 N	117·10 W
155	Pulog (Mtn.) (po͞o'lôg)	Phil. (Manila In.)	16·38 N	120·53 E
112	Pultusk (po͞ol'to͝osk)	Pol.	52·40 N	21·09 E
67	Pumpkin Cr. (pŭmp'kĭn)	Mont.	45·47 N	105·35 W
142	Punakhapo͝o-nŭk'ŭ)	Bhu.	27·45 N	89·59 E
98	Punata (po͞o-nä'tä)	Bol.	17·43 S	65·43 W
142	Punjab (State) (pŭn'jäb')	India	35·50 N	75·20 E
98	Puno (po͞o'nô)	Peru	15·58 S	7·02 W
100	Punta Arenas (po͞o'n-tă-rĕ'năs)	Chile	53·09 S	70·48 W
99	Punta de Piedras (po͞o'n-tä dĕ pyĕ'drăs)	Ven. (In.)	10·54 N	64·06 W
92	Punta Gorda (po͝on'tă gôr'dă)	Br. Hond.	16·07 N	88·50 W
79	Punta Gorda (pŭn'tȧ gôr'dȧ)	Fla. (In.)	26·55 N	82·02 W
93	Punta Gorda, Rio (R.) (po͞o'n-tä gô'r-dă)	Nic.	11·34 N	84·13 W
101	Punta Indio, Can. (po͞o'n-tä ē'n-dyô)	Arg. (Buenos Aires In.)	34·56 S	57·20 W
93	Puntarenas (po͝ont-ă-rā'näs)	C. R.	9·59 N	84·49 W
98	Punto Fijo (po͞o'n-tô fē'ĸô)	Ven.	11·48 N	70·14 W
164	Punto Grande (grä'n-dĕ)	C. V. Is. (In.)	16·53 N	25·00 W
81	Punxsutawney (pŭnk-sŭ-tô'nē)	Pa.	40·55 N	79·00 W
98	Puquio (po͞o'kyô)	Peru	14·43 S	74·02 W
134	Pur (R.)	Sov. Un.	65·30 N	77·30 E
73	Purcell (pûr-sĕl')	Okla.	35·01 N	97·22 W
65	Purdy (pûr'dē)	Wash. (Seattle In.)	47·23 N	122·37 W
90	Purépero (po͞o-rā'pȧ-rō)	Mex.	19·56 N	102·02 W
72	Purgatoire (R.) (pûr-gȧ-twär')	Colo.	37·25 N	103·53 W
142	Puri (po͝o'rē)	India	19·52 N	85·51 E
95	Purial, Sierra de (Mts.) (sē-ĕ'r-rȧ-dĕ-po͞o-rē-äl')	Cuba	20·15 N	74·40 W
98	Purificacion (po͞o-rē-fē-kä-syōn')	Col. (In.)	3·52 N	74·54 W
90	Purificación (po͞o-rē-fē-kä-syô'n)	Mex.	19·44 N	104·38 W
90	Purificación (R.)	Mex.	19·30 N	104·54 W
111	Purkersdorf	Aus. (Vienna In.)	48·13 N	16·11 E
154	Pursat (po͝or-sät')	Camb.	12·33 N	103·51 E
90	Puruandiro (po͝o-ro͞o-än'dē-rō)	Mex.	20·04 N	101·33 W
98	Purús (R.) (po͞o-ro͞o's)	Braz.	6·45 S	64·34 W
152	Pusan	Kor.	35·08 N	129·05 E
136	Pushkin (po͝osh'kĭn)	Sov. Un. (Leningrad In.)	59·43 N	30·25 E
136	Pushkino (po͝osh'kē-nô)	Sov. Un. (Moscow In.)	56·01 N	37·51 E
128	Pustoshka (pûs-tôsh'kȧ)	Sov. Un.	56·20 N	29·33 E
91	Pustunich (po͞os-to͞o'nēch)	Mex.	19·10 N	90·29 W
101	Putaendo (po͞o-tä-ĕn-dô)	Chile (Santiago In.)	32·37 S	70·42 W
123	Puteaux (pü-tō')	Fr. (Paris In.)	48·52 N	2·12 E
167	Putfontein (po͝ot'fŏn-tān)	S. Afr. (Johannesburg & Pretoria In.)	26·08 S	28·24 E
151	P'ut'ien	China	25·40 N	119·02 E
129	Putivl' (po͞o-tēv'l')	Sov. Un.	51·22 N	33·24 E
91	Putla de Guerrero (po͞o'tlä-dĕ-gĕr-rĕ'rō)	Mex.	17·03 N	97·55 W
81	Putnam (pŭt'năm)	Conn.	41·55 N	71·55 W
134	Putorana, Gory (Mts.)	Sov. Un.	68·45 N	93·15 E
143	Puttālām	Ceylon	8·02 N	79·44 E
98	Putumayo (R.) (po͝o-to͞o-mä'yō)	Col.-Peru	1·02 S	73·50 W
149	Putung (po͞o'to͝ong')	China (Shanghai In.)	31·14 N	121·29 E
154	Putung, Tandjung (C.)	Indon.	3·35 S	111·50 E
119	Puulavesi (L.)	Fin.	61·49 N	27·10 E
65	Puyallup (pū-ăl'ŭp)	Wash. (Seattle In.)	47·12 N	122·18 W
148	P'uyang (po͞o'yäng)	China	35·42 N	114·58 E
166	Pweto (pwā'tō)	Con. L.	8·29 S	28·58 E
134	Pyasina (R.) (pyä-sē'nȧ)	Sov. Un.	72·45 N	87·37 E
133	Pyatigorsk (pyȧ-tē-gôrsk')	Sov. Un.	44·00 N	43·00 E
119	Pyhäjärvi (L.)	Fin.	60·57 N	21·50 E
146	Pyinmana (pyēn-mä'nŭ)	Bur.	19·47 N	96·15 E
80	Pymatuning Res. (pī-mȧ-tûn'ĭng)	Pa.	41·40 N	80·30 W
152	Pyŏnggang (pyŭng'gäng')	Kor.	38·21 N	127·18 E
152	P'yŏngyang	Kor.	39·03 N	125·48 E
68	Pyramid (L.) (pĭ'rȧ-mĭd)	Nev.	40·02 N	119·50 W
68	Pyramid Lake Ind. Res.	Nev.	40·17 N	119·52 W
168	Pyramids	U. A. R. (Nile In.)	29·53 N	31·10 E
125	Pyrenees (Mts.) (pĭr-e-nēz')	Fr.-Sp.	43·00 N	0·05 E
120	Pyrzyce (pĕzhĭ'tsĕ)	Pol.	53·09 N	14·53 E
168	Qana el Suweis (Suez Can.)	U. A. R. (Suez In.)	30·53 N	32·21 E
115	Qārah (Oasis)	U. A. R.	29·28 N	26·29 E
133	Qareh Sū (R.)	Iran	38·50 N	47·10 E
168	Qārūn, Birket (L.)	U. A. R. (Nile In.)	29·34 N	30·34 E
144	Qaryat al Ulya	Sau. Ar.	27·43 N	47·43 E
165	Qasr Banī Walid	Libya	31·45 N	14·04 E
138	Qatar (kä'tȧr)	Asia	25·00 N	52·45 E
115	Qattarah, Munkhafad al (Dep.)	U. A. R.	30·07 N	27·30 E
144	Qāyen	Iran	33·45 N	59·08 E
168	Qena, Wadi (val.)	U. A. R. (Nile In.)	26·38 N	32·53 E
144	Qeshm	Qeshm (Isl.)	26·51 N	56·10 E
144	Qeshm (I.)	Iran	26·52 N	56·15 E
144	Qezel Owzan	Iran	37·00 N	48·23 E

ăt; finăl; rāte; senāte; ärm; ȧsk; sofȧ; fâre; ch-choose; dh-as th in other; bē; ēvent; bĕt; recĕnt; cratẽr; g-go; gh-guttural g; bĭt; ĭ-short neutral; rīde; ĸ-guttural k as ch in German ich;

Page	Name Pronunciation Region	Lat. °′	Long. °′
133	Qezel Owzan (R.) . . . . . Iran	37·00 N	47·35 E
139	Qiblîya, el (cliff) U. A. R. (Palestine In.)	28·47 N	32·22 E
168	Qifṭ (kêft) . . . U. A. R. (Nile In.)	25·58 N	32·52 E
168	Qinā (kā'nȧ) . . . U. A. R. (Nile In.)	26·10 N	32·48 E
139	Qiraiya (R.) U. A. R. (Palestine In.)	30·14 N	34·21 E
144	Qom . . . . . Iran	34·28 N	50·53 E
	Qomul, see Hami		
81	Quabbin Res. (kwā'bĭn) . . . Mass	42·20 N	72·10 W
73	Quachita, L. (kwä shĭ'tô) . . . Ark.	34·47 N	93·37 W
81	Quakertown (kwā'kēr-toun) . . . Pa.	40·30 N	75·20 W
72	Quanah (kwā'nȧ) . . . Tex.	34·19 N	99·43 W
151	Quang Ngai (kwäng n'gä'ē) . . Viet.	15·05 N	108·58 E
151	Quang Ngai (Mtn.) . . . Viet.	15·10 N	108·20 E
154	Quang Tri (kwäng'trē') . . . Viet.	16·39 N	107·05 E
86	Qu'Appelle (R.) (kȧ-pĕl') . . . Can.	50·55 N	104·12 W
126	Quartu Sant' Elena (kwär-tōō' sänt a'lâ-nä) . It.	39·16 N	9·12 E
85	Quebec (kwê-bĕk') (kȧ-bĕk') Can. (Quebec In.)	46·49 N	71·14 W
87	Quebec (Prov.) . . . Can.	51·07 N	70·25 W
120	Quedlinburg (kvĕd'lĕn-bōōrgh) Ger.	51·49 N	11·10 E
86	Queen Charlotte Is. (kwēn shär'lŏt) . Can.	53·40 N	132·50 W
86	Queen Charlotte Str. (strāt) . Can.	51·19 N	128·42 W
49	Queen Elizabeth Is. (ê-lĭz'ȧ-bĕth) Can.	78·20 N	110·00 W
86	Queen Maud G. (mäd) . . . Can.	68·27 N	102·55 W
47	Queen Maud Land . . . Ant.	75·00 S	10·00 E
47	Queen Maud Ra . . . Ant.	85·00 S	179·00 W
158	Queens Chan. (kwēnz) . . . Austl.	14·25 S	129·10 E
161	Queenscliff . Austl. (Melbourne In.)	38·16 S	144·39 E
159	Queensland (State) (kwēnz'lȧnd) Austl.	22·45 S	141·01 E
160	Queenstown (kwēnz'toun) . . Austl.	42·00 S	145·40 E
167	Queenstown . . . S. Afr. (Natal In.)	31·54 S	26·53 E
124	Queija, Sierra de (Mts.) (sē-ĕ'r-rä-dĕ-kĕ'y-kä) . Sp.	42·08 N	7·23 W
100	Queimados (kā-mȧ'dôs) Braz. (In.)	22·42 S	43·34 W
166	Quelimane (kā lê-mä'nĕ) . . . Moz.	17·48 S	37·05 E
	Quelpart, see Cheju		
94	Quemado de Güines (kā-mä'dhā-dĕ-gwē'nĕs) . . . Cuba	22·45 N	80·20 W
151	Quemoy (Chinmen) . . . Taiwan	24·30 N	118·20 E
93	Quepos (kā'pôs) . . . C. R.	9·26 N	84·10 W
93	Quepos, Punta (pt.) (pōō'n-tä) . C. R.	9·23 N	84·20 W
166	Que Que (kwĕ'kwĕ) . . . S. Rh.	18·49 S	29·45 E
90	Querétaro (kȧ-rā'tä-rō) . . . Mex.	20·37 N	100·25 W
124	Quesada (kȧ-sä'dhä) . . . Sp.	37·51 N	3·04 W
86	Quesnel (kā-nĕl') . . . Can.	53·00 N	122·28 W
86	Quesnel (L.) . . . Can.	52·28 N	121·40 W
98	Quetame (kĕ-tä'mĕ) . . . Col. (In.)	4·20 N	73·50 W
87	Quetico Park (kwĕ'tĭ-kō) . . . Can.	48·29 N	91·50 W
142	Quetta (kwĕt'ȧ) . . . W. Pak.	30·19 N	67·01 E
92	Quezaltenango (kȧ-zäl'tȧ-näŋ'gō) Guat.	14·50 N	91·30 W
92	Quezaltepeque (kȧ-zäl'tȧ-pā'kȧ) Guat.	14·39 N	89·26 W
92	Quezaltepeque (kĕ-zäl'tĕ'pĕ-kĕ) Sal.	13·50 N	89·17 W
155	Quezon City (kā-zōn) Phil. (Manila In.)	14·40 N	121·02 E
98	Quibdo (kēb'dō) . . . Col. (In.)	5·42 N	76·41 W
122	Quiberon (kê-bē-rôn') . . . Fr.	47·29 N	3·08 W
92	Quiché (kē-shā') . . . Guat.	15·05 N	91·08 W
111	Quicksborn (kvĕks'bōrn) Ger. (Hamburg In.)	53·44 N	9·54 E
65	Quilcene (kwĭl-sēn') Wash. (Seattle In.)	47·50 N	122·53 W
101	Quilimari (kē-lē-mȧ'rē) Chile (Santiago In.)	32·06 S	71·28 W
86	Quill (L.) (kwĭl) . . . Can.	52·10 N	103·34 W
122	Quillan (kê-yäN') . . . Fr.	43·53 N	2·13 E
101	Quillota (kēl-yō'tä) Chile (Santiago In.)	32·52 S	71·14 W
100	Quilmes (kēl'mâs) . . . Arg. (In.)	34·28 S	58·16 W
143	Quilon (kwê-lōn') . . . India	8·58 N	76·16 E
160	Quilpie (kwĭl'pê) . . . Austl.	26·34 S	149·20 E
101	Quilpué (kēl-pōō ĕ') Chile (Santiago In.)	33·03 S	71·22 W
98	Quimbaya (kēm-bä'yä) . Col. (In.)	4·38 N	75·46 W
122	Quimper (käN-pĕr') . . . Fr.	47·59 N	4·04 W
155	Quinabucasan Pt. (kē-nä-bōō-kä'sän) Phil. (Manila In.)	14·09 N	123·33 E
66	Quinalt R. . . . Wash.	47·23 N	124·10 W
66	Quinault Ind. Res. . . . Wash.	47·27 N	124·34 W
78	Quincy (kwĭn'sê) . . . Fla.	30·35 N	84·35 W
73	Quincy . . . Ill.	39·55 N	91·23 W
83	Quincy . . . Mass. (Boston In.)	42·15 N	71·00 W
80	Quincy . . . Mich.	42·00 N	84·50 W
65	Quincy . . . Ore. (Portland In.)	46·08 N	123·10 W
154	Qui Nhon (kwĭnyôn) . . . Viet.	13·51 N	109·03 E
66	Quinn R. (kwĭn) . . . Nev.	41·42 N	117·45 W
124	Quintana de la Serena (kēn-tä'nä dā lä sȧ-rā'nä) . Sp.	38·45 N	5·39 W
124	Quintanar (kēn-tä-när') . . . Sp.	39·36 N	3·02 W
88	Quintana Roo (Ter.) (rô'ô) . . Mex.	19·30 N	88·35 W
101	Quintero (kēn-tĕ'rō) Chile (Santiago In.)	32·48 S	71·30 W
90	Quiroga (kē-rō'gä) . . . Mex.	19·39 N	101·30 W
124	Quiroga (kē-rō'gä) . . . Sp.	42·28 N	7·18 W
78	Quitman (kwĭt'mȧn) . . . Ga.	30·46 N	83·35 W
78	Quitman . . . Miss.	33·02 N	88·43 W
98	Quito (kē'tō) . . . Ec.	0·17 S	78·32 W
99	Quixadá (kê-shä-dä') . . . Braz.	4·58 S	38·58 W
168	Qulūṣanā (kōō-lōōs'nā) U. A. R. (Nile In.)	28·22 N	30·44 E
167	Qumbu (kōōm'bōō) S. Afr. (Natal In.)	29·12 S	28·53 E
139	Qumran . . . Jordan (Palestine In.)	31·45 N	35·28 E

Page	Name Pronunciation Region	Lat. °′	Long. °′
84	Quonset Point (kwŏn'sĕt) R. I. (Providence In.)	41·36 N	71·25 W
160	Quorn (kwôrn) . . . Austl.	32·20 S	138·00 E
168	Qūs (kōōs) . . . U. A. R. (Nile In.)	25·53 N	32·48 E
167	Quthing . . . Bas. (Natal In.)	30·35 S	27·42 E
159	Quvea (I.) . . . N. Cal.	20·43 S	166·48 E
144	Quzvīn . . . Iran	36·10 N	49·59 E
120	Raab R. (räp) . . . Aus.	46·55 N	15·55 E
112	Raahe (rä'ĕ) . . . Fin.	64·39 N	24·22 E
126	Rab (I.) (räb) . . . Yugo.	44·45 N	14·40 E
154	Raba . . . Indon.	8·32 S	118·49 E
121	Raba R. . . . Hung.	47·28 N	17·12 E
164	Rabat (rȧ-bät') . . . Mor.	33·59 N	6·47 W
155	Rabaul (rä'boul) . . . N. Gui. Ter.	4·15 S	152·19 E
127	Rača (rä'chȧ) . . . Yugo.	44·13 N	21·01 E
71	Raccoon (R.) (ră-kōōn') . . . Iowa	42·07 N	94·45 W
95	Raccoon Cay (I.) . . . Ba. Is.	22·25 N	75·50 W
83	Race, C. (rās) . . . Can.	46·37 N	52·55 W
139	Rachado, C. Mala. (Singapore In.)	2·26 N	101·29 E
121	Racibórz (rä-chē'bōōzh) . . . Pol.	50·06 N	18·14 E
75	Racine (rȧ-sēn') Wis. (Milwaukee In.)	42·43 N	87·49 W
74	Raco (rȧ cō) Mich. (Sault Ste. Marie In.)	46·22 N	84·43 W
121	Rădăuti (rŭ-dŭ-ōōts'') . . . Rom.	47·53 N	25·55 E
110	Radcliffe (răd'klĭf) . . . Eng.	53·34 N	2·20 W
123	Radevormwald (rä'dĕ-fōrm-väld) Ger. (Ruhr In.)	51·12 N	7·22 E
79	Radford (răd'fērd) . . . Va.	37·06 N	81·33 W
142	Rādhanpur . . . India	23·57 N	71·38 E
74	Radio Center (ra'dĭ-ō cĕn'tēr) Minn. (Minneapolis, St. Paul In.)	44·50 N	93·06 W
168	Radium (rā'dĭ-ŭm) . . . S. Afr. (Johannesburg & Pretoria In.)	25·06 S	28·18 E
116	Radnor Forest (răd'nôr) . . . Wales	52·11 N	3·25 W
121	Radom (rä'dôm) . . . Pol.	51·24 N	21·11 E
127	Radomir (rä'dô-mêr) . . . Bul.	42·33 N	22·58 E
121	Radomsko (rä-dôm'skô) . . . Pol.	51·04 N	19·27 E
129	Radomyshl (rä-dô-mēsh''l) Sov. Un.	50·30 N	29·13 E
127	Radoviš (rä'dô-vêsh) . . . Yugo.	41·39 N	22·28 E
118	Radöy (I.) (räd-ûê) . . . Nor.	60·43 N	4·40 E
129	Radul' (rä'dōōl) . . . Sov. Un.	51·52 N	30·46 E
119	Radviliškis (räd'vê-lēsh'kēs) Sov. Un.	55·49 N	23·31 E
144	Radwah, Jabal (Mtn.) . . . Sau. Ar.	24·44 N	38·14 E
121	Radzyń Podlaski (räd'zēn-y' pŭd-lä'skĭ) . Pol.	51·49 N	22·40 E
79	Raeford (rā'fērd) . . . N. C.	34·57 N	79·15 W
123	Raesfeld (räz'fĕld) Ger. (Ruhr In.)	51·46 N	6·50 E
158	Raeside (rā'sīd) . . . Austl.	29·20 S	122·30 E
86	Rae Str. (rā) . . . Can.	68·40 N	95·03 W
100	Rafaela (rä-fä-ā'lä) . . . Arg.	31·15 S	61·21 W
115	Rafah (rä'fä) . . . U. A. R.	31·14 N	34·12 E
165	Rafai (rä-fī') . . . Cen. Afr. Rep.	4·59 N	23·58 E
144	Rafhā . . . Sau. Ar.	29·43 N	43·13 E
67	Raft R. (răft) . . . Idaho	42·20 N	113·17 W
142	Raga . . . China	29·31 N	85·52 E
155	Ragay (rä-gī') . Phil. (Manila In.)	13·49 N	122·45 E
155	Ragay G. . . . Phil. (Manila In.)	13·44 N	122·38 E
133	Ragga . . . U. A. R.	36·00 N	39·00 E
118	Ragunda (rä-gōōn'dä) . . . Swe.	63·07 N	16·24 E
113	Ragusa (rä-gōō'sä) . . . It.	36·58 N	14·41 E
	Ragusa, see Dubrovnik		
84	Rahway (rô'wā) N. J. (New York In.)	40·37 N	74·16 W
143	Raichur (rä'ê-chōōr') . . . India	16·23 N	77·18 E
142	Raigarh (rī'gŭr) . . . India	21·57 N	83·32 E
69	Rainbow Bridge Natl. Mon. (rān'bō) . Utah	37·05 N	111·00 W
88	Rainbow City . . . C. Z. (Panama Canal In.)	9.20 N	79·23 W
65	Rainier . . . Ore. (Portland In.)	46·05 N	122·56 W
66	Rainier, Mt. (rā-nēr') . . . Wash.	46·52 N	121·46 W
71	Rainy (L.) (rān'ê) . . . Can.-Minn.	48·50 N	93·06 W
71	Rainy (R.) . . . Can.-Minn.	48·36 N	94·14 W
87	Rainy River . . . Can.	48·42 N	94·29 W
142	Raipur (rä'jŭ-bōō-rê') . . . India	21·25 N	81·37 E
80	Raisin (R.) (rā'zĭn) . . . Mich.	42·00 N	83·35 W
84	Raitan (rā-tăn) N. J. (New York In.)	40·34 N	74·40 W
154	Raja, Bukit (Mtn.) . . . Indon.	0·45 S	112·11 E
143	Rajahmundry (räj-ŭ-mŭn'drê) India	17·03 N	81·51 E
154	Rajang, Balang (strm.) . . . Mala.	2·10 N	113·30 E
142	Rājasthān (State) (rä'jŭs-tän) India	31·20 N	72·00 E
142	Rājkot (räj'kôt) . . . India	22·20 N	70·48 E
142	Rakers Tal (L.) . . . China	30·42 N	80·40 E
121	Rakhov (rä'kôf) . . . Sov. Un.	48·02 N	24·13 E
136	Rakh'ya (räk'yȧ) Sov. Un. (Leningrad In.)	60·06 N	30·50 E
129	Rakitnoye (rȧ-kēt'nô-yĕ) . Sov. Un.	50·51 N	35·53 E
120	Rakovnik (rä'kôv-nyĕk) . . . Czech.	50·07 N	13·45 E
128	Rakvere (räk'vĕ-rĕ) . . . Sov. Un.	59·22 N	26·14 E
79	Raleigh (rô'lȧ) . . . N. C.	35·45 N	78·39 W
79	Raleigh, B. . . . N. C.	34·50 N	76·15 W
93	Rama (rä'mä) . . . Nic.	12·11 N	84·14 W
101	Ramallo (rä-mä'l-yô) Arg. (Buenos Aires In.)	33·28 S	60·02 W
123	Rambouillet (räN-bōō-yĕ') Fr. (Paris In.)	48·39 N	1·49 E
167	Rame Hd. . . . S. Afr. (Natal In.)	31·48 S	29·22 E
136	Ramenskoye (rá'mĕn-skô-yĕ) Sov. Un. (Moscow In.)	55·34 N	38·15 E
144	Ramlat As Sab Atayn (Reg.) Sau. Ar.	16·02 N	45·30 E
139	Ramm, Jabal (Mts.) Jordan (Palestine In.)	29·37 N	35·32 E
143	Rāmnād . . . India	9·13 N	78·52 E
90	Ramos (rä'mōs) . . . Mex.	22·46 N	101·52 W
76	Ramos Arizpe (ä-rēz'pȧ) . . . Mex.	25·33 N	100·57 W
64	Rampart (răm'pärt) . . . Alaska	65·28 N	150·18 W
84	Rampo Mts. (răm'pō) N. J.-N. Y. (New York In.)	41·06 N	74·12 W

Page	Name Pronunciation Region	Lat. °′	Long. °′
142	Rāmpur (räm'pōōr) . . . India	28·53 N	79·03 E
142	Rāmpur-Boālia (bō-ä'lē-ä) E. Pak.	24·26 N	88·39 E
154	Ramree (I.) (räm'rē') . . . Bur.	19·01 N	93·23 E
85	Ramsayville (răm'zê vĭl) Can. (Ottawa In.)	45·23 N	75·34 W
110	Ramsbottom (rămz'bŏt-ŭm) Eng.	53·39 N	2·20 W
116	Ramsey (răm'zê) . . . Isle of Man	54·20 N	4·25 W
84	Ramsey . . . N. J. (New York In.)	41·03 N	74·09 W
117	Ramsgate (rămz''gāt) . . . Eng.	51·19 N	1·20 E
118	Ramsjö (räm'shû) . . . Swe.	62·11 N	15·44 E
155	Ramu (R.) (rä'mōō) . . N. Gui. Ter.	5·35 S	145·16 E
154	Ranau, L. (rä-nä'ōō) . . . Indon.	4·52 S	103·52 E
101	Rancagua (rän-kä'gwä) Chile (Santiago In.)	34·10 S	70·43 W
122	Rance (räNs) . . . Fr.	48·17 N	2·30 W
142	Rānchi (rän'chē) . . . India	23·24 N	85·18 E
95	Rancho Boyeros (rä'n-chô-bô-yĕ'rôs) Cuba (Havana In.)	23·00 N	82·23 W
84	Randallstown (răn'dȧlz-toun) Md. (Baltimore In.)	39·22 N	76·48 W
118	Randers (rän'ĕrs) . . . Den.	56·28 N	10·03 E
167	Randfontein (rănt'fŏn-tān) . S. Afr. (Johannesburg & Pretoria In.)	26·10 S	27·42 E
79	Randleman (răn'd'l-mȧn) . . . N. C.	35·49 N	79·50 W
83	Randolph (răn'dôlf) Mass. (Boston In.)	42 10 N	71·03 W
70	Randolph . . . Nebr.	42·22 N	97·22 W
81	Randolph . . . Vt.	43·55 N	72·40 W
83	Random I. (răn'dŭm) . . . Can.	48·12 N	53·25 W
118	Rands Fd. (räns' fyôr) . . . Nor.	60·35 N	10·10 E
82	Rangeley (rānj'lê) . . . Maine	44·56 N	70·38 W
81	Rangeley (L.) . . . Maine	44·55 N	70·40 W
76	Ranger (rān'jēr) . . . Tex.	32·26 N	98·41 W
142	Rangia . . . India	26·32 N	91·39 E
154	Rangoon (răŋ-gōōn') . . . Bur.	16·46 N	96·09 E
142	Rangpur (rŭng'pōōr) . . . E. Pak.	25·48 N	89·19 E
139	Rangsang, Palau (I.) (räng'säng') Indon. (Singapore In.)	1·03 N	102·54 E
111	Rangsdorf (rängs'dōrf) Ger. (Berlin In.)	52·17 N	13·25 E
142	Raniganj (rä-nē-gŭnj') . . . India	23·40 N	87·08 E
86	Rankin Inlet (răŋ'kĕn) . . . Can.	62·45 N	94·27 W
128	Ranova (R.) (rä'nô-vȧ) . . Sov. Un.	53·55 N	40·03 E
75	Ransomville (răn'sum-vĭl) N. Y. (Buffalo In.)	43·15 N	78·54 W
139	Rantau . . . Mala. (Singapore In.)	2·35 N	101·58 E
154	Rantemario, Bulu (Mtn.) . . Indon.	3·22 S	119·50 E
80	Rantoul (răn-tōōl') . . . Ill.	40·25 N	88·05 W
126	Rapallo (rä-päl'lô) . . . It.	44·21 N	9·14 E
157	Rapa Nui (Easter) (I.) (rä'pä nōō'ê) (ēs'tēr) . Chile	26·50 S	109·00 W
101	Rapel (rä-pȧl') (R.) Chile (Santiago In.)	34·05 S	71·30 W
71	Rapid (R.) (răp'ĭd) . . . Minn.	48·21 N	94·50 W
70	Rapid City . . . S. D.	44·06 N	103·14 W
119	Rapla (räp'lȧ) . . . Sov. Un.	59·02 N	24·46 E
81	Rappahannock (R.) (răp'ȧ-hăn'ŭk) . Va.	38·20 N	75·25 W
81	Raquette (L.) (răk'ĕt) . . . N. Y.	43·50 N	74·35 W
81	Raquette (R.) . . . N. Y.	44·20 N	74·50 W
121	Rara Mazowiecka (rä'rä mä-zō-vyĕts'kä) . Pol.	51·46 N	20·17 E
84	Raritan R. (răr'ĭ-tăn) N. J. (New York In.)	40·32 N	74·27 W
157	Rarotonga (rä'rō-tôŋ'gȧ) . Cook Is.	20·40 S	163·00 W
144	Ras Al Hadd (C.) . . . Mus. & Om.	22·29 N	59·46 E
139	Ra's an Naqb Jordan (Palestine In.)	30·00 N	35·29 E
163	Ras Dashan (Mtn.) (räs dä-shän') Eth.	12·49 N	38·14 E
119	Raseiniai (rä-syā'nyĭ) . . Sov. Un.	55·23 N	23·04 E
144	Ras Fartak (C.) . . . Aden	15·43 N	52·17 E
139	Rashayya . . . Leb. (Palestine In.)	33·30 N	35·50 E
168	Rashīd (Rosetta) (rȧ-shēd') (rō-zĕt'ȧ) U. A. R. (Nile In.)	31·22 N	30·25 E
168	Rashîd, Masabb (R. Mth.) U. A. R. (Nile In.)	31·30 N	29·58 E
136	Rashkina (rȧsh'kĭ-nȧ) Sov. Un. (Urals In.)	59·57 N	61·30 E
129	Rashkov (räsh'kôf) . . . Sov. Un.	47·55 N	28·51 E
144	Rasht . . . Iran	37·13 N	49·45 E
127	Raška (räsh'kȧ) . . . Yugo.	43·16 N	20·40 E
142	Ras Kuh Mt. . . . W. Pak.	34·03 N	65·10 E
144	Ras Madrakah (C.) . . Mus. & Om.	18·53 N	57·48 E
133	Rasskazovo (räs-kä'sô-vô) Sov. Un.	52·40 N	41·40 E
144	Ra's Tannūrah . . . Sau. Ar.	26·45 N	49·59 E
120	Rastatt (rä-shtät) . . . Ger.	48·51 N	8·12 E
136	Rastes (räs'tĕs) Sov. Un. (Urals In.)	59·24 N	58·49 E
136	Rastunovo (rȧs-tōō'nô-vô) Sov. Un. (Moscow In.)	55·15 N	37·50 E
124	Ras Uarc (C.) . . . Mor.	35·28 N	2·58 W
142	Ratangarh (rŭ-tŭn'gŭr) . . . India	28·10 N	74·30 E
154	Rat Buri . . . Thai.	13·30 N	99·46 E
77	Ratcliff (răt'klĭf) . . . Tex.	31·22 N	95·09 W
120	Rathenow (rä'tē-nō) . . . Ger.	52·36 N	12·20 E
116	Rathlin (I.) (răth-lĭn) . . . Ire.	54·80 N	6·10 W
123	Ratingen (rä'tēn-gĕn) Ger. (Ruhr In.)	51·18 N	6·51 E
64	Rat Is. (răt) . . . Alaska	51·35 N	176·48 E
142	Ratlam . . . India	23·19 N	75·05 E
143	Ratnāgir . . . India	17·04 N	73·24 E
72	Raton (rȧ-tōn') . . . N. Mex.	36·52 N	104·26 W
66	Rattlesnake Cr. (răt''l snāk) . Ore.	42·38 N	117·39 W
118	Rättvik (rĕt'vēk) . . . Swe.	60·54 N	15·07 E
120	Ratzeburger See (L.) (rä'tzĕ-bōōr-gĕr-zā) . Ger.	53·48 N	11·02 E
101	Rauch (rá'ōōch) Arg. (Buenos Aires In.)	36·47 S	59·05 W
118	Raufoss (rou'fôs) . . . Nor.	60·44 N	10·30 E
101	Raúl Soares (rä-ōō'l-sôä'rĕs) Braz. (Rio de Janeiro In.)	20·05 S	42·28 W

ng-sing; ŋ-baŋk; N-nasalized n; nŏd; cŏmmit; ōld; ôbey; ôrder; fōōd; fŏŏt; ou-out; s-soft; sh-dish; th-thin; pūre; ûnite; ûrn; stŭd; circŭs; ü-as "y" in study; '-indeterminate vowel.

Page	Name Pronunciation Region	Lat. °′	Long. °′
119	Rauma (rä'ōō-mȧ) . . . Fin.	61·07 N	21·31 E
119	Rauna (rȧū'-nȧ) . . . Sov. Un.	57·21 N	25·31 E
154	Raung, Gunung (Mtn.) . . . Indon.	8·15 S	113·56 E
119	Rautalampi (rä'ōō-tē-lăm'pô) . Fin.	62·39 N	26·25 E
121	Rava-Russkaya (rä'vȧ rōōs'kȧ-yȧ) Sov. Un.	50·14 N	23·40 E
126	Ravenna (rä-vĕn'nä) . . . It.	44·27 N	12·13 E
70	Ravenna (rȧ-vĕn'ȧ) . . . Nebr.	41·20 N	98·50 W
80	Ravenna . . . Ohio	41·10 N	81·20 W
120	Ravensburg (rä'vĕns-bōōrgh) . Ger.	47·48 N	9·35 E
65	Ravensdale (rā'vĕnz-dāl) Wash. (Seattle In.)	47·22 N	121·58 W
158	Ravensthorpe (rā'vĕns-thôrp) Austl.	33·30 S	120·20 E
80	Ravenswood (rā'vĕnz-wŏŏd) W. Va.	38·55 N	81·50 W
142	Rawalpindi (rä-wŭl-pēn'dē) W. Pak.	33·42 N	73·04 E
144	Rawanduz . . . Iraq	36·37 N	44·30 E
120	Rawicz (rä'vēch) . . . Pol.	51·36 N	16·51 E
158	Rawlina (rôr-lēnȧ) . . . Austl.	31·13 S	125·45 E
67	Rawlins (rô'lĭnz) . . . Wyo.	41·46 N	107·15 W
100	Rawson (rô'sŭn) . . . Arg.	43·16 S	65·09 W
101	Rawson . . . Arg. (Buenos Aires In.)	34·36 S	60·03 W
110	Rawtenstall (rô'tĕn-stôl) . . . Eng.	53·42 N	2·17 W
83	Ray, C. (rā) . . . Can.	47·38 N	59·25 W
135	Raychikinsk (rī'chĭ-kēnsk) Sov. Un.	49·52 N	129·17 E
110	Rayleigh (rā'lē) Eng. (London In.)	51·35 N	0·36 E
86	Raymond (rā'mŭnd) . . . Can.	49·32 N	112·38 W
66	Raymond . . . Wash.	46·41 N	123·42 W
77	Raymondville (rā'mŭnd-vĭl) . . Tex.	26·30 N	97·46 W
64	Ray Mts. . . . Alaska	65·40 N	151·45 W
77	Rayne (rān) . . . La.	30·12 N	92·15 W
90	Rayón (rä-yōn') . . . Mex.	21·49 N	99·39 W
167	Rayton (rā'tŭn) . . . S. Afr. (Johannesburg & Pretoria In.)	25·45 S	28·33 E
74	Raytown (rā'toun) Mo. (Kansas City In.)	39·01 N	94·48 W
77	Rayville (rā-vĭl) . . . La.	32·28 N	91·46 W
122	Raz, Pte. du (Pt.) (pwănt dū rä) . Fr.	48·02 N	4·43 W
129	Razdel'naya (räz-dĕl'nä-yȧ) Sov. Un.	46·47 N	30·08 E
152	Razdol'noye (räz-dôl'nô-yĕ) Sov. Un.	43·38 N	131·58 E
127	Razgrad . . . Bulg.	43·32 N	26·32 E
127	Razlog (räz'lôk) . . . Bul.	41·54 N	23·32 E
122	Ré, Île de (I.) (ēl dē rā') . . . Fr.	46·10 N	1·53 W
110	Rea (R.) (rē) . . . Eng.	52·25 N	2·31 W
85	Reaburn (rā'bûrn) Can. (Winnipeg In.)	50·06 N	97·53 W
110	Reading (rĕd'ĭng) Eng. (London In.)	51·25 N	0·58 W
83	Reading . . . Mass. (Boston In.)	42·32 N	71·07 W
80	Reading . . . Mich.	41·45 N	84·45 W
75	Reading . . . Ohio (Cincinnati In.)	39·14 N	84·26 W
81	Reading . . . Pa.	40·20 N	75·55 W
100	Realango (rĕ-ä-län-gô) . Braz. (In.)	22·25 S	43·25 W
165	Rebiana (Oasis) . . . Libya	24·10 N	22·03 E
152	Rebun (I.) (rē'bōōn) . . . Jap.	45·25 N	140·54 E
126	Recanati (rā-kä-nä'tē) . . . It.	43·25 N	13·35 E
158	Recherche, Arch. of the (rē-shârsh') . Austl.	34·17 S	122·30 E
128	Rechitsa (ryĕ'chēt-sȧ) . . . Sov. Un.	52·22 N	30·24 E
99	Recife (Pernambuco) (rȧ-sē'fĕ) (pĕr-năm-bōō'kô) . Braz.	8.09 S	34·59 W
167	Recife, C. (rȧ-sē'fĕ) S. Afr. (Natal In.)	34·03 S	25·43 E
100	Reconquista (rā-kôn-kēs'tä) . Arg.	29·01 S	59·41 W
73	Rector (rĕk'tẽr) . . . Ark.	36·16 N	90·21 W
78	Red (R.) . . . Tenn.	36·30 N	87·10 W
72	Red (R.), North Fk. . . . Tex.	35·20 N	100·08 W
63	Red. (R.) . . . U. S.	31·40 N	92·55 W
62	Red (R.) (rĕd) . . . U. S.-Can.	48·10 N	97·00 W
84	Redan (rē-dăn') (rĕd'ăn) Ga. (Atlanta In.)	33·44 N	84·09 W
84	Red Bank (băngk) N. J. (New York In.)	40·21 N	74·06 W
68	Red Bluff (blŭf) . . . Calif.	40·10 N	122·14 W
76	Red Bluff Res. . . . Tex.	32·03 N	103·52 W
71	Redby (rĕd'bē) . . . Minn.	47·52 N	94·55 W
71	Red Cedar (R.) (sē'dẽr) . . . Wis.	45·03 N	91·48 W
86	Redcliff (rĕd'clĭf) . . . Can.	50·10 N	111·09 W
71	Red Cliff Ind. Res. . . . Wis.	46·48 N	91·22 W
160	Redcliffe (rĕd'clĭf) . . . Austl.	27·20 S	153·12 E
72	Red Cloud (kloud) . . . Nebr.	40·06 N	98·32 W
86	Red Deer (dēr) . . . Can.	52·12 N	113·52 W
86	Red Deer (R.) . . . Can.	50·55 N	111·32 W
75	Reddick (rĕd'dĭk) Ill. (Chicago In.)	41·06 N	88·16 W
84	Redding (rĕd'ĭng) Ala. (Birmingham In.)	33·27 N	86·54 W
66	Redding . . . Calif.	40·36 N	122·25 W
101	Redenção da Serra (rĕ-dĕn-souɴ-dä-sĕ'r-rä) Braz. (Rio de Janeiro In.)	23·17 S	45·31 W
70	Redfield (rĕd'fēld) . . . S. D.	44·53 N	98·30 W
77	Red Fish Bar . . . Tex. (In.)	29·29 N	94·53 W
83	Red Indian L. (ĭn'dĭ-ăn) . . . Can.	48·42 N	56·40 W
123	Redklinghausen (rĕk'lĭng-hou-zĕn) Ger. (Ruhr In.)	51·36 N	7·13 E
87	Red Lake (lāk) . . . Can.	51·01 N	93·55 W
70	Red Lake (R.) . . . Minn.	48·02 N	96·04 W
70	Red Lake Falls (lāk fôls) . . . Minn.	47·52 N	96·17 W
70	Red Lake Ind. Res. . . . Minn.	48·09 N	95·55 W
74	Redlands (rĕd'lăndz) Calif. (Los Angeles In.)	34·04 N	117·11 W
81	Red Lion (lī'ŭn) . . . Pa.	39·55 N	76·30 W
67	Red Lodge . . . Mont.	45·13 N	107·16 W
65	Redmond (rĕd'mŭnd) Wash. (Seattle In.)	47·40 N	122·07 W
120	Rednitz R. (rĕd'nētz) . . . Ger.	49·49 N	10·57 E
70	Red Oak (ōk) . . . Iowa	41·00 N	95·12 W
122	Redon (rē-dôɴ') . . . Fr.	47·42 N	2·03 W
100	Redonda, Isla (ē's-lä-rĕ-dô'n-dä) Braz. (In.)	23·05 S	43·11 W
93	Redonda I. N. A. (Le. & Wind. Is. In.)	16·55 N	62·28 W
124	Redondela (rā-dhôn-dā'lä) . . . Sp.	42·16 N	8·34 W
124	Redondo (rā-dôn'dōō) . . . Port.	38·40 N	7·32 W
65	Redondo (rē-dŏn'dō) Wash. (Seattle In.)	47·21 N	122·19 W
74	Redondo Beach Calif. (Los Angeles In.)	33·50 N	118·23 W
72	Red R., Prairie Dog Town Fk. (prā'rĭ) . Tex.	34·54 N	101·31 W
72	Red R., Salt Fk. . . . Tex.	35·04 N	100·31 W
146	Red R. . . . Viet.	22·25 N	103·50 E
67	Red Rock Cr. . . . Mont.	44·54 N	112·44 W
165	Red Sea . . . Afr.-Asia	23·15 N	37·00 E
67	Redwater Cr. (rĕd-wô'tẽr) . . Mont.	47·37 N	105·25 W
72	Red Willow Cr. . . . Nebr.	40·34 N	100·48 W
71	Red Wing . . . Minn.	44·34 N	92·35 W
65	Redwood City (rĕd' wŏŏd) Calif. (San Francisco In.)	37·29 N	122·13 W
71	Redwood Falls . . . Minn.	44·32 N	95·06 W
116	Ree, Lough (B.) (lŏĸ'rē') . . . Ire.	53·30 N	7·45 W
80	Reed City (rēd) . . . Mich.	43·50 N	85·35 W
68	Reedley (rēd'lē) . . . Calif.	36·37 N	119·27 W
71	Reedsburg (rēdz'bûrg) . . . Wis.	43·32 N	90·01 W
66	Reedsport (rēdz'pôrt) . . . Ore.	43·42 N	124·08 W
78	Reelfoot (R.) (rēl'fŏŏt) . . . Tenn.	36·18 N	89·20 W
123	Rees (rĕz) . . . Ger. (Ruhr In.)	51·46 N	6·25 E
74	Reese (rēs) Utah (Salt Lake City In.)	41·15 N	112·09 W
160	Reeves, Mt. (rēv's) . . . Austl.	33·50 S	149·56 E
78	Reform (rē-fôrm') . . . Ala.	33·23 N	88·00 W
77	Refugio (rȧ-fōō'hyô) (rĕ-fū'jō) . Tex.	28·18 N	97·15 W
120	Rega (R.) (rĕ-gä) . . . Pol.	53·48 N	15·30 E
120	Regen R. (rā'ghĕn) . . . Ger.	49·09 N	12·21 E
120	Regensburg (rā'ghĕns-bōōrgh) . Ger.	49·02 N	12·06 E
126	Reggio (rĕ'jô) . . . It.	44·43 N	10·34 E
84	Reggio (rĕg'jĭ-ō) La. (New Orleans In.)	29·50 N	89·46 W
126	Reggio di Calabria (rĕ'jō dē kä-lä'brē-ä) . It.	38·07 N	15·42 E
121	Reghin (rȧ-gēn') . . . Rom.	46·47 N	24·44 E
86	Regina (rē-jī'nȧ) . . . Can.	50·31 N	104·30 W
144	Registan (Reg.) . . . Afg.	30·53 N	64·42 E
95	Regla (rāg'lä) Cuba (Havana In.)	23·08 N	82·20 W
124	Reguengos de Monsaraz (rȧ-gĕŋ'gōzh dā mōn-sä-räzh') Port.	38·26 N	7·30 W
84	Rehoboth (rē-hō'bŏth) Mass. (Providence In.)	41·50 N	71·13 W
166	Rehoboth . . . S. W. Afr.	23·10 S	17·15 E
139	Rehovoth . . . Isr. (Palestine In.)	31·53 N	34·49 E
120	Reichenbach (rī'kĕn-bäĸ) . . . Ger.	50·36 N	12·18 E
79	Reidsville (rēdz'vĭl) . . . N. C.	36·20 N	79·37 W
110	Reigate (rī'gāt) . Eng. (London In.)	51·12 N	0·12 W
122	Reims (răɴs) . . . Fr.	49·16 N	4·00 E
100	Reina Adelaida, Arch. (är-chē'-pyĕ'lȧ-gō-rā'nä-ä-dĕ-lī'dä) Chile	52·00 S	74·15 W
71	Reinbeck (rīn'bĕk) . . . Iowa	42·22 N	92·34 W
86	Reindeer (L.) (rān'dẽr) . . . Can.	57·36 N	101·23 W
124	Reinosa (rȧ-ē-nō'sȧ) . . . Sp.	43·01 N	4·08 W
84	Reistertown (rēs'tẽr-toun) Md. (Baltimore In.)	39·28 N	76·50 W
168	Reitz . . . S. Afr. (Johannesburg & Pretoria In.)	27·48 S	28·25 E
84	Relay (rē'lā) . . Md. (Baltimore In.)	39·14 N	76·44 W
125	Relizane (rē-lē-zän') . . . Alg.	35·43 N	0·34 E
139	Rembau . . . Mala. (Singapore In.)	2·36 N	102·06 E
98	Remedios (rĕ-mĕ'dyôs) . . Col. (In.)	7·03 N	74·42 W
94	Remedios (rā-mā'dhē-ōs) . . . Cuba	22·30 N	79·35 W
93	Remedios (rĕ-mĕ'dyōs) . . . Pan.	8·14 N	81·46 W
123	Remiremont (rē-mēr-môɴ') . . . Fr.	48·01 N	6·35 E
139	Rempang I. Indon. (Singapore In.)	0·51 N	104·04 E
123	Remscheid (rĕm'shīt) Ger. (Ruhr In.)	51·10 N	7·11 E
159	Rendova (I.) (rĕn'dô-vȧ) . Sol. Is.	8·38 S	156·26 E
120	Rendsburg (rĕnts'bōōrgh) . . . Ger.	54·19 N	9·39 E
81	Renfrew (rĕn'frōō) . . . Can.	45·30 N	76·30 W
139	Rengam (rĕn'gäm') Mala. (Singapore In.)	1·53 N	103·24 E
101	Rengo (rĕn'gō) Chile (Santiago In.)	34·22 S	70·50 W
129	Reni (ran') . . . Sov. Un.	45·26 N	28·18 E
160	Renmark (rĕn'märk) . . . Austl.	34·10 S	140·50 E
159	Rennel (I.) (rĕn-nĕl') . . . Sol. Is.	11·50 S	160·38 E
122	Rennes (rĕn) . . . Fr.	48·07 N	1·02 W
81	Rensselaer (rĕn'sĕ-lâr) . . . N. Y.	42·40 N	73·45 W
68	Reno (rē'nō) . . . Nev.	39·32 N	119·49 W
126	Reno (R.) (rā'nô) . . . It.	44·10 N	10·55 E
81	Renovo (rē-nō'vō) . . . Pa.	41·20 N	77·50 W
80	Rensselaer (rĕn'sē-lâr) . . . Ind.	41·00 N	87·10 W
74	Rentchler (rĕnt'chlẽr) Ill. (St. Louis In.)	38·30 N	89·52 W
65	Renton (rĕn'tŭn) Wash. (Seattle In.)	47·29 N	122·13 W
71	Renville (rĕn'vĭl) . . . Minn.	44·44 N	95·13 W
84	Republic (rē-pŭb'lĭk) Ala. (Birmingham In.)	33·37 N	86·54 W
66	Republic . . . Wash.	48·38 N	118·44 W
72	Republican (R.), South Fk. (rē-pŭb'lĭ-kăn) . Colo.	39·35 N	102·28 W
73	Republican (R.) . . . Kans.	39·22 N	97·14 W
159	Repulse B. (rē-pŭls') . . . Austl.	20·56 S	149·22 E
124	Requena (rȧ-kā'nä) . . . Sp.	39·29 N	1·03 W
101	Resende (rĕ-sĕ'n-dĕ) Braz. (Rio de Janeiro In.)	22·30 S	44·26 W
101	Resende Costa (kôs-tä) Braz. (Rio de Janeiro In.)	20·55 S	44·12 W
129	Reshetilovka (ryĕ' shĕ-tē-lôf-kȧ) Sov. Un.	49·34 N	34·04 E
100	Resistencia (rā-sēs-tĕn'syä) . . . Arg.	27·24 S	58·54 W
127	Reşita (rā'shē-tä) . . . Rom.	45·18 N	21·56 E
87	Resolution (I.) (rĕz-ô-lū'shŭn) Can.	61·30 N	63·58 W
159	Resolution (I.) (rĕz-ŏl-ûshŭn) N. Z. (In.)	45·43 S	166·00 E
82	Restigouche (R.) (rĕs-tē-gōōsh') Can.	47·35 N	67·35 W
98	Restrepo (rĕs-trĕ'pô) . . . Col. (In.)	3·49 N	76·31 W
98	Restrepo . . . Col. (In.)	4·16 N	73·32 W
92	Retalhuleu (rā-täl-ōō-lān') . . Guat.	14·31 N	91·41 W
122	Rethel (r-tl') . . . Fr.	49·34 N	4·20 E
126	Réthimnon . . . Grc. (In.)	35·21 N	24·30 E
111	Retie . . . Bel. (Brussels In.)	51·16 N	5·08 E
65	Retsil (rĕt'sĭl) . Wash. (Seattle In.)	47·33 N	122·37 W
47	Reunion I. (rā-ü-nyôn') . . . Afr.	21·06 S	55·36 E
125	Reus (rā'ōōs) . . . Sp.	41·08 N	1·05 E
120	Reutlingen (roit'lĭng-ĕn) . . . Ger.	48·29 N	9·14 E
136	Reutov (rĕ-ōōt'ôf) Sov. Un. (Moscow In.)	55·45 N	37·52 E
	Reval, see Tallinn		
136	Revda (ryâv'dá) Sov. Un. (Urals In.)	56·48 N	59·57 E
86	Revelstoke (rĕv'ĕl-stōk) . . . Can.	51·02 N	118·19 W
93	Reventazon, R. (rā-vĕn-tä-zōn') C. R.	10·10 N	83·30 W
83	Revere (rē-vēr') Mass. (Boston In.)	42·24 N	71·01 W
88	Revillagigedo, Islas De (I.) (ē's-läs-dĕ-rĕ-vēl-yä-hē'gĕ-dô) Mex.	18·45 N	111·00 W
122	Revin (rē-văɴ') . . . Fr.	49·56 N	4·34 E
142	Rewa (rā'wä) . . . India	24·41 N	81·11 E
142	Rewāri . . . India	28·19 N	76·39 E
67	Rexburg (rĕks'bûrg) . . . Idaho	43·50 N	111·48 W
76	Rey, L. (rā) . . . Mex.	27·00 N	103·33 W
93	Rey, Isla del (I.) (ē's-lä-dĕl-rā'ē) . Pan.	8·20 N	78·40 W
98	Reyes (rā'yĕs) . . . Bol.	14·19 S	67·16 W
68	Reyes, Pt. . . . Calif.	38·00 N	123·00 W
102	Reykjanes (C.) (rā'kyȧ-nĕs) . . . Ice.	63·37 N	24·33 W
112	Reykjavik (rā'kyȧ-vēk) . . . Ice.	64·09 N	21·39 W
76	Reynosa (rā-ē-nō'sä) . . . Mex.	26·05 N	98·21 W
144	Rezā'īyeh (Urmia) (rĕ-zī'ä) (ōōr'mē-ä) . Iran	37·30 N	45·15 E
128	Rēzekne (rā'zĕk-nĕ) . . . Sov. Un.	56·31 N	27·19 E
136	Rezh (rĕzh') . . Sov. Un. (Urals In.)	57·22 N	61·23 E
129	Rezina (ryĕzh'ĕ-nĭ) . . . Sov. Un.	47·44 N	28·56 E
126	Rhaetien Alps (Mts.) . . . It.	46·22 N	10·33 E
117	Rheden (rā'dĕn) . . . Neth.	52·02 N	6·02 E
123	Rheinberg (rīn'bĕrgh) Ger. (Ruhr In.)	51·33 N	6·37 E
120	Rheine (rī'nĕ) . . . Ger.	52·16 N	7·26 E
120	Rheinland-Pfalz (Rhineland-Palatinate) (State) . Ger.	50·05 N	6·40 E
120	Rhein R. (rīn) . . . Ger.	50·34 N	7·21 E
123	Rheydt (rĕ'yt) . . . Ger. (Ruhr In.)	51·10 N	6·28 E
71	Rhinelander (rīn'lăn-dẽr) . . . Wis.	45·39 N	89·25 W
111	Rhin Kanal (Can.) (rēn kä-näl') Ger. (Berlin In.)	52·47 N	12·40 E
111	Rhin R. (rēn) . . . Ger. (Berlin In.)	52·52 N	12·49 E
63	Rhode Island (State) (rōd ī'lănd) U. S.	41·35 N	71·40 W
167	Rhodes (rôdz) . . S. Afr. (Natal In.)	30·48 S	27·56 E
127	Rhodope Mts. (rô'dô-pĕ) . . . Bul.	42·00 N	24·08 E
116	Rhondda (rŏn'dhȧ) . . . Wales	51·40 N	3·40 W
122	Rhône (R.) (rōn) . . . Fr.	45·14 N	4·53 E
111	Rhoon . . . Neth. (Amsterdam In.)	51·52 N	4·24 E
116	Rhum (I.) (rŭm) . . . Scot.	56·63 N	6·20 W
99	Riachão (rē-ä-chouɴ') . . . Braz.	6·55 S	46·33 W
74	Rialto (rē-ăl'tō) Calif. (Los Angeles In.)	34·06 N	117·23 W
124	Riaza (R.) (rē-ä'thä) . . . Sp.	41·25 N	3·25 W
124	Ribadavia (rē-bä-dhä'vē-ä) . . . Sp.	42·18 N	8·06 W
124	Ribadeo (rē-bä-dhā'ō) . . . Sp.	37·32 N	7·05 W
124	Ribadesella (rē'bä-dā-säl'yä) . . Sp.	43·30 N	5·02 W
116	Ribble, R. (rĭb''l) . . . Eng.	53·10 N	3·15 W
118	Ribe (rē'bĕ) . . . Den.	55·20 N	8·45 E
101	Ribeirão Prêto (rē-bā-rouɴ-prĕ'tô) Braz. (Rio de Janeiro In.)	21·11 S	47·47 W
72	Ribera (rē-bĕ'rä) . . . N. Mex.	35·23 N	105·27 W
98	Riberalta (rē-bā-räl'tä) . . . Bol.	11·06 S	66·02 W
71	Rib Lake (rĭb lāk) . . . Wis.	45·20 N	90·11 W
68	Rice (rīs) . . . Calif.	34·05 N	114·50 W
81	Rice (L.) . . . Can.	44·05 N	78·10 W
74	Rice L. . . . Minn. (Minneapolis, St. Paul In.)	45·10 N	93·09 W
71	Rice Lake . . . Wis.	45·30 N	91·44 W
64	Richards I. (rĭch'ẽrds) . . . Can.	69·45 N	135·30 W
74	Richards Landing (lănd'ĭng) Can. (Sault Ste. Marie In.)	46·18 N	84·02 W
74	Richardson (rĭch'ẽrd-sŭn) Tex. (Dallas, Fort Worth In.)	32·56 N	96·44 W
65	Richardson . . . Wash. (Seattle In.)	48·27 N	122·54 W
86	Richardson Mts. . . . Can.	66·58 N	136·19 W
84	Richardson Park (pärk) . . . Del.	39·45 N	75·35 W
81	Richelieu (R.) (rĕsh'lyû') . . . Can.	45·05 N	73·25 W
74	Richfield (rĭch'fēld) Minn. (Minneapolis, St. Paul In.)	44·53 N	93·17 W
75	Richfield . . . Ohio (Cleveland In.)	41·14 N	81·38 W
69	Richfield . . . Utah	38·45 N	112·05 W
81	Richford (rĭch'fẽrd) . . . Vt.	45·00 N	72·35 W
73	Rich Hill (rĭch hĭl) . . . Mo.	38·05 N	94·21 W
82	Richibucto (rĭ-chĭ-bŭk'tō) . . . Can.	46·42 N	64·55 W
78	Richland (rĭch'lănd) . . . Ga.	32·05 N	84·40 W
66	Richland . . . Wash.	46·17 N	119·19 W
71	Richland Center (sĕn'tẽr) . . . Wis.	43·20 N	90·25 W
159	Richmond (rĭch'mŭnd) . . . Austl.	20·47 S	143·14 E
161	Richmond . . . Austl. (Sydney In.)	33·36 S	150·45 E
65	Richmond Calif. (San Francisco In.)	37·56 N	122·21 W
82	Richmond . . . Can.	45·40 N	72·07 W
85	Richmond . . . Can. (Ottawa In.)	45·12 N	75·49 W
75	Richmond . . . Ill. (Chicago In.)	42·29 N	88·18 W
80	Richmond . . . Ind.	39·50 N	85·00 W
80	Richmond . . . Ky.	37·45 N	84·20 W
73	Richmond . . . Mo.	39·16 N	93·58 W

ăt; finȧl; rāte; senâte; ärm; àsk; sofȧ; fâre; ch-choose; dh-as th in other; bē; ēvent; bĕt; recĕnt; cratẽr; g-go; gh-guttural g; bĭt; ĭ-short neutral; rīde; ĸ-guttural k as ch in German ich;

Page	Name Pronunciation Region	Lat. °′	Long. °′
77	Richmond . . . . Tex.	29·35 N	95·45 W
167	Richmond . . . . . S. Afr. (Natal In.)	29·52 S	30·17 E
167	Richmond . . . . . S. Afr. (Natal In.)	33·44 S	26·36 E
67	Richmond . . . . Utah	41·55 N	111·50 W
81	Richmond . . . . Va.	37·35 N	77·30 W
65	Richmond Beach Wash. (Seattle In.)	47·47 N	122·23 W
74	Richmond Heights Mo. (St. Louis In.)	38·38 N	90·20 W
85	Richmond Hill (hĭl) Can. (Toronto In.)	43·53 N	79·26 W
93	Richmond Pk. St. Vincent (Le. & Wind. Is. In.)	13·19 N	61·12 W
78	Richton (rĭch'tŭn) . . . . Miss.	31·20 N	89·54 W
80	Richwood (rĭch'wŏŏd) . . . . . W. Va.	38·10 N	80·30 W
111	Ridderkerk Neth. (Amsterdam In.)	51·52 N	4·35 E
81	Rideau L. (rē-dō') . . . . Can.	44·40 N	76·20 W
85	Rideau R. . . . . . Can. (Ottawa In.)	45·17 N	75·41 W
84	Ridgefield (rĭj'fēld) Conn. (New York In.)	41·16 N	73·30 W
65	Ridgefield . . . Wash. (Portland In.)	45·49 N	122·40 W
81	Ridgeley (rĭj'lē) . . . . W. Va.	39·40 N	78·45 W
75	Ridgeway (rĭj'wā) Can. (Buffalo In.)	42·53 N	79·02 W
81	Ridgeway . . . . Pa.	41·25 N	78·40 W
84	Ridgewood (ridj'wŏŏd) N. J. (New York In.)	40·59 N	74·08 W
86	Riding Mountain Natl. Park (rīd'ĭng) . Can.	50·59 N	99·19 W
94	Riding Rocks (Is.) . . . . Ba. Is.	25·20 N	79·10 W
167	Riebeek-Oos . . . S. Afr. (Natal In.)	33·14 S	26·09 E
120	Ried (rēd) . . . . Aus.	48·13 N	13·30 E
120	Riesa (rē'zȧ) . . . . Ger.	51·17 N	13·17 E
167	Riet (R.) (rēt) . . . . S. Afr. (Johannesburg & Pretoria In.)	25·54 S	27·54 E
126	Rieti (rē-ā'tē) . . . . It.	42·25 N	12·51 E
167	Rievleidam (L.) . . . . S. Afr. (Johannesburg & Pretoria In.)	25·52 S	28·18 E
69	Rifle (rī'f'l) . . . . Colo.	39·35 N	107·50 W
119	Riga (rē'gȧ) . . . . Sov. Un.	56·55 N	24·05 E
119	Riga, G. of . . . . Sov. Un.	57·56 N	23·05 E
144	Rīgān . . . . Iran	28·45 N	58·55 E
85	Rigaud (rê-gō') Can. (Montreal In.)	45·29 N	74·18 W
67	Rigby (rĭg'bē) . . . . Idaho	43·40 N	111·55 W
87	Rigolet (rĭg-ō-lā') . . . . Can.	54·10 N	58·40 W
126	Rijeka (Fiume) (rĭ-yĕ'kȧ) . . . Yugo.	45·22 N	14·24 E
111	Rijkevorsel . . . . Bel. (Brussels In.)	51·21 N	4·46 E
111	Rijswijk . . Neth. (Amsterdam In.)	52·03 N	4·19 E
121	Rika R. (rē'kȧ) . . . . Sov. Un.	48·21 N	23·37 E
122	Rille (R.) (rēl) . . . . Fr.	49·12 N	0·43 E
144	Rimach, Wādī ar (R.) . . . . Sau. Ar.	26·17 N	41·13 E
121	Rimavska Sobota (rē'máf-skȧ sô'bô-tȧ) . Czech.	48·25 N	20·01 E
118	Rimbo (rēm'bōō) . . . . Swe.	59·45 N	18·22 E
126	Rimini (rē'mē-nē) . . . . It.	44·03 N	12·33 E
127	Rîmnicul Sărat . . . . Rom.	45·24 N	27·06 E
127	Rîmnicu Valcea . . . . Rom.	45·07 N	24·22 E
82	Rimouski (rê-mōōs'kē) . . . . . . Can.	48·27 N	68·32 W
90	Rincón de Romos (rên-kōn dā rô-mōs') . Mex.	22·13 N	102·21 W
154	Rindjani, Gunung (Mtn.) . . Indon.	8·39 S	116·22 E
118	Ringkøbing (rĭng'kûb-ĭng) . . . Den.	56·06 N	8·14 E
118	Ringkøbing Fd . . . . Den.	55·55 N	8·04 E
118	Ringsaker (rĭngs'äk-ĕr) . . . . . . Nor.	60·55 N	10·40 E
118	Ringsted (rĭng'stĕdh) . . . . Den.	55·27 N	11·49 E
112	Ringvassöy (I.) (rĭng'väs-ûê) . Nor.	69·58 N	16·43 E
161	Ringwood . Austl. (Melbourne In.)	37·49 S	145·14 E
88	Rio Abajo (rê'ō-ä-bä'kō) Pan. (Panama Canal In.)	9·01 N	78·30 W
90	Rio Balsas (rê'ō-bäl-säs) . . . . Mex.	17·59 N	99·45 W
98	Riobamba (rē'ō-bäm'bä) . . . . . . Ec.	1·45 S	78·37 W
101	Rio Bonito (rē'ōō bō-nē'tōō) Braz. (Rio de Janeiro In.)	22·44 S	42·38 W
98	Rio Branco (rē'ōō brăŋ'kōō) . Braz.	9·57 S	67·50 W
99	Rio Branco (Ter.) . . . . Braz.	2·35 N	61·25 W
101	Rio Casca (rē'ō-kä's-kä) Braz. (Rio de Janeiro In.)	20·15 S	42·39 W
99	Rio Chico (rê'ō chê'kō) . Ven. (In.)	10·20 N	65·58 W
101	Rio Claro (rē'ōō klä'rōō) Braz. (Rio de Janeiro In.)	21·25 S	47·33 W
100	Río Cuarto (rē'ō kwär'tō) . . . . Arg.	33·05 S	64·15 W
101	Rio das Flores (rē-ō-däs-flô-rĕs) Braz. (Rio de Janeiro In.)	22·10 S	43·35 W
100	Rio de Janeiro (rē'ōō dā zhä-nâ'ê-rōō) Braz. (In.)	22·50 S	43·20 W
99	Rio de Janeiro (State) . . . . . . Braz.	22·27 S	42·43 W
93	Río de Jesús (rê'ō-dĕ-kĕ-sōō's) Pan.	7·54 N	80·59 W
164	Rio del Rey (rē'ō dĕl rā'ê) . . . Nig.	4·41 N	8·38 E
164	Rio de Oro (Ter.) (rē'ō dā ō'rō) Sp. Sah.	23·11 N	14·15 W
100	Río Dercero (rê'ō dĕr-sĕ'rô) . . Arg.	32·12 S	63·59 W
91	Río Frío (rê'ō-frē'ō) Mex. (Mexico City In.)	19·21 N	98·40 W
100	Río Gallegos (rē'ō gä-lā'gōs) . . Arg.	51·43 S	69·15 W
100	Rio Grande (rē'ōō grän'dĕ) . . Braz.	31·04 S	52·14 W
90	Rio Grande (rē'ō grän'dā) . . . Mex.	23·51 N	102·59 W
76	Riogrande (rē'ō grän'dā) . . . . . Tex.	26·23 N	98·48 W
69	Rio Grande (R.) (rē'ōō grän'dĕ) Colo.	37·44 N	106·51 W
99	Rio Grande do Norte (State) (rē'ōō grän'dĕ dōō nôr'tĕ) . Braz.	5·26 S	37·20 W
100	Rio Grande do Sul (State) (rē'ōō grän'dĕ-dô-sōō'l) . Braz.	29·00 S	54·00 W
98	Ríohacha (rē'ō-ä'chä) . . . . Col.	11·30 N	72·54 W
93	Río Hato (rē'ō-ä'tō) . . . . Pan.	8·19 N	80·11 W
122	Riom (rê-ôN') . . . . Fr.	45·54 N	3·08 E
163	Rio Muni (Col.) (rē'ō mōō'nê) . Afr.	1·47 N	8·33 E
98	Ríonegro (rê'ō-nĕ'grō) . . . Col. (In.)	6·09 N	75·22 W
100	Río Negro (Prov.) (rē'ō nā'grō) Arg.	40·15 S	68·15 W
101	Río Negro (Dept.) (rê'ō-nĕ'grō) Ur. (Buenos Aires In.)	32·48 S	57·45 W
100	Rio Negro, Embalse del (Res.) (ĕm-bä'l-sĕ-dĕl-rê'ō-nĕ'grō) . Ur.	32·45 S	55·50 W
126	Rionero (rē-ō-nā'rô) . . . . It.	40·55 N	15·42 E
101	Rio Novo (rē'ō-nô'vô) Braz. (Rio de Janeiro In.)	21·30 S	43·08 W
99	Rio Pardo de Minas (rē'ō pär'dō-dĕ-mē'näs) . Braz.	15·43 S	42·24 W
101	Rio Pombo (rē'ō pôm'bä) Braz. (Rio de Janeiro In.)	21·17 S	43·09 W
101	Rio Sorocaba, Represado (Res.) (rĕ-prĕ-sä-dô-rē'ō-sô-rō-kä'bä) Braz. (Rio de Janeiro In.)	23·37 S	47·19 W
98	Ríosucio (rē'ō-sōō'syō) . . Col. (In.)	5·25 N	75·41 W
125	Riou, Oued (R.) (ōō-ĕd rĭ-ōō) Alg.	35·45 N	1·18 E
139	Riouw Arch. Indon. (Singapore In.)	0·49 N	103·45 E
154	Riouw, Pulau-Pulau (Is.) . . Indon.	0·30 N	104·55 E
139	Riouw, Selat (Str.) Indon. (Singapore In.)	0·49 N	104·24 E
99	Rio Verde (vĕr'dĕ) . . . . Braz.	17·47 S	50·49 W
90	Ríoverde (rē'ō-vĕr'dȧ) . . . . . . Mex.	21·54 N	99·59 W
110	Ripley (rĭp'lē) . . . . Eng.	53·03 N	1·24 W
78	Ripley . . . . Miss.	34·44 N	88·55 W
78	Ripley . . . . Tenn.	35·44 N	89·34 W
125	Ripoll (rê-pōl'') . . . . Sp.	42·10 N	2·10 E
71	Ripon (rĭp'ŏn) . . . . Wis.	43·49 N	88·50 W
158	Ripon (I.) . . . . Austl.	20·05 S	118·10 E
165	Ripon Falls . . . . Ug.	0·38 N	33·02 E
159	Risdon (rĭz'dŭn) . . . . Austl.	42·37 S	147·32 E
152	Rishiri (I.) (rē-shē'rē) . . . . Jap.	45·10 N	141·08 E
139	Rishon le Zion . Isr. (Palestine In.)	31·57 N	34·48 E
80	Rising Sun (rīz'ĭng sŭn) . . . . . . Ind.	38·55 N	84·55 W
118	Risor (rēs'ûr) . . . . Nor.	58·44 N	9·10 E
98	Ritacuva, Alto (Mtn.) (ȧ'l-tô-rē-tä-kōō'vä) . Col.	6·22 N	72·13 W
75	Rittman (rĭt'măn) Ohio (Cleveland In.)	40·58 N	81·47 W
66	Ritzville (rĭts'vĭl) . . . . Wash.	47·08 N	118·23 W
118	Riuvenfjeld (Mts.) (rĭû-vĕn-fyĕl') Nor.	59·20 N	6·55 E
95	Riva (rē'vä) . . . . Dom. Rep.	19·10 N	69·55 W
126	Riva (rē'vä) . . . . It.	45·54 N	10·49 E
92	Rivas (rē'väs) . . . . Nic.	11·25 N	85·51 W
122	Rive-de-Gier (rēv-dĕ-zhē-ā') . . . Fr.	45·32 N	4·37 E
100	Rivera (rê-vā'rä) . . . . Ur.	30·52 S	55·32 W
164	River Cess (rĭv'ĕr sĕs) . . . . Lib.	5·46 N	9·52 W
75	Riverdale (rĭv'ĕr dāl) Ill. (Chicago In.)	41·38 N	87·36 W
74	Riverdale Utah (Salt Lake City In.)	41·11 N	112·00 W
78	River Falls . . . . Ala.	31·20 N	86·25 W
71	River Falls . . . . Wis.	44·48 N	92·38 W
81	Riverhead (rĭv'ĕr hĕd) . . . . . . N. Y.	40·55 N	72·40 W
160	Riverina (Reg.) (rĭv-ĕr-ē'nȧ) . Austl.	34·55 S	144·30 E
65	River Jordan (jôr'dăn) Can. (Seattle In.)	48·26 N	124·02 W
74	River Oaks (ōkz) Tex. (Dallas, Fort Worth In.)	32·47 N	97·24 W
75	River Rouge (rōōzh) Mich. (Detroit In.)	42·16 N	83·09 W
74	Riverside (rĭv'ĕr-sīd) Calif. (Los Angeles In.)	33·59 N	117·21 W
75	Riverside . . . . . Can. (Detroit In.)	42·20 N	82·57 W
84	Riverside . N. J. (Philadelphia In.)	40·02 N	74·58 W
161	Riverstone . . . . Austl. (Sydney In.)	33·41 S	150·52 E
86	Riverton (rĭv'ĕr-tăn) . . . . Can.	51·02 N	97·12 W
81	Riverton . . . . Va.	39·00 N	78·15 W
67	Riverton . . . . Wyo.	43·02 N	108·24 W
122	Rivesaltes (rēv'zält') . . . . Fr.	42·48 N	2·48 E
79	Riviera Beach (rĭv-ĭ-ĕr'ȧ bēch) Fla. (In.)	26·46 N	80·04 W
82	Riviere (rê-vyâr') . . . . Can.	46·43 N	72·00 W
82	Riviere (R.) . . . . Can.	49·05 N	72·04 W
85	Rivie're Beaudette (bō-dĕt') Can. (Montreal In.)	45·14 N	74·20 W
82	Riviere du Loup (rê-vyâr' dü lōō') Can.	47·50 N	69·34 W
85	Rivie're-Qui-Barre (rēv-yĕr' kē-bär) Can. (Edmonton In.)	53·47 N	113·51 W
133	Rize (rē'zĕ) . . . . Tur.	41·00 N	40·30 E
127	Rizzuto, C. (rēt-sōō'tô) . . . . It.	38·53 N	17·05 E
118	Rjukan (ryōō'kän) . . . . Nor.	59·53 N	8·30 E
122	Roanne (rō-än') . . . . Fr.	46·02 N	4·04 E
78	Roanoke (rō'á-nōk) . . . . Ala.	33·08 N	85·21 W
79	Roanoke . . . . Va.	37·16 N	79·55 W
79	Roanoke (R.) . . . . N. C.-Va.	36·17 N	77·22 W
79	Roanoke Rapids . . . . N. C.	36·25 N	77·40 W
79	Roanoke Rapids, L. . . . . N. C.	36·28 N	77·37 W
69	Roan Plat. (rōn) . . . . Colo.	39·25 N	108·50 W
92	Roatan (rō-ä-tän') . . . . Hond.	16·18 N	86·33 W
92	Roatan I. . . . . Hond.	16·19 N	86·46 W
166	Robben Island S. Afr. (Cape Town In.)	33·48 S	18·22 E
75	Robbins (rŏb'ĭnz) . Ill. (Chicago In.)	41·39 N	87·42 W
74	Robbinsdale (rŏb'ĭnz-dāl) Minn. (Minneapolis, St. Paul In.)	45·03 N	93·22 W
65	Robe (rōb) . . . . Wash. (Seattle In.)	48·06 N	121·50 W
159	Roberts, Mt. (rŏb'ērts) . . . . . Austl.	32·05 S	152·30 E
65	Roberts, Pt. (rŏb'ērts) Wash. (Vancouver In.)	48·58 N	123·05 W
83	Robertson (rŏb'ērt-sŭn) . . . . . Can.	51·05 N	59·07 W
164	Robertsport (rŏb'ērts-pōrt) . . . Lib.	6·45 N	11·31 W
82	Roberval (rŏb'ēr-văl) (rô-bĕr-väl') Can.	48·32 N	72·15 W
80	Robinson (rŏb'ĭn-sŭn) . . . . Ill.	39·00 N	87·45 W
83	Robinson's . . . . Can.	48·16 N	58·50 W
160	Robinvale (rŏb-ĭn'văl) . . . . . . Austl.	34·45 S	142·45 E
86	Robson, Mt. (rŏb'sŭn) . . . . Can.	53·13 N	119·02 W
77	Robstown (rŏbz'toun) . . . . Tex.	27·46 N	97·41 W
125	Roca, Cabo da (C.) (kȧ'bō-dȧ-rô'kȧ) Port. (Lisbon In.)	38·47 N	9·30 W
99	Rocas, Atol das (Atoll) (ȧ-tôl-däs-rō'käs) . Braz.	3·50 S	33·46 W
168	Rocca Littotorio Som. (Horn of Afr. In.)	7·00 N	47·30 E
96	Rocedos São Pedro E São Paulo (I.) (rô-zĕ'dôs-souN-pĕ'drô-ĕ-souN-päōō-lô) . Braz.	1·50 N	30·00 W
100	Rocha (rō'chȧs) . . . . Ur.	34·26 S	54·14 W
110	Rochdale (rŏch'dāl) . . . . Eng.	53·37 N	2·09 W
95	Roche à Bateau (rôsh á bȧ-tō') Hai.	18·10 N	74·00 W
122	Rochefort (rôsh-fŏr') . . . . Fr.	45·55 N	0·57 W
71	Rochelle (rô-shĕl') . . . . Ill.	41·53 N	89·06 W
80	Rochester (rŏch'ĕs-tēr) . . . . Ind.	41·05 N	86·20 W
75	Rochester . . . . . Mich. (Detroit In.)	42·41 N	83·09 W
71	Rochester . . . . Minn.	44·01 N	92·30 W
81	Rochester . . . . N. H.	43·20 N	71·00 W
81	Rochester . . . . N. Y.	43·15 N	77·35 W
75	Rochester . . . . Pa. (Pittsburgh In.)	40·42 N	80·16 W
71	Rock (R.) . . . . Ill.	41·40 N	89·52 W
70	Rock (R.) . . . . Iowa	43·17 N	96·13 W
65	Rock (R.) . . . . . Ore. (Portland In.)	45·34 N	122·52 W
65	Rock (R.) . . . . . Ore. (Portland In.)	45·52 N	123·14 W
84	Rockaway (rŏck'á-wā) N. J. (New York In.)	40·54 N	74·30 W
161	Rockbank . Austl. (Melbourne In.)	37·44 S	144·40 E
85	Rockcliffe Park (rok'klĭf pärk) Can. (Ottawa In.)	45·27 N	75·40 W
75	Rock Cr. (rŏk) . . . Ill. (Chicago In.)	41·16 N	87·54 W
67	Rock Cr. . . . . Mont.	46·25 N	113·40 W
66	Rock Cr. . . . . Ore.	45·30 N	120·06 W
66	Rock Cr. . . . . Wash.	47·09 N	117·50 W
77	Rockdale (rŏck'dāl) . . . . Tex.	30·39 N	97·00 W
71	Rock Falls (rŏck fôlz) . . . . Ill.	41·45 N	89·42 W
71	Rockford (rŏck'fērd) . . . . Ill.	42·16 N	89·07 W
159	Rockhampton (rŏk-hămp'tăn) Austl.	23·26 S	150·29 E
79	Rockhill (rŏk'hĭl) . . . . S. C.	34·55 N	81·01 W
79	Rockingham (rŏk'ĭng-hăm) . . N. C.	34·54 N	79·45 W
110	Rockingham For. (rok'ĭng-hăm) Eng.	52·29 N	0·43 W
71	Rock Island . . . . Ill.	41·31 N	90·37 W
66	Rock Island Dam (ī lănd) . . Wash.	47·17 N	120·33 W
85	Rockland (rŏk'lănd) Can. (Ottawa In.)	45·33 N	75·17 W
82	Rockland . . . . Maine	44·06 N	69·09 W
83	Rockland . . . . . Mass. (Boston In.)	42·07 N	70·55 W
160	Rockland Res. . . . . Austl.	36·55 S	142·20 E
78	Rockmart (rŏk'märt) . . . . Ga.	33·58 N	85·00 W
74	Rockmont (rŏk'mŏnt) Wis. (Duluth In.)	46·34 N	91·54 W
80	Rockport (rŏk'pōrt) . . . . Ind.	38·20 N	87·00 W
83	Rockport . . . . . Mass. (Boston In.)	42·39 N	70·37 W
73	Rockport . . . . Mo.	40·25 N	95·30 W
77	Rockport . . . . Tex.	28·03 N	97·03 W
70	Rock Rapids (răp'ĭdz) . . . . Iowa	43·26 N	96·10 W
95	Rock Sd. . . . . Ba. Is.	24·50 N	76·05 W
76	Rocksprings (rŏk sprĭngs) . . . . Tex.	30·02 N	100·12 W
67	Rock Springs . . . . Wyo.	41·35 N	109·13 W
99	Rockstone (rŏk'stōn) . . . . . Br. Gu.	5·55 N	57·27 W
85	Rockton (rŏk'tŭn) Can. (Toronto In.)	43·18 N	80·08 W
70	Rock Valley (văl'ĭ) . . . . Iowa	43·13 N	96·17 W
80	Rockville (rŏk'vĭl) . . . . Ind.	39·45 N	87·15 W
84	Rockville Centre (sĕn'tēr) N. Y. (New York In.)	40·39 N	73·39 W
73	Rockwall (rŏk'wôl) . . . . Tex.	32·55 N	96·23 W
71	Rockwell City (rŏk'wĕl) . . . . . Iowa	42·22 N	94·37 W
85	Rockwood (rŏk-wŏŏd) Can. (Toronto In.)	43·37 N	80·08 W
82	Rockwood . . . . Maine	45·39 N	69·45 W
78	Rockwood . . . . Tenn.	35·51 N	84·41 W
67	Rocky Boys Ind. Res. . . . . . . Mont.	48·08 N	109·34 W
72	Rocky Ford . . . . Colo.	38·02 N	103·43 W
84	Rocky Hill (hĭl) N. J. (New York In.)	40·24 N	74·38 W
79	Rocky Mount . . . . N. C.	35·55 N	77·47 W
72	Rocky Mountain Natl. Park. Colo.	40·29 N	106·06 W
49	Rocky Mts. (rŏk'ē) . . . . N. A.	50·00 N	114·00 W
75	Rocky River . Ohio (Cleveland In.)	41·29 N	81·51 W
75	Rocky R., E. Br. Ohio (Cleveland In.)	41·13 N	81·43 W
75	Rocky R., W. Br. Ohio (Cleveland In.)	41·17 N	81·54 W
95	Rodas (rō'dhȧs) . . . . Cuba	22·20 N	80·35 W
110	Roden (R.) (rō'dĕn) . . . . Eng.	52·49 N	2·38 W
65	Rodeo (rō'dēō) Calif. (San Francisco In.)	38·02 N	122·16 W
76	Rodeo (rô-dā'ō) . . . . Mex.	25·12 N	104·34 W
122	Rodez (rô-dĕz') . . . . Fr.	44·22 N	2·34 E
115	Rōdhos . . . . Grc.	36·24 N	28·15 E
115	Ródhos (I.) . . . . Grc.	36·00 N	28·29 E
121	Rodnei, Muntii (Mts.) (rôd'nĕ-ê) Rom.	47·41 N	24·05 E
128	Rodniki (rôd'nê-kê) . . . . . Sov. Un.	57·08 N	41·48 E
127	Rodonit, Kep I (C.) . . . . Alb.	41·38 N	19·01 E
	Rodosto, see Tekirdağ		
84	Roebling (rōb'lĭng) N. J. (Philadelphia In.)	40·07 N	74·48 W
158	Roebourne (rō'bŭrn) . . . . Austl.	20·50 S	117·15 E
158	Roebuck, B. (rō'bŭck) . . . . . Austl.	18·15 S	121·10 E
168	Roedtan . . . . S. Afr. (Johannesburg & Pretoria In.)	24·37 S	29·08 E
117	Roermond (rōōr'mônt) . . . . . . Neth.	41·11 N	5·59 E
117	Roeselare . . . . Bel.	50·55 N	3·05 E
65	Roesiger (L.) (rōz'ĭ-gēr) Wash. (Seattle In.)	47·59 N	121·56 W
87	Roes Welcome Sd. (rōz) . . . . . Can.	64·10 N	87·23 W
128	Rogachëv (rôg'á-chyôf) . . Sov. Un.	53·07 N	30·04 E
127	Rogatica (rô-gä'tē-tsä) . . . . . . Yugo.	43·46 N	19·00 E
121	Rogatin (rō-gä'tĭn) . . . . Sov. Un.	49·22 N	24·37 E
73	Rogers (rŏj-ērz) . . . . Ark.	36·19 N	94·07 W
80	Rogers City . . . . Mich.	45·30 N	83·50 W
78	Rogersville (rŏj'ērz-vĭl) . . . . . Tenn.	36·21 N	83·00 W
122	Rognac (rŏn-yȧk') Fr. (Marseille In.)	43·29 N	5·15 E
98	Rogoaguado (L.) (rō'gō-ȧ-gwȧ'dō) Bol.	12·42 S	66·46 W

Page	Name Pronunciation Region	Lat. °′	Long. °′
129	Rogovskaya (rô-gôf'skȧ-yȧ) Sov. Un.	45·43 N	38·42 E
120	Rogózno (rô'gôzh-nô) Pol.	52·44 N	16·53 E
66	Rogue R. (rōg) Ore.	42·32 N	124·13 W
118	Röikenviken (rûē'kĕn-vêk-ĕn) Nor.	60·27 N	10·26 E
101	Rojas (rō'hās) Arg. (Buenos Aires In.)	34·11 S	60·42 W
91	Rojo, Cabo (C.) (rō'hō) Mex.	21·35 N	97·16 W
89	Rojo, Cabo (C.) (rō'hō) P. R. (Puerto Rico In.)	17·55 N	67·14 W
153	Rokkō-Zan (Mtn.) (rôk'kō zän) Jap. (Osaka In.)	34·46 N	135·16 E
120	Rokycany (rô'kĭ'tsȧ-nĭ) Czech.	49·44 N	13·37 E
98	Roldanillo (rôl-dȧ-nē'l-yō) Col. (In.)	4·24 N	76·09 W
73	Rolla (rŏl'ȧ) Mo.	37·56 N	91·45 W
70	Rolla N. D.	48·52 N	99·32 W
118	Rollag (rōō'lăgh) Nor.	59·55 N	8·48 E
95	Rolleville Ba. Is.	23·40 N	76·00 W
160	Roma (rō'mȧ) Austl.	26·30 S	148·48 E
167	Roma Bas. (Natal In.)	29·28 S	27·43 E
125	Roma (Rome) (rō'mä) (rōm) It. (Rome In.)	41·52 N	12·37 E
126	Romagna (Reg.) (rô-mä'n-yȧ) It.	44·18 N	10·48 E
83	Romaine (rô-mĕn') Can.	50·12 N	60·38 W
87	Romaine (R.) Can.	51·22 N	63·23 W
121	Roman (rō'măn) Rom.	46·56 N	26·57 E
102	Romania (rō-mā'nē-ȧ) Eur.	46·18 N	22·53 E
79	Romano, C. (rō-mä'nō) Fla. (In.)	25·48 N	82·00 W
94	Romano, Cayo (I.) (kä'yō-rô-mȧ'nô) Cuba	22·15 N	78·00 W
136	Romanovo (rô-mä'nô-vô) Sov. Un. (Urals In.)	59·09 N	61·24 E
122	Romans-sur-Isère (rô-mäN'-sür-ē-sĕr') Fr.	45·04 N	4·49 E
64	Romanzof, C. (rō'măn zôf) Alaska	62·00 N	167·18 W
155	Romblon (rōm-blōn') Phil. (Manila In.)	12·34 N	122·16 E
155	Romblon (I.) Phil. (Manila In.)	12·33 N	122·17 E
78	Rome (rōm) Ga.	34·14 N	85·10 W
81	Rome N. Y.	43·15 N	75·25 W
	Rome, see Roma		
80	Romeo (rō'mē-ō) Mich.	42·50 N	83·00 W
110	Romford (rŭm'fērd) Eng. (London In.)	51·35 N	0·11 E
122	Romilly-sur-Seine (rô-mē-yē'sür-sān') Fr.	48·32 N	3·41 E
90	Romita (rō-mē'tä) Mex.	20·53 N	101·32 W
129	Romny (rôm'nĭ) Sov. Un.	50·46 N	33·31 E
118	Rømø (I.) (rûm'û) Den.	55·08 N	8·17 E
74	Romoland (rō'mō'lănd) Calif. (Los Angeles In.)	33·44 N	117·11 W
122	Romorantin (rô-mô-räN-täN') Fr.	47·24 N	1·46 E
139	Rompin Mala. (Singapore In.)	2·42 N	102·30 E
139	Rompin (R.) Mala. (Singapore In.)	2·54 N	103·10 E
75	Romulus (rom'ū lŭs) Mich. (Detroit In.)	42·14 N	83·24 W
116	Ronaldsay, North (I.) Scot.	59·21 N	2·23 W
116	Ronaldsay, South (I.) (rŏn'ăld-s'ā) Scot.	59·48 N	2·55 W
67	Ronan (rō'năn) Mont.	47·28 N	114·03 W
99	Roncador, Serra do (Mts.) (sĕr'rȧ dōō rôn-kȧ-dôr') Braz.	12·44 S	52·19 W
124	Roncesvalles (rôn-sĕs-vȧ'l-yĕs) Sp.	43·00 N	1·17 W
80	Ronceverte (rŏn'sē-vûrt) W. Va.	37·45 N	80·30 W
124	Ronda (rōn'dä) Sp.	37·45 N	5·10 W
98	Rondônia (Ter.) Braz.	10·15 S	63·07 W
86	Ronge, Lac la (L.) Can.	55·16 N	104·16 W
118	Rønne (rûn'ĕ) Den.	55·08 N	14·46 E
118	Ronneby (rōn'ĕ-bü) Swe.	56·13 N	15·17 E
72	Ront Ra. (Mts.) (rŏnt) Colo.	40·59 N	105·29 W
167	Roodepoort (rō'dĕ-pōrt) S. Afr. (Johannesburg & Pretoria In.)	26·10 S	27·52 E
73	Roodhouse (rōōd'hous) Ill.	39·29 N	90·21 W
168	Rooiberg S. Afr. (Johannesburg & Pretoria In.)	24·46 S	27·42 E
111	Roosendaal (rō'zĕn-däl) Neth. (Amsterdam In.)	51·32 N	4·27 E
69	Roosevelt (rōz'vĕlt) Utah	40·20 N	110·00 W
69	Roosevelt (R.) Ariz.	33·45 N	111·00 W
99	Roosevelt (R.) (rô'sĕ-vĕlt) Braz.	9·22 S	60·28 W
47	Roosevelt I. Ant.	79·30 S	168·00 W
75	Root R. (rōōt) Wis. (Milwaukee In.)	42·49 N	87·54 W
158	Roper (R.) (rōp'ēr) Austl.	14·50 S	134·00 E
136	Ropsha (rôp'shȧ) Sov. Un. (Leningrad In.)	59·44 N	29·53 E
122	Roquefort Fr.	43·59 N	3·00 E
98	Roques, Islas los (Is.) Ven.	21·25 N	67·40 W
101	Roque Pérez (rô'kĕ-pĕ'rĕz) Arg. (Buenos Aires In.)	35·23 S	59·22 W
125	Roquetas (rô-kā'tās) Sp.	40·50 N	0·32 E
99	Roraima, Mtn. (rô-rä-ē'mä) Ven.-Br. Gu.	5·12 N	60·52 W
118	Röros (rûr'ôs) Nor.	62·36 N	11·25 E
120	Rorschach (rōr'shäk) Switz.	47·27 N	9·28 E
129	Ros' (R.) (rôs) Sov. Un.	49·40 N	30·22 E
120	Rosa, Monte (Mt.) (mōn'tä rō'zä) It.	45·56 N	7·51 E
76	Rosales (rō-zä'lās) Mex.	28·15 N	100·43 W
155	Rosales (rô-sä'lĕs) Phil. (Manila In.)	15·54 N	120·38 E
90	Rosamorada (rō'zä-mō-rä'dhä) Mex.	22·06 N	105·16 W
91	Rosaria, Laguna (L.) (lä-gōō'nä-rô-sȧ'ryä) Mex.	17·50 N	93·51 W
101	Rosario (rō-zä'rē-ō) Arg. (Buenos Aires In.)	32·58 S	60·42 W
99	Rosario (rô-zȧ'rē-ōō) Braz.	2·49 S	44·15 W
90	Rosario Mex.	22·58 N	105·54 W
155	Rosario Phil. (Manila In.)	13·49 N	121·13 E
101	Rosario Ur. (Buenos Aires In.)	34·19 S	57·24 W
94	Rosario, Cayo (I.) (kä'yō-rō-sä'ryō) Cuba	21·40 N	81·55 W
100	Rosário do Sul (rô-zä'rê-ōō-dô-sōō'l) Braz.	30·17 S	54·52 W
99	Rosário Oeste (ō'ĕst'ĕ) Braz.	14·47 S	56·20 W
65	Rosario Str. Wash. (Seattle In.)	48·27 N	122·45 W
125	Rosas, Golfo de (G.) (gôl-fô-dĕ-rō'zäs) Sp.	42·10 N	3·20 E
123	Rosbach (rōz'bäk) Ger. (Ruhr In.)	50·47 N	7·38 E
76	Roscoe (rôs'kō) Tex.	32·26 N	100·38 W
70	Roseau (rô-zō') Minn.	48·52 N	95·47 W
93	Roseau Dominica (Le. & Wind. Is. In.)	15·17 N	61·23 W
70	Roseau (R.) Minn.	48·52 N	96·11 W
66	Roseberg (rōz'bûrg) Ore.	43·13 N	123·20 W
67	Rosebud Cr. Mont.	45·48 N	106·34 W
70	Rosebud Ind. Res. (rōz'bud) S. D.	43·13 N	100·42 W
78	Rosedale (rōz'dāl) Miss.	33·49 N	90·56 W
65	Rosedale Wash. (Seattle In.)	47·20 N	122·39 W
75	Roselle (rō-zĕl') Ill. (Chicago In.)	41·59 N	88·05 W
85	Rosemere (rōz'mēr) Can. (Montreal In.)	45·38 N	73·48 W
74	Rosemount (rōz'mount) Minn. (Minneapolis, St. Paul In.)	44·44 N	93·08 W
168	Rosendal (rô-sĕn'täl) S. Afr. (Johannesburg & Pretoria In.)	28·32 S	27·56 E
120	Rosenheim (rō'zĕn-hīm) Ger.	47·52 N	12·06 E
86	Rosetown (rōz'toun) Can.	51·37 N	108·10 W
	Rosetta, see Rashīd		
167	Rosettenville S. Afr. (Johannesburg & Pretoria In.)	26·15 S	28·04 E
68	Roseville (rōz'vĭl) Calif.	38·44 N	121·19 W
75	Roseville Mich. (Detroit In.)	42·30 N	82·55 W
74	Roseville Minn. (Minneapolis, St. Paul In.)	45·01 N	93·10 W
80	Rosiclare (rōz'ĭ-klâr) Ill.	37·30 N	88·15 W
99	Rosignol (rŏs-ĭg-nŏl) Br. Gu.	6·16 N	57·37 W
127	Rosiorii de Vede (rô-shôr'ê dĕ vĕ-dĕ) Rom.	44·06 N	25·00 E
118	Roskilde (rôs'kĕl-dĕ) Den.	55·39 N	12·04 E
128	Roslavl' (rôs'läv'l) Sov. Un.	53·56 N	32·52 E
66	Roslyn (rŏz'lĭn) Wash.	47·14 N	121·00 W
129	Rosovka Sov. Un.	47·14 N	36·35 E
123	Rösrath (rûz'rät) Ger. (Ruhr In.)	50·53 N	7·11 E
75	Ross (rôs) Ohio (Cincinnati In.)	39·19 N	84·39 W
126	Rossano (rô-sä'nō) It.	39·34 N	16·38 E
85	Ross Cr. Can. (Edmonton In.)	53·50 N	113·08 W
66	Ross Dam Wash.	48·40 N	121·07 W
83	Rosseau (L.) (rôs-sō') Can.	45·15 N	79·30 W
159	Rossel (I.) (rô-sĕl') Austl.	11·31 S	154·00 E
85	Rosser (rôs'sēr) Can. (Winnipeg In.)	49·59 N	97·27 W
82	Rossignol (rô-sē-nyôl') Can.	44·15 N	65·25 W
86	Rossland (rôs'lănd) Can.	49·00 N	118·08 W
129	Rossosh' (rôs'sŭsh) Sov. Un.	50·12 N	39·32 E
167	Rossouw S. Afr. (Natal In.)	31·12 S	27·18 E
47	Ross Sea Ant.	76·00 S	178·00 W
47	Ross Shelf Ice Ant.	81·30 S	175·00 W
78	Rossville (rôs'vĭl) Ga.	34·57 N	85·22 W
120	Rostock (rôs'tŭk) Ger.	54·04 N	12·06 E
128	Rostov Sov. Un.	57·13 N	39·23 E
129	Rostov (Oblast) Sov. Un.	47·38 N	39·15 E
133	Rostov-na-Donu (rôstôv-nȧ-dô-nōō) Sov. Un.	47·16 N	39·47 E
112	Rösvatn (L.) (rûs-vät'n) Nor.	65·36 N	13·08 E
78	Roswell (rŏz'wĕl) Ga.	34·02 N	84·21 W
72	Roswell N. Mex.	33·23 N	104·32 W
72	Rotan (rô-tăn') Tex.	32·51 N	100·27 W
120	Rothenburg Ger.	49·20 N	10·10 E
110	Rotherham (rŏdh'ēr-ăm) Eng.	53·26 N	1·21 W
82	Rothesay Can.	45·25 N	65·59 W
116	Rothesay (rôth'sȧ) Scot.	55·50 N	3·14 W
110	Rothwell (rôth'wĕl) Eng.	53·44 N	1·30 W
154	Roti (I.) (rō'tê) Indon.	10·30 S	122·52 E
160	Roto (rō'tô) Austl.	33·07 S	145·30 E
111	Rotterdam (rŏt'ēr-däm') Neth. (Amsterdam In.)	51·55 N	4·27 E
120	Rottweil (rōt'vīl) Ger.	48·10 N	8·36 E
122	Roubaix (rōō-bĕ') Fr.	50·42 N	3·10 E
122	Rouen (rōō-äN') Fr.	49·25 N	1·05 E
75	Rouge, R. Mich. (Detroit In.)	42·30 N	83·15 W
85	Rouge R. (rōōzh) Can. (Toronto In.)	43·53 N	79·21 W
75	Round Lake Ill. (Chicago In.)	42·21 N	88·05 W
82	Round Pd. (round) Can.	48·12 N	53·50 W
65	Round Top (Mtn.) (tŏp) Ore. (Portland In.)	45·41 N	123·22 W
67	Roundup (round'ŭp) Mont.	46·25 N	108·35 W
116	Rousay (I.) (rōō'zȧ) Scot.	59·10 N	3·04 W
87	Rouyn (rōōn) Can.	48·22 N	79·03 W
112	Rovaniemi (rô'vȧ-nyĕ'mĭ) Fin.	66·29 N	25·45 E
126	Rovato (rō-vä'tō) It.	45·33 N	10·00 E
129	Roven'ki (rō-vĕn'kĭ') Sov. Un.	48·06 N	39·44 E
129	Roven'ki Sov. Un.	49·54 N	38·54 E
126	Rovereto (rō-vā-rā'tō) It.	45·53 N	11·05 E
126	Rovigo (rô-vē'gô) It.	45·05 N	11·48 E
126	Rovinj (rô'vēn') Yugo.	45·05 N	13·40 E
98	Rovira (rô-vē'rä) Col. (In.)	4·14 N	75·13 W
121	Rovno (rôv'nô) Sov. Un.	50·37 N	26·17 E
129	Rovno (Oblast) Sov. Un.	50·55 N	27·00 E
129	Rovnoye (rôv'nô-yĕ) Sov. Un.	48·11 N	31·46 E
83	Rowley (rou'lē) Mass. (Boston In.)	42·43 N	70·53 W
74	Roxana (rŏks'ăn-nȧ) Ill. (St. Louis In.)	38·51 N	90·05 W
154	Roxas (rô-xäs) Phil.	11·30 N	122·47 E
79	Roxboro (rŏks' bŭr-ō) N. C.	36·22 N	78·58 W
72	Roy (roi) N. Mex.	35·54 N	104·09 W
74	Roy Utah (Salt Lake City In.)	41·10 N	112·02 W
94	Royal (I.) Ba. Is.	25·30 N	76·50 W
116	Royal Can. (roi-ăl) Ire.	53·28 N	6·45 W
167	Royal Natal Natl. Pk. (roi'ăl) S. Afr. (Natal In.)	28·35 S	28·54 E
65	Royal Oak (roi'ăl ōk) Can. (Seattle In.)	48·30 N	123·24 W
75	Royal Oak Mich. (Detroit In.)	42·29 N	83·09 W
80	Royalton (roi'ăl-tŭn) Mich.	42·00 N	86·25 W
122	Royan (rwä-yäN') Fr.	45·40 N	1·02 W
122	Roye (rwä) Fr.	49·43 N	2·40 E
84	Royersford (rô' yĕrz-fērd) Pa. (Philadelphia In.)	40·11 N	75·32 W
78	Royston (roiz'tŭn) Ga.	34·15 N	83·06 W
110	Royton (roi'tŭn) Eng.	53·34 N	2·07 W
123	Rozay-en-Brie (rô-zā-ĕN-brē') Fr. (Paris In.)	48·41 N	2·57 E
136	Rozhaya R. (rô'zhȧ-yȧ) Sov. Un. (Moscow In.)	55·20 N	37·37 E
121	Rožňava (rôzh'nyȧ-vȧ) Czech.	48·39 N	20·32 E
133	Rtishchevo ('r-tĭsh'chĕ-vô) Sov. Un.	52·15 N	43·40 E
167	Ruaha (R.) (rwä'hȧ) Tan.	7·51 S	37·00 E
159	Ruapehu (Mtn.) (rōō-ȧ-pā'hōō) N. Z. (In.)	39·15 S	175·37 E
139	Ruâq (R.) U. A. R. (Palestine In.)	29·48 N	33·59 E
134	Rubtsovak Sov. Un.	51·31 N	81·17 E
64	Ruby (rōō'bē) Alaska	64·38 N	155·22 W
68	Ruby (L.) Nev.	40·11 N	115·20 W
68	Ruby Mts. Nev.	40·11 N	115·36 W
67	Ruby R. Mont.	45·06 N	112·10 W
95	Rucilla, Loma (Hill) (lô'mä-rōō-sē'l-yä) Dom. Rep.	19·05 N	70·55 W
144	Rūd-E-Kar (R.) Iran	33·15 N	47·31 E
118	Rudkøbing (rōōdh'kûb-ĭng) Den.	54·56 N	10·44 E
111	Rüdnitz (rüd'nētz) Ger. (Berlin In.)	52·44 N	13·38 E
142	Rudok (rōō'dŏk) China	33·42 N	79·56 E
165	Rudolf, L. (rōō'dŏlf) Ken.-Eth.	3·43 N	35·49 E
117	Rudolstadt (rōō'dôl-shtät) Ger.	50·46 N	13·30 E
165	Rufa'a (rōō-fä'ä) Sud.	14·52 N	33·30 E
122	Ruffec (rü-fĕk') Fr.	46·03 N	0·11 E
167	Rufiji (R.) (rōō-fē'jē) Tan.	8·29 S	37·39 E
164	Rufisque (rü-fēsk') Senegal	14·41 N	17·13 W
66	Rufus Woods Wash.	48·02 N	119·33 W
110	Rugby (rŭg'bē) Eng.	52·22 N	1·15 W
70	Rugby N. D.	48·22 N	100·00 W
110	Rugeley (rōōj'lē) Eng.	52·46 N	1·56 W
120	Rügen (Pen.) (rü'ghĕn) Ger.	54·28 N	13·47 E
119	Ruhnu-Saar (I.) (rōōnōō-sȧ'ȧr) Sov. Un.	57·46 N	23·15 E
120	Ruhr R. (rōōr) Ger.	51·18 N	8·17 E
90	Ruiz (rōōē'z) Mex.	21·55 N	105·09 W
98	Ruiz, Nevado del (Pk.) (nĕ-vȧ'dô-dĕl-rōōē'z) Col. (In.)	4·52 N	75·20 W
119	Rūjiena (rōō'yĭ-ă-nȧ) Sov. Un.	57·54 N	25·19 E
166	Rukwa (L.) (rōōk-wä') Tan.	8·15 S	33·14 E
71	Rum (R.) (rŭm) Minn.	45·52 N	93·45 W
127	Ruma (rōō'mȧ) Yugo.	45·00 N	19·53 E
165	Rumbek (rŭm'bĕk) Sud.	6·52 N	29·43 E
95	Rum Cay (I.) Ba. Is.	23·40 N	74·50 W
82	Rumford (rŭm'fērd) Maine	44·32 N	70·35 W
139	Rummānah U. A. R. (Palestine In.)	31·01 N	32·39 E
110	Runcorn (rŭŋ'kôrn) Eng.	53·20 N	2·44 W
139	Rupat, Palau (I.) (rōō'pät) Indon. (Singapore In.)	1·55 N	101·35 E
139	Rupat, Selat (Str.) Indon. (Singapore In.)	1·55 N	101·17 E
67	Rupert (rōō'pērt) Idaho	42·36 N	113·41 W
87	Rupert (R.) Can.	76·27 N	77·47 W
127	Ruse (Russe) (rōō'sĕ) (rōō'sĕ) Bul.	43·50 N	25·59 E
71	Rush City Minn.	45·40 N	92·59 W
65	Rushton (rŭsh'tŭn) Wash. (Seattle In.)	47·18 N	122·30 W
73	Rushville (rŭsh'vĭl) Ill.	40·08 N	90·34 W
80	Rushville Ind.	39·35 N	85·30 W
70	Rushville Nebr.	42·43 N	102·27 W
77	Rusk (rŭsk) Tex.	31·49 N	95·09 W
65	Ruskin (rŭs'kĭn) Can. (Vancouver In.)	49·10 N	122·25 W
111	Russ (R.) Aus. (Vienna In.)	48·12 N	16·55 E
99	Russas (rōō's-säs) Braz.	4·48 S	37·50 W
	Russe, see Ruse		
65	Russell Calif. (San Francisco In.)	37·39 N	122·08 W
86	Russell (rŭs'ĕl) Can.	50·47 N	101·20 W
85	Russell Can. (Ottawa In.)	45·15 N	75·22 W
72	Russell Kans.	38·51 N	98·51 W
80	Russell Ky.	38·30 N	82·45 W
159	Russell N. Z. (In.)	35·38 S	174·13 E
159	Russell Is Sol. Is.	9·16 S	158·30 E
78	Russellville (rŭs'ĕl-vĭl) Ala.	34·29 N	87·44 W
73	Russellville Ark.	35·16 N	93·08 W
78	Russelville Ky.	36·48 N	86·51 W
130	Russian S. F. S. R. Sov. Un.	61·00 N	60·00 E
68	Russian (R.) (rŭsh'ăn) Calif.	38·59 N	123·10 W
168	Rustenburg (rŭs'tĕn-bûrg) S. Afr. (Johannesburg & Pretoria In.)	25·40 S	26·15 E
77	Ruston (rŭs'tŭn) La.	32·32 N	92·39 W
129	Rutchenkovo (rōō-chĕn'kô-vô) Sov. Un.	47·54 N	37·36 E
124	Rute (rōō'tä) Sp.	37·20 N	4·34 W
68	Ruth (rōōth) Nev.	39·17 N	115·00 W
121	Ruthenia (Reg.) Sov. Un.	48·25 N	23·00 E
79	Rutherfordton (rŭdh'ēr-fērd-tŭn) N. C.	35·23 N	81·58 W
81	Rutland (rŭt'lănd) Vt.	43·35 N	72·55 W
110	Rutland (Co.) Eng.	52·40 N	0·37 W
166	Rutshuru (rōōt-shōō'rōō) Con. L.	1·13 S	29·15 E
126	Ruvo (rōō'vô) It.	41·07 N	16·32 E
163	Ruwenzori Ra. (rōō-wĕn-zō'rē) Afr.	0·53 N	30·00 E
128	Ruza (rōō'zȧ) Sov. Un.	55·42 N	36·12 E
121	Ruzhany (rōō-zhän'ĭ) Sov. Un.	52·49 N	24·54 E
166	Rwanda Afr.	2·10 S	29·37 E
136	Ryabovo (ryä'bô-vô) Sov. Un. (Leningrad In.)	59·24 N	31·08 E
128	Ryazan' (ryä-zän'') Sov. Un.	54·37 N	39·43 E
128	Ryazan' (Oblast) Sov. Un.	54·10 N	39·37 E
128	Ryazhsk (ryäzh'sk') Sov. Un.	53·43 N	40·04 E
132	Rybachiy, P-Ov. (Pen.) Sov. Un.	69·50 N	33·20 E
136	Rybatskoye (rĭ-bät'skô-yĕ) Sov. Un. (Leningrad In.)	59·50 N	30·31 E

ăt; finăl; rāte; senâte; ärm; åsk; sofȧ; fâre; ch-choose; dh-as th in other; bē; ēvent; bĕt; recĕnt; cratēr; g-go; gh-guttural g; bĭt; ĭ-short neutral; rīde; K-guttural k as ch in German ich;

Page	Name	Pronunciation	Region	Lat. °'	Long. °'
128	Rybinsk (ry-bĭ′nsk)	Sov. Un.	58·02 N	38·52 E
	Rybinsk, L., see Rybinskoye Vodokhranilishche			
128	Rybinskoye Vodokhranilishche (Rybinsk) (L.)	Sov. Un.	58·23 N	38·15 E
121	Rybnik (rĭb′nĕk)	Pol.	50·06 N	18·37 E
129	Rybnitsa (rĭb′nĕt-sá)	Sov. Un.	47·45 N	29·02 E
116	Ryde (rīd)	Eng.	50·43 N	1·16 W
84	Rye (rī)	N. Y. (New York In.)	40·58 N	73·42 W
129	Ryl′sk (rēl′′sk)	Sov. Un.	51·33 N	34·42 E
152	Ryōtsu (ryŏt′sōō)	Jap.	38·02 N	138·23 E
121	Rypin (rĭ′pên)	Pol.	53·04 N	19·25 E
156	Ryūkyū Rettō (Is.) (ryōō′kyōō)	Asia	26·00 N	119·00 E
121	Rzeszów (zhá′shōōf)	Pol.	50·02 N	22·00 E
128	Rzhev (′r-zhěf)	Sov. Un.	56·16 N	34·17 E
129	Rzhishchëv (′r-zhĭsh′chěf)	Sov. Un.	49·58 N	31·05 E
120	Saale R. (sä′lě)	Ger.	51·14 N	11·52 E
120	Saalfeld (säl′fĕlt)	Ger.	50·38 N	11·20 E
120	Saar (State) (zär)	Ger.	49·25 N	6·50 E
120	Saarbrücken (zähr′brü-kěn)	Ger.	49·15 N	7·01 E
119	Saaremaa (Ezel) (I.) (sä′rě-mä)	Sov. Un.	58·28 N	21·30 E
100	Saavedra (sä-ä-vä′drä)	Arg.	37·45 S	62·23 W
127	Šabac (shä′báts)	Yugo.	44·45 N	19·49 E
125	Sabadell (sä-bä-dhäl′)	Sp.	41·32 N	2·07 E
154	Sabah (Reg.)	Asia	5·10 N	116·25 E
93	Saba I. (sä′bä)	N. A. (Le. & Wind. Is. In.)	17·39 N	63·20 W
154	Sabalana (I.)	Indon.	6·56 S	118·10 E
94	Sabana, Arch. de (är-chě-pyě′lä-gô dě sä-bä′nä)	Cuba	23·05 N	80·00 W
93	Sabana, R. (sä-bä′nä)	Pan.	8·40 N	78·02 W
95	Sabana de la Mar (sä-bä′nä dä lä mär′)	Dom. Rep.	19·05 N	69·30 W
99	Sabana de Uchire (sä-bä′nä dě ōō-chē′rě)	Ven. (In.)	10·02 N	65·32 W
92	Sabanagrande (sä-bä′nä-grä′n-dě)	Hond.	13·47 N	87·16 W
98	Sabanalarga (sä-bä′nä-lär′gä)	Col.	10·38 N	75·02 W
98	Sabanas Páramo (Mtn.) (sä-bä′näs pá′rä-mô)	Col. (In.)	6·28 N	76·08 W
91	Sabancuy (sä-bän-kwē′)	Mex.	18·58 N	91·09 W
154	Sabang (sä′bäng)	Indon.	5·52 N	95·26 E
126	Sabaudia (sä-bou′dě-ä)	It.	41·19 N	13·00 E
165	Sabderat (säb-dä-rät′)	Eth.	15·30 N	36·45 E
73	Sabetha (sá-běth′á)	Kans.	39·54 N	95·49 W
166	Sabi (sä′bě)	S. Rh.	20·18 S	32·07 E
119	Sabile (sá′bě-lě)	Sov. Un.	57·03 N	22·34 E
76	Sabinal (sá-bī′nál)	Tex.	29·19 N	99·27 W
94	Sabinal, Cayo (I.) (ká′yō sä-bē-näl′)	Cuba	21·40 N	77·20 W
88	Sabinas	Mex.	28·05 N	102·30 W
76	Sabinas, R. (sä-bē′näs)	Mex.	26·37 N	99·52 W
76	Sabinas, Rio (R.) (rē′ō sä-bē′näs)	Mex.	27·25 N	100·33 W
76	Sabinas Hidalgo (ē-däl′gô)	Mex.	26·30 N	100·10 W
77	Sabine (sá-bēn′)	Tex.	29·44 N	93·54 W
47	Sabine, Mt.	Ant.	72·05 S	169·10 E
63	Sabine (R.)	U. S.	31·35 N	94·00 W
77	Sabine L.	La.-Tex.	29·53 N	93·41 W
155	Sablayan (säb-lä-yän′)	Phil. (Manila In.)	12·49 N	120·47 E
82	Sable, C. (sä′b′l)	Can.	43·25 N	65·24 W
79	Sable, C.	Fla. (In.)	25·12 N	81·10 W
122	Sablé-sur-Sarthe (säb-lā-sür-särt′)	Fr.	47·50 N	0·17 W
132	Sablya, Gora (Mtn.)	Sov. Un.	64·50 N	59·00 E
124	Sàbor (R.) (sä-bōr′)	Port.	41·18 N	6·54 W
73	Sac (R.) (sôk)	Mo.	38·11 N	93·45 W
81	Sacandaga Res. (sä-kăn-dä′gá)	N. Y.	43·10 N	74·15 W
125	Sacavém (sä-kä-věn′)	Port. (Lisbon In.)	38·47 N	9·06 W
125	Sacavem (R.)	Port. (Lisbon In.)	38·52 N	9·06 W
71	Sac City (sŏk)	Iowa	42·25 N	95·00 W
120	Sachsen (Reg.) (zäk′sĕn)	Ger.	50·45 N	12·17 E
81	Sacketts Harbor (săk′ĕts)	N. Y.	43·55 N	76·05 W
82	Sackville (săk′vĭl)	Can.	45·54 N	64·26 W
82	Saco (sô′kô)	Maine	43·30 N	70·28 W
100	Saco (R.) (sä′kô)	Braz. (In.)	22·20 S	43·26 W
82	Saco (R.)	Maine	43·53 N	70·46 W
100	Sacra Familia do Tinguá (sä-krä fä-mä′lyä dô těn-gwä′)	Braz. (In.)	22·29 S	43·36 W
68	Sacramento (săk-rá-měn′tō)	Calif.	38·35 N	121·30 W
76	Sacramento	Mex.	25·45 N	103·22 W
76	Sacramento	Mex.	27·05 N	101·45 W
68	Sacramento (R.)	Calif.	40·20 N	122·07 W
166	Sa′da Bandeira (sä′dá bän-dā′rá)	Ang.	14·50 S	13·30 E
65	Saddle Mtn. (săd′′l)	Ore. (Portland In.)	45·58 N	123·40 W
145	Sadiya (sŭ-dē′yä)	India	27·53 N	95·35 E
152	Sado (I.) (sä′dō)	Jap.	38·05 N	138·26 E
124	Sado (R.) (sä′dōō)	Port.	38·15 N	8·20 W
118	Saeby (sě′bü)	Den.	57·21 N	10·29 E
153	Saeki (sä′ä-kě)	Jap.	32·56 N	131·51 E
139	Safad (sä′fäd)	Isr. (Palestine In.)	32·58 N	35·30 E
69	Safford (säf′ferd)	Ariz.	32·50 N	109·45 W
164	Safi (Asfi) (äs′fē) (äs′fě)	Mor.	32·24 N	9·09 W
133	Safid Rud (R.)	Iran	36·50 N	49·40 E
153	Saga (sä′gä)	Jap.	33·15 N	130·18 E
153	Sagami-Nada (Sea) (sä′gä′mě nä-dä)	Jap.	35·06 N	139·24 E
75	Sagamore Hills (săg′á-môr hĭlz)	Ohio (Cleveland In.)	41·19 N	81·34 W
71	Saganaga (L.) (sä-gä-nä′gá)	Can.-Minn.	48·13 N	91·17 W
80	Saginaw (săg′ĭ-nô)	Mich.	43·25 N	84·00 W
74	Saginaw	Minn. (Duluth In.)	46·51 N	92·26 W

Page	Name	Pronunciation	Region	Lat. °'	Long. °'
74	Saginaw	Tex. (Dallas, Fort Worth In.)	32·52 N	97·22 W
80	Saginaw B.	Mich.	43·50 N	83·40 W
133	Sagiz (R.) (sä′gēz)	Sov. Un.	48·30 N	56·10 E
69	Saguache (sá-wäch′) (sá-gwä′chě)	Colo.	38·05 N	106·10 W
69	Saguache Cr.	Colo.	38·05 N	106·40 W
95	Sagua de Tánamo (sä-gwä dě tá′nä-mō)	Cuba	20·40 N	75·15 W
94	Sagua la Grande (sä-gwä lä grä′n-dě)	Cuba	22·45 N	80·05 W
69	Saguaro Natl. Mon. (säg-wä′rō)	Ariz.	32·12 N	110·40 W
87	Saguenay (R.) (săg-ē-nā′)	Can.	48·05 N	70·26 W
164	Saguia el Hamra (Ter.) (säg-yä ĕl häm′rä)	Sp. Sah.	27·01 N	10·58 W
125	Sagunto (sä-gōōn′tō)	Sp.	39·40 N	0·17 W
163	Sahara Des. (sá-hä′rá)	Afr.	23·44 N	1·40 W
114	Saharan Atlas (Mts.)	Mor.-Alg.	32·51 N	1·02 E
142	Sahāranpur (sŭ-hä′rŭn-pōōr′)	India	29·58 N	77·41 E
74	Sahara Village (sá-hä′rá)	Utah (Salt Lake City In.)	41·06 N	111·58 W
139	Saheira (R.)	U. A. R. (Palestine In.)	29·55 N	33·18 E
90	Sahuayo (sä-wä′yō)	Mex.	20·03 N	102·43 W
164	Saïda (sä′ē-dä)	Alg.	34·51 N	00·07 E
144	Sa′īdabād (sä′ē-dä-bät′)	Iran	29·30 N	55·43 E
154	Saigon (sä-ê-gŏn′) (sī-gōn′)	Viet.	10·46 N	106·34 E
153	Saijō (sä′ê-jō)	Jap.	33·55 N	133·13 E
119	Saimaa (sä′ī-mä)	Fin.	61·24 N	28·45 E
90	Sain Alto (sä-ēn′ äl′tō)	Mex.	23·35 N	103·13 W
85	St. Adolphe (sänt a′dôlf) (sä′′ tá-dôlf′)	Can. (Winnipeg In.)	49·40 N	97·07 W
122	St. Affrique (sä′′ tä-frēk′)	Fr.	43·58 N	2·52 E
161	St. Albans (sänt ôl′bănz)	Austl. (Melbourne In.)	37·44 S	144·47 E
110	St. Albans	Eng. (London In.)	51·44 N	0·20 W
81	St. Albans	Vt.	44·50 N	73·05 W
80	St. Albans	W. Va.	38·20 N	81·50 W
116	St. Albans Hd.	Eng.	50·34 N	2·00 W
85	St. Albert (sänt ăl′bert)	Can. (Edmonton In.)	53·38 N	113·38 W
122	St. Amand Montrond (sä′′ tä-män′ môn-rôn′)	Fr.	46·44 N	2·28 E
167	St. André, Cap (C.) (sä′′ tän-drā′)	Malag. Rep.	16·15 S	44·31 E
78	St. Andrew, B.	Fla.	30·20 N	85·45 W
83	St. Andrew Chan.	Can.	46·06 N	60·28 W
82	St. Andrews (än′drōōz)	Can.	43·42 N	65·05 W
116	St. Andrews	Scot.	56·20 N	2·40 W
85	St. Andrews East	Can. (Montreal In.)	45·33 N	74·19 W
85	Ste. Angele-de-Laval (sănt′ än-zhěl′-dē-läväl′)	Can. (Montreal In.)	45·33 N	73·42 W
85	Ste. Anicet (sĕnt ä-nē-sě′)	Can. (Montreal In.)	45·07 N	74·23 W
74	St. Ann (sänt än′)	Mo. (St. Louis In.)	38·44 N	90·23 W
82	Ste. Anne (sănt′ án′) (sänt ăn′)	Can.	46·55 N	71·46 W
85	Ste. Anne	Can. (Montreal In.)	45·24 N	73·57 W
75	Ste. Anne	Ill. (Chicago In.)	41·01 N	87·44 W
93	Ste. Anne	Grande Terre (Le. & Wind. Is. In.)	16·15 N	61·23 W
85	Ste. Anne, R.	Can. (Quebec In.)	47·07 N	70·50 W
85	Ste. Anne-de-Beaupré (dě bō-prā′)	Can. (Quebec In.)	47·01 N	70·56 W
82	St. Anne de la Pocatière (dě lä pô-kä-tyär′)	Can.	47·24 N	70·01 W
85	Ste. Anne-des-Plaines	Can. (Montreal In.)	45·46 N	73·49 W
83	St. Anns B. (ănz)	Can.	46·28 N	60·10 W
94	St. Ann's Bay	Jam.	18·25 N	77·15 W
85	St. Anselme (sän′ tän-sělm′)	Can. (Quebec In.)	46·37 N	70·58 W
83	St. Anthony (sän′ ăn′thô-ně)	Can.	51·24 N	55·35 W
67	St. Anthony (sänt ăn′thô-ně)	Idaho	43·59 N	111·42 W
155	St. Antonio, Mt.	Phil. (Manila In.)	13·23 N	122·00 E
85	St. Apollinaire (sän′ tä-pôl-ê-nâr′)	Can. (Quebec In.)	46·36 N	71·30 W
123	St. Arnoult-en-Yvelines (sän-tär-nōō′ĕn-nēv-lēn′)	Fr. (Paris In.)	48·33 N	1·55 E
85	St. Augustin (sänt ô′gŭs-těn)	Can. (Montreal In.)	45·38 N	73·59 W
85	St. Augustin (sän′ tô-gŭs-tăn′)	Can. (Quebec In.)	46·45 N	71·27 W
79	St. Augustine (sänt ô′gŭs-tēn)	Fla.	29·53 N	81·21 W
85	Ste. Barbe (sänt bärb′)	Can. (Montreal In.)	45·14 N	74·12 W
125	Ste. Barbe du Tlelat (sänt bärb′ dü tlě-lä′)	Alg.	35·33 N	0·28 W
82	St. Barthélémy (sän′ bár-tā-lě-me)	Can.	46·09 N	73·10 W
93	St. Barthelemy I.	N. A. (Le. & Wind. Is. In.)	17·55 N	62·32 W
116	St. Bees Hd. (sänt bēz′ hěd)	Eng.	54·30 N	3·40 W
85	St. Benoit (sĕn bě-nōō-ä′)	Can. (Montreal In.)	45·34 N	74·05 W
84	St. Bernard (běr-närd′)	La. (New Orleans In.)	29·52 N	89·52 W
75	St. Bernard	Ohio (Cincinnati In.)	39·10 N	84·30 W
85	St. Boniface (bŏn′ĭ fás)	Can. (Winnipeg In.)	49·53 N	97·06 W
116	St. Brides B. (sänt brīdz′)	Wales	51·17 N	4·45 W
122	St. Brieuc (sän′ brěs′)	Fr.	48·32 N	2·47 W
85	St. Bruno (brü′nō)	Can. (Montreal In.)	45·31 N	73·20 W
85	St. Canut (sän′ kä-nü′)	Can. (Montreal In.)	45·43 N	74·04 W
82	St. Casimir (ká-zě-mēr′)	Can.	46·45 N	72·34 W

Page	Name	Pronunciation	Region	Lat. °'	Long. °'
85	St. Catharines (kăth′á-rĭnz)	Can. (Toronto In.)	43·10 N	79·14 W
93	St. Catherine, Mt.	Grenada (Le. & Wind. Is. In.)	12·10 N	62·42 W
122	St. Chamas (sän-shä-mä′)	Fr. (Marseille In.)	43·32 N	5·03 E
122	St. Chamond (sän′ shä-môn′)	Fr.	45·30 N	4·17 E
85	St. Charles (sän′ shärlz′)	Can. (Quebec In.)	46·47 N	70·57 W
75	St. Charles (sänt chärlz′)	Ill. (Chicago In.)	41·55 N	88·19 W
80	St. Charles	Mich.	43·20 N	84·10 W
71	St. Charles	Minn.	43·56 N	92·05 W
74	St. Charles	Mo. (St. Louis In.)	38·47 N	90·29 W
93	St. Christopher I. (St. Kitts) (sänt kĭts′) St. Kitts-Nevis-Anguilla	(Le. & Wind. Is. In.)	17·24 N	62·25 W
80	St. Clair (sänt klâr′)	Mich.	42·55 N	82·30 W
80	St. Clair (L.)	Mich.-Can.	42·25 N	82·30 W
80	St. Clair (R.)	Mich.-Can.	42·45 N	82·25 W
85	Ste. Claire	Can. (Quebec In.)	46·36 N	70·52 W
75	St. Clair Shores	Mich. (Detroit In.)	42·30 N	82·54 W
123	St. Claude (sän′ klōd′)	Fr.	46·24 N	5·53 E
85	St. Clet (sănt′ klä′)	Can. (Montreal In.)	45·22 N	74·21 W
79	St. Cloud (sänt kloud′)	Fla. (In.)	28·13 N	81·17 W
71	St. Cloud	Minn.	45·33 N	94·08 W
85	St. Constant (kŏn′stänt)	Can. (Montreal In.)	45·22 N	73·35 W
167	St. Croix (I.) (sän krwä′)	S. Afr. (Natal In.)	33·48 S	25·45 E
89	Saint Croix (I.) (sänt kroi′)	Vir. Is. (U. S. A.) (Puerto Rico In.)	17·40 N	64·43 W
82	St. Croix (R.) (kroi′)	Can.	45·17 N	67·32 W
71	St. Croix Ind. Res.	Wis.	45·40 N	92·21 W
71	St. Croix R. (sänt kroi′)	Minn.-Wis.	45·00 N	92·44 W
85	St. Damien (sänt dä′mě-ĕn)	Can. (Quebec In.)	46·37 N	70·39 W
85	St. David (dä′vĭd)	Can. (Quebec In.)	46·47 N	71·11 W
116	St. David's Hd.	Wales	51·54 N	5·25 W
123	St.-Denis (sän′dě-ně′)	Fr. (Paris In.)	48·26 N	2·22 E
123	St. Dié (dě-ā′)	Fr.	48·18 N	6·55 E
122	St. Dizier (dě-zyä′)	Fr.	48·49 N	4·55 E
85	St. Dominique (sĕn dō-mē-nēk′)	Can. (Montreal In.)	45·19 N	74·09 W
85	St. Edouard (sěn-tě-dōō-är′)	Can. (Montreal In.)	45·14 N	73·31 W
64	St. Elias, Mt. (sěn-tě-lī′ás)	Can.	60·25 N	141·00 W
85	St. Elzear (sěn-těl-zě-âr′)	Can. (Montreal In.)	45·36 N	73·44 W
85	St. Etienne (sän′ tä-tyěn′)	Can. (Montreal In.)	45·15 N	73·55 W
85	St. Etienne	Can. (Quebec In.)	46·39 N	71·19 W
122	St.-Étienne	Fr.	45·26 N	4·22 E
85	Ste. Euphémie (sěnt û-fě-mě′)	Can. (Quebec In.)	46·47 N	70·27 W
85	St. Eustache (sän′ tû-stäsh′)	Can. (Montreal In.)	45·34 N	73·54 W
85	St. Eustache	Can. (Winnipeg In.)	49·58 N	97·47 W
85	St. Eustache sur le Lac (sĕn tû-stäsh′ sür lě läk)	Can. (Montreal In.)	45·33 N	73·54 W
93	St. Eustatius I. (sänt u-stä′shŭs)	N. A. (Le. & Wind. Is. In.)	17·32 N	62·45 W
85	Ste. Famille (sănt′ fä-mě′y′)	Can. (Quebec In.)	46·58 N	70·58 W
82	St. Felicien (sän fä-lě-syän′)	Can.	48·39 N	72·30 W
82	Ste. Felicite	Can.	48·54 N	67·22 W
85	St. Féréol (fä-rä-ôl′)	Can. (Quebec In.)	47·07 N	70·52 W
126	St. Florent, Golfe de (G.)	Cor.	42·55 N	9·08 E
122	St. Florent-sur-Cher (sän′ flô-rän′sür-shâr′)	Fr.	46·58 N	2·15 E
122	St. Flour (sän flōōr′)	Fr.	45·02 N	3·09 E
85	Ste. Foy (sänt fwä)	Can. (Quebec In.)	46·45 N	71·20 W
73	St. Francis (R.) (sänt frăn′sĭs)	Ark.	35·56 N	90·27 W
82	St. Francis (frän′sĭs)	Can.	45·55 N	72·25 W
81	St. Francis L. (sän frän′sĭs)	Can.	45·00 N	74·20 W
85	St. François (sän′frän-swä′)	Can. (Quebec In.)	47·01 N	70·49 W
122	St. Gaudens (gō-dăns′)	Fr.	43·07 N	0·43 E
73	Ste. Genevieve (sänt jěn′ě-věv)	Mo.	37·58 N	90·02 W
160	St. George (sänt jôrj′)	Austl.	28·02 S	148·40 E
82	St. George (sän jôrj′)	Can.	45·08 N	66·49 W
85	St. George (sän′zhôrzh′)	Can. (Toronto In.)	43·14 N	80·15 W
79	St. George (sänt jôrj′)	S. C.	33·11 N	80·35 W
69	St. George	Utah	37·05 N	113·40 W
64	St. George (I.)	Alaska	56·30 N	169·40 W
83	St. George, C.	Can.	48·28 N	59·24 W
78	St. George, C.	Fla.	29·35 N	85·20 W
82	St. Georges (jôrj′ěs)	Can.	46·09 N	70·42 W
83	St. George's	Can.	48·26 N	58·26 W
99	St. Georges	Fr. Gu.	3·48 N	51·47 W
93	St. Georges	Grenada (Le. & Wind. Is. In.)	12·02 N	61·57 W
83	St. Georges B.	Can.	48·28 N	59·00 W
116	St. George's Chan.	Eng.-Ire.	51·45 N	6·30 W
123	St. Germain-en-Laye (sän′ zhěr-män-än-lä′)	Fr. (Paris In.)	48·53 N	2·05 E
85	St. Gervais (zhěr-vě′)	Can. (Quebec In.)	46·43 N	70·53 W
122	St. Girons (zhē-rôn′)	Fr.	42·58 N	1·08 E

Page	Name	Pronunciation	Region	Lat. °'	Long. °'

120 St. Gotthard Tun.
(sȧnt gŏthȧrd) (săN gô-tȧr′)
Switz. 46·38 N 8·55 E
83 St. Gregory, Mt. (sȧnt grĕg′ēr-ė̇)
Can. 49·29 N 58·14 W
163 St. Helena (I.)........Atl. O. 16·01 S 5·16 W
166 St. Helena B..............Afr. 32·25 S 17·15 E
110 St. Helens (sȧnt hĕl′ĕnz).....Eng. 53·27 N 2·44 W
65 St. Helens (hĕl′ĕnz)
Ore. (Portland In.) 45·52 N 122·49 W
66 St. Helens, Mt.........Wash. 46·13 N 122·10 W
122 St. Hélier (hyĕl′yēr)....Chan. Is. 49·12 N 2·06 W
85 St. Henri (săN′ hĕn′rė̇)
Can. (Quebec In.) 46·41 N 71·04 W
85 St. Hermas (hĕr′mȧs)
Can. (Montreal In.) 45·37 N 74·11 W
81 St. Hyacinthe
(săN′ tê-ȧ-săNt′) (sȧnt hī′ȧ-sĭnth)
Can. 45·35 N 72·55 W
71 St. Ignace (sȧnt ĭg′nȧs)....Mich. 45·51 N 84·39 W
71 St. Ignace (I.) (săN′ ĭg′nȧs)..Can. 48·47 N 88·14 W
82 St. Irenee (săN′ tē-rȧ-nā′)....Can. 47·34 N 70·15 W
85 St. Isidore
(saN′ tē-zė̇-dōr′) (săNt ĭz′ĭ-dôr)
Can. (Montreal In.) 45·18 N 73·41 W
85 St. Isidore-de-Prescott
(săN′ ĭz′ĭ-dôr-prĕs-kŏt)
Can. (Ottawa In.) 45·23 N 74·54 W
85 St. Isidore-Dorchester
(dôr-chĕs′tēr).Can. (Quebec In.) 46·35 N 71·05 W
74 St. Jacob (jā-kŏb)
Ill. (St. Louis In.) 38·43 N 89·46 W
85 St. Jacques-le-Mineur
(sĕN zhȧk-lĕ-mē-nûr)
Can. (Montreal In.) 45·16 N 73·25 W
71 St. James (sȧnt jāmz′).....Minn. 43·58 N 94·37 W
73 St. James.................Mo. 37·59 N 91·37 W
85 St. Janvier (săN′ zhän-vyā′)
Can. (Montreal In.) 45·43 N 73·56 W
81 St. Jean (săN′ zhän′).......Can. 45·20 N 73·15 W
82 St. Jean..............Can. 48·51 N 67·07 W
85 St. Jean....Can. (Quebec In.) 46·55 N 70·54 W
85 St. Jean Chrysostome
(krĭ′zōs-tōm′).Can. (Quebec In.) 46·43 N 71·12 W
122 St. Jean-d'Angely (dän-zhȧ-lē′)
Fr. 45·56 N 0·33 W
122 St. Jean de Luz (dē lüz′)......Fr. 43·23 N 1·40 W
85 St. Jerome
(sȧnt jĕ-rōm′) (săN zhä-rōm′)
Can. (Montreal In.) 45·47 N 74·00 W
85 St. Joachim (sȧnt jō′ȧ-kĭm)
Can. (Quebec In.) 47·04 N 70·51 W
82 St. John..................Can. 45·19 N 66·04 W
75 St. John (sȧnt jŏn)
Ind. (Chicago In.) 41·27 N 87·29 W
72 St. John.................Kans. 37·59 N 98·44 W
70 St. John................N. D. 48·57 N 99·42 W
82 St. John (R.)............Can. 46·39 N 67·40 W
83 St. John, C...............Can. 49·59 N 55·20 W
89 St. John (I.)....Vir. Is. (U. S. A.)
(Puerto Rico In.) 18·16 N 64·48 W
82 St. John, L..............Can. 48·45 N 71·40 W
69 St. Johns (jŏnz)........Ariz. 34·30 N 109·25 W
83 St. John's (jŏns)........Can. 47·34 N 52·40 W
80 St. Johns...............Mich. 43·05 N 84·35 W
93 St. Johns
Antigua (Le. & Wind. Is. In.) 17·07 N 61·50 W
79 St. Johns (R.)...........Fla. 30·24 N 81·32 W
81 St. Johnsbury (jŏnz′bĕr-ė̇)...Vt. 44·25 N 72·00 W
82 St. Joseph (jō′zŭf)........Can. 46·17 N 70·52 W
80 St. Joseph................Mich. 42·05 N 86·30 W
73 St. Joseph (sȧnt jô-sĕf′)......Mo. 39·44 N 94·49 W
53 St. Joseph
Dominica (Le. & Wind. Is. In.) 15·25 N 61·26 W
80 St. Joseph (I.)...........Can. 46·15 N 83·55 W
87 St. Joseph (L.) (jō′zhŭf)....Can. 51·31 N 90·40 W
78 St. Joseph, B. (jō′zhŭf).....Fla. 29·48 N 85·26 W
80 St. Joseph (R.) (sȧnt jô′sĕf) Mich. 41·45 N 85·50 W
85 St. Joseph du Lac
(sĕN zhō-zĕf′ dü lȧk)
Can. (Montreal In.) 45·32 N 74·00 W
77 St. Joseph I. (sȧnt jô-sĕf′)....Tex. 27·58 N 96·50 W
122 St. Junien (săN′zhü-nyăN′)....Fr. 45·53 N 0·54 E
85 Ste. Justine (sȧnt jŭs-tēn′)
Can. (Montreal In.) 45·22 N 74·22 W
116 St. Kilda (I.) (kĭl′dȧ)......Scot. 57·10 N 8·32 W
St. Kitts I., see St. Christopher I.
85 St. Lambert
(săN′ läN-bĕr′) (sȧnt lăm′bĕrt)
Can. (Montreal In.) 45·29 N 73·29 W
85 St. Lambert....Can. (Quebec In.) 46·35 N 71·12 W
85 St. Laurent (săN′ lō-ränt′)
Can. (Montreal In.) 45·31 N 73·41 W
85 St. Laurent....Can. (Quebec In.) 46·52 N 71·00 W
99 St. Laurent..........Fr. Gu. 5·27 N 53·56 W
83 St. Lawrence (sȧnt lô′rĕns)....Can. 46·54 N 55·23 W
64 St. Lawrence (I.) (sȧnt lô′rĕns)
Alaska 63·10 N 172·12 W
87 St. Lawrence Is. Natl. Park..Can. 44·30 N 75·38 W
87 St. Lawrence R. (sȧnt lô′rĕns)
Can.-U. S. A. 48·24 N 69·03 W
85 St. Lazare (săN′ lȧ-zȧr′)
Can. (Montreal In.) 45·24 N 74·08 W
85 St. Lazare....Can. (Quebec In.) 46·39 N 70·48 W
123 St. Léger-en-Yvelines
(săN-lā-zhĕ′ĕN-nēv-lēn′)
Fr. (Paris In.) 48·43 N 1·45 E
82 St. Leonard (sȧnt lĕn′ȧrd)..Can. 47·09 N 67·53 W
122 St. Léonard-de-Noblat
(săN′ lā-ô-nȧr′dĕ-nô-blä′).Fr. 45·51 N 1·30 E
85 St. Lin (săN′ lăn′)
Can. (Montreal In.) 45·51 N 73·46 W
122 Saint-Lô (săN′lō′)........Fr. 49·08 N 1·07 W
85 St. Louis (săN′ lōō-ē′)
Can. (Montreal In.) 45·13 N 74·00 W
80 St. Louis (sȧnt lōō′ĭs)......Mich. 43·25 N 84·35 W

74 St. Louis (sȧnt lōō′ĭs) (lōō′ē)
Mo. (St. Louis In.) 38·39 N 90·15 W
164 St. Louis.............Senegal 16·08 N 16·29 W
85 St. Louis, Lac (L.) (săN′ lōō-ē′)
Can. (Montreal In.) 45·24 N 73·51 W
71 St. Louis (R.) (sȧnt lōō′ĭs)..Minn. 46·57 N 92·58 W
74 St. Louis Park...........Minn.
(Minneapolis, St. Paul In.) 44·56 N 93·21 W
93 St. Lucia Chan. (lū′shĭ-ȧ)
N. A. (Le. & Wind. Is. In.) 14·15 N 61·00 W
93 St. Lucia I.
N. A. (Le. & Wind. Is. In.) 13·54 N 60·40 W
79 St. Lucie Can. (lū′sē).....Fla. (In.) 26·57 N 80·25 W
116 St. Magnus B. (măg′nŭs)....Scot. 60·25 N 2·09 W
122 St. Maixent (săN′ mĕk-säN′)...Fr. 46·25 N 0·12 W
122 St. Malo (săN′ mȧ-lō′)......Fr. 48·40 N 2·02 W
122 St. Malo, Golfe de (G.)
(gōlf-dĕ-săN-mȧ-lō′).Fr. 48·50 N 2·49 W
95 St. Marc (săN′ mȧrk′).......Hai. 19·10 N 72·40 W
95 St.-Marc, Canal de (Chan.)..Hai. 19·05 N 73·15 W
123 St. Marcellin (mȧr-sĕ-lăN′)....Fr. 45·08 N 5·15 E
82 Ste. Marie (sȧnt′ mȧ-rē′)....Can. 46·27 N 71·03 W
167 Ste. Marie (I.)....Malag. Rep. 16·58 N 50·15 W
167 Ste. Marie, Cap (C.) Malag. Rep. 25·31 S 45·00 E
123 Ste. Marie aux Mines
(săN′tĕ-mȧ-rē′ō-mēn′).Fr. 48·14 N 7·08 E
66 St. Maries (sȧnt mȧ′rēs)....Idaho 47·18 N 116·34 W
82 St. Margarets (sȧnt mȧr′gȧ-rĕts)
Can. 44·25 N 63·35 W
85 Ste. Martine..Can. (Montreal In.) 45·14 N 73·37 W
93 St. Martin I. (mȧr′tĭn)
N. A. (Le. & Wind. Is. In.) 18·06 N 62·54 W
82 St. Martins (mȧr′tĭnz).......Can. 45·24 N 65·32 W
77 St. Martinville (mȧr′tĭn-vĭl)...La. 30·08 N 91·50 W
82 St. Mary B. (mā′rē).........Can. 44·22 N 66·09 W
160 St. Marys (mā′rēz)........Austl. 41·40 S 148·10 E
80 St. Marys................Ga. 43·15 N 81·10 W
79 St. Marys................Ga. 30·43 N 81·35 W
73 St. Mary's..............Kans. 39·12 N 96·03 W
80 St. Marys................Ohio 40·30 N 84·25 W
81 St. Marys................Pa. 41·25 N 78·30 W
80 St. Marys (mā′rēz)........W. Va. 39·20 N 81·15 W
79 St. Marys (R.).........Ga.-Fla. 30·37 N 82·05 W
83 St. Mary's B..............Can. 46·52 N 53·53 W
83 St. Marys................Can. 50·19 N 59·17 W
74 St. Marys R.
Can.-U. S. (Sault Ste. Marie In.) 46·27 N 84·33 W
79 St. Mathew (măth′ū).......S. C. 33·40 N 80·46 W
85 St. Mathieu (sĕN măt-yû)
Can. (Montreal In.) 45·19 N 73·32 W
64 St. Matthew (I.)........Alaska 60·25 N 172·10 W
75 St. Matthews (măth′ūz)
Ky. (Louisville In.) 38·15 N 85·39 W
123 St. Maur-des-Fossés
Fr. (Paris In.) 48·48 N 2·29 E
82 St. Maurice (R.)
(săN′ mô-rēs′) (sȧnt mô′rĭs)
Can. 47·20 N 72·55 W
64 St. Michael (sȧnt mĭ′kĕl)..Alaska 63·22 N 162·20 W
85 St. Michel (săN′ mė̇-shĕl′)
Can. (Montreal In.) 45·14 N 73·34 W
85 St. Michel....Can. (Quebec In.) 46·52 N 70·54 W
85 St. Michel, Bras (R.)
Can. (Quebec In.) 46·48 N 70·51 W
95 St. Michel-de-l'Atalaye......Hai. 19·25 N 72·20 W
123 St. Mihiel (săN′ mē-yĕl′)......Fr. 48·53 N 5·30 E
122 St. Mitre (săN mēt-rĕ′)
Fr. (Marseille In.) 43·27 N 5·02 E
120 St. Moritz
(sȧnt mō′rĭts) (zäNkt mō′rĕts)
Switz. 46·31 N 9·50 E
122 St. Nazaire-Trignac
(săN′nȧ-zȧr′trēn-yȧĸ).Fr. 47·18 N 2·13 W
85 St. Nérée (nā-rā′)
Can. (Quebec In.) 46·43 N 70·43 W
85 St. Nicolas (ne-kô-lȧ′)
Can. (Quebec In.) 46·42 N 71·23 W
95 St. Nicolas, Cap (C.)......Haí. 19·45 N 73·35 W
85 St. Norbert (sȧnt nôr′bĕrt)
Can. (Winnipeg In.) 49·46 N 97·09 W
122 St. Omer (săN′tô-mâr′).......Fr. 50·44 N 2·16 E
82 St. Pascal................Can. 47·30 N 69·49 W
86 St. Paul (sȧnt pôl′).........Can. 53·58 N 111·30 W
74 St. Paul.................Minn.
(Minneapolis, St. Paul In.) 44·57 N 93·05 W
70 St. Paul.................Nebr. 41·13 N 98·28 W
64 St. Paul (I.)............Alaska 57·10 N 170·20 W
83 St. Paul (I.)............Can. 47·14 N 60·08 W
47 St. Paul I.............Ind. O. 38·43 S 77·31 E
74 St. Paul Park (pȧrk).......Minn.
(Minneapolis, St. Paul In.) 44·51 N 93·00 W
79 St. Pauls (pôls)..........N. C. 34·47 N 78·57 W
71 St. Peter (pē′tēr).........Minn. 44·20 N 93·56 W
82 St. Peter, L. (pē′tēr)......Can. 46·07 N 72·42 W
83 St. Peters...............Can. 45·43 N 60·50 W
79 St. Petersburg (pē′tērz-bûrg)
Fla. (In.) 27·47 N 82·38 W
85 Ste. Pétronille (sĕNt pĕt-rō-nēl′)
Can. (Quebec In.) 46·51 N 71·08 W
85 St. Philémon (sĕN fēl-mōN′)
Can. (Quebec In.) 46·41 N 70·28 W
85 Ste. Philomene (sȧNt fē-lô-mân′)
Can. (Quebec In.) 45·19 N 73·45 W
85 St. Philippe (săN′ fė̇-lēp′)
Can. (Montreal In.) 45·19 N 73·28 W
85 St. Philippe..Can. (Montreal In.) 45·38 N 74·25 W
85 St. Pierre (săN′ pyâr′)
Can. (Quebec In.) 46·53 N 71·04 W
85 St. Pierre....Can. (Quebec In.) 46·55 N 70·37 W
122 St. Pierre (sȧnt pyâr′) (săN′ pyâr′)
Chan. Is. 49·27 N 2·35 W
93 St. Pierre
N. A. (Le. & Wind. Is. In.) 14·45 N 61·12 W
83 St. Pierre (I.)...........Can. 46·46 N 56·14 W
85 St. Placide (plȧs′ĭd)
Can. (Montreal In.) 45·32 N 74·11 W

122 St. Pol-de-Léon (săN-pô′dĕ-lā-ôN′)
Fr. 48·41 N 4·00 W
120 St. Pölten (zäNkt-pûl′tĕn)....Aus. 48·12 N 15·38 E
122 St. Quentin (săN′kän-tăN′)....Fr. 49·52 N 3·16 E
85 St. Raphaél (rȧ-fȧ-él′)
Can. (Quebec In.) 46·48 N 70·46 W
82 St. Raymond
(săN′ rā-môN′) (sȧnt rā′mŭnd)
Can. 46·50 N 71·51 W
85 St. Rédempteur (săN rā-dāNp-tûr′)
Can. (Montreal In.) 45·26 N 74·23 W
85 St. Rédempteur
Can. (Quebec In.) 46·42 N 71·18 W
85 St. Rémi (sĕN rĕ-mē′)
Can. (Montreal In.) 45·15 N 73·36 W
85 St. Romuald (săN′ rô-mü-àl′)
Can. (Quebec In.) 46·45 N 71·14 W
84 St. Rosalie (sȧnt rŏz′ȧ-lē)
La. (New Orleans In.) 29·40 N 89·58 W
85 Ste. Rose (săNt rōz′)
Can. (Montreal In.) 45·37 N 73·47 W
93 Ste. Rose
Basse Terre (Le. & Wind. Is. In.) 16·19 N 61·45 W
122 Saintes.................Fr. 45·44 N 0·41 W
85 Ste. Scholastique (skô-làs-tēk′)
Can. 45·39 N 74·05 W
122 St. Servan-sur-Mer (sĕr-väN′)..Fr. 48·37 N 1·59 W
82 St. Simeon................Can. 47·51 N 69·55 W
85 St. Stanislas-de Kostka
(sĕN stȧ-nēs-lȧz′ de kŏst′kȧ)
Can. (Montreal In.) 45·11 N 74·08 W
82 St. Stephen (stē′vĕn).......Can. 45·12 N 65·17 W
85 St. Sulpice..Can. (Montreal In.) 45·50 N 73·21 W
85 St. Therese de Blainville
(tĕ-rĕz′ dĕ blĕN-vēl′)
Can. (Monteral In.) 45·38 N 73·51 W
80 St. Thomas (tŏm′ȧs)........Can. 42·45 N 81·15 W
St. Thomas, see Charlotte
Amalie
89 St. Thomas (I.).........Vir. Is.
(U. S. A.) (St. Thomas In.) 18·22 N 64·57 W
89 St. Thomas Hbr. (tŏm′ȧs). Vir. Is.
(U. S. A.) (St. Thomas In.) 18·19 N 64·56 W
85 St. Timothee (tĕ-mô-tā′)
Can. (Montreal In.) 45·17 N 74·03 W
123 St. Tropez (trô-pĕ′).........Fr. 43·15 N 6·42 E
85 St. Urbain....Can. (Montreal In.) 45·14 N 73·44 W
85 St. Valentin (văl-ĕn-tĭn)
Can. (Montreal In.) 45·07 N 73·19 W
122 St. Valéry (vȧ-lā-rē′)........Fr. 50·10 N 1·39 E
85 St. Vallier (văl-yā′)
Can. (Quebec In.) 46·54 N 70·49 W
120 St. Veit (zäNkt vīt′)........Aus. 46·46 N 14·20 E
82 St. Victor (vĭk′tēr)........Can. 46·09 N 70·56 W
160 St. Vincent, G. (vĭn′sĕnt)...Austl. 34·55 S 138·00 E
85 St. Vincent-de-Paul
(săN′ văn-săN′ dĕ pôl′)
Can. (Montreal In.) 45·37 N 73·39 W
93 St. Vincent I.
N. A. (Le. & Wind. Is. In.) 13·14 N 60·50 W
93 St. Vincent Pass.
N. A. (Le. & Wind. Is. In.) 13·35 N 61·10 W
86 St. Walburg..............Can. 53·40 N 109·10 W
69 St. Xavier Ind. Res. (x-ā′vĭ′ēr)
Ariz. 32·07 N 111·12 W
122 St. Yrieix (ē-rē-ĕ′).........Fr. 45·30 N 1·08 E
153 Saitama (Pref.) (sī′tä-mä)
Jap. (Tōkyō In.) 35·52 N 139·40 E
136 Saitbaba (sä-ĕt′bá-bà)
Sov. Un. (Urals In.) 54·06 N 56·42 E
98 Sajama, Nevada (Pk.)
(nĕ-vá′dä-sä-hä′mä) Bol. 18·13 S 68·53 W
153 Sakai (sä′kä-ē)...Jap. (Ōsaka In.) 34·34 N 135·28 E
144 Sakākah................Sau. Ar. 29·58 N 40·03 E
166 Sakania (sä-kä′nĭ-ȧ)......Con. L. 12·41 S 28·39 E
133 Sakarya (sä-kär′yȧ)......Tur. 40·10 N 31·00 E
152 Sakata (sä′kä-tä)..........Jap. 38·56 N 139·57 E
152 Sakchu (säk′chōō).........Kor. 40·29 N 125·09 E
135 Sakhalin (I.) (sä-kä-lēn′).Sov. Un. 51·52 N 144·15 E
119 Šakiai (sä`kĭ-ī).........Sov. Un. 54·59 N 23·05 E
151 Sakishima-Gunto (Is.)
(sä′kė̇-shē′ma gōōn′tō′)
Ryūkyū Is. 24·25 N 125·00 E
133 Sakmara (R.)............Sov. Un. 52·00 N 56·10 E
84 Sakomet R. (sä-kō′mĕt)
R. I. (Providence In.) 41·32 N 71·11 W
165 Sak'ot'ā.................Eth. 12·47 N 38·59 E
94 Sal, Cay (I.) (kē sàl)....Ba. Is. 23·45 N 80·25 W
133 Sal (R.) (säl)...........Sov. Un. 47·20 N 42·10 E
118 Sala (sö′lä)..............Swe. 59·56 N 16·34 E
126 Sala Consilina (sä′lä kôn-sē-lē′nä)
It. 40·24 N 15·38 E
68 Salada, Laguna (L.)
(lä-gōō′nä-sä-lä′dä) Mex. 32·34 N 115·45 W
101 Saladillo
Arg. (Buenos Aires In.) 35·38 S 59·48 W
92 Salado (sä-lä′dhō)........Hond. 15·44 N 87·03 W
100 Salado (sä-lä′dō) (R.)......Arg. 26·05 S 63·35 W
101 Salado (R.)
Arg. (Buenos Aires In.) 35·53 S 58·12 W
91 Salado (R.) (sä-lä′dō).....Mex. 18·30 N 97·29 W
76 Salado, Rio (R.) (rē′ō).....Mex. 26·55 N 99·36 W
74 Salado Cr.
Tex. (San Antonio In.) 29·23 N 98·25 W
76 Salado de los Nadadores Rio (R.)
(dĕ-lôs-nä-dä-dō′rĕs) Mex. 27·26 N 101·35 W
154 Salajar (I.)............Indon. 6·15 S 121·15 E
92 Salamá (sä-lä-mä′)........Guat. 15·06 N 90·19 W
92 Salamá (sä-lä-mä′)........Hond. 14·43 N 86·30 W
101 Salamanca
Chile (Santiago In.) 31·48 S 70·57 W
90 Salamanca................Chile 20·36 N 101·10 W
81 Salamanca (săl-ȧ-măn′kȧ)..N. Y. 42·10 N 78·45 W
124 Salamanca (sä-lä-mä′n-kä)....Sp. 40·54 N 5·42 W

ăt; fĭnȧl; rāte; senȧte; ȧrm; ȧsk; sofȧ; fâre; ch-choose; dh-as th in other; bē; ĕvent; bĕt; recĕnt; cratēr; g-go; gh-guttural g; bĭt; ĭ-short neutral; rīde; ĸ-guttural k as ch in German ich;

Page	Name Pronunciation Region	Lat. °′	Long. °′
165	Salamat, Bahr (R.) (bär sä-lä-mät').Chad.	10·06 N	19·16 E
155	Salamaua (sä-lä-mä'wȧ) N. Gui. Ter.	6·50 S	146·55 E
98	Salamina (sä-lä-mē'-nä).Col. (In.)	5·25 N	75·29 W
127	Salamis (săl'ȧ-mĭs)..........Grc.	37·58 N	23·30 E
98	Salaverry (sä-lä-vā'rê).......Peru	8·16 S	78·54 W
155	Salawati (I.) (sä-lä-wä'tê) W. Irian	1·22 S	130·15 E
157	Sala-y-Gómez (I.)..........Chile	26·50 S	105·50 W
95	Salcedo (säl-sā'dō)....Dom. Rep.	19·25 N	70·30 W
98	Saldaña (R.) (säl-dȧ'n-yä) Col. (In.)	3·42 N	75·16 W
166	Saldanha................S. Afr.	32·55 S	18·05 E
119	Saldus (sȧl'dŏŏs)........Sov. Un.	56·39 N	22·30 E
160	Sale (sāl).................Austl.	38·10 S	147·07 E
110	Sale.......................Eng.	53·24 N	2·20 W
164	Salé (sȧ-lā').................Mor.	34·09 N	6·42 W
85	Sale, Riviére (R.) (sȧl'rê-vyâr') Can. (Winnipeg In.)	49·44 N	97·11 W
132	Salekhard (sŭ-lyĭ-kärt)...Sov. Un.	66·35 N	66·50 E
80	Salem (sā'lĕm)...............Ill.	38·40 N	89·00 W
143	Salem.....................India	11·39 N	78·11 E
80	Salem......................Ind.	38·35 N	86·00 W
83	Salem........Mass. (Boston In.)	42·31 N	70·54 W
73	Salem......................Mo.	37·36 N	91·33 W
83	Salem........N. H. (Boston In.)	42·46 N	71·16 W
81	Salem......................N. J.	39·35 N	75·30 W
80	Salem.....................Ohio	40·55 N	80·50 W
66	Salem......................Ore.	44·55 N	123·03 W
70	Salem......................S. D.	43·43 N	97·23 W
167	Salem.........S. Afr. (Natal In.)	33·29 S	26·30 E
79	Salem......................Va.	37·16 N	80·05 W
80	Salem....................W. Va.	39·15 N	80·35 W
126	Salemi (sä-lâ'mē).............It.	37·48 N	38·50 E
125	Salerno (sä-lĕr'nô) It. (Naples In.)	40·27 N	14·46 E
126	Salerno, Golfo di (G.) (gôl-fô-dē) It.	40·30 N	14·40 E
110	Salford (săl'fẽrd)...........Eng.	53·26 N	2·19 W
129	Salgir (R.) (sȧl'gēr)......Sov. Un.	45·25 N	34·22 E
121	Salgōtarjan (shôl'gô-tôr-yăn) Hung.	48·06 N	19·50 E
72	Salida (sȧ-lī'dȧ)............Colo.	38·31 N	106·01 W
122	Salies (sȧ-lēs')...............Fr.	43·27 N	0·58 W
73	Salina (sȧ-lī'nȧ)...........Kans.	38·50 N	97·37 W
69	Salina.....................Utah	39·00 N	111·55 W
126	Salina (I.) (sä-lē'nă)..........It.	38·35 N	14·48 E
95	Salina Pt................Ba. Is.	22·10 N	74·20 W
91	Salina Cruz (sä-lē'nä krōōz').Mex.	16·10 N	95·12 W
68	Salinas (sȧ-lē'nȧs)..........Calif.	36·41 N	121·40 W
90	Salinas....................Mex.	22·38 N	101·42 W
89	Salinas...P. R. (Puerto Rico In.)	17·58 N	66·16 W
68	Salinas (R.)...............Calif.	36·33 N	121·29 W
91	Salinas (R.) (sä-lê'nȧs)......Mex.	16·15 N	90·31 W
92	Salinas, Bahia de (B.) (bä-ē'ä-dĕ-sȧ-lē'nȧs).Nic.-C. R.	11·05 N	85·55 W
125	Salinas, Cape (sä-lênȁs)......Sp..	39·14 N	1·02 E
76	Salinas Victoria (sä-lē'näs vêk-tō'rê-ȁ).Mex.	25·59 N	100·19 W
73	Saline (R.) (sȧ-lēn').........Ark.	34·06 N	92·30 W
72	Saline (R.)................Kans.	39·05 N	99·43 W
123	Salins-les-Bains (sȧ-lȧN'-lā-bȧN') Fr.	46·55 N	5·54 E
166	Salisbury................S. Rh.	17·49 S	30·52 E
116	Salisbury (sôlz'bē-rê)........Eng.	50·35 N	1·51 W
82	Salisbury.................Can.	46·03 N	65·05 W
81	Salisbury..................Md.	38·20 N	75·40 W
73	Salisbury..................Mo.	39·24 N	92·47 W
79	Salisbury.................N. C.	35·40 N	80·29 W
87	Salisbury (I.)..............Can.	63·36 N	76·20 W
116	Salisbury Plain............Eng.	51·15 N	1·52 W
164	Sal I. (säal).......C. V. Is. (In.)	16·45 N	22·39 W
79	Salkehatchie (R.) (sô-kê-hăch'ê) S. C.	33·09 N	81·10 W
73	Sallisaw (săl'ĭ-sô)...........Okla.	35·27 N	94·48 W
67	Salmon (săm'ŭn)...........Idaho	45·11 N	113·54 W
66	Salmon Falls R............Idaho	42·22 N	114·53 W
158	Salmon Gums (gŭmz)......Austl.	33·00 S	122·00 E
82	Salmon (R.)...............Can.	46·19 N	65·36 W
81	Salmon (R.)...............N. Y.	44·35 N	74·15 W
65	Salmon (R.).Wash. (Portland In.)	45·44 N	122·36 W
66	Salmon R..................Idaho	45·30 N	115·45 W
66	Salmon R., Middle Fork....Idaho	44·54 N	114·50 W
66	Salmon R., South Fork.....Idaho	44·51 N	115·47 W
66	Salmon River Mts.........Idaho	44·15 N	115·44 W
123	Salon-de-Provence (sȧ-lôN-dē-prô-văNs').Fr.	43·48 N	5·09 E
121	Salonta (sä-lôn'tă).........Rom.	46·46 N	21·38 E
133	Sal'sk (sälsk)...........Sov. Un.	46·30 N	41·20 E
69	Salt, (R.) (sôlt)............Ariz.	33·28 N	111·35 W
73	Salt (R.)....................Mo.	39·54 N	92·11 W
100	Salta (säl'tä)................Arg.	24·50 S	65·16 W
100	Salta (Prov.)...............Arg.	25·15 S	65·00 W
74	Saltair (sôlt'âr) Utah (Salt Lake City In.)	40·46 N	112·09 W
95	Salt Cay (I.)...Turks & Caicos Is.	21·20 N	71·15 W
75	Salt Cr. (sôlt)...Ill. (Chicago In.)	42·01 N	88·01 W
76	Saltillo (säl-tēl'yō)..........Mex.	25·24 N	100·59 W
74	Salt Lake City (sôlt lāk sĭ'tĭ) Utah (Salt Lake City In.)	40·45 N	111·52 W
101	Salto (säl'tō) Arg. (Buenos Aires In.)	34·17 S	60·15 W
100	Salto......................Ur.	31·18 S	57·45 W
101	Salto, Serra do (Mtn.) (sĕ'r-rä-dô) Braz. (Rio de Janeiro In.)	20·26 S	43·28 W
90	Salto (R.).................Mex.	22·16 N	99·18 W
99	Salto Grande (grän'dā).....Braz.	22·57 S	49·58 W
68	Salton Sea (sôlt'ŭn)........Calif.	33·28 N	115·43 W
164	Saltpond.................Ghana	5·16 N	1·07 W
69	Salt River Ind. Res. (sôlt rĭv'ẽr) Ariz.	33·40 N	112·01 W
95	Saltrou (sȧl-trōō')...........Hai.	18·15 N	72·00 W
118	Saltsjöbaden (sält'shû-bäd'ĕn) Swe.	59·15 N	18·20 E
79	Saltville (sôlt'vĭl)............Va.	36·50 N	81·45 W
136	Saltykovka (sȧl-tē'kôf-kȧ) Sov. Un. (Moscow In.)	55·45 N	37·56 E
88	Salud, Mt. (sä-lōō'th) Pan. (Panama Canal In.)	9·14 N	79·42 W
79	Saluda (sȧ-lōō'dȧ)..........S. C.	34·02 N	81·46 W
79	Saluda (R.)................S. C.	34·07 N	81·48 W
126	Saluzzo (sä-lōōt'sō)...........It.	44·39 N	7·31 E
99	Salvador (Bahia) (säl-vă-dōr') (bă-ē'ȧ).Braz.	12·59 S	38·27 W
77	Salvador L..................La.	29·45 N	90·20 W
94	Salvador Pt..............Ba. Is.	24·30 N	77·45 W
90	Salvatierra (säl-vä-tyĕr'rä)..Mex.	20·13 N	100·52 W
146	Salween R. (săl-wēn')........Bur.	26·46 N	98·19 E
133	Sal'yany...............Sov. Un.	39·40 N	49·10 E
120	Salzburg (sälts'bŏŏrgh)......Aus.	47·48 N	13·04 E
120	Salzburg (State)............Aus.	47·30 N	13·18 E
120	Salzwedel (sälts-vā'dĕl)......Ger.	52·51 N	11·10 E
168	Samālūt (sä-mä-lōōt') U. A. R. (Nile In.)	28·17 N	30·43 E
95	Samaná (sä-mä-nä')...Dom. Rep.	19·15 N	69·25 W
95	Samana, Cabo (C.) (kȧ'bô) Dom. Rep.	19·20 N	69·00 W
95	Samana or Atwood Cay (I.) Ba. Is.	23·05 N	73·45 W
155	Samar (I.) (sä'mär).........Phil.	11·30 N	126·07 E
133	Samara (R.)............Sov. Un.	52·50 N	50·35 E
129	Samara (R.) (sȧ-mä'rȧ)..Sov. Un.	48·47 N	35·30 E
155	Samarai (sä-mä-rä'ê)........Pap.	10·45 S	150·49 E
134	Samarkand (sȧ-mȧr-kănt') Sov. Un.	39·42 N	67·00 E
142	Sambalpur (sŭm'bŭl-pŏŏr)..India	21·30 N	84·05 E
142	Sāmbhar (R.)..............India	27·00 N	74·58 E
121	Sambor (säm'bôr).......Sov. Un.	49·31 N	23·12 E
101	Samborombón, Bahia (B.) (bä-ē'ä-säm-bô-rôm-bô'n) Arg. (Buenos Aires In.)	35·57 S	57·05 W
101	Samborombón (R.) Arg. (Buenos Aires In.)	35·20 S	57·52 W
117	Sambre (R.) (säN'br')........Bel.	50·20 N	4·15 E
65	Sammamish, L. (sȧ-măm'ĭsh) Wash. (Seattle In.)	47·35 N	122·02 W
65	Sammamish (R.) Wash. (Seattle In.)	47·43 N	122·08 W
127	Samokov (sä'mô-kôf)........Bul.	42·20 N	23·33 E
125	Samora Correia (sä-mô'rä-kôr-rĕ'yă) Port. (Lisbon In.)	38·55 N	8·52 W
134	Samorovo (sȧ-mȧ-rô'vô).Sov. Un.	60·47 N	69·13 E
127	Sámos (I.) (să'mŏs).........Grc.	37·53 N	26·35 E
127	Samothráki (I.).............Grc.	40·23 N	25·10 E
155	Sampaloc Pt. (säm-pă'lôk) Phil. (Manila In.)	14·43 N	119·56 E
118	Samsø (I.) (săm'sû).........Den.	55·49 N	10·47 E
78	Samson (săm'sŭn)...........Ala.	31·06 N	86·02 W
152	Samsu (säm'sōō')...........Kor.	41·12 N	128·00 E
133	Samsun (sȧm'sōōn')..........Tur.	41·20 N	36·05 E
133	Samtredia (sȧm'trĕ-dê)..Sov. Un.	42·18 N	42·25 E
65	Samuel (I.) (sȧm'ū-ĕl) Can. (Vancouver In.)	48·50 N	123·10 W
133	Samur (R.) (sä-mōōr')...Sov. Un.	41·40 N	47·20 E
164	San (sän)...................Mali	13·37 N	4·45 W
144	San'a (sän'ä)............Yemen	15·45 N	44·00 E
164	Sanaga R. (sä-nä'gä).......Cam.	4·33 N	11·50 E
96	San Ambrosio, Isla de (I.) (ê's-lä-dĕ-sän äm-brō'zê-ō).Chile	26·40 S	80·00 W
155	Sanana (I.)...............Indon.	2·15 S	126·38 E
144	Sanandaj..................Iran	36·44 N	46·43 E
68	San Andreas (săn ăn'drê-ăs).Calif.	38·10 N	120·42 W
65	San Andreas (L.) Calif. (San Francisco In.)	37·36 N	122·26 W
98	San Andrés (sän-än-drĕ's) Col. (In.)	6·57 N	75·41 W
91	San Andrés (sän än-drās') Mex. (Mexico City In.)	19·15 N	99·10 W
91	San Andres, Laguna de (L.).Mex.	22·40 N	97·50 W
62	San Andres, Mts. (săn ăn'drê-ăs) U. S.	33·00 N	106·40 W
	San Andrés, see Petén, Laguna de		
101	San Andrés de Giles (sän-än-drĕ's-dĕ-gē'lĕs) Arg. (Buenos Aires In.)	34·26 S	59·28 W
93	San Andres I..............Col.	12·32 N	81·34 W
69	San Andres Mts.........N. Mex.	23·45 N	106·40 W
91	San Andrés Tuxtla (sän-än-drā's-tōōs'tlä).Mex.	18·27 N	95·12 W
76	San Angelo (săn ăn'jĕ-lō)....Tex.	31·28 N	100·22 W
126	San Antioco, I. di (ê'sō-lä-dē-sän-ăn-tyŏ'kô).It.	39·00 N	8·25 E
101	San Antonio (sän-ȧn-tô'nyō) Chile (Santiago In.)	33·34 S	71·36 W
98	San Antonio..........Col. (In.)	2·57 N	75·06 W
98	San Antonio..........Col. (In.)	3·55 N	75·38 W
155	San Antonio....Phil. (Manila In.)	14·57 N	120·05 E
74	San Antonio (săn ăn-tō'nê-ô) Tex. (San Antonio In.)	29·25 N	98·30 W
68	San Antonio (R.)..........Calif.	36·00 N	121·13 W
94	San Antonio, Cabo (C.) (kȧ'bô-sän-än-tô'nyô).Cuba	21·55 N	84·55 W
125	San Antonio Abad (sän än-tō'nyô ä-bädh').Sp.	38·59 N	1·17 E
77	San Antonio B.............Tex.	28·20 N	97·08 W
101	San Antonio de Areco (dā ä-rā'kô) Arg. (Buenos Aires In.)	34·16 S	59·30 W
95	San Antonio de las Vegas (sän än-tô'nyô-dĕ-läs-vĕ'gäs) Cuba (Havana In.)	22·07 N	82·16 W
95	San Antonio de los Baños (dȧ lōs bän'yōs) Cuba (Havana In.)	22·08 N	82·30 W
100	San Antonio de los Cobres (dȧ lōs kō'brȧs).Arg.	24·15 S	66·29 W
101	San Antônio de Pádua (dĕ-pȧ'dwä) Braz. (Rio de Janeiro In.)	21·32 S	42·09 W
99	San Antonio de Tamanaco (sän-ȧn-tô-nyō-dĕ-tȧ-mä-nȧ'kô) Ven. (In.)	9·42 N	66·03 W
100	San Antonio Oeste (sän-än-tō'nyô ô-ĕs'tȧ).Arg.	40·49 S	64·56 W
74	San Antonio Pk. (săn ăn-tō'nĭ-ô) Calif. (Los Angeles In.)	34·17 N	117·39 W
76	San Antonio R.............Tex.	29·00 N	97·58 W
92	Sanarate (sä-nä-rä'tĕ)......Guat.	14·47 N	90·12 W
77	San Augustine (săn ô'gŭs-tên) Tex.	31·33 N	94·08 W
76	San Bartolo...............Mex.	24·43 N	103·12 W
91	San Bartolo (sän bär-tō'lô) Mex. (Mexico City In.)	19·36 N	99·43 W
126	San Bartolomeo (bär-tô-lô-mā'ô) It.	41·25 N	15·04 E
126	San Benedetto del Tronto (bā'nȧ-dĕt'tô dĕl trōn'tô).It.	42·58 N	13·54 E
77	San Benito (săn bĕ-nē'tô)....Tex.	26·07 N	97·37 W
68	San Benito (R.)...........Calif.	36·40 N	121·20 W
74	San Bernardino (bûr-när-dē'nô) Calif. (Los Angeles In.)	34·07 N	117·19 W
68	San Bernardino Mts.......Calif.	34·05 N	116·23 W
101	San Bernardo (sän bĕr-när'dô) Chile (Santiago In.)	33·35 S	70·42 W
90	San Blas (sän bläs')........Mex.	21·33 N	105·19 W
78	San Blas, C.................Fla.	29·38 N	85·38 W
93	San Blas, Cord. de (Mts.) (kôr-dēl-yĕ'rä-dĕ).Pan.	9·17 N	78·20 W
93	San Blas, Golfo de (G.)......Pan.	9·33 N	78·42 W
93	San Blas, Punta (Pt.).......Pan.	9·35 N	78·55 W
65	San Bruno (sän brū-nô) Calif. (San Francisco In.)	37·38 N	122·25 W
76	San Buenaventura (bwā'nȧ-vĕn-tōō'rȧ).Mex.	27·07 N	101·30 W
65	San Carlos (sän kär'lōs) Calif. (San Francisco In.)	37·30 N	122·15 W
100	San Carlos (sän-kȧ'r-lŏs)....Chile	36·23 S	71·58 W
98	San Carlos............Col. (In.)	6·11 N	74·58 W
91	San Carlos (sän Kär'lōs).....Mex.	17·49 N	92·33 W
76	San Carlos................Mex.	24·36 N	98·52 W
93	San Carlos (sän-kä'r-lôs).....Nic.	11·08 N	84·48 W
155	San Carlos.....Phil. (Manila In.)	15·56 N	120·20 E
98	San Carlos................Ven.	9·36 N	68·35 W
100	San Carlos de Bariloche (sän-kȧ'r lŏs-dĕ-bä-rē-lô'chĕ) Arg.	41·15 S	71·26 W
69	San Carlos Ind. Res. (sän kär'lōs) Ariz.	33·27 N	110·15 W
69	San Carlos Res............Ariz.	33·05 N	110·29 W
93	San Carlos R..............C. R.	10·36 N	84·18 W
99	San Casimiro (kä-sē-mê'rô) Ven. (In.)	10·01 N	67·02 W
126	San Cataldo (kä-täl'dō).......It.	37·30 N	13·59 E
95	Sanchez (sän'chĕz)....Dom. Rep.	19·15 N	69·40 W
90	Sanchez, Río de los (R.) (rê'ō-dĕ-lôs).Mex.	20·31 N	102·29 W
90	Sánchez Román (Tlaltenango) (rô-mȧ'n) (tlä'l-tĕ-nän-gô).Mex.	21·48 N	103·20 W
124	San Clemente (sän klȧ-mĕn'tȧ).Sp.	39·25 N	2·24 W
68	San Clemente (I.).........Calif.	33·02 N	118·36 W
95	San Cristobal (krēs-tô'bäl) Dom. Rep.	18·25 N	70·05 W
92	San Cristóbal.............Guat.	15·22 N	90·26 W
98	San Cristóbal.............Ven.	7·43 N	72·15 W
98	San Cristobal (I.)............Ec.	1·05 S	89·15 W
159	San Cristobal (I.)........Sol. Is.	10·47 S	162·17 E
126	San Croce, C. (krô'chā)..... It.	37·15 N	15·18 E
94	Sancti Spíritus (säŋk'tê spē'rê-tōōs).Cuba	21·55 N	79·25 W
122	Sancy, Puy de (Pk.) (pwē-dĕ-sȧN-sē').Fr.	45·30 N	2·53 E
65	Sand (I.) (sănd) Ore. (Portland In.)	46·16 N	124·01 W
71	Sand (I.)..................Wis.	46·03 N	91·09 W
168	Sand (R.) S. Afr. (Johannesburg & Pretoria In.)	28·09 S	26·46 E
153	Sanda (sän'dä)...Jap. (Ōsaka In.)	34·53 N	135·14 E
154	Sandakan (sȧn-dä'kȧn).....Mala.	5·51 N	118·03 E
116	Sanday (I.) (sănd'ā)........Scot.	59·17 N	2·25 W
110	Sandbach (sănd'băch).......Scot.	53·08 N	2·22 W
118	Sandefjord (sän'dĕ-fyôr')....Nor.	59·09 N	10·14 E
65	San de Fuca (de-fōō-cä) Wash. (Seattle In.)	48·14 N	122·44 W
76	Sanderson (săn'dẽr-sŭn).....Tex.	30·09 N	102·24 W
78	Sandersville (săn'dẽrz-vĭl).....Ga.	32·57 N	82·50 W
167	Sandflats (sănd-flăts) S. Afr. (Natal In.)	33·26 S	25·57 E
118	Sandhammar, C. (sänt'häm-mȧr) Swe.	55·24 N	14·37 E
70	Sand Hills (Reg.) (sănd)....Nebr.	41·57 N	101·29 W
84	Sand Hook (sănd hŏŏk) N. J. (New York In.)	40·29 N	74·05 W
110	Sandhurst (sănd'hûrst) Eng. (London In.)	51·20 N	0·48 W
68	San Diego (săn dê-ā'gô) Calif. (San Diego In.)	32·43 N	117·10 W
76	San Diego.................Tex.	27·47 N	98·13 W
68	San Diego (R.)............Calif.	32·53 N	116·57 W
90	San Diego de la Unión (sän dê-ȧ'gô dȧ lä ōō-nyōn') Mex.	21·27 N	100·52 W
77	Sandies Cr. (sănd'ēz)........Tex.	29·13 N	97·34 W
74	San Dimas (săn dĕ'mȧs) Calif. (Los Angeles In.)	34·07 N	117·49 W
90	San Dimas (dê-mäs')........Mex.	24·08 N	105·57 W
118	Sandnes (sänd'nĕs)..........Nor.	58·52 N	5·44 E
166	Sandoa (sän-dō'ȧ)........Con. L.	9·39 S	23·00 E
121	Sandomierz (sȧn-dô'myĕzh)...Pol.	50·39 N	21·45 E
126	San Donà di Piave (sän dô-nȧ' dê pyä'vĕ).It.	45·38 N	12·34 E
146	Sandoway (sän-dô-wī')......Bur.	18·24 N	94·28 E
66	Sandpoint (sănd point).....Idaho	48·17 N	116·34 W
161	Sandringham (săn'drĭng-ăm) Austl. (Melbourne In.)	37·57 S	145·01 E
126	Sandrio (sä'n-dryô)...........It.	46·11 N	9·53 E
73	Sand Springs (sănd sprĭnz)..Okla.	36·08 N	96·06 W

ng-sing; ŋ-baŋk; N-nasalized n; nŏd; cŏmmit; ōld; ôbey; ôrder; fōōd; fŏŏt; ou-out; s-soft; sh-dish; th-thin; pūre; ûnite; ûrn; stŭd; circŭs; ü-as "y" in study; '-indeterminate vowel.

Page	Name Pronunciation Region	Lat. °′	Long. °′
158	Sandstone (sănd'stōn) . . . . . . Austl.	28·25 S	119·25 E
71	Sandstone . . . . Minn.	46·08 N	92·53 W
84	Sandusky (săn-dŭs'kē) Ala. (Birmingham In.)	33·32 N	86·50 W
80	Sandusky . . . . Mich.	43·25 N	82·50 W
80	Sandusky . . . . Ohio	41·25 N	82·45 W
80	Sandusky (R.) . . . . Ohio	41·10 N	83·20 W
80	Sandwich (sănd'wĭch) . . . . Ill.	42·35 N	88·35 W
65	Sandy (sănd'ē) . Ore. (Portland In.)	45·24 N	122·16 W
74	Sandy . . Utah (Salt Lake City In.)	40·36 N	111·53 W
83	Sandy (I.) . . . . Can.	51·13 N	58·10 W
65	Sandy (R.) . . . . Ore. (Portland In.)	45·28 N	122·17 W
160	Sandy C. . . . . Austl.	24·25 S	153·10 E
67	Sandy Cr. . . . . Mont.	48·20 N	110·08 W
67	Sandy Cr. . . . . Wyo.	42·08 N	109·35 W
84	Sandy Hook (hŏŏk) Conn. (New York In.)	41·25 N	73·17 W
85	Sandy L. . . . Can. (Edmonton In.)	53·46 N	113·58 W
77	Sandy Point . . . . Tex. (In.)	29·22 N	95·27 W
65	Sandy Pt. . Wash. (Vancouver In.)	48·48 N	122·42 W
84	Sandy Springs (sprinz) Ga. (Atlanta In.)	33·55 N	84·23 W
101	San Enrique (sän-ĕn-rē'kĕ) Arg. (Buenos Aires In.)	35·47 S	60·22 W
100	San Estanislao (ĕs-tä-nēs-lä'ô) Par.	24·38 S	56·20 W
92	San Esteban (ĕs-tĕ'bän) . . . . Hond.	15·13 N	85·53 W
155	San Fabian (fä-byä'n) Phil. (Manila In.)	16·14 N	120·28 E
101	San Felipe (fâ-lē'pâ) Chile (Santiago In.)	32·45 S	70·43 W
90	San Felipe (fĕ-lē'pĕ) . . . . Mex.	21·29 N	101·13 W
90	San Felipe . . . . Mex.	22·21 N	105·26 W
98	San Felipe (fĕ-lē'pĕ) . . . . Ven.	10·13 N	68·45 W
	San Felipe, see Jalapa de Diaz		
68	San Felipe, Cr. (săn fê-lēp'â) Calif.	33·10 N	116·03 W
94	San Felipe, Cayos de (Is.) (kä'yōs-dĕ-sän-fĕ-lē'pĕ) . Cuba	22·00 N	83·30 W
125	San Felíu de Guixols (sän fâ-lē'ōō dâ gê-hôls) . Sp.	41·45 N	3·01 E
96	San Felix, Isla de (I.) (ē's-lä-dĕ-sän fâ-lēks') . Chile	26·20 S	80·10 W
124	San Fernanda (fĕr-nä'n-dä) . . . . Sp.	36·28 N	6·13 W
100	San Fernando (fĕr-nà'n-dô) Arg. (In.)	34·11 S	58·34 W
74	San Fernando (fĕr-năn'dô) Calif. (Los Angeles In.)	34·17 N	118·27 W
101	San Fernando . Chile (Santiago In.)	36·36 S	70·58 W
76	San Fernando (fĕr-nän'dô) . . Mex.	24·52 N	98·10 W
155	San Fernando (sän fĕr-nä'n-dô) Phil. (Manila In.)	16·38 N	120·19 E
98	San Fernando de Apure (sän-fĕr-nä'n-dō-dĕ-ä-pōō'râ) Ven.	7·46 N	67·29 W
98	San Fernando de Atabapo (dĕ-ä-tä-bä'pô) . Ven.	3·58 N	67·41 W
125	San Fernando de Henares (dĕ-ā-nä'râs) . Sp. (Madrid In.)	40·23 N	3·31 W
76	San Fernando R. (sän fĕr-nän'dô) . Mex.	25·07 N	98·25 W
118	Sånfjället (Mtn.) . . . . Swe.	62·19 N	13·30 E
85	Sanford (săn'fērd) Can. (Winnipeg In.)	49·41 N	97·27 W
79	Sanford (săn'fôrd) . . . . Fla. (In.)	28·46 N	80·18 W
82	Sanford (săn'fērd) . . . . Maine	43·26 N	70·47 W
79	Sanford . . . . N. C.	35·26 N	79·10 W
100	San Francisco (săn frăn-sĭs'kô) Arg.	31·23 S	62·09 W
65	San Francisco Calif. (San Francisco In.)	37·45 N	122·26 W
92	San Francisco . . . . Sal.	13·48 N	88·11 W
	San Francisco, see Ixhuatán		
69	San Francisco (R.) . . . . . . N. Mex.	33·35 N	108·55 W
65	San Francisco B. (săn frăn-sĭs'kô) Calif. (San Francisco In.)	37·45 N	122·21 W
88	San Francisco del Oro (dĕl ō'rō) Mex.	27·00 N	106·37 W
90	San Francisco del Rincón (dĕl rēn-kōn') . Mex.	21·01 N	101·51 W
99	San Francisco de Macaira (dĕ-mä-kī'rä) . Ven. (In.)	9·58 N	66·17 W
95	San Francisco de Macoris (dā-mä-kō'rēs) . Dom. Rep.	19·20 N	70·15 W
95	San Francisco de Paula (dä pou'lä) . Cuba (Havana In.)	23·04 N	82·18 W
62	San Francisco Mts . . . . U. S.	35·30 N	112·35 W
74	San Gabriel (săn gä-brê-ĕl') (gā'brê-ĕl) Calif. (Los Angeles In.)	34·06 N	118·06 W
90	San Gabriel Chilac (sän-gä-brē-ĕl-chê-läk') . Mex.	18·19 N	97·22 W
74	San Gabriel Mts. Calif. (Los Angeles In.)	34·17 N	118·03 W
74	San Gabriel Res. Calif. (Los Angeles In.)	34·14 N	117·48 W
74	San Gabriel R. Calif. (Los Angeles In.)	33·47 N	118·06 W
73	Sangamon (R.) (săn'gà-mŭn) . . Ill.	40·08 N	90·08 W
165	Sanga R. (säŋ-gä) . . . . Afr.	3·41 N	16·12 E
68	Sanger (săng'ēr) . . . . Calif.	36·42 N	119·33 W
120	Sangerhausen (säng'ĕr-hou-zĕn) Ger.	51·28 N	11·17 E
155	Sangihe (I.) (säŋ'gê-ē) . . . . . Indon.	3·30 N	125·30 E
98	San Gil (sän-ĸē'l) . . . . Col.	6·32 N	73·13 W
126	San Giovanni in Fiore (sän jô-vän'nē ēn fyō'rä) . It.	39·15 N	16·40 E
125	San Giuseppe Vesuviano (sän-zhēōō-sĕ'p-pĕ-vĕ-sōō-vyä'nô) It. (Naples In.)	40·36 N	14·31 E
152	Sangju (säng'jōō') . . . . Kor.	36·20 N	128·07 E
124	Sangonera (R.) (säŋ-gō-nä'rä) . Sp.	37·43 N	1·58 W
74	San Gorgonio Mt. (săn gôr-gō'nĭ-ō) Calif. (Los Angeles In.)	34·06 N	116·50 W
62	Sangre De Cristo, Mts. (săng'ẽr-de-krēs-tō) . U. S.	37·45 N	105·50 W
65	San Gregoria (săn grĕ-gôr'ä) Calif. (San Francisco In.)	37·20 N	122·23 W
126	Sangro (R.) (säŋ'grô) . . . . It.	41·38 N	13·56 E
124	Sangüesa (sän-gwĕ'sä) . . . . Sp.	42·36 N	1·15 W
148	Sanho (sän'hō) . . . . China	39·59 N	117·06 E
79	Sanibel I. (săn'ĭ-bĕl) . . . . Fla. (In.)	26·26 N	82·15 W
	San Ildefonso, see Villa Alta		
155	San Ildefonso, C. (sän-ēl-dĕ-fôn-sô) Phil. (Manila In.)	16·03 N	122·10 E
124	San Ildefonso o la Granja (ō lä grän'khä) . Sp.	40·54 N	4·02 W
100	San Isidro (ē-sē'drô) . . . . Arg. (In.)	34·13 S	58·31 W
93	San Isidro . . . . C. R.	9·24 N	83·43 W
74	San Jacinto (săn jȧ-sĭn'tô) Calif. (Los Angeles In.)	33·47 N	116·57 W
155	San Jacinto (sän hä-sēn'tô) Phil. (Manila In.)	12·33 N	123·43 E
77	San Jacinto (R.), West Fork . Tex.	30·35 N	95·37 W
74	San Jacinto R. (săn jȧ-sĭn'tô) Calif. (Los Angeles In.)	33·44 N	117·14 W
77	San Jacinto R. . . . . Tex.	30·25 N	95·05 W
101	San Javier (sän-hä-vē-ĕr) Chile (Santiago In.)	35·35 S	71·43 W
91	San Jerónimo Mex. (Mexico City In.)	19·31 N	98·46 W
90	San Jerónimo de Juárez (hâ-rō'nê-mô dâ hwä'râz) . Mex.	17·08 N	100·30 W
99	San Joaquin (hô-ä-kē'n) Ven. (In.)	10·16 N	67·47 W
68	San Joaquin (R.) (săn hwä-kēn') Calif.	37·10 N	120·51 W
68	San Joaquin Valley . . . . Calif.	36·45 N	120·30 W
100	San Jorge, Golfo (G.) (gôl-fô-sän-ĸô'r-kĕ) . Arg.	46·15 S	66·45 W
99	San José (sän hô-sā') . . . . Bol.	17·54 S	60·42 W
65	San Jose (săn hô-zā') Calif. (San Francisco In.)	37·20 N	121·54 W
93	San Jose (sän hô-sā') . . . . C. R.	9·57 N	84·05 W
92	San José . . . . Guat.	13·56 N	90·49 W
155	San Jose . . . . . Phil. (Manila In.)	12·22 N	121·04 E
155	San Jose (sän-ĸô-sĕ') Phil. (Manila In.)	13·52 N	121·07 E
155	San José . . . . Phil. (Manila In.)	14·49 N	120·47 E
155	San Jose . . . . Phil. (Manila In.)	15·49 N	120·57 E
101	San José (hô-sĕ') Ur. (Buenos Aires In.)	34·20 S	56·43 W
101	San José (Dept.) Ur. (Buenos Aires In.)	34·17 S	56·23 W
88	San Jose (I.) (ĸô-sĕ') . . . . Mex.	25·00 N	110·35 W
69	San Jose (R.) (săn hō-zā') N. Mex.	35·15 N	108·10 W
93	San Jose, Isla de (I.) (ē's-lä-dĕ-sän hô-sā') . Pan.	8·17 N	79·20 W
101	San José (R.) (sän-hô-sĕ') Ur. (Buenos Aires In.)	34·05 S	56·47 W
100	San José de Feliciano (dâ lä ĕs-kē'nȧ) . Arg.	30·26 S	58·44 W
99	San José de Gauribe (sän-hô-sĕ'dĕ-gȧōō-rē'bĕ) Ven. (In.)	9·51 N	65·49 W
95	San Jose de las Lajas (sän-ĸô-sĕ'dĕ-läs-lä'käs) Cuba (Havana In.)	22·13 N	82·10 W
90	San José Iturbide (ē-tōōr-bē'dĕ) Mex.	21·00 N	100·24 W
100	San Juan (hwän') . . . . Arg.	31·36 S	68·29 W
98	San Juan (hōōà'n) . . . . . Col. (In.)	3·23 N	73·48 W
95	San Juan (săn hwän') . . Dom. Rep.	18·50 N	71·15 W
155	San Juan (sän-ĸōōà'n) Phil. (Manila In.)	14·30 N	121·14 E
155	San Juan . . . . . . Phil. (Manila In.)	16·41 N	120·20 E
89	San Juan (săn hwän') P. R. (Puerto Rico In.)	18·30 N	66·10 W
	San Juan, see Guichicovi		
	San Juan, see Mazatlán		
100	San Juan (Prov.) . . . . Arg.	31·00 S	69·30 W
89	San Juan, Cabezas de (C.) P. R. (Puerto Rico In.)	18·29 N	65·30 W
94	San Juan, Pico (Pk.) (pē'kô-sän-kōōà'n) . Cuba	21·55 N	80·00 W
91	San Juan (R.) (sän-hōō-än') . Mex.	18·10 N	95·23 W
76	San Juan, Rio (R.) (rē'ō-sän hwän) . Mex.	25·35 N	99·15 W
69	San Juan (R.) . . . . Utah	37·10 N	110·30 W
100	San Juan Bautista (sän hwän' bou-tēs'tä) . Par.	26·48 S	57·09 W
90	San Juan Capistrano (sän-hōō-än' kä-pēs-trä'nô) Mex.	22·41 N	104·07 W
68	San Juan Cr. (săn hwän') . . . Calif.	35·24 N	120·12 W
76	San Juan de Guadalupe (sän hwan dā gwä-dhä-lōō'pä) Mex.	24·37 N	102·43 W
93	San Juan del Norte (Greytown) (dĕl nôr-tā) (grā'toun) . Nic.	10·55 N	83·44 W
93	San Juan del Norte Bahia de (B.) (bä-ē'ä-dĕ-sän hwän dĕl nôr'tā) Nic.	11·12 N	83·40 W
90	San Juan de los Lagos (sän-hōō-än'dā lōs lä'gôs) . Mex.	21·15 N	102·18 W
90	San Juan de los Lagos (R.) (dā lōs lä'gôs) . Mex.	21·13 N	102·12 W
99	San Juan de los Morros (dĕ-lôs-mô'r-rôs) . Ven. (In.)	9·54 N	67·22 W
90	San Juan del Rio (dĕl rē'ô) . . Mex.	20·21 N	99·59 W
76	San Juan del Rio (sän hwän del rē'ô) . Mex.	24·47 N	104·29 W
92	San Juan del Sur (dĕl sōōr) . . . Nic.	11·15 N	85·53 W
76	San Juan de Sabinas (dĕ-sä-bē'näs) . Mex.	27·56 N	101·23 W
91	San Juan Evangelista (sän-hōō-ä'n-å-väŋ-kå-lēs'ta') Mex.	17·57 N	95·08 W
74	San Juan Hot Springs (săn hwän') . Calif. (Los Angeles In.)	33·37 N	117·28 W
65	San Juan I. . . . Wash. (Seattle In.)	48·28 N	123·08 W
65	San Juan Is. (săn hwän) Can. (Vancouver In.)	48·49 N	123·14 W
91	San Juan Ixtenco (ēx-tĕ'n-kô) Mex.	19·14 N	97·52 W
94	San Juan Martinez (sän kōō à'n-mär-tē'nĕz) . Cuba	22·15 N	83·50 W
69	San Juan Mts. (săn hwän') . . Colo.	37·50 N	107·30 W
93	San Juan R. . . . . Nic.	10·58 N	84·18 W
100	San Julián (sän hōō-lyà'n) . . . Arg.	49·17 S	68·02 W
100	San Justo (hōōs'tô) . . . . . Arg. (In.)	34·25 S	58·33 W
164	Sankarani R. (sän'kä-rä'nē) Mali-Gui.	11·15 N	8·01 W
120	Sankt Gallen . . . . Switz.	47·25 N	9·22 E
166	Sankuru (R.) (sän-kōō'rōō) Con. L.	4·12 S	22·08 E
88	San Lazaro, C. (sän-lä'zä-rō) Mex.	24·58 N	113·30 W
65	San Leandro (săn lê-ăn'drô) Calif. (San Francisco In.)	37·43 N	122·10 W
101	San Lorenzo (sän lô-rĕn'zô) Arg. (Buenos Aires In.)	32·46 S	60·44 W
65	San Lorenzo (săn lô-rĕn'zô) Calif. (San Francisco In.)	37·41 N	122·08 W
92	San Lorenzo (sän lô-rĕn'zô) . Hond.	13·24 N	87·24 W
125	San Lorenzo de El Escorial (sän lô-rĕn'tho dĕl ĕs-kō-rê-äl') Sp. (Madrid In.)	40·36 N	4·09 W
124	Sanlúcar (sän-lōō'kär) . . . . Sp.	36·46 N	6·21 W
98	San Lucas (lōō'kàs) . . . . Bol.	20·12 S	65·06 W
	San Lucas, see Ojitlán		
88	San Lucas, C. . . . . Mex.	22·45 N	109·45 W
100	San Luis (lōō-ēs') . . . . Arg.	33·16 S	66·15 W
98	San Luis (lōōē's) . . . . . . Col. (In.)	6·03 N	74·57 W
95	San Luis . . . . Cuba	20·15 N	75·50 W
92	San Luis . . . . Guat.	14·38 N	89·42 W
100	San Luis (Prov.) . . . . Arg.	32·45 S	66·00 W
88	San Luis (State) . . . . Mex.	22·45 N	101·45 W
90	San Luis de la Paz (dā lä päz') Mex.	21·17 N	100·32 W
76	San Luis del Cordero (dĕl kôr-dā'rô) . Mex.	25·25 N	104·20 W
68	San Luis Obispo (ō-bĭs'pō) . . Calif.	35·18 N	120·40 W
68	San Luis Obispo, B. . . . . Calif.	35·07 N	121·05 W
90	San Luis Potosi (pō-tô-sē') . . Mex.	22·08 N	100·58 W
68	San Luis Rey (R.) (rā'ē) . . . . Calif.	33·22 N	117·06 W
69	San Manuel (săn măn'ū-ĕl) . . Ariz.	32·30 N	110·45 W
69	San Marcial (săn mär-shäl') N. Mex.	33·40 N	107·00 W
126	San Marco (sän mär'kô) . . . . It.	41·53 N	15·50 E
92	San Marcos (mär'kôs) . . . . . . Guat.	14·57 N	91·49 W
90	San Marcos . . . . Mex.	16·46 N	99·23 W
76	San Marcos (săn mär'kôs) . . . Tex.	29·53 N	97·56 W
92	San Marcos de Colón (sän-mà'r-kōs-dĕ-kô-lô'n) . Hond.	13·17 N	86·50 W
76	San Marcos R. . . . . Tex.	30·08 N	98·15 W
92	San Maria (Vol.) (sän-mä-rē'ä) Guat.	14·45 N	91·33 W
127	San Maria di Léuca, C. (dē-lĕ'ōō-kä) . It.	39·47 N	18·20 E
155	San Mariano (sän mä-rê-ä'nô) Phil. (Manila In.)	17·00 N	121·58 E
74	San Marino (săn mēr-ē'nô) Calif. (Los Angeles In.)	34·07 N	118·06 W
126	San Marino (sän mä-rē'nô) . . . Eur.	43·52 N	12·38 E
126	San Marino . . . . San Marino	44·55 N	12·26 E
98	San Martín (sän mär-tē'n) Col. (In.)	3·42 N	73·44 W
91	San Martín (mär-tē'n) . . . . . . Mex.	18·36 N	95·11 W
100	San Martín (L.) . . . . Arg.-Chile	48·15 S	72·30 W
90	San Martin Chalchicuautla (sän mär-tē'n chäl-chē-kwä-ōō'tlä) . Mex.	21·22 N	98·39 W
125	San Martin de la Vega (sän mär ten' dā lä vā'gä) Sp. (Madrid In.)	40·12 N	3·34 W
90	San Martín Hidalgo (sän mär-tē'n-ē-däl'gô) . Mex.	20·27 N	103·55 W
65	San Mateo (săn mä-tā'ô) Calif. (San Francisco In.)	37·34 N	122·20 W
91	San Mateo (Etlatongo) (sän-mä-tĕ'ô) (ĕ-tlä-tô'n-gō) Mex.	16·59 N	97·04 W
125	San Mateo (sän mä-tā'ō) . . . . . . Sp.	40·26 N	0·09 E
99	San Mateo (sän mà-tĕ'ô) Ven. (In.)	9·45 N	64·34 W
100	San Matías, Golfo (G.) (sän mä-tē'äs) . Arg	41·30 S	63·45 W
151	Sanmen Wan (B.) . . . . China	29·00 N	122·15 E
100	San Miguel (sän mē-gĕ'l) Arg. (In.)	34·17 S	58·43 W
91	San Miguel (sän mê-gâl') . . . . Mex.	18·18 N	97·09 W
93	San Miguel . . . . Pan.	8·26 N	78·55 W
155	San Miguel (sän mē-gĕ'l) Phil. (Manila In.)	15·09 N	120·56 E
92	San Miguel (sän mê-gâl') . . . . . Sal.	13·28 N	88·11 W
99	San Miguel (sän mē-gĕ'l) Ven. (In.)	9·56 N	64·58 W
	San Miguel, see Sola de Vega		
	San Miguel, see Talea de Castro		
93	San Miguel, Bahia (B.) (bä-ē'ä-sän mê-gâl') . Pan.	8·17 N	78·26 W
68	San Miguel (I.) . . . . Calif.	34·03 N	120·23 W
98	San Miguel (R.) (sän-mē-gĕl') Bol.	13·34 S	63·58 W
69	San Miguel (R.) (săn mê-gĕl') Colo.	38·15 N	108·40 W
91	San Miguel (R.) (sän mê-gâl') Mex.	15·27 N	92·00 W
92	San Miguel (Vol.) . . . . Sal.	13·27 N	88·17 W
155	San Miguel B. . Phil. (Manila In.)	13·55 N	123·12 E
90	San Miguel de Allende (dā ä-lyĕn'dā) . Mex.	20·54 N	100·44 W

ăt; finăl; rāte; senâte; ärm; åsk; sofȧ; fâre; ch-choose; dh-as th in other; bē; ēvent; bĕt; recĕnt; cratẽr; g-go; gh-guttural g; bĭt; ĭ-short neutral; rīde; ĸ-guttural k as ch in German ich;

Page	Name Pronunciation Region	Lat. °′	Long. °′
90	San Miguel el Alto (ĕl äl'tō) . Mex.	21·03 N	102·26 W
168	Sanmur, Wadi (Val.) U. A. R. (Nile In.)	28·48 N	31·12 E
155	San Narcisco . . . Phil. (Manila In.)	15·01 N	120·05 E
155	San Narciso (sän när-sē'sō) Phil. (Manila In.)	13·34 N	123·33 E
101	San Nicolás (sän nē-kō-lä's) Arg. (Buenos Aires In.)	33·20 S	60·14 W
155	San Nicolas (nē-kō-läs') Phil. (Manila In.)	16·05 N	120·45 E
68	San Nicolas (I.) (săn nĭ'kō-là) Calif.	33·14 N	119·10 W
90	San Nicolás (R.) Mex.	19·40 N	105·08 W
121	Sanok (sä'nôk) Pol.	49·31 N	22·13 E
65	San Pablo (săn păb'lō) Calif. (San Francisco In.)	37·58 N	122·21 W
155	San Pablo (sän-pä-blō) Phil. (Manila In.)	14·05 N	121·20 E
155	San Pablo . . . Phil. (Manila In.)	17·29 N	121·49 E
99	San Pablo (sän-pä'blō) . Ven. (In.)	9·46 N	65·04 W
65	San Pablo B. (săn păb'lō) Calif (San Francisco In.)	38·04 N	122·25 W
65	San Pablo Res. Calif. (San Francisco In.)	37·55 N	122·12 W
93	San Pablo R. (sän päb'lō) . . . . Pan.	8·12 N	81·12 W
155	San Pascual (päs-kwäl') Phil. (Manila In.)	13·08 N	122·59 E
100	San Pedro (sän pā'drō) . . . . Arg.	24·15 S	64·51 W
101	San Pedro. Arg. (Buenos Aires In.)	33·41 S	59·42 W
74	San Pedro (săn pē'drō) Calif. (Los Angeles In.)	33·44 N	118·17 W
101	San Pedro (sän pĕ'drō) Chile (Santiago In.)	33·54 S	71·27 W
91	San Pedro (sän pā'drō) . . . . Mex.	18·38 N	92·25 W
100	San Pedro (sän-pĕ'drō) . . . . Par.	24·13 S	57·00 W
92	San Pedro (sän pā'drō) . . . . Sal.	13·49 N	88·58 W
	San Pedro, see Amusgos		
	San Pedro, see Pochutla		
69	San Pedro (R.) Ariz.	32·48 N	110·37 W
94	San Pedro (R.) (sän-pĕ'drō) . Cuba	21·05 N	78·15 W
91	San Pedro, Rio de (R.) (rē'ō-dĕ-sän-pĕ'drō) . Mex.	18·23 N	92·13 W
90	San Pedro, Río de (R.) . . . . Mex.	21·51 N	102·24 W
90	San Pedro (R.) (sän pā'drō) . Mex.	22·08 N	104·59 W
74	San Pedro B. (săn pē'drō) Calif. (Los Angeles In.)	33·42 N	118·12 W
76	San Pedro de las Colonias (dĕ-läs-kō-lō'nyäs) . Mex.	25·47 N	102·58 W
95	San Pedro de Macorís (sän-pĕ'drō-dä mä-kō-rēs') Dom. Rep.	18·30 N	69·30 W
90	San Pedro Lagunillas (sän pā'drō lä-gōō-nēl'yäs) . Mex.	21·12 N	104·47 W
92	San Pedro R. (sän pā'drō) Guat. (Yucatan In.)	17·11 N	90·23 W
76	San Pedro R. Mex.	27·56 N	105·50 W
92	San Pedro Sula (sän pā'drō sōō'lä) Hond.	15·29 N	88·01 W
	San Pedro y San Pablo, see Teposcolula		
126	San Pietro, I. di (ē'sō-lä-dē-sän pyā'trō) . It.	39·09 N	8·15 E
65	San Quentin (săn kwĕn-tēn') Calif. (San Francisco In.)	37·57 N	122·29 W
155	San Quintin (sän kēn-tēn') Phil. (Manila In.)	15·59 N	120·47 E
100	San Rafael (sän rä-fä-äl') . . . . Arg.	34 30 S	68·13 W
65	San Rafael (săn rá-fĕl) Calif. (San Francisco In.)	37·58 N	122·31 W
98	San Rafael (sän-rä-fä-ĕ'l) Col. (In.)	6·18 N	75·02 W
69	San Rafael (R.) (săn rà-fĕl') Utah	39·05 N	110·50 W
95	San Rafael, Cabo (C.) (kà'bō) Dom. Rep.	19·00 N	68·50 W
65	San Ramon (săn rä-mōn') Calif. (San Francisco In.)	37·47 N	122·59 W
93	San Ramōn C. R.	10·07 N	84·30 W
126	San Remo (sän rā'mō) It.	43·48 N	7·46 E
121	San R. Pol.	50·33 N	22·12 E
89	San Roman, C. (sän-rō-mä'n) Ven.	12·00 N	69·45 W
98	San Roque (sän-rō'kĕ) . . Col. (In.)	6·29 N	75·00 W
124	San Roque Sp.	36·13 N	5·23 W
76	San Saba (săn sä'bà) Tex.	31·12 N	98·43 W
76	San Saba R. Tex.	30·58 N	99·12 W
92	San Salvador (sän säl-vä-dōr') . Sal.	13·45 N	89·11 W
98	San Salvador (I.) Ec.	0·14 S	90·50 W
95	San Salvador (Watling) (I.) (săn săl'và-dôr) . Ba. Is.	24·05 N	74·30 W
101	San Salvador (R.) (sän-säl-vä-dō'r) Ur. (Buenos Aires In.)	33·42 S	58·04 W
164	Sansanné-Mango (sän-sà-nā' mäɴ'gō) . Togo	10·31 N	0·23 E
164	San Sebastian (sän sä-bäs-tyän') Can. Is.	28·09 N	17·11 W
124	San Sebastian Sp.	43·19 N	1·59 W
99	San Sebastián (sän-sĕ-bäs-tyà'n) Ven. (In.)	9·58 N	67·11 W
125	San Sebastián de los Reyes (sän sä-bäs-tyän'dä lōs rā'yĕs) Sp. (Madrid In.)	40·33 N	3·38 W
126	San Severo (sän sĕ-vâ'rō) It.	41·43 N	15·24 E
150	San She (Mtn.) China	33·00 N	103·50 E
147	San Shui China	23·14 N	112·51 E
69	San Simon Cr. (săn sī-mōn') Ariz.	32·45 N	109·30 W
74	Santa Ana (săn'tà ăn'à) Calif. (Los Angeles In.)	33·45 N	117·52 W
90	Santa Ana (sän'tä ä'nä) Mex.	19·18 N	98·10 W
92	Santa Ana Sal.	14·02 N	89·35 W
74	Santa Ana Mts. Calif. (Los Angeles In.)	33·44 N	117·36 W
74	Santa Ana R. Calif. (Los Angeles In.)	33·41 N	117·57 W
76	Santa Anna Tex.	31·44 N	99·18 W
100	Santa Anna, Cochilha de (Mts.) (kō-chē'lä dĕ sän-tä-nä) . Braz.	30·30 S	56·30 W
125	Sant' Antimo . . . It. (Naples In.)	40·40 N	14·11 E
101	Santa Bárbara (sän-tä-bä'r-bä-rä) Braz. (Rio de Janeiro In.)	19·57 S	43·25 W
68	Santa Barbara (săn'tȧ bär'bȧ-rȧ) Calif.	34·26 N	119·43 W
92	Santa Barbara (sän'tä bär'bä-rä) Hond.	14·52 N	88·20 W
76	Santa Barbara Mex.	26·48 N	105·50 W
68	Santa Barbara (I.) Calif.	33·30 N	113·01 W
68	Santa Barbara (Is.) Calif.	33·45 N	119·46 W
68	Santa Barbara Chan. Calif.	34·15 N	120·00 W
101	Santa Branca (sän-tä-brä'ɴ-kä) Braz. (Rio de Janeiro In.)	23·25 S	45·52 W
68	Santa Catalina (I.) Calif.	33·29 N	118·37 W
93	Santa Catalina, Cerro de (Mt.) (sĕ'r-rō-dĕ-sän-tä-kä-tä-lē'nä) Pan.	8·39 N	81·36 W
68	Santa Catalina, G. of (săn'tȧ kă-tȧ-lē'nȧ) . Calif.	33·00 N	117·58 W
76	Santa Catarina (sän'tä kä-tä-rē'nä) Mex.	25·41 N	100·27 W
	Sta. Catarina, see Loxicha		
	Sta. Catarina, see Yosonotú		
100	Santa Catarina (State) (sän-tä-kä-tä-rē'nä) . Braz.	27·15 S	50·30 W
90	Santa Catarina (R.) Mex.	16·31 N	98·39 W
65	Santa Clara (săn'tȧ klâr'ȧ) Calif. (San Francisco In.)	37·21 N	121·56 W
94	Santa Clara (sän'tä klä'rä) . . Cuba	22·25 N	80·00 W
76	Santa Clara Mex.	24·29 N	103·22 W
100	Santa Clara Ur.	32·46 S	54·51 W
68	Santa Clara (R.) (săn'tȧ klă'rȧ) Calif.	34·22 N	118·53 W
92	Santa Clara, (Vol.) Nic.	12·44 N	87·00 W
94	Santa Clara, Bahía de (B.) (bä-ē'ä-dĕ-sän-tä-klä-rä) . . Cuba	23·05 N	80·50 W
88	Santa Clara, Sierra, (Mts.) (sē-ĕ'r-rä-sän'tä klä'rä) . Mex.	27·30 N	113·50 W
98	Santa Cruz (sän'tä krōōz') . . . Bol.	17·45 S	63·03 W
100	Santa Cruz (sän-tä-krōō's) . . Braz.	29·43 S	52·15 W
100	Santa Cruz Braz. (In.)	22·55 S	43·41 W
68	Santa Cruz (săn'tȧ krōōz') . . Calif.	36·59 N	122·02 W
101	Santa Cruz . . . Chile (Santiago In.)	34·38 S	71·21 W
92	Santa Cruz C. R.	10·16 N	85·37 W
76	Santa Cruz Mex.	25·50 N	105·25 W
155	Santa Cruz . . . . Phil. (Manila In.)	13·28 N	122·02 E
155	Santa Cruz . . . . Phil. (Manila In.)	14·17 N	121·25 E
155	Santa Cruz . . . . Phil. (Manila In.)	15·46 N	119·53 E
155	Santa Cruz . . . . Phil. (Manila In.)	17·06 N	120·27 E
100	Santa Cruz (Prov.) Arg.	48·00 S	70·00 W
68	Santa Cruz (I.) (săn'tȧ krōōz') Calif.	34·05 N	119·55 W
98	Santa Cruz (I.) (sän-tä-krōō'z) . Ec.	0·38 S	90·20 W
69	Santa Cruz (R.) (săn'tȧ krōōz') Ariz.	32·30 N	111·30 W
100	Santa Cruz (R.) (sän'tä krōōz') Arg.	50·05 S	66·30 W
92	Santa Cruz Barillas (sän-tä-krōō'z-bä-rē'l-yäs) Guat.	15·47 N	91·22 W
	Santa Cruz Chico, see Pedro Antonio Santos		
94	Santa Cruz del Sur (sän-tä-krōō's-dĕl-sōō'r) . Cuba	20·45 N	78·00 W
164	Santa Cruz de Tenerife (sän'tä krōōz dä tā-nå-rē'fä) Can. Is.	28·07 N	15·27 W
159	Santa Cruz Is. Sol. Is.	10·58 S	166·47 E
65	Santa Cruz Mts. (săn'tȧ krōōz') Calif. (San Francisco In.)	37·30 N	122·19 W
95	Santa Domingo, Cay (I.) . . Ba. Is.	21·50 N	75·45 W
126	Sant'Eufemia, Golfo di (G.) (gôl-fō-dē-sän-tĕ'ōō-fĕ'myä) . . It.	38·53 N	15·53 E
124	Santa Eugenia de Ribeira (sän-tä-ĕōō-hĕ'nyä-dĕ-rē-bĕ'y-rä) Sp.	42·34 N	8·55 W
125	Santa Eulalia del Rio (sän'ta ä-ōō-lä'lē-ä dĕl rē'ō) . Sp.	38·58 N	1·29 E
100	Santa Fe (sän'tä fā') Arg.	31·33 S	60·45 W
94	Santa Fe (sän-tä-fĕ') Cuba	21·45 N	82·40 W
69	Santa Fe (săn'tȧ fā') . . . . N. Mex.	35·10 N	106·00 W
124	Santafé (sän'tä-fā') Sp.	37·12 N	3·43 W
100	Santa Fe (Prov.) (sän'tä fā') . Arg.	32·00 S	61·15 W
99	Santa Filomena (sän-tä-fē-lō-mĕ'nä) . Braz.	9·09 S	44·45 W
88	Santa Genoveva, (Mtn.) (sän-tä-hĕ-nō-vĕ'vä) . Mex.	23·30 N	110·00 W
151	Sant'ai China	31·02 N	105·02 E
99	Santa Inés (sän'tä ē-nĕ's) Ven. (In.)	9·54 N	64·21 W
100	Santa Inés (I.) (sän'tä ē-näs') Chile	53·45 S	74·15 W
164	Santa Isabel (ē-sä-bĕl') Fernando Poo	3·43 N	8·42 E
159	Santa Isabel, (I.) Sol. Is.	7·57 S	159·28 E
94	Santa Lucia (sän'tä lōō-sē'ä) . Cuba	21·50 N	77·30 W
101	Santa Lucia (sän-tä-lōō-sē'ä) Ur. (Buenos Aires In.)	34·27 S	56·23 W
99	Santa Lucia Ven. (In.)	10·18 N	66·40 W
101	Santa Lucia (R.) (sän-tä-lōō-sē'ä) Ur. (Buenos Aires In.)	34·19 S	56·13 W
94	Santa Lucia B. (sän'tä lōō-sē'ä) Cuba	22·55 N	84·20 W
88	Santa Magarita (I.) (sän'tä mär-gä-rē'tä) . Mex.	24·15 N	112·00 W
100	Santa Maria (sän'tä mä-rē'ä) Braz.	29·40 S	28·45 W
68	Santa Maria (săn-tȧ mȧ-rē'ȧ) Calif.	34·57 N	120·28 W
126	Santa Maria (sän-tä mä-rē'ä) . . It.	41·05 N	14·15 E
155	Santa Maria (sän-tä-mä-rē'ä) Phil. (Manila In.)	14·48 N	120·57 E
	Santa Maria, see Huazolotitlán		
90	Santa Maria (R.) (sän'tä mä-rē'ä) . Mex.	21·33 N	100·17 W
95	Santa Maria, C. Ba. Is.	23·45 N	75·30 W
124	Santa Maria, Cabo de (C.) (kä'bō-dĕ-sän-tä-mä-rē'ä) . Port.	36·58 N	7·54 W
94	Santa Maria, Cayo (I.) (kä'yō-săn'tȧ mȧ-rē'ȧ) . Cuba	22·40 N	79·00 W
90	Santa María del Oro (sän'tä-mä-rē'ä-dĕl-ô-rō) . Mex.	21·21 N	104·35 W
90	Santa Maria de los Angeles (dĕ-lôs-ä'n-hĕ-lĕs) . Mex.	22·10 N	103·34 W
90	Santa María del Rio (sän'tä mä-rē'ä dĕl rē'ō) . Mex.	21·46 N	100·43 W
90	Santa Maria de Ocotán (sän'tä-mä-rê'ä-dĕ-ô-kô-tà'n) Mex.	22·56 N	104·30 W
164	Santa Maria I. (sän-tä-mä-rē'ä) Azores (In.)	37·09 N	26·02 W
101	Santa Maria Madalena (sän-tä-mä-rē'ä-mä-dä-lĕ-nä) Braz. (Rio de Janeiro In.)	22·00 S	42·00 W
98	Santa Marta (sän'tä mär'tä) . Col.	11·15 N	74·13 W
74	Santa Monica (săn'tȧ mŏn'ĭ-kȧ) Calif. (Los Angeles In.)	34·01 N	118·29 W
74	Santa Monica Mts. Calif. (Los Angeles In.)	34·08 N	118·38 W
100	Santana (R.) (sän-tä'nä) Braz. (In.)	22·33 S	43·37 W
98	Santander (sän-tän-dĕr') Col. (In.)	3·00 N	76·25 W
124	Santander (sän-tän-dâr') Sp.	43·27 N	3·50 W
125	Sant'Angelo Romano (sän-tä'n-gzhĕ-lō-rō-mä'nō) It. (Rome In.)	42·02 N	12·45 E
125	Sant' Antimo . . . . It. (Naples In.)	40·40 N	14·11 E
125	Santañy (sän-tän'yē) Sp.	39·21 N	3·08 E
68	Santa Paula (săn'tȧ pô'lȧ) . . Calif.	34·24 N	119·05 W
99	Santarém (sän-tä-rĕɴ') Braz.	2·28 S	54·37 W
124	Santarém Port.	39·18 N	8·48 W
94	Santaren Chan. (sän-tȧ-rĕn') Ba. Is.	24·15 N	79·30 W
69	Santa Rita (săn'tȧ rē'tä) . N. Mex.	32·45 N	108·05 W
101	Santa Rita do Passo Quatro (sän-tä-rĕ'tä-dô-pä'sô-kwà'trô) Braz. (Rio de Janeiro In.)	21·43 S	47·27 W
101	Santa Rita do Sapucai (sä-pōō-kà'ē) Braz. (Rio de Janeiro In.)	22·15 S	45·41 W
100	Santa Rosa (sän-tä-rô-sä) . . . . Arg.	36·45 S	64·10 W
68	Santa Rosa (săn'tȧ rō'zȧ) . . . Calif.	38·27 N	122·42 W
98	Santa Rosa (sän-tä-rô-sä) Col. (In.)	6·38 N	75·26 W
98	Santa Rosa Ec.	3·29 S	78·55 W
92	Santa Rosa (sän'tä rō'sä) . . . Guat.	14·21 N	90·16 W
92	Santa Rosa Hond.	14·45 N	88·51 W
72	Santa Rosa (săn'tȧ rō'sȧ) N. Mex.	34·55 N	104·41 W
155	Santa Rosa (sän'tä rō'sä) Phil. (Manila In.)	14·18 N	121·07 E
99	Santa Rosa (sän-tä-rô-sä) Ven. (In.)	9·37 N	64·10 W
98	Santa Rosa de Cabal (sän-tä-rô-sä-dĕ-kä-bä'l) Col. (In.)	4·53 N	75·38 W
101	Santa Rosa de Viterbo (sän-tä-rô-sä-dĕ-vē-tĕr'-bô) Braz. (Rio de Janeiro In.)	21·30 S	47·21 W
68	Santa Rosa Ind. Res. (săn'tȧ rō'zȧ') . Calif.	33·28 N	116·50 W
88	Santa Rosalía (sän'tä rô-zä'lē-ä) Mex.	27·13 N	112·15 W
	Santa Rosalia, see Ciudad Camargo		
66	Santa Rosa Mts. (săn'tȧ rō'zȧ) Nev.	41·33 N	117·50 W
74	Santa Susana (săn'tȧ sōō-ză'nȧ) Calif. (Los Angeles In.)	34·16 N	118·42 W
	Santa Tecla, see Nueva San Salvador		
101	Santa Teresa (sän-tä-tĕ-rĕ'sä) Arg. (Buenos Aires In.)	33·27 S	60·47 W
99	Santa Teresa Ven. (In.)	10·14 N	66·40 W
100	Santa Vitória do Palmar (sän-tä-vē-tô'ryä-dô-päl-màr) Braz.	33·30 S	53·16 W
68	Santa Ynez (R.) (săn'tȧ ē-nĕz') Calif.	34·40 N	120·20 W
68	Santa Ysabel Ind. Res. (săn-tȧ ĭ-zȧ-bĕl') . Calif.	33·05 N	116·46 W
68	Santee (săn-tē') Calif. (San Diego In.)	32·50 N	116·58 W
79	Santee (R.) S. C.	33·27 N	80·02 W
100	Santiago (sän-tyà'gō) Braz.	29·05 S	54·46 W
101	Santiago (sän-tê-à'gō) Chile (Santiago In.)	33·26 S	70·40 W
93	Santiago Pan.	8·07 N	80·58 W
155	Santiago (sän-tyä'gō) Phil. (Manila In.)	16·42 N	121·33 E
124	Santiago Sp.	42·52 N	8·32 W
	Santiago, see Tejupan		
	Santiago, see Zacatepec		
101	Santiago (Prov.) (sän-tyà'gō) Chile (Santiago In.)	33·28 S	70·55 W
90	Santiago, Rio Grande de (R.) (rê'ō-grä'n-dĕ-dĕ-sän-tyà'gō) Mex.	21·15 N	104·05 W
155	Santiago (I.) . . . Phil. (Manila In.)	16·29 N	120·03 E
95	Santiago de los Cabelleros (sän-tyà'gô-dä lōs kä-bä-yā'rōs) Dom. Rep.	19·30 N	70·45 W
95	Santiago de Cuba (sän-tyà'gô-dä kōō'bä) . . . . Cuba	20·00 N	75·50 W
95	Santiago de las Vegas (sän-tyà'gô-dĕ-läs-vĕ'gäs) Cuba (Havana In.)	22·13 N	82·23 W
100	Santiago del Estero (sän-tē-à'gō-dĕl ĕs-tā'rō) . Arg.	27·50 S	64·14 W

ng-sing; ŋ-baŋk; ɴ-nasalized n; nŏd; cŏmmit; ōld; ôbey; ôrder; fōōd; fŏŏt; ou-out; s-soft; sh-dish; th-thin; pūre; ûnite; ûrn; stŭd; circŭs; ü-as "y" in study; '-indeterminate vowel.

Page Name Pronunciation Region Lat. °′ Long. °′

100 Santiago del Estero (Prov.) (sän-tē-ä'gō-dĕl ĕs-tä'rō). Arg. 27·15 s 63·30 w
76 Santiago Mts. (sän-tē-ä'gō) . . Tex. 30·00 N 103·30 w
74 Santiago Res. Calif. (Los Angeles In.) 33·47 N 117·42 w
95 Santiago Rodriguez (sän-tyȧ'gō-rō-drē'gĕz) Dom. Rep. 19·30 N 71·25 w
91 Santiago Tuxtla (sän-tyȧ'gō-tōō'x-tlä). Mex. 18·28 N 95·18 w
76 Santiaguillo, Laguna de (L.) (lä-ōō'nä-dĕ-sän-tē-ä-gēl'yō) Mex. 24·51 N 104·43 w
66 Santiam R. (săn'tyȧm) . . . . . . Ore. 44·42 N 122·26 w
124 Santisteban del Puerto (sän'tē stȧ-bän'dĕl pwĕr'tō) . Sp. 38·15 N 3·12 w
148 Santo (sän'tō) . . . . China 32·49 N 119·39 E
99 Santo Amaro (sän'tōō ä-mä'rōō) Braz. 12·32 s 38·33 w
101 Santo Amaro de Campos (sän-tō-ä-mä'rō-dĕ-kȧm'pōs) Braz. (Rio de Janeiro In.) 22·01 s 41·05 w
101 Santo André (sän-tō-än-drĕ') Braz. (Rio de Janeiro In.) 23·40 s 46·31 w
100 Santo Angelo (sän-tō-ä'n-zhĕ-lō) Braz. 28·16 s 53·59 w
164 Santo Antào I. (sän-tō-än-tä-ō) C. V. Is. (In.) 17·20 N 26·05 w
166 Santo Antonio (sän'tōō än-tō'nē-ōō). Ang. 6·10 s 12·25 E
101 Santo Antônio do Monte (sän-tō-än-tō'nyō-dō-môn'tĕ) Braz. (Rio de Janeiro In.) 20·06 s 45·18 w
94 Santo Domingo (sän'tō-dōmĭn'gō) Cuba 22·35 N 80·20 w
92 Santo Domingo (sän-tō-dō-mē'n-gō) . Nic. 12·15 N 84·56 w
155 Santo Domingo . Phil. (Manila In.) 17·39 N 120·24 E
95 Santo Domingo (sän'tō dō-mĭn'gō) Dom. Rep. 18·30 N 69·55 w
Santo Domingo, see Zanatepec
124 Santo Domingo de la Caızada (dā lä käl-thä'dä) . Sp. 42·27 N 2·55 w
124 Santoña (sän-tō'nyä) . . . . Sp. 43·25 N 3·27 w
101 Santos (sän'tozh) Braz. (Rio de Janeiro In.) 23·58 s 46·20 w
101 Santos Dumont (sän'tôs-dōō-mô'nt) Braz. (Rio de Janeiro In.) 21·28 s 43·33 w
155 Santo Thomas (sän-tō-tō-mä's) Phil. (Manila In.) 14·07 N 121·09 E
155 Santo Tomas (Mtn.) Phil. (Manila In.) 16·23 N 120·32 E
100 Santo Tomé (sän-tō-tō-mĕ') . . Arg. 28·32 s 56·04 w
153 Sanuki (sä'nōō-kē) Jap. (Tōkyō In.) 35·16 N 139·53 E
101 San Urbano (sän-ōōr-bä'nō) Arg. (Buenos Aires In.) 33·39 s 61·28 w
100 San Valentin, M. (Mtn.) (sän-vȧ-lĕn-tē'n) . Chile 46·41 s 73·30 w
122 Sanvic (sȧn-vēk') . . . . Fr. 49·34 N 0·08 E
101 San Vicente (sän-vē-sĕn'tĕ) Arg. (Buenos Aires In.) 35·00 s 58·26 w
101 San Vicente . . Chile (Santiago In.) 34·25 s 71·06 w
92 San Vicente (sän vē-sĕn'tä) . . . Sal. 13·41 N 88·43 w
124 San Vincente de Alcántara (sän vē-thĕn'tȧ dȧ äl-kän'tä-rä) Sp. 39·24 N 7·08 w
126 San Vito (sän vē'tō) . . . . It. 45·53 N 12·52 E
151 Sanya . . . . China 18·10 N 109·32 E
166 Sanyati (R.) (sän-yä'tē) . . . . S. Rh. 17·08 s 29·11 E
149 Sanyüanli . . . . . China (Canton In.) 23·11 N 113·16 E
68 San Ysidro (sän ysĭ-drō') Calif. (San Diego In.) 32·33 N 117·02 w
101 São Bernardo do Campo (souN-bĕr-när'dō-dô-kä'm-pō) Braz. (Rio de Janeiro In.) 23·44 s 46·33 w
100 São Borja (souN-bôr-zhä) . . . Braz. 28·44 s 55·59 w
101 São Carlos (souN kär'lōzh) Braz. (Rio de Janeiro In.) 22·02 s 47·54 w
99 São Cristovão (souN-krês-tō-vouN) Braz. 11·04 s 37·11 w
101 São Fidélis (souN-fē-dĕ'lēs) Braz. (Rio de Janeiro In.) 21·41 s 41·45 w
99 São Francisco (souN frän-sēsh'kōō) Braz. 15·59 s 44·42 w
99 São Francisco, Rio (R.) (rē'ō-sän-frän-sē's-kō) . Braz. 8·56 s 40·20 w
100 São Francisco do Sul (souN frän-sēsh'kōō-dô-sōō'l) Braz. 26·15 s 48·42 w
100 São Gabriel (souN'gä-brē-ĕl') Braz. 30·28 s 54·11 w
101 São Geraldo (souN-zhĕ-rä'l-dô) Braz. (Rio de Janeiro In.) 21·01 s 42·49 w
101 São Gonçalo (souN'gōŋ-sä'lōō) Braz. (In.) 22·55 s 43·04 w
101 São Gonçalo do Sapucaí (souN-gôn-sä'lō-dô-sä-pōō-kī') Braz. (Rio de Janeiro In.) 21·55 s 45·34 w
101 São João da Barra (souN-zhôuN-dä-bȧ'rä) Braz. (Rio de Janeiro In.) 21·40 s 41·03 w
101 São João da Boa Vista (souN-zhôuN-dä-bôä-vē's-tä) Braz. (Rio de Janeiro In.) 21·58 s 46·45 w
101 São João del Rei (souN zhô-ouN'dĕl-rā) Braz. (Rio de Janeiro In.) 21·08 s 44·14 w
100 São João de Meriti (souN-zhôuN-dĕ-mĕ-rē-tê) Braz. (In.) 22·47 s 43·22 w
99 São João do Araguaia (souN zhô-ouN'dô-ä-rä-gwä'yä) Braz. 5·29 s 48·44 w
125 São João dos Lampas (souN' zhô-ouN' dōzh län-päzh') Port. (Lisboa In.) 38·52 N 9·24 w
101 São João Nepomuceno (souN-zhôuN-nĕ-pô-mōō-sĕ-nō) Braz. (Rio de Janeiro In.) 21·33 s 43·00 w
164 São Jorge I. (souN zhôr' zhĕ) Azores (In.) 38·28 N 27·34 w
101 São José do Rio Pardo (souN-zhô-sĕ'dô-rē'ō-pȧ'r-dō) Braz. (Rio de Janeiro In.) 21·36 s 46·50 w
99 São José do Rio Prêto (souN zhô-zĕ'dô-rē'ō-prĕ-tō) Braz. 20·57 s 49·12 w
101 São José dos Campos (souN zhô-zā'dōzh kȧN pōzh') Braz. (Rio de Janeiro In.) 23·12 s 45·53 w
100 São Leopoldo (souN-lĕ-ô-pôl'dô) Braz. 29·46 s 51·09 w
99 São Luis (Maranhão) (souN-lōōē's-mä-rän-youN').Braz. 2·31 s 43·14 w
101 São Luis do Paraitinga (souN-lōōē's-dô-pä-rä-ē-tē'n-gä) Braz. (Rio de Janeiro In.) 23·15 s 44·18 w
99 São Mateus (souN mä-tā'ōōzh) Braz. 18·44 s 39·45 w
101 São Miguel Arcanjo (souN-mē-gĕ'l-är-kän-zhō) Braz. (Rio de Janeiro In.) 23·54 s 47·59 w
164 São Miguel I. . . . . Azores (In.) 37·59 N 26·38 w
95 Saona (I.) (sä-ō'nä) . . . Dom. Rep. 18·10 N 68·55 w
122 Saône (R.) (sōn) . . . . Fr. 46·27 N 4·58 E
164 São Nicolau (souN' nē-kô-louN') C. V. Is. (In.) 16·19 N 25·19 w
101 São Paulo (souN' pou'lōō) Braz. (Rio de Janeiro In.) 23·34 s 46·38 w
99 São Paulo (State) (souN pou'lōō) Braz. 21·45 s 50·47 w
98 São Paulo de Olivença (souN'pou'lōōdä ô-lē-vĕn'sȧ) Braz. 3·32 s 68·46 w
101 São Pedro (souN-pĕ'drō) Braz. (Rio de Janeiro In.) 22·34 s 47·54 w
101 São Pedro de Aldeia (souN-pĕ'drô-dĕ-äl-dĕ'yä) Braz. (Rio de Janeiro In.) 22·50 s 42·04 w
99 São Raimundo Nonato (souN' rī-mōō'n-do nô-nä'tōō) Braz. 9·09 s 42·32 w
101 São Roque (souN' rō'kĕ) Braz. (Rio de Janeiro In.) 23·32 s 47·08 w
99 São Roque, Cabo de (C) (kä'bo-dē-souN' rō'kĕ) . Braz. 5·06 s 35·11 w
166 São Salvador (souN säl-vȧ-dôr) Ang. 6·30 s 14·10 E
101 São Sebastião (souN sȧ-bäs-tē-ouN') Braz. (Rio de Janeiro In.) 23·48 s 45·25 w
101 São Sebastião, Ilha de (I.) (ēl'yȧ dä souN' sȧ-bäs-tē-ouN') Braz. (Rio de Janeiro In.) 23·52 s 45·22 w
101 São Sebastião do Paraíso (souN-sĕ-bäs-tē-ouN-dô-pä-rä-ē'sō) . Braz. (Rio de Janeiro In.) 20·54 s 46·58 w
101 São Simão (souN-sē-mouN) Braz. (Rio de Janeiro In.) 21·30 s 47·33 w
164 São Tiago I. (souN tē-ä'gōō) C. V. Is. (In.) 15·09 N 24·45 w
164 São Tomé (souN tô-mā') . . . . . Afr. 0·16 N 6·44 E
101 São Tomé, Cabo de (C.) (kä'bō-dĕ-souN-tô-mĕ') Braz. (Rio de Janeiro In.) 22·00 s 40·00 w
164 São Tomé, Ilhade (I.) (ē'lä-dĕ) . Afr. 0·41 N 6·01 E
114 Saoura, Oued (R.) . . . . Alg. 29·39 N 1·42 w
124 São Vinente, Cabo de (C.) (kä'bō-dĕ-sän-vē-sĕ'n-tĕ) . Port. 37·03 N 9·31 w
101 São Vicente (souN ve-se'n-tĕ) Braz. (Rio de Janeiro In.) 23·57 s 46·25 w
164 Sao Vincente I. (souN vē-sĕn'tȧ) C. V. Is. (In.) 16·51 N 24·35 w
164 Sapele (sä-pā'lā) . . . . Nig. 5·57 N 5·22 E
128 Sapozhok (sä-pô-zhôk') . . Sov. Un. 53·58 N 40·44 E
152 Sapporo (säp-pô'rô) . . . . Jap. 43·02 N 141·29 E
136 Sapronovo (säp-rô'nô-vô) Sov. Un. (Moscow In.) 55·13 N 38·25 E
101 Sapucaí (R.) (sä-pōō-kä-ē') Braz. (Rio de Janeiro In.) 21·07 s 45·53 w
101 Sapucaia (sä-pōō-kä'yȧ) Braz. (Rio de Janeiro In.) 22·01 s 42·54 w
101 Sapucaí Mirim (R.) (sä-pōō-kä-ē'mē-rēN) Braz. (Rio de Janeiro In.) 21·06 s 47·03 w
73 Sapulpa (sȧ-pŭl'pȧ) . . . . Okla. 36·01 N 96·05 w
101 Saquarema (sä-kwä-rĕ-mä) Braz. (Rio de Janeiro In.) 22·56 s 42·32 w
65 Sara (sä'rä) . . Wash. (Portland In.) 45·45 N 122·42 w
127 Sara, Bahr (R.) (bär) Chad-Cen. Afr. Rep. 8·19 N 17·44 E
127 Sarajevo (sȧ-rȧ-yĕv'ô) (sä-rä'ya-vô).Yugo. 43·15 N 18·26 E
136 Sarana (sá-rä'nȧ) Sov. Un. (Urals In.) 56·31 N 57·44 E
81 Saranac Lake . . . . N. Y. 44·20 N 74·05 w
81 Saranac L. (săr'ȧ-năk) . . . . . . N. Y. 44·15 N 74·20 w
100 Sarandi (sä-rän'dē) . . . . . Arg. (In.) 34·26 s 58·21 w
101 Sarandi Grande (sä-rän'dē-grän'dĕ) Ur. (Buenos Aires In.) 33·42 s 56·21 w
142 Sarangpur . . . . India 23·39 N 76·32 E
132 Saransk (sá-ränsk') . . . . . Sov. Un. 54·10 N 45·10 E
136 Sarany (sá-rä'nĭ) Sov. Un. (Urals In.) 58·33 N 58·48 E
132 Sarapul (sä-räpōōl') . . . . . Sov. Un. 56·28 N 53·50 E
79 Sarasota (săr-ȧ-sōtȧ) . . . . . Fla. (In.) 27·27 N 82·30 w
77 Saratoga (săr-ȧ-tō'gȧ) . . . . Tex. 30·17 N 94·31 w
65 Saratoga . . . . . . Wash. (Seattle In.) 48·04 N 122·29 w
65 Saratoga Pass . Wash. (Seattle In.) 48·09 N 122·33 w
81 Saratoga Springs (sprĭngz) . . N. Y. 43·05 N 74·50 w
133 Saratov (sá rä'tôf) . . . . Sov. Un. 51·50 N 45·00 E
151 Saravane . . . . Laos 15·48 N 106·40 E
154 Sarawak (Reg.) (sá-rä'wäk) . . Asia 2·30 N 112·45 E
121 Sárbogárd (shär'bô-gärd) . . . Hung. 46·53 N 18·38 E
85 Sarcee Ind. Res. (sär'sē) Can. (Calgary In.) 50·58 N 114·23 w
164 Sardalas . . . . Libya 25·59 N 10·33 E
126 Sardinia (I.) (sär-dĭn'ĭȧ) . . . . It. 40·08 N 9·05 E
78 Sardis (sär'dĭs) . . . . Miss. 34·26 N 89·55 w
70 Sargent (sär'jĕnt) . . . . Nebr. 41·40 N 99·38 w
133 Sarıkamis . . . . Tur. 40·30 N 42·40 E
125 Sariñena (sä-rēn-yĕ'nä) . . . . Sp. 41·46 N 0·11 w
150 Sariwŏn (sä'rē-wŭn') . . . . Korea 38·40 N 125·45 E
122 Sark (I.) (särk) . . . . Chan. Is. 49·28 N 2·22 w
127 Şarkoy (shär'kû-ê) . . . . Tur. 40·39 N 27·07 E
122 Sarlat (sär-lä') . . . . Fr. 44·52 N 1·13 E
100 Sarmiento, Monte (Mt.) (mô'n-tĕ-sär-myĕn'tō) . Chile 54·28 s 70·40 w
80 Sarnia (sär'nē-ȧ) . . . . Can. 43·00 N 82·25 w
125 Sarno (sä'r-nô) . . . It. (Naples In.) 40·35 N 14·38 E
121 Sarny (sär'nē) . . . . Sov. Un. 51·17 N 26·39 E
127 Saronikós Kólpos (G.) . . . . Grc. 37·51 N 23·30 E
127 Saros Körfezi (G.) (sä'rôs) . . . Tur. 40·30 N 26·20 E
121 Sárospatak (shä'rôsh-pô'tôk) Hung. 48·19 N 21·35 E
127 Šar Planina (Mts.) (shär plä'nê-na) . Yugo. 42·07 N 21·54 E
118 Sarpsborg (särps'bôrg) . . . . Nor. 59·17 N 11·07 E
123 Sarrebourg (sär-bōōr') . . . . Fr. 48·44 N 7·02 E
123 Sarreguemines (sär-gē-mēn') . . . Fr. 49·06 N 7·05 E
124 Sarria (sär'ē-ä) . . . . Sp. 42·14 N 7·17 w
92 Sarstun R. (särs-tōō'n) . . . . . Guat. 15·50 N 89·26 w
126 Sartène (sär-tĕn') . . . . Fr. 41·36 N 8·59 E
122 Sarthe (R.) (särt) . . . . Fr. 47·44 N 0·32 w
Sartor, see Store Sotra
120 Sárvár (shär'vär) . . . . Hung. 47·14 N 16·55 E
133 Sarych, Mys (C.) (mĭs sȧ-rēch') Sov. Un. 44·25 N 33·00 E
134 Sary Ishikotrau, Peski (des.) (sä'rē ē' shĕk-ō'trou) . Sov. Un. 46·12 N 75·30 E
134 Sarysu (R.) (sä'rê-sōō) . . . Sov. Un. 47·47 N 69·14 E
142 Sasaram (sŭs-ŭ-räm') . . . . India 25·00 N 84·00 E
153 Sasayama (sä'sä-yä'mä) . . . . . . Jap. 35·05 N 135·14 E
153 Sasebo (sä'sä-bô) . . . . Jap. 33·12 N 129·43 E
Saseno, see Sazan
120 Sašice . . . . Czech. 49·14 N 13·31 E
86 Saskatchewan (Prov.) . . . . Can. 54·46 N 107·40 w
86 Saskatchewan (R.) (săs-kăch'ē-wăn) . Can. 53·30 N 103·41 w
86 Saskatoon (săs-kȧ-tōōn') . . . . . Can. 52·11 N 106·42 w
119 Saslauka (sȧs-lä'û-kȧ) . . . . Sov. Un. 57·22 N 22·34 E
168 Sasolburg S. Afr. (Johannesburg & Pretoria In.) 26·52 s 27·47 E
132 Sasovo (sȧs'ô-vô) . . . . Sov. Un. 54·20 N 42·00 E
74 Saspamco (săs-păm'cō) Tex. (San Antonio In.) 29·13 N 98·18 w
164 Sassandra R. (sȧs-săn'drȧ) Ivory Coast 6·23 N 6·52 w
126 Sassari (säs'sä-rē) . . . . It. 40·44 N 8·33 E
120 Sassnitz (säs'nēts) . . . . Ger. 54·31 N 13·37 E
164 Satadougou (sä-tȧ-dōō-gōō') . . Mali 12·31 N 11·26 w
118 Säter (sĕ'tĕr) . . . . Swe. 60·21 N 15·50 E
79 Satilla (R.) (sȧ-tĭl'ȧ) . . . . Ga. 31·15 N 82·13 w
136 Satka (sät'kȧ) Sov. Un. (Urals In.) 55·03 N 59·02 E
121 Sátoraljaujhely (shä'tô-rô-lyô-ōō'yĕl') . Hung. 48·24 N 21·40 E
121 Satu-Mare (sȧ'tōō-mȧ'rĕ) . . . Rom. 47·50 N 22·53 E
65 Saturna (sȧ-tûr'nȧ) Can. (Vancouver In.) 48·48 N 123·12 w
65 Saturna (I.) . Can. (Vancouver In.) 48·47 N 123·03 w
118 Saude (sou'dĕ) . . . . Nor. 59·40 N 6·21 E
112 Saudhárkrokur . . . . Ice. 65·41 N 19·38 w
138 Saudi Arabia (sȧ-ōō'dĭ ȧ-rä'bĭ-ȧ) Asia 22·40 N 46·00 E
111 Sauerlach (zou'ĕr-läk) Ger. (Munich In.) 47·58 N 11·39 E
80 Saugatuck (sô'gȧ-tŭk) . . . . . . Mich. 42·40 N 86·10 w
80 Saugeen Pen. (sô'gēn) . . . . Can. 44·55 N 81·20 w
80 Saugeer (R.) (sô'gēr) . . . . Can. 44·20 N 81·20 w
81 Saugerties (sô'gēr-tēz) . . . . . . N. Y. 42·05 N 73·55 w
142 Saugor (sä-gŭr') (sô-gôr') . . . India 23·55 N 78·45 E
83 Saugus (sô'gŭs) . Mass. (Boston In.) 42·28 N 71·01 w
71 Sauk (R.) (sôk) . . . . Minn. 45·30 N 94·45 w
71 Sauk Centre . . . . Minn. 45·43 N 94·58 w
71 Sauk City . . . . Wis. 43·16 N 89·45 w
71 Sauk Rapids (răp'ĭd) . . . . Minn. 45·35 N 94·08 w
Saulai, see Shyaulyay
82 Sault-au-Mouton . . . . Can. 48·34 N 69·20 w
74 Sault Ste. Marie (sōō sānt mȧ-rē') Mich. (Sault Ste. Marie In.) 46·29 N 84·21 w
95 Saumatre, Etang (L.) . . . . Hai. 18·40 N 72·10 w
159 Saunders, C. (sôrn'dĕrs) . N. Z. (In.) 45·55 s 170·50 E
85 Saunders L. (săn'dĕrs) Can. (Edmonton In.) 53·18 N 113·25 w
65 Sausalito (sô-sȧ-lē'tô) Calif. (San Francisco In.) 37·51 N 122·29 w
122 Sausset-les-Pins (sō-sĕ'lā-pȧN') Fr. (Marseille In.) 43·20 N 5·08 E
65 Sauvie I. (sô'vē) Ore. (Portland In.) 45·43 N 123·49 w
127 Sava (R.) (sä'vä) . . . . Yugo. 44·50 N 19·07 E
84 Savage (să'vĕj) Md. (Baltimore In.) 39·07 N 76·49 w
74 Savage . . . . . . Minn. (Minneapolis, St. Paul In.) 44·47 N 93·20 w
133 Savalan (Mtn.) . . . . Iran 38·20 N 48·00 E
164 Savalou . . . . Dahomey 7·58 N 2·00 E
71 Savanna (sȧ-văn'ȧ) . . . . Ill. 42·05 N 90·09 w
79 Savannah (sȧ-văn'ȧ) . . . . Ga. 32·04 N 81·07 w
73 Savannah . . . . Mo. 39·58 N 94·49 w
78 Savannah . . . . Tenn. 35·13 N 88·14 w
79 Savannah (R.) . . . . Ga.-S. C. 33·11 N 81·51 w

ăt; finăl; rāte; senâte; ärm; ȧsk; sofȧ; fâre; ch-choose; dh-as th in other; bē; ēvent; bĕt; recĕnt; cratẽr; g-go; gh-guttural g; bĭt; ĭ-short neutral; rīde; K-guttural k as ch in German ich;

Page	Name Pronunciation Region	Lat. °′	Long. °′
94	Savanna la Mar (sȧ-văn'ȧ lȧ mär') Jam.	18·10 N	78·10 W
120	Sávava R. Czech.	49·36 N	15·24 E
164	Savé (sȧ-vā') Dahomey	8·09 N	2·30 E
122	Save (R.) Fr.	43·32 N	0·50 E
166	Save, Rio (R.) (rē'ō-sȧ'vĕ) Moz.	21·28 S	34·14 E
123	Saverne (sȧ-vĕrn') Fr.	48·40 N	7·22 E
126	Savigliano (sä-vēl-yä'nô) It.	44·38 N	7·42 E
126	Savona (sä-vō'nä) It.	44·19 N	8·28 E
119	Savonlinna (sȧ'vôn-lēn'nȧ) Fin.	61·53 N	28·49 E
129	Savran' (säv-rän') Sov. Un.	48·07 N	30·09 E
154	Savu Sea (sä'vōō) Indon.	9·15 S	122·15 E
154	Sawahlunto Indon.	0·37 S	100·50 E
154	Sawankhalok Thai.	17·16 N	99·48 E
165	Sawda, Jabal as (Mts.) Libya	28·14 N	13·46 E
114	Sawfjjin, Wadi (R.) Libya	31·18 N	13·16 E
168	Sawhāj U. A. R. (Nile In.)	26·34 N	31·40 E
165	Sawknah Libya	29·04 N	15·53 E
154	Sawu (I.) Indon.	10·15 S	122·00 E
65	Sawyer (L.) (sô'yēr) Wash. (Seattle In.)	47·20 N	122·02 W
164	Say (sä'ē) Niger	13·09 N	2·16 E
134	Sayan Khrebet (Mts.) (sŭ-yän') Sov. Un.	51·30 N	90·00 E
139	Sayda (Sidon) (sä'ē-dä) (sī'dŏn) Leb. (Palestine In.)	33·34 N	35·23 E
74	Sayers (sā'ērs) Tex. (San Antonio In.)	29·22 N	98·18 W
144	Sayhūt Aden	15·23 N	51·28 E
72	Sayre (sā'ēr) Okla.	35·19 N	99·40 W
81	Sayre Pa.	41·55 N	76·30 W
84	Sayreton (sā'ēr-tŭn) Ala. (Birmingham In.)	33·34 N	86·51 W
84	Sayreville (sâr'vĭl) N. J. (New York In.)	40·28 N	74·21 W
146	Sayr Usa Mong.	44·51 N	107·00 E
91	Sayula (sä-yōō'lä) Mex.	17·51 N	94·56 W
90	Sayula Mex.	19·50 N	101·33 W
90	Sayula, Luguna de (L.) (lä-gōō'nä-dĕ) Mex.	20·00 N	103·33 W
144	Say'ūn Aden	16·00 N	48·59 E
81	Sayville (sā'vĭl) N. Y.	40·45 N	73·10 W
127	Sazan (Saseno) (I.) Alb.	40·30 N	19·17 E
136	Sazhino (sȧz-hē'nô) Sov. Un. (Urals In.)	56·20 N	58·15 E
118	Scäffle Swe.	59·10 N	12·55 E
138	Scandinavian Pen. Eur.	62·00 N	14·00 E
74	Scanlon (skăn'lôn) Minn. (Duluth In.)	46·27 N	92·26 W
65	Scappoose (skă-pōōs') Ore. (Portland In.)	45·46 N	122·53 W
65	Scappoose (R.) Ore. (Portland In.)	45·47 N	122·57 W
85	Scarborough (skär'bēr-ô) Can. (Toronto In.)	43·45 N	79·12 W
116	Scarborough (skär'bŭr-ô) Eng.	54·16 N	0·19 W
85	Scarborough Junction Can. (Toronto In.)	43·43 N	79·15 W
84	Scarsdale (skärz'dāl) N. Y. (New York In.)	41·01 N	73·47 W
165	Sceui Ghimira Eth.	7·13 N	35·49 E
111	Schaerbeek (skär'bāk) Bel. (Brussels In.)	50·53 N	4·23 E
120	Schaffhausen (shäf'hou-zĕn) Switz.	47·43 N	8·38 E
87	Schefferville Can.	54·52 N	67·01 W
117	Schelde, R. Bel.	51·04 N	3·55 E
81	Schenectady (skĕ-nĕk'tȧ-dē) N. Y.	42·50 N	73·55 W
111	Scheveningen Neth. (Amsterdam In.)	52·06 N	4·15 E
111	Schiedam Neth. (Amsterdam In.)	51·55 N	4·23 E
123	Schiltigheim (shēl'tegh-hīm) Fr.	48·48 N	7·47 E
126	Schio (skē'ô) It.	45·43 N	11·23 E
120	Schleswig (shlĕs'vēgh) Ger.	54·32 N	9·32 E
120	Schleswig-Holstein (State) (shlĕs'vēgh-hōl'shtīn) Ger.	54·40 N	9·10 E
120	Schmalkalden (shmäl'käl-dĕn) Ger.	50·41 N	10·25 E
75	Schneider (schnīd'ēr) Ind. (Chicago In.)	41·12 N	87·26 W
71	Schofield (skō'fēld) Wis.	44·52 N	89·37 W
120	Schönebeck (shû'nĕ-bergh) Ger.	52·01 N	11·44 E
111	Schoonhoven Neth. (Amsterdam In.)	51·56 N	4·51 E
155	Schouten (I.) (skou'tĕn) W. Irian	0·45 S	136·40 E
120	Schramberg (shräm'bĕrgh) Ger.	48·14 N	8·24 E
81	Schroon (L.) (skrōōn) N. Y.	43·50 N	73·50 W
111	Schultzendorf (shōōl'tzĕn-dōrf) Ger. (Berlin In.)	52·21 N	13·35 E
70	Schuyler (skī'ler) Nebr.	41·28 N	97·05 W
81	Schuylkill (skōōl'kĭl) Pa.	40·35 N	76·10 W
120	Schwabach (shvä'bäk) Ger.	49·19 N	11·02 E
120	Schwäbische Alb (Mts.) (shvă'bē-shĕ älb) Ger.	48·11 N	9·09 E
120	Schwäbisch Gmünd (shvă'bēsh gmünd) Ger.	48·47 N	9·49 E
120	Schwäbisch Hall (häl) Ger.	49·08 N	9·44 E
120	Schwandorf (shvän'dôrf) Ger.	49·19 N	12·08 E
154	Schwaner Mts. (skvän'ēr) Indon.	1·38 S	111·08 E
120	Schwarzwald (For.) (shvärts' väld) Ger.	47·54 N	7·57 E
120	Schwaz Aus.	47·20 N	11·45 E
111	Schwechat (shvĕk'ät) Aus. (Vienna In.)	48·09 N	16·29 E
120	Schwedt (shvĕt) Ger.	53·04 N	14·17 E
120	Schweinfurt (shvīn'fōōrt) Ger.	50·03 N	10·14 E
123	Schwelm (shvĕlm) Ger. (Ruhr In.)	51·17 N	7·18 E
120	Schwenningen (shvĕn'ĭng-ĕn) Ger.	48·04 N	8 33 E
120	Schwerin (shvĕ-rēn') Ger.	53·36 N	11·25 E
120	Schweriner See (L.) (shvĕ'rē-nĕr zā) Ger.	53·40 N	11·06 E
123	Schwerte (shvĕr'tĕ) Ger. (Ruhr In.)	51·26 N	7·34 E
111	Schwielow L. (shvē'lōv) Ger. (Berlin In.)	52·20 N	12·52 E
120	Schwyz (shvēts) Switz.	47·01 N	8·38 E

Page	Name Pronunciation Region	Lat. °′	Long. °′
126	Sciacca (shē-äk'kä) It.	37·30 N	13·09 E
116	Scilly (Is.) (sĭl'ē) Eng.	49·56 N	6·50 W
80	Scioto (R.) (sī-ō'tō) Ohio	39·10 N	82·55 W
83	Scituate (sĭt'ū-āt) Mass. (Boston In.)	42·12 N	70·45 W
67	Scobey (skō'bē) Mont.	48·48 N	105·29 W
65	Scoggin (skŏ'gĭn) Ore. (Portland In.)	45·28 N	123·14 W
85	Scotch R. (skŏch) Can. (Ottawa In.)	45·21 N	74·56 W
66	Scotia (skō'shȧ) Calif.	40·29 N	124·06 W
116	Scotland (skŏt'lȧnd) U. K.	57·05 N	5·10 W
70	Scotland S. D.	43·08 N	97·43 W
79	Scotland Neck (nĕk) N. C.	36·06 N	77·25 W
81	Scotstown (skŏts'toun) Can.	45·35 N	71·15 W
86	Scott, C. (skŏt) Can.	50·48 N	129·34 W
66	Scott, Mt. Ore.	42·55 N	122·00 W
65	Scott, Mt. Ore. (Portland In.)	45·27 N	122·33 W
74	Scott Air Force Base Ill. (St. Louis In.)	38·33 N	89·52 W
167	Scottburgh (skŏt'bŭr-ô) S. Afr. (Natal In.)	30·18 S	30·42 E
72	Scott City Kans.	38·28 N	100·54 W
84	Scottdale (skŏt' dāl) Ga. (Atlanta In.)	33·47 N	84·16 W
47	Scott Is. Ant.	67·24 S	179·55 W
47	Scott Ra. Ant.	68·00 S	55·00 E
70	Scottsbluff (skŏts'blŭf) Nebr.	41·52 N	103·40 W
70	Scotts Bluff Natl. Mon. Nebr.	41·45 N	103·47 W
78	Scottsboro (skŏts'bŭro) Ala.	34·40 N	86·03 W
80	Scottsburg (skŏts' bûrg) Ind.	38·40 N	85·50 W
160	Scottsdale (skŏts'dāl) Austl.	41·12 S	147·37 E
78	Scottsville (skŏts'vĭl) Ky.	36·45 N	86·10 W
80	Scottville Mich.	44·00 N	86·20 W
81	Scranton (skrăn'tŭn) Pa.	41·45 N	75·45 W
81	Scugog (L.) (skū'gôg) Can.	44·05 N	78·55 W
110	Scunthorpe (skŭn'thôrp) Eng.	53·36 N	0·38 W
	Scutari, see Shkodër		
127	Scutari (R.) (skōō'tä-rē) Alb.	42·14 N	19·33 E
79	Sea, Is. (sē) Ga.-S. C.	31·21 N	81·05 W
65	Seabeck (sē'bĕck) Wash. (Seattle In.)	47·38 N	122·50 W
65	Seabold (sē'bōld) Wash. (Seattle In.)	47·42 N	122·33 W
84	Sea Bright (sē brīt) N. J. (New York In.)	40·22 N	73·58 W
77	Seabrook (sē'brŏŏk) Tex. (In.)	29·34 N	95·01 W
81	Seaford (sē'fērd) Del.	38·35 N	75·40 W
72	Seagraves (sē'grāvs) Tex.	32·51 N	102·38 W
86	Seal (R.) Can.	59·08 N	96·37 W
74	Seal Beach Calif. (Los Angeles In.)	33·44 N	118·06 W
95	Seal Cays (Is.) Turks & Caicos Is.	21·10 N	71·45 W
95	Seal Cays (Is.) Ba. Is.	22·40 N	75·55 W
166	Seal I. (sēl) S. Afr. (Cape Town In.)	34·07 S	18·36 E
77	Sealy (sē'lē) Tex.	29·46 N	96·10 W
166	Sea Point (sē point) S. Afr. (Cape Town In.)	33·55 S	18·23 E
73	Searcy (sûr'sē) Ark.	35·13 N	91·43 W
68	Searles (L.) (sûrl's) Calif.	35·44 N	117·22 W
82	Searsport (sērz'pōrt) Maine	44·28 N	68·55 W
66	Seaside (sē'sīd) Ore.	45·59 N	123·55 W
65	Seattle (sē-ăt''l) Wash. (Seattle In.)	47·36 N	122·20 W
92	Sebaco (sĕ-bä'kô) Nic.	12·50 N	86·03 W
82	Sebago (sē-bā'gō) Maine	43·52 N	70·20 W
88	Sebastion Vizcaino, Bahia (B.) (bä-ē'ä-sĕ-bäs-tyô'n-vēs-kä-ē'nô) Mex.	28·45 N	115·15 W
68	Sebastopol (sē-bȧs'tō-pōl) Calif.	38·27 N	122·50 W
154	Sebatik (I.) Indon.	3·52 N	118·14 E
127	Sebes Rom.	45·58 N	23·34 E
80	Sebewaing (se'bē-wăng) Mich.	43·45 N	83·25 W
128	Sebezh (syĕ'bĕzh) Sov. Un.	56·16 N	28·29 E
133	Sebinkarahisar Tur.	40·15 N	38·10 E
124	Sebkha bou Areg (Marsh) Mor.	35·09 N	3·02 W
125	Sebkhan d'Oran (L.) Alg.	35·28 N	0·28 W
120	Sebnitz (zĕb'nēts) Ger.	51·01 N	14·16 E
125	Seborbe (sĕ-bōr-dĕ) Sp.	39·50 N	0·30 W
114	Sebou, Oued R. Mor.	34·23 N	5·18 W
80	Sebree (sē-brē') Ky.	37·35 N	87·30 W
79	Sebring (sē'brĭng) Fla. (In.)	27·30 N	81·26 W
80	Sebring Ohio	40·55 N	81·05 W
126	Secchia (R.) (sĕ'kyä) It.	44·25 N	10·25 E
91	Seco (R.) (sĕ'kô) Mex.	18·11 N	93·18 W
165	Second Cataract Sud.	21·52 N	31·18 E
73	Sedalia (sē-dā'lē-ȧ) Mo.	38·42 N	93·12 W
122	Sedan (sē-däN') Fr.	49·49 N	4·55 E
73	Sedan (sē-dăn') Kans.	37·07 N	96·08 W
110	Sedgley (sĕdj'lĭ) Eng.	52·32 N	2·07 W
139	Sedom Isr. (Palestine In.)	31·04 N	35·24 E
65	Sedro Woolley (sē'drô-wŏŏl'ē) Wash. (Seattle In.)	48·30 N	122·14 W
119	Šeduva (shĕ'dŏŏ-vá) Sov. Un.	55·46 N	23·45 E
166	Seekoevlei (L.) (zā'kŏŏf-lī) S. Afr. (Cape Town In.)	34·04 S	18·33 E
111	Seestall (zā'shtäl) Ger. (Munich In.)	47·58 N	10·52 E
114	Sefrou (sĕ-frōō') Mor.	33·49 N	4·46 W
132	Seg (L.) (syĕgh) Sov. Un.	64·00 N	33·30 E
139	Segamat (sā'gȧ-mȧt) Mala. (Singapore In.)	2·30 N	102·49 E
164	Ségou (sā-gōō') Mali	13·24 N	6·20 W
98	Segovia (sĕ-gō'vēä) Col. (In.)	7·08 N	74·42 W
124	Segovia (sĕ-gō'vē-ä) Sp.	40·58 N	4·05 W
	Segovia, see Coco		
125	Segre (R.) (sā'grä) Sp.	41·54 N	1·10 E
64	Seguam (I.) (sē'gwäm) Alaska	52·16 N	172·10 W
64	Seguam P. Alaska	52·20 N	173·00 W
164	Séguela (sā-gā-lä') Ivory Coast	8·03 N	7·05 W
76	Seguin (sĕ-gēn') Tex.	29·35 N	97·58 W
64	Segula (I.) (sē-gū'lȧ) Alaska	52·08 N	178·35 E
125	Segura (R.) (sā-gōō'rä) Sp.	38·07 N	0·33 W
124	Segura, Sierra de (Mts.) (sē-ĕ'r-rä-dĕ) Sp.	38·05 N	2·45 W

Page	Name Pronunciation Region	Lat. °′	Long. °′
124	Segura (R.) Sp.	38·24 N	2·12 W
142	Sehwān W. Pak.	26·33 N	67·51 E
95	Seibo (sĕ'y-bō) Dom. Rep.	18·45 N	69·05 W
119	Seinäjoki (sā'ē-nĕ-yô'kē) Fin.	62·47 N	22·50 E
122	Seine, Baie de la (B.) (bī dĕ lä sĕn) Fr.	49·37 N	0·53 W
71	Seine (R.) (sān) Can.	49·04 N	91·00 W
122	Seine, Rivière (R.) (rēv-yâr') Fr.	49·21 N	1·17 E
85	Seine R. (sān) Can. (Winnipeg In.)	49·48 N	97·04 W
100	Seio do Venus (Mtn.) (sĕ-yô-dô-vĕ'nōōs) Braz. (In.)	22·28 S	43·12 W
125	Seixal (sā-ē-shäl') Port. (Lisbon In.)	38·38 N	9·06 W
164	Sekondi-Takoradi (sĕ-kôn'dē tä-kô-rä'dē) Ghana	4·55 N	1·53 W
139	Selangor (State) (sā-län'gōr) Mala. (Singapore In.)	2·53 N	101·29 E
127	Selanoutsi (sâl'ä-nôv-tsĭ) Bul.	43·42 N	24·05 E
155	Selaru (I.) Indon.	8·30 S	130·30 E
154	Selatan, Tandjung (C.) (sȧ-lä'tän) Indon.	4·09 S	114·40 E
64	Selawik (sē-lȧ-wĭk) Alaska	66·30 N	160·09 W
118	Selbu (L.) (sĕl'bōō) Nor.	63·18 N	11·55 E
110	Selby (sĕl'bē) Eng.	53·47 N	1·03 W
64	Seldovia (sĕl-dō'vē-ȧ) Alaska	59·26 N	151·42 W
135	Selemdzha (R.) (sȧ-lĕmt-zhä') Sov. Un.	52·28 N	131·50 E
135	Selenga (R.) (sĕ lĕŋ gä') Sov. Un.	51·00 N	106·40 E
146	Selenge Gol (R.) Mong.	49·04 N	102·23 E
135	Selennyakh (R.) (sĕl-yĭn-yäk) Sov. Un.	67·42 N	141·45 E
123	Sélestat (sē-lē-stä') Fr.	48·16 N	7·27 E
164	Selibaby (sȧ-lē-bȧ-bē') Mauritania	15·21 N	12·11 W
128	Seliger (L.) (sĕl'lē-gĕr) Sov. Un.	57·14 N	33·18 E
142	Seling Tsho (L.) China	31·55 N	89·00 E
142	Selipuk Gömpa China	31·37 N	82·42 E
128	Selizharovo (sâ'lē-zhä'rô-vô) Sov. Un.	56·51 N	33·28 E
86	Selkirk (sĕl'kûrk) Can.	50·13 N	97·07 W
86	Selkirk Mts. Can.	50·14 N	116·42 W
65	Selleck (sĕl'ĕck) Wash. (Seattle In.)	47·22 N	121·52 W
75	Sellersburg (sĕl'ērs-bûrg) Ind. (Louisville In.)	38·25 N	85·45 W
135	Sellya Khskaya, Guba (B.) (sĕl-yäk'skȧ-yȧ) Sov. Un.	72·30 N	136·00 E
78	Selma (sĕl'mȧ) Ala.	32·25 N	87·00 W
68	Selma Calif.	36·34 N	119·37 W
79	Selma N. C.	35·33 N	78·16 W
74	Selma Tex. (San Antonio In.)	29·33 N	98·19 W
111	Selsingen (zĕl'zĕn-gĕn) Ger. (Hamburg In.)	53·22 N	9·13 E
166	Selukwe (sē-lŭk'wē) S. Rh.	19·34 S	30·03 E
66	Selway R. (sĕl'wȧ) Idaho	46·07 N	115·12 W
86	Selwyn (L.) (sĕl'wĭn) Can.	59·41 N	104·30 W
127	Seman (R.) Alb.	40·48 N	19·53 E
154	Semarang (sĕ-mä'räng) Indon.	7·03 S	110·27 E
154	Semarinda Indon.	0·30 S	117·10 E
	Semendria, see Smederevo		
129	Semënovka (sĕ-myôn'ôf-kȧ) Sov. Un.	52·10 N	32·34 E
65	Semiahmoo Ind. Res. Can. (Vancouver In.)	49·01 N	122·43 W
65	Semiahmoo Spit (sĕm'ī-ȧ-mōō) Wash. (Vancouver In.)	48·59 N	122·52 W
64	Semichi Is. (sē mē'chī) Alaska	52·40 N	174·50 E
67	Seminoe Res. (sĕm'ĭ nô) Wyo.	42·08 N	107·10 W
73	Seminole (sĕm'ĭ-nōl) Okla.	35·13 N	96·41 W
79	Seminole Ind. Res. Fla. (In.)	26·19 N	81·11 W
79	Seminole Ind. Res. Fla. (In.)	27·05 N	81·25 W
78	Seminole, L. Fla.-Ga.	30·57 N	84·46 W
134	Semipalatinsk (sĕ'mē-pȧ-lȧ-tyĕnsk') Sov. Un.	50·28 N	80·29 E
64	Semisopochnoi (I.) (sĕ-mē-sȧ-pōsh' noi) Alaska	51·45 N	179·25 E
134	Semiyarskoye (sĕ'mē-yär'skô-yĕ) Sov. Un.	51·03 N	78·28 E
165	Semliki R. (sĕm'lē-kē) Con. L.-Ug.	0·45 N	29·36 E
	Semlin, see Zemun		
120	Semmering P. (sĕm'ĕr-ĭng) Aus.	47·39 N	15·50 E
133	Semnān Iran	35·30 N	53·30 E
99	Senador Pompeu (sĕ-nä-dōr-pôm-pĕ'ōō) Braz.	5·34 S	39·18 W
78	Senatobia (sĕ-nȧ-tō'bē-ȧ) Miss.	34·36 N	89·56 W
152	Sendai (sĕn-dī') Jap.	38·18 N	141·02 E
73	Seneca (sĕn'ē-kȧ) Kans.	39·49 N	96·03 W
78	Seneca S. C.	34·40 N	82·58 W
81	Seneca (L.) N. Y.	42·30 N	76·55 W
81	Seneca Falls N. Y.	42·55 N	76·55 W
163	Senegal (sĕn-ĕ-gôl') Afr.	14·53 N	14·58 W
164	Senegal R. Senegal-Mauritania	16·45 N	14·37 W
168	Senekal (sĕn'ĕ-kȧl) S. Afr. (Johannesburg & Pretoria In.)	28·20 S	27·37 E
120	Senftenberg (zĕnf'tĕn-bĕrgh) Ger.	51·32 N	14·00 E
99	Senhor do Bonfim (sĕn-yôr dô bôN-fē'N) Braz.	5·21 S	40·09 W
126	Senigallia (sä-nē-gäl'lyä) It.	43·42 N	13·16 E
126	Senj (sĕn') Yugo.	44·58 N	14·55 E
112	Senja (I.) (sĕnyä) Nor.	69·28 N	16·10 E
123	Senlis (säN-lēs') Fr. (Paris In.)	49·13 N	2·35 E
165	Sennar (sĕn-när') Sud.	13·34 N	33·32 E
165	Sennar Dam Sud.	13·38 N	33·38 E
87	Senneterre Can.	48·20 N	77·22 W
128	Senno (syĕ'nô) Sov. Un.	54·48 N	29·43 E
122	Sens (säNs) Fr.	48·05 N	3·18 E
92	Sensuntepeque (sĕn-sōōn-tȧ-pä'kȧ) Sal.	13·53 N	88·34 W
127	Senta (sĕn'tä) Yugo.	45·54 N	20·05 E
153	Senzaki (sĕn'zä-kē) Jap.	34·22 N	131·09 E
	Seoul, see Sŏul		
139	Sepang Mala. (Singapore In.)	2·43 N	101·45 E
100	Sepetiba, Baia de (B.) (bäē'ä dĕ sä-pȧ-tē'bȧ) Braz. (In.)	23·01 S	43·42 W
155	Sepik (R.) (sĕp-ēk') N. Gui. Ter.	4·07 S	142·40 E

Page Name Pronunciation Region Lat. °' Long. °'

122 Septèmes-les-Vallons (sĕ-tâm'la-vä-ôN') Fr. (Marseille In.) 43·25 N 5·23 E
95 Septentrional, Cordillera (Mts.) (kôr-dēl-yĕ'rä sĕp-tĕn-tryō-nä'l) Dom. Rep. 19·50 N 71·15 W
123 Septeuil (sĕ-tû') Fr. (Paris In.) 48·53 N 1·40 E
82 Sept-Iles Can. 50·11 N 66·21 W
78 Sequatchie (R.) (sē-kwăch'ē) Tenn 35·33 N 85·14 W
65 Sequim (sē'kwĭm) Wash. (Seattle In.) 48·05 N 123·07 W
65 Sequim B. Wash. (Seattle In.) 48·04 N 122·58 W
68 Sequoia Natl. Park (sē-kwoi'á) Calif. 36·34 N 118·37 W
117 Seraing (sē-răN') Bel. 50·38 N 5·28 E
155 Seram (I.) Indon. 2·45 S 129·30 E
142 Serampore India (Calcutta In.) 22·44 N 88·21 E
154 Serang (så-răng') Indon. 6·13 S 106·10 E
139 Seranggung Indon. (Singapore In.) 0·49 N 104·11 E
Serbia (Reg.), see Srbija
133 Serdobsk (sĕr-dôpsk') Sov. Un. 52·30 N 44·20 E
129 Seredina-Buda (sĕ-rå-dē'ná-bōō'dá) Sov. Un. 52·11 N 34·03 E
139 Seremban (sĕr-ĕm-bän') Mala. (Singapore In.) 2·44 N 101·57 E
166 Serenje (sē-rĕn'yē) N. Rh. 13·12 S 30·49 E
168 Serenli (så-rĕn'lē) Som. (Horn of Afr. In.) 2·28 N 42·15 E
Seres, see Sérrai
121 Seret Czech. 48·17 N 17·43 E
121 Seret Rom. 47·58 N 26·01 E
121 Seret R. (sĕr'ĕt) Sov. Un. 49·45 N 25·30 E
134 Sergeya Kirova (I.) (sĕr-gyĕ'yà kē'rô-vá) Sov. Un. 77·30 N 86·10 E
99 Sergipe (State) (sĕr-zhē'pĕ) Braz. 10·27 S 37·04 W
132 Sergiyevsk Sov. Un. 53·58 N 51·00 E
127 Sérifos Grc. 37·10 N 24·32 E
127 Sérifos (I.) Grc. 37·42 N 24·17 E
101 Serodino (sĕ-rô-dē'nō) Arg. (Buenos Aires In.) 32·36 S 60·56 W
100 Seropédica (sĕ-rô-pĕ'dē-kä) Braz. (In.) 22·44 S 43·43 W
136 Serov (syĕ-rôf') Sov. Un. (Urals In.) 59·36 N 60·30 E
166 Serowe (sĕ-rō'wĕ) Bech. 22·18 S 26·39 E
124 Serpa (sĕr-pä) Port. 37·56 N 7·38 W
128 Serpukhov (syĕr'pōō-kôf) Sov. Un. 54·53 N 37·27 E
127 Sérrai (Seres) (sĕr'rĕ) (sĕr'ĕs) Grc. 41·06 N 23·36 E
76 Serranias Del Burro (sĕr-rä-nē'äs dĕl bōō'r-rô) Mex. 29·39 N 102·07 W
99 Serrinha (sĕr-rēn'yá) Braz. 11·43 S 38·49 W
124 Serta (sĕr'tà) Port. 39·48 N 8·01 W
99 Sertânia (sĕr-tà'nyä) Braz. 8·28 S 37·13 W
101 Sertãozinho (sĕr-touN-zē'n-yô) Braz. (Rio de Janeiro In.) 21·10 S 47·58 W
139 Serting (R.) Mala. (Singapore In.) 3·01 N 102·32 E
100 Seruí (sĕ-rōō-ē') Braz. (In.) 22·40 S 43·08 W
126 Sesia (R.) (såz'yä) It. 45·33 N 8·25 E
125 Sesimbra (sĕ-sē'm-brä) Port. (Lisbon In.) 38·27 N 9·06 W
167 Sesmyl (R.) S. Afr. (Johannesburg & Pretoria In.) 25·51 S 28·06 E
126 Sestri Levante (sĕs'trē lå-vän'tå) It. 44·15 N 9·24 E
136 Sestroretsk (sĕs-trô'rĕtsk) Sov. Un. (Leningrad In.) 60·06 N 29·58 E
136 Sestroretskiy Razliv, Ozero (L.) (ô'zĕ-rô sĕs-trô' rĕts-kĭ räz'lĭf) Sov. Un. (Leningrad In.) 60·05 N 30·07 E
153 Seta (sĕ'tä) Jap. (Ōsaka In.) 34·58 N 135·56 E
122 Sète (Cette) (sĕt) Fr. 43·24 N 3·42 E
99 Sete Lagoas (sĕ-tĕ lä-gô'äs) Braz. 19·23 S 43·58 W
164 Setif (så-tēf') Alg. 36·18 N 5·21 E
153 Seto (sē'tō) Jap. 35·11 N 137·07 E
153 Seto-Naikai (Sea) (sĕ'tô nī'kī) Jap. 33·50 N 132·25 E
164 Settat (sĕt-ät') (sē-tà') Mor. 33·02 N 7·30 W
166 Setté-Cama (sĕ-tĕ-kä-mä') Gabon 2·29 S 9·40 E
94 Settlement Pt. (sĕt'l-mĕnt) Ba. Is. 26·40 N 79·00 W
168 Settlers (sĕt'lĕrs) S. Afr. (Johannesburg & Pretoria In.) 24·57 S 28·33 E
125 Setúbal (så-tōō'bäl) Port. (Lisbon In.) 30·32 N 8·54 W
124 Setúbal, B. de (bä-ē'ä) Port. 38·27 N 9·08 W
87 Seul, Lac (L.) (låk sûl) Can. 50·28 N 91·26 W
118 Sevalen (L.) (sĕ'vä-lĕn) Nor. 62·19 N 10·15 E
133 Sevan (L.) (syĭ-vän') Sov. Un. 40·10 N 45·20 E
129 Sevastopol' (Akhiar) (syĕ-vås-tô'pôl'') (äK'yår) Sov. Un. 44·34 N 33·34 E
Seven Is., see Shichitō
110 Sevenoaks (sĕ-vĕn-ôks') Eng. (London In.) 51·16 N 0·12 E
136 Severka R. (sâ'vĕr-kà) Sov. Un. (Moscow In.) 55·11 N 38·41 E
87 Severn (R.) (sĕv'ĕrn) Can. 55·21 N 88·42 W
116 Severn (R.) Eng. 51·42 N 2·25 W
84 Severna Park (sĕv'ĕrn-å) Md. (Baltimore In.) 39·04 N 76·33 W
132 Severnaya Dvina (Northern Dvina) (R.) Sov. Un. 63·00 N 42·40 E
130 Severnaya Zemlya (Northern Land) (Is.) (sĕ-vyĭr-nī'u zĭ-m'lyä') Sov. Un. 79·33 N 101·15 E
136 Severoural'sk (sĕ-vyĭ-rŭ-ōō-rälsk') Sov. Un. (Urals In.) 60·08 N 59·53 E
69 Sevier (L.) (sē-vēr') Utah 38·55 N 113·10 W
69 Sevier R. Utah 39·25 N 112·20 W
69 Sevier R., East Fork Utah 37·45 N 112·10 W
98 Sevilla (sĕ-vē'l-yä) Col. (In.) 4·16 N 75·56 W
124 Sevilla (så-vēl'yä) Sp. 37·29 N 5·58 W
75 Seville (sĕ'vĭl) Ohio (Cleveland In.) 41·01 N 81·54 W
127 Sevlievo (sĕv'lyĕ-vô) Bul. 41·02 N 25·05 E
122 Sèvre Nantaise (R.) (så'vrĕ näN-tàz') Fr. 47·00 N 1·02 W
122 Sèvre Niortaise (R.) (så'vr' nyôr-tâz') Fr. 46·23 N 1·05 W
128 Sevsk (syĕfsk) Sov. Un. 52·08 N 34·28 E
64 Seward (sū'ārd) Alaska 60·18 N 149·28 W
73 Seward Nebr. 40·55 N 97·06 W
64 Seward Pen Alaska 65·40 N 164·00 W
100 Sewell (sĕ'ōō-ĕl) Chile 34·01 S 70·18 W
75 Sewickley (sē-wĭk'lē) Pa. (Pittsburg In.) 40·33 N 80·11 W
91 Seybaplaya (sā-ē-bä-plä'yä) Mex. 19·38 N 90·40 W
47 Seychelles (Is.) (sā-shĕl') Afr. 5·20 S 55·10 E
112 Seydhisfjördhur (sā'dês-fyûr-dōōr) Ice. 65·21 N 14·08 W
92 Seyé (sĕ-yĕ') Mex. (Yucatan In.) 20·51 N 89·22 W
115 Seyhan (R.) Tur. 37·28 N 35·40 E
129 Seym (R.) (sĕym) Sov. Un. 51·23 N 33·22 E
80 Seymour (sē'mōr) Ind. 38·55 N 85·55 W
71 Seymour Iowa 40·41 N 93·03 W
72 Seymour Tex. 33·35 N 99·16 W
167 Seymour (sē'môr) S. Afr. (Natal In.) 32·33 S 26·48 E
167 Sezela S. Afr. (Natal In.) 30·33 S 30·37 W
126 Sezze (sĕt'så) It. 41·32 N 13·03 E
127 Sfântul-Gheorghe Rom. 45·53 N 25·49 E
164 Sfax (sfäks) Tun. 34·51 N 10·45 E
111 's Gravenhage (The Hague) ('s Krä'vĕn-hä'Kĕ) (hāg) Neth. (Amsterdam In.) 52·05 N 4·16 E
147 Sha (R.) (shä) China 33·33 N 114·30 E
148 Sha (R.) China 34·47 N 118·27 E
148 Sha (R.) China 39·26 N 122·08 E
166 Shabani S. Rh. 20·15 S 30·28 E
136 Shablykino (sháb-lē'kĭ-nô) Sov. Un. (Moscow In.) 56·22 N 38·37 E
149 Shaching China (Canton In.) 22·44 N 113·48 E
47 Shackleton Shelf Ice (shăk''l-tŭn) Ant. 65·00 S 100·00 E
84 Shades Cr. (shādz) Ala. (Birmingham In.) 33·20 N 86·55 W
84 Shades Mtn. Ala. (Birmingham In.) 33·22 N 86·51 W
144 Shagrā (shäg'rä) Sau. Ar. 25·13 N 45·15 E
144 Shahdād Iran 30·45 N 57·45 E
142 Shah Fuladi (Mt.) Afg. 39·33 N 67·38 E
165 Shahhāt Libya 32·49 N 21·46 E
142 Shāhjahānpur (shä-jŭ-hän'pōōr) India 27·58 N 79·58 E
150 Shaho (shä-hō') China (Peking In.) 40·08 N 116·16 E
144 Shahrezā (shä-rā'zä) Iran 31·47 N 51·47 E
133 Shahsavār Iran 36·40 N 51·00 E
75 Shaker Hts. (shā'kĕr) Ohio (Cleveland In.) 41·28 N 81·34 W
129 Shakhty (shäK'tē) Sov. Un. 47·41 N 40·11 E
74 Shakopee (shăk'ô-pe) Minn. (Minneapolis, St. Paul In.) 44·48 N 93·31 W
165 Shala L. (shä'lä) Eth. 7·34 N 39·00 E
144 Sham, Jabal ash (Mtn.) Mus. & Om. 23·01 N 57·45 E
165 Shambe (shäm'bå) Sud. 7·08 N 30·46 E
144 Shammar, Jabal (Mts.) (jĕb'ĕl shŭm'år) Sau. Ar. 27·13 N 40·16 E
81 Shamokin (shá-mō'kĭn) Pa. 40·45 N 76·30 W
72 Shamrock (shăm'rŏk) Tex. 35·14 N 100·12 W
166 Shamva (shäm'vå) S. Rh. 17·18 S 31·35 E
75 Shandon (shăn-dŭn) Ohio (Cincinnati In.) 39·20 N 84·13 W
148 Shangch'eng (shäng'chĕng) China 31·47 N 115·22 E
148 Shangchialin (shäng'jĭä'lĭn) China 38·20 N 116·05 E
148 Shangch'iu (shäng'chĭō) China 34·24 N 115·39 E
149 Shanghai (shäng'hī') China (Shanghai In.) 31·14 N 121·27 E
149 Shanghaihsien China (Shanghai In.) 31·02 N 121·24 E
148 Shanghai Shih (Prov.) China 31·30 N 121·45 E
148 Shangho (shäng'hŏ) China 37·18 N 117·10 E
151 Shangjao China 28·25 N 117·58 E
148 Shangts'ai (shäng'tsī) China 33·16 N 114·16 E
150 Shangtu China 41·38 N 113·22 E
147 Shanhsi (Shansi) (Prov.) China 37·31 N 111·30 E
148 Shanhsien (shän'hsyĕn') China 34·47 N 116·04 E
84 Shannon (shăn'ŭn) Ala. (Birmingham In.) 33·23 N 86·52 W
116 Shannon R. (shăn'ŏn) Ire. 52·30 N 9·58 W
146 Shanshan (shän'shän') China 42·51 N 89·53 E
Shansi, see Shanhsi
135 Shantar (I.) (shän'tär) Sov. Un. 55·13 N 138·42 E
151 Shant'ou (Swatow) (swä'tō') China 23·20 N 116·40 E
147 Shantung (Prov.) China 36·08 N 117·09 E
151 Shantung Pantao (Pen.) China 37·00 N 120·10 E
151 Shantung Pt. (shän'tōōng') China 37·28 N 122·40 E
151 Shaohsing China 30·00 N 120·40 E
148 Shaopo (shou'pō') China 32·33 N 119·30 E
148 Shaopo Hu (L.) (shou'pō' hōō) China 32·07 N 119·13 E
136 Shapki (shäp'kĭ) Sov. Un. (Leningrad In.) 59·36 N 31·11 E
158 Shark B. (shärk) Austl. 25·30 S 113·00 E
83 Sharon (shăr'ŏn) Mass. (Boston In.) 42·07 N 71·11 W
80 Sharon Pa. 41·15 N 80·30 W
72 Sharon Springs Kan. 38·51 N 101·45 W
75 Sharonville (shăr'ŏn vĭl) Ohio (Cincinnati In.) 39·16 N 84·24 W
75 Sharpsburg (shärps'bûrg) Pa. (Pittsburgh In.) 40·30 N 79·54 W
144 Sharr, Jabal (Mtn.) Sau. Ar. 28·00 N 36·07 E
151 Shashih China 30·20 N 112·18 E
66 Shasta, Mt. Calif. 41·35 N 122·12 W
66 Shasta L. (shăs'tà) Calif. 40·51 N 122·32 W
132 Shatsk (shàtsk) Sov. Un. 54·00 N 41·40 E
72 Shattuck (shăt'ŭk) Okla. 36·16 N 99·53 W
86 Shaunavon Can. 49·37 N 108·29 W
78 Shaw (shô) Miss. 33·36 N 90·44 W
71 Shawano (shá-wô'nō) Wis. 44·41 N 88·13 W
87 Shawinigan Falls Can. 46·32 N 72·46 W
74 Shawnee (shô-nē') Mo. (Kansas City In.) 39·01 N 94·43 W
73 Shawnee Okla. 35·20 N 96·54 W
80 Shawneetown (shô'nē-toun) Ill. 37·40 N 88·05 W
151 Shayang China 31·00 N 112·38 E
121 Shchara (R.) (sh-chä'rå) Sov. Un. 53·17 N 25·12 E
136 Shchëlkovo (shchĕl'kô-vô) Sov. Un. (Moscow In.) 55·55 N 38·00 E
129 Shchëtovo (shchĕ'tô-vô) Sov. Un. 48·11 N 39·13 E
129 Shchigry (shchē'grē) Sov. Un. 51·52 N 36·54 E
129 Shchors (shchôrs) Sov. Un. 51·38 N 31·58 E
136 Shchuch'ye Ozero (shchōōch'yĕ ô'zĕ-rō) Sov. Un. (Urals In.) 56·31 N 56·35 E
142 Sheakhala India (Calcutta In.) 22·47 N 88·10 E
168 Shebeli R. (shā'bå-lē) Eth. (Horn of Afr. In.) 6·07 N 43·10 E
71 Sheboygan (shē-boi'gǎn) Wis. 43·45 N 87·44 W
71 Sheboygan Falls Wis. 43·43 N 87·51 W
164 Shebshi Mts. Nig.-Cam. 8·22 N 12·14 E
82 Shediac (shĕ'dē-ăk) Can. 46·16 N 64·33 W
116 Sheelin (L.) (shēlĭn) Ire. 53·46 N 7·34 W
110 Sheerness (shēr'nĕs) Eng. (London In.) 51·26 N 0·46 E
78 Sheffield (shĕf'fēld) Ala. 35·42 N 87·42 W
85 Sheffield Can. (Toronto In.) 43·20 N 80·13 W
110 Sheffield Eng. 53·23 N 1·28 W
75 Sheffield Ohio (Cleveland In.) 41·26 N 82·05 W
75 Sheffield Lake Ohio (Cleveland In.) 41·30 N 82·03 W
148 Shehsien (shĕ'hsyĕn') China 36·34 N 113·42 E
116 Shehy, Mts. Ire. 51·46 N 9·35 W
132 Sheksna (R.) (shĕks'nà) Sov. Un. 59·50 N 38·40 E
135 Shelagskiy, Mys (C.) (shĭ-läg'skē) Sov. Un. 70·08 N 170·52 E
73 Shelbina (shĕl-bī'nȧ) Ark. 39·41 N 92·03 W
82 Shelbourne (shĕl'bǔrn) Can. 43·46 N 65·20 W
80 Shelburn (shĕl'bǔrn) Ind. 39·10 N 87·30 W
81 Shelburne Can. 44·05 N 80·05 W
75 Shelby (shĕl'bē) Ind. (Chicago In.) 41·12 N 87·21 W
80 Shelby Mich. 43·35 N 86·20 W
78 Shelby Miss. 33·56 N 90·44 W
67 Shelby Mont. 48·26 N 111·50 W
79 Shelby N. C. 35·16 N 81·35 W
80 Shelby Ohio 40·50 N 82·40 W
80 Shelbyville (shĕl'bē-vĭl) Ill. 39·20 N 88·45 W
80 Shelbyville Ind. 39·30 N 85·45 W
80 Shelbyville Ky. 38·10 N 85·15 W
78 Shelbyville Tenn. 35·30 N 86·28 W
70 Sheldon (shĕl'dǔn) Iowa 43·10 N 95·50 W
77 Sheldon Tex. (In.) 29·52 N 95·07 W
135 Shelekhova, Zaliv (B.) Sov. Un. 60·00 N 156·00 E
64 Shelikof Str. (shĕ'lē-kôf) Alaska 57·56 N 154·20 W
84 Shell Beach (bĕch) La. (New Orleans In.) 29·52 N 89·41 W
67 Shelley (shĕl'lē) Idaho 43·24 N 112·06 W
84 Shell I. (shĕl) La. (New Orleans In.) 29·17 N 89·42 W
71 Shellrock (R.) (shĕl'rŏk) Iowa 43·25 N 93·19 W
128 Shelon' (R.) (shâ'lôn) Sov. Un. 57·50 N 29·40 E
81 Shelton (shĕl'tǔn) Conn. 41·15 N 73·05 W
72 Shelton Nebr. 40·46 N 98·41 W
66 Shelton Wash. 47·14 N 123·05 W
136 Shemakha (shĕ-mà-kä') Sov. Un. (Urals In.) 56·16 N 59·19 E
133 Shemakha Sov. Un. 40·35 N 48·40 E
73 Shenandoah (shĕn-ǎn-dō'ȧ) Iowa 40·46 N 95·23 W
81 Shenandoah Pa. 40·50 N 76·15 W
81 Shenandoah Va. 38·30 N 78·30 W
81 Shenandoah Natl. Park Va. 38·35 N 78·25 W
81 Shenandoah (R.) Va. 38·55 N 78·05 W
148 Shenchiu (shenchĭō) China 33·11 N 115·06 E
165 Shendi (shĕn'dē) Sud. 16·44 N 33·29 E
148 Shengfang (shengfäng) China 39·05 N 116·40 E
146 Shenhsi (Shensi) (Prov.) (shĕn'sē') China 35·04 N 108·45 E
148 Shenhsien (shen'sĭän) China 38·02 N 115·33 E
132 Shenkursk (shĕn-kōōrsk') Sov. Un. 62·10 N 43·08 E
150 Shenmu China 38·55 N 110·35 E
Shensi, see Shenhsi
148 Shentse (shen'zhŏ) China 38·12 N 115·12 E
150 Shenyang (Mukden) (shĕn'yäng') (mōōk'dĕn) China 41·45 N 123·22 E
142 Sheopur India 25·37 N 78·10 E
85 Shepard (shĕ'pȧrd) Can. (Calgary In.) 50·57 N 113·54 W
129 Shepetovka (shĕ-pĕ-tôf'kȧ) Sov. Un. 50·10 N 27·01 E
160 Shepparton (shĕp'ȧr-tǔn) Austl. 36·15 S 145·25 E
83 Sherborn (shûr'bǔrn) Mass. (Boston In.) 42·15 N 71·22 W
81 Sherbrooke (shûr'brŏŏk) Can. 45·25 N 72·00 W
110 Sherburn (shûr'bǔrn) Eng. 53·47 N 1·15 W
121 Shereshevo (shĕ-rĕ-shĕ-vô) Sov. Un. 52·31 N 24·08 E
73 Sheridan (shĕr'ĭ-dǎn) Ark. 34·19 N 92·21 W
66 Sheridan Ore. 45·06 N 123·22 W
67 Sheridan Wyo. 44·48 N 106·56 W
73 Sherman (shĕr'mǎn) Tex. 33·39 N 96·37 W
136 Sherna R. (shĕr'nȧ) Sov. Un. (Moscow In.) 56·08 N 38·45 E
86 Sherridon Can. 55·08 N 101·00 W
111 's Hertogenbosch (sĕr-tō'ghĕn-bôs) Neth. (Amsterdam In.) 51·41 N 5·19 E
65 Sherwood (shûr'wŏŏd) Ore. (Portland In.) 45·21 N 122·50 W
110 Sherwood For. Eng. 53·11 N 1·07 W
116 Shetland (Is.) (shĕt'lǎnd) Scot. 60·35 N 2·10 W
139 Sheva R. Isr. (Palestine In.) 31·15 N 34·38 E
70 Sheyenne (R.) (shī-ĕn') N. D. 46·42 N 97·52 W
80 Shiawassee (R.) (shī-ȧ-wôs'ē) Mich. 43·15 N 84·05 W
144 Shibām (shē'bäm) Aden 16·02 N 48·40 E
168 Shibeli R. Som. (Horn of Afr. In.) 1·38 N 43·50 E

ăt; finǎl; rāte; senāte; ärm; åsk; sofȧ; fâre; ch-choose; dh-as th in other; bē; ēvent; bĕt; recĕnt; cratĕr; g-go; gh-guttural g; bĭt; ĭ-short neutral; rīde; K-guttural k as ch in German ich;

Page	Name Pronunciation Region	Lat. °′	Long. °′
168	Shibīn al Kawn (shē-bēn′ĕl kōm′) U. A. R. (Nile In.)	30·31 N	31·01 E
168	Shībin al Qanāţir (kȧ-nä′têr) U. A. R. (Nile In.)	30·18 N	31·21 E
153	Shichitō (Seven Is.) (shē′chē-tō) Jap.	34·18 N	139·28 E
67	Shields R. (shēldz) Mont.	45·54 N	110·40 W
110	Shifnal (shĭf′nȧl) Eng.	52·40 N	2·22 W
148	Shih (R.) (shē hŏ) China	32·09 N	114·11 E
148	Shihchiangchen (shē′kĭäng′zhen) China	32·16 N	120·59 E
149	Shihch′iao China (Canton In.)	22·56 N	113·22 E
148	Shihchiu Hu (L.) (shē′jĭō′ho͞o) China	31·29 N	119·07 E
	Shihkiachwang, see Shihmen		
151	Shihlung China	23·05 N	113·58 E
148	Shihmen (Shihkiachwang) (shē mĕn) (shē′jĭȧ′zho͞oäng) China	38·04 N	114·31 E
148	Shihohienfou China	31·27 N	117·51 E
144	Shihr Aden	14·45 N	49·32 E
149	Shiht′ou China (Canton In.)	23·01 N	113·23 E
148	Shihts′un (shē′cho͞oen) China	33·47 N	117·18 E
148	Shihtzu Shan (Mts.) (shē′jĕ shän) China	37·17 N	121·38 E
149	Shihwan China (Canton In.)	23·01 N	113·04 E
151	Shihwanta Shan (Mtns.) China	22·10 N	107·30 E
150	Shihwei Pk China	47·11 N	119·59 E
142	Shikarpur W. Pak.	27·51 N	68·52 E
153	Shiki (shē′kē) Jap. (Tōkyō In.)	35·50 N	139·35 E
153	Shikoku (I.) (shē′kō′ko͞o) Jap.	33·43 N	133·33 E
135	Shilka (R.) (shĭl′kȧ) Sov. Un.	53·00 N	118·45 E
142	Shilla (Mt.) India	37·18 N	78·17 E
142	Shillong (shēl-lông′) India	25·39 N	91·58 E
74	Shiloh (shī′lō) Ill. (St. Louis In.)	38·34 N	89·54 W
153	Shimabara (shē′mä-bä′rä) Jap.	32·46 N	130·22 E
153	Shimada (shē′mä-dä) Jap.	34·49 N	138·13 E
153	Shimizu (shē′mē-zo͞o) Jap.	35·00 N	138·29 E
153	Shimminato (shēm′mē′nä-tō) Jap.	36·47 N	137·05 E
153	Shimoda (shē′mō-dȧ) Jap.	34·41 N	138·58 E
143	Shimoga India	13·59 N	75·38 E
153	Shimonoseki (shē′mō-nō-sĕ′kē) (shē-mō-nō′sĕ-kĭ) Jap.	33·58 N	130·55 E
153	Shimo-Saga (shē′mō sä′gä) Jap. (Ōsaka In.)	35·01 N	135·41 E
116	Shin, Loch (L.) (lŏk shĭn) Scot.	58·08 N	4·20 W
153	Shinagawa-Wan (B.) (shē′nä-gä′wä wän) Jap. (Tōkyō In.)	35·37 N	139·49 E
153	Shinano-Gawa (Strm.) (shē-nä′nō gä′wä) Jap.	36·43 N	138·22 E
65	Shine (shīn) Wash. (Seattle In.)	47·52 N	122·40 W
153	Shingū (shĭn′go͞o) Jap.	33·43 N	135·59 E
153	Shinji (L.) (shĭn′jē) Jap.	35·23 N	133·05 E
165	Shinko R. (shĭn′kō) Cen. Afr. Rep.	6·37 N	24·31 E
166	Shinyanga (shĭn-yäŋ′gä) Tan.	3·35 S	33·07 E
152	Shiono Misaki (C.) (shē-ō′nō mē′sä-kē) Jap.	33·20 N	136·10 E
94	Ship Channel Cay (I.) (shĭp chă-nĕl kē) Ba. Is.	24·50 N	76·50 W
110	Shipley (shĭp′lē) Eng.	53·50 N	1·47 W
82	Shippegan Can.	47·44 N	64·45 W
82	Shippegan (I.) Can.	47·50 N	64·38 W
81	Shippenburg (shĭp′ĕn bûrg) Pa.	40·00 N	77·30 W
82	Shipshaw (R.) (shĭp′shô) Can.	48·50 N	71·03 W
139	Shiqma (R.) Isr. (Palestine In.)	31·31 N	34·40 E
153	Shirane-san (Mtn.) (shē′rä′nā-sän′) Jap.	35·44 N	138·14 E
152	Shira Saki (C.) (shē′rä sä′kē) Jap.	41·25 N	142·10 E
166	Shirati (shē-rä′tē) Tan.	1·15 S	34·02 E
144	Shiraz (shē-räz′) Iran	29·32 N	52·27 E
166	Shire (R.) (shē′rā) Nya.	15·10 S	34·58 E
129	Shirokoye (shē′rô-kō-yĕ) Sov. Un.	47·40 N	33·18 E
142	Shirpuri India	25·31 N	77·46 E
64	Shishaldin Vol. (shī-shăl′dĭn) Alaska	54·48 N	164·00 W
75	Shively (shīv′lē) Ky. (Louisville In.)	38·11 N	85·47 W
139	Shivta Isr. (Palestine In.)	30·53 N	34·38 E
69	Shivwits (Shebit) Ind. Res. (shĭv′wĭts) (shĕ′bĭt) Utah	37·10 N	113·50 W
69	Shivwits Plat Ariz.	36·13 N	113·42 W
83	Shirley (shûr′lē) Mass. (Boston In.)	42·33 N	71·39 W
153	Shizuki (shĭ′zo͞o-kē) Jap.	34·29 N	134·51 E
153	Shizuoka (shē′zo͞o′ōkȧ) Jap.	34·58 N	138·24 E
128	Shklov (shklôf) Sov. Un.	54·11 N	30·23 E
127	Shkodër (Scutari) (shkô′dûr) (sko͞o′tȧrē) Alb.	42·04 N	19·30 E
152	Shkotovo (shkô′tô-vô) Sov. Un.	43·15 N	132·21 E
73	Shoal Cr. (shōl) Ill.	38·37 N	89·25 W
80	Shoals (shōlz) Ind.	38·40 N	86·45 W
142	Shoapur India	25·53 N	76·45 E
153	Shodo (I.) (shō′dō) Jap.	34·27 N	134·27 E
143	Sholāpur (shō′lä-po͞or) India	17·42 N	75·51 E
139	Shoniron Jordan (Palestine In.)	32·18 N	35·14 E
75	Shorewood (shōr′wo͝od) Wis. (Milwaukee In.)	43·05 N	77·54 W
67	Shoshone (shō-shōn′ē) Idaho	42·56 N	114·24 W
67	Shoshone L Wyo.	44·17 N	110·50 W
67	Shoshone R Wyo.	44·20 N	109·28 W
129	Shostka (shôst′kȧ) Sov. Un.	51·51 N	33·31 E
148	Sh′ouchang (shō′zhäng) China	35·59 N	115·52 E
148	Shouhsien China	32·36 N	116·45 E
148	Shoukuang (shō′go͞oäng) China	36·53 N	118·45 E
129	Shpola (shpō′lȧ) Sov. Un.	49·01 N	31·36 E
77	Shreveport (shrēv′pōrt) La.	32·30 N	93·46 W
110	Shrewsbury (shro͞oz′bēr-ĭ) Eng.	52·43 N	2·44 W
83	Shrewsbury Mass. (Boston In.)	42·18 N	71·43 W
110	Shropshire (Co.) (shrŏp′shēr) Eng.	52·36 N	2·45 W
94	Shroud Cay (I.) (shroud) Ba. Is.	24·20 N	76·40 W
150	Shuangch′eng China	45·18 N	126·18 E
148	Shuangho (sho͞oäng hŏ) China	31·33 N	116·48 E
148	Shuanglunho (sho͞oäng′lo͝oĕn′hŏ) China	31·50 N	115·07 E
150	Shuangyang China	43·28 N	125·45 E
71	Shullsburg (shŭlz′bûrg) Wis.	42·35 N	90·16 W
148	Shulyehehen (sho͞olĭĕhŭhĕn) China	36·08 N	114·07 E
64	Shumagin (Is.) (sho͞o′mȧ-gēn) Alaska	55·22 N	159·20 W
151	Shunan (sho͞o′nän′) China	29·38 N	119·00 E
64	Shungnak (shŭng′nȧk) Alaska	66·55 N	157·20 W
150	Shuni (sho͞on′yĭ′) China (Peking In.)	40·09 N	116·38 E
146	Shunning (shŭ′nĭng′) China	24·34 N	99·49 E
149	Shunte China (Canton In.)	22·50 N	113·15 E
136	Shunut, ′Gora (Mt.) (gȧ-rä sho͞o′no͝ot) Sov. Un. (Urals In.)	56·33 N	59·45 E
144	Shuqrah Aden	13·32 N	46·02 E
144	Shūrāb (R.) (sho͞o rāb) Iran	31·02 N	55·43 E
152	Shuri (sho͞o′rē) Ryūkyū Is.	26·10 N	127·48 E
133	Shur R. (sho͞or) Iran	35·40 N	50·10 E
144	Shūstar (sho͞osh′tŭr) Iran	31·50 N	48·46 E
128	Shuya (sho͞o′yȧ) Sov. Un.	56·52 N	41·23 E
148	Shuyang (sho͞o yäng) China	34·09 N	118·47 E
145	Shweba Bur.	22·23 N	96·13 E
	Shyaulyay, see Šiauliai		
152	Siakin (L.) (sĭä′jĭn) China	42·25 N	132·45 E
139	Siak Ketjil (R.) Indon. (Singapore In.)	1·01 N	101·45 E
139	Siak Sri Indrapura (sē-äks′rĭ ēn′drȧ-po͞o′rä) Indon. (Singapore In.)	0·48 N	102·05 E
142	Sialkot (sē-äl′kōt) W. Pak.	32·39 N	74·30 E
	Siam, see Thailand		
154	Siam, G. of (sī-ăm′) Thai.	11·37 N	100·46 E
150	Sian (Hsian) (syän′) China	34·20 N	109·00 E
148	Siaowu Shan (Mts.) (sĭou′wo͞o shän) China	39·48 N	114·52 E
127	Siátista (syä′tĭs-ta) Grc.	40·15 N	21·32 E
155	Siau (I.) Indon.	2·40 N	126·00 E
119	Šiauliai (Shyaulyay) (shē-ou′lē-ī) Sov. Un.	55·57 N	23·19 E
136	Sibay (sē′báy) Sov. Un. (Urals In.)	52·41 N	58·40 E
126	Šibenik (shē-bā′nēk) Yugo.	43·44 N	15·55 E
138	Siberia (Reg.) Asia	57·00 N	97·00 E
154	Siberut (I.) (sē′bā-ro͞ot) Indon.	1·22 S	99·45 E
142	Sibī W. Pak.	29·41 N	67·52 E
166	Sibiti (sē-bē-tē′) Con. B.	3·35 S	13·10 E
127	Sibiu (sē-bĭ-o͞o′) Rom.	45·47 N	24·09 E
70	Sibley (sĭb′lē) Iowa	43·24 N	95·33 W
154	Sibolga (sē-bō′gā) Indon.	1·45 N	98·45 E
145	Sibsagar (sēb-sŭ′gŭr) India	26·47 N	94·45 E
154	Sibuti Phil.	4·40 N	119·30 E
155	Sibuyan (I.) (sē-bo͞o-yän′) Phil. (Manila In.)	12·19 N	122·25 E
154	Sibuyan Sea Phil.	12·43 N	122·38 E
154	Sicapoo (Mtn.) (sē-kä-po͞o′) Phil.	18·05 N	121·03 E
113	Sicily (I.) (sĭs′ĭ-lē) It.	37·38 N	13·30 E
92	Sico R. (sē′kō) Hond.	15·32 N	85·42 W
98	Sicuaní (sē-kwä′nē) Peru	14·12 S	71·12 W
165	Sidamo (Prov.) (sē-dä′mō) Eth.	5·08 N	37·45 E
126	Siderno Marina (sē-dĕr′nō mä-rē′nä) It.	38·18 N	16·19 E
126	Sídheros, Akr. (C.) Grc. (Inset)	35·19 N	26·20 E
127	Sidhiró Kastron Grc.	41·13 N	23·27 E
125	Sidi-Aïsa Alg.	35·53 N	3·44 E
165	Sīdī Barrānī U. A. R.	31·41 N	26·09 E
164	Sidi-bel Abbès (sē′dē-bĕl ȧ-bĕs′) Alg.	35·15 N	0·43 W
164	Sidi Ifni (ēf′nē) Ifni	29·22 N	10·15 W
47	Sidley, Mt. (sĭd′lē) Ant.	77·25 S	129·00 W
67	Sidney (sĭd′nē) Mont.	47·43 N	104·07 W
70	Sidney Nebr.	41·10 N	103·00 W
80	Sidney Ohio	40·20 N	84·10 W
78	Sidney Lanier, L. (lăn′yēr) Ga.	34·27 N	83·56 W
	Sidon, see Sayda		
121	Siedlce (syĕd′′l-tsĕ) Pol.	52·09 N	22·20 E
123	Siegburg (zēg′bo͞orgh) Ger. (Ruhr In.)	50·48 N	7·13 E
123	Siegen (zē′ghĕn) Ger. (Ruhr In.)	50·52 N	8·01 E
111	Sieghartskirchen Aus. (Vienna In.)	48·16 N	16·00 E
120	Sieg R. (zēg) Ger.	50·51 N	7·53 E
121	Siemiatycze (syĕm′yä′tē-chĕ) Pol.	52·26 N	22·52 E
121	Siemionówka (sēĕ-mēŏ′-nôf-kȧ) Pol.	52·53 N	43·50 E
154	Siem Reap (syĕm′rā′ȧp) Camb.	13·32 N	103·54 E
126	Siena (sē-ĕn′ä) It.	43·19 N	11·21 E
121	Sieradz (syĕ′rädz) Pol.	51·35 N	18·45 E
124	Siero (syā′rō) Sp.	43·24 N	5·39 W
121	Sierpc (syĕrpts) Pol.	52·51 N	19·42 E
76	Sierra Blanca (sē-ĕ′rȧ blaŋ-kȧ) Tex.	31·10 N	105·20 W
69	Sierra Blanca Pk. (blăn′kȧ) N. Mex.	33·25 N	105·50 W
163	Sierra Leone (sē-ĕr′rä lā-ō′nā) Afr.	8·48 N	12·30 E
74	Sierra Madre (mă′drē) Calif. (Los Angeles In.)	34·10 N	118·03 W
76	Sierra Mojada (sē-ĕ′r-rä-mō-кä′dä) Mex.	27·22 N	103·42 W
127	Sífnos (I.) Grc.	36·58 N	24·30 E
118	Sigdal (sēgh′däl) Nor.	60·01 N	9·35 E
122	Sigean (sē-zhŏɴ′) Fr.	43·02 N	2·56 E
71	Sigeurney (sē-gûr-nĭ) Iowa	41·16 N	92·10 W
121	Sighet (sē-gāt′) Rom.	47·57 N	23·55 E
121	Sighisoara (sē-gē-shwä′rȧ) Rom.	46·11 N	24·48 E
112	Siglufjördhur Ice.	66·06 N	18·45 W
133	Signakhi Sov. Un.	41·45 N	45·50 E
74	Signal Hill (sĭg′nȧl hĭl) Calif. (Los Angeles In.)	33·48 N	118·11 W
98	Sigsig (sēg-sēg′) Ec.	3·05 S	78·44 W
118	Sigtuna (sēgh-to͞o′nȧ) Swe.	59·40 N	17·39 E
94	Siguanea, Ensenada de la (B.) (ĕn-sĕ-nä-dä-dĕ-lä-sē-gwä-nā′ä) Cuba	21·45 N	83·15 W
92	Siguatepeque (sē-gwȧ′tĕ-pĕ-kĕ) Hond.	14·33 N	87·51 W
124	Sigüenza (sē-gwĕ′n-zä) Sp.	41·03 N	2·38 W
164	Siguiri (sē-gē-rē′) Gui.	11·30 N	9·04 W
133	Siirt (sĭ-ērt′) Tur.	38·00 N	42·00 E
164	Sikasso (sē-käs′sō) Mali	11·15 N	5·43 W
73	Sikeston (sīks′tŭn) Mo.	36·50 N	89·35 W
135	Sikhote Alin′, Khrebet (Mts.) (se-кô′ta a-lēn′) Sov. Un.	45·00 N	135·45 E
127	Sikinos (I.) (sĭ′kĭ-nōs) Grc.	36·45 N	24·55 E
142	Sikkim Asia	27·42 N	88·25 E
121	Siklós (sĭ′klōsh) Hung.	45·51 N	18·18 E
124	Sil (R.) (sē′l) Sp.	42·20 N	7·13 W
155	Silang (sē-läng′) Phil. (Manila In.)	14·14 N	120·58 E
90	Silao (sē-lä′ō) Mex.	20·56 N	101·25 W
142	Silchar (sĭl-chär′) India	24·52 N	92·50 E
168	Silent Valley (sī′lĕnt vă′lē) S. Afr. (Johannesburg & Pretoria In.)	24·32 S	26·40 E
79	Siler City (sī′lēr) N. C.	35·45 N	79·29 W
121	Silesia (Reg.) (sĭ-lē′shȧ) Pol.	50·58 N	16·53 E
133	Silifke Tur.	36·20 N	34·00 E
115	Silistra (sē-lēs′trȧ) Bul.	44·01 N	27·13 E
118	Siljan (R.) (sēl′yän) Swe.	60·48 N	14·28 E
118	Silkeborg (sĭl′kĕ-bôr′) Den.	56·10 N	9·33 E
85	Sillery (sēl′-re′) Can. (Quebec In.)	46·46 N	71·15 W
73	Siloam Springs (sī-lōm) Ark.	36·10 N	94·32 W
90	Silocayoápan (sē-lō-kä-yō-ȧ′pän) Mex.	17·29 N	98·09 W
77	Silsbee (sĭlz′ bē) Tex.	30·19 N	94·09 W
119	Šilutė (shĭ-lo͞o′tā) Sov. Un.	55·23 N	21·26 E
101	Silva Jardim (sē′l-vä-zhär-dēɴ) Braz. (Rio de Janeiro In.)	22·40 S	42·24 W
65	Silvana (sĭl-vän′ȧ) Wash. (Seattle In.)	48·12 N	122·16 W
99	Silvânia (sēl-vȧ′nyä) Braz.	16·43 S	48·33 W
166	Silva Porto (sĭl′vȧ pōr′to͝o) Ang.	12·20 S	17·05 E
73	Silver (L.) Mo.	39·38 N	93·12 W
74	Silverado (sĭl-vēr-ä′dō) Calif. (Los Angeles In.)	33·45 N	117·40 W
95	Silver Bk. Ba. Is.	20·40 N	69·40 W
95	Silver Bank Passage (Str.) Ba. Is.	20·40 N	70·20 W
71	Silver Bay Minn.	47·24 N	91.07 W
69	Silver City (sĭl′vēr sĭ′tĭ) N. Mex.	32·45 N	108·20 W
93	Silver City Pan.	9·20 N	79·54 W
81	Silver Creek (crēk) N. Y.	42·35 N	79·10 W
69	Silver Cr. Ariz.	34·30 N	110·05 W
75	Silver Cr. Ind. (Louisville In.)	38·20 N	85·45 W
75	Silver Cr., Muddy Fk. Ind. (Louisville In.)	38·26 N	85·52 W
65	Silverdale (sĭl′vēr-dāl) Wash. (Seattle In.)	49·39 N	122·42 W
75	Silver Lake (lāk) Wis. (Milwaukee In.)	42·33 N	88·10 W
75	Silver L. Wis. (Milwaukee In.)	42·35 N	88·08 W
81	Silver Spring (sprĭng) Md.	39·00 N	77·00 W
65	Silver Star Mtn. Wash. (Portland In.)	45·45 N	122·15 W
69	Silverton (sĭl′vēr-tŭn) Colo.	37·50 N	107·40 W
75	Silverton Ohio (Cincinnati In.)	39·12 N	84·24 W
66	Silverton Ore.	45·02 N	122·46 W
167	Silverton S. Afr. (Johannesburg & Pretoria In.)	25·45 S	28·13 E
124	Silves (sēl′vĕzh) Port.	37·15 N	8·24 W
66	Silvies R. (sĭl′vēz) Ore.	43·44 N	119·15 W
168	Silwá (Baḩrī) U. A. R. (Nile In.)	24·43 N	32·58 E
136	Sim (sĭm) Sov. Un. (Urals In.)	55·00 N	57·42 E
80	Simcoe (sĭm′kō) Can.	42·50 N	80·20 W
81	Simcoe (L.) Can.	44·30 N	79·20 W
154	Simeuloee (I.) Indon.	2·27 N	95·30 E
129	Simferopol′ (Akmechet) (sēm-fĕ-rô′pōl′) (ȧk-mĕch′ĕt) Sov. Un.	44·58 N	34·04 E
115	Simi (I.) Grc.	36·27 N	27·41 E
65	Similk Beach (sē′mĭlk) Wash. (Seattle In.)	48·27 N	122·35 W
142	Simla (sĭm′lȧ) India	31·09 N	77·15 E
121	Simleul-Silvaniei (shēm-lā′o͞ol-sēl-vă′nyĕ-ē) Rom.	47·14 N	22·46 E
94	Simms Pt. Ba. Is.	25·00 N	77·40 W
91	Simojovel (sē-mō-hō-vĕl′) Mex.	17·12 N	92·43 W
119	Simola (sē′mō-lȧ) Fin.	60·55 N	28·06 E
101	Simonésia (sē-mō-nĕ′syä) Braz. (Rio de Janeiro In.)	20·04 S	41·53 W
166	Simonstown (sī′mŭnztoun) S. Afr. (Cape Town In.)	34·11 S	18·25 E
120	Simplon P. (sĭm′plŏn) (săɴ-plôɴ′) Switz.	46·13 N	7·53 E
120	Simplon Tun. It.-Switz.	46·16 N	8·20 E
71	Simpson (I.) Can.	48·43 N	87·44 W
158	Simpson Des. (sĭmp-sŭn) Austl.	24·40 S	136·40 E
86	Simpson Pen. Can.	68·58 N	89·20 W
118	Simrishamn (sēm′rēs-hăm′n) Swe.	55·35 N	14·19 E
136	Sim R. Sov Un. (Urals In.)	55·00 N	57·42 E
77	Sims Bay, (sĭmz bī-yo͞o′) Tex. (In.)	29·37 N	95·23 W
135	Simushir (I.) (se-mo͞o′shēr) Sov. Un.	47·15 N	150·47 E
127	Sinaia (sĭ-nä′yȧ) Rom.	45·20 N	25·30 E
165	Sinai Pen. (sī′nī) U. A. R.	29·24 N	33·29 E
155	Sinait (sē-nä′ēt) Phil. (Manila In.)	15·54 N	120·28 E
88	Sinaloa (State) (sē-nä-lô-ä) Mex.	25·15 N	107·45 W
152	Sinanju (sĭ′nän-jo͝o′) Kor.	39·39 N	125·41 E
133	Sinap Tur.	42·00 N	35·05 E
98	Sincé (sēn′sā) Col.	9·15 N	75·14 W
98	Sincelejo (sēn-sā-lā′hō) Col.	9·12 N	75·30 W
65	Sinclair Inlet (sĭn-klâr′) Wash. (Seattle In.)	47·31 N	122·41 W
119	Sindi (sēn′dē) Sov. Un.	58·20 N	24·40 E
129	Sinel′nikovo (sē′nyĕl-nē′kô′vō) Sov. Un.	49·19 N	35·33 E
124	Sines (sē′nāzh) Port.	37·57 N	8·50 W
165	Singa (sĭŋ′gȧ) Sud.	13·09 N	33·52 E
139	Singapore (sĭn′gȧ-pōr′) Singapore I. (Singapore In.)	1·18 N	103·52 E
139	Singapore I. Asia (Singapore In.)	1·22 N	103·45 E
139	Singapore Str. Indon. (Singapore In.)	1·14 N	104·20 E

ng-sing; ŋ-baŋk; ɴ-nasalized n; nŏd; cŏmmit; ōld; ôbey; ôrder; fo͞od; fo͝ot; ou-out; s-soft; sh-dish; th-thin; pūre; ûnite; ûrn; stŭd; circŭs; ü-as "y" in study; ′-indeterminate vowel.

Page	Name Pronunciation Region	Lat. °′	Long. °′
154	Singaradjac (sĭŋ'gȧ-rä'jä) Indon.	8·15 S	115·03 E
127	Singitikós Kólpos (G.) Grc.	40·15 N	24·00 E
146	Singu (sĭn'gŭ) Bur.	22·37 N	96·04 E
167	Singunyane (R.) Bas. (Natal In.)	29·35 S	28·08 E
129	Siniye Lipyagi (sēn'ē-ĕ lēp'yȧ-gē) Sov. Un.	51·24 N	38·29 E
126	Sinj (sēn') Yugo.	43·42 N	16·39 E
146	Sinkiang Uighur (Aut. Reg.) China	40·15 N	82·15 E
136	Sin'kovo (sĭn-kô'vô) Sov. Un. (Moscow In.)	56·23 N	37·19 E
99	Sinnamary Fr. Gu.	5·15 N	57·52 W
126	Sinni (R.) (sēn'nē) It.	40·05 N	16·15 E
168	Sinnūris U. A. R. (Nile In.)	29·25 N	30·52 E
100	Sino, Pedra do (Mtn.) (pĕ'drä-dô-sē'nô) Braz. (In.)	22·27 S	43·02 W
166	Sinoia (sĭ-noi'ȧ) S. Rh.	17·17 S	30·09 E
111	Sint Niklaas Bel. (Brussels In.)	51·10 N	4·07 E
77	Sinton (sĭn'tŭn) Tex.	28·03 N	97·30 W
125	Sintra (sēn'trȧ) Port. (Lisbon In.)	38·48 N	9·23 W
111	Sint Truiden Bel. (Brussels In.)	50·49 N	5·14 E
152	Sinŭiju (sĭ'nŏŏĭ-jōō) Kor.	40·04 N	124·33 E
136	Sinyavino (sĭn-yä'vĭ-nô) Sov. Un. (Leningrad In.)	59·50 N	31·07 E
128	Sinyaya (R.) (sėn'yȧ-yȧ) Sov. Un.	56·40 N	28·20 E
129	Sinyukha (R.) (sē'nyōō-kȧ) Sov. Un.	48·34 N	30·49 E
120	Sion (sē'ôN') Switz.	46·15 N	7·17 E
70	Sioux City (sōō) Iowa	42·30 N	96·25 W
70	Sioux Falls (fôlz) S. D.	43·33 N	96·43 W
87	Sioux Lookout Can.	50·11 N	91·42 W
98	Sipí (sē-pē') Col. (In.)	4·39 N	76·38 W
86	Sipiwesk Can.	55·36 N	97·24 W
78	Sipsey (R.) (sĭp'sē) Ala.	33·26 N	87·42 W
154	Sipura (I.) Indon.	2·15 S	99·33 E
90	Siqueros (sē-kā'rōs) Mex.	23·19 N	106·14 W
93	Siquia, R. (sē-kē'ä) Nic.	12·23 N	84·36 W
113	Siracusa (sē-rä-koo'sä) It.	37·02 N	15·19 E
142	Sirājganj (sĭ-räj'gŭnj) E. Pak.	24·23 N	89·43 E
92	Sirama (sē-rä-mä) Sal.	13·23 N	87·55 W
158	Sir Edward Pellew Group (Is.) (pĕl'ū) Austl.	15·15 S	137·15 E
121	Siretul R. Rom.	46·10 N	27·18 E
144	Sirham, Wadi (R.) Sau. Ar.	31·02 N	37·16 E
127	Síros (Ermoúpolis) Grc.	37·30 N	24·56 E
127	Síros (I.) Grc.	37·23 N	24·55 E
142	Sirsa India	29·39 N	75·02 E
119	Širvintos (shēr'vĭn-tôs) Sov. Un.	55·02 N	24·59 E
91	Sisal (sē-säl') Mex.	21·09 N	90·03 W
126	Siska (sē'säk) Yugo.	45·29 N	16·20 E
68	Sisquoc (R.) (sĭs'kwŏk) Calif.	34·47 N	120·13 W
70	Sisseton (sĭs'tŭn) S. D.	45·39 N	97·04 W
144	Sistān, Daryacheh-ye (L.) Iran-Afg.	31·45 N	61·15 E
123	Sisteron (sēst'rôN') Fr.	44·10 N	5·55 E
80	Sisterville (sĭs'tēr-vĭl) W. Va.	39·30 N	81·00 W
126	Sitía (sē'tĭ-ȧ) Grc. (In.)	26·10 N	35·09 E
64	Sitka (sĭt'kȧ) Alaska	57·08 N	135·18 W
64	Sitka Natl. Mon. Alaska	57·20 N	136·10 W
110	Sittingbourne (sĭt-ĭng-bôrn) Eng. (London In.)	51·20 N	0·44 E
133	Sivas (sē'väs) Tur.	39·50 N	36·50 E
129	Sivash (L.) (sē'vȧsh) Sov. Un.	45·55 N	34·42 E
133	Siverek (sē'vĕ-rĕk) Tur.	37·50 N	39·20 E
119	Siverskaya (sē'vĕr-skȧ-yȧ) Sov. Un.	59·17 N	30·03 E
165	Sīwah (Oasis) (sē'wä) U. A. R.	29·33 N	25·11 E
93	Sixaola R. (sē-kä-ō'lä) (sĕk-sȧ-ō'lȧ) C. R.	9·31 N	83·07 W
165	Sixth Cataract Sud.	16·26 N	32·44 E
118	Sjaelland (I.) (shĕl'lăn') Den.	55·34 N	11·35 E
127	Sjenica (syĕ'nē-tsȧ) Yugo.	43·15 N	20·02 E
129	Skadovsk (skä'dôfsk) Sov. Un.	46·08 N	32·54 E
118	Skagen (skä'ghĕn) Den.	57·43 N	10·32 E
118	Skagen (Pt.) Den.	57·43 N	10·31 E
118	Skagerrak (Str.) (skä-ghĕ-räk') Eur.	57·43 N	8·28 E
65	Skagit B. (skăg'ĭt) Wash. (Seattle In.)	48·20 N	122·32 W
66	Skagit R. Wash.	48·29 N	121·52 W
64	Skagway (skăg-wā) Alaska	59·30 N	135·28 W
118	Skälderviken (B.) Swe.	56·20 N	12·25 E
135	Skalistyy, Golets (Mtn.) Sov. Un.	57·28 N	119·48 E
65	Skamania (skȧ-mā'nĭ-ȧ) Wash. (Portland In.)	45·37 N	122·03 W
65	Skamokawa (skȧ-mä'nĭ-ȧ) Wash. (Portland In.)	46·16 N	123·27 W
118	Skanderborg (skän'ĕr-bôr') Den.	56·04 N	9·55 E
81	Skaneateles (skăn-ĕ-ăt'lĕs) N. Y.	42·55 N	76·25 W
81	Skaneateles (L.) N. Y.	42·50 N	76·20 W
118	Skänninge (shĕn'ĭng-ĕ) Swe.	58·24 N	15·02 E
118	Skanör (skän'ûr) Swe.	55·24 N	12·49 E
127	Skantzoúra (Is.) (skän'tsōō-rä) Grc.	39·03 N	24·05 E
118	Skara (skä'rȧ) Swe.	58·25 N	13·24 E
86	Skeena (R.) Can.	54·31 N	129·21 W
167	Skeerpoort S. Afr. (Johannesburg & Pretoria In.)	25·49 S	27·45 E
167	Skeerpoort (R.) S. Afr. (Johannesburg & Pretoria In.)	25·58 S	27·41 E
99	Skeldon (skĕl'dŭn) Br. Gu.	5·49 N	57·15 W
112	Skellefte (R.) (shĕl'ĕf-tē) Swe.	65·18 N	19·08 E
112	Skellefteå (shĕl'ĕf-tē-å') Swe.	64·47 N	20·48 E
118	Skern (R.) (skĕrn) Den.	55·56 N	8·52 E
116	Skerries (Is.) (skĕr'ēz) Wales	53·30 N	4·59 W
136	Skhodnya R. (skôd'nyȧ) Sov. Un. (Moscow In.)	55·55 N	37·16 E
127	Skíathos (I.) (skē'ȧ-thôs) Grc.	39·15 N	23·25 E
116	Skibbereen (skĭb'ēr-ēn) Ire.	51·32 N	9·25 W
77	Skidmore (skĭd'mōr) Tex.	28·16 N	97·40 W
118	Skien (skē'ĕn) Nor.	59·13 N	9·35 E
121	Skierniewice (skyĕr-nyĕ-vēt'sĕ) Pol.	51·58 N	20·13 E
168	Skilpadfontein S. Afr. (Johannesburg & Pretoria In.)	25·02 S	28·50 E
127	Skíros Grc.	38·53 N	24·32 E
127	Skíros (I.) Grc.	38·50 N	24·43 E
118	Skive (skē'vĕ) Den.	56·34 N	8·56 E
112	Skjalfandá (R.) (skyäl'fänd-ô) Ice.	65·24 N	16·40 W
112	Skjerstad (skyĕr-städ) Nor.	67·12 N	15·37 E
126	Škofja Loka (shkôf'yȧ lō'kȧ) Yugo.	46·10 N	14·20 E
75	Skokie (skō'kē) Ill. (Chicago In.)	42·02 N	87·45 W
65	Skokomish Ind. Res. (skŏ-kō'mĭsh) Wash. (Seattle In.)	47·22 N	123·07 W
121	Skole (skô'lĕ) Sov. Un.	49·03 N	23·32 E
127	Skópelos (I.) (skô'pȧ-lôs) Grc.	39·04 N	23·31 E
128	Skopin (skô'pēn) Sov. Un.	53·49 N	39·35 E
127	Skopje (skôp'yĕ) Yugo.	42·02 N	21·26 E
118	Skövde (shûv'dĕ) Swe.	58·25 N	13·48 E
135	Skovorodino (skô'vô-rô'dĭ-nô) Sov. Un.	53·53 N	123·56 E
82	Skowhegan (skou-hē'gȧn) Maine	44·45 N	69·27 W
126	Skradin (skrä'dēn) Yugo.	43·49 N	17·58 E
118	Skreia (skrā'ȧ) Nor.	60·40 N	10·55 E
118	Skudeneshavn (skōō'dĕ-nes-houn') Nor.	59·10 N	5·19 E
118	Skulerud (skōō'lĕ-rōōdh) Nor.	59·40 N	11·30 E
69	Skull Valley Ind. Res. (skŭl) Utah	40·25 N	112·50 W
78	Skuna, (R.) (skû'nȧ) Miss.	33·57 N	89·36 W
71	Skunk (R.) (skŭnk) Iowa	41·12 N	92·14 W
119	Skuodas (skwô'dȧs) Sov. Un.	56·16 N	21·32 E
118	Skurup (skû'rōōp) Swe.	55·29 N	13·27 E
129	Skvira (skvē'rȧ) Sov. Un.	49·43 N	29·41 E
100	Skvring, Seno (B.) (sĕ'nô-s-krē'ng) Chile	52·35 S	72·30 W
120	Skwierzyna (skvē-ĕr'zhĭ-nȧ) Pol.	52·35 N	15·30 E
116	Skye (I.) (skī) Scot.	57·25 N	6·17 W
65	Skykomish (R.) (skī'kō-mĭsh) Wash. (Seattle In.)	47·50 N	121·55 W
118	Slagese Den.	55·25 N	11·19 E
154	Slamet, Gunung (Mtn.) (slä'mĕt) Indon.	7·15 S	109·15 E
127	Slanic (slŭ'nēk) Rom.	45·13 N	25·56 E
71	Slate (I.) (slāt) Can.	48·38 N	87·14 W
73	Slater (slāt'ēr) Mo.	39·13 N	93·03 W
127	Slatina (slä'tē-nä) Rom.	44·26 N	24·21 E
72	Slaton (slā'tŭn) Tex.	33·26 N	101·38 W
86	Slave (R.) (slāv) Can.	59·40 N	111·21 W
134	Slavgorod (slȧf'gô-rôt) Sov. Un.	52·58 N	78·43 E
127	Slavonija (Reg.) (slä-vô'nê-yä) Yugo.	45·29 N	17·31 E
126	Slavonska Požega (slä-vôn'skä pô'zhĕ-gä) Yugo.	45·18 N	17·42 E
127	Slavonski Brod (slä-vôn'skē brôd) Yugo.	45·10 N	18·01 E
129	Slavuta (slȧ-vōō'tȧ) Sov. Un.	50·18 N	27·01 E
129	Slavyansk (slȧv'yänsk') Sov. Un.	48·52 N	37·34 E
129	Slavyanskaya (slȧv-yȧn'skȧ-yȧ) Sov. Un.	45·14 N	38·09 E
70	Slayton (slā'tŭn) Minn.	44·00 N	95·44 W
110	Sleaford (slē'fērd) Eng.	53·00 N	0·25 W
71	Sleepy Eye (slēp'ĭ ī) Minn.	44·17 N	94·44 W
77	Slidell (slī-dĕl') La.	30·17 N	89·47 W
111	Sliedrecht Neth (Amsterdam In.)	51·49 N	4·46 E
116	Sligo (slī'gō) Ire.	54·17 N	8·19 W
118	Slite (slē'tĕ) Swe.	57·41 N	18·47 E
127	Sliven (slē'vĕn) Bul.	42·41 N	26·20 E
84	Sloatsburg (slōts'bŭrg) N. Y. (New York In.)	41·09 N	74·11 W
119	Slobodka (slô'bôd-kȧ) Sov. Un.	54·34 N	26·12 E
132	Slobodskoy (slô'bôt-skoi) Sov. Un.	58·48 N	50·02 E
119	Sloka (slô'kȧ) Sov. Un.	56·57 N	23·37 E
121	Slonim (swō'nēm) Sov. Un.	53·05 N	25·19 E
110	Slough (slou) Eng. (London In.)	51·29 N	0·36 W
	Slovakia, see Slovensko		
126	Slovenija (Reg.) (slô-vĕ'nē-yä) Yugo.	45·58 N	14·43 E
121	Slovensko (Slovakia) (Prov.) (slô-vĕn'skô) (slô-vȧk'ĭ-ȧ) Czech.	48·40 N	19·00 E
121	Sluch' (R.) Sov. Un.	50·56 N	26·48 E
126	Sluderno (slōō-dĕr'nô) It.	46·38 N	10·37 E
126	Slunj (slōōn') Yugo.	45·08 N	15·46 E
121	Slupsk (swōōpsk) Pol.	54·28 N	17·02 E
128	Slutsk (slōōtsk) Sov. Un.	53·02 N	27·34 E
116	Slyne Head (slīn) Ire.	53·25 N	10·05 W
73	Smackover (smăk'ô-vēr) Ark.	33·22 N	92·42 W
127	Smederevo (Semendria) (smĕ'dĕ-rĕ-vô) (sĕ-mĕn'drĭ-ȧ) Yugo.	44·39 N	20·54 E
127	Smederevska Palanka (smĕ-dĕ-rĕv'skä pä-län'kä) Yugo.	44·21 N	21·00 E
118	Smedjebacken (smĭ'tyĕ-bä-kĕn) Swe.	60·09 N	15·19 E
129	Smela (smyā'lȧ) Sov. Un.	49·14 N	31·52 E
129	Smeloye (smyā'lô-ĕ) Sov. Un.	50·55 N	33·36 E
81	Smethport (smĕth'pōrt) Pa.	41·50 N	78·25 W
128	Smiltene (smēl'tĕ-nĕ) Sov. Un.	57·26 N	25·57 E
86	Smith (smĭth) Can.	55·10 N	113·53 W
65	Smith (I.) Wash. (Seattle In.)	48·20 N	122·53 W
72	Smith Center (sĕn'tēr) Kans.	39·45 N	98·46 W
86	Smithers (smĭth'ērs) Can.	54·13 N	127·22 W
79	Smithfield (smĭth'fēld) N. C.	35·30 N	78·21 W
74	Smithfield Tex. (Dallas, Fort Worth In.)	32·52 N	97·12 W
67	Smithfield Utah	41·50 N	111·49 W
80	Smithland (smĭth'lănd) Ky.	37·10 N	88·25 W
77	Smith Point Tex. (In.)	29·32 N	94·45 W
67	Smith R. Mont.	47·00 N	111·20 W
81	Smiths Falls (smĭths) Can.	44·55 N	76·05 W
83	Smith Sd. Can.	48·15 N	53·50 W
160	Smithton (smĭth'tŭn) Austl.	40·55 S	145·12 E
74	Smithton Ill. (St. Louis In.)	38·24 N	89·59 W
77	Smithville (smĭth'vĭl) Tex.	30·00 N	97·08 W
167	Smits (R.) S. Afr. (Natal In.)	31·45 S	26·33 E
166	Smitswinkel Flats S. Afr. (Cape Town In.)	34·16 S	18·25 E
68	Smoke Creek Des. (smōk crēk) Nev.	40·28 N	119·40 W
73	Smoky Hill (R.) (smōk'ĭ hĭl) Kans.	38·40 N	97·32 W
118	Smöla (I.) (smûlȧ) Nor.	63·16 N	7·40 E
128	Smolensk (smô-lyĕnsk') Sov. Un.	54·46 N	32·03 E
128	Smolensk (Oblast) Sov. Un.	55·00 N	32·18 E
127	Smyadovo Bul.	43·04 N	27·00 E
81	Smyrna (smûr'nȧ) Del.	39·20 N	75·35 W
84	Smyrna Ga. (Atlanta In.)	33·53 N	84·31 W
	Smyrna, see Izmir		
64	Snag (snăg) Can.	62·18 N	140·30 W
71	Snake (R.) (snāk) Minn.	45·58 N	93·20 W
69	Snake Ra. Nev.	39·20 N	114·15 W
67	Snake R., Henrys Fork Idaho	43·52 N	111·55 W
66	Snake R. Wash.	46·33 N	118·18 W
66	Snake River Pln. (rĭv'ēr) Idaho	43·08 N	114·46 W
94	Snap Pt. Ba. Is.	23·45 N	77·30 W
69	Sneffels Pk. (snĕf'ĕlz) Colo.	38·00 N	107·50 W
85	Snelgrove (snĕl'grōv) Can. (Toronto In.)	43·44 N	79·50 W
121	Sniardwy L. (snyärt'vĭ) Pol.	53·46 N	21·59 E
118	Snöhetta (Mtn.) (snû-hĕttä) Nor.	62·18 N	9·12 E
65	Snohomish (snô-hō'mĭsh) Wash. (Seattle In.)	47·55 N	122·05 W
65	Snohomish (R.) Wash. (Seattle In.)	47·53 N	122·04 W
65	Snoqualmie (snō qwäl'mē) Wash. (Seattle In.)	47·32 N	121·50 W
66	Snoqualmie R. Wash.	47·32 N	121·53 W
129	Snov (R.) (snôf) Sov. Un.	51·38 N	31·38 E
116	Snowdon, Mt. (snō'dŭn) Wales	53·05 N	4·04 W
81	Snow Hill (hĭl) Md.	38·15 N	75·20 W
159	Snowy Mts. (snō'ē) Austl.	36·17 S	148·30 E
72	Snyder (snī'dēr) Okla.	34·40 N	98·57 W
76	Snyder Tex.	32·48 N	100·53 W
110	Soar (R.) (sōr) Eng.	52·44 N	1·09 W
165	Sobat R. (sō'bät) Sud.	9·04 N	32·02 E
128	Sobinka (sô-bĭŋ'kȧ) Sov. Un.	55·59 N	40·02 E
153	Sobo Zan (Mt.) (sō'bô zän) Jap.	32·47 N	131·27 E
99	Sobral (sô-brä'l) Braz.	3·39 S	40·16 W
121	Sochaczew (sô-kä'chĕf) Pol.	52·14 N	20·18 E
146	Soché (Yarkand) (sō'chĕ) (yär-känt') China	38·15 N	77·15 E
133	Sochi (sôch'ĭ) Sov. Un.	43·35 N	39·50 E
157	Society Is. (sô-sī'ĕ-tē) Fr. Polynesia	15·00 S	157·30 W
84	Socola (sŏ-kō'lȧ) La. (New Orleans In.)	29·32 N	89·46 W
91	Socoltenango (sô-kôl-tĕ-näŋ'gō) Mex.	16·17 N	92·20 W
101	Socorro (sŏ-kô'r-rō) Braz. (Rio de Janeiro In.)	22·35 S	46·32 W
98	Socorro (sô-kôr'rō) Col.	6·23 N	73·19 W
69	Socorro N. Mex.	34·05 N	106·55 W
168	Socotra I. (sô-kō'trȧ) Som. (Horn of Afr. In.)	13·00 N	52·30 E
124	Socuellamos (sô-kōō-āl'yä-môs) Sp.	39·18 N	2·48 W
68	Soda (L.) (sō'dȧ) Calif.	35·12 N	116·25 W
65	Soda Pk. Wash. (Portland In.)	45·53 N	122·04 W
67	Soda Springs (sprĭngz) Idaho	42·39 N	111·37 W
118	Söderhamn (sû-dĕr-häm''n) Swe.	61·20 N	17·00 E
118	Söderköping Swe.	58·30 N	16·14 E
118	Södertälje (sû-dĕr-tĕl'yĕ) Swe.	59·12 N	17·35 E
150	Sodi Soruksum (Mtn.) China	37·20 N	102·00 E
165	Sodo Eth.	7·03 N	37·46 E
118	Södra Dellen (L.) Swe.	61·45 N	16·30 E
120	Soest (zōst) Ger.	51·35 N	8·05 E
	Sofia, see Sofiya		
127	Sofiya (Sofia) (sô'fê-yȧ) (sô'fê-ȧ) Bul.	42·43 N	23·20 E
129	Sofiyevka (sô-fē'yĕf-kȧ) Sov. Un.	48·03 N	33·53 E
153	Soga (sô'gä) Jap. (Tōkyō In.)	35·35 N	140·08 E
98	Sogamoso (sô-gä-mō'sō) Col.	5·42 N	72·51 W
118	Sogndal (sôghn'dȧl) Nor.	58·20 N	6·17 E
118	Sogndal Nor.	61·14 N	7·04 E
118	Sogne Fd. (sôgn'ĕ fyôrd) Nor.	61·09 N	5·30 E
128	Sogozha (R.) (sô'gô-zhȧ) Sov. Un.	58·35 N	39·08 E
122	Soissons (swä-sôN') Fr.	49·23 N	3·17 E
153	Sōka (sō'kä) Jap. (Tōkyō In.)	35·50 N	139·49 E
121	Sokal (sô'käl') Sov. Un.	50·28 N	24·20 E
133	Soke (sû'kĕ) Tur.	37·40 N	27·10 E
164	Sokodé (sô-kô-dā') Togo	8·56 N	1·08 E
121	Sokolka (sô-kōōl'kȧ) Pol.	53·23 N	23·30 E
164	Sokolo (sô-kô-lō') Mali	14·51 N	6·09 W
164	Sokoto (sō'kô-tō) Nig.	13·03 N	5·14 E
164	Sokoto (Reg.) Nig.	12·29 N	6·34 E
121	Sokotów Podlaski (sô-kô-wōōf' pŭd-lä'skĭ) Pol.	52·24 N	22·15 E
91	Sola de Vega (San Miguel) (sō'lä dā vā'gä) (sän mē-gāl') Mex.	16·31 N	96·58 W
155	Solana (sō-lä'nä) Phil. (Manila In.)	17·40 N	121·41 E
161	Solander, C. Austl. (Sydney In.)	34·03 S	151·16 E
155	Solano (sō-lä'nō) Phil. (Manila In.)	16·31 N	121·11 E
98	Soledad (sŏ-lĕ-dä'd) Col.	10·47 N	75·00 W
90	Soledad Díez Gutierrez (sô-lȧ-dhädh'dē'äz gōō-tyā'rĕz) Mex.	22·19 N	100·54 W
66	Soleduck R. (sōl'dŭk) Wash.	47·59 N	124·28 W
92	Solentiname, Islas de (Is.) (ē's-läs-dĕ-sô-lĕn-tĕ-nä'mä) Nic.	11·15 N	85·16 W
110	Solihull (sō'lĭ-hŭl) Eng.	52·25 N	1·46 W
136	Solikamsk (sô-lē-kȧmsk') Sov. Un. (Urals In.)	59·38 N	56·48 E
98	Solimões, Rio (R.) (rē'ō-sô-lē-mô'ĕs) Braz.	2·45 S	67·44 W
123	Solingen (zō'lĭng-ĕn) Ger. (Ruhr In.)	51·10 N	7·05 E
118	Sollefteå (sôl-lĕf'tĕ-ô) Swe.	63·06 N	17·17 E
125	Sóller (sō'lyĕr) Sp.	39·45 N	2·40 E
133	Sol'-Iletsk Sov. Un.	51·10 N	55·05 E
122	Sologne (Reg.) (sō-lŏn'yĕ) Fr.	47·36 N	1·53 E
92	Sololá (sō-lō'lä) Guat.	14·45 N	91·12 W
159	Solomon Is. Prot. (sŏ'ô-mŭn) Oceania	8·50 S	157·52 E
156	Solomon Is. Oceania	7·00 S	148·00 E
72	Solomon R. Kans.	39·24 N	98·19 W
72	Solomon R. North Fk. Kans.	39·34 N	99·52 W
72	Solomon R., South Fk. Kans.	39·19 N	99·52 W

ăt; finăl; rāte; senâte; ärm; ȧsk; sofȧ; fâre; ch-choose; dh-as th in other; bē; ēvent; bĕt; recĕnt; cratēr; g-go; gh-guttural g; bĭt; ĭ-short neutral; rīde; K-guttural k as ch in German ich;

Page	Name Pronunciation Region	Lat. °′	Long. °′
75	Solon (sō'lŭn) Ohio (Cleveland In.)	41·23 N	81·26 W
120	Solothurn (zô'lō-thōōrn) Switz.	47·13 N	7·30 E
132	Solov'etskiy (I.) Sov. Un.	65·10 N	35·40 E
126	Šolta (I.) (shôl'tä) Yugo.	43·20 N	16·15 E
144	Soltānābād Iran	28·06 N	55·24 E
120	Soltau (sôl'tou) Ger.	53·00 N	9·50 E
128	Sol'tsy (sôl'tsė) Sov. Un.	58·04 N	30·13 E
150	Solun (sô-lōōn') China	47·32 N	121·18 E
81	Solvay (sŏl'vā) N. Y.	43·05 N	76·10 W
118	Sölvesborg (sûl'vĕs-bôrg) Swe.	56·04 N	14·35 E
132	Sol'vychegodsk (sôl'vê-chĕ-gôtsk') Sov. Un.	61·18 N	46·58 E
116	Solway Firth (sŏl'wāfûrth') Eng.-Scot.	54·42 N	3·55 W
163	Somali Republic (sō-mä'lē) Afr.	3·28 N	44·47 E
127	Sombor (sôm'bôr) Yugo.	45·45 N	19·10 E
90	Sombrerete (sōm-brå-rā'tå) Mex.	23·38 N	103·37 W
99	Sombrero, Cayo (C.) (kä-yô-sôm-brĕ'rô) Ven. (In.)	10·52 N	68·12 W
78	Somerset (sŭm'ēr-sĕt) Ky.	37·05 N	84·35 W
84	Somerset Mass. (Providence In.)	41·46 N	71·05 W
81	Somerset Pa.	40·00 N	79·05 W
74	Somerset Tex. (San Antonio In.)	29·13 N	98·39 W
167	Somerset East S. Afr. (Natal In.)	32·44 S	25·36 E
82	Somersworth (sŭm'ērz-wûrth) N. H.	43·16 N	70·53 W
68	Somerton (sŭm'ēr-tŭn) Ariz.	32·36 N	114·43 W
83	Somerville (sŭm'ēr-vĭl) Mass. (Boston In.)	42·23 N	71·06 W
84	Somerville N.J. (New York In.)	40·34 N	74·37 W
78	Somerville Tenn.	35·14 N	89·21 W
77	Somerville Tex.	30·21 N	96·31 W
121	Somesul R. (sô-mâ'shōōl) Rom.	47·43 N	23·09 E
125	Somma Vesuviana (sôm'mä vā-zōō-vê-ä'nä) It. (Naples In.)	40·38 N	14·27 E
122	Somme (R.) (sŏm) Fr.	50·02 N	2·04 E
111	Sommerfeld (zō'mĕr-fĕld) Ger. (Berlin In.)	52·48 N	13·02 E
161	Sommerville Austl. (Melbourne In.)	38·14 S	145·10 E
92	Somoto (sô-mō'tō) Nic.	13·28 N	86·37 W
100	Somuncurá, Meseta de (Plat.) (mĕ-sĕ'tä-dĕ-sô-mōō'n-kōō-rá') Arg.	41·15 S	68·00 W
142	Son (R.) (sōn) India	24·40 N	82·35 E
93	Soná (sō'nä) Pan.	8·00 N	81·19 W
152	Sŏnchŏn (sŭn'shŭn) Kor.	39·49 N	124·56 E
118	Sønderborg (sûn''er-bôrgh) Den.	54·55 N	9·47 E
120	Sondershausen (zōn'dērz-hou'zĕn) Ger.	51·17 N	10·45 E
151	Song Ca (R.) Viet.	19·15 N	105·00 E
166	Songea (sôn-gā'ä) Tan.	10·39 S	35·44 E
152	Sŏngjin (sŭng'jĭn') Kor.	40·38 N	129·10 E
154	Songkhla (sông'klä') Thai.	7·09 N	100·34 E
120	Sonneberg (sôn'ē-bĕrgh) Ger.	50·20 N	11·14 E
68	Sonora (sô-nō'rá) Calif.	37·58 N	120·22 W
76	Sonora Tex.	30·33 N	100·38 W
88	Sonora (State) Mex.	29·45 N	111·15 W
88	Sonora (R.) Mex.	28·45 N	111·35 W
68	Sonora Pk. Calif.	38·22 N	119·39 W
124	Sonseca (sôn-sā'kä) Sp.	39·41 N	3·56 W
98	Sonsón (sôn-sôn') Col. (In.)	5·42 N	75·28 W
92	Sonsonate (sōn-sô-nä'tå) Sal.	13·46 N	89·43 W
155	Sonsorol Is. (sŏn-sô-rōl') Pac. Is. Trust Ter.	5·03 N	132·33 E
148	Soochow (Wuhsien) (sōō'jō) (wōō'sĭän) China	31·19 N	120·37 E
65	Sooke Basin (sŏŏk) Can. (Seattle In.)	48·21 N	123·47 W
74	Soo Locks (sōō lŏks) U. S.-Can.	46·30 N	84·30 W
98	Sopetrán (sô-pĕ-trä'n) Col. (In.)	6·30 N	75·44 W
118	Sopot (sô'pôt) Pol.	54·26 N	18·25 E
120	Sopron (shŏp'rōn) Hung.	47·41 N	16·36 E
126	Sora (sô'rä) It.	41·43 N	13·37 E
118	Sör Aurdal (sûr äür-däl) Nor.	60·54 N	9·24 E
124	Sorbas (sôr'bäs) Sp.	37·05 N	2·07 W
91	Sordo (R.) (sô'r-dō) Mex.	16·39 N	97·33 W
82	Sorel (sô-rĕl') Can.	46·01 N	73·07 W
160	Sorell, C. Austl.	42·10 S	144·50 E
126	Soresina (sō-rā-zē'nä) It.	45·17 N	9·51 E
124	Soria (sō'rē-ä) Sp.	41·46 N	2·28 W
101	Soriano (sō-rēä'nō) (Dept.) Ur. (Buenos Aires In.)	33·25 S	58·00 W
101	Sorocaba (sô-rô-kä'bá) Braz. (Rio de Janeiro In.)	23·29 S	47·27 W
129	Soroki (sô-rō'kē) Sov. Un.	48·09 N	28·17 E
155	Sorong (sō-rông') W. Irian	1·15 S	131·30 E
128	Sorot' (R.) (sō-rō'tzh) Sov. Un.	57·08 N	29·23 E
165	Soroti (sō-rō'tē) Ug.	1·51 N	33·33 E
112	Söröy (I.) (sûr-ûê) Nor.	70·37 N	20·58 E
124	Sorraia (R.) (sôr-rī'ä) Port.	38·55 N	8·42 W
125	Sorrento (sôr-rĕn'tō) It. (Naples In.)	40·23 N	14·23 E
155	Sorsogon (sôr-sōgōn') Phil.	12·51 N	124·02 E
119	Sortavala (sôr'tä-vä-lä) Sov. Un.	61·43 N	30·40 E
150	Sŏsan (sŭ'sän) Korea	36·40 N	126·25 E
129	Sosna (R.) (sôs'nà) Sov. Un.	50·33 N	38·15 E
129	Sosnitsa (sôs-nē'tsä) Sov. Un.	51·30 N	32·29 E
134	Sosnogorsk Sov. Un.	63·13 N	54·09 E
121	Sosnowiec (sôs-nô'vyĕts) Pol.	50·17 N	19·10 E
152	Sosunova, Mys (Pt.) (mĭs sô'sōō-nôf'à) Sov. Un.	46·28 N	138·06 E
136	Sos'va R. (sôs'vá) Sov. Un. (Urals In.)	59·55 N	60·40 E
132	Sos'va (R.) (sôs'vá) Sov. Un.	63·10 N	63·30 E
90	Sota la Marina (sô-tä-lä-mä-rē'nä) Mex.	22·45 N	98·11 W
91	Soteapan (sō-tå-ä'pän) Mex.	18·14 N	94·51 W
90	Soto la Marina, Rio (R.) (rē'ō-sō'tō lä mä-rē'nä) Mex.	23·55 N	98·30 W
92	Sotuta (sô-tōō'tä) Mex. (Yucatan In.)	20·35 N	89·00 W
99	Soublette (sŏ-ōō-blĕ'tĕ) Ven. (In.)	9·55 N	66·06 W
126	Soúdhas, Kólpos (G.) Grc. (Inset)	35·33 N	24·22 E
115	Soueïda Syr.	32·41 N	36·41 E
127	Souflion Grc.	41·12 N	26·17 E
93	Soufrière (sōō-frê-âr') St. Lucia (Le. & Wind. Is. In.)	13·50 N	61·03 W
93	Soufrière (Vol.) Basse Terre (Le. & Wind. Is. In.)	16·02 N	61·41 W
93	Soufrière Vol. Montserrat (Le. & Wind. Is. In.)	16·43 N	62·10 W
113	Souk-Ahras (sōōk-ä-räs') Alg.	36·18 N	8·19 E
152	Sŏul (Seoul) Kor.	37·35 N	127·03 E
167	Sources, Mt. aux (mōN'tō sōōrs') Bas. (Natal In.)	28·47 S	29·04 E
124	Soure (sōr-ĕ) Port.	40·04 N	8·37 W
83	Souris (sōō-rē') Can.	46·20 N	62·17 W
86	Souris Can.	49·32 N	100·23 W
86	Souris (R.) Can.	48·46 N	101·32 W
77	Sourlake (sour'läk) Tex.	30·09 N	94·24 W
164	Sousse (sōōs) Tun.	36·00 N	10·39 E
122	Soustons (sōōs-tôN') Fr.	43·46 N	1·22 W
79	South (R.) N. C.	34·49 N	78·33 W
167	South Africa Afr. (Natal In.)	31·50 S	28·05 E
84	South Amboy (south'ăm'boi) N. J. (New York In.)	40·28 N	74·17 W
6	South America		
116	Southampton (south-ămp'tŭn) Eng.	50·54 N	1·30 W
87	Southampton I. Can.	64·38 N	84·00 W
154	South Andaman I. (ăn-dá-măn') India	11·57 N	93·24 E
158	South Australia (State) (ôs-trā'lĭ-á) Austl.	29·45 S	132·00 E
95	South B. Ba. Is.	20·55 N	73·35 W
80	South Bend (bĕnd) Ind.	41·40 N	86·20 W
66	South Bend (bĕnd) Wash.	46·39 N	123·48 W
94	South Bight (B.) Ba. Is.	24·20 N	77·35 W
94	South Bimini (I.) (bē'mê-nê) Ba. Is.	25·40 N	79·20 W
83	Southboro (south'bŭr-ô) Mass. (Boston In.)	42·18 N	71·33 W
79	South Boston (bôs'tŭn) Va.	36·41 N	78·55 W
81	Southbridge (south'brĭj) Mass.	42·05 N	72·00 W
95	South Caicos (I.) (kī'kōs) Caicos	21·30 N	71·35 W
155	South C. Pap.	10·40 S	149·00 E
63	South Carolina (State) (kăr-ô-lī'ná) U. S.	34·15 N	81·10 W
110	South Cave (cāv) Eng.	53·45 N	0·35 W
80	South Charleston (south chärlz'tŭn) W. Va.	38·20 N	81·40 W
154	South China Sea (chī'ná) Asia	15·23 N	114·12 E
161	South Cr. Austl. (Sydney In.)	33·43 S	167·00 E
62	South Dakota (State) (dá-kō'tá) U. S.	44·20 N	101·55 W
116	South Downs (dounz) Eng.	50·55 N	1·13 W
159	Southeast, C. Austl.	43·47 S	146·03 E
110	Southend-on-Sea (south-ĕnd') Eng. (London In.)	51·33 N	0·41 E
159	Southern Alps (Mts.) (sŭ-thûrn ălps) N. Z. (In.)	44·08 S	169·18 E
158	Southern Cross Austl.	31·13 S	119·30 E
86	Southern Indian (L.) (sŭth'ērn ĭn'dĭ-ăn) Can.	57·20 N	99·29 W
79	Southern Pines (sŭth'ērn pīnz) N. C.	35·10 N	79·23 W
166	Southern Rhodesia (rô-dē'zhĭ-à) Afr.	17·50 S	29·30 E
116	Southern Uplands (ŭp'lándz) Scot.	55·15 N	4·28 W
69	Southern Ute Ind. Res. (ūt) Colo.	37·05 N	108·23 W
75	South Euclid (ū'klĭd) Ohio (Cleveland In.)	41·30 N	81·34 W
80	South Fox (I.) (fŏks) Mich.	45·25 N	85·55 W
74	South Gate (gāt) Calif. (Los Angeles In.)	33·57 N	118·13 W
96	South Georgia (I.) (jôr'jă) Falk. Is.	54·00 S	37·00 W
80	South Haven (hāv''n) Mich.	42·25 N	86·15 W
81	Southington (sŭdh'ĭng-tŭn) Conn.	41·35 N	72·55 W
159	South I. N. Z. (In.)	43·15 S	167·00 E
70	South Loup (R.) (lōōp) Nebr.	41·21 N	100·08 W
83	South Merrimack (mĕr'ĭ-măk) N. H. (Boston In.)	42·47 N	71·36 W
75	South Milwaukee (mĭl-wô'kê) Wis. (Milwaukee In.)	42·55 N	87·52 W
94	South Negril Pt. (nå-grēl') Jam.	18·15 N	78·25 W
84	South Norfolk (nôr'fŏk) Va. (Norfolk In.)	36·48 N	76·16 W
74	South Ogden (ŏg'dĕn) Utah (Salt Lake City In.)	41·12 N	111·58 W
82	South Paris (păr'ĭs) Maine	44·13 N	70·32 W
75	South Park (pärk) Ky. (Louisville In.)	38·06 N	85·43 W
74	South Pasadena (păs-à-dē'ná) Calif. (Los Angeles In.)	34·06 N	118·08 W
72	South Pease (R.) (pēz) Tex.	33·54 N	100·45 W
65	South Pender (I.) (pĕn'dēr) Can. (Vancouver In.)	48·45 N	123·09 W
78	South Pittsburg (pĭts'bûrg) Tenn.	35·00 N	85·42 W
62	South Platte (R.) (plăt) U. S.	40·40 N	102·40 W
80	South Pt. Mich.	44·50 N	83·20 W
93	South Pt. W. I. F. (Le. & Wind. Is. In.)	13·00 N	59·43 W
47	South Polar Plat Ant.	87·00 S	2·00 W
160	Southport (south'pōrt) Austl.	27·57 S	153·27 E
79	Southport N. C.	35·55 N	78·02 W
110	Southport (south'pôrt) Eng.	53·38 N	3·00 W
75	Southport Ind. (Indianapolis In.)	39·40 N	86·07 W
82	South Portland (pōrt-lănd) Maine	43·37 N	70·15 W
65	South Prairie (prā'rĭ) Wash. (Seattle In.)	47·08 N	122·06 W
74	South Range (rānj) Wis. (Duluth In.)	46·37 N	91·59 W
84	South River (rĭv'ēr) N. J. (New York In.)	40·27 N	74·23 W
84	South R. Ga. (Atlanta In.)	33·40 N	84·15 W
74	South St. Paul Minn. (Minneapolis, St. Paul In.)	44·54 N	93·02 W
74	South Salt Lake (sôlt lāk) Utah (Salt Lake City In.)	40·44 N	111·53 W
96	South Sandwich Is. (sănd'wĭch) Falk. Is.	58·00 S	27·00 W
96	South Sandwich Trench S. A.-Ant.	55·00 S	27·00 W
65	South San Francisco (săn frăn-sĭs'kô) Calif. (San Francisco In.)	37·39 N	122·24 W
86	South Saskatchewan (R.) (săs-kăch'ē-wăn) Can.	50·29 N	110·25 W
116	South Shields (shēldz) Eng.	55·00 N	1·22 W
116	South Shropshire Hills (shrŏp'shĭr) Eng.	52·30 N	3·02 W
70	South Sioux City (sōō sĭt'ē) Nebr.	42·28 N	96·26 W
159	South Taranaki Bght. (tä-rä-nä'kê) N. Z. (In.)	39·27 S	171·44 E
74	Southton (south'tŭn) Tex. (San Antonio In.)	29·18 N	98·26 W
116	South Uist (I.) (ū'ĭst) Scot.	56·83 N	6·64 W
66	South Umpqua R. (ŭmp'kwå) Ore.	43·00 N	122·54 W
110	Southwell (south'wĕl) Eng.	53·04 N	0·56 W
163	South-West Africa (ăf'rĭ-kä) Afr.	19·30 S	16·13 E
159	Southwest C. N. Z. (In.)	47·17 S	167.12 E
65	South Westminster (wĕst'mĭn-stēr) Can. (Vancouver In.)	49·12 N	122·53 W
95	Southwest Pt. Ba. Is.	23·55 N	74·30 W
94	Southwest Pt. Ba. Is.	25·50 N	77·10 W
94	Southwest Pt. Ba. Is.	26·35 N	78·35 W
119	Sovetsk (Tilsit) (sô-vyĕtsk') Sov. Un.	55·04 N	21·54 E
135	Sovetskaya Gavan' (sŭ-vyĕt'skĭ-u gä'vŭn') Sov. Un.	48·59 N	140·14 E
138	Soviet Union (sō-vĭ-ĕt') Eur.-Asia	60·30 N	64·00 E
110	Sow (R.) (sou) Eng.	52·45 N	2·12 W
152	Sōya Kaikyō (Str.) (sō'ya kī'kyō) Jap.-Sov. Un.	45·45 N	141·38 E
152	Sōya Misaki (C.) (sō'yä mē'sä-kē) Jap.	45·35 N	141·25 E
128	Sozh (R.) (sôzh) Sov. Un.	52·17 N	31·00 E
127	Sozopol (sôz'ô-pôl') Bul.	42·18 N	27·50 E
117	Spa (spä) Bel.	50·30 N	5·50 E
74	Spadra (spăd'rå) Calif. (Los Angeles In.)	34·03 N	117·48 W
102	Spain (spān) Eur.	40·15 N	4·30 W
70	Spalding (spôl'dĭng) Nebr.	41·43 N	98·23 W
65	Spanaway (spăn'á-wā) Wash. (Seattle In.)	47·06 N	122·26 W
81	Spangler (spăng'lēr) Pa.	40·40 N	78·50 W
69	Spanish Fork (spăn'ĭsh fôrk) Utah	40·10 N	111·40 W
163	Spanish Sahara (sá hä'rá) Afr.	23·05 N	15·33 W
94	Spanish Town Jam.	18·00 N	76·55 W
68	Sparks (spärks) Nev.	39·34 N	119·45 W
84	Sparrows Point (spăr'ōz) Md. (Baltimore In.)	39·13 N	76·29 W
78	Sparta (spär'tá) Ga.	33·16 N	82·59 W
73	Sparta Ill.	38·07 N	89·42 W
80	Sparta Mich.	43·10 N	85·45 W
78	Sparta Tenn.	35·54 N	85·26 W
71	Sparta Wis.	43·56 N	90·50 W
	Sparta, see Spárti		
84	Sparta Mts. N. J. (New York In.)	41·00 N	74·38 W
79	Spartanburg (spär'tăn-bûrg) S. C.	34·57 N	82·13 W
124	Spartel (C.) (spär-tĕl') Mor.	35·48 N	5·50 W
127	Spárti (Sparta) Grc.	37·07 N	22·28 E
126	Spartivento, C. (spär-tê-vĕn'tô) It.	37·55 N	16·09 E
126	Spartivento, C It.	38·54 N	8·52 E
128	Spas-Demensk (spås dyĕ-mĕnsk') Sov. Un.	54·24 N	34·02 E
128	Spas-Klepiki (spås klĕp'ê-kê) Sov. Un.	55·09 N	40·11 E
135	Spassk-Dal'niy (spŭsk'däl'nyē) Sov. Un.	44·30 N	133·00 E
128	Spassk-Ryazanskiy (ryä-zän'skĭ) Sov. Un.	54·24 N	40·21 E
126	Spátha, Akr. (C.) Grc. (Inset)	35·42 N	23·45 E
84	Spaulding (spôl'dĭng) Ala. (Birmingham In.)	33·27 N	86·50 W
83	Spear, C. (spēr) Can.	47·28 N	52·30 W
70	Spearfish (spēr'fĭsh) S. D.	44·28 N	103·52 W
75	Speed (spēd) Ind. (Louisville In.)	38·25 N	85·45 W
75	Speedway (spēd'wā) Ind. (Indianapolis In.)	39·47 N	86·14 W
111	Speicher L. (shpī'kĕr) Ger. (Munich In.)	48·12 N	11·47 E
80	Spencer (spĕn'sēr) Ind.	39·15 N	86·45 W
71	Spencer Iowa	43 09 N	95·08 W
79	Spencer N. C.	35·43 N	80·25 W
80	Spencer W. Va.	38·55 N	81·20 W
160	Spencer G. (spĕn'sĕr) Austl.	34·20 S	136·55 E
111	Sperenberg (shpĕ'rĕn-bĕrgh) Ger. (Berlin In.)	52·09 N	13·22 E
127	Sperkhiós (R.) Grc.	38·54 N	22·02 E
116	Sperrin Mts. (spĕr'ĭn) N. Ire.	54·55 N	6·45 E
120	Spessart (Mts.) (shpĕ'särt) Ger.	50·07 N	9·32 E
116	Spey (L.) (spā) Scot.	57·25 N	3·29 W
120	Speyer (shpī'ĕr) Ger.	49·18 N	8·26 E
168	Sphinx (Pyramid) (sfĭnks) U. A. R. (Nile In.)	29·57 N	31·08 E
111	Spijkenisse Neth. (Amsterdam In.)	51·51 N	4·18 E
126	Spinazzola (spē-nät'zô-lä) It.	40·58 N	16·05 E
66	Spirit Lake (spĭr'ĭt) Idaho	47·58 N	116·51 W
71	Spirit Lake (lāk) Iowa	43·25 N	95·08 W
86	Spirit River Can.	55·50 N	118·50 W
121	Spišská Nová Ves (spēsh'skä nō'vä vĕs) Czech.	48·56 N	20·35 E
120	Spittal (shpē-tāl') Aus.	46·48 N	13·28 E
	Spitzbergen (Is.), see Svalbard		
126	Split (splĕt) Yugo.	43·30 N	16·28 E
66	Spokane (spō-kăn') Wash.	47·39 N	117·25 W
66	Spokane R. Wash.	47·47 N	118·00 W
126	Spoleto (spô-lā'tō) It.	42·44 N	12·44 E
73	Spoon (R.) (spōōn) Ill.	40·36 N	90·22 W
71	Spooner (spōōn'ēr) Wis.	45·50 N	91·53 W

ng-sing; ŋ-baŋk; N-nasalized n; nŏd; cŏmmit; ōld; ôbey; ôrder; fōōd; fŏŏt; ou-out; s-soft; sh-dish; th-thin; pūre; ūnite; ûrn; stŭd; circŭs; ü-as "y" in study; '-indeterminate vowel.

Page	Name Pronunciation Region	Lat. °'	Long. °'
127	Sporádhes (Is.) . . . . Grc.	38·55 N	24·05 E
84	Spotswood (spŏtz'wŏŏd) N. J. (New York In.)	40·23 N	74·22 W
66	Sprague R. (sprāg) . . . . Ore.	42·30 N	121·42 W
154	Spratly (I.) (sprăt'lē) . . . . . . China	8·38 N	11·54 E
79	Spray (sprā) . . . . N. C.	36·30 N	79·44 W
120	Spree R. (shprā) . . . . Ger.	51·53 N	14·08 E
120	Spremberg (shprĕm'bĕrgh) . . . Ger.	51·35 N	14·23 E
73	Spring (R.) . . . . Ark.	36·25 N	91·35 W
166	Springbok (sprĭng'bŏk) . . . . S. Afr.	29·35 S	17·55 E
68	Spring, Cr. (sprĭng) . . . . Nev.	40·18 N	117·45 W
77	Spring Cr. . . . . Tex.	30·03 N	95·43 W
76	Spring Cr. . . . . Tex.	31·08 N	100·50 W
73	Springdale (sprĭng'dāl) . . . . . . Ark.	36·10 N	94·07 W
83	Springdale . . . . Can.	49·30 N	56·05 W
84	Springdale . Conn. (New York In.)	41·05 N	73·31 W
75	Springdale . . . Pa. (Pittsburgh In.)	40·33 N	79·46 W
72	Springer (sprĭng'ĕr) . . . . . . N. Mex.	36·21 N	104·37 W
72	Springfield (sprĭng'fēld) . . . . . Colo.	37·24 N	102·40 W
71	Springfield . . . . Minn.	44·14 N	94·59 W
66	Springfield . . . . Ore.	44·01 N	123·02 W
73	Springfield . . . . Ill.	39·46 N	89·37 W
80	Springfield . . . . Ky.	37·35 N	85·10 W
81	Springfield . . . . Mass.	42·05 N	72·35 W
73	Springfield . . . . Mo.	37·13 N	93·17 W
80	Springfield . . . . Ohio	39·55 N	83·50 W
78	Springfield . . . . Tenn.	36·30 N	86·53 W
81	Springfield . . . . Vt.	43·20 N	72·35 W
166	Springfontein (sprĭng'fŏn-tīn) S. Afr.	30·16 S	25·45 E
82	Springhill (sprĭng-hĭl') . . . . Can.	45·39 N	64·04 W
68	Spring Mts. . . . . Nev.	36·18 N	115·49 W
167	Springs (sprĭngs) . . . . S. Afr. (Johannesburg & Pretoria In.)	26·16 S	28·27 E
85	Springstein (sprĭng'stīn) Can. (Winnipeg In.)	49·49 N	97·29 W
84	Springton Res. (sprĭng-tŭn) Pa. (Philadelphia In.)	39·57 N	75·26 W
161	Springvale Austl. (Melbourne In.)	37·57 S	145·09 E
68	Spring Valley Calif. (San Diego In.)	32·46 N	117·01 W
80	Springvalley (sprĭng-văl'ĭ) . . . . . Ill.	41·20 N	89·15 W
71	Spring Valley . . . . Minn.	43·41 N	92·26 W
84	Spring Valley N. Y. (New York In.)	41·07 N	74·03 W
69	Springville (sprĭng-vĭl) . . . . . . Utah	40·10 N	111·40 W
161	Springwood . . . Austl. (Sydney In.)	33·42 S	150·34 E
85	Spruce Grove (sprōōs grōv) Can. (Edmonton In.)	53·33 N	113·55 W
72	Spur (spûr) . . . . Tex.	33·29 N	100·51 W
81	Squam (L.) (skwôm) . . . . N. H.	43·45 N	71·30 W
126	Squillace, Gulfo di (G.) (gōō'l-fō-dē skwēl-lä'chā) . . . . It.	38·44 N	16·47 E
127	Srbija (Serbia) (Reg.) (sr bē-yä) (sĕr'bē-ȧ) . Yugo.	44·05 N	20·35 E
127	Srbobran (s'r'bô-brän') . . . . . Yugo.	45·32 N	19·50 E
135	Sredne-Kolymsk (s'rĕd'nyĕ kô-lēmsk') . Sov. Un.	67·49 N	154·55 E
136	Sredne Rogartka (s'red'nȧ-ya) (rô gär'tkȧ) Sov. Un. (Leningrad In.)	59·49 N	30·20 E
136	Sredniy Ik (R.) (srĕd'nĭ ĭk) Sov. Un. (Urals In.)	55·46 N	58·50 E
136	Sredniy Ural (Mts.) (ōō'rȧl) Sov. Un. (Urals In.)	57·47 N	59·00 E
121	Śrem (shrĕm) . . . . Pol.	52·06 N	17·01 E
127	Sremska Karlovci (srĕm'skê kär'lov-tsē) . Yugo.	45·10 N	19·57 E
127	Sremska Mitrovica (srĕm'skä mē'trô-vê-tsä') . Yugo.	44·59 N	19·39 E
135	Sretensk (s'rĕ'tĕnsk) . . . . . Sov. Un.	52·13 N	117·39 E
142	Srinagar (srē-nŭg'ŭr) . . . . India	34·11 N	74·49 E
121	Sroda (shrô'dȧ) . . . . Pol	52·14 N	17·17 E
146	Ssuch'uan (Szechwan) (Prov.) China	31·30 N	102·52 E
151	Ssuen . . . . China	24·50 N	108·18 E
148	Ssuhsien (sü'sĭän) . . . . China	33·29 N	116·57 E
146	Ssumao . . . . China	22·56 N	101·07 E
151	Ssŭnan . . . . China	27·50 N	108·30 E
150	Ssup'ing . . . . China	43·05 N	124·24 E
148	Ssushui (sĕ'sōōĭ) . . . . China	35·40 N	117·17 E
149	Ssut'uan China (Shanghai In.)	30·57 N	121·43 E
111	Stabroek . . . . . . Bel. (Brussels In.)	51·20 N	4·21 E
111	Stade (shtä'dĕ) Ger. (Hamburg In.)	53·36 N	9·28 E
112	Stadhur . . . . Ice.	65·08 N	20·56 W
118	Städjan (Mtn.) (stĕd'yän) . . . Swe.	61·53 N	12·50 E
110	Stafford (stăf'fĕrd) . . . . Eng.	52·48 N	2·06 W
72	Stafford . . . . Kans.	37·58 N	78·37 W
110	Stafford (Co.) . . . . Eng.	52·45 N	2·00 W
111	Stahnsdorf (shtäns'dôrf) Ger. (Berlin In.)	52·22 N	13·10 E
	Stalin, see Varna		
	Stalinabad, see Dushanbe		
	Stalingrad, see Volgograd		
	Stalino, see Donetsk		
129	Stalino (Oblast) (stä'lĭ-nô) (ôb'lȧst) . Sov. Un.	47·54 N	37·13 E
134	Stalino, Pik (Mtn.) . . . . . . Sov. Un.	39·00 N	72·15 E
128	Stalinogorsk (stä'lyin-ŭ-gôrsk') Sov. Un.	54·06 N	38·08 E
	Stalinsk, see Novokuznetsk		
110	Stalybridge (stā'lē-brĭj) . . . . . . Eng.	53·29 N	2·03 W
71	Stambaugh (stăm'bô) . . . . . . Mich.	46·03 N	88·38 W
84	Stamford (stăm'fĕrd) Conn. (New York In.)	41·03 N	73·32 W
110	Stamford . . . . Eng.	52·39 N	0·28 W
72	Stamford . . . . Tex.	32·57 N	99·48 W
111	Stammersdorf (shtäm'ĕrs-dôrf) Aus. (Vienna In.)	48·19 N	16·25 E
73	Stamps (stămps) . . . . Ark.	33·22 N	93·31 W
73	Stanberry (stan'bĕr-ē) . . . . Mo.	40·12 N	94·34 W
168	Standerton (stăn'dĕr-tŭn) . . S. Afr. (Johannesburg & Prestoria In.)	26·57 S	29·17 E
70	Standing Rock Ind. Res. (stănd'ĭng rŏk) . N. D.	47·07 N	101·05 W
110	Standish (stăn'dĭsh) . . . . Eng.	53·36 N	2·39 W
78	Stanford (stăn'fĕrd) . . . . Ky.	37·29 N	84·40 W
167	Stanger (stăŋ-ger) S. Afr. (Natal In.)	29·22 S	31·18 E
118	Stangvik Fd. (stang'vēk fyôrd) Nor.	62·54 N	8·55 E
94	Staniard Creek . . . . Ba. Is.	24·50 N	77·55 W
68	Stanislaus (R.) (stăn'ĭs-lô) . Calif.	38·10 N	120·16 W
82	Stanley (stăn'lē) . . . . Can.	46·19 N	66·45 W
70	Stanley . . . . N. D.	48·20 N	102·25 W
71	Stanley . . . . Wis.	44·56 N	90·56 W
165	Stanley Falls . . . . Con. L.	0·12 N	25·34 E
166	Stanley Pool (L.) . . . . Con. L.	4·15 S	16·00 E
142	Stanley Res. (stăn'lē) . . . . India	12·07 N	77·27 E
165	Stanleyville (stan'lē-vĭl) . . . Con.L.	0·32 N	25·14 E
92	Stann Creek (stăn krēk) Br. Hond. (Yucatan In.)	17·01 N	88·14 W
135	Stanovoy Khrebet (Mts.) (stŭn-ȧ-voi') . Sov. Un.	56·12 N	127·12 E
74	Stanton (stăn'tŭn) Calif. (Los Angeles In.)	33·48 N	118·00 W
70	Stanton . . . . Nebr.	41·57 N	97·15 W
76	Stanton . . . . Tex.	32·08 N	101·46 W
65	Stanwood (stăn'wŏŏd) Wash. (Seattle In.)	48·14 N	122·23 W
71	Staples (stā'p'lz) . . . . Minn.	46·21 N	94·48 W
127	Stara Planina (Balkan Mts.) . Bul.	42·50 N	24·45 E
136	Staraya Kupavna (stä'rȧ-yȧ kû-päf'nȧ) Sov. Un. (Moscow In.)	55·48 N	38·10 E
128	Staraya Russa (stä'rȧ-yȧ rōōsȧ) Sov. Un.	57·58 N	31·21 E
127	Stara Zagora (zä'gô-rȧ) . . . . . . Bul.	42·26 N	25·37 E
85	Starbuck (stär'bŭk) Can. (Winnipeg In.)	49·46 N	97·38 W
120	Stargard Szczecinski (shtär'gärt shchĕ-chyn'skē) . Pol.	53·19 N	15·03 E
128	Staritsa (stä'rē-tsȧ) . . . . . . Sov. Un.	56·29 N	34·58 E
79	Starke (stärk) . . . . Fla.	29·55 N	82·07 W
72	Starkville (stärk'vĭl) . . . . Colo.	37·06 N	104·34 W
78	Starkville . . . . Miss.	33·27 N	88·47 W
111	Starnberg (shtärn-bĕrgh) Ger. (Munich In.)	47·59 N	11·20 E
129	Starobel'sk (stä-rô-byĕlsk') Sov. Un.	49·19 N	38·57 E
128	Starodub (stä-rô-drōōp') . Sov. Un.	52·25 N	32·49 E
121	Starogard Gdenski (stä'rō-gärd gdĕn'skē) . . . . . Pol.	53·58 N	18·33 E
129	Staro-Konstantinov (stä'rô kôn-stán-tē'nôf) Sov. Un.	49·45 N	27·12 E
129	Staro-Minskaya (stä'rô mĭn'skȧ-yȧ) . Sov. Un.	46·19 N	38·51 E
129	Staro-Shcherbinovskaya . Sov. Un.	46·38 N	38·38 E
136	Staro-Subkhangulovo (stäro-sōōb-kan-gōō'lōvō) Sov. Un. (Urals In.)	53·08 N	57·24 E
136	Staroutkinsk (stä-rô-ōōt'kĭnsk) Sov. Un. (Urals In.)	57·14 N	59·21 E
129	Staroverovka . . . . Sov. Un.	49·31 N	35·48 E
116	Start Pt. (stärt) . . . . Eng.	50·14 N	3·34 W
121	Stary Sącz (stä-rē sônch') . . . . Pol.	49·32 N	20·36 E
129	Staryy Oskol (stä'rē ôs-kôl') Sov. Un.	51·18 N	37·51 E
120	Stassfurt (shtäs'fōōrt) . . . . Ger.	51·52 N	11·35 E
121	Staszów (stä'shŏŏf) . . . . Pol.	50·32 N	21·13 E
81	State College (stāt kŏl'ĕj) . . . . . Pa.	40·50 N	77·55 W
74	State Line (līn) Minn. (Duluth In.)	46·36 N	92·18 W
84	Staten I. (stăt'ĕn) N. Y. (New York In.)	40·35 N	74·10 W
79	Statesboro (stāts'bŭr-ô) . . . . . . Ga.	32·26 N	81·47 W
79	Statesville (stāts'vĭl) . . . . N. C.	35·45 N	80·54 W
74	Staunton (stôn'tŭn) Ill. (St. Louis In.)	39·01 N	89·47 W
81	Staunton . . . . Va.	38·10 N	79·05 W
118	Stavanger (stä'väng'ĕr) . . . . . Nor.	58·59 N	5·44 E
65	Stave (R.) (stāv) Can. (Vancouver In.)	49·12 N	122·24 W
110	Staveley (stāv'lē) . . . . Eng.	53·17 N	1·21 W
111	Stavenisse . . Neth.(Amsterdam In.)	51·35 N	3·59 E
132	Stavropol' (stäv'rô-pôl') . Sov. Un.	53·30 N	49·10 E
133	Stavropol' . . . . Sov. Un.	45·05 N	41·50 E
120	Stawno (swav'nō) . . . . Pol.	54·21 N	16·38 E
72	Steamboat Springs (stēm'bōt') Colo.	40·30 N	106·48 W
129	Steblëv (styĕp'lyôf) . . . . . Sov. Un.	49·23 N	31·03 E
71	Steel (R.) (stēl) . . . . Can.	49·08 N	86·55 W
81	Steelton (stēl'tŭn) . . . . Pa.	40·15 N	76·45 W
111	Steenbergen Neth. (Amsterdam In.)	51·35 N	4·18 E
66	Steens Mts. (stēnz) . . . . Ore.	42·15 N	118·52 W
158	Steep Pt. (stēp) . . . . Austl.	26·15 S	112·05 E
165	Stefanie L. (stĕf-ȧ-nē') . . . . Eth.	4·46 N	37·31 E
75	Steger (stē'gĕr) . Ill. (Chicago In.)	41·28 N	87·38 W
120	Steiermark (Styria) (state) (shtī'ĕr-märk) . Aus.	47·22 N	14·40 E
86	Steinbach . . . . Can.	49·28 N	96·52 W
112	Steinkjer (stĕĭn-kyĕr) . . . . Nor.	64·00 N	11·19 E
65	Stella (stĕl'ȧ) Wash. (Portland In.)	46·11 N	123·12 W
83	Stellarton (stĕl'ȧr-tŭn) . . . . . . Can.	45·34 N	62·41 W
120	Stendal (shtĕn'dăl) . . . . Ger.	52·37 N	11·51 E
133	Stepanakert (styĕ'pän-ȧ-kĕrt) Sov. Un.	39·50 N	46·40 E
160	Stephens, Port (stē'fĕns) . . . Austl.	32·43 S	152·55 E
83	Stephenville (stē'vĕn-vĭl) . . . . Can.	48·31 N	58·38 W
84	Stepney Depot (stĕp-nē) Conn. (New York In.)	41·17 N	73·15 W
134	Stepnyak (styĭp-nyäk') . . Sov. Un.	52·37 N	70·43 E
123	Sterkrade (shtĕr'krädĕ) Ger. (Ruhr In.)	51·31 N	6·51 E
167	Sterkstroom . . . S. Afr. (Natal In.)	31·33 S	26·36 E
72	Sterling (stûr'lĭng) . . . . Colo.	40·38 N	103·14 W
71	Sterling . . . . Ill.	41·48 N	89·42 W
72	Sterling . . . . Kans.	38·11 N	98·11 W
83	Sterling . . . . . . Mass. (Boston In.)	42·26 N	71·41 W
76	Sterling . . . . Tex.	31·53 N	100·58 W
136	Sterlitamak (styĕr'lē-ta-mȧk') Sov. Un. (Urals In.)	53·38 N	55·56 E
121	Sternberk (shtĕrn'bĕrk) . . . . Czech.	49·44 N	17·18 E
	Stettin, see Szczec'in		
120	Stettiner Haff (L.) (shtĕ'tē-nĕr häf) . Ger.	53·47 N	14·02 E
86	Stettler . . . . Can.	52·19 N	112·50 W
80	Steubenville (stū'bĕn-vĭl) . . . . Ohio	40·20 N	80·40 W
65	Stevens (L.) (stē'vĕnz) Wash. (Seattle In.)	47·59 N	122·06 W
71	Stevens Point . . . . Wis.	44·30 N	89·35 W
67	Stevensville (stē'vĕnz-vĭl) . . Mont.	46·31 N	114·03 W
65	Steveston (stēvz'tŭn) Can. (Vancouver In.)	49·08 N	123·11 W
86	Stewart (R.) (stū'ĕrt) . . . . Can.	63·27 N	138·48 W
159	Stewart I. . . . . N. Z. (In.)	46·50 S	168·06 E
82	Stewiacke (stū'wē-ăk) . . . . Can.	45·08 N	63·22 W
168	Steynsrus (stīns'rōōs) . . . . . . S. Afr. (Johannesburg & Pretoria In.)	27·58 S	27·33 E
120	Steyr (shtīr) . . . . Aus.	48·03 N	14·24 E
86	Stikine (R.) (stĭ-kēn') . . . . Can.	58·17 N	103·10 W
86	Stikine Mts. . . . . Can.	59·24 N	129·12 W
65	Stillaguamish (R.) Wash. (Seattle In.)	48·11 N	122·18 W
65	Stillaguamish (R.), South Fk. (stĭl-ȧ-gwä'mĭsh) Wash. (Seattle In.)	48·05 N	121·59 W
74	Stillwater (stĭl'wô-tĕr) Minn. (Minneapolis, St. Paul In.)	45·04 N	92·48 W
67	Stillwater . . . . Mont.	45·23 N	109·45 W
73	Stillwater . . . . Okla.	36·06 N	97·03 W
68	Stillwater Ra. . . . . Nev.	39·43 N	118·11 W
66	Stillwater R. . . . . Mont.	48·47 N	114·40 W
127	Štip (shtĭp) . . . . Yugo.	41·43 N	22·07 E
116	Stirling (stûr'lĭng) . . . . Scot.	56·05 N	3·59 W
85	Stittsville (stĭts'vĭl) Can. (Ottawa In.)	45·15 N	75·54 W
118	Stjördalshalsen (styûr-dåls-hälsĕn) . Nor.	63·26 N	11·00 E
71	Stockbridge Munsee Ind. Res. (stŏk'brĭdj mŭn-sē) . Wis.	44·49 N	89·00 W
111	Stockerau (shtô'kĕ-rou) Aus. (Vienna In.)	48·24 N	16·13 E
82	Stockholm (stŏk'hōlm) . . . . . Maine	47·05 N	68·08 W
118	Stockholm (stôk'hôlm') . . . . . . Swe.	59·23 N	18·00 E
110	Stockport (stŏk'pôrt) . . . . Eng.	53·24 N	2·09 W
68	Stockton (stŏk'tŭn) . . . . Calif.	37·56 N	121·16 W
116	Stockton . . . . Eng.	54·35 N	1·25 W
72	Stockton . . . . Kans.	39·26 N	99·16 W
71	Stockton (I.) . . . . Wis.	46·56 N	90·25 W
76	Stockton Plat . . . . Tex.	30·34 N	102·35 W
118	Stöde (stû'dĕ) . . . . Swe.	62·26 N	16·35 E
110	Stoke-on-Trent (stōk-ŏn-trĕnt) Eng.	53·01 N	2·12 W
121	Stokhod (R.) (stō-kōd) . . Sov. Un.	51·24 N	25·20 E
127	Stolac (stô'läts) . . . . Yugo.	43·03 N	17·59 E
135	Stolbovoy (Is.) (stôl-bô-voi') Sov. Un.	73·43 N	133·05 E
121	Stolin (stô'lĕn) . . . . Sov. Un.	51·54 N	26·52 E
123	Stommeln (shtō'mĕln) Ger. (Ruhr In.)	51·01 N	6·46 E
118	Stömstad . . . . Swe.	58·58 N	11·09 E
110	Stone . . . . Eng.	52·54 N	2·09 W
85	Stoneham (stōn'ăm) Can. (Quebec In.)	46·59 N	71·22 W
83	Stoneham . . . . . Mass. (Boston In.)	42·30 N	71·05 W
116	Stonehaven (stōn'hā-v'n) . . . . Scot.	56·57 N	2·09 W
84	Stone Mountain (stōn) Ga. (Atlanta In.)	33·49 N	84·10 W
85	Stonewall (stōn'wôl) Can. (Winnipeg In.)	50·08 N	97·19 W
78	Stonewall . . . . Miss.	32·08 N	88·44 W
85	Stoney Creek (stō'nē) Can. (Toronto In.)	43·13 N	79·45 W
85	Stoney Ind. Res. Can (Calgary In.)	51·10 N	114·45 W
81	Stonington (stōn'ĭng-tŭn) . . . Conn.	41·20 N	71·55 W
68	Stony Cr. (stō'nē) . . . . Calif.	39·28 N	122·35 W
85	Stony Mountain Can. (Winnipeg In.)	50·05 N	97·13 W
85	Stony Plain (stō'nē plān) Can. (Edmonton In.)	53·23 N	114·00 W
84	Stony Point . N. Y. (New York In.)	41·13 N	73·58 W
118	Storå (R.) . . . . Den.	56·22 N	8·35 E
132	Stora Lule (R.) (stōō'rȧ lōō'lĕ) Swe.	67·00 N	19·30 E
118	Stord (I.) (stôrd) . . . . Nor.	59·54 N	5·15 E
118	Store Baelt (Str.) . . . . Den.	55·25 N	10·50 E
112	Stören (stûrĕn) . . . . Nor.	62·58 N	10·21 E
118	Store Sotra (Sartor) (stô-rĕ-sô'-trȧ) (sär'tôr) . Nor.	60·24 N	4·35 E
118	Stor Fd. (stôr fyôrd) . . . . Nor.	62·17 N	6·19 E
167	Stormberg (Mts.) (stôrm'bûrg) S. Afr. (Natal In.)	31·28 S	26·35 E
71	Storm Lake . . . . Iowa	42·39 N	95·12 W
89	Stormy Pt. (stôrm'ē) Vir. Is. (U. S. A.) (St. Thomas In.)	18·22 N	65·01 W
116	Stornoway (stôr'nô-wā) . . . . . Scot.	58·13 N	6·21 W
121	Storozhinets (stō-rô'zhĕn-yĕts) Sov. Un.	48·10 N	25·44 E
118	Storsjö (stôr'shû) . . . . Swe.	62·49 N	13·08 E
118	Storsjöen (L.) (stôr-syûĕn) . . . Nor.	61·32 N	11·30 E
118	Storsjön (L.) . . . . Swe.	63·06 N	14·00 E
118	Storvik (stôr'vēk) . . . . Swe.	60·37 N	16·31 E
83	Stoughton (stō'tŭn) Mass. (Boston In.)	42·07 N	71·06 W
71	Stoughton . . . . Wis.	42·54 N	89·15 W
117	Stour (R.) (stour) . . . . Eng.	52·09 N	0·29 E
110	Stourbridge (stour'brĭj) . . . . . . Eng.	52·27 N	2·08 W
83	Stow (stō) . . . . Mass. (Boston In.)	42·56 N	71·31 W
75	Stow . . . . Ohio (Cleveland In.)	41·09 N	81·26 W

ăt; finăl; rāte; senâte; ärm; ȧsk; sofȧ; fâre; ch-choose; dh-as th in other; bē; ēvent; bĕt; recĕnt; cratĕr; g-go; gh-guttural g; bĭt; ĭ-short neutral· rīde; K-guttural k as ch in German ich;

Page	Name Pronunciation Region	Lat. °′	Long. °′
168	Straatsdrif...S. Afr. (Johannesburg & Pretoria In.)	25·19 S	26·22 E
116	Strabane (stră-băn')...N. Ire.	54·52 N	6·60 W
159	Stradbroke Is. (străd'brōk). Austl.	27·45 S	154·18 E
123	Straelen (shtră'lĕn) Ger. (Ruhr In.)	51·26 N	6·16 E
159	Strahan (strā'ăn)...Austl.	42·08 S	145·28 E
120	Strakonice (strä'kô-nyê-tsĕ) Czech.	49·18 N	13·52 E
127	Straldzha (strāl'dzhà)...Bul.	42·37 N	26·44 E
120	Stralsund (shrāl'sŏŏnt)...Ger.	54·18 N	13·04 E
118	Strand (strănd)...Nor.	59·05 N	5·59 E
116	Strangford, Lough (B.) (lŏk străng'fērd). Ire.	54·30 N	5·34 W
118	Strängnas (strĕng'nĕs)...Swe.	59·23 N	16·59 E
116	Stranraer (străn-rär')...Scot.	54·55 N	5·05 W
123	Strasbourg (stràs-bōōr')...Fr.	48·36 N	7·49 E
80	Stratford (străt'fērd)...Can.	43·20 N	81·05 W
81	Stratford...Conn.	41·10 N	73·05 W
116	Stratford...Eng.	52·13 N	1·41 W
71	Stratford...Wis.	44·16 N	90·02 W
120	Straubing (strou'bĭng)...Ger.	48·52 N	12·36 E
120	Strausberg (strous'bĕrgh)...Ger.	52·35 N	13·50 E
69	Strawberry (R.)...Utah	40·05 N	110·55 W
66	Strawberry Mts. (strô'bĕr'ĭ)..Ore.	44·19 N	119·20 W
76	Strawn (strôn)...Tex.	32·38 N	98·28 W
80	Streator (strē'tēr)...Ill.	41·05 N	88·50 W
70	Streeter...N. D.	46·40 N	99·22 W
85	Streetsville (strētz'vĭl) Can. (Toronto In.)	43·34 N	79·43 W
127	Strehaia (strĕ-ĸä'yà)...Rom.	44·37 N	23·13 E
136	Strel'na (strĕl'nà) Sov. Un. (Leningrad In.)	59·52 N	30·01 E
110	Stretford (strĕt'fērd)...Eng.	53·25 N	2·19 W
155	Strickland (R.) (strĭk'lănd)..Pap.	6·15 S	142·00 E
111	Strijen...Neth. (Amsterdam In.)	51·44 N	4·32 E
127	Strimonikós Kólpos (G.)...Grc.	40·40 N	23·55 E
126	Strómboli (Vol.) (strôm'bô-lē)..It.	38·46 N	15·16 E
136	Stromyn (strô'mĭn) Sov. Un. (Moscow In.)	56·02 N	38·29 E
78	Strong (R.) (strông)...Miss.	32·03 N	89·42 W
75	Strongsville (strôŋgz'vĭl) Ohio (Cleveland In.)	41·19 N	81·50 W
116	Stronsay (I.) (strŏn'sā)...Scot.	59·09 N	2·35 W
81	Stroudsburg (stroudz'bûrg)...Pa.	41·00 N	75·15 W
118	Struer...Den.	56·29 N	8·34 E
128	Strugi Krasnyye (strōō'gĭ krä's-ny'yĕ). Sov. Un.	58·14 N	29·10 E
127	Struma (R.) (strōō'mà)...Bul.	41·55 N	23·05 E
127	Strumica (strōō'mĭ-tsà)...Yugo.	41·26 N	22·38 E
80	Struthers (strŭdh'ērz)...Ohio	41·00 N	80·35 W
111	Struvenhütten (shtrōō'vĕn-hü-tĕn) Ger. (Hamburg In.)	53·52 N	10·04 E
168	Strydpoortberg (Mts.)...S. Afr. (Johannesburg & Pretoria In.)	24·08 S	29·18 E
121	Stryy (strē')...Sov. Un.	49·16 N	23·51 E
121	Strzelce Opolskie (stzhĕl'tsĕ o-pōl'skyĕ). Pol.	50·31 N	18·20 E
121	Strzelin (stzhĕ-lĭn)...Pol.	50·48 N	17·06 E
121	Strzelno (stzhål'nō)...Pol.	52·37 N	18·10 E
79	Stuart (stū'ērt)...Fla. (In.)	27·10 N	80·14 W
71	Stuart...Iowa	41·31 N	94·20 W
64	Stuart (I.)...Alaska	63·25 N	162·45 W
65	Stuart (I.). Wash. (Vancouver In.)	48·42 N	123·10 W
158	Stuart Ra...Austl.	29·00 S	134·30 E
154	Stung Treng (stŏŏng'trĕng') Camb.	13·36 N	106·00 E
111	Stupava...Czech. (Vienna In.)	48·17 N	17·02 E
121	Stupsk (swōōpsk)...Pol.	54·28 N	17·02 E
71	Sturgeon (R.)...Mich.	46·43 N	88·43 W
71	Sturgeon Bay...Wis.	44·50 N	87·22 W
87	Sturgeon Falls...Can.	46·19 N	79·49 W
85	Sturgeon R. (stûr'jŭn) Can. (Edmonton In.)	53·41 N	113·46 W
80	Sturgis...Ky.	37·35 N	88·00 W
80	Sturgis (stûr'jĭs)...Mich.	41·45 N	85·25 W
70	Sturgis...S. D.	44·25 N	103·31 W
158	Sturt Cr...Austl.	19·40 S	127·40 E
75	Sturtevant (stŭr'tĕ-vănt) Wis. (Milwaukee In.)	42·42 N	87·54 W
167	Stutterheim (stŭrt'ēr-hīm) S. Afr. (Natal In.)	32·34 S	27·27 E
73	Stuttgart (stŭt'gärt)...Ark.	34·30 N	91·33 W
120	Stuttgart (shtōōt'gärt)...Ger.	48·48 N	9·15 E
112	Stykkisholmur...Ice.	65·00 N	21·48 W
121	Styr' R. (stêr)...Sov. Un.	51·44 N	26·07 E
	Styria, see Steiermark		
165	Suakin (swä'kĕn)...Sud.	19·02 N	37·19 E
151	Suao (sōō'ou)...Taiwan	24·35 N	121·45 E
142	Subarnarakha (R.)...India	22·38 N	86·26 E
119	Subata (sōō'bà-tà)...Sov. Un.	56·02 N	25·54 E
155	Subic (sōō'bĭk). Phil. (Manila In.)	14·52 N	120·15 E
155	Subic B...Phil. (Manila In.)	14·41 N	120·11 E
127	Subotica (sōō'bô'tē-tsà)...Yugo.	46·06 N	19·41 E
84	Succasunna (sŭk'kȧ-sŭn'nȧ) N. J. (New York In.)	40·52 N	74·37 W
121	Suceava (sōō-chȧ-ä'và)...Rom.	47·39 N	26·17 E
121	Suceava R...Rom.	47·45 N	26·10 E
121	Sucha (sōō'ĸȧ)...Pol.	49·44 N	19·40 E
135	Suchan (sōō-chän')...Sov. Un.	43·15 N	133·19 E
91	Suchiapa (sōō-chê-ä'pä)...Mex.	16·38 N	93·08 W
91	Suchiapa (R.)...Mex.	16·27 N	93·26 W
148	Such'ien (sü'chĭän)...China	33·57 N	118·17 E
92	Suchitoto (sōō-chê-tō'tō)...Sal.	13·58 N	89·03 W
	Süchow, see Hsüchou		
	Süchow, see Ipin		
65	Sucia Is. (sōō'sē-ȧ) Wash. (Vancouver In.)	48·46 N	122·54 W
98	Sucio (R.) (sōō'syô)...Col. (In.)	6·55 N	76·15 W
116	Suck (sŭk)...Ire.	53·34 N	8·16 W
98	Sucre (sōō'krā)...Bol.	19·06 S	65·16 W
99	Sucre (State) (sōō'krĕ)..Ven. (In.)	10·18 N	64·12 W
99	Suçuapara (sōō-sōōà-pá'rä)..Braz.	16·57 S	48·47 W
95	Sud, Canal du (Chan.)...Hai.	18·40 N	73·15 W
85	Sud, Rivière du (rê-vyâr'dü süd') Can. (Quebec In.)	46·56 N	70·35 W
136	Suda (sōō'dá)..Sov. Un. (Urals In.)	56·58 N	56·45 E
128	Suda (R.) (sōō'dà)...Sov. Un.	59·24 N	36·40 E
144	Sudair (sŭ-dä'ēr)...Sau. Ar.	25·48 N	46·28 E
163	Sudan...Afr.	14·00 N	28·00 E
163	Sudan (Reg.) (sōō-dän')...Afr.	16·48 N	3·11 E
87	Sudbury (sŭd'bēr-ê)...Can.	46·28 N	81·00 W
83	Sudbury...Mass. (Boston In.)	42·23 N	71·25 W
120	Sudetes (Mts.)...Czech.	50·41 N	15·37 E
128	Sudogda (sōō'dôk-dà)...Sov. Un.	55·57 N	40·29 E
128	Sudost' (R.) (sōō-dôst')..Sov. Un.	52·43 N	33·13 E
139	Sudr (R.). U. A. R. (Palestine In.)	29·46 N	32·57 E
129	Sudzha (sŏŏd'zhà)...Sov. Un.	51·14 N	35·11 E
125	Sueca (swā'kä)...Sp.	39·12 N	0·18 W
	Suez, see As Suways		
	Suez Canal, see Qana el Suweis		
168	Suez, G. of (sōō-ĕz') U. A. R. (Suez In.)	29·53 N	32·33 E
84	Suffern (sŭf'fērn) N. Y. (New York In.)	41·07 N	74·09 W
84	Suffolk (sŭf'ŭk)..Va. (Norfolk In.)	36·43 N	76·35 W
146	Sufu (Kashgar)...China	39·29 N	76·00 E
134	Sufu...Sov. Un.	39·47 N	76·17 E
80	Sugar (Cr.)...Ind.	39·55 N	87·10 W
72	Sugar City...Colo.	38·12 N	103·42 W
74	Sugar Creek Mo. (Kansas City In.)	39·07 N	94·27 W
73	Sugar Cr. (shŏŏg'ēr)...Ill.	40·14 N	89·28 W
74	Sugar I. Mich. (Sault Ste. Marie In.)	46·31 N	84·12 W
77	Sugarland Jct. (shŏŏg'ēr-lănd) Tex. (In.)	29·29 N	95·31 W
160	Sugarloaf Pt. (sŏŏgēr'lōf)...Austl.	32·19 S	153·04 E
142	Suget Pass (sōō'gĕt)...China	36·35 N	77·40 E
120	Suhl (zōōl)...Ger.	50·37 N	10·41 E
148	Suhsien (sōō'sĭän)...China	33·37 N	117·51 E
151	Suichuan (Mtn.)...China	26·25 N	114·10 E
148	Suichung (sōōĭ'jōōng)...China	40·22 N	120·20 E
135	Suifenho (swā'fŭn'hŭ')...Sov. Un.	44·47 N	131·13 E
150	Suihua (Peilintzu)...China	41·38 N	126·42 E
146	Suilai (sōō'ê-lī')...China	44·30 N	86·00 E
148	Suining (sōō'ê-nĭng')...China	33·54 N	117·57 E
101	Suipacha (swê-pä'chä) Arg. (Buenos Aires In.)	34·45 S	59·43 W
148	Suip'ing (sōō'ê-pĭng)...China	33·09 N	113·58 E
116	Suir R. (sūr)...Ire.	52·20 N	7·32 W
65	Suisun B. (sōō-ê-sōōn') Calif. (San Francisco In.)	38·07 N	122·02 W
153	Suita (sōō'ē-tä)..Jap. (Ōsaka In.)	34·45 N	135·32 E
150	Suite...China	37·32 N	110·12 E
146	Suiyuan (Prov.) (sōō'ê-yän') China	41·31 N	107·04 E
154	Sukabumi...Indon.	6·52 S	106·56 E
154	Sukadana...Indon.	1·15 S	110·30 E
153	Sukagawa (sōō'kä-gä'wä)...Jap.	37·08 N	140·07 E
128	Sukhinichi (sōō'ĸē'nê-chê) Sov. Un.	54·07 N	35·18 E
132	Sukhona (R.) (sŏŏ-ĸô'nà) Sov. Un.	59·30 N	42·20 E
136	Sukhoy Log (sōō'kôy lôg) Sov. Un. (Urals In.)	56·55 N	62·03 E
133	Sukhumi (sŏŏ-kŏŏm')...Sov. Un.	43·00 N	41·00 E
142	Sukkur (sŭk'ŭr)...W. Pak.	27·49 N	68·50 E
136	Suksun (sŏŏk'sŏŏn) Sov. Un. (Urals In.)	57·08 N	57·22 E
153	Sukumo (sōō'kōō-mô)...Jap.	32·58 N	132·45 E
153	Sukurai (sōō'kōō-rī) Jap. (Ōsaka In.)	34·31 N	135·51 E
155	Sula (I.)...Indon.	2·20 S	125·20 E
129	Sula (R.) (sōō-là')...Sov. Un.	50·36 N	33·13 E
92	Sulaco R. (sōō-lä'kō)...Hond.	14·55 N	87·31 W
142	Sulaiman Ra. (sōō-lä-ê-män') W. Pak.	34·22 N	69·10 E
133	Sulak (R.) (sōō-làk')...Sov. Un.	43·30 N	47·00 E
154	Sulawesi (Prov.)...Indon.	1·30 S	120·22 E
118	Suldals Vand (L.) (sŭl-däls vän) Nor.	59·35 N	6·59 E
136	Suleya (sōō-lĕ'yá) Sov. Un. (Urals In.)	55·12 N	58·52 E
111	Sulfeld (zōōl'fĕld) Ger. (Hamburg In.)	53·48 N	10·13 E
129	Sulina (sōō-lē'nà)...Rom.	45·08 N	29·38 E
112	Sulitjema (Mtn.) (sōō-lê-tyĕl'mà) Nor.-Swe.	67·03 N	16·09 E
98	Sullana (sōō-lyä'nä)...Peru	4·57 N	80·47 W
78	Sulligent (sŭl'ĭ-jĕnt)...Ala.	33·52 N	88·06 W
80	Sullivan (sŭl'ĭ-văn)...Ill.	41·35 N	88·35 W
80	Sullivan...Ind.	39·05 N	87·20 W
73	Sullivan...Mo.	38·13 N	91·09 W
126	Sulmona (sōōl-mō'nä)...It.	42·02 N	13·58 E
146	Sulo...China	41·29 N	80·15 E
146	Sulo Ho (R.)...China	40·53 N	94·55 E
73	Sulphur (sŭl'fŭr)...Okla.	34·31 N	96·58 W
73	Sulphur (R.)...Tex.	33·26 N	95·06 W
73	Sulphur Springs (sprĭngz)...Tex.	33·09 N	95·36 W
65	Sultan (sŭl'tăn) Wash. (Seattle In.)	47·52 N	121·49 W
65	Sultan (R.)...Wash. (Seattle In.)	47·55 N	121·49 W
90	Sultepec (sōōl-tà-pĕk')...Mex.	18·50 N	99·51 W
154	Sulu Arch. (sōō'lōō)...Phil.	5·52 N	122·00 E
115	Suluntah...Libya	32·39 N	21·49 E
115	Sulūq...Libya	31·41 N	20·23 E
154	Sulu Sea...Phil.	8·25 N	119·00 E
153	Suma (sōō'mä)...Jap. (Ōsaka In.)	34·39 N	135·08 E
65	Sumas (sū'mȧs) Wash. (Vancouver In.)	49·00 N	122·16 W
154	Sumatera (Sumatra) (I.) (sōō-mä-tĕr'ȧ). Indon.	2·06 N	99·40 E
139	Sumatera Tenga (Prov.) Indon. (Singapore In.)	0·56 N	101 25 E
154	Sumba (I.) (sŭm'bà)...Indon.	9·52 S	119·00 E
154	Sumbawa (I.) (sŏŏm-bä'wä) Indon.	9·00 S	118·18 E
154	Sumbawa-Besar...Indon.	8·32 S	117·20 E
121	Sümeg (shü'mĕg)...Hung.	46·59 N	17·19 E
153	Sumida (R.) (sōō'mê-dä)...Jap.	36·01 N	139·24 E
101	Sumidouro (sōō-mê-dō'rōō) Braz. (Rio de Janeiro In.)	22·04 S	42·41 W
153	Sumiyoshi (sōō'mê-yō'shê) Jap. (Ōsaka In.)	34·43 N	135·16 E
66	Summer L. (sŭm'ēr)...Ore.	42·50 N	120·35 W
82	Summerside (sŭm'ēr-sīd)...Can.	46·25 N	63·47 W
79	Summerton (sŭm'ēr-tŭn)...S. C.	33·37 N	80·22 W
79	Summerville (sŭm'ēr-vĭl)...S. C.	33·00 N	80·10 W
75	Summit (sŭm'mĭt) Ill. (Chicago In.)	41·47 N	87·48 W
84	Summit...N. J. (New York In.)	40·43 N	74·21 W
66	Summit Lake Ind. Res...Nev.	41·35 N	119·30 W
69	Summit Pk...Colo.	37·20 N	106·40 W
65	Sumner (sŭm'nēr) Wash. (Seattle In.)	47·12 N	122·14 W
120	Šumperk (shŏŏm'pĕrk)...Czech.	49·57 N	17·02 E
78	Sumrall (sŭm'rôl)...Miss.	31·25 N	89·34 W
79	Sumter (sŭm'tēr)...S. C.	33·55 N	80·21 W
129	Sumy (sōō'mĭ)...Sov. Un.	50·54 N	34·47 E
129	Sumy (Oblast)...Sov. Un.	51·02 N	34·05 E
81	Sunbury (sŭn'bēr-ê)...Pa.	40·50 N	76·45 W
154	Sunda Is...Indon.	9·00 S	108·40 E
118	Sundals Fd. (sŏŏn'däls)...Nor.	62·50 N	7·55 E
67	Sundance (sŭn'dăns)...Wyo.	44·24 N	104·27 W
142	Sundarbans (Swp.) (sŏŏn'dēr-bŭns). E. Pak.-India	21·50 N	89·00 E
154	Sunda Selat (Str.)...Indon.	5·45 S	106·15 E
154	Sunda Trench (sōōn'dä)...Indon.	9·45 S	107·30 E
167	Sundays (R.) (sŭn'dās) S. Afr. (Natal In.)	33·17 S	25·14 E
158	Sunday Str. (sŭn'dā)...Austl.	15·50 S	122·45 E
118	Sundbyberg (sŏŏn'bü-bĕrgh). Swe.	59·24 N	17·56 E
116	Sunderland (sŭn'dēr-lănd)...Eng.	54·55 N	1·25 W
118	Sundsvall (sŏŏnds'väl)...Swe.	62·24 N	19·19 E
78	Sunflower, (R.) (sŭn-flou'ēr). Miss.	32·57 N	90·40 W
150	Sungari Res. (sŏŏn'gȧ-rē)...China	42·55 N	127·50 E
	Sungari, see Sung Hua (R.)		
149	Sungchiang..China (Shanghai In.)	31·01 N	121·14 E
147	Sung Hua (R.) (Sungari) (sŏŏn'gȧ-rē) China	46·09 N	127·53 E
150	Sungtzu (Mtn.)...China	39·40 N	114·50 E
133	Sungurlu (sōōn'gŏŏr-lōō')...Tur.	40·08 N	34·20 E
142	Sun Kosi (R.)...Nepal	27·13 N	85·52 E
74	Sunland (sŭn-lănd) Calif. (Los Angeles In.)	34·16 N	118·18 W
118	Sunne (sŏŏn'ĕ)...Swe.	59·51 N	13·07 E
110	Sunninghill (sŭnĭng'hĭl) Eng. (London In.)	51·23 N	0·40 W
65	Sunnydale (sŭn-nê-dāl) Calif. (San Francisco In.)	37·23 N	122·02 W
74	Sunnymead (sŭn'ĭ-mēd) Calif. (Los Angeles In.)	33·56 N	117·15 W
69	Sunnyside (sŭn'ĭ-sīd)...Utah	39·35 N	110·20 W
66	Sunnyside...Wash.	46·19 N	120·00 W
65	Sunol (sōō'nŭl) Calif. (San Francisco In.)	37·36 N	122·53 W
67	Sun R. (sŭn)...Mont.	47·34 N	111·53 W
74	Sunset (sŭn-sĕt) Utah (Salt Lake City In.)	41·08 N	112·02 W
69	Sunset Crater Natl. Mon. (krā'tēr). Ariz.	35·20 N	111·30 W
161	Sunshine..Austl. (Melbourne In.)	37·47 S	144·50 E
135	Suntar (sŏŏn-tàr')...Sov. Un.	62·14 N	117·49 E
119	Suoyarvi (sōō'ô-yĕr'vê)..Sov. Un.	62·12 N	32·29 E
69	Superior (su-pē'rĭ-ēr)...Ariz.	33·15 N	111·10 W
72	Superior...Nebr.	40·04 N	98·05 W
74	Superior...Wis. (Duluth In.)	46·44 N	92·06 W
67	Superior...Wyo.	41·45 N	108·57 W
91	Superior, Laguna (L.) (lä-gōō'nà sōō-pā-rê-ōr'). Mex.	16·20 N	94·55 W
63	Superior, L...U. S.-Can.	47·38 N	89·20 W
74	Superior Village. Wis. (Duluth In.)	46·38 N	92·07 W
152	Sup'ung Res. (sōō'pōōng) Kor.-China	40·35 N	126·00 E
65	Suquamish (sōō-gwä'mĭsh) Wash. (Seattle In.)	47·44 N	122·34 W
139	Sūr (Tyre) (sōōr) (tīr) Leb. (Palestine In.)	33·16 N	35·13 E
144	Şūr...Muscat and Oman	22·23 N	59·28 E
154	Surabaja...Indon.	7·23 S	112·45 E
168	Surad Ad (Mt.) (sōō'răd-ăd) Som. (Horn of Afr. In.)	10·40 N	47·23 E
154	Surakarta...Indon.	7·35 S	110·45 E
121	Šurany (shōō'rá-nü')...Czech.	48·05 N	18·11 E
160	Surat (sŭ-răt)...Austl.	27·18 S	149·00 E
142	Surat (sōō'rŭt)...India	21·08 N	73·22 E
154	Surat Thani...Thai.	8·59 N	99·14 E
128	Surazh (sōō-ràzh')...Sov. Un.	53·02 N	32·27 E
128	Surazh...Sov. Un.	55·24 N	30·46 E
122	Surgères (sür-zhâr')...Fr.	46·06 N	0·51 W
134	Surgut (sŏŏr-gŏŏt')...Sov. Un.	61·18 N	73·38 E
154	Surin...Thai.	14·59 N	103·57 E
99	Surinam (Neth. Guiana) (sōō-rē-näm') (gē-än'ȧ). S. A.	3·45 N	56·30 W
99	Suriname (R.)...Sur.	4·15 N	55·38 W
119	Sur-Sari (I.) (sŏŏr-sä'rĭ)..Sov. Un.	60·04 N	26·55 E
153	Suruga-Wan (B.) (sōō'rōō-gä wän). Jap.	34·52 N	138·36 E
165	Surt...Libya	31·14 N	16·37 E
115	Surt, Khalij (G.)...Afr.	31·30 N	18·28 E
126	Susa (sōō'sä)...It.	45·01 N	7·09 E
153	Susa...Jap.	34·40 N	131·39 E
126	Sušac (sōō'shàts)...Yugo.	44·31 N	14·15 E
126	Sušak (sōō'shàk)...Yugo.	45·20 N	14·24 E
126	Sušak (I.)...Yugo.	42·45 N	16·30 E
153	Susaki (sōō'sä-kê)...Jap.	33·23 N	133·16 E
64	Susitna (sōō-sĭt'nȧ)...Alaska	61·28 N	150·28 W
64	Susitna (R.)...Alaska	62·00 N	150·28 W
81	Susquehanna (sŭs'kwê-hăn'ȧ). Pa.	41·55 N	75·35 W
81	Susquehanna (R.)...Pa.	39·50 N	76·20 W
75	Sussex...Wis. (Milwaukee In.)	43·08 N	88·12 W
82	Sussex (sŭs'ĕks)...Can.	45·42 N	65·32 W
84	Sussex...N. J. (New York In.)	41·12 N	74·36 W
151	Susung (sōō'sōōng')...China	30·18 N	116·08 E

ng-sing; ŋ-baŋk: ĸ-nasalized n; nŏd; cŏmmit; ōld; ôbey; ôrder; fōōd; fŏŏt; ou-out; s-soft; sh-dish; th-thin; pūre; ûnite; ûrn; stŭd; circŭs; ü-as "y" in study; '-indeterminate vowel.

Page	Name Pronunciation Region	Lat. °′	Long. °′
161	Sutherland (sŭdh' ēr-lănd) Austl. (Sydney In.)	34·02 S	151·04 E
166	Sutherland (sŭ'thēr-lănd) S. Afr.	32·25 S	20·40 E
142	Sutlej (R.) (sŭt'lĕj) Pak.-India	29·53 N	72·25 E
110	Sutton (sut''n) Eng. (London In.)	51·21 N	0·12 W
83	Sutton Mass. (Boston In)	42·09 N	71·46 W
110	Sutton Coldfield (kōld'fēld) Eng.	52·34 N	1·49 W
110	Sutton-in-Ashfield (ĭn-ăsh'fēld) Eng.	53·07 N	1·15 W
153	Suwa (sōō'wä) Jap.	36·03 N	138·08 E
121	Suwatki (sōō-vou'kê) Pol.	54·05 N	22·58 E
78	Suwannee (R.) (sōō-wô'nê) Fla.-Ga.	29·42 N	83·00 W
128	Suzdal' (sōōz'dál) Sov. Un.	56·26 N	40·29 E
152	Suzu Misaki (C.) (sōō'zōō mê'sä-kê) Jap.	37·30 N	137·35 E
130	Svalbard (Spitzbergen) (Is.) (sväl'bärt) (spĭts'bûr-gĕn) Eur.	77·00 N	20·00 E
118	Svaneke (svä'nĕ-kĕ) Den.	55·08 N	15 07 E
129	Svatovo (svä'tô-vô) Sov. Un.	49·23 N	38·10 E
118	Svedala (svĕ'dä-lä) Swe.	55·29 N	13·11 E
118	Sveg Swe.	62·03 N	14·22 E
118	Svelvik (svĕl'vêk) Nor.	59·37 N	10·18 E
118	Svendborg (svĕn-bôrgh) Den.	55·05 N	10·35 E
65	Svensen (svĕn'sĕn) Ore. (Portland In.)	46·10 N	123·39 W
136	Sverdlovsk (svĕrd-lôfsk') Sov. Un. (Urals In.)	56·48 N	60·37 E
152	Svetlaya (svyĕt'là-yà) Sov. Un.	46·09 N	137·53 E
127	Svilajnac (svē'là-ê-nàts) Yugo.	44·12 N	21·14 E
127	Svilengrad (svĕl'ĕn-gràt) Bul.	41·44 N	26·11 E
132	Svir' (R.) Sov. Un.	60·55 N	33·40 E
119	Svir Kanal (can.) (kà-näl') Sov. Un.	60·10 N	32·40 E
127	Svishtov (svēsh'tôf) Bul.	43·36 N	25·21 E
128	Svisloch' (svēs'lôk) Sov. Un.	53·38 N	28·10 E
120	Svitavy Czech.	49·46 N	16·28 E
121	Svitsa (R.) (svĭ-tsà) Sov. Un.	49·09 N	24·10 E
135	Svobodnyy (svô-bôd'nĭ) Sov. Un.	51·28 N	128·28 E
112	Svolvaer (svôl'vĕr) Nor.	68·15 N	14·29 E
135	Svyatoy Nos, Mys (C.) (svyŭ'toi nôs) Sov. Un.	72·18 N	139·28 E
119	Svyentsyany (shvyĕn'tsyà-nĭ) Sov. Un.	55·09 N	26·09 E
110	Swadlincote (swŏd'lĭn-kôt) Eng.	52·46 N	1·33 W
159	Swain Rfs. (swān) Austl.	22·12 S	152·08 E
79	Swainsboro (swānz'bŭr-ô) Ga.	32·37 N	82·21 W
166	Swakopmund (svä'kôp-mōōnt) (swä'kôp-mōōnd) S. W. Afr.	22·40 S	14·30 E
116	Swale (R.) (swāl) Eng.	54·12 N	1·30 W
110	Swallowfield (swŏl'ô-fēld) Eng. (London In.)	51·21 N	0·58 W
83	Swampscott (swômp'skŏt) Mass. (Boston In.)	42·28 N	70·55 W
161	Swan, I. (swŏn) Austl. (Melbourne In.)	38·15 S	144·41 E
158	Swan (R.) Austl.	31·30 S	126·30 E
160	Swan Hill Austl.	35·20 S	143·30 E
86	Swan Hills (hĭlz) Can.	54·50 N	118·10 W
158	Swanland (Reg.) (swŏn'lănd) Austl.	31·45 S	119·15 E
86	Swan River (swŏn rĭv'ēr) Can.	52·01 N	101·29 W
67	Swan R. Mont.	47·40 N	113·45 W
85	Swansea (swän'sē) Can. (Toronto In.)	43·38 N	79·28 W
116	Swansea Wales	51·37 N	3·59 W
74	Swansea (swŏn'sē) Ill. (St. Louis In.)	38·32 N	89·59 W
84	Swansea Mass. (Providence In.)	41·45 N	71·09 W
116	Swansea B. Wales	51·25 N	4·12 W
72	Swanson Res. (swŏn'sŭn) Nebr.	40·13 N	101·30 W
166	Swartkop (Mtn.) S. Afr. (Cape Town In.)	34·13 S	18·27 E
168	Swartruggens S. Afr. (Johannesburg & Pretoria In.)	25·59 S	26·40 E
167	Swartspruit S. Afr. (Johannesburg & Pretoria In.)	25·44 S	28·01 E
	Swatow, see Shant'ou		
166	Swaziland (Swä'zē-lănd) Afr.	26·45 S	31·30 E
102	Sweden (swē'dĕn) Eur.	60·10 N	14·10 E
84	Swedesboro (swēdz'bē-rô) N. J. (Philadelphia In.)	39·45 N	75·22 W
78	Sweetwater (swēt'wô-tēr) Tenn.	35·36 N	84·29 W
76	Sweetwater Tex.	32·28 N	100·25 W
70	Sweetwater (L.) N. D.	48·15 N	98·35 W
168	Sweetwater (can.) U. A. R. (Suez In.)	30·14 N	32·25 E
68	Sweetwater Res. Calif. (San Diego In.)	32·42 N	116·54 W
67	Sweetwater R. Wyo.	42·19 N	108·35 W
120	Świdnica (shvĭd-nē'tsä) Pol.	50·50 N	16·30 E
120	Swidwin (shvĭd'vĭn) Pol.	53·46 N	15·48 E
120	Swiebodziec (shvyĕN-bo' jĕts) Pol.	52·16 N	15·36 E
120	Swiebodzin (shvyăN-bôd'jĕn) Pol.	50·51 N	16·17 E
120	Swiecie (shvyăN'tsyĕ) Pol.	53·23 N	18·26 E
121	Swietokrzyskie Góry (Mts.) (shvyĕN-tô-kzhĭ'skyĕ gōō'rĭ) Pol.	50·57 N	21·02 E
110	Swift (R.) Eng.	52·26 N	1·08 W
82	Swift (R.) (swĭft) Maine	44·42 N	70·40 W
86	Swift Current (swĭft kûr'ĕnt) Can.	50·20 N	107·59 W
66	Swift Res Wash.	46·03 N	122·10 W
116	Swilly, Lough (B.) (lŏk swĭ-lē) Ire.	54·84 N	8·04 W
116	Swindon (swĭn'dŭn) Eng.	51·35 N	1·55 W
65	Swinomish Ind. Res. (swĭ-nō'mĭsh) Wash. (Seattle In.)	48·25 N	122·27 W
120	Swinoujscie (shvĭ-nĭ-ô-wēsh'chyĕ) Pol.	53·56 N	14·14 E
110	Swinton (swĭn'tŭn) Eng.	53·30 N	1·19 W
75	Swissvale (swĭs'vāl) Pa. (Pittsburgh In.)	40·25 N	79·53 W
102	Switzerland (swĭt'zēr-lănd) Eur.	46·30 N	7·43 E
128	Syas' (R.) (syäs) Sov. Un.	59·28 N	33·24 E
71	Sycamore (sĭk'à-mōr) Ill.	42·00 N	88·42 W
128	Sychëvka (sē-chôf'kà) Sov. Un.	55·52 N	34·18 E
161	Sydney (sĭd'nê) Austl. (Sydney In.)	33·55 S	151·17 E
83	Sydney Can.	46·08 N	60·11 W
	Syene, see Aswān		
83	Sydney Mines Can.	46·15 N	60·15 W
132	Syktyvkar (sük-tüf'kär) Sov.Un.	61·35 N	50·40 E
78	Sylacauga (sĭl-à-kô'gà) Ala.	33·10 N	86·15 W
118	Sylfjällen (Mtn.) (sül'fyĕl-ĕn) Swe.	63·00 N	12·10 E
118	Sylling (sül'lĭng) Nor.	59·52 N	10·12 E
120	Sylt I. (sĭlt) Ger.	54·55 N	8·30 E
79	Sylvania (sĭl-vā'nĭ-à) Ga.	32·44 N	81·40 W
78	Sylvester (sĭl-vĕs'tēr) Ga.	31·32 N	83·50 W
81	Syracuse N. Y.	43·05 N	76·10 W
72	Syracuse (sĭr'à-kūs) Kans.	37·59 N	101·44 W
74	Syracuse Utah (Salt Lake City In.)	41·06 N	112·04 W
115	Syra I. Grc.	37·19 N	25·10 E
103	Syr-Dar'ya (R.) Sov. Un.	44·15 N	65·45 E
165	Syria (sĭr'ĭ-à) Asia	35·00 N	37·15 E
144	Syrian Des. (sĭr'ĭ-ăn) Asia	32·03 N	39·30 E
136	Sysert' (sĕ'sĕrt) Sov. Un. (Urals In.)	56·30 N	60·48 E
132	Syso'la (R.) Sov. Un.	60·50 N	50·40 E
133	Syzran' (sĕz-rän'') Sov. Un.	53·10 N	48·10 E
121	Szabadszallas (sô'bôd-sà'lāsh) Hung.	46·52 N	19·15 E
120	Szamotuty (shà-mô-tōō'wē) Pol.	52·36 N	16·34 E
121	Szarvas (sôr'vôsh) Hung.	46·51 N	20·36 E
121	Szczebrzeszyn (shchĕ-bzhä'shĕn) Pol.	50·41 N	22·58 E
120	Szczecin (Stettin) (shchĕ'tsĭn) (shtĕ-tēn') Pol.	53·25 N	14·35 E
120	Szczecinek (shchĕ'tsĭ-nĕk) Pol.	53·42 N	16·42 E
121	Szczuczyn (shchōō'chĕn) Pol.	53·32 N	22·17 E
121	Szczytno (shchĭt'nô) Pol.	53·33 N	21 00 E
	Szechwan, see Ssuchuan		
121	Szeged (sĕ'gĕd) Hung.	46·15 N	20·12 E
121	Székesfehérvar (sā'kĕsh-fĕ'hăr-vär) Hung.	47·12 N	18·26 E
121	Szekszard (sĕk'särd) Hung.	46·19 N	18·42 E
146	Szengen China	23·39 N	107·45 E
121	Szentendre (sĕnt'ĕn-drĕ) Hung.	47·40 N	19·07 E
121	Szentes (sĕn'tĕsh) Hung.	46·38 N	20·18 E
121	Szigetvar (sĕ'gĕt-vär) Hung.	46·05 N	17·50 E
121	Szolnok (sôl'nôk) Hung.	47·11 N	20·12 E
120	Szombathely (sôm'bôt-hĕl') Hung.	47·13 N	16·35 E
120	Szprotawa Pol.	51·34 N	15·29 E
121	Sztálinváros Hung.	46·57 N	18·55 E
121	Szydlowiec (shid-wô'vyets) Pol.	51·13 N	20·53 E
155	Taal (L.) (tä-äl') Phil. (Manila In.)	13·58 N	121·06 E
155	Tabaco (tä-bä'kō) Phil. (Manila In.)	13·27 N	123·40 E
167	Tabankulu (tä-bän-kōō'la) S. Afr. (Natal In.)	30·56 S	29·19 E
93	Tabasara, Serrania de (Ra.) (sĕr-rä-nē'ä dā tä-bä-sä'rä) Pan.	8·29 N	81·22 W
90	Tabasco (tä-bäs'kô) Mex.	21·47 N	103·04 W
86	Taber Can.	49·47 N	112·20 W
155	Tablas (I.) (tä'bläs) Phil. (Manila In.)	12·26 N	112·15 E
155	Tablas Str. Phil. (Manila In.)	12·17 N	121·41 E
166	Table B. (tā'b'l) S. Afr. (Cape Town In.)	33·41 S	18·27 E
166	Table Mt. S. Afr. (Cape Town In.)	33·58 S	18·26 E
73	Table Rock Lake Mo.	36·37 N	93·29 W
	Tabletop, see Jacques Cartier, Mt.		
88	Taboga (I.) (tä-bō'gä) Pan. (Panama Canal In.)	8·48 N	79·35 W
88	Taboguilla (I.) (tä-bô-gē'l-yä) Pan. (Panama Canal In.)	8·48 N	79·31 W
99	Taboleiro (Plat.) (tä-bô-lā'rô) Braz.	9·34 S	39·22 W
120	Tábor (tä'bôr) Czech.	49·25 N	14·40 E
166	Tabora (tä-bō'rä) Tan.	5·07 S	32·47 E
164	Tabou (tä-bōō') Ivory Coast	4·30 N	7·25 W
144	Tabrīz (tä-brēz') Iran	38·00 N	46·13 E
90	Tacámbaro (R.) (tä-käm'bä-rō) Mex.	18·55 N	101·25 W
90	Tacambaro de Codallos (dä kô-däl'yōs) Mex.	19·12 N	101·28 W
92	Tacaná (Vol.) (tä-kä-nä') Mex.-Guat.	15·09 N	92·07 W
99	Tacarigua, Laguna de la (L.) (lä-gōō'nä-dĕ-lä-tä-kä-rē'gwä) Ven. (In.)	10·18 N	65·43 W
93	Tacarouna, Cerro (Mt.) (sĕ'r-rô-tä-kä-rô-ōō'nä) Pan.	8·07 N	77·18 W
149	Tach'ang China (Shanghai In.)	31·18 N	121·25 E
148	Tach'angshan Tao (I.) (dá'chäng'shän dou) China	39·21 N	122·31 E
146	T'ach'eng (Chuguchak) (tä'chĕng') China	46·50 N	83·24 E
148	Tach'iao (dá'chĭou) China	32·23 N	119·41 E
148	Tach'in Tao (I.) (dá'chĭn dou) China	38·18 N	120·50 E
155	Tacloban (tä-klō'bän) Phil.	11·06 N	124·58 E
98	Tacna (täk'nä) Peru	18·34 S	70·16 W
65	Tacoma (tà-kō'mà) Wash. (Seattle In.)	47·14 N	122·27 W
81	Taconic Ra. (tà-kŏn'ĭk) N. Y.	41·55 N	73·40 W
91	Tacotalpa (tä-kô-täl'pä) Mex.	17·37 N	92·51 W
91	Tacotalpa (R.) Mex.	17·24 N	92·38 W
100	Tacuarembó (tä-kwä-rĕm'bô) Ur.	31·44 S	55·56 W
164	Tademaït, Plat. du (tä-dē-mä'ēt) Alg.	28·00 N	2·15 E
168	Tadjoura (tàd-zhōō'rà) Fr. Som. (Horn of Afr. In.)	11·48 N	42·54 E
110	Tadley (tăd'lê) Eng. (London In.)	51·19 N	1·08 W
98	Tadó (tä-dō') Col. (In.)	5·15 N	76·30 W
153	Tadotsu (tä'dô-tsōō) Jap.	34·14 N	133·43 E
82	Tadoussac (tá-dōō-sák') Can.	48·09 N	69·44 W
130	Tadzhik (S. S. R.) (tàt'zhêk) Sov. Un.	39·22 N	69·30 E
152	Taebaek Sanmaek (Mts.) (tī-bĭk' sän-mĭk') Kor.	37·20 N	128·50 E
152	Taedong R. (tī-dŏng) Kor.	38·38 N	124·32 E
152	Taegu (tī'gōō') Kor.	35·49 N	128·41 E
124	Tafalla (tä-fäl'yä) Sp.	42·30 N	1·42 W
149	Tafan China (Canton In.)	23·27 N	113·06 E
114	Tafilelt (Oasis) (tä-fē'lĕlt) Mor.	31·49 N	4·44 W
125	Tafna (R.) (täf'nä) Alg.	35·28 N	1·00 W
68	Taft (tăft) Calif.	35·09 N	119·27 W
129	Taganrog (tà-gàn-rôk') Sov. Un.	47·13 N	38·44 E
129	Taganrogskiy Zaliv (B.) (tà-gàn-rôk'skĭ zä'lĭf) Sov. Un.	46·55 N	38·17 E
126	Tagliamento (R.) (täl-yä-mĕn'tō) It.	46·11 N	12·53 E
159	Tagula (I.) (tä'gōō-lä) Austl.	11·45 S	153·46 E
	Tagus, see Tajo, Río		
154	Tahan, Gunong (Pk.) Mala.	4·33 N	101·52 E
164	Tahat, Mt. (tä-hät') Alg.	23·22 N	5·21 E
148	Taheishan Tao (I.) (dá'hā'shän dou) China	37·57 N	120·37 E
157	Tahiti (I.) (tä-hē'tē) (tä'ē-tē') Fr. Polynesia	17·30 S	149·30 W
119	Tahkuna Nina (tàh-kōō'nà nē'nà) Sov. Un.	59·08 N	22·03 E
73	Tahlequah (tă-lĕ-kwä') Okla.	35·54 N	94·58 W
68	Tahoe (L.) (tä'hō) Calif.-Nev.	39·09 N	120·18 W
164	Tahoua (tä'ōō-ä) Niger	14·52 N	5·16 E
151	Tahsien China	31·12 N	107·30 E
148	Tahsien Shan (Mts.) (dá'sĭän shän) China	36·28 N	117·42 E
150	Tahsing China (Peking In.)	39·44 N	116·19 E
150	Tahsingaling Shanmo (Greater Khingan Mts.) China	46·30 N	120·00 E
168	Ṭahṭā (tä'tä) U. A. R. (Nile In.)	26·48 N	31·29 E
65	Tahuya (tà-hū-yā') Wash. (Seattle In.)	47·23 N	123·03 W
65	Tahuya (R.) Wash. (Seattle In.)	47·28 N	122·55 W
148	T'aian (tī'ăn') China	36·13 N	117·08 E
148	Taich'iao (dăĭ'chĭou) China	31·43 N	120·40 E
151	T'aichung (tī'chōōng) Taiwan	24·10 N	120·42 E
148	T'aierhchuang (tăĭ'ē'jōōäng) China	34·34 N	117·44 E
148	Taifou (dăĭ'fōō) China	31·22 N	119·29 E
	Taigones, see Taygonos		
150	T'aihang Shan (Mts.) (tī'häng' shän') China	35·45 N	112·00 E
148	T'aiho (tăĭ'hŭ) China	33·10 N	115·38 E
148	Taihsien (tăĭ'sĭän) China	32·31 N	119·54 E
148	T'aihsing (tăĭ'sĭng) China	32·12 N	119·58 E
148	T'ai Hu (L.) (tăĭ'hōō) China	31·13 N	120·00 E
150	Taiku China	37·25 N	112·35 E
146	Tailagein Khara (Reg.) (tĭ'lä-gän' kä'rä) Mong.	43·39 N	105·54 E
150	T'ailai China	46·20 N	123·10 E
160	Tailem Bend (tā-lĕm) Austl.	35·15 S	139·30 E
	Taimyr, see Taymyr		
151	T'ainan (tī'nan') Taiwan	23·08 N	120·18 E
115	Tainaron, Akra (C.) Grc.	36·20 N	21·20 E
151	Taining (tĭ'nĭng') China	26·58 N	117·15 E
150	T'aipai Shan (Mtn.) China	33·42 N	107·25 E
151	T'aipei (tī'pā') Taiwan	25·02 N	121·38 E
154	Taiping Mala.	4·56 N	100·39 E
152	Taira (tī'rä) Jap.	37·03 N	140·57 E
153	Taisha (tī'shä) Jap.	35·23 N	132·40 E
151	T'aishan China	22·15 N	112·50 E
148	T'ai Shan (Mtn.) (tăĭ' shän) China	36·16 N	117·05 E
	Taishet, see Tayshet		
100	Taitao, Peninsula de (pĕ-nē'ng-sōō-lä-dĕ-tä-ê-tä'ō) Chile	46·20 S	77·15 W
149	T'aits'ang (tī'tsäng') China (Shanghai In.)	31·26 N	121·06 E
151	T'aitung (tī'tōōng') Taiwan	22·45 N	121·02 E
150	Taiwan (Formosa) (I.) (tī-wän) (fŏr-mō'sà) Asia	23·30 N	122·20 E
150	T'aiyüan (tī'yü-än') China	37·32 N	112·38 E
151	Taiyün (Mtn.) (tī'yü-än') China	25·40 N	118·08 E
101	Tajano de Morais (tĕ-zhä'nô-dĕ-mô-rä'ĕs) Braz. (Rio de Janeiro In.)	22·05 S	42·04 W
124	Tajo, Río (Tagus) (R.) (rê'ō-tä'hō) (tā'gŭs) Sp.	39·43 N	5·52 W
92	Tajumulco (Vol.) (tä-hōō-mōōl'kō) Guat.	15·03 N	91·53 W
124	Tajuña (R.) (tä-kōō'n-yä) Sp.	40·23 N	2·36 W
114	Tājūrā Libya	32·56 N	13·24 W
154	Tak Thai.	16·57 N	99·12 E
153	Taka (I.) (tä'kä) Jap.	30·47 N	130·23 E
153	Takada (tä'kä-dä) Jap.	37·08 N	138·30 E
153	Takahashi (tä'kä'hä-shĭ') Jap.	34·47 N	133·35 E
153	Takamatsu (tä'kä'mä-tsōō') Jap.	34·20 N	134·02 E
153	Takamori (tä'kä'mô-rē') Jap.	32·50 N	131·08 E
149	Takang China (Canton In.)	22·48 N	113·24 E
153	Takaoka (ta'kä'ô-kä') Jap.	36·45 N	136·59 E
153	Takarazuka (tä'kä-rä-zōō'kä) Jap. (Ōsaka In.)	34·48 N	135·22 E
153	Takasaki (tä'kät'sōō-kē') Jap.	36·20 N	139·00 E
153	Takatsu (Mizonokuchi) (tä-kät'sōō) (mē'zō-nô-kōō'chê) Jap. (Tōkyō In.)	35·36 N	139·37 E
153	Takatsuki (tä'kät'sōō-kē') Jap. (Ōsaka In.)	34·51 N	135·38 E
167	Takaungu (tä'kä'ōōn-gōō') Ken.	3·41 S	39·48 E
153	Takayama (tä'kä'yä'mä) Jap.	36·11 N	137·16 E
153	Takefu (tä'kĕ-fōō) Jap.	35·57 N	136·09 E
165	Takkaze R. (täk'kä-zâ) Eth.	13·38 N	38·00 E
86	Takla (L.) (tăk'lă) Can.	55·33 N	125·22 W
146	Takla Makan (Des.) (mä-kän') China	39·22 N	82·34 E
148	Taku China	39·00 N	117·42 E
148	Taku (R.) (dä'gōō) China	37·07 N	120·14 E
90	Tala (tä'lä) Mex.	20·39 N	103·42 W
101	Talagante (tä-lä-gà'n-tĕ) Chile (Santiago In.)	33·39 S	70·54 W
150	Tal'ai China	45·25 N	124·22 E

ăt; finăl; rāte; senâte; ärm; àsk; sofà; fâre; ch-choose; dh-as th in other; bē; ēvent; bĕt; recĕnt; cratēr; g-go; gh-guttural g; bĭt; ĭ-short neutral; rīde; K-guttural k as ch in German ich;

Page	Name Pronunciation Region	Lat. °′	Long. °′
154	Talakmau, Gunung (Mtn.) . Indon.	0·12 N	100·05 E
165	Tala Mt. . . . . Eth.	11·00 N	38·41 E
92	Talanga (tä-lä'n-gä) . . . . Hond.	14·21 N	87·09 W
98	Talara (tä-lä'rä) . . . . Peru	4·32 N	81·17 W
155	Talasea (tä-lä-sā'ä) . . N. Gui. Ter.	5·20 S	150·00 E
155	Talaud, Pulau-Pulau (Is.) (tä-lout') . Indon.	4·17 N	127·30 E
124	Talavera de la Reina (tä-lä-vā'rä dā lä rā-ē'nä) . Sp.	39·58 N	4·51 W
74	Talbert (tôl'bûrt) Calif. (Los Angeles In.)	33·42 N	117·57 W
101	Talca (täl'kä) . Chile (Santiago In.)	35·25 S	71·39 W
101	Talca (Prov.) . Chile (Santiago In.)	35·23 S	71·15 W
101	Talca, Punta (Pt.) (pōō'n-tä-täl'kä) Chile (Santiago In.)	33·25 S	71·42 W
100	Talcahuano (täl-kä-wä'nō) . . Chile	36·41 S	73·05 W
128	Taldom (täl-dôm) . . . . Sov. Un.	56·44 N	37·33 E
134	Taldy-Kurgan (tál'dĭ-kōōr-gän') Sov. Un.	45·03 N	77·18 E
91	Talea de Çastro (San Miguel) (tä'lā-ä dā käs'trō) . Mex.	17·22 N	96·14 W
122	Talence (tȧ-lôɴs) . . . . Fr.	44·48 N	0·38 W
146	Tali (tä'lē) . . . . China	26·00 N	100·08 E
155	Taliabu (tä-lê-ä'bōō) . . . . . . Indon.	1·30 S	125·00 E
148	Talichi (dä'lē'jē) . . . . China	33·47 N	117·47 E
148	Talien (Daíren) (dä'lĭän) . . . China	38·54 N	121·35 E
148	Talien Wan (B.) (wän) . . . . . China	38·55 N	121·50 E
155	Talim (I.) (tä-lēm') Phil. (Manila In.)	14·21 N	121·14 E
155	Talisay (tä-lē'sī) . Phil. (Manila In.)	14·08 N	122·56 E
64	Talkeetna (tăl-kēt'nȧ) . . . . . Alaska	62·18 N	150·02 W
133	Talkheh Rūd (R.) . . . . Iran	38·00 N	46·50 E
78	Talladega (tăl-ȧ-dē'gȧ) . . . . . . Ala.	33·25 N	86·06 W
78	Tallahassee (tăl-ȧ-hăs'ē) . . . . . . Fla.	30·25 N	84·17 W
78	Tallahatchie (R.) (tal-ȧ hăch'ē) Miss.	34·21 N	90·03 W
78	Tallapoosa (tăl-ȧ-pōō'sȧ) . . . . . Ga.	33·44 N	85·15 W
78	Tallapoosa (R.) . . . . Ala.	32·22 N	86·08 W
78	Tallassee (tăl'ȧ-sē) . . . . Ala.	32·30 N	85·54 W
119	Tallinn (Reval) (tȧl'lĕn) (rā'väl) Sov. Un.	59·26 N	24·44 E
75	Tallmadge (tăl'mĭj) Ohio (Cleveland In.)	41·06 N	81·26 W
77	Tallulah (tă-lōō'lȧ) . . . . La.	32·25 N	91·13 W
93	Talmanca, Cord. de (Mts.) (kôr-dēl-yĕ'rä-dĕ-tâl-mä'n-kä) C. R.	9·37 N	83·55 W
129	Tal'noye (tȧl'nô-yĕ) . . . . . Sov. Un.	48·52 N	30·43 E
165	Talōdi (tä-lō'dê) . . . . Sud.	10·41 N	30·21 E
143	Taloje Budrukh India (Bombay In.)	19·05 N	73·05 E
90	Talpa de Allende (täl'pä dā äl-yĕn'dȧ) . Mex.	20·25 N	104·48 W
119	Talsi (tal'sĭ) . . . . Sov. Un.	57·16 N	22·35 E
100	Taltal (täl-täl') . . . . Chile	25·26 S	70·32 W
129	Taly (täl'ĭ) . . . . Sov. Un.	49·51 N	40·07 E
71	Tama (tā'mȧ) . . . . Iowa	41·57 N	92·36 W
153	Tama (R.) . . . . . . Jap. (Tōkyō In.)	35·38 N	139·35 E
164	Tamale (tä-mä'lȧ) . . . . Ghana	9·16 N	00·53 W
129	Taman' (tȧ-män'') . . . . . . Sov. Un.	45·13 N	36·46 E
98	Tamaná, Cerro (Mtn.) (sĕ'r-rô-tä-mä-nȧ') . Col. (In.)	5·06 N	76·10 W
99	Tamanaco (tä-mä-nä'kō) (R.) Ven. (In.)	9·32 N	66·00 W
164	Tamanr'aset R. (tä-män-räs'sĕt) Alg.	22·15 N	2·51 E
	Tamanrasset, see Fort Laperrine		
81	Tamaqua (tȧ-mô'kwȧ) . . . . Pa.	40·45 N	75·50 W
116	Tamar (R.) (tā'mär) . . . . Eng.	50·35 N	4·15 W
125	Tamarite (tä-mä-rē'tä) . . . . Sp.	41·52 N	0·24 E
167	Tamatave (tä-mȧ-täv') Malag. Rep.	18·14 S	49·25 E
90	Tamaulipas (State) (tä-mä-ōō-lē'päs') . Mex.	23·45 N	98·30 W
90	Tamazula de Gordiano (tä-mä-zōō'lä dā gôr-dê-ä'nô) Mex.	19·44 N	103·09 W
91	Tamazulapan del Progreso (tä-mä-zōō-lä'päm-dĕl-prô-grĕ-sō) . Mex.	17·41 N	97·34 W
90	Tamazunchale (tä-mä-zōōn-chä'lȧ) Mex.	21·16 N	98·46 W
164	Tambacounda (täm-bä-kōōn'dä) Senegal	13·45 N	13·52 W
99	Tambador, Serra do (Mts.) (sĕ'r-rä-dô-täm'bä-dōr) . Braz.	10·33 S	41·16 W
153	Tambaichi (täm'bī'chê) Jap. (Ōsaka In.)	34·36 N	135·50 E
154	Tambelan, Pulau-Pulau (Is.) (täm-bȧ-län') . Indon.	0·38 N	107·38 E
160	Tambo (tăm'bō) . . . . Austl.	24·50 S	146·15 E
133	Tambov (tȧm-bôf') . . . . . . Sov. Un.	52·45 N	41·10 E
128	Tambov (Oblast) . . . . Sov. Un.	52·50 N	40·42 E
124	Tambre (R.) (täm'brā) . . . . Sp.	42·59 N	8·33 W
165	Tambura (täm-bōō'rä) . . . . Sud.	5·34 N	27·30 E
110	Tame (R.) (tām) . . . . Eng.	52·41 N	1·42 W
124	Tamega (R.) (tä-mā'gä) . . . . . Port.	41·30 N	7·45 W
90	Tamesí (R.) (tä-mĕ-sē') . . . . . Mex.	22·36 N	98·32 W
164	Tamgak, Monts (Mt.) (tam-gäk') Niger	19·06 N	8·31 E
114	Tamgrout (täm-grōōt') . . . . . . Mor.	30·12 N	5·46 W
164	Tamgue, M. du (Mt.) . . . . Gui.	12·13 N	12·28 W
91	Tamiahua (tä-myä-wä) . . . . . Mex.	21·17 N	97·26 W
91	Tamiahua, Laguna (L.) (lä-gōō'nä-tä-myä-wä) . Mex.	21·38 N	97·33 W
79	Tamiami, can. (tă-mī-ăm'ĭ) Fla. (In.)	25·52 N	80·08 W
148	Taming (dä'mĭng) . . . . China	36·15 N	115·09 E
119	Tammela (tám'ĕ-lä) . . . . Fin.	60·49 N	23·45 E
	Tammisaari, see Ekenäs		
79	Tampa (tăm'pȧ) . . . . Fla. (In.)	27·57 N	82·25 W
79	Tampa B. . . . . Fla. (In.)	27·35 N	82·38 W
112	Tampere (tám'pĕ-rĕ) . . . . Fin.	61·21 N	23·39 E
91	Tampico (täm-pē'kō) . . . . Mex.	22·14 N	97·51 W
91	Tampico Alto (täm-pē'kō äl'tō) Mex.	22·07 N	97·48 W
139	Tampin . . . . Mala. (Singapore In.)	2·28 N	102·15 E
155	Tamrau (Mtn.) . . . . W. Irian	0·45 S	132·26 E
90	Tamuín (tä-mōō-ē'n) . . . . Mex.	22·04 N	98·47 W
160	Tamworth (tăm'wûrth) . . . . Austl.	31·01 S	151·00 E
110	Tamworth . . . . Eng.	52·58 N	1·41 W
167	Tana (R.) (tä'nä) . . . . Ken.	0·22 S	39·33 E
159	Tana (I.) . . . . New Hebr.	19·32 S	169·27 E
112	Tana (R.) . . . . Nor.-Fin.	69·20 N	24·54 E
153	Tanabe (tä-nä'bā) . . . . Jap.	33·45 N	135·21 E
153	Tanabe . . . . Jap. (Ōsaka In.)	34·49 N	135·46 E
64	Tanacross (tă'nȧ-crōs) . . . . . Alaska	63·20 N	143·30 W
64	Tanaga (I.) (tä-nä'gä) . . . . . Alaska	51·28 N	178·10 W
154	Tanahbala (I.) (tȧ-nä-bä'lä) Indon.	0·30 S	98·22 E
154	Tanahmasa (I.) (tȧ-nä-mä'sä) Indon.	0·03 S	97·30 E
142	Tanakpur (tŭn'ăk-pōōr) . . . . . India	29·10 N	80·07 E
165	Tana L. . . . . Eth.	12·09 N	36·41 E
158	Tanami (tȧ-nā'mê) . . . . Austl.	19·45 S	129·50 E
64	Tanana (tă'nȧ-nô) . . . . Alaska	65·18 N	152·20 W
64	Tanana (R.) . . . . Alaska	64·26 N	148·40 W
167	Tananarive (tȧ-nä-nä-rēv') Malag. Rep.	18·51 S	47·40 E
126	Tanaro (R.) (tä-nä'rô) . . . . It.	44·45 N	8·02 E
155	Tanauan (tä-nä'wän) Phil. (Manila In.)	14·04 N	121·10 E
148	T'anch'eng (tän'chĕng) . . . . . China	34·37 N	118·22 E
152	Tanchŏn (tän'chŭn) . . . . Kor.	40·29 N	128·50 E
90	Tancítaro (tän-sē'tä-rō) . . . . . Mex.	19·16 N	102·24 W
90	Tancítaro, Cerro de (sĕ'r-rô-dĕ) Mex.	19·24 N	102·19 W
91	Tancoco (tän-kō'kō) . . . . Mex.	21·16 N	99·45 W
100	Tandil (tän-dēl') . . . . Arg.	36·16 S	59·01 W
100	Tandil, Sierra del (Mts.) . . . . Arg.	38·40 S	59·40 W
154	Tandjungbalai (tän'jông-bä'lä') Indon.	2·52 N	99·43 E
139	Tandjungbalai Indon. (Singapore In.)	1·00 N	103·26 E
139	Tandjung Berakit (C.) Indon. (Singapore In.)	1·16 N	104·44 E
154	Tandjungpandan . . . . Indon.	2·47 S	107·51 E
139	Tandjungpinang (tän'jŏng-pē'näng) Indon. (Singapore In.)	0·55 N	104·29 E
153	Tanega (I.) (tä'nȧ-gä') . . . . Jap.	30·36 N	131·11 E
164	Tanezrouft (Reg.) (tä'nĕz-rōōft) Alg.	24·17 N	0·30 W
148	T'ang (R.) (täng) . . . . China	33·38 N	117·29 E
167	Tanga (tăŋ'gȧ) . . . . Tan.	5·07 S	39·06 E
90	Tangancícuaro (täŋ-gän-sē'kwä rô) . Mex.	19·52 N	102·13 W
163	Tanganyika (tăŋ-găn-yē'kȧ) . . Afr.	6·48 S	33·58 E
166	Tanganyika, L. . . . . Tan.	6·00 S	30·15 E
148	T'angchiacha (täng'jēä'jä) . . China	32·06 N	120·48 E
149	Tangchiaochen China (Shanghai In.)	31·13 N	121·30 E
164	Tanger (tăn-jēr') . . . . Mor.	35·52 N	5·55 W
120	Tangermünde (täŋ'ĕr-mün'de) Ger.	52·33 N	11·58 E
150	Tangho . . . . China	32·40 N	112·50 E
148	T'anghsien (täng'sĭän) . . . . . China	38·09 N	115·00 E
77	Tangipahoa R. (tăn'jê-pȧ-hō'ȧ) La.	30·48 N	90·28 W
148	T'angku (täŋ'kōō') . . . . China	39·04 N	117·41 E
142	Tangra Tsho (L.) . . . . China	30·38 N	85·40 E
148	Tangt'u (däng'tōō) . . . . China	31·35 N	118·28 E
148	Tangshan (täng'shän') . . . . China	34·27 N	116·27 E
148	T'angshan . . . . China	39·38 N	118·11 E
155	Tanimbar, Pulau-Pulau (Is.) Indon.	8·00 S	132·00 E
139	Tanjong (C.) . Mala. (Singapore In.)	1·53 N	102·29 E
139	Tanjong Piai (I.) Mala. (Singapore In.)	1·16 N	103·11 E
139	Tanjong Ramunia (C.) Mala. (Singapore In.)	1·27 N	104·44 E
143	Tanjore (tăn-jôr') . . . . India	10·51 N	79·11 E
131	Tannu-Ola (Mts.) . . . . Sov. Un.	51·00 N	94·00 E
155	Tañong (tän-yōn') Phil. (Manila In.)	14·46 N	120·52 E
149	T'anpu . . . . China (Canton In.)	23·20 N	113·06 E
91	Tanquijo, Arrecife (Reef) (är-rĕ-sē'fĕ-tän-kē'kô) . Mex.	21·07 N	97·16 W
168	Ţanţā (tän'tä) . U. A. R. (Nile In.)	30·50 N	31·00 E
90	Tantoyuca (tän-tō-yōō'kä) . . Mex.	21·22 N	98·13 W
148	Tanyang (dän'yäng) . . . . China	32·01 N	119·32 E
152	Tanyang . . . . Kor.	36·53 N	128·20 E
152	Taoan (tä'ō-än') . . . . China	45·41 N	123·00 E
148	T'aoch'ichen (tou'chē'jĕn) . . China	31·33 N	117·01 E
150	Taoerh (R.) . . . . China	45·40 N	122·00 E
150	Táo Ho' (R.) (tä'ō hō') . . . . China	35·30 N	103·40 E
148	Tao Hu (L.) (tou'hōō) . . . . . China	31·37 N	119·29 E
148	T'aok'ou (tou'kō) . . . . China	35·34 N	114·32 E
150	T'aonan (tä'ō-nän') . . . . China	45·15 N	122·45 E
126	Taormina (tä-ôr-mē'nä) . . . . It.	37·53 N	15·18 E
69	Taos (tä'ôs) . . . . N. Mex.	36·25 N	105·35 W
164	Taoudenni (tä'ōō-dĕ-nē') . . . . Mali	22·57 N	3·37 W
164	Taoudenni (Oasis) . . . . Mali	23·00 N	3·48 W
164	Taoulo (tä'ōō-lō) . . . . Lib.	6·30 N	8·49 W
164	Taourirt (tä-ōō-rērt') . . . . Alg.	27·08 N	0·06 E
151	Taoyüan (tä'ō-yü-än') . . . . . . China	29·00 N	111·15 E
119	Tapa (tȧ'pȧ) . . . . Sov. Un.	59·16 N	25·56 E
92	Tapachula . . . . Guat.	14·55 N	92·20 W
150	Tapa Shan (Mts.) . . . . China	32·25 N	108·20 E
99	Tapajós (R.) (tä-pä-zhô's) . . Braz.	3·27 S	55·33 W
101	Tapalqué (tä-päl-kĕ') Arg. (Buenos Aires In.)	36·22 S	60·05 W
91	Tapanatepec (tä-pä-nä-tĕ-pĕk) Mex.	16·22 N	94·19 W
166	Tapepo (Mtn.) . . . . Tan.	7·57 S	31·28 E
151	Tapieh Shan (Mts.) . . . . China	31·40 N	114·50 E
148	Tapingi (dä'pĭng'yē) . . . . China	35·30 N	117·38 E
152	Tappi Saki (C.) (täp'pê sä'kê) Jap.	41·05 N	139·40 E
65	Tapps (L.) (tăpz) Wash. (Seattle In.)	47·20 N	122·12 W
142	Tāpti (R.) (tăp'tê) . . . . India	21·38 N	74·10 E
149	Tapuhsü . . . . . China (Canton In.)	23·17 N	113·34 E
99	Taquara, Serra de (Mts.) (sĕ'r-rä-dĕ-tä-kwä'rä) . Braz.	15·28 S	54·33 W
99	Taquari (R.) (tä-kwä'rĭ) . . . . Braz.	18·35 S	56·50 W
79	Tar (R.) (tär) . . . . N. C.	35·58 N	78·06 W
134	Tara (tä'rȧ) . . . . Sov. Un.	56·58 N	74·13 E
155	Tara (I.) (tä'rä) . Phil. (Manila In.)	12·18 N	120·28 E
134	Tara (R.) (tä'rȧ) . . . . Sov. Un.	56·32 N	76·13 E
139	T'arābulus (Tripoli) (tȧ-rä'bōō-lōōs) Leb. (Palestine In.)	34·25 N	35·50 E
165	Tarābulus (Tripoli) . . . . Libya	32·50 N	13·13 E
165	Tarābulus (Tripolitania) (Prov.) Libya	31·00 N	12·26 E
154	Tarakan (Bunju) . . . . Indon.	3·17 N	118·04 E
124	Tarancón (tä-rän-kōn') . . . . Sp.	40·01 N	3·00 W
126	Taranto (tä'rän-tô) . . . . It.	40·30 N	17·15 E
126	Taranto, Golfo di (G.) (gôl-fô-dē tä'rän-tô) . It.	40·03 N	17·10 E
98	Tarapoto (tä-rä-pô'tō) . . . . Peru	6·29 S	76·26 W
122	Tarare (tȧ-rär') . . . . Fr.	45·55 N	4·23 E
122	Tarascon (tȧ-räs-kôɴ') . . . . Fr.	42·53 N	1·35 E
122	Tarascon-sur-Rhône (tȧ-räs-kôɴ-sür-rōn') . Fr.	43·47 N	4·41 E
129	Tarashcha (tä'rȧsh-chȧ) . Sov. Un.	49·34 N	30·52 E
98	Tarata (tä-rä'tä) . . . . Bol.	17·43 S	66·00 W
126	Taravo (R.) . . . . Fr.	41·54 N	8·58 E
124	Tarazona (tä-rä-thō'nä) . . . . . . Sp.	41·54 N	1·45 W
124	Tarazona de la Mancha (tä-rä-zô'nä-dĕ-lä-mä'n-chȧ) . Sp.	39·13 N	1·50 W
116	Tarbat Ness (Hd.) (tȧr'bát) . Scot.	57·51 N	3·50 W
122	Tarbes (tȧrb) . . . . Fr.	43·04 N	0·05 E
79	Tarboro (tär'bŭr-ô) . . . . N. C.	35·53 N	77·34 W
165	Tarbū . . . . Libya	26·07 N	15·49 E
160	Taree (tă-rē') . . . . Austl.	31·52 S	152·21 E
139	Tareifiya (R.) U. A. R. (Palestine In.)	29·34 N	33·41 E
75	Tarentum (tȧ-rĕn'tŭm) Pa. (Pittsburgh In.)	40·36 N	79·44 W
168	Tarfa, Wadi el (Val.) U. A. R. (Nile In.)	28·14 N	31·00 E
164	Tarhmanant (Well) (tär-mä-nänt') . Mali	24·32 N	4·58 W
124	Tarifa (tä-rē'fä) . . . . Sp.	36·02 N	5·35 W
98	Tarija (tär-rē'hä) . . . . Bol.	21·42 S	64·52 W
144	Tarīm (tȧ-rīm') . . . . Aden	16·13 N	49·08 E
146	Tarim (R.) (tȧ-rĭm') . . . . China	40·45 N	85·39 E
146	Tarim Basin (tȧ-rĭm') . . . . . . China	39·52 N	82·34 E
167	Tarka (R.) (tä'kȧ) S. Afr. (Natal In.)	32·15 S	26·00 E
167	Tarkastad . . . . . S. Afr. (Natal In.)	32·01 S	26·18 E
129	Tarkhankut, Mys (C.) (mĭs tȧr-kän'kōōt) . Sov. Un.	45·18 N	32·08 E
73	Tarkio (tär'kĭ-ō) . . . . Mo.	40·27 N	95·22 W
164	Tarkwa (tärk'wä) . . . . Ghana	5·16 N	2·03 W
155	Tarlac (tär'läk) Phil. (Manila In.)	15·29 N	120·36 E
167	Tarlton (tärl'tŭn) . . . . S. Afr. (Johannesburg & Pretoria In.)	26·05 S	27·38 E
98	Tarma (tär'mä) . . . . Peru	11·26 S	75·40 W
122	Tarn (R.) (tärn) . . . . Fr.	44·03 N	2·41 E
121	Târnava Mica R. (tĕr-nä'vȧ mē'kŏ) . Rom.	46·17 N	24·20 E
121	Tarnów (tär'nōōf) . . . . Pol.	50·02 N	21·00 E
126	Taro (R.) (tä'rō) . . . . It.	44·41 N	10·03 E
164	Taroudant (tȧ-rōō-dänt') . . . . Mor.	30·39 N	8·52 W
79	Tarpon Springs (tär'pŏn) Fla. (In.)	28·07 N	82·44 W
110	Tarporley (tär'pēr-lê) . . . . Eng.	53·09 N	2·40 W
95	Tarpum B. (tär'pŭm) . . . . Ba. Is.	25·05 N	76·20 W
126	Tarquinia (Corneto) (tär-kwē'nê-ä) (kôr-nā'tô) . It.	42·16 N	11·46 E
125	Tarragona (tär-rä-gō'nä) . . . . . . Sp.	41·05 N	1·15 E
84	Tarrant (tăr'ănt) Ala. (Birmingham In.)	33·35 N	86·46 W
125	Tarrasa (tär-rä'sä) . . . . Sp.	41·34 N	2·01 E
125	Tárrega (tä rȧ-gä) . . . . Sp.	41·40 N	1·09 E
125	Tarrejón de Ardoz (tär-rĕ-кō'n-dĕ-är-dôz) Sp. (Madrid In.)	40·28 N	3·29 W
84	Tarrytown (tăr'ĭ-toun) N. Y. (New York In.)	41·04 N	73·52 W
133	Tarsus (tȧr'sōōs) (tär'sŭs) . . . . Tur.	37·00 N	34·50 E
100	Tartagal (tär-tä-gä'l) . . . . Arg.	23·31 S	63·47 W
115	Tartous (tȧr-tōōs') . . . . U. A. R.	34·54 N	35·59 E
128	Tartu (Dorpat) (tär'tōō) (dôr'pät) Sov. Un.	58·23 N	26·44 E
153	Tarumi (tä'rōō-mê) Jap. (Ōsaka In.)	34·38 N	135·04 E
128	Tarusa (tä-rōōs'ȧ) . . . . Sov. Un.	54·43 N	37·11 E
74	Tarzana (tär-ză'ȧ) Calif. (Los Angeles In.)	34·10 N	118·32 W
148	Tashanchen (dä'shän'jĕn) . China	34·17 N	119·17 E
103	Tashauz (tŭ-shŭ-ōōs') . . . Sov. Un.	41·50 N	59·45 E
142	Tashi-Chho Dzong (Thimbu) . Bhu.	27·33 N	89·42 E
134	Tashkent (tȧsh'kĕnt) . . . . Sov. Un.	41·23 N	69·04 E
159	Tasman B. (tăz'măn) . N. Z. (In.)	39·11 S	173·22 E
159	Tasmania (I.) (tăz-mā'nĭ-ȧ) Austl.	41·28 S	142·30 E
160	Tasman Pen. . . . . Austl.	43·00 S	148·30 E
156	Tasman Sea . . . . Oceania	29·30 S	155·00 E
90	Tasquillo (täs-kē'lyō) . . . . Mex.	20·34 N	99·21 W
164	Tassili-n-Ajjer (Plat.) (tȧs'ē-lē ȧ'jĕr) . Alg.	25·40 N	6·57 E
132	Tatar (A. S. S. R.) (tȧ-tär') Sov. Un.	55·30 N	51·00 E
134	Tatarsk (tȧ-tärsk') . . . . . . Sov. Un.	55·15 N	75·00 E
135	Tatar Str. . . . . Sov. Un.	51·00 N	141·45 E
65	Tater Hill (Mtn.) (tāt'ĕr hĭl) Ore. (Portland In.)	45·47 N	123·02 W
153	Tateyama (tä'tē-yä'mä) . . . . . . Jap.	35·04 N	139·52 E
166	Tati (tä'tê) . . . . Bech.	21·18 S	27·43 E
121	Tatra Mts. . . . . Czech.-Pol.	49·15 N	19·40 E

ng-sing; ŋ-baŋŋ; ɴ-nasalized n; nŏd; cŏmmit; ōld; ôbey; ôrder; fōōd; fŏŏt; ou-out; s-soft; sh-dish; th-thin; pūre; ûnite; ûrn; stŭd; circŭs; ü-as "y" in study; '-indeterminate vowel.

Page	Name Pronunciation Region	Lat. °′	Long. °′
151	Tattien Ting (Mtn.) China	22·25 N	111·20 E
151	Tatu Ho (R.) China	29·20 N	103·30 E
101	Tatuí (tä-tōō-ē') Braz. (Rio de Janeiro In.)	23·21 S	47·49 W
150	Tat'ung (tä'tōōng') China	40·00 N	113·30 E
101	Taubaté (tou-bà-tā') Braz. (Rio de Janeiro In.)	23·03 S	45·32 W
120	Tauern Tun Aus.	47·12 N	13·17 E
165	Taufikia (tou-fēk'yà) Sud.	9·30 N	31·47 E
166	Taungs (tä'ōōngs) S. Afr.	27·25 S	29·45 E
84	Taunton (tän'tŭn) Mass. (Providence In.)	41·54 N	71·03 W
84	Taunton R. R. I. (Providence In.)	41·50 N	71·02 W
117	Taunus (Mts.) (tou'nōōz) Ger.	50·15 N	8·33 E
159	Taupo, L. (tä'ōō-pō) N. Z. (In.)	38·38 S	175·27 E
119	Taurage (tou'rà-gä) Sov. Un.	55·15 N	22·18 E
	Taurus Mts., see Toros Dağlari		
124	Tauste (tä-ōōs'tå) Sp.	41·55 N	1·15 W
134	Tavda (tàv-dà') Sov. Un.	58·00 N	64·44 E
132	Tavda (R.) Sov. Un.	59·20 N	63·28 E
123	Taverny (tá-vĕr-nē') Fr. (Paris In.)	49·02 N	2·13 E
91	Taviche (tä-vē'chĕ) Mex.	16·43 N	96·35 W
124	Tavira (tä-vē'rá) Port.	37·09 N	7·42 W
154	Tavoy Bur.	14·04 N	98·19 E
133	Tavşanli (tàv'shän-lĭ) Tur.	39·30 N	29·30 E
77	Tawakoni (L.) Tex.	32·51 N	95·59 W
153	Tawaramoto (tä'wä-rä-mô-tô) Jap. (Ōsaka In.)	34·33 N	135·48 E
80	Tawas City Mich.	44·15 N	83·30 W
80	Tawas Pt. (tô'wȧs) Mich.	44·15 N	83·25 W
148	Tawen (R.) (dä'wĕn) China	35·58 N	116·53 E
154	Tawitawi Group (Is.) (tä'wê-tä'wê) Phil.	4·52 N	120·35 E
90	Taxco de Alarcón (täs'kō dĕ ä-lär-kô'n) Mex.	18·34 N	99·37 W
116	Tay, Firth of (fûrth ŏv tā) Scot.	56·26 N	2·45 W
116	Tay (L.) Scot.	56·25 N	5·07 W
116	Tay (R.) Scot.	56·35 N	3·37 W
155	Tayabas B. (tä-yä'bäs) Phil. (Manila In.)	13·44 N	121·40 E
134	Tayga (tī'gä) Sov. Un.	56·12 N	85·47 E
135	Taygonos, Mys (Taigonos) (C.) Sov. Un.	60·37 N	160·17 E
77	Taylor (tā'lēr) Tex.	30·35 N	97·25 W
69	Taylor, Mt. N. Mex.	35·20 N	107·40 W
80	Taylorville (tā'lēr-vĭl) Ill.	39·30 N	89·20 W
144	Taymā Sau. Ar.	27·45 N	38·55 E
135	Taymyr (Taimyr) (L.) (tī-mĭr') Sov. Un.	74·13 N	100·45 E
134	Taymyr, P-Ov (Taimyr) (Pen.) Sov. Un.	75·15 N	95·00 E
134	Tayshet (Taishet) (tī-shĕt') Sov. Un.	56·09 N	97·49 E
154	Taytay (tī-tī) Phil.	10·37 N	119·10 E
151	Tayü China	25·20 N	114·20 E
155	Tayung (tā-yōōng') Phil. (Manila In.)	16·01 N	120·45 E
134	Taz (B.) (tàz) Sov. Un.	67·15 N	80·45 E
164	Taza (tä'zä) Mor.	34·08 N	4·00 W
134	Tazovskoye Sov. Un.	66·58 N	78·28 E
133	Tbilisi ('tbĭl-yē'sē) Sov. Un.	41·40 N	44·45 E
166	Tchibanga (chê-bäŋ'gä) Gabon	2·48 S	10·50 E
121	Tczew (t'chĕf') Pol.	54·06 N	18·48 E
92	Teabo (tĕ-ä'bô) Mex. (Yucatan In.)	20·25 N	89·14 W
77	Teague (tēg) Tex.	31·39 N	96·16 W
91	Teapa (tā-ä'pä) Mex.	17·35 N	92·56 W
164	Tébessa (tā'bĕs'ä) Alg.	35·27 N	8·13 E
139	Tebingtinggi, Palau (I.) (teb'ĭng-tĭng'gä) Indon. (Singapore In.	0·54 N	102·39 E
90	Tecalitlán (tā-kä-lē-tlän') Mex.	19·28 N	103·17 W
90	Tecoanapa (tāk-wä-nä-pä') Mex.	16·33 N	98·46 W
92	Tecoh (tĕ-kô) Mex. (Yucatan In.)	20·46 N	89·27 W
90	Tecolotlán (tā-kô-lô-tlän') Mex.	20·13 N	103·57 W
91	Tecolutla (tā-kô-lōō'tlä) Mex.	20·33 N	97·00 W
91	Tecolutla (R.) Mex.	20·16 N	97·14 W
90	Tecomán (tā-kô-män') Mex.	18·53 N	103·53 W
91	Tecómitl (tĕ-kŏ'mētl) Mex. (Mexico City In.)	19·13 N	98·59 W
90	Tecozautla (tā'kô-zä-ōō'tlä) Mex.	20·33 N	99·38 W
90	Tecpan de Galeana (tĕk-pän' dā gä-lā-ä'nä) Mex.	17·13 N	100·41 W
91	Tecpatán (tĕk-pä-tä'n) Mex.	17·08 N	93·18 W
90	Tecuala (tĕ-kwä-lä) Mex.	22·24 N	105·29 W
121	Tecuci (ta-kōōch') Rom.	45·51 N	27·30 E
75	Tecumseh (tê-kŭm'sĕ) Can. (Detroit In.)	42·19 N	82·53 W
80	Tecumseh Mich.	42·00 N	84·00 W
76	Tecumseh Nebr.	40·21 N	96·09 W
73	Tecumseh Okla.	35·18 N	96·55 W
116	Tees (R.) (tēz) Eng.	54·40 N	2·10 W
98	Tefé (těf-ā') Braz.	3·27 S	64·43 W
153	Teganuna (L.) (tā'gä-nōō'nä) Jap. (Tōkyō In.)	35·50 N	140·02 E
92	Tegucigalpa (tå-gōō-sê-gäl'pä) Hond.	14·08 N	87·15 W
68	Tehachapi Mts. (tĕ-hă-shă'pĭ) Calif.	34·50 N	118·55 W
144	Tehrān (tĕ-hrän') Iran	35·45 N	51·30 E
148	Tehsien (dŭ'siän) China	37·28 N	116·17 E
151	Tehua China	25·30 N	118·15 E
91	Tehuacan (tā-wä-kän') Mex.	18·27 N	97·23 W
91	Tehuantepec (Sto. Domingo) (tå-wän-tå-pĕk') (sän-tô dô-mĕ'n-gô) Mex.	16·20 N	95·14 W
88	Tehuantepec, Golfo de (G.) (gôl-fô dĕ) Mex.	15·45 N	95·00 W
91	Tehuantepec, Istmo de (Isth.) (ē'st-mô dĕ) Mex.	17·55 N	94·35 W
91	Tehuantepec (R.) Mex.	16·30 N	95·23 W
90	Tehuehuetla Arroyo (R.) (tĕ-wĕ-wĕ'tlä är-rô-yô) Mex.	17·54 N	100·26 W
90	Tehuitzingo (tā-wê-tzĭŋ'gō) Mex.	18·21 N	98·16 W
124	Tejeda, Sierra de. (Mts.) (sē-ĕ'r-rä dĕ tĕ-kĕ'dä) Sp.	36·55 N	5·57 W
124	Tejo, Rio (R.) (rē-ōtä'hōō) Port.	39·23 N	8·01 W
91	Tejúpan (Santiago) (tĕ-ĸōō-pä'n) (sän-tyà'gô) Mex.	17·39 N	97·34 W
90	Tejúpan, Punta (Pt.) (pōō'n-tä) Mex.	18·19 N	103·30 W
90	Tejupilco de Hidalgo (tå-hōō-pēl'kô dä ê-dhäl'gō) Mex.	18·52 N	100·07 W
70	Tekamah (tê-kā'mȧ) Nebr.	41·46 N	96·13 W
92	Tekax de Alvaro Obregon (tĕ-kä'x dĕ ä'l-vä-rô-brĕ-gô'n) Mex. (Yucatan In.)	20·12 N	89·11 W
127	Tekirdağ (Rodosto) (tĕ-kēr'dägh') Tur.	41·00 N	27·28 E
92	Tekit (tĕ-kĕ't). Mex. (Yucatan In.)	20·35 N	89·18 W
66	Tekoa (tê-kō'ȧ) Wash.	47·15 N	117·03 W
92	Tela (tā'lä) Hond.	15·45 N	87·25 W
92	Tela, Bahía de (B.) (bä-ē'ä dĕ) Hond.	15·53 N	87·29 W
139	Telapa Burok, Gunong (Mt.) Mala. (Singapore In.)	2·51 N	102·04 E
133	Telavi Sov. Un.	42·00 N	45·20 E
139	Tel Aviv-Jaffa (tĕl-ä-vēv'jä'fȧ) Isr. (Palestine In.)	32·03 N	34·46 E
86	Telegraph Creek (tĕl'ê-gràf) Can.	57·59 N	131·22 W
129	Teleneshty (tyĕ-le-nĕsht'i) Sov. Un.	47·31 N	28·22 E
68	Telescope Pk. (tĕl'ê skōp) Calif.	36·12 N	117·05 W
99	Teles Pirez (R.) (tĕ-lĕs pē'rĕz) Braz.	8·28 S	57·07 W
139	Telesung Indon. (Singapore In.)	1·07 N	102·53 E
92	Telica (Vol.) (tå-lē'kä) Nic.	12·38 N	86·52 W
146	Telii Nuur (L.) China	45·49 N	86·08 E
80	Tell City (tĕl) Ind.	38·00 N	86·45 W
64	Teller (tĕl'ēr) Alaska	65·17 N	166·28 W
98	Tello (tĕ'l-yô) Col. (In.)	3·05 N	75·08 W
69	Telluride (tĕl'ū-rīd) Colo.	37·55 N	107·50 W
139	Telok Datok Mala. (Singapore In.)	2·51 N	101·33 E
90	Teloloapan (tā'lō-lô-ä'pän) Mex.	18·19 N	99 54 W
132	Tel'pos-Iz, Gora (Mtn.) (tyĕl'pôs-ēz') Sov. Un.	63·50 N	59·20 E
139	Tel Sharuhea Isr. (Palestine In.)	31·16 N	34·29 E
119	Telšiai (tĕl'-shä'ê) Sov. Un.	55·59 N	22·17 E
111	Teltow (tĕl'tō) Ger. (Berlin In.)	52·24 N	13·12 E
154	Telukbetung Indon.	5·30 S	105·04 E
139	Telukletjak Indon. (Singapore In.)	1·53 N	101·45 E
164	Tema (tē'mȧ) Ghana	5·45 N	0.00
90	Temascalcingo (tā'mäs-käl-sĭŋ'gō) Mex.	19·55 N	100·00 W
90	Temascaltepec (tā'mäs-käl-tå pĕk) Mex.	19·00 N	100·03 W
92	Temax (tĕ'mäx) Mex. (Yucatan In.)	21·10 N	88·51 W
133	Temir (tyĕ'mêr) Sov. Un.	49·10 N	57·15 E
134	Temir-Tau Sov. Un.	50·08 N	73·13 E
82	Temiscouata (L.) (tĕ'mĭs-kōō-ä'tä) Can.	47·46 N	69·10 W
91	Temoaya (tĕ-mô-ä-yä) Mex. (Mexico City In.)	19·28 N	99·36 W
100	Temperley (tĕ'm-pĕr-lā) Arg. (In.)	34·32 S	58·24 W
126	Tempio Pausania (tĕm'pê-ō pou-sä'nê-ä) Sard.	40·55 N	9·05 E
77	Temple (tĕm'p'l) Tex.	31·06 N	97·20 W
74	Temple City Calif. (Los Angeles In.)	34·07 N	118·02 W
85	Templeton (tĕm'p'l-tŭn) Can. (Ottawa In.)	45·29 N	75·37 W
120	Templin (tĕm-plēn') Ger.	53·08 N	13·30 E
90	Tempoal (R.) (tĕm-pô-ä'l) Mex.	21·38 N	98·23 W
129	Temryuk (tyĕm-ryōōk') Sov. Un.	45·17 N	37·21 E
100	Temuco (tå-mōō'kō) Chile	38·46 S	72·38 W
136	Temyasovo (tĕm-yä'sô-vô) Sov. Un. (Urals In.)	53·00 N	58·06 E
92	Tenabó (tĕ-nä-bŏ') Mex. (Yucatan In.)	20·05 N	90·11 W
90	Tenamaxtlán (tā'nä-mäs-tlän') Mex.	20·13 N	104·06 W
90	Tenancingo (tå-nän-sēn'gō) Mex.	18·54 N	99·36 W
91	Tenango (tå-näŋ'gō) Mex. (Mexico City In.)	19·09 N	98·51 W
154	Tenasserim (tĕn-ăs'ēr-ĭm) Bur.	12·09 N	99·01 E
129	Tenderovskaya Kosa (C.) (tĕn-dĕ-rôf'skä-yä kô-sä') Sov. Un.	46·12 N	31·17 E
	Tenedos, see Bozcaada		
164	Ténéré (Reg.) Niger	18·45 N	11·16 E
164	Tenerife I. (tå-nå-rē'fä) (tĕn-ēr-ĭf') Can. Is.	28·41 N	17·02 W
113	Ténés (tā-nĕs') Alg.	36·28 N	1·22 E
148	T'enghsien (tĕng'hsê-ĕn') China	35·07 N	117·08 E
134	Tengiz (L.) (tyĭn-gĕs') Sov. Un.	50·45 N	68·39 E
146	Tengri Khan (tĕŋ'grê kän') China	42·10 N	80·20 E
153	Tenjin (tĕn'jĕn) Jap. (Ōsaka In.)	34·54 N	135·04 E
166	Tenke (tĕŋ'kå) Con. L.	10·36 S	26·12 E
73	Tenkiller Ferry Res. (tĕn-kĭl'ēr) Okla.	35·42 N	94·47 W
164	Tenkodogo (tĕŋ-kô-dō'gô) Upper Volta	11·42 N	0·30 W
65	Tenmile (R.) (tĕn mīl) Wash. (Vancouver In.)	48·52 N	122·32 W
158	Tennant Creek (tĕn'ănt) Austl.	19·45 S	134·00 E
63	Tennessee (State) (tĕn-ĕ-sē') U. S.	35·50 N	88·00 W
63	Tennessee (L.) U. S.	35·35 N	88·20 W
78	Tennessee (R.) U. S.	35·10 N	88·20 W
78	Tennille (tĕn'ĭl) Ga.	32·55 N	86·50 W
101	Teno (tĕ'nô) (R.) Chile (Santiago In.)	34·55 S	71·00 W
160	Tenora (tĕn-ôrȧ) Austl.	34·23 S	147·33 E
91	Tenosique (tā-nô-sē'kå) Mex.	17·27 N	91·25 W
153	Tenryū-Gawa (Strm.) (tĕn'ryōō'gä'wä) Jap.	35·16 N	137·54 E
77	Tensas R. (tĕn'sô) La.	31·54 N	91·30 W
78	Tensaw (R.) (tĕn'sô) Ala.	30·45 N	87·52 W
160	Tenterfield (tĕn'tēr-fēld) Austl.	29·00 S	52·06 E
79	Ten Thousand, Is. (tĕn thou'zănd) Fla (In.)	25·45 N	81·35 W
90	Teocaltiche (tā'ô-käl-tē'chå) Mex.	21·27 N	102·38 W
91	Teocelo (tā-ô-sā'lō) Mex.	19·22 N	96·57 W
90	Teocuitatlán de Corona (tā'ô-kwē'tä-tlän' dä kô-rō'nä) Mex.	20·06 N	103·22 W
99	Teófilo Otoni (tĕ-ô'fē-lō-tô'nê) Braz.	17·49 S	41·18 W
90	Teoloyucan (tā'ô-lô-yōō'kän) Mex.	19·43 N	99·12 W
91	Teopisca (tā-ô-pēs'kä) Mex.	16·30 N	92·33 W
91	Teotihuacán (tĕ-ō-tē-wä-kà'n) Mex. (Mexico City In.)	19·40 N	98·52 W
91	Teotitlán del Camino (tā-ô-tē-tlän' dĕl kä-mē'nô) Mex.	18·07 N	97·04 W
90	Tepalcatepec (tā'päl-kä-tå'pĕk) Mex.	19·11 N	102·51 W
90	Tepalcatepec (R.) Mex.	18·54 N	102·25 W
90	Tepalcingo (tā-päl-sĕŋ'gô) Mex.	18·34 N	98·49 W
90	Tepatitlan de Morelos (tā-pä-tê-tlän' dā mô-rā'los) Mex.	20·15 N	102·47 W
91	Tepeaca (tā-pà-ä'kä) Mex.	18·57 N	97·54 W
90	Tepecoacuilco de Trujano (tā'pà-kō'ä-kwēl'kō dä trōō-hä'nō) Mex.	19·15 N	99·29 W
90	Tepeji del Rio (tā-pà-ĸe' dĕl rē'ō) Mex.	19·55 N	99·22 W
91	Tepelmeme (tā'pĕl-mä'må) Mex.	17·51 N	97·23 W
91	Tepetlaoxtoc (tā'pā-tlä'ôs-tōk') Mex. (Mexico City In.)	19·34 N	98·49 W
90	Tepezala (tā-pà-zä-lä') Mex.	22·12 N	102·12 W
90	Tepic (tā-pēk') Mex.	21·32 N	104·53 W
148	Tep'ing (dŭ'pĭng) China	37·28 N	116·57 E
136	Tëplaya Gora (tyôp'lȧ-yȧ gô-rȧ) Sov. Un. (Urals In.)	58·32 N	59·08 E
120	Teplice Sanov (tĕp'li-tsĕ shä'nôf) Czech.	50·39 N	13·50 E
91	Teposcolula (San Pedro y San Pablo) (tā-pôs-kô-lōō'lä) (sän pā'drō ē sän pä'blō) Mex.	17·33 N	97·29 W
98	Tequendama, Salto de (Falls) (sä'l-tô dĕ tĕ-kĕn-dä'mä) Col. (In.)	4·34 N	74·18 W
90	Tequila (tå-kē'lä) Mex.	20·53 N	103·48 W
91	Tequisistlán (R.) (tĕ-kē-sēs-tlä'n) Mex.	16·20 N	95·40 W
90	Tequisquiapan (tå-kēs-kê-ä'pän) Mex.	20·33 N	99·57 W
125	Ter (R.) (tĕr) Sp.	42·04 N	2·52 E
124	Tera (R.) (tā'rä) Sp.	42·05 N	6·24 W
126	Teramo (tā'rä-mô) It.	42·40 N	13·41 E
123	Terborg (tĕr'bōrg) Neth. (Ruhr In.)	51·55 N	6·23 E
133	Tercan (tĕr'jän) Tur.	39·40 N	40·12 E
164	Terceira I. (tĕr-sā'rä) Azores (In.)	38·49 N	26·36 W
121	Terebovlya (tĕ-rä'bôv-lyä) Sov. Un.	49·18 N	25·43 E
133	Terek (R.) Sov. Un.	43·30 N	45·10 E
136	Terenkul' (tĕ-rĕn'kōōl) Sov. Un. (Urals In.)	55·38 N	62·18 E
99	Teresina (tĕr-ā-sē'nȧ) Braz.	5·04 S	42·42 W
100	Teresópolis (tĕr-ā-sô'pō-lēzh) Braz. (In.)	22·25 S	42·59 W
132	Teribërka (tyĕr-ê-byôr'kȧ) Sov. Un.	69·00 N	35·15 E
133	Terme (tĕr'mĕ) Tur.	41·05 N	42·00 E
142	Termez (tyĕr'mĕz) Sov. Un.	37·19 N	67·20 E
126	Termini (tĕr'mê-nê) It.	37·58 N	13·39 E
91	Términos, Laguna de (L.) (lä-gōō'nä dĕ ĕ'r-mē-nôs) Mex.	18·37 N	91·32 W
126	Termoli (tĕr'mô-lê) It.	42·00 N	15·01 E
110	Tern (R.) (tûrn) Eng.	52·49 N	2·31 W
155	Ternate (tĕr-nä'tä) Indon.	0·52 N	127·25 E
126	Terni (tĕr'nê) It.	42·38 N	12·41 E
121	Ternopol' (tĕr-nō-pōl') Sov. Un.	49·32 N	25·36 E
152	Terpeniya, Zaliv (B.) (zä'lĭf tĕr-pä'nĭ-yä) Sov. Un.	49·10 N	143·05 E
135	Terpeniya, Mys (C.) Sov. Un.	48·44 N	144·42 E
86	Terrace (tĕr'ĭs) Can.	54·36 N	128·38 W
126	Terracina (tĕr-rä-chē'nä) It.	41·18 N	13·14 E
83	Terra Nova Natl. Park Can.	48·37 N	54·15 W
85	Terrebonne (tĕr-bŏn') Can. (Montreal In.)	45·42 N	73·38 W
77	Terrebonne B. La.	28·55 N	90·30 W
80	Terre Haute (tĕr-ê hōt') Ind.	39·25 N	87·25 W
77	Terrell (tĕr'ĕl) Tex.	32·44 N	96·15 W
65	Terrell Wash. (Vancouver In.)	48·53 N	122·44 W
74	Terrell Hills (tĕr'ĕl hĭlz) Tex. (San Antonio In.)	29·28 N	98·27 W
117	Terschelling (I.) (tĕr-sĸĕl'ĭng) Neth.	53·25 N	5·12 E
124	Teruel (tå-rōō-ĕl') Sp.	40·20 N	1·05 W
127	Tešanj (tĕ'shän') Yugo.	44·36 N	17·59 E
111	Teschendorf (tĕ'shĕn-dōrf) Ger. (Berlin In.)	52·51 N	13·10 E
91	Tesecheacan (tĕ-sĕ-chĕ-ä-kà'n) Mex.	18·10 N	95·41 W
64	Teshekpuk (L.) (tē-shĕk'pŭk) Alaska	70·18 N	152·36 W
152	Teshio Dake (Mt.) (tĕsh'ē-ō-dä'kä) Jap.	44·00 N	142·50 E
152	Teshio Gawa (R.) (tĕsh'ê-ô gä'wä) Jap.	44·35 N	114·55 E
86	Teslin (L.) (tĕs-lĭn) Can.	60·12 N	132·08 W
86	Teslin (R.) Can.	61·18 N	134·14 W
146	Tesiin Gol (R.) Mong.	50·14 N	94·30 E
164	Tessaoua (tĕs-sä'ōō-ä) Niger	13·53 N	7·53 E
111	Tessenderlo Bel. (Brussels In.)	51·04 N	5·08 E
116	Test (R.) (tĕst) Eng.	51·10 N	2·20 W
126	Testa del Gargano (Pt.) (tās'tä dĕl gär-gä'nō) It.	41·48 N	16·13 E

Page	Name Pronunciation Region	Lat. °′	Long. °′
166	Tete (tā'tĕ) Moz.	15·13 S	33·40 E
129	Teterev (R.) (tyĕ'tyĕ-rĕf) Sov. Un.	50·35 N	29·18 E
120	Teterow (tā'tĕ-rō) Ger.	53·46 N	12·33 E
127	Teteven (tĕt'ĕ-ven') Bul.	42·57 N	24·15 E
67	Teton R. (tē'tŏn) Mont.	47·54 N	111·37 W
127	Tetovo (tā'tô-vô) Yugo.	42·01 N	21·00 E
110	Tettenhall (tĕt'ĕn-hôl) Eng.	52·36 N	2·10 W
164	Tetuán (tā-twän') Mor.	35·42 N	5·34 W
152	Tetyukhe-Pristan (tĕt-yōō'ĸĕ prĭ-stän') Sov. Un.	44·21 N	135·44 E
132	Tetyushi (tyĕt-yōō'shĭ) Sov. Un.	54·58 N	48·40 E
111	Teupitz (toi'pētz) Ger. (Berlin In.)	52·08 N	13·37 E
126	Tevere (Tiber) (R.) (tā'vā-rā) (tī'bēr) It.	42·30 N	12·14 E
83	Tewksbury (tūks'bēr-ĭ) Mass. (Boston In.)	42·37 N	71·14 W
73	Texarkana (tĕk-sär-kăn'ȧ) Ark.	33·26 N	94·02 W
73	Texarkana Tex.	33·26 N	94·04 W
73	Texarkana Dam Tex.	33·18 N	94·09 W
84	Texas (tĕk'sȧs) Md. (Baltimore In.)	39·28 N	76·40 W
62	Texas (State) U. S.	31·00 N	101·00 W
77	Texas City Tex. (In.)	29·23 N	94·54 W
90	Texcaltitlán (tās-käl'tē-tlän') Mex.	18·54 N	99·51 W
117	Texel (I.) (tĕk'sĕl) Neth.	53·10 N	4·45 E
91	Texcoco (tās-kō'kō) Mex. (Mexico City In.)	19·31 N	98·53 W
90	Texcoco, Lago de (L.) (lä'gô-dĕ) Mex.	19·28 N	98·59 W
91	Texistepec (tĕk-sēs-tā-pĕk') Mex.	17·51 N	94·46 W
91	Texmelucan (tās-mȧ-lōō'kän) Mex. (Mexico City In.)	19·17 N	98·26 W
73	Texoma, L. (tĕk'ō-mă) Okla.	34·03 N	96·28 W
167	Teyateyaneng Bas. (Natal In.)	29·11 S	27·43 E
128	Teykovo (tĕy-kô-vô) Sov. Un.	56·52 N	40·34 E
91	Teziutlán (tā-zē-ōō-tlän') Mex.	19·48 N	97·21 W
90	Tezontepec (tā-zōn-tā-pĕk') Mex.	19·52 N	98·48 W
90	Tezontepec de Aldama (dā äl-dä'mä) Mex.	20·19 N	99·19 W
142	Tezpur India	26·42 N	92·52 E
86	Tha-anne (R.) Can.	60·50 N	96·56 W
167	Thaba Putsua (Mtn.) Bas. (Natal In.)	29·44 S	27·58 E
168	Thabazimbi S. Afr. (Johannesburg & Pretoria In.)	24·36 S	27·22 E
138	Thailand (Siam) Asia	16·30 N	101·00 E
154	Thale Luang (L.) Thai.	7·51 N	99·39 E
110	Thame (tām) Eng. (London In.)	51·43 N	0·59 W
80	Thames (R.) (tĕmz) Can.	42·40 N	81·45 W
117	Thames, R. Eng.	51·26 N	0·54 E
115	Thamit R. Libya	30·39 N	16·23 E
143	Thāna (thä'nŭ) India (Bombay In.)	19·13 N	72·58 E
143	Thāna Cr. India (Bombay In.)	19·03 N	72·58 E
146	Thang Ha Ri (Mts.) China	33·15 N	89·07 E
151	Thanh-Hoa (tän'hō'ä) Viet.	19·46 N	105·42 E
123	Thann (tän) Fr.	47·49 N	7·05 E
123	Thaon-les-Vosges (tȧ-ŏN-lā-vōzh') Fr.	48·16 N	6·24 E
160	Thargomindah (thär'gō-mĭn'dȧ) Austl.	27·58 S	143·57 E
127	Thásos (I.) (thă'sôs) Grc.	40·41 N	24·53 E
89	Thatch Cay (I.) (thăch) Vir. Is. (U. S. A.) (St. Thomas In.)	18·22 N	64·53 W
120	Thaya R. (tä'yȧ) Aus.-Czech.	48·48 N	15·40 E
73	Thayer (thâ'ēr) Mo.	36·30 N	91·34 W
	Thebes, see Thivai		
168	Thebes (Ruins) (thēbz) U. A. R. (Nile In.)	25·47 N	32·39 E
65	The Brothers (Mtn.) (brŭth'ērs) Wash. (Seattle In.)	47·39 N	123·08 W
66	The Dalles (dălz) Ore.	45·36 N	121·10 W
155	The Father, (Mtn.) N. Gui. Ter.	5·10 S	151·55 E
	The Hague, see 's Gravenhage		
142	Thelum W. Pak.	32·59 N	73·43 E
161	The Oaks Austl. (Sydney In.)	34·04 S	150·36 E
160	Theodore (thēō'dôr) Austl.	24·51 S	150·09 E
69	Theodore Roosevelt Dam (thē-ô-dōr rōō-sȧ-vĕlt) Ariz.	33·46 N	111·25 W
70	Theodore Roosevelt Natl. Mem. Park N. D.	47·20 N	103·42 W
86	The Pas (pä) Can.	53·48 N	101·17 W
67	Thermopolis (thēr-mŏp'ô-lĭs) Wyo.	43·38 N	108·11 W
160	The Round Mtn. Austl.	30·17 S	152·19 E
127	Thessalía (Reg.) Grc.	39·50 N	22·09 E
87	Thessalon Can.	46·11 N	83·37 W
127	Thessaloníki (thĕs-sȧ-lô-nē'kē) Grc.	40·38 N	22·59 E
82	Thetford Mines (thĕt'fērd mīns) Can.	46·05 N	71·20 W
167	The Twins (Mtn.) (twĭnz) S. Afr. (Natal In.)	30·09 S	28·29 E
168	Theunissen S. Afr. (Johannesburg & Pretoria In.)	28·25 S	26·44 E
77	Thibodaux (tē-bô-dō') La.	29·48 N	90·48 W
86	Thickwood Hills (thĭk'wŏŏd) Can.	53·28 N	108·30 W
70	Thief (L.) (thēf) Minn.	48·32 N	95·46 W
70	Thief (R.) Minn.	48·18 N	96·07 W
70	Thief River Falls (thēf rĭv'ēr fôlz) Minn.	48·07 N	96·11 W
84	Thiells (thēlz) N. Y. (New York In.)	41·12 N	74·01 W
122	Thiers (tyâr) Fr.	45·51 N	3·32 E
164	Thiès (tē-ĕs') Senegal	14·43 N	16·56 W
146	Thimbu Bhu.	27·31 N	89·45 E
112	Thingvallavatn (L.) Ice.	64·12 N	20·22 W
123	Thionville (tyôN-vēl') Fr.	49·23 N	6·31 E
165	Third Cataract Sud.	19·53 N	30·11 E
118	Thisted (tēs'tĕdh) Den.	56·57 N	8·38 E
112	Thistil Fd. (tēs'tĕl) Ice.	66·29 N	14·59 W
160	Thistle (I.) (thĭs''l) Austl.	34·55 S	136·11 E
127	Thivai (Thebes) Grc.	38·20 N	23·18 E
112	Thjörsá (R.) (tyûr'sȧ) Ice.	64·23 N	19·18 W
111	Tholen Neth. (Amsterdam In.)	51·32 N	4·11 E
72	Thomas (tŏm'ȧs) Okla.	35·44 N	98·43 W
81	Thomas W. Va.	39·15 N	79·30 W
78	Thomaston (tŏm'ȧs-tŭn) Ga.	32·51 N	84·17 W
78	Thomasville (tŏm'ȧs-vĭl) Ala.	31·55 N	87·43 W
79	Thomasville N. C.	35·52 N	80·05 W
86	Thompson (tŏmp'sŭn) Can.	55·48 N	97·59 W
73	Thompson (R.) Mo.	40·32 N	93·49 W
66	Thompson Falls Mont.	47·35 N	115·20 W
75	Thompsonville (tomp'sŭn-vĭl) Wis. (Milwaukee In.)	42·47 N	87·57 W
79	Thomson (tŏm'sŭn) Ga.	33·28 N	82·29 W
159	Thomson (R.) (tŏm-sŏn) Austl.	29·30 S	143·07 E
123	Thonon-les-Bains (tô-nôN'lā-băN') Fr.	46·22 N	6·27 E
112	Thórisvatn (L.) Ice.	64·02 N	19·09 W
110	Thorne (thôrn) Eng.	53·37 N	0·58 W
85	Thornhill (thôrn-hĭl) Can. (Toronto In.)	43·49 N	79·25 W
80	Thorntown (thôrn'tŭn) Ind.	40·05 N	86·35 W
85	Thorold (thō'rōld) Can. (Toronto In.)	43·13 N	79·12 W
122	Thouars (tōō-är') Fr.	47·00 N	0·17 W
81	Thousand Is. (thou'zănd) N. Y.-Can.	44·15 N	76·10 W
127	Thrace (Reg.) (thrās) Grc.-Tur.	41·20 N	26·07 E
110	Thrapston (thrăp'stŭn) Eng.	52·23 N	0·32 W
67	Three Forks (thrē fôrks) Mont.	45·56 N	111·35 W
80	Three Oaks (thrē ōks) Mich.	41·50 N	86·40 W
164	Three Points, C. Ghana	4·27 N	2·29 W
80	Three Rivers Mich.	42·00 N	83·40 W
120	Thun (tōōn) Switz.	46·46 N	7·34 E
71	Thunder B. (thŭn'dēr) Can.	48·29 N	88·52 W
120	Thuner See (L.) Switz.	46·40 N	7·30 E
76	Thurber (thûr'bēr) Tex.	32·30 N	98·23 W
120	Thüringen (Thuringia) (former state or region) (tü'rĭng-ĕn) Ger.	51·07 N	10·45 E
116	Thurles (thûrlz) Ire.	52·44 N	7·45 W
110	Thurrock (thŭ'rŏk) Eng. (London In.)	51·28 N	0·19 E
159	Thursday (I.) (thûrz-dā) Austl.	10·17 S	142·23 E
85	Thurso (thŭr'sô) Can. (Ottawa In.)	45·36 N	75·15 W
116	Thurso Scot.	58·35 N	3·40 W
47	Thurston Pen. (thûrs'tŭn) Ant.	71·20 S	98·00 W
166	Thysville (tēs-vēl') Con. L.	5·08 S	14·58 E
155	Tiaong (tē-ä-ông') Phil. (Manila In.)	13·56 N	121·20 E
164	Tiaret (tyä-rĕ') Alg.	35·28 N	1·15 E
100	Tibagi (tē-bä-zhē) Braz.	24·40 S	50·35 W
165	Tibasti, Sarir (Des.) Chad	24·00 N	16·30 E
	Tiber (R.), see Tévere		
139	Tiberias (tī-bē'rĭ-ȧs) Isr. (Palestine In.)	32·48 N	35·32 E
165	Tibesti Massif (Mts.) Chad	20·43 N	17·16 E
146	Tibet Aut. Reg. (tĭ-bĕt') China	31·15 N	84·48 E
146	Tibet, Plat. of China	32·22 N	83·30 E
139	Tibnīn Leb. (Palestine In.)	33·12 N	35·23 E
65	Tiburon (tē-bōō-rōn') Calif. (San Francisco In.)	37·53 N	122·27 W
95	Tiburon Hai.	18·35 N	74·25 W
88	Tiburón (I.) Mex.	28·45 N	113·10 W
93	Tiburon, Cabo (C.) (kä'bô) Pan.	8·42 N	77·19 W
65	Tiburon I. Calif. (San Francisco In.)	37·52 N	122·26 W
155	Ticaco Pass (tē-kä-kō) Phil. (Manila In.)	12·38 N	123·50 E
155	Ticao (I.) (tē-kä'ō) Phil. (Manila In.)	12·40 N	123·30 E
110	Tickhill (tĭk'ĭl) Eng.	53·26 N	1·06 W
81	Ticonderaga (tī-kŏn-dēr-ō'gȧ) N. Y.	43·50 N	73·30 W
92	Ticul (tē-kōō'l) Mex. (Yucatan In.)	20·22 N	89·32 W
118	Tidaholm (tē'dȧ-hōlm) Swe.	58·11 N	13·53 E
110	Tideswell (tīdz'wĕl) Eng.	53·17 N	1·47 W
164	Tidikelt (Reg.) (tē-dē-kĕlt') Alg.	25·53 N	2·11 E
164	Tidjikdja (tē-jĭk'jä) Mauritania	18·37 N	11·30 W
150	T'iehling (tyâ'lĭng) China	42·18 N	123·50 E
125	Tielmes (tyâl-màs') Sp. (Madrid In.)	40·15 N	3·20 W
151	Tien Ch'ih (L.) (tyĕn) China	24·58 N	103·18 E
148	T'ienching (Tientsin) (tyĕn'tsĕn') China	39·08 N	117·14 E
111	Tienen Bel. (Brussels In.)	50·49 N	4·58 E
148	Tienerhwan (dĭän'ĕ'hōōän) China	31·39 N	114·08 E
148	Tienfou (dĭän'fōō) China	31·53 N	117·28 E
148	T'ienma Shan (Mts.) (tĭän'mä shän) China	36·02 N	117·57 E
151	Tienmen (tyĕn'mĕn') China	30·40 N	113·10 E
151	Tienpai China	21·30 N	111·20 E
151	T'ienpao China	23·18 N	106·40 E
	Tien-Shan (Mts.), see Tyan' Shan'		
148	Tienshan Hu (L.) (dĭän'shän'hōō) China	31·08 N	120·30 E
150	T'ienshui China	34·25 N	105·40 E
150	T'ientsaokang China	45·58 N	126·00 E
	Tientsin, see T'ienching		
151	T'ientung China	23·32 N	107·10 E
118	Tierp (tyĕrp) Swe.	60·21 N	17·28 E
167	Tierpoort S. Afr. (Johannesburg & Pretoria In.)	25·53 S	28·26 E
91	Tierra Blanca (tyĕ'r-rä-blä'n-kä) Mex.	18·28 N	96·19 W
100	Tierra del Fuego (Reg.) (tyĕr'rä dĕl fwä'gō) Chile-Arg.	53·50 S	68·45 W
124	Tiétar (R.) (tē-ā'tär) Sp.	39·56 N	5·44 W
101	Tietê (tyā-tā') Braz. (Rio de Janeiro In.)	23·08 S	47·42 W
99	Tieté (R.) Braz.	20·46 S	50·46 W
80	Tiffin (tĭf'ĭn) Ohio	41·10 N	83·15 W
78	Tifton (tĭf'tŭn) Ga.	31·25 N	83·34 W
65	Tigard (tī'gärd) Ore. (Portland In.)	45·25 N	122·46 W
82	Tignish (tĭg'nĭsh) Can.	46·56 N	64·03 W
136	Tigoda R. (tē'gô-dȧ) Sov. Un. (Leningrad In.)	59·29 N	31·15 E
100	Tigre (tē'grĕ) Arg. (In.)	34·09 S	58·35 W
98	Tigre (R.) Peru	2·20 S	75·41 W
166	Tigres, Peninsula dos (Pen.) (pĕ-nē'ŋ-sōō-lä-dôs-tē'grĕs) Ang.	16·30 S	11·45 E
144	Tigris, R. Asia	34·30 N	44·00 E
139	Tīh, Gebel el (Mts.) U. A. R. (Palestine In.)	29·24 N	33·42 E
146	Tihua (Urumchi) (ōō-rōōm'chē) China	43·49 N	87·43 E
91	Tihuatlán (tē-wä-tlän') Mex.	20·43 N	97·34 W
68	Tijuana (tē-hwä'nä) Mex. (San Diego In.)	32·32 N	117·02 W
100	Tijuca, Pico da (Mtn.) (pē'kō-dä-tē-zhōō'kä) Braz. (In.)	22·56 S	43·17 W
92	Tikal (Ruins) (tē-käl') Guat. (Yucatan In.)	17·16 N	89·49 W
133	Tikhoretsk (tē kôr-yĕtsk') Sov. Un.	45·55 N	40·05 E
128	Tikhvin (têĸ-vēn') Sov. Un.	59·36 N	33·38 E
144	Tikrīt Iraq	34·36 N	43·31 E
135	Tiksi (têk-sē') Sov. Un.	71·42 N	128·32 E
111	Tilburg (tĭl'bûrg) Neth. (Amsterdam In.)	51·33 N	5·05 E
164	Tilemsi, Vallée du (Valley) Mali	18·09 N	0·02 W
135	Tilichiki (tyĭ-le-chĭ-kê) Sov. Un.	60·49 N	166·14 E
129	Tiligul (R.) (tē'lĭ-gûl) Sov. Un.	47·25 N	30·27 E
164	Tillabéri (tē-yȧ-bā-rē') Niger	14·14 N	1·30 E
66	Tillamook (tĭl'ȧ-mŏŏk) Ore.	45·27 N	123·50 W
66	Tillamook B. Ore.	45·32 N	124·26 W
118	Tillberga (tēl-bĕr'ghȧ) Swe.	59·40 N	16·34 E
80	Tillsonburg (tĭl'sŭn-bûrg) Can.	42·50 N	80·50 W
	Tilsit, see Sovetsk		
129	Tim (têm) Sov. Un.	51·39 N	37·07 E
159	Timaru (tĭm'ȧ-rōō) N. Z. (In.)	44·26 S	171·17 E
129	Timashevskaya (tēmä-shĕfs-kȧ'yȧ) Sov. Un.	45·47 N	38·57 E
77	Timbalier B. (tĭm'bȧ-lēr) La.	28·55 N	90·14 W
65	Timber (tĭm'bēr) Ore. (Portland In.)	45·43 N	123·17 W
164	Timbo (tĭm'bō) Gui.	10·41 N	11·51 W
	Timbuktu, see Tombouctou		
118	Time (tē'mĕ) Nor.	58·45 N	5·39 E
164	Timimoun (tē-mê-mōōn') Alg.	29·14 N	0·22 E
164	Timiris, Cap (C.) Mauritania	19·37 N	17·38 W
127	Timiş (R.) Rom.	45·28 N	21·06 E
87	Timiskaming (L.) Can.	47·27 N	81·00 W
87	Timiskaming Station (tē-mĭs'kȧ-mĭng) Can.	46·41 N	79·01 W
87	Timmins (tĭm'ĭnz) Can.	48·25 N	81·22 W
164	Timmissao (tē-mē-sä'ō) Alg.	22·03 N	2·56 E
79	Timmonsville (tĭm'ŭnz-vĭl) S. C.	34·09 N	79·55 W
155	Timor (I.) (tê-mōr') Indon.	10·08 S	125·00 E
156	Timor Sea Asia	12·40 S	125·00 E
127	Timoşoara Rom.	45·44 N	21·21 E
69	Timpanogos Cave Natl. Mon. (tĭ-măn'ō-gŏz) Utah	40·25 N	111·45 W
77	Timpson (tĭmp'sŭn) Tex.	31·55 N	94·24 W
135	Timpton (R.) (têmp'tôn) Sov. Un.	57·15 N	126·35 E
168	Timsāh (L.) (tĭm'sä) U. A. R. (Suez In.)	30·34 N	32·22 E
95	Tina, Monte (Mtn.) (mô'n-tĕ-tē'nä) Dom. Rep.	18·50 N	70·40 W
167	Tina (R.) (tē'nȧ) S. Afr. (Natal In.)	30·50 S	28·44 E
99	Tinaguillo (tē-nä-gē'l-yō) Ven. (In.)	9·55 N	68·18 W
164	Tindouf (tēn-dōōf') Alg.	27·43 N	7·44 W
139	Tinggi, Palau (I.) Mala. (Singapore In.)	2·16 N	104·16 E
148	T'ingho (dĭng'hŭ) China	37·45 N	118·29 E
148	Tinghsien (dĭng'sĭän) China	38·30 N	115·00 E
148	Tinghsing (dĭng'sĭng) China	39·18 N	115·50 E
149	Tinglin China (Shanghai In.)	30·53 N	121·18 E
98	Tingo María (tē'ngō-mä-rē'ä) Peru	9·15 S	76·04 W
118	Tingsryd (tĭngs'rüd) Swe.	56·32 N	14·58 E
148	Tingtzu Wan (B.) (dĭng'tze wän) China	36·33 N	121·06 E
90	Tinguindio Paracho (tēn-kē'n-dyō-pärä-chō) Mex.	19·38 N	102·02 W
101	Tinguiririca (R.) (tē'n-gē-rē-rē'kä) Chile (Santiago In.)	36·48 S	70·45 W
148	Tingyüan (tĭng'yü-än') China	32·32 N	117·40 E
75	Tinley Park (tĭn'lē) Ill. (Chicago In.)	41·34 N	87·47 W
118	Tinnosset (tĕn'nôs'sĕt) Nor.	49·44 N	9·00 E
118	Tinnsjö (tĭnnsyû) Nor.	59·55 N	8·49 E
100	Tinogasta (tē-nô-gäs'tä) Arg.	28·07 S	67·30 W
127	Tínos (I.) Grc.	37·45 N	25·12 E
145	Tinsukia (tin-sōō'kĭ-ȧ) India	27·18 N	95·29 E
69	Tintic (tĭn'tĭk) Utah	39·55 N	112·15 W
165	Tin Toumma Steppe (Plat.) (tĭn tōōm'ȧ) Niger	16·16 N	13·06 E
139	Tioman (I.) Mala. (Singapore In.)	2·25 N	104·30 E
92	Tipitapa (tē-pē-tä'pä) Nic.	12·14 N	86·05 W
92	Tipitapa R. Nic.	12·13 N	85·57 W
78	Tippah Cr., (R.) (tĭp'pȧ) Miss.	34·43 N	88·15 W
80	Tippecanoe (R.) (tĭp-ē-kȧ-nōō') Ind.	40·55 N	86·45 W
166	Tipperary (tĭ-pē-râ'rē) Ire.	52·28 N	8·13 W
73	Tippo Bay. (tĭp'ō bīōō') Miss.	33·35 N	90·06 W
110	Tipton (tĭp'tŭn) Eng.	52·32 N	2·04 W
80	Tipton Ind.	40·15 N	86·00 W
71	Tipton Iowa	41·46 N	91·10 W
127	Tiranë (tē-rä'nä) Alb.	41·18 N	19·50 E
126	Tirano (tē-rä'nō) It.	46·12 N	10·09 E
129	Tiraspol' (tē-räs'pôl') Sov. Un.	46·52 N	29·38 E
168	Tir'at el'Abbāsîya R. U. A. R. (Suez In.)	32·45 N	32·15 E
133	Tire (tē'rĕ) Tur.	38·05 N	27·48 E
116	Tiree (I.) (tī-rē') Scot.	56·34 N	6·30 W
127	Tîrgovişte Rom.	44·54 N	25·29 E
121	Tîrgu-Mures Rom.	46·33 N	24·35 E
121	Tîrgu Neamt Rom.	47·14 N	26·23 E
121	Tîrgu-Ocna Rom.	46·18 N	26·38 E

ng-sing; ŋ-baŋk; ɴ-nasalized n; nŏd; cŏmmit; ōld; ōbey; ôrder; fōōd; fŏŏt; ou-out; s-soft; sh-dish; th-thin; pūre; ûnite; ûrn; stŭd; circŭs; ü-a "y" in study; '-indeterminate vowel.

Page	Name Pronunciation Region	Lat. °'	Long. °'
121	Tîrgu Săcuesc . . . Rom.	46·04 N	26·06 E
142	Tirich Mir (Mt.) . . . Afg.	41·06 N	71·48 E
136	Tirlyanskiy (tĭr-lyän'skĭ) Sov. Un. (Urals In.)	54·13 N	58·37 E
121	Tîrnava Sinmartin . . . Rom.	46·19 N	24·18 E
127	Tírnavos . . . Grc.	39·50 N	22·14 E
120	Tirol (State) (tē-rōl') . . . Aus.	47·13 N	11·10 E
126	Tirso (R.) (tēr'sō) . . . It.	40·15 N	9·03 E
143	Tiruchchirāppalli (tĭr'ōō-chĭ-rä'pà-lĭ) . India	10·49 N	78·48 E
143	Tirunelveli . . . India	8·48 N	77·49 E
143	Tiruppūr . . . India	11·11 N	77·08 E
86	Tisdale (tĭz'dāl) . . . Can.	52·55 N	103·56 W
142	Tista (R.) . . . India	26·03 N	88·52 E
127	Tisza (R.) (tē'sä) . . . Yugo.	45·50 N	20·13 E
121	Tisza R. (tē'sä) . . . Hung.	46·30 N	20·08 E
142	Titagarh . . . India (Calcutta In.)	22·44 N	88·23 E
98	Titicaca, Lago (L.) (lä'gô-tē-tē-kä'kä) . Bol.-Peru	16·12 S	70·33 W
98	Titiribí (tē-tē-rē-bē') . . . Col. (In.)	6·05 N	75·47 W
127	Titograd . . . Yugo.	42·25 N	20·42 E
127	Titovo Užice (tē'tô-vô ōō'zhē-tsĕ) Yugo.	43·51 N	19·53 E
127	Titov Veles (tē'tôv vĕ'lĕs) . . Yugo.	41·42 N	21·50 E
79	Titusville (tī'tŭs-vĭl) . . . Fla. (In.)	28·37 N	80·44 W
81	Titusville . . . Pa.	40·40 N	79·40 W
123	Titz (tētz) . . . Ger. (Ruhr In.)	51·00 N	6·26 E
84	Tiverton (tĭv'ēr-tŭn) R. I. (Providence In.)	41·38 N	71·11 W
125	Tívoli (tē'vô-lē) . . . It. (Rome In.)	41·58 N	12·48 E
92	Tixkokob (tēx-kō-kō'b) Mex. (Yucatan In.)	21·01 N	89·23 W
90	Tixtla de Guerrero (tē'x-tlä-dĕ-gĕr-rĕ'rô) . Mex.	17·36 N	99·24 W
154	Tizard Bk. and Rf. (tĭz'ărd) . China	10·51 N	113·20 E
92	Tizimín (tē-zē-mē'n) Mex. (Yucatan In.)	21·08 N	88·10 W
164	Tizi-Ouzou (tē'zē-ōō-zōō') . . . Alg.	36·44 N	4·04 E
99	Tiznados (R.) (tēz-nä'dôs) Ven. (In.)	9·53 N	67·49 W
164	Tiznit (tēz-nēt) . . . Mor.	29·52 N	9·39 W
154	Tjirebon . . . Indon.	6·50 S	108·33 E
91	Tlacolula de Matamoros (tlä-kô-lōō'lä dā mätä-mō'rôs) Mex.	16·56 N	96·29 W
91	Tlacotálpan (tlä-kô-täl'pän) . Mex.	18·39 N	95·40 W
90	Tlacotepec (tlä-kô-tå-pĕ'k) . Mex.	17·46 N	99·57 W
91	Tlacotepec . . . Mex.	18·41 N	97·40 W
90	Tlacotepec . . . Mex.	19·11 N	99·41 W
91	Tláhuac (tlä-wäk') Mex. (Mexico City In.)	19·16 N	99·00 W
90	Tlajomulca de Zúñiga (tlä-hô-mōō'l-kä-dĕ-zōō'n-yē-gä) Mex.	20·30 N	103·27 W
90	Tlalchapa (tläl-chä'pä) . . . Mex.	18·26 N	100·29 W
91	Tlalixcoyan (tlä-lēs'kō-yän') . Mex.	18·53 N	96·04 W
91	Tlalmanalco (tläl-mä-nä'l-kô) Mex. (Mexico City In.)	19·12 N	98·48 W
91	Tlalnepantia (tläl-nĕ-pà'n-tyä) Mex. (Mexico City In.)	19·32 N	99·13 W
91	Tlalnepantla (tläl-nå-pän'tlä) Mex. (Mexico City In.)	18·59 N	99·01 W
91	Tlalpan (tläl-pä'n) Mex. (Mexico City In.)	19·17 N	99·10 W
90	Tlalpujahua (tläl-pōō-kä'wä) . Mex.	19·50 N	100·10 W
	Tlaltenango, see Sanchez Román		
90	Tlapa (tlä'pä) . . . Mex.	17·30 N	98·09 W
90	Tlapa (tlä'pä) . . . Mex.	17·30 N	98·09 W
91	Tlapacoyan (tlä-pä-kô-yä'n) . Mex.	19·57 N	97·11 W
90	Tlapaneco (R.) (tlä-pä-nĕ'kô) Mex.	17·59 N	98·44 W
90	Tlapehuala (tlä-pä-wä'lä) . . . Mex.	18·17 N	100·30 W
90	Tlaquepaque (tlä-kĕ-pä'kĕ) . . Mex.	20·39 N	103·17 W
90	Tlatlaya (tlä-tlä'yä) . . . Mex.	18·36 N	100·14 W
90	Tlaxcala (tläs-kä'lä) . . . Mex.	19·16 N	98·14 W
90	Tlaxco (tläs'kō) . . . Mex.	19·37 N	98·06 W
91	Tlaxiaco Sta. María Asunción (tläk-sē-ä'kō sän'tä mä-rē'ä ä-sōōn-syōn') . Mex.	17·16 N	95·41 W
91	Tlayacapan (tlä-yä-kä-pä'n) Mex. (Mexico City In.)	18·57 N	99·00 W
164	Tlemcen (tlĕm-sĕn') . . . Alg.	34·53 N	1·21 W
121	Tlumach (t'lû-māch') . . . Sov. Un.	48·47 N	25·00 E
95	Toa (R.) (tō'ä) . . . Cuba	20·25 N	74·35 W
67	Toano Ra. (Mts.) (tō-ȧ-nō') . Nev.	40·45 N	114·11 W
95	Toar, Cuchillas de (Mtn.) (kōō-chē'l-lyäs-dĕ-tô-ä'r) . Cuba	18·20 N	74·50 W
153	Toba (tō'bä) . . . Jap.	34·27 N	136·51 E
89	Tobago (I.) (tô-bā'gō) . . . N. A.	11·15 N	60·30 W
124	Tobarra (tô-bär'rä) . . . Sp.	38·37 N	1·42 W
153	Tobata (tō-bä'tä) . . . Jap.	33·55 N	130·48 E
134	Tobol (R.) (tô-bôl') . . . Sov. Un.	56·02 N	65·30 E
134	Tobol'sk (tô-bôlsk') . . . Sov. Un.	58·09 N	68·28 E
	Tobruk, see Tubruq		
98	Tocaima (tô-kä'y-mä) . . . Col. (In.)	4·28 N	74·38 W
99	Tocantinópolis (tō-kän-tē-nō'pō-lēs) Braz.	6·27 S	47·18 W
99	Tocantins (R.) (tō-kän-tēns') . Braz.	3·28 S	49·22 W
78	Toccoa (tŏk'ō-ȧ) . . . Ga.	34·35 N	83·20 W
78	Toccoa (R.) . . . Ga.	34·53 N	84·24 W
153	Tochigi (tō'chē-gĭ) . . . Jap.	36·25 N	139·45 E
148	T'ochi Tao (I.) (tōōŭ'jē dou) China	38·11 N	120·45 E
92	Tocoa (tō-kō'ä) . . . Hond.	15·37 N	86·01 W
100	Tocopilla (tō-kô-pēl'yä) . . . Chile	22·03 S	70·08 W
99	Tocuyo de la Costa (tô-kōō'yō-dĕ-lä-kôs'tä) Ven. (In.)	11·03 N	68·24 W
110	Todmorden (tŏd'môr-dĕn) . . . Eng.	53·43 N	2·05 W
118	Töfsingdalens (Natl. Park) . . . Swe.	62·09 N	13·05 E
153	Tōgane (tō'gä-nä) . . . Jap.	35·29 N	140·16 E
163	Togo (tō'gō) . . . Afr.	8·00 N	0·52 E
136	Toguzak R. (tô'gōō-zák) Sov. Un. (Urals In.)	53·40 N	61·42 E
79	Tohopekaliga (L.) (tō'hō-pē'kà-lĭ'gȧ) . Fla. (In.)	28·16 N	81·09 W

Page	Name Pronunciation Region	Lat. °'	Long. °'
148	To'Hu (L.) (tōōŭ'hōō) . . . China	33·07 N	117·25 E
119	Toijala (toi'yȧ-lȧ) . . . Fin.	61·11 N	21·46 E
153	Toi-Misaki (C.) (toi mē'sä-kē) . Jap.	31·20 N	131·20 E
68	Toiyabe Ra. (toi'yă-bē) . . . Nev.	38·59 N	117·22 W
152	Tokachi Gawa (R.) (tō-kä'chē gä'wä) . Jap.	43·10 N	142·30 E
121	Tokaj (tô'kô-ē) . . . Hung.	48·06 N	21·24 E
165	Tokar (tō'kär) . . . Sud.	18·28 N	37·46 E
152	Tokara Guntō (Is.) (tō-kä'rä gōōn'tō') . Jap.	29·45 N	129·15 E
152	Tokara Kaikyo (Str.) (tō'kä-rä kī'kyō) . Jap.	30·20 N	129·50 E
133	Tokat (tô-kät') . . . Tur.	40·20 N	36·30 E
156	Tokelau Is. (tō-kē-lä'ōō) . . Oceania	8·00 S	176·00 W
134	Tokmak (tôk'mȧk) . . . Sov. Un.	42·44 N	75·41 E
153	Tokorozawa (tô'kô-rô-zä'wä) Jap. (Tōkyō In.)	35·47 N	139·29 E
152	Tokuno (I.) (tô-kōō'nō) . . . Jap.	27·42 N	129·25 E
153	Tokushima (tō'kōō'shē-mä) . . . Jap.	34·06 N	134·31 E
153	Tokuyama (tō'kōō'yä-mä) . . . Jap.	34·04 N	131 49 E
153	Tōkyō (tō'kē-ō) . Jap. (Tōkyō In.)	35·41 N	139·44 E
153	Tōkyō (Pref.) . . . Jap. (Tōkyō In.)	35·42 N	139·40 E
153	Tōkyō-Wan (B.) (tō'kyō wän) Jap. (Tōkyō In.)	35·32 N	139·56 E
127	Tolbukhin . . . Bul.	43·33 N	27·52 E
90	Tolcayuca (tôl-kä-yōō'kä) . . . Mex.	19·55 N	98·54 W
71	Toledo (tô-lē'dō) . . . Iowa	41·59 N	92·35 W
80	Toledo . . . Ohio	41·40 N	83·35 W
66	Toledo . . . Ore.	44·37 N	123·58 W
124	Toledo (tô-lĕ'dô) . . . Sp.	39·53 N	4·02 W
124	Toledo, Montes de (Mts.) (mô'n-tĕs-dĕ-tô-lĕ'dô) . Sp.	39·33 N	4·40 W
98	Tolima (Dept.) (tô-lē'mä) Col. (In.)	4·07 N	75·20 W
98	Tolima, Nevado del (Pk.) (nĕ-vä-dô-dĕl-tô-lē'mä) . Col. (In.)	4·40 N	75·20 W
90	Tolimán (tô-lē-män') . . . Mex.	20·54 N	99·54 W
110	Tollesbury (tōl'z-bĕrĭ) Eng. (London In.)	51·46 N	0·49 E
126	Tolmezzo (tôl-mĕt'sô) . . . It.	46·25 N	13·03 E
126	Tolmin (tôl'mēn) . . . Yugo.	46·12 N	13·45 E
121	Tolna (tôl'nô) . . . Hung.	46·25 N	18·47 E
154	Tolo, Teluk (B.) (tō'lō) . . . Indon.	2·00 S	122·06 E
124	Tolosa (tô-lō'sä) . . . Sp.	43·10 N	2·05 W
65	Tolt (R.) (tōlt) Wash. (Seattle In.)	47·13 N	121·49 W
80	Toluca (tô-lōō'kȧ) . . . Ill.	41·00 N	89·10 W
91	Toluca (tô-lōō'kä) Mex. (Mexico City In.)	19·17 N	99·40 W
91	Toluca, Nevado de (Zinántecatl) Mtn. (nĕ-vä-dô-dĕ-tô-lōō'kä) (zē-nä'n-tĕ-kä'tl) Mex. (Mexico City In.)	19·09 N	99·42 W
150	Tolun . . . China	42·12 N	116·15 E
134	Tom' (R.) . . . Sov. Un.	55·33 N	85·00 E
71	Tomah (tō'mȧ) . . . Wis.	43·58 N	90·31 W
71	Tomahawk (tŏm'ȧ-hôk) . . . Wis.	45·27 N	89·44 W
129	Tomakovka (tô-mä'kôf-kä) Sov. Un.	47·49 N	34·43 E
124	Tomar (tō-mär') . . . Port.	39·36 N	8·26 W
121	Tomaszewica (tô-mä'shĕf-kä) Sov. Un.	51·34 N	23·37 E
121	Tomaszow Lubelski (tô-mä'shōōf lōō-bĕl'skĭ) . Pol.	50·20 N	23·27 E
121	Tomaszów Mazowiecki (tô-mä'shōōf mä-zō'vyĕt-skĭ) Pol.	51·33 N	20·00 E
90	Tomatlán (tô-mä-tlä'n) . . . Mex.	19·54 N	105·14 W
90	Tomatlán (R.) . . . Mex.	19·56 N	105·14 W
99	Tombador, Serra do (Mts.) (sĕr'rȧ dōō tōm-bä-dôr') . . Braz.	11·31 S	57·33 W
78	Tombigbee (R.) (tŏm-bĭg'bē) . Ala.	31·45 N	88·02 W
101	Tombos (tô'm-bōs) Braz. (Rio de Janeiro In.)	20·53 S	42·00 W
164	Tombouctou (Timbuktu) (tôm-bōōk-tōō') . Mali	16·52 N	2·53 W
69	Tombstone (tōōm'stōn) . . . Ariz.	31·40 N	110·00 W
118	Tomelilla (tô'mĕ-lēl-lä) . . . Swe.	55·34 N	13·55 E
124	Tomelloso (tō-mäl-lyō'sō) . . . Sp.	39·09 N	3·02 W
154	Tomini, Teluk (B.) (tô-mē'nē) Indon.	0·10 N	121·00 E
135	Tommot (tŏm-mŏt') . . . Sov. Un.	59·13 N	126·22 E
134	Tomsk (tŏmsk) . . . Sov. Un.	56·29 N	84·57 E
91	Tonalá (tō-nä-lä') . . . Mex.	16·05 N	93·45 W
90	Tonala . . . Mex.	20·38 N	103·14 W
91	Tonalá (R.) . . . Mex.	18·05 N	94·08 W
75	Tonawanda (tôn-ȧ-wŏn'dȧ) N. Y. (Buffalo In.)	43·01 N	78·53 W
75	Tonawanda Cr. N. Y. (Buffalo In.)	43·05 N	78·43 W
110	Tonbridge (tŭn-brij) Eng. (London In.)	51·11 N	0·17 E
153	Tonda (tôn'dä) . Jap. (Ōsaka In.)	34·51 N	135·38 E
153	Tondabayashi (tôn'dä-bä'yä-shē) Jap. (Osaka In.)	34·29 N	135·36 E
155	Tondano (tôn-dä'nō) . . . Indon.	1·15 N	124·50 E
118	Tønder (tûn'nēr) . . . Den.	54·47 N	8·49 E
91	Tondlá . . . Mex.	16·04 N	93·57 W
153	Tone (R.) (tō'nē) Jap. (Tōkyō In.)	35·55 N	139·57 E
153	Tone-Gawa (Strm.) (tō'nē gä'wa) Jap.	36·12 N	139·19 E
156	Tonga Is. (tŏŋ'gȧ) . . . Oceania	18·50 S	175·20 W
100	Tongoy (tōn-goi') . . . Chile	30·16 S	71·29 W
	Tongue of Arabat, see Arabatskaya Strelka (Spit)		
94	Tongue of the Ocean (Chan.) (tŭng ŏv thē ōshŭn) . Ba. Is.	24·05 N	77·20 W
67	Tongue R. (tŭng) . . . Mont.	45·08 N	106·40 W
67	Tongue River Ind. Res. . . . Mont.	45·32 N	106·43 W
165	Tonj R. (tônj) . . . Sud.	6·18 N	28·33 E
142	Tonk (tŏŋk) . . . India	26·13 N	75·45 E
73	Tonkawa (tŏŋ'kȧ-wô) . . . Okla.	36·42 N	97·19 W
151	Tonkin, Gulf of (tôn-kăn') . . . Viet.	20·30 N	108·10 E
154	Tonle Sap (L.) (tôn'lā sȧp') . Camb.	13·03 N	102·49 E

Page	Name Pronunciation Region	Lat. °'	Long. °'
122	Tonneins (tô-năn') . . . Fr.	44·24 N	0·18 E
120	Tönning (tû'nēng) . . . Ger.	54·20 N	8·55 E
68	Tonopah (tō-nō-pä') . . . Nev.	38·04 N	117·15 W
118	Tönsberg (tûns'bĕrgh) . . . Nor.	59·19 N	10·25 E
91	Tonto (R.) (tōn'tō) . . . Mex.	18·15 N	96·13 W
69	Tonto Cr. . . . Ariz.	34·05 N	111·15 W
69	Tonto Natl. Mon. (tôn'tô) . . Ariz.	33·33 N	111·08 W
74	Tooele (tōō-ĕl'ē) Utah (Salt Lake City In.)	40·33 N	112·17 W
151	Toohsien . . . China	25·30 N	111·32 E
160	Toowoomba (tōō wōōm'bȧ) . Austl.	27·32 S	152·10 E
74	Topanga (tō'păn-gȧ) Calif. (Los Angeles In.)	34·05 N	118·36 W
73	Topeka (tô-pē'kȧ) . . . Kans.	39·02 N	95·41 W
91	Topilejo (tō-pē-lĕ'hô) Mex. (Mexico City In.)	19·12 N	99·09 W
121	Topol'čany (tô-pôl'chä-nü) . Czech.	48·38 N	18·10 E
88	Topolobampo (tō-pō-lô-bä'm-pô) Mex.	25·45 N	109·00 W
127	Topolovgrad . . . Bul.	42·05 N	26·19 E
66	Toppenish (tôp'ĕn-ĭsh) . . . Wash.	46·22 N	120·00 W
83	Torbay (tôr-bā') . . . Can.	47·41 N	52·38 W
160	Torbreck, Mt. (tôr-brĕk) . . . Austl.	37·05 S	146·55 E
80	Torch (L.) (tôrch) . . . Mich.	45·00 N	85·30 W
118	Töreboda (tû'rē-bō'dä) . . . Swe.	58·44 N	14·04 E
117	Torhout . . . Bel.	51·01 N	3·04 E
98	Toribío (tô-rē-bē'ō) . . . Col. (In.)	2·58 N	76·14 W
153	Toride (tô'rē-dä) . Jap. (Tōkyō In.)	35·54 N	140·04 E
126	Torino (Turin) (tô-rē'no) (tū'rĭn) It.	45·05 N	7·44 E
112	Torino (R.) (tôr'nĭ-ô) . . Fin.-Swe.	67·00 N	23·50 E
124	Tormes (R.) (tōr'mās) . . . Sp.	41·12 N	6·15 W
112	Torne (R.) (tôr'nĕ) . . . Swe.	67·29 N	21·44 E
112	Torne Träsk (L.) (tôr'nĕ trĕsk) Swe.	68·10 N	20·36 E
87	Torngat Mts. . . . Can.	59·18 N	64·35 W
112	Tornio (tôr'nĭ-ô) . . . Fin.	65·55 N	24·09 E
82	Toro, Lac (L.) . . . Can.	46·53 N	73·46 W
127	Toronaíos Kólpos (G.) . . . Grc.	40·10 N	23·35 E
85	Toronto (tô-rŏn'tō) Can. (Toronto In.)	43·40 N	79·23 W
80	Toronto . . . Ohio	40·30 N	80·35 W
76	Toronto, L. (lä'gô-tô-rô'n-tō) Mex.	27·35 N	105·37 W
128	Toropets (tô'rô-pyĕts) . . . Sov. Un.	56·31 N	31·37 E
133	Toros Dağlari (Taurus Mts.) (tô'rŭs) . Tur.	37·00 N	32·40 E
125	Torote (R.) (tô-rō'tä) Sp. (Madrid In.)	40·36 N	3·24 W
118	Torp (tôrp) . . . Swe.	62·30 N	16·04 E
	Torpen, see Åmot		
116	Torquay (tôr-kē') . . . Eng.	50·30 N	3·26 W
98	Torra, Cerro (Mtn.) (sĕ'r-rô-tô'r-rä) . Col. (In.)	4·41 N	76·22 W
74	Torrance (tŏr'rănc) Calif. (Los Angeles In.)	33·50 N	118·20 W
125	Torre Annunziata (tôr'rä ä-nōōn-tsē-ä'tä) It. (Naples In.)	40·31 N	14·27 E
124	Torre de Cerredo (Mtn.) (tôr'rā dä thä-rä'dhō) . Sp.	43·10 N	4·47 W
125	Torre del Greco (tôr'rā dĕl grā'kô) It. (Naples In.)	40·32 N	14·23 E
124	Torrejoncillo (tôr'rā-hōn-thē'lyō) Sp.	39·54 N	6·26 W
124	Torrelavega (tôr-rā'lä-vā'gä) . . Sp.	43·22 N	4·02 W
126	Torre Maggiore (tôr'rā mäd-jō'rā) It.	40·41 N	15·18 E
160	Torrens, L. (tŏr-ĕns) . . . Austl.	30·07 S	137·40 E
125	Torrente (tôr-rĕn'tä) . . . Sp.	39·25 N	0·28 W
76	Torreon (tôr-rā-ōn') . . . Mex.	25·32 N	103·26 W
125	Torre-Pacheco (tôr-rĕ-pä-chĕ'kô) Sp.	37·44 N	0·58 W
159	Torres Is. (tôr'rĕs) (tŏr'ĕz) New Hebr.	13·18 S	165·59 E
68	Torres Martinez Ind. Res. (tôr'ĕz mär-tē'nĕz) . Calif.	33·33 N	116·21 W
124	Tôrres Novas (tôr'rĕzh nō'väzh) Port.	39·28 N	8·37 W
155	Torres Str. (tôr'rĕs) . . . Austl.	10·30 S	141·30 E
124	Tôrres Vedras (tôr'rĕzh vā'dräzh) Port.	39·08 N	9·18 W
125	Torrevieja (tôr-rā-vyā'hä) . . . Sp.	37·58 N	0·40 W
155	Torrijos (tôr-rē'hōs) Phil. (Manila In.)	13·19 N	122·06 E
81	Torrington (tŏr'ĭng-tŭn) . . . Conn.	41·50 N	73·10 W
70	Torrington . . . Wyo.	42·04 N	104·11 W
124	Torro (tô'r-rō) . . . Sp.	41·27 N	5·23 W
118	Torsby (tôrs'bü) . . . Swe.	60·07 N	12·56 E
118	Torshälla (tôrs'hĕl-ä) . . . Swe.	59·26 N	16·21 E
112	Tórshavn (tôrs-houn') . . . Faer.	62·00 N	6·55 W
89	Tortola (I.) (tôr-tō'lä) Vir. Is. (Br.) (Puerto Rico In.)	18·34 N	64·40 W
126	Tortona (tôr-tō'nä) . . . It.	44·52 N	8·52 E
125	Tortosa (tôr-tō'sä) . . . Sp.	40·59 N	0·33 E
125	Tortosa, Cabo de (C.) (kä'bô-dĕ-tôr-tō-sä) . Sp.	40·42 N	0·55 E
95	Tortue, Canal de la (Chan.) (tôr-tü') . Hai.	20·05 N	73·20 W
95	Tortue, Ile de la (I.) . . . Hai.	20·10 N	73·00 W
99	Tortuga, Isla la (I.) (ē's-lä-lä-tôr-tōō'gä) . Ven. (In.)	10·55 N	65·18 W
121	Toruń (tō'rōōn') . . . Pol.	53·01 N	18·37 E
128	Tôrva (t'r'vȧ) . . . Sov. Un.	58·02 N	25·56 E
116	Tory (I.) (tō'rē) . . . Ire.	54·77 N	8·08 W
128	Torzhok (tôr'zhôk) . . . Sov. Un.	57·03 N	34·53 E
153	Tosa-Wan (B.) (tô'sä wän) . . Jap.	33·14 N	133·39 E
126	Toscana (Reg.) (tôs-kä'nä) . . . It.	43·23 N	11·08 E
136	Tosna R. Sov. Un. (Leningrad In.)	59·38 N	30·52 E
136	Tosno (tôs'nô) Sov. Un. (Leningrad In.)	59·32 N	30·52 E
100	Tostado (tōs-tä'dō) . . . Arg.	29·10 S	61·43 W
133	Tosya (tōz'yä) . . . Tur.	41·00 N	34·00 E
124	Totana (tō-tä-nä) . . . Sp.	37·45 N	1·28 W
132	Tot'ma (tôt'mä) . . . Sov. Un.	60·00 N	42·20 E

Page	Name Pronunciation Region	Lat. °′	Long. °′
92	Totonicapán (tô-tō-nê-kä'pän) Guat.	14·55 N	91·20 W
101	Totoras (tô-tô'räs) Arg. (Buenos Aires In.)	32·33 S	61·13 W
153	Totsuka (tōt'sōō-kä) Jap.	35·24 N	139·32 E
110	Tottenham (tŏt'ĕn-ǎm) Eng. (London In.)	51·35 N	0·06 W
153	Tottori (tô'tô-rê) Jap.	35·30 N	134·15 E
164	Touat (Oases) (tōō'ät) Alg.	27·22 N	00·38 W
164	Toubkal Pk. Mor.	31·15 N	7·46 W
164	Touggourt (tōō-gōōrt') (tōō-gōōr') Alg.	33·09 N	6·07 E
114	Touil R. (tōō-ēl') Alg.	34·42 N	2·16 E
123	Toul (tōōl) Fr.	48·39 N	5·51 E
82	Toulnustouc, Riviere (R.) Can.	50·30 N	67·55 W
123	Toulon (tōō-lôN') Fr.	43·09 N	5·54 E
122	Toulouse (tōō-lōōz') Fr.	43·37 N	1·27 E
154	Toungoo (tŏ-ōōŋ-gōō') Bur.	19·00 N	96·29 E
151	Tourane (tōō-rän') Viet.	16·08 N	108·22 E
122	Tourcoing (tōōr-kwaN') Fr.	50·44 N	3·06 E
123	Tournan-en-Brie (tōōr-näN-ĕN-brē') Fr. (Paris In.)	48·45 N	2·47 E
122	Tours (tōōr) Fr.	47·23 N	0·39 E
165	Toussidé, Pic (Pk.) (tōō-sē-dā') Chad	21·10 N	16·30 E
118	Tovdalselv (R.) (tôv-däls-ĕlv) Nor.	58·23 N	8·16 E
81	Towanda (tô-wän'dȧ) Pa.	41·45 N	76·30 W
70	Towner (tou'nẽr) N. D.	48·21 N	100·24 W
83	Townsend (toun'zĕnd) Mass. (Boston In.)	42·41 N	71·42 W
67	Townsend Mont.	46·19 N	111·35 W
65	Townsend, Mt. Wash. (Seattle In.)	47·52 N	123·03 W
159	Townsville (tounz'vĭl) Austl.	19·18 S	146·50 E
84	Towson (tou'sŭn) Md. (Baltimore In.)	39·24 N	76·36 W
154	Towuti, Danau (L.) (tô-wōō'tê) Indon.	3·00 S	121·45 E
76	Toyah (tô'yȧ) Tex.	31·19 N	103·46 W
153	Toyama (tō'yä-mä) Jap.	36·42 N	137·14 E
153	Toyama-Wan (B.) Jap.	36·58 N	137·16 E
153	Toyohashi (tō'yô-hä'shê) Jap.	34·44 N	137·21 E
153	Toyonaka (tō'yô-nä'kä) Jap. (Ōsaka In.)	34·47 N	135·28 E
114	Tozeur (tô-zûr') Tun.	33·59 N	8·11 E
124	Trabancos (R.) (trä-bäŋ'kōs) Sp.	41·15 N	5·13 W
133	Trabzon (träb'zôn) Tur.	41·00 N	39·45 E
68	Tracy (trā'sê) Calif.	37·45 N	121·27 W
70	Tracy Minn.	44·13 N	95·37 W
78	Tracy City Tenn.	35·15 N	85·44 W
124	Trafalgar, Cabo de (C.) (kä'bô-dĕ-trä-fäl-gä'r) Sp.	36·10 N	6·02 W
167	Trafonomby (Mtn.) Malag. Rep.	24·32 S	46·35 E
86	Trail (trāl) Can.	49·04 N	117·56 W
111	Traisen (R.) Aus. (Vienna In.)	48·15 N	15·55 E
111	Traiskirchen Aus. (Vienna In.)	48·01 N	16·18 E
119	Trakai (trä-kāy) Sov. Un.	54·38 N	24·59 E
121	Trakiszki (trä-kē'-sh-kê) Pol.	54·16 N	23·07 E
116	Tralee (trȧ-lē') Ire.	52·16 N	9·20 W
118	Trälleborg (trĕl'ĕ-bôrg) Swe.	55·24 N	13·07 E
118	Tranas (trän'ōs) Swe.	58·03 N	14·56 E
142	Tranbonsha (Mt.) China	35·27 N	86·25 E
124	Trancoso (träŋ-kō'sōō) Port.	40·46 N	7·23 W
155	Trangan (I.) (träŋ'gän) Indon.	6·52 S	133·30 E
126	Trani (trä'nē) It.	41·15 N	16·25 E
103	Transcaucasia (Reg.) Sov. Un.	41·17 N	44·30 E
85	Transcona (trăns-kō'nȧ) Can. (Winnipeg In.)	49·54 N	97·00 W
146	Trans-Himalays Mts. (trăns'hĭ-mä'lȧ-yȧ) China	31·15 N	81·56 E
166	Transvaal (Prov.) (trăns-väl') S. Afr.	24·21 S	28·18 E
121	Transylvania (Reg.) (trăn-sĭl-vā'nĭ-ȧ) Rom.	46·30 N	22·35 E
	Transylvanian Alps (Mts.), see Carpatii Meridionali		
126	Trapani (trä'pä-nê) It.	38·02 N	14·34 E
123	Trappes (tràp) Fr. (Paris In.)	48·47 N	2·01 E
160	Traralgon (trȧ'răl-gŏn) Austl.	38·15 S	146·33 E
126	Trasimeno, Lago (L.) (lä'gō trä-sê-mā'nō) It.	43·00 N	12·12 E
124	Tras os Montes (Mts.) (träzh'ōzh mōn'tāzh) Port.	41·33 N	7·13 W
124	Trasparga (träs-pär-gä) Sp.	43·13 N	7·50 W
120	Traun R. (troun) Aus.	48·10 N	14·15 E
120	Traunstein (troun'stīn) Ger.	47·52 N	12·38 E
70	Traverse, L. (trăv'ẽrs) Minn.-S. D.	45·46 N	96·53 W
80	Traverse City Mich.	44·45 N	85·40 W
126	Travnik (träv'nēk) Yugo.	44·13 N	17·43 E
65	Treasure I. (trĕzh'ẽr) Calif. (San Francisco In.)	37·49 N	122·22 W
111	Trebbin (trĕ'bēn) Ger. (Berlin In.)	52·13 N	13·13 E
120	Třebíč (t'rzhĕ'bēch) Czech.	49·13 N	15·53 E
127	Trebinje (trĕ'bēn-yĕ) Yugo.	42·43 N	18·21 E
121	Trebisow (trĕ'bê-shôf) Czech.	48·36 N	21·32 E
120	Třeboň (t'rzhĕ'bôn') Czech.	49·00 N	14·48 E
159	Tregrosse Is. (trê-grōs') Austl.	18·08 S	150·53 E
100	Treinta y Tres (trā-ēn'tä ē träs') Ur.	33·14 S	54·17 W
122	Trélazé (trā-là-zā') Fr.	47·27 N	0·32 W
100	Trelew (trē'lū) Arg.	43·15 S	65·25 W
116	Tremadoc B. (trĕ-mă'dŏk) Wales	52·43 N	4·27 W
126	Tremiti, Isole di (Is.) (ē'sō-lĕ dē trā-mē'tē) It.	42·07 N	16·33 E
121	Trenčín (trĕn'chēn) Czech.	48·52 N	18·02 E
154	Trengganu (State) (trĕng-gä'nōō) Mala.	4·53 N	102·26 E
100	Trenque Lauquén (trĕn'kĕ-lä'ōō-kĕ'n) Arg.	35·50 S	62·44 W
81	Trent (R.) (trĕnt) Can.	44·15 N	77·55 W
116	Trent (R.) Eng.	53·05 N	1·00 W
110	Trent and Mersey Can. (trĕnt) (mûr'zē) Eng.	53·11 N	2·24 W
126	Trento (trĕn'tô) It.	46·04 N	11·07 E
126	Trento (Reg.) It.	46·16 N	10·47 E
81	Trenton (trĕn'tŭn) Can.	44·05 N	77·35 W
83	Trenton Can.	45·39 N	62·40 W
75	Trenton Mich. (Detroit In.)	42·08 N	83·12 W
73	Trenton Mo.	40·05 N	93·36 W
84	Trenton N. J. (New York In.)	40·13 N	74·46 W
78	Trenton Tenn.	35·57 N	88·55 W
83	Trepassey (trê-păs'ê) Can.	46·47 N	53·20 W
83	Trepassey B. Can.	46·35 N	53·25 W
100	Tres Arroyos (träs'är-rō'yōs) Arg.	38·18 S	60·16 W
101	Três Coraçoes (trĕ's kō-rä-zô'ĕs) Braz. (Rio de Janeiro In.)	21·41 S	45·14 W
91	Tres Cumbres (trĕ's kōō'm-brĕs) Mex. (Mexico City In.)	19·03 N	99·14 W
99	Três Lagoas (trĕ's lä-gô'äs) Braz.	20·48 S	51·42 W
99	Três Marias, Represa (Res.) (rĕ-prā'sä trĕs' mä-rē'äs) Braz.	18·15 S	45·30 W
98	Tres Morros, Alto de (Mtn.) (ä'l-tō dĕ trĕ's mô'r-rôs) Col. (In.)	7·08 N	76·10 W
101	Três Pontas (trĕ's pô'n-täs) Braz. (Rio de Janeiro In.)	21·22 S	45·30 W
101	Três Rios (trĕ's rē'ōs) Braz. (Rio de Janeiro In.)	22·07 S	43·13 W
111	Treuenbrietzen (troi'ĕn-brē-tzĕn) Ger. (Berlin In.)	52·06 N	12·52 E
126	Treviglio (trā-vē'lyô) It.	45·30 N	9·34 E
126	Treviso (trĕ-vē'sō) It.	45·39 N	12·15 E
146	Triangle, The (Reg.) Asia	26·00 N	98·00 E
168	Trichardt (trĭ-kärt') S. Afr. (Johannesburg & Pretoria In.)	26·32 S	29·16 E
126	Trieste (Trst) (trê-ĕs'tä) It.	45·39 N	13·48 E
126	Trieste, G. of It.	45·38 N	13·40 E
124	Trigueros (trê-gā'rōs) Sp.	37·23 N	6·50 W
142	Trigu Tsho (L.) China	28·47 N	91·37 E
127	Tríkkala Grc.	39·33 N	21·49 E
75	Trim Cr. (trĭm) Ill. (Chicago In.)	41·19 N	87·39 W
143	Trincomalee (trĭŋ-kô-mȧ-lē') Ceylon	8·39 N	81·12 E
110	Tring (trĭng) Eng. (London In.)	51·46 N	0·40 W
98	Trinidad (trē-nê-dhädh') Bol.	14·48 S	64·43 W
72	Trinidad (trĭn'ĭ-dăd) Colo.	37·11 N	104·31 W
94	Trinidad (trē-nê-dhädh') Cuba	21·50 N	80·00 W
101	Trinidad Ur. (Buenos Aires In.)	33·29 S	56·55 W
94	Trinidad, Sierra de (Mts.) (sē-ĕ'r-rä dĕ trē-nê-dä'd) Cuba	21·50 N	79·55 W
99	Trinidad (I.) (trĭn'ĭ-dăd) Trin.	10·00 N	61·00 W
89	Trinidad and Tobago (trĭn'ĭ-dăd) (tô-bā'gō) N. A.	11·00 N	61·00 W
96	Trinidade, Ilha de (I.) (ē'lä dĕ trê-nē-dä-dĕ) Braz.	21·00 S	32·00 W
88	Trinidad R. Pan. (Panama Canal In.)	8·55 N	80·01 W
91	Trinitaria (trē-nē-tä'ryä) Mex.	16·09 N	92·04 W
93	Trinité Mart. (Le. & Wind. Is. In.)	14·47 N	61·00 W
83	Trinity (trĭn'ĭ-tê) Can.	48·22 N	53·24 W
77	Trinity Tex.	30·52 N	95·27 W
64	Trinity (Is.) Alaska	56·25 N	153·15 W
72	Trinity (R.), West Fk. Tex.	33·22 N	98·26 W
73	Trinity (R.), East Fk. Tex.	33·24 N	96·42 W
83	Trinity B. Can.	47·55 N	53·30 W
66	Trinity Res. Calif.	40·51 N	122·41 W
66	Trinity R. Calif.	40·50 N	123·20 W
77	Trinity R. Tex.	30·50 N	95·09 W
126	Trino (trē'nô) It.	45·11 N	8·16 E
78	Trion (trī'ŏn) Ga.	34·32 N	85·18 W
	Tripoli, see T'arābulus		
	Tripoli, see Tarābulus		
127	Tripolis (trĭ'pô-lĭs) Grc.	37·32 N	22·32 E
	Tripolitania, see Tarābulus		
70	Tripp (trĭp) S. D.	43·13 N	97·58 W
142	Tripura (Mts.) W. Pak.	28·38 N	91·37 E
47	Tristan da Cunha Is. (três-tän'dä kōō'nyȧ) Atl. O.	35·30 S	12·15 W
99	Triste, Golfo (G.) (gôl-fô trĕ's-tĕ) Ven. (In.)	10·40 N	68·05 W
84	Triticus Res. (trī tĭ-cŭs) N. Y. (New York In.)	41·20 N	73·36 W
84	Triumph (trī'ŭmf) La. (New Orleans In.)	29·21 N	89·29 W
143	Trivandrum (trê-vŭn'drŭm) India	8·34 N	76·58 E
121	Trnava (t'r'nȧ-vȧ) Czech.	48·22 N	17·34 E
155	Trobriand Is. (trō-brê-ănd') Pap.	8·25 S	151·45 E
126	Trogir (trô'gēr) Yugo.	43·32 N	16·17 E
82	Trois Pistoles (trwä' pĕs-tôl') Can.	48.07 N	69·10 W
82	Trois-Riviéres (rê-vyâr') Can.	46·21 N	72·35 W
136	Troitsk (trô'ētsk) Sov. Un. (Urals In.)	54·06 N	61·34 E
134	Troitsko-Pechorsk (trô'ĭtsk-ô-pyĕ-chôrsk') Sov. Un.	62·18 N	56·07 E
129	Troitskoye Sov. Un.	47·39 N	30·16 E
118	Trollhättan (trôl'hĕt-ĕn) Swe.	58·17 N	12·17 E
118	Trollheim (Mts.) (trôll-hĕĭm) Nor.	62·48 N	9·05 E
112	Tromsö (trôm'sû) Nor.	69·38 N	19·12 E
68	Trona (trō'nȧ) Calif.	35·49 N	117·20 W
100	Tronador, Cerro (Mtn.) (sĕ'r-rô trō-nä'dôr) Arg.	41·17 S	71·56 W
90	Troncoso (trôn-kô'sō) Mex.	22·43 N	102·22 W
118	Trondheim (Nidaros) (trôn'hām) (nē'dhä-rôs) Nor.	63·25 N	11·35 E
139	Troodos, Mt. Cyprus (Palestine In.)	34·56 N	32·52 E
118	Trosa (trô'sä) Swe.	58·54 N	17·25 E
87	Trout (L.) Can.	51·16 N	92·46 W
66	Trout Cr. Ore.	42·18 N	118·31 W
65	Troutdale (trout'dāl) Ore. (Portland In.)	45·32 N	122·23 W
122	Trouville-sur-Mer (trōō-vēl'sür-mâr') Fr.	49·23 N	0·05 E
78	Troy (troi) Ala.	31·47 N	85·46 W
74	Troy Ill. (St. Louis In.)	38·44 N	89·53 W
73	Troy Kans.	39·46 N	95·07 W
73	Troy Mo.	38·56 N	90·57 W
66	Troy Mont.	48·28 N	115·56 W
81	Troy N. Y.	42·45 N	73·45 W
79	Troy N. C.	35·21 N	79·58 W
80	Troy Ohio	40·00 N	84·10 W
127	Troy (Ruins) Tur.	39·59 N	26·14 E
122	Troyes (trwä) Fr.	48·18 N	4·03 E
	Trst, see Trieste		
127	Trstenik (t'r'stĕ-nêk) Yugo.	43·36 N	20·00 E
128	Trubchëvsk (trōōp'chĕfsk) Sov. Un.	52·36 N	32·46 E
138	Trucial Coast (trōō'shăl) Asia	23·30 N	53·00 E
68	Truckee (trŭk'ē) Calif.	39·20 N	120·12 W
68	Truckee (R.) Calif.-Nev.	39·25 N	120·07 W
161	Truganina Austl. (Melbourne In.)	37·49 S	144·44 E
98	Trujillo (trōō-kĕ'l-yō) Col. (In.)	4·10 N	76·20 W
92	Trujillo (trōō-kēl'yō) Hond.	15·55 N	85·58 W
98	Trujillo Peru	8·08 S	79·00 W
124	Trujillo (trōō-kĕ'l-yô) Sp.	39·27 N	5·50 W
98	Trujillo Ven.	9·15 N	70·28 W
90	Trujillo (R.) Mex.	23·12 N	103·10 W
95	Trujin, L. (trōō-kēn') Dom. Rep.	17·45 N	71·25 W
73	Trumann (trōō'măn) Ark.	35·41 N	90·31 W
127	Trŭn (trŭn) Bul.	42·49 N	22·39 E
82	Truro (trōō'rō) Can.	45·22 N	63·20 W
116	Truro Eng.	50·17 N	5·05 W
84	Trussville (trŭs'vĭl) Ala. (Birmingham In.)	33·37 N	86·37 W
69	Truth or Consequences (trōōth ŏr kŏn'sê-kwĕn-sĭs) N. Mex.	33·10 N	107·20 W
120	Trutnov (trōōt'nôf) Czech.	50·36 N	15·36 E
120	Trzcianka (tchyän'kȧ) Pol.	53·02 N	16·27 E
120	Trzebiatowo (tchĕ-byä'tōō-vô) Pol.	54·03 N	15·16 E
146	Tsaidam Swp. (tsī'dàm) China	37·19 N	94·08 E
150	Ts'aiyü China (Peking In.)	39·39 N	116·36 E
79	Tsala Apopka (R.) (tsä'lȧ ă-pŏp'kȧ) Fla.	28·57 N	82·11 W
148	Ts'anghsien (chäng'sĭän) China	38·21 N	116·53 E
149	Ts'angmen China (Canton In.)	22·42 N	113·09 E
	Tsangwu, see Wuchou		
148	Tsaochuang (jou'jōōäng) China	34·51 N	117·34 E
148	Ts'aohsien (tsou'sĭän) China	34·48 N	115·33 E
146	Tsasata Bogda Uula (Mt.) Mong.	46·44 N	92·34 E
65	Tsawwassen Ind. Res. Can. (Vancouver In.)	49·03 N	123·11 W
134	Tselinograd (tsĕ'lĕ-nô-grä'd) Sov. Un.	51·10 N	71·43 E
149	Tsengch'en China (Canton In.)	23·18 N	113·49 E
136	Tsentral'nyy-Kospashskiy (tsĕn-träl'nyĭ-kôs-päsh'skĭ) Sov. Un. (Urals In.)	59·03 N	57·48 E
142	Tsethang China	29·20 N	91·49 E
166	Tshela (tshā'lä) Con. L.	4·50 S	13·05 E
166	Tshikapa (tshê-kä'pä) Con. L.	6·29 S	20·53 E
166	Tshilongo (tshê-lôŋ'gō) Con. L.	10·28 S	26·09 E
166	Tshuapa (R.) Con. L.	0·25 S	22·07 E
167	Tsiafajovona (Mtn.) Malag. Rep.	19·17 S	47·27 E
167	Tsiandra (tsē-än-drō') Malag. Rep.	18·46 S	44·58 E
133	Tsimlyanskiy (Res.) (tsym-lyä'ns-kēē) Sov. Un.	47·50 N	43·40 E
139	Tsin (R.) Isr. (Palestine In.)	30·52 N	35·05 E
148	Tsinan (Chinan) (je'nän) China	36·40 N	117·01 E
	Tsinghai (Prov.), see Chinghai		
	Tsingtao, see Ch'ingtao		
167	Tsiribihina (R.) (tsē'rê-bē-hê-nä') Malag. Rep.	19·45 S	43·30 E
167	Tsitsa (R.) (tsê'tsä) S. Afr. (Natal In.)	31·28 S	28·53 E
	Tsitsihar, see Ch'ich'ihaerh		
167	Tsolo (tsō'lō) S. Afr. (Natal In.)	31·19 S	28·47 E
167	Tsomo S. Afr. (Natal In.)	32·03 S	27·49 E
167	Tsomo (R.) S. Afr. (Natal In.)	31·53 S	27·48 E
153	Tsu (tsōō) Jap.	34·42 N	136·31 E
153	Tsuchiura (tsōō'chê-ōō-rä) Jap.	36·04 N	140·09 E
153	Tsuda (tsōō'dä) Jap. (Ōsaka In.)	34·48 N	135·43 E
152	Tsugaru Kaikyō (str.) (tsōō'gä-rōō kī'kyō) Jap.	41·25 N	140·20 E
166	Tsumeb (tsōō'mĕb) S. W. Afr.	19·10 S	17·45 E
153	Tsunashima (tsōō'nä-shê'mä) Jap. (Tōkyō In.)	35·32 N	139·37 E
151	Ts'unghua China	23·30 N	113·40 E
148	Tsunhua (zhōōn'hooä) China	40·12 N	117·55 E
153	Tsuruga (tsōō'rōō-gä) Jap.	35·39 N	136·04 E
153	Tsurugi San (Mtn.) (tsōō'rōō-gê sän) Jap.	33·52 N	134·07 E
152	Tsuruoka (tsōō'rōō-ō'kä) Jap.	38·43 N	139·51 E
153	Tsurusaki (tsōō'rōō-sä'kê) Jap.	33·15 N	131·42 E
153	Tsu Shima (I.) (tsōō shē'mä) Jap.	34·28 N	129·30 E
153	Tsushima Kaikyō (Str.) (tsōō'shē-mä kī'kyō) Asia	33·52 N	129·30 E
153	Tsuwano (tsōō'wȧ-nō') Jap.	34·28 N	131·47 E
153	Tsuyama (tsōō'yä-mä') Jap.	35·05 N	134·00 E
124	Tua (R.) (tōō'ä) Port.	41·23 N	7·18 W
65	Tualatin (R.) (tōō'ȧ-lā-tĭn) Ore. (Portland In.)	45·25 N	122·54 W
157	Tuamotu (Low), Arch. (tōō-ä-mō'tōō) Fr. Polynesia	19·00 S	141·20 W
155	Tuao (tōō-ä'ō) Phil. (Manila In.)	17·44 N	121·26 E
133	Tuapse (tōō'äp-sĕ) Sov. Un.	44·00 N	39·10 E
164	Tuareg (Reg.) Alg.	21·26 N	2·51 E
164	Tuayq, Jabal (Mts.) Sau. Ar.	20·45 N	46·30 E
100	Tubarão (tōō-bä-rouN') Braz.	28·23 S	48·56 W
120	Tübingen (tü'bĭng-ĕn) Ger.	48·33 N	9·05 E
136	Tubinskiy (tû bĭn'skĭ) Sov. Un. (Urals In.)	52·53 N	58·15 E
165	Tubruq (Tobruk) Libya	32·03 N	24·04 E
99	Tucacas (tōō-kä'käs) Ven. (In.)	10·48 N	68·20 W
84	Tucker (tŭk'ẽr) Ga (Atlanta In.)	33·51 N	84·13 W
69	Tucson (tōō-sŏn') Ariz.	32·15 N	111·00 W
100	Tucumán (tōō-kōō-män') Arg.	26·52 S	65·08 W
100	Tucumán (Prov.) Arg.	26·30 S	65·30 W
72	Tucumcari (tōō'kŭm-kâr-ē) N. Mex.	35·11 N	103·43 W
98	Tucupita (tōō-kōō-pē'tä) Ven.	9·00 N	62·09 W
99	Tucuruí (tōō-kōō-tōō-ē') Braz.	3·34 S	49·44 W
124	Tudela (tōō-dhä'lä) Sp.	42·03 N	1·37 W

ng-sing; ŋ-baŋk; N-nasalized n; nŏd; cŏmmit; ōld; ôbey; ôrder; fōōd; fŏŏt; ou-out; s-soft; sh-dish; th-thin; pūre; ûnite; ûrn; stŭd; circŭs; ü-as "y" in study; '-indeterminate vowel.

Page	Name Pronunciation Region	Lat. °′	Long. °′
78	Tugaloo (R.) (tŭg′ȧ-lōō). Ga.-S. C.	34·35 N	83·05 W
167	Tugela (R.) (tōō-gel′ȧ) S. Afr. (Natal In.)	28·50 S	30·52 E
167	Tugela Ferry . . S. Afr. (Natal In.)	29·16 S	30·24 E
80	Tug Fork (R.) (tŭg) . . . . . . W. Va.	37·50 N	82·30 W
155	Tuguegarao (tōō-gā-gá-rä′ō) Phil. (Manila In.)	17·37 N	121·44 E
148	T'uhsieh (R.) (tōō′hăi) . . . . . China	37·05 N	116·56 E
168	Tuinplaas . . . . S. Afr. (Johannesburg & Pretoria In.)	24·54 S	28·46 E
74	Tujunga (tōō-jŭŋ′gȧ) Calif. (Los Angeles In.)	34·15 N	118·16 W
136	Tukan (tōō′kȧn) Sov. Un. (Urals In.)	53·52 N	57·25 E
155	Tukengbesi, Palau-Palau (Is.) Indon.	6·00 S	124·15 E
165	Tukrah . . . . Libya	32·34 N	20·47 E
86	Tuktoyaktuk (tōōk-tō-yăk′tōōk) Can.	69·32 N	132·37 W
132	Tukum (tōō′kōōm) . . . . . . Sov. Un.	57·00 N	22·50 E
119	Tukums (tōō′kōōms) . . . . Sov. Un.	56·57 N	23·09 E
166	Tukuyu (tōō-kōō′yȧ) . . . . Tan.	9·13 S	33·43 E
65	Tukwila (tŭk′wĭ-lȧ) Wash. (Seattle In.)	47·28 N	122·16 W
90	Tula (tōō′lä) . . . . Mex.	20·04 N	99·22 W
128	Tula (tōō′lȧ) . . . . Sov. Un.	54·12 N	37·37 E
128	Tula (Oblast) . . . . Sov. Un.	53·45 N	37·19 E
90	Tula (R.) (tōō′lä) . . . . Mex.	20·40 N	99·27 W
159	Tulagi (I.) (tōō-lä′gē) . . . . . Sol. Is.	9·15 S	160·17 E
65	Tulalip (tū-lă′lĭp) Wash. (Seattle In.)	48·04 N	122·18 W
65	Tulalip Ind. Res. Wash. (Seattle In.)	48·06 N	122·16 W
90	Tulancingo (tōō-län-sĭŋ′gō) . . Mex.	20·04 N	98·24 W
68	Tulare (tōō-lä′rȧ) (tŭl-âr′) . . Calif.	36·12 N	119·22 W
68	Tulare Basin . . . . Calif.	35·57 N	120·18 W
69	Tularosa (tōō-lȧ-rō′zȧ) . . . N. Mex.	33·05 N	106·05 W
98	Tulcán (tōōl-kän′) . . . . Ec.	0·44 N	77·52 W
129	Tulcea (tōōl′chȧ) . . . . Rom.	45·10 N	28·47 E
129	Tul'chin (tōōl′chĕn) . . . . . Sov. Un.	48·42 N	28·53 E
90	Tulcingo (tōōl-sĭŋ′gō) . . . . Mex.	18·03 N	98·27 W
68	Tule (R.) (tōō′lȧ) . . . . Calif.	36·08 N	118·50 W
167	Tuléar (tōō-lā-är′) . . . Malag. Rep.	20·16 S	43·44 E
68	Tule River Ind. Res. (tōō′lȧ) Calif.	36·05 N	118·35 W
166	Tuli (tōō′lē) . . . . S. Rh.	20·58 S	29·12 E
72	Tulia (tōō′lĭ-ȧ) . . . . Tex.	34·32 N	101·46 W
91	Tulijá (R.) (tōō-lē-ĸȧ′) . . . . . . Mex.	17·28 N	92·11 W
64	Tulik Vol. (tōō′lĭk) . . . . Alaska	53·28 N	168·10 W
139	Tūl Karm (tōōl kärm) Jordan (Palestine In.)	32·19 N	35·02 E
78	Tullahoma (tŭl-ȧ-hō′mȧ) . . . Tenn.	35·21 N	86·12 W
116	Tullamore (tŭl-ȧ-mōr′) . . . . Ire.	53·15 N	7·29 W
122	Tulle (tūl) . . . . Fr.	45·15 N	1·45 E
111	Tulln (tōōln) . . . Aus. (Vienna In.)	48·21 N	16·04 E
111	Tullner Feld (Reg.) Aus. (Vienna In.)	48·20 N	15·59 E
165	Tulmaythah . . . . Libya	32·44 N	21·08 E
91	Tulpetlac (tōōl-pȧ-tlăk′) Mex. (Mexico City In.)	19·33 N	99·04 W
73	Tulsa (tŭl′sȧ) . . . . Okla.	36·08 N	95·58 W
98	Tuluá (tōō-lōō-ȧ′) . . . . . . Col. (In.)	4·06 N	76·12 W
146	T'ulufan (Turfan) (tōō′lōō-fän′) (tōōr-fän′) . China	43·06 N	88·41 E
92	Tulum (tōō-lōō′m) Mex. (Yucatan In.)	20·17 N	87·26 W
134	Tulun (tōō-lōōn′) . . . . Sov. Un.	54·29 N	100·43 E
69	Tumacacori Natl. Mon. (tōō-mä-kä′kō-rē) . Ariz.	31·36 N	110·20 W
98	Tumaco (tōō-mä′kō) . . . . Col.	1·41 N	78·44 W
92	Tuma R. (tōō′mä) . . . . Nic.	13·07 N	85·32 W
166	Tumba (L.) (tōōm′bä) . . . . Con. L.	1·03 S	18·28 E
98	Tumbes (tōō′m-bĕs) . . . . Peru	3·39 S	80·27 W
90	Tumbiscatío (tōōm-bē-skä-tē′ō) Mex.	18·32 N	102·23 W
65	Tumbo (I.) . . Can. (Vancouver In.)	48·49 N	123·04 W
150	T'umen (tōō′mĕn) . . . . China	43·00 N	129·50 E
152	Tumen (R.) . . . . China	42·08 N	128·40 E
99	Tumeremo (tōō-mȧ-rä′mō) . . . . Ven.	7·15 N	61·28 W
99	Tumuc-Humac Mts. (tōō-mōōk′ōō-măk′) . S. A.	2·15 N	54·50 W
94	Tunas de Zaza (tōō′näs dā zä′zä) Cuba	21·40 N	79·35 W
116	Tunbridge Wells (tŭn′brĭj welz′) Eng.	51·05 N	0·09 E
134	Tundra (Reg.) . . . . Sov. Un.	70·45 N	84·00 E
147	Tung (R.) . . . . China	24·13 N	115·08 E
148	Tunga (dōōng′ä) . . . . China	36·11 N	116·16 E
142	Tungabhadra Res . . . . India	15·26 N	75·57 E
151	T'ungan (tōōn′gän′) . . . . China	24·48 N	118·02 E
148	T'ungch'engi (tōōng′chĕng′yē) China	36·21 N	116·14 E
147	T'ungchiang . . . . China	47·38 N	132·54 E
148	Tungeh'angshou (tōōng′chăng′shō) China	38·21 N	114·41 E
148	Tunghai (dōōng′hăi) . . . . China	34·35 N	119·05 E
150	T'ungho . . . . China	45·58 N	128·40 E
151	Tunghsiang . . . . China	28·18 N	116·38 E
150	Tunghsien . . . . . China (Peking In.)	39·55 N	116·40 E
148	Tung Hu (L.) (tōōng′ hōō′) . China	32·22 N	116·32 E
151	Tungjen (tōōng′jĕn′) . . . . China	27·45 N	109·12 E
149	Tungkuan . . . . China (Canton In.)	23·03 N	113·14 E
150	T'ung-Kuan . . . . China	34·48 N	110·25 E
148	Tungkuang (dōōng′gōōăng) . China	37·54 N	116·33 E
151	T'ungku Chiao (Pt.) . . . . China	19·40 N	111·15 E
150	Tungliao (Payintala) . . . . China	43·30 N	122·15 E
148	Tungming (tōōng′mĭng′) . . . . China	35·16 N	115·06 E
148	Tungpa (tōōng′bä) . . . . China	31·40 N	119·02 E
148	Tungpa . . . . China	35·56 N	116·19 E
150	T'ungpei (tōōng′pā) . . . . China	48·00 N	126·48 E
148	Tungping (tōōng′pĭng) . . . . . . China	35·50 N	116·24 E
148	Tungp'ing Hu (L.) (hōō) . . . . China	36·06 N	116·24 E
148	Tungt'antien (dōōng′tän′dĭăn) China	35·26 N	116·54 E
151	Tungt'ing Hŭ (L.) (tōōng′tĕng′ hōō) . China	29·10 N	112·30 E
148	Tungwen (R.) (dōōng′wĕn) . China	36·24 N	119·00 E
150	Tunhua . . . . China	48·18 N	128·10 E
143	Tuni . . . . India	17·29 N	82·38 E
78	Tunica (tū′nĭ-kȧ) . . . . Miss.	34·41 N	90·23 W
164	Tunis (tū′nĭs) . . . . Tun.	36·59 N	10·06 E
113	Tunis, Golfe de (G.) . . . . Tun.	37·06 N	10·43 E
163	Tunisia (tū-nĭzh′ē-ȧ) . . . . Afr.	35·00 N	10·11 E
98	Tunja (tōō′n-hä) . . . . Col.	5·32 N	73·19 W
81	Tunkhannock (tŭnk-hăn′ŭk) . . Pa.	41·35 N	75·55 W
65	Tunnel (R.) (tŭn′ĕl) Wash. (Seattle In.)	47·48 N	123·04 W
68	Tuolumne (R.) (twô-lŭm′nē) . Calif.	37·35 N	120·37 W
135	Tuostakh (R.) . . . . Sov. Un.	67·09 N	137·30 E
99	Tupã (tōō-pȧ) . . . . Braz.	21·47 S	50·33 W
78	Tupelo (tū′pē-lō) . . . . Miss.	34·14 N	88·43 W
99	Tupinambaranas, Ilha (I.) (ē′lȧ-tōō-pē-nȧɴ-bȧ-rȧ′nȧs) . Braz.	3·04 S	58·09 W
98	Tupiza (tōō-pē′zä) . . . . Bol.	21·26 S	65·43 W
81	Tupper Lake (tŭp′ẽr) . . . . . . N. Y.	44·15 N	74·25 W
98	Tuquerres (tōō-kĕ′r-rĕs) . . . . . . Col.	1·12 N	77·44 W
134	Tura (tōōr′ȧ) . . . . Sov. Un.	64·08 N	99·58 E
103	Tura (R.) . . . . Sov. Un.	57·15 N	64·23 E
144	Turayf . . . . Sau. Ar.	31·32 N	38·30 E
90	Turbio (R.) (tōōr-byô) . . . . . . Mex.	20·28 N	101·40 W
98	Turbo (tōō′bō) . . . . Col.	8·02 N	76·43 W
121	Turciansky Sväty Martin (tōōr′chyȧn-skū′svä′tū′ mär′tyĕn) . Czech.	49·02 N	18·48 E
121	Turda (tōōr′dȧ) . . . . Rom.	46·35 N	23·47 E
	Turfan, see T'ulufan		
146	Turfan Depression . . . . China	42·16 N	90·00 E
167	Turffontein . . . . S. Afr. (Johannesburg & Pretoria In.)	26·15 S	28·03 E
134	Turgay (tōōr′gī) . . . . Sov. Un.	49·42 N	63·39 E
103	Turgayka (R.) (tōōr-gī′kȧ) Sov. Un.	49·44 N	66·15 E
127	Tŭrgovishte . . . . Bul.	43·14 N	26·36 E
133	Turgutlu . . . . Tur.	38·30 N	27·20 E
119	Türi (tü′rĭ) . . . . Sov. Un.	58·49 N	25·29 E
124	Turia (R.) (tōō′ryä) . . . . Sp.	40·12 N	1·18 W
90	Turicato (tōō-rē-kä′tō) . . . . . . Mex.	19·03 N	101·24 W
94	Turiguano (I.) (tōō-rê-gwä′nō) Cuba	22·20 N	78·35 W
	Turin, see Torino		
121	Turka (tōōr′kȧ) . . . . Sov. Un.	49·10 N	23·02 E
134	Turkestan (tûr-kĕ-stăn′) (tōōr-kĕ-stan′) . Sov. Un.	42·40 N	65·00 E
130	Turkestan (Reg.) . . . . Sov. Un.	43·27 N	62·14 E
138	Turkey . . . . Eur.-Asia	38·45 N	32·00 E
71	Turkey (R.) (tûrk′ē) . . . . Iowa	43·20 N	92·16 W
130	Turkmen (S. S. R.) (tōōrk-mĕn′) Sov. Un.	40·46 N	56·01 E
95	Turks I. Pass . . Turks & Caicos Is.	21·15 N	71·25 W
95	Turks Is. (tûrks) Turks & Caicos Is.	21·25 N	71·10 W
119	Turku (Åbo) (tōōr′kōō) (ô′bô) . Fin.	60·28 N	22·12 E
68	Turlock (tûr′lŏk) . . . . Calif.	37·30 N	120·51 W
92	Turneffe I. (tûr-nĕf′fē) Br. Hond. (Yucatan In.)	17·25 N	87·43 W
74	Turner (tûr′nẽr) Mo. (Kansas City In.)	39·05 N	94·42 W
94	Turner Sd . . . . Ba. Is.	24·20 N	78·05 W
111	Turnhout (tŭrn-hout′) Bel. (Brussels In.)	51·19 N	4·58 E
120	Turnov (tōōr′nôf) . . . . Czech.	50·36 N	15·12 E
127	Tŭrnovo . . . . Bul.	43·06 N	25·38 E
127	Turnu Măgurele (tōōr′nōō mŭ-gōō-rĕ′ly′) . Rom.	43·54 N	24·49 E
127	Turnu-Severin (sĕ-vĕ-rēn′) . . Rom.	44·37 N	22·38 E
94	Turquino, Pico de (Pk.) (pē′kō dā tōōr-kē′nō) . Cuba	20·00 N	76·50 W
93	Turrialba (tōōr-ryä′l-bä) . . . . C. R.	9·54 N	83·41 W
127	Turski Trstenik . . . . Bul.	43·26 N	24·50 E
103	Turtkul' (tōōrt-kōōl′) . . . Sov. Un.	41·28 N	61·02 E
77	Turtle B. (tûr′t′l) . . . . . . Tex. (In.)	29·48 N	94·38 W
70	Turtle Cr . . . . S. D.	44·40 N	98·53 W
70	Turtle Mountain Ind. Res . . N. D.	48·45 N	99·57 W
70	Turtle Mts . . . . N. D.	48·57 N	100·11 W
134	Turukhansk (tōō-rōō-kȧnsk′) Sov. Un.	66·03 N	88·39 E
121	Turya R. (tōōr′yȧ) . . . . Sov. Un.	51·18 N	24·55 E
78	Tuscaloosa (tŭs-kȧ-lōō′sȧ) . . . . Ala.	33·10 N	87·35 W
66	Tuscarora (tŭs-kȧ-rō′rȧ) . . . . . Nev.	41·18 N	116·15 W
75	Tuscarora Ind. Res. N. Y. (Buffalo In.)	43·10 N	78·51 W
80	Tuscola (tŭs-kō′lȧ) . . . . Ill.	39·50 N	88·20 W
78	Tuscumbia (tŭs-kŭm′bĭ-ȧ) . . . . . Ala.	35·41 N	87·42 W
151	Tushan (dōō′shän) . . . . China	25·50 N	107·42 E
148	Tushan . . . . China	31·38 N	116·16 E
136	Tushino (tōō′shĭ-nô) Sov. Un. (Moscow In.)	55·51 N	37·22 E
78	Tuskegee (tŭs-kē′gē) . . . . Ala.	32·25 N	85·40 W
148	T'ussuk'ou (tōō′sē′kō) . . . . . . China	36·19 N	117·37 E
74	Tustin (tŭs′tĭn) Calif. (Los Angeles In.)	33·44 N	117·49 W
128	Tutayev (tōō-tȧ-yĕf′) . . . . Sov. Un.	57·53 N	39·34 E
110	Tutbury (tŭt′bẽr-ē) . . . . Eng.	52·52 N	1·51 W
143	Tuticorin (tōō-tē-kō-rĭn′) . . . . India	8·51 N	78·09 E
91	Tutitlan (tōō-tē-tlä′n) Mex. (Mexico City In.)	19·38 N	99·10 W
99	Tutóia (tōō-tō′yȧ) . . . . Braz.	2·42 S	42·21 W
127	Tutrakan . . . . Bul.	44·02 N	26·36 E
73	Tuttle Creek Res . . . . Kans.	39·30 N	96·38 W
120	Tuttlingen (tōōt′lĭng-ĕn) . . . . . Ger.	47·58 N	8·50 E
78	Tutwiler (tŭt′wĭ-lẽr) . . . . Miss.	34·01 N	90·25 W
134	Tuva Aut. Oblast . . . . Sov. Un.	51·15 N	90·45 E
85	Tuxedo (tŭk-sē′dō) Can. (Winnipeg In.)	49·51 N	97·13 W
84	Tuxedo Park (tŭk-sē′dō pärk) N. Y. (New York In.)	41·11 N	74·11 W
110	Tuxford (tŭks′fẽrd) . . . . Eng.	53·14 N	0·54 W
90	Tuxpan (tōōs′pän) . . . . Mex.	19·34 N	103·22 W
91	Túxpan . . . . Mex.	20·57 N	97·26 W
91	Túxpan (R.) (tōōs′pän) . . . . . Mex.	20·55 N	97·52 W
91	Túxpan, Arrecife (Rf.) (är-rē-sē′fē-tōō′x-pä′n) . Mex.	21·01 N	97·12 W
91	Tuxtepec (tōōs-tȧ-pĕk′) . . . . . Mex.	18·06 N	96·09 W
91	Tuxtla Gutiérrez (tōōs′tlä gōō-tyȧr′rĕs) . Mex.	16·44 N	93·08 W
112	Tuy . . . . Sp.	42·07 N	8·49 W
99	Tuy (tōō′ē) (R.) . . . . Ven. (In.)	10·15 N	66·03 W
93	Tuyra R. (tōō-ē′rȧ) . . . . Pan.	7·55 N	77·37 W
151	Tuyün (tōō′yün′) . . . . China	26·18 N	107·40 E
133	Tuz Gölü (L.) . . . . Tur.	39·00 N	33·30 E
127	Tuzla (tōōz′lȧ) . . . . Yugo.	44·33 N	18·46 E
118	Tvedestrand (tvĭ′dhĕ-stränd) . Nor.	58·39 N	8·54 E
118	Tveitsund (tvåt′sōōnd) . . . . . . Nor.	59·03 N	8·29 E
	Tver, see Kalinin		
128	Tvertsa (L.) (tvĕr′tsȧ) . . . Sov. Un.	56·58 N	35·22 E
116	Tweed (R.) (twēd) . . . . Scot.	55·32 N	2·35 W
168	Tweeling (twē′lĭng) . . . . S. Afr. (Johannesburg & Pretoria In.)	27·34 S	28·31 E
75	Twelvemile Cr. (twĕlv′mīl) N. Y. (Buffalo In.)	43·13 N	78·58 W
85	Twenty Mile Cr. (twĕn′tĭ mīl) Can. (Toronto In.)	43·09 N	79·49 W
110	Twickenham (twĭk″n-ȧm) Eng. (London In.)	51·26 N	0·20 W
83	Twillingate (twĭl′ĭn-gāt) . . . . . Can.	49·41 N	54·49 W
67	Twin Bridges (twĭn brĭ-jĕz) . Mont.	45·34 N	112·17 W
67	Twin Falls (fôls) . . . . Idaho	42·33 N	114·29 W
75	Twinsburg (twĭnz′bûrg) Ohio (Cleveland In.)	41·19 N	81·26 W
72	Two Butte Cr. (tōō būt) . . . . Colo.	37·39 N	102·45 W
71	Two Harbors . . . . Minn.	47·00 N	91·42 W
73	Two Prairie Bay. (prâ′rĭ bī ōō′) Ark.	34·48 N	92·07 W
71	Two Rivers (rĭv′ẽrz) . . . . Wis.	44·09 N	87·36 W
161	Tyabb . . . . Austl. (Melbourne In.)	38·16 S	145·11 E
121	Tyachev (tyä′chĕf) . . . . . Sov. Un.	48·01 N	23·42 E
146	Tyan' Shan' (Tien-Shan) (Mts.) Sov. Un.-China	42·00 N	78·46 E
129	Tyasmin (R.) (tyȧs-mĭn′) Sov. Un.	49·14 N	32·23 E
167	Tylden (tĭl-dĕn) . S. Afr. (Natal In.)	32·08 S	27·06 E
110	Tyldesley (tĭldz′lē) . . . . Eng.	53·32 N	2·28 W
70	Tyler (tī′lẽr) . . . . Minn.	44·18 N	96·08 W
77	Tyler . . . . Tex.	32·21 N	95·19 W
78	Tylertown (tī′lẽr-toun) . . . . . . Miss.	31·08 N	90·06 W
70	Tyndall (tĭn′dȧl) . . . . S. D.	42·58 N	97·52 W
135	Tyndinskiy . . . . Sov. Un.	55·22 N	124·45 E
116	Tyne (R.) (tīn) . . . . Eng.	54·59 N	1·56 W
116	Tynemouth (tīn′mŭth) . . . . . . Eng.	55·04 N	1·39 W
118	Tynest (tün′sĕt) . . . . Nor.	62·17 N	10·45 E
83	Tyngsboro (tĭnj-bŭr′ô) Mass. (Boston In.)	42·40 N	71·27 W
	Tyre, see Sūr		
118	Tyri Fd. (tü′rē) . . . . Nor.	60·03 N	10·25 E
69	Tyrone (tī′rōn) . . . . N. Mex.	32·40 N	108·20 W
81	Tyrone . . . . Pa.	40·40 N	78·15 W
160	Tyrrell, L. (tĭr′ĕl) . . . . Austl.	35·12 S	143·00 E
113	Tyrrhenian Sea (tĭr-rē′nĭ-ȧn) . . . It.	40·10 N	12·15 E
119	Tyrvää (tür′vȧ) . . . . Fin.	61·19 N	22·51 E
133	Tyub-Karagan, Mys (C.) Sov. Un.	44·30 N	50·10 E
134	Tyukalinsk (tyōō-kȧ-lĭnsk′) Sov. Un.	56·03 N	71·43 E
135	Tyukyan (R.) (tyōōk′yȧn) Sov. Un.	65·42 N	116·09 E
133	Tyuleniy (I.) . . . . Sov. Un.	44·30 N	48·00 E
134	Tyumen' (tyōō-mĕn′) . . . Sov. Un.	57·02 N	65·28 E
134	Tyura-Tam . . . . Sov. Un.	46·00 N	63·15 E
92	Tzucacab (tzōō-kä-kä′b) Mex. (Yucatan In.)	20·06 N	89·03 W
148	Tz'uhsien (tsĕ′sĭăn) . . . . China	36·22 N	114·23 E
151	Tzu Shui (R.) (tsōō) . . . . China	26·50 N	111·00 E
148	Tzuya (R.) (zhĕ′yä) . . . . China	38·38 N	116·31 E
148	Tzuyang (tsĕ′yäng) . . . . China	35·35 N	116·50 E
114	Uarc, Ras (C.) . . . . Mor.	35·31 N	2·45 W
98	Uaupés (wä-ōō′päs) . . . . Braz.	0·02 S	67·03 W
101	Ubá (ōō-bä′) Braz. (Rio de Janeiro In.)	21·08 S	42·55 W
163	Ubangi R. (ōō-bäŋ′gē) . . . . Afr.	0·45 N	17·28 E
101	Ubatuba (ōō-bȧ-tōō′bȧ) Braz. (Rio de Janeiro In.)	23·25 S	45·06 W
153	Ube (ōō′bā) . . . . Jap.	33·57 N	131·18 E
124	Ubeda (ōō′bā-dä) . . . . Sp.	38·01 N	3·23 W
99	Uberaba (ōō-bȧ-rä′bȧ) . . . . . . Braz.	19·47 S	47·47 W
99	Uberlândia (ōō-bĕr-lȧ′n-dyȧ) . Braz.	18·54 S	48·11 W
166	Ubombo (ōō-bôm′bō) . . . . . . S. Afr.	27·33 S	32·13 E
154	Ubon Ratchathani (ōō′bŭn rä′chätá-nē) . Thai	15·15 N	104·52 E
129	Ubort' (R.) (ōō-bôrt′) . . . Sov. Un.	51·18 N	27·43 E
124	Ubrique (ōō-brē′kȧ) . . . . Sp.	36·43 N	5·36 W
146	Ubsa Nuur (L.) . . . . Mong.	50·29 N	93·32 E
98	Ucayali (R.) (ōō′kä-yä′lē) . . . . Peru	8·58 S	74·13 W
111	Uccle (ū′kl′) . . . . Bel. (Brussels In.)	50·48 N	4·17 E
136	Uchaly (û-chä′lĭ) Sov. Un. (Urals In.)	54·22 N	59·28 E
134	Uch-Aral (ōōch′ȧ-ral′) . . . Sov. Un.	46·14 N	80·58 E
153	Uchiko (ōō′chē-kō) . . . . Jap.	33·30 N	132·39 E
153	Uchinoura (ōō′chē-nō-ōō′rȧ) . . Jap.	31·16 N	131·03 E
136	Uchinskoye Vodokhranilishche L. (ōōch-ĕn′skô-yĕ vô-dô-ĸrȧ-nĭ′lĭ-shchĕ) Sov. Un. (Moscow In.)	56·08 N	37·44 E
152	Uchiura-Wan (B.) (ōō′chē-ōō′rä wän) . Jap.	42·20 N	140·44 E
142	Uch-Korgon . . . . Sov. Un.	37·22 N	68·41 E
	Uch Turfan, see Wushih		
135	Uchur (R.) (ōō-chōōr′) . . . Sov. Un.	58·27 N	131·34 E
135	Uda (R.) (ōō′dȧ) . . . . Sov. Un.	52·28 N	110·51 E
135	Uda (R.) . . . . Sov. Un.	53·54 N	131·29 E
142	Udaipur (ōō-dŭ′ē-pōōr) . . . . . India	24·41 N	73·41 E
129	Uday (R.) (ōō-dĭ′) . . . . . . Sov. Un.	50·45 N	32·13 E
118	Uddevalla (ōōd′dē-väl-ȧ) . . . . Swe.	58·21 N	11·55 E
126	Udine (ōō′dē-nȧ) . . . . It.	46·05 N	13·14 E
134	Udmurt (A. S. S. R.) . . . . Sov. Un.	57·00 N	52·17 E
154	Udon Thani . . . . Thai.	17·31 N	102·51 E
135	Udskaya Guba (B.) . . . . . Sov. Un.	55·00 N	136·30 E
165	Ueb Gestro R. (wĕb gĕs′tro) . . Eth.	6·25 N	41·21 E
120	Ueckermünde (ü′kĕr-mün-dĕ) . Ger.	53·43 N	14·01 E

ăt; finăl; rāte; senâte; ärm; àsk; sofȧ; fâre; ch-choose; dh-as th in other; bē; êvent; bĕt; recĕnt; craterẽ; g-go; gh-guttural g; bĭt; ĭ-short neutral; rīde: ĸ-guttural k as ch in German ich;

Page	Name Pronunciation Region	Lat. °′	Long. °′
153	Ueda (wä'dä) Jap.	36·26 N	138·16 E
135	Uelen (wĕ-lĕn') Sov. Un.	66·23 N	179·58 E
165	Uele R. (wä'lå) Con. L.	3·34 N	23·23 E
136	Ufa (ōō'fá) Sov. Un. (Urals In.)	54·45 N	55·57 E
132	Ufa (R.) Sov. Un.	56·00 N	57·05 E
166	Ugab (R.) (ōō'gäb) S. W. Afr.	21·10 S	14·00 E
166	Ugalla (R.) (ōō-gä'lä) Tan.	6·09 S	32·30 E
163	Uganda (ōō-gän'dä) (û-găn'dȧ) Afr.	2·00 N	32·28 E
64	Ugashik L. (ōō'gà-shĕk) Alaska	57·36 N	157·10 W
167	Ugie (ōō'jē) S. Afr. (Natal In.)	31·13 S	28·14 E
135	Uglegorsk (ōō-glĕ-gôrsk) Sov. Un.	49·00 N	142·31 E
136	Ugleural'sk (ōōg-lĕ-ōō-rálsk') Sov. Un. (Urals In.)	58·58 N	57·35 E
128	Uglich (ōōg-lēch') Sov. Un.	57·33 N	38·19 E
136	Uglitskiy (ōōg-lĭt'skĭ) Sov. Un. (Urals In.)	53·50 N	60·18 E
128	Uglovka (ōōg-lôf'kȧ) Sov. Un.	58·14 N	33·24 E
128	Ugra (R.) (ōōg'rȧ) Sov. Un.	54·43 N	34·20 E
127	Ugŭrchin Bul.	43·06 N	24·23 E
121	Uherske Hradiště (ōō-hĕr'skyĕ hrä-dĕsh'tyĕ) Czech.	49·01 N	17·28 E
80	Uhrichsville (ū'rĭks-vĭl) Ohio	40·25 N	81·20 W
152	Uiju (ōō'ējōō) Kor.	40·09 N	124·33 E
133	Uil (R.) (ōō-ēl') Sov. Un.	49·30 N	55·10 E
69	Uinkaret Plat. (ū-ĭn'kâr-ĕt) Ariz.	36·43 N	113·15 W
136	Uinskoye (ōō-ĭn'skô-yĕ) Sov. Un. (Urals In.)	56·53 N	56·25 E
69	Uinta (R.) (ū-ĭn'tȧ) Utah	40·25 N	109·55 W
74	Uintah (ū-ĭn'tȧ) Utah (Salt Lake City In.)	41·09 N	111·56 W
69	Uintah and Ouray Ind. Res. Utah	39·55 N	109·20 W
167	Uitenhage S. Afr. (Natal In.)	33·46 S	25·26 E
111	Uithorn Neth. (Amsterdam In.)	52·13 N	4·49 E
153	Uji (ōō'jē) Jap. (Ōsaka In.)	34·53 N	135·49 E
166	Ujiji (ōō-jē'jē) Tan.	4·57 S	29·43 E
153	Uji-Yamada (ōō'jē yä'mä-dä) Jap.	34·30 N	136·43 E
142	Ujjain (ōō-jŭēn) India	23·13 N	75·49 E
68	Ukiah (ū-kī'ȧ) Calif.	35·09 N	122·12 W
134	Ukhta Sov. Un.	63·08 N	53·42 E
132	Ukhta (ōōk'tȧ) Sov. Un.	65·22 N	31·30 E
119	Ukmergė (ōōk'mĕr-ghȧ) Sov. Un.	55·16 N	24·45 E
130	Ukrainian (S. S. R.) (ū'krān) Sov. Un.	49·15 N	30·15 E
153	Uku (I.) (ōōk'ōō) Jap.	33·18 N	129·02 E
146	Ulaan Baatar Mong.	47·56 N	107·00 E
146	Ulaan Goom Mong.	50·23 N	92·14 E
135	Ulan Ude (ōō'lan ōō'dȧ) Sov. Un.	51·59 N	107·41 E
152	Ulchin (ōōl'chĕn') Kor.	36·57 N	129·26 E
127	Ulcinj (Dulcigno) (ōōl'tsēn') Yugo.	41·56 N	19·15 E
143	Ulhās (R.) India (Bombay In.)	19·13 N	73·03 E
166	Ulindi (R.) (ōō-lĭn'dē) Con. L.	1·47 S	26·29 E
128	Ulla (ōōl'ȧ) Sov. Un.	55·14 N	29·15 E
128	Ulla (R.) Sov. Un.	54·58 N	29·03 E
124	Ulla (R.) (ōō'lä) Sp.	42·45 N	8·33 W
152	Ullŭng (I.) (ōōl'lōōng') Kor.	37·29 N	130·50 E
120	Ulm (ōōlm) Ger.	48·24 N	9·59 E
47	Ulmer, Mt. (ŭl'mûr') Ant.	77·30 S	86·00 W
118	Ulricehamn (ōōl-rē'sĕ-häm) Swe.	57·49 N	13·23 E
152	Ulsan (ōōl'sän') Kor.	35·35 N	129·22 E
116	Ulster (Reg.) (ŭl'stẽr) Ire.-N. Ire.	54·41 N	7·10 W
92	Ulua R. (ōō-lōō'ȧ) Hond.	15·49 N	87·45 W
133	Ulukisla (ōō-lōō-kēsh'lȧ) Tur.	36·40 N	34·30 E
152	Ulunga (ōō-lōōn'gȧ) Sov. Un.	46·16 N	136·29 E
136	Ulu-Telyak (ōō lōō'tĕlyăk) Sov. Un. (Urals In.)	54·54 N	57·01 E
160	Ulverstone (ŭl'vẽr-stŭn) Austl.	41·20 S	146·22 E
118	Ulvik (ōōl'vĕk) Nor.	60·35 N	6·53 E
136	Ul'yanovka (ōō-lyä'nôf-kȧ) Sov. Un. (Leningrad In.)	59·38 N	30·47 E
132	Ul'yanovsk (ōō-lyä'nôfsk) Sov. Un.	54·20 N	53·05 E
72	Ulysses (ū-lĭs'ēz) Kans.	37·34 N	101·25 W
120	Ülzen (ült'sĕn) Ger.	52·58 N	10·34 E
91	Umán (ōō-män') Mex.	20·52 N	89·44 W
129	Uman' (ōō-män'') Sov. Un.	48·44 N	30·13 E
66	Umatilla Ind. Res. (ū-mȧ-tĭl'ȧ) Ore.	45·38 N	118·35 W
82	Umbagog (L.) (ŭm-bā'gôg) Maine	44·44 N	71·20 W
143	Umberpādā India (Bombay In.)	19·28 N	73·04 E
126	Umbria (Reg.) (ŭm'brĭ-ȧ) It.	42·53 N	12·22 E
112	Ume (R.) (ōō'mĕ) Swe.	64·57 N	18·51 E
112	Umeå (ōō'mĕ-ô) Swe.	63·48 N	20·29 E
167	Umgeni (R.) (ōōm-gä'nē) S. Afr. (Natal In.)	29·38 S	30·53 E
167	Umhlatuzi (R.) (ōōm'hlȧ-tōō'zĭ) S. Afr. (Natal In.)	28·47 S	31·17 E
64	Umiat (ōō'mĭ-ăt) Alaska	69·20 N	152·28 W
167	Umkomaas (ōōm-kō'mäs) S. Afr. (Natal In.)	30·12 S	30·48 E
167	Umkomaas (R.) S. Afr. (Natal In.)	30·10 S	30·30 E
167	Umlazi (R.) S. Afr. (Natal In.)	29·52 S	30·42 E
64	Umnak (I.) (ōōm'näk) Alaska	53·10 N	169·08 W
64	Umnak P. Alaska	53·10 N	168·04 W
66	Umpqua R. (ŭmp'kwȧ) Ore.	43·42 N	123·50 W
166	Umtali (ōōm-tä'lē) S. Rh.	18·49 S	32·39 E
167	Umtamvuna (R.) (ōōm-täm-vōō'nȧ) S. Afr. (Natal In.)	30·43 S	29·53 E
167	Umtata (ōōm-tä'tȧ) S. Afr. (Natal In.)	31·36 S	28·47 E
167	Umtata (R.) S. Afr. (Natal In.)	31·48 S	29·03 E
167	Umtentweni S. Afr. (Natal In.)	30·41 S	30·29 E
167	Umvoti (R.) (ōōm-vō'tĭ) S. Afr. (Natal In.)	29·18 S	30·52 E
167	Umzimkulu (ōōm-zēm-kōō'lōō) S. Afr. (Natal In.)	30·12 S	29·53 E
167	Umzimkulu (R.) S. Afr. (Natal In.)	30·12 S	29·57 E
167	Umzimvubu (R.) (ōōm-zēm-vōō'bōō) S. Afr. (Natal In.)	31·22 S	29·20 E

Page	Name Pronunciation Region	Lat. °′	Long. °′
167	Umzinto (ōōm-zĭn'tō) S. Afr. (Natal In.)	30·19 S	30·41 E
126	Una (R.) (ōō'nȧ) Yugo.	44·38 N	16·10 E
64	Unalakleet (ū-nȧ-lăk'lēt) Alaska	63·50 N	160·42 W
64	Unalaska (ū-nȧ-lăs'kȧ) Alaska	53·30 N	166·20 W
99	Unare (R.) Ven. (In.)	9·45 N	65·12 W
99	Unare, Laguna de (L.) (lä-gōō'nä-de-ōō-nä'rĕ) Ven. (In.)	10·07 N	65·23 W
144	Unayzah Sau. Ar.	25·50 N	44·02 E
85	Uncas (ŭŋ'kȧs) Can. (Edmonton In.)	53·30 N	113·02 W
98	Uncía (ōōn'sē-ä) Bol.	18·28 S	66·32 W
69	Uncompahgre (R.) Colo.	38·20 N	107·45 W
69	Uncompahgre Pk. (ŭn-kŭm-pä'grē) Colo.	38·00 N	107·30 W
69	Uncompahgre Plat. Colo.	38·40 N	108·40 W
167	Underberg (ŭn'dẽr-bûrg) S. Afr. (Natal In.)	29·51 S	29·32 E
165	Undo Eth.	6·37 N	38·29 E
128	Unecha (ōō-nĕ'chȧ) Sov. Un.	32·51 N	32·44 E
80	Ungava B. (ŭŋ-gä'vȧ) Can.	59·46 N	67·18 W
87	Ungava Pen. Can.	60·38 N	74·00 W
100	União da Vitória (ōō-nê-ouN' dä vē-tô'ryä) Braz.	26·17 S	51·13 W
126	Unije (I.) (ōō'nê-yĕ) Yugo.	44·39 N	14·10 E
64	Unimak (I.) (ōō-nê-mäk') Alaska	54·30 N	163·35 W
64	Unimak P. Alaska	54·22 N	165·22 W
78	Union (ūn'yŭn) Miss.	32·35 N	89·07 W
73	Union Mo.	38·28 N	90·59 W
79	Union N. C.	34·42 N	81·40 W
66	Union Ore.	45·13 N	117·52 W
65	Union City Calif. (San Francisco In.)	37·36 N	122·01 W
80	Union City Ind.	40·10 N	85·00 W
80	Union City Mich.	42·00 N	85·10 W
81	Union City Pa.	41·50 N	79·50 W
78	Union City Tenn.	36·25 N	89·04 W
94	Union de Reves (ōō-nyō'n-dĕ-rĕ-vĕ's) Cuba	22·45 N	81·30 W
90	Union de San Antonio (săn ăn-tō'nyō) Mex.	21·07 N	101·56 W
90	Union de Tula (tōō'lä) Mex.	19·57 N	104·14 W
75	Union Grove (ūn'yȧn grōv) Wis. (Milwaukee In.)	42·41 N	88·03 W
91	Unión Hidalgo (ê-dä'l-gô) Mex.	16·29 N	94·51 W
75	Union Hill Ill. (Chicago In.)	41·06 N	88·09 W
78	Union Point Ga.	33·37 N	83·08 W
78	Union Springs (sprĭngz) Ala.	32·08 N	85·43 W
78	Uniontown (ūn'yȧn-toun) Ala.	32·26 N	87·30 W
75	Uniontown Ohio (Cleveland In.)	40·58 N	81·25 W
81	Uniontown Pa.	39·55 N	79·45 W
85	Unionville (ūn'yȧn-vĭl) Can. (Toronto In.)	43·52 N	79·19 W
73	Unionville Mo.	40·28 N	92·58 W
155	Unisan (ōō-nē'sän) Phil. (Manila In.)	13·50 N	121·59 E
62	Unitas, Mts. (ū-nĭ'tăs) U. S.	40·35 N	111·00 W
163	United Arab Republic (Egypt) (ē'jĭpt) Afr.	26·58 N	27·01 E
69	United Pueblo Ind. Res. (u-nĭt'ĕd pōō-ĕb'lō) (pwā'blō) N. Mex.	35·30 N	107·00 W
49	United States N. A.	38·00 N	110·00 W
75	Unity (ū'nĭ-tĭ) Pa. (Pittsburgh In.)	40·49 N	79·46 W
80	Universal (ū-nĭ-vûr'săl) Ind.	39·35 N	87·30 W
124	Universales, Montes (Mts.) (mōn'tås ōō-nē-vĕr-sä'lås) Sp.	40·21 N	1·43 W
74	University City (ū'nĭ-vûr'sĭ-tĭ) Mo. (St. Louis In.)	38·40 N	90·19 W
74	University Park Tex. (Dallas, Fort Worth In.)	32·51 N	96·48 W
123	Unna (ōō'nä) Ger. (Ruhr In.)	51·32 N	7·41 E
116	Unst (I.) (ōōnst) Scot.	60·50 N	1·24 W
111	Unterhaching (ōōn'tĕr-hä-kĕng) Ger. (Munich In.)	48·03 N	11·38 E
133	Unye (ün'yĕ) Tur.	41·00 N	37·10 E
132	Unzha (R.) (ōōn'zhȧ) Sov. Un.	57·45 N	44·10 E
165	Uorra Ilu (vō'rä) Eth.	10·39 N	39·21 E
128	Upa (R.) (ōō'pȧ) Sov. Un.	53·54 N	36·48 E
163	Upanda, Sierra do (Mts.) (sē-ĕ'r-rä-dô-ōō-pä'n-dä) Ang.	13·15 S	14·15 E
98	Upata (ōō-pä'tä) Ven.	7·58 N	62·27 W
166	Upington (ŭp'ĭng-tŭn) S. Afr.	28·25 S	21·15 E
74	Upland (ŭp'lănd) Calif. (Los Angeles In.)	34·06 N	117·38 W
157	Upolu Pt. (ōō-pô'lōō) Hawaii (In.)	20·15 N	155·48 W
86	Upper Arrow (L.) Can.	50·28 N	117·29 W
84	Upper Darby (där'bĭ) Pa. (Philadelphia In.)	39·58 N	75·16 W
70	Upper de Lacs (R.) (dĕ lăk) N. D.	48·58 N	101·55 W
84	Upper Falls (fôlz') Md. (Baltimore In.)	39·26 N	76·24 W
154	Upper Kapuas Mts. Mala.	1·45 N	112·06 E
167	Upper Kubusi (kōō-bōō'sĭ) S. Afr. (Natal In.)	32·37 S	27·31 E
66	Upper L. (ŭp'ẽr) Nev.	41·42 N	119·59 W
65	Upper Mill (mĭl) Wash. (Seattle In.)	47·11 N	121·55 W
71	Upper Red L. (rĕd) Minn.	48·14 N	94·53 W
80	Upper Sandusky (săn-dŭs'kē) Ohio	40·50 N	83·20 W
65	Upper San Leandro Res. (ŭp'ẽr săn lē-ăn'drō) Calif. (San Francisco In.)	37·47 N	122·04 W
163	Upper Volta (vôl'tȧ) Afr.	11·46 N	3·18 E
110	Uppingham (ŭp'ĭng-ȧm) Eng.	52·35 N	0·43 W
118	Uppsala (ōōp'sȧ-lä) Swe.	59·53 N	17·39 E
83	Uptown (ŭp'toun) Mass. (Boston In.)	42·10 N	71·36 W
153	Uraga (ōō'rȧ-gä') Jap. (Tōkyō In.)	35·15 N	139·43 E
153	Uraga-Kaikyō (Str.) (ōō'rä-gä kī'kyō) Jap. (Tōkyō In.)	35·11 N	139·44 E

Page	Name Pronunciation Region	Lat. °′	Long. °′
133	Ural (R.) (ōō-räl'') (ū-rôl) Sov. Un.	49·50 N	51·30 E
130	Urals (Mts.) Sov. Un.	56·28 N	58·13 E
133	Ural'sk (ōō-rálsk') Sov. Un.	51·15 N	51·10 E
143	Uran (ōō-răn') India (Bombay In.)	18·53 N	72·56 E
86	Uranium City Can.	59·34 N	108·59 W
153	Urawa (ōō'rä-wä') Jap. (Tōkyō In.)	35·52 N	139·39 E
153	Urayasu (ōō'rä-yä'sōō) Jap. (Tōkyō In.)	35·40 N	139·54 W
129	Urazovo (ōō-rȧ'zô-vô) Sov. Un.	50·08 N	38·03 E
80	Urbana (ûr-băn'ȧ) Ill.	40·10 N	88·15 W
80	Urbana Ohio	40·05 N	83·50 W
126	Urbino (ōōr-bē'nô) It.	43·43 N	12·37 E
133	Urda (ōōr'dȧ) Sov. Un.	48·50 N	47·30 E
155	Urdaneta (ōōr-dä-nā'tä) Phil. (Manila In.)	15·59 N	120·34 E
101	Urdinarrain (ōōr-dē-när-rȧē'n) Arg. (Buenos Aires In.)	32·43 S	58·53 W
134	Urdzhar (ōōrd-zhär') Sov. Un.	47·28 N	82·00 E
133	Urfa (ōōr'fȧ) Tur.	37·20 N	38·45 E
103	Urgench (ōōr-gĕnch') Sov. Un.	41·32 N	60·33 E
136	Uritsk (ōō'rĭtsk) Sov. Un. (Leningrad In.)	59·50 N	30·11 E
127	Urla (ōōr'lȧ) Tur.	38·20 N	26·44 E
136	Urman (ōōr'mán) Sov. Un. (Urals In.)	54·53 N	56·52 E
152	Urmi (R.) (ōōr'mē) Sov. Un.	48·50 N	134·00 E
98	Urrao (ōōr-rä'ô) Col. (In.)	6·19 N	76·11 W
128	Urshel'skiy (ōōr-shĕl'skēē) Sov. Un.	55·50 N	40·11 E
98	Urubamba (R.) (ōō-rōō-bäm'bä) Peru	11·48 S	72·34 W
100	Uruguaianá (ōō-rōō-gwī-ä'nȧ) Braz.	29·45 S	57·00 W
96	Uruguay (ōō-rōō-gwī') (ū'rōō-gwä) S. A.	32·45 S	56·00 W
100	Uruguay, Rio (R.) (rē'ō-ōō-rōō-gwī) Braz.	27·05 S	55·15 W
	Urumchi, see Tihua		
146	Urungu R. (ōō-rōōŋ'gōō') China	46·31 N	87·44 E
135	Urup (I.) (ōō'rōōp') Sov. Un.	46·08 N	151·00 E
133	Uryupinsk (ōōr'yōō-pēn-sk') Sov. Un.	50·50 N	42·00 E
142	Urzan W. Pak.	33·03 N	70·39 E
127	Urziceni (ōō-zē-chĕn'') Rom.	44·45 N	26·42 E
132	Usa (R.) (ōō'sȧ) Sov. Un.	66·00 N	58·20 E
133	Uş ak (ōō'shȧk) Tur.	39·50 N	29·15 E
166	Usakos (ōō-sä'kōs) S. W. Afr.	22·00 S	15·40 E
136	Ushaki (ōō'shá-kĭ) Sov. Un. (Leningrad In.)	59·28 N	31·00 E
136	Ushakovskoye (ōō-shá-kôv'skô-yĕ) Sov. Un. (Urals In.)	56·18 N	62·23 E
153	Ushiku (ōō'shê-kōō) Jap. (Tōkyō In.)	35·24 N	140·09 E
153	Ushimado (ōō'shē-mä'dō) Jap.	34·37 N	134·09 E
100	Ushuaia (ōō-shōō-ī'ä) Arg.	54·46 S	68·24 W
133	Üsküdar Tur.	40·55 N	29·00 E
128	Usman' (ōōs-mán') Sov. Un.	52·03 N	39·40 E
136	Usol'ye (ōō-sô'lyĕ) Sov. Un. (Urals In.)	59·24 N	56·40 E
134	Usol'ye-Sibirskoye (ōō-sô'lyĕsĭ' bēr'skô-yĕ) Sov. Un.	52·44 N	103·46 E
100	Uspallata P. (ōōs-pä-lyä'tä) Arg.-Chile	32·47 S	70·08 W
91	Uspanapa (R.) (ōōs-pä-nä'pä) Mex.	17·43 N	94·14 W
122	Ussel (üs'ĕl) Fr.	45·33 N	2·17 E
147	Ussuri (R.) (ōō-sōō'rē) China	46·30 N	133·56 E
135	Ussuriysk Sov. Un.	43·48 N	132·09 E
135	Ust'-Bol'sheretsk Sov. Un.	52·41 N	157·00 E
126	Ustica, I. di (ē'sō-lä-dē-ōōs'tē-kä) It.	38·43 N	12·11 E
120	Usti nad Labem (Aussig) (ōōs'tē) Czech.	50·39 N	14·02 E
129	Ustinovka (ōōs-tē'nôf-kä) Sov. Un.	47·59 N	32·31 E
136	Ust'-Izhora (ōōst-ēz'hô-rȧ) Sov. Un. (Leningrad In.)	59·49 N	30·35 E
120	Ustka (ōōst'kȧ) Pol.	54·34 N	16·52 E
135	Ust'-Kamchatsk Sov. Un.	56·13 N	162·18 E
134	Ust'-Kamenogorsk Sov. Un.	49·58 N	80·43 E
136	Ust'-Katav (ōōst kȧ'tȧf) Sov. Un. (Urals In.)	54·55 N	58·12 E
136	Ust'-Kishert' (ōōst kē'shĕrt) Sov. Un. (Urals In.)	57·21 N	57·13 E
132	Ust'-Kulom (kōō'lŭn) Sov. Un.	61·38 N	54·00 E
135	Ust'-Maya (mä'yȧ) Sov. Un.	60·33 N	134·43 E
135	Ust' Olenëk Sov. Un.	72·52 N	120·15 E
135	Ust-Ordynskiy (ōōst-ôr-dyĕnsk'ĭ) Sov. Un.	52·47 N	104·39 E
135	Ust' Penzhimo Sov. Un.	63·00 N	165·10 E
134	Ust' Port (ōōst'pôrt') Sov. Un.	69·20 N	83·41 E
132	Ust'-Tsil'ma (tsĭl'mȧ) Sov. Un.	65·25 N	52·10 E
135	Ust'-Tyrma (tor'mȧ) Sov. Un.	50·27 N	131·17 E
136	Ust'Uls (ōōls) Sov. Un. (Urals In.)	60·35 N	58·32 E
130	Ust'-Urt, Plato (Plat.) (ōōrt) Sov. Un.	44·03 N	54·58 E
128	Ustyuzhna (yōōzh'nȧ) Sov. Un.	58·49 N	36·19 E
153	Usuki (ōō'sōō-kē') Jap.	33·06 N	131·47 E
92	Usulutan (ōō-sōō-lä-tän') Sal.	13·22 N	88·25 W
91	Usumacinta (R.) (ōō'sōō-mä-sēn'tō) Mex.	18·24 N	92·30 W
166	Usumbura (ōō-sōōm-bōō'rȧ) Burundi	3·19 S	29·28 E
136	Us'va (ōōs'vȧ) Sov. Un. (Urals In.)	58·41 N	57·38 E
62	Utah (State) (ū'tô) U. S.	39·25 N	112·40 W
69	Utah (L.) Utah	40·10 N	111·55 W
143	Utan India (Bombay In.)	19·27 N	72·43 E
69	Ute Mtn. Ind. Res. N. Mex.	36·57 N	108·34 W
119	Utena (ōō'tā-nä) Sov. Un.	55·32 N	25·40 E
167	Utete (ōō-tā'tȧ) Tan.	8·05 S	38·47 E

ng-sing; ŋ-baŋk; N-nasalized n; nŏd; cŏmmit; ōld; ôbey; ôrder; fōōd; fŏŏt; ou-out; s-soft; sh-dish; th-thin; pūre; ûnite; ûrn; stŭd; circŭs; ü-as "y" in study; '-indeterminate vowel.

Page Name Pronunciation Region Lat. °′ Long. °′

75 Utica (ū′tĭ-kȧ) Ind. (Louisville In.) 38·20 N 85·39 W
81 Utica .... N. Y. 43·05 N 75·10 W
124 Utiel (ōō-tyål′) .... Sp. 39·34 N 1·13 W
75 Utika (ū′tĭ-kȧ) Mich. (Detroit In.) 42·37 N 83·02 W
92 Utila I. (ōō-tē′lä) .... Hond. 16·07 N 87·05 W
153 Uto (ōō′tō′) .... Jap. 32·43 N 130·39 E
111 Utrecht (ū′trĕkt) (ü′trĕkt) Neth. (Amsterdam In.) 52·05 N 5·06 E
124 Utrera (ōō-trä′rä) .... Sp. 37·12 N 5·48 W
118 Utsira (I.) (ŭtsĭrä) .... Nor. 59·21 N 4·50 E
153 Utsunomiya (ōōt′sŏŏ-nō′mē-yȧ′) Jap. 36·35 N 139·52 E
154 Uttaradit .... Thai. 17·47 N 100·10 E
142 Uttar Pradesh (State) (ŏŏt-tär-prä-dĕsh) . India 34·19 N 78·40 E
110 Uttoxeter (ŭt-tôk′sē-tẽr) ..... Eng. 52·54 N 1·52 W
89 Utuado (ōō-tōō-ä′dhō) P. R. (Puerto Rico In.) 18·16 N 66·40 W
119 Uusikaupunki (Nystad) (ōō′sĭ-kou′pŏŏŋ-kĭ) (nü′städh) Fin. 60·48 N 21·24 E
76 Uvalde (ū-văl′dē) .... Tex. 29·14 N 99·47 W
136 Uvel′skiy (ŏŏ-vyĕl′skĭ) Sov. Un. (Urals In.) 54·27 N 60·22 E
166 Uvira (ōō-vē′rä) .... Con. L. 3·28 S 29·03 E
128 Uvod′ (R.) (ŏŏ-vôd′) .... Sov. Un. 56·52 N 41·03 E
167 Uvongo .... S. Afr. (Natal In.) 30·49 S 30·23 E
153 Uwajima (ōō-wä′jē-mä) .... Jap. 33·12 N 132·35 E
83 Uxbridge (ŭks′brĭj) Mass. (Boston In.) 42·05 N 71·38 W
92 Uxmal (Ruins) (ōō′x-mä′l) Mex. (Yucatan In.) 20·22 N 89·44 W
136 Uy R. (ōōy) . . Sov. Un. (Urals In.) 54·05 N 62·11 E
136 Uyskoye (ûy′skô-yĕ) Sov. Un. (Urals In.) 54·22 N 60·01 E
98 Uyuni (ōō-yōō′nē) .... Bol. 20·28 S 66·45 W
98 Uyuni, Salar de (Salt Flat) (sä-lär-dĕ) . Bol. 20·58 S 67·09 W
130 Uzbek S. S. R. (ŏŏz-bĕk′) . Sov. Un. 42·42 N 60·00 E
133 Uzen, Bol′shoy (R.) ..... Sov. Un. 49·50 N 49·35 E
129 Uzh (R.) (ŏŏzh) .... Sov. Un. 51·07 N 29·05 E
121 Uzhgorod (ŏŏzh′gô-rôt) . . Sov. Un. 48·38 N 22·18 E
127 Uzunköpru (ōō′zōōn′kû-prü) . . Tur. 41·17 N 26·42 E
166 Vaal (R.) (väl) .... S. Afr. 28·15 S 24·30 E
168 Vaaldam (L.) .... S. Afr. (Johannesburg & Pretoria In.) 26·58 S 28·37 E
168 Vaalplaas .... S. Afr. (Johannesburg & Pretoria In.) 25·39 S 28·56 E
168 Vaalwater .... S. Afr. (Johannesburg & Pretoria In.) 24·17 S 28·08 E
119 Vaasa (vä′så) .... Fin. 63·06 N 21·39 E
121 Vác (väts) .... Hung. 47·46 N 19·10 E
95 Vache, Ile À (I.) (väsh) ...... Hai. 18·05 N 73·40 W
112 Vadsö (vädh′sû) .... Nor. 70·08 N 29·52 E
118 Vadstena (väd′stĭ′nå) .... Swe. 58·27 N 14·53 E
120 Vaduz (vä′dŏŏts) .... Liech. 47·10 N 9·32 E
132 Vaga (R.) (va′gȧ) .... Sov. Un. 61·55 N 42·30 E
118 Vågsöy (I.) .... Nor. 61·58 N 4·44 E
121 Váh R. (väk) .... Czech. 48·07 N 17·52 E
142 Vaigai (R.) .... India 10·20 N 78·13 E
134 Vakh (R.) (vak) .... Sov. Un. 61·30 N 81·33 E
127 Valachia (Reg.) .... Rom. 44·45 N 24·17 E
85 Valcartier-Village (väl-kärt-yĕ′ vē-läzh′) Can. (Quebec In.) 46·56 N 71·28 W
128 Valdai Hills (vål-dī′ gô′rĭ) Sov. Un. 57·50 N 32·35 E
128 Valday (Valdai) (vål-dī′) . Sov. Un. 57·58 N 33·13 E
125 Valdemorillo (väl-då-mô-rēl′yō) Sp. (Madrid In.) 40·30 N 4·04 W
124 Valdepeñas (väl-då-pān′yäs) . . . Sp. 38·46 N 3·22 W
124 Valderaduey (R.) (väl-dĕ-rä-dwĕ′y) . Sp. 41·39 N 5·35 W
100 Valdés, Pen. (väl-dĕ′s) .... Arg. 42·15 S 63·15 W
64 Valdez (văl′dĕz) .... Alaska 61·10 N 146·18 W
125 Valdilecha (väl-dē-lā′chä) Sp. (Madrid In.) 40·17 N 3·19 W
100 Valdivia (väl-dē′vä) .... Chile 39·47 S 73·13 W
98 Valdivia (väl-dē′vēä) .... Col. (In.) 7·10 N 75·26 W
87 Val d′ Or .... Can. 48·03 N 77·50 W
78 Valdosta (văl-dŏs′tȧ) .... Ga. 30·50 N 83·18 W
124 Valdovino (väl-dô-vē′nō) ...... Sp. 43·36 N 8·05 W
66 Vale (vāl) .... Ore. 43·59 N 117·14 W
99 Valença (vä-lĕn′sȧ) .... Braz. 13·43 S 38·58 W
122 Valence-sur-Rhône (vä-lĕns-sür-rōn′) . Fr. 44·56 N 4·54 E
124 Valencia (vä-lĕ′n-syä) .... Port. 42·03 N 8·36 W
125 Valencia (vä-lĕn′thē-ä) .... Sp. 39·26 N 0·23 W
124 Valencia .... Sp. 39·34 N 7·13 W
99 Valencia (vä-lĕn′syä) . . . Ven. (In.) 10·11 N 68·00 W
125 Valencia (Reg.) (vä-lĕn′thē-ä) . Sp. 39·08 N 0·43 W
116 Valencia (I.) (vȧ-lĕn′shȧ) ..... Ire. 51·55 N 10·26 W
99 Valencia, Lago de (L.) . . Ven. (In.) 10·11 N 67·45 W
122 Valenciennes (vå-län-syĕn′) . . . . Fr. 50·24 N 3·36 E
70 Valentine (vȧ lăn-tē-nyē′) . . . Nebr. 42·52 N 100·34 W
98 Valera (vä-lĕ′rä) .... Ven. 9·12 N 70·45 W
136 Valerianovsk (vå-lĕ-rĭ-ä′nôvsk) Sov. Un. (Urals In.) 58·47 N 59·34 E
128 Valga (väl′gȧ) .... Sov. Un. 57·47 N 26·03 E
167 Valhalla (văl-hăl-ȧ) .... S. Afr. (Johannesburg & Pretoria In.) 25·49 S 28·09 E
67 Valier (vă-lēr′) .... Mont. 48·17 N 112·14 W
127 Valjevo (väl′yå-vô) .... Yugo. 44·17 N 19·57 E
129 Valki (väl′kē) .... Sov. Un. 49·49 N 35·40 E
92 Valladolid (väl-yä-dhô-lēdh′) Mex. (Yucatan In.) 20·39 N 88·13 W
124 Valladolid (väl-yä-dhô-lēdh′) . . Sp. 41·41 N 4·41 W
125 Vall de Uxo′ (väl-dĕ-ōōx-ŏ′) . . . Sp. 39·50 N 0·15 W
98 Valle (Dept.) (vä′l-yĕ) . . Col. (In.) 4·03 N 76·13 W
68 Valle, Arroyo del (ä-rō′yō dĕl väl′yȧ) . Calif. 37·36 N 121·43 W
125 Vallecas (väl-yä′käs) Sp. (Madrid In.) 40·23 N 3·37 W
76 Valle de Allende (väl′yä dä äl-yĕn′då) . Mex. 26·55 N 105·25 W
90 Valle de Bravo (brä′vô) ..... Mex. 19·12 N 100·07 W
99 Valle de Guanape (vä′l-yĕ-dĕ-gwä-nä′pĕ) Ven. (In.) 9·54 N 65·41 W
98 Valle de la Pascua (lä-pä′s-kōōä) Ven. 9·12 N 65·08 W
90 Valle de Santiago (sän-tē-ä′gô) Mex. 20·23 N 101·11 W
98 Valledupar (dōō-pär′) .... Col. 10·13 N 73·39 W
98 Valle Grande (grän′dä) .... Bol. 18·27 S 64·03 W
65 Vallejo (vä-yä′hō) (vă-lā′hō) Calif. (San Francisco In.) 38·06 N 122·15 W
90 Vallejo, Sierra de (Mts.) (sē-ĕ′r-rä-dĕ-väl-yĕ′kô) . Mex. 21·00 N 105·10 W
100 Vallenar (väl-yå-när′) .... Chile 28·39 S 70·52 W
125 Vallerano (R.) (vä-lĕ-rä′nô) It. (Rome In.) 41·46 N 12·29 E
114 Valletta (väl-lĕt′ä) .... Malta 35·50 N 14·29 E
74 Valle Vista (văl′yȧ vĭs′tȧ) Calif. (Los Angeles In.) 33·45 N 116·53 W
70 Valley City .... N. D. 46·55 N 97·59 W
75 Valley City (văl′ĭ) Ohio (Cleveland In.) 41·14 N 81·56 W
73 Valley Falls .... Kans. 39·21 N 95·26 W
84 Valley Falls (fôls) R. I. (Providence In.) 41·55 N 71·23 W
85 Valleyfield (văl′ē-fēld) Can. (Montreal In.) 45·16 N 74·09 W
74 Valley Park (văl′ē pärk) Mo. (St. Louis In.) 38·33 N 90·30 W
84 Valley Stream (văl′ĭ strēm) N. Y. (New York In.) 40·39 N 73·42 W
126 Valli di Comácchio (L.) (vä′lē-dē-kô-mä′chyô) . It. 44·38 S 12·15 E
95 Vallière (väl-yâr′) .... Hai. 19·30 N 71·55 W
101 Vallimanca (R.) (väl-yē-mä′n-kä) Arg. (Buenos Aires In.) 36·21 S 60·55 W
125 Valls (väls) .... Sp. 41·15 N 1·15 E
86 Val Marie .... Can. 49·10 N 107·59 W
119 Valmiera (väl′myĕ-rä) . . . Sov. Un. 57·34 N 25·54 E
122 Valognes (vå-lôn′y′) .... Fr. 49·32 N 1·30 W
Valona, see Vlorë
101 Valparaíso (väl′pä-rä-ē′sô) Chile (Santiago In.) 33·02 S 71·32 W
80 Valparaiso (văl-pȧ-rā′zô) ..... Ind. 41·25 N 87·05 W
90 Valparaiso .... Mex. 22·49 N 103·33 W
101 Valpariso (Prov.) Chile (Santiago In.) 32·58 S 71·23 W
122 Valréas (vål-rà-ä′) .... Fr. 45·25 N 4·56 E
Valsbaai, see False B.
155 Valsch, Kap (C.) (välsh) . W. Irian 8·30 S 137·15 E
168 Valsch R. .... S. Afr. (Johannesburg & Pretoria In.) 27·32 S 26·51 E
136 Valuyevo (vå-lōō′yĕ-vô) Sov. Un. (Moscow In.) 55·34 N 37·21 E
129 Valuyki (vå-lōō-ē′kē) . . . . Sov. Un. 50·14 N 38·04 E
74 Val Verde (văl vûr′dē) Calif. (Los Angeles In.) 33·51 N 117·15 W
95 Valverde (väl-vĕ′r-dĕ) . Dom. Rep. 19·35 N 71·10 W
124 Valverde del Camino (väl-vĕr-dĕ-dĕl-kä-mē′nō) . Sp. 37·34 N 6·44 W
142 Vambanād (R.) .... India 10·00 N 76·03 E
133 Van (vȧn) .... Tur. 38·04 N 43·10 E
73 Van Buren (văn bū′rĕn) ..... Ark. 35·26 N 94·20 W
82 Van Buren .... Maine 47·09 N 67·58 W
80 Vanceburg (văns′bûrg) .... Ky. 38·35 N 83·20 W
65 Vancouver (văn-kōō′vẽr) Can. (Vancouver In.) 49·16 N 123·06 W
65 Vancouver . . Wash. (Portland In.) 45·37 N 122·40 W
86 Vancouver I. .... Can. 49·47 N 128·23 W
80 Vandalia (văn-dā′lĭ-ȧ) .... Ill. 39·00 N 89·00 W
73 Vandalia .... Mo. 39·19 N 91·30 W
168 Vanderbijlpark .... S. Afr. (Johannesburg & Pretoria In.) 26·43 S 27·50 E
86 Vanderhoof .... Can. 53·59 N 124·10 W
Van Diemen, see Ōsumi Kaikyō
158 Van Diemen, C. (văndē′mĕn) . Austl. 11·05 S 130·15 E
158 Van Diemen G. .... Austl. 11·50 S 131·30 E
75 Van Dyke (văn dīk) Mich. (Detroit In.) 42·27 N 83·01 W
90 Vanegas (vä-nĕ′gäs) .... Mex. 23·54 N 100·54 W
118 Vänern (L.) .... Swe. 58·52 N 13·17 E
118 Vänersborg (vĕ′nĕrs-bôr′) .... Swe. 58·24 N 12·15 E
167 Vanga (väŋ′gä) .... Ken. 4·38 S 39·10 E
143 Vangani . . . . . India (Bombay In.) 19·07 N 73·15 E
133 Van Gölü (L.) .... Tur. 38·45 N 43·00 E
80 Van Lear (văn lēr′) .... Ky. 37·45 N 82·50 W
122 Vannes (vȧn) .... Fr. 47·42 N 2·46 W
74 Van Nuys (văn nīz′) Calif. (Los Angeles In.) 34·11 N 118·27 W
119 Vantaan (R.) .... Fin. 60·25 N 24·43 E
80 Van Wert (văn wûrt′) .... Ohio 40·50 N 84·35 W
118 Vara (vä′rä) .... Swe. 58·17 N 12·55 E
128 Varaklāni .... Sov. Un. 56·38 N 26·46 E
126 Varallo (vä-räl′lô) .... It. 45·44 N 8·14 E
142 Vārānasi (Banaras) .... India 25·25 N 83·00 E
112 Varanger Fd. (vä-räng′gẽr) . . Nor. 70·05 N 30·53 E
126 Varano, Lago di (L.) (lä′gō-dē-vä-rä′nô) . It. 41·52 N 15·55 E
126 Varaždin (vä′räzh′dĕn) ..... Yugo. 46·17 N 16·20 E
126 Varazze (vä-rät′sä) .... It. 44·23 N 8·34 E
118 Varberg (vär′bĕrg) .... Swe. 57·06 N 12·16 E
127 Vardar (R.) (vär′där) ...... Yugo. 41·40 N 21·50 E
118 Varde (vär′dĕ) .... Den. 55·39 N 8·28 E
112 Vardö (vărd′û) .... Nor. 70·23 N 30·43 E
154 Varella, C. .... Viet. 12·58 N 109·50 E
119 Varĕna (vä-rā′nȧ) . . . . . Sov. Un. 54·16 N 24·35 E
85 Varennes (vȧ-rĕn′) Can. (Montreal In.) 45·41 N 73·27 W
127 Varĕs (vä′rĕsh) .... Yugo. 44·10 N 18·20 E
126 Varese (vä-rā′så) .... It. 45·45 N 8·49 E
101 Varginha (vär-zhē′n-yä) Braz. (Rio de Janeiro In.) 21·33 S 45·25 W
119 Varkaus (vär′kous) .... Fin. 62·19 N 27·51 E
136 Varlamovo (vár-lá′mô-vô) Sov. Un. (Urals In.) 54·37 N 60·41 E
127 Varna (Stalin) (vär′nȧ) (stä′lĭn) Bul. 43·14 N 27·58 E
136 Varna .... Sov. Un. (Urals In.) 53·22 N 60·59 E
118 Värnamo (vĕr′nȧ-mô) .... Swe. 57·11 N 13·45 E
120 Varnsdorf (värns′dôrf) ..... Czech. 50·54 N 14·36 E
79 Varnville (värn′vĭl) .... S. C. 32·49 N 81·05 W
85 Vars (värz) . . . . Can. (Ottawa In.) 45·21 N 75·21 W
129 Varvaropolye (vȧr′vȧr′ô-pô-lyĕ) Sov. Un. 48·38 N 38·37 E
124 Vascongadas (Reg.) (väs-kôn-gä′däs) . Sp. 42·35 N 2·46 W
132 Vashka (R.) .... Sov. Un. 63·20 N 47·50 E
65 Vashon (văsh′ŭn) Wash. (Seattle In.) 47·27 N 122·28 W
65 Vashon Heights (hītz) Wash. (Seattle In.) 47·30 N 122·28 W
65 Vashon I. . . . . Wash. (Seattle In.) 47·27 N 122·27 W
129 Vasil′kov (vå-sēl′-kôf′) . . . Sov. Un. 50·10 N 30·22 E
121 Vaslui (vȧs-lōō′ē) .... Rom. 46·39 N 27·49 E
80 Vassar (văs′ẽr) .... Mich. 43·25 N 83·35 W
100 Vassouras (väs-sō′räzh) . Braz. (In.) 22·25 S 43·40 W
118 Västanfors (vĕst′ån-fôrs) ..... Swe. 59·59 N 15·49 E
118 Västerås (vĕs′tĕr-ôs) .... Swe. 59·39 N 16·30 E
118 Väster-dalälven (R.) .... Swe. 61·06 N 13·10 E
118 Västervik (vĕs′tĕr-vēk) ...... Swe. 57·45 N 16·35 E
126 Vasto (väs′tô) .... It. 42·06 N 12·42 E
134 Vasyugan (R.) (vås-yōō-gȧn′) Sov. Un. 58·52 N 77·30 E
125 Vatican City (Cittádel Vaticano) (văt′ĭ-kăn sĭt′ē) (chē-tà′del vä-tē-kä′nô) . Eur. (Rome In.) 41·54 N 12·22 E
126 Vaticano, C. (vä-tē-kä′nô) ..... It. 38·38 N 15·52 E
112 Vatnajökull (Gl.) (vät′nȧ-yû-kōōl) Ice. 64·34 N 16·41 W
167 Vatomandry (vä-tōō-män′drē) Malag. Rep. 18·53 S 48·13 E
121 Vatra Dornei (vät′rȧ dôr′nā′) Rom. 47·22 N 25·20 E
118 Vättern (L.) .... Swe. 58·15 N 14·24 E
85 Vaudreuil (vô-drû′y′) Can. (Montreal In.) 45·24 N 74·02 W
65 Vaugh (vôn) . . Wash. (Seattle In.) 47·21 N 122·47 W
72 Vaughn .... N. Mex. 34·37 N 105·13 W
98 Vaupés (R.) (vå′ōō-pĕ′s) ..... Col. 1·18 N 71·14 W
118 Vaxholm (väks′hôlm) .... Swe. 59·26 N 18·19 E
118 Växjo (vĕks′shû) .... Swe. 56·53 N 14·46 E
132 Vaygach (I.) (vī-gäch′) . . Sov. Un. 70·00 N 59·00 E
99 Veadeiros, Chapadas dos (Mts.) (shä-pä′däs-dôs-vĕ-å-dā′rōs) Braz. 15·20 S 48·43 W
118 Veblungsnares (vib′lōōngs-nĕs) Nor. 62·33 N 7·46 E
127 Vedea (R.) (vå′dyȧ) .... Rom. 44·25 N 24·45 E
101 Vedia (vĕ′dyä) Arg. (Buenos Aires In.) 34·29 S 61·30 W
80 Veedersburg (vē′dẽrz-bûrg) . . . Ind. 40·05 N 87·15 W
91 Vega de Alatorre (vä′gä dä ä-lä-tōr′rå) . Mex. 20·02 N 96·39 W
95 Vega Real (Mts.) (vĕ′gä-rĕ-ä′l) Dom. Rep. 19·30 N 71·05 W
112 Vegen (I.) (vĕ′ghĕn) .... Nor. 65·38 N 10·51 E
86 Vegreville .... Can. 53·26 N 112·27 W
143 Vehār L. . . . . . India (Bombay In.) 19·11 N 72·50 E
101 Veinticinco de Mayo (vå-ēn′tē-sēn′kō dä mä′yō) Arg. (Buenos Aires In.) 35·26 S 60·09 W
124 Vejer (vā-kĕr′) .... Sp. 36·15 N 5·58 W
118 Vejle (vī′lĕ) .... Den. 55·41 N 9·29 E
123 Velbert (fĕl′bĕrt) . . Ger. (Ruhr In.) 51·20 N 7·03 E
126 Velebit (Mts.) (vā′lĕ-bēt) . . . Yugo. 44·25 N 15·23 E
123 Velen (fĕ′lĕn) . . . . . Ger. (Ruhr In.) 51·54 N 7.00 E
124 Vélez-Málaga (vā′lāth-mä′lä-gä) Sp. 36·48 N 4·05 W
124 Vélez Rubio (rōō′bē-ô) .... Sp. 37·38 N 2·05 W
126 Velika Kapela (Mts.) (vĕ′lē-kä kä-pĕ′lä) . Yugo. 45·03 N 15·20 E
127 Velika Morava (R.) (mô′rä-vä) Yugo. 44·20 N 21·10 E
128 Velikaya (R.) (vå-lē′kȧ-yȧ) Sov. Un. 57·25 N 28·07 E
121 Velikiy Bychkov (vĕ-lē′kē bōōch-kôf′) . Sov. Un. 47·59 N 24·01 E
128 Velikiye Luki (vyē-lē′-kyē lōō′ke) Sov. Un. 56·19 N 30·32 E
132 Velikiy Ustyug (vå-lē′kĭ ōōs-tyōōg′) . Sov. Un. 60·45 N 46·38 E
128 Velikoye (vå-lē′kô-yĕ) . . . Sov. Un. 57·21 N 39·45 E
128 Velikoye (L.) .... Sov. Un. 57·00 N 36·53 E
128 Velizh (vå′lēzh) .... Sov. Un. 55·37 N 31·11 E
120 Velke Meziřičí (vĕl′kä mĕzh′′r-zhyĭ-chĭ) . Czech. 49·21 N 16·01 E
159 Vella (I.) (văl′yä) .... Sol. Is. 8·00 S 156·42 E
125 Velletri (vĕl-lā′trē) . It. (Rome In.) 41·42 N 12·48 E
143 Vellore (vĕl-lōr′) .... India 12·57 N 79·09 E
136 Vels (vĕls) . . . Sov. Un. (Urals In.) 60·35 N 58·47 E
132 Vel′sk (vĕlsk) .... Sov. Un. 61·00 N 42·18 E
111 Velten (fel′tĕn) . . Ger. (Berlin In.) 52·41 N 13·11 E
136 Velya R. (vĕl′yȧ) Sov. Un. (Moscow In.) 56·23 N 37·54 E
98 Venadillo (vĕ-nä-dē′l-yō) Col. (In.) 4·43 N 74·55 W
90 Venado (vå-nä′dō) .... Mex. 22·54 N 101·07 W
100 Venado Tuerto (vĕ-nä′dô-tōōĕ′r-tô) . Arg. 33·28 S 61·47 W
122 Vendée, Collines de (hills) (kō-lēn′ dĕ vĕn-dā′) . Fr. 46·44 N 0·17 W
122 Vendôme (väN-dōm′) .... Fr. 47·46 N 1·05 E
126 Veneto (Reg.) (vĕ-nĕ′tô) .... It. 45·58 N 11·24 E
128 Venëv (vĕn-ĕf′) .... Sov. Un. 54·19 N 38·14 E
126 Venezia (Venice) (vå-nāt′sē-ä) . It. 45·25 N 12·18 E
126 Venezia, Golfo di (G.) (gôl-fô-dē-vå-nāt′sē-ä) . It. 45·23 N 13·00 E

Page	Name Pronunciation Region	Lat. °'	Long. °'
96	Venezuela (vĕn-ĕ-zwē'lȧ) S. A.	8·00 N	65·00 W
98	Venezuela, Golfo de (G.) (gôl-fô-dĕ) . Ven.	11·34 N	71·02 W
64	Veniaminof, Mt. Alaska	56·12 N	159·20 W
74	Venice (vĕn'ĭs) Calif. (Los Angeles In.)	33·59 N	118·28 W
74	Venice Ill. (St. Louis In.)	38·40 N	90·10 W
84	Venice La. (New Orleans In.)	29·17 N	89·22 W
	Venice, see Venezia		
123	Venlo Neth. (Ruhr In.)	51·22 N	6·11 E
119	Venta (R.) (vĕn'tȧ) Sov. Un.	57·05 N	21·45 E
100	Ventana, Sierra de la (Mts.) (sē-ĕ'r-rä-dĕ-lä-vĕn-tä'nä) . Arg.	38·00 S	63·00 W
168	Ventersburg (vĕn-tērs'bûrg) S. Afr. (Johannesburg & Pretoria In.)	28·06 S	27·10 E
168	Ventersdorp (vĕn-tērs'dôrp) S. Afr. (Johannesburg & Pretoria In.)	26·20 S	26·48 E
126	Ventimiglia (vĕn-tê-mēl'yä) It.	43·46 N	7·37 E
81	Ventnor (vĕnt'nēr) N. J.	39·20 N	74·25 W
119	Ventspils (vĕnt'spēls) Sov. Un.	57·24 N	21·41 E
98	Ventuari (R.) (vĕn-tōōä'rē) Ven.	4·47 N	65·56 W
68	Ventura (vĕn-tōō'rȧ) Calif.	34·18 N	119·18 W
136	Venukovsky (vĕ-nōō'kôv-skĭ) Sov. Un. (Moscow In.)	55·10 N	37·26 E
90	Venustiano Carranza (vĕ-nōōs-tyä'nō-kär-rä'n-zä) Mex.	19·44 N	103·48 W
91	Venustiano Carranzo (kär-rä'n-zō) Mex.	16·21 N	92·36 W
100	Vera (vĕ-rä) Arg.	29·22 S	60·09 W
124	Vera (vā'rä) Sp.	37·18 N	1·53 W
88	Vera Cruz (State) (vā-rä-krōōz') Mex.	20·30 N	97·15 W
91	Veracruz Llave (l-yä'vĕ) Mex.	19·13 N	96·07 W
142	Verāval (vĕr'ŭ-väl) India	20·59 N	70·49 E
126	Vercelli (vĕr-chĕl'lē) It.	45·18 N	8·27 E
85	Verchères (vĕr-shâr') Can. (Montreal In.)	45·46 N	73·21 W
69	Verde (R.) (vûrd) Ariz.	34·04 N	111·40 W
95	Verde, Cap (C.) Ba. Is.	22·50 N	75·00 W
95	Verde, Cay (I.) Ba. Is.	22·00 N	75·05 W
91	Verde (R.) Mex.	16·05 N	97·44 W
90	Verde (R.) Mex.	20·50 N	103·00 W
90	Verde (R.) Mex.	21·48 N	99·50 W
155	Verde (I.) (vĕr'dā) Phil. (Manila In.)	13·34 N	121·11 E
155	Verde Island Pass. (vĕr'dē) Phil. (Manila In.)	13·36 N	120·39 E
74	Verdemont (vûr'dē-mŏnt) Calif. (Los Angeles In.)	34·12 N	117·22 W
120	Verden (fĕr'dĕn) Ger.	52·55 N	9·15 E
73	Verdigris (R.) (vûr'dē-grēs) . Okla.	36·50 N	95·29 W
85	Verdun (vĕr'dŭn) Can. (Montreal In.)	45·27 N	73·34 W
122	Verdun-sur-Meuse (vâr-dûn'sür-mûz') . Fr.	49·09 N	5·21 E
168	Vereeniging (vĕ-rā'nĭ-gĭng) . S. Afr. (Johannesburg & Pretoria In.)	26·40 S	27·56 E
168	Verena (vĕr-ĕn ȧ) S. Afr. (Johannesburg & Pretoria In.)	25·30 S	29·02 E
128	Vereya (vĕ-rā'yȧ) Sov. Un.	55·21 N	36·08 E
124	Vergara (vĕr-gä'rä) Sp.	43·08 N	2·23 W
124	Verin (vâ-rēn') Sp.	41·56 N	7·26 W
136	Verkhne Chusovskiye Gorodki (vyĕrk'nyĕ chōō-sôv'skĭ-ye gȧ-rôd'ki) . Sov. Un. (Urals In.)	58·13 N	75·06 E
135	Verkhne-Kamchatsk (vyĕrk'nyĕ kȧm-chatsk') Sov. Un.	54·42 N	158·41 E
136	Verkhne Neyvinskiy (nā-vĭn'skĭ) Sov. Un. (Urals In.)	57·17 N	60·10 E
136	Verkhne Ural'sk (ōō-ralsk') Sov. Un. (Urals In.)	53·53 N	59·15 E
129	Verkhneye (vyĕrk'nĕ-yĕ) Sov. Un.	48·53 N	38·29 E
136	Verkhniy Avzyan (vyĕrk'nyĕ ȧv-zyȧn') Sov. Un. (Urals In.)	53·32 N	57·30 E
136	Verkhniye Kigi (vyĕrk'nĭ-yĕ kĭ'gĭ) Sov. Un. (Urals In.)	55·23 N	58·37 E
136	Verkhniy Ufaley (ōō-fá'lā) Sov. Un. (Urals In.)	56·04 N	60·15 E
121	Verkhniy Yasenov (vyĕ'rk-nēē yȧ'syĕ-ŋĕf) . Sov. Un.	48·17 N	24·21 E
136	Verkhnyaya Pyshma (vyĕrk'nyä-yä pōōsh'mȧ) Sov. Un. (Urals In.)	56·57 N	60·37 E
136	Verkhnyaya Salda (säl'dȧ) Sov. Un. (Urals In.)	58·03 N	60·33 E
134	Verkhnyaya Tunguska (Angara) (R.) (tōōn-gōōs'kȧ) . Sov. Un.	58·13 N	97·00 E
136	Verkhnyaya Tura (tōō'rȧ) Sov. Un. Urals. In.)	58·22 N	59·51 E
136	Verkhnyaya Yayva (yäy'vȧ) Sov. Un. (Urals In.)	59·28 N	59·38 E
136	Verkhotur'ye (vyĕr-kô-tōōr'yĕ) Sov. Un. (Urals In.)	58·52 N	60·47 E
135	Verkhoyansk (vyĕr-kô-yänsk') Sov. Un.	67·43 N	133·33 E
135	Verkhoyanskiy Khrebet (Mts.) (vyĕr-kô-yänsk') . Sov. Un.	67·45 N	128·00 E
86	Vermilion (vēr-mĭl'yŭn) Can.	53·19 N	110·53 W
82	Vermilion (R.) Can.	47·30 N	73·15 W
80	Vermilion (R.) Ill.	41·05 N	89·00 W
71	Vermilion (L.) Minn.	47·49 N	92·35 W
71	Vermilion Ra Minn.	47·55 N	91·59 W
71	Vermilion (R.) Minn.	48·09 N	92·31 W
70	Vermillion S. D.	42·46 N	96·56 W
70	Vermillion (R.) S. D.	43·54 N	97·14 W
77	Vermillion B. La.	29·47 N	92·00 W
63	Vermont (State) (vēr-mŏnt') U. S.	43·50 N	72·50 W
67	Vernal (vûr'nȧl) Utah	40·29 N	109·40 W
166	Verneuk Pan (L.) (vĕr-nŭk') S. Afr.	30·10 S	21·46 E
74	Vernon (vûr'nŭn) Calif. (Los Angeles In.)	34·01 N	118·12 W
86	Vernon (vĕr-nôn') Can.	50·18 N	119·15 W
85	Vernon Can. (Ottawa In.)	45·10 N	75·27 W
80	Vernon (vûr'nŭn) Ind.	39·00 N	85·40 W
84	Vernon N. J. (New York In.)	41·12 N	74·29 W
72	Vernon Tex.	34·09 N	99·16 W
79	Vero Beach (vē'rō) Fla. (In.)	27·36 N	80·25 W
127	Véroia Grc.	40·30 N	22·13 E
126	Verona (vä-rō'nä) It.	45·28 N	11·02 E
65	Vernonia (vûr-nō'nyȧ) Ore. (Portland In.)	45·52 N	123·12 W
123	Versailles (vĕr-sī'y') Fr. (Paris In.)	48·48 N	2·07 E
80	Versailles (vēr-sālz') Ky.	38·05 N	84·45 W
73	Versailles Mo.	38·27 N	92·52 W
82	Verte, B. (vûrt) Can.	46·03 N	63·57 W
164	Vert, Cap (C.) Senegal	14·52 N	17·49 W
167	Verulam (vĕ-rōō-lăm) S. Afr. (Natal In.)	29·39 S	31·08 E
117	Verviers (vĕr-vyā') Bel.	50·35 N	5·57 E
129	Vesëloye (vĕ-syô'lô-yĕ) . . Sov. Un.	46·59 N	34·56 E
119	Vesijärvi (L.) Fin.	61·09 N	25·10 E
123	Vesoul (vē-sōōl') Fr.	47·38 N	6·11 E
112	Vester Aalen (Is.) (vĕs'tēr ô'lĕn) Nor.	68·54 N	14·03 E
112	Vestfjord Nor.	67·33 N	12·59 E
112	Vestmannaeyjar (vĕst'män-ā-ā'yär) . Ice.	63·12 N	20·17 W
125	Vesuvio (vesuvius) (Mtn.) (vĕ-sōō'vyä) . It. (Naples In.)	40·35 N	14·26 E
128	Ves'yegonsk (vĕ-syĕ-gônsk') Sov. Un.	58·42 N	37·09 E
121	Veszprem (vĕs'prām) Hung.	47·05 N	17·53 E
121	Vesztö (vĕs'tû) Hung.	46·55 N	21·18 E
128	Vetka (vyĕt'kȧ) Sov. Un.	52·36 N	31·05 E
118	Vetlanda (vĕt-län'dä) Swe.	57·26 N	15·05 E
132	Vetluga (vyĕt-lōō'gȧ) Sov. Un.	57·50 N	45·42 E
132	Vetluga (R.) Sov. Un.	56·50 N	45·50 E
127	Vetovo (vä'tô-vô) Bul.	43·42 N	26·18 E
127	Vetren (vĕt'rĕn') Bul.	42·16 N	24·04 E
168	Vet R. (vĕt) S. Afr. (Johannesburg & Pretoria In.)	28·25 S	26·37 E
80	Vevay (vē'vā) Ind.	38·45 N	85·05 W
123	Veynes (vān'') Fr.	44·31 N	5·47 E
122	Vézère (R.) (vā-zer') Fr.	45·01 N	1·00 E
98	Viacha (vēä'chä) Bol.	16·43 S	68·16 W
126	Viadana (vē-ä-dä'nä) It.	44·55 N	10·30 E
73	Vian (vī'ăn) Okla.	35·30 N	95·00 W
99	Viana (vē-ä'nä) Braz.	3·09 S	44·44 W
124	Viana del Bollo (vē-ä'nä dĕl bôl'yô) Sp.	42·10 N	7·07 W
124	Viana do Alentejo (vē-ä'nȧ dōō ä-lĕn-tā'hōō) . Port.	38·20 N	8·02 W
124	Viana do Castélo (dōō käs-tă'lōō) Port.	41·41 N	8·45 W
124	Viar (R.) (vē-ä'rä) Sp.	38·15 N	6·08 W
126	Viareggio (vē-ä-rĕd'jô) It.	43·52 N	10·14 E
118	Viborg (vē'bôr) Den.	56·27 N	9·22 E
126	Vibo Valentia (vē'bō-vä-lĕ'n-tyä) It.	38·47 N	16·06 E
125	Vicálvero (vē-kä'l-vĕ-rō) Sp. (Madrid In.)	40·25 N	3·37 W
100	Vicente López (vē-sĕ'n-tĕ-lō'pĕz) Arg. (In.)	34·15 S	58·29 W
126	Vicenza (vē-chĕnt'sä) It.	45·33 N	11·33 E
125	Vich (vēch) Sp.	41·55 N	2·14 E
128	Vichuga (vē-chōō'gȧ) Sov. Un.	57·13 N	41·58 E
122	Vichy (vē-shē') Fr.	46·06 N	3·28 E
80	Vicksburg (vĭks'bûrg) Mich.	42·10 N	85·30 W
78	Vicksburg Miss.	32·20 N	90·50 W
101	Viçosa (vē-sô'sä) Braz. (Rio de Janeiro In.)	23·46 S	42·51 W
101	Victoria (vēk-tô'rēä) Arg. (Buenos Aires In.)	32·36 S	60·09 W
65	Victoria (vĭk-tō'rĭ-ȧ) Can. (Seattle In.)	48·26 N	123·23 W
100	Victoria (vēk-tô-rēä) Chile	38·15 S	72·16 W
149	Victoria (vĭk-tō'rĭ-ȧ) Hong Kong	22·10 N	114·18 E
98	Victoria (vēk-tô'rēä) Col. (In.)	5·19 N	74·54 W
164	Victoria (vĭk-tō'rĭ-ȧ) Nig.	4·06 N	9·13 E
155	Victoria (vēk-tô-ryä) Phil. (Manila In.)	15·34 N	120·41 E
77	Victoria (vĭk-tō'rĭ-ȧ) Tex.	28·48 N	97·00 W
79	Victoria Va.	36·57 N	78·13 W
159	Victoria (State) Austl.	36·46 S	143·15 E
158	Victoria (R.) Austl.	17·25 S	130·50 E
146	Victoria, Mt. Bur.	21·26 N	93·59 E
155	Victoria, Mt. Pap.	9·35 S	147·45 E
166	Victoria (L.) Tan.	2·00 S	32·16 E
90	Victoria de Durango (vēk-tō'ryä-dĕ-dōō-rä'n-gô) Mex.	24·02 N	104·42 W
94	Victoria de las Tunas (vēk-tō'rē-ä dā läs tōō'näs) Cuba	20·55 N	77·05 W
166	Victoria Falls S. Rh.	18·15 S	25·35 E
86	Victoria I. Can.	70·13 N	107·45 W
47	Victoria Land Ant.	75·00 S	160·00 E
92	Victoria Pk. (vēk-tōrĭ'ä) Br. Hond. (Yucatan In.)	16·47 N	88·40 W
158	Victoria River Downs (vĭc-tōr'ĭȧ) Austl.	16·30 S	131·10 E
86	Victoria Str. (vĭk-tō'rĭ-ȧ) Can.	69·10 N	100·58 E
82	Victoriaville (vĭk-tō'rĭ-ȧ-vĭl) . Can.	46·04 N	71·59 W
166	Victoria West (wĕst) S. Afr.	31·25 S	23·10 E
79	Vidalia (vĭ-dā'lĭ-ȧ) Ga.	32·10 N	82·26 W
77	Vidalia La.	31·33 N	91·28 W
127	Vidin (vĭ'dĕn) Bul.	44·00 N	22·53 E
128	Vidzy (vē'dzĭ) Sov. Un.	55·23 N	26·46 E
100	Viedma (vyād'mä) Arg.	40·55 S	63·03 W
100	Viedma (L.) Arg.	49·40 S	72·35 W
92	Viejo R. (vyā'hō) Nic.	12·45 N	86·19 W
78	Vienna (vē-ĕn'ȧ) Ga.	32·03 N	83·50 W
73	Vienna Ill.	37·24 N	88·50 W
	Vienna, see Wien		
122	Vienne (vyĕn') Fr.	45·31 N	4·54 E
122	Vienne (R.) Fr.	47·06 N	0·20 E
154	Vientiane (vyăn'tyän') Laos	18·07 N	102·33 E
89	Vieques (vyā'kâs) P. R. (Puerto Rico In.)	18·09 N	65·27 W
89	Vieques (I.) (vyā'kâs) P. R. (Puerto Rico In.)	18·05 N	65·28 W
168	Vierfontien (vĕr'fôn-tān) . . . S. Afr. (Johannesburg & Pretoria In.)	27·06 S	26·45 E
123	Viersen (fēr'zĕn) . Ger. (Ruhr In.)	51·15 N	6·24 E
120	Vierwaldstätter See (L.) Switz.	46·54 N	8·36 E
122	Vierzon (vyâr-zôn') Fr.	47·14 N	2·04 E
76	Viesca (vē-âs'kä) Mex.	25·21 N	102·47 W
76	Viesca, Laguna de (L.) (lä-ōō'nä-dĕ) . Mex.	25·30 N	102·40 W
126	Vieste (vyĕs'tâ) It.	41·52 N	16·10 E
139	Vietnam (vyĕt'năm') Asia	18·00 N	106·20 E
155	Vigan (vēgän) . . Phil. (Manila In.)	17·36 N	120·22 E
126	Vigevano (vē-jȧ-vä'nô) It.	45·18 N	8·52 E
123	Vigny (vēn-y'ē') . . . Fr. (Paris In.)	49·05 N	1·54 E
124	Vigo (vē'gō) Sp.	42·18 N	8·42 W
119	Vihti (vē'tĭ) Fin.	60·27 N	24·18 E
	Viipuri, see Vyborg		
127	Vijosë (R.) Alb.	40·15 N	20·30 E
112	Vik Ice.	63·22 N	18·58 W
118	Vik (vĭk) Nor.	61·06 N	6·35 E
159	Vila New Hebr.	18·00 S	168·30 E
166	Vila de João Belo (vē'lä-dĕ-zho'un-bĕ'lô) . Moz.	25·00 S	33·45 E
166	Vila de Manica (vē'lä dä mä-nē'kȧ) . Moz.	18·48 S	32·49 E
124	Vila de Rei (vē'lȧ dä rā'ĭ) . . . Port.	39·42 N	8·03 W
124	Vila do Conde (vē'lä dōō kôn'dĕ) Port.	41·21 N	8·44 W
124	Vila Franca de Xira (fräŋ'kä dä shē'rä) . Port.	38·58 N	8·59 W
166	Vila Henrique De Carvalho (vē'lä-ĕn-rē'kĕ-dĕ-kär-vä'lô) Ang.	9·25 S	20·30 E
122	Vilaine (R.) (vē-lân') Fr.	47·34 N	0·20 W
166	Vila Luso (vē'lä-lōō'sô) Ang.	11·45 S	19·55 E
166	Vila Marechal Carmona (mä-rĕ-zhäl-kär-mō-nä) . Ang.	7·30 S	15·05 E
166	Vilanculos (vē-län-kōō'lôs) . . Moz.	22·03 S	35·13 E
128	Vilāni (vē'lȧ-nĭ) Sov. Un.	56·31 N	27·00 E
124	Vila Nova de Fozcoa (nō'vȧ dä fôz-kō'ȧ) . Port.	41·08 N	7·11 W
124	Vila Nova de Gaia (vē'lä nō'vȧ dä gä'yȧ) . Port.	41·08 N	8·40 W
124	Vila Nova de Milfontes (nō'vȧ dä mēl-fôn'tāzh) . Port.	37·44 N	8·48 W
124	Vila Real (rä-äl') Port.	41·18 N	7·48 W
124	Vila Real de Santo Antonio (vē'lä-rĕ-ä'l-dĕ-sän-tô-än-tô'nyô) Port.	37·14 N	7·25 W
166	Vila Rocadas (rô-kä'däs) Ang.	16·50 S	15·05 E
124	Vila Vicosa (vē-sō'zȧ) Port.	38·47 N	7·24 W
128	Vileyka (vē-lā'ē-kȧ) Sov. Un.	54·19 N	26·58 E
112	Vilhelmina Swe.	64·37 N	16·30 E
119	Viljandi (vēl'yȧn-dē) Sov. Un.	58·24 N	25·34 E
168	Viljoenskroon S. Afr. (Johannesburg & Pretoria In.)	27·13 S	26·58 E
119	Vilkaviškis (vêl-kȧ-vēsh'kēs) Sov. Un.	54·40 N	23·08 E
119	Vilkija (vêl-kē'ēȧ) Sov. Un.	55·04 N	23·30 E
134	Vil'kitskogo (I.) (vyl-kēts-kōgō) Sov. Un.	73·25 N	76·00 E
133	Vilkovo (vĭl-kô-vô) Sov. Un.	45·24 N	29·36 E
76	Villa Acuña (vĕl'yä-kōō'n-yä) Mex.	29·20 N	100·56 W
76	Villa Ahumada (ä-ōō-mä'dä) . Mex.	30·43 N	106·30 W
91	Villa Alta (San Ildefonso) (äl'tä) (sän ēl-dā-fōn'sō) . Mex.	17·20 N	96·08 W
100	Villa Angela (vē'l-yä ä'n-kĕ-lä) Arg.	27·31 S	60·42 W
124	Villaba (vēl-yä'bä) Sp.	43·18 N	7·43 W
100	Villa Ballester (vē'l-yä-bäl-yĕs-tĕr) Arg. (In.)	34·18 S	58·33 W
98	Villa Bella (bĕ'l-yä) Bol.	10·25 S	65·22 W
164	Villa Bens (bĕns) Mor.	27·54 N	12·41 W
124	Villablino (vēl-yä-blē'nô) Sp.	42·58 N	6·18 W
124	Villacañas (vēl-yä-kän'yäs) Sp.	39·39 N	3·20 W
124	Villacarrillo (vēl-yä-kä-rēl'yô) Sp.	38·09 N	3·07 W
120	Villach (fē'läk) Aus.	46·38 N	13·50 E
126	Villacidro (vē-lä-chē'drô) It.	39·28 N	8·41 E
164	Villa Cisneros (vēl'yä thēs-nā'rôs) Sp. Sah.	23·45 N	16·04 W
101	Villa Constitución (kōn-stē-tōō-syōn') Arg. (Buenos Aires In.)	33·15 S	60·19 W
76	Villa Coronado (kō-rō-nä'dhō) Mex.	26·45 N	105·10 W
91	Villa Cuauhtémoc (vē'l-yä-kōō-äōō-tĕ'mōk) . Mex.	22·11 N	97·50 W
76	Villa de Allende (vēl'yä dä äl-yĕn'dä) . Mex.	25·18 N	100·01 W
90	Villa de Alvarez (vēl'yä-dĕ-ä'l-vä-rĕz) . Mex.	19·17 N	103·44 W
99	Villa de Cura (dĕ-kōō'rä) Ven. (In.)	10·03 N	67·29 W
90	Villa de Guadalupe (dĕ-gwä-dhä-lōō'pä) . Mex.	23·22 N	100·44 W
90	Villa de Reyes (dä rā'yĕs) . . . Mex.	21·45 N	100·55 W
100	Villa Dolores (vēl'yä dō-lō'räs) Arg.	31·50 S	65·05 W
90	Villa Escalante (vēl'yä-ĕs-kä-län'tĕ) Mex.	19·24 N	101·36 W
125	Villafamés (vēl'yä-fä-mās') . . . Sp.	40·07 N	0·05 W
91	Villa Flores (vēl'yä-flō'räs) . . . Mex.	16·13 N	93·17 W
126	Villafranca (vĕl-lä-fräŋ'kä) . . . It.	45·22 N	10·53 E
124	Villafranca del Bierzo (vēl-yä-fräŋ'kä dĕl byĕr'thō) . Sp.	42·37 N	6·49 W

ng-sing; ŋ-baŋk; N-nasalized n; nŏd; cŏmmit; ōld; ôbey; ôrder; fōōd; fŏŏt; ou-out; s-soft; sh-dish; th-thin; pūre; ûnite; ûrn; stŭd; circŭs; ü-as "y" in study; '-indeterminate vowel.

Page	Name Pronunciation Region	Lat. °′	Long. °′
124	Villafranca de los Barros (vēl-yä-fräŋ′kä dā lōs bär′rōs) Sp.	38·34 N	6·22 W
125	Villafranca del Panadés (vēl-yä frän′kä dĕl pä-nä-dās′) Sp.	41·20 N	1·40 E
90	Villa García (gär-sē′ä) . . . . . . Mex.	22·07 N	101·55 W
124	Villagarcia (vēl′yä-gär-thē′ä) . . Sp.	42·38 N	8·43 W
168	Villaggio Duca degli Abruzzi Som. (Horn of Afr. In.)	2·40 N	45·20 E
76	Villagran (vēl-yä-grän′) . . . . . Mex.	24·28 N	99·30 W
80	Villa Grove (vĭl′ȧ grōv′) . . . . Ill.	39·55 N	88·15 W
100	Villaguay (vê′l-yä-gwī) . . . . . . Arg.	31·47 N	58·53 W
100	Villa Hayes (vēl′yä äyȧs) (hāz) Par.	25·07 S	57·31 W
91	Villahermosa (vēl′yä-ĕr-mō′sä) Mex.	17·59 N	92·56 W
90	Villa Hidalgo (vēl′yäē-däl′gō) Mex.	21·39 N	102·41 W
125	Villajoyosa (vēl′yä-hô-yō′sä) . . Sp.	38·30 N	0·14 W
76	Villaldama (vēl-yäl-dä′mä) . . Mex.	26·30 N	100·26 W
76	Villa Lopez (vēl′yä lō′pĕz) . . . Mex.	27·00 N	105·02 W
124	Villalpando (vēl-yäl-pän′dō) . . . Sp.	41·54 N	5·24 W
100	Villa Maria (vê′l-yä-mä-rē′ä) . Arg.	32·17 S	63·08 W
124	Villamatín (vēl-yä-mä-tê′n) . . . Sp.	36·50 N	5·38 W
100	Villa Mercedes (mĕr-sā′dȧs) . . Arg.	33·38 S	65·16 W
98	Villa Montes (vê′l-yä-mô′n-tĕs) Bol.	21·13 S	63·26 W
90	Villa Morelos (mô-rĕ′lōs) . . . . Mex.	20·01 N	101·24 W
98	Villanueva (vê′l-yä-nōōĕ′vä) . . Col.	10·44 N	73·08 W
92	Villanueva (vēl′yä-nwā′vä) . Hond.	15·19 N	88·02 W
90	Villanueva (vêl′yä-nōōĕ′vä) . . Mex.	22·25 N	102·53 W
124	Villanueva de Córdoba (vêl-yä-nwĕ′vä-dā kôr′dô-bä) Sp.	38·18 N	4·38 W
124	Villanueva de la Serena (lä sā-rā′nä) . Sp.	38·59 N	5·56 W
125	Villanueva y Geltrú (ēKĕl-trōō′) Sp.	41·13 N	1·44 E
91	Villa Obregón (vē′l-yä-ô-brĕ-gô′n) Mex. (Mexico City In.)	19·21 N	99·11 W
76	Villa Ocampo (ô-käm′pō) . . . . Mex.	26·26 N	105·30 W
90	Villa Pedro Montoya (vêl′yä-pĕ′drô-môn-tô′yȧ) . Mex.	21·38 N	99·51 W
123	Villard-Bonnot (vēl-yär′bôn-nō′) Fr.	45·15 N	5·53 E
125	Villarreal (vêl-yär-rĕ-äl) . . . . . . Sp.	39·55 N	0·07 W
100	Villarrica (vēl-yä-rē′kä) . . . . . . Par.	25·55 S	56·23 W
124	Villarrobledo (vēl-yär-rô-blā′dhō) Sp.	39·15 N	2·37 W
124	Villa Sanjurjo (vêl-yä-sän-Kōō′r-Kô) . Sp.	35·15 N	3·55 W
90	Villa Union (vêl′yä-ōō-nyōn′) Mex.	23·10 N	106·14 W
98	Villavicencio (vê′l-yä-vē-sĕ′n-syō) Col. (In.)	4·09 N	73·38 W
125	Villaviciosa de Odón (vēl′yä-vê-thê-ō′sä dā ō-dōn′) Sp. (Madrid In.)	40·22 N	3·54 W
98	Villavieja (vê′l-yä-vē-ĕ′Kȧ) Col. (In.)	3·13 N	75·13 W
100	Villazón (vê′l-yä-zô′n) . . . . Bol.	22·02 S	65·42 W
122	Villefranche-de-Lauragais (vēl-fränsh′dĕ-lô-rä-gā′) . . . . . Fr.	43·25 N	1·41 E
122	Villefranche-de-Rouergue (dē-rōō-ĕrg′) . Fr.	44·21 N	2·02 E
122	Villefranche sur-Saône (sür-sä-ōn′) . Fr.	45·59 N	4·43 E
123	Villejuif (vēl′zhüst′) Fr. (Paris In.)	48·48 N	2·22 E
87	Ville Marie . . . . Can.	47·18 N	79·22 W
125	Villena (vē-lyā′nȧ) . . . . Sp.	38·37 N	0·52 W
85	Villeneuve (vēl′nûv′) Can. (Edmonton In.)	53·40 N	113·49 W
123	Villeneuve-St. Georges (săN-zhôrzh′) . Fr. (Paris In.)	48·43 N	2·27 E
122	Villeneuve-sur-Lot (sür-lō′) . . . . Fr.	44·25 N	0·41 E
77	Ville Platte (vēl plȧt′) . . . . La.	30·41 N	92·17 W
122	Villers Cotterêts (vē-ār′kô-trā′) Fr. (Paris In.)	49·15 N	3·05 E
123	Villerupt (vēl′rüp′) . . . . Fr.	49·28 N	6·16 E
98	Villeta (vē′l-yĕ′tȧ) . . . . . . Col. (In.)	5·02 N	74·29 W
122	Villeurbanne (vēl-ûr-bän′) . . . . . Fr.	45·43 N	4·55 E
168	Villiers (vĭl′ĭ-ērs) . . . . S. Afr. (Johannesburg & Pretoria In.)	27·03 S	28·38 E
120	Villingen (fĭl′ĭng-ĕn) . . . . Ger.	48·04 N	8·28 E
71	Villisca (vĭ-lĭs′kȧ) . . . . Iowa	40·56 N	94·56 W
143	Villupuram . . . . India	11·59 N	79·33 E
119	Vilnius (Wilno) (vĭl′nê-ōōs) Sov. Un.	54·40 N	25·26 E
119	Vilppula (vĭl′pŭ-lȧ) . . . . Fin.	62·01 N	24·24 E
111	Vilvoorde . . . . . . Bel. (Brussels In.)	50·56 N	4·25 E
135	Vilyuy (R.) (vēl′yȧ) . . . . . Sov. Un.	65·22 N	108·45 E
135	Vilyuysk (vê-lyōō′ĭsk′) . . . Sov. Un.	63·41 N	121·47 E
135	Vilyuyskiye Gory (Mts.) (vê-lyōōs-kê-yĕ) . Sov. Un.	67·45 N	109·45 E
118	Vimmerby (vĭm′ĕr-bü) . . . . . . Swe.	57·41 N	15·51 E
120	Vimperk (vĭm-pĕrk′) . . . . . . Czech.	49·04 N	13·41 E
101	Viña del Mar (vē′nyä dĕl mär′) Chile (Santiago In.)	33·00 S	71·33 W
82	Vinalhaven (vī-năl-hā′vĕn) . Maine	44·03 N	68·49 W
125	Vinaroz (vē-nä′rōth) . . . . Sp.	40·29 N	0·27 E
123	Vincennes (văN-sĕn′) Fr. (Paris In.)	48·51 N	2·27 E
80	Vincennes (vĭn-zĕnz′) . . . . Ind.	38·40 N	87·30 W
78	Vincent (vĭn′sĕnt) . . . . Ala.	33·21 N	86·25 W
112	Vindelälven (R.) . . . . Swe.	65·02 N	18·30 E
112	Vindeln (vĭn′dĕln) . . . . Swe.	64·10 N	19·52 E
142	Vindhya Ra. (vĭnd′yä) . . . . . . India	22·30 N	75·50 E
81	Vineland (vīn′lănd) . . . . N. J.	39·30 N	75·00 W
151	Vinh (vên′y′) . . . . Viet.	18·38 N	105·42 E
124	Vinhais (vēn-yä′ēzh) . . . . Port.	41·51 N	7·00 W
84	Vinings (vī′nĭngz) Ga. (Atlanta In.)	33·52 N	84·28 W
73	Vinita (vĭ-nē′tȧ) . . . . Okla.	36·38 N	95·09 W
127	Vinkovci (vēn′kôv-tsê) . . . . . Yugo.	45·17 N	18·47 E
129	Vinnitsa (vê′nêt-sȧ) . . . . . Sov. Un.	49·13 N	28·31 E
129	Vinnitsa (Oblast) . . . . Sov. Un.	48·45 N	28·01 E
136	Vinogradovo (vĭ-nô-grä′do-vô) Sov. Un. (Moscow In.)	55·25 N	38·33 E
47	Vinson Massif (Mtn.) . . . . Ant.	77·40 S	87·00 W
71	Vinton (vĭn′tŭn) . . . . Iowa	42·08 N	92·01 W
77	Vinton . . . . La.	30·12 N	93·35 W
143	Vinukonda . . . . India	16·05 N	79·48 E
84	Violet (vī′ô-lĕt) La. (New Orleans In.)	29·54 N	89·54 W
151	Virac (vê-räk′) . . . . Phil.	13·38 N	124·20 E
119	Virbalis (vêr′bȧ-lês) . . . . . Sov. Un.	54·38 N	22·55 E
86	Virden (vûr′dĕn) . . . . Can.	49·48 N	101·00 W
73	Virden . . . . Ill.	39·28 N	89·46 W
69	Virgin (R.) . . . . . . Ariz.-Nev.-Utah	36·51 N	113·50 W
71	Virginia (vēr-jĭn′yȧ) . . . . Minn.	47·32 N	92 36 W
168	Virginia . . . . S. Afr. (Johannesburg & Pretoria In.)	28·07 S	26·54 E
63	Virginia (State) . . . . U. S.	37·00 N	80·45 W
84	Virginia Beach . . Va. (Norfolk In.)	36·50 N	75·58 W
68	Virginia City . . . . Nev.	39·18 N	119·40 W
89	Virgin Is. (vûr′jĭn) . . . . N. A.	18·15 N	64·00 W
119	Virmo (vĭr′mô) . . . . Fin.	60·41 N	21·58 E
71	Viroqua (vĭ-rō′kwȧ) . . . . Wis.	43·33 N	90·54 W
126	Virovitica (vê-rô-vē′tê-tsȧ) . Yugo.	45·50 N	17·24 E
127	Virpazar (vêr′pä-zär′) . . . . . . Yugo.	42·16 N	19·06 E
119	Virrat (vĭr′ät) . . . . , ... Fin.	62·15 N	23·45 E
118	Virserum (vĭr′sĕ-rōōm) . . . . . . Swe.	57·22 N	15·35 E
126	Vis (vês) . . . . Yugo.	43·03 N	16·11 E
126	Vis (I.) . . . . Yugo.	43·00 N	16·10 E
126	Visa, Mt. (Mtn.) (vê′sä) . . . . It.	45·42 N	7·08 E
143	Visākhapatnan (vī-zä′kȧ-pŭt′nȧn) India	17·48 N	83·21 E
68	Visalia (vĭ-sā′lĭ-ȧ) . . . . Calif.	36·20 N	119·18 W
118	Visby (vĭs′bü) . . . . Swe.	57·39 N	18·19 E
49	Viscount Mellville Sound (vī′kount′) . Can.	74·80 N	110·00 W
127	Višegrad (vē′shĕ-gräd) . . . . . . Yugo.	43·45 N	19·19 E
136	Vishera R. (vĭ′shĕ-rȧ) Sov. Un. (Urals In.)	60·40 N	58·46 E
136	Visim (vē′sĭm) . Sov. Un. (Urals In.)	57·38 N	59·32 E
118	Viskan (R.) . . . . Swe.	57·20 N	12·25 E
128	Viški (vēs′kĭ) . . . . Sov. Un.	56·02 N	26·47 E
127	Visoko (vē′sô-kô) . . . . Yugo.	43·59 N	18·10 E
127	Vistonís (L.) (vês′tô-nĭs) . . . . . Grc.	40·58 N	25·12 E
	Vistula, see Wisla		
127	Vitanovac (vê′tä′nô-vȧts) . . . Yugo.	43·44 N	20·50 E
128	Vitebsk (vē′tyĕpsk) . . . . . Sov. Un.	55·12 N	30·16 E
128	Vitebsk (Oblast) . . . . Sov. Un.	55·05 N	29·18 E
126	Viterbo (vê-tĕr′bō) . . . . It.	42·24 N	12·08 E
135	Vitim (vē′têm) . . . . Sov. Un.	59·22 N	112·43 E
135	Vitim (R.) (vē′têm) . . . . . Sov. Un.	56·12 N	115·30 E
136	Vitino (vē′tĭ-nô) Sov. Un. (Leningrad In.)	59·40 N	29·51 E
99	Vitória (vê-tō′rê-ä) . . . . Braz.	20·09 S	40·17 W
124	Vitoria (vē-tô-ryä) . . . . Sp.	42·43 N	2·43 W
99	Vitória da Conquista (-dä-kōn-kwē′s-tä) . Braz.	14·51 S	40·44 W
122	Vitré (vê-trā′) . . . . Fr.	48·09 N	1·15 W
122	Vitrolles (vē-trōl′) Fr. (Marseille In.)	43·27 N	5·15 E
122	Vitry-le-François (vê-trē′lĕ-fräN-swȧ′) . Fr.	48·44 N	4·34 E
113	Vittoria (vê-tô′rê-ô) . . . . It.	37·01 N	14·31 E
126	Vittorio (vê-tô′rê-ô) . . . . It.	45·59 N	12·17 E
155	Vitu Is. (vē′tōō) . . . . N. Gui. Ter.	4·45 S	149·50 E
124	Vivero (vê-vā′rō) . . . . Sp.	43·39 N	7·37 W
77	Vivian (vĭv′ĭ-ȧn) . . . . La.	32·51 N	93·59 W
127	Vize (vē′zĕ) . . . . Tur.	41·34 N	27·46 E
143	Vizianagram (vē-zê-ȧ-nŭ′grȧm′) India	18·10 N	83·29 E
111	Vlaardingen (vlär′dĭng-ĕn) Neth. (Amsterdam In.)	51·54 N	4·20 E
128	Vladimir (vlȧ-dyē′mēr) . . Sov. Un.	56·08 N	40·24 E
128	Vladimir (Oblast) (vlä-dyē′mēr) Sov. Un.	56·08 N	39·53 E
152	Vladimiro-Aleksandrovskoye (vlȧ-dyē′mē-rô ȧ-lĕk-sän′drôf-skô-yĕ) . Sov. Un.	42·50 N	133·00 E
121	Vladimir-Volynskiy (vlȧ-dyē′mēr vô-lēn′skĭ) Sov. Un.	50·50 N	24·20 E
135	Vladivostok (vlȧ-dê-vôs-tôk′) Sov. Un.	43·06 N	131·47 E
127	Vlasenica (vlä′sĕ-nêt′sȧ) . . . . Yugo.	44·11 N	18·58 E
127	Vlasotinci (vlä′sô-tên-tsĕ) . . . Yugo.	42·58 N	22·08 E
117	Vlieland (I.) (vlē′länt) . . . . . . Neth.	53·19 N	4·55 E
117	Vlissingen (vlĭs′sĭng-ĕn) . . . . . Neth.	51·30 N	3·34 E
127	Vlorë (Valona) (vlō′rŭ) . . . . . . Alb.	40·28 N	19·31 E
120	Vltana R. . . . . Czech.	49·24 N	14·18 E
132	Vodl (L.) (vôd′′l) . . . . Sov. Un.	62·20 N	37·20 E
167	Vogel (R.) (vô′gĕl) S. Afr. (Natal In.)	32·52 S	25·12 E
155	Vogelkop Pen. (fō′gĕl-kôp) W. Irian	1·25 S	133·15 E
126	Voghera (vô-gā′rä) . . . . It.	44·58 N	9·02 E
167	Vohémar (vô-ā-mär′) . Malag. Rep.	13·35 S	50·05 E
65	Voight (R.) . . . Wash. (Seattle In.)	47·03 N	122·08 W
123	Voiron (vwȧ-rôN′) . . . . Fr.	45·23 N	5·48 E
127	Voïviïs (L.) . . . . Grc.	39·34 N	22·50 E
129	Volchansk (vôl-chänsk′) . . Sov. Un.	50·18 N	36·56 E
129	Volch′ya (R.) (vôl-chyä′) . Sov. Un.	49·42 N	34·39 E
133	Volga (R.) (vôl′gä) . . . . . . Sov. Un.	47·30 N	46·20 E
133	Volga, Mouths of the . . . . Sov. Un.	46·00 N	49·10 E
113	Volgograd (Stalingrad) (vŏl′gō-gră′t) (stȧ′lên-grat) Sov. Un.	48·40 N	42·20 E
133	Volgogradskoye (Res.) (vôl-gô-grad′skô-yĕ) . Sov. Un.	51·10 N	45·10 E
128	Volkhov (vôl′kôf) . . . . Sov. Un.	59·54 N	32·21 E
128	Volkhov (R.) . . . . Sov. Un.	58·45 N	31·40 E
121	Volkovysk (vôl-kô-vêsk′) . Sov. Un.	53·11 N	24·29 E
85	Volmer (vŏl′mĕr) Can. (Edmonton In.)	53·43 N	113·40 W
136	Volodarskiy (vô-lô-där′skĭ) Sov. Un. (Leningrad In.)	59·49 N	30·06 E
128	Vologda (vô′lôg-dȧ) . . . . . Sov. Un.	59·12 N	39·52 E
128	Vologda (Oblast) . . . . Sov. Un.	59·00 N	37·26 E
129	Volokonovka (vô-lô-kô′nôf-kȧ) Sov. Un.	50·28 N	37·52 E
128	Volokolamsk (vô-lô-kôlȧmsk) Sov. Un.	56·02 N	35·58 E
127	Vólos (vô′lôs) . . . . Grc.	39·23 N	22·56 E
128	Volozhin (vô′lô-shên) . . . . Sov. Un.	54·04 N	26·38 E
133	Vol′sk (vôl′sk) . . . . Sov. Un.	52·10 N	47·00 E
164	Volta R. (vôl′tȧ) . . . . Ghana	8·15 N	0·57 W
101	Volta Redonda (vōl′tä-rā-dôn′dä) Braz. (Rio de Janeiro In.)	22·32 S	44·05 W
126	Volterra (vôl-tĕr′rä) . . . . It.	43·22 N	10·51 E
126	Voltri (vōl′trē) . . . . It.	44·25 N	8·45 E
126	Volturno (R.) (vôl-tōōr′nô) . . . . It.	41·12 N	14·20 E
128	Volzhskoye (L.) (vôl′sh-skô-yĕ) Sov. Un.	56·43 N	36·18 E
74	Von Ormy (vŏn ôr′mê) Tex. (San Antonio In.)	29·18 N	98·36 W
128	Võõpsu (vōōp′-sōō) . . . . . . Sov. Un.	58·06 N	27·30 E
111	Voorberg . . Neth. (Amsterdam In.)	52·04 N	4·21 E
167	Voortrekkerhoogte . . . . S. Afr. (Johannesburg & Pretoria In.)	25·48 S	28·10 E
168	Voortrekkerspos (vôr′trĕ-kērs-pŏs) . S. Afr. (Johannesburg & Pretoria In.)	24·12 S	27·00 E
128	Vop′ (R.) (vôp) . . . . Sov. Un.	55·20 N	32·40 E
112	Vopnafjördhur . . . . Ice.	65·43 N	14·58 W
120	Vorarlberg (Prov.) . . . . Aus.	47·20 N	9·55 E
118	Vordingborg (vôr′dĭng-bôr) . . Den.	55·10 N	11·55 E
127	Voríai (Is.) . . . . Grc.	39·12 N	24·03 E
127	Vorios Evvïkós Kólpos (G.) . . Grc.	38·48 N	23·02 E
132	Vorkuta (vôr-kōō′tȧ) . . . . Sov. Un.	67·28 N	63·40 E
119	Vormsi (I.) (vôrm′sĭ) . . . . Sov. Un.	59·06 N	23·05 E
133	Vorona (R.) (vô-rô′nă) . . Sov. Un.	51·50 N	42·00 E
132	Voron′ya (R.) (vô-rô′nyȧ) Sov. Un.	68·20 N	35·20 E
129	Voronezh (vô-rô′nyĕzh) . . Sov. Un.	51·39 N	39·11 E
129	Voronezh (Oblast) . . . . . . Sov. Un.	51·10 N	39·13 E
128	Voronezh (R.) . . . . Sov. Un.	52·17 N	39·32 E
121	Voronovo (vô′rô-nô-vô) . . Sov. Un.	54·07 N	25·16 E
136	Vorontsovka (vô-rônt′sôv-kȧ) Sov. Un. (Urals In.)	59·40 N	60·14 E
128	Võrts-Järv (L.) (vôrts yärv) Sov. Un.	58·15 N	26·12 E
128	Võru (vô′rû) . . . . Sov. Un.	57·50 N	26·58 E
136	Vorya R. (vôr′yȧ) Sov. Un. (Moscow In.)	55·55 N	38·15 E
123	Vosges (Mts.) (vōzh) . . . . Fr.	48·09 N	6·57 E
136	Voskresensk (vôs-krĕ-sĕnsk′) Sov. Un. (Moscow In.)	55·20 N	38·42 E
118	Voss (vôs) . . . . Nor.	60·40 N	6·24 E
132	Votkinsk (vôt-kēnsk′) . . . Sov. Un.	57·00 N	54·00 E
124	Vouga (R.) (vō′gȧ) . . . . Port.	40·43 N	7·51 W
122	Vouziers (vōō-zyā′) . . . . Fr.	49·25 N	4·40 E
118	Voxna älv (R.) . . . . Swe.	61·30 N	15·24 E
132	Vozhe (L.) (vôzh′yĕ) . . . . Sov. Un.	60·40 N	39·00 E
129	Voznesensk (vôz-nyĕ-sĕnsk′) Sov. Un.	47·34 N	31·22 E
130	Vrangelya (Wrangel) (I.) . Sov. Un.	71·25 N	173·38 E
127	Vranje (vrän′yĕ) . . . . Yugo.	42·33 N	21·55 E
127	Vratsa (vrät′tsȧ) . . . . Bul.	43·12 N	23·31 E
127	Vrbas (v′r′bäs) . . . . Yugo.	45·34 N	19·43 E
126	Vrbas (R.) . . . . Yugo.	44·25 N	17·17 E
120	Vrchlabi (v′r′chlä-bê) . . . . . . Czech.	50·32 N	15·51 E
168	Vrede (vrĭ′dĕ) (vrēd) . . . . . . S. Afr. (Johannesburg & Pretoria In.)	27·25 S	29·11 E
168	Vredefort (vrĭ′dĕ-fôrt) (vrēd′fōrt) S. Afr. (Johannesburg & Pretoria In.)	27·00 S	27·21 E
111	Vreeswijk . Neth. (Amsterdam In.)	52·00 N	5·06 E
127	Vršac (v′r′shȧts) . . . . Yugo.	45·08 N	21·18 E
121	Vrutky (vrōōt′kê) . . . . Czech.	49·09 N	18·55 E
166	Vryburg (vrī′bûrg) . . . . S. Afr.	26·55 S	29·45 E
166	Vryheid (vrī′hīt) . . . . S. Afr.	27·43 S	30·58 E
121	Vsetín (fsĕt′yēn) . . . . Czech.	49·21 N	18·01 E
136	Vsevolozhskiy (vsyĕ′vôlô′zh-skēê) Sov. Un. (Leningrad In.)	60·01 N	30·41 E
94	Vuelta Abajo (Mts.) (vwĕl′tä ä-bä′hō) . Cuba	22·20 N	83·45 W
111	Vught . . . . Neth. (Amsterdam In.)	51·38 N	5·18 E
127	Vukovar (vōō′kô-vär) . . . . . . Yugo.	45·20 N	19·00 E
80	Vulcan (vŭl′kăn) . . . . Mich.	45·45 N	87·50 W
126	Vulcano (I.) (vōōl-kä′nô) . . . . . . It.	38·23 N	15·00 E
127	Vŭlchedrŭm . . . . Bul.	43·43 N	23·29 E
119	Vyartsilya (vyȧr-tsē′lyȧ) . Sov. Un.	62·10 N	30·40 E
132	Vyatka (R.) (vyȧt′kȧ) . . . Sov. Un.	58·25 N	51·25 E
152	Vyazemskiy (vyȧ-zĕm′skĭ) Sov. Un.	47·29 N	134·39 E
128	Vyaz′ma (vyȧz′mȧ) . . . . . Sov. Un.	55·12 N	34·17 E
132	Vyazniki (vyȧz′nê-kê) . . . Sov. Un.	56·10 N	42·10 E
119	Vyborg (Viipuri) (vwē′bôrk) Sov. Un.	60·43 N	28·46 E
132	Vychegda (R.) (vê′chĕg-dȧ) Sov. Un.	61·40 N	48·00 E
132	Vyg (L.) . . . . Sov. Un.	63·40 N	35·00 E
132	Vym (R.) (vwēm) . . . . Sov. Un.	63·15 N	51·20 E
136	Vyritsa (vē′rĭ-tsȧ) Sov. Un. (Leningrad In.)	59·24 N	30·20 E
128	Vyshnevolotskoye (L.) (vŭy′sh-ŋê′vōlôt′s-kô′yĕ) Sov. Un.	57·30 N	34·27 E
128	Vyshniy Volochëk (vêsh′nyĭ vôl-ô-chĕk′) . Sov. Un.	57·34 N	34·35 E
120	Výškov (vēsh′kôf) . . . . Czech.	49·17 N	16·58 E
120	Vysoké Myto (vû′sô-kā mû′tô) Czech.	49·58 N	16·07 E
128	Vysokovsk (vĭ-sô′kôfsk) . . Sov. Un.	56·16 N	36·32 E
132	Vytegra (vû′tĕg-rȧ) . . . . . . Sov. Un.	61·00 N	36·20 E
132	Vyur . . . . Sov. Un.	57·55 N	27·00 E
117	Waal (L.) (väl) . . . . Neth.	51·46 N	5·00 E
111	Waalwijk . Neth. (Amsterdam In.)	51·41 N	5·05 E
87	Wabana (wä bä-nä) Can. (Newfoundland In.)	47·32 N	52·29 W
80	Wabash (wô′băsh) . . . . Ind.	40·45 N	85·50 W
80	Wabash (R.) . . . . Ill.-Ind.	38·00 N	88·00 W

ăt; finăl; rāte; senâte; ärm; ȧsk; sofȧ; fâre; ch-choose; dh-as th in other; bē; êvent; bĕt; recĕnt; cratẽr; g-go; gh-guttural g; bĭt; ĭ-short neutral; rīde; K-guttural k as ch in German ich;

Page	Name Pronunciation Region	Lat. °′	Long. °′
71	Wabasha (wä'bȧ-shô) Minn.	44·24 N	92·04 W
121	Wabrzeźno (vôŋ-bzĕzh'nô) Pol.	53·17 N	18·59 E
79	Waccamaw (R.) (wăk'ȧ-mô) S. C.	33·47 N	78·55 W
78	Waccasassa B. (wă-kȧ-să'sȧ) Fla.	29·02 N	83·10 W
111	Wachow (vä'kōv) Ger. (Berlin In.)	52·32 N	12·46 E
77	Waco (wā'kō) Tex.	31·35 N	97·06 W
153	Wadayama (wä'dä'yä-mä) Jap.	35·19 N	134·49 E
117	Waddenzee (Sea) Neth.	53·00 N	4·50 E
86	Waddington, Mt. (wŏd'dĭng-tŭn) Can.	51·30 N	125·23 W
165	Wadelai (wä-dĕ-lä'ē) Ug.	2·45 N	31·34 E
71	Wadena (wŏ-dē'nȧ) Minn.	46·26 N	95·09 W
79	Wadesboro (wādz'bŭr-ô) N. C.	34·57 N	80·05 W
165	Wādi Halfa (wä'dē häl'fä) Sud.	21·58 N	31·23 E
139	Wadī Musa Jordan (Palestine In.)	30·19 N	35·29 E
79	Wadley (wŏd'lē) Ga.	32·54 N	82·25 W
165	Wad Medani (wäd mĕ-dä'nē) Sud.	14·27 N	33·31 E
121	Wadowice (vȧ-dô'vēt-sĕ) Pol.	49·53 N	19·31 E
87	Wager B. (wā'jẽr) Can.	65·48 N	88·19 W
160	Wagga Wagga (wôg'ȧ wôg'ȧ) Austl.	35·10 S	147·30 E
73	Wagoner (wăg'ŭn-ẽr) Okla.	35·58 N	95·22 W
72	Wagon Mound (wăg'ŭn mound) N. Mex.	35·59 N	104·45 W
121	Wagrowiec (vôŋ-grô'vyĕts) Pol.	52·47 N	17·14 E
70	Wahoo (wä-hōō') Nebr.	41·14 N	96·39 W
70	Wahpeton (wô'pē-tŭn) N. D.	46·17 N	96·38 W
157	Waialua (wä'ē-ä-lōō'ä) Hawaii (In.)	21·33 N	158·08 W
157	Waianae (wä'ē-ȧ-nä'ä) Hawaii (In.)	21·25 N	158·11 W
120	Waidhofen (vīd'hôf-ĕn) Aus.	47·58 N	14·46 E
155	Waigeo (I.) (wä-ē-gä'ô) W. Irian	0·07 N	131·00 E
149	Waikang (wäī'käng) China (Shanghai In.)	31·23 N	121·11 E
159	Waikato (R.) (wä'ē-kä'to) N. Z. (In.)	38·00 S	175·47 E
160	Waikerie (wā'kẽr-ē) Austl.	34·15 S	140·00 E
157	Wailuku (wä'ē-lōō'kōō) Hawaii (In.)	20·55 N	156·30 W
157	Waimanalo (wä-ē-mä'nä-lô) Hawaii (In.)	21·19 N	157·53 W
157	Waimea (wä-ē-mā'ä) Hawaii (In.)	20·01 N	155·40 W
157	Waimea Hawaii (In.)	21·56 N	159·38 W
142	Wainganga (R.) (wä-ēn-gŭŋ'gä) India	20·24 N	79·41 E
154	Waingapu Indon.	9·32 S	120·00 E
64	Wainwright (wān-rīt) Alaska	74·40 N	159·00 W
86	Wainwright Can.	52·53 N	110·40 W
157	Waipahu (wä'ē-pä'hōō) Hawaii (In.)	21·20 N	158·02 W
74	Waiska R. (wȧ-ĭz-kȧ) Mich. (Sault Ste. Marie In.)	46·20 N	84·38 W
66	Waitsburg (wāts'bûrg) Wash.	46·17 N	118·08 W
153	Wajima (wä'jē-mä) Jap.	37·23 N	136·56 E
153	Wakamatsu (wä-kä'mät-sōō) Jap.	33·54 N	130·44 E
153	Wakamatsu Jap.	37·27 N	139·51 E
153	Wakasa-Wan (B.) (wä'kä-sä wän) Jap.	35·43 N	135·39 E
159	Wakatipu (R.) (wä-kä-tē'pōō) N. Z. (In.)	44·24 S	169·00 E
153	Wakayama (wä-kä'yä-mä) Jap.	34·14 N	135 11 E
156	Wake (I.) (wāk) Oceania	19·25 N	165·00 E
72	Wakeeney (wô-kē'nē) Kans.	39·01 N	99·53 W
85	Wakefield (wāk-fēld) Can. (Ottawa In.)	45·39 N	75·55 W
110	Wakefield Eng.	53·41 N	1·25 W
83	Wakefield Mass. (Boston In.)	42·31 N	71·05 W
71	Wakefield Mich.	46·28 N	89·55 W
70	Wakefield Nebr.	42·15 N	96·52 W
84	Wakefield R. I. (Providence In.)	41·26 N	71·30 W
79	Wake Forest (wāk fŏr'ĕst) N. C.	35·58 N	78·31 W
153	Waki (wä'kē) Jap.	34·05 N	134·10 E
152	Wakkanai (wä'kä-nä'ē) Jap.	45·19 N	141·43 E
166	Wakkerstroom (vȧk'ẽr-strōm) (wăk'ẽr-strōōm) S. Afr.	27·19 S	30·04 E
120	Walbrzych (väl'bzhûk) Pol.	50·46 N	16·16 E
82	Waldoboro (wôl'dô-bŭr-ô) Maine	44·06 N	69·22 W
66	Waldo L. (wôl'dō) Ore.	43·46 N	122·10 W
74	Waldron (wôl'drŭn) Mo. (Kansas City In.)	39·14 N	94·47 W
65	Waldron (I.) Wash. (Vancouver In.)	48·42 N	123·02 W
64	Wales (wālz) Alaska	65·35 N	168·14 W
116	Wales U. K.	52·12 N	3·40 W
120	Wałez (välch) Pol.	53·16 N	16·30 E
160	Walgett (wôl'gĕt) Austl.	30·00 S	148·10 E
47	Walgreen Coast (wôl'grēn) Ant.	73·00 S	110·00 W
78	Walhalla (wŏl-hăl'ȧ) S. C.	34·45 N	83·04 W
71	Walker (wôk'ẽr) Minn.	47·06 N	94·37 W
68	Walker (R.) Nev.	39·07 N	119·10 W
65	Walker, Mt. Wash. (Seattle In.)	47·47 N	122·54 W
68	Walker L. Nev.	38·46 N	118·30 W
68	Walker River Ind. Res. Nev.	39·06 N	118·20 W
67	Walkerville (wôk'ẽr-vĭl) Mont.	46·20 N	112·32 W
66	Wallace (wŏl'ås) Idaho	47·27 N	115·55 W
161	Wallacia Austl. (Sydney In.)	33·52 S	150·40 E
66	Wallapa B. (wŏl ȧ pä) Wash.	46·39 N	124·30 W
160	Wallaroo (wŏl-ȧ-rōō) Austl.	33·52 S	137·45 E
110	Wallasey (wŏl'ȧ-sē) Eng.	53·25 N	3·03 W
66	Walla Walla (wŏl'ȧ wŏl'ȧ) Wash.	46·03 N	118·20 W
75	Walled Lake (wôl'd lāk) Mich. (Detroit In.)	42·32 N	83·29 W
165	Wallel, Tulu (Mt.) Eth.	9·00 N	34·52 E
110	Wallingford (wŏl'ĭng-fẽrd) Eng. (London In.)	51·34 N	1·08 W
81	Wallingford Vt.	43·30 N	72·55 W
156	Wallis Is. Oceania	13·00 S	183·50 E
77	Wallisville (wŏl'ĭs-vĭl) Tex. (In.)	29·50 N	94·44 W
66	Wallowa (wôl'ô-wȧ) Ore.	45·34 N	117·32 W
66	Wallowa Mts. Ore.	45·10 N	117·22 W
66	Wallowa R. Ore.	45·28 N	117·28 W
116	Walney (C.) (wôl'nē) Eng.	54·04 N	3·13 W
74	Walnut (wôl'nŭt) Calif. (Los Angeles In.)	34·00 N	117·51 W
73	Walnut (R.) Kans.	37·28 N	97·06 W
69	Walnut Canyon Natl. Mon. Ariz.	35·10 N	111·30 W
65	Walnut Creek Calif. (San Francisco In.)	37·54 N	122·04 W
74	Walnut Cr. Tex. (Dallas, Fort Worth In.)	32·37 N	97·03 W
73	Walnut Ridge (rĭj) Ark.	36·04 N	90·56 W
83	Walpole (wôl'pōl) Mass. (Boston In.)	42·09 N	71·15 W
81	Walpole N. H.	43·05 N	72·25 W
110	Walsall (wôl-sôl) Eng.	52·35 N	1·58 W
72	Walsenburg (wôl'sĕn-bûrg) Colo.	37·38 N	104·46 W
72	Walters (wôl'tẽrz) Okla.	34·21 N	98·19 W
83	Waltham (wôl'thȧm) Mass. (Boston In.)	42·22 N	71·14 W
110	Walthamstow (wôl'tȧm-stō) Eng. (London In.)	51·34 N	0·01 W
81	Walton (wôl'tŭn) N. Y.	42·10 N	75·05 W
110	Walton-le-Dale (lē-dāl') Eng.	53·44 N	2·40 W
166	Walvis Bay (wôl'vĭs) S. Afr.	22·50 S	14·30 E
71	Walworth (wôl'wûrth) Wis.	42·33 N	88·39 W
165	Wamba (wäm'bä) Con. L.	2·15 N	28·05 E
166	Wamba (R.) Con. L.	6·45 S	17·51 E
73	Wamego (wŏ-mē'gō) Kans.	39·13 N	96·17 W
167	Wami (R.) (wä'mē) Tan.	6·31 S	37·17 E
84	Wanaque (wŏn'ȧ-kū) N. J. (New York In.)	41·03 N	74·16 W
84	Wanaque Res. N. J. (New York In.)	41·06 N	74·20 W
148	Wanchih (wän'chĭ') China	31·11 N	118·31 E
111	Wandsbek (vånds'bĕk) Ger. (Hamburg In.)	53·34 N	10·07 E
110	Wandsworth (wôndz'wûrth) Eng.	51·26 N	0·12 W
159	Wanganui (wôŋ'gȧ-nōō'ē) N. Z. (In.)	39·53 S	175·01 E
160	Wangaratta (wŏŋ'gȧ-răt'ȧ) Austl.	36·23 S	146·18 E
152	Wangching (wäng'chĕng) China	43·14 N	129·33 E
148	Wangch'ingt'o (wäng'chĭng'tōōŭ) China	39·14 N	116·56 E
120	Wangeroog I. (vän'gĕ-rōg) Ger.	53·49 N	7·57 E
151	Wanhsien (wän'hsyĕn') China	30·48 N	108·22 E
148	Wanhsien (wän'sĭän) China	38·51 N	115·10 E
166	Wankie (wăŋ'kē) S. Rh.	18·27 S	26·30 E
110	Wantage (wŏn'tȧj) Eng. (London In.)	51·33 N	1·26 W
151	Wantsai China	28·05 N	114·25 E
160	Waodoan (wŏd'ŏn) Austl.	26·12 S	149·52 E
80	Wapakoneta (wä'pȧ-kô-nĕt'ȧ) Ohio	40·35 N	84·10 W
71	Wapello (wŏ-pĕl'ō) Iowa	41·10 N	91·11 W
73	Wappapello Res. (wă'pȧ-pĕl-lō) Mo.	37·07 N	90·10 W
81	Wappingers Falls (wŏp'ĭn-jẽrz) N. Y.	41·35 N	73·55 W
71	Wapsipinicon (R.) (wŏp'sĭ-pĭn'ĭ-kŏn) Iowa	42·16 N	91·35 W
153	Warabi (wä'rä-bē) Jap. (Tōkyō In.)	35·50 N	139·41 E
143	Warangal (wŭ'răŋ-gȧl) India	18·03 N	17·39 E
158	Warburton, The (R.) (wŏr'bûr-tŭn) Austl.	27·30 S	138·45 E
139	Wardan (R.) U. A. R. (Egypt) (Palestine In.)	29·29 N	32·52 E
168	Warden (wŏr'dĕn) S. Afr. (Johannesburg & Pretoria In.)	27·52 S	28·59 E
142	Wardha (wŭr'dä) India	20·46 N	78·42 E
75	Wardsworth (wôrdz'wûrth) Ohio (Cleveland In.)	41·01 N	81·44 W
80	War Eagle (wôr ē'g'l) W. Va.	37·30 N	81·50 W
120	Waren (vä'rĕn) Ger.	53·32 N	12·43 E
123	Warendorf (vä'rĕn-dōrf) Ger. (Ruhr In.)	51·57 N	7·59 E
166	Warmbad (värm'bȧd) (wôrm'băd) S. W. Afr.	28·25 S	18·45 E
168	Warmbad S. Afr. (Johannesburg & Pretoria In.)	24·52 S	28·18 E
65	Warm Beach (wôrm) Wash. (Seattle In.)	48·10 N	122·22 W
66	Warm Springs Ind. Res. (wôrm sprĭngz) Ore.	44·55 N	121·30 W
66	Warm Springs Res. Ore.	43·42 N	118·40 W
118	Warnemünde (vär'nĕ-mün-dĕ) Ger.	54·11 N	12·04 E
66	Warner Ra. (Mts.) (wôrn'ẽr) Calif.-Ore.	41·30 N	120·17 W
120	Warnow R. (vär'nō) Ger.	53·51 N	11·55 E
160	Warracknabeal Austl.	36·20 S	142·28 E
161	Warragamba (R.) Austl. (Sydney In.)	33·55 S	150·32 E
159	Warrego (R.) (wôr'ē-gō) Austl.	27·13 S	145·58 E
73	Warren (wŏr'ĕn) Ark.	33·37 N	92·03 W
80	Warren Ind.	40·40 N	85·25 W
75	Warren Mich. (Detroit In.)	42·33 N	83·03 W
70	Warren Minn.	48·11 N	96·44 W
80	Warren Ohio	41·15 N	80·50 W
65	Warren Ore. (Portland In.)	45·49 N	122·51 W
81	Warren Pa.	41·50 N	79·10 W
84	Warren R. I. (Providence In.)	41·44 N	71·14 W
75	Warrendale (wŏr'ĕn-dāl) Pa. (Pittsburgh In.)	40·39 N	80·04 W
73	Warrensburg (wŏr'ĕnz-bûrg) Mo.	38·45 N	93·42 W
85	Warrenton (wŏr'ĕn-tŭn) Can. (Winnipeg In.)	50·08 N	97·32 W
79	Warrenton Ga.	33·26 N	82·37 W
65	Warrenton Ore. (Portland In.)	46·10 N	123·56 W
81	Warrenton Va.	38·45 N	77·50 W
164	Warri (wär'ē) Nig.	5·33 N	5·43 E
110	Warrington Eng.	53·22 N	2·30 W
78	Warrington (wŏr'ĭng-tŭn) Fla.	30·21 N	87·15 W
160	Warrnambool (wôr'nȧm-bōōl) Austl.	36·20 S	142·28 E
71	Warroad (wôr'rōd) Minn.	48·55 N	95·20 W
159	Warrumbungle Ra. (wôr'ŭm-bŭŋ-g'l) Austl.	31·18 S	150·00 E
73	Warsaw (wôr'sô) Ill.	40·21 N	91·26 W
80	Warsaw Ind.	41·15 N	85·50 W
81	Warsaw N. Y.	42·45 N	78·10 W
79	Warsaw N. C.	35·00 N	78·07 W
	Warsaw, see Warszawa		
110	Warsop (wôr'sŭp) Eng.	53·13 N	1·05 W
121	Warszawa (Warsaw) (vár-shä'vá) Pol.	52·15 N	21·05 E
120	Warta R. (vär'tȧ) Pol.	52·35 N	15·07 E
167	Wartburg S. Afr. (Natal In.)	29·26 S	30·39 E
160	Warwick (wŏr'ĭk) Austl.	28·05 S	152·10 E
82	Warwick Can.	45·58 N	71·57 W
116	Warwick Eng.	52·19 N	1·46 W
84	Warwick N. Y. (New York In.)	41·15 N	74·22 W
84	Warwick R. I. (Providence In.)	41·42 N	71·27 W
110	Warwick (Co.) Eng.	52·22 N	1·34 W
74	Wasatch Mts. (wô'săch) Utah (Salt Lake City In.)	40·45 N	111·46 W
69	Wasatch Plat. Utah	38·55 N	111·40 W
62	Wasatch Ra. U. S.	39·10 N	111·30 W
167	Wasbank S. Afr. (Natal In.)	28·27 S	30·09 E
167	Waschbank Pk. (Mtn.) (văsh'bȧnk) S. Afr. (Natal In.)	31·17 S	27·26 E
66	Wasco (wăs'kō) Ore.	45·36 N	120·42 W
71	Waseca (wô-sē'kȧ) Minn.	44·04 N	93·31 W
117	Wash, The (Est.) (wŏsh) Eng.	53·00 N	0·20 E
82	Washburn (wŏsh'bŭrn) Maine	46·46 N	68·10 W
71	Washburn Wis.	46·41 N	90·55 W
67	Washburn, Mt. Wyo.	44·55 N	110·10 W
81	Washington (wŏsh'ĭng-tŭn) D. C.	38·50 N	77·00 W
78	Washington Ga.	33·43 N	82·46 W
80	Washington Ind.	38·40 N	87·10 W
71	Washington Iowa	41·17 N	91·42 W
73	Washington Kans.	39·48 N	97·04 W
73	Washington Mo.	38·33 N	91·00 W
79	Washington N. C.	35·32 N	77·01 W
75	Washington Pa. (Pittsburgh In.)	40·10 N	80·14 W
62	Washington (State) U. S.	47·30 N	121·10 W
81	Washington, Mt. N. H.	44·15 N	71·15 W
65	Washington, L. Wash. (Seattle In.)	47·34 N	122·12 W
71	Washington (I.) Wis.	45·18 N	86·42 W
80	Washington Court House Ohio	39·30 N	83·25 W
74	Washington Park Ill. (St. Louis In.)	38·38 N	90·06 W
72	Washita (R.) (wŏsh'ĭ-tô) Okla.	35·33 N	99·16 W
65	Washougal (wŏ-shōō'gȧl) Wash. (Portland In.)	45·35 N	122·21 W
65	Washougal (R.) Wash. (Portland In.)	45·38 N	122·17 W
121	Wasilkow (vȧ-sēl'kōōf) Pol.	53·12 N	23·13 E
123	Wassenberg (vä'sĕn-bĕrgh) Ger. (Ruhr In.)	51·06 N	6·07 E
68	Wassuk Ra. (wȧs'sŭk) Nev.	38·58 N	119·00 W
74	Watauga (wȧ tō gā') Tex. (Dallas, Fort Worth In.)	32·51 N	97·16 W
89	Water (I.) (wô'tẽr) Vir. Is. (U. S. A.) (St. Thomas In.)	18·20 N	64·57 W
168	Waterberg (Mts.) (wôrtẽr'bûrg) S. Afr. (Johannesburg & Pretoria In.)	24·25 S	27·53 E
79	Waterboro (wô'tẽr-bûr-ō) S. C.	32·50 N	80·40 W
81	Waterbury (wô'tẽr-bĕr-ē) Conn.	41·30 N	73·00 W
82	Waterbury Vt.	44·20 N	72·44 W
95	Water Cay (I.) Ba. Is.	22·55 N	75·50 W
85	Waterdown (wô'tẽr-doun) Can. (Toronto In.)	43·20 N	79·54 W
79	Wateree (R.) (wô'tẽr-ē) S. C.	34·40 N	80·48 W
116	Waterford (wô'tẽr-fẽrd) Ire.	52·20 N	7·03 W
75	Waterford Wis. (Milwaukee In.)	42·46 N	88·13 W
167	Waterkloof S. Afr. (Johannesburg & Pretoria In.)	25·48 S	28·15 E
111	Waterloo Bel. (Brussels In.)	50·44 N	4·24 E
80	Waterloo (wô-tẽr-lōō') Can.	43·30 N	80·40 W
81	Waterloo Can.	45·25 N	72·30 W
73	Waterloo Ill.	38·19 N	90·08 W
71	Waterloo Iowa	42·30 N	92·22 W
81	Waterloo N. Y.	42·55 N	76·50 W
67	Waterton-Glacier Intl. Peace Park (wô'ter-tŭn-glā'shûr) Mont.-Can.	48·55 N	114·10 W
83	Watertown (wô'tẽr-toun) Mass. (Boston In.)	42·22 N	71·11 W
81	Watertown N. Y.	44·00 N	75·55 W
70	Watertown S. D.	44·53 N	97·07 W
71	Watertown Wis.	43·13 N	88·40 W
78	Water Valley (văl'ē) Miss.	34·08 N	89·38 W
82	Waterville (wô'tẽr-vĭl) Maine	44·34 N	69·37 W
71	Waterville Minn.	44·10 N	93·35 W
66	Waterville Wash.	47·38 N	120·04 W
81	Watervliet (wô'tẽr-vlēt') N. Y.	42·45 N	73·45 W
110	Watford (wŏt'fŏrd) Eng. (London In.)	51·38 N	0·24 W
	Watling I., see San Salvador I.		
110	Watlington (wŏt'lĭng-tŭn) Eng. (London In.)	51·37 N	1·01 W
72	Watonga (wŏ-tôŋ'gȧ) Okla.	35·50 N	98·26 W
86	Watrous Can.	51·40 N	105·32 W
165	Watsa (wät'sä) Con. L.	3·02 N	29·30 E
80	Watseka (wŏt-sē'kȧ) Ill.	40·45 N	87·45 W
75	Watson (wŏt'sŭn) Ind. (Louisville In.)	38·21 N	85·42 W
86	Watson Lake Can.	60·18 N	128·50 W
68	Watsonville (wŏt'sŭn-vĭl) Calif.	36·55 N	121·46 W
123	Wattenscheid (vä'tĕn-shīd) Ger. (Ruhr In.)	51·30 N	7·07 E
74	Watts (wŏts) Calif. (Los Angeles In.)	33·56 N	118·15 W
78	Watts Bar (R.) (bär) Tenn.	35·45 N	84·49 W
165	Wau (wä'ōō) Sud.	7·41 N	28·00 E
165	Wāu al Kebir Libya	25·23 N	16·52 E
70	Waubay (wô'bā) S. D.	45·19 N	97·18 W
79	Wauchula (wô-chōō'lȧ) Fla. (In.)	27·32 N	81·48 W
75	Wauconda (wô-kŏn'dȧ) Ill. (Chicago In.)	42·15 N	88·08 W
75	Waukegan (wŏ-kē'gȧn) Ill. (Chicago In.)	42·22 N	87·51 W

Page Name Pronunciation Region Lat. °' Long. °'

75 Waukesha (wô'kê-shô) Wis. (Milwaukee In.) 43·01 N 88·13 W
71 Waukon (wô kŏn) Iowa 43·15 N 91·30 W
65 Wauna (wȧ-nȧ) Ore. (Portland In.) 46·09 N 123·25 W
71 Waupaca (wô-păk'ȧ) Wis. 44·22 N 89·06 W
71 Waupun (wô-pŭn') Wis. 43·37 N 88·45 W
72 Waurika (wô-rē'kȧ) Okla. 34·09 N 97·59 W
71 Wausau (wô'sô) Wis. 44·58 N 89·40 W
71 Wausaukee (wô-sô'kê) Wis. 45·22 N 87·58 W
80 Wauseon (wô'sê-ŏn) Ohio 41·30 N 84·10 W
71 Wautoma (wô-tō'mȧ) Wis. 44·04 N 89·11 W
75 Wauwatosa (wô-wȧ-tō'sȧ) Wis. (Milwaukee In.) 43·03 N 88·00 W
117 Waveney (R.) (wāv'nê) Eng. 52·27 N 1·17 E
167 Waverley S. Afr. (Natal In.) 31·54 S 26·29 E
71 Waverly (wā'vẽr-lê) Iowa 42·43 N 92·29 W
78 Waverly Tenn. 36·04 N 87·46 W
80 Wawasee (L.) (wô-wô-sē') Ind. 41·25 N 85·45 W
77 Waxahachie (wăk-sȧ-hăch'ê) Tex. 32·23 N 96·50 W
79 Waycross (wā'krôs) Ga. 31·11 N 82·24 W
78 Wayland (wā'lȧnd) Ky. 37·25 N 82·47 W
83 Wayland Mass. (Boston In.) 42·23 N 71·22 W
75 Wayne Mich. (Detroit In.) 42·17 N 83·23 W
70 Wayne (wān) Nebr. 42·13 N 97·03 W
84 Wayne Pa. (Philadelphia In.) 40·03 N 75·22 W
79 Waynesboro (wānz'bŭr-ô) Ga. 33·05 N 82·02 W
81 Waynesboro Pa. 39·45 N 77·35 W
81 Waynesboro Va. 38·05 N 78·50 W
81 Waynesburg (wānz'bûrg) Pa. 39·55 N 80·10 W
78 Waynesville (wānz'vĭl) N. C. 35·28 N 82·58 W
72 Waynoka (wā-nō'kȧ) Okla. 36·34 N 98·52 W
74 Wayzata (wā-zä-tȧ) Minn. (Minneapolis, St. Paul In.) 44·58 N 93·31 W
142 Wazīrbad W. Pak. 32·39 N 74·11 E
116 Weald, The (Reg.) (wēld) Eng. 50·58 N 0·15 W
72 Weatherford (wĕ-dhẽr-fẽrd) Okla. 85·32 N 98·41 W
77 Weatherford Tex. 32·45 N 97·46 W
110 Weaver (R.) (wē'vẽr) Eng. 53·09 N 2·31 W
66 Weaverville (wē'vẽr-vĭl) Calif. 40·44 N 122·55 W
73 Webb City (wĕb) Mo. 37·10 N 94·26 W
74 Weber R. (wĕb'ẽr) Utah (Salt Lake City In.) 41·13 N 112·07 W
83 Webster (wĕb'stẽr) Mass. (Boston In.) 42·04 N 71·52 W
70 Webster S. D. 45·19 N 97·30 W
77 Webster Tex. (In.) 29·32 N 95·07 W
71 Webster City Iowa 42·28 N 93·49 W
74 Webster Groves (grōvz) Mo. (St. Louis In.) 38·36 N 90·22 W
81 Webster Springs (sprĭngz) W. Va. 38·30 N 80·20 W
47 Weddell Sea (wĕd'ĕl) Ant. 73·00 S 45·00 W
111 Wedel (vā'dĕl) Ger. (Hamburg In.) 53·35 N 9·42 E
82 Wedgeport (wĕj'pōrt) Can. 43·46 N 65·58 W
110 Wednesbury (wĕd''nz-bŭr-ê) Eng. 52·33 N 2·01 W
110 Wednesfield (wĕd''nz-fēld) Eng. 52·36 N 2·04 W
66 Weed (wēd) Calif. 41·35 N 122·21 W
85 Weed Cr. Can. (Edmonton In.) 53·18 N 114·01 W
167 Weenen (vā'nĕn) S. Afr. (Natal In.) 28·52 S 30·05 E
117 Weert Neth. 51·16 N 5·39 E
111 Weesp Neth. (Amsterdam In.) 52·18 N 5·01 E
87 Weggs, C. Can. 62·14 N 73·43 W
121 Wegorzewo (vôŋ-gô'zhĕ-vô) Pol. 54·14 N 21·46 E
121 Wegrow (vôŋ'grōōf) Pol. 52·23 N 22·02 E
148 Wei (R.) (wā) China 35·47 N 114·27 E
150 Weich'ang (wā'chăng') China 41·50 N 118·00 E
148 Weihaiwei (wa'hăĭ'wā) China 37·30 N 122·05 E
150 Wei Ho (R.) China 34·00 N 108·10 E
146 Weihsi (wā'hsē') China 27·27 N 99·30 E
148 Weihsien (wā'hsyĕn') China 36·43 N 119·08 E
148 Weihsien China 36·59 N 115·17 E
120 Weilheim (vīl'hīm') Ger. 47·50 N 11·06 E
120 Weimar (vī'mär) Ger. 50·59 N 11·20 E
150 Weinan China 34·32 N 109·40 E
159 Weipa Austl. 12·25 S 141·54 E
80 Weirton (wẽr'tŭn) W. Va. 40·25 N 80·35 W
66 Weiser (wē'zẽr) Idaho 44·15 N 116·58 W
66 Weiser R. Idaho 44·26 N 116·40 W
148 Weishih (wā'shē) China 34·23 N 114·12 E
120 Weissenburg (vī'sĕn-bōōrgh) Ger. 49·04 N 11·20 E
120 Weissenfels (vī'sĕn-fĕlz) Ger. 51·13 N 11·58 E
121 Wejherowo (vā-hĕ-rō'vô) Pol. 54·36 N 18·15 E
79 Welch (wĕlch) W. Va. 37·24 N 81·28 W
79 Weldon (wĕl'dŭn) N. C. 36·24 N 77·36 W
73 Weldon (R.) Mo. 40·22 N 93·39 W
73 Weleetka (wê-lēt'kȧ) Okla. 35·19 N 96·08 W
160 Welford (wĕl'fẽrd) Austl. 25·08 S 144·43 E
168 Welkom (wĕl'kŏm) S. Afr. (Johannesburg & Pretoria In.) 27·57 S 26·45 E
75 Welland (wĕl'ȧnd) Can. (Buffalo In.) 42·59 N 79·13 W
116 Welland (R.) Eng. 52·38 N 0·40 W
83 Wellesley (wĕlz'lê) Mass. (Boston In.) 42·18 N 71·17 W
158 Wellesley Is. Austl. 16·15 S 139·25 E
160 Wellington (wĕl'lĭng-tŭn) Austl. 32·40 S 148·50 E
110 Wellington Eng. 52·42 N 2·30 W
73 Wellington Kans. 37·16 N 97·24 W
159 Wellington N. Z. (In.) 41·15 S 174·45 E
80 Wellington Ohio 41·10 N 82·10 W
72 Wellington Tex. 34·51 N 100·12 W
100 Wellington (I.) (ŏŏĕ'lĕng-tŏn) Chile 49·30 S 76·30 W
158 Wells (wĕlz) Austl. 26·35 S 123·40 E
86 Wells Can. 54·11 N 121·40 W
80 Wells Mich. 45·50 N 87·00 W
71 Wells Minn. 43·44 N 93·43 W
66 Wells Nev. 41·07 N 115·04 W
81 Wellsboro (wĕlz'bŭ-rô) Pa. 41·45 N 77·15 W
80 Wellsburg (wĕlz'bûrg) W. Va. 40·10 N 80·40 W
74 Wellston (wĕlz'tŭn) Mo. (St. Louis In.) 38·41 N 90·18 W
80 Wellston Ohio 39·05 N 82·30 W
73 Wellsville (wĕlz'vĭl) Mo. 39·04 N 91·33 W
81 Wellsville N. Y. 42·10 N 78·00 W
80 Wellsville Ohio 40·35 N 80·40 W
67 Wellsville Utah 41·38 N 111·57 W
120 Wels (vĕls) Aus. 48·10 N 14·01 E
116 Welshpool (wĕlsh'pōōl) Wales 52·44 N 3·10 W
168 Welverdiend (vĕl-vẽr-dēnd') S. Afr. (Johannesburg & Pretoria In.) 26·23 S 27·16 E
110 Welwyn Garden City (wĕl'ĭn) Eng. (London In.) 51·46 N 0·17 W
110 Wem (wĕm) Eng. 52·51 N 2·44 W
148 Wenan Wa (Swp.) (wĕn'än' wä) China 38·56 N 116·29 E
66 Wenatchee (wê-năch'ê) Wash. 47·24 N 120·18 W
66 Wenatchee Mts. Wash. 47·28 N 121·10 W
151 Wench'ang China 19·32 N 110·42 E
151 Wenchow (Yungchia) (wĕn'chō') China 28·00 N 120·40 E
150 Wenchüan (Halunrshan) China 47·10 N 120·00 E
67 Wendorer Utah 40·47 N 114·01 W
85 Wendover (wĕn-dōv'ẽr) Can. (Ottawa In.) 45·34 N 75·07 W
110 Wendover Eng. (London In.) 51·44 N 0·45 W
83 Wenham (wĕn'ȧm) Mass. (Boston In.) 42·36 N 70·53 W
84 Wenonah (wĕn'ō-nä) N. J. (Philadelphia In.) 39·48 N 75·08 W
151 Wenshan China 23·20 N 104·15 E
148 Wenshang (wĕn'shäng) China 35·43 N 116·31 E
148 Wenshussu (wĕn'shōō'sē) China 31·55 N 114·47 E
146 Wensu (Aksu) (wĕn'sōō') (äk'sōō') China 41·45 N 79·54 E
117 Wensum (R.) (wĕn'sŭm) Eng. 52·45 N 1·08 E
110 Went (R.) (wĕnt) Eng. 53·38 N 1·08 W
148 Wenteng (wĕn'tĕng') China 37·14 N 122·03 E
160 Wentworth (wĕnt'wûrth) Austl. 34·03 S 141·53 E
166 Wepener (wē'pĕn-ẽr) (vā'pĕn-ẽr) S. Afr. 29·43 S 27·04 E
111 Werder (vĕr'dĕr) Ger. (Berlin In.) 52·23 N 12·56 E
123 Werl (vĕrl) Ger. (Ruhr In.) 51·33 N 7·55 E
123 Werne (vĕr'nĕ) Ger. (Ruhr In.) 51·39 N 7·38 E
111 Werneuchen (vĕr'hoi-ĸĕn) Ger. (Berlin In.) 52·38 N 13·44 E
120 Werra R. (vĕr'ä) Ger. 51·16 N 9·54 E
161 Werribee Austl. (Melbourne In.) 37·54 S 144·40 E
161 Werribee (R.) Austl. (Melbourne In.) 37·40 S 144·37 E
120 Wertach R. (vĕr'täk) Ger. 48·12 N 10·40 E
123 Weseke (vĕ'zĕ-kĕ) Ger. (Ruhr In.) 51·54 N 6·51 E
123 Wesel (vā'zĕl) Ger. (Ruhr In.) 51·39 N 6·37 E
120 Weser R. (vā'zẽr) Ger. 53·08 N 8·35 E
76 Weslaco (wĕs-lā'kō) Tex. 26·10 N 97·59 W
83 Wesleyville (wĕs'lē-vĭl) Can. 49·09 N 53·33 W
158 Wessel (Is.) (wĕs'ĕl) Austl. 11·45 S 36·25 E
168 Wesselsbron (wĕs'ĕl-brŏn) S. Afr. (Johannesburg & Pretoria In.) 27·51 S 26·22 E
70 Wessington Springs (wĕs'ĭng-tŭn) S. D. 44·06 N 98·35 W
88 West, Mt C. Z. (Panama Canal In.) 9·10 N 79·52 W
75 West Allis (wĕst-ăl'ĭs) Wis. (Milwaukee In.) 43·01 N 88·01 W
74 West Alton (ôl'tŭn) Mo. (St. Louis In.) 38·52 N 90·13 W
77 West B. Tex. (In.) 29·11 N 95·03 W
71 West Bend (wĕst bĕnd) Wis. 43·25 N 88·13 W
142 West Bengal (State) (bĕn-gôl') India 28·00 N 87·42 E
111 West Berlin (bĕr-lēn') Ger. (Berlin In.) 52·31 N 13·20 E
78 West Blocton (blŏk'tŭn) Ala. 33·05 N 87·05 W
83 Westboro (wĕst'bŭr-ô) Mass. (Boston In.) 42·17 N 71·37 W
83 West Boyleston (boil'stŭn) Mass. (Boston In.) 42·22 N 71·46 W
80 West Branch (wĕst brȧnch) Mich. 44·15 N 84·10 W
110 West Bridgford (brĭj'fẽrd) Eng. 52·55 N 1·08 W
110 West Bromwich (wĕst brŭm'ĭj) Eng. 52·32 N 1·59 W
82 Westbrook (wĕst'brŏŏk) Maine 43·41 N 70·23 W
71 Westby (wĕst'bê) Wis. 43·40 N 90·52 W
95 West Caicos (I.) (käē'kōs) Caicos 21·40 N 72·30 W
158 West Cape Howe (C.) Austl. 35·15 S 117·30 E
75 West Chester (chĕs'tẽr) Ohio (Cincinnati In.) 39·20 N 84·24 W
84 West Chester Pa. (Philadelphia In.) 39·57 N 75·36 W
75 West Chicago (chĭ-kȧ'gō) Ill. (Chicago In.) 41·53 N 88·12 W
79 West Columbia (cŏl'ŭm-bē-ȧ) S. C. 33·58 N 81·05 W
77 West Columbia Tex. 29·08 N 95·39 W
77 West Cote Blanche B. (kōt blănch) La. 29·30 N 92·17 W
74 West Covina (wĕst kô-vē'nȧ) Calif. (Los Angeles In.) 34·04 N 117·55 W
71 West Des Moines (dē moin') Iowa 41·35 N 93·42 W
71 West Des Moines (R.) Iowa 42·52 N 94·32 W
94 West End Ba. Is. 26·40 N 78·55 W
110 Westerham (wĕ'stẽr'ŭm) Eng. (London In.) 51·15 N 0·05 E
111 Westerhorn (vĕs'tĕr-hŏrn) Ger. (Hamburg In.) 53·52 N 9·41 E
111 Westerlo Bel. (Brussels In.) 51·05 N 4·57 E
81 Westerly (wĕs'tẽr-lê) Conn. 41·25 N 71·50 W
120 Western Alps (Mts.) Switz.-Fr. 46·19 N 7·03 E
158 Western Australia (State) (ôs-trā'lĭ-ȧ) Austl. 24·15 S 121·30 E
Western Dvina, see Zapadnaya Dvina
116 Western Downs Eng. 50·50 N 2·25 W
143 Western Ghats (Mts.) India 22·09 N 74·15 E
81 Western Port (wĕs'tẽrn pōrt) Md. 39·30 N 79·00 W
164 Western Region (Div.) Nig. 8·54 N 3·30 E
156 Western Samoa Oceania 14·30 S 172·00 W
66 Western Shoshone Ind. Res. (wĕst'ẽrn shô-shōn'ē) Idaho 42·02 N 115·49 W
130 Western Siberian Lowland Sov. Un. 63·37 N 72·45 E
80 Westerville (wĕs'tẽr-vĭl) Ohio 40·10 N 83·00 W
120 Westerwald (For.) (vĕs'tĕr-väld) Ger. 50·35 N 7·45 E
84 Westfield (wĕst'fēld) Ala. (Birmingham In.) 33·29 N 86·57 W
81 Westfield Mass. 42·05 N 72·45 W
84 Westfield N. J. (New York In.) 40·39 N 74·21 W
81 Westfield (wĕst'fēld) N. Y. 42·20 N 79·40 W
83 Westford (wĕst'fẽrd) Mass. (Boston In.) 42·35 N 71·26 W
80 West Frankfort (frăŋk'fŭrt) Ill. 37·55 N 88·55 W
110 West Ham Eng. (London In.) 51·30 N 0·00
81 West Hartford (härt'fẽrd) Conn. 41·45 N 72·45 W
116 West Hartlepool (här't'l-pōōl) Eng. 54·40 N 1·12 W
73 West Helena (hĕl'ĕn-ȧ) Ark. 34·32 N 90·39 W
85 West Hill Can. (Toronto In.) 43·46 N 79·09 W
89 West Indies (Reg.) (ĭn'dēz) N. A. 19·00 N 78·30 W
155 West Irian (ĭr'ē-ȧn) Asia 3·05 S 135·00 E
74 West Jordan (jôr'dȧn) Utah (Salt Lake City In.) 40·37 N 111·56 W
110 West Kirby (kûr'bê) Eng. 53·22 N 3·11 W
80 West Lafayette (lä-fâ-yĕt') Ind. 40·25 N 86·55 W
75 Westlake Ohio (Cleveland In.) 41·27 N 81·55 W
168 Westleigh (wĕst-lē) S. Afr. (Johannesburg & Pretoria In.) 27·39 S 27·18 E
71 West Liberty (wĕst lĭb'ẽr-tĭ) Iowa 41·34 N 91·15 W
65 West Linn (lĭn) Ore. (Portland In.) 45·22 N 122·37 W
74 Westminster (wĕst'mĭn-stẽr) Calif. (Los Angeles In.) 33·45 N 117·59 W
81 Westminster Md. 39·40 N 76·55 W
78 Westminster S. C. 34·38 N 83·10 W
85 Westmount (wĕst'mount) Can. (Montreal In.) 45·29 N 73·36 W
83 West Newbury (nū'bẽr-ê) Mass. (Boston In.) 42·47 N 70·57 W
75 West Newton (nū'tŭn) Pa. (Pittsburgh In.) 40·12 N 79·45 W
84 West New York (nū yŏrk) N. J. (New York In.) 40·47 N 74·01 W
73 West Nishnabotna (R.) (nĭsh-nȧ-bŏt'nȧ) Iowa 40·56 N 95·37 W
84 West Norfolk (nôr'fŏk) Va. (Norfolk In.) 36·52 N 76·20 W
85 Weston (wĕs'tŭn) Can. (Toronto In.) 43·40 N 79·30 W
83 Weston Mass. (Boston In.) 42·22 N 71·18 W
80 Weston W. Va. 39·00 N 80·30 W
168 Westonaria S. Afr. (Johannesburg & Pretoria In.) 26·19 S 27·38 E
116 Weston-super-Mare (wĕs'tŭn sū'pẽr-mā'rê) Eng. 51·23 N 3·00 W
84 West Orange (wĕst ŏr'ĕnj) N. J. (New York In.) 40·46 N 74·14 W
79 West Palm Beach (päm bēch) Fla. (In.) 26·44 N 80·04 W
78 West Pensacola (pĕn-sȧ-kō'lȧ) Fla. 30·24 N 87·18 W
65 West Pittsburg (pĭts'bûrg) Calif. (San Francisco In.) 38·02 N 121·56 W
73 Westplains (wĕst-plānz') Mo. 36·42 N 91·51 W
78 West Point Ga. 32·52 N 85·10 W
78 West Point Miss. 33·36 N 88·39 W
70 Westpoint Nebr. 41·50 N 96·00 W
84 West Point N. Y. (New York In.) 41·23 N 73·58 W
74 West Point Utah (Salt Lake City In.) 41·07 N 112·05 W
81 West Point Va. 37·35 N 76·50 W
82 West Pt. (wĕst' point) Can. 49·53 N 64·35 W
84 Westport (wĕst'pōrt) Conn. (New York In.) 41·07 N 73·22 W
116 Westport Ire. 53·44 N 9·36 W
65 Westport (wĕst'pôrt) Ore. (Portland In.) 46·08 N 123·22 W
116 Westray (I.) (wĕs'trā) Scot. 59·19 N 3·05 W
110 West Riding (Co.) (rīd'ĭng) Eng. 53·37 N 1·30 W
74 West Riverside (wĕst rĭv'ẽr-sīd) Calif. (Los Angeles In.) 33·59 N 117·24 W
74 West St. Paul (sȧnt pôl') Minn. (Minneapolis, St. Paul In.) 44·55 N 93·05 W
95 West Sand Spit (I.) Ba. Is. 21·25 N 72·10 W
117 West Schelde (R.) Neth. 51·25 N 3·30 E
69 West Tavaputs Plat. (wĕst tăv'ȧ-pŏŏts) Utah 39·45 N 110·35 W
80 West Terre Haute (tĕr-ê hōt') Ind. 39·30 N 87·30 W
71 West Union (ūn'yŭn) Iowa 42·58 N 91·48 W
75 Westview (wĕst'vū) Ohio (Cleveland In.) 41·21 N 81·54 W
75 West View Pa. (Pittsburgh In.) 40·31 N 80·02 W
83 Westville (wĕst'vĭl) Can. 45·35 N 62·45 W
80 Westville Ill. 40·00 N 87·40 W
63 West Virginia (State) (wĕst vẽr-jĭn'ĭ-ȧ) U. S. 39·00 N 80·50 W
68 West Walker (R.) (wôk'ẽr) Calif. 38·25 N 119·25 W
84 West Warwick (wŏr'ĭk) R. I. (Providence In.) 41·42 N 71·31 W
84 Westwego (wĕst-wē'gō) La. (New Orleans In.) 29·55 N 90·09 W
68 Westwood (wĕst'wŏŏd) Calif. 40·18 N 121·00 W
83 Westwood Mass. (Boston In.) 42·13 N 71·14 W
74 Westwood Mo. (Kansas City In.) 39·03 N 94·37 W
84 Westwood N. J. (New York In.) 40·59 N 74·02 W
160 West Wyalong (wī'ȧlông) Austl. 34·00 S 147·20 E
155 Wetar (I.) (wĕt'ȧr) Indon. 7·34 S 126·00 E
86 Wetaskiwin (wĕ-tăs'kê-wŏn) Can. 53·01 N 113·24 W
74 Wetmore (wĕt'mōr) Tex. (San Antonio In.) 29·34 N 98·25 W
123 Wettin (vĕ'tĕn) Ger. (Ruhr In.) 51·23 N 7·23 E
78 Wetumpka (wê-tŭmp'kȧ) Ala. 32·33 N 86·12 W
123 Wetzlar (vĕts'lär) Ger. 50·35 N 8·30 E
155 Wewak (wā-wäk') N. Gui. Ter. 3·19 S 143·30 E
73 Wewoka (wê-wō'kȧ) Okla. 35·09 N 96·30 W
116 Wexford (wĕks'fẽrd) Ire. 52·20 N 6·30 W
110 Weybridge (wā'brĭj) Eng. (London In.) 51·20 N 0·26 W
86 Weyburn Can. 49·31 N 103·50 W
116 Weymouth (wā'mŭth) Eng. 50·37 N 2·34 W
83 Weymouth Mass. (Boston In.) 42·44 N 70·57 W

ăt; finăl; rāte; senâte; ärm; åsk; sofȧ; fâre; ch-choose; dh-as th in other; bē; ēvent; bĕt; recĕnt; cratẽr; g-go; gh-guttural g; bĭt; ĭ-short neutral; rīde; ĸ-guttural k as ch in German ich;

Page	Name Pronunciation Region	Lat. °′	Long. °′
75	Weymouth . . Ohio (Cleveland In.)	41·11 N	81·48 W
94	Whale Cay (I.) . . . . Ba. Is.	24·50 N	77·45 W
94	Whale Cay Chans . . . . Ba. Is.	26·45 N	77·10 W
116	Wharfe (R.) (hwôr'fê) . . . . Eng.	54·01 N	1·53 W
84	Wharton (hwôr'tŭn) N. J. (New York In.)	40·54 N	74·35 W
77	Wharton . . . . Tex.	29·19 N	96·06 W
71	What Cheer (hwŏt chēr) . . . . Iowa	41·23 N	92·24 W
65	Whatcom, L. (hwăt'kŭm) Wash. (Portland In.)	48·44 N	123·34 W
75	Wheatland (hwēt'lănd) Wis. (Milwaukee In.)	42·36 N	88·12 W
67	Wheatland . . . . Wyo.	42·04 N	104·52 W
75	Wheaton (hwē'tŭn) Ill. (Chicago In.)	41·52 N	88·06 W
81	Wheaton . . . . Md.	39·05 N	77·05 W
70	Wheaton . . . . Minn.	45·48 N	96·29 W
69	Wheeler Pk. (hwē'lẽr) . . . . Nev.	38·58 N	114·15 W
75	Wheeling (hwēl'ĭng) Ill. (Chicago In.)	42·08 N	87·54 W
80	Wheeling . . . . W. Va.	40·05 N	80·45 W
101	Wheelwright (ŏŏē'l-rē'gt) Arg. (Buenos Aires In.)	33·46 S	61·14 W
65	Whidbey I. (hwĭd'bê) Wash. (Seattle In.)	48·13 N	122·50 W
84	Whippany (hwĭp'á-nē) N. J. (New York In.)	40·49 N	74·25 W
78	Whistler (hwĭs'lẽr) . . . . Ala.	30·46 N	88·07 W
81	Whitby (hwĭt'bê) . . . . Can.	43·50 N	79·00 W
110	Whitchurch (hwĭt'chûrch) . . . Eng.	52·58 N	79·00 W
73	White (R.) . . . . Ark.	34·32 N	91·11 W
68	White Mt . . . . Calif.	37·38 N	118·13 W
81	White (L.) . . . . Can.	45·15 N	76·35 W
71	White (L.) . . . . Can.	48·47 N	85·50 W
71	White (R.) . . . . Can.	48·34 N	85·46 W
69	White (R.) . . . . Colo.	40·10 N	108·55 W
80	White (R.) . . . . Ind.	39·15 N	86·45 W
70	White (R.) . . . . S. D.	43·41 N	99·48 W
70	White (R.), South Fork . . . . . S. D.	43·13 N	101·04 W
72	White (R.) . . . . Tex.	36·25 N	102·20 W
81	White (R.) . . . . Vt.	43·45 N	72·35 W
83	White B . . . . Can.	50·07 N	56·24 W
83	White Bear B . . . . Can.	47·28 N	57·55 W
74	White Bear Lake . . . . Minn. (Minneapolis, St. Paul In.)	45·05 N	93·01 W
74	White Bear L . . . . Minn. (Minneapolis, St. Paul In.)	45·04 N	92·58 W
77	White Castle . . . . La.	30·10 N	91·09 W
80	White Cloud . . . . Mich.	43·35 N	85·45 W
86	White Court . . . . Can.	54·09 N	115·34 W
70	White Earth (R.) . . . . N. D.	48·30 N	102·44 W
70	White Earth Ind. Res . . . . . . Minn.	47·18 N	95·42 W
71	Whiteface (R.) (whīt'fās) . . . . Minn.	47·12 N	92·13 W
81	Whitefield (hwĭt'fēld) . . . . . . N. H.	44·20 N	71·35 W
67	Whitefish (hwĭt'fĭsh) . . . . Mont.	48·24 N	114·25 W
71	Whitefish (B.) . . . . Mich.	46·36 N	84·50 W
71	Whitefish (R.) . . . . Mich.	46·12 N	86·56 W
75	Whitefish Bay Wis. (Milwaukee In.)	43·07 N	77·54 W
73	White Hall . . . . Ill.	39·26 N	90·23 W
80	Whitehall (hwĭt'hôl) . . . . Mich.	43·20 N	86·20 W
81	Whitehall . . . . N. Y.	43·30 N	73·25 W
116	Whitehaven (hwĭt'hā-vĕn) . . . Eng.	54·35 N	3·30 W
65	Whitehorn, Pt. (hwĭt'hôrn) Wash. (Vancouver In.)	48·54 N	122·48 W
86	Whitehorse (whīt'hôrs) . . . . . . Can.	60·39 N	135·01 W
84	White House . N. J. (New York In.)	40·37 N	74·46 W
77	White L . . . . La.	29·40 N	92·35 W
82	White Mts . . . . Maine	44·22 N	71·15 W
81	White Mts . . . . N. H.	42·20 N	71·05 W
70	Whitemouth (L.) (hwĭt'mŭth) Can.	49·18 N	95·50 W
	White Nile, see El Abyad, Bahr		
71	White Otter (L.) . . . . Can.	49·15 N	91·48 W
86	White P . . . . Alaska-Can.	59·35 N	135·03 W
84	White Plains N. Y. (New York In.)	41·02 N	73·47 W
80	White R., East Fork . . . . Ind.	38·45 N	86·20 W
66	White R . . . . Wash.	47·07 N	121·48 W
69	White River Plat . . . . Colo.	39·45 N	107·50 W
65	White Rock . Can. (Vancouver In.)	49·01 N	122·49 W
74	Whiterock Res. (hwĭt'rŏk) Tex. (Dallas, Fort Worth In.)	32·51 N	96·40 W
168	Whites (wĭts) . . . . S. Afr. (Johannesburg & Pretoria In.)	28·02 S	27·00 E
69	White Sands Natl. Mon . . N. Mex.	32·50 N	106·20 W
132	White Sea . . . . Sov. Un.	66·00 N	40·00 E
74	White Settlement Tex. (Dallas, Fort Worth In.)	32·45 N	97·28 W
67	White Sulphur Springs . . . . . Mont.	46·32 N	110·49 W
167	White Umfolosi (R.) (ŭm-fô-lō'zê) S. Afr. (Natal In.)	28·12 S	30·55 E
79	Whiteville (hwĭt'vĭl) . . . . N. C.	34·18 N	78·45 W
71	Whitewater (whīt-wŏt'ẽr) . . . . Wis.	42·49 N	88·40 W
70	Whitewater (L.) . . . . Can.	49·14 N	100·39 W
79	Whitewater B . . . . Fla. (In.)	25·16 N	80·21 W
67	Whitewater Cr . . . . Mont.	48·50 N	107·50 W
75	Whitewater R. Ind. (Cincinnati In.)	39·19 N	84·55 W
78	Whitewell (hwĭt'wĕl) . . . . Tenn.	35·11 N	85·31 W
73	Whitewright (hwĭt'rīt) . . . . Tex.	33·33 N	96·25 W
116	Whitham (R.) (wĭth'ŭm) . . . . Eng.	53·08 N	0·15 W
75	Whiting (hwĭt'ĭng) Ind. (Chicago In.)	41·41 N	87·30 W
83	Whitinsville (hwĭt'ĕns-vĭl) Mass. (Boston In.)	42·06 N	71·40 W
83	Whitman (hwĭt'măn) Mass. (Boston In.)	42·05 N	70·57 W
66	Whitman Natl. Mon . . . . Ore.	45·58 N	118·10 W
79	Whitmire (hwĭt'mīr) . . . . S. C.	34·30 N	81·40 W
68	Whitney, Mt . . . . Calif.	36·34 N	118·18 W
77	Whitney L. (hwĭt'nê) . . . . Tex.	32·02 N	97·36 W
110	Whitstable (wĭt'stăb'l) Eng. (London In.)	51·22 N	1·03 E
159	Whitsunday (I.) (hwĭt's'n-dā) Austl.	20·16 S	149·00 E
74	Whittier (hwĭt'ĭ-ẽr) Calif. (Los Angeles In.)	33·58 N	118·02 W
167	Whittlesea (wĭt'l'sē) S. Afr. (Natal In.)	32·11 S	26·51 E
110	Whitworth (hwĭt'wŭrth) . . . . . Eng.	53·40 N	2·10 W
160	Whyalla (hwī-ăl'á) . . . . Austl.	33·00 S	137·32 E
80	Wiarton (wī'ár-tŭn) . . . . Can.	44·45 N	80·45 W
73	Wichita (wĭch'ĭ-tô) . . . . Kans.	37·42 N	97·21 W
72	Wichita (R.) . . . . Tex.	33·50 N	99·38 W
72	Wichita Falls (fôls) . . . . Tex.	33·54 N	98·29 W
72	Wichita Mts . . . . Okla.	34·48 N	98·43 W
116	Wick (wĭk) . . . . Scot.	58·25 N	3·05 W
84	Wickatunk (wĭk'á-tŭnk) N. J. (New York In.)	40·21 N	74·15 W
84	Wickford (wĭk'fẽrd) R. I. (Providence In.)	41·34 N	71·26 W
75	Wickliffe (wĭk'klĭf) Ohio (Cleveland In.)	41·37 N	81·29 W
	Wicklow, see Cill Mantainn		
116	Wicklow Mts. (wĭk'lō) . . . . Ire.	52·49 N	6·20 W
65	Wickup Mtn. (wĭk'ŭp) Ore. (Portland In.)	46·06 N	123·35 W
81	Wiconisco (wĭ-kŏn'ĭs-kō) . . . . . . Pa.	40·35 N	76·45 W
80	Widen (wī'dĕn) . . . . W. Va.	38·25 N	80·55 W
110	Widnes (wĭd'nĕs) . . . . Eng.	53·21 N	2·44 W
120	Wieden (vē'dĕn) . . . . Ger.	49·41 N	12·09 E
121	Wieliczka (vyĕ-lēch'kà) . . . . Pol.	49·58 N	20·06 E
121	Wieluń (vyĕ'lōōn') . . . . Pol.	51·13 N	18·33 E
111	Wien (Vienna) (vēn) (vê-ĕn'ă) Aus. (Vienna In.)	48·13 N	16·22 E
111	Wien (State) . . . Aus. (Vienna In.)	48·11 N	16·23 E
120	Wiener Neustadt (vē'nẽr noi'shtät) . . Aus.	47·48 N	16·15 E
111	Wiener Wald (For.) Aus. (Vienna In.)	48·09 N	16·05 E
121	Wieprz, R. (vyĕpzh) . . . . Pol.	51·25 N	22·45 E
77	Wiergate (wẽr'gāt) . . . . Tex.	31·00 N	93·42 W
120	Wiesbaden (vēs'bä-dĕn) . . . . . . Ger.	50·05 N	8·15 E
110	Wigan (wĭg'ăn) . . . . Eng.	53·33 N	2·37 W
78	Wiggins (wĭg'ĭnz) . . . . Miss.	30·51 N	89·05 W
116	Wight, Isle of (I.) (wīt) . . . . . Eng.	50·44 N	1·17 W
73	Wilber (wĭl'bẽr) . . . . Nebr.	40·29 N	96·57 W
73	Wilburton (wĭl'bẽr-tŭn) . . . . . . Okla.	34·54 N	95·18 W
160	Wilcannia (wĭl-căn-ĭá) . . . . . . Austl.	31·30 S	143·30 E
111	Wildau (vēl'dou) . Ger. (Berlin In.)	52·20 N	13·39 E
111	Wildberg (vēl'bĕrgh) Ger. (Berlin In.)	52·52 N	12·39 E
74	Wildomar (wĭl'dô-mär) Calif. (Los Angeles In.)	33·35 N	117·17 W
70	Wild Rice (R.) . . . . Minn.	47·10 N	96·40 W
70	Wild Rice (R.) . . . . N. D.	46·10 N	97·12 W
74	Wild Rice L . . Minn. (Duluth In.)	46·54 N	92·10 W
120	Wild Spitze Pk . . . . Aus.	46·49 N	10·50 E
81	Wildwood (wīld'wŏŏd) . . . . N. J.	39·00 N	74·50 W
72	Wiley (wī'lê) . . . . Colo.	38·08 N	102·41 W
168	Wilge R. (wĭl'jê) . . . . S. Afr. (Johannesburg & Pretoria In.)	25·38 S	29·09 E
168	Wilge R . . . . S. Afr. (Johannesburg & Pretoria In.)	27·27 S	28·46 E
155	Wilhelm, Mt . . . . N. Gui. Ter.	5·58 S	144·58 E
99	Wilhelmina Gebergte (Mts.) . . Sur.	4·30 N	57·00 W
155	Wilhelmina-Top (Pk.) (vēl-hĕl-mē'nà) . W. Irian	3·55 S	138·26 E
120	Wilhelmshaven (vêl-hĕlms-hä'fĕn) Ger.	53·30 N	8·10 E
111	Wilhemina, Kanal (can.) Neth. (Amsterdam In.)	51·37 N	4·55 E
81	Wilkes-Barre (wĭlks'băr-ê) . . . . Pa.	41·15 N	75·50 W
47	Wilkes Land . . . . Ant.	71·00 S	126·00 E
65	Wilkeson (wĭl-kē'sŭn) Wash. (Seattle In.)	47·06 N	122·03 W
86	Wilkie (wĭlk'ē) . . . . Can.	52·29 N	108·50 W
75	Wilkinsburg (wĭl'kĭnz-bûrg) Pa. (Pittsburgh In.)	40·26 N	79·53 W
66	Willamette R . . . . Ore.	44·15 N	123·13 W
80	Willard (wĭl'ărd) . . . . Ohio	41·00 N	82·50 W
74	Willard . Utah (Salt Lake City In.)	41·24 N	112·02 W
69	Willcox (wĭl'kŏks) . . . . Ariz.	32·15 N	109·50 W
98	Willemstad . . . . Curaçao	12·12 N	68·58 W
110	Willenhall (wĭl'ĕn-hôl) . . . . . . Eng.	52·35 N	2·03 W
110	Willesden (wĭlz'dĕn) Eng. (London In.)	51·31 N	0·17 W
158	William Creek (wĭl'yăm) . . . Austl.	28·45 S	136·20 E
69	Williams (wĭl'yămz) . . . . Ariz.	35·15 N	112·15 W
94	Williams (I.) . . . . Ba. Is.	25·30 N	78·30 W
78	Williamsburg (wĭl'yămz-bûrg) . Ky.	36·42 N	84·09 W
75	Williamsburg Ohio (Cincinnati In.)	39·04 N	84·02 W
79	Williamsburg . . . . Va.	37·15 N	76·41 W
80	Williamson (wĭl'yăm-sŭn) . . W. Va.	37·40 N	82·15 W
81	Williamsport (wĭl'yămz-pōrt) . Md.	39·35 N	77·45 W
81	Williamsport . . . . Pa.	41·15 N	77·05 W
79	Williamston (wĭl'yămz-tŭn) . N. C.	35·50 N	77·04 W
79	Williamston . . . . S. C.	34·36 N	82·30 W
80	Williamstown (wĭl'yămz-toun) W. Va.	39·20 N	81·30 W
75	Williamsville (wĭl'yăm-vĭl) N. Y. (Buffalo In.)	42·58 N	78·46 W
81	Willimantic (wĭl-ĭ-măn'tĭk) . Conn.	41·40 N	72·10 W
77	Willis (wĭl'ĭs) . . . . Tex.	30·24 N	95·29 W
159	Willis Is . . . . Austl.	16·15 S	150·30 E
70	Williston (wĭl'ĭs-tŭn) . . . . N. D.	48·08 N	103·38 W
75	Willoughby (wĭl'ô-bê) Ohio (Cleveland In.)	41·39 N	81·25 W
67	Willow Cr. (wĭl'ô) . . . . Mont.	48·45 N	111·34 W
66	Willow Cr . . . . Ore.	44·21 N	117·34 W
85	Willowdale (wĭl'ô-dāl) Can. (Toronto In.)	43·47 N	79·25 W
84	Willow Grove Pa. (Philadelphia In.)	40·07 N	75·07 W
74	Willowick (wĭl'ô-wĭk) Calif. (Los Angeles In.)	33·45 N	117·55 W
75	Willowick . . . Ohio (Cleveland In.)	41·39 N	81·28 W
166	Willowmore (wĭl'ô-mōr) . . . S. Afr.	33·15 S	23·37 E
75	Willow Run (wĭl'ô rŭn) Mich. (Detroit In.)	42·16 N	83·34 W
68	Willows (wĭl'ōz) . . . . Calif.	39·32 N	122·11 W
73	Willow Springs (sprĭngz) . . . . . Mo.	36·59 N	91·56 W
167	Willowvale (wĭ-lô'văl) S. Afr. (Natal In.)	32·17 S	28·32 E
77	Wills Point (wĭlz point) . . . . . Tex.	32·42 N	96·02 W
71	Wilmar (wĭl'mär) . . . . Minn.	45·07 N	95·05 W
74	Wilmer (wĭl'mẽr) Tex. (Dallas, Fort Worth In.)	32·35 N	96·40 W
75	Wilmette (wĭl-mĕt') Ill. (Chicago In.)	42·04 N	87·42 W
74	Wilmington (wĭl'mĭng-tŭn) Calif. (Los Angeles In.)	33·46 N	118·16 W
84	Wilmington . Del. (Philadelphia In.)	39·45 N	75·33 W
75	Wilmington . . . . Ill. (Chicago In.)	41·19 N	88·09 W
83	Wilmington . . . Mass. (Boston In.)	42·34 N	71·10 W
79	Wilmington . . . . N. C.	34·12 N	77·56 W
80	Wilmington . . . . Ohio	39·20 N	83·50 W
80	Wilmore (wĭl'mōr) . . . . Ky.	37·50 N	84·35 W
110	Wilmslow (wĭlmz' lō) . . . . Eng.	53·19 N	2·14 W
	Wilno, see Vilnius		
73	Wilson (wĭl'sŭn) . . . . Ark.	35·35 N	90·02 W
79	Wilson . . . . N. C.	35·42 N	77·55 W
73	Wilson . . . . Okla.	34·09 N	97·27 W
78	Wilson, L . . . . Ala.	34·45 N	86·58 W
78	Wilson (R.) . . . . Ala.	34·53 N	87·28 W
161	Wilson, Pt . . Austl. (Melbourne In.)	38·05 S	144·31 E
74	Wilson, Mt. Calif. (Los Angeles In.)	34·15 N	118·06 W
71	Wilson (I.) . . . . Can.	48·48 N	87·23 W
67	Wilson Pk . . . . Utah	40·46 N	110·27 W
160	Wilson's Prom. (wĭl'sŭnz) . . . Austl.	39·05 S	146·50 E
74	Wilsonville (wĭl'sŭn-vĭl) Ill. (St. Louis In.)	39·04 N	89·52 W
111	Wilstedt (vēl'shtĕt) Ger. (Hamburg In.)	53·45 N	10·04 E
111	Wilster (vēl'stĕr) Ger. (Hamburg In.)	53·55 N	9·23 E
84	Wilton (wĭl'tŭn) Conn. (New York In.)	41·11 N	73·25 W
70	Wilton . . . . N. D.	47·90 N	100·47 W
158	Wiluna (wĭ-lōō'ná) . . . . Austl.	26·35 S	120·25 E
80	Winamac (wĭn'á măk) . . . . Ind.	41·05 N	86·40 W
169	Winburg (wĭn'bûrg) . . . . S. Afr. (Johannesburg & Pretoria In.)	28·31 S	27·02 E
74	Winchester (wĭn'chĕs-tẽr) Calif. (Los Angeles In.)	33·41 N	117·06 W
116	Winchester . . . . Eng.	3·03 N	1·20 W
66	Winchester . . . . Idaho	46·14 N	116·39 W
80	Winchester . . . . Ind.	40·10 N	84·50 W
80	Winchester . . . . Ky.	38·00 N	84·15 W
83	Winchester . . . . Mass. (Boston In.)	42·28 N	71·09 W
81	Winchester . . . . N. H.	42·45 N	72·25 W
78	Winchester . . . . Tenn.	35·11 N	86·06 W
81	Winchester . . . . Va.	39·40 N	78·10 W
81	Windber (wĭnd'bẽr) . . . . Pa.	40·15 N	78·45 W
70	Wind Cave Natl. Park . . . . . . S. D.	43·36 N	103·53 W
78	Winder (wīn'dẽr) . . . . Ga.	33·58 N	83·43 W
116	Windermere (wĭn'dẽr-mẽr) . . . Eng.	54·25 N	2·59 W
81	Windham (wĭnd'ăm) . . . . Conn.	41·45 N	72·05 W
83	Windham . . . . . N. H. (Boston In.)	42·49 N	71·21 W
166	Windhoek (vĭnt'hŏŏk) . . S. W. Afr.	22·05 S	17·10 E
75	Wind L . . . . . Wis. (Milwaukee In.)	42·49 N	88·06 W
76	Wind Mtn . . . . N. Mex.	32·02 N	105·30 W
71	Windom (wĭn'dŭm) . . . . Minn.	43·50 N	95·04 W
160	Windora (wĭn-dō'rá) . . . . Austl.	25·15 S	142·50 E
67	Wind R . . . . Wyo.	43·17 N	109·02 W
67	Wind River Ind Res . . . . Wyo.	43·07 N	109·08 W
67	Wind River Ra . . . . Wyo.	43·19 N	109·47 W
161	Windsor (wĭn'zẽr) Austl. (Sydney In.)	33·37 S	150·49 E
75	Windsor . . . . Can. (Detroit In.)	42·19 N	83·00 W
82	Windsor . . . . Can.	44·59 N	64·07 W
83	Windsor . . . . Can.	49·00 N	55·39 W
72	Windsor . . . . Colo.	40·27 N	104·51 W
110	Windsor . . . . Eng. (London In.)	51·27 N	0·37 W
73	Windsor . . . . Mo.	38·32 N	93·31 W
82	Windsor . . . . Vt.	43·30 N	72·25 W
79	Windsor . . . . N. C.	35·58 N	76·57 W
89	Windward Is. (wĭnd'wẽrd) . . N. A.	12·45 N	61·40 W
95	Windward Pass . . . . N. A.	19·30 N	74·20 W
73	Winfield (wĭn'fēld) . . . . Kans.	37·14 N	97·00 W
87	Wingham (wĭn'găm) . . . . Can.	43·48 N	81·23 W
67	Winifred (wĭn ĭ frĕd) . . . . Mont.	47·35 N	109·20 W
76	Wink (wĭŋk) . . . . Tex.	31·48 N	103·06 W
164	Winneba (wĭn'ē-bà) . . . . Ghana	5·29 N	0·43 W
71	Winnebago (wĭn'ê-bā'gō) . . . Minn.	43·45 N	94·08 W
71	Winnebago, L . . . . Wis.	44·09 N	88·10 W
70	Winnebago Ind. Res . . . . Nebr.	42·15 N	96·06 W
66	Winnemucca (wĭn-ê-mŭk'á) . . Nev.	40·59 N	117·43 W
68	Winnemucca (L.) . . . . Nev.	40·06 N	119·07 W
70	Winner (wĭn'ẽr) . . . . S. D.	43·22 N	99·50 W
75	Winnetka (wĭ-nĕt'ká) Ill. (Chicago In.)	42·07 N	87·44 W
67	Winnett (wĭn'ĕt) . . . . Mont.	47·01 N	108·20 W
77	Winnfield (wĭn'fēld) . . . . La.	31·56 N	92·39 W
71	Winnibigoshish (L.) (wĭn'ĭ-bĭ-gō'shĭsh) . Minn.	47·30 N	93·45 W
85	Winnipeg (wĭn'ĭ-pĕg) Can. (Winnipeg In.)	49·55 N	97·09 W
86	Winnipeg, L . . . . Can.	53·29 N	98·41 W
86	Winnipeg (R.) . . . . Can.	50·30 N	95·34 W
86	Winnipegosis (wĭn'ĭ-pê-gō'sĭs) Can.	51·40 N	100·01 W
86	Winnipegosis (L.) . . . . Can.	52·19 N	101·40 W
81	Winnipesaukee (L.) (wĭn'ê-pê-sô'kê) . N. H.	43·40 N	71·20 W
77	Winnsboro (wĭnz'bŭr-ô) . . . . La.	32·09 N	91·42 W
79	Winnsboro . . . . S. C.	34·29 N	81·05 W
73	Winnsboro . . . . Tex.	32·56 N	95·15 W
85	Winona (wĭ-nō'ná) Can. (Toronto In.)	43·13 N	79·39 W
71	Winona . . . . Minn.	44·03 N	91·40 W
78	Winona . . . . Miss.	33·29 N	89·43 W
81	Winooski (wĭ-nōōs'kê) . . . . Vt.	44·30 N	73·10 W
111	Winsen (Luhe) (vēn'zĕn) (lōō'hĕ) Ger. (Hamburg In.)	53·22 N	10·13 E
110	Winsford (wĭnz'fẽrd) . . . . Eng.	53·11 N	2·30 W

ng-sing; ŋ-baŋk; N-nasalized n; nŏd; cŏmmit; ōld; ôbey; ôrder; fōōd; fŏŏt; ou-out; s-soft; sh-dish; th-thin; pūre; ûnite; ûrn; stŭd; circŭs; ŭ-as "y" in study; '-indeterminate vowel.

Page	Name Pronunciation Region	Lat. °'	Long. °'
69	Winslow (wĭnz'lō) . . . Ariz.	35·00 N	110·45 W
65	Winslow . . . Wash. (Seattle In.)	47·38 N	122·31 W
81	Winsted (wĭn'stĕd) . . . Conn.	41·55 N	73·05 W
110	Winster (wĭn'stẽr) . . . Eng.	53·08 N	1·38 W
79	Winston-Salem (wĭn stŭn-sā'lĕm) N. C.	36·05 N	80·15 W
167	Winterberg (Mts.) S. Afr. (Natal In.)	32·18 S	26·25 E
79	Winter Garden (wĭn'tẽr gär'd'n) Fla. (In.)	28·32 N	81·35 W
79	Winter Haven (hā'vĕn) . . Fla. (In.)	28·01 N	81·38 W
79	Winter Park (pärk) . . . Fla. (In.)	28·35 N	81·21 W
76	Winters (wĭn'tẽrz) . . . Tex.	31·59 N	99·58 W
71	Winterset (wĭn'tẽr-sĕt) . . . Iowa	41·19 N	94·03 W
123	Winterswijk . . . Neth. (Ruhr In.)	51·58 N	6·44 E
120	Winterthur (vĭn'tẽr-tōōr) . . . Switz.	47·30 N	8·32 E
167	Winterton (wĭn-tẽr-tŏn) S. Afr. (Natal In.)	28·51 S	29·33 E
82	Winthrop (wĭn'thrŭp) . . . Maine	44·19 N	70·00 W
83	Winthrop . . . Mass. (Boston In.)	42·23 N	70·59 W
71	Winthrop . . . Minn.	44·31 N	94·20 W
159	Winton (wĭn-tŭn) . . . Austl.	22·17 S	143·08 E
123	Wipperfürth (vē'pẽr-fürt) Ger. (Ruhr In.)	51·07 N	7·23 E
110	Wirksworth (wûrks'wûrth) . . . Eng.	53·05 N	1·35 W
63	Wisconsin (State) (wĭs-kŏn'sĭn) U. S.	44·30 N	91·00 W
71	Wisconsin (R.) . . . Wis.	43·14 N	90·34 W
71	Wisconsin Dells . . . Wis.	43·38 N	89·46 W
71	Wisconsin Rapids . . . Wis.	44·24 N	89·50 W
70	Wishek (wĭsh'ĕk) . . . N. D.	46·15 N	99·34 W
121	Wisla (Vistula) R. (vēs'wà) (vĭs'tū-là) . Pol.	52·48 N	19·02 E
121	Wisloka R. (vēs-wô'kà) . . . Pol.	49·55 N	21·26 E
99	Wismar (wĭs'mȧr) . . . Br. Gu.	5·58 N	58·15 W
120	Wismar (vĭs'mär) . . . Ger.	53·53 N	11·28 E
70	Wisner (wĭz'nẽr) . . . Nebr.	42·00 N	96·55 W
123	Wissembourg (vē-sän-bōōr') . . . Fr.	49·03 N	7·58 E
166	Wissmann Pool (L.) . . . Con. L.	3·18 S	17·28 E
73	Wister Res. (vĭs'tẽr) . . . Okla.	35·02 N	94·52 W
168	Witbank (wĭt-bănk) . . . S. Afr. (Johannesburg & Pretoria In.)	25·53 S	29·14 E
110	Witham (wĭdh'ăm) Eng. (London In.)	51·48 N	0·37 E
110	Witham (R.) . . . Eng.	53·11 N	0·20 W
75	Withamsville (wĭdh'ămz-vĭl) Ohio (Cincinnati In.)	39·04 N	84·16 W
79	Withlacoochee (R.) (wĭth-là-kōō'chē) . Fla. (In.)	28·58 N	82·30 W
78	Withlacoochee (R.) . . . Ga.	31·15 N	83·30 W
74	Withrow (wĭdh'rō) . . . Minn. (Minneapolis, St. Paul In.)	45·08 N	92·54 W
110	Witney (wĭt'nē) Eng. (London In.)	51·45 N	1·30 W
168	Witpoort S. Afr. (Johannesburg & Pretoria In.)	26·57 S	26·17 E
168	Witsieshoek (wĭt'sēz-hŏŏk) S. Afr. (Johannesburg & Pretoria In.)	28·33 S	28·48 E
80	Witt (vĭt) . . . Ill.	39·10 N	89·15 W
123	Witten (vē'tĕn) . . . Ger. (Ruhr In.)	51·26 N	7·19 E
120	Wittenberg (vē'tĕn-bĕrgh) . . . Ger.	51·53 N	12·40 E
120	Wittenberge (vĭt-ĕn-bĕr'gē) . . . Ger.	52·59 N	11·45 E
120	Wittlich (vĭt'lĭk) . . . Ger.	49·58 N	6·54 E
167	Witu (wē'tōō) . . . Ken.	2·18 S	40·28 E
167	Witwatersberg (Mts.) (wĭt-wôr-tẽrz-bûrg) . S. Afr. (Johannesburg & Pretoria In.)	25·58 S	27·43 E
168	Witwatersrand (Ridge) (wĭt-wôr'tẽrs-rănd) . S. Afr. (Johannesburg & Pretoria In.)	25·55 S	26·27 E
121	Wkra R. (f'krà) . . . Pol.	52·40 N	20·35 E
121	Włocławek (vwô-tswä'vĕk) . . . Pol.	52·38 N	19·08 E
121	Włodawa (vwô-dä'vä) . . . Pol.	51·33 N	23·33 E
121	Włoszczowa (vwôsh-chô'vä) . . Pol.	50·51 N	19·58 E
83	Woburn (wōō'bŭrn) (wō'bŭrn) Mass. (Boston In.)	42·29 N	71·10 W
111	Woerden . . Neth. (Amsterdam In.)	52·05 N	4·52 E
110	Woking (wô'kĭng) Eng. (London In.)	51·18 N	0·33 W
110	Wokingham (wô'kĭng-hăm) Eng. (London In.)	51·23 N	0·50 W
74	Wolcott (wŏl'kŏt) Kans. (Kansas City In.)	39·12 N	94·47 W
81	Wolf (I.) (wŏŏlf) . . . Can.	44·10 N	76·25 W
78	Wolf (R.) . . . Miss.	30·45 N	89·36 W
71	Wolf (R.) . . . Wis.	45·14 N	88·45 W
120	Wolfenbüttel (vŏl'fĕn-büt-ĕl) . Ger.	52·10 N	10·32 E
75	Wolf L. . . . Ill. (Chicago In.)	41·39 N	87·33 W
67	Wolf Point (wŏŏlf point) . . . Mont.	48·07 N	105·40 W
111	Wolfratshausen (vŏlf'räts-hou-zĕn) Ger. (Munich In.)	47·55 N	11·25 E
120	Wolfsburg (vŏlfs'bŏŏrgh) . . . Ger.	52·30 N	10·37 E
82	Wolfville (wŏŏlf'vĭl) . . . Can.	45·06 N	64·02 W
120	Wolgast (vŏl'gäst) . . . Ger.	54·04 N	13·46 E
167	Wolhuterskop . . . S. Afr. (Johannesburg & Pretoria In.)	25·41 S	27·40 E
111	Wolkersdorf . . . Aus. (Vienna In.)	48·24 N	16·31 E
86	Wollaston (L.) (wŏŏl'ȧs-tŭn) . Can.	58·03 N	105·00 W
86	Wollaston Pen. . . . Can.	69·55 N	115·13 W
160	Wollongong (wŏŏl'ŭn-gŏng) . Austl.	34·26 S	151·05 E
121	Wołomin (vô-wō'mēn) . . . Pol.	52·19 N	21·17 E
110	Wolstanton (wŏŏl-stăn'tŭn) . . Eng.	53·02 N	2·13 W
111	Woltersdorf (vŏl'tẽrs-dōrf) Ger. (Berlin In.)	52·07 N	13·13 E
110	Wolverhampton (wŏŏl'vẽr-hămp-tŭn) . Eng.	52·35 N	2·07 W
168	Wolwehoek . . . S. Afr. (Johannesburg & Pretoria In.)	26·55 S	27·50 E
152	Wŏnsan (wŭn'sän') . . . Kor.	39·08 N	127·24 E
160	Wonthaggi (wŏnt-hăg'ē) . . . Austl.	38·45 S	145·42 E
70	Wood (wŏŏd) . . . S. D.	43·26 N	100·25 W
70	Woodbine (wŏŏd'bīn) . . . Iowa	41·44 N	95·42 W
85	Woodbridge (wŏŏd'brĭj') Can. (Toronto In.)	43·47 N	79·36 W
84	Woodbridge . N. J. (New York In.)	40·33 N	74·18 W
86	Wood Buffalo Natl. Park . . . Can.	59·50 N	118·53 W
74	Woodburn (wŏŏd'bûrn) Ill. (St. Louis In.)	39·03 N	90·01 W
66	Woodburn . . . Ore.	45·10 N	122·51 W
84	Woodbury (wŏŏd'bẽr-ē) N. J. (Philadelphia In.)	39·50 N	75·14 W
74	Woodcrest (wŏŏd'krĕst) Calif. (Los Angeles In.)	33·53 N	117·18 W
65	Woodinville (wŏŏd'ĭn-vĭl) Wash. (Seattle In.)	47·46 N	122·09 W
68	Woodland (wŏŏd'lănd) . . . Calif.	38·41 N	121·47 W
65	Woodland . . . Wash. (Portland In.)	45·54 N	122·45 W
74	Woodland Hills Calif. (Los Angeles In.)	34·10 N	118·36 W
155	Woodlark (I.) (wŏŏd'lärk) . . . Pap.	9·07 S	152·00 E
75	Woodlawn Beach (wŏŏd'lôn bēch) N. Y. (Buffalo In.)	42·48 N	78·51 W
74	Wood River . . . Ill. (St. Louis In.)	38·52 N	90·06 W
158	Woodroffe, Mt. (wŏŏd'rŭf) . . Austl.	26·05 S	132·00 E
79	Woodruff (wŏŏd'rŭf) . . . S. C.	34·43 N	82·03 W
75	Woodruff Place Ind. (Indianapolis In.)	39·47 N	86·07 W
158	Woods (L.) (wŏŏdz) . . . Austl.	18·00 S	133·18 E
63	Woods, L. of the . . . Can.-Minn.	49·25 N	93·25 W
74	Woods Cross (krôs) Utah (Salt Lake City In.)	40·53 N	111·54 W
80	Woodsfield (wŏŏdz-fēld) . . . Ohio	39·45 N	81·10 W
65	Woodson (wŏŏdsŭn) Ore. (Portland In.)	46·07 N	123·20 W
80	Woodstock (wŏŏd'stŏk) . . . Can.	43·10 N	80·50 W
82	Woodstock . . . Can.	46·09 N	67·36 W
110	Woodstock . . . Eng. (London In.)	51·49 N	1·22 W
71	Woodstock . . . Ill.	42·20 N	88·29 W
81	Woodstock . . . Va.	38·55 N	78·25 W
81	Woodsville (wŏŏdz'vĭl) . . . N. H.	44·10 N	72·00 W
78	Woodville (wŏŏd'vĭl) . . . Miss.	31·06 N	91·11 W
77	Woodville . . . Tex.	30·48 N	94·25 W
72	Woodward (wŏŏd'wôrd) . . . Okla.	36·25 N	99·24 W
110	Woolwich (wŏŏl'ĭj) Eng. (London In.)	51·28 N	0·05 E
160	Woomera (wŏŏm'ērȧ) . . . Austl.	31·15 S	136·43 E
84	Woonsocket (wōōn-sŏk'ĕt) R. I. (Providence In.)	42·00 N	71·30 W
70	Woonsocket . . . S. D.	44·03 N	98·17 W
80	Wooster (wŏŏs'tẽr) . . . Ohio	40·50 N	81·55 W
116	Worcester (wŏŏ-stẽr) . . . Eng.	52·09 N	2·14 W
166	Worcester (wŏŏs'tẽr) . . . S. Afr.	33·35 S	19·31 E
110	Worcester (Co.) (wŏŏ'stẽr) . . . Eng.	52·24 N	2·15 W
83	Worcester (wôr'chĕs-tẽr) Mass. (Boston In.)	42·16 N	71·49 W
74	Worden (wôr'dĕn) Ill. (St. Louis In.)	38·56 N	89·50 W
116	Workington (wûr'kĭng-tŭn) . . Eng.	54·40 N	3·30 W
110	Worksop (wûrk'sŏp) (wûr'sŭp) Eng.	53·18 N	1·07 W
67	Worland (wûr'lănd) . . . Wyo.	44·02 N	107·56 W
120	Worms (vōrms) . . . Ger.	49·37 N	8·22 E
161	Worona Res. . Austl. (Sydney In.)	34·12 S	150·55 E
75	Worth (wûrth) . . Ill. (Chicago In.)	41·42 N	87·47 W
74	Worth L. Tex. (Dallas, Fort Worth In.)	32·48 N	97·32 W
77	Wortham (wûr'dhăm) . . . Tex.	31·46 N	96·22 W
116	Worthing (wûr'dhĭng) . . . Eng.	50·48 N	0·29 W
80	Worthington (wûr'dhĭng-tŭn) . Ind.	39·05 N	87·00 W
70	Worthington . . . Minn.	43·38 N	95·36 W
155	Wowoni (I.) (wō-wō'nē) . . . Indon.	4·05 S	123·45 E
110	Wragby (răg'bē) . . . Eng.	53·17 N	0·19 W
64	Wrangell (răn'gĕl) . . . Alaska	56·28 N	132·25 W
64	Wrangell, Mt. . . . Alaska	61·58 N	143·50 W
64	Wrangell Mts. . . . Alaska-Can.	62·28 N	142·40 W
116	Wrath, C. (răth) . . . Scot.	58·34 N	5·01 W
72	Wray (rā) . . . Colo.	40·06 N	102·14 W
101	Wreak (R.) (rēk) . . . Eng.	52·45 N	0·59 W
159	Wreck Rfs. (rĕk) . . . Austl.	22·00 S	155·52 E
110	Wrekin, The (Mt.) (rĕk'ĭn) . . Eng.	52·40 N	2·33 W
79	Wrens (rĕnz) . . . Ga.	33·15 N	82·25 W
83	Wrentham (rĕn'thăm) Mass. (Boston In.)	42·04 N	71·20 W
110	Wrexham (rĕk'săm) . . . Wales	53·03 N	3·00 W
75	Wrights Corners (rītz kôr'nẽrz) N. Y. (Buffalo In.)	43·14 N	78·42 W
79	Wrightsville (rīts'vĭl) . . . Ga.	32·44 N	82·44 W
121	Wrocław (Breslau) (vrô'tsläv) (brĕs'lou) . Pol.	51·07 N	17·10 E
110	Wrotham (rōōt'ŭm) Eng. (London In.)	51·18 N	0·19 E
121	Września (vzhäsh'nyȧ) . . . Pol.	52·19 N	17·33 E
151	Wuch'ang (wōō'chăng') . . . China	30·32 N	114·25 E
150	Wuch'ang . . . China	44·59 N	127·00 E
148	Wuchi (wōō'jē) . . . China	38·12 N	114·57 E
148	Wuchiang (wōō'jĭăng) . . . China	31·10 N	120·38 E
148	Wuch'iao (wōō'chĭou) . . . China	37·37 N	116·29 E
148	Wuchin (wōō'jĭn) . . . China	31·47 N	119·56 E
150	Wuching (wōō'chĭng') China (Peking In.)	39·32 N	116·51 E
151	Wu Chin Shan . . . China	18·48 N	109·30 E
151	Wuchou (Tsangwu) (wōō'chō') China	23·32 N	111·25 E
151	Wuhan . . . China	30·30 N	114·15 E
148	Wuhsi (wōō'sē) . . . China	31·36 N	120·17 E
	Wuhsien, see Soochow		
151	Wuhsing . . . China	30·38 N	120·10 E
148	Wuhu (wōō'hōō') . . . China	31·22 N	118·22 E
151	Wui Shan (Mts.) . . . China	26·38 N	116·35 E
147	Wukung Shan (Mts.) (wōō'kōōng'shän') . China	26·45 N	115·19 E
152	Wulachieh (wōō'lä-kē'ä) . . . China	44·08 N	126·25 E
	Wulanhata, see Ch'ihfeng		
154	Wu Liang Shan (Mts.) . . . China	23·07 N	100·45 E
148	Wulitien (wōō'lē'dĭăn) . . . China	32·09 N	114·17 E
111	Wünsdorf (vüns'dōrf) Ger. (Berlin In.)	52·10 N	13·29 E
69	Wupatki Natl. Mon. (wōō-pät'kē) . Ariz.	35·36 N	111·45 W
151	Wup'ing (wōō'pĭng') . . . China	25·05 N	116·01 E
123	Wuppertal (vŏŏp'ẽr-täl) Ger. (Ruhr In.)	51·16 N	7·14 E
151	Wu R. (wōō') . . . China	27·30 N	108·00 E
111	Würm (R.) . . . Ger.	48·50 N	11·17 E
120	Würm See (L.) (vürm zā) . . . Ger.	47·58 N	11·30 E
123	Würselen (vür'zĕ-lĕn) Ger. (Ruhr In.)	50·49 N	6·09 E
120	Würzburg (vürts'bŏŏrgh) . . . Ger.	49·48 N	9·57 E
120	Wurzen (vŏŏrt'sĕn) . . . Ger.	51·22 N	12·45 E
146	Wushih (Uch Turfan) (wōō'shĭ) (ōōch' tōōr-fän') . China	41·13 N	79·08 E
111	Wustermark (vōōs'tẽr-märk) Ger. (Berlin In.)	52·33 N	12·57 E
111	Wustrau (vōōst'rou) Ger. (Berlin In.)	52·51 N	12·51 E
146	Wusu (Kweitun) (wōō'sōō') (kwā'tōōn') . China	44·28 N	84·07 E
149	Wusung (wōō'sōōng) China (Shanghai In.)	31·23 N	121 29 E
111	Wuustwezel . . . Bel. (Brussels In.)	51·23 N	4·36 E
148	Wuwei (wōō'wā') . . . China	31·19 N	117·53 E
148	Wuyang (wōō'yăng) . . . China	33·16 N	113·37 E
148	Wuyuch'ang . . . China	33·18 N	120·15 E
147	Wuyün (wōō-yün') . . . China	48·51 N	130·06 E
75	Wyandotte (wī'ăn-dŏt) Mich. (Detroit In.)	42·12 N	83·10 W
110	Wye (wī) . . . Eng. (London In.)	51·12 N	0·57 E
110	Wye (R.) . . . Eng.	53·14 N	1·46 W
73	Wymore (wī'mōr) . . . Nebr.	40·09 N	96·41 W
166	Wynberg (wĭn'bĕrg) S. Afr. (Cape Town In.)	34·00 S	18·28 E
158	Wyndham (wĭnd'ăm) . . . Austl.	15·30 S	128·15 E
73	Wynne (wĭn) . . . Ark.	35 12 N	90·46 W
73	Wynnewood (wĭn'wŏŏd) . . . Okla.	34·39 N	97·10 W
73	Wynona (wī-nō'nȧ) . . . Okla.	36·33 N	96·19 W
86	Wynyard (wĭn'yẽrd) . . . Can.	51·48 N	104·13 W
75	Wyoming (wī-ō'mĭng) Ohio (Cincinnati In.)	39·14 N	84·28 W
62	Wyoming (State) . . . U. S.	42·50 N	108·30 W
67	Wyoming Ra. . . . Wyo.	42·43 N	110·35 W
110	Wyre Fon. (wīr) . . . Eng.	52·24 N	2·24 W
121	Wysokie Mazowieckie (vē-sô'kyĕ mä-zô-vyĕts'kyĕ) . Pol.	52·55 N	22·42 E
121	Wyszków (vĕsh'kŏŏf) . . . Pol.	52·35 N	21·29 E
79	Wytheville (wĭth'vĭl) . . . Va.	36·55 N	81·06 W
94	Xagua, Banco (Bk.) (bä'n-kô-sä'gwä) . Cuba	21·35 N	80·50 W
123	Xanten (ksän'tĕn) . Ger. (Ruhr In.)	51·40 N	6·28 E
127	Xanthi . . . Grc.	41·08 N	24·53 E
92	Xcalak (sä-lä'k) Mex. (Yucatan In.)	18·15 N	87·50 W
80	Xenia (zē'nĭ-ȧ) . . . Ohio	39·40 N	83·55 W
90	Xicotencatl (sē-kô-tĕn-kät''l) . Mex.	23·00 N	98·58 W
90	Xilitla (sē-lē'tlä) . . . Mex.	21·24 N	98·59 W
99	Xingú (R.) (zhĕn-gōō') . . . Braz.	6·20 S	52·34 W
90	Xochihuehuetlán (sô-chē-wĕ-wĕ-tlä'n) . Mex.	17·53 N	98·29 W
91	Xochimilco (sō-chē-mēl'kô) Mex. (Mexico City In.)	19·15 N	99·06 W
151	Yaan . . . China	30·00 N	103·20 E
121	Yablonitskiy Pereval (P.) (yȧb-lô'nĭt-skĭ pĕ-rĕ-väl') . Sov. Un.	48·20 N	24·25 E
135	Yablonovyy Khrebet (Mts.) (yȧ-blô-nô-vē') . Sov. Un.	51·15 N	111·30 E
65	Yacolt (yă'kōlt) Wash. (Portland In.)	45·52 N	122·24 W
65	Yacolt (Mt.) . Wash. (Portland In.)	45·52 N	122·27 W
78	Yacona (R.) (yá'cō nă) . . . Miss.	34·13 N	89·30 W
100	Yacuiba (yȧ-kōō-ē'bä) . . . Arg.	22·02 S	63·44 W
79	Yadkin (R.) (yăd'kĭn) . . . N. C.	36·12 N	80·40 W
153	Yagi (yä'gē) . . . Jap. (Ōsaka In.)	34·31 N	135·48 E
129	Yagotin (yä'gô-tēn) . . . Sov. Un.	50·18 N	31·46 E
94	Yaguajay (yä-guä-hä'ē) . . . Cuba	22·20 N	79·20 W
153	Yahagi-Gawa (Strm.) (yä'hä-gē gä'wä) . Jap.	35·16 N	137·22 E
153	Yahata (yä'hä-tä) . . . Jap.	33·50 N	131·48 E
149	Yahu . . . China (Canton In.)	23·19 N	113·17 E
90	Yahualica (yä-wä-lē'kä) . . . Mex.	21·08 N	102·53 W
148	Yahungch'iao (yä'hōōng'chĭou) China	39·45 N	117·52 E
151	Yaihsien . . . China	18·20 N	109·10 E
91	Yajalón (yä-hä-lōn') . . . Mex.	17·16 N	92·20 W
136	Yakhroma (yäk'rô-mȧ) Sov. Un. (Moscow In.)	56·17 N	37·30 E
136	Yakhroma R. Sov. Un. (Moscow In.)	56·15 N	37·38 E
66	Yakima (yăk'ĭ-mȧ) . . . Wash.	46·35 N	120·30 W
66	Yakima R. (yăk'ĭ-mȧ) . . . Wash.	46·48 N	120·22 W
153	Yaku (I.) (yä'kōō) . . . Jap.	30·15 N	130·41 E
135	Yakut A.S.S.R. . . . Sov. Un.	65·21 N	117·13 E
64	Yakutat (yăk'ōō-tăt) . . . Alaska	59·32 N	139·35 W
135	Yakutsk (yȧ-kōōtsk') . . . Sov. Un.	62·13 N	129·49 E
152	Yal (R.) (yäl) . . . China	48·20 N	122·35 E
80	Yale . . . Mich.	43·05 N	82·45 W
73	Yale . . . Okla.	36·07 N	96·42 W
66	Yale Res. . . . Wash.	46·00 N	122·20 W
165	Yalinga (yȧ-lĭŋ'gȧ) . Cen. Afr. Rep.	6·56 N	23·22 E
78	Yalobusha (R.) (yȧ-lô-bŏŏsh'ȧ) Miss.	33·48 N	90·02 W
129	Yalta (Krasnoarmeisk) (yäl'tȧ) (kräs-nô-är-mäsk') . Sov. Un.	44·29 N	34·12 E
152	Yalu (Amnok) (R.) . . . China-Kor.	41·20 N	126·35 E
146	Yalung Chiang (R.) (yä'lōōng') China	32·29 N	98·41 E
134	Yalutorovsk (yä-lōō-tô'rôfsk) Sov. Un.	56·42 N	66·32 E
153	Yamada (yä'mȧ-dȧ) . . . Jap.	33·37 N	133·39 E
152	Yamagata (yä-mä'gä-tȧ) . . . Jap.	38·12 N	140·24 E
153	Yamaguchi (yä-mȧ'gōō-chē) . . Jap.	34·10 N	131·30 E
134	Yamal, P-ov (Pen.) (yȧ-mäl') Sov. Un.	71·15 N	70·00 E
136	Yamantau, Gora (Mt.) (gȧ-rä' yä'măn-tȧw) . Sov. Un. (Urals In.)	54·16 N	58·08 E
95	Yamasá (yä-mä'sä) . . . Dom. Rep.	18·50 N	70·00 W
153	Yamasaki (yä'mä'sä-kē) . . . Jap.	35·01 N	134·33 E
153	Yamasaki . . . Jap. (Ōsaka In.)	34·53 N	135·41 E

ăt; finăl; rāte; senāte; ärm; ȧsk; sofȧ; fâre; ch-choose; dh-as th in other: bē: ēvent; bĕt; recĕnt; cratẽr; g-go; gh-guttural g; bĭt; ĭ-short neutral; rīde; K-guttural k as ch in German ich;

Page	Name	Pronunciation	Region	Lat. °′	Long. °′
153	Yamashina	(yä′mä-shė̇′nä)	Jap. (Ōsaka In.)	34·59 N	135·50 E
153	Yamashita	(yä′mä-shė̇′tä)	Jap. (Ōsaka In.)	34·53 N	135·25 E
153	Yamato-takada	(yä′mä-tō̇ tä′kä-dä)	Jap. (Ōsaka In.)	34·31 N	135·45 E
98	Yambi, Mesa de	(mĕ′sä-dĕ-yȧ′m-bē)	Col.	1·55 N	71·45 W
146	Yamdrog Tsho (L.)		China	29·11 N	91·26 E
146	Yamethin	(yŭ-mē′thĕn)	Bur.	20·14 N	96·27 E
65	Yamhill	(yăm′hĭl)	Ore. (Portland In.)	45·20 N	123·11 W
136	Yamkino	(yäm′kĭ-nô)	Sov. Un. (Moscow In.)	55·56 N	38·25 E
160	Yamma Yamma, L.	(yäm′ȧ yäm′ȧ)	Austl.	26·15 S	141·30 E
67	Yampa R.	(yăm′pȧ)	Colo.	40·29 N	108·12 W
135	Yamsk	(yämsk)	Sov. Un.	59·41 N	154·09 E
142	Yamuna (R.)		India	26·50 N	79·45 E
135	Yana (R.)	(yä′nȧ)	Sov. Un.	69·42 N	135·45 E
160	Yanac	(yăn′ȧk)	Austl.	36·10 S	141·30 E
153	Yanagawa	(yä-nä′gä-wä)	Jap.	33·11 N	130·24 E
143	Yanam	(yŭnŭm′)	India	16·48 N	82·15 E
144	Yanbu al Bahr		Sau. Ar.	23·57 N	38·02 E
148	Yangch'eng Hu (L.)	(yäng′chĕng′hōō)	China	31·30 N	120·31 E
151	Yangchiang		China	21·52 N	111·58 E
148	Yangchiaokou	(yang′jēou′gō)	China	37·16 N	118·53 E
148	Yangchiat'an	(yäng′jēä′tän)	China	31·43 N	115·53 E
148	Yangch'uanchan		China	37·52 N	113·36 E
151	Yangch'un	(yäng′chōōn′)	China	22·08 N	111·48 E
148	Yangerhchuang	(yäng′ẽ′jōōäng)	China	38·18 N	117·31 E
148	Yangho	(yäng′hŭ)	China	33·48 N	118·23 E
148	Yanghsin	(yäng′sĭn)	China	37·39 N	117·34 E
150	Yangkochuang		China (Peking In.)	40·10 N	116·48 E
148	Yangku	(yäng′kōō′)	China	36·06 N	115·46 E
148	Yangsanmu	(yäng′sän′mōō)	China	38·28 N	117·18 E
147	Yangtze (R.)	(yäng′tsĕ)	China	30·30 N	117·25 E
152	Yangyang	(yäng′yäng′)	Kor.	38·02 N	128·38 E
70	Yankton	(yănk′tŭn)	S. D.	42·51 N	97·24 W
	Yannina, see Ioánnina				
136	Yanychi	(yä′nĭ-chĭ)	Sov. Un. (Urals In.)	57·42 N	56·24 E
165	Yao	(yä′ō)	Chad	13·00 N	17·38 E
153	Yao		Jap. (Ōsaka In.)	34·37 N	135·36 E
164	Yaounde	(yȧ-ōōn-dā′)	Cam.	3·58 N	11·45 E
156	Yap	(yăp) (I.)	Pac. Is. Trust Ter.	11·00 N	138·00 E
95	Yaque del Norte (R.)	(yä′kȧ dĕl nôr′tȧ)	Dom. Rep.	19·40 N	71·25 W
95	Yaque del Sur (R.)	(yä-kĕ-dĕl-sōō′r)	Dom. Rep.	18·35 N	71·05 W
88	Yaqui (R.)	(yä′kē)	Mex.	28·15 N	109·40 W
99	Yaracuy (State)	(yä-rä-kōō′ē)	Ven. (In.)	10·10 N	68·31 W
160	Yaraka	(yȧ-răk′ȧ)	Austl.	24·50 S	144·08 E
132	Yaransk	(yä-ränsk′)	Sov. Un.	57·18 N	48·05 E
165	Yarda (Well)	(yär′dȧ)	Chad	18·29 N	19·13 E
	Yarkand, see Soch'e				
142	Yarkand (R.)	(yär-känt′)	India	36·11 N	76·10 E
82	Yarmouth	(yär′mŭth)	Can.	43·49 N	66·08 W
136	Yaroslavka	(yȧ-rô-släv′kȧ)	Sov. Un. (Urals In.)	55·52 N	57·59 E
128	Yaroslavl'	(yȧ-rô-släv″l)	Sov. Un.	57·57 N	39·54 E
128	Yaroslavl' (Oblast)		Sov. Un.	58·05 N	38·05 E
132	Yarra-to (L.)	(yȧ′rô-tô′)	Sov. Un.	68·30 N	71·30 E
128	Yartsevo	(yär′tsyė̇-vô)	Sov. Un.	55·04 N	32·38 E
134	Yartsevo		Sov. Un.	60·13 N	89·52 E
98	Yarumal	(yä-rōō-mäl′)	Col. (In.)	6·57 N	75·24 W
121	Yasel'da R.	(yä-syŭl′dȧ)	Sov. Un.	52·13 N	25·53 E
95	Yateras	(yä-tā′räs)	Cuba	20·00 N	75·00 W
73	Yates Center	(yāts)	Kans.	37·53 N	95·44 W
86	Yathkyed (L.)	(yȧth-kī-ĕd′)	Can.	62·38 N	97·12 W
153	Yatsuga-dake (Mtn.)	(yät′sōō-gä dä′kā)	Jap.	36·01 N	138·21 E
153	Yatsushiro	(yät′sōō′shė̇-rô)	Jap.	32·30 N	130·35 E
90	Yautepec	(yä-ōō-tȧ-pĕk′)	Mex.	18·53 N	99·04 W
121	Yavoroy	(yă′vō-rō′yė̇)	Sov. Un.	49·56 N	23·24 E
153	Yawata	(yä′wä-tä)	Jap. (Osaka In.)	34·52 N	135·43 E
153	Yawatahama	(yä′wä′tä′hä-mä)	Jap.	33·24 N	132·25 E
144	Yazd		Iran	31·59 N	54·03 E
78	Yazoo (R.)	(yă′zōō)	Miss.	32·32 N	90·40 W
78	Yazoo City		Miss.	32·50 N	90·18 W
154	Ye	(yā)	Bur.	15·13 N	97·52 E
84	Yeadon	(yē′dŭn)	Pa. (Philadelphia In.)	39·56 N	75·16 W
124	Yecla	(yā′klä)	Sp.	38·35 N	1·09 W
128	Yefremov	(yĕ-fră′môf)	Sov. Un.	53·08 N	38·04 E
128	Yegor'yevsk	(yĕ-gôr′yĕfsk)	Sov. Un.	55·23 N	38·59 E
148	Yehch'eng (Karghalik)	(yĕ′chĕng′)	China	37·30 N	79·26 E
148	Yehhsien	(yĕ′sĭän)	China	33·37 N	113·23 E
132	Yelabuga	(yĕ-lä′bŏŏ-gȧ)	Sov. Un.	55·50 N	52·18 E
133	Yelan		Sov. Un.	50·50 N	44·00 E
128	Yelets	(yĕ-lyĕts′)	Sov. Un.	52·35 N	38·28 E
136	Yelizavetpol'skiy	(yĕ′lĭ-za-vĕt-pôl-skĭ)	Sov. Un. (Urals In.)	52·51 N	60·38 E
135	Yelizavety, Mys (C.)	(yĕ-lyē-sȧ-vyĕ′tȧ)	Sov. Un.	54·28 N	142·59 E
116	Yell (I.)	(yĕl)	Scot.	60·35 N	1·27 W
78	Yellow (R.)	(yĕl′ô)	Fla.	30·33 N	86·53 W
86	Yellowknife	(yĕl′ô-nīf)	Can.	62·29 N	114·38 W
	Yellow R., see Hwang Ho				
150	Yellow Sea		China	35·20 N	122·15 E
67	Yellowstone L.		Wyo.	44·27 N	110·03 W
67	Yellowstone Natl. Park	(yĕl′ô-stōn)	Wyo.	44·45 N	110·35 W
67	Yellowstone R.		Mont.	46·28 N	105·39 W
67	Yellowstone R., Clark Fk.		Wyo.	44·55 N	109·05 W
128	Yel'nya	(yĕl′nyȧ)	Sov. Un.	54·34 N	33·12 E
164	Yelwa	(yĕl′wä)	Nig.	8·57 N	9·44 E
136	Yemanzhelinsk	(yĕ-mȧn-zhâ′lĭnsk)	Sov. Un. (Urals In.)	54·47 N	61·24 E
138	Yemen	(yĕm′ĕn)	Asia	15·45 N	44·30 E
132	Yemetsk		Sov. Un.	63·28 N	41·28 E
129	Yenakiyevo	(yĕ-nä′kĭ-yĕ-vô)	Sov. Un.	48·14 N	38·12 E
150	Yenan	(yĕn′än′)	China	36·35 N	109·32 E
145	Yenangyaung	(yā′nän-d oung)	Bur.	20·27 N	94·59 E
148	Yench'eng	(yĕn′chĕng)	China	33·23 N	120·11 E
148	Yencheng	(yĕn′chĕng)	China	33·38 N	113·59 E
146	Yench'i	(yĕn′chĭ′)	China	42·14 N	86·28 E
150	Yenchi		China	42·55 N	129·35 E
148	Yenchiaha	(yen′jēä′hŭ)	China	31·47 N	114·50 E
148	Yenchianchi	(yĕn′jēä′jē)	China	31·52 N	115·57 E
148	Yenching	(yĕn′jĭn)	China	35·09 N	114·13 E
148	Yenchuang	(yĕn′jŏŏäng)	China	36·08 N	117·47 E
164	Yendi	(yĕn′dė̇)	Ghana	9·21 N	0·02 E
133	Yenice (R.)		Tur.	41·10 N	33·00 E
134	Yenisey (R.)	(yĕ-nė̇-sĕ′ė̇)	Sov. Un.	67·48 N	87·15 E
134	Yeniseysk	(yĕ-nĭ-sā′ĭsk)	Sov. Un.	58·27 N	90·28 E
148	Yenling	(yĕn′lĭng′)	China	34·07 N	114·12 E
148	Yenshan	(yĕn′shän′)	China	38·05 N	117·15 E
150	Yenshou		China	45·25 N	128·43 E
148	Yent'ai (Chefoo)		China	37·32 N	121·22 E
158	Yeo (I.)	(yō)	Austl.	28·15 S	124·00 E
133	Yerevan	(yĕ-rĕ-vän′)	Sov. Un.	40·10 N	44·30 E
116	Yerington	(yė̇′rĭng-tŭn)	Nev.	38·59 N	119·10 W
132	Yermak (I.)		Sov. Un.	66·30 N	71·30 E
124	Yeste	(yĕs′tȧ)	Sp.	38·23 N	2·19 W
122	Yeu, Île d' (I.)	(ēl dyû)	Fr.	46·43 N	2·45 W
129	Yevpatoriya	(yĕf-pä′tô-rĭ-yȧ)	Sov. Un.	45·13 N	33·22 E
129	Yeya (R.)	(yă′yȧ)	Sov. Un.	46·25 N	39·17 E
135	Yevrey Aut. Oblast		Sov Un.	48·45 N	132·00 E
129	Yeysk	(yĕysk)	Sov. Un.	46·41 N	38·13 E
	Yg, see Yug				
127	Yiannitsá		Grc.	40·47 N	22·26 E
150	Yinch'uan (Nīnghsia)		China	38·22 N	106·22 E
146	Yingchisha		China	39·01 N	75·29 E
150	Yingk'ou	(yĭng′kō′)	China	40·35 N	122·10 E
149	Yinhang		China (Shanghai In.)	31·20 N	121·30 E
150	Yin Shan (Mtn.)	(yĭng′shän′)	China	40·50 N	110·30 E
	Yinhsien, see Ningpo				
127	Yioúra (I.)		Grc.	37·52 N	24·42 E
127	Yíthion		Grc.	36·50 N	22·37 E
153	Ynasa	(yōō′ä-sä)	Jap.	34·02 N	135·10 E
77	Yoakum	(yō′kŭm)	Tex.	29·18 N	97·09 W
78	Yockanookany, (R.)	(yŏk′ȧ-nōō-kă-nī)	Miss.	32·47 N	89·38 W
153	Yodo-Gawa (Str.)	(yō′dō′gä-wä)	Jap. (Ōsaka In.)	34·46 N	135·35 E
151	Yog Pt.	(yōg)	Phil.	14·00 N	124·30 E
86	Yoho Natl. Park	(yō′hō)	Can.	51·32 N	117·06 W
92	Yojoa, Lago de (L.)	(lä′gô dĕ yô-hō′ä)	Hond.	14·49 N	87·53 W
153	Yokkaichi	(yô′kä′ė̇-chė̇)	Jap.	34·58 N	136·35 E
153	Yokohama	(yō′kô-hä′mȧ)	Jap. (Tōkyō In.)	35·37 N	139·40 E
153	Yokosuka	(yô-kō′sōō-kä)	Jap. (Tōkyō In.)	35·17 N	139·40 E
153	Yokota	(yō-kō′tȧ)	Jap. (Tōkyō In.)	35·23 N	140·02 E
164	Yola	(yō′lä)	Nig.	9·13 N	12·27 E
93	Yolaina, Cord. de (Mts.)	(kôr-dēl-yĕ′rä dĕ yō-lä-ē′nä)	Nic.	11·34 N	84·34 W
98	Yolombó	(yô-lôm-bŏ′)	Col. (In.)	6·37 N	74·59 W
153	Yonago	(yō′nä-gō)	Jap.	35·27 N	133·19 E
152	Yonezawa	(yō′nĕ′zȧ-wä)	Jap.	37·50 N	140·07 E
152	Yŏngdŏk	(yŭng′dŭk′)	Kor.	36·28 N	129·25 E
152	Yŏnghŭng	(yŭng′hŏŏng′)	Kor.	39·31 N	127·11 E
152	Yonghŭng Man (B.)		Kor.	39·10 N	128·00 E
84	Yonkers	(yŏŋ′kẽrz)	N. Y. (New York In.)	40·57 N	73·54 W
122	Yonne (R.)	(yôn)	Fr.	48·18 N	3·15 E
153	Yono	(yō′nō)	Jap. (Tōkyō In.)	35·53 N	139·36 E
74	Yorba Linda	(yôr′bă lĭn′dȧ)	Calif. (Los Angeles In.)	33·55 N	117·51 W
78	York	(yôrk)	Ala.	32·33 N	88·16 W
158	York		Austl.	32·00 S	117·00 E
116	York		Eng.	53·58 N	1·10 W
73	York		Nebr.	40·52 N	97·36 W
81	York		Pa.	40·00 N	76·40 W
79	York		S. C.	34·59 N	81·14 W
159	York, C.		Austl.	10·45 S	142·35 E
49	York, Kap (C.)		Grnld.	75·30 N	73·00 W
160	Yorketown		Austl.	35·00 S	137·28 E
87	York Factory	(făk′tô-rĭ)	Can.	56·59 N	92·27 W
160	York Pen		Austl.	34·24 S	137·20 E
116	Yorkshire Wolds (Hills)	(yôrk′shĭr)	Eng.	54·00 N	0·35 W
86	Yorkton	(yôrk′tŭn)	Can.	51·11 N	102·40 W
77	Yorktown	(yôrk′toun)	Tex.	28·57 N	97·30 W
79	Yorktown		Va.	37·12 N	76·31 W
92	Yoro	(yō′rô)	Hond.	15·09 N	87·05 W
68	Yosemite Natl. Park	(yô-sĕm′ĭ-tė̇)	Calif.	38·03 N	119·36 W
153	Yoshida	(yō′shė̇-dȧ)	Jap.	34·39 N	132·41 E
153	Yoshikawa	(yō-shė̇′kä′wä′)	Jap. (Tōkyō In.)	35·53 N	139·51 E
153	Yoshino (R.)	(yō′shē-nō)	Jap.	34·04 N	133·57 E
153	Yoshiwara	(yō-shė̇′wä′rä′)	Jap.	35·11 N	138·44 E
132	Yoshkar-Ola	(yôsh-kär′ô-lä′)	Sov. Un.	56·35 N	48·05 E
91	Yosonotú (Santa Catarina)	(yô-sō-nô-tōō′) (sän′tä kä-tä-rē′nä)	Mex.	16·51 N	97·37 W
152	Yŏsu	(yŭ′sōō′)	Kor.	34·42 N	127·42 E
116	Youghal B.	(yōō′ôl) (yôl)	Ire.	51·52 N	7·46 W
116	Youhal		Ire.	51·58 N	7·57 W
165	Youkadouma	(yōō-kȧ-dōō′mä)	Cam.	3·29 N	15·04 E
160	Young	(yŭng)	Austl.	34·15 S	148·18 E
101	Young	(yô-ōō′ng)	Ur. (Buenos Aires In.)	32·42 S	57·38 W
65	Youngs (L.)	(yŭngz)	Wash. (Seattle In.)	47·25 N	122·08 W
75	Youngstown	(yŭngz′toun)	N. Y. (Buffalo In.)	43·15 N	79·02 W
80	Youngstown		Ohio	41·05 N	80·40 W
133	Yozgat	(yôz′gȧd)	Tur.	39·50 N	34·50 E
75	Ypsilanti	(ĭp-sĭ-lăn′tĭ)	Mich. (Detroit In.)	42·15 N	83·37 W
66	Yreka	(wī-rē′kȧ)	Calif.	41·43 N	122·36 W
84	Yscloskey	(ĭs-klŏs′kĕ)	La. (New Orleans In.)	29·51 N	89·42 W
76	Ysleta	(ė̇z-lĕ′tȧ)	Tex.	31·42 N	106·18 W
122	Yssingeaux	(ē-săɴ-zhō′)	Fr.	45·09 N	4·08 E
118	Ystad	(ü′städ)	Swe.	55·29 N	13·28 E
118	Ytre Solund (I.)	(ü′trĕ sōō′lĕn)	Nor.	61·01 N	4·25 E
151	Yüan (R.)	(yōō′än′)	China	28·50 N	110·50 E
151	Yüanan	(yōō′ä-nän′)	China	31·08 N	111·28 E
151	Yüanling		China	28·30 N	110·18 E
148	Yüanshih		China	37·45 N	114·32 E
68	Yuba City	(yōō′bȧ)	Calif.	39·08 N	121·38 W
164	Yubi C.	(yōō′bė̇)	Mor.	28·01 N	13·21 W
74	Yucaipa	(yŭ-kȧ-ē′pȧ)	Calif. (Los Angeles In.)	34·02 N	117·02 W
88	Yucatan (State)	(yōō-kä-tän′)	Mex.	20·45 N	89·00 W
88	Yucatán Chan		Mex.	22·30 N	87·00 W
151	Yu Chiang (R.)	(yōō)	China	23·55 N	106·50 E
148	Yüch'eng	(yü′chĕng′)	China	34·31 N	115·54 E
148	Yuch'eng		China	36·55 N	116·39 E
135	Yudoma (R.)	(yōō-dō′mȧ)	Sov. Un.	59·13 N	137·00 E
148	Yüehchuang	(yüĕ′jŏŏäng)	China	36·13 N	118·17 E
151	Yüehyang		China	29·25 N	113·05 E
132	Yug (R.)	(yŏŏg)	Sov. Un.	59·50 N	45·55 E
102	Yugoslavia	(yōō-gô-slä-vĭ-ȧ)	Eur.	44·48 N	17·29 E
148	Yühsien	(yüsĭän)	China	34·09 N	113·25 E
150	Yühsien	(yōō′hsyĕn′)	China	39·40 N	114·38 E
128	Yukhnov	(yŏŏk′-nof)	Sov. Un.	54·44 N	35·15 E
86	Yukon (Ter.)	(yōō′kŏn)	Can.	63·16 N	135·30 W
64	Yukon R.		Alaska	62·10 N	163·10 W
64	Yukutat B.	(yōō-kū tăt′)	Alaska	59·34 N	140·50 W
136	Yuldybayevo	(yŏŏld′-bä′yĕ-vô)	Sov. Un. (Urals In.)	52·20 N	57·52 E
151	Yülin		China	22·38 N	110·10 E
150	Yülin	(yōō′lĭn′)	China	38·18 N	109·45 E
69	Yuma	(yōō′mä)	Ariz.	32·40 N	114·40 W
72	Yuma		Colo.	40·08 N	102·50 W
95	Yuma, Bahia de (B.)	(bä-ē′ä-dĕ-yōō′mä)	Dom. Rep.	18·20 N	68·05 W
95	Yuma (R.)		Dom. Rep.	19·05 N	70·05 W
146	Yümen	(yü′mĕn′)	China	40·14 N	96·56 E
150	Yünch'eng	(yün′chĕng)	China	35·00 N	110·40 E
151	Yüngan	(yŏŏn′gän′)	China	26·00 N	117·22 E
	Yungchia, see Wenchow				
150	Yungch'ing	(yŏŏng′chĭng′)	China (Peking In.)	39·18 N	116·27 E
	Yungchow, see Lingling				
148	Yungnien	(yōōng′nĭän)	China	36·41 N	114·46 E
151	Yungshun	(yŏŏng′shōōn′)	China	29·05 N	109·58 E
150	Yungting Ho (R.)	(yŏŏng′tĭng′ hō′)	China	40·25 N	115·00 E
148	Yün Ho (R.) (Grand Canal)	(yün′hŭ)	China	34·23 N	117·57 E
151	Yünhsiao		China	24·00 N	117·20 E
150	Yünhsien		China	32·50 N	110·55 E
147	Yün Ling Shan (Mts.)	(yün lĭng shän)	China	26·35 N	117·15 E
146	Yünnan (Prov.)	(yün′nän′)	China	24·23 N	101·03 E
	Yünnanfu, see K'unming				
146	Yünnan Plat		China	26·03 N	101·26 E
153	Yura	(yōō′rä)	Jap.	34·18 N	134·54 E
90	Yurécuaro	(yōō-rā′kwä-rô)	Mex.	20·21 N	102·16 W
98	Yurimaguas	(yōō-rė̇-mä′gwäs)	Peru	5·59 S	76·12 W
90	Yuriria	(yōō′rė̇-rē′ä)	Mex.	20·11 N	101·08 W
132	Yur'yevets		Sov. Un.	57·15 N	43·08 E
136	Yuryuzan'	(yŏŏr-yŏŏ-zän′)	Sov. Un. (Urals In.)	54·47 N	58·45 E
92	Yuscarán	(yōōs-kä-rän′)	Hond.	13·57 N	86·48 W
151	Yüshan	(yōō′shän′)	China	28·42 N	118·20 E
150	Yüshu		China	44·58 N	126·32 E
142	Yutien (Keriya)	(yōō′tĕn′)	China	36·55 N	81·39 E
148	Yut'ien	(yü′tyĕn′)	China	39·54 N	117·45 E
100	Yuty	(yōō-tē′)	Par.	26·45 S	56·13 W
150	Yützu		China	37·32 N	112·40 E
148	Yuwangcheng	(yü′wäng′chĕng)	China	31·32 N	114·26 E
132	Yuzha	(yōō′zhȧ)	Sov. Un.	56·38 N	42·20 E
136	Yuzhnny Ural (Mts.)	(yōō′zhnĭ ŏŏ-räl′)	Sov. Un. (Urals In.)	52·51 N	57·48 E
135	Yuzhno-Sakhalinsk	(yōōzh′nô-sä-ĸä-lĭnsk′)	Sov. Un.	47·11 N	143·04 E
136	Yuzhnoural'skiy	(yōōzh-nô-ŏŏ-rál′skĭ)	Sov. Un. (Urals In.)	54·26 N	61·17 E
120	Yverdon	(ė̇-vĕr-dôn)	Switz.	46·46 N	6·35 E
122	Yvetot	(ēv-tō′)	Fr.	49·39 N	0·45 E
114	Za R.		Mor.	34·19 N	2·23 W
91	Zaachila	(sä-ä-chē′lȧ)	Mex.	16·56 N	96·45 W
111	Zaandam	(zän′dȧm)	Neth. (Amsterdam In.)	52·25 N	4·49 E
139	Zabdānī		Syr. (Palestine In.)	33·45 N	36·06 E
120	Zabkowice	(zaɴb′kô-vē′tsĕ)	Pol.	50·35 N	16·48 E
121	Zabrze	(zäb′zhĕ)	Pol.	50·18 N	18·48 E
92	Zacapa	(sä-kä′pä)	Guat.	14·56 N	89·30 W
91	Zacapoaxtla	(sä-kä-pō-äs′tlä)	Mex.	19·51 N	97·34 W
90	Zacatecas	(sä-kä-tā′käs)	Mex.	22·44 N	102·32 W
88	Zacatecas (State)		Mex.	24·00 N	102·45 W
92	Zacatecoluca	(sä-kä-tȧ-kô-lōō′kä)	Sal.	13·31 N	88·50 W
90	Zacateko	(zä-kȧ-tĕ′kō)	Mex.	19·12 N	98·12 W
91	Zacatepec (Santiago)	(sä-kä-tȧ-pĕk′) (sän-tė̇-ä′gô)	Mex.	17·10 N	95·53 W
91	Zacatlán	(sä-kä-tlän′)	Mex.	19·55 N	97·57 W
90	Zacoalco de Torres	(sä-kô-äl′kô dā tōr′rĕs)	Mex.	20·12 N	103·33 W
90	Zacualpan	(sä-kŏŏ-äl-pän′)	Mex.	18·43 N	99·46 W

ng-sing; ŋ-baŋk; ɴ-nasalized n; nŏd; cŏmmit; ōld; ôbey; ôrder; fōōd; fŏŏt; ou-out; s-soft; sh-dish; th-thin; pūre; ûnite; ûrn; stŭd; circŭs; ü-as "y" in study; ′-indeterminate vowel.

Page	Name Pronunciation	Region	Lat. °′	Long. °′
90	Zacualtipan (sä-kōō-äl-tē-pän′)	Mex.	20·38 N	98·39 W
126	Zadar (zä′där)	Yugo.	44·08 N	15·16 E
128	Zadonsk (zä-dônsk′)	Sov. Un.	52·22 N	38·55 E
139	Za'farānah	U. A. R. (Egypt) (Palestine In.)	29·07 N	32·38 E
120	Zagan (zhä′gan′)	Pol.	51·34 N	15·32 E
125	Zagarolo (tzä-gä-rô′lô)	It. (Rome In.)	41·51 N	12·53 E
119	Žagare (zhȧgȧrĕ)	Sov. Un.	56·21 N	23·14 E
139	Zaghartā	Leb. (Palestine In.)	34·24 N	35·53 E
164	Zaghouan (zȧ-gwäN′)	Tun.	36·30 N	10·04 E
127	Zagorá (zä′gô-rä)	Grc.	39·29 N	23·04 E
136	Zagorsk (zä-gôrsk′)	Sov. Un. (Moscow In.)	56·18 N	38·08 E
126	Zagreb (zä′grĕb)	Yugo.	45·50 N	15·58 E
144	Zagro Mts.	Iran	33·30 N	46·30 E
144	Zahedān (zä′hȧ-dän)	Iran	29·37 N	60·31 E
139	Zahlah (zä-lä′)	Leb. (Palestine In.)	33·50 N	35·54 E
111	Zahorska-Ves	Czech. (Vienna In.)	48·24 N	16·51 E
125	Zahrez Chergui (L.)	Alg.	35·10 N	2·17 E
127	Zaječar (zä′yĕ-chär′)	Yugo.	43·54 N	22·16 E
127	Zákinthos	Grc.	37·48 N	20·55 E
127	Zákinthos (Zante) (I.)	Grc.	37·45 N	20·32 E
121	Zakopane (zȧ-kô-pä′nĕ)	Pol.	49·18 N	19·57 E
120	Zalaegerszeg (zŏ′lŏ-ĕ′gĕr-sĕg)	Hung.	46·50 N	16·50 E
121	Zalău (zȧ-lŭ′ōō)	Rom.	47·11 N	23·06 E
111	Zaltbommel	Neth. (Amsterdam In.)	51·48 N	5·15 E
166	Zambezi (R.) (zȧm-bā′zē)	Afr.	16·33 S	29·22 E
154	Zamboanga (säm-bô-aŋ′gä)	Phil.	6·58 N	122·02 E
121	Zambrów (zäm′brōōf)	Pol.	52·59 N	22·17 E
90	Zamora (sä-mō′rä)	Mex.	19·59 N	102·16 W
124	Zamora (thä-mō′rä)	Sp.	41·32 N	5·43 W
121	Zamość (zä′môshch)	Pol.	50·42 N	23·17 E
91	Zanatepec (Sto. Domingo) (sä-nä-tȧ-pek′) (sän-tô dō-miŋ′gō)	Mex.	16·30 N	94·22 W
111	Zandvoort	Neth. (Amsterdam In.)	52·22 N	4·30 E
80	Zanesville (zānz′vĭl)	Ohio	39·55 N	82·00 W
144	Zanjān	Iran	36·26 N	48·24 E
167	Zanzibar (zăn′zĭ-bär)	Zan.	6·13 S	39·12 E
167	Zanzibar (I.)	Afr.	6·00 S	39·30 E
165	Zanzūr (zän-zōōr′)	Libya	32·40 N	12·49 E
128	Zapadnaya Dvina (R.) (zä′pȧd-nȧ-yȧ dvē′nȧ)	Sov. Un.	55·30 N	28·27 E
100	Zapala (zä-pä′lä)	Arg.	38·53 S	70·02 W
119	Zapa-naya Dvina (R.) (zä′pȧd-nä-yȧ dvē nȧ)	Sov. Un.	56·40 N	24·40 E
76	Zapata (sȧ-pä′tȧ)	Tex.	26·52 N	99·18 W
94	Zapata, Ciénaga de (Swp.) (syĕ′nä-gä-dĕ-zä-pä′tȧ)	Cuba	22·30 N	81·20 W
94	Zapata, Península de (pĕ-nē′n-sōō-lä-dĕ-zä-pä′tȧ)	Cuba	22·20 N	81·30 W
92	Zapatera, Isla (I.) (ē′s-lä-sä-pä-tā′rō)	Nic.	11·45 N	85·45 W
90	Zapopan (sä-pō′pän)	Mex.	20·42 N	103·23 W
119	Zaporoshskoye (zȧ-pô-rôsh′skô-yĕ)	Sov. Un.	60·36 N	30·31 E
129	Zaporozh'ye (zä-pô-rôzh′yĕ)	Sov. Un.	47·53 N	35·25 E
129	Zaporozhye (Oblast) (zä-pô-rôzh′yĕ ôb′lȧst)	Sov. Un.	47·20 N	35·05 E
90	Zapotiltic (sä-pô-tēl-tēk′)	Mex.	19·37 N	103·25 W
90	Zapotitlán (sä-pô-tē-tlän′)	Mex.	17·13 N	98·58 W
91	Zapotitlán, Punta (Pt.)	Mex.	18·34 N	94·48 W
90	Zapotlanejo (sä-pô-tlä-nā′hō)	Mex.	20·38 N	103·05 W
90	Zaragoza (sä-rä-gō′sä)	Mex.	23·59 N	99·45 W
90	Zaragoza	Mex.	22·02 N	100·45 W
125	Zaragoza (thä-rä-gō′thä)	Sp.	41·39 N	0·53 W
121	Zărandului, Muntii (Mts.)	Rom.	46·07 N	22·21 E
119	Zarasay (zȧ-rȧ-sī′)	Sov. Un.	55·45 N	26·18 E
101	Zárate (zä-rä′tä)	Arg. (Buenos Aires In.)	34·05 S	59·05 W
128	Zaraysk (zȧ-rä′ēsk)	Sov. Un.	54·46 N	38·53 E
142	Zardālu	W. Pak.	30·20 N	67·40 E
164	Zaria (zä′rē-ä)	Nig.	11·08 N	7·45 E
133	Zarineh, Rūd-é (R.)	Iran	36·40 N	46·35 E
139	Zarga (R.)	Jordan (Palestine In.)	32·13 N	35·43 E
120	Zary (zhä′rē)	Pol.	51·38 N	15·08 E
98	Zarzal (zär-zä′l)	Col. (In.)	4·23 N	76·04 W
135	Zashiversk (zä′shĭ-vĕrsk′)	Sov. Un.	67·08 N	144·02 E
121	Zastavna (zȧs-tăf′nȧ)	Sov. Un.	48·32 N	25·50 E
167	Zastron (zȧs′trŭn)	S. Afr. (Natal In.)	30·19 S	27·07 E
120	Žatec (zhä′tĕts)	Czech.	50·19 N	13·32 E
135	Zavitinsk	Sov. Un.	50·12 N	129·44 E
121	Zawiercie (zȧ-vyĕr′tsyĕ)	Pol.	50·28 N	19·25 E
144	Zāyantleh Rud (R.)	Iran	32·16 N	50·48 E
134	Zaysan (zī′sȧn)	Sov. Un.	47·43 N	84·44 E
134	Zaysan (L.)	Sov. Un.	48·16 N	84·05 E
94	Zaza (R.) (zä′zä)	Cuba	21·40 N	79·25 W
121	Zbarazh (zbä-räzh′)	Sov. Un.	49·39 N	25·48 E
121	Zbruch R (zbrōōch)	Sov. Un.	48·56 N	26·18 E
121	Zdolbunov (zdôl-bōō′nōōf)	Sov. Un.	50·31 N	26·17 E
121	Zdunska Wola (zdōōn″skä vō′lä)	Pol.	51·36 N	18·27 E
168	Zebediela	S. Afr. (Johannesburg & Pretoria In.)	24·19 S	29·21 E
117	Zeebrugge (zā′brōōg′gĕ)	Bel.	51·20 N	3·00 W
80	Zeeland (zē′lȧnd)	Mich.	42·50 N	86·00 W
111	Zehdenick (tsā′dē-nēk)	Ger. (Berlin In.)	52.59 N	13·20 E
111	Zehlendorf (tsā′lĕn-dôrf)	Ger. (Berlin In.)	52·47 N	13·23 E
168	Zeila (zā′lä)	Som. (Horn of Afr. In.)	11·19 N	43·20 E
111	Zeist	Neth. (Amsterdam In.)	52·05 N	5·14 E
121	Zelechów (zhĕ-lĕ′kōōf)	Pol.	51·48 N	21·55 E
119	Zelenogorsk (zĕ-lă′nô-gôrsk)	Sov. Un.	60·13 N	29·39 E
120	Zella-Mehlis (tsĕl′ȧ-mā′lēs)	Ger.	50·40 N	10·38 E
165	Zémio (za-myō′)	Cen. Afr. Rep.	5·03 N	25·11 E
130	Zemlya Frantsa Iosifa (Franz Josef Land) (Is.)	Sov. Un.	81·32 N	40·00 E
91	Zempoala, Punta (Pt.) (pōō′n-tä-sĕm-pô-ä′lä)	Mex.	19·30 N	96·18 W
91	Zempoatlépetl (Mtn.) (sĕm-pô-ä-tlā′pĕt′l)	Mex.	17·13 N	95·59 W
127	Zemun (Semlin) (zĕ′mōōn) (sĕm′lĭn)	Yugo.	44·50 N	20·25 E
127	Zenica (zĕ′nēt-sä)	Yugo.	44·10 N	17·54 E
153	Zeni-Su (Is.) (zĕ′nē sōō)	Jap.	33·55 N	138·55 E
129	Zen'kov (zĕn-kof′)	Sov. Un.	50·13 N	34·23 E
127	Žepče (zhĕp′chĕ)	Yugo.	44·26 N	18·01 E
111	Zepernick (tsĕ′pĕr-nēk)	Ger. (Berlin In.)	52·39 N	13·32 E
103	Zeravshan (R.) (zĕ-räf-shän′)	Sov. Un.	40·00 N	65·42 E
120	Zerbst (tsĕrbst)	Ger.	51·58 N	12·03 E
111	Zerpenschleuse (tsĕr′pĕn-shloi-zĕ)	Ger. (Berlin In.)	52·51 N	13·30 E
111	Zeuthen (tsoi′tĕn)	Ger. (Berlin In.)	52·21 N	13·38 E
123	Zevenaar	Neth. (Ruhr In.)	51·56 N	6·06 E
111	Zevenbergen	Neth. (Amsterdam In.)	51·38 N	4·36 E
135	Zeya (zâ′yȧ)	Sov. Un.	53·43 N	127·29 E
135	Zeya (R.)	Sov. Un.	52·31 N	128·30 E
133	Zeytun (zā-tōōn′)	Tur.	38·00 N	36·40 E
124	Zezere (R.) (zĕ′zȧ-rĕ)	Port.	39·54 N	8·12 W
121	Zgierz (zgyĕzh)	Pol.	51·51 N	19·26 E
129	Zgurovka (zgōō′rôf-kä)	Sov. Un.	50·31 N	31·43 E
129	Zhdanov (zhdä′nôf)	Sov. Un.	47·07 N	37·32 E
134	Zhelaniya, Mys (C.) (zhĕ′lä-nĭ-yȧ)	Sov. Un.	75·43 N	69·10 E
135	Zhigalovo (zhē-gä′lô-vô)	Sov. Un.	54·52 N	105·05 E
135	Zhigansk (zhē-gänsk′)	Sov. Un.	66·45 N	123·20 E
142	Zhikatse	China	29·22 N	88·57 E
129	Zhitomir (zhē′tô′mēr)	Sov. Un.	50·15 N	28·40 E
129	Zhitomir (Oblast)	Sov. Un.	50·40 N	28·07 E
128	Zhizdra (zhēz′drȧ)	Sov. Un.	53·47 N	34·41 E
128	Zhizhitskoye (R.) (zhē-zhĕt′skô-yĕ)	Sov. Un.	56·08 N	31·34 E
129	Zhmerinka (zhmyĕ′rĕŋ-kȧ)	Sov. Un.	49·02 N	28·09 E
136	Zhukovskiy (zhōō-kôf′skĭ)	Sov. Un. (Moscow In.)	55·33 N	38·09 E
158	Ziel, Mt. (zēl)	Austl.	23·15 S	132·45 E
120	Zietona Gora (zhyĕ-lô′nȧ gōō′rä)	Pol.	51·56 N	15·30 E
136	Zigazinskiy (zĭ-gazinskēē)	Sov. Un. (Urals In.)	53·50 N	57·18 E
164	Ziguichor	Senegal	12·28 N	16·27 W
136	Zilair (zē′lȧ-ĭr)	Sov. Un. (Urals In.)	52·12 N	57·23 E
133	Zile (zē-lĕ′)	Tur.	40·20 N	35·50 E
121	Žilina (zhē′lĭ-nä)	Czech.	49·14 N	18·45 E
165	Zillah	Libya	28·26 N	17·52 E
134	Zima (zē′mȧ)	Sov. Un.	53·58 N	102·08 E
90	Zimapan (sē-mä′pän)	Mex.	20·43 N	99·23 W
91	Zimatlán de Alvarez (sē-mä-tlän′ dā äl′vä-rāz)	Mex.	16·52 N	96·47 W
127	Zimnicea (zēm-nē′chȧ)	Rom.	43·39 N	25·22 E
91	Zinacatepec (zē-nä-kä-tĕ′pĕk)	Mex.	18·19 N	97·15 W
	Zinántectl, see Toluca, Nevado de			
90	Zinapécuaro (sē-nä-pā′kwȧ-rô)	Mex.	19·50 N	100·49 W
164	Zinder (zĭn′dĕr)	Niger	13·49 N	8·54 E
75	Zion (zī′ŭn)	Ill. (Chicago In.)	42·27 N	87·50 W
69	Zion Natl. Park	Utah	37·20 N	113·00 W
75	Zionsville (zīŭnz-vĭl)	Ind. (Indianapolis In.)	39·57 N	86·15 W
98	Zipaquirá (sē-pä-kē-rä′)	Col. (In.)	5·01 N	74·01 W
90	Zirandaro (sē-rän-dä′rō)	Mex.	18·28 N	101·02 W
90	Zitacuaro (sē-tä-kwä′rō)	Mex.	19·25 N	100·22 W
90	Zitlala (sē-tlä′lä)	Mex.	17·38 N	99·09 W
120	Zittau (tsē′tou)	Ger.	50·55 N	14·48 E
127	Zlatograd	Bul.	41·24 N	25·05 E
136	Zlatoust (zlȧ-tô-ōōst′)	Sov. Un. (Urals In.)	55·13 N	59·39 E
165	Zlitan	Libya	32·27 N	14·33 E
121	Złoczew (zwô′chĕf)	Pol.	51·23 N	18·34 E
128	Zlynka (zlĕŋ′kȧ)	Sov. Un.	52·28 N	31·39 E
129	Znamenka (znä′mĕn-kä)	Sov. Un.	48·43 N	32·35 E
119	Znamensk (znä′mĕnsk)	Sov. Un.	54·39 N	21·49 E
120	Znojomo (znoi′mô)	Czech.	48·52 N	16·03 E
111	Zoetermeer	Neth. (Amsterdam In.)	52·03 N	4·29 E
111	Zoeterwoude	Neth. (Amsterdam In.)	52·03 N	4·29 E
111	Zohor	Czech. (Vienna In.)	48·20 N	17·00 E
121	Zolochëv (zô′lô-chĕf)	Sov. Un.	49·48 N	24·55 E
129	Zolotonosha (zô′lô-tô-nô′shȧ)	Sov. Un.	49·41 N	32·03 E
152	Zolotoy, Mys (Pt.) (mĭs zô-lô-tôy′)	Sov. Un.	47·24 N	139·10 E
166	Zomba (zōm′bȧ)	Nya.	15·19 S	35·17 E
165	Zongo (zŏŋ′gō)	Con. L.	4·19 N	18·36 E
133	Zonguldak (zôn′gōōl′dȧk)	Tur.	41·25 N	31·50 E
111	Zonhoven	Bel. (Brussels In.)	50·59 N	5·24 E
91	Zoquitlán (sô-kēt-län′)	Mex.	18·09 N	97·02 W
124	Zorita (thō-rē′tä)	Sp.	39·18 N	5·41 W
111	Zossen (tsō′sĕn)	Ger. (Berlin In.)	52·13 N	13·27 E
128	Zubtsov (zōōp-tsôf′)	Sov. Un.	56·13 N	34·34 E
125	Zuera (thwā′rä)	Sp.	41·40 N	0·48 W
120	Zuger See (L.) (tsōōg)	Switz.	47·10 N	8·40 E
120	Zugspitze Pk.	Aus.-Ger.	47·25 N	11·00 E
124	Zújar (R.) (zōō′kär)	Sp.	38·55 N	5·05 W
94	Zulueta (zōō-lōō-ĕ′tä)	Cuba	22·20 N	79·35 W
166	Zululand (Reg.) (zōō′lōō-lănd)	S. Afr.	27·45 S	31·29 E
166	Zumbo (zōōm′bōō)	Moz.	15·32 S	30·30 E
71	Zumbro (R.) (zŭm′brō)	Minn.	44·18 N	92·14 W
71	Zumbrota (zŭm-brō′tȧ)	Minn.	44·16 N	92·39 W
90	Zumpango (sōōm-päŋ-gō)	Mex.	19·48 N	99·06 W
111	Zundert	Neth. (Amsterdam In.)	51·28 N	4·39 E
164	Zungeru (zōōŋ-gä′rōō)	Nig.	9·45 N	6·13 E
69	Zuni (R.)	Ariz.-N. Mex.	34·40 N	109·30 W
69	Zuni Ind. Res. (zōō′nē)	N. Mex.	35·10 N	108·40 W
69	Zuni Mts.	N. Mex.	35·10 N	108·10 W
120	Zürich (tsü′rĭk)	Switz.	47·22 N	8·32 E
120	Zürich See (L.)	Switz.	47·18 N	8·47 E
153	Zushi (zōō′shē)	Jap. (Tōkyō In.)	35·17 N	139·35 E
167	Zuurberg (Mts.) (zōō′bûrg)	S. Afr. (Natal In.)	33·15 S	25·32 E
165	Zuwārah	Libya	32·58 N	12·07 E
139	Zuwayzā	Jordan (Palestine In.)	31·42 N	35·58 E
128	Zvenigorod (zvā-nē′gô-rôt)	Sov. Un.	55·46 N	36·54 E
129	Zvenigorodka (zvā-nē′gô-rôt′kä)	Sov. Un.	49·07 N	30·59 E
121	Zvolen (zvô′lĕn)	Czech.	48·35 N	19·10 E
127	Zvornik (zvôr′nēk)	Yugo.	44·24 N	19·08 E
165	Zwai L. (zwä′ē)	Eth.	8·08 N	39·11 E
167	Zwartberg (Mtn.) (zvärt-bĕrk)	S. Afr. (Natal In.)	30·08 S	29·34 E
120	Zwickau (tsvĭk′ou)	Ger.	50·43 N	12·30 E
120	Zwiebrücken (tsvī-brük′ĕn)	Ger.	49·16 N	7·20 E
117	Zwolle (zvôl′ĕ)	Neth.	52·33 N	6·05 E
121	Zyrardow (zhē-rär′dōōf)	Pol.	52·04 N	20·28 E
135	Zyryanka (zē-ryän′kȧ)	Sov. Un.	65·45 N	151·15 E
134	Zyryanovsk (zē-ryä′nôfsk)	Sov. Un.	49·43 N	83·52 E
121	Zywiec (zhĭ′vyĕts)	Pol.	49·42 N	19·14 E

ăt: finăl; rāte; senāte; ärm; ȧsk; sofȧ; fâre; ch-choose; dh-as th in other; bē; ēvent; bĕt; recĕnt; cratẽr; g-go; gh-guttural g; bĭt; ĭ-short neutral; rīde; K-guttural k as ch in German ich;

STRASBURG, VA. 1:62 500
U.S. GEOLOGICAL SURVEY